CONNECT FEATURES

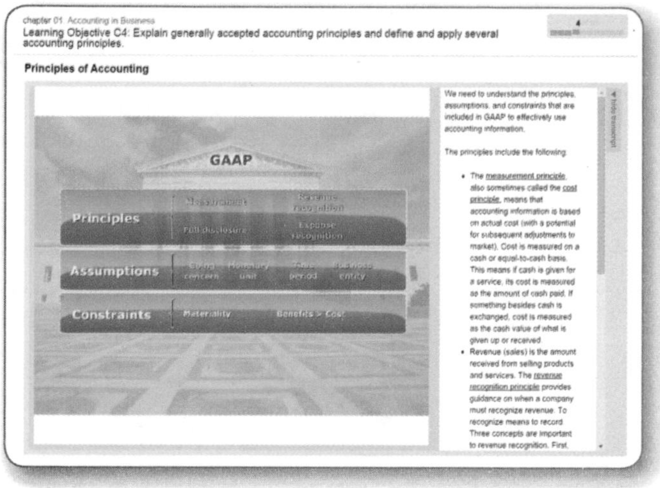

Interactive Presentations

Interactive Presentations cover each chapter's core learning objectives with narrated, animated presentations that pause frequently to check for comprehension. Interactive Presentations harness the full power of technology to appeal to all learning styles. Interactive Presentations are a great way to improve online or hybrid sections, but also extend the learning opportunity for traditional classes, such as in facilitating a "flipped classroom."

Guided Examples

Guided Examples provide narrated and animated step-by-step walkthroughs of algorithmic versions of assigned exercises. This allows students to identify, review, or reinforce the concepts and activities covered in class. Guided Examples provide immediate feedback and focus on the areas where students need the most guidance.

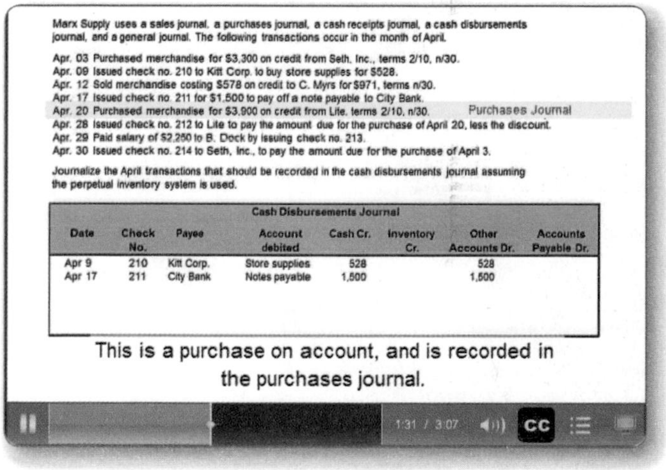

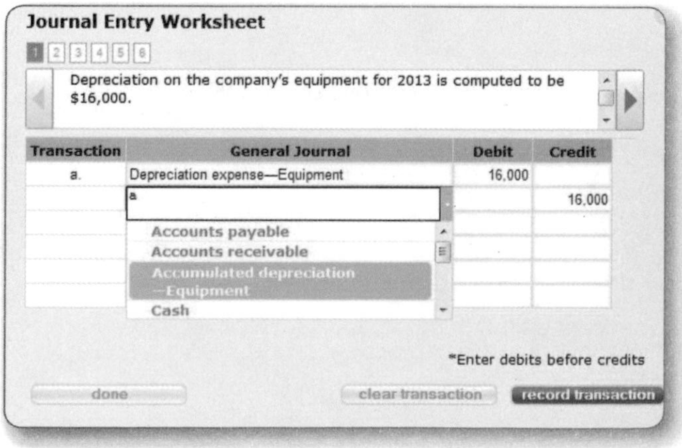

End-of-Chapter Material

McGraw-Hill Education redesigned the student interface for our end-of-chapter assessment content. The new interface provides improved answer acceptance to reduce students' frustration with formatting issues (such as rounding) and, for select questions, provides an expanded table that guides students through the process of solving the problem. Many questions have been redesigned to more fully test students' mastery of the content.

General Ledger

New to 6e are General Ledger problems that offer students the ability to see how transactions post from the general journal all the way through the financial statements. General Ledger (GL) questions provide auto-grading in the same intelligent design as our end-of-chapter content. Critical thinking and analysis components are added to each GL problem to ensure understanding of the entire process.

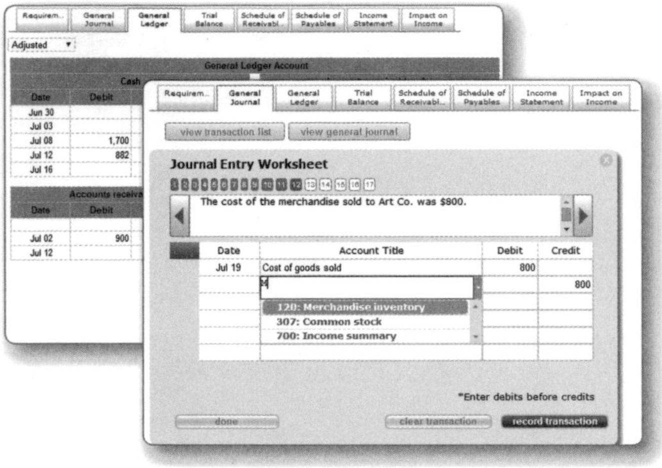

Excel Simulations

Assignable within Connect Accounting, Excel Simulations allow students to practice their Excel skills—such as basic formulas and formatting—within the context of accounting. These questions feature animated, narrated Help and Show Me tutorials (when enabled). These simulations are auto-graded and provide instant feedback to the student.

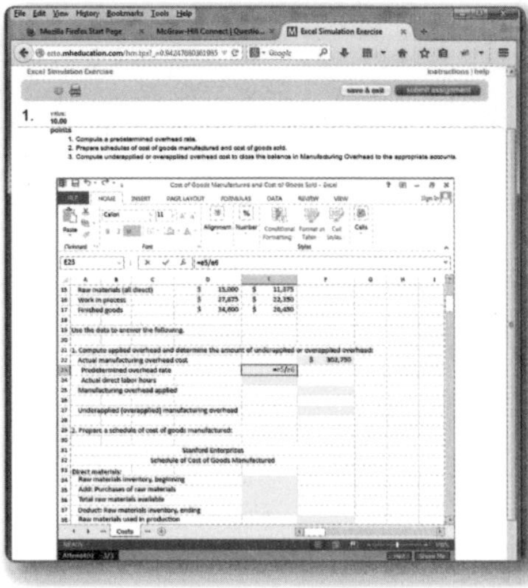

POWERFUL PERFORMANCE REPORTING

Connect generates comprehensive reports and graphs that provide instructors with an instant view of the performance of individual students, a specific section, or multiple sections. Since all content is mapped to learning objectives, Connect reporting is ideal for accreditation or other administrative documentation.

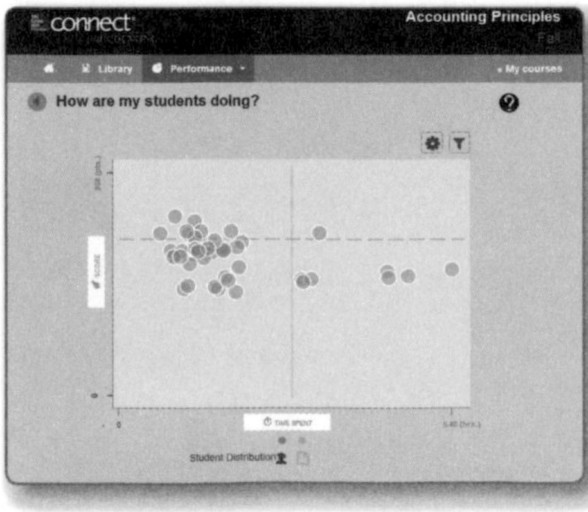

Connect Insight

The first and only analytics tool of its kind, Connect Insight is a series of visual data displays that are each framed by an intuitive question and provide at-a-glance information regarding how an instructor's class is performing. Connect Insight is available through Connect titles.

Financial and Managerial Accounting

6th edition

INFORMATION FOR DECISIONS

John J. Wild

University of Wisconsin at Madison

Ken W. Shaw

University of Missouri at Columbia

Barbara Chiappetta

Nassau Community College

Mc Graw Hill Education

To my students and family, especially **Kimberly, Jonathan, Stephanie** and **Trevor.**
To my wife **Linda** and children **Erin, Emily** and **Jacob.**
To my mother, husband **Bob** and sons **Michael** and **David.**

FINANCIAL AND MANAGERIAL ACCOUNTING: INFORMATION FOR DECISIONS, SIXTH EDITION
Published by McGraw-Hill Education, 2 Penn Plaza, New York, NY 10121.

This book is printed on acid-free paper.

4 5 6 7 8 9 LWI 21 20 19 18 17

ISBN 978-0-07-802576-1
MHID 0-07-802576-1

Senior Vice President, Products & Markets: *Kurt L. Strand*
Vice President, General Manager, Products & Markets: *Marty Lange*
Vice President, Content Design & Delivery: *Kimberly Meriwether David*
Managing Director: *Tim Vertovec*
Marketing Director: *Brad Parkins*
Brand Manager: *Steve Schuetz*
Director, Product Development: *Rose Koos*
Director of Digital Content: *Patricia Plumb*
Lead Product Developer: *Ann Torbert*
Product Developer: *Lindsey Schauer*
Marketing Manager: *Michelle Nolte*
Digital Product Analyst: *Xin Lin*
Director, Content Design & Delivery: *Linda Avenarius*
Program Manager: *Daryl Horrocks*
Content Project Managers: *Lori Koetters, Brian Nacik*
Buyer: *Carol A. Bielski*
Design: *Debra Kubiak*
Content Licensing Specialists: *DeAnna Dausener, Keri Johnson*
Cover Image: *Ascent Xmedia/Getty Images*
Compositor: *Aptara®, Inc.*
Printer: *LSC Communications*

Library of Congress Control Number: 2014954119

www.mhhe.com

Adapting to the Needs of Today's Students

Financial and Managerial Accounting, 6e

Enhancements in technology have changed how we live and learn. Working with learning resources across devices, whether smartphones, tablets, or laptop computers, empowers students to drive their own learning by putting increasingly intelligent technology into their hands.

Whether the goal is to become an accountant, a businessperson, or simply an informed consumer of accounting information, *Financial and Managerial Accounting (FinMan)* has helped generations of students succeed. Its leading-edge accounting content, paired with state-of-the-art technology, supports student learning and elevates understanding of key accounting principles.

FinMan excels at **engaging students** with content that will help them see the relevance of accounting. Its chapter-opening vignettes showcase dynamic, successful entrepreneurial individuals and companies and **highlight the usefulness of accounting to business owners**. This edition's featured companies—**Apple, Google,** and **Samsung**—capture student interest with their products, and their annual reports serve as a pathway for learning financial statements. New in this edition, Need-to-Know illustrations in each chapter demonstrate how to apply key accounting procedures. They are supported by guided video presentations.

FinMan also delivers innovative technology to help student performance. ***Connect Accounting*** provides students with a media-rich eBook version of the textbook and offers instant grading and feedback for assignments that are completed online. Our system for completing exercise and problem material takes accounting content to the next level, delivering assessment material in a **more intuitive, less restrictive** format that adapts to the needs of today's students.

This technology features:

- **a general journal interface** that looks and feels more like that found in practice.
- **an auto-calculation** feature that allows students to focus on concepts rather than rote tasks.
- **a smart (auto-fill) drop-down design**.

The end result is content that better prepares students for the real world.

Connect Accounting also includes digitally based, interactive, adaptive learning tools that provide an opportunity to engage students more effectively by offering varied instructional methods and more personalized learning paths that build on different learning styles, interests, and abilities.

The revolutionary technology of the LearnSmart Advantage Series—consisting of **LearnSmart®** and **SmartBook®**—is available only from McGraw-Hill Education. These products are based on an intelligent learning system that uses a series of adaptive questions to pinpoint each student's knowledge gaps and then provides an optimal learning path. Students spend less time in areas they already know and more time in areas they don't. The result: Students study more efficiently, learn faster, and retain more knowledge. Valuable reports provide insights into how students are progressing through textbook content and information useful for shaping in-class time or assessment.

Interactive Presentations teach each chapter's core learning objectives in a rich, multimedia format, bringing the content to life. Your students will come to class prepared when you assign Interactive Presentations. Students can also review the Interactive Presentations as they study. Further, **Guided Examples** provide students with narrated, animated, step-by-step walk-throughs of algorithmic versions of assigned exercises. Students appreciate the Guided Examples, which help them learn accounting and complete assignments outside of class.

A **General Ledger (GL) application,** new to 6e, offers students the ability to see how transactions post from the general journal all the way through the financial statements. It uses the intuitive, less restrictive format used for other homework, and it adds critical thinking components to each GL question, to ensure understanding of the entire process.

The first and only analytics tool of its kind, **Connect Insight®** is a series of visual data displays—each framed by an intuitive question—to provide at-a-glance information about how your class is doing. Connect Insight provides a quick analysis on five key dimensions, available at a moment's notice from a tablet device: *How are my students doing? How is my section doing? How is this student doing? How are my assignments going?* and *How is this assignment going?*

> "This is an excellent book that is well-written and contains excellent illustrations. It has the best online supplements of any of the texts that I have reviewed. . . . This is an excellent book that I would recommend to all of my colleagues."
>
> **—KAREN CRISONINO, County College of Morris**

About the Authors

JOHN J. WILD is a distinguished professor of accounting at the University of Wisconsin at Madison. He previously held appointments at Michigan State University and the University of Manchester in England. He received his BBA, MS, and PhD from the University of Wisconsin.

Professor Wild teaches accounting courses at both the undergraduate and graduate levels. He has received numerous teaching honors, including the Mabel W. Chipman Excellence-in-Teaching Award, the departmental Excellence-in-Teaching Award, and the Teaching Excellence Award from the 2003 and 2005 business graduates at the University of Wisconsin. He also received the Beta Alpha Psi and Roland F. Salmonson Excellence-in-Teaching Award from Michigan State University. Professor Wild has received several research honors and is a past KPMG Peat Marwick National Fellow and is a recipient of fellowships from the American Accounting Association and the Ernst and Young Foundation.

Professor Wild is an active member of the American Accounting Association and its sections. He has served on several committees of these organizations, including the Outstanding Accounting Educator Award, Wildman Award, National Program Advisory, Publications, and Research Committees. Professor Wild is author of *Fundamental Accounting Principles, Financial Accounting, Managerial Accounting,* and *College Accounting*, each published by McGraw-Hill Education. His research articles on accounting and analysis appear in *The Accounting Review; Journal of Accounting Research; Journal of Accounting and Economics; Contemporary Accounting Research; Journal of Accounting, Auditing and Finance; Journal of Accounting and Public Policy;* and other journals. He is past associate editor of *Contemporary Accounting Research* and has served on several editorial boards including *The Accounting Review*.

In his leisure time, Professor Wild enjoys hiking, sports, travel, people, and spending time with family and friends.

KEN W. SHAW is an associate professor of accounting and the Deloitte Professor of Accounting at the University of Missouri. He previously was on the faculty at the University of Maryland at College Park. He has also taught in international programs at the University of Bergamo (Italy) and the University of Alicante (Spain). He received an accounting degree from Bradley University and an MBA and PhD from the University of Wisconsin. He is a Certified Public Accountant with work experience in public accounting.

Professor Shaw teaches accounting at the undergraduate and graduate levels. He has received numerous School of Accountancy, College of Business and university-level teaching awards. He was voted the "Most Influential Professor" by three School of Accountancy graduating classes, and is a two-time recipient of the O'Brien Excellence in Teaching Award. He is the advisor to his school's chapter of the Association of Certified Fraud Examiners.

Professor Shaw is an active member of the American Accounting Association and its sections. He has served on many committees of these organizations and presented his research papers at national and regional meetings. Professor Shaw's research appears in the *Journal of Accounting Research*; *The Accounting Review; Contemporary Accounting Research; Journal of Financial and Quantitative Analysis; Journal of the American Taxation Association; Strategic Management Journal; Journal of Accounting, Auditing, and Finance; Journal of Financial Research;* and other journals. He has served on the editorial boards of *Issues in Accounting Education; Journal of Business Research;* and *Research in Accounting Regulation.* Professor Shaw is co-author of *Fundamental Accounting Principles, Managerial Accounting,* and *College Accounting,* all published by McGraw-Hill Education.

In his leisure time, Professor Shaw enjoys tennis, cycling, music, and coaching his children's sports teams.

BARBARA CHIAPPETTA received her BBA in Accountancy and MS in Education from Hofstra University and is a tenured full professor at Nassau Community College. For the past two decades, she has been an active executive board member of the Teachers of Accounting at Two-Year Colleges (TACTYC), serving 10 years as vice president and as president from 1993 through 1999. As an active member of the American Accounting Association, she has served on the Northeast Regional Steering Committee, chaired the Curriculum Revision Committee of the Two-Year Section, and participated in numerous national committees. Professor Chiappetta has been inducted into the American Accounting Association Hall of Fame for the Northeast Region. She has also received the Nassau Community College dean of instruction's Faculty Distinguished Achievement Award. Professor Chiappetta was honored with the State University of New York Chancellor's Award for Teaching Excellence in 1997. As a confirmed believer in the benefits of the active learning pedagogy, Professor Chiappetta has authored *Student Learning Tools,* an active learning workbook for a first-year accounting course, published by McGraw-Hill Education.

In her leisure time, Professor Chiappetta enjoys tennis and participates on a U.S.T.A. team. She also enjoys the challenge of bridge. Her husband, Robert, is an entrepreneur in the leisure sport industry. She has two sons—Michael, a lawyer, specializing in intellectual property law in New York, and David, a composer, pursuing a career in music for film in Los Angeles.

Dear Colleagues and Friends,

As we roll out the new edition of *Financial and Managerial Accounting,* we thank each of you who provided suggestions to improve the textbook and its teaching resources. This new edition reflects the advice and wisdom of many dedicated reviewers, symposium and workshop participants, students, and instructors. Throughout the revision process, we steered this textbook and its teaching tools in the manner you directed. As you'll find, the new edition offers a rich set of features—especially digital features—to improve student learning and assist instructor teaching and grading. We believe you and your students will like what you find in this new edition.

Many talented educators and professionals have worked hard to create the materials for this product, and for their efforts, we're grateful. **We extend a special thank-you to our contributing and technology supplement authors,** who have worked so diligently to support this product:

Contributing Author: Kathleen O'Donnell, *Onondaga Community College*

Accuracy Checkers: Dave Krug, *Johnson County Community College;* Mark McCarthy, *East Carolina University;* Helen Roybark, *Radford University;* Barbara Schnathorst; and Beth Woods

LearnSmart Author: April Mohr, *Jefferson Community and Technical College, SW*

Interactive Presentations: Jeannie Folk, *College of DuPage*

PowerPoint Presentations: Beth Kane, *Northwestern University*

Instructor Resource Manual: Patricia Walczak, *Lansing Community College*

Test Bank Contributors: Anna Boulware, *St. Charles Community College,* and Brenda J. McVey, *University of Mississippi*

Digital Contributor, Connect Content, General Ledger Problems, and Exercise PowerPoints: Kathleen O'Donnell, *Onondaga Community College*

In addition to the invaluable help from the colleagues listed above, we thank the entire *FinMan,* 6e team at McGraw-Hill Education: Tim Vertovec, Steve Schuetz, Michelle Nolte, Lindsey Schauer, Lori Koetters, Ann Torbert, Brad Parkins, Patricia Plumb, Xin Lin, Kevin Moran, Debra Kubiak, Carol Bielski, Keri Johnson, DeAnna Dausener, Sarah Evertson, Ben Pearsall, Brian Nacik, Ron Nelms, and Daryl Horrocks. We could not have published this new edition without your efforts.

John J. Wild *Ken W. Shaw* *Barbara Chiappetta*

connect | ACCOUNTING Easy to Use. Proven Effective.

McGraw-Hill *CONNECT ACCOUNTING*

McGraw-Hill *Connect Accounting* is a digital teaching and learning environment that gives students the means to better connect with their coursework, with their instructors, and with the important concepts they will need to know for success now and in the future. With *Connect Accounting,* instructors can easily deliver assignments, quizzes, and tests online. Students can review course material and practice important skills.

McGraw-Hill *Connect Accounting* provides all of the following learning and teaching resources:

- SmartBook, powered by LearnSmart
- Auto-graded online homework
- General ledger problems
- Auto-graded Excel simulations
- Interactive Presentations
- Guided Examples

In short, *Connect Accounting* offers students powerful tools and features that optimize their time and energy, enabling them to focus on learning.

SmartBook, Powered by LearnSmart

SMARTBOOK® McGraw-Hill LearnSmart® is the market-leading adaptive study resource that is proven to strengthen memory recall, increase class retention, and boost grades. LearnSmart allows students to study more efficiently because they are made aware of what they know and don't know.

SmartBook®, which is powered by LearnSmart, is the first and only adaptive reading experience designed to change the way students read and learn. It creates a personalized reading experience by highlighting the most impactful concepts a student needs to learn at that moment in time. As a student engages with SmartBook, the reading experience continuously adapts by highlighting content based on what the student knows and doesn't know. This ensures that the focus is on the content he or she needs to learn, while simultaneously promoting long-term retention of material.

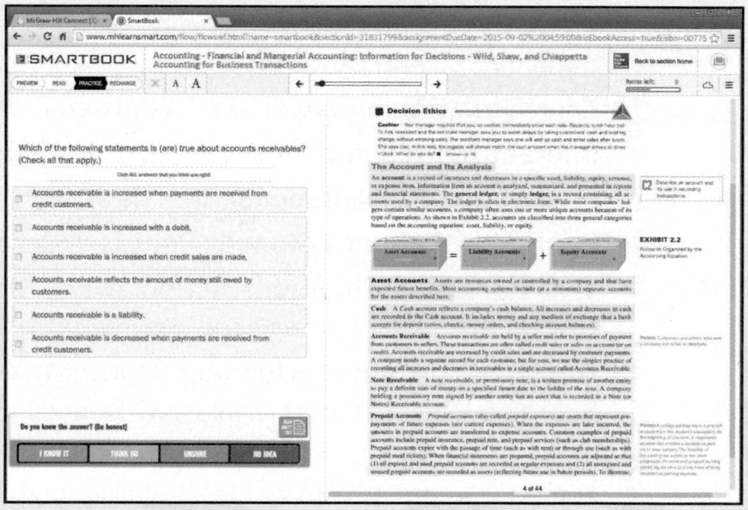

Use SmartBook's real-time reports to quickly identify the concepts that require more attention from individual students—or the entire class. The end result? Students are more engaged with course content, can better prioritize their time, and come to class ready to participate.

Tailored to You.

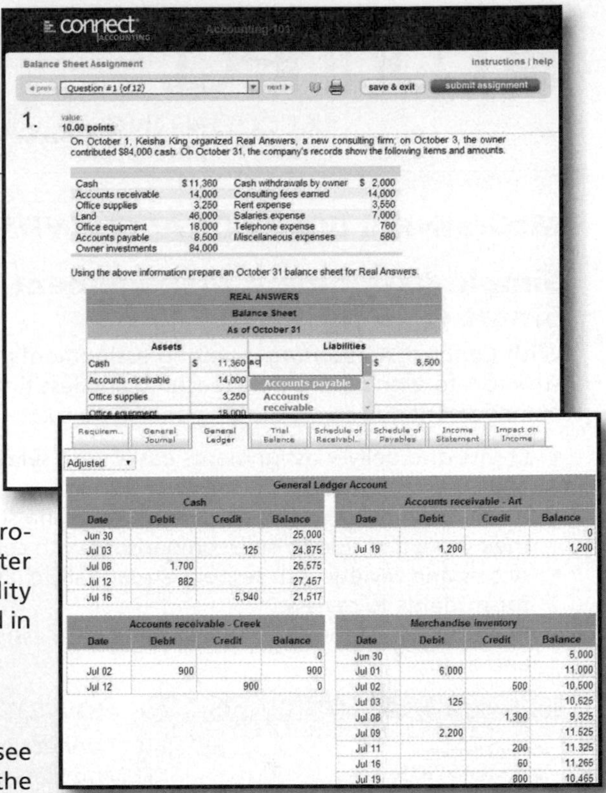

Online Assignments

Connect Accounting helps students learn more efficiently by providing feedback and practice material when they need it, where they need it. *Connect* grades homework automatically and gives immediate feedback on any questions students may have missed. Our assignable, gradable end-of-chapter content includes a general journal application that looks and feels more like what you would find in a general ledger software package. Also, select questions have been redesigned to test students' knowledge more fully. They now include tables for students to work through rather than requiring that all calculations be done off-line. McGraw-Hill's redesigned student interface provides a real-world feel to interactive assignments and end-of-chapter assessment content. This robust accounting software allows for flexibility in learning styles and provides opportunities for courses to be delivered in traditional, online, and blended settings.

General Ledger Problems

New General Ledger problems for select questions enable students to see how transactions post from the general journal all the way through the financial statements. It provides a much-improved experience for students working with accounting cycle questions. Students' work in the general journal is automatically posted to the ledger, navigation is much simpler, scrolling is no longer an issue, and students can easily link back to their original entries simply by clicking the ledger if edits are needed. Many questions now have critical thinking components added, to maximize students' foundational knowledge of accounting concepts and principles.

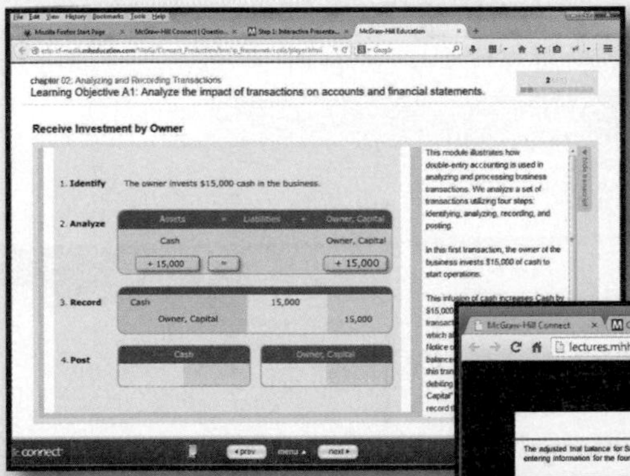

Interactive Presentations

Interactive Presentations provide engaging narratives of all chapter learning objectives in an assignable interactive online format. They follow the structure of the text and are organized to match the specific learning objectives within each chapter. While the Interactive Presentations are not meant to replace the textbook, they provide additional explanation and enhancement of material from the text chapter, allowing students to learn, study, and practice at their own pace, with instant feedback.

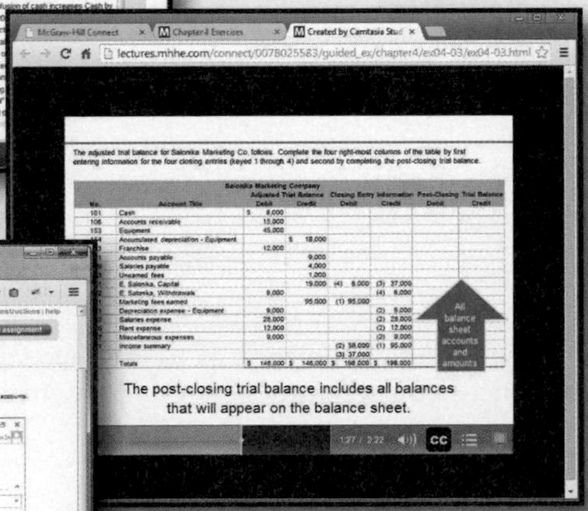

Guided Examples

The Guided Examples in *Connect Accounting* provide a narrated, animated, step-by-step walk-through of select exercises similar to those assigned. These short presentations, which can be turned on or off by instructors, provide reinforcement when students need it most.

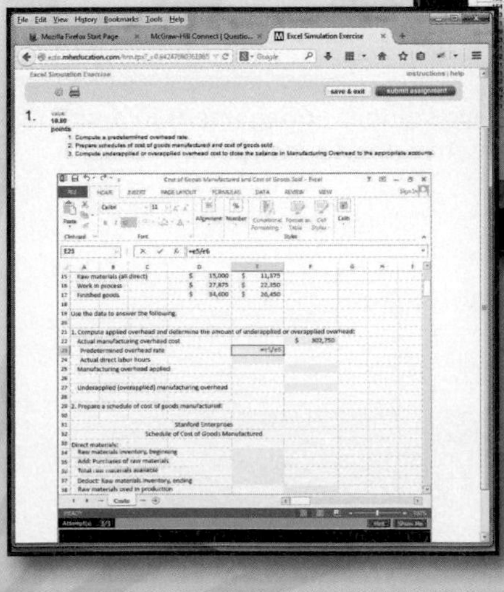

Excel Simulations

Simulated Excel questions, assignable within *Connect Accounting,* allow students to practice their Excel skills—such as basic formulas and formatting—within the context of accounting. These questions feature animated, narrated Help and Show Me tutorials (when enabled), as well as automatic feedback and grading for both students and professors.

connect® | ACCOUNTING

Easy to Use. Proven Effective.

McGraw-Hill *CONNECT ACCOUNTING* Features

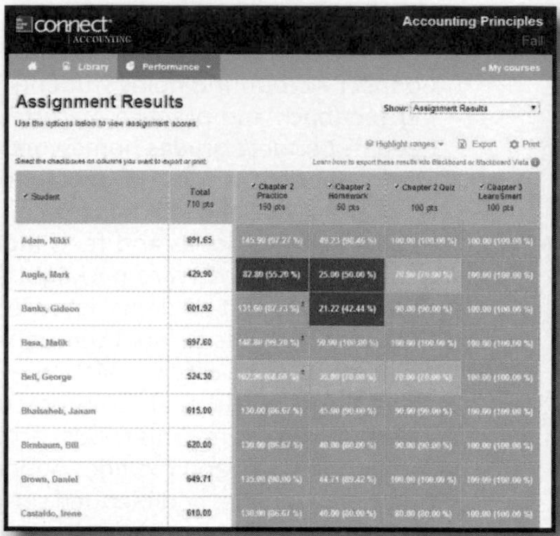

Simple Assignment Management and Smart Grading

With *Connect Accounting,* creating assignments is easier than ever, enabling instructors to spend more time teaching and less time managing. Simple assignment management and smart grading allow you to:

- Create and deliver assignments easily with selectable end-of-chapter questions and Test Bank items.
- Have assignments scored automatically, giving students immediate feedback on their work and side-by-side comparisons with correct answers.
- Access and review each response, manually change grades, or leave comments for students to review.
- Reinforce classroom concepts with practice assignments and instant quizzes and exams.

Powerful Instructor and Student Reports

Connect Accounting keeps instructors informed about how each student, section, and class is performing, allowing for more productive use of lecture and office hours. The progress-tracking function enables you to:

- View scored work immediately and track individual or group performance with assignment and grade reports.
- Access an instant view of student or class performance relative to learning objectives.
- Collect data and generate reports required by many accreditation organizations, such as AACSB and AICPA.

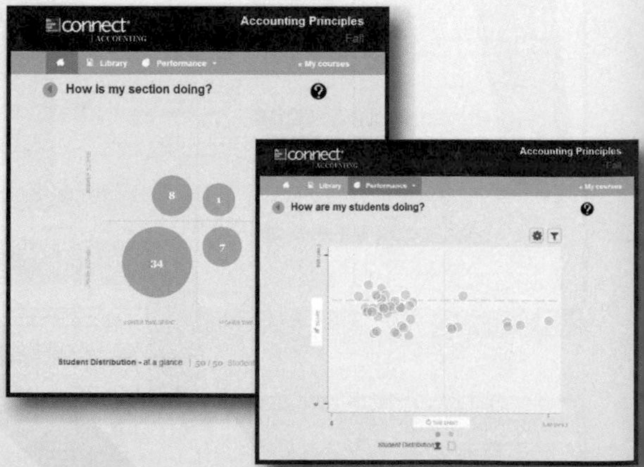

Connect Insight

The first and only analytics tool of its kind, McGraw-Hill Connect® Insight is a series of visual data displays—each framed by an intuitive question—to provide at-a-glance information about how your class is doing.

Connect Insight provides a quick analysis on five key insights, available at a moment's notice from your tablet device:

- How are my students doing?
- How is my section doing?
- How is this student doing?
- How are my assignments going?
- How is this assignment going?

Instructor Library

The *Connect Accounting* Instructor Library is a repository for additional resources to improve student engagement in and out of class. You can select and use any asset that enhances your lecture. The *Connect Accounting* Instructor Library includes:

- Presentation slides.
- Animated PowerPoint exhibits and exercises.
- Solutions Manual.
- Test Bank.
- Instructor's Resource Manual.

The *Connect Accounting* Instructor Library also allows you to upload your own files.

For more information about *Connect Accounting,* go to **http://connect.mheducation.com,** or contact your local McGraw-Hill Higher Education representative.

Tailored to You.

Other Technology Offered by McGraw-Hill

Tegrity Campus: Lectures 24/7

Tegrity Campus is a service that makes class time available 24/7 by automatically capturing every lecture. With a simple one-click start-and-stop process, you capture all computer screens and corresponding audio in a format that is easily searchable, frame by frame. Students can replay any part of any recorded class with easy-to-use browser-based viewing on a PC, Mac, or mobile device.

Help turn your students' study time into learning moments immediately supported by your lecture. With Tegrity Campus, you also increase intent listening and class participation by easing students' concerns about note-taking.

To learn more about Tegrity, watch a two-minute Flash demo at **http://tegritycampus.mhhe.com.**

McGraw-Hill Campus

McGraw-Hill Campus® is a new one-stop teaching and learning experience available to users of any learning management system. This institutional service allows faculty and students to enjoy single sign-on (SSO) access to all McGraw-Hill Higher Education materials, including the award-winning McGraw-Hill *Connect* platform, from directly within the institution's website. To learn more about McGraw-Hill Campus, visit **http://mhcampus.mhhe.com.**

Custom Publishing through Create

McGraw-Hill Create™ is a self-service website that allows instructors to create custom course materials by drawing upon McGraw-Hill's comprehensive, cross-disciplinary content. Instructors can add their own content quickly and easily and tap into other rights-secured, third-party sources as well, then arrange the content in a way that makes the most sense for their course.

Through Create, you can:

- Combine material from different sources and even upload your own content.
- Personalize your product with the course name and information.
- Choose the best format for your students—color print, black-and-white print, or eBook.
- Edit and update your course materials as often as you'd like.

Begin creating now at **www.mcgrawhillcreate.com.**

ALEKS: A Superior, Student-Friendly Accounting Experience

Artificial intelligence: Fills knowledge gaps.

Cycle of learning and assessment: Increases learning momentum and engages students.

Customizable curriculum: Aligns with your course syllabi and textbooks.

Dynamic, automated reports: Monitors detailed student and class progress.

To learn more, visit **www.aleks.com/highered/business.**

CourseSmart

CourseSmart is a way for faculty to find and review eTextbooks. It's also a great option for students who are interested in accessing their course materials digitally and saving money.

CourseSmart offers thousands of the most commonly adopted textbooks across hundreds of courses from a wide variety of higher education publishers. With the CourseSmart eTextbook, students can save up to 45 percent off the cost of a print book, reduce their impact on the environment, and access powerful web tools for learning. CourseSmart is an online eTextbook, which means users access and view their textbook online when connected to the Internet. Students can also print sections of the book for maximum portability. CourseSmart eTextbooks are available in one standard online reader with full text search, notes and highlighting, and e-mail tools for sharing notes between classmates. For more information on CourseSmart, go to **www.coursesmart.com.**

McGraw-Hill Customer Experience Group Contact Information

At McGraw-Hill, we understand that getting the most from new technology can be challenging. That's why our services don't stop after you purchase our products. You can contact our Product Specialists 24 hours a day to get product training online. Or you can search the knowledge bank of Frequently Asked Questions on our support website. For customer support, call **800-331-5094** or visit **www.mhhe.com/support.**

Innovative Textbook Features . . .

Using Accounting for Decisions

Whether we prepare, analyze, or apply accounting information, one skill remains essential: decision making. To help develop good decision-making habits and to illustrate the relevance of accounting, we use a pedagogical framework we call the Decision Center. This framework encompasses a variety of approaches and subject areas, giving students insight into every aspect of business decision making; see the four nearby examples for the different types of decision boxes, including those that relate to fraud. Answers to Decision Maker and Ethics boxes are at the end of each chapter.

Decision Insight

Women Entrepreneurs SPANX has given more than $20 million to charity. The Center for Women's Business Research reports that women-owned businesses, such as SPANX (owner Sara Blakely in photo), are growing and that they:

- Total approximately 11 million and employ nearly 20 million workers.
- Generate $2.5 trillion in annual sales and tend to embrace technology.
- Are philanthropic—70% of owners volunteer at least once per month.
- Are more likely funded by individual investors (73%) than venture firms (15%). ■

Paul Morigi/Getty Images for FORTUNE

Decision Ethics

Payables Manager As a new accounts payable manager, you are being trained by the outgoing manager. She explains that the system prepares checks for amounts net of favorable cash discounts, and the checks are dated the last day of the discount period. She also tells you that checks are not mailed until five days later, adding that "the company gets free use of cash for an extra five days, and our department looks better. When a supplier complains, we blame the computer system and the mailroom." Do you continue this payment policy? ■ [Answers follow the chapter's Summary.]

Profit Margin and Current Ratio **Decision Analysis**

Profit Margin

A useful measure of a company's operating results is the ratio of its net income to net sales. This ratio is called **profit margin,** or *return on sales,* and is computed as in Exhibit 3.22.

$$\text{Profit margin} = \frac{\text{Net income}}{\text{Net sales}}$$

EXHIBIT 3.22
Profit Margin

This ratio is interpreted as reflecting the percent of profit in each dollar of sales. To illustrate how we compute and use profit margin, let's look at the results of **Limited Brands, Inc.,** in Exhibit 3.23 for its fiscal years 2009 through 2013.

A1 Compute profit margin and describe its use in analyzing company performance.

Decision Maker

Supplier A retailer requests to purchase supplies on credit from your company. You have no prior experience with this retailer. The retailer's current ratio is 2.1, its acid-test ratio is 0.5, and inventory makes up most of its current assets. Do you extend credit? ■ [Answers follow the chapter's Summary.]

> "Authors do a good job of relating material to real-life situations and putting students in the decision-maker role."
>
> **—MORGAN ROCKETT, Moberly Area Community College**

Chapter Preview

Each chapter opens with a visual chapter preview. Students can begin their reading with a clear understanding of what they will learn and when, allowing them to stay more focused and organized along the way. Learning objective numbers highlight the location of related content.

Chapter Preview

MERCHANDISING ACTIVITIES	MERCHANDISING PURCHASES	MERCHANDISING SALES	MERCHANDISE REPORTING AND ANALYSIS
C1 Reporting income and inventory	P1 Accounting for:	P2 Accounting for:	P3 Adjusting and closing for merchandisers
C2 Operating cycles and inventory system	Purchase discounts	Sales of merchandise	P4 Multiple-step and single-step income statements
	Purchase returns and allowances	Sales discounts	A1 Acid-test analysis
	Transportation costs	Sales returns and allowances	A2 Gross margin analysis

CAP Model

The Conceptual/Analytical/Procedural (CAP) Model allows courses to be specially designed to meet the teaching needs of a diverse faculty. This model identifies learning objectives, textual materials, assignments, and test items by C, A, or P, allowing different instructors to teach from the same materials, yet easily customize their courses toward a conceptual, analytical, or procedural approach (or a combination thereof) based on personal preferences.

Learning Objectives

CONCEPTUAL

C1 Explain the steps in processing transactions and the role of source documents.

C2 Describe an account and its use in recording transactions.

C3 Describe a ledger and a chart of accounts.

C4 Define *debits* and *credits* and explain double-entry accounting.

ANALYTICAL

A1 Analyze the impact of transactions on accounts and financial statements.

A2 Compute the debt ratio and describe its use in analyzing financial condition.

PROCEDURAL

P1 Record transactions in a journal and post entries to a ledger.

P2 Prepare and explain the use of a trial balance.

P3 Prepare financial statements from business transactions.

Bring Accounting to Life

NEED-TO-KNOW 1-5

Financial Statements

P2

Prepare the (a) income statement, (b) statement of owner's equity, and (c) balance sheet, for **Apple** using the following condensed data from its fiscal year ended September 28, 2013. (All $s are in millions.)

Accounts payable	$ 22,367	Investments and other assets	$163,042
Other liabilities	61,084	Land and equipment	16,597
Cost of sales and other expenses	119,724	Selling and other expenses	14,149
Cash	14,259	Accounts receivable	13,102
Owner, Capital, Sep. 29, 2012	118,210	Net income	37,037
Withdrawals in fiscal year 2013	31,698	Owner, Capital, Sep. 28, 2013	123,549
Revenues	170,910		

Solution

APPLE
Income Statement
For Fiscal Year Ended September 28, 2013

Revenues		$170,910
Expenses		
Cost of sales and other expenses	119,724	
Selling and other expenses	14,149	

Need-to-Know Illustrations

New in this edition are several Need-to-Know illustrations located at key junctures in each chapter. These illustrations pose questions about the material just presented—content that students "need to know" to successfully learn accounting. Accompanying solutions walk students through key procedures and analysis necessary to be successful with homework and test materials. Need-to-Know illustrations are supplemented with narrated, animated, step-by-step walk-through videos led by an instructor and available via *Connect*.

Global View

The Global View section explains international accounting practices relating to the material covered in that chapter. The aim of this section is to describe accounting practices and to identify the similarities and differences in international accounting practices versus those in the United States. As we move toward global convergence in accounting practices, and as we witness the likely convergence of U.S. GAAP to IFRS, the importance of student familiarity with international accounting grows. This innovative section helps us begin down that path. This section is purposefully located at the end of each chapter so that each instructor can decide what emphasis, if at all, is to be assigned to it.

GLOBAL VIEW

This section discusses similarities and differences between U.S. GAAP and IFRS in accounting and reporting for merchandise purchases and sales, and for the income statement.

Accounting for Merchandise Purchases and Sales Both U.S. GAAP and IFRS include broad and similar guidance for the accounting of merchandise purchases and sales. Specifically, all of the transactions presented and illustrated in this chapter are accounted for identically under the two systems. The closing process for merchandisers also is identical for U.S. GAAP and IFRS. In the next chapter we describe how inventory valuation can, in some cases, be different for the two systems.

Income Statement Presentation We explained that net income, profit, and earnings refer to the same (*bottom line*) item. However, IFRS tends to use the term *profit* more than any other term, whereas U.S. statements tend to use *net income* more than any other term. Both U.S. GAAP and IFRS income statements begin with the net sales or net revenues (*top line*) item. For merchandisers and manufacturers, this is followed by cost of goods sold. The presentation is similar for the remaining items with the following differences.

- U.S. GAAP offers little guidance about the presentation or order of expenses. IFRS requires separate disclosures for financing costs (interest expense), income tax expense, and some other special items.
- Both systems require separate disclosure of items when their size, nature, or frequency are important.
- IFRS permits expenses to be presented by their function or their nature. U.S. GAAP provides no direction but the SEC requires presentation by function.
- Neither U.S. GAAP nor IFRS define *operating* income, which results in latitude in reporting.
- IFRS permits alternative income measures on the income statement; U.S. GAAP does not.

VOLKSWAGEN **Volkswagen Group** provides the following example of income statement reporting. We see the separate disclosure of finance costs, taxes, and other items. We also see the unusual practice of using the minus

Sustainability and Accounting The founders of **Proof Eyewear**, as introduced in this chapter's opening feature, assert that "sustainability is a key test in every product decision . . . it has to have an aspect of sustainability to it or we just won't develop it." This level of commitment to sustainability is impressive. The founders also impose a "three-pillar foundation" in everything they do, which is graphically portrayed below. Some of their recent activities include: (1) planting a tree for each pair of sunglasses sold on Earth Day, (2) financing a portion of sight-saving surgeries for each pair of frames purchased, (3) using only wood from sustainably managed forests and rejecting endangered wood, and (4) contributing to reforestation efforts.

Sustainability and Accounting

New in this edition are brief sections that highlight the importance of sustainability within the broader context of global accounting (and accountability). Companies increasingly address sustainability in their public reporting and consider the sustainability accounting standards (from the Sustainability Accounting Standards Board) and the expectations of our global society. These boxes, located near the end of the Global View section, cover different aspects of sustainability, often within the context of the chapter's featured entrepreneurial company.

"I like the layout of the text and the readability. The illustrations and comics in the book make the text seem less intimidating and boring for students. The PowerPoint slides are easy to understand and use, the pictorials are great, and the text has great coverage of accounting material. The addition of IFRS information and the updates to the opening stories are great. I like that the decision insights are about businesses the students can relate to (i.e., Facebook, women start-up businesses, etc.)."

—JEANNIE LIU, Chaffey College

Outstanding Assignment Material . . .

Once a student has finished reading the chapter, how well he or she retains the material can depend greatly on the questions, exercises, and problems that reinforce it. This book leads the way in comprehensive, accurate assignments.

Comprehensive Need-to-Know Problems present both a problem and a complete solution, allowing students to review the entire problem-solving process and achieve success.

Water Sports Company (WSC) patented and successfully test-marketed a new product. To expand its ability to produce and market the new product, WSC needs to raise \$800,000 of financing. On January 1, 2015, the company obtained the money in two ways:

NEED-TO-KNOW
COMPREHENSIVE

a. WSC signed a \$400,000, 10% installment note to be repaid with five equal annual installments to be made on December 31 of 2015 through 2019.
b. WSC issued five-year bonds with a par value of \$400,000. The bonds have a 12% annual contract rate and pay interest on June 30 and December 31. The bonds' annual market rate is 10% as of January 1, 2015.

Required

1. For the installment note, (*a*) compute the size of each annual payment, (*b*) prepare an amortization table such as Exhibit 14.14, and (*c*) prepare the journal entry for the first payment.
2. For the bonds, (*a*) compute their issue price; (*b*) prepare the January 1, 2015, journal entry to record their issuance; (*c*) prepare an amortization table using the straight-line method; (*d*) prepare the June 30, 2015, journal entry to record the first interest payment; and (*e*) prepare a journal entry to record retiring the bonds at a \$416,000 call price on January 1, 2017.
3.[B] Redo parts 2(*c*), 2(*d*), and 2(*e*) assuming the bonds are amortized using the effective interest method.

PLANNING THE SOLUTION

- For the installment note, divide the borrowed amount by the annuity factor (from Table B.3) using the 10% rate and five payments to compute the amount of each payment. Prepare a table similar to Exhibit 14.14 and use the numbers in the table's first line for the journal entry.
- Compute the bonds' issue price by using the market rate to find the present value of their cash flows (use tables found in Appendix B). Then use this result to record the bonds' issuance. Next, prepare an amortization table like Exhibit 14.11 (and Exhibit 14B.2) and use it to get the numbers needed for the journal entry. Also use the table to find the carrying value as of the date of the bonds' retirement that you need for the journal entry.

SOLUTION

Part 1: Installment Note

a. Annual payment = Note balance/PV Annuity factor = \$400,000/3.7908 = \$105,519 (The present value annuity factor is for five payments and a rate of 10%.)
b. An amortization table for the long-term note payable follows.

Chapter Summaries provide students with a review organized by learning objectives. Chapter Summaries are a component of the CAP model (see page x), which recaps each conceptual, analytical, and procedural objective.

Key Terms

Account	Debit	Posting
Account balance	Debt ratio	Posting reference (PR) column
Balance column account	Double-entry accounting	Source documents
Chart of accounts	General journal	T-account
Compound journal entry	General ledger	Trial balance
Credit	Journal	Unearned revenue
Creditors	Journalizing	

Key Terms are bolded in the text and repeated at the end of the chapter. A complete glossary of key terms is available online through *Connect Accounting.*

Multiple Choice Quiz Answers at end of chapter

1. A company forgot to record accrued and unpaid employee wages of \$350,000 at period-end. This oversight would
   a. Understate net income by \$350,000.
   b. Overstate net income by \$350,000.
   c. Have no effect on net income.
   d. Overstate assets by \$350,000.
   e. Understate assets by \$350,000.
2. Prior to recording adjusting entries, the Supplies account has a \$450 debit bal...

4. On November 1, 2015, Stockton Co. receives \$3,600 cash from Hans Co. for consulting services to be provided evenly over the period November 1, 2015, to April 30, 2016—at which time Stockton credited \$3,600 to Unearned Consulting Fees. The adjusting entry on December 31, 2015 (Stockton's year-end) would include a
   a. Debit to Unearned Consulting Fees for \$1,200.
   b. Debit to Unearned Consulting Fees for \$2,400.
   c. Credit to Consulting Fees Earned for \$2,400.

Multiple Choice Quiz questions quickly test chapter knowledge before a student moves on to complete Quick Studies, Exercises, and Problems.

connect

QUICK STUDY

QS 3-1
Periodic reporting
C1

Choose from the following list of terms/phrases to best complete the statements below.

a. Fiscal year	d. Accounting period	g. Natural business year
b. Timeliness	e. Annual financial statements	h. Time period assumption
c. Calendar year	f. Interim financial statements	i. Quarterly statements

1. ______ presumes that an organization's activities can be divided into specific time periods.
2. Financial reports covering a one-year period are known as ______.
3. A ______ consists of any 12 consecutive months.
4. A ______ consists of 12 consecutive months ending on December 31.
5. The value of information is often linked to its ______.

Quick Study assignments are short exercises that often focus on one learning objective. Most are included in *Connect Accounting.* There are at least 10–15 Quick Study assignments per chapter.

Exercises are one of this book's many strengths and a competitive advantage. There are at least 10–15 per chapter, and most are included in *Connect Accounting.*

connect

EXERCISES

Exercise 1-1
Classifying activities reflected in the accounting system
C1

Accounting is an information and measurement system that identifies, records, and communicates relevant, reliable, and comparable information about an organization's business activities. Classify the following activities as part of the identifying (I), recording (R), or communicating (C) aspects of accounting.

______ 1. Analyzing and interpreting reports.	______ 5. Preparing financial statements.
______ 2. Presenting financial information.	______ 6. Seeing revenues generated from a service.
______ 3. Keeping a log of service costs.	______ 7. Observing employee tasks behind a product.
______ 4. Measuring the costs of a product.	______ 8. Registering cash sales of products sold.

PROBLEM SET A

Problem 2-1A
Preparing and posting journal entries; preparing a trial balance
C3 C4 A1 P1 P2

Karla Tanner opens a w...
in its first month of ope...
April 1 Tanner inves...

PROBLEM SET B

Problem 2-1B
Preparing and posting journal entries; preparing a trial balance
C3 C4 A1 P1 P2

...hese transactions in September.
...th office equipment valued at \$15,000
...for office space. (*Hint:* Debit Prepaid
...equipment and \$2,400 in office sup-
...ly received \$3,280 cash.

Problem Sets A & B are proven problems that can be assigned as homework or for in-class projects. All problems are coded according to the CAP model (see page x), and Set A is included in *Connect Accounting.*

Helps Students Master Key Concepts

Beyond the Numbers exercises ask students to use accounting figures and understand their meaning. Students also learn how accounting applies to a variety of business situations. These creative and fun exercises are all new or updated and are divided into sections:

- Reporting in Action
- Comparative Analysis
- Ethics Challenge
- Communicating in Practice
- Taking It to the Net
- Teamwork in Action
- Hitting the Road
- Entrepreneurial Decision
- Global Decision

Beyond the Numbers

REPORTING IN ACTION
A1 P4

APPLE

BTN 3-1 Refer to Apple's financial statements in Appendix A to answer the following.

1. Identify and write down the revenue recognition principle as explained in the chapter.
2. Review Apple's footnotes (in Appendix A and/or from its 10-K on its website) to discover how it applies the revenue recognition principle and when it recognizes revenue. Report what you discover.
3. What is Apple's profit margin for fiscal years ended September 28, 2013, and September 29, 2012.
4. For the fiscal year ended September 28, 2013, what amount is credited to Income Summary to summarize its revenues earned?
5. For the fiscal year ended September 28, 2013, what amount is debited to Income Summary to summarize its expenses incurred?
6. For the fiscal year ended September 28, 2013, what is the balance of its Income Summary account before it is closed?

Serial Problems use a continuous running case study to illustrate chapter concepts in a familiar context. The Serial Problem can be followed continuously from the first chapter or picked up at any later point in the book; enough information is provided to ensure students can get right to work.

This serial problem began in Chapter 1 and continues through most of the book. If previous chapter segments were not completed, the serial problem can still begin at this point. It is helpful, but not necessary, to use the Working Papers that accompany the book.

SERIAL PROBLEM
Business Solutions
P1 P2 P3 P4 P5

SP 3 After the success of the company's first two months, Santana Rey continues to operate Business Solutions. (Transactions for the first two months are described in the Chapter 2 serial problem.) The November 30, 2015, unadjusted trial balance of Business Solutions (reflecting its transactions for October and November of 2015) follows.

No.	Account Title	Debit	Credit
101	Cash	$38,264	
106	Accounts receivable	12,618	
126	Computer supplies	2,545	
128	Prepaid insurance	2,220	
131	Prepaid rent	3,300	
163	Office equipment	8,000	
164	Accumulated depreciation—Office equipment		$ 0

"The serial problems are excellent.... I like the continuation of the same problem to the next chapters if applicable. I use the Quick Studies as practice problems. . . . Students have commented that this really works for them if they work (these questions) before attempting the assigned exercises and problems. I also like the discussion (questions) and make this an assignment. You have done an outstanding job presenting accounting to our students."

—JERRI TITTLE, Rose State College

General Ledger Problems New General Ledger problems enable students to see how transactions post. Students can track an amount in any financial statement all the way back to the original journal entry. Critical thinking components then challenge students to analyze the business activities in the problem.

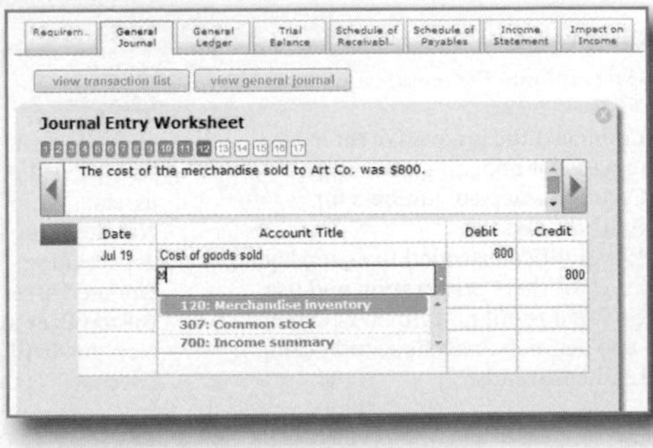

Using transactions from the following assignments, prepare journal entries for each transaction and identify the financial statement impact of each entry. The financial statements are automatically generated based on the journal entries recorded.

GENERAL LEDGER PROBLEM
Available in Connect
connect | ACCOUNTING

GL 2-1 Transactions from the FastForward illustration in this chapter
GL 2-2 Based on Exercise 2-9
GL 2-3 Based on Exercise 2-12
GL 2-4 Based on Problem 2-1A

Using transactions from the following assignments, record journal entries, create financial statements, and assess the impact of each transaction on financial statements.

The End of the Chapter Is Only the Beginning Our valuable and proven assignments aren't just confined to the book. From problems that require technological solutions to materials found exclusively online, this book's end-of-chapter material is fully integrated with its technology package.

connect | ACCOUNTING

- Quick Studies, Exercises, and Problems available in *Connect* are marked with an icon.
- Assignments that focus on global accounting practices and companies are often identified with an icon.
- Assignments that involve decision analysis are identified with an icon.

Content Revisions Enhance Learning

This edition's revisions are driven by feedback from instructors and students.

- Many new, revised, and updated assignments throughout, including serial problem and entrepreneurial assignments.
- New Need-to-Know illustrations added to each chapter, at key junctures to reinforce key topics.
- New Sustainability section for each chapter, with examples linked to the company featured in the chapter opener.
- New annual reports and comparison assignments: Apple, Google, and Samsung.
- New streamlined opening layout for each chapter.
- Revised art program, visual infographics, and text layout.
- Updated ratio/tool analysis, using data from well-known firms.
- New General Ledger questions added to most chapters.
- New material on International Financial Reporting Standards (IFRS).
- New and revised entrepreneurial examples and elements.
- New technology content integrated and referenced in the book.
- Revised terminology from *goods in process* to *work in process*.
- Changed the title of *Manufacturing Statement* to *Schedule of Cost of Goods Manufactured* due to its use in practice.

Chapter 1

Apple **NEW opener.**
Added titles to revenue and expense entries in columnar layout of transaction analysis.
Streamlined section on Dodd-Frank.
Bulleted presentation of accounting principles and fraud triangle.
Deleted world map of IFRS coverage.
Updated salary information.
New discussion of FASB and IASB convergence.
Updated return on assets for Dell.

Chapter 2

Akola Project **NEW opener.**
New layout showing financial statements drawn from trial balance.
New preliminary coverage of classified and unclassified balance sheets.
Changed selected numbers for FastForward.
Revised Piaggio's (IFRS) balance sheet.
Updated debt ratio section using Skechers.

Chapter 3

International Princess Project **NEW opener.**
Enhanced the innovative three-step process for adjusting accounts.
Changed selected numbers for FastForward.
New multicolor-coded five-step layout for work sheet preparation and use.
Updated profit margin and current ratio decision analysis section using Limited Brands.

Chapter 4

Sseko Designs **NEW opener.**
Enhanced exhibit on transportation costs and FOB terms.
New T-accounts to highlight inventory flow.
Enhanced two-step process for recording merchandise sales.
Updated gross margin and quick ratios section using JCPenney.

Chapter 5

Proof Eyewear **NEW opener.**
Streamlined inventory presentation.
Added several new T-accounts to facilitate learning of inventory flow.
New explanatory notes added to exhibits as learning aids.
Updated inventory ratios section using Toys "R" Us.
Simplified presentation and exhibits for periodic inventory methods.

Chapter 6

Dandelion Chocolate **NEW opener.**
New learning notes added to bank reconciliation.
New chart for timing differences for bank reconciliation.
Updated receivables analysis using Hasbro and Mattel.

Chapter 7

Skai Blue Media **NEW opener.**
Enhanced three-step process for estimating allowance for uncollectibles.
New T-accounts to enhance learning of receivables.
Enhanced infographic on methods to estimate bad debts.
New notes on pros/cons of allowance vs. direct write-off.
Updated receivables analysis using Dell and HP.

Chapter 8

New Glarus Brewing Co. **NEW opener.**
Rearranged presentation of plant assets.
New learning notes on book value and depreciation.
Updated asset turnover analysis using Boston Beer and Molson Coors.
New goodwill example using Facebook's purchase of WhatsApp.

Chapter 9

Uncharted Play **NEW opener.**
Updated payroll rates to 2014.
New explanation of *Additional Medicare Tax*.
Updated FUTA rate.
Clarified bonus explanation and computations.
Enhanced payroll reports and exhibits.

Chapter 10

Stone + Cloth **NEW opener.**
New learning notes for bond interest computations.
New color highlighting for learning amortization.
New T-accounts for bond amortization.
Updated debt-to-equity analysis using Amazon.

Chapter 11

Alibaba Group **NEW opener.**
New dividend taxation information.
New learning notes for computations.
Updated PE and dividend yield ratios for Amazon and Altria.

Chapter 12

LSTN **NEW opener.**
New infographics for operating, investing, and financing activities.
New linkage of cash flow classifications to balance sheet.
Simplified discussion of noncash investing and financing.
New, simplified preparation steps for statement of cash flows.
New, overall summary T-account for preparing statement of cash flows.
New reconstruction entries to help determine cash.
Updated cash flow analysis using Nike.
3 new Quick Studies and 3 revised Exercises.

Chapter 13

Motley Fool **REVISED opener.**
New companies—Apple, Google, and Samsung—throughout the text and exhibits.
New boxed discussion of the role of financial statement analysis to fight and prevent fraud.
Enhanced horizontal and vertical ratio analysis using new companies and industry data.
New analysis for segment data.

Chapter 14

SunSaluter **NEW opener.**
Revised discussions of the purpose of managerial accounting and cost classifications and their uses.
Reduced number of cost classifications from five to three.
Revised exhibit and example of direct vs. indirect costs.
Added new exhibit comparing the balance sheet and income statement for different types of companies.
Reduced level of detail in exhibit on income statement reporting.
Revised discussion of the flow of manufacturing costs.
New four-step process to illustrate the schedule of cost of goods manufactured (COGM).
Added T-accounts to show the flow of costs for the COGM.
Added a third column to the schedule of COGM, for enhanced presentation.
Simplified exhibit on cost flows across the financial statements.
New discussion of corporate social responsibility.
Added 6 Quick Studies and 4 Exercises.

Chapter 15

Middleton Made Knives **NEW opener.**
New discussion of differences between job order and process operations.
Moved discussion of job order costing for services to later in chapter.
Revised/simplified discussions of cost flows and job cost sheets.
Simplified journal entries for labor costs.
New exhibits to show postings of product cost journal entries to general ledger accounts and to job cost sheets.
Revised exhibits on materials and labor cost flows.
Revised text and new exhibit on four-step process to record overhead.
Revised discussion of applying overhead and recording actual overhead.
Added new discussion and presentation of journal entries for indirect materials and indirect labor.
Added new exhibit showing calculations for overhead applied to individual jobs.
Added new exhibit on the flow of costs to general ledger accounts, the manufacturing statement, and the financial statements.
Added new schedule of cost of goods manufactured exhibit.
Added 2 Quick Studies and 2 Exercises.

Chapter 16

Kar's Nuts NEW opener.
Major change: Revised the overview exhibit of process operations and expanded the illustration to show *two departments.*
Major change: Combined coverage of direct labor and overhead into *conversion costs.*
Revised exhibits/examples to show fewer processes and simpler, more engaging products (tennis balls and trail mix).
Added discussion, with journal entries, of transfers of costs across departments.
Added discussion of multiple work in process (WIP) inventory accounts.
Revised discussion of job order vs. process costing.
Revised discussion, with new exhibit, on computation of equivalent units.
Added conversion costs per unit to equivalent units discussion.
Added a section differentiating the weighted-average and FIFO methods.
New exhibit showing units transferred out and units remaining in ending work in process inventory.
Added formula for computing equivalent units under the weighted-average method.
Moved discussion of journal entries to later in the chapter.
Revised the process costing summary report to focus on direct materials and conversion costs.
Revised journal entries to show two WIP Inventory accounts and to eliminate the Factory Payroll account.
Added discussion of Volkswagen's use of robotics in process operations.
Revised and added Comprehensive Need-to-Knows to reflect changes in chapter (including *two processes*).
New exhibits showing transfer of units and costs across departments, using T-accounts.
In the FIFO method appendix:

- Added discussion of differences between FIFO and weighted-average approaches to computing equivalent units.
- Added exhibits on computing equivalent units and cost per equivalent unit under FIFO.
- Revised discussion of applying four-step process using FIFO.

Added 16 Quick Studies and 7 Exercises.

Chapter 17

Suja Juice Company NEW opener.
Clarified departmental overhead rate method and ABC methods as four-step processes.
Re-graded heading levels to highlight plantwide and departmental overhead rate method topics.
Expanded discussion of examples used in the ABC application, to enhance clarity.
Revised Exhibit 17.16, separating Costs of Good Quality from Costs of Poor Quality, thus highlighting the Cost of Quality Report.
4 new Quick Studies, and some old Quick Studies repurposed to Exercises.

Chapter 18

Fast Yeti Custom Tees NEW opener.
Revised discussion of fixed and variable costs.
Revised discussion of *relevant range.*
Reorganized discussion of the high-low method as a three-step process.
Enhanced exhibit on high-low method.
Revised discussion of how changes in estimates affect break-even points.
Revised *target income* discussion to focus on pretax income.
Simplified exhibit on using the contribution margin income statement to compute sales needed for target income.
Revised discussion of sensitivity analyses, with examples of buying a new machine or increasing advertising.
Added exhibit on using the contribution margin income statement in sensitivity analysis.
Eliminated the *weighted-average contribution margin* method of computing multiproduct break-even.
Added two exhibits on calculations of *operating leverage.*
Added appendix on variable costing.
Added 5 Quick Studies and 6 Exercises.

Chapter 19

Happy Family Brands UPDATED opener.
Added new discussion of the three-step process to determine product selling price in the "Setting Prices" section.
Added short section on sources of data for CVP Analysis when preparing income statement under variable costing versus absorption costing.
Replaced previous break-even Decision Analysis example with special-order example using IceAge Company.
3 new Quick Studies and 4 new Exercises.

Chapter 20

Solben NEW opener.
Major change: Uses a *manufacturing company* as the example within the chapter. Budgeting for a *merchandising company* now appears in the chapter-end appendix.
Shortened/tightened section on budget process and administration.
Added section on the benefits of budgeting.
New section on the master budget differences between manufacturers and merchandisers.
Revised exhibit on the sequence of preparing the master budget for a *manufacturer.*
Reformatted sales budget exhibit.
Streamlined and reformatted several exhibits in Excel format.
Rewrote sections on preparing the direct materials, direct labor, and factory overhead budgets.
Clarified explanation of capital expenditures budget.
Slightly expanded section on preparation of the cash budget.
Added section on using the master budget.
In appendix, added new exhibit on the master budget sequence for a merchandiser.
Added 5 Quick Studies and 6 Exercises.

Chapter 21

Niner Bikes NEW opener.
Revised discussions of fixed and flexible budget performance reports.
Revised several flexible budget exhibits.
Revised discussion of setting standard costs.
Revised discussion of computing and analyzing cost variances.
Revised exhibits on computing direct materials and direct labor variances.
Revised sections on analyzing materials, labor, and overhead variances.
Simplified discussion of setting overhead standards.
Revised discussion of computing the predetermined overhead rate.
Revised exhibits on overhead variances and overhead variance report.
Revised discussion of sales variances in Decision Analysis.
Added learning objective for overhead spending and efficiency variances (in appendix).
In the appendix, added discussion, with an exhibit, on the standard costing income statement.
Added 7 Exercises.

Chapter 22

United by Blue UPDATED opener.
Added discussion of advantages and disadvantages of decentralization.
Reorganized discussion of cost, profit, and investment centers into a bulleted list, with examples using Kraft Foods Group.
Revised discussion and exhibit of responsibility accounting for cost centers.
Streamlined and clarified discussion and exhibits in the allocation of indirect expenses example.
Added discussion of the usefulness of departmental income statements in decision making.
Revised discussion of the use of return on investment and residual income in decision making.
Revised example of profit margin and investment turnover calculations, using Walt Disney Company
Added 3 Quick Studies, 5 Exercises, and 1 Problem.

Chapter 23

Charlie's Brownies UPDATED opener.
Expanded discussion and exhibits for short-term decisions, including additional business, make or buy, scrap or rework, sell or process further, sales mix, and segment elimination.
Added a Need-to-Know illustration for each short-term decision.
New Global View on segment elimination.
Added 3 Quick Studies.

Chapter 24

Adafruit Industries NEW opener.
Revised separate discussions of the accounting rate of return, net present value, and internal rate of return.
Updated graphic showing cost of capital estimates by industry.
Revised discussion of profitability index, with new exhibit.
Added 7 Quick Studies and 6 Exercises.

Appendix C

New three-step process for fair value adjustment.
New learning note for investee vs. investor securities.
New Google example for comprehensive income.
Updated return analysis using Gap.

Appendix D

New LLC example using STARZ.
New T-accounts to enhance learning of partnership capital.

Appendix E

Streamlined several sections.
Updated segment analysis using Callaway Golf.

Instructor Resources

Connect is your all-in-one location for a variety of instructor resources. You can create custom presentations from your own materials and access all of the following. Here's what you'll find there:

- **Instructor's Resource Manual**
  Written by April Mohr, Jefferson Community and Technical College, SW.
  This manual contains (for each chapter) a Lecture Outline, a chart linking all assignment materials to learning objectives, and additional visuals with transparency masters.
- **Solutions Manual**
  Written by John J. Wild, University of Wisconsin–Madison, and Ken W. Shaw, University of Missouri–Columbia.
- **Test Bank, Computerized Test Bank**
  Revised by James Racic, Lakeland Community College
- **PowerPoint® Presentations**
  Prepared by Anna Boulware, St. Charles Community College.
  Presentations allow for revision of lecture slide, and include a viewer, allowing screens to be shown with or without the software.
- **Exercise PowerPoints**
  Prepared by Kathleen O'Donnell, Onandaga Community College.
  Exercise PowerPoints are animated walk-throughs of end-of-chapter exercises that you can edit and customize for your classroom use. These presentations are a powerful tool for the smart classroom, allowing you to spend more time teaching and less time writing on the board.

Student Supplements

Working Papers
Vol. 1, Chapters 1–13
Available on demand through Create.

Vol. 2, Chapters 12–24
Available on demand through Create.

Written by John J. Wild.

***Connect Accounting* with LearnSmart Access Code Card**
ISBN: 9780077633059
MHID: 0077633059

"This textbook does address many learning styles and at the same time allows for many teaching styles ... our faculty have been very pleased with the continued revisions and supplements. From paper working papers ... to continually improved homework sites and ebooks. I'm a 'Wild' fan!"

—RITA HAYS, Southwestern Oklahoma State University

Meeting Accreditation Needs

Assurance of Learning Ready

Many educational institutions today are focused on the notion of assurance of learning, an important element of some accreditation standards. *Financial and Managerial Accounting* is designed specifically to support your assurance of learning initiatives with a simple, yet powerful solution. Each test bank question for *Financial and Managerial Accounting* maps to a specific chapter learning objective listed in the text. You can use our test bank software, EZ Test Online, or *Connect Accounting* to easily query for learning objectives that directly relate to the learning objectives for your course. You can then use the EZ Test reporting features to aggregate student results in similar fashion, making the collection and presentation of assurance of learning data simple and easy.

"*Connect* certainly offers so much for the students and at the same time helps the professors. The professors can offer more learning opportunities to the students without intensive time investment."

—**CONSTANCE HYLTON, George Mason University**

AACSB Statement

The McGraw-Hill Companies is a proud corporate member of AACSB International. Understanding the importance and value of AACSB accreditation, *Financial and Managerial Accounting* recognizes the curricula guidelines detailed in the AACSB standards for business accreditation by connecting selected questions in the test bank to the general knowledge and skill guidelines in the AACSB standards. The statements contained in *Financial and Managerial Accounting* are provided only as a guide for the users of this textbook. The AACSB leaves content coverage and assessment within the purview of individual schools, the mission of the school, and the faculty. While *Financial and Managerial Accounting* and the teaching package make no claim of any specific AACSB qualification or evaluation, we have within *Financial and Managerial Accounting* labeled select questions according to the general knowledge and skills areas.

Acknowledgments

John J. Wild, Ken W. Shaw, Barbara Chiappetta, and McGraw-Hill Education recognize the following instructors for their valuable feedback and involvement in the development of *Financial and Managerial Accounting,* 6e. We are thankful for their suggestions, counsel, and encouragement.

Khaled Abdou, Penn State University–Berks
Anne Marie Anderson, Raritan Valley Community College
Elaine Anes, Heald College–Fresno
Jerome Apple, University of Akron
Jack Aschkenazi, American Intercontinental University
Sidney Askew, Borough of Manhattan Community College
Lawrence Awopetu, University of Arkansas–Pine Bluff
Jon Backman, Spartanburg Community College
Charles Baird, University of Wisconsin–Stout
Michael Barendse, Grossmont College
Richard Barnhart, Grand Rapids Community College
Beverly R. Beatty, Anne Arundel Community College
Anna Beavers, Laney College
Judy Benish, Fox Valley Technical College
Patricia Bentley, Keiser University
Teri Bernstein, Santa Monica College
Jaswinder Bhangal, Chabot College
Sandra Bitenc, University of Texas at Arlington
Susan Blizzard, San Antonio College
Marvin Blye, Wor-Wic Community College
Patrick Borja, Citrus College
Anna Boulware, St. Charles Community College
Gary Bower, Community College of Rhode Island–Flanagan
Leslee Brock, Southwest Mississippi Community College
Gregory Brookins, Santa Monica College
Regina Brown, Eastfield College
Tracy L. Bundy, University of Louisiana at Lafayette
Roy Carson, Anne Arundel Community College
Deborah Carter, Coahoma Community College
Roberto Castaneda, DeVry University Online
Martha Cavalaris, Miami Dade College
Amy Chataginer, Mississippi Gulf Coast Community College
Gerald Childs, Waukesha County Technical College
Colleen Chung, Miami Dade College–Kendall
Shifei Chung, Rowan University
Robert Churchman, Harding University
Marilyn Ciolino, Delgado Community College
Thomas Clement, University of North Dakota
Oyinka Coakley, Broward College
Susan Cockrell, Birmingham-Southern College
Lisa Cole, Johnson County Community College
Robbie R. Coleman, Northeast Mississippi Community College
Christie Comunale, Long Island University–C.W. Post Campus
Jackie Conrecode, Florida Gulf Coast University
Debora Constable, Georgia Perimeter College
Susan Cordes, Johnson County Community College
Anne Cordozo, Broward College
Cheryl Corke, Genesee Community College
James Cosby, John Tyler Community College
Ken Couvillion, Delta College
Loretta Darche, Southwest Florida College
Judy Daulton, Piedmont Technical College
Annette Davis, Glendale Community College
Dorothy Davis, University of Louisiana–Monroe
Walter DeAguero, Saddleback College
Mike Deschamps, MiraCosta College
Pamela Donahue, Northern Essex Community College
Steve Doster, Shawnee State University
Larry Dragosavac, Edison Community College
Samuel Duah, Bowie State University
Robert Dunlevy, Montgomery County Community College
Jerrilyn Eisenhauer, Tulsa Community College–Southeast
Ronald Elders, Virginia College
Terry Elliott, Morehead State University
Patricia Feller, Nashville State Community College
Albert Fisher, College of Southern Nevada
Annette Fisher, Glendale Community College
Ron Fitzgerald, Santa Monica College
David Flannery, Bryant and Stratton College
Hollie Floberg, Tennessee Wesleyan College
Linda Flowers, Houston Community College
Jeannie Folk, College of DuPage
Rebecca Foote, Middle Tennessee State University
Paul Franklin, Kaplan University
Tim Garvey, Westwood College
Barbara Gershman, Northern Virginia Community College–Woodbridge
Barbara Gershowitz, Nashville State Technical Community College
Mike Glasscock, Amarillo College
Diane Glowacki, Tarrant County College
Ernesto Gonzalez, Florida National College
Lori Grady, Bucks County Community College
Gloria Grayless, Sam Houston State University
Ann Gregory, South Plains College
Rameshwar Gupta, Jackson State University
Amy Haas, Kingsborough Community College
Pat Halliday, Santa Monica College
Keith Hallmark, Calhoun Community College
Rebecca Hancock, El Paso Community College–Valley Verde
Mechelle Harris, Bossier Parish Community College
Tracey Hawkins, University of Cincinnati–Clermont College
Thomas Hayes, University of Arkansas–Ft. Smith
Laurie Hays, Western Michigan University
Roger Hehman, University of Cincinnati–Clermont College
Cheri Hernandez, Des Moines Area Community College
Margaret Hicks, Howard University
Melanie Hicks, Liberty University
James Higgins, Holy Family University
Patricia Holmes, Des Moines Area Community College
Barbara Hopkins, Northern Virginia Community College–Manassas
Wade Hopkins, Heald College
Aileen Huang, Santa Monica College
Les Hubbard, Solano College
Deborah Hudson, Gaston College
James Hurst, National College

Constance Hylton, George Mason University
Christine Irujo, Westfield State University
Tamela Jarvais, Prince George's Community College
Fred Jex, Macomb Community College
Gina M. Jones, Aims Community College
Jeff Jones, College of Southern Nevada
Rita Jones, Columbus State University
Odessa Jordan, Calhoun Community College
Dmitriy Kalyagin, Chabot College
Thomas Kam, Hawaii Pacific University
Naomi Karolinski, Monroe Community College
Shirly A. Kleiner, Johnson County Community College
Kenneth A. Koerber, Bucks County Community College
Jill Kolody, Anne Arundel Community College
Tamara Kowalczyk, Appalachian State University
Anita Kroll, University of Wisconsin–Madison
David Krug, Johnson County Community College
Christopher Kwak, DeAnza College
Tara Laken, Joliet Junior College
Jeanette Landin, Empire College
Beth Lasky, Delgado Community College
Neal Leviton, Santa Monica College
Danny Litt, University of California Los Angeles
James L. Lock, Northern Virginia Community College
Steve Ludwig, Northwest Missouri State University
Debra Luna, El Paso Community College
Amado Mabul, Heald College
Lori Major, Luzerne County Community College
Jennifer Malfitano, Delaware County Community College
Maria Mari, Miami Dade College–Kendall
Thomas S. Marsh, Northern Virginia Community College–Annandale
Karen Martinson, University of Wisconsin–Stout
Brenda Mattison, Tri-County Technical College
Stacie Mayes, Rose State College
Clarice McCoy, Brookhaven College
Tammy Metzke, Milwaukee Area Technical College
Jeanine Metzler, Northampton Community College
Theresa Michalow, Moraine Valley Community College
Julie Miller, Chippewa Valley Tech College
Tim Miller, El Camino College
John Minchin, California Southern University
Edna C. Mitchell, Polk State College
Jill Mitchell, Northern Virginia Community College
Lynn Moore, Aiken Technical College
Angela Mott, Northeast Mississippi Community College
Andrea Murowski, Brookdale Community College
Timothy Murphy, Diablo Valley College
Kenneth F. O'Brien, Farmingdale State College
Kathleen O'Donnell, Onondaga Community College
Ahmed Omar, Burlington County College
Robert A. Pacheco, Massasoit Community College
Margaret Parilo, Cosumnes River College
Paige Paulsen, Salt Lake Community College
Yvonne Phang, Borough of Manhattan Community College
Gary Pieroni, Diablo Valley College
Debbie Porter, Tidewater Community College, Virginia Beach
Kristen Quinn, Northern Essex Community College
James Racic, Lakeland Community College
David Ravetch, University of California Los Angeles
Ruthie Reynolds, Howard University
Cecile Roberti, Community College of Rhode Island
Morgan Rockett, Moberly Area Community College
Patrick Rogan, Cosumnes River College
Paul Rogers, Community College of Beaver County
Brian Routh, Washington State University–Vancouver
Helen Roybark, Radford University
Alphonse Ruggiero, Suffolk County Community College
Joan Ryan, Clackamas Community College
Martin Sabo, Community College of Denver
Arjan Sadhwani, South University
Gary K. Sanborn, Northwestern Michigan College
Kin Kin Sandhu, Heald College
Marcia Sandvold, Des Moines Area Community College
Gary Schader, Kean University
Barbara Schnathorst, The Write Solution, Inc.
Darlene Schnuck, Waukesha County Technical College
Elizabeth Serapin, Columbia Southern University
Geeta Shankhar, University of Dayton
Regina Shea, Community College of Baltimore County–Essex
James Shelton, Liberty University
Jay Siegel, Union County College
Gerald Singh, New York City College of Technology
Lois Slutsky, Broward College–South
Gerald Smith, University of Northern Iowa
Kathleen Sobieralski, University of Maryland University College
Charles Spector, State University of New York at Oswego
Diane Stark, Phoenix College
Thomas Starks, Heald College
Carolyn L. Strauch, Crowder College
Latazia Stuart, Fortis University Online
Gene Sullivan, Liberty University
David Sulzen, Ferrum College
Dominique Svarc, William Rainey Harper College
Linda Sweeney, Sam Houston State University
Carl Swoboda, Southwest Tennessee Community College, Macon
Margaret Tanner, University of Arkansas–Ft. Smith
Ulysses Taylor, Fayetteville State University
Anthony Teng, Saddleback College
Paula Thomas, Middle Tennessee State University
Teresa Thompson, Chaffey Community College
Leslie Thysell, John Tyler Community College
Melanie Torborg, Globe University
Shafi Ullah, Broward College
Bob Urell, Irvine Valley College
Adam Vitalis, Georgia Tech
Patricia Walczak, Lansing Community College
Terri Walsh, Seminole State College–Oviedo
Shunda Ware, Atlanta Technical College
Janis Weber, University of Louisiana–Monroe
Dave Welch, Franklin University
Jean Wells-Jessup, Howard University
Christopher Widmer, Tidewater Community College
Andrew Williams, Edmonds Community College
Jonathan M. Wild, University of Wisconsin–Madison
Wanda Wong, Chabot College
John Woodward, Polk State College
Patricia Worsham, Norco College, Riverside Community College
Gail E. Wright, Stevenson University
Lynnette Yerbury, Salt Lake Community College
Judy Zander, Grossmont College
Mary Zenner, College of Lake County
Jane Zlojutro, Northwestern Michigan College

Brief Contents

*Appendixes D & E are available in McGraw-Hill *Connect* and as print copies from a McGraw-Hill representative.

Contents

20 Master Budgets and Performance Planning 870

21 Flexible Budgets and Standard Costs 922

22 Performance Measurement and Responsibility Accounting 970

23 Relevant Costing for Managerial Decisions 1014

*Appendixes D & E are available in McGraw-Hill *Connect* and as print copies from a McGraw-Hill representative.

Financial and Managerial Accounting

INFORMATION FOR DECISIONS

chapter 1

Accounting in Business

Chapter Preview

IMPORTANCE OF ACCOUNTING	FUNDAMENTALS OF ACCOUNTING	TRANSACTION ANALYSIS	FINANCIAL STATEMENTS
C1 Purpose of accounting	**C3** Ethics—key concept	**A1** Accounting equation and its components	**P2** Income statement
C2 Accounting information users	**C4** Generally accepted accounting principles	**P1** Transaction analysis—illustrated	Statement of retained earnings
Opportunities in accounting	International standards		Balance sheet
	Conceptual framework		Statement of cash flows
			A2 Financial analysis

Chapter Preview *is organized by key topics and includes learning objectives*
Learning Objectives *are classified as conceptual, analytical, or procedural*

Learning Objectives

CONCEPTUAL

C1 Explain the purpose and importance of accounting.

C2 Identify users and uses of, and opportunities in, accounting.

C3 Explain why ethics are crucial to accounting.

C4 Explain generally accepted accounting principles and define and apply several accounting principles.

C5 *Appendix 1B*—Identify and describe the three major activities of organizations.

ANALYTICAL

A1 Define and interpret the accounting equation and each of its components.

A2 Compute and interpret return on assets.

A3 *Appendix 1A*—Explain the relation between return and risk.

PROCEDURAL

P1 Analyze business transactions using the accounting equation.

P2 Identify and prepare basic financial statements and explain how they interrelate.

Christof Stache/AFP/Getty Images

Big Apple

*A **Decision Feature** launches each chapter showing the relevance of accounting for a real entrepreneur. An **Entrepreneurial Decision** assignment returns to this feature with a mini-case*

CUPERTINO, CA—"When I designed the Apple stuff," says Steve Wozniak (a.k.a. the *Wizard of Woz*), "I never thought in my life I would have enough money to fly to Hawaii or make a down payment on a house." But some dreams do come true. Woz, along with Steve Jobs and Ron Wayne, founded Apple on April 1, 1976. Today, **Apple** (**Apple.com**) boasts a value of over $500 billion and revenues of over $170 billion. Along the way, the young entrepreneurs faced many challenges, including accounting issues such as how to properly read and interpret accounting data. The first challenge was how to finance the new company, which they did by selling some of their prized possessions, such as Woz's Hewlett-Packard scientific calculator and Jobs's Volkswagen van. The $1,300 they raised helped them purchase the electronic equipment Woz used to build the first Apple computer.

> *"Wherever smart people work, doors are unlocked"*
> **—Steve Wozniak**

In setting up their company, the two young entrepreneurs also had to decide what type of entity to form—a partnership or a corporation. They decided on a partnership, and Ron Wayne "sat down at a typewriter and typed our partnership contract right out of his head," recalls Woz. "He did an etching of Newton under the apple tree for the cover of our Apple I manual [and] he wrote the manual." The original partnership agreement included Wayne as a third partner with 10% ownership. However, a few days later, Wayne had a change of heart when he considered the unlimited liability of a partnership. He pulled out, leaving Woz and Jobs holding 50 percent each. Within nine months, Woz and Jobs identified some advantages to the corporate form of business organization, and they converted Apple to a corporation on January 3, 1977.

As their company grew, Woz and Jobs had to learn more accounting, along with details of preparing and interpreting financial statements. Important questions involving transaction analysis and financial reporting arose, and the owners took care to do things right. "Everything we did," asserts Woz, "we were setting the tone for the world." Still, there were some doubters, including Woz's father who worried about his cash controls. "A person like him shouldn't have that much money," said his father after finding $250,000 worth of uncashed checks lying around in Woz's Porsche.

Woz and Jobs tightened the accounting system and focused it on providing information for Apple's business decisions. Today, Woz believes that Apple is integral to the language of technology, just as accounting is the language of business. In retrospect, Woz says, "Every dream I have ever had in life has come true ten times over." He adds: "In the end, I hope there's a little note somewhere that says I designed a good computer."

Sources: *Woz website,* Woz.org, January 2015; *iWoz: From Computer Geek to Cult Icon,* W.W. Norton & Co., 2006; *Founders at Work,* Apress, 2007; *Apple website,* September 2014

IMPORTANCE OF ACCOUNTING

C1 Explain the purpose and importance of accounting.

Why is accounting so popular on campus? Why are there so many openings for accounting jobs? Why is accounting so important to companies? Why do politicians and business leaders focus on accounting regulations? The answer is that we live in an information age, where that information, and its reliability, impacts us all.

Accounting is an information and measurement system that identifies, records, and communicates relevant, reliable, and comparable information about an organization's business activities. *Identifying* business activities requires that we select relevant transactions and events. Examples are the sale of iPhones by **Apple** and the receipt of ticket money by **TicketMaster**. *Recording* business activities requires that we keep a chronological log of transactions and events measured in dollars. *Communicating* business activities requires that we prepare accounting reports such as financial statements, which we analyze and interpret. (The financial statements and notes of Apple are shown in Appendix A near the end of this book. This appendix also shows the financial statements of **Google** and **Samsung**.) Exhibit 1.1 summarizes accounting activities.

***Real company names** are printed in bold magenta*

EXHIBIT 1.1
Accounting Activities

Accounting is part of our everyday lives. Our most common contact with accounting is through credit approvals, checking accounts, tax forms, and payroll. These experiences tend to focus on the recordkeeping parts of accounting. **Recordkeeping,** or **bookkeeping,** is the recording of transactions and events, either manually or electronically. This is just one part of accounting. Accounting also identifies and communicates information on transactions and events, and it includes the crucial processes of analysis and interpretation.

Technology is a key part of modern business and plays a major role in accounting. Technology reduces the time, effort, and cost of recordkeeping while improving clerical accuracy. Some small organizations continue to perform various accounting tasks manually, but even they are impacted by technology. As technology makes more information available, the demand for accounting increases and so too the skills for applying that information. Consulting, planning, and other financial services are now closely linked to accounting. These services require sorting through data, interpreting their meaning, identifying key factors, and analyzing their implications.

Point: Technology is only as useful as the accounting data available, and users' decisions are only as good as their understanding of accounting. The best software and recordkeeping cannot make up for lack of accounting knowledge.

Users of Accounting Information

C2 Identify users and uses of, and opportunities in, accounting.

Accounting is called the *language of business* because all organizations set up an accounting information system to communicate data to help people make better decisions. Exhibit 1.2 shows that accounting serves many users (this is a partial listing) who can be divided into two groups: external users and internal users.

External Information Users **External users** of accounting information are *not* directly involved in running the organization. They include shareholders (investors), lenders, directors, customers, suppliers, regulators, lawyers, brokers, and the press. External users have limited access to an organization's information. Yet their business decisions depend on information that is reliable, relevant, and comparable. **Financial accounting** is the area of accounting aimed at serving external users by providing them with *general-purpose financial statements*. The term

EXHIBIT 1.2

Users of Accounting Information

External users

- Lenders
- Shareholders
- Governments
- Consumer groups
- External auditors
- Customers

Internal users

- Officers
- Managers
- Internal auditors
- Sales staff
- Budget officers
- Controllers

Infographics reinforce key concepts through visual learning

general-purpose refers to the broad range of purposes for which external users rely on these statements. Following is a partial list of external users and some decisions they make with accounting information.

- *Lenders* (creditors) loan money or other resources to an organization. Banks, savings and loans, co-ops, and mortgage and finance companies are lenders. Lenders look for information to help them assess whether an organization is likely to repay its loans with interest.
- *Shareholders* (*investors*) are the owners of a corporation. They use accounting reports in deciding whether to buy, hold, or sell stock.
- *Directors* are typically elected to a *board of directors* to oversee their interests in an organization. Since directors are responsible to shareholders, their information needs are similar.
- *External* (independent) *auditors* examine financial statements to verify that they are prepared according to generally accepted accounting principles.
- *Nonexecutive employees* and *labor unions* use financial statements to judge the fairness of wages, assess job prospects, and bargain for better wages.
- *Regulators* often have legal authority over certain activities of organizations. For example, the Internal Revenue Service (IRS) and other tax authorities require organizations to file accounting reports in computing taxes. Other regulators include utility boards that use accounting information to set utility rates and securities regulators that require reports for companies that sell their stock to the public.
- *Voters, legislators,* and *government officials* use accounting information to monitor and evaluate government receipts and expenses.
- *Contributors* to nonprofit organizations use accounting information to evaluate the use and impact of their donations.
- *Suppliers* use accounting information to judge the soundness of a customer before making sales on credit.
- *Customers* use financial reports to assess the staying power of potential suppliers.

Internal Information Users **Internal users** of accounting information are those directly involved in managing and operating an organization such as the chief executive officer (CEO), chief financial officer (CFO), chief audit executive (CAE), treasurer, and other executive and managerial-level employees. They use the information to help improve the efficiency and effectiveness of an organization. **Managerial accounting** is the area of accounting that serves the decision-making needs of internal users. Internal reports are not subject to the same rules as external reports and instead are designed with the special needs of internal users in mind. Following is a partial list of internal users and some decisions they make with accounting information.

- *Research and development managers* need information about projected costs and revenues of any proposed changes in products and services.
- *Purchasing managers* need to know what, when, and how much to purchase.

- *Human resource managers* need information about employees' payroll, benefits, performance, and compensation.
- *Production managers* depend on information to monitor costs and ensure quality.
- *Distribution managers* need reports for timely, accurate, and efficient delivery of products and services.
- *Marketing managers* use reports about sales and costs to target consumers, set prices, and monitor consumer needs, tastes, and price concerns.
- *Service managers* require information on the costs and benefits of looking after products and services.

Opportunities in Accounting

Accounting information is in all aspects of our lives. When we earn money, pay taxes, invest savings, budget earnings, and plan for the future, we use accounting. Accounting has four broad areas of opportunities: financial, managerial, taxation, and accounting-related. Exhibit 1.3 lists selected opportunities in each area.

EXHIBIT 1.3

Accounting Opportunities

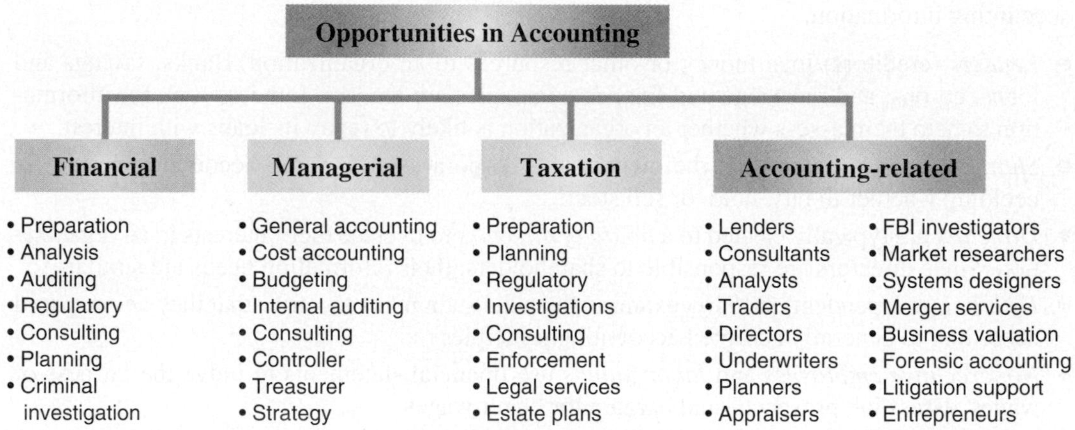

Exhibit 1.4 shows that the majority of opportunities are in *private accounting,* which are employees working for businesses. *Public accounting* offers the next largest number of opportunities, which involve services such as auditing and tax advice. Still other opportunities exist in government and not-for-profit agencies, including business regulation and investigation of law violations.

EXHIBIT 1.4

Accounting Jobs by Area

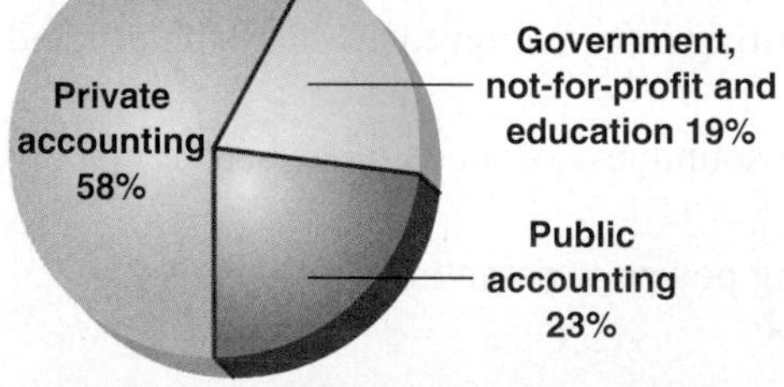

Accounting specialists are highly regarded and their professional standing is often denoted by a certificate. Certified public accountants (CPAs) must meet education and experience requirements, pass an examination, and exhibit ethical character. Many accounting specialists hold certificates in addition to or instead of the CPA. Two of the most common are the certificate in management accounting (CMA) and the certified internal auditor (CIA). Employers also look for specialists with designations such as certified bookkeeper (CB), certified payroll professional (CPP), personal financial specialist (PFS), certified fraud examiner (CFE), and certified forensic accountant (CrFA).

Point: The largest accounting firms are EY, KPMG, PwC, and Deloitte.

Margin notes further enhance textual material

Point: Census Bureau (2011) reports that for workers 25 and over, higher education yields higher average pay:

Advanced degree	$81,568
Bachelor's degree	57,326
High school degree	36,876
No high school degree	26,124

Demand for accounting specialists is strong. Exhibit 1.5 reports average annual salaries for several accounting positions. Salary variation depends on location, company size, professional designation, experience, and other factors. For example, salaries for chief financial officers (CFOs) range from under $100,000 to more than $1 million per year. Likewise, salaries for bookkeepers range from under $30,000 to more than $80,000.

EXHIBIT 1.5

Accounting Salaries for Selected Fields

Field	Title (experience)	2014 Salary	2019 Estimate*
Public Accounting	Partner	$239,000	$264,000
	Manager (6–8 years)	107,500	118,500
	Senior (3–5 years)	84,000	92,500
	Junior (0–2 years)	59,500	65,500
Private Accounting	CFO	282,000	311,500
	Controller/Treasurer	177,500	196,000
	Manager (6–8 years)	95,500	105,500
	Senior (3–5 years)	79,500	88,000
	Junior (0–2 years)	57,000	63,000
Recordkeeping	Full-charge bookkeeper	59,500	65,500
	Accounts manager	57,000	63,000
	Payroll manager	58,500	64,500
	Accounting clerk (0–2 years)	38,500	42,500

* Estimates assume a 2% compounded annual increase over current levels (rounded to nearest $500).

Point: U.S. Bureau of Labor (June 2011) reports higher education is linked to a lower unemployment rate:
Bachelor's degree or more . . 4.4%
High school degree 10.0%
No high school degree 14.3%

Point: For updated salary info:
Abbott-Langer.com
www.AICPA.org
Kforce.com

***NEED-TO-KNOWs** highlight key procedures and concepts in learning accounting*

NEED-TO-KNOW 1-1

Accounting Users
C1 C2

Identify the following users of accounting information as either an (a) external or (b) internal user.

1. ____ Regulator
2. ____ CEO
3. ____ Shareholder
4. ____ Controller
5. ____ Executive employee
6. ____ External auditor
7. ____ Production manager
8. ____ Nonexecutive employee

Solution

1. a **2.** b **3.** a **4.** b **5.** b **6.** a **7.** b **8.** a

Do More: QS 1-1, QS 1-2, E 1-1, E 1-2, E 1-3

QC1

***QC icon** indicates Quick Check self-review questions available in the eBook*

FUNDAMENTALS OF ACCOUNTING

Accounting is guided by principles, standards, concepts, and assumptions. This section describes several of these key fundamentals of accounting.

Ethics—A Key Concept

C3

Explain why ethics are crucial to accounting.

The goal of accounting is to provide useful information for decisions. For information to be useful, it must be trusted. This demands ethics in accounting. **Ethics** are beliefs that distinguish right from wrong. They are accepted standards of good and bad behavior.

Identifying the ethical path is sometimes difficult. The preferred path is a course of action that avoids casting doubt on one's decisions. For example, accounting users are less likely to trust an auditor's report if the auditor's pay depends on the client's success. To avoid such concerns, ethics rules are often set. For example, auditors are banned from direct investment in their client and cannot accept pay that depends on figures in the client's reports. Exhibit 1.6 gives a three-step process for making ethical decisions.

Point: Sarbanes-Oxley Act requires each issuer of securities to disclose whether it has adopted a code of ethics for its senior officers and the contents of that code.

EXHIBIT 1.6

Guidelines for Ethical Decision Making

Point: The American Institute of Certified Public Accountants' *Code of Professional Conduct* is available at **www.AICPA.org**.

Accountants face many ethical choices as they prepare financial reports. These choices can affect the price a buyer pays and the wages paid to workers. They can even affect the success of products and services. Misleading information can lead to a wrongful closing of a division that harms workers, customers, and suppliers. There is an old saying: *Good ethics are good business.*

Fraud Triangle

The fraud triangle is a model created by a criminologist that asserts the following *three* factors must exist for a person to commit fraud: opportunity, pressure, and rationalization.

- *Opportunity.* A person must envision a way to commit fraud with a low perceived risk of getting caught. Employers can directly reduce this risk. An example of some control on opportunity is a pre-employment background check.
- *Pressure,* or incentive. A person must have some pressure to commit fraud. Examples are unpaid bills and addictions.
- *Rationalization,* or attitude. A person who rationalizes fails to see the criminal nature of the fraud or justifies the action.

It is important to recognize that all three factors of the fraud triangle must usually exist for fraud to occur. The absence of one or more factors suggests fraud is unlikely. The key to dealing with fraud is to focus on prevention. It is less expensive and more effective to prevent fraud from happening than it is to try to detect the crime. By the time the fraud is discovered, the money is gone and chances are slim that it will be recovered. Additionally, it is costly and time-consuming to investigate a fraud.

Both internal and external users rely on internal controls to reduce the likelihood of fraud. *Internal controls* are procedures set up to protect company property and equipment, ensure reliable accounting reports, promote efficiency, and encourage adherence to company policies. Examples are good records, physical controls (locks, passwords, guards), and independent reviews.

__Decision Insight__ boxes highlight relevant items from practice

Decision Insight

Cooking the Books Our economic and social welfare depends on reliable accounting. Some individuals forgot that and are now paying their dues. They include Tsuyoshi Kikukawa of **Olympus**, guilty of hiding $1.7 billion in losses; Bernard Madoff of **Madoff Investment Securities**, convicted of falsifying securities records; Bernard Ebbers of **WorldCom**, convicted of an $11 billion accounting scandal; Andrew Fastow of **Enron**, guilty of hiding debt and inflating income; and Ramalinga Raju of **Satyam Computers**, accused of overstating assets by $1.5 billion. ■

Comstock/Stockbyte/Getty Images

Generally Accepted Accounting Principles

C4 Explain generally accepted accounting principles and define and apply several accounting principles.

Financial accounting is governed by concepts and rules known as **generally accepted accounting principles (GAAP).** We must understand these principles to best use accounting data. GAAP aims to make information *relevant, reliable,* and *comparable*. Relevant information affects decisions of users. Reliable information is trusted by users. Comparable information is helpful in contrasting organizations.

In the United States, the **Securities and Exchange Commission (SEC),** a government agency, has the legal authority to set GAAP. The SEC also oversees proper use of GAAP by companies that raise money from the public through issuances of their stock and debt. Those companies that issue their stock on U.S. exchanges include both *U.S. SEC registrants* (companies incorporated in the United States) and *non-U.S. SEC registrants* (companies incorporated under non-U.S. laws). The SEC has largely delegated the task of setting U.S. GAAP to the **Financial Accounting Standards Board (FASB),** which is a private-sector group that sets both broad and specific principles.

Point: State ethics codes require CPAs who audit financial statements to disclose areas where those statements fail to comply with GAAP. If CPAs fail to report noncompliance, they can lose their licenses and be subject to criminal and civil actions and fines.

International Standards

In today's global economy, there is increased demand by external users for comparability in accounting reports. This demand often arises when companies wish to raise money from lenders and investors in different countries. To that end, the **International Accounting Standards Board (IASB),** an independent group (consisting of individuals from many countries), issues **International Financial Reporting Standards (IFRS)** that identify preferred accounting practices.

If standards are harmonized, one company can potentially use a single set of financial statements in all financial markets. Differences between U.S. GAAP and IFRS are decreasing as the FASB and IASB pursue a *convergence* process aimed to achieve a single set of accounting standards for global use. More than 115 countries now require or permit companies to prepare financial reports following IFRS. Further, non-U.S. SEC registrants can use IFRS in financial reports filed with the SEC (with no reconciliation to U.S. GAAP). This means there are *two* sets of accepted accounting principles in the United States: (1) U.S. GAAP for U.S. SEC registrants and (2) either IFRS or U.S. GAAP for non-U.S. SEC registrants.

The SEC is encouraging the FASB to change U.S. GAAP over a period of several years by endorsing, and thereby incorporating, individual IFRS standards into U.S. GAAP. This *endorsement process* would still allow the FASB to modify IFRS when necessary. The SEC would:

- Maintain its statutory oversight of the FASB, including authority to prescribe accounting principles and standards for U.S. issuers.
- Contribute to oversight and governance of the IASB through its involvement on the IFRS Foundation Monitoring Board.

The FASB would continue, but its role would be to provide input and support to the IASB in crafting high-quality, global standards. The FASB is to develop a transition plan to effect these changes over the next five years or so. For updates on this roadmap, we can check with the AICPA (**IFRS.com**), FASB (**FASB.org**), and IASB (**ifrs.org**).

IFRS

Like the FASB, the IASB uses a conceptual framework to aid in revising or drafting new standards. However, unlike the FASB, the IASB's conceptual framework is used as a reference when specific guidance is lacking. The IASB also requires that transactions be accounted for according to their substance (not only their legal form), and that financial statements give a fair presentation, whereas the FASB narrows that scope to fair presentation *in accordance with U.S. GAAP.* ■

Conceptual Framework and Convergence

The FASB and IASB are attempting to converge and enhance the **conceptual framework** that guides standard setting. The FASB framework consists broadly of the following:

- **Objectives**—to provide information useful to investors, creditors, and others.
- **Qualitative Characteristics**—to require information that is *relevant, reliable,* and *comparable.*
- **Elements**—to define items that financial statements can contain.
- **Recognition and Measurement**—to set criteria that an item must meet for it to be recognized as an element; and how to measure that element.

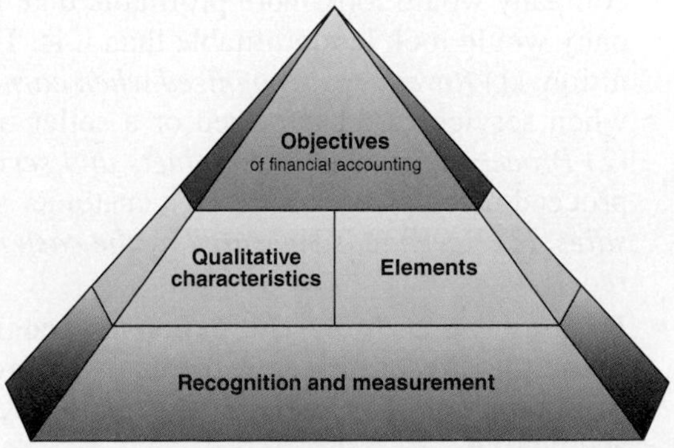

For updates on this joint FASB and IASB conceptual framework convergence we can check the **FASB.org** or **ifrs.org** websites. We must remember that U.S. GAAP and IFRS are two similar, but not identical, systems. However, their similarities greatly outweigh any differences. The remainder of this section describes key principles and assumptions of accounting.

Principles and Assumptions of Accounting Accounting principles (and assumptions) are of two types. *General principles* are the basic assumptions, concepts, and guidelines for preparing financial statements. *Specific principles* are detailed rules used in reporting business transactions and events. General principles stem from long-used accounting practices. Specific principles arise more often from the rulings of authoritative groups.

EXHIBIT 1.7

Building Blocks for GAAP

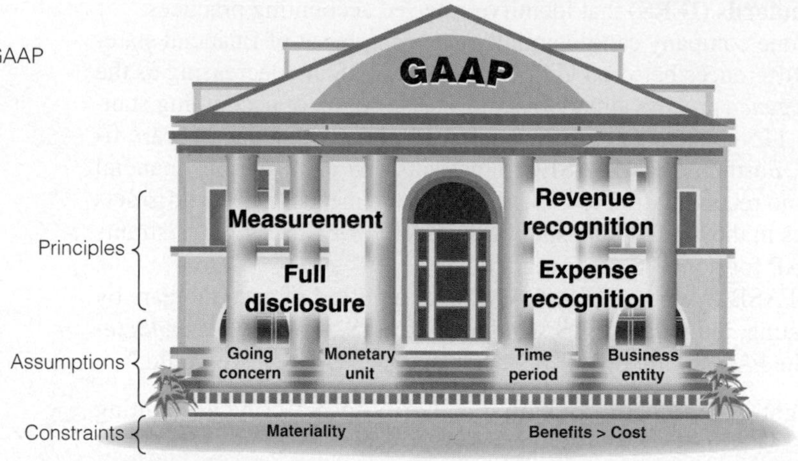

We need to understand both general and specific principles to effectively use accounting information. Several general principles are described in this section that are relied on in later chapters. General principles (in purple font with white shading) and assumptions (in red font with white shading) are portrayed as building blocks of GAAP in Exhibit 1.7. The specific principles are described as we encounter them in the book.

Accounting Principles General principles consist of at least four basic principles, four assumptions, and two constraints.

Point: The cost principle is also called the *historical cost principle.*

- *Measurement* The **measurement principle,** also called the **cost principle,** usually prescribes that accounting information is based on actual cost (with a potential for subsequent adjustments to market). Cost is measured on a cash or equal-to-cash basis. This means if cash is given for a service, its cost is measured as the amount of cash paid. If something besides cash is exchanged (such as a car traded for a truck), cost is measured as the cash value of what is given up or received. The cost principle emphasizes reliability and verifiability, and information based on cost is considered objective. *Objectivity* means that information is supported by independent, unbiased evidence; it demands more than a person's opinion. To illustrate, suppose a company pays $5,000 for equipment. The cost principle requires that this purchase be recorded at $5,000. It makes no difference if the owner thinks this equipment is worth $7,000. Later in the book we introduce *fair value* measures.

Example: A lawn service bills a customer $1,000 on June 1 for two months of mowing (June and July). The customer pays the bill on July 1. When is revenue recorded? *Answer:* Revenue is recorded over time as it is earned; if monthly reports are prepared, then record $500 revenue for June and $500 for July.

- *Revenue recognition* Revenue (sales) is the amount received from selling products and services. The **revenue recognition principle** provides guidance on when a company must recognize revenue. To *recognize* means to record it. If revenue is recognized too early, a company would look more profitable than it is. If revenue is recognized too late, a company would look less profitable than it is. Three concepts are important to revenue recognition. (1) *Revenue is recognized when earned.* The earnings process is normally complete when services are performed or a seller transfers ownership of products to the buyer. (2) *Proceeds from selling products and services need not be in cash.* A common noncash proceed received by a seller is a customer's promise to pay at a future date, called *credit sales.* (3) *Revenue is measured by the cash received plus the cash value of any other items received.*

Example: Credit cards are used to pay $400 in gas for a lawn mowing business during June and July. The cards are paid off in August. When is expense recorded? *Answer:* Expense is recorded when the revenue it helped generate is recorded. Assuming revenue is earned over time and monthly reports are prepared, then record $200 expense in June and $200 in July.

- *Expense recognition* The **expense recognition principle,** also called the **matching principle,** prescribes that a company record the expenses it incurred to generate the revenue reported. The principles of matching and revenue recognition are key to modern accounting.
- *Full disclosure* The **full disclosure principle** prescribes that a company report the details behind financial statements that would impact users' decisions. Those disclosures are often in footnotes to the statements.

Decision Insight

Revenues for the **New York Giants**, **Green Bay Packers**, and other professional football teams include ticket sales, television and cable broadcasts, radio rights, concessions, and advertising. Revenues from ticket sales are earned when the NFL team plays each game. Advance ticket sales are not revenues; instead, they represent a liability until the NFL team plays the game for which the ticket was sold. At that point, the liability is removed and revenues are reported. ■

Scott Boehm/Getty Images

Accounting Assumptions There are four accounting assumptions: the going-concern assumption, the monetary unit assumption, the time period assumption, and the business entity assumption.

- *Going concern* The **going-concern assumption** means that accounting information reflects a presumption that the business will continue operating instead of being closed or sold. This implies, for example, that property is reported at cost instead of, say, liquidation values that assume closure.

*Key **terms** are printed in bold and defined again in the **glossary***

- *Monetary unit* The **monetary unit assumption** means that we can express transactions and events in monetary, or money, units. Money is the common denominator in business. Examples of monetary units are the dollar in the United States, Canada, Australia, and Singapore; and the peso in Mexico, the Philippines, and Chile. The monetary unit a company uses in its accounting reports usually depends on the country where it operates, but many companies today are expressing reports in more than one monetary unit.

Point: For currency conversion: xe.com

- *Time period* The **time period assumption** presumes that the life of a company can be divided into time periods, such as months and years, and that useful reports can be prepared for those periods.
- *Business entity* The **business entity assumption** means that a business is accounted for separately from other business entities, including its owner. The reason for this assumption is that separate information about each business is necessary for good decisions. A business entity can take one of three legal forms: *proprietorship, partnership,* or *corporation.*

Point: Abuse of the entity assumption was a main culprit in **Enron**'s collapse.

1. A **sole proprietorship,** or simply **proprietorship,** is a business owned by one person. The business is a separate entity for accounting purposes. However, the business is *not* a separate legal entity from its owner. This means, for example, that a court can order an owner to sell personal belongings to pay a proprietorship's debt. This *unlimited liability* of a proprietorship is a disadvantage. However, an advantage is that a proprietorship's income is not subject to a business income tax but is instead reported and taxed on the owner's personal income tax return. Proprietorship attributes are summarized in Exhibit 1.8, including those for partnerships and corporations.

EXHIBIT 1.8

Attributes of Businesses

Attribute Present	Proprietorship	Partnership	Corporation
One owner allowed	yes	no	yes
Business taxed	no	no	yes
Limited liability	no*	no*	yes
Business entity	yes	yes	yes
Legal entity	no	no	yes
Unlimited life	no	no	yes

* Proprietorships and partnerships that are set up as LLCs provide limited liability.

2. A **partnership** is a business owned by two or more people, called *partners,* which are jointly liable for tax and other obligations. Like a proprietorship, no special legal requirements must be met in starting a partnership. The only requirement is an agreement between partners to run a business together. The agreement can be either oral or written and

Point: Proprietorships and partnerships are usually managed by their owners. In a corporation, the owners (shareholders) elect a board of directors who appoint managers to run the business.

usually indicates how income and losses are to be shared. A partnership, like a proprietorship, is *not* legally separate from its owners. This means that each partner's share of profits is reported and taxed on that partner's tax return. It also means *unlimited liability* for its partners. However, at least three types of partnerships limit liability. A *limited partnership* (*LP*) includes a general partner(s) with unlimited liability and a limited partner(s) with liability restricted to the amount invested. A *limited liability partnership* (*LLP*) restricts partners' liabilities to their own acts and the acts of individuals under their control. This protects an innocent partner from the negligence of another partner, yet all partners remain responsible for partnership debts. A *limited liability company* (*LLC*) offers the limited liability of a corporation and the tax treatment of a partnership (and proprietorship). Most proprietorships and partnerships are now organized as LLCs.

3. A **corporation,** also called a *C corporation,* is a business legally separate from its owner or owners, meaning it is responsible for its own acts and its own debts. Separate legal status means that a corporation can conduct business with the rights, duties, and responsibilities of a person. A corporation acts through its managers, who are its legal agents. Separate legal status also means that its owners, who are called **shareholders** (or **stockholders**), are not personally liable for corporate acts and debts. This limited liability is its main advantage. A main disadvantage is what's called *double taxation*—meaning that (1) the corporation income is taxed and (2) any distribution of income to its owners through dividends is taxed as part of the owners' personal income, usually at the individual's income tax rate. (For "qualified" dividends, the tax rate is 0%, 15%, or 20%, depending on the individual's tax bracket.) An *S corporation,* a corporation with special attributes, does not owe corporate income tax. Owners of S corporations report their share of corporate income with their personal income. Ownership of all corporations is divided into units called **shares** or **stock.** When a corporation issues only one class of stock, we call it **common stock** (or *capital stock*).

Decision Ethics boxes are role-playing exercises that stress ethics in accounting

Decision Ethics

Entrepreneur You and a friend develop a new design for in-line skates that improves speed by 25% to 30%. You plan to form a business to manufacture and market those skates. You and your friend want to minimize taxes, but your prime concern is potential lawsuits from individuals who might be injured on these skates. What form of organization do you set up? ■ [Answers follow the chapter's Summary.]

Accounting Constraints There are two basic constraints on financial reporting.

- *Materiality* The **materiality constraint** prescribes that only information that would influence the decisions of a reasonable person need be disclosed. This constraint looks at both the importance and relative size of an amount.
- *Benefit exceeds cost* The **cost-benefit constraint** prescribes that only information with benefits of disclosure greater than the costs of providing it need be disclosed.

Conservatism and *industry practices* are also sometimes referred to as accounting constraints.

Sarbanes-Oxley (SOX)

Point: An **audit** examines whether financial statements are prepared using GAAP. It does *not* attest to absolute accuracy of the statements.

Congress passed the **Sarbanes-Oxley Act,** also called *SOX,* to help curb financial abuses at companies that issue their stock to the public. SOX requires that these public companies apply both accounting oversight and stringent internal controls. The desired results include more transparency, accountability, and truthfulness in reporting transactions.

Compliance with SOX requires documentation and verification of internal controls and increased emphasis on internal control effectiveness. Failure to comply can yield financial penalties, stock market delisting, and criminal prosecution of executives. Management must issue a report stating that internal controls are effective. CEOs and CFOs who knowingly sign off on bogus accounting reports risk millions of dollars in fines and years in prison. **Auditors** also must verify the effectiveness of internal controls.

Point: *BusinessWeek* reports that external audit costs run about $35,000 for start-ups, up from $15,000 pre-SOX.

A listing of some of the more publicized accounting scandals in recent years follows.

Company	Alleged Accounting Abuses
Enron	Inflated income, hid debt, and bribed officials
WorldCom	Understated expenses to inflate income and hid debt
Fannie Mae	Inflated income
Adelphia Communications	Understated expenses to inflate income and hid debt
AOL Time Warner	Inflated revenues and income
Xerox	Inflated income
Bristol-Myers Squibb	Inflated revenues and income
Nortel Networks	Understated expenses to inflate income
Global Crossing	Inflated revenues and income
Tyco	Hid debt and CEO evaded taxes
Halliburton	Inflated revenues and income
Qwest Communications	Inflated revenues and income

To reduce the risk of accounting fraud, companies set up *governance systems.* A company's governance system includes its owners, managers, employees, board of directors, and other important stakeholders, who work together to reduce the risk of accounting fraud and increase confidence in accounting reports.

The impact of SOX regulations for accounting and business is discussed throughout this book. Ethics and investor confidence are key to company success. Lack of confidence in accounting numbers impacts company value as evidenced by huge stock price declines for **Enron**, **WorldCom**, **Tyco**, and **ImClone** after accounting misconduct was uncovered.

Dodd-Frank

Congress passed the **Dodd-Frank Wall Street Reform and Consumer Protection Act,** or *Dodd-Frank,* to (1) promote accountability and transparency in the financial system, (2) put an end to the notion of "too big to fail," (3) protect the taxpayer by ending bailouts, and (4) protect consumers from abusive financial services. It includes provisions whose impacts are unknown until regulators set detailed rules. However, a few proposals are notable, such as the following:

- *Exemption* Exemption from Section 404(b) of SOX for smaller public entities from the requirement to obtain an external audit on effectiveness of internal control over financial reporting.
- *Independence* Independence for all members of the compensation committee (including additional disclosures); in the event of an accounting restatement, an entity must set policies mandating recovery ("clawback") of excess incentive compensation.
- *Whistleblower* Requires the SEC, when sanctions exceed $1 million, to pay whistleblowers between 10% and 30% of the sanction.

NEED-TO-KNOW 1-2

Accounting Guidance

C3 C4

Part 1: Identify each of the following terms/phrases as either an accounting (a) principle, (b) assumption, or (c) constraint.

1. ____ Materiality
2. ____ Measurement
3. ____ Business entity
4. ____ Going concern
5. ____ Expense recognition
6. ____ Time period
7. ____ Full disclosure
8. ____ Revenue recognition

Solution

1. c **2.** a **3.** b **4.** b **5.** a **6.** b **7.** a **8.** a

Part 2: Complete the following table with either a yes or a no regarding the attributes of a partnership and a corporation.

Attribute Present	Partnership	Corporation
Business taxed.	a. ____	e. ____
Limited liability	b. ____	f. ____
Legal entity	c. ____	g. ____
Unlimited life.	d. ____	h. ____

Do More: QS 1-3, QS 1-4, QS 1-5, QS 1-6, E 1-4, E 1-5, E 1-7

QC2

Solution

a. no **b.** no **c.** no **d.** no **e.** yes **f.** yes **g.** yes **h.** yes

TRANSACTION ANALYSIS AND THE ACCOUNTING EQUATION

A1

Define and interpret the accounting equation and each of its components.

To understand accounting information, we need to know how an accounting system captures relevant data about transactions, and then classifies, records, and reports data.

Accounting Equation

The accounting system reflects two basic aspects of a company: what it owns and what it owes. *Assets* are resources a company owns or controls. Examples are cash, supplies, equipment, and land, where each carries expected benefits. The claims on a company's assets—what it owes—are separated into owner and nonowner claims. *Liabilities* are what a company owes its nonowners (creditors) in future payments, products, or services. *Equity* (also called stockholders' equity or capital) refers to the claims of its owner(s). Together, liabilities and equity are the source of funds to acquire assets. The relation of assets, liabilities, and equity is reflected in the following **accounting equation:**

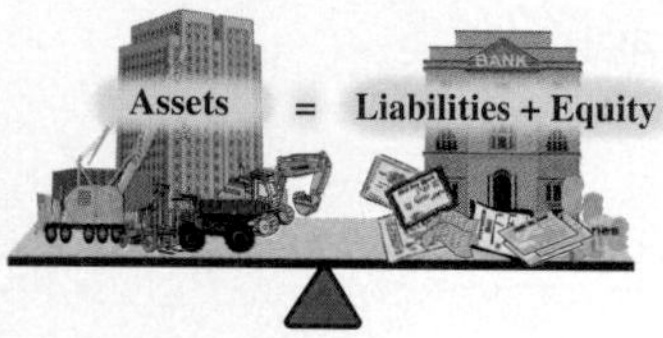

Assets = Liabilities + Equity

Liabilities are usually shown before equity in this equation because creditors' claims must be paid before the claims of owners. (The terms in this equation can be rearranged; for example, Assets − Liabilities = Equity.) The accounting equation applies to all transactions and events, to all companies and forms of organization, and to all points in time. For example, **Apple**'s assets equal $207,000, its liabilities equal $83,451, and its equity equals $123,549 ($ in millions). Let's now look at the accounting equation in more detail.

Point: The phrases "on credit" and "on account" imply that cash payment will occur at a future date.

Assets **Assets** are resources a company owns or controls. These resources are expected to yield future benefits. Examples are web servers for an online services company, musical instruments for a rock band, and land for a vegetable grower. The term *receivable* is used to refer to an asset that promises a future inflow of resources. A company that provides a service or product on credit is said to have an account receivable from that customer.

Liabilities **Liabilities** are creditors' claims on assets. These claims reflect company obligations to provide assets, products, or services to others. The term *payable* refers to a liability that promises a future outflow of resources. Examples are wages payable to workers, accounts payable to suppliers, notes payable to banks, and taxes payable to the government.

Equity **Equity** is the owner's claim on assets, and is equal to assets minus liabilities. This is the reason equity is also called *net assets* or *residual equity*.

Equity increases from owner investments, called stock issuances, and from revenues. It decreases from dividends and expenses. Specifically, a corporation's equity—also called *stockholders'* or *shareholders' equity*—consists of four elements.

Contributed capital →

- ***Common Stock*** **Common stock,** which is part of contributed capital, reflects inflows of resources such as cash and other net assets from stockholders in exchange for stock (later chapters identify other parts of contributed capital).

- ***Dividends*** The outflow of resources such as cash and other assets to stockholders is called **dividends,** which reduce equity.
- ***Revenues*** **Revenues** increase equity (via net income) from sales of products and services to customers; examples are sales of products, consulting services provided, facilities rented to others, and commissions from services.
- ***Expenses*** **Expenses** decrease equity (via net income) from costs of providing products and services to customers; examples are costs of employee time, use of supplies, advertising, utilities, and insurance fees.

Retained earnings

More generally, **contributed capital** refers to the amount stockholders invest in the company, and **retained earnings** is the accumulated revenues *less* the accumulated expenses and dividends since the company began. This breakdown of equity yields the following **expanded accounting equation:**

Equity

Assets = Liabilities + Contributed Capital + Retained Earnings

= Liabilities + Common Stock − Dividends + Revenues − Expenses

Net income occurs when revenues exceed expenses. Net income increases equity. A **net loss** occurs when expenses exceed revenues, which decreases equity.

Decision Insight

Big Data Most organizations offer access to large accounting databases—see **Apple Inc. (Apple.com)** as an example. The SEC keeps an online database called **EDGAR (www.SEC.gov/edgar.shtml),** which has accounting information for thousands of companies that issue stock to the public. The annual report filing for most publicly traded U.S. companies is known as Form 10-K, and the quarterly filing is Form 10-Q. Information services such as **Finance.Google.com** and **Finance.Yahoo.com** offer online data and analysis. ■

Yasuyoshi Chiba/AFP/Getty Images

NEED-TO-KNOW 1-3

Accounting Equation

A1

Part 1: Use the *accounting equation* to compute the missing financial statement amounts.

Company	Assets	Liabilities	Equity
BOSE	$150	$ 30	$__(a)__
VOGUE	$__(b)__	$100	$300

Solution

a. $120 **b.** $400

Part 2: Use the *expanded accounting equation* to compute the missing financial statement amounts.

Company	Assets	Liabilities	Common Stock	Dividends	Revenues	Expenses
Nikon	$200	$ 80	$100	$0	__(a)__	$40
YouTube	$400	$160	$220	__(b)__	$120	$90

Solution

a. $60 **b.** $10

Do More: QS 1-7, QS 1-8, E 1-8, E 1-9

Transaction Analysis

P1

Analyze business transactions using the accounting equation.

Business activities can be described in terms of transactions and events. **External transactions** are exchanges of value between two entities, which yield changes in the accounting equation. An example is the sale of the *AppleCare Protection Plan* by **Apple**. **Internal transactions** are exchanges within an entity, which may or may not affect the accounting equation. An example is Twitter's use of its supplies, which are reported as expenses when used. **Events** refer to happenings that affect the accounting equation *and* are reliably measured. They include business events such as changes in the market value of certain assets and liabilities and natural events such as floods and fires that destroy assets and create losses. They do not include, for example, the signing of service or product contracts, which by themselves do not impact the accounting equation.

This section uses the accounting equation to analyze 11 selected transactions and events of FastForward, a start-up consulting (service) business, in its first month of operations. Remember that each transaction and event leaves the equation in balance and that assets *always* equal the sum of liabilities and equity.

Transaction 1: Investment by Owner On December 1, Chas Taylor forms a consulting business, named FastForward and set up as a corporation, that focuses on assessing the performance of footwear and accessories. Taylor owns and manages the business. The marketing plan for the business is to focus primarily on publishing online reviews and consulting with clubs, athletes, and others who place orders for footwear and accessories with manufacturers. Taylor personally invests $30,000 cash in the new company and deposits the cash in a bank account opened under the name of FastForward. After this transaction, the cash (an asset) and the stockholders' equity each equal $30,000. The source of increase in equity is the owner's investment (stock issuance), which is included in the column titled Common Stock. The effect of this transaction on FastForward is reflected in the accounting equation as follows (we label the equity entries):

Point: There are 3 basic types of company operations: (1) **Services**—providing customer services for profit, (2) **Merchandisers**—buying products and reselling them for profit, and (3) **Manufacturers**—creating products and selling them for profit.

	Assets	=	Liabilities	+	Equity
	Cash	=			**Common Stock**
(1)	**+$30,000**	=			**+$30,000** Owner investment

Transaction 2: Purchase Supplies for Cash FastForward uses $2,500 of its cash to buy supplies of brand name footwear for performance testing over the next few months. This transaction is an exchange of cash, an asset, for another kind of asset, supplies. It merely changes the form of assets from cash to supplies. The decrease in cash is exactly equal to the increase in supplies. The supplies of footwear are assets because of the expected future benefits from the test results of their performance. This transaction is reflected in the accounting equation as follows:

	Assets			=	Liabilities	+	Equity
	Cash	+	**Supplies**	=			**Common Stock**
Old Bal.	$30,000			=			$30,000
(2)	**−2,500**	+	**$2,500**				
New Bal.	$27,500	+	$ 2,500	=			$30,000
	$30,000				$30,000		

Transaction 3: Purchase Equipment for Cash FastForward spends $26,000 to acquire equipment for testing footwear. Like transaction 2, transaction 3 is an exchange of one asset, cash, for another asset, equipment. The equipment is an asset because of its expected future benefits from testing footwear. This purchase changes the makeup of assets but does not change the asset total. The accounting equation remains in balance.

	Assets					=	Liabilities	+	Equity
	Cash	+	**Supplies**	+	**Equipment**	=			**Common Stock**
Old Bal.	$27,500	+	$2,500			=			$30,000
(3)	**−26,000**			+	**$26,000**				
New Bal.	$ 1,500	+	$2,500	+	$ 26,000	=			$30,000
			$30,000				$30,000		

Transaction 4: Purchase Supplies on Credit Taylor decides more supplies of footwear and accessories are needed. These additional supplies total $7,100, but as we see from the accounting equation in transaction 3, FastForward has only $1,500 in cash. Taylor arranges to purchase them on credit from CalTech Supply Company. Thus, FastForward acquires supplies in exchange for a promise to pay for them later. This purchase increases assets by $7,100 in supplies, and liabilities (called *accounts payable* to CalTech Supply) increase by the same amount. The effects of this purchase follow:

Example: If FastForward pays $500 cash in transaction 4, how does this partial payment affect the liability to CalTech? What would be FastForward's cash balance? *Answers:* The liability to CalTech would be reduced to $6,600 and the cash balance would be reduced to $1,000.

	Assets					=	Liabilities	+	Equity
	Cash	+	**Supplies**	+	**Equipment**	=	**Accounts Payable**	+	**Common Stock**
Old Bal.	$1,500	+	$2,500	+	$26,000	=			$30,000
(4)		**+**	**7,100**				**+$7,100**		
New Bal.	$1,500	+	$9,600	+	$26,000	=	$ 7,100	+	$30,000
			$37,100					$37,100	

Transaction 5: Provide Services for Cash FastForward plans to earn revenues by selling online ad space to manufacturers and by consulting with clients about test results on footwear and accessories. It earns net income only if its revenues are greater than its expenses incurred in earning them. In one of its first jobs, FastForward provides consulting services to a power-walking club and immediately collects $4,200 cash. The accounting equation reflects this increase in cash of $4,200 and in equity of $4,200. This increase in equity is identified in the far right column under Revenues because the cash received is earned by providing consulting services.

Point: Revenue recognition principle requires that revenue is recognized when work is performed.

	Assets					=	Liabilities	+	Equity		
	Cash	+	**Supplies**	+	**Equipment**	=	**Accounts Payable**	+	**Common Stock**	+	**Revenues**
Old Bal.	$1,500	+	$9,600	+	$26,000	=	$7,100	+	$30,000		
(5)	**+4,200**									**+**	**$4,200** Consulting
New Bal.	$5,700	+	$9,600	+	$26,000	=	$7,100	+	$30,000	+	$ 4,200
			$41,300						$41,300		

Transactions 6 and 7: Payment of Expenses in Cash FastForward pays $1,000 rent to the landlord of the building where its facilities are located. Paying this amount allows FastForward to occupy the space for the month of December. The rental payment is reflected in the following accounting equation as transaction 6. FastForward also pays the biweekly $700 salary of the company's only employee. This is reflected in the accounting equation as transaction 7. Both transactions 6 and 7 are December expenses for FastForward. The costs of both rent and salary are expenses, as opposed to assets, because their benefits are used in December (they have no future benefits after December). These transactions also use up an asset (cash) in carrying out FastForward's operations. The accounting equation shows that both transactions reduce cash and equity. The far right column identifies these decreases as Expenses.

Point: Expense recognition principle requires that expenses are recognized when the revenue they help generate is recorded. Expenses are outflows of net assets, which decrease equity.

By definition, increases in expenses yield decreases in equity.

	Assets					=	Liabilities	+	Equity				
	Cash	+	**Supplies**	+	**Equipment**	=	**Accounts Payable**	+	**Common Stock**	+	**Revenues**	−	**Expenses**
Old Bal.	$5,700	+	$9,600	+	$26,000	=	$7,100	+	$30,000	+	$4,200		
(6)	**−1,000**											**−**	**$1,000** Rent
Bal.	4,700	+	9,600	+	26,000	=	7,100	+	30,000	+	4,200	−	1,000
(7)	**− 700**											**−**	**700** Salaries
New Bal.	$4,000	+	$9,600	+	$26,000	=	$7,100	+	$30,000	+	$4,200	−	$ 1,700
			$39,600						$39,600				

Point: Transaction 8, like 5, records revenue when work is performed, not necessarily when cash is received.

Transaction 8: Provide Services and Facilities for Credit FastForward provides consulting services of $1,600 and rents its test facilities for $300 to a podiatric services center. The rental involves allowing members to try recommended footwear and accessories at FastForward's testing area. The center is billed for the $1,900 total. This transaction results in a new asset, called *accounts receivable,* from this client. It also yields an increase in equity from the two revenue components reflected in the Revenues column of the accounting equation:

	Assets				= Liabilities +	Equity		
	Cash	**+ Accounts Receivable**	**+ Supplies**	**+ Equipment**	**= Accounts Payable**	**+ Common Stock**	**+ Revenues**	**− Expenses**
Old Bal.	$4,000	+	+ $9,600	+ $26,000	= $7,100	+ $30,000	+ $4,200	− $1,700
(8)		**+ $1,900**					**+ 1,600** Consulting	
							+ 300 Rental	
New Bal.	$4,000	+ $ 1,900	+ $9,600	+ $26,000	= $7,100	+ $30,000	+ $6,100	− $1,700
	$41,500				$41,500			

Point: Transaction 9 involved no added client work, so no added revenue was recorded.

Point: Receipt of cash is not always a revenue.

Transaction 9: Receipt of Cash from Accounts Receivable The client in transaction 8 (the podiatric center) pays $1,900 to FastForward 10 days after it is billed for consulting services. This transaction 9 does not change the total amount of assets and does not affect liabilities or equity. It converts the receivable (an asset) to cash (another asset). It does not create new revenue. Revenue was recognized when FastForward rendered the services in transaction 8, not when the cash is now collected. This emphasis on the earnings process instead of cash flows is a goal of the revenue recognition principle and yields useful information to users. The new balances follow:

	Assets				= Liabilities +	Equity		
	Cash	**+ Accounts Receivable**	**+ Supplies**	**+ Equipment**	**= Accounts Payable**	**+ Common Stock**	**+ Revenues**	**− Expenses**
Old Bal.	$4,000	+ $1,900	+ $9,600	+ $26,000	= $7,100	+ $30,000	+ $6,100	− $1,700
(9)	**+1,900**	**− 1,900**						
New Bal.	$5,900	+ $ 0	+ $9,600	+ $26,000	= $7,100	+ $30,000	+ $6,100	− $1,700
	$41,500				$41,500			

Transaction 10: Payment of Accounts Payable FastForward pays CalTech Supply $900 cash as partial payment for its earlier $7,100 purchase of supplies (transaction 4), leaving $6,200 unpaid. The accounting equation shows that this transaction decreases FastForward's cash by $900 and decreases its liability to CalTech Supply by $900. Equity does not change. This event does not create an expense even though cash flows out of FastForward (instead the expense is recorded when FastForward derives the benefits from these supplies).

	Assets				= Liabilities +	Equity		
	Cash	**+ Accounts Receivable**	**+ Supplies**	**+ Equipment**	**= Accounts Payable**	**+ Common Stock**	**+ Revenues**	**− Expenses**
Old Bal.	$5,900	+ $ 0	+ $9,600	+ $26,000	= $7,100	+ $30,000	+ $6,100	− $1,700
(10)	**− 900**				**−900**			
New Bal.	$5,000	+ $ 0	+ $9,600	+ $26,000	= $6,200	+ $30,000	+ $6,100	− $1,700
	$40,600				$40,600			

Transaction 11: Payment of Cash Dividend FastForward declares and pays a $200 cash dividend to its owner (the sole shareholder). Dividends (decreases in equity) are not reported as expenses because they are not part of the company's earnings process. Since dividends are not company expenses, they are not used in computing net income.

By definition, increases in dividends yield decreases in equity.

	Assets				= Liabilities +	Equity			
	Cash	+ Accounts Receivable	+ Supplies	+ Equipment	= Accounts Payable	+ Common Stock	− Dividends	+ Revenues	− Expenses
Old Bal.	$5,000	+ $ 0	+ $9,600	+ $26,000	= $6,200	+ $30,000		+ $6,100	− $1,700
(11)	− 200						− $200 Dividends		
New Bal.	$4,800	+ $ 0	+ $9,600	+ $26,000	= $6,200	+ $30,000	− $200	+ $6,100	− $1,700
	$40,400				$40,400				

Summary of Transactions

We summarize in Exhibit 1.9 the effects of these 11 transactions of FastForward using the accounting equation. First, we see that the accounting equation remains in balance after each transaction. Second, transactions can be analyzed by their effects on components of the accounting equation. For example, in transactions 2, 3, and 9, one asset increased while another asset decreased by equal amounts.

Point: Knowing how financial statements are prepared improves our analysis of them.

EXHIBIT 1.9

Summary of Transactions Using the Accounting Equation

	Assets				= Liabilities +	Equity			
	Cash	+ Accounts Receivable	+ Supplies	+ Equipment	= Accounts Payable	+ Common Stock	− Dividends	+ Revenues	− Expenses
(1)	$30,000				=	$30,000			
(2)	− 2,500		+ $2,500						
Bal.	27,500		+ 2,500		=	30,000			
(3)	−26,000			+ $26,000					
Bal.	1,500		+ 2,500	+ 26,000	=	30,000			
(4)			+ 7,100		+$7,100				
Bal.	1,500		+ 9,600	+ 26,000	= 7,100	+ 30,000			
(5)	+ 4,200							+ $4,200	
Bal.	5,700		+ 9,600	+ 26,000	= 7,100	+ 30,000		+ 4,200	
(6)	− 1,000								− $1,000
Bal.	4,700		+ 9,600	+ 26,000	= 7,100	+ 30,000		+ 4,200	− 1,000
(7)	− 700								− 700
Bal.	4,000		+ 9,600	+ 26,000	= 7,100	+ 30,000		+ 4,200	− 1,700
(8)		+ $1,900						+ 1,600 + 300	
Bal.	4,000	+ 1,900	+ 9,600	+ 26,000	= 7,100	+ 30,000		+ 6,100	− 1,700
(9)	+ 1,900	− 1,900							
Bal.	5,900	+ 0	+ 9,600	+ 26,000	= 7,100	+ 30,000		+ 6,100	− 1,700
(10)	− 900				− 900				
Bal.	5,000	+ 0	+ 9,600	+ 26,000	= 6,200	+ 30,000		+ 6,100	− 1,700
(11)	− 200						− $200		
Bal.	$ 4,800	+ $ 0	+ $ 9,600	+ $ 26,000	= $ 6,200	+ $ 30,000	− $200	+ $6,100	− $ 1,700

NEED-TO-KNOW 1-4

Transaction Analysis

P1

QC3

Assume Tata Company began operations on January 1 and completed the following transactions during its first month of operations. Arrange the following asset, liability, and equity titles in a table like Exhibit 1.9: Cash; Accounts Receivable; Equipment; Accounts Payable; Common Stock; Dividends; Revenues; and Expenses.

Jan. 1 Jamsetji Tata invested $4,000 cash in Tata Company in exchange for its common stock.
5 The company purchased $2,000 of equipment on credit.
14 The company provided $540 of services for a client on credit.
21 The company paid $250 cash for an employee's salary.

Do More: QS 1-10, QS 1-11, E 1-10, E 1-11, E 1-13

Solution

	Assets				Liabilities +	Equity			
	Cash +	Accounts Receivable +	Equipment	=	Accounts Payable +	Common Stock −	Dividends +	Revenues −	Expenses
Jan. 1	**$4,000**			=		**$4,000**			
Jan. 5			**+$2,000**		**+$2,000**				
Bal.	4,000		2,000	=	2,000	4,000			
Jan. 14		**+$540**						**+$540**	
Bal.	4,000	540	2,000	=	2,000	4,000		540	
Jan. 21	**−250**							−	**$250**
Bal.	3,750	540	2,000	=	2,000	4,000		540 −	250
	$6,290				$6,290				

FINANCIAL STATEMENTS

P2 Identify and prepare basic financial statements and explain how they interrelate.

This section introduces us to how financial statements are prepared from the analysis of business transactions. The four financial statements and their purposes are:

1. **Income statement**—describes a company's revenues and expenses along with the resulting net income or loss over a period of time due to earnings activities.
2. **Statement of retained earnings**—explains changes in equity from net income (or loss) and from any dividends over a period of time.
3. **Balance sheet**—describes a company's financial position (types and amounts of assets, liabilities, and equity) at a point in time.
4. **Statement of cash flows**—identifies cash inflows (receipts) and cash outflows (payments) over a period of time.

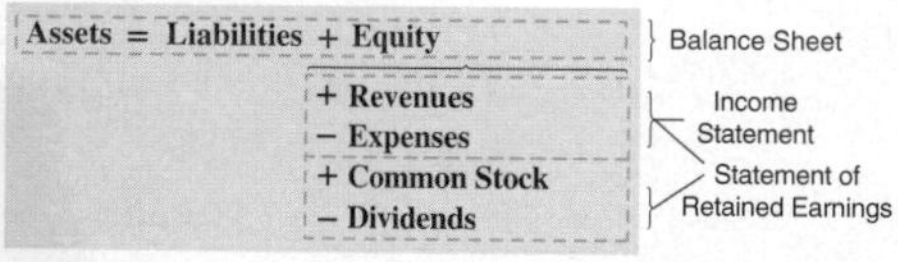

We prepare these financial statements, in this order, using the 11 selected transactions of FastForward. (These statements are technically called *unadjusted*—we explain this in Chapters 2 and 3.) The graphic to the side shows that financial statements reflect different parts of the expanded accounting equation.

Income Statement

FastForward's income statement for December is shown at the top of Exhibit 1.10. Information about revenues and expenses is conveniently taken from the Equity columns of Exhibit 1.9. Revenues are reported first on the income statement. They include consulting revenues of $5,800 from transactions 5 and 8 and rental revenue of $300 from transaction 8. Expenses are reported after revenues. (For convenience in this chapter, we list larger amounts first, but we can sort expenses in different ways.) Rent and salary expenses are from transactions 6 and 7. Expenses reflect the costs to generate the revenues reported. Net income (or loss) is reported at the bottom of the statement and is the amount earned in December. Stockholders' investments and dividends are *not* part of income.

Point: Total revenues
− Total expenses
= Net income (or loss)

Point: Net income is sometimes called *earnings* or *profit*.

Statement of Retained Earnings

The statement of retained earnings reports information about how retained earnings changes over the reporting period. This statement shows beginning retained earnings, events that increase it (net income), and events that decrease it (dividends and net loss). Ending retained earnings is computed in this statement and is carried over and reported on the balance sheet. FastForward's statement of retained earnings is the second report in Exhibit 1.10. The beginning balance is measured as of the start of business on December 1. It is zero because FastForward did not exist before then. An existing business reports the beginning balance equal to that as of the end of the prior reporting period (such as from November 30). FastForward's statement shows the $4,400 of net income earned during the period. This links the income statement to the statement of retained earnings (see line ①). The statement also reports the $200 cash dividend and FastForward's end-of-period retained earnings balance.

Point: The statement of retained earnings is also called the *statement of changes in retained earnings*. Note: Beg. Retained Earnings + Net Income − Dividends = End. Retained Earnings

EXHIBIT 1.10

Financial Statements and Their Links

FASTFORWARD
Income Statement
For Month Ended December 31, 2015

Revenues		
Consulting revenue ($4,200 + $1,600)	$ 5,800	
Rental revenue	300	
Total revenues		$ 6,100
Expenses		
Rent expense	1,000	
Salaries expense	700	
Total expenses		1,700
Net income		**$ 4,400**

FASTFORWARD
Statement of Retained Earnings
For Month Ended December 31, 2015

Retained earnings, December 1, 2015	$ 0
Plus: Net income	**4,400** ①
	4,400
Less: Dividends	200
Retained earnings, December 31, 2015	**$ 4,200**

FASTFORWARD
Balance Sheet
December 31, 2015

Assets		**Liabilities**	
Cash	**$ 4,800**	Accounts payable	$ 6,200 ②
Supplies	9,600	Total liabilities	6,200
Equipment	26,000	**Equity**	
		Common stock	30,000
		Retained earnings	**4,200**
		Total equity	34,200
Total assets	$ 40,400	Total liabilities and equity	$ 40,400

FASTFORWARD
Statement of Cash Flows
For Month Ended December 31, 2015

Cash flows from operating activities		
Cash received from clients ($4,200 + $1,900)	$ 6,100	
③ Cash paid for supplies ($2,500 + $900)	(3,400)	
Cash paid for rent	(1,000)	
Cash paid to employee	(700)	
Net cash provided by operating activities		$ 1,000
Cash flows from investing activities		
Purchase of equipment	(26,000)	
Net cash used by investing activities		(26,000)
Cash flows from financing activities		
Investments from stockholder	30,000	
Dividends to stockholder	(200)	
Net cash provided by financing activities		29,800
Net increase in cash		$ 4,800
Cash balance, December 1, 2015		0
Cash balance, December 31, 2015		**$ 4,800**

Point: A statement's heading identifies the company, the statement title, and the date or time period.

Point: Arrow lines show how the statements are linked. ① Net income is used to compute equity. ② Retained earnings is used to prepare the balance sheet. ③ Cash from the balance sheet is used to reconcile the statement of cash flows.

Point: The income statement, the statement of retained earnings, and the statement of cash flows are prepared for a *period* of time. The balance sheet is prepared as of a *point* in time.

Point: A single ruled line denotes an addition or subtraction. Final totals are double underlined. Negative amounts are often in parentheses.

Balance Sheet

FastForward's balance sheet is the third report in Exhibit 1.10. This statement refers to FastForward's financial condition at the close of business on December 31. The left side of the balance sheet lists FastForward's assets: cash, supplies, and equipment. The upper right side of the balance sheet shows that FastForward owes $6,200 to creditors. Any other liabilities (such as a bank loan) would be listed here. The equity balance is $34,200. Line ② shows the link between the ending balance of the statement of retained earnings and the retained earnings balance on the balance sheet. (This presentation of the balance sheet is called the *account form:* assets on the left and liabilities and equity on the right. Another presentation is the *report form:* assets on top, followed by liabilities and then equity at the bottom. Either presentation is acceptable.) As always, we see the accounting equation applies: Assets of $40,400 = Liabilities of $6,200 + Equity of $34,200.

Statement of Cash Flows

Point: Statement of cash flows has three main sections: operating, investing, and financing.

Point: Payment for supplies is an operating activity because supplies are expected to be used up in short-term operations (typically less than one year).

Point: Investing activities refer to long-term asset investments by the company, *not* to owner investments.

FastForward's statement of cash flows is the final report in Exhibit 1.10. The first section reports cash flows from *operating activities*. It shows the $6,100 cash received from clients and the $5,100 cash paid for supplies, rent, and employee salaries. Outflows are in parentheses to denote subtraction. Net cash provided by operating activities for December is $1,000. If cash paid exceeded the $5,100 cash received, we would call it "cash used by operating activities." The second section reports *investing activities,* which involve buying and selling assets such as land and equipment that are held for *long-term use* (typically more than one year). The only investing activity is the $26,000 purchase of equipment. The third section shows cash flows from *financing activities,* which include the *long-term* borrowing and repaying of cash from lenders and the cash investments from, and dividends to, stockholders. FastForward reports $30,000 from the owner's initial investment and the $200 cash dividend. The net cash effect of all financing transactions is a $29,800 cash inflow. The final part of the statement shows FastForward increased its cash balance by $4,800 in December. Since it started with no cash, the ending balance is also $4,800—see line ③. We see that cash flow numbers are different from income statement (*accrual*) numbers, which is common.

NEED-TO-KNOW 1-5

Financial Statements

P2

Prepare the (a) income statement, (b) statement of retained earnings, and (c) balance sheet, for **Apple** using the following *condensed* data from its fiscal year ended September 28, 2013 ($ in millions).

Accounts payable	$ 22,367	Investments and other assets	$163,042
Other liabilities	61,084	Land and equipment (net)	16,597
Cost of sales and other expenses	119,724	Selling and other expenses	14,149
Cash	14,259	Accounts receivable	13,102
Retained earnings, Sep. 29, 2012	101,289	Net income	37,037
Dividends in fiscal year 2013	34,070	Retained earnings, Sep. 28, 2013	104,256
Revenues	170,910	Common stock	19,293

Solution ($ in millions)

APPLE
Income Statement
For Fiscal Year Ended September 28, 2013

Revenues		$170,910
Expenses		
Cost of sales and other expenses	119,724	
Selling and other expenses	14,149	
Total expenses		133,873
Net income		$ 37,037

To next page statement of retained earnings

APPLE
Statement of Retained Earnings
For Fiscal Year Ended September 28, 2013

Retained earnings, Sep. 29, 2012	$101,289
Plus: Net income	37,037
	138,326
Less: Dividends	34,070
Retained earnings, Sep. 28, 2013	$104,256

From prior page income statement

APPLE
Balance Sheet
September 28, 2013

Assets		**Liabilities**	
Cash	$ 14,259	Accounts payable	$ 22,367
Accounts receivable	13,102	Other liabilities	61,084
Land and equipment (net)	16,597	Total liabilities	83,451
Investments and other assets	163,042	**Equity**	
		Common stock	19,293
		Retained earnings	104,256
		Total equity	123,549
Total assets	$207,000	Total liabilities and equity	$207,000

Do More: QS 1-12, QS 1-13, QS 1-14, E 1-15, E 1-16, E 1-17

QC4

GLOBAL VIEW

Accounting according to U.S. GAAP is similar, but not identical, to IFRS. Throughout the book we use this last section to identify major similarities and differences between IFRS and U.S. GAAP for the materials in each chapter.

Basic Principles Both U.S. GAAP and IFRS include broad and similar guidance for accounting. However, neither system specifies particular account names nor the detail required. (A typical *chart of accounts* is shown near the end of this book.) IFRS does require certain minimum line items be reported in the balance sheet along with other minimum disclosures that U.S. GAAP does not. On the other hand, U.S. GAAP requires disclosures for the current and prior two years for the income statement, statement of cash flows, and statement of retained earnings (equity), while IFRS requires disclosures for the current and prior year. Still, the basic principles behind these two systems are similar.†

Transaction Analysis Both U.S. GAAP and IFRS apply transaction analysis identically as shown in this chapter. Although some variations exist in revenue and expense recognition and other principles, all of the transactions in this chapter are accounted for identically under these two systems. It is often said that U.S. GAAP is more *rules-based* whereas IFRS is more *principles-based*. The main difference on the rules versus principles focus is with the approach in deciding how to account for certain transactions. Under U.S. GAAP, the approach is more focused on strictly following the accounting rules; under IFRS, the approach is more focused on a review of the situation and how accounting can best reflect it. This difference typically impacts advanced topics beyond the introductory course.

Financial Statements Both U.S. GAAP and IFRS prepare the same four basic financial statements. To illustrate, a condensed version of **Samsung**'s income statement follows (numbers here are in thousands of U.S. dollars). Similar condensed versions can be prepared for the other three statements (see Appendix A).

Samsung

†The FASB and the IASB completed a joint project in 2014 to clarify the principles for recognizing revenue and to develop a common revenue standard for U.S. GAAP and IFRS. The FASB amended the FASB Accounting Standards Codification® and created a new Topic 606, *Revenue from Contracts with Customers,* and the IASB issued IFRS 15, *Revenue from Contracts with Customers.* The core principle is that "an entity should recognize revenue to depict the transfer of promised goods or services to customers in an amount that reflects the consideration to which the entity expects to be entitled in exchange for those goods or services." All discussions and presentations in this book are consistent with this new standard.

SAMSUNG Income Statement (in $ thousands) For Year Ended December 31, 2013	
Revenues	$216,708,677
Cost of sales	130,480,725
Cost of selling, wages, depreciation, and other expenses, net	49,874,044
Tax expense	7,476,087
Net income (profit)	$ 28,877,821

Status of IFRS Accounting impacts companies across the world, which requires us to take a global view. IFRS is now adopted or accepted in over 115 countries, including over 30 member-states of the EU. The FASB and IASB continue to work on the convergence of IFRS and U.S. GAAP.

Sustainability and Accounting The **Sustainability Accounting Standards Board (SASB)** is a nonprofit entity engaged in creating and disseminating sustainability accounting standards for use by companies. Sustainability refers to *environmental*, *social*, and *governance* (*ESG*) dimensions of a company. An example of a company's social dimension is donations to hospitals, colleges, community programs, and law enforcement. It can also include programs to reduce pollution, increase product safety, improve worker conditions, and support continuing education. Other programs include discounts to students and senior citizens, and sponsoring events such as Special Olympics and summer reading programs.

Sustainability accounting standards are intended to complement financial accounting standards. The SASB has a *Conceptual Framework* to guide the development of sustainability standards. It has also developed a set of *principles,* which serve as a set of minimum criteria. In the case of **Apple**, it asserts that "we're still the only company in our industry whose data centers are powered by 100 percent renewable energy and whose entire product line not only meets but far exceeds strict ENERGY STAR guidelines. And . . . even though we're manufacturing and shipping more products, our carbon emissions per product are dropping."

Decision Insight

Sustainability Returns Virtue is not always its own reward. Compare the S&P 500 with the Domini Social Index (DSEFX), which covers 400 companies that have especially good records for sustainability. We see that returns for companies with sustainable behavior are roughly on par with, or better than, those of the S&P 500 for the recent five-year period. Varying, but similar, results are evident over several recent time periods. ■

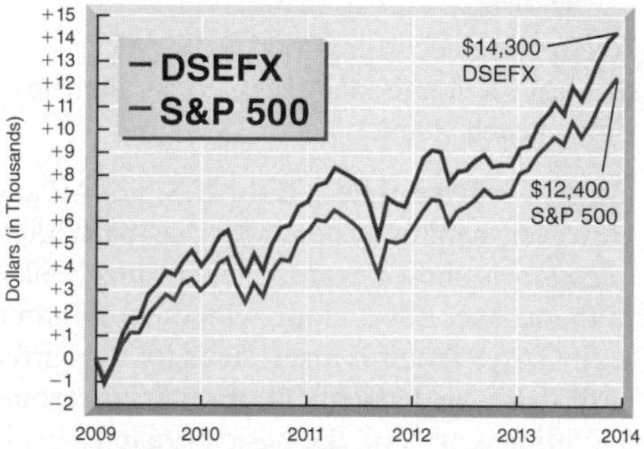

Decision Analysis (a section at the end of each chapter) introduces and explains ratios for decision making using real company data. Instructors can skip this section and cover all ratios in Chapter 13

Decision Analysis — Return on Assets

A2 Compute and interpret return on assets.

A *Decision Analysis* section at the end of each chapter is devoted to financial statement analysis. We organize financial statement analysis into four areas: (1) liquidity and efficiency, (2) solvency, (3) profitability, and (4) market prospects—Chapter 13 has a ratio listing with definitions and groupings by area. When analyzing ratios, we need benchmarks to identify good, bad, or average levels. Common benchmarks include the company's prior levels and those of its competitors.

This chapter presents a profitability measure: return on assets. Return on assets is useful in evaluating management, analyzing and forecasting profits, and planning activities. **Dell** has its marketing department compute return on assets for *every* order. **Return on assets (ROA),** also called *return on investment* (*ROI*), is defined in Exhibit 1.11.

EXHIBIT 1.11
Return on Assets

$$\textbf{Return on assets} = \frac{\textbf{Net income}}{\textbf{Average total assets}}$$

Net income is from the annual income statement, and average total assets is computed by adding the beginning and ending amounts for that same period and dividing by 2. To illustrate, **Dell** reports net income of $2,372 million for fiscal year 2013. At the beginning of fiscal 2013, its total assets are $44,533 million and at the end of fiscal 2013, they total $47,540 million. Dell's return on assets for fiscal 2013 is:

$$\text{Return on assets} = \frac{\$2{,}372 \text{ million}}{(\$47{,}540 \text{ million} + \$44{,}533 \text{ million})/2} = 5.2\%$$

Is a 5.2% return on assets good or bad for Dell? To help answer this question, we compare (benchmark) Dell's return with its prior performance, the returns of competitors (such as **Hewlett-Packard**, **IBM**, and **Lenovo**), and the returns from alternative investments. Dell's return for each of the prior five years is in the second column of Exhibit 1.12, which ranges from 4.8% to 9.2%.

EXHIBIT 1.12

Dell and Industry Returns

	Return on Assets	
Fiscal Year	**Dell**	**Industry**
2013	5.2%	4.9%
2012	8.4	6.9
2011	7.3	6.5
2010	4.8	4.7
2009	9.2	7.2

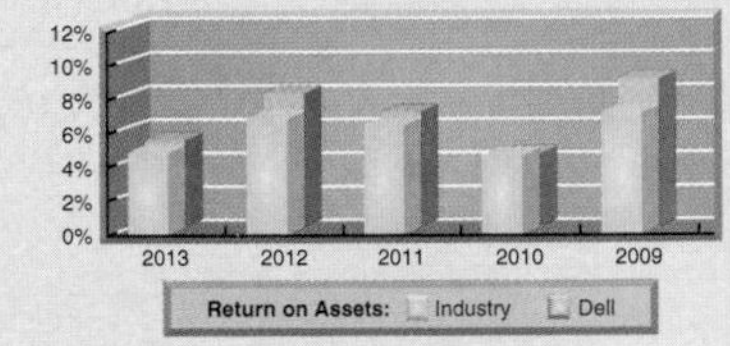

Dell shows a fairly stable pattern of good returns that reflect its productive use of assets. There is a decline in its 2013 return reflecting a more competitive environment. We compare Dell's return to the normal return for similar manufacturers of computers (third column). Industry averages are available from services such as **Dun & Bradstreet**'s *Industry Norms and Key Ratios* and **The Risk Management Association** *Annual Statement Studies*. When compared to the industry, Dell performs slightly above average.

*Each **Decision Analysis** section ends with a role-playing scenario to show the usefulness of ratios*

Decision Maker

Business Owner You own a small winter ski resort that earns a 21% return on its assets. An opportunity to purchase a winter ski equipment manufacturer is offered to you. This manufacturer earns a 19% return on its assets. The industry return for this manufacturer is 14%. Do you purchase this manufacturer? ■ [Answers follow the chapter's Summary.]

*The **Comprehensive Need-to-Know** is a review of key chapter content. The* Planning the Solution *offers strategies in solving the problem*

NEED-TO-KNOW COMPREHENSIVE

After several months of planning, Jasmine Worthy started a haircutting business called Expressions. The following events occurred during its first month of business.

a. On August 1, Worthy invested $3,000 cash and $15,000 of equipment in Expressions in exchange for its common stock.
b. On August 2, Expressions paid $600 cash for furniture for the shop.
c. On August 3, Expressions paid $500 cash to rent space in a strip mall for August.
d. On August 4, it purchased $1,200 of equipment on credit for the shop (using a long-term note payable).
e. On August 5, Expressions opened for business. Cash received from haircutting services in the first week and a half of business (ended August 15) was $825.
f. On August 15, it provided $100 of haircutting services on account.
g. On August 17, it received a $100 check for services previously rendered on account.
h. On August 17, it paid $125 cash to an assistant for hours worked during the grand opening.
i. Cash received from services provided during the second half of August was $930.
j. On August 31, it paid a $400 installment toward principal on the note payable entered into on August 4.
k. On August 31, it paid $900 cash in dividends to Worthy (sole shareholder).

Required

1. Arrange the following asset, liability, and equity titles in a table similar to the one in Exhibit 1.9: Cash; Accounts Receivable; Furniture; Store Equipment; Note Payable; Common Stock; Dividends; Revenues; and Expenses. Show the effects of each transaction using the accounting equation.
2. Prepare an income statement for August.
3. Prepare a statement of retained earnings for August.
4. Prepare a balance sheet as of August 31.
5. Prepare a statement of cash flows for August.
6. Determine the return on assets ratio for August.

PLANNING THE SOLUTION

- Set up a table like Exhibit 1.9 with the appropriate columns for accounts.
- Analyze each transaction and show its effects as increases or decreases in the appropriate columns. Be sure the accounting equation remains in balance after each transaction.
- Prepare the income statement, and identify revenues and expenses. List those items on the statement, compute the difference, and label the result as *net income* or *net loss*.
- Use information in the Equity columns to prepare the statement of retained earnings.
- Use information in the last row of the transactions table to prepare the balance sheet.
- Prepare the statement of cash flows; include all events listed in the Cash column of the transactions table. Classify each cash flow as operating, investing, or financing.
- Calculate return on assets by dividing net income by average assets.

SOLUTION

1.

	Assets							=	Liabilities	+	Equity						
	Cash	+	Accounts Receivable	+	Furniture	+	Store Equipment	=	Note Payable	+	Common Stock	−	Dividends	+	Revenues	−	Expenses
a.	$3,000						$15,000				$18,000						
b.	− 600			+	$600												
Bal.	2,400	+		+	600	+	15,000	=			18,000						
c.	− 500															−	$500
Bal.	1,900	+		+	600	+	15,000	=			18,000					−	500
d.						+	1,200		+$1,200								
Bal.	1,900	+		+	600	+	16,200	=	1,200	+	18,000					−	500
e.	+ 825													+	$ 825		
Bal.	2,725	+		+	600	+	16,200	=	1,200	+	18,000			+	825	−	500
f.		+	$100											+	100		
Bal.	2,725	+	100	+	600	+	16,200	=	1,200	+	18,000			+	925	−	500
g.	+ 100	−	100														
Bal.	2,825	+	0	+	600	+	16,200	=	1,200	+	18,000			+	925	−	500
h.	− 125															−	125
Bal.	2,700	+	0	+	600	+	16,200	=	1,200	+	18,000			+	925	−	625
i.	+ 930													+	930		
Bal.	3,630	+	0	+	600	+	16,200	=	1,200	+	18,000			+	1,855	−	625
j.	− 400								− 400								
Bal.	3,230	+	0	+	600	+	16,200	=	800	+	18,000			+	1,855	−	625
k.	− 900											−	$900				
Bal.	$ 2,330	+	0	+	$600	+	$ 16,200	=	$ 800	+	$ 18,000	−	$900	+	$1,855	−	$625

2.

EXPRESSIONS
Income Statement
For Month Ended August 31

Revenues		
Haircutting services revenue		$1,855
Expenses		
Rent expense	$500	
Wages expense	125	
Total expenses		625
Net income		$1,230

3.

EXPRESSIONS
Statement of Retained Earnings
For Month Ended August 31

Retained earnings, August 1*	$ 0
Plus: Net income	1,230
	1,230
Less: Dividend to owner	900
Retained earnings, August 31	$ 330

*If Expressions had been an existing business from a prior period, the beginning retained earnings balance would equal the retained earnings balance from the end of the prior period.

4.

EXPRESSIONS
Balance Sheet
August 31

Assets		**Liabilities**	
Cash	$ 2,330	Note payable	$ 800
Furniture	600	**Equity**	
Store equipment	16,200	Common stock	18,000
		Retained earnings	330
		Total equity	18,330
Total assets	$19,130	Total liabilities and equity	$19,130

5.

EXPRESSIONS
Statement of Cash Flows
For Month Ended August 31

Cash flows from operating activities		
Cash received from customers	$1,855	
Cash paid for rent	(500)	
Cash paid for wages	(125)	
Net cash provided by operating activities		$1,230
Cash flows from investing activities		
Cash paid for furniture		(600)
Cash flows from financing activities		
Cash investments from stockholders	3,000	
Cash dividends to stockholders	(900)	
Partial repayment of (long-term) note payable	(400)	
Net cash provided by financing activities		1,700
Net increase in cash		$2,330
Cash balance, August 1		0
Cash balance, August 31		$2,330

6. Return on assets $= \frac{\text{Net income}}{\text{Average assets}} = \frac{\$1{,}230}{(\$18{,}000^* + \$19{,}130)/2} = \frac{\$1{,}230}{\$18{,}565} = \underline{\underline{6.63\%}}$

*Uses the initial $18,000 investment as the beginning balance for the *start-up period only*.

APPENDIX

1A Return and Risk Analysis

A3 Explain the relation between return and risk.

This appendix explains return and risk analysis and its role in business and accounting.

Net income is often linked to **return.** Return on assets (ROA) is stated in ratio form as income divided by assets invested. For example, banks report return from a savings account in the form of an interest return such as 4%. If we invest in a savings account or in U.S. Treasury bills, we expect a return of around 2% to 7%. We could also invest in a company's stock, or even start our own business. How do we decide among these investment options? The answer depends on our trade-off between return and risk.

Risk is the uncertainty about the return we will earn. All business investments involve risk, but some investments involve more risk than others. The lower the risk of an investment, the lower is our expected return. The reason that savings accounts pay such a low return is the low risk of not being repaid with interest (the government guarantees most savings accounts from default). If we buy a share of eBay or any other company, we might obtain a large return. However, we have no guarantee of any return; there is even the risk of loss.

EXHIBIT 1A.1

Average Returns for Bonds with Different Risks

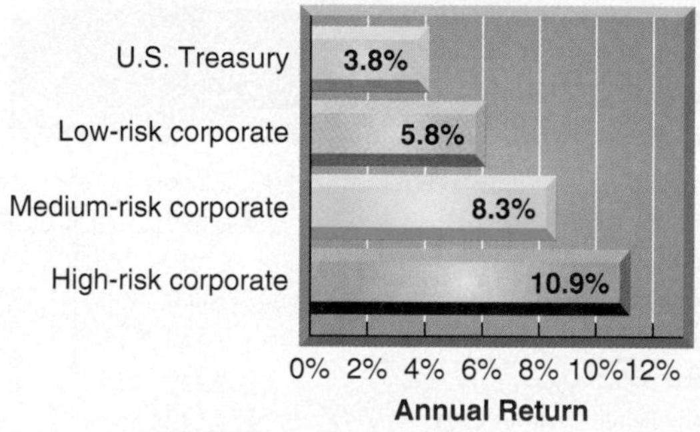

The bar graph in Exhibit 1A.1 shows recent returns for 10-year bonds with different risks. *Bonds* are written promises by organizations to repay amounts loaned with interest. U.S. Treasury bonds provide a low expected return, but they also offer low risk since they are backed by the U.S. government. High-risk corporate bonds offer a much larger potential return but with much higher risk.

The trade-off between return and risk is a normal part of business. Higher risk implies higher, but riskier, expected returns. To help us make better decisions, we use accounting information to assess both return and risk.

APPENDIX

1B Business Activities and the Accounting Equation

C5 Identify and describe the three major activities of organizations.

This appendix explains how the accounting equation is derived from business activities.

There are three major types of business activities: financing, investing, and operating. Each of these requires planning. *Planning* involves defining an organization's ideas, goals, and actions. Most public corporations use the *Management Discussion and Analysis* section in their annual reports to communicate plans. However, planning is not cast in stone. This adds *risk* to both setting plans and analyzing them.

Financing *Financing activities* provide the means organizations use to pay for resources such as land, buildings, and equipment to carry out plans. Organizations are careful in acquiring and managing financing activities because they can determine success or failure. The two sources of financing are owner and nonowner. *Owner financing* refers to resources contributed by the owner along with any income the owner leaves in the organization. *Nonowner* (or *creditor*) *financing* refers to resources contributed by creditors (lenders). *Financial management* is the task of planning how to obtain these resources and to set the right mix between owner and creditor financing.

Point: Management must understand accounting data to set financial goals, make financing and investing decisions, and evaluate operating performance.

Investing *Investing activities* are the acquiring and disposing of resources (assets) that an organization uses to acquire and sell its products or services. Assets are funded by an organization's financing. Organizations differ on the amount and makeup of assets. Some require land and factories to operate. Others need only an office. Determining the amount and type of assets for operations is called *asset management.* Invested amounts are referred to as *assets.* Financing is made up of creditor and owner financing, which hold claims on assets. Creditors' claims are called *liabilities,* and the owner's claim is called *equity.* This basic equality is called the *accounting equation* and can be written as: Assets = Liabilities + Equity.

Point: Investing (assets) and financing (liabilities plus equity) totals are *always* equal.

Operating *Operating activities* involve using resources to research, develop, purchase, produce, distribute, and market products and services. Sales and revenues are the inflow of assets from selling products and services. Costs and expenses are the outflow of assets to support operating activities. *Strategic management* is the process of determining the right mix of operating activities for the type of organization, its plans, and its market.

Exhibit 1B.1 summarizes business activities. Planning is part of each activity and gives them meaning and focus. Investing (assets) and financing (liabilities and equity) are set opposite each other to stress their balance. Operating activities are below investing and financing activities to show that operating activities are the result of investing and financing.

EXHIBIT 1B.1

Activities of Organizations

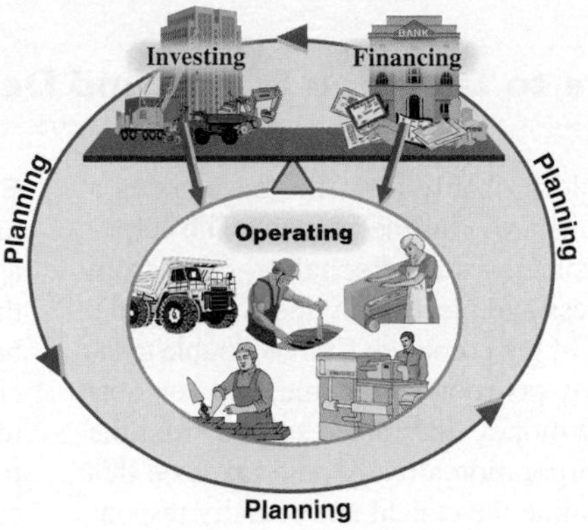

Summary

*A **Summary** organized by learning objectives concludes each chapter*

C1 Explain the purpose and importance of accounting. Accounting is an information and measurement system that aims to identify, record, and communicate relevant, reliable, and comparable information about business activities. It helps assess opportunities, products, investments, and social and community responsibilities.

C2 Identify users and uses of, and opportunities in, accounting. Users of accounting are both internal and external. Some users and uses of accounting include (a) managers in controlling, monitoring, and planning; (b) lenders for measuring the risk and return of loans; (c) shareholders for assessing the return and risk of stock; (d) directors for overseeing management; and (e) employees for judging employment opportunities. Opportunities in accounting include financial, managerial, and tax accounting. They also include accounting-related fields such as lending, consulting, managing, and planning.

C3 Explain why ethics are crucial to accounting. The goal of accounting is to provide useful information for decision making. For information to be useful, it must be trusted. This demands ethical behavior in accounting.

C4 Explain generally accepted accounting principles and define and apply several accounting principles. Generally accepted accounting principles are a common set of standards applied by accountants. Accounting principles aid in producing relevant, reliable, and comparable information. Four principles underlying financial statements were introduced: cost, revenue recognition, matching, and full disclosure. Financial statements also reflect four assumptions: going-concern, monetary unit, time period, and business entity.

C5[B] Identify and describe the three major activities of organizations. Organizations carry out three major activities: financing, investing, and operating. Financing is the means used to pay for resources such as land, buildings, and machines. Investing refers to the buying and selling of resources used in acquiring and selling products and services. Operating activities are those necessary for carrying out the organization's plans.

A1 Define and interpret the accounting equation and each of its components. The accounting equation is: Assets = Liabilities + Equity. Assets are resources owned by a company. Liabilities are creditors' claims on assets. Equity is the owner's claim on assets (*the residual*). The expanded accounting equation is: Assets = Liabilities + [Common Stock − Dividends + Revenues − Expenses].

A2 Compute and interpret return on assets. Return on assets is computed as net income divided by average assets. For example, if we have an average balance of $100 in a savings account and it earns $5 interest for the year, the return on assets is $5/$100, or 5%.

A3[A] Explain the relation between return and risk. *Return* refers to income, and *risk* is the uncertainty about the return we hope to make. All investments involve risk. The lower the risk of an investment, the lower is its expected return. Higher risk implies higher, but riskier, expected return.

P1 Analyze business transactions using the accounting equation. A *transaction* is an exchange of economic consideration between two parties. Examples include exchanges of products, services, money, and rights to collect money. Transactions always have at least two effects on one or more components of the accounting equation. This equation is always in balance.

P2 Identify and prepare basic financial statements and explain how they interrelate. Four financial statements report on an organization's activities: balance sheet, income statement, statement of retained earnings, and statement of cash flows.

Guidance Answers to Decision Maker and Decision Ethics

Entrepreneur You should probably form the business as a corporation if potential lawsuits are of prime concern. The corporate form of organization protects your personal property from lawsuits directed at the business and places only the corporation's resources at risk. A downside of the corporate form is double taxation: The corporation must pay taxes on its income, and you normally must pay taxes on any money distributed to you from the business (even though the corporation already paid taxes on this money). You should also examine the ethical and socially responsible aspects of starting a business in which you anticipate injuries to others. Formation as an LLC or S corp. should also be explored.

Business Owner The 19% return on assets for the manufacturer exceeds the 14% industry return (and many others). This is a positive factor for a potential purchase. Also, the purchase of this manufacturer is an opportunity to spread your risk over two businesses as opposed to one. Still, you should hesitate to purchase a business whose return of 19% is lower than your current resort's return of 21%. You are probably better off directing efforts to increase investment in your resort, assuming you can continue to earn a 21% return.

A list of key terms concludes each chapter (a complete glossary is also available)

Key Terms

Accounting
Accounting equation
Assets
Audit
Auditors
Balance sheet
Bookkeeping
Business entity assumption
Common stock
Conceptual framework
Contributed capital
Corporation
Cost-benefit constraint
Cost principle
Dividends
Dodd-Frank Wall Street Reform and Consumer Protection Act
Equity
Ethics
Events
Expanded accounting equation
Expense recognition principle
Expenses
External transactions
External users
Financial accounting
Financial Accounting Standards Board (FASB)
Full disclosure principle
Generally accepted accounting principles (GAAP)
Going-concern assumption
Income statement
Internal transactions
Internal users
International Accounting Standards Board (IASB)
International Financial Reporting Standards (IFRS)
Liabilities
Managerial accounting
Matching principle
Materiality constraint
Measurement principle
Monetary unit assumption
Net income
Net loss
Partnership
Proprietorship
Recordkeeping
Retained earnings
Return
Return on assets (ROA)
Revenue recognition principle
Revenues
Risk
Sarbanes-Oxley Act (SOX)
Securities and Exchange Commission (SEC)
Shareholders
Shares
Sole proprietorship
Statement of cash flows
Statement of retained earnings
Stock
Stockholders
Sustainability Accounting Standards Board (SASB)
Time period assumption

Multiple Choice Quiz Answers at end of chapter

1. A building is offered for sale at $500,000 but is currently assessed at $400,000. The purchaser of the building believes the building is worth $475,000, but ultimately purchases the building for $450,000. The purchaser records the building at:
a. $50,000
b. $400,000
c. $450,000
d. $475,000
e. $500,000

2. On December 30, 2014, **KPMG** signs a $150,000 contract to provide accounting services to one of its clients in 2015. KPMG has a December 31 year-end. Which accounting principle or assumption requires KPMG to record the accounting services revenue from this client in 2015 and not 2014?
a. Business entity assumption
b. Revenue recognition principle
c. Monetary unit assumption
d. Cost principle
e. Going-concern assumption

3. If the assets of a company increase by $100,000 during the year and its liabilities increase by $35,000 during the same year, then the change in equity of the company during the year must have been:
a. An increase of $135,000.
b. A decrease of $135,000.
c. A decrease of $65,000.
d. An increase of $65,000.
e. An increase of $100,000.

4. **Brunswick** borrows $50,000 cash from Third National Bank. How does this transaction affect the accounting equation for Brunswick?
a. Assets increase by $50,000; liabilities increase by $50,000; no effect on equity.
b. Assets increase by $50,000; no effect on liabilities; equity increases by $50,000.
c. Assets increase by $50,000; liabilities decrease by $50,000; no effect on equity.
d. No effect on assets; liabilities increase by $50,000; equity increases by $50,000.
e. No effect on assets; liabilities increase by $50,000; equity decreases by $50,000.

5. **Geek Squad** performs services for a customer and bills the customer for $500. How would Geek Squad record this transaction?
a. Accounts receivable increase by $500; revenues increase by $500.
b. Cash increases by $500; revenues increase by $500.
c. Accounts receivable increase by $500; revenues decrease by $500.
d. Accounts receivable increase by $500; accounts payable increase by $500.
e. Accounts payable increase by $500; revenues increase by $500.

A(B) *Superscript letter A (B) denotes assignments based on Appendix 1A (1B).*
Icon denotes assignments that involve decision making.

Discussion Questions

1. What is the purpose of accounting in society?
2. Technology is increasingly used to process accounting data. Why then must we study and understand accounting?
3. Identify four kinds of external users and describe how they use accounting information.
4. What are at least three questions business owners and managers might be able to answer by looking at accounting information?
5. Identify three actual businesses that offer services and three actual businesses that offer products.
6. Describe the internal role of accounting for organizations.
7. Identify three types of services typically offered by accounting professionals.
8. What type of accounting information might be useful to the marketing managers of a business?
9. Why is accounting described as a service activity?
10. What are some accounting-related professions?
11. How do ethics rules affect auditors' choice of clients?
12. What work do tax accounting professionals perform in addition to preparing tax returns?
13. What does the concept of *objectivity* imply for information reported in financial statements? Why?
14. A business reports its own office stationery on the balance sheet at its $400 cost, although it cannot be sold for more than $10 as scrap paper. Which accounting principle and/or assumption justifies this treatment?
15. Why is the revenue recognition principle needed? What does it demand?
16. Describe the three basic forms of business organization and their key attributes.
17. Define (*a*) *assets,* (*b*) *liabilities,* (*c*) *equity,* and (*d*) *net assets.*
18. What events or transactions change equity?
19. Identify the two main categories of accounting principles.
20. What do accountants mean by the term *revenue*?
21. Define *net income* and explain its computation.

22. Identify the four basic financial statements of a business.

23. What information is reported in an income statement?

24. Give two examples of expenses a business might incur.

25. What is the purpose of the statement of retained earnings?

26. What information is reported in a balance sheet?

27. The statement of cash flows reports on what major activities?

28. Define and explain return on assets.

29.[A] Define return and risk. Discuss the trade-off between them.

30.[B] Describe the three major business activities in organizations.

31.[B] Explain why investing (assets) and financing (liabilities and equity) totals are always equal.

32. Refer to the financial statements of **Apple** in Appendix A near the end of the book. To what level of significance are dollar amounts rounded? What time period does its income statement cover? **APPLE**

33. Identify the dollar amounts of **Google**'s 2013 assets, liabilities, and equity as reported in its statements in Appendix A near the end of the book. **GOOGLE**

34. Refer to **Samsung**'s 2013 balance sheet in Appendix A near the end of the book. Confirm that its total assets equal its total liabilities plus total equity. **Samsung**

35. Access the SEC EDGAR database (**www.SEC.gov**) and retrieve **Apple**'s 2013 10-K (filed October 29, 2013). Identify its auditor. What responsibility does its independent auditor claim regarding Apple's financial statements? **APPLE**

Quick Study exercises offer a brief test of key elements

Connect reproduces assignments online, in static or algorithmic mode, which allows instructors to monitor, promote, and assess student learning. It can be used for practice, homework, or exams

connect

QUICK STUDY

QS 1-1
Understanding accounting
C1

Choose from the following list of terms/phrases to best complete the following statements.

a. Accounting	**c.** Recording	**e.** Recordkeeping (bookkeeping)	**g.** Language of business
b. Identifying	**d.** Communicating	**f.** Technology	**h.** Governmental

______ **1.** reduces the time, effort, and cost of recordkeeping while improving clerical accuracy.

______ **2.** business activities requires that we keep a chronological log of transactions and events measured in dollars.

______ **3.** is the recording of transactions and events, either manually or electronically.

QS 1-2
Identifying accounting users
C2

Identify the following users as either external users (E) or internal users (I).

______ **a.** Customers	______ **e.** Managers	______ **i.** Controllers
______ **b.** Suppliers	______ **f.** District attorney	______ **j.** FBI and IRS
______ **c.** Brokers	______ **g.** Shareholders	______ **k.** Consumer group
______ **d.** Business press	______ **h.** Lenders	______ **l.** Sales clerks

QS 1-3
Identifying ethical concerns
C3

a. Accounting professionals must sometimes choose between two or more acceptable methods of accounting for business transactions and events. Explain why these situations can involve difficult matters of ethical concern.

b. An important responsibility of many accounting professionals is to design and implement internal control procedures for organizations. Explain the purpose of internal control procedures. Provide two examples of internal controls applied by companies.

QS 1-4
Identifying principles, assumptions and constraints C4

Identify each of the following terms/phrases as either an accounting: (a) principle, (b) assumption, or (c) constraint.

______ **1.** Materiality	______ **3.** Benefit exceeds cost
______ **2.** Time period	______ **4.** Revenue recognition

QS 1-5
Identifying attributes of businesses
C4

Complete the following table with either a yes or no regarding the attributes of a proprietorship, partnership and corporation.

Attribute Present	Proprietorship	Partnership	Corporation
1. Business taxed.	____	____	____
2. Business entity.	____	____	____
3. Legal entity	____	____	____

QS 1-6
Identifying accounting principles C4

This icon highlights assignments that enhance decision-making skills

Identify which accounting principle or assumption best describes each of the following practices:

a. In December 2014, Chavez Landscaping received a customer's order and cash prepayment to install sod at a new house that would not be ready for installation until March 2015. Chavez should record the revenue from the customer order in March 2015, not in December 2014.

b. If $51,000 cash is paid to buy land, the land is reported on the buyer's balance sheet at $51,000.

c. Jo Keene owns both Sailing Passions and Dockside Supplies. In preparing financial statements for Dockside Supplies, Keene makes sure that the expense transactions of Sailing Passions are kept separate from Dockside's transactions and financial statements.

QS 1-7
Applying the accounting equation A1

a. Total assets of Charter Company equal $700,000 and its equity is $420,000. What is the amount of its liabilities?

b. Total assets of Martin Marine equal $500,000 and its liabilities and equity amounts are equal to each other. What is the amount of its liabilities? What is the amount of its equity?

QS 1-8
Applying the accounting equation
A1

1. Use the accounting equation to compute the missing financial statement amounts (*a*), (*b*), and (*c*).

	A	B		C		D
1	**Company**	**Assets**	=	**Liabilities**	+	**Equity**
2	1	$ 75,000		$ (*a*)		$ 40,000
3	2	(*b*)		25,000		70,000
4	3	85,000		20,000		(*c*)
5						

2. Use the expanded accounting equation to compute the missing financial statement amounts (*a*) and (*b*).

	A	B	C	D	E	F	G
1				**Common**			
2	**Company**	**Assets**	**Liabilities**	**Stock**	**Dividends**	**Revenues**	**Expenses**
3	1	$ 40,000	$ 16,000	$ 20,000	$ 0	(*a*)	$ 8,000
4	2	$ 80,000	$ 32,000	$ 44,000	(*b*)	$ 24,000	$ 18,000
5							

QS 1-9
Identifying and computing assets, liabilities, and equity A1

Samsung

Use **Samsung**'s December 31, 2013, financial statements, in Appendix A near the end of the book, to answer the following:

a. Identify the amounts (in millions of Korean won) of its 2013 (1) assets, (2) liabilities, and (3) equity.

b. Using amounts from part *a*, verify that Assets = Liabilities + Equity.

QS 1-10
Identifying effects of transactions using accounting equation—Revenues and Expenses
P1

Create a table like the one in Exhibit 1.9, using the following headings for columns: Cash; Accounts Receivable; Accounts Payable; Common Stock; Dividends; Revenues; and Expenses. Then use additions and subtractions to show the effects of each transaction on individual items of the accounting equation (identify each revenue and expense type, such as commissions revenue or rent expense).

a. The company completed consulting work for a client and immediately collected $5,500 cash earned.
b. The company completed commission work for a client and sent a bill for $4,000 to be received within 30 days.
c. The company paid an assistant $1,400 cash as wages for the period.
d. The company collected $1,000 cash as a partial payment for the amount owed by the client in transaction *b*.
e. The company paid $700 cash for this period's cleaning services.

QS 1-11
Identifying effects of transactions using accounting equation—Assets and Liabilities
P1

Create a table like the one in Exhibit 1.9, using the following headings for columns: Cash; Supplies; Equipment; Land; Accounts Payable; Notes Payable; Common Stock; Dividends; Revenues; and Expenses. Then use additions and subtractions to show the effects of each transaction on individual items of the accounting equation.

a. The owner (Alex Carr) invested $15,000 cash in the company in exchange for its common stock.
b. The company purchased supplies for $500 cash.
c. The company purchased $10,000 in equipment on credit (record liability as Note Payable).
d. The company purchased $200 of additional supplies on credit.
e. The company purchased land for $9,000 cash.

QS 1-12
Identifying items with financial statements
P2

Indicate in which financial statement each item would most likely appear: income statement (I), balance sheet (B), statement of retained earnings (E), or statement of cash flows (CF).

_____ **a.** Assets
_____ **b.** Cash from operating activities
_____ **c.** Dividends
_____ **d.** Equipment
_____ **e.** Expenses
_____ **f.** Liabilities
_____ **g.** Net decrease (or increase) in cash
_____ **h.** Revenues
_____ **i.** Total liabilities and equity

QS 1-13
Identifying income and equity accounts P2

Classify each of the following items as revenues (R), expenses (EX), or dividends (D).

_____ **1.** Cost of sales (expense)
_____ **2.** Service revenue
_____ **3.** Wages expense
_____ **4.** Dividends

QS 1-14
Identifying assets, liabilities, and equity P2

Classify each of the following items as assets (A), liabilities (L), or equity (EQ).

_____ **1.** Land
_____ **2.** Common stock
_____ **3.** Equipment
_____ **4.** Accounts payable
_____ **5.** Accounts receivable

QS 1-15
Computing and interpreting return on assets A2

In a recent year's financial statements, **Home Depot** reported the following results. Compute and interpret Home Depot's return on assets (assume competitors average an 8.0% return on assets).

Sales	$67,997 million
Net income	3,338 million
Average total assets	40,501 million

QS 1-16
International accounting standards C4

Answer each of the following questions related to international accounting standards.

a. The International Accounting Standards Board (IASB) issues preferred accounting practices that are referred to as what?
b. The FASB and IASB are working on a convergence process for what purpose?

This icon highlights assignments that focus on IFRS-related content

QS 1-17
Sustainability accounting
C4

Match each of the numbered descriptions with the term or phrase it best reflects. Indicate your answer by writing the letter for the term or phrase in the blank provided.

A. SASB **C.** Social dimension **E.** Conceptual framework **G.** Sustainability standards
B. Principles **D.** Sustainability **F.** Environmental dimension **H.** Domini Social Index

_____ **1.** Refers to the environmental, social, and governance dimensions of an entity.
_____ **2.** A structure to help guide development of sustainability standards.
_____ **3.** An entity that creates and publishes sustainability accounting standards.
_____ **4.** Facet of an entity involved with donations to hospitals, colleges, and community programs.

connect

EXERCISES

Exercise 1-1
Classifying activities reflected in the accounting system
C1

Accounting is an information and measurement system that identifies, records, and communicates relevant, reliable, and comparable information about an organization's business activities. Classify the following activities as part of the identifying (I), recording (R), or communicating (C) aspects of accounting.

_____ **1.** Analyzing and interpreting reports.
_____ **2.** Presenting financial information.
_____ **3.** Keeping a log of service costs.
_____ **4.** Measuring the costs of a product.
_____ **5.** Preparing financial statements.
_____ **6.** Seeing revenues generated from a service.
_____ **7.** Observing employee tasks behind a product.
_____ **8.** Registering cash sales of products sold.

Exercise 1-2
Identifying accounting users and uses
C2

Part A. Identify the following questions as most likely to be asked by an internal (I) or an external (E) user of accounting information.

_____ **1.** What are reasonable payroll benefits and wages?
_____ **2.** Should we make a five-year loan to that business?
_____ **3.** What are the costs of our product's ingredients?
_____ **4.** Do income levels justify the current stock price?
_____ **5.** Should we spend additional money for redesign of our product?
_____ **6.** Which firm reports the highest sales and income?
_____ **7.** What are the costs of our service to customers?

Part B. Identify the following users of accounting information as either an internal (I) or an external (E) user.

_____ **1.** Research and development director
_____ **2.** Human resources director
_____ **3.** Nonexecutive employee
_____ **4.** Shareholders
_____ **5.** Distribution managers
_____ **6.** Creditors
_____ **7.** Production supervisors
_____ **8.** Purchasing manager

Exercise 1-3
Describing accounting responsibilities
C2

Many accounting professionals work in one of the following three areas:

A. Financial accounting **B.** Managerial accounting **C.** Tax accounting

Identify the area of accounting that is most involved in each of the following responsibilities:

_____ **1.** Internal auditing
_____ **2.** External auditing
_____ **3.** Cost accounting
_____ **4.** Budgeting
_____ **5.** Investigating violations of tax laws
_____ **6.** Planning transactions to minimize taxes
_____ **7.** Preparing external financial statements
_____ **8.** Reviewing reports for SEC compliance

Exercise 1-4
Learning the language of business
C1 C2 C3

Match each of the numbered descriptions with the term or phrase it best reflects. Indicate your answer by writing the letter for the term or phrase in the blank provided.

A. Audit **C.** Ethics **E.** SEC **G.** Net income
B. GAAP **D.** Tax accounting **F.** Public accountants **H.** IASB

_____ **1.** An examination of an organization's accounting system and records that adds credibility to financial statements.
_____ **2.** Amount a business earns in excess of all expenses and costs associated with its sales and revenues.
_____ **3.** An accounting area that includes planning future transactions to minimize taxes paid.
_____ **4.** Accounting professionals who provide services to many clients.
_____ **5.** Principles that determine whether an action is right or wrong.

Exercise 1-5
Identifying ethical concerns
C3

Assume the following role and describe a situation in which ethical considerations play an important part in guiding your decisions and actions:

a. You are an accounting professional with audit clients that are competitors in business.
b. You are an accounting professional preparing tax returns for clients.
c. You are a manager with responsibility for several employees.
d. You are a student in an introductory accounting course.

Exercise 1-6
Distinguishing business organizations
C4

The following describe several different business organizations. Determine whether the description refers to a sole proprietorship (SP), partnership (P), or corporation (C).

______ **a.** Micah Douglas and Nathan Logan own Financial Services, a financial services provider. Neither Douglas nor Logan has personal responsibility for the debts of Financial Services.
______ **b.** Riley and Kay own Speedy Packages, a courier service. Both are personally liable for the debts of the business.
______ **c.** IBC Services does not have separate legal existence apart from the one person who owns it.
______ **d.** Trent Company is owned by Trent Malone, who is personally liable for the company's debts.
______ **e.** Ownership of Zander Company is divided into 1,000 shares of stock.
______ **f.** Physio Products does not pay income taxes and has one owner.
______ **g.** AJ Company pays its own income taxes and has two owners.

Exercise 1-7
Identifying accounting principles and assumptions
C4

Match each of the numbered descriptions with the principle or assumption it best reflects. Enter the letter for the appropriate principle or assumption in the blank space next to each description.

A. General accounting principle
B. Cost principle
C. Business entity assumption
D. Revenue recognition principle
E. Specific accounting principle
F. Matching (expense recognition) principle
G. Going-concern assumption
H. Full disclosure principle

______ **1.** A company reports details behind financial statements that would impact users' decisions.
______ **2.** Financial statements reflect the assumption that the business continues operating.
______ **3.** A company records the expenses incurred to generate the revenues reported.
______ **4.** Derived from long-used and generally accepted accounting practices.
______ **5.** Every business is accounted for separately from its owner or owners.
______ **6.** Revenue is recorded only when the earnings process is complete.
______ **7.** Usually created by a pronouncement from an authoritative body.
______ **8.** Information is based on actual costs incurred in transactions.

Exercise 1-8
Using the accounting equation
A1

Determine the missing amount from each of the separate situations *a*, *b*, and *c* below.

	A		B		C
1	**Assets**	=	**Liabilities**	+	**Equity**
2	(a) $?		$ 20,000		$ 45,000
3	(b) 100,000		34,000		?
4	(c) 154,000		?		40,000
5					

Exercise 1-9
Using the accounting equation
A1

Answer the following questions. (*Hint:* Use the accounting equation.)

a. At the beginning of the year, Addison Company's assets are $300,000 and its equity is $100,000. During the year, assets increase $80,000 and liabilities increase $50,000. What is the equity at the end of the year?
b. Office Store has assets equal to $123,000 and liabilities equal to $47,000 at year-end. What is the total equity for Office Store at year-end?
c. At the beginning of the year, Quaker Company's liabilities equal $70,000. During the year, assets increase by $60,000, and at year-end assets equal $190,000. Liabilities decrease $5,000 during the year. What are the beginning and ending amounts of equity?

Check (c) Beg. equity, $60,000

Exercise 1-10
Analysis using the accounting equation
P1

Zen began a new consulting firm on January 5. The accounting equation showed the following balances after each of the company's first five transactions. Analyze the accounting equation for each transaction and describe each of the five transactions with their amounts.

	Assets								=	Liabilities	+	Equity		
Transaction	Cash	+	Accounts Receivable	+	Office Supplies	+	Office Furniture		=	Accounts Payable	+	Common Stock	+	Revenues
a.	$40,000	+	$ 0	+	$ 0	+	$ 0		=	$ 0	+	$40,000	+	$ 0
b.	38,000	+	0	+	3,000	+	0		=	1,000	+	40,000	+	0
c.	30,000	+	0	+	3,000	+	8,000		=	1,000	+	40,000	+	0
d.	30,000	+	6,000	+	3,000	+	8,000		=	1,000	+	40,000	+	6,000
e.	31,000	+	6,000	+	3,000	+	8,000		=	1,000	+	40,000	+	7,000

Exercise 1-11
Identifying effects of transactions on the accounting equation
P1

The following table shows the effects of five transactions (*a* through *e*) on the assets, liabilities, and equity of Mulan's Boutique. Write short descriptions of the probable nature of each transaction.

	Assets							=	Liabilities	+	Equity		
	Cash	+	Accounts Receivable	+	Office Supplies	+	Land	=	Accounts Payable	+	Common Stock	+	Revenues
	$ 21,000	+	$ 0	+	$3,000	+	$19,000	=	$ 0	+	$43,000	+	$ 0
a.	− 4,000					+	4,000						
b.				+	1,000				+1,000				
c.		+	1,900									+	1,900
d.	− 1,000								−1,000				
e.	+ 1,900	−	1,900										
	$ 17,900	+	$ 0	+	$4,000	+	$23,000	=	$ 0	+	$43,000	+	$1,900

Exercise 1-12
Identifying effects of transactions on the accounting equation
P1

Provide an example of a transaction that creates the described effects for the separate cases *a* through *g*.

a. Decreases an asset and decreases equity.
b. Increases an asset and increases a liability.
c. Decreases a liability and increases a liability.
d. Decreases an asset and decreases a liability.
e. Increases an asset and decreases an asset.
f. Increases a liability and decreases equity.
g. Increases an asset and increases equity.

Exercise 1-13
Identifying effects of transactions using the accounting equation
P1

Ming Chen began a professional practice on June 1 and plans to prepare financial statements at the end of each month. During June, Ming Chen (the owner) completed these transactions:

a. Owner invested $60,000 cash in the company along with equipment that had a $15,000 market value in exchange for its common stock.
b. The company paid $1,500 cash for rent of office space for the month.
c. The company purchased $10,000 of additional equipment on credit (payment due within 30 days).
d. The company completed work for a client and immediately collected the $2,500 cash earned.
e. The company completed work for a client and sent a bill for $8,000 to be received within 30 days.
f. The company purchased additional equipment for $6,000 cash.
g. The company paid an assistant $3,000 cash as wages for the month.
h. The company collected $5,000 cash as a partial payment for the amount owed by the client in transaction *e*.
i. The company paid $10,000 cash to settle the liability created in transaction *c*.
j. The company paid $1,000 cash in dividends to the owner (sole shareholder).

Required

Create a table like the one in Exhibit 1.9, using the following headings for columns: Cash; Accounts Receivable; Equipment; Accounts Payable; Common Stock; Dividends; Revenues; and Expenses. Then use additions and subtractions to show the effects of the transactions on individual items of the accounting equation. Show new balances after each transaction.

Check Net income, $6,000

Exercise 1-14
Analysis of return on assets A2

Swiss Group reports net income of $40,000 for 2015. At the beginning of 2015, Swiss Group had $200,000 in assets. By the end of 2015, assets had grown to $300,000. What is Swiss Group's 2015 return on assets? How would you assess its performance if competitors average a 10% return on assets?

Exercise 1-15
Preparing an income statement
P2

On October 1, Ebony Ernst organized Ernst Consulting; on October 3, the owner contributed $84,000 in assets to launch the business. On October 31, the company's records show the following items and amounts. Use this information to prepare an October income statement for the business.

Cash	$11,360	Cash dividends	$ 2,000
Accounts receivable	14,000	Consulting fees earned	14,000
Office supplies	3,250	Rent expense	3,550
Land	46,000	Salaries expense	7,000
Office equipment	18,000	Telephone expense	760
Accounts payable	8,500	Miscellaneous expenses	580
Common stock	84,000		

Check Net income, $2,110

Exercise 1-16
Preparing a statement of retained earnings P2

Use the information in Exercise 1-15 to prepare an October statement of retained earnings for Ernst Consulting.

Exercise 1-17
Preparing a balance sheet P2

Use the information in Exercise 1-15 (if completed, you can also use your solution to Exercise 1-16) to prepare an October 31 balance sheet for Ernst Consulting.

Exercise 1-18
Preparing a statement of cash flows
P2

Use the information in Exercise 1-15 to prepare an October 31 statement of cash flows for Ernst Consulting. Also assume the following:

a. The owner's initial investment consists of $38,000 cash and $46,000 in land in exchange for its common stock.
b. The company's $18,000 equipment purchase is paid in cash.
c. The accounts payable balance of $8,500 consists of the $3,250 office supplies purchase and $5,250 in employee salaries yet to be paid.
d. The company's rent, telephone, and miscellaneous expenses are paid in cash.
e. No cash has been collected on the $14,000 consulting fees earned.

Check Net increase in cash, $11,360

Exercise 1-19
Identifying sections of the statement of cash flows
P2

Indicate the section where each of the following would appear on the statement of cash flows.

O. Cash flows from operating activity
I. Cash flows from investing activity
F. Cash flows from financing activity

______ **1.** Cash purchase of equipment
______ **2.** Cash paid for dividends
______ **3.** Cash paid for advertising
______ **4.** Cash paid for wages
______ **5.** Cash paid on account payable to supplier
______ **6.** Cash received from clients
______ **7.** Cash investment from stockholders
______ **8.** Cash paid for rent

Exercise 1-20
Preparing an income statement for a global company
P2

BMW Group, one of Europe's largest manufacturers, reports the following income statement accounts for the year ended December 31, 2013 (euros in millions).

Revenues	€68,821
Cost of sales	54,276
Sales and administrative costs	6,177
Other expenses	3,487

Use this information to prepare BMW's income statement for the year ended December 31, 2013.

Exercise 1-21[B]
Identifying business activities
C5

Match each transaction or event to one of the following activities of an organization: financing activities (F), investing activities (I), or operating activities (O).

_______ **a.** An owner contributes resources to the business in exchange for its common stock.
_______ **b.** The organization borrows money from a bank.
_______ **c.** An organization advertises a new product.
_______ **d.** An organization sells some of its land.
_______ **e.** An organization purchases equipment.

***Problem Set B** located at the end of **Problem Set A** is provided for each problem to reinforce the learning process*

connect

PROBLEM SET A

Problem 1-1A
Identifying effects of transactions on financial statements
A1 P1

Identify how each of the following separate transactions affects financial statements. For the balance sheet, identify how each transaction affects total assets, total liabilities, and total equity. For the income statement, identify how each transaction affects net income. For the statement of cash flows, identify how each transaction affects cash flows from operating activities, cash flows from investing activities, and cash flows from financing activities. For increases, place a "+" in the column or columns. For decreases, place a "−" in the column or columns. If both an increase and a decrease occur, place a "+/−" in the column or columns. The first transaction is completed as an example.

		Balance Sheet			Income Statement	Statement of Cash Flows		
	Transaction	Total Assets	Total Liab.	Total Equity	Net Income	Operating Activities	Investing Activities	Financing Activities
1	Owner invests cash for its stock	+		+				+
2	Receives cash for services provided							
3	Pays cash for employee wages							
4	Incurs legal costs on credit							
5	Borrows cash by signing long-term note payable							
6	Buys office equipment for cash							
7	Buys land by signing note payable							
8	Provides services on credit							
9	Pays cash dividend							
10	Collects cash on receivable from (8)							

Problem 1-2A
Computing missing information using accounting knowledge
A1 P1

The following financial statement information is from five separate companies:

	Company A	Company B	Company C	Company D	Company E
December 31, 2014					
Assets	$55,000	$34,000	$24,000	$60,000	$119,000
Liabilities	24,500	21,500	9,000	40,000	?
December 31, 2015					
Assets	58,000	40,000	?	85,000	113,000
Liabilities	?	26,500	29,000	24,000	70,000
During year 2015					
Stock issuances	6,000	1,400	9,750	?	6,500
Net income (loss)	8,500	?	8,000	14,000	20,000
Cash dividends	3,500	2,000	5,875	0	11,000

Required

1. Answer the following questions about Company A:
   a. What is the amount of equity on December 31, 2014?
   b. What is the amount of equity on December 31, 2015?
   c. What is the amount of liabilities on December 31, 2015?
2. Answer the following questions about Company B:
   a. What is the amount of equity on December 31, 2014?
   b. What is the amount of equity on December 31, 2015?
   c. What is net income for year 2015?
3. Calculate the amount of assets for Company C on December 31, 2015.
4. Calculate the amount of stock issuances for Company D during year 2015.
5. Calculate the amount of liabilities for Company E on December 31, 2014.

Check (1*b*) $41,500

(2*c*) $1,600

(3) $55,875

Problem 1-3A
Preparing a balance sheet
P2

The following is selected financial information for Armani Company as of December 31, 2015: liabilities, $44,000; equity, $46,000; assets, $90,000.

Required

Prepare the balance sheet for Armani Company as of December 31, 2015.

Problem 1-4A
Preparing an income statement
P2

The following is selected financial information for Edison Energy Company for the year ended December 31, 2015: revenues, $55,000; expenses, $40,000; net income, $15,000.

Required

Prepare the 2015 calendar-year income statement for Edison Energy Company.

Problem 1-5A
Preparing a statement of retained earnings
P2

Following is selected financial information for Kojo Company for the year ended December 31, 2015.

Retained earnings, Dec. 31, 2015	$14,000	Cash dividends	$1,000
Net income	8,000	Retained earnings, Dec. 31, 2014	7,000

Required

Prepare the 2015 statement of retained earnings for Kojo Company.

Problem 1-6A
Preparing a statement of cash flows
P2

Following is selected financial information of Kia Company for the year ended December 31, 2015.

Cash used by investing activities	$(2,000)
Net increase in cash	1,200
Cash used by financing activities	(2,800)
Cash from operating activities	6,000
Cash, December 31, 2014	2,300

Required

Prepare the 2015 statement of cash flows for Kia Company.

Check Cash balance, Dec. 31, 2015, $3,500

Problem 1-7A
Analyzing transactions and preparing financial statements
C4 P1 P2

Gabi Gram started The Gram Co., a new business that began operations on May 1. The Gram Co. completed the following transactions during its first month of operations.

May 1 G. Gram invested $40,000 cash in the company in exchange for its common stock.
1 The company rented a furnished office and paid $2,200 cash for May's rent.
3 The company purchased $1,890 of office equipment on credit.
5 The company paid $750 cash for this month's cleaning services.
8 The company provided consulting services for a client and immediately collected $5,400 cash.
12 The company provided $2,500 of consulting services for a client on credit.
15 The company paid $750 cash for an assistant's salary for the first half of this month.
20 The company received $2,500 cash payment for the services provided on May 12.
22 The company provided $3,200 of consulting services on credit.
25 The company received $3,200 cash payment for the services provided on May 22.

26 The company paid $1,890 cash for the office equipment purchased on May 3.
27 The company purchased $80 of advertising in this month's (May) local paper on credit; cash payment is due June 1.
28 The company paid $750 cash for an assistant's salary for the second half of this month.
30 The company paid $300 cash for this month's telephone bill.
30 The company paid $280 cash for this month's utilities.
31 The company paid $1,400 cash in dividends to the owner (sole shareholder).

Required

1. Arrange the following asset, liability, and equity titles in a table like Exhibit 1.9: Cash; Accounts Receivable; Office Equipment; Accounts Payable; Common Stock; Dividends; Revenues; and Expenses.
2. Show effects of the transactions on the accounts of the accounting equation by recording increases and decreases in the appropriate columns. Do not determine new account balances after each transaction. Determine the final total for each account and verify that the equation is in balance.
3. Prepare an income statement for May, a statement of retained earnings for May, a May 31 balance sheet, and a statement of cash flows for May.

Check (2) Ending balances: Cash, $42,780; Expenses, $5,110

(3) Net income, $5,990; Total assets, $44,670

Problem 1-8A
Analyzing effects of transactions
C4 P1 P2 A1

Lita Lopez started Biz Consulting, a new business, and completed the following transactions during its first year of operations.

a. Lita Lopez invests $70,000 cash and office equipment valued at $10,000 in the company in exchange for its common stock.
b. The company purchased a $150,000 building to use as an office. Biz Consulting paid $20,000 in cash and signed a note payable promising to pay the $130,000 balance over the next 10 years.
c. The company purchased office equipment for $15,000 cash.
d. The company purchased $1,200 of office supplies and $1,700 of office equipment on credit.
e. The company paid a local newspaper $500 cash for printing an announcement of the office's opening.
f. The company completed a financial plan for a client and billed that client $2,800 for the service.
g. The company designed a financial plan for another client and immediately collected a $4,000 cash fee.
h. The company paid $3,275 cash in dividends to the owner (sole shareholder).
i. The company received $1,800 cash as partial payment from the client described in transaction *f*.
j. The company made a partial payment of $700 cash on the equipment purchased in transaction *d*.
k. The company paid $1,800 cash for the office secretary's wages for this period.

Required

1. Create a table like the one in Exhibit 1.9, using the following headings for the columns: Cash; Accounts Receivable; Office Supplies; Office Equipment; Building; Accounts Payable; Notes Payable; Common Stock; Dividends; Revenues; and Expenses.
2. Use additions and subtractions within the table created in part 1 to show the dollar effects of each transaction on individual items of the accounting equation. Show new balances after each transaction.
3. Once you have completed the table, determine the company's net income.

Check (2) Ending balances: Cash, $34,525; Expenses, $2,300; Notes Payable, $130,000

(3) Net income, $4,500

Problem 1-9A
Analyzing transactions and preparing financial statements
C4 P1 P2

Sanyu Sony started a new business and completed these transactions during December.

Dec. 1 Sanyu Sony transferred $65,000 cash from a personal savings account to a checking account in the name of Sony Electric in exchange for its common stock.
2 The company rented office space and paid $1,000 cash for the December rent.
3 The company purchased $13,000 of electrical equipment by paying $4,800 cash and agreeing to pay the $8,200 balance in 30 days.
5 The company purchased office supplies by paying $800 cash.
6 The company completed electrical work and immediately collected $1,200 cash for these services.
8 The company purchased $2,530 of office equipment on credit.
15 The company completed electrical work on credit in the amount of $5,000.
18 The company purchased $350 of office supplies on credit.
20 The company paid $2,530 cash for the office equipment purchased on December 8.
24 The company billed a client $900 for electrical work completed; the balance is due in 30 days.
28 The company received $5,000 cash for the work completed on December 15.
29 The company paid the assistant's salary of $1,400 cash for this month.
30 The company paid $540 cash for this month's utility bill.
31 The company paid $950 cash in dividends to the owner (sole shareholder).

Required

1. Arrange the following asset, liability, and equity titles in a table like Exhibit 1.9: Cash; Accounts Receivable; Office Supplies; Office Equipment; Electrical Equipment; Accounts Payable; Common Stock; Dividends; Revenues; and Expenses.
2. Use additions and subtractions to show the effects of each transaction on the accounts in the accounting equation. Show new balances after each transaction.
3. Use the increases and decreases in the columns of the table from part 2 to prepare an income statement, a statement of retained earnings, and a statement of cash flows—each of these for the current month. Also prepare a balance sheet as of the end of the month.

Check (2) Ending balances: Cash, $59,180, Accounts Payable, $8,550

(3) Net income, $4,160; Total assets, $76,760

Analysis Component

4. Assume that the owner investment transaction on December 1 was $49,000 cash instead of $65,000 and that Sony Electric obtained another $16,000 in cash by borrowing it from a bank. Explain the effect of this change on total assets, total liabilities, and total equity.

Problem 1-10A
Determining expenses, liabilities, equity, and return on assets
A1 A2

Kyzera manufactures, markets, and sells cellular telephones. The average total assets for Kyzera is $250,000. In its most recent year, Kyzera reported net income of $65,000 on revenues of $475,000.

Required

1. What is Kyzera's return on assets?
2. Does return on assets seem satisfactory for Kyzera given that its competitors average a 12% return on assets?
3. What are total expenses for Kyzera in its most recent year?
4. What is the average total amount of liabilities plus equity for Kyzera?

Check (3) $410,000

(4) $250,000

Problem 1-11A
Computing and interpreting return on assets
A2

Coca-Cola and **PepsiCo** both produce and market beverages that are direct competitors. Key financial figures (in $ millions) for these businesses for a recent year follow.

Key Figures ($ millions)	Coca-Cola	PepsiCo
Sales	$46,542	$66,504
Net income	8,634	6,462
Average assets	76,448	70,518

Required

1. Compute return on assets for (*a*) Coca-Cola and (*b*) PepsiCo.
2. Which company is more successful in its total amount of sales to consumers?
3. Which company is more successful in returning net income from its assets invested?

Check (1*a*) 11.3%; (1*b*) 9.2%

Analysis Component

4. Write a one-paragraph memorandum explaining which company you would invest your money in and why. (Limit your explanation to the information provided.)

Problem 1-12A[A]
Identifying risk and return
A3

All business decisions involve aspects of risk and return.

Required

Identify both the risk and the return in each of the following activities:

1. Investing $2,000 in a 5% savings account.
2. Placing a $2,500 bet on your favorite sports team.
3. Investing $10,000 in Yahoo! stock.
4. Taking out a $15,000 college loan toward earning an accounting degree.

Problem 1-13A^B
Describing organizational activities
C5

A start-up company often engages in the following transactions in its first year of operations. Classify those transactions in one of the three major categories of an organization's business activities.

F. Financing **I.** Investing **O.** Operating

______ **1.** Owner investing land in business.
______ **2.** Purchasing a building.
______ **3.** Purchasing land.
______ **4.** Borrowing cash from a bank.
______ **5.** Purchasing equipment.
______ **6.** Selling and distributing products.
______ **7.** Paying for advertising.
______ **8.** Paying employee wages.

Problem 1-14A^B
Describing organizational activities C5

An organization undertakes various activities in pursuit of business success. Identify an organization's three major business activities, and describe each activity.

PROBLEM SET B

Problem 1-1B
Identifying effects of transactions on financial statements
A1 P1

Identify how each of the following separate transactions affects financial statements. For the balance sheet, identify how each transaction affects total assets, total liabilities, and total equity. For the income statement, identify how each transaction affects net income. For the statement of cash flows, identify how each transaction affects cash flows from operating activities, cash flows from investing activities, and cash flows from financing activities. For increases, place a "+" in the column or columns. For decreases, place a "−" in the column or columns. If both an increase and a decrease occur, place "+/−" in the column or columns. The first transaction is completed as an example.

		Balance Sheet			Income Statement	Statement of Cash Flows		
	Transaction	Total Assets	Total Liab.	Total Equity	Net Income	Operating Activities	Investing Activities	Financing Activities
1	Owner invests cash for its stock	+		+				+
2	Buys building by signing note payable							
3	Buys store equipment for cash							
4	Provides services for cash							
5	Pays cash for rent incurred							
6	Incurs utilities costs on credit							
7	Pays cash for salaries incurred							
8	Pays cash dividend							
9	Provides services on credit							
10	Collects cash on receivable from (9)							

Problem 1-2B
Computing missing information using accounting knowledge
A1 P1

The following financial statement information is from five separate companies.

	Company V	Company W	Company X	Company Y	Company Z
December 31, 2014					
Assets	$54,000	$80,000	$141,500	$92,500	$144,000
Liabilities	25,000	60,000	68,500	51,500	?
December 31, 2015					
Assets	59,000	100,000	186,500	?	170,000
Liabilities	36,000	?	65,800	42,000	42,000
During year 2015					
Stock issuances	5,000	20,000	?	48,100	60,000
Net income or (loss)	?	40,000	18,500	24,000	32,000
Cash dividends	5,500	2,000	0	20,000	8,000

Required

1. Answer the following questions about Company V:
   a. What is the amount of equity on December 31, 2014?
   b. What is the amount of equity on December 31, 2015?
   c. What is the net income or loss for the year 2015?
2. Answer the following questions about Company W:
   a. What is the amount of equity on December 31, 2014?
   b. What is the amount of equity on December 31, 2015?
   c. What is the amount of liabilities on December 31, 2015?
3. Calculate the amount of stock issuances for Company X during 2015.
4. Calculate the amount of assets for Company Y on December 31, 2015.
5. Calculate the amount of liabilities for Company Z on December 31, 2014.

Check (1*b*) $23,000

(2*c*) $22,000

(4) $135,100

Problem 1-3B
Preparing a balance sheet
P2

The following is selected financial information for Safari Company as of December 31, 2015.

Liabilities	$64,000	Equity	$50,000	Assets	$114,000

Required

Prepare the balance sheet for Safari Company as of December 31, 2015.

Problem 1-4B
Preparing an income statement
P2

Selected financial information for Solar Company for the year ended December 31, 2015, follows.

Revenues	$68,000	Expenses	$40,000	Net income	$28,000

Required

Prepare the 2015 income statement for Solar Company.

Problem 1-5B
Preparing a statement of retained earnings
P2

Following is selected financial information of Audi Company for the year ended December 31, 2015.

Retained earnings, Dec. 31, 2015	$47,000	Cash dividends	$ 7,000
Net income	5,000	Retained earnings, Dec. 31, 2014........	49,000

Required

Prepare the 2015 statement of retained earnings for Audi Company.

Problem 1-6B
Preparing a statement of cash flows
P2

Selected financial information of Banji Company for the year ended December 31, 2015, follows.

Cash from investing activities	$1,600
Net increase in cash	400
Cash from financing activities	1,800
Cash used by operating activities	(3,000)
Cash, December 31, 2014	1,300

Required

Prepare the 2015 statement of cash flows for Banji Company.

Problem 1-7B
Analyzing transactions and preparing financial statements
C4 P1 P2

Nina Niko launched a new business, Niko's Maintenance Co., that began operations on June 1. The following transactions were completed by the company during that first month.

June 1 Nina Niko invested $130,000 cash in the company in exchange for its common stock.
2 The company rented a furnished office and paid $6,000 cash for June's rent.
4 The company purchased $2,400 of equipment on credit.
6 The company paid $1,150 cash for this month's advertising of the opening of the business.
8 The company completed maintenance services for a customer and immediately collected $850 cash.
14 The company completed $7,500 of maintenance services for City Center on credit.
16 The company paid $800 cash for an assistant's salary for the first half of the month.
20 The company received $7,500 cash payment for services completed for City Center on June 14.
21 The company completed $7,900 of maintenance services for Paula's Beauty Shop on credit.
24 The company completed $675 of maintenance services for Build-It Coop on credit.
25 The company received $7,900 cash payment from Paula's Beauty Shop for the work completed on June 21.
26 The company made payment of $2,400 cash for equipment purchased on June 4.
28 The company paid $800 cash for an assistant's salary for the second half of this month.
29 The company paid $4,000 cash in dividends to the owner (sole shareholder).
30 The company paid $150 cash for this month's telephone bill.
30 The company paid $890 cash for this month's utilities.

Required

1. Arrange the following asset, liability, and equity titles in a table like Exhibit 1.9: Cash; Accounts Receivable; Equipment; Accounts Payable; Common Stock; Dividends; Revenues; and Expenses.
2. Show the effects of the transactions on the accounts of the accounting equation by recording increases and decreases in the appropriate columns. Do not determine new account balances after each transaction. Determine the final total for each account and verify that the equation is in balance.
3. Prepare a June income statement, a June statement of retained earnings, a June 30 balance sheet, and a June statement of cash flows.

Check (2) Ending balances: Cash, $130,060; Expenses, $9,790

(3) Net income, $7,135; Total assets, $133,135

Problem 1-8B
Analyzing effects of transactions
C4 P1 P2 A1

Neva Nadal started a new business, Nadal Computing, and completed the following transactions during its first year of operations.

a. Neva Nadal invests $90,000 cash and office equipment valued at $10,000 in the company in exchange for its common stock.
b. The company purchased a $150,000 building to use as an office. It paid $40,000 in cash and signed a note payable promising to pay the $110,000 balance over the next 10 years.
c. The company purchased office equipment for $25,000 cash.
d. The company purchased $1,200 of office supplies and $1,700 of office equipment on credit.
e. The company paid a local newspaper $750 cash for printing an announcement of the office's opening.
f. The company completed a financial plan for a client and billed that client $2,800 for the service.
g. The company designed a financial plan for another client and immediately collected a $4,000 cash fee.
h. The company paid $11,500 cash in dividends to the owner (sole shareholder).
i. The company received $1,800 cash from the client described in transaction *f*.
j. The company made a payment of $700 cash on the equipment purchased in transaction *d*.
k. The company paid $2,500 cash for the office secretary's wages.

Required

1. Create a table like the one in Exhibit 1.9, using the following headings for the columns: Cash; Accounts Receivable; Office Supplies; Office Equipment; Building; Accounts Payable; Notes Payable; Common Stock; Dividends; Revenues; and Expenses.
2. Use additions and subtractions within the table created in part 1 to show the dollar effects of each transaction on individual items of the accounting equation. Show new balances after each transaction.
3. Once you have completed the table, determine the company's net income.

Check (2) Ending balances: Cash, $15,350; Expenses, $3,250; Notes Payable, $110,000

(3) Net income, $3,550

Problem 1-9B
Analyzing transactions and preparing financial statements
C4 P1 P2

Rivera Roofing Company, owned by Reyna Rivera, began operations in July and completed these transactions during that first month of operations.

July	1	Reyna Rivera invested $80,000 cash in the company in exchange for its common stock.
	2	The company rented office space and paid $700 cash for the July rent.
	3	The company purchased roofing equipment for $5,000 by paying $1,000 cash and agreeing to pay the $4,000 balance in 30 days.
	6	The company purchased office supplies for $600 cash.
	8	The company completed work for a customer and immediately collected $7,600 cash for the work.
	10	The company purchased $2,300 of office equipment on credit.
	15	The company completed work for a customer on credit in the amount of $8,200.
	17	The company purchased $3,100 of office supplies on credit.
	23	The company paid $2,300 cash for the office equipment purchased on July 10.
	25	The company billed a customer $5,000 for work completed; the balance is due in 30 days.
	28	The company received $8,200 cash for the work completed on July 15.
	30	The company paid an assistant's salary of $1,560 cash for this month.
	31	The company paid $295 cash for this month's utility bill.
	31	The company paid $1,800 cash in dividends to the owner (sole shareholder).

Required

1. Arrange the following asset, liability, and equity titles in a table like Exhibit 1.9: Cash; Accounts Receivable; Office Supplies; Office Equipment; Roofing Equipment; Accounts Payable; Common Stock; Dividends; Revenues; and Expenses.
2. Use additions and subtractions to show the effects of each transaction on the accounts in the accounting equation. Show new balances after each transaction.
3. Use the increases and decreases in the columns of the table from part 2 to prepare an income statement, a statement of retained earnings, and a statement of cash flows—each of these for the current month. Also prepare a balance sheet as of the end of the month.

Check (2) Ending balances: Cash, $87,545; Accounts Payable, $7,100

(3) Net income, $18,245; Total assets, $103,545

Analysis Component

4. Assume that the $5,000 purchase of roofing equipment on July 3 was financed from an owner investment of another $5,000 cash in the business in exchange for more common stock (instead of the purchase conditions described in the transaction). Explain the effect of this change on total assets, total liabilities, and total equity.

Problem 1-10B
Determining expenses, liabilities, equity, and return on assets
A1 A2

Ski-Doo Company manufactures, markets, and sells snowmobiles and snowmobile equipment and accessories. The average total assets for Ski-Doo is $3,000,000. In its most recent year, Ski-Doo reported net income of $201,000 on revenues of $1,400,000.

Required

1. What is Ski-Doo Company's return on assets?
2. Does return on assets seem satisfactory for Ski-Doo given that its competitors average a 9.5% return on assets?
3. What are the total expenses for Ski-Doo Company in its most recent year?
4. What is the average total amount of liabilities plus equity for Ski-Doo Company?

Check (3) $1,199,000

(4) $3,000,000

Problem 1-11B
Computing and interpreting return on assets
A2

AT&T and **Verizon** produce and market telecommunications products and are competitors. Key financial figures (in $ millions) for these businesses for a recent year follow.

Key Figures ($ millions)	AT&T	Verizon
Sales	$126,723	$110,875
Net income	4,184	10,198
Average assets	269,868	225,233

Required

1. Compute return on assets for (*a*) AT&T and (*b*) Verizon.
2. Which company is more successful in the total amount of sales to consumers?
3. Which company is more successful in returning net income from its assets invested?

Check (1*a*) 1.6%; (1*b*) 4.5%

Analysis Component

4. Write a one-paragraph memorandum explaining which company you would invest your money in and why. (Limit your explanation to the information provided.)

Problem 1-12B[A]
Identifying risk and return
A3

All business decisions involve aspects of risk and return.

Required

Identify both the risk and the return in each of the following activities:

1. Stashing $500 cash under your mattress.
2. Placing a $250 bet on a horse running in the Kentucky Derby.
3. Investing $20,000 in Nike stock.
4. Investing $35,000 in U.S. Savings Bonds.

Problem 1-13B[B]
Describing organizational activities
C5

A start-up company often engages in the following activities during its first year of operations. Classify each of the following activities into one of the three major activities of an organization.

F. Financing **I.** Investing **O.** Operating

______	**1.** Providing client services.	______	**5.** Supervising workers.
______	**2.** Obtaining a bank loan.	______	**6.** Owner investing money in business.
______	**3.** Purchasing machinery.	______	**7.** Renting office space.
______	**4.** Research for its products.	______	**8.** Paying utilities expenses.

Problem 1-14B[B]
Describing organizational activities C5

Identify in outline format the three major business activities of an organization. For each of these activities, identify at least two specific transactions or events normally undertaken by the business's owners or its managers.

This serial problem starts here and continues throughout most chapters of the book. It is most readily solved if you use the Working Papers that accompany this book (but working papers are not required)

SERIAL PROBLEM

Business Solutions
C4 P1

SP 1 On October 1, 2015, Santana Rey launched a computer services company, **Business Solutions,** that is organized as a corporation and provides consulting services, computer system installations, and custom program development. Rey adopts the calendar year for reporting purposes and expects to prepare the company's first set of financial statements on December 31, 2015.

Required

Create a table like the one in Exhibit 1.9 using the following headings for columns: Cash; Accounts Receivable; Computer Supplies; Computer System; Office Equipment; Accounts Payable; Common Stock; Dividends; Revenues; and Expenses. Then use additions and subtractions within the table created to show the dollar effects for each of the following October transactions for Business Solutions on the individual items of the accounting equation. Show new balances after each transaction.

Oct.	1	S. Rey invested $45,000 cash, a $20,000 computer system, and $8,000 of office equipment in the company in exchange for its common stock.
	3	The company purchased $1,420 of computer supplies on credit from Harris Office Products.
	6	The company billed Easy Leasing $4,800 for services performed in installing a new web server.
	8	The company paid $1,420 cash for the computer supplies purchased from Harris Office Products on October 3.

10 The company hired Lyn Addie as a part-time assistant for $125 per day, as needed.
12 The company billed Easy Leasing another $1,400 for services performed.
15 The company received $4,800 cash from Easy Leasing as partial payment toward its account.
17 The company paid $805 cash to repair computer equipment damaged when moving it.
20 The company paid $1,728 cash for advertisements published in the local newspaper.
22 The company received $1,400 cash from Easy Leasing toward its account.
28 The company billed IFM Company $5,208 for services performed.
31 The company paid $875 cash for Lyn Addie's wages for seven days of work this month.
31 The company paid $3,600 cash in dividends to the owner (sole shareholder).

Check Ending balances: Cash, $42,772; Revenues, $11,408; Expenses, $3,408

GL GENERAL LEDGER PROBLEM

Available in Connect

connect ACCOUNTING

Accounting professionals apply many technology tools to aid them in their everyday tasks and decision making. The **General Ledger** tool in *Connect* automates several of the procedural steps in the accounting cycle so that the accounting professional can focus on the impacts of each transaction on the full set of financial statements. Chapter 2 is the first chapter to exploit this tool in helping students see the advantages of technology and, in particular, the power of the General Ledger tool in accounting practice, including financial analysis and "what if" scenarios.

***Beyond the Numbers (BTN)** is a special problem section aimed to refine communication, conceptual, analysis, and research skills. It includes many activities helpful in developing an active learning environment*

Beyond the Numbers

REPORTING IN ACTION

A1 A2 A3

APPLE

BTN 1-1 Key financial figures for **Apple**'s fiscal year ended September 28, 2013, follow.

Key Figure	In Millions
Liabilities + Equity.........	$207,000
Net income	37,037
Revenues	170,910

Required

1. What is the total amount of assets invested in Apple?
2. What is Apple's return on assets for fiscal year 2013? Its assets at September 29, 2012, equal $176,064 (in millions).
3. How much are total expenses for Apple for the year ended September 28, 2013?
4. Does Apple's return on assets for fiscal 2013 seem satisfactory if competitors average a 10% return?

Check (2) 19.3%

Fast Forward

5. Access Apple's financial statements (Form 10-K) for years ending after September 28, 2013, from its website (Apple.com) or from the SEC website (www.SEC.gov) and compute its return on assets for those years. Compare the September 28, 2013, year-end return on assets to any subsequent years' returns you are able to compute, and interpret the results.

COMPARATIVE ANALYSIS

A1 A2 A3

APPLE
GOOGLE

BTN 1-2 Key comparative figures ($ millions) for both **Apple** and **Google** follow.

Key Figure	Apple	Google
Liabilities + Equity.........	$207,000	$110,920
Net income	37,037	12,920
Revenues and sales.........	170,910	59,825

Required

1. What is the total amount of assets invested in (*a*) Apple and (*b*) Google?
2. What is the return on assets for (*a*) Apple and (*b*) Google? Apple's beginning-year assets equal $176,064 (in millions) and Google's beginning-year assets equal $93,798 (in millions).
3. How much are expenses for (*a*) Apple and (*b*) Google?
4. Is return on assets satisfactory for (*a*) Apple and (*b*) Google? (Assume competitors average a 10% return.)
5. What can you conclude about Apple and Google from these computations?

Check (2*b*) 12.6%

ETHICS CHALLENGE
C3 C4

BTN 1-3 Craig Thorne works in a public accounting firm and hopes to eventually be a partner. The management of Allnet Company invites Thorne to prepare a bid to audit Allnet's financial statements. In discussing the audit fee, Allnet's management suggests a fee range in which the amount depends on the reported profit of Allnet. The higher its profit, the higher will be the audit fee paid to Thorne's firm.

Required

1. Identify the parties potentially affected by this audit and the fee plan proposed.
2. What are the ethical factors in this situation? Explain.
3. Would you recommend that Thorne accept this audit fee arrangement? Why or why not?
4. Describe some ethical considerations guiding your recommendation.

COMMUNICATING IN PRACTICE
A1 C2

APPLE

BTN 1-4 Refer to this chapter's opening feature about **Apple**. Assume that the owners, sometime during their first five years of business, desire to expand their computer product services to meet people's demands regarding technical support. They eventually decide to meet with their banker to discuss a loan to allow Apple to expand and offer computing services.

Required

1. Prepare a half-page report outlining the information you would request from the owners if you were the loan officer.
2. Indicate whether the information you request and your loan decision are affected by the form of business organization for Apple.

TAKING IT TO THE NET
A2

BTN 1-5 Visit the EDGAR database at **www.SEC.gov**. Access the Form 10-K report of **Rocky Mountain Chocolate Factory** (ticker RMCF) filed on May 29, 2013, covering its 2013 fiscal year.

Required

1. Item 6 of the 10-K report provides comparative financial highlights of RMCF for the years 2009–2013. How would you describe the revenue trend for RMCF over this five-year period?
2. Has RMCF been profitable (see net income) over this five-year period? Support your answer.

TEAMWORK IN ACTION
C1

BTN 1-6 Teamwork is important in today's business world. Successful teams schedule convenient meetings, maintain regular communications, and cooperate with and support their members. This assignment aims to establish support/learning teams, initiate discussions, and set meeting times.

Required

1. Form teams and open a team discussion to determine a regular time and place for your team to meet between each scheduled class meeting. Notify your instructor via a memorandum or e-mail message as to when and where your team will hold regularly scheduled meetings.
2. Develop a list of telephone numbers and/or e-mail addresses of your teammates.

ENTREPRENEURIAL DECISION

A1 P1

APPLE

BTN 1-7 Refer to this chapter's opening feature about **Apple**. Assume that the owners decide to open a new company with an innovative mobile app devoted to microblogging for accountants and those learning accounting. This new company will be called **AccountApp**.

Required

1. AccountApp obtains a $500,000 loan and the two owners contribute $250,000 in total from their own savings in exchange for common stock in the new company.
   a. What is the new company's total amount of liabilities plus equity?
   b. What is the new company's total amount of assets?
2. If the new company earns $80,250 in net income in the first year of operation, compute its return on assets (assume average assets equal $750,000). Assess its performance if competitors average a 10% return.

Check (2) 10.7%

HITTING THE ROAD

C2

BTN 1-8 You are to interview a local business owner. (This can be a friend or relative.) Opening lines of communication with members of the business community can provide personal benefits of business networking. If you do not know the owner, you should call ahead to introduce yourself and explain your position as a student and your assignment requirements. You should request a 30-minute appointment for a face-to-face or phone interview to discuss the form of organization and operations of the business. Be prepared to make a good impression.

Required

1. Identify and describe the main operating activities and the form of organization for this business.
2. Determine and explain why the owner(s) chose this particular form of organization.
3. Identify any special advantages and/or disadvantages the owner(s) experiences in operating with this form of business organization.

GLOBAL DECISION

A1 A2 A3

Samsung
APPLE
GOOGLE

BTN 1-9 **Samsung** (Samsung.com) is a leading global manufacturer, and it competes to varying degrees with both **Apple** and **Google**. Key financial figures for Samsung follow.

Key Figure*	Korean Won in Millions
Average assets	₩197,573,294
Net income	₩ 30,474,764
Revenue	₩228,692,667
Return on assets	15.4%

* Figures prepared in accordance with International Financial Reporting Standards as adopted by the Republic of Korea.

Required

1. Identify any concerns you have in comparing Samsung's income and revenue figures to those of Apple and Google (in BTN 1-2) for purposes of making business decisions.
2. Identify any concerns you have in comparing Samsung's return on assets ratio to those of Apple and Google (computed for BTN 1-2) for purposes of making business decisions.

ANSWERS TO MULTIPLE CHOICE QUIZ

1. c; $450,000 is the actual cost incurred.
2. b; revenue is recorded when earned.
3. d;

Assets	=	Liabilities	+	Equity
+$100,000	=	+$35,000	+	?

Change in equity = $100,000 − $35,000 = $65,000

4. a
5. a

chapter 2

Accounting for Business Transactions

Chapter Preview

ANALYZING AND RECORDING PROCESS	ANALYZING AND PROCESSING TRANSACTIONS	TRIAL BALANCE AND THE FINANCIAL STATEMENTS
C1 Source documents	**C3** General ledger	**P2** Trial balance preparation and use
C2 The account and its analysis	**C4** Double-entry accounting	**P3** Financial statement preparation
Types of accounts	**P1** Journalizing and posting	**A2** Analysis of financing sources
Unclassified vs. classified	**A1** Processing transactions—an illustration	

Learning Objectives

CONCEPTUAL

C1 Explain the steps in processing transactions and the role of source documents.

C2 Describe an account and its use in recording transactions.

C3 Describe a ledger and a chart of accounts.

C4 Define *debits* and *credits* and explain double-entry accounting.

ANALYTICAL

A1 Analyze the impact of transactions on accounts and financial statements.

A2 Compute the debt ratio and describe its use in analyzing financial condition.

PROCEDURAL

P1 Record transactions in a journal and post entries to a ledger.

P2 Prepare and explain the use of a trial balance.

P3 Prepare financial statements from business transactions.

Courtesy of Akola Project

Work of Art

DALLAS—Brittany Merrill Underwood had no idea that her summer teaching job in Uganda during her second year in college would change her life forever. Brittany was deeply moved by a Ugandan woman who struggled to care for 24 children who slept on her floor. After graduating college, Brittany launched **Akola Project (AkolaProject.org)**, which is a handmade jewelry and accessories business focused on empowering Ugandan women to support their families and communities through economic means.

"Akola is unique . . . because we are a social business," explains Brittany. "This means that 100% of the net revenue from all of our products goes directly back into development projects benefiting the women who make them." Brittany's website explains that she runs "a no handout policy," and instead, "provides vocational skills and [then] monthly income" to the hundreds of women teaming with her jewelry company. Her site says that she has "helped elevate lives of 1,400 women and children out of extreme poverty . . . [by] equipping women to become entrepreneurs."

"Dream without limitations"
—Brittany Merrill Underwood

Akola trains women in rural villages to fashion quality jewelry and handbags and facilitates savings associations to encourage the women to invest their monthly revenues in small local business initiatives and to reliably account for expenses and revenues. "We partner with women in rural villages who have never had access to training or educational opportunities and spend five years training them to become artisans to unlock their potential," explains Brittany. The products are now sold in over 250 boutiques, national department stores, and online.

Brittany applies that same commitment to succeed to her business, where she relies on recordkeeping processes, transaction analysis, inventory accounting, and financial reporting. She hopes that reliable accounting for all activities will help sustain her business and the business of her artisans. Brittany insists that accounting is crucial to track and account for all revenues and expenses, including what is invested in her business and non-profit. She maintains that effective accounting helps keep the dream alive for both her and her artisans.

"In addition to creating a thriving social business for women," insists Brittany. "We have built an orphanage home to house over 200 street children, drilled 23 clean water wells in displaced communities, and provided educational programs for women." The artisans, however, are the real winners. "By employing women and giving them a reliable income, we could care for thousands of children."

Still, Brittany says that if she had to do it over, she would have "gone to business school!" She adds that the greatest obstacle to launching Akola was "not having a business background."

Sources: *Akola website*, January 2015; *ltd Daily*, March 2014; *FOXBusiness*, April 2014; *Fieldnotes Magazine*, February 2014

ANALYZING AND REPORTING ACCOUNTS

C1 Explain the steps in processing transactions and the role of source documents.

The accounting process identifies business transactions and events, analyzes and records their effects, and summarizes and presents information in reports and financial statements. These reports and statements are used for making investing, lending, and other business decisions. The steps in the accounting process that focus on *analyzing and recording* transactions and events are shown in Exhibit 2.1.

EXHIBIT 2.1

The Analyzing and Recording Process

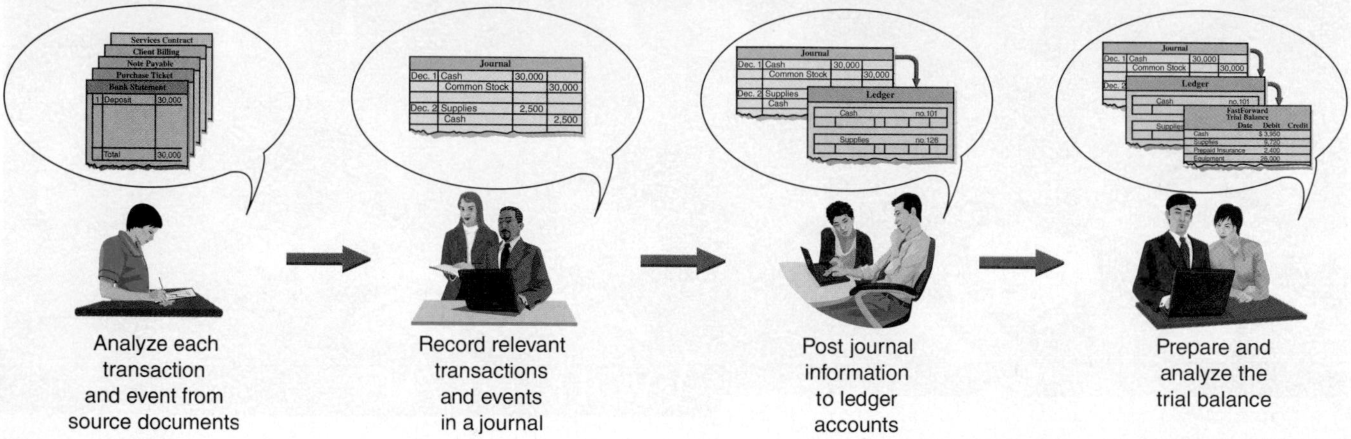

Business transactions and events are the starting points. Relying on source documents, the transactions and events are analyzed using the accounting equation to understand how they affect company performance and financial position. These effects are recorded in accounting records, informally referred to as the *accounting books,* or simply the *books*. Additional steps such as posting and then preparing a trial balance help summarize and classify the effects of transactions and events. Ultimately, the accounting process provides information in useful reports or financial statements to decision makers.

Source Documents

Source documents identify and describe transactions and events entering the accounting process. They are the sources of accounting information and can be in either hard copy or electronic form. Examples are sales tickets, checks, purchase orders, bills from suppliers, employee earnings records, and bank statements. To illustrate, when an item is purchased on credit, the seller usually prepares at least two copies of a sales invoice. One copy is given to the buyer. Another copy, often sent electronically, results in an entry in the seller's information system to record the sale. Sellers use invoices for recording sales and for control; buyers use them for recording purchases and for monitoring purchasing activity. Many cash registers record information for each sale on a tape or electronic file locked inside the register. This record can be used as a source document for recording sales in the accounting records. Source documents, especially if obtained from outside the organization, provide objective and reliable evidence about transactions and events and their amounts.

Point: To ensure that all sales are rung up on the register, most sellers require customers to have their receipts to exchange or return purchased items.

Decision Ethics

Cashier Your manager requires that you, as cashier, immediately enter each sale. Recently, lunch hour traffic has increased and the assistant manager asks you to avoid delays by taking customers' cash and making change without entering sales. The assistant manager says she will add up cash and enter sales after lunch. She says that, in this way, the register will always match the cash amount when the manager arrives at three o'clock. What do you do? ■ [Answers follow the chapter's Summary.]

The Account and Its Analysis

An **account** is a record of increases and decreases in a specific asset, liability, equity, revenue, or expense item. Information from an account is analyzed, summarized, and presented in reports and financial statements. The **general ledger,** or simply **ledger,** is a record containing all accounts used by a company. The ledger is often in electronic form. While most companies' ledgers contain similar accounts, a company often uses one or more unique accounts because of its type of operations. An *unclassified balance sheet* broadly groups accounts into assets, liabilities, and equity. Exhibit 2.2 shows typical asset, liability, and equity accounts.

C2 Describe an account and its use in recording transactions.

EXHIBIT 2.2

Accounts Organized by the Accounting Equation

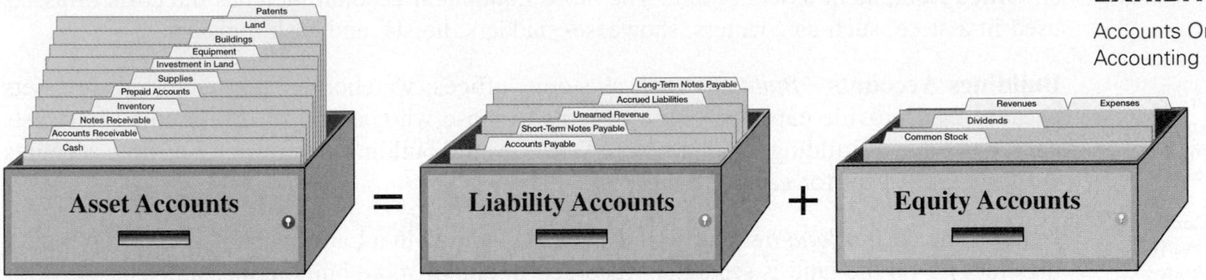

Asset Accounts Assets are resources owned or controlled by a company, and those resources have expected future benefits. Most accounting systems include (at a minimum) separate accounts for the assets described here.

Cash A *Cash* account reflects a company's cash balance. All increases and decreases in cash are recorded in the Cash account. It includes money and any medium of exchange that a bank accepts for deposit (coins, checks, money orders, and checking account balances).

Accounts Receivable *Accounts receivable* are held by a seller and refer to promises of payment from customers to sellers. These transactions are often called *credit sales* or *sales on account* (or *on credit*). Accounts receivable are increased by credit sales and billings to customers, but are decreased by customer payments. A company needs a separate record for each customer, but for now, we use the simpler practice of recording all increases and decreases in receivables in a single account called Accounts Receivable.

Point: Customers and others who owe a company are called its **debtors.**

Note Receivable A *note receivable,* or promissory note, is a written promise of another entity to pay a definite sum of money on a specified future date to the holder of the note. A company holding a promissory note signed by another entity has an asset that is recorded in a Note (or Notes) Receivable account.

Point: A college parking fee is a prepaid account from the student's standpoint. At the beginning of the term, it represents an asset that entitles a student to park on or near campus. The benefits of the parking fee expire as the term progresses. At term-end, prepaid parking (asset) equals zero as it has been entirely recorded as parking expense.

Prepaid Accounts *Prepaid accounts* (also called *prepaid expenses*) are assets that represent prepayments of future expenses (expenses expected to be incurred in one or more future accounting periods). When the expenses are later incurred, the amounts in prepaid accounts are transferred to expense accounts. Common examples of prepaid accounts include prepaid insurance, prepaid rent, and prepaid services (such as club memberships). Prepaid accounts expire with the passage of time (such as with rent) or through use (such as with prepaid meal tickets). When financial statements are prepared, prepaid accounts are adjusted so that (1) all expired and used prepaid accounts are recorded as expenses and (2) all unexpired and unused prepaid accounts are recorded as assets (reflecting future use in future periods). To illustrate, when an insurance fee, called a *premium,* is paid in advance, the cost is typically recorded in the asset account titled Prepaid Insurance. Over time, the expiring portion of the insurance cost is removed from this asset account and reported in expenses on the income statement. Any unexpired portion remains in Prepaid Insurance and is reported on the balance sheet as an asset.

Point: Prepaid accounts that apply to current and future periods are assets. These assets are adjusted at the end of each period to reflect only those amounts that have not yet expired, and to record as expenses those amounts that have expired.

Supplies Accounts *Supplies* are assets until they are used. When they are used up, their costs are reported as expenses. The costs of unused supplies are recorded in a Supplies asset account.

Supplies are often grouped by purpose—for example, office supplies and store supplies. *Office supplies* include stationery, paper, toner, and pens. *Store supplies* include packaging materials, plastic and paper bags, gift boxes and cartons, and cleaning materials. The costs of these unused supplies can be recorded in an Office Supplies or a Store Supplies asset account. When supplies are used, their costs are transferred from the asset accounts to expense accounts.

Equipment Accounts *Equipment* is an asset. When equipment is used and gets worn down, its cost is gradually reported as an expense (called depreciation). Equipment is often grouped by its purpose—for example, office equipment and store equipment. *Office equipment* includes computers, printers, desks, chairs, and shelves. Costs incurred for these items are recorded in an Office Equipment asset account. The *Store Equipment* account includes the costs of assets used in a store, such as counters, showcases, ladders, hoists, and cash registers.

Point: Some assets are described as *intangible* because they do not have physical existence or their benefits are highly uncertain. A recent balance sheet for **Coca-Cola Company** shows nearly $1 billion in intangible assets.

Buildings Accounts *Buildings* such as stores, offices, warehouses, and factories are assets because they provide expected future benefits to those who control or own them. Their costs are recorded in a Buildings asset account. When several buildings are owned, separate accounts are sometimes kept for each of them.

Land The cost of *land* owned by a business is recorded in a Land account. The cost of buildings located on the land is separately recorded in one or more building accounts.

Decision Insight

Women Entrepreneurs **SPANX** has given more than $20 million to charity. The Center for Women's Business Research reports that women-owned businesses, such as SPANX (owner Sara Blakely in photo), are growing and that they:

- Total approximately 11 million and employ nearly 20 million workers.
- Generate $2.5 trillion in annual sales and tend to embrace technology.
- Are philanthropic—70% of owners volunteer at least once per month.
- Are more likely funded by individual investors (73%) than venture firms (15%). ■

Paul Morigi/Getty Images for FORTUNE

Liability Accounts Liabilities are claims (by creditors) against assets, which means they are obligations to transfer assets or provide products or services to others. **Creditors** are individuals and organizations that have rights to receive payments from a company. If a company fails to pay its obligations, the law gives creditors a right to force the sale of that company's assets to obtain the money to meet creditors' claims. When assets are sold under these conditions, creditors are paid first, but only up to the amount of their claims. Any remaining money, the residual, goes to the owners of the company. Creditors often use a balance sheet to help decide whether to loan money to a company. A loan is less risky if the borrower's liabilities are small in comparison to assets because this means there are more resources than claims on resources. Common liability accounts are described here.

Point: Accounts payable are also called *trade payables*.

Accounts Payable *Accounts payable* refer to oral or implied promises to pay later, which usually arise from purchases of merchandise. Payables can also arise from purchases of supplies, equipment, and services. Accounting systems keep separate records about each creditor. We describe these individual records in Chapter 4.

Note Payable A *note payable* refers to a formal promise, usually denoted by the signing of a promissory note, to pay a future amount. It is recorded in either a short-term Note Payable account or a long-term Note Payable account, depending on when it must be repaid. We explain details of short- and long-term classification in the next two chapters.

Point: Two words that almost always identify liability accounts: "Payable" meaning liabilities that must be paid, and "Unearned" meaning liabilities that must be fulfilled.

Unearned Revenue Accounts **Unearned revenue** refers to a liability that is settled in the future when a company delivers its products or services. When customers pay in advance for products or services (before revenue is earned), the revenue recognition principle requires that the seller consider this receipt as unearned revenue. Examples of unearned revenue include magazine subscriptions collected in advance by a publisher, rent collected in advance by a landlord, and season ticket sales by sports teams. The seller would record these in liability accounts such as Unearned Subscriptions, Unearned Rent, and Unearned Ticket Revenue. When products and services are later delivered, the earned portion of the unearned revenue is transferred to revenue accounts such as Subscription Fees Revenue, Rent Revenue, and Ticket Revenue.[1]

Point: If a subscription is canceled, the publisher is expected to refund the unused portion to the subscriber.

Accrued Liabilities *Accrued liabilities* are amounts owed that are not yet paid. Examples are wages payable, taxes payable, and interest payable. These are often recorded in separate liability accounts by the same title. If they are not large in amount, one or more ledger accounts can be added and reported as a single amount on the balance sheet. (Financial statements often have amounts reported that are a summation of several ledger accounts.)

Decision Insight

Revenue Spread The **Seattle Seahawks** have *Unearned Revenues* of over $100 million in advance ticket sales. When the team plays its home games, it settles this liability to its ticket holders and then transfers the amount earned to *Ticket Revenues*. Other teams have similar unearned revenues. ■

Jeff Gross/Getty Images

Equity Accounts The owner's claim on a company's assets is called *equity, stockholders' equity,* or *shareholders' equity.* Equity is the owner's *residual interest* in the assets of a business after deducting liabilities. In its simple form, equity is impacted by four types of accounts as follows: **Equity = Common stock − Dividends + Revenues − Expenses.** We show this visually in Exhibit 2.3 by expanding the accounting equation. We also organize assets and liabilities into subgroups that have similar attributes. An important subgroup for both assets and liabilities is the *current* items. Current items are usually those expected to come due (either collected or owed) within the next year. The next chapter explains this in detail. At this point, know that a *classified balance sheet* reports current assets before noncurrent assets and current liabilities before noncurrent liabilities.

Point: Equity is also called *net assets.*

EXHIBIT 2.3

Expanded Accounting Equation

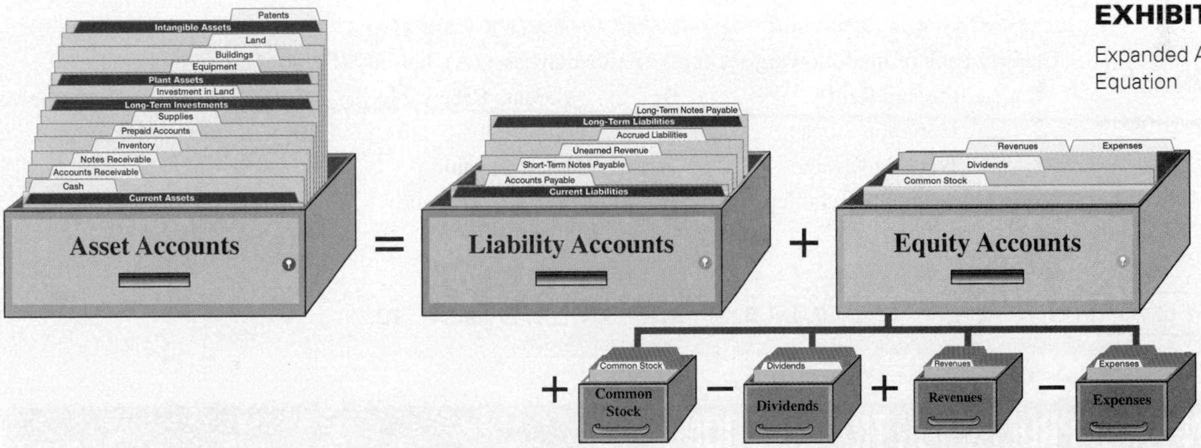

Owner Investments When an owner invests in a company in exchange for its common stock, it increases both assets and equity of the company. The increase to equity is recorded in an account titled Common Stock. Any further owner investments are also recorded in this account.

[1]In practice, account titles vary. As one example, Subscription Fees Revenue is sometimes called Subscription Fees, Subscription Fees Earned, or Earned Subscription Fees. As another example, Rent Revenue is sometimes called Rent Earned, Rental Revenue, or Earned Rent Revenue. We must use good judgment when reading financial statements because titles can differ even within the same industry. For example, product sales are called *net sales* at **Apple**, *revenues* at **Google**, and *revenue* at **Samsung**. Generally, the term *revenues* or *fees* is more commonly used with service businesses, and *net sales* or *sales* with product businesses.

Point: The Dividends account is sometimes referred to as a *contra equity* account because it reduces the normal balance of equity.

Point: The withdrawal of assets by the owners of a corporation is called a *dividend.*

Owner Distributions When a corporation distributes assets to its owner it decreases both company assets and total equity. The decrease to equity is recorded in an account titled Dividends. Dividends are not expenses of the business; they are simply the opposite of owner investments.

Revenue Accounts The inflow of net assets from providing products and services to customers increases equity through increases in revenue accounts. Examples of revenue accounts are Sales, Commissions Earned, Professional Fees Earned, Rent Revenue, and Interest Revenue. *Revenues always increase equity.*

Expense Accounts The outflow of net assets in helping generate revenues decreases equity through increases in expense accounts. Examples of expense accounts are Advertising Expense, Store Supplies Expense, Office Salaries Expense, Office Supplies Expense, Rent Expense, Utilities Expense, and Insurance Expense. *Expenses always decrease equity.*

The variety of revenues and expenses can be seen by looking at the *chart of accounts* that follows the index at the back of this book. (Different companies sometimes use different account titles than those in this book's chart of accounts. For example, some might use Interest Revenue instead of Interest Earned, or Rental Expense instead of Rent Expense. It is important only that an account title describe the item it represents.)

Decision Insight

Sporting Accounts The **Miami Heat**, **San Antonio Spurs**, **Indiana Pacers**, **Los Angeles Lakers**, and other NBA teams have the following major revenue and expense accounts:

Revenues	Expenses
Basketball ticket sales	Team salaries
TV & radio broadcast fees	Game costs
Advertising revenues	NBA franchise costs
Basketball playoff receipts	Promotional costs ■

Andrew D. Bernstein/NBAE/Getty Images

NEED-TO-KNOW 2-1

Classifying Accounts

C1 C2

Classify each of the following accounts as either an asset (A), liability (L), or equity (EQ).

1. ____ Prepaid Rent
2. ____ Common Stock
3. ____ Note Receivable
4. ____ Accounts Payable
5. ____ Accounts Receivable
6. ____ Equipment
7. ____ Interest Payable
8. ____ Unearned Revenue
9. ____ Land
10. ____ Prepaid Insurance

Solution

1. A **2.** EQ **3.** A **4.** L **5.** A **6.** A **7.** L **8.** L **9.** A **10.** A

Do More: QS 2-2, QS 2-3

ANALYZING AND PROCESSING TRANSACTIONS

This section explains several tools and processes that comprise an accounting system. These include a ledger, T-account, debits and credits, double-entry accounting, journalizing, and posting.

Ledger and Chart of Accounts

C3 Describe a ledger and a chart of accounts.

The collection of all accounts and their balances for an information system is called a *ledger* (or *general ledger*). If accounts are in files on a hard drive, the sum of those files is the ledger. If the accounts are pages in a file, that file is the ledger. A company's size and diversity of operations affect the number of accounts needed. A small company can get by with as few as 20 or 30 accounts; a large company can require several thousand. The **chart of accounts** is a list of all ledger accounts and includes an identification number assigned to each account. A small business might use the following numbering system for its accounts:

Chart of Accounts

101–199	Asset accounts
201–299	Liability accounts
301–399	Equity accounts
401–499	Revenue accounts
501–699	Expense accounts

These numbers provide a three-digit code that is useful in recordkeeping. In this case, the first digit assigned to asset accounts is a 1, the first digit assigned to liability accounts is a 2, and so on. The second and third digits relate to the accounts' subcategories. Exhibit 2.4 shows a partial chart of accounts for FastForward, the focus company of Chapter 1. (Please review the more complete chart of accounts that follows the index at the back of this book.)

EXHIBIT 2.4

Partial Chart of Accounts for FastForward

Chart of Accounts

Acct. No.	Account Name	Acct. No.	Account Name	Acct. No.	Account Name
101	Cash	236	Unearned consulting revenue	406	Rental revenue
106	Accounts receivable	307	Common stock	622	Salaries expense
126	Supplies	318	Retained earnings	637	Insurance expense
128	Prepaid insurance	319	Dividends	640	Rent expense
167	Equipment	403	Consulting revenue	652	Supplies expense
201	Accounts payable			690	Utilities expense

Debits and Credits

C4 Define *debits* and *credits* and explain double-entry accounting.

A **T-account** represents a ledger account and is a tool used to understand the effects of one or more transactions. Its name comes from its shape like the letter **T**. The layout of a T-account, shown in Exhibit 2.5, is (1) the account title on top; (2) a left, or debit, side; and (3) a right, or credit, side.

EXHIBIT 2.5

The T-Account

Account Title	
(Left side) **Debit**	(Right side) **Credit**

The left side of an account is called the **debit** side, often abbreviated *Dr.* The right side is called the **credit** side, abbreviated *Cr.*[2] To enter amounts on the left side of an account is to *debit* the account. To enter amounts on the right side is to *credit* the account. Do not make the error of thinking that the terms *debit* and *credit* mean increase or decrease. Whether a debit or a credit is an increase or decrease depends on the account. For an account where a debit is an increase, the credit is a decrease; for an account where a debit is a decrease, the credit is an increase. The difference between total debits and total credits for an account, including any beginning balance, is the **account balance.** When the sum of debits exceeds the sum of credits, the account has a *debit balance*. It has a *credit balance* when the sum of credits exceeds the sum of debits. When the sum of debits equals the sum of credits, the account has a *zero balance.*

Point: Think of *debit* and *credit* as accounting directions for left and right.

Double-Entry Accounting

Double-entry accounting demands the accounting equation remain in balance and thus requires that for each transaction:

- At least two accounts are involved, with at least one debit and one credit.
- The total amount debited must equal the total amount credited.

[2] These abbreviations are remnants of 18th-century English recordkeeping practices where the terms *debitor* and *creditor* were used instead of *debit* and *credit*. The abbreviations use the first and last letters of these terms, just as we still do for Saint (St.) and Doctor (Dr.).

This means the sum of the debits for all entries must equal the sum of the credits for all entries, and the sum of debit account balances in the ledger must equal the sum of credit account balances.

The system for recording debits and credits follows from the usual accounting equation—see Exhibit 2.6. Two points are important here. First, like any simple mathematical relation, net increases or decreases on one side have equal net effects on the other side. For example, a net increase in assets must be accompanied by an identical net increase on the liabilities and equity side. Recall that some transactions affect only one side of the equation, meaning that two or more accounts on one side are affected, but their net effect on this one side is zero. Second, the left side is the *normal balance* side for assets, and the right side is the *normal balance* side for liabilities and equity. This matches their layout in the accounting equation where assets are on the left side of this equation, and liabilities and equity are on the right.

Point: Assets are on the left-hand side of the equation and thus increase on the left. Liabilities and Equity are on the right-hand side of the equation and thus increase on the right.

EXHIBIT 2.6

Debits and Credits in the Accounting Equation

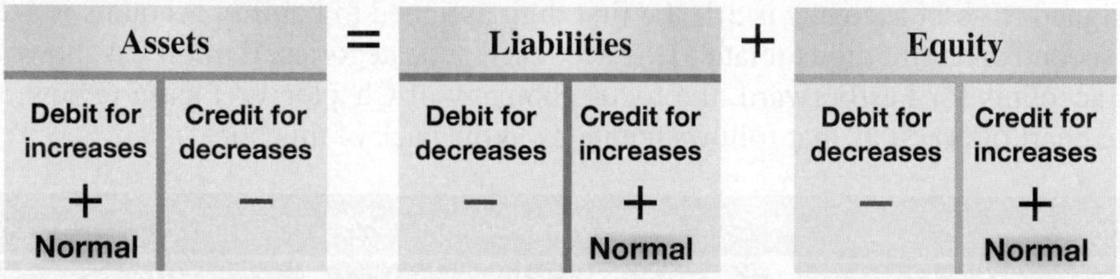

Recall that equity increases from revenues and owner investments (stock issuances) and it decreases from expenses and dividends. These important equity relations are conveyed by expanding the accounting equation to include debits and credits in double-entry form as shown in Exhibit 2.7.

Point: Equity increases from owner investments and revenues; it decreases from dividends and expenses.

EXHIBIT 2.7

Debit and Credit Effects for Component Accounts

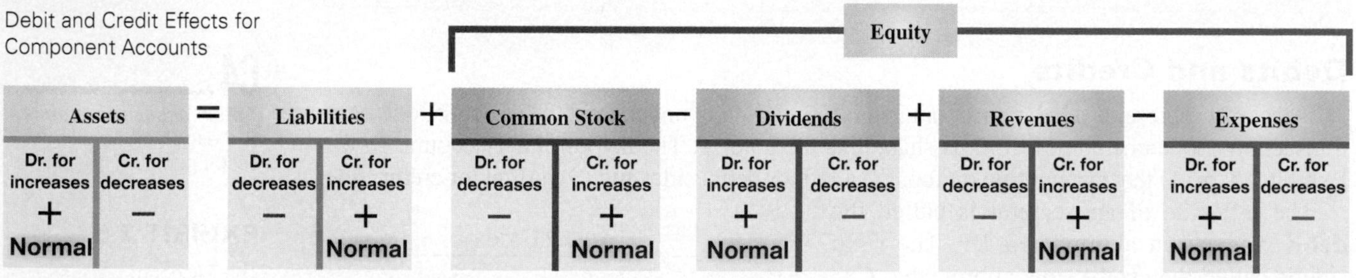

Increases (credits) to common stock and revenues *increase* equity; increases (debits) to dividends and expenses *decrease* equity. The normal balance of each account (asset, liability, common stock, dividends, revenue, or expense) refers to the left or right (debit or credit) side where *increases* are recorded. Understanding these diagrams and rules is required to prepare, analyze, and interpret financial statements.

Point: Debits and credits do not mean favorable or unfavorable. A debit to an asset increases it, as does a debit to an expense. A credit to a liability increases it, as does a credit to a revenue.

The T-account for FastForward's Cash account, reflecting its first 11 transactions (from Exhibit 1.9), is shown in Exhibit 2.8. The total increases (debits) in its Cash account are $36,100, and the total decreases (credits) are $31,300. Total debits exceed total credits by $4,800; thus, Cash has an ending debit balance of $4,800. (We illustrate use of T-accounts later in this chapter.)

EXHIBIT 2.8

Computing the Balance for a T-Account

Cash			
Receive investment by owner for stock	30,000	Purchase of supplies	2,500
Consulting services revenue earned	4,200	Purchase of equipment	26,000
Collection of account receivable	1,900	Payment of rent	1,000
		Payment of salary	700
		Payment of account payable	900
		Payment of cash dividend	200
Balance	**4,800**		

Point: The ending balance is on the side with the larger dollar amount. Also, a plus (+) and minus (−) are not used in a T-account.

NEED-TO-KNOW 2-2

Normal Account Balance

C3 C4

Identify the normal balance (debit [Dr] or credit [Cr]) for each of the following accounts.

1. ____ Prepaid Rent	**5.** ____ Accounts Receivable	**9.** ____ Land
2. ____ Common Stock	**6.** ____ Equipment	**10.** ____ Prepaid Insurance
3. ____ Note Receivable	**7.** ____ Interest Payable	**11.** ____ Dividends
4. ____ Accounts Payable	**8.** ____ Unearned Revenue	

Solution

1. Dr. **2.** Cr. **3.** Dr. **4.** Cr. **5.** Dr. **6.** Dr. **7.** Cr. **8.** Cr. **9.** Dr. **10.** Dr. **11.** Dr.

Do More: QS 2-4, QS 2-5, QS 2-6, E 2-4

QC1

Journalizing and Posting Transactions

P1 Record transactions in a journal and post entries to a ledger.

Processing transactions is a crucial part of accounting. The four usual steps of this process are depicted in Exhibit 2.9. Steps 1 and 2—involving transaction analysis and the accounting equation—were introduced in prior sections. This section extends that discussion and focuses on steps 3 and 4 of the accounting process. Step 3 is to record each transaction chronologically in a journal. A **journal** gives a complete record of each transaction in one place. It also shows debits and credits for each transaction. The process of recording transactions in a journal is called **journalizing.** Step 4 is to transfer (or *post*) entries from the journal to the ledger. The process of transferring journal entry information to the ledger is called **posting.**

EXHIBIT 2.9

Steps in Processing Transactions

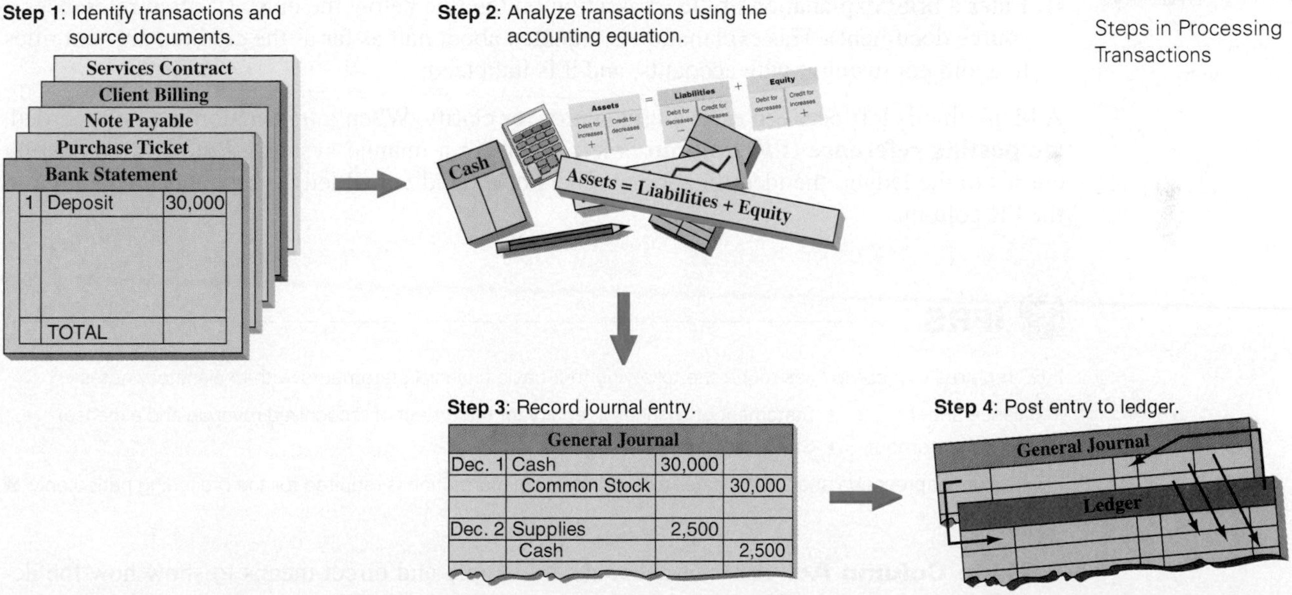

Journalizing Transactions The process of journalizing transactions requires an understanding of a journal. While companies can use various journals, every company uses a **general journal.** It can be used to record any transaction and includes the following information about each transaction: ⓐ date of transaction, ⓑ titles of affected accounts, ⓒ dollar amount of each debit and credit, and ⓓ explanation of the transaction. Exhibit 2.10 shows how the first two transactions of FastForward are recorded in a general journal. This process is similar for manual and computerized systems. Computerized journals are often designed to look like a manual journal page, and also include error-checking routines that ensure debits equal credits for each entry. Shortcuts allow recordkeepers to select account names and numbers from pull-down menus.

EXHIBIT 2.10

Partial General Journal for FastForward

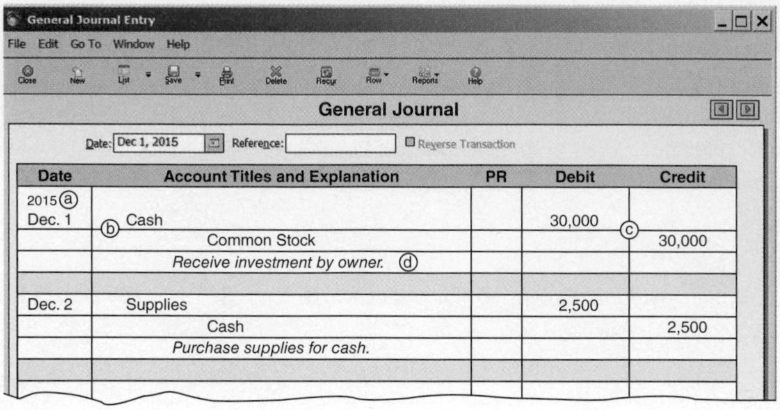

Date	Account Titles and Explanation	PR	Debit	Credit
2015 (a)				
Dec. 1	(b) Cash		30,000 (c)	
	Common Stock			30,000
	Receive investment by owner. (d)			
Dec. 2	Supplies		2,500	
	Cash			2,500
	Purchase supplies for cash.			

To record entries in a general journal, apply these steps; refer to the entries in Exhibit 2.10 when reviewing these steps.

a. Date the transaction: Enter the year at the top of the first column and the month and day on the first line of each journal entry.

b. Enter titles of accounts debited and then enter amounts in the Debit column on the same line. Account titles are taken from the chart of accounts and are aligned with the left margin of the Account Titles and Explanation column.

c. Enter titles of accounts credited and then enter amounts in the Credit column on the same line. Account titles are from the chart of accounts and are indented from the left margin of the Account Titles and Explanation column to distinguish them from debited accounts.

d. Enter a brief explanation of the transaction on the line below the entry (it often references a source document). This explanation is indented about half as far as the credited account titles to avoid confusing it with accounts, and it is italicized.

Point: There are no exact rules for writing journal entry explanations. An explanation should be short yet describe why an entry is made.

A blank line is left between each journal entry for clarity. When a transaction is first recorded, the **posting reference (PR) column** is left blank (in a manual system). Later, when posting entries to the ledger, the identification numbers of the individual ledger accounts are entered in the PR column.

IFRS

IFRS requires that companies report the following four basic financial statements with explanatory notes:

- Balance sheet
- Income statement
- Statement of changes in equity (or statement of recognized revenue and expense)
- Statement of cash flows

IFRS does not prescribe specific formats, and comparative information is required for the preceding period only. ■

Balance Column Account T-accounts are simple and direct means to show how the accounting process works. However, actual accounting systems need more structure and therefore use **balance column accounts,** such as that in Exhibit 2.11.

EXHIBIT 2.11

Cash Account in Balance Column Format

General Ledger					
Cash				Account No. 101	
Date	Explanation	PR	Debit	Credit	Balance
2015					
Dec. 1		G1	30,000		30,000
Dec. 2		G1		2,500	27,500
Dec. 3		G1		26,000	1,500
Dec. 10		G1	4,200		5,700

The balance column account format is similar to a T-account in having columns for debits and credits. It is different in including transaction date and explanation columns. It also has a column with the balance of the account after each entry is recorded. To illustrate, FastForward's Cash account in Exhibit 2.11 is debited on December 1 for the $30,000 owner investment, yielding a $30,000 debit balance. The account is credited on December 2 for $2,500, yielding a $27,500 debit balance. On December 3, it is credited again, this time for $26,000, and its debit balance is reduced to $1,500. The Cash account is debited for $4,200 on December 10, and its debit balance increases to $5,700; and so on.

Point: Explanations are typically included in ledger accounts only for unusual transactions or events.

The heading of the Balance column does not show whether it is a debit or credit balance. Instead, an account is assumed to have a *normal balance*. Unusual events can sometimes temporarily give an account an abnormal balance. An *abnormal balance* refers to a balance on the side where decreases are recorded. For example, a customer might mistakenly overpay a bill. This gives that customer's account receivable an abnormal (credit) balance. An abnormal balance is often identified by circling it, setting it in brackets, or by entering it in red or some other unusual color. A zero balance for an account is usually shown by writing zeros or a dash in the Balance column to avoid confusion between a zero balance and one omitted in error.

Posting Journal Entries Step 4 of processing transactions is to post journal entries to ledger accounts (see Exhibit 2.9). To ensure that the ledger is up to date, entries are posted as soon as possible. This might be daily, weekly, or when time permits. All entries must be posted to the ledger before financial statements are prepared to ensure that account balances are up to date. When entries are posted to the ledger, the debits in journal entries are transferred into ledger accounts as debits, and credits are transferred into ledger accounts as credits. Exhibit 2.12 shows the *four steps to post a journal entry*. First, identify the ledger account that is debited in the entry; then, in the ledger, enter the entry date, the journal and page in its PR column, the debit amount, and the new balance of the ledger account. (The letter *G* shows it came from the

Point: Computerized systems often provide a code beside a balance such as *dr.* or *cr.* to identify its balance. Posting is automatic and immediate with accounting software.

Point: A journal is often referred to as the *book of original entry*. The ledger is referred to as the *book of final entry* because financial statements are prepared from it.

EXHIBIT 2.12

Posting an Entry to the Ledger

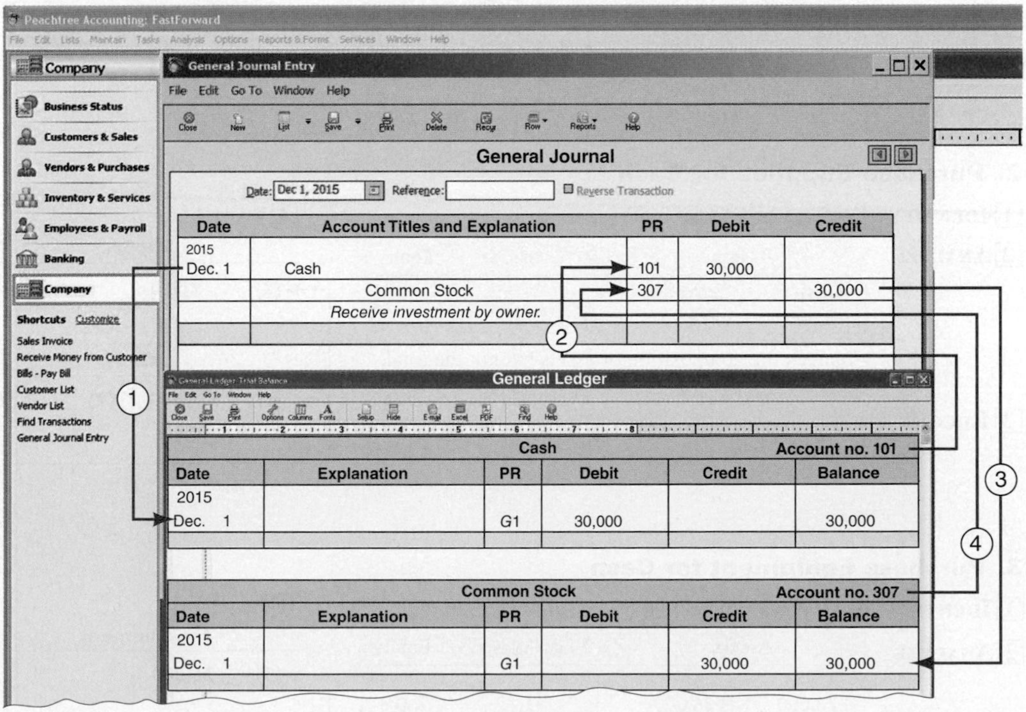

Key:
① Identify debit account in Ledger: enter date, journal page, amount, and balance.
② Enter the debit account number from the Ledger in the PR column of the journal.
③ Identify credit account in Ledger: enter date, journal page, amount, and balance.
④ Enter the credit account number from the Ledger in the PR column of the journal.

Point: The fundamental concepts of a manual (pencil-and-paper) system are identical to those of a computerized information system.

General Journal.) Second, enter the ledger account number in the PR column of the journal. Steps 3 and 4 repeat the first two steps for credit entries and amounts. The posting process creates a link between the ledger and the journal entry. This link is a useful cross-reference for tracing an amount from one record to another.

Analyzing Transactions—An Illustration

A1 Analyze the impact of transactions on accounts and financial statements.

We return to the activities of FastForward to show how double-entry accounting is useful in analyzing and processing transactions. Analysis of each transaction follows the four steps of Exhibit 2.9.

Step 1 Identify the transaction and any source documents.

Step 2 Analyze the transaction using the accounting equation.

Step 3 Record the transaction in journal entry form applying double-entry accounting.

Step 4 Post the entry (for simplicity, we use T-accounts to represent ledger accounts).

Point: In the Comprehensive Need-To-Know at the chapter end we show how to use "balance column accounts" for the ledger.

Study each transaction thoroughly before proceeding to the next. The first 11 transactions are from Chapter 1, and we analyze five additional December transactions of FastForward (numbered 12 through 16) that were omitted earlier.

FASTForward

1. Receive Investment by Owner

1 Identify FastForward receives $30,000 cash from Chas Taylor in exchange for common stock.

2 Analyze

Assets	=	Liabilities	+	Equity
Cash				Common Stock
+30,000	=	0		+30,000

3 Record

Date	Account Titles and Explanation	PR	Debit	Credit
(1)	Cash	101	30,000	
	Common Stock	307		30,000

4 Post

Cash			101
(1)	30,000		

Common Stock			307
		(1)	30,000

2. Purchase Supplies for Cash

1 Identify FastForward pays $2,500 cash for supplies.

2 Analyze

Assets		=	Liabilities	+	Equity
Cash	Supplies				
−2,500	+2,500	=	0	+	0

Changes the composition of assets but not the total.

3 Record

Date	Account Titles and Explanation	PR	Debit	Credit
(2)	Supplies	126	2,500	
	Cash	101		2,500

4 Post

Supplies			126
(2)	2,500		

Cash			101
(1)	30,000	(2)	2,500

3. Purchase Equipment for Cash

1 Identify FastForward pays $26,000 cash for equipment.

2 Analyze

Assets		=	Liabilities	+	Equity
Cash	Equipment				
−26,000	+26,000	=	0	+	0

Changes the composition of assets but not the total.

3 Record

Date	Account Titles and Explanation	PR	Debit	Credit
(3)	Equipment	167	26,000	
	Cash	101		26,000

4 Post

Equipment			167
(3)	26,000		

Cash			101
(1)	30,000	(2)	2,500
		(3)	26,000

4. Purchase Supplies on Credit

1 IDENTIFY FastForward purchases $7,100 of supplies on credit from a supplier.

2 ANALYZE

Assets	=	Liabilities	+	Equity
Supplies		**Accounts Payable**		
+7,100	=	+7,100	+	0

3 RECORD

Date	Account Titles and Explanation	PR	Debit	Credit
(4)	Supplies	126	7,100	
	Accounts Payable	201		7,100

4 POST

Supplies			126
(2)	2,500		
(4)	**7,100**		

Accounts Payable			201
		(4)	**7,100**

5. Provide Services for Cash

1 IDENTIFY FastForward provides consulting services and immediately collects $4,200 cash.

2 ANALYZE

Assets	=	Liabilities	+	Equity
Cash				**Consulting Revenue**
+4,200	=	0		+4,200

3 RECORD

Date	Account Titles and Explanation	PR	Debit	Credit
(5)	Cash	101	4,200	
	Consulting Revenue	403		4,200

4 POST

Cash			101
(1)	30,000	(2)	2,500
(5)	**4,200**	(3)	26,000

Consulting Revenue			403
		(5)	**4,200**

6. Payment of Expense in Cash

1 IDENTIFY FastForward pays $1,000 cash for December rent.

2 ANALYZE

Assets	=	Liabilities	+	Equity
Cash				**Rent Expense**
−1,000	=	0		−1,000

3 RECORD

Date	Account Titles and Explanation	PR	Debit	Credit
(6)	Rent Expense	640	1,000	
	Cash	101		1,000

4 POST

Rent Expense			640
(6)	**1,000**		

Cash			101
(1)	30,000	(2)	2,500
(5)	4,200	(3)	26,000
		(6)	**1,000**

7. Payment of Expense in Cash

1 IDENTIFY FastForward pays $700 cash for employee salary.

2 ANALYZE

Assets	=	Liabilities	+	Equity
Cash				**Salaries Expense**
−700	=	0		−700

3 RECORD

Date	Account Titles and Explanation	PR	Debit	Credit
(7)	Salaries Expense	622	700	
	Cash	101		700

4 POST

Salaries Expense			622
(7)	**700**		

Cash			101
(1)	30,000	(2)	2,500
(5)	4,200	(3)	26,000
		(6)	1,000
		(7)	**700**

Point: *Salary* usually refers to compensation for an employee who receives a fixed amount for a given time period, whereas *wages* usually refers to compensation based on time worked.

Point: The *revenue recognition principle* requires revenue to be recognized when earned, which is when the company provides products and services to a customer. This is not necessarily the same time that the customer pays. A customer can pay before or after products or services are provided.

Point: Transaction 8 is a **compound journal entry,** which affects three or more accounts.

8. Provide Consulting and Rental Services on Credit

1 IDENTIFY FastForward provides consulting services of $1,600 and rents its test facilities for $300. The customer is billed $1,900 for these services.

2 ANALYZE

Assets	=	Liabilities	+	Equity	
Accounts Receivable				**Consulting Revenue**	**Rental Revenue**
+1,900	=	0		+1,600	+300

3 RECORD

Date	Account Titles and Explanation	PR	Debit	Credit
(8)	Accounts Receivable	106	1,900	
	Consulting Revenue	403		1,600
	Rental Revenue	406		300

4 POST

Accounts Receivable	106		
(8)	**1,900**		

Consulting Revenue	403		
		(5)	4,200
		(8)	**1,600**

Rental Revenue	406		
		(8)	**300**

9. Receipt of Cash on Account

1 IDENTIFY FastForward receives $1,900 cash from the client billed in transaction 8.

2 ANALYZE

Assets		=	Liabilities	+	Equity
Cash	**Accounts Receivable**				
+1,900	−1,900	=	0	+	0

3 RECORD

Date	Account Titles and Explanation	PR	Debit	Credit
(9)	Cash	101	1,900	
	Accounts Receivable	106		1,900

4 POST

Cash	101		
(1)	30,000	(2)	2,500
(5)	4,200	(3)	26,000
(9)	**1,900**	(6)	1,000
		(7)	700

Accounts Receivable	106		
(8)	1,900	**(9)**	**1,900**

10. Partial Payment of Accounts Payable

1 IDENTIFY FastForward pays CalTech Supply $900 cash toward the payable of transaction 4.

2 ANALYZE

Assets	=	Liabilities	+	Equity
Cash		**Accounts Payable**		
−900	=	−900	+	0

3 RECORD

Date	Account Titles and Explanation	PR	Debit	Credit
(10)	Accounts Payable	201	900	
	Cash	101		900

4 POST

Accounts Payable	201		
(10)	**900**	(4)	7,100

Cash	101		
(1)	30,000	(2)	2,500
(5)	4,200	(3)	26,000
(9)	1,900	(6)	1,000
		(7)	700
		(10)	**900**

11. Payment of Cash Dividend

Point: Dividends always decrease equity.

1 IDENTIFY FastForward pays $200 cash for dividends.

2 ANALYZE

Assets	=	Liabilities	+	Equity
Cash				**Dividends**
−200	=	0		−200

3 RECORD

Date	Account Titles and Explanation	PR	Debit	Credit
(11)	Dividends	319	200	
	Cash	101		200

4 POST

Dividends	319		
(11)	**200**		

Cash	101		
(1)	30,000	(2)	2,500
(5)	4,200	(3)	26,000
(9)	1,900	(6)	1,000
		(7)	700
		(10)	900
		(11)	**200**

12. Receipt of Cash for Future Services

1 IDENTIFY FastForward receives $3,000 cash in advance of providing consulting services to a customer.

2 ANALYZE

Assets	=	Liabilities	+	Equity
Cash		**Unearned Consulting Revenue**		
+3,000	=	+3,000	+	0

Accepting $3,000 cash obligates FastForward to perform future services and is a liability. No revenue is earned until services are provided.

3 RECORD

Date	Account Titles and Explanation	PR	Debit	Credit
(12)	Cash	101	3,000	
	Unearned Consulting Revenue	236		3,000

4 POST

Cash			101
(1)	30,000	(2)	2,500
(5)	4,200	(3)	26,000
(9)	1,900	(6)	1,000
(12)	**3,000**	(7)	700
		(10)	900
		(11)	200

Unearned Consulting Revenue			236
		(12)	**3,000**

Point: "Unearned" accounts are liabilities that must be fulfilled.

Point: Luca Pacioli, a 15th-century monk, is considered a pioneer in accounting and the first to devise double-entry accounting.

13. Pay Cash for Future Insurance Coverage

1 IDENTIFY FastForward pays $2,400 cash (insurance premium) for a 24-month insurance policy. Coverage begins on December 1.

2 ANALYZE

Assets		=	Liabilities	+	Equity
Cash	**Prepaid Insurance**				
−2,400	+2,400	=	0	+	0

Changes the composition of assets from cash to prepaid insurance. Expense is incurred as insurance coverage expires.

3 RECORD

Date	Account Titles and Explanation	PR	Debit	Credit
(13)	Prepaid Insurance	128	2,400	
	Cash	101		2,400

4 POST

Prepaid Insurance			128
(13)	**2,400**		

Cash			101
(1)	30,000	(2)	2,500
(5)	4,200	(3)	26,000
(9)	1,900	(6)	1,000
(12)	3,000	(7)	700
		(10)	900
		(11)	200
		(13)	**2,400**

14. Purchase Supplies for Cash

1 IDENTIFY FastForward pays $120 cash for supplies.

2 ANALYZE

Assets		=	Liabilities	+	Equity
Cash	**Supplies**				
−120	+120	=	0	+	0

3 RECORD

Date	Account Titles and Explanation	PR	Debit	Credit
(14)	Supplies	126	120	
	Cash	101		120

4 POST

Supplies			126
(2)	2,500		
(4)	7,100		
(14)	**120**		

Cash			101
(1)	30,000	(2)	2,500
(5)	4,200	(3)	26,000
(9)	1,900	(6)	1,000
(12)	3,000	(7)	700
		(10)	900
		(11)	200
		(13)	2,400
		(14)	**120**

15. Payment of Expense in Cash

1 IDENTIFY FastForward pays $305 cash for December utilities expense.

Point: Expenses always decrease equity.

2 ANALYZE

Assets	=	Liabilities	+	Equity
Cash				Utilities Expense
−305	=	0		−305

3 RECORD

Date	Account Titles and Explanation	PR	Debit	Credit
(15)	Utilities Expense	690	305	
	Cash	101		305

4 POST

Utilities Expense			690
(15)	**305**		

Cash			101
(1)	30,000	(2)	2,500
(5)	4,200	(3)	26,000
(9)	1,900	(6)	1,000
(12)	3,000	(7)	700
		(10)	900
		(11)	200
		(13)	2,400
		(14)	120
		(15)	**305**

16. Payment of Expense in Cash

Point: We could merge transactions 15 and 16 into one *compound entry.*

1 IDENTIFY FastForward pays $700 cash in employee salary for work performed in the latter part of December.

2 ANALYZE

Assets	=	Liabilities	+	Equity
Cash				Salaries Expense
−700	=	0		−700

3 RECORD

Date	Account Titles and Explanation	PR	Debit	Credit
(16)	Salaries Expense	622	700	
	Cash	101		700

4 POST

Salaries Expense			622
(7)	700		
(16)	**700**		

Cash			101
(1)	30,000	(2)	2,500
(5)	4,200	(3)	26,000
(9)	1,900	(6)	1,000
(12)	3,000	(7)	700
		(10)	900
		(11)	200
		(13)	2,400
		(14)	120
		(15)	305
		(16)	**700**

Accounting Equation Analysis

Point: Technology does not provide the judgment required to analyze most business transactions. Analysis requires the expertise of skilled and ethical professionals.

Exhibit 2.13 shows the ledger accounts (in T-account form) of FastForward after all 16 transactions are recorded and posted and the balances computed. The accounts are grouped into three major columns corresponding to the accounting equation: assets, liabilities, and equity. Note several important points. First, as with each transaction, the totals for the three columns must obey the accounting equation. Specifically, assets equal $42,395 ($4,275 + $0 + $9,720 + $2,400 + $26,000); liabilities equal $9,200 ($6,200 + $3,000); and equity equals $33,195 ($30,000 − $200 + $5,800 + $300 − $1,400 − $1,000 − $305). These numbers prove the accounting equation: Assets of $42,395 = Liabilities of $9,200 + Equity of $33,195. Second, the common stock, dividends, revenue, and expense accounts reflect the transactions that change equity. These account categories underlie the statement of retained earnings. Third, the revenue and expense account balances will be summarized and reported in the income statement. Fourth, increases and decreases in the Cash account make up the elements reported in the statement of cash flows.

Debit and Credit Rules

Accounts	Increase (normal bal.)	Decrease
Asset	Debit	Credit
Liability	Credit	Debit
Common Stock	Credit	Debit
Dividends	Debit	Credit
Revenue	Credit	Debit
Expense	Debit	Credit

EXHIBIT 2.13

Ledger for FastForward (in T-Account Form)

General Ledger

Assets = Liabilities + Equity

Assets

Cash			101
(1)	30,000	(2)	2,500
(5)	4,200	(3)	26,000
(9)	1,900	(6)	1,000
(12)	3,000	(7)	700
		(10)	900
		(11)	200
		(13)	2,400
		(14)	120
		(15)	305
		(16)	700
Balance	**4,275**		

Accounts Receivable			106
(8)	1,900	(9)	1,900
Balance	**0**		

Supplies			126
(2)	2,500		
(4)	7,100		
(14)	120		
Balance	**9,720**		

Prepaid Insurance			128
(13)	**2,400**		

Equipment			167
(3)	**26,000**		

Liabilities

Accounts Payable			201
(10)	900	(4)	7,100
		Balance	**6,200**

Unearned Consulting Revenue			236
		(12)	**3,000**

Equity

Common Stock			307
		(1)	**30,000**

Dividends			319
(11)	**200**		

Consulting Revenue			403
		(5)	4,200
		(8)	1,600
		Balance	**5,800**

Rental Revenue			406
		(8)	**300**

Salaries Expense			622
(7)	700		
(16)	700		
Balance	**1,400**		

Rent Expense			640
(6)	**1,000**		

Utilities Expense			690
(15)	**305**		

Accounts in this white area reflect those reported on the income statement.

$42,395 = **$9,200** + **$33,195**

NEED-TO-KNOW 2-3

Recording Transactions

P1 A1

Assume Tata Company began operations on January 1 and completed the following transactions during its first month of operations. For each transaction, (a) analyze the transaction using the accounting equation, (b) record the transaction in journal entry form, and (c) post the entry using T-accounts to represent ledger accounts. Tata Company has the following (partial) chart of accounts—account numbers in parentheses: Cash (101); Accounts Receivable (106); Equipment (167); Accounts Payable (201); Common Stock (307); Dividends (319); Services Revenue (403); and Wages Expense (601).

Jan. 1 Jamsetji Tata invested $4,000 cash in the Tata Company in exchange for common stock.

5 Tata Company purchased $2,000 of equipment on credit.

14 Tata Company provided $540 of services for a client on credit.

Solution

Jan. 1 Receive Investment by Owner

a ANALYZE

Assets	=	Liabilities	+	Equity
Cash				**Common Stock**
+4,000	=	0		+4,000

b RECORD

Date	Account Titles and Explanation	PR	Debit	Credit
Jan. 1	Cash	101	4,000	
	Common Stock	307		4,000

c POST

Cash			101
Jan. 1	4,000		

Common Stock			307
		Jan. 1	4,000

Jan. 5 Purchase Equipment on Credit

a ANALYZE

Assets	=	Liabilities	+	Equity
Equipment		**Accounts Payable**		
+2,000	=	+2,000	+	0

b RECORD

Date	Account Titles and Explanation	PR	Debit	Credit
Jan. 5	Equipment	167	2,000	
	Accounts Payable	201		2,000

c POST

Equipment			167
Jan. 5	2,000		

Accounts Payable			201
		Jan. 5	2,000

Jan. 14 Provide Services on Credit

a ANALYZE

Assets	=	Liabilities	+	Equity
Accounts Receivable				**Services Revenue**
+540	=	0		+540

b RECORD

Date	Account Titles and Explanation	PR	Debit	Credit
Jan. 14	Accounts Receivable	106	540	
	Services Revenue	403		540

c POST

Accounts Receivable			106
Jan. 14	540		

Services Revenue			403
		Jan. 14	540

Do More: QS 2-7, E 2-7, E 2-9, E 2-11, E 2-12

QC2

TRIAL BALANCE

P2 Prepare and explain the use of a trial balance.

Double-entry accounting requires the sum of debit account balances to equal the sum of credit account balances. A trial balance is used to confirm this. A **trial balance** is a list of accounts and their balances at a point in time. Account balances are reported in their appropriate debit or credit columns of a trial balance. A trial balance can be used to confirm this and to follow up on any abnormal or unusual balances. Exhibit 2.14 shows the trial balance for FastForward after its 16 entries have been posted to the ledger. (This is an *unadjusted* trial balance—Chapter 3 explains the necessary adjustments.)

Preparing a Trial Balance

Preparing a trial balance involves three steps:

1. List each account title and its amount (from ledger) in the trial balance. If an account has a zero balance, list it with a zero in its normal balance column (or omit it entirely).
2. Compute the total of debit balances and the total of credit balances.
3. Verify (*prove*) total debit balances equal total credit balances.

Point: A trial balance is *not* a financial statement but a mechanism for checking equality of debits and credits in the ledger. Financial statements do not have debit and credit columns.

The total of debit balances equals the total of credit balances for the trial balance in Exhibit 2.14. Equality of these two totals does not guarantee that no errors were made. For example, the column totals still will be equal when a debit or credit of a correct amount is made to

EXHIBIT 2.14

Trial Balance (Unadjusted)

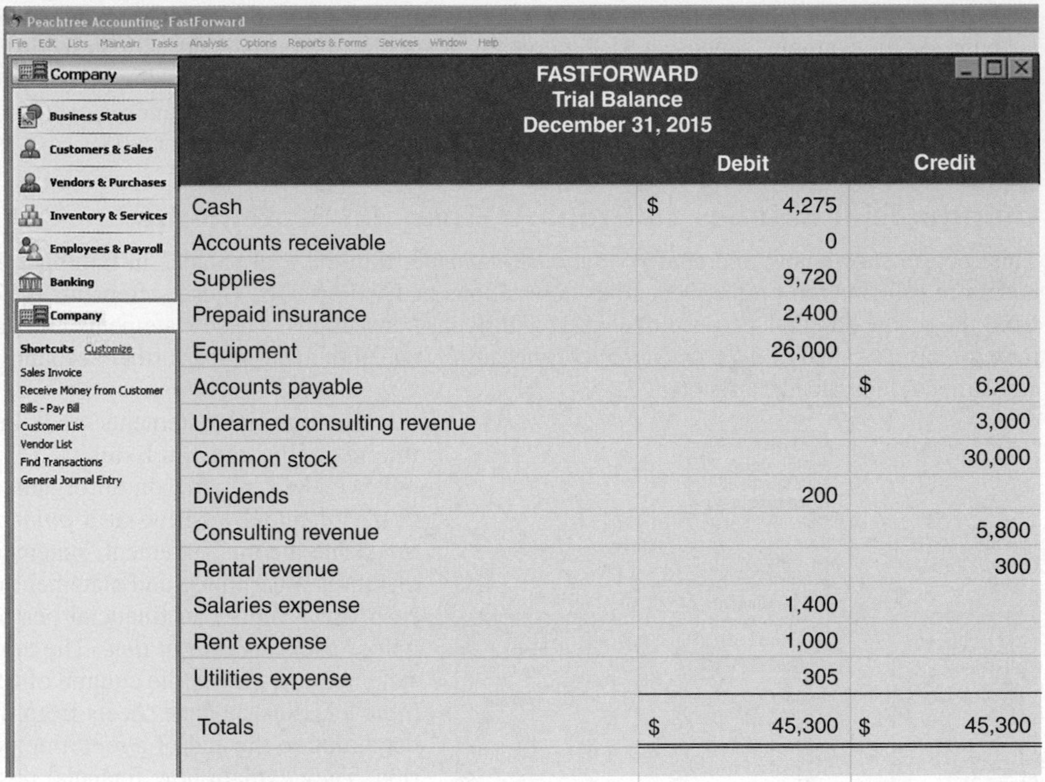

FASTFORWARD
Trial Balance
December 31, 2015

	Debit	Credit
Cash	$ 4,275	
Accounts receivable	0	
Supplies	9,720	
Prepaid insurance	2,400	
Equipment	26,000	
Accounts payable		$ 6,200
Unearned consulting revenue		3,000
Common stock		30,000
Dividends	200	
Consulting revenue		5,800
Rental revenue		300
Salaries expense	1,400	
Rent expense	1,000	
Utilities expense	305	
Totals	$ 45,300	$ 45,300

Point: The ordering of accounts in a trial balance follows their identification number from the chart of accounts, which is in the following order: asset, liability, equity, revenue, and expense accounts.

a wrong account. Another error that does not cause unequal column totals occurs when equal debits and credits of an incorrect amount are entered.

Searching for and Correcting Errors If the trial balance does not balance (when its columns are not equal), the error (or errors) must be found and corrected. An efficient way to search for an error is to check the journalizing, posting, and trial balance preparation in *reverse order*. Step 1 is to verify that the trial balance columns are correctly added. If step 1 fails to find the error, Step 2 is to verify that account balances are accurately entered from the ledger. Step 3 is to see whether a debit (or credit) balance is mistakenly listed in the trial balance as a credit (or debit). A clue to this error is when the difference between total debits and total credits equals twice the amount of the incorrect account balance. If the error is still undiscovered, Step 4 is to recompute each account balance in the ledger. Step 5 is to verify that each journal entry is properly posted. Step 6 is to verify that the original journal entry has equal debits and credits. At this point, the errors should be uncovered.[3]

Example: If a credit to Unearned Revenue was incorrectly posted from the journal as a credit to the Revenue ledger account, would the ledger still balance? Would the financial statements be correct? *Answers:* The ledger would balance, but liabilities would be understated, equity would be overstated, and income would be overstated (all because of overstated revenues).

If an error in a journal entry is discovered before the error is posted, it can be corrected in a manual system by drawing a line through the incorrect information. The correct information is written above it to create a record of change for the auditor. Many computerized systems do not allow journal entries to be changed or deleted as part of a good system of internal controls. One approach is to "reverse" the original entry and then input the correct entry.

Point: The IRS requires companies to keep records that can be audited.

If an error in a journal entry is not discovered until after it is posted, we do not strike through both erroneous entries in the journal and ledger. Instead, we correct this error by creating a

[3] *Transposition* occurs when two digits are switched, or transposed, within a number. If transposition is the only error, it yields a difference between the two trial balance totals that is evenly divisible by 9. For example, assume that a $691 debit in an entry is incorrectly posted to the ledger as $619. Total credits in the trial balance are then larger than total debits by $72 ($691 − $619). The $72 error is *evenly* divisible by 9 (72/9 = 8). The first digit of the quotient (in our example it is 8) equals the difference between the digits of the two transposed numbers (the 9 and the 1). The number of digits in the quotient also tells the location of the transposition, starting from the right. The quotient in our example had only one digit (8), so it tells us the transposition is in the first digit. Consider another example where a transposition error involves posting $961 instead of the correct $691. The difference in these numbers is $270, and its quotient is 30 (270/9). The quotient has two digits, so it tells us to check the second digit from the right for a transposition of two numbers that have a difference of 3.

correcting entry that removes the amount from the wrong account and records it to the correct account. As an example, suppose a $100 purchase of supplies is journalized with an incorrect debit to Equipment, and then this incorrect entry is posted to the ledger. The Supplies ledger account balance is understated by $100, and the Equipment ledger account balance is overstated by $100. The correcting entry is: debit Supplies and credit Equipment (both for $100).

Using a Trial Balance to Prepare Financial Statements

P3 Prepare financial statements from business transactions.

This section shows how to prepare *financial statements* from the trial balance in Exhibit 2.14 and from information on the December transactions of FastForward. These statements differ from those in Chapter 1 because of several additional transactions. These statements are also more precisely called *unadjusted statements* because we need to make some further accounting adjustments (described in Chapter 3).

EXHIBIT 2.15

Links between Financial Statements across Time

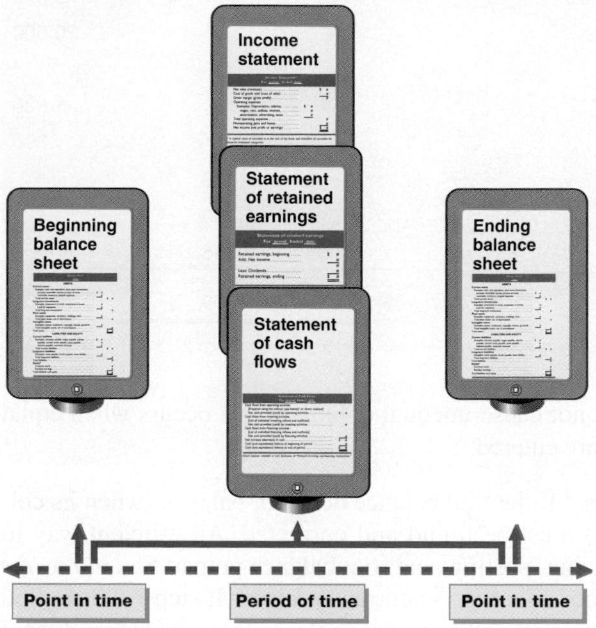

How financial statements are linked in time is illustrated in Exhibit 2.15. A balance sheet reports on an organization's financial position at a *point in time*. The income statement, statement of retained earnings, and statement of cash flows report on financial performance over a *period of time*. The three statements in the middle column of Exhibit 2.15 link balance sheets from the beginning to the end of a reporting period. They explain how financial position changes from one point to another.

Preparers and users (including regulatory agencies) determine the length of the reporting period. A one-year, or annual, reporting period is common, as are semiannual, quarterly, and monthly periods. The one-year reporting period is known as the *accounting,* or *fiscal, year*. Businesses whose accounting year begins on January 1 and ends on December 31 are known as *calendar-year* companies. **Google** is a calendar-year company. Many companies choose a fiscal year ending on a date other than December 31. **Apple** is a *noncalendar-year* company as reflected in the headings of its September 28, 2013, year-end financial statements in Appendix A near the end of the book.

Point: A statement's heading lists the 3 W's: **W**ho—name of organization, **W**hat—name of statement, **W**hen—statement's point in time or period of time.

Income Statement An income statement reports the revenues earned less the expenses incurred by a business over a period of time. FastForward's income statement for December is shown at the top of Exhibit 2.16. Information about revenues and expenses is conveniently taken from the trial balance in Exhibit 2.14. Net income of $3,395 is reported at the bottom of the statement. Owner investments and dividends are *not* part of income.

Point: An income statement is also called an *earnings statement, a statement of operations,* or a *P&L* (profit and loss) *statement.* A balance sheet is also called a *statement of financial position.*

Statement of Retained Earnings The statement of retained earnings reports information about how retained earnings change over the reporting period. FastForward's statement of retained earnings is the second report in Exhibit 2.16. It shows the $3,395 of net income, the $200 dividend, and the $3,195 end-of-period balance. (The beginning balance in the statement of retained earnings is rarely zero; an exception is for the first period of operations. The beginning balance in January 2016 is $3,195, which is December 2015's ending balance.)

Point: While revenues increase equity, and expenses decrease equity, the amounts are not reported in detail in the statement of retained earnings. Instead, their effects are reflected through net income.

Balance Sheet The balance sheet reports the financial position of a company at a point in time, usually at the end of a month, quarter, or year. FastForward's balance sheet is the third report in Exhibit 2.16. This statement refers to financial condition at the close of business on

EXHIBIT 2.16

Financial Statements Prepared from Trial Balance

FASTFORWARD
Trial Balance
December 31, 2015

	Debit	Credit
Cash	$ 4,275	
Accounts receivable	0	
Supplies	9,720	
Prepaid insurance	2,400	
Equipment	26,000	
Accounts payable		$ 6,200
Unearned consulting revenue		3,000
Common stock		30,000
Dividends	200	
Consulting revenue		5,800
Rental revenue		300
Salaries expense	1,400	
Rent expense	1,000	
Utilities expense	305	
Totals	$45,300	$45,300

Each account on the trial balance is either an asset (to balance sheet), liability (to balance sheet), or equity (to income statement or to statement of retained earnings).

FASTFORWARD
Income Statement
For Month Ended December 31, 2015

Revenues		
Consulting revenue ($4,200 + $1,600)	$ 5,800	
Rental revenue	300	
Total revenues		$ 6,100
Expenses		
Salaries expense	1,400	
Rent expense	1,000	
Utilities expense	305	
Total expenses		2,705
Net income		$ 3,395

FASTFORWARD
Statement of Retained Earnings
For Month Ended December 31, 2015

Retained earnings, December 1, 2015	$ 0
Plus: Net income	3,395
	3,395
Less: Cash dividends	200
Retained earnings, December 31, 2015	$ 3,195

FASTFORWARD
Balance Sheet
December 31, 2015

Assets		Liabilities	
Cash	$ 4,275	Accounts payable	$ 6,200
Supplies	9,720	Unearned consult. revenue	3,000
Prepaid insurance	2,400	Total liabilities	9,200
Equipment	26,000	**Equity**	
		Common stock	30,000
		Retained earnings	3,195
		Total equity	33,195
Total assets	$42,395	Total liabilities and equity	$42,395

Point: Arrow lines show how the statements are linked.

Point: To *foot* a column of numbers is to add them.

December 31. The left side of the balance sheet lists its assets: cash, supplies, prepaid insurance, and equipment. The upper right side of the balance sheet shows that it owes $6,200 to creditors and $3,000 in services to customers who paid in advance. The equity section shows an ending balance of $33,195. Note the link between the ending balance of the statement of retained earnings and the retained earnings balance. (Recall that this presentation of the balance sheet is called the *account form:* assets on the left and liabilities and equity on the right. Another presentation is the *report form:* assets on top, followed by liabilities and then equity. Either presentation is acceptable.)

Point: Knowing how financial statements are prepared improves our analysis of them.

Decision Maker

Entrepreneur You open a wholesale business selling entertainment equipment to retail outlets. You find that most of your customers demand to buy on credit. How can you use the balance sheets of these customers to decide which ones to extend credit to? ■ [Answers follow the chapter's Summary.]

Presentation Issues Dollar signs are not used in journals and ledgers. They do appear in financial statements and other reports such as trial balances. The usual practice is to put dollar signs beside only the first and last numbers in a column. **Apple**'s financial statements in Appendix A show this. When amounts are entered in a journal, ledger, or trial balance, commas are optional to indicate thousands, millions, and so forth. However, commas are always used in financial statements. Companies also commonly round amounts in reports to the nearest dollar, or even to a higher level. Apple is typical of many companies in that it rounds its financial statement amounts to the nearest million (or thousand). This decision is based on the perceived impact of rounding for users' business decisions.

Point: The terms "Debit" and "Credit" do not appear on financial statements.

NEED-TO-KNOW 2-4

Preparing Trial Balance

P2

Prepare a trial balance for **Apple** using the following *condensed* data from its fiscal year ended September 29, 2012 ($ in millions).

Common stock	$ 16,422	Dividends	$ 2,523
Accounts payable	21,175	Securities investments and other assets	138,936
Other liabilities	36,679	Land and equipment (net)	15,452
Cost of sales (and other expenses)	101,876	Selling and other expense	12,899
Cash	10,746	Accounts receivable	10,930
Revenues	156,508	Retained earnings	62,578

Solution ($ in millions)

APPLE
Trial Balance
September 29, 2012

	Debit	Credit
Cash	$ 10,746	
Accounts receivable	10,930	
Land and equipment (net)	15,452	
Securities investments and other assets	138,936	
Accounts payable		$ 21,175
Other liabilities		36,679
Common stock		16,422
Retained earnings		62,578
Dividends	2,523	
Revenues		156,508
Cost of sales and other expenses	101,876	
Selling and other expense	12,899	
Totals	$293,362	$293,362

Do More: E 2-8, E 2-10

QC3

GLOBAL VIEW

Financial accounting according to U.S. GAAP is similar, but not identical, to IFRS. This section discusses differences in analyzing and recording transactions, and with the preparation of financial statements.

Analyzing and Recording Transactions Both U.S. GAAP and IFRS include broad and similar guidance for financial accounting. As the FASB and IASB work toward a common conceptual framework over the next few years, even those differences will fade. Further, both U.S. GAAP and IFRS apply transaction analysis and recording as shown in this chapter—using the same debit and credit system and accrual accounting. Although some variations exist in revenue and expense recognition and other accounting principles, all of the transactions in this chapter are accounted for identically under these two systems.

Financial Statements Both U.S. GAAP and IFRS prepare the same four basic financial statements. A few differences within each statement do exist and we will discuss those throughout the book.

For example, both U.S. GAAP and IFRS require balance sheets to separate current items from noncurrent items. However, while U.S. GAAP balance sheets report current items first, IFRS balance sheets normally (but are not required to) present noncurrent items first, and equity before liabilities. To illustrate, a condensed version of **Piaggio**'s balance sheet follows (numbers using Euros in thousands).

PIAGGIO

PIAGGIO
Balance Sheet (in thousands of Euros)
December 31, 2012

Assets		Equity and Liabilities	
Noncurrent assets	€1,052,797	Total equity	€ 439,873
Current assets	427,428	Noncurrent liabilities	453,272
		Current liabilities	587,080
Total assets	€1,480,225	Total equity and liabilities	€1,480,225

Accounting Controls and Assurance Accounting systems depend on control procedures that assure the proper principles were applied in processing accounting information. The passage of SOX legislation strengthened U.S. control procedures in recent years. However, global standards for control are diverse and so are enforcement activities. Consequently, while global accounting standards are converging, their application in different countries can yield different outcomes depending on the quality of their auditing standards and enforcement.

Decision Insight

Accounting Control Recording valid transactions, and not recording fraudulent transactions, enhances the quality of financial statements. The graph here shows the percentage of employees in information technology that report observing specific types of misconduct [Source: KPMG 2009]. ■

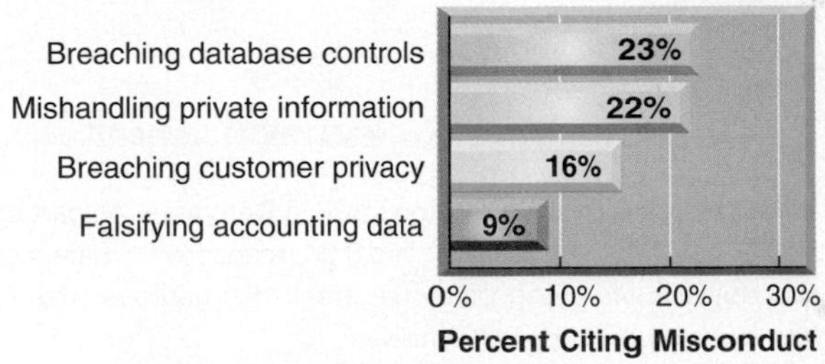

Sustainability and Accounting **Akola Project**, as introduced in this chapter's opening feature, emphasizes the building of an infrastructure within the poorest communities for purposes of sustainability. That social aim is the overriding theme for all of its business activities. This theme is communicated to its customers in a desire to enhance sales and to better the lives of artisans working for Akola. This is a win-win scenario according to its entrepreneurial owner, Brittany Merrill Underwood. Importantly, accounting is used both to track the costs for the artisans and to record revenues from product sales, which are then shared 100% with artisans. Brittany's site includes the model shown here and explains that her "sustainable model transforms the . . . livelihoods of our artisans-in-training, their families, and communities through empowering vocational training and income-generating opportunities."

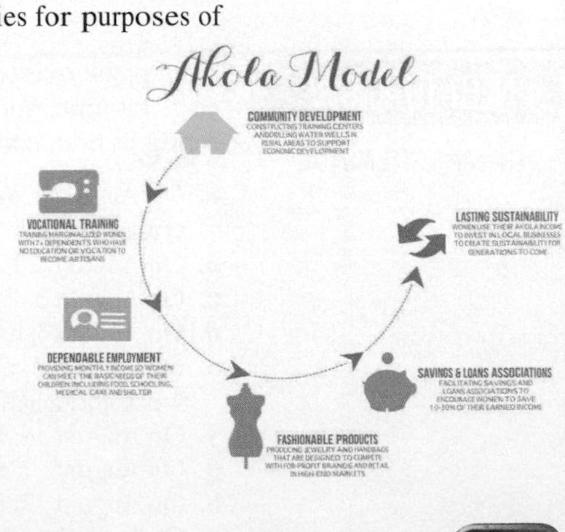

Both images: Courtesy of Akola Project

Debt Ratio — Decision Analysis

A2 Compute the debt ratio and describe its use in analyzing financial condition.

An important business objective is gathering information to help assess a company's risk of failing to pay its debts. Companies finance their assets with either liabilities or equity. A company that finances a relatively large portion of its assets with liabilities is said to have a high degree of *financial leverage*. Higher financial leverage involves greater risk because liabilities must be repaid and often require regular interest payments (equity financing does not). The risk that a company might not be able to meet such required payments is higher if it has more liabilities (is more highly leveraged). One way to assess the risk associated with a company's use of liabilities is to compute the **debt ratio** as in Exhibit 2.17.

EXHIBIT 2.17

Debt Ratio

$$\textbf{Debt ratio} = \frac{\textbf{Total liabilities}}{\textbf{Total assets}}$$

Point: Compare the equity amount to the liability amount to assess the extent of owner versus nonowner financing.

To see how to apply the debt ratio, let's look at **Skechers**'s liabilities and assets. The company designs, markets, and sells footwear for men, women, and children under the Skechers brand. Exhibit 2.18 computes and reports its debt ratio at the end of each year from 2009 to 2013.

EXHIBIT 2.18

Computation and Analysis of Debt Ratio

$ in millions	2013	2012	2011	2010	2009
Total liabilities	$ 429	$ 421	$ 389	$ 359	$246
Total assets	$1,409	$1,340	$1,282	$1,305	$996
Debt ratio	**0.30**	**0.31**	**0.30**	**0.28**	**0.25**
Industry debt ratio	0.47	0.46	0.47	0.49	0.51

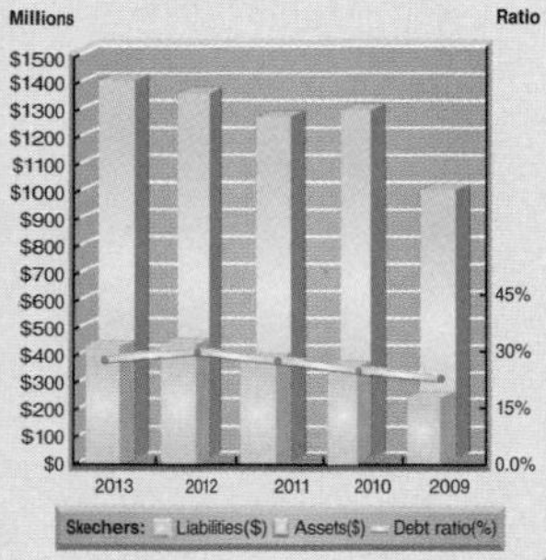

Skechers's debt ratio ranges from a low of 0.25 to a high of 0.31—also, see graph in margin. Its ratio is lower, compared with the industry ratio. This analysis implies a lower risk from its financial leverage. Is financial leverage good or bad for Skechers? To answer that question we need to compare the company's return on the borrowed money to the rate it is paying creditors. If the company's return is higher, it is successfully borrowing money to make more money. A company's success with making money from borrowed money can quickly turn unprofitable if its own return drops below the rate it is paying creditors.

Decision Maker

Investor You consider buying stock in **Converse.** As part of your analysis, you compute its debt ratio for 2013, 2014, and 2015 as: 0.35, 0.74, and 0.94, respectively. Based on the debt ratio, is Converse a low-risk investment? Has the risk of buying Converse stock changed over this period? (The industry debt ratio averages 0.40.) ■

[Answers follow the chapter's Summary.]

NEED-TO-KNOW COMPREHENSIVE

(This problem extends the Comprehensive Need-To-Know of Chapter 1.) After several months of planning, Jasmine Worthy started a haircutting business called Expressions. The following events occurred during its first month.

a. On August 1, Worthy invested $3,000 cash and $15,000 of equipment in Expressions in exchange for common stock.
b. On August 2, Expressions paid $600 cash for furniture for the shop.
c. On August 3, Expressions paid $500 cash to rent space in a strip mall for August.
d. On August 4, it purchased $1,200 of equipment on credit for the shop (using a long-term note payable).
e. On August 5, Expressions opened for business. Cash received from haircutting services in the first week and a half of business (ended August 15) was $825.
f. On August 15, it provided $100 of haircutting services on account.
g. On August 17, it received a $100 check for services previously rendered on account.
h. On August 17, it paid $125 to an assistant for hours worked during the grand opening.
i. Cash received from services provided during the second half of August was $930.
j. On August 31, it paid a $400 installment toward principal on the note payable entered into on August 4.
k. On August 31, it paid $900 cash in dividends to Worthy (sole shareholder).

Required

1. Open the following ledger accounts in balance column format (account numbers are in parentheses): Cash (101); Accounts Receivable (102); Furniture (161); Store Equipment (165); Note Payable (240); Common Stock (307); Dividends (319); Haircutting Services Revenue (403); Wages Expense (623); and Rent Expense (640). Prepare general journal entries for the transactions.

2. Post the journal entries from (1) to the ledger accounts.
3. Prepare a trial balance as of August 31.
4. Prepare an income statement for August.
5. Prepare a statement of retained earnings for August.
6. Prepare a balance sheet as of August 31.
7. Determine the debt ratio as of August 31.

Extended Analysis

8. In the coming months, Expressions will experience a greater variety of business transactions. Identify which accounts are debited and which are credited for the following transactions. (*Hint:* We must use some accounts not opened in part 1.)
   a. Purchase supplies with cash.
   b. Pay cash for future insurance coverage.
   c. Receive cash for services to be provided in the future.
   d. Purchase supplies on account.

PLANNING THE SOLUTION

- Analyze each transaction and use the debit and credit rules to prepare a journal entry for each.
- Post each debit and each credit from journal entries to their ledger accounts and cross-reference each amount in the posting reference (PR) columns of the journal and ledger.
- Calculate each account balance and list the accounts with their balances on a trial balance.
- Verify that total debits in the trial balance equal total credits.
- To prepare the income statement, identify revenues and expenses. List those items on the statement, compute the difference, and label the result as *net income* or *net loss*.
- Use information in the ledger to prepare the statement of retained earnings.
- Use information in the ledger to prepare the balance sheet.
- Calculate the debt ratio by dividing total liabilities by total assets.
- Analyze the future transactions to identify the accounts affected and apply debit and credit rules.

SOLUTION

1. General journal entries:

General Journal — Page 1

Date	Account Titles and Explanation	PR	Debit	Credit
Aug. 1	Cash	101	3,000	
	Store Equipment	165	15,000	
	Common Stock	307		18,000
	Owner's investment in exchange for stock.			
2	Furniture	161	600	
	Cash	101		600
	Purchased furniture for cash.			
3	Rent Expense	640	500	
	Cash	101		500
	Paid rent for August.			
4	Store Equipment	165	1,200	
	Note Payable	240		1,200
	Purchased additional equipment on credit.			
15	Cash	101	825	
	Haircutting Services Revenue	403		825
	Cash receipts from first half of August.			

[continued on next page]

[continued from previous page]

15	Accounts Receivable	102	100	
	Haircutting Services Revenue	403		100
	To record revenue for services provided on account.			
17	Cash	101	100	
	Accounts Receivable	102		100
	To record cash received as payment on account.			
17	Wages Expense	623	125	
	Cash	101		125
	Paid wages to assistant.			
31	Cash	101	930	
	Haircutting Services Revenue	403		930
	Cash receipts from second half of August.			
31	Note Payable	240	400	
	Cash	101		400
	Paid an installment on the note payable.			
31	Dividends	319	900	
	Cash	101		900
	Paid cash for dividends.			

2. Post journal entries from part 1 to the ledger accounts:

General Ledger

Cash **Account No. 101**

Date	PR	Debit	Credit	Balance
Aug. 1	G1	3,000		3,000
2	G1		600	2,400
3	G1		500	1,900
15	G1	825		2,725
17	G1	100		2,825
17	G1		125	2,700
31	G1	930		3,630
31	G1		400	3,230
31	G1		900	2,330

Accounts Receivable **Account No. 102**

Date	PR	Debit	Credit	Balance
Aug. 15	G1	100		100
17	G1		100	0

Furniture **Account No. 161**

Date	PR	Debit	Credit	Balance
Aug. 2	G1	600		600

Store Equipment **Account No. 165**

Date	PR	Debit	Credit	Balance
Aug. 1	G1	15,000		15,000
4	G1	1,200		16,200

Note Payable **Account No. 240**

Date	PR	Debit	Credit	Balance
Aug. 4	G1		1,200	1,200
31	G1	400		800

Common Stock **Account No. 307**

Date	PR	Debit	Credit	Balance
Aug. 1	G1		18,000	18,000

Dividends **Account No. 319**

Date	PR	Debit	Credit	Balance
Aug. 31	G1	900		900

Haircutting Services Revenue Account No. 403

Date	PR	Debit	Credit	Balance
Aug. 15	G1		825	825
15	G1		100	925
31	G1		930	1,855

Wages Expense **Account No. 623**

Date	PR	Debit	Credit	Balance
Aug. 17	G1	125		125

Rent Expense **Account No. 640**

Date	PR	Debit	Credit	Balance
Aug. 3	G1	500		500

3. Prepare a trial balance from the ledger:

EXPRESSIONS
Trial Balance
August 31

	Debit	Credit
Cash	$ 2,330	
Accounts receivable	0	
Furniture	600	
Store equipment	16,200	
Note payable		$ 800
Common stock		18,000
Dividends	900	
Haircutting services revenue		1,855
Wages expense	125	
Rent expense	500	
Totals	$20,655	$20,655

4.

EXPRESSIONS
Income Statement
For Month Ended August 31

Revenues		
Haircutting services revenue		$1,855
Operating expenses		
Rent expense	$500	
Wages expense	125	
Total operating expenses		625
Net income		$1,230

5.

EXPRESSIONS
Statement of Retained Earnings
For Month Ended August 31

Retained earnings, August 1	$ 0
Plus: Net income	1,230
	1,230
Less: Cash dividends	900
Retained earnings, August 31	$ 330

6.

EXPRESSIONS
Balance Sheet
August 31

Assets		Liabilities	
Cash	$ 2,330	Note payable	$ 800
Furniture	600	**Equity**	
Store equipment	16,200	Common stock	18,000
		Retained earnings	330
		Total equity	18,330
Total assets	$19,130	Total liabilities and equity	$19,130

7. $$\text{Debt ratio} = \frac{\text{Total liabilities}}{\text{Total assets}} = \frac{\$800}{\$19{,}130} = \underline{\underline{\mathbf{4.18\%}}}$$

8a. Supplies *debited*
Cash *credited*

8b. Prepaid Insurance *debited*
Cash *credited*

8c. Cash *debited*
Unearned Services Revenue *credited*

8d. Supplies *debited*
Accounts Payable *credited*

Summary

C1 Explain the steps in processing transactions and the role of source documents. The accounting process identifies business transactions and events, analyzes and records their effects, and summarizes and prepares information useful in making decisions. Transactions and events are the starting points in the accounting process. Source documents identify and describe transactions and events. Examples are sales tickets, checks, purchase orders, bills, and bank statements. Source documents provide objective and reliable evidence, making information more useful. The effects of transactions and events are recorded in journals. Posting along with a trial balance helps summarize and classify these effects.

C2 Describe an account and its use in recording transactions. An account is a detailed record of increases and decreases in a specific asset, liability, equity, revenue, or expense. Information from accounts is analyzed, summarized, and presented in reports and financial statements for decision makers.

C3 Describe a ledger and a chart of accounts. The ledger (or general ledger) is a record containing all accounts used by a company and their balances. It is referred to as the *books*. The chart of accounts is a list of all accounts and usually includes an identification number assigned to each account.

C4 Define *debits* and *credits* and explain double-entry accounting. *Debit* refers to left, and *credit* refers to right. Debits increase assets, expenses, and dividends while credits decrease them. Credits increase liabilities, common stock, and revenues; debits decrease them. Double-entry accounting means each transaction affects at least two accounts and has at least one debit and one credit. The system for recording debits and credits follows from the accounting equation. The left side of an account is the normal balance for assets, dividends, and expenses, and the right side is the normal balance for liabilities, common stock, and revenues.

A1 Analyze the impact of transactions on accounts and financial statements. We analyze transactions using concepts of double-entry accounting. This analysis is performed by determining a transaction's effects on accounts. These effects are recorded in journals and posted to ledgers.

A2 Compute the debt ratio and describe its use in analyzing financial condition. A company's debt ratio is computed as total liabilities divided by total assets. It reveals how much of the assets are financed by creditor (nonowner) financing. The higher this ratio, the more risk a company faces because liabilities must be repaid at specific dates.

P1 Record transactions in a journal and post entries to a ledger. Transactions are recorded in a journal. Each entry in a journal is posted to the accounts in the ledger. This provides information that is used to produce financial statements. Balance column accounts are widely used and include columns for debits, credits, and the account balance.

P2 Prepare and explain the use of a trial balance. A trial balance is a list of accounts from the ledger showing their debit or credit balances in separate columns. The trial balance is a summary of the ledger's contents and is useful in preparing financial statements and in revealing recordkeeping errors.

P3 Prepare financial statements from business transactions. The balance sheet, the statement of retained earnings, the income statement, and the statement of cash flows use data from the trial balance (and other financial statements) for their preparation.

Guidance Answers to Decision Maker and Decision Ethics

Cashier The advantages to the process proposed by the assistant manager include improved customer service, fewer delays, and less work for you. However, you should have serious concerns about internal control and the potential for fraud. In particular, the assistant manager could steal cash and simply enter fewer sales to match the remaining cash. You should reject her suggestion without the manager's approval. Moreover, you should have an ethical concern about the assistant manager's suggestion to ignore store policy.

Entrepreneur We can use the accounting equation (Assets = Liabilities + Equity) to help us identify risky customers to whom we would likely not want to extend credit. A balance sheet provides amounts for each of these key components. The lower a customer's equity is relative to liabilities, the less likely you would extend credit. A low equity means the business has little value that does not already have creditor claims to it.

Investor The debt ratio suggests the stock of Converse is of higher risk than normal and that this risk is rising. The average industry ratio of 0.40 further supports this conclusion. The 2015 debt ratio for Converse is twice the industry norm. Also, a debt ratio approaching 1.0 indicates little to no equity.

Key Terms

Account
Account balance
Balance column account
Chart of accounts
Compound journal entry
Credit
Creditors
Debit
Debt ratio
Double-entry accounting
General journal
General ledger
Journal
Journalizing
Ledger
Posting
Posting reference (PR) column
Source documents
T-account
Trial balance
Unearned revenue

Multiple Choice Quiz

Answers at end of chapter

1. Amalia Company received its utility bill for the current period of $700 and immediately paid it. Its journal entry to record this transaction includes a
   - a. Credit to Utility Expense for $700.
   - b. Debit to Utility Expense for $700.
   - c. Debit to Accounts Payable for $700.
   - d. Debit to Cash for $700.
   - e. Credit to Common Stock for $700.
2. On May 1, Mattingly Lawn Service collected $2,500 cash from a customer in advance of five months of lawn service. Mattingly's journal entry to record this transaction includes a
   - a. Credit to Unearned Lawn Service Fees for $2,500.
   - b. Debit to Lawn Service Fees Earned for $2,500.
   - c. Credit to Cash for $2,500.
   - d. Debit to Unearned Lawn Service Fees for $2,500.
   - e. Credit to Common Stock for $2,500.
3. Liang Shue contributed $250,000 cash and land worth $500,000 to open his new business, Shue Consulting Corporation. Which of the following journal entries does Shue Consulting make to record this transaction?

a. Cash Assets	750,000	
Common Stock		750,000
b. Common Stock	750,000	
Assets		750,000
c. Cash	250,000	
Land	500,000	
Common Stock		750,000
d. Common Stock	750,000	
Cash		250,000
Land		500,000

4. A trial balance prepared at year-end shows total credits exceed total debits by $765. This discrepancy could have been caused by
   - a. An error in the general journal where a $765 increase in Accounts Payable was recorded as a $765 decrease in Accounts Payable.
   - b. The ledger balance for Accounts Payable of $7,650 being entered in the trial balance as $765.
   - c. A general journal error where a $765 increase in Accounts Receivable was recorded as a $765 increase in Cash.
   - d. The ledger balance of $850 in Accounts Receivable was entered in the trial balance as $85.
   - e. An error in recording a $765 increase in Cash as a credit.
5. Bonaventure Company has total assets of $1,000,000, liabilities of $400,000, and equity of $600,000. What is its debt ratio (rounded to a whole percent)?
   - a. 250%
   - b. 167%
   - c. 67%
   - d. 150%
   - e. 40%

[I] Icon denotes assignments that involve decision making.

Discussion Questions

1. Provide the names of two (*a*) asset accounts, (*b*) liability accounts, and (*c*) equity accounts.
2. What is the difference between a note payable and an account payable?
3. [I] Discuss the steps in processing business transactions.
4. What kinds of transactions can be recorded in a general journal?
5. Are debits or credits typically listed first in general journal entries? Are the debits or the credits indented?
6. Should a transaction be recorded first in a journal or the ledger? Why?
7. If assets are valuable resources and asset accounts have debit balances, why do expense accounts also have debit balances?
8. [I] Why does the recordkeeper prepare a trial balance?
9. If an incorrect amount is journalized and posted to the accounts, how should the error be corrected?
10. Identify the four financial statements of a business.
11. [I] What information is reported in a balance sheet?
12. [I] What information is reported in an income statement?
13. [I] Why does the user of an income statement need to know the time period that it covers?

14. Define (*a*) *assets,* (*b*) *liabilities,* (*c*) *equity,* and (*d*) *net assets.*

15. Which financial statement is sometimes called the *statement of financial position*?

16. Review the **Apple** balance sheet in Appendix A. Identify three accounts on its balance sheet that carry debit balances and three accounts on its balance sheet that carry credit balances. **APPLE**

17. Review the **Google** balance sheet in Appendix A. Identify an asset with the word *receivable* in its account title and a liability with the word *payable* in its account title. **GOOGLE**

18. Review the **Samsung** balance sheet in Appendix A. Identify three current liabilities and three noncurrent liabilities in its balance sheet. **Samsung**

connect

QUICK STUDY

QS 2-1
Identifying source documents C1

Identify the items from the following list that are likely to serve as source documents.

a. Sales ticket
b. Trial balance
c. Balance sheet
d. Telephone bill
e. Invoice from supplier
f. Company revenue account
g. Income statement
h. Bank statement
i. Prepaid insurance

QS 2-2
Identifying financial statement accounts C2

Classify each of the following accounts as an asset (A), liability (L), or equity (EQ) account.

a. Cash
b. Prepaid Rent
c. Office Supplies
d. Prepaid Insurance
e. Office Equipment
f. Common Stock
g. Accounts Payable
h. Unearned Rent Revenue
i. Dividends

QS 2-3
Reading a chart of accounts C3

A chart of accounts is a list of all ledger accounts and an identification number for each. One example of a chart of accounts is near the end of the book on pages CA and CA-1. Using that chart, identify the following accounts as either an asset (A), liability (L), equity (EQ), revenue (R), or expense (E) account, along with its identification number.

a. Advertising Expense
b. Rent Revenue
c. Rent Receivable
d. Patents
e. Rent Payable
f. Furniture
g. Notes Payable
h. Common Stock
i. Utilities Expense

QS 2-4
Identifying normal balance C4

Identify the normal balance (debit or credit) for each of the following accounts.

a. Fees Earned (Revenues)
b. Office Supplies
c. Dividends
d. Wages Expense
e. Accounts Receivable
f. Prepaid Rent
g. Wages Payable
h. Building
i. Common Stock

QS 2-5
Linking debit or credit with normal balance C4

Indicate whether a debit or credit *decreases* the normal balance of each of the following accounts.

a. Interest Payable
b. Service Revenue
c. Salaries Expense
d. Accounts Receivable
e. Common Stock
f. Prepaid Insurance
g. Buildings
h. Interest Revenue
i. Dividends
j. Unearned Revenue
k. Accounts Payable
l. Land

QS 2-6
Analyzing transactions and preparing journal entries P1

For each transaction, (1) analyze the transaction using the accounting equation, (2) record the transaction in journal entry form, and (3) post the entry using T-accounts to represent ledger accounts. Use the following (partial) chart of accounts—account numbers in parentheses: Cash (101); Accounts Receivable (106); Office Supplies (124); Trucks (153); Equipment (167); Accounts Payable (201); Unearned Landscaping Revenue (236); Common Stock (307); Dividends (319); Landscaping Revenue (403); Wages Expense (601), and Landscaping Expense (696).

a. On May 15, DeShawn Tyler opens a landscaping company called Elegant Lawns by investing $7,000 in cash along with equipment having a $3,000 value in exchange for common stock.
b. On May 21, Elegant Lawns purchases office supplies on credit for $500.
c. On May 25, Elegant Lawns receives $4,000 cash for performing landscaping services.
d. On May 30, Elegant Lawns receives $1,000 cash in advance of providing landscaping services to a customer.

QS 2-7
Analyzing debit or credit by account
A1

Identify whether a debit or credit yields the indicated change for each of the following accounts.

a. To increase Land
b. To decrease Cash
c. To increase Fees Earned (Revenues)
d. To increase Office Expense
e. To decrease Unearned Revenue
f. To decrease Prepaid Rent
g. To increase Notes Payable
h. To decrease Accounts Receivable
i. To increase Common Stock
j. To increase Store Equipment

QS 2-8
Identifying a posting error
P2

A trial balance has total debits of $20,000 and total credits of $24,500. Which one of the following errors would create this imbalance? Explain.

a. A $2,250 debit to Utilities Expense in a journal entry is incorrectly posted to the ledger as a $2,250 credit, leaving the Utilities Expense account with a $3,000 debit balance.
b. A $4,500 debit to Salaries Expense in a journal entry is incorrectly posted to the ledger as a $4,500 credit, leaving the Salaries Expense account with a $750 debit balance.
c. A $2,250 credit to Consulting Fees Earned (Revenues) in a journal entry is incorrectly posted to the ledger as a $2,250 debit, leaving the Consulting Fees Earned account with a $6,300 credit balance.
d. A $2,250 debit posting to Accounts Receivable was posted mistakenly to Land.
e. A $4,500 debit posting to Equipment was posted mistakenly to Cash.
f. An entry debiting Cash and crediting Accounts Payable for $4,500 was mistakenly not posted.

QS 2-9
Classifying accounts in financial statements
P3

Indicate the financial statement on which each of the following items appears. Use I for income statement, E for statement of retained earnings, and B for balance sheet.

a. Services Revenue
b. Interest Payable
c. Accounts Receivable
d. Salaries Expense
e. Equipment
f. Prepaid Insurance
g. Buildings
h. Rental Revenue
i. Dividends
j. Office Supplies
k. Interest Expense
l. Insurance Expense

QS 2-10
International accounting standards C4

Answer each of the following questions related to international accounting standards.

a. What type of journal entry system is applied when accounting follows IFRS?
b. Identify the number and usual titles of the financial statements prepared under IFRS.
c. How do differences in accounting controls and enforcement impact accounting reports prepared across different countries?

connect

EXERCISES

Exercise 2-1
Steps in analyzing and recording transactions C1

Order the following steps in the accounting process that focus on analyzing and recording transactions.

_____ **a.** Prepare and analyze the trial balance.
_____ **b.** Analyze each transaction from source documents.
_____ **c.** Record relevant transactions in a journal.
_____ **d.** Post journal information to ledger accounts.

Exercise 2-2
Identifying and classifying accounts
C2

Enter the number for the item that best completes each of the descriptions below.

1. Asset
2. Equity
3. Account
4. Liability
5. Three

a. Accounts are arranged into _____ general categories.
b. Common Stock and Dividends are examples of _____ accounts.
c. Accounts Payable, Unearned Revenue, and Note Payable are examples of _____ accounts.
d. Accounts Receivable, Prepaid Accounts, Supplies, and Land are examples of _____ accounts.
e. An _____ is a record of increases and decreases in a specific asset, liability, equity, revenue, or expense item.

Exercise 2-3
Identifying a ledger and chart of accounts
C3

Enter the number for the item that best completes each of the descriptions below.

1. Chart
2. General ledger

a. A _____ of accounts is a list of all accounts a company uses.
b. The _____ is a record containing all accounts used by a company.

Exercise 2-4
Identifying type and normal balances of accounts
C4

For each of the following (1) identify the type of account as an asset, liability, equity, revenue, or expense, (2) identify the normal balance of the account, and (3) enter *debit* (*Dr.*) or *credit* (*Cr.*) to identify the kind of entry that would increase the account balance.

a. Land
b. Cash
c. Legal Expense
d. Prepaid Insurance
e. Accounts Receivable
f. Dividends
g. License Fee Revenue
h. Unearned Revenue
i. Fees Earned
j. Equipment
k. Notes Payable
l. Common Stock

Exercise 2-5
Analyzing effects of transactions on accounts
A1

Groro Co. bills a client $62,000 for services provided and agrees to accept the following three items in full payment: (1) $10,000 cash, (2) computer equipment worth $80,000, and (3) to assume responsibility for a $28,000 note payable related to the computer equipment. The entry Groro makes to record this transaction includes which one or more of the following?

a. $28,000 increase in a liability account
b. $10,000 increase in the Cash account
c. $10,000 increase in a revenue account
d. $62,000 increase in an asset account
e. $62,000 increase in a revenue account
f. $62,000 increase in an equity account

Exercise 2-6
Analyzing account entries and balances
A1

Use the information in each of the following separate cases to calculate the unknown amount.

a. Corentine Co. had $152,000 of accounts payable on September 30 and $132,500 on October 31. Total purchases on account during October were $281,000. Determine how much cash was paid on accounts payable during October.

b. On September 30, Valerian Co. had a $102,500 balance in Accounts Receivable. During October, the company collected $102,890 from its credit customers. The October 31 balance in Accounts Receivable was $89,000. Determine the amount of sales on account that occurred in October.

c. During October, Alameda Company had $102,500 of cash receipts and $103,150 of cash disbursements. The October 31 Cash balance was $18,600. Determine how much cash the company had at the close of business on September 30.

Exercise 2-7
Preparing general journal entries
P1

Prepare general journal entries for the following transactions of a new company called Pose-for-Pics.

Aug.	1	Madison Harris, the owner, invested $6,500 cash and $33,500 of photography equipment in the company in exchange for common stock.
	2	The company paid $2,100 cash for an insurance policy covering the next 24 months.
	5	The company purchased office supplies for $880 cash.
	20	The company received $3,331 cash in photography fees earned.
	31	The company paid $675 cash for August utilities.

Exercise 2-8
Preparing T-accounts (ledger) and a trial balance P2

Use the information in Exercise 2-7 to prepare an August 31 trial balance for Pose-for-Pics. Begin by opening these T-accounts: Cash; Office Supplies; Prepaid Insurance; Photography Equipment; Common Stock; Photography Fees Earned; and Utilities Expense. Then, post the general journal entries to these T-accounts (which will serve as the ledger), and prepare the trial balance.

Exercise 2-9
Recording effects of transactions in T-accounts
A1

Prepare general journal entries to record the transactions below for Spade Company by using the following accounts: Cash; Accounts Receivable; Office Supplies; Office Equipment; Accounts Payable; Common Stock; Dividends; Fees Earned; and Rent Expense. Use the letters beside each transaction to identify entries. After recording the transactions, post them to T-accounts, which serves as the general ledger for this assignment. Determine the ending balance of each T-account.

a. Kacy Spade, owner, invested $100,750 cash in the company in exchange for common stock.
b. The company purchased office supplies for $1,250 cash.
c. The company purchased $10,050 of office equipment on credit.
d. The company received $15,500 cash as fees for services provided to a customer.
e. The company paid $10,050 cash to settle the payable for the office equipment purchased in transaction *c*.
f. The company billed a customer $2,700 as fees for services provided.
g. The company paid $1,225 cash for the monthly rent.
h. The company collected $1,125 cash as partial payment for the account receivable created in transaction *f*.
i. The company paid $10,000 cash in dividends to the owner (sole shareholder).

Check Cash ending balance, $94,850

Exercise 2-10
Preparing a trial balance
P2

After recording the transactions of Exercise 2-9 in T-accounts and calculating the balance of each account, prepare a trial balance. Use May 31, 2015, as its report date.

Exercise 2-11
Analyzing and journalizing expense transactions
A1 P1

Examine the following transactions and identify those that create expenses for Valdez Services. Prepare general journal entries to record those expense transactions and explain why the other transactions did not create expenses.

a. The company paid $12,200 cash for payment on a 16-month-old liability for office supplies.
b. The company paid $1,233 cash for the just completed two-week salary of the receptionist.
c. The company paid $39,200 cash for equipment purchased.
d. The company paid $870 cash for this month's utilities.
e. The company paid $4,500 cash in dividends to the owner (sole shareholder).

Exercise 2-12
Analyzing and journalizing revenue transactions
A1 P1

Examine the following transactions and identify those that create revenues for Valdez Services, a company owned by Brina Valdez. Prepare general journal entries to record those revenue transactions and explain why the other transactions did not create revenues.

a. Brina Valdez invests $39,350 cash in the company in exchange for common stock.
b. The company provided $2,300 of services on credit.
c. The company provided services to a client and immediately received $875 cash.
d. The company received $10,200 cash from a client in payment for services to be provided next year.
e. The company received $3,500 cash from a client in partial payment of an account receivable.
f. The company borrowed $120,000 cash from the bank by signing a promissory note.

Exercise 2-13
Interpreting and describing transactions from T-accounts
A1

Assume the following T-accounts reflect Belle Co.'s general ledger and that seven transactions *a* through *g* are posted to them. Provide a short description of each transaction. Include the amounts in your descriptions.

Cash

(a)	6,000	(b)	4,800
(e)	4,500	(c)	900
		(f)	1,600
		(g)	820

Office Supplies

(c)	900		
(d)	300		

Prepaid Insurance

(b)	4,800		

Equipment

(a)	7,600		
(d)	9,700		

Automobiles

(a)	12,000		

Accounts Payable

(f)	1,600	(d)	10,000

Common Stock

		(a)	25,600

Delivery Services Revenue

		(e)	4,500

Gas and Oil Expense

(g)	820		

Exercise 2-14
Preparing general journal entries P1

Use information from the T-accounts in Exercise 2-13 to prepare general journal entries for each of the seven transactions *a* through *g*.

Exercise 2-15
Computing net income
A1

A corporation had the following assets and liabilities at the beginning and end of this year.

	Assets	Liabilities
Beginning of the year	$ 60,000	$20,000
End of the year	105,000	36,000

Determine the net income earned or net loss incurred by the business during the year for each of the following *separate* cases:

a. Owner made no investments in the business, and no dividends were paid during the year.
b. Owner made no investments in the business, but dividends were $1,250 cash per month.
c. No dividends were paid during the year, but the owner did invest an additional $55,000 cash in exchange for common stock.
d. Dividends were $1,250 cash per month, and the owner invested an additional $35,000 cash in exchange for common stock.

Exercise 2-16
Preparing an income statement
C3 P3

Carmen Camry operates a consulting firm called Help Today, which began operations on August 1. On August 31, the company's records show the following accounts and amounts for the month of August. Use this information to prepare an August income statement for the business.

Cash	$25,360	Consulting fees earned	$ 27,000
Accounts receivable	22,360	Rent expense	9,550
Office supplies	5,250	Salaries expense...........................	5,600
Land	44,000	Telephone expense	860
Office equipment	20,000	Miscellaneous expenses.....................	520
Accounts payable	10,500	Common stock	102,000
Dividends	6,000		

Check Net income, $10,470

Exercise 2-17
Preparing a statement of retained earnings P3

Use the information in Exercise 2-16 to prepare an August statement of retained earnings for Help Today. (The owner invested $102,000 cash in the company on August 1 in exchange for common stock.)

Check End. Ret. Earnings, $4,470

Exercise 2-18
Preparing a balance sheet P3

Use the information in Exercise 2-16 (if completed, use the solution to Exercise 2-17) to prepare an August 31 balance sheet for Help Today.

Exercise 2-19
Analyzing changes in a company's equity
P3

Compute the missing amount for each of the following separate companies *a* through *d*.

	A	B	C	D	E
1		(a)	(b)	(c)	(d)
2	Equity, December 31, 2014	$ 0	$ 0	$ 0	$ 0
3	Owner investments for stock during the year	110,000	?	87,000	210,000
4	Dividends during the year	?	(47,000)	(10,000)	(55,000)
5	Net income (loss) for the year	22,000	90,000	(4,000)	?
6	Equity, December 31, 2015	104,000	85,000	?	110,000
7					

Exercise 2-20
Identifying effects of posting errors on the trial balance
A1 P2

Posting errors are identified in the following table. In column (1), enter the amount of the difference between the two trial balance columns (debit and credit) due to the error. In column (2), identify the trial balance column (debit or credit) with the larger amount if they are not equal. In column (3), identify the account(s) affected by the error. In column (4), indicate the amount by which the account(s) in column (3) is under- or overstated. Item (a) is completed as an example.

	Description of Posting Error	(1) Difference between Debit and Credit Columns	(2) Column with the Larger Total	(3) Identify Account(s) Incorrectly Stated	(4) Amount that Account(s) Is Over- or Understated
a.	$3,600 debit to Rent Expense is posted as a $1,340 debit.	$2,260	Credit	Rent Expense	Rent Expense understated $2,260
b.	$6,500 credit to Cash is posted twice as two credits to Cash.				
c.	$10,900 debit to the Dividends account is debited to Common Stock.				
d.	$2,050 debit to Prepaid Insurance is posted as a debit to Insurance Expense.				
e.	$38,000 debit to Machinery is posted as a debit to Accounts Payable.				
f.	$5,850 credit to Services Revenue is posted as a $585 credit.				
g.	$1,390 debit to Store Supplies is not posted.				

Exercise 2-21
Analyzing a trial balance error
A1 P2

You are told the column totals in a trial balance are not equal. After careful analysis, you discover only one error. Specifically, a correctly journalized credit purchase of an automobile for $18,950 is posted from the journal to the ledger with an $18,950 debit to Automobiles and another $18,950 debit to Accounts Payable. The Automobiles account has a debit balance of $37,100 on the trial balance. Answer each of the following questions and compute the dollar amount of any misstatement.

a. Is the Debit column total of the trial balance overstated, understated, or correctly stated?

b. Is the Credit column total of the trial balance overstated, understated, or correctly stated?

c. Is the Automobiles account balance overstated, understated, or correctly stated in the trial balance?

d. Is the Accounts Payable account balance overstated, understated, or correctly stated in the trial balance?

e. If the Debit column total of the trial balance is $200,000 before correcting the error, what is the total of the Credit column before correction?

Exercise 2-22
Preparing a balance sheet following IFRS
P3

Heineken N.V., a global brewer domiciled in the Netherlands, reports the following balance sheet accounts for the year ended December 31, 2013 (euro in millions). Prepare the balance sheet for this company as of December 31, 2013, following the usual IFRS format.

Current liabilities	€ 8,003	Noncurrent liabilities	€12,978
Current assets	5,495	Noncurrent assets	27,842
Total equity	12,356		

Exercise 2-23
Interpreting the debt ratio and return on assets
A2

a. Calculate the debt ratio and the return on assets using the year-end information for each of the following six separate companies ($ thousands).

	Case	Assets	Liabilities	Average Assets	Net Income
2	Company 1	$90,500	$11,765	$100,000	$20,000
3	Company 2	64,000	46,720	40,000	3,800
4	Company 3	32,500	26,650	50,000	650
5	Company 4	147,000	55,860	200,000	21,000
6	Company 5	92,000	31,280	40,000	7,520
7	Company 6	104,500	52,250	80,000	12,000
8					

b. Of the six companies, which business relies most heavily on creditor financing?
c. Of the six companies, which business relies most heavily on equity financing?
d. Which two companies indicate the greatest risk?
e. Which two companies earn the highest return on assets?
f. Which one company would investors likely prefer based on the risk-return relation?

connect

PROBLEM SET A

Karla Tanner opens a web consulting business called Linkworks and completes the following transactions in its first month of operations.

Problem 2-1A
Preparing and posting journal entries; preparing a trial balance
C3 C4 A1 P1 P2

April	1	Tanner invests $80,000 cash along with office equipment valued at $26,000 in the company in exchange for common stock.
	2	The company prepaid $9,000 cash for twelve months' rent for office space. (*Hint:* Debit Prepaid Rent for $9,000.)
	3	The company made credit purchases for $8,000 in office equipment and $3,600 in office supplies. Payment is due within 10 days.
	6	The company completed services for a client and immediately received $4,000 cash.
	9	The company completed a $6,000 project for a client, who must pay within 30 days.
	13	The company paid $11,600 cash to settle the account payable created on April 3.
	19	The company paid $2,400 cash for the premium on a 12-month insurance policy. (*Hint:* Debit Prepaid Insurance for $2,400.)
	22	The company received $4,400 cash as partial payment for the work completed on April 9.
	25	The company completed work for another client for $2,890 on credit.
	28	The company paid $5,500 cash in dividends.
	29	The company purchased $600 of additional office supplies on credit.
	30	The company paid $435 cash for this month's utility bill.

Required

1. Prepare general journal entries to record these transactions (use account titles listed in part 2).
2. Open the following ledger accounts—their account numbers are in parentheses (use the balance column format): Cash (101); Accounts Receivable (106); Office Supplies (124); Prepaid Insurance (128); Prepaid Rent (131); Office Equipment (163); Accounts Payable (201); Common Stock (307); Dividends (319); Services Revenue (403); and Utilities Expense (690). Post journal entries from part 1 to the ledger accounts and enter the balance after each posting.
3. Prepare a trial balance as of April 30.

Check (2) Ending balances: Cash, $59,465; Accounts Receivable, $4,490; Accounts Payable, $600

(3) Total debits, $119,490

Problem 2-2A
Preparing and posting journal entries; preparing a trial balance
C3 C4 A1 P1 P2

Aracel Engineering completed the following transactions in the month of June.

a. Jenna Aracel, the owner, invested $100,000 cash, office equipment with a value of $5,000, and $60,000 of drafting equipment to launch the company in exchange for common stock.
b. The company purchased land worth $49,000 for an office by paying $6,300 cash and signing a long-term note payable for $42,700.
c. The company purchased a portable building with $55,000 cash and moved it onto the land acquired in *b*.
d. The company paid $3,000 cash for the premium on an 18-month insurance policy.
e. The company completed and delivered a set of plans for a client and collected $6,200 cash.
f. The company purchased $20,000 of additional drafting equipment by paying $9,500 cash and signing a long-term note payable for $10,500.
g. The company completed $14,000 of engineering services for a client. This amount is to be received in 30 days.
h. The company purchased $1,150 of additional office equipment on credit.
i. The company completed engineering services for $22,000 on credit.
j. The company received a bill for rent of equipment that was used on a recently completed job. The $1,333 rent cost must be paid within 30 days.
k. The company collected $7,000 cash in partial payment from the client described in transaction *g*.
l. The company paid $1,200 cash for wages to a drafting assistant.
m. The company paid $1,150 cash to settle the account payable created in transaction *h*.
n. The company paid $925 cash for minor maintenance of its drafting equipment.

o. The company paid $9,480 cash in dividends.
p. The company paid $1,200 cash for wages to a drafting assistant.
q. The company paid $2,500 cash for advertisements on the web during June.

Required

1. Prepare general journal entries to record these transactions (use the account titles listed in part 2).
2. Open the following ledger accounts—their account numbers are in parentheses (use the balance column format): Cash (101); Accounts Receivable (106); Prepaid Insurance (108); Office Equipment (163); Drafting Equipment (164); Building (170); Land (172); Accounts Payable (201); Notes Payable (250); Common Stock (307); Dividends (319); Engineering Fees Earned (402); Wages Expense (601); Equipment Rental Expense (602); Advertising Expense (603); and Repairs Expense (604). Post the journal entries from part 1 to the accounts and enter the balance after each posting.
3. Prepare a trial balance as of the end of June.

Check (2) Ending balances: Cash, $22,945; Accounts Receivable, $29,000; Accounts Payable, $1,333

(3) Trial balance totals, $261,733

Problem 2-3A
Preparing and posting journal entries; preparing a trial balance
C3 C4 A1 P1 P2

Denzel Brooks opens a web consulting business called Venture Consultants and completes the following transactions in March.

March 1 Brooks invested $150,000 cash along with $22,000 in office equipment in the company in exchange for common stock.
2 The company prepaid $6,000 cash for six months' rent for an office. (*Hint:* Debit Prepaid Rent for $6,000.)
3 The company made credit purchases of office equipment for $3,000 and office supplies for $1,200. Payment is due within 10 days.
6 The company completed services for a client and immediately received $4,000 cash.
9 The company completed a $7,500 project for a client, who must pay within 30 days.
12 The company paid $4,200 cash to settle the account payable created on March 3.
19 The company paid $5,000 cash for the premium on a 12-month insurance policy. (*Hint:* Debit Prepaid Insurance for $5,000.)
22 The company received $3,500 cash as partial payment for the work completed on March 9.
25 The company completed work for another client for $3,820 on credit.
29 The company paid $5,100 cash in dividends.
30 The company purchased $600 of additional office supplies on credit.
31 The company paid $500 cash for this month's utility bill.

Required

1. Prepare general journal entries to record these transactions (use the account titles listed in part 2).
2. Open the following ledger accounts—their account numbers are in parentheses (use the balance column format): Cash (101); Accounts Receivable (106); Office Supplies (124); Prepaid Insurance (128); Prepaid Rent (131); Office Equipment (163); Accounts Payable (201); Common Stock (307); Dividends (319); Services Revenue (403); and Utilities Expense (690). Post the journal entries from part 1 to the ledger accounts and enter the balance after each posting.
3. Prepare a trial balance as of the end of March.

Check (2) Ending balances: Cash, $136,700; Accounts Receivable, $7,820; Accounts Payable, $600

(3) Total debits, $187,920

Problem 2-4A
Recording transactions; posting to ledger; preparing a trial balance
C3 A1 P1 P2

Business transactions completed by Hannah Venedict during the month of September are as follows.

a. Venedict invested $60,000 cash along with office equipment valued at $25,000 in exchange for common stock of a new company named HV Consulting.
b. The company purchased land valued at $40,000 and a building valued at $160,000. The purchase is paid with $30,000 cash and a long-term note payable for $170,000.
c. The company purchased $2,000 of office supplies on credit.
d. Venedict invested her personal automobile in the company in exchange for more common stock. The automobile has a value of $16,500 and is to be used exclusively in the business.
e. The company purchased $5,600 of additional office equipment on credit.
f. The company paid $1,800 cash salary to an assistant.
g. The company provided services to a client and collected $8,000 cash.
h. The company paid $635 cash for this month's utilities.
i. The company paid $2,000 cash to settle the account payable created in transaction *c*.
j. The company purchased $20,300 of new office equipment by paying $20,300 cash.

k. The company completed $6,250 of services for a client, who must pay within 30 days.
l. The company paid $1,800 cash salary to an assistant.
m. The company received $4,000 cash in partial payment on the receivable created in transaction *k*.
n. The company paid $2,800 cash in dividends.

Required

1. Prepare general journal entries to record these transactions (use account titles listed in part 2).
2. Open the following ledger accounts—their account numbers are in parentheses (use the balance column format): Cash (101); Accounts Receivable (106); Office Supplies (108); Office Equipment (163); Automobiles (164); Building (170); Land (172); Accounts Payable (201); Notes Payable (250); Common Stock (307); Dividends (319); Fees Earned (402); Salaries Expense (601); and Utilities Expense (602). Post the journal entries from part 1 to the ledger accounts and enter the balance after each posting.
3. Prepare a trial balance as of the end of September.

Check (2) Ending balances: Cash, $12,665; Office Equipment, $50,900

(3) Trial balance totals, $291,350

Problem 2-5A
Computing net income from equity analysis, preparing a balance sheet, and computing the debt ratio
C2 A1 A2 P3

The accounting records of Nettle Distribution show the following assets and liabilities as of December 31, 2014 and 2015.

December 31	2014	2015
Cash	$ 64,300	$ 15,640
Accounts receivable	26,240	19,390
Office supplies	3,160	1,960
Office equipment	44,000	44,000
Trucks	148,000	157,000
Building	0	80,000
Land	0	60,000
Accounts payable	3,500	33,500
Note payable	0	40,000

Late in December 2015, the business purchased a small office building and land for $140,000. It paid $100,000 cash toward the purchase and a $40,000 note payable was signed for the balance. Mr. Nettle had to invest $35,000 cash in the business (in exchange for common stock) to enable it to pay the $100,000 cash. The business also pays $3,000 cash per month for dividends.

Required

1. Prepare balance sheets for the business as of December 31, 2014 and 2015. (*Hint:* Report only total equity on the balance sheet and remember that total equity equals the difference between assets and liabilities.)
2. By comparing equity amounts from the balance sheets and using the additional information presented in this problem, prepare a calculation to show how much net income was earned by the business during 2015.
3. Compute the 2015 year-end debt ratio (in percent and rounded to one decimal).

Check (2) Net income, $23,290

(3) Debt ratio, 19.4%

Problem 2-6A
Analyzing account balances and reconstructing transactions
C1 C3 A1 P2

Yi Min started an engineering firm called Min Engineering. He began operations and completed seven transactions in May, which included his initial investment of $18,000 cash. After those seven transactions, the ledger included the following accounts with normal balances.

Cash	$37,641
Office supplies	890
Prepaid insurance	4,600
Office equipment	12,900
Accounts payable	12,900
Common stock	18,000
Dividends	3,329
Engineering fees earned	36,000
Rent expense	7,540

Required

1. Prepare a trial balance for this business as of the end of May.

Check (1) Trial balance totals, $66,900

Analysis Components

2. Analyze the accounts and their balances and prepare a list that describes each of the seven most likely transactions and their amounts.
3. Prepare a report of cash received and cash paid showing how the seven transactions in part 2 yield the $37,641 ending Cash balance.

(3) Cash paid, $16,359

PROBLEM SET B

Problem 2-1B
Preparing and posting journal entries; preparing a trial balance
C3 C4 A1 P1 P2

Humble Management Services opens for business and completes these transactions in September.

Sept.	1	Henry Humble, the owner, invests $38,000 cash along with office equipment valued at $15,000 in the company in exchange for common stock.
	2	The company prepaid $9,000 cash for 12 months' rent for office space. (*Hint:* Debit Prepaid Rent for $9,000.)
	4	The company made credit purchases for $8,000 in office equipment and $2,400 in office supplies. Payment is due within 10 days.
	8	The company completed work for a client and immediately received $3,280 cash.
	12	The company completed a $15,400 project for a client, who must pay within 30 days.
	13	The company paid $10,400 cash to settle the payable created on September 4.
	19	The company paid $1,900 cash for the premium on an 18-month insurance policy. (*Hint:* Debit Prepaid Insurance for $1,900.)
	22	The company received $7,700 cash as partial payment for the work completed on September 12.
	24	The company completed work for another client for $2,100 on credit.
	28	The company paid $5,300 cash in dividends.
	29	The company purchased $550 of additional office supplies on credit.
	30	The company paid $860 cash for this month's utility bill.

Required

1. Prepare general journal entries to record these transactions (use account titles listed in part 2).
2. Open the following ledger accounts—their account numbers are in parentheses (use the balance column format): Cash (101); Accounts Receivable (106); Office Supplies (124); Prepaid Insurance (128); Prepaid Rent (131); Office Equipment (163); Accounts Payable (201); Common Stock (307); Dividends (319); Services Revenue (401); and Utilities Expense (690). Post journal entries from part 1 to the ledger accounts and enter the balance after each posting.
3. Prepare a trial balance as of the end of September.

Check (2) Ending balances: Cash, $21,520; Accounts Receivable, $9,800; Accounts Payable, $550

(3) Total debits, $74,330

Problem 2-2B
Preparing and posting journal entries; preparing a trial balance
C3 C4 A1 P1 P2

At the beginning of April, Bernadette Grechus launched a custom computer solutions company called Softworks. The company had the following transactions during April.

a. Bernadette Grechus invested $65,000 cash, office equipment with a value of $5,750, and $30,000 of computer equipment in the company in exchange for common stock.
b. The company purchased land worth $22,000 for an office by paying $5,000 cash and signing a long-term note payable for $17,000.
c. The company purchased a portable building with $34,500 cash and moved it onto the land acquired in *b*.
d. The company paid $5,000 cash for the premium on a two-year insurance policy.
e. The company provided services to a client and immediately collected $4,600 cash.
f. The company purchased $4,500 of additional computer equipment by paying $800 cash and signing a long-term note payable for $3,700.
g. The company completed $4,250 of services for a client. This amount is to be received within 30 days.
h. The company purchased $950 of additional office equipment on credit.
i. The company completed client services for $10,200 on credit.
j. The company received a bill for rent of a computer testing device that was used on a recently completed job. The $580 rent cost must be paid within 30 days.
k. The company collected $5,100 cash in partial payment from the client described in transaction *i*.
l. The company paid $1,800 cash for wages to an assistant.

m. The company paid $950 cash to settle the payable created in transaction *h*.
n. The company paid $608 cash for minor maintenance of the company's computer equipment.
o. The company paid $6,230 cash in dividends.
p. The company paid $1,800 cash for wages to an assistant.
q. The company paid $750 cash for advertisements on the web during April.

Required

1. Prepare general journal entries to record these transactions (use account titles listed in part 2).
2. Open the following ledger accounts—their account numbers are in parentheses (use the balance column format): Cash (101); Accounts Receivable (106); Prepaid Insurance (108); Office Equipment (163); Computer Equipment (164); Building (170); Land (172); Accounts Payable (201); Notes Payable (250); Common Stock (307); Dividends (319); Fees Earned (402); Wages Expense (601); Computer Rental Expense (602); Advertising Expense (603); and Repairs Expense (604). Post the journal entries from part 1 to the accounts and enter the balance after each posting.
3. Prepare a trial balance as of the end of April.

Check (2) Ending balances: Cash, $17,262; Accounts Receivable, $9,350; Accounts Payable, $580

(3) Trial balance totals, $141,080

Problem 2-3B
Preparing and posting journal entries; preparing a trial balance
C3 C4 A1 P1 P2

Zucker Management Services opens for business and completes these transactions in November.

Nov. 1 Matt Zucker, the owner, invested $30,000 cash along with $15,000 of office equipment in the company in exchange for common stock.
2 The company prepaid $4,500 cash for six months' rent for an office. (*Hint:* Debit Prepaid Rent for $4,500.)
4 The company made credit purchases of office equipment for $2,500 and of office supplies for $600. Payment is due within 10 days.
8 The company completed work for a client and immediately received $3,400 cash.
12 The company completed a $10,200 project for a client, who must pay within 30 days.
13 The company paid $3,100 cash to settle the payable created on November 4.
19 The company paid $1,800 cash for the premium on a 24-month insurance policy.
22 The company received $5,200 cash as partial payment for the work completed on November 12.
24 The company completed work for another client for $1,750 on credit.
28 The company paid $5,300 cash in dividends.
29 The company purchased $249 of additional office supplies on credit.
30 The company paid $831 cash for this month's utility bill.

Required

1. Prepare general journal entries to record these transactions (use account titles listed in part 2).
2. Open the following ledger accounts—their account numbers are in parentheses (use the balance column format): Cash (101); Accounts Receivable (106); Office Supplies (124); Prepaid Insurance (128); Prepaid Rent (131); Office Equipment (163); Accounts Payable (201); Common Stock (307); Dividends (319); Services Revenue (403); and Utilities Expense (690). Post the journal entries from part 1 to the ledger accounts and enter the balance after each posting.
3. Prepare a trial balance as of the end of November.

Check (2) Ending balances: Cash, $23,069; Accounts Receivable, $6,750; Accounts Payable, $249

(3) Total debits, $60,599

Problem 2-4B
Recording transactions; posting to ledger; preparing a trial balance
C3 A1 P1 P2

Nuncio Consulting completed the following transactions during June.

a. Armand Nuncio, the owner, invested $35,000 cash along with office equipment valued at $11,000 in the new company in exchange for common stock.
b. The company purchased land valued at $7,500 and a building valued at $40,000. The purchase is paid with $15,000 cash and a long-term note payable for $32,500.
c. The company purchased $500 of office supplies on credit.
d. A. Nuncio invested his personal automobile in the company in exchange for more common stock. The automobile has a value of $8,000 and is to be used exclusively in the business.
e. The company purchased $1,200 of additional office equipment on credit.
f. The company paid $1,000 cash salary to an assistant.
g. The company provided services to a client and collected $3,200 cash.
h. The company paid $540 cash for this month's utilities.
i. The company paid $500 cash to settle the payable created in transaction *c*.

j. The company purchased $3,400 of new office equipment by paying $3,400 cash.
k. The company completed $4,200 of services for a client, who must pay within 30 days.
l. The company paid $1,000 cash salary to an assistant.
m. The company received $2,200 cash in partial payment on the receivable created in transaction *k*.
n. The company paid $1,100 cash in dividends.

Required

1. Prepare general journal entries to record these transactions (use account titles listed in part 2).
2. Open the following ledger accounts—their account numbers are in parentheses (use the balance column format): Cash (101); Accounts Receivable (106); Office Supplies (108); Office Equipment (163); Automobiles (164); Building (170); Land (172); Accounts Payable (201); Notes Payable (250); Common Stock (307); Dividends (319); Fees Earned (402); Salaries Expense (601); and Utilities Expense (602). Post the journal entries from part 1 to the ledger accounts and enter the balance after each posting.
3. Prepare a trial balance as of the end of June.

Check (2) Ending balances: Cash, $17,860; Office Equipment, $15,600

(3) Trial balance totals, $95,100

Problem 2-5B
Computing net income from equity analysis, preparing a balance sheet, and computing the debt ratio
C2 A1 A2 P3

The accounting records of Tama Co. show the following assets and liabilities as of December 31, 2014 and 2015.

December 31	2014	2015
Cash	$20,000	$ 5,000
Accounts receivable	35,000	25,000
Office supplies	8,000	13,500
Office equipment	40,000	40,000
Machinery	28,500	28,500
Building	0	250,000
Land	0	50,000
Accounts payable	4,000	12,000
Note payable	0	250,000

Late in December 2015, the business purchased a small office building and land for $300,000. It paid $50,000 cash toward the purchase and a $250,000 note payable was signed for the balance. Joe Tama, the owner, had to invest an additional $15,000 cash (in exchange for common stock) to enable it to pay the $50,000 cash toward the purchase. The business also pays $250 cash per month for dividends.

Required

1. Prepare balance sheets for the business as of December 31, 2014 and 2015. (*Hint:* Report only total equity on the balance sheet and remember that total equity equals the difference between assets and liabilities.)
2. By comparing equity amounts from the balance sheets and using the additional information presented in the problem, prepare a calculation to show how much net income was earned by the business during 2015.
3. Calculate the December 31, 2015, debt ratio (in percent and rounded to one decimal).

Check (2) Net income, $10,500

(3) Debt ratio, 63.6%

Problem 2-6B
Analyzing account balances and reconstructing transactions
C1 C3 A1 P2

Roshaun Gould started a web consulting firm called Gould Solutions. He began operations and completed seven transactions in April that resulted in the following accounts, which all have normal balances.

Cash	$19,982
Office supplies	760
Prepaid rent	1,800
Office equipment	12,250
Accounts payable	12,250
Common stock	15,000
Dividends	5,200
Consulting fees earned	20,400
Operating expenses	7,658

Required

1. Prepare a trial balance for this business as of the end of April.

Check (1) Trial balance totals, $47,650

Analysis Component

2. Analyze the accounts and their balances and prepare a list that describes each of the seven most likely transactions and their amounts.
3. Prepare a report of cash received and cash paid showing how the seven transactions in part 2 yield the $19,982 ending Cash balance.

(3) Cash paid, $15,418

SERIAL PROBLEM

Business Solutions

A1 P1 P2

(This serial problem started in Chapter 1 and continues through most of the chapters. If the Chapter 1 segment was not completed, the problem can begin at this point. It is helpful, but not necessary, to use the Working Papers that accompany this book.)

SP 2 On October 1, 2015, Santana Rey launched a computer services company called **Business Solutions,** which provides consulting services, computer system installations, and custom program development. Rey adopts the calendar year for reporting purposes and expects to prepare the company's first set of financial statements on December 31, 2015. The company's initial chart of accounts follows.

Account	No.	Account	No.
Cash	101	Common Stock	307
Accounts Receivable	106	Dividends	319
Computer Supplies	126	Computer Services Revenue	403
Prepaid Insurance	128	Wages Expense	623
Prepaid Rent	131	Advertising Expense	655
Office Equipment	163	Mileage Expense	676
Computer Equipment	167	Miscellaneous Expenses	677
Accounts Payable	201	Repairs Expense—Computer	684

Required

1. Prepare journal entries to record each of the following transactions for Business Solutions.

Oct. 1 S. Rey invested $45,000 cash, a $20,000 computer system, and $8,000 of office equipment in the company in exchange for its common stock.
2 The company paid $3,300 cash for four months' rent. (*Hint:* Debit Prepaid Rent for $3,300.)
3 The company purchased $1,420 of computer supplies on credit from Harris Office Products.
5 The company paid $2,220 cash for one year's premium on a property and liability insurance policy. (*Hint:* Debit Prepaid Insurance for $2,220.)
6 The company billed Easy Leasing $4,800 for services performed in installing a new web server.
8 The company paid $1,420 cash for the computer supplies purchased from Harris Office Products on October 3.
10 The company hired Lyn Addie as a part-time assistant for $125 per day, as needed.
12 The company billed Easy Leasing another $1,400 for services performed.
15 The company received $4,800 cash from Easy Leasing as partial payment on its account.
17 The company paid $805 cash to repair computer equipment that was damaged when moving it.
20 The company paid $1,728 cash for advertisements published in the local newspaper.
22 The company received $1,400 cash from Easy Leasing on its account.
28 The company billed IFM Company $5,208 for services performed.
31 The company paid $875 cash for Lyn Addie's wages for seven days' work.
31 The company paid $3,600 cash in dividends.

Nov. 1 The company reimbursed S. Rey in cash for business automobile mileage allowance (Rey logged 1,000 miles at $0.32 per mile).
2 The company received $4,633 cash from Liu Corporation for computer services performed.
5 The company purchased computer supplies for $1,125 cash from Harris Office Products.
8 The company billed Gomez Co. $5,668 for services performed.
13 The company received notification from Alex's Engineering Co. that Business Solutions' bid of $3,950 for an upcoming project is accepted.
18 The company received $2,208 cash from IFM Company as partial payment of the October 28 bill.
22 The company donated $250 cash to the United Way in the company's name.

24 The company completed work for Alex's Engineering Co. and sent it a bill for $3,950.
25 The company sent another bill to IFM Company for the past-due amount of $3,000.
28 The company reimbursed S. Rey in cash for business automobile mileage (1,200 miles at $0.32 per mile).
30 The company paid $1,750 cash for Lyn Addie's wages for 14 days' work.
30 The company paid $2,000 cash in dividends.

2. Open ledger accounts (in balance column format) and post the journal entries from part 1 to them.
3. Prepare a trial balance as of the end of November.

Check (2) Cash, Nov. 30 bal., $38,264
(3) Trial bal. totals, $98,659

GENERAL LEDGER PROBLEM

Available in Connect

connect ACCOUNTING

Using transactions from the following assignments, prepare journal entries for each transaction and identify the financial statement impact of each entry. The financial statements are automatically generated based on the journal entries recorded.

GL 2-1 Transactions from the FastForward illustration in this chapter

GL 2-2 Based on Exercise 2-9

GL 2-3 Based on Exercise 2-12

GL 2-4 Based on Problem 2-1A

Using transactions from the following assignments, record journal entries, create financial statements, and assess the impact of each transaction on financial statements.

GL 2-5 Based on Problem 2-2A

GL 2-6 Based on Problem 2-3A

GL 2-7 Based on Problem 2-4A

GL 2-8 Based on the Serial Problem SP 2

Beyond the Numbers

REPORTING IN ACTION
A1 A2

APPLE

BTN 2-1 Refer to **Apple**'s financial statements in Appendix A for the following questions.

Required

1. What amount of total liabilities does it report for each of the fiscal years ended September 28, 2013, and September 29, 2012?
2. What amount of total assets does it report for each of the fiscal years ended September 28, 2013, and September 29, 2012?
3. Compute its debt ratio for each of the fiscal years ended September 28, 2013, and September 29, 2012. (Report ratio in percent and round it to one decimal.)
4. In which fiscal year did it employ more financial leverage (September 28, 2013, or September 29, 2012)? Explain.

Fast Forward

5. Access its financial statements (10-K report) for a fiscal year ending after September 28, 2013, from its website (**Apple.com**) or the SEC's EDGAR database (**www.SEC.gov**). Recompute its debt ratio for any subsequent year's data and compare it with the debt ratio for 2013 and 2012.

COMPARATIVE ANALYSIS
A1 A2

APPLE
GOOGLE

BTN 2-2 Key comparative figures for **Apple** and **Google** follow.

	Apple		Google	
(in millions)	Current Year	Prior Year	Current Year	Prior Year
Total liabilities	$ 83,451	$ 57,854	$ 23,611	$22,083
Total assets	207,000	176,064	110,920	93,798

1. What is the debt ratio for Apple in the current year and for the prior year?
2. What is the debt ratio for Google in the current year and for the prior year?
3. Which of the two companies has the higher degree of financial leverage? What does this imply?

ETHICS CHALLENGE
C1

BTN 2-3 Review the *Decision Ethics* case from the first part of this chapter involving the cashier. The guidance answer suggests that you should not comply with the assistant manager's request.

Required

Propose and evaluate two other courses of action you might consider, and explain why.

COMMUNICATING IN PRACTICE
C1 C2 A1 P3

BTN 2-4 Lila Corentine is an aspiring entrepreneur and your friend. She is having difficulty understanding the purposes of financial statements and how they fit together across time.

Required

Write a one-page memorandum to Corentine explaining the purposes of the four financial statements and how they are linked across time.

TAKING IT TO THE NET
A1

BTN 2-5 Access EDGAR online (**www.SEC.gov**) and locate the 2013 10-K report of **Amazon.com** (ticker AMZN) filed on January 30, 2014. Review its financial statements reported for years ended 2013, 2012, and 2011 to answer the following questions.

Required

1. What are the amounts of its net income or net loss reported for each of these three years?
2. Does Amazon's operating activities provide cash or use cash for each of these three years?
3. If Amazon has a 2013 net income of $274 million and 2013 operating cash flows of $5,475 million, how is it possible that its cash balance at December 31, 2013, increases by only $574 million relative to its balance at December 31, 2012?

TEAMWORK IN ACTION
C1 C2 C4 A1

BTN 2-6 The expanded accounting equation consists of assets, liabilities, common stock, dividends, revenues, and expenses. It can be used to reveal insights into changes in a company's financial position.

Required

1. Form *learning teams* of six (or more) members. Each team member must select one of the six components and each team must have at least one expert on each component: (*a*) assets, (*b*) liabilities, (*c*) common stock, (*d*) dividends, (*e*) revenues, and (*f*) expenses.
2. Form *expert teams* of individuals who selected the same component in part 1. Expert teams are to draft a report that each expert will present to his or her learning team addressing the following:
   a. Identify for its component the (i) increase and decrease side of the account and (ii) normal balance side of the account.
   b. Describe a transaction, with amounts, that increases its component.
   c. Using the transaction and amounts in (b), verify the equality of the accounting equation and then explain any effects on the income statement and statement of cash flows.
   d. Describe a transaction, with amounts, that decreases its component.
   e. Using the transaction and amounts in (d), verify the equality of the accounting equation and then explain any effects on the income statement and statement of cash flows.
3. Each expert should return to his/her learning team. In rotation, each member presents his/her expert team's report to the learning team. Team discussion is encouraged.

ENTREPRENEURIAL DECISION
A1 A2 P3

BTN 2-7 Assume that Brittany Merrill Underwood of **Akola Project** plans on expanding her business to accommodate more product lines. She is considering financing her expansion in one of two ways: (1) contributing more of her own funds to the business or (2) borrowing the funds from a bank.

Required

Identify at least two issues that Brittany should consider when trying to decide on the method for financing her expansion.

BTN 2-8 Angel Martin is a young entrepreneur who operates Martin Music Services, offering singing lessons and instruction on musical instruments. Martin wishes to expand but needs a $30,000 loan. The bank requests that Martin prepare a balance sheet and key financial ratios. Martin has not kept formal records but is able to provide the following accounts and their amounts as of December 31, 2015.

ENTREPRENEURIAL DECISION
A1 A2 P3

Cash	$ 3,600	Accounts Receivable	$ 9,600	Prepaid Insurance	$ 1,500
Prepaid Rent	9,400	Store Supplies	6,600	Equipment	50,000
Accounts Payable	2,200	Unearned Lesson Fees	15,600	Total Equity*	62,900
Annual net income	40,000				

* The total equity amount reflects all owner investments, dividends, revenues, and expenses as of December 31, 2015.

Required

1. Prepare a balance sheet as of December 31, 2015, for Martin Music Services. (Report only the total equity amount on the balance sheet.)
2. Compute Martin's debt ratio and its return on assets (the latter ratio is defined in Chapter 1). Assume average assets equal its ending balance.
3. Do you believe the prospects of a $30,000 bank loan are good? Why or why not?

BTN 2-9 Obtain a recent copy of the most prominent newspaper distributed in your area. Research the classified section and prepare a report answering the following questions (attach relevant classified clippings to your report). Alternatively, you may want to search the web for the required information. One suitable website is **CareerOneStop (www.CareerOneStop.org)**. For documentation, you should print copies of websites accessed.

HITTING THE ROAD
C1

1. Identify the number of listings for accounting positions and the various accounting job titles.
2. Identify the number of listings for other job titles, with examples, that require or prefer accounting knowledge/experience but are not specifically accounting positions.
3. Specify the salary range for the accounting and accounting-related positions if provided.
4. Indicate the job that appeals to you, the reason for its appeal, and its requirements.

BTN 2-10 **Samsung (www.Samsung.com)** is a market leader in high-tech electronics manufacturing and digital media, and it competes to some extent with both **Apple** and **Google**. Key financial ratios for the current fiscal year follow.

GLOBAL DECISION
A2

Samsung
APPLE
GOOGLE

Key Figure	Samsung	Apple	Google
Return on assets	15.4%	19.3%	12.6%
Debt ratio	29.9%	40.3%	21.3%

Required

1. Which company is most profitable according to its return on assets?
2. Which company is most risky according to the debt ratio?
3. Which company deserves increased investment based on a joint analysis of return on assets and the debt ratio? Explain.

ANSWERS TO MULTIPLE CHOICE QUIZ

1. b; debit Utility Expense for $700, and credit Cash for $700.
2. a; debit Cash for $2,500, and credit Unearned Lawn Service Fees for $2,500.
3. c; debit Cash for $250,000, debit Land for $500,000, and credit Common Stock for $750,000.
4. d
5. e; Debt ratio = $400,000/$1,000,000 = 40%

chapter 3 Adjusting Accounts for Financial Statements

Chapter Preview

PERIODIC REPORTS AND ADJUSTING ACCOUNTS	FINANCIAL STATEMENTS AND CLOSING PROCESS	CLASSIFIED BALANCE SHEET AND ANALYSIS
C1 Timing and accruals	**P3** Preparing financial statements	**C3** Classified balance sheet—Structure and categories
P1 Accounting adjustments	**P4** Closing entries	**A1** Profit margin analysis
Prepaid expenses	**P5** Post-closing trial balance	**A2** Current ratio analysis
Unearned revenues	**C2** Accounting cycle	
Accrued expenses		
Accrued revenues		
P2 Adjusted trial balance		

Learning Objectives

CONCEPTUAL

C1 Explain the importance of periodic reporting and the role of accrual accounting.

C2 Identify steps in the accounting cycle.

C3 Explain and prepare a classified balance sheet.

ANALYTICAL

A1 Compute profit margin and describe its use in analyzing company performance.

A2 Compute the current ratio and describe what it reveals about a company's financial condition.

PROCEDURAL

P1 Prepare and explain adjusting entries.

P2 Explain and prepare an adjusted trial balance.

P3 Prepare financial statements from an adjusted trial balance.

P4 Describe and prepare closing entries.

P5 Explain and prepare a post-closing trial balance.

P6 *Appendix 3A*—Explain the alternatives in accounting for prepaids.

P7 *Appendix 3B*—Prepare a work sheet and explain its usefulness.

P8 *Appendix 3C*—Prepare reversing entries and explain their purpose.

Courtesy of International Princess Project

Princess of Fashion

COSTA MESA, CA—Life would never be the same for Shannon Keith after she witnessed modern-day slavery. She was volunteering her time to work with women in a red-light area of India when she saw young girls sold into the sex trade by their families, orphans taken off the streets by pimps, and young mothers prostituting to feed their children. "I was exposed to the issue of human trafficking and forced prostitution," explains Shannon. "I felt a deep calling and responsibility to bring my gifts to bear on this issue."

That deep calling led Shannon to launch the **International Princess Project** (**Punjammies.com**), which aims to empower these girls and young mothers. Shannon quickly realized that a business solution was necessary for them to survive outside of brothels. Her idea was to set up an e-commerce site to sell pajamas, aka *punjammies*, which are made by the victims. Shannon began in a single room with six women who made 300 punjammies the first year. Today, she has three sewing centers staffed by nearly 200 women who make more than 20,000 punjammies a year.

"Dignity, humility and authenticity are necessary virtues"
—Shannon Keith

Shannon explains how she set up an accounting system early on to account for all business activities, including cash, revenues, receivables, and payables. She also had to learn about the deferral and accrual of revenues and expenses. Setting up a reliable accounting system was part of her success. Her website explains, "each woman not only receives a wage higher than fair trade along with housing options, medical care and, where applicable, education for her children," but the women "are also part of a loving, restorative community of other women who were formerly trafficked."

Financial reporting and analysis are tasks that Shannon emphasizes. She insists on timely and accurate accounting reports, but admits she is happily surprised with how business has blossomed. To achieve that growth, Shannon took time to understand accounting adjustments and their effects on business. "We're poised to hit $1 million in sales this year," proclaims Shannon. Her commitment, however, is first and foremost to the women: "We have a highly traumatized workforce. They come to us with low skills. If their sewing isn't that great, we're not going to fire them. We're going to find something else for them to do."

It is the bigger picture that is important to Shannon. "I'm learning that social justice is not a cause, it's a lifestyle and complete worldview," explains Shannon. "My dream for the future would be to have my children live in a slave-free world, where every human life is valued and free."

Sources: *International Princess Project website,* January 2015; *Orange County Register,* May 2012; *Crest,* February 2014

TIMING AND REPORTING

C1 Explain the importance of periodic reporting and the role of accrual accounting.

This section describes the importance of reporting accounting information at regular intervals and its impact for recording revenues and expenses.

The Accounting Period

The value of information is often linked to its timeliness. Useful information must reach decision makers frequently and promptly. To provide timely information, accounting systems prepare reports at regular intervals. This results in an accounting process impacted by the time period (or periodicity) assumption. The **time period assumption** presumes that an organization's activities can be divided into specific time periods such as a month, a three-month quarter, a six-month interval, or a year. Exhibit 3.1 shows various **accounting,** or *reporting,* **periods.** Most organizations use a year as their primary accounting period. Reports covering a one-year period are known as **annual financial statements.** Many organizations also prepare **interim financial statements** covering one, three, or six months of activity.

"Apple announces annual income of . . ."

EXHIBIT 3.1
Accounting Periods

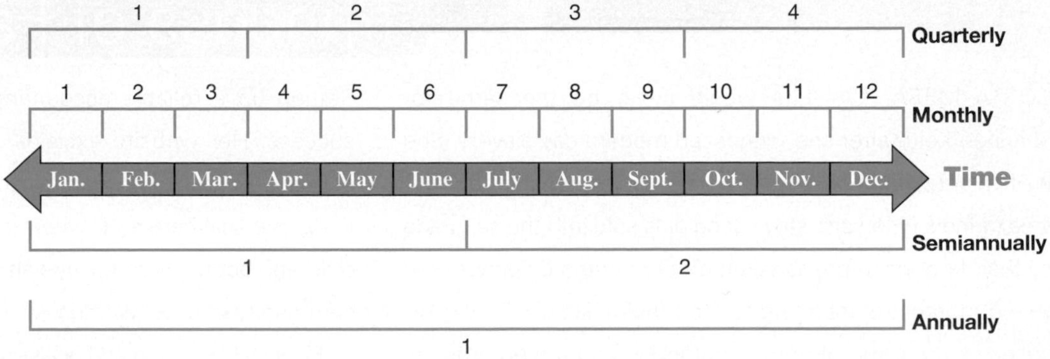

C Flanigan/Wirelmage/Getty Images

The annual reporting period is not always a calendar year ending on December 31. An organization can adopt a **fiscal year** consisting of any 12 consecutive months. It is also acceptable to adopt an annual reporting period of 52 weeks. For example, **Gap**'s fiscal year consistently ends the final week of January or the first week of February each year.

Companies with little seasonal variation in sales often choose the calendar year as their fiscal year. **Facebook, Inc.**, uses calendar year reporting. However, the financial statements of **The Kellogg Company** (the company that controls characters such as Tony the Tiger, Snap! Crackle! Pop!, and Keebler Elf) reflect a fiscal year that ends on the Saturday nearest December 31. Companies experiencing seasonal variations in sales often choose a **natural business year** end, which is when sales activities are at their lowest level for the year. The natural business year for retailers such as **Walmart**, **Target**, and **Macy's** usually ends around January 31, after the holiday season.

Accrual Basis versus Cash Basis

After external transactions and events are recorded, several accounts still need adjustments before their balances appear in financial statements. This need arises because internal transactions and events remain unrecorded. **Accrual basis accounting** uses the adjusting process to recognize revenues when earned and expenses when incurred (matched with revenues).

Cash basis accounting recognizes revenues when cash is received and records expenses when cash is paid. This means that cash basis net income for a period is the difference between cash receipts and cash payments. Cash basis accounting is not consistent with generally accepted accounting principles (neither U.S. GAAP nor IFRS).

It is commonly held that accrual accounting better reflects business performance than information about cash receipts and payments. Accrual accounting also increases the *comparability* of financial statements from one period to another. Yet cash basis accounting is useful for several business decisions—which is the reason companies must report a statement of cash flows.

To see the difference between these two accounting systems, let's consider FastForward's Prepaid Insurance account. FastForward paid $2,400 for 24 months of insurance coverage that began on December 1, 2015. Accrual accounting requires that $100 of insurance expense be reported each month, from December 2015 through November 2017. (This means expenses are $100 in 2015, $1,200 in 2016, and $1,100 in 2017.) Exhibit 3.2 illustrates this allocation of insurance cost across these three years. Any unexpired premium is reported as a Prepaid Insurance asset on the accrual basis balance sheet.

EXHIBIT 3.2

Accrual Accounting for Allocating Prepaid Insurance to Expense

Point: Annual income statements for Exhibit 3.2 follow:

Accrual Basis	2015	2016	2017
Revenues	$ #	$ #	$ #
Insur. exp. ...	$100	$1,200	$1,100

Alternatively, a cash basis income statement for December 2015 reports insurance expense of $2,400, as shown in Exhibit 3.3. The cash basis income statements for years 2016 and 2017 report no insurance expense. The cash basis balance sheet never reports an insurance asset because it is immediately expensed. This shows that cash basis income for 2015–2017 fails to match the cost of insurance with the insurance benefits received for those years and months.

EXHIBIT 3.3

Cash Accounting for Allocating Prepaid Insurance to Expense

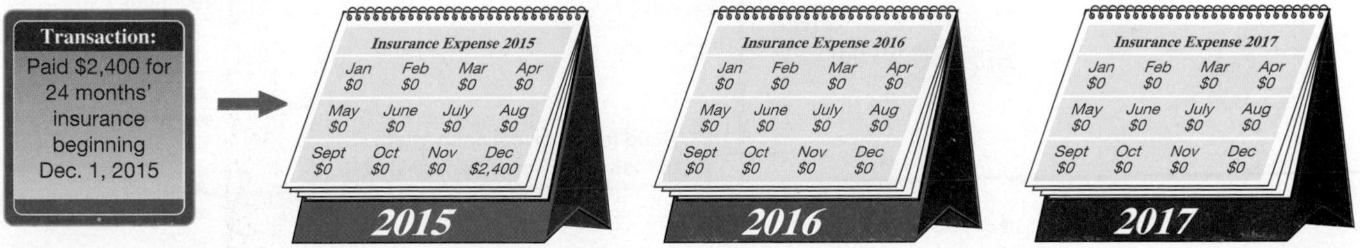

Point: Annual income statements for Exhibit 3.3 follow:

Cash Basis	2015	2016	2017
Revenues	$ #	$#	$#
Insur. exp.	$2,400	$0	$0

Recognizing Revenues and Expenses

We use the time period assumption to divide a company's activities into specific time periods, but not all activities are complete when financial statements are prepared. Thus, adjustments often are required to get correct account balances.

We rely on two principles in the adjusting process: revenue recognition and expense recognition (the latter is often referred to as *matching*). Chapter 1 explained that the *revenue recognition principle* requires that revenue be recorded when earned, not before and not after. Most companies earn revenue when they provide services and products to customers. A major goal of the adjusting process is to have revenue recognized (reported) in the time period when it is earned. The **expense recognition** (or **matching**) **principle** aims to record expenses in the same accounting period as the revenues that are earned as a result of those expenses. This matching of expenses with the revenue benefits is a major part of the adjusting process.

Point: Recording revenue early overstates current-period revenue and income; recording it late understates current-period revenue and income.

Point: Recording expense early overstates current-period expense and understates current-period income; recording it late understates current-period expense and overstates current-period income.

Matching expenses with revenues often requires us to predict certain events. When we use financial statements, we must understand that they require estimates and therefore include measures that are not precise. **Walt Disney**'s annual report explains that its production costs from movies, such as its *Pirates of the Caribbean* series, are matched to revenues based on a ratio of current revenues from the movie divided by its predicted total revenues.

Decision Insight

QC1

Diamond Foods, Inc., a popular snack maker, was charged by the SEC in 2014 in an accounting scheme to falsify walnut costs to boost income. This alleged late expense recognition caused income to be overstated. The SEC further alleges that its former CFO misled Diamond's independent auditors by giving false and incomplete information to justify its accounting treatment. (For more details, see SEC release 2014-4 from January 9, 2014.) ■

©The McGraw-Hill Companies, Inc./ Jill Braaten, photographer

ADJUSTING ACCOUNTS

P1 Prepare and explain adjusting entries.

Adjusting accounts is a 3-step process:

Step 1: Determine what the current account balance *equals.*

Step 2: Determine what the current account balance *should equal.*

Step 3: Record an adjusting entry to get from step *1* to step 2.

Framework for Adjustments

Adjustments are necessary for transactions and events that extend over more than one period. It is helpful to group adjustments by the timing of cash receipt or cash payment in relation to the recognition of the related revenues or expenses. Exhibit 3.4 identifies four types of adjustments.

EXHIBIT 3.4

Types of Adjustments

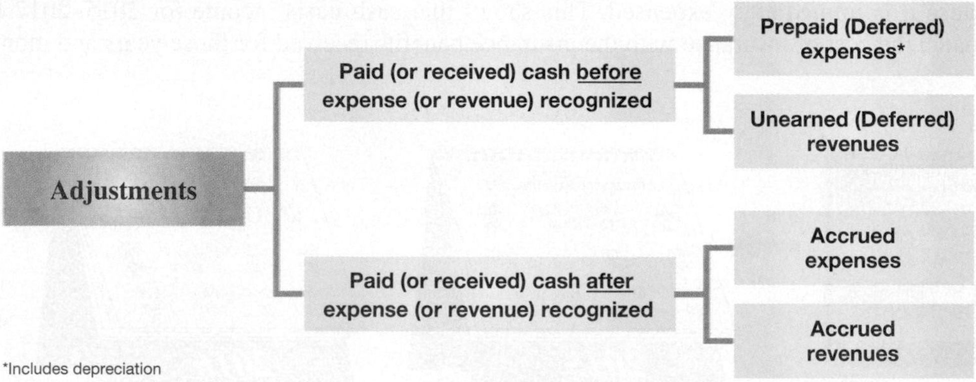

*Includes depreciation

Point: Source documents provide information for most daily transactions, and in many businesses the recordkeepers record them. Adjustments require more knowledge and are usually handled by senior accounting professionals.

The upper half of this exhibit shows prepaid expenses (including depreciation) and unearned revenues, which reflect transactions when cash is paid or received *before* a related expense or revenue is recognized. They are also called *deferrals* because the recognition of an expense (or revenue) is *deferred* until after the related cash is paid (or received). The lower half of this exhibit shows accrued expenses and accrued revenues, which reflect transactions when cash is paid or received *after* a related expense or revenue is recognized. Adjusting entries are necessary for each of these so that revenues, expenses, assets, and liabilities are correctly reported. Specifically, an **adjusting entry** is made at the end of an accounting period to reflect a transaction or event that is not yet recorded. Each adjusting entry affects one or more income statement accounts *and* one or more balance sheet accounts (but never the Cash account). The four types of adjusting entries follow:

	Adjusting Entry Required	
Adjustment Type	Balance Sheet Effect	Income Statement Effect
Prepaid expenses	Cr. (decrease) Asset	Dr. (increase) Expense
Unearned revenues	Dr. (decrease) Liability	Cr. (increase) Revenue
Accrued expenses	Cr. (increase) Liability	Dr. (increase) Expense
Accrued revenues	Dr. (increase) Asset	Cr. (increase) Revenue

Prepaid (Deferred) Expenses

Prepaid expenses refer to items *paid for* in advance of receiving their benefits. Prepaid expenses are assets. When these assets are used, their costs become expenses. Adjusting entries for prepaids increase expenses and decrease assets as shown in the T-accounts of Exhibit 3.5. Such adjustments reflect transactions and events that use up prepaid expenses (including passage of time). To illustrate the accounting for prepaid expenses, we look at prepaid insurance, supplies, and depreciation. In each case we decrease an asset (balance sheet) account, and increase an expense (income statement) account.

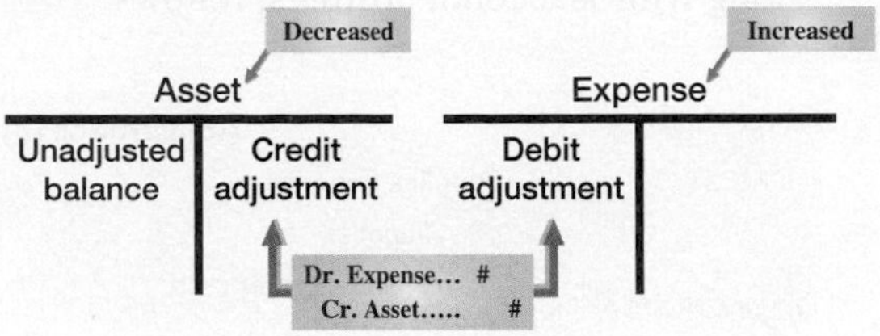

EXHIBIT 3.5

Adjusting for Prepaid Expenses (decrease an asset and record an expense)

Prepaid Insurance We use our 3-step process for this and all accounting adjustments.

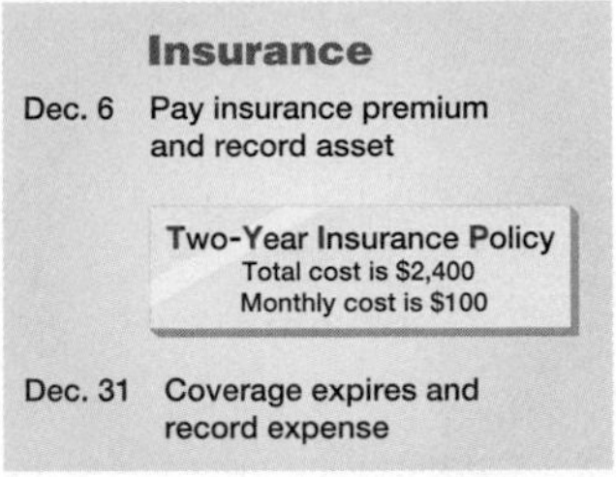

Step 1: We determine that the current balance of FastForward's prepaid insurance is equal to its $2,400 payment for 24 months of insurance benefits that began on December 1, 2015.

Step 2: With the passage of time, the benefits of the insurance gradually expire and a portion of the Prepaid Insurance asset becomes expense. For instance, one month's insurance coverage expires by December 31, 2015. This expense is $100, or 1/24 of $2,400, which leaves $2,300.

Step 3: The adjusting entry to record this expense and reduce the asset, along with T-account postings, follows:

	Adjustment (*a*)		
Dec. 31	Insurance Expense	100	
	Prepaid Insurance		100
	To record first month's expired insurance.		

Assets = Liabilities + Equity
−100 −100

Insurance Expense	**637**		
Dec. 31	**100**		

Prepaid Insurance			**128**
Dec. 6	2,400	**Dec. 31**	**100**
Balance	2,300		

Explanation After adjusting and posting, the $100 balance in Insurance Expense and the $2,300 balance in Prepaid Insurance are ready for reporting in financial statements. *Not* making the adjustment on or before December 31 would (1) understate expenses by $100 and overstate net income by $100 for the December income statement and (2) overstate both prepaid insurance (assets) and equity (because of net income) by $100 in the December 31 balance sheet. (Exhibit 3.2 showed that 2016's adjustments must transfer a total of $1,200 from Prepaid Insurance to Insurance Expense, and 2017's adjustments must transfer the remaining $1,100 to Insurance Expense.) The following table highlights the December 31, 2015, adjustment for prepaid insurance.

Point: Many companies record adjusting entries only at the end of each year because of the time and cost necessary.

Before Adjustment	Adjustment	After Adjustment
Prepaid Insurance = $2,400	**Deduct $100 from Prepaid Insurance** **Add $100 to Insurance Expense**	**Prepaid Insurance = $2,300**
Reports $2,400 policy for 24-months' coverage.	Record current month's $100 insurance expense and $100 reduction in prepaid amount.	Reports $2,300 in coverage for remaining 23 months.

Supplies Supplies are a prepaid expense requiring adjustment.

Step 1: FastForward purchased $9,720 of supplies in December and some of them were used during this month. When financial statements are prepared at December 31, the cost of supplies used during December must be recognized.

Assets = Liabilities + Equity
−1,050 −1,050

Step 2: When FastForward computes (takes physical count of) its remaining unused supplies at December 31, it finds $8,670 of supplies remaining of the $9,720 total supplies. The $1,050 difference between these two amounts is December's supplies expense.

Step 3: The adjusting entry to record this expense and reduce the Supplies asset account, along with T-account postings, follows:

	Adjustment (*b*)		
Dec. 31	Supplies Expense	1,050	
	Supplies		1,050
	To record supplies used.		

Supplies Expense		652
Dec. 31	**1,050**	

Supplies			126
Dec. 2	2,500	**Dec. 31**	**1,050**
6	7,100		
26	120		
Balance	8,670		

Explanation The balance of the Supplies account is $8,670 after posting—equaling the cost of the remaining supplies. *Not* making the adjustment on or before December 31 would (1) understate expenses by $1,050 and overstate net income by $1,050 for the December income statement and (2) overstate both supplies and equity (because of net income) by $1,050 in the December 31 balance sheet. The following table highlights the adjustment for supplies.

Before Adjustment	Adjustment	After Adjustment
Supplies = $9,720	**Deduct $1,050 from Supplies** **Add $1,050 to Supplies Expense**	**Supplies = $8,670**
Reports $9,720 in supplies.	Record $1,050 in supplies used and $1,050 as supplies expense.	Reports $8,670 in supplies.

Point: We assume that prepaid and unearned items are recorded in balance sheet accounts. An alternative is to record them in income statement accounts; Appendix 3A discusses this alternative. The adjusted financial statements are identical.

Other Prepaid Expenses Other prepaid expenses, such as Prepaid Rent, are accounted for exactly as Insurance and Supplies are. We should note that some prepaid expenses are both paid for and fully used up within a single accounting period. One example is when a company pays monthly rent on the first day of each month. This payment creates a prepaid expense on the first day of each month that fully expires by the end of the month. In these special cases, we can record the cash paid with a debit to an expense account instead of an asset account. This practice is described more completely later in the chapter.

Decision Maker

Investor A small publishing company signs an aspiring Olympic gymnast to write a book. The company pays the gymnast $500,000 to sign plus future book royalties. A note to the company's financial statements says that "prepaid expenses include $500,000 in author signing fees to be matched against future expected sales." Is this accounting for the signing bonus acceptable? How does it affect your analysis? ■ [Answers follow the chapter's Summary.]

Point: Plant assets are also called *Plant & Equipment*, or *Property, Plant & Equipment*.

Point: Depreciation does not necessarily measure decline in market value.

Point: An asset's expected value at the end of its useful life is called *salvage value*.

Depreciation A special category of prepaid expenses is **plant assets,** which refers to long-term tangible assets used to produce and sell products and services. Plant assets are expected to provide benefits for more than one period. Examples of plant assets are buildings, machines, vehicles, and fixtures. All plant assets, with a general exception for land, eventually wear out or decline in usefulness. The costs of these assets are deferred but are gradually reported as expenses in the income statement over the assets' useful lives (benefit periods). **Depreciation** is the process of allocating the costs of these assets over their expected useful lives. Depreciation expense is recorded with an adjusting entry similar to that for other prepaid expenses.

Depreciation

Dec. 3 Purchase equipment and record asset

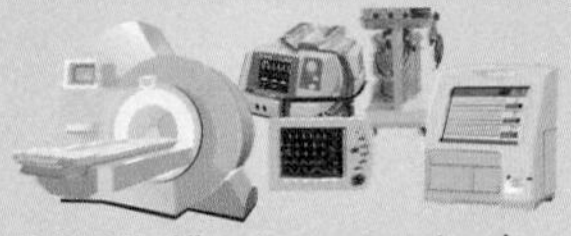

Dec. 31 Allocate asset cost and record depreciation

Step 1: Recall that FastForward purchased equipment for $26,000 in early December to use in earning revenue. This equipment's cost must be depreciated.

Step 2: The equipment is expected to have a useful life (benefit period) of five years and to be worth about $8,000 at the end of five years. This means the *net* cost of this equipment over its useful life is $18,000 ($26,000 − $8,000). We can use any of several methods to allocate this $18,000 net cost to expense. FastForward uses a method called **straight-line depreciation,** which allocates equal amounts of the asset's net cost to depreciation during its useful life. Dividing the $18,000 net cost by the 60 months in the asset's useful life gives a monthly cost of $300 ($18,000/60).

Step 3: The adjusting entry to record monthly depreciation expense, along with T-account postings, follows:

Adjustment (c)

Dec. 31	Depreciation Expense	300	
	Accumulated Depreciation—Equipment		300
	To record monthly equipment depreciation.		

Assets = Liabilities + Equity
−300 −300

Depreciation Expense—Equipment 612

Dec. 31	**300**	

Equipment 167

Dec. 3	26,000	

Accumulated Depreciation—Equipment 168

	Dec. 31	**300**

Explanation After posting the adjustment, the Equipment account ($26,000) less its Accumulated Depreciation ($300) account equals the $25,700 net cost (made up of $17,700 for the 59 remaining months in the benefit period plus the $8,000 value at the end of that time). The $300 balance in the Depreciation Expense account is reported in the December income statement. *Not* making the adjustment at December 31 would (1) understate expenses by $300 and overstate net income by $300 for the December income statement and (2) overstate both assets and equity (because of income) by $300 in the December 31 balance sheet. The following table highlights the adjustment for depreciation.

Before Adjustment	Adjustment	After Adjustment
Equipment, net = $26,000	**Deduct $300 from Equipment, net Add $300 to Depreciation Expense**	**Equipment, net = $25,700**
Reports $26,000 in equipment.	Record $300 in depreciation and $300 as accumulated depreciation, which is deducted from equipment.	Reports $25,700 in equipment, net of accumulated depreciation.

Accumulated depreciation is kept in a separate contra account. A **contra account** is an account linked with another account, it has an opposite normal balance, and it is reported as a subtraction from that other account's balance. For instance, FastForward's contra account of Accumulated Depreciation—Equipment is subtracted from the Equipment account in the balance sheet (see Exhibit 3.7). This contra account allows balance sheet readers to know both the full costs of assets and the total depreciation.

Point: Accumulated Depreciation has a normal credit balance; it decreases the asset's reported value.

EXHIBIT 3.6

Accounts after Three Months of Depreciation Adjustments

Equipment 167

Dec. 3	26,000	

Accumulated Depreciation—Equipment 168

	Dec. 31	300
	Jan. 31	300
	Feb. 28	300
	Balance	**900**

Point: The cost principle requires an asset to be initially recorded at acquisition cost. Depreciation causes the asset's book value (cost less accumulated depreciation) to decline over time.

Point: The net cost of equipment is also called the *depreciable basis*.

The title of the contra account, *Accumulated Depreciation,* reveals that this account includes total depreciation expense for all prior periods for which the asset was used. To illustrate, the Equipment and the Accumulated Depreciation accounts appear as in Exhibit 3.6 on February 28, 2016, after three months of adjusting entries. The $900 balance in the Accumulated Depreciation account can be subtracted from its related $26,000 asset cost. The difference ($25,100) between these two balances is the cost of the asset that has not yet been depreciated. This difference is called the **book value,** or the *net amount,* which equals the asset's costs less its accumulated depreciation.

These account balances are reported in the assets section of the February 28 balance sheet in Exhibit 3.7.

EXHIBIT 3.7

Equipment and Accumulated Depreciation on February 28 Balance Sheet

Assets (at February 28, 2016)		
Cash		$
⋮		
Equipment	**$26,000**	
Less accumulated depreciation	**900**	**25,100** ← Commonly titled *Equipment, net*
Total Assets		$

NEED-TO-KNOW 3-1

Prepaid Expenses

P1

For each separate case below, follow the three-step process for adjusting the prepaid asset account at December 31. Step 1: Determine what the current account balance equals. Step 2: Determine what the current account balance should equal. Step 3: Record the December 31 adjusting entry to get from step 1 to step 2. *Assume no other adjusting entries are made during the year.*

1. **Prepaid Insurance.** The Prepaid Insurance account has a $5,000 debit balance to start the year, and no insurance payments were made during the year. A review of insurance policies and payments shows that $1,000 of unexpired insurance remains at its December 31 year-end.
2. **Prepaid Rent.** On October 1 of the current year, the company prepaid $12,000 for one year of rent for facilities being occupied from that day forward. The company debited Prepaid Rent and credited Cash for $12,000. December 31 year-end statements must be prepared.
3. **Supplies.** The Supplies account has a $1,000 debit balance to start the year. Supplies of $2,000 were purchased during the current year and debited to the Supplies account. A December 31 physical count shows $500 of supplies remaining.
4. **Accumulated Depreciation.** The company has only one fixed asset (equipment) that it purchased at the start of this year. That asset had cost $38,000, had an estimated life of 10 years, and is expected to be valued at $8,000 at the end of the 10-year life. December 31 year-end statements must be prepared.

Solution

1. Step 1: Prepaid Insurance equals $5,000 (before adjustment)
   Step 2: Prepaid Insurance should equal $1,000 (the unexpired part)
   Step 3: Adjusting entry to get from step 1 to step 2

Dec. 31	Insurance Expense	4,000	
	Prepaid Insurance		4,000
	To record insurance coverage that expired ($5,000 − $1,000).		

2. Step 1: Prepaid Rent equals $12,000 (before adjustment)
   Step 2: Prepaid Rent should equal $9,000 (the unexpired part)*
   Step 3: Adjusting entry to get from step 1 to step 2

Dec. 31	Rent Expense	3,000	
	Prepaid Rent		3,000
	To record prepaid rent that expired. *($12,000 − $3,000 = $9,000) where $3,000 is from: ($12,000/12 months) × 3 months*		

3. Step 1: Supplies equal $3,000 (from $1,000 + $2,000; before adjustment)
Step 2: Supplies should equal $500 (what's left)
Step 3: Adjusting entry to get from step 1 to step 2*

Dec. 31	Supplies Expense	2,500	
	Supplies		2,500
	*To record supplies used. *$1,000 + $2,000 purchased − Supplies used = $500 remaining*		

4. Step 1: Accumulated Depreciation equals $0 (before adjustment)
Step 2: Accumulated Depreciation should equal $3,000 (after current period depreciation of $3,000)*
Step 3: Adjusting entry to get from step 1 to step 2

Dec. 31	Depreciation Expense—Equipment	3,000	
	Accumulated Depreciation—Equipment		3,000
	*To record depreciation expense for the period. *($38,000 − $8,000)/10 years*		

Do More: QS 3-5, QS 3-6, QS 3-7, QS 3-8, QS 3-9

Unearned (Deferred) Revenues

The term **unearned revenues** refers to cash received in advance of providing products and services. Unearned revenues, also called *deferred revenues,* are liabilities. When cash is accepted, an obligation to provide products or services is accepted. As products or services are provided, the liability decreases, and the unearned revenues become *earned* revenues. Adjusting entries for unearned items decrease the unearned (balance sheet) account, and increase the revenue (income statement) account, as shown in Exhibit 3.8.

Point: To *defer* is to postpone. We postpone reporting amounts received as revenues until they are earned.

EXHIBIT 3.8

Adjusting for Unearned Revenues (decrease a liability and record revenue)

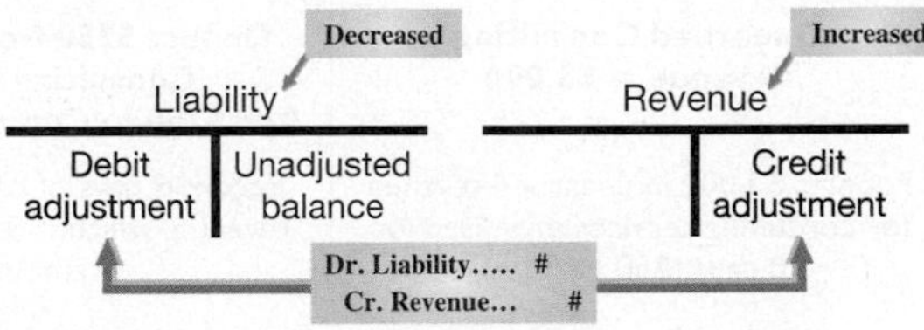

An example of unearned revenues is from **Gannett Co., Inc.**, publisher of *USA TODAY*, which reports unexpired (unearned subscriptions) of $224 million: "Revenue is recognized in the period in which it is earned (as newspapers are delivered)." Unearned revenues are nearly 25% of the current liabilities for Gannett. Another example comes from the **Boston Celtics**. When the Celtics receive cash from advance ticket sales and broadcast fees, they record it in an unearned revenue account called *Deferred Game Revenues.* The Celtics recognize this unearned revenue with adjusting entries on a game-by-game basis. Since the NBA regular season begins in October and ends in April, revenue recognition is mainly limited to this period. For a recent season, the Celtics' quarterly revenues were $0 million for July–September; $34 million for October–December; $48 million for January–March; and $17 million for April–June.

Returning to FastForward, it also has unearned revenues. It agreed on December 26 to provide consulting services to a client for a fixed fee of $3,000 for 60 days.

Step 1: On December 26, the client paid the 60-day fee in advance, covering the period December 27 to February 24. The entry to record the cash received in advance is

Dec. 26	Cash	3,000	
	Unearned Consulting Revenue		3,000
	Received advance payment for services over the next 60 days.		

Assets = Liabilities + Equity
+3,000 +3,000

This advance payment increases cash and creates an obligation to do consulting work over the next 60 days (5 days this year and 55 days next year).

Step 2: As time passes, FastForward earns this payment through consulting. By December 31, it has provided five days' service and earned 5/60 of the $3,000 unearned revenue. This amounts to $250 ($3,000 × 5/60). The *revenue recognition principle* implies that $250 of unearned revenue must be reported as revenue on the December income statement.

Step 3: The adjusting entry to reduce the liability account and recognize earned revenue, along with T-account postings, follows:

Assets = Liabilities + Equity
−250 +250

Adjustment (d)

Dec. 31	Unearned Consulting Revenue.	250	
	Consulting Revenue		250
	To record earned revenue that was received in advance ($3,000 × 5/60).		

Unearned Consulting Revenue 236

Dec. 31	**250**	Dec. 26	3,000
		Balance	2,750

Consulting Revenue 403

		Dec. 5	4,200
		12	1,600
		31	**250**
		Balance	6,050

Explanation The adjusting entry transfers $250 from unearned revenue (a liability account) to a revenue account. *Not* making the adjustment (1) understates revenue and net income by $250 in the December income statement and (2) overstates unearned revenue and understates equity by $250 on the December 31 balance sheet. The following highlights the adjustment for unearned revenue.

Before Adjustment	Adjustment	After Adjustment
Unearned Consulting Revenue = $3,000	**Deduct $250 from Unearned Consulting Revenue** **Add $250 to Consulting Revenue**	**Unearned Consulting Revenue = $2,750**
Reports $3,000 in unearned revenue for consulting services promised for 60 days ($50 per day).	Record 5 days of earned consulting revenue, which is 5/60 of unearned amount.	Reports $2,750 in unearned revenue for consulting services owed over next 55 days (55 days × $50 = $2,750).

Accounting for unearned revenues is crucial to many companies. For example, the **National Retail Federation** reports that gift card sales, which are unearned revenues for sellers, exceed $20 billion annually. Gift cards are now the top selling holiday gift; roughly 60% of all gift givers planned to give at least one gift card within the next year (source: NRF website).

NEED-TO-KNOW 3-2

Unearned Revenues

P1

For each separate case below, follow the three-step process for adjusting the unearned revenue liability account at December 31. Step 1: Determine what the current account balance equals. Step 2: Determine what the current account balance should equal. Step 3: Record the December 31 adjusting entry to get from step 1 to step 2. *Assume no other adjusting entries are made during the year.*

a. Unearned Rent Revenue. The company collected $24,000 rent in advance on September 1, debiting Cash and crediting Unearned Rent Revenue. The tenant was paying 12 months' rent in advance and occupancy began September 1.

b. Unearned Services Revenue. The company charges $100 per month to spray a house for insects. A customer paid $600 on November 1 in advance for six treatments, which was recorded with a debit to Cash and a credit to Unearned Services Revenue. At year-end, the company has applied two treatments for the customer.

Solution

a. Step 1: Unearned Rent Revenue equals $24,000 (before adjustment)
Step 2: Unearned Rent Revenue should equal $16,000 (current period earned revenue is $8,000*)
Step 3: Adjusting entry to get from step 1 to step 2

Dec. 31	Unearned Rent Revenue	8,000	
	Rent Revenue		8,000
	To record earned portion of rent received in advance. **($24,000/12 months) × 4 months' rental usage*		

b. Step 1: Unearned Services Revenue equals $600 (before adjustment)
Step 2: Unearned Services Revenue should equal $400 (current period earned revenue is $200*)
Step 3: Adjusting entry to get from step 1 to step 2

Dec. 31	Unearned Services Revenue.	200	
	Services Revenue		200
	To record earned portion of revenue received in advance.		
	**$100 × 2 treatments = Services revenue*		

Do More: QS 3-10, QS 3-11

Accrued Expenses

Accrued expenses refer to costs that are incurred in a period but are both unpaid and unrecorded. Accrued expenses must be reported on the income statement for the period when incurred. Adjusting entries for recording accrued expenses increase the expense (income statement) account, and increase a liability (balance sheet) account, as shown in Exhibit 3.9. This adjustment recognizes expenses incurred in a period but not yet paid. Common examples of accrued expenses are salaries, interest, rent, and taxes. We use salaries and interest to show how to adjust accounts for accrued expenses.

Point: Accrued expenses are also called *accrued liabilities*.

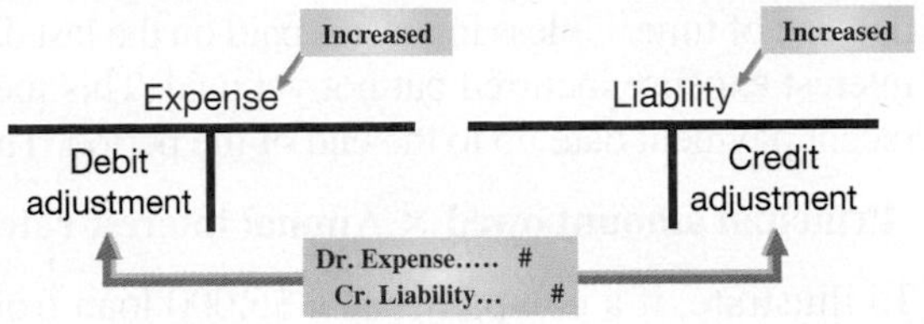

EXHIBIT 3.9

Adjusting for Accrued Expenses (increase a liability and record an expense)

Accrued Salaries Expense FastForward's employee earns $70 per day, or $350 for a five-day workweek beginning on Monday and ending on Friday.

Step 1: Its employee is paid every two weeks on Friday. On December 12 and 26, the wages are paid, recorded in the journal, and posted to the ledger.

Step 2: The calendar in Exhibit 3.10 shows three working days after the December 26 payday (29, 30, and 31). This means the employee has earned three days' salary by the close of business

EXHIBIT 3.10

Salary Accrual and Paydays

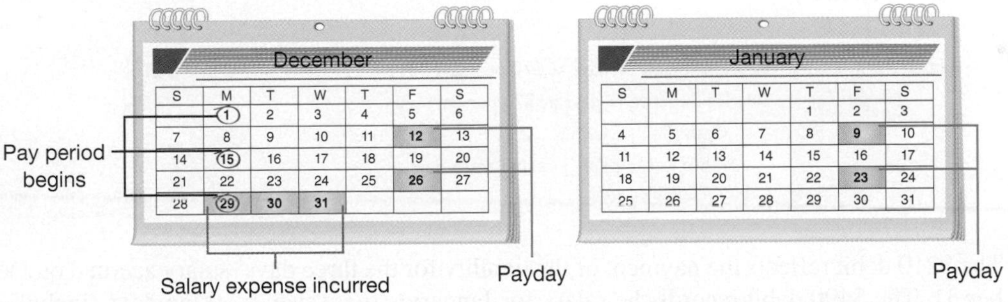

on Wednesday, December 31, yet this salary cost has not been paid or recorded. The financial statements would be incomplete if FastForward failed to report the added expense and liability to the employee for unpaid salary from December 29, 30, and 31.

Point: An employer records salaries expense and a vacation pay liability when employees earn vacation pay.

Step 3: The adjusting entry to account for accrued salaries, along with T-account postings, follows:

Adjustment (e)

Dec. 31	Salaries Expense	210	
	Salaries Payable		210
	To record three days' accrued salary (3 × $70).		

Assets = Liabilities + Equity
+210 −210

Salaries Expense		622
Dec. 12	700	
26	700	
31	**210**	
Balance	1,610	

Salaries Payable		209
	Dec. 31	**210**

Explanation Salaries expense of $1,610 is reported on the December income statement and $210 of salaries payable (liability) is reported in the balance sheet. *Not* making the adjustment (1) understates salaries expense and overstates net income by $210 in the December income statement and (2) understates salaries payable (liabilities) and overstates equity by $210 on the December 31 balance sheet. The following highlights the adjustment for salaries incurred.

Before Adjustment	Adjustment	After Adjustment
Salaries Payable = $0	**Add $210 to Salaries Payable** **Add $210 to Salaries Expense**	**Salaries Payable = $210**
Reports $0 from employee salaries incurred but not yet paid in cash.	Record 3 days' salaries owed to employee, but not yet paid, at $70 per day.	Reports $210 salaries payable to employee but not yet paid.

Accrued Interest Expense Companies commonly have accrued interest expense on notes payable and other long-term liabilities at the end of a period. Interest expense is incurred with the passage of time. Unless interest is paid on the last day of an accounting period, we need to adjust for interest expense incurred but not yet paid. This means we must accrue interest cost from the most recent payment date up to the end of the period. The formula for computing accrued interest is:

Principal amount owed × Annual interest rate × Fraction of year since last payment date.

Point: Interest computations assume a 360-day year; known as the *bankers' rule.*

To illustrate, if a company has a $6,000 loan from a bank at 6% annual interest, then 30 days' accrued interest expense is $30—computed as $6,000 × 0.06 × 30/360. The adjusting entry would be to debit Interest Expense for $30 and credit Interest Payable for $30.

Future Payment of Accrued Expenses Adjusting entries for accrued expenses foretell cash transactions in future periods. Specifically, accrued expenses at the end of one accounting period result in *cash payment* in a *future period*(s). To illustrate, recall that FastForward recorded accrued salaries of $210. On January 9, the first payday of the next period, the following entry settles the accrued liability (salaries payable) and records salaries expense for seven days of work in January:

Assets	=	Liabilities	+	Equity
−700		−210		−490

Jan. 9	Salaries Payable (3 days at $70 per day)	210	
	Salaries Expense (7 days at $70 per day)	490	
	Cash		700
	Paid two weeks' salary including three days accrued in December.		

The $210 debit reflects the payment of the liability for the three days' salary accrued on December 31. The $490 debit records the salary for January's first seven working days (including the New Year's Day holiday) as an expense of the new accounting period. The $700 credit records the total amount of cash paid to the employee.

NEED-TO-KNOW 3-3

Accrued Expenses

P1

For each separate case below, follow the three-step process for adjusting the accrued expense account at December 31. Step 1: Determine what the current account balance equals. Step 2: Determine what the current account balance should equal. Step 3: Record the December 31 adjusting entry to get from step 1 to step 2. *Assume no other adjusting entries are made during the year.*

a. Salaries Payable. At year-end, salaries expense of $5,000 has been incurred by the company, but is not yet paid to employees.

b. Interest Payable. At its December 31 year-end, the company holds a mortgage payable that has incurred $1,000 in annual interest that is neither recorded nor paid. The company intends to pay the interest on January 3 of the next year.

Solution

a. Step 1: Salaries Payable equals $0 (before adjustment)
Step 2: Salaries Payable should equal $5,000 (not yet recorded)
Step 3: Adjusting entry to get from step 1 to step 2

Dec. 31	Salaries Expense	5,000	
	Salaries Payable		5,000
	To record employee salaries earned but not yet paid.		

b. Step 1: Interest Payable equals $0 (before adjustment)
Step 2: Interest Payable should equal $1,000 (not yet recorded)
Step 3: Adjusting entry to get from step 1 to step 2

Dec. 31	Interest Expense	1,000	
	Interest Payable		1,000
	To record interest incurred but not yet paid.		

Do More: QS 3-12, QS 3-13, E 3-1, E 3-2

Accrued Revenues

The term **accrued revenues** refers to revenues earned in a period that are both unrecorded and not yet received in cash (or other assets). An example is a technician who bills customers only when the job is done. If one-third of a job is complete by the end of a period, then the technician must record one-third of the expected billing as revenue in that period—even though there is no billing or collection. The adjusting entries for accrued revenues increase a revenue (income statement) account, and increase an asset (balance sheet) account, as shown in Exhibit 3.11. Accrued revenues commonly arise from services, products, interest, and rent. We use service fees and interest to show how to adjust for accrued revenues.

Point: Accrued revenues are also called *accrued assets.*

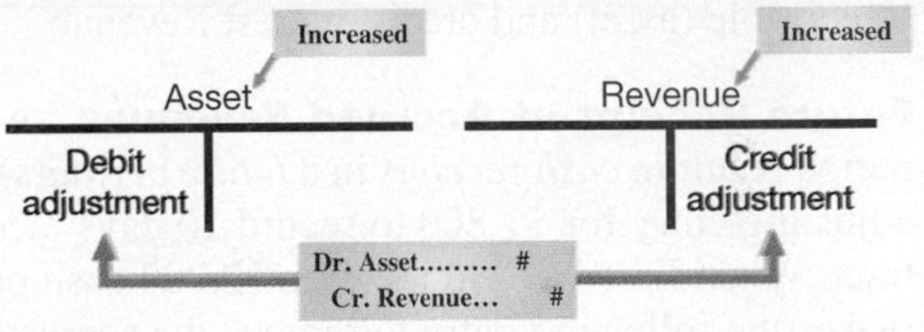

EXHIBIT 3.11
Adjusting for Accrued Revenues (increase an asset and record revenue)

Accrued Services Revenue Accrued revenues are not recorded until adjusting entries are made at the end of the accounting period. These accrued revenues are earned but unrecorded because either the buyer has not yet paid for them or the seller has not yet billed the buyer. FastForward provides an example.

Accrued Revenues
Dec. 31 Record revenue and receivable for services provided but unbilled

Jan. 10 Receive cash and reduce receivable

Step 1: In the second week of December, it agreed to provide 30 days of consulting services to a local fitness club for a fixed fee of $2,700 (or $90 per day). The terms of the initial agreement call for FastForward to provide services from December 12, 2015, through January 10, 2016, or 30 days of service. The club agrees to pay FastForward $2,700 on January 10, 2016, when the service period is complete.

Step 2: At December 31, 2015, 20 days of services have already been provided. Since the contracted services have not yet been entirely provided, FastForward has neither billed the club nor recorded the services already provided. Still, FastForward has earned two-thirds of the 30-day fee, or $1,800 ($2,700 × 20/30). The *revenue recognition principle* implies that it must report the $1,800 on the December income statement. The balance sheet also must report that the club owes FastForward $1,800.

Step 3: The year-end adjusting entry to account for accrued services revenue is

Adjustment (*f*)

Dec. 31	Accounts Receivable	1,800	
	Consulting Revenue		1,800
	To record 20 days' accrued revenue.		

Assets = Liabilities + Equity
+1,800 +1,800

Accounts Receivable			106
Dec. 12	1,900	Dec. 22	1,900
31	**1,800**		
Balance	1,800		

Consulting Revenue			403
		Dec. 5	4,200
		12	1,600
		31	250
		31	**1,800**
		Balance	7,850

Example: What is the adjusting entry if the 30-day consulting period began on December 22? *Answer:* One-third of the fee is earned:
Accounts Receivable . . 900
Consulting Rev. 900

Explanation Accounts receivable are reported on the balance sheet at $1,800, and the $7,850 total of consulting revenue is reported on the income statement. *Not* making the adjustment would understate (1) both consulting revenue and net income by $1,800 in the December income statement and (2) both accounts receivable (assets) and equity by $1,800 on the December 31 balance sheet. The following table highlights the adjustment for accrued revenue.

Before Adjustment	Adjustment	After Adjustment
Accounts Receivable = $0	**Add $1,800 to Accounts Receivable** **Add $1,800 to Consulting Revenue**	**Accounts Receivable = $1,800**
Reports $0 from revenue earned but not yet received in cash.	Record 20 days of earned consulting revenue, which is 20/30 of total contract amount.	Reports $1,800 in accounts receivable from consulting services provided.

Accrued Interest Revenue In addition to the accrued interest expense we described earlier, interest can yield an accrued revenue when a debtor owes money (or other assets) to a company. If a company is holding notes or accounts receivable that produce interest revenue, we must adjust the accounts to record any earned and yet uncollected interest revenue. The adjusting entry is similar to the one for accruing services revenue. Specifically, we debit Interest Receivable (asset) and credit Interest Revenue.

Future Receipt of Accrued Revenues Accrued revenues at the end of one accounting period result in *cash receipts* in a *future period*(s). To illustrate, recall that FastForward made an adjusting entry for $1,800 to record 20 days' accrued revenue earned from its consulting contract. When FastForward receives $2,700 cash on January 10 for the entire contract amount, it makes the following entry to remove the accrued asset (accounts receivable) and recognize the revenue earned in January. The $2,700 debit reflects the cash received. The $1,800 credit reflects the removal of the receivable, and the $900 credit records the revenue earned in January.

Assets	=	Liabilities	+	Equity
+2,700				+900
−1,800				

Jan. 10	Cash	2,700	
	Accounts Receivable (20 days at $90 per day)		1,800
	Consulting Revenue (10 days at $90 per day)		900
	Received cash for the accrued asset and recorded earned consulting revenue for January.		

Decision Maker

Loan Officer The owner of a custom audio, video, and home theater store applies for a business loan. The store's financial statements reveal large increases in current-year revenues and income. Analysis shows that these increases are due to a promotion that let consumers buy now and pay nothing until January 1 of next year. The store recorded these sales as accrued revenue. Does your analysis raise any concerns? ■ [Answers follow the chapter's Summary.]

NEED-TO-KNOW 3-4

Accrued Revenues

P1

For each separate case below, follow the three-step process for adjusting the accrued revenue account at December 31. Step 1: Determine what the current account balance equals. Step 2: Determine what the current account balance should equal. Step 3: Record the December 31 adjusting entry to get from step 1 to step 2. *Assume no other adjusting entries are made during the year.*

a. Accounts Receivable. At year-end, the company has completed services of $1,000 for a client, but the client has not yet been billed for those services.

b. Interest Receivable. At year-end, the company has earned, but not yet recorded, $500 of interest earned from its investments in government bonds.

Solution

a. Step 1: Accounts Receivable equals $0 (before adjustment)
Step 2: Accounts Receivable should equal $1,000 (not yet recorded)
Step 3: Adjusting entry to get from step 1 to step 2

Dec. 31	Accounts Receivable	1,000	
	Services Revenue		1,000
	To record services revenue earned but not yet received.		

b. Step 1: Interest Receivable equals $0 (before adjustment)
Step 2: Interest Receivable should equal $500 (not yet recorded)
Step 3: Adjusting entry to get from step 1 to step 2

Dec. 31	Interest Receivable	500	
	Interest Revenue		500
	To record interest earned but not yet received.		

Do More: QS 3-3, QS 3-14

Links to Financial Statements

The process of adjusting accounts is intended to bring an asset or liability account balance to its correct amount. It also updates a related expense or revenue account. These adjustments are necessary for transactions and events that extend over more than one period. (Adjusting entries are posted like any other entry.)

Exhibit 3.12 summarizes the four types of transactions requiring adjustment. Understanding this exhibit is important to understanding the adjusting process and its importance to financial statements. Remember that each adjusting entry affects one or more income statement accounts *and* one or more balance sheet accounts (but never the Cash account).

EXHIBIT 3.12

Summary of Adjustments and Financial Statement Links

	BEFORE Adjusting		
Category	**Balance Sheet**	**Income Statement**	**Adjusting Entry**
Prepaid expenses†	Asset overstated Equity overstated	Expense understated	**Dr. Expense** **Cr. Asset***
Unearned revenues†	Liability overstated Equity understated	Revenue understated	**Dr. Liability** **Cr. Revenue**
Accrued expenses	Liability understated Equity overstated	Expense understated	**Dr. Expense** **Cr. Liability**
Accrued revenues	Asset understated Equity understated	Revenue understated	**Dr. Asset** **Cr. Revenue**

* For depreciation, the credit is to Accumulated Depreciation (contra asset).

† Exhibit assumes that prepaid expenses are initially recorded as assets and that unearned revenues are initially recorded as liabilities.

Information about some adjustments is not always available until several days or even weeks after the period-end. This means that some adjusting and closing entries are recorded later than, but dated as of, the last day of the period. One example is a company that receives a utility bill on January 10 for costs incurred for the month of December. When it receives the bill, the company records the expense and the payable as of December 31. Other examples include long-distance phone usage and costs of many web billings. The December income statement reflects these additional expenses incurred, and the December 31 balance sheet includes these payables, although the amounts were not actually known on December 31.

Point: CFOs often feel pressure to pursue fraudulent accounting due to pressure applied by their superiors, such as overbearing CEOs or aggressive boards.

Decision Ethics

Financial Officer At year-end, the president instructs you, the financial officer, not to record accrued expenses until next year because they will not be paid until then. The president also directs you to record in current-year sales a recent purchase order from a customer that requires merchandise to be delivered two weeks after the year-end. Your company would report a net income instead of a net loss if you carry out these instructions. What do you do? ■ [Answers follow the chapter's Summary.]

QC2

Adjusted Trial Balance

P2 Explain and prepare an adjusted trial balance.

An **unadjusted trial balance** is a list of accounts and balances prepared *before* adjustments are recorded. An **adjusted trial balance** is a list of accounts and balances prepared *after* adjusting entries have been recorded and posted to the ledger.

Exhibit 3.13 shows both the unadjusted and the adjusted trial balances for FastForward at December 31, 2015. The order of accounts in the trial balance is usually set up to match the order in the chart of accounts. Several new accounts arise from the adjusting entries.

EXHIBIT 3.13

Unadjusted and Adjusted Trial Balances

FASTFORWARD
Trial Balances
December 31, 2015

		Unadjusted Trial Balance		Adjustments		Adjusted Trial Balance	
Acct. No.	Account Title	Dr.	Cr.	Dr.	Cr.	Dr.	Cr.
101	Cash	$ 4,275				$ 4,275	
106	Accounts receivable	0		(f) $1,800		1,800	
126	Supplies	9,720			(b) $1,050	8,670	
128	Prepaid insurance	2,400			(a) 100	2,300	
167	Equipment	26,000				26,000	
168	Accumulated depreciation—Equip.		$ 0		(c) 300		$ 300
201	Accounts payable		6,200				6,200
209	Salaries payable		0		(e) 210		210
236	Unearned consulting revenue		3,000	(d) 250			2,750
307	Common stock		30,000				30,000
318	Retained earnings		0				0
319	Dividends	200				200	
403	Consulting revenue		5,800		(d) 250		7,850
					(f) 1,800		
406	Rental revenue		300				300
612	Depreciation expense—Equip.	0		(c) 300		300	
622	Salaries expense	1,400		(e) 210		1,610	
637	Insurance expense	0		(a) 100		100	
640	Rent expense	1,000				1,000	
652	Supplies expense	0		(b) 1,050		1,050	
690	Utilities expense	305				305	
	Totals	$45,300	$45,300	$3,710	$3,710	$47,610	$47,610

Point: Sarbanes-Oxley Act requires that financial statements filed with the SEC be certified by the CEO and CFO, including a declaration that the statements fairly present the issuer's operations and financial condition. Violators can receive fines and/or prison terms.

Each adjustment (see middle columns) is identified by a letter in parentheses that links it to an adjusting entry explained earlier. Each amount in the Adjusted Trial Balance columns is computed by taking that account's amount from the Unadjusted Trial Balance columns and adding or subtracting any adjustment(s). To illustrate, Supplies has a $9,720 Dr. balance in the unadjusted columns. Subtracting the $1,050 Cr. amount shown in the Adjustments columns yields an adjusted $8,670 Dr. balance for Supplies. An account can have more than one adjustment, such as for Consulting Revenue. Also, some accounts might not require adjustment for this period, such as Accounts Payable.

PREPARING FINANCIAL STATEMENTS

P3 Prepare financial statements from an adjusted trial balance.

We can prepare financial statements directly from information in the *adjusted* trial balance. An adjusted trial balance (see the right-most columns in Exhibit 3.13) includes all accounts and balances appearing in financial statements, and is easier to work from than the entire ledger when preparing financial statements.

Exhibit 3.14 shows how revenue and expense balances are transferred from the adjusted trial balance to the income statement (red lines). The net income and the dividends amount are then used to prepare the statement of retained earnings (black lines). Asset and liability balances on the adjusted trial balance are then transferred to the balance sheet (blue lines). The ending retained earnings is determined on the statement of retained earnings and transferred to the balance sheet (green line).

EXHIBIT 3.14

Preparing Financial Statements (Adjusted Trial Balance from Exhibit 3.13)

FASTFORWARD
Adjusted Trial Balance
December 31, 2015

Acct. No.	Account Title	Debit	Credit
101	Cash	$ 4,275	
106	Accounts receivable	1,800	
126	Supplies	8,670	
128	Prepaid insurance	2,300	
167	Equipment	26,000	
168	Accumulated depreciation—Equip.		$ 300
201	Accounts payable		6,200
209	Salaries payable		210
236	Unearned consulting revenue		2,750
307	Common stock		30,000
318	Retained earnings		0
319	Dividends	200	
403	Consulting revenue		7,850
406	Rental revenue		300
612	Depreciation expense—Equip.	300	
622	Salaries expense	1,610	
637	Insurance expense	100	
640	Rent expense	1,000	
652	Supplies expense	1,050	
690	Utilities expense	305	
	Totals	$47,610	$47,610

Step 3 Prepare balance sheet

FASTFORWARD
Balance Sheet
December 31, 2015

Assets		
Cash		$ 4,275
Accounts receivable		1,800
Supplies		8,670
Prepaid insurance		2,300
Equipment	$26,000	
Less accumulated depreciation	300	25,700
Total assets		$ 42,745
Liabilities		
Accounts payable		$ 6,200
Salaries payable		210
Unearned consulting revenue		2,750
Total liabilities		9,160
Equity		
Common stock		30,000
Retained earnings		3,585
Total equity		33,585
Total liabilities and equity		$ 42,745

Step 2 Prepare statement of retained earnings

FASTFORWARD
Statement of Retained Earnings
For Month Ended December 31, 2015

Retained earnings, December 1	$ 0
Plus: Net income	3,785
	3,785
Less: Cash dividends	200
Retained earnings, December 31	$3,585

Step 1 Prepare income statement

FASTFORWARD
Income Statement
For Month Ended December 31, 2015

Revenues		
Consulting revenue	$7,850	
Rental revenue	300	
Total revenues		$8,150
Expenses		
Depreciation expense — Equip.	300	
Salaries expense	1,610	
Insurance expense	100	
Rent expense	1,000	
Supplies expense	1,050	
Utilities expense	305	
Total expenses		4,365
Net income		$3,785

Steps to Prepare Financial Statements

Step 1	Prepare income statement using revenue and expense accounts from trial balance
Step 2	Prepare statement of retained earnings using retained earnings and dividends from trial balance; and pull net income from step 1
Step 3	Prepare balance sheet using asset and liability accounts and common stock from trial balance; and pull updated retained earnings from step 2
Step 4	Prepare statement of cash flows from changes in cash flows for the period (illustrated later in the book)

We prepare financial statements in the following order: income statement, statement of retained earnings, and balance sheet. This order makes sense because the balance sheet uses information from the statement of retained earnings, which in turn uses information from the income statement. The statement of cash flows is usually the final statement prepared.

Point: Each trial balance amount is used in only *one* financial statement and, when financial statements are completed, each account will have been used once.

NEED-TO-KNOW 3-5

Preparing Financial Statements from a Trial Balance

P3

Use the following adjusted trial balance of Magic Company to prepare its (1) income statement, (2) statement of retained earnings, and (3) balance sheet (unclassified) for the year ended, or date of, December 31, 2015. The Retained Earnings account balance is $45,000 at December 31, 2014.

MAGIC COMPANY
Adjusted Trial Balance
December 31, 2015

Account Title	Debit	Credit
Cash	$ 13,000	
Accounts receivable	17,000	
Land	85,000	
Accounts payable		$ 12,000
Long-term notes payable		33,000
Common stock		30,000
Retained earnings		45,000
Dividends	20,000	
Fees earned		79,000
Salaries expense	56,000	
Office supplies expense	8,000	
Totals	$199,000	$199,000

Solution

Step 1

MAGIC COMPANY
Income Statement
For Year Ended December 31, 2015

Fees earned		$79,000
Expenses		
Salaries expense	$56,000	
Office supplies expense	8,000	
Total expenses		64,000
Net income		$15,000

Step 2

MAGIC COMPANY
Statement of Retained Earnings
For Year Ended December 31, 2015

Retained earnings, December 31, 2014	$ 45,000
Add: Net income	15,000
	60,000
Less: Dividends	(20,000)
Retained earnings, December 31, 2015	$ 40,000

Step 3

MAGIC COMPANY
Balance Sheet
December 31, 2015

Assets	
Cash	$ 13,000
Accounts receivable	17,000
Land	85,000
Total assets	$115,000
Liabilities	
Accounts payable	$ 12,000
Long-term notes payable	33,000
Total liabilities	45,000
Equity	
Common stock	30,000
Retained earnings	40,000
Total equity	70,000
Total liabilities and equity	$115,000

Do More: E 3-7, P 3-5, P 3-8

QC3

CLOSING PROCESS

P4 Describe and prepare closing entries.

The **closing process** is an important step at the end of an accounting period *after* financial statements have been completed. It prepares accounts for recording the transactions and the events of the *next* period. In the closing process we must (1) identify accounts for closing, (2) record and post the closing entries, and (3) prepare a post-closing trial balance. The purpose of the closing process is twofold. First, it resets revenue, expense, and dividends account balances to zero at the end of each period (which also updates the Retained Earnings account for inclusion on the balance sheet). This is done so that these accounts can properly measure income and dividends for the next period. Second, it helps in summarizing a period's revenues and expenses. This section explains the closing process.

Temporary and Permanent Accounts

Temporary (or *nominal*) **accounts** accumulate data related to one accounting period. They include all income statement accounts, the Dividends account, and the Income Summary account. They are temporary because the accounts are opened at the beginning of a period, used to record transactions and events for that period, and then closed at the end of the period. *The closing process applies only to temporary accounts.* **Permanent** (or *real*) **accounts** report on activities related to one or more future accounting periods. They carry their ending balances into the next period and generally consist of all balance sheet accounts. These asset, liability, and equity accounts are not closed (balance sheet accounts are permanent).

Temporary Accounts
(closed at period-end)
Revenues
Expenses
Dividends
Income Summary

Permanent Accounts
(not closed at period-end)
Assets
Liabilities
Common Stock
Retained Earnings

Recording Closing Entries

To record and post **closing entries** is to transfer the end-of-period balances in revenue, expense, and dividends accounts to the permanent Retained Earnings account. Closing entries are necessary at the end of each period after financial statements are prepared because

- Revenue, expense, and dividends accounts must begin each period with zero balances.
- Retained earnings must reflect prior periods' revenues, expenses, and dividends.

An income statement aims to report revenues and expenses for a *specific accounting period*. The statement of retained earnings reports similar information, including dividends. Since revenue, expense, and dividends accounts must accumulate information separately for each period, they must start each period with zero balances. To close these accounts, we transfer their balances first to an account called *Income Summary*. **Income Summary** is a temporary account (only used for the closing process) that contains a credit for the sum of all revenues (and gains) and a debit for the sum of all expenses (and losses). Its balance equals net income or net loss and it is transferred to retained earnings. Next the Dividends account balance is transferred to retained earnings. After these closing entries are posted, the revenue, expense, dividends, and Income Summary accounts have zero balances. These accounts are then said to be *closed* or *cleared*.

Point: To understand the closing process, focus on its *outcomes—updating* the Retained Earnings account balance to its proper ending balance, and getting *temporary accounts* to show *zero balances* for purposes of accumulating data for the next period.

Exhibit 3.15 uses the adjusted account balances of FastForward (from the left side of Exhibit 3.14) to show the four steps necessary to close its temporary accounts. We explain each step.

EXHIBIT 3.15
Four-Step Closing Process

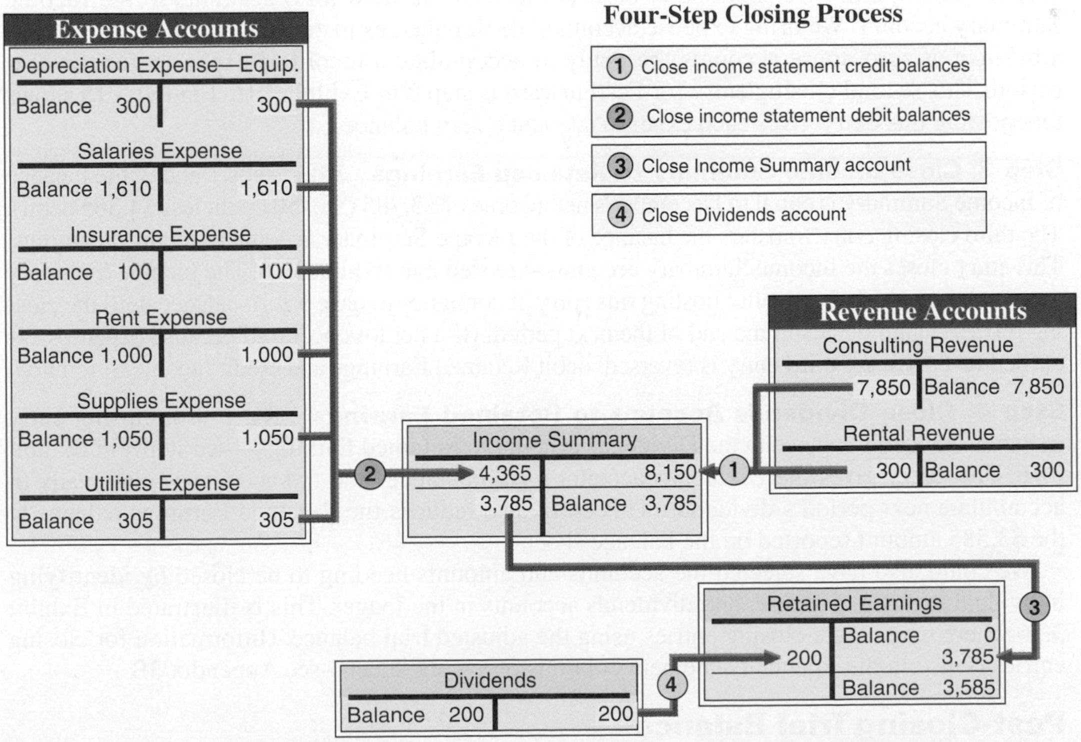

Point: Retained Earnings is the only *permanent account* in Exhibit 3.15.

Step 1: Close Credit Balances in Revenue Accounts to Income Summary The first closing entry transfers credit balances in revenue (and gain) accounts to the Income Summary account. We bring accounts with credit balances to zero by debiting them. For FastForward, this

FASTFORWARD
Adjusted Trial Balance
December 31, 2015

	Debit	Credit
Cash	$ 4,275	
Accounts receivable	1,800	
Supplies	8,670	
Prepaid insurance	2,300	
Equipment	26,000	
Accumulated depreciation—Equip.		$ 300
Accounts payable		6,200
Salaries payable		210
Unearned consulting revenue		2,750
Common stock		30,000
Retained earnings		0
Dividends	200	
Consulting revenue		7,850
Rental revenue		300
Depreciation expense—Equip.	300	
Salaries expense	1,610	
Insurance expense	100	
Rent expense	1,000	
Supplies expense	1,050	
Utilities expense	305	
Totals	$47,610	$47,610

General Journal

Step 1:			
Dec. 31	Consulting Revenue	7,850	
	Rental Revenue	300	
	Income Summary		8,150
	To close revenue accounts.		
Step 2:			
Dec. 31	Income Summary	4,365	
	Depreciation Expense—Equipment		300
	Salaries Expense		1,610
	Insurance Expense		100
	Rent Expense		1,000
	Supplies Expense		1,050
	Utilities Expense		305
	To close expense accounts.		
Step 3:			
Dec. 31	Income Summary	3,785	
	Retained Earnings		3,785
	To close Income Summary account.		
Step 4:			
Dec. 31	Retained Earnings	200	
	Dividends		200
	To close the Dividends account.		

EXHIBIT 3.16

Preparing Closing Entries

Point: It is possible to close revenue and expense accounts directly to Retained Earnings. Computerized accounting systems do this.

journal entry is step 1 in Exhibit 3.16. This entry closes revenue accounts and leaves them with zero balances. The accounts are now ready to record revenues when they occur in the next period. The $8,150 credit entry to Income Summary equals total revenues for the period.

Step 2: Close Debit Balances in Expense Accounts to Income Summary The second closing entry transfers debit balances in expense (and loss) accounts to the Income Summary account. We bring expense accounts' debit balances to zero by crediting them. With a balance of zero, these accounts are ready to accumulate a record of expenses for the next period. This second closing entry for FastForward is step 2 in Exhibit 3.16. Exhibit 3.15 shows that posting this entry gives each expense account a zero balance.

Step 3: Close Income Summary to Retained Earnings After steps 1 and 2, the balance of Income Summary is equal to December's net income of $3,785 ($8,150 credit less $4,365 debit). The third closing entry transfers the balance of the Income Summary account to retained earnings. This entry closes the Income Summary account—see step 3 in Exhibit 3.16. The Income Summary account has a zero balance after posting this entry. It continues to have a zero balance until the closing process again occurs at the end of the next period. (If a net loss occurred because expenses exceeded revenues, the third entry is reversed: debit Retained Earnings and credit Income Summary.)

Step 4: Close Dividends Account to Retained Earnings The fourth closing entry transfers any debit balance in the Dividends account to Retained Earnings—see step 4 in Exhibit 3.16. This entry gives the Dividends account a zero balance, and the account is now ready to accumulate next period's dividends. This entry also reduces the Retained Earnings balance to the $3,585 amount reported on the balance sheet.

We could also have selected the accounts and amounts needing to be closed by identifying individual revenue, expense, and dividends accounts in the ledger. This is illustrated in Exhibit 3.16 where we prepare closing entries using the adjusted trial balance. (Information for closing entries is also in the financial statement columns of a work sheet—see Appendix 3B.)

Post-Closing Trial Balance

P5 Explain and prepare a post-closing trial balance.

Exhibit 3.17 shows the entire ledger of FastForward as of December 31 after adjusting and closing entries are posted. (The transaction entries are in Chapter 2.) The temporary accounts (revenues, expenses, and dividends) have ending balances equal to zero.

EXHIBIT 3.17

General Ledger after the Closing Process for FastForward

Asset Accounts

Cash Acct. No. 101

Date	Explan.	PR	Debit	Credit	Balance
2015					
Dec. 1	(1)	G1	30,000		30,000
2	(2)	G1		2,500	27,500
3	(3)	G1		26,000	1,500
5	(5)	G1	4,200		5,700
6	(13)	G1		2,400	3,300
12	(6)	G1		1,000	2,300
12	(7)	G1		700	1,600
22	(9)	G1	1,900		3,500
24	(10)	G1		900	2,600
24	(11)	G1		200	2,400
26	(12)	G1	3,000		5,400
26	(14)	G1		120	5,280
26	(15)	G1		305	4,975
26	(16)	G1		700	**4,275**

Accounts Receivable Acct. No. 106

Date	Explan.	PR	Debit	Credit	Balance
2015					
Dec. 12	(8)	G1	1,900		1,900
22	(9)	G1		1,900	0
31	Adj.(f)	G1	1,800		**1,800**

Supplies Acct. No. 126

Date	Explan.	PR	Debit	Credit	Balance
2015					
Dec. 2	(2)	G1	2,500		2,500
6	(4)	G1	7,100		9,600
26	(14)	G1	120		9,720
31	Adj.(b)	G1		1,050	**8,670**

Prepaid Insurance Acct. No. 128

Date	Explan.	PR	Debit	Credit	Balance
2015					
Dec. 6	(13)	G1	2,400		2,400
31	Adj.(a)	G1		100	**2,300**

Equipment Acct. No. 167

Date	Explan.	PR	Debit	Credit	Balance
2015					
Dec. 3	(3)	G1	26,000		**26,000**

Accumulated Depreciation—Equipment Acct. No. 168

Date	Explan.	PR	Debit	Credit	Balance
2015					
Dec. 31	Adj.(c)	G1		300	**300**

Liability and Equity Accounts

Accounts Payable Acct. No. 201

Date	Explan.	PR	Debit	Credit	Balance
2015					
Dec. 6	(4)	G1		7,100	7,100
24	(10)	G1	900		**6,200**

Salaries Payable Acct. No. 209

Date	Explan.	PR	Debit	Credit	Balance
2015					
Dec. 31	Adj.(e)	G1		210	**210**

Unearned Consulting Revenue Acct. No. 236

Date	Explan.	PR	Debit	Credit	Balance
2015					
Dec. 26	(12)	G1		3,000	3,000
31	Adj.(d)	G1	250		**2,750**

Common Stock Acct. No. 307

Date	Explan.	PR	Debit	Credit	Balance
2015					
Dec. 1	(1)	G1		30,000	30,000

Retained Earnings Acct. No. 318

Date	Explan.	PR	Debit	Credit	Balance
2015					
Dec. 31	**Clos.(3)**	**G1**		**3,785**	**3,785**
31	**Clos.(4)**	**G1**	**200**		**3,585**

Dividends Acct. No. 319

Date	Explan.	PR	Debit	Credit	Balance
2015					
Dec. 24	(11)	G1	200		200
31	**Clos.(4)**	**G1**		**200**	**0**

Revenue and Expense Accounts (Including Income Summary)

Consulting Revenue Acct. No. 403

Date	Explan.	PR	Debit	Credit	Balance
2015					
Dec. 5	(5)	G1		4,200	4,200
12	(8)	G1		1,600	5,800
31	Adj.(d)	G1		250	6,050
31	Adj.(f)	G1		1,800	**7,850**
31	**Clos.(1)**	**G1**	**7,850**		**0**

Rental Revenue Acct. No. 406

Date	Explan.	PR	Debit	Credit	Balance
2015					
Dec. 12	(8)	G1		300	**300**
31	**Clos.(1)**	**G1**	**300**		**0**

Depreciation Expense—Equipment Acct. No. 612

Date	Explan.	PR	Debit	Credit	Balance
2015					
Dec. 31	Adj.(c)	G1	300		**300**
31	**Clos.(2)**	**G1**		**300**	**0**

Salaries Expense Acct. No. 622

Date	Explan.	PR	Debit	Credit	Balance
2015					
Dec. 12	(7)	G1	700		700
26	(16)	G1	700		1,400
31	Adj.(e)	G1	210		**1,610**
31	**Clos.(2)**	**G1**		**1,610**	**0**

Insurance Expense Acct. No. 637

Date	Explan.	PR	Debit	Credit	Balance
2015					
Dec. 31	Adj.(a)	G1	100		**100**
31	**Clos.(2)**	**G1**		**100**	**0**

Rent Expense Acct. No. 640

Date	Explan.	PR	Debit	Credit	Balance
2015					
Dec. 12	(6)	G1	1,000		**1,000**
31	**Clos.(2)**	**G1**		**1,000**	**0**

Supplies Expense Acct. No. 652

Date	Explan.	PR	Debit	Credit	Balance
2015					
Dec. 31	Adj.(b)	G1	1,050		**1,050**
31	**Clos.(2)**	**G1**		**1,050**	**0**

Utilities Expense Acct. No. 690

Date	Explan.	PR	Debit	Credit	Balance
2015					
Dec. 26	(15)	G1	305		**305**
31	**Clos.(2)**	**G1**		**305**	**0**

Income Summary Acct. No. 901

Date	Explan.	PR	Debit	Credit	Balance
2015					
Dec. 31	**Clos.(1)**	**G1**		**8,150**	**8,150**
31	**Clos.(2)**	**G1**	**4,365**		**3,785**
31	**Clos.(3)**	**G1**	**3,785**		**0**

A **post-closing trial balance** is a list of permanent accounts and their balances from the ledger after all closing entries have been journalized and posted. It lists the balances for all accounts not closed. These accounts comprise a company's assets, liabilities, and equity, which are identical to those in the balance sheet. The aim of a post-closing trial balance is to verify that (1) total debits equal total credits for permanent accounts and (2) all temporary accounts have zero balances. FastForward's post-closing trial balance is shown in Exhibit 3.18. The post-closing trial balance usually is the last step in the accounting process.

EXHIBIT 3.18
Post-Closing Trial Balance

FASTFORWARD
Post-Closing Trial Balance
December 31, 2015

	Debit	Credit
Cash	$ 4,275	
Accounts receivable	1,800	
Supplies	8,670	
Prepaid insurance	2,300	
Equipment	26,000	
Accumulated depreciation—Equipment		$ 300
Accounts payable		6,200
Salaries payable		210
Unearned consulting revenue		2,750
Common stock		30,000
Retained earnings		3,585
Totals	$43,045	$43,045

Point: Only balance sheet (permanent) accounts are on a post-closing trial balance.

Accounting Cycle

C2 Identify steps in the accounting cycle.

The term **accounting cycle** refers to the steps in preparing financial statements. It is called a *cycle* because the steps are repeated each reporting period. Exhibit 3.19 shows the 10 steps in the cycle, beginning with analyzing transactions and ending with a post-closing trial balance or

EXHIBIT 3.19
Steps in the Accounting Cycle*

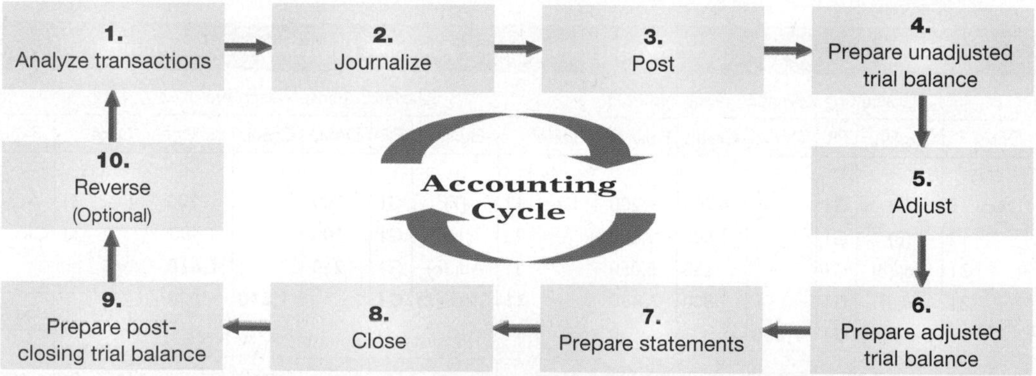

Explanations

1. Analyze transactions	Analyze transactions to prepare for journalizing.
2. Journalize	Record accounts, including debits and credits, in a journal.
3. Post	Transfer debits and credits from the journal to the ledger.
4. Prepare unadjusted trial balance	Summarize unadjusted ledger accounts and amounts.
5. Adjust	Record adjustments to bring account balances up to date; journalize and post adjustments.
6. Prepare adjusted trial balance	Summarize adjusted ledger accounts and amounts.
7. Prepare statements	Use adjusted trial balance to prepare financial statements.
8. Close	Journalize and post entries to close temporary accounts.
9. Prepare post-closing trial balance	Test clerical accuracy of the closing procedures.
10. Reverse (optional)	Reverse certain adjustments in the next period—optional step; see Appendix 3C.

* Steps 4, 6, and 9 can be done on a work sheet. A work sheet is useful in planning adjustments, but adjustments (step 5) must always be journalized and posted. Steps 3, 4, 6, and 9 are automatic with a computerized system.

reversing entries. Steps 1 through 3 usually occur regularly as a company enters into transactions. Steps 4 through 9 are done at the end of a period. *Reversing entries* in step 10 are optional and are explained in Appendix 3C.

NEED-TO-KNOW 3-6

Closing Entries

P4

Use the adjusted trial balance solution for Magic Company from Need-To-Know 3-5 to prepare its closing entries.

Dec. 31	Fees Earned	79,000	
	Income Summary		79,000
	To close the revenue account.		
31	Income Summary	64,000	
	Salaries Expense		56,000
	Office Supplies Expense		8,000
	To close the expense accounts.		
31	Income Summary	15,000	
	Retained Earnings		15,000
	To close Income Summary.		
31	Retained Earnings	20,000	
	Dividends		20,000
	To close the Dividends account.		

Do More: QS 3-21, E 3-8

QC4

CLASSIFIED BALANCE SHEET

C3 Explain and prepare a classified balance sheet.

Our discussion to this point has been limited to unclassified financial statements. This section describes a classified balance sheet. The next chapter describes a classified income statement. An **unclassified balance sheet** is one whose items are broadly grouped into assets, liabilities, and equity. One example is FastForward's balance sheet in Exhibit 3.14. A **classified balance sheet** organizes assets and liabilities into important subgroups that provide more information to decision makers.

Classification Structure

A classified balance sheet has no required layout, but it usually contains the categories in Exhibit 3.20. One of the more important classifications is the separation between current and noncurrent items for both assets and liabilities. Current items are those expected to come due (either collected or owed) within one year or the company's operating cycle, whichever is longer. The **operating cycle** is the time span from when *cash is used* to acquire goods and services until *cash is received* from the sale of goods and services. "Operating" refers to company operations and "cycle" refers to the circular flow of cash used for company inputs and then cash received from its outputs. The length of a company's operating cycle depends on its activities. For a service company, the operating cycle is the time span between (1) paying employees who perform the services and (2) receiving cash from customers. For a merchandiser selling products, the operating cycle is the time span between (1) paying suppliers for merchandise and (2) receiving cash from customers.

Point: Current and noncurrent are also referred to as short-term and long-term, respectively.

EXHIBIT 3.20

Typical Categories in a Classified Balance Sheet

Assets	Liabilities and Equity
Current assets	Current liabilities
Noncurrent assets	Noncurrent liabilities
Long-term investments	Equity
Plant assets	
Intangible assets	

Most operating cycles are less than one year. This means most companies use a one-year period in deciding which assets and liabilities are current. A few companies have an operating cycle

Cameron Spencer/Getty Images

longer than one year. For instance, producers of certain beverages (wine) and products (ginseng) that require aging for several years have operating cycles longer than one year. A balance sheet lists current assets before noncurrent assets and current liabilities before noncurrent liabilities. This consistency in presentation allows users to quickly identify current assets that are most easily converted to cash and current liabilities that are shortly coming due. Items in current assets and current liabilities are listed in the order of how quickly they will be converted to, or paid in, cash.

Classification Categories

This section describes the most common categories in a classified balance sheet. The balance sheet for Snowboarding Components in Exhibit 3.21 shows the typical categories. Its assets are classified as either current or noncurrent. Its noncurrent assets include three main categories: long-term investments, plant assets, and intangible assets. Its liabilities are classified as either current or long-term. Not all companies use the same categories of assets and liabilities for their balance sheets. **K2 Sports**, a manufacturer of snowboards, reported a balance sheet with only three asset classes: current assets; property, plant and equipment; and other assets.

EXHIBIT 3.21

Example of a Classified Balance Sheet

SNOWBOARDING COMPONENTS
Balance Sheet
January 31, 2015

Assets		
Current assets		
Cash	$ 6,500	
Short-term investments	2,100	
Accounts receivable, net	4,400	
Merchandise inventory	27,500	
Prepaid expenses	2,400	
Total current assets		$ 42,900
Long-term investments		
Notes receivable	1,500	
Investments in stocks and bonds	18,000	
Land held for future expansion	48,000	
Total long-term investments		67,500
Plant assets		
Equipment and buildings	203,200	
Less accumulated depreciation	53,000	
Equipment and buildings, net		150,200
Land		73,200
Total plant assets		223,400
Intangible assets		10,000
Total assets		$343,800
Liabilities		
Current liabilities		
Accounts payable	$ 15,300	
Wages payable	3,200	
Notes payable	3,000	
Current portion of long-term liabilities	7,500	
Total current liabilities		$ 29,000
Long-term liabilities (net of current portion)		150,000
Total liabilities		179,000
Equity		
Common stock		50,000
Retained earnings		114,800
Total equity		164,800
Total liabilities and equity		$343,800

Current Assets **Current assets** are cash and other resources that are expected to be sold, collected, or used within one year or the company's operating cycle, whichever is longer. Examples are cash, short-term investments, accounts receivable, short-term notes receivable, goods for sale (called *merchandise* or *inventory*), and prepaid expenses. The individual prepaid expenses of a company are usually small in amount compared to many other assets and are often combined and shown as a single item. The prepaid expenses likely include items such as prepaid insurance, prepaid rent, office supplies, and store supplies. Prepaid expenses are usually listed last because they will not be converted to cash (instead, they are used).

©Stephen D. Cannerelli/Syracuse Newspapers/The Image Works

Long-Term Investments A second major balance sheet classification is **long-term** (or *non-current*) **investments.** Notes receivable and investments in stocks and bonds are long-term assets when they are expected to be held for more than the longer of one year or the operating cycle. Land held for future expansion is a long-term investment because it is *not* used in operations.

Plant Assets Plant assets are tangible assets that are both *long-lived* and *used to produce or sell products and services*. Examples are equipment, machinery, buildings, and land that are used to produce or sell products and services. The order listing for plant assets is usually from most liquid to least liquid such as equipment and machinery to buildings and land.

Point: Plant assets are also called *fixed assets; property, plant and equipment;* or *long-lived assets.*

Intangible Assets **Intangible assets** are long-term resources that benefit business operations, usually lack physical form, and have uncertain benefits. Examples are patents, trademarks, copyrights, franchises, and goodwill. Their value comes from the privileges or rights granted to or held by the owner. **K2 Sports** reported intangible assets of $228 million, which is nearly 20 percent of its total assets. Its intangibles included trademarks, patents, and licensing agreements.

Point: Furniture and fixtures are referred to as F&F, which are classified as noncurrent assets.

Current Liabilities **Current liabilities** are obligations due to be paid or settled within one year or the operating cycle, whichever is longer. They are usually settled by paying out current assets such as cash. Current liabilities often include accounts payable, notes payable, wages payable, taxes payable, interest payable, and unearned revenues. Also, any portion of a long-term liability due to be paid within one year or the operating cycle, whichever is longer, is a current liability. Unearned revenues are current liabilities when they will be settled by delivering products or services within one year or the operating cycle, whichever is longer. Current liabilities are reported in the order of those to be settled first.

Point: Many financial ratios are distorted if accounts are not classified correctly.

Long-Term Liabilities **Long-term liabilities** are obligations *not* due within one year or the operating cycle, whichever is longer. Notes payable, mortgages payable, bonds payable, and lease obligations are common long-term liabilities. If a company has both short- and long-term items in each of these categories, they are commonly separated into two accounts in the ledger.

Point: Only assets and liabilities (not equity) are classified as current or noncurrent.

Equity Equity is the owner's claim on assets. The equity section for a corporation is divided into two main subsections, common stock (contributed capital) and retained earnings.

NEED-TO-KNOW 3-7

Classified Balance Sheet

C3

Use the adjusted trial balance solution for Magic Company from Need-To-Know 3-5 to prepare its classified balance sheet as of December 31, 2015. (*Hint:* The Retained Earnings account balance is $40,000 at December 31, 2015.)

MAGIC COMPANY
Balance Sheet
December 31, 2015

Assets		**Liabilities**	
Current assets		Current liabilities	
Cash	$ 13,000	Accounts payable	$ 12,000
Accounts receivable	17,000	Total current liabilities	12,000
Total current assets	30,000	Long-term notes payable	33,000
Plant assets		Total liabilities	45,000
Land	85,000	**Equity**	
Total plant assets	85,000	Common stock	30,000
		Retained earnings	40,000
		Total equity	70,000
Total assets	$115,000	Total liabilities and equity	$115,000

Do More: QS 3-24, E 3-9, P 3-7

QC5

GLOBAL VIEW

We explained that accounting under U.S. GAAP is similar, but not identical, to that under IFRS. This section discusses differences in adjusting accounts, preparing financial statements, and reporting assets and liabilities on a balance sheet.

Adjusting Accounts Both U.S. GAAP and IFRS include broad and similar guidance for adjusting accounts. Although some variations exist in revenue and expense recognition and other principles, all of the adjustments in this chapter are accounted for identically under the two systems. In later chapters we describe how certain assets and liabilities can result in different adjusted amounts using fair value measurements.

Preparing Financial Statements Both U.S. GAAP and IFRS prepare the same four basic financial statements following the same process discussed in this chapter. Chapter 2 explained how both U.S. GAAP and IFRS require current items to be separated from noncurrent items on the balance sheet (yielding a classified balance sheet). U.S. GAAP balance sheets report current items first. Assets are listed from most liquid to least liquid, where liquid refers to the ease of converting an asset to cash. Liabilities are listed from nearest to maturity to furthest from maturity, where maturity refers to the nearness of paying off the liability. IFRS balance sheets normally present noncurrent items first (and equity before liabilities), but this is not a requirement. Other differences with financial statements exist, which we identify in later chapters. **Piaggio** provides the following example of IFRS reporting for its assets, liabilities, and equity within the balance sheet:

PIAGGIO

Point: IASB and FASB are working to improve financial statements. One proposal would reorganize the balance sheet to show assets and liabilities classified as operating, investing, or financing.

IFRS: New revenue recognition rules proposed by the FASB and the IASB reduce variation between U.S. GAAP and IFRS when accounting for revenue.

PIAGGIO
Balance Sheet (in thousands of euros)
December 31, 2011

Assets		Equity and Liabilities	
Noncurrent assets		Total equity	€ 446,218
Intangible assets	€ 649,420	Noncurrent liabilities	
Property, plant and equipment	274,871	Financial liabilities falling due after one year	329,200
Other noncurrent assets	86,185	Other long-term liabilities	100,489
Total noncurrent assets	1,010,476	Total noncurrent liabilities	429,689
Current assets		Current liabilities	
Trade, tax and other receivables	120,833	Financial liabilities falling due within one year	170,261
Inventories	236,988	Trade, tax and other payables	460,901
Cash and cash equivalents	151,887	Current portion of other long-term provisions	13,115
Total current assets	509,708	Total current liabilities	644,277
Total assets	€1,520,184	Total equity and liabilities	€1,520,184

Closing Process The closing process is identical under U.S. GAAP and IFRS. Although unique accounts can arise under either system, the closing process remains the same.

IFRS

Revenue and expense recognition are key to recording accounting adjustments. IFRS tends to be more *principles-based* relative to U.S. GAAP, which is viewed as more *rules-based.* A principles-based system depends heavily on control procedures to reduce the potential for fraud or misconduct. Failure in judgment led to improper accounting adjustments at **Fannie Mae**, **Xerox**, **WorldCom**, and others. A KPMG survey of accounting and finance employees found that more than 10% of them had witnessed falsification or manipulation of accounting data within the past year. Internal controls and governance processes are directed at curtailing such behavior. Yet, a 2011 KPMG fraud survey found that one in seven frauds was uncovered by chance, which emphasizes our need to improve internal controls and governance. ■

Sustainability and Accounting **International Princess Project**, as introduced in this chapter's opening feature, emphasizes the social aspects of its business for its sustainability. Its entrepreneurial founder, Shannon Keith, explained that "because economics and abject poverty is a root issue to sex slavery, it was inherent in the business model to bring an economic solution for long-term freedom for the victims and their children." That business model and its social dimensions are key to her business's success and its sustainability.

Courtesy of International Princess Project

Profit Margin and Current Ratio — **Decision Analysis**

Profit Margin

A useful measure of a company's operating results is the ratio of its net income to net sales. This ratio is called **profit margin,** or *return on sales,* and is computed as in Exhibit 3.22.

EXHIBIT 3.22

Profit Margin

$$\textbf{Profit margin} = \frac{\textbf{Net income}}{\textbf{Net sales}}$$

A1 Compute profit margin and describe its use in analyzing company performance.

This ratio is interpreted as reflecting the percent of profit in each dollar of sales. To illustrate how we compute and use profit margin, let's look at the results of **Limited Brands, Inc.**, in Exhibit 3.23 for its fiscal years 2009 through 2013.

EXHIBIT 3.23

Limited Brands' Profit Margin

$ in millions	2013	2012	2011	2010	2009
Net income	$ 753	$ 850	$ 805	$ 448	$ 220
Net sales	$10,459	$10,364	$9,613	$8,632	$9,043
Profit margin	**7.2%**	**8.2%**	**8.4%**	**5.2%**	**2.4%**
Industry profit margin	1.7%	1.9%	2.1%	0.9%	0.3%

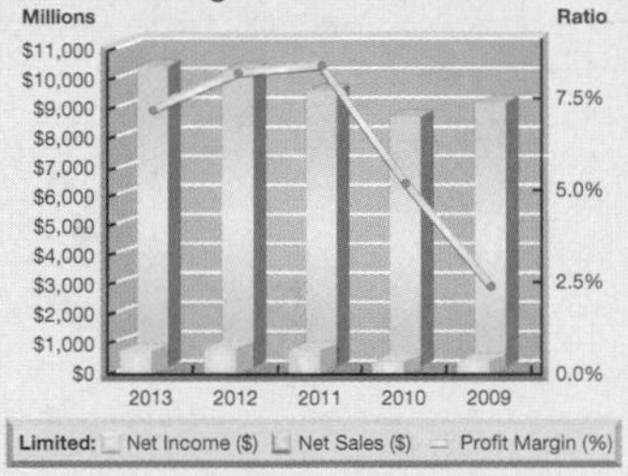

Limited's average profit margin is 6.3% during this 5-year period. This favorably compares to the average industry profit margin of 1.4%. Moreover, we see that Limited's profit margin has rebounded from the recent recessionary period and is at the 7% to 8% margin for the past three years (see margin graph). Future success depends on Limited maintaining its market share and increasing its profit margin.

Current Ratio

A2 Compute the current ratio and describe what it reveals about a company's financial condition.

An important use of financial statements is to help assess a company's ability to pay its debts in the near future. Such analysis affects decisions by suppliers when allowing a company to buy on credit. It also affects decisions by creditors when lending money to a company, including loan terms such as interest rate, due date, and collateral requirements. It can also affect a manager's decisions about using cash to pay debts when they come due. The **current ratio** is one measure of a company's ability to pay its short-term obligations. It is defined in Exhibit 3.24 as current assets divided by current liabilities.

EXHIBIT 3.24

Current Ratio

$$\textbf{Current ratio} = \frac{\textbf{Current assets}}{\textbf{Current liabilities}}$$

Using financial information from **Limited Brands, Inc.**, we compute its current ratio for the recent six-year period. The results are in Exhibit 3.25.

EXHIBIT 3.25

Limited Brands' Current Ratio

$ in millions	2013	2012	2011	2010	2009	2008
Current assets	$2,205	$2,368	$2,592	$3,250	$2,867	$2,919
Current liabilities	$1,538	$1,526	$1,504	$1,322	$1,255	$1,374
Current ratio	**1.4**	**1.6**	**1.7**	**2.5**	**2.3**	**2.1**
Industry current ratio	1.5	1.6	1.7	1.9	2.0	2.1

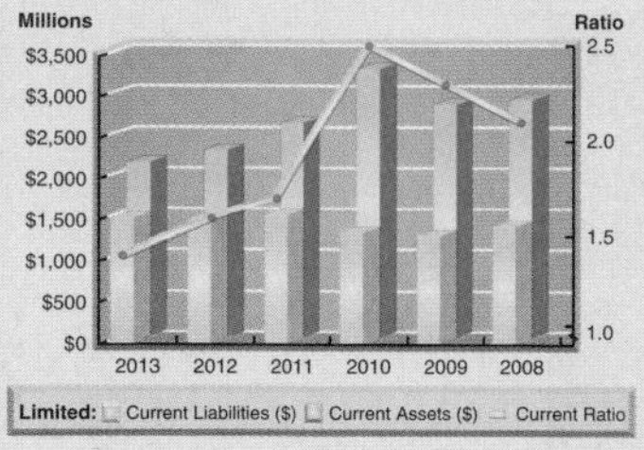

Limited Brands' current ratio averaged 1.9 for its fiscal years 2008 through 2013. The current ratio for each of these years suggests that the company's short-term obligations can be covered with its short-term assets. However, if its ratio would approach 1.0, Limited would expect to face challenges in covering liabilities. If the ratio were *less* than 1.0, current liabilities would exceed current assets, and the company's ability to pay short-term obligations could be in doubt. Limited Brands' liquidity, as evidenced by its current ratio, declined in 2011, 2012, and 2013, which roughly matches the industry decline.

Decision Maker

Analyst You are analyzing the financial condition of a company to assess its ability to meet upcoming loan payments. You compute its current ratio as 1.2. You also find that a major portion of accounts receivable is due from one client who has not made any payments in the past 12 months. Removing this receivable from current assets lowers the current ratio to 0.7. What do you conclude? ■ [Answers follow the chapter's Summary.]

NEED-TO-KNOW

COMPREHENSIVE 1

The following information relates to Fanning's Electronics on December 31, 2015. The company, which uses the calendar year as its annual reporting period, initially records prepaid and unearned items in balance sheet accounts (assets and liabilities, respectively).

a. The company's weekly payroll is $8,750, paid each Friday for a five-day workweek. Assume December 31, 2015, falls on a Monday, but the employees will not be paid their wages until Friday, January 4, 2016.

b. Eighteen months earlier, on July 1, 2014, the company purchased equipment that cost $20,000. Its useful life is predicted to be five years, at which time the equipment is expected to be worthless (zero salvage value).

c. On October 1, 2015, the company agreed to work on a new housing development. The company is paid $120,000 on October 1 in advance of future installation of similar alarm systems in 24 new homes. That amount was credited to the Unearned Services Revenue account. Between October 1 and December 31, work on 20 homes was completed.

d. On September 1, 2015, the company purchased a 12-month insurance policy for $1,800. The transaction was recorded with an $1,800 debit to Prepaid Insurance.

e. On December 29, 2015, the company completed a $7,000 service that has not been billed and not recorded as of December 31, 2015.

Required

1. Prepare any necessary adjusting entries on December 31, 2015, in relation to transactions and events *a* through *e*.
2. Prepare T-accounts for the accounts affected by adjusting entries, and post the adjusting entries. Determine the adjusted balances for the Unearned Revenue and the Prepaid Insurance accounts.
3. Complete the following table and determine the amounts and effects of your adjusting entries on the year 2015 income statement and the December 31, 2015, balance sheet. Use up (down) arrows to indicate an increase (decrease) in the Effect columns.

Entry	Amount in the Entry	Effect on Net Income	Effect on Total Assets	Effect on Total Liabilities	Effect on Total Equity

PLANNING THE SOLUTION

- Analyze each situation to determine which accounts need to be updated with an adjustment.
- Calculate the amount of each adjustment and prepare the necessary journal entries.
- Show the amount of each adjustment in the designated accounts, determine the adjusted balance, and identify the balance sheet classification of the account.
- Determine each entry's effect on net income for the year and on total assets, total liabilities, and total equity at the end of the year.

SOLUTION

1. Adjusting journal entries.

(*a*) Dec. 31	Wages Expense	1,750	
	Wages Payable		1,750
	To accrue wages for the last day of the year ($8,750 × 1/5).		
(*b*) Dec. 31	Depreciation Expense—Equipment	4,000	
	Accumulated Depreciation—Equipment		4,000
	To record depreciation expense for the year ($20,000/5 years = $4,000 per year).		
(*c*) Dec. 31	Unearned Services Revenue	100,000	
	Services Revenue		100,000
	To recognize services revenue earned ($120,000 × 20/24).		
(*d*) Dec. 31	Insurance Expense	600	
	Prepaid Insurance		600
	To adjust for expired portion of insurance ($1,800 × 4/12).		
(e) Dec. 31	Accounts Receivable	7,000	
	Services Revenue		7,000
	To record services revenue earned.		

2. T-accounts for adjusting journal entries *a* through *e*.

Wages Expense

Debit		Credit	
(*a*)	1,750		

Wages Payable

Debit		Credit	
		(*a*)	1,750

Depreciation Expense—Equipment

Debit		Credit	
(*b*)	4,000		

Accumulated Depreciation—Equipment

Debit		Credit	
		(*b*)	4,000

Unearned Services Revenue

Debit		Credit	
		Unadj. Bal.	120,000
(*c*)	100,000		
		Adj. Bal.	20,000

Services Revenue

Debit		Credit	
		(*c*)	100,000
		(e)	7,000
		Adj. Bal.	107,000

Insurance Expense

Debit		Credit	
(*d*)	600		

Prepaid Insurance

Debit		Credit	
Unadj. Bal.	1,800		
		(*d*)	600
Adj. Bal.	1,200		

Accounts Receivable

Debit		Credit	
(e)	7,000		

3. Financial statement effects of adjusting journal entries.

Entry	Amount in the Entry	Effect on Net Income	Effect on Total Assets	Effect on Total Liabilities	Effect on Total Equity
a	$ 1,750	$ 1,750 ↓	No effect	$ 1,750 ↑	$ 1,750 ↓
b	4,000	4,000 ↓	$4,000 ↓	No effect	4,000 ↓
c	100,000	100,000 ↑	No effect	$100,000 ↓	100,000 ↑
d	600	600 ↓	$ 600 ↓	No effect	600 ↓
e	7,000	7,000 ↑	$7,000 ↑	No effect	7,000 ↑

NEED-TO-KNOW

COMPREHENSIVE 2

Use the following adjusted trial balance to answer questions 1–3.

CHOI COMPANY Adjusted Trial Balance December 31	Debit	Credit
Cash	$ 3,050	
Accounts receivable	400	
Prepaid insurance	830	
Supplies	80	
Equipment	217,200	
Accumulated depreciation—Equipment		$ 29,100
Wages payable		880
Interest payable		3,600
Unearned rent		460
Long-term notes payable		150,000
Common stock		10,000
Retained earnings		30,340
Dividends	21,000	
Rent earned		57,500
Wages expense	25,000	
Utilities expense	1,900	
Insurance expense	3,200	
Supplies expense	250	
Depreciation expense—Equipment	5,970	
Interest expense	3,000	
Totals	$281,880	$281,880

1. Prepare the annual income statement from the adjusted trial balance of Choi Company.

Answer:

CHOI COMPANY Income Statement For Year Ended December 31		
Revenues		
Rent earned		$57,500
Expenses		
Wages expense	$25,000	
Utilities expense	1,900	
Insurance expense	3,200	
Supplies expense	250	
Depreciation expense—Equipment	5,970	
Interest expense	3,000	
Total expenses		39,320
Net income		$18,180

2. Prepare a statement of retained earnings from the adjusted trial balance of Choi Company.

Answer:

CHOI COMPANY Statement of Retained Earnings For Year Ended December 31	
Retained earnings, December 31 prior year-end	$30,340
Plus: Net income	18,180
	48,520
Less: Dividends	21,000
Retained earnings, December 31 current year-end	$27,520

3. Prepare a balance sheet (unclassified) from the adjusted trial balance of Choi Company.

Answer:

CHOI COMPANY Balance Sheet December 31		
Assets		
Cash		$ 3,050
Accounts receivable		400
Prepaid insurance		830
Supplies		80
Equipment	$217,200	
Less accumulated depreciation	29,100	188,100
Total assets		$192,460
Liabilities		
Wages payable		$ 880
Interest payable		3,600
Unearned rent		460
Long-term notes payable		150,000
Total liabilities		154,940
Equity		
Common stock		10,000
Retained earnings		27,520
Total equity		37,520
Total liabilities and equity		$192,460

APPENDIX

Alternative Accounting for Prepayments 3A

This appendix explains an alternative in accounting for prepaid expenses and unearned revenues.

RECORDING PREPAYMENT OF EXPENSES IN EXPENSE ACCOUNTS

P6 Explain the alternatives in accounting for prepaids.

An alternative method is to record *all* prepaid expenses with debits to expense accounts. If any prepaids remain unused or unexpired at the end of an accounting period, then adjusting entries must transfer the cost of the unused portions from expense accounts to prepaid expense (asset) accounts. This alternative method is acceptable. The financial statements are identical under either method, but the adjusting entries are different. To illustrate the differences between these two methods, let's look at FastForward's cash payment of December 6 for 24 months of insurance coverage beginning on December 1. FastForward recorded that payment with a debit to an asset account, but it could have recorded a debit to an expense account. These alternatives are shown in Exhibit 3A.1.

EXHIBIT 3A.1

Alternative Initial Entries for Prepaid Expenses

		Payment Recorded as Asset		Payment Recorded as Expense	
Dec. 6	Prepaid Insurance	2,400			
	Cash		2,400		
Dec. 6	Insurance Expense			2,400	
	Cash				2,400

At the end of its accounting period on December 31, insurance protection for one month has expired. This means $100 ($2,400/24) of insurance coverage expired and is an expense for December. The adjusting entry depends on how the original payment was recorded. This is shown in Exhibit 3A.2.

EXHIBIT 3A.2

Adjusting Entry for Prepaid Expenses for the Two Alternatives

		Payment Recorded as Asset		Payment Recorded as Expense	
Dec. 31	Insurance Expense	100			
	Prepaid Insurance		100		
Dec. 31	Prepaid Insurance			2,300	
	Insurance Expense				2,300

When these entries are posted to the accounts in the ledger, we can see that these two methods give identical results. The December 31 adjusted account balances in Exhibit 3A.3 show Prepaid Insurance of $2,300 and Insurance Expense of $100 for both methods.

EXHIBIT 3A.3

Account Balances under Two Alternatives for Recording Prepaid Expenses

Payment Recorded as Asset

Prepaid Insurance			128
Dec. 6	2,400	Dec. 31	100
Balance	**2,300**		

Insurance Expense			637
Dec. 31	**100**		

Payment Recorded as Expense

Prepaid Insurance			128
Dec. 31	**2,300**		

Insurance Expense			637
Dec. 6	2,400	Dec. 31	2,300
Balance	**100**		

RECORDING PREPAYMENT OF REVENUES IN REVENUE ACCOUNTS

As with prepaid expenses, an alternative method is to record *all* unearned revenues with credits to revenue accounts. If any revenues are unearned at the end of an accounting period, then adjusting entries must transfer the unearned portions from revenue accounts to unearned revenue (liability) accounts. This alternative method is acceptable. The adjusting entries are different for these two alternatives, but the financial statements are identical. To illustrate the accounting differences between these two methods, let's look at FastForward's December 26 receipt of $3,000 for consulting services covering the period December 27 to February 24. FastForward recorded this transaction with a credit to a liability account. The alternative is to record it with a credit to a revenue account, as shown in Exhibit 3A.4.

EXHIBIT 3A.4

Alternative Initial Entries for Unearned Revenues

		Receipt Recorded as Liability		Receipt Recorded as Revenue	
Dec. 26	Cash	3,000			
	Unearned Consulting Revenue		3,000		
Dec. 26	Cash			3,000	
	Consulting Revenue				3,000

By the end of its accounting period on December 31, FastForward has earned $250 of this revenue. This means $250 of the liability has been satisfied. Depending on how the initial receipt is recorded, the adjusting entry is as shown in Exhibit 3A.5.

EXHIBIT 3A.5

Adjusting Entry for Unearned Revenues for the Two Alternatives

		Receipt Recorded as Liability		Receipt Recorded as Revenue	
Dec. 31	Unearned Consulting Revenue	250			
	Consulting Revenue		250		
Dec. 31	Consulting Revenue			2,750	
	Unearned Consulting Revenue				2,750

After adjusting entries are posted, the two alternatives give identical results. The December 31 adjusted account balances in Exhibit 3A.6 show unearned consulting revenue of $2,750 and consulting revenue of $250 for both methods.

EXHIBIT 3A.6

Account Balances under Two Alternatives for Recording Unearned Revenues

Receipt Recorded as Liability

Unearned Consulting Revenue			236
Dec. 31	250	Dec. 26	3,000
		Balance	**2,750**

Consulting Revenue			403
		Dec. 31	**250**

Receipt Recorded as Revenue

Unearned Consulting Revenue			236
		Dec. 31	**2,750**

Consulting Revenue			403
Dec. 31	2,750	Dec. 26	3,000
		Balance	**250**

APPENDIX

Work Sheet as a Tool 3B

P7 Prepare a work sheet and explain its usefulness.

Information preparers use various analyses and internal documents when organizing information for internal and external decision makers. Internal documents are often called **working papers.** One widely used working paper is the **work sheet,** which is a useful tool for preparers in working with accounting information. It is usually not available to external decision makers such as investors.

BENEFITS OF A WORK SHEET (SPREADSHEET)

A work sheet is *not* a required report, yet using a manual or electronic work sheet has several potential benefits. Specifically, a work sheet

- Aids the preparation of financial statements.
- Reduces the possibility of errors when working with many accounts and adjustments.
- Links accounts and adjustments to their impacts in financial statements.
- Assists in planning and organizing an audit of financial statements—as it can be used to reflect any adjustments necessary.
- Helps in preparing interim (monthly and quarterly) financial statements when the journalizing and posting of adjusting entries are postponed until year-end.
- Shows the effects of proposed or "what-if" transactions.

USE OF A WORK SHEET

When a work sheet is used to prepare financial statements, it is constructed at the end of a period before the adjusting process. The complete work sheet includes a list of the accounts, their balances and adjustments, and their sorting into financial statement columns. It provides two columns each for the unadjusted trial balance, the adjustments, the adjusted trial balance, the income statement, and the balance sheet. To describe and interpret the work sheet, we use the information from FastForward. Preparing the work sheet has five important steps. Each step, 1 through 5, is color-coded and explained with reference to Exhibit 3B.1.

Point: Since a work sheet is *not* a required report or an accounting record, its format is flexible and can be modified by its user to fit his/her preferences.

1 Step 1. Enter Unadjusted Trial Balance

Refer to Exhibit 3B.1—green section. The first step in preparing a work sheet is to list the title of every account and its account number that is expected to appear on its financial statements. This includes all accounts in the ledger plus any new ones from adjusting entries. Most adjusting entries—including expenses from salaries, supplies, depreciation, and insurance—are predictable and recurring. The unadjusted balance for each account is then entered in the appropriate Debit or Credit column of the unadjusted trial balance columns. The totals of these two columns must be equal. The light green section of Exhibit 3B.1 shows FastForward's work sheet after completing this first step (dark green rows reflect accounts expected to arise as part of the adjustments). Sometimes blank lines are left on the work sheet based on past experience to indicate where lines will be needed for adjustments to certain accounts. Exhibit 3B.1 shows Consulting Revenue as one example. An alternative is to squeeze adjustments on one line or to combine the effects of two or more adjustments in one amount. In the unusual case when an account is not predicted, we can add a new line for such an account following the *Totals* line.

2 Step 2. Enter Adjustments

Point: A recordkeeper often can complete the procedural task of journalizing and posting adjusting entries by using a work sheet and the guidance that *keying* provides.

Refer to Exhibit 3B.1—yellow section. The second step in preparing a work sheet is to enter adjustments in the Adjustments columns. The adjustments shown are the same ones shown in Exhibit 3.13. An identifying letter links the debit and credit of each adjustment. This is called *keying* the adjustments. After preparing a work sheet, adjustments must still be entered in the journal and posted to the ledger. The Adjustments columns provide the information for adjusting entries in the journal.

3 Step 3. Prepare Adjusted Trial Balance

Refer to Exhibit 3B.1—blue section. The adjusted trial balance is prepared by combining the adjustments with the unadjusted balances for each account. As an example, the Prepaid Insurance account has a $2,400 debit balance in the Unadjusted Trial Balance columns. This $2,400 debit is combined with the $100 credit in the Adjustments columns to give Prepaid Insurance a $2,300 debit in the Adjusted Trial Balance columns. The totals of the Adjusted Trial Balance columns confirm the equality of debits and credits.

Point: To avoid omitting the transfer of an account balance, start with the first line (Cash) and continue in account order.

4 Step 4. Sort Adjusted Trial Balance Amounts to Financial Statements

Refer to Exhibit 3B.1—orange section. This step involves sorting account balances from the adjusted trial balance to their proper financial statement columns. Expenses go to the Income Statement Debit column and revenues to the Income Statement Credit column. Assets and dividends go to the Balance Sheet Debit column. Liabilities, retained earnings, and common stock go to the Balance Sheet Credit column.

5 Step 5. Total Statement Columns, Compute Income or Loss, and Balance Columns

Refer to Exhibit 3B.1—purple section. Each financial statement column (from step 4) is totaled. The difference between the totals of the Income Statement columns is net income or net loss. This occurs because revenues are entered in the Credit column and expenses in the Debit column. If the Credit total exceeds the Debit total, there is net income. If the Debit total exceeds the Credit total, there is a net loss. For FastForward, the Credit total exceeds the Debit total, giving a $3,785 net income.

The net income from the Income Statement columns is then entered in the Balance Sheet Credit column. Adding net income to the last Credit column implies that it is to be added to retained earnings. If a loss occurs, it is added to the Debit column. This implies that it is to be subtracted from retained earnings. The ending balance of retained earnings does not appear in the last two columns as a single amount, but it is computed in the statement of retained earnings using these account balances. When net income or net loss is added to the proper Balance Sheet column, the totals of the last two columns must balance. If they do not, one or more errors have been made. The error can either be mathematical or involve sorting one or more amounts to incorrect columns.

WORK SHEET APPLICATIONS AND ANALYSIS

A work sheet does not substitute for financial statements. It is a tool we can use at the end of an accounting period to help organize data and prepare financial statements. FastForward's financial statements are shown in Exhibit 3.14. Its income statement amounts are taken from the Income Statement columns of the work sheet. Similarly, amounts for its balance sheet and its statement of retained earnings are taken from the Balance Sheet columns of the work sheet.

Information from the Adjustments columns of a work sheet can be used to journalize adjusting entries. It is important to remember that a work sheet is not a journal. This means that even when a work sheet is prepared, it is necessary to both journalize adjustments and post them to the ledger.

EXHIBIT 3B.1

Work Sheet with Five-Step Process for Completion

FastForward
Work Sheet
For Month Ended December 31, 2015

No.	Account	Unadjusted Trial Balance Dr.	Unadjusted Trial Balance Cr.	Adjustments Dr.	Adjustments Cr.	Adjusted Trial Balance Dr.	Adjusted Trial Balance Cr.	Income Statement Dr.	Income Statement Cr.	Balance Sheet Dr.	Balance Sheet Cr.
101	Cash	4,275				4,275				4,275	
106	Accounts receivable	0		(f)1,800		1,800				1,800	
126	Supplies	9,720			(b)1,050	8,670				8,670	
128	Prepaid insurance	2,400			(a) 100	2,300				2,300	
167	Equipment	26,000				26,000				26,000	
168	Accumulated depreciation—Equip.				(c) 300		300				300
201	Accounts payable		6,200				6,200				6,200
209	Salaries payable				(e) 210		210				210
236	Unearned consulting revenue		3,000	(d) 250			2,750				2,750
307	Common stock		30,000				30,000				30,000
318	Retained earnings		0				0				0
319	Dividends	200				200				200	
403	Consulting revenue		5,800		(d) 250		7,850		7,850		
					(f)1,800						
406	Rental revenue		300				300		300		
612	Depreciation expense—Equip.			(c) 300		300		300			
622	Salaries expense	1,400		(e) 210		1,610		1,610			
637	Insurance expense			(a) 100		100		100			
640	Rent expense	1,000				1,000		1,000			
652	Supplies expense			(b)1,050		1,050		1,050			
690	Utilities expense	305				305		305			
	Totals	45,300	45,300	3,785	3,785	47,685	47,685	4,365	8,150	43,320	39,535
	Net income							3,785			3,785
	Totals							8,150	8,150	43,320	43,320

- (1a) List all accounts from the ledger; include those accounts (shaded in dark green) necessary to make accounting adjustments.
- (1b) Enter all amounts available from ledger accounts. Column totals must be equal.
- (2) Enter adjustment amounts and use letters to cross-reference debit and credit adjustments. Column totals must be equal.
- (3) Combine unadjusted trial balance amounts with the adjustments to get the adjusted trial balance amounts. Column totals must be equal.
- (4a) Extend all revenue and expense amounts to the income statement columns.
- (4b) Extend all asset, liability, equity, and dividends amounts to these columns.
- (5a) Enter two new lines for the (1) net income or loss (2) totals.
- (5b) First "Totals" row for income statement columns differ by the amount of net income or net loss.
- (5c) Net income (loss) is extended to the credit (debit) column.

APPENDIX

Reversing Entries 3C

P8 Prepare reversing entries and explain their purpose.

Reversing entries are optional. They are recorded in response to accrued assets and accrued liabilities that were created by adjusting entries at the end of a reporting period. The purpose of reversing entries is to simplify a company's recordkeeping. Exhibit 3C.1 shows an example of FastForward's reversing entries. The top of the exhibit shows the adjusting entry FastForward recorded on December 31 for its

Point: As a general rule, adjusting entries that create new asset or liability accounts are likely candidates for reversing.

employee's earned but unpaid salary. The entry recorded three days' salary of $210, which increased December's total salary expense to $1,610. The entry also recognized a liability of $210. The expense is reported on December's income statement. The expense account is then closed. The ledger on January 1, 2016, shows a $210 liability and a zero balance in the Salaries Expense account. At this point, the choice is made between using or not using reversing entries.

Accounting *without* Reversing Entries The path down the left side of Exhibit 3C.1 is described in the chapter. To summarize here, when the next payday occurs on January 9, we record payment with a compound entry that debits both the expense and liability accounts and credits Cash. Posting that entry creates a $490 balance in the expense account and reduces the liability account balance to zero

EXHIBIT 3C.1

Reversing Entries for an Accrued Expense

Accrue salaries expense on December 31, 2015

Salaries Expense 210
    Salaries Payable 210

Salaries Expense

Date	Expl.	Debit	Credit	Balance
2015				
Dec. 12	(7)	700		700
26	(16)	700		1,400
31	*(e)*	210		1,610

Salaries Payable

Date	Expl.	Debit	Credit	Balance
2015				
Dec. 31	*(e)*		210	210

WITHOUT Reversing Entries — OR — **WITH Reversing Entries**

WITHOUT Reversing Entries

No reversing entry recorded on January 1, 2016

NO ENTRY

Salaries Expense

Date	Expl.	Debit	Credit	Balance
2016				

Salaries Payable

Date	Expl.	Debit	Credit	Balance
2015				
Dec. 31	*(e)*		210	210
2016				

WITH Reversing Entries

Reversing entry recorded on January 1, 2016

Salaries Payable 210
    Salaries Expense 210

Salaries Expense*

Date	Expl.	Debit	Credit	Balance
2016				
Jan. 1			210	(210)

Salaries Payable

Date	Expl.	Debit	Credit	Balance
2015				
Dec. 31	*(e)*		210	210
2016				
Jan. 1		210		0

Pay the accrued and current salaries on January 9, the first payday in 2016

WITHOUT Reversing Entries

Salaries Expense 490
Salaries Payable 210
    Cash 700

Salaries Expense

Date	Expl.	Debit	Credit	Balance
2016				
Jan. 9		490		**490**

Salaries Payable

Date	Expl.	Debit	Credit	Balance
2015				
Dec. 31	*(e)*		210	210
2016				
Jan. 9		210		**0**

WITH Reversing Entries

Salaries Expense 700
    Cash 700

Salaries Expense*

Date	Expl.	Debit	Credit	Balance
2016				
Jan. 1			210	(210)
Jan. 9		700		**490**

Salaries Payable

Date	Expl.	Debit	Credit	Balance
2015				
Dec. 31	*(e)*		210	210
2016				
Jan. 1		210		**0**

Under both approaches, the expense and liability accounts have identical balances after the cash payment on January 9.

Salaries Expense $490
Salaries Payable .... $ 0

*Circled numbers in the *Balance* column indicate abnormal balances.

because the debt has been settled. The disadvantage of this approach is the slightly more complex entry required on January 9. Paying the accrued liability means that this entry differs from the routine entries made on all other paydays. To construct the proper entry on January 9, we must recall the effect of the December 31 adjusting entry. Reversing entries overcome this disadvantage.

Point: Firms that use reversing entries hope that this simplification will reduce errors.

Accounting *with* Reversing Entries The right side of Exhibit 3C.1 shows how a reversing entry on January 1 overcomes the disadvantage of the January 9 entry when not using reversing entries. A reversing entry is the exact opposite of an adjusting entry. For FastForward, the Salaries Payable liability account is debited for $210, meaning that this account now has a zero balance after the entry is posted. The Salaries Payable account temporarily understates the liability, but this is not a problem since financial statements are not prepared before the liability is settled on January 9. The credit to the Salaries Expense account is unusual because it gives the account an *abnormal credit balance.* We highlight an abnormal balance by circling it. Because of the reversing entry, the January 9 entry to record payment is straightforward. This entry debits the Salaries Expense account and credits Cash for the full $700 paid. It is the same as all other entries made to record 10 days' salary for the employee. Notice that after the payment entry is posted, the Salaries Expense account has a $490 balance that reflects seven days' salary of $70 per day (see the lower right side of Exhibit 3C.1). The zero balance in the Salaries Payable account is now correct. The lower section of Exhibit 3C.1 shows that the expense and liability accounts have exactly the same balances whether reversing entries are used or not. This means that both approaches yield identical results.

Summary

C1 Explain the importance of periodic reporting and the time period assumption. The value of information is often linked to its timeliness. To provide timely information, accounting systems prepare periodic reports at regular intervals. The time period assumption presumes that an organization's activities can be divided into specific time periods for periodic reporting. Accrual accounting recognizes revenue when earned and expenses when incurred—not necessarily when cash inflows and outflows occur.

C2 Identify steps in the accounting cycle. The accounting cycle consists of 10 steps: (1) analyze transactions, (2) journalize, (3) post, (4) prepare an unadjusted trial balance, (5) adjust accounts, (6) prepare an adjusted trial balance, (7) prepare statements, (8) close, (9) prepare a post-closing trial balance, and (10) prepare (optional) reversing entries.

C3 Explain and prepare a classified balance sheet. Classified balance sheets report assets and liabilities in two categories: current and noncurrent. Noncurrent assets often include long-term investments, plant assets, and intangible assets. A corporation separates equity into common stock and retained earnings.

A1 Compute profit margin and describe its use in analyzing company performance. *Profit margin* is defined as the reporting period's net income divided by its net sales. Profit margin reflects on a company's earnings activities by showing how much income is in each dollar of sales.

A2 Compute the current ratio and describe what it reveals about a company's financial condition. A company's current ratio is defined as current assets divided by current liabilities. We use it to evaluate a company's ability to pay its current liabilities out of current assets.

P1 Prepare and explain adjusting entries. Accounting adjustments bring an asset or liability account balance to its correct amount. They also update related expense or revenue accounts. *Prepaid expenses* refer to items paid for in advance of receiving their benefits. Prepaid expenses are assets. Adjusting entries for prepaids involve increasing (debiting) expenses and decreasing (crediting) assets. *Unearned* (or *prepaid*) *revenues* refer to cash received in advance of providing products and services. Unearned revenues are liabilities. Adjusting entries for unearned revenues involve increasing (crediting) revenues and decreasing (debiting) unearned revenues. *Accrued expenses* refer to costs incurred in a period that are both unpaid and unrecorded. Adjusting entries for recording accrued expenses involve increasing (debiting) expenses and increasing (crediting) liabilities. *Accrued revenues* refer to revenues earned in a period that are both unrecorded and not yet received in cash. Adjusting entries for recording accrued revenues involve increasing (debiting) assets and increasing (crediting) revenues.

P2 Explain and prepare an adjusted trial balance. An adjusted trial balance is a list of accounts and balances prepared after recording and posting adjusting entries. Financial statements are often prepared from the adjusted trial balance.

P3 Prepare financial statements from an adjusted trial balance. Revenue and expense balances are reported on the income statement. Asset, liability, and equity balances are reported on the balance sheet. We usually prepare statements in the following order: income statement, statement of retained earnings, balance sheet, and statement of cash flows.

P4 Describe and prepare closing entries. Closing entries involve four steps: (1) close credit balances in revenue (and gain) accounts to Income Summary, (2) close debit balances in expense (and loss) accounts to Income Summary, (3) close Income Summary to the Retained Earnings account, and (4) close the Dividends account to Retained Earnings.

P5 Explain and prepare a post-closing trial balance. A post-closing trial balance is a list of permanent accounts and their balances after all closing entries have been journalized and posted. Its purpose is to verify that (1) total debits equal total credits for permanent accounts and (2) all temporary accounts have zero balances.

P6A Explain the alternatives in accounting for prepaids. Charging all prepaid expenses to expense accounts when they are purchased is acceptable. When this is done, adjusting entries must transfer any unexpired amounts from expense accounts to asset accounts. Crediting all unearned revenues to revenue accounts when cash is received is also acceptable. In this case, the adjusting entries must transfer any unearned amounts from revenue accounts to unearned revenue accounts.

P7B Prepare a work sheet and explain its usefulness. A work sheet can be a useful tool in preparing and analyzing financial statements. It is helpful at the end of a period in preparing adjusting entries, an adjusted trial balance, and financial statements. A work sheet usually contains five pairs of columns: Unadjusted Trial Balance, Adjustments, Adjusted Trial Balance, Income Statement, and Balance Sheet.

P8C Prepare reversing entries and explain their purpose. Reversing entries are an optional step. They are applied to accrued expenses and revenues. The purpose of reversing entries is to simplify subsequent journal entries. Financial statements are unaffected by the choice to use or not use reversing entries.

Guidance Answers to Decision Maker and Decision Ethics

Investor Prepaid expenses are items paid for in advance of receiving their benefits. They are assets and are expensed as they are used up. The publishing company's treatment of the signing bonus is acceptable provided future book sales can at least match the $500,000 expense. As an investor, you are concerned about the risk of future book sales. The riskier the likelihood of future book sales is, the more likely your analysis is to treat the $500,000, or a portion of it, as an expense, not a prepaid expense (asset).

Loan Officer Your concern in lending to this store arises from analysis of current-year sales. While increased revenues and income are fine, your concern is with collectibility of these promotional sales. If the owner sold products to customers with poor records of paying bills, then collectibility of these sales is low. Your analysis must assess this possibility and recognize any expected losses.

Financial Officer Omitting accrued expenses and recognizing revenue early can mislead financial statement users. One action is to request a second meeting with the president so you can explain that accruing expenses when incurred and recognizing revenue when earned are required practices. If the president persists, you might discuss the situation with legal counsel and any auditors involved. Your ethical action might cost you this job, but the potential pitfalls for falsification of statements, reputation and personal integrity loss, and other costs are too great.

Analyst A current ratio of 1.2 suggests that current assets are sufficient to cover current liabilities, but it implies a minimal buffer in case of errors in measuring current assets or current liabilities. Removing the past due receivable reduces the current ratio to 0.7. Your assessment is that the company will have some difficulty meeting its loan payments.

Key Terms

Accounting cycle
Accounting periods
Accrual basis accounting
Accrued expenses
Accrued revenues
Adjusted trial balance
Adjusting entry
Annual financial statements
Book value
Cash basis accounting
Classified balance sheet
Closing entries
Closing process
Contra account
Current assets
Current liabilities
Current ratio
Depreciation
Expense recognition (or matching) **principle**
Fiscal year
Income Summary
Intangible assets
Interim financial statements
Long-term investments
Long-term liabilities
Natural business year
Operating cycle
Permanent accounts
Plant assets
Post-closing trial balance
Prepaid expenses
Profit margin
Reversing entries
Straight-line depreciation method
Temporary accounts
Time period assumption
Unadjusted trial balance
Unclassified balance sheet
Unearned revenues
Work sheet
Working papers

Multiple Choice Quiz

Answers at end of chapter

1. A company forgot to record accrued and unpaid employee wages of $350,000 at period-end. This oversight would

a. Understate net income by $350,000.
b. Overstate net income by $350,000.
c. Have no effect on net income.
d. Overstate assets by $350,000.
e. Understate assets by $350,000.

2. Prior to recording adjusting entries, the Supplies account has a $450 debit balance. A physical count of supplies shows $125 of unused supplies still available. The required adjusting entry is:

a. Debit Supplies $125; Credit Supplies Expense $125.
b. Debit Supplies $325; Credit Supplies Expense $325.
c. Debit Supplies Expense $325; Credit Supplies $325.
d. Debit Supplies Expense $325; Credit Supplies $125.
e. Debit Supplies Expense $125; Credit Supplies $125.

3. On May 1, 2015, a two-year insurance policy was purchased for $24,000 with coverage to begin immediately. What is the amount of insurance expense that appears on the company's income statement for the year ended December 31, 2015?

a. $4,000 **b.** $8,000 **c.** $12,000 **d.** $20,000 **e.** $24,000

4. On November 1, 2015, Stockton Co. receives $3,600 cash from Hans Co. for consulting services to be provided evenly over the period November 1, 2015, to April 30, 2016—at which time Stockton credited $3,600 to Unearned Consulting Fees. The adjusting entry on December 31, 2015 (Stockton's year-end) would include a

a. Debit to Unearned Consulting Fees for $1,200.
b. Debit to Unearned Consulting Fees for $2,400.
c. Credit to Consulting Fees Earned for $2,400.
d. Debit to Consulting Fees Earned for $1,200.
e. Credit to Cash for $3,600.

5. If a company had $15,000 in net income for the year, and its sales were $300,000 for the same year, what is its profit margin?

a. 20% **b.** 2,000% **c.** $285,000 **d.** $315,000 **e.** 5%

6. Based on the following information from Repicor Company's balance sheet, what is Repicor Company's current ratio?

Current assets . . .	$ 75,000	Current liabilities	$ 50,000
Investments	30,000	Long-term liabilities . . .	60,000
Plant assets	300,000	Common stock	295,000

a. 2.10 **b.** 1.50 **c.** 1.00 **d.** 0.95 **e.** 0.67

A(B, C) *Superscript letter A(B, C) denotes assignments based on Appendix 3A (3B, 3C).*
Icon denotes assignments that involve decision making.

Discussion Questions

1. What is the difference between the cash basis and the accrual basis of accounting?

2. Why is the accrual basis of accounting generally preferred over the cash basis?

3. What type of business is most likely to select a fiscal year that corresponds to its natural business year instead of the calendar year?

4. What is a prepaid expense and where is it reported in the financial statements?

5. What type of assets requires adjusting entries to record depreciation?

6. What contra account is used when recording and reporting the effects of depreciation? Why is it used?

7. Assume **Samsung** has unearned revenue. What is unearned revenue and where is it reported in financial statements?

8. What is an accrued revenue? Give an example.

9.[A] If a company initially records prepaid expenses with debits to expense accounts, what type of account is debited in the adjusting entries for those prepaid expenses?

10. Review the balance sheet of **Apple** in Appendix A. Identify one asset account that requires adjustment before annual financial statements can be prepared. What would be the effect on the income statement if this asset account were not adjusted? (Number not required, but comment on over- or understating of net income.)

11. Review the balance sheet of **Google** in Appendix A. Identify the amount for property and equipment. What adjusting entry is necessary (no numbers required) for this account when preparing financial statements?

12. Refer to **Samsung**'s balance sheet in Appendix A. If it made an adjustment for unpaid wages at year-end, where would the accrued wages be reported on its balance sheet?

13. What are the steps in recording closing entries?

14. What accounts are affected by closing entries? What accounts are not affected?

15. What two purposes are accomplished by recording closing entries?

16. What is the purpose of the Income Summary account?

17. Explain whether an error has occurred if a post-closing trial balance includes a Depreciation Expense account.

18. What tasks are aided by a work sheet?

19. Why are the debit and credit entries in the Adjustments columns of the work sheet identified with letters?

20. What is a company's operating cycle?

21. What classes of assets and liabilities are shown on a typical classified balance sheet?

22. How is unearned revenue classified on the balance sheet?

23. What are the characteristics of plant assets?

24.[C] How do reversing entries simplify recordkeeping?

25.[C] If a company recorded accrued salaries expense of $500 at the end of its fiscal year, what reversing entry could be made? When would it be made?

26. Refer to the most recent balance sheet for **Apple** in Appendix A. What five main noncurrent asset categories are used on its classified balance sheet? **APPLE**

27. Refer to **Samsung**'s most recent balance sheet in Appendix A. Identify and list its nine current assets. **Samsung**

28. Refer to **Google**'s most recent balance sheet in Appendix A. Identify the eight accounts listed as current liabilities. **GOOGLE**

29. Refer to **Samsung**'s financial statements in Appendix A. What journal entry was likely recorded as of December 31, 2013, to close its Income Summary account? **Samsung**

connect

QUICK STUDY

QS 3-1
Periodic reporting
C1

Choose from the following list of terms/phrases to best complete the statements below.

a. Fiscal year	**d.** Accounting period	**g.** Natural business year
b. Timeliness	**e.** Annual financial statements	**h.** Time period assumption
c. Calendar year	**f.** Interim financial statements	**i.** Quarterly statements

1. ______ presumes that an organization's activities can be divided into specific time periods.
2. Financial reports covering a one-year period are known as ______.
3. A ______ consists of any 12 consecutive months.
4. A ______ consists of 12 consecutive months ending on December 31.
5. The value of information is often linked to its ______.

QS 3-2
Computing accrual and cash income C1

In its first year of operations, Roma Co. earned $45,000 in revenues and received $37,000 cash from these customers. The company incurred expenses of $25,500 but had not paid $5,250 of them at year-end. The company also prepaid $6,750 cash for costs that will not be expensed until the next year. Calculate the first year's net income under both the cash basis and the accrual basis of accounting.

QS 3-3
Identifying accounting adjustments
P1

Classify the following adjusting entries as involving prepaid expenses (PE), unearned revenues (UR), accrued expenses (AE), or accrued revenues (AR).

______ **a.** To record revenue earned that was previously received as cash in advance.
______ **b.** To record wages expense incurred but not yet paid (nor recorded).
______ **c.** To record revenue earned but not yet billed (nor recorded).
______ **d.** To record expiration of prepaid insurance.
______ **e.** To record annual depreciation expense.

QS 3-4
Concepts of adjusting entries P1

During the year, a company recorded prepayments of expenses in asset accounts, and cash receipts of unearned revenues in liability accounts. At the end of its annual accounting period, the company must make three adjusting entries: (1) accrue salaries expense, (2) adjust the Unearned Services Revenue account to recognize earned revenue, and (3) record services revenue earned for which cash will be received the following period. For each of these adjusting entries (1), (2), and (3), indicate the account from *a* through *i* to be debited and the account to be credited.

a. Prepaid Salaries	**d.** Unearned Services Revenue	**g.** Accounts Receivable
b. Cash	**e.** Salaries Expense	**h.** Accounts Payable
c. Salaries Payable	**f.** Services Revenue	**i.** Equipment

QS 3-5
Prepaid (deferred) expenses adjustments
P1

For each separate case below, follow the 3-step process for adjusting the prepaid asset account at December 31. Step 1: Determine what the current account balance equals. Step 2: Determine what the current account balance should equal. Step 3: Record the December 31 adjusting entry to get from step 1 to step 2. *Assume no other adjusting entries are made during the year.*

a. Prepaid Insurance. The Prepaid Insurance account has a $4,700 debit balance to start the year. A review of insurance policies and payments shows that $900 of unexpired insurance remains at year-end.

b. Prepaid Insurance. The Prepaid Insurance account has a $5,890 debit balance at the start of the year. A review of insurance policies and payments shows $1,040 of insurance has expired by year-end.

c. Prepaid Rent. On September 1 of the current year, the company prepaid $24,000 for 2 years of rent for facilities being occupied that day. The company debited Prepaid Rent and credited Cash for $24,000.

QS 3-6
Prepaid (deferred) expenses adjustments
P1

For each separate case below, follow the 3-step process for adjusting the supplies asset account at December 31. Step 1: Determine what the current account balance equals. Step 2: Determine what the current account balance should equal. Step 3: Record the December 31 adjusting entry to get from step 1 to step 2. *Assume no other adjusting entries are made during the year.*

a. Supplies. The Supplies account has a $300 debit balance to start the year. No supplies were purchased during the current year. A December 31 physical count shows $110 of supplies remaining.

b. Supplies. The Supplies account has an $800 debit balance to start the year. Supplies of $2,100 were purchased during the current year and debited to the Supplies account. A December 31 physical count shows $650 of supplies remaining.

c. Supplies. The Supplies account has a $4,000 debit balance to start the year. During the current year, supplies of $9,400 were purchased and debited to the Supplies account. The inventory of supplies available at December 31 totaled $2,660.

QS 3-7
Adjusting prepaid expenses
P1

a. On July 1, 2015, Lopez Company paid $1,200 for six months of insurance coverage. No adjustments have been made to the Prepaid Insurance account, and it is now December 31, 2015. Prepare the journal entry to reflect expiration of the insurance as of December 31, 2015.

b. Zim Company has a Supplies account balance of $5,000 on January 1, 2015. During 2015, it purchased $2,000 of supplies. As of December 31, 2015, a supplies inventory shows $800 of supplies available. Prepare the adjusting journal entry to correctly report the balance of the Supplies account and the Supplies Expense account as of December 31, 2015.

QS 3-8
Accumulated depreciation adjustments
P1

For each separate case below, follow the 3-step process for adjusting the accumulated depreciation account at December 31. Step 1: Determine what the current account balance equals. Step 2: Determine what the current account balance should equal. Step 3: Record the December 31 adjusting entry to get from step 1 to step 2. *Assume no other adjusting entries are made during the year.*

a. Accumulated Depreciation. The Krug Company's Accumulated Depreciation account has a $13,500 balance to start the year. A review of depreciation schedules reveals that $14,600 of depreciation expense must be recorded for the year.

b. Accumulated Depreciation. The company has only one fixed asset (truck) that it purchased at the start of this year. That asset had cost $44,000, had an estimated life of five years, and is expected to have zero value at the end of the five years.

c. Accumulated Depreciation. The company has only one fixed asset (equipment) that it purchased at the start of this year. That asset had cost $32,000, had an estimated life of seven years, and is expected to be valued at $4,000 at the end of the seven years.

QS 3-9
Adjusting for depreciation
P1

a. Barga Company purchases $20,000 of equipment on January 1, 2015. The equipment is expected to last five years and be worth $2,000 at the end of that time. Prepare the entry to record one year's depreciation expense of $3,600 for the equipment as of December 31, 2015.

b. Welch Company purchases $10,000 of land on January 1, 2015. The land is expected to last indefinitely. What depreciation adjustment, if any, should be made with respect to the Land account as of December 31, 2015?

QS 3-10
Unearned (deferred) revenues adjustments
P1

For each separate case below, follow the 3-step process for adjusting the unearned revenue liability account at December 31. Step 1: Determine what the current account balance equals. Step 2: Determine what the current account balance should equal. Step 3: Record the December 31 adjusting entry to get from step 1 to step 2. *Assume no other adjusting entries are made during the year.*

a. Unearned Rent Revenue. The Krug Company collected $6,000 rent in advance on November 1, debiting Cash and crediting Unearned Rent Revenue. The tenant was paying 12 months' rent in advance and occupancy began November 1.

b. Unearned Services Revenue. The company charges $75 per month to spray a house for insects. A customer paid $300 on October 1 in advance for four treatments, which was recorded with a debit to Cash and a credit to Unearned Services Revenue. At year-end, the company has applied three treatments for the customer.

c. Unearned Rent Revenue. On September 1, a client paid the company $24,000 cash for six months of rent in advance (the client leased a building and took occupancy immediately). The company recorded the cash as Unearned Rent Revenue.

QS 3-11
Adjusting for unearned revenues
P1

a. Tao Co. receives $10,000 cash in advance for 4 months of legal services on October 1, 2015, and records it by debiting Cash and crediting Unearned Revenue both for $10,000. It is now December 31, 2015, and Tao has provided legal services as planned. What adjusting entry should Tao make to account for the work performed from October 1 through December 31, 2015?

b. A. Caden started a new publication called *Contest News*. Its subscribers pay $24 to receive 12 monthly issues. With every new subscriber, Caden debits Cash and credits Unearned Subscription Revenue for the amounts received. The company has 100 new subscribers as of July 1, 2015. It sends *Contest News* to each of these subscribers every month from July through December. Assuming no changes in subscribers, prepare the journal entry that Caden must make as of December 31, 2015, to adjust the Subscription Revenue account and the Unearned Subscription Revenue account.

QS 3-12
Accrued expenses adjustments
P1

For each separate case below, follow the 3-step process for adjusting the accrued expense account at December 31. Step 1: Determine what the current account balance equals. Step 2: Determine what the current account balance should equal. Step 3: Record the December 31 adjusting entry to get from step 1 to step 2. *Assume no other adjusting entries are made during the year.*

a. Salaries Payable. At year-end, salaries expense of $15,500 has been incurred by the company, but is not yet paid to employees.

b. Interest Payable. At its December 31 year-end, the company owes $250 of interest on a line-of-credit loan. That interest will not be paid until sometime in January of the next year.

c. Interest Payable. At its December 31 year-end, the company holds a mortgage payable that has incurred $875 in annual interest that is neither recorded nor paid. The company intends to pay the interest on January 7 of the next year.

QS 3-13
Accruing salaries
P1

Molly Mocha employs one college student every summer in her coffee shop. The student works the five weekdays and is paid on the following Monday. (For example, a student who works Monday through Friday, June 1 through June 5, is paid for that work on Monday, June 8.) The coffee shop adjusts its books *monthly,* if needed, to show salaries earned but unpaid at month-end. The student works the last week of July—Friday is August 1. If the student earns $100 per day, what adjusting entry must the coffee shop make on July 31 to correctly record accrued salaries expense for July?

QS 3-14
Accrued revenues adjustments
P1

For each separate case below, follow the 3-step process for adjusting the accrued revenue account at December 31. Step 1: Determine what the current account balance equals. Step 2: Determine what the current account balance should equal. Step 3: Record the December 31 adjusting entry to get from step 1 to step 2. *Assume no other adjusting entries are made during the year.*

a. Accounts Receivable. At year-end, the Krug Company has completed services of $19,000 for a client, but the client has not yet been billed for those services.

b. Interest Receivable. At year-end, the company has earned, but not yet recorded, $390 of interest earned from its investments in government bonds.

c. Accounts Receivable. A painting company collects fees when jobs are complete. The work for one customer, whose job was bid at $1,300, has been completed, but the customer has not yet been billed.

QS 3-15
Recording and analyzing adjusting entries
P1

Adjusting entries affect at least one balance sheet account and at least one income statement account. For the following entries, identify the account to be debited and the account to be credited. Indicate which of the accounts is the income statement account and which is the balance sheet account.

a. Entry to record revenue earned that was previously received as cash in advance.
b. Entry to record wage expenses incurred but not yet paid (nor recorded).
c. Entry to record revenue earned but not yet billed (nor recorded).
d. Entry to record expiration of prepaid insurance.
e. Entry to record annual depreciation expense.

QS 3-16
Determining effects of adjusting entries
P1

In making adjusting entries at the end of its accounting period, Chao Consulting failed to record $3,200 of insurance coverage that had expired. This $3,200 cost had been initially debited to the Prepaid Insurance account. The company also failed to record accrued salaries expense of $2,000. As a result of these two oversights, the financial statements for the reporting period will [choose one] (1) understate assets by $3,200; (2) understate expenses by $5,200; (3) understate net income by $2,000; or (4) overstate liabilities by $2,000.

QS 3-17
Interpreting adjusting entries
P2

The following information is taken from Camara Company's unadjusted and adjusted trial balances.

	Unadjusted		Adjusted	
	Debit	Credit	Debit	Credit
Prepaid insurance.........	$4,100		$3,700	
Interest payable		$ 0		$800

Given this information, which of the following is likely included among its adjusting entries?

a. A $400 debit to Insurance Expense and an $800 debit to Interest Payable.
b. A $400 debit to Insurance Expense and an $800 debit to Interest Expense.
c. A $400 credit to Prepaid Insurance and an $800 debit to Interest Payable.

QS 3-18
International accounting standards
P3

Answer each of the following questions related to international accounting standards.

a. Do financial statements prepared under IFRS normally present assets from least liquid to most liquid or vice versa?
b. Do financial statements prepared under IFRS normally present liabilities from furthest from maturity to nearest to maturity or vice versa?

QS 3-19
Analyzing profit margin
A1

Damita Company reported net income of $48,025 and net sales of $425,000 for the current year. Calculate the company's profit margin and interpret the result. Assume that its competitors earn an average profit margin of 15%.

QS 3-20^A
Preparing adjusting entries
P6

Cal Consulting initially records prepaid and unearned items in income statement accounts. Given this company's accounting practices, which of the following applies to the preparation of adjusting entries at the end of its first accounting period?

a. Unearned fees (on which cash was received in advance earlier in the period) are recorded with a debit to Consulting Fees Earned of $500 and a credit to Unearned Consulting Fees of $500.
b. Unpaid salaries of $400 are recorded with a debit to Prepaid Salaries of $400 and a credit to Salaries Expense of $400.
c. Office supplies purchased for the period were $1,000. The cost of unused office supplies of $650 is recorded with a debit to Supplies Expense of $650 and a credit to Office Supplies of $650.
d. Earned but unbilled (and unrecorded) consulting fees for the period were $1,200, which are recorded with a debit to Unearned Consulting Fees of $1,200 and a credit to Consulting Fees Earned of $1,200.

QS 3-21
Prepare closing entries from the ledger P4

The ledger of Mai Company includes the following accounts with normal balances: Common Stock $9,000; Dividends $800; Services Revenue $13,000; Wages Expense $8,400; and Rent Expense $1,600. Prepare the necessary closing entries from the available information at December 31.

QS 3-22
Identify post-closing accounts P5

Identify which of the following accounts would be included in a post-closing trial balance.

_____ **a.** Accounts Receivable
_____ **b.** Salaries Expense
_____ **c.** Goodwill
_____ **d.** Land
_____ **e.** Income Tax Expense
_____ **f.** Salaries Payable

QS 3-23
Identifying the accounting cycle C2

List the following steps of the accounting cycle in their proper order.

_____ **a.** Posting the journal entries.
_____ **b.** Journalizing and posting adjusting entries.
_____ **c.** Preparing the adjusted trial balance.
_____ **d.** Journalizing and posting closing entries.
_____ **e.** Analyzing transactions and events.
_____ **f.** Preparing the financial statements.
_____ **g.** Preparing the unadjusted trial balance.
_____ **h.** Journalizing transactions and events.
_____ **i.** Preparing the post-closing trial balance.

QS 3-24
Classifying balance sheet items C3

The following are common categories on a classified balance sheet.

A. Current assets
B. Long-term investments
C. Plant assets
D. Intangible assets
E. Current liabilities
F. Long-term liabilities

For each of the following items, select the letter that identifies the balance sheet category where the item typically would best appear.

_____ **1.** Land not currently used in operations
_____ **2.** Notes payable (due in five years)
_____ **3.** Accounts receivable
_____ **4.** Trademarks
_____ **5.** Accounts payable
_____ **6.** Store equipment
_____ **7.** Wages payable
_____ **8.** Cash

QS 3-25
Identifying current accounts and computing the current ratio A2

Compute Chavez Company's current ratio using the following information.

Accounts receivable	$18,000	Long-term notes payable	$21,000
Accounts payable	11,000	Office supplies	2,800
Buildings	45,000	Prepaid insurance	3,560
Cash	7,000	Unearned services revenue	3,000

QS 3-26[B]
Extending accounts in a work sheet P7
Check Net income, $17,800

The Adjusted Trial Balance columns of a 10-column work sheet for Planta Company follow. Complete the work sheet by extending the account balances into the appropriate financial statement columns and by entering the amount of net income for the reporting period.

	A	B	C	D	E	F	G	H	I	J	K	L
1			Unadjusted				Adjusted		Income			
2			Trial Balance		Adjustments		Trial Balance		Statement		Balance Sheet	
3	No.	Account Title	Dr.	Cr.	Dr.	Cr.	Dr.	Cr.	Dr.	Cr.	Dr.	Cr.
4	101	Cash					$ 7,000					
5	106	Accounts receivable					27,200					
6	153	Trucks					42,000					
7	154	Accumulated depreciation—Trucks						$ 17,500				
8	183	Land					32,000					
9	201	Accounts payable						15,000				
10	209	Salaries payable						4,200				
11	233	Unearned fees						3,600				
12	307	Common stock						20,000				
13	318	Retained earnings						45,500				
14	319	Dividends					15,400					
15	401	Plumbing fees earned						84,000				
16	611	Depreciation expense—Trucks					6,500					
17	622	Salaries expense					38,000					
18	640	Rent expense					13,000					
19	677	Miscellaneous expenses					8,700					
20		Totals					$189,800	$189,800				
21												

QS 3-27^C
Reversing entries
P8

On December 31, 2014, Yates Co. prepared an adjusting entry for $12,000 of earned but unrecorded management fees. On January 16, 2015, Yates received $26,700 cash in management fees, which included the accrued fees earned in 2014. Assuming the company uses reversing entries, prepare the January 1, 2015, reversing entry and the January 16, 2015, cash receipt entry.

connect

EXERCISES

Exercise 3-1
Adjusting and paying accrued wages
P1

Pablo Management has five part-time employees, each of whom earns $250 per day. They are normally paid on Fridays for work completed Monday through Friday of the same week. Assume that December 28, 2015, was a Friday, and that they were paid in full on that day. The next week, the five employees worked only four days because New Year's Day was an unpaid holiday. (*a*) Assuming that December 31, 2015, was a Monday, prepare the adjusting entry that would be recorded at the close of that day. (*b*) Assuming that January 4, 2016, was a Friday, prepare the journal entry that would be made to record payment of the employees' wages.

Exercise 3-2
Adjusting and paying accrued expenses
P1

The following three separate situations require adjusting journal entries to prepare financial statements as of April 30. For each situation, present both the April 30 adjusting entry and the subsequent entry during May to record the payment of the accrued expenses.

a. On April 1, the company retained an attorney for a flat monthly fee of $3,500. Payment for April legal services was made by the company on May 12.

b. A $900,000 note payable requires 12% annual interest, or $9,000 to be paid at the 20th day of each month. The interest was last paid on April 20 and the next payment is due on May 20. As of April 30, $3,000 of interest expense has accrued.

c. Total weekly salaries expense for all employees is $10,000. This amount is paid at the end of the day on Friday of each five-day workweek. April 30 falls on Tuesday of this year, which means that the employees had worked two days since the last payday. The next payday is May 3.

Check (*b*) May 20 Dr. Interest Expense, $6,000

Exercise 3-3
Preparing adjusting entries
P1

Prepare adjusting journal entries for the year ended (date of) December 31, 2015, for each of these separate situations. Assume that prepaid expenses are initially recorded in asset accounts. Also assume that fees collected in advance of work are initially recorded as liabilities.

a. Depreciation on the company's equipment for 2015 is computed to be $18,000.

b. The Prepaid Insurance account had a $6,000 debit balance at December 31, 2015, before adjusting for the costs of any expired coverage. An analysis of the company's insurance policies showed that $1,100 of unexpired insurance coverage remains.

c. The Office Supplies account had a $700 debit balance on December 31, 2014; and $3,480 of office supplies were purchased during the year. The December 31, 2015, physical count showed $300 of supplies available.

d. Two-thirds of the work related to $15,000 of cash received in advance was performed this period.

e. The Prepaid Insurance account had a $6,800 debit balance at December 31, 2015, before adjusting for the costs of any expired coverage. An analysis of insurance policies showed that $5,800 of coverage had expired.

f. Wage expenses of $3,200 have been incurred but are not paid as of December 31, 2015.

Check (*c*) Dr. Office Supplies Expense, $3,880; (*e*) Dr. Insurance Expense, $5,800

Exercise 3-4
Preparing adjusting entries
P1

For each of the following separate cases, prepare adjusting entries required for financial statements for the year ended (date of) December 31, 2015. (Assume that prepaid expenses are initially recorded in asset accounts and that fees collected in advance of work are initially recorded as liabilities.)

a. One-third of the work related to $15,000 cash received in advance is performed this period.

b. Wages of $8,000 are earned by workers but not paid as of December 31, 2015.

c. Depreciation on the company's equipment for 2015 is $18,000.

d. The Office Supplies account had a $240 debit balance on December 31, 2014. During 2015, $5,200 of office supplies are purchased. A physical count of supplies at December 31, 2015, shows $440 of supplies available.

e. The Prepaid Insurance account had a $4,000 balance on December 31, 2014. An analysis of insurance policies shows that $1,200 of unexpired insurance benefits remain at December 31, 2015.

f. The company has earned (but not recorded) $1,050 of interest from investments in CDs for the year ended December 31, 2015. The interest revenue will be received on January 10, 2016.

g. The company has a bank loan and has incurred (but not recorded) interest expense of $2,500 for the year ended December 31, 2015. The company must pay the interest on January 2, 2016.

Check (*e*) Dr. Insurance Expense, $2,800; (*f*) Cr. Interest Revenue, $1,050

Exercise 3-5
Analyzing and preparing adjusting entries
P1 P3

Following are two income statements for Alexis Co. for the year ended December 31. The left column is prepared before any adjusting entries are recorded, and the right column includes the effects of adjusting entries. The company records cash receipts and payments related to unearned and prepaid items in balance sheet accounts. Analyze the statements and prepare the eight adjusting entries that likely were recorded. (*Note:* 30% of the $7,000 adjustment for Fees Earned has been earned but not billed, and the other 70% has been earned by performing services that were paid for in advance.)

ALEXIS CO.
Income Statements
For Year Ended December 31

	Unadjusted	Adjusted
Revenues		
Fees earned	$18,000	$25,000
Commissions earned	36,500	36,500
Total revenues	54,500	61,500
Expenses		
Depreciation expense—Computers	0	1,600
Depreciation expense—Office furniture	0	1,850
Salaries expense	13,500	15,750
Insurance expense	0	1,400
Rent expense	3,800	3,800
Office supplies expense	0	580
Advertising expense	2,500	2,500
Utilities expense	1,245	1,335
Total expenses	21,045	28,815
Net income	$33,455	$32,685

Exercise 3-6
Preparing a balance sheet following IFRS
P3

adidas AG reports the following balance sheet accounts for the year ended December 31, 2013 (euros in millions). Prepare the balance sheet for this company as of December 31, 2013, following usual IFRS practices.

Tangible and other assets	€ 304	Intangible assets	€ 148
Total equity	2,489	Total current liabilities	794
Receivables and other assets	1,928	Inventories	29
Total noncurrent liabilities	3,411	Total liabilities	4,205
Cash and cash equivalents	736	Other current assets	73
Total current assets	2,766	Total noncurrent assets	3,928
Other noncurrent assets	3,476		

Exercise 3-7
Preparing financial statements
P3

Use the following adjusted trial balance of Wilson Trucking Company to prepare the (1) income statement and (2) statement of retained earnings for the year ended December 31, 2015. The Retained Earnings account balance is $155,000 at December 31, 2014.

Account Title	Debit	Credit
Cash	$ 8,000	
Accounts receivable	17,500	
Office supplies	3,000	
Trucks	172,000	
Accumulated depreciation—Trucks		$ 36,000
Land	85,000	
Accounts payable		12,000
Interest payable		4,000
Long-term notes payable		53,000
Common stock		20,000
Retained earnings		155,000
Dividends	20,000	
Trucking fees earned		130,000
Depreciation expense—Trucks	23,500	
Salaries expense	61,000	
Office supplies expense	8,000	
Repairs expense—Trucks	12,000	
Totals	$410,000	$410,000

Exercise 3-8
Preparing closing entries
P4

Following are **Nintendo**'s revenue and expense accounts for a recent calendar year (yen in millions). Prepare the company's closing entries for its revenues and its expenses.

Net sales	¥1,014,345
Cost of sales	626,379
Advertising expense	96,359
Other expense, net	213,986

Exercise 3-9
Preparing a classified balance sheet
C3

Use the information in the adjusted trial balance reported in Exercise 3-7 to prepare Wilson Trucking Company's classified balance sheet as of December 31, 2015.

Check Total assets, $249,500

Exercise 3-10
Computing and interpreting profit margin
A1

Use the following information to compute profit margin for each separate company *a* through *e*.

	Net Income	Net Sales		Net Income	Net Sales
a.	$ 4,361	$ 44,500	**d.**	$65,646	$1,458,800
b.	97,706	398,800	**e.**	80,132	435,500
c.	111,281	257,000			

Which of the five companies is the most profitable according to the profit margin ratio? Interpret that company's profit margin ratio.

Exercise 3-11
Computing and analyzing the current ratio
A2

Calculate the current ratio in each of the following separate cases (round the ratio to two decimals). Identify the company case with the strongest liquidity position. (These cases represent competing companies in the same industry.)

	Current Assets	Current Liabilities
Case 1	$ 79,040	$ 32,000
Case 2	104,880	76,000
Case 3	45,080	49,000
Case 4	85,680	81,600
Case 5	61,000	100,000

Exercise 3-12^A
Adjusting for prepaids recorded as expenses and unearned revenues recorded as revenues
P6

Ricardo Construction began operations on December 1. In setting up its accounting procedures, the company decided to debit expense accounts when it prepays its expenses and to credit revenue accounts when customers pay for services in advance. Prepare journal entries for items *a* through *d* and the adjusting entries as of its December 31 period-end for items *e* through *g*.

a. Supplies are purchased on December 1 for $2,000 cash.

b. The company prepaid its insurance premiums for $1,540 cash on December 2.

c. On December 15, the company receives an advance payment of $13,000 cash from a customer for remodeling work.

d. On December 28, the company receives $3,700 cash from another customer for remodeling work to be performed in January.

e. A physical count on December 31 indicates that the Company has $1,840 of supplies available.

f. An analysis of the insurance policies in effect on December 31 shows that $340 of insurance coverage had expired.

g. As of December 31, only one remodeling project has been worked on and completed. The $5,570 fee for this project had been received in advance and recorded as remodeling fees earned.

Check (*f*) Cr. Insurance Expense, $1,200; (*g*) Dr. Remodeling Fees Earned, $11,130

Exercise 3-13^A
Recording and reporting revenues received in advance
P6

Costanza Company experienced the following events and transactions during July.

July	1	Received $3,000 cash in advance of performing work for Vivian Solana.
	6	Received $7,500 cash in advance of performing work for Iris Haru.
	12	Completed the job for Solana.
	18	Received $8,500 cash in advance of performing work for Amina Jordan.
	27	Completed the job for Haru.
	31	None of the work for Jordan has been performed.

a. Prepare journal entries (including any adjusting entries as of the end of the month) to record these events using the procedure of initially crediting the Unearned Fees account when payment is received from a customer in advance of performing services.

b. Prepare journal entries (including any adjusting entries as of the end of the month) to record these events using the procedure of initially crediting the Fees Earned account when payment is received from a customer in advance of performing services.

c. Under each method, determine the amount of earned fees reported on the income statement for July and the amount of unearned fees reported on the balance sheet as of July 31.

Check (*c*) Fees Earned—using entries from part *b*, $10,500

Exercise 3-14^B
Completing a work sheet
P7

The following data are taken from the unadjusted trial balance of the Westcott Company at December 31, 2015. Each account carries a normal balance and the accounts are shown here.

Accounts Payable	$ 6	Prepaid Insurance	$18	Retained earnings	$32
Accounts Receivable................	12	Revenue	75	Dividends	6
Accumulated Depreciation—Equip.	15	Salaries Expense........	18	Unearned Revenue	12
Cash..............................	21	Supplies	24	Utilities Expense	12
Equipment.........................	39	Common stock	10		

1. Use the data above to prepare a work sheet. Enter the accounts in proper order and enter their balances in the correct Debit or Credit column.

2. Use the following adjustment information to complete the work sheet.

a. Depreciation on equipment, $3
b. Accrued salaries, $6
c. The $12 of unearned revenue has been earned
d. Supplies available at December 31, 2015, $15
e. Expired insurance, $15

Exercise 3-15^C
Preparing reversing entries
P8

The following two events occurred for Trey Co. on October 31, 2015, the end of its fiscal year.

a. Trey rents a building from its owner for $2,800 per month. By prearrangement, the company delayed paying October's rent until November 5. On this date, the company paid the rent for both October and November.

b. Trey rents space in a building it owns to a tenant for $850 per month. By prearrangement, the tenant delayed paying the October rent until November 8. On this date, the tenant paid the rent for both October and November.

Required

1. Prepare adjusting entries that the company must record for these events as of October 31.

2. Assuming Trey does *not* use reversing entries, prepare journal entries to record Trey's payment of rent on November 5 and the collection of the tenant's rent on November 8.

3. Assuming that the company uses reversing entries, prepare reversing entries on November 1 and the journal entries to record Trey's payment of rent on November 5 and the collection of the tenant's rent on November 8.

connect

PROBLEM SET A

Problem 3-1A
Identifying adjusting entries with explanations
P1

For each of the following entries, enter the letter of the explanation that most closely describes it in the space beside each entry. (You can use letters more than once.)

A. To record receipt of unearned revenue.
B. To record this period's earning of prior unearned revenue.
C. To record payment of an accrued expense.
D. To record receipt of an accrued revenue.
E. To record an accrued expense.
F. To record an accrued revenue.
G. To record this period's use of a prepaid expense.
H. To record payment of a prepaid expense.
I. To record this period's depreciation expense.

		Account	Debit	Credit
____	1.	Interest Expense	1,000	
		Interest Payable		1,000
____	2.	Depreciation Expense	4,000	
		Accumulated Depreciation		4,000
____	3.	Unearned Professional Fees	3,000	
		Professional Fees Earned		3,000
____	4.	Insurance Expense	4,200	
		Prepaid Insurance		4,200
____	5.	Salaries Payable	1,400	
		Cash		1,400
____	6.	Prepaid Rent	4,500	
		Cash		4,500
____	7.	Salaries Expense	6,000	
		Salaries Payable		6,000
____	8.	Interest Receivable	5,000	
		Interest Revenue		5,000
____	9.	Cash	9,000	
		Accounts Receivable (from consulting)		9,000
____	10.	Cash	7,500	
		Unearned Professional Fees		7,500
____	11.	Cash	2,000	
		Interest Receivable		2,000
____	12.	Rent Expense	2,000	
		Prepaid Rent		2,000

Problem 3-2A
Preparing adjusting and subsequent journal entries
A1 P1

Arnez Co. follows the practice of recording prepaid expenses and unearned revenues in balance sheet accounts. The company's annual accounting period ends on December 31, 2015. The following information concerns the adjusting entries to be recorded as of that date.

a. The Office Supplies account started the year with a $4,000 balance. During 2015, the company purchased supplies for $13,400, which was added to the Office Supplies account. The inventory of supplies available at December 31, 2015, totaled $2,554.

b. An analysis of the company's insurance policies provided the following facts.

Policy	Date of Purchase	Months of Coverage	Cost
A	April 1, 2013	24	$14,400
B	April 1, 2014	36	12,960
C	August 1, 2015	12	2,400

The total premium for each policy was paid in full (for all months) at the purchase date, and the Prepaid Insurance account was debited for the full cost. (Year-end adjusting entries for Prepaid Insurance were properly recorded in all prior years.)

c. The company has 15 employees, who earn a total of $1,960 in salaries each working day. They are paid each Monday for their work in the five-day workweek ending on the previous Friday. Assume that December 31, 2015, is a Tuesday, and all 15 employees worked the first two days of that week. Because New Year's Day is a paid holiday, they will be paid salaries for five full days on Monday, January 6, 2016.

d. The company purchased a building on January 1, 2015. It cost $960,000 and is expected to have a $45,000 salvage value at the end of its predicted 30-year life. Annual depreciation is $30,500.

e. Since the company is not large enough to occupy the entire building it owns, it rented space to a tenant at $3,000 per month, starting on November 1, 2015. The rent was paid on time on November 1, and the amount received was credited to the Rent Earned account. However, the tenant has not paid the December rent. The company has worked out an agreement with the tenant, who has promised to pay both December and January rent in full on January 15. The tenant has agreed not to fall behind again.

f. On November 1, the company rented space to another tenant for $2,800 per month. The tenant paid five months' rent in advance on that date. The payment was recorded with a credit to the Unearned Rent account.

Check (1*b*) Dr. Insurance Expense, $7,120 (1*d*) Dr. Depreciation Expense, $30,500

Required

1. Use the information to prepare adjusting entries as of December 31, 2015.

2. Prepare journal entries to record the first subsequent cash transaction in 2016 for parts *c* and *e*.

Problem 3-3A
Preparing adjusting entries, adjusted trial balance, and financial statements
P1 P2 P3

Wells Technical Institute (WTI), a school owned by Tristana Wells, provides training to individuals who pay tuition directly to the school. WTI also offers training to groups in off-site locations. Its unadjusted trial balance as of December 31, 2015, follows. WTI initially records prepaid expenses and unearned revenues in balance sheet accounts. Descriptions of items *a* through *h* that require adjusting entries on December 31, 2015, follow.

Additional Information Items

a. An analysis of WTI's insurance policies shows that $2,400 of coverage has expired.

b. An inventory count shows that teaching supplies costing $2,800 are available at year-end 2015.

c. Annual depreciation on the equipment is $13,200.

d. Annual depreciation on the professional library is $7,200.

e. On November 1, WTI agreed to do a special six-month course (starting immediately) for a client. The contract calls for a monthly fee of $2,500, and the client paid the first five months' fees in advance. When the cash was received, the Unearned Training Fees account was credited. The fee for the sixth month will be recorded when it is collected in 2016.

f. On October 15, WTI agreed to teach a four-month class (beginning immediately) for an individual for $3,000 tuition per month payable at the end of the class. The class started on October 15, but no payment has yet been received. (WTI's accruals are applied to the nearest half-month; for example, October recognizes one-half month accrual.)

g. WTI's two employees are paid weekly. As of the end of the year, two days' salaries have accrued at the rate of $100 per day for each employee.

h. The balance in the Prepaid Rent account represents rent for December.

	WELLS TECHNICAL INSTITUTE Unadjusted Trial Balance December 31, 2015		
2		Debit	Credit
3	Cash	$ 34,000	
4	Accounts receivable	0	
5	Teaching supplies	8,000	
6	Prepaid insurance	12,000	
7	Prepaid rent	3,000	
8	Professional library	35,000	
9	Accumulated depreciation—Professional library		$ 10,000
10	Equipment	80,000	
11	Accumulated depreciation—Equipment		15,000
12	Accounts payable		26,000
13	Salaries payable		0
14	Unearned training fees		12,500
15	Common stock		10,000
16	Retained earnings		80,000
17	Dividends	50,000	
18	Tuition fees earned		123,900
19	Training fees earned		40,000
20	Depreciation expense—Professional library	0	
21	Depreciation expense—Equipment	0	
22	Salaries expense	50,000	
23	Insurance expense	0	
24	Rent expense	33,000	
25	Teaching supplies expense	0	
26	Advertising expense	6,000	
27	Utilities expense	6,400	
28	Totals	$ 317,400	$ 317,400
29			

Required

1. Prepare T-accounts (representing the ledger) with balances from the unadjusted trial balance.
2. Prepare the necessary adjusting journal entries for items *a* through *h* and post them to the T-accounts. Assume that adjusting entries are made only at year-end.
3. Update balances in the T-accounts for the adjusting entries and prepare an adjusted trial balance.
4. Prepare Wells Technical Institute's income statement and statement of retained earnings for the year 2015 and prepare its balance sheet as of December 31, 2015.

Check (2*e*) Cr. Training Fees Earned, $5,000; (2*f*) Cr. Tuition Fees Earned, $7,500; (3) Adj. trial balance totals, $345,700; (4) Net income, $49,600

Problem 3-4A
Interpreting unadjusted and adjusted trial balances, and preparing financial statements
P1 P2 P3

A six-column table for JKL Company follows. The first two columns contain the unadjusted trial balance for the company as of July 31, 2015. The last two columns contain the adjusted trial balance as of the same date.

Required

Analysis Component

1. Analyze the differences between the unadjusted and adjusted trial balances to determine the eight adjustments that likely were made. Show the results of your analysis by inserting these adjustment amounts in the table's two middle columns. Label each adjustment with a letter *a* through *h* and provide a short description of it at the bottom of the table.

Preparation Component

2. Use the information in the adjusted trial balance to prepare the company's (*a*) income statement and its statement of retained earnings for the year ended July 31, 2015 (*Note:* Retained earnings at July 31, 2014, was $25,000, and the current-year dividends were $5,000), and (*b*) the balance sheet as of July 31, 2015.

Check (2) Net income, $4,960; Total assets, $124,960

	Unadjusted Trial Balance		Adjustments		Adjusted Trial Balance	
Cash	$ 34,000				$ 34,000	
Accounts receivable	14,000				22,000	
Office supplies	16,000				2,000	
Prepaid insurance	8,540				2,960	
Office equipment	84,000				84,000	
Accum. depreciation—Office equip.		$ 14,000				$ 20,000
Accounts payable		9,100				10,000
Interest payable		0				1,000
Salaries payable		0				7,000
Unearned consulting fees		18,000				15,000
Long-term notes payable		52,000				52,000
Common stock		15,000				15,000
Retained earnings		25,000				25,000
Dividends	5,000				5,000	
Consulting fees earned		123,240				134,240
Depreciation expense—Office equip.	0				6,000	
Salaries expense	67,000				74,000	
Interest expense	1,200				2,200	
Insurance expense	0				5,580	
Rent expense	14,500				14,500	
Office supplies expense	0				14,000	
Advertising expense	12,100				13,000	
Totals	$256,340	$256,340			$279,240	$279,240

Problem 3-5A
Preparing financial statements from the adjusted trial balance and calculating profit margin
P3 A1

The adjusted trial balance for Chiara Company as of December 31, 2015, follows.

	Debit	Credit
Cash	$ 30,000	
Accounts receivable	52,000	
Interest receivable	18,000	
Notes receivable (due in 90 days)	168,000	
Office supplies	16,000	
Automobiles	168,000	
Accumulated depreciation—Automobiles		$ 50,000
Equipment	138,000	
Accumulated depreciation—Equipment		18,000
Land	78,000	
Accounts payable		96,000
Interest payable		20,000
Salaries payable		19,000
Unearned fees		30,000
Long-term notes payable		138,000
Common stock		20,000
Retained earnings		235,800
Dividends	46,000	
Fees earned		484,000
Interest earned		24,000
Depreciation expense—Automobiles	26,000	
Depreciation expense—Equipment	18,000	
Salaries expense	188,000	
Wages expense	40,000	
Interest expense	32,000	
Office supplies expense	34,000	
Advertising expense	58,000	
Repairs expense—Automobiles	24,800	
Totals	$1,134,800	$1,134,800

Required

1. Use the information in the adjusted trial balance to prepare (*a*) the income statement for the year ended December 31, 2015; (*b*) the statement of retained earnings for the year ended December 31, 2015; and (*c*) the balance sheet as of December 31, 2015.
2. Calculate the profit margin for year 2015.

Check (1) Total assets, $600,000

Problem 3-6A
Applying the accounting cycle
P1 P2 P3 P4 P5

On April 1, 2015, Jiro Nozomi created a new travel agency, Adventure Travel. The following transactions occurred during the company's first month.

April 1 Nozomi invested $30,000 cash and computer equipment worth $20,000 in the company in exchange for common stock.
2 The company rented furnished office space by paying $1,800 cash for the first month's (April) rent.
3 The company purchased $1,000 of office supplies for cash.
10 The company paid $2,400 cash for the premium on a 12-month insurance policy. Coverage begins on April 11.
14 The company paid $1,600 cash for two weeks' salaries earned by employees.
24 The company collected $8,000 cash on commissions from airlines on tickets obtained for customers.
28 The company paid $1,600 cash for two weeks' salaries earned by employees.
29 The company paid $350 cash for minor repairs to the company's computer.
30 The company paid $750 cash for this month's telephone bill.
30 The company paid $1,500 cash in dividends.

The company's chart of accounts follows:

101	Cash	405	Commissions Earned
106	Accounts Receivable	612	Depreciation Expense—Computer Equip.
124	Office Supplies	622	Salaries Expense
128	Prepaid Insurance	637	Insurance Expense
167	Computer Equipment	640	Rent Expense
168	Accumulated Depreciation—Computer Equip.	650	Office Supplies Expense
209	Salaries Payable	684	Repairs Expense
307	Common Stock	688	Telephone Expense
318	Retained Earnings	901	Income Summary
319	Dividends		

Required

1. Use the balance column format to set up each ledger account listed in its chart of accounts.
2. Prepare journal entries to record the transactions for April and post them to the ledger accounts. The company records prepaid and unearned items in balance sheet accounts.
3. Prepare an unadjusted trial balance as of April 30.
4. Use the following information to journalize and post adjusting entries for the month:
   a. Two-thirds (or $133) of one month's insurance coverage has expired.
   b. At the end of the month, $600 of office supplies are still available.
   c. This month's depreciation on the computer equipment is $500.
   d. Employees earned $420 of unpaid and unrecorded salaries as of month-end.
   e. The company earned $1,750 of commissions that are not yet billed at month-end.
5. Prepare the adjusted trial balance as of April 30. Prepare the income statement and the statement of retained earnings for the month of April and the balance sheet at April 30, 2015.
6. Prepare journal entries to close the temporary accounts and post these entries to the ledger.
7. Prepare a post-closing trial balance.

Check (3) Unadj. trial balance totals, $58,000

(4*a*) Dr. Insurance Expense, $133

(5) Net income, $2,197; Total assets, $51,117

(7) P-C trial balance totals, $51,617

Problem 3-7A
Determining balance sheet classifications
C3

In the blank space beside each numbered balance sheet item, enter the letter of its balance sheet classification. If the item should not appear on the balance sheet, enter a *Z* in the blank.

A. Current assets
B. Long-term investments
C. Plant assets
D. Intangible assets
E. Current liabilities
F. Long-term liabilities
G. Equity

_____ **1.** Long-term investment in stock
_____ **2.** Depreciation expense—Building
_____ **3.** Prepaid rent
_____ **4.** Interest receivable
_____ **5.** Taxes payable
_____ **6.** Automobiles
_____ **7.** Notes payable (due in 3 years)
_____ **8.** Accounts payable
_____ **9.** Prepaid insurance
_____ **10.** Common stock
_____ **11.** Unearned services revenue
_____ **12.** Accumulated depreciation—Trucks
_____ **13.** Cash
_____ **14.** Buildings
_____ **15.** Store supplies
_____ **16.** Office equipment
_____ **17.** Land (used in operations)
_____ **18.** Repairs expense
_____ **19.** Office supplies
_____ **20.** Current portion of long-term note payable

Problem 3-8A
Preparing closing entries, financial statements, and ratios
A1 A2 P3 P4

The adjusted trial balance for Tybalt Construction as of December 31, 2015, follows.

TYBALT CONSTRUCTION
Adjusted Trial Balance
December 31, 2015

No.	Account Title	Debit	Credit
101	Cash	$ 5,000	
104	Short-term investments	23,000	
126	Supplies	8,100	
128	Prepaid insurance	7,000	
167	Equipment	40,000	
168	Accumulated depreciation—Equipment		$ 20,000
173	Building	150,000	
174	Accumulated depreciation—Building		50,000
183	Land	55,000	
201	Accounts payable		16,500
203	Interest payable		2,500
208	Rent payable		3,500
210	Wages payable		2,500
213	Property taxes payable		900
233	Unearned professional fees		7,500
251	Long-term notes payable		67,000
307	Common stock		5,000
318	Retained earnings		121,400
319	Dividends	13,000	
401	Professional fees earned		97,000
406	Rent earned		14,000
407	Dividends earned		2,000
409	Interest earned		2,100
606	Depreciation expense—Building	11,000	
612	Depreciation expense—Equipment	6,000	
623	Wages expense	32,000	
633	Interest expense	5,100	
637	Insurance expense	10,000	
640	Rent expense	13,400	
652	Supplies expense	7,400	
682	Postage expense	4,200	
683	Property taxes expense	5,000	
684	Repairs expense	8,900	
688	Telephone expense	3,200	
690	Utilities expense	4,600	
	Totals	$411,900	$411,900

The December 31, 2014, credit balance of the Retained Earnings account was $121,400. Tybalt Construction is required to make a $7,000 payment on its long-term notes payable during 2016.

Required

1. Prepare the income statement and the statement of retained earnings for the calendar year 2015 and the classified balance sheet at December 31, 2015.
2. Prepare the necessary closing entries at December 31, 2015.
3. Use the information in the financial statements to compute these ratios: (*a*) return on assets (total assets at December 31, 2014, was $200,000), (*b*) debt ratio, (*c*) profit margin ratio (use total revenues as the denominator), and (*d*) current ratio. Round ratios to three decimals for parts *a* and *c*, and to two decimals for parts *b* and *d*.

Check (1) Total assets (12/31/2015), $218,100; Net income, $4,300

PROBLEM SET B

Problem 3-1B
Identifying adjusting entries with explanations
P1

For each of the following entries, enter the letter of the explanation that most closely describes it in the space beside each entry. (You can use letters more than once.)

A. To record payment of a prepaid expense.
B. To record this period's use of a prepaid expense.
C. To record this period's depreciation expense.
D. To record receipt of unearned revenue.
E. To record this period's earning of prior unearned revenue.
F. To record an accrued expense.
G. To record payment of an accrued expense.
H. To record an accrued revenue.
I. To record receipt of accrued revenue.

______	1.	Interest Receivable	3,500	
		Interest Revenue		3,500
______	2.	Salaries Payable	9,000	
		Cash		9,000
______	3.	Depreciation Expense	8,000	
		Accumulated Depreciation		8,000
______	4.	Cash	9,000	
		Unearned Professional Fees		9,000
______	5.	Insurance Expense	4,000	
		Prepaid Insurance		4,000
______	6.	Interest Expense	5,000	
		Interest Payable		5,000
______	7.	Cash	1,500	
		Accounts Receivable (from services)		1,500
______	8.	Salaries Expense	7,000	
		Salaries Payable		7,000
______	9.	Cash	1,000	
		Interest Receivable		1,000
______	10.	Prepaid Rent	3,000	
		Cash		3,000
______	11.	Rent Expense	7,500	
		Prepaid Rent		7,500
______	12.	Unearned Professional Fees	6,000	
		Professional Fees Earned		6,000

Problem 3-2B
Preparing adjusting and subsequent journal entries
P1

Natsu Co. follows the practice of recording prepaid expenses and unearned revenues in balance sheet accounts. The company's annual accounting period ends on October 31, 2015. The following information concerns the adjusting entries that need to be recorded as of that date.

a. The Office Supplies account started the fiscal year with a $600 balance. During the fiscal year, the company purchased supplies for $4,570, which was added to the Office Supplies account. The supplies available at October 31, 2015, totaled $800.

b. An analysis of the company's insurance policies provided the following facts.

Policy	Date of Purchase	Months of Coverage	Cost
A	April 1, 2014	24	$6,000
B	April 1, 2015	36	7,200
C	August 1, 2015	12	1,320

The total premium for each policy was paid in full (for all months) at the purchase date, and the Prepaid Insurance account was debited for the full cost. (Year-end adjusting entries for Prepaid Insurance were properly recorded in all prior fiscal years.)

c. The company has four employees, who earn a total of $1,000 for each workday. They are paid each Monday for their work in the five-day workweek ending on the previous Friday. Assume that October 31, 2015, is a Monday, and all four employees worked the first day of that week. They will be paid salaries for five full days on Monday, November 7, 2015.

d. The company purchased a building on November 1, 2012, that cost $175,000 and is expected to have a $40,000 salvage value at the end of its predicted 25-year life. Annual depreciation is $5,400.

e. Since the company does not occupy the entire building it owns, it rented space to a tenant at $1,000 per month, starting on September 1, 2015. The rent was paid on time on September 1, and the amount received was credited to the Rent Earned account. However, the October rent has not been paid. The company has worked out an agreement with the tenant, who has promised to pay both October and November rent in full on November 15. The tenant has agreed not to fall behind again.

f. On September 1, the company rented space to another tenant for $725 per month. The tenant paid five months' rent in advance on that date. The payment was recorded with a credit to the Unearned Rent account.

Required

Check (1*b*) Dr. Insurance Expense, $4,730; (1*d*) Dr. Depreciation Expense, $5,400

1. Use the information to prepare adjusting entries as of October 31, 2015.

2. Prepare journal entries to record the first subsequent cash transaction in November 2015 for parts *c* and *e*.

Problem 3-3B
Preparing adjusting entries, adjusted trial balance, and financial statements
P1 P2 P3

Following is the unadjusted trial balance for Alonzo Institute as of December 31, 2015, which initially records prepaid expenses and unearned revenues in balance sheet accounts. The Institute provides one-on-one training to individuals who pay tuition directly to the business and offers extension training to groups in off-site locations. Shown after the trial balance are items *a* through *h* that require adjusting entries as of December 31, 2015.

	A	B	C
1	**ALONZO INSTITUTE** **Unadjusted Trial Balance** **December 31, 2015**		
2		**Debit**	**Credit**
3	Cash	$ 60,000	
4	Accounts receivable	0	
5	Teaching supplies	70,000	
6	Prepaid insurance	19,000	
7	Prepaid rent	3,800	
8	Professional library	12,000	
9	Accumulated depreciation—Professional library		$ 2,500
10	Equipment	40,000	
11	Accumulated depreciation—Equipment		20,000
12	Accounts payable		11,200
13	Salaries payable		0
14	Unearned training fees		28,600
15	Common stock		11,000
16	Retained earnings		60,500
17	Dividends	20,000	
18	Tuition fees earned		129,200
19	Training fees earned		68,000
20	Depreciation expense—Professional library	0	
21	Depreciation expense—Equipment	0	
22	Salaries expense	44,200	
23	Insurance expense	0	
24	Rent expense	29,600	
25	Teaching supplies expense	0	
26	Advertising expense	19,000	
27	Utilities expense	13,400	
28	Totals	$ 331,000	$331,000
29			

Additional Information Items

a. An analysis of the Institute's insurance policies shows that $9,500 of coverage has expired.
b. An inventory count shows that teaching supplies costing $20,000 are available at year-end 2015.
c. Annual depreciation on the equipment is $5,000.
d. Annual depreciation on the professional library is $2,400.
e. On November 1, the Institute agreed to do a special five-month course (starting immediately) for a client. The contract calls for a $14,300 monthly fee, and the client paid the first two months' fees in advance. When the cash was received, the Unearned Training Fees account was credited. The last two months' fees will be recorded when collected in 2016.
f. On October 15, the Institute agreed to teach a four-month class (beginning immediately) to an individual for $2,300 tuition per month payable at the end of the class. The class started on October 15, but no payment has yet been received. (The Institute's accruals are applied to the nearest half-month; for example, October recognizes one-half month accrual.)
g. The Institute's only employee is paid weekly. As of the end of the year, three days' salaries have accrued at the rate of $150 per day.
h. The balance in the Prepaid Rent account represents rent for December.

Required

1. Prepare T-accounts (representing the ledger) with balances from the unadjusted trial balance.
2. Prepare the necessary adjusting journal entries for items *a* through *h*, and post them to the T-accounts. Assume that adjusting entries are made only at year-end.
3. Update balances in the T-accounts for the adjusting entries and prepare an adjusted trial balance.
4. Prepare the company's income statement and statement of retained earnings for the year 2015, and prepare its balance sheet as of December 31, 2015.

Check (2*e*) Cr. Training Fees Earned, $28,600; (2*f*) Cr. Tuition Fees Earned, $5,750; (3) Adj. trial balance totals, $344,600; (4) Net income, $54,200

Problem 3-4B
Interpreting unadjusted and adjusted trial balances, and preparing financial statements
P1 P2 P3

A six-column table for Yan Consulting Company follows. The first two columns contain the unadjusted trial balance for the company as of December 31, 2015, and the last two columns contain the adjusted trial balance as of the same date.

	Unadjusted Trial Balance		Adjustments		Adjusted Trial Balance	
Cash	$ 45,000				$ 45,000	
Accounts receivable	60,000				66,660	
Office supplies	40,000				17,000	
Prepaid insurance	8,200				3,600	
Office equipment	120,000				120,000	
Accumulated depreciation—Office equip.		$ 20,000				$ 30,000
Accounts payable		26,000				32,000
Interest payable		0				2,150
Salaries payable		0				16,000
Unearned consulting fees		40,000				27,800
Long-term notes payable		75,000				75,000
Common stock		4,000				4,000
Retained earnings		76,200				76,200
Dividends	20,000				20,000	
Consulting fees earned		234,600				253,460
Depreciation expense—Office equip.	0				10,000	
Salaries expense	112,000				128,000	
Interest expense	8,600				10,750	
Insurance expense	0				4,600	
Rent expense	20,000				20,000	
Office supplies expense	0				23,000	
Advertising expense	42,000				48,000	
Totals	$475,800	$475,800			$516,610	$516,610

Required

Analysis Component

1. Analyze the differences between the unadjusted and adjusted trial balances to determine the eight adjustments that likely were made. Show the results of your analysis by inserting these adjustment amounts in the table's two middle columns. Label each adjustment with a letter *a* through *h* and provide a short description of it at the bottom of the table.

Preparation Component

Check (2) Net income, $9,110; Total assets, $222,260

2. Use the information in the adjusted trial balance to prepare this company's (*a*) income statement and its statement of retained earnings for the year ended December 31, 2015 (*Note:* Retained earnings at December 31, 2014, was $76,200, and the current-year dividends were $20,000), and (*b*) the balance sheet as of December 31, 2015.

Problem 3-5B
Preparing financial statements from the adjusted trial balance and calculating profit margin
P3 A1

The adjusted trial balance for Speedy Courier as of December 31, 2015, follows.

	Debit	Credit
Cash	$ 58,000	
Accounts receivable	120,000	
Interest receivable	7,000	
Notes receivable (due in 90 days)	210,000	
Office supplies	22,000	
Trucks	134,000	
Accumulated depreciation—Trucks		$ 58,000
Equipment	270,000	
Accumulated depreciation—Equipment		200,000
Land	100,000	
Accounts payable		134,000
Interest payable		20,000
Salaries payable		28,000
Unearned delivery fees		120,000
Long-term notes payable		200,000
Common stock		15,000
Retained earnings		110,000
Dividends	50,000	
Delivery fees earned		611,800
Interest earned		34,000
Depreciation expense—Trucks	29,000	
Depreciation expense—Equipment	48,000	
Salaries expense	74,000	
Wages expense	300,000	
Interest expense	15,000	
Office supplies expense	31,000	
Advertising expense	27,200	
Repairs expense—Trucks	35,600	
Totals	$1,530,800	$1,530,800

Required

Check (1) Total assets, $663,000

1. Use the information in the adjusted trial balance to prepare (*a*) the income statement for the year ended December 31, 2015, (*b*) the statement of retained earnings for the year ended December 31, 2015, and (*c*) the balance sheet as of December 31, 2015.
2. Calculate the profit margin for year 2015.

Problem 3-6B
Applying the accounting cycle
P1 P2 P3 P4 P5

On July 1, 2015, Lula Plume created a new self-storage business, Safe Storage Co. The following transactions occurred during the company's first month.

July 1 Plume invested $30,000 cash and buildings worth $150,000 in the company in exchange for common stock.
2 The company rented equipment by paying $2,000 cash for the first month's (July) rent.
5 The company purchased $2,400 of office supplies for cash.
10 The company paid $7,200 cash for the premium on a 12-month insurance policy. Coverage begins on July 11.

14 The company paid an employee $1,000 cash for two weeks' salary earned.
24 The company collected $9,800 cash for storage fees from customers.
28 The company paid $1,000 cash for two weeks' salary earned by an employee.
29 The company paid $950 cash for minor repairs to a leaking roof.
30 The company paid $400 cash for this month's telephone bill.
31 The company paid $2,000 cash in dividends.

The company's chart of accounts follows:

101	Cash	401	Storage Fees Earned
106	Accounts Receivable	606	Depreciation Expense—Buildings
124	Office Supplies	622	Salaries Expense
128	Prepaid Insurance	637	Insurance Expense
173	Buildings	640	Rent Expense
174	Accumulated Depreciation—Buildings	650	Office Supplies Expense
209	Salaries Payable	684	Repairs Expense
307	Common Stock	688	Telephone Expense
318	Retained Earnings	901	Income Summary
319	Dividends		

Required

1. Use the balance column format to set up each ledger account listed in its chart of accounts.
2. Prepare journal entries to record the transactions for July and post them to the ledger accounts. Record prepaid and unearned items in balance sheet accounts.
3. Prepare an unadjusted trial balance as of July 31.
4. Use the following information to journalize and post adjusting entries for the month:
   a. Two-thirds of one month's insurance coverage has expired.
   b. At the end of the month, $1,525 of office supplies are still available.
   c. This month's depreciation on the buildings is $1,500.
   d. An employee earned $100 of unpaid and unrecorded salary as of month-end.
   e. The company earned $1,150 of storage fees that are not yet billed at month-end.
5. Prepare the adjusted trial balance as of July 31. Prepare the income statement and the statement of retained earnings for the month of July and the balance sheet at July 31, 2015.
6. Prepare journal entries to close the temporary accounts and post these entries to the ledger.
7. Prepare a post-closing trial balance.

Check (3) Unadj. trial balance totals, $189,800

(4*a*) Dr. Insurance Expense, $400

(5) Net income, $2,725; Total assets, $180,825

(7) P-C trial balance totals, $182,325

Problem 3-7B
Determining balance sheet classifications
C3

In the blank space beside each numbered balance sheet item, enter the letter of its balance sheet classification. If the item should not appear on the balance sheet, enter a *Z* in the blank.

A. Current assets
B. Long-term investments
C. Plant assets
D. Intangible assets
E. Current liabilities
F. Long-term liabilities
G. Equity

______ **1.** Commissions earned
______ **2.** Interest receivable
______ **3.** Long-term investment in stock
______ **4.** Prepaid insurance
______ **5.** Machinery
______ **6.** Notes payable (due in 15 years)
______ **7.** Copyrights
______ **8.** Current portion of long-term note payable
______ **9.** Accumulated depreciation—Trucks
______ **10.** Office equipment
______ **11.** Rent receivable
______ **12.** Salaries payable
______ **13.** Income taxes payable
______ **14.** Common stock
______ **15.** Office supplies
______ **16.** Interest payable
______ **17.** Rent revenue
______ **18.** Notes receivable (due in 120 days)
______ **19.** Land (used in operations)
______ **20.** Depreciation expense—Trucks

Problem 3-8B
Preparing closing entries, financial statements, and ratios
A1 A2 P3 P4

The adjusted trial balance for Anara Co. as of December 31, 2015, follows.

ANARA COMPANY
Adjusted Trial Balance
December 31, 2015

No.	Account Title	Debit	Credit
101	Cash	$ 7,400	
104	Short-term investments	11,200	
126	Supplies	4,600	
128	Prepaid insurance	1,000	
167	Equipment	24,000	
168	Accumulated depreciation—Equipment		$ 4,000
173	Building	100,000	
174	Accumulated depreciation—Building		10,000
183	Land	30,500	
201	Accounts payable		3,500
203	Interest payable		1,750
208	Rent payable		400
210	Wages payable		1,280
213	Property taxes payable		3,330
233	Unearned professional fees		750
251	Long-term notes payable		40,000
307	Common stock		30,000
318	Retained earnings		62,800
319	Dividends	8,000	
401	Professional fees earned		59,600
406	Rent earned		4,500
407	Dividends earned		1,000
409	Interest earned		1,320
606	Depreciation expense—Building	2,000	
612	Depreciation expense—Equipment	1,000	
623	Wages expense	18,500	
633	Interest expense	1,550	
637	Insurance expense	1,525	
640	Rent expense	3,600	
652	Supplies expense	1,000	
682	Postage expense	410	
683	Property taxes expense	4,825	
684	Repairs expense	679	
688	Telephone expense	521	
690	Utilities expense	1,920	
	Totals	$224,230	$224,230

The December 31, 2014, credit balance of the Retained Earnings account was $62,800. Anara Company is required to make an $8,400 payment on its long-term notes payable during 2016.

Required

Check (1) Total assets (12/31/2015), $164,700; Net income, $28,890

1. Prepare the income statement and the statement of retained earnings for the calendar year 2015 and the classified balance sheet at December 31, 2015.
2. Prepare the necessary closing entries at December 31, 2015.
3. Use the information in the financial statements to calculate these ratios: (*a*) return on assets (total assets at December 31, 2014, were $160,000), (*b*) debt ratio, (*c*) profit margin ratio (use total revenues as the denominator), and (*d*) current ratio. Round ratios to three decimals for parts *a* and *c*, and to two decimals for parts *b* and *d*.

This serial problem began in Chapter 1 and continues through most of the book. If previous chapter segments were not completed, the serial problem can still begin at this point. It is helpful, but not necessary, to use the Working Papers that accompany the book.

SERIAL PROBLEM

Business Solutions

P1 P2 P3 P4 P5

SP 3 After the success of the company's first two months, Santana Rey continues to operate Business Solutions. (Transactions for the first two months are described in the Chapter 2 serial problem.) The November 30, 2015, unadjusted trial balance of Business Solutions (reflecting its transactions for October and November of 2015) follows.

No.	Account Title	Debit	Credit
101	Cash	$38,264	
106	Accounts receivable	12,618	
126	Computer supplies	2,545	
128	Prepaid insurance	2,220	
131	Prepaid rent	3,300	
163	Office equipment	8,000	
164	Accumulated depreciation—Office equipment		$ 0
167	Computer equipment	20,000	
168	Accumulated depreciation—Computer equipment		0
201	Accounts payable		0
210	Wages payable		0
236	Unearned computer services revenue		0
307	Common stock		73,000
318	Retained earnings		0
319	Dividends	5,600	
403	Computer services revenue		25,659
612	Depreciation expense—Office equipment	0	
613	Depreciation expense—Computer equipment	0	
623	Wages expense	2,625	
637	Insurance expense	0	
640	Rent expense	0	
652	Computer supplies expense	0	
655	Advertising expense	1,728	
676	Mileage expense	704	
677	Miscellaneous expenses	250	
684	Repairs expense—Computer	805	
	Totals	$98,659	$98,659

Business Solutions had the following transactions and events in December 2015.

Dec. 2 Paid $1,025 cash to Hillside Mall for Business Solutions' share of mall advertising costs.
3 Paid $500 cash for minor repairs to the company's computer.
4 Received $3,950 cash from Alex's Engineering Co. for the receivable from November.
10 Paid cash to Lyn Addie for six days of work at the rate of $125 per day.
14 Notified by Alex's Engineering Co. that Business Solutions' bid of $7,000 on a proposed project has been accepted. Alex's paid a $1,500 cash advance to Business Solutions.
15 Purchased $1,100 of computer supplies on credit from Harris Office Products.
16 Sent a reminder to Gomez Co. to pay the fee for services recorded on November 8.
20 Completed a project for Liu Corporation and received $5,625 cash.
22–26 Took the week off for the holidays.
28 Received $3,000 cash from Gomez Co. on its receivable.
29 Reimbursed S. Rey for business automobile mileage (600 miles at $0.32 per mile).
31 The company paid $1,500 cash in dividends.

The following additional facts are collected for use in making adjusting entries prior to preparing financial statements for the company's first three months:

a. The December 31 inventory count of computer supplies shows $580 still available.

b. Three months have expired since the 12-month insurance premium was paid in advance.

c. As of December 31, Lyn Addie has not been paid for four days of work at $125 per day.
d. The computer system, acquired on October 1, is expected to have a four-year life with no salvage value.
e. The office equipment, acquired on October 1, is expected to have a five-year life with no salvage value.
f. Three of the four months' prepaid rent has expired.

Required

1. Prepare journal entries to record each of the December transactions and events for Business Solutions. Post those entries to the accounts in the ledger.
2. Prepare adjusting entries to reflect *a* through *f*. Post those entries to the accounts in the ledger.
3. Prepare an adjusted trial balance as of December 31, 2015.
4. Prepare an income statement for the three months ended December 31, 2015.
5. Prepare a statement of retained earnings for the three months ended December 31, 2015.
6. Prepare a balance sheet as of December 31, 2015.
7. Record and post the necessary closing entries for Business Solutions.
8. Prepare a post-closing trial balance as of December 31, 2015.

Check (3) Adjusted trial balance totals, $109,034

(6) Total assets, $83,460

(8) Post-closing trial balance totals, $85,110

GENERAL LEDGER PROBLEM

Available in Connect

connect ACCOUNTING

The General Ledger tool in Connect allows students to immediately see the financial statements as of a specific date. Each of the following questions begins with an unadjusted trial balance. Using transactions from the following assignment, prepare the necessary adjustments, and determine the impact each adjustment has on net income. The financial statements are automatically populated.

GL 3-1 Based on the FastForward illustration in this chapter

Using transactions from the following assignments, prepare the necessary adjustments, create the financial statements, and determine the impact each adjustment has on net income.

GL 3-2 Based on Problem 3-3A

GL 3-3 Extension of Problem 2-1A

GL 3-4 Extension of Problem 2-2A

GL 3-5 Based on Problem 3-6A

GL 3-6 Based on Serial Problem SP 3

Beyond the Numbers

REPORTING IN ACTION

A1 P4

APPLE

BTN 3-1 Refer to **Apple**'s financial statements in Appendix A to answer the following.

1. Identify and write down the revenue recognition principle as explained in the chapter.
2. Review Apple's footnotes (in Appendix A and/or from its 10-K on its website) to discover how it applies the revenue recognition principle and when it recognizes revenue. Report what you discover.
3. What is Apple's profit margin for fiscal years ended September 28, 2013, and September 29, 2012.
4. For the fiscal year ended September 28, 2013, what amount is credited to Income Summary to summarize its revenues earned?
5. For the fiscal year ended September 28, 2013, what amount is debited to Income Summary to summarize its expenses incurred?
6. For the fiscal year ended September 28, 2013, what is the balance of its Income Summary account before it is closed?

Fast Forward

7. Access Apple's annual report (10-K) for fiscal years ending after September 28, 2013, at its website (Apple.com) or the SEC's EDGAR database (www.SEC.gov). Assess and compare the September 28, 2013, fiscal year profit margin to any subsequent year's profit margin that you compute.

COMPARATIVE ANALYSIS

A1 A2

APPLE

GOOGLE

BTN 3-2 Key figures for the recent two years of both **Apple** and **Google** follow.

	Apple		Google	
($ millions)	Current Year	Prior Year	Current Year	Prior Year
Net income	$ 37,037	$ 41,733	$12,920	$10,737
Net sales	170,910	156,508	59,825	50,175
Current assets	73,286	57,653	72,886	60,454
Current liabilities	43,658	38,542	15,908	14,337

Required

1. Compute profit margins for (*a*) Apple and (*b*) Google for the two years of data shown.
2. Which company is more successful on the basis of profit margin? Explain.
3. Compute the current ratio for both years for both companies.
4. Which company has the better ability to pay short-term obligations according to the current ratio?
5. Analyze and comment on each company's current ratios for the past two years.
6. How do Apple's and Google's current ratios compare to their industry (assumed) average ratio of 2.0?

ETHICS CHALLENGE

C1

BTN 3-3 Jessica Boland works for Sea Biscuit Co. She and Farah Smith, her manager, are preparing adjusting entries for annual financial statements. Boland computes depreciation and records it as

Depreciation Expense—Equipment	123,000	
Accumulated Depreciation—Equipment		123,000

Smith agrees with her computation but says the credit entry should be directly to the Equipment account. Smith argues that while accumulated depreciation is technically correct, "it is less hassle not to use a contra account and just credit the Equipment account directly. And besides, the balance sheet shows the same amount for total assets under either method."

Required

1. How should depreciation be recorded? Do you support Boland or Smith?
2. Evaluate the strengths and weaknesses of Smith's reasons for preferring her method.
3. Indicate whether the situation Boland faces is an ethical problem. Explain.

COMMUNICATING IN PRACTICE

P4

BTN 3-4 Assume that one of your classmates states that a company's books should be ongoing and therefore not closed until that business is terminated. Write a half-page memo to this classmate explaining the concept of the closing process by drawing analogies between (1) a scoreboard for an athletic event and the revenue and expense accounts of a business or (2) a sports team's record book and retained earnings. (*Hint:* Think about what would happen if the scoreboard is not cleared before the start of a new game.)

TAKING IT TO THE NET

A1

BTN 3-5 Access EDGAR online (www.SEC.gov) and locate the 10-K report of **The Gap, Inc.**, (ticker GPS) filed on March 26, 2012. Review its financial statements reported for the year ended January 28, 2012, to answer the following questions.

Required

1. What are Gap's main brands?
2. What is Gap's fiscal year-end?
3. What is Gap's net sales for the period ended January 28, 2012?
4. What is Gap's net income for the period ended January 28, 2012?
5. Compute Gap's profit margin for the year ended January 28, 2012.
6. Do you believe Gap's decision to use a year-end of late January or early February relates to its natural business year? Explain.

TEAMWORK IN ACTION

P1

BTN 3-6 Four types of adjustments are described in the chapter: (1) prepaid expenses, (2) unearned revenues, (3) accrued expenses, and (4) accrued revenues.

Required

1. Form *learning teams* of four (or more) members. Each team member must select one of the four adjustments as an area of expertise (each team must have at least one expert in each area).
2. Form *expert teams* from the individuals who have selected the same area of expertise. Expert teams are to discuss and write a report that each expert will present to his or her learning team addressing the following:
   a. Description of the adjustment and why it's necessary.
   b. Example of a transaction or event, with dates and amounts, that requires adjustment.
   c. Adjusting entry(ies) for the example in requirement *b*.
   d. Status of the affected account(s) before and after the adjustment in requirement *c*.
   e. Effects on financial statements of not making the adjustment.
3. Each expert should return to his or her learning team. In rotation, each member should present his or her expert team's report to the learning team. Team discussion is encouraged.

ENTREPRENEURIAL DECISION

C1 A1

BTN 3-7 Review the opening feature of this chapter dealing with **International Princess Project** and its entrepreneurial owner, Shannon Keith.

Required

1. Assume that International Princess Project sells a $300 gift certificate to a customer, collecting the $300 cash in advance. Prepare the journal entry for the (*a*) collection of the cash for delivery of the gift certificate to the customer and (*b*) revenue from the subsequent delivery of merchandise when the gift certificate is used.
2. How can keeping less inventory help to improve International Princess Project's profit margin?
3. Shannon Keith understands that many companies carry considerable inventory, and she is thinking of carrying additional inventory of merchandise for sale. Shannon desires your advice on the pros and cons of carrying such inventory. Provide at least one reason for, and one reason against, carrying additional inventory.

HITTING THE ROAD

C1

BTN 3-8 Select a company that you can visit in person or interview on the telephone. Call ahead to the company to arrange a time when you can interview an employee (preferably an accountant) who helps prepare the annual financial statements. Inquire about the following aspects of its *accounting cycle:*

1. Does the company prepare interim financial statements? What time period(s) is used for interim statements?
2. Does the company use the cash or accrual basis of accounting?
3. Does the company use a work sheet in preparing financial statements? Why or why not?
4. Does the company use a spreadsheet program? If so, which software program is used?
5. How long does it take after the end of its reporting period to complete annual statements?

GLOBAL DECISION

A1 C1

Samsung
APPLE
GOOGLE

BTN 3-9 **Samsung (Samsung.com)** is a leading manufacturer of consumer electronic products. The following selected information is available from Samsung's financial statements along with that from **Apple** and **Google**.

(millions)	Samsung	Apple	Google
Net income	₩ 30,474,764	$ 37,037	$12,920
Net sales	228,692,667	170,910	59,825

Required

1. Compute profit margin for the current year for Samsung, Apple, and Google.
2. Which company has the higher profit margin? For that company, how much net income does it receive for each $1 or ₩1 of sales?

ANSWERS TO MULTIPLE CHOICE QUIZ

1. b; the forgotten adjusting entry is: *dr*. Wages Expense, *cr*. Wages Payable.
2. c; Supplies used = $450 − $125 = $325
3. b; Insurance expense = $24,000 × (8/24) = $8,000; adjusting entry is: *dr.* Insurance Expense for $8,000, *cr.* Prepaid Insurance for $8,000.
4. a; Consulting fees earned = $3,600 × (2/6) = $1,200; adjusting entry is: *dr.* Unearned Consulting Fee for $1,200, *cr.* Consulting Fees Earned for $1,200.
5. e; Profit margin = $15,000/$300,000 = 5%
6. b

chapter 4

Accounting for Merchandising Operations

Chapter Preview

MERCHANDISING ACTIVITIES	MERCHANDISING PURCHASES	MERCHANDISING SALES	MERCHANDISE REPORTING AND ANALYSIS
C1 Reporting income and inventory **C2** Operating cycles and inventory system	**P1** Accounting for: Purchase discounts Purchase returns and allowances Transportation costs	**P2** Accounting for: Sales of merchandise Sales discounts Sales returns and allowances	**P3** Adjusting and closing for merchandisers **P4** Multiple-step and single-step income statements **A1** Acid-test analysis **A2** Gross margin analysis

Learning Objectives

CONCEPTUAL

C1 Describe merchandising activities and identify income components for a merchandising company.

C2 Identify and explain the inventory asset and cost flows of a merchandising company.

ANALYTICAL

A1 Compute the acid-test ratio and explain its use to assess liquidity.

A2 Compute the gross margin ratio and explain its use to assess profitability.

PROCEDURAL

P1 Analyze and record transactions for merchandise purchases using a perpetual system.

P2 Analyze and record transactions for merchandise sales using a perpetual system.

P3 Prepare adjustments and close accounts for a merchandising company.

P4 Define and prepare multiple-step and single-step income statements.

P5 *Appendix 4A*—Record and compare merchandising transactions using both periodic and perpetual inventory systems.

Courtesy of Sseko

Fashioning a Future

PORTLAND—"I'm passionate about social entrepreneurship," exclaims Liz Forkin Bohannon, "and dreaming about the way business can be an incredibly powerful force for positive social change." For Liz, her dream began with a postcollege trip to Uganda for a new job. What she discovered were young women who were unable to earn enough money to pay for their college tuition. "These women saw the education they were receiving as such a gift," explains Liz. "All they needed was an opportunity."

"Assume a posture of asking 'why not?'"
—Liz Forkin Bohannon

Armed with her passion, Liz launched **Sseko (SsekoDesigns.com)**—inspiration for its name derives from *enseko*, the Lugandan word for "laughter." Sseko's mission, explains Liz, is "to provide employment to vulnerable groups of women." She hires young women who need money for college. The women make products from materials Liz acquires, and Liz then exports the finished products. Liz began with sandals and has expanded into scarves and leather bags.

Her start-up, however, was a struggle. "I spent a few weeks scouring the country for the materials we needed," admits Liz. She recalls how the business required a merchandising accounting system to account for purchases and sales transactions and to effectively track materials. Inventory was especially important to account for and monitor. Liz admits that early on, soon after her sandals made it into Martha Stewart's holiday gift guide, she ran out of sandals. While a nice problem on one hand, Liz knew she had to get her accounting in order.

Liz ultimately set up an accounting system to capture and communicate costs and sales information. Tracking merchandising activities was necessary to set prices and to manage discounts, allowances, and returns for both sales and purchases. A perpetual inventory system enabled her to stock the right kind and amount of merchandise and to avoid the costs of out-of-stock and excess inventory. "I am still learning. I am making mistakes," admits Liz. "But, it is a beautiful adventure!"

Mastering accounting for merchandising is important to Liz. "We needed to generate income," says Liz. "I had committed to these young women . . . I owed it to them to push as hard as I could to make it work." And push she has. "All they needed was an opportunity; an opportunity to work; an opportunity to succeed and earn and save," insists Liz. "There is nothing better than . . . the opportunity to work hard in a dignified way."

Sources: *Sseko Designs website,* January 2015; *Trend Hunter,* February 2012; *FOXBusiness,* March 2014; *The Oregonian,* January 2012

MERCHANDISING ACTIVITIES

C1 Describe merchandising activities and identify income components for a merchandising company.

Previous chapters emphasized the accounting and reporting activities of service companies. A merchandising company's activities differ from those of a service company. **Merchandise** consists of products, also called *goods,* that a company acquires to resell to customers. A **merchandiser** earns net income by buying and selling merchandise. Merchandisers are often identified as either wholesalers or retailers. A **wholesaler** is an *intermediary* that buys products from manufacturers or other wholesalers and sells them to retailers or other wholesalers. A **retailer** is an intermediary that buys products from manufacturers or wholesalers and sells them to consumers. Many retailers sell both products and services.

Reporting Income for a Merchandiser

Net income for a merchandiser equals revenues from selling merchandise minus both the cost of merchandise sold to customers and the cost of other expenses for the period; see Exhibit 4.1. The usual accounting term for revenues from selling merchandise is *sales,* and the term used for the expense of buying and preparing the merchandise is **cost of goods sold.** (Some service companies use the term *sales* instead of revenues; and cost of goods sold is also called *cost of sales.*)

EXHIBIT 4.1

Computing Income for a Merchandising Company versus a Service Company

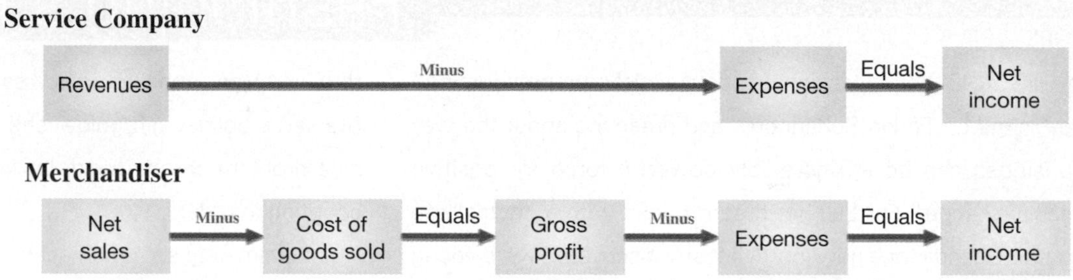

Point: Fleming, SuperValu, and SYSCO are wholesalers. Aeropostale, Coach, Target, and Walmart are retailers.

The income statement for Z-Mart in Exhibit 4.2 illustrates these key components of a merchandiser's net income. The first two lines show that products are acquired at a cost of $230,400 and sold for $314,700. The third line shows an $84,300 **gross profit,** also called **gross margin,** which equals net sales less cost of goods sold. Additional expenses of $71,400 are reported, which leaves $12,900 in net income.

EXHIBIT 4.2

Merchandiser's Income Statement

Z-MART
Income Statement
For Year Ended December 31, 2015

Net sales	$314,700
Cost of goods sold	**230,400**
Gross profit	**84,300**
Expenses	71,400
Net income	$ 12,900

C2 Identify and explain the inventory asset and cost flows of a merchandising company.

Reporting Inventory for a Merchandiser

A merchandiser's balance sheet includes a current asset called *merchandise inventory,* an item not on a service company's balance sheet. **Merchandise inventory,** or simply *inventory,* refers to products that a company owns and intends to sell. The cost of this asset includes the cost incurred to buy the goods, ship them to the store, and make them ready for sale.

Operating Cycle for a Merchandiser

A merchandising company's operating cycle begins by purchasing merchandise and ends by collecting cash from selling the merchandise. The length of an operating cycle differs across the types of businesses. Department stores often have operating cycles of two to five months. Operating cycles for grocery merchants usually range from two to eight weeks. A grocer has more operating cycles in a year than, say, clothing or electronics retailers.

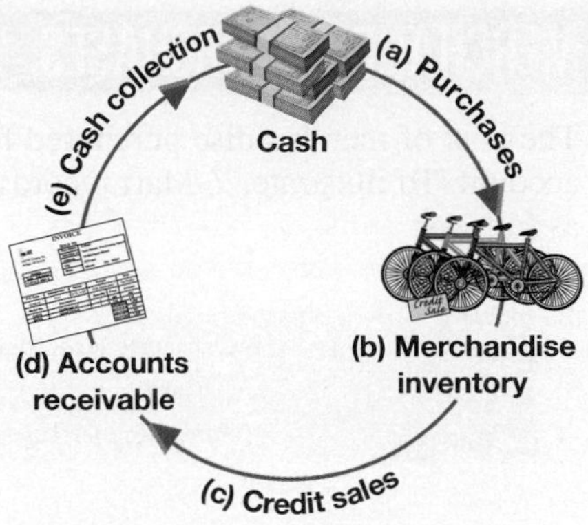

EXHIBIT 4.3

Merchandiser's Operating Cycle

Exhibit 4.3 illustrates an operating cycle for a merchandiser with credit sales. The cycle moves from (*a*) cash purchases of merchandise to (*b*) inventory for sale to (*c*) credit sales to (*d*) accounts receivable to (*e*) cash. Companies try to keep their operating cycles short because assets tied up in inventory and receivables are not productive. Cash sales shorten operating cycles.

Inventory Systems

Cost of goods sold is the cost of merchandise sold to customers during a period. It is often the largest single expense on a merchandiser's income statement. **Inventory** refers to products a company owns and expects to sell in its normal operations. Exhibit 4.4 shows that a company's merchandise available for sale consists of what it begins with (beginning inventory) and what it purchases (net purchases). The merchandise available is either sold (cost of goods sold) or kept for future sales (ending inventory).

Merchandise Inventory

Beg. inventory	#		
Net purchases	#		
Merchandise avail. for sale	#		
		COGS	#
End. inventory	#		

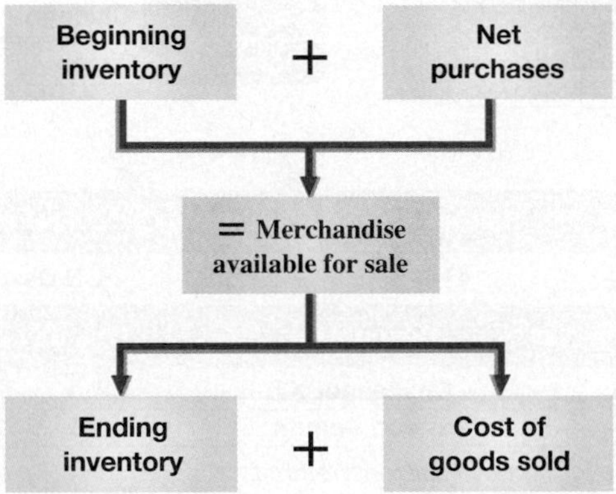

EXHIBIT 4.4

Merchandiser's Cost Flow for a Single Time Period

Point: Mathematically, Exhibit 4.4 says
BI + NP = MAS,
where BI is beginning inventory, NP is net purchases, and MAS is merchandise available for sale. Exhibit 4.4 also says
MAS = EI + COGS,
which can be rewritten as MAS − EI = COGS or MAS − COGS = EI, where EI is ending inventory and COGS is cost of goods sold. In both equations above, if we know two of the three values, we can solve for the third.

Two alternative inventory accounting systems can be used to collect information about cost of goods sold and cost of inventory: *perpetual system* or *periodic system*. The **perpetual inventory system** continually updates accounting records for merchandising transactions—specifically, for those records of inventory available for sale and inventory sold. The **periodic inventory system** updates the accounting records for merchandise transactions only at the *end of a period*. Technological advances and competitive pressures have dramatically increased the use of the perpetual system. It gives managers immediate access to detailed information on sales and inventory levels, where they can strategically react to sales trends, cost changes, consumer tastes, and so forth, to increase gross profit. (Some companies use a *hybrid* system where the perpetual system is used for tracking units available and the periodic system is used to compute cost of sales.)

Point: Growth of superstores such as **Costco** and **Sam's** is fueled by efficient use of perpetual inventory. Such large stores evolved only after scannable UPC codes to help control inventory were invented.

QC1

The following sections, consisting of the next 11 pages on purchasing, selling, and adjusting merchandise, use the perpetual system. Appendix 4A uses the periodic system (with the perpetual results on the side). An instructor can choose to cover either one or both inventory systems.

ACCOUNTING FOR MERCHANDISE PURCHASES

P1 Analyze and record transactions for merchandise purchases using a perpetual system.

The cost of merchandise purchased for resale is recorded in the Merchandise Inventory asset account. To illustrate, Z-Mart records a $1,200 cash purchase of merchandise on November 2 as follows:

Assets = Liabilities + Equity
+1,200
−1,200

Nov. 2	Merchandise Inventory.	1,200	
	Cash		1,200
	Purchased merchandise for cash.		

Point: The Merchandise Inventory account reflects the cost of goods available for resale. Costs recorded in Merchandise Inventory are sometimes called *inventoriable costs.*

The invoice for this merchandise is shown in Exhibit 4.5. The buyer usually receives the original invoice, and the seller keeps a copy. This *source document* serves as the purchase invoice of Z-Mart (buyer) and the sales invoice for Trex (seller). The amount recorded for merchandise inventory includes its purchase cost, shipping fees, taxes, and any other costs necessary to make it ready for sale. This section explains how we compute the recorded cost of merchandise purchases.

EXHIBIT 4.5
Invoice

INVOICE

(1) TREX
W9797 Cherry Rd.
Antigo, WI 54409

(2) Invoice Date: 11/2/15 — Invoice Number: 4657-2

SOLD TO (3)

Firm Name	Z-Mart
Attention of	Tom Novak, Purchasing Agent
Address	10 Michigan Street
City	Chicago
State	Illinois — Zip 60521

P.O. Date (4)	Salesperson	Terms (5)	Freight (6)	Ship
10/30/15	#141	2/10, n/30	FOB Destination	Via FedEx

Model No. (7)	Description	Quantity	Price	Amount
CH015	Challenger X7	1	490	490
SD099	Speed Demon	1	710	710
See reverse for terms of sale and returns.			Subtotal	1,200
			Shipping	—
			Tax	—
			(8) Total	1,200

Key: (1) Seller (2) Invoice date (3) Purchaser (4) Order date (5) Credit terms (6) Freight terms (7) Goods (8) Total invoice amount

Decision Insight

Trade Discounts When a manufacturer or wholesaler prepares a catalog of items it has for sale, it usually gives each item a **list price,** also called a *catalog price.* However, an item's intended *selling price* equals list price minus a given percent called a **trade discount.** The amount of trade discount usually depends on whether a buyer is a wholesaler, retailer, or final consumer. A wholesaler buying in large quantities is often granted a larger discount than a retailer buying in smaller quantities. A buyer records the net amount of list price minus trade discount. For example, in the November 2 purchase of merchandise by Z-Mart, the merchandise was listed in the seller's catalog at $2,000 and Z-Mart received a 40% trade discount. This meant that Z-Mart's purchase price was $1,200, computed as $2,000 − (40% × $2,000). ■

Point: Lowes and Home Depot offer trade discounts to construction companies and contractors. Trade discounts help create loyalty among customers. Trade discounts are not journalized; purchases are recorded based on the invoice amount.

Purchase Discounts

The purchase of goods on credit requires a clear statement of expected future payments and dates to avoid misunderstandings. **Credit terms** for a purchase include the amounts and timing of payments from a buyer to a seller. Credit terms usually reflect an industry's practices. To illustrate, when sellers require payment within 10 days after the end of the month of the invoice date, the invoice will show credit terms as "n/10 EOM," which stands for net 10 days after end of month (**EOM**). When sellers require payment within 30 days after the invoice date, the invoice shows credit terms of "n/30," which stands for *net 30 days*.

Exhibit 4.6 portrays credit terms. The amount of time allowed before full payment is due is called the **credit period.** Sellers can grant a **cash discount** to encourage buyers to pay earlier. A buyer views a cash discount as a **purchase discount.** A seller views a cash discount as a **sales discount.** Any cash discounts are described in the credit terms on the invoice. For example, credit terms of "2/10, n/60" mean that full payment is due within a 60-day credit period, but the buyer can deduct 2% of the invoice amount if payment is made within 10 days of the invoice date. This reduced payment applies only for the **discount period.**

Point: Since both the buyer and seller know the invoice date, this date is used in setting the discount and credit periods.

EXHIBIT 4.6

Credit Terms

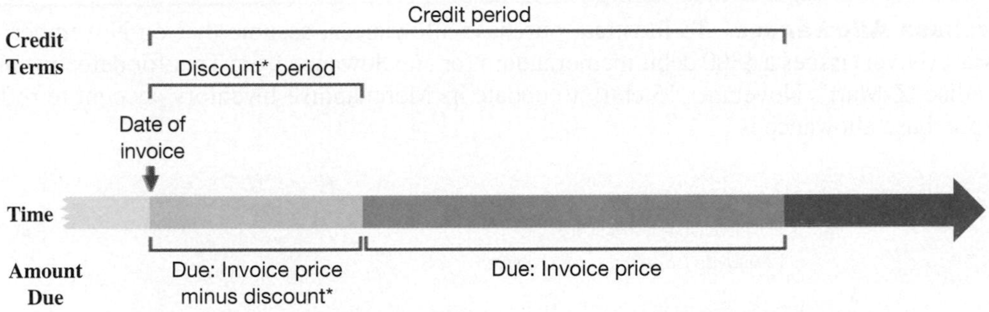

*Discount refers to a purchase discount for a buyer and a sales discount for a seller.

To illustrate how a buyer accounts for a purchase discount, assume that Z-Mart's $1,200 purchase of merchandise is on credit with terms of 2/10, n/30. Its entry is

Point: Appendix 4A repeats journal entries *a* through *f* using a periodic inventory system.

(*a*) Nov. 2	Merchandise Inventory	1,200	
	Accounts Payable		1,200
	Purchased merchandise on credit, invoice dated Nov. 2, terms 2/10, n/30.		

Assets = Liabilities + Equity
+1,200 +1,200

If Z-Mart pays the amount due on (or before) November 12, the entry is

(*b*) Nov. 12	Accounts Payable	1,200	
	Merchandise Inventory		24
	Cash		1,176
	Paid for the $1,200 purchase of Nov. 2 less the discount of $24 (2% × $1,200).		

Assets = Liabilities + Equity
−24 −1,200
−1,176

The Merchandise Inventory account after these entries reflects the net cost of merchandise purchased, and the Accounts Payable account shows a zero balance. Both ledger accounts, in T-account form, follow:

Point: These entries illustrate what is called the *gross method* of accounting for purchases with discount terms.

Merchandise Inventory			
Nov. 2	1,200	Nov. 12	24
Balance	1,176		

Accounts Payable			
Nov. 12	1,200	Nov. 2	1,200
		Balance	0

Point: Inventory balance of $1,176 equals the cash paid for it (*measurement principal*).

Point: Buyers sometimes make partial payments toward amounts owed. Assume that credit terms apply to both partial and full payments.

A buyer's failure to pay within a discount period can be expensive. To illustrate, if Z-Mart does not pay within the 10-day 2% discount period, it can delay payment by 20 more days. This delay costs Z-Mart $24, computed as 2% × $1,200. Most buyers take advantage of a purchase discount because of the usually high interest rate implied from not taking it.[1] Also, good cash management means that no invoice is paid until the last day of the discount or credit period.

Decision Maker

Entrepreneur You purchase a batch of products on terms of 3/10, n/90, but your company has limited cash and you must borrow funds at an 11% annual rate if you are to pay within the discount period. Is it to your advantage to take the purchase discount? Explain. ■ [Answers follow the chapter's Summary.]

Purchase Returns and Allowances

Point: The sender (maker) of a *debit memorandum* will debit the account payable of the memo's receiver. The memo's receiver will credit the sender's account receivable.

Purchase returns refer to merchandise a buyer acquires but then returns to the seller. A *purchase allowance* is a reduction in the cost of defective or unacceptable merchandise that a buyer acquires. Buyers often keep defective but still marketable merchandise if the seller grants an acceptable allowance. When a buyer returns or takes an allowance on merchandise, the buyer issues a **debit memorandum** to inform the seller of a debit made to the account payable in the buyer's records (debits reduce liabilities).

Purchase Allowances To illustrate purchase allowances, assume that on November 15, Z-Mart (buyer) issues a $300 debit memorandum for an allowance from Trex for defective merchandise. Z-Mart's November 15 entry to update its Merchandise Inventory account to reflect the purchase allowance is

Assets = Liabilities + Equity
−300 −300

(c) Nov. 15	Accounts Payable	300	
	Merchandise Inventory		300
	Allowance for defective merchandise.		

The buyer's allowance for defective merchandise is usually offset against the buyer's current account payable balance to the seller. When cash is refunded, the Cash account is debited instead of Accounts Payable.

Point: In the perpetual system, all purchases, purchase discounts, purchase returns, and cost of sales are recorded in the Merchandise Inventory account. This is different from the periodic system as explained in Appendix 4A.

Purchase Returns Returns are recorded at the net costs charged to buyers. To illustrate the accounting for returns, suppose Z-Mart purchases $1,000 of merchandise on June 1 with terms 2/10, n/60. Two days later, Z-Mart returns $100 of goods before paying the invoice. When Z-Mart later pays on June 11, it takes the 2% discount only on the $900 remaining balance. When goods are returned, a buyer can take a purchase discount on only the remaining balance of the invoice. The resulting discount is $18 (2% × $900) and the cash payment is $882 ($900 − $18). The following entries reflect this illustration.

Merchandise Inventory

Debit	Credit
Purch. 1,000	Returns 100
	Discount 18
Net purch. 882	

June 1	Merchandise Inventory	1,000	
	Accounts Payable		1,000
	Purchased merchandise, invoice dated June 1, terms 2/10, n/60.		
June 3	Accounts Payable	100	
	Merchandise Inventory		100
	Returned merchandise to seller.		
June 11	Accounts Payable	900	
	Merchandise Inventory		18
	Cash		882
	Paid for $900 merchandise ($1,000 − $100) less $18 discount (2% × $900).		

Example: Assume Z-Mart pays $980 cash for $1,000 of merchandise purchased within its 2% discount period. Later, it returns $100 of the original $1,000 merchandise. The return entry is
Cash 98
Merch. Inv. 98

[1] The *implied annual interest rate* formula is:

[365 days ÷ (Credit period − Discount period)] × Cash discount rate.

For terms of 2/10, n/30, missing the 2% discount for an additional 20 days is equal to an annual interest rate of 36.5%, computed as [365 days/(30 days − 10 days)] × 2% discount rate. *Favorable purchase discounts* are those with implied annual interest rates that exceed the purchaser's annual rate for borrowing money.

Decision Ethics

Payables Manager As a new accounts payable manager, you are being trained by the outgoing manager. She explains that the system prepares checks for amounts net of favorable cash discounts, and the checks are dated the last day of the discount period. She also tells you that checks are not mailed until five days later, adding that "the company gets free use of cash for an extra five days, and our department looks better. When a supplier complains, we blame the computer system and the mailroom." Do you continue this payment policy? ■ [Answers follow the chapter's Summary.]

Transportation Costs and Ownership Transfer

The buyer and seller must agree on who is responsible for paying any freight costs and who bears the risk of loss during transit for merchandising transactions. This is essentially the same as asking at what point ownership transfers from the seller to the buyer. The point of transfer is called the **FOB** (*free on board*) point, which determines who pays transportation costs (and often other incidental costs of transit such as insurance). Whoever owns the goods in transit takes on the shipping cost.

Exhibit 4.7 identifies two alternative points of transfer. (1) *FOB shipping point,* also called *FOB factory,* means the buyer accepts ownership when the goods depart the seller's place of business. The buyer is then responsible for paying shipping costs and bearing the risk of damage or loss when goods are in transit. The goods are part of the buyer's inventory when they are in transit since ownership has transferred to the buyer. **1-800-FLOWERS.COM**, a floral and gift merchandiser, and **Bare Escentuals**, a cosmetic manufacturer, both use FOB shipping point. (2) *FOB destination* means ownership of goods transfers to the buyer when the goods arrive at the buyer's place of business. The seller is responsible for paying shipping charges and bears the risk of damage or loss in transit. The seller does not record revenue from this sale until the goods arrive at the destination because this transaction is not complete before that point. **Kyocera**, a manufacturer, uses FOB destination.

Point: The party not responsible for shipping cost sometimes pays shipping cost. In these cases, the party paying this cost either bills the party responsible or, more commonly, adjusts its account payable or account receivable with the other party. For example, a buyer paying shipping cost when terms are FOB destination can decrease its account payable to the seller by the amount of shipping cost. Assume that any freight payments to carriers are *not* applied in computing merchandise discounts.

EXHIBIT 4.7

Ownership Transfer and Transportation Costs

Shipping Terms	Ownership Transfers at	Goods in Transit Owned by	Transportation Costs Paid by
FOB shipping point	Shipping point	Buyer	**Buyer** Merchandise Inventory . . . # Cash . . . . #
FOB destination	Destination	Seller	**Seller** Delivery Expense . . . . # Cash . . . . #

Point: If we place an order online and receive free shipping, we have terms FOB destination.

© Royalty Free/Corbis

Z-Mart's $1,200 purchase on November 2 is on terms of FOB destination. This means Z-Mart is not responsible for paying transportation costs. When a buyer is responsible for paying transportation costs, the payment is made to a carrier or directly to the seller depending on the agreement. The cost principle requires that any necessary transportation costs of a buyer (often called *transportation-in* or *freight-in*) be included as part of the cost of purchased merchandise. To illustrate, Z-Mart's entry to record a $75 freight charge from an independent carrier for merchandise purchased FOB shipping point is

(d) Nov. 24	Merchandise Inventory	75	
	Cash		75
	Paid freight costs on purchased merchandise.		

Assets = Liabilities + Equity
+75
−75

Point: INcoming freight costs are charged to INventory; when inventory EXits it is charged to EXpense.

A seller records the costs of shipping goods to customers in a Delivery Expense account when the seller is responsible for these costs. Delivery expense, also called *transportation-out* or *freight-out,* is reported as a selling expense in the seller's income statement.

Point: With *tracking numbers* it is possible to know the exact time shipped goods arrive at their destination.

In summary, purchases are recorded as debits to Merchandise Inventory. Any later purchase discounts, returns, and allowances are credited (decreases) to Merchandise Inventory. Transportation-in is debited (added) to Merchandise Inventory. Z-Mart's itemized costs of merchandise purchases for year 2015 are in Exhibit 4.8.

EXHIBIT 4.8

Itemized Costs of Merchandise Purchases

Z-MART
Itemized Costs of Merchandise Purchases
For Year Ended December 31, 2015

Invoice cost of merchandise purchases	$ 235,800
Less: Purchase discounts received	(4,200)
Purchase returns and allowances	(1,500)
Add: Costs of transportation-in	2,300
Total net cost of merchandise purchases	**$232,400**

Point: Some companies have separate accounts for purchase discounts, returns and allowances, and transportation-in. These accounts are then transferred to Merchandise Inventory at period-end. This is a *hybrid system* of perpetual and periodic. That is, Merchandise Inventory is updated on a perpetual basis but only for purchases and cost of goods sold.

The accounting system described here does not provide separate records (accounts) for total purchases, total purchase discounts, total purchase returns and allowances, and total transportation-in. Yet nearly all companies collect this information in supplementary records because managers need this information to evaluate and control each of these cost elements. **Supplementary records,** also called *supplemental records,* refer to information outside the usual general ledger accounts.

NEED-TO-KNOW 4-1

Merchandise Purchases

P1

Prepare journal entries to record each of the following purchases transactions of a merchandising company. Show supporting calculations and assume a perpetual inventory system.

Oct. 1 Purchased 125 units of a product at a cost of $4 per unit. Terms of the sale are 2/10, n/30, and FOB shipping point; the invoice is dated October 1.
Oct. 3 Paid $30 cash for freight charges from UPS for the October 1 purchase.
Oct. 7 Returned 50 defective units from the October 1 purchase and received full credit.
Oct. 11 Paid the amount due from the October 1 purchase, less the return on October 7.
Oct. 31 *Assume the October 11 payment was never made* and, instead, payment of the amount due on the October 1 purchase, less the return on October 7, occurred on October 31.

Solution

Oct. 1	Merchandise Inventory	500	
	Accounts Payable		500
	To record credit purchase (125 units × $4).		
Oct. 1	Merchandise Inventory	30	
	Cash		30
	Paid freight costs on goods purchased FOB shipping point.		
Oct. 7	Accounts Payable	200	
	Merchandise Inventory		200
	Returned defective units (50 units × $4).		
Oct. 11	Accounts Payable	300	
	Cash		294
	Merchandise Inventory*		6
	*Paid for purchases less cash discount *[($500 − $200) × 2%].*		
Oct. 31	Accounts Payable	300	
	Cash		300
	Paid for purchases (no cash discount received).		

Do More: QS 4-4, QS 4-5, QS 4-16, E 4-4, E 4-6

QC2

ACCOUNTING FOR MERCHANDISE SALES

P2 Analyze and record transactions for merchandise sales using a perpetual system.

Merchandising companies also must account for sales, sales discounts, sales returns and allowances, and cost of goods sold. A merchandising company such as Z-Mart reflects these items in its gross profit computation, as shown in Exhibit 4.9. This section explains how this information is derived from transactions.

EXHIBIT 4.9 Gross Profit Computation

Z-MART
Computation of Gross Profit
For Year Ended December 31, 2015

Sales.		$321,000
Less: Sales discounts.	$4,300	
Sales returns and allowances	2,000	6,300
Net sales		314,700
Cost of goods sold		230,400
Gross profit		**$ 84,300**

Sales of Merchandise

Each sales transaction for a seller of merchandise involves two parts.

1. **Revenue received in the form of an asset from the customer.**
2. **Cost of goods sold incurred for merchandise sold to the customer.**

Accounting for a sales transaction under the perpetual system requires recording information about both parts. This means that each sales transaction for merchandisers, whether for cash or on credit, requires *two entries:* one for revenue and one for cost. To illustrate, Z-Mart sold $2,400 of merchandise on credit on November 3. The revenue part of this transaction is recorded as

(e) Nov. 3	Accounts Receivable	2,400	
	Sales		2,400
	Sold merchandise on credit.		

Assets = Liabilities + Equity
+2,400 +2,400

This entry reflects an increase in Z-Mart's assets in the form of accounts receivable. It also shows the increase in revenue (Sales). If the sale is for cash, the debit is to Cash instead of Accounts Receivable. We explain accounting for credit card sales in Chapter 7.

The cost part of each sales transaction ensures that the Merchandise Inventory account under a perpetual inventory system reflects the updated cost of the merchandise available for sale. For example, the cost of the merchandise Z-Mart sold on November 3 is $1,600, and the entry to record the cost part of this sales transaction follows. (This shows the *expense recognition principle* as expense is recorded when sales are; and, when a UPC code is scanned using point-of-sale software, the sale and cost are both recorded, and inventory is reduced.)

(e) Nov. 3	Cost of Goods Sold	1,600	
	Merchandise Inventory		1,600
	To record the cost of Nov. 3 sale.		

Assets = Liabilities + Equity
−1,600 −1,600

Decision Insight

Suppliers and Demands Large merchandising companies often bombard suppliers with demands. These include discounts for bar coding and technology support systems, and fines for shipping errors. Merchandisers' goals are to reduce inventories, shorten lead times, and eliminate errors. Many colleges now offer programs in supply chain management and logistics to train future employees to help merchandisers meet such goals. ■

Sales Discounts

Point: Radio-frequency identification (RFID) tags attach to objects for tracking purposes. Such tags help employees find items in a store, monitor shipments, and check on production progress.

Sales discounts on credit sales can benefit a seller by decreasing the delay in receiving cash and reducing future collection efforts. At the time of a credit sale, a seller does not know whether a customer will pay within the discount period and take advantage of a discount. This means the seller usually does not record a sales discount until a customer actually pays within the discount period. To illustrate, Z-Mart completes a credit sale for $1,000 on November 12 with terms of 2/10, n/60. The entry to record the revenue part of this sale is

Assets = Liabilities + Equity
+1,000 +1,000

Nov. 12	Accounts Receivable	1,000	
	Sales		1,000
	*Sold merchandise under terms of 2/10, n/60.**		
	**The entry to record cost of this sale is not shown here.*		

This entry records the receivable and the revenue as if the customer will pay the full amount. The customer has two options, however. One option is to wait 60 days until January 11 and pay the full $1,000. In this case, Z-Mart records that payment as

Assets = Liabilities + Equity
+1,000
−1,000

Jan. 11	Cash	1,000	
	Accounts Receivable		1,000
	Received payment for Nov. 12 sale.		

The customer's second option is to pay $980 within a 10-day period ending November 22. If the customer pays on (or before) November 22, Z-Mart records the payment as

Assets = Liabilities + Equity
+980 −20
−1,000

Nov. 22	Cash ($1,000 × 0.98).	980	
	Sales Discounts ($1,000 × 0.02).	20	
	Accounts Receivable		1,000
	Received payment for Nov. 12 sale less discount.		

Sales Discounts is a contra revenue account, meaning the Sales Discounts account is deducted from the Sales account when computing a company's net sales (see Exhibit 4.9). Management monitors Sales Discounts to assess the effectiveness and cost of its discount policy.

Sales Returns and Allowances

Point: Published income statements rarely disclose sales discounts, returns, and allowances. Instead, net sales are reported.

Sales returns refer to merchandise that customers return to the seller after a sale. Many companies allow customers to return merchandise for a full refund. *Sales allowances* refer to reductions in the selling price of merchandise sold to customers. This can occur with damaged or defective merchandise that a customer is willing to purchase with a decrease in selling price. Sales returns and allowances usually involve dissatisfied customers and the possibility of lost future sales, and managers monitor information about returns and allowances.

Sales Returns To illustrate, recall Z-Mart's sale of merchandise on November 3 for $2,400 that had cost $1,600. Assume that the customer returns part of the merchandise on November 6, and the returned items sell for $800 and cost $600. The revenue part of this transaction must reflect the decrease in sales from the customer's return of merchandise as follows:

Assets = Liabilities + Equity
−800 −800

(f) Nov. 6	Sales Returns and Allowances	800	
	Accounts Receivable		800
	Customer returns merchandise from Nov. 3 sale.		

If the merchandise returned to Z-Mart is not defective and can be resold to another customer, Z-Mart returns these goods to its inventory. The entry to restore the cost of such goods to the Merchandise Inventory account is

Assets = Liabilities + Equity
+600 +600

Nov. 6	Merchandise Inventory	600	
	Cost of Goods Sold		600
	Returned goods added to inventory.		

This entry changes if the goods returned are defective. In this case, the returned inventory is recorded at its estimated value, not its cost. To illustrate, if the goods (costing $600) returned to Z-Mart are defective and estimated to be worth $150, the following entry is made: Dr. Merchandise Inventory for $150, Dr. Loss from Defective Merchandise for $450, and Cr. Cost of Goods Sold for $600.

Point: Some sellers charge buyers a restocking fee for returns.

Sales Allowances To illustrate sales allowances, assume that $800 of the merchandise Z-Mart sold on November 3 is defective but the buyer decides to keep it because Z-Mart offers a $100 price reduction. Z-Mart records this allowance as follows:

Nov. 6	Sales Returns and Allowances	100	
	Accounts Receivable		100
	To record sales allowance on Nov. 3 sale.		

Assets = Liabilities + Equity
−100 −100

Sales Returns and Allowances is a contra revenue account, meaning it is deducted from sales when computing net sales. The seller usually prepares a credit memorandum to confirm a buyer's return or allowance. A seller's **credit memorandum** informs a buyer of the seller's credit to the buyer's Account Receivable (on the seller's books). In summary, net sales equals sales minus sales discounts and minus sales returns and allowances. This means net sales is the amount customers paid for goods kept.

Point: The sender (maker) of a credit memorandum will *credit* the account of the receiver. The receiver of a credit memorandum will *debit* the sender's account.

NEED-TO-KNOW 4-2

Merchandise Sales

P2

Prepare journal entries to record each of the following sales transactions of a merchandising company. Show supporting calculations and assume a perpetual inventory system.

June 1 Sold 500 units of merchandise to a customer for $14 per unit under credit terms of 2/10, n/30, FOB shipping point, and the invoice is dated June 1. The merchandise had cost $10 per unit.

June 7 The customer returns 20 units because those units did not fit the customer's needs. The seller restores those units to its inventory.

June 8 The customer discovers that 30 units are damaged but are still of some use and, therefore, keeps the units because the seller sends the buyer a credit memorandum for $90 to compensate for the damage.

June 11 The customer discovers that 10 units are the wrong color, but keeps 8 of these units because the seller sends a $12 credit memorandum to compensate. The customer returns the remaining 2 units to the seller. The seller restores the 2 returned units to its inventory.

Solution

June 1	Accounts Receivable	7,000	
	Sales		7,000
	Sold merchandise on credit (500 × $14).		
June 1	Cost of Goods Sold	5,000	
	Merchandise Inventory		5,000
	To record cost of sale (500 × $10).		
June 7	Sales Returns and Allowances	280	
	Accounts Receivable		280
	Accepted a return from a customer (20 × $14).		
June 7	Merchandise Inventory	200	
	Cost of Goods Sold		200
	Returned merchandise to inventory (20 × $10).		
June 8	Sales Returns and Allowances	90	
	Accounts Receivable		90
	Granted allowance for damaged merchandise.		
June 11	Sales Returns and Allowances	40	
	Accounts Receivable		40
	Granted allowance for miscolored merchandise and accepted a return from a customer for the miscolored merchandise [$12 + (2 × $14)].		
June 11	Merchandise Inventory	20	
	Cost of Goods Sold		20
	Returned merchandise to inventory (2 × $10).		

Do More: QS 4-7, E 4-5

QC3

COMPLETING THE ACCOUNTING CYCLE

Exhibit 4.10 shows the flow of merchandising costs during a period and where these costs are reported at period-end. Specifically, beginning inventory plus the net cost of purchases is the merchandise available for sale. As inventory is sold, its cost is recorded in cost of goods sold on the income statement; what remains is ending inventory on the balance sheet. A period's ending inventory is the next period's beginning inventory.

EXHIBIT 4.10

Merchandising Cost Flow in the Accounting Cycle

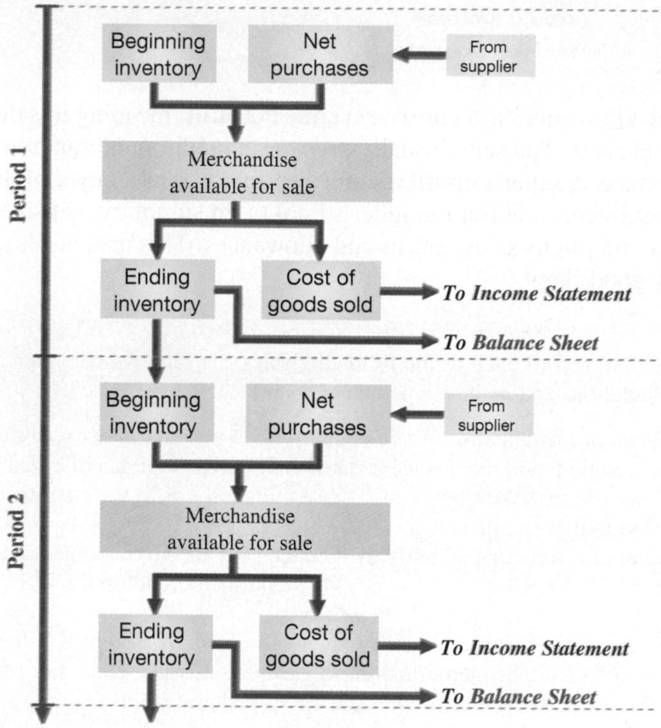

Adjusting Entries for Merchandisers

P3 Prepare adjustments and close accounts for a merchandising company.

Each of the steps in the accounting cycle described in the prior chapter for a service company applies to a merchandiser. This section and the next two further explain three steps of the accounting cycle for a merchandiser—adjustments, statement preparation, and closing.

Adjusting entries are generally the same for merchandising companies and service companies, including those for prepaid expenses (including depreciation), accrued expenses, unearned revenues, and accrued revenues. However, a merchandiser using a perpetual inventory system is usually required to make another adjustment to update the Merchandise Inventory account to reflect any loss of merchandise, including theft and deterioration. **Shrinkage** is the term used to refer to the loss of inventory, and it is computed by comparing a physical count of inventory with recorded amounts. A physical count is usually performed at least once annually.

Point: About two-thirds of shoplifting losses are thefts by employees.

To illustrate, Z-Mart's Merchandise Inventory account at the end of year 2015 has a balance of $21,250, but a physical count reveals that only $21,000 of inventory exists. The adjusting entry to record this $250 shrinkage is

Assets	=	Liabilities	+	Equity
−250				−250

Dec. 31	Cost of Goods Sold	250	
	Merchandise Inventory		250
	To adjust for $250 shrinkage revealed by a physical count of inventory.		

Preparing Financial Statements

The financial statements of a merchandiser, and their preparation, are similar to those for a service company described in Chapters 2 and 3. The income statement mainly differs by the inclusion of *cost of goods sold* and *gross profit.* Also, net sales is affected by discounts, returns, and allowances, and some additional expenses are possible such as delivery expense and loss from defective merchandise. The balance sheet mainly differs by the inclusion of *merchandise inventory* as part of current assets. The statement of retained earnings is unchanged. A work sheet can be used to help prepare these statements, and one for Z-Mart is illustrated in Appendix 4B.

Point: Staples's costs of shipping merchandise to its stores is included in its costs of inventories as required by the cost principle.

Closing Entries for Merchandisers

Closing entries are similar for service companies and merchandising companies using a perpetual system. The difference is that we must close some new temporary accounts that arise from merchandising activities. Z-Mart has several temporary accounts unique to merchandisers: Sales (of goods), Sales Discounts, Sales Returns and Allowances, and Cost of Goods Sold. Their existence in the ledger means that the first two closing entries for a merchandiser are slightly different from the ones described in the prior chapter for a service company. These differences are set in **red boldface** in the closing entries of Exhibit 4.11.

Point: The Inventory account is not affected by the closing process under a perpetual system.

EXHIBIT 4.11

Closing Entries for a Merchandiser

Step 1: Close Credit Balances in Temporary Accounts to Income Summary.

Dec. 31	**Sales**	**321,000**	
	Income Summary		321,000
	To close credit balances in temporary accounts.		

Step 2: Close Debit Balances in Temporary Accounts to Income Summary.

Dec. 31	Income Summary	308,100	
	Sales Discounts		**4,300**
	Sales Returns and Allowances		**2,000**
	Cost of Goods Sold		**230,400**
	Depreciation Expense		3,700
	Salaries Expense		43,800
	Insurance Expense		600
	Rent Expense		9,000
	Supplies Expense		3,000
	Advertising Expense		11,300
	To close debit balances in temporary accounts.		

Step 3: Close Income Summary to Retained Earnings.

The third closing entry is identical for a merchandising company and a service company. The $12,900 amount is net income reported on the income statement.

Dec. 31	Income Summary	12,900	
	Retained Earnings		12,900
	To close the Income Summary account.		

Step 4: Close Dividends Account to Retained Earnings.

The fourth closing entry is identical for a merchandising company and a service company. It closes the Dividends account and adjusts the Retained Earnings account to the amount shown on the balance sheet.

Dec. 31	Retained Earnings	4,000	
	Dividends		4,000
	To close the Dividends account.		

Summary of Merchandising Entries

Exhibit 4.12 summarizes the key adjusting and closing entries of a merchandiser (using a perpetual inventory system) that are different from those of a service company described in prior chapters (**Need-To-Know Comprehensive 2** illustrates these merchandising entries).

EXHIBIT 4.12

Summary of Merchandising Entries

	Merchandising Transactions	Merchandising Entries	Dr.	Cr.
Purchases	Purchasing merchandise for resale.	Merchandise Inventory	#	
		Cash or Accounts Payable		#
	Paying freight costs on purchases; FOB shipping point.	Merchandise Inventory	#	
		Cash		#
	Paying within discount period.	Accounts Payable	#	
		Merchandise Inventory		#
		Cash		#
	Recording purchase returns or allowances.	Cash or Accounts Payable	#	
		Merchandise Inventory		#
Sales	Selling merchandise.	Cash or Accounts Receivable	#	
		Sales		#
		Cost of Goods Sold	#	
		Merchandise Inventory		#
	Receiving payment within discount period.	Cash	#	
		Sales Discounts	#	
		Accounts Receivable		#
	Granting sales returns or allowances.	Sales Returns and Allowances	#	
		Cash or Accounts Receivable		#
		Merchandise Inventory	#	
		Cost of Goods Sold		#
	Paying freight costs on sales; FOB destination.	Delivery Expense	#	
		Cash		#

	Merchandising Events	Adjusting and Closing Entries	Dr.	Cr.
Adjusting	Adjusting due to shrinkage (occurs when recorded amount larger than physical inventory).	Cost of Goods Sold	#	
		Merchandise Inventory		#
Closing	Closing temporary accounts with credit balances.	Sales	#	
		Income Summary		#
	Closing temporary accounts with debit balances.	Income Summary	#	
		Sales Returns and Allowances		#
		Sales Discounts		#
		Cost of Goods Sold		#
		Delivery Expense		#
		"Other Expenses"		#

Merchandise Inventory	
Beginning inventory	
Purchases	Pur. returns
Freight-in (FOB shp pt)	Pur. allowances
Customer returns	Pur. discounts
	Shrinkage
Goods avail. for sale	
	COGS
Ending inventory	

NEED-TO-KNOW 4-3

Recording Shrinkage and Closing Process

P3

A merchandising company's ledger on May 31, its fiscal year-end, includes the following selected accounts that have normal balances (it uses the perpetual inventory system). A physical count of its May 31 year-end inventory reveals that the cost of the merchandise inventory still available is $718. (a) Prepare the entry to record any inventory shrinkage. (b) Prepare journal entries to close the balances in temporary revenue and expense accounts.

Merchandise inventory	$ 756	Sales returns and allowances	$ 130
Retained Earnings	2,306	Cost of goods sold	2,100
Dividends	140	Depreciation expense	206
Sales	3,204	Salaries expense	650
Sales discounts	94	Other operating expenses	100

Solution

May 31	Cost of Goods Sold	38	
	Merchandise Inventory		38
	To adjust for shrinkage based on physical count [$756 − $718].		
May 31	Sales	3,204	
	Income Summary		3,204
	To close temporary accounts with credit balances.		

[continued on next page]

[continued from previous page]

May 31	Income Summary	3,318	
	Sales Discounts		94
	Sales Returns and Allowances		130
	Cost of Goods Sold*		2,138
	Depreciation Expense		206
	Salaries Expense		650
	Other Operating Expenses		100
	To close temporary accounts with debit balances.		
	**$2,100 (pre-adjustment bal.) + $38 (from shrinkage)*		

Do More: QS 4-8, QS 4-9, E 4-9, E 4-11, P 4-4

QC4

FINANCIAL STATEMENT FORMATS

Generally accepted accounting principles do not require companies to use any one presentation format for financial statements so we see many different formats in practice. This section describes two common income statement formats: multiple-step and single-step. The classified balance sheet of a merchandiser is also explained.

P4 Define and prepare multiple-step and single-step income statements.

Multiple-Step Income Statement

A **multiple-step income statement** format shows detailed computations of net sales and other costs and expenses, and reports subtotals for various classes of items. Exhibit 4.13 shows a multiple-step income statement for Z-Mart. The statement has three main parts: (1) *gross profit,* determined by net sales less cost of goods sold, (2) *income from operations,* determined by

EXHIBIT 4.13

Multiple-Step Income Statement

Z-MART
Income Statement
For Year Ended December 31, 2015

Sales		$321,000	Gross profit computation
Less: Sales discounts	$ 4,300		
Sales returns and allowances	2,000	6,300	
Net sales		314,700	
Cost of goods sold*		230,400	
Gross profit		84,300	
Operating Expenses			Income from operations computation
Selling expenses			
Depreciation expense—Store equipment	3,000		
Sales salaries expense	18,500		
Rent expense—Selling space	8,100		
Store supplies expense	1,200		
Advertising expense	11,300		
Total selling expenses	42,100		
General and administrative expenses			
Depreciation expense—Office equipment	700		
Office salaries expense	25,300		
Insurance expense	600		
Rent expense—Office space	900		
Office supplies expense	1,800		
Total general and administrative expenses	29,300		
Total operating expenses		71,400	
Income from operations		12,900	
Other revenues and gains (expenses and losses)			Nonoperating activities computation
Interest revenue	1,000		
Gain on sale of building	2,500		
Interest expense	(1,500)		
Total other revenue and gains (expenses and losses)		2,000	
Net income		$ 14,900	

*Cost of goods sold consists of the following:

Beginning inventory	$ 19,000
Net cost of purchases	232,400
Goods available for sale	251,400
Less ending inventory	21,000
Cost of goods sold	$230,400

Point: Z-Mart did not have any nonoperating activities; however, Exhibit 4.13 includes some for illustrative purposes.

Point: Many companies report interest expense and interest revenue in separate categories after operating income and before subtracting income tax expense. As one example, see **Samsung**'s income statement in Appendix A.

Example: Sometimes interest revenue and interest expense are reported on the income statement as *interest, net.* To illustrate, if a company has $1,000 of interest expense and $600 of interest revenue, it might report $400 as *interest, net.*

gross profit less operating expenses, and (3) *net income,* determined by income from operations adjusted for nonoperating items.

Operating expenses are classified into two sections. **Selling expenses** include the expenses of promoting sales by displaying and advertising merchandise, making sales, and delivering goods to customers. **General and administrative expenses** support a company's overall operations and include expenses related to accounting, human resource management, and financial management. Expenses are allocated between sections when they contribute to more than one. Z-Mart allocates rent expense of $9,000 from its store building between two sections: $8,100 to selling expense and $900 to general and administrative expense.

Nonoperating activities consist of other expenses, revenues, losses, and gains that are unrelated to a company's operations. *Other revenues and gains* commonly include interest revenue, dividend revenue, rent revenue, and gains from asset disposals. *Other expenses and losses* commonly include interest expense, losses from asset disposals, and casualty losses. When a company has no reportable nonoperating activities, its income from operations is simply labeled net income.

Single-Step Income Statement

A **single-step income statement** is another widely used format and is shown in Exhibit 4.14 for Z-Mart. It lists cost of goods sold as another expense and shows only one subtotal for total expenses. Expenses are grouped into very few, if any, categories. Many companies use formats that combine features of both the single- and multiple-step statements. Provided that income statement items are shown sensibly, management can choose the format. (In later chapters, we describe some items, such as extraordinary gains and losses, that must be reported in certain locations on the income statement.) Similar presentation options are available for the statement of retained earnings and statement of cash flows.

EXHIBIT 4.14

Single-Step Income Statement

Z-MART
Income Statement
For Year Ended December 31, 2015

Revenues		
Net sales		$314,700
Interest revenue		1,000
Gain on sale of building		2,500
Total revenues		318,200
Expenses		
Cost of goods sold	$230,400	
Selling expenses	42,100	
General and administrative expenses	29,300	
Interest expense	1,500	
Total expenses		303,300
Net income		$ 14,900

Point: Net income is identical under the single-step and multiple-step formats.

Classified Balance Sheet

The merchandiser's classified balance sheet reports merchandise inventory as a current asset, usually after accounts receivable according to an asset's nearness to liquidity. Inventory is usually less liquid than accounts receivable because inventory must first be sold before cash can be received; but it is more liquid than supplies and prepaid expenses. Exhibit 4.15 shows

EXHIBIT 4.15

Classified Balance Sheet (partial) of a Merchandiser

Z-MART
Balance Sheet (partial)
December 31, 2015

Current assets	
Cash	$ 8,200
Accounts receivable	11,200
Merchandise inventory	**21,000**
Office supplies	550
Store supplies	250
Prepaid insurance	300
Total current assets	$ 41,500

the current asset section of Z-Mart's classified balance sheet (other sections are as shown and explained in our previous chapter).

Decision Insight

Merchandising Shenanigans Accurate invoices are important to both sellers and buyers. Merchandisers rely on invoices to make certain they receive all monies for products provided—no more, no less. To achieve this, controls are set up. Still, failures arise. A survey reports that 9% of employees in sales and marketing witnessed false or misleading invoices sent to customers. Another 14% observed employees violating contract terms with customers (KPMG 2009). ■

NEED-TO-KNOW 4-4

Multiple- and Single-Step Income Statements

P4

Assume Target's adjusted trial balance on April 30, 2015, its fiscal year-end, follows. (a) Prepare a multiple-step income statement that includes separate categories for selling expenses and for general and administrative expenses. (b) Prepare a single-step income statement that includes these expense categories: cost of goods sold, selling expenses, and general and administrative expenses.

Merchandise inventory	$ 820	
Other (noninventory) assets	2,608	
Total liabilities		$ 500
Common stock		400
Retained earnings		1,691
Dividends	160	
Sales		4,512
Sales discounts	45	
Sales returns and allowances	240	
Cost of goods sold	1,490	
Sales salaries expense	640	
Rent expense—Selling space	160	
Store supplies expense	30	
Advertising expense	260	
Office salaries expense	570	
Rent expense—Office space	72	
Office supplies expense	8	
Totals	$7,103	$7,103

Solution

a. Multiple-step income statement

TARGET
Income Statement
For Year Ended April 30, 2015

Sales		$4,512
Less: Sales discounts	$ 45	
Sales returns and allowances	240	285
Net sales		4,227
Cost of goods sold		1,490
Gross profit		2,737
Expenses		
Selling expenses		
Sales salaries expense	640	
Rent expense—Selling space	160	
Store supplies expense	30	
Advertising expense	260	
Total selling expenses		1,090
General and administrative expenses		
Office salaries expense	570	
Rent expense—Office space	72	
Office supplies expense	8	
Total general and administrative expenses		650
Total expenses		1,740
Net income		$ 997

b. Single-step income statement

TARGET
Income Statement
For Year Ended April 30, 2015

Net sales		$4,227
Expenses		
Cost of goods sold	$1,490	
Selling expenses	1,090	
General and administrative expenses	650	
Total expenses		3,230
Net income		$ 997

Do More: QS 4-14, E 4-20, P 4-3

GLOBAL VIEW

This section discusses similarities and differences between U.S. GAAP and IFRS in accounting and reporting for merchandise purchases and sales, and for the income statement.

Accounting for Merchandise Purchases and Sales Both U.S. GAAP and IFRS include broad and similar guidance for the accounting of merchandise purchases and sales. Specifically, all of the transactions presented and illustrated in this chapter are accounted for identically under the two systems. The closing process for merchandisers also is identical for U.S. GAAP and IFRS. In the next chapter we describe how inventory valuation can, in some cases, be different for the two systems.

Income Statement Presentation We explained that net income, profit, and earnings refer to the same (*bottom line*) item. However, IFRS tends to use the term *profit* more than any other term, whereas U.S. statements tend to use *net income* more than any other term. Both U.S. GAAP and IFRS income statements begin with the net sales or net revenues (*top line*) item. For merchandisers and manufacturers, this is followed by cost of goods sold. The presentation is similar for the remaining items with the following differences.

- U.S. GAAP offers little guidance about the presentation or order of expenses. IFRS requires separate disclosures for financing costs (interest expense), income tax expense, and some other special items.
- Both systems require separate disclosure of items when their size, nature, or frequency are important.
- IFRS permits expenses to be presented by their function or their nature. U.S. GAAP provides no direction but the SEC requires presentation by function.
- Neither U.S. GAAP nor IFRS define *operating* income, which results in latitude in reporting.
- IFRS permits alternative income measures on the income statement; U.S. GAAP does not.

VOLKSWAGEN

Volkswagen Group provides the following example of income statement reporting. We see the separate disclosure of finance costs, taxes, and other items. We also see the unusual practice of using the minus symbol in an income statement.

VOLKSWAGEN GROUP
Income Statement (in euros million)
For Year Ended December 31, 2013

Sales revenue	€ 197,007
Cost of sales	−161,407
Gross profit	35,600
Distribution expenses	−19,655
Administrative expenses	−6,888
Other operating income (net of other expenses)	2,613
Operating profit	11,671
Finance costs	−2,366
Other financial results (including equity investments)	3,123
Profit before tax	12,428
Income tax	−3,283
Profit	€ 9,145

Balance Sheet Presentation Chapters 2 and 3 explained how both U.S. GAAP and IFRS require current items to be separated from noncurrent items on the balance sheet (yielding a *classified balance sheet*). As discussed, U.S. GAAP balance sheets report current items first. Assets are listed from most liquid to least liquid, whereas liabilities are listed from nearest to maturity to furthest from maturity. IFRS balance sheets normally present noncurrent items first (and equity before liabilities), but this is *not* a requirement as evidenced in **Samsung**'s balance sheet in Appendix A.

Courtesy of Sseko

Sustainability and Accounting **Sseko Designs**, as introduced in this chapter's opening feature, places great emphasis on creating opportunities for young women. Sseko's model is in contrast to some other social businesses that offer to give some portion of their products or income to underprivileged communities. Sseko's founder, Liz Forkin Bohannon, explains, "We've seen firsthand the effects of brands that donate products to impoverished communities. Although the immediate need may be met, local economies often suffer. Economies simply cannot thrive when the market is flooded with free product." Liz explains Sseko's approach as follows: "Instead of donating product to help meet immediate needs, we try to go back further into the cycle of poverty and ask how we can empower and enable communities to take care of themselves and one another. We believe that job creation is a key component to that. Give her the opportunity and she will do the rest!" Her model is portrayed here.

Reprinted by permission of Sseko Designs

Acid-Test and Gross Margin Ratios **Decision Analysis**

Acid-Test Ratio

A1 Compute the acid-test ratio and explain its use to assess liquidity.

For many merchandisers, inventory makes up a large portion of current assets. Inventory must be sold and any resulting accounts receivable must be collected before cash is available. Chapter 3 explained that the current ratio, defined as current assets divided by current liabilities, is useful in assessing a company's ability to pay current liabilities. Because it is sometimes unreasonable to assume that inventories are a source of payment for current liabilities, we look to other measures.

One measure of a merchandiser's ability to pay its current liabilities (referred to as its *liquidity*) is the acid-test ratio. It differs from the current ratio by excluding less liquid current assets such as inventory and prepaid expenses that take longer to be converted to cash. The **acid-test ratio,** also called *quick ratio,* is defined as *quick assets* (cash, short-term investments, and current receivables) divided by current liabilities—see Exhibit 4.16.

EXHIBIT 4.16

Acid-Test (Quick) Ratio

$$\textbf{Acid-test ratio} = \frac{\textbf{Cash and cash equivalents + Short-term investments + Current receivables}}{\textbf{Current liabilities}}$$

Exhibit 4.17 shows both the acid-test and current ratios of retailer **JCPenney** for fiscal years 2009 through 2014—also see margin graph. JCPenney's acid-test ratio reveals an increase from 2009 through 2011 that exceeds the industry average, and then a marked decline in 2012 and 2013, with a slight rebound in 2014. Further, JCPenney's current ratio shows a marked decline in 2012 to 1.84, and even more in 2013 to 1.43 (with a slight rebound in 2014). This suggests that its short-term obligations are less confidently covered with short-term assets compared with prior years (especially in 2013).

EXHIBIT 4.17

JCPenney's Acid-Test and Current Ratios

($ millions)	2014	2013	2012	2011	2010	2009
Total quick assets	$1,519	$ 987	$1,920	$2,956	$3,406	$2,704
Total current assets	$4,833	$3,683	5,081	$6,370	$6,652	$6,220
Total current liabilities	$2,846	$2,568	2,756	$2,647	$3,249	$2,794
Acid-test ratio	**0.53**	**0.38**	**0.70**	**1.12**	**1.05**	**0.97**
Current ratio	**1.70**	**1.43**	**1.84**	**2.41**	**2.05**	**2.23**
Industry acid-test ratio	0.50	0.51	0.54	0.61	0.59	0.63
Industry current ratio	1.99	1.94	2.01	2.27	2.15	2.31

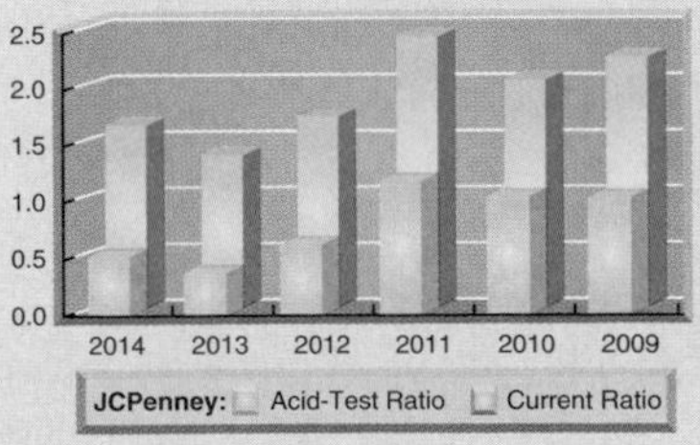

An acid-test ratio less than 1.0 means that current liabilities exceed quick assets. A rule of thumb is that the acid-test ratio should have a value near, or higher than, 1.0 to conclude that a company is unlikely to face near-term liquidity problems. A value much less than 1.0 raises liquidity concerns unless a company can generate enough cash from inventory sales or if much of its liabilities are not due until late in the next period. Similarly, a value slightly larger than 1.0 can hide a liquidity problem if payables are due shortly and receivables are not collected until late in the next period. Analysis of JCPenney shows some need for concern regarding its liquidity as its acid-test ratio is less than one. However, retailers such as JCPenney pay many current liabilities from inventory sales and in all years except 2013, JCPenney's acid-test ratios exceed the industry norm (and its inventory is fairly liquid).

Point: Successful use of a just-in-time inventory system can narrow the gap between the acid-test ratio and the current ratio.

Decision Maker

Supplier A retailer requests to purchase supplies on credit from your company. You have no prior experience with this retailer. The retailer's current ratio is 2.1, its acid-test ratio is 0.5, and inventory makes up most of its current assets. Do you extend credit? ■ [Answers follow the chapter's Summary.]

Gross Margin Ratio

A2 Compute the gross margin ratio and explain its use to assess profitability.

The cost of goods sold makes up much of a merchandiser's expenses. Without sufficient gross profit, a merchandiser will likely fail. Users often compute the gross margin ratio to help understand this relation. It differs from the profit margin ratio in that it excludes all costs except cost of goods sold. The **gross margin ratio** (also called *gross profit ratio*) is defined as *gross margin* (net sales minus cost of goods sold) divided by net sales—see Exhibit 4.18.

EXHIBIT 4.18
Gross Margin Ratio

$$\textbf{Gross margin ratio} = \frac{\textbf{Net sales} - \textbf{Cost of goods sold}}{\textbf{Net sales}}$$

Point: The power of a ratio is often its ability to identify areas for more detailed analysis.

Exhibit 4.19 shows the gross margin ratio of **JCPenney** for fiscal years 2009 through 2014. For JCPenney, each $1 of sales in 2014 yielded about 29.4¢ in gross margin to cover all other expenses and still produce a net income. This 29.4¢ margin is down from 37.4¢ in 2009. This decrease is not a favorable development. Success for merchandisers such as JCPenney depends on adequate gross margin. For example, the 8.0¢ decrease in the gross margin ratio, computed as 29.4¢ − 37.4¢, means that JCPenney has $948.72 million less in gross margin! (This is computed as net sales of $11,859 million multiplied by the 8.0% decrease in gross margin.) Management's discussion in its annual report attributes this decline "to sales of clearance merchandise at lower margins . . . including additional markdowns taken to sell through inventory associated with our previous strategy, as well as our transition back to a promotional pricing strategy."

EXHIBIT 4.19
JCPenney's Gross Margin Ratio

($ millions)	2014	2013	2012	2011	2010	2009
Gross margin	$ 3,492	$ 4,066	$ 6,218	$ 6,960	$ 6,910	$ 6,915
Net sales	$11,859	$12,985	$17,260	$17,759	$17,556	$18,486
Gross margin ratio	**29.4%**	**31.3%**	**36.0%**	**39.2%**	**39.4%**	**37.4%**

Decision Maker

Financial Officer Your company has a 36% gross margin ratio and a 17% net profit margin ratio. Industry averages are 44% for gross margin and 16% for net profit margin. Do these comparative results concern you? ■ [Answers follow the chapter's Summary.]

NEED-TO-KNOW

COMPREHENSIVE 1

Use the following adjusted trial balance and additional information to complete the requirements.

KC ANTIQUES
Adjusted Trial Balance
December 31, 2015

	Debit	Credit
Cash	$ 7,000	
Accounts receivable	13,000	
Merchandise inventory	60,000	
Store supplies	1,500	
Equipment	45,600	
Accumulated depreciation—Equipment		$ 16,600
Accounts payable		9,000
Salaries payable		2,000
Common stock		20,000
Retained earnings		59,000
Dividends	10,000	
Sales		343,250
Sales discounts	5,000	
Sales returns and allowances	6,000	
Cost of goods sold	159,900	
Depreciation expense—Store equipment	4,100	
Depreciation expense—Office equipment	1,600	
Sales salaries expense	30,000	
Office salaries expense	34,000	
Insurance expense	11,000	
Rent expense (70% is store, 30% is office)	24,000	
Store supplies expense	5,750	
Advertising expense	31,400	
Totals	$449,850	$449,850

KC Antiques's *supplementary records* for 2015 reveal the following itemized costs for merchandising activities:

Invoice cost of merchandise purchases	$150,000
Purchase discounts received	2,500
Purchase returns and allowances	2,700
Cost of transportation-in	5,000

Required

1. Use the supplementary records to compute the total cost of merchandise purchases for 2015.
2. Prepare a 2015 multiple-step income statement. (Inventory at December 31, 2014, is $70,100.)
3. Prepare a single-step income statement for 2015.
4. Prepare closing entries for KC Antiques at December 31, 2015.
5. Compute the acid-test ratio and the gross margin ratio. Explain the meaning of each ratio and interpret them for KC Antiques.

PLANNING THE SOLUTION

- Compute the total cost of merchandise purchases for 2015.
- To prepare the multiple-step statement, first compute net sales. Then, to compute cost of goods sold, add the net cost of merchandise purchases for the year to beginning inventory and subtract the cost of ending inventory. Subtract cost of goods sold from net sales to get gross profit. Then classify expenses as selling expenses or general and administrative expenses.
- To prepare the single-step income statement, begin with net sales. Then list and subtract the expenses.
- The first closing entry debits all temporary accounts with credit balances and opens the Income Summary account. The second closing entry credits all temporary accounts with debit balances. The

third entry closes the Income Summary account to the Retained Earnings account, and the fourth entry closes the Dividends account to the Retained Earnings account.

- Identify the quick assets on the adjusted trial balance. Compute the acid-test ratio by dividing quick assets by current liabilities. Compute the gross margin ratio by dividing gross profit by net sales.

SOLUTION

1.

Invoice cost of merchandise purchases	$150,000
Less: Purchases discounts received	2,500
Purchase returns and allowances	2,700
Add: Cost of transportation-in	5,000
Total cost of merchandise purchases	$149,800

2. Multiple-step income statement

KC ANTIQUES
Income Statement
For Year Ended December 31, 2015

Sales		$343,250
Less: Sales discounts	$ 5,000	
Sales returns and allowances	6,000	11,000
Net sales		332,250
Cost of goods sold*		159,900
Gross profit		172,350
Expenses		
Selling expenses		
Depreciation expense—Store equipment	4,100	
Sales salaries expense	30,000	
Rent expense—Selling space	16,800	
Store supplies expense	5,750	
Advertising expense	31,400	
Total selling expenses	88,050	
General and administrative expenses		
Depreciation expense—Office equipment	1,600	
Office salaries expense	34,000	
Insurance expense	11,000	
Rent expense—Office space	7,200	
Total general and administrative expenses	53,800	
Total operating expenses		141,850
Net income		$ 30,500

Tax Expense for a corporation appears immediately before net income in its own category.

* Cost of goods sold can also be directly computed (applying concepts from Exhibit 4.4):

Merchandise inventory, December 31, 2014	$ 70,100
Total cost of merchandise purchases (from part 1)	149,800
Goods available for sale	219,900
Merchandise inventory, December 31, 2015	60,000
Cost of goods sold	$159,900

3. Single-step income statement

KC ANTIQUES
Income Statement
For Year Ended December 31, 2015

Net sales		$332,250
Expenses		
Cost of goods sold	$159,900	
Selling expenses	88,050	
General and administrative expenses	53,800	
Total expenses		301,750
Net income		$ 30,500

4.

Dec. 31	Sales	343,250	
	Income Summary		343,250
	To close credit balances in temporary accounts.		
Dec. 31	Income Summary	312,750	
	Sales Discounts		5,000
	Sales Returns and Allowances		6,000
	Cost of Goods Sold		159,900
	Depreciation Expense—Store Equipment		4,100
	Depreciation Expense—Office Equipment		1,600
	Sales Salaries Expense		30,000
	Office Salaries Expense		34,000
	Insurance Expense		11,000
	Rent Expense		24,000
	Store Supplies Expense		5,750
	Advertising Expense		31,400
	To close debit balances in temporary accounts.		
Dec. 31	Income Summary	30,500	
	Retained Earnings		30,500
	To close the Income Summary account.		
Dec. 31	Retained Earnings	10,000	
	Dividends		10,000
	To close the Dividends account.		

5. Acid-test ratio = (Cash and equivalents + Short-term investments + Current receivables)/ Current liabilities

= (Cash + Accounts receivable/(Accounts payable + Salaries payable)

= ($7,000 + $13,000)/($9,000 + $2,000) = $20,000/$11,000 = 1.82

Gross margin ratio = Gross profit/Net sales = $172,350/$332,250 = 0.52 (or 52%)

KC Antiques has a healthy acid-test ratio of 1.82. This means it has more than $1.80 in liquid assets to satisfy each $1.00 in current liabilities. The gross margin of 0.52 shows that KC Antiques spends 48¢ ($1.00 − $0.52) of every dollar of net sales on the costs of acquiring the merchandise it sells. This leaves 52¢ of every dollar of net sales to cover other expenses incurred in the business and to provide a net profit.

NEED-TO-KNOW

COMPREHENSIVE 2

Prepare journal entries to record the following merchandising transactions for both the seller (BMX) and buyer (Sanuk).

May 4	BMX sold $1,500 of merchandise on account to Sanuk, terms FOB shipping point, n/45, invoice dated May 4. The cost of the merchandise was $900.
May 6	Sanuk paid transportation charges of $30 on the May 4 purchase from BMX.
May 8	BMX sold $1,000 of merchandise on account to Sanuk, terms FOB destination, n/30, invoice dated May 8. The cost of the merchandise was $700.
May 10	BMX paid transportation costs of $50 for delivery of merchandise sold to Sanuk on May 8.
May 16	BMX issued Sanuk a $200 credit memorandum for merchandise returned. The merchandise was purchased by Sanuk on account on May 8. The cost of the merchandise returned was $140.
May 18	BMX received payment from Sanuk for purchase of May 8.
May 21	BMX sold $2,400 of merchandise on account to Sanuk, terms FOB shipping point, 2/10, n/EOM. BMX prepaid transportation costs of $100, which were added to the invoice. The cost of the merchandise was $1,440.
May 31	BMX received payment from Sanuk for purchase of May 21, less discount (2% × $2,400).

SOLUTION

BMX (Seller)

Date	Account	Debit	Credit
May 4	Accounts Receivable—Sanuk	1,500	
	Sales		1,500
	Cost of Goods Sold	900	
	Merchandise Inventory		900
6	No entry.		
8	Accounts Receivable—Sanuk	1,000	
	Sales		1,000
	Cost of Goods Sold	700	
	Merchandise Inventory		700
10	Delivery Expense	50	
	Cash		50
16	Sales Returns & Allowances	200	
	Accounts Receivable—Sanuk		200
	Merchandise Inventory	140	
	Cost of Goods Sold		140
18	Cash	800	
	Accounts Receivable—Sanuk		800
21	Accounts Receivable—Sanuk	2,400	
	Sales		2,400
	Accounts Receivable—Sanuk	100	
	Cash		100
	Cost of Goods Sold	1,440	
	Merchandise Inventory		1,440
31	Cash	2,452	
	Sales Discounts	48	
	Accounts Receivable—Sanuk		2,500

Sanuk (Buyer)

Date	Account	Debit	Credit
May 4	Merchandise Inventory	1,500	
	Accounts Payable—BMX		1,500
6	Merchandise Inventory	30	
	Cash		30
8	Merchandise Inventory	1,000	
	Accounts Payable—BMX		1,000
10	No entry.		
16	Accounts Payable—BMX	200	
	Merchandise Inventory		200
18	Accounts Payable—BMX	800	
	Cash		800
21	Merchandise Inventory	2,500	
	Accounts Payable—BMX		2,500
31	Accounts Payable—BMX	2,500	
	Merchandise Inventory		48
	Cash		2,452

APPENDIX

4A Periodic Inventory System

A periodic inventory system requires updating the inventory account only at the *end of a period* to reflect the quantity and cost of both the goods available and the goods sold. Thus, during the period, the Merchandise Inventory balance remains unchanged. It reflects the beginning inventory balance until it is updated at the end of the period. During the period the cost of merchandise is recorded in a temporary *Purchases* account. When a company sells merchandise, it records revenue ***but not the cost of the goods sold.*** At the end of the period when a company prepares financial statements, it takes a *physical count of inventory* by counting the quantities and costs of merchandise available. The cost of goods sold is then computed by subtracting the ending inventory amount from the cost of merchandise available for sale.

P5 Record and compare merchandising transactions using both periodic and perpetual inventory systems.

Recording Merchandise Transactions Under a periodic system, purchases, purchase returns and allowances, purchase discounts, and transportation-in transactions are recorded in separate temporary accounts. At period-end, each of these temporary accounts is closed and the Merchandise Inventory account is updated. To illustrate, journal entries under the periodic inventory system are shown for the most common transactions (codes ***a*** through ***f*** link these transactions to those in the chapter, and we drop explanations for simplicity). For comparison, perpetual system journal entries are shown to the right of each periodic entry, where differences are highlighted in yellow.

Purchases The periodic system uses a temporary *Purchases* account that accumulates the cost of all purchase transactions during each period. Z-Mart's November 2 entry to record the purchase of merchandise for $1,200 on credit with terms of 2/10, n/30 is (*a*) Periodic / Perpetual

Periodic			Perpetual		
Purchases	1,200		Merchandise Inventory	1,200	
Accounts Payable		1,200	Accounts Payable		1,200

Purchase Discounts The periodic system uses a temporary *Purchase Discounts* account that accumulates discounts taken on purchase transactions during the period. If payment in (*a*) is delayed until after the discount period expires, the entry is to debit Accounts Payable and credit Cash for $1,200 each. However, if Z-Mart pays the supplier for the previous purchase in (*a*) within the discount period, the required payment is $1,176 ($1,200 × 98%) and is recorded as

(*b*)

Periodic			Perpetual		
Accounts Payable	1,200		Accounts Payable	1,200	
Purchase Discounts		24	Merchandise Inventory		24
Cash		1,176	Cash		1,176

Purchase Returns and Allowances Z-Mart returned merchandise purchased on November 2 because of defects. In the periodic system, the temporary *Purchase Returns and Allowances* account accumulates the cost of all returns and allowances during a period. The recorded cost (including discounts) of the defective merchandise is $300, and Z-Mart records the November 15 return with this entry:

Point: Purchase Discounts and Purchase Returns and Allowances are both classified as contra purchases accounts *and* have normal credit balances.

(*c*)

Periodic			Perpetual		
Accounts Payable	300		Accounts Payable	300	
Purchase Returns and Allowances		300	Merchandise Inventory		300

Transportation-In Z-Mart paid a $75 freight charge to transport merchandise to its store. In the periodic system, this cost is charged to a temporary *Transportation-In* account.

(*d*)

Periodic			Perpetual		
Transportation-In	75		Merchandise Inventory	75	
Cash		75	Cash		75

Sales Under the periodic system, the cost of goods sold is *not* recorded at the time of each sale. (We later show how to compute total cost of goods sold at the end of a period.) Z-Mart's November 3 entry to record sales of $2,400 in merchandise on credit (when its cost is $1,600) is:

(*e*)

Periodic			Perpetual		
Accounts Receivable	2,400		Accounts Receivable	2,400	
Sales		2,400	Sales		2,400
			Cost of Goods Sold	1,600	
None			Merchandise Inventory		1,600

Sales Returns A customer returned part of the merchandise from the transaction in (*e*), where the returned items sell for $800 and cost $600. (*Recall:* The periodic system records only the revenue effect, not the cost effect, for sales transactions.) Z-Mart restores the merchandise to inventory and records the November 6 return as

(*f*)

Periodic			Perpetual		
Sales Returns and Allowances	800		Sales Returns and Allowances	800	
Accounts Receivable		800	Accounts Receivable		800
			Merchandise Inventory	600	
None			Cost of Goods Sold		600

Sales Discounts To illustrate sales discounts, assume that the remaining $1,600 of receivables (computed as $2,400 from ***e*** less $800 for ***f***) has credit terms of 3/10, n/90 and that customers all pay within the discount period. Z-Mart records this payment as

Periodic			*Perpetual*		
Cash	1,552		Cash	1,552	
Sales Discounts ($1,600 × 0.03)	48		Sales Discounts ($1,600 × 0.03)	48	
Accounts Receivable		1,600	Accounts Receivable		1,600

Adjusting and Closing Entries The periodic and perpetual inventory systems have slight differences in adjusting and closing entries. The period-end Merchandise Inventory balance (unadjusted) is $19,000 under the periodic system. Since the periodic system does not update the Merchandise Inventory balance during the period, the $19,000 amount is the beginning inventory.

A physical count of inventory taken at the end of the period reveals $21,000 of merchandise available. The adjusting and closing entries for the two systems are shown in Exhibit 4A.1. Recording the periodic inventory balance is a two-step process. The ending inventory balance of $21,000 (which includes shrinkage) is entered by debiting the inventory account in the first closing entry. The beginning inventory balance of $19,000 is deleted by crediting the inventory account in the second closing entry.[2]

EXHIBIT 4A.1

Comparison of Adjusting and Closing Entries—Periodic and Perpetual

PERIODIC			PERPETUAL		
Adjusting Entry—Shrinkage			Adjusting Entry—Shrinkage		
None			Cost of Goods Sold	250	
			Merchandise Inventory		250
Closing Entries			Closing Entries		
(1) Sales	321,000		(1) Sales	321,000	
Merchandise Inventory (ending)	**21,000**				
Purchase Discounts	**4,200**				
Purchase Returns and Allowances	**1,500**				
Income Summary		347,700	Income Summary		321,000
(2) Income Summary	334,800		(2) Income Summary	308,100	
Sales Discounts		4,300	Sales Discounts		4,300
Sales Returns and Allowances		2,000	Sales Returns and Allowances		2,000
Merchandise Inventory (beginning)		**19,000**			
Purchases		**235,800**	**Cost of Goods Sold**		**230,400**
Transportation-In		**2,300**			
Depreciation Expense		3,700	Depreciation Expense		3,700
Salaries Expense		43,800	Salaries Expense		43,800
Insurance Expense		600	Insurance Expense		600
Rent Expense		9,000	Rent Expense		9,000
Supplies Expense		3,000	Supplies Expense		3,000
Advertising Expense		11,300	Advertising Expense		11,300
(3) Income Summary	12,900		(3) Income Summary	12,900	
Retained Earnings		12,900	Retained Earnings		12,900
(4) Retained Earnings	4,000		(4) Retained Earnings	4,000	
Dividends		4,000	Dividends		4,000

By updating Merchandise Inventory and closing Purchases, Purchase Discounts, Purchase Returns and Allowances, and Transportation-In, the periodic system transfers the cost of goods sold amount to Income Summary. Review the periodic side of Exhibit 4A.1 and notice that the **red boldface** items affect Income Summary as follows.

[2] This approach is called the *closing entry method.* An alternative approach, referred to as the *adjusting entry method,* would not make any entries to Merchandise Inventory in the closing entries of Exhibit 4A.1, but instead would make two adjusting entries. Using Z-Mart data, the two adjusting entries would be: (1) Dr. Income Summary and Cr. Merchandise Inventory for $19,000 each, and (2) Dr. Merchandise Inventory and Cr. Income Summary for $21,000 each. The first entry removes the beginning balance of Merchandise Inventory, and the second entry records the actual ending balance.

Credit to Income Summary in the first closing entry includes amounts from:	
Merchandise inventory (ending)	$ 21,000
Purchase discounts	4,200
Purchase returns and allowances	1,500
Debit to Income Summary in the second closing entry includes amounts from:	
Merchandise inventory (beginning)	(19,000)
Purchases	(235,800)
Transportation-in	(2,300)
Net effect on Income Summary (net debit = cost of goods sold)	**$(230,400)**

This $230,400 effect on Income Summary is the cost of goods sold amount. The periodic system transfers cost of goods sold to the Income Summary account but without using a Cost of Goods Sold account. Also, the periodic system does not separately measure shrinkage. Instead, it computes cost of goods available for sale, subtracts the cost of ending inventory, and defines the difference as cost of goods sold, which includes shrinkage.

Preparing Financial Statements The financial statements of a merchandiser using the periodic system are similar to those for a service company described in prior chapters. The income statement mainly differs by the inclusion of *cost of goods sold* and *gross profit*—of course, net sales is affected by discounts, returns, and allowances. The cost of goods sold section under the periodic system follows.

Calculation of Cost of Goods Sold
For Year Ended December 31, 2015

Beginning inventory	$ 19,000
Net cost of purchases	232,400
Cost of goods available for sale	251,400
Less ending inventory	21,000
Cost of goods sold	$230,400

QC5

The balance sheet mainly differs by the inclusion of *merchandise inventory* in current assets—see Exhibit 4.15. The statement of retained earnings is unchanged. A work sheet can be used to help prepare these statements. The only differences under the periodic system from the work sheet illustrated in Appendix 4B using the perpetual system are highlighted as follows in **blue boldface** font.

	A	B	C	D	E	F	G	H	I	J	K	L
1			Unadjusted Trial Balance		Adjustments		Adjusted Trial Balance		Income Statement		Balance Sheet and Statement of Equity	
2	No.	Account	Dr.	Cr.	Dr.	Cr.	Dr.	Cr.	Dr.	Cr.	Dr.	Cr.
3	101	Cash	8,200				8,200				8,200	
4	106	Accounts receivable	11,200				11,200				11,200	
5	**119**	**Merchandise inventory**	**19,000**				**19,000**		**19,000**	**21,000**	**21,000**	
6	126	Supplies	3,800			*(b)* 3,000	800				800	
7	128	Prepaid insurance	900			*(a)* 600	300				300	
8	167	Equipment	34,200				34,200				34,200	
9	168	Accumulated depr.—Equip.		3,700		*(c)* 3,700		7,400				7,400
10	201	Accounts payable		16,000				16,000				16,000
11	209	Salaries payable				*(d)* 800		800				800
12	307	Common stock		10,000				10,000				10,000
13	318	Retained earnings		32,600				32,600				32,600
14	319	Dividends	4,000				4,000				4,000	
15	413	Sales		321,000				321,000		321,000		
16	414	Sales returns and allowances	2,000				2,000		2,000			
17a	415	Sales discounts	4,300				4,300		4,300			
17b	**505**	**Purchases**	**235,800**				**235,800**		**235,800**			
17c	**506**	**Purchases returns & allowance**		**1,500**				**1,500**		**1,500**		
17d	**507**	**Purchases discounts**		**4,200**				**4,200**		**4,200**		
18	**508**	**Transportation-in**	**2,300**				**2,300**		**2,300**			
19	612	Depreciation expense—Equip.			*(c)* 3,700		3,700		3,700			
20	622	Salaries expense	43,000		*(d)* 800		43,800		43,800			
21	637	Insurance expense			*(a)* 600		600		600			
22	640	Rent expense	9,000				9,000		9,000			
23	652	Supplies expense			*(b)* 3,000		3,000		3,000			
24	655	Advertising expense	11,300				11,300		11,300			
25		Totals	389,000	389,000	8,100	8,100	393,500	393,500	334,800	347,700	79,700	66,800
26		Net income							12,900			12,900
27		Totals							347,700	347,700	79,700	79,700
28												

APPENDIX

4B Work Sheet—Perpetual System

Exhibit 4B.1 shows the work sheet for preparing financial statements of a merchandiser. It differs slightly from the work sheet layout in Chapter 3—the differences are in **red boldface**. Also, the adjustments in the work sheet reflect the following: (*a*) expiration of $600 of prepaid insurance, (*b*) use of $3,000 of supplies, (*c*) depreciation of $3,700 for equipment, (*d*) accrual of $800 of unpaid salaries, and (*e*) inventory shrinkage of $250. Once the adjusted amounts are extended into the financial statement columns, the information is used to develop financial statements. We also see that the far-right Balance Sheet and Statement of Equity columns are identical under the perpetual and periodic methods.

EXHIBIT 4B.1

Work Sheet for Merchandiser (using a perpetual system)

	A	B	C	D	E	F	G	H	I	J	K	L
1			Unadjusted Trial Balance		Adjustments		Adjusted Trial Balance		Income Statement		Balance Sheet and Statement of Equity	
2	No.	Account	Dr.	Cr.	Dr.	Cr.	Dr.	Cr.	Dr.	Cr.	Dr.	Cr.
3	101	Cash	8,200				8,200				8,200	
4	106	Accounts receivable	11,200				11,200				11,200	
5	**119**	**Merchandise inventory**	**21,250**			(*e*) 250	**21,000**				**21,000**	
6	126	Supplies	3,800			(*b*) 3,000	800				800	
7	128	Prepaid insurance	900			(*a*) 600	300				300	
8	167	Equipment	34,200				34,200				34,200	
9	168	Accumulated depr.—Equip.		3,700		(*c*) 3,700		7,400				7,400
10	201	Accounts payable		16,000				16,000				16,000
11	209	Salaries payable				(*d*) 800		800				800
12	307	Common stock		10,000				10,000				10,000
13	318	Retained earnings		32,600				32,600				32,600
14	319	Dividends	4,000				4,000				4,000	
15	**413**	**Sales**		**321,000**				**321,000**		**321,000**		
16	**414**	**Sales returns and allowances**	**2,000**				**2,000**		**2,000**			
17	**415**	**Sales discounts**	**4,300**				**4,300**		**4,300**			
18	**502**	**Cost of goods sold**	**230,150**		(*e*) 250		**230,400**		**230,400**			
19	612	Depreciation expense—Equip.			(*c*) 3,700		3,700		3,700			
20	622	Salaries expense	43,000		(*d*) 800		43,800		43,800			
21	637	Insurance expense			(*a*) 600		600		600			
22	640	Rent expense	9,000				9,000		9,000			
23	652	Supplies expense			(*b*) 3,000		3,000		3,000			
24	655	Advertising expense	11,300				11,300		11,300			
25		Totals	383,300	383,300	8,350	8,350	387,800	387,800	308,100	321,000	79,700	66,800
26		Net income							12,900			12,900
27		Totals							321,000	321,000	79,700	79,700
28												

Summary

C1 Describe merchandising activities and identify income components for a merchandising company. Merchandisers buy products and resell them. Examples of merchandisers include Walmart, Home Depot, The Limited, and Barnes & Noble. A merchandiser's costs on the income statement include an amount for cost of goods sold. Gross profit, or gross margin, equals sales minus cost of goods sold.

C2 Identify and explain the inventory asset and cost flows of a merchandising company. The current asset section of a merchandising company's balance sheet includes *merchandise inventory,* which refers to the products a merchandiser sells and are available for sale at the balance sheet date. Cost of merchandise purchases flows into Merchandise Inventory and from there to Cost of Goods Sold on the income statement. Any remaining inventory is reported as a current asset on the balance sheet.

A1 Compute the acid-test ratio and explain its use to assess liquidity. The acid-test ratio is computed as quick assets (cash, short-term investments, and current receivables) divided by current liabilities. It indicates a company's ability to pay its current liabilities with its existing quick assets. An acid-test ratio equal to or greater than 1.0 is often adequate.

A2 Compute the gross margin ratio and explain its use to assess profitability. The gross margin ratio is computed as gross margin (net sales minus cost of goods sold) divided by net sales. It indicates a company's profitability before considering other expenses.

P1 Analyze and record transactions for merchandise purchases using a perpetual system. For a perpetual inventory system, purchases of inventory (net of trade discounts) are added to the Merchandise Inventory account. Purchase discounts and purchase returns and allowances are subtracted from Merchandise Inventory, and transportation-in costs are added to Merchandise Inventory.

P2 Analyze and record transactions for merchandise sales using a perpetual system. A merchandiser records sales at list price less any trade discounts. The cost of items sold is transferred from Merchandise Inventory to Cost of Goods Sold. Refunds or credits given to customers for unsatisfactory merchandise are recorded in Sales Returns and Allowances, a contra account to Sales. If merchandise is returned and restored to inventory, the cost of this merchandise is removed from Cost of Goods Sold and transferred back to Merchandise Inventory. When cash discounts from the sales price are offered and customers pay within the discount period, the seller records this in Sales Discounts, a contra account to Sales.

P3 Prepare adjustments and close accounts for a merchandising company. With a perpetual system, it is often necessary to make an adjustment for inventory shrinkage. This is computed by comparing a physical count of inventory with the Merchandise Inventory balance. Shrinkage is normally charged to Cost of Goods Sold. Temporary accounts closed to Income Summary for a merchandiser include Sales, Sales Discounts, Sales Returns and Allowances, and Cost of Goods Sold.

P4 Define and prepare multiple-step and single-step income statements. Multiple-step income statements include greater detail for sales and expenses than do single-step income statements. They also show details of net sales and report expenses in categories reflecting different activities.

P5A Record and compare merchandising transactions using both periodic and perpetual inventory systems. A perpetual inventory system continuously tracks the cost of goods available for sale and the cost of goods sold. A periodic system accumulates the cost of goods purchased during the period and does not compute the amount of inventory or the cost of goods sold until the end of a period. Transactions involving the sale and purchase of merchandise are recorded and analyzed under both the periodic and perpetual inventory systems. Adjusting and closing entries for both inventory systems are illustrated and explained.

Guidance Answers to Decision Maker and Decision Ethics

Entrepreneur For terms of 3/10, n/90, missing the 3% discount for an additional 80 days equals an implied annual interest rate of 13.69%, computed as (365 days ÷ 80 days) × 3%. Since you can borrow funds at 11% (assuming no other processing costs), it is better to borrow and pay within the discount period. You save 2.69% (13.69% − 11%) in interest costs by paying early.

Payables Manager Your decision is whether to comply with prior policy or to create a new policy and not abuse discounts offered by suppliers. Your first step should be to meet with your superior to find out if the late payment policy is the actual policy and, if so, its rationale. If it is the policy to pay late, you must apply your own sense of ethics. One point of view is that the late payment policy is unethical. A deliberate plan to make late payments means the company lies when it pretends to make payment within the discount period. Another view is that the late payment policy is acceptable. In some markets, attempts to take discounts through late payments are accepted as a continued phase of "price negotiation." Also, your company's suppliers can respond by billing your company for the discounts not accepted because of late payments. However, this is a dubious viewpoint, especially since the prior manager proposes that you dishonestly explain late payments as computer or mail problems and since some suppliers have complained.

Supplier A current ratio of 2.1 suggests sufficient current assets to cover current liabilities. An acid-test ratio of 0.5 suggests, however, that quick assets can cover only about one-half of current liabilities. This implies that the retailer depends on money from sales of inventory to pay current liabilities. If sales of inventory decline or profit margins decrease, the likelihood that this retailer will default on its payments increases. Your decision is probably not to extend credit. If you do extend credit, you are likely to closely monitor the retailer's financial condition. (It is better to hold unsold inventory than uncollectible receivables.)

Financial Officer Your company's net profit margin is about equal to the industry average and suggests typical industry performance. However, gross margin reveals that your company is paying far more in cost of goods sold or receiving far less in sales price than competitors. Your attention must be directed to finding the problem with cost of goods sold, sales, or both. One positive note is that your company's expenses make up 19% of sales (36% − 17%). This favorably compares with competitors' expenses that make up 28% of sales (44% − 16%).

Key Terms

Acid-test ratio
Cash discount
Cost of goods sold
Credit memorandum
Credit period
Credit terms
Debit memorandum
Discount period
EOM

FOB
General and administrative expenses
Gross margin
Gross margin ratio
Gross profit
Inventory
List price
Merchandise
Merchandise inventory
Merchandiser
Multiple-step income statement
Periodic inventory system
Perpetual inventory system
Purchase discount
Retailer
Sales discount
Selling expenses
Shrinkage
Single-step income statement
Supplementary records
Trade discount
Wholesaler

Multiple Choice Quiz

Answers at end of chapter

1. A company has $550,000 in net sales and $193,000 in gross profit. This means its cost of goods sold equals
a. $743,000 **c.** $357,000 **e.** $(193,000)
b. $550,000 **d.** $193,000

2. A company purchased $4,500 of merchandise on May 1 with terms of 2/10, n/30. On May 6, it returned $250 of that merchandise. On May 8, it paid the balance owed for merchandise, taking any discount it is entitled to. The cash paid on May 8 is
a. $4,500 **c.** $4,160 **e.** $4,410
b. $4,250 **d.** $4,165

3. A company has cash sales of $75,000, credit sales of $320,000, sales returns and allowances of $13,700, and sales discounts of $6,000. Its net sales equal
a. $395,000 **c.** $300,300 **e.** $414,700
b. $375,300 **d.** $339,700

4. A company's quick assets are $37,500, its current assets are $80,000, and its current liabilities are $50,000. Its acid-test ratio equals
a. 1.600 **c.** 0.625 **e.** 0.469
b. 0.750 **d.** 1.333

5. A company's net sales are $675,000, its cost of goods sold is $459,000, and its net income is $74,250. Its gross margin ratio equals
a. 32% **c.** 47% **e.** 34%
b. 68% **d.** 11%

A(B) *Superscript letter A (B) denotes assignments based on Appendix 4A (4B).*
Icon denotes assignments that involve decision making.

Discussion Questions

1. What items appear in financial statements of merchandising companies but not in the statements of service companies?

2. In comparing the accounts of a merchandising company with those of a service company, what additional accounts would the merchandising company likely use, assuming it employs a perpetual inventory system?

3. Explain how a business can earn a positive gross profit on its sales and still have a net loss.

4. Why do companies offer a cash discount?

5. How does a company that uses a perpetual inventory system determine the amount of inventory shrinkage?

6. Distinguish between cash discounts and trade discounts. Is the amount of a trade discount on purchased merchandise recorded in the accounts?

7. What is the difference between a sales discount and a purchase discount?

8. Why would a company's manager be concerned about the quantity of its purchase returns if its suppliers allow unlimited returns?

9. Does the sender (maker) of a debit memorandum record a debit or a credit in the recipient's account? What entry (debit or credit) does the recipient record?

10. What is the difference between the single-step and multiple-step income statement formats?

11. Refer to the balance sheet and income statement for **Apple** in Appendix A. What does the company title its inventory account? Does the company present a detailed calculation of its cost of goods sold?

12. Refer to **Google**'s income statement in Appendix A. What title does it use for cost of goods sold?

13. Refer to the income statement for **Samsung** in Appendix A. What does Samsung title its cost of goods sold account?

14. Refer to the income statement of **Samsung** in Appendix A. Does its income statement report a gross profit figure? If yes, what is the amount?

15. Buyers negotiate purchase contracts with suppliers. What type of shipping terms should a buyer attempt to negotiate to minimize freight-in costs?

connect

QUICK STUDY

QS 4-1
Applying merchandising terms
C1

Enter the letter for each term in the blank space beside the definition that it most closely matches.

A. Sales discount	**E.** FOB shipping point	**H.** Purchase discount
B. Credit period	**F.** Gross profit	**I.** Cash discount
C. Discount period	**G.** Merchandise inventory	**J.** Trade discount
D. FOB destination		

_____ **1.** Goods a company owns and expects to sell to its customers.
_____ **2.** Time period that can pass before a customer's payment is due.
_____ **3.** Seller's description of a cash discount granted to buyers in return for early payment.
_____ **4.** Reduction below list or catalog price that is negotiated in setting the price of goods.
_____ **5.** Ownership of goods is transferred when the seller delivers goods to the carrier.
_____ **6.** Purchaser's description of a cash discount received from a supplier of goods.
_____ **7.** Reduction in a receivable or payable if it is paid within the discount period.
_____ **8.** Difference between net sales and the cost of goods sold.
_____ **9.** Time period in which a cash discount is available.
_____ **10.** Ownership of goods is transferred when delivered to the buyer's place of business.

QS 4-2
Identifying inventory costs
C2

Costs of $5,000 were incurred to acquire goods and make them ready for sale. The goods were shipped to the buyer (FOB shipping point) for a cost of $200. Additional necessary costs of $400 were incurred to acquire the goods. What is the buyer's total cost of merchandise inventory?

a. $5,000 **b.** $5,200 **c.** $5,400 **d.** $5,600

QS 4-3
Merchandise equations and flows
C2

Use the following information (in random order) from a service company and from a merchandiser to compute net income. For the merchandiser, also compute gross profit, the goods available for sale, and the cost of goods sold. *Hint:* Not all information may be necessary.

Krug Service Company		Kleiner Merchandising Company	
Expenses	$ 8,500	Accumulated depreciation	$ 700
Revenues	14,000	Beginning inventory	5,000
Dividends	1,600	Common stock	50
Cash	700	Retained earnings	900
Prepaid rent	800	Ending inventory	1,700
Accounts payable	200	Operating expenses	1,450
Common stock	500	Purchases	3,900
Retained earnings	2,500	Sales	9,500
Equipment	1,300	Dividends	1,600

QS 4-4
Recording purchases—perpetual system
P1

Prepare journal entries to record each of the following purchases transactions of a merchandising company. Show supporting calculations and assume a perpetual inventory system.

Nov. 5 Purchased 600 units of product at a cost of $10 per unit. Terms of the sale are 2/10, n/60; the invoice is dated November 5.
Nov. 7 Returned 25 defective units from the November 5 purchase and received full credit.
Nov. 15 Paid the amount due from the November 5 purchase, less the return on November 7.

QS 4-5
Recording discounts taken—perpetual P1

On August 1, Gilmore Company purchased merchandise from Hendren with an invoice price of $60,000 and credit terms of 2/10, n/30. Gilmore Company paid Hendren on August 11. Prepare any required journal entry(ies) for Gilmore Company (the purchaser) on: (*a*) August 1, and (*b*) August 11. Assume Gilmore uses the perpetual inventory method.

QS 4-6
Recording discounts missed—perpetual P1

On September 15, Krug Company purchased merchandise inventory from Makarov with an invoice price of $35,000 and credit terms of 2/10, n/30. Krug Company paid Makarov on September 28. Prepare any required journal entry(ies) for Krug Company (the purchaser) on: (*a*) September 15, and (*b*) September 28. Assume Krug uses the perpetual inventory method.

QS 4-7
Recording sales—perpetual system
P2

Prepare journal entries to record each of the following sales transactions of a merchandising company. Show supporting calculations and assume a perpetual inventory system.

Apr. 1	Sold merchandise for $3,000, granting the customer terms of 2/10, EOM; invoice dated April 1. The cost of the merchandise is $1,800.
Apr. 4	The customer in the April 1 sale returned merchandise and received credit for $600. The merchandise, which had cost $360, is returned to inventory.
Apr. 11	Received payment for the amount due from the April 1 sale less the return on April 4.

QS 4-8
Accounting for shrinkage—perpetual system
P3

Nix'It Company's ledger on July 31, its fiscal year-end, includes the following selected accounts that have normal balances (Nix'It uses the perpetual inventory system).

Merchandise inventory	$ 37,800	Sales returns and allowances	$ 6,500
Retained earnings	115,300	Cost of goods sold	105,000
Dividends	7,000	Depreciation expense	10,300
Sales	160,200	Salaries expense	32,500
Sales discounts	4,700	Miscellaneous expenses	5,000

A physical count of its July 31 year-end inventory discloses that the cost of the merchandise inventory still available is $35,900. Prepare the entry to record any inventory shrinkage.

QS 4-9
Closing entries P3

Refer to QS 4-8 and prepare journal entries to close the balances in temporary revenue and expense accounts. Remember to consider the entry for shrinkage that is made to solve QS 4-8.

QS 4-10
Multiple-step income statement
P4

For each item below indicate whether the statement describes a multiple-step income statement or a single-step income statement.

a. Multiple-step income statement **b.** Single-step income statement

_____ **1.** Shows detailed computations of net sales and other costs and expenses.
_____ **2.** Statement limited to two main categories (revenues and expenses).
_____ **3.** Reports gross profit as a separate line item.
_____ **4.** Reports net income equal to income from operations adjusted for any nonoperating items.

QS 4-11
Computing and interpreting acid-test ratio
A1

Use the following information on current assets and current liabilities to compute and interpret the acid-test ratio. Explain what the acid-test ratio of a company measures.

Cash	$1,490	Prepaid expenses	$ 700
Accounts receivable	2,800	Accounts payable	5,750
Inventory	6,000	Other current liabilities	850

QS 4-12
Contrasting liquidity ratios A1

Identify similarities and differences between the acid-test ratio and the current ratio. Compare and describe how the two ratios reflect a company's ability to meet its current obligations.

QS 4-13
Computing and analyzing gross margin
A2

Compute net sales, gross profit, and the gross margin ratio for each separate case *a* through *d*. Interpret the gross margin ratio for case *a*.

	a	b	c	d
Sales	$150,000	$550,000	$38,700	$255,700
Sales discounts	5,000	17,500	600	4,800
Sales returns and allowances	20,000	6,000	5,100	900
Cost of goods sold	79,750	329,589	24,453	126,500

QS 4-14
IFRS income statement presentation
P4

Income statement information for **adidas Group**, a German footwear, apparel, and accessories manufacturer, for the year ended December 31, 2013, follows. The company applies IFRS, as adopted by the European Union, and reports its results in millions of euros. Prepare its calendar year 2013 (1) multiple-step income statement and (2) single-step income statement.

Net income	€ 790
Financial income	26
Financial expenses	94
Operating profit	1,202
Cost of sales	7,352
Income taxes	344
Income before taxes	1,134
Gross profit	7,140
Royalty and commission income	104
Other operating income	143
Other operating expenses	6,185
Net sales	14,492

QS 4-15^A
Contrasting periodic and perpetual systems
P5

Identify whether each description best applies to a periodic or a perpetual inventory system.

_____ **a.** Updates the inventory account only at period-end.
_____ **b.** Requires an adjusting entry to record inventory shrinkage.
_____ **c.** Markedly increased in frequency and popularity in business within the past decade.
_____ **d.** Records cost of goods sold each time a sales transaction occurs.
_____ **e.** Provides more timely information to managers.

QS 4-16^A
Recording purchases—periodic system P5

Refer to QS 4-4 and prepare journal entries to record each of the merchandising transactions assuming that the periodic inventory system is used.

QS 4-17^A
Recording purchases—periodic system P5

Refer to QS 4-7 and prepare journal entries to record each of the merchandising transactions assuming that the periodic inventory system is used.

QS 4-18
International accounting standards
C1

Answer each of the following questions related to international accounting standards.

a. Explain how the accounting for merchandise purchases and sales is different between accounting under IFRS versus U.S. GAAP.

b. Income statements prepared under IFRS usually report an item titled *finance costs*. What do finance costs refer to?

c. U.S. GAAP prohibits alternative measures of income reported on the income statement. Does IFRS permit such alternative measures on the income statement?

connect

EXERCISES

Exercise 4-1
Computing revenues, expenses, and income
C1 C2

Using your accounting knowledge, fill in the blanks in the following separate income statements *a* through *e*. Identify any negative amount by putting it in parentheses.

	a	b	c	d	e
Sales	$62,000	$43,500	$46,000	$?	$25,600
Cost of goods sold					
Merchandise inventory (beginning)	8,000	17,050	7,500	8,000	4,560
Total cost of merchandise purchases	38,000	?	?	32,000	6,600
Merchandise inventory (ending)	?	(3,000)	(9,000)	(6,600)	?
Cost of goods sold	34,050	16,000	?	?	7,000
Gross profit	?	?	3,750	45,600	?
Expenses	10,000	10,650	12,150	3,600	6,000
Net income (loss)	$?	$16,850	$ (8,400)	$42,000	$?

Exercise 4-2
Operating cycle for merchandiser
C2

The operating cycle of a merchandiser with credit sales includes the following five activities. Starting with merchandise acquisition, identify the chronological order of these five activities.

_____ **a.** Inventory made available for sale.
_____ **b.** Cash collections from customers.
_____ **c.** Credit sales to customers.
_____ **d.** Purchases of merchandise.
_____ **e.** Accounts receivable accounted for.

Exercise 4-3
Sales returns and allowances C1

Business decision makers desire information on sales returns and allowances. (1) Explain why a company's manager wants the accounting system to record customers' returns of unsatisfactory goods in the Sales Returns and Allowances account instead of the Sales account. (2) Explain whether this information would be useful for external decision makers.

Exercise 4-4
Recording entries for merchandise purchases
P1

Prepare journal entries to record the following transactions for a retail store. Assume a perpetual inventory system.

Apr. 2	Purchased merchandise from Lyon Company under the following terms: $4,600 price, invoice dated April 2, credit terms of 2/15, n/60, and FOB shipping point.
3	Paid $300 for shipping charges on the April 2 purchase.
4	Returned to Lyon Company unacceptable merchandise that had an invoice price of $600.
17	Sent a check to Lyon Company for the April 2 purchase, net of the discount and the returned merchandise.
18	Purchased merchandise from Frist Corp. under the following terms: $8,500 price, invoice dated April 18, credit terms of 2/10, n/30, and FOB destination.
21	After negotiations, received from Frist a $1,100 allowance on the April 18 purchase.
28	Sent check to Frist paying for the April 18 purchase, net of the discount and allowance.

Check April 28, Cr. Cash $7,252

Exercise 4-5
Recording sales returns and allowances
P2

Allied Parts was organized on May 1, 2015, and made its first purchase of merchandise on May 3. The purchase was for 2,000 units at a price of $10 per unit. On May 5, Allied Parts sold 1,500 of the units for $14 per unit to Baker Co. Terms of the sale were 2/10, n/60. Prepare entries for Allied Parts to record the May 5 sale and each of the following separate transactions *a* through *c* using a perpetual inventory system.

a. On May 7, Baker returns 200 units because they did not fit the customer's needs. Allied Parts restores the units to its inventory.

b. On May 8, Baker discovers that 300 units are damaged but are still of some use and, therefore, keeps the units. Allied Parts sends Baker a credit memorandum for $600 to compensate for the damage.

c. On May 15, Baker discovers that 100 units are the wrong color. Baker keeps 60 of these units because Allied Parts sends a $120 credit memorandum to compensate. Baker returns the remaining 40 units to Allied Parts. Allied Parts restores the 40 returned units to its inventory.

Check (*c*) Dr. Merchandise Inventory $400

Exercise 4-6
Recording purchase returns and allowances
P1

Refer to Exercise 4-5 and prepare the appropriate journal entries for Baker Co. to record the May 5 purchase and each of the three separate transactions *a* through *c*. Baker is a retailer that uses a perpetual inventory system and purchases these units for resale.

Exercise 4-7
Analyzing and recording merchandise transactions—both buyer and seller
P1 P2

Santa Fe Company purchased merchandise for resale from Mesa Company with an invoice price of $24,000 and credit terms of 3/10, n/60. The merchandise had cost Mesa $16,000. Santa Fe paid within the discount period. Assume that both buyer and seller use a perpetual inventory system.

1. Prepare entries that the buyer should record for (*a*) the purchase and (*b*) the cash payment.

2. Prepare entries that the seller should record for (*a*) the sale and (*b*) the cash collection.

3. Assume that the buyer borrowed enough cash to pay the balance on the last day of the discount period at an annual interest rate of 8% and paid it back on the last day of the credit period. Compute how much the buyer saved by following this strategy. (Assume a 365-day year and round dollar amounts to the nearest cent, including computation of interest per day.)

Check (3) $465 savings

Exercise 4-8
Analyzing and recording merchandise transactions—both buyer and seller
P1 P2

On May 11, Sydney Co. accepts delivery of $40,000 of merchandise it purchases for resale from Troy Corporation. With the merchandise is an invoice dated May 11, with terms of 3/10, n/90, FOB shipping point. The goods cost Troy $30,000. When the goods are delivered, Sydney pays $345 to Express Shipping for delivery charges on the merchandise. On May 12, Sydney returns $1,400 of goods to Troy, who receives them one day later and restores them to inventory. The returned goods had cost Troy $800. On May 20, Sydney mails a check to Troy Corporation for the amount owed. Troy receives it the following day. (Both Sydney and Troy use a perpetual inventory system.)

1. Prepare journal entries that Sydney Co. records for these transactions.
2. Prepare journal entries that Troy Corporation records for these transactions.

Check (1) May 20, Cr. Cash $37,442

Exercise 4-9
Recording effects of merchandising activities
P1 P2

The following supplementary records summarize Tosca Company's merchandising activities for year 2015. Set up T-accounts for Merchandise Inventory and Cost of Goods Sold. Then record the summarized activities in those T-accounts and compute account balances.

Cost of merchandise sold to customers in sales transactions	$196,000
Merchandise inventory, December 31, 2014	25,000
Invoice cost of merchandise purchases	192,500
Shrinkage determined on December 31, 2015	800
Cost of transportation-in	2,900
Cost of merchandise returned by customers and restored to inventory	2,100
Purchase discounts received	1,700
Purchase returns and allowances	4,000

Check Year-end Merchandise Inventory, Dec. 31, $20,000

Exercise 4-10
Preparing journal entries—perpetual system
P1 P2

Journalize the following merchandising transactions for Chilton Systems assuming it uses a perpetual inventory system.

1. On November 1, Chilton Systems purchases merchandise for $1,500 on credit with terms of 2/5, n/30, FOB shipping point; invoice dated November 1.
2. On November 5, Chilton Systems pays cash for the November 1 purchase.
3. On November 7, Chilton Systems discovers and returns $200 of defective merchandise purchased on November 1 for a cash refund.
4. On November 10, Chilton Systems pays $90 cash for transportation costs with the November 1 purchase.
5. On November 13, Chilton Systems sells merchandise for $1,600 on credit. The cost of the merchandise is $800.
6. On November 16, the customer returns merchandise from the November 13 transaction. The returned items are priced at $300 and cost $130; the items were not damaged and were returned to inventory.

Exercise 4-11
Preparing adjusting and closing entries for a merchandiser
P3

The following list includes selected permanent accounts and all of the temporary accounts from the December 31, 2015, unadjusted trial balance of Emiko Co., a business owned by Kumi Emiko. Use these account balances along with the additional information to journalize (*a*) adjusting entries and (*b*) closing entries. Emiko Co. uses a perpetual inventory system.

	Debit	Credit
Merchandise inventory	$ 30,000	
Prepaid selling expenses	5,600	
Dividends	33,000	
Sales		$529,000
Sales returns and allowances	17,500	
Sales discounts	5,000	
Cost of goods sold	212,000	
Sales salaries expense	48,000	
Utilities expense	15,000	
Selling expenses	36,000	
Administrative expenses	105,000	

Additional Information

Accrued sales salaries amount to $1,700. Prepaid selling expenses of $3,000 have expired. A physical count of year-end merchandise inventory shows $28,450 of goods still available.

Check Entry to close Income Summary: Cr. Retained Earnings $84,250

Exercise 4-12
Multiple-step income statement P4

A company reports the following sales-related information. Prepare the net sales portion only of this company's multiple-step income statement.

Sales, gross	$200,000	Sales returns and allowances	$16,000
Sales discounts	4,000	Sales salaries expense	10,000

Exercise 4-13
Interpreting a physical count error as inventory shrinkage
A1

A retail company recently completed a physical count of ending merchandise inventory to use in preparing adjusting entries. In determining the cost of the counted inventory, company employees failed to consider that $3,000 of incoming goods had been shipped by a supplier on December 31 under an FOB shipping point agreement. These goods had been recorded in Merchandise Inventory as a purchase, but they were not included in the physical count because they were in transit. Explain how this overlooked fact affects the company's financial statements and the following ratios: return on assets, debt ratio, current ratio, and acid-test ratio.

Exercise 4-14
Physical count error and profits A2

Refer to the information in Exercise 4-13 and explain how the error in the physical count affects the company's gross margin ratio and its profit margin ratio.

Exercise 4-15
Computing and analyzing acid-test and current ratios
A1

Compute the current ratio and acid-test ratio for each of the following separate cases. (Round ratios to two decimals.) Which company case is in the best position to meet short-term obligations? Explain.

	Case X	Case Y	Case Z
Cash	$2,000	$ 110	$1,000
Short-term investments	50	0	580
Current receivables	350	470	700
Inventory	2,600	2,420	4,230
Prepaid expenses	200	500	900
Total current assets	$5,200	$3,500	$7,410
Current liabilities	$2,000	$1,000	$3,800

Exercise 4-16^A
Recording purchases—periodic system P5

Refer to Exercise 4-4 and prepare journal entries to record each of the merchandising transactions assuming that the periodic inventory system is used.

Exercise 4-17^A
Recording purchases and sales—periodic system
P5

Refer to Exercise 4-7 and prepare journal entries to record each of the merchandising transactions assuming that the periodic inventory system is used by both the buyer and the seller. (Skip the part 3 requirement.)

Exercise 4-18^A
Buyer and seller transactions—periodic system P5

Refer to Exercise 4-8 and prepare journal entries to record each of the merchandising transactions assuming that the periodic inventory system is used by both the buyer and the seller.

Exercise 4-19^A
Recording purchases—periodic system P5

Refer to Exercise 4-10 and prepare journal entries to record each of the merchandising transactions assuming that the periodic inventory system is used.

Exercise 4-20
Preparing an income statement following IFRS
P4

L'Oréal reports the following income statement accounts for the year ended December 31, 2013 (euros in millions). Prepare the income statement for this company for the year ended December 31, 2013, following usual IFRS practices.

Net profit	€ 2,961.4	Income tax expense	€1,063.0
Finance costs	29.1	Profit before tax expense	4,024.4
Net sales	22,976.6	Research and development expense	857.0
Gross profit	16,374.8	Selling, general and administrative expense	4,756.8
Other income	145.2	Advertising and promotion expense	6,886.2
Cost of sales	6,601.8	Finance income	33.5

connect

PROBLEM SET A

Problem 4-1A
Preparing journal entries for merchandising activities—perpetual system P1 P2

Prepare journal entries to record the following merchandising transactions of Blink Company, which applies the perpetual inventory system. (*Hint:* It will help to identify each receivable and payable; for example, record the purchase on July 1 in Accounts Payable—Boden.)

July 1 Purchased merchandise from Boden Company for $6,000 under credit terms of 1/15, n/30, FOB shipping point, invoice dated July 1.
2 Sold merchandise to Creek Co. for $900 under credit terms of 2/10, n/60, FOB shipping point, invoice dated July 2. The merchandise had cost $500.
3 Paid $125 cash for freight charges on the purchase of July 1.
8 Sold merchandise that had cost $1,300 for $1,700 cash.
9 Purchased merchandise from Leight Co. for $2,200 under credit terms of 2/15, n/60, FOB destination, invoice dated July 9.
11 Received a $200 credit memorandum from Leight Co. for the return of part of the merchandise purchased on July 9.
12 Received the balance due from Creek Co. for the invoice dated July 2, net of the discount.
16 Paid the balance due to Boden Company within the discount period.
19 Sold merchandise that cost $800 to Art Co. for $1,200 under credit terms of 2/15, n/60, FOB shipping point, invoice dated July 19.
21 Issued a $200 credit memorandum to Art Co. for an allowance on goods sold on July 19.
24 Paid Leight Co. the balance due after deducting the discount.
30 Received the balance due from Art Co. for the invoice dated July 19, net of discount.
31 Sold merchandise that cost $4,800 to Creek Co. for $7,000 under credit terms of 2/10, n/60, FOB shipping point, invoice dated July 31.

Check July 12, Dr. Cash $882
July 16, Cr. Cash $5,940
July 24, Cr. Cash $1,960
July 30, Dr. Cash $980

Problem 4-2A
Preparing journal entries for merchandising activities—perpetual system
P1 P2

Prepare journal entries to record the following merchandising transactions of Sheng Company, which applies the perpetual inventory system. (*Hint:* It will help to identify each receivable and payable; for example, record the purchase on August 1 in Accounts Payable—Arotek.)

Aug. 1 Purchased merchandise from Arotek Company for $7,500 under credit terms of 1/10, n/30, FOB destination, invoice dated August 1.
5 Sold merchandise to Laird Corp. for $5,200 under credit terms of 2/10, n/60, FOB destination, invoice dated August 5. The merchandise had cost $4,000.
8 Purchased merchandise from Waters Corporation for $5,400 under credit terms of 1/10, n/45, FOB shipping point, invoice dated August 8. The invoice showed that at Sheng's request, Waters paid the $140 shipping charges and added that amount to the bill. (*Hint:* Discounts are not applied to freight and shipping charges.)
9 Paid $125 cash for shipping charges related to the August 5 sale to Laird Corp.
10 Laird returned merchandise from the August 5 sale that had cost Sheng $400 and been sold for $600. The merchandise was restored to inventory.
12 After negotiations with Waters Corporation concerning problems with the merchandise purchased on August 8, Sheng received a credit memorandum from Waters granting a price reduction of $700.

Check Aug. 9, Dr. Delivery Expense, $125

14 At Arotek's request, Sheng paid $200 cash for freight charges on the August 1 purchase, reducing the amount owed to Arotek.

15 Received balance due from Laird Corp. for the August 5 sale less the return on August 10.

Aug. 18, Cr. Cash $4,793

18 Paid the amount due Waters Corporation for the August 8 purchase less the price reduction granted.

19 Sold merchandise to Tux Co. for $4,800 under credit terms of 1/10, n/30, FOB shipping point, invoice dated August 19. The merchandise had cost $2,400.

22 Tux requested a price reduction on the August 19 sale because the merchandise did not meet specifications. Sheng sent Tux a $500 credit memorandum to resolve the issue.

Aug. 29, Dr. Cash $4,257

29 Received Tux's cash payment for the amount due from the August 19 sale.

30 Paid Arotek Company the amount due from the August 1 purchase.

Problem 4-3A
Computing merchandising amounts and formatting income statements
C2 P4

Valley Company's adjusted trial balance on August 31, 2015, its fiscal year-end, follows.

	Debit	Credit
Merchandise inventory	$ 41,000	
Other (noninventory) assets	130,400	
Total liabilities		$ 25,000
Common stock		10,000
Retained earnings		94,550
Dividends	8,000	
Sales		225,600
Sales discounts	2,250	
Sales returns and allowances	12,000	
Cost of goods sold	74,500	
Sales salaries expense	32,000	
Rent expense—Selling space	8,000	
Store supplies expense	1,500	
Advertising expense	13,000	
Office salaries expense	28,500	
Rent expense—Office space	3,600	
Office supplies expense	400	
Totals	$355,150	$355,150

On August 31, 2014, merchandise inventory was $25,400. Supplementary records of merchandising activities for the year ended August 31, 2015, reveal the following itemized costs.

Invoice cost of merchandise purchases	$92,000
Purchase discounts received	2,000
Purchase returns and allowances	4,500
Costs of transportation-in	4,600

Required

1. Compute the company's net sales for the year.
2. Compute the company's total cost of merchandise purchased for the year.
3. Prepare a multiple-step income statement that includes separate categories for selling expenses and for general and administrative expenses.
4. Prepare a single-step income statement that includes these expense categories: cost of goods sold, selling expenses, and general and administrative expenses.

Check (2) $90,100
(3) Gross profit, $136,850; Net income, $49,850
(4) Total expenses, $161,500

Problem 4-4A
Preparing closing entries and interpreting information about discounts and returns

C2 P3

Use the data for Valley Company in Problem 4-3A to complete the following requirements.

Required

1. Prepare closing entries as of August 31, 2015 (the perpetual inventory system is used).

Analysis Component

2. The company makes all purchases on credit, and its suppliers uniformly offer a 3% sales discount. Does it appear that the company's cash management system is accomplishing the goal of taking all available discounts? Explain.
3. In prior years, the company experienced a 4% returns and allowance rate on its sales, which means approximately 4% of its gross sales were eventually returned outright or caused the company to grant allowances to customers. How do this year's results compare to prior years' results?

Check (1) $49,850 Dr. to close Income Summary
(3) Current-year rate, 5.3%

Problem 4-5A
Preparing adjusting entries and income statements; and computing gross margin, acid-test, and current ratios

A1 A2 P3 P4

The following unadjusted trial balance is prepared at fiscal year-end for Nelson Company.

	A	B	C
	NELSON COMPANY **Unadjusted Trial Balance** **January 31, 2015**		
1		**Debit**	**Credit**
2	Cash	$ 1,000	
3	Merchandise inventory	12,500	
4	Store supplies	5,800	
5	Prepaid insurance	2,400	
6	Store equipment	42,900	
7	Accumulated depreciation—Store equipment		$ 15,250
8	Accounts payable		10,000
9	Common stock		5,000
10	Retained earnings		27,000
11	Dividends	2,200	
12	Sales		111,950
13	Sales discounts	2,000	
14	Sales returns and allowances	2,200	
15	Cost of goods sold	38,400	
16	Depreciation expense—Store equipment	0	
17	Salaries expense	35,000	
18	Insurance expense	0	
19	Rent expense	15,000	
20	Store supplies expense	0	
21	Advertising expense	9,800	
22	Totals	$169,200	$169,200
23			

Rent expense and salaries expense are equally divided between selling activities and the general and administrative activities. Nelson Company uses a perpetual inventory system.

Required

1. Prepare adjusting journal entries to reflect each of the following:
   a. Store supplies still available at fiscal year-end amount to $1,750.
   b. Expired insurance, an administrative expense, for the fiscal year is $1,400.
   c. Depreciation expense on store equipment, a selling expense, is $1,525 for the fiscal year.
   d. To estimate shrinkage, a physical count of ending merchandise inventory is taken. It shows $10,900 of inventory is still available at fiscal year-end.
2. Prepare a multiple-step income statement for fiscal year 2015.
3. Prepare a single-step income statement for fiscal year 2015.
4. Compute the current ratio, acid-test ratio, and gross margin ratio as of January 31, 2015. (Round ratios to two decimals.)

Check (2) Gross profit, $67,750
(3) Total expenses, $106,775; Net income, $975

Problem 4-6A[B]
Preparing a work sheet for a merchandiser
P3

Refer to the data and information in Problem 4-5A.

Required

Prepare and complete the entire 10-column work sheet for Nelson Company. Follow the structure of Exhibit 4B.1 in Appendix 4B.

PROBLEM SET B

Problem 4-1B
Preparing journal entries for merchandising activities—perpetual system
P1 P2

Prepare journal entries to record the following merchandising transactions of Yarvelle Company, which applies the perpetual inventory system. (*Hint:* It will help to identify each receivable and payable; for example, record the purchase on May 2 in Accounts Payable—Havel.)

May 2 Purchased merchandise from Havel Co. for $10,000 under credit terms of 1/15, n/30, FOB shipping point, invoice dated May 2.
4 Sold merchandise to Heather Co. for $11,000 under credit terms of 2/10, n/60, FOB shipping point, invoice dated May 4. The merchandise had cost $5,600.
5 Paid $250 cash for freight charges on the purchase of May 2.
9 Sold merchandise that had cost $2,000 for $2,500 cash.
10 Purchased merchandise from Duke Co. for $3,650 under credit terms of 2/15, n/60, FOB destination, invoice dated May 10.
12 Received a $400 credit memorandum from Duke Co. for the return of part of the merchandise purchased on May 10.
14 Received the balance due from Heather Co. for the invoice dated May 4, net of the discount.
17 Paid the balance due to Havel Co. within the discount period.
20 Sold merchandise that cost $1,450 to Tameron Co. for $2,800 under credit terms of 2/15, n/60, FOB shipping point, invoice dated May 20.
22 Issued a $400 credit memorandum to Tameron Co. for an allowance on goods sold from May 20.
25 Paid Duke Co. the balance due after deducting the discount.
30 Received the balance due from Tameron Co. for the invoice dated May 20, net of discount and allowance.
31 Sold merchandise that cost $3,600 to Heather Co. for $7,200 under credit terms of 2/10, n/60, FOB shipping point, invoice dated May 31.

Check May 14, Dr. Cash $10,780
May 17, Cr. Cash $9,900
May 30, Dr. Cash $2,352

Problem 4-2B
Preparing journal entries for merchandising activities—perpetual system
P1 P2

Prepare journal entries to record the following merchandising transactions of Mason Company, which applies the perpetual inventory system. (*Hint:* It will help to identify each receivable and payable; for example, record the purchase on July 3 in Accounts Payable—OLB.)

July 3 Purchased merchandise from OLB Corp. for $15,000 under credit terms of 1/10, n/30, FOB destination, invoice dated July 3.
7 Sold merchandise to Brill Co. for $11,500 under credit terms of 2/10, n/60, FOB destination, invoice dated July 7. The merchandise had cost $7,750.
10 Purchased merchandise from Rupert Corporation for $14,200 under credit terms of 1/10, n/45, FOB shipping point, invoice dated July 10. The invoice showed that at Mason's request, Rupert paid the $500 shipping charges and added that amount to the bill. (*Hint:* Discounts are not applied to freight and shipping charges.)
11 Paid $300 cash for shipping charges related to the July 7 sale to Brill Co.
12 Brill returned merchandise from the July 7 sale that had cost Mason $1,450 and been sold for $1,850. The merchandise was restored to inventory.
14 After negotiations with Rupert Corporation concerning problems with the merchandise purchased on July 10, Mason received a credit memorandum from Rupert granting a price reduction of $2,000.
15 At OLB's request, Mason paid $150 cash for freight charges on the July 3 purchase, reducing the amount owed to OLB.
17 Received balance due from Brill Co. for the July 7 sale less the return on July 12.
20 Paid the amount due Rupert Corporation for the July 10 purchase less the price reduction granted.
21 Sold merchandise to Brown for $11,000 under credit terms of 1/10, n/30, FOB shipping point, invoice dated July 21. The merchandise had cost $7,000.
24 Brown requested a price reduction on the July 21 sale because the merchandise did not meet specifications. Mason sent Brown a credit memorandum for $1,300 to resolve the issue.
30 Received Brown's cash payment for the amount due from the July 21 sale.
31 Paid OLB Corp. the amount due from the July 3 purchase.

Check July 17, Dr. Cash $9,457
July 20, Cr. Cash $12,578
July 30, Dr. Cash $9,603

Problem 4-3B
Computing merchandising amounts and formatting income statements
C1 C2 P4

Barkley Company's adjusted trial balance on March 31, 2015, its fiscal year-end, follows.

	Debit	Credit
Merchandise inventory	$ 56,500	
Other (noninventory) assets	202,600	
Total liabilities		$ 42,500
Common stock		10,000
Retained earnings		154,425
Dividends	3,000	
Sales		332,650
Sales discounts	5,875	
Sales returns and allowances	20,000	
Cost of goods sold	115,600	
Sales salaries expense	44,500	
Rent expense—Selling space	16,000	
Store supplies expense	3,850	
Advertising expense	26,000	
Office salaries expense	40,750	
Rent expense—Office space	3,800	
Office supplies expense	1,100	
Totals	$539,575	$539,575

On March 31, 2014, merchandise inventory was $37,500. Supplementary records of merchandising activities for the year ended March 31, 2015, reveal the following itemized costs.

Invoice cost of merchandise purchases	$138,500
Purchase discounts received	2,950
Purchase returns and allowances	6,700
Costs of transportation-in	5,750

Required

1. Calculate the company's net sales for the year.
2. Calculate the company's total cost of merchandise purchased for the year.
3. Prepare a multiple-step income statement that includes separate categories for selling expenses and for general and administrative expenses.
4. Prepare a single-step income statement that includes these expense categories: cost of goods sold, selling expenses, and general and administrative expenses.

Check (2) $134,600
(3) Gross profit, $191,175; Net income, $55,175
(4) Total expenses, $251,600

Problem 4-4B
Preparing closing entries and interpreting information about discounts and returns
C2 P3

Use the data for Barkley Company in Problem 4-3B to complete the following requirements.

Required

1. Prepare closing entries as of March 31, 2015 (the perpetual inventory system is used).

Analysis Component

2. The company makes all purchases on credit, and its suppliers uniformly offer a 3% sales discount. Does it appear that the company's cash management system is accomplishing the goal of taking all available discounts? Explain.
3. In prior years, the company experienced a 5% returns and allowance rate on its sales, which means approximately 5% of its gross sales were eventually returned outright or caused the company to grant allowances to customers. How do this year's results compare to prior years' results?

Check (1) $55,175 Dr. to close Income Summary
(3) Current-year rate, 6.0%

Problem 4-5B
Preparing adjusting entries and income statements; and computing gross margin, acid-test, and current ratios

A1 A2 P3 P4

The following unadjusted trial balance is prepared at fiscal year-end for Foster Products Company.

	A	B	C
1	**FOSTER PRODUCTS COMPANY** **Unadjusted Trial Balance** **October 31, 2015**	**Debit**	**Credit**
2	Cash	$ 7,400	
3	Merchandise inventory	24,000	
4	Store supplies	9,700	
5	Prepaid insurance	6,600	
6	Store equipment	81,800	
7	Accumulated depreciation—Store equipment		$ 32,000
8	Accounts payable		18,000
9	Common stock		3,000
10	Retained earnings		40,000
11	Dividends	2,000	
12	Sales		227,100
13	Sales discounts	1,000	
14	Sales returns and allowances	5,000	
15	Cost of goods sold	75,800	
16	Depreciation expense—Store equipment	0	
17	Salaries expense	63,000	
18	Insurance expense	0	
19	Rent expense	26,000	
20	Store supplies expense	0	
21	Advertising expense	17,800	
22	Totals	$320,100	$320,100
23			

Rent expense and salaries expense are equally divided between selling activities and the general and administrative activities. Foster Products Company uses a perpetual inventory system.

Required

1. Prepare adjusting journal entries to reflect each of the following.
   a. Store supplies still available at fiscal year-end amount to $3,700.
   b. Expired insurance, an administrative expense, for the fiscal year is $2,800.
   c. Depreciation expense on store equipment, a selling expense, is $3,000 for the fiscal year.
   d. To estimate shrinkage, a physical count of ending merchandise inventory is taken. It shows $21,300 of inventory is still available at fiscal year-end.
2. Prepare a multiple-step income statement for fiscal year 2015.
3. Prepare a single-step income statement for fiscal year 2015.
4. Compute the current ratio, acid-test ratio, and gross margin ratio as of October 31, 2015. (Round ratios to two decimals.)

Check (2) Gross profit, $142,600
(3) Total expenses, $197,100; Net income, $24,000

Problem 4-6B[B]
Preparing a work sheet for a merchandiser

P3

Refer to the data and information in Problem 4-5B.

Required

Prepare and complete the entire 10-column work sheet for Foster Products Company. Follow the structure of Exhibit 4B.1 in Appendix 4B.

SERIAL PROBLEM
Business Solutions

P1 P2 P3 P4

(This serial problem began in Chapter 1 and continues through most of the book. If previous chapter segments were not completed, the serial problem can begin at this point. It is helpful, but not necessary, to use the Working Papers that accompany the book.)

SP 4 Santana Rey created Business Solutions on October 1, 2015. The company has been successful, and its list of customers has grown. To accommodate the growth, the accounting system is modified to set up separate accounts for each customer. The following chart of accounts includes the account number used for each account and any balance as of December 31, 2015. Santana Rey decided to add a fourth digit with a decimal point to the 106 account number that had been used for the single Accounts Receivable account. This change allows the company to continue using the existing chart of accounts.

No.	Account Title	Dr.	Cr.
101	Cash	$48,372	
106.1	Alex's Engineering Co.	0	
106.2	Wildcat Services	0	
106.3	Easy Leasing	0	
106.4	IFM Co.	3,000	
106.5	Liu Corp.	0	
106.6	Gomez Co.	2,668	
106.7	Delta Co.	0	
106.8	KC, Inc.	0	
106.9	Dream, Inc.	0	
119	Merchandise inventory	0	
126	Computer supplies	580	
128	Prepaid insurance	1,665	
131	Prepaid rent	825	
163	Office equipment	8,000	
164	Accumulated depreciation—Office equipment		$ 400
167	Computer equipment	20,000	
168	Accumulated depreciation—Computer equipment		1,250
201	Accounts payable		1,100

No.	Account Title	Dr.	Cr.
210	Wages payable		$ 500
236	Unearned computer services revenue		1,500
307	Common stock		73,000
318	Retained earnings		7,360
319	Dividends	$0	
403	Computer services revenue		0
413	Sales		0
414	Sales returns and allowances	0	
415	Sales discounts	0	
502	Cost of goods sold	0	
612	Depreciation expense—Office equipment	0	
613	Depreciation expense—Computer equipment	0	
623	Wages expense	0	
637	Insurance expense	0	
640	Rent expense	0	
652	Computer supplies expense	0	
655	Advertising expense	0	
676	Mileage expense	0	
677	Miscellaneous expenses	0	
684	Repairs expense—Computer	0	

In response to requests from customers, S. Rey will begin selling computer software. The company will extend credit terms of 1/10, n/30, FOB shipping point, to all customers who purchase this merchandise. However, no cash discount is available on consulting fees. Additional accounts (Nos. 119, 413, 414, 415, and 502) are added to its general ledger to accommodate the company's new merchandising activities. Also, Business Solutions does not use reversing entries and, therefore, all revenue and expense accounts have zero beginning balances as of January 1, 2016. Its transactions for January through March follow:

Jan. 4 The company paid cash to Lyn Addie for five days' work at the rate of $125 per day. Four of the five days relate to wages payable that were accrued in the prior year.

5 Santana Rey invested an additional $25,000 cash in the company in exchange for more common stock.

7 The company purchased $5,800 of merchandise from Kansas Corp. with terms of 1/10, n/30, FOB shipping point, invoice dated January 7.

9 The company received $2,668 cash from Gomez Co. as full payment on its account.

11 The company completed a five-day project for Alex's Engineering Co. and billed it $5,500, which is the total price of $7,000 less the advance payment of $1,500.

Check Jan. 11, Dr. Unearned Computer Services Revenue $1,500

13 The company sold merchandise with a retail value of $5,200 and a cost of $3,560 to Liu Corp., invoice dated January 13.

15 The company paid $600 cash for freight charges on the merchandise purchased on January 7.

16 The company received $4,000 cash from Delta Co. for computer services provided.

17 The company paid Kansas Corp. for the invoice dated January 7, net of the discount.

20 Liu Corp. returned $500 of defective merchandise from its invoice dated January 13. The returned merchandise, which had a $320 cost, is discarded. (The policy of Business Solutions is to leave the cost of defective products in Cost of Goods Sold.)

Check Jan. 20, No entry to Cost of Goods Sold

22 The company received the balance due from Liu Corp., net of both the discount and the credit for the returned merchandise.

24 The company returned defective merchandise to Kansas Corp. and accepted a credit against future purchases. The defective merchandise invoice cost, net of the discount, was $496.

26 The company purchased $9,000 of merchandise from Kansas Corp. with terms of 1/10, n/30, FOB destination, invoice dated January 26.
26 The company sold merchandise with a $4,640 cost for $5,800 on credit to KC, Inc., invoice dated January 26.
31 The company paid cash to Lyn Addie for 10 days' work at $125 per day.
Feb. 1 The company paid $2,475 cash to Hillside Mall for another three months' rent in advance.
3 The company paid Kansas Corp. for the balance due, net of the cash discount, less the $496 amount in the credit memorandum.
5 The company paid $600 cash to the local newspaper for an advertising insert in today's paper.
11 The company received the balance due from Alex's Engineering Co. for fees billed on January 11.
15 The company paid $4,800 cash for dividends.
23 The company sold merchandise with a $2,660 cost for $3,220 on credit to Delta Co., invoice dated February 23.
26 The company paid cash to Lyn Addie for eight days' work at $125 per day.
27 The company reimbursed Santana Rey for business automobile mileage (600 miles at $0.32 per mile).
Mar. 8 The company purchased $2,730 of computer supplies from Harris Office Products on credit, invoice dated March 8.
9 The company received the balance due from Delta Co. for merchandise sold on February 23.
11 The company paid $960 cash for minor repairs to the company's computer.
16 The company received $5,260 cash from Dream, Inc., for computing services provided.
19 The company paid the full amount due to Harris Office Products, consisting of amounts created on December 15 (of $1,100) and March 8.
24 The company billed Easy Leasing for $9,047 of computing services provided.
25 The company sold merchandise with a $2,002 cost for $2,800 on credit to Wildcat Services, invoice dated March 25.
30 The company sold merchandise with a $1,048 cost for $2,220 on credit to IFM Company, invoice dated March 30.
31 The company reimbursed Santana Rey for business automobile mileage (400 miles at $0.32 per mile).

The following additional facts are available for preparing adjustments on March 31 prior to financial statement preparation:

a. The March 31 amount of computer supplies still available totals $2,005.
b. Three more months have expired since the company purchased its annual insurance policy at a $2,220 cost for 12 months of coverage.
c. Lyn Addie has not been paid for seven days of work at the rate of $125 per day.
d. Three months have passed since any prepaid rent has been transferred to expense. The monthly rent expense is $825.
e. Depreciation on the computer equipment for January 1 through March 31 is $1,250.
f. Depreciation on the office equipment for January 1 through March 31 is $400.
g. The March 31 amount of merchandise inventory still available totals $704.

Required

1. Prepare journal entries to record each of the January through March transactions.
2. Post the journal entries in part 1 to the accounts in the company's general ledger. (*Note:* Begin with the ledger's post-closing adjusted balances as of December 31, 2015.)
3. Prepare a partial work sheet consisting of the first six columns (similar to the one shown in Exhibit 4B.1) that includes the unadjusted trial balance, the March 31 adjustments (*a*) through (*g*), and the adjusted trial balance. Do not prepare closing entries and do not journalize the adjustments or post them to the ledger.
4. Prepare an income statement (from the adjusted trial balance in part 3) for the three months ended March 31, 2016. Use a single-step format. List all expenses without differentiating between selling expenses and general and administrative expenses.
5. Prepare a statement of retained earnings (from the adjusted trial balance in part 3) for the three months ended March 31, 2016.
6. Prepare a classified balance sheet (from the adjusted trial balance) as of March 31, 2016.

Check (2) Ending balances at March 31: Cash, $68,057; Sales, $19,240
(3) Unadj. TB totals, $151,557; Adj. TB totals, $154,082
(4) Net income, $18,833
(6) Total assets, $120,268

The **General Ledger** tool in *Connect Plus* automates several of the procedural steps in the accounting cycle so that the accounting professional can focus on the impacts of each transaction on the various financial reports. The following General Ledger questions highlight the operating cycle of a merchandising company. In each case, the trial balance is automatically updated from the journal entries recorded.

GL 4-1 Based on Problem 4-1A

GL 4-2 Based on Problem 4-2A

GL 4-3 Based on Problem 4-5A

GENERAL LEDGER PROBLEM

Available in Connect

connect ACCOUNTING

Beyond the Numbers

REPORTING IN ACTION

A1

APPLE

BTN 4-1 Refer to **Apple**'s financial statements in Appendix A to answer the following.

Required

1. Assume that the amounts reported for inventories and cost of sales reflect items purchased in a form ready for resale. Compute the net cost of goods purchased for the year ended September 28, 2013.
2. Compute the current ratio and acid-test ratio as of September 28, 2013, and September 29, 2012. Interpret and comment on the ratio results. How does Apple compare to the industry average of 1.5 for the current ratio and 1.25 for the acid-test ratio?

Fast Forward

3. Access Apple's financial statements (form 10-K) for fiscal years ending after September 28, 2013, from its website (Apple.com) or the SEC's EDGAR database (www.SEC.gov). Recompute and interpret the current ratio and acid-test ratio for these current fiscal years.

COMPARATIVE ANALYSIS

A2

APPLE

GOOGLE

BTN 4-2 Key comparative figures for both **Apple** and **Google** follow.

	Apple		Google	
($ millions)	Current Year	Prior Year	Current Year	Prior Year
Net sales	$170,910	$156,508	$59,825	$50,175
Cost of sales	106,606	87,846	25,858	20,634

Required

1. Compute the dollar amount of gross margin and the gross margin ratio for the two years shown for each of these companies.
2. Which company earns more in gross margin for each dollar of net sales? How do they compare to the industry average of 45.0%?
3. Did the gross margin ratio improve or decline for these companies?

ETHICS CHALLENGE

C1 P2

BTN 4-3 Amy Martin is a student who plans to attend approximately four professional events a year at her college. Each event necessitates a financial outlay of $100 to $200 for a new suit and accessories. After incurring a major hit to her savings for the first event, Amy developed a different approach. She buys the suit on credit the week before the event, wears it to the event, and returns it the next week to the store for a full refund on her charge card.

Required

1. Comment on the ethics exhibited by Amy and possible consequences of her actions.
2. How does the merchandising company account for the suits that Amy returns?

COMMUNICATING IN PRACTICE

C2 P3 P5

BTN 4-4 You are the financial officer for Music Plus, a retailer that sells goods for home entertainment needs. The business owner, Vic Velakturi, recently reviewed the annual financial statements you prepared and sent you an e-mail stating that he thinks you overstated net income. He explains that although he has invested a great deal in security, he is sure shoplifting and other forms of inventory shrinkage have occurred, but he does not see any deduction for shrinkage on the income statement. The store uses a perpetual inventory system.

Required

Prepare a brief memorandum that responds to the owner's concerns.

TAKING IT TO THE NET

A2 C1

BTN 4-5 Access the SEC's EDGAR database (**www.SEC.gov**) and obtain the March 24, 2014, filing of its fiscal 2014 10-K report (for year ended February 1, 2014) for **J. Crew Group, Inc.** (ticker: JCG).

Required

Prepare a table that reports the gross margin ratios for J. Crew using the revenues and cost of goods sold data from J. Crew's income statement for each of its most recent three years. Analyze and comment on the trend in its gross margin ratio.

TEAMWORK IN ACTION

C1 C2

BTN 4-6 Official Brands' general ledger and supplementary records at the end of its current period reveal the following.

Sales	$600,000	Merchandise inventory (beginning of period)	$ 98,000
Sales returns & allowances	20,000	Invoice cost of merchandise purchases	360,000
Sales discounts	13,000	Purchase discounts received	9,000
Cost of transportation-in	22,000	Purchase returns and allowances	11,000
Operating expenses	50,000	Merchandise inventory (end of period)	84,000

Required

1. *Each* member of the team is to assume responsibility for computing *one* of the following items. You are not to duplicate your teammates' work. Get any necessary amounts to compute your item from the appropriate teammate. Each member is to explain his or her computation to the team in preparation for reporting to the class.
   a. Net sales
   b. Total cost of merchandise purchases
   c. Cost of goods sold
   d. Gross profit
   e. Net income
2. Check your net income with the instructor. If correct, proceed to step 3.
3. Assume that a physical inventory count finds that actual ending inventory is $76,000. Discuss how this affects previously computed amounts in step 1.

Point: In teams of four, assign the same student *a* and e. Rotate teams for reporting on a different computation and the analysis in step 3.

ENTREPRENEURIAL DECISION

C1 C2 P4

BTN 4-7 Refer to the opening feature about **Sseko Designs**. Assume that Liz Forkin Bohannon reports current annual sales at approximately $1 million and prepares the following income statement.

SSEKO DESIGNS Income Statement For Year Ended January 31, 2014	
Net sales	$1,000,000
Cost of sales	610,000
Expenses (other than cost of sales)	200,000
Net income	$ 190,000

Liz Forkin Bohannon sells to individuals and retailers, ranging from small shops to large chains. Assume that she currently offers credit terms of 1/15, n/60, and ships FOB destination. To improve her cash flow, she is considering changing credit terms to 3/10, n/30. In addition, she proposes to change shipping terms to FOB shipping point. She expects that the increase in discount rate will increase net sales by 9%, but the gross margin ratio (and ratio of cost of sales divided by net sales) is expected to remain unchanged. She also expects that delivery expenses will be zero under this proposal; thus, expenses other than cost of sales are expected to increase only 6%.

Required

1. Prepare a forecasted income statement for the year ended January 31, 2015, based on the proposal.
2. Based on the forecasted income statement alone (from your part 1 solution), do you recommend that Liz implement the new sales policies? Explain.
3. What else should Liz consider before deciding whether or not to implement the new policies? Explain.

HITTING THE ROAD

C1

BTN 4-8 Arrange an interview (in person or by phone) with the manager of a retail shop in a mall or in the downtown area of your community. Explain to the manager that you are a student studying merchandising activities and the accounting for sales returns and sales allowances. Ask the manager what the store policy is regarding returns. Also find out if sales allowances are ever negotiated with customers. Inquire whether management perceives that customers are abusing return policies and what actions management takes to counter potential abuses. Be prepared to discuss your findings in class.

Point: This activity complements the Ethics Challenge assignment.

GLOBAL DECISION

A2 P4

Samsung
APPLE
GOOGLE

BTN 4-9 **Samsung** (www.Samsung.com), **Apple**, and **Google** are competitors in the global marketplace. Key comparative figures for each company follow.

	Net Sales	Cost of Sales
Samsung*	₩228,692,667	₩137,696,309
Apple†	$ 170,910	$ 106,606
Google†	$ 59,825	$ 25,858

* Millions of Korean won for Samsung.
† Millions of dollars for Apple and Google.

Required

1. Rank the three companies (highest to lowest) based on the gross margin ratio.
2. Which of the companies uses a multiple-step income statement format? (These companies' income statements are in Appendix A.)

ANSWERS TO MULTIPLE CHOICE QUIZ

1. c; Gross profit = $550,000 − $193,000 = $357,000
2. d; ($4,500 − $250) × (100% − 2%) = $4,165
3. b; Net sales = $75,000 + $320,000 − $13,700 − $6,000 = $375,300
4. b; Acid-test ratio = $37,500/$50,000 = 0.750
5. a; Gross margin ratio = ($675,000 − $459,000)/$675,000 = 32%

chapter 5

Inventories and Cost of Sales

Chapter Preview

INVENTORY BASICS	INVENTORY COSTING	INVENTORY VALUATION, ERRORS, AND ANALYSIS
C1 Determining inventory items **C2** Determining inventory costs Internal control of inventory and taking a physical count	**P1** Cost flow assumptions using: Specific identification First-in, first-out Last-in, first-out Weighted average **A1** Effects on financial statements	**P2** Inventory valuation at lower of cost or market **A2** Financial statement effects of inventory errors **A3** Inventory management **P3** Periodic system **P4** Inventory estimation

Learning Objectives

CONCEPTUAL

C1 Identify the items making up merchandise inventory.

C2 Identify the costs of merchandise inventory.

ANALYTICAL

A1 Analyze the effects of inventory methods for both financial and tax reporting.

A2 Analyze the effects of inventory errors on current and future financial statements.

A3 Assess inventory management using both inventory turnover and days' sales in inventory.

PROCEDURAL

P1 Compute inventory in a perpetual system using the methods of specific identification, FIFO, LIFO, and weighted average.

P2 Compute the lower of cost or market amount of inventory.

P3 *Appendix 5A*—Compute inventory in a periodic system using the methods of specific identification, FIFO, LIFO, and weighted average.

P4 *Appendix 5B*—Apply both the retail inventory and gross profit methods to estimate inventory.

Courtesy of Proof

Out of the Woods

BOISE—"We make the world's best handcrafted eyewear and boast the largest sustainable eyewear line in the industry," exclaims Brooks Dame. Brooks, along with his brothers Taylor and Tanner, launched **Proof Eyewear (IWantProof.com)** out of their garage in 2010 making wooden glasses for family and friends. They targeted surfers and skateboarders such as themselves, but quickly found that the market was much larger. "Wood adds a fresh take on sunglasses and makes them a little more edgy," explains Brooks. "Wood eyewear is a crazy idea [and] that crazy idea has become a business and a passion."

"Don't sleep on your dreams"
—Brooks Dame

The company's launch, however, was a challenge. "We had to get our financials in order," admits Brooks. "We really hadn't run any numbers." The brothers also had to confront inventory production and sales planning, and had to deal with discounts and allowances. A major challenge was identifying the appropriate inventories while controlling costs. "We didn't know what to expect," recalls Brooks. "We had money in the bank and our savings was growing and we felt good about it."

Applying inventory management, and old-fashioned trial and error, the brothers learned to fill orders, collect money, and maintain the right level and mix of inventory. To help, they set up an inventory system to account for sales and purchases in real time. The brothers insist that while it is important to stay on the cutting edge, business success demands sound inventory management. "We needed cash to fund inventory and cover new orders coming in," explains Brooks. Nevertheless, success requires more than perpetual inventory management. "We swam with the sharks and made it out and we did it our way," says Brooks.

Although the brothers continue to measure, monitor, and manage inventories and costs, their success and growth are pushing them into new products and opportunities. "We are never satisfied; we're always looking for ways to improve our products and to make things better," explains Tanner. "We are hungry and never stop exploring and pushing the envelope."

Their inventory procedures and accounting systems contribute to their lean business model. "We get things done quickly and efficiently working as brothers," insists Brooks. Sustainability is also part of their success. "Sustainability is a key test in every product decision that we make," explains Brooks. "Making a product that would not harm Mother Nature was just a given. It is part of our constitution as a company." Now that is timeless.

Sources: *Proof Eyewear website,* January 2015; *Trend Hunter,* February 2012; *Outlier Magazine,* April 2013; *StartUp FASHION,* February 2014

INVENTORY BASICS

This section identifies the items and costs making up merchandise inventory. It also describes the importance of internal controls in taking a physical count of inventory.

Determining Inventory Items

C1
Identify the items making up merchandise inventory.

Merchandise inventory includes all goods that a company owns and holds for sale. This rule holds regardless of where the goods are located when inventory is counted. Certain inventory items require special attention, including goods in transit, goods on consignment, and goods that are damaged or obsolete.

Goods in Transit Does a purchaser's inventory include goods in transit from a supplier? The answer is that if ownership has passed to the purchaser, the goods are included in the purchaser's inventory. We determine this by reviewing the shipping terms: *FOB destination* or *FOB shipping point.* Goods purchased FOB shipping point are included in the buyer's inventory when the items are shipped. Goods purchased FOB destination are not included in the buyer's inventory until they arrive at their destination.

Point: FOB shipping point is also called *FOB origin* or *FOB supplier's warehouse.*

Goods on Consignment Goods on consignment are goods shipped by the owner, called the **consignor,** to another party, the **consignee.** A consignee sells goods for the owner. The consignor continues to own the consigned goods and reports them in its inventory. **Upper Deck**, for instance, pays sports celebrities such as Aaron Rodgers of the Green Bay Packers to sign memorabilia, which are offered to shopping networks on consignment. Upper Deck, the consignor, must report these items in its inventory until sold. The consignee never includes consigned goods in inventory.

Goods Damaged or Obsolete Damaged and obsolete (and deteriorated) goods are not counted in inventory if they cannot be sold. If these goods can be sold at a reduced price, they are included in inventory at a conservative estimate of their **net realizable value.** Net realizable value is sales price minus the cost of making the sale. The period when damage or obsolescence (or deterioration) occurs is the period when the loss in value is reported.

Decision Insight

A wireless portable device with a two-way radio allows clerks to quickly record inventory by scanning bar codes and to instantly send and receive inventory data. It gives managers access to up-to-date information on inventory and its location. Bar codes have influenced nearly all aspects of inventory control and management. The use of bar codes makes accounting for inventory simpler, more accurate, and more efficient. ■

Clerkenwell/Getty Images

Determining Inventory Costs

C2
Identify the costs of merchandise inventory.

Merchandise inventory includes costs of expenditures necessary, directly or indirectly, to bring an item to a salable condition and location. This means that the cost of an inventory item includes its invoice cost minus any discount, and plus any incidental costs necessary to put it in a place and condition for sale. Incidental costs can include import tariffs, freight, storage, insurance, and costs incurred in an aging process (for example, aging wine or cheese).

Accounting principles prescribe that incidental costs be added to inventory. Also, the *matching (expense recognition) principle* states that inventory costs should be recorded against revenue in the period when inventory is sold. However, some companies use the *materiality constraint* (*cost-to-benefit constraint*) to avoid assigning some incidental costs of acquiring merchandise to inventory. Instead, they expense them to cost of goods sold when incurred. These companies argue either that those incidental costs are immaterial or that the effort in assigning them outweighs the benefit.

Internal Controls and Taking a Physical Count

Events can cause the Inventory account balance to differ from the actual inventory available. Such events include theft, loss, damage, and errors. Thus, nearly all companies take a *physical count of inventory* at least once each year—informally called *taking an inventory.* This often occurs at the end of a fiscal year or when inventory amounts are low. This physical count is used to adjust the Inventory account balance to the actual inventory available.

Fraud: Auditors commonly observe employees as they take a physical inventory. Auditors take their own test counts to monitor the accuracy of a company's count.

Fraud

A company applies internal controls when taking a physical count of inventory that usually include the following procedures to minimize fraud and to increase reliability:

- *Prenumbered inventory tickets* are distributed to *counters*—each ticket must be accounted for.
- Counters of inventory are assigned and do not include those responsible for inventory.
- Counters confirm the validity of inventory, including its existence, amount, and quality.
- A second count is taken by a different counter.
- A manager confirms that all inventories are ticketed once, and only once.

Point: The Inventory account is a controlling account for the inventory subsidiary ledger. This *subsidiary ledger* contains a separate record (units and costs) for each separate product, and it can be in electronic or paper form. Subsidiary records assist managers in planning and monitoring inventory.

NEED-TO-KNOW 5-1

Inventory Items and Costs

C1 C2

1. A master carver of wooden birds operates her business out of a garage. At the end of the current period, the carver has 17 units (carvings) in her garage, three of which were damaged by water and cannot be sold. The distributor also has another five units in her truck, ready to deliver per a customer order, terms FOB destination, and another 11 units out on consignment at several small retail stores. How many units does the carver include in the business's period-end inventory?
2. A distributor of artistic iron-based fixtures acquires a piece for $1,000, terms FOB shipping point. Additional costs in obtaining it and offering it for sale include $150 for transportation-in, $300 for import duties, $100 for insurance during shipment, $200 for advertising, a $50 voluntary gratuity to the delivery person, $75 for enhanced store lighting, and $250 for sales staff salaries. For computing inventory, what cost is assigned to this artistic piece?

Solutions

1.

Units in ending inventory	
Units in storage	17 units
Less damaged (unsalable) units	(3)
Plus units in transit	5
Plus units on consignment	11
Total units in ending inventory	30 units

2.

Merchandise cost	$1,000
Plus	
Transportation-in	150
Import duties	300
Insurance	100
Total inventory cost	$1,550

Do More: QS 5-1, QS 5-2, E 5-1, E 5-2

QC1

INVENTORY COSTING UNDER A PERPETUAL SYSTEM

Accounting for inventory affects both the balance sheet and the income statement. A major goal in accounting for inventory is to properly match costs with sales. We use the *expense recognition* (or *matching*) *principle* to decide how much of the cost of the goods available for sale is deducted from sales and how much is carried forward as inventory and matched against future sales.

Management decisions in accounting for inventory involve the following:

- Items included in inventory and their costs.
- Costing method (specific identification, FIFO, LIFO, or weighted average).
- Inventory system (perpetual or periodic).
- Use of market values or other estimates.

The first point was explained on the prior two pages. The second and third points will be addressed now. The fourth point is the focus at the end of this chapter. Decisions on these points affect the reported amounts for inventory, cost of goods sold, gross profit, income, current assets, and other accounts.

One of the most important issues in accounting for inventory is determining the per unit costs assigned to inventory items. When all units are purchased at the same unit cost, this process is simple. When identical items are purchased at different costs, however, a question arises as to which amounts to record in cost of goods sold and which amounts remain in inventory.

EXHIBIT 5.1

Frequency in Use of Inventory Methods

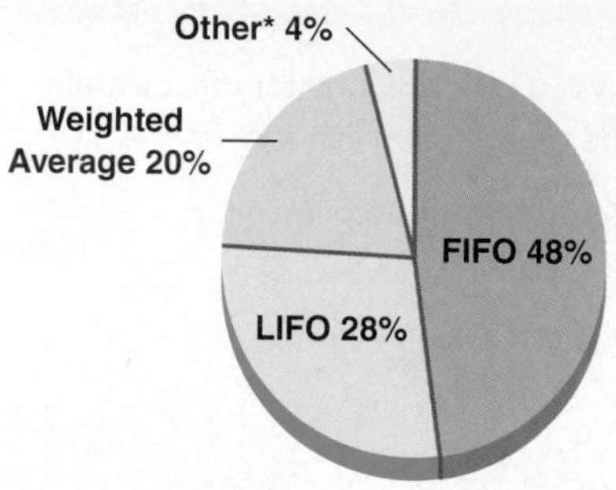

*Includes specific identification.

Four methods are commonly used to assign costs to inventory and to cost of goods sold: (1) specific identification; (2) first-in, first-out (FIFO); (3) last-in, first-out (LIFO); and (4) weighted average. Exhibit 5.1 shows the frequency in the use of these methods.

Each method assumes a particular pattern for how costs flow through inventory. Each of these four methods is acceptable whether or not the actual physical flow of goods follows the cost flow assumption. Physical flow of goods depends on the type of product and the way it is stored. (Perishable goods such as fresh fruit demand that a business attempt to sell them in a first-in, first-out physical flow. Other products such as crude oil and minerals such as coal, gold, and decorative stone can be sold in a last-in, first-out physical flow.) With the exception of specific identification, the **physical flow and cost flow need not be the same**.

Inventory Cost Flow Assumptions

Point: Cost of goods sold is abbreviated COGS.

This section introduces inventory cost flow assumptions. For this purpose, assume that three identical units are purchased separately at the following three dates and costs: May 1 at $45, May 3 at $65, and May 6 at $70. One unit is then sold on May 7 for $100. Exhibit 5.2 gives a visual layout of the flow of costs to either the gross profit section of the income statement or the inventory reported on the balance sheet for FIFO, LIFO, and weighted average.

(1) *FIFO assumes costs flow in the order incurred.* The unit purchased on May 1 for $45 is the earliest cost incurred—it is sent to cost of goods sold on the income statement first. The remaining two units ($65 and $70) are reported in inventory on the balance sheet.

(2) *LIFO assumes costs flow in the reverse order incurred.* The unit purchased on May 6 for $70 is the most recent cost incurred—it is sent to cost of goods sold on the income

EXHIBIT 5.2

Cost Flow Assumptions

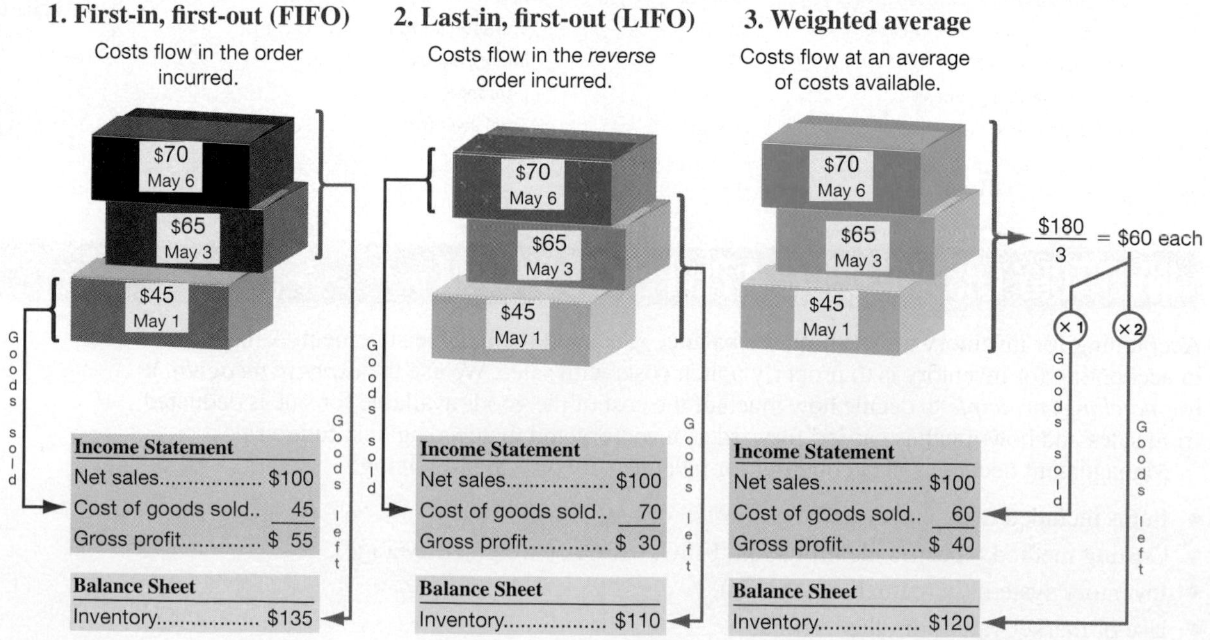

statement. The remaining two units ($45 and $65) are reported in inventory on the balance sheet.

(3) *Weighted average assumes costs flow at an average of the costs available.* The units available at the May 7 sale average $60 in cost, computed as ($45 + $65 + $70)/3. One unit's $60 average cost is sent to cost of goods sold on the income statement. The remaining two units' average costs are reported in inventory at $120 on the balance sheet.

Cost flow assumptions can markedly impact gross profit and inventory numbers. Exhibit 5.2 shows that gross profit as a percent of net sales ranges from 30% to 55% due to nothing else but the cost flow assumption.

Point: It is helpful to recall the cost flow of inventory.

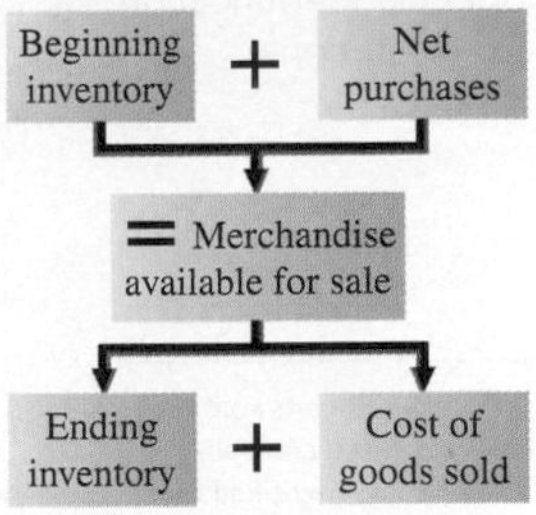

The following 5 pages on inventory costing use the perpetual system. Appendix 5A uses the periodic system. An instructor can choose to cover either one or both systems. If the perpetual system is skipped, then read Appendix 5A and return to the Decision Maker box (5 pages ahead) titled "Cost Analyst."

Inventory Costing Illustration

P1 Compute inventory in a perpetual system using the methods of specific identification, FIFO, LIFO, and weighted average.

This section provides a comprehensive illustration of inventory costing methods. We use information from Trekking, a sporting goods store. Among its many products, Trekking carries one type of mountain bike whose sales are directed at resorts that provide inexpensive mountain bikes for complimentary guest use. We use Trekking's data from August. Its mountain bike (unit) inventory at the beginning of August and its purchases and sales during August are shown in Exhibit 5.3. It ends August with 12 bikes remaining in inventory.

EXHIBIT 5.3

Purchases and Sales of Goods

Date	Activity	Units Acquired at Cost	Units Sold at Retail	Unit Inventory
Aug. 1	Beginning inventory	10 units @ $ 91 = $ 910		10 units
Aug. 3	Purchases	15 units @ $106 = $ 1,590		25 units
Aug. 14	Sales		20 units @ $130	5 units
Aug. 17	Purchases	20 units @ $115 = $ 2,300		25 units
Aug. 28	Purchases	10 units @ $119 = $ 1,190		35 units
Aug. 31	Sales		23 units @ $150	**12 units** (Units left)
	Totals	**55 units** (Units available for sale) **$5,990** (Goods available for sale)	**43 units** (Units sold)	

Trekking uses the perpetual inventory system, which means that its Merchandise Inventory account is continually updated to reflect purchases and sales. **(Appendix 5A describes the assignment of costs to inventory using a periodic system.)** Regardless of what inventory method or system is used, cost of goods available for sale must be allocated between cost of goods sold and ending inventory.

Point: The perpetual inventory system is the most dominant system for U.S. businesses.

Specific Identification

When each item in inventory can be identified with a specific purchase and invoice, we can use **specific identification** or **SI** (also called *specific invoice inventory pricing*) to assign costs. We also need sales records that identify exactly which items were sold and when. For example, each bike's serial number could be used to track costs and compute cost of goods sold. Trekking's internal documents reveal the following specific unit sales:

August 14	Sold 8 bikes costing $91 each and 12 bikes costing $106 each
August 31	Sold 2 bikes costing $91 each, 3 bikes costing $106 each, 15 bikes costing $115 each, and 3 bikes costing $119 each

Applying specific identification, and using the information above and from Exhibit 5.3, we prepare Exhibit 5.4. This exhibit starts with 10 bikes at $91 each in beginning inventory. On August 3,

Point: Three key variables determine the value assigned to ending inventory: (1) inventory quantity, (2) unit costs of inventory, and (3) cost flow assumption.

EXHIBIT 5.4

Specific Identification Computations

"goods in" "goods out" "what's left"

Date	Goods Purchased	Cost of Goods Sold	Inventory Balance
Aug. 1	Beginning balance		10 @ $ 91 = $ 910
Aug. 3	15 @ $106 = $1,590		10 @ $ 91 15 @ $106 } = $2,500
Aug. 14		8 @ $ 91 = $ 728 12 @ $106 = $1,272 } = $2,000*	2 @ $ 91 3 @ $106 } = $ 500
Aug. 17	20 @ $115 = $2,300		2 @ $ 91 3 @ $106 20 @ $115 } = $2,800
Aug. 28	10 @ $119 = $1,190		2 @ $ 91 3 @ $106 20 @ $115 10 @ $119 } = $3,990
Aug. 31		2 @ $ 91 = $ 182 3 @ $106 = $ 318 15 @ $115 = $1,725 3 @ $119 = $ 357 } = $2,582*	5 @ $115 7 @ $119 } = **$1,408**
		$4,582	

For the 20 units sold on Aug. 14, the company specifically identified that 8 of those had cost $91 and 12 had cost $106.

For the 23 units sold on Aug. 31, the company specifically identified each bike sold and its acquisition cost from prior purchases.

* Identification of items sold (and their costs) is obtained from internal documents that track each unit from its purchase to its sale.

Merchandise Inventory (SI)

Aug. 1 910	
Aug. 3 1,590	
	Aug. 14 2,000
Aug. 17 2,300	
Aug. 28 1,190	
	Aug. 31 2,582
Aug. 31 1,408	

Point: Specific identification is usually practical for companies with expensive or custom-made inventory. Examples include car dealerships, implement dealers, jewelers, and fashion designers.

Point: The assignment of costs to goods sold and to inventory using specific identification is the same for both the perpetual and periodic systems.

15 more bikes are purchased at $106 each for $1,590. Inventory available now consists of 10 bikes at $91 each and 15 bikes at $106 each, for a total of $2,500. On August 14 (see sales data on previous page), 20 bikes costing $2,000 are sold—leaving 5 bikes costing $500 in inventory. On August 17, 20 bikes costing $2,300 are purchased, and on August 28, another 10 bikes costing $1,190 are purchased, for a total of 35 bikes costing $3,990 in inventory. On August 31 (see sales data on previous page), 23 bikes costing $2,582 are sold, which leaves 12 bikes costing $1,408 in ending inventory. Carefully study this exhibit and the boxed explanations to see the flow of costs both in and out of inventory. Each unit, whether sold or remaining in inventory, has its own specific cost attached to it.

When using specific identification, Trekking's cost of goods sold reported on the income statement totals **$4,582**, the sum of $2,000 and $2,582 from the third column of Exhibit 5.4. Trekking's ending inventory reported on the balance sheet is **$1,408**, which is the final inventory balance from the fourth column of Exhibit 5.4.

First-In, First-Out

The **first-in, first-out (FIFO)** method of assigning costs to both inventory and cost of goods sold assumes that inventory items are sold in the order acquired. When sales occur, the costs of the earliest units acquired are charged to cost of goods sold. This leaves the costs from the most recent purchases in ending inventory. Use of FIFO for computing the cost of inventory and cost of goods sold is shown in Exhibit 5.5.

Point: "Goods Purchased" column is identical for all methods. Data are taken from Exhibit 5.3.

Point: Under FIFO, a unit sold is assigned the earliest (oldest) cost from inventory. This leaves the most recent costs in ending inventory.

This exhibit starts with beginning inventory of 10 bikes at $91 each. On August 3, 15 more bikes costing $106 each are bought for $1,590. Inventory now consists of 10 bikes at $91 each and 15 bikes at $106 each, for a total of $2,500. On August 14, 20 bikes are sold—applying FIFO, the first 10 sold cost $91 each and the next 10 sold cost $106 each, for a total cost of $1,970. This leaves 5 bikes costing $106 each, or $530, in inventory. On August 17, 20 bikes costing $2,300 are purchased, and on August 28, another 10 bikes costing $1,190 are purchased, for a total of 35 bikes costing $4,020 in inventory. On August 31, 23 bikes are sold—applying FIFO, the first 5 bikes sold cost $530 and the next 18 sold cost $2,070, which leaves 12 bikes costing $1,420 in ending inventory.

EXHIBIT 5.5

FIFO Computations—Perpetual System

Date	Goods Purchased	Cost of Goods Sold	Inventory Balance
Aug. 1	Beginning balance		10 @ $ 91 = $ 910
Aug. 3	15 @ $106 = $1,590		10 @ $ 91 15 @ $106 } = $2,500
Aug. 14		10 @ $ 91 = $ 910 10 @ $106 = $1,060 } = **$1,970**	5 @ $106 = $ 530
Aug. 17	20 @ $115 = $2,300		5 @ $106 20 @ $115 } = $2,830
Aug. 28	10 @ $119 = $1,190		5 @ $106 20 @ $115 10 @ $119 } = $4,020
Aug. 31		5 @ $106 = $ 530 18 @ $115 = $2,070 } = **$2,600**	2 @ $115 10 @ $119 } = **$1,420**
		$4,570	

For the 20 units sold on Aug. 14, the first 10 sold are assigned the earliest cost of $91 (from beg. bal.). The next 10 sold are assigned the next earliest cost of $106.

For the 23 units sold on Aug. 31, the first 5 sold are assigned the earliest available cost of $106 (from Aug. 3 purchase). The next 18 sold are assigned the next earliest cost of $115 (from Aug. 17 purchase).

Merchandise Inventory (FIFO)	
Aug. 1 910	
Aug. 3 1,590	
	Aug. 14 1,970
Aug. 17 2,300	
Aug. 28 1,190	
	Aug. 31 2,600
Aug. 31 1,420	

Trekking's FIFO cost of goods sold reported on its income statement (reflecting the 43 units sold) is **$4,570** ($1,970 + $2,600), and its ending inventory reported on the balance sheet (reflecting the 12 units unsold) is **$1,420**.

Last-In, First-Out

The **last-in, first-out (LIFO)** method of assigning costs assumes that the most recent purchases are sold first. These more recent costs are charged to the goods sold, and the costs of the earliest purchases are assigned to inventory. As with other methods, LIFO is acceptable even when the physical flow of goods does not follow a last-in, first-out pattern. One appeal of LIFO is that by assigning costs from the most recent purchases to cost of goods sold, LIFO comes closest to matching current costs of goods sold with revenues (compared to FIFO or weighted average).

Point: Under LIFO, a unit sold is assigned the most recent (latest) cost from inventory. This leaves the oldest costs in inventory.

Exhibit 5.6 shows the LIFO computations. It starts with beginning inventory of 10 bikes at $91 each. On August 3, 15 more bikes costing $106 each are bought for $1,590. Inventory now consists of 10 bikes at $91 each and 15 bikes at $106 each, for a total of $2,500. On August 14, 20 bikes are sold—applying LIFO, the first 15 sold are from the most recent purchase costing $106 each, and

EXHIBIT 5.6

LIFO Computations—Perpetual System

Date	Goods Purchased	Cost of Goods Sold	Inventory Balance
Aug. 1	Beginning balance		10 @ $ 91 = $ 910
Aug. 3	15 @ $106 = $1,590		10 @ $ 91 15 @ $106 } = $ 2,500
Aug. 14		15 @ $106 = $1,590 5 @ $ 91 = $ 455 } = **$2,045**	5 @ $ 91 = $ 455
Aug. 17	20 @ $115 = $2,300		5 @ $ 91 20 @ $115 } = $ 2,755
Aug. 28	10 @ $119 = $1,190		5 @ $ 91 20 @ $115 10 @ $119 } = $ 3,945
Aug. 31		10 @ $119 = $1,190 13 @ $115 = $1,495 } = **$2,685**	5 @ $ 91 7 @ $115 } = **$1,260**
		$4,730	

For the 20 units sold on Aug. 14, the first 15 sold are assigned the most recent cost of $106. The next 5 sold are assigned the next most recent cost of $91.

For the 23 units sold on Aug. 31, the first 10 sold are assigned the most recent cost of $119. The next 13 sold are assigned the next most recent cost of $115.

Merchandise Inventory (LIFO)	
Aug. 1 910	
Aug. 3 1,590	
	Aug. 14 2,045
Aug. 17 2,300	
Aug. 28 1,190	
	Aug. 31 2,685
Aug. 31 1,260	

the next 5 sold are from the next most recent purchase costing $91 each, for a total cost of $2,045. This leaves 5 bikes costing $91 each, or $455, in inventory. On August 17, 20 bikes costing $2,300 are purchased, and on August 28, another 10 bikes costing $1,190 are purchased, for a total of 35 bikes costing $3,945 in inventory. On August 31, 23 bikes are sold—applying LIFO, the first 10 bikes sold are from the most recent purchase costing $1,190, and the next 13 sold are from the next most recent purchase costing $1,495, which leaves 12 bikes costing $1,260 in ending inventory.

Trekking's LIFO cost of goods sold reported on the income statement is **$4,730** ($2,045 + $2,685), and its ending inventory reported on the balance sheet is **$1,260**.

Weighted Average

The **weighted average** (also called **average cost**) method of assigning cost requires that we use the weighted average cost per unit of inventory at the time of each sale. Weighted average cost per unit at the time of each sale equals the cost of goods available for sale divided by the units available. The results using weighted average (WA) for Trekking are shown in Exhibit 5.7.

EXHIBIT 5.7

Weighted Average Computations—Perpetual System

For the 20 units sold on Aug. 14, the cost assigned is the $100 *average cost* per unit from the Inventory Balance column at the time of sale.

For the 23 units sold on Aug. 31, the cost assigned is the $114 *average cost* per unit from the Inventory Balance column at the time of sale.

Date	Goods Purchased	Cost of Goods Sold	Inventory Balance	
Aug. 1	Beginning balance		10 @ $ 91	= $ 910
Aug. 3	15 @ $106 = $1,590		10 @ $ 91 15 @ $106	= $2,500 (or $100 per unit)[a]
Aug. 14		20 @ $100 = **$2,000**	5 @ $100	= $ 500 (or $100 per unit)[b]
Aug. 17	20 @ $115 = $2,300		5 @ $100 20 @ $115	= $2,800 (or $112 per unit)[c]
Aug. 28	10 @ $119 = $1,190		5 @ $100 20 @ $115 10 @ $119	= $3,990 (or $114 per unit)[d]
Aug. 31		23 @ $114 = **$2,622**	12 @ $114	= **$1,368** (or $114 per unit)[e]
		$4,622		

[a] $100 per unit = ($2,500 inventory balance ÷ 25 units in inventory).
[b] $100 per unit = ($500 inventory balance ÷ 5 units in inventory).
[c] $112 per unit = ($2,800 inventory balance ÷ 25 units in inventory).
[d] $114 per unit = ($3,990 inventory balance ÷ 35 units in inventory).
[e] $114 per unit = ($1,368 inventory balance ÷ 12 units in inventory).

Merchandise Inventory (WA)	
Aug. 1 910	
Aug. 3 1,590	
	Aug. 14 2,000
Aug. 17 2,300	
Aug. 28 1,190	
	Aug. 31 2,622
Aug. 31 1,368	

This exhibit starts with beginning inventory of 10 bikes at $91 each. On August 3, 15 more bikes costing $106 each are bought for $1,590. Inventory now consists of 10 bikes at $91 each and 15 bikes at $106 each, for a total of $2,500. The average cost per bike for that inventory is $100, computed as $2,500/(10 bikes + 15 bikes). On August 14, 20 bikes are sold—applying WA, the 20 sold are assigned the $100 average cost, for a total cost of $2,000. This leaves 5 bikes with an average cost of $100 each, or $500, in inventory. On August 17, 20 bikes costing $2,300 are purchased, and on August 28, another 10 bikes costing $1,190 are purchased, for a total of 35 bikes costing $3,990 in inventory at August 28. The average cost per bike for the August 28 inventory is $114, computed as $3,990/(5 bikes + 20 bikes + 10 bikes). On August 31, 23 bikes are sold—applying WA, the 23 sold are assigned the $114 average cost, for a total cost of $2,622. This leaves 12 bikes costing $1,368 in ending inventory.

Trekking's cost of goods sold reported on the income statement (reflecting the 43 units sold) is **$4,622** ($2,000 + $2,622), and its ending inventory reported on the balance sheet (reflecting the 12 units unsold) is **$1,368**.

This completes computations under the four most common perpetual inventory costing methods. Advances in technology have greatly reduced the cost of a perpetual inventory system. Many companies now ask whether they can afford *not* to have a perpetual inventory system because timely access to inventory information is a competitive advantage and it can help reduce the amount of inventory, which reduces costs.

Point: Under weighted average, a unit sold is assigned the average cost of all items currently available for sale at the date of each sale. This means a new average cost is computed after each purchase.

Point: Cost of goods available for sale, units available for sale, and units in ending inventory are identical for all methods.

Decision Insight

Inventory Control Inventory safeguards include restricted access, use of authorized requisitions, security measures, and controlled environments to prevent damage. Proper accounting includes matching inventory received with purchase order terms and quality requirements, preventing misstatements, and controlling access to inventory records. A study reports that 23% of employees in purchasing and procurement observed inappropriate kickbacks or gifts from suppliers. Another study reports that submission of fraudulent supplier invoices is now common, and perpetrators are often employees (KPMG 2011). ■

Financial Statement Effects of Costing Methods

When purchase prices do not change, each inventory costing method assigns the same cost amounts to inventory and to cost of goods sold. When purchase prices are different, however, the methods nearly always assign different cost amounts. We show these differences in Exhibit 5.8 using Trekking's data.

A1 Analyze the effects of inventory methods for both financial and tax reporting.

EXHIBIT 5.8

Financial Statement Effects of Inventory Costing Methods

TREKKING COMPANY For Month Ended August 31	Specific Identification	FIFO	LIFO	Weighted Average
Income Statement				
Sales	$ 6,050	$ 6,050	$ 6,050	$ 6,050
Cost of goods sold	4,582	4,570	4,730	4,622
Gross profit	1,468	1,480	1,320	1,428
Expenses	450	450	450	450
Income before taxes	1,018	1,030	870	978
Income tax expense (30%)	305	309	261	293
Net income	**$ 713**	**$ 721**	**$ 609**	**$ 685**
Balance Sheet				
Inventory	**$1,408**	**$1,420**	**$1,260**	**$1,368**

This exhibit reveals two important results. First, when purchase costs *regularly rise,* as in Trekking's case, the following occurs:

- FIFO assigns the lowest amount to cost of goods sold—yielding the highest gross profit and net income.
- LIFO assigns the highest amount to cost of goods sold—yielding the lowest gross profit and net income, which also yields a temporary tax advantage by postponing payment of some income tax.
- Weighted average yields results between FIFO and LIFO.
- Specific identification always yields results that depend on which units are sold.

Point: Managers prefer FIFO when costs are rising *and* incentives exist to report higher income for reasons such as bonus plans, job security, and reputation.

Second, when costs *regularly decline,* the reverse occurs for FIFO and LIFO. Namely, FIFO gives the highest cost of goods sold—yielding the lowest gross profit and income. However, LIFO then gives the lowest cost of goods sold—yielding the highest gross profit and income.

All four inventory costing methods are acceptable. However, a company must disclose the inventory method it uses in its financial statements or notes. Each method offers certain advantages as follows:

Point: LIFO inventory is often less than the inventory's replacement cost because LIFO inventory is valued using the oldest inventory purchase costs.

- FIFO assigns an amount to inventory on the balance sheet that approximates its current cost; it also mimics the actual flow of goods for most businesses.
- LIFO assigns an amount to cost of goods sold on the income statement that approximates its current cost; it also better matches current costs with revenues in computing gross profit.
- Weighted average tends to smooth out erratic changes in costs.
- Specific identification exactly matches the costs of items with the revenues they generate.

Decision Maker

Cost Analyst Your supervisor says she finds managing product costs easier if the balance sheet reflects inventory values that closely reflect replacement cost. Which inventory costing method do you advise adopting? ■ [Answers follow the chapter's Summary.]

Tax Effects of Costing Methods Trekking's segment income statement in Exhibit 5.8 includes income tax expense (at a rate of 30%) because it was formed as a corporation. Since inventory costs affect net income, they have potential tax effects. Trekking gains a temporary tax advantage by using LIFO. Many companies use LIFO for this reason.

Point: *LIFO conformity rule* may be revised if IFRS is adopted for U.S. companies as IFRS currently does not permit LIFO (see Global View).

Companies can and often do use different costing methods for financial reporting and tax reporting. *The only exception is when LIFO is used for tax reporting; in this case, the IRS requires that it also be used in financial statements*—called the LIFO conformity rule.

Consistency in Using Costing Methods

The **consistency concept** prescribes that a company use the same accounting methods period after period so that financial statements are comparable across periods—the only exception is when a change from one method to another will improve its financial reporting. The *full-disclosure principle* prescribes that the notes to the statements report this type of change, its justification, and its effect on income.

The consistency concept does *not* require a company to use one method exclusively. For example, it can use different methods to value different categories of inventory.

Decision Ethics

Inventory Manager Your compensation as inventory manager includes a bonus plan based on gross profit. Your superior asks your opinion on changing the inventory costing method from FIFO to LIFO. Since costs are expected to continue to rise, your superior predicts that LIFO would match higher current costs against sales, thereby lowering taxable income (and gross profit). What do you recommend? ■ [Answers follow the chapter's Summary.]

NEED-TO-KNOW 5-2

Perpetual SI, FIFO, LIFO, and WA

P3

A company reported the following December purchases and sales data for its only product.

Date	Activities	Units Acquired at Cost		Units Sold at Retail
Dec. 1	Beginning inventory........	5 units @ $3.00 =	$ 15.00	
Dec. 8	Purchase	10 units @ $4.50 =	45.00	
Dec. 9	Sales....................			8 units @ $7.00
Dec. 19	Purchase	13 units @ $5.00 =	65.00	
Dec. 24	Sales....................			18 units @ $8.00
Dec. 30	Purchase	8 units @ $5.30 =	42.40	
Totals	....	36 units	$167.40	26 units

The company uses a *perpetual inventory system.* Determine the cost assigned to ending inventory and to cost of goods sold using (*a*) specific identification, (*b*) FIFO, (*c*) LIFO, and (*d*) weighted average. (Round per unit costs and inventory amounts to cents.) For specific identification, ending inventory consists of 10 units, where 8 are from the December 30 purchase and 2 are from the December 8 purchase.

Solutions

a. Specific identification: Ending inventory—eight units from December 30 purchase and two units from December 8 purchase

Specific Identification	Ending Inventory	Cost of Goods Sold
(8 × $5.30) + (2 × $4.50)	$51.40	
(5 × $3.00) + (8 × $4.50) + (13 × $5.00) + (0 × $5.30)		$116.00
or $167.40 [Total Goods Available] − $51.40 [Ending Inventory]		$116.00

Merchandise Inventory (SI)			
Beg. inventory	15.00		
Net purchases	152.40		
Avail. for sale	167.40		
		COGS	116.00
End. inventory	51.40		

b. FIFO—Perpetual

Date	Goods Purchased	Cost of Goods Sold	Inventory Balance
12/1			5 @ $3.00 = $15.00
12/8	10 @ $4.50		5 @ $3.00 10 @ $4.50 } = $60.00
12/9		5 @ $3.00 3 @ $4.50 } = $ 28.50	7 @ $4.50 = $31.50
12/19	13 @ $5.00		7 @ $4.50 13 @ $5.00 } = $96.50
12/24		7 @ $4.50 11 @ $5.00 } = $ 86.50	2 @ $5.00 = $10.00
12/30	8 @ $5.30	$115.00	2 @ $5.00 8 @ $5.30 } = $52.40

Merchandise Inventory (FIFO)			
Beg. inventory	15.00		
Net purchases	152.40		
Avail. for sale	167.40		
		COGS	115.00
End. inventory	52.40		

OR "short-cut" FIFO—Perpetual

FIFO	Ending Inventory	Cost of Goods Sold
(8 × $5.30) + (2 × $5.00)	$52.40	
(5 × $3.00) + (10 × $4.50) + (11 × $5.00)		$115.00
or $167.40 [Total Goods Available] − $52.40 [Ending Inventory]		$115.00

c. LIFO—Perpetual

Date	Goods Purchased	Cost of Goods Sold	Inventory Balance
12/1			5 @ $3.00 = $15.00
12/8	10 @ $4.50		5 @ $3.00 10 @ $4.50 } = $60.00
12/9		8 @ $4.50 = $ 36.00	5 @ $3.00 2 @ $4.50 } = $24.00
12/19	13 @ $5.00		5 @ $3.00 2 @ $4.50 13 @ $5.00 } = $89.00
12/24		13 @ $5.00 2 @ $4.50 3 @ $3.00 } = $ 83.00	2 @ $3.00 = $ 6.00
12/30	8 @ $5.30	$119.00	2 @ $3.00 8 @ $5.30 } = $48.40

Merchandise Inventory (LIFO)			
Beg. inventory	15.00		
Net purchases	152.40		
Avail. for sale	167.40		
		COGS	119.00
End. inventory	48.40		

d. Weighted Average—Perpetual

Date	Goods Purchased	Cost of Goods Sold		Inventory Balance
12/1				5 @ $3.00 = $15.00
12/8	10 @ $4.50			5 @ $3.00 } 10 @ $4.50 } = $60.00
				($60.00/15 units = $4.00 avg. cost)
12/9		8 @ $4.00	= $ 32.00	7 @ $4.00 = $28.00
12/19	13 @ $5.00			7 @ $4.00 } 13 @ $5.00 } = $93.00
				($93.00/20 units = $4.65 avg. cost)
12/24		18 @ $4.65	= $ 83.70	2 @ $4.65 = $ 9.30
12/30	8 @ $5.30		$115.70	2 @ $4.65 } 8 @ $5.30 } = $51.70
				($51.70/10 units = $5.17 avg. cost)

Merchandise Inventory (WA)

Beg. inventory	15.00		
Net purchases	152.40		
Avail. for sale	167.40		
		COGS	115.70
End. inventory	51.70		

Do More: QS 5-4, QS 5-5, QS 5-6, QS 5-10, QS 5-11, QS 5-12, QS 5-13

QC2

VALUING INVENTORY AT LCM AND THE EFFECTS OF INVENTORY ERRORS

This section examines the role of market costs in determining inventory on the balance sheet and also the financial statement effects of inventory errors.

Lower of Cost or Market

P2 Compute the lower of cost or market amount of inventory.

We explained how to assign costs to ending inventory and cost of goods sold using one of four costing methods (FIFO, LIFO, weighted average, or specific identification). However, *accounting principles require that inventory be reported at the market value (cost) of replacing inventory when market value is lower than cost.* Merchandise inventory is then said to be reported on the balance sheet at the **lower of cost or market (LCM).**

Computing the Lower of Cost or Market *Market* in the term *LCM* is defined as the current replacement cost of purchasing the same inventory items in the usual manner. A decline in replacement cost reflects a loss of value in inventory. When the recorded cost of inventory is higher than the replacement cost, a loss is recognized. When the recorded cost is lower, no adjustment is made.

LCM is applied in one of three ways: (1) to each individual item separately, (2) to major categories of items, or (3) to the whole of inventory. The less similar the items that make up inventory, the more likely companies are to apply LCM to individual items or categories. With the increasing application of technology and inventory tracking, companies increasingly apply LCM to each individual item separately. Accordingly, we show that method only; however, advanced courses cover the other two methods. To illustrate LCM, we apply it to the ending inventory of a motorsports retailer in Exhibit 5.9.

Point: LCM applied to each individual item always yields the lowest inventory.

EXHIBIT 5.9

Lower of Cost or Market Computations

Inventory Items	Units	Per Unit Cost	Per Unit Market	Total Cost	Total Market	LCM Applied to Items
Cycles						
Roadster	20	$8,000	$7,000	$160,000	$140,000	$ 140,000
Sprint	10	5,000	6,000	50,000	60,000	50,000
Off-Road						
Trax-4	8	5,000	6,500	40,000	52,000	40,000
Blazer	5	9,000	7,000	45,000	35,000	35,000
Totals				$295,000		**$265,000**

$140,000 is the lower of $160,000 or $140,000.

Market amount of $265,000 is lower than the $295,000 recorded cost.

LCM Applied to Individual Items When LCM is applied to individual *items* of inventory, the number of comparisons equals the number of items. For Roadster, $140,000 is the lower of the $160,000 cost and the $140,000 market. For Sprint, $50,000 is the lower of the $50,000 cost and the $60,000 market. For Trax-4, $40,000 is the lower of the $40,000 cost and the $52,000 market. For Blazer, $35,000 is the lower of the $45,000 cost and the $35,000 market. This yields a $265,000 reported inventory, computed from $140,000 for Roadster plus $50,000 for Sprint plus $40,000 for Trax-4 plus $35,000 for Blazer.

The retailer **The Buckle** applies LCM and reports that its "inventory is stated at the lower of cost or market. Cost is determined using the average cost method."

Point: Advances in technology encourage the individual-item approach for LCM.

Global: IFRS requires that LCM be applied to individual items; this results in the most conservative inventory amount.

Recording the Lower of Cost or Market Inventory must be adjusted downward when market is less than cost. To illustrate, if LCM is applied to the individual items of inventory in Exhibit 5.9, the Merchandise Inventory account must be adjusted from the $295,000 recorded cost down to the $265,000 market amount as follows.

Cost of Goods Sold	30,000	
Merchandise Inventory		30,000
To adjust inventory cost to market.		

Accounting rules require that inventory be adjusted to market when market is less than cost, but inventory normally cannot be written up to market when market exceeds cost. If recording inventory down to market is acceptable, why are companies not allowed to record inventory up to market? One view is that a gain from a market increase should not be realized until a sales transaction verifies the gain. However, this view also applies when market is less than cost. A second and primary reason is the **conservatism constraint,** which prescribes the use of the less optimistic amount when more than one estimate of the amount to be received or paid exists and these estimates are about equally likely.

NEED-TO-KNOW 5-3

LCM Method

P2

A company has the following products in its ending inventory, along with cost and market values. (a) Compute the lower of cost or market for its inventory when applied *separately to each product.* (b) If the market amount is less than the recorded cost of the inventory, then record the December 31 LCM adjustment to the Merchandise Inventory account.

		Per Unit	
	Units	Cost	Market
Road bikes	5	$1,000	$800
Mountain bikes	4	500	600
Town bikes	10	400	450

Solution

a.

		Per Unit				
Inventory Items	**Units**	**Cost**	**Market**	**Total Cost**	**Total Market**	**LCM Items**
Road bikes	5	$1,000	$800	$ 5,000	$4,000	$ 4,000
Mountain bikes	4	500	600	2,000	2,400	2,000
Town bikes	10	400	450	4,000	4,500	4,000
				$11,000		$ 10,000
LCM applied to each product						**$10,000**

b.

Dec. 31	Cost of Goods Sold	1,000	
	Merchandise Inventory		1,000
	To adjust inventory cost to market ($11,000 − $10,000).		

Do More: QS 5-19, E 5-10

Financial Statement Effects of Inventory Errors

A2 Analyze the effects of inventory errors on current and future financial statements.

Companies must take care in both taking a physical count of inventory and in assigning a cost to it. An inventory error causes misstatements in cost of goods sold, gross profit, net income, current assets, and equity. It also causes misstatements in the next period's statements because ending inventory of one period is the beginning inventory of the next. As we consider the financial statement effects in this section, it is helpful if we recall the following *inventory relation.*

Beginning inventory + Net purchases − Ending inventory = Cost of goods sold

Income Statement Effects Exhibit 5.10 shows the effects of inventory errors on key amounts in the current and next periods' income statements. Let's look at row 1 and year 1. We see that understating ending inventory overstates cost of goods sold. This can be seen from the above inventory relation where we subtract a smaller ending inventory amount in computing cost of goods sold. Then a higher cost of goods sold yields a lower income.

To understand year 2 of row 1, remember that an understated ending inventory for year 1 becomes an understated beginning inventory for year 2. Using the above inventory relation, we see that if beginning inventory is understated, then cost of goods sold is understated (because we are starting with a smaller amount). A lower cost of goods sold yields a higher income.

Turning to overstatements, let's look at row 2 and year 1. If ending inventory is overstated, we use the inventory relation to see that cost of goods sold is understated. A lower cost of goods sold yields a higher income.

For year 2 of row 2, we again recall that an overstated ending inventory for year 1 becomes an overstated beginning inventory for year 2. If beginning inventory is overstated, we use the inventory relation to see that cost of goods sold is overstated. A higher cost of goods sold yields a lower income.

EXHIBIT 5.10

Effects of Inventory Errors on the Income Statement

	Year 1		Year 2	
Ending Inventory	Cost of Goods Sold	Net Income	Cost of Goods Sold	Net Income
Understated ↓	Overstated ↑	Understated ↓	Understated ↓	Overstated ↑
Overstated* ↑	Understated ↓	Overstated ↑	Overstated ↑	Understated ↓

* This error is less likely under a perpetual system versus a periodic because it implies more inventory than is recorded (or less shrinkage than expected). Management will normally follow up and discover and correct this error before it impacts any accounts.

To illustrate, consider an inventory error for a company with $100,000 in sales for each of the years 2013, 2014, and 2015. If this company maintains a steady $20,000 inventory level during this period and makes $60,000 in purchases in each of these years, its cost of goods sold is $60,000 and its gross profit is $40,000 each year.

Ending Inventory Understated—Year 1 Assume that this company errs in computing its 2013 ending inventory and reports $16,000 instead of the correct amount of $20,000. The effects of this error are shown in Exhibit 5.11. The $4,000 understatement of 2013 ending inventory causes a $4,000 overstatement in 2013 cost of goods sold and a $4,000 understatement in both gross profit and net income for 2013. We see that these effects match the effects predicted in Exhibit 5.10.

Example: If 2013 ending inventory in Exhibit 5.11 is overstated by $3,000 (not understated by $4,000), what is the effect on cost of goods sold, gross profit, assets, and equity? *Answer:* Cost of goods sold is understated by $3,000 in 2013 and overstated by $3,000 in 2014. Gross profit and net income are overstated in 2013 and understated in 2014. Assets and equity are overstated in 2013.

Ending Inventory Understated—Year 2 The 2013 understated ending inventory becomes the 2014 understated *beginning* inventory. We see in Exhibit 5.11 that this error causes an understatement in 2014 cost of goods sold and a $4,000 overstatement in both gross profit and net income for 2014.

Ending Inventory Understated—Year 3 Exhibit 5.11 shows that the 2013 ending inventory error affects only that period and the next. It does not affect 2015 results or any period thereafter. An inventory error is said to be *self-correcting* because it always yields an offsetting error in the

EXHIBIT 5.11

Effects of Inventory Errors on Three Periods' Income Statements

Income Statements	2013		2014		2015	
Sales		$100,000		$100,000		$100,000
Cost of goods sold						
Beginning inventory	$20,000		→ $16,000*		→ $20,000	
Cost of goods purchased	60,000		60,000		60,000	
Goods available for sale	80,000		76,000		80,000	
Ending inventory	16,000*		20,000		20,000	
Cost of goods sold		64,000†		56,000†		60,000
Gross profit		36,000		44,000		40,000
Expenses		10,000		10,000		10,000
Net income		$ 26,000		$ 34,000		$ 30,000

Correct income is $30,000 for each year.

* Correct amount is $20,000. † Correct amount is $60,000.

next period. This does not reduce the severity of inventory errors. Managers, lenders, owners, and others make important decisions from analysis of income and costs.

We can also do an analysis of beginning inventory errors. The income statement effects are the opposite of those for ending inventory.

Point: A former internal auditor at **Coca-Cola** alleges that just before midnight at a prior calendar year-end, fully loaded Coke trucks were ordered to drive about 2 feet away from the loading dock so that Coke could record millions of dollars in extra sales.

Balance Sheet Effects Balance sheet effects of an inventory error can be seen by considering the accounting equation: Assets = Liabilities + Equity. For example, understating ending inventory understates both current and total assets. An understatement in ending inventory also yields an understatement in equity because of the understatement in net income. Exhibit 5.12 shows the effects of inventory errors on the current period's balance sheet amounts. Errors in *beginning* inventory do not yield misstatements in the end-of-period balance sheet, but they do affect that current period's income statement.

EXHIBIT 5.12

Effects of Inventory Errors on Current Period's Balance Sheet

Ending Inventory	Assets	Equity
Understated ↓	Understated ↓	Understated ↓
Overstated ↑	Overstated ↑	Overstated ↑

NEED-TO-KNOW 5-4

Effects of Inventory Errors

A2

A company had $10,000 of sales in each of three consecutive years, 2012–2014, and it purchased merchandise costing $7,000 in each of those years. It also maintained a $2,000 physical inventory from the beginning to the end of that three-year period. In accounting for inventory, it made an error at the end of year 2012 that caused its year-end 2012 inventory to appear on its statements as $1,600 rather than the correct $2,000. (a) Determine the correct amount of the company's gross profit in each of the years 2012–2014. (b) Prepare comparative income statements as in Exhibit 5.11 to show the effect of this error on the company's cost of goods sold and gross profit for each of the years 2012–2014.

Solution

a. Correct gross profit = $10,000 − $7,000 = $3,000 (for each year).

b. Cost of goods sold and gross profit figures follow:

	Year 2012		Year 2013		Year 2014	
Sales		$10,000		$10,000		$10,000
Cost of goods sold						
Beginning inventory	$2,000		**$1,600**		$2,000	
Cost of purchases	7,000		7,000		7,000	
Goods available for sale	9,000		8,600		9,000	
Ending inventory	**1,600**		2,000		2,000	
Cost of goods sold		7,400		6,600		7,000
Gross profit		$ 2,600		$ 3,400		$ 3,000

See that combined income for the 3 years is $9,000 ($2,600 + $3,400 + $3,000); which is correct, meaning the inventory error is "self-correcting" (even though individual year's inventory amounts are in error).

Do More: QS 5-20, E 5-12

QC3

GLOBAL VIEW

This section discusses differences between U.S. GAAP and IFRS in the items and costs making up merchandise inventory, in the methods to assign costs to inventory, and in the methods to estimate inventory values.

Items and Costs Making Up Inventory Both U.S. GAAP and IFRS include broad and similar guidance for the items and costs making up merchandise inventory. Specifically, under both accounting systems, merchandise inventory includes all items that a company owns and holds for sale. Further, merchandise inventory includes costs of expenditures necessary, directly or indirectly, to bring those items to a salable condition and location.

Assigning Costs to Inventory Both U.S. GAAP and IFRS allow companies to use specific identification in assigning costs to inventory. Further, both systems allow companies to apply a *cost flow assumption*. The usual cost flow assumptions are: FIFO, weighted average, and LIFO. However, IFRS does not (currently) allow use of LIFO. As the convergence project progresses, this prohibition may or may not persist.

Estimating Inventory Costs The value of inventory can change while it awaits sale to customers. That value can decrease or increase.

Decreases in Inventory Value Both U.S. GAAP and IFRS require companies to write down (reduce the cost recorded for) inventory when its value falls below the cost recorded. This is referred to as the *lower of cost or market* method explained in this chapter. U.S. GAAP prohibits any later increase in the recorded value of that inventory even if that decline in value is reversed through value increases in later periods. However, IFRS allows reversals of those write-downs up to the original acquisition cost. For example, if **Apple** wrote down its 2013 inventory from $1,764 million to $1,700 million, it could not reverse this in future periods even if its value increased to more than $1,764 million. However, if Apple applied IFRS, it could reverse that previous loss. (Another difference is that value refers to *replacement cost* under U.S. GAAP, but *net realizable value* under IFRS.)

APPLE

Increases in Inventory Value Neither U.S. GAAP nor IFRS allow inventory to be adjusted upward beyond the original cost. (One exception is that IFRS requires agricultural assets such as animals, forests, and plants to be measured at fair value less point-of-sale costs.)

NOKIA

Nokia provides the following description of its inventory valuation procedures:

> Inventories are stated at the lower of cost or net realizable value. Cost . . . approximates actual cost on a FIFO (first-in first-out) basis. Net realizable value is the amount that can be realized from the sale of the inventory in the normal course of business after allowing for the costs of realization.

Sustainability and Accounting The founders of **Proof Eyewear**, as introduced in this chapter's opening feature, assert that "sustainability is a key test in every product decision . . . it has to have an aspect of sustainability to it or we just won't develop it." This level of commitment to sustainability is impressive. The founders also impose a "three-pillar foundation" in everything they do, which is graphically portrayed below. Some of their recent activities include: (1) planting a tree for each pair of sunglasses sold on Earth Day, (2) financing a portion of sight-saving surgeries for each pair of frames purchased, (3) using only wood from sustainably managed forests and rejecting endangered wood, and (4) contributing to reforestation efforts.

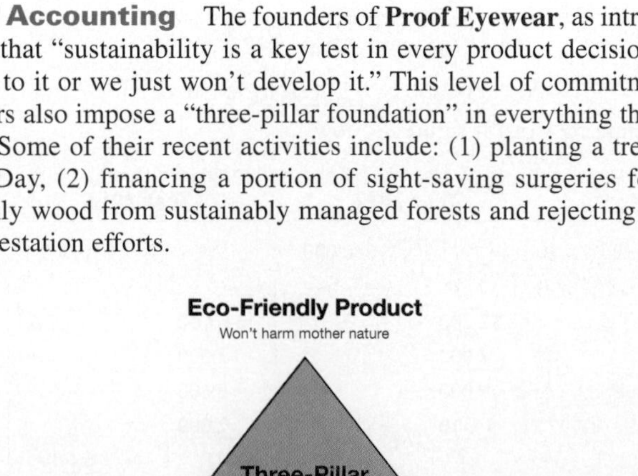

Inventory Turnover and Days' Sales in Inventory **Decision Analysis**

Inventory Turnover

Earlier chapters described two important ratios useful in evaluating a company's short-term liquidity: current ratio and acid-test ratio. A merchandiser's ability to pay its short-term obligations also depends on how quickly it sells its merchandise inventory. **Inventory turnover,** also called *merchandise inventory turnover* or, simply, *turns,* is one ratio used to assess this and is defined in Exhibit 5.13.

A3 Assess inventory management using both inventory turnover and days' sales in inventory.

$$\text{Inventory turnover} = \frac{\text{Cost of goods sold}}{\text{Average inventory}}$$

EXHIBIT 5.13

Inventory Turnover

This ratio reveals how many *times* a company turns over (sells) its inventory during a period. If a company's inventory greatly varies within a year, average inventory amounts can be computed from interim periods such as quarters or months.

Users apply inventory turnover to help analyze short-term liquidity and to assess whether management is doing a good job controlling the amount of inventory available. A low ratio compared to that of competitors suggests inefficient use of assets. The company may be holding more inventory than it needs to support its sales volume. Similarly, a very high ratio compared to that of competitors suggests inventory might be too low. This can cause lost sales if customers must back-order merchandise. Inventory turnover has no simple rule except to say *a high ratio is preferable provided inventory is adequate to meet demand.*

Point: We must take care when comparing turnover ratios across companies that use different costing methods (such as FIFO and LIFO).

Point: Companies with low inventory turnover can be susceptible to losses due to obsolescence and trend changes.

Days' Sales in Inventory

To better interpret inventory turnover, many users measure the adequacy of inventory to meet sales demand. **Days' sales in inventory,** also called *days' stock on hand,* is a ratio that reveals how much inventory is available in terms of the number of days' sales. It can be interpreted as the number of days one can sell from inventory if no new items are purchased. This ratio is often viewed as a measure of the buffer against out-of-stock inventory and is useful in evaluating liquidity of inventory. It is defined in Exhibit 5.14.

Point: Inventory turnover is higher and days' sales in inventory is lower for industries such as foods and other perishable products. The reverse holds for nonperishable product industries.

$$\text{Days' sales in inventory} = \frac{\text{Ending inventory}}{\text{Cost of goods sold}} \times 365$$

EXHIBIT 5.14

Days' Sales in Inventory

Days' sales in inventory focuses on ending inventory and it estimates how many days it will take to convert inventory at the end of a period into accounts receivable or cash. Days' sales in inventory focuses on *ending* inventory whereas inventory turnover focuses on *average* inventory.

Analysis of Inventory Management

Inventory management is a major emphasis for merchandisers. They must both plan and control inventory purchases and sales. **Toys "R" Us** is one of those merchandisers. Its inventory in fiscal year 2014 was \$2,171 million. This inventory constituted 67% of its current assets and 29% of its total assets. We apply the analysis tools in this section to Toys "R" Us, as shown in Exhibit 5.15—also see margin graph.

($ millions)	2014	2013	2012	2011	2010	2009
Cost of goods sold	\$8,154	\$8,592	\$8,939	\$8,939	\$8,790	\$8,976
Ending inventory	\$2,171	\$2,229	\$2,232	\$2,104	\$1,810	\$1,781
Inventory turnover	**3.7** times	**3.9** times	**4.1** times	**4.6** times	**4.9** times	**4.8** times
Industry inventory turnover	3.4 times	3.2 times	3.4 times	3.3 times	3.5 times	3.2 times
Days' sales in inventory	**97** days	**95** days	**91** days	**86** days	**75** days	**72** days
Industry days' sales in inventory	129 days	132 days	128 days	132 days	129 days	124 days

EXHIBIT 5.15

Inventory Turnover and Days' Sales in Inventory for Toys "R" Us

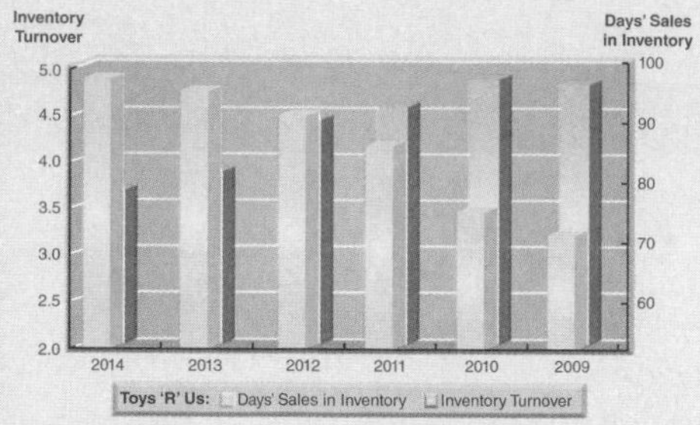

Its 2014 inventory turnover of 3.7 times means that Toys "R" Us turns over its inventory 3.7 times per year, or once every 99 days (365 days ÷ 3.7). We prefer inventory turnover to be high provided inventory is not out of stock and the company is not losing customers. The second metric computed, the 2014 days' sales in inventory of 97 days, reveals that it is carrying 97 days of sales in inventory. This inventory buffer seems more than adequate. The increased days' sales in inventory suggests that Toys "R" Us would benefit from management efforts to increase inventory turnover and to especially reduce inventory levels.

Decision Maker

Entrepreneur Analysis of your retail store yields an inventory turnover of 5.0 and a days' sales in inventory of 73 days. The industry norm for inventory turnover is 4.4 and for days' sales in inventory is 74 days. What is your assessment of inventory management? ■ [Answers follow the chapter's Summary.]

NEED-TO-KNOW

COMPREHENSIVE 1

Perpetual Method

Craig Company buys and sells one product. Its beginning inventory, purchases, and sales during calendar year 2015 follow:

Date	Activity	Units Acquired at Cost	Units Sold at Retail	Unit Inventory
Jan. 1	Beg. inventory	400 units @ $14 = $ 5,600		400 units
Jan. 15	Sale		200 units @ $30	200 units
March 10	Purchase	200 units @ $15 = $ 3,000		400 units
April 1	Sale		200 units @ $30	200 units
May 9	Purchase	300 units @ $16 = $ 4,800		500 units
Sept. 22	Purchase	250 units @ $20 = $ 5,000		750 units
Nov. 1	Sale		300 units @ $35	450 units
Nov. 28	Purchase	100 units @ $21 = $ 2,100		550 units
	Totals	1,250 units $20,500	700 units	

Additional tracking data for specific identification: (1) January 15 sale—200 units @ $14, (2) April 1 sale—200 units @ $15, and (3) November 1 sale—200 units @ $14 and 100 units @ $20.

Required

1. Calculate the cost of goods available for sale.
2. Apply the four different methods of inventory costing (FIFO, LIFO, weighted average, and specific identification) to calculate ending inventory and cost of goods sold under each method using the perpetual system.
3. Compute gross profit earned by the company for each of the four costing methods in part 2. Also, report the inventory amount reported on the balance sheet for each of the four methods.
4. In preparing financial statements for year 2015, the financial officer was instructed to use FIFO but failed to do so and instead computed cost of goods sold according to LIFO, which led to a $1,400 overstatement in cost of goods sold from using LIFO. Determine the impact on year 2015's income from the error. Also determine the effect of this error on year 2016's income. Assume no income taxes.

5. Management wants a report that shows how changing from FIFO to another method would change net income. Prepare a table showing (1) the cost of goods sold amount under each of the four methods, (2) the amount by which each cost of goods sold total is different from the FIFO cost of goods sold, and (3) the effect on net income if another method is used instead of FIFO.

PLANNING THE SOLUTION

- Compute cost of goods available for sale by multiplying the units of beginning inventory and each purchase by their unit costs to determine the total cost of goods available for sale.
- Prepare a perpetual FIFO table starting with beginning inventory and showing how inventory changes after each purchase and after each sale (see Exhibit 5.5).
- Prepare a perpetual LIFO table starting with beginning inventory and showing how inventory changes after each purchase and after each sale (see Exhibit 5.6).
- Make a table of purchases and sales recalculating the average cost of inventory prior to each sale to arrive at the weighted average cost of ending inventory. Total the average costs associated with each sale to determine cost of goods sold (see Exhibit 5.7).
- Prepare a table showing the computation of cost of goods sold and ending inventory using the specific identification method (see Exhibit 5.4).
- Compare the year-end 2015 inventory amounts under FIFO and LIFO to determine the misstatement of year 2015 income that results from using LIFO. The errors for year 2015 and 2016 are equal in amount but opposite in effect.
- Create a table showing cost of goods sold under each method and how net income would differ from FIFO net income if an alternate method were adopted.

SOLUTION

1. Cost of goods available for sale (this amount is the same for all methods).

Date		Units	Unit Cost	Cost
Jan. 1	Beg. inventory	400	$14	$ 5,600
March 10	Purchase	200	15	3,000
May 9	Purchase	300	16	4,800
Sept. 22	Purchase	250	20	5,000
Nov. 28	Purchase	100	21	2,100
Total goods available for sale		1,250		$20,500

2a. FIFO perpetual method.

Date	Goods Purchased	Cost of Goods Sold	Inventory Balance	
Jan. 1	Beginning balance		400 @ $14	= $ 5,600
Jan. 15		200 @ $14 = $2,800	200 @ $14	= $ 2,800
Mar. 10	200 @ $15 = $3,000		200 @ $14 200 @ $15	= $ 5,800
April 1		200 @ $14 = $2,800	200 @ $15	= $ 3,000
May 9	300 @ $16 = $4,800		200 @ $15 300 @ $16	= $ 7,800
Sept. 22	250 @ $20 = $5,000		200 @ $15 300 @ $16 250 @ $20	= $12,800
Nov. 1		200 @ $15 = $3,000 100 @ $16 = $1,600	200 @ $16 250 @ $20	= $ 8,200
Nov. 28	100 @ $21 = $2,100		200 @ $16 250 @ $20 100 @ $21	= $10,300
Total cost of goods sold		$10,200		

Point: Students often mistakenly assume that the costing acronym refers to what remains in inventory. For example, it is important to realize that FIFO refers to costs that are assumed to flow into COGS; namely, the first units purchased are assumed to be the first ones to flow out to cost of goods sold. For FIFO, this means that the goods purchased most recently are assumed to be in ending inventory.

Note to students: **In a classroom situation,** once we compute cost of goods available for sale, we can compute the amount for either cost of goods sold or ending inventory—it is a matter of preference. **In practice,** the costs of items sold are identified as sales are made and immediately transferred from the Inventory account to the Cost of Goods Sold account. The previous solution showing the line-by-line approach illustrates actual application in practice. The following alternate solutions illustrate that, once the concepts are understood, other solution approaches are available. Although this is only shown for FIFO, it could be shown for all methods.

Alternate Methods to Compute FIFO Perpetual Numbers

[FIFO Alternate No. 1: Computing cost of goods sold first]

Cost of goods available for sale (from part 1)			$ 20,500
Cost of goods sold			
Jan. 15	Sold (200 @ $14)	$2,800	
April 1	Sold (200 @ $14)	2,800	
Nov. 1	Sold (200 @ $15 and 100 @ $16)	4,600	10,200
Ending inventory			**$10,300**

[FIFO Alternate No. 2: Computing ending inventory first]

Cost of goods available for sale (from part 1)			$ 20,500
Ending inventory*			
Nov. 28	Purchase (100 @ $21)	$2,100	
Sept. 22	Purchase (250 @ $20)	5,000	
May 9	Purchase (200 @ $16)	3,200	
Ending inventory			10,300
Cost of goods sold			**$10,200**

* Since FIFO assumes that the earlier costs are the first to flow out, we determine ending inventory by assigning the most recent costs to the remaining items.

2b. LIFO perpetual method.

Date	Goods Purchased	Cost of Goods Sold	Inventory Balance
Jan. 1	Beginning balance		400 @ $14 = $ 5,600
Jan. 15		200 @ $14 = $2,800	200 @ $14 = $ 2,800
Mar. 10	200 @ $15 = $3,000		200 @ $14 200 @ $15 } = $ 5,800
April 1		200 @ $15 = $3,000	200 @ $14 = $ 2,800
May 9	300 @ $16 = $4,800		200 @ $14 300 @ $16 } = $ 7,600
Sept. 22	250 @ $20 = $5,000		200 @ $14 300 @ $16 250 @ $20 } = $12,600
Nov. 1		250 @ $20 = $5,000 50 @ $16 = $ 800	200 @ $14 250 @ $16 } = $ 6,800
Nov. 28	100 @ $21 = $2,100		200 @ $14 250 @ $16 100 @ $21 } = $ 8,900
Total cost of goods sold		**$11,600**	

2c. Weighted average perpetual method.

Date	Goods Purchased	Cost of Goods Sold	Inventory Balance
Jan. 1	Beginning balance		400 @ $14 = $ 5,600 ($5,600/400 units = $14.00 avg. cost)
Jan. 15		200 @ $14 = $2,800	200 @ $14 = $ 2,800
Mar. 10	200 @ $15 = $3,000		200 @ $14 200 @ $15 } = $ 5,800 ($5,800/400 units = $14.50 avg. cost)
April 1		200 @ $14.5 = $2,900	200 @ $14.5 = $ 2,900
May 9	300 @ $16 = $4,800		200 @ $14.5 300 @ $16 } = $ 7,700 ($7,700/500 units = $15.40 avg. cost)
Sept. 22	250 @ $20 = $5,000		200 @ $14.5 300 @ $16 250 @ $20 } = $ 12,700 ($12,700/750 units = $16.93** avg. cost)
Nov. 1		300 @ $16.93 = $5,079	450 @ $16.93 = $ 7,618.5
Nov. 28	100 @ $21 = $2,100		450 @ $16.93 100 @ $21 } = **$9,718.5**
Total cost of goods sold*		**$10,779**	

* Cost of goods sold ($10,779) plus ending inventory ($9,718.5) is $2.5 less than the cost of goods available for sale ($20,500) due to rounding.

** Rounded to 2 decimal places.

2d. Specific identification method.

Date	Goods Purchased	Cost of Goods Sold	Inventory Balance
Jan. 1	Beginning balance		400 @ $14 = $ 5,600
Jan. 15		200 @ $14 = $2,800	200 @ $14 = $ 2,800
Mar. 10	200 @ $15 = $3,000		200 @ $14 200 @ $15 } = $ 5,800
April 1		200 @ $15 = $3,000	200 @ $14 = $ 2,800
May 9	300 @ $16 = $4,800		200 @ $14 300 @ $16 } = $ 7,600
Sept. 22	250 @ $20 = $5,000		200 @ $14 300 @ $16 250 @ $20 } = $ 12,600
Nov. 1		200 @ $14 = $2,800 100 @ $20 = $2,000	300 @ $16 150 @ $20 } = $ 7,800
Nov. 28	100 @ $21 = $2,100		300 @ $16 150 @ $20 100 @ $21 } = **$ 9,900**
Total cost of goods sold		**$10,600**	

3.

	FIFO	LIFO	Weighted Average	Specific Identification
Income Statement				
Sales*	$ 22,500	$22,500	$ 22,500	$22,500
Cost of goods sold	**10,200**	**11,600**	**10,779**	**10,600**
Gross profit	$ 12,300	$10,900	$ 11,721	$11,900
Balance Sheet				
Inventory	**$10,300**	**$ 8,900**	**$9,718.5**	**$ 9,900**

* Sales = (200 units × $30) + (200 units × $30) + (300 units × $35) = $22,500

4. Mistakenly using LIFO when FIFO should have been used overstates cost of goods sold in year 2015 by $1,400, which is the difference between the FIFO and LIFO amounts of ending inventory. It understates income in 2015 by $1,400. In year 2016, income is overstated by $1,400 because of the understatement in beginning inventory.

5. Analysis of the effects of alternative inventory methods.

	Cost of Goods Sold	Difference from FIFO Cost of Goods Sold	Effect on Net Income If Adopted Instead of FIFO
FIFO	$10,200	—	—
LIFO	11,600	+$1,400	$1,400 lower
Weighted average	10,779	+ 579	579 lower
Specific identification	10,600	+ 400	400 lower

NEED-TO-KNOW

COMPREHENSIVE 2

Periodic Method

Refer to the information in **Need-To-Know Comprehensive 1** to answer the following requirements.

Required

1. Calculate the cost of goods available for sale.

2. Apply the four different methods of inventory costing (FIFO, LIFO, weighted average, and specific identification) to calculate ending inventory and cost of goods sold under each method using the periodic system.

3. Compute gross profit earned by the company for each of the four costing methods in part 2. Also, report the inventory amount reported on the balance sheet for each of the four methods.

4. In preparing financial statements for year 2015, the financial officer was instructed to use FIFO but failed to do so and instead computed cost of goods sold according to LIFO. Determine the impact of the error on year 2015's income. Also determine the effect of this error on year 2016's income. Assume no income taxes.

SOLUTION

1. The solution is identical to the solution for part 1 of **Need-To-Know Comprehensive 1.**

2a. FIFO periodic method (FIFO under periodic and perpetual yields identical results).

Cost of goods available for sale (from part 1)			$ 20,500
Ending inventory*			
Nov. 28	Purchase (100 @ $21)	$2,100	
Sept. 22	Purchase (250 @ $20)	5,000	
May 9	Purchase (200 @ $16)	3,200	
Ending inventory			**10,300**
Cost of goods sold			**$10,200**

* Since FIFO assumes that the earlier costs are the first to flow out, we determine ending inventory by assigning the most recent costs to the remaining items.

2b. LIFO periodic method.

Cost of goods available for sale (from part 1)			$ 20,500
Ending inventory*			
January 1	Beg. inventory (400 @ $14)	$5,600	
March 10	Purchase (150 @ $15)	2,250	
Ending inventory			**7,850**
Cost of goods sold			**$12,650**

* Since LIFO assumes that the most recent (newest) costs are the first to flow out, we determine ending inventory by assigning the earliest (oldest) costs to the remaining items.

2c. Weighted average periodic method.

Step 1:	400 units @ $14 =	$ 5,600
	200 units @ $15 =	3,000
	300 units @ $16 =	4,800
	250 units @ $20 =	5,000
	100 units @ $21 =	2,100
	1,250	**$20,500**

Step 2: $20,500/1,250 units = **$16.40** weighted average cost per unit

Step 3:	Total cost of 1,250 units available for sale	$20,500
	Less **ending inventory** priced on a weighted average cost basis: 550 units at $16.40 each	9,020
	Cost of goods sold (700 units at $16.40 each)	**$11,480**

2d. Specific identification method.

The solution is identical to the solution shown in part 2d of **Need-To-Know Comprehensive 1.** This is because specific identification is *not* a cost flow assumption; instead, this method specifically identifies each item in inventory and each item that is sold.

3.

	FIFO	LIFO	Weighted Average	Specific Identification
Income Statement				
Sales*	$ 22,500	$22,500	$ 22,500	$22,500
Cost of goods sold	**10,200**	**12,650**	**11,480**	**10,600**
Gross profit	$ 12,300	$ 9,850	$ 11,020	$11,900
Balance Sheet				
Inventory	**$10,300**	**$ 7,850**	**$ 9,020**	**$ 9,900**

* Sales = (200 units × $30) + (200 units × $30) + (300 units × $35) = $22,500

4. Mistakenly using LIFO, when FIFO should have been used, overstates cost of goods sold in year 2015 by $2,450, which is the difference between the FIFO and LIFO amounts of ending inventory. It understates income in 2015 by $2,450. In year 2016, income is overstated by $2,450 because of the understatement in beginning inventory.

APPENDIX

Inventory Costing under a Periodic System 5A

P3 Compute inventory in a periodic system using the methods of specific identification, FIFO, LIFO, and weighted average.

This section illustrates inventory costing methods. We use information from Trekking, a sporting goods store. Among its products, Trekking carries one type of mountain bike whose sales are directed at resorts that provide inexpensive mountain bikes for complimentary guest use. These resorts usually purchase in amounts of 10 or more bikes. We use Trekking's data from August. Its mountain bike (unit) inventory at the beginning of August and its purchases and sales during August are in Exhibit 5A.1. It ends August with 12 bikes in inventory. Trekking uses the **periodic inventory system**, which means that its

EXHIBIT 5A.1

Purchases and Sales of Goods

Date	Activity	Units Acquired at Cost		Units Sold at Retail	Unit Inventory
Aug. 1	Beginning inventory	10 units @ $ 91 =	$ 910		10 units
Aug. 3	Purchases	15 units @ $106 =	$ 1,590		25 units
Aug. 14	Sales			20 units @ $130	5 units
Aug. 17	Purchases	20 units @ $115 =	$ 2,300		25 units
Aug. 28	Purchases	10 units @ $119 =	$ 1,190		35 units
Aug. 31	Sales			23 units @ $150	**12 units**
	Totals	**55 units**	**$5,990**	**43 units**	
		Units available for sale	Goods available for sale	Units sold	Units left

Merchandise Inventory account is updated at the end of each period (monthly for Trekking) to reflect purchases and sales. Regardless of what inventory method or system is used, cost of goods available for sale must be allocated between cost of goods sold and ending inventory.

Point: Three key variables determine the value assigned to ending inventory: (1) inventory quantity, (2) unit costs of inventory, and (3) cost flow assumption.

Specific Identification When each item in inventory can be identified with a specific purchase and invoice, we can use **specific identification** or **SI** (also called *specific invoice inventory pricing*) to assign costs. We also need sales records that identify exactly which items were sold and when. Trekking's internal documents reveal the following specific unit sales:

August 14	Sold 8 bikes costing $91 each and 12 bikes costing $106 each
August 31	Sold 2 bikes costing $91 each, 3 bikes costing $106 each, 15 bikes costing $115 each, and 3 bikes costing $119 each

Applying specific identification, and using the information above and from Exhibit 5A.1, we prepare Exhibit 5A.2. This exhibit begins with the $5,990 in total units available for sale—this is from Exhibit 5A.1. Applying specific identification, we know that for the 20 units sold on August 14, the company specifically identified that 8 of them had cost $91 each and 12 had cost $106 each, resulting in an August 14 cost of sales of $2,000. Next, for the 23 units sold on August 31, the company specifically identified that 2 of them had cost $91 each, that 3 had cost $106 each, that 15 had cost $115 each, and 3 had cost $119 each, resulting in an August 31 cost of sales of $2,582. This yields a total cost of sales for the period of $4,582. We then subtract this $4,582 in cost of goods sold from the $5,990 in cost of goods available to get $1,408 in ending inventory. Carefully study this exhibit and the explanations to see the flow of costs. Each unit, whether sold or remaining in inventory, has its own specific cost attached to it.

EXHIBIT 5A.2

Specific Identification Computations

Total cost of 55 units available for sale (from Exhibit 5A.1)		$5,990
Cost of goods sold*		
Aug. 14 (8 @ $91) + (12 @ $106)	$2,000	
Aug. 31 (2 @ $91) + (3 @ $106) + (15 @ $115) + (3 @ $119)	2,582	4,582
Ending inventory		**$1,408**

* Identification of items sold (and their costs) is obtained from internal documents that track each unit from its purchase to its sale.

Point: SI yields identical results under both periodic and perpetual.

Point: Specific identification is usually practical for companies with expensive or custom-made inventory. Examples include car dealerships, implement dealers, jewelers, and fashion designers.

When using specific identification, Trekking's cost of goods sold reported on the income statement totals **$4,582**, the sum of $2,000 and $2,582 from the cost of goods sold section of Exhibit 5A.2. Trekking's ending inventory reported on the balance sheet is **$1,408**, which is the final inventory balance from Exhibit 5A.2. The following graphic visually reflects the computations under specific identification.

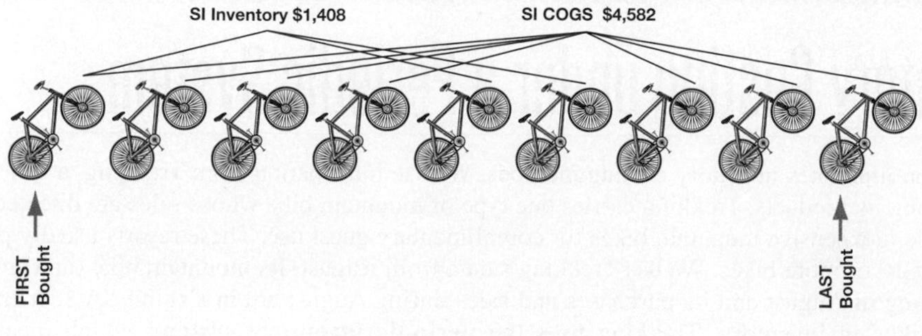

First-In, First-Out The **first-in, first-out (FIFO)** method of assigning costs to both inventory and cost of goods sold assumes that inventory items are sold in the order acquired. When sales occur, the costs of the earliest units acquired are charged to cost of goods sold. This leaves the costs from the most recent purchases in ending inventory. Use of FIFO for computing the cost of inventory and cost of goods sold is shown in Exhibit 5A.3.

This exhibit starts with computing $5,990 in total units available for sale—this is from Exhibit 5A.1. Applying FIFO, we know that the 12 units in ending inventory will be reported at the cost of the most recent 12 purchases. Reviewing purchases in reverse order, we assign costs to the 12 bikes in ending inventory as follows: $119 cost to 10 bikes and $115 cost to 2 bikes. This yields 12 bikes costing $1,420 in ending inventory. We then subtract this $1,420 in ending inventory from $5,990 in cost of goods available to get $4,570 in cost of goods sold.

Point: Under FIFO, a unit sold is assigned the earliest (oldest) cost from inventory. This leaves the most recent costs in ending inventory.

EXHIBIT 5A.3

FIFO Computations—Periodic System

Total cost of 55 units available for sale (from Exhibit 5A.1)		$5,990
Less ending inventory priced using FIFO		
10 units from August 28 purchase at $119 each	$1,190	
2 units from August 17 purchase at $115 each	230	
Ending inventory		1,420
Cost of goods sold		$4,570

Exhibit 5A.1 shows that the 12 units in ending inventory consist of 10 units from the latest purchase on Aug. 28 and 2 units from the next latest purchase on Aug. 17.

Trekking's ending inventory reported on the balance sheet is **$1,420**, and its cost of goods sold reported on the income statement is **$4,570**. The following graphic visually reflects the computations under FIFO.

Point: The assignment of costs to goods sold and to inventory using FIFO is the same for both the periodic and perpetual systems.

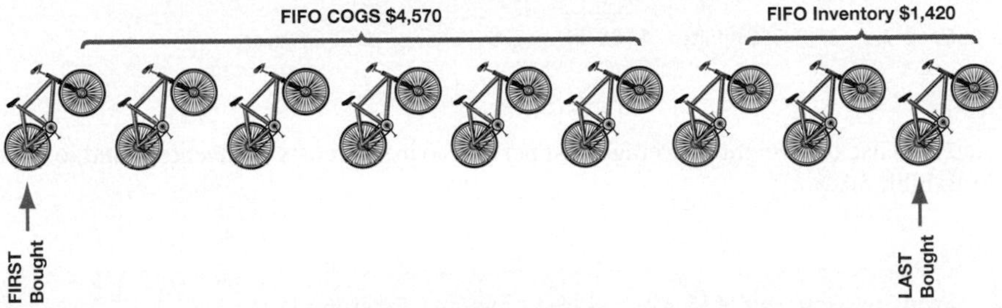

Last-In, First-Out The **last-in, first-out (LIFO)** method of assigning costs assumes that the most recent purchases are sold first. These more recent costs are charged to goods sold, and the costs of the earliest purchases are assigned to inventory. LIFO results in costs of the most recent purchases being assigned to cost of goods sold, which means that LIFO comes close to matching current costs of goods sold with revenues. Use of LIFO for computing cost of inventory and cost of goods sold is shown in Exhibit 5A.4.

This exhibit starts with computing $5,990 in total units available for sale—this is from Exhibit 5A.1. Applying LIFO, we know that the 12 units in ending inventory will be reported at the cost of the earliest 12 purchases. Reviewing the earliest purchases in order, we assign costs to the 12 bikes in ending inventory as follows: $91 cost to 10 bikes and $106 cost to 2 bikes. This yields 12 bikes costing $1,122 in ending inventory. We then subtract this $1,122 in ending inventory from $5,990 in cost of goods available to get $4,868 in cost of goods sold.

Point: Under LIFO, a unit sold is assigned the most recent (latest) cost from inventory. This leaves the oldest costs in inventory.

EXHIBIT 5A.4

LIFO Computations—Periodic System

Total cost of 55 units available for sale (from Exhibit 5A.1)		$5,990
Less ending inventory priced using LIFO		
10 units in beginning inventory at $91 each	$910	
2 units from August 3 purchase at $106 each	212	
Ending inventory		1,122
Cost of goods sold		$4,868

Exhibit 5A.1 shows that the 12 units in ending inventory consist of 10 units from the earliest purchase (beg. inv.) and 2 units from the next earliest purchase on Aug. 3.

Trekking's ending inventory reported on the balance sheet is **$1,122**, and its cost of goods sold reported on the income statement is **$4,868**. The following graphic visually reflects the computations under LIFO.

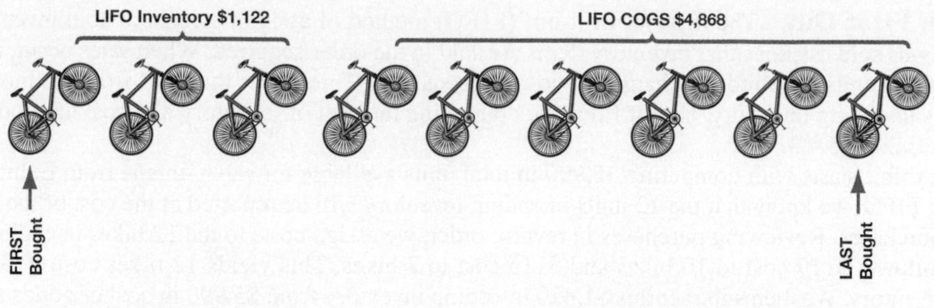

Weighted Average The **weighted average** or **WA** (also called **average cost**) method of assigning cost requires that we use the average cost per unit of inventory at the end of the period. Weighted average cost per unit equals the cost of goods available for sale divided by the units available. The weighted average method of assigning cost involves three important steps. The first two steps are shown in Exhibit 5A.5. First, multiply the per unit cost for beginning inventory and each particular purchase by the corresponding number of units (from Exhibit 5A.1). Second, add these amounts and divide by the total number of units available for sale to find the weighted average cost per unit.

EXHIBIT 5A.5

Weighted Average Cost per Unit

Example: In Exhibit 5A.5, if 5 more units had been purchased at $120 each, what would be the weighted average cost per unit?

Answer: $109.83 ($6,590/60)

Step 1:	10 units @ $ 91 =	$ 910
	15 units @ $106 =	1,590
	20 units @ $115 =	2,300
	10 units @ $119 =	1,190
	55	**$5,990**
Step 2:	$5,990/55 units = **$108.91** weighted average cost per unit	

The third step is to use the weighted average cost per unit to assign costs to inventory and to the units sold as shown in Exhibit 5A.6.

EXHIBIT 5A.6

Weighted Average Computations—Periodic

Step 3:	Total cost of 55 units available for sale (from Exhibit 5A.1).	$ 5,990
	Less **ending inventory** priced on a weighted average cost basis: 12 units at $108.91 each (from Exhibit 5A.5).	**1,307**
	Cost of goods sold (43 units at $108.91 each)	**$4,683**

Trekking's ending inventory reported on the balance sheet is **$1,307**, and its cost of goods sold reported on the income statement is **$4,683** when using the weighted average (periodic) method. The following graphic visually reflects the computations under weighted average.

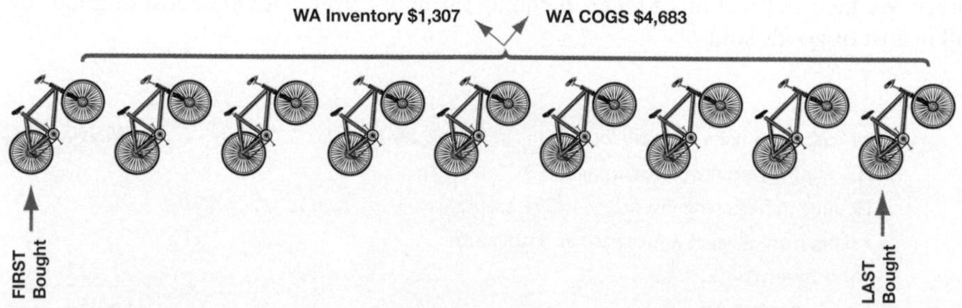

A1

Analyze the effects of inventory methods for both financial and tax reporting.

Financial Statement Effects of Costing Methods When purchase prices do not change, each inventory costing method assigns the same cost amounts to inventory and to cost of goods sold. When purchase prices are different, however, the methods nearly always assign different cost amounts. We show these differences in Exhibit 5A.7 using Trekking's data.

EXHIBIT 5A.7

Financial Statement Effects of Inventory Costing Methods

TREKKING COMPANY For Month Ended August 31	Specific Identification	FIFO	LIFO	Weighted Average
Income Statement				
Sales	$ 6,050	$ 6,050	$ 6,050	$ 6,050
Cost of goods sold	**4,582**	**4,570**	**4,868**	**4,683**
Gross profit	1,468	1,480	1,182	1,367
Expenses	450	450	450	450
Income before taxes	1,018	1,030	732	917
Income tax expense (30%)	305	309	220	275
Net income	**$ 713**	**$ 721**	**$ 512**	**$ 642**
Balance Sheet				
Inventory	**$1,408**	**$1,420**	**$1,122**	**$1,307**

This exhibit reveals two important results. First, when purchase costs *regularly rise,* as in Trekking's case, observe the following:

- FIFO assigns the lowest amount to cost of goods sold—yielding the highest gross profit and net income.
- LIFO assigns the highest amount to cost of goods sold—yielding the lowest gross profit and net income, which also yields a temporary tax advantage by postponing payment of some income tax.
- Weighted average yields results between FIFO and LIFO.
- Specific identification always yields results that depend on which units are sold.

Point: Managers prefer FIFO when costs are rising *and* incentives exist to report higher income for reasons such as bonus plans, job security, and reputation.

Second, when costs *regularly decline,* the reverse occurs for FIFO and LIFO. FIFO gives the highest cost of goods sold—yielding the lowest gross profit and income. And LIFO gives the lowest cost of goods sold—yielding the highest gross profit and income.

All four inventory costing methods are acceptable in practice. A company must disclose the inventory method it uses. Each method offers certain advantages as follows:

- FIFO assigns an amount to inventory on the balance sheet that approximates its current cost; it also mimics the actual flow of goods for most businesses.
- LIFO assigns an amount to cost of goods sold on the income statement that approximates its current cost; it also better matches current costs with revenues in computing gross profit.
- Weighted average tends to smooth out erratic changes in costs.
- Specific identification exactly matches the costs of items with the revenues they generate.

Point: LIFO inventory is often less than the inventory's replacement cost because LIFO inventory is valued using the oldest inventory purchase costs.

NEED-TO-KNOW 5-5

Periodic SI, FIFO, LIFO, and WA

P1

A company reported the following December purchases and sales data for its only product.

Date	Activities	Units Acquired at Cost		Units Sold at Retail
Dec. 1	Beginning inventory	5 units @ $3.00 =	$ 15.00	
Dec. 8	Purchase	10 units @ $4.50 =	45.00	
Dec. 9	Sales			8 units @ $7.00
Dec. 19	Purchase	13 units @ $5.00 =	65.00	
Dec. 24	Sales			18 units @ $8.00
Dec. 30	Purchase	8 units @ $5.30 =	42.40	
Totals		36 units	$167.40	26 units

The company uses a *periodic inventory system.* Determine the cost assigned to ending inventory and to cost of goods sold using (*a*) specific identification, (*b*) FIFO, (*c*) LIFO, and (*d*) weighted average. (Round per unit costs and inventory amounts to cents.) For specific identification, ending inventory consists of 10 units, where eight are from the December 30 purchase and two are from the December 8 purchase.

Solutions

a. Specific identification: Ending inventory—eight units from December 30 purchase and two units from December 8 purchase

Specific Identification	Ending Inventory	Cost of Goods Sold
(8 × $5.30) + (2 × $4.50)	$51.40	
(5 × $3.00) + (8 × $4.50) + (13 × $5.00) + (0 × $5.30)		$116.00
or $167.40 [Total Goods Available] − $51.40 [Ending Inventory]		$116.00

b. FIFO—Periodic

FIFO	Ending Inventory	Cost of Goods Sold
(8 × $5.30) + (2 × $5.00)	$52.40	
(5 × $3.00) + (10 × $4.50) + (11 × $5.00)		$115.00
or $167.40 [Total Goods Available] − $52.40 [Ending Inventory]		$115.00

c. LIFO—Periodic

LIFO	Ending Inventory	Cost of Goods Sold
(5 × $3.00) + (5 × $4.50)	$37.50	
(8 × $5.30) + (13 × $5.00) + (5 × $4.50)		$129.90
or $167.40 [Total Goods Available] − $37.50 [Ending Inventory]		$129.90

d. WA—Periodic

WA	Ending Inventory	Cost of Goods Sold
10 × $4.65 (computed from $167.40/36)	$46.50	
26 × $4.65 (computed from $167.40/36)		$120.90
or $167.40 [Total Goods Available] − $46.50 [Ending Inventory]		$120.90

Do More: QS 5-7, QS 5-8, QS 5-9, QS 5-14, QS 5-15, QS 5-16, QS 5-17

APPENDIX

5B Inventory Estimation Methods

P4 Apply both the retail inventory and gross profit methods to estimate inventory.

Inventory sometimes requires estimation for two reasons. First, companies often require **interim statements** (financial statements prepared for periods of less than one year), but they only annually take a physical count of inventory. Second, companies may require an inventory estimate if some casualty such as fire or flood makes taking a physical count impossible. Estimates are usually only required for companies that use the periodic system. Companies using a perpetual system would presumably have updated inventory data.

This appendix describes two methods to estimate inventory.

Point: When a retailer takes a physical inventory, it can restate the retail value of inventory to a cost basis by applying the cost-to-retail ratio. It can also estimate the amount of shrinkage by comparing the inventory computed with the amount from a physical inventory.

Retail Inventory Method To avoid the time-consuming and expensive process of taking a physical inventory each month or quarter, some companies use the **retail inventory method** to estimate cost of goods sold and ending inventory. Some companies even use the retail inventory method to prepare the annual statements. **Home Depot**, for instance, says in its annual report: "Inventories are stated at the lower of cost (first-in, first-out) or market, as determined by the retail inventory method." A company may also estimate inventory for audit purposes or when inventory is damaged or destroyed.

The retail inventory method uses a three-step process to estimate ending inventory. We need to know the amount of inventory a company had at the beginning of the period in both *cost* and *retail* amounts. We already explained how to compute the cost of inventory. The *retail amount of inventory* refers to its dollar amount measured using selling prices of inventory items. We also need to know the net amount of goods purchased (minus returns, allowances, and discounts) in the period, both at cost and at retail. The amount of net sales at retail is also needed. The process is shown in Exhibit 5B.1.

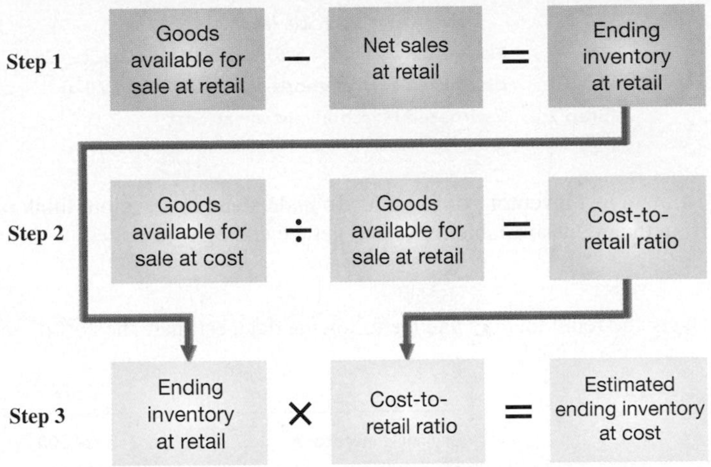

EXHIBIT 5B.1

Retail Inventory Method of Inventory Estimation

The reasoning behind the retail inventory method is that if we can get a good estimate of the cost-to-retail ratio, we can multiply ending inventory at retail by this ratio to estimate ending inventory at cost. We show in Exhibit 5B.2 how these steps are applied to estimate ending inventory for a typical company. First, we find that $100,000 of goods (at retail selling prices) were available for sale. We see that $70,000 of these goods were sold, leaving $30,000 (retail value) of merchandise in ending inventory. Second, the cost of these goods is 60% of the $100,000 retail value. Third, since cost for these goods is 60% of retail, the estimated cost of ending inventory is $18,000.

Example: What is the cost of ending inventory in Exhibit 5B.2 if the cost of beginning inventory is $22,500 and its retail value is $34,500? *Answer:* $30,000 × 62% = $18,600

EXHIBIT 5B.2

Estimated Inventory Using the Retail Inventory Method

		At Cost	At Retail
	Goods available for sale		
	Beginning inventory	$ 20,500	$ 34,500
	Cost of goods purchased	39,500	65,500
Step 1:	Goods available for sale	60,000	100,000
	Deduct net sales at retail		**70,000**
	Ending inventory at retail		**$ 30,000**
Step 2:	**Cost-to-retail ratio: ($60,000 ÷ $100,000) = 60%**		
Step 3:	**Estimated ending inventory at cost ($30,000 × 60%)**	**$18,000**	

Point: A retailer such as Target can speed up its year-end physical count by using the retail inventory method. Inventory counters can record the item's retail price without having to look up the cost of each item.

Gross Profit Method The **gross profit method** estimates the cost of ending inventory by applying the gross profit ratio to net sales (at retail). This type of estimate often is needed when inventory is destroyed, lost, or stolen. These cases require an inventory estimate so that a company can file a claim with its insurer. Users also apply this method to see whether inventory amounts from a physical count are reasonable. This method uses the historical relation between cost of goods sold and net sales to estimate the proportion of cost of goods sold making up current sales. This cost of goods sold estimate is then subtracted from cost of goods available for sale to estimate the ending inventory at cost. These two steps are shown in Exhibit 5B.3.

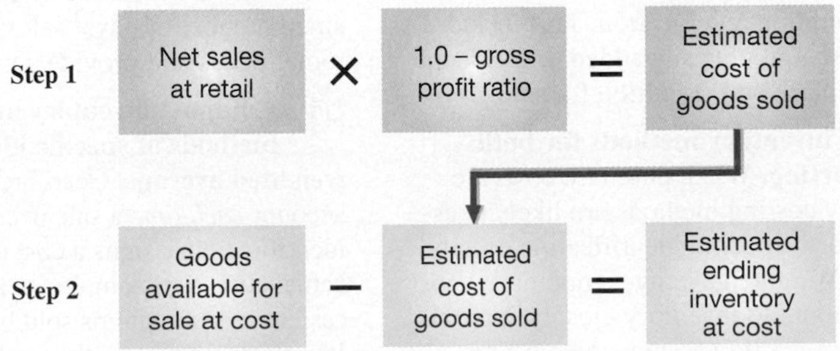

EXHIBIT 5B.3

Gross Profit Method of Inventory Estimation

To illustrate, assume that a company's inventory is destroyed by fire in March 2015. When the fire occurs, the company's accounts show the following balances for January through March: Sales, $31,500; Sales Returns, $1,500; Inventory (January 1, 2015), $12,000; and Cost of Goods Purchased, $20,500. If this company's gross profit ratio is 30%, then 30% of each net sales dollar is gross profit and 70% is cost of goods sold. We show in Exhibit 5B.4 how this 70% is used to

Point: A fire or other catastrophe can result in an insurance claim for lost inventory or income. Backup and off-site storage of data help ensure coverage for such losses.

Point: Reliability of the gross profit method depends on an accurate and stable estimate of the gross profit ratio.

EXHIBIT 5B.4

Estimated Inventory Using the Gross Profit Method

	Goods available for sale		
	Inventory, January 1, 2015	$12,000	
	Cost of goods purchased	20,500	
	Goods available for sale (at cost)	32,500	
	Net sales at retail ($31,500 − $1,500)		$30,000
Step 1:	**Estimated cost of goods sold ($30,000 × 70%)**	**(21,000)**	← × 0.70
Step 2:	**Estimated March inventory at cost**	**$11,500**	

estimate lost inventory of $11,500. To understand this exhibit, think of subtracting the cost of goods sold from the goods available for sale to get the ending inventory.

NEED-TO-KNOW 5-6

Retail Inventory Estimation

P4

Using the retail method and the following data, estimate the cost of ending inventory.

	Cost	Retail
Beginning inventory	$324,000	$530,000
Cost of goods purchased	195,000	335,000
Net sales		320,000

Solution

Estimated ending inventory (at cost) is $327,000. It is computed as follows:

Step 1: ($530,000 + $335,000) − $320,000 = $545,000

Step 2: $\frac{\$324{,}000 + \$195{,}000}{\$530{,}000 + \$335{,}000} = 60\%$

Step 3: $545,000 × 60% = $327,000

Do More: QS 5-22, E 5-16, E 5-17

Summary

C1 Identify the items making up merchandise inventory. Merchandise inventory refers to goods owned by a company and held for resale. Three special cases merit our attention. Goods in transit are reported in inventory of the company that holds ownership rights. Goods on consignment are reported in the consignor's inventory. Goods damaged or obsolete are reported in inventory at their net realizable value.

C2 Identify the costs of merchandise inventory. Costs of merchandise inventory include expenditures necessary to bring an item to a salable condition and location. This includes its invoice cost minus any discount plus any added or incidental costs necessary to put it in a place and condition for sale.

A1 Analyze the effects of inventory methods for both financial and tax reporting. When purchase costs are rising or falling, the inventory costing methods are likely to assign different costs to inventory. Specific identification exactly matches costs and revenues. Weighted average smooths out cost changes. FIFO assigns an amount to inventory closely approximating current replacement cost. LIFO assigns the most recent costs incurred to cost of goods sold and likely better matches current costs with revenues.

A2 Analyze the effects of inventory errors on current and future financial statements. An error in the amount of ending inventory affects assets (inventory), net income (cost of goods sold), and equity for that period. Since ending inventory is next period's beginning inventory, an error in ending inventory affects next period's cost of goods sold and net income. Inventory errors in one period are offset in the next period.

A3 Assess inventory management using both inventory turnover and days' sales in inventory. We prefer a high inventory turnover, provided that goods are not out of stock and customers are not turned away. We use days' sales in inventory to assess the likelihood of goods being out of stock. We prefer a small number of days' sales in inventory if we can serve customer needs and provide a buffer for uncertainties.

P1 Compute inventory in a perpetual system using the methods of specific identification, FIFO, LIFO, and weighted average. Costs are assigned to the Cost of Goods Sold account *each time* a sale occurs in a perpetual system. Specific identification assigns a cost to each item sold by referring to its actual cost (for example, its net invoice cost). Weighted average assigns a cost to items sold by dividing the current balance in the Inventory account by the total items available for sale to determine cost per unit. We then multiply the number of units sold by this cost per unit to get the cost of each sale. FIFO assigns cost to items sold assuming that the earliest units purchased are the first units sold. LIFO assigns cost to items sold assuming that the most recent units purchased are the first units sold.

P2 Compute the lower of cost or market amount of inventory. Inventory is reported at market cost when market is *lower* than recorded cost, called the *lower of cost or market (LCM) inventory.* Market is typically measured as replacement cost. Lower of cost or market can be applied separately to each item, to major categories of items, or to the entire inventory.

P3^A Compute inventory in a periodic system using the methods of specific identification, FIFO, LIFO, and weighted average. Periodic inventory systems allocate the cost of goods available for sale between cost of goods sold and ending inventory *at the end of a period.* Specific identification and FIFO give identical results whether the periodic or perpetual system is used. LIFO assigns costs to cost of goods sold assuming the last units purchased for the period are the first units sold. The weighted average cost per unit is computed by dividing the total cost of beginning inventory and net purchases for the period by the total number of units available. Then, it multiplies cost per unit by the number of units sold to give cost of goods sold.

P4^B Apply both the retail inventory and gross profit methods to estimate inventory. The retail inventory method involves three steps: (1) goods available at retail minus net sales at retail equals ending inventory at retail, (2) goods available at cost divided by goods available at retail equals the cost-to-retail ratio, and (3) ending inventory at retail multiplied by the cost-to-retail ratio equals estimated ending inventory at cost. The gross profit method involves two steps: (1) net sales at retail multiplied by 1 minus the gross profit ratio equals estimated cost of goods sold, and (2) goods available at cost minus estimated cost of goods sold equals estimated ending inventory at cost.

Guidance Answers to Decision Maker and Decision Ethics

Cost Analyst Explain to your supervisor that when inventory costs are increasing, FIFO results in an inventory valuation that approximates replacement cost. The most recently purchased goods are assigned to ending inventory under FIFO and are likely closer to replacement values than earlier costs that would be assigned to inventory if LIFO were used.

Inventory Manager It seems your company can save (or at least postpone) taxes by switching to LIFO, but the switch is likely to reduce bonus money that you think you have earned and deserve. Since the U.S. tax code requires companies that use LIFO for tax reporting also to use it for financial reporting, your options are further constrained. Your best decision is to tell your superior about the tax savings with LIFO. You also should discuss your bonus plan and how this is likely to hurt you unfairly. You might propose to compute inventory under the LIFO method for reporting purposes but use the FIFO method for your bonus calculations. Another solution is to revise the bonus plan to reflect the company's use of the LIFO method.

Entrepreneur Your inventory turnover is markedly higher than the norm, whereas days' sales in inventory approximates the norm. Since your turnover is already 14% better than average, you are probably best served by directing attention to days' sales in inventory. You should see whether you can reduce the level of inventory while maintaining service to customers. Given your higher turnover, you should be able to hold less inventory.

Key Terms

Average cost
Conservatism constraint
Consignee
Consignor
Consistency concept
Days' sales in inventory
First-in, first-out (FIFO)
Gross profit method
Interim statements
Inventory turnover
Last-in, first-out (LIFO)
Lower of cost or market (LCM)
Net realizable value
Retail inventory method
Specific identification
Weighted average

Multiple Choice Quiz

Answers at end of chapter

Use the following information from Marvel Company for the month of July to answer questions 1 through 4.

July 1	Beginning inventory	75 units @ $25 each
July 3	Purchase	348 units @ $27 each
July 8	Sale	300 units
July 15	Purchase	257 units @ $28 each
July 23	Sale	275 units

1. Perpetual: Assume that Marvel uses a *perpetual* FIFO inventory system. What is the dollar value of its ending inventory?

a. $2,940
b. $2,685
c. $2,625
d. $2,852
e. $2,705

2. **Perpetual:** Assume that Marvel uses a *perpetual* LIFO inventory system. What is the dollar value of its ending inventory?
a. $2,940 **c.** $2,625 **e.** $2,705
b. $2,685 **d.** $2,852

3. **Perpetual:** Assume that Marvel uses a *perpetual* specific identification inventory system. Its ending inventory consists of 20 units from beginning inventory, 40 units from the July 3 purchase, and 45 units from the July 15 purchase. What is the dollar value of its ending inventory?
a. $2,940 **c.** $2,625 **e.** $2,840
b. $2,685 **d.** $2,852

4. **Periodic:** Assume that Marvel uses a *periodic* FIFO inventory system. What is the dollar value of its ending inventory?
a. $2,940 **c.** $2,625 **e.** $2,705
b. $2,685 **d.** $2,852

5. **Periodic:** A company reports the following beginning inventory and purchases, and it ends the period with 30 units in inventory.

Beginning inventory	100 units at $10 cost per unit
Purchase 1..............	40 units at $12 cost per unit
Purchase 2..............	20 units at $14 cost per unit

a. Compute ending inventory using the FIFO *periodic* system.
b. Compute cost of goods sold using the LIFO *periodic* system.

6. A company has cost of goods sold of $85,000 and ending inventory of $18,000. Its days' sales in inventory equals:
a. 49.32 days **d.** 77.29 days
b. 0.21 days **e.** 1,723.61 days
c. 4.72 days

Superscript letter A (B) denotes assignments based on Appendix 5A (5B).
Icon denotes assignments that involve decision making.

Discussion Questions

1. Describe how costs flow from inventory to cost of goods sold for the following methods: (*a*) FIFO and (*b*) LIFO.
2. Where is the amount of merchandise inventory disclosed in the financial statements?
3. Why are incidental costs sometimes ignored in inventory costing? Under what accounting constraint is this permitted?
4. If costs are declining, will the LIFO or FIFO method of inventory valuation yield the lower cost of goods sold? Why?
5. What does the full-disclosure principle prescribe if a company changes from one acceptable accounting method to another?
6. Can a company change its inventory method each accounting period? Explain.
7. Does the accounting concept of consistency preclude any changes from one accounting method to another?
8. If inventory errors are said to correct themselves, why are accounting users concerned when such errors are made?
9. Explain the following statement: "Inventory errors correct themselves."
10. What is the meaning of *market* as it is used in determining the lower of cost or market for inventory?
11. What guidance does the accounting constraint of conservatism offer?
12. What factors contribute to (or cause) inventory shrinkage?
13.[B] When preparing interim financial statements, what two methods can companies utilize to estimate cost of goods sold and ending inventory?
14. Refer to **Google**'s financial statements in Appendix A. On December 31, 2013, what percent of current assets are represented by inventory? **GOOGLE**
15. Refer to **Apple**'s financial statements in Appendix A and compute its cost of goods available for sale for the year ended September 28, 2013. **APPLE**
16. Refer to **Samsung**'s financial statements in Appendix A. Compute its cost of goods available for sale for the year ended December 31, 2013. **Samsung**
17. Refer to **Samsung**'s financial statements in Appendix A. What percent of its current assets are inventory as of December 31, 2013 and 2012? **Samsung**

connect

QUICK STUDY

QS 5-1
Inventory ownership C1

Homestead Crafts, a distributor of handmade gifts, operates out of owner Emma Finn's house. At the end of the current period, Emma reports she has 1,300 units (products) in her basement, 20 of which were damaged by water and cannot be sold. She also has another 350 units in her van, ready to deliver per a customer order, terms FOB destination, and another 80 units out on consignment to a friend who owns a retail store. How many units should Emma include in her company's period-end inventory?

QS 5-2
Inventory costs C2

A car dealer acquires a used car for $14,000, terms FOB shipping point. Additional costs in obtaining and offering the car for sale include $250 for transportation-in, $900 for import duties, $300 for insurance during shipment, $150 for advertising, and $1,250 for sales staff salaries. For computing inventory, what cost is assigned to the used car?

QS 5-3
Computing goods available for sale P1

Wattan Company reports beginning inventory of 10 units at $60 each. Every week for four weeks it purchases an additional 10 units at respective costs of $61, $62, $65, and $70 per unit for weeks 1 through 4. Calculate the cost of goods available for sale and the units available for sale for this four-week period. Assume that no sales occur during those four weeks.

QS 5-4
Perpetual: Inventory costing with FIFO
P1

A company reports the following beginning inventory and purchases for the month of January. On January 26, the company sells 350 units. 150 units remain in ending inventory at January 31.

	Units	Unit Cost
Beginning inventory on January 1	320	$3.00
Purchase on January 9	80	3.20
Purchase on January 25	100	3.34

Required

Assume the perpetual inventory system is used and then determine the costs assigned to ending inventory when costs are assigned based on the FIFO method. (Round per unit costs and inventory amounts to cents.)

QS 5-5
Perpetual: Inventory costing with LIFO P1

Refer to the information in QS 5-4 and assume the perpetual inventory system is used. Determine the costs assigned to ending inventory when costs are assigned based on LIFO. (Round per unit costs and inventory amounts to cents.)

QS 5-6
Perpetual: Inventory costing with weighted average P1
Check End. inv., $465

Refer to the information in QS 5-4 and assume the perpetual inventory system is used. Determine the costs assigned to ending inventory when costs are assigned based on the weighted average method. (Round per unit costs and inventory amounts to cents.)

QS 5-7^A
Periodic: Inventory costing with FIFO P3

Refer to the information in QS 5-4 and assume the periodic inventory system is used. Determine the costs assigned to ending inventory when costs are assigned based on the FIFO method. (Round per unit costs and inventory amounts to cents.)

QS 5-8^A
Periodic: Inventory costing with LIFO P3

Refer to the information in QS 5-4 and assume the periodic inventory system is used. Determine the costs assigned to ending inventory when costs are assigned based on the LIFO method. (Round per unit costs and inventory amounts to cents.)

QS 5-9^A
Periodic: Inventory costing with weighted average P3

Refer to the information in QS 5-4 and assume the periodic inventory system is used. Determine the costs assigned to ending inventory when costs are assigned based on the weighted average method. (Round per unit costs and inventory amounts to cents.)

QS 5-10
Perpetual: Assigning costs with FIFO
P1

Trey Monson starts a merchandising business on December 1 and enters into the following three inventory purchases. Also, on December 15, Monson sells 15 units for $20 each.

Purchases on December 7	10 units @ $ 6.00 cost
Purchases on December 14	20 units @ $12.00 cost
Purchases on December 21	15 units @ $14.00 cost

Required

Monson uses a perpetual inventory system. Determine the costs assigned to the December 31 ending inventory based on the FIFO method. (Round per unit costs and inventory amounts to cents.)

QS 5-11
Perpetual: Inventory costing with LIFO P1

Refer to the information in QS 5-10 and assume the perpetual inventory system is used. Determine the costs assigned to ending inventory when costs are assigned based on the LIFO method. (Round per unit costs and inventory amounts to cents.)

QS 5-12
Perpetual: Inventory costing with weighted average P1

Check End. inv., $360

Refer to the information in QS 5-10 and assume the perpetual inventory system is used. Determine the costs assigned to ending inventory when costs are assigned based on the weighted average method. (Round per unit costs and inventory amounts to cents.)

QS 5-13
Perpetual: Inventory costing with specific identification P1

Refer to the information in QS 5-10 and assume the perpetual inventory system is used. Determine the costs assigned to ending inventory when costs are assigned based on specific identification. Of the units sold, eight are from the December 7 purchase and seven are from the December 14 purchase. (Round per unit costs and inventory amounts to cents.)

QS 5-14A
Periodic: Inventory costing with FIFO P3

Refer to the information in QS 5-10 and assume the periodic inventory system is used. Determine the costs assigned to ending inventory when costs are assigned based on the FIFO method. (Round per unit costs and inventory amounts to cents.)

QS 5-15
Periodic: Inventory costing with LIFO P3

Refer to the information in QS 5-10 and assume the periodic inventory system is used. Determine the costs assigned to ending inventory when costs are assigned based on the LIFO method. (Round per unit costs and inventory amounts to cents.)

QS 5-16A
Periodic: Inventory costing with weighted average P3

Refer to the information in QS 5-10 and assume the periodic inventory system is used. Determine the costs assigned to ending inventory when costs are assigned based on the weighted average method. (Round per unit costs and inventory amounts to cents.)

QS 5-17A
Periodic: Inventory costing with specific identification P3

Refer to the information in QS 5-10 and assume the periodic inventory system is used. Determine the costs assigned to ending inventory when costs are assigned based on specific identification. Of the units sold, eight are from the December 7 purchase and seven are from the December 14 purchase. (Round per unit costs and inventory amounts to cents.)

QS 5-18
Contrasting inventory costing methods
A1

Identify the inventory costing method best described by each of the following separate statements. Assume a period of increasing costs.

_______ **1.** Yields a balance sheet inventory amount often markedly less than its replacement cost.
_______ **2.** Results in a balance sheet inventory amount approximating replacement cost.
_______ **3.** Provides a tax advantage (deferral) to a corporation when costs are rising.
_______ **4.** Recognizes (matches) recent costs against net sales.
_______ **5.** The preferred method when each unit of product has unique features that markedly affect cost.

QS 5-19
Applying LCM to inventories
P2

Ames Trading Co. has the following products in its ending inventory. Compute lower of cost or market for inventory applied separately to each product.

Product	Quantity	Cost per Unit	Market per Unit
Mountain bikes	11	$600	$550
Skateboards	13	350	425
Gliders	26	800	700

QS 5-20
Inventory errors
A2

In taking a physical inventory at the end of year 2015, Grant Company forgot to count certain units. Explain how this error affects the following: (*a*) 2015 cost of goods sold, (*b*) 2015 gross profit, (*c*) 2015 net income, (*d*) 2016 net income, (*e*) the combined two-year income, and (*f*) income for years after 2016.

QS 5-21
Analyzing inventory A3

Endor Company begins the year with $140,000 of goods in inventory. At year-end, the amount in inventory has increased to $180,000. Cost of goods sold for the year is $1,200,000. Compute Endor's inventory turnover and days' sales in inventory. Assume that there are 365 days in the year.

QS 5-22B
Estimating inventories—gross profit method
P4

Confucius Bookstore's inventory is destroyed by a fire on September 5, 2015. The following data for year 2015 are available from the accounting records. Estimate the cost of the inventory destroyed.

Jan. 1 inventory	$190,000
Jan. 1 through Sept. 5 purchases (net)	$352,000
Jan. 1 through Sept. 5 sales (net)	$685,000
Year 2015 estimated gross profit rate	44%

QS 5-23
International accounting standards
C1 C2 P2

Answer each of the following questions related to international accounting standards.

a. Explain how the accounting for items and costs making up merchandise inventory is different between IFRS and U.S. GAAP.

b. Can companies reporting under IFRS apply a cost flow assumption in assigning costs to inventory? If yes, identify at least two acceptable cost flow assumptions.

c. Both IFRS and U.S. GAAP apply the lower of cost or market method for reporting inventory values. If inventory is written down from applying the lower of cost or market method, explain in general terms how IFRS and U.S. GAAP differ in accounting for any subsequent period reversal of that reported decline in inventory value.

connect

EXERCISES

Exercise 5-1
Inventory ownership C1

1. At year-end, Harris Co. had shipped $12,500 of merchandise FOB destination to Harlow Co. Which company should include the $12,500 of merchandise in transit as part of its year-end inventory?

2. Harris Company has shipped $20,000 of goods to Harlow Co., and Harlow Co. has arranged to sell the goods for Harris. Identify the consignor and the consignee. Which company should include any unsold goods as part of its inventory?

Exercise 5-2
Inventory costs
C2

Walberg Associates, antique dealers, purchased the contents of an estate for $75,000. Terms of the purchase were FOB shipping point, and the cost of transporting the goods to Walberg Associates' warehouse was $2,400. Walberg Associates insured the shipment at a cost of $300. Prior to putting the goods up for sale, they cleaned and refurbished them at a cost of $980. Determine the cost of the inventory acquired from the estate.

Exercise 5-3
Perpetual: Inventory costing methods
P1

Laker Company reported the following January purchases and sales data for its only product.

Date	Activities	Units Acquired at Cost		Units Sold at Retail
Jan. 1	Beginning inventory	140 units @ $6.00 =	$ 840	
Jan. 10	Sales			100 units @ $15
Jan. 20	Purchase	60 units @ $5.00 =	300	
Jan. 25	Sales			80 units @ $15
Jan. 30	Purchase	180 units @ $4.50 =	810	
	Totals	380 units	$1,950	180 units

Required

The company uses a perpetual inventory system. Determine the cost assigned to ending inventory and to cost of goods sold using (*a*) specific identification, (*b*) weighted average, (*c*) FIFO, and (*d*) LIFO. (Round per unit costs and inventory amounts to cents.) For specific identification, ending inventory consists of 200 units, where 180 are from the January 30 purchase, 5 are from the January 20 purchase, and 15 are from beginning inventory.

Check Ending inventory: LIFO, $930; WA, $918

Exercise 5-4
Perpetual: Income effects of inventory methods
A1

Use the data in Exercise 5-3 to prepare comparative income statements for the month of January for Laker Company similar to those shown in Exhibit 5.8 for the four inventory methods. Assume expenses are $1,250, and that the applicable income tax rate is 40%. (Round amounts to cents.)

1. Which method yields the highest net income?
2. Does net income using weighted average fall between that using FIFO and LIFO?
3. If costs were rising instead of falling, which method would yield the highest net income?

Exercise 5-5A
Periodic: Inventory costing P3

Refer to the information in Exercise 5-3 and assume the periodic inventory system is used. Determine the costs assigned to ending inventory and to cost of goods sold using (*a*) specific identification, (*b*) weighted average, (*c*) FIFO, and (*d*) LIFO. (Round per unit costs and inventory amounts to cents.)

Exercise 5-6A
Periodic: Income effects of inventory methods
A1

Use the data and results from Exercise 5-5 to prepare comparative income statements for the month of January for the company similar to those shown in Exhibit 5.8 for the four inventory methods. Assume expenses are $1,250, and that the applicable income tax rate is 40%. (Round amounts to cents.)

Required

1. Which method yields the highest net income?
2. Does net income using weighted average fall between that using FIFO and LIFO?
3. If costs were rising instead of falling, which method would yield the highest net income?

Exercise 5-7
Perpetual: Inventory costing methods—FIFO and LIFO
P1

Hemming Co. reported the following current-year purchases and sales for its only product.

Date	Activities	Units Acquired at Cost		Units Sold at Retail
Jan. 1	Beginning inventory	200 units @ $10 =	$ 2,000	
Jan. 10	Sales			150 units @ $40
Mar. 14	Purchase	350 units @ $15 =	5,250	
Mar. 15	Sales			300 units @ $40
July 30	Purchase	450 units @ $20 =	9,000	
Oct. 5	Sales			430 units @ $40
Oct. 26	Purchase	100 units @ $25 =	2,500	
	Totals	1,100 units	$18,750	880 units

Required

Hemming uses a perpetual inventory system. Determine the costs assigned to ending inventory and to cost of goods sold using (*a*) FIFO and (*b*) LIFO. Compute the gross margin for each method. (Round amounts to cents.)

Check Ending inventory: LIFO, $4,150

Exercise 5-8
Specific identification P1

Refer to the information in Exercise 5-7. Ending inventory consists of 45 units from the March 14 purchase, 75 units from the July 30 purchase, and all 100 units from the October 26 purchase. Using the specific identification method, calculate (*a*) the cost of goods sold and (*b*) the gross profit. (Round amounts to cents.)

Exercise 5-9A
Periodic: Inventory costing P3

Refer to the information in Exercise 5-7 and assume the periodic inventory system is used. Determine the costs assigned to ending inventory and to cost of goods sold using (*a*) FIFO and (*b*) LIFO. Then (*c*) compute the gross margin for each method.

Exercise 5-10
Lower of cost or market
P2

Martinez Company's ending inventory includes the following items. Compute the lower of cost or market for ending inventory applied separately to each product.

		Per Unit	
Product	Units	Cost	Market
Helmets	24	$50	$54
Bats	17	78	72
Shoes	38	95	91
Uniforms	42	36	36

Check LCM = $7,394

Exercise 5-11
Comparing LIFO numbers to FIFO numbers; ratio analysis
A1 A3

Cruz Company uses LIFO for inventory costing and reports the following financial data. It also recomputed inventory and cost of goods sold using FIFO for comparison purposes.

	2015	2014
LIFO inventory	$160	$110
LIFO cost of goods sold	740	680
FIFO inventory	240	110
FIFO cost of goods sold	660	645
Current assets (using LIFO)	220	180
Current liabilities	200	170

1. Compute its current ratio, inventory turnover, and days' sales in inventory for 2015 using (*a*) LIFO numbers and (*b*) FIFO numbers. (Round answers to one decimal.)
2. Comment on and interpret the results of part 1.

Check (1) FIFO: Current ratio, 1.5; Inventory turnover, 3.8 times

Exercise 5-12
Analysis of inventory errors
A2

Vibrant Company had $850,000 of sales in each of three consecutive years 2014–2016, and it purchased merchandise costing $500,000 in each of those years. It also maintained a $250,000 physical inventory from the beginning to the end of that three-year period. In accounting for inventory, it made an error at the end of year 2014 that caused its year-end 2014 inventory to appear on its statements as $230,000 rather than the correct $250,000.

1. Determine the correct amount of the company's gross profit in each of the years 2014–2016.
2. Prepare comparative income statements as in Exhibit 5.11 to show the effect of this error on the company's cost of goods sold and gross profit for each of the years 2014–2016.

Check 2014 reported gross profit, $330,000

Exercise 5-13
Inventory turnover and days' sales in inventory
A3

Use the following information for Palmer Co. to compute inventory turnover for 2015 and 2014, and its days' sales in inventory at December 31, 2015 and 2014. (Round answers to one decimal.) Comment on Palmer's efficiency in using its assets to increase sales from 2014 to 2015.

	2015	2014	2013
Cost of goods sold	$643,825	$426,650	$391,300
Ending inventory	97,400	87,750	92,500

Exercise 5-14^A
Periodic: Cost flow assumptions
P3

Lopez Company reported the following current-year data for its only product. The company uses a periodic inventory system, and its ending inventory consists of 150 units—50 from each of the last three purchases. Determine the cost assigned to ending inventory and to cost of goods sold using (*a*) specific identification, (*b*) weighted average, (*c*) FIFO, and (*d*) LIFO. (Round per unit costs and inventory amounts to cents.) Which method yields the highest net income?

Jan. 1	Beginning inventory	96 units @ $2.00 =	$ 192
Mar. 7	Purchase	220 units @ $2.25 =	495
July 28	Purchase	544 units @ $2.50 =	1,360
Oct. 3	Purchase	480 units @ $2.80 =	1,344
Dec. 19	Purchase	160 units @ $2.90 =	464
	Totals	1,500 units	$3,855

Check Inventory; LIFO, $313.50; FIFO, $435.00

Exercise 5-15
Periodic: Cost flow assumptions
P3

Flora's Gifts reported the following current-month data for its only product. The company uses a periodic inventory system, and its ending inventory consists of 60 units—50 units from the January 6 purchase, and 10 units from the January 25 purchase. Determine the cost assigned to ending inventory and to cost of goods sold using (*a*) specific identification, (*b*) weighted average, (*c*) FIFO, and (*d*) LIFO. (Round per unit costs and inventory amounts to cents.) Which method yields the lowest net income?

Jan. 1	Beginning inventory	138 units @ $3.00 =	$	414
Jan. 6	Purchase	300 units @ $2.80 =		840
Jan. 17	Purchase	540 units @ $2.30 =		1,242
Jan. 25	Purchase	22 units @ $2.00 =		44
	Totals	1,000 units		$2,540

Check Inventory: LIFO, $180.00; FIFO, $131.40

Exercise 5-16B
Estimating ending inventory—retail method
P4

In 2015, Dakota Company had net sales (at retail) of $260,000. The following additional information is available from its records at the end of 2015. Use the retail inventory method to estimate Dakota's 2015 ending inventory at cost.

	At Cost	At Retail
Beginning inventory	$ 63,800	$128,400
Cost of goods purchased	115,060	196,800

Check End. inventory at cost, $35,860

Exercise 5-17B
Estimating ending inventory—gross profit method P4

On January 1, JKR Shop had $225,000 of inventory at cost. In the first quarter of the year, it purchased $795,000 of merchandise, returned $11,550, and paid freight charges of $18,800 on purchased merchandise, terms FOB shipping point. The company's gross profit averages 30%, and the store had $1,000,000 of net sales (at retail) in the first quarter of the year. Use the gross profit method to estimate its cost of inventory at the end of the first quarter.

Exercise 5-18
Accounting for inventory following IFRS
P2

Samsung Electronics reports the following regarding its accounting for inventories.

> Inventories are stated at the lower of cost or net realizable value. Cost is determined using the average cost method, except for materials-in-transit. Inventories are reduced for the estimated losses arising from excess, obsolescence, and the decline in value. This reduction is determined by estimating market value based on future customer demand. The losses on inventory obsolescence are recorded as a part of cost of sales.

1. What cost flow assumption(s) does Samsung apply in assigning costs to its inventories?
2. If at year-end 2013 there was an increase in the value of its inventories such that there was a reversal of ₩550 (₩ is Korean won) million for the 2012 write-down, how would Samsung account for this under IFRS? Would Samsung's accounting be different for this reversal if it reported under U.S. GAAP? Explain.

connect

PROBLEM SET A

Problem 5-1A
Perpetual: Alternative cost flows
P1

Warnerwoods Company uses a perpetual inventory system. It entered into the following purchases and sales transactions for March. (For specific identification, the March 9 sale consisted of 80 units from beginning inventory and 340 units from the March 5 purchase; the March 29 sale consisted of 40 units from the March 18 purchase and 120 units from the March 25 purchase.)

Date	Activities	Units Acquired at Cost	Units Sold at Retail
Mar. 1	Beginning inventory	100 units @ $50.00 per unit	
Mar. 5	Purchase	400 units @ $55.00 per unit	
Mar. 9	Sales		420 units @ $85.00 per unit
Mar. 18	Purchase	120 units @ $60.00 per unit	
Mar. 25	Purchase	200 units @ $62.00 per unit	
Mar. 29	Sales		160 units @ $95.00 per unit
	Totals	820 units	580 units

Required

1. Compute cost of goods available for sale and the number of units available for sale.
2. Compute the number of units in ending inventory.
3. Compute the cost assigned to ending inventory using (*a*) FIFO, (*b*) LIFO, (*c*) weighted average, and (*d*) specific identification. (Round all amounts to cents.)
4. Compute gross profit earned by the company for each of the four costing methods in part 3.

Check (3) Ending inventory: FIFO, $14,800; LIFO, $13,680, WA, $14,352
(4) LIFO gross profit, $17,980

Problem 5-2A^A
Periodic: Alternative cost flows
P1

Refer to the information in Problem 5-1A and assume the periodic inventory system is used.

Required

1. Compute cost of goods available for sale and the number of units available for sale.
2. Compute the number of units in ending inventory.
3. Compute the cost assigned to ending inventory using (*a*) FIFO, (*b*) LIFO, (*c*) weighted average, and (*d*) specific identification. (Round all amounts to cents.)
4. Compute gross profit earned by the company for each of the four costing methods in part 3.

Problem 5-3A
Perpetual: Alternative cost flows
P1

Montoure Company uses a perpetual inventory system. It entered into the following calendar-year 2015 purchases and sales transactions. (For specific identification, units sold consist of 600 units from beginning inventory, 300 from the February 10 purchase, 200 from the March 13 purchase, 50 from the August 21 purchase, and 250 from the September 5 purchase.)

Date	Activities	Units Acquired at Cost	Units Sold at Retail
Jan. 1	Beginning inventory	600 units @ $45.00 per unit	
Feb. 10	Purchase	400 units @ $42.00 per unit	
Mar. 13	Purchase	200 units @ $27.00 per unit	
Mar. 15	Sales		800 units @ $75.00 per unit
Aug. 21	Purchase	100 units @ $50.00 per unit	
Sept. 5	Purchase	500 units @ $46.00 per unit	
Sept. 10	Sales		600 units @ $75.00 per unit
	Totals	1,800 units	1,400 units

Required

1. Compute cost of goods available for sale and the number of units available for sale.
2. Compute the number of units in ending inventory.
3. Compute the cost assigned to ending inventory using (*a*) FIFO, (*b*) LIFO, (*c*) weighted average, and (*d*) specific identification. (Round all amounts to cents.)
4. Compute gross profit earned by the company for each of the four costing methods in part 3.

Check (3) Ending inventory: FIFO, $18,400; LIFO, $18,000; WA, $17,760
(4) LIFO gross profit, $45,800

Analysis Component

5. If the company's manager earns a bonus based on a percent of gross profit, which method of inventory costing will the manager likely prefer?

Problem 5-4A^A
Periodic: Alternative cost flows
P1

Refer to the information in Problem 5-3A and assume the periodic inventory system is used.

Required

1. Compute cost of goods available for sale and the number of units available for sale.
2. Compute the number of units in ending inventory.
3. Compute the cost assigned to ending inventory using (*a*) FIFO, (*b*) LIFO, (*c*) weighted average, and (*d*) specific identification. (Round all amounts to cents.)
4. Compute gross profit earned by the company for each of the four costing methods in part 3.

Analysis Component

5. If the company's manager earns a bonus based on a percentage of gross profit, which method of inventory costing will the manager likely prefer?

Problem 5-5A
Lower of cost or market
P2

A physical inventory of Liverpool Company taken at December 31 reveals the following.

	A	B	C	D
1			Per Unit	
2	Item	Units	Cost	Market
3	Audio equipment			
4	Receivers	345	$ 90	$ 98
5	CD players	260	111	100
6	MP3 players	326	86	95
7	Speakers	204	52	41
8	Video equipment			
9	Handheld LCDs	480	150	125
10	VCRs	291	93	84
11	Camcorders	212	310	322
12	Car audio equipment			
13	Satellite radios	185	70	84
14	CD/MP3 radios	170	97	105
15				

Required

Check (1) $273,054

1. Calculate the lower of cost or market for the inventory applied separately to each item.
2. If the market amount is less than the recorded cost of the inventory, then record the LCM adjustment to the Merchandise Inventory account.

Problem 5-6A
Analysis of inventory errors
A2

Navajo Company's financial statements show the following. The company recently discovered that in making physical counts of inventory, it had made the following errors: Inventory on December 31, 2014, is understated by $56,000, and inventory on December 31, 2015, is overstated by $20,000.

For Year Ended December 31	2014	2015	2016
(*a*) Cost of goods sold	$ 615,000	$ 957,000	$ 780,000
(*b*) Net income	230,000	285,000	241,000
(*c*) Total current assets	1,255,000	1,365,000	1,200,000
(*d*) Total equity	1,387,000	1,530,000	1,242,000

Required

1. For each key financial statement figure—(*a*), (*b*), (*c*), and (*d*) above—prepare a table similar to the following to show the adjustments necessary to correct the reported amounts.

Figure: ______	2014	2015	2016
Reported amount			
Adjustments for: 12/31/2014 error			
12/31/2015 error			
Corrected amount			

Check (1) Corrected net income: 2014, $286,000; 2015, $209,000; 2016, $261,000

Analysis Component

2. What is the error in total net income for the combined three-year period resulting from the inventory errors? Explain.
3. Explain why the understatement of inventory by $56,000 at the end of 2014 results in an understatement of equity by the same amount in that year.

Problem 5-7A[A]
Periodic: Alternative cost flows P3

Seminole Company began year 2015 with 23,000 units of product in its January 1 inventory costing $15 each. It made successive purchases of its product in year 2015 as follows. The company uses a periodic inventory system. On December 31, 2015, a physical count reveals that 40,000 units of its product remain in inventory.

Mar. 7	30,000 units @ $18.00 each
May 25	39,000 units @ $20.00 each
Aug. 1	23,000 units @ $25.00 each
Nov. 10	35,000 units @ $26.00 each

Required

1. Compute the number and total cost of the units available for sale in year 2015.
2. Compute the amounts assigned to the 2015 ending inventory and the cost of goods sold using (*a*) FIFO, (*b*) LIFO, and (*c*) weighted average. (Round all amounts to cents.)

Check (2) Cost of goods sold: FIFO, $2,115,000; LIFO, $2,499,000; WA, $2,310,000

Problem 5-8A^A
Periodic: Income comparisons and cost flows
A1 P3

QP Corp. sold 4,000 units of its product at $50 per unit in year 2015 and incurred operating expenses of $5 per unit in selling the units. It began the year with 700 units in inventory and made successive purchases of its product as follows.

Jan. 1	Beginning inventory	700 units @ $18.00 per unit
Feb. 20	Purchase	1,700 units @ $19.00 per unit
May 16	Purchase	800 units @ $20.00 per unit
Oct. 3	Purchase	500 units @ $21.00 per unit
Dec. 11	Purchase	2,300 units @ $22.00 per unit
	Total	6,000 units

Required

1. Prepare comparative income statements similar to Exhibit 5.8 for the three inventory costing methods of FIFO, LIFO, and weighted average. (Round all amounts to cents.) Include a detailed cost of goods sold section as part of each statement. The company uses a periodic inventory system, and its income tax rate is 40%.
2. How would the financial results from using the three alternative inventory costing methods change if the company had been experiencing declining costs in its purchases of inventory?
3. What advantages and disadvantages are offered by using (*a*) LIFO and (*b*) FIFO? Assume the continuing trend of increasing costs.

Check (1) Net income: FIFO, $61,200; LIFO, $57,180; WA, $59,196

Problem 5-9A^B
Retail inventory method
P4

The records of Alaska Company provide the following information for the year ended December 31.

	At Cost	At Retail
January 1 beginning inventory	$ 469,010	$ 928,950
Cost of goods purchased	3,376,050	6,381,050
Sales		5,595,800
Sales returns		42,800

Required

1. Use the retail inventory method to estimate the company's year-end inventory at cost.
2. A year-end physical inventory at retail prices yields a total inventory of $1,686,900. Prepare a calculation showing the company's loss from shrinkage at cost and at retail.

Check (1) Inventory, $924,182 cost
(2) Inventory shortage at cost, $36,873

Problem 5-10A^B
Gross profit method
P4

Wayward Company wants to prepare interim financial statements for the first quarter. The company wishes to avoid making a physical count of inventory. Wayward's gross profit rate averages 34%. The following information for the first quarter is available from its records.

January 1 beginning inventory	$ 302,580
Cost of goods purchased	941,040
Sales	1,211,160
Sales returns	8,410

Required

Use the gross profit method to estimate the company's first quarter ending inventory.

Check Estimated ending inventory, $449,805

PROBLEM SET B

Problem 5-1B
Perpetual: Alternative cost flows
P1

Ming Company uses a perpetual inventory system. It entered into the following purchases and sales transactions for April. (For specific identification, the April 9 sale consisted of 8 units from beginning inventory and 27 units from the April 6 purchase; the April 30 sale consisted of 12 units from beginning inventory, 3 units from the April 6 purchase, and 10 units from the April 25 purchase.)

Date	Activities	Units Acquired at Cost	Units Sold at Retail
Apr. 1	Beginning inventory	20 units @ $3,000.00 per unit	
Apr. 6	Purchase	30 units @ $3,500.00 per unit	
Apr. 9	Sales		35 units @ $12,000.00 per unit
Apr. 17	Purchase	5 units @ $4,500.00 per unit	
Apr. 25	Purchase	10 units @ $4,800.00 per unit	
Apr. 30	Sales		25 units @ $14,000.00 per unit
	Total	65 units	60 units

Required

1. Compute cost of goods available for sale and the number of units available for sale.
2. Compute the number of units in ending inventory.
3. Compute the cost assigned to ending inventory using (*a*) FIFO, (*b*) LIFO, (*c*) weighted average, and (*d*) specific identification. (Round all amounts to cents.)
4. Compute gross profit earned by the company for each of the four costing methods in part 3.

Check (3) Ending inventory: FIFO, $24,000; LIFO, $15,000; WA, $20,000
(4) LIFO gross profit, $549,500

Problem 5-2B[A]
Periodic: Alternative cost flows
P1

Refer to the information in Problem 5-1B and assume the periodic inventory system is used.

Required

1. Compute cost of goods available for sale and the number of units available for sale.
2. Compute the number of units in ending inventory.
3. Compute the cost assigned to ending inventory using (*a*) FIFO, (*b*) LIFO, (*c*) weighted average, and (*d*) specific identification. (Round all amounts to cents.)
4. Compute gross profit earned by the company for each of the four costing methods in part 3.

Problem 5-3B
Perpetual: Alternative cost flows
P1

Aloha Company uses a perpetual inventory system. It entered into the following calendar-year 2015 purchases and sales transactions. (For specific identification, the May 9 sale consisted of 80 units from beginning inventory and 100 units from the May 6 purchase; the May 30 sale consisted of 200 units from the May 6 purchase and 100 units from the May 25 purchase.)

Date	Activities	Units Acquired at Cost	Units Sold at Retail
May 1	Beginning inventory	150 units @ $300.00 per unit	
May 6	Purchase	350 units @ $350.00 per unit	
May 9	Sales		180 units @ $1,200.00 per unit
May 17	Purchase	80 units @ $450.00 per unit	
May 25	Purchase	100 units @ $458.00 per unit	
May 30	Sales		300 units @ $1,400.00 per unit
	Total	680 units	480 units

Required

1. Compute cost of goods available for sale and the number of units available for sale.
2. Compute the number of units in ending inventory.
3. Compute the cost assigned to ending inventory using (*a*) FIFO, (*b*) LIFO, (*c*) weighted average, and (*d*) specific identification. (Round all amounts to cents.)
4. Compute gross profit earned by the company for each of the four costing methods in part 3.

Check (3) Ending inventory: FIFO, $88,800; LIFO, $62,500; WA, $75,600
(4) LIFO gross profit, $449,200

Analysis Component

5. If the company's manager earns a bonus based on a percent of gross profit, which method of inventory costing will the manager likely prefer?

Problem 5-4B[A]
Periodic: Alternative cost flows
P1

Refer to the information in Problem 5-3B and assume the periodic inventory system is used.

Required

1. Compute cost of goods available for sale and the number of units available for sale.
2. Compute the number of units in ending inventory.
3. Compute the cost assigned to ending inventory using (*a*) FIFO, (*b*) LIFO, (*c*) weighted average, and (*d*) specific identification. (Round all amounts to cents.)
4. Compute gross profit earned by the company for each of the four costing methods in part 3.

Analysis Component

5. If the company's manager earns a bonus based on a percentage of gross profit, which method of inventory costing will the manager likely prefer?

Problem 5-5B
Lower of cost or market
P2

A physical inventory of Office Necessities Company taken at December 31 reveals the following.

	A	B	C	D
1			Per Unit	
2	**Item**	**Units**	**Cost**	**Market**
3	Office furniture			
4	Desks	536	$261	$305
5	Credenzas	395	227	256
6	Chairs	687	49	43
7	Bookshelves	421	93	82
8	Filing cabinets			
9	Two-drawer	114	81	70
10	Four-drawer	298	135	122
11	Lateral	75	104	118
12	Office equipment			
13	Fax machines	370	168	200
14	Copiers	475	317	288
15	Telephones	302	125	117
16				

Required

1. Compute the lower of cost or market for the inventory applied separately to each item.
2. If the market amount is less than the recorded cost of the inventory, then record the LCM adjustment to the Merchandise Inventory account.

Check (1) $580,054

Problem 5-6B
Analysis of inventory errors
A2

Hallam Company's financial statements show the following. The company recently discovered that in making physical counts of inventory, it had made the following errors: Inventory on December 31, 2014, is overstated by $18,000, and inventory on December 31, 2015, is understated by $26,000.

For Year Ended December 31	2014	2015	2016
(*a*) Cost of goods sold	$207,200	$213,800	$197,030
(*b*) Net income	175,800	212,270	184,910
(*c*) Total current assets	276,000	277,500	272,950
(*d*) Total equity	314,000	315,000	346,000

Required

1. For each key financial statement figure—(*a*), (*b*), (*c*), and (*d*) above—prepare a table similar to the following to show the adjustments necessary to correct the reported amounts.

Check (1) Corrected net income: 2014, $157,800; 2015, $256,270; 2016, $158,910

Figure: ______	2014	2015	2016
Reported amount			
Adjustments for: 12/31/2014 error			
12/31/2015 error			
Corrected amount			

Analysis Component

2. What is the error in total net income for the combined three-year period resulting from the inventory errors? Explain.
3. Explain why the overstatement of inventory by $18,000 at the end of 2014 results in an overstatement of equity by the same amount in that year.

Problem 5-7B^A
Periodic: Alternative cost flows
P3

Seneca Co. began year 2015 with 6,500 units of product in its January 1 inventory costing $35 each. It made successive purchases of its product in year 2015 as follows. The company uses a periodic inventory system. On December 31, 2015, a physical count reveals that 8,500 units of its product remain in inventory.

Jan. 4	11,500 units @ $33 each
May 18	13,400 units @ $32 each
July 9	11,000 units @ $29 each
Nov. 21	7,600 units @ $27 each

Required

Check (2) Cost of goods sold: FIFO, $1,328,700; LIFO, $1,266,500; WA, $1,294,800

1. Compute the number and total cost of the units available for sale in year 2015.
2. Compute the amounts assigned to the 2015 ending inventory and the cost of goods sold using (*a*) FIFO, (*b*) LIFO, and (*c*) weighted average. (Round all amounts to cents.)

Problem 5-8B^A
Periodic: Income comparisons and cost flows
A1 P3

Shepard Company sold 4,000 units of its product at $100 per unit in year 2015 and incurred operating expenses of $15 per unit in selling the units. It began the year with 840 units in inventory and made successive purchases of its product as follows.

Jan. 1	Beginning inventory	840 units @ $58 per unit
April 2	Purchase	600 units @ $59 per unit
June 14	Purchase	1,205 units @ $61 per unit
Aug. 29	Purchase	700 units @ $64 per unit
Nov. 18	Purchase	1,655 units @ $65 per unit
	Total	5,000 units

Required

Check (1) Net income: LIFO, $52,896; FIFO, $57,000; WA, $55,200

1. Prepare comparative income statements similar to Exhibit 5.8 for the three inventory costing methods of FIFO, LIFO, and weighted average. (Round all amounts to cents.) Include a detailed cost of goods sold section as part of each statement. The company uses a periodic inventory system, and its income tax rate is 40%.
2. How would the financial results from using the three alternative inventory costing methods change if the company had been experiencing decreasing prices in its purchases of inventory?
3. What advantages and disadvantages are offered by using (*a*) LIFO and (*b*) FIFO? Assume the continuing trend of increasing costs.

Problem 5-9B[B]
Retail inventory method
P4

The records of Macklin Co. provide the following information for the year ended December 31.

	At Cost	At Retail
January 1 beginning inventory	$ 90,022	$115,610
Cost of goods purchased	502,250	761,830
Sales		782,300
Sales returns		3,460

Required

1. Use the retail inventory method to estimate the company's year-end inventory.
2. A year-end physical inventory at retail prices yields a total inventory of $80,450. Prepare a calculation showing the company's loss from shrinkage at cost and at retail.

Check (1) Inventory, $66,555 cost
(2) Inventory shortage at cost, $12,251.25

Problem 5-10B[B]
Gross profit method
P4

Otingo Equipment Co. wants to prepare interim financial statements for the first quarter. The company wishes to avoid making a physical count of inventory. Otingo's gross profit rate averages 35%. The following information for the first quarter is available from its records.

January 1 beginning inventory	$ 802,880
Cost of goods purchased	2,209,636
Sales	3,760,260
Sales returns	79,300

Required

Use the gross profit method to estimate the company's first-quarter ending inventory.

Check Est. ending inventory, $619,892

SERIAL PROBLEM
Business Solutions
P2 A3

(This serial problem began in Chapter 1 and continues through most of the book. If previous chapter segments were not completed, the serial problem can begin at this point.)

SP 5

Part A

Santana Rey of Business Solutions is evaluating her inventory to determine whether it must be adjusted based on lower of cost or market rules. Business Solutions has three different types of software in its inventory and the following information is available for each.

		Per Unit	
Inventory Items	Units	Cost	Market
Office productivity	3	$ 76	$ 74
Desktop publishing	2	103	100
Accounting	3	90	96

Required

1. Compute the lower of cost or market for ending inventory assuming Rey applies the lower of cost or market rule to inventory as a whole. Must Rey adjust the reported inventory value? Explain.
2. Assume that Rey had instead applied the lower of cost or market rule to each product in inventory. Under this assumption, must Rey adjust the reported inventory value? Explain.

Part B

Selected accounts and balances for the three months ended March 31, 2016, for Business Solutions follow.

January 1 beginning inventory	$ 0
Cost of goods sold	14,052
March 31 ending inventory	704

Required

1. Compute inventory turnover and days' sales in inventory for the three months ended March 31, 2016.
2. Assess the company's performance if competitors average 15 times for inventory turnover and 25 days for days' sales in inventory.

Beyond the Numbers

REPORTING IN ACTION

C2 A3

APPLE

BTN 5-1 Refer to **Apple**'s financial statements in Appendix A to answer the following.

Required

1. What amount of inventories did Apple report as a current asset on September 28, 2013? On September 29, 2012?
2. Inventories represent what percent of total assets on September 28, 2013? On September 29, 2012?
3. Comment on the relative size of Apple's inventories compared to its other types of assets.
4. What accounting method did Apple use to compute inventory amounts on its balance sheet?
5. Compute inventory turnover for fiscal year ended September 28, 2013, and days' sales in inventory as of September 28, 2013.

Fast Forward

6. Access Apple's financial statements for fiscal years ended after September 28, 2013, from its website (Apple.com) or the SEC's EDGAR database (www.SEC.gov). Answer questions 1 through 5 using the current Apple information and compare results to those prior years.

COMPARATIVE ANALYSIS

A3

APPLE
GOOGLE

BTN 5-2 Comparative figures for **Apple** and **Google** follow.

	Apple			Google		
($ millions)	Current Year	One Year Prior	Two Years Prior	Current Year	One Year Prior	Two Years Prior
Inventory	$ 1,764	$ 791	$ 776	$ 426	$ 505	$ 35
Cost of sales	106,606	87,846	64,431	25,858	20,634	13,188

Required

1. Compute inventory turnover for each company for the most recent two years shown.
2. Compute days' sales in inventory for each company for the three years shown.
3. Comment on and interpret your findings from parts 1 and 2. Assume an industry average for inventory turnover of 40.

ETHICS CHALLENGE

A1

BTN 5-3 Golf Challenge Corp. is a retail sports store carrying golf apparel and equipment. The store is at the end of its second year of operation and is struggling. A major problem is that its cost of inventory has continually increased in the past two years. In the first year of operations, the store assigned inventory costs using LIFO. A loan agreement the store has with its bank, its prime source of financing, requires the store to maintain a certain profit margin and current ratio. The store's owner is currently looking over Golf Challenge's preliminary financial statements for its second year. The numbers are not favorable. The only way the store can meet the required financial ratios agreed on with the bank is to change from LIFO to FIFO. The store originally decided on LIFO because of its tax advantages. The owner recalculates ending inventory using FIFO and submits those numbers and statements to the loan officer at the bank for the required bank review. The owner thankfully reflects on the available latitude in choosing the inventory costing method.

Required

1. How does Golf Challenge's use of FIFO improve its net profit margin and current ratio?
2. Is the action by Golf Challenge's owner ethical? Explain.

BTN 5-4 You are a financial adviser with a client in the wholesale produce business that just completed its first year of operations. Due to weather conditions, the cost of acquiring produce to resell has escalated during the later part of this period. Your client, Javonte Gish, mentions that because her business sells perishable goods, she has striven to maintain a FIFO flow of goods. Although sales are good, the increasing cost of inventory has put the business in a tight cash position. Gish has expressed concern regarding the ability of the business to meet income tax obligations.

COMMUNICATING IN PRACTICE

A1

Required

Prepare a memorandum that identifies, explains, and justifies the inventory method you recommend your client, Ms. Gish, adopt.

BTN 5-5 Access the September 28, 2013, 10-K report for **Apple, Inc.** (Ticker AAPL), filed on October 29, 2013, from the EDGAR filings at **www.SEC.gov**.

TAKING IT TO THE NET

A3

APPLE

Required

1. What products are manufactured by Apple?
2. What inventory method does Apple use? (*Hint:* See the Note 1 to its financial statements.)
3. Compute its gross margin and gross margin ratio for the 2013 fiscal year. Comment on your computations—assume an industry average of 40% for the gross margin ratio.
4. Compute its inventory turnover and days' sales in inventory for the year ended September 28, 2013. Comment on your computations—assume an industry average of 40 for inventory turnover and 9 for days' sales in inventory.

BTN 5-6 Each team member has the responsibility to become an expert on an inventory method. This expertise will be used to facilitate teammates' understanding of the concepts relevant to that method.

TEAMWORK IN ACTION

A1 P1

Point: Step 1 allows four choices or areas for expertise. Larger teams will have some duplication of choice, but the specific identification method should not be duplicated.

1. Each learning team member should select an area for expertise by choosing one of the following inventory methods: specific identification, LIFO, FIFO, or weighted average.
2. Form expert teams made up of students who have selected the same area of expertise. The instructor will identify where each expert team will meet.
3. Using the following data, each expert team must collaborate to develop a presentation that illustrates the relevant concepts and procedures for its inventory method. Each team member must write the presentation in a format that can be shown to the learning team.

Data

The company uses a *perpetual* inventory system. It had the following beginning inventory and current-year purchases of its product.

Jan. 1	Beginning inventory.........	50 units @ $100 =	$ 5,000
Jan. 14	Purchase	150 units @ $120 =	18,000
Apr. 30	Purchase	200 units @ $150 =	30,000
Sept. 26	Purchase	300 units @ $200 =	60,000

The company transacted sales on the following dates at a $350 per unit sales price.

Jan. 10	30 units	(specific cost: 30 @ $100)
Feb. 15	100 units	(specific cost: 100 @ $120)
Oct. 5	350 units	(specific cost: 100 @ $150 and 250 @ $200)

Concepts and Procedures to Illustrate in Expert Presentation

a. Identify and compute the costs to assign to the units sold. (Round per unit costs to three decimals.)
b. Identify and compute the costs to assign to the units in ending inventory. (Round inventory balances to the dollar.)
c. How likely is it that this inventory costing method will reflect the actual physical flow of goods? How relevant is that factor in determining whether this is an acceptable method to use?
d. What is the impact of this method versus others in determining net income and income taxes?
e. How closely does the ending inventory amount reflect replacement cost?

4. Re-form learning teams. In rotation, each expert is to present to the team the presentation developed in part 3. Experts are to encourage and respond to questions.

ENTREPRENEURIAL DECISION

A3

BTN 5-7 Review the chapter's opening feature highlighting the Dame brothers (Brooks, Taylor, and Tanner) and their company, **Proof Eyewear**. Assume that Proof Eyewear consistently maintains an inventory level of $30,000, meaning that its average and ending inventory levels are the same. Also assume its annual cost of sales is $120,000. To cut costs, the Dame brothers propose to slash inventory to a constant level of $15,000 with no impact on cost of sales. They plan to work with suppliers to get quicker deliveries and to order smaller quantities more often.

Required

1. Compute the company's inventory turnover and its days' sales in inventory under (*a*) current conditions and (*b*) proposed conditions.
2. Evaluate and comment on the merits of their proposal given your analysis for part 1. Identify any concerns you might have about the proposal.

HITTING THE ROAD

C1 C2

BTN 5-8 Visit four retail stores with another classmate. In each store, identify whether the store uses a bar coding system to help manage its inventory. Try to find at least one store that does not use bar coding. If a store does not use bar coding, ask the store's manager or clerk whether he or she knows which type of inventory method the store employs. Create a table that shows columns for the name of store visited, type of merchandise sold, use or nonuse of bar coding, and the inventory method used if bar coding is not employed. You might also inquire as to what the store's inventory turnover is and how often physical inventory is taken.

GLOBAL DECISION

A3

Samsung
APPLE
GOOGLE

BTN 5-9 Following are key figures (in millions of Korean won) for **Samsung** (www.Samsung.com), which is a leading manufacturer of consumer electronics products.

₩ in millions	Current Year	One Year Prior	Two Years Prior
Inventory	₩ 19,134,868	₩ 17,747,413	₩ 15,716,715
Cost of sales	137,696,309	126,651,931	112,145,120

Required

1. Use these data and those from BTN 5-2 to compute (*a*) inventory turnover and (*b*) days' sales in inventory for the most recent two years shown for **Samsung**, **Apple**, and **Google**.
2. Comment on and interpret your findings from part 1.

ANSWERS TO MULTIPLE CHOICE QUIZ

1. a; FIFO perpetual

Date	Goods Purchased	Cost of Goods Sold	Inventory Balance
July 1			75 units @ $25 = $ 1,875
July 3	348 units @ $27 = $9,396		75 units @ $25 348 units @ $27 } = $11,271
July 8		75 units @ $25 225 units @ $27 } = $ 7,950	123 units @ $27 = $ 3,321
July 15	257 units @ $28 = $7,196		123 units @ $27 257 units @ $28 } = $10,517
July 23		123 units @ $27 152 units @ $28 } = $ 7,577	105 units @ $28 = **$ 2,940**
		$15,527	

2. b; LIFO perpetual

Date	Goods Purchased	Cost of Goods Sold	Inventory Balance
July 1			75 units @ $25 = $ 1,875
July 3	348 units @ $27 = $9,396		75 units @ $25 348 units @ $27 } = $11,271
July 8		300 units @ $27 = $ 8,100	75 units @ $25 48 units @ $27 } = $ 3,171
July 15	257 units @ $28 = $7,196		75 units @ $25 48 units @ $27 257 units @ $28 } = $10,367
July 23		257 units @ $28 18 units @ $27 } = $ 7,682	75 units @ $25 30 units @ $27 } = **$ 2,685**
		$15,782	

3. e; Specific identification (perpetual and periodic are identical for specific identification). Ending inventory computation:

20 units @ $25	$ 500
40 units @ $27	1,080
45 units @ $28	1,260
105 units	$2,840

4. a; FIFO periodic. Ending inventory computation: 105 units @ $28 each = $2,940; The FIFO periodic inventory computation is identical to the FIFO perpetual inventory computation (see question 1).

5. a; FIFO periodic inventory = (20 × $14) + (10 × $12) = $400

a; LIFO periodic cost of goods sold = (20 × $14) + (40 × $12) + (70 × $10) = $1,460

6. d; Days' sales in inventory = (Ending inventory/Cost of goods sold × 365) = ($18,000/$85,000) × 365 = 77.29 days

chapter 6

Cash and Internal Controls

Chapter Preview

INTERNAL CONTROL	CONTROL OF CASH	TOOLS OF CONTROL AND ANALYSIS
C1 Purpose and Principles of controls Technology and controls Limitations of controls	C2 Definition and reporting of cash P1 Control of cash receipts and cash disbursements	P2 Control of petty cash P3 Bank reconciliation as a control tool A1 Assessing liquidity

Learning Objectives

CONCEPTUAL

C1 Define internal control and identify its purpose and principles.

C2 Define cash and cash equivalents and explain how to report them.

ANALYTICAL

A1 Compute the days' sales uncollected ratio and use it to assess liquidity.

PROCEDURAL

P1 Apply internal control to cash receipts and disbursements.

P2 Explain and record petty cash fund transactions.

P3 Prepare a bank reconciliation.

P4 *Appendix 6A*—Describe the use of documentation and verification to control cash disbursements.

P5 *Appendix 6B—Apply the net method to control purchase discounts.*

Courtesy of Molly DeCoudreaux/Dandelion Chocolate

Chocoholics

SAN FRANCISCO—"We spent about two years in a garage roasting beans, building machines, and figuring out how to make chocolate from the bean," explains Todd Masonis. "When we shared our chocolate with friends and family, they were surprised by the unique and distinct flavors of each bean." Soon thereafter Todd, along with Cameron Ring, launched **Dandelion Chocolate (DandelionChocolate.com)**. "Our business model is pretty simple—we make great chocolate and people buy it."

"It's really fun to make chocolate"
—Todd Masonis

"We don't really have any gimmicks," insists Todd. "We believe that if you start with great cocoa beans and take the time to process them carefully, you can find some amazing flavors." Amazing flavors translate to business success. Todd and Cam presently sell more than 10,000 chocolate bars and 3,000 hot chocolate drinks per month. "It's a really exciting time for chocolate," proclaims Todd. "What happened to coffee, microbrew, and wine, is all happening to chocolate right now."

Although the chocolate experience is key to their success, Todd and Cam's management of internal controls and cash is equally impressive. Several control procedures monitor business activities and safeguard assets. An example is their inventory control system. Explains Todd, quality ingredients are crucial to customer satisfaction, and monitoring controls ensure the quality of their ingredients. "In the kitchen we have an iPad where the pastry team tracks every brownie and cookie sold." Similar controls are applied throughout their factory and retail store. The owners explain that such controls raise productivity, cut expenses, and enhance the customer experience.

Their store's cash management practices are equally impressive, including controls over cash receipts, disbursements, and petty cash. The use of bank reconciliations further helps with the company's control and management of cash. "All the tools play nicely together, "explains Todd. "For instance, when someone orders online, it goes straight into our accounting software and a shipping label pops out of the shipping printer. The demand dashboard updates and the fulfillment team gets a notification. Each application is being attacked in its own niche way." The owners explain that they take advantage of available banking services to enhance further controls over cash.

Internal controls are crucial when on a busy day their business transacts with hundreds of customers. "It's a challenge with having to keep up production to meet the demand," explains Todd. "There's something very magical about that."

Sources: *Dandelion Chocolate website,* January 2015; *Eater,* January 2014; *Trend Hunter,* April 2012; *Mercury News,* March 2012; *Hunter Walk,* February 2014

INTERNAL CONTROL

C1 Define internal control and identify its purpose and principles.

This section describes internal control and its fundamental principles. We also discuss the impact of technology on internal control and the limitations of control procedures.

Purpose of Internal Control

Managers (or owners) of small businesses often control the entire operation. These managers usually purchase all assets, hire and manage employees, negotiate all contracts, and sign all checks. They know from personal contact and observation whether the business is actually receiving the assets and services paid for. Most companies, however, cannot maintain this close personal supervision. They must delegate responsibilities and rely on formal procedures rather than personal contact in controlling business activities.

Andre Kudyusov/Photodisc/Alamy

Internal Control System Managers use an internal control system to monitor and control business activities. An **internal control system** consists of the policies and procedures managers use to

- Protect assets.
- Ensure reliable accounting.
- Promote efficient operations.
- Urge adherence to company policies.

A properly designed internal control system is a key part of systems design, analysis, and performance. Managers place a high priority on internal control systems because they can prevent avoidable losses, help managers plan operations, and monitor company and employee performance. For example, internal controls for health care must protect patient records and privacy. Internal controls do not provide guarantees, but they lower the company's risk of loss.

Sarbanes-Oxley Act (SOX) The **Sarbanes-Oxley Act (SOX)** requires the managers and auditors of companies whose stock is traded on an exchange (called *public companies*) to document and certify the system of internal controls. Following are some of the specific requirements:

- Auditors must evaluate internal controls and issue an internal control report.
- Auditors of a client are restricted as to what consulting services they can provide that client.
- The person leading an audit can serve no more than seven years without a two-year break.
- Auditors' work is overseen by the *Public Company Accounting Oversight Board* (PCAOB).
- Harsh penalties exist for violators—sentences up to 25 years in prison with severe fines.

SOX has markedly impacted companies, and the costs of its implementation are high. Importantly, **Section 404** of SOX requires that managers document and assess the effectiveness of all internal control processes that can impact financial reporting. The benefits include greater confidence in accounting systems and their related reports. However, the public continues to debate the costs versus the benefits of SOX as nearly all business activities of these companies are impacted by SOX. Section 404 of SOX requires that managers document and assess their internal controls *and* that auditors provide an opinion on managers' documentation and assessment. Costs of complying with Section 404 for companies is reported to average $4 million (Financial Executives Institute).

Principles of Internal Control

Internal control policies and procedures vary from company to company according to such factors as the nature of the business and its size. Certain fundamental internal control principles apply to all companies. The **principles of internal control** are to

1. Establish responsibilities.
2. Maintain adequate records.
3. Insure assets and bond key employees.
4. Separate recordkeeping from custody of assets.
5. Divide responsibility for related transactions.
6. Apply technological controls.
7. Perform regular and independent reviews.

This section explains these seven principles and describes how internal control procedures minimize the risk of fraud and theft. These procedures also increase the reliability and accuracy of accounting records. A framework for how these seven principles improve the quality of financial reporting is provided by the **Committee of Sponsoring Organizations (COSO) (www.COSO.org)**. Specifically, these principles link to five aspects of internal control: control activities, control environment, risk assessment, monitoring, and communication.

Point: Sarbanes-Oxley Act (SOX) requires that each annual report contain an *internal control report,* which must: (1) state managers' responsibility for establishing and maintaining adequate internal controls for financial reporting and (2) assess the effectiveness of those controls.

Establish Responsibilities Proper internal control means that responsibility for a task is clearly established and assigned to one person. When a problem occurs in a company where responsibility is not identified, determining who is at fault is difficult. For instance, if two salesclerks share the same cash register and there is a cash shortage, neither clerk can be held accountable. To prevent this problem, one clerk might be given responsibility for handling all cash sales. Alternately, a company can use a register with separate cash drawers for each clerk. Most of us have waited at a retail counter during a shift change while employees swap cash drawers.

Point: Many companies have a mandatory vacation policy for employees who handle cash. When another employee must cover for the one on vacation, it is more difficult to hide cash frauds.

Maintain Adequate Records Good recordkeeping is part of an internal control system. It helps protect assets and ensures that employees use prescribed procedures. Reliable records are also a source of information that managers use to monitor company activities. When detailed records of equipment are kept, for instance, items are unlikely to be lost or stolen without detection. Similarly, transactions are less likely to be entered in wrong accounts if a chart of accounts is set up and carefully used. Many preprinted forms and internal documents are also designed for use in a good internal control system. When sales slips are properly designed, for instance, sales personnel can record needed information efficiently with less chance of errors or delays to customers. When sales slips are prenumbered and controlled, each one issued is the responsibility of one salesperson, preventing the salesperson from pocketing cash by making a sale and destroying the sales slip. Computerized point-of-sale systems achieve the same control results.

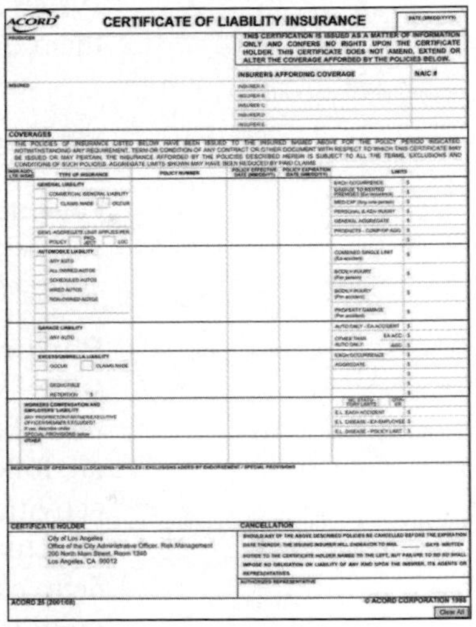

Insure Assets and Bond Key Employees Good internal control means that assets are adequately insured against casualty and that employees handling large amounts of cash and easily transferable assets are bonded. An employee is *bonded* when a company purchases an insurance policy, or a bond, against losses from theft by that employee. Bonding reduces the risk of loss. It also discourages theft because bonded employees know an independent bonding company will be involved when theft is uncovered and is unlikely to be sympathetic with an employee involved in theft. (A common question on job applications is whether you are bonded or bondable.)

Decision Insight

Asset Theft Control A novel technique exists for marking physical assets. It involves embedding a less than one-inch-square tag of fibers that creates a unique optical signature recordable by scanners. Manufacturers hope to embed tags in everything from compact discs and credit cards to designer clothes for purposes of internal control and efficiency. ■

Ingram Publishing

Separate Recordkeeping from Custody of Assets A person who controls or has access to an asset must not keep that asset's accounting records. This principle reduces the risk of theft or waste of an asset because the person with control over it knows that another person keeps its records. Also, a recordkeeper who does not have access to the asset has no reason to falsify records. This means that to steal an asset and hide the theft from the records, two or more people must *collude*—or agree in secret to commit the fraud. Some payroll cash checking services require fingerprint ID before the payroll check is cashed.

Point: The Association of Certified Fraud Examiners (acfe.com) estimates that employee fraud costs companies more than $140,000 per incident.

Divide Responsibility for Related Transactions Good internal control divides responsibility for a transaction or a series of related transactions between two or more individuals or departments. This is to ensure that the work of one individual acts as a check on the other. This principle, often called *separation of duties,* is not a call for duplication of work. Each employee or department should perform unduplicated effort. Examples of transactions with divided responsibility are placing purchase orders, receiving merchandise, and paying vendors. These tasks should not be given to one individual or department. Assigning responsibility for two or more of these tasks to one party increases mistakes and perhaps fraud. Having an independent person, for example, check incoming goods for quality and quantity encourages more care and attention to detail than having the person who placed the order do the checking. Added protection can result from identifying a third person to approve payment of the invoice. A company can even designate a fourth person with authority to write checks as another protective measure.

Point: There's a new security device—a person's ECG (electrocardiogram) reading—that is as unique as a fingerprint and a lot harder to lose or steal than a PIN. ECGs can be read through fingertip touches. An ECG also shows that a living person is actually there, whereas fingerprint and facial recognition software can be fooled.

Apply Technological Controls Cash registers, check protectors, time clocks, and personal identification scanners are examples of devices that can improve internal control. Technology often improves the effectiveness of controls. A cash register with a locked-in tape or electronic file makes a record of each cash sale. A check protector perforates the amount of a check into its face and makes it difficult to alter the amount. A time clock registers the exact time an employee both arrives at and departs from the job. Mechanical change and currency counters quickly and accurately count amounts, and personal scanners limit access to only authorized individuals. Each of these and other technological controls are an effective part of many internal control systems. Some companies video record workers as they clock in and out, which discourages them from clocking in or out for others.

Decision Insight

Face Reading Face-recognition software snaps a digital picture of the face and converts key facial features—say, the distance between the eyes—into a series of numerical values. These can be stored on an ID or ATM card as a simple bar code to prohibit unauthorized access. ■

Point: COSO organizes control components into five types:
- Control environment
- Control activities
- Risk assessment
- Monitoring
- Information and communication

Perform Regular and Independent Reviews Changes in personnel, stress of time pressures, and technological advances present opportunities for shortcuts and lapses. To counter these factors, regular reviews of internal control systems are needed to ensure that procedures are followed. These reviews are preferably done by internal auditors not directly involved in the activities. Their impartial perspective encourages an evaluation of the efficiency as well as the effectiveness of the internal control system. Many companies also pay for audits by independent, external auditors. These external auditors test the company's financial records to give an opinion as to whether its financial statements are presented fairly. Before external auditors decide on how much testing is needed, they evaluate the effectiveness of the internal control system. This evaluation is often helpful to a client. Independent, external audits are usually performed by auditors who work for public accounting firms.

Decision Maker

Entrepreneur As owner of a start-up information services company, you hire a systems analyst. The analyst sees that your company employs only two workers. She recommends you improve controls and says that as owner you must serve as a compensating control. What does the analyst mean? ■ [Answers follow the chapter's Summary.]

Technology and Internal Control

Point: Information on Internet fraud can be found at these websites:
sec.gov/investor/pubs/cyberfraud.htm
consumer.ftc.gov
www.fraud.org

The fundamental principles of internal control are relevant no matter what the technological state of the accounting system, from purely manual to fully automated systems. Technology impacts an internal control system in several important ways. Perhaps the most obvious is that technology allows us quicker access to databases and information. Used effectively, technology greatly improves managers' abilities to monitor and control business activities. This section describes some technological impacts we must be alert to.

Point: Evidence of any internal control failure for a company reduces user confidence in its financial statements.

Reduced Processing Errors Technologically advanced systems reduce the number of errors in processing information. Provided the software and data entry are correct, the risk of mechanical and mathematical errors is nearly eliminated. However, we must remember that erroneous software or data entry does exist. Also, less human involvement in data processing can cause data entry errors to go undiscovered. Moreover, errors in software can produce consistent but erroneous processing of transactions. Continually checking and monitoring all types of systems are important.

More Extensive Testing of Records A company's review and audit of electronic records can include more extensive testing when information is easily and rapidly accessed. When accounting records are kept manually, auditors and others likely select only small samples of data to test. When data are accessible with computer technology, however, auditors can quickly analyze large samples or even the entire database.

Limited Evidence of Processing Many data processing steps are increasingly done by computer. Accordingly, fewer hard-copy items of documentary evidence are available for review. Yet technologically advanced systems can provide new evidence. They can, for instance, record who made the entries, the date and time, the source of the entry, and so on. Technology can also be designed to require the use of passwords or other identification before access to the system is granted. This means that internal control depends more on the design and operation of the information system and less on the analysis of its resulting documents.

Point: We look to several sources when assessing a company's internal controls. Sources include the auditor's report, management report on controls (if available), management discussion and analysis, and financial press.

Crucial Separation of Duties Technological advances in accounting information systems often yield some job eliminations or consolidations. While those who remain have the special skills necessary to operate advanced programs and equipment, a company with a reduced workforce risks losing its crucial separation of duties. The company must establish ways to control and monitor employees to minimize risk of error and fraud. For instance, the person who designs and programs the information system must not be the one who operates it. The company must also separate control over programs and files from the activities related to cash receipts and disbursements. For instance, a computer operator should not control check-writing activities. Achieving acceptable separation of duties can be especially difficult and costly in small companies with few employees.

Increased E-Commerce Technology has encouraged the growth of e-commerce. **Amazon.com** and **eBay** are examples of companies that have successfully exploited e-commerce. Most companies have some e-commerce transactions. All such transactions involve at least three risks. (1) *Credit card number theft* is a risk of using, transmitting, and storing such data online. This increases the cost of e-commerce. (2) *Computer viruses* are malicious programs that attach themselves to innocent files for purposes of infecting and harming other files and programs. (3) *Impersonation* online can result in charges of sales to bogus accounts, purchases of inappropriate materials, and the unknowing giving up of confidential information to hackers. Companies use both firewalls and encryption to combat some of these risks—firewalls are points of entry to a system that require passwords to continue, and encryption is a mathematical process to rearrange contents that cannot be read without the process code. Nearly 5% of Americans already report being victims of identity theft, and roughly 10 million say their privacy has been compromised.

"Worst case of identity theft I've ever seen!"

Decision Insight

Winnings and Controls Certified Fraud Examiners website reports the following: Andrew Cameron stole Jacqueline Boanson's credit card. Cameron headed to the racetrack and promptly charged two bets for $150 on the credit card—winning $400. Unfortunately for Cameron, the racetrack refused to pay him cash as its internal control policy is to credit winnings from bets made on a credit card to that same card. Cameron was later nabbed; and the racetrack let Ms. Boanson keep the winnings. ■

Limitations of Internal Control

All internal control policies and procedures have limitations that usually arise from either (1) the human element or (2) the cost-benefit principle.

Internal control policies and procedures are applied by people. This human element creates several potential limitations that we can categorize as either (1) human error or (2) human fraud. *Human error* can occur from negligence, fatigue, misjudgment, or confusion. *Human fraud* involves intent by people to defeat internal controls, such as *management override,* for personal gain. Fraud also includes collusion to thwart the separation of duties. The human element highlights the importance of establishing an *internal control environment* to convey management's commitment to internal control policies and procedures. Human fraud is driven by the *triple-threat* of fraud:

- **Opportunity**—refers to internal control deficiencies in the workplace.
- **Pressure**—refers to financial, family, society, and other stresses to succeed.
- **Rationalization**—refers to employees justifying fraudulent behavior.

The second major limitation on internal control is the *cost-benefit principle,* which dictates that the costs of internal controls must not exceed their benefits. Analysis of costs and benefits must consider all factors, including the impact on morale. Most companies, for instance, have a legal right to read employees' e-mails, yet companies seldom exercise that right unless they are confronted with evidence of potential harm to the company. The same holds for drug testing, phone tapping, and hidden cameras. The bottom line is that managers must establish internal control policies and procedures with a net benefit to the company.

Point: Cybercrime.gov pursues computer and intellectual property crimes, including that of e-commerce.

Hacker's Guide to Cyberspace

Pharming Viruses attached to e-mails and websites load software onto your PC that monitors keystrokes; when you sign on to financial websites, it steals your passwords.

Phishing Hackers send e-mails to you posing as banks; you are asked for information using fake websites where they reel in your passwords and personal data.

Wi-Phishing Cybercrooks set up wireless networks hoping you will use them to connect to the web; your passwords and data are stolen as you use their network.

Bot-Networking Hackers send remote-control programs to your PC that take control to send out spam and viruses; they even rent your bot to other cybercrooks.

Typo-Squatting Hackers set up websites with addresses similar to legit outfits; when you make a typo and hit their sites, they infect your PC with viruses or take them over as bots.

Hackers also have their own self-identification system:

- *Hackers,* or *external attackers,* crack systems and take data for illicit gains (as unauthorized users).
- *Rogue insiders,* or *internal attackers,* crack systems and take data for illicit gains or revenge (as authorized users).
- *Ethical hackers,* or *good-guys* or *white-hat hackers,* crack systems and reveal vulnerabilities to enhance controls.
- *Crackers,* or *criminal hackers,* crack systems illegally for illicit gains, fame, or revenge.

NEED-TO-KNOW 6-1

Internal Controls

C1

Identify the following phrases/terms as best associated with the (a) purposes of an internal control system, (b) principles of internal control, or (c) limitations of internal control.

1. ____ Protect assets
2. ____ Establish responsibilities
3. ____ Human error
4. ____ Maintain adequate records
5. ____ Apply technological controls
6. ____ Ensure reliable accounting
7. ____ Insure assets and bond key employees
8. ____ Human fraud
9. ____ Separate recordkeeping from custody of assets
10. ____ Divide responsibility for related transactions
11. ____ Cost-benefit principle
12. ____ Promote efficient operations
13. ____ Perform regular and independent reviews
14. ____ Urge adherence to company policies

Do More: QS 6-1, E 6-1, E 6-4, P 6-1

QC1

Solution

1. a **2.** b **3.** c **4.** b **5.** b **6.** a **7.** b **8.** c **9.** b **10.** b **11.** c **12.** a **13.** b **14.** a

CONTROL OF CASH

Cash is a necessary asset of every company. Most companies also own *cash equivalents* (defined below), which are assets similar to cash. Cash and cash equivalents are the most liquid of all assets and are easily hidden and moved. Cash is also the most desired asset as other assets must be *fenced* (sold in a secondary market). An effective system of internal controls protects cash assets and it should meet three basic guidelines:

1. Handling cash is separate from recordkeeping of cash.
2. Cash receipts are promptly deposited in a bank.
3. Cash disbursements are made by check (or electronic funds transfer, EFT).

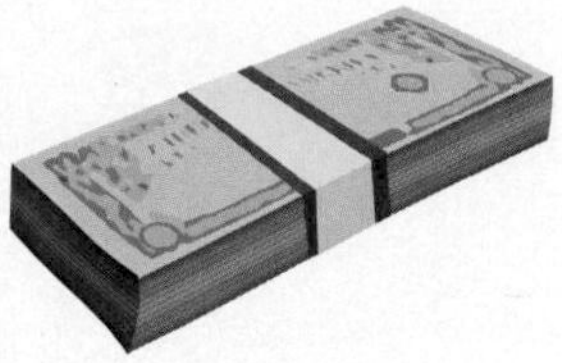

The first guideline applies separation of duties to minimize errors and fraud. When duties are separated, two or more people must collude to steal cash and conceal this action in the accounting records. The second guideline uses immediate (say, daily) deposits of all cash receipts to produce a timely independent record of the cash received. It also reduces the likelihood of cash theft (or loss) and the risk that an employee could personally use the money before depositing it. The third guideline uses payments by check to develop an independent bank record of cash disbursements. This guideline also reduces the risk of cash theft (or loss).

This section begins with definitions of cash and cash equivalents. Discussion then focuses on controls and accounting for both cash receipts and disbursements. The exact procedures used to achieve control over cash vary across companies. They depend on factors such as company size, number of employees, volume of cash transactions, and sources of cash.

Cash, Cash Equivalents, and Liquidity

C2 Define cash and cash equivalents and explain how to report them.

Good accounting systems help in managing the amount of cash and controlling who has access to it. Cash is the usual means of payment when paying for assets, services, or liabilities. **Liquidity** refers to a company's ability to pay for its near-term obligations. Cash and similar assets are called **liquid assets** because they can be readily used to settle such obligations. A company needs liquid assets to effectively operate.

Cash includes currency and coins along with the amounts on deposit in bank accounts, checking accounts (called *demand deposits*), and many savings accounts (called *time deposits*). Cash also includes items that are acceptable for deposit in these accounts such as customer checks, cashier's checks, certified checks, and money orders. **Cash equivalents** are short-term, highly liquid investment assets meeting two criteria: (1) readily convertible to a known cash amount and (2) sufficiently close to their due date so that their market value is not sensitive to interest rate changes. Only investments purchased within three months of their due date usually satisfy these criteria. Examples of cash equivalents are short-term investments in assets such as U.S. Treasury bills and money market funds. To increase their return, many companies invest idle cash in cash equivalents. Most companies combine cash equivalents with cash as a single item on the balance sheet.

Point: The most-liquid assets are usually reported first on a balance sheet; the least-liquid assets are reported last.

Cash Management

When companies fail, one of the most common causes is their inability to manage cash. Companies must plan both cash receipts and cash payments. The goals of cash management are twofold:

1. Plan cash receipts to meet cash payments when due.
2. Keep a minimum level of cash necessary to operate.

The *treasurer* of the company is responsible for cash management. Effective cash management involves applying the following cash management principles.

- **Encourage collection of receivables.** The more quickly customers and others pay the company, the more quickly that company can use the money. Some companies have cash-only sales policies. Others might offer discounts for payments received early.
- **Delay payment of liabilities.** The more delayed a company is in paying others, the more time it has to use the money. Some companies regularly wait to pay their bills until the last possible day allowed—although, a company must take care not to hurt its credit standing.
- **Keep only necessary levels of assets.** The less money tied up in idle assets, the more money to invest in productive assets. Some companies maintain *just-in-time* inventory; meaning they plan inventory to be available at the same time orders are filled. Others might lease out excess warehouse space or rent equipment instead of buying it.
- **Plan expenditures.** Money should be spent only when it is available. Companies must look at seasonal and business cycles to plan expenditures.

- **Invest excess cash.** Excess cash earns no return and should be invested. Excess cash from seasonal cycles can be placed in a bank account or other short-term investment for income. Excess cash beyond what's needed for regular business should be invested in productive assets like factories and inventories.

Decision Insight

Days' Cash Expense Coverage The ratio of *cash (and cash equivalents) to average daily cash expenses* indicates the number of days a company can operate without additional cash inflows. It reflects on company liquidity and on the potential of excess cash. ■

Control of Cash Receipts

P1 Apply internal control to cash receipts and disbursements.

Internal control of cash receipts ensures that cash received is properly recorded and deposited. Cash receipts can arise from transactions such as cash sales, collections of customer accounts, receipts of interest earned, bank loans, sales of assets, and owner investments. This section explains internal control over two important types of cash receipts: over-the-counter and by mail.

Over-the-Counter Cash Receipts For purposes of internal control, over-the-counter cash receipts from sales should be recorded on a cash register at the time of each sale. To help ensure that correct amounts are entered, each register should be located so customers can read the amounts entered. Clerks also should be required to enter each sale before wrapping merchandise and to give the customer a receipt for each sale. The design of each cash register should provide a permanent, locked-in record of each transaction. In many systems, the register is directly linked with computing and accounting services. Less advanced registers simply print a record of each transaction on a paper tape or electronic file locked inside the register.

Proper internal control prescribes that custody over cash should be separate from its recordkeeping. For over-the-counter cash receipts, this separation begins with the cash sale. The clerk who has access to cash in the register should not have access to its locked-in record. At the end of the clerk's work period, the clerk should count the cash in the register, record the amount, and turn over the cash and a record of its amount to the company cashier. The cashier, like the clerk, has access to the cash but should not have access to accounting records (or the register tape or file). A third employee, often a supervisor, compares the record of total register transactions (or the register tape or file) with the cash receipts reported by the cashier. This record is the basis for a journal entry recording over-the-counter cash receipts. The third employee has access to the records for cash but not to the actual cash. The clerk and the cashier have access to cash but not to the accounting records. None of them can make a mistake or divert cash without the difference being revealed—see the following diagram.

Point: Convenience stores sometimes display a sign: *Cashier has no access to cash in locked floor (or wall) safe.* Such signs help deter theft and holdups.

Point: Many businesses have signs that read: If you receive no receipt, your purchase is free! This helps ensure that clerks ring up all transactions on registers.

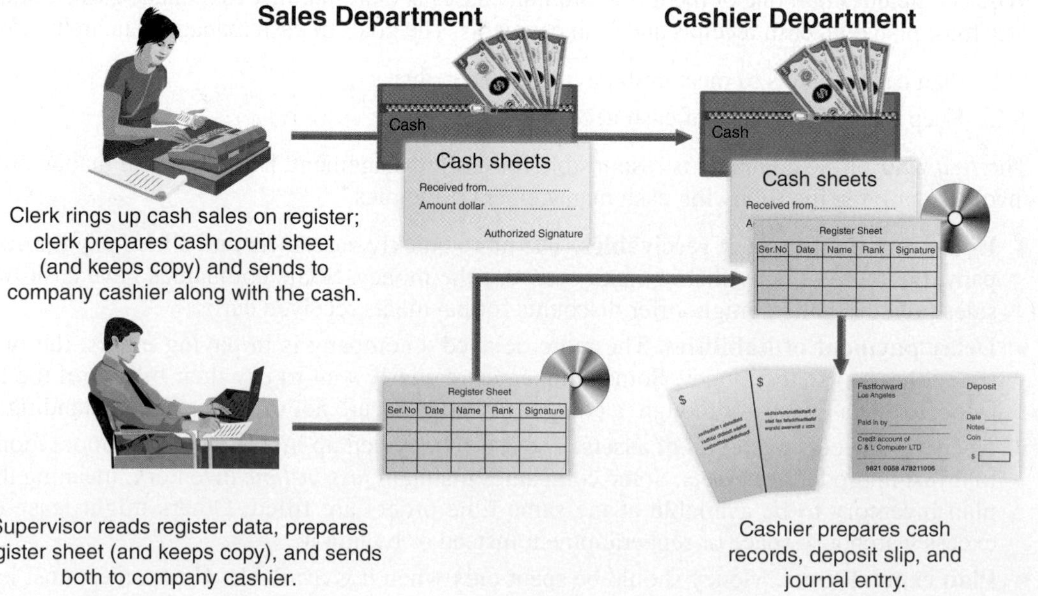

Cash over and short. Sometimes errors in making change are discovered from differences between the cash in a cash register and the record of the amount of cash receipts. Although a clerk is careful, one or more customers can be given too much or too little change. This means that at the end of a work period, the cash in a cash register might not equal the record of cash receipts. This difference is reported in the **Cash Over and Short** account, also called *Cash Short and Over,* which is an income statement account recording the income effects of cash overages and cash shortages. To illustrate, if a cash register's record shows $550 but the count of cash in the register is $555, the entry to record cash sales and its overage is

Point: Retailers often require cashiers to restrictively endorse checks immediately on receipt by stamping them "For deposit only."

Cash	555	
Cash Over and Short		5
Sales		550
To record cash sales and a cash overage.		

Assets	= Liabilities	+ Equity
+555		+5
		+550

On the other hand, if a cash register's record shows $625 but the count of cash in the register is $621, the entry to record cash sales and its shortage is

Cash	621	
Cash Over and Short	4	
Sales		625
To record cash sales and a cash shortage.		

Assets	= Liabilities	+ Equity
+621		−4
		+625

Since customers are more likely to dispute being shortchanged than being given too much change, the Cash Over and Short account usually has a debit balance at the end of an accounting period. A debit balance reflects an expense. It is reported on the income statement as part of selling, general and administrative expenses. (Since the amount is usually small, it is often combined with other small expenses and reported as part of *miscellaneous expenses*—or as part of *miscellaneous revenues* if it has a credit balance.)

Point: Merchants begin a business day with a *change fund* in their cash register. The accounting for a change fund is similar to that for petty cash, including that for cash shortages or overages.

Cash Receipts by Mail Control of cash receipts that arrive through the mail starts with the person who opens the mail. Preferably, two people are assigned the task of, and are present for, opening the mail. In this case, theft of cash receipts by mail requires collusion between these two employees. Specifically, the person(s) opening the mail enters a list (in triplicate) of money received. This list should contain a record of each sender's name, the amount, and an explanation of why the money is sent. The first copy is sent with the money to the cashier. A second copy is sent to the recordkeeper in the accounting area. A third copy is kept by the clerk(s) who opened the mail. The cashier deposits the money in a bank, and the recordkeeper records the amounts received in the accounting records.

Point: Collusion implies that two or more individuals are knowledgeable about or involved with the activities of the other(s).

This process reflects good internal control. That is, when the bank balance is reconciled by another person (explained later in the chapter), errors or acts of fraud by the mail clerks, the cashier, or the recordkeeper are revealed. They are revealed because the bank's record of cash deposited must agree with the records from each of the three. Moreover, if the mail clerks do not report all receipts correctly, customers will question their account balances. If the cashier does not deposit all receipts, the bank balance does not agree with the recordkeeper's cash balance. The recordkeeper and the person who reconciles the bank balance do not have access to cash and therefore have no opportunity to divert cash to themselves. This system makes errors and fraud highly unlikely. The exception is employee collusion.

Decision Insight

Rapid Accounting **Walmart** uses a network of information links with its point-of-sale cash registers to coordinate sales, purchases, and distribution. Its stores ring up tens of thousands of separate sales on heavy days. By using cash register information, the company can fix pricing mistakes quickly and capitalize on sales trends. Interestingly, Sam Walton, the founder, was a self-described distruster of computers. ■

Control of Cash Disbursements

Control of cash disbursements is especially important as most large thefts occur from payment of fictitious invoices. One key to controlling cash disbursements is to require all expenditures to be made by check. The only exception is small payments made from petty cash. Another key is to deny access to the accounting records to anyone other than the owner who has the authority to sign checks. A small-business owner often signs checks and knows from personal contact that the items being paid for are actually received. This arrangement is impossible in large businesses. Instead, internal control procedures must be substituted for personal contact. Such procedures are designed to assure the check signer that the obligations recorded are properly incurred and should be paid. This section describes these and other internal control procedures, including the voucher system and petty cash system. A method for management of cash disbursements for purchases is described in Appendix 6B.

Cash Budget Projected cash receipts and cash disbursements are often summarized in a *cash budget.* Provided that sufficient cash exists for effective operations, companies wish to minimize the cash they hold because of its risk of theft and its low return versus other investment opportunities.

Decision Insight

Lock Box Some companies do not receive cash in the mail but, instead, elect to have customers send deposits directly to the bank using a *lock box* system. Bank employees are charged with receipting the cash and depositing it in the correct business bank account. ■

Voucher System of Control A **voucher system** is a set of procedures and approvals designed to control cash disbursements and the acceptance of obligations. The voucher system of control establishes procedures for

- Verifying, approving, and recording obligations for eventual cash disbursement.
- Issuing checks for payment of verified, approved, and recorded obligations.

A reliable voucher system follows standard procedures for every transaction. This applies even when multiple purchases are made from the same supplier.

A voucher system's control over cash disbursements begins when a company incurs an obligation that will result in payment of cash. A key factor in this system is that only approved departments and individuals are authorized to incur such obligations. The system often limits the type of obligations that a department or individual can incur. In a large retail store, for instance, only a purchasing department should be authorized to incur obligations for merchandise inventory. Another key factor is that procedures for purchasing, receiving, and paying for merchandise are divided among several departments (or individuals). These departments include the one requesting the purchase, the purchasing department, the receiving department, and the accounting department. To coordinate and control responsibilities of these departments, a company uses several different business documents. Exhibit 6.1 shows how documents are accumulated in a **voucher,** which is an internal document (or file) used to accumulate information to control cash disbursements and to ensure that a transaction is properly recorded. This specific example begins with a *purchase requisition* and concludes with a *check* drawn against cash. Appendix 6A describes the documentation and verification necessary for a voucher system of control. It also describes the internal control objective served by each document.

Point: MCI, formerly **WorldCom,** paid a whopping $500 million in SEC fines for accounting fraud. Among the charges were that it inflated earnings by as much as $10 billion. Its CEO, Bernard Ebbers, was sentenced to 25 years.

Point: A *voucher* is an internal document (or file).

Point: The basic purposes of paper and electronic documents are similar. However, the internal control system must change to reflect different risks, including confidential and competitive-sensitive information that is at greater risk in electronic systems.

A voucher system should be applied not only to purchases of inventory but to all expenditures. To illustrate, when a company receives a monthly telephone bill, it should review and verify the charges, prepare a voucher (file), and insert the bill. This transaction is then recorded with a journal entry. If the amount is currently due, a check is issued. If not, the voucher is filed for payment on its due date. If no voucher is prepared, verifying the invoice and its amount after several days or weeks can be difficult. Also, without records, a dishonest employee could collude with a dishonest supplier to get more than one payment for an obligation, payment for excessive amounts, or payment for goods and services not received. An effective voucher system helps prevent such frauds.

EXHIBIT 6.1

Document Flow in a Voucher System

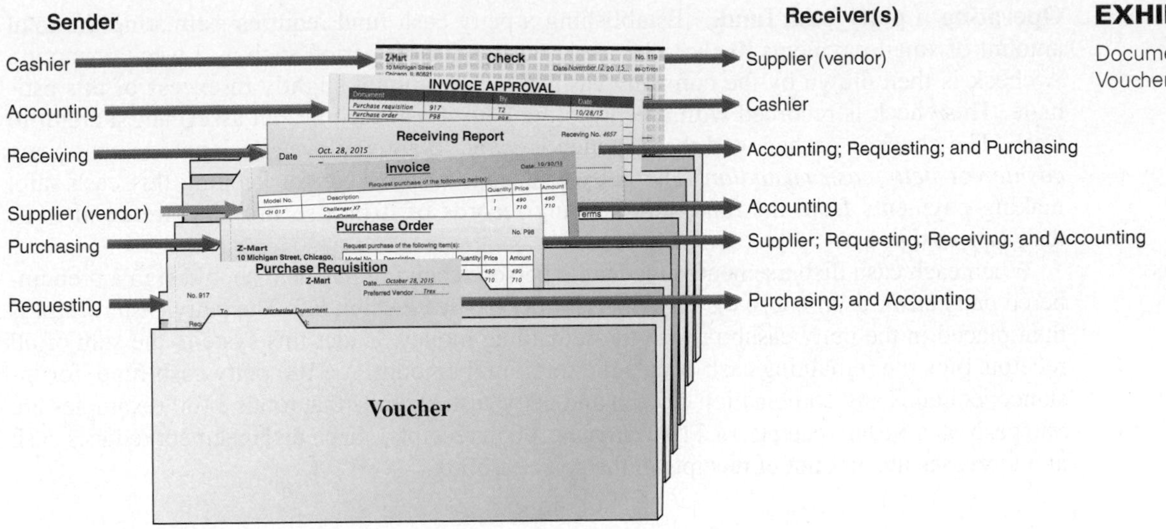

Decision Insight

Cyber Setup The FTC is on the cutting edge of cybersleuthing. Opportunists in search of easy money are lured to **www.wemarket4u.net/sundaestation/** and **www.wemarket4u.net/fatfoe/**. Take the bait and you get warned. The top five fraud complaints as compiled by the Federal Trade Commission are shown to the right. ■

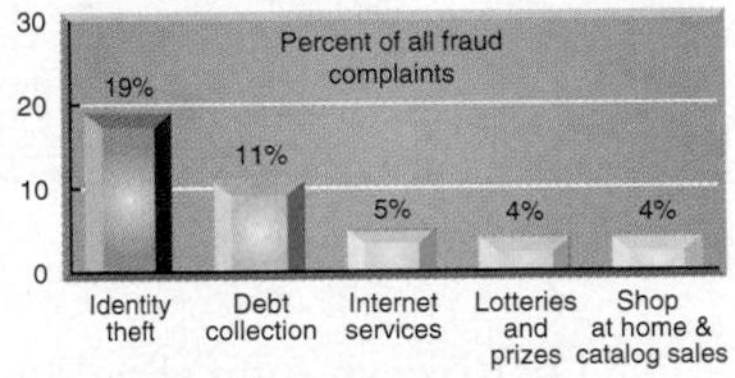

NEED-TO-KNOW 6-2

Control of Cash Receipts and Payments

P1 C2

A good system of internal control for cash provides adequate procedures for protecting both cash receipts and cash disbursements. Which of the following statements is true regarding the control of cash receipts and cash disbursements?

____ **1.** Over-the-counter cash receipts from sales should be recorded on a cash register at the time of each sale.

____ **2.** Custody over cash should be separate from the recordkeeping of cash.

____ **3.** For control of cash receipts that arrive through the mail, two people should be assigned the task of, and be present for, opening that mail.

____ **4.** One key to controlling cash disbursements is to require that no expenditures be made by check; instead, all expenditures should be made from petty cash.

____ **5.** A voucher system of control should be applied only to purchases of inventory and never to other expenditures.

Do More: QS 6-3, E 6-2, E 6-4

QC2

Solution

1. True **2.** True **3.** True **4.** False **5.** False

P2

Explain and record petty cash fund transactions.

Petty Cash System of Control A basic principle for controlling cash disbursements is that all payments must be made by check. An exception to this rule is made for *petty cash disbursements,* which are the small payments required for items such as postage, courier fees, minor repairs, and low-cost supplies. To avoid the time and cost of writing checks for small amounts, a company sets up a petty cash fund to make small payments. (**Petty cash** activities are part of an *imprest system,* which designates advance money to establish the fund, to withdraw from the fund, and to reimburse the fund.)

Operating a petty cash fund. Establishing a petty cash fund requires estimating the total amount of small payments likely to be made during a short period such as a week or month. A check is then drawn by the company cashier for an amount slightly in excess of this estimate. This check is recorded with a debit to the Petty Cash account (an asset) and a credit to Cash. The check is cashed, and the currency is given to an employee designated as the *petty cashier* or *petty cash custodian*. The petty cashier is responsible for keeping this cash safe, making payments from the fund, and keeping records of it in a secure place referred to as the *petty cashbox*.

Point: A petty cash fund is used only for business expenses.

When each cash disbursement is made, the person receiving payment should sign a prenumbered *petty cash receipt,* also called *petty cash ticket*—see Exhibit 6.2. The petty cash receipt is then placed in the petty cashbox with the remaining money. Under this system, the sum of all receipts plus the remaining cash equals the total fund amount. A $100 petty cash fund, for instance, contains any combination of cash and petty cash receipts that totals $100 (examples are $80 cash plus $20 in receipts, or $10 cash plus $90 in receipts). Each disbursement reduces cash and increases the amount of receipts in the petty cashbox.

EXHIBIT 6.2

Petty Cash Receipt

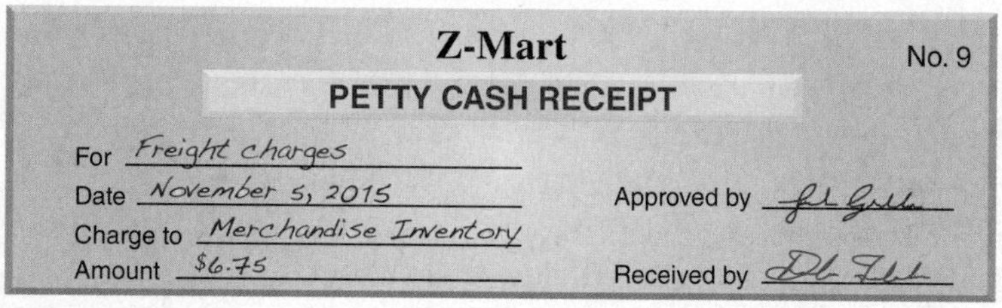
Z-Mart
No. 9
PETTY CASH RECEIPT
For Freight charges
Date November 5, 2015
Charge to Merchandise Inventory
Amount $6.75
Approved by
Received by

Point: Petty cash receipts with either no signature or a forged signature usually indicate misuse of petty cash. Companies respond with surprise petty cash counts for verification.

The petty cash fund should be reimbursed when it is nearing zero and at the end of an accounting period when financial statements are prepared. For this purpose, the petty cashier sorts the paid receipts by the type of expense or account and then totals the receipts. The petty cashier presents all paid receipts to the company cashier, who stamps all receipts *paid* so they cannot be reused, files them for recordkeeping, and gives the petty cashier a check for their sum. When this check is cashed and the money placed in the cashbox, the total money in the cashbox is restored to its original amount. The fund is now ready for a new cycle of petty cash payments.

Illustrating a petty cash fund. To illustrate, assume Z-Mart establishes a petty cash fund on November 1 and designates one of its office employees as the petty cashier. A $75 check is drawn, cashed, and the proceeds given to the petty cashier. The entry to record the setup of this petty cash fund is

Assets = Liabilities + Equity
+75
−75

Nov. 1	Petty Cash	75	
	Cash		75
	To establish a petty cash fund.		

Point: Reducing or eliminating a petty cash fund requires a credit to Petty Cash.

Point: Although *individual* petty cash disbursements are not evidenced by a check, the initial petty cash fund is evidenced by a check, and later petty cash expenditures are evidenced by a check to replenish them *in total.*

After the petty cash fund is established, the Petty Cash account is not debited or credited again unless the amount of the fund is changed. (A fund should be increased if it requires reimbursement too frequently. On the other hand, if the fund is too large, some of its money should be redeposited in the Cash account.)

Next, assume that Z-Mart's petty cashier makes several November payments from petty cash. Each person who received payment is required to sign a receipt. On November 27, after making a $26.50 cash payment for tile cleaning, only $3.70 cash remains in the fund. The petty cashier then summarizes and totals the petty cash receipts as shown in Exhibit 6.3.

EXHIBIT 6.3

Petty Cash Payments Report

Z-MART Petty Cash Payments Report			
Miscellaneous Expenses			
Nov. 2	Cleaning of LCD panels	$20.00	
Nov. 27	Tile cleaning	26.50	$ 46.50
Merchandise Inventory (transportation-in)			
Nov. 5	Transport of merchandise purchased	6.75	
Nov. 20	Transport of merchandise purchased	8.30	15.05
Delivery Expense			
Nov. 18	Customer's package delivered		5.00
Office Supplies Expense			
Nov. 15	Purchase of office supplies immediately used		4.75
Total			$71.30

Point: This report can also include receipt number and names of those who approved and received cash payment (see **Need-To-Know 6.3**).

The petty cash payments report and all receipts are given to the company cashier in exchange for a $71.30 check to reimburse the fund. The petty cashier cashes the check and puts the $71.30 cash in the petty cashbox. The company records this reimbursement as follows.

Nov. 27	Miscellaneous Expenses	46.50	
	Merchandise Inventory	15.05	
	Delivery Expense	5.00	
	Office Supplies Expense	4.75	
	Cash*		71.30
	*To reimburse petty cash. *$75 fund bal. − $3.70 cash rem.*		

Assets = Liabilities + Equity
−71.30 −46.50
−15.05
− 5.00
− 4.75

A petty cash fund is usually reimbursed at the end of an accounting period so that expenses are recorded in the proper period, even if the fund is not low on money. If the fund is not reimbursed at the end of a period, the financial statements would show both an overstated cash asset and understated expenses (or assets) that were paid out of petty cash. Some companies do not reimburse the petty cash fund at the end of each period under the notion that this amount is immaterial to users of financial statements.

Point: To avoid errors in recording petty cash reimbursement, follow these steps: (1) prepare payments report, (2) compute cash needed by subtracting cash remaining from total fund amount, (3) record entry, and (4) check "Dr. = Cr." in entry. Any difference is Cash Over and Short.

Increasing or decreasing a petty cash fund. A decision to increase or decrease a petty cash fund is often made when reimbursing it. To illustrate, assume Z-Mart decides to *increase* its petty cash fund from $75 to $100 on November 27 when it reimburses the fund. The entries required are to (1) reimburse the fund as usual (see the preceding November 27 entry) and (2) increase the fund amount as follows.

Nov. 27	Petty Cash	25	
	Cash		25
	To increase the petty cash fund amount.		

Alternatively, if Z-Mart *decreases* the petty cash fund from $75 to $55 on November 27, the entry is to (1) credit Petty Cash for $20 (decreasing the fund from $75 to $55) and (2) debit Cash for $20 (reflecting the $20 transfer from Petty Cash to Cash).

Summary of Petty Cash Accounting

Event	Petty Cash	Cash	Expenses
Set up fund	Dr.	Cr.	—
Reimburse fund	—	Cr.	Dr.
Increase fund	Dr.	Cr.	—
Decrease fund	Cr.	Dr.	—

Cash over and short. Sometimes a petty cashier fails to get a receipt for payment or overpays for the amount due. When this occurs and the fund is later reimbursed, the petty cash payments report plus the cash remaining will not total to the fund balance. This mistake causes the fund to be *short*. This shortage is recorded as an expense in the reimbursing entry with a debit to the Cash Over and Short account. (An overage in the petty cash fund is recorded with a credit to Cash Over and Short in the reimbursing entry.) To illustrate,

$200 Petty Cash Fund

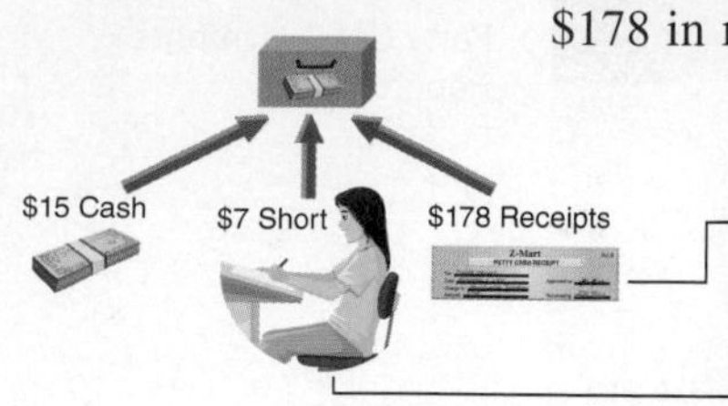

prepare the June 1 entry to reimburse a $200 petty cash fund when its payments report shows $178 in miscellaneous expenses and $15 cash remains.

June 1	Miscellaneous Expenses	178	
	Cash Over and Short	**7**	
	Cash*		185
	*To reimburse petty cash. *$200 fund bal. − $15 cash rem.*		

Decision Insight

Warning Signs There are clues to internal control violations. Warning signs from accounting include (1) an increase in customer refunds—could be fake, (2) missing documents—could be used for fraud, (3) differences between bank deposits and cash receipts—could be cash embezzled, and (4) delayed recording—could reflect fraudulent records. Warning signs from employees include (1) lifestyle change—could be embezzlement, (2) too close with suppliers—could signal fraudulent transactions, and (3) failure to leave job, even for vacations—could conceal fraudulent activities. ■

NEED-TO-KNOW 6-3

Petty Cash System

P2

Bacardi Company established a $150 petty cash fund with Eminem as the petty cashier. When the fund balance reached $19 cash, Eminem prepared a petty cash payments report, which follows.

Petty Cash Payments Report

Receipt No.	Account Charged		Approved by	Received by
12	Delivery Expense	$ 29	Eminem	A. Smirnoff
13	Merchandise Inventory	18	Eminem	J. Daniels
15	(Omitted)	32	Eminem	C. Carlsberg
16	Miscellaneous Expense	41	(Omitted)	J. Walker
	Total	$120		

Required

1. Identify four internal control weaknesses from the petty cash payments report.
2. Prepare general journal entries to record:
   a. Establishment of the petty cash fund.
   b. Reimbursement of the fund. (Assume for this part only that petty cash receipt no. 15 was issued for miscellaneous expenses.)
3. What is the Petty Cash account balance immediately before reimbursement? Immediately after reimbursement?

Solution

1. Four internal control weaknesses that are apparent from the payments report include:
   a. Petty cash ticket no. 14 is missing. Its omission raises questions about the petty cashier's management of the fund.
   b. The $19 cash balance means that $131 has been withdrawn ($150 − $19 = $131). However, the total amount of the petty cash receipts is only $120 ($29 + $18 + $32 + $41). The fund is $11 short of cash ($131 − $120 = $11). Was petty cash receipt no. 14 issued for $11? Management should investigate.
   c. The petty cashier (Eminem) did not sign petty cash receipt no. 16. This omission could have been an oversight on his part or he might not have authorized the payment. Management should investigate.
   d. Petty cash receipt no. 15 does not indicate which account to charge. This omission could have been an oversight on the petty cashier's part. Management could check with C. Carlsberg and the petty cashier (Eminem) about the transaction. Without further information, debit Miscellaneous Expense.

2. Petty cash general journal entries.

a. Entry to establish the petty cash fund.

Petty Cash	150	
Cash		150

b. Entry to reimburse the fund.

Delivery Expense	29	
Merchandise Inventory	18	
Miscellaneous Expense ($41 + $32)	73	
Cash Over and Short	11	
Cash ($150 fund bal. − $19 cash rem.)		131

Do More: QS 6-4, E 6-5, E 6-6, P 6-2

3. The Petty Cash account balance *always* equals its fund balance, in this case $150. This account balance does not change unless the fund is increased or decreased.

QC3

BANKING ACTIVITIES AS CONTROLS

Banks (and other financial institutions) provide many services, including helping companies control cash. Banks safeguard cash, provide detailed and independent records of cash transactions, and are a source of cash financing. This section describes these services and the documents provided by banking activities that increase managers' control over cash.

Basic Bank Services

This section explains basic bank services—such as the bank account, the bank deposit, and checking—that contribute to the control of cash.

Bank Account, Deposit, and Check A *bank account* is a record set up by a bank for a customer. It permits a customer to deposit money for safekeeping and helps control withdrawals. To limit access to a bank account, all persons authorized to write checks on the account must sign a **signature card,** which bank employees use to verify signatures on checks. Many companies have more than one bank account to serve different needs and to handle special transactions such as payroll.

Each bank deposit is supported by a **deposit ticket,** which lists items such as currency, coins, and checks deposited along with their corresponding dollar amounts. The bank gives the customer a copy of the deposit ticket or a deposit receipt as proof of the deposit. Exhibit 6.4 shows one type of deposit ticket.

Point: Online banking services include the ability to stop payment on a check, move money between accounts, get up-to-date balances, and identify cleared checks and deposits.

EXHIBIT 6.4

Deposit Ticket

Front

DEPOSIT TICKET

VideoBuster Company
901 Main Street
Hillcrest, NY 11749

Date October 2, 20 15

		Dollars	Cents
CASH	CURRENCY	36	50
	COIN		
LIST CHECKS SINGLY			
TOTAL FROM OTHER SIDE		203	50
TOTAL		240	00
NET DEPOSIT		240	00

USE OTHER SIDE FOR ADDITIONAL LISTINGS. BE SURE EACH ITEM IS PROPERLY ENDORSED.

Deposit checks
(Memo)

99-DT/101

FN First National
Hillcrest, New York 11750

Checks and other items are received for deposit subject to the provisions of the uniform commercial code or any applicable collection agreement.

|:012410497|: 457923 • 02 75

Back

	CHECKS LIST SINGLY	DOLLARS	CENTS
1	14-287/939	90	50
2	82-759/339	82	80
3	76-907/919	30	20
4			
5			
6			
7			
8			
9			
10			
11			
12			
13			
14			
15			
16			
17			
18			
19			
20			
21			
22			
	TOTAL	203	50

ENTER TOTAL ON THE FRONT OF THIS TICKET

To withdraw money from an account, the depositor can use a **check,** which is a document signed by the depositor instructing the bank to pay a specified amount of money to a designated recipient. A check involves three parties: a *maker* who signs the check, a *payee* who is the recipient, and a *bank* (or *payer*) on which the check is drawn. The bank provides a depositor the checks that are serially numbered and imprinted with the name and address of both the depositor and bank. Both checks and deposit tickets are imprinted with identification codes in magnetic ink for computer processing. Exhibit 6.5 shows one type of check. It is accompanied with an optional *remittance advice* explaining the payment. When a remittance advice is unavailable, the *memo* line is often used for a brief explanation.

EXHIBIT 6.5

Check with Remittance Advice

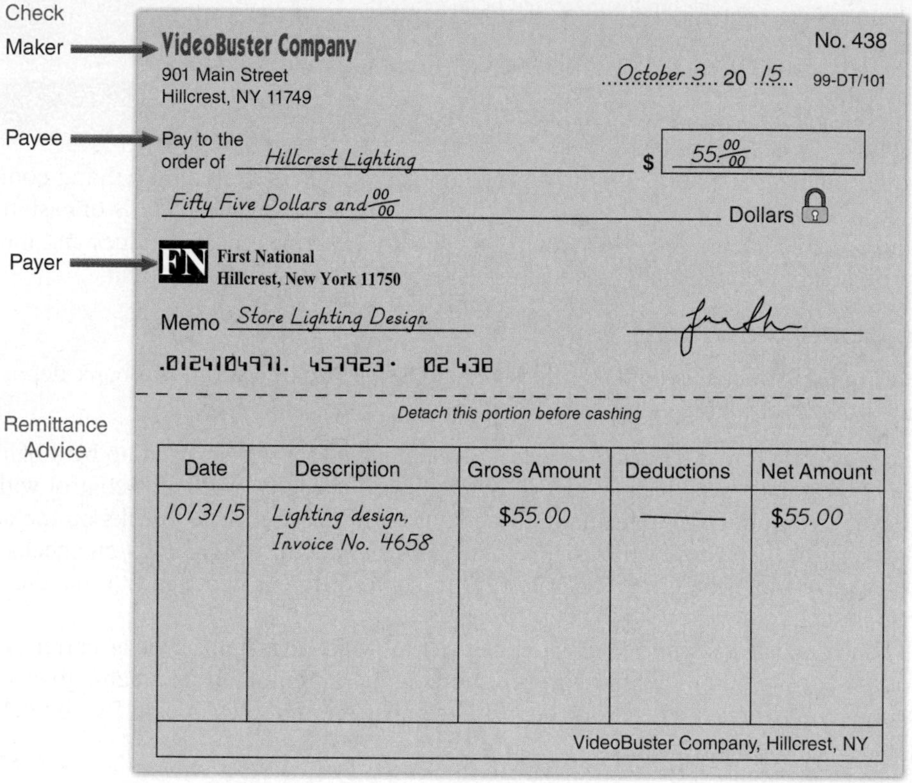

Electronic Funds Transfer **Electronic funds transfer (EFT)** is the electronic transfer of cash from one party to another. No paper documents are necessary. Banks simply transfer cash from one account to another with a journal entry. Companies are increasingly using EFT because of its convenience and low cost. For instance, it can cost up to 50 cents to process a check through the banking system, whereas EFT cost is near zero. We now commonly see items such as payroll, rent, utilities, insurance, and interest payments being handled by EFT. The bank statement lists cash withdrawals by EFT with the checks and other deductions. Cash receipts by EFT are listed with deposits and other additions. A bank statement is sometimes a depositor's only notice of an EFT.

Bank Statement

Usually once a month, the bank sends each depositor a **bank statement** showing the activity in the account. Although a monthly statement is common, companies often regularly access information on their banking transactions. (Companies can choose to record any accounting adjustments required from the bank statement immediately or later, say, at the end of each day, week, month, or when reconciling a bank statement.) Different banks use different formats for their bank statements, but all of them include the following items of information:

1. Beginning-of-period balance of the depositor's account.
2. Checks and other debits decreasing the account during the period.
3. Deposits and other credits increasing the account during the period.
4. End-of-period balance of the depositor's account.

Point: Good internal control is to deposit all cash receipts daily and make all payments for goods and services by check. This controls access to cash and creates an independent record of all cash activities. Another good control is to send a copy of the bank statement directly to a party without access to cash or recordkeeping.

EXHIBIT 6.6

Bank Statement

FN First National
Hillcrest, New York 11750

Bank Statement

Member FDIC

VideoBuster Company
901 Main Street
Hillcrest, NY 11749

October 31, 2015
Statement Date

494 504 2
Account Number

Ⓐ

Previous Balance	Total Checks and Debits	Total Deposits and Credits	Current Balance
1,609.58	723.00	1,163.42	2,050.00

Ⓑ Checks and Debits

Date	No.	Amount
10/03	119	55.00
10/09	120	200.00
10/10	121	120.00
10/12		23.00 DM
10/14	122	70.00
10/16	123	25.00 EFT
10/23	125	15.00
10/25		20.00 NSF
		10.00 DM
10/26	127	50.00
10/29	128	135.00

Debits decrease bank's liability to depositor

Ⓒ Deposits and Credits

Date	Amount
10/02	240.00
10/09	180.00
10/15	100.00 EFT
10/16	150.00
10/23	485.00 CM
10/31	8.42 IN

Credits increase bank's liability to depositor

Ⓓ Daily Balance

Date	Amount
10/01	1,609.58
10/02	1,849.58
10/03	1,794.58
10/09	1,774.58
10/10	1,654.58
10/12	1,631.58
10/14	1,561.58
10/15	1,661.58
10/16	1,786.58
10/23	2,256.58
10/25	2,226.58
10/26	2,176.58
10/29	2,041.58
10/31	2,050.00

Symbols: CM–Credit Memo EC–Error Correction NSF–Non-Sufficient Funds SC–Service Charge
DM–Debit Memo IN–Interest Earned EFT–Electronic Funds Transfer OD–Overdraft

< Reconcile the account immediately. >

Bank's Liability to Video Buster

		9/30 bal.	1,609.58
		CRs	1,163.42
DRs	723.00		
		10/31 bal.	2,050.00

Point: Many banks separately report other debits and credits apart from checks and deposits.

This information reflects the bank's records. Exhibit 6.6 shows one type of bank statement. Identify each of these four items in that statement. Part Ⓐ of Exhibit 6.6 summarizes changes in the account. Part Ⓑ lists paid checks along with other debits. Part Ⓒ lists deposits and credits to the account, and part Ⓓ shows the daily account balances.

In reading a bank statement note that a depositor's account is a liability on the bank's records. This is because the money belongs to the depositor, not the bank. When a depositor increases the account balance, the bank records it with a *credit* to that liability account. This means that **debit memos from the bank produce *credits* on the depositor's books, and credit memos from the bank produce *debits* on the depositor's books.**

Enclosed with a bank statement is a list of the depositor's canceled checks (or the actual canceled checks) along with any debit or credit memoranda affecting the account. Increasingly, banks are showing canceled checks electronically via online access to accounts. **Canceled checks** are checks the bank has paid and deducted from the customer's account during the period. We say such checks have *cleared the bank.* Other deductions that can appear on a bank statement include (1) service charges and fees assessed by the bank, (2) checks deposited that are uncollectible, (3) corrections of previous errors, (4) withdrawals through automated teller machines (ATMs), and (5) periodic payments arranged in advance by a depositor. (Most company checking accounts do not allow ATM withdrawals because of the company's desire to make all disbursements by check.) Except for service charges, the bank notifies the depositor of each deduction with a debit memorandum when the bank reduces the balance. A copy of each debit memorandum is usually sent with the statement (again, this information is often available earlier via online access and notifications).

Transactions that increase the depositor's account include amounts the bank collects on behalf of the depositor and the corrections of previous errors. Credit memoranda notify the depositor of all increases when they are recorded. A copy of each credit memorandum is often sent with the bank statement. Banks that pay interest on checking accounts often compute the amount of interest earned on the average cash balance and credit it to the depositor's account each period. In Exhibit 6.6, the bank credits $8.42 of interest to the account.

Point: Your checking account is a liability from the bank's perspective (but an asset from yours). Credits increase the bank's liability to you. When you make a deposit, they "credit your account." Debits decrease the bank's liability to you. When you write a check, or use your debit card for a purchase, the bank decreases its liability to you; they "debit your account."

Global: If cash is in more than one currency, a company usually translates these amounts into U.S. dollars using the exchange rate as of the balance sheet date. Also, a company must disclose any restrictions on cash accounts located outside the U.S.

Bank Reconciliation

P3 Prepare a bank reconciliation.

When a company deposits all cash receipts and makes all cash payments (except petty cash) by check, it can use the bank statement for proving the accuracy of its cash records. This is done using a **bank reconciliation,** which is a report explaining any differences between the checking account balance according to the depositor's records and the balance reported on the bank statement. The figure below reflects this process, which we describe in the following sections.

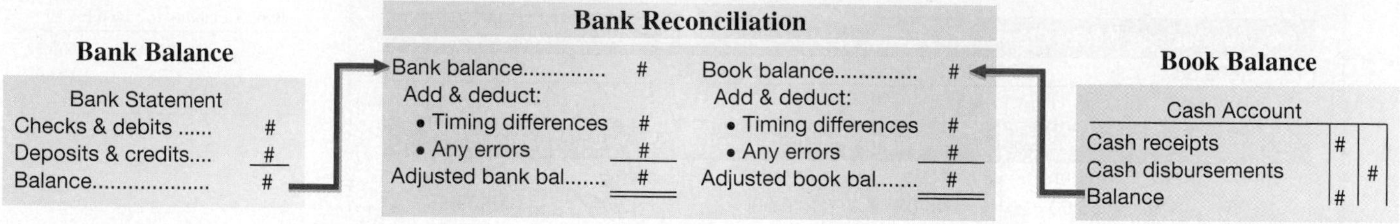

Purpose of Bank Reconciliation The balance of a checking account reported on the bank statement rarely equals the balance in the depositor's accounting records. This is usually due to information that one party has that the other does not. We must therefore prove the accuracy of both the depositor's records and those of the bank. This means we must *reconcile* the two balances and explain or account for any differences in them. Among the factors causing the bank statement balance to differ from the depositor's book balance are these:

- **Outstanding checks.** [Adjust bank balance.] **Outstanding checks** are checks written (or drawn) by the depositor, deducted on the depositor's records, and sent to the payees but not yet received by the bank for payment at the bank statement date.
- **Deposits in transit** (also called **outstanding deposits**). [Adjust bank balance.] **Deposits in transit** are deposits made and recorded by the depositor but not yet recorded on the bank statement. For example, companies can make deposits (in the night depository) at the end of a business day after the bank is closed. If such a deposit occurred on a bank statement date, it would not appear on this period's statement. The bank would record such a deposit on the next business day, and it would appear on the next period's bank statement. Deposits mailed to the bank near the end of a period also can be in transit and unrecorded when the statement is prepared.
- **Deductions for uncollectible items and for services.** [Adjust book balance.] A company sometimes deposits another party's check that is uncollectible (usually meaning the balance in that party's account is not large enough to cover the check). This check is called a *nonsufficient funds (NSF)* check. The bank would have initially credited the depositor's account for the amount of the check. When the bank learns the check is uncollectible, it debits (reduces) the depositor's account for the amount of that check. The bank may also charge the depositor a fee for processing an uncollectible check and notify the depositor of the deduction by sending a debit memorandum. The depositor should record each deduction when a debit memorandum is received, but an entry is sometimes not made until the bank reconciliation is prepared. Other possible bank charges to a depositor's account that are first reported on a bank statement include printing new checks and service fees.
- **Additions for collections and for interest.** [Adjust book balance.] Banks sometimes act as collection agents for their depositors by collecting notes and other items. Banks can also receive electronic funds transfers to the depositor's account. When a bank collects an item, it is added to the depositor's account, less any service fee. The bank also sends a credit memorandum to notify the depositor of the transaction. When the memorandum is received, the depositor should record it; yet it sometimes remains unrecorded until the bank reconciliation is prepared. The bank statement also includes a credit for any interest earned.
- **Errors.** [Adjust bank or book balance.] Both banks and depositors can make errors. Bank errors might not be discovered until the depositor prepares the bank reconciliation. Also, depositor errors are sometimes discovered when the bank balance is reconciled. Error testing includes: (a) comparing deposits on the bank statement with deposits in the accounting records and (b) comparing canceled checks on the bank statement with checks recorded in the accounting records.

Forms of Check Fraud (CkFraud.org)

- Forged signatures—legitimate blank checks with fake payer signature
- Forged endorsements—stolen check that is endorsed and cashed by someone other than the payee
- Counterfeit checks—fraudulent checks with fake payer signature
- Altered checks—legitimate check altered (such as changed payee or amount) to benefit perpetrator
- Check kiting—deposit check from one bank account (without sufficient funds) into a second bank account

Point: Small businesses with few employees often allow recordkeepers to both write checks and keep the general ledger. If this is done, it is essential that the owner do the bank reconciliation.

Point: The person preparing the bank reconciliation should not be responsible for processing cash receipts, managing checks, or maintaining cash records.

Timing differences. The following lists common timing differences. Each of these items has already been recorded by either the bank, or the company, but not both.

Reconciling Item	Has Already Been:	Included on Bank Reconciliation as:
Outstanding checks	Subtracted from book balance	Subtraction from bank balance
Deposits in transit	Added to book balance	Addition to bank balance
Bank fees.................	Subtracted from bank balance	Subtraction from book balance
NSF checks	Subtracted from bank balance	Subtraction from book balance
Interest earned	Added to bank balance	Addition to book balance

Illustration of a Bank Reconciliation We follow nine steps in preparing the bank reconciliation. It is helpful to refer to the bank reconciliation in Exhibit 6.7 when studying steps 1 through 9.

EXHIBIT 6.7

Bank Reconciliation

VIDEOBUSTER
Bank Reconciliation
October 31, 2015

①	Bank statement balance		$ 2,050.00	⑤	Book balance		$ 1,404.58
②	Add			⑥	Add		
	Deposit of Oct. 31 in transit		145.00		Collect $500 note less $15 fee	$485.00	
			2,195.00		Interest earned	8.42	493.42
③	Deduct						1,898.00
	Outstanding checks			⑦	Deduct		
	No. 124..................	$150.00			Check printing charge	23.00	
	No. 126..................	200.00	350.00		NSF check plus service fee........	30.00	53.00
④	**Adjusted bank balance**		**$1,845.00**	⑧	**Adjusted book balance**		**$1,845.00**

⑨ Balances are equal (reconciled)

1 Identify the bank statement balance of the Cash account (*balance per bank*). VideoBuster's bank balance is $2,050.

2 Identify and list any unrecorded deposits and any bank errors understating the bank balance. Add them to the bank balance. VideoBuster's $145 deposit placed in the bank's night depository on October 31 is not recorded on its bank statement.

3 Identify and list any outstanding checks and any bank errors overstating the bank balance. Deduct them from the bank balance. VideoBuster's comparison of canceled checks with its books shows two checks outstanding: No. 124 for $150 and No. 126 for $200.

4 Compute the *adjusted bank balance,* also called the *corrected* or *reconciled balance.*

5 Identify the company's book balance of the Cash account (*balance per book*). VideoBuster's book balance is $1,404.58.

6 Identify and list any unrecorded credit memoranda from the bank, any interest earned, and errors understating the book balance. Add them to the book balance. VideoBuster's bank statement includes a credit memorandum showing the bank collected a note receivable for the company on October 23. The note's proceeds of $500 (minus a $15 collection fee) are credited to the company's account. VideoBuster's bank statement also shows a credit of $8.42 for interest earned on the average cash balance. There was no prior notification of this item, and it is not yet recorded.

7 Identify and list any unrecorded debit memoranda from the bank, any service charges, and errors overstating the book balance. Deduct them from the book balance. Debits on VideoBuster's bank statement that are not yet recorded include (a) a $23 charge for check printing and (b) an NSF check for $20 plus a related $10 processing fee. (The NSF check is dated October 16 and was included in the book balance.)

8 Compute the *adjusted book balance,* also called *corrected* or *reconciled balance.*

9 Verify that the two adjusted balances from steps 4 and 8 are equal. If so, they are reconciled. If not, check for accuracy and missing data to achieve reconciliation.

Point: Outstanding checks are identified by comparing canceled checks on the bank statement with checks recorded. This includes identifying any outstanding checks listed on the *previous* period's bank reconciliation that are not included in the canceled checks on this period's bank statement.

Point: Adjusting entries can be combined into one compound entry.

Adjusting Entries from a Bank Reconciliation A bank reconciliation often identifies unrecorded items that need recording by the company. In VideoBuster's reconciliation, the adjusted balance of $1,845 is the correct balance as of October 31. But the company's accounting records show a $1,404.58 balance. We must prepare journal entries to adjust the book balance to the correct balance. **It is important to remember that only the items reconciling the *book balance* require adjustment.** A review of Exhibit 6.7 indicates that four entries are required for VideoBuster.

Collection of note. The first entry is to record the proceeds of its note receivable collected by the bank less the expense of having the bank perform that service.

Assets = Liabilities + Equity
+485 −15
−500

Oct. 31	Cash	485	
	Collection Expense	15	
	Notes Receivable		500
	To record the collection fee and proceeds for a note collected by the bank.		

Interest earned. The second entry records interest credited to its account by the bank.

Assets = Liabilities + Equity
+8.42 +8.42

Oct. 31	Cash	8.42	
	Interest Revenue.		8.42
	To record interest earned on the cash balance in the checking account.		

Check printing. The third entry records expenses for the check printing charge.

Assets = Liabilities + Equity
−23 −23

Oct. 31	Miscellaneous Expenses	23	
	Cash		23
	Check printing charge.		

NSF check. The fourth entry records the NSF check that is returned as uncollectible. The $20 check was originally received from T. Woods in payment of his account and then deposited. The bank charged $10 for handling the NSF check and deducted $30 total from VideoBuster's account. This means the entry must reverse the effects of the original entry made when the check was received and must record (add) the $10 bank fee.

Point: The company will try to collect the entire NSF amount of $30 from customer.

Assets = Liabilities + Equity
+30
−30

Oct. 31	Accounts Receivable—T. Woods.	30	
	Cash		30
	To charge Woods' account for $20 NSF check and $10 bank fee.		

Point: Need-To-Know 6-4 shows an adjusting entry for an error correction.

Cash			
Unadj. bal.	1,404.58		
⑥	485.00	⑦	23.00
⑥	8.42	⑦	30.00
Adj. bal.	1,845.00		

After these four entries are recorded, the book balance of cash is adjusted to the correct amount of $1,845 (the adjusted book balance). The Cash T-account to the side shows the same computation, where entries are keyed to the numerical codes in Exhibit 6.7.

Decision Insight

Fraud A survey reports that 74% of employees had "personally seen" or had "first-hand knowledge of" fraud or misconduct within the past year. Another survey found that fraudsters exploited weak internal controls in 74% of the frauds—up from 49% four years earlier—see graphic (KPMG 2011). ■

Percent Citing These Root Causes to Override Controls

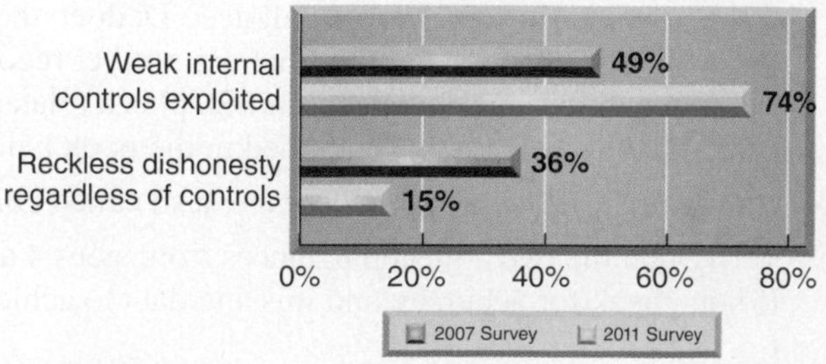

NEED-TO-KNOW 6-4

Bank Reconciliation

P3

The following information is available to reconcile Gucci's book balance of cash with its bank statement cash balance as of December 31, 2016.

a. The December 31 cash balance according to the accounting records is $1,610, and the bank statement cash balance for that date is $1,900.

b. Gucci's December 31 daily cash receipts of $800 were placed in the bank's night depository on December 31 but do not appear on the December 31 bank statement.

c. Check No. 6273 for $400 and Check No. 6282 for $100, both written and entered in the accounting records in December, are not among the canceled checks. Two checks, No. 6231 for $2,000 and No. 6242 for $200, were outstanding on the most recent November 30 reconciliation. Check No. 6231 is listed with the December canceled checks, but Check No. 6242 is not.

d. When the December checks are compared with entries in the accounting records, it is found that Check No. 6267 had been correctly drawn for $340 to pay for office supplies but was erroneously entered in the accounting records as $430.

e. A credit memorandum indicates that the bank collected $500 cash on a note receivable for the company, deducted a $30 collection fee, and credited the balance to the company's Cash account. Gucci had not recorded this transaction before receiving the statement.

f. Two debit memoranda are enclosed with the statement and are unrecorded at the time of the reconciliation. One debit memorandum is for $150 and dealt with an NSF check for $140 received from a customer, Prada Inc., in payment of its account. The bank assessed a $10 fee for processing it. The second debit memorandum is a $20 charge for check printing. Gucci had not recorded these transactions before receiving the statement.

Required

1. Prepare the bank reconciliation for this company as of December 31, 2016.
2. Prepare the journal entries necessary to bring Gucci's book balance of cash into conformity with the reconciled cash balance as of December 31, 2016.

Solutions

Part 1

GUCCI
Bank Reconciliation
December 31, 2016

Bank statement balance			$1,900	Book balance		$1,610
Add				Add		
Deposit of Dec. 31			800	Error (Ck 6267)	$ 90	
			2,700	Proceeds of note less $30 fee	470	560
						2,170
Deduct				Deduct		
Outstanding Checks No.	6242	$200		NSF check	$150	
	6273	400		Printing fee	20	
	6282	100	700			170
Adjusted bank balance			$2,000	Adjusted book balance		$2,000

Part 2

Dec. 31	Cash	90	
	Office Supplies		90
	To correct an entry error.		
Dec. 31	Cash	470	
	Collection Expense	30	
	Notes Receivable		500
	To record note collection less fees.		
Dec. 31	Accounts Receivable—Prada Inc.	150	
	Cash		150
	To charge account for NSF check plus fees.		
Dec. 31	Miscellaneous Expenses	20	
	Cash		20
	To record check printing charge.		

Do More: QS 6-5, QS 6-6, QS 6-7, E 6-8, E 6-9, E 6-10, E 6-11

QC4

GLOBAL VIEW

This section discusses similarities and differences between U.S. GAAP and IFRS regarding internal controls and in the accounting and reporting of cash.

Internal Control Purposes, Principles, and Procedures Both U.S. GAAP and IFRS aim for high-quality financial reporting. That aim translates into enhanced internal controls worldwide. Specifically, the purposes and principles of internal control systems are fundamentally the same across the globe. However, culture and other realities suggest different emphases on the mix of control procedures, and some sensitivity to different customs and environments when establishing that mix. Nevertheless, the discussion in this chapter applies internationally. **Nokia** provides the following description of its control activities.

NOKIA

> Nokia has an internal audit function that acts as an independent appraisal function by examining and evaluating the adequacy and effectiveness of the company's system of internal control.

Control of Cash Accounting definitions for cash are similar for U.S. GAAP and IFRS. The need for control of cash is universal and applies globally. This means that companies worldwide desire to apply cash management procedures as explained in this chapter and aim to control both cash receipts and disbursements. Accordingly, systems that employ tools such as cash monitoring mechanisms, verification of documents, and petty cash processes are applied worldwide. The basic techniques explained in this chapter are part of those control procedures.

Banking Activities as Controls There is a global demand for banking services, bank statements, and bank reconciliations. To the extent feasible, companies utilize banking services as part of their effective control procedures. Further, bank statements are similarly used along with bank reconciliations to control and monitor cash.

IFRS

Internal controls are crucial to companies that convert from U.S. GAAP to IFRS. Major risks include misstatement of financial information and fraud. Other risks are ineffective communication of the impact of this change for investors, creditors and others, and management's inability to certify the effectiveness of controls over financial reporting. ■

Courtesy of Molly DeCoudreaux/Dandelion Chocolate

Sustainability and Accounting The founders, Todd and Cam, of **Dandelion Chocolate**, as introduced in this chapter's opening feature, explain that their entrepreneurial efforts include sustainable initiatives on two fronts. First, they support sustainable agricultural practices among the farmers who grow their cocoa beans. In this way they also focus on creating sustainable economies in those farming communities through dignified jobs with fair wages. Second, they support community nonprofits that help the disadvantaged and poor to achieve sustainable incomes and lifestyles.

Decision Analysis — Days' Sales Uncollected

A1 Compute the days' sales uncollected ratio and use it to assess liquidity.

An important part of cash management is monitoring the receipt of cash from receivables. If customers and others who owe money to a company are delayed in payment, then that company can find it difficult to pay its obligations when they are due. A company's customers are crucial partners in its cash management. Many companies attract customers by selling to them on credit. This means that cash receipts from customers are delayed until accounts receivable are collected.

One measure of how quickly a company can convert its accounts receivable into cash is the **days' sales uncollected,** also called *days' sales in receivables*. This measure is computed by dividing the current balance of receivables by net credit sales over the year just completed and then multiplying by 365 (number of days in a year). Since net credit sales usually are not reported to external users, the net sales (or revenues) figure is commonly used in the computation as in Exhibit 6.8.

EXHIBIT 6.8

Days' Sales Uncollected

$$\textbf{Days' sales uncollected} = \frac{\textbf{Accounts receivable}}{\textbf{Net sales}} \times 365$$

We use days' sales uncollected to estimate how much time is likely to pass before the current amount of accounts receivable is received in cash. For evaluation purposes, we need to compare this estimate to that for other companies in the same industry. We also make comparisons between current and prior periods.

To illustrate, we select data from the annual reports of two toy manufacturers, **Hasbro** and **Mattel**. Their days' sales uncollected figures are shown in Exhibit 6.9.

EXHIBIT 6.9

Analysis Using Days' Sales Uncollected

Company	Figure ($ millions)	2013	2012	2011	2010	2009
Hasbro	Accounts receivable	$1,094	$1,030	$1,035	$961	$1,039
	Net sales	$4,082	$4,089	$4,286	$4,002	$4,068
	Days' sales uncollected	**98 days**	**92 days**	**88 days**	**88 days**	**93 days**
Mattel	Accounts receivable	$1,260	$1,227	$1,247	$1,146	$749
	Net sales	$6,485	$6,421	$6,266	$5,856	$5,431
	Days' sales uncollected	**71 days**	**70 days**	**73 days**	**71 days**	**50 days**

Days' sales uncollected for Hasbro in 2013 is computed as ($1,094/$4,082) × 365 days = 98 days. This means that it will take about 98 days to collect cash from ending accounts receivable. This number reflects one or more of the following factors: a company's ability to collect receivables, customer financial health, customer payment strategies, and discount terms. To further assess days' sales uncollected for Hasbro, we compare it to its own four prior years and to those of Mattel. We see that Hasbro's days' sales uncollected has worsened since 2012 as it takes much longer to collect its receivables relative to all its prior years. In comparison, Mattel has also worsened from 50 days in 2009 up to 71 days in 2013. For all years, Mattel is superior to Hasbro on this measure of cash management. The less time that money is tied up in receivables often translates into increased profitability.

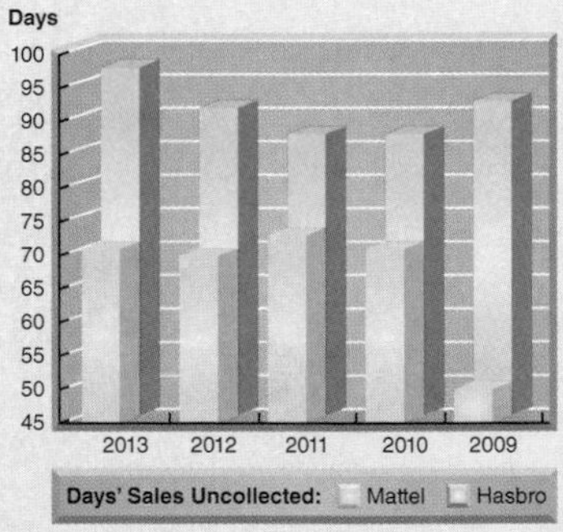

Decision Maker

Sales Representative The sales staff is told to take action to help reduce days' sales uncollected for cash management purposes. What can you, a salesperson, do to reduce days' sales uncollected? ■ [Answers follow the chapter's Summary.]

NEED-TO-KNOW

COMPREHENSIVE

Prepare a bank reconciliation for Jamboree Enterprises for the month ended November 30, 2015. The following information is available to reconcile Jamboree Enterprises's book balance of cash with its bank statement balance as of November 30, 2015:

a. After all posting is complete on November 30, the company's book balance of Cash has a $16,380 debit balance, but its bank statement shows a $38,520 balance.

b. Checks No. 2024 for $4,810 and No. 2026 for $5,000 are outstanding.

c. In comparing the canceled checks on the bank statement with the entries in the accounting records, it is found that Check No. 2025 in payment of rent is correctly drawn for $1,000 but is erroneously entered in the accounting records as $880.

Point: Generally, the party that is not the initial recorder of an item, but is later informed, includes that item on its "book" of the bank reconciliation. For example, the bank records an NSF check and then informs the company. The company, as not the initial recorder of the item, reports it on the book side of its reconciliation.

d. The November 30 deposit of $17,150 was placed in the night depository after banking hours on that date, and this amount does not appear on the bank statement.

e. In reviewing the bank statement, a check written by Jumbo Enterprises in the amount of $160 was erroneously drawn against Jamboree's account.

f. A credit memorandum enclosed with the bank statement indicates that the bank collected a $30,000 note and $900 of related interest on Jamboree's behalf. This transaction was not recorded by Jamboree prior to receiving the statement.

g. A debit memorandum for $1,100 lists a $1,100 NSF check received from a customer, Marilyn Welch. Jamboree had not recorded the return of this check before receiving the statement.

h. Bank service charges for November total $40. These charges were not recorded by Jamboree before receiving the statement.

PLANNING THE SOLUTION

- Set up a bank reconciliation with a bank side and a book side (as in Exhibit 6.7). Leave room to both add and deduct items. Each column will result in a reconciled, equal balance.
- Examine each item *a* through *h* to determine whether it affects the book or the bank balance and whether it should be added or deducted from the bank or book balance.
- After all items are analyzed, complete the reconciliation and arrive at a reconciled balance between the bank side and the book side.
- For each reconciling item on the book side, prepare an adjusting entry. Additions to the book side require an adjusting entry that debits Cash. Deductions on the book side require an adjusting entry that credits Cash.

SOLUTION

JAMBOREE ENTERPRISES
Bank Reconciliation
November 30, 2015

Bank statement balance		$ 38,520	Book balance		$ 16,380
Add			Add		
Deposit of Nov. 30	$17,150		Collection of note	$30,000	
Bank error (Jumbo)	160	17,310	Interest earned	900	30,900
		55,830			47,280
Deduct			Deduct		
Outstanding checks			NSF check (M. Welch)	1,100	
No. 2024	4,810		Recording error (# 2025) ...	120	
No. 2026	5,000	9,810	Service charge	40	1,260
Adjusted bank balance ...		**$46,020**	**Adjusted book balance**		**$46,020**

Required Adjusting Entries for Jamboree

Nov. 30	Cash	30,900	
	Notes Receivable		30,000
	Interest Earned		900
	To record collection of note with interest.		
Nov. 30	Accounts Receivable—M. Welch..................	1,100	
	Cash		1,100
	To reinstate account due from an NSF check.		
Nov. 30	Rent Expense	120	
	Cash		120
	To correct recording error on Check No. 2025.		
Nov. 30	Bank Service Charges	40	
	Cash		40
	To record bank service charges.		

Point: Error correction can alternatively involve (1) reversing the error entry, and (2) recording the correct entry. Auditors prefer this alternative.

APPENDIX

Documentation and Verification 6A

This appendix describes the important business documents of a voucher system of control.

P4 Describe the use of documentation and verification to control cash disbursements.

Purchase Requisition Department managers are usually not allowed to place orders directly with suppliers for control purposes. Instead, a department manager must inform the purchasing department of its needs by preparing and signing a **purchase requisition,** which lists the merchandise needed and requests that it be purchased—see Exhibit 6A.1. Two copies of the purchase requisition are sent to the purchasing department, which then sends one copy to the accounting department. When the accounting department receives a purchase requisition, it creates and maintains a voucher for this transaction. The requesting department keeps the third copy.

EXHIBIT 6A.1

Purchase Requisition

Z-Mart

PURCHASE REQUISITION No. 917

From: Sporting Goods Department
To: Purchasing Department

Date: October 28, 2015
Preferred Vendor: Trex

Request purchase of the following item(s):

MODEL NO.	DESCRIPTION	QUANTITY
CH 015	Challenger X7	1
SD 099	SpeedDemon	1

Reason for Request: Replenish inventory
Approval for Request: T.Z.
For Purchasing Department use only: Order Date 10/30/15 P.O. No. P98

Purchase Order A **purchase order** is a document the purchasing department uses to place an order with a **vendor** (seller or supplier). A purchase order authorizes a vendor to ship ordered merchandise at the stated price and terms—see Exhibit 6A.2. When the purchasing department receives a purchase requisition, it prepares at least five copies of a purchase order. The copies are distributed as follows: *copy 1* to the vendor as a purchase request and as authority to ship merchandise; *copy 2,* along with a copy of the purchase requisition, to the accounting department, where it is entered in the voucher and used in approving payment of the invoice; *copy 3* to the requesting department to inform its manager that action is being taken; *copy 4* to the receiving department without order quantity so it can compare with goods received and provide independent count of goods received; and *copy 5* retained on file by the purchasing department.

Point: A voucher system is designed to uniquely meet the needs of a specific business. Thus, we should read this appendix as one example of a common voucher system design, but *not* the only design.

EXHIBIT 6A.2

Purchase Order

Point: Shipping terms and credit terms are shown on the purchase order.

Z-Mart
10 Michigan Street
Chicago, Illinois 60521

PURCHASE ORDER
No. P98

To: Trex
W9797 Cherry Road
Antigo, Wisconsin 54409

Date: 10/30/15
FOB: Destination
Ship by: As soon as possible
Terms: 2/15, n/30

Request shipment of the following item(s):

Model No.	Description	Quantity	Price	Amount
CH 015	Challenger X7	1	490	490
SD 099	SpeedDemon	1	710	710

All shipments and invoices must include purchase order number

J.W.
ORDERED BY

Invoice An **invoice** is an itemized statement of goods prepared by the vendor listing the customer's name, items sold, sales prices, and terms of sale. An invoice is also a bill sent to the buyer from the supplier. From the vendor's point of view, it is a *sales invoice*. The buyer, or **vendee,** treats it as a *purchase invoice*. When receiving a purchase order, the vendor ships the ordered merchandise to the buyer and includes or mails a copy of the invoice covering the shipment to the buyer. The invoice is sent to the buyer's accounting department where it is placed in the voucher. (Refer back to Exhibit 4.5, which shows Z-Mart's purchase invoice.)

Receiving Report Many companies maintain a separate department to receive all merchandise and purchased assets. When each shipment arrives, this receiving department counts the goods and checks them for damage and agreement with the purchase order. It then prepares four or more copies of a **receiving report,** which is used within the company to notify the appropriate persons that ordered goods have been received and to describe the quantities and condition of the goods. One copy is sent to accounting and placed in the voucher. Copies are also sent to the requesting department and the purchasing department to notify them that the goods have arrived. The receiving department retains a copy in its files.

Invoice Approval When a receiving report arrives, the accounting department should have copies of the following documents in the voucher: purchase requisition, purchase order, and invoice. With the information in these documents, the accounting department can record the purchase and approve its payment. In approving an invoice for payment, it checks and compares information across all documents. To facilitate this checking and to ensure that no step is omitted, it often uses an **invoice approval,** also called *check authorization*—see Exhibit 6A.3. An invoice approval is a checklist of steps necessary for approving an invoice for recording and payment. It is a separate document either filed in the voucher or preprinted (or stamped) on the voucher.

EXHIBIT 6A.3

Invoice Approval

INVOICE APPROVAL

DOCUMENT		BY	DATE
Purchase requisition	*917*	*TZ*	*10/28/15*
Purchase order	*P98*	*JW*	*10/30/15*
Receiving report	*R85*	*SK*	*11/03/15*
Invoice:	*4657*		*11/12/15*
Price		*JK*	*11/12/15*
Calculations		*JK*	*11/12/15*
Terms		*JK*	*11/12/15*
Approved for payment		*BC*	

Point: Recording a purchase is initiated by an invoice approval, not an invoice. An invoice approval verifies that the amount is consistent with that requested, ordered, and received. This controls and verifies purchases and related liabilities.

Point: Auditors, when auditing inventory, check a sampling of purchases by reviewing the purchase order, receiving report, and invoice.

As each step in the checklist is approved, the person initials the invoice approval and records the current date. Final approval implies the following steps have occurred:

1. **Requisition check:** Items on invoice are requested per purchase requisition.
2. **Purchase order check:** Items on invoice are ordered per purchase order.
3. **Receiving report check:** Items on invoice are received per receiving report.
4. **Invoice check: Price:** Invoice prices are as agreed with the vendor.
   Calculations: Invoice has no mathematical errors.
   Terms: Terms are as agreed with the vendor.

Voucher Once an invoice has been checked and approved, the voucher is complete. A complete voucher is a record summarizing a transaction. Once the voucher certifies a transaction, it authorizes recording an obligation. A voucher also contains approval for paying the obligation on an appropriate date. The physical form of a voucher varies across companies. Many are designed so that the invoice and other related source documents are placed inside the voucher, which can be a folder.

Completion of a voucher usually requires a person to enter certain information on both the inside and outside of the voucher. Typical information required on the inside of a voucher is shown in Exhibit 6A.4, and that for the outside is shown in Exhibit 6A.5. This information is taken from the invoice and the supporting documents filed in the voucher. A complete voucher is sent to an authorized individual (often called an *auditor*). This person performs a final review, approves the accounts and amounts for debiting (called the *accounting distribution*), and authorizes recording of the voucher.

EXHIBIT 6A.4

Inside of a Voucher

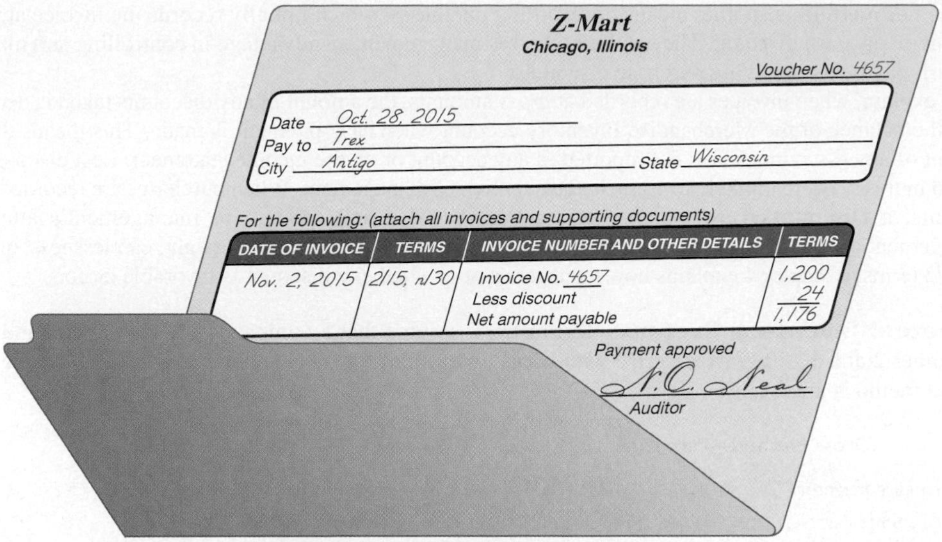

EXHIBIT 6A.5

Outside of a Voucher

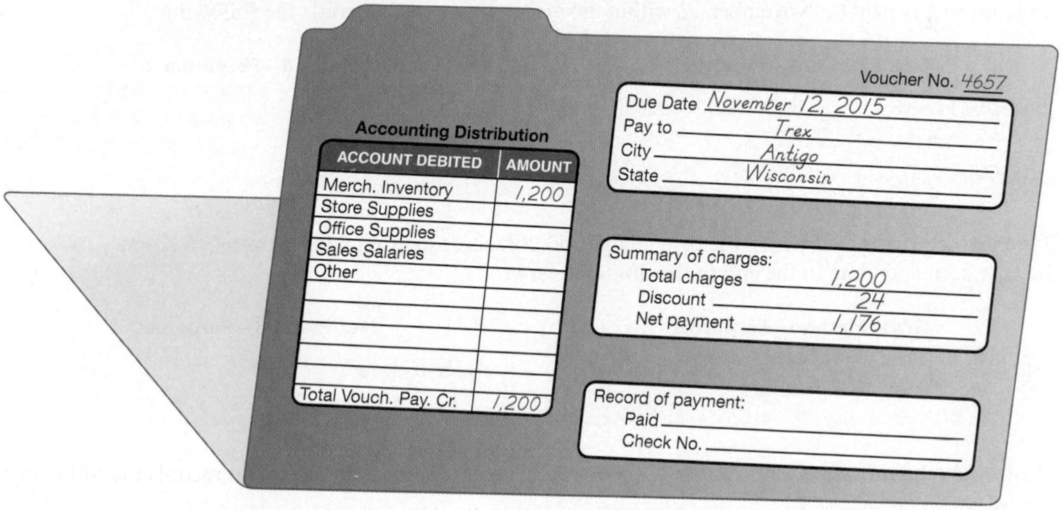

After a voucher is approved and recorded (in a journal called a **voucher register**), it is filed by its due date. A check is then sent on the payment date from the cashier, the voucher is marked "paid," and the voucher is sent to the accounting department and recorded (in a journal called the **check register**). The person issuing checks relies on the approved voucher and its signed supporting documents as proof that an obligation has been incurred and must be paid. The purchase requisition and purchase order confirm the purchase was authorized. The receiving report shows that items have been received, and the invoice approval form verifies that the invoice has been checked for errors. There is little chance for error and even less chance for fraud without collusion unless all the documents and signatures are forged.

APPENDIX

Control of Purchase Discounts 6B

P5 Apply the net method to control purchase discounts.

This appendix explains how a company can better control its cash *disbursements* to take advantage of favorable purchases discounts. Chapter 4 described the entries to record the receipt and payment of an invoice for a merchandise purchase with and without discount terms. Those entries were prepared under what is called the **gross method** of recording purchases, which initially records the invoice at its *gross* amount ignoring any cash discount.

The **net method** is another means of recording purchases, which initially records the invoice at its *net* amount of any cash discount. The net method gives management an advantage in controlling and monitoring cash payments involving purchase discounts.

Point: Most firms use the gross method as it is less expensive to administer and makes it easier to communicate with vendors.

To explain, when invoices are recorded at *gross* amounts, the amount of any discounts taken is deducted from the balance of the Merchandise Inventory account when cash payment is made. This means that the amount of any discounts lost is not reported in any account or on the income statement. Lost discounts recorded in this way are unlikely to come to the attention of management. When purchases are recorded at *net* amounts, a **Discounts Lost** expense account is recorded and brought to management's attention. Management can then seek to identify the reason for discounts lost such as oversight, carelessness, or unfavorable terms. (Chapter 4 explains how managers assess whether a discount is favorable or not.)

Perpetual Inventory System To illustrate, assume that a company purchases merchandise on November 2 at a $1,200 invoice price with terms of 2/10, n/30. Its November 2 entries under the gross and net methods are

Gross Method—Perpetual

Merchandise Inventory	1,200	
Accounts Payable		1,200

Net Method—Perpetual

Merchandise Inventory	1,176	
Accounts Payable		1,176

If the invoice is paid on November 12 within the discount period, it records the following:

Gross Method—Perpetual

Accounts Payable	1,200	
Merchandise Inventory		24
Cash		1,176

Net Method—Perpetual

Accounts Payable	1,176	
Cash		1,176

If the invoice is *not* paid within the discount period, it records the following November 12 entry (which is the date corresponding to the end of the discount period):

Gross Method—Perpetual

No entry		

Net Method—Perpetual

Discounts Lost	24	
Accounts Payable		24

Then, when the invoice is later paid on December 2, outside the discount period, it records the following:

Gross Method—Perpetual

Accounts Payable	1,200	
Cash		1,200

Net Method—Perpetual

Accounts Payable	1,200	
Cash		1,200

(The discount lost can be recorded when the cash payment is made with a single entry. However, in this case, when financial statements are prepared after a discount is lost and before the cash payment is made, an adjusting entry is required to recognize any unrecorded discount lost in the period when incurred.)

Periodic Inventory System The preceding entries assume a perpetual inventory system. If a company is using a periodic system, its November 2 entries under the gross and net methods are

Gross Method—Periodic

Purchases	1,200	
Accounts Payable		1,200

Net Method—Periodic

Purchases	1,176	
Accounts Payable		1,176

If the invoice is paid on November 12 within the discount period, it records the following:

Gross Method—Periodic

Accounts Payable	1,200	
Purchases Discounts		24
Cash		1,176

Net Method—Periodic

Accounts Payable	1,176	
Cash		1,176

If the invoice is *not* paid within the discount period, it records the following November 12 entry:

Gross Method—Periodic			Net Method—Periodic		
No entry			**Discounts Lost**	24	
			Accounts Payable		24

Then, when the invoice is later paid on December 2, outside the discount period, it records the following:

Gross Method—Periodic			Net Method—Periodic		
Accounts Payable	1,200		Accounts Payable	1,200	
Cash		1,200	Cash		1,200

Summary

C1 Define internal control and identify its purpose and principles. An internal control system consists of the policies and procedures managers use to protect assets, ensure reliable accounting, promote efficient operations, and urge adherence to company policies. It can prevent avoidable losses and help managers both plan operations and monitor company and human performance. Principles of good internal control include establishing responsibilities, maintaining adequate records, insuring assets and bonding employees, separating recordkeeping from custody of assets, dividing responsibilities for related transactions, applying technological controls, and performing regular independent reviews.

C2 Define cash and cash equivalents and explain how to report them. Cash includes currency, coins, and amounts on (or acceptable for) deposit in checking and savings accounts. Cash equivalents are short-term, highly liquid investment assets readily convertible to a known cash amount and sufficiently close to their maturity date so that market value is not sensitive to interest rate changes. Cash and cash equivalents are liquid assets because they are readily converted into other assets or can be used to pay for goods, services, or liabilities.

A1 Compute the days' sales uncollected ratio and use it to assess liquidity. Many companies attract customers by selling to them on credit. This means that cash receipts from customers are delayed until accounts receivable are collected. Users want to know how quickly a company can convert its accounts receivable into cash. The days' sales uncollected ratio, one measure reflecting company liquidity, is computed by dividing the ending balance of receivables by annual net sales, and then multiplying by 365.

P1 Apply internal control to cash receipts and disbursements. Internal control of cash receipts ensures that all cash received is properly recorded and deposited. Attention focuses on two important types of cash receipts: over-the-counter and by mail. Good internal control for over-the-counter cash receipts includes use of a cash register, customer review, use of receipts, a permanent transaction record, and separation of the custody of cash from its recordkeeping. Good internal control for cash receipts by mail includes at least two people assigned to open mail and a listing of each sender's name, amount, and explanation. (Banks offer several services that promote the control and safeguarding of cash.)

P2 Explain and record petty cash fund transactions. Petty cash disbursements are payments of small amounts for items such as postage, courier fees, minor repairs, and supplies. A company usually sets up one or more petty cash funds. A petty cash fund cashier is responsible for safekeeping the cash, making payments from this fund, and keeping receipts and records. A Petty Cash account is debited only when the fund is established or increased in amount. When the fund is replenished, petty cash disbursements are recorded with debits to expense (or asset) accounts and a credit to Cash.

P3 Prepare a bank reconciliation. A bank reconciliation proves the accuracy of the depositor's and the bank's records. The bank statement balance is adjusted for items such as outstanding checks and unrecorded deposits made on or before the bank statement date but not reflected on the statement. The book balance is adjusted for items such as service charges, bank collections for the depositor, and interest earned on the account.

P4A Describe the use of documentation and verification to control cash disbursements. A voucher system is a set of procedures and approvals designed to control cash disbursements and acceptance of obligations. The voucher system of control relies on several important documents, including the voucher and its supporting files. A key factor in this system is that only approved departments and individuals are authorized to incur certain obligations.

P5B Apply the net method to control purchase discounts. The net method aids management in monitoring and controlling purchase discounts. When invoices are recorded at gross amounts, the amount of discounts taken is deducted from the balance of the Inventory account. This means that the amount of any discounts lost is not reported in any account and is unlikely to come to the attention of management. When purchases are recorded at net amounts, a Discounts Lost account is brought to management's attention as an operating expense. Management can then seek to identify the reason for discounts lost, such as oversight, carelessness, or unfavorable terms.

Guidance Answers to Decision Maker

Entrepreneur To achieve proper separation of duties, a minimum of three employees are required. Transaction authorization, recording, and asset custody are ideally handled by three employees. Many small businesses do not employ three workers. In such cases, an owner must exercise more oversight to make sure that the lack of separation of duties does not result in fraudulent transactions.

Sales Representative A salesperson can take several steps to reduce days' sales uncollected. These include (1) decreasing the ratio of sales on account to total sales by encouraging more cash sales, (2) identifying customers most delayed in their payments and encouraging earlier payments or cash sales, and (3) applying stricter credit policies to eliminate credit sales to customers that never pay.

Key Terms

Bank reconciliation
Bank statement
Canceled checks
Cash
Cash equivalents
Cash Over and Short
Check
Check register
Committee of Sponsoring Organizations (COSO)
Days' sales uncollected
Deposit ticket
Deposits in transit
Discounts lost
Electronic funds transfer (EFT)
Gross method
Internal control system
Invoice
Invoice approval
Liquid assets
Liquidity
Net method
Outstanding checks
Petty cash
Principles of internal control
Purchase order
Purchase requisition
Receiving report
Sarbanes-Oxley Act
Section 404 (of SOX)
Signature card
Vendee
Vendor
Voucher
Voucher register
Voucher system

Multiple Choice Quiz   Answers at end of chapter

1. A company needs to replenish its $500 petty cash fund. Its petty cash box has $75 cash and petty cash receipts of $420. The journal entry to replenish the fund includes
a. A debit to Cash for $75.
b. A credit to Cash for $75.
c. A credit to Petty Cash for $420.
d. A credit to Cash Over and Short for $5.
e. A debit to Cash Over and Short for $5.

2. The following information is available for Hapley Company:
- The November 30 bank statement shows a $1,895 balance.
- The general ledger shows a $1,742 balance at November 30.
- A $795 deposit placed in the bank's night depository on November 30 does not appear on the November 30 bank statement.
- Outstanding checks amount to $638 at November 30.
- A customer's $335 note was collected by the bank in November. A collection fee of $15 was deducted by the bank and the difference deposited in Hapley's account.
- A bank service charge of $10 is deducted by the bank and appears on the November 30 bank statement.

How will the customer's note appear on Hapley's November 30 bank reconciliation?
a. $320 appears as an addition to the book balance of cash.
b. $320 appears as a deduction from the book balance of cash.
c. $320 appears as an addition to the bank balance of cash.
d. $320 appears as a deduction from the bank balance of cash.
e. $335 appears as an addition to the bank balance of cash.

3. Using the information from question 2, what is the reconciled balance on Hapley's November 30 bank reconciliation?
a. $2,052 **c.** $1,742 **e.** $1,184
b. $1,895 **d.** $2,201

4. A company had net sales of $84,000 and accounts receivable of $6,720. Its days' sales uncollected is
a. 3.2 days **c.** 230.0 days **e.** 12.5 days
b. 18.4 days **d.** 29.2 days

5[B] A company records its purchases using the net method. On August 1, it purchases merchandise on account for $6,000 with terms of 2/10, n/30. The August 1 journal entry to record this transaction includes a
a. Debit to Merchandise Inventory for $6,000.
b. Debit to Merchandise Inventory for $5,880.
c. Debit to Merchandise Inventory for $120.
d. Debit to Accounts Payable for $5,880.
e. Credit to Accounts Payable for $6,000.

A(B) *Superscript letter A (B) denotes assignments based on Appendix 6A (6B).*
Icon denotes assignments that involve decision making.

Discussion Questions

1. List the seven broad principles of internal control.
2. Internal control procedures are important in every business, but at what stage in the development of a business do they become especially critical?
3. Why should responsibility for related transactions be divided among different departments or individuals?
4. Why should the person who keeps the records of an asset not be the person responsible for its custody?
5. When a store purchases merchandise, why are individual departments not allowed to directly deal with suppliers?
6. What are the limitations of internal controls?
7. Which of the following assets—inventory, building, accounts receivable, or cash—is most liquid? Which is least liquid?
8. What is a petty cash receipt? Who should sign it?
9. Why should cash receipts be deposited on the day of receipt?
10. **Apple**'s statement of cash flows in Appendix A describes changes in cash and cash equivalents for the year ended September 28, 2013. What total amount is provided (used) by investing activities? What amount is provided (used) by financing activities? **APPLE**
11. Refer to **Google**'s financial statements in Appendix A. Identify Google's net earnings (income) for the year ended December 31, 2013. Is its net earnings equal to the increase in cash and cash equivalents for the year? Explain the difference between net earnings and the increase in cash and cash equivalents. **GOOGLE**
12. Refer to **Samsung**'s balance sheet in Appendix A. How does its cash (titled "Cash and cash equivalents") compare with its other current assets (both in amount and percent) as of December 31, 2013? Compare and assess its cash at December 31, 2013, with its cash at December 31, 2012. **Samsung**
13. **Samsung**'s balance sheet in Appendix A reports the change in cash and equivalents for the year ended December 31, 2013. Identify the cash generated (or used) by operating activities, by investing activities, and by financing (funding) activities. **Samsung**

connect

QUICK STUDY

QS 6-1
Internal control objectives
C1

An internal control system consists of all policies and procedures used to protect assets, ensure reliable accounting, promote efficient operations, and urge adherence to company policies. Evaluate each of the following statements and indicate which are true and which are false regarding the objectives of an internal control system.

____ 1. Separation of recordkeeping for assets from the custody over assets is intended to reduce theft and fraud.

____ 2. The primary objective of internal control procedures is to safeguard the business against theft from government agencies.

____ 3. The main objective of internal control procedures is best accomplished by designing an operational system with managerial policies that protect the assets from waste, fraud, and theft.

____ 4. Separating the responsibility for a transaction between two or more individuals or departments will not help prevent someone from creating a fictitious invoice and paying the money to herself or himself.

QS 6-2
Cash and equivalents
C2

Choose from the following list of terms/phrases to best complete the following statements.

a. Cash	**c.** Outstanding check	**e.** Bank reconciliation
b. Cash equivalents	**d.** Liquidity	**f.** Current assets

____ 1. The ________ category includes currency and coins along with amounts on deposit in bank accounts, checking accounts, and savings accounts.

____ 2. The term ________ refers to a company's ability to pay for its near-term obligations.

____ 3. The ________ category includes short-term, highly liquid investment assets that are readily convertible to a known cash amount and sufficiently close to their due dates so that their market value is not sensitive to interest rate changes.

QS 6-3
Internal control for cash
P1

A good system of internal control for cash provides adequate procedures for protecting both cash receipts and cash disbursements. Identify each of the following statements as either true or false regarding this protection.

____ **a.** A basic guideline for safeguarding cash is that all cash receipts be deposited weekly or monthly.
____ **b.** A voucher system of control is a control system exclusively for cash receipts.
____ **c.** A basic guideline for safeguarding cash is to separate the duties of those who have custody of cash from those who keep cash records.
____ **d.** A petty cash system is not a control procedure for safeguarding cash.

QS 6-4
Petty cash accounting
P2

1. The petty cash fund of the Brooks Agency is established at $150. At the end of the current period, the fund contained $28 and had the following receipts: film rentals, $24; refreshments for meetings, $46 (both expenditures to be classified as Entertainment Expense); postage, $30; and printing, $22. Prepare journal entries to record (*a*) establishment of the fund and (*b*) reimbursement of the fund at the end of the current period.

2. Identify the two events from the following that cause a Petty Cash account to be credited in a journal entry.

____ **a.** Fund amount is being reduced ____ **c.** Fund is being eliminated
____ **b.** Fund amount is being increased ____ **d.** Fund is being established

QS 6-5
Bank reconciliation
P3

For each of the following items *a* through *g*, indicate whether its amount (1) affects the bank or book side of a bank reconciliation, (2) represents an addition or a subtraction in a bank reconciliation, and (3) requires an adjusting journal entry.

	Bank or Book Side	Add or Subtract	Adj. Entry or Not
a. Interest on cash balance	______	______	______
b. Bank service charges	______	______	______
c. Debit memos	______	______	______
d. Outstanding checks	______	______	______
e. Credit memos	______	______	______
f. NSF checks	______	______	______
g. Outstanding deposits	______	______	______

QS 6-6
Bank reconciliation
P3

Nolan Company deposits all cash receipts on the day when they are received and it makes all cash payments by check. At the close of business on June 30, 2015, its Cash account shows a $22,352 debit balance. Nolan's June 30 bank statement shows $21,332 on deposit in the bank. Prepare a bank reconciliation for the company using the following information.

a. Outstanding checks as of June 30 total $3,713.

b. The June 30 bank statement included a $41 debit memorandum for bank services; the company has not yet recorded the cost of these services.

c. In reviewing the bank statement, a $90 check written by the company was mistakenly recorded in the company's books at $99.

d. June 30 cash receipts of $4,724 were placed in the bank's night depository after banking hours and were not recorded on the June 30 bank statement.

e. The bank statement included a $23 credit for interest earned on the cash in the bank.

QS 6-7
Reviewing bank statements
P3

An entrepreneur commented that a bank reconciliation may not be necessary as she regularly reviews her online bank statement for any unusual items and errors.

a. Describe how a bank reconciliation and an online review (or reading) of the bank statement are not equivalent.

b. Identify and explain at least two frauds or errors that would be uncovered through a bank reconciliation and that would *not* be uncovered through an online review of the bank statement.

QS 6-8
Days' sales uncollected
A1

The following annual account balances are taken from Armour Sports at December 31.

	2015	2014
Accounts receivable	$ 100,000	$ 85,000
Net sales	2,500,000	2,000,000

What is the change in the number of days' sales uncollected between years 2014 and 2015? (Round the number of days to one decimal.) According to this analysis, is the company's collection of receivables improving? Explain.

QS 6-9[A]
Documents in a voucher system
P4

Management uses a voucher system to help control and monitor cash disbursements. Which of the four documents listed below are prepared as part of a voucher system of control?

____ **a.** Purchase order ____ **b.** Outstanding check ____ **c.** Invoice ____ **d.** Voucher

QS 6-10[B]
Purchase discounts
P5

An important part of cash management is knowing when, and if, to take purchase discounts.

a. Which accounting method uses a Discounts Lost account?

b. What is the advantage of this method for management?

QS 6-11
International accounting and internal controls
C1 P1

Answer each of the following related to international accounting standards.

a. Explain how the purposes and principles of internal controls are different between accounting systems reporting under IFRS versus U.S. GAAP.

b. Cash presents special internal control challenges. How do internal controls for cash differ for accounting systems reporting under IFRS versus U.S. GAAP? How do the procedures applied differ across those two accounting systems?

connect

EXERCISES

Exercise 6-1
Analyzing internal control
C1

Franco Company is a rapidly growing start-up business. Its recordkeeper, who was hired six months ago, left town after the company's manager discovered that a large sum of money had disappeared over the past three months. An audit disclosed that the recordkeeper had written and signed several checks made payable to her fiancé and then recorded the checks as salaries expense. The fiancé, who cashed the checks but never worked for the company, left town with the recordkeeper. As a result, the company incurred an uninsured loss of $184,000. Evaluate Franco's internal control system and indicate which principles of internal control appear to have been ignored.

Exercise 6-2
Internal control recommendations
C1

What internal control procedures would you recommend in each of the following situations?

1. A concession company has one employee who sells towels, coolers, and sunglasses at the beach. Each day, the employee is given enough towels, coolers, and sunglasses to last through the day and enough cash to make change. The money is kept in a box at the stand.

2. An antique store has one employee who is given cash and sent to garage sales each weekend. The employee pays cash for any merchandise acquired that the antique store resells.

Exercise 6-3
Cash, liquidity, and return
C2

Good accounting systems help with the management and control of cash and cash equivalents.

1. Define and contrast the terms *liquid asset* and *cash equivalent.*

2. Why would companies invest their idle cash in cash equivalents?

3. Identify five principles of effective cash management.

Exercise 6-4
Control of cash receipts by mail
P1

Some of Crown Company's cash receipts from customers are received by the company with the regular mail. The company's recordkeeper opens these letters and deposits the cash received each day.

a. Identify any internal control problem(s) in this arrangement.

b. What changes to its internal control system do you recommend?

Exercise 6-5
Petty cash fund with a shortage P2

Check (2) Cr. Cash $246 and (3) Cr. Cash $50

Waupaca Company establishes a $350 petty cash fund on September 9. On September 30, the fund shows $104 in cash along with receipts for the following expenditures: transportation-in, $40; postage expenses, $123; and miscellaneous expenses, $80. The petty cashier could not account for a $3 shortage in the fund. The company uses the perpetual system in accounting for merchandise inventory. Prepare (1) the September 9 entry to establish the fund, (2) the September 30 entry to reimburse the fund, and (3) an October 1 entry to increase the fund to $400.

Exercise 6-6
Petty cash fund accounting P2

Check (3) Cr. Cash $162 & $250

Palmona Co. establishes a $200 petty cash fund on January 1. On January 8, the fund shows $38 in cash along with receipts for the following expenditures: postage, $74; transportation-in, $29; delivery expenses, $16; and miscellaneous expenses, $43. Palmona uses the perpetual system in accounting for merchandise inventory. Prepare journal entries to (1) establish the fund on January 1, (2) reimburse it on January 8, and (3) both reimburse the fund and increase it to $450 on January 8, assuming no entry in part 2. (*Hint*: Make two separate entries for part 3.)

Exercise 6-7
Voucher system
P1

The voucher system of control is designed to control cash disbursements and the acceptance of obligations.

1. The voucher system of control establishes procedures for what two processes?

2. What types of expenditures should be overseen by a voucher system of control?

3. When is the voucher initially prepared? Explain.

Exercise 6-8
Bank reconciliation and adjusting entries
P3

Prepare a table with the following headings for a monthly bank reconciliation dated September 30.

Bank Balance		Book Balance			Not Shown on the Reconciliation
Add	Deduct	Add	Deduct	Adjust	

For each item 1 through 12, place an *x* in the appropriate column to indicate whether the item should be added to or deducted from the book or bank balance, or whether it should not appear on the reconciliation. If the book balance is to be adjusted, place a *Dr.* or *Cr.* in the Adjust column to indicate whether the Cash balance should be debited or credited. At the left side of your table, number the items to correspond to the following list.

1. NSF check from customer is returned on September 25 but not yet recorded by this company.

2. Interest earned on the September cash balance in the bank.

3. Deposit made on September 5 and processed by the bank on September 6.

4. Checks written by another depositor but charged against this company's account.

5. Bank service charge for September.

6. Checks outstanding on August 31 that cleared the bank in September.

7. Check written against the company's account and cleared by the bank; erroneously not recorded by the company's recordkeeper.

8. Principal and interest on a note receivable to this company is collected by the bank but not yet recorded by the company.

9. Checks written and mailed to payees on October 2.

10. Checks written by the company and mailed to payees on September 30.

11. Night deposit made on September 30 after the bank closed.

12. Special bank charge for collection of note in part 8 on this company's behalf.

Exercise 6-9
Bank reconciliation
P3

Del Gato Clinic deposits all cash receipts on the day when they are received and it makes all cash payments by check. At the close of business on June 30, 2015, its Cash account shows an $11,589 debit balance. Del Gato Clinic's June 30 bank statement shows $10,555 on deposit in the bank. Prepare a bank reconciliation for Del Gato Clinic using the following information:

a. Outstanding checks as of June 30 total $1,829.

b. The June 30 bank statement included a $16 debit memorandum for bank services.

c. Check No. 919, listed with the canceled checks, was correctly drawn for $467 in payment of a utility bill on June 15. Del Gato Clinic mistakenly recorded it with a debit to Utilities Expense and a credit to Cash in the amount of $476.

d. The June 30 cash receipts of $2,856 were placed in the bank's night depository after banking hours and were not recorded on the June 30 bank statement.

Check Reconciled bal., $11,582

Exercise 6-10
Adjusting entries from bank reconciliation P3

Prepare the adjusting journal entries that Del Gato Clinic must record as a result of preparing the bank reconciliation in Exercise 6-9.

Exercise 6-11
Bank reconciliation
P3

Wright Company deposits all cash receipts on the day when they are received and it makes all cash payments by check. At the close of business on May 31, 2015, its Cash account shows a $27,500 debit balance. The company's May 31 bank statement shows $25,800 on deposit in the bank. Prepare a bank reconciliation for the company using the following information.

a. The May 31 bank statement included a $100 debit memorandum for bank services; the company has not yet recorded the cost of these services.

b. Outstanding checks as of May 31 total $5,600.

c. May 31 cash receipts of $6,200 were placed in the bank's night depository after banking hours and were not recorded on the May 31 bank statement.

d. In reviewing the bank statement, a $400 check written by Smith Company was mistakenly drawn against Wright's account.

e. A debit memorandum for $600 refers to a $600 NSF check from a customer; the company has not yet recorded this NSF check.

Check Reconciled bal., $26,800

Exercise 6-12
Liquid assets and accounts receivable
A1

Barga Co. reported net sales for 2014 and 2015 of $730,000 and $1,095,000, respectively. Its year-end balances of accounts receivable follow: December 31, 2014, $65,000; and December 31, 2015, $123,000.

a. Calculate its days' sales uncollected at the end of each year. Round the number of days to one decimal.

b. Evaluate and comment on any changes in the amount of liquid assets tied up in receivables.

Exercise 6-13^A
Documents in a voucher system
P4

Match each document in a voucher system in column one with its description in column two.

Document	Description
1. Purchase requisition	____ **A.** An itemized statement of goods prepared by the vendor listing the customer's name, items sold, sales prices, and terms of sale.
2. Purchase order	____ **B.** An internal file used to store documents and information to control cash disbursements and to ensure that a transaction is properly authorized and recorded.
3. Invoice	____ **C.** A document used to place an order with a vendor that authorizes the vendor to ship ordered merchandise at the stated price and terms.
4. Receiving report	____ **D.** A checklist of steps necessary for the approval of an invoice for recording and payment; also known as a check authorization.
5. Invoice approval	____ **E.** A document used by department managers to inform the purchasing department to place an order with a vendor.
6. Voucher	____ **F.** A document used to notify the appropriate persons that ordered goods have arrived, including a description of the quantities and condition of goods.

Exercise 6-14[B]
Record invoices at gross or net amounts
P5

Piere Imports uses the perpetual system in accounting for merchandise inventory and had the following transactions during the month of October. Prepare entries to record these transactions assuming that Piere Imports records invoices (*a*) at gross amounts and (*b*) at net amounts.

Oct. 2 Purchased merchandise at a $3,000 price, invoice dated October 2, terms 2/10, n/30.
10 Received a $500 credit memorandum (at full invoice price) for the return of merchandise that it purchased on October 2.
17 Purchased merchandise at a $5,400 price, invoice dated October 17, terms 2/10, n/30.
27 Paid for the merchandise purchased on October 17, less the discount.
31 Paid for the merchandise purchased on October 2. Payment was delayed because the invoice was mistakenly filed for payment today. This error caused the discount to be lost.

connect

PROBLEM SET A

Problem 6-1A
Analyzing internal control
C1

For each of these five separate cases, identify the principle(s) of internal control that is violated. Recommend what the business should do to ensure adherence to principles of internal control.

1. Chi Han records all incoming customer cash receipts for her employer and posts the customer payments to their respective accounts.
2. At Tico Company, Julia and Trevor alternate lunch hours. Julia is the petty cash custodian, but if someone needs petty cash when she is at lunch, Trevor fills in as custodian.
3. Nori Nozumi posts all patient charges and payments at the Hopeville Medical Clinic. Each night Nori backs up the computerized accounting system to a tape and stores the tape in a locked file at her desk.
4. Benedict Shales prides himself on hiring quality workers who require little supervision. As office manager, Benedict gives his employees full discretion over their tasks and for years has seen no reason to perform independent reviews of their work.
5. Carla Farah's manager has told her to reduce costs. Carla decides to raise the deductible on the plant's property insurance from $5,000 to $10,000. This cuts the property insurance premium in half. In a related move, she decides that bonding the plant's employees is a waste of money since the company has not experienced any losses due to employee theft. Carla saves the entire amount of the bonding insurance premium by dropping the bonding insurance.

Problem 6-2A
Establish, reimburse, and adjust petty cash
P2

Kiona Co. set up a petty cash fund for payments of small amounts. The following transactions involving the petty cash fund occurred in May (the last month of the company's fiscal year).

May 1 Prepared a company check for $300 to establish the petty cash fund.
15 Prepared a company check to replenish the fund for the following expenditures made since May 1.
a. Paid $88 for janitorial services.
b. Paid $53.68 for miscellaneous expenses.
c. Paid postage expenses of $53.50.
d. Paid $47.15 to *The County Gazette* (the local newspaper) for an advertisement.
e. Counted $62.15 remaining in the petty cash box.
16 Prepared a company check for $200 to increase the fund to $500.
31 The petty cashier reports that $288.20 cash remains in the fund. A company check is drawn to replenish the fund for the following expenditures made since May 15.
f. Paid postage expenses of $147.36.
g. Reimbursed the office manager for business mileage, $23.50.
h. Paid $34.75 to deliver merchandise to a customer, terms FOB destination.
31 The company decides that the May 16 increase in the fund was too large. It reduces the fund by $100, leaving a total of $400.

Required

1. Prepare journal entries (in dollars and cents) to establish the fund on May 1, to replenish it on May 15 and on May 31, and to reflect any increase or decrease in the fund balance on May 16 and May 31.

Check (1) Cr. to Cash: May 15, $237.85; May 16, $200.00

Analysis Component

2. Explain how the company's financial statements are affected if the petty cash fund is not replenished and no entry is made on May 31.

Problem 6-3A
Establish, reimburse, and increase petty cash
P2

Nakashima Gallery had the following petty cash transactions in February of the current year.

Feb. 2 Wrote a $400 check, cashed it, and gave the proceeds and the petty cashbox to Chloe Addison, the petty cashier.
5 Purchased bond paper for the copier for $14.15 that is immediately used.
9 Paid $32.50 COD shipping charges on merchandise purchased for resale, terms FOB shipping point. Nakashima uses the perpetual system to account for merchandise inventory.
12 Paid $7.95 postage to express mail a contract to a client.
14 Reimbursed Adina Sharon, the manager, $68 for business mileage on her car.
20 Purchased stationery for $67.77 that is immediately used.
23 Paid a courier $20 to deliver merchandise sold to a customer, terms FOB destination.
25 Paid $13.10 COD shipping charges on merchandise purchased for resale, terms FOB shipping point.
27 Paid $54 for postage expenses.
28 The fund had $120.42 remaining in the petty cash box. Sorted the petty cash receipts by accounts affected and exchanged them for a check to reimburse the fund for expenditures.
28 The petty cash fund amount is increased by $100 to a total of $500.

Required

1. Prepare the journal entry to establish the petty cash fund.

2. Prepare a petty cash payments report for February with these categories: delivery expense, mileage expense, postage expense, merchandise inventory (for transportation-in), and office supplies expense. Sort the payments into the appropriate categories and total the expenditures in each category.

3. Prepare the journal entries (in dollars and cents) for part 2 to both (*a*) reimburse and (*b*) increase the fund amount.

Check (3*a* & 3*b*) Total Cr. to Cash $379.58

Problem 6-4A
Prepare a bank reconciliation and record adjustments
P3

The following information is available to reconcile Branch Company's book balance of cash with its bank statement cash balance as of July 31, 2015.

a. On July 31, the company's Cash account has a $27,497 debit balance, but its July bank statement shows a $27,233 cash balance.

b. Check No. 3031 for $1,482 and Check No. 3040 for $558 were outstanding on the June 30 bank reconciliation. Check No. 3040 is listed with the July canceled checks, but Check No. 3031 is not. Also, Check No. 3065 for $382 and Check No. 3069 for $2,281, both written in July, are not among the canceled checks on the July 31 statement.

c. In comparing the canceled checks on the bank statement with the entries in the accounting records, it is found that Check No. 3056 for July rent was correctly written and drawn for $1,270 but was erroneously entered in the accounting records as $1,250.

d. A credit memorandum enclosed with the July bank statement indicates the bank collected $8,000 cash on a noninterest-bearing note for Branch, deducted a $45 collection fee, and credited the remainder to its account. Branch had not recorded this event before receiving the statement.

e. A debit memorandum for $805 lists a $795 NSF check plus a $10 NSF charge. The check had been received from a customer, Evan Shaw. Branch has not yet recorded this check as NSF.

f. Enclosed with the July statement is a $25 debit memorandum for bank services. It has not yet been recorded because no previous notification had been received.

g. Branch's July 31 daily cash receipts of $11,514 were placed in the bank's night depository on that date but do not appear on the July 31 bank statement.

Required

1. Prepare the bank reconciliation for this company as of July 31, 2015.

2. Prepare the journal entries necessary to bring the company's book balance of cash into conformity with the reconciled cash balance as of July 31, 2015.

Check (1) Reconciled balance, $34,602; (2) Cr. Notes Receivable $8,000

Analysis Component

3. Assume that the July 31, 2015, bank reconciliation for this company is prepared and some items are treated incorrectly. For each of the following errors, explain the effect of the error on (i) the adjusted bank statement cash balance and (ii) the adjusted Cash account book balance.

a. The company's unadjusted Cash account balance of $27,497 is listed on the reconciliation as $27,947.

b. The bank's collection of the $8,000 note less the $45 collection fee is added to the bank statement cash balance on the reconciliation.

Problem 6-5A
Prepare a bank reconciliation and record adjustments
P3

Chavez Company most recently reconciled its bank statement and book balances of cash on August 31 and it reported two checks outstanding, No. 5888 for $1,028.05 and No. 5893 for $494.25. The following information is available for its September 30, 2015, reconciliation.

From the September 30 Bank Statement

PREVIOUS BALANCE	TOTAL CHECKS AND DEBITS	TOTAL DEPOSITS AND CREDITS	CURRENT BALANCE
16,800.45	9,620.05	11,272.85	18,453.25

CHECKS AND DEBITS			DEPOSITS AND CREDITS		DAILY BALANCE	
Date	No.	Amount	Date	Amount	Date	Amount
09/03	5888	1,028.05	09/05	1,103.75	08/31	16,800.45
09/04	5902	719.90	09/12	2,226.90	09/03	15,772.40
09/07	5901	1,824.25	09/21	4,093.00	09/04	15,052.50
09/17		600.25 NSF	09/25	2,351.70	09/05	16,156.25
09/20	5905	937.00	09/30	12.50 IN	09/07	14,332.00
09/22	5903	399.10	09/30	1,485.00 CM	09/12	16,558.90
09/22	5904	2,090.00			09/17	15,958.65
09/28	5907	213.85			09/20	15,021.65
09/29	5909	1,807.65			09/21	19,114.65
					09/22	16,625.55
					09/25	18,977.25
					09/28	18,763.40
					09/29	16,955.75
					09/30	18,453.25

From Chavez Company's Accounting Records

Cash Receipts Deposited

Date			Cash Debit
Sept.	5		1,103.75
	12		2,226.90
	21		4,093.00
	25		2,351.70
	30		1,682.75
			11,458.10

Cash Disbursements

Check No.		Cash Credit
5901		1,824.25
5902		719.90
5903		399.10
5904		2,060.00
5905		937.00
5906		982.30
5907		213.85
5908		388.00
5909		1,807.65
		9,332.05

Cash — Acct. No. 101

Date		Explanation	PR	Debit	Credit	Balance
Aug.	31	Balance				15,278.15
Sept.	30	Total receipts	R12	11,458.10		26,736.25
	30	Total disbursements	D23		9,332.05	17,404.20

Additional Information

Check No. 5904 is correctly drawn for $2,090 to pay for computer equipment; however, the recordkeeper misread the amount and entered it in the accounting records with a debit to Computer Equipment and a credit to Cash of $2,060. The NSF check shown in the statement was originally received from a customer, S. Nilson, in payment of her account. Its return has not yet been recorded by the company. The credit memorandum is from the collection of a $1,500 note for Chavez Company by the bank. The bank deducted a $15 collection fee. The collection and fee are not yet recorded.

Required

1. Prepare the September 30, 2015, bank reconciliation for this company.
2. Prepare the journal entries (in dollars and cents) to adjust the book balance of cash to the reconciled balance.

Check (1) Reconciled balance, $18,271.45; (2) Cr. Notes Receivable $1,500.00

Analysis Component

3. The bank statement reveals that some of the prenumbered checks in the sequence are missing. Describe three situations that could explain this.

PROBLEM SET B

Problem 6-1B
Analyzing internal control
C1

For each of these five separate cases, identify the principle(s) of internal control that is violated. Recommend what the business should do to ensure adherence to principles of internal control.

1. Latisha Tally is the company's computer specialist and oversees its computerized payroll system. Her boss recently asked her to put password protection on all office computers. Latisha has put a password in place that allows only the boss access to the file where pay rates are changed and personnel are added or deleted from the payroll.
2. Marker Theater has a computerized order-taking system for its tickets. The system is active all week and backed up every Friday night.
3. Sutton Company has two employees handling acquisitions of inventory. One employee places purchase orders and pays vendors. The second employee receives the merchandise.
4. The owner of Super Pharmacy uses a check protector to perforate checks, making it difficult for anyone to alter the amount of the check. The check protector is on the owner's desk in an office that contains company checks and is normally unlocked.
5. Lavina Company is a small business that has separated the duties of cash receipts and cash disbursements. The employee responsible for cash disbursements reconciles the bank account monthly.

Problem 6-2B
Establishing, reimbursing, and adjusting petty cash
P2

Moya Co. establishes a petty cash fund for payments of small amounts. The following transactions involving the petty cash fund occurred in January (the last month of the company's fiscal year).

Jan. 3 A company check for $150 is written and made payable to the petty cashier to establish the petty cash fund.

14 A company check is written to replenish the fund for the following expenditures made since January 3.
- *a.* Purchased office supplies for $14.29 that are immediately used up.
- *b.* Paid $19.60 COD shipping charges on merchandise purchased for resale, terms FOB shipping point. Moya uses the perpetual system to account for inventory.
- *c.* Paid $38.57 to All-Tech for minor repairs to a computer.
- *d.* Paid $12.82 for items classified as miscellaneous expenses.
- *e.* Counted $62.28 remaining in the petty cash box.

15 Prepared a company check for $50 to increase the fund to $200.

31 The petty cashier reports that $17.35 remains in the fund. A company check is written to replenish the fund for the following expenditures made since January 14.
- *f.* Paid $50 to *The Smart Shopper* for an advertisement in January's newsletter.
- *g.* Paid $48.19 for postage expenses.
- *h.* Paid $78 to Smooth Delivery for delivery of merchandise, terms FOB destination.

31 The company decides that the January 15 increase in the fund was too little. It increases the fund by another $50, leaving a total of $250.

Required

1. Prepare journal entries (in dollars and cents) to establish the fund on January 3, to replenish it on January 14 and January 31, and to reflect any increase or decrease in the fund balance on January 15 and 31.

Check (1) Cr. to Cash: Jan. 14, $87.72; Jan. 31 (total), $232.65

Analysis Component

2. Explain how the company's financial statements are affected if the petty cash fund is not replenished and no entry is made on January 31.

Problem 6-3B
Establish, reimburse, and increase petty cash
P2

Blues Music Center had the following petty cash transactions in March of the current year.

March	5	Wrote a $250 check, cashed it, and gave the proceeds and the petty cashbox to Jen Rouse, the petty cashier.
	6	Paid $12.50 COD shipping charges on merchandise purchased for resale, terms FOB shipping point. Blues uses the perpetual system to account for merchandise inventory.
	11	Paid $10.75 delivery charges on merchandise sold to a customer, terms FOB destination.
	12	Purchased file folders for $14.13 that are immediately used.
	14	Reimbursed Bob Geldof, the manager, $11.65 for office supplies purchased and used.
	18	Purchased printer paper for $20.54 that is immediately used.
	27	Paid $45.10 COD shipping charges on merchandise purchased for resale, terms FOB shipping point.
	28	Paid postage expenses of $18.
	30	Reimbursed Geldof $56.80 for business car mileage.
	31	Cash of $61.53 remained in the fund. Sorted the petty cash receipts by accounts affected and exchanged them for a check to reimburse the fund for expenditures.
	31	The petty cash fund amount is increased by $50 to a total of $300.

Required

1. Prepare the journal entry to establish the petty cash fund.
2. Prepare a petty cash payments report for March with these categories: delivery expense, mileage expense, postage expense, merchandise inventory (for transportation-in), and office supplies expense. Sort the payments into the appropriate categories and total the expenses in each category.
3. Prepare the journal entries (in dollars and cents) for part 2 to both (*a*) reimburse and (*b*) increase the fund amount.

Check (2) Total expenses $189.47

(3*a* & 3*b*) Total Cr. to Cash $238.47

Problem 6-4B
Prepare a bank reconciliation and record adjustments
P3

The following information is available to reconcile Severino Co.'s book balance of cash with its bank statement cash balance as of December 31, 2015.

a. The December 31 cash balance according to the accounting records is $32,878.30, and the bank statement cash balance for that date is $46,822.40.

b. Check No. 1273 for $4,589.30 and Check No. 1282 for $400, both written and entered in the accounting records in December, are not among the canceled checks. Two checks, No. 1231 for $2,289 and No. 1242 for $410.40, were outstanding on the most recent November 30 reconciliation. Check No. 1231 is listed with the December canceled checks, but Check No. 1242 is not.

c. When the December checks are compared with entries in the accounting records, it is found that Check No. 1267 had been correctly drawn for $3,456 to pay for office supplies but was erroneously entered in the accounting records as $3,465.

d. Two debit memoranda are enclosed with the statement and are unrecorded at the time of the reconciliation. One debit memorandum is for $762.50 and dealt with an NSF check for $745 received from a customer, Titus Industries, in payment of its account. The bank assessed a $17.50 fee for processing it. The second debit memorandum is a $99 charge for check printing. Severino did not record these transactions before receiving the statement.

e. A credit memorandum indicates that the bank collected $19,000 cash on a note receivable for the company, deducted a $20 collection fee, and credited the balance to the company's Cash account. Severino did not record this transaction before receiving the statement.

f. Severino's December 31 daily cash receipts of $9,583.10 were placed in the bank's night depository on that date but do not appear on the December 31 bank statement.

Required

1. Prepare the bank reconciliation for this company as of December 31, 2015.
2. Prepare the journal entries (in dollars and cents) necessary to bring the company's book balance of cash into conformity with the reconciled cash balance as of December 31, 2015.

Check (1) Reconciled balance, $51,005.80; (2) Cr. Notes Receivable $19,000.00

Analysis Component

3. Explain the nature of the communications conveyed by a bank when the bank sends the depositor (*a*) a debit memorandum and (*b*) a credit memorandum.

Problem 6-5B
Prepare a bank reconciliation and record adjustments
P3

Shamara Systems most recently reconciled its bank balance on April 30 and reported two checks outstanding at that time, No. 1771 for $781 and No. 1780 for $1,425.90. The following information is available for its May 31, 2015, reconciliation.

From the May 31 Bank Statement

PREVIOUS BALANCE	TOTAL CHECKS AND DEBITS	TOTAL DEPOSITS AND CREDITS	CURRENT BALANCE
18,290.70	13,094.80	16,566.80	21,762.70

CHECKS AND DEBITS			DEPOSITS AND CREDITS		DAILY BALANCE	
Date	No.	Amount	Date	Amount	Date	Amount
05/01	1771	781.00	05/04	2,438.00	04/30	18,290.70
05/02	1783	382.50	05/14	2,898.00	05/01	17,509.70
05/04	1782	1,285.50	05/22	1,801.80	05/02	17,127.20
05/11	1784	1,449.60	05/25	7,350.00 CM	05/04	18,279.70
05/18		431.80 NSF	05/26	2,079.00	05/11	16,830.10
05/25	1787	8,032.50			05/14	19,728.10
05/26	1785	63.90			05/18	19,296.30
05/29	1788	654.00			05/22	21,098.10
05/31		14.00 SC			05/25	20,415.60
					05/26	22,430.70
					05/29	21,776.70
					05/31	21,762.70

From Shamara Systems's Accounting Records

Cash Receipts Deposited

Date			Cash Debit
May	4		2,438.00
	14		2,898.00
	22		1,801.80
	26		2,079.00
	31		2,727.30
			11,944.10

Cash Disbursements

Check No.		Cash Credit
1782		1,285.50
1783		382.50
1784		1,449.60
1785		63.90
1786		353.10
1787		8,032.50
1788		644.00
1789		639.50
		12,850.60

Cash — Acct. No. 101

Date		Explanation	PR	Debit	Credit	Balance
Apr.	30	Balance				16,083.80
May	31	Total receipts	R7	11,944.10		28,027.90
	31	Total disbursements	D8		12,850.60	15,177.30

Additional Information

Check No. 1788 is correctly drawn for $654 to pay for May utilities; however, the recordkeeper misread the amount and entered it in the accounting records with a debit to Utilities Expense and a credit to Cash for $644. The bank paid and deducted the correct amount. The NSF check shown in the statement was originally received from a customer, W. Sox, in payment of her account. The company has not yet recorded its return. The credit memorandum is from a $7,400 note that the bank collected for the company. The bank deducted a $50 collection fee and deposited the remainder in the company's account. The collection and fee have not yet been recorded.

Required

Check (1) Reconciled balance, $22,071.50; (2) Cr. Notes Receivable $7,400.00

1. Prepare the May 31, 2015, bank reconciliation for Shamara Systems.
2. Prepare the journal entries (in dollars and cents) to adjust the book balance of cash to the reconciled balance.

Analysis Component

3. The bank statement reveals that some of the prenumbered checks in the sequence are missing. Describe three possible situations to explain this.

SERIAL PROBLEM

Business Solutions

P3

(This serial problem began in Chapter 1 and continues through most of the book. If previous chapter segments were not completed, the serial problem can begin at this point. It is helpful, but not necessary, to use the Working Papers that accompany the book.)

SP 6 Santana Rey receives the March bank statement for Business Solutions on April 11, 2016. The March 31 bank statement shows an ending cash balance of $67,566. A comparison of the bank statement with the general ledger Cash account, No. 101, reveals the following.

a. S. Rey notices that the bank erroneously cleared a $500 check against her account in March that she did not issue. The check documentation included with the bank statement shows that this check was actually issued by a company named Business Systems.

b. On March 25, the bank issued a $50 debit memorandum for the safety deposit box that Business Solutions agreed to rent from the bank beginning March 25.

c. On March 26, the bank issued a $102 debit memorandum for printed checks that Business Solutions ordered from the bank.

d. On March 31, the bank issued a credit memorandum for $33 interest earned on Business Solutions's checking account for the month of March.

e. S. Rey notices that the check she issued for $128 on March 31, 2016, has not yet cleared the bank.

f. S. Rey verifies that all deposits made in March do appear on the March bank statement.

g. The general ledger Cash account, No. 101, shows an ending cash balance per books of $68,057 as of March 31 (prior to any reconciliation).

Required

Check (1) Adj. bank bal. $67,938

1. Prepare a bank reconciliation for Business Solutions for the month ended March 31, 2016.
2. Prepare any necessary adjusting entries. Use Miscellaneous Expenses, No. 677, for any bank charges. Use Interest Revenue, No. 404, for any interest earned on the checking account for the month of March.

GL GENERAL LEDGER PROBLEM

Available in Connect

Connect | ACCOUNTING

The **General Ledger** tool in *Connect* automates several of the procedural steps in the accounting cycle so that the financial professional can focus on the impacts of each transaction on the various financial reports.

GL 6-1 General Ledger assignment GL 6-1, based on Problem 6-2A, focuses on transactions related to the petty cash fund and highlights the impact each transaction has on net income, if any. Prepare the journal entries related to the petty cash fund and assess the impact of each transaction on the company's net income, if any.

Beyond the Numbers

REPORTING IN ACTION
C2 A1

APPLE

BTN 6-1 Refer to **Apple**'s financial statements in Appendix A to answer the following.

1. For both fiscal years ended September 28, 2013, and September 29, 2012, identify the total amount of cash and cash equivalents. Determine the percent (rounded to one decimal) that this amount represents of total current assets, total current liabilities, total shareholders' equity, and total assets for both years. Comment on any trends.
2. For fiscal years ended September 28, 2013, and September 29, 2012, use the information in the statement of cash flows to determine the percent change (rounded to one decimal) between the beginning and ending year amounts of cash and cash equivalents.
3. Compute the days' sales uncollected (rounded to two decimals) as of September 28, 2013, and September 29, 2012. Has the collection of receivables improved? Are accounts receivable an important asset for Apple? Explain.

Fast Forward

4. Access Apple's financial statements for fiscal years ending after September 28, 2013, from its website (Apple.com) or the SEC's EDGAR database (www.SEC.gov). Recompute its days' sales uncollected for years ending after September 28, 2013. Compare this to the days' sales uncollected for fiscal years ended September 28, 2013, and September 29, 2012.

COMPARATIVE ANALYSIS
A1

APPLE
GOOGLE

BTN 6-2 Key comparative figures for **Apple** and **Google** follow.

	Apple		Google	
($ millions)	Current Year	Prior Year	Current Year	Prior Year
Accounts receivable	$ 13,102	$ 10,930	$ 8,882	$ 7,885
Net sales	170,910	156,508	59,825	50,175

Required

Compute days' sales uncollected (rounded to two decimals) for these companies for each of the two years shown. Comment on any trends for the companies. Which company has the largest percent change (rounded to two decimals) in days' sales uncollected?

ETHICS CHALLENGE
C1

BTN 6-3 Harriet Knox, Ralph Patton, and Marcia Diamond work for a family physician, Dr. Gwen Conrad, who is in private practice. Dr. Conrad is knowledgeable about office management practices and has segregated the cash receipt duties as follows. Knox opens the mail and prepares a triplicate list of money received. She sends one copy of the list to Patton, the cashier, who deposits the receipts daily in the bank. Diamond, the recordkeeper, receives a copy of the list and posts payments to patients' accounts. About once a month the office clerks have an expensive lunch they pay for as follows. First, Patton endorses a patient's check in Dr. Conrad's name and cashes it at the bank. Knox then destroys the remittance advice accompanying the check. Finally, Diamond posts payment to the customer's account as a miscellaneous credit. The three justify their actions by their relatively low pay and knowledge that Dr. Conrad will likely never miss the money.

Required

1. Who is the best person in Dr. Conrad's office to reconcile the bank statement?
2. Would a bank reconciliation uncover this office fraud?
3. What are some procedures to detect this type of fraud?
4. Suggest additional internal controls that Dr. Conrad could implement.

COMMUNICATING IN PRACTICE

P5

BTN 6-4[B] Assume you are a business consultant. The owner of a company sends you an e-mail expressing concern that the company is not taking advantage of its discounts offered by vendors. The company currently uses the gross method of recording purchases. The owner is considering a review of all invoices and payments from the previous period. Due to the volume of purchases, however, the owner recognizes that this is time-consuming and costly. The owner seeks your advice about monitoring purchase discounts in the future. Provide a response in memorandum form.

TAKING IT TO THE NET

C1 P1

BTN 6-5 Visit the Association of Certified Fraud Examiners website at **acfe.com**. Find and open the file "2014 Report to the Nation." Read the two-page Executive Summary and fill in the following blanks. (The report is under its *Fraud Resources* tab or use the *Search* tab.)

1. The median loss caused by the frauds in our study was ______. Additionally, ______ of the cases involved losses of at least $1 million.
2. The typical organization loses ______ of revenues each year to fraud; this translates to a potential projected global fraud loss of nearly ______.
3. The median duration—the amount of time from when the fraud commenced until it was detected—for the fraud cases reported to us was ______.
4. Asset misappropriations are the most common fraud, occurring in ______ of the cases in our study, as well as the least costly, causing a median loss of ______.
5. Only ______ of cases involved financial statement fraud, but those cases had the greatest financial impact, with a median loss of ______. Corruption schemes fell in the middle in terms of both frequency (______ of cases) and median loss (______).
6. Over ______ of all cases were detected by a tip—more than twice the rate of any other detection method.
7. Owners/executives only accounted for ______ of all cases, but they caused a median loss of ______. Employees committed ______ of occupational frauds but only caused a median loss of ______. Managers ranked in the middle, committing ______ of frauds with a median loss of ______.
8. Approximately ______ of the frauds in our study were committed by individuals working in one of seven departments: accounting, operations, sales, executive/upper management, customer service, purchasing, and finance.
9. The vast majority of occupational fraudsters are first-time offenders; only ______ had been convicted of a fraud-related offense prior to committing the crimes in our study. Furthermore, ______ of fraudsters had never previously been punished or terminated by an employer for fraud-related conduct.

TEAMWORK IN ACTION

C1

BTN 6-6 Organize the class into teams. Each team must prepare a list of 10 internal controls a consumer could observe in a typical retail department store. When called upon, the team's spokesperson must be prepared to share controls identified by the team that have not been shared by another team's spokesperson.

ENTREPRENEURIAL DECISION

C1 P1

BTN 6-7 Review the opening feature of this chapter that highlights Todd Masonis and Cameron Ring and their company **Dandelion Chocolate**. Their company has one retail store with plans to open at least one additional kiosk in the Ferry Building in San Francisco. Other retail outlets and expansion plans may be in the works.

Required

1. List the seven principles of internal control and explain how a retail outlet might implement each of the principles in its store.
2. Do you believe that a retail outlet will need to add controls to the business as it expands? Explain.

BTN 6-8 Visit an area of your college that serves the student community with either products or services. Some examples are food services, libraries, and bookstores. Identify and describe between four and eight internal controls being implemented.

HITTING THE ROAD
C1

BTN 6-9 The following information is from **Samsung** (www.Samsung.com or its financial statements in Appendix A), which is a leading manufacturer of consumer electronic products.

GLOBAL DECISION
C2 A1

Samsung

₩ in millions	Current Year	Prior Year
Cash	₩ 16,284,780	₩ 18,791,460
Accounts receivable	27,875,934	26,674,596
Current assets	110,760,271	87,269,017
Total assets	214,075,018	181,071,570
Current liabilities	51,315,409	46,933,052
Shareholders' equity	150,016,010	121,480,206
Net sales	228,692,667	201,103,613

Required

1. For each year, compute the percentage (rounded to one decimal) that cash represents of current assets, total assets, current liabilities, and shareholders' equity. Comment on any trends in these percentages.
2. Determine the percentage change (rounded to one decimal) between the current and prior year cash balances.
3. Compute the days' sales uncollected (rounded to one decimal) at the end of both the current year and the prior year. Has the collection of receivables improved? Explain.

ANSWERS TO MULTIPLE CHOICE QUIZ

1. e; The entry follows.

Debits to expenses (or assets)	420	
Cash Over and Short	5	
Cash		425

2. a; recognizes cash collection of note by bank.
3. a; the bank reconciliation follows.

Bank Reconciliation November 30			
Balance per bank statement	$1,895	Balance per books	$1,742
Add: Deposit in transit	795	Add: Note collected less fee	320
Deduct: Outstanding checks	(638)	Deduct: Service charge	(10)
Reconciled balance	$2,052	Reconciled balance	$2,052

4. d; ($6,720/$84,000) × 365 = 29.2 days
5. b; The entry follows.

Merchandise Inventory*	5,880	
Accounts Payable		5,880

*$6,000 × 98%

chapter 7

Accounting for Receivables

Chapter Preview

ACCOUNTS RECEIVABLE	NOTES RECEIVABLE	DISPOSAL AND ANALYSIS OF RECEIVABLES
C1 Recognizing accounts receivable	**C2** Computing maturity and interest	**C3** Selling and pledging receivables
P1 Valuing accounts receivable	Recognizing notes receivable	**A1** Assessing accounts receivable turnover
P2 Estimating and recording bad debts	**P3** Valuing and settling notes receivable	

Learning Objectives

CONCEPTUAL

C1 Describe accounts receivable and how they occur and are recorded.

C2 Describe a note receivable, the computation of its maturity date, and the recording of its existence.

C3 Explain how receivables can be converted to cash before maturity.

ANALYTICAL

A1 Compute accounts receivable turnover and use it to help assess financial condition.

PROCEDURAL

P1 Apply the direct write-off method to account for accounts receivable.

P2 Apply the allowance method and estimate uncollectibles based on sales and accounts receivable.

P3 Record the honoring and dishonoring of a note and adjustments for interest.

Courtesy of Skai Blue Media

PR Maven

"Love what you do, live what you love"

—Rakia Reynolds

PHILADELPHIA—"My parents were blue-collar workers and told me I could reach for the stars and do anything I wanted to do," explains Rakia Reynolds. With that backdrop, Rakia set out on a journey, a journey that included work as a college residential advisor, TV producer, and magazine editorial writer. "I want to be living proof that you can do everything you put your mind to."

Rakia eventually put her mind to launching **Skai Blue Media** (**SkaiBlueMedia.com**), a multimedia public relations agency with an emphasis on lifestyle, technology, and fashion. As sales grew, she struggled. "I wish I could have found someone who could have guided me," says Rakia, "especially concerning the financial aspects of running a business." She spent many evenings and weekends learning about accounting and managing expenses. "It's exhausting for sure," admits Rakia. "But it's also super rewarding." Rakia's attention to detail carried over when she learned to monitor receivables, including decisions on credit sales and policies for extending credit.

"I was always more intrigued by the business side," explains Rakia. That business focus helped ensure that her credit sales were extended to customers in good credit standing. Rakia knows her clients, including who pays and when. Explains Rakia, we understand our customers—inside and out—including cash payment patterns that allow us to estimate uncollectibles and minimize bad debts. "Look at financial projections," insists Rakia. "Looking at projections is one of the key things for growing your business." Adding clients who are projected to pay is part of the recipe for success.

A commitment to quality customers is propelling Skai Blue Media's sales and shattering Rakia's most optimistic goals. "Every year you want to be bigger, you want to be better, you want to be more effective and efficient," explains Rakia. "When I took a risk, it was not a great feeling." Accordingly, Rakia manages all accounts and notes receivables, and reviews the allowance for doubtful accounts regularly. "Reconcile finances and cash flows," says Rakia. "See where you can improve."

When asked what her favorite tip is for a budding entrepreneur, Rakia says: "QuickBooks, QuickBooks, and QuickBooks." She explains that accounting provides discipline for decisions and the information to make them. "When you're an entrepreneur, it is the most lonely road."

Sources: *Skai Blue Media website,* January 2015; *Startup Collective,* 2013; *IdeaMensch,* 2012; *Empowerment Group,* September 2011; *Rad Girls,* March 2014

ACCOUNTS RECEIVABLE

C1 Describe accounts receivable and how they occur and are recorded.

A *receivable* is an amount due from another party. The two most common receivables are accounts receivable and notes receivable. Other receivables include interest receivable, rent receivable, tax refund receivable, and receivables from employees. **Accounts receivable** are amounts due from customers for credit sales. This section begins by describing how accounts receivable occur. It includes receivables that occur when customers use credit cards issued by third parties and when a company gives credit directly to customers. When a company does extend credit directly to customers, it (1) maintains a separate account receivable for each customer and (2) accounts for bad debts from credit sales.

Recognizing Accounts Receivable

Accounts receivable occur from credit sales to customers. The amount of credit sales has increased in recent years, reflecting several factors including an efficient financial system. Retailers such as **Costco** and **Best Buy** hold millions of dollars in accounts receivable. Similar amounts are held by wholesalers such as **SUPERVALU** and **SYSCO**. Exhibit 7.1 shows recent dollar amounts of receivables and their percent of total assets for four well-known companies.

EXHIBIT 7.1

Accounts Receivable for Selected Companies

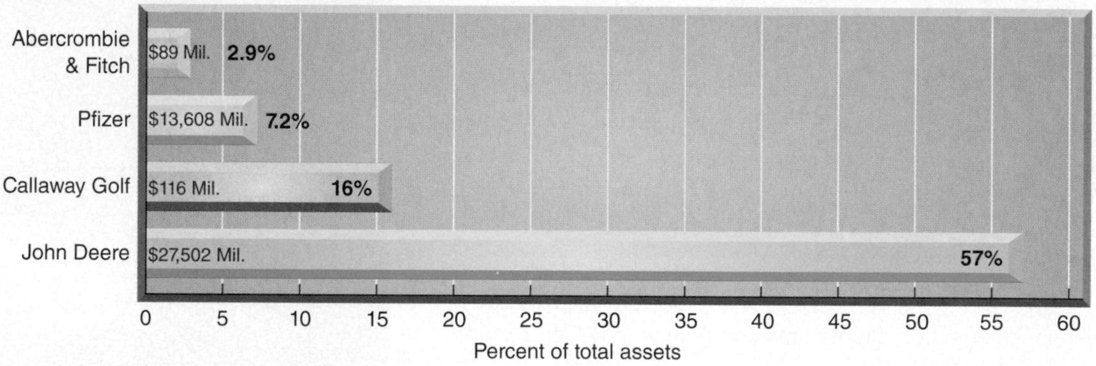

Sales on Credit Credit sales are recorded by increasing (debiting) Accounts Receivable. A company must also maintain a separate account for each customer that tracks how much that customer purchases, has already paid, and still owes. This information provides the basis for sending bills to customers and for other business analyses. To maintain this information, companies that extend credit directly to their customers keep a separate account receivable for each one of them. The general ledger continues to have a single Accounts Receivable account (called a *control* account) along with the other financial statement accounts, but a supplementary record is created to maintain a separate account for each customer. This supplementary record is called the *accounts receivable ledger* (or *accounts receivable subsidiary ledger*).

Exhibit 7.2 shows the relation between the Accounts Receivable account in the general ledger and its individual customer accounts in the accounts receivable ledger for TechCom, a small electronics wholesaler. This exhibit reports a $3,000 ending balance of TechCom's accounts receivable for June 30. TechCom's transactions are mainly in cash, but it has two major credit

EXHIBIT 7.2

General Ledger and the Accounts Receivable Ledger (before July 1 transactions)

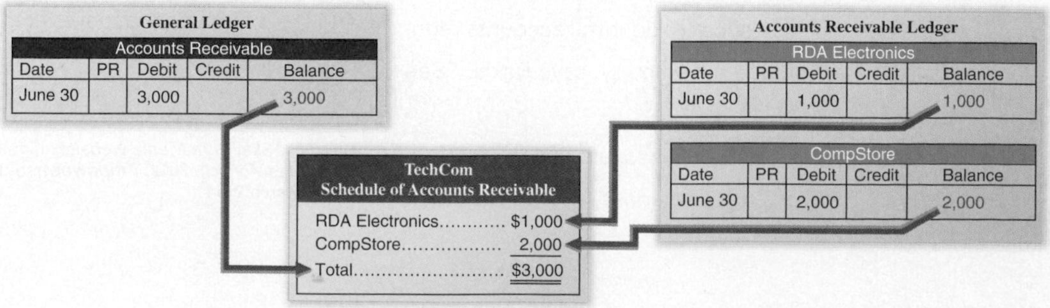

customers: CompStore and RDA Electronics. Its *schedule of accounts receivable* shows that the $3,000 balance of the Accounts Receivable account in the general ledger equals the total of its two customers' balances in the accounts receivable ledger.

To see how accounts receivable from credit sales are recognized in the accounting records, we look at two transactions on July 1 between TechCom and its credit customers—see Exhibit 7.3. The first is a credit sale of $950 to CompStore. A credit sale is posted with both a debit to the Accounts Receivable account in the general ledger and a debit to the customer account in the accounts receivable ledger. The second transaction is a collection of $720 from RDA Electronics from a prior credit sale. Cash receipts from a credit customer are posted with a credit to the Accounts Receivable account in the general ledger and flow through to credit the customer account in the accounts receivable ledger. (Posting debits or credits to Accounts Receivable in two separate ledgers does not violate the requirement that debits equal credits. The equality of debits and credits is maintained in the general ledger. The accounts receivable ledger is a *supplementary* record providing information on each customer.)

EXHIBIT 7.3

Accounts Receivable Transactions

July 1	Accounts Receivable—CompStore................	950	
	Sales		950
	*To record credit sales.**		
July 1	Cash	720	
	Accounts Receivable—RDA Electronics		720
	To record collection of credit sales.		

Assets = Liabilities + Equity
+ 950 +950

Assets = Liabilities + Equity
+720
−720

* We omit the entry to Dr. Cost of Sales and Cr. Merchandise Inventory to focus on sales and receivables.

Exhibit 7.4 shows the general ledger and the accounts receivable ledger after recording the two July 1 transactions. The general ledger shows the effects of the sale, the collection, and the resulting balance of $3,230. These events are also reflected in the individual customer accounts: RDA Electronics has an ending balance of $280, and CompStore's ending balance is $2,950. The $3,230 sum of the individual accounts equals the debit balance of the Accounts Receivable account in the general ledger.

EXHIBIT 7.4

General Ledger and the Accounts Receivable Ledger (after July 1 transactions)

General Ledger

Accounts Receivable

Date	PR	Debit	Credit	Balance
June 30		3,000		3,000
July 1		950		3,950
July 1			720	3,230

Accounts Receivable Ledger

RDA Electronics

Date	PR	Debit	Credit	Balance
June 30		1,000		1,000
July 1			720	280

CompStore

Date	PR	Debit	Credit	Balance
June 30		2,000		2,000
July 1		950		2,950

TechCom
Schedule of Accounts Receivable

RDA Electronics............	$ 280
CompStore..................	2,950
Total........................	$3,230

Like TechCom, many large retailers such as **Target** and **JCPenney** sell on credit. Many also maintain their own credit cards to grant credit to approved customers and to earn interest on any balance not paid within a specified period of time. This allows them to avoid the fee charged by credit card companies. The entries in this case are the same as those for TechCom except for the possibility of added interest revenue. If a customer owes interest on a bill, we debit Interest Receivable and credit Interest Revenue for that amount. (Many retailers require clerks to ask customers during checkout if they wish to apply for a store credit card—sweeteners are often used such as: *save 10% off today's purchases if you apply now.*)

Ken Reid/Photographer's Choice/Getty Images

Credit Card Sales Many companies allow their customers to pay for products and services using third-party credit cards such as **Visa**, **MasterCard**, or **American Express**, and debit cards (also called ATM or bank cards). This practice gives customers the ability to make purchases without cash or checks. Once credit is established with a credit card company or bank, the customer does not have to open an account with each store. Customers using these cards can make single monthly payments instead of several payments to different creditors and can defer their payments.

Point: Visa USA now transacts more than $1 trillion from its credit, debit, and prepaid cards.

Many sellers allow customers to use third-party credit cards and debit cards instead of granting credit directly for several reasons. First, the seller does not have to evaluate each customer's credit standing or make decisions about who gets credit and how much. Second, the seller avoids the risk of extending credit to customers who cannot or do not pay. This risk is transferred to the card company. Third, the seller typically receives cash from the card company sooner than had it granted credit directly to customers. Fourth, a variety of credit options for customers offers a potential increase in sales volume. **Sears** historically offered credit only to customers using a Sears card but later changed its policy to permit customers to charge purchases to third-party credit card companies in a desire to increase sales. It reported: "SearsCharge increased its share of Sears retail sales even as the company expanded the payment options available to its customers with the acceptance . . . of Visa, MasterCard, and American Express in addition to the [Sears] Card."

There are guidelines for how companies account for credit card and debit card sales. Some credit cards, but nearly all debit cards, credit a seller's Cash account immediately upon deposit, via electronic funds transfer. The majority of credit cards, however, require the seller to remit a copy electronically of each receipt to the card company. Until payment is received, the seller has an account receivable from the card company. In both cases, the seller pays a fee for services provided by the card company, often ranging from 1% to 5% of card sales. This charge is deducted from the credit to the seller's account or the cash payment to the seller. (Many retailers accept MasterCard and Visa, but not American Express. The reason is that American Express usually charges retailers a higher percentage fee than other credit card companies.)

Decision Insight

Debit Card vs. Credit Card A buyer's debit card purchase reduces the buyer's cash account balance at the card company, which is often a bank. Since the buyer's cash account balance is a liability (with a credit balance) for the card company to the buyer, the card company would debit that account for a buyer's purchase—hence, the term *debit card.* A credit card reflects authorization by the card company of a line of credit for the buyer with preset interest rates and payment terms—hence, the term *credit card.* Most card companies waive interest charges if the buyer pays its balance each month. ■

Point: Web merchants pay twice as much in credit card association fees as other retailers because they suffer 10 times as much fraud.

The procedures used in accounting for credit card sales depend on whether cash is received immediately on deposit or cash receipt is delayed until the credit card company makes the payment.

Cash Received Immediately on Deposit To illustrate, if TechCom has $100 of credit card sales with a 4% fee, and its $96 cash is received immediately on deposit, the entry is

Assets = Liabilities + Equity
+96 +100
−4

July 15	Cash	96	
	Credit Card Expense	4	
	Sales		100
	*To record credit card sales less a 4% credit card expense.**		

* We omit the entry to Dr. Cost of Sales and Cr. Merchandise Inventory to focus on credit card expense.

Point: *Expense recognition principle* requires that we record credit card expense when we record sales.

Cash Received Sometime after Deposit However, if instead TechCom must remit electronically the credit card sales receipts to the credit card company and wait for the $96 cash payment, the entry on the date of sale is

Assets = Liabilities + Equity
+96 +100
−4

July 15	**Accounts Receivable—Credit Card Co.**	96	
	Credit Card Expense	4	
	Sales		100
	*To record credit card sales less 4% credit card expense.**		

* We omit the entry to Dr. Cost of Sales and Cr. Merchandise Inventory to focus on credit card expense.

When cash is later received from the credit card company, usually through electronic funds transfer, the entry is

Assets = Liabilities + Equity
+96
−96

July 20	Cash	96	
	Accounts Receivable—Credit Card Co.		96
	To record cash receipt.		

Some firms report credit card expense in the income statement as a type of discount deducted from sales to get net sales. Other companies classify it as a selling expense or even as an administrative expense. Arguments can be made for each approach. In this book we classify credit card expense as a selling expense.

Point: Third-party credit card costs can be large. JCPenney reported third-party credit card costs exceeding $10 million.

Installment Sales and Receivables Many companies allow their credit customers to make periodic payments over several months. For example, **Ford Motor Company** reports more than $70 billion in installment receivables. The seller refers to such assets as *installment accounts* (or *finance*) *receivable,* which are amounts owed by customers from credit sales for which payment is required in periodic amounts over an extended time period. Source documents for installment accounts receivable include sales slips or invoices describing the sales transactions. The customer is usually charged interest. Although installment accounts receivable can have credit periods of more than one year, they are classified as current assets if the seller regularly offers customers such terms.

Robert Laberge/NASCAR via Getty Images

Decision Maker

Entrepreneur As a small retailer, you are considering allowing customers to buy merchandise using credit cards. Until now, your store accepted only cash and checks. What analysis do you use to make this decision? ■ [Answers follow the chapter's Summary.]

NEED-TO-KNOW 7-1

Credit Card Sales

C1

A small retailer allows customers to use two different credit cards in charging purchases. With the AA Bank Card, the retailer receives an immediate credit to its account when it deposits sales receipts. AA Bank assesses a 5% service charge for credit card sales. The second credit card that the retailer accepts is the VIZA Card. The retailer sends its accumulated receipts to VIZA on a weekly basis and is paid by VIZA about a week later. VIZA assesses a 3% charge on sales for using its card. Prepare journal entries to record the following selected credit card transactions for the retailer. (The retailer uses the perpetual inventory system for recording sales.)

Jan. 2 Sold merchandise for $1,000 (that had cost $600) and accepted the customer's AA Bank Card. The AA receipts are immediately deposited in the retailer's bank account.

Jan. 6 Sold merchandise for $400 (that had cost $300) and accepted the customer's VIZA Card. Transferred $400 of credit card receipts to VIZA, requesting payment.

Jan. 16 Received VIZA's check for the January 6 billing, less the service charge.

Solution

Jan. 2	Cash	950	
	Credit Card Expense*	50	
	Sales		1,000
	*To record credit card sales less 5% fee. *($1,000 × 0.05)*		
Jan. 2	Cost of Goods Sold	600	
	Merchandise Inventory		600
	To record cost of sales.		
Jan. 6	Accounts Receivable—VIZA	388	
	Credit Card Expense*	12	
	Sales		400
	*To record credit card sales less 3% fee. *($400 × 0.03)*		
Jan. 6	Cost of Goods Sold	300	
	Merchandise Inventory		300
	To record cost of sales.		
Jan. 16	Cash	388	
	Accounts Receivable—VIZA		388
	To record cash received on credit sales less fees.		

Do More: QS 7-1, E 7-2

QC1

Valuing Accounts Receivable—Direct Write-Off Method

P1 Apply the direct write-off method to account for accounts receivable.

When a company directly grants credit to its customers, it expects that some customers will not pay what they promised. The accounts of these customers are *uncollectible accounts,* commonly called **bad debts.** The total amount of uncollectible accounts is an expense of selling on credit. Why do companies sell on credit if they expect some accounts to be uncollectible? The answer is that companies believe that granting credit will increase total sales and net income enough to offset bad debts. Companies use two methods to account for uncollectible accounts: (1) direct write-off method and (2) allowance method. We describe both.

Point: Managers realize that some portion of credit sales will be uncollectible, but which credit sales are uncollectible is unknown.

Recording and Writing Off Bad Debts The **direct write-off method** of accounting for bad debts records the loss from an uncollectible account receivable when it is determined to be uncollectible. No attempt is made to predict bad debts expense. To illustrate, if TechCom determines on January 23 that it cannot collect $520 owed to it by its customer J. Kent, it recognizes the loss using the direct write-off method as follows:

Assets = Liabilities + Equity
−520 −520

Jan. 23	Bad Debts Expense	520	
	Accounts Receivable—J. Kent		520
	To write off an uncollectible account.		

Point: If a customer fails to pay within the credit period, most companies send out repeated billings and make other efforts to collect.

The debit in this entry charges the uncollectible amount directly to the current period's Bad Debts Expense account. The credit removes its balance from the Accounts Receivable account in the general ledger (and its subsidiary ledger).

Point: Recovery of a bad debt always requires two journal entries.

Recovering a Bad Debt Although uncommon, sometimes an account written off is later collected. This can be due to factors such as continual collection efforts or a customer's good fortune. If the account of J. Kent that was written off directly to Bad Debts Expense is later collected in full, the following two entries record this recovery:

Assets = Liabilities + Equity
+520 +520

Assets = Liabilities + Equity
+520
−520

Mar. 11	Accounts Receivable—J. Kent	520	
	Bad Debts Expense		520
	To reinstate account previously written off.		
Mar. 11	Cash	520	
	Accounts Receivable—J. Kent		520
	To record full payment of account.		

Direct write-off method
Advantages:
- Simple
- No estimates required

Disadvantages:
- Receivables and income temporarily overstated
- Bad debts expense often not matched with sales

Assessing the Direct Write-Off Method Examples of companies that use the direct write-off method include **Rand Medical Billing, Gateway Distributors, Microwave Satellite Technologies, First Industrial Realty, New Frontier Energy,** and **Sub Surface Waste Management**. The following disclosure by **Pharma-Bio Serv** is typical of the justification for this method: Bad debts are accounted for using the direct write-off method whereby an expense is recognized only when a specific account is determined to be uncollectible. The effect of using this method approximates that of the allowance method. Companies must weigh at least two accounting concepts when considering the use of the direct write-off method: the (1) matching principle and (2) materiality constraint.

Matching principle applied to bad debts. The **matching (expense recognition) principle** requires expenses to be reported in the same accounting period as the sales they helped produce. This means that if extending credit to customers helped produce sales, the bad debts expense linked to those sales is matched and reported in the same period. The direct write-off method usually does *not* best match sales and expenses because bad debts expense is not recorded until an account becomes uncollectible, which often occurs in a period after that of the credit sale. To match bad debts expense with the sales it produces therefore requires a company to estimate future uncollectibles.

Point: Under direct write-off, expense is recorded each time an account is written off. Under the allowance method, expense is recorded with an adjusting entry equal to the total estimated uncollectibles for that period's sales.

Materiality constraint applied to bad debts. The **materiality constraint** states that an amount can be ignored if its effect on the financial statements is unimportant to users' business decisions. The materiality constraint permits the use of the direct write-off method when bad debts expenses are very small in relation to a company's other financial statement items such as sales and net income.

NEED-TO-KNOW 7-2

Entries under Direct Write-Off Method

P1

A retailer applies the direct write-off method in accounting for uncollectible accounts. Prepare journal entries to record its following selected transactions.

Feb. 14 The retailer determines that it cannot collect $400 of its accounts receivable from a customer named ZZZ Companay.

Apr. 1 ZZZ Company unexpectedly pays its account in full to the retailer, which then records its recovery of this bad debt.

Solution

Feb. 14	Bad Debts Expense.	400	
	Accounts Receivable—ZZZ Co.		400
	To write off an account.		
Apr. 1	Accounts Receivable—ZZZ Co.	400	
	Bad Debts Expense		400
	To reinstate an account previously written off.		
Apr. 1	Cash	400	
	Accounts Receivable—ZZZ Co.		400
	To record cash received on account.		

Do More: QS 7-2, QS 7-3, E 7-3

Valuing Accounts Receivable—Allowance Method

P2 Apply the allowance method and estimate uncollectibles based on sales and accounts receivable.

The **allowance method** of accounting for bad debts matches the *estimated* loss from uncollectible accounts receivable against the sales they helped produce. We must use estimated losses because when sales occur, management does not know which customers will not pay their bills. This means that at the end of each period, the allowance method requires an estimate of the total bad debts expected to result from that period's sales. This method has two advantages over the direct write-off method: (1) it records estimated bad debts expense in the period when the related sales are recorded and (2) it reports accounts receivable on the balance sheet at the estimated amount of cash to be collected.

	Bad Debts Expense Recognized in
Direct write-off method	The future when account is deemed uncollectible.
Allowance method	Current period to yield realizable Accts. Rec. bal.

Recording Bad Debts Expense The allowance method estimates bad debts expense at the end of each accounting period and records it with an adjusting entry. TechCom, for instance, had credit sales of $300,000 during its first year of operations. At the end of the first year, $20,000 of credit sales remained uncollected. Based on the experience of similar businesses, TechCom estimated that $1,500 of its accounts receivable would be uncollectible. This estimated expense is recorded with the following adjusting entry:

Dec. 31	Bad Debts Expense	1,500	
	Allowance for Doubtful Accounts.		1,500
	To record estimated bad debts.		

Assets	=	Liabilities	+	Equity
−1,500				−1,500

Allowance method

Advantages:
- Receivables fairly stated
- Bad debts expense is matched with sales
- Writing off bad debt does not affect net receivables nor net income

Disadvantages:
- Estimates required

The estimated bad debts expense of $1,500 is reported on the income statement (as either a selling expense or an administrative expense) and offsets the $300,000 credit sales it helped produce. The **Allowance for Doubtful Accounts** is a contra asset account. A contra account is used instead of reducing accounts receivable directly because at the time of the adjusting entry, the company does not know which customers will not pay. After the bad debts adjusting entry is posted, TechCom's account balances (in T-account form) for Accounts Receivable and its Allowance for Doubtful Accounts are as shown in Exhibit 7.5.

EXHIBIT 7.5

General Ledger after Bad Debts Adjusting Entry

Accounts Receivable			
Dec. 31	20,000		

Allowance for Doubtful Accounts			
		Dec. 31	1,500

The Allowance for Doubtful Accounts credit balance of $1,500 has the effect of reducing accounts receivable to its estimated realizable value. **Realizable value** refers to the expected proceeds from converting an asset into cash. Although credit customers owe $20,000 to TechCom, only $18,500 is expected to be realized in cash collections from these customers. (TechCom continues to bill its customers a total of $20,000, the amounts from the subsidiary ledger.) In the balance sheet, the Allowance for Doubtful Accounts is subtracted from Accounts Receivable and is often reported as shown in Exhibit 7.6.

EXHIBIT 7.6

Balance Sheet for the Allowance for Doubtful Accounts

Current assets		
Accounts receivable	**$20,000**	
Less allowance for doubtful accounts	**1,500**	**$18,500**

Sometimes the Allowance for Doubtful Accounts is not reported separately. This alternative presentation is shown in Exhibit 7.7 (also see Appendix A).

EXHIBIT 7.7

Alternative Presentation of the Allowance for Doubtful Accounts

Current assets	
Accounts receivable (net of $1,500 doubtful accounts)	**$18,500**

Writing Off a Bad Debt When specific accounts are identified as uncollectible, they are written off against the Allowance for Doubtful Accounts. To illustrate, TechCom decides that J. Kent's $520 account is uncollectible and makes the following entry to write it off.

Assets = Liabilities + Equity
+520
−520

Jan. 23	Allowance for Doubtful Accounts	520	
	Accounts Receivable—J. Kent		520
	To write off an uncollectible account.		

Point: The Bad Debts Expense is not debited in the write-off because it was recorded in the period when sales occurred.

Posting this write-off entry to the Accounts Receivable account removes the amount of the bad debt from the general ledger (it is also posted to the accounts receivable subsidiary ledger). The general ledger accounts now appear as in Exhibit 7.8 (assuming no other transactions affecting these accounts).

EXHIBIT 7.8

General Ledger after Write-Off

Accounts Receivable			
Dec. 31	20,000		
		Jan. 23	**520**

Allowance for Doubtful Accounts			
		Dec. 31	1,500
Jan. 23	**520**		

Point: In posting a write-off, the ledger's Explanation column indicates the reason for this credit so it is not misinterpreted as payment in full.

The write-off does *not* affect the realizable value of accounts receivable as shown in Exhibit 7.9. Neither total assets nor net income is affected by the write-off of a specific account. Instead, both assets and net income are affected in the period when bad debts expense is predicted and recorded with an adjusting entry.

EXHIBIT 7.9

Realizable Value before and after Write-Off of a Bad Debt

	Before Write-Off	After Write-Off
Accounts receivable	$ 20,000	$ 19,480
Less allowance for doubtful accounts	1,500	980
Estimated realizable accounts receivable	**$18,500**	**$18,500**

Recovering a Bad Debt When a customer fails to pay and the account is written off as uncollectible, his or her credit standing is jeopardized. To help restore credit standing, a customer sometimes volunteers to pay all or part of the amount owed. A company makes two entries when collecting an account previously written off by the allowance method. The first is to reverse the write-off and reinstate the customer's account. The second entry records the collection of the reinstated account. To illustrate, if on March 11 Kent pays in full his account previously written off, the entries are

Point: Recovery of a bad debt always requires two journal entries.

Assets = Liabilities + Equity
+520
−520

Assets = Liabilities + Equity
+520
−520

Mar. 11	Accounts Receivable—J. Kent	520	
	Allowance for Doubtful Accounts		520
	To reinstate account previously written off.		
Mar. 11	Cash	520	
	Accounts Receivable—J. Kent		520
	To record full payment of account.		

In this illustration, Kent paid the entire amount previously written off, but sometimes a customer pays only a portion of the amount owed. A question then arises as to whether the entire balance of the account or just the amount paid is returned to accounts receivable. This is a matter of judgment. If we believe this customer will later pay in full, we return the entire amount owed to accounts receivable, but if we expect no further collection, we return only the amount paid.

Example: If TechCom used a collection agency and paid a 35% commission on $520 collected from Kent, how is this recorded? *Answer:*

Cash	338	
Collection Expense	182	
Accts. Rec.—J. Kent		520

Point: Bad Debts Expense is also called *Uncollectible Accounts Expense.* The Allowance for Doubtful Accounts is also called *Allowance for Uncollectible Accounts.*

Decision Insight

PayPal PayPal is legally just a money transfer agent, but it is increasingly challenging big credit card brands—see chart. PayPal is successful because: (1) online credit card processing fees can exceed $0.15 per dollar, but PayPal's fees are under $0.10 per dollar. (2) PayPal's merchant fraud losses are under 0.2% of revenues, which compares to nearly 2% for online merchants using credit cards. ■

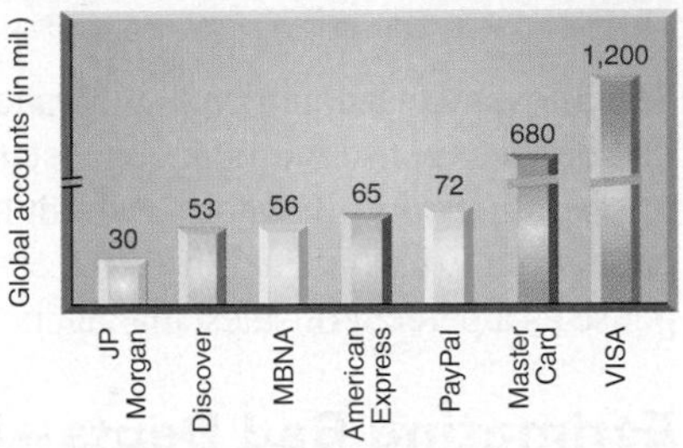

NEED-TO-KNOW 7-3

Entries under Allowance Method

P2

A retailer applies the allowance method in accounting for uncollectible accounts. Prepare journal entries to record its following selected transactions.

2014

Dec. 31 The retailer estimates $3,000 of its accounts receivable are uncollectible.

2015

Feb. 14 The retailer determines that it cannot collect $400 of its accounts receivable from a customer named ZZZ Company.

Apr. 1 ZZZ Company unexpectedly pays its account in full to the retailer, which then records its recovery of this bad debt.

Solution

2014			
Dec. 31	Bad Debts Expense	3,000	
	Allowance for Doubtful Accounts		3,000
	To record estimated bad debts.		
2015			
Feb. 14	Allowance for Doubtful Accounts	400	
	Accounts Receivable—ZZZ Co.		400
	To write off an account.		
Apr. 1	Accounts Receivable—ZZZ Co.	400	
	Allowance for Doubtful Accounts		400
	To reinstate an account previously written off.		
Apr. 1	Cash	400	
	Accounts Receivable—ZZZ Co.		400
	To record cash received on account.		

Do More: QS 7-5

Estimating Bad Debts—Percent of Sales Method

The allowance method requires an estimate of bad debts expense to prepare an adjusting entry at the end of each accounting period. There are two common methods. One is based on the income statement relation between bad debts expense and sales. The second is based on the balance sheet relation between accounts receivable and the allowance for doubtful accounts.

The *percent of sales method,* also referred to as the *income statement method,* is based on the idea that a given percent of a company's credit sales for the period is uncollectible. To illustrate, assume that Musicland has credit sales of $400,000 in year 2015. Based on past experience, Musicland estimates 0.6% of credit sales to be uncollectible. This implies that Musicland

Point: Focus is on *credit* sales because cash sales do not produce bad debts. If cash sales are a small or stable percent of credit sales, total sales can be used.

expects $2,400 of bad debts expense from its sales (computed as $400,000 × 0.006). The adjusting entry to record this estimated expense is

Assets = Liabilities + Equity
−2,400 −2,400

Dec. 31*	Bad Debts Expense	2,400	
	Allowance for Doubtful Accounts		2,400
	To record estimated bad debts.		

*The adjusting entry above applies our 3-step adjusting entry process from Chapter 3:
Step 1: Current balance for Bad Debts Expense is $0 debit (as the expense account was closed in prior period).
Step 2: Current balance for Bad Debts Expense should be $2,400 debit.
Step 3: Record entry to get from Step 1 to Step 2.

Bad Debts Expense	
Unadj. 0	
Adj. (% Sales) 2,400	
Est. bal. 2,400	

Point: When using the *percent of sales method* for estimating uncollectibles, and because the unadj. bal. in Bad Debts Expense is always $0, the adjusting entry amt. always equals the % of sales.

The allowance account ending balance on the balance sheet for this method would rarely equal the bad debts expense on the income statement. This is because unless a company is in its first period of operations, its allowance account has a zero balance only if the prior amounts written off as uncollectible *exactly* equal the prior estimated bad debts expenses. (When computing bad debts expense as a percent of sales, managers monitor and adjust the percent so it is not too high or too low.)

Estimating Bad Debts—Percent of Receivables Method

The *accounts receivable methods,* also referred to as *balance sheet methods,* use balance sheet relations to estimate bad debts—mainly the relation between accounts receivable and the allowance amount. The goal of the bad debts adjusting entry for these methods is to make the Allowance for Doubtful Accounts balance equal to the portion of accounts receivable that is estimated to be uncollectible. The estimated balance for the allowance account is obtained in one of two ways: (1) computing the percent uncollectible from the total accounts receivable or (2) aging accounts receivable.

The *percent of accounts receivable method* assumes that a given percent of a company's receivables is uncollectible. This percent is based on past experience and is impacted by current conditions such as economic trends and customer difficulties. The total dollar amount of all receivables is multiplied by this percent to get the estimated dollar amount of uncollectible accounts—reported in the balance sheet as the Allowance for Doubtful Accounts.

Point: When using an accounts receivable method for estimating uncollectibles, the allowance account balance is adjusted to equal the estimate of uncollectibles.

To illustrate, assume that Musicland has $50,000 of accounts receivable on December 31, 2015. Experience suggests 5% of its receivables is uncollectible. This means that *after* the adjusting entry is posted, we want the Allowance for Doubtful Accounts to show a $2,500 credit balance (5% of $50,000). We are also told that its beginning balance is $2,200, which is 5% of the $44,000 accounts receivable on December 31, 2014—see Exhibit 7.10.

EXHIBIT 7.10

Allowance for Doubtful Accounts after Bad Debts Adjusting Entry

Allowance for Doubtful Accounts				
		Dec. 31, 2014, bal.	2,200	← Prior-year estimate of allowance for doubtful accounts
Current-year write-offs → Feb. 6	800			
July 10	700			
Nov. 20	500			
		Unadjusted bal.	200	
		Dec. 31 adjustment	**2,300**	← Adjusting entry
		Dec. 31, 2015, bal.	2,500	← Current-year estimate of allowance for doubtful accounts

During 2015, accounts of customers are written off on February 6, July 10, and November 20. Thus, the account has a $200 credit balance *before* the December 31, 2015, adjustment. The adjusting entry to give the allowance account the estimated $2,500 balance is

Assets = Liabilities + Equity
−2,300 −2,300

Dec. 31*	Bad Debts Expense	2,300	
	Allowance for Doubtful Accounts		2,300
	To record estimated bad debts.		

*The adjusting entry above applies our 3-step adjusting entry process from Chapter 3:
Step 1: Current balance for Allowance account is $200 credit.
Step 2: Current balance for Allowance account should be $2,500 credit.
Step 3: Record entry to get from Step 1 to Step 2.

Decision Insight

Aging Pains Unlike wine, accounts receivable do not improve with age. Experience shows that the longer a receivable is past due, the lower is the likelihood of its collection. An *aging schedule* uses this knowledge to estimate bad debts. The chart here is from a survey that reported estimates of bad debts for receivables grouped by how long they were past their due dates. Each company sets its own estimates based on its customers and its experiences with those customers' payment patterns. ■

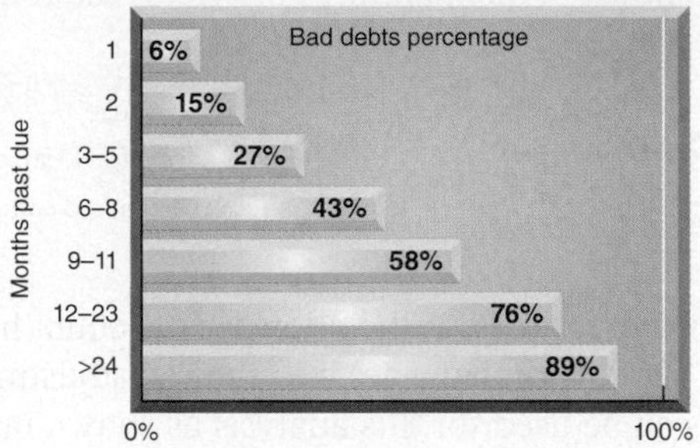

Estimating Bad Debts—Aging of Receivables Method

The **aging of accounts receivable** method uses both past and current receivables information to estimate the allowance amount. Specifically, each receivable is classified by how long it is past its due date. Then estimates of uncollectible amounts are made assuming that the longer an amount is past due, the more likely it is to be uncollectible. Classifications are often based on 30-day periods. After the amounts are classified (or aged), experience is used to estimate the percent of each uncollectible class. These percents are applied to the amounts in each class and then totaled to get the estimated balance of the Allowance for Doubtful Ac-counts. This computation is performed by setting up a schedule such as Exhibit 7.11.

EXHIBIT 7.11
Aging of Accounts Receivable

MUSICLAND
Schedule of Accounts Receivable by Age
December 31, 2015

Customer	Totals	Not Yet Due	1 to 30 Days Past Due	31 to 60 Days Past Due	61 to 90 Days Past Due	Over 90 Days Past Due
Carlie Abbott..............	$ 5,890	$ 5,890				
Jamie Allen..................	710			$ 710		
Chavez Andres.............	10,500	10,300	$ 200			
Balicia Company...........	2,800				$1,900	$ 900
Texas Rawhide.............	9,100		6,110	2,990		
Zamora Services...........	21,000	20,810	190			
Total receivables*......	$50,000	$37,000	$6,500	$3,700	$1,900	$ 900
Percent uncollectible......		× 2%	× 5%	× 10%	× 25%	× 40%
Estimated uncollectible...	$ 2,270	$ 740	$ 325	$ 370	$ 475	$ 360

Each receivable is grouped by how long it is past its due date.

Each age group is multiplied by its estimated bad debts percent.

Estimated bad debts for each group are totaled.

Exhibit 7.11 lists each customer's individual balances assigned to one of five classes based on its days past due. The amounts in each class are totaled and multiplied by the estimated percent of uncollectible accounts for each class. The percents used are regularly reviewed to reflect changes in the company and economy.

To explain, Musicland has $3,700 in accounts receivable that are 31 to 60 days past due. Its management estimates 10% of the amounts in this age class are uncollectible, or a total of $370 (computed as $3,700 × 10%). Similar analysis is done for each of the other four classes. The final total of $2,270 ($740 + $325 + 370 + $475 + $360) shown in the first column is the estimated balance for the Allowance for Doubtful Accounts. Exhibit 7.12 shows that since the

EXHIBIT 7.12
Computation of the Required Adjustment for the Accounts Receivable Method

Step 1: Current account balance equals	Unadjusted balance	$ 200 credit
Step 2: Determine what account balance should be	Estimated balance	2,270 credit
Step 3: Make adjustment to get from step 1 to step 2	**Required adjustment**	**$2,070 credit**

Allowance for Doubtful Accounts	
	Unadj. bal. 200
	Req. adj. 2,070
	Estim. bal. 2,270

Assets = Liabilities + Equity
−2,070 −2,070

allowance account has an unadjusted credit balance of $200, the required adjustment to the Allowance for Doubtful Accounts is $2,070. (We could also use a T-account for this analysis as shown in the margin.) This yields the following end-of-period adjusting entry:

Dec. 31	Bad Debts Expense	2,070	
	Allowance for Doubtful Accounts		2,070
	To record estimated bad debts.		

Point: A debit balance implies that write-offs for that period exceed the total allowance.

Alternatively, if the allowance account had an unadjusted *debit* balance of $500 (instead of the $200 credit balance), its required adjustment would be computed as follows. (Again, a T-account can be used for this analysis as shown in the margin.)

Allowance for Doubtful Accounts	
Unadj. bal. 500	
	Req. adj. 2,770
	Estim. bal. 2,270

Step 1: Current account balance equals	Unadjusted balance	$ 500 debit
Step 2: Determine what account balance should be	Estimated balance	2,270 credit ← Current-year estimate of allowance for doubtful accounts
Step 3: Make adjustment to get from step 1 to step 2	**Required adjustment**	**$ 2,770 credit**

Adjusting entry amount

The entry to record the end-of-period adjustment for this alternative case is

Assets = Liabilities + Equity
−2,770 −2,770

Dec. 31	Bad Debts Expense	2,770	
	Allowance for Doubtful Accounts		2,770
	To record estimated bad debts.		

Point: Credit approval is usually not assigned to the selling dept. because its goal is to increase sales, and it may approve customers at the cost of increased bad debts. Instead, approval is assigned to a separate credit-granting or administrative dept.

The aging of accounts receivable method is an examination of specific accounts and is usually the most reliable of the estimation methods.

Estimating Bad Debts—Summary of Methods Exhibit 7.13 summarizes the principles guiding all three estimation methods and their focus of analysis. Percent of sales, with its income statement focus, does a good job at matching bad debts expense with sales. The accounts receivable methods, with their balance sheet focus, do a better job at reporting accounts receivable at realizable value.

EXHIBIT 7.13

Methods to Estimate Bad Debts

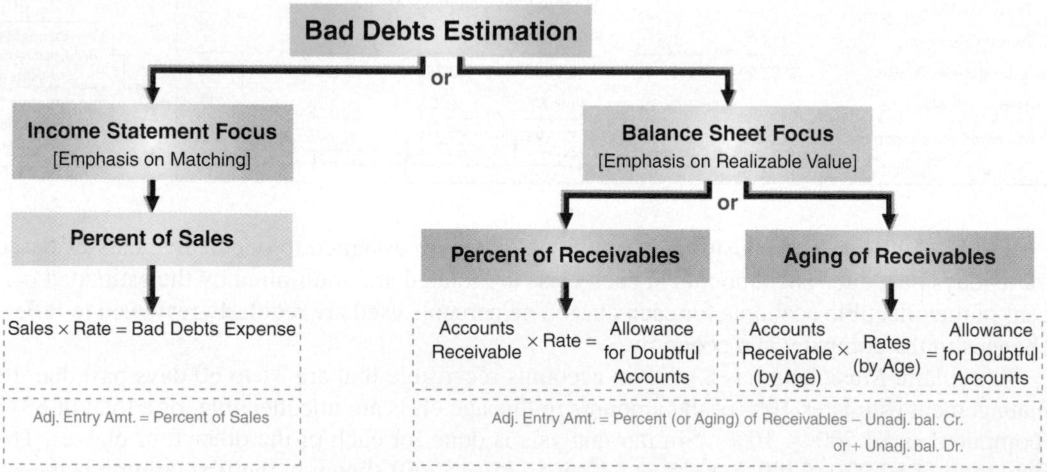

Decision Maker

Labor Union Chief One week prior to labor contract negotiations, financial statements are released showing no income growth. A 10% growth was predicted. Your analysis finds that the company increased its allowance for uncollectibles from 1.5% to 4.5% of receivables. Without this change, income would show a 9% growth. Does this analysis impact negotiations? ■ [Answers follow the chapter's Summary.]

At its December 31 year-end, a company estimates uncollectible accounts using the allowance method.

NEED-TO-KNOW 7-4

Estimating Bad Debts

P2

1. It prepared the following aging of receivables analysis. (a) Estimate the balance of the Allowance for Doubtful Accounts using the aging of accounts receivable method. (b) Prepare the adjusting entry to record bad debts expense using the estimate from part *a*. Assume the unadjusted balance in the Allowance for Doubtful Accounts is a $10 debit.

		Days Past Due				
	Total	**0**	**1 to 30**	**31 to 60**	**61 to 90**	**Over 90**
Accounts receivable	$2,600	$2,000	$300	$80	$100	$120
Percent uncollectible		1%	2%	5%	7%	10%

2. (a) Estimate the balance of the Allowance for Doubtful Accounts assuming the company uses 2% of total accounts receivable to estimate uncollectibles, instead of the aging of receivables method in question 1. (b) Prepare the adjusting entry to record bad debts expense using the estimate from part *a*. Assume the unadjusted balance in the Allowance for Doubtful Accounts is a $4 credit.
3. (a) Estimate the balance of the uncollectibles assuming the company uses 0.5% of annual credit sales (annual credit sales were $10,000). (b) Prepare the adjusting entry to record bad debts expense using the estimate from part *a*. Assume the unadjusted balance in the Allowance for Doubtful Accounts is a $4 credit.

Solutions

1a. Computation of the estimated balance of the allowance for uncollectibles:

Not due:	$2,000 × 0.01 =	$20	
1 to 30:	300 × 0.02 =	6	
31 to 60:	80 × 0.05 =	4	
61 to 90:	100 × 0.07 =	7	
Over 90:	120 × 0.10 =	12	
		$49	credit

Do More: QS 7-6, E 7-4, E 7-5, E 7-6, E 7-7, E 7-8, E 7-9

QC2

1b.

Dec. 31	*Bad Debts Expense*	59	
	Allowance for Doubtful Accounts...........		59
	*To record estimated bad debts.**		

Step 1: Current account balance equals	*Unadjusted balance	$10 debit
Step 2: Determine what account balance should be	Estimated balance	49 credit
Step 3: Make adjustment to get from step 1 to step 2	Required adjustment	$59 credit

Allowance for Doubtful Accounts

Unadj. Dec. 31	10		
		Adj. Dec. 31	**59**
		Est. bal. Dec. 31	49

2a. Computation of the estimated balance of the allowance for uncollectibles:

$2,600 × 0.02 = $52 credit

2b.

Dec. 31	*Bad Debts Expense*	48	
	Allowance for Doubtful Accounts		48
	*To record estimated bad debts.**		

Step 1: Current account balance equals	*Unadjusted balance	$ 4 credit
Step 2: Determine what account balance should be	Estimated balance	52 credit
Step 3: Make adjustment to get from step 1 to step 2	Required adjustment	$48 credit

Allowance for Doubtful Accounts

		Unadj. Dec. 31	4
		Adj. Dec. 31	**48**
		Est. bal. Dec. 31	52

3a. Computation of the estimated balance of the bad debts expense:

$10,000 × 0.005 = $50 credit

3b.

Dec. 31	*Bad Debts Expense*	50	
	Allowance for Doubtful Accounts		50
	To record estimated bad debts.		

Bad Debts Expense

Unadj. Dec. 31	0		
Adj. Dec. 31	**50**		
Est. bal. Dec. 31	50		

NOTES RECEIVABLE

C2

Describe a note receivable, the computation of its maturity date, and the recording of its existence.

A **promissory note** is a written promise to pay a specified amount of money, usually with interest, either on demand or at a definite future date. Promissory notes are used in many transactions, including paying for products and services, and lending and borrowing money. Sellers sometimes ask for a note to replace an account receivable when a customer requests additional time to pay a past-due account. For legal reasons, sellers generally prefer to receive notes when the credit period is long and when the receivable is for a large amount. If a lawsuit is needed to collect from a customer, a note is the buyer's written acknowledgment of the debt, its amount, and its terms.

Exhibit 7.14 shows a simple promissory note dated July 10, 2015. For this note, Julia Browne promises to pay TechCom or to its order (according to TechCom's instructions) a specified amount of money ($1,000), called the **principal of a note,** at a definite future date (October 8, 2015). As the one who signed the note and promised to pay it at maturity, Browne is the **maker of the note.** As the person to whom the note is payable, TechCom is the **payee of the note.** To Browne, the note is a liability called a *note payable*. To TechCom, the same note is an asset called a *note receivable*. This note bears interest at 12%, as written on the note. **Interest** is the charge for using the money until its due date. To a borrower, interest is an expense. To a lender, it is revenue.

EXHIBIT 7.14

Promissory Note

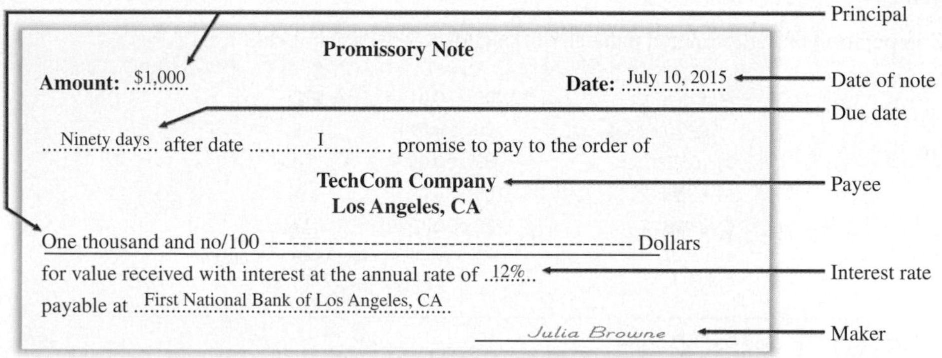
Promissory Note

Amount: $1,000 Date: July 10, 2015

Ninety days after date I promise to pay to the order of

TechCom Company
Los Angeles, CA

One thousand and no/100 -- Dollars

for value received with interest at the annual rate of 12%

payable at First National Bank of Los Angeles, CA

Julia Browne

Computing Maturity and Interest

This section describes key computations for notes including the determination of maturity date, period covered, and interest computation.

Maturity Date and Period The **maturity date of a note** is the day the note (principal and interest) must be repaid. The *period* of a note is the time from the note's (contract) date to its maturity date. Many notes mature in less than a full year, and the period they cover is often expressed in days. When the time of a note is expressed in days, its maturity date is the specified number of days after the note's date. As an example, a five-day note dated June 15 matures and is due on June 20. A 90-day note dated July 10 matures on October 8. This October 8 due date is computed as shown in Exhibit 7.15. The period of a note is sometimes expressed in months or years. When months are used, the note matures and is payable in the month of its maturity on the *same day of the month* as its original date. A nine-month note dated July 10, for instance, is payable on April 10. The same analysis applies when years are used.

EXHIBIT 7.15

Maturity Date Computation

Days in July	31		
Minus the date of the note	10		
Days remaining in July		21	July 11–31
Add days in August		31	Aug. 1–31
Add days in September		30	Sept. 1–30
Days to equal 90 days, or **maturity date of October 8**		8	Oct. 1–8
Period of the note in days		90	

Interest Computation *Interest* is the cost of borrowing money for the borrower or, alternatively, the profit from lending money for the lender. Unless otherwise stated, the rate of interest on a note is the rate charged for the use of the principal for one year. The formula for computing interest on a note is shown in Exhibit 7.16.

EXHIBIT 7.16

Computation of Interest Formula

$$\text{Principal of the note} \times \text{Annual interest rate} \times \text{Time expressed in fraction of year} = \text{Interest}$$

To simplify interest computations, a year is commonly treated as having 360 days (called the *banker's rule* in the business world and widely used in commercial transactions). **We treat a year as having 360 days for interest computations in the examples and assignments**. Using the promissory note in Exhibit 7.14 where we have a 90-day, 12%, $1,000 note, the total interest is computed as follows:

$$\$1{,}000 \times 12\% \times \frac{90}{360} = \$1{,}000 \times 0.12 \times 0.25 = \$30$$

Point: If the *banker's rule* is not followed, interest is computed as:

$1,000 × 12% × 90/365 = $29.589041

The *banker's rule* would yield $30, which is easier to account for than $29.589041.

Recognizing Notes Receivable

Notes receivable are usually recorded in a single Notes Receivable account to simplify recordkeeping. The original notes are kept on file, including information on the maker, rate of interest, and due date. (When a company holds a large number of notes, it sometimes sets up a controlling account and a subsidiary ledger for notes. This is similar to the handling of accounts receivable.) To illustrate the recording for the receipt of a note, we use the $1,000, 90-day, 12% promissory note in Exhibit 7.14. TechCom received this note at the time of a product sale to Julia Browne. This transaction is recorded as follows:

July 10*	Notes Receivable	1,000	
	Sales		1,000
	Sold goods in exchange for a 90-day, 12% note.		

* We omit the entry to Dr. Cost of Sales and Cr. Merchandise Inventory to focus on sales and receivables.

Assets = Liabilities + Equity
+1,000 +1,000

When a seller accepts a note from an overdue customer as a way to grant a time extension on a past-due account receivable, it will often collect part of the past-due balance in cash. This partial payment forces a concession from the customer, reduces the customer's debt (and the seller's risk), and produces a note for a smaller amount. To illustrate, assume that TechCom agreed to accept $232 in cash along with a $600, 60-day, 15% note from Jo Cook to settle her $832 past-due account. TechCom made the following entry to record receipt of this cash and note:

Oct. 5	Cash	232	
	Notes Receivable	600	
	Accounts Receivable—J. Cook		832
	Received cash and note to settle account.		

Assets = Liabilities + Equity
+232
+600
−832

Valuing and Settling Notes

P3 Record the honoring and dishonoring of a note and adjustments for interest.

Recording an Honored Note The principal and interest of a note are due on its maturity date. The maker of the note usually *honors* the note and pays it in full. To illustrate, when J. Cook pays the note above on its due date, TechCom records it as follows:

Dec. 4	Cash	615	
	Notes Receivable		600
	Interest Revenue		15
	Collect note with interest of $600 × 15% × 60/360.		

Assets = Liabilities + Equity
+615 +15
−600

Interest revenue, also called *interest earned,* is reported on the income statement.

Recording a Dishonored Note When a note's maker is unable or refuses to pay at maturity, the note is *dishonored.* The act of dishonoring a note does not relieve the maker of the obligation to pay. The payee should use every legitimate means to collect. How do companies report this event? The balance of the Notes Receivable account should include only those notes that have not matured. Thus, when a note is dishonored, we remove the amount of this note from the Notes Receivable account and charge it back to an account receivable from its maker. To illustrate, assume that J. Cook dishonors the note above at maturity. The journal entry to record the dishonoring of the note follows:

Point: When posting a dishonored note to a customer's account, an explanation is included so as not to misinterpret the debit as a sale on account.

Assets	= Liabilities +	Equity
+615		+15
−600		

Dec. 4	Accounts Receivable—J. Cook	615	
	Interest Revenue		15
	Notes Receivable		600
	To charge account of J. Cook for a dishonored note and interest of $600 × 15% × 60/360.		

Point: Reporting the details of notes is consistent with the **full disclosure principle,** which requires financial statements (including footnotes) to report all relevant information.

Charging a dishonored note back to the account of its maker serves two purposes. First, it removes the amount of the note from the Notes Receivable account and records the dishonored note in the maker's account. Second, and more important, if the maker of the dishonored note applies for credit in the future, his or her account will reveal all past dealings, including the dishonored note. Restoring the account also reminds the company to continue collection efforts from Hart for both principal and interest. The entry records the full amount, including interest, to ensure that it is included in collection efforts.

Recording End-of-Period Interest Adjustment When notes receivable are outstanding at the end of a period, any accrued interest earned is computed and recorded. To illustrate, on December 16, TechCom accepts a $3,000, 60-day, 12% note from a customer in granting an extension on a past-due account. When TechCom's accounting period ends on December 31, $15 of interest has accrued on this note ($3,000 × 12% × 15/360). The following adjusting entry records this revenue:

Assets	= Liabilities +	Equity
+15		+15

Dec. 31	Interest Receivable	15	
	Interest Revenue		15
	To record accrued interest earned.		

Point: Assume reversing entries are not made unless otherwise stated.

Interest revenue appears on the income statement, and interest receivable appears on the balance sheet as a current asset. When the December 16 note is collected on February 14, TechCom's entry to record the cash receipt is

Assets	= Liabilities +	Equity
+3,060		+45
−15		
−3,000		

Feb. 14	Cash	3,060	
	Interest Revenue		45
	Interest Receivable		15
	Notes Receivable		3,000
	Received payment of note and its interest.		

Total interest earned on the 60-day note is $60. The $15 credit to Interest Receivable on February 14 reflects the collection of the interest accrued from the December 31 adjusting entry. The $45 interest earned reflects TechCom's revenue from holding the note from January 1 to February 14 of the current period.

a. AA Company purchases $1,400 of merchandise from ZZ on December 16, 2014. ZZ accepts AA's $1,400, 90-day, 12% note as payment. ZZ's accounting period ends on December 31, and it does not make reversing entries. Prepare entries for ZZ on December 16, 2014, and December 31, 2014. (Assume reversing entries are not made.)

b. Using the information in part *a*, prepare ZZ's March 16, 2015, entry if AA dishonors the note.

c. Instead of the facts in part *b*, prepare ZZ's March 16, 2015, entry if AA honors the note.

d. Assume the facts in part *b* above. Then, on March 31, ZZ decides to write-off the receivable from AA Company. Prepare that write-off entry assuming that ZZ uses the allowance method.

NEED-TO-KNOW 7-5

Honoring and Dishonoring Notes

C2 P3

Solution

a.

Dec. 16	Note Receivable — AA	1,400	
	Sales		1,400
Dec. 31	Interest Receivable	7	
	Interest Revenue		7
	($1,400 × 12% × 15/360)		

b.

Mar. 16	Accounts Receivable — AA	1,442	
	Interest Revenue		35
	Interest Receivable		7
	Notes Receivable—AA		1,400

c.

Mar. 16	Cash	1,442	
	Interest Revenue		35
	Interest Receivable		7
	Notes Receivable—AA		1,400

Do More: QS 7-8, QS 7-9, QS 7-10, E 7-12, E 7-13, E 7-10, E 7-11

d.

Mar. 31	Allowance for Doubtful Accounts	1,442	
	Accounts Receivable—AA Company		1,442

QC3

DISPOSAL OF RECEIVABLES

Companies can convert receivables to cash before they are due. Reasons for this include the need for cash or the desire not to be involved in collection activities. Converting receivables is usually done either by (1) selling them or (2) using them as security for a loan. A recent survey shows that about 20% of companies obtain cash from either selling receivables or pledging them as security. In some industries such as textiles, apparel, and furniture, this is common practice.

C3 Explain how receivables can be converted to cash before maturity.

Selling Receivables

A company can sell all or a portion of its receivables to a finance company or bank. The buyer, called a *factor,* charges the seller a *factoring fee* and then the buyer takes ownership of the receivables and receives cash when they come due. By incurring a factoring fee, the seller receives cash earlier and can pass the risk of bad debts to the factor. The seller can also choose to avoid costs of billing and accounting for the receivables. To illustrate, if TechCom sells $20,000 of its accounts receivable and is charged a 4% factoring fee, it records this sale as follows:

Global: Firms in export sales increasingly sell their receivables to factors.

Aug. 15	Cash	19,200	
	Factoring Fee Expense	800	
	Accounts Receivable		20,000
	Sold accounts receivable for cash, less 4% fee.		

Assets	=	Liabilities	+	Equity
+19,200				−800
−20,000				

The accounting for sales of notes receivable is similar to that for accounts receivable. The detailed entries are covered in advanced courses. *Remember:* When factoring receivables, the company selling receivables always receives less cash than the amount of receivables sold due to factoring fees.

Pledging Receivables

A company can raise cash by borrowing money and *pledging* its receivables as security for the loan. Pledging receivables does not transfer the risk of bad debts to the lender because the borrower retains ownership of the receivables. If the borrower defaults on the loan, the lender has a right to be paid from the cash receipts of the receivable when collected. To illustrate, when TechCom borrows $35,000 and pledges its receivables as security, it records this transaction as follows:

Assets = Liabilities + Equity
+35,000 +35,000

Aug. 20	Cash	35,000	
	Notes Payable		35,000
	To borrow with a note secured by pledging receivables.		

Since pledged receivables are committed as security for a specific loan, the borrower's financial statements disclose the pledging of them. TechCom, for instance, includes the following note with its statements: Accounts receivable of $40,000 are pledged as security for a $35,000 note payable. Inventory and accounts receivable are two assets commonly demanded by bankers as collateral when making business loans.

Decision Maker

Analyst/Auditor You are reviewing accounts receivable. Over the past five years, the allowance account as a percentage of gross accounts receivable shows a steady downward trend. What does this finding suggest? ■

[Answers follow the chapter's Summary.]

GLOBAL VIEW

This section discusses similarities and differences between U.S. GAAP and IFRS regarding the recognition, measurement, and disposition of receivables.

Recognition of Receivables Both U.S. GAAP and IFRS have similar asset criteria that apply to recognition of receivables. Further, receivables that arise from revenue-generating activities are subject to broadly similar criteria for U.S. GAAP and IFRS. Specifically, both refer to the realization principle and an earnings process. The realization principle under U.S. GAAP implies an *arm's-length transaction* occurs, whereas under IFRS this notion is applied in terms of reliable measurement and likelihood of economic benefits. Regarding U.S. GAAP's reference to an earnings process, IFRS instead refers to risk transfer and ownership reward. While these criteria are broadly similar, differences do exist, and they arise mainly from industry-specific guidance under U.S. GAAP, which is very limited under IFRS.

Valuation of Receivables Both U.S. GAAP and IFRS require that receivables be reported net of estimated uncollectibles. Further, both systems require that the expense for estimated uncollectibles be recorded in the same period when any revenues from those receivables are recorded. This means that for accounts receivable, both U.S. GAAP and IFRS require the allowance method for uncollectibles (unless uncollectibles are immaterial). The allowance method using percent of sales, percent of receivables, and aging was explained in this chapter. **Nokia** reports the following for its allowance for uncollectibles:

NOKIA

Management specifically analyzes accounts receivables and historical bad debt, customer concentrations, customer creditworthiness, current economic trends and changes in our customer payment terms when evaluating the adequacy of the allowance.

Disposition of Receivables Both U.S. GAAP and IFRS apply broadly similar rules in recording dispositions of receivables. Those rules are discussed in this chapter. We should be aware of an important difference in terminology. Companies reporting under U.S. GAAP disclose Bad Debts Expense, which is also referred to as *Provision for Bad Debts* or the *Provision for Uncollectible Accounts*. For U.S. GAAP, *provision* here refers to expense. Under IFRS, the term *provision* usually refers to a liability whose amount or timing (or both) is uncertain.

Sustainability and Accounting The entrepreneur, Rakia Reynolds, of **Skai Blue Media**, as introduced in this chapter's opening feature, explains that her company's focus includes a sustainable initiative that involves helping others. "When someone comes to me, I need to make sure that I am paying that forward and helping other people," explains Rakia. "I would say that mentorship is probably one of the most important things in a successful business." Accordingly, Rakia works hard to instill a team attitude in her workforce, and a mentorship attitude with others. "Teamwork makes the dream work," insists Rakia. And, "you're a blessing to be a blessing to others."

Courtesy of Skai Blue Media

Accounts Receivable Turnover — Decision Analysis

A1 Compute accounts receivable turnover and use it to help assess financial condition.

For a company selling on credit, we want to assess both the quality and liquidity of its accounts receivable. *Quality* of receivables refers to the likelihood of collection without loss. Experience shows that the longer receivables are outstanding beyond their due date, the lower the likelihood of collection. *Liquidity* of receivables refers to the speed of collection. **Accounts receivable turnover** is a measure of both the quality and liquidity of accounts receivable. It indicates how often, on average, receivables are received and collected during the period. The formula for this ratio is shown in Exhibit 7.17.

EXHIBIT 7.17 Accounts Receivable Turnover

$$\textbf{Accounts receivable turnover} = \frac{\textbf{Net sales}}{\textbf{Average accounts receivable, net}}$$

We prefer to use net *credit* sales in the numerator because cash sales do not create receivables. However, since financial statements rarely report net credit sales, our analysis uses net sales. The denominator is the *average* accounts receivable balance, computed as (Beginning balance + Ending balance) ÷ 2. TechCom has an accounts receivable turnover of 5.1. This indicates its average accounts receivable balance is converted into cash 5.1 times during the period. Exhibit 7.18 shows graphically this turnover activity for TechCom.

EXHIBIT 7.18 Rate of Accounts Receivable Turnover for TechCom

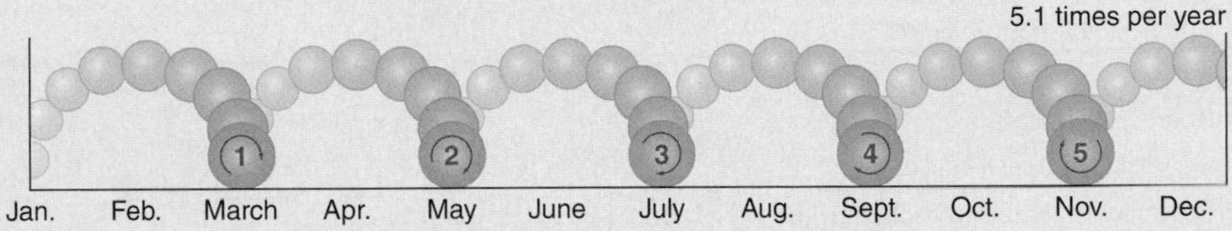

Accounts receivable turnover also reflects how well management is doing in granting credit to customers in a desire to increase sales. A high turnover in comparison with competitors suggests that management should consider using more liberal credit terms to increase sales. A low turnover suggests management should consider stricter credit terms and more aggressive collection efforts to avoid having its resources tied up in accounts receivable.

Point: Credit risk ratio is computed by dividing the Allowance for Doubtful Accounts by Accounts Receivable. The higher this ratio, the higher is credit risk.

To illustrate, we take fiscal year data from two competitors: **Dell** and **Hewlett-Packard** (HP). Exhibit 7.19 shows accounts receivable turnover for both companies.

EXHIBIT 7.19 Analysis Using Accounts Receivable Turnover

Company	Figure ($ millions)	2013	2012	2011	2010
Dell	Net sales	$ 56,940	$ 62,071	$ 61,494	$ 52,902
	Average accounts receivable, net	$ 6,553	$ 6,485	$ 6,165	$ 5,284
	Accounts receivable turnover	**8.7**	**9.6**	**10.0**	**10.0**
Hewlett-Packard	Net sales	$112,298	$120,357	$127,245	$126,033
	Average accounts receivable, net	$ 16,142	$ 17,316	$ 18,353	$ 17,509
	Accounts receivable turnover	**7.0**	**7.0**	**6.9**	**7.2**

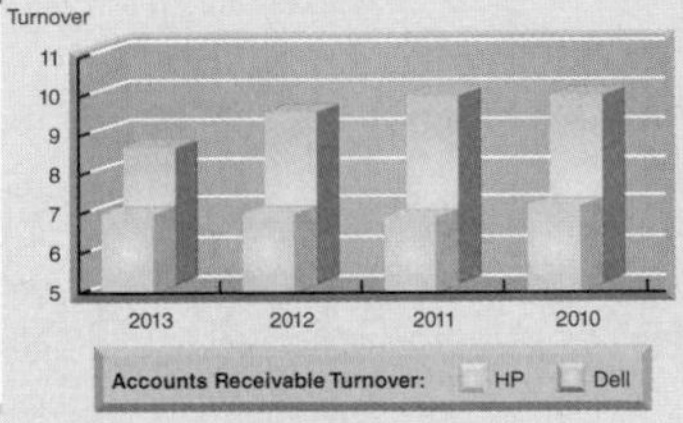

Dell's 2013 turnover is 8.7, computed as $56,940/$6,553 ($ millions). This means that Dell's average accounts receivable balance was converted into cash 8.7 times in 2013. Its turnover declined in 2013 (8.7) compared with 2012 (9.6) and 2011 (10.0). However, Dell's turnover exceeds that for HP in each of the past four years. Is either company's turnover too high? Since sales are relatively flat over this time period, neither company's turnover rate appears to be too high. Instead, both Dell and HP seem to be doing an adequate job of managing receivables.[1]

Decision Maker

Family Physician Your medical practice is barely profitable, so you hire a health care analyst. The analyst highlights several points including the following: *"Accounts receivable turnover is too low. Tighter credit policies are recommended along with discontinuing service to those most delayed in payments."* How do you interpret these recommendations? What actions do you take? ■ [Answers follow the chapter's Summary.]

NEED-TO-KNOW

COMPREHENSIVE

Clayco Company completes the following selected transactions during year 2015.

July 14 Writes off a $750 account receivable arising from a sale to Briggs Company that dates to 10 months ago. (Clayco Company uses the allowance method.)

30 Clayco Company receives a $1,000, 90-day, 10% note in exchange for merchandise sold to Sumrell Company (the merchandise cost $600).

Aug. 15 Receives $2,000 cash plus a $10,000 note from JT Co. in exchange for merchandise that sells for $12,000 (its cost is $8,000). The note is dated August 15, bears 12% interest, and matures in 120 days.

Nov. 1 Completed a $200 credit card sale with a 4% fee (the cost of sales is $150). The cash is received immediately from the credit card company.

3 Sumrell Company refuses to pay the note that was due to Clayco Company on October 28. Prepare the journal entry to charge the dishonored note plus accrued interest to Sumrell Company's accounts receivable.

5 Completed a $500 credit card sale with a 5% fee (the cost of sales is $300). The payment from the credit card company is received on Nov. 9.

15 Received the full amount of $750 from Briggs Company that was previously written off on July 14. Record the bad debts recovery.

Dec. 13 Received payment of principal plus interest from JT for the August 15 note.

Required

1. Prepare journal entries to record these transactions on Clayco Company's books.

2. Prepare an adjusting journal entry as of December 31, 2015, assuming the following:

a. Bad debts are estimated to be $20,400 by aging accounts receivable. The unadjusted balance of the Allowance for Doubtful Accounts is $1,000 debit.

b. Alternatively, assume that bad debts are estimated using the percent of sales method. The Allowance for Doubtful Accounts had a $1,000 debit balance before adjustment, and the company estimates bad debts to be 1% of its credit sales of $2,000,000.

PLANNING THE SOLUTION

- Examine each transaction to determine the accounts affected, and then record the entries.
- For the year-end adjustment, record the bad debts expense for the two approaches.

[1] As an estimate of *average days' sales uncollected,* we compute how many days (*on average*) it takes to collect receivables as follows: 365 days ÷ accounts receivable turnover. An increase in this *average collection period* can signal a decline in customers' financial condition.

SOLUTION

1.

July 14	Allowance for Doubtful Accounts	750	
	Accounts Receivable—Briggs Co.		750
	Wrote off an uncollectible account.		
July 30	Notes Receivable—Sumrell Co.	1,000	
	Sales		1,000
	Sold merchandise for a 90-day, 10% note.		
July 30	Cost of Goods Sold	600	
	Merchandise Inventory		600
	To record the cost of July 30 sale.		
Aug. 15	Cash	2,000	
	Notes Receivable—JT Co.	10,000	
	Sales		12,000
	Sold merchandise to customer for $2,000 cash and $10,000 note.		
Aug. 15	Cost of Goods Sold	8,000	
	Merchandise Inventory		8,000
	To record the cost of Aug. 15 sale.		
Nov. 1	Cash	192	
	Credit Card Expense	8	
	Sales		200
	To record credit card sale less a 4% credit card expense.		
Nov. 1	Cost of Goods Sold	150	
	Merchandise Inventory		150
	To record the cost of Nov. 1 sale.		
Nov. 3	Accounts Receivable—Sumrell Co.	1,025	
	Interest Revenue		25
	Notes Receivable—Sumrell Co.		1,000
	To charge account of Sumrell Company for a $1,000 dishonored note and interest of $1,000 × 10% × 90/360.		
Nov. 5	Accounts Receivable—Credit Card Co.	475	
	Credit Card Expense	25	
	Sales		500
	To record credit card sale less a 5% credit card expense.		
Nov. 5	Cost of Goods Sold	300	
	Merchandise Inventory		300
	To record the cost of Nov. 5 sale.		
Nov. 9	Cash	475	
	Accounts Receivable—Credit Card Co.		475
	To record cash receipt from Nov. 5 sale.		
Nov. 15	Accounts Receivable—Briggs Co.	750	
	Allowance for Doubtful Accounts		750
	To reinstate the account of Briggs Company previously written off.		
Nov. 15	Cash	750	
	Accounts Receivable—Briggs Co.		750
	Cash received in full payment of account.		
Dec. 13	Cash	10,400	
	Interest Revenue		400
	Note Receivable—JT Co.		10,000
	Collect note with interest of $10,000 × 12% × 120/360.		

2a. Aging of accounts receivable method.

Dec. 31	Bad Debts Expense	21,400	
	Allowance for Doubtful Accounts		21,400
	To adjust allowance account from a $1,000 debit balance to a $20,400 credit balance.		

2b. Percent of sales method.*

Dec. 31	Bad Debts Expense	20,000	
	Allowance for Doubtful Accounts		20,000
	To provide for bad debts as 1% × $2,000,000 in credit sales.		

*For the income statement approach, which requires estimating bad debts as a percent of sales or credit sales, the Allowance account balance is *not* considered when making the adjusting entry.

Summary

C1 Describe accounts receivable and how they occur and are recorded. Accounts receivable are amounts due from customers for credit sales. A subsidiary ledger lists amounts owed by each customer. Credit sales arise from at least two sources: (1) sales on credit and (2) credit card sales. *Sales on credit* refers to a company's granting credit directly to customers. Credit card sales involve customers' use of third-party credit cards.

C2 Describe a note receivable, the computation of its maturity date, and the recording of its existence. A note receivable is a written promise to pay a specified amount of money at a definite future date. The maturity date is the day the note (principal and interest) must be repaid. Interest rates are normally stated in annual terms. The amount of interest on the note is computed by expressing time as a fraction of one year and multiplying the note's principal by this fraction and the annual interest rate. A note received is recorded at its principal amount by debiting the Notes Receivable account. The credit amount is to the asset, product, or service provided in return for the note.

C3 Explain how receivables can be converted to cash before maturity. Receivables can be converted to cash before maturity in at least two ways. First, a company can sell accounts receivable to a factor, who charges a factoring fee. Second, a company can borrow money by signing a note payable that is secured by pledging the accounts receivable.

A1 Compute accounts receivable turnover and use it to help assess financial condition. Accounts receivable turnover is a measure of both the quality and liquidity of accounts receivable. The accounts receivable turnover measure indicates how often, on average, receivables are received and collected during the period. Accounts receivable turnover is computed as net sales divided by average accounts receivable.

P1 Apply the direct write-off method to account for accounts receivable. The direct write-off method charges Bad Debts Expense when accounts are written off as uncollectible. This method is acceptable only when the amount of bad debts expense is immaterial.

P2 Apply the allowance method and estimate uncollectibles based on sales and accounts receivable. Under the allowance method, bad debts expense is recorded with an adjustment at the end of each accounting period that debits the Bad Debts Expense account and credits the Allowance for Doubtful Accounts. The uncollectible accounts are later written off with a debit to the Allowance for Doubtful Accounts. Uncollectibles are estimated by focusing on either (1) the income statement relation between bad debts expense and credit sales or (2) the balance sheet relation between accounts receivable and the allowance for doubtful accounts. The first approach emphasizes the matching principle using the income statement. The second approach emphasizes realizable value of accounts receivable using the balance sheet.

P3 Record the honoring and dishonoring of a note and adjustments for interest. When a note is honored, the payee debits the money received and credits both Notes Receivable and Interest Revenue. Dishonored notes are credited to Notes Receivable and debited to Accounts Receivable (to the account of the maker in an attempt to collect), and Interest Revenue is recorded for interest earned for the time the note is held.

Guidance Answers to Decision Maker

Entrepreneur Analysis of credit card sales should weigh the benefits against the costs. The primary benefit is the potential to increase sales by attracting customers who prefer the convenience of credit cards. The primary cost is the fee charged by the credit card company for providing this service. Analysis should therefore estimate the expected increase in dollar sales from allowing credit card sales and then subtract (1) the normal costs and expenses and (2) the credit card fees associated with this expected increase in dollar sales. If your analysis shows an increase in profit from allowing credit card sales, your store should probably accept them.

Labor Union Chief Yes, this information is likely to impact your negotiations. The obvious question is why the company markedly increased this allowance. The large increase in this allowance means a substantial increase in bad debts expense *and* a decrease in earnings. This change (coming immediately prior to labor contract discussions) also raises concerns since it reduces the union's bargaining power for increased compensation. You want to ask management for supporting documentation justifying this increase. You also want data for two or three prior years and similar data from competitors. These data should give you some sense of whether the change in the allowance for uncollectibles is justified.

Analyst/Auditor The downward trend suggests the company is reducing the relative amount charged to bad debts expense each year. This may reflect the company's desire to increase net income. On the other hand, it might be that collections have improved and the lower provision for bad debts is justified. If this is not the case, the lower allowances might be insufficient for bad debts.

Family Physician The recommendations are twofold. First, the analyst suggests more stringent screening of patients' credit standing. Second, the analyst suggests dropping patients who are most overdue in payments. You are likely bothered by both suggestions. They are probably financially wise recommendations, but you are troubled by eliminating services to those less able to pay. One alternative is to follow the recommendations while implementing a care program directed at patients less able to pay for services. This allows you to continue services to patients less able to pay and lets you discontinue services to patients able but unwilling to pay.

Key Terms

Accounts receivable
Accounts receivable turnover
Aging of accounts receivable
Allowance for Doubtful Accounts
Allowance method
Bad debts
Direct write-off method
Interest
Maker of the note
Matching (expense recognition) principle
Materiality constraint
Maturity date of a note
Payee of the note
Principal of a note
Promissory note (or note)
Realizable value

Multiple Choice Quiz

Answers at end of chapter

1. A company's Accounts Receivable balance at its December 31 year-end is $125,650, and its Allowance for Doubtful Accounts has a credit balance of $328 before year-end adjustment. Its net sales are $572,300. It estimates that 4% of outstanding accounts receivable are uncollectible. What amount of bad debts expense is recorded at December 31?

a. $5,354 **c.** $5,026 **e.** $34,338
b. $328 **d.** $4,698

2. A company's Accounts Receivable balance at its December 31 year-end is $489,300, and its Allowance for Doubtful Accounts has a debit balance of $554 before year-end adjustment. Its net sales are $1,300,000. It estimates that 6% of outstanding accounts receivable are uncollectible. What amount of bad debts expense is recorded at December 31?

a. $29,912 **c.** $78,000 **e.** $554
b. $28,804 **d.** $29,358

3. Total interest to be earned on a $7,500, 5%, 90-day note is

a. $93.75 **c.** $1,125.00 **e.** $125.00
b. $375.00 **d.** $31.25

4. A company receives a $9,000, 8%, 60-day note. The maturity value of the note is

a. $120 **c.** $9,120 **e.** $9,720
b. $9,000 **d.** $720

5. A company has net sales of $489,600 and average accounts receivable of $40,800. What is its accounts receivable turnover?

a. 0.08 **c.** 1,341.00 **e.** 111.78
b. 30.41 **d.** 12.00

Icon denotes assignments that involve decision making.

Discussion Questions

1. How do sellers benefit from allowing their customers to use credit cards?

2. Why does the direct write-off method of accounting for bad debts usually fail to match revenues and expenses?

3. Explain the accounting constraint of materiality.

4. Why might a business prefer a note receivable to an account receivable?

5. Explain why writing off a bad debt against the Allowance for Doubtful Accounts does not reduce the estimated realizable value of a company's accounts receivable.

6. Why does the Bad Debts Expense account usually not have the same adjusted balance as the Allowance for Doubtful Accounts?

7. Refer to the financial statements and notes of **Apple** in Appendix A. In its presentation of accounts receivable on the balance sheet, how does it title accounts receivable? What does it report for its allowance as of September 28, 2013?

8. Refer to the balance sheet of **Google** in Appendix A. Does it use the direct write-off method or allowance method in accounting for its accounts receivable? What is the realizable value of its receivables balance as of December 31, 2013?

9. Refer to the financial statements of **Samsung** in Appendix A. What does Samsung title its accounts receivable on its consolidated balance sheet? What are Samsung's accounts receivable at December 31, 2013?

10. Refer to the December 31, 2013, financial statements of **Samsung** in Appendix A. Does Samsung report its accounts receivable as a current or noncurrent asset? Does Samsung report its accounts receivable net of an allowance?

QUICK STUDY

QS 7-1
Credit card sales
C1

Prepare journal entries for the following credit card sales transactions (the company uses the perpetual inventory system).

1. Sold $20,000 of merchandise, that cost $15,000, on MasterCard credit cards. The net cash receipts from sales are immediately deposited in the seller's bank account. MasterCard charges a 5% fee.

2. Sold $5,000 of merchandise, that cost $3,000, on an assortment of credit cards. Net cash receipts are received 5 days later, and a 4% fee is charged.

QS 7-2
Direct write-off method
P1

Solstice Company determines on October 1 that it cannot collect $50,000 of its accounts receivable from its customer P. Moore. Apply the direct write-off method to record this loss as of October 1.

QS 7-3
Recovering a bad debt
P1

Solstice Company determines on October 1 that it cannot collect $50,000 of its accounts receivable from its customer P. Moore. It uses the direct write-off method to record this loss as of October 1. On October 30, P. Moore unexpectedly paid his account in full to Solstice Company. Record Solstice's entry(ies) to reflect recovery of this bad debt.

QS 7-4
Distinguish between the allowance method and direct write-off method
P1 P2

The following list describes aspects of either the allowance method or the direct write-off method to account for bad debts. For each item listed, indicate if the statement best describes either the allowance method or the direct write-off method.

____ **1.** No attempt is made to predict bad debts expense.
____ **2.** Accounts receivable on the balance sheet is reported at net realizable value.
____ **3.** The write-off of a specific account does not affect net income.
____ **4.** When an account is written off, the debit is to bad debts expense.
____ **5.** Sales and any bad debt expense are usually not recorded in the same period, thus proper matching (of revenue and expense recognition) does not consistently occur.
____ **6.** Requires a company to estimate bad debt expense related to the sales recorded in that period.

QS 7-5
Allowance method for bad debts
P2

Gomez Corp. uses the allowance method to account for uncollectibles. On January 31, it wrote off an $800 account of a customer, C. Green. On March 9, it receives a $300 payment from Green.

1. Prepare the journal entry or entries for January 31.

2. Prepare the journal entry or entries for March 9; assume no additional money is expected from Green.

QS 7-6
Percent of accounts receivable method
P2

Warner Company's year-end unadjusted trial balance shows accounts receivable of $99,000, allowance for doubtful accounts of $600 (credit), and sales of $280,000. Uncollectibles are estimated to be 1.5% of accounts receivable.

1. Prepare the December 31 year-end adjusting entry for uncollectibles.

2. What amount would have been used in the year-end adjusting entry if the allowance account had a year-end unadjusted debit balance of $300?

Warner Company's year-end unadjusted trial balance shows accounts receivable of $99,000, allowance for doubtful accounts of $600 (credit), and sales of $280,000. Uncollectibles are estimated to be 0.5% of sales. Prepare the December 31 year-end adjusting entry for uncollectibles.

QS 7-7
Percent of sales method
P2

On August 2, 2015, Jun Co. receives a $6,000, 90-day, 12% note from customer Ryan Albany as payment on his $6,000 account. (1) Compute the maturity date for this note. (2) Prepare Jun's journal entry for August 2.

QS 7-8
Note receivable C2

On August 2, 2015, Jun Co. receives a $6,000, 90-day, 12% note from customer Ryan Albany as payment on his $6,000 account. Prepare Jun's journal entry assuming the note is honored by the customer on October 31, 2015.

QS 7-9
Note receivable honored P3

Daw Company's December 31 year-end unadjusted trial balance shows a $10,000 balance in Notes Receivable. This balance is from one 6% note dated December 1, with a period of 45 days. Prepare any necessary journal entries for December 31 and for the note's maturity date assuming it is honored.

QS 7-10
Note receivable P3

Record the sale by Balus Company of $125,000 in accounts receivable on May 1. Balus is charged a 2.5% factoring fee.

QS 7-11
Disposing receivables C3

The following data are taken from the comparative balance sheets of Ruggers Company. Compute and interpret its accounts receivable turnover for year 2015 (competitors average a turnover of 7.5).

	2015	2014
Accounts receivable, net	$153,400	$138,500
Net sales	861,105	910,600

QS 7-12
Accounts receivable turnover
A1

Answer each of the following related to international accounting standards.

a. Explain (in general terms) how the accounting for recognition of receivables is different between IFRS and U.S. GAAP.

b. Explain (in general terms) how the accounting for valuation of receivables is different between IFRS and U.S. GAAP.

QS 7-13
International accounting standards
C1

connect

EXERCISES

Vail Company recorded the following selected transactions during November 2015.

Nov. 5	Accounts Receivable—Ski Shop	4,615	
	Sales		4,615
10	Accounts Receivable—Welcome Enterprises	1,350	
	Sales		1,350
13	Accounts Receivable—Zia Natara	832	
	Sales		832
21	Sales Returns and Allowances	209	
	Accounts Receivable—Zia Natara		209
30	Accounts Receivable—Ski Shop	2,713	
	Sales		2,713

Exercise 7-1
Accounts receivable subsidiary ledger; schedule of accounts receivable
C1

1. Open a general ledger having T-accounts for Accounts Receivable, Sales, and Sales Returns and Allowances. Also open an accounts receivable subsidiary ledger having a T-account for each customer. Post these entries to both the general ledger and the accounts receivable ledger.

2. Prepare a schedule of accounts receivable (see Exhibit 7.4) and compare its total with the balance of the Accounts Receivable controlling account as of November 30.

Check Accounts Receivable ending balance, $9,301

Exercise 7-2
Accounting for credit card sales
C1

Levine Company uses the perpetual inventory system and allows customers to use two credit cards in charging purchases. With the Suntrust Bank Card, Levine receives an immediate credit to its account when it deposits sales receipts. Suntrust assesses a 4% service charge for credit card sales. The second credit card that Levine accepts is the Continental Card. Levine sends its accumulated receipts to Continental on a weekly basis and is paid by Continental about a week later. Continental assesses a 2.5% charge on sales for using its card. Prepare journal entries to record the following selected credit card transactions of Levine Company.

Apr. 8 Sold merchandise for $8,400 (that had cost $6,000) and accepted the customer's Suntrust Bank Card. The Suntrust receipts are immediately deposited in Levine's bank account.
12 Sold merchandise for $5,600 (that had cost $3,500) and accepted the customer's Continental Card. Transferred $5,600 of credit card receipts to Continental, requesting payment.
20 Received Continental's check for the April 12 billing, less the service charge.

Exercise 7-3
Direct write-off method
P1

Dexter Company applies the direct write-off method in accounting for uncollectible accounts. Prepare journal entries to record the following selected transactions of Dexter.

March 11 Dexter determines that it cannot collect $45,000 of its accounts receivable from its customer Lester Company.
29 Lester Company unexpectedly pays its account in full to Dexter Company. Dexter records its recovery of this bad debt.

Exercise 7-4
Percent of sales method; write-off
P2

At year-end (December 31), Chan Company estimates its bad debts as 0.5% of its annual credit sales of $975,000. Chan records its bad debts expense for that estimate. On the following February 1, Chan decides that the $580 account of P. Park is uncollectible and writes it off as a bad debt. On June 5, Park unexpectedly pays the amount previously written off. Prepare the journal entries of Chan to record these transactions and events of December 31, February 1, and June 5.

Exercise 7-5
Percent of accounts receivable method
P2

At each calendar year-end, Mazie Supply Co. uses the percent of accounts receivable method to estimate bad debts. On December 31, 2015, it has outstanding accounts receivable of $55,000, and it estimates that 2% will be uncollectible. Prepare the adjusting entry to record bad debts expense for year 2015 under the assumption that the Allowance for Doubtful Accounts has (*a*) a $415 credit balance before the adjustment and (*b*) a $291 debit balance before the adjustment.

Exercise 7-6
Aging of receivables method
P2

Daley Company estimates uncollectible accounts using the allowance method at December 31. It prepared the following aging of receivables analysis.

		Days Past Due				
	Total	0	1 to 30	31 to 60	61 to 90	Over 90
Accounts receivable	$570,000	$396,000	$90,000	$36,000	$18,000	$30,000
Percent uncollectible		1%	2%	5%	7%	10%

a. Estimate the balance of the Allowance for Doubtful Accounts using the aging of accounts receivable method.

b. Prepare the adjusting entry to record bad debts expense using the estimate from part *a*. Assume the unadjusted balance in the Allowance for Doubtful Accounts is a $3,600 credit.

c. Prepare the adjusting entry to record bad debts expense using the estimate from part *a*. Assume the unadjusted balance in the Allowance for Doubtful Accounts is a $100 debit.

Exercise 7-7
Percent of receivables method
P2

Refer to the information in Exercise 7-6 to complete the following requirements.

a. Estimate the balance of the Allowance for Doubtful Accounts assuming the company uses 4.5% of total accounts receivable to estimate uncollectibles, instead of the aging of receivables method.

b. Prepare the adjusting entry to record bad debts expense using the estimate from part *a*. Assume the unadjusted balance in the Allowance for Doubtful Accounts is a $12,000 credit.

c. Prepare the adjusting entry to record bad debts expense using the estimate from part *a*. Assume the unadjusted balance in the Allowance for Doubtful Accounts is a $1,000 debit.

Exercise 7-8
Writing off receivables
P2

Refer to the information in Exercise 7-6 to complete the following requirements.

a. On February 1 of the next period, the company determined that $6,800 in customer accounts is uncollectible; specifically, $900 for Oakley Co. and $5,900 for Brookes Co. Prepare the journal entry to write off those accounts.

b. On June 5 of that next period, the company unexpectedly received a $900 payment on a customer account, Oakley Company, that had previously been written off in part *a*. Prepare the entries necessary to reinstate the account and to record the cash received.

Exercise 7-9
Estimating bad debts
P2

At December 31, Folgeys Coffee Company reports the following results for its calendar year.

Cash sales	$900,000
Credit sales	300,000

Its year-end unadjusted trial balance includes the following items.

Accounts receivable	$125,000 debit
Allowance for doubtful accounts	5,000 debit

a. Prepare the adjusting entry to record bad debts expense assuming uncollectibles are estimated to be 3% of credit sales.

b. Prepare the adjusting entry to record bad debts expense assuming uncollectibles are estimated to be 1% of total sales.

c. Prepare the adjusting entry to record bad debts expense assuming uncollectibles are estimated to be 6% of year-end accounts receivable.

Check Dr. Bad Debts Expense: (*a*) $9,000

(*c*) $12,500

Exercise 7-10
Notes receivable transactions
C2

Prepare journal entries for the following selected transactions of Danica Company for 2014.

2014

Dec. 13 Accepted a $9,500, 45-day, 8% note dated December 13 in granting Miranda Lee a time extension on her past-due account receivable.

31 Prepared an adjusting entry to record the accrued interest on the Lee note.

Check Dec. 31, Cr. Interest Revenue $38

Exercise 7-11
Notes receivable transactions P3

Refer to the information in Exercise 7-10 and prepare the journal entries for the following selected transactions of Danica Company for 2015.

2015

Jan. 27 Received Lee's payment for principal and interest on the note dated December 13.

Mar. 3 Accepted a $5,000, 10%, 90-day note dated March 3 in granting a time extension on the past-due account receivable of Tomas Company.

17 Accepted a $2,000, 30-day, 9% note dated March 17 in granting H. Cheng a time extension on his past-due account receivable.

Apr. 16 Cheng dishonors his note when presented for payment.

May 1 Wrote off the Cheng account against the Allowance for Doubtful Accounts.

June 1 Received the Tomas payment for principal and interest on the note dated March 3.

Check Jan. 27, Dr. Cash $9,595

June 1, Dr. Cash $5,125

Exercise 7-12
Honoring a note
P3

Prepare journal entries to record these selected transactions for Vitalo Company (assume that no reversing entries are recorded).

Nov. 1 Accepted a $6,000, 180-day, 8% note dated November 1 from Kelly White in granting a time extension on her past-due account receivable.

Dec. 31 Adjusted the year-end accounts for the accrued interest earned on the White note.

Apr. 30 White honors her note when presented for payment; February has 28 days for the current year.

Exercise 7-13
Dishonoring a note
P3

Prepare journal entries to record the following selected transactions of Ridge Company.

Mar. 21 Accepted a $9,500, 180-day, 8% note dated March 21 from Tamara Jackson in granting a time extension on her past-due account receivable.
Sept. 17 Jackson dishonors her note when it is presented for payment.
Dec. 31 After exhausting all legal means of collection, Ridge Company writes off Jackson's account against the Allowance for Doubtful Accounts.

Exercise 7-14
Selling and pledging accounts receivable
C3

On June 30, Petrov Co. has $128,700 of accounts receivable. Prepare journal entries to record the following selected July transactions. Also prepare any footnotes to the July 31 financial statements that result from these transactions. (The company uses the perpetual inventory system.)

July 4 Sold $7,245 of merchandise (that had cost $5,000) to customers on credit.
9 Sold $20,000 of accounts receivable to Main Bank. Main charges a 4% factoring fee.
17 Received $5,859 cash from customers in payment on their accounts.
27 Borrowed $10,000 cash from Main Bank, pledging $12,500 of accounts receivable as security for the loan.

Exercise 7-15
Accounts receivable turnover
A1

The following information is from the annual financial statements of Raheem Company. Compute its accounts receivable turnover for 2014 and 2015. Compare the two years' results and give a possible explanation for any change (competitors average a turnover of 11).

	2015	2014	2013
Net sales	$405,140	$335,280	$388,000
Accounts receivable, net (year-end)	44,800	41,400	34,800

Exercise 7-16
Accounting for bad debts following IFRS
P2

Hitachi, Ltd., reports total revenues of ¥9,041,071 million for its fiscal year ending March 31, 2013, and its March 31, 2013, unadjusted trial balance reports a debit balance for trade receivables (gross) of ¥2,500,000 million.

a. Prepare the adjusting entry to record its bad debts expense assuming uncollectibles are estimated to be 0.4% of total revenues and its unadjusted trial balance reports a credit balance of ¥10,000 million for the allowance for doubtful accounts.

b. Prepare the adjusting entry to record bad debts expense assuming uncollectibles are estimated to be 2.0% of year-end trade receivables (gross) and its unadjusted trial balance reports a credit balance of ¥10,000 million for the allowance for doubtful accounts.

connect

PROBLEM SET A

Problem 7-1A
Sales on account and credit card sales
C1

Mayfair Co. allows select customers to make purchases on credit. Its other customers can use either of two credit cards: Zisa or Access. Zisa deducts a 3% service charge for sales on its credit card and credits the bank account of Mayfair immediately when credit card receipts are deposited. Mayfair deposits the Zisa credit card receipts each business day. When customers use Access credit cards, Mayfair accumulates the receipts for several days before submitting them to Access for payment. Access deducts a 2% service charge and usually pays within one week of being billed. Mayfair completes the following transactions in June. (The terms of all credit sales are 2/15, n/30, and all sales are recorded at the gross price.)

June 4 Sold $650 of merchandise (that had cost $400) on credit to Natara Morris.
5 Sold $6,900 of merchandise (that had cost $4,200) to customers who used their Zisa cards.
6 Sold $5,850 of merchandise (that had cost $3,800) to customers who used their Access cards.
8 Sold $4,350 of merchandise (that had cost $2,900) to customers who used their Access cards.
10 Submitted Access card receipts accumulated since June 6 to the credit card company for payment.
13 Wrote off the account of Abigail McKee against the Allowance for Doubtful Accounts. The $429 balance in McKee's account stemmed from a credit sale in October of last year.
17 Received the amount due from Access.
18 Received Morris's check in full payment for the purchase of June 4.

Check June 17, Dr. Cash $9,996

Required

Prepare journal entries to record the preceding transactions and events. (The company uses the perpetual inventory system. Round amounts to the nearest dollar.)

Problem 7-2A
Estimating and reporting bad debts
P2

At December 31, 2015, Hawke Company reports the following results for its calendar year.

Cash sales	$1,905,000
Credit sales	5,682,000

In addition, its unadjusted trial balance includes the following items.

Accounts receivable	$1,270,100 debit
Allowance for doubtful accounts	16,580 debit

Required

1. Prepare the adjusting entry for this company to recognize bad debts under each of the following independent assumptions.
   a. Bad debts are estimated to be 1.5% of credit sales.
   b. Bad debts are estimated to be 1% of total sales.
   c. An aging analysis estimates that 5% of year-end accounts receivable are uncollectible.
2. Show how Accounts Receivable and the Allowance for Doubtful Accounts appear on its December 31, 2015, balance sheet given the facts in part 1*a*.
3. Show how Accounts Receivable and the Allowance for Doubtful Accounts appear on its December 31, 2015, balance sheet given the facts in part 1*c*.

Check Bad Debts Expense: (1*a*) $85,230, (1*c*) $80,085

Problem 7-3A
Aging accounts receivable and accounting for bad debts
P2

Jarden Company has credit sales of $3.6 million for year 2015. On December 31, 2015, the company's Allowance for Doubtful Accounts has an unadjusted credit balance of $14,500. Jarden prepares a schedule of its December 31, 2015, accounts receivable by age. On the basis of past experience, it estimates the percent of receivables in each age category that will become uncollectible. This information is summarized here.

	A	B	C
1 2	**December 31, 2015 Accounts Receivable**	**Age of Accounts Receivable**	**Expected Percent Uncollectible**
3	$830,000	Not yet due	1.25%
4	254,000	1 to 30 days past due	2.00
5	86,000	31 to 60 days past due	6.50
6	38,000	61 to 90 days past due	32.75
7	12,000	Over 90 days past due	68.00
8			

Required

1. Estimate the required balance of the Allowance for Doubtful Accounts at December 31, 2015, using the aging of accounts receivable method.
2. Prepare the adjusting entry to record bad debts expense at December 31, 2015.

Check (2) Dr. Bad Debts Expense $27,150

Analysis Component

3. On June 30, 2016, Jarden Company concludes that a customer's $4,750 receivable (created in 2015) is uncollectible and that the account should be written off. What effect will this action have on Jarden's 2016 net income? Explain.

Problem 7-4A
Accounts receivable transactions and bad debts adjustments
C1 P2

Liang Company began operations on January 1, 2014. During its first two years, the company completed a number of transactions involving sales on credit, accounts receivable collections, and bad debts. These transactions are summarized as follows:

2014

a. Sold $1,345,434 of merchandise (that had cost $975,000) on credit, terms n/30.
b. Wrote off $18,300 of uncollectible accounts receivable.
c. Received $669,200 cash in payment of accounts receivable.
d. In adjusting the accounts on December 31, the company estimated that 1.5% of accounts receivable will be uncollectible.

Check (*d*) Dr. Bad Debts Expense $28,169

2015

e. Sold $1,525,634 of merchandise (that had cost $1,250,000) on credit, terms n/30.

f. Wrote off $27,800 of uncollectible accounts receivable.

g. Received $1,204,600 cash in payment of accounts receivable.

(h) Dr. Bad Debts Expense $32,199

h. In adjusting the accounts on December 31, the company estimated that 1.5% of accounts receivable will be uncollectible.

Required

Prepare journal entries to record Liang's 2014 and 2015 summarized transactions and its year-end adjustments to record bad debts expense. (The company uses the perpetual inventory system and it applies the allowance method for its accounts receivable. Round amounts to the nearest dollar.)

Problem 7-5A
Analyzing and journalizing notes receivable transactions
C2 C3 P3

The following selected transactions are from Ohlm Company.

2014

Dec. 16 Accepted a $10,800, 60-day, 8% note dated this day in granting Danny Todd a time extension on his past-due account receivable.

31 Made an adjusting entry to record the accrued interest on the Todd note.

2015

Check Feb. 14, Cr. Interest Revenue $108

Feb. 14 Received Todd's payment of principal and interest on the note dated December 16.

Mar. 2 Accepted a $6,100, 8%, 90-day note dated this day in granting a time extension on the past-due account receivable from Midnight Co.

17 Accepted a $2,400, 30-day, 7% note dated this day in granting Ava Privet a time extension on her past-due account receivable.

Apr. 16 Privet dishonored her note when presented for payment.

May 31, Cr. Interest Revenue $122

May 31 Midnight Co. refuses to pay the note that was due to Ohlm Co. on May 31. Prepare the journal entry to charge the dishonored note plus accrued interest to Midnight Co.'s accounts receivable.

July 16 Received payment from Midnight Co. for the maturity value of its dishonored note plus interest for 46 days beyond maturity at 8%.

Aug. 7 Accepted a $7,450, 90-day, 10% note dated this day in granting a time extension on the past-due account receivable of Mulan Co.

Sept. 3 Accepted a $2,100, 60-day, 10% note dated this day in granting Noah Carson a time extension on his past-due account receivable.

Nov. 2, Cr. Interest Revenue $35

Nov. 2 Received payment of principal plus interest from Carson for the September 3 note.

Nov. 5 Received payment of principal plus interest from Mulan for the August 7 note.

Dec. 1 Wrote off the Privet account against Allowance for Doubtful Accounts.

Required

1. Prepare journal entries to record these transactions and events. (Round amounts to the nearest dollar.)

Analysis Component

2. What reporting is necessary when a business pledges receivables as security for a loan and the loan is still outstanding at the end of the period? Explain the reason for this requirement and the accounting principle being satisfied.

PROBLEM SET B

Problem 7-1B
Sales on account and credit card sales
C1

Archer Co. allows select customers to make purchases on credit. Its other customers can use either of two credit cards: Commerce Bank or Aztec. Commerce Bank deducts a 3% service charge for sales on its credit card and immediately credits the bank account of Archer when credit card receipts are deposited. Archer deposits the Commerce Bank credit card receipts each business day. When customers use the Aztec card, Archer accumulates the receipts for several days and then submits them to Aztec for payment. Aztec deducts a 2% service charge and usually pays within one week of being billed. Archer completed the following transactions in August (terms of all credit sales are 2/10, n/30; and all sales are recorded at the gross price).

Aug. 4 Sold $3,700 of merchandise (that had cost $2,000) on credit to McKenzie Carpenter.

10 Sold $5,200 of merchandise (that had cost $2,800) to customers who used their Commerce Bank credit cards.

11 Sold $1,250 of merchandise (that had cost $900) to customers who used their Aztec cards.
14 Received Carpenter's check in full payment for the purchase of August 4.
15 Sold $3,240 of merchandise (that had cost $1,758) to customers who used their Aztec cards.
18 Submitted Aztec card receipts accumulated since August 11 to the credit card company for payment.
22 Wrote off the account of Craw Co. against the Allowance for Doubtful Accounts. The $498 balance in Craw Co.'s account stemmed from a credit sale in November of last year.
25 Received the amount due from Aztec.

Check Aug. 25, Dr. Cash $4,400

Required

Prepare journal entries to record the preceding transactions and events. (The company uses the perpetual inventory system. Round amounts to the nearest dollar.)

Problem 7-2B
Estimating and reporting bad debts
P2

At December 31, 2015, Ingleton Company reports the following results for the year:

Cash sales	$1,025,000
Credit sales	1,342,000

In addition, its unadjusted trial balance includes the following items:

Accounts receivable	$575,000 debit
Allowance for doubtful accounts	7,500 credit

Required

1. Prepare the adjusting entry for Ingleton Co. to recognize bad debts under each of the following independent assumptions.
   a. Bad debts are estimated to be 2.5% of credit sales.
   b. Bad debts are estimated to be 1.5% of total sales.
   c. An aging analysis estimates that 6% of year-end accounts receivable are uncollectible.

Check Dr. Bad debts expense: (1*b*) $35,505, (1*c*) $27,000

2. Show how Accounts Receivable and the Allowance for Doubtful Accounts appear on its December 31, 2015, balance sheet given the facts in part 1*a*.

3. Show how Accounts Receivable and the Allowance for Doubtful Accounts appear on its December 31, 2015, balance sheet given the facts in part 1*c*.

Problem 7-3B
Aging accounts receivable and accounting for bad debts
P2

Hovak Company has credit sales of $4.5 million for year 2015. At December 31, 2015, the company's Allowance for Doubtful Accounts has an unadjusted debit balance of $3,400. Hovak prepares a schedule of its December 31, 2015, accounts receivable by age. On the basis of past experience, it estimates the percent of receivables in each age category that will become uncollectible. This information is summarized here.

	A	B	C
1–2	December 31, 2015 Accounts Receivable	Age of Accounts Receivable	Expected Percent Uncollectible
3	$396,400	Not yet due	2.0%
4	277,800	1 to 30 days past due	4.0
5	48,000	31 to 60 days past due	8.5
6	6,600	61 to 90 days past due	39.0
7	2,800	Over 90 days past due	82.0
8			

Required

1. Compute the required balance of the Allowance for Doubtful Accounts at December 31, 2015, using the aging of accounts receivable method.

2. Prepare the adjusting entry to record bad debts expense at December 31, 2015.

Check (2) Dr. Bad Debts Expense $31,390

Analysis Component

3. On July 31, 2016, Hovak concludes that a customer's $3,455 receivable (created in 2015) is uncollectible and that the account should be written off. What effect will this action have on Hovak's 2016 net income? Explain.

Problem 7-4B
Accounts receivable transactions and bad debts adjustments
C1 P2

Sherman Co. began operations on January 1, 2014, and completed several transactions during 2014 and 2015 that involved sales on credit, accounts receivable collections, and bad debts. These transactions are summarized as follows.

2014

a. Sold $685,350 of merchandise (that had cost $500,000) on credit, terms n/30.

b. Received $482,300 cash in payment of accounts receivable.

c. Wrote off $9,350 of uncollectible accounts receivable.

d. In adjusting the accounts on December 31, the company estimated that 1% of accounts receivable will be uncollectible.

Check (*d*) Dr. Bad Debts Expense $11,287

2015

e. Sold $870,220 of merchandise (that had cost $650,000) on credit, terms n/30.

f. Received $990,800 cash in payment of accounts receivable.

g. Wrote off $11,090 of uncollectible accounts receivable.

h. In adjusting the accounts on December 31, the company estimated that 1% of accounts receivable will be uncollectible.

(*h*) Dr. Bad Debts Expense $9,773

Required

Prepare journal entries to record Sherman's 2014 and 2015 summarized transactions and its year-end adjusting entry to record bad debts expense. (The company uses the perpetual inventory system and it applies the allowance method for its accounts receivable. Round amounts to the nearest dollar.)

Problem 7-5B
Analyzing and journalizing notes receivable transactions
C2 C3 P3

The following selected transactions are from Springer Company.

2014

Nov. 1 Accepted a $4,800, 90-day, 8% note dated this day in granting Steve Julian a time extension on his past-due account receivable.

Dec. 31 Made an adjusting entry to record the accrued interest on the Julian note.

2015

Jan. 30 Received Julian's payment for principal and interest on the note dated November 1.

Feb. 28 Accepted a $12,600, 30-day, 8% note dated this day in granting a time extension on the past-due account receivable from King Co.

Mar. 1 Accepted a $6,200, 60-day, 12% note dated this day in granting Myron Shelley a time extension on his past-due account receivable.

30 The King Co. dishonored its note when presented for payment.

Apr. 30 Received payment of principal plus interest from M. Shelley for the March 1 note.

June 15 Accepted a $2,000, 72-day, 8% note dated this day in granting a time extension on the past-due account receivable of Ryder Solon.

21 Accepted a $9,500, 90-day, 8% note dated this day in granting J. Felton a time extension on his past-due account receivable.

Aug. 26 Received payment of principal plus interest from R. Solon for the note of June 15.

Sep. 19 Received payment of principal plus interest from J. Felton for the June 21 note.

Nov. 30 Wrote off King's account against Allowance for Doubtful Accounts.

Check Jan. 30, Cr. Interest Revenue $32

April 30, Cr. Interest Revenue $124

Sep. 19, Cr. Interest Revenue $190

Required

1. Prepare journal entries to record these transactions and events. (Round amounts to the nearest dollar.)

Analysis Component

2. What reporting is necessary when a business pledges receivables as security for a loan and the loan is still outstanding at the end of the period? Explain the reason for this requirement and the accounting principle being satisfied.

SERIAL PROBLEM

Business Solutions

P1 P2

(This serial problem began in Chapter 1 and continues through most of the book. If previous chapter segments were not completed, the serial problem can begin at this point. It is helpful, but not necessary, to use the Working Papers that accompany the book.)

SP 7 Santana Rey, owner of Business Solutions, realizes that she needs to begin accounting for bad debts expense. Assume that Business Solutions has total revenues of $44,000 during the first three months of 2016, and that the Accounts Receivable balance on March 31, 2016, is $22,867.

Required

1. Prepare the adjusting entry needed for Business Solutions to recognize bad debts expense on March 31, 2016, under each of the following independent assumptions (assume a zero unadjusted balance in the Allowance for Doubtful Accounts at March 31).
   - **a.** Bad debts are estimated to be 1% of total revenues. (Round amounts to the dollar.)
   - **b.** Bad debts are estimated to be 2% of accounts receivable. (Round amounts to the dollar.)
2. Assume that Business Solutions' Accounts Receivable balance at June 30, 2016, is $20,250 and that one account of $100 has been written off against the Allowance for Doubtful Accounts since March 31, 2016. If S. Rey uses the method prescribed in part 1*b*, what adjusting journal entry must be made to recognize bad debts expense on June 30, 2016?
3. Should S. Rey consider adopting the direct write-off method of accounting for bad debts expense rather than one of the allowance methods considered in part 1? Explain.

Check (2) Dr. Bad Debts Expense, $48

GENERAL LEDGER PROBLEM

Available in Connect

The **General Ledger** tool in *Connect* automates several of the procedural steps in accounting so that the financial professional can focus on the impacts of each transaction on various financial reports and performance measures.

GL 7-1 General Ledger assignment GL 7-1, based on Problem 7-5A, focuses on transactions related to accounts and notes receivable and highlights the impact each transaction has on interest revenue, if any. Prepare the journal entries related to accounts and notes receivable; the schedules of accounts receivable and notes receivable are automatically completed using the General Ledger tool. Next, compute both the amount and timing of interest revenue for each note receivable.

connect ACCOUNTING

Beyond the Numbers

REPORTING IN ACTION

A1

APPLE

BTN 7-1 Refer to **Apple**'s financial statements in Appendix A to answer the following.

1. What is the amount of Apple's accounts receivable as of September 28, 2013?
2. Compute Apple's accounts receivable turnover as of September 28, 2013.
3. How long does it take, *on average,* for the company to collect receivables?
4. Apple's most liquid assets include (*a*) cash and cash equivalents, (*b*) short-term marketable securities, (*c*) receivables, and (*d*) inventory. Compute the percentage that these liquid assets make up of current liabilities as of September 28, 2013. Do the same computations for September 29, 2012. Comment on the company's ability to satisfy its current liabilities as of its fiscal 2013 year-end compared to its fiscal 2012 year-end.
5. What criteria did Apple use to classify items as cash equivalents? (*Hint:* Refer to Apple's footnotes describing cash equivalents in Appendix A.)

Fast Forward

6. Access Apple's financial statements for fiscal years after September 28, 2013, at its website (www.Apple.com) or the SEC's EDGAR database (www.SEC.gov). Recompute parts 2 and 4 and comment on any changes since September 28, 2013.

COMPARATIVE ANALYSIS

A1 P2

APPLE
GOOGLE

BTN 7-2 Comparative figures for **Apple** and **Google** follow.

($ millions)	Apple			Google		
	Current Year	One Year Prior	Two Years Prior	Current Year	One Year Prior	Two Years Prior
Accounts receivable, net . .	$ 13,102	$ 10,930	$ 5,369	$ 8,882	$ 7,885	$ 5,427
Net sales	170,910	156,508	108,249	59,825	50,175	37,905

Required

1. Compute the accounts receivable turnover for Apple and Google for each of the two most recent years using the data shown.
2. Using results from part 1, compute how many days it takes each company, *on average,* to collect receivables. Compare the collection periods for Apple and Google, and suggest at least one explanation for the difference.
3. Which company is more efficient in collecting its accounts receivable? Explain.

Hint: Average collection period equals 365 divided by the accounts receivable turnover.

ETHICS CHALLENGE

P2

BTN 7-3 Anton Blair is the manager of a medium-size company. A few years ago, Blair persuaded the owner to base a part of his compensation on the net income the company earns each year. Each December he estimates year-end financial figures in anticipation of the bonus he will receive. If the bonus is not as high as he would like, he offers several recommendations to the accountant for year-end adjustments. One of his favorite recommendations is for the controller to reduce the estimate of doubtful accounts.

Required

1. What effect does lowering the estimate for doubtful accounts have on the income statement and balance sheet?
2. Do you believe Blair's recommendation to adjust the allowance for doubtful accounts is within his rights as manager, or do you believe this action is an ethics violation? Justify your response.
3. What type of internal control(s) might be useful for this company in overseeing the manager's recommendations for accounting changes?

COMMUNICATING IN PRACTICE

P2

BTN 7-4 As the accountant for Pure-Air Distributing, you attend a sales managers' meeting devoted to a discussion of credit policies. At the meeting, you report that bad debts expense is estimated to be $59,000 and accounts receivable at year-end amount to $1,750,000 less a $43,000 allowance for doubtful accounts. Sid Omar, a sales manager, expresses confusion over why bad debts expense and the allowance for doubtful accounts are different amounts. Write a one-page memorandum to him explaining why a difference in bad debts expense and the allowance for doubtful accounts is not unusual. The company estimates bad debts expense as 2% of sales.

TAKING IT TO THE NET

C1

BTN 7-5 Access **eBay**'s, January 31, 2014, filing of its 10-K report for the year ended December 31, 2013, at www.SEC.gov.

Required

1. What is the amount of eBay's net accounts receivable at December 31, 2013, and at December 31, 2012?
2. "Financial Statement Schedule II" to its financial statements lists eBay's allowance for doubtful accounts (including authorized credits). For the two years ended December 31, 2013 and 2012, compute its allowance for doubtful accounts (including authorized credits) as a percent of gross accounts receivable.
3. Do you believe that these percentages are reasonable based on what you know about eBay? Explain.

TEAMWORK IN ACTION

P2

BTN 7-6 Each member of a team is to participate in estimating uncollectibles using the aging schedule and percents shown in Problem 7-3A. The division of labor is up to the team. Your goal is to accurately complete this task as soon as possible. After estimating uncollectibles, check your estimate with the instructor. If the estimate is correct, the team then should prepare the adjusting entry and the presentation of accounts receivable (net) for the December 31, 2015, balance sheet.

BTN 7-7 Rakia Reynolds of **Skai Blue Media** is introduced in the chapter's opening feature. Rakia has a client that currently sells his products through multiple outlets. The client asks Rakia for guidance as he is considering two possible plans, A or B, for expanding sales for his merchandising company.

ENTREPRENEURIAL DECISION

C1

Plan A. The client would begin selling additional products online directly to customers, which are only currently sold directly to stores. These new online customers would use their credit cards. It currently has the capability of selling through its website with no additional investment in hardware or software. Credit sales are expected to increase by $250,000 per year. Costs associated with this plan are: cost of these sales will be $135,500, credit card fees will be 4.75% of sales, and additional recordkeeping and shipping costs will be 6% of sales. These online sales will reduce the sales to stores by $35,000 because some customers will now purchase items online. Sales to stores have a 25% gross margin percentage.

Plan B. The client would expand its market to more stores. It would make additional credit sales of $500,000 to those stores. Costs associated with those sales are: cost of sales will be $375,000, additional recordkeeping and shipping will be 4% of sales, and uncollectible accounts will be 6.2% of sales.

Required

1. Compute the additional annual net income or loss expected under (a) Plan A and (b) Plan B.
2. Should the client pursue either plan? Discuss both the financial and nonfinancial factors relevant to this decision.

Check (1*b*) Additional net income, $74,000

BTN 7-8 Many commercials include comments similar to the following: "We accept **VISA**" or "We do not accept **American Express.**" Conduct your own research by contacting at least five companies via interviews, phone calls, or the Internet to determine the reason(s) companies discriminate in their use of credit cards. Collect information on the fees charged by the different cards for the companies contacted. (The instructor can assign this as a team activity.)

HITTING THE ROAD

C1

BTN 7-9 Key information from **Samsung (www.Samsung.com)**, which is a leading manufacturer of consumer electronic products, follows.

GLOBAL DECISION

C1 P2

Samsung
APPLE
GOOGLE

₩ in millions	Current Year	One Year Prior	Two Years Prior
Accounts receivable, net*	₩ 27,875,934	₩ 26,674,596	₩ 24,153,028
Sales	228,692,667	201,103,613	165,001,771

*Samsung refers to it as "Trade and other receivables."

1. Compute the accounts receivable turnover for the current year.
2. How long does it take on average for Samsung to collect receivables?
3. Refer to BTN 7-2. How does Samsung compare to **Apple** and **Google** in terms of its accounts receivable turnover and its collection period?

ANSWERS TO MULTIPLE CHOICE QUIZ

1. d; Desired balance in Allowance for Doubtful Accounts = $ 5,026 cr.
   ($125,650 $\times$ 0.04)
   Current balance in Allowance for Doubtful Accounts = (328) cr.
   Bad Debts Expense to be recorded = $ 4,698
2. a; Desired balance in Allowance for Doubtful Accounts = $29,358 cr.
   ($489,300 $\times$ 0.06)
   Current balance in Allowance for Doubtful Accounts = 554 dr.
   Bad Debts Expense to be recorded = $29,912
3. a; $7,500 $\times$ 0.05 $\times$ 90/360 = $93.75
4. c; Principal amount $9,000
   Interest accrued . . . . 120 ($9,000 $\times$ 0.08 $\times$ 60/360)
   Maturity value $9,120
5. d; $489,600/$40,800 = 12

chapter 8

Accounting for Long-Term Assets

Chapter Preview

PLANT ASSETS	NATURAL RESOURCES	INTANGIBLE ASSETS
C1 Cost determination	P3 Cost determination	P4 Cost determination
P1 Depreciation	Depletion	Amortization
C2 Partial-years and changes in estimates	Presentation	Types of intangibles
C3 Additional expenditures	Plant assets tied into extracting resources	A1 Analyze asset usage
P2 Disposal		

Learning Objectives

CONCEPTUAL

C1 Explain the cost principle for computing the cost of plant assets.

C2 Explain depreciation for partial years and changes in estimates.

C3 Distinguish between revenue and capital expenditures, and account for them.

ANALYTICAL

A1 Compute total asset turnover and apply it to analyze a company's use of assets.

PROCEDURAL

P1 Compute and record depreciation using the straight-line, units-of-production, and declining-balance methods.

P2 Account for asset disposal through discarding or selling an asset.

P3 Account for natural resource assets and their depletion.

P4 Account for intangible assets.

P5 *Appendix 8A*—Account for asset exchanges.

Casper Hedberg/Bloomberg via Getty Images

Crafting the Dream

NEW GLARUS, WI—"When I was 10, I was walking around saying, 'Geez, I'd like to own a brewery,'" jokes Deb Carey. All kidding aside, Deb explains that "At a certain point I thought, I'll start a brewery." Deb describes how "One day, we were talking to a maltster in Wisconsin, and the person asked if we were bidding on the equipment for sale in Appleton. It was equipment for a 20-barrel stainless system for a brew pub." She soon decided, "I'm going to bid on it!" Her husband Dan reminded her, "But we don't have any money." Deb then declared, "I'm going to sell the house." Soon, she explains, "I put all the listing stuff together to sell the house, then I got on a train." Such was the launch of **New Glarus Brewing Co. (NewGlarusBrewing.com)**.

> *"Constantly strive to surpass yourself, not the competition"*
> **—Deb Carey**

From those modest beginnings, Deb has persevered. "In that first year, we took home $16,000, with no health insurance and no time off," explains Deb. "We had no money, and we were working from 5 a.m. to midnight. We were renting a house with no dishwasher where the basement leaked and the heater went out." Moreover, long-term assets in the brewery such as brew houses, packaging lines, and fermentation cellars are expensive. Deb explains that financing that equipment, buildings, and other assets was challenging. She explains that one must be a little creative. For example, in the case of one of her new buildings, she "got a grant for $1.7 million for energy savings." Creative indeed!

New Glarus Brewing is currently on a roll—employing nearly 100 workers, offering unique products such as Spotted Cow, and generating over 100,000 barrels of beer annually with more than $31 million in yearly sales. Still, a constant challenge for Deb is maintaining the right kind and amount of assets to meet business demands and be profitable. "Machinery cannot be divorced from the process," insists Dan. "Machinery has its own personality, its own temperament, and its own foibles. So you have to work with the strengths and weaknesses of your machinery."

Deb explains that New Glarus Brewing Co.'s success depends on continued monitoring and control of the types and costs of long-term assets. Each of her tangible and intangible assets commands Deb's attention. She accounts for, manages, and focuses on recovering all costs of those acquisitions, including her current $11 million expansion plan. "It really is like having a big family," says Deb. "I feel like I am giving something back to the community. The people who work here are the best on the planet, and I try to take care of them."

Sources: *New Glarus Brewing Co. website,* January 2015; *The Daily Page,* August 2013; *Wisconsin State Journal,* July 2011; *The Business Journal,* June 2013

Section 1—Plant Assets

Plant assets are tangible assets used in a company's operations that have a useful life of more than one accounting period. Plant assets are also called *plant and equipment; property, plant and equipment;* or *fixed assets.* For many companies, plant assets make up the single largest class of assets they own. Exhibit 8.1 shows plant assets as a percent of total assets for several companies. Not only do they make up a large percent of many companies' assets, but their dollar values are large. **McDonald's** plant assets, for instance, are reported at more than $22 billion, and **Walmart** reports plant assets of more than $107 billion.

EXHIBIT 8.1

Plant Assets of Selected Companies

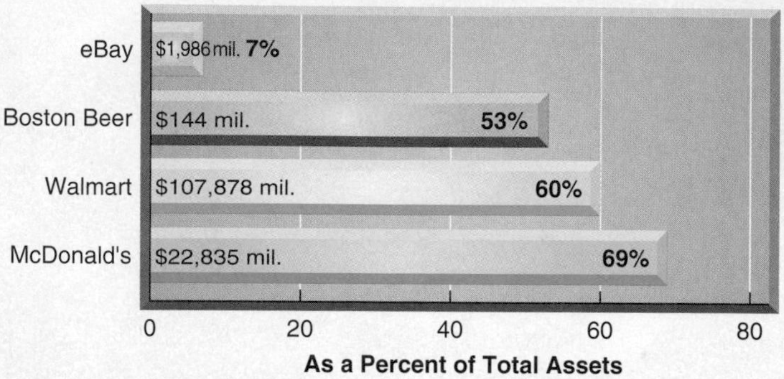

Plant assets are set apart from other assets by two important features. First, *plant assets are used in operations.* This makes them different from, for instance, inventory that is held for sale and not used in operations. The distinctive feature here is use, not type of asset. A company that purchases a computer to resell it reports it on the balance sheet as inventory. If the same company purchases this computer to use in operations, however, it is a plant asset. Another example is land held for future expansion, which is reported as a long-term investment. However, if this land holds a factory used in operations, the land is part of plant assets. Another example is equipment held for use in the event of a breakdown or for peak periods of production, which is reported in plant assets. If this same equipment is removed from use and held for sale, however, it is not reported in plant assets.

Point: The phrase *capital-intensive* refers to companies with large amounts invested in plant assets.

The second important feature is that *plant assets have useful lives extending over more than one accounting period.* This makes plant assets different from current assets such as supplies that are normally consumed in a short time period after they are placed in use.

Point: It can help to view plant assets as prepaid expenses that benefit several future accounting periods.

The accounting for plant assets reflects these two features. Since plant assets are used in operations, we try to match their costs against the revenues they generate. Also, since their useful lives extend over more than one period, our matching of costs and revenues must extend over several periods. Specifically, we value plant assets (balance sheet effect) and then, for many of them, we allocate their costs to periods benefiting from their use (income statement effect). An important exception is land; land cost is not allocated to expense when we expect it to have an indefinite life.

Exhibit 8.2 shows four main issues in accounting for plant assets: (1) computing the costs of plant assets, (2) allocating the costs of most plant assets (less any salvage amounts) against

EXHIBIT 8.2

Issues in Accounting for Plant Assets

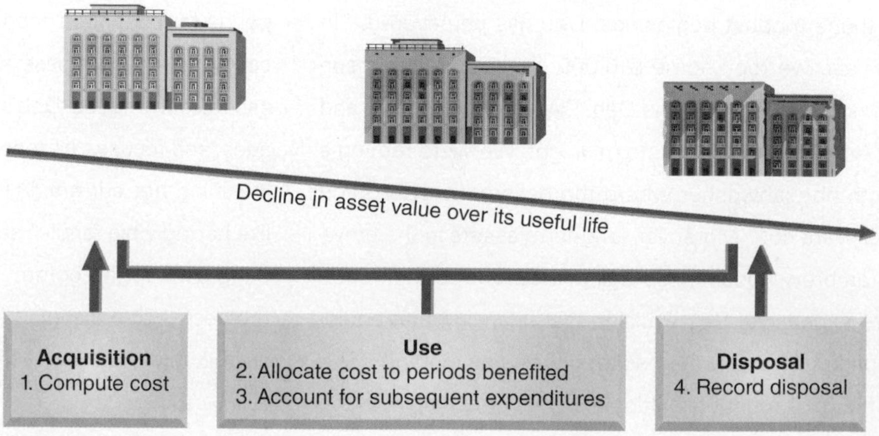

revenues for the periods they benefit, (3) accounting for expenditures such as repairs and improvements to plant assets, and (4) recording the disposal of plant assets. The following sections discuss these issues.

COST DETERMINATION

C1 Explain the cost principle for computing the cost of plant assets.

Plant assets are recorded at cost when acquired. This is consistent with the *cost principle.* **Cost** includes all normal and reasonable expenditures necessary to get the asset in place and ready for its intended use. The cost of a factory machine, for instance, includes its invoice cost less any cash discount for early payment, plus any necessary freight, unpacking, assembling, installing, and testing costs. Examples are the costs of building a base or foundation for a machine, providing electrical hookups, and testing the asset before using it in operations.

To be recorded as part of the cost of a plant asset, an expenditure must be normal, reasonable, and necessary in preparing it for its intended use. If an asset is damaged during unpacking, the repairs are not added to its cost. Instead, they are charged to an expense account. Nor is a paid traffic fine for moving heavy machinery on city streets without a proper permit part of the machinery's cost; but payment for a proper permit is included in the cost of machinery. Charges are sometimes incurred to modify or customize a new plant asset. These charges are added to the asset's cost. We explain in this section how to determine the cost of plant assets for each of its four major classes.

Machinery and Equipment

The costs of machinery and equipment consist of all costs normal and necessary to purchase them and prepare them for their intended use. These include the purchase price, taxes, transportation charges, insurance while in transit, and the installing, assembling, and testing of the machinery and equipment.

Buildings

A Building account is charged for the costs of purchasing or constructing a building that is used in operations. When purchased, a building's costs usually include its purchase price, brokerage fees, taxes, title fees, and attorney fees. Its costs also include all expenditures to ready it for its intended use, including any necessary repairs or renovations such as wiring, lighting, flooring, and wall coverings. When a company constructs a building or any plant asset for its own use, its costs include materials and labor plus a reasonable amount of indirect overhead cost. Overhead includes the costs of items such as heat, lighting, power, and depreciation on machinery used to construct the asset. Costs of construction also include design fees, building permits, and insurance during construction. However, costs such as insurance to cover the asset *after* it is placed in use are operating expenses.

PhotoLink/Getty Images

Land Improvements

Land improvements are additions to land and have limited useful lives. Examples are parking lot surfaces, driveways, walkways, fences, landscaping, and sprinkling and lighting systems. Costs of land improvements include expenditures necessary to make those improvements ready for their intended use. While the costs of these improvements increase the usefulness of the land, they are charged to a separate Land Improvement account so that their costs can be allocated to the periods they benefit.

Land

Land is the earth's surface and has an indefinite (unlimited) life. Costs of land include expenditures necessary to make that property ready for its intended use. When land is purchased for a building site, its cost includes the total amount paid for thc land, including any real estate commissions, title insurance fees, legal fees, and any accrued property taxes paid by the purchaser. Payments for surveying, clearing, grading, and draining also are included in the cost of land. Other costs include government assessments, whether incurred at the time of purchase or later, for items such as public roadways, sewers, and sidewalks. These assessments are included because they permanently add to the land's value. Land purchased as a building site sometimes includes structures that must be removed. In such cases, the total purchase price is charged to the Land account as is the cost of removing the structures, less any amounts recovered through sale of salvaged materials. To illustrate, assume that **Starbucks** paid $167,000 cash to acquire land for a retail store. This land had an old service garage that was removed at a net cost of $13,000 ($15,000 in costs less $2,000 proceeds from salvaged materials). Additional closing costs total $10,000, consisting of brokerage fees ($8,000), legal fees ($1,500), and title costs ($500). The cost of this land to Starbucks is $190,000 and is computed as shown in Exhibit 8.3.

EXHIBIT 8.3

Computing Cost of Land

Cash price of land	$ 167,000
Net cost of garage removal	13,000
Closing costs	10,000
Cost of land	**$190,000**

Example: If appraised values in Exhibit 8.4 are building, $84,000; land improvements, $12,000; and land, $24,000, what cost is assigned to the building? *Answer:*
(1) $84,000 + $12,000 + $24,000 = $120,000 (total appraisal)
(2) $84,000/$120,000 = 70% (building's percent of total)
(3) 70% × $90,000 = $63,000 (building's apportioned cost)

Lump-Sum Purchase

Plant assets sometimes are purchased as a group in a single transaction for a lump-sum price. This transaction is called a *lump-sum purchase,* or *group, bulk,* or *basket purchase.* When this occurs, we allocate the cost of the purchase among the different types of assets acquired based on their *relative market values,* which can be estimated by appraisal or by using the tax-assessed valuations of the assets. To illustrate, assume **CarMax** paid $90,000 cash to acquire a group of items consisting of a building appraised at $60,000, land improvements appraised at $10,000, and land appraised at $30,000. The $90,000 cost is allocated on the basis of these appraised values as shown in Exhibit 8.4.

EXHIBIT 8.4

Computing Costs in a Lump-Sum Purchase

	Appraised Value	Percent of Total	Apportioned Cost
Building	$ 60,000	60% ($60,000/$100,000)	**$54,000** ($90,000 × 60%)
Land improvements	10,000	10 ($10,000/$100,000)	**9,000** ($90,000 × 10%)
Land	30,000	30 ($30,000/$100,000)	**27,000** ($90,000 × 30%)
Totals	$100,000	100%	$ 90,000

NEED-TO-KNOW 8-1

Cost Determination
C1

Compute the amount recorded as the cost of a new machine given the following payments related to its purchase: gross purchase price, $700,000; sales tax, $49,000; purchase discount taken, $21,000; freight cost—terms FOB shipping point, $3,500; normal assembly costs, $3,000; cost of necessary machine platform, $2,500; cost of parts used in maintaining machine, $4,200.

Solution

$737,000 = $700,000 + $49,000 − $21,000 + $3,500 + $3,000 + $2,500

Do More: QS 8-1, QS 8-2, E 8-1, E 8-2, E 8-3

QC1

DEPRECIATION

Point: Depreciation is cost allocation, not asset valuation.

Depreciation is the process of allocating the cost of a plant asset to expense in the accounting periods benefiting from its use. Depreciation does not measure the decline in the asset's market value each period, nor does it measure the asset's physical deterioration. Since depreciation reflects the cost of using a plant asset, depreciation charges are only recorded when the asset is actually in service. This section describes the factors we must consider in computing depreciation, the depreciation methods used, revisions in depreciation, and depreciation for partial periods.

Factors in Computing Depreciation

P1 Compute and record depreciation using the straight-line, units-of-production, and declining-balance methods.

Factors that determine depreciation are (1) cost, (2) salvage value, and (3) useful life.

Cost The **cost** of a plant asset consists of all necessary and reasonable expenditures to acquire it and to prepare it for its intended use.

Salvage Value The total amount of depreciation to be charged off over an asset's benefit period equals the asset's cost minus its salvage value. **Salvage value,** also called *residual value* or *scrap value,* is an estimate of the asset's value at the end of its benefit period. This is the amount the owner expects to receive from disposing of the asset at the end of its benefit period. If the asset is expected to be traded in on a new asset, its salvage value is the expected trade-in value.

Point: If we expect additional costs in preparing a plant asset for disposal, the salvage value equals the expected amount from disposal less any disposal costs.

Useful Life The **useful life** of a plant asset is the length of time it is productively used in a company's operations. Useful life, also called *service life,* might not be as long as the asset's total productive life. For example, the productive life of a computer can be eight years or more. Some companies, however, trade in old computers for new ones every two years. In this case, these computers have a two-year useful life, meaning the cost of these computers (less their expected trade-in values) is charged to depreciation expense over a two-year period.

Point: Useful life and salvage value are estimates. Estimates require judgment based on all available information.

Several variables often make the useful life of a plant asset difficult to predict. A major variable is the wear and tear from use in operations. Two other variables, inadequacy and obsolescence, also require consideration. **Inadequacy** refers to the insufficient capacity of a company's plant assets to meet its growing productive demands. **Obsolescence** refers to the condition of a plant asset that is no longer useful in producing goods or services with a competitive advantage because of new inventions and improvements. Both inadequacy and obsolescence are difficult to predict because of demand changes, new inventions, and improvements. A company usually disposes of an inadequate or obsolete asset before it wears out.

A company is often able to better predict a new asset's useful life when it has past experience with a similar asset. When it has no such experience, a company relies on the experience of others or on engineering studies and judgment. In note 1 of its annual report, **Tootsie Roll**, a snack food manufacturer, reports the following useful lives:

Point: Land is recorded at cost but not depreciated because it is assumed to have an indefinite life.

Buildings	20–35 years
Machinery and Equipment	5–20 years

Decision Insight

Life Line Life expectancy of plant assets is often in the eye of the beholder. For instance, **Hershey Foods** and **Tootsie Roll** are competitors and apply similar manufacturing processes, yet their equipment's life expectancies are different. Hershey depreciates equipment over 3 to 15 years, but Tootsie Roll depreciates them over 5 to 20 years. Such differences markedly impact financial statements. ■

Sergey Lavrentev/iStock/360/Getty Images

Depreciation Methods

Depreciation methods are used to allocate a plant asset's cost over the accounting periods in its useful life. The most frequently used method of depreciation is the straight-line method. Another common depreciation method is the units-of-production method. We explain both of these methods in this section. This section also describes accelerated depreciation methods, with a focus on the declining-balance method.

The computations in this section use information about a machine that inspects athletic shoes before packaging. Manufacturers such as **Converse**, **Reebok**, **adidas**, and **Fila** use this machine. Data for this machine are in Exhibit 8.5.

EXHIBIT 8.5

Data for Athletic Shoe–Inspecting Machine

Cost	$10,000	Useful life	
Salvage value	1,000	Accounting periods	5 years
Depreciable cost	$ 9,000	Units inspected	36,000 shoes

Straight-Line Method **Straight-line depreciation** charges the same amount of expense to each period of the asset's useful life. A two-step process is used. We first compute the *depreciable cost* of the asset, also called the *cost to be depreciated.* It is computed by subtracting the asset's salvage value from its total cost. Second, depreciable cost is divided by the number of accounting periods in the asset's useful life. The formula for straight-line depreciation, along with its computation for the inspection machine just described, is shown in Exhibit 8.6.

EXHIBIT 8.6

Straight-Line Depreciation Formula and Example

$$\frac{\textbf{Cost} - \textbf{Salvage value}}{\textbf{Useful life in periods}} = \frac{\$10{,}000 - \$1{,}000}{5 \text{ years}} = \$1{,}800 \text{ per year}$$

If this machine is purchased on December 31, 2014, and used throughout its predicted useful life of five years, the straight-line method allocates an equal amount of depreciation to each of the years 2015 through 2019. We make the following adjusting entry at the end of each of the five years to record straight-line depreciation of this machine.

Assets = Liabilities + Equity
−1,800 −1,800

Dec. 31	Depreciation Expense	1,800	
	Accumulated Depreciation—Machinery		1,800
	To record annual depreciation.		

The $1,800 Depreciation Expense is reported on the income statement among operating expenses. The $1,800 Accumulated Depreciation is a contra asset account to the Machinery account in the balance sheet. The graph on the left in Exhibit 8.7 shows the $1,800 per year expenses reported in each of the five years. The graph on the right shows the amounts reported on each of the six December 31 balance sheets.

Example: If salvage value of the machine is $2,500, what is the annual depreciation? *Answer:* ($10,000 − $2,500)/5 years = $1,500

EXHIBIT 8.7

Financial Statement Effects of Straight-Line Depreciation

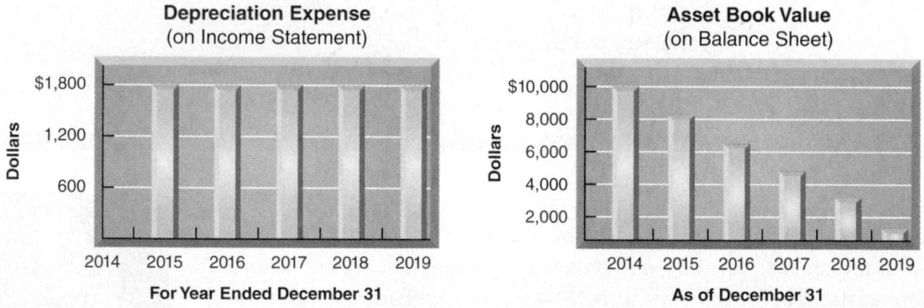

Book value = Cost − Accumulated depreciation

The net balance sheet amount is the **asset book value,** or simply *book value,* and is computed as the asset's total cost less its accumulated depreciation. For example, at the end of year 2 (December 31, 2016), its book value is $6,400 and is reported in the balance sheet as follows:

Machinery	$10,000	
Less accumulated depreciation	3,600	$6,400 ← Book value

The book value of this machine declines by $1,800 each year due to depreciation. The left-side graphic in Exhibit 8.7 reveals why this method is called straight-line.

Point: Once an asset's book value equals its salvage value, depreciation stops.

We also can compute the *straight-line depreciation rate,* defined as 100% divided by the number of periods in the asset's useful life. For the inspection machine, this rate is

20% (100% ÷ 5 years, or 1/5 per period). We use this rate, along with other information, to compute the machine's *straight-line depreciation schedule* shown in Exhibit 8.8. Note three points in this exhibit. First, depreciation expense is the same each period. Second, accumulated depreciation is the sum of current and prior periods' depreciation expense. Third, book value declines each period until it equals salvage value at the end of the machine's useful life.

EXHIBIT 8.8

Straight-Line Depreciation Schedule

	Depreciation for the Period			End of Period	
Annual Period	Depreciable Cost*	Depreciation Rate	Depreciation Expense	Accumulated Depreciation	Book Value†
2014	—	—	—	—	$10,000
2015	$9,000	20%	**$1,800**	$1,800	8,200
2016	9,000	20	**1,800**	3,600	6,400
2017	9,000	20	**1,800**	5,400	4,600
2018	9,000	20	**1,800**	7,200	2,800
2019	9,000	20	**1,800**	9,000	**1,000** ← Salvage value is not depreciated
			$9,000 ← ($10,000 cost − $1,000 salvage)		

* $10,000 − $1,000. † Book value is total cost minus accumulated depreciation.

Units-of-Production Method The straight-line method charges an equal share of an asset's cost to each period. If plant assets are used up in about equal amounts each accounting period, this method produces a reasonable matching of expenses with revenues. However, the use of some plant assets varies greatly from one period to the next. A builder, for instance, might use a piece of construction equipment for a month and then not use it again for several months. When equipment use varies from period to period, the units-of-production depreciation method can better match expenses with revenues. **Units-of-production depreciation** charges a varying amount to expense for each period of an asset's useful life depending on its *usage*.

A two-step process is used to compute units-of-production depreciation. We first compute *depreciation per unit* by subtracting the asset's salvage value from its total cost and then dividing by the total number of units expected to be produced during its useful life. Units of production can be expressed in product or other units such as hours used or miles driven. The second step is to compute depreciation expense for the period by multiplying the units produced in the period by the depreciation per unit. The formula for units-of-production depreciation, along with its computation for the machine described in Exhibit 8.5, is shown in Exhibit 8.9. (7,000 shoes are inspected and sold in its first year.)

EXHIBIT 8.9

Units-of-Production Depreciation Formula and Example

Step **1**

$$\textbf{Depreciation per unit} = \frac{\textbf{Cost} - \textbf{Salvage value}}{\textbf{Total units of production}} = \frac{\$10{,}000 - \$1{,}000}{36{,}000 \text{ shoes}} = \$0.25 \text{ per shoe}$$

Step **2**

$$\textbf{Depreciation expense} = \textbf{Depreciation per unit} \times \textbf{Units produced in period}$$

$$\$0.25 \text{ per shoe} \times 7{,}000 \text{ shoes} = \$1{,}750$$

Using data on the number of shoes inspected by the machine, we can compute the *units-of-production depreciation schedule* shown in Exhibit 8.10. For example, depreciation for the first year is $1,750 (7,000 shoes at $0.25 per shoe). Depreciation for the second year is $2,000 (8,000 shoes at $0.25 per shoe). Other years are similarly computed. Exhibit 8.10 shows that (1) depreciation expense depends on unit output, (2) accumulated depreciation is the sum of current and prior periods' depreciation expense, and (3) book value declines each period until it

Example: Refer to Exhibit 8.10. If the number of shoes inspected in 2019 is 5,500, what is depreciation for 2019? *Answer:* $1,250 (never depreciate below salvage value)

equals salvage value at the end of the asset's useful life. **Deltic Timber** is one of many companies using the units-of-production depreciation method. It reports that depreciation "is calculated over the estimated useful lives of the assets by using the units of production method for machinery and equipment."

EXHIBIT 8.10

Units-of-Production Depreciation Schedule

	Depreciation for the Period			End of Period	
Annual Period	**Number of Units**	**Depreciation per Unit**	**Depreciation Expense**	**Accumulated Depreciation**	**Book Value**
2014	—	—	—	—	$10,000
2015	7,000	$0.25	**$1,750**	$1,750	8,250
2016	8,000	0.25	**2,000**	3,750	6,250
2017	9,000	0.25	**2,250**	6,000	4,000
2018	7,000	0.25	**1,750**	7,750	2,250
2019	5,000	0.25	**1,250**	9,000	**1,000**
	36,000 units		**$9,000**		

($10,000 cost − $1,000 salvage)

Salvage value is not depreciated

Declining-Balance Method An **accelerated depreciation method** yields larger depreciation expenses in the early years of an asset's life and less depreciation in later years. The most common accelerated method is the **declining-balance method** of depreciation, which uses a depreciation rate that is a multiple of the straight-line rate and applies it to the asset's beginning-of-period book value. The amount of depreciation declines each period because book value declines each period.

A common depreciation rate for the declining-balance method is double the straight-line rate. This is called the *double-declining-balance (DDB)* method. This method is applied in three steps: (1) compute the asset's straight-line depreciation rate, (2) double the straight-line rate, and (3) compute depreciation expense by multiplying this rate by the asset's beginning-of-period book value. To illustrate, let's return to the machine in Exhibit 8.5 and apply the double-declining-balance method to compute depreciation expense. Exhibit 8.11 shows the first-year depreciation computation for the machine. The three-step process is to (1) divide 100% by five years to determine the straight-line rate of 20%, or 1/5, per year, (2) double this 20% rate to get the declining-balance rate of 40%, or 2/5, per year, and (3) compute depreciation expense as 40%, or 2/5, multiplied by the beginning-of-period book value.

Point: In the DDB method, *double* refers to the rate and *declining balance* refers to book value. The rate is applied to beginning book value each period.

EXHIBIT 8.11

Double-Declining-Balance Depreciation Formula*

Step 1

Straight-line rate = 100% ÷ Useful life = 100% ÷ 5 years = 20%

Step 2

Double-declining-balance rate = 2 × Straight-line rate = 2 × 20% = 40%

Step 3

Depreciation expense = Double-declining-balance rate × Beginning-period book value

40% × $10,000 = $4,000 (for 2015)

* To simplify: DDB depreciation = (2 × Beginning-period book value)/Useful life.

$$\text{SL rate} = \frac{100\%}{\text{Useful life}}$$

$$\text{DDB rate} = \frac{200\%}{\text{Useful life}}$$

Example: What is the DDB depreciation in year 2018 if salvage value is $2,000? *Answer:* $2,160 − $2,000 = $160

The *double-declining-balance depreciation schedule* is shown in Exhibit 8.12. The schedule follows the formula except for year 2019, when depreciation expense is $296. This $296 is not equal to 40% × $1,296, or $518.40. If we had used the $518.40 for depreciation expense in 2019, the ending book value would equal $777.60, which is less than the $1,000 salvage value. Instead, the $296 is computed by subtracting the $1,000 salvage value from the $1,296 book value at the beginning of the fifth year (the year when DDB depreciation cuts into salvage value).

EXHIBIT 8.12

Double-Declining-Balance Depreciation Schedule

	Depreciation for the Period			End of Period	
Annual Period	Beginning of Period Book Value	Depreciation Rate	Depreciation Expense	Accumulated Depreciation	Book Value
2014	—	—	—	—	$10,000
2015	$10,000	40%	**$4,000**	$4,000	6,000
2016	6,000	40	**2,400**	6,400	3,600
2017	3,600	40	**1,440**	7,840	2,160
2018	2,160	40	**864**	8,704	1,296
2019	1,296	40	**296***	9,000	**1,000** ← Salvage value is not depreciated
			$9,000 ← ($10,000 cost − $1,000 salvage)		

* Year 2019 depreciation is $1,296 − $1,000 = $296 (never depreciate book value below salvage value).

Comparing Depreciation Methods Exhibit 8.13 shows depreciation expense for each year of the machine's useful life under each of the three depreciation methods. While depreciation expense per period differs for different methods, total depreciation expense of $9,000 is the same over the machine's useful life.

EXHIBIT 8.13

Depreciation Expense for the Different Methods

	A	B	C	D
1	**Period**	**Straight-Line**	**Units-of-Production**	**Double-Declining-Balance**
2	2015	$1,800	$1,750	$4,000
3	2016	1,800	2,000	2,400
4	2017	1,800	2,250	1,440
5	2018	1,800	1,750	864
6	2019	1,800	1,250	296
7	Totals	**$9,000**	**$9,000**	**$9,000**
8				

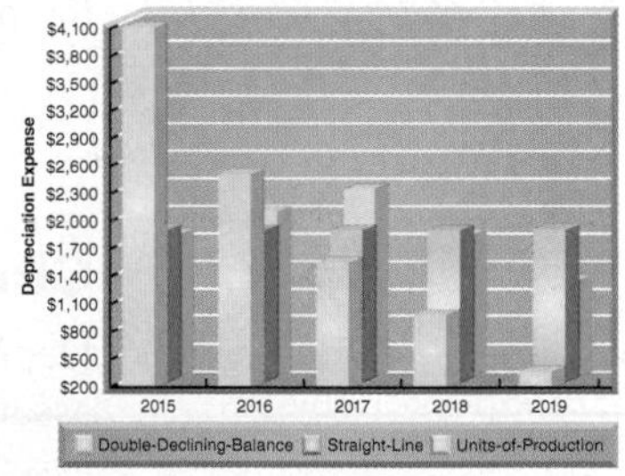

Each method starts with a total cost of $10,000 and ends with a salvage value of $1,000. The difference is the pattern in depreciation expense over the useful life. The book value of the asset when using straight-line is always greater than the book value from using double-declining-balance, except at the beginning and end of the asset's useful life, when it is the same. Also, the straight-line method yields a steady pattern of depreciation expense while the units-of-production depreciation depends on the number of units produced. Each of these methods is acceptable because it allocates cost in a systematic and rational manner.

Decision Insight

In Vogue About 85% of companies use straight-line depreciation for plant assets, 5% use units-of-production, and 4% use declining-balance. Another 6% use an unspecified accelerated method—most likely declining-balance. ■

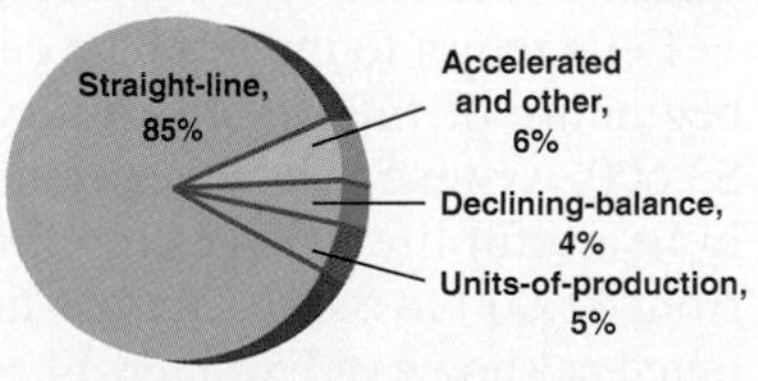

Depreciation for Tax Reporting The records a company keeps for financial accounting purposes are usually separate from the records it keeps for tax accounting purposes. This is so because financial accounting aims to report useful information on financial performance and position, whereas tax accounting reflects government objectives in raising revenues. Differences between these two accounting systems are normal and expected. Depreciation is a common example of how the records differ. For example, many companies use accelerated depreciation in computing taxable income. Reporting higher depreciation expense in the early years of an asset's life reduces the company's taxable income in those years and increases it in later years, when the depreciation expense is lower. The company's goal here is to *postpone* its tax payments.

Point: Understanding depreciation for financial accounting will help in learning MACRS for tax accounting. Rules for MACRS are available from www.IRS.gov.

The U.S. federal income tax law has rules for depreciating assets. These rules include the **Modified Accelerated Cost Recovery System (MACRS),** which allows straight-line depreciation for some assets but requires accelerated depreciation for most kinds of assets. MACRS separates depreciable assets into different classes and defines the depreciable life and rate for each class. MACRS is *not* acceptable for financial reporting because it often allocates costs over an arbitrary period that is less than the asset's useful life and it fails to estimate salvage value. Details of MACRS are covered in tax accounting courses.

Partial-Year Depreciation

C2 Explain depreciation for partial years and changes in estimates.

Plant assets are purchased and disposed of at various times. When an asset is purchased (or disposed of) at a time other than the beginning or end of an accounting period, depreciation is recorded for part of a year. This is done so that the year of purchase or the year of disposal is charged with its share of the asset's depreciation.

Point: Assets purchased on days 1 through 15 of a month are usually recorded as purchased on the 1st of that month. Assets purchased on days 16 to the month-end are recorded as if purchased on the 1st of the next month.

Point: Many firms use a "half-year convention," which records 6 months' depreciation in the year of purchase, regardless of the purchase date.

To illustrate, assume that the machine in Exhibit 8.5 is purchased and placed in service on October 8, 2014, and the annual accounting period ends on December 31. Since this machine is purchased and used for nearly three months in 2014, the calendar-year income statement should report depreciation expense on the machine for that part of the year. Normally, depreciation assumes that the asset is purchased on the first day of the month nearest the actual date of purchase. In this case, since the purchase occurred on October 8, we assume an October 1 purchase date. This means that three months' depreciation is recorded in 2014. Using straight-line depreciation, we compute three months' depreciation of $450 as follows.

$$\frac{\$10{,}000 - \$1{,}000}{5 \text{ years}} \times \frac{3}{12} = \$450$$

Example: If the machine's salvage value is zero and purchase occurs on Oct. 8, 2014, how much depreciation is recorded at Dec. 31, 2014? *Answer:* $10,000/5 × 3/12 = $500

A similar computation is necessary when an asset disposal occurs during a period. To illustrate, assume that the machine is sold on June 24, 2019. Depreciation is recorded for the period January 1 through June 24 when it is disposed of. This partial year's depreciation, computed to the nearest whole month, is

$$\frac{\$10{,}000 - \$1{,}000}{5 \text{ years}} \times \frac{6}{12} = \$900$$

Change in Estimates for Depreciation

Point: Remaining depreciable cost equals book value less revised salvage value at the point of revision.

Depreciation is based on estimates of salvage value and useful life. During the useful life of an asset, new information may indicate that these estimates are inaccurate. If our estimate of an asset's useful life and/or salvage value changes, what should we do? The answer is to use the new estimate to compute depreciation for current and future periods. This means that we revise the depreciation expense computation by spreading the cost yet to be depreciated over the remaining useful life. This approach is used for all depreciation methods.

Let's return to the machine described in Exhibit 8.8 using straight-line depreciation. At the beginning of this asset's third year, its book value is $6,400, computed as $10,000 minus $3,600. Assume that at the beginning of its third year, the estimated number of years remaining in its useful life changes from three to four years *and* its estimate of salvage value changes from $1,000 to $400. Straight-line depreciation for each of the four remaining years is computed as shown in Exhibit 8.14.

EXHIBIT 8.14

Computing Revised Straight-Line Depreciation

$$\frac{\textbf{Book value} - \textbf{Revised salvage value}}{\textbf{Revised remaining useful life}} = \frac{\$6{,}400 - \$400}{4 \text{ years}} = \$1{,}500 \text{ per year}$$

Example: If at the start of its second year the machine's remaining useful life changes from 4 to 3 years and salvage value from $1,000 to $400, how much straight-line depreciation is recorded in remaining years? *Answer:* Revised depreciation = ($8,200 − $400)/3 = $2,600

Thus, $1,500 of depreciation expense is recorded for the machine at the end of the third through sixth years—each year of its remaining useful life. Since this asset was depreciated at $1,800 per year for the first two years, it is tempting to conclude that depreciation expense was overstated in the first two years. However, these expenses reflected the best information available at that time. We do not go back and restate prior years' financial statements for this type of new information. Instead, we adjust the current and future periods' statements to reflect this new information. Revising an estimate of the useful life or salvage value of a plant asset is referred to as a **change in an accounting estimate** and is reflected in current and future financial statements, not in prior statements.

Reporting Depreciation

Both the cost and accumulated depreciation of plant assets are reported on the balance sheet or in its notes. **Dale Jarrett Racing Adventure**, for instance, reports the following.

Race vehicles and other	$1,027,026
Furniture, software, DJ Graphics, and equipment	105,478
Shop and track equipment	173,739
Property and equipment, gross	1,306,243
Less accumulated depreciation	901,767
Property and equipment, net	$ 404,476

Chris Trotman/NASCAR/Getty Images

Many companies also show plant assets on one line with the net amount of cost less accumulated depreciation. When this is done, the amount of accumulated depreciation is disclosed in a note. **Apple** reports only the net amount of its property, plant and equipment in its balance sheet. To satisfy the full-disclosure principle, Apple describes its depreciation methods in its Note 1 and the amounts comprising plant assets in its Note 3—see its 10-K at **www.SEC.gov**.

Point: A company usually keeps records for each asset showing its cost and depreciation to date. The combined records for individual assets are a type of *plant asset subsidiary ledger.*

Reporting both the cost and accumulated depreciation of plant assets helps users compare the assets of different companies. For example, a company holding assets costing $50,000 and accumulated depreciation of $40,000 is likely in a situation different from a company with new assets costing $10,000. While the net undepreciated cost of $10,000 is the same in both cases, the first company may have more productive capacity available but likely is facing the need to replace older assets. These insights are not provided if the two balance sheets report only the $10,000 book values.

Users must remember that plant assets are reported on a balance sheet at their undepreciated costs (book value), not at fair (market) values. This emphasis on costs rather than fair values is based on the *going-concern assumption* described in Chapter 1. This assumption states that, unless there is evidence to the contrary, we assume that a company continues in business. This implies that plant assets are held and used long enough to recover their cost through the sale of products and services. Because plant assets are not for sale, their fair values are not reported. An exception is when there is a *permanent decline* in the fair value of an asset relative to its book value, called an asset **impairment.** In this case the company writes the asset down to this fair value (details for the two-step process for assessing and computing the impairment loss are in advanced courses).

Accumulated Depreciation is a contra asset account with a normal credit balance. It does *not* reflect funds accumulated to buy new assets when the assets currently owned are replaced. If a company has funds available to buy assets, the funds are shown on the balance sheet among liquid assets such as cash or investments.

Example: Assume equipment carries a book value of $800 ($900 cost less $100 accumulated depreciation) and a fair (market) value of $750, *and* this $50 decline in value meets the 2-step impairment test. The entry to record this impairment is:

Impairment Loss	$50	
Accum Depr-Equip.		$50

Decision Ethics

Controller You are the controller for a struggling company. Its operations require regular investments in equipment, and depreciation is its largest expense. Its competitors frequently replace equipment—often depreciated over three years. The company president instructs you to revise useful lives of equipment from three to six years and to use a six-year life on all new equipment. What actions do you take? ■ [Answers follow the chapter's Summary.]

NEED-TO-KNOW 8-2

Depreciation Computations

P1 C2

Part 1. A machine costing $22,000 with a five-year life and an estimated $2,000 salvage value is installed on January 1. The manager estimates the machine will produce 1,000 units of product during its life. It actually produces the following units: 200 in 1st year, 400 in 2nd year, 300 in 3rd year, 80 in 4th year, 30 in 5th year. The total units produced by the end of year 5 exceeds the original estimate—this difference was not predicted. (The machine must not be depreciated below its estimated salvage value.) Prepare a table with the following column headings—Year, Straight-Line, Units-of-Production, Double-Declining-Balance—and then compute depreciation expense for each year (and total depreciation for all years combined) under each method.

Part 2. In early January 2013, a company acquires equipment for $3,800. The company estimates this equipment to have a useful life of three years and a salvage value of $200. Early in 2015, the company changes its estimates to a total four-year useful life and zero salvage value. Using the straight-line method, what is depreciation expense for the year ended 2015?

Solution—Part 1

Year	Straight-Line[a]	Units-of-Production[b]	Double-Declining-Balance[c]
1	$ 4,000	$ 4,000	$ 8,800
2	4,000	8,000	5,280
3	4,000	6,000	3,168
4	4,000	1,600	1,901
5	4,000	400	851
Totals	$20,000	$20,000	$20,000

[a]Straight-line: Cost per year = ($22,000 − $2,000)/5 years = $4,000 per year
[b]Units-of-production: Cost per unit = ($22,000 − $2,000)/1,000 units = $20 per unit

Year	Units	Depreciation per Unit	Depreciation
1	200	$20	$ 4,000
2	400	20	8,000
3	300	20	6,000
4	80	20	1,600
5	30	20	400*
Total			$20,000

*Set depreciation in year 5 to reduce book value to the $20,000 salvage value; namely, instead of $600 (30 × $20), we use the maximum of $400 ($20,000 − $19,600 accum depr).

[c]Double-declining-balance: (100%/5) × 2 = 40% depreciation rate

Year	Beginning Book Value	Annual Depreciation (40% of Book Value)	Accumulated Depreciation at the End of the Year	Ending Book Value ($22,000 Cost less Accumulated Depreciation)
1	$22,000	$ 8,800	$ 8,800	$13,200
2	13,200	5,280	14,080	7,920
3	7,920	3,168	17,248	4,752
4	4,752	1,901*	19,149	2,851
5	2,851	851**	20,000	2,000
Total		$20,000		

*Rounded to the nearest dollar.
**Set depreciation in year 5 to reduce book value to the $20,000 salvage value; namely, instead of $1,140 (2,851 × 40%), we use the maximum of $851 ($2,851 − $2,000).

Solution—Part 2

Do More: QS 8-3 through QS 8-7, E 8-4 through E 8-13

($3,800 − $200)/3 years = $1,200 (original depreciation per year)

$1,200 × 2 years = $2,400 (accumulated depreciation at date of change in estimate)

QC2

($3,800 − $2,400)/2 years = **$700** (revised depreciation)

ADDITIONAL EXPENDITURES

C3
Distinguish between revenue and capital expenditures, and account for them.

After a company acquires a plant asset and puts it into service, it often makes additional expenditures for that asset's operation, maintenance, repair, and improvement. In recording these expenditures, it must decide whether to capitalize or expense them (to capitalize an expenditure is to debit the asset account). The issue is whether these expenditures are reported as current-period expenses or added to the plant asset's cost and depreciated over its remaining useful life.

Revenue expenditures, also called *income statement expenditures,* are additional costs of plant assets that do not materially increase the asset's life or productive capabilities. They are recorded as expenses and deducted from revenues in the current period's income statement. Examples of revenue expenditures are cleaning, repainting, adjustments, and lubricants. **Capital expenditures,** also called *balance sheet expenditures,* are additional costs of plant assets that provide benefits extending beyond the current period. They are debited to asset accounts and reported on the balance sheet. Capital expenditures increase or improve the type or amount of service an asset provides. Examples are roofing replacement, plant expansion, and major overhauls of machinery and equipment.

	Financial Statement Effect	
	Accounting	Expense Timing
Revenue expenditure	Income stmt. account debited	Expensed currently
Capital expenditure	Balance sheet account debited	Expensed in future

Financial statements are affected for several years by the accounting choice of recording costs as either revenue expenditures or capital expenditures. This decision is based on whether the expenditures are identified as ordinary repairs or as betterments and extraordinary repairs.

Decision Maker

Entrepreneur Your start-up Internet services company needs cash, and you are preparing financial statements to apply for a short-term loan. A friend suggests that you treat as many expenses as possible as capital expenditures. What are the impacts on financial statements of this suggestion? What do you think is the aim of this suggestion? ■ [Answers follow the chapter's Summary.]

Ordinary Repairs

Ordinary repairs are expenditures to keep an asset in normal, good operating condition. They are necessary if an asset is to perform to expectations over its useful life. Ordinary repairs do not extend an asset's useful life beyond its original estimate or increase its productivity beyond original expectations. Examples are normal costs of cleaning, lubricating, adjusting, oil changing, and replacing small parts of a machine. Ordinary repairs are treated as *revenue expenditures.* This means their costs are reported as expenses on the current-period income statement. Following this rule, **Brunswick** reports that "maintenance and repair costs are expensed as incurred." If Brunswick's current-year repair costs are $9,500, it makes the following entry.

Point: Many companies apply the *materiality constraint* to treat *low-cost plant assets* (say, less than $500) as revenue expenditures. This practice is referred to as a "capitalization policy."

Dec. 31	Repairs Expense	9,500	
	Cash		9,500
	To record ordinary repairs of equipment.		

Assets = Liabilities + Equity
−9,500 −9,500

Betterments and Extraordinary Repairs

Accounting for betterments and extraordinary repairs is similar—both are treated as *capital expenditures.*

Betterments (Improvements) **Betterments,** also called *improvements,* are expenditures that make a plant asset more efficient or productive. A betterment often involves adding a component to an asset or replacing one of its old components with a better one and does not always increase an asset's useful life. An example is replacing manual controls on a machine with automatic controls. One special type of betterment is an *addition,* such as adding a new wing or dock to a warehouse. Since a betterment benefits future periods, it is debited to the asset account as a capital expenditure. The new book value (less salvage value) is then depreciated over the asset's remaining useful life. To illustrate, suppose a company pays $8,000 for a machine with an eight-year useful life and no salvage value. After three years and $3,000 of depreciation, it adds an automated control system to the machine at a cost of $1,800. This results in reduced labor costs in future periods. The cost of the betterment is added to the Machinery account with this entry.

Example: Assume a firm owns a web server. Identify each cost as a revenue or capital expenditure: (1) purchase price, (2) necessary wiring, (3) platform for operation, (4) circuits to increase capacity, (5) cleaning after each month of use, (6) repair of a faulty switch, and (7) replaced a worn fan. *Answer:* Capital expenditures: 1, 2, 3, 4; revenue expenditures: 5, 6, 7.

Jan. 2	Machinery	1,800	
	Cash		1,800
	To record installation of automated system.		

Assets = Liabilities + Equity
+1,800
−1,800

After the betterment is recorded, the remaining cost to be depreciated is $6,800, computed as $8,000 − $3,000 + $1,800. Depreciation expense for the remaining five years is $1,360 per year, computed as $6,800/5 years.

Point: Both extraordinary repairs and betterments require revising future depreciation.

Extraordinary Repairs (Replacements) **Extraordinary repairs** are expenditures extending the asset's useful life beyond its original estimate. Extraordinary repairs are *capital expenditures* because they benefit future periods. Their costs are debited to the asset account (or to accumulated depreciation). For example, **Delta Air Lines** reports, "modifications that . . . extend the useful lives of airframes or engines are capitalized and amortized [depreciated] over the remaining estimated useful life of the asset."

Decision Insight

Extraordinary Bombers If we owned a 20-year-old truck and planned to use it in our work for another 40 years, we would expect some extraordinary repairs in future years. A similar situation confronts Whiteman Air Force Base, home to the B-2 stealth bomber, which rolled out of a **Northrop Grumman** hangar in the 1980s. The plan is to keep those bat-winged bombers flying until 2058. The Pentagon is moving forward with a $2 billion, 10-year effort to modernize the bombers' defensive capabilities. ■

Purestock/Superstock

DISPOSALS OF PLANT ASSETS

P2 Account for asset disposal through discarding or selling an asset.

Plant assets are disposed of for several reasons. Some are discarded because they wear out or become obsolete. Others are sold because of changing business plans. Regardless of the reason, disposals of plant assets occur in one of three basic ways: discarding, sale, or exchange. The general steps in accounting for a disposal of plant assets are described in Exhibit 8.15.

EXHIBIT 8.15

Accounting for Disposals of Plant Assets

1. Record depreciation up to the date of disposal—this also updates Accumulated Depreciation.
2. Record the removal of the disposed asset's account balances—including its Accumulated Depreciation.
3. Record any cash (and/or other assets) received or paid in the disposal.
4. Record any gain or loss—computed by comparing the disposed asset's book value with the market value of any assets received.*

* An exception to step 4 is the case of an exchange that lacks *commercial substance*—see Appendix 8A.

Discarding Plant Assets

A plant asset is *discarded* when it is no longer useful to the company and it has no market value. To illustrate, assume that a machine costing $9,000 with accumulated depreciation of $9,000 is discarded. When accumulated depreciation equals the asset's cost, it is said to be *fully depreciated* (zero book value). The entry to record the discarding of this asset is

Assets = Liabilities + Equity
+9,000
−9,000

June 5	Accumulated Depreciation—Machinery	9,000	
	Machinery		9,000
	To discard fully depreciated machinery.		

This entry reflects all four steps of Exhibit 8.15. Step 1 is unnecessary since the machine is fully depreciated. Step 2 is reflected in the debit to Accumulated Depreciation and credit to Machinery. Since no other asset is involved, step 3 is irrelevant. Finally, since book value is zero and no other asset is involved, no gain or loss is recorded in step 4.

How do we account for discarding an asset that is not fully depreciated or one whose depreciation is not up-to-date? To answer this, consider equipment costing $8,000 with accumulated depreciation of $6,000 on December 31 of the prior fiscal year-end. This equipment is being depreciated using the straight-line method over eight years with zero salvage. On July 1 of the current year it is discarded. Step 1 is to bring depreciation up-to-date.

Point: Recording depreciation expense up-to-date gives an up-to-date book value for determining gain or loss.

Assets = Liabilities + Equity
−500 −500

July 1	Depreciation Expense	500	
	Accumulated Depreciation—Equipment		500
	To record 6 months' depreciation ($1,000 × 6/12).		

Steps 2 through 4 of Exhibit 8.15 are reflected in the second (and final) entry.

July 1	Accumulated Depreciation—Equipment	6,500	
	Loss on Disposal of Equipment	1,500	
	Equipment		8,000
	To discard equipment with a $1,500 book value.		

Assets = Liabilities + Equity
+6,500 −1,500
−8,000

This loss is computed by comparing the equipment's $1,500 book value ($8,000 − $6,000 − $500) with the zero net cash proceeds. The loss is reported in the Other Expenses and Losses section of the income statement. Discarding an asset can sometimes require a cash payment that would increase the loss.

Point: Gain or loss is determined by comparing "value given" (book value) to "value received."

Selling Plant Assets

Companies often sell plant assets when they restructure or downsize operations. To illustrate the accounting for selling plant assets, we consider BTO's March 31 sale of equipment that cost $16,000 and has accumulated depreciation of $12,000 at December 31 of the prior calendar year-end. Annual depreciation on this equipment is $4,000 computed using straight-line depreciation. Step 1 of this sale is to record depreciation expense and update accumulated depreciation to March 31 of the current year.

March 31	Depreciation Expense	1,000	
	Accumulated Depreciation—Equipment		1,000
	To record 3 months' depreciation ($4,000 × 3/12).		

Assets = Liabilities + Equity
−1,000 −1,000

Steps 2 through 4 of Exhibit 8.15 can be reflected in one final entry that depends on the amount received from the asset's sale. We consider three different possibilities.

Sale at Book Value If BTO receives $3,000 cash, an amount equal to the equipment's book value as of March 31 (book value = $16,000 − $12,000 − $1,000), no gain or loss occurs on disposal. The entry is

Sale price = Book value → No gain or loss

March 31	Cash	3,000	
	Accumulated Depreciation—Equipment	13,000	
	Equipment		16,000
	To record sale of equipment for no gain or loss.		

Assets = Liabilities + Equity
+3,000
+13,000
−16,000

Sale above Book Value If BTO receives $7,000, an amount that is $4,000 above the equipment's $3,000 book value as of March 31, a gain on disposal occurs. The entry is

Sale price > Book value → Gain

March 31	Cash	7,000	
	Accumulated Depreciation—Equipment	13,000	
	Gain on Disposal of Equipment		4,000
	Equipment		16,000
	To record sale of equipment for a $4,000 gain.		

Assets = Liabilities + Equity
+7,000 +4,000
+13,000
−16,000

Sale below Book Value If BTO receives $2,500, an amount that is $500 below the equipment's $3,000 book value as of March 31, a loss on disposal occurs. The entry is

Sale price < Book value → Loss

March 31	Cash	2,500	
	Loss on Disposal of Equipment	500	
	Accumulated Depreciation—Equipment	13,000	
	Equipment		16,000
	To record sale of equipment for a $500 loss.		

Assets = Liabilities + Equity
+2,500 −500
+13,000
−16,000

IFRS

Unlike U.S. GAAP, IFRS requires an annual review of useful life and salvage value estimates. IFRS also permits revaluation of plant assets to market value if market value is reliably determined. ■

NEED-TO-KNOW 8-3

Additional Expenditures and Asset Disposals

C3 P2

Part 1. A company pays $1,000 for equipment expected to last four years and have a $200 salvage value. Prepare journal entries to record the following costs related to the equipment.

a. During the second year of the equipment's life, $400 cash is paid for a new component expected to increase the equipment's productivity by 20% a year.

b. During the third year, $250 cash is paid for normal repairs necessary to keep the equipment in good working order.

c. During the fourth year, $500 is paid for repairs expected to increase the useful life of the equipment from four to five years.

Part 2. A company owns a machine that cost $500 and has accumulated depreciation of $400. Prepare the entry to record the disposal of the machine on January 2 under each of the following independent situations.

a. The machine needed extensive repairs, and it was not worth repairing. The company disposed of the machine, receiving nothing in return.

b. The company sold the machine for $80 cash.

c. The company sold the machine for $100 cash.

d. The company sold the machine for $110 cash.

Solutions—Part 1

a.

Year 2	Equipment.	400	
	Cash		400
	To record betterment.		

b.

Year 3	Repairs Expense	250	
	Cash		250
	To record ordinary repairs.		

c.

Year 4	Equipment	500	
	Cash		500
	To record extraordinary repairs.		

Solutions—Part 2 [Note: Book value of machine = $500 − $400 = $100]

a. Disposed of at no value

Jan. 2	Loss on Disposal of Machine.	100	
	Accumulated Depreciation—Machine	400	
	Machine		500
	To record disposal of machine.		

b. Sold for $80 cash

Jan. 2	Cash	80	
	Loss on Sale of Machine	20	
	Accumulated Depreciation—Machine	400	
	Machine.		500
	To record cash sale of machine (below book value).		

c. Sold for $100 cash

Jan. 2	Cash	100	
	Accumulated Depreciation—Machine	400	
	Machine.		500
	To record cash sale of machine (at book value).		

d. Sold for $110 cash

Jan. 2	Cash	110	
	Accumulated Depreciation—Machine	400	
	Gain on Sale of Machine		10
	Machine		500
	To record cash sale of machine (above book value).		

Do More: QS 8-8, QS 8-9, E 8-14, E 8-15, E 8-16, E 8-17

QC3

Section 2—Natural Resources

P3 Account for natural resource assets and their depletion.

Natural resources are assets that are physically consumed when used. Examples are standing timber, mineral deposits, and oil and gas fields. Since they are consumed when used, they are often called *wasting assets*. These assets represent soon-to-be inventories of raw materials that will be converted into one or more products by cutting, mining, or pumping. Until that conversion takes place, they are noncurrent assets and are shown in a balance sheet using titles such as *Timberlands, Mineral deposits,* or *Oil reserves*. Natural resources are reported under either plant assets or their own separate category. **Alcoa**, for instance, reports its natural resources under the balance sheet title *Properties, plants and equipment.* In a note to its financial statements, Alcoa reports a separate amount for *Land and land rights, including mines.* **Weyerhaeuser**, on the other hand, reports its timber holdings in a separate balance sheet category titled *Timber and timberlands.*

Cost Determination and Depletion

Natural resources are recorded at cost, which includes all expenditures necessary to acquire the resource and prepare it for its intended use. **Depletion** is the process of allocating the cost of a natural resource to the period when it is consumed. Natural resources are reported on the balance sheet at cost less *accumulated depletion.* The depletion expense per period is usually based on units extracted from cutting, mining, or pumping. This is similar to units-of-production depreciation. **Exxon Mobil** uses this approach to amortize the costs of discovering and operating its oil wells.

Digital Vision/Getty Images

To illustrate depletion of natural resources, let's consider a mineral deposit with an estimated 250,000 tons of available ore. It is purchased for $500,000, and we expect zero salvage value. The depletion charge per ton of ore mined is $2, computed as $500,000 ÷ 250,000 tons. If 85,000 tons are mined and sold in the first year, the depletion charge for that year is $170,000. These computations are detailed in Exhibit 8.16.

EXHIBIT 8.16 Depletion Formula and Example

Step 1

$$\textbf{Depletion per unit} = \frac{\textbf{Cost} - \textbf{Salvage value}}{\textbf{Total units of capacity}} = \frac{\$500{,}000 - \$0}{250{,}000 \text{ tons}} = \$2 \text{ per ton}$$

Step 2

$$\textbf{Depletion expense} = \textbf{Depletion per unit} \times \textbf{Units extracted and sold in period}$$
$$= \$2 \times 85{,}000 = \$170{,}000$$

Depletion expense for the first year is recorded as follows.

Dec. 31	Depletion Expense—Mineral Deposit	170,000	
	Accumulated Depletion—Mineral Deposit		170,000
	To record depletion of the mineral deposit.		

Assets = Liabilities + Equity
−170,000 −170,000

The period-end balance sheet reports the mineral deposit as shown in Exhibit 8.17.

EXHIBIT 8.17 Balance Sheet Presentation of Natural Resources

Mineral deposit	$500,000	
Less accumulated depletion	**170,000**	$330,000

Since all 85,000 tons of the mined ore are sold during the year, the entire $170,000 of depletion is reported on the income statement. If some of the ore remains unsold at year-end, however, the depletion related to the unsold ore is carried forward on the balance sheet and reported as Ore Inventory, a current asset. To illustrate, and continuing with our example, assume that 40,000 tons are mined in the second year, but only 34,000 tons are sold. We record depletion of $68,000 (34,000 tons × $2 depletion per unit) and the remaining Ore Inventory of $12,000 (6,000 tons × $2 depletion per unit) as follows.

Assets	= Liabilities	+ Equity
−80,000		−68,000
+12,000		

Dec. 31	Depletion Expense—Mineral Deposit	68,000	
	Ore Inventory	12,000	
	Accumulated Depletion—Mineral Deposit		80,000
	To record depletion and inventory of mineral deposit.		

Plant Assets Tied into Extracting

The conversion of natural resources by mining, cutting, or pumping usually requires machinery, equipment, and buildings. When the usefulness of these plant assets is directly related to the depletion of a natural resource, their costs are depreciated using the units-of-production method in proportion to the depletion of the natural resource. For example, if a machine is permanently installed in a mine and 10% of the ore is mined and sold in the period, then 10% of the machine's cost (less any salvage value) is allocated to depreciation expense. The same procedure is used when a machine is abandoned once resources have been extracted. If, however, a machine will be moved to and used at another site when extraction is complete, the machine is depreciated over its own useful life.

Decision Insight

Asset Control Long-term assets must be safeguarded against theft, misuse, and other damages. Controls take many forms depending on the asset, including use of security tags, the legal monitoring of rights infringements, and approvals of all asset disposals. A study reports that 43% of employees in operations and service areas witnessed the wasting, mismanaging, or abusing of assets in the past year (KPMG 2011). ■

NEED-TO-KNOW 8-4

Depletion Accounting

P3

A company acquires a zinc mine at a cost of $750,000 on January 1. At that same time it incurs additional costs of $100,000 to access the mine, which is estimated to hold 200,000 tons of zinc. The estimated value of the land after the zinc is removed is $50,000.

1. Prepare the January 1 entry(ies) to record the cost of the zinc mine.
2. Prepare the December 31 year-end adjusting entry if 50,000 tons of zinc are mined, but only 40,000 tons are sold the first year.

Solution

1.

Jan. 1	Zinc Mine	850,000	
	Cash		850,000
	To record cost of zinc mine.		

2. Depletion per unit = ($750,000 + $100,000 − $50,000)/200,000 tons = $4.00 per ton

Dec. 31	Depletion Expense—Zinc Mine	160,000	
	Zinc Inventory	40,000	
	Accumulated Depletion—Zinc Mine		200,000
	To record depletion of zinc mine (50,000 × $4.00).		

Do More: QS 8-10, E 8-18

Section 3—Intangible Assets

P4

Account for intangible assets.

Intangible assets are nonphysical assets (used in operations) that confer on their owners long-term rights, privileges, or competitive advantages. Examples are patents, copyrights, licenses, leaseholds, franchises, goodwill, and trademarks. Lack of physical substance does not necessarily imply an intangible asset. Notes and accounts receivable, for instance, lack physical substance, but they are not intangibles. This section identifies the more common types of intangible assets and explains the accounting for them.

Cost Determination and Amortization

An intangible asset is recorded at cost when purchased. Intangibles are then separated into those with limited lives or indefinite lives. If an intangible has a **limited life,** its cost is systematically allocated to expense over its estimated useful life through the process of **amortization.** If an intangible asset has an **indefinite life**—meaning that no legal, regulatory, contractual, competitive, economic, or other factors limit its useful life—it should not be amortized. (If an intangible with an indefinite life is later judged to have a limited life, it is amortized over that limited life.) Amortization of intangible assets is similar to depreciation of plant assets and the depletion of natural resources in that it is a process of cost allocation. However, only the straight-line method is used for amortizing intangibles *unless* the company can show that another method is preferred. The effects of amortization are recorded in a contra account (Accumulated Amortization). The gross acquisition cost of intangible assets is disclosed in the balance sheet along with their accumulated amortization (these disclosures are new). The eventual disposal of an intangible asset involves removing its book value, recording any other asset(s) received or given up, and recognizing any gain or loss for the difference.

Point: Depreciation, depletion, and amortization are related in that each describes cost allocation.

Many intangibles have limited lives due to laws, contracts, or other asset characteristics. Examples are patents, copyrights, and leaseholds. Other intangibles such as goodwill, trademarks, and trade names have lives that cannot be easily determined. The cost of intangible assets is amortized over the periods expected to benefit by their use, but in no case can this period be longer than the asset's legal existence. The values of some intangible assets such as goodwill continue indefinitely into the future and are not amortized. (An intangible asset that is not amortized is tested annually for **impairment**—if necessary, an impairment loss is recorded. Details for this test are in advanced courses.)

Point: Goodwill is not amortized; instead, it is annually tested for impairment.

Hunter Martin/Getty Images

Intangible assets are often shown in a separate section of the balance sheet immediately after plant assets. **Callaway Golf**, for instance, follows this approach in reporting nearly $90 million of intangible assets in its balance sheet, plus nearly $30 million in goodwill. Companies usually disclose their amortization periods for intangibles. The remainder of our discussion focuses on accounting for specific types of intangible assets.

Types of Intangibles

Patents The federal government grants patents to encourage the invention of new technology, mechanical devices, and production processes. A **patent** is an exclusive right granted to its owner to manufacture and sell a patented item or to use a process for 20 years. When patent rights are purchased, the cost to acquire the rights is debited to an account called Patents. If the owner engages in lawsuits to successfully defend a patent, the cost of lawsuits is debited to the Patents account; if the defense was unsuccessful, the book value of the patent is expensed. However, the costs of research and development leading to a new patent are expensed when incurred.

A patent's cost is amortized over its estimated useful life (not to exceed 20 years). If we purchase a patent costing $25,000 with a useful life of 10 years, we make the following adjusting entry at the end of each of the 10 years to amortize one-tenth of its cost.

Dec. 31	Amortization Expense—Patents	2,500	
	Accumulated Amortization—Patents		2,500
	To amortize patent costs over its useful life.		

Assets = Liabilities + Equity
−2,500 −2,500

The $2,500 debit to Amortization Expense appears on the income statement as a cost of the product or service provided under protection of the patent. The Accumulated Amortization—Patents account is a contra asset account to Patents.

Decision Insight

Mention "drug war" and most people think of illegal drug trade. But another drug war is under way: Brand-name drugmakers are fighting to stop generic copies of their products from hitting the market once patents expire. Delaying a generic rival can yield millions in extra sales. One way drugmakers fight patent expirations is to alter *drug delivery.* The first patent might require a patient to take a pill 4×/day. When that patent expires, the drugmaker can "improve" the drug's delivery release system to 2×/day, and then 1×/day, and so forth. ■

Prescriptions That Specify Generics

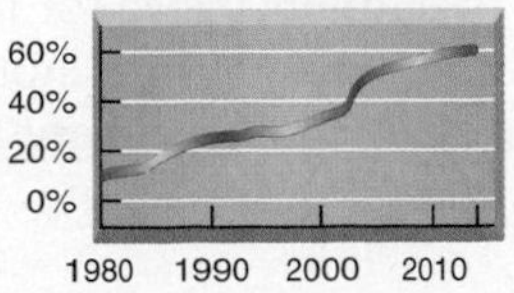

Copyrights A **copyright** gives its owner the exclusive right to publish and sell a musical, literary, or artistic work during the life of the creator plus 70 years, although the useful life of most copyrights is much shorter. The costs of a copyright are amortized over its useful life. The only identifiable cost of many copyrights is the fee paid to the Copyright Office of the federal government or international agency granting the copyright. If this fee is immaterial, it is charged directly to an expense account; but if the identifiable costs of a copyright are material, they are capitalized (recorded in an asset account) and periodically amortized by debiting an account called Amortization Expense—Copyrights.

Decision Insight

Mickey Mouse Protection Act The Walt Disney Company successfully lobbied Congress to extend copyright protection from the life of the creator plus 50 years to life of the creator plus 70 years. This extension allows the company to protect its characters for 20 additional years before the right to use them enters the public domain. Mickey Mouse is now protected by copyright law until 2023. The law is officially termed the Copyright Term Extension Act (CTEA) but it is also known as the Mickey Mouse Protection Act. ■

Yoshikazu Tsuno/AFP/Getty Images

Franchises and Licenses **Franchises** and **licenses** are rights that a company or government grants an entity to deliver a product or service under specified conditions. Many organizations grant franchise and license rights—**McDonald's**, **Pizza Hut**, and **Major League Baseball** are just a few examples. The costs of franchises and licenses are debited to a Franchises and Licenses asset account and are amortized over the lives of the agreements. If an agreement is for an indefinite or perpetual period, those costs are not amortized.

Trademarks and Trade Names Companies often adopt unique symbols or select unique names and brands in marketing their products. A **trademark** or **trade (brand) name** is a symbol, name, phrase, or jingle identified with a company, product, or service. Examples are Nike swoosh, Marlboro Man, Big Mac, Coca-Cola, and Corvette. Ownership and exclusive right to use a trademark or trade name is often established by showing that one company used it before another. Ownership is best established by registering a trademark or trade name with the government's Patent Office. The cost of developing, maintaining, or enhancing the value of a trademark or trade name (such as advertising) is charged to expense when incurred. If a trademark or trade name is purchased, however, its cost is debited to an asset account and then amortized over its expected life. If the company plans to renew indefinitely its right to the trademark or trade name, the cost is not amortized.

Point: McDonald's "golden arches" are one of the world's most valuable trademarks, yet this asset is not shown on McDonald's balance sheet.

Goodwill **Goodwill** has a specific meaning in accounting. Goodwill is the amount by which a company's value exceeds the value of its individual assets and liabilities. This usually implies that the company as a whole has certain valuable attributes not measured among its individual assets and liabilities. These can include superior management, skilled workforce, good supplier or customer relations, quality products or services, good location, or other competitive advantages.

To keep accounting information from being too subjective, goodwill is not recorded unless an entire company or business segment is purchased. Purchased goodwill is measured by taking the purchase price of the company and subtracting the market value of its individual net assets (excluding goodwill). For instance, **Google** paid $1.19 billion to acquire **YouTube**; about $1.13 of the $1.19 billion was for goodwill. Goodwill was also a major portion of the $19 billion that **Facebook** paid to acquire **WhatsApp**.

Goodwill is measured as the excess of the cost of an acquired entity over the value of the acquired net assets. Goodwill is recorded as an asset, and it is *not* amortized. Instead, goodwill is annually tested for impairment. If the book value of goodwill does not exceed its fair (market) value, goodwill is not impaired. However, if the book value of goodwill does exceed its fair value, an impairment loss is recorded equal to that excess. (Details of this test are in advanced courses.)

Point: Amortization of goodwill is different for financial accounting and tax accounting. The IRS requires the amortization of goodwill over 15 years.

Example: Assume goodwill carries a book value of $500 and has an implied fair value of $475, *and* this $25 decline in value meets the 2-step impairment test. The entry to record this impairment is:

Impairment Loss. . . .	$25	
Goodwill.		$25

Leaseholds Property is rented under a contract called a **lease.** The property's owner, called the **lessor,** grants the lease. The one who secures the right to possess and use the property is called the **lessee.** A **leasehold** refers to the rights the lessor grants to the lessee under the terms of the lease. A leasehold is an intangible asset for the lessee.

Certain leases require no advance payment from the lessee but require monthly rent payments. In this case, we do not set up a Leasehold account. Instead, the monthly payments are debited to a Rent Expense account. If a long-term lease requires the lessee to pay the final period's rent in advance when the lease is signed, the lessee records this advance payment with a debit to the Leasehold account. Since the advance payment is not used until the final period, the Leasehold account balance remains intact until that final period when its balance is transferred to Rent Expense. (Some long-term leases give the lessee essentially the same rights as a purchaser. This results in a tangible asset and a liability reported by the lessee. Chapter 10 describes these so-called *capital leases.*)

A long-term lease can increase in value when current rental rates for similar property rise while the required payments under the lease remain constant. This increase in value of a lease is not reported on the lessee's balance sheet. However, if the property is subleased and the new tenant makes a cash payment to the original lessee for the rights under the old lease, the new tenant debits this payment to a Leasehold account, which is amortized to Rent Expense over the remaining life of the lease.

Point: A leasehold account implies existence of future benefits that the lessee controls because of a prepayment. It also meets the definition of an asset.

Leasehold Improvements A lessee sometimes pays for alterations or improvements to the leased property such as partitions, painting, and storefronts. These alterations and improvements are called **leasehold improvements,** and the lessee debits these costs to a Leasehold Improvements account. Since leasehold improvements become part of the property and revert to the lessor at the end of the lease, the lessee amortizes these costs over the life of the lease or the life of the improvements, whichever is shorter. The amortization entry debits Amortization Expense—Leasehold Improvements and credits Accumulated Amortization—Leasehold Improvements.

Other Intangibles There are other types of intangible assets such as *software, noncompete covenants, customer lists,* and so forth. Our accounting for them is the same. First, we record the intangible asset's costs. Second, we determine whether the asset has a limited or indefinite life. If limited, we allocate its costs over that period. If indefinite, its costs are not amortized.

NEED-TO-KNOW 8-5

Accounting for Intangibles

P4

Part 1. A publisher purchases the copyright on a book for $1,000 on January 1 of this year. The copyright legally protects its owner for five more years. The company plans to market and sell prints of the original for seven years. Prepare entries to record the purchase of the copyright on January 1 of this year, and its annual amortization on December 31 of this year.

Part 2. On January 3 of this year, a retailer incurs a $9,000 cost to modernize its store. Improvements include lighting, partitions, and sound system. These improvements are estimated to yield benefits for five years. The retailer leases its store and has three years remaining on its lease. Prepare the entry to record (a) the cost of modernization and (b) amortization at the end of this current year.

Part 3. On January 6 of this year, a company pays $6,000 for a patent with a remaining 12-year legal life to produce a supplement expected to be marketable for 3 years. Prepare entries to record its acquisition and the December 31 amortization entry for this current year.

Solution—Part 1

Jan. 1	Copyright	1,000	
	Cash		1,000
	To record purchase of copyright.		
Dec. 31	Amortization Expense—Copyright	200	
	Accumulated Amortization—Copyright		200
	To record amortization of copyright [$1,000/5 years].		

Solution—Part 2

a.

Jan. 3	Leasehold Improvements	9,000	
	Cash		9,000
	To record leasehold improvements.		

b.

Dec. 31	Amortization Expense–Leasehold Improvements	3,000	
	Accumulated Amortization—Leasehold Improvements		3,000
	*To record amortization of leasehold over remaining lease life.**		

*Amortization = $9,000/3-year-lease-term = $3,000 per year

Solution—Part 3

Jan. 6	Patents	6,000	
	Cash		6,000
	To record purchase of patent.		
Dec. 31	Amortization Expense*	2,000	
	Accumulated Amortization—Patents		2,000
	*To record amortization of patent. *$6,000/3 years = $2,000*		

Do More: QS 8-12, E 8-19, E 8-20

QC4

GLOBAL VIEW

This section discusses similarities and differences between U.S. GAAP and IFRS in accounting and reporting for plant assets and intangible assets.

Accounting for Plant Assets Issues involving cost determination, depreciation, additional expenditures, and disposals of plant assets are subject to broadly similar guidance for both U.S. GAAP and IFRS. Although differences exist, the similarities vastly outweigh the differences. **Nokia** describes its accounting for plant assets as follows:

NOKIA

> Property, plant and equipment are stated at cost less accumulated depreciation. Depreciation is recorded on a straight-line basis over the expected useful lives of the assets. Maintenance, repairs and renewals are generally charged to expense during the financial period in which they are incurred. However, major renovations are capitalized and included in the carrying amount of the asset . . . Major renovations are depreciated over the remaining useful life of the related asset.

One area where notable differences exist is in accounting for changes in the value of plant assets (between the time they are acquired and when disposed of). Namely, how do IFRS and U.S. GAAP treat decreases and increases in the value of plant assets subsequent to acquisition?

Decreases in the Value of Plant Assets When the value of plant assets declines after acquisition, but before disposition, both U.S. GAAP and IFRS require companies to record those decreases as *impairment losses*. While the *test for impairment* uses a different base between U.S. GAAP and IFRS, a more fundamental difference is that U.S. GAAP revalues impaired plant assets to *fair value* whereas IFRS revalues them to a *recoverable amount* (defined as fair value less costs to sell).

Increases in the Value of Plant Assets U.S. GAAP prohibits companies from recording increases in the value of plant assets. However, IFRS permits upward *asset revaluations*. Namely, under IFRS, if an impairment was previously recorded, a company would reverse that impairment to the extent necessary and record that increase in income. If the increase is beyond the original cost, that increase is recorded in comprehensive income.

Accounting for Intangible Assets For intangible assets, the accounting for cost determination, amortization, additional expenditures, and disposals is subject to broadly similar guidance for U.S. GAAP and IFRS. Although differences exist, the similarities vastly outweigh differences. Again, and consistent with the accounting for plant assets, U.S. GAAP and IFRS handle decreases and increases in the value of intangible assets differently. However, IFRS requirements for recording increases in the value of intangible assets are so restrictive that such increases are rare. **Nokia** describes its accounting for intangible assets as follows:

> [Intangible assets] are capitalized and amortized using the straight-line method over their useful lives. Where an indication of impairment exists, the carrying amount of the related intangible asset is assessed for recoverability. Any resulting impairment losses are recognized immediately in the income statement.

Sustainability and Accounting Entrepreneur Deb Carey, of **New Glarus Brewing Co.**, as introduced in this chapter's opening feature, explains that her company is committed to a green footprint. For example, five years ago, she put in her own on-site wastewater treatment system that reduced the demands placed on the community's sewer system. She then uses the treated wastewater for irrigation. She is currently attempting to reroute the brewery's cooling system outside during the winter season to take advantage of nature's cooling system. This would save considerable refrigeration costs. Her goal is to be in the top 10% of most energy-efficient breweries in the world.

Total Asset Turnover — Decision Analysis

A1 Compute total asset turnover and apply it to analyze a company's use of assets.

A company's assets are important in determining its ability to generate sales and earn income. Managers devote much attention to deciding what assets a company acquires, how much it invests in assets, and how to use assets most efficiently and effectively. One important measure of a company's ability to use its assets is **total asset turnover,** defined in Exhibit 8.18.

EXHIBIT 8.18 Total Asset Turnover

$$\textbf{Total asset turnover} = \frac{\textbf{Net sales}}{\textbf{Average total assets}}$$

The numerator reflects the net amounts earned from the sale of products and services. The denominator reflects the average total resources devoted to operating the company and generating sales.

To illustrate, let's look at total asset turnover in Exhibit 8.19 for two competing companies: **Molson Coors** and **Boston Beer**.

EXHIBIT 8.19 Analysis Using Total Asset Turnover

Company	Figure ($ millions)	2013	2012	2011	2010	2009
Molson Coors	Net sales	$ 4,206.1	$ 3,916.5	$ 3,515.7	$ 3,254.4	$ 3,032.4
	Average total assets	$15,896.2	$14,318.0	$12,560.7	$12,359.4	$11,203.9
	Total asset turnover	**0.26**	**0.27**	**0.28**	**0.26**	**0.27**
Boston Beer	Net sales	$ 739.1	$ 580.2	$ 513.0	$ 463.8	$ 415.1
	Average total assets	$ 401.8	$ 316.0	$ 265.5	$ 260.7	$ 241.3
	Total asset turnover	**1.84**	**1.84**	**1.93**	**1.78**	**1.72**

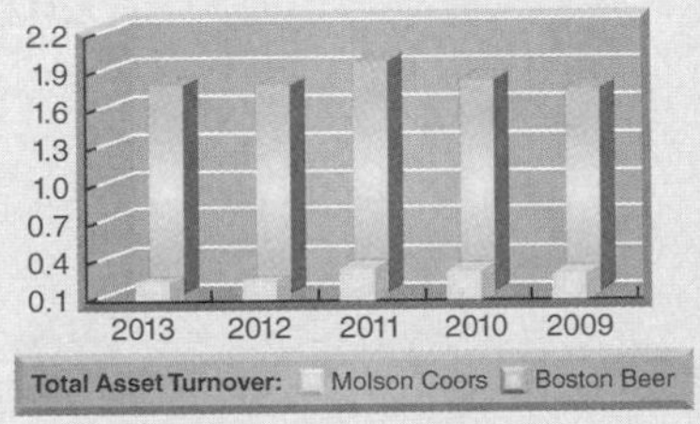

To show how we use total asset turnover, let's look at Molson Coors. We express Molson Coors's use of assets in generating net sales by saying "it turned its assets over 0.26 times during 2013." This means that each $1.00 of assets produced $0.26 of net sales. Is a total asset turnover of 0.26 good or bad? It is safe to say that all companies desire a high total asset turnover. Like many ratio analyses, however, a company's total asset turnover must be interpreted in comparison with those of prior years and of its competitors. Interpreting the total asset turnover also requires an understanding of the company's operations. Some operations are capital-intensive, meaning that a relatively large amount is invested in assets to generate sales. This suggests a relatively lower total asset turnover. Other companies' operations are labor-intensive, meaning that they generate sales more by the efforts of people than the use of assets. In that case, we expect a higher total asset turnover. Companies with low total asset turnover require higher profit margins (examples are hotels and real estate); companies with high total asset turnover can succeed with lower profit margins (examples are food stores and toy merchandisers). Molson Coors's turnover is much lower than that for Boston Beer and many other competitors. Total asset turnover for Molson Coors's competitors, available in industry publications such as Dun & Bradstreet, is generally in the range of 0.5 to 1.0 over this same period. Overall, Molson Coors must improve relative to its competitors on total asset turnover.

Point: An estimate of **plant asset useful life** equals the plant asset cost divided by depreciation expense.

Point: The plant asset age is estimated by dividing accumulated depreciation by depreciation expense. Older plant assets can signal needed asset replacements; they may also signal less efficient assets.

Decision Maker

Environmentalist A paper manufacturer claims it cannot afford more environmental controls. It points to its low total asset turnover of 1.9 and argues that it cannot compete with companies whose total asset turnover is much higher. Examples cited are food stores (5.5) and auto dealers (3.8). How do you respond? ■ [Answers follow the chapter's Summary.]

NEED-TO-KNOW

COMPREHENSIVE

On July 14, 2015, Tulsa Company pays $600,000 to acquire a fully equipped factory. The purchase involves the following assets and information.

Asset	Appraised Value	Salvage Value	Useful Life	Depreciation Method
Land	$160,000			Not depreciated
Land improvements	80,000	$ 0	10 years	Straight-line
Building	320,000	100,000	10 years	Double-declining-balance
Machinery	240,000	20,000	10,000 units	Units-of-production*
Total	$800,000			

* The machinery is used to produce 700 units in 2015 and 1,800 units in 2016.

Required

1. Allocate the total $600,000 purchase cost among the separate assets.
2. Compute the 2015 (six months) and 2016 depreciation expense for each asset, and compute the company's total depreciation expense for both years.
3. On the last day of calendar year 2017, Tulsa discarded machinery that had been on its books for five years. The machinery's original cost was $12,000 (estimated life of five years) and its salvage value was $2,000. No depreciation had been recorded for the fifth year when the disposal occurred. Journalize the fifth year of depreciation (straight-line method) and the asset's disposal.
4. At the beginning of year 2017, Tulsa purchased a patent for $100,000 cash. The company estimated the patent's useful life to be 10 years. Journalize the patent acquisition and its amortization for the year 2017.
5. Late in the year 2017, Tulsa acquired an ore deposit for $600,000 cash. It added roads and built mine shafts for an additional cost of $80,000. Salvage value of the mine is estimated to be $20,000. The company estimated 330,000 tons of available ore. In year 2017, Tulsa mined and sold 10,000 tons of ore. Journalize the mine's acquisition and its first year's depletion.

6^A (This question applies this chapter's Appendix coverage.) On the first day of 2017, Tulsa exchanged the machinery that was acquired on July 14, 2015, along with $5,000 cash for machinery with a $210,000 market value. Journalize the exchange of these assets assuming the exchange lacked commercial substance. (Refer to background information in parts 1 and 2.)

PLANNING THE SOLUTION

- Complete a three-column table showing the following amounts for each asset: appraised value, percent of total value, and apportioned cost.
- Using allocated costs, compute depreciation for 2015 (only one-half year) and 2016 (full year) for each asset. Summarize those computations in a table showing total depreciation for each year.
- Depreciation must be recorded up-to-date before discarding an asset. Calculate and record depreciation expense for the fifth year using the straight-line method. Since salvage value is not received at the end of a discarded asset's life, the salvage value becomes a loss on disposal. Record the loss on the disposal as well as the removal of the discarded asset and its related accumulated depreciation.
- Record the patent (an intangible asset) at its purchase price. Use straight-line amortization over its useful life to calculate amortization expense.
- Record the ore deposit (a natural resource asset) at its cost, including any added costs to ready the mine for use. Calculate depletion per ton using the depletion formula. Multiply the depletion per ton by the amount of tons mined and sold to calculate depletion expense for the year.
- Remember that gains and losses on asset exchanges that lack commercial substance are not recognized. Make a journal entry to add the acquired machinery to the books and to remove the old machinery, along with its accumulated depreciation, and to record the cash given in the exchange.

SOLUTION

1. Allocation of the total cost of $600,000 among the separate assets.

Asset	Appraised Value	Percent of Total Value	Apportioned Cost
Land	$160,000	20%	**$120,000** ($600,000 × 20%)
Land improvements	80,000	10	**60,000** ($600,000 × 10%)
Building	320,000	40	**240,000** ($600,000 × 40%)
Machinery	240,000	30	**180,000** ($600,000 × 30%)
Total	$800,000	100%	$ 600,000

2. Depreciation for each asset. (Land is not depreciated.)

Land Improvements	
Cost	$ 60,000
Salvage value	0
Depreciable cost	$ 60,000
Useful life	10 years
Annual depreciation expense ($60,000/10 years)	$ 6,000
2015 depreciation ($6,000 × 6/12)	**$ 3,000**
2016 depreciation	**$ 6,000**
Building	
Straight-line rate = 100%/10 years = 10%	
Double-declining-balance rate = 10% × 2 = 20%	
2015 depreciation ($240,000 × 20% × 6/12)	**$ 24,000**
2016 depreciation [($240,000 − $24,000) × 20%]	**$ 43,200**
Machinery	
Cost	$180,000
Salvage value	20,000
Depreciable cost	$160,000
Total expected units of production	10,000 units
Depreciation per unit ($160,000/10,000 units)	$ 16
2015 depreciation ($16 × 700 units)	**$ 11,200**
2016 depreciation ($16 × 1,800 units)	**$ 28,800**

Total depreciation expense for each year:

	2015	2016
Land improvements	$ 3,000	$ 6,000
Building	24,000	43,200
Machinery	11,200	28,800
Total	$38,200	$78,000

3. Record the depreciation up-to-date on the discarded asset.

	Debit	Credit
Depreciation Expense—Machinery	2,000	
Accumulated Depreciation—Machinery		2,000
To record depreciation on date of disposal: ($12,000 − $2,000)/5		

Record the removal of the discarded asset and its loss on disposal.

	Debit	Credit
Accumulated Depreciation—Machinery	10,000	
Loss on Disposal of Machinery	2,000	
Machinery		12,000
To record the discarding of machinery with a $2,000 book value.		

4.

Patent	100,000	
Cash		100,000
To record patent acquisition.		

Amortization Expense—Patent	10,000	
Accumulated Amortization—Patent		10,000
To record amortization expense: $100,000/10 years = $10,000.		

5.

Ore Deposit	680,000	
Cash		680,000
To record ore deposit acquisition and its related costs.		

Depletion Expense—Ore Deposit	20,000	
Accumulated Depletion—Ore Deposit		20,000
To record depletion expense: ($680,000 − $20,000)/330,000 tons = $2 per ton. 10,000 tons mined and sold × $2 = $20,000 depletion.		

6. Record the asset exchange: The book value on the exchange date is $180,000 (cost) − $40,000 (accumulated depreciation). The book value of the machinery given up in the exchange ($140,000) plus the $5,000 cash paid is less than the $210,000 value of the machine acquired. The entry to record this exchange of assets that lacks commercial substance does not recognize the $65,000 "gain."

Machinery (new)	145,000*	
Accumulated Depreciation—Machinery (old)	40,000	
Machinery (old)		180,000
Cash		5,000
To record asset exchange that lacks commercial substance.		

* Market value of the acquired asset of $210,000 minus $65,000 "gain."

APPENDIX

8A Exchanging Plant Assets

P5^A Account for asset exchanges.

Many plant assets such as machinery, automobiles, and office equipment are disposed of by exchanging them for newer assets. In a typical exchange of plant assets, a *trade-in allowance* is received on the old asset and the balance is paid in cash. Accounting for the exchange of assets depends on whether the transaction has *commercial substance* (per *SFAS 153,* commercial substance implies that it alters the company's future cash flows). If an asset exchange has commercial substance, a gain or loss is recorded based on the difference between the book value of the asset(s) given up and the market value of the asset(s) received. If an asset exchange lacks commercial substance, no gain or loss is recorded, and the asset(s) received is recorded based on the book value of the asset(s) given up. An exchange has commercial substance if the company's future cash flows change as a result of the transaction. This section describes the accounting for the exchange of assets.

Exchange with Commercial Substance: A Loss A company acquires $42,000 in new equipment. In exchange, the company pays $33,000 cash and trades in old equipment. The old equipment originally cost $36,000 and has accumulated depreciation of $20,000, which implies a $16,000 book value at the time of exchange. We are told this exchange has commercial substance and that the old equipment has a trade-in allowance of $9,000. This exchange yields a loss as computed in the middle (Loss) columns of Exhibit 8A.1; the loss is computed as Asset received − Assets given = $42,000 − $49,000 = $(7,000). We can also compute the loss as Trade-in allowance − Book value of asset given = $9,000 − $16,000 = $(7,000).

EXHIBIT 8A.1

Computing Gain or Loss on Asset Exchange with Commercial Substance

Asset Exchange Has Commercial Substance	Loss		Gain	
Market value of asset received		$42,000		$52,000
Book value of assets given:				
Equipment ($36,000 − $20,000)	$16,000		$16,000	
Cash	33,000	49,000	33,000	49,000
Gain (loss) on exchange		**$(7,000)**		**$ 3,000**

The entry to record this asset exchange is

Jan. 3	Equipment (**new**)	42,000	
	Loss on Exchange of Assets	7,000	
	Accumulated Depreciation—Equipment (**old**)	20,000	
	Equipment (**old**)		36,000
	Cash		33,000
	To record exchange (with commercial substance) of old equipment and cash for new equipment.		

Assets	= Liabilities +	Equity
+42,000		−7,000
+20,000		
−36,000		
−33,000		

Point: Parenthetical notes to "new" and "old" equipment are for illustration only. Both the debit and credit are to the same Equipment account.

Exchange with Commercial Substance: A Gain Let's assume the same facts as in the preceding asset exchange *except* that the new equipment received has a market value of $52,000 instead of $42,000. We are told that this exchange has commercial substance and that the old equipment has a trade-in allowance of $19,000. This exchange yields a gain as computed in the right-most (Gain) columns of Exhibit 8A.1; the gain is computed as Asset received − Assets given = $52,000 − $49,000 = $3,000. We can also compute the gain as Trade-in allowance − Book value of asset given = $19,000 − $16,000 = $3,000. The entry to record this asset exchange is

Jan. 3	Equipment (**new**)	52,000	
	Accumulated Depreciation—Equipment (**old**)	20,000	
	Equipment (**old**)		36,000
	Cash		33,000
	Gain on Exchange of Assets		3,000
	To record exchange (with commercial substance) of old equipment and cash for new equipment.		

Assets	= Liabilities +	Equity
+52,000		+3,000
+20,000		
−36,000		
−33,000		

Exchanges without Commercial Substance Let's assume the same facts as in the preceding asset exchange involving new equipment received with a market value of $52,000, but let's instead assume the transaction *lacks commercial substance.* The entry to record this asset exchange is

Jan. 3	Equipment (**new**)	49,000	
	Accumulated Depreciation—Equipment (**old**)	20,000	
	Equipment (**old**)		36,000
	Cash		33,000
	To record exchange (without commercial substance) of old equipment and cash for new equipment.		

Assets	= Liabilities +	Equity
+49,000		
+20,000		
−36,000		
−33,000		

The $3,000 gain recorded when the transaction has commercial substance is *not* recognized in this entry because of the rule prohibiting recording a gain or loss on asset exchanges without commercial substance. The $49,000 recorded for the new equipment equals its cash price ($52,000) less the unrecognized gain ($3,000) on the exchange. The $49,000 cost recorded is called the *cost basis* of the new machine. This cost basis is the amount we use to compute depreciation and its book value. The cost basis of the new asset also can be computed by summing the book values of the assets given up as shown in Exhibit 8A.2. The same analysis and approach are taken for a loss on an asset exchange without commercial substance.

Point: No gain or loss is recorded for exchanges *without* commercial substance.

EXHIBIT 8A.2

Cost Basis of New Asset When Gain Not Recorded on Asset Exchange without Commercial Substance

Cost of old equipment	$ 36,000
Less accumulated depreciation	20,000
Book value of old equipment	16,000
Cash paid in the exchange	33,000
Cost recorded for new equipment	**$49,000**

NEED-TO-KNOW 8-6

Asset Exchange

P5

A company trades an old web server for a new one. The cost of the old server is $30,000, and its accumulated depreciation at the time of the trade is $23,400. The new server has a cash price of $45,000. Prepare entries to record the trade under two different assumptions where the company receives a trade-in allowance of (*a*) $3,000 and the exchange has commercial substance, and (*b*) $7,000 and the exchange lacks commercial substance.

Solution

(*a*) Equipment (new)	45,000	
Loss on Exchange of Assets	3,600	
Accumulated Depreciation—Equipment (old)	23,400	
Equipment (old)		30,000
Cash ($45,000 − $3,000)		42,000

(*b*) Equipment (new)*	44,600	
Accumulated Depreciation—Equipment (old)	23,400	
Equipment (old)		30,000
Cash ($45,000 − $7,000)		38,000

* Includes $400 unrecognized gain.

Do More: QS 8-23

Summary

C1 Explain the cost principle for computing the cost of plant assets. Plant assets are set apart from other tangible assets by two important features: use in operations and useful lives longer than one period. Plant assets are recorded at cost when purchased. Cost includes all normal and reasonable expenditures necessary to get the asset in place and ready for its intended use. The cost of a lump-sum purchase is allocated among its individual assets.

C2 Explain depreciation for partial years and changes in estimates. Partial-year depreciation is often required because assets are bought and sold throughout the year. Depreciation is revised when changes in estimates such as salvage value and useful life occur. If the useful life of a plant asset changes, for instance, the remaining cost to be depreciated is spread over the remaining (revised) useful life of the asset.

C3 Distinguish between revenue and capital expenditures, and account for them. Revenue expenditures expire in the current period and are debited to expense accounts and matched with current revenues. Ordinary repairs are an example of revenue expenditures. Capital expenditures benefit future periods and are debited to asset accounts. Examples of capital expenditures are extraordinary repairs and betterments.

A1 Compute total asset turnover and apply it to analyze a company's use of assets. Total asset turnover measures a company's ability to use its assets to generate sales. It is defined as net sales divided by average total assets. While all companies desire a high total asset turnover, it must be interpreted in comparison with those for prior years and its competitors.

P1 Compute and record depreciation using the straight-line, units-of-production, and declining-balance methods. *Depreciation* is the process of allocating to expense the cost of a plant asset over the accounting periods that benefit from its use. Depreciation does not measure the decline in a plant asset's market value or its physical deterioration. Three factors determine depreciation: cost, salvage value, and useful life. Salvage value is an estimate of the asset's value at the end of its benefit period. Useful (service) life is the length of time an asset is productively used. The straight-line method divides cost less salvage value by the asset's useful life to determine depreciation expense per period. The units-of-production method divides cost less salvage value by the estimated number of units the asset will produce over its life to determine depreciation per unit. The declining-balance method multiplies the asset's beginning-of-period book value by a factor that is often double the straight-line rate.

P2 Account for asset disposal through discarding or selling an asset. When a plant asset is discarded or sold, its cost and accumulated depreciation are removed from the accounts. Any cash proceeds from discarding or selling an asset are recorded and compared to the asset's book value to determine gain or loss.

P3 Account for natural resource assets and their depletion. The cost of a natural resource is recorded in a noncurrent asset account. Depletion of a natural resource is recorded by allocating its cost to depletion expense using the units-of-production method. Depletion is credited to an Accumulated Depletion account.

P4 Account for intangible assets. An intangible asset is recorded at the cost incurred to purchase it. The cost of an intangible asset with a definite useful life is allocated to expense using the straight-line method, and is called *amortization*. Goodwill and intangible assets with an indefinite useful life are not amortized— they are annually tested for impairment. Intangible assets include patents, copyrights, leaseholds, goodwill, and trademarks.

P5A **Account for asset exchanges.** For an asset exchange with commercial substance, a gain or loss is recorded based on the difference between the book value of the asset given up and the market value of the asset received. For an asset exchange without commercial substance, no gain or loss is recorded, and the asset received is recorded based on the book value of the asset given up.

Guidance Answers to Decision Maker and Decision Ethics

Controller The president's instructions may reflect an honest and reasonable prediction of the future. Since the company is struggling financially, the president may have concluded that the normal pattern of replacing assets every three years cannot continue. Perhaps the strategy is to avoid costs of frequent replacements and stretch use of equipment a few years longer until financial conditions improve. However, if you believe the president's decision is unprincipled, you might confront the president with your opinion that it is unethical to change the estimate to increase income. Another possibility is to wait and see whether the auditor will prohibit this change in estimate. In either case, you should insist that the statements be based on reasonable estimates.

Entrepreneur Treating an expense as a capital expenditure means that reported expenses will be lower and income higher in the short run. This is so because a capital expenditure is not expensed immediately but is spread over the asset's useful life. Treating an expense as a capital expenditure also means that asset and equity totals are reported at larger amounts in the short run. This continues until the asset is fully depreciated. Your friend is probably trying to help, but the suggestion is misguided. Only an expenditure benefiting future periods is a capital expenditure.

Environmentalist The paper manufacturer's comparison of its total asset turnover with food stores and auto dealers is misdirected. These other industries' turnovers are higher because their profit margins are lower (about 2%). Profit margins for the paper industry are usually 3% to 3.5%. You need to collect data from competitors in the paper industry to show that a 1.9 total asset turnover is about the norm for this industry. You might also want to collect data on this company's revenues and expenses, along with compensation data for its high-ranking officers and employees.

Key Terms

Accelerated depreciation method
Amortization
Asset book value
Betterments
Capital expenditures
Change in an accounting estimate
Copyright
Cost
Declining-balance method
Depletion
Depreciation
Extraordinary repairs
Franchises
Goodwill
Impairment
Inadequacy
Indefinite life
Intangible assets
Land improvements
Lease
Leasehold
Leasehold improvements
Lessee
Lessor
Licenses
Limited life
Modified Accelerated Cost Recovery System (MACRS)
Natural resources
Obsolescence
Ordinary repairs
Patent
Plant asset age
Plant assets
Revenue expenditures
Salvage value
Straight-line depreciation
Total asset turnover
Trademark or trade (brand) name
Units-of-production depreciation
Useful life

Multiple Choice Quiz

Answers at end of chapter

1. A company paid $326,000 for property that included land, land improvements, and a building. The land was appraised at $175,000, the land improvements were appraised at $70,000, and the building was appraised at $105,000. What is the allocation of property costs to the three assets purchased?
   a. Land, $150,000; Land Improvements, $60,000; Building, $90,000
   b. Land, $163,000; Land Improvements, $65,200; Building, $97,800
   c. Land, $150,000; Land Improvements, $61,600; Building, $92,400
   d. Land, $159,000; Land Improvements, $65,200; Building, $95,400
   e. Land, $175,000; Land Improvements, $70,000; Building, $105,000

2. A company purchased a truck for $35,000 on January 1, 2015. The truck is estimated to have a useful life of four years and an estimated salvage value of $1,000. Assuming that the company uses straight-line depreciation, what is the depreciation expense on the truck for the year ended December 31, 2016?
a. $8,750 **c.** $8,500 **e.** $25,500
b. $17,500 **d.** $17,000

3. A company purchased machinery for $10,800,000 on January 1, 2015. The machinery has a useful life of 10 years and an estimated salvage value of $800,000. What is the depreciation expense on the machinery for the year ended December 31, 2016, assuming that the double-declining-balance method is used?
a. $2,160,000 **c.** $1,728,000 **e.** $1,600,000
b. $3,888,000 **d.** $2,000,000

4. A company sold a machine that originally cost $250,000 for $120,000 when accumulated depreciation on the machine was $100,000. The gain or loss recorded on the sale of this machine is
a. $0 gain or loss. **d.** $30,000 gain.
b. $120,000 gain. **e.** $150,000 loss.
c. $30,000 loss.

5. A company had average total assets of $500,000, gross sales of $575,000, and net sales of $550,000. The company's total asset turnover is
a. 1.15 **d.** 0.87
b. 1.10 **e.** 1.05
c. 0.91

A Superscript letter A denotes assignments based on Appendix 8A.
Icon denotes assignments that involve decision making.

Discussion Questions

1. What characteristics of a plant asset make it different from other assets?
2. What is the general rule for cost inclusion for plant assets?
3. What is different between land and land improvements?
4. Why is the cost of a lump-sum purchase allocated to the individual assets acquired?
5. Does the balance in the Accumulated Depreciation—Machinery account represent funds to replace the machinery when it wears out? If not, what does it represent?
6. Why is the Modified Accelerated Cost Recovery System not generally accepted for financial accounting purposes?
7. What accounting concept justifies charging low-cost plant asset purchases immediately to an expense account?
8. What is the difference between ordinary repairs and extraordinary repairs? How should each be recorded?
9. Identify events that might lead to disposal of a plant asset.
10. What is the process of allocating the cost of natural resources to expense as they are used?
11. Is the declining-balance method an acceptable way to compute depletion of natural resources? Explain.
12. What are the characteristics of an intangible asset?
13. What general procedures are applied in accounting for the acquisition and potential cost allocation of intangible assets?
14. When do we know that a company has goodwill? When can goodwill appear in a company's balance sheet?
15. Assume that a company buys another business and pays for its goodwill. If the company plans to incur costs each year to maintain the value of the goodwill, must it also amortize this goodwill?
16. How is total asset turnover computed? Why would a financial statement user be interested in total asset turnover?
17. On its recent balance sheet in Appendix A, **Apple** lists its plant assets as "Property, plant and equipment, net." What does "net" mean in this title?
18. Refer to **Google**'s recent balance sheet in Appendix A. What property, plant and equipment assets does Google list on its balance sheet? What is the book value of its total net property, plant and equipment assets at December 31, 2013?
19. Refer to **Samsung**'s balance sheet in Appendix A. What does it title its plant assets? What is the book value of its plant assets at December 31, 2013?
20. Refer to the December 31, 2013, balance sheet of **Samsung** in Appendix A. What long-term assets discussed in this chapter are reported by the company?
21. Identify the main difference between (a) plant assets and current assets, (b) plant assets and inventory, and (c) plant assets and long-term investments.

QUICK STUDY

QS 8-1
Cost of plant assets
C1

Kegler Bowling installs automatic scorekeeping equipment with an invoice cost of $190,000. The electrical work required for the installation costs $20,000. Additional costs are $4,000 for delivery and $13,700 for sales tax. During the installation, a component of the equipment is carelessly left on a lane and hit by the automatic lane-cleaning machine. The cost of repairing the component is $1,850. What is the total recorded cost of the automatic scorekeeping equipment?

QS 8-2
Assigning costs to plant assets
C1

Listed below are certain costs (or discounts) incurred in the purchase or construction of new plant assets. (1) Indicate whether the costs should be *expensed* or *capitalized* (meaning they are included in the cost of the plant assets on the balance sheet). (2) For costs that should be included in plant assets, indicate in which category of plant assets (Equipment, Building, or Land) the related costs should be recorded on the balance sheet.

Expensed or Capitalized	Asset Category	
_____	_____	**1.** Charges incurred to train employees to use new equipment
_____	_____	**2.** Invoice cost to purchase new equipment
_____	_____	**3.** Deduction for an early payment discount taken on the purchase of new equipment
_____	_____	**4.** Real estate commissions incurred on land purchased for a new plant
_____	_____	**5.** Property taxes on land incurred after it was purchased
_____	_____	**6.** Costs of tune-up for the truck used to deliver new equipment
_____	_____	**7.** Costs to lay foundation for a new building
_____	_____	**8.** Insurance on a new building during the construction phase

QS 8-3
Straight-line depreciation
P1

On January 2, 2015, the Matthews Band acquires sound equipment for concert performances at a cost of $65,800. The band estimates it will use this equipment for four years, during which time it anticipates performing about 200 concerts. It estimates that after four years it can sell the equipment for $2,000. During year 2015, the band performs 45 concerts. Compute the year 2015 depreciation using the straight-line method.

QS 8-4
Units-of-production depreciation P1

On January 2, 2015, the Matthews Band acquires sound equipment for concert performances at a cost of $65,800. The band estimates it will use this equipment for four years, during which time it anticipates performing about 200 concerts. It estimates that after four years it can sell the equipment for $2,000. During year 2015, the band performs 45 concerts. Compute the year 2015 depreciation using the units-of-production method.

QS 8-5
Computing revised depreciation C2

On January 2, 2015, the Matthews Band acquires sound equipment for concert performances at a cost of $65,800. The band estimates it will use this equipment for four years. It estimates that after four years it can sell the equipment for $2,000. Matthews Band uses straight-line depreciation but realizes at the start of the second year that due to concert bookings beyond expectations, this equipment will last only a total of three years. The salvage value remains unchanged. Compute the revised depreciation for both the second and third years.

QS 8-6
Double-declining-balance method P1

A fleet of refrigerated delivery trucks is acquired on January 5, 2015, at a cost of $830,000 with an estimated useful life of eight years and an estimated salvage value of $75,000. Compute the depreciation expense for the first three years using the double-declining-balance method.

QS 8-7
Recording plant asset impairment C2

Assume a company's equipment carries a book value of $16,000 ($16,500 cost less $500 accumulated depreciation) and a fair value of $14,750, *and* that the $1,250 decline in fair value in comparison to the book value meets the two-step impairment test. Prepare the entry to record this $1,250 impairment.

QS 8-8
Revenue and capital expenditures
C3

1. Classify the following as either a revenue expenditure or a capital expenditure.

_____ **a.** Paid $40,000 cash to replace a compressor on a refrigeration system that extends its useful life by four years.

_____ **b.** Paid $200 cash per truck for the cost of their annual tune-ups.

_____ **c.** Paid $175 for the monthly cost of replacement filters on an air-conditioning system.

_____ **d.** Completed an addition to an office building for $225,000 cash.

2. Prepare the journal entries to record transactions *a* and *d* of part 1.

QS 8-9
Disposal of assets P2

Garcia Co. owns equipment that cost $76,800, with accumulated depreciation of $40,800. Garcia sells the equipment for cash. Record the sale of the equipment assuming Garcia sells the equipment for (1) $47,000 cash, (2) $36,000 cash, and (3) $31,000 cash.

QS 8-10
Natural resources and depletion
P3

Perez Company acquires an ore mine at a cost of $1,400,000. It incurs additional costs of $400,000 to access the mine, which is estimated to hold 1,000,000 tons of ore. The estimated value of the land after the ore is removed is $200,000.

1. Prepare the entry(ies) to record the cost of the ore mine.
2. Prepare the year-end adjusting entry if 180,000 tons of ore are mined and sold the first year.

QS 8-11
Classify assets
P3 P4

Identify the following assets *a* through *h* as reported on the balance sheet as intangible assets (IA), natural resources (NR), or other (O).

____ **a.** Oil well	____ **d.** Gold mine	____ **g.** Franchise
____ **b.** Trademark	____ **e.** Building	____ **h.** Timberland
____ **c.** Leasehold	____ **f.** Copyright	

QS 8-12
Intangible assets and amortization
P4

On January 4 of this year, Diaz Boutique incurs a $105,000 cost to modernize its store. Improvements include new floors, ceilings, wiring, and wall coverings. These improvements are estimated to yield benefits for 10 years. Diaz leases its store and has eight years remaining on the lease. Prepare the entry to record (1) the cost of modernization and (2) amortization at the end of this current year.

QS 8-13
Computing total asset turnover A1

Aneko Company reports the following ($000s): net sales of $14,800 for 2015 and $13,990 for 2014; end-of-year total assets of $19,100 for 2015 and $17,900 for 2014. Compute its total asset turnover for 2015, and assess its level if competitors average a total asset turnover of 2.0 times.

QS 8-14A
Asset exchange
P5

Caleb Co. owns a machine that costs $42,400 with accumulated depreciation of $18,400. Caleb exchanges the machine for a newer model that has a market value of $52,000. (1) Record the exchange assuming Caleb paid $30,000 cash and the exchange has commercial substance. (2) Record the exchange assuming Caleb pays $22,000 cash and the exchange lacks commercial substance.

QS 8-15
International accounting standards
C1 C3

Answer each of the following related to international accounting standards.

a. Accounting for plant assets involves cost determination, depreciation, additional expenditures, and disposals. Is plant asset accounting broadly similar or dissimilar between IFRS and U.S. GAAP? Identify one notable difference between IFRS and U.S. GAAP in accounting for plant assets.

b. Describe how IFRS and U.S. GAAP treat increases in the value of plant assets subsequent to their acquisition (but before their disposition).

connect

EXERCISES

Exercise 8-1
Cost of plant assets
C1

Rizio Co. purchases a machine for $12,500, terms 2/10, n/60, FOB shipping point. The seller prepaid the $360 freight charges, adding the amount to the invoice and bringing its total to $12,860. The machine requires special steel mounting and power connections costing $895. Another $475 is paid to assemble the machine and get it into operation. In moving the machine to its steel mounting, $180 in damages occurred. Materials costing $40 are used in adjusting the machine to produce a satisfactory product. The adjustments are normal for this machine and are not the result of the damages. Compute the cost recorded for this machine. (Rizio pays for this machine within the cash discount period.)

Exercise 8-2
Recording costs of assets
C1

Cala Manufacturing purchases a large lot on which an old building is located as part of its plans to build a new plant. The negotiated purchase price is $280,000 for the lot plus $110,000 for the old building. The company pays $33,500 to tear down the old building and $47,000 to fill and level the lot. It also pays a total of $1,540,000 in construction costs—this amount consists of $1,452,200 for the new building and $87,800 for lighting and paving a parking area next to the building. Prepare a single journal entry to record these costs incurred by Cala, all of which are paid in cash.

Exercise 8-3
Lump-sum purchase of plant assets C1

Rodriguez Company pays $375,280 for real estate plus $20,100 in closing costs. The real estate consists of land appraised at $157,040; land improvements appraised at $58,890; and a building appraised at $176,670. Allocate the total cost among the three purchased assets and prepare the journal entry to record the purchase.

Exercise 8-4
Straight-line depreciation P1

Ramirez Company installs a computerized manufacturing machine in its factory at the beginning of the year at a cost of $43,500. The machine's useful life is estimated at 10 years, or 385,000 units of product, with a $5,000 salvage value. During its second year, the machine produces 32,500 units of product. Determine the machine's second-year depreciation under the straight-line method.

Exercise 8-5
Units-of-production depreciation P1

Ramirez Company installs a computerized manufacturing machine in its factory at the beginning of the year at a cost of $43,500. The machine's useful life is estimated at 10 years, or 385,000 units of product, with a $5,000 salvage value. During its second year, the machine produces 32,500 units of product. Determine the machine's second-year depreciation using the units-of-production method.

Exercise 8-6
Double-declining-balance depreciation P1

Ramirez Company installs a computerized manufacturing machine in its factory at the beginning of the year at a cost of $43,500. The machine's useful life is estimated at 10 years, or 385,000 units of product, with a $5,000 salvage value. During its second year, the machine produces 32,500 units of product. Determine the machine's second-year depreciation using the double-declining-balance method.

Exercise 8-7
Straight-line depreciation P1

In early January 2015, NewTech purchases computer equipment for $154,000 to use in operating activities for the next four years. It estimates the equipment's salvage value at $25,000. Prepare a table showing depreciation and book value for each of the four years assuming straight-line depreciation.

Exercise 8-8
Double-declining-balance depreciation P1

In early January 2015, NewTech purchases computer equipment for $154,000 to use in operating activities for the next four years. It estimates the equipment's salvage value at $25,000. Prepare a table showing depreciation and book value for each of the four years assuming double-declining-balance depreciation.

Exercise 8-9
Straight-line depreciation and income effects P1

Tory Enterprises pays $238,400 for equipment that will last five years and have a $43,600 salvage value. By using the equipment in its operations for five years, the company expects to earn $88,500 annually, after deducting all expenses except depreciation. Prepare a table showing income before depreciation, depreciation expense, and net (pretax) income for each year and for the total five-year period, assuming straight-line depreciation.

Exercise 8-10
Double-declining-balance depreciation P1

Check Year 3 NI, $54,170

Tory Enterprises pays $238,400 for equipment that will last five years and have a $43,600 salvage value. By using the equipment in its operations for five years, the company expects to earn $88,500 annually, after deducting all expenses except depreciation. Prepare a table showing income before depreciation, depreciation expense, and net (pretax) income for each year and for the total five-year period, assuming double-declining-balance depreciation is used.

Exercise 8-11
Straight-line, partial-year depreciation C2

On April 1, 2014, Cyclone's Backhoe Co. purchases a trencher for $280,000. The machine is expected to last five years and have a salvage value of $40,000. Compute depreciation expense for both 2014 and 2015 assuming the company uses the straight-line method.

Exercise 8-12
Double-declining-balance, partial-year depreciation C2

On April 1, 2014, Cyclone's Backhoe Co. purchases a trencher for $280,000. The machine is expected to last five years and have a salvage value of $40,000. Compute depreciation expense for both 2014 and 2015 assuming the company uses the double-declining-balance method.

Exercise 8-13
Revising depreciation C2

Check (2) $3,710

Apex Fitness Club uses straight-line depreciation for a machine costing $23,860, with an estimated four-year life and a $2,400 salvage value. At the beginning of the third year, Apex determines that the machine has three more years of remaining useful life, after which it will have an estimated $2,000 salvage value. Compute (1) the machine's book value at the end of its second year and (2) the amount of depreciation for each of the final three years given the revised estimates.

Exercise 8-14
Ordinary repairs, extraordinary repairs, and betterments C3

Oki Company pays $264,000 for equipment expected to last four years and have a $29,000 salvage value. Prepare journal entries to record the following costs related to the equipment.

1. During the second year of the equipment's life, $22,000 cash is paid for a new component expected to increase the equipment's productivity by 10% a year.
2. During the third year, $6,250 cash is paid for normal repairs necessary to keep the equipment in good working order.
3. During the fourth year, $14,870 is paid for repairs expected to increase the useful life of the equipment from four to five years.

Exercise 8-15
Extraordinary repairs; plant asset age
C3

Martinez Company owns a building that appears on its prior year-end balance sheet at its original $572,000 cost less $429,000 accumulated depreciation. The building is depreciated on a straight-line basis assuming a 20-year life and no salvage value. During the first week in January of the current calendar year, major structural repairs are completed on the building at a $68,350 cost. The repairs extend its useful life for 5 years beyond the 20 years originally estimated.

1. Determine the building's age (plant asset age) as of the prior year-end balance sheet date.
2. Prepare the entry to record the cost of the structural repairs that are paid in cash.
3. Determine the book value of the building immediately after the repairs are recorded.
4. Prepare the entry to record the current calendar year's depreciation.

Check (3) $211,350

Exercise 8-16
Disposal of assets
P2

Diaz Company owns a milling machine that cost $250,000 and has accumulated depreciation of $182,000. Prepare the entry to record the disposal of the milling machine on January 3 under each of the following independent situations.

1. The machine needed extensive repairs, and it was not worth repairing. Diaz disposed of the machine, receiving nothing in return.
2. Diaz sold the machine for $35,000 cash.
3. Diaz sold the machine for $68,000 cash.
4. Diaz sold the machine for $80,000 cash.

Exercise 8-17
Partial-year depreciation; disposal of plant asset
P2

Rayya Co. purchases and installs a machine on January 1, 2015, at a total cost of $105,000. Straight-line depreciation is taken each year for four years assuming a seven-year life and no salvage value. The machine is disposed of on July 1, 2019, during its fifth year of service. Prepare entries to record the partial year's depreciation on July 1, 2019, and to record the disposal under the following separate assumptions:

1. The machine is sold for $45,500 cash.
2. An insurance settlement of $25,000 is received due to the machine's total destruction in a fire.

Exercise 8-18
Depletion of natural resources
P1 P3

On April 2, 2015, Montana Mining Co. pays $3,721,000 for an ore deposit containing 1,525,000 tons. The company installs machinery in the mine costing $213,500, with an estimated seven-year life and no salvage value. The machinery will be abandoned when the ore is completely mined. Montana begins mining on May 1, 2015, and mines and sells 166,200 tons of ore during the remaining eight months of 2015. Prepare the December 31, 2015, entries to record both the ore deposit depletion and the mining machinery depreciation. Mining machinery depreciation should be in proportion to the mine's depletion.

Exercise 8-19
Amortization of intangible assets P4

Milano Gallery purchases the copyright on an oil painting for $418,000 on January 1, 2015. The copyright legally protects its owner for 10 more years. The company plans to market and sell prints of the original for 11 years. Prepare entries to record the purchase of the copyright on January 1, 2015, and its annual amortization on December 31, 2015.

Exercise 8-20
Goodwill
P4

On January 1, 2015, Robinson Company purchased Franklin Company at a price of $2,500,000. The fair market value of the net assets purchased equals $1,800,000.

1. What is the amount of goodwill that Robinson records at the purchase date?
2. Explain how Robinson would determine the amount of goodwill amortization for the year ended December 31, 2015.
3. Robinson Company believes that its employees provide superior customer service, and through their efforts, Robinson Company believes it has created $900,000 of goodwill. How would Robinson Company record this goodwill?

Exercise 8-21
Cash flows related to assets C1
GOOGLE

Refer to the statement of cash flows for **Google** in Appendix A for the fiscal year ended December 31, 2013, to answer the following.

1. What amount of cash is used to purchase property and equipment?
2. How much depreciation and amortization of property and equipment are recorded?
3. What total amount of net cash is used in investing activities?

Exercise 8-22
Evaluating efficient use of assets A1

Lok Co. reports net sales of $5,856,480 for 2014 and $8,679,690 for 2015. End-of-year balances for total assets are 2013, $1,686,000; 2014, $1,800,000; and 2015, $1,982,000. (*a*) Compute Lok's total asset turnover for 2014 and 2015. (*b*) Comment on Lok's efficiency in using its assets if its competitors average a total asset turnover of 3.0.

Exercise 8-23^A
Exchanging assets
P5

Gilly Construction trades in an old tractor for a new tractor, receiving a $29,000 trade-in allowance and paying the remaining $83,000 in cash. The old tractor had cost $96,000, and straight-line accumulated depreciation of $52,500 had been recorded to date under the assumption that it would last eight years and have a $12,000 salvage value. Answer the following questions assuming the exchange has commercial substance.

1. What is the book value of the old tractor at the time of exchange?
2. What is the loss on this asset exchange?
3. What amount should be recorded (debited) in the asset account for the new tractor?

Check (2) $14,500

Exercise 8-24^A
Recording plant asset disposals P2 P5

On January 2, 2015, Bering Co. disposes of a machine costing $44,000 with accumulated depreciation of $24,625. Prepare the entries to record the disposal under each of the following separate assumptions.

1. The machine is sold for $18,250 cash.
2. The machine is traded in for a newer machine having a $60,200 cash price. A $25,000 trade-in allowance is received, and the balance is paid in cash. Assume the asset exchange lacks commercial substance.
3. The machine is traded in for a newer machine having a $60,200 cash price. A $15,000 trade-in allowance is received, and the balance is paid in cash. Assume the asset exchange has commercial substance.

Check (2) Dr. Machinery (new), $54,575

Exercise 8-25
Accounting for plant assets under IFRS
C2 P1 P2

Volkswagen Group reports the following information for property, plant, and equipment as of December 31, 2013, along with additions, disposals, depreciation, and impairments for the year ended December 31, 2013 (euros in millions):

Property, plant, and equipment, net	€42,389
Additions to property, plant, and equipment	11,061
Disposals of property, plant, and equipment	2,362
Depreciation on property, plant, and equipment	6,689
Impairments to property, plant, and equipment	118

1. Prepare Volkswagen's journal entry to record its depreciation for 2013.
2. Prepare Volkswagen's journal entry to record its additions for 2013 assuming they are paid in cash and are treated as "betterments (improvements)" to the assets.
3. Prepare Volkswagen's journal entry to record its €2,362 in disposals for 2013 assuming it receives €700 cash in return and the accumulated depreciation on the disposed assets totals €1,162.
4. Volkswagen reports €118 of impairments. Do these impairments increase or decrease the Property, Plant and Equipment account? By what amount?

connect

PROBLEM SET A

Problem 8-1A
Plant asset costs; depreciation methods
C1 P1

Timberly Construction negotiates a lump-sum purchase of several assets from a company that is going out of business. The purchase is completed on January 1, 2015, at a total cash price of $900,000 for a building, land, land improvements, and four vehicles. The estimated market values of the assets are building, $508,800; land, $297,600; land improvements, $28,800; and four vehicles, $124,800. The company's fiscal year ends on December 31.

Required

1. Prepare a table to allocate the lump-sum purchase price to the separate assets purchased (round percents to the nearest 1%). Prepare the journal entry to record the purchase.
2. Compute the depreciation expense for year 2015 on the building using the straight-line method, assuming a 15-year life and a $27,000 salvage value.
3. Compute the depreciation expense for year 2015 on the land improvements assuming a five-year life and double-declining-balance depreciation.

Check (2) $30,000

(3) $10,800

Analysis Component

4. Defend or refute this statement: Accelerated depreciation results in payment of less taxes over the asset's life.

Problem 8-2A
Depreciation methods
P1

A machine costing $257,500 with a four-year life and an estimated $20,000 salvage value is installed in Luther Company's factory on January 1. The factory manager estimates the machine will produce 475,000 units of product during its life. It actually produces the following units: 220,000 in 1st year, 124,600 in 2nd year, 121,800 in 3rd year, 15,200 in 4th year. The total number of units produced by the end of year 4 exceeds the original estimate—this difference was not predicted. (The machine must not be depreciated below its estimated salvage value.)

Required

Prepare a table with the following column headings and compute depreciation for each year (and total depreciation of all years combined) for the machine under each depreciation method.

Check Year 4: units-of-production depreciation, $4,300; DDB depreciation, $12,187

Year	Straight-Line	Units-of-Production	Double-Declining-Balance

Problem 8-3A
Asset cost allocation; straight-line depreciation
C1 P1

In January 2015, Mitzu Co. pays $2,600,000 for a tract of land with two buildings on it. It plans to demolish Building 1 and build a new store in its place. Building 2 will be a company office; it is appraised at $644,000, with a useful life of 20 years and a $60,000 salvage value. A lighted parking lot near Building 1 has improvements (Land Improvements 1) valued at $420,000 that are expected to last another 12 years with no salvage value. Without the buildings and improvements, the tract of land is valued at $1,736,000. The company also incurs the following additional costs:

Cost to demolish Building I	$ 328,400
Cost of additional land grading	175,400
Cost to construct new building (Building 3), having a useful life of 25 years and a $392,000 salvage value	2,202,000
Cost of new land improvements (Land Improvements 2) near Building 2 having a 20-year useful life and no salvage value	164,000

Required

Check (1) Land costs, $2,115,800; Building 2 costs, $598,000

1. Prepare a table with the following column headings: Land, Building 2, Building 3, Land Improvements 1, and Land Improvements 2. Allocate the costs incurred by Mitzu to the appropriate columns and total each column (round percents to the nearest 1%).
2. Prepare a single journal entry to record all the incurred costs assuming they are paid in cash on January 1, 2015.
3. Using the straight-line method, prepare the December 31 adjusting entries to record depreciation for the 12 months of 2015 when these assets were in use.

(3) Depr.—Land Improv. 1 and 2, $32,500 and $8,200

Problem 8-4A
Computing and revising depreciation; revenue and capital expenditures
C1 C2 C3

Champion Contractors completed the following transactions and events involving the purchase and operation of equipment in its business.

2014

Jan. 1	Paid $287,600 cash plus $11,500 in sales tax and $1,500 in transportation (FOB shipping point) for a new loader. The loader is estimated to have a four-year life and a $20,600 salvage value. Loader costs are recorded in the Equipment account.
Jan. 3	Paid $4,800 to enclose the cab and install air-conditioning in the loader to enable operations under harsher conditions. This increased the estimated salvage value of the loader by another $1,400.
Dec. 31	Recorded annual straight-line depreciation on the loader.

Check Dec. 31, 2014, Dr. Depr. Expense—Equip., $70,850

2015

Jan. 1	Paid $5,400 to overhaul the loader's engine, which increased the loader's estimated useful life by two years.
Feb. 17	Paid $820 to repair the loader after the operator backed it into a tree.
Dec. 31	Recorded annual straight-line depreciation on the loader.

Check Dec. 31, 2015, Dr. Depr. Expense—Equip., $43,590

Required

Prepare journal entries to record these transactions and events.

Problem 8-5A
Computing and revising depreciation; selling plant assets
C2 P1 P2

Yoshi Company completed the following transactions and events involving its delivery trucks.

2014

Jan. 1 Paid $20,515 cash plus $1,485 in sales tax for a new delivery truck estimated to have a five-year life and a $2,000 salvage value. Delivery truck costs are recorded in the Trucks account.

Dec. 31 Recorded annual straight-line depreciation on the truck.

2015

Dec. 31 Due to new information obtained earlier in the year, the truck's estimated useful life was changed from five to four years, and the estimated salvage value was increased to $2,400. Recorded annual straight-line depreciation on the truck.

Check Dec. 31, 2015, Dr. Depr. Expense—Trucks, $5,200

2016

Dec. 31 Recorded annual straight-line depreciation on the truck.

Dec. 31 Sold the truck for $5,300 cash.

Dec. 31, 2016, Dr. Loss on Disposal of Trucks, $2,300

Required

Prepare journal entries to record these transactions and events.

Problem 8-6A
Disposal of plant assets
C1 P1 P2

Onslow Co. purchases a used machine for $178,000 cash on January 2 and readies it for use the next day at an $2,840 cost. On January 3, it is installed on a required operating platform costing $1,160, and it is further readied for operations. The company predicts the machine will be used for six years and have a $14,000 salvage value. Depreciation is to be charged on a straight-line basis. On December 31, at the end of its fifth year in operations, it is disposed of.

Required

1. Prepare journal entries to record the machine's purchase and the costs to ready and install it. Cash is paid for all costs incurred.
2. Prepare journal entries to record depreciation of the machine at December 31 of (*a*) its first year in operations and (*b*) the year of its disposal.
3. Prepare journal entries to record the machine's disposal under each of the following separate assumptions: (*a*) it is sold for $15,000 cash; (*b*) it is sold for $50,000 cash; and (*c*) it is destroyed in a fire and the insurance company pays $30,000 cash to settle the loss claim.

Check (2*b*) Depr. Exp., $28,000

(3*c*) Dr. Loss from Fire, $12,000

Problem 8-7A
Natural resources
P3

On July 23 of the current year, Dakota Mining Co. pays $4,715,000 for land estimated to contain 5,125,000 tons of recoverable ore. It installs machinery costing $410,000 that has a 10-year life and no salvage value and is capable of mining the ore deposit in eight years. The machinery is paid for on July 25, seven days before mining operations begin. The company removes and sells 480,000 tons of ore during its first five months of operations ending on December 31. Depreciation of the machinery is in proportion to the mine's depletion as the machinery will be abandoned after the ore is mined.

Required

Prepare entries to record (*a*) the purchase of the land, (*b*) the cost and installation of machinery, (*c*) the first five months' depletion assuming the land has a net salvage value of zero after the ore is mined, and (*d*) the first five months' depreciation on the machinery.

Check (*c*) Depletion, $441,600

(*d*) Depreciation, $38,400

Analysis Component

Describe both the similarities and differences in amortization, depletion, and depreciation.

Problem 8-8A
Intangible assets
P4

On July 1, 2010, Falk Company signed a contract to lease space in a building for 15 years. The lease contract calls for annual (prepaid) rental payments of $80,000 on each July 1 throughout the life of the lease and for the lessee to pay for all additions and improvements to the leased property. On June 25, 2015, Falk decides to sublease the space to Ryan & Associates for the remaining 10 years of the lease—Ryan pays $200,000 to Falk for the right to sublease and it agrees to assume the obligation to pay the $80,000 annual rent to the building owner beginning July 1, 2015. After taking possession of the leased space, Ryan pays for improving the office portion of the leased space at a $130,000 cost. The improvements are paid for by Ryan on July 5, 2015, and are estimated to have a useful life equal to the 16 years remaining in the life of the building.

Required

1. Prepare entries for Ryan to record (*a*) its payment to Falk for the right to sublease the building space, (*b*) its payment of the 2015 annual rent to the building owner, and (*c*) its payment for the office improvements.
2. Prepare Ryan's year-end adjusting entries required at December 31, 2015, to (*a*) amortize the $200,000 cost of the sublease, (*b*) amortize the office improvements, and (*c*) record rent expense.

Check Dr. Rent Expense for (2*a*) $10,000, (2*c*) $40,000

PROBLEM SET B

Problem 8-1B
Plant asset costs; depreciation methods
C1 P1

Nagy Company negotiates a lump-sum purchase of several assets from a contractor who is relocating. The purchase is completed on January 1, 2015, at a total cash price of $1,800,000 for a building, land, land improvements, and five trucks. The estimated market values of the assets are building, $890,000; land, $427,200; land improvements, $249,200; and five trucks, $213,600. The company's fiscal year ends on December 31.

Required

1. Prepare a table to allocate the lump-sum purchase price to the separate assets purchased (round percents to the nearest 1%). Prepare the journal entry to record the purchase.
2. Compute the depreciation expense for year 2015 on the building using the straight-line method, assuming a 12-year life and a $120,000 salvage value.
3. Compute the depreciation expense for year 2015 on the land improvements assuming a 10-year life and double-declining-balance depreciation.

Check (2) $65,000

(3) $50,400

Analysis Component

4. Defend or refute this statement: Accelerated depreciation results in payment of more taxes over the asset's life.

Problem 8-2B
Depreciation methods
P1

On January 2, Manning Co. purchases and installs a new machine costing $324,000 with a five-year life and an estimated $30,000 salvage value. Management estimates the machine will produce 1,470,000 units of product during its life. Actual production of units is as follows: 355,600 in 1st year, 320,400 in 2nd year, 317,000 in 3rd year, 343,600 in 4th year, 138,500 in 5th year. The total number of units produced by the end of year 5 exceeds the original estimate—this difference was not predicted. (The machine must not be depreciated below its estimated salvage value.)

Required

Prepare a table with the following column headings and compute depreciation for each year (and total depreciation of all years combined) for the machine under each depreciation method.

Check DDB Depreciation, year 3, $46,656; U-of-P Depreciation, year 4, $68,720

Year	Straight-Line	Units-of-Production	Double-Declining-Balance

Problem 8-3B
Asset cost allocation; straight-line depreciation
C1 P1

In January 2015, ProTech Co. pays $1,550,000 for a tract of land with two buildings. It plans to demolish Building A and build a new shop in its place. Building B will be a company office; it is appraised at $482,800, with a useful life of 15 years and a $99,500 salvage value. A lighted parking lot near Building B has improvements (Land Improvements B) valued at $142,000 that are expected to last another five years with no salvage value. Without the buildings and improvements, the tract of land is valued at $795,200. The company also incurs the following additional costs.

Cost to demolish Building A	$ 122,000
Cost of additional land grading	174,500
Cost to construct new building (Building C), having a useful life of 20 years and a $258,000 salvage value	1,458,000
Cost of new land improvements (Land Improvements C) near Building C, having a 10-year useful life and no salvage value	103,500

Required

1. Prepare a table with the following column headings: Land, Building B, Building C, Land Improvements B, and Land Improvements C. Allocate the costs incurred by ProTech to the appropriate columns and total each column (round percents to the nearest 1%).
2. Prepare a single journal entry to record all incurred costs assuming they are paid in cash on January 1, 2015.
3. Using the straight-line method, prepare the December 31 adjusting entries to record depreciation for the 12 months of 2015 when these assets were in use.

Check (1) Land costs, $1,164,500; Building B costs, $527,000

(3) Depr.—Land Improv. B and C, $31,000 and $10,350

Problem 8-4B
Computing and revising depreciation; revenue and capital expenditures
C1 C2 C3

Mercury Delivery Service completed the following transactions and events involving the purchase and operation of equipment for its business.

2014

Jan. 1	Paid $25,860 cash plus $1,810 in sales tax for a new delivery van that was estimated to have a five-year life and a $3,670 salvage value. Van costs are recorded in the Equipment account.
Jan. 3	Paid $1,850 to install sorting racks in the van for more accurate and quicker delivery of packages. This increases the estimated salvage value of the van by another $230.
Dec. 31	Recorded annual straight-line depreciation on the van.

2015

Jan. 1	Paid $2,064 to overhaul the van's engine, which increased the van's estimated useful life by two years.
May 10	Paid $800 to repair the van after the driver backed it into a loading dock.
Dec. 31	Record annual straight-line depreciation on the van. (Round to the nearest dollar.)

Check Dec. 31, 2014, Dr. Depr. Expense—Equip., $5,124

Check Dec. 31, 2015, Dr. Depr. Expense—Equip., $3,760

Required

Prepare journal entries to record these transactions and events.

Problem 8-5B
Computing and revising depreciation; selling plant assets
C2 P1 P2

York Instruments completed the following transactions and events involving its machinery.

2014

Jan. 1	Paid $107,800 cash plus $6,470 in sales tax for a new machine. The machine is estimated to have a six-year life and a $9,720 salvage value.
Dec. 31	Recorded annual straight-line depreciation on the machinery.

2015

Dec. 31	Due to new information obtained earlier in the year, the machine's estimated useful life was changed from six to four years, and the estimated salvage value was increased to $14,345. Recorded annual straight-line depreciation on the machinery.

Check Dec. 31, 2015, Dr. Depr. Expense—Machinery, $27,500

2016

Dec. 31	Recorded annual straight-line depreciation on the machinery.
Dec. 31	Sold the machine for $25,240 cash.

Dec. 31, 2016, Dr. Loss on Disposal of Machinery, $16,605

Required

Prepare journal entries to record these transactions and events.

Problem 8-6B
Disposal of plant assets
C1 P1 P2

On January 1, Walker purchases a used machine for $150,000 and readies it for use the next day at a cost of $3,510. On January 4, it is mounted on a required operating platform costing $4,600, and it is further readied for operations. Management estimates the machine will be used for seven years and have an $18,110 salvage value. Depreciation is to be charged on a straight-line basis. On December 31, at the end of its sixth year of use, the machine is disposed of.

Required

1. Prepare journal entries to record the machine's purchase and the costs to ready and install it. Cash is paid for all costs incurred.
2. Prepare journal entries to record depreciation of the machine at December 31 of (*a*) its first year in operations and (*b*) the year of its disposal.
3. Prepare journal entries to record the machine's disposal under each of the following separate assumptions: (*a*) it is sold for $28,000 cash; (*b*) it is sold for $52,000 cash; and (*c*) it is destroyed in a fire and the insurance company pays $25,000 cash to settle the loss claim.

Check (2*b*) Depr. Exp., $20,000

(3*c*) Dr. Loss from Fire, $13,110

Problem 8-7B
Natural resources
P3

On February 19 of the current year, Quartzite Co. pays $5,400,000 for land estimated to contain 4 million tons of recoverable ore. It installs machinery costing $400,000 that has a 16-year life and no salvage value and is capable of mining the ore deposit in 12 years. The machinery is paid for on March 21, eleven days before mining operations begin. The company removes and sells 254,000 tons of ore during its first nine months of operations ending on December 31. Depreciation of the machinery is in proportion to the mine's depletion as the machinery will be abandoned after the ore is mined.

Required

Check (c) Depletion, $342,900; (d) Depreciation, $25,400

Prepare entries to record (*a*) the purchase of the land, (*b*) the cost and installation of the machinery, (*c*) the first nine months' depletion assuming the land has a net salvage value of zero after the ore is mined, and (*d*) the first nine months' depreciation on the machinery.

Analysis Component

Describe both the similarities and differences in amortization, depletion, and depreciation.

Problem 8-8B
Intangible assets
P4

On January 1, 2008, Mason Co. entered into a 12-year lease on a building. The lease contract requires (1) annual (prepaid) rental payments of $36,000 each January 1 throughout the life of the lease and (2) for the lessee to pay for all additions and improvements to the leased property. On January 1, 2015, Mason decides to sublease the space to Stewart Co. for the remaining five years of the lease—Stewart pays $40,000 to Mason for the right to sublease and agrees to assume the obligation to pay the $36,000 annual rent to the building owner beginning January 1, 2015. After taking possession of the leased space, Stewart pays for improving the office portion of the leased space at a $20,000 cost. The improvements are paid for by Stewart on January 3, 2015, and are estimated to have a useful life equal to the 13 years remaining in the life of the building.

Required

1. Prepare entries for Stewart to record (*a*) its payment to Mason for the right to sublease the building space, (*b*) its payment of the 2015 annual rent to the building owner, and (*c*) its payment for the office improvements.

Check Dr. Rent Expense: (2*a*) $8,000, (2*c*) $36,000

2. Prepare Stewart's year-end adjusting entries required on December 31, 2015, to (*a*) amortize the $40,000 cost of the sublease, (*b*) amortize the office improvements, and (*c*) record rent expense.

SERIAL PROBLEM
Business Solutions
P1 A1

(This serial problem began in Chapter 1 and continues through most of the book. If previous chapter segments were not completed, the serial problem can begin at this point. It is helpful, but not necessary, to use the Working Papers that accompany the book.)

SP 8 Selected ledger account balances for Business Solutions follow.

	For Three Months Ended December 31, 2015	For Three Months Ended March 31, 2016
Office equipment	$ 8,000	$ 8,000
Accumulated depreciation—Office equipment	400	800
Computer equipment	20,000	20,000
Accumulated depreciation—Computer equipment	1,250	2,500
Total revenue	31,284	44,000
Total assets	83,460	120,268

Required

1. Assume that Business Solutions does not acquire additional office equipment or computer equipment in 2016. Compute amounts for *the year ended* December 31, 2016, for Depreciation Expense—Office Equipment and for Depreciation Expense—Computer Equipment (assume use of the straight-line method).
2. Given the assumptions in part 1, what is the book value of both the office equipment and the computer equipment as of December 31, 2016?

Check (3) Three-month (annual) turnover = 0.43 (1.73 annual)

3. Compute the three-month total asset turnover for Business Solutions as of March 31, 2016. Use total revenue for the numerator and average the December 31, 2015, total assets and the March 31, 2016, total assets for the denominator. Interpret its total asset turnover if competitors average 2.5 for annual periods. (Round turnover to two decimals.)

Beyond the Numbers

REPORTING IN ACTION

A1

APPLE

BTN 8-1 Refer to the financial statements of **Apple** in Appendix A to answer the following.

1. What percent of the original cost of Apple's property and equipment remains to be depreciated as of September 28, 2013 and September 29, 2012? Assume these assets have no salvage value.
2. Over what length(s) of time is Apple depreciating its major categories of property and equipment?
3. What is the change in total property, plant, and equipment (before accumulated depreciation) for the year ended September 28, 2013? What is the amount of cash provided (used) by investing activities for property and equipment for the year ended September 28, 2013? What is one possible explanation for the difference between these two amounts?
4. Compute its total asset turnover for the year ended September 28, 2013, and the year ended September 29, 2012. Assume total assets at September 24, 2011, are $116,371 ($ millions).

Fast Forward

5. Access Apple's financial statements for fiscal years ending after September 28, 2013, at its website (Apple.com) or the SEC's EDGAR database (www.SEC.gov). Recompute Apple's total asset turnover for the additional years' data you collect. Comment on any differences relative to the turnover computed in part 4.

COMPARATIVE ANALYSIS

A1

APPLE
GOOGLE

BTN 8-2 Comparative figures for **Apple** and **Google** follow.

	Apple			Google		
($ millions)	Current Year	One Year Prior	Two Years Prior	Current Year	One Year Prior	Two Years Prior
Total assets	$207,000	$176,064	$116,371	$110,920	$93,798	$72,574
Net sales	170,910	156,508	108,249	59,825	50,175	37,905

Required

1. Compute total asset turnover for the most recent two years for Apple and Google using the data shown.
2. Which company is more efficient in generating net sales given the total assets it employs? Assume an industry average of 1.0 for asset turnover.

ETHICS CHALLENGE

C1

BTN 8-3 Flo Choi owns a small business and manages its accounting. Her company just finished a year in which a large amount of borrowed funds was invested in a new building addition as well as in equipment and fixture additions. Choi's banker requires her to submit semiannual financial statements so he can monitor the financial health of her business. He has warned her that if profit margins erode, he might raise the interest rate on the borrowed funds to reflect the increased loan risk from the bank's point of view. Choi knows profit margin is likely to decline this year. As she prepares year-end adjusting entries, she decides to apply the following depreciation rule: All asset additions are considered to be in use on the first day of the following month. (The previous rule assumed assets are in use on the first day of the month nearest to the purchase date.)

Required

1. Identify decisions that managers like Choi must make in applying depreciation methods.
2. Is Choi's rule an ethical violation, or is it a legitimate decision in computing depreciation?
3. How will Choi's new depreciation rule affect the profit margin of her business?

COMMUNICATING IN PRACTICE

A1

BTN 8-4 Teams are to select an industry, and each team member is to select a different company in that industry. Each team member is to acquire the financial statements (Form 10-K) of the company selected—see the company's website or the SEC's EDGAR database (www.SEC.gov). Use the financial statements to compute total asset turnover. Communicate with teammates via a meeting, e-mail, or telephone to discuss the meaning of this ratio, how different companies compare to each other, and the industry norm. The team must prepare a one-page report that describes the ratios for each company and identifies the conclusions reached during the team's discussion.

TAKING IT TO THE NET

P4

BTN 8-5 Access the **Yahoo!** (ticker: YHOO) 10-K report for the year ended December 31, 2013, filed on February 28, 2014, at **www.SEC.gov**.

Required

1. What amount of goodwill is reported on Yahoo!'s balance sheet? What percentage of total assets does its goodwill represent? Is goodwill a major asset for Yahoo!? Explain.
2. Locate Note 5 to its financial statements. Identify the change in goodwill from December 31, 2012, to December 31, 2013. Comment on the change in goodwill over this period.
3. Locate Note 6 to its financial statements. What are the three categories of intangible assets that Yahoo! reports at December 31, 2013? What proportion of total assets do the intangibles represent?
4. What does Yahoo! indicate is the life of "Trade names, trademarks, and domain names" according to its Note 6? Comment on the difference between the estimated useful life and the legal life of Yahoo!'s trademark.

TEAMWORK IN ACTION

P1

BTN 8-6 Each team member is to become an expert on one depreciation method to facilitate teammates' understanding of that method. Follow these procedures:

a. Each team member is to select an area for expertise from one of the following depreciation methods: straight-line, units-of-production, or double-declining-balance.

b. Expert teams are to be formed from those who have selected the same area of expertise. The instructor will identify the location where each expert team meets.

c. Using the following data, expert teams are to collaborate and develop a presentation answering the requirements. Expert team members must write the presentation in a format they can show to their learning teams.

Point: This activity can follow an overview of each method. Step 1 allows for three areas of expertise. Larger teams will have some duplication of areas, but the straight-line choice should not be duplicated. Expert teams can use the book and consult with the instructor.

Data and Requirements On January 8, 2013, Whitewater Riders purchases a van to transport rafters back to the point of departure at the conclusion of the rafting adventures they operate. The cost of the van is $44,000. It has an estimated salvage value of $2,000 and is expected to be used for four years and driven 60,000 miles. The van is driven 12,000 miles in 2013, 18,000 miles in 2014, 21,000 in 2015, and 10,000 in 2016.

1. Compute the annual depreciation expense for each year of the van's estimated useful life.
2. Explain when and how annual depreciation is recorded.
3. Explain the impact on income of this depreciation method versus others over the van's life.
4. Identify the van's book value for each year of its life and illustrate the reporting of this amount for any one year.

d. Re-form original learning teams. In rotation, experts are to present to their teams the results from part *c*. Experts are to encourage and respond to questions.

ENTREPRENEURIAL DECISION

A1

BTN 8-7 Review the chapter's opening feature involving Deb Carey and her company, **New Glarus Brewing Co.**. Assume that the company currently has net sales of $8,000,000, and that it is planning an expansion that will increase net sales by $4,000,000. To accomplish this expansion, New Glarus Brewing Co. must increase its average total assets from $2,500,000 to $3,000,000.

Required

1. Compute the company's total asset turnover under (*a*) current conditions and (*b*) proposed conditions.
2. Evaluate and comment on the merits of the proposal given your analysis in part 1. Identify any concerns you would express about the proposal.

HITTING THE ROAD

P3 P4

BTN 8-8 Team up with one or more classmates for this activity. Identify companies in your community or area that must account for at least one of the following assets: natural resource; patent; lease; leasehold improvement; copyright; trademark; or goodwill. You might find a company having more than one type of asset. Once you identify a company with a specific asset, describe the accounting this company uses to allocate the cost of that asset to the periods benefited from its use.

BTN 8-9 **Samsung** (www.Samsung.com), **Apple**, and **Google** are all competitors in the global marketplace. Comparative figures for these companies' recent annual accounting periods follow.

GLOBAL DECISION

A1

(in millions, except turnover)	Samsung (KRW millions)			Apple		Google	
	Current Year	Prior Year	Two Years Prior	Current Year	Prior Year	Current Year	Prior Year
Total assets	₩214,075,018	₩181,071,570	₩155,800,263	$207,000	$176,064	$110,920	$93,798
Net sales	228,692,667	201,103,613	165,001,771	170,910	156,508	59,825	50,175
Total asset turnover	?	?	—	0.89	1.07	0.58	0.60

Required

1. Compute total asset turnover for the most recent two years for Samsung using the data shown.
2. Which company is most efficient in generating net sales given the total assets it employs?

Samsung
APPLE
GOOGLE

ANSWERS TO MULTIPLE CHOICE QUIZ

1. b;

	Appraisal Value	%	Total Cost	Allocated
Land	$175,000	50%	$326,000	$163,000
Land improvements	70,000	20	326,000	65,200
Building	105,000	30	326,000	97,800
Totals	$350,000			$326,000

2. c; ($35,000 − $1,000)/4 years = $8,500 per year
3. c; 2015: $10,800,000 × (2 × 10%) = $2,160,000
   2016: ($10,800,000 − $2,160,000) × (2 × 10%) = $1,728,000
4. c;

Cost of machine	$250,000
Accumulated depreciation	100,000
Book value	150,000
Cash received	120,000
Loss on sale	$ 30,000

5. b; $550,000/$500,000 = 1.10

chapter 9

Accounting for Current Liabilities

Chapter Preview

CHARACTERISTICS OF LIABILITIES	KNOWN LIABILITIES	ESTIMATED LIABILITIES	CONTINGENCIES AND ANALYSIS
C1 Reporting liabilities based on: Definition Classification Uncertainty	**C2** Accounts payable, sales taxes payable, and unearned revenues **P1** Short-term notes **P2** Employee deductions **P3** Employer payroll	**P4** Reporting for: Health and pension benefits Vacation benefits Bonus plans Warranty liabilities	**C3** Accounting for contingencies based on notions of probable, possible, remote **A1** Times interest earned ratio

Learning Objectives

CONCEPTUAL

C1 Describe current and long-term liabilities and their characteristics.

C2 Identify and describe known current liabilities.

C3 Explain how to account for contingent liabilities.

ANALYTICAL

A1 Compute the times interest earned ratio and use it to analyze liabilities.

PROCEDURAL

P1 Prepare entries to account for short-term notes payable.

P2 Compute and record *employee* payroll deductions and liabilities.

P3 Compute and record *employer* payroll expenses and liabilities.

P4 Account for estimated liabilities, including warranties and bonuses.

P5 *Appendix 9A*—Identify and describe the details of payroll reports, records, and procedures.

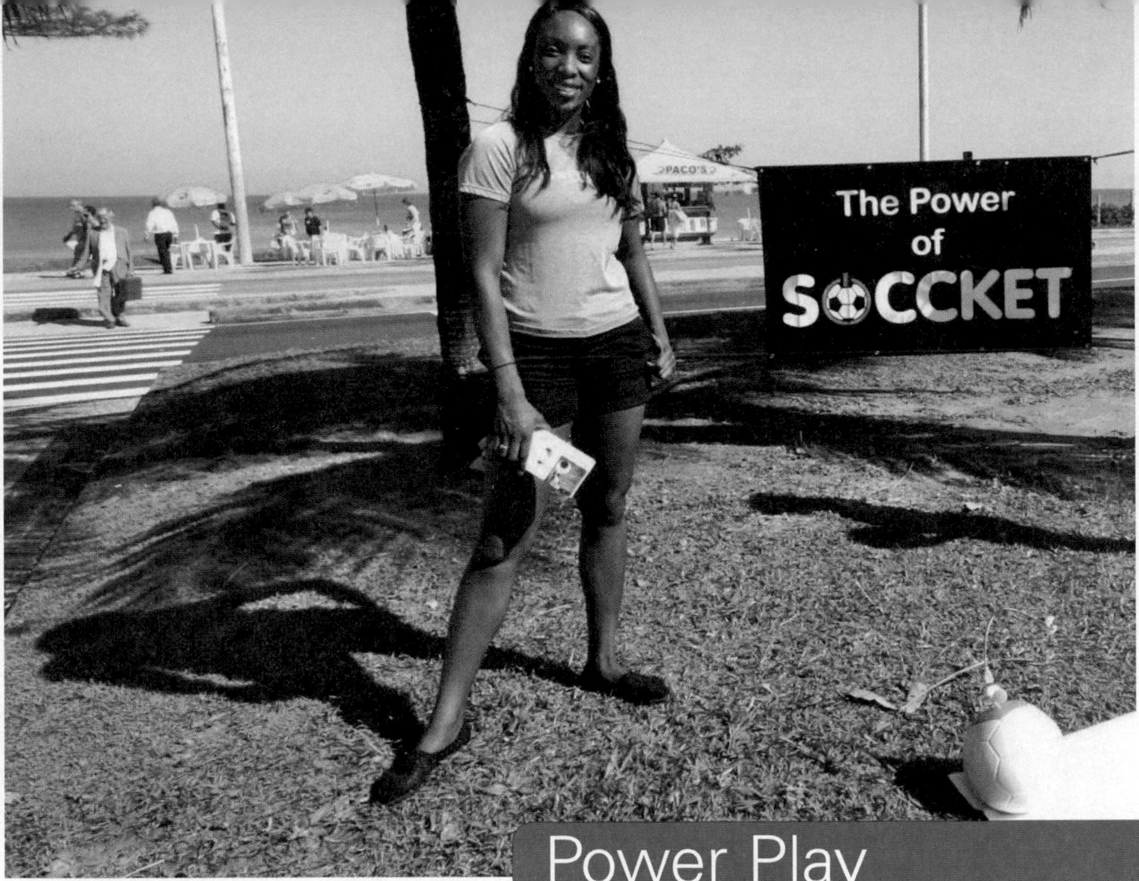

Courtesy of Uncharted Play

Power Play

NEW YORK—"I knew it would be a good product," insists Jessica O. Matthews. "I was very persistent in my belief the SOCCKET would matter to people in a way that made it worth continuing." The "SOCCKET" is a soccer ball that contains a gyroscope that generates and stores energy. "Each SOCCKET comes with an LED lamp that can be plugged into the ball when the sun goes down." The ball is ideal for use in the developing world where use of kerosene lamps and diesel generators presents many risks. With 30 minutes of play, it provides about three hours of light. Jessica's start-up, **Uncharted Play (UnchartedPlay.com)**, has produced more than 10,000 SOCCKETs for Africa and Central/South America.

Jessica's commitment to help people in the developing world better manage their lives carries over to her own business. "I taught myself accounting," explains Jessica. "I find understanding numbers and the financial system as valuable skills." To increase her odds of success, she applies those skills to the important task of managing liabilities for payroll, supplies, employee wages, training, and taxes. Jessica insists that effective management of liabilities, especially payroll and employee benefits, is crucial. "During the initial start-up," says Jessica, "my team worked for free for several months." She stresses that monitoring and controlling liabilities in creative ways is a must.

"Work hard and be authentic"
—Jessica O. Matthews

To help control liabilities, Jessica points to how she began by working out of office space donated by her father. "The world of business is not a playground," explains Jessica. "Sometimes things were inefficient, money was periodically lost, and on occasion, relationships were ruined. Not everyone that was involved knew what it would take to run an effective business." By focusing on efficiencies and controlling liabilities, she was able to grow her company and witness financial success. Creative reduction of liabilities has been part of that success.

Jessica continues to monitor liabilities and payment patterns. "Working on an international scale with international vendors and clients can lead to unexpected barriers in communication and scheduling," explains Jessica. She insists that accounting for and monitoring liabilities is a key to a successful start-up. Her company now generates sufficient income to pay for liabilities and it produces revenue growth for expansion. "We want to create the Google of factories," insists Jessica. "[A plant] where people love to be there and are learning to be innovators regardless of where they are in the company." And she adds: "It's not a power company, it's a play company."

Sources: *Uncharted Play website,* January 2015; *Birchbox,* 2013; *OIC,* November 2013; *Huffington Post,* November 2011; *Shero of the Week,* February 2014; *Forbes,* January 2014; *Spur,* December 2013

CHARACTERISTICS OF LIABILITIES

C1 Describe current and long-term liabilities and their characteristics.

This section discusses important characteristics of liabilities and how liabilities are classified and reported.

Defining Liabilities

A *liability* is a probable future payment of assets or services that a company is presently obligated to make as a result of past transactions or events. This definition includes three crucial factors:

1. A past transaction or event.
2. A present obligation.
3. A future payment of assets or services.

These three important elements are portrayed visually in Exhibit 9.1. Liabilities reported in financial statements exhibit those characteristics. No liability is reported when one or more of those characteristics is absent. For example, most companies expect to pay wages to their employees in upcoming months and years, but these future payments are *not* liabilities because no past event such as employee work resulted in a present obligation. Instead, such liabilities arise when employees perform their work and earn the wages.

EXHIBIT 9.1

Characteristics of a Liability

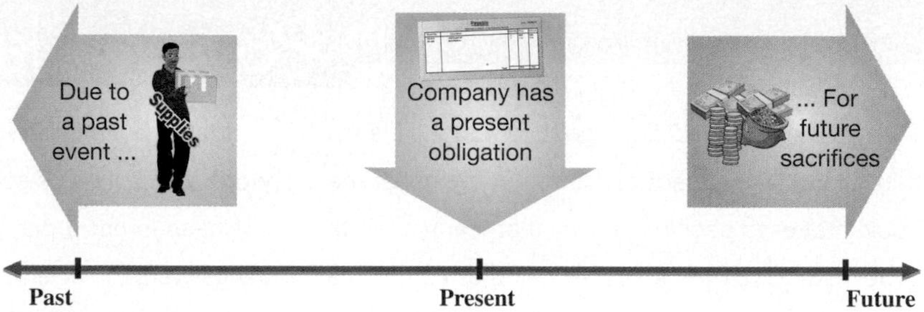

Classifying Liabilities

Point: Account titles using "payable" and "unearned" refer to liabilities. Unearned accounts are liabilities that must be fulfilled, rather than repaid.

Point: Improper classification of liabilities can distort ratios used in financial statement analysis and business decisions.

Information about liabilities is more useful when the balance sheet identifies them as either current or long term. Decision makers need to know when obligations are due so they can plan for them and take appropriate action.

Current Liabilities **Current liabilities,** also called *short-term liabilities,* are obligations due within one year or the company's operating cycle, whichever is longer. They are expected to be paid using current assets or by creating other current liabilities. Common examples of current liabilities are accounts payable, short-term notes payable, wages payable, warranty liabilities, lease liabilities, taxes payable, and unearned revenues.

Current liabilities differ across companies because they depend on the type of company operations. **MGM Resorts**, for instance, included the following current liabilities related to its gaming, hospitality, and entertainment operations ($000s):

Advance deposits and ticket sales	$104,504
Casino outstanding chip liability	409,917
Casino front money deposits	125,180

Harley-Davidson reports a much different set of current liabilities. It discloses current liabilities made up of items such as warranty, recall, and dealer incentive liabilities.

Long-Term Liabilities A company's obligations not expected to be paid within the longer of one year or the company's operating cycle are reported as **long-term liabilities.** They can include long-term notes payable, warranty liabilities, lease liabilities, and bonds payable. They are sometimes reported on the balance sheet in a single long-term liabilities total or in multiple categories.

Domino's Pizza, for instance, reports long-term liabilities of $1,584 million. They are reported after current liabilities. A single liability also can be divided between the current and noncurrent sections if a company expects to make payments toward it in both the short and long term. Domino's reports long-term debt, $1,536 million; and current portion of long-term debt, $24 million, which is less than 2%. The second item is reported in current liabilities. We sometimes see liabilities that do not have a fixed due date but instead are payable on the creditor's demand. These are reported as current liabilities because of the possibility of payment in the near term. Exhibit 9.2 shows amounts of current liabilities and as a percent of total liabilities for selected companies.

Point: The current portion of any long-term debt is a current liability.

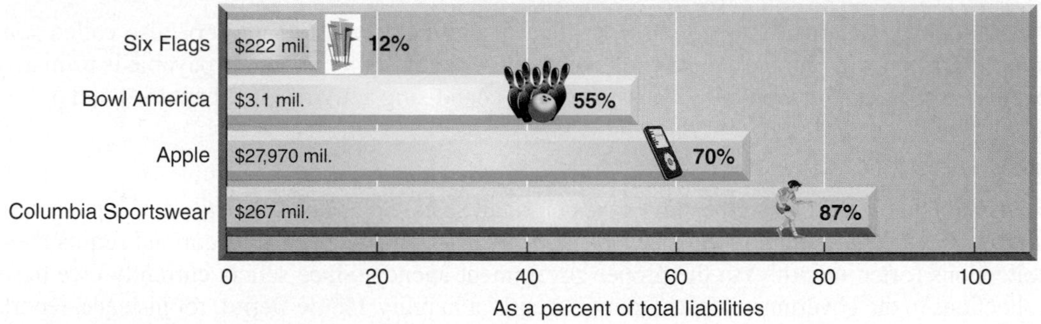

EXHIBIT 9.2

Current Liabilities of Selected Companies

Uncertainty in Liabilities

Accounting for liabilities involves addressing three important questions: Whom to pay? When to pay? How much to pay? Answers to these questions are often decided when a liability is incurred. For example, if a company has a $100 account payable to a specific individual, payable on March 15, the answers are clear. The company knows whom to pay, when to pay, and how much to pay. However, the answers to one or more of these questions are uncertain for some liabilities.

Uncertainty in Whom to Pay Liabilities can involve uncertainty in whom to pay. For instance, a company can create a liability with a known amount when issuing a note that is payable to its holder. In this case, a specific amount is payable to the note's holder at a specified date, but the company does not know who the holder is until that date. Despite this uncertainty, the company reports this liability on its balance sheet.

Point: An *accrued expense* is an unpaid expense and is also called an *accrued liability*.

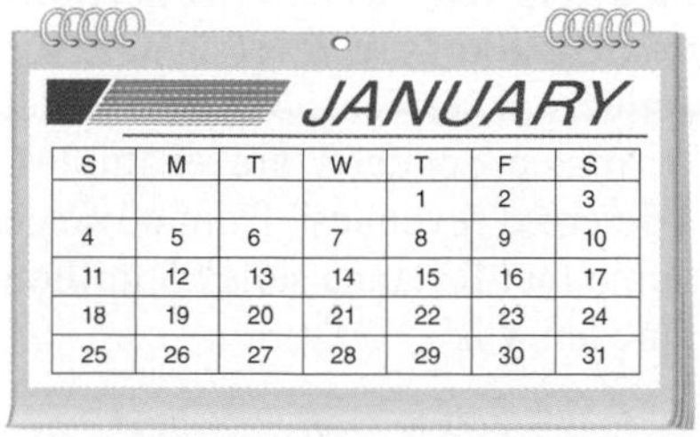

Uncertainty in When to Pay A company can have an obligation of a known amount to a known creditor but not know when it must be paid. For example, a legal services firm can accept fees in advance from a client who plans to use the firm's services in the future. This means that the firm has a liability that it settles by providing services at an unknown future date. Although this uncertainty exists, the legal firm's balance sheet must report this liability. These types of obligations are reported as current liabilities because they are likely to be settled in the short term.

Uncertainty in How Much to Pay A company can be aware of an obligation but not know how much will be required to settle it. For example, a company using electrical power is billed only after the meter has been read. This cost is incurred and the liability created before a bill is received. A liability to the power company is reported as an estimated amount if the balance sheet is prepared before a bill arrives.

IFRS

IFRS records a contingent liability when an obligation exists from a past event if there is a "probable" outflow of resources and the amount can be estimated reliably. However, IFRS defines probable as "more likely than not" while U.S. GAAP defines it as "likely to occur." ■

QC1

KNOWN LIABILITIES

C2 Identify and describe known current liabilities.

Most liabilities arise from situations with little uncertainty. They are set by agreements, contracts, or laws and are measurable. These liabilities are **known liabilities,** also called *definitely determinable liabilities.* Known liabilities include accounts payable, notes payable, payroll, sales taxes, unearned revenues, and leases. We describe how to account for these known liabilities in this section.

Accounts Payable

Accounts payable, or trade accounts payable, are amounts owed to suppliers, also called *vendors,* for products or services purchased on credit. Accounting for accounts payable is primarily explained and illustrated in our discussion of merchandising activities in Chapters 4 and 5.

Sales Taxes Payable

Nearly all states and many cities levy taxes on retail sales. Sales taxes are stated as a percent of selling prices. The seller collects sales taxes from customers when sales occur and remits these collections (often monthly) to the proper government agency. Since sellers currently owe these collections to the government, this amount is a current liability. **Home Depot**, for instance, reports sales taxes payable of $396 million in its recent annual report. To illustrate, if Home Depot sells materials on August 31 for $6,000 cash that are subject to a 5% sales tax, the revenue portion of this transaction is recorded as follows. (The entry for cost of sales is omitted for simplicity.)

Assets = Liabilities + Equity
+6,300 +300 +6,000

Aug. 31	Cash	6,300	
	Sales		6,000
	Sales Taxes Payable ($6,000 × 0.05)		300
	To record cash sales and 5% sales tax.		

Sales Taxes Payable is debited and Cash credited when it remits these collections to the government. Sales Taxes Payable is not an expense. It arises because laws require sellers to collect this cash from customers for the government.[1]

Cameron Spencer/Getty Images

Unearned Revenues

Point: To *defer* a revenue means to postpone recognition of a revenue collected in advance until it is earned. Sports teams must defer recognition of ticket sales until games are played.

Unearned revenues (also called *deferred revenues, collections in advance,* and *prepayments*) are amounts received in advance from customers for future products or services. Advance ticket sales for sporting events or music concerts are examples. **Rihanna**, for instance, has "deferred revenues" from advance ticket sales. To illustrate, assume that Rihanna sells $5 million in tickets for eight concerts; the entry is

Assets = Liabilities + Equity
+5,000,000 +5,000,000

June 30	Cash	5,000,000	
	Unearned Ticket Revenue		5,000,000
	To record sale of concert tickets.		

When a concert is played, Rihanna would record revenue for the portion earned.

Assets = Liabilities + Equity
−625,000 +625,000

Oct. 31	Unearned Ticket Revenue	625,000	
	Ticket Revenue[a]		625,000
	To record concert ticket revenues earned. [a]*$5,000,000 × 1/8*		

[1] Sales taxes can be computed from total sales receipts when sales taxes are not separately identified on the register. To illustrate, assume a 5% sales tax and $420 in total sales receipts (which includes sales taxes). Sales are computed as follows:

$$\text{Sales} = \text{Total sales receipts}/(1 + \text{Sales tax percentage}) = \$420/1.05 = \$400$$

Thus, the sales tax amount equals total sales receipts minus sales, or $420 − $400 = $20. Sellers are required to act as "agents" for the government and collect sales tax. This extra work can be offset by the sellers' ability to use or invest that cash until it must be paid to the government.

Unearned Ticket Revenue is an unearned revenue account and is reported as a current liability. Unearned revenues also arise with airline ticket sales, magazine subscriptions, construction projects, hotel reservations, gift card sales, and custom orders.

Decision Insight

Reward Programs Gift card sales now exceed $100 billion annually, and reward (also called loyalty) programs are growing. There are no exact rules for how retailers account for rewards. When **Best Buy** launched its "Reward Zone," shoppers earned $5 on each $125 spent and had 90 days to spend it. Retailers make assumptions about how many reward program dollars will be spent and how to report it. Best Buy sets up a liability and reduces revenue by the same amount. **Talbots** does not reduce revenue but instead increases selling expense. **Men's Wearhouse** records rewards in cost of goods sold, whereas **Neiman Marcus** subtracts them from revenue. The FASB continues to review reward programs. ■

Short-Term Notes Payable

P1 Prepare entries to account for short-term notes payable.

A **short-term note payable** is a written promise to pay a specified amount on a definite future date within one year or the company's operating cycle, whichever is longer. These promissory notes are negotiable (as are checks), meaning they can be transferred from party to party by endorsement. The written documentation provided by notes is helpful in resolving disputes and for pursuing legal actions involving these liabilities. Most notes payable bear interest to compensate for use of the money until payment is made. Short-term notes payable can arise from many transactions. A company that purchases merchandise on credit can sometimes extend the credit period by signing a note to replace an account payable. Such notes also can arise when money is borrowed from a bank. We describe both of these cases.

Point: Required characteristics for negotiability of a note: (1) unconditional promise, (2) in writing, (3) specific amount, and (4) definite due date.

Note Given to Extend Credit Period A company can replace an account payable with a note payable. A common example is a creditor that requires the substitution of an interest-bearing note for an overdue account payable that does not bear interest. A less common situation occurs when a debtor's weak financial condition motivates the creditor to accept a note, sometimes for a lesser amount, and to close the account to ensure that this customer makes no additional credit purchases.

To illustrate, let's assume that on August 23, Brady Company asks to extend its past-due $600 account payable to McGraw. After some negotiations, McGraw agrees to accept $100 cash and a 60-day, 12%, $500 note payable to replace the account payable. Brady records the transaction with this entry:

Aug. 23	Accounts Payable—McGraw	600	
	Cash		100
	Notes Payable—McGraw		500
	Gave $100 cash and a 60-day, 12% note for payment on account.		

Assets	=	Liabilities	+	Equity
−100		−600		
		+500		

Signing the note does not resolve Brady's debt. Instead, the form of debt is changed from an account payable to a note payable. McGraw prefers the note payable over the account payable because it earns interest and it is written documentation of the debt's existence, term, and amount. When the note comes due, Brady pays the note and interest by giving McGraw a check for $510. Brady records that payment with this entry:

Point: Accounts payable are detailed in a subsidiary ledger, but notes payable sometimes are not. A file with copies of notes can serve as a subsidiary ledger.

Oct. 22	Notes Payable—McGraw	500	
	Interest Expense	10	
	Cash		510
	Paid note with interest ($500 × 12% × 60/360).		

Assets	=	Liabilities	+	Equity
−510		−500		−10

Interest expense is computed by multiplying the principal of the note ($500) by the annual interest rate (12%) for the fraction of the year the note is outstanding (60 days/360 days).

Point: Commercial companies commonly compute interest using a 360-day year. This is known as the *banker's rule.*

Note Given to Borrow from Bank A bank nearly always requires a borrower to sign a promissory note when making a loan. When the note matures, the borrower repays the note with an amount larger than the amount borrowed. The difference between the amount borrowed and the amount repaid is *interest*. This section considers a type of note whose signer promises to pay

Point: When money is borrowed from a bank, the loan is reported as an asset (receivable) on the bank's balance sheet.

principal (the amount borrowed) plus interest. In this case, the *face value* of the note equals principal. Face value is the value shown on the face (front) of the note. To illustrate, assume that a company needs $2,000 for a project and borrows this money from a bank at 12% annual interest. The loan is made on September 30, 2015, and is due in 60 days. Specifically, the borrowing company signs a note with a face value equal to the amount borrowed. The note includes a statement similar to this: *"I promise to pay $2,000 plus interest at 12% within 60 days after September 30."* This simple note is shown in Exhibit 9.3.

EXHIBIT 9.3

Note with Face Value Equal to Amount Borrowed

Promissory Note

$2,000 — Face Value

Sept. 30, 2015 — Date

Sixty days after date, I promise to pay to the order of

National Bank
Boston, MA

Two thousand and no/100 ---------------------------- Dollars

plus interest at the annual rate of 12%.

Janet Lee

The borrower records its receipt of cash and the new liability with this entry:

Assets = Liabilities + Equity
+2,000 +2,000

Sept. 30	Cash	2,000	
	Notes Payable		2,000
	Borrowed $2,000 cash with a 60-day, 12%, $2,000 note.		

When principal and interest are paid, the borrower records payment with this entry:

Assets = Liabilities + Equity
−2,040 −2,000 −40

Nov. 29	Notes Payable	2,000	
	Interest Expense	40	
	Cash		2,040
	Paid note with interest ($2,000 × 12% × 60/360).		

End-of-period interest adjustment. When the end of an accounting period occurs between the signing of a note payable and its maturity date, the *expense recognition (matching) principle* requires us to record the accrued but unpaid interest on the note. To illustrate, return to the note in Exhibit 9.3, but assume that the company borrows $2,000 cash on December 16, 2015, instead of September 30. This 60-day note matures on February 14, 2016, and the company's fiscal year ends on December 31. Thus, we need to record interest expense for the final 15 days in December. This means that one-fourth (15 days/60 days) of the $40 total interest is an expense of year 2015. The borrower records this expense (assuming no reversing entries were made) with the following adjusting entry:

Assets = Liabilities + Equity
+10 −10

2015			
Dec. 31	Interest Expense	10	
	Interest Payable		10
	To record accrued interest ($2,000 × 12% × 15/360).		

Example: If this note is dated Dec. 1 instead of Dec. 16, how much expense is recorded on Dec. 31? *Answer:* $2,000 × 12% × 30/360 = $20

When this note matures on February 14, the borrower must recognize 45 days of interest expense for year 2016 and remove the balances of the two liability accounts:

Assets = Liabilities + Equity
−2,040 −10 −30
−2,000

2016			
Feb. 14	Interest Expense*	30	
	Interest Payable	10	
	Notes Payable	2,000	
	Cash		2,040
	*Paid note with interest. *$2,000 × 12% × 45/360*		

Decision Insight

Many franchisors, such as **Baskin-Robbins**, **Dunkin' Donuts**, and **Cold Stone Creamery**, use notes to help entrepreneurs acquire their own franchises, including using notes to pay for the franchise fee and any equipment. Payments on these notes are usually collected monthly and often are secured by the franchisees' assets. For example, a **McDonald's** franchise can cost from under $200,000 to over $2 million, depending on the type selected, see **FranchiseFoundations.com**. ■

Adam Gault/OJO Images/Getty Images

NEED-TO-KNOW 9-1

Accounting for Known Liabilities

P1 C2

Part 1. A retailer sells merchandise for $500 cash on June 30 (cost of merchandise is $300). The sales tax law requires the retailer to collect 7% sales tax on every dollar of merchandise sold. Record the entry for the $500 sale and its applicable sales tax. Also record the entry that shows the remittance of the 7% tax on this sale to the state government on July 15.

Part 2. A ticket agency receives $40,000 cash in advance ticket sales for a four-date tour of Haim. Record the advance ticket sales on April 30. Record the revenue earned for the first concert date of May 15, assuming it represents one-fourth of the advance ticket sales.

Part 3. On November 25 of the current year, a company borrows $8,000 cash by signing a 90-day, 5% note payable with a face value of $8,000. (a) Compute the accrued interest payable on December 31 of the current year, (b) prepare the journal entry to record the accrued interest expense at December 31 of the current year, and (c) prepare the journal entry to record payment of the note at maturity.

Solution—Part 1

June 30	Cash	535	
	Sales		500
	Sales Taxes Payable		35
	To record cash sales and 5% sales tax.		
June 30	Cost of Goods Sold	300	
	Merchandise Inventory		300
	To record cost of June 30 sales.		
July 15	Sales Taxes Payable	35	
	Cash		35
	To record remittance of sales taxes to govt.		

Solution—Part 2

April 30	Cash	40,000	
	Unearned Ticket Revenue		40,000
	To record sales in advance of concerts.		
May 15	Unearned Ticket Revenue	10,000	
	Earned Ticket Revenue		10,000
	To record concert revenues earned.		

Solution—Part 3

a.

Computation of interest payable at December 31:

Days from November 25 to December 31	36 days
Accrued interest (5% × $8,000 × 36/360)	$40

b.

Dec. 31	Interest Expense	40	
	Interest Payable		40
	To record accrued interest (5% × $8,000 × 36/360).		

c.

Feb. 23	Interest Expense	60	
	Interest Payable	40	
	Notes Payable	8,000	
	Cash		8,100
	To record payment of note plus interest		
	(5% × $8,000 × 90/360 = $100 total interest).		
	(5% × $8,000 × 54/360 = $60 interest expense).		

Point: Feb. 23 entry assumes no reversing entry was made.

Do More: QS 9-2, QS 9-3, QS 9-4, E 9-2, E 9-3, E 9-4

Payroll Liabilities

An employer incurs several expenses and liabilities from having employees. These expenses and liabilities are often large and arise from salaries and wages earned, from employee benefits, and from payroll taxes levied on the employer. **Boston Beer**, for instance, reports payroll-related current liabilities of more than $14.8 million from accrued "**employee wages, benefits and reimbursements.**" We discuss payroll liabilities and related accounts in this section. Appendix 9A describes details about payroll reports, records, and procedures.

P2

Compute and record *employee* payroll deductions and liabilities.

Employee Payroll Deductions **Gross pay** is the total compensation an employee earns including wages, salaries, commissions, bonuses, and any compensation earned before deductions such as taxes. (Wages usually refer to payments to employees at an hourly rate. *Salaries* usually refer to payments to employees at a monthly or yearly rate.) **Net pay,** also called *take-home pay,* is gross pay less all deductions. **Payroll deductions,** commonly called *withholdings,* are amounts withheld from an employee's gross pay, either required or voluntary. Required deductions result from laws and include income taxes and Social Security taxes. Voluntary deductions, at an employee's option, include pension and health contributions, health and life insurance premiums, union dues, and charitable giving. Exhibit 9.4 shows the typical payroll deductions of an employee. The employer withholds payroll deductions from employees' pay and is obligated to transmit this money to the designated organization. The employer records payroll deductions as current liabilities until these amounts are transmitted. This section discusses the major payroll deductions.

Point: Deductions at some companies, such as those for insurance coverage, are "required" under its own labor contracts.

EXHIBIT 9.4

Payroll Deductions

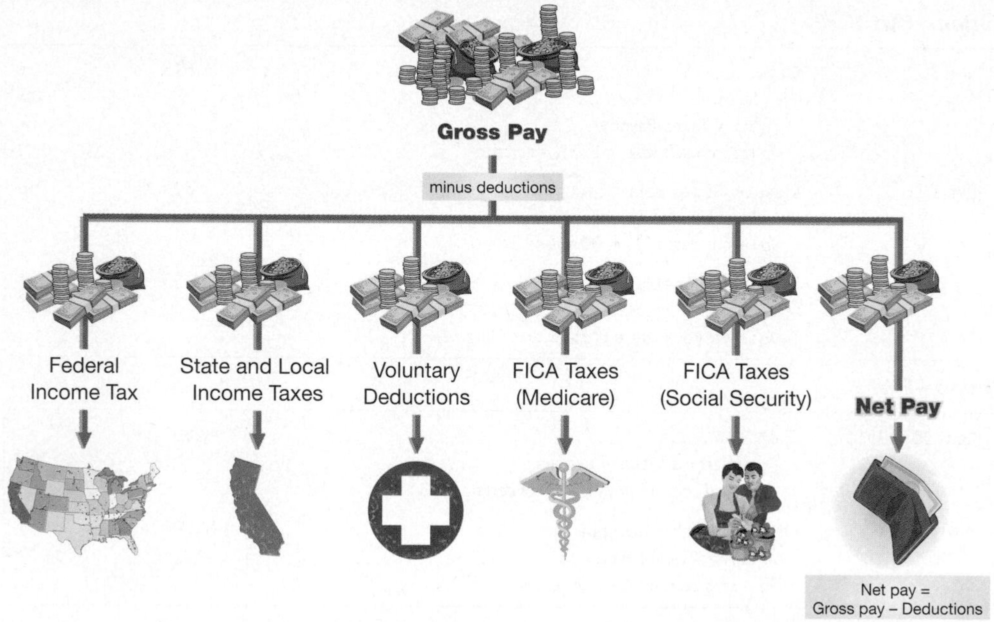

Employee FICA taxes. The federal Social Security system provides retirement, disability, survivorship, and medical benefits to qualified workers. Laws *require* employers to withhold **Federal Insurance Contributions Act (FICA) taxes** from employees' pay to cover costs of the system. Employers usually separate FICA taxes into two groups: (1) retirement, disability, and survivorship and (2) medical. For the first group, the Social Security system provides monthly cash payments to qualified retired workers for the rest of their lives. These payments are often called *Social Security benefits.* Taxes related to this group are often called *Social Security taxes.* For the second group, the system provides monthly payments to deceased workers' surviving families and to disabled workers who qualify for assistance. These payments are commonly called *Medicare benefits;* like those in the first group, they are paid with *Medicare taxes* (part of FICA taxes).

Law requires employers to withhold FICA taxes from each employee's salary or wages on each payday. The taxes for Social Security and Medicare are computed separately. For example, for 2014, the amount scheduled to be withheld from each employee's pay for Social Security tax is 6.2% of the first $117,000 the employee earns in the calendar year. The Medicare tax is 1.45% of *all* amounts the employee earns; there is no maximum limit to Medicare tax. A 0.9%

Additional Medicare Tax is imposed on the employee for pay in excess of $200,000 (this additional tax is *not* imposed on the employer).

Employers must pay withheld taxes to the Internal Revenue Service (IRS) on specific filing dates during the year. Employers who fail to send the withheld taxes to the IRS on time can be assessed substantial penalties. Until all the taxes are sent to the IRS, they are included in employers' current liabilities. For any changes in rates or with the maximum earnings level, check the IRS website at www.IRS.gov or the SSA website at www.SSA.gov.

Point: The sources of U.S. tax receipts are roughly as follows:
50% Personal income tax
35 FICA and FUTA taxes
10 Corporate income tax
5 Other taxes

Employee income tax. Most employers are required to withhold federal income tax from each employee's paycheck. The amount withheld is computed using tables published by the IRS. The amount depends on the employee's annual earnings rate and the number of *withholding allowances* the employee claims. Allowances reduce the amount of taxes one owes the government. The more allowances one claims, the less tax the employer will withhold. Employees can claim allowances for themselves and their dependents. They also can claim additional allowances if they expect major declines in their taxable income for medical expenses. (An employee who claims more allowances than appropriate is subject to a fine.) Most states and many local governments require employers to withhold income taxes from employees' pay and to remit them promptly to the proper government agency. Until they are paid, withholdings are reported as a current liability on the employer's balance sheet.

Point: Part-time employees may claim "exempt from withholding" if they did not have any income tax liability in the prior year and do not expect any in the current year.

Point: IRS withholding tables are based on projecting weekly (or other period) pay into an annual figure.

Point: Is there a maximum to the withholding allowances one can claim? Recall, the more allowances, the lower the withholding. However, an employee that claims, say, over 10 allowances on the W-4 is likely to receive an IRS inquiry asking to justify the number of allowances.

Employee voluntary deductions. Beyond Social Security, Medicare, and income taxes, employers often withhold other amounts from employees' earnings. These withholdings arise from employee requests, contracts, unions, or other agreements. They can include amounts for charitable giving, medical and life insurance premiums, pension contributions, and union dues. Until they are paid, such withholdings are reported as part of employers' current liabilities.

Recording employee payroll deductions. Employers must accrue payroll expenses and liabilities at the end of each pay period. To illustrate, assume that an employee earns a salary of $2,000 per month. At the end of January, the employer's entry to accrue payroll expenses and liabilities for this employee is

Jan. 31	Salaries Expense	2,000	
	FICA—Social Security Taxes Payable (6.2%)		124
	FICA—Medicare Taxes Payable (1.45%)		29
	Employee Federal Income Taxes Payable*		213
	Employee Medical Insurance Payable*		85
	Employee Union Dues Payable*		25
	Salaries Payable		1,524
	To record accrued payroll for January.		

* Amounts taken from employer's accounting records.

Assets	=	Liabilities	+	Equity
		+124		−2,000
		+29		
		+213		
		+85		
		+25		
		+1,524		

Salaries Expense (debit) shows that the employee earns a gross salary of $2,000. The first five payables (credits) show the liabilities the employer owes on behalf of this employee to cover FICA taxes, income taxes, medical insurance, and union dues. The Salaries Payable account (credit) records the $1,524 net pay the employee receives from the $2,000 gross pay earned. When the employee is paid, another entry (or a series of entries) is required to record the check written and distributed (or funds transferred). The entry to record cash payment to this employee is to debit Salaries Payable and credit Cash for $1,524.

Salaries Payable	1,524	
Cash		1,524

Decision Insight

Pay or Else "Failure to pay employment taxes is stealing from the employees of the business," alleges former IRS Commissioner Mark W. Everson. "The IRS pursues business owners who don't follow the law, and those who embrace these schemes face civil or criminal sanctions." There are many reasons employers do not withhold or pay employment taxes. Some attempt to use the government as a "bank to borrow money for a short time," some collect the taxes and keep it, and still others object to U.S. tax laws. Regardless, federal law requires employment tax withholding and payment by employers (IRS.gov/newsroom). ■

P3

Compute and record *employer* payroll expenses and liabilities.

Employer Payroll Taxes Employers must pay payroll taxes in addition to those required of employees. Employer taxes include FICA and unemployment taxes.

Employer FICA tax. Employers must pay FICA taxes on their payroll to employees. For 2014, the employer must pay Social Security tax of 6.2% on the first $117,000 earned by each employee, and 1.45% Medicare tax on all earnings of each employee. An employer's tax is credited to the same FICA Taxes Payable accounts used to record the Social Security and Medicare taxes withheld from employees. (A self-employed person must pay both the employee and employer FICA taxes.)

Federal and state unemployment taxes. The federal government participates with states in a joint federal and state unemployment insurance program. Each state administers its program. These programs provide unemployment benefits to qualified workers. The federal government approves state programs and pays a portion of their administrative expenses.

Federal Unemployment Tax Act (FUTA). Employers are subject to a federal unemployment tax on wages and salaries paid to their employees. For the recent year, employers were required to pay FUTA taxes of as much as 6.0% of the first $7,000 earned by each employee. This federal tax can be reduced by a credit of up to 5.4% for taxes paid to a state program. As a result, the net federal unemployment tax is often only 0.6%.

State Unemployment Tax Act (SUTA). All states support their unemployment insurance programs by placing a payroll tax on employers. (A few states require employees to make a contribution. In the book's assignments, we assume that this tax is only on the employer.) In most states, the base rate for SUTA taxes is 5.4% of the first $7,000 paid each employee. This base rate is adjusted according to an employer's merit rating. The state assigns a **merit rating** that reflects a company's stability or instability in employing workers. A good rating reflects stability in employment and means an employer can pay less than the 5.4% base rate. A low rating reflects high turnover or seasonal hirings and layoffs. To illustrate, an employer with 50 employees, each of whom earns $7,000 or more per year, saves $15,400 annually if it has a merit rating of 1.0% versus 5.4%. This is computed by comparing taxes of $18,900 at the 5.4% rate to only $3,500 at the 1.0% rate.

Recording employer payroll taxes. Employer payroll taxes are an added expense beyond the wages and salaries earned by employees. These taxes are often recorded in an entry separate from the one recording payroll expenses and deductions. To illustrate, assume that the $2,000 recorded salaries expense from the previous example is earned by an employee whose earnings have not yet reached $5,000 for the year. This means the entire salaries expense for this period is subject to tax because year-to-date pay is under $7,000. Also assume that the federal unemployment tax rate is 0.6% and the state unemployment tax rate is 5.4%. Consequently, the FICA portion of the employer's tax is $153, computed by multiplying both the 6.2% and 1.45% by the $2,000 gross pay. Moreover, state unemployment (SUTA) taxes are $108 (5.4% of the $2,000 gross pay), and federal unemployment (FUTA) taxes are $12 (0.6% of $2,000). The entry to record the employer's payroll tax expense and related liabilities is

Example: If the employer's merit rating in this example reduces its SUTA rate to 2.9%, what is its SUTA liability? *Answer:* SUTA payable = $2,000 × 2.9% = $58

Assets	=	Liabilities	+	Equity
		+124		−273
		+29		
		+108		
		+12		

Jan. 31	Payroll Taxes Expense	273	
	FICA—Social Security Taxes Payable (6.2%)		124
	FICA—Medicare Taxes Payable (1.45%)		29
	State Unemployment Taxes Payable		108
	Federal Unemployment Taxes Payable		12
	To record employer payroll taxes.		

Point: Internal control is important for payroll accounting. Managers must monitor (1) employee hiring, (2) timekeeping, (3) payroll listings, and (4) payroll payments. Poor controls led the U.S. Army to pay nearly $10 million to deserters, fictitious soldiers, and other unauthorized entities.

Decision Ethics

Web Designer You take a summer job working for a family friend who runs a small IT service. On your first payday, the owner slaps you on the back, gives you full payment in cash, winks, and adds: "No need to pay those high taxes, eh." What action, if any, do you take? ■ [Answers follow the chapter's Summary.]

Multi-Period Known Liabilities

Many known liabilities extend over multiple periods. These often include unearned revenues and notes payable. For example, if **Sports Illustrated** sells a four-year magazine subscription, it records amounts received for this subscription in an Unearned Subscription Revenues account. Amounts in this account are liabilities, but are they current or long term? They are *both.* The portion of the Unearned Subscription Revenues account that will be fulfilled in the next year is reported as a current liability. The remaining portion is reported as a long-term liability.

The same analysis applies to notes payable. For example, a borrower reports a three-year note payable as a long-term liability in the first two years it is outstanding. In the third year, the borrower reclassifies this note as a current liability since it is due within one year or the operating cycle, whichever is longer. The **current portion of long-term debt** refers to that part of long-term debt due within one year or the operating cycle, whichever is longer. Long-term debt is reported under long-term liabilities, but the *current portion due* is reported under current liabilities. To illustrate, assume that a $7,500 debt is paid in installments of $1,500 per year for five years. The $1,500 due within the year is reported as a current liability. No journal entry is necessary for this reclassification. Instead, we simply classify the amounts for debt as either current or long term when the balance sheet is prepared.

Some known liabilities are rarely reported in long-term liabilities. These include accounts payable, sales taxes, and wages and salaries.

Point: If *Sports Illustrated* offers you a sweatshirt of your favorite team if you subscribe, it must account for the sweatshirts using a *Promotions Liability account* if, and when, you subscribe.

Point: Some accounting systems do make an entry to transfer the current amount due out of Long-Term Debt and into the Current Portion of Long-Term Debt as follows:

Long-Term Debt . .	1,500	
Current Portion of L-T Debt . .		1,500

Decision Insight

Liability Limits Probably the greatest number of frauds involve payroll. Companies must safeguard payroll activities. Controls include proper approvals and processes for employee additions, deletions, and pay rate changes. A common fraud is a manager adding a fictitious employee to the payroll and then cashing the fictitious employee's check. A study reports that 28% of employees in operations and service areas witnessed violations of employee wage, overtime, or benefit rules in the past year (KPMG 2009). Another 21% observed falsifying of time and expense reports. ■

Ceridian Connection reports:
8.5% of fraud is tied to payroll.
$72,000 is the median loss per payroll fraud.
24 months is the median time to uncover payroll fraud.

NEED-TO-KNOW 9-2

Payroll Liabilities

P2 P3

A company's first weekly pay period of the year ends on January 8. On that date, the column totals in its payroll register show that sales employees earned $30,000 and office employees earned $20,000 in salaries. The employees are to have withheld from their salaries FICA Social Security taxes at the rate of 6.2%, FICA Medicare taxes at the rate of 1.45%, $9,000 of federal income taxes, $2,000 of medical insurance deductions, and $1,000 of pension contributions. No employee earned more than $7,000 in the first pay period.

Part 1. Compute FICA Social Security taxes payable and FICA Medicare taxes payable. Prepare the journal entry to record the company's January 8 (employee) payroll expenses and liabilities. (Round amounts to cents.)

Part 2. Prepare the journal entry to record the company's (employer) payroll taxes resulting from the January 8 payroll. Its merit rating reduces its state unemployment tax rate to 3.4% of the first $7,000 paid to each employee. The federal unemployment tax rate is 0.6%. (Round amounts to cents.)

Solution—Part 1

Jan. 8	Sales Salaries Expense	30,000.00	
	Office Salaries Expense	20,000.00	
	FICA—Social Security Taxes Payable*		3,100.00
	FICA—Medicare Taxes Payable**		725.00
	Employee Fed. Income Taxes Payable		9,000.00
	Employee Med. Insurance Payable		2,000.00
	Employee Pensions Payable		1,000.00
	Salaries Payable		34,175.00
	To record payroll for period.		

*$50,000 × 6.2% = $3,100.00
**$50,000 × 1.45% = $725.00

Solution—Part 2

Jan. 8	Payroll Taxes Expense	5,825.00	
	FICA—Social Security Taxes Payable		3,100.00
	FICA—Medicare Taxes Payable		725.00
	State Unemployment Taxes Payable*		1,700.00
	Federal Unemployment Taxes Payable**		300.00
	To record employer payroll taxes.		

*$50,000 × 0.034 = $1,700.00
**$50,000 × 0.006 = $300.00

Do More: QS 9-5, QS 9-6, E 9-5, E 9-6, E 9-7, E 9-8, E 9-9

QC2

ESTIMATED LIABILITIES

P4
Account for estimated liabilities, including warranties and bonuses.

An **estimated liability** is a known obligation that is of an uncertain amount but that can be reasonably estimated. Common examples are employee benefits such as pensions, health care and vacation pay, and warranties offered by a seller. We discuss each of these in this section. Other examples of estimated liabilities include property taxes and certain contracts to provide future services.

Health and Pension Benefits

Many companies provide **employee benefits** beyond salaries and wages. An employer often pays all or part of medical, dental, life, and disability insurance. Many employers also contribute to *pension plans,* which are agreements by employers to provide benefits (payments) to employees after retirement. Many companies also provide medical care and insurance benefits to their retirees. When payroll taxes and charges for employee benefits are totaled, payroll cost often exceeds employees' gross earnings by 25% or more.

To illustrate, assume that an employer agrees to (1) pay an amount for medical insurance equal to $8,000 and (2) contribute an additional 10% of the employees' $120,000 gross salaries to a retirement program. The entry to record these accrued benefits is

Assets = Liabilities + Equity
+8,000 −20,000
+12,000

Dec. 31	Employee Benefits Expense	20,000	
	Employee Medical Insurance Payable		8,000
	Employee Retirement Program Payable		12,000
	To record costs of employee benefits.		

Decision Insight

Postgame Spoils Baseball was the first pro sport to set up a pension, originally up to $100 per month depending on years played. Many former players now take home six-figure pensions. Cal Ripken Jr.'s pension when he reaches 62 is estimated at $160,000 per year (he played 21 seasons). The requirement is only 43 games for a full pension and just one game for full medical benefits. ■

Jeff Zelevansky/Getty Images

Vacation Benefits

Many employers offer paid vacation benefits, also called *paid absences* or *compensated absences.* To illustrate, assume that salaried employees earn 2 weeks' vacation per year. This benefit increases employers' payroll expenses because employees are paid for 52 weeks but work for only 50 weeks. Total annual salary is the same, but the cost per week worked is greater than the amount paid per week. For example, if an employee is paid $20,800 for 52 weeks but works only 50 weeks, the total weekly expense to the employer is $416 ($20,800/50 weeks) instead of the $400 cash paid weekly to the employee ($20,800/52 weeks). The $16 difference between these two amounts is recorded weekly as follows:

Assets = Liabilities + Equity
+16 −16

	Vacation Benefits Expense	16	
	Vacation Benefits Payable		16
	To record vacation benefits accrued.		

Vacation Benefits Expense is an operating expense, and Vacation Benefits Payable is a current liability. When the employee takes a vacation, the employer reduces (debits) the Vacation Benefits Payable and credits Cash (no additional expense is recorded).

Vacation Benefits Payable. .	#
Cash	#

Bonus Plans

Many companies offer bonuses to employees, and many of the bonuses depend on net income. To illustrate, assume that an employer offers a bonus to its employees equal to 5% of the company's annual net income (to be equally shared by all). The company's expected annual *pre-bonus* net income is $210,000. The year-end adjusting entry to record this benefit is

Dec. 31	Employee Bonus Expense*	10,000	
	Bonus Payable		10,000
	To record expected bonus costs.		

Assets = Liabilities + Equity
+10,000 −10,000

* Bonus Expense (B) equals 5% of net income, where net income equals $210,000 minus the bonus; the bonus is computed as:

$$B = 0.05\,(\$210{,}000 - B)$$
$$B = \$10{,}500 - 0.05B$$
$$1.05B = \$10{,}500$$
$$\mathbf{B = \$10{,}500/1.05 = \$10{,}000}$$

When the bonus is paid, Bonus Payable is debited and Cash is credited for $10,000.

Warranty Liabilities

A **warranty** is a seller's obligation to replace or correct a product (or service) that fails to perform as expected within a specified period. Most new cars, for instance, are sold with a warranty covering parts for a specified period of time. **Ford Motor Company** reported almost $8 billion in "dealer and dealers' customer allowances and claims" in its annual report. To comply with the *full disclosure* and *matching principles,* the seller reports the expected warranty expense in the period when revenue from the sale of the product or service is reported. The seller reports this warranty obligation as a liability, although the existence, amount, payee, and date of future sacrifices are uncertain. This is because such warranty costs are probable and the amount can be estimated using, for instance, past experience with warranties.

Point: **Fiat**, maker of the Ferrari, recently reported about $5 billion in warranty claims.

To illustrate, a dealer sells a used car for $16,000 on December 1, 2015, with a maximum one-year or 12,000-mile warranty covering parts. This dealer's experience shows that warranty expense averages about 4% of a car's selling price, or $640 in this case ($16,000 × 4%). The dealer records the estimated expense and liability related to this sale with this entry:

2015			
Dec. 1	Warranty Expense	640	
	Estimated Warranty Liability		640
	To record estimated warranty expense.		

Assets = Liabilities + Equity
+640 −640

This entry alternatively could be made as part of end-of-period adjustments. Either way, the estimated warranty expense is reported on the 2015 income statement and the warranty liability on the 2015 balance sheet. To further extend this example, suppose the customer returns the car for warranty repairs on January 9, 2016. The dealer performs this work by replacing parts costing $200. The entry to record partial settlement of the estimated warranty liability is

Point: Recognition of warranty liabilities is necessary to comply with the expense recognition (matching) and full disclosure principles.

2016			
Jan. 9	Estimated Warranty Liability	200	
	Auto Parts Inventory		200
	To record costs of warranty repairs.		

Assets = Liabilities + Equity
−200 −200

This entry reduces the balance of the estimated warranty liability. Warranty expense was previously recorded in 2015, the year the car was sold with the warranty. Finally, what happens if total warranty expenses are more or less than the estimated 4%, or $640? The answer is that management should monitor actual warranty expenses to see whether the 4% rate is accurate. If experience reveals a large difference from the estimate, the rate for current and future sales should be changed. Differences are expected, but they should be small.

Point: Both U.S. GAAP and IFRS account for restructuring costs in a manner similar to accounting for warranties.

Decision Insight

Warranty Profits When we purchase a new laptop at **Best Buy**, a sales clerk commonly asks: *"Want the Geek Squad Protection Plan?"* Best Buy earns about a 60% profit margin on such warranty contracts, and those contracts are a large part of its profit—see table to the side [*BusinessWeek*]. ■

Warranty contracts as a percentage of sales	4%
Warranty contracts as a percentage of operating profit	45%
Profit margin on warranty contracts	60%

Multi-Period Estimated Liabilities

QC3

Estimated liabilities can be both current and long term. For example, pension liabilities to employees are long term to workers who will not retire within the next period. For employees who are retired or will retire within the next period, a portion of pension liabilities is current. Other examples include employee health benefits and warranties. Specifically, many warranties are for 30 or 60 days in length. Estimated costs under these warranties are properly reported in current liabilities. Many other automobile warranties are for three years or 36,000 miles. A portion of these warranties is reported as long term.

CONTINGENT LIABILITIES

C3

Explain how to account for contingent liabilities.

A **contingent liability** is a potential obligation that depends on a future event arising from a past transaction or event. An example is a pending lawsuit. Here, a past transaction or event leads to a lawsuit whose result depends on the outcome of the suit. Future payment of a contingent liability depends on whether an uncertain future event occurs.

Accounting for Contingent Liabilities

Accounting for contingent liabilities depends on the likelihood that a future event will occur and the ability to estimate the future amount owed if this event occurs. Three different possibilities are identified in the following chart: record liability, disclose in notes, or no disclosure.

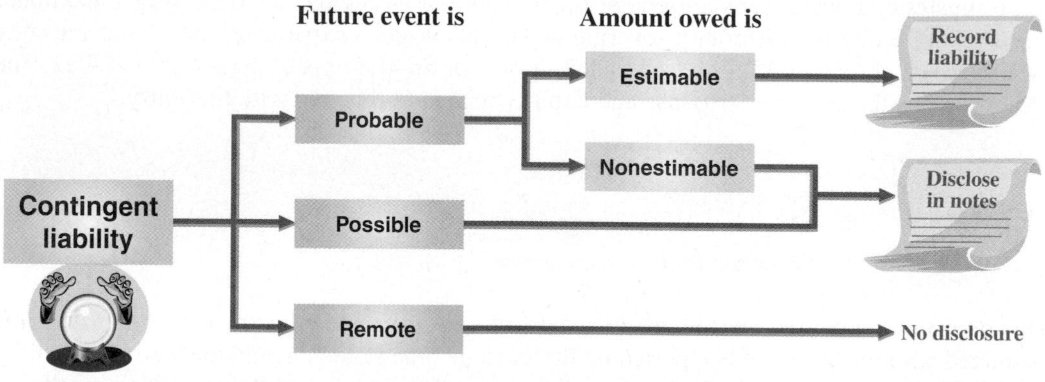

The conditions that determine each of these three possibilities follow:

1. The future event is *probable* (likely) and the amount owed can be *reasonably estimated.* We then record this amount as a liability. Examples are the estimated liabilities described earlier such as warranties, vacation pay, and income taxes.
2. The future event is *reasonably possible* (could occur). We disclose information about this type of contingent liability in notes to the financial statements.
3. The future event is *remote* (unlikely). We do not record or disclose information on remote contingent liabilities.

Point: A contingency is an *if.* Namely, if a future event occurs, then financial consequences are likely for the entity.

Reasonably Possible Contingent Liabilities

This section identifies and discusses contingent liabilities that commonly fall in the second category—when the future event is reasonably possible. Disclosing information about contingencies in this category is motivated by the *full disclosure principle,* which requires information relevant to decision makers be reported and not ignored.

Potential Legal Claims Many companies are sued or at risk of being sued. The accounting issue is whether the defendant should recognize a liability on its balance sheet or disclose a contingent liability in its notes while a lawsuit is outstanding and not yet settled. The answer is that a potential claim is recorded in the accounts *only* if payment for damages is probable and the amount can be reasonably estimated. If the potential claim cannot be reasonably estimated or is less than probable but reasonably possible, it is disclosed. **Ford Motor Company**, for example, includes the following note in its annual report: "Various legal actions, proceedings, and claims are pending . . . arising out of alleged defects in our products."

Point: A sale of a note receivable "with recourse" is a contingent liability. It becomes a liability if the original signer of the note fails to pay it at maturity.

Debt Guarantees Sometimes a company guarantees the payment of debt owed by a supplier, customer, or another company. The guarantor usually discloses the guarantee in its financial statement notes as a contingent liability. If it is probable that the debtor will default, the guarantor needs to record and report the guarantee in its financial statements as a liability. The **Boston Celtics** report a unique guarantee when it comes to coaches and players: "Certain of the contracts provide for guaranteed payments which must be paid even if the employee [player] is injured or terminated."

Other Contingencies Other examples of contingencies include environmental damages, possible tax assessments, insurance losses, and government investigations. **Sunoco**, for instance, reports that "federal, state and local laws . . . result in liabilities and loss contingencies. Sunoco accrues . . . cleanup costs [that] are probable and reasonably estimable. Management believes it is reasonably possible (i.e., less than probable but greater than remote) that additional . . . losses will be incurred." Many of Sunoco's contingencies are revealed only in notes.

Point: Auditors and managers often have different views about whether a contingency is recorded, disclosed, or omitted.

Decision Insight

Pricing Priceless What's it worth to see from one side of the Grand Canyon to the other? What's the cost when Gulf Coast beaches are closed due to an oil well disaster? A method to measure environmental liabilities is *contingent valuation,* by which people answer such questions. Regulators use their answers to levy fines and assess punitive damages. ■

John Burcham/National Geographic/Getty Images

Uncertainties That Are Not Contingencies

All organizations face uncertainties from future events such as natural disasters and the development of new competing products or services. These uncertainties are not contingent liabilities because they are future events *not* arising from past transactions. Accordingly, they are not disclosed.

NEED-TO-KNOW 9-3

Estimated and Contingent Liabilities

P4 C3

Part 1. A company's salaried employees earn two weeks' vacation per year. It pays $208,000 in total employee salaries for 52 weeks, but its employees work only 50 weeks. This means its total weekly expense is $4,160 ($208,000/50 weeks) instead of the $4,000 cash paid weekly to the employees ($208,000/52 weeks). Record the company's regular weekly vacation benefits expense.

Part 2. For the current year ended December 31, a company has implemented an employee bonus program equal to 5% of its net income, which employees share equally. Its net income (pre-bonus) is expected to be $840,000, and bonus expense is deducted in computing net income. (a) Compute the bonus payable to the employees at year-end using the method described in the chapter and round to the nearest dollar; then prepare the journal entry at December 31 of the current year to record the bonus due. (b) Prepare the journal entry at January 20 of the following year to record payment of that bonus to employees.

Part 3. On June 11 of the current year, a retailer sells a trimmer for $400 with a one-year warranty that covers parts. Warranty expense is estimated at 5% of sales. On March 24 of the next year, the trimmer is brought in for repairs covered under the warranty requiring $15 in materials taken from the Repair Parts

Inventory. Prepare the (a) June 11 entry to record the trimmer sale—ignore the cost of sales part of this sales entry, and (b) March 24 entry to record warranty repairs.

Part 4. The following legal claims exist for a company. Identify the accounting treatment for each claim as either (i) a liability that is recorded or (ii) an item described in notes to its financial statements. If an item is to be recorded, prepare the entry (date any entry Dec. 31).

a. The company (defendant) estimates that a pending lawsuit could result in damages of $500,000; it is reasonably possible that the plaintiff will win the case.

b. The company faces a probable loss on a pending lawsuit; the amount is not reasonably estimable.

c. The company estimates environmental damages in a pending case at $900,000 with a high probability of losing the case.

Solution—Part 1

Weekly	Vacation Benefits Expense*	160	
	Vacation Benefits Payable		160
	To record vacation benefits accrued. **$4,160 − $4,000*		

Solution—Part 2

a.
$$B = 0.05\,(\$840{,}000 - B)$$
$$B = \$42{,}000 - 0.05B$$
$$1.05B = \$42{,}000$$
$$B = \underline{\underline{\$40{,}000}}$$

Dec. 31	Employee Bonus Expense	40,000	
	Bonus Payable		40,000
	To record expected bonus costs.		

b.

Jan. 20	Bonus Payable	40,000	
	Cash		40,000
	To record payment of bonus.		

Solution—Part 3

June 11	Cash	400	
	Sales		400
	To record trimmer sales.		
June 11	Warranty Expense	20	
	Estimated Warranty Liability		20
	To record estimated warranty expense ($400 × 5%).		
March 24	Estimated Warranty Liability	15	
	Repair Parts Inventory		15
	To record cost of warranty repairs.		

Solution—Part 4

a. (ii); reason—is reasonably estimated but not a probable loss.

b. (ii); reason—probable loss but cannot be reasonably estimated.

c. (i); reason—can be reasonably estimated and loss is probable. The journal entry follows:

Dec. 31	Environmental Contingent Expense	900,000	
	Environmental Contingent Liability		900,000
	To record environmental contingent liability.		

Do More: QS 9-7, QS 9-8, QS 9-9, QS 9-10, E 9-10, E 9-11, E 9-12, E 9-13

QC4

GLOBAL VIEW

This section discusses similarities and differences between U.S. GAAP and IFRS in accounting and reporting for current liabilities.

Characteristics of Liabilities The definitions and characteristics of current liabilities are broadly similar for both U.S. GAAP and IFRS. Although differences exist, the similarities vastly outweigh any differences. Remembering that "provision" is typically used under IFRS to refer to what is titled "liability" under U.S. GAAP, **Nokia** describes its recognition of liabilities as follows:

> Provisions are recognized when the Group has a present legal or constructive obligation as a result of past events, it is probable that an outflow of resources will be required to settle the obligation and a reliable estimate of the amount can be made.

NOKIA

Known (Determinable) Liabilities When there is little uncertainty surrounding current liabilities, both U.S. GAAP and IFRS require companies to record them in a similar manner. This correspondence in accounting applies to accounts payable, sales taxes payable, unearned revenues, short-term notes, and payroll liabilities. Of course, tax regulatory systems of countries are different, which implies use of different rates and levels. Still, the basic approach is the same.

Estimated Liabilities When there is a known current obligation that involves an uncertain amount, but one that can be reasonably estimated, both U.S. GAAP and IFRS require similar treatment. This treatment extends to many obligations such as those arising from vacations, warranties, restructurings, pensions, and health care. Both accounting systems require that companies record estimated expenses related to these obligations when they can reasonably estimate the amounts. **Nokia** reports wages, salaries, and bonuses of €6,080 million. It also reports pension expenses of €375 million.

Sustainability and Accounting Entrepreneur Jessica O. Matthews of **Uncharted Play**, as introduced in this chapter's opening feature, explains that her company's focus involves a sustainable initiative. "As people start seeing that this means long-term economic and environmental sustainability, the global community will start to wholly embrace the concept." Jessica goes on to articulate her own "Impact Model," which follows:

- Joyful, renewable sources of power for resource-poor communities.
- An inspirational product to inspire social invention.
- Tangible, fun tools for STEM education globally.
- A platform to motivate organic physical activity.

Courtesy of Uncharted Play

Times Interest Earned Ratio — Decision Analysis

A company incurs interest expense on many of its current and long-term liabilities. Examples extend from its short-term notes and the current portion of long-term liabilities to its long-term notes and bonds. Interest expense is often viewed as a *fixed expense* because the amount of these liabilities is likely to remain in one form or another for a substantial period of time. This means that the amount of interest is unlikely to vary due to changes in sales or other operating activities. While fixed expenses can be advantageous when a company is growing, they create risk. This risk stems from the possibility that a company might be unable to pay fixed expenses if sales decline. To illustrate, consider Diego Co.'s results for 2015 and two possible outcomes for year 2016 in Exhibit 9.5.

A1 Compute the times interest earned ratio and use it to analyze liabilities.

EXHIBIT 9.5 Actual and Projected Results

		2016 Projections	
($ thousands)	2015	Sales Increase	Sales Decrease
Sales	$600	$900	$300
Expenses (75% of sales)	450	675	225
Income before interest	150	225	75
Interest expense (fixed)	60	60	60
Net income	$ 90	$165	$ 15

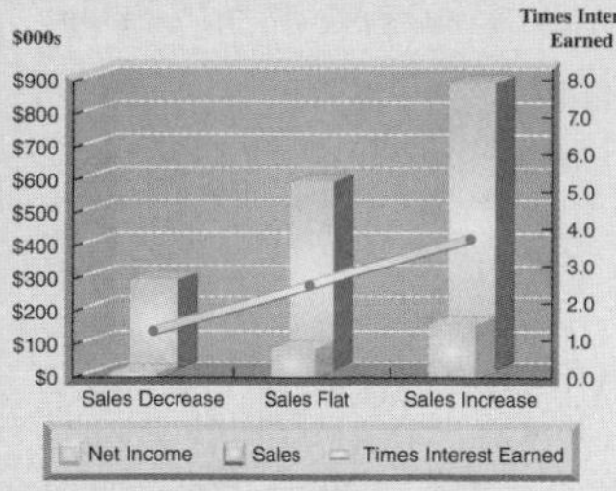

Expenses excluding interest are at, and expected to remain at, 75% of sales. Expenses such as these that change with sales volume are called *variable expenses.* However, interest expense is at, and expected to remain at, $60,000 per year due to its fixed nature.

The middle numerical column of Exhibit 9.5 shows that Diego's income increases by 83% to $165,000 if sales increase by 50% to $900,000. In contrast, the far right column shows that income decreases by 83% if sales decline by 50%. These results reveal that the amount of fixed interest expense affects a company's risk of its ability to pay interest, which is numerically reflected in the **times interest earned** ratio in Exhibit 9.6.

EXHIBIT 9.6

Times Interest Earned

$$\textbf{Times interest earned} = \frac{\textbf{Income before interest expense and income taxes}}{\textbf{Interest expense}}$$

For 2015, Diego's times interest earned is computed as $150,000/$60,000, or 2.5 times. This ratio suggests that Diego faces low to moderate risk because its sales must decline sharply before it would be unable to cover its interest expenses. (Diego is an LLC and does not pay income taxes.)

Experience shows that when times interest earned falls below 1.5 to 2.0 and remains at that level or lower for several periods, the default rate on liabilities increases sharply. This reflects increased risk for companies and their creditors. We also must interpret the times interest earned ratio in light of information about the variability of a company's income before interest. If income is stable from year to year or if it is growing, the company can afford to take on added risk by borrowing. If its income greatly varies from year to year, fixed interest expense can increase the risk that it will not earn enough income to pay interest.

Decision Maker

Entrepreneur You wish to invest in a franchise for either one of two national chains. Each franchise has an expected annual net income *after* interest and taxes of $100,000. Net income for the first franchise includes a regular fixed interest charge of $200,000. The fixed interest charge for the second franchise is $40,000. Which franchise is riskier to you if sales forecasts are not met? Does your decision change if the first franchise has more variability in its income stream? ■ [Answers follow the chapter's Summary.]

NEED-TO-KNOW

COMPREHENSIVE

The following transactions and events took place at Kern Company during its recent calendar-year reporting period (Kern does not use reversing entries).

a. In September 2015, Kern sold $140,000 of merchandise covered by a 180-day warranty. Prior experience shows that costs of the warranty equal 5% of sales. Compute September's warranty expense and prepare the adjusting journal entry for the warranty liability as recorded at September 30. Also prepare the journal entry on October 8 to record a $300 cash expenditure to provide warranty service on an item sold in September.

b. On October 12, 2015, Kern arranged with a supplier to replace Kern's overdue $10,000 account payable by paying $2,500 cash and signing a note for the remainder. The note matures in 90 days and has a 12% interest rate. Prepare the entries recorded on October 12, December 31, and January 10, 2016, related to this transaction.

c. In late December, Kern learns it is facing a product liability suit filed by an unhappy customer. Kern's lawyer advises that although it will probably suffer a loss from the lawsuit, it is not possible to estimate the amount of damages at this time.

d. Sally Bline works for Kern. For the pay period ended November 30, her gross earnings are $3,000. Bline has $800 deducted for federal income taxes and $200 for state income taxes from each paycheck. Additionally, a $35 premium for her health care insurance and a $10 donation to the United Way are deducted. Bline pays FICA Social Security taxes at a rate of 6.2% and FICA Medicare taxes at a rate of 1.45%. She has not earned enough this year to be exempt from any FICA taxes. Journalize the accrual of salaries expense of Bline's wages by Kern.

e. On November 1, Kern borrows $5,000 cash from a bank in return for a 60-day, 12%, $5,000 note. Record the note's issuance on November 1 and its repayment with interest on December 31.

f[B] *(Part f covers Appendix 9B.)* Kern has estimated and recorded its quarterly income tax payments. In reviewing its year-end tax adjustments, it identifies an additional $5,000 of income tax expense that should be recorded. A portion of this additional expense, $1,000, is deferrable to future years. Record this year-end income taxes expense adjusting entry.

g. For this calendar year, Kern's net income is $1,000,000, its interest expense is $275,000, and its income taxes expense is $225,000. Calculate Kern's times interest earned ratio.

PLANNING THE SOLUTION

- For *a,* compute the warranty expense for September and record it with an estimated liability. Record the October expenditure as a decrease in the liability.
- For *b,* eliminate the liability for the account payable and create the liability for the note payable. Compute interest expense for the 80 days that the note is outstanding in 2015 and record it as an additional liability. Record the payment of the note, being sure to include the interest for the 10 days in 2016.
- For *c,* decide whether the company's contingent liability needs to be disclosed or accrued (recorded) according to the two necessary criteria: probable loss and reasonably estimable.
- For *d,* set up payable accounts for all items in Bline's paycheck that require deductions. After deducting all necessary items, credit the remaining amount to Salaries Payable.
- For *e,* record the issuance of the note. Calculate 60 days' interest due using the 360-day convention in the interest formula.
- For *f,* determine how much of the income taxes expense is payable in the current year and how much needs to be deferred.
- For *g,* apply and compute times interest earned.

SOLUTION

a. Warranty expense = 5% × $140,000 = $7,000

Sept. 30	Warranty Expense	7,000	
	Estimated Warranty Liability		7,000
	To record warranty expense for the month.		
Oct. 8	Estimated Warranty Liability	300	
	Cash		300
	To record the cost of the warranty service.		

b. Interest expense for 2015 = 12% × $7,500 × 80/360 = $200
Interest expense for 2016 = 12% × $7,500 × 10/360 = $25

Oct. 12	Accounts Payable	10,000	
	Notes Payable		7,500
	Cash		2,500
	Paid $2,500 cash and gave a 90-day, 12% note to extend the due date on the account.		
Dec. 31	Interest Expense	200	
	Interest Payable		200
	To accrue interest on note payable.		
Jan. 10	Interest Expense	25	
	Interest Payable	200	
	Notes Payable	7,500	
	Cash		7,725
	Paid note with interest, including the accrued interest payable.		

c. Disclose the pending lawsuit in the financial statement notes. Although the loss is probable, no liability can be accrued since the loss cannot be reasonably estimated.

d.

Nov. 30	Salaries Expense	3,000.00	
	FICA—Social Security Taxes Payable (6.2%)		186.00
	FICA—Medicare Taxes Payable (1.45%)		43.50
	Employee Federal Income Taxes Payable		800.00
	Employee State Income Taxes Payable		200.00
	Employee Medical Insurance Payable		35.00
	Employee United Way Payable		10.00
	Salaries Payable		1,725.50
	To record Bline's accrued payroll.		

e.

Nov. 1	Cash	5,000	
	Notes Payable		5,000
	Borrowed cash with a 60-day, 12% note.		

When the note and interest are paid 60 days later, Kern Company records this entry:

Dec. 31	Notes Payable	5,000	
	Interest Expense	100	
	Cash		5,100
	Paid note with interest ($5,000 × 12% × 60/360).		

f.

Dec. 31	Income Taxes Expense	5,000	
	Income Taxes Payable		4,000
	Deferred Income Tax Liability		1,000
	To record added income taxes expense and the deferred tax liability.		

g. $$\text{Times interest earned} = \frac{\$1{,}000{,}000 + \$275{,}000 + \$225{,}000}{\$275{,}000} = \underline{\underline{5.45 \text{ times}}}$$

APPENDIX

9A Payroll Reports, Records, and Procedures

Understanding payroll procedures and keeping adequate payroll reports and records are essential to a company's success. This appendix focuses on payroll accounting and its reports, records, and procedures.

P5

Identify and describe the details of payroll reports, records, and procedures.

Payroll Reports Most employees and employers are required to pay local, state, and federal payroll taxes. Payroll expenses involve liabilities to individual employees, to federal and state governments, and to other organizations such as insurance companies. Beyond paying these liabilities, employers are required to prepare and submit reports explaining how they computed these payments.

Reporting FICA Taxes and Income Taxes The Federal Insurance Contributions Act (FICA) requires each employer to file an Internal Revenue Service (IRS) **Form 941,** the *Employer's Quarterly Federal Tax Return,* within one month after the end of each calendar quarter. A sample Form 941 is shown in Exhibit 9A.1 for Phoenix Sales & Service, a landscape design company. Accounting information and software are helpful in tracking payroll transactions and reporting the accumulated information on Form 941. Specifically, the employer reports total wages subject to income tax withholding on line 2 of Form 941. (For simplicity, this appendix uses *wages* to refer to both wages and salaries.) The income tax withheld is reported on line 3. The combined amount of employee and employer FICA (Social Security) taxes for Phoenix Sales & Service is reported on line 5a (taxable Social Security wages,

EXHIBIT 9A.1

Form 941

Form **941** **Employer's QUARTERLY Federal Tax Return**

Department of the Treasury — Internal Revenue Service

(EIN) Employer identification number: 8 6 – 3 2 1 4 5 8 7

Name *(not your trade name)*: Phoenix Sales & Service

Trade name *(if any)*:

Address: 1214 (Number) Mill Road (Street) Suite or room number

Phoenix (City) AZ (State) 85621 (ZIP code)

Report for this Quarter ... (Check one.)

- ☐ 1: January, February, March
- ☐ 2: April, May, June
- ☐ 3: July, August, September
- ☒ 4: October, November, December

Part 1: Answer these questions for this quarter.

1 Number of employees who received wages, tips, or other compensation for the pay period including: *Mar. 12* (Quarter 1), *June 12* (Quarter 2), *Sept. 12* (Quarter 3), *Dec. 12* (Quarter 4)	1	2
2 Wages, tips, and other compensation	2	36,599.00
3 Total income tax withheld from wages, tips, and other compensation	3	3,056.47
4 If no wages, tips, and other compensation are subject to social security or Medicare tax		☐ Check and go to line 6.

5 Taxable social security and Medicare wages and tips:

	Column 1		Column 2
5a Taxable social security wages	36,599.00	× .124 =	4,538.28
5b Taxable social security tips	.	× .124 =	.
5c Taxable Medicare wages & tips	36,599.00	× .029 =	1,061.37

5d Total social security and Medicare taxes (*Column 2*, lines 5a + 5b + 5c = line 5d)	5d	5,599.65
6 Total taxes before adjustments (lines 3 + 5d = line 6)	6	8,656.12

7 **TAX ADJUSTMENTS** (Read the instructions for line 7 before completing lines 7a through 7h.):

7a Current quarter's fractions of cents	.
7b Current quarter's sick pay	.
7c Current quarter's adjustments for tips and group-term life insurance	.
7d Current year's income tax withholding (attach Form 941c)	.
7e Prior quarters' social security and Medicare taxes (attach Form 941c)	.
7f Special additions to federal income tax (attach Form 941c)	.
7g Special additions to social security and Medicare (attach Form 941c)	.

7h **TOTAL ADJUSTMENTS** (Combine all amounts: lines 7a through 7g.)	7h	0.00
8 Total taxes after adjustments (Combine lines 6 and 7h.)	8	8,656.12
9 Advance earned income credit (EIC) payments made to employees	9	.
10 Total taxes after adjustment for advance EIC (lines 8 – line 9 = line 10)	10	8,656.12
11 Total deposits for this quarter, including overpayment applied from a prior quarter	11	8,656.12
12 Balance due (If line 10 is more than line 11, write the difference here.) Make checks payable to *United States Treasury.*	12	0.00

13 Overpayment (If line 11 is more than line 10, write the difference here.) 0.00 Check one ☐ Apply to next return. ☐ Send a refund.

Part 2: Tell us about your deposit schedule and tax liability for this quarter.

If you are unsure about whether you are a monthly schedule depositor or a semiweekly schedule depositor, see *Pub. 15 (Circular E)*, section 11.

14 A Z Write the state abbreviation for the state where you made your deposits OR write "MU" if you made your deposits in *multiple* states.

15 Check one: ☐ Line 10 is less than $2,500. Go to Part 3.

☒ You were a monthly schedule depositor for the entire quarter. Fill out your tax liability for each month. Then go to Part 3.

Tax liability:	
Month 1	3,079.11
Month 2	2,049.77
Month 3	3,527.24
Total liability for quarter	8,656.12

Total must equal line 10.

☐ You were a semiweekly schedule depositor for any part of this quarter. Fill out *Schedule B (Form 941): Report of Tax Liability for Semiweekly Schedule Depositors*, and attach it to this form.

Part 3: Tell us about your business. If a question does NOT apply to your business, leave it blank.

16 If your business has closed or you stopped paying wages ☐ Check here, and

enter the final date you paid wages / /

17 If you are a seasonal employer and you do not have to file a return for every quarter of the year ☐ Check here.

Part 4: May we speak with your third-party designee?

Do you want to allow an employee, a paid tax preparer, or another person to discuss this return with the IRS? See the instructions for details.

☐ Yes. Designee's name

Phone ( ) – Personal Identification Number (PIN)

☒ No.

Part 5: Sign here. You MUST fill out both sides of this form and SIGN it.

Under penalties of perjury, I declare that I have examined this return, including accompanying schedules and statements, and to the best of my knowledge and belief, it is true, correct, and complete.

✗ Sign your name here

Print name and title

Date / / Phone ( ) –

Point: Line 5a shows the matching nature of the FICA tax as 6.2% × 2, or 12.4%; which is shown as 0.124.

Point: Auditors rely on the four 941 forms filed during a year when auditing a company's annual wages and salaries expense account.

$36,599 × 12.4% = $4,538.28). The 12.4% is the sum of the Social Security tax withheld, computed as 6.2% tax withheld from the employee wages for the quarter plus the 6.2% tax levied on the employer. The combined amount of employee Medicare wages is reported on line 5c. The 2.9% is the sum of 1.45% withheld from employee wages for the quarter plus 1.45% tax levied on the employer. Total FICA taxes are reported on line 5d and are added to the total income taxes withheld of $3,056.47 to yield a total of $8,656.12. For this year, assume that income up to $117,000 is subject to Social Security tax. There is no income limit on amounts subject to Medicare tax. Congress sets rates owed for Social Security tax (and it typically changes each year).

Point: Deposits for federal payroll taxes must be made by electronic funds transfer (EFT).

Federal depository banks are authorized to accept deposits of amounts payable to the federal government. Deposit requirements depend on the amount of tax owed. For example, when the sum of FICA taxes plus the employee income taxes is less than $2,500 for a quarter, the taxes can be paid when Form 941 is filed. Companies with large payrolls are often required to pay monthly or even semiweekly.

Reporting FUTA Taxes and SUTA Taxes An employer's federal unemployment taxes (FUTA) are reported on an annual basis by filing an *Annual Federal Unemployment Tax Return,* IRS **Form 940.** It must be mailed on or before January 31 following the end of each tax year. Ten more days are allowed if all required tax deposits are filed on a timely basis and the full amount of tax is paid on or before January 31. FUTA payments are made quarterly to a federal depository bank if the total amount due exceeds $500. If $500 or less is due, the taxes are remitted annually. Requirements for paying and reporting state unemployment taxes (SUTA) vary depending on the laws of each state. Most states require quarterly payments and reports.

Reporting Wages and Salaries Employers are required to give each employee an annual report of his or her wages subject to FICA and federal income taxes along with the amounts of these taxes withheld. This report is called a *Wage and Tax Statement,* or **Form W-2.** It must be given to employees before January 31 following the year covered by the report. Exhibit 9A.2 shows Form W-2 for one of the employees at Phoenix Sales & Service. Copies of the W-2 Form must be sent to the Social Security Administration, where the amount of the employee's wages subject to FICA taxes and FICA taxes withheld are posted to each employee's Social Security account. These posted amounts become the basis for determining an employee's retirement and survivors' benefits. The Social Security Administration also transmits to the IRS the amount of each employee's wages subject to federal income taxes and the amount of taxes withheld.

EXHIBIT 9A.2

Form W-2

Form **W-2** Wage and Tax Statement
Copy 1–For State, City, or Local Tax Department
Department of Treasury—Internal Revenue Service

a Control number: AR101 | 22222 | OMB No. 1545-0006

b Employer identification number (EIN): 86-3214587

c Employer's name, address and ZIP code:
Phoenix Sales & Service
1214 Mill Road
Phoenix, AZ 85621

d Employee's social security number: 333-22-9999

e Employee's first name and initial: Robert J. Last name: Austin

f Employee's address and ZIP code:
18 Roosevelt Blvd., Apt. C
Tempe, AZ 86322

1 Wages, tips, other compensation: 4,910.00	2 Federal income tax withheld: 333.37
3 Social security wages: 4,910.00	4 Social security tax withheld: 304.42
5 Medicare wages and tips: 4,910.00	6 Medicare tax withheld: 71.20
7 Social security tips	8 Allocated tips
9 Advance EIC payment	10 Dependent care benefits
11 Nonqualified plans	12a Code
13 Statutory employee / Retirement plan / Third-party sick pay	12b Code
14 Other	12c Code
	12d Code

15 State	Employer's state ID number	16 State wages, tips, etc.	17 State income tax	18 Local wages, tips, etc.	19 Local income tax	20 Locality name
AZ	13-902319	4,910.00	26.68			

Payroll Records Employers must keep payroll records in addition to reporting and paying taxes. These records usually include a payroll register and an individual earnings report for each employee.

EXHIBIT 9A.3

Payroll Register

	A	B	C	D	E	F	G	H	I
1	Phoenix Sales & Service								
2	Payroll Register								
3	For Week Ended Jan. 8, 2015								
4	Employee ID	Gross Pay			FIT	SIT	FICA-SS_EE	FICA-Med_EE	
5	Employee				[blank]	[blank]	[blank]	[blank]	
6	SS No.	Pay	Pay	Gross	FUTA	SUTA	FICA-SS_ER	FICA-Med_ER	Net
7	Refer., Date	Type	Hours	Pay					Pay
8	AR101	Regular	40.00	400.00	−28.99	−2.32	−24.80	−5.80	338.09
9	Robert Austin	Overtime	0.00	0.00					
10	333-22-9999			400.00	−2.40	−10.80	−24.80	−5.80	
11	9001, 1/8/15								
12	CJ102	Regular	40.00	560.00	−52.97	−4.24	−36.02	−8.42	479.35
13	Judy Cross	Overtime	1.00	21.00					
14	299-11-9201			581.00	−3.49	−15.69	−36.02	−8.42	
15	9002, 1/8/15								
16	DJ103	Regular	40.00	560.00	−48.33	−3.87	−37.32	−8.73	503.75
17	John Diaz	Overtime	2.00	42.00					
18	444-11-9090			602.00	−3.61	−16.25	−37.32	−8.73	
19	9003, 1/8/15								
20	KK104	Regular	40.00	560.00	−68.57	−5.49	−34.72	−8.12	443.10
21	Kay Keife	Overtime	0.00	0.00					
22	909-11-3344			560.00	−3.36	−15.12	−34.72	−8.12	
23	9004, 1/8/15								
24	ML105	Regular	40.00	560.00	−34.24	−2.74	−34.72	−8.12	480.18
25	Lee Miller	Overtime	0.00	0.00					
26	444-56-3211			560.00	−3.36	−15.12	−34.72	−8.12	
27	9005, 1/8/15								
28	SD106	Regular	40.00	560.00	−68.57	−5.49	−34.72	−8.12	443.10
29	Dale Sears	Overtime	0.00	0.00					
30	909-33-1234			560.00	−3.36	−15.12	−34.72	−8.12	
31	9006, 1/8/15								
32	Totals	Regular	240.00	3,200.00	−301.67	−24.15	−202.30	−47.31	2,687.57
33		Overtime	3.00	63.00					
34				3,263.00	−19.58	−88.10	−202.30	−47.31	
35									
36									

Payroll Register A **payroll register** usually shows the pay period dates, hours worked, gross pay, deductions, and net pay of each employee for each pay period. Exhibit 9A.3 shows a payroll register for Phoenix Sales & Service. It is organized into nine columns:

Col. 1 Employee identification (ID); Employee name; Social Security number (SS No.); Reference (check number); and Date (date check issued)
Col. 2 Pay Type (regular and overtime)
Col. 3 Pay Hours (number of hours worked as regular and overtime)
Col. 4 Gross Pay (amount of gross pay)[2]
Col. 5 FIT (federal income taxes withheld); FUTA (federal unemployment taxes)
Col. 6 SIT (state income taxes withheld); SUTA (state unemployment taxes)
Col. 7 FICA-SS_EE (social security taxes withheld, employee); FICA-SS_ER (social security taxes, employer)
Col. 8 FICA-Med_EE (medicare tax withheld, employee); FICA-Med_ER (medicare tax, employer)
Col. 9 Net pay (Gross pay less amounts withheld from employees)

Net pay for each employee is computed as gross pay minus the items on the first line of columns 5–8. The employer's payroll tax for each employee is computed as the sum of items on the third line of columns 5–8. A payroll register includes all data necessary to record payroll. In some software programs the entries to record payroll are made in a special *payroll journal.*

---

[2] The Gross Pay column shows regular hours worked on the first line multiplied by the regular pay rate—this equals regular pay. Overtime hours multiplied by the overtime premium rate equals overtime premium pay reported on the second line. If employers are engaged in interstate commerce, federal law sets a minimum overtime rate of pay to employees. For this company, workers earn 150% of their regular rate for hours in excess of 40 per week.

Payroll Check Payment of payroll is usually done by check or electronic funds transfer. Exhibit 9A.4 shows a *payroll check* for a Phoenix employee. This check is accompanied with a detachable *statement of earnings* (at top) showing gross pay, deductions, and net pay.

EXHIBIT 9A.4

Check and Statement of Earnings

EMPLOYEE NO.	EMPLOYEE NAME	SOCIAL SECURITY NO.	PAY PERIOD END	CHECK DATE
AR101	Robert Austin	333-22-9999	1/8/15	1/8/15

ITEM	RATE	HOURS	TOTAL	ITEM	THIS CHECK	YEAR TO DATE
Regular	10.00	40.00	400.00	Gross	400.00	400.00
Overtime	15.00			Fed. Income tax	-28.99	-28.99
				FICA-Soc. Sec.	-24.80	-24.80
				FICA-Medicare	-5.80	-5.80
				State Income tax	-2.32	-2.32

HOURS WORKED	GROSS THIS PERIOD	GROSS YEAR TO DATE	NET CHECK	CHECK NO.
40.00	400.00	400.00	$338.09	9001

(Detach and retain for your records)

PHOENIX SALES & SERVICE
1214 Mill Road
Phoenix, AZ 85621
602-555-8900

Phoenix Bank and Trust
Phoenix, AZ 85621
3312-87044

No. 9001

DATE January 8, 20 15

Check No. 9001

Amount Three Hundred Thirty-Eight and 9/100 Dollars $ **************$338.09*

Pay to the order of
Robert Austin
18 Roosevelt Blvd., Apt C
Tempe, AZ 86322

Mary Wills
AUTHORIZED SIGNATURE

Employee Earnings Report An **employee earnings report** is a cumulative record of an employee's hours worked, gross earnings, deductions, and net pay. Payroll information on this report is taken from the payroll register. The employee earnings report for R. Austin at Phoenix Sales & Service is shown in Exhibit 9A.5. An employee earnings report accumulates information that can show when an employee's earnings reach the tax-exempt points for FICA, FUTA, and SUTA taxes. It also gives data an employer needs to prepare Form W-2.

Payroll Procedures

Employers must be able to compute federal income tax for payroll purposes. This section explains how we compute this tax and how to use a payroll bank account.

Computing Federal Income Taxes To compute the amount of taxes withheld from each employee's wages, we need to determine both the employee's wages earned and the employee's number of *withholding allowances.* Each employee records the number of withholding allowances claimed on a withholding allowance certificate, **Form W-4,** filed with the employer. When the number of withholding allowances increases, the amount of income taxes withheld decreases.

Employers often use a **wage bracket withholding table** similar to the one shown in Exhibit 9A.6 to compute the federal income taxes withheld from each employee's gross pay. The table in Exhibit 9A.6 is for a single employee paid weekly. Tables are also provided for married employees and for biweekly, semimonthly, and monthly pay periods (most payroll software includes these tables). When using a wage bracket withholding table to compute federal income tax withheld from an employee's gross wages, we need to locate an employee's wage bracket within the first two columns. We then find the amount withheld by looking in the Withholding Allowance column for that employee.

Payroll Bank Account Companies with few employees often pay them with checks drawn on the company's regular bank account. Companies with many employees often use a special **payroll bank account** to pay employees. When this account is used, a company either (1) draws one check for total payroll on the regular bank account and deposits it in the payroll bank account or (2) executes an *electronic funds transfer* to the payroll bank account. Individual payroll checks are then drawn on this payroll bank account. Since only one check for the total payroll is drawn on the regular bank account each payday, use of a special payroll bank account helps with internal control. It also helps in reconciling the regular bank account. When companies use a payroll bank account, they usually include check numbers in the payroll register. The payroll register in Exhibit 9A.3 shows check numbers in column 1. For instance, Check No.

	A	B	C	D	E	F	G	H
1	Phoenix Sales & Service							
2	Employee Earnings Report							
3	For Month Ended Dec. 31, 2015							
4	Employee ID			FIT	SIT	FICA-SS_EE	FICA-Med_EE	
5	Employee	Date	Gross	[blank]	[blank]	[blank]	[blank]	Net
6	SS No.	Reference	Pay	FUTA	SUTA	FICA-SS_ER	FICA-Med_ER	Pay
7	Beginning	11/26/15	2,910.00	−188.42	−15.08	−180.42	−42.20	2,483.88
8	Balance for	(balance)						
9	Robert Austin			−17.46	−78.57	−180.42	−42.20	
10	AR101	12/03/15	400.00	−28.99	−2.32	−24.80	−5.80	338.09
11	Robert Austin	9049						
12	333-22-9999			−2.40	−10.80	−24.80	−5.80	
13	AR101	12/10/15	400.00	−28.99	−2.32	−24.80	−5.80	338.09
14	Robert Austin	9055						
15	333-22-9999			−2.40	−10.80	−24.80	−5.80	
16	AR101	12/17/15	400.00	−28.99	−2.32	−24.80	−5.80	338.09
17	Robert Austin	9061						
18	333-22-9999			−2.40	−10.80	−24.80	−5.80	
19	AR101	12/24/15	400.00	−28.99	−2.32	−24.80	−5.80	338.09
20	Robert Austin	9067						
21	333-22-9999			−2.40	−10.80	−24.80	−5.80	
22	AR101	12/31/15	400.00	−28.99	−2.32	−24.80	−5.80	338.09
23	Robert Austin	9073						
24	333-22-9999			−2.40	−10.80	−24.80	−5.80	
25	Total 5-wk month		2,000.00	−144.95	−11.60	−124.00	−29.00	1,690.45
26	thru 12/31/15							
27				−12.00	−54.00	−124.00	−29.00	
28	Year-to-date	12/31/15	4,910.00	−333.37	−26.68	−304.42	−71.20	4,174.33
29	Total for Robert	(balance)						
30	Austin			−29.46	−132.57	−304.42	−71.20	
31								

EXHIBIT 9A.5

Employee Earnings Report

Point: Year-end balances agree with W-2.

SINGLE Persons—WEEKLY Payroll Period

If the wages are–		And the number of withholding allowances claimed is—										
At least	But less than	0	1	2	3	4	5	6	7	8	9	10
		The amount of income tax to be withheld is—										
$600	$610	$76	$67	$58	$49	$39	$30	$21	$12	$6	$0	$0
610	620	79	69	59	50	41	32	22	13	7	1	0
620	630	81	70	61	52	42	33	24	15	8	2	0
630	640	84	72	62	53	44	35	25	16	9	3	0
640	650	86	73	64	55	45	36	27	18	10	4	0
650	660	89	75	65	56	47	38	28	19	11	5	0
660	670	91	76	67	58	48	39	30	21	12	6	0
670	680	94	78	68	59	50	41	31	22	13	7	1
680	690	96	81	70	61	51	42	33	24	14	8	2
690	700	99	83	71	62	53	44	34	25	16	9	3
700	710	101	86	73	64	54	45	35	27	17	10	4
710	720	104	88	74	65	56	47	37	28	19	11	5
720	730	106	91	76	67	57	48	39	30	20	12	6
730	740	109	93	78	68	59	50	40	31	22	13	7
740	750	111	96	80	70	60	51	42	33	23	14	8

EXHIBIT 9A.6

Wage Bracket Withholding Table

9001 is issued to Robert Austin. With this information, the payroll register serves as a supplementary record of wages earned by and paid to employees.

Who Pays What Payroll Taxes and Benefits We conclude this appendix with the following table identifying who pays which payroll taxes and which common employee benefits such as medical, disability, pension, charitable, and union costs. Who pays which employee benefits, and what portion, is subject to agreements between companies and their workers. Also, self-employed workers must pay both the employer and employee FICA taxes for Social Security and Medicare.

QC5

Point: IRS Statistics of Income Bulletin (Winter 2012) reports the following average (effective) income tax rate for different categories of U.S. income earners:

Top 1%	24%
Top 5%	20%
Top 10%	18%
Bottom 50%	1.85%

Employer Payroll Taxes and Costs	Employee Payroll Deductions
• FICA—Social Security taxes	• FICA—Social Security taxes
• FICA—Medicare taxes	• FICA—Medicare taxes
• FUTA (federal unemployment taxes)	• Federal income taxes
• SUTA (state unemployment taxes)	• State and local income taxes
• Share of medical coverage, if any	• Share of medical coverage, if any
• Share of pension coverage, if any	• Share of pension coverage, if any
• Share of other benefits, if any	• Share of other benefits, if any

APPENDIX

9B Corporate Income Taxes

This appendix explains current liabilities involving income taxes for corporations.

Income Tax Liabilities Corporations are subject to income taxes and must estimate their income tax liability when preparing financial statements. Since income tax expense is created by earning income, a liability is incurred when income is earned. This tax must be paid quarterly under federal regulations. To illustrate, consider a corporation that prepares monthly financial statements. Based on its income in January 2015, this corporation estimates that it owes income taxes of $12,100. The following adjusting entry records this estimate:

Assets = Liabilities + Equity
+12,100 −12,100

Jan. 31	Income Taxes Expense	12,100	
	Income Taxes Payable		12,100
	To accrue January income taxes.		

The tax liability is recorded each month until the first quarterly payment is made. If the company's estimated taxes for this first quarter total $30,000, the entry to record its payment is

Assets = Liabilities + Equity
−30,000 −30,000

Apr. 10	Income Taxes Payable	30,000	
	Cash		30,000
	Paid estimated quarterly income taxes based on first-quarter income.		

This process of accruing and then paying estimated income taxes continues through the year. When annual financial statements are prepared at year-end, the corporation knows its actual total income and the actual amount of income taxes it must pay. This information allows it to properly record income taxes expense for the fourth quarter so that the total of the four quarters' expense amounts equals the actual taxes paid to the government.

Deferred Income Tax Liabilities An income tax liability for corporations can arise when the amount of income before taxes that the corporation reports on its income statement is not the same as the amount of income reported on its income tax return. This difference occurs because income tax laws and GAAP measure income differently. (Differences between tax laws and GAAP arise because Congress uses tax laws to generate receipts, stimulate the economy, and influence behavior, whereas GAAP are intended to provide financial information useful for business decisions. Also, tax accounting often follows the cash basis, whereas GAAP follows the accrual basis.)

Some differences between tax laws and GAAP are temporary. *Temporary differences* arise when the tax return and the income statement report a revenue or expense in different years. As an example, companies are often able to deduct higher amounts of depreciation in the early years of an asset's life and smaller amounts in later years for tax reporting in comparison to GAAP. This means that in the early years, depreciation for tax reporting is often more than depreciation on the income statement. In later years, depreciation for tax reporting is often less than depreciation on the income statement. When temporary differences exist between taxable income on the tax return and the income before taxes on the income statement, corporations compute income taxes expense based on the income reported on the income statement. The result is that income taxes expense reported in the income statement is often different from the amount of income taxes payable to the government. This difference is the **deferred income tax liability.**

To illustrate, assume that in recording its usual quarterly income tax payments, a corporation computes $25,000 of income taxes expense. It also determines that only $21,000 is currently due and $4,000 is deferred to future years (a timing difference). The entry to record this end-of-period adjustment is

Dec. 31	Income Taxes Expense	25,000	
	Income Taxes Payable		21,000
	Deferred Income Tax Liability		4,000
	To record tax expense and deferred tax liability.		

Assets	=	Liabilities	+	Equity
		+21,000		−25,000
		+4,000		

The credit to Income Taxes Payable reflects the amount currently due to be paid. The credit to Deferred Income Tax Liability reflects tax payments deferred until future years when the temporary difference reverses.

Temporary differences also can cause a company to pay income taxes *before* they are reported on the income statement as expense. If so, the company reports a *Deferred Income Tax Asset* on its balance sheet.

Summary

C1 Describe current and long-term liabilities and their characteristics. Liabilities are probable future payments of assets or services that past transactions or events obligate an entity to make. Current liabilities are due within one year or the operating cycle, whichever is longer. All other liabilities are long term.

C2 Identify and describe known current liabilities. Known (determinable) current liabilities are set by agreements or laws and are measurable with little uncertainty. They include accounts payable, sales taxes payable, unearned revenues, notes payable, payroll liabilities, and the current portion of long-term debt.

C3 Explain how to account for contingent liabilities. If an uncertain future payment depends on a probable future event and the amount can be reasonably estimated, the payment is recorded as a liability. The uncertain future payment is reported as a contingent liability (in the notes) if (*a*) the future event is reasonably possible but not probable or (*b*) the event is probable but the payment amount cannot be reasonably estimated.

A1 Compute the times interest earned ratio and use it to analyze liabilities. Times interest earned is computed by dividing a company's net income before interest expense and income taxes by the amount of interest expense. The times interest earned ratio reflects a company's ability to pay interest obligations.

P1 Prepare entries to account for short-term notes payable. Short-term notes payable are current liabilities; most bear interest. When a short-term note's face value equals the amount borrowed, it identifies a rate of interest to be paid at maturity.

P2 Compute and record *employee* payroll deductions and liabilities. Employee payroll deductions include FICA taxes, income taxes, and voluntary deductions such as for pensions and charities. They make up the difference between gross and net pay.

P3 Compute and record *employer* payroll expenses and liabilities. An employer's payroll expenses include employees' gross earnings, any employee benefits, and the payroll taxes levied on the employer. Payroll liabilities include employees' net pay amounts, withholdings from employee wages, any employer-promised benefits, and the employer's payroll taxes.

P4 Account for estimated liabilities, including warranties and bonuses. Liabilities for health and pension benefits, warranties, and bonuses are recorded with estimated amounts. These items are recognized as expenses when incurred and matched with revenues generated.

P5A Identify and describe the details of payroll reports, records, and procedures. Employers report FICA taxes and federal income tax withholdings using Form 941. FUTA taxes are reported on Form 940. Earnings and deductions are reported to each employee and the federal government on Form W-2. An employer's payroll records often include a payroll register for each pay period, payroll checks and statements of earnings, and individual employee earnings reports.

Guidance Answers to Decision Maker and Decision Ethics

Web Designer You need to be concerned about being an accomplice to unlawful payroll activities. Not paying federal and state taxes on wages earned is illegal and unethical. Such payments also will not provide the employee with Social Security and some Medicare credits. The best course of action is to request payment by check. If this fails to change the owner's payment practices, you must consider quitting this job.

Entrepreneur Risk is partly reflected by the times interest earned ratio. This ratio for the first franchise is 1.5 [($100,000 + $200,000)/$200,000], whereas the ratio for the second franchise is 3.5 [($100,000 + $40,000)/$40,000]. This analysis shows that the first franchise is more at risk of incurring a loss if its sales decline. The second question asks about variability of income. If income greatly varies, this increases the risk an owner will not earn sufficient income to cover interest. Since the first franchise has the greater variability, it is a riskier investment.

Key Terms

Contingent liability
Current liabilities
Current portion of long-term debt
Deferred income tax liability
Employee benefits
Employee earnings report
Estimated liability
Federal depository bank
Federal Insurance Contributions Act (FICA) taxes
Federal Unemployment Tax Act (FUTA)
Form 940
Form 941
Form W-2
Form W-4
Gross pay
Known liabilities
Long-term liabilities
Merit rating
Net pay
Payroll bank account
Payroll deductions
Payroll register
Short-term note payable
State Unemployment Tax Act (SUTA)
Times interest earned
Wage bracket withholding table
Warranty

Multiple Choice Quiz Answers at end of chapter

1. On December 1, a company signed a $6,000, 90-day, 5% note payable, with principal plus interest due on March 1 of the following year. What amount of interest expense should be accrued at December 31 on the note?
a. $300 **c.** $100 **e.** $0
b. $25 **d.** $75

2. An employee earned $50,000 during the year. FICA tax for Social Security is 6.2% and FICA tax for Medicare is 1.45%. The employer's share of FICA taxes is
a. Zero, since the employee's pay exceeds the FICA limit.
b. Zero, since FICA is not an employer tax.
c. $3,100
d. $725
e. $3,825

3. Assume the FUTA tax rate is 0.6% and the SUTA tax rate is 5.4%. Both taxes are applied to the first $7,000 of an employee's pay. What is the total unemployment tax an employer must pay on an employee's annual wages of $40,000?
a. $2,400
b. $420
c. $42
d. $378
e. Zero; the employee's wages exceed the $7,000 maximum.

4. A company sells big-screen televisions for $3,000 each. Each television has a two-year warranty that covers the replacement of defective parts. It is estimated that 1% of all televisions sold will be returned under warranty at an average cost of $250 each. During July, the company sold 10,000 big screen televisions, and 80 were serviced under the warranty during July at a total cost of $18,000. The credit balance in the Estimated Warranty Liability account at July 1 was $26,000. What is the company's warranty expense for the month of July?
a. $51,000 **c.** $25,000 **e.** $18,000
b. $1,000 **d.** $33,000

5. Employees earn vacation pay at the rate of one day per month. During October, 150 employees qualify for one vacation day each. Their average daily wage is $175 per day. What is the amount of vacation benefit expense for October?
a. $26,250 **c.** $2,100 **e.** $150
b. $175 **d.** $63,875

A(B) *Superscript letter A (B) denotes assignments based on Appendix 9A (9B).*
I Icon denotes assignments that involve decision making.

Discussion Questions

1. I What is the difference between a current and a long-term liability?

2. What is an estimated liability?

3. I What are the three important questions concerning the uncertainty of liabilities?

4. If $988 is the total of a sale that includes its sales tax of 4%, what is the selling price of the item only?

5. What is the combined amount (in percent) of the employee and employer Social Security tax rate? (Assume wages do not exceed $200,000 per year.)

6. What is the current Medicare tax rate? This rate is applied to what maximum level of salary and wages?

7. Which payroll taxes are the employee's responsibility and which are the employer's responsibility?

8. What determines the amount deducted from an employee's wages for federal income taxes?

9. What is an employer's unemployment merit rating? How are these ratings assigned to employers?

10. Why are warranty liabilities usually recognized on the balance sheet as liabilities even when they are uncertain?

11. Suppose that a company has a facility located where disastrous weather conditions often occur. Should it report a probable loss from a future disaster as a liability on its balance sheet? Explain.

12.[A] What is a wage bracket withholding table?

13.[A] What amount of income tax is withheld from the salary of an employee who is single with two withholding allowances and earning $725 per week? What if the employee earned $625 and has no withholding allowances? (Use Exhibit 9A.6.)

14. Refer to **Apple**'s balance sheet in Appendix A. What is the amount of Apple's accounts payable as of September 28, 2013? **APPLE**

15. Refer to **Google**'s balance sheet in Appendix A. What accrued expenses (liabilities) does Google report at December 31, 2013? **GOOGLE**

16. Refer to **Samsung**'s balance sheet in Appendix A. List Samsung's current liabilities as of December 31, 2013. **Samsung**

17. Refer to **Samsung**'s recent balance sheet in Appendix A. What current liabilities related to income taxes are on its balance sheet? Explain the meaning of each income tax account identified. **Samsung**

connect

QUICK STUDY

QS 9-1
Classifying liabilities
C1

Which of the following items are normally classified as current liabilities for a company that has a 15-month operating cycle?

____ **1.** Portion of long-term note due in 15 months.
____ **2.** Note payable maturing in 2 years.
____ **3.** Note payable due in 18 months.
____ **4.** Note payable due in 11 months.
____ **5.** FICA taxes payable.
____ **6.** Salaries payable.

QS 9-2
Accounting for sales taxes
C2

Dextra Computing sells merchandise for $6,000 cash on September 30 (cost of merchandise is $3,900). The sales tax law requires Dextra to collect 5% sales tax on every dollar of merchandise sold. Record the entry for the $6,000 sale and its applicable sales tax. Also record the entry that shows the remittance of the 5% tax on this sale to the state government on October 15.

QS 9-3
Unearned revenue C2

Ticketsales, Inc., receives $5,000,000 cash in advance ticket sales for a four-date tour of Bon Jovi. Record the advance ticket sales on October 31. Record the revenue earned for the first concert date of November 5, assuming it represents one-fourth of the advance ticket sales.

QS 9-4
Interest-bearing note transactions P1

On November 7, 2015, Mura Company borrows $160,000 cash by signing a 90-day, 8% note payable with a face value of $160,000. (1) Compute the accrued interest payable on December 31, 2015, (2) prepare the journal entry to record the accrued interest expense at December 31, 2015, and (3) prepare the journal entry to record payment of the note at maturity.

QS 9-5
Record employee payroll taxes
P2

On January 15, the end of the first biweekly pay period of the year, North Company's payroll register showed that its employees earned $35,000 of sales salaries. Withholdings from the employees' salaries include FICA Social Security taxes at the rate of 6.2%, FICA Medicare taxes at the rate of 1.45%, $6,500 of federal income taxes, $772.50 of medical insurance deductions, and $120 of union dues. No employee earned more than $7,000 in this first period. Prepare the journal entry to record North Company's January 15 (employee) payroll expenses and liabilities. (Round amounts to cents.)

QS 9-6
Record employer payroll taxes
P3

Merger Co. has 10 employees, each of whom earns $2,000 per month and has been employed since January 1. FICA Social Security taxes are 6.2% of the first $117,000 paid to each employee, and FICA Medicare taxes are 1.45% of gross pay. FUTA taxes are 0.6% and SUTA taxes are 5.4% of the first $7,000 paid to each employee. Prepare the March 31 journal entry to record the March payroll taxes expenses. (Round amounts to cents.)

QS 9-7
Accounting for bonuses
P4

Noura Company offers an annual bonus to employees if the company meets certain net income goals. Prepare the journal entry to record a $15,000 bonus owed to its workers (to be shared equally) at calendar year-end.

QS 9-8
Accounting for vacations
P4

Chavez Co.'s salaried employees earn four weeks' vacation per year. It pays $312,000.00 in total employee salaries for 52 weeks, but its employees work only 48 weeks. This means Chavez's total weekly expense is $6,500 ($312,000/48 weeks) instead of the $6,000 cash paid weekly to the employees ($312,000/52 weeks). Record Chavez's weekly vacation benefits expense.

QS 9-9
Recording warranty repairs P4

On September 11, 2014, Home Store sells a mower for $500 with a one-year warranty that covers parts. Warranty expense is estimated at 8% of sales. On July 24, 2015, the mower is brought in for repairs covered under the warranty requiring $35 in materials taken from the Repair Parts Inventory. Prepare the September 11, 2014, entry to record the mower sale, and the July 24, 2015, entry to record the warranty repairs.

QS 9-10
Accounting for contingent liabilities
C3

The following legal claims exist for Huprey Co. Identify the accounting treatment for each claim as either (*a*) a liability that is recorded or (*b*) an item described in notes to its financial statements.

____ **1.** Huprey (defendant) estimates that a pending lawsuit could result in damages of $1,250,000; it is reasonably possible that the plaintiff will win the case.

____ **2.** Huprey faces a probable loss on a pending lawsuit; the amount is not reasonably estimable.

____ **3.** Huprey estimates damages in a case at $3,500,000 with a high probability of losing the case.

QS 9-11
Times interest earned A1

Compute the times interest earned for Park Company, which reports income before interest expense and income taxes of $1,885,000 and interest expense of $145,000. Interpret its times interest earned (assume that its competitors average a times interest earned of 4.0).

QS 9-12[A]
Net pay and tax computations
P5

The payroll records of Speedy Software show the following information about Marsha Gottschalk, an employee, for the weekly pay period ending September 30, 2015. Gottschalk is single and claims one allowance. Compute her Social Security tax (6.2%), Medicare tax (1.45%), federal income tax withholding, state income tax (1.0%), and net pay for the current pay period. (Use the withholding table in Exhibit 9A.6 and round tax amounts to the nearest cent.)

Total (gross) earnings for current pay period..........	$ 740
Cumulative earnings of previous pay periods..........	$9,700

Check Net pay, $579.99

QS 9-13[B]
Record deferred income tax liability P4

Sera Corporation has made and recorded its quarterly income tax payments. After a final review of taxes for the year, the company identifies an additional $40,000 of income tax expense that should be recorded. A portion of this additional expense, $6,000, is deferred for payment in future years. Record Sera's year-end adjusting entry for income tax expense.

QS 9-14
International accounting standards
C1 C2

Answer each of the following related to international accounting standards.

a. In general, how similar or different are the definitions and characteristics of current liabilities between IFRS and U.S. GAAP?

b. Companies reporting under IFRS often reference a set of current liabilities with the title *financial liabilities.* Identify two current liabilities that would be classified under financial liabilities per IFRS. (*Hint:* **Nokia** provides examples in this chapter.)

connect

EXERCISES

Exercise 9-1
Classifying liabilities
C1

The following items appear on the balance sheet of a company with a two-month operating cycle. Identify the proper classification of each item as follows: *C* if it is a current liability, *L* if it is a long-term liability, or *N* if it is not a liability.

______ **1.** Notes payable (due in 13 to 24 months).
______ **2.** Notes payable (due in 6 to 12 months).
______ **3.** Notes payable (mature in five years).
______ **4.** Current portion of long-term debt.
______ **5.** Notes payable (due in 120 days).
______ **6.** FUTA taxes payable.
______ **7.** Accounts receivable.
______ **8.** Sales taxes payable.
______ **9.** Salaries payable.
______ **10.** Wages payable.

Exercise 9-2
Recording known current liabilities
C2

Prepare any necessary entries at December 31, 2015, for Piper Company in preparation for year-end financial statements for each of the following separate transactions and events.

1. Piper Company records a year-end entry for $10,000 of previously unrecorded cash sales (costing $5,000) and its sales taxes at a rate of 4%.

2. The company earned $50,000 of $125,000 previously received in advance and originally recorded as unearned services revenue.

Sylvestor Systems borrows $110,000 cash on May 15, 2015, by signing a 60-day, 12% note.

1. On what date does this note mature?

2. Suppose the face value of the note equals $110,000, the principal of the loan. Prepare the journal entries to record (*a*) issuance of the note and (*b*) payment of the note at maturity.

Exercise 9-3
Accounting for note payable P1

Check (2*b*) Interest expense, $2,200

Keesha Co. borrows $200,000 cash on November 1, 2015, by signing a 90-day, 9% note with a face value of $200,000.

1. On what date does this note mature?

2. How much interest expense results from this note in 2015? (Assume a 360-day year.)

3. How much interest expense results from this note in 2016? (Assume a 360-day year.)

4. Prepare journal entries to record (*a*) issuance of the note, (*b*) accrual of interest at the end of 2015, and (*c*) payment of the note at maturity. (Assume no reversing entries are made.)

Exercise 9-4
Interest-bearing notes payable with year-end adjustments P1

Check (2) $3,000
(3) $1,500

BMX Company has one employee. FICA Social Security taxes are 6.2% of the first $117,000 paid to its employee, and FICA Medicare taxes are 1.45% of gross pay. For BMX, its FUTA taxes are 0.6% and SUTA taxes are 2.9% of the first $7,000 paid to its employee. Compute BMX's amounts for each of these four taxes as applied to the employee's gross earnings for September under each of three separate situations (*a*), (*b*), and (*c*). (Round amounts to cents.)

Exercise 9-5
Computing payroll taxes
P2 P3

	Gross Pay through August	Gross Pay for September
a.	$ 6,400	$ 800
b.	18,200	2,100
c.	110,700	8,000

Check (*a*) FUTA, $3.60; SUTA, $17.40

Using the data in *situation a* of Exercise 9-5, prepare the employer's September 30 journal entries to record salary expense and its related payroll liabilities for this employee. The employee's federal income taxes withheld by the employer are $80 for this pay period. (Round amounts to cents.)

Exercise 9-6
Payroll-related journal entries P2

Using the data in *situation a* of Exercise 9-5, prepare the employer's September 30 journal entries to record the *employer's* payroll taxes expense and its related liabilities. (Round amounts to cents.)

Exercise 9-7
Payroll-related journal entries P3

The following monthly data are taken from Ramirez Company at July 31: sales salaries, $200,000; office salaries, $160,000; federal income taxes withheld, $90,000; state income taxes withheld, $20,000; Social Security taxes withheld, $22,320; Medicare taxes withheld, $5,220; medical insurance premiums, $7,000; life insurance premiums, $4,000; union dues deducted, $1,000; and salaries subject to unemployment taxes, $50,000. The employee pays 40% of medical and life insurance premiums.

Prepare journal entries to record: (1) accrued payroll, including employee deductions, for July; (2) cash payment of the net payroll (salaries payable) for July; (3) accrued employer payroll taxes, and other related employment expenses, for July—assume that FICA taxes are identical to those on employees and that SUTA taxes are 5.4% and FUTA taxes are 0.6%; and (4) cash payment of all liabilities related to the July payroll.

Exercise 9-8
Recording payroll
P2 P3

Mester Company has 10 employees. FICA Social Security taxes are 6.2% of the first $117,000 paid to each employee, and FICA Medicare taxes are 1.45% of gross pay. FUTA taxes are 0.6% and SUTA taxes are 5.4% of the first $7,000 paid to each employee. Cumulative pay for the current year for each of its employees follows.

Exercise 9-9
Computing payroll taxes
P2 P3

Employee	Cumulative Pay	Employee	Cumulative Pay	Employee	Cumulative Pay
Ken S.	$ 6,000	Ann T.	$146,500	Lori K.	$119,500
Tim V.	60,200	Kathleen K.	106,900	Kitty O.	36,900
Steve S.	87,000	Michelle H.	117,000	John W.	4,000

a. Prepare a table with the following column headings: Employee; Cumulative Pay; Pay Subject to FICA Social Security Taxes; Pay Subject to FICA Medicare Taxes; Pay Subject to FUTA Taxes; Pay Subject to SUTA Taxes. Compute the amounts in this table for each employee and total the columns.

b. For the company, compute each total for: FICA Social Security taxes, FICA Medicare taxes, FUTA taxes, and SUTA taxes. (*Hint:* Remember to include in those totals any employee share of taxes that the company must collect.) (Round amounts to cents.)

Exercise 9-10
Warranty expense and liability computations and entries P4

Check (1) $240

(4) $31

Hitzu Co. sold a copier costing $4,800 with a two-year parts warranty to a customer on August 16, 2015, for $6,000 cash. Hitzu uses the perpetual inventory system. On November 22, 2016, the copier requires on-site repairs that are completed the same day. The repairs cost $209 for materials taken from the Repair Parts Inventory. These are the only repairs required in 2016 for this copier. Based on experience, Hitzu expects to incur warranty costs equal to 4% of dollar sales. It records warranty expense with an adjusting entry at the end of each year.

1. How much warranty expense does the company report in 2015 for this copier?
2. How much is the estimated warranty liability for this copier as of December 31, 2015?
3. How much warranty expense does the company report in 2016 for this copier?
4. How much is the estimated warranty liability for this copier as of December 31, 2016?
5. Prepare journal entries to record (*a*) the copier's sale; (*b*) the adjustment on December 31, 2015, to recognize the warranty expense; and (*c*) the repairs that occur in November 2016.

Exercise 9-11
Computing and recording bonuses P4

Check (1) $14,563

For the year ended December 31, 2015, Lopez Company has implemented an employee bonus program equal to 3% of Lopez's net income, which employees will share equally. Lopez's net income (pre-bonus) is expected to be $500,000, and bonus expense is deducted in computing net income.

1. Compute the amount of the bonus payable to the employees at year-end (use the method described in the chapter and round to the nearest dollar).
2. Prepare the journal entry at December 31, 2015, to record the bonus due the employees.
3. Prepare the journal entry at January 19, 2016, to record payment of the bonus to employees.

Exercise 9-12
Accounting for estimated liabilities
P4

Prepare any necessary adjusting entries at December 31, 2015, for Maxum Company's year-end financial statements for each of the following separate transactions and events.

1. Employees earn vacation pay at a rate of one day per month. During December, 20 employees qualify for one vacation day each. Their average daily wage is $160 per employee.
2. During December, Maxum Company sold 12,000 units of a product that carries a 60-day warranty. December sales for this product total $460,000. The company expects 10% of the units to need warranty repairs, and it estimates the average repair cost per unit will be $15.

Exercise 9-13
Accounting for contingent liabilities
C3

Prepare any necessary adjusting entries at December 31, 2015, for Melbourn Company's year-end financial statements for each of the following separate transactions and events.

1. Melbourn Company guarantees the $100,000 debt of a supplier. The supplier will probably not default on the debt.
2. A disgruntled employee is suing Melbourn Company. Legal advisers believe that the company will probably need to pay damages, but the amount cannot be reasonably estimated.

Exercise 9-14
Computing and interpreting times interest earned A1

Check (*b*) 11.00

Use the following information from separate companies *a* through *f* to compute times interest earned. Which company indicates the strongest ability to pay interest expense as it comes due? (Round ratios to two decimals.)

	Net Income (Loss)	Interest Expense	Income Taxes
a.	$115,000	$44,000	$ 35,000
b.	110,000	16,000	50,000
c.	100,000	12,000	70,000
d.	235,000	14,000	130,000
e.	59,000	14,000	30,000
f.	(5,000)	10,000	0

Exercise 9-15[B]
Accounting for income taxes
P4

Nishi Corporation prepares financial statements for each month-end. As part of its accounting process, estimated income taxes are accrued each month for 30% of the current month's net income. The income taxes are paid in the first month of each quarter for the amount accrued for the prior quarter. The following information is available for the fourth quarter of year 2015. When tax computations are completed on January 20, 2016, Nishi determines that the quarter's Income Taxes Payable account balance should be $28,300 on December 31, 2015 (its unadjusted balance is $24,690).

October 2015 net income.	$28,600
November 2015 net income	19,100
December 2015 net income	34,600

1. Determine the amount of the accounting adjustment (dated as of December 31, 2015) to produce the proper ending balance in the Income Taxes Payable account.

2. Prepare journal entries to record (*a*) the December 31, 2015, adjustment to the Income Taxes Payable account and (*b*) the January 20, 2016, payment of the fourth-quarter taxes.

Check (1) $3,610

Exercise 9-16ᴬ
Gross and net pay computation
P5

Lenny Florita, an unmarried employee, works 48 hours in the week ended January 12. His pay rate is $14 per hour, and his wages are subject to no deductions other than FICA Social Security, FICA Medicare, and federal income taxes. He claims two withholding allowances. Compute his regular pay, overtime pay (for this company, workers earn 150% of their regular rate for hours in excess of 40 per week), and gross pay. Then compute his FICA tax deduction (use 6.2% for the Social Security portion and 1.45% for the Medicare portion), income tax deduction (use the wage bracket withholding table from Exhibit 9A.6), total deductions, and net pay. (Round tax amounts to the nearest cent.)

Check Net pay, $596.30

Exercise 9-17
Preparing payroll register and related entries
P5

Stark Company has five employees. Employees paid by the hour receive a $10 per hour pay rate for the regular 40-hour workweek plus one and one-half times the hourly rate for each overtime hour beyond the 40 hours per week. Hourly employees are paid every two weeks, but salaried employees are paid monthly on the last biweekly payday of each month. FICA Social Security taxes are 6.2% of the first $117,000 paid to each employee, and FICA Medicare taxes are 1.45% of gross pay. FUTA taxes are 0.6% and SUTA taxes are 5.4% of the first $7,000 paid to each employee. The company has a benefits plan that includes medical insurance, life insurance, and retirement funding for employees. Under this plan, employees must contribute 5 percent of their gross income as a payroll withholding, which the company matches with double the amount. Following is the partially completed payroll register for the biweekly period ending August 31, which is the last payday of August.

Employee	Cumulative Pay (Excludes Current Period)	Current Period Gross Pay: Pay Type	Pay Hours	Gross Pay	FIT / SIT	FUTA / SUTA	FICA-SS_EE / FICA-SS_ER	FICA-Med_EE / FICA-Med_ER	EE-Ben_Plan Withholding / ER-Ben_Plan Expense	Employee Net Pay
Kathleen	$115,200.00	Salary	---	$7,000.00	$2,000.00					
					300.00					
Anthony	6,800.00	Salary	---	500.00	80.00					
					20.00					
Nichole	15,000.00	Regular	80		110.00					
		Overtime	8		25.00					
Zoey	6,500.00	Regular	80		100.00					
		Overtime	4		22.00					
Gracie	5,000.00	Regular	74	740.00	90.00					
		Overtime	0	0.00	21.00					
Totals	$148,500.00				2,380.00					
					388.00					

* Table abbreviations follow those in Exhibit 9A.3; and "Ben_Plan" refers to employee (EE) withholding or the employer (ER) expense for the benefits plan.

a. Complete this payroll register by filling in all cells for the pay period ended August 31. *Hint:* See Exhibit 9A.5 for guidance. (Round amounts to cents.)

b. Prepare the August 31 journal entry to record the accrued biweekly payroll and related liabilities for deductions.

c. Prepare the August 31 journal entry to record the employer's cash payment of the net payroll of part *b*.

d. Prepare the August 31 journal entry to record the employer's payroll taxes including the contribution to the benefits plan.

e. Prepare the August 31 journal entry to pay all liabilities (except for the net payroll in part *c*) for this biweekly period.

Exercise 9-18
Accounting for current liabilities under IFRS
P4

Volvo Group reports the following information for its product warranty costs as of December 31, 2013, along with provisions and utilizations of warranty liabilities for the year ended December 31, 2013 (SEK in millions).

Provision for product warranty Warranty provisions are estimated with consideration of historical claims statistics, the warranty period, the average time-lag between faults occurring and claims to the company and anticipated changes in quality indexes. Estimated costs for product warranties are recognized as cost of sales when the products are sold . . . Differences between actual warranty claims and the estimated claims generally affect the recognized expense and provisions in future periods. Refunds from suppliers, that decrease the Volvo Group's warranty costs, are recognized to the extent these are considered to be certain. As of December 31, 2013 (2012) warranty cost provisions amount to 9,881 (8,852).

Product warranty liabilities, December 31, 2012	SEK 8,852
Additional provisions to product warranty liabilities	7,706
Utilizations and reductions of product warranty liabilities	(6,677)
Product warranty liabilities, December 31, 2013	9,881

1. Prepare Volvo's journal entry to record its estimated warranty liabilities (provisions) for 2013.
2. Prepare Volvo's journal entry to record its costs (utilizations) related to its warranty program for 2013. Assume those costs involve replacements taken out of Inventory, with no cash involved.
3. How much warranty expense does Volvo report for 2013?

connect

PROBLEM SET A

Problem 9-1A
Short-term notes payable transactions and entries

P1

Tyrell Co. entered into the following transactions involving short-term liabilities in 2014 and 2015.

2014

Apr. 20	Purchased $40,250 of merchandise on credit from Locust, terms are 1/10, n/30. Tyrell uses the perpetual inventory system.
May 19	Replaced the April 20 account payable to Locust with a 90-day, $35,000 note bearing 10% annual interest along with paying $5,250 in cash.
July 8	Borrowed $80,000 cash from National Bank by signing a 120-day, 9% interest-bearing note with a face value of $80,000.
___?___	Paid the amount due on the note to Locust at the maturity date.
___?___	Paid the amount due on the note to National Bank at the maturity date.
Nov. 28	Borrowed $42,000 cash from Fargo Bank by signing a 60-day, 8% interest-bearing note with a face value of $42,000.
Dec. 31	Recorded an adjusting entry for accrued interest on the note to Fargo Bank.

2015

___?___	Paid the amount due on the note to Fargo Bank at the maturity date.

Required

1. Determine the maturity date for each of the three notes described.
2. Determine the interest due at maturity for each of the three notes. (Assume a 360-day year.)
3. Determine the interest expense to be recorded in the adjusting entry at the end of 2014.
4. Determine the interest expense to be recorded in 2015.
5. Prepare journal entries for all the preceding transactions and events for years 2014 and 2015.

Check (2) Locust, $875

(3) $308

(4) $252

Problem 9-2A
Entries for payroll transactions

P2 P3

On January 8, the end of the first weekly pay period of the year, Regis Company's payroll register showed that its employees earned $22,760 of office salaries and $65,840 of sales salaries. Withholdings from the employees' salaries include FICA Social Security taxes at the rate of 6.2%, FICA Medicare taxes at the rate of 1.45%, $12,860 of federal income taxes, $1,340 of medical insurance deductions, and $840 of union dues. No employee earned more than $7,000 in this first period.

Required

1. Calculate FICA Social Security taxes payable and FICA Medicare taxes payable. Prepare the journal entry to record Regis Company's January 8 (employee) payroll expenses and liabilities. (Round amounts to cents.)
2. Prepare the journal entry to record Regis's (employer) payroll taxes resulting from the January 8 payroll. Regis's merit rating reduces its state unemployment tax rate to 4% of the first $7,000 paid each employee. The federal unemployment tax rate is 0.6%. (Round amounts to cents.)

Check (1) Cr. Salaries Payable, $66,782.10

(2) Dr. Payroll Taxes Expense, $10,853.50

Problem 9-3A
Payroll expenses, withholdings, and taxes
P2 P3

Paloma Co. Stars has four employees. FICA Social Security taxes are 6.2% of the first $117,000 paid to each employee, and FICA Medicare taxes are 1.45% of gross pay. Also, for the first $7,000 paid to each employee, the company's FUTA taxes are 0.6% and SUTA taxes are 2.15%. The company is preparing its payroll calculations for the week ended August 25. Payroll records show the following information for the company's four employees.

	A	B	C	D
1		Gross Pay		Current Week
2	Name	through Aug. 18	Gross Pay	Income Tax Withholding
3	Dahlia	$115,900	$2,000	$284
4	Trey	116,100	900	145
5	Kiesha	7,100	450	39
6	Chee	1,050	400	30
7				

In addition to gross pay, the company must pay one-half of the $60 per employee weekly health insurance; each employee pays the remaining one-half. The company also contributes an extra 8% of each employee's gross pay (at no cost to employees) to a pension fund.

Required

Compute the following for the week ended August 25 (round amounts to the nearest cent):

1. Each employee's FICA withholdings for Social Security.
2. Each employee's FICA withholdings for Medicare.
3. Employer's FICA taxes for Social Security.
4. Employer's FICA taxes for Medicare.
5. Employer's FUTA taxes.
6. Employer's SUTA taxes.
7. Each employee's net (take-home) pay.
8. Employer's total payroll-related expense for each employee.

Check (3) $176.70
(4) $54.38
(5) $2.40
(7) Total net pay, $2,900.92

Problem 9-4A
Warranty expense and liability estimation
P4

On October 29, 2014, Lobo Co. began operations by purchasing razors for resale. Lobo uses the perpetual inventory method. The razors have a 90-day warranty that requires the company to replace any nonworking razor. When a razor is returned, the company discards it and mails a new one from Merchandise Inventory to the customer. The company's cost per new razor is $20 and its retail selling price is $75 in both 2014 and 2015. The manufacturer has advised the company to expect warranty costs to equal 8% of dollar sales. The following transactions and events occurred.

2014

Nov. 11 Sold 105 razors for $7,875 cash.
30 Recognized warranty expense related to November sales with an adjusting entry.
Dec. 9 Replaced 15 razors that were returned under the warranty.
16 Sold 220 razors for $16,500 cash.
29 Replaced 30 razors that were returned under the warranty.
31 Recognized warranty expense related to December sales with an adjusting entry.

2015

Jan. 5 Sold 150 razors for $11,250 cash.
17 Replaced 50 razors that were returned under the warranty.
31 Recognized warranty expense related to January sales with an adjusting entry.

Required

1. Prepare journal entries to record these transactions and adjustments for 2014 and 2015.
2. How much warranty expense is reported for November 2014 and for December 2014?
3. How much warranty expense is reported for January 2015?
4. What is the balance of the Estimated Warranty Liability account as of December 31, 2014?
5. What is the balance of the Estimated Warranty Liability account as of January 31, 2015?

Check (3) $900
(4) $1,050 Cr.
(5) $950 Cr.

Problem 9-5A
Computing and analyzing times interest earned
A1

Shown here are condensed income statements for two different companies (both are organized as LLCs and pay no income taxes).

Miller Company	
Sales	$1,000,000
Variable expenses (80%)	800,000
Income before interest	200,000
Interest expense (fixed)	60,000
Net income	$ 140,000

Weaver Company	
Sales	$1,000,000
Variable expenses (60%)	600,000
Income before interest	400,000
Interest expense (fixed)	260,000
Net income	$ 140,000

Required

1. Compute times interest earned for Miller Company.
2. Compute times interest earned for Weaver Company.
3. What happens to each company's net income if sales increase by 30%?
4. What happens to each company's net income if sales increase by 50%?
5. What happens to each company's net income if sales increase by 80%?
6. What happens to each company's net income if sales decrease by 10%?
7. What happens to each company's net income if sales decrease by 20%?
8. What happens to each company's net income if sales decrease by 40%?

Check (3) Miller net income, $200,000 (43% increase)

(6) Weaver net income, $100,000 (29% decrease)

Analysis Component

9. Comment on the results from parts 3 through 8 in relation to the fixed-cost strategies of the two companies and the ratio values you computed in parts 1 and 2.

Problem 9-6A[A]
Entries for payroll transactions
P2 P3 P5

Francisco Company has 10 employees, each of whom earns $2,800 per month and is paid on the last day of each month. All 10 have been employed continuously at this amount since January 1. On March 1, the following accounts and balances exist in its general ledger:

a. FICA—Social Security Taxes Payable, $3,472; FICA—Medicare Taxes Payable, $812. (The balances of these accounts represent total liabilities for *both* the employer's and employees' FICA taxes for the February payroll only.)
b. Employees' Federal Income Taxes Payable, $4,000 (liability for February only).
c. Federal Unemployment Taxes Payable, $336 (liability for January and February together).
d. State Unemployment Taxes Payable, $2,240 (liability for January and February together).

During March and April, the company had the following payroll transactions.

Mar. 15 Issued check payable to Swift Bank, a federal depository bank authorized to accept employers' payments of FICA taxes and employee income tax withholdings. The $8,284 check is in payment of the February FICA and employee income taxes.

31 Recorded the journal entry for the March salaries payable. Then recorded the cash payment of the March payroll (the company issued checks payable to each employee in payment of the March payroll). The payroll register shows the following summary totals for the March pay period.

Check March 31: Salaries Payable, $21,858

Salaries: Office Salaries	Salaries: Shop Salaries	Gross Pay	FICA Taxes*	Federal Income Taxes	Net Pay
$11,200	$16,800	$28,000	$1,736 $ 406	$4,000	$21,858

* FICA taxes are Social Security and Medicare, respectively.

31 Recorded the employer's payroll taxes resulting from the March payroll. The company has a merit rating that reduces its state unemployment tax rate to 4.0% of the first $7,000 paid each employee. The federal rate is 0.6%.

March 31: Dr. Payroll Taxes Expenses, $2,786

Apr. 15 Issued check to Swift Bank in payment of the March FICA and employee income taxes.

April 15: Cr. Cash, $8,284 (Swift Bank)

15 Issued check to the State Tax Commission for the January, February, and March state unemployment taxes. Mailed the check and the first-quarter tax return to the Commission.

30 Issued check payable to Swift Bank in payment of the employer's FUTA taxes for the first quarter of the year.

30 Mailed Form 941 to the IRS, reporting the FICA taxes and the employees' federal income tax withholdings for the first quarter.

Required

Prepare journal entries to record the transactions and events for both March and April.

PROBLEM SET B

Problem 9-1B
Short-term notes payable transactions and entries
P1

Warner Co. entered into the following transactions involving short-term liabilities in 2014 and 2015.

2014

Apr. 22	Purchased $5,000 of merchandise on credit from Fox Products, terms are 1/10, n/30. Warner uses the perpetual inventory system.
May 23	Replaced the April 22 account payable to Fox Products with a 60-day, $4,600 note bearing 15% annual interest along with paying $400 in cash.
July 15	Borrowed $12,000 cash from Spring Bank by signing a 120-day, 10% interest-bearing note with a face value of $12,000.
?	Paid the amount due on the note to Fox Products at maturity.
?	Paid the amount due on the note to Spring Bank at maturity.
Dec. 6	Borrowed $8,000 cash from City Bank by signing a 45-day, 9% interest-bearing note with a face value of $8,000.
31	Recorded an adjusting entry for accrued interest on the note to City Bank.

2015

?	Paid the amount due on the note to City Bank at maturity.

Required

1. Determine the maturity date for each of the three notes described.
2. Determine the interest due at maturity for each of the three notes. (Assume a 360-day year.)
3. Determine the interest expense to be recorded in the adjusting entry at the end of 2014.
4. Determine the interest expense to be recorded in 2015.
5. Prepare journal entries for all the preceding transactions and events for years 2014 and 2015.

Check (2) Fox, $115
(3) $50
(4) $40

Problem 9-2B
Entries for payroll transactions
P2 P3

Tavella Company's first weekly pay period of the year ends on January 8. On that date, the column totals in Tavella's payroll register indicate its sales employees earned $34,745, its office employees earned $21,225, and its delivery employees earned $1,030 in salaries. The employees are to have withheld from their salaries FICA Social Security taxes at the rate of 6.2%, FICA Medicare taxes at the rate of 1.45%, $8,625 of federal income taxes, $1,160 of medical insurance deductions, and $138 of union dues. No employee earned more than $7,000 in the first pay period.

Required

1. Calculate FICA Social Security taxes payable and FICA Medicare taxes payable. Prepare the journal entry to record Tavella Company's January 8 (employee) payroll expenses and liabilities. (Round amounts to cents.)
2. Prepare the journal entry to record Tavella's (employer) payroll taxes resulting from the January 8 payroll. Tavella's merit rating reduces its state unemployment tax rate to 3.4% of the first $7,000 paid each employee. The federal unemployment tax rate is 0.6%. (Round amounts to cents.)

Check (1) Cr. Salaries Payable, $42,716.50

(2) Dr. Payroll Taxes Expense, $6,640.50

Problem 9-3B
Payroll expenses, withholdings, and taxes
P2 P3

Fishing Guides Co. has four employees. FICA Social Security taxes are 6.2% of the first $117,000 paid to each employee, and FICA Medicare taxes are 1.45% of gross pay. Also, for the first $7,000 paid to each employee, the company's FUTA taxes are 0.6% and SUTA taxes are 1.75%. The company is preparing its payroll calculations for the week ended September 30. Payroll records show the following information for the company's four employees.

	A	B	C	D
1		Gross Pay		Current Week
2	Name	through Sep. 23	Gross Pay	Income Tax Withholding
3	Ahmed	$115,400	$2,500	$198
4	Carlos	115,485	1,515	182
5	June	6,650	475	32
6	Marie	22,200	1,000	68
7				

In addition to gross pay, the company must pay one-half of the $50 per employee weekly health insurance; each employee pays the remaining one-half. The company also contributes an extra 5% of each employee's gross pay (at no cost to employees) to a pension fund.

Required

Compute the following for the week ended September 30 (round amounts to the nearest cent):

1. Each employee's FICA withholdings for Social Security.
2. Each employee's FICA withholdings for Medicare.
3. Employer's FICA taxes for Social Security.
4. Employer's FICA taxes for Medicare.
5. Employer's FUTA taxes.
6. Employer's SUTA taxes.
7. Each employee's net (take-home) pay.
8. Employer's total payroll-related expense for each employee.

Check (3) $284.58
(4) $79.61
(5) $2.10
(7) Total net pay, $4,545.81

Problem 9-4B
Warranty expense and liability estimation
P4

On November 10, 2015, Lee Co. began operations by purchasing coffee grinders for resale. Lee uses the perpetual inventory method. The grinders have a 60-day warranty that requires the company to replace any nonworking grinder. When a grinder is returned, the company discards it and mails a new one from Merchandise Inventory to the customer. The company's cost per new grinder is $24 and its retail selling price is $50 in both 2015 and 2016. The manufacturer has advised the company to expect warranty costs to equal 10% of dollar sales. The following transactions and events occurred.

2015

Nov.	16	Sold 50 grinders for $2,500 cash.
	30	Recognized warranty expense related to November sales with an adjusting entry.
Dec.	12	Replaced six grinders that were returned under the warranty.
	18	Sold 200 grinders for $10,000 cash.
	28	Replaced 17 grinders that were returned under the warranty.
	31	Recognized warranty expense related to December sales with an adjusting entry.

2016

Jan.	7	Sold 40 grinders for $2,000 cash.
	21	Replaced 36 grinders that were returned under the warranty.
	31	Recognized warranty expense related to January sales with an adjusting entry.

Required

1. Prepare journal entries to record these transactions and adjustments for 2015 and 2016.
2. How much warranty expense is reported for November 2015 and for December 2015?
3. How much warranty expense is reported for January 2016?
4. What is the balance of the Estimated Warranty Liability account as of December 31, 2015?
5. What is the balance of the Estimated Warranty Liability account as of January 31, 2016?

Check (3) $200
(4) $698 Cr.
(5) $34 Cr.

Problem 9-5B
Computing and analyzing times interest earned
A1

Shown here are condensed income statements for two different companies (both are organized as LLCs and pay no income taxes).

Ellis Company	
Sales	$240,000
Variable expenses (50%)	120,000
Income before interest	120,000
Interest expense (fixed)	90,000
Net income	$ 30,000

Seidel Company	
Sales	$240,000
Variable expenses (75%)	180,000
Income before interest	60,000
Interest expense (fixed)	30,000
Net income	$ 30,000

Required

1. Compute times interest earned for Ellis Company.
2. Compute times interest earned for Seidel Company.
3. What happens to each company's net income if sales increase by 10%?
4. What happens to each company's net income if sales increase by 40%?
5. What happens to each company's net income if sales increase by 90%?
6. What happens to each company's net income if sales decrease by 20%?
7. What happens to each company's net income if sales decrease by 50%?
8. What happens to each company's net income if sales decrease by 80%?

Check (4) Ellis net income, $78,000 (160% increase)
(6) Seidel net income, $18,000 (40% decrease)

Analysis Component

9. Comment on the results from parts 3 through 8 in relation to the fixed-cost strategies of the two companies and the ratio values you computed in parts 1 and 2.

Problem 9-6BA
Entries for payroll transactions
P2 P3 P5

MLS Company has five employees, each of whom earns $1,600 per month and is paid on the last day of each month. All five have been employed continuously at this amount since January 1. On June 1, the following accounts and balances exist in its general ledger:

a. FICA—Social Security Taxes Payable, $992; FICA—Medicare Taxes Payable, $232. (The balances of these accounts represent total liabilities for *both* the employer's and employees' FICA taxes for the May payroll only.)
b. Employees' Federal Income Taxes Payable, $1,050 (liability for May only).
c. Federal Unemployment Taxes Payable, $66 (liability for April and May together).
d. State Unemployment Taxes Payable, $440 (liability for April and May together).

During June and July, the company had the following payroll transactions.

June 15 Issued check payable to Security Bank, a federal depository bank authorized to accept employers' payments of FICA taxes and employee income tax withholdings. The $2,274 check is in payment of the May FICA and employee income taxes.

30 Recorded the journal entry for the June salaries payable. Then recorded the cash payment of the June payroll (the company issued checks payable to each employee in payment of the June payroll). The payroll register shows the following summary totals for the June pay period.

Check June 30: Cr. Salaries Payable, $6,338

Salaries					
Office Salaries	Shop Salaries	Gross Pay	FICA Taxes*	Federal Income Taxes	Net Pay
$3,800	$4,200	$8,000	$496 $116	$1,050	$6,338

* FICA taxes are Social Security and Medicare, respectively.

30 Recorded the employer's payroll taxes resulting from the June payroll. The company has a merit rating that reduces its state unemployment tax rate to 4.0% of the first $7,000 paid each employee. The federal rate is 0.6%.

July 15 Issued check payable to Security Bank in payment of the June FICA and employee income taxes.

15 Issued check to the State Tax Commission for the April, May, and June state unemployment taxes. Mailed the check and the second-quarter tax return to the State Tax Commission.

31 Issued check payable to Security Bank in payment of the employer's FUTA taxes for the first quarter of the year.

31 Mailed Form 941 to the IRS, reporting the FICA taxes and the employees' federal income tax withholdings for the second quarter.

Check June 30: Dr. Payroll Taxes Expenses, $612
July 15: Cr. Cash $2,274 (Security Bank)

Required

Prepare journal entries to record the transactions and events for both June and July.

SERIAL PROBLEM

Business Solutions

P2 P3 C2

(This serial problem began in Chapter 1 and continues through most of the book. If previous chapter segments were not completed, the serial problem can begin at this point. It is helpful, but not necessary, to use the Working Papers that accompany the book.)

SP 9 Review the February 26 and March 25 transactions for Business Solutions (SP 4) from Chapter 4.

Required

1. Assume that Lyn Addie is an unmarried employee. Her $1,000 of wages are subject to no deductions other than FICA Social Security taxes, FICA Medicare taxes, and federal income taxes. Her federal income taxes for this pay period total $159. Compute her net pay for the eight days' work paid on February 26. (Round amounts to the nearest cent.)
2. Record the journal entry to reflect the payroll payment to Lyn Addie as computed in part 1.
3. Record the journal entry to reflect the (employer) payroll tax expenses for the February 26 payroll payment. Assume Lyn Addie has not met earnings limits for FUTA and SUTA—the FUTA rate is 0.6% and the SUTA rate is 4% for Business Solutions. (Round amounts to the nearest cent.)
4. Record the entry(ies) for the merchandise sold on March 25 if a 4% sales tax rate applies.

COMPREHENSIVE PROBLEM

Bug-Off Exterminators

(Review of Chapters 1–9)

CP 9 Bug-Off Exterminators provides pest control services and sells extermination products manufactured by other companies. The following six-column table contains the company's unadjusted trial balance as of December 31, 2015.

BUG-OFF EXTERMINATORS
December 31, 2015

	Unadjusted Trial Balance		Adjustments		Adjusted Trial Balance	
Cash	$ 17,000					
Accounts receivable	4,000					
Allowance for doubtful accounts		$ 828				
Merchandise inventory	11,700					
Trucks	32,000					
Accum. depreciation—Trucks		0				
Equipment	45,000					
Accum. depreciation—Equipment		12,200				
Accounts payable		5,000				
Estimated warranty liability		1,400				
Unearned services revenue		0				
Interest payable		0				
Long-term notes payable		15,000				
Common stock		10,000				
Retained earnings		49,700				
Dividends	10,000					
Extermination services revenue		60,000				
Interest revenue		872				
Sales (of merchandise)		71,026				
Cost of goods sold	46,300					
Depreciation expense—Trucks	0					
Depreciation expense—Equipment	0					
Wages expense	35,000					
Interest expense	0					
Rent expense	9,000					
Bad debts expense	0					
Miscellaneous expense	1,226					
Repairs expense	8,000					
Utilities expense	6,800					
Warranty expense	0					
Totals	$226,026	$226,026				

The following information in *a* through *h* applies to the company at the end of the current year.

a. The bank reconciliation as of December 31, 2015, includes the following facts.

Cash balance per bank	$15,100
Cash balance per books	17,000
Outstanding checks	1,800
Deposit in transit	2,450
Interest earned (on bank account)	52
Bank service charges (miscellaneous expense)	15

Reported on the bank statement is a canceled check that the company failed to record. (Information from the bank reconciliation allows you to determine the amount of this check, which is a payment on an account payable.)

b. An examination of customers' accounts shows that accounts totaling $679 should be written off as uncollectible. Using an aging of receivables, the company determines that the ending balance of the Allowance for Doubtful Accounts should be $700.

c. A truck is purchased and placed in service on January 1, 2015. Its cost is being depreciated with the straight-line method using the following facts and estimates.

Original cost	$32,000
Expected salvage value	8,000
Useful life (years)	4

d. Two items of equipment (a sprayer and an injector) were purchased and put into service in early January 2013. They are being depreciated with the straight-line method using these facts and estimates.

	Sprayer	Injector
Original cost	$27,000	$18,000
Expected salvage value	3,000	2,500
Useful life (years)	8	5

e. On August 1, 2015, the company is paid $3,840 cash in advance to provide monthly service for an apartment complex for one year. The company began providing the services in August. When the cash was received, the full amount was credited to the Extermination Services Revenue account.

f. The company offers a warranty for the services it sells. The expected cost of providing warranty service is 2.5% of the extermination services revenue of $57,760 for 2015. No warranty expense has been recorded for 2015. All costs of servicing warranties in 2015 were properly debited to the Estimated Warranty Liability account.

g. The $15,000 long-term note is an 8%, five-year, interest-bearing note with interest payable annually on December 31. The note was signed with First National Bank on December 31, 2015.

h. The ending inventory of merchandise is counted and determined to have a cost of $11,700. Bug-Off uses a perpetual inventory system.

Required

1. Use the preceding information to determine amounts for the following items.

a. Correct (reconciled) ending balance of Cash, and the amount of the omitted check.

Check (1*a*) Cash bal. $15,750

b. Adjustment needed to obtain the correct ending balance of the Allowance for Doubtful Accounts.

(1*b*) $551 credit

c. Depreciation expense for the truck used during year 2015.

d. Depreciation expense for the two items of equipment used during year 2015.

e. The adjusted 2015 ending balances of the Extermination Services Revenue and Unearned Services Revenue accounts.

f. The adjusted 2015 ending balances of the accounts for Warranty Expense and Estimated Warranty Liability.

(1*f*) Estimated Warranty Liability, $2,844 Cr.

g. The adjusted 2015 ending balances of the accounts for Interest Expense and Interest Payable. (Round amounts to nearest whole dollar.)

(2) Adjusted trial balance totals, $238,207

2. Use the results of part 1 to complete the six-column table by first entering the appropriate adjustments for items *a* through *g* and then completing the adjusted trial balance columns. (*Hint:* Item *b* requires two adjustments.)
3. Prepare journal entries to record the adjustments entered on the six-column table. Assume Bug-Off's adjusted balance for Merchandise Inventory matches the year-end physical count.

(4) Net income, $9,274; Total assets, $82,771

4. Prepare a single-step income statement, a statement of retained earnings (cash dividends during 2015 were $10,000), and a classified balance sheet.

GL GENERAL LEDGER PROBLEM

Available in Connect

connect ACCOUNTING

GL 9-1 General Ledger assignment GL 9-1, based on Problem 9-1A, focuses on transactions related to accounts and notes payable and highlights the impact each transaction has on interest expense, if any. Prepare the journal entries related to accounts and notes payable; the schedules for accounts payable and notes payable are automatically completed using the General Ledger tool. Compute both the amount and timing of interest expense for each note. Prepare the subsequent period journal entries related to accrued interest.

Beyond the Numbers

REPORTING IN ACTION

A1 P4

APPLE

BTN 9-1 Refer to the financial statements of **Apple** in Appendix A to answer the following.

1. Compute times interest earned for the fiscal years ended 2013, 2012, and 2011. Apple reports that 2013 interest expense was $136 million, and during 2012 and 2011 it "had no debt outstanding and accordingly did not incur any related interest expense"; however, for purposes of learning from this assignment, assume that Apple had interest expense of $100 million for each of 2012 and 2011. Comment on Apple's ability to cover its interest expense for this period. Assume an industry average of 10 for times interest earned.
2. Apple's current liabilities include "Deferred revenue"; assume that this account reflects "Loyalty reward liabilities." Is this a known or an estimated liability? Explain how this liability is created.
3. Identify its total of accrued expenses and search its footnotes to list the six accounts that make up accrued expenses.

Fast Forward

4. Access Apple's financial statements for fiscal years ending after September 28, 2013, at its website (Apple.com) or the SEC's EDGAR database (www.SEC.gov). Compute its times interest earned for years ending after September 28, 2013, and compare your results to those in part 1. If no interest expense is reported, assume $100 million of interest expense in each year.

COMPARATIVE ANALYSIS

A1

APPLE

GOOGLE

BTN 9-2 Key figures for **Apple** and **Google** follow.

	Apple			Google		
($ millions)	Current Year	One Year Prior	Two Years Prior	Current Year	One Year Prior	Two Years Prior
Net income	$37,037	$41,733	$25,922	$12,920	$10,737	$9,737
Income taxes	13,118	14,030	8,283	2,282	2,598	2,589
Interest expense	136	100*	100*	83	84	58

*Apple did not report interest expense for these periods. Amounts included here are assumed for purposes of this analysis.

Required

1. Compute times interest earned for the three years' data shown for each company.
2. Comment on which company appears stronger in its ability to pay interest obligations if income should decline. Assume an industry average of 10.

ETHICS CHALLENGE

P4

BTN 9-3 Cameron Bly is a sales manager for an automobile dealership. He earns a bonus each year based on revenue from the number of autos sold in the year less related warranty expenses. Actual warranty expenses have varied over the prior 10 years from a low of 3% of an automobile's selling price to a high of 10%. In the past, Bly has tended to estimate warranty expenses on the high end to be conservative. He must work with the dealership's accountant at year-end to arrive at the warranty expense accrual for cars sold each year.

1. Does the warranty accrual decision create any ethical dilemma for Bly?
2. Since warranty expenses vary, what percent do you think Bly should choose for the current year? Justify your response.

COMMUNICATING IN PRACTICE

C3

BTN 9-4 Dusty Johnson is the accounting and finance manager for a manufacturer. At year-end, he must determine how to account for the company's contingencies. His manager, Tom Pretti, objects to Johnson's proposal to recognize an expense and a liability for warranty service on units of a new product introduced in the fourth quarter. Pretti comments, "There's no way we can estimate this warranty cost. We don't owe anyone anything until a product fails and it is returned. Let's report an expense if and when we do any warranty work."

Required

Prepare a one-page memorandum for Johnson to send to Pretti defending his proposal.

TAKING IT TO THE NET

C1 A1

BTN 9-5 Access the February 24, 2014, filing of the December 31, 2013, annual 10-K report of **McDonald's Corporation** (Ticker: MCD), which is available from www.SEC.gov.

Required

1. Identify the current liabilities on McDonald's balance sheet as of December 31, 2013.
2. What portion (in percent) of McDonald's long-term debt matures within the next 12 months?
3. Use the consolidated statement of income for the year ended December 31, 2013, to compute McDonald's times interest earned ratio. Comment on the result. Assume an industry average of 15.0.

TEAMWORK IN ACTION

C2 P1

BTN 9-6 Assume that your team is in business and you must borrow $6,000 cash for short-term needs. You have been shopping banks for a loan, and you have the following two options.

A. Sign a $6,000, 90-day, 10% interest-bearing note dated June 1.

B. Sign a $6,000, 120-day, 8% interest-bearing note dated June 1.

Required

1. Discuss these two options and determine the best choice. Ensure that all teammates concur with the decision and understand the rationale.
2. Each member of the team is to prepare *one* of the following journal entries.
   a. Option A—at date of issuance.
   b. Option B—at date of issuance.
   c. Option A—at maturity date.
   d. Option B—at maturity date.
3. In rotation, each member is to explain the entry he or she prepared in part 2 to the team. Ensure that all team members concur with and understand the entries.

4. Assume that the funds are borrowed on December 1 (instead of June 1) and your business operates on a calendar-year reporting period. Each member of the team is to prepare *one* of the following entries.
   a. Option A—the year-end adjustment.
   b. Option B—the year-end adjustment.
   c. Option A—at maturity date.
   d. Option B—at maturity date.
5. In rotation, each member is to explain the entry he or she prepared in part 4 to the team. Ensure that all team members concur with and understand the entries.

ENTREPRENEURIAL DECISION

A1

BTN 9-7 Review the chapter's opening feature about Jessica Matthews and her start-up company, **Uncharted Play**. Assume that she is considering expanding her business to open a location in Europe. Assume her current income statement appears as follows.

UNCHARTED PLAY Income Statement For Year Ended December 31, 2015	
Sales	$1,000,000
Operating expenses (55%)	550,000
Net income	$ 450,000

Uncharted Play currently has no interest-bearing debt. If it expands to open a European location, it will require a $300,000 loan. Uncharted Play has found a bank that will loan it the money on a 7% note payable. The company believes that, at least for the first few years, sales at its European location will equal $250,000, and that all expenses at both locations will continue to equal 55% of sales.

Required

1. Prepare an income statement (showing three separate columns for current operations, European, and total) for the company assuming that it borrows the funds and expands to Europe. Annual revenues for current operations are expected to remain at $1,000,000.
2. Compute the company's times interest earned under the expansion assumptions in part 1.
3. Assume sales at its European location are $400,000. Prepare an income statement (with columns for current operations, European, and total) for the company and compute times interest earned.
4. Assume sales at its European location are $100,000. Prepare an income statement (with columns for current operations, European, and total) for the company and compute times interest earned.
5. Comment on your results from parts 1 through 4.

HITTING THE ROAD

P2

BTN 9-8 Check your phone book or the Social Security Administration website (**www.SSA.gov**) to locate the Social Security office near you. Visit the office to request a personal earnings and estimate form. Fill out the form and mail according to the instructions. You will receive a statement from the Social Security Administration regarding your earnings history and future Social Security benefits you can receive. (Formerly the request could be made online. The online service has been discontinued and is now under review by the Social Security Administration due to security concerns.) It is good to request an earnings and benefit statement every 5 to 10 years to make sure you have received credit for all wages earned and for which you and your employer have paid taxes into the system.

GLOBAL DECISION

A1

Samsung
APPLE
GOOGLE

BTN 9-9 **Samsung**, **Apple**, and **Google** are all competitors in the global marketplace. Comparative figures for Samsung (**www.Samsung.com**), along with selected figures from Apple and Google, follow.

	Samsung (₩ millions)		Apple		Google	
Key Figures	Current Year	Prior Year	Current Year	Prior Year	Current Year	Prior Year
Net income	₩30,474,764	₩23,845,285	—	—	—	—
Income taxes	7,889,515	6,069,732	—	—	—	—
Interest expense	7,754,972	7,934,450	—	—	—	—
Times interest earned	?	?	369.79	558.63	184.16	159.75

Required

1. Compute the times interest earned ratio for the most recent two years for Samsung using the data shown.
2. Which company of the three presented provides the best coverage of interest expense? Explain.

ANSWERS TO MULTIPLE CHOICE QUIZ

1. b; $6,000 × 0.05 × 30/360 = $25
2. e; $50,000 × (0.062 + 0.0145) = $3,825
3. b; $7,000 × (0.006 + 0.054) = $420
4. c; 10,000 television sets × 0.01 × $250 = $25,000
5. a; 150 employees × $175 per day × 1 vacation day earned = $26,250

chapter 10

Accounting for Long-Term Liabilities

Chapter Preview

BOND BASICS	BOND ISSUANCES	BOND RETIREMENT	LONG-TERM NOTES
A1 Fundamentals of: Bond financing Bond trading Bond issuance procedures	**P1** Issuance at par **P2** Issuance at a discount **P3** Issuance at a premium Bond pricing	**P4** Accounting for bond retirement: At maturity Before maturity By conversion	**C1** Types of notes Recording notes **DEBT ANALYSIS** **A2** Debt features **A3** Debt-to-equity

Learning Objectives

CONCEPTUAL

C1 Explain the types of notes and prepare entries to account for notes.

C2 *Appendix 10A*—Explain and compute the present value of an amount(s) to be paid at a future date(s).

C3 *Appendix 10C*—Describe interest accrual when bond payment periods differ from accounting periods.

C4 *Appendix 10D*—Describe accounting for leases and pensions.

ANALYTICAL

A1 Compare bond financing with stock financing.

A2 Assess debt features and their implications.

A3 Compute the debt-to-equity ratio and explain its use.

PROCEDURAL

P1 Prepare entries to record bond issuance and interest expense.

P2 Compute and record amortization of bond discount using straight-line method.

P3 Compute and record amortization of bond premium using straight-line method.

P4 Record the retirement of bonds.

P5 *Appendix 10B*—Compute and record amortization of bond discount using effective interest method.

P6 *Appendix 10B*—Compute and record amortization of bond premium using effective interest method.

Kristian Punturere/Courtesy of stone + cloth

Inspiration Mountain

"It's better to take action and course correct"
—Matthew Clough

LOS ANGELES—A trip to Tanzania changed Matthew Clough's life forever. "I took a trip to Africa to hike Mt. Kilimanjaro," recalls Matthew. "As I descended from the summit, I learned my friendly and hardworking porter, named Benson, only earns between $1 to $2 per day. This isn't enough to put a child through school. It was an epiphany trip for me." Matthew decided to pursue a business where he would donate a portion of each sale toward the education of a child in Tanzania.

"We carry backpacks for school and a rucksack to climb, so creating a mountain-inspired bag to tie the two together seemed like the natural solution," explains Matthew. The result was **Stone + Cloth (StoneCloth.com),** an American-made backpack line, where Matthew pledges to give 10% of profits to educating children in Tanzania.

"I started by finding an old sewing machine on Craigslist," recounts Matthew. "I drove out to this trailer park in the middle of nowhere to pick it up. After that I just started making bags with zero resources and a wild imagination." Launching his fledgling business presented challenges. He especially needed to focus on managing liabilities to suppliers, shippers, and other creditors that help him sustain the business.

Matthew insists that effective management of liabilities, especially long-term financing from sources such as bonds and notes, is crucial to achieving his dream through business success. In his case, he launched Stone + Cloth with limited loans, or notes payable. "Starting a business can be scary," admits Matthew. Interest payments, principal repayments, and operating expenses must be controlled. "If there's one thing I've learned from starting this project," says Matthew, "I know I can't do it alone."

Matthew continues to monitor liabilities and their payment patterns, and he is not shy about striving to better learn the accounting side. "We're super small, so I manage everything," explains Matthew. "Some days I'll be down at our cut-and-sew shop, checking on the quality of the backpacks that are being produced, and I'll spend other days looking at where we've been so we can use that knowledge to make decisions for the future." He insists that accounting for and monitoring liabilities of long-term financing are important ingredients to a successful start-up. His company now generates sufficient income to pay for interest and principal on long-term liabilities.

Still, the larger message of Stone + Cloth is education. "Education is valued in Tanzania. They understand how important it is and I want to help them achieve what they want to achieve," explains Matthew. "Your purchase [of a backpack] helps provide scholarships for students in need."

Sources: *Stone + Cloth website,* January 2015; *Trendhunter,* February 2012; *The State Press,* January 2012; *TOMS website,* February 2012; *el ay made,* May 2013

BASICS OF BONDS

This section explains the basics of bonds and a company's motivation for issuing them.

Bond Financing

A1 Compare bond financing with stock financing.

Projects that demand large amounts of money often are funded from bond issuances. (Both for-profit and nonprofit companies, as well as governmental units, such as nations, states, cities, and school districts, issue bonds.) A **bond** is its issuer's written promise to pay an amount identified as the par value of the bond with interest. The **par value of a bond,** also called the *face amount* or *face value,* is paid at a specified future date known as the bond's *maturity date.* Most bonds also require the issuer to make semiannual interest payments. The amount of interest paid each period is determined by multiplying the par value of the bond by the bond's contract rate of interest for that same period. This section explains both advantages and disadvantages of bond financing.

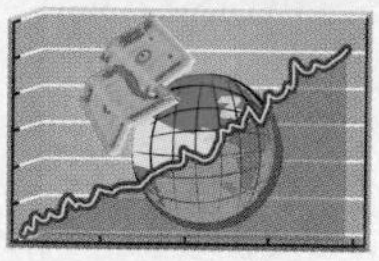

Advantages of Bonds There are three main advantages of bond financing:

1. *Bonds do not affect owner control.* Equity financing reflects ownership in a company, whereas bond financing does not. A person who contributes $1,000 of a company's $10,000 equity financing typically controls one-tenth of all owner decisions. A person who owns a $1,000, 11%, 20-year bond has no ownership right. This person, or bondholder, is to receive from the bond issuer 11% interest, or $110, each year the bond is outstanding and $1,000 when it matures in 20 years.
2. *Interest on bonds is tax deductible.* Bond interest payments are tax deductible for the issuer, but equity payments (distributions) to owners are not. To illustrate, assume that a corporation with no bond financing earns $15,000 in income *before* paying taxes at a 40% tax rate, which amounts to $6,000 ($15,000 × 40%) in taxes. If a portion of its financing is in bonds, however, the resulting bond interest is deducted in computing taxable income. That is, if bond interest expense is $10,000, the taxes owed would be $2,000 ([$15,000 − $10,000] × 40%), which is less than the $6,000 owed with no bond financing.
3. *Bonds can increase return on equity.* A company that earns a higher return with borrowed funds than it pays in interest on those funds increases its return on equity. This process is called *financial leverage* or *trading on the equity.*

Point: Financial leverage reflects issuance of bonds, notes, and preferred stock.

To illustrate the third point, consider Magnum Co., which has $1 million in equity and is planning a $500,000 expansion to meet increasing demand for its product. Magnum predicts the $500,000 expansion will yield $125,000 in additional income before paying any interest. It currently earns $100,000 per year and has no interest expense. Magnum is considering three plans. Plan A is to not expand. Plan B is to expand and raise $500,000 from equity financing. Plan C is to expand and issue $500,000 of bonds that pay 10% annual interest ($50,000). Exhibit 10.1 shows how these three plans affect Magnum's net income, equity, and return on equity (net income/equity). The owner(s) will earn a higher return on equity if expansion occurs. Moreover, the preferred expansion plan is to issue bonds. Projected net income under Plan C ($175,000) is smaller than under Plan B ($225,000), but the return on equity is larger because of less equity investment. Plan C has another advantage if income is taxable. This illustration reflects a general rule: *Return on equity increases when the expected rate of return from the new assets is higher than the rate of interest expense on the debt financing.*

Example: Compute return on equity for all three plans if Magnum is subject to a 40% income tax. *Answer* ($ 000s):
A = 6.0% ($100[1 − 0.4]/$1,000)
B = 9.0% ($225[1 − 0.4]/$1,500)
C = 10.5% ($175[1 − 0.4]/$1,000)

EXHIBIT 10.1

Financing with Bonds versus Equity

	Plan A: Do Not Expand	Plan B: Equity Financing	Plan C: Bond Financing
Income before interest expense	$ 100,000	$ 225,000	$ 225,000
Interest expense	—	—	(50,000)
Net income	**$ 100,000**	**$ 225,000**	**$ 175,000**
Equity	$1,000,000	$1,500,000	$1,000,000
Return on equity	**10.0%**	**15.0%**	**17.5%**

Disadvantages of Bonds The two main disadvantages of bond financing are these:

1. *Bonds can decrease return on equity*. When a company earns a lower return with the borrowed funds than it pays in interest, it decreases its return on equity. This downside risk of financial leverage is more likely to arise when a company has periods of low income or net losses.
2. *Bonds require payment of both periodic interest and the par value at maturity*. Bond payments can be especially burdensome when income and cash flow are low. Equity financing, in contrast, does not require any payments because cash withdrawals (dividends) are paid at the discretion of the owner (or board).

A company must weigh the risks and returns of the disadvantages and advantages of bond financing when deciding whether to issue bonds to finance operations.

Point: There are nearly 5 million individual U.S. bond issues, ranging from huge treasuries to tiny municipalities. This compares to about 12,000 individual U.S. stocks that are traded.

Point: Debt financing is desirable when interest is tax deductible, when owner control is preferred, and when return on equity exceeds the debt's interest rate.

Point: The phrase: *debt is cheaper than equity,* refers in part to interest expense on bonds being tax deductible whereas dividends on stock are not.

Bond Trading

Bonds are securities that can be readily bought and sold. A large number of bonds trade on both the New York Exchange and the American Exchange. A bond *issue* consists of a number of bonds, usually in denominations of $1,000 or $5,000, and is sold to many different lenders. After bonds are issued, they often are bought and sold by investors, meaning that any particular bond probably has a number of owners before it matures. Since bonds are exchanged (bought and sold) in the market, they have a market value (price). For convenience, bond market values are expressed as a percent of their par (face) value. For example, a company's bonds might be trading at 103½, meaning they can be bought or sold for 103.5% of their par value. Bonds can also trade below par value. For instance, if a company's bonds are trading at 95, they can be bought or sold at 95% of their par value.

Point: The largest bond issuances in history occurred in 2013:

Verizon . . . . $49 billion.
Apple . . . . $17 billion.

Decision Insight

Bonds	Rate	Mat	Yld	Vol	Close	Chg
IBM	5.7	17	4.7	130	121.18	+0.24%

Quotes The **IBM** bond quote here is interpreted (left to right) as **Bonds,** issuer name; **Rate,** contract interest rate (5.7%); **Mat,** matures in year 2017 when principal is paid; **Yld,** yield rate (4.7%) of bond at current price; **Vol,** daily dollar worth ($130,000) of trades (in 1,000s); **Close,** closing price (121.18) for the day as percentage of par value; **Chg,** change (+0.24%) in closing price from prior day's close. ■

Point: A bond with a par value of $1,000 trading at 103½ sells for $1,035 ($1,000 × 1.035). A bond with a par value of $1,000 trading at 95½ sells for $955 ($1,000 × 0.955).

Bond-Issuing Procedures

EXHIBIT 10.2

Bond Certificate

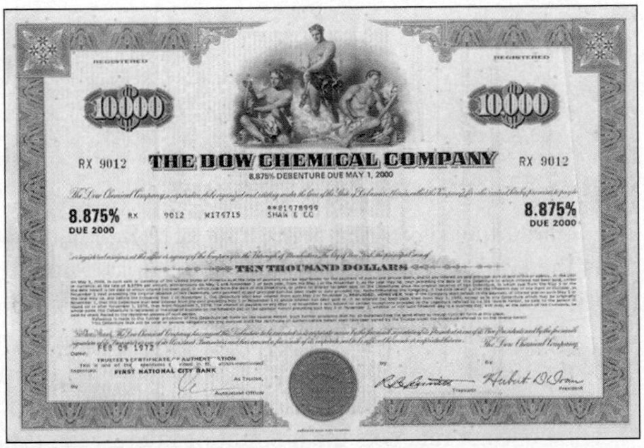

Courtesy of Dow Chemicals

State and federal laws govern bond issuances. Bond issuers also want to ensure that they do not violate any of their existing contractual agreements when issuing bonds. Authorization of bond issuances includes the number of bonds authorized, their par value, and the contract interest rate. The legal document identifying the rights and obligations of both the bondholders and the issuer is called the **bond indenture,** which is the legal contract between the issuer and the bondholders (and specifies how often interest is paid). A bondholder may also receive a bond certificate as evidence of the company's debt. A **bond certificate,** such as that shown in Exhibit 10.2, includes specifics such as the issuer's name, the par value, the contract interest rate, and the maturity date. Many companies reduce costs by not issuing paper certificates to bondholders.[1]

Point: *Indenture* refers to a bond's legal contract; *debenture* refers to an unsecured bond.

Point: The *spread* between the dealer's cost and what buyers pay can be huge. Dealers earn more than $25 billion in annual spread revenue.

Global: In the United Kingdom, government bonds are called *gilts*—short for gilt-edged investments.

[1] The issuing company normally sells its bonds to an investment firm called an *underwriter,* which resells them to the public. An issuing company can also sell bonds directly to investors. When an underwriter sells bonds to a large number of investors, a *trustee* represents and protects the bondholders' interests. The trustee monitors the issuer to ensure that it complies with the obligations in the bond indenture. Most trustees are large banks or trust companies. The trustee writes and accepts the terms of a bond indenture before it is issued. When bonds are offered to the public, called *floating an issue,* they must be registered with the Securities and Exchange Commission (SEC). SEC registration requires the issuer to file certain financial information. Most company bonds are issued in par value units of $1,000 or $5,000. *A baby bond* has a par value of less than $1,000, such as $100.

BOND ISSUANCES

This section explains accounting for bond issuances at par, below par (discount), and above par (premium). It also describes how to amortize a discount or premium and record bonds issued between interest payment dates.

Issuing Bonds at Par

P1 Prepare entries to record bond issuance and interest expense.

To illustrate an issuance of bonds at par value, suppose a company receives authorization to issue $800,000 of 9%, 20-year bonds dated January 1, 2015, that mature on December 31, 2034, and pay interest semiannually on each June 30 and December 31. After accepting the bond indenture on behalf of the bondholders, the trustee can sell all or a portion of the bonds to an underwriter. If all bonds are sold at par value, the issuer records the sale as follows.

Assets = Liabilities + Equity
+800,000 +800,000

2015			
Jan. 1	Cash	800,000	
	Bonds Payable		800,000
	Sold bonds at par.		

This entry reflects increases in the issuer's cash *and* long-term liabilities.

The issuer records the first semiannual interest payment as follows.

Assets = Liabilities + Equity
−36,000 −36,000

2015			
June 30	Bond Interest Expense	36,000	
	Cash		36,000
	Paid semiannual interest (9% × $800,000 × ½ year).		

The issuer pays and records its semiannual interest obligation every six months until the bonds mature. When they mature, the issuer records its payment of principal as follows.

Assets = Liabilities + Equity
−800,000 −800,000

2034			
Dec. 31	Bonds Payable	800,000	
	Cash		800,000
	Paid bond principal at maturity.		

Bond Discount or Premium

The bond issuer pays the interest rate specified in the indenture, the **contract rate,** also referred to as the *coupon rate, stated rate,* or *nominal rate*. The annual interest paid is determined by multiplying the bond par value by the contract rate. The contract rate is usually stated on an annual basis, even if interest is paid semiannually. For example, if a company issues a $1,000, 8% bond paying interest semiannually, it pays annual interest of $80 (8% × $1,000) in two semiannual payments of $40 each.

The contract rate sets the amount of interest the issuer pays in *cash,* which is not necessarily the *bond interest expense* actually incurred by the issuer. Bond interest expense depends on the bond's market value at issuance, which is determined by market expectations of the risk of lending to the issuer. The bond's **market rate** of interest is the rate that borrowers are willing to pay and lenders are willing to accept for a particular bond and its risk level. As the risk level increases, the rate increases to compensate purchasers for the bonds' increased risk. Also, the market rate is generally higher when the time period until the bond matures is longer due to the risk of adverse events occurring over a longer time period.

QC1

Many bond issuers try to set a contract rate of interest equal to the market rate they expect as of the bond issuance date. When the contract rate and market rate are equal, a bond sells at par value, but when they are not equal, a bond does not sell at par value. Instead, it is sold at a *premium* above par value or at a *discount* below par value. Exhibit 10.3 shows the relation between the contract rate, market rate, and a bond's issue price.

EXHIBIT 10.3

Relation between Bond Issue Price, Contract Rate, and Market Rate

Bond Sets	Market Sets	Bond Price Determined	
Contract rate	Market rate	Contract rate > Market rate	Bond sells at premium
		Contract rate = Market rate	Bond sells at par
		Contract rate < Market rate	Bond sells at discount

Issuing Bonds at a Discount

P2 Compute and record amortization of bond discount using straight-line method.

A **discount on bonds payable** occurs when a company issues bonds with a contract rate less than the market rate. This means that the issue price is less than par value. To illustrate, assume that **Fila** announces an offer to issue bonds with a $100,000 par value, an 8% annual contract rate (paid semiannually), and a two-year life. Also assume that the market rate for Fila bonds is 10%. These bonds then will sell at a discount since the contract rate is less than the market rate. The exact issue price for these bonds is stated as 96.454 (implying 96.454% of par value, or $96,454); we show how to compute this issue price later in the chapter. These bonds obligate the issuer to pay two separate types of future cash flows:

Point: The difference between the contract rate and the market rate of interest on a new bond issue is usually a fraction of a percent. We use a difference of 2% to emphasize the effects.

1. Par value of $100,000 cash at the end of the bonds' two-year life.
2. Cash interest payments of $4,000 ($100,000 × 8% × 1/2 year) at the end of each semiannual period during the bonds' two-year life.

The exact pattern of cash flows for the Fila bonds is shown in Exhibit 10.4.

EXHIBIT 10.4

Cash Flows for Fila Bonds

0	6 mo.	12 mo.	18 mo.	24 mo.	
	$4,000	**$4,000**	**$4,000**	**$100,000**	**$116,000 total**
				$4,000	

When Fila accepts $96,454 cash for its bonds on the issue date of December 31, 2015, it records the sale as follows.

Dec. 31	Cash	96,454	
	Discount on Bonds Payable	3,546	
	Bonds Payable		100,000
	Sold bonds at a discount on their issue date.		

Assets	=	Liabilities	+	Equity
+96,454		+100,000		
		−3,546		

These bonds are reported in the long-term liability section of the issuer's December 31, 2015, balance sheet as shown in Exhibit 10.5. A discount is deducted from the par value of bonds to yield the **carrying (book) value of bonds.** Discount on Bonds Payable is a contra liability account.

Point: Book value at issuance always equals the issuer's cash borrowed.

EXHIBIT 10.5

Balance Sheet Presentation of Bond Discount

Long-term liabilities		
Bonds payable, 8%, due December 31, 2017	$100,000	
Less discount on bonds payable	**3,546**	$96,454 ← carrying (book) value

Amortizing a Bond Discount Fila receives $96,454 for its bonds; in return it must pay bondholders $100,000 after two years (plus semiannual interest payments). The $3,546 discount is paid to bondholders at maturity and is part of the cost of using the $96,454 for two years. The upper portion of panel A in Exhibit 10.6 shows that total bond interest expense of $19,546 is the difference between the total amount repaid to bondholders ($116,000) and the amount borrowed from bondholders ($96,454). Alternatively, we can compute total bond interest expense as the sum of the four interest payments and the bond discount. This alternative computation is shown in the lower portion of panel A.

The total $19,546 bond interest expense must be allocated across the four semiannual periods in the bonds' life, and the bonds' carrying value must be updated at each balance sheet

EXHIBIT 10.6

Interest Computation and Entry for Bonds Issued at a Discount

Panel A: Interest Computations

Amount repaid to bondholders	
Four interest payments of $4,000 (4 pymts × [$100,000 × 0.08 × 1/2 yr]) . . .	$ 16,000
Par value at maturity . . .	100,000
Total repaid to bondholders . . .	116,000
Less amount borrowed from bondholders . . .	(96,454)
Total bond interest expense . . .	**$ 19,546**
Alternative Computation	
Four payments of $4,000 (4 pymts × [$100,000 × 0.08 × 1/2 yr]) . . .	$ 16,000
Plus discount . . .	3,546
Total bond interest expense . . .	**$ 19,546**

Equal

$$\frac{\text{Bond interest expense}}{\text{(per interest period)}} = \frac{\text{Total bond interest expense}}{\text{Number of interest periods}} = \frac{\$19{,}546}{4} = \$4{,}887$$

Panel B: Entry to Record Interest Payment and Amortization

2016–2017			
June 30 and Dec. 31	Bond Interest Expense . . .	4,887	
	Discount on Bonds Payable . . .		887
	Cash . . .		4,000
	To record semiannual interest and discount amortization (straight-line method).		

Discount ÷ periods

Par value × contract rate

date. This is accomplished using the straight-line method (or the effective interest method in Appendix 10B). Both methods systematically reduce the bond discount to zero over the two-year life. This process is called *amortizing a bond discount.*

The following section on discount amortization uses the straight-line method. Appendix 10B uses the effective interest method. An instructor can choose to cover either one or both methods. If the straight-line method is skipped, then jump two pages ahead to the section titled "Issuing Bonds at a Premium."

Straight-Line Method The **straight-line bond amortization** method allocates an equal portion of the total bond interest expense to each interest period. To apply the straight-line method to Fila's bonds, we divide the total bond interest expense of $19,546 by 4 (the number of semiannual periods in the bonds' life). This gives a bond interest expense of $4,887 per period, which is $4,886.5 rounded to the nearest dollar per period (all computations, including those for assignments, are rounded to the nearest whole dollar). Alternatively, we can find this number by first dividing the $3,546 discount by 4, which yields the $887 amount of discount to be amortized each interest period. When the $887 is added to the $4,000 cash payment, the bond interest expense for each period is $4,887. Panel B of Exhibit 10.6 shows how the issuer records bond interest expense and updates the balance of the bond liability account at the end of *each* of the four semiannual interest periods (June 30, 2016, through December 31, 2017).

Point: Amortization always results in the carrying value of a bond moving closer to its par value.

EXHIBIT 10.7

Straight-Line Amortization of Bond Discount

Semiannual Period-End	Unamortized Discount*	Carrying Value†
(0) 12/31/2015	$3,546	$ 96,454
(1) 6/30/2016	2,659	97,341
(2) 12/31/2016	1,772	98,228
(3) 6/30/2017	885	99,115
(4) **12/31/2017**	**0‡**	**100,000**

The two columns always sum to par value for a discount bond.

* Total bond discount (of $3,546) less accumulated periodic amortization ($887 per semiannual interest period).

† Bond par value (of $100,000) less unamortized discount.

‡ Adjusted for rounding.

Exhibit 10.7 shows the pattern of decreases in the Discount on Bonds Payable account and the pattern of increases in the bonds' carrying value. The following points summarize the discount bonds' straight-line amortization:

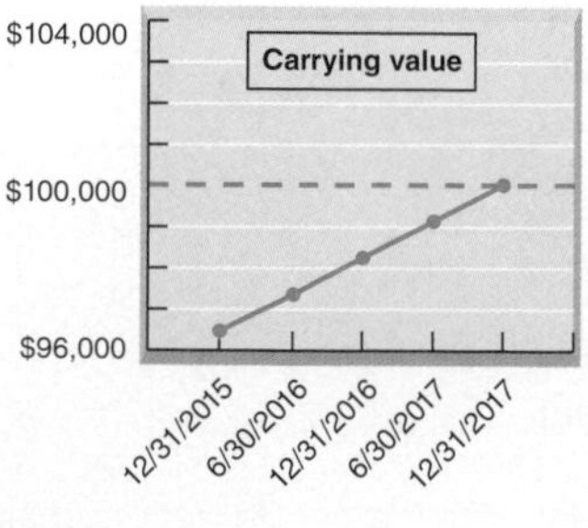

1. At issuance, the $100,000 par value consists of the $96,454 cash received by the issuer plus the $3,546 discount.
2. During the bonds' life, the (unamortized) discount decreases each period by the $887 amortization ($3,546/4), and the carrying value (par value less unamortized discount) increases each period by $887.
3. At maturity, the unamortized discount equals zero, and the carrying value equals the $100,000 par value that the issuer pays the holder.

We see that the issuer incurs a $4,887 bond interest expense each period but pays only $4,000 cash. The $887 unpaid portion of this expense is added to the bonds' carrying value. (The total $3,546 unamortized discount is "paid" when the bonds mature; $100,000 is paid at maturity but only $96,454 was received at issuance.)

Bonds Payable

Debit	Credit
	12/31/2015 100,000
	6/30/2016 —
	12/31/2016 —
	6/30/2017 —
	12/31/2017 **100,000**

Discount on Bonds Payable

Debit	Credit
12/31/2015 3,546	
	6/30/2016 887
	12/31/2016 887
	6/30/2017 887
	12/31/2017 885
	12/31/2017 **0**

Decision Insight

Ratings Game Many bond buyers rely on rating services to assess bond risk. The best known are **Standard & Poor's**, **Moody's**, and **Fitch**. These services focus on the issuer's financial statements and other factors in setting ratings. Standard & Poor's ratings, from best quality to default, are AAA, AA, A, BBB, BB, B, CCC, CC, C, and D. Ratings can include a plus (+) or minus (−) to show relative standing within a category. Bonds rated in the A and B range are referred to as *investment grade;* lower-rated bonds are considered much riskier. ■

NEED-TO-KNOW 10-1

Recording Discount Bonds

P1 P2

A company issues 8%, two-year bonds on December 31, 2015, with a par value of $7,000 and semiannual interest payments. On the issue date, the annual market rate for these bonds is 10%, which implies a selling price of 96.46 or $6,752. (*a*) Prepare an amortization table such as Exhibit 10.7 for these bonds; use the straight-line method to amortize the discount. Then, prepare journal entries to record (*b*) the issuance of bonds on December 31, 2015; (*c*) the first through fourth interest payments on each June 30 and December 31; and (*d*) the maturity of the bond on December 31, 2017.

Solution

a.

Semiannual Period-End	Unamortized Discount	Carrying Value
(0) 12/31/2015	$248	$6,752
(1) 6/30/2016	186	6,814
(2) 12/31/2016	124	6,876
(3) 6/30/2017	62	6,938
(4) 12/31/2017	0	7,000

Interest computations for solutions *a, b,* and *c*

Amount repaid to bondholders:	
Four interest payments of $280	
[4 pymts × ($7,000 × 0.08 × 1/2 yr)]	$1,120
Par value at maturity	7,000
Total repaid to bondholders	$8,120
Less amount borrowed from bondholders	
($7,000 × 0.9646)	6,752
Total bond interest expense	$1,368
Divided by number of periods	÷ 4
Bond interest expense per period	$ 342

b.

Date	Account	Debit	Credit
2015 Dec. 31	Cash	6,752	
	Discount on Bonds Payable	248	
	Bonds Payable		7,000
	Sold bonds at discount.		

c.

Date	Account	Debit	Credit
2016 June 30	Bond Interest Expense	342	
	Discount on Bonds Payable*		62
	Cash**		280
	To pay semiannual interest and record amortization.		
2016 Dec. 31	Bond Interest Expense	342	
	Discount on Bonds Payable*		62
	Cash**		280
	To pay semiannual interest and record amortization.		
2017 June 30	Bond Interest Expense	342	
	Discount on Bonds Payable*		62
	Cash**		280
	To pay semiannual interest and record amortization.		
2017 Dec. 31	Bond Interest Expense	342	
	Discount on Bonds Payable*		62
	Cash**		280
	To pay semiannual interest and record amortization.		

*$248/4 **$7,000 × 8% × ½

Bonds Payable

Debit	Credit
	12/31/2015 7,000
	6/30/2016 —
	12/31/2016 —
	6/30/2017 —
	12/31/2017 **7,000**

Discount on Bonds Payable

Debit	Credit
12/31/2015 248	
	6/30/2016 62
	12/31/2016 62
	6/30/2017 62
	12/31/2017 62
	12/31/2017 **0**

d.

Date	Account	Debit	Credit
2017 Dec. 31	Bonds Payable	7,000	
	Cash		7,000
	To record maturity and payment of bonds.		

Do More: QS 10-2, QS 10-6, QS 10-7, E 10-1, E 10-2, E 10-4, E 10-5

QC2

Issuing Bonds at a Premium

P3 Compute and record amortization of bond premium using straight-line method.

When the contract rate of bonds is higher than the market rate, the bonds sell at a price higher than par value. The amount by which the bond price exceeds par value is the **premium on bonds.** To illustrate, assume that **Adidas** issues bonds with a $100,000 par value, a 12% annual contract rate, semiannual interest payments, and a two-year life. Also assume that the market rate for Adidas bonds is 10% on the issue date. The Adidas bonds will sell at a premium because the contract rate is higher than the market rate. The issue price for these bonds is stated as 103.546 (implying 103.546% of par value, or $103,546); we show how to compute this issue price later in the chapter. These bonds obligate the issuer to pay out two separate future cash flows:

Premium bond:
Contract rate → Cash int. pymt.
Market rate → Interest expense

If Cash int. pymt. > Int. expense:
- Bond sells at premium
- Carrying value > par value
- Carrying value declines over time

1. Par value of $100,000 cash at the end of the bonds' two-year life.
2. Cash interest payments of $6,000 ($100,000 × 12% × 1/2 year) at the end of each semiannual period during the bonds' two-year life.

The exact pattern of cash flows for the Adidas bonds is shown in Exhibit 10.8.

EXHIBIT 10.8
Cash Flows for Adidas Bonds

				$100,000	
	$6,000	**$6,000**	**$6,000**	**$6,000**	} **$124,000 total**
0	6 mo.	12 mo.	18 mo.	24 mo.	

When Adidas accepts $103,546 cash for its bonds on the issue date of December 31, 2015, it records this transaction as follows.

Assets	= Liabilities	+ Equity
+103,546	+100,000	
	+3,546	

Dec. 31	Cash	103,546	
	Premium on Bonds Payable		3,546
	Bonds Payable		100,000
	Sold bonds at a premium on their issue date.		

These bonds are reported in the long-term liability section of the issuer's December 31, 2015, balance sheet as shown in Exhibit 10.9. A premium is added to par value to yield the carrying (book) value of bonds. Premium on Bonds Payable is an adjunct liability account.

EXHIBIT 10.9
Balance Sheet Presentation of Bond Premium

Long-term liabilities		
Bonds payable, 12%, due December 31, 2017	$100,000	
Plus premium on bonds payable	**3,546**	$103,546

Amortizing a Bond Premium Adidas receives $103,546 for its bonds; in return, it pays bondholders $100,000 after two years (plus semiannual interest payments). The $3,546 premium not repaid to issuer's bondholders at maturity goes to reduce the issuer's expense of using the $103,546 for two years. The upper portion of panel A of Exhibit 10.10 shows that total bond interest expense of $20,454 is the difference between the total amount repaid to bondholders ($124,000) and the amount borrowed from bondholders ($103,546). Alternatively, we can compute total bond interest expense as the sum of the four interest payments less the bond premium. The premium is subtracted because it will not be paid to bondholders when the bonds mature; see the lower portion of panel A. Total bond interest expense must be allocated over the four semiannual periods using the straight-line method (or the effective interest method in Appendix 10B).

Point: The phrase *ability to service debt* refers to making interest and principal payments on time.

EXHIBIT 10.10

Interest Computation and Entry for Bonds Issued at a Premium

Panel A: Interest Computations

Amount repaid to bondholders	
Four interest payments of $6,000 (4 pymts × [$100,000 × 0.12 × 1/2 yr])	$ 24,000
Par value at maturity	100,000
Total repaid to bondholders	124,000
Less amount borrowed from bondholders	(103,546)
Total bond interest expense	**$20,454**
Alternative Computation	
Four payments of $6,000 (4 pymts × [$100,000 × 0.12 × 1/2 yr])	$ 24,000
Less premium	(3,546)
Total bond interest expense	**$20,454**

(The two totals are marked "Equal".)

$$\frac{\text{Bond interest expense}}{\text{(per interest period)}} = \frac{\text{Total bond interest expense}}{\text{Number of interest periods}} = \frac{\$20{,}454}{4} = \$5{,}113$$

Panel B: Entry to Record Interest Payment and Amortization

2016–2017			
June 30 and Dec. 31	Bond Interest Expense	5,113	
	Premium on Bonds Payable	887	
	Cash		6,000
	To record semiannual interest and premium amortization (straight-line method).		

Premium ÷ periods (887); Par value × contract rate (6,000)

Bonds Payable

	12/31/2015 100,000
	6/30/2016 —
	12/31/2016 —
	6/30/2017 —
	12/31/2017 **100,000**

Premium on Bonds Payable

	12/31/2015 3,546
6/30/2016 887	
12/31/2016 887	
6/30/2017 887	
12/31/2017 885	
	12/31/2017 0

The following section on premium amortization uses the straight-line method. Appendix 10B uses the effective interest method. An instructor can choose to cover either one or both methods. If the straight-line method is skipped, then jump two pages ahead to the section titled "Bond Pricing."

Straight-Line Method The straight-line method allocates an equal portion of total bond interest expense to each of the bonds' semiannual interest periods. To apply this method to Adidas bonds, we divide the two years' total bond interest expense of $20,454 by 4 (the number of semiannual periods in the bonds' life). This gives a total bond interest expense of $5,113 per period, which is $5,113.5 rounded down so that the journal entry balances and for simplicity in presentation (alternatively, one could carry cents). Panel B of Exhibit 10.10 shows how the issuer records bond interest expense and updates the balance of the bond liability account for *each* semiannual period (June 30, 2016, through December 31, 2017).

Point: A premium decreases Bond Interest Expense; a discount increases it.

EXHIBIT 10.11

Straight-Line Amortization of Bond Premium

Semiannual Period-End	Unamortized Premium*	Carrying Value†
(0) 12/31/2015	$3,546	$103,546
(1) 6/30/2016	2,659	102,659
(2) 12/31/2016	1,772	101,772
(3) 6/30/2017	885	100,885
(4) 12/31/2017	0‡	**100,000**

* Total bond premium (of $3,546) less accumulated periodic amortization ($887 per semiannual interest period).

† Bond par value (of $100,000) plus unamortized premium.

‡ Adjusted for rounding.

During the bond life, carrying value is adjusted to par and the amortized premium to zero.

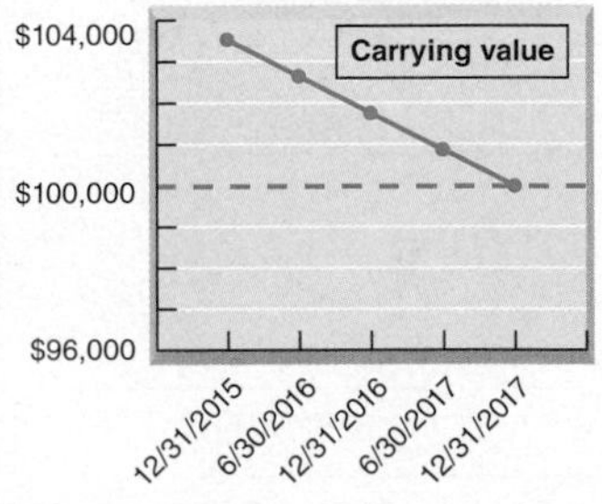

Exhibit 10.11 shows the pattern of decreases in the unamortized Premium on Bonds Payable account and in the bonds' carrying value. The following points summarize straight-line amortization of the premium bonds:

1. At issuance, the $100,000 par value plus the $3,546 premium equals the $103,546 cash received by the issuer.
2. During the bonds' life, the (unamortized) premium decreases each period by the $887 amortization ($3,546/4), and the carrying value decreases each period by the same $887.
3. At maturity, the unamortized premium equals zero, and the carrying value equals the $100,000 par value that the issuer pays the holder.

NEED-TO-KNOW 10-2

Recording Premium Bonds

P3

A company issues 8%, two-year bonds on December 31, 2015, with a par value of $7,000 and semiannual interest payments. On the issue date, the annual market rate for these bonds is 6%, which implies a selling price of 103.71 or $7,260. (*a*) Prepare an amortization table such as Exhibit 10.11 for these bonds; use the straight-line method to amortize the premium. Then, prepare journal entries to record (*b*) the issuance of bonds on December 31, 2015; (*c*) the first through fourth interest payments on each June 30 and December 31; and (*d*) the maturity of the bond on December 31, 2017.

Solution

a.

Semiannual Period-End	Unamortized Premium	Carrying Value
(0) 12/31/2015	$260	$7,260
(1) 6/30/2016	195	7,195
(2) 12/31/2016	130	7,130
(3) 6/30/2017	65	7,065
(4) 12/31/2017	0	7,000

Interest computations for solutions *a*, *b*, and *c*

Amount repaid to bondholders:	
Four interest payments of $280 [4 pymts × ($7,000 × 0.08 × 1/2 yr)]	$1,120
Par value at maturity	7,000
Total repaid to bondholders	$8,120
Less amount borrowed from bondholders ($7,000 × 1.0371)	7,260
Total bond interest expense	$ 860
Divided by number of periods	÷ 4
Bond interest expense per period	$ 215

b.

Date	Account	Debit	Credit
2015			
Dec. 31	Cash	7,260	
	Premium on Bonds Payable		260
	Bonds Payable		7,000
	Sold bonds at premium.		

c.

Date	Account	Debit	Credit
2016			
June 30	Bond Interest Expense	215	
	Premium on Bonds Payable*	65	
	Cash**		280
	To pay semiannual interest and record amortization.		
2016			
Dec. 31	Bond Interest Expense	215	
	Premium on Bonds Payable*	65	
	Cash**		280
	To pay semiannual interest and record amortization.		
2017			
June 30	Bond Interest Expense	215	
	Premium on Bonds Payable*	65	
	Cash**		280
	To pay semiannual interest and record amortization.		
2017			
Dec. 31	Bond Interest Expense	215	
	Premium on Bonds Payable*	65	
	Cash**		280
	To pay semiannual interest and record amortization.		

*$260/4 **$7,000 × 8% × ½

Bonds Payable

Debit	Credit
	12/31/2015 7,000
	6/30/2016 —
	12/31/2016 —
	6/30/2017 —
	12/31/2017 **7,000**

Premium on Bonds Payable

Debit	Credit
	12/31/2015 260
6/30/2016 65	
12/31/2016 65	
6/30/2017 65	
12/31/2017 65	
	12/31/2017 **0**

d.

Date	Account	Debit	Credit
2017			
Dec. 31	Bonds Payable	7,000	
	Cash		7,000
	To record maturity and payment of bonds.		

Do More: QS 10-8, E 10-6, E 10-7, P 10-3, P 10-4

QC3

The next section describes bond pricing. An instructor can choose to cover bond pricing or not. Assignments requiring the "Bond Pricing" section are Quick Study 10-3 and Exercises 10-3 and 10-8.

Point: *Zero-coupon bonds* do not pay periodic interest (contract rate is zero). These bonds always sell at a discount because their 0% contract rate is always below the market rate.

Bond Pricing

Prices for bonds traded on an organized exchange are often published in newspapers and through online services. This information normally includes the bond price (called *quote*), its contract rate, and its current market (called *yield*) rate. However, only a fraction of bonds are traded on organized exchanges. To compute the price of a bond, we apply present value concepts. This section explains how to use *present value concepts* to price the Fila discount bond and the Adidas premium bond described earlier.

Point: InvestingInBonds.com is a bond research and learning source.

Present Value of a Discount Bond The issue price of bonds is found by computing the present value of the bonds' cash payments, discounted at the bonds' market rate. When computing the present value of the Fila bonds, we work with *semiannual* compounding periods because this is the time between interest payments; the annual market rate of 10% is considered a semiannual rate of 5%. Also, the two-year bond life is viewed as four semiannual periods. The price computation is twofold: (1) Find the present value of the $100,000 par value paid at maturity and (2) find the present value of the series of four semiannual payments of $4,000 each; see Exhibit 10.4. These present values can be found by using *present value tables*. Appendix B at the end of this book shows present value tables and describes their use. Table B.1 at the end of Appendix B is used for the single $100,000 maturity payment, and Table B.3 in Appendix B is used for the $4,000 series of interest payments. Specifically, we go to Table B.1, row 4, and across to the 5% column to identify the present value factor of 0.8227 for the maturity payment. Next, we go to Table B.3, row 4, and across to the 5% column, where the present value factor is 3.5460 for the series of interest payments. We compute bond price by multiplying the cash flow payments by their corresponding present value factors and adding them together; see Exhibit 10.12.

Point: A bond's market value (price) at issuance equals the present value of its future cash payments, where the interest (discount) rate used is the bond's market rate.

Point: Many calculators have present value functions for computing bond prices.

EXHIBIT 10.12

Computing Issue Price for the Fila Discount Bonds

Cash Flow	Table	Present Value Factor		Amount		Present Value
$100,000 par (maturity) value	B.1 (PV of 1)	0.8227	×	$100,000	=	$ 82,270
$4,000 interest payments	B.3 (PV of ann.)	3.5460	×	4,000	=	14,184
Price of bond						**$96,454**

Calculator
N = 4 PMT = 4,000
I/Yr = 5 FV = 100,000
PV = **96,454**

Present Value of a Premium Bond We find the issue price of the Adidas bonds by using the market rate to compute the present value of the bonds' future cash flows. When computing the present value of these bonds, we again work with *semiannual* compounding periods because this is the time between interest payments. The annual 10% market rate is applied as a semiannual rate of 5%, and the two-year bond life is viewed as four semiannual periods. The computation is twofold: (1) Find the present value of the $100,000 par value paid at maturity and (2) find the present value of the series of four payments of $6,000 each; see Exhibit 10.8. These present values can be found by using present value tables. First, go to Table B.1, row 4, and across to the 5% column where the present value factor is 0.8227 for the maturity payment. Second, go to Table B.3, row 4, and across to the 5% column, where the present value factor is 3.5460 for the series of interest payments. The bonds' price is computed by multiplying the cash flow payments by their corresponding present value factors and adding them together; see Exhibit 10.13.

Point: Calculator inputs defined:
- N Number of semiannual periods
- I/Yr Market rate per semiannual period
- FV Future (maturity) value
- PMT Payment (interest) per semiannual period
- PV Price (present value)

EXHIBIT 10.13

Computing Issue Price for the Adidas Premium Bonds

Cash Flow	Table	Present Value Factor		Amount		Present Value
$100,000 par (maturity) value	B.1 (PV of 1)	0.8227	×	$100,000	=	$ 82,270
$6,000 interest payments	B.3 (PV of ann.)	3.5460	×	6,000	=	21,276
Price of bond						**$103,546**

Calculator
N = 4 PMT = 6,000
I/Yr = 5 FV = 100,000
PV = **103,546**

Decision Insight

Equivalent Payments Concept Business decisions frequently involve concepts using the time value of money. To help in those decisions, the present value factors can be thought of as *equivalent payments.* For example, using the data in Exhibit 10.12, one payment of $100,000 scheduled two years from today is the *equivalent* of a 0.8227 payment of $100,000 today (assuming a market with 10% return). Similarly, four semiannual payments of $4,000 over the next two years are the equivalent of 3.5460 payments of $4,000 today (again, assuming a 10% return). ■

BOND RETIREMENT

P4 Record the retirement of bonds.

This section describes the retirement of bonds (1) at maturity, (2) before maturity, and (3) by conversion to stock.

Bond Retirement at Maturity

The carrying value of bonds at maturity always equals par value. For example, both Exhibits 10.7 (a discount) and 10.11 (a premium) show that the carrying value of bonds at the end of their lives equals par value ($100,000). The retirement of these bonds at maturity, assuming interest is already paid and entered, is recorded as follows:

Assets	= Liabilities	+ Equity
−100,000	−100,000	

2017			
Dec. 31	Bonds Payable	100,000	
	Cash		100,000
	To record retirement of bonds at maturity.		

Bond Retirement before Maturity

Point: Bond retirement is also referred to as *bond redemption.*

Point: Gains and losses from retiring bonds were *previously* reported as extraordinary items. New standards require that they now be judged by the "unusual and infrequent" criteria for reporting purposes.

Issuers sometimes wish to retire some or all of their bonds prior to maturity. For instance, if interest rates decline greatly, an issuer may wish to replace high-interest-paying bonds with new low-interest bonds. Two common ways to retire bonds before maturity are to (1) exercise a call option or (2) purchase them on the open market. In the first instance, an issuer can reserve the right to retire bonds early by issuing callable bonds. The bond indenture can give the issuer an option to *call* the bonds before they mature by paying the par value plus a *call premium* to bondholders. In the second case, the issuer retires bonds by repurchasing them on the open market at their current price. Whether bonds are called or repurchased, the issuer is unlikely to pay a price that exactly equals their carrying value. When a difference exists between the bonds' carrying value and the amount paid, the issuer records a gain or loss equal to the difference.

To illustrate the accounting for retiring callable bonds, assume that a company issued callable bonds with a par value of $100,000. The call option requires the issuer to pay a call premium of $3,000 to bondholders in addition to the par value. Next, assume that after the June 30, 2015, interest payment, the bonds have a carrying value of $104,500. Then on July 1, 2015, the issuer calls these bonds and pays $103,000 to bondholders. The issuer recognizes a $1,500 gain from the difference between the bonds' carrying value of $104,500 and the retirement price of $103,000. The issuer records this bond retirement as follows.

Assets	= Liabilities	+ Equity
−103,000	−100,000	+1,500
	−4,500	

July 1	Bonds Payable	100,000	
	Premium on Bonds Payable	4,500	
	Gain on Bond Retirement		1,500
	Cash		103,000
	To record retirement of bonds before maturity.		

An issuer usually must call all bonds when it exercises a call option. However, to retire as many or as few bonds as it desires, an issuer can purchase them on the open market. If it retires less than the entire class of bonds, it recognizes a gain or loss for the difference between the carrying value of those bonds retired and the amount paid to acquire them.

Bond Retirement by Conversion

Holders of convertible bonds have the right to convert their bonds to stock. When conversion occurs, the bonds' carrying value is transferred to equity accounts and no gain or loss is recorded. (We further describe convertible bonds in the Decision Analysis section of this chapter.)

Convertible Bond

To illustrate, assume that on January 1 the $100,000 par value bonds of **Converse**, with a carrying value of $100,000, are converted to 15,000 shares of $2 par value common stock. The entry to record this conversion follows (the market prices of the bonds and stock are *not* relevant to this entry; the material in Chapter 11 is helpful in understanding this transaction):

Jan. 1	Bonds Payable	100,000	
	Common Stock		30,000
	Paid-In Capital in Excess of Par Value		70,000
	To record retirement of bonds by conversion.		

Assets	=	Liabilities	+	Equity
		−100,000		+30,000
				+70,000

QC4

Decision Insight

Junk Bonds Junk bonds are company bonds with low credit ratings due to a higher than average likelihood of default. On the upside, the high risk of junk bonds can yield high returns if the issuer survives and repays its debt. Investors in junk bonds identify and buy bonds with low credit ratings when they believe those bonds will survive and payoff their obligations. ■

LONG-TERM NOTES PAYABLE

C1 Explain the types of notes and prepare entries to account for notes.

Like bonds, notes are issued to obtain assets such as cash. Unlike bonds, notes are typically transacted with a *single* lender such as a bank. An issuer initially records a note at its selling price—that is, the note's face value minus any discount or plus any premium. Over the note's life, the amount of interest expense allocated to each period is computed by multiplying the market rate (at issuance of the note) by the beginning-of-period note balance. The note's carrying (book) value at any time equals its face value minus any unamortized discount or plus any unamortized premium; carrying value is also computed as the present value of all remaining payments, discounted using the market rate at issuance.

Installment Notes

An **installment note** is an obligation requiring a series of payments to the lender. Installment notes are common for franchises and other businesses when lenders and borrowers agree to spread payments over several periods. To illustrate, assume that Foghog borrows $60,000 from a bank to purchase equipment. It signs an 8% installment note requiring six annual payments of principal plus interest and it records the note's issuance at January 1, 2015, as follows.

Assets = Liabilities + Equity
+60,000 +60,000

Jan. 1	Cash	60,000	
	Notes Payable		60,000
	Borrowed $60,000 by signing an 8%, six-year installment note.		

Payments on an installment note normally include the accrued interest expense plus a portion of the amount borrowed (the *principal*). This section describes an installment note with equal payments.

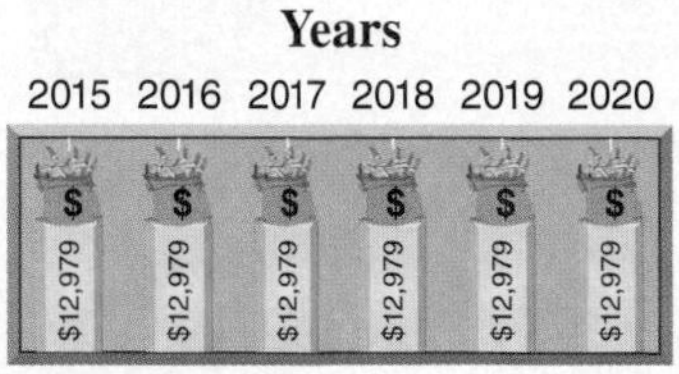

The equal total payments pattern consists of changing amounts of both interest and principal. To illustrate, assume that Foghog borrows $60,000 by signing a $60,000 note that requires six *equal payments* of $12,979 at the end of each year. (The present value of an annuity of six annual payments of $12,979, discounted at 8%, equals $60,000; we show this computation in footnote 2.) The $12,979 includes both interest and principal, the amounts of which change with each payment. Exhibit 10.14 shows the pattern of equal total payments and its two parts, interest and principal. Column A shows the note's beginning balance. Column B shows accrued interest for each year at 8% of the beginning note balance. Column C shows the impact on the note's principal, which equals the difference between the total payment in column D and the interest expense in column B. Column E shows the note's year-end balance.

Point: Most consumer notes are installment notes that require equal total payments.

EXHIBIT 10.14

Installment Note: Equal Total Payments Amortization Schedule

		Payments					
Period Ending Date	(A) Beginning Balance	(B) *Debit* Interest Expense 8% × (A)	+	(C) *Debit* Notes Payable (D) − (B)	=	(D) *Credit* Cash (computed)	(E) Ending Balance (A) − (C)
(1) **12/31/2015**	**$60,000**	**$ 4,800**		**$ 8,179**		**$12,979**	**$51,821**
(2) 12/31/2016	51,821	4,146		8,833		12,979	42,988
(3) 12/31/2017	42,988	3,439		9,540		12,979	33,448
(4) 12/31/2018	33,448	2,676		10,303		12,979	23,145
(5) 12/31/2019	23,145	1,852		11,127		12,979	12,018
(6) 12/31/2020	12,018	961		12,018		12,979	0
		$17,874		**$60,000**		**$77,874**	

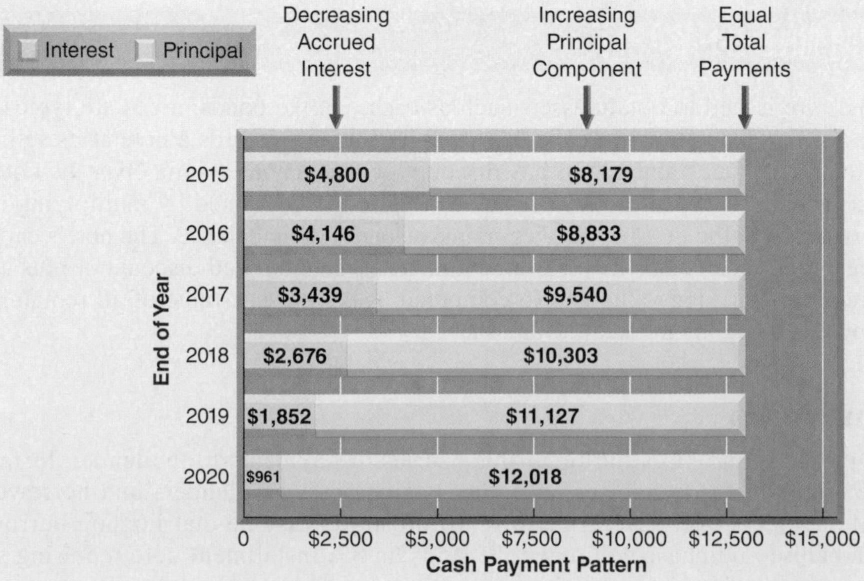

Although the six cash payments are equal, accrued interest decreases each year because the principal balance of the note declines. As the amount of interest decreases each year, the portion of each payment applied to principal increases. This pattern is graphed in the lower part of Exhibit 10.14. Foghog uses the amounts in Exhibit 10.14 to record its first two payments (for years 2015 and 2016) as follows:

2015			
Dec. 31	Interest Expense	4,800	
	Notes Payable	8,179	
	Cash		12,979
	To record first installment payment.		

Assets = Liabilities + Equity
−12,979 −8,179 −4,800

2016			
Dec. 31	Interest Expense	4,146	
	Notes Payable	8,833	
	Cash		12,979
	To record second installment payment.		

Assets = Liabilities + Equity
−12,979 −8,833 −4,146

Foghog records similar entries but with different amounts for each of the remaining four payments. After six years, the Notes Payable account balance is zero.[2]

Mortgage Notes and Bonds

A **mortgage** is a legal agreement that helps protect a lender if a borrower fails to make required payments on notes or bonds. A mortgage gives the lender a right to be paid from the cash proceeds of the sale of a borrower's assets identified in the mortgage. A legal document, called a *mortgage contract,* describes the mortgage terms.

Mortgage notes carry a mortgage contract pledging title to specific assets as security for the note. Mortgage notes are especially popular in the purchase of homes and the acquisition of plant assets. Less common *mortgage bonds* are backed by the issuer's assets. Accounting for mortgage notes and bonds is similar to that for unsecured notes and bonds, except that the mortgage agreement must be disclosed. For example, **TIBCO Software** reports that its "mortgage note payable . . . is collateralized by the commercial real property acquired [corporate headquarters]."

Point: The Truth in Lending Act requires lenders to provide information about loan costs including finance charges and interest rate.

Global: Countries vary in the preference given to debtholders vs. stockholders when a company is in financial distress. Some countries such as Germany, France, and Japan give preference to stockholders over debtholders.

Decision Maker

Entrepreneur You are a furniture retailer planning a Super Bowl sale on a home theater system that requires no payments for two years. At the end of two years, buyers must pay the full amount. The system's suggested retail price is $4,100, but you are willing to sell it today for $3,000 cash. What is your sale price if payment will not occur for two years and the market interest rate is 10%? ■ [Answers follow the chapter's Summary.]

---

[2] Table B.3 in Appendix B is used to compute the dollar amount of the six payments that equal the initial note balance of $60,000 at 8% interest. We go to Table B.3, row 6, and across to the 8% column, where the present value factor is 4.6229. The dollar amount is then computed by solving this equation:

Table	Present Value Factor		Dollar Amount		Present Value
B.3	4.6229	×	?	=	$60,000

The dollar amount is computed by dividing $60,000 by 4.6229, yielding $12,979.

Example: Suppose the $60,000 installment loan has an 8% interest rate with eight equal annual payments. What is the annual payment? *Answer* (using Table B.3): $60,000/5.7466 = $10,441

NEED-TO-KNOW 10-3

Recording Installment Note

C1 P5

On January 1, 2015, a company borrows $1,000 cash by signing a four-year, 5% installment note. The note requires four equal total payments of accrued interest and principal on December 31 of each year from 2015 through 2018.

1. Compute the amount of each of the four equal total payments.
2. Prepare an amortization table for this installment note like the one in Exhibit 10.14.
3. Prepare journal entries to record the loan on January 1, 2015, and the four payments from December 31, 2015, through December 31, 2018.

Solution

1. Amount of each payment = Initial note balance/PV of annuity (from Table B.3)
   = $1,000/3.5460 = $282 (rounded)

2. Amortization table for loan

		Payments					
Period Ending Date	(A) Beginning Balance [Prior (E)]	(B) *Debit* Interest Expense [5% × (A)]	+	(C) *Debit* Notes Payable [(D) − (B)]	=	(D) *Credit* Cash [computed]	(E) Ending Balance [(A) − (C)]
2015	$1,000	$ 50		$ 232		$ 282	$768
2016	768	38		244		282	524
2017	524	26		256		282	268
2018	268	14*		268		282	0
		$128		$1,000		$1,128	

*Adjusted for rounding.

3.

2015 Jan. 1	Cash	1,000	
	Notes Payable		1,000
	Borrowed $1,000 by signing a 5% installment note.		
2015 Dec. 31	Interest Expense	50	
	Notes Payable	232	
	Cash		282
	To record first installment payment.		
2016 Dec. 31	Interest Expense	38	
	Notes Payable	244	
	Cash		282
	To record second installment payment.		
2017 Dec. 31	Interest Expense	26	
	Notes Payable	256	
	Cash		282
	To record third installment payment.		
2018 Dec. 31	Interest Expense	14	
	Notes Payable	268	
	Cash		282
	To record fourth installment payment.		

Do More: QS 10-11, E 10-10, E 10-11

QC5

GLOBAL VIEW

This section discusses similarities and differences between U.S. GAAP and IFRS in accounting and reporting for long-term liabilities such as bonds and notes.

Accounting for Bonds and Notes The definitions and characteristics of bonds and notes are broadly similar for both U.S. GAAP and IFRS. Although slight differences exist, accounting for bonds and notes under U.S. GAAP and IFRS is similar. Specifically, the accounting for issuances (including recording discounts and premiums), market pricing, and retirement of both bonds and notes follows the procedures in this chapter. **Nokia** describes its accounting for bonds, which follows the amortized cost approach explained in this chapter (and in Appendix 10B), as follows: Loans payable [bonds] are recognized initially at fair value, net of transaction costs incurred. In the subsequent periods, loans payable are measured at amortized cost using the effective interest method.

NOKIA

Both U.S. GAAP and IFRS allow companies to account for bonds and notes using fair value (different from the amortized value described in this chapter). This method is referred to as the **fair value option.** This method is similar to that applied in measuring and accounting for debt and equity securities. *Fair value* is the amount a company would receive if it settled a liability (or sold an asset) in an orderly transaction as of the balance sheet date. Companies can use several sources of inputs to determine fair value, and those inputs fall into the following three classes (ranked in order of preference). The procedures for marking liabilities to fair value at each balance sheet date are in advanced courses.

Level 1: Observable quoted market prices in active markets for identical items.
Level 2: Observable inputs other than those in Level 1 such as prices from inactive markets or from similar, but not identical, items.
Level 3: Unobservable inputs reflecting a company's assumptions about value.

Point: Lease accounting is expected to change over the next year or so.

Accounting for Leases and Pensions Both U.S. GAAP and IFRS require companies to distinguish between operating leases and capital leases; the latter is referred to as *finance leases* under IFRS. The accounting and reporting for leases are broadly similar for both U.S. GAAP and IFRS. The main difference is the criteria for identifying a lease as a capital lease are more general under IFRS. However, the basic approach applies.

For pensions, both U.S. GAAP and IFRS require companies to record costs of retirement benefits as employees work and earn them. The basic methods are similar in accounting and reporting for pensions.

Kristian Punturere/Courtesy of stone + cloth

Sustainability and Accounting Matthew Clough, the founder of **Stone + Cloth**, as introduced in this chapter's opening feature, is a *social entrepreneur*. Matthew dedicates his business activities to help provide scholarships for students in need. Partnered with The Knock Foundation, they invest 10% of their profits into their scholarship program. As their business grows, they plan to advocate and invest in education on a global scale as they identify needs in other areas of the world.

Decision Analysis

Debt Features and the Debt-to-Equity Ratio

Collateral agreements can reduce the risk of loss for both bonds and notes. Unsecured bonds and notes are riskier because the issuer's obligation to pay interest and principal has the same priority as all other unsecured liabilities in the event of bankruptcy. If a company is unable to pay its debts in full, the unsecured creditors (including the holders of debentures) lose all or a portion of their balances. These types of legal agreements and other characteristics of long-term liabilities are crucial for effective business decisions. The first part of this section describes the different types of features sometimes included with bonds and notes. The second part explains and applies the debt-to-equity ratio.

Features of Bonds and Notes

A2 Assess debt features and their implications.

This section describes common features of debt securities.

Secured or Unsecured **Secured bonds** (and notes) have specific assets of the issuer pledged (or *mortgaged*) as collateral. This arrangement gives holders added protection against the issuer's default. If the issuer fails to pay interest or par value, the secured holders can demand that the collateral be sold and the proceeds used to pay the obligation.

Secured Debt

Unsecured Debt

Point: More than a million municipal bonds, or "munis," exist, and many are tax exempt. Munis are issued by state, city, town, and county governments to pay for public projects including schools, libraries, roads, bridges, and stadiums.

Unsecured bonds (and notes), also called *debentures,* are backed by the issuer's general credit standing. Unsecured debt is riskier than secured debt. *Subordinated debentures* are liabilities that are not repaid until the claims of the more senior, unsecured (and secured) liabilities are settled.

Term or Serial **Term bonds** (and notes) are scheduled for maturity on one specified date. **Serial bonds** (and notes) mature at more than one date (often in series) and thus are usually repaid over a number of periods. For instance, $100,000 of serial bonds might mature at the rate of $10,000 each year from 6 to 15 years after they are issued. Many bonds are **sinking fund bonds,** which to reduce the holder's risk require the issuer to create a *sinking fund* of assets set aside at specified amounts and dates to repay the bonds.

Registered or Bearer Bonds issued in the names and addresses of their holders are **registered bonds.** The issuer makes bond payments by sending checks (or cash transfers) to registered holders. A registered holder must notify the issuer of any ownership change. Registered bonds offer the issuer the practical advantage of not having to actually issue bond certificates. Bonds payable to whoever holds them (the *bearer*) are called **bearer bonds** or *unregistered bonds.* Sales or exchanges might not be recorded, so the holder of a bearer bond is presumed to be its rightful owner. As a result, lost bearer bonds are difficult to replace. Many bearer bonds are also **coupon bonds.** This term reflects interest coupons that are attached to the bonds. When each coupon matures, the holder presents it to a bank or broker for collection. At maturity, the holder follows the same process and presents the bond certificate for collection. Issuers of coupon bonds cannot deduct the related interest expense for taxable income. This is to prevent abuse by taxpayers who own coupon bonds but fail to report interest income on their tax returns.

Convertible Debt

Callable Debt

Convertible and/or Callable **Convertible bonds** (and notes) can be exchanged for a fixed number of shares of the issuing corporation's common stock. Convertible debt offers holders the potential to participate in future increases in stock price. Holders still receive periodic interest while the debt is held and the par value if they hold the debt to maturity. In most cases, the holders decide whether and when to convert debt to stock. **Callable bonds** (and notes) have an option exercisable by the issuer to retire them at a stated dollar amount before maturity.

Decision Insight

Collateral Lenders prefer that more liquid assets serve as collateral for loans. These usually are current assets such as accounts receivable or inventory. The reason is if borrowers default and collateral must be seized, then lenders desire assets that are easily sold to recover losses. ■

Debt-to-Equity Ratio

A3 Compute the debt-to-equity ratio and explain its use.

Beyond assessing different characteristics of debt as just described, we want to know the level of debt, especially in relation to total equity. Such knowledge helps us assess the risk of a company's financing structure. A company financed mainly with debt is more risky because liabilities must be repaid—usually with periodic interest—whereas equity financing does not. A measure to assess the risk of a company's financing structure is the **debt-to-equity ratio** (see Exhibit 10.15).

EXHIBIT 10.15 Debt-to-Equity Ratio

$$\text{Debt-to-equity} = \frac{\text{Total liabilities}}{\text{Total equity}}$$

The debt-to-equity ratio varies across companies and industries. To apply the debt-to-equity ratio, let's look at this measure for **Amazon.com** in Exhibit 10.16.

EXHIBIT 10.16 Amazon's Debt-to-Equity Ratio

($ millions)	2013	2012	2011	2010
Total liabilities	$30,413	$24,363	$17,521	$11,933
Total equity	$ 9,746	$ 8,192	$ 7,757	$ 6,864
Debt-to-equity	3.1	3.0	2.3	1.7
Industry debt-to-equity	**1.6**	**1.5**	**1.5**	**1.4**

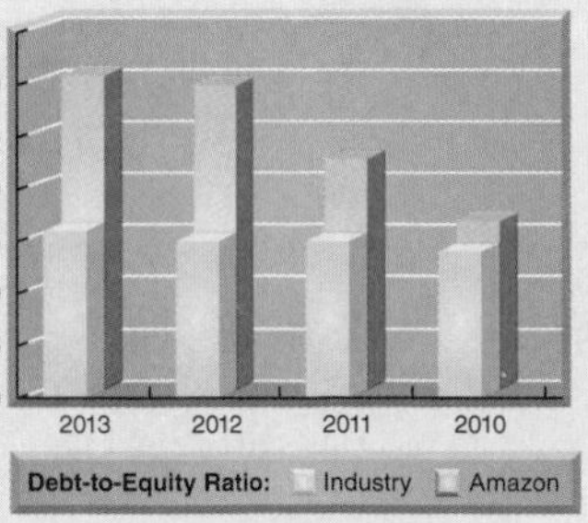

Amazon's 2013 debt-to-equity ratio is 3.1, meaning that debtholders contributed $3.10 for each $1 contributed by equity holders. This implies a riskier than usual financing structure for Amazon. A similar concern is drawn from a comparison of Amazon with its competitors, where the 2013 industry ratio is 1.6. Analysis across the years shows that Amazon's financing structure has risen to a riskier level in recent years. Given its growth in revenues and innovative past, investors have been patient in waiting for income. However, debtholders will grow increasingly concerned if income doesn't rise in the near future.

Decision Maker

Bond Investor You plan to purchase debenture bonds from one of two companies in the same industry that are similar in size and performance. The first company has $350,000 in total liabilities and $1,750,000 in equity. The second company has $1,200,000 in total liabilities and $1,000,000 in equity. Which company's debenture bonds are less risky based on the debt-to-equity ratio? ■ [Answers follow the chapter's Summary.]

NEED-TO-KNOW

COMPREHENSIVE

Water Sports Company (WSC) patented and successfully test-marketed a new product. To expand its ability to produce and market the new product, WSC needs to raise $800,000 of financing. On January 1, 2015, the company obtained the money in two ways:

a. WSC signed a $400,000, 10% installment note to be repaid with five equal annual installments to be made on December 31 of 2015 through 2019.

b. WSC issued five-year bonds with a par value of $400,000. The bonds have a 12% annual contract rate and pay interest on June 30 and December 31. The bonds' annual market rate is 10% as of January 1, 2015.

Required

1. For the installment note, (*a*) compute the size of each annual payment, (*b*) prepare an amortization table such as Exhibit 10.14, and (*c*) prepare the journal entry for the first payment.

2. For the bonds, (*a*) compute their issue price; (*b*) prepare the January 1, 2015, journal entry to record their issuance; (*c*) prepare an amortization table using the straight-line method; (*d*) prepare the June 30, 2015, journal entry to record the first interest payment; and (*e*) prepare a journal entry to record retiring the bonds at a $416,000 call price on January 1, 2017.

3[B]. Redo parts 2(*c*), 2(*d*), and 2(*e*) assuming the bonds are amortized using the effective interest method.

PLANNING THE SOLUTION

- For the installment note, divide the borrowed amount by the annuity factor (from Table B.3) using the 10% rate and five payments to compute the amount of each payment. Prepare a table similar to Exhibit 10.14 and use the numbers in the table's first line for the journal entry.
- Compute the bonds' issue price by using the market rate to find the present value of their cash flows (use tables found in Appendix B). Then use this result to record the bonds' issuance. Next, prepare an amortization table like Exhibit 10.11 (and Exhibit 10B.2) and use it to get the numbers needed for the journal entry. Also use the table to find the carrying value as of the date of the bonds' retirement that you need for the journal entry.

SOLUTION

Part 1: Installment Note

a. Annual payment = Note balance/PV Annuity factor = $400,000/3.7908 = $105,519 (The present value annuity factor is for five payments and a rate of 10%.)

b. An amortization table for the long-term note payable follows.

Annual Period Ending	(a) Beginning Balance	(b) Debit Interest Expense 10% × (a)		(c) Debit Notes Payable (d) − (b)		(d) Credit Cash (computed)	(e) Ending Balance (a) − (c)
		Payments					
(1) 12/31/2015	$400,000	$ 40,000	+	$ 65,519	=	$105,519	$334,481
(2) 12/31/2016	334,481	33,448		72,071		105,519	262,410
(3) 12/31/2017	262,410	26,241		79,278		105,519	183,132
(4) 12/31/2018	183,132	18,313		87,206		105,519	95,926
(5) 12/31/2019	95,926	9,593		95,926		105,519	0
		$127,595		$400,000		$527,595	

c. Journal entry for December 31, 2015, payment.

Dec. 31	Interest Expense	40,000	
	Notes Payable	65,519	
	Cash		105,519
	To record first installment payment.		

Part 2: Bonds (Straight-Line Amortization)

a. Compute the bonds' issue price.

Cash Flow	Table	Present Value Factor*	Amount	Present Value
Par (maturity) value	B.1 in App. B (PV of 1)	0.6139	× 400,000	= $245,560
Interest payments	B.3 in App. B (PV of annuity)	7.7217	× 24,000	= 185,321
Price of bond				$430,881

* Present value factors are for 10 payments using a semiannual market rate of 5%.

b. Journal entry for January 1, 2015, issuance.

Jan. 1	Cash	430,881	
	Premium on Bonds Payable		30,881
	Bonds Payable		400,000
	Sold bonds at a premium.		

c. Straight-line amortization table for premium bonds.

	A	B	C
1–2	Semiannual Period-End	Unamortized Premium	Carrying Value
3	(0) 1/1/2015	$ 30,881	$ 430,881
4	(1) 6/30/2015	27,793	427,793
5	(2) 12/31/2015	24,705	424,705
6	(3) 6/30/2016	21,617	421,617
7	(4) 12/31/2016	18,529	418,529
8	(5) 6/30/2017	15,441	415,441
9	(6) 12/31/2017	12,353	412,353
10	(7) 6/30/2018	9,265	409,265
11	(8) 12/31/2018	6,177	406,177
12	(9) 6/30/2019	3,089	403,089
13	(10) 12/31/2019	0*	400,000
14			

* Adjusted for rounding.

d. Journal entry for June 30, 2015, bond payment.

June 30	Bond Interest Expense	20,912	
	Premium on Bonds Payable	3,088	
	Cash		24,000
	Paid semiannual interest on bonds.		

e. Journal entry for January 1, 2017, bond retirement.

Jan. 1	Bonds Payable	400,000	
	Premium on Bonds Payable	18,529	
	Cash		416,000
	Gain on Retirement of Bonds		2,529
	To record bond retirement (carrying value as of Dec. 31, 2016).		

Part 3: Bonds (Effective Interest Amortization)—Appendix 10B

c. The effective interest amortization table for premium bonds.

	A	B	C	D	E	F
1–4	Semiannual Interest Period	(A) Cash Interest Paid 6% × $400,000	(B) Interest Expense 5% × Prior (E)	(C) Premium Amortization (A) − (B)	(D) Unamortized Premium Prior (D) − (C)	(E) Carrying Value $400,000 + (D)
5	(0) 1/1/2015				$30,881	$430,881
6	(1) 6/30/2015	$ 24,000	$ 21,544	$ 2,456	28,425	428,425
7	(2) 12/31/2015	24,000	21,421	2,579	25,846	425,846
8	(3) 6/30/2016	24,000	21,292	2,708	23,138	423,138
9	(4) 12/31/2016	24,000	21,157	2,843	20,295	420,295
10	(5) 6/30/2017	24,000	21,015	2,985	17,310	417,310
11	(6) 12/31/2017	24,000	20,866	3,134	14,176	414,176
12	(7) 6/30/2018	24,000	20,709	3,291	10,885	410,885
13	(8) 12/31/2018	24,000	20,544	3,456	7,429	407,429
14	(9) 6/30/2019	24,000	20,371	3,629	3,800	403,800
15	(10) 12/31/2019	24,000	20,200*	3,800	0	400,000
16		$240,000	$209,119	$30,881		
17						

* Adjusted for rounding.

d. Journal entry for June 30, 2015, bond payment.

June 30	Bond Interest Expense	21,544	
	Premium on Bonds Payable	2,456	
	Cash		24,000
	Paid semiannual interest on bonds.		

e. Journal entry for January 1, 2017, bond retirement.

Jan. 1	Bonds Payable	400,000	
	Premium on Bonds Payable	20,295	
	Cash		416,000
	Gain on Retirement of Bonds		4,295
	To record bond retirement (carrying value as of December 31, 2016).		

APPENDIX

Present Values of Bonds and Notes

10A

C2 Explain and compute the present value of an amount(s) to be paid at a future date(s).

This appendix explains how to apply present value techniques to measure a long-term liability when it is created and to assign interest expense to the periods until it is settled. Appendix B at the end of the book provides additional discussion of present value concepts.

Present Value Concepts The basic present value concept is that cash paid (or received) in the future has less value now than the same amount of cash paid (or received) today. To illustrate, if we must pay $1 one year from now, its present value is less than $1. To see this, assume that we borrow $0.9259 today that must be paid back in one year with 8% interest. Our interest expense for this loan is computed as $0.9259 × 8%, or $0.0741. When the $0.0741 interest is added to the $0.9259 borrowed, we get the $1 payment necessary to repay our loan with interest. This is formally computed in Exhibit 10A.1. The

EXHIBIT 10A.1

Components of a One-Year Loan

Amount borrowed	**$0.9259**
Interest for one year at 8%	0.0741
Amount owed after 1 year	$ 1.0000

$0.9259 borrowed is the present value of the $1 future payment. More generally, an amount borrowed equals the present value of the future payment. (This same interpretation applies to an investment. If $0.9259 is invested at 8%, it yields $0.0741 in revenue after one year. This amounts to $1, made up of principal and interest.)

Point: Benjamin Franklin is said to have described compounding as "the money, money makes, makes more money."

To extend this example, assume that we owe $1 two years from now instead of one year, and the 8% interest is compounded annually. *Compounded* means that interest during the second period is based on the total of the amount borrowed plus the interest accrued from the first period. The second period's interest is then computed as 8% multiplied by the sum of the amount borrowed plus interest earned in the first period. Exhibit 10A.2 shows how we compute the present value of $1 to be paid in two years. This amount is $0.8573. The first year's interest of $0.0686 is added to the principal so that the second year's interest is based on $0.9259. Total interest for this two-year period is $0.1427, computed as $0.0686 plus $0.0741.

EXHIBIT 10A.2

Components of a Two-Year Loan

Amount borrowed	**$0.8573**
Interest for first year ($0.8573 × 8%)	0.0686
Amount owed after 1 year	0.9259
Interest for second year ($0.9259 × 8%)	0.0741
Amount owed after 2 years	$ 1.0000

Present Value Tables The present value of $1 that we must repay at some future date can be computed by using this formula: $1/(1 + i)^n$. The symbol i is the interest rate per period and n is the number of periods until the future payment must be made. Applying this formula to our two-year loan, we get $\$1/(1.08)^2$, or $0.8573. This is the same value shown in Exhibit 10A.2. We can use this formula to find any present value. However, a simpler method is to use a *present value table,* which lists present values computed with this formula for various interest rates and time periods. Many people find it helpful in learning present value concepts to first work with the table and then move to using a calculator.

EXHIBIT 10A.3

Present Value of 1

	Rate		
Periods	6%	8%	10%
1	0.9434	**0.9259**	0.9091
2	0.8900	**0.8573**	0.8264
3	0.8396	0.7938	0.7513
4	0.7921	0.7350	0.6830
5	0.7473	0.6806	0.6209
6	0.7050	0.6302	0.5645
7	0.6651	0.5835	0.5132
8	0.6274	0.5403	0.4665
9	0.5919	0.5002	0.4241
10	0.5584	0.4632	0.3855

Exhibit 10A.3 shows a present value table for a future payment of 1 for up to 10 periods at three different interest rates. Present values in this table are rounded to four decimal places. This table is drawn from the larger and more complete Table B.1 in Appendix B at the end of the book. Notice that the first value in the 8% column is 0.9259, the value we computed earlier for the present value of a $1 loan for one year at 8% (see Exhibit 10A.1). Go to the second row in the same 8% column and find the present value of 1 discounted at 8% for two years, or 0.8573. This $0.8573 is the present value of our obligation to repay $1 after two periods at 8% interest (see Exhibit 10A.2).

Example: Use Exhibit 10A.3 to find the present value of $1 discounted for 2 years at 6%. *Answer:* $0.8900

EXHIBIT 10A.4

Present Value of a Series of Unequal Payments

Periods	Payments	Present Value of 1 at 10%	Present Value of Payments
1	$2,000	0.9091	$ 1,818
2	3,000	0.8264	2,479
3	5,000	0.7513	3,757
Present value of all payments			**$8,054**

Applying a Present Value Table To illustrate how to measure a liability using a present value table, assume that a company plans to borrow cash and repay it as follows: $2,000 after one year, $3,000 after two years, and $5,000 after three years. How much does this company receive today if the interest rate on this loan is 10%? To answer, we need to compute the present value of the three future payments, discounted at 10%. This computation is shown in Exhibit 10A.4 using present values from Exhibit 10A.3. The company can borrow $8,054 today at 10% interest in exchange for its promise to make these three payments at the scheduled dates.

Present Value of an Annuity The $8,054 present value for the loan in Exhibit 10A.4 equals the sum of the present values of the three payments. When payments are not equal, their combined present value is best computed by adding the individual present values as shown in Exhibit 10A.4. Sometimes payments follow an **annuity,** which is a series of *equal* payments at equal time intervals. The present value of an annuity is readily computed.

To illustrate, assume that a company must repay a 6% loan with a $5,000 payment at each year-end for the next four years. This loan amount equals the present value of the four payments discounted at 6%. Exhibit 10A.5 shows how to compute this loan's present value of $17,326 by multiplying each payment by its matching present value factor taken from Exhibit 10A.3.

EXHIBIT 10A.5

Present Value of a Series of Equal Payments (Annuity) by Discounting Each Payment

Periods	Payments	Present Value of 1 at 6%	Present Value of Payments
1	$5,000	0.9434	$ 4,717
2	5,000	0.8900	4,450
3	5,000	0.8396	4,198
4	5,000	0.7921	3,961
Present value of all payments		**3.4651**	**$17,326**

Point: Four payments of $5,000 at the end of each of the next 4 years is the equivalent of 3.4651 payments of $5,000 today.

However, the series of $5,000 payments is an annuity, so we can compute its present value with either of two shortcuts. First, the third column of Exhibit 10A.5 shows that the sum of the present values of 1 at 6% for periods 1 through 4 equals 3.4651. One shortcut is to multiply this total of 3.4651 by the $5,000 annual payment to get the combined present value of $17,326. It requires one multiplication instead of four.

The second shortcut uses an *annuity table* such as the one shown in Exhibit 10A.6, which is drawn from the more complete Table B.3 in Appendix B. We go directly to the annuity table to get the present value factor for a specific number of payments and interest rate. We then multiply this factor by the amount of the payment to find the present value of the annuity. Specifically, find the row for four periods and go across to the 6% column, where the factor is 3.4651. This factor equals the present value of an annuity with four payments of 1, discounted at 6%. We then multiply 3.4651 by $5,000 to get the $17,326 present value of the annuity.

EXHIBIT 10A.6

Present Value of an Annuity of 1

	Rate		
Periods	6%	8%	10%
1	0.9434	0.9259	0.9091
2	1.8334	1.7833	1.7355
3	2.6730	2.5771	2.4869
4	**3.4651**	3.3121	3.1699
5	4.2124	3.9927	3.7908
6	4.9173	4.6229	4.3553
7	5.5824	5.2064	4.8684
8	6.2098	5.7466	5.3349
9	6.8017	6.2469	5.7590
10	7.3601	6.7101	6.1446

Example: Use Exhibit 10A.6 to find the present value of an annuity of eight $15,000 payments with an 8% interest rate. *Answer:* $15,000 × 5.7466 = $86,199

Compounding Periods Shorter Than a Year The present value examples all involved periods of one year. In many situations, however, interest is compounded over shorter periods. For example, the interest rate on bonds is usually stated as an annual rate but interest is often paid every six months (semiannually). This means that the present value of interest payments from such bonds must be computed using interest periods of six months.

QC6

Assume that a borrower wants to know the present value of a series of 10 *semiannual payments* of $4,000 made over five years at an *annual interest rate* of 12%. The interest rate is stated as an annual rate of 12%, but it is actually a rate of 6% per semiannual interest period. To compute the present value of this series of $4,000 payments, go to row 10 of Exhibit 10A.6 and across to the 6% column to find the factor 7.3601. The present value of this annuity is $29,440 (7.3601 × $4,000).

Example: If this borrower makes five semiannual payments of $8,000, what is the present value of this annuity at a 12% rate? *Answer:* 4.2124 × $8,000 = $33,699

Appendix B further describes present value concepts and includes more complete present value tables and assignments.

APPENDIX

10B Effective Interest Amortization

P5 Compute and record amortization of bond discount using effective interest method.

Effective Interest Amortization of a Discount Bond The straight-line method yields changes in the bonds' carrying value while the amount for bond interest expense remains constant. This gives the impression of a changing interest rate when users divide a constant bond interest expense over a changing carrying value. As a result, accounting standards allow use of the straight-line method only when its results do not differ materially from those obtained using the effective interest method. The **effective interest method,** or simply *interest method,* allocates total bond interest expense over the bonds'

Point: The effective interest method computes bond interest expense using the market rate at issuance. This rate is applied to a changing carrying value.

life in a way that yields a constant rate of interest. This constant rate of interest is the market rate at the issue date. Thus, bond interest expense for a period equals the carrying value of the bond at the beginning of that period multiplied by the market rate when issued.

Exhibit 10B.1 shows an effective interest amortization table for the Fila bonds (as described in Exhibit 10.4). The key difference between the effective interest and straight-line methods lies in computing bond interest expense. Instead of assigning an equal amount of bond interest expense to each period, the effective interest method assigns a bond interest expense amount that increases over the life of a discount bond. **Both methods allocate the *same* $19,546 of total bond interest expense to the bonds' life, but in different patterns.** Specifically, the amortization table in Exhibit 10B.1 shows that the balance of the discount (column D) is amortized until it reaches zero. Also, the bonds' carrying value (column E) changes each period until it equals par value at maturity. Compare columns D and E to the corresponding columns in Exhibit 10.7 to see the amortization patterns. Total bond interest expense is $19,546, consisting of $16,000 of semiannual cash payments and $3,546 of the original bond discount, the same for both methods.

Point: Contract rate determines cash interest paid, but the market rate determines the actual interest expense.

EXHIBIT 10B.1

Effective Interest Amortization of Bond Discount

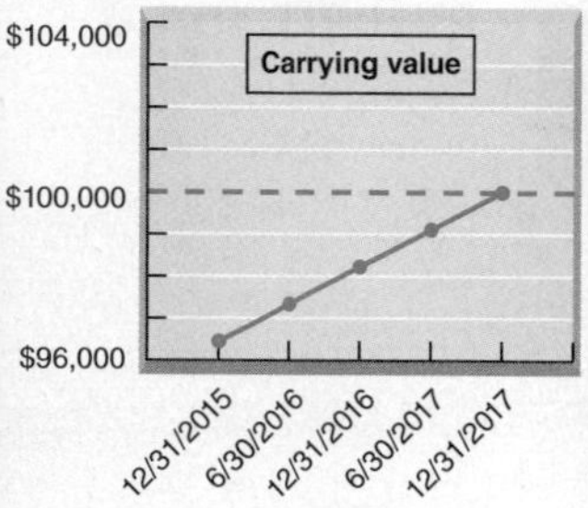

Bonds: $100,000 Par Value, Semiannual Interest Payments, Two-Year Life, 4% Semiannual Contract Rate, 5% Semiannual Market Rate

Semiannual Interest Period-End	(A) Cash Interest Paid 4% × $100,000	(B) Bond Interest Expense 5% × Prior (E)	(C) Discount Amortization (B) − (A)	(D) Unamortized Discount Prior (D) − (C)	(E) Carrying Value $100,000 − (D)
(0) **12/31/2015**				**$3,546**	**$ 96,454**
(1) **6/30/2016**	**$4,000**	**$4,823**	**$ 823**	**2,723**	**97,277**
(2) 12/31/2016	4,000	4,864	864	1,859	98,141
(3) 6/30/2017	4,000	4,907	907	952	99,048
(4) 12/31/2017	4,000	4,952	952	**0**	**100,000**
	$16,000	$19,546	$3,546		

Column (**A**) is the par value ($100,000) multiplied by the semiannual contract rate (4%).
Column (**B**) is the prior period's carrying value multiplied by the semiannual market rate (5%).
Column (**C**) is the difference between interest paid and bond interest expense, or [(B) − (A)].
Column (**D**) is the prior period's unamortized discount less the current period's discount amortization.
Column (**E**) is the par value less unamortized discount, or [$100,000 − (D)].

Except for differences in amounts, journal entries recording the expense and updating the liability balance are the same under the effective interest method and the straight-line method. We can use the numbers in Exhibit 10B.1 to record each semiannual entry during the bonds' two-year life (June 30, 2016, through December 31, 2017). For instance, we record the interest payment at the end of the first semiannual period as follows:

2016			
June 30	Bond Interest Expense	4,823	
	Discount on Bonds Payable		823
	Cash		4,000
	To record semiannual interest and discount amortization (effective interest method).		

Assets = Liabilities + Equity
−4,000 +823 −4,823

P6 Compute and record amortization of bond premium using effective interest method.

Effective Interest Amortization of a Premium Bond Exhibit 10B.2 shows the amortization table using the effective interest method for the Adidas bonds (as described in Exhibit 10.8). Column A lists the semiannual cash payments. Column B shows the amount of bond interest expense, computed as the 5% semiannual market rate at issuance multiplied by the beginning-of-period carrying value. The amount of cash paid in column A is larger than the bond interest expense because the cash payment is based on the higher 6% semiannual contract rate. The excess cash payment over the interest expense reduces the principal. These amounts are shown in column C. Column E shows the carrying

EXHIBIT 10B.2

Effective Interest Amortization of Bond Premium

	A	B	C	D	E	F
1–2	**Bonds: $100,000 Par Value, Semiannual Interest Payments, Two-Year Life, 6% Semiannual Contract Rate, 5% Semiannual Market Rate**					
3–5	**Semiannual Interest Period-End**	**(A) Cash Interest Paid**	**(B) Bond Interest Expense**	**(C) Premium Amortization**	**(D) Unamortized Premium**	**(E) Carrying Value**
6		6% × $100,000	5% × Prior (E)	(A) − (B)	Prior (D) − (C)	$100,000 + (D)
7	(0) **12/31/2015**				**$3,546**	**$103,546**
8	(1) **6/30/2016**	**$6,000**	**$5,177**	**$ 823**	**2,723**	**102,723**
9	(2) 12/31/2016	6,000	5,136	864	1,859	101,859
10	(3) 6/30/2017	6,000	5,093	907	952	100,952
11	(4) 12/31/2017	6,000	5,048	952	**0**	**100,000**
12		$24,000	$20,454	$3,546		
13						

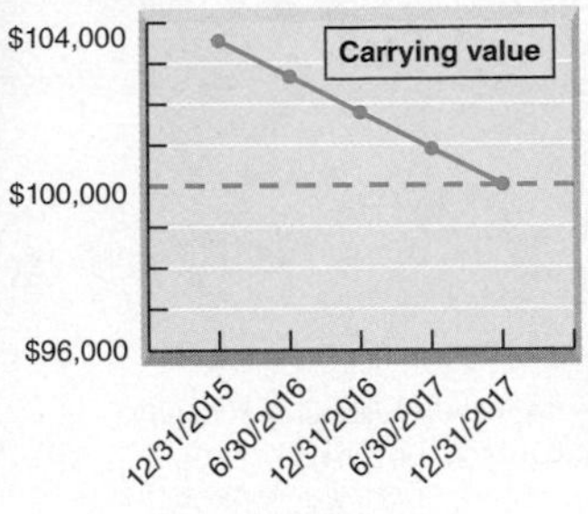

Column (**A**) is the par value ($100,000) multiplied by the semiannual contract rate (6%).
Column (**B**) is the prior period's carrying value multiplied by the semiannual market rate (5%).
Column (**C**) is the difference between interest paid and bond interest expense, or [(A) − (B)].
Column (**D**) is the prior period's unamortized premium less the current period's premium amortization.
Column (**E**) is the par value plus unamortized premium, or [$100,000 + (D)].

Bonds Payable

Debit		Credit	
		12/31/2015	100,000
		6/30/2016	—
		12/31/2016	—
		6/30/2017	—
		12/31/2017	**100,000**

Premium on Bonds Payable

Debit		Credit	
		12/31/2015	3,546
6/30/2016	823		
12/31/2016	864		
6/30/2017	907		
12/31/2017	952		
		12/31/2017	**0**

value after deducting the amortized premium in column C from the prior period's carrying value. Column D shows the premium's reduction by periodic amortization. When the issuer makes the first semiannual interest payment, the effect of premium amortization on bond interest expense and bond liability is recorded as follows:

2016			
June 30	Bond Interest Expense	5,177	
	Premium on Bonds Payable	823	
	Cash		6,000
	To record semiannual interest and premium amortization (effective interest method).		

Assets	=	Liabilities	+	Equity
−6,000		−823		−5,177

Similar entries with different amounts are recorded at each payment date until the bond matures at the end of 2017. The effective interest method yields decreasing amounts of bond interest expense and increasing amounts of premium amortization over the bonds' life.

IFRS

Unlike U.S. GAAP, IFRS requires that interest expense be computed using the effective interest method with *no* exceptions. ■

APPENDIX

Issuing Bonds between Interest Dates **10C**

C3 Describe interest accrual when bond payment periods differ from accounting periods.

An issuer can sell bonds at a date other than an interest payment date. When this occurs, the buyers normally pay the issuer the purchase price plus any interest accrued since the prior interest payment date. This accrued interest is then repaid to these buyers on the next interest payment date. To illustrate, suppose **Avia** sells $100,000 of its 9% bonds at par on March 1, 2015, 60 days after the stated issue date. The interest on Avia bonds is payable semiannually on each June 30 and December 31. Since 60 days have passed, the issuer collects accrued interest from the buyers at the time of issuance. This amount is $1,500 ($100,000 × 9% × $^{60}/_{360}$ year). This case is reflected in Exhibit 10C.1.

EXHIBIT 10C.1

Accruing Interest between Interest Payment Dates

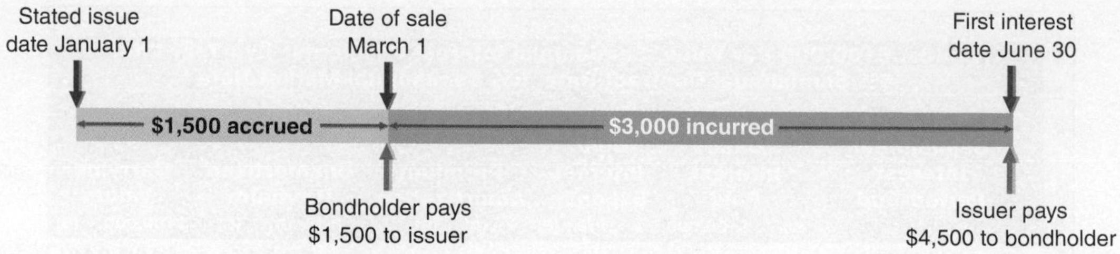

Avia records the issuance of these bonds on March 1, 2015, as follows:

Assets = Liabilities + Equity
+101,500 +100,000
+1,500

Mar. 1	Cash	101,500	
	Interest Payable		1,500
	Bonds Payable.		100,000
	Sold bonds at par with accrued interest.		

Example: How much interest is collected from a buyer of $50,000 of Avia bonds sold at par 150 days after the contract issue date? *Answer:* $1,875 (computed as $50,000 × 9% × 150/360 year)

Liabilities for interest payable and bonds payable are recorded in separate accounts. When the June 30, 2015, semiannual interest date arrives, Avia pays the full semiannual interest of $4,500 ($100,000 × 9% × ½ year) to the bondholders. This payment includes the four months' interest of $3,000 earned by the bondholders from March 1 to June 30 *plus* the repayment of the 60 days' accrued interest collected by Avia when the bonds were sold. Avia records this first semiannual interest payment as follows:

Assets = Liabilities + Equity
−4,500 −1,500 −3,000

June 30	Interest Payable	1,500	
	Bond Interest Expense.	3,000	
	Cash		4,500
	Paid semiannual interest on the bonds.		

The practice of collecting and then repaying accrued interest with the next interest payment is to simplify the issuer's administrative efforts. To explain, suppose an issuer sells bonds on 15 or 20 different dates between the stated issue date and the first interest payment date. If the issuer does not collect accrued interest from buyers, it needs to pay different amounts of cash to each of them according to the time that passed after purchasing the bonds. The issuer needs to keep detailed records of buyers and the dates they bought bonds. Issuers avoid this recordkeeping by having each buyer pay accrued interest at purchase. Issuers then pay the full semiannual interest to all buyers, regardless of when they bought bonds.

Accruing Bond Interest Expense If a bond's interest period does not coincide with the issuer's accounting period, an adjusting entry is needed to recognize bond interest expense accrued since the most recent interest payment. To illustrate, assume that the stated issue date for Adidas bonds described in Exhibit 10.10 is September 1, 2015, instead of December 31, 2015, and that the bonds are sold on September 1, 2015. As a result, four months' interest (and premium amortization) accrue before the end of the 2015 calendar year. Interest for this period equals $3,409, or 4/6 of the first six months' interest of $5,113. Also, the premium amortization is $591, or 4/6 of the first six months' amortization of $887. The sum of the bond interest expense and the amortization is $4,000 ($3,409 + $591), which equals 4/6 of the $6,000 cash payment due on February 28, 2016. Adidas records these effects with an adjusting entry at December 31, 2015.

Point: Computation of accrued bond interest may use months instead of days for simplicity purposes. For example, the accrued interest computation for the Adidas bonds is based on months.

Assets = Liabilities + Equity
−591 −3,409
+4,000

Dec. 31	Bond Interest Expense ($5,113 × 4/6).	3,409	
	Premium on Bonds Payable ($887 × 4/6)	591	
	Interest Payable ($6,000 × 4/6)		4,000
	To record four months' accrued interest and premium amortization.		

Similar entries are made on each December 31 throughout the bonds' two-year life. When the $6,000 cash payment occurs on each February 28 interest payment date, Adidas must recognize bond interest expense and amortization for January and February. It must also eliminate the interest payable liability created by the December 31 adjusting entry. For example, Adidas records its payment on February 28, 2016, as follows:

Feb. 28	Interest Payable	4,000	
	Bond Interest Expense ($5,113 × ⅓)	1,704	
	Premium on Bonds Payable ($887 × ⅓)	296	
	Cash		6,000
	To record 2 months' interest and amortization, and eliminate accrued interest liability.		

Assets	=	Liabilities	+	Equity
−6,000		−4,000		−1,704
		−296		

QC7

The interest payments made each August 31 are recorded as usual because the entire six-month interest period is included within this company's calendar-year reporting period.

Decision Maker

Bond Rater You work for **Moody's** rating service and it's your job to assist in assigning a rating to a bond that reflects its risk to bondholders. Identify factors you consider in assessing bond risk. Indicate the likely levels (relative to the norm) for the factors you identify for a bond that sells at a discount. ■ [Answers follow the chapter's Summary.]

APPENDIX

Leases and Pensions

10D

This appendix briefly explains the accounting and analysis for both leases and pensions.

C4 Describe accounting for leases and pensions.

Lease Liabilities A **lease** is a contractual agreement between a *lessor* (asset owner) and a *lessee* (asset renter or tenant) that grants the lessee the right to use the asset for a period of time in return for cash (rent) payments. Nearly one-fourth of all equipment purchases are financed with leases. The advantages of lease financing include the lack of an immediate large cash payment and the potential to deduct rental payments in computing taxable income. From an accounting perspective, leases can be classified as either operating or capital leases. (Lease accounting will change over the next few years, whereby operating leases are likely to be accounted for similar to capital leases . . . stay tuned!)

Operating Leases **Operating leases** are short-term (or cancelable) leases in which the lessor retains the risks and rewards of ownership. Examples include most car and apartment rental agreements. The lessee records such lease payments as expenses; the lessor records them as revenue. The lessee does not report the leased item as an asset or a liability (it is the lessor's asset). To illustrate, if an employee of Amazon leases a car for $300 at an airport while on company business, Amazon (lessee) records this cost as follows:

Point: Home Depot reports that its rental expenses from operating leases total more than $900 million.

July 4	Rental Expense	300	
	Cash		300
	To record lease rental payment.		

Assets	=	Liabilities	+	Equity
−300				−300

Capital Leases **Capital leases** are long-term (or noncancelable) leases by which the lessor transfers substantially all risks and rewards of ownership to the lessee.[3] Examples include most leases of airplanes and department store buildings. The lessee records the leased item as its own asset along with a lease liability at the start of the lease term; the amount recorded equals the present value of all lease payments. To illustrate, assume that K2 Co. enters into a six-year lease of a building in which it will sell sporting

[3] A *capital lease* meets any one or more of four criteria: (1) transfers title of leased asset to lessee, (2) contains a bargain purchase option, (3) has a lease term that is 75% or more of the leased asset's useful life, or (4) has a present value of lease payments that is 90% or more of the leased asset's market value.

equipment. The lease transfers all building ownership risks and rewards to K2 (the present value of its $12,979 annual lease payments is $60,000). K2 records this transaction as follows:

Assets = Liabilities + Equity
+60,000 +60,000

2015			
Jan. 1	Leased Asset—Building.	60,000	
	Lease Liability		60,000
	To record leased asset and lease liability.		

Point: Home Depot reports *"certain locations . . . are leased under capital leases."* The net present value of this lease liability is about $400 million.

K2 reports the leased asset as a plant asset and the lease liability as a long-term liability. The portion of the lease liability expected to be paid in the next year is reported as a current liability.[4] At each year-end, K2 records depreciation on the leased asset (assume straight-line depreciation, six-year lease term, no bargain purchase option, and no salvage value) as follows:

Assets = Liabilities + Equity
−10,000 −10,000

Dec. 31	Depreciation Expense—Leased Asset, Building.	10,000	
	Accumulated Depreciation—Leased Asset, Building		10,000
	To record depreciation on leased asset.		

K2 also accrues interest on the lease liability at each year-end. Interest expense is computed by multiplying the remaining lease liability by the interest rate on the lease. Specifically, K2 records its annual interest expense as part of its annual lease payment ($12,979) as follows (for its first year):

Assets = Liabilities + Equity
−12,979 −8,179 −4,800

2015			
Dec. 31	Interest Expense	4,800	
	Lease Liability	8,179	
	Cash.		12,979
	*To record first annual lease payment.**		

* These numbers are computed from a *lease payment schedule.* For simplicity, we use the same numbers from Exhibit 10.14 for this lease payment schedule—with different headings as follows:

		Payments			
	(A)	(B) *Debit*	(C) *Debit*	(D) *Credit*	(E)
Period Ending Date	Beginning Balance of Lease Liability	Interest on Lease Liability 8% × (A)	+ Lease Liability (D) − (B)	= Cash Lease Payment	Ending Balance of Lease Liability (A) − (C)
12/31/2015	**$60,000**	**$ 4,800**	**$ 8,179**	**$12,979**	**$51,821**
12/31/2016	51,821	4,146	8,833	12,979	42,988
12/31/2017	42,988	3,439	9,540	12,979	33,448
12/31/2018	33,448	2,676	10,303	12,979	23,145
12/31/2019	23,145	1,852	11,127	12,979	12,018
12/31/2020	12,018	961	12,018	12,979	0
		$17,874	**$60,000**	**$77,874**	

Point: Fringe benefits are often 40% or more of salaries and wages, and pension benefits make up nearly 15% of fringe benefits.

Point: Two types of pension plans are (1) *defined benefit plan*—the retirement benefit is defined and the employer estimates the contribution necessary to pay these benefits—and (2) *defined contribution plan*—the pension contribution is defined and the employer and/or employee contributes amounts specified in the pension agreement.

Pension Liabilities A **pension plan** is a contractual agreement between an employer and its employees for the employer to provide benefits (payments) to employees after they retire. Most employers pay the full cost of the pension, but sometimes employees pay part of the cost. An employer records its payment into a pension plan with a debit to Pension Expense and a credit to Cash. A *plan administrator* receives payments from the employer, invests them in pension assets, and makes benefit payments to *pension recipients* (retired employees). Insurance and trust companies often serve as pension plan administrators.

Many pensions are known as *defined benefit plans* that define future benefits; the employer's contributions vary, depending on assumptions about future pension assets and liabilities. Several disclosures are necessary in this case. Specifically, a pension liability is reported when the accumulated benefit obligation is *more than* the plan assets, a so-called *underfunded plan.* The accumulated benefit obligation is the present value of promised future pension payments to retirees. *Plan assets* refer to the market value of assets the plan

[4] Most lessees try to keep leased assets and lease liabilities off their balance sheets by failing to meet any one of the four criteria of a capital lease. This is because a lease liability increases a company's total liabilities, making it more difficult to obtain additional financing. The acquisition of assets without reporting any related liabilities (or other asset outflows) on the balance sheet is called **off-balance-sheet financing.**

administrator holds. A pension asset is reported when the accumulated benefit obligation is *less than* the plan assets, a so-called *overfunded plan.* An employer reports pension expense when it receives the benefits from the employees' services, which is sometimes decades before it pays pension benefits to employees. (*Other Postretirement Benefits* refer to nonpension benefits such as health care and life insurance benefits. Similar to a pension, costs of these benefits are estimated and liabilities accrued when the employees earn them.)

Summary

C1 Explain the types of notes and prepare entries to account for notes. Notes repaid over a period of time are called *installment notes* and usually follow one of two payment patterns: (1) decreasing payments of interest plus equal amounts of principal or (2) equal total payments. Mortgage notes also are common. Interest is allocated to each period in a note's life by multiplying its beginning–period carrying value by its market rate at issuance. If a note is repaid with equal payments, the payment amount is computed by dividing the borrowed amount by the present value of an annuity factor (taken from a present value table) using the market rate and the number of payments.

C2A Explain and compute the present value of an amount(s) to be paid at a future date(s). The basic concept of present value is that an amount of cash to be paid or received in the future is worth less than the same amount of cash to be paid or received today. Another important present value concept is that interest is compounded, meaning interest is added to the balance and used to determine interest for succeeding periods. An annuity is a series of equal payments occurring at equal time intervals. An annuity's present value can be computed using the present value table for an annuity (or a calculator).

C3C Describe interest accrual when bond payment periods differ from accounting periods. Issuers and buyers of debt record the interest accrued when issue dates or accounting periods do not coincide with debt payment dates.

C4D Describe accounting for leases and pensions. A lease is a rental agreement between the lessor and the lessee. When the lessor retains the risks and rewards of asset ownership (an *operating lease*), the lessee debits Rent Expense and credits Cash for its lease payments. When the lessor substantially transfers the risks and rewards of asset ownership to the lessee (a *capital lease*), the lessee capitalizes the leased asset and records a lease liability. Pension agreements can result in either pension assets or pension liabilities.

A1 Compare bond financing with stock financing. Bond financing is used to fund business activities. Advantages of bond financing versus stock include (1) no effect on owner control, (2) tax savings, and (3) increased earnings due to financial leverage. Disadvantages include (1) interest and principal payments and (2) amplification of poor performance.

A2 Assess debt features and their implications. Certain bonds are secured by the issuer's assets; other bonds, called *debentures,* are unsecured. Serial bonds mature at different points in time; term bonds mature at one time. Registered bonds have each bondholder's name recorded by the issuer; bearer bonds are payable to the holder. Convertible bonds are exchangeable for shares of the issuer's stock. Callable bonds can be retired by the issuer at a set price. Debt features alter the risk of loss for creditors.

A3 Compute the debt-to-equity ratio and explain its use. Both creditors and equity holders are concerned about the relation between the amount of liabilities and the amount of equity. A company's financing structure is at less risk when the debt-to-equity ratio is lower, as liabilities must be paid and usually with periodic interest.

P1 Prepare entries to record bond issuance and interest expense. When bonds are issued at par, Cash is debited and Bonds Payable is credited for the bonds' par value. At bond interest payment dates (usually semiannual), Bond Interest Expense is debited and Cash credited—the latter for an amount equal to the bond par value multiplied by the bond contract rate.

P2 Compute and record amortization of bond discount using straight-line method. Bonds are issued at a discount when the contract rate is less than the market rate, making the issue (selling) price less than par. When this occurs, the issuer records a credit to Bonds Payable (at par) and debits both Discount on Bonds Payable and Cash. The amount of bond interest expense assigned to each period is computed using the straight-line method.

P3 Compute and record amortization of bond premium using straight-line method. Bonds are issued at a premium when the contract rate is higher than the market rate, making the issue (selling) price greater than par. When this occurs, the issuer records a debit to Cash and credits both Premium on Bonds Payable and Bonds Payable (at par). The amount of bond interest expense assigned to each period is computed using the straight-line method. The Premium on Bonds Payable is allocated to reduce bond interest expense over the life of the bonds.

P4 Record the retirement of bonds. Bonds are retired at maturity with a debit to Bonds Payable and a credit to Cash at par value. The issuer can retire the bonds early by exercising a call option or purchasing them in the market. Bondholders can also retire bonds early by exercising a conversion feature on convertible bonds. The issuer recognizes a gain or loss for the difference between the amount paid and the bond carrying value.

P5B Compute and record amortization of bond discount using effective interest method. Bonds are issued at a discount when the contract rate is less than the market rate, making the issue (selling) price less than par. The amount of bond interest expense assigned to each period, including amortization of the discount, is computed using the effective interest method.

P6B Compute and record amortization of bond premium using effective interest method. Bonds are issued at a premium when the contract rate is higher than the market rate, making the issue (selling) price greater than par. The amount of bond interest expense assigned to each period, including amortization of the premium, is computed using the effective interest method.

Guidance Answers to Decision Maker

Entrepreneur This is a "present value" question. The market interest rate (10%) and present value ($3,000) are known, but the payment required two years later is unknown. This amount ($3,630) can be computed as $3,000 × 1.10 × 1.10. Thus, the sale price is $3,630 when no payments are received for two years. The $3,630 received two years from today is equivalent to $3,000 cash today.

Bond Investor The debt-to-equity ratio for the first company is 0.2 ($350,000/$1,750,000) and for the second company is 1.2 ($1,200,000/$1,000,000), suggesting that the financing structure of the second company is more risky than that of the first company. Consequently, as a buyer of unsecured debenture bonds, you prefer the first company (all else equal).

Bond Rater Bonds with longer repayment periods (life) have higher risk. Also, bonds issued by companies in financial difficulties or facing higher than normal uncertainties have higher risk. Moreover, companies with higher than normal debt and large fluctuations in earnings are considered to be higher risk. Discount bonds are more risky on one or more of these factors.

Key Terms

Annuity
Bearer bonds
Bond
Bond certificate
Bond indenture
Callable bonds
Capital leases
Carrying (book) value of bonds
Contract rate
Convertible bonds
Coupon bonds
Debt-to-equity ratio
Discount on bonds payable
Effective interest method
Fair value option
Installment note
Lease
Market rate
Mortgage
Off-balance-sheet financing
Operating leases
Par value of a bond
Pension plan
Premium on bonds
Registered bonds
Secured bonds
Serial bonds
Sinking fund bonds
Straight-line bond amortization
Term bonds
Unsecured bonds

Multiple Choice Quiz

Answers at end of chapter

1. A bond traded at 97½ means that
- **a.** The bond pays 97½% interest.
- **b.** The bond trades at $975 per $1,000 bond.
- **c.** The market rate of interest is below the contract rate of interest for the bond.
- **d.** The bonds can be retired at $975 each.
- **e.** The bond's interest rate is 2½%.

2. A bondholder that owns a $1,000, 6%, 15-year bond has
- **a.** The right to receive $1,000 at maturity.
- **b.** Ownership rights in the bond-issuing entity.
- **c.** The right to receive $60 per month until maturity.
- **d.** The right to receive $1,900 at maturity.
- **e.** The right to receive $600 per year until maturity.

3. A company issues 8%, 20-year bonds with a par value of $500,000. The current market rate for the bonds is 8%. The amount of interest owed to the bondholders for each semiannual interest payment is
- **a.** $40,000
- **b.** $0
- **c.** $20,000
- **d.** $800,000
- **e.** $400,000

4. A company issued five-year, 5% bonds with a par value of $100,000. The company received $95,735 for the bonds. Using the straight-line method, the company's interest expense for the first semiannual interest period is
- **a.** $2,926.50
- **b.** $5,853.00
- **c.** $2,500.00
- **d.** $5,000.00
- **e.** $9,573.50

5. A company issued eight-year, 5% bonds with a par value of $350,000. The company received proceeds of $373,745. Interest is payable semiannually. The amount of premium amortized for the first semiannual interest period, assuming straight-line bond amortization, is
- **a.** $2,698
- **b.** $23,745
- **c.** $8,750
- **d.** $9,344
- **e.** $1,484

B(C,D) *Superscript letter B(C, D) denotes assignments based on Appendix 10B(10C, 10D).*

Icon denotes assignments that involve decision making.

Discussion Questions

1. What is the main difference between notes payable and bonds payable?
2. What is the main difference between a bond and a share of stock?
3. What is the advantage of issuing bonds instead of obtaining financing from the company's owners?
4. What is a bond indenture? What provisions are usually included in it?
5. What are the duties of a trustee for bondholders?
6. What are the *contract* rate and the *market* rate for bonds?
7. What factors affect the market rates for bonds?
8.[B] Does the straight-line or effective interest method produce an interest expense allocation that yields a constant rate of interest over a bond's life? Explain.
9.[C] Why does a company that issues bonds between interest dates collect accrued interest from the bonds' purchasers?
10. If you know the par value of bonds, the contract rate, and the market rate, how do you compute the bonds' price?
11. What is the issue price of a $2,000 bond sold at 98¼? What is the issue price of a $6,000 bond sold at 101½?
12. Describe the debt-to-equity ratio and explain how creditors and owners would use this ratio to evaluate a company's risk.
13. What obligation does an entrepreneur (owner) have to investors that purchase bonds to finance the business?
14. Refer to **Apple**'s annual report in Appendix A. Is there any indication that Apple has issued long-term debt? **APPLE**
15. By what amount did **Samsung**'s long-term borrowings increase or decrease in 2013? **Samsung**
16. Refer to the statement of cash flows for **Samsung** in Appendix A. For the year ended December 31, 2013, what was the amount for repayment of long-term borrowings and debentures? **Samsung**
17. Refer to the statements for **Google** in Appendix A. For the year ended December 31, 2013, what is its debt-to-equity ratio? What does this ratio tell us? **GOOGLE**
18.[D] When can a lease create both an asset and a liability for the lessee?
19.[D] Compare and contrast an operating lease with a capital lease.
20.[D] Describe the two basic types of pension plans.

connect

Round dollar amounts to the nearest whole dollar.

QUICK STUDY

QS 10-1 Bond financing A1

Identify the following as either an advantage (A) or a disadvantage (D) of bond financing.

____ **a.** Bonds do not affect owner control.
____ **b.** A company earns a lower return with borrowed funds than it pays in interest.
____ **c.** A company earns a higher return with borrowed funds than it pays in interest.
____ **d.** Bonds require payment of periodic interest.
____ **e.** Interest on bonds is tax deductible.
____ **f.** Bonds require payment of par value at maturity.

QS 10-2 Journalize bond issuance P1

Enviro Company issues 8%, 10-year bonds with a par value of $250,000 and semiannual interest payments. On the issue date, the annual market rate for these bonds is 10%, which implies a selling price of 87½. Prepare the journal entries for the issuance of the bonds. Assume the bonds are issued for cash on January 1, 2015.

QS 10-3 Computing bond price P1

Using the bond details in QS 10-2, confirm that the bonds' selling price is approximately correct (within $100). Use the present value tables B.1 and B.3 in Appendix B.

QS 10-4 Journalize bond issuance P1

Garcia Company issues 10%, 15-year bonds with a par value of $240,000 and semiannual interest payments. On the issue date, the annual market rate for these bonds is 8%, which implies a selling price of 117¼. Prepare the journal entry for the issuance of these bonds. Assume the bonds are issued for cash on January 1, 2015.

QS 10-5
Computing bond price
P1

Using the bond details in QS 10-4, confirm that the bonds' selling price is approximately correct (within $100). Use the present value tables B.1 and B.3 in Appendix B.

QS 10-6
Straight-Line: Bond computations
P2

Enviro Company issues 8%, 10-year bonds with a par value of $250,000 and semiannual interest payments. On the issue date, the annual market rate for these bonds is 10%, which implies a selling price of 87½. The straight-line method is used to allocate interest expense.

1. What are the issuer's cash proceeds from issuance of these bonds?
2. What total amount of bond interest expense will be recognized over the life of these bonds?
3. What is the amount of bond interest expense recorded on the first interest payment date?

QS 10-7
Recording bond issuance and discount amortization
P1 P2

Sylvestor Company issues 10%, five-year bonds, on December 31, 2014, with a par value of $100,000 and semiannual interest payments. Use the following bond amortization table and prepare journal entries to record (*a*) the issuance of bonds on December 31, 2014; (*b*) the first interest payment on June 30, 2015; and (*c*) the second interest payment on December 31, 2015.

Semiannual Period-End	Unamortized Discount	Carrying Value
(0) 12/31/2014	$7,360	$92,640
(1) 6/30/2015	6,624	93,376
(2) 12/31/2015	5,888	94,112

QS 10-8
Straight-Line: Bond computations
P3

Enviro Company issues 8%, 10-year bonds with a par value of $250,000 and semiannual interest payments. On the issue date, the annual market rate for these bonds is 5%, which implies a selling price of 123⅜. The straight-line method is used to allocate interest expense.

1. What are the issuer's cash proceeds from issuance of these bonds?
2. What total amount of bond interest expense will be recognized over the life of these bonds?
3. What is the amount of bond interest expense recorded on the first interest payment date?

QS 10-9
Bond retirement by call option P4

On July 1, 2015, Advocate Company exercises an $8,000 call option (plus par value) on its outstanding bonds that have a carrying value of $416,000 and par value of $400,000. The company exercises the call option after the semiannual interest is paid on June 30, 2015. Record the entry to retire the bonds.

QS 10-10
Bond retirement by stock conversion P4

On January 1, 2015, the $2,000,000 par value bonds of Spitz Company with a carrying value of $2,000,000 are converted to 1,000,000 shares of $1.00 par value common stock. Record the entry for the conversion of the bonds.

QS 10-11
Computing payments for an installment note C1

Murray Company borrows $340,000 cash from a bank and in return signs an installment note for five annual payments of equal amount, with the first payment due one year after the note is signed. Use Table B.3 in Appendix B to compute the amount of the annual payment for each of the following annual market rates: (*a*) 4%, (*b*) 8%, and (*c*) 12%.

QS 10-12
Bond features and terminology
A2

Enter the letter of the description *A* through *H* that best fits each term or phrase 1 through 8.

A. Records and tracks the bondholders' names.
B. Is unsecured; backed only by the issuer's credit standing.
C. Has varying maturity dates for amounts owed.
D. Identifies rights and responsibilities of the issuer and the bondholders.
E. Can be exchanged for shares of the issuer's stock.
F. Is unregistered; interest is paid to whoever possesses them.
G. Maintains a separate asset account from which bondholders are paid at maturity.
H. Pledges specific assets of the issuer as collateral.

1. ______ Registered bond
2. ______ Serial bond
3. ______ Secured bond
4. ______ Bearer bond
5. ______ Convertible bond
6. ______ Bond indenture
7. ______ Sinking fund bond
8. ______ Debenture

QS 10-13
Debt-to-equity ratio
A3

Compute the debt-to-equity ratio for each of the following companies. Which company appears to have a riskier financing structure? Explain.

	Atlanta Company	Spokane Company
Total liabilities	$429,000	$ 549,000
Total equity	572,000	1,830,000

QS 10-14B
Effective Interest: Bond discount computations
P5

Garcia Company issues 10%, 15-year bonds with a par value of $240,000 and semiannual interest payments. On the issue date, the annual market rate for these bonds is 14%, which implies a selling price of 75¼. The effective interest method is used to allocate interest expense.

1. What are the issuer's cash proceeds from issuance of these bonds?
2. What total amount of bond interest expense will be recognized over the life of these bonds?
3. What amount of bond interest expense is recorded on the first interest payment date?

QS 10-15B
Effective Interest: Bond premium computations
P6

Garcia Company issues 10%, 15-year bonds with a par value of $240,000 and semiannual interest payments. On the issue date, the annual market rate for these bonds is 8%, which implies a selling price of 117¼. The effective interest method is used to allocate interest expense.

1. What are the issuer's cash proceeds from issuance of these bonds?
2. What total amount of bond interest expense will be recognized over the life of these bonds?
3. What amount of bond interest expense is recorded on the first interest payment date?

QS 10-16C
Issuing bonds between interest dates C3

Madrid Company plans to issue 8% bonds on January 1, 2015, with a par value of $4,000,000. The company sells $3,600,000 of the bonds on January 1, 2015. The remaining $400,000 sells at par on March 1, 2015. The bonds pay interest semiannually as of June 30 and December 31. Record the entry for the March 1 cash sale of bonds.

QS 10-17D
Recording operating leases C4

Jin Li, an employee of ETrain.com, leases a car at O'Hare airport for a three-day business trip. The rental cost is $250. Prepare the entry by ETrain.com to record Jin Li's short-term car lease cost.

QS 10-18D
Recording capital leases
C4

Algoma, Inc., signs a five-year lease for office equipment with Office Solutions. The present value of the lease payments is $15,499. Prepare the journal entry that Algoma records at the inception of this capital lease.

QS 10-19
International liabilities disclosures
P1

Vodafone Group Plc reports the following information among its bonds payable as of March 31, 2013 (pounds in millions).

Financial Long-Term Liabilities Measured at Amortized Cost			
(£ millions)	Nominal (par) Value	Carrying Value	Fair Value
4.625% (US dollar 500 million) bond due July 2018.....	£313	£367	£354

a. What is the par value of the 4.625% bond issuance? What is its book (carrying) value?
b. Was the 4.625% bond sold at a discount or a premium? Explain.

QS 10-20
International liabilities disclosures and interpretations
P1

Refer to the information in QS 10-19 for **Vodafone Group Plc**. The following price quotes (from Yahoo! Finance Bond Center) relate to its bonds payable. The price quote indicates that the 4.625% bonds have a market price of 111.67 (111.67% of par value), resulting in a yield to maturity of 1.710%.

Price	Contract Rate (coupon)	Maturity Date	Market Rate (YTM)
111.67	4.625%	15-Jul-2018	1.710%

a. Assuming that the 4.625% bonds were originally issued at par value, what does the market price reveal about interest rate changes since bond issuance? (Assume that Vodafone's credit rating has remained the same.)

b. Does the change in market rates since the issuance of these bonds affect the amount of interest expense reported on Vodafone's income statement? Explain.

c. How much cash would Vodafone need to pay to repurchase the 4.625% bonds at the quoted market price of 111.67? (Assume no interest is owed when the bonds are repurchased.)

d. Assuming that the 4.625% bonds remain outstanding until maturity, at what market price will the bonds sell on the due date in 2018?

connect

EXERCISES

Round dollar amounts to the nearest whole dollar. Assume no reversing entries are used.

Exercise 10-1
Recording bond issuance and interest
P1

On January 1, 2015, Boston Enterprises issues bonds that have a $3,400,000 par value, mature in 20 years, and pay 9% interest semiannually on June 30 and December 31. The bonds are sold at par.

1. How much interest will Boston pay (in cash) to the bondholders every six months?

2. Prepare journal entries to record (*a*) the issuance of bonds on January 1, 2015; (*b*) the first interest payment on June 30, 2015; and (*c*) the second interest payment on December 31, 2015.

3. Prepare the journal entry for issuance assuming the bonds are issued at (*a*) 98 and (*b*) 102.

Exercise 10-2
Straight-Line: Amortization of bond discount
P2

Tano issues bonds with a par value of $180,000 on January 1, 2015. The bonds' annual contract rate is 8%, and interest is paid semiannually on June 30 and December 31. The bonds mature in three years. The annual market rate at the date of issuance is 10%, and the bonds are sold for $170,862.

1. What is the amount of the discount on these bonds at issuance?

2. How much total bond interest expense will be recognized over the life of these bonds?

3. Prepare an amortization table like the one in Exhibit 10.7 for these bonds; use the straight-line method to amortize the discount.

Exercise 10-3
Computing bond interest and price; recording bond issuance
P2

Bringham Company issues bonds with a par value of $800,000 on their stated issue date. The bonds mature in 10 years and pay 6% annual interest in semiannual payments. On the issue date, the annual market rate for the bonds is 8%.

1. What is the amount of each semiannual interest payment for these bonds?

2. How many semiannual interest payments will be made on these bonds over their life?

3. Use the interest rates given to determine whether the bonds are issued at par, at a discount, or at a premium.

Check (4) $691,287

4. Compute the price of the bonds as of their issue date.

5. Prepare the journal entry to record the bonds' issuance.

Exercise 10-4
Straight-Line: Recording bond issuance and discount amortization
P1 P2

Paulson Company issues 6%, four-year bonds, on December 31, 2015, with a par value of $200,000 and semiannual interest payments. Use the following bond amortization table and prepare journal entries to record (*a*) the issuance of bonds on December 31, 2015; (*b*) the first interest payment on June 30, 2016; and (*c*) the second interest payment on December 31, 2016.

Semiannual Period-End	Unamortized Discount	Carrying Value
(0) 12/31/2015	$13,466	$186,534
(1) 6/30/2016	11,782	188,218
(2) 12/31/2016	10,098	189,902

Exercise 10-5
Straight-Line: Recording bond issuance and discount amortization
P1 P2

Dobbs Company issues 5%, two-year bonds, on December 31, 2015, with a par value of $200,000 and semiannual interest payments. Use the following bond amortization table and prepare journal entries to record (*a*) the issuance of bonds on December 31, 2015; (*b*) the first through fourth interest payments on each June 30 and December 31; and (*c*) the maturity of the bond on December 31, 2017.

Semiannual Period-End	Unamortized Discount	Carrying Value
(0) 12/31/2015	$12,000	$188,000
(1) 6/30/2016	9,000	191,000
(2) 12/31/2016	6,000	194,000
(3) 6/30/2017	3,000	197,000
(4) 12/31/2017	0	200,000

Exercise 10-6
Straight-Line: Recording bond issuance and premium amortization
P1 P3

Woodwick Company issues 10%, five-year bonds, on December 31, 2014, with a par value of $200,000 and semiannual interest payments. Use the following bond amortization table and prepare journal entries to record (*a*) the issuance of bonds on December 31, 2014; (*b*) the first interest payment on June 30, 2015; and (*c*) the second interest payment on December 31, 2015.

Semiannual Period-End	Unamortized Premium	Carrying Value
(0) 12/31/2014	$16,222	$216,222
(1) 6/30/2015	14,600	214,600
(2) 12/31/2015	12,978	212,978

Exercise 10-7
Straight-Line: Amortization of bond premium
P3

Quatro Co. issues bonds dated January 1, 2015, with a par value of $400,000. The bonds' annual contract rate is 13%, and interest is paid semiannually on June 30 and December 31. The bonds mature in three years. The annual market rate at the date of issuance is 12%, and the bonds are sold for $409,850.

1. What is the amount of the premium on these bonds at issuance?
2. How much total bond interest expense will be recognized over the life of these bonds?
3. Prepare an amortization table like the one in Exhibit 10.11 for these bonds; use the straight-line method to amortize the premium.

Exercise 10-8
Computing bond interest and price; recording bond issuance
P3

Citywide Company issues bonds with a par value of $150,000 on their stated issue date. The bonds mature in five years and pay 10% annual interest in semiannual payments. On the issue date, the annual market rate for the bonds is 8%.

1. What is the amount of each semiannual interest payment for these bonds?
2. How many semiannual interest payments will be made on these bonds over their life?
3. Use the interest rates given to determine whether the bonds are issued at par, at a discount, or at a premium.
4. Compute the price of the bonds as of their issue date.
5. Prepare the journal entry to record the bonds' issuance.

Check (4) $162,172

Exercise 10-9
Straight-Line: Bond computations, amortization, and bond retirement
P4 P2

On January 1, 2015, Shay issues $700,000 of 10%, 15-year bonds at a price of 97¾. Six years later, on January 1, 2021, Shay retires 20% of these bonds by buying them on the open market at 104½. All interest is accounted for and paid through December 31, 2020, the day before the purchase. The straight-line method is used to amortize any bond discount.

1. How much does the company receive when it issues the bonds on January 1, 2015?
2. What is the amount of the discount on the bonds at January 1, 2015?
3. How much amortization of the discount is recorded on the bonds for the entire period from January 1, 2015, through December 31, 2020?
4. What is the carrying (book) value of the bonds as of the close of business on December 31, 2020? What is the carrying value of the 20% soon-to-be-retired bonds on this same date?
5. How much did the company pay on January 1, 2021, to purchase the bonds that it retired?
6. What is the amount of the recorded gain or loss from retiring the bonds?
7. Prepare the journal entry to record the bond retirement at January 1, 2021.

Check (6) $8,190 loss

Exercise 10-10
Installment note with equal total payments C1

On January 1, 2015, Eagle borrows $100,000 cash by signing a four-year, 7% installment note. The note requires four equal total payments of accrued interest and principal on December 31 of each year from 2015 through 2018.

1. Compute the amount of each of the four equal total payments.
2. Prepare an amortization table for this installment note like the one in Exhibit 10.14.

Check (1) $29,523

Exercise 10-11
Installment note entries
C1

Use the information in Exercise 10-10 to prepare the journal entries for Eagle to record the loan on January 1, 2015, and the four payments from December 31, 2015, through December 31, 2018.

Exercise 10-12
Applying debt-to-equity ratio
A3

Montclair Company is considering a project that will require a $500,000 loan. It presently has total liabilities of $220,000 and total assets of $620,000.

1. Compute Montclair's (*a*) present debt-to-equity ratio and (*b*) the debt-to-equity ratio assuming it borrows $500,000 to fund the project.
2. Evaluate and discuss the level of risk involved if Montclair borrows the funds to pursue the project.

Exercise 10-13[B]
Effective Interest: Amortization of bond discount
P5

Stanford issues bonds dated January 1, 2015, with a par value of $500,000. The bonds' annual contract rate is 9%, and interest is paid semiannually on June 30 and December 31. The bonds mature in three years. The annual market rate at the date of issuance is 12%, and the bonds are sold for $463,140.

1. What is the amount of the discount on these bonds at issuance?
2. How much total bond interest expense will be recognized over the life of these bonds?
3. Prepare an amortization table like the one in Exhibit 10B.1 for these bonds; use the effective interest method to amortize the discount.

Exercise 10-14[B]
Effective Interest: Amortization of bond premium
P6

Quatro Co. issues bonds dated January 1, 2015, with a par value of $400,000. The bonds' annual contract rate is 13%, and interest is paid semiannually on June 30 and December 31. The bonds mature in three years. The annual market rate at the date of issuance is 12%, and the bonds are sold for $409,850.

1. What is the amount of the premium on these bonds at issuance?
2. How much total bond interest expense will be recognized over the life of these bonds?
3. Prepare an amortization table like the one in Exhibit 10B.2 for these bonds; use the effective interest method to amortize the premium.

Exercise 10-15
Straight-Line: Amortization and accrued bond interest expense
C3 P2

Duval Co. issues four-year bonds with a $100,000 par value on June 1, 2015, at a price of $95,948. The annual contract rate is 7%, and interest is paid semiannually on November 30 and May 31.

1. Prepare an amortization table like the one in Exhibit 10.7 for these bonds. Use the straight-line method of interest amortization.
2. Prepare journal entries to record the first two interest payments and to accrue interest as of December 31, 2015.

Exercise 10-16[C]
Recording bond issuance with accrued interest
C3 P1
Check (1) $102,000

On May 1, 2015, Brussels Enterprises issues bonds dated January 1, 2015, that have a $3,400,000 par value, mature in 20 years, and pay 9% interest semiannually on June 30 and December 31. The bonds are sold at par plus four months' accrued interest.

1. How much accrued interest do the bond purchasers pay Brussels on May 1, 2015?
2. Prepare Brussels' journal entries to record (*a*) the issuance of bonds on May 1, 2015; (*b*) the first interest payment on June 30, 2015; and (*c*) the second interest payment on December 31, 2015.

Exercise 10-17[D]
Identifying capital and operating leases
C4

Indicate whether the company in each separate case 1 through 3 has entered into an operating lease or a capital lease.

1. The lessor retains title to the asset, and the lease term is three years on an asset that has a five-year useful life.
2. The title is transferred to the lessee, the lessee can purchase the asset for $1 at the end of the lease, and the lease term is five years. The leased asset has an expected useful life of six years.
3. The present value of the lease payments is 95% of the leased asset's market value, and the lease term is 70% of the leased asset's useful life.

Exercise 10-18[D]
Accounting for capital lease
C4

Harbor (lessee) signs a five-year capital lease for office equipment with a $10,000 annual lease payment. The present value of the five annual lease payments is $41,000, based on a 7% interest rate.

1. Prepare the journal entry Harbor will record at inception of the lease.
2. If the leased asset has a five-year useful life with no salvage value, prepare the journal entry Harbor will record each year to recognize depreciation expense related to the leased asset.

Exercise 10-19D
Analyzing lease options
C4

General Motors advertised three alternatives for a 25-month lease on a new Tahoe: (1) zero dollars down and a lease payment of $1,750 per month for 25 months, (2) $5,000 down and $1,500 per month for 25 months, or (3) $38,500 down and no payments for 25 months. Use the present value Table B.3 in Appendix B to determine which is the best alternative for the customer (assume you have enough cash to accept any alternative and the annual interest rate is 12% compounded monthly).

Exercise 10-20
Accounting for long-term liabilities under IFRS
C1

Heineken N.V. reports the following information for its loans and borrowings as of December 31, 2013, including proceeds and repayments for the year ended December 31, 2013 (euros in millions).

Loans and borrowings (noncurrent liabilities)	
Loans and borrowings, December 31, 2013	€ 9,112
Proceeds (cash) from issuances of loans and borrowings	1,663
Repayments (in cash) of loans and borrowings	(2,474)

1. Prepare Heineken's journal entry to record its cash proceeds from issuances of its loans and borrowings for 2013. Assume that the par value of these issuances is €1,700.
2. Prepare Heineken's journal entry to record its cash repayments of its loans and borrowings for 2013. Assume that the par value of these issuances is €2,400, and the premium on them is €24.
3. Compute the discount or premium on its loans and borrowings as of December 31, 2013, assuming that the par value of these liabilities is €9,000.
4. Given the facts in part 3 and viewing the entirety of loans and borrowings as one issuance, was the contract rate on these loans and borrowings higher or lower than the market rate at the time of issuance? Explain. (Assume that Heineken's credit rating has remained the same.)

connect

PROBLEM SET A

Round dollar amounts to the nearest whole dollar. Assume no reversing entries are used.

Problem 10-1A
Computing bond price and recording issuance
P1

Hartford Research issues bonds dated January 1, 2015, that pay interest semiannually on June 30 and December 31. The bonds have a $40,000 par value and an annual contract rate of 10%, and they mature in 10 years.

Required

For each of the following three separate situations, (*a*) determine the bonds' issue price on January 1, 2015, and (*b*) prepare the journal entry to record their issuance.

1. The market rate at the date of issuance is 8%.
2. The market rate at the date of issuance is 10%.
3. The market rate at the date of issuance is 12%.

Check (1) Premium, $5,437

(3) Discount, $4,588

Problem 10-2A
Straight-Line: Amortization of bond discount
P1 P2

Hillside issues $4,000,000 of 6%, 15-year bonds dated January 1, 2015, that pay interest semiannually on June 30 and December 31. The bonds are issued at a price of $3,456,448.

Required

1. Prepare the January 1, 2015, journal entry to record the bonds' issuance.
2. For each semiannual period, compute (*a*) the cash payment, (*b*) the straight-line discount amortization, and (*c*) the bond interest expense.
3. Determine the total bond interest expense to be recognized over the bonds' life.
4. Prepare the first two years of an amortization table like Exhibit 10.7 using the straight-line method.
5. Prepare the journal entries to record the first two interest payments.

Check (3) $4,143,552

(4) 12/31/2016 carrying value, $3,528,920

Problem 10-3A
Straight Line: Amortization of bond premium
P1 P3

Refer to the bond details in Problem 10-2A, *except* assume that the bonds are issued at a price of $4,895,980.

Required

1. Prepare the January 1, 2015, journal entry to record the bonds' issuance.
2. For each semiannual period, compute (*a*) the cash payment, (*b*) the straight-line premium amortization, and (*c*) the bond interest expense.

[continued on next page]

Check (3) $2,704,020

(4) 12/31/2016 carrying value, $4,776,516

3. Determine the total bond interest expense to be recognized over the bonds' life.

4. Prepare the first two years of an amortization table like Exhibit 10.11 using the straight-line method.

5. Prepare the journal entries to record the first two interest payments.

Problem 10-4A
Straight-Line: Amortization of bond premium P1 P3

Ellis issues 6.5%, five-year bonds dated January 1, 2015, with a $250,000 par value. The bonds pay interest on June 30 and December 31 and are issued at a price of $255,333. The annual market rate is 6% on the issue date.

Required

1. Calculate the total bond interest expense over the bonds' life.

2. Prepare a straight-line amortization table like Exhibit 10.11 for the bonds' life.

3. Prepare the journal entries to record the first two interest payments.

Check (2) 6/30/2017 carrying value, $252,668

Problem 10-5A
Straight-Line: Amortization of bond premium and discount P1 P2 P3

Legacy issues $325,000 of 5%, four-year bonds dated January 1, 2015, that pay interest semiannually on June 30 and December 31. They are issued at $292,181 and their market rate is 8% at the issue date.

Required

1. Prepare the January 1, 2015, journal entry to record the bonds' issuance.

2. Determine the total bond interest expense to be recognized over the bonds' life.

3. Prepare a straight-line amortization table like the one in Exhibit 10.7 for the bonds' first two years.

4. Prepare the journal entries to record the first two interest payments.

Check (2) $97,819

(3) 12/31/2016 carrying value, $308,589

Analysis Component

5. Assume the market rate on January 1, 2015, is 4% instead of 8%. Without providing numbers, describe how this change affects the amounts reported on Legacy's financial statements.

Problem 10-6A
Installment notes C1

On November 1, 2015, Norwood borrows $200,000 cash from a bank by signing a five-year installment note bearing 8% interest. The note requires equal total payments each year on October 31.

Required

1. Compute the total amount of each installment payment.

2. Complete an amortization table for this installment note similar to the one in Exhibit 10.14.

3. Prepare the journal entries in which Norwood records (*a*) accrued interest as of December 31, 2015 (the end of its annual reporting period) and (*b*) the first annual payment on the note.

Check (2) 10/31/2019 ending balance, $46,382

Problem 10-7A
Applying the debt-to-equity ratio A3

At the end of the current year, the following information is available for both Pulaski Company and Scott Company.

	Pulaski Company	Scott Company
Total assets	$860,000	$440,000
Total liabilities	360,000	240,000
Total equity	500,000	200,000

Required

1. Compute the debt-to-equity ratios for both companies.

2. Comment on your results and discuss the riskiness of each company's financing structure.

Problem 10-8A[B]
Effective Interest: Amortization of bond discount P1 P5

Refer to the bond details in Problem 10-5A.

Required

1. Prepare the January 1, 2015, journal entry to record the bonds' issuance.

2. Determine the total bond interest expense to be recognized over the bonds' life.

3. Prepare an effective interest amortization table like the one in Exhibit 10B.1 for the bonds' first two years.

4. Prepare the journal entries to record the first two interest payments.

Check (2) $97,819

(3) 12/31/2016 carrying value, $307,308

Problem 10-9A^B
Effective Interest: Amortization of bond premium; computing bond price P1 P6

Refer to the bond details in Problem 10-4A.

Required

1. Compute the total bond interest expense over the bonds' life.
2. Prepare an effective interest amortization table like the one in Exhibit 10B.2 for the bonds' life.
3. Prepare the journal entries to record the first two interest payments.
4. Use the market rate at issuance to compute the present value of the remaining cash flows for these bonds as of December 31, 2017. Compare your answer with the amount shown on the amortization table as the balance for that date (from part 2) and explain your findings.

Check (2) 6/30/2017 carrying value, $252,865
(4) $252,326

Problem 10-10A^B
Effective Interest: Amortization of bond; retiring bonds
P1 P4 P5 P6

Ike issues $180,000 of 11%, three-year bonds dated January 1, 2015, that pay interest semiannually on June 30 and December 31. They are issued at $184,566. Their market rate is 10% at the issue date.

Required

1. Prepare the January 1, 2015, journal entry to record the bonds' issuance.
2. Determine the total bond interest expense to be recognized over the bonds' life.
3. Prepare an effective interest amortization table like Exhibit 10B.2 for the bonds' first two years.
4. Prepare the journal entries to record the first two interest payments.
5. Prepare the journal entry to record the bonds' retirement on January 1, 2017, at 98.

Check (3) 6/30/2016 carrying value, $182,448
(5) $5,270 gain

Analysis Component

6. Assume that the market rate on January 1, 2015, is 12% instead of 10%. Without presenting numbers, describe how this change affects the amounts reported on Ike's financial statements.

Problem 10-11A^D
Capital lease accounting
C4

Rogers Company signs a five-year capital lease with Packer Company for office equipment. The annual year-end lease payment is $10,000, and the interest rate is 8%.

Required

1. Compute the present value of Rogers's five-year lease payments.
2. Prepare the journal entry to record Rogers's capital lease at its inception.
3. Complete a lease payment schedule for the five years of the lease with the following headings. Assume that the beginning balance of the lease liability (present value of lease payments) is $39,927. (*Hint:* To find the amount allocated to interest in year 1, multiply the interest rate by the beginning-of-year lease liability. The amount of the annual lease payment not allocated to interest is allocated to principal. Reduce the lease liability by the amount allocated to principal to update the lease liability at each year-end.)

Check (1) $39,927
(3) Year 3 ending balance, $17,833

Period Ending Date	Beginning Balance of Lease Liability	Interest on Lease Liability	Reduction of Lease Liability	Cash Lease Payment	Ending Balance of Lease Liability

4. Use straight-line depreciation and prepare the journal entry to depreciate the leased asset at the end of year 1. Assume zero salvage value and a five-year life for the office equipment.

PROBLEM SET B

Round dollar amounts to the nearest whole dollar. Assume no reversing entries are used.

Problem 10-1B
Computing bond price and recording issuance
P1

Flagstaff Systems issues bonds dated January 1, 2015, that pay interest semiannually on June 30 and December 31. The bonds have a $90,000 par value and an annual contract rate of 12%, and they mature in five years.

Required

For each of the following three separate situations, (*a*) determine the bonds' issue price on January 1, 2015, and (*b*) prepare the journal entry to record their issuance.

1. The market rate at the date of issuance is 10%.
2. The market rate at the date of issuance is 12%.
3. The market rate at the date of issuance is 14%.

Check (1) Premium, $6,948
(3) Discount, $6,326

Problem 10-2B
Straight-Line:
Amortization of bond discount
P1 P2

Romero issues $3,400,000 of 10%, 10-year bonds dated January 1, 2015, that pay interest semiannually on June 30 and December 31. The bonds are issued at a price of $3,010,000.

Required

1. Prepare the January 1, 2015, journal entry to record the bonds' issuance.
2. For each semiannual period, compute (*a*) the cash payment, (*b*) the straight-line discount amortization, and (*c*) the bond interest expense.
3. Determine the total bond interest expense to be recognized over the bonds' life.
4. Prepare the first two years of an amortization table like Exhibit 10.7 using the straight-line method.
5. Prepare the journal entries to record the first two interest payments.

Check (3) $3,790,000
(4) 6/30/2016 carrying value, $3,068,500

Problem 10-3B
Straight-line:
Amortization of bond premium
P1 P3

Refer to the bond details in Problem 10-2B, *except* assume that the bonds are issued at a price of $4,192,932.

Required

1. Prepare the January 1, 2015, journal entry to record the bonds' issuance.
2. For each semiannual period, compute (*a*) the cash payment, (*b*) the straight-line premium amortization, and (*c*) the bond interest expense.
3. Determine the total bond interest expense to be recognized over the bonds' life.
4. Prepare the first two years of an amortization table like Exhibit 10.11 using the straight-line method.
5. Prepare the journal entries to record the first two interest payments.

Check (3) $2,607,068
(4) 6/30/2016 carrying value, 4,073,991

Problem 10-4B
Straight-Line:
Amortization of bond premium
P1 P3

Ripkin Company issues 9%, five-year bonds dated January 1, 2015, with a $320,000 par value. The bonds pay interest on June 30 and December 31 and are issued at a price of $332,988. Their annual market rate is 8% on the issue date.

Required

1. Calculate the total bond interest expense over the bonds' life.
2. Prepare a straight-line amortization table like Exhibit 10.11 for the bonds' life.
3. Prepare the journal entries to record the first two interest payments.

Check (2) 6/30/2017 carrying value, $326,493

Problem 10-5B
Straight-Line:
Amortization of bond discount
P1 P2

Gomez issues $240,000 of 6%, 15-year bonds dated January 1, 2015, that pay interest semiannually on June 30 and December 31. They are issued at $198,494, and their market rate is 8% at the issue date.

Required

1. Prepare the January 1, 2015, journal entry to record the bonds' issuance.
2. Determine the total bond interest expense to be recognized over the life of the bonds.
3. Prepare a straight-line amortization table like the one in Exhibit 10.7 for the bonds' first two years.
4. Prepare the journal entries to record the first two interest payments.

Check (2) $257,506
(3) 6/30/2016 carrying value, $202,646

Problem 10-6B
Installment notes
C1

On October 1, 2015, Gordon Enterprises borrows $150,000 cash from a bank by signing a three-year installment note bearing 10% interest. The note requires equal total payments each year on September 30.

Required

1. Compute the total amount of each installment payment.
2. Complete an amortization table for this installment note similar to the one in Exhibit 10.14.
3. Prepare the journal entries to record (*a*) accrued interest as of December 31, 2015 (the end of its annual reporting period) and (*b*) the first annual payment on the note.

Check (2) 9/30/2017 ending balance, $54,836

Problem 10-7B
Applying the debt-to-equity ratio
A3

At the end of the current year, the following information is available for both Atlas Company and Bryan Company.

	Atlas Company	Bryan Company
Total assets	$180,000	$750,000
Total liabilities	80,000	562,500
Total equity	100,000	187,500

Required

1. Compute the debt-to-equity ratios for both companies.
2. Comment on your results and discuss what they imply about the relative riskiness of these companies.

Problem 10-8B[B]
Effective Interest: Amortization of bond discount P1 P5

Refer to the bond details in Problem 10-5B.

Required

1. Prepare the January 1, 2015, journal entry to record the bonds' issuance.
2. Determine the total bond interest expense to be recognized over the bonds' life.
3. Prepare an effective interest amortization table like the one in Exhibit 10B.1 for the bonds' first two years.
4. Prepare the journal entries to record the first two interest payments.

Check (2) $257,506; (3) 6/30/2016 carrying value, $200,803

Problem 10-9B[B]
Effective Interest: Amortization of bond premium; computing bond price P1 P6

Refer to the bond details in Problem 10-4B.

Required

1. Compute the total bond interest expense over the bonds' life.
2. Prepare an effective interest amortization table like the one in Exhibit 10B.2 for the bonds' life.
3. Prepare the journal entries to record the first two interest payments.
4. Use the market rate at issuance to compute the present value of the remaining cash flows for these bonds as of December 31, 2017. Compare your answer with the amount shown on the amortization table as the balance for that date (from part 2) and explain your findings.

Check (2) 6/30/2017 carrying value, $327,136
(4) $325,807

Problem 10-10B[B]
Effective Interest: Amortization of bond; retiring bonds
P1 P4 P5 P6

Valdez issues $450,000 of 13%, four-year bonds dated January 1, 2015, that pay interest semiannually on June 30 and December 31. They are issued at $493,608, and their market rate is 10% at the issue date.

Required

1. Prepare the January 1, 2015, journal entry to record the bonds' issuance.
2. Determine the total bond interest expense to be recognized over the bonds' life.
3. Prepare an effective interest amortization table like the one in Exhibit 10B.2 for the bonds' first two years.
4. Prepare the journal entries to record the first two interest payments.
5. Prepare the journal entry to record the bonds' retirement on January 1, 2017, at 106.

Analysis Component

6. Assume that the market rate on January 1, 2015, is 14% instead of 10%. Without presenting numbers, describe how this change affects the amounts reported on Valdez's financial statements.

Check (3) 6/30/2016 carrying value, $479,202
(5) $3,088 loss

Problem 10-11B[D]
Capital lease accounting
C4

Braun Company signs a five-year capital lease with Verdi Company for office equipment. The annual year-end lease payment is $20,000, and the interest rate is 10%.

Required

1. Compute the present value of Braun's lease payments.
2. Prepare the journal entry to record Braun's capital lease at its inception.
3. Complete a lease payment schedule for the five years of the lease with the following headings. Assume that the beginning balance of the lease liability (present value of lease payments) is $75,816. (*Hint:* To find

Check (1) $75,816
(3) Year 3 ending balance, $34,712

the amount allocated to interest in year 1, multiply the interest rate by the beginning-of-year lease liability. The amount of the annual lease payment not allocated to interest is allocated to principal. Reduce the lease liability by the amount allocated to principal to update the lease liability at each year-end.)

Period Ending Date	Beginning Balance of Lease Liability	Interest on Lease Liability	Reduction of Lease Liability	Cash Lease Payment	Ending Balance of Lease Liability

4. Use straight-line depreciation and prepare the journal entry to depreciate the leased asset at the end of year 1. Assume zero salvage value and a five-year life for the office equipment.

SERIAL PROBLEM

Business Solutions

A1 A3

(This serial problem began in Chapter 1 and continues through most of the book. If previous chapter segments were not completed, the serial problem can begin at this point. It is helpful, but not necessary, to use the Working Papers that accompany the book.)

SP 10 Santana Rey has consulted with her local banker and is considering financing an expansion of her business by obtaining a long-term bank loan. Selected account balances at March 31, 2016, for Business Solutions follow.

Total assets	$120,268	Total liabilities.......	$875	Total equity.......	$119,393

Required

Check (1) $94,639

1. The bank has offered a long-term secured note to Business Solutions. The bank's loan procedures require that a client's debt-to-equity ratio not exceed 0.8. As of March 31, 2016, what is the maximum amount that Business Solutions could borrow from this bank (rounded to nearest dollar)?
2. If Business Solutions borrows the maximum amount allowed from the bank, what percentage of assets would be financed (*a*) by debt and (*b*) by equity?
3. What are some factors Santana Rey should consider before borrowing the funds?

Beyond the Numbers

REPORTING IN ACTION

A1 A2

APPLE

BTN 10-1 Refer to **Apple**'s financial statements in Appendix A to answer the following.

1. Identify the items, if any, that make up Apple's long-term debt as reported on its balance sheet at September 28, 2013.
2. Assume that Apple has $100 million in convertible debentures that carry a 4.25% contract rate of interest. How much annual cash interest must be paid on those convertible debentures?
3. Assume that the convertible bonds discussed in part 2 are convertible into 20,000 shares of Apple's stock. If the carrying value of these bonds is $100 million, what is the entry recorded by Apple upon conversion?

Fast Forward

4. Access Apple's financial statements for the years ending after September 28, 2013, from its website (Apple.com) or the SEC's EDGAR database (www.SEC.gov). Has it issued additional long-term debt since the year-end September 28, 2013? If yes, identify the amount(s).

COMPARATIVE ANALYSIS

A3

APPLE
GOOGLE

BTN 10-2 Key figures for **Apple** and **Google** follow.

	Apple		Google	
($ millions)	Current Year	Prior Year	Current Year	Prior Year
Total assets............	$207,000	$176,064	$110,920	$93,798
Total liabilities	83,451	57,854	23,611	22,083
Total equity	123,549	118,210	87,309	71,715

Required

1. Compute the debt-to-equity ratios for Apple and Google for both the current year and the prior year.
2. Use the ratios you computed in part 1 to determine which company's financing structure is least risky. Assume an industry average of 0.44 for debt-to-equity.

ETHICS CHALLENGE

C4 A1

BTN 10-3 Traverse County needs a new county government building that would cost $10 million. The politicians feel that voters will not approve a municipal bond issue to fund the building since it would increase taxes. They opt to have a state bank issue $10 million of tax-exempt securities to pay for the building construction. The county then will make yearly lease payments (of principal and interest) to repay the obligation. Unlike conventional municipal bonds, the lease payments are not binding obligations on the county and, therefore, require no voter approval.

Required

1. Do you think the actions of the politicians and the bankers in this situation are ethical?
2. In terms of risk, how do the tax-exempt securities used to pay for the building compare to a conventional municipal bond issued by Traverse County?

COMMUNICATING IN PRACTICE

P3

BTN 10-4 Your business associate mentions that she is considering investing in corporate bonds currently selling at a premium. She says that since the bonds are selling at a premium, they are highly valued and her investment will yield more than the going rate of return for the risk involved. Reply with a memorandum to confirm or correct your associate's interpretation of premium bonds.

TAKING IT TO THE NET

A2

BTN 10-5 Access the March 27, 2014, filing of the 10-K report of **Home Depot** for the year ended February 2, 2014, from www.SEC.gov (Ticker: HD). Refer to Home Depot's balance sheet, including its note 3 (on debt).

Required

1. Identify Home Depot's long-term liabilities and the amounts for those liabilities from Home Depot's balance sheet at February 2, 2014.
2. Review Home Depot's note 3. The note reports that as of February 2, 2014, it had $2.962 billion of "5.875% Senior Notes; due December 16, 2036; interest payable semiannually on June 16 and December 16." These notes have a face value of $3.0 billion and were originally issued at $2.958 billion.
   a. Why would Home Depot issue $3.0 billion of its notes for only $2.958 billion?
   b. How much cash interest must Home Depot pay each June 16 and December 16 on these notes?

TEAMWORK IN ACTION

P2 P3

BTN 10-6[B] Break into teams and complete the following requirements related to *effective interest* amortization for a premium bond.

1. Each team member is to independently prepare a blank table with proper headings for amortization of a bond premium. When all have finished, compare tables and ensure that all are in agreement.

Parts 2 and 3 require use of these facts: On January 1, 2015, McElroy issues $100,000, 9%, five-year bonds at 104.1. The market rate at issuance is 8%. McElroy pays interest semiannually on June 30 and December 31.

2. In rotation, *each* team member must explain how to complete *one* line of the bond amortization table, including all computations for his or her line. (Round amounts to the nearest dollar.) All members are to fill in their tables during this process. You need not finish the table; stop after all members have explained a line.
3. In rotation, *each* team member is to identify a separate column of the table and indicate what the final number in that column will be and explain the reasoning.

[continued on next page]

Hint: Rotate teams to report on parts 4 and 5. Consider requiring entries for issuance and interest payments.

4. Reach a team consensus as to what the total bond interest expense on this bond issue will be if the bond is not retired before maturity.
5. As a team, prepare a list of similarities and differences between the amortization table just prepared and the amortization table if the bond had been issued at a discount.

ENTREPRENEURIAL DECISION

A1

BTN 10-7 Matthew Clough is the founder of **Stone + Cloth**. Assume that his company currently has $250,000 in equity, and he is considering a $100,000 expansion to meet increased demand. The $100,000 expansion would yield $16,000 in additional annual income before interest expense. Assume that the business currently earns $40,000 annual income before interest expense of $10,000, yielding a return on equity of 12% ($30,000/$250,000). To fund the expansion, he is considering the issuance of a 10-year, $100,000 note with annual interest payments (the principal due at the end of 10 years).

Required

1. Using return on equity as the decision criterion, show computations to support or reject the expansion if interest on the $100,000 note is (*a*) 10%, (*b*) 15%, (*c*) 16%, (*d*) 17%, and (*e*) 20%.
2. What general rule do the results in part 1 illustrate?

HITTING THE ROAD

A1

BTN 10-8 Visit your city or county library. Ask the librarian to help you locate the most recent financial records of your city or county government. Examine those records.

Required

1. Determine the amount of long-term bonds and notes currently outstanding.
2. Read the supporting information to your municipality's financial statements and record
   a. The market interest rate(s) when the bonds and/or notes were issued.
   b. The date(s) when the bonds and/or notes will mature.
   c. Any rating(s) on the bonds and/or notes received from **Moody's**, **Standard & Poor's**, or another rating agency.

GLOBAL DECISION

A3

Samsung
APPLE
GOOGLE

BTN 10-9 **Samsung** (www.Samsung.com), **Apple**, and **Google** are competitors in the global marketplace. Selected results from these companies follow.

	Samsung (₩ millions)		Apple ($ millions)		Google ($ millions)	
Key Figures	Current Year	Prior Year	Current Year	Prior Year	Current Year	Prior Year
Total assets.	₩214,075,018	₩181,071,570	$207,000	$176,064	$110,920	$93,798
Total liabilities	64,059,008	59,591,364	83,451	57,854	23,611	22,083
Total equity	150,016,010	121,480,206	123,549	118,210	87,309	71,715
Debt-to-equity ratio	?	?	0.68	0.49	0.27	0.31

Required

1. Compute Samsung's debt-to-equity ratio for the current year and the prior year.
2. Use the data provided and the ratios computed in part 1 to determine which company's financing structure is least risky.

ANSWERS TO MULTIPLE CHOICE QUIZ

1. b
2. a
3. c; $500,000 × 0.08 × ½ year = $20,000
4. a; Cash interest paid = $100,000 × 5% × ½ year = $2,500
   Discount amortization = ($100,000 − $95,735)/10 periods = $426.50
   Interest expense = $2,500.00 + $426.50 = $2,926.50
5. e; ($373,745 − $350,000)/16 periods = $1,484

chapter 11

Corporate Reporting and Analysis

Chapter Preview

COMMON STOCK	DIVIDENDS	PREFERRED STOCK	TREASURY STOCK	REPORTING AND ANALYSIS
C1 Stock basics **P1** Issuance at: Par value No-par value Stated value Noncash assets	**P2** Cash dividends Stock dividends Stock splits	**C2** Issuance Dividend preferences Convertible and callable Rationale	**P3** Purchasing treasury stock Reissuing treasury stock Retiring stock	**C3** Statements of retained earnings and equity **A1** EPS **A2** PE ratio **A3** Dividend yield **A4** Book value

Learning Objectives

CONCEPTUAL

C1 Identify characteristics of corporations and their organization.

C2 Explain characteristics of, and distribute dividends between, common and preferred stock.

C3 Explain the items reported in retained earnings.

ANALYTICAL

A1 Compute earnings per share and describe its use.

A2 Compute price-earnings ratio and describe its use in analysis.

A3 Compute dividend yield and explain its use in analysis.

A4 Compute book value and explain its use in analysis.

PROCEDURAL

P1 Record the issuance of corporate stock.

P2 Record transactions involving cash dividends, stock dividends, and stock splits.

P3 Record purchases and sales of treasury stock and the retirement of stock.

AP Images/Imaginechina

Open Sesame

HANGZHOU, CHINA—"In 1995 a friend showed me the Internet for the first time," recalls Jack Ma. "We searched the word *beer* . . . [then we] discovered that there was no data about China. We decided to launch a website." Jack never looked back. "My dream was to set up my own e-commerce company," explains Jack. "I gathered 17 people in my apartment and spoke to them for two hours about my vision. Everyone put their money on the table."

"Think about what social problem you could solve"

—Jack Ma

Jack then needed a company name. "I was in San Francisco in a coffee shop, and I was thinking *Alibaba* is a good name. Then a waitress came, and I said do you know about Alibaba? And she said yes. I said what do you know about Alibaba, and she said 'Open Sesame.' And I said yes, this is the name! Then I went onto the street and found 30 people and asked them, 'Do you know Alibaba?' People from India, people from Germany, people from Tokyo and China . . . They all knew about Alibaba." Thus, the **Alibaba Group (AlibabaGroup.com)** was born.

The success of Alibaba would not have been possible without good decisions regarding creditor vs. equity financing. To make it happen, the new company had to deal with corporate formation, equity issuance, stock types, retaining earnings, and dividend policies. Jack eventually set up the Alibaba Group as a corporate-type entity. With his structure in place, Jack was ready to attack the market. "You've got to make your team have value, innovation, and vision," insists Jack. "When you are small, you have to be very focused and rely on your brain."

The success of Alibaba's corporate-type structure and its mix of creditor vs. equity financing brought both opportunities and challenges. Jack explains the empowering of consumers. "It's customers number one, employees two, and shareholders three," declares Jack. "It's the shareholders who when the crisis comes . . . ran away. My customers and my people stayed." The challenge is staying the course. "Nobody believed in me," admits Jack. "[Moreover] do not allow your colleagues and employees to work for you. Instead, let them work for a common goal."

There are new challenges on the horizon for Jack. One is effectively leveraging accounting knowledge to achieve his current task: managing Alibaba stock on the NYSE. This demands knowledge of corporate formation, stock types, and equity transactions. Jack's company recently achieved the largest initial public offering of stock in history.

Through it all, Jack remains humble. "I call myself 'blind man riding on the back of a blind tiger.'"

Sources: *Alibaba website,* January 2015; *Inc.*, January 2008; *Upstart Business Journal*, September 2011; *Talk Asia*, April 2006; *South China Morning Post,* July 2013; *Jungle News,* May 2014; *Vulcan Post,* February 2014

CORPORATE FORM OF ORGANIZATION

C1 Identify characteristics of corporations and their organization.

A **corporation** is an entity created by law that is separate from its owners. It has most of the rights and privileges granted to individuals. Owners of corporations are called *stockholders* or *shareholders.* Corporations can be separated into two types. A *privately held* (or *closely held*) corporation does not offer its stock for public sale and usually has few stockholders. A *publicly held* corporation offers its stock for public sale and can have thousands of stockholders. *Public sale* usually refers to issuance of stock and trading on an organized stock market.

Characteristics of Corporations

Corporations represent an important type of organization. Their unique characteristics offer advantages and disadvantages.

Advantages of Corporate Form

- **Separate legal entity:** A corporation conducts its affairs with the same rights, duties, and responsibilities of a person. It takes actions through its agents, who are its officers and managers.
- **Limited liability of stockholders:** Stockholders are liable for neither corporate acts nor corporate debt.
- **Transferable ownership rights:** The transfer of shares from one stockholder to another usually has no effect on the corporation or its operations except when this causes a change in the directors who control or manage the corporation.
- **Continuous life:** A corporation's life continues indefinitely because it is not tied to the physical lives of its owners.
- **Lack of mutual agency for stockholders:** A corporation acts through its agents, who are its officers and managers. Stockholders, who are not its officers and managers, do not have the power to bind the corporation to contracts—referred to as *lack of mutual agency.*
- **Ease of capital accumulation:** Buying stock is attractive to investors because (1) stockholders are not liable for the corporation's acts and debts, (2) stocks usually are transferred easily, (3) the life of the corporation is unlimited, and (4) stockholders are not corporate agents. These advantages enable corporations to accumulate large amounts of capital from the combined investments of many stockholders.

Point: The *business entity assumption* requires a corporation to be accounted for separately from its owners (shareholders).

Disadvantages of Corporate Form

- **Government regulation:** A corporation must meet requirements of a state's incorporation laws, which subject the corporation to state regulation and control. Proprietorships and partnerships avoid many of these regulations and governmental reports.
- **Corporate taxation:** Corporations are subject to the same property and payroll taxes as proprietorships and partnerships plus *additional* taxes. The most burdensome of these are federal and state income taxes that together can take 40% or more of corporate pretax income. Moreover, corporate income is usually taxed a second time as part of stockholders' personal income when they receive cash distributed as dividends. This is called *double taxation.* (Dividends are normally taxed at the individual's income tax rate; for "qualified" dividends, the tax rate is 0%, 15%, or 20%, depending on the individual's tax bracket.)

Point: Proprietorships and partnerships are not subject to income taxes. Their income is taxed as the personal income of their owners.

Point: Double taxation is less severe when a corporation's owner-manager collects a salary that is taxed only once as part of his or her personal income. At year-end, many small corporations distribute *bonuses* to owner-managers equal to the corporation's income. This reduces corporate income to $0 and avoids double taxation.

Decision Insight

Stock Financing Mark Zuckerberg took his company, **Facebook**, public by issuing its first shares on the Nasdaq exchange. The initial public offering (IPO) of Facebook shares raised billions in equity financing. It also raised the importance of accounting reports versus market hype. The IPO of Facebook shares came eight years after the company was founded by Zuckerberg in his college dorm room. ■

AP Images/Nasdaq via Facebook, Zef Nikolla

Corporate Organization and Management

This section describes the incorporation, costs, and management of corporate organizations.

Incorporation A corporation is created by obtaining a charter from a state government. A charter application usually must be signed by the prospective stockholders called *incorporators* or *promoters* and then filed with the proper state official. When the application process is complete and fees paid, the charter is issued and the corporation is formed. Investors then purchase the corporation's stock, meet as stockholders, and elect a board of directors. Directors oversee a corporation's affairs.

Point: A corporation is not required to have an office in its state of incorporation. Delaware is viewed as having favorable corporate laws and about half of all corporations listed on the NYSE are incorporated there.

Organization Expenses **Organization expenses** (also called *organization costs*) are the costs to organize a corporation; they include legal fees, promoters' fees, and amounts paid to obtain a charter. The corporation records (debits) these costs to an expense account called *Organization Expenses*. Organization costs are expensed as incurred because it is difficult to determine the amount and timing of their future benefits.

Management of a Corporation The ultimate control of a corporation rests with stockholders who control a corporation by electing its *board of directors,* or simply, *directors*. Each stockholder usually has one vote for each share of stock owned. This control relation is shown in Exhibit 11.1. Directors are responsible for and have final authority for managing corporate activities. A board can act only as a collective body and usually limits its actions to setting general policy.

EXHIBIT 11.1

Corporate Structure

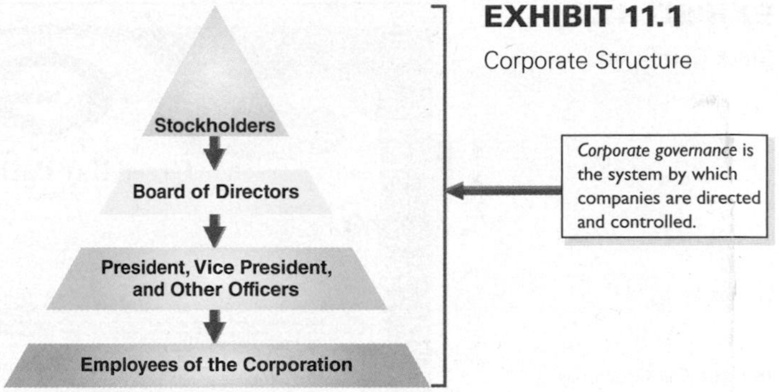

A corporation usually holds a stockholder meeting at least once a year to elect directors and transact business as its bylaws require. A group of stockholders owning or controlling votes of more than a 50% share of a corporation's stock can elect the board and control the corporation. Stockholders who do not attend stockholders' meetings must have an opportunity to delegate their voting rights to an agent by signing a **proxy,** a document that gives a designated agent the right to vote the stock.

Day-to-day direction of corporate business is delegated to executive officers appointed by the board. A corporation's chief executive officer (CEO) is often its president. Several vice presidents, who report to the president, are commonly assigned specific areas of management responsibility such as finance, production, and marketing. One person often has the dual role of chairperson of the board of directors and CEO. In this case, the president is usually designated the chief operating officer (COO).

Point: *Bylaws* are guidelines that govern the behavior of individuals employed by and managing the corporation.

Decision Insight

Seed Money Sources for start-up money include (1) "angel" investors such as family, friends, or anyone who believes in a company, (2) employees, investors, and even suppliers who can be paid with stock, and (3) venture capitalists (investors) who have a record of entrepreneurial success. See the National Venture Capital Association (**NVCA.org**) for information. ■

Global: Some corporate labels are:

Country	Label
United States	Inc.
France	SA
United Kingdom	
Public	PLC
Private	Ltd
Germany & Austria	
Public	AG
Private	GmbH
Sweden & Finland	AB
Italy	SpA
Netherlands	NV
Australia	AG
Mexico	SA
Bahamas	IBC

Stockholders of Corporations

This section explains stockholder rights, stock purchases and sales, and the role of registrars and transfer agents.

Rights of Stockholders When investors buy stock, they acquire all *specific* rights the corporation's charter grants to stockholders. They also acquire *general* rights granted stockholders by the laws of the state in which the company is incorporated. When a corporation has only one class of stock, it is identified as **common stock.** State laws vary, but common stockholders usually have the general right to

1. Vote at stockholders' meetings (or register proxy votes electronically).
2. Sell or otherwise dispose of their stock.
3. Purchase their proportional share of any common stock later issued by the corporation. This **preemptive right** protects stockholders' proportionate interest in the corporation. For example, a stockholder who owns 25% of a corporation's common stock has the first opportunity to buy 25% of any new common stock issued.
4. Receive the same dividend, if any, on each common share of the corporation.
5. Share in any assets remaining after creditors and preferred stockholders are paid when, and if, the corporation is liquidated. Each common share receives the same amount.

Stockholders also have the right to receive timely financial reports.

Stock Certificates and Transfer Investors who buy a corporation's stock sometimes receive a *stock certificate* as proof of share ownership. Many corporations issue only one certificate for each block of stock purchased. A certificate can be for any number of shares. Exhibit 11.2 shows a stock certificate of the **Green Bay Packers.** A certificate shows the company name, stockholder name, number of shares, and other crucial information. Issuance of certificates is becoming less common. Instead, many stockholders maintain accounts with the corporation or their stockbrokers and never receive actual certificates.

EXHIBIT 11.2

Stock Certificate

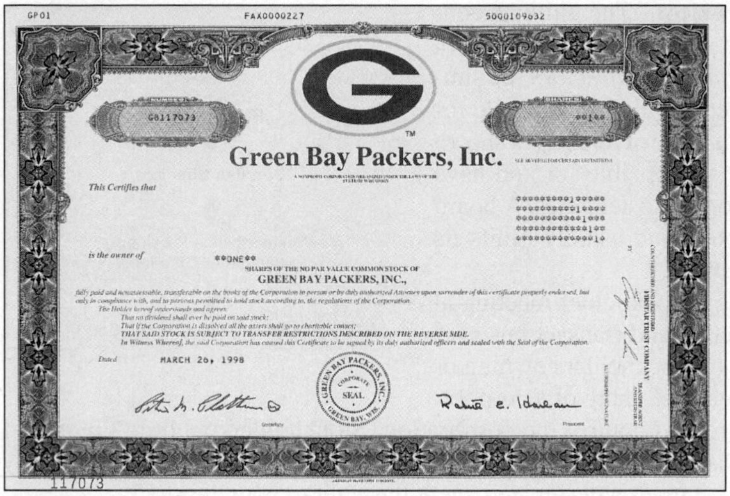

Courtesy of JJW Images

Point: The Green Bay Packers is the only nonprofit, community-owned major league professional sports team. The NFL now prohibits any other teams from becoming community-owned.

Registrar and Transfer Agents If a corporation's stock is traded on a major stock exchange, the corporation must have a registrar and a transfer agent. A *registrar* keeps stockholder records and prepares official lists of stockholders for stockholder meetings and dividend payments. A *transfer agent* assists with purchases and sales of shares by receiving and issuing certificates as necessary. Registrars and transfer agents are usually large banks or trust companies with computer facilities and staff to do this work.

Decision Insight

Pricing Stock A prospectus accompanies a stock's initial public offering (IPO), giving financial information about the company issuing the stock. A prospectus should help answer these questions to price an IPO: (1) Is the underwriter reliable? (2) Is there growth in revenues, profits, and cash flows? (3) What is management's view of operations? (4) Are current owners selling? (5) What are the risks? ■

Basics of Capital Stock

Capital stock is a general term that refers to any shares issued to obtain capital (owner financing). This section introduces terminology and accounting for capital stock.

Authorized Stock **Authorized stock** is the number of shares that a corporation's charter allows it to sell. The number of authorized shares usually exceeds the number of shares issued (and outstanding), often by a large amount. (*Outstanding stock* refers to issued stock held by stockholders.) No formal journal entry is required for stock authorization. A corporation must apply to the state for a change in its charter if it wishes to issue more shares than previously authorized. A corporation discloses the number of shares authorized in the equity section of its balance sheet or notes. **Apple**'s balance sheet reports 1.8 billion common shares authorized as of the start of its 2014 fiscal year.

Subcategories of Authorized Stock

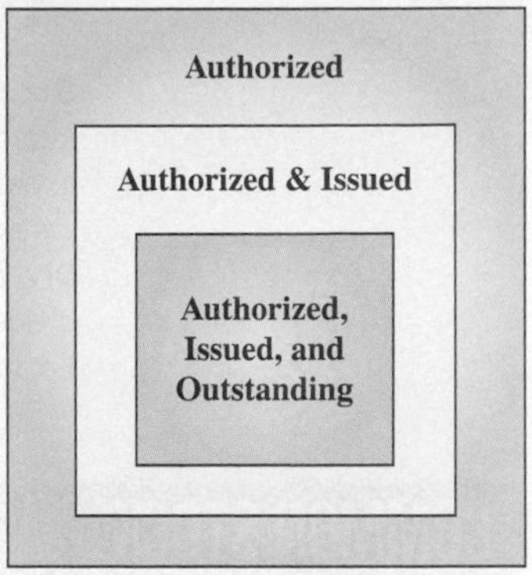

The innermost box shows that shares issued decline if a company buys back its previously issued stock.

Selling (Issuing) Stock A corporation can sell stock directly or indirectly. To *sell directly,* it advertises its stock issuance to potential buyers. This type of issuance is most common with privately held corporations. To *sell indirectly,* a corporation pays a brokerage house (investment banker) to issue its stock. Some brokerage houses *underwrite* an indirect issuance of stock; that is, they buy the stock from the corporation and take all gains or losses from its resale.

Market Value of Stock **Market value per share** is the price at which a stock is bought and sold. Expected future earnings, dividends, growth, and other company and economic factors influence market value. Traded stocks' market values are available daily in newspapers such as *The Wall Street Journal* and online. The current market value of previously issued shares (for example, the price of stock in trades between investors) does not impact the issuing corporation's stockholders' equity.

Classes of Stock When all authorized shares have the same rights and characteristics, the stock is called *common stock.* A corporation is sometimes authorized to issue more than one class of stock, including preferred stock and different classes of common stock. **American Greetings**, for instance, has two types of common stock: Class A stock has 1 vote per share and Class B stock has 10 votes per share.

Par Value Stock **Par value stock** is stock that is assigned a **par value,** which is an amount assigned per share by the corporation in its charter. For example, **Monster Worldwide, Inc.**'s common stock has a par value of $0.001. Other commonly assigned par values are $10, $5, $1 and $0.01. There is no restriction on the assigned par value. In many states, the par value of a stock establishes **minimum legal capital,** which refers to the least amount that the buyers of stock must contribute to the corporation or be subject to paying at a future date. For example, if a corporation issues 1,000 shares of $10 par value stock, the corporation's minimum legal capital in these states would be $10,000. Minimum legal capital is intended to protect a corporation's creditors. Since creditors cannot demand payment from stockholders' personal assets, their claims are limited to the corporation's assets and any minimum legal capital. At liquidation, creditor claims are paid before any amounts are distributed to stockholders.

Point: Managers are motivated to set a low par value when minimum legal capital or state issuance taxes are based on par value.

Point: Minimum legal capital was intended to protect creditors by requiring a minimum level of net assets.

No-Par Value Stock **No-par value stock,** or simply *no-par stock,* is stock *not* assigned a value per share by the corporate charter. Its advantage is that it can be issued at any price without the possibility of a minimum legal capital deficiency.

Point: Par, no-par, and stated value do *not* set the stock's market value.

Stated Value Stock **Stated value stock** is no-par stock to which the directors assign a "stated" value per share. Stated value per share becomes the minimum legal capital per share in this case.

Stockholders' Equity A corporation's equity is known as **stockholders' equity,** also called *shareholders' equity* or *corporate capital.* Stockholders' equity consists of (1) paid-in (or contributed) capital and (2) retained earnings; see Exhibit 11.3. **Paid-in capital** is the total amount of cash and other assets the corporation receives from its stockholders in exchange for its stock. **Retained earnings** is the cumulative net income (and loss) not distributed as dividends to its stockholders.

EXHIBIT 11.3

Equity Composition

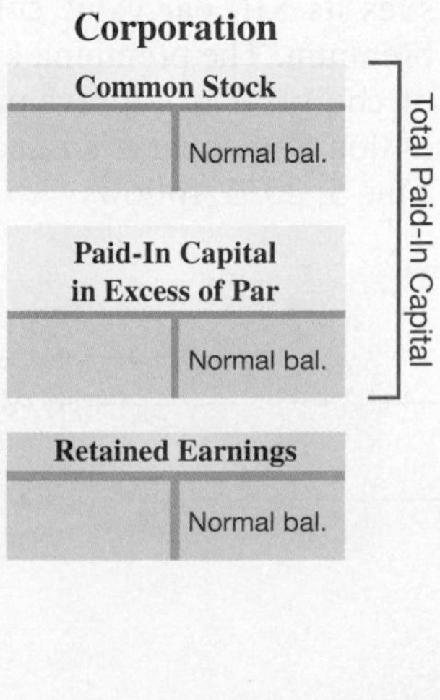

Point: Paid-in capital comes from stock-related transactions, whereas retained earnings comes from operations; if Retained Earnings has a debit balance, it is often titled *Accumulated Deficit.*

Decision Insight

Stock Quote The **Target** stock quote is interpreted as (left to right): **Hi,** highest price in past 52 weeks; **Lo,** lowest price in past 52 weeks; **Sym,** company exchange symbol; **Div,** dividends paid per share in past year; **Yld %,** dividend divided by closing price; **PE,** stock price per share divided by earnings per share; **Vol mil.,** number (in millions) of shares traded; **Hi,** highest price for the day; **Lo,** lowest price for the day; **Close,** closing price for the day; **Net Chg,** change in closing price from prior day. ■

52 Weeks				Yld		Vol				Net
Hi	Lo	Sym	Div	%	PE	mil.	Hi	Lo	Close	Chg
58.95	45.28	TGT	1.20	2.07	13.5	668	58.06	57.40	57.63	−0.30

QC1

COMMON STOCK

P1 Record the issuance of corporate stock.

Accounting for the issuance of common stock affects only paid-in (contributed) capital accounts; no retained earnings accounts are affected.

Issuing Par Value Stock

Par value stock can be issued at par, at a premium (above par), or at a discount (below par). In each case, stock can be exchanged for either cash or noncash assets.

Issuing Par Value Stock at Par When common stock is issued at par value, we record amounts for both the asset(s) received and the par value stock issued. To illustrate, the entry to record Dillon Snowboards's issuance of 30,000 shares of $10 par value stock for $300,000 cash on June 5, 2015, follows:

Assets	= Liabilities	+ Equity
+300,000		+300,000

$10 par value × 30,000 shares

		Debit	Credit
June 5	Cash	300,000	
	Common Stock, $10 Par Value		300,000
	Issued 30,000 shares of $10 par value common stock at par.		

Exhibit 11.4 shows the stockholders' equity of Dillon Snowboards at year-end 2015 (its first year of operations) after income of $65,000 and no dividend payments.

EXHIBIT 11.4

Stockholders' Equity for Stock Issued at Par

Stockholders' Equity	
Common Stock—$10 par value; 50,000 shares authorized; 30,000 shares issued and outstanding	$300,000
Retained earnings	65,000
Total stockholders' equity	$365,000

Point: A *premium* is the amount by which issue price exceeds par (or stated) value. It is recorded in the "Paid-In Capital in Excess of Par Value, Common Stock" account; also called "Additional Paid-In Capital, Common Stock."

Issuing Par Value Stock at a Premium A **premium on stock** occurs when a corporation sells its stock for more than par (or stated) value. To illustrate, if Dillon Snowboards issues its $10 par value common stock at $12 per share, its stock is sold at a $2 per share premium. The premium, known as **paid-in capital in excess of par value,** is reported as part of equity; it is not revenue and is not listed on the income statement. The entry to record Dillon Snowboards's issuance of 30,000 shares of $10 par value stock for $12 per share on June 5, 2015, follows:

Assets	= Liabilities	+ Equity
+360,000		+300,000
		+60,000

$10 par value × 30,000 shares

[$12 issue price − $10 par value] × 30,000 shares

		Debit	Credit
June 5	Cash	360,000	
	Common Stock, $10 Par Value		300,000
	Paid-In Capital in Excess of Par Value, Common Stock		**60,000**
	Sold and issued 30,000 shares of $10 par value common stock at $12 per share.		

The Paid-In Capital in Excess of Par Value account is added to the par value of the stock in the equity section of the balance sheet as shown in Exhibit 11.5.

Point: The *paid-in capital* terminology is interchangeable with *contributed capital.*

EXHIBIT 11.5

Stockholders' Equity for Stock Issued at a Premium

Stockholders' Equity	
Common Stock—$10 par value; 50,000 shares authorized; 30,000 shares issued and outstanding	$300,000
Paid-in capital in excess of par value, common stock	**60,000**
Retained earnings	65,000
Total stockholders' equity	$425,000

Issuing Par Value Stock at a Discount A **discount on stock** occurs when a corporation sells its stock for less than par (or stated) value. Most states prohibit the issuance of stock at a discount. In states that allow stock to be issued at a discount, its buyers usually become contingently liable to creditors for the discount. If stock is issued at a discount, the amount by which issue price is less than par is debited to a *Discount on Common Stock* account, a contra to the Common Stock account, and its balance is subtracted from the par value of stock in the equity section of the balance sheet. This discount is not an expense and does not appear on the income statement.

Point: Retained earnings can be negative, reflecting accumulated losses. **Pandora Media** had an accumulated deficit of $167 million at the start of 2014.

Issuing No-Par Value Stock

When no-par stock is issued and is not assigned a stated value, the amount the corporation receives becomes legal capital and is recorded as common stock. This means that the entire proceeds are credited to a no-par stock account. To illustrate, a corporation records its October 20 issuance of 1,000 shares of no-par stock for $40 cash per share as follows:

Oct. 20	Cash	40,000	
	Common Stock, No-Par Value		40,000
	Issued 1,000 shares of no-par value common stock at $40 per share.		

Assets	= Liabilities +	Equity
+40,000		+40,000

$40 issue price × 1,000 no-par shares

Issuing Stated Value Stock

When no-par stock is issued and assigned a stated value, its stated value becomes legal capital and is credited to a stated value stock account. Assuming that stated value stock is issued at an amount in excess of stated value (the usual case), the excess is credited to Paid-In Capital in Excess of Stated Value, Common Stock, which is reported in the stockholders' equity section. To illustrate, a corporation that issues 1,000 shares of no-par common stock having a stated value of $40 per share in return for $50 cash per share records this as follows:

Frequency of Stock Types

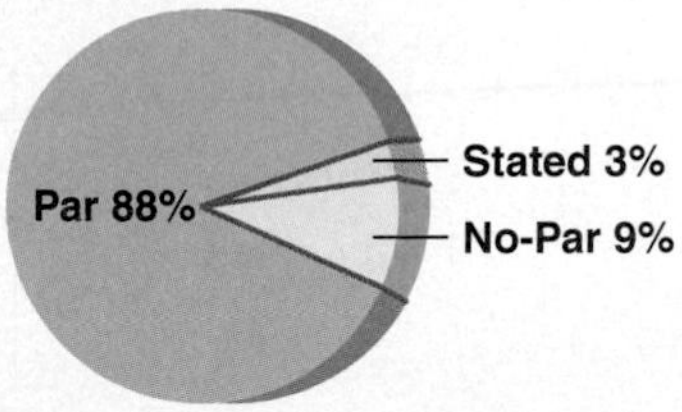

Oct. 20	Cash	50,000	
	Common Stock, $40 Stated Value		40,000
	Paid-In Capital in Excess of Stated Value, Common Stock		10,000
	Issued 1,000 shares of $40 per share stated value stock at $50 per share.		

Assets	= Liabilities +	Equity
+50,000		+40,000
		+10,000

$40 stated value × 1,000 shares

[$50 issue price − $40 stated value] × 1,000 shares

Issuing Stock for Noncash Assets

A corporation can receive assets other than cash in exchange for its stock. (It can also assume liabilities on the assets received such as a mortgage on property received.) The corporation records the assets received at their market values as of the date of the transaction. The stock given in exchange is recorded at its par (or stated) value with any excess recorded in the Paid-In Capital in Excess of Par (or Stated) Value account. (If no-par stock is issued, the stock is

Point: Stock issued for noncash assets should be recorded at the market value of either the stock or the noncash asset, whichever is more clearly determinable.

recorded at the assets' market value.) To illustrate, the entry to record receipt of land valued at $105,000 in return for issuance of 4,000 shares of $20 par value common stock on June 10 is

Assets	= Liabilities	+ Equity
+105,000		+80,000
		+25,000

$20 par value × 4,000 shares

$105,000 asset value − $80,000 par value

June 10	Land	105,000	
	Common Stock, $20 Par Value		80,000
	Paid-In Capital in Excess of Par Value, Common Stock		25,000
	Exchanged 4,000 shares of $20 par value common stock for land.		

A corporation sometimes gives shares of its stock to promoters in exchange for their services in organizing the corporation, which the corporation records as organization expenses. The entry to record receipt of services valued at $12,000 in organizing the corporation in return for 600 shares of $15 par value common stock on June 5 is

Point: Any type of stock can be issued for noncash assets.

Assets	= Liabilities	+ Equity
		−12,000
		+9,000
		+3,000

$15 par value × 600 shares

$12,000 services value − $9,000 par value

June 5	Organization Expenses	12,000	
	Common Stock, $15 Par Value		9,000
	Paid-In Capital in Excess of Par Value, Common Stock		3,000
	Gave promoters 600 shares of $15 par value common stock in exchange for their services.		

NEED-TO-KNOW 11-1

Recording Stock Issuance

P1

Prepare journal entries to record the following four separate (independent) issuances of stock.

1. A corporation issued 80 shares of $5 par value common stock for $700 cash.
2. A corporation issued 40 shares of no-par common stock to its promoters in exchange for their efforts, estimated to be worth $800. The stock has a $1 per share stated value.
3. A corporation issued 40 shares of no-par common stock in exchange for land, estimated to be worth $800. The stock has no stated value.
4. A corporation issued 20 shares of $30 par value preferred stock for $900 cash.

Solution

1.

Cash	700	
Common Stock, $5 Par Value*		400
Paid-In Capital in Excess of Par Value, Common Stock**		300
Issued common stock for cash.		
*80 shares × $5 per share = $400 **$700 − $400 = $300		

2.

Organization Expenses	800	
Common Stock, $1 Stated Value		40
Paid-In Capital in Excess of Stated Value, Common Stock		760
Issued stock to promoters.		

3.

Land	800	
Common Stock, No-Par Value		800
Issued stock in exchange for land.		

4.

Cash	900	
Preferred Stock, $30 Par Value*		600
Paid-In Capital in Excess of Par Value, Preferred Stock**		300
Issued preferred stock for cash.		
*20 shares × $30 per share = $600 **$900 − $600 = $300		

Do More: QS 11-2, QS 11-3, QS 11-4, QS 11-5, E 11-2, E 11-3, E 11-4

QC2

DIVIDENDS

This section describes both cash and stock dividend transactions.

P2 Record transactions involving cash dividends, stock dividends, and stock splits.

Cash Dividends

The decision to pay cash dividends rests with the board of directors and involves more than evaluating the amounts of retained earnings and cash. The directors, for instance, may decide to keep the cash to invest in the corporation's growth, to meet emergencies, to take advantage of unexpected opportunities, or to pay off debt. Alternatively, many corporations pay cash dividends to their stockholders at regular dates. These cash flows provide a return to investors and almost always affect the stock's market value.

Percent of Corporations Paying Dividends

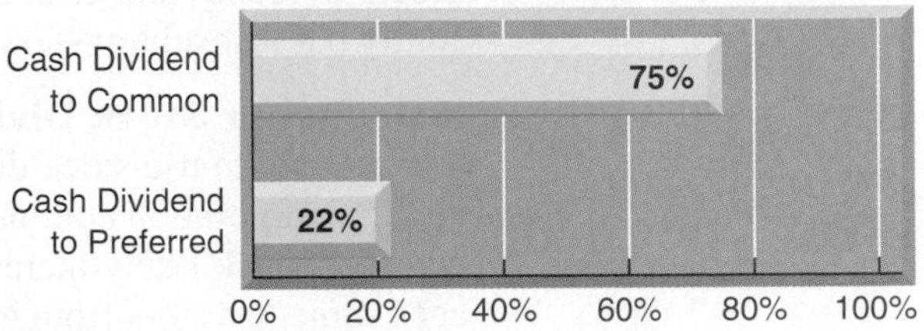

Accounting for Cash Dividends Dividend payment involves three important dates: declaration, record, and payment. **Date of declaration** is the date the directors vote to declare and pay a dividend. This creates a legal liability of the corporation to its stockholders. **Date of record** is the future date specified by the directors for identifying those stockholders listed in the corporation's records to receive dividends. The date of record usually follows the date of declaration by at least two weeks. Persons who own stock on the date of record receive dividends. **Date of payment** is the date when the corporation makes payment; it follows the date of record by enough time to allow the corporation to arrange checks, money transfers, or other means to pay dividends.

To illustrate, the entry to record a January 9 declaration of a $1 per share cash dividend by the directors of Z-Tech, Inc., with 5,000 outstanding shares is

Date of Declaration

Jan. 9	Retained Earnings	5,000	
	Common Dividend Payable		5,000
	Declared $1 per common share cash dividend.[1]		

Assets = Liabilities + Equity
+5,000 −5,000

$1 per share declared dividend × 5,000 outstanding shares

Common Dividend Payable is a current liability. The date of record for the Z-Tech dividend is January 22. *No formal journal entry is needed on the date of record.* The February 1 date of payment requires an entry to record both the settlement of the liability and the reduction of the cash balance, as follows:

Date of Payment

Feb. 1	Common Dividend Payable	5,000	
	Cash		5,000
	Paid $1 per common share cash dividend.		

Assets = Liabilities + Equity
−5,000 −5,000

Deficits and Cash Dividends A corporation with a debit (abnormal) balance for Retained Earnings is said to have a **retained earnings deficit,** which arises when a company incurs cumulative losses and/or pays more dividends than total earnings from current and prior years. A deficit is reported as a deduction on the balance sheet, as shown in Exhibit 11.6. Most states prohibit a corporation with a deficit from paying a cash dividend to its stockholders. This legal restriction is designed to protect creditors by preventing distribution of assets to stockholders when the company may be in financial difficulty.

Point: It is often said a dividend is a distribution of retained earnings, but it is more precise to describe a dividend as a distribution of assets to satisfy stockholder claims.

Point: The Retained Earnings Deficit account is also called *Accumulated Deficit.*

[1] An alternative entry is to debit Dividends instead of Retained Earnings. The balance in Dividends is then closed to Retained Earnings at the end of the reporting period. The effect is the same: Retained Earnings is decreased and a Dividend Payable is increased. For simplicity, all assignments in this chapter use the Retained Earnings account to record dividend declarations.

EXHIBIT 11.6

Stockholders' Equity with a Deficit

Common stock—$10 par value, 5,000 shares authorized, issued, and outstanding	$50,000
Retained earnings deficit	**(6,000)**
Total stockholders' equity	$44,000

Point: Amazon.com has never declared a cash dividend.

QC3

Some state laws allow cash dividends to be paid by returning a portion of the capital contributed by stockholders. This type of dividend is called a **liquidating cash dividend,** or simply *liquidating dividend,* because it returns a part of the original investment back to the stockholders. This requires a debit entry to one of the contributed capital accounts instead of Retained Earnings at the declaration date.

Stock Dividends

A **stock dividend,** declared by a corporation's directors, is a distribution of additional shares of the corporation's own stock to its stockholders without the receipt of any payment in return. Stock dividends and cash dividends are different. A stock dividend does not reduce assets and equity but instead transfers a portion of equity from retained earnings to contributed capital.

Reasons for Stock Dividends Stock dividends exist for at least two reasons. First, directors are said to use stock dividends to keep the market price of the stock affordable. For example, if a corporation continues to earn income but does not issue cash dividends, the price of its common stock likely increases. The price of such a stock may become so high that it discourages some investors from buying the stock (especially in lots of 100 and 1,000). When a corporation has a stock dividend, it increases the number of outstanding shares and lowers the per share stock price. Another reason for a stock dividend is to provide evidence of management's confidence that the company is doing well and will continue to do well.

Accounting for Stock Dividends A stock dividend affects the components of equity by transferring part of retained earnings to contributed capital accounts, sometimes described as *capitalizing* retained earnings. Accounting for a stock dividend depends on whether it is a small or large stock dividend. A **small stock dividend** is a distribution of 25% or less of previously outstanding shares. It is recorded by capitalizing retained earnings for an amount equal to the market value of the shares to be distributed. A **large stock dividend** is a distribution of more than 25% of previously outstanding shares. A large stock dividend is recorded by capitalizing retained earnings for the minimum amount required by state law governing the corporation. Most states require capitalizing retained earnings equal to the par or stated value of the stock.

Five Steps to Record Stock Dividends

Step 1: Identify number of shares outstanding

Step 2: Identify the stock dividend percentage

Step 3: Compute number of new shares (Step 1 × Step 2)

Step 4: Value new shares at market (small stock dividend) *or* par (large stock dividend)

Step 5: Determine debit (reduction) to Retained Earnings (Step 3 × Step 4)

To illustrate stock dividends, we use the equity section of Quest's balance sheet shown in Exhibit 11.7 just *before* its declaration of a stock dividend on December 31.

EXHIBIT 11.7

Stockholders' Equity *before* a Stock Dividend

Stockholders' Equity	**Before Dividend**
Common stock—$10 par value, 15,000 shares authorized, 10,000 shares issued and outstanding	$100,000
Paid-in capital in excess of par value, common stock	8,000
Retained earnings	35,000
Total stockholders' equity	$143,000

Point: Small stock dividends are recorded at market value.

Assets = Liabilities + Equity
−15,000
+10,000
+5,000

Recording a small stock dividend. Assume that Quest's directors declare a 10% stock dividend on December 31. This stock dividend of 1,000 shares, computed as 10% of its 10,000 outstanding shares, is to be distributed on January 20 to the stockholders of record on January 15. Since the market price of Quest's stock on December 31 is $15 per share, this small stock dividend declaration is recorded as follows:

Date of Declaration—Small Stock Dividend

Dec. 31	Retained Earnings	15,000	
	Common Stock Dividend Distributable		10,000
	Paid-In Capital in Excess of Par Value, Common Stock		5,000
	Declared a 1,000-share (10%) stock dividend.		

10% dividend × 10,000 outstanding shares × $10 par value

10% dividend × 10,000 outstanding shares × [$15 market price − $10 par value]

The $10,000 credit in the declaration entry equals the par value of the shares and is recorded in *Common Stock Dividend Distributable,* an equity account. Its balance exists only until the shares are issued. The $5,000 credit equals the amount by which market value exceeds par value. This amount increases the Paid-In Capital in Excess of Par Value account in anticipation of the issuance of shares. In general, the balance sheet changes in three ways when a stock dividend is declared. First, the amount of equity attributed to common stock increases; for Quest, from $100,000 to $110,000 for 1,000 additional declared shares. Second, paid-in capital in excess of par increases by the excess of market value over par value for the declared shares. Third, retained earnings decreases, reflecting the transfer of amounts to both common stock and paid-in capital in excess of par. The impact on stockholders' equity of Quest is shown in Exhibit 11.8 when its 10% stock dividend is declared on December 31— see the "declaration" column.

Point: The term *Distributable* (not *Payable*) is used for stock dividends. A stock dividend is never a liability because it never reduces assets.

Point: The credit to Paid-In Capital in Excess of Par Value is recorded when the stock dividend is declared. This account is not affected when stock is later distributed.

EXHIBIT 11.8

Stockholders' Equity *after* a Stock Dividend

Stockholders' Equity	Before Dividend	Declaration	Issuance	After Dividend
Common stock—$10 par value, 15,000 shares authorized, 10,000 shares issued and outstanding	$100,000	$ —	$ 10,000	$110,000
Common stock dividend distributable—1,000 shares	—	10,000	(10,000)	0
Paid-in capital in excess of par value, common stock	8,000	5,000	—	13,000
Retained earnings	35,000	(15,000)	—	20,000
Total stockholders' equity	$143,000	$ 0	$ 0	$143,000

No entry is made on the date of record for a stock dividend. On January 20, the date of payment, Quest distributes the new shares to stockholders and records this entry (this entry is reflected in the "issuance" column of Exhibit 11.8):

Date of Payment—Small Stock Dividend

Jan. 20	Common Stock Dividend Distributable	10,000	
	Common Stock, $10 Par Value		10,000
	To record issuance of common stock dividend.		

Assets = Liabilities + Equity
−10,000
+10,000

The combined effect of these stock dividend entries is to transfer (or capitalize) $15,000 of retained earnings to paid-in capital accounts (see far-right column of Exhibit 11.8). The amount of capitalized retained earnings equals the market value of the 1,000 issued shares ($15 × 1,000 shares). A stock dividend has no effect on the ownership percentage of individual stockholders.

Point: A stock dividend does not affect total assets nor total equity.

Recording a large stock dividend. A corporation capitalizes retained earnings equal to the minimum amount required by state law for a large stock dividend. For most states, this amount is the par or stated value of the newly issued shares. To illustrate, suppose Quest's board declares a stock dividend of 30% instead of 10% on December 31. Since this dividend is more than 25%, it is treated as a large stock dividend. Thus, the par value of the 3,000 (computed as 10,000 outstanding shares × 30%) dividend shares is capitalized at the date of declaration with this entry:

Point: Large stock dividends are recorded at par or stated value.

Date of Declaration—Large Stock Dividend

Dec. 31	Retained Earnings	30,000	
	Common Stock Dividend Distributable		30,000
	Declared a 3,000-share (30%) stock dividend.		

Assets = Liabilities + Equity
−30,000
+30,000

30% dividend × 10,000 outstanding shares × $10 par value

This transaction decreases retained earnings and increases contributed capital by $30,000. On the date of payment the company debits Common Stock Dividend Distributable and credits Common Stock for $30,000. The effects from a large stock dividend on balance sheet accounts are similar to those for a small stock dividend except for the absence of any effect on paid-in capital in excess of par.

Stock Splits

A **stock split** is the distribution of additional shares to stockholders according to their percent ownership. When a stock split occurs, the corporation "calls in" its outstanding shares and issues more than one new share in exchange for each old share. Splits can be done in any ratio,

Before 5:1 Split: 1 share, $50 par

After 5:1 Split: 5 shares, $10 par

including 2-for-1, 3-for-1, or higher. In 2012, **Google** directors approved a 2-for-1 stock split. Stock splits reduce the par or stated value per share. The reasons for stock splits are similar to those for stock dividends.

To illustrate, CompTec has 100,000 outstanding shares of $20 par value common stock with a current market value of $88 per share. A 2-for-1 stock split cuts par value in half as it replaces 100,000 shares of $20 par value stock with 200,000 shares of $10 par value stock. Market value is reduced from $88 per share to about $44 per share. The split does not affect any equity amounts reported on the balance sheet or any individual stockholder's percent ownership. Both the Paid-In Capital and Retained Earnings accounts are unchanged by a split, and *no journal entry is made*. The only effect on the accounts is a change in the stock account description. CompTec's 2-for-1 split on its $20 par value stock means that after the split, it changes its stock account title to *Common Stock, $10 Par Value*. This stock's description on the balance sheet also changes to reflect the additional authorized, issued, and outstanding shares and the new par value.

The difference between stock splits and large stock dividends is often blurred. Many companies report stock splits in their financial statements without calling in the original shares by simply changing their par value. This type of "split" is really a large stock dividend and results in additional shares issued to stockholders by capitalizing retained earnings or transferring other paid-in capital to Common Stock. This approach avoids administrative costs of splitting the stock. **Harley-Davidson** recently declared a 2-for-1 stock split executed in the form of a 100% stock dividend.

Point: Berkshire Hathaway has resisted a stock split. Its recent stock price was $170,000 per share.

Point: A **reverse stock split** is the opposite of a stock split. It increases both the market value per share and the par or stated value per share with a split ratio less than 1-for-1, such as 1-for-2. A reverse split results in fewer shares. Markets often read bad news into reverse splits.

Decision Maker

Entrepreneur A company you co-founded and own stock in announces a 50% stock dividend. Has the value of your stock investment increased, decreased, or remained the same? Would it make a difference if it was a 3-for-2 stock split executed in the form of a dividend? ■ [Answers follow the chapter's Summary.]

NEED-TO-KNOW 11-2

Recording Dividends

P2

A company began the current year with the following balances in its stockholders' equity accounts.

Common stock—$10 par, 500 shares authorized, 200 shares issued and outstanding	$2,000
Paid-in capital in excess of par, common stock	1,000
Retained earnings	5,000
Total	$8,000

All outstanding common stock was issued for $15 per share when the company was created. Prepare journal entries to account for the following transactions during the current year.

Jan. 10 The board declared a $0.10 cash dividend per share to shareholders of record Jan. 28.
Feb. 15 Paid the cash dividend declared on January 10.
Mar. 31 Declared a 20% stock dividend. The market value of the stock is $18 per share.
May 1 Distributed the stock dividend declared on March 31.
Dec. 1 Declared a 40% stock dividend. The market value of the stock is $25 per share.
Dec. 31 Distributed the stock dividend declared on December 1.

Jan. 10	Retained Earnings[a]	20	
	Common Dividend Payable		20
	Declared a $0.10 per share cash dividend.		
	[a]200 outstanding shares × $0.10		
Feb. 15	Common Dividend Payable	20	
	Cash		20
	Paid $0.10 per share cash dividend.		

[continued on next page]

[continued from previous page]

Mar. 31	Retained Earnings[b]	720	
	Common Stock Dividend Distributable[c]		400
	Paid-In Capital in Excess of Par Value, Common Stock		320
	Declared a small stock dividend of 20% or 40 shares; market value is $18 per share.		
	[b]200 outstanding shares × 20% × $18 market		
	[c]40 new shares × $10 par		
May 1	Common Stock Dividend Distributable	400	
	Common Stock		400
	Distributed 40 shares of common stock.		
Dec. 1	Retained Earnings[d]	960	
	Common Stock Dividend Distributable		960
	Declared a large stock dividend of 40% or 96 shares (40% × [200 + 40]); par value is $10 per share.		
	[d]240 outstanding shares × 40% × $10 par		
Dec. 31	Common Stock Dividend Distributable	960	
	Common Stock		960
	Distributed 96 shares of common stock.		

Do More: QS 11-6, QS 11-7, QS 11-8, E 11-5, E 11-6

QC4

PREFERRED STOCK

C2 Explain characteristics of, and distribute dividends between, common and preferred stock.

A corporation can issue two basic kinds of stock, common and preferred. **Preferred stock** has special rights that give it priority (or senior status) over common stock in one or more areas. Special rights typically include a preference for receiving dividends and for the distribution of assets if the corporation is liquidated. Preferred stock carries all rights of common stock unless the corporate charter nullifies them. Most preferred stock, for instance, does not confer the right to vote. Exhibit 11.9 shows that preferred stock is issued by about one-fourth of corporations. All corporations issue common stock. (While rare, not all common stock carries voting rights; Google's C Class common shares are nonvoting.)

EXHIBIT 11.9

Corporations and Preferred Stock

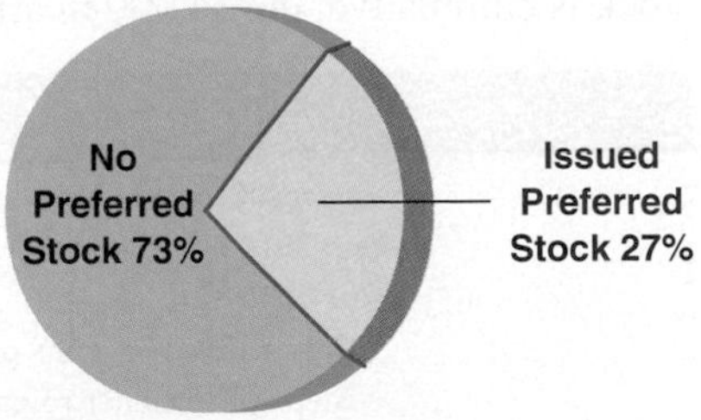

Issuance of Preferred Stock

Preferred stock usually has a par value. Like common stock, it can be sold at a price different from par. Preferred stock is recorded in its own separate capital accounts. To illustrate, if Dillon Snowboards issues 50 shares of $100 par value preferred stock for $6,000 cash on July 1, 2015, the entry is

July 1	Cash	6,000	
	Preferred Stock, $100 Par Value		5,000
	Paid-In Capital in Excess of Par Value, Preferred Stock		1,000
	Issued preferred stock for cash.		

Assets	= Liabilities	+ Equity
+6,000		+5,000
		+1,000

$100 par value × 50 shares

$6,000 cash − [$100 par value × 50 shares]

The equity section of the year-end balance sheet for Dillon Snowboards, including preferred stock, is shown in Exhibit 11.10. (This exhibit assumes that common stock was issued at par.) Issuing no-par preferred stock is similar to issuing no-par common stock. Also, the entries for issuing preferred stock for noncash assets are similar to those for common stock.

EXHIBIT 11.10

Stockholders' Equity with Common and Preferred Stock

Stockholders' Equity	
Common stock—$10 par value; 50,000 shares authorized; 30,000 shares issued and outstanding	$300,000
Preferred stock—$100 par value; 1,000 shares authorized; 50 shares issued and outstanding	**5,000**
Paid-in capital in excess of par value, preferred stock	**1,000**
Retained earnings	65,000
Total stockholders' equity	$371,000

Dividend Preference of Preferred Stock

Preferred stock usually carries a preference for dividends, meaning that preferred stockholders are allocated their dividends before any dividends are allocated to common stockholders. The dividends allocated to preferred stockholders are usually expressed as a dollar amount per share or a percent applied to par value. A preference for dividends does *not* ensure dividends. If the directors do not declare a dividend, neither the preferred nor the common stockholders receive one.

Point: Dividend preference does not imply that preferred stockholders receive more dividends than common stockholders, nor does it guarantee a dividend.

Cumulative or Noncumulative Dividend Most preferred stocks carry a cumulative dividend right. **Cumulative preferred stock** gives its owners a right to be paid both the current and all prior periods' unpaid dividends before any dividend is paid to common stockholders. When preferred stock is cumulative and the directors either do not declare a dividend to preferred stockholders or declare one that does not cover the total amount of cumulative dividend, the unpaid dividend amount is called **dividend in arrears.** Accumulation of dividends in arrears on cumulative preferred stock does not guarantee they will be paid. **Noncumulative preferred stock** confers no right to prior periods' unpaid dividends if they were not declared in those prior periods.

To illustrate the difference between cumulative and noncumulative preferred stock, assume that a corporation's outstanding stock includes (1) 1,000 shares of $100 par, 9% preferred stock—yielding $9,000 per year (1,000 shares × $100 par × 9%) in potential dividends, and (2) 4,000 shares of $50 par value common stock. During 2014, the first year of operations, the directors declare cash dividends of $5,000. In year 2015, they declare cash dividends of $42,000. See Exhibit 11.11 for the allocation of dividends for these two years. Allocation of year 2015 dividends depends on whether the preferred stock is noncumulative or cumulative. With noncumulative preferred, the preferred stockholders never receive the $4,000 skipped in 2014. If the preferred stock is cumulative, the $4,000 in arrears is paid in 2015 before any other dividends are paid.

EXHIBIT 11.11

Allocation of Dividends (noncumulative vs. cumulative preferred stock)

	Preferred	Common
Preferred Stock Is Noncumulative		
Year 2014	$ 5,000	$ 0
Year 2015		
Step 1: Current year's preferred dividend	$ 9,000	
Step 2: Remainder to common		$33,000
Totals for 2014–2015	$14,000	$33,000
Preferred Stock Is Cumulative		
Year 2014	$ 5,000	$ 0
Year 2015		
Step 1: Dividend in arrears	$ 4,000	
Step 2: Current year's preferred dividend	9,000	
Step 3: Remainder to common		$29,000
Totals for year 2015	$13,000	$29,000
Totals for 2014–2015	$18,000	$29,000

Example: What dividends do cumulative preferred stockholders receive in 2015 if the corporation paid only $2,000 of dividends in 2014? How does this affect dividends to common stockholders in 2015? *Answers:* $16,000 ($7,000 dividends in arrears, plus $9,000 current preferred dividends). Dividends to common stockholders decrease to $26,000.

A liability for a dividend does not exist until the directors declare a dividend. If a preferred dividend date passes and the corporation's board fails to declare the dividend on its cumulative preferred stock, the dividend in arrears is not a liability. The *full disclosure principle* requires a corporation to report (usually in a note) the amount of preferred dividends in arrears as of the balance sheet date.

Participating or Nonparticipating Dividend **Nonparticipating preferred stock** has a feature that limits dividends to a maximum amount each year. This maximum is often stated as a percent of the stock's par value or as a specific dollar amount per share. Once preferred stockholders receive this amount, the common stockholders receive any and all additional dividends. **Participating preferred stock** has a feature allowing preferred stockholders to share with common stockholders in any dividends paid in excess of the percent or dollar amount stated on the preferred stock. This participation feature does not apply until common stockholders receive dividends equal to the preferred stock's dividend percent. Many corporations are authorized to issue participating preferred stock but rarely do, and most managers never expect to issue it.[2]

Convertible Preferred Stock

Preferred stock is more attractive to investors if it carries a right to exchange preferred shares for a fixed number of common shares. **Convertible preferred stock** gives holders the option to exchange their preferred shares for common shares at a specified rate. When a company prospers and its common stock increases in value, convertible preferred stockholders can share in this success by converting their preferred stock into more valuable common stock.

Callable Preferred Stock

Callable preferred stock gives the issuing corporation the right to purchase (retire) this stock from its holders at specified future prices and dates. The amount paid to call and retire a preferred share is its **call price,** or *redemption value,* and is set when the stock is issued. The call price normally includes the stock's par value plus a premium giving holders additional return on their investment. When the issuing corporation calls and retires a preferred stock, the terms of the agreement often require it to pay the call price *and* any dividends in arrears.

Point: The issuing corporation has the right, or option, to retire its callable preferred stock.

IFRS

Like U.S. GAAP, IFRS requires that preferred stocks be classified as debt or equity based on analysis of the stock's contractual terms. However, IFRS uses different criteria for such classification. ■

Reasons for Issuing Preferred Stock

Corporations issue preferred stock for several reasons. One is to raise capital without sacrificing control. For example, suppose a company's organizers have $100,000 cash to invest and organize a corporation that needs $200,000 of capital to start. If they sell $200,000 worth of common stock (with $100,000 to the organizers), they would have only 50% control and would need to negotiate extensively with other stockholders in making policy. However, if they issue $100,000 worth of common stock to themselves and sell outsiders $100,000 of 8%, cumulative preferred stock with no voting rights, they retain control.

A second reason to issue preferred stock is to boost the return earned by common stockholders. To illustrate, suppose a corporation's organizers expect to earn an annual after-tax income of $24,000 on an investment of $200,000. If they sell and issue $200,000 worth of common stock, the $24,000 income produces a 12% return on the $200,000 of common stockholders' equity. However, if they issue $100,000 of 8% preferred stock to outsiders and $100,000 of common stock to themselves, their own return increases to 16% per year, as shown in Exhibit 11.12.

EXHIBIT 11.12

Return to Common Stockholders When Preferred Stock Is Issued

Net (after-tax) income	$24,000
Less preferred dividends at 8%	(8,000)
Balance to common stockholders	$16,000
Return to common stockholders ($16,000/$100,000)	16%

[2] Participating preferred stock is usually authorized as a defense against a possible corporate *takeover* by an "unfriendly" investor (or a group of investors) who intends to buy enough voting common stock to gain control. Taking a term from spy novels, the financial world refers to this type of plan as a *poison pill* that a company swallows if enemy investors threaten its capture. A poison pill usually works as follows: A corporation's common stockholders on a given date are granted the right to purchase a large amount of participating preferred stock at a very low price. This right to purchase preferred shares is *not* transferable. If an unfriendly investor buys a large block of common shares (whose right to purchase participating preferred shares does *not* transfer to this buyer), the board can issue preferred shares at a low price to the remaining common shareholders who retained the right to purchase. Future dividends are then divided between the newly issued participating preferred shares and the common shares. This usually transfers value from common shares to preferred shares, causing the unfriendly investor's common stock to lose much of its value and reducing the potential benefit of a hostile takeover.

Point: Financial leverage also occurs when debt is issued and the interest rate paid on it is less than the rate earned from using the assets the creditors lend the company.

Common stockholders earn 16% instead of 12% because assets contributed by preferred stockholders are invested to earn $12,000 while the preferred dividend is only $8,000. Use of preferred stock to increase return to common stockholders is an example of **financial leverage** (also called *trading on the equity*). As a general rule, when the dividend rate on preferred stock is less than the rate the corporation earns on its assets, the effect of issuing preferred stock is to increase (or *lever)* the rate earned by common stockholders.

Other reasons for issuing preferred stock include its appeal to some investors who believe that the corporation's common stock is too risky or that the expected return on common stock is too low.

Decision Maker

Concert Organizer Assume that you alter your business strategy from organizing concerts targeted at under 1,000 people to those targeted at between 5,000 and 20,000 people. You also incorporate because of increased risk of lawsuits and a desire to issue stock for financing. It is important that you control the company for decisions on whom to schedule. What types of stock do you offer? ■ [Answers follow the chapter's Summary.]

NEED-TO-KNOW 11-3

Allocating Cash Dividends

C2

A company's outstanding stock consists of 80 shares of *noncumulative* 5% preferred stock with a $5 par value and also 200 shares of common stock with a $1 par value. During its first three years of operation, the corporation declared and paid the following total cash dividends:

2015 total cash dividends	$ 15
2016 total cash dividends	5
2017 total cash dividends	200

Part 1. Determine the amount of dividends paid each year to each of the two classes of stockholders: preferred and common. Also compute the total dividends paid to each class for the three years combined.

Part 2. Determine the amount of dividends paid each year to each of the two classes of stockholders assuming that the preferred stock is *cumulative.* Also determine the total dividends paid to each class for the three years combined.

Solution—Part 1

	Non-Cumulative Preferred	Common
2015 ($15 paid)		
Preferred*	$15	
Common—remainder		$ 0
Total for the year	$15	$ 0
2016 ($5 paid)		
Preferred*	$ 5	
Common—remainder		$ 0
Total for the year	$ 5	$ 0
2017 ($200 paid)		
Preferred*	$20	
Common—remainder		$180
Total for the year	$20	$180
2015–2017 (combined $220 paid)		
Total for three years	$40	$180

* Holders of noncumulative preferred stock are entitled to no more than $20 of dividends in any one year (5% × $5 × 80 shares).

Solution—Part 2

	Cumulative Preferred	Common
2015 ($15 paid)		
Preferred*	$15	
Common—remainder	—	$ 0
Total for the year	$15	$ 0
(Note: $5 in preferred dividends in arrears; ($20 × 1 yr) − $15 paid.)		
2016 ($5 paid)		
Preferred—arrears from 2015	$ 5	
Preferred*	0	
Common—remainder	—	$ 0
Total for the year	$ 5	$ 0
(Note: $20 in preferred dividends in arrears; ($20 × 2 yrs) − $15 paid − $5 paid.)		
2017 ($200 paid)		
Preferred—arrears from 2016	$20	
Preferred*	20	
Common—remainder	—	$160
Total for the year	$40	$160
(Note: $0 in preferred dividends in arrears; ($20 × 3 yrs) − $15 paid − $5 paid − $40 paid.)		
2015–2017 (combined $220 paid)		
Total for three years	$60	$160

* Holders of cumulative preferred stock are entitled to no more than $20 of dividends declared in any year (5% × $5 × 80 shares) plus any dividends in arrears.

Do More: QS 11-9, QS 11-10, E 11-7, E 11-8, E 11-9

QC5

TREASURY STOCK

P3 Record purchases and sales of treasury stock and the retirement of stock.

Corporations acquire shares of their own stock for several reasons: (1) to use their shares to acquire another corporation, (2) to purchase shares to avoid a hostile takeover of the company, (3) to reissue them to employees as compensation, and (4) to maintain a strong market for their stock or to show management confidence in the current price.

A corporation's reacquired shares are called **treasury stock,** which is similar to unissued stock in several ways: (1) neither treasury stock nor unissued stock is an asset, (2) neither receives cash dividends or stock dividends, and (3) neither allows the exercise of voting rights. However, treasury stock does differ from unissued stock in one major way: The corporation can resell treasury stock at less than par without having the buyers incur a liability, provided it was originally issued at par value or higher. Treasury stock purchases also require management to exercise ethical sensitivity because funds are being paid to specific stockholders instead of all stockholders. Managers must be sure the purchase is in the best interest of all stockholders. These concerns cause companies to fully disclose treasury stock transactions.

Corporations and Treasury Stock

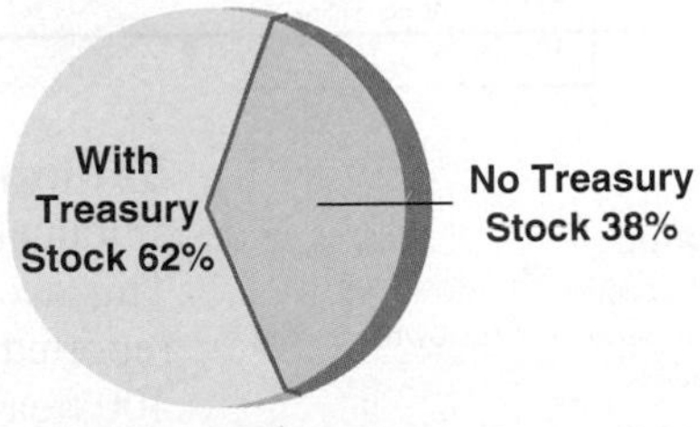

Purchasing Treasury Stock

Purchasing treasury stock reduces the corporation's assets and equity by equal amounts. (We describe the *cost method* of accounting for treasury stock, which is the most widely used method. The *par value* method is another method explained in advanced courses.) To illustrate, Exhibit 11.13 shows Cyber Corporation's account balances *before* any treasury stock purchase (Cyber has no liabilities).

EXHIBIT 11.13

Account Balances *before* Purchasing Treasury Stock

Assets		Stockholders' Equity	
Cash	$ 30,000	Common stock—$10 par; 10,000 shares authorized, issued, and outstanding	$100,000
Other assets	95,000	Retained earnings	25,000
Total assets	$125,000	Total stockholders' equity	$125,000

Cyber then purchases 1,000 of its own shares for $11,500 on May 1, which is recorded as follows:

Assets = Liabilities + Equity
−11,500 −11,500

$11.50 cost per share × 1,000 shares

May 1	Treasury Stock, Common	11,500	
	Cash		11,500
	Purchased 1,000 treasury shares at $11.50 per share.		

This entry reduces equity through the debit to the Treasury Stock account, which is a contra equity account. Exhibit 11.14 shows account balances *after* this transaction.

EXHIBIT 11.14

Account Balances *after* Purchasing Treasury Stock

Assets		Stockholders' Equity	
Cash	$ 18,500	Common stock—$10 par; 10,000 shares authorized and issued; 1,000 shares in treasury	$100,000
Other assets	95,000	Retained earnings, $11,500 restricted by treasury stock purchase	25,000
		Less cost of treasury stock	**(11,500)**
Total assets	$113,500	Total stockholders' equity	$113,500

Point: The Treasury Stock account is *not* an asset. Treasury stock does not carry voting or dividend rights.

Point: A treasury stock purchase is also called a *stock buyback*.

The treasury stock purchase reduces Cyber's cash, total assets, and total equity by $11,500 but does not reduce the balance of either the Common Stock or the Retained Earnings account. The equity reduction is reported by deducting the cost of treasury stock in the equity section. Also, two disclosures are evident. First, the stock description reveals that 1,000 issued shares are in treasury, leaving only 9,000 shares still outstanding. Second, the description for retained earnings reveals that it is partly restricted.

Reissuing Treasury Stock

Treasury stock can be reissued by selling it at cost, above cost, or below cost.

Selling Treasury Stock at Cost If treasury stock is reissued at cost, the entry is the reverse of the one made to record the purchase. For instance, if on May 21 Cyber reissues 100 of the treasury shares purchased on May 1 at the same $11.50 per share cost, the entry is

Assets = Liabilities + Equity
+1,150 +1,150

$11.50 cost per share × 100 shares

May 21	Cash	1,150	
	Treasury Stock, Common		1,150
	Received $11.50 per share for 100 treasury shares costing $11.50 per share.		

Point: Treasury stock does not represent ownership. A company cannot own a part of itself.

Selling Treasury Stock *above* Cost If treasury stock is sold for more than cost, the amount received in excess of cost is credited to the Paid-In Capital, Treasury Stock account. This account is reported as a separate item in the stockholders' equity section. No gain is ever reported from the sale of treasury stock. To illustrate, if Cyber receives $12 cash per share for 400 treasury shares costing $11.50 per share on June 3, the entry is

Assets = Liabilities + Equity
+4,800 +4,600
+200

$11.50 cost per share × 400 shares

[$12 issue price − $11.50 cost per share] × 400 shares

June 3	Cash	4,800	
	Treasury Stock, Common		4,600
	Paid-In Capital, Treasury Stock		**200**
	Received $12 per share for 400 treasury shares costing $11.50 per share.		

Point: The phrase *treasury stock* is believed to arise from the fact that reacquired stock is held in a corporation's treasury.

Point: The Paid-In Capital, Treasury Stock account can have a zero or credit balance but never a debit balance.

Selling Treasury Stock *below* Cost When treasury stock is sold below cost, the entry to record the sale depends on whether the Paid-In Capital, Treasury Stock account has a credit balance. If it has a zero balance, the excess of cost over the sales price is debited to Retained Earnings. If the Paid-In Capital, Treasury Stock account has a credit balance, it is debited for the excess of the cost over the selling price but not to exceed the balance in this account. When the credit balance in this paid-in capital account is eliminated, any remaining difference between the cost and selling price is debited to Retained Earnings. To illustrate, if Cyber sells its remaining 500 shares of treasury stock at $10 per share on July 10, equity is reduced by $750 (500 shares × $1.50 per share excess of cost over selling price), as shown in this entry:

July 10	Cash	5,000	
	Paid-In Capital, Treasury Stock	**200**	
	Retained Earnings	**550**	
	Treasury Stock, Common		5,750
	Received $10 per share for 500 treasury shares costing $11.50 per share.		

Assets = Liabilities + Equity
+5,000 −200
−550
+5,750

[$10 issue price − $11.50 cost per share] × 500 shares; not to exceed $200

For any amount exceeding $200 PIC from TS

$11.50 cost per share × 500 shares

This entry eliminates the $200 credit balance in the paid-in capital account created on June 3 and then reduces the Retained Earnings balance by the remaining $550 excess of cost over selling price. A company never reports a loss (or gain) from the sale of treasury stock.

Retiring Stock

A corporation can purchase its own stock and retire it. Retiring stock reduces the number of issued shares. Retired stock is the same as authorized and unissued shares. Purchases and retirements of stock are permissible under state law only if they do not jeopardize the interests of creditors and stockholders. When stock is purchased for retirement, we remove all capital amounts related to the retired shares. If the purchase price exceeds the net amount removed, this excess is debited to Retained Earnings. If the net amount removed from all capital accounts exceeds the purchase price, this excess is credited to the Paid-In Capital from Retirement of Stock account. A company's assets and equity are always reduced by the amount paid for the retiring stock.

Point: Recording stock retirement results in canceling the equity from the original issuance of the shares.

NEED-TO-KNOW 11-4

Recording Treasury Stock

P3

A company began the current year with the following balances in its stockholders' equity accounts.

Common stock—$10 par, 500 shares authorized, 200 shares issued and outstanding	$2,000
Paid-in capital in excess of par, common stock	1,000
Retained earnings	5,000
Total	$8,000

All outstanding common stock was issued for $15 per share when the company was created. Prepare journal entries to account for the following transactions during the current year.

July 1 Purchased 30 shares of treasury stock at $20 per share.
Sept. 1 Sold 20 treasury shares at $26 cash per share.
Dec. 1 Sold the remaining 10 shares of treasury stock at $7 cash per share.

July 1	Treasury Stock, Common[a]	600	
	Cash		600
	Purchased 30 common shares at $20 per share.		
	[a]30 shares × $20 cost		
Sept. 1	Cash[b]	520	
	Treasury Stock, Common[c]		400
	Paid-In Capital, Treasury Stock		120
	Sold 20 treasury shares at $26 per share.		
	[b]20 shares × $26 reissue price [c]20 shares × $20 cost		
Dec. 1	Cash[d]	70	
	Paid-In Capital, Treasury Stock[e]	120	
	Retained Earnings	10	
	Treasury Stock, Common[f]		200
	Sold 10 treasury shares at $7 per share.		
	[d]10 shares × $7 reissue price		
	[e]Not to exceed existing balance [f]10 shares × $20 cost		

Do More: QS 11-11, E 11-10

QC6

REPORTING OF EQUITY

C3

Explain the items reported in retained earnings.

Statement of Retained Earnings

Retained earnings generally consist of a company's cumulative net income less any net losses and dividends declared since its inception. Retained earnings are part of stockholders' claims on the company's net assets, but this does *not* imply that a certain amount of cash or other assets is available to pay stockholders. For example, **Abercrombie & Fitch** has $2,320,571 thousand in retained earnings, but only $583,495 thousand in cash. This section describes events and transactions affecting retained earnings and how retained earnings are reported.

Restrictions and Appropriations The term **restricted retained earnings** refers to both statutory and contractual restrictions. A common *statutory* (or *legal*) *restriction* is to limit treasury stock purchases to the amount of retained earnings. The balance sheet in Exhibit 11.14 provides an example. A common *contractual restriction* involves loan agreements that restrict paying dividends beyond a specified amount or percent of retained earnings. Restrictions are usually described in the notes. The term **appropriated retained earnings** refers to a voluntary transfer of amounts from the Retained Earnings account to the Appropriated Retained Earnings account to inform users of special activities that require funds.

Prior Period Adjustments **Prior period adjustments** are corrections of material errors in prior period financial statements. These errors include arithmetic mistakes, unacceptable accounting, and missed facts. Prior period adjustments are reported in the *statement of retained earnings* (or the statement of stockholders' equity), net of any income tax effects. Prior period adjustments result in changing the beginning balance of retained earnings for events occurring prior to the earliest period reported in the current set of financial statements. To illustrate, assume that ComUS makes an error in a 2013 journal entry for the purchase of land by incorrectly debiting an expense account. When this is discovered in 2015, the statement of retained earnings includes a prior period adjustment, as shown in Exhibit 11.15. This exhibit also shows the usual format of the statement of retained earnings.

Point: If a year 2013 error is discovered in 2014, the company records the adjustment in 2014. But if the financial statements include 2013 and 2014 figures, the statements report the correct amounts for 2013, and a note describes the correction.

EXHIBIT 11.15

Statement of Retained Earnings with a Prior Period Adjustment

ComUS Statement of Retained Earnings For Year Ended December 31, 2015	
Retained earnings, Dec. 31, 2014, as previously reported	$4,745,000
Prior period adjustment	
Cost of land incorrectly expensed (net of $63,000 of income tax benefit)	**147,000**
Retained earnings, Dec. 31, 2014, as adjusted	4,892,000
Plus net income	1,224,300
Less cash dividends declared	(301,800)
Retained earnings, Dec. 31, 2015	$5,814,500

Many items reported in financial statements are based on estimates. Future events are certain to reveal that some of these estimates were inaccurate even when based on the best data available at the time. These inaccuracies are *not* considered errors and are *not* reported as prior period adjustments. Instead, they are identified as **changes in accounting estimates** and are accounted for in current and future periods. To illustrate, we know that depreciation is based on estimated useful lives and salvage values. As time passes and new information becomes available, managers may need to change these estimates and the resulting depreciation expense for current and future periods.

Point: Accounting for changes in estimates is sometimes criticized as two wrongs to make a right. Consider a change in an asset's life. Depreciation neither before nor after the change is the amount computed if the revised estimate were originally selected. Regulators chose this approach to avoid restating prior period numbers.

Closing Process The closing process was explained earlier in the book as: (1) Close credit balances in revenue accounts to Income Summary, (2) Close debit balances in expense accounts to Income Summary, and (3) Close Income Summary to Retained Earnings. If dividends are recorded in a Dividends account, and not as an immediate reduction to Retained Earnings (as shown in this chapter), a fourth step is necessary to close the Dividends account to Retained Earnings.

Statement of Stockholders' Equity

Instead of a separate statement of retained earnings, companies commonly report a statement of stockholders' equity that includes changes in retained earnings. A **statement of stockholders' equity** lists the beginning and ending balances of key equity accounts and describes the changes that occur during the period. The companies in Appendix A report such a statement. The usual format is to provide a column for each component of equity and use the rows to describe events occurring in the period. Exhibit 11.16 shows a condensed statement for **Apple**.

EXHIBIT 11.16
Statement of Stockholders' Equity

APPLE

APPLE
Statement of Stockholders' Equity

($ millions, shares in thousands)	Common Stock Shares	Common Stock Amount	Retained Earnings	Other	Total Equity
Balance, Sept. 29, 2012	**939,208**	**$16,422**	**$101,289**	**$ 499**	**$118,210**
Net income	—	—	37,037	—	37,037
Issuance of common stock	6,981	(143)	(444)	—	(587)
Repurchase of common stock and other	(46,976)	3,485	(22,950)	(970)	(20,435)
Cash dividends ($11.40 per share)	—	—	(10,676)	—	(10,676)
Balance, Sept. 28, 2013	**899,213**	**$19,764**	**$104,256**	**$(471)**	**$123,549**

Reporting Stock Options

Many corporations whose shares are publicly traded issue **stock options,** which are rights to purchase common stock at a fixed price over a specified period. As the stock's price rises, the option's value increases. **Starbucks** and **Home Depot** offer stock options to both full- and part-time employees. Stock options are said to motivate managers and employees to (1) focus on company performance, (2) take a long-run perspective, and (3) remain with the company. A stock option is like having an investment with no risk ("a carrot with no stick").

To illustrate, Quantum grants each of its employees the option to purchase 100 shares of its $1 par value common stock at its current market price of $50 per share anytime within the next 10 years. If the stock price rises to $70 per share, an employee can exercise the option at a gain of $20 per share (acquire a $70 stock at the $50 option price). With 100 shares, a single employee would have a total gain of $2,000, computed as $20 × 100 shares. Companies report the cost of stock options in the income statement. Measurement of this cost is explained in advanced courses.

Decision Insight

Pump 'n Dump Fraudulent information can be used by the owners of a company's stock to pump it up and claim it is undervalued, which causes naïve investors to seek to acquire the stock and drive up its price. After that, those behind the release of fraudulent information dump the stock at an inflated price. When later information reveals that the stock is overvalued, its price declines and investors still holding the stock lose value. This scheme is called *pump 'n dump*. Jonathan Lebed, at 15 years old, allegedly made about $1 million in one of the most infamous cases of pump 'n dump. ■

GLOBAL VIEW

This section discusses similarities and differences between U.S. GAAP and IFRS in accounting and reporting for equity.

Accounting for Common Stock The accounting for and reporting of common stock under U.S. GAAP and IFRS are similar. Specifically, procedures for issuing common stock at par, at a premium, at a discount, and for noncash assets are similar across the two systems. However, we must be aware of legal and cultural differences across the world that can impact the rights and responsibilities of common shareholders. **Samsung**'s terminology is a bit different as it uses the phrase "share premium" in reference to what U.S. GAAP would title "paid-in capital in excess of par value" (see Appendix A).

Samsung

Accounting for Dividends Accounting for and reporting of dividends under U.S. GAAP and IFRS are consistent. This applies to cash dividends, stock dividends, and stock splits. **Samsung**, "declared cash dividends to shareholders of common stock and preferred stock as interim dividends for the six-month periods . . . and as year-end dividends." Samsung, like many other companies, follows a dividend policy set by management and its board.

Accounting for Preferred Stock Accounting and reporting for preferred stock are similar for U.S. GAAP and IFRS, but there are some important differences. First, preferred stock that is redeemable at the option of the preferred stockholders is reported *between* liabilities and equity in U.S. GAAP balance sheets. However, that same stock is reported as a liability in IFRS balance sheets. Second, the issue price of convertible preferred stock (and bonds) is recorded entirely under preferred stock (or bonds) *and none is assigned to the conversion feature* under U.S. GAAP. However, IFRS requires that a portion of the issue price be allocated to the conversion feature when it exists. Samsung has preferred stock, which is noncumulative and nonvoting.

Accounting for Treasury Stock Both U.S. GAAP and IFRS apply the principle that companies do not record gains or losses on transactions involving their own stock. This applies to purchases, reissuances, and retirements of treasury stock. Consequently, the accounting for treasury stock explained in this chapter is consistent with that under IFRS. However, IFRS in this area is less detailed than U.S. GAAP.

Bloomberg via Getty Images

Sustainability and Accounting The founder, Jack Ma, of **Alibaba Group**, as introduced in this chapter's opening feature, explains that sustainability is an important part of his company's mission. Jack explains: "I always believe we shouldn't build an 'empire;' instead, we should build an 'ecosystem.' Every empire will be toppled someday, but an ecosystem is sustainable." Jack points to his company's website, which has set aside "0.3% of our annual revenue to fund efforts designed to encourage environmental awareness and conservation." The site also states that they ban "all product postings related to shark fins, ivory, bear bile, cat and dog fur and meat, and various other products made from endangered animals."

Decision Analysis — Earnings per Share, Price-Earnings Ratio, Dividend Yield, and Book Value per Share

Earnings per Share

A1 Compute earnings per share and describe its use.

The income statement reports **earnings per share,** also called *EPS* or *net income per share,* which is the amount of income earned per share of a company's outstanding common stock. The **basic earnings per share** formula is shown in Exhibit 11.17. When a company has no preferred stock, then preferred dividends are zero. The weighted-average common shares outstanding is measured over the income reporting period; its computation is explained in advanced courses.

EXHIBIT 11.17

Basic Earnings per Share

$$\textbf{Basic earnings per share} = \frac{\textbf{Net income} - \textbf{Preferred dividends}}{\textbf{Weighted-average common shares outstanding}}$$

To illustrate, assume that Quantum Co. earns $40,000 net income in 2015 and declares dividends of $7,500 on its noncumulative preferred stock. (If preferred stock is *non*cumulative, the income available [numerator] is the current-period net income less any preferred dividends *declared* in that same period. If preferred stock is cumulative, the income available [numerator] is the current-period net income less the preferred dividends whether declared or not.) Quantum has 5,000 weighted-average common shares outstanding during 2015. Its basic EPS[3] is

$$\text{Basic earnings per share} = \frac{\$40{,}000 - \$7{,}500}{5{,}000 \text{ shares}} = \$6.50$$

[3]A corporation can be classified as having either a simple or complex capital structure. The term **simple capital structure** refers to a company with only common stock and nonconvertible preferred stock outstanding. The term **complex capital structure** refers to companies with dilutive securities. **Dilutive securities** include options, rights to purchase common stock, and any bonds or preferred stock that are convertible into common stock. A company with a complex capital structure must often report two EPS figures: basic and diluted. **Diluted earnings per share** is computed by adding all dilutive securities to the denominator of the basic EPS computation. It reflects the decrease in basic EPS *assuming* that all dilutive securities are converted into common shares.

Price-Earnings Ratio

A stock's market value is determined by its *expected* future cash flows. A comparison of a company's EPS and its market value per share reveals information about market expectations. This comparison is traditionally made using a **price-earnings (or PE) ratio,** expressed also as *price earnings, price to earnings,* or *PE*. Some analysts interpret this ratio as what price the market is willing to pay for a company's current earnings stream. Price-earnings ratios can differ across companies that have similar earnings because of either higher or lower expectations of future earnings. The price-earnings ratio is defined in Exhibit 11.18.

A2 Compute price-earnings ratio and describe its use in analysis.

Point: The average PE ratio of stocks in the 1950–2014 period is about 14.

EXHIBIT 11.18

Price-Earnings Ratio

$$\textbf{Price-earnings ratio} = \frac{\textbf{Market value (price) per share}}{\textbf{Earnings per share}}$$

This ratio is often computed using EPS from the most recent period (for **Amazon**, its PE is 138; for **Altria**, its PE is 19). However, many users compute this ratio using *expected* EPS for the next period.

Some analysts view stocks with high PE ratios (higher than 20 to 25) as more likely to be overpriced and stocks with low PE ratios (less than 5 to 8) as more likely to be underpriced. These investors prefer to sell or avoid buying stocks with high PE ratios and to buy or hold stocks with low PE ratios. However, investment decision making is rarely so simple as to rely on a single ratio. For instance, a stock with a high PE ratio can prove to be a good investment if its earnings continue to increase beyond current expectations. Similarly, a stock with a low PE ratio can prove to be a poor investment if its earnings decline below expectations.

Point: Average PE ratios for U.S. stocks increased over the past two decades. Some analysts interpret this as a signal the market is overpriced. But higher ratios can at least partly reflect accounting changes that have reduced reported earnings.

Decision Maker

Money Manager You plan to invest in one of two companies identified as having identical future prospects. One has a PE of 19 and the other a PE of 25. Which do you invest in? Does it matter if your *estimate* of PE for these two companies is 29 as opposed to 22? ■ [Answers follow the chapter's Summary.]

Dividend Yield

Investors buy shares of a company's stock in anticipation of receiving a return from either or both cash dividends and stock price increases. Stocks that pay large dividends on a regular basis, called *income stocks,* are attractive to investors who want recurring cash flows from their investments. In contrast, some stocks pay little or no dividends but are still attractive to investors because of their expected stock price increases. The stocks of companies that distribute little or no cash but use their cash to finance expansion are called *growth stocks*. One way to help identify whether a stock is an income stock or a growth stock is to analyze its dividend yield. **Dividend yield,** defined in Exhibit 11.19, shows the annual amount of cash dividends distributed to common shares relative to their market value.

A3 Compute dividend yield and explain its use in analysis.

EXHIBIT 11.19

Dividend Yield

$$\textbf{Dividend yield} = \frac{\textbf{Annual cash dividends per share}}{\textbf{Market value per share}}$$

Dividend yield can be computed for current and prior periods using actual dividends and stock prices and for future periods using expected values. Exhibit 11.20 shows recent dividend and stock price data for **Amazon** and **Altria Group** to compute dividend yield.

EXHIBIT 11.20

Dividend and Stock Price Information

Company	Cash Dividends per Share	Market Value per Share	Dividend Yield
Amazon	$0.00	$300	0.0%
Altria Group.	$1.84	$ 35	5.3%

Dividend yield is zero for Amazon, implying it is a growth stock. An investor in Amazon would look for increases in stock prices (and eventual cash from the sale of stock). Altria has a dividend yield of 5.3%, implying it is an income stock for which dividends are important in assessing its value.

Point: The *payout ratio* equals cash dividends declared on common stock divided by net income. A low payout ratio suggests that a company is retaining earnings for future growth.

Book Value per Share

Case 1: Common Stock (Only) Outstanding. **Book value per common share,** defined in Exhibit 11.21, reflects the amount of equity applicable to *common* shares on a per share basis. To illustrate, we use Dillon Snowboards's data from Exhibit 11.4. Dillon has 30,000 outstanding common shares, and the stockholders'

A4 Compute book value and explain its use in analysis.

equity applicable to common shares is $365,000. Dillon's book value per common share is $12.17, computed as $365,000 divided by 30,000 shares.

EXHIBIT 11.21

Book Value per Common Share

$$\text{Book value per common share} = \frac{\text{Stockholders' equity applicable to common shares}}{\text{Number of common shares outstanding}}$$

Point: Book value per share is also referred to as *stockholders' claim to assets on a per share basis.*

Case 2: Common and Preferred Stock Outstanding. To compute book value when both common and preferred shares are outstanding, we allocate total equity between the two types of shares. The **book value per preferred share** is computed first; its computation is shown in Exhibit 11.22.

EXHIBIT 11.22

Book Value per Preferred Share

$$\text{Book value per preferred share} = \frac{\text{Stockholders' equity applicable to preferred shares}}{\text{Number of preferred shares outstanding}}$$

The equity applicable to preferred shares equals the preferred share's call price (or par value if the preferred is not callable) plus any cumulative dividends in arrears. The remaining equity is the portion applicable to common shares. To illustrate, consider LTD's equity in Exhibit 11.23. Its preferred stock is callable at $108 per share, and two years of cumulative preferred dividends are in arrears.

EXHIBIT 11.23

Stockholders' Equity with Preferred and Common Stock

Stockholders' Equity	
Preferred stock—$100 par value, 7% cumulative, 2,000 shares authorized, 1,000 shares issued and outstanding	$100,000
Common stock—$25 par value, 12,000 shares authorized, 10,000 shares issued and outstanding	250,000
Paid-in capital in excess of par value, common stock	15,000
Retained earnings	82,000
Total stockholders' equity	$447,000

The book value computations are in Exhibit 11.24. Equity is first allocated to preferred shares before the book value of common shares is computed.

EXHIBIT 11.24

Computing Book Value per Preferred and Common Share

Total stockholders' equity		$447,000
Less equity applicable to preferred shares		
Call price (1,000 shares × $108)	$108,000	
Dividends in arrears ($100,000 × 7% × 2 years)	14,000	(122,000)
Equity applicable to common shares		$325,000
Book value per preferred share ($122,000/1,000 shares)		**$ 122.00**
Book value per common share ($325,000/10,000 shares)		**$ 32.50**

Book value per share reflects the value per share if a company is liquidated at balance sheet amounts. Book value is also the starting point in many stock valuation models, merger negotiations, price setting for public utilities, and loan contracts. The main limitation in using book value is the potential difference between recorded value and market value for assets and liabilities. Investors often adjust their analysis for estimates of these differences.

Decision Maker

Investor You are considering investing in **BMX**, whose book value per common share is $4 and price per common share on the stock exchange is $7. From this information, are BMX's net assets priced higher or lower than its recorded values? ■ [Answers follow the chapter's Summary.]

NEED-TO-KNOW

COMPREHENSIVE

Barton Corporation began operations on January 1, 2014. The following transactions relating to stockholders' equity occurred in the first two years of the company's operations.

2014

Jan. 1 Authorized the issuance of 2 million shares of $5 par value common stock and 100,000 shares of $100 par value, 10% cumulative, preferred stock.

Jan. 2 Issued 200,000 shares of common stock for $12 cash per share.

Jan. 3 Issued 100,000 shares of common stock in exchange for a building valued at $820,000 and merchandise inventory valued at $380,000.

Jan. 4 Paid $10,000 cash to the company's founders for organization activities.

Jan. 5 Issued 12,000 shares of preferred stock for $110 cash per share.

2015

June 4 Issued 100,000 shares of common stock for $15 cash per share.

Required

1. Prepare journal entries to record these transactions.
2. Prepare the stockholders' equity section of the balance sheet as of December 31, 2014, and December 31, 2015, based on these transactions.
3. Prepare a table showing dividend allocations and dividends per share for 2014 and 2015 assuming Barton declares the following cash dividends: 2014, $50,000, and 2015, $300,000.
4. Prepare the January 2, 2014, journal entry for Barton's issuance of 200,000 shares of common stock for $12 cash per share assuming
   a. Common stock is no-par stock without a stated value.
   b. Common stock is no-par stock with a stated value of $10 per share.

PLANNING THE SOLUTION

- Record journal entries for the transactions for 2014 and 2015.
- Determine the balances for the 2014 and 2015 equity accounts for the balance sheet.
- Prepare the contributed capital portion of the 2014 and 2015 balance sheets.
- Prepare a table similar to Exhibit 11.11 showing dividend allocations for 2014 and 2015.
- Record the issuance of common stock under both specifications of no-par stock.

SOLUTION

1. Journal entries.

2014 Jan. 2	Cash	2,400,000	
	Common Stock, $5 Par Value		1,000,000
	Paid-In Capital in Excess of Par Value, Common Stock		1,400,000
	Issued 200,000 shares of common stock.		
Jan. 3	Building	820,000	
	Merchandise Inventory	380,000	
	Common Stock, $5 Par Value		500,000
	Paid-In Capital in Excess of Par Value, Common Stock		700,000
	Issued 100,000 shares of common stock.		
Jan. 4	Organization Expenses	10,000	
	Cash		10,000
	Paid founders for organization costs.		
Jan. 5	Cash	1,320,000	
	Preferred Stock, $100 Par Value		1,200,000
	Paid-In Capital in Excess of Par Value, Preferred Stock		120,000
	Issued 12,000 shares of preferred stock.		
2015 June 4	Cash	1,500,000	
	Common Stock, $5 Par Value		500,000
	Paid-In Capital in Excess of Par Value, Common Stock		1,000,000
	Issued 100,000 shares of common stock.		

2. Balance sheet presentations (at December 31 year-end).

	2015	2014
Stockholders' Equity		
Preferred stock—$100 par value, 10% cumulative, 100,000 shares authorized, 12,000 shares issued and outstanding	$1,200,000	$1,200,000
Paid-in capital in excess of par value, preferred stock	120,000	120,000
Total paid-in capital by preferred stockholders	1,320,000	1,320,000
Common stock—$5 par value, 2,000,000 shares authorized, 300,000 shares issued and outstanding in 2014, and 400,000 shares issued and outstanding in 2015	2,000,000	1,500,000
Paid-in capital in excess of par value, common stock	3,100,000	2,100,000
Total paid-in capital by common stockholders	5,100,000	3,600,000
Total paid-in capital	$6,420,000	$4,920,000

3. Dividend allocation table.

	Common	Preferred
2014 ($50,000)		
Preferred—current year (12,000 shares × $10 = $120,000)	$ 0	$ 50,000
Common—remainder (300,000 shares outstanding)	0	0
Total for the year	$ 0	$ 50,000
2015 ($300,000)		
Preferred—dividend in arrears from 2014 ($120,000 − $50,000)	$ 0	$ 70,000
Preferred—current year	0	120,000
Common—remainder (400,000 shares outstanding)	110,000	0
Total for the year	$110,000	$190,000
Dividends per share		
2014	$ 0.00	$ 4.17
2015	$ 0.28	$ 15.83

4. Journal entries.

a. For 2014 (no-par stock without a stated value):

Jan. 2	Cash	2,400,000	
	Common Stock, No-Par Value		2,400,000
	Issued 200,000 shares of no-par common stock at $12 per share.		

b. For 2014 (no-par stock with a stated value):

Jan. 2	Cash	2,400,000	
	Common Stock, $10 Stated Value		2,000,000
	Paid-In Capital in Excess of Stated Value, Common Stock		400,000
	Issued 200,000 shares of $10 stated value common stock at $12 per share.		

Summary

C1 Identify characteristics of corporations and their organization. Corporations are legal entities whose stockholders are not liable for its debts. Stock is easily transferred, and the life of a corporation does not end with the incapacity of a stockholder. A corporation acts through its agents, who are its officers and managers. Corporations are regulated and subject to income taxes. Authorized stock is the stock that a corporation's charter authorizes it to sell. Issued stock is the portion of authorized shares sold. Par value stock is a value per share assigned by the charter. No-par value stock is stock *not* assigned a value per share by the charter. Stated value stock is no-par stock to which the directors assign a value per share.

C2 Explain characteristics of, and distribute dividends between, common and preferred stock. Preferred stock has a priority (or senior status) relative to common stock in one or more areas, usually (1) dividends and (2) assets in case of liquidation. Preferred stock usually does not carry voting rights and can be convertible or callable. Convertibility permits the holder to convert preferred to common. Callability permits the issuer to buy back preferred stock under specified conditions. Preferred stockholders usually hold the right to dividend distributions before common stockholders. When preferred stock is cumulative and in arrears, the amount in arrears must be distributed to preferred before any dividends are distributed to common.

C3 Explain the items reported in retained earnings. Stockholders' equity is made up of (1) paid-in capital and (2) retained earnings. Paid-in capital consists of funds raised by stock issuances. Retained earnings consists of cumulative net income (losses) not distributed. Many companies face statutory and contractual restrictions on retained earnings. Corporations can voluntarily appropriate retained earnings to inform others about their disposition. Prior period adjustments are corrections of errors in prior financial statements.

A1 Compute earnings per share and describe its use. A company with a simple capital structure computes basic EPS by dividing net income less any preferred dividends by the weighted-average number of outstanding common shares. A company with a complex capital structure must usually report both basic and diluted EPS.

A2 Compute price-earnings ratio and describe its use in analysis. A common stock's price-earnings (PE) ratio is computed by dividing the stock's market value (price) per share by its EPS. A stock's PE is based on expectations that can prove to be better or worse than eventual performance.

A3 Compute dividend yield and explain its use in analysis. Dividend yield is the ratio of a stock's annual cash dividends per share to its market value (price) per share. Dividend yield can be compared with the yield of other companies to determine whether the stock is expected to be an income or growth stock.

A4 Compute book value and explain its use in analysis. Book value per common share is equity applicable to common shares divided by the number of outstanding common shares. Book value per preferred share is equity applicable to preferred shares divided by the number of outstanding preferred shares.

P1 Record the issuance of corporate stock. When stock is issued, its par or stated value is credited to the stock account and any excess is credited to a separate contributed capital account. If a stock has neither par nor stated value, the entire proceeds are credited to the stock account. Stockholders must contribute assets equal to minimum legal capital or be potentially liable for the deficiency.

P2 Record transactions involving cash dividends, stock dividends, and stock splits. Cash dividends involve three events. On the date of declaration, the directors bind the company to pay the dividend. A dividend declaration reduces retained earnings and creates a current liability. On the date of record, recipients of the dividend are identified. On the date of payment, cash is paid to stockholders and the current liability is removed. Neither a stock dividend nor a stock split alters the value of the company. However, the value of each share is less due to the distribution of additional shares. The distribution of additional shares is according to individual stockholders' ownership percentage. Small stock dividends ($\leq$25%) are recorded by capitalizing retained earnings equal to the market value of distributed shares. Large stock dividends ($>$25%) are recorded by capitalizing retained earnings equal to the par or stated value of distributed shares. Stock splits do not necessitate journal entries but do necessitate changes in the description of stock.

P3 Record purchases and sales of treasury stock and the retirement of stock. When a corporation purchases its own previously issued stock, it debits the cost of these shares to Treasury Stock. Treasury stock is subtracted from equity in the balance sheet. If treasury stock is reissued, any proceeds in excess of cost are credited to Paid-In Capital, Treasury Stock. If the proceeds are less than cost, they are debited to Paid-In Capital, Treasury Stock to the extent a credit balance exists. Any remaining amount is debited to Retained Earnings. When stock is retired, all accounts related to the stock are removed.

Guidance Answers to Decision Maker

Entrepreneur The 50% stock dividend provides you no direct income. A stock dividend often reveals management's optimistic expectations about the future and can improve a stock's marketability by making it affordable to more investors. Accordingly, a stock dividend usually reveals "good news" and because of this, it likely increases (slightly) the market value for your stock. The same conclusions apply to the 3-for-2 stock split.

Concert Organizer You have two basic options: (1) different classes of common stock or (2) common and preferred stock. Your objective is to issue to yourself stock that has all or a majority of the voting power. The other class of stock would carry limited or no voting rights. In this way, you maintain control and are able to raise the necessary funds.

Money Manager Since one company requires a payment of \$19 for each \$1 of earnings, and the other requires \$25, you would prefer the stock with the PE of 19; it is a better deal given identical prospects. You should make sure these companies' earnings computations are roughly the same, for example, no extraordinary items, unusual events, and so forth. Also, your PE estimates for these companies do matter. If you are willing to pay

$29 for each $1 of earnings for these companies, you obviously expect both to exceed current market expectations.

Investor Book value reflects recorded values. BMX's book value is $4 per common share. Stock price reflects the market's expectation of net asset value (both tangible and intangible items). BMX's market value is $7 per common share. Comparing these figures suggests BMX's market value of net assets is higher than its recorded values (by an amount of $7 versus $4 per share).

Key Terms

Appropriated retained earnings
Authorized stock
Basic earnings per share
Book value per common share
Book value per preferred share
Call price
Callable preferred stock
Capital stock
Changes in accounting estimates
Common stock
Complex capital structure
Convertible preferred stock
Corporation
Cumulative preferred stock
Date of declaration
Date of payment
Date of record
Diluted earnings per share
Dilutive securities
Discount on stock
Dividend in arrears
Dividend yield
Earnings per share (EPS)
Financial leverage
Large stock dividend
Liquidating cash dividend
Market value per share
Minimum legal capital
Noncumulative preferred stock
Nonparticipating preferred stock
No-par value stock
Organization expenses
Paid-in capital
Paid-in capital in excess of par value
Par value
Par value stock
Participating preferred stock
Preemptive right
Preferred stock
Premium on stock
Price-earnings (PE) ratio
Prior period adjustments
Proxy
Restricted retained earnings
Retained earnings
Retained earnings deficit
Reverse stock split
Simple capital structure
Small stock dividend
Stated value stock
Statement of stockholders' equity
Stock dividend
Stock options
Stock split
Stockholders' equity
Treasury stock

Multiple Choice Quiz Answers at end of chapter

1. A corporation issues 6,000 shares of $5 par value common stock for $8 cash per share. The entry to record this transaction includes:
   - a. A debit to Paid-In Capital in Excess of Par Value for $18,000.
   - b. A credit to Common Stock for $48,000.
   - c. A credit to Paid-In Capital in Excess of Par Value for $30,000.
   - d. A credit to Cash for $48,000.
   - e. A credit to Common Stock for $30,000.
2. A company reports net income of $75,000. Its weighted-average common shares outstanding is 19,000. It has no other stock outstanding. Its earnings per share is:
   - a. $4.69
   - b. $3.95
   - c. $3.75
   - d. $2.08
   - e. $4.41
3. A company has 5,000 shares of $100 par preferred stock and 50,000 shares of $10 par common stock outstanding. Its total stockholders' equity is $2,000,000. Its book value per common share is:
   - a. $100.00
   - b. $10.00
   - c. $40.00
   - d. $30.00
   - e. $36.36
4. A company paid cash dividends of $0.81 per share. Its earnings per share is $6.95 and its market price per share is $45.00. Its dividend yield is:
   - a. 1.8%
   - b. 11.7%
   - c. 15.4%
   - d. 55.6%
   - e. 8.6%
5. A company's shares have a market value of $85 per share. Its net income is $3,500,000, and its weighted-average common shares outstanding is 700,000. Its price-earnings ratio is:
   - a. 5.9
   - b. 425.0
   - c. 17.0
   - d. 10.4
   - e. 41.2

Icon denotes assignments that involve decision making.

Discussion Questions

1. What are organization expenses? Provide examples.
2. How are organization expenses reported?
3. Who is responsible for directing a corporation's affairs?
4. What is the difference between authorized shares and outstanding shares?
5. What is the preemptive right of common stockholders?
6. List the general rights of common stockholders.
7. What is the difference between the market value per share and the par value per share?
8. What is the difference between the par value and the call price of a share of preferred stock?
9. Why would an investor find convertible preferred stock attractive?
10. Identify and explain the importance of the three dates relevant to corporate dividends.
11. Why is the term *liquidating dividend* used to describe cash dividends debited against paid-in capital accounts?
12. How does declaring a stock dividend affect the corporation's assets, liabilities, and total equity? What are the effects of the eventual distribution of that stock?
13. What is the difference between a stock dividend and a stock split?
14. Courts have ruled that a stock dividend is not taxable income to stockholders. What justifies this decision?
15. How does the purchase of treasury stock affect the purchaser's assets and total equity?
16. Why do laws place limits on treasury stock purchases?
17. How are EPS results computed for a corporation with a simple capital structure?
18. What is a stock option?
19. How is book value per share computed for a corporation with no preferred stock? What is the main limitation of using book value per share to value a corporation?
20. Refer to **Apple**'s fiscal 2013 balance sheet in Appendix A. How many shares of common stock are authorized? How many shares of voting common stock are issued? **APPLE**
21. Refer to the 2013 balance sheet for **Google** in Appendix A. What is the par value per share of its preferred stock? Suggest a rationale for the amount of par value it assigned. **GOOGLE**
22. Refer to the financial statements for **Samsung** in Appendix A. How much were its cash payments for treasury stock purchases for the year ended December 31, 2013? **Samsung**

connect

QUICK STUDY

QS 11-1
Characteristics of corporations
C1

Of the following statements, which are true for the corporate form of organization?

____ 1. Ownership rights cannot be easily transferred.
____ 2. Owners have unlimited liability for corporate debts.
____ 3. Capital is more easily accumulated than with most other forms of organization.
____ 4. Corporate income that is distributed to shareholders is usually taxed twice.
____ 5. It is a separate legal entity.
____ 6. It has a limited life.
____ 7. Owners are not agents of the corporation.

QS 11-2
Issuance of common stock
P1

Prepare the journal entry to record Zende Company's issuance of 75,000 shares of $5 par value common stock assuming the shares sell for:

a. $5 cash per share.
b. $6 cash per share.

QS 11-3
Issuance of par and stated value common stock P1

Prepare the journal entry to record Jevonte Company's issuance of 36,000 shares of its common stock assuming the shares have a:

a. $2 par value and sell for $18 cash per share.
b. $2 stated value and sell for $18 cash per share.

QS 11-4
Issuance of no-par common stock
P1

Prepare the journal entry to record Autumn Company's issuance of 63,000 shares of no-par value common stock assuming the shares:

a. Sell for $29 cash per share.
b. Are exchanged for land valued at $1,827,000.

QS 11-5
Issuance of common stock P1

Prepare the issuer's journal entry for each of the following separate transactions.

a. On March 1, Atlantic Co. issues 42,500 shares of $4 par value common stock for $297,500 cash.
b. On April 1, OP Co. issues no-par value common stock for $70,000 cash.
c. On April 6, MPG issues 2,000 shares of $25 par value common stock for $45,000 of inventory, $145,000 of machinery, and acceptance of a $94,000 note payable.

QS 11-6
Accounting for cash dividends
P2

Prepare journal entries to record the following transactions for Emerson Corporation.

July 15 Declared a cash dividend payable to common stockholders of $165,000.
Aug. 15 Date of record is August 15 for the cash dividend declared on July 15.
Aug. 31 Paid the dividend declared on July 15.

QS 11-7
Accounting for small stock dividend
P2

The stockholders' equity section of Jun Company's balance sheet as of April 1 follows. On April 2, Jun declares and distributes a 10% stock dividend. The stock's per share market value on April 2 is $20 (prior to the dividend). Prepare the stockholders' equity section immediately after the stock dividend.

Common stock—$5 par value, 375,000 shares authorized, 200,000 shares issued and outstanding	$1,000,000
Paid-in capital in excess of par value, common stock	600,000
Retained earnings	833,000
Total stockholders' equity	$2,433,000

QS 11-8
Accounting for dividends
P2

Which of the following statements are true regarding dividends?

____ **1.** Cash and stock dividends reduce retained earnings.
____ **2.** Dividends payable is recorded at the time a cash dividend is declared.
____ **3.** The date of record refers to the date a cash dividend is paid to stockholders.
____ **4.** Stock dividends are a mechanism to keep the market price of stock affordable.

QS 11-9
Preferred stock issuance and dividends C2

1. Prepare the journal entry to record Tamasine Company's issuance of 5,000 shares of $100 par value, 7% cumulative preferred stock for $102 cash per share.
2. Assuming the facts in part 1, if Tamasine declares a year-end cash dividend, what is the amount of dividend paid to preferred shareholders? (Assume no dividends in arrears.)

QS 11-10
Dividend allocation between classes of shareholders
C2

Stockholders' equity of Ernst Company consists of 80,000 shares of $5 par value, 8% cumulative preferred stock and 250,000 shares of $1 par value common stock. Both classes of stock have been outstanding since the company's inception. Ernst did not declare any dividends in the prior year, but it now declares and pays a $110,000 cash dividend at the current year-end. Determine the amount distributed to each class of stockholders for this two-year-old company.

QS 11-11
Purchase and sale of treasury stock P3

On May 3, Zirbal Corporation purchased 4,000 shares of its own stock for $36,000 cash. On November 4, Zirbal reissued 850 shares of this treasury stock for $8,500. Prepare the May 3 and November 4 journal entries to record Zirbal's purchase and reissuance of treasury stock.

QS 11-12
Impacts of stock issuances, dividends, splits, and treasury transactions P2 P3

Listed below are various transactions that a company incurred during the current year. Indicate the impact on total stockholders' equity for each scenario. Specifically state whether stockholders' equity would "Increase," "Decrease," or have "No Effect" as a result of each transaction listed below. Consider each transaction independently.

____ **1.** A stock dividend equal to 30% of the previously outstanding shares is declared.
____ **2.** New shares of common stock are issued for cash.
____ **3.** Treasury shares of common stock are purchased (assume the cost method).
____ **4.** Cash dividends are paid to shareholders.

QS 11-13
Accounting for changes in estimates; error adjustments
C3

Answer the following questions related to a company's activities for the current year:

1. A review of the notes payable files discovers that three years ago the company reported the entire amount of a payment (principal and interest) on an installment note payable as interest expense. This mistake had a material effect on the amount of income in that year. How should the correction be reported in the current-year financial statements?
2. After using an expected useful life of seven years and no salvage value to depreciate its office equipment over the preceding three years, the company decided early this year that the equipment will last only two more years. How should the effects of this decision be reported in the current-year financial statements?

QS 11-14
Basic earnings per share
A1

Murray Company reports net income of $770,000 for the year. It has no preferred stock, and its weighted-average common shares outstanding is 280,000 shares. Compute its basic earnings per share.

QS 11-15
Basic earnings per share
A1

Epic Company earned net income of $900,000 this year. The number of common shares outstanding during the entire year was 400,000, and preferred shareholders received a $20,000 cash dividend. Compute Epic Company's basic earnings per share.

QS 11-16
Price-earnings ratio
A2

Compute Topp Company's price-earnings ratio if its common stock has a market value of $20.54 per share and its EPS is $3.95. Would an analyst likely consider this stock potentially overpriced, underpriced, or neither? Explain.

QS 11-17
Dividend yield A3

Foxburo Company expects to pay a $2.34 per share cash dividend this year on its common stock. The current market value of Foxburo stock is $32.50 per share. Compute the expected dividend yield on the Foxburo stock. Would you classify the Foxburo stock as a growth or an income stock? Explain.

QS 11-18
Book value per common share
A4

The stockholders' equity section of Montel Company's balance sheet follows. The preferred stock's call price is $40. Determine the book value per share of the common stock.

Preferred stock—5% cumulative, $10 par value, 20,000 shares authorized, issued, and outstanding	$ 200,000
Common stock—$5 par value, 200,000 shares authorized, 150,000 shares issued and outstanding	750,000
Retained earnings	900,000
Total stockholders' equity	$1,850,000

QS 11-19
International equity disclosures
P1

Air France-KLM reports the following equity information for its fiscal year ended March 31, 2014 (euros in millions). Prepare its journal entry, using its account titles, to record the issuance of capital stock assuming that its entire par value stock was issued on March 31, 2014, for cash.

March 31	2014
Issued capital	€ 300
Additional paid-in capital	2,971

connect

EXERCISES

Exercise 11-1
Characteristics of corporations
C1

Describe how each of the following characteristics of organizations applies to a corporation.

1. Owner authority and control	5. Duration of life
2. Ease of formation	6. Owner liability
3. Transferability of ownership	7. Legal status
4. Ability to raise large capital amounts	8. Tax status of income

Exercise 11-2
Accounting for par, stated, and no-par stock issuances P1

Rodriguez Corporation issues 19,000 shares of its common stock for $152,000 cash on February 20. Prepare journal entries to record this event under each of the following separate situations.

1. The stock has a $2 par value.
2. The stock has neither par nor stated value.
3. The stock has a $5 stated value.

Exercise 11-3
Recording stock issuances
P1

Prepare journal entries to record the following four separate issuances of stock.

1. A corporation issued 4,000 shares of $5 par value common stock for $35,000 cash.
2. A corporation issued 2,000 shares of no-par common stock to its promoters in exchange for their efforts, estimated to be worth $40,000. The stock has a $1 per share stated value.
3. A corporation issued 2,000 shares of no-par common stock to its promoters in exchange for their efforts, estimated to be worth $40,000. The stock has no stated value.
4. A corporation issued 1,000 shares of $50 par value preferred stock for $60,000 cash.

Exercise 11-4
Stock issuance for noncash assets P1

Sudoku Company issues 7,000 shares of $7 par value common stock in exchange for land and a building. The land is valued at $45,000 and the building at $85,000. Prepare the journal entry to record issuance of the stock in exchange for the land and building.

Exercise 11-5
Stock dividends and splits
P2

On June 30, 2015, Sharper Corporation's common stock is priced at $62 per share before any stock dividend or split, and the stockholders' equity section of its balance sheet appears as follows.

Common stock—$10 par value, 120,000 shares authorized, 50,000 shares issued and outstanding	$ 500,000
Paid-in capital in excess of par value, common stock	200,000
Retained earnings	660,000
Total stockholders' equity	$1,360,000

1. Assume that the company declares and immediately distributes a 50% stock dividend. This event is recorded by capitalizing retained earnings equal to the stock's par value. Answer these questions about stockholders' equity as it exists *after* issuing the new shares.
   a. What is the retained earnings balance?
   b. What is the amount of total stockholders' equity?
   c. How many shares are outstanding?
2. Assume that the company implements a 3-for-2 stock split instead of the stock dividend in part 1. Answer these questions about stockholders' equity as it exists *after* issuing the new shares.
   a. What is the retained earnings balance?
   b. What is the amount of total stockholders' equity?
   c. How many shares are outstanding?
3. Explain the difference, if any, to a stockholder from receiving new shares distributed under a large stock dividend versus a stock split.

Check (1*b*) $1,360,000

(2*a*) $660,000

Exercise 11-6
Stock dividends and per share book values
P2

The stockholders' equity of TVX Company at the beginning of the day on February 5 follows:

Common stock—$10 par value, 150,000 shares authorized, 60,000 shares issued and outstanding	$ 600,000
Paid-in capital in excess of par value, common stock	425,000
Retained earnings	550,000
Total stockholders' equity	$1,575,000

On February 5, the directors declare a 20% stock dividend distributable on February 28 to the February 15 stockholders of record. The stock's market value is $40 per share on February 5 before the stock dividend. The stock's market value is $33.40 per share on February 28.

1. Prepare entries to record both the dividend declaration and its distribution.
2. One stockholder owned 800 shares on February 5 before the dividend. Compute the book value per share and total book value of this stockholder's shares immediately before *and* after the stock dividend of February 5.
3. Compute the total market value of the investor's shares in part 2 as of February 5 and February 28.

Check (2) Book value per share: before, $26.250; after, $21.875

Exercise 11-7
Identifying characteristics of preferred stock
C2

Match each description 1 through 6 with the characteristic of preferred stock that it best describes by writing the letter of that characteristic in the blank next to each description.

A. Callable **B.** Convertible **C.** Cumulative
D. Noncumulative **E.** Nonparticipating **F.** Participating

_______ **1.** Holders of the stock are entitled to receive current and all past dividends before common stockholders receive any dividends.
_______ **2.** The issuing corporation can retire the stock by paying a prespecified price.
_______ **3.** Holders of the stock can receive dividends exceeding the stated rate under certain conditions.
_______ **4.** Holders of the stock are not entitled to receive dividends in excess of the stated rate.
_______ **5.** Holders of this stock can exchange it for shares of common stock.
_______ **6.** Holders of the stock lose any dividends that are not declared in the current year.

Exercise 11-8
Dividends on common and noncumulative preferred stock
C2

York's outstanding stock consists of 80,000 shares of *noncumulative* 7.5% preferred stock with a $5 par value and also 200,000 shares of common stock with a $1 par value. During its first four years of operation, the corporation declared and paid the following total cash dividends:

2015 total cash dividends	$ 20,000
2016 total cash dividends	28,000
2017 total cash dividends	200,000
2018 total cash dividends	350,000

Determine the amount of dividends paid each year to each of the two classes of stockholders: preferred and common. Also compute the total dividends paid to each class for the four years combined.

Check 4-year total paid to preferred, $108,000

Exercise 11-9
Dividends on common and cumulative preferred stock C2

Use the data in Exercise 11-8 to determine the amount of dividends paid each year to each of the two classes of stockholders assuming that the preferred stock is *cumulative*. Also determine the total dividends paid to each class for the four years combined.

Exercise 11-10
Recording and reporting treasury stock transactions
P3

On October 10, the stockholders' equity of Sherman Systems appears as follows:

Common stock—$10 par value, 72,000 shares authorized, issued, and outstanding	$ 720,000
Paid-in capital in excess of par value, common stock	216,000
Retained earnings	864,000
Total stockholders' equity	$1,800,000

1. Prepare journal entries to record the following transactions for Sherman Systems.
   a. Purchased 5,000 shares of its own common stock at $25 per share on October 11.
   b. Sold 1,000 treasury shares on November 1 for $31 cash per share.
   c. Sold all remaining treasury shares on November 25 for $20 cash per share.
2. Explain how the company's equity section changes after the October 11 treasury stock purchase, and prepare the revised equity section of its balance sheet at that date.

Check (1*c*) Dr. Retained Earnings, $14,000

Exercise 11-11
Preparing a statement of retained earnings
C3

The following information is available for Amos Company for the year ended December 31, 2015.

a. Balance of retained earnings, December 31, 2014, prior to discovery of error, $1,375,000.
b. Cash dividends declared and paid during 2015, $43,000.
c. It neglected to record 2013 depreciation expense of $55,500, which is net of $4,500 in tax benefits.
d. The company earned $126,000 in 2015 net income.

Prepare a 2015 statement of retained earnings for Amos Company.

Exercise 11-12
Earnings per share
A1

Ecker Company reports $2,700,000 of net income for 2015 and declares $388,020 of cash dividends on its preferred stock for 2015. At the end of 2015, the company had 678,000 weighted-average shares of common stock.

1. What amount of net income is available to common stockholders for 2015?
2. What is the company's basic EPS for 2015?

Check (2) $3.41

Exercise 11-13
Earnings per share
A1

Kelley Company reports $960,000 of net income for 2015 and declares $120,000 of cash dividends on its preferred stock for 2015. At the end of 2015, the company had 400,000 weighted-average shares of common stock.

1. What amount of net income is available to common stockholders for 2015?
2. What is the company's basic EPS for 2015? Round your answer to the nearest whole cent.

Check (2) $2.10

Exercise 11-14
Price-earnings ratio computation and interpretation
A2

Compute the price-earnings ratio for each of these four separate companies. Which stock might an analyst likely investigate as being potentially undervalued by the market? Explain.

	A	B	C
1–2	Company	Earnings per Share	Market Value per Share
3	1	$12.00	$176.40
4	2	10.00	96.00
5	3	7.50	93.75
6	4	50.00	250.00
7			

Exercise 11-15
Dividend yield computation and interpretation
A3

Compute the dividend yield for each of these four separate companies. Which company's stock would probably *not* be classified as an income stock? Explain.

	A	B	C
1–2	Company	Annual Cash Dividend per Share	Market Value per Share
3	1	$16.06	$220.00
4	2	13.86	132.00
5	3	3.96	72.00
6	4	0.96	80.00
7			

Exercise 11-16
Book value per share
A4

The equity section of Cyril Corporation's balance sheet shows the following:

Preferred stock—6% cumulative, $25 par value, $30 call price, 10,000 shares issued and outstanding	$ 250,000
Common stock—$10 par value, 80,000 shares issued and outstanding	800,000
Retained earnings	535,000
Total stockholders' equity	$1,585,000

[continued on next page]

Determine the book value per share of the preferred and common stock under two separate situations.

1. No preferred dividends are in arrears.
2. Three years of preferred dividends are in arrears.

Check (1) Book value of common, $16.06 per share

Exercise 11-17
Accounting for equity under IFRS
C3 P1

Unilever Group reports the following equity information for the years ended December 31, 2013 and 2012 (euros in millions).

December 31	2013	2012
Share capital	€ 484	€ 484
Share premium	138	140
Other reserves	(6,746)	(6,196)
Retained profit	20,468	20,964
Shareholders' equity	€14,344	€15,392

1. Match each of the three account titles—*share capital, share premium,* and *retained profit*—with the usual account title applied under U.S. GAAP from the following options:
   _____ **a.** Paid-in capital in excess of par value, common stock
   _____ **b.** Retained earnings
   _____ **c.** Common stock, par value
2. Prepare Unilever's journal entry, using its account titles, to record the issuance of capital stock assuming that its entire par value stock was issued on December 31, 2012, for cash.
3. What were Unilever's 2013 dividends assuming that only dividends and income impacted retained profit for 2013 and that its 2013 income totaled €5,263?

Exercise 11-18
Cash dividends, treasury stock, and statement of retained earnings
C3 P2 P3

Alexander Corporation reports the following components of stockholders' equity on December 31, 2015:

Common stock—$25 par value, 50,000 shares authorized, 30,000 shares issued and outstanding	$ 750,000
Paid-in capital in excess of par value, common stock	50,000
Retained earnings	340,000
Total stockholders' equity	$1,140,000

In year 2016, the following transactions affected its stockholders' equity accounts.

Jan. 2	Purchased 3,000 shares of its own stock at $25 cash per share.
Jan. 7	Directors declared a $1.50 per share cash dividend payable on Feb. 28 to the Feb. 9 stockholders of record.
Feb. 28	Paid the dividend declared on January 7.
July 9	Sold 1,200 of its treasury shares at $30 cash per share.
Aug. 27	Sold 1,500 of its treasury shares at $20 cash per share.
Sept. 9	Directors declared a $2 per share cash dividend payable on October 22 to the September 23 stockholders of record.
Oct. 22	Paid the dividend declared on September 9.
Dec. 31	Closed the $52,000 credit balance (from net income) in the Income Summary account to Retained Earnings.

Required

1. Prepare journal entries to record each of these transactions for 2016.
2. Prepare a statement of retained earnings for the year ended December 31, 2016.
3. Prepare the stockholders' equity section of the company's balance sheet as of December 31, 2016.

connect

PROBLEM SET A

Problem 11-1A
Stockholders' equity transactions and analysis
C2 P1

Kinkaid Co. is incorporated at the beginning of this year and engages in a number of transactions. The following journal entries impacted its stockholders' equity during its first year of operations.

a.	Cash	300,000	
	Common Stock, $25 Par Value		250,000
	Paid-In Capital in Excess of Par Value, Common Stock		50,000
b.	Organization Expenses	150,000	
	Common Stock, $25 Par Value		125,000
	Paid-In Capital in Excess of Par Value, Common Stock		25,000
c.	Cash	43,000	
	Accounts Receivable	15,000	
	Building	81,500	
	Notes Payable		59,500
	Common Stock, $25 Par Value		50,000
	Paid-In Capital in Excess of Par Value, Common Stock		30,000
d.	Cash	120,000	
	Common Stock, $25 Par Value		75,000
	Paid-In Capital in Excess of Par Value, Common Stock		45,000

Required

1. Explain the transaction(s) underlying each journal entry (*a*) through (*d*).
2. How many shares of common stock are outstanding at year-end?
3. What is the amount of minimum legal capital (based on par value) at year-end?
4. What is the total paid-in capital at year-end?
5. What is the book value per share of the common stock at year-end if total paid-in capital plus retained earnings equals $695,000?

Check (2) 20,000 shares
(3) $500,000
(4) $650,000

Problem 11-2A
Cash dividends, treasury stock, and statement of retained earnings
C3 P2 P3

Kohler Corporation reports the following components of stockholders' equity on December 31, 2015:

Common stock—$10 par value, 100,000 shares authorized, 40,000 shares issued and outstanding	$400,000
Paid-in capital in excess of par value, common stock	60,000
Retained earnings	270,000
Total stockholders' equity	$730,000

In year 2016, the following transactions affected its stockholders' equity accounts.

Jan. 1	Purchased 4,000 shares of its own stock at $20 cash per share.
Jan. 5	Directors declared a $2 per share cash dividend payable on Feb. 28 to the Feb. 5 stockholders of record.
Feb. 28	Paid the dividend declared on January 5.
July 6	Sold 1,500 of its treasury shares at $24 cash per share.
Aug. 22	Sold 2,500 of its treasury shares at $17 cash per share.
Sept. 5	Directors declared a $2 per share cash dividend payable on October 28 to the September 25 stockholders of record.
Oct. 28	Paid the dividend declared on September 5.
Dec. 31	Closed the $388,000 credit balance (from net income) in the Income Summary account to Retained Earnings.

Required

1. Prepare journal entries to record each of these transactions for 2016.
2. Prepare a statement of retained earnings for the year ended December 31, 2016.
3. Prepare the stockholders' equity section of the company's balance sheet as of December 31, 2016.

Check (2) Retained earnings, Dec. 31, 2016, $504,500

Problem 11-3A
Equity analysis—journal entries and account balances

P2

At September 30, the end of Beijing Company's third quarter, the following stockholders' equity accounts are reported.

Common stock, $12 par value	$360,000
Paid-in capital in excess of par value, common stock	90,000
Retained earnings	320,000

In the fourth quarter, the following entries related to its equity are recorded:

Oct. 2	Retained Earnings	60,000	
	Common Dividend Payable		60,000
Oct. 25	Common Dividend Payable	60,000	
	Cash		60,000
Oct. 31	Retained Earnings	75,000	
	Common Stock Dividend Distributable		36,000
	Paid-In Capital in Excess of Par Value, Common Stock		39,000
Nov. 5	Common Stock Dividend Distributable	36,000	
	Common Stock, $12 Par Value		36,000
Dec. 1	Memo — Change the title of the Common Stock account to reflect the new par value of $4.		
Dec. 31	Income Summary	210,000	
	Retained Earnings		210,000

Required

1. Explain the transaction(s) underlying each journal entry.
2. Complete the following table showing the equity account balances at each indicated date (include the balances from September 30).

	Oct. 2	Oct. 25	Oct. 31	Nov. 5	Dec. 1	Dec. 31
Common stock	$ ____	$ ____	$ ____	$ ____	$ ____	$ ____
Common stock dividend distributable	____	____	____	____	____	____
Paid-in capital in excess of par, common stock	____	____	____	____	____	____
Retained earnings	____	____	____	____	____	____
Total equity	$ ____	$ ____	$ ____	$ ____	$ ____	$ ____

Check Total equity: Oct. 2, $710,000; Dec. 31, $920,000

Problem 11-4A
Analysis of changes in stockholders' equity accounts

C3 P2 P3

The equity sections from Atticus Group's 2015 and 2016 year-end balance sheets follow.

Stockholders' Equity (December 31, 2015)	
Common stock—$4 par value, 100,000 shares authorized, 40,000 shares issued and outstanding	$160,000
Paid-in capital in excess of par value, common stock	120,000
Retained earnings	320,000
Total stockholders' equity	$600,000

Stockholders' Equity (December 31, 2016)	
Common stock—$4 par value, 100,000 shares authorized, 47,400 shares issued, 3,000 shares in treasury	$189,600
Paid-in capital in excess of par value, common stock	179,200
Retained earnings ($30,000 restricted by treasury stock)	400,000
	768,800
Less cost of treasury stock	(30,000)
Total stockholders' equity	$738,800

The following transactions and events affected its equity during year 2016.

Jan. 5	Declared a $0.50 per share cash dividend, date of record January 10.
Mar. 20	Purchased treasury stock for cash.
Apr. 5	Declared a $0.50 per share cash dividend, date of record April 10.
July 5	Declared a $0.50 per share cash dividend, date of record July 10.
July 31	Declared a 20% stock dividend when the stock's market value is $12 per share.
Aug. 14	Issued the stock dividend that was declared on July 31.
Oct. 5	Declared a $0.50 per share cash dividend, date of record October 10.

Required

1. How many common shares are outstanding on each cash dividend date?
2. What is the total dollar amount for each of the four cash dividends?
3. What is the amount of the capitalization of retained earnings for the stock dividend?
4. What is the per share cost of the treasury stock purchased?
5. How much net income did the company earn during year 2016?

Check (3) $88,800

(4) $10

(5) $248,000

Problem 11-5A
Computation of book values and dividend allocations

C2 A4

Raphael Corporation's common stock is currently selling on a stock exchange at $85 per share, and its current balance sheet shows the following stockholders' equity section:

Preferred stock—5% cumulative, $___ par value, 1,000 shares authorized, issued, and outstanding	$ 50,000
Common stock—$___ par value, 4,000 shares authorized, issued, and outstanding	80,000
Retained earnings	150,000
Total stockholders' equity	$280,000

Required (Round per share amounts to cents.)

1. What is the current market value (price) of this corporation's common stock?
2. What are the par values of the corporation's preferred stock and its common stock?
3. If no dividends are in arrears, what are the book values per share of the preferred stock and the common stock?
4. If two years' preferred dividends are in arrears, what are the book values per share of the preferred stock and the common stock?
5. If two years' preferred dividends are in arrears and the preferred stock is callable at $55 per share, what are the book values per share of the preferred stock and the common stock?
6. If two years' preferred dividends are in arrears and the board of directors declares cash dividends of $11,500, what total amount will be paid to the preferred and to the common shareholders? What is the amount of dividends per share for the common stock?

Check (4) Book value of common, $56.25

(5) Book value of common, $55.00

(6) Dividends per common share, $1.00

Analysis Component

7. What are some factors that can contribute to a difference between the book value of common stock and its market value (price)?

PROBLEM SET B

Problem 11-1B
Stockholders' equity transactions and analysis
C2 P1

Weiss Company is incorporated at the beginning of this year and engages in a number of transactions. The following journal entries impacted its stockholders' equity during its first year of operations.

a.	Cash	120,000	
	Common Stock, $1 Par Value		3,000
	Paid-In Capital in Excess of Par Value, Common Stock		117,000
b.	Organization Expenses	40,000	
	Common Stock, $1 Par Value		1,000
	Paid-In Capital in Excess of Par Value, Common Stock		39,000
c.	Cash	13,300	
	Accounts Receivable	8,000	
	Building	37,000	
	Notes Payable		18,300
	Common Stock, $1 Par Value		800
	Paid-In Capital in Excess of Par Value, Common Stock		39,200
d.	Cash	60,000	
	Common Stock, $1 Par Value		1,200
	Paid-In Capital in Excess of Par Value, Common Stock		58,800

Required

1. Explain the transaction(s) underlying each journal entry (*a*) through (*d*).
2. How many shares of common stock are outstanding at year-end?
3. What is the amount of minimum legal capital (based on par value) at year-end?
4. What is the total paid-in capital at year-end?
5. What is the book value per share of the common stock at year-end if total paid-in capital plus retained earnings equals $283,000?

Check (2) 6,000 shares
(3) $6,000
(4) $260,000

Problem 11-2B
Cash dividends, treasury stock, and statement of retained earnings
C3 P2 P3

Balthus Corp. reports the following components of stockholders' equity on December 31, 2015:

Common stock—$1 par value, 320,000 shares authorized, 200,000 shares issued and outstanding	$ 200,000
Paid-in capital in excess of par value, common stock	1,400,000
Retained earnings	2,160,000
Total stockholders' equity	$3,760,000

It completed the following transactions related to stockholders' equity in year 2016:

Jan. 10 Purchased 40,000 shares of its own stock at $12 cash per share.
Mar. 2 Directors declared a $1.50 per share cash dividend payable on March 31 to the March 15 stockholders of record.
Mar. 31 Paid the dividend declared on March 2.
Nov. 11 Sold 24,000 of its treasury shares at $13 cash per share.
Nov. 25 Sold 16,000 of its treasury shares at $9.50 cash per share.
Dec. 1 Directors declared a $2.50 per share cash dividend payable on January 2 to the December 10 stockholders of record.
Dec. 31 Closed the $1,072,000 credit balance (from net income) in the Income Summary account to Retained Earnings.

Required

1. Prepare journal entries to record each of these transactions for 2016.
2. Prepare a statement of retained earnings for the year ended December 31, 2016.
3. Prepare the stockholders' equity section of the company's balance sheet as of December 31, 2016.

Check (2) Retained earnings, Dec. 31, 2016, $2,476,000

Problem 11-3B
Equity analysis—journal entries and account balances
P2

At December 31, the end of Chilton Communication's third quarter, the following stockholders' equity accounts are reported:

Common stock, $10 par value	$ 960,000
Paid-in capital in excess of par value, common stock	384,000
Retained earnings	1,600,000

In the fourth quarter, the following entries related to its equity are recorded:

Jan. 17	Retained Earnings	96,000	
	Common Dividend Payable		96,000
Feb. 5	Common Dividend Payable	96,000	
	Cash		96,000
Feb. 28	Retained Earnings	252,000	
	Common Stock Dividend Distributable		120,000
	Paid-In Capital in Excess of Par Value, Common Stock		132,000
Mar. 14	Common Stock Dividend Distributable	120,000	
	Common Stock, $10 Par Value		120,000
Mar. 25	Memo—Change the title of the Common Stock account to reflect the new par value of $5.		
Mar. 31	Income Summary	720,000	
	Retained Earnings		720,000

Required

1. Explain the transaction(s) underlying each journal entry.
2. Complete the following table showing the equity account balances at each indicated date (include the balances from December 31).

	Jan. 17	Feb. 5	Feb. 28	Mar. 14	Mar. 25	Mar. 31
Common stock	$____	$____	$____	$____	$____	$____
Common stock dividend distributable	____	____	____	____	____	____
Paid-in capital in excess of par, common stock	____	____	____	____	____	____
Retained earnings	____	____	____	____	____	____
Total equity	$____	$____	$____	$____	$____	$____

Check Total equity: Jan. 17, $2,848,000; Mar. 31, $3,568,000

Problem 11-4B
Analysis of changes in stockholders' equity accounts
C3 P2 P3

The equity sections from Hovo Corporation's 2015 and 2016 balance sheets follow.

Stockholders' Equity (December 31, 2015)	
Common stock—$20 par value, 30,000 shares authorized, 17,000 shares issued and outstanding	$340,000
Paid-in capital in excess of par value, common stock	60,000
Retained earnings	270,000
Total stockholders' equity	$670,000

Stockholders' Equity (December 31, 2016)	
Common stock—$20 par value, 30,000 shares authorized, 19,000 shares issued, 1,000 shares in treasury	$380,000
Paid-in capital in excess of par value, common stock	104,000
Retained earnings ($40,000 restricted by treasury stock)	295,200
	779,200
Less cost of treasury stock	(40,000)
Total stockholders' equity	$739,200

The following transactions and events affected its equity during year 2016.

Feb. 15 Declared a $0.40 per share cash dividend, date of record five days later.
Mar. 2 Purchased treasury stock for cash.
May 15 Declared a $0.40 per share cash dividend, date of record five days later.
Aug. 15 Declared a $0.40 per share cash dividend, date of record five days later.
Oct. 4 Declared a 12.5% stock dividend when the stock's market value is $42 per share.
Oct. 20 Issued the stock dividend that was declared on October 4.
Nov. 15 Declared a $0.40 per share cash dividend, date of record five days later.

Required

1. How many common shares are outstanding on each cash dividend date?
2. What is the total dollar amount for each of the four cash dividends?
3. What is the amount of the capitalization of retained earnings for the stock dividend?
4. What is the per share cost of the treasury stock purchased?
5. How much net income did the company earn during year 2016?

Check (3) $84,000

(4) $40

(5) $136,000

Problem 11-5B
Computation of book values and dividend allocations
C2 A4

Soltech Company's common stock is currently selling on a stock exchange at $90 per share, and its current balance sheet shows the following stockholders' equity section.

Preferred stock—8% cumulative, $___ par value, 1,500 shares authorized, issued, and outstanding	$ 375,000
Common stock—$___ par value, 18,000 shares authorized, issued, and outstanding	900,000
Retained earnings	1,125,000
Total stockholders' equity	$2,400,000

Required (Round per share amounts to cents.)

1. What is the current market value (price) of this corporation's common stock?
2. What are the par values of the corporation's preferred stock and its common stock?
3. If no dividends are in arrears, what are the book values per share of the preferred stock and the common stock? (Round per share values to the nearest cent.)
4. If two years' preferred dividends are in arrears, what are the book values per share of the preferred stock and the common stock? (Round per share values to the nearest cent.)
5. If two years' preferred dividends are in arrears and the preferred stock is callable at $280 per share, what are the book values per share of the preferred stock and the common stock? (Round per share values to the nearest cent.)
6. If two years' preferred dividends are in arrears and the board of directors declares cash dividends of $100,000, what total amount will be paid to the preferred and to the common shareholders? What is the amount of dividends per share for the common stock? (Round per share values to the nearest cent.)

Check (4) Book value of common, $109.17

(5) Book value of common, $106.67

(6) Dividends per common share, $0.56

Analysis Component

7. Discuss why the book value of common stock is not always a good estimate of its market value.

SERIAL PROBLEM

Business Solutions

P1 C1 C2

(This serial problem began in Chapter 1 and continues through most of the book. If previous chapter segments were not completed, the serial problem can begin at this point. It is helpful, but not necessary, to use the Working Papers that accompany the book.)

SP 11 Santana Rey created Business Solutions on October 1, 2015. The company has been successful, and Santana plans to expand her business. She believes that an additional $86,000 is needed and is investigating three funding sources.

a. Santana's sister Cicely is willing to invest $86,000 in the business as a common shareholder. Since Santana currently has about $129,000 invested in the business, Cicely's investment will mean that Santana will maintain about 60% ownership, and Cicely will have 40% ownership of Business Solutions.

b. Santana's uncle Marcello is willing to invest $86,000 in the business as a preferred shareholder. Marcello would purchase 860 shares of $100 par value, 7% preferred stock.

c. Santana's banker is willing to lend her $86,000 on a 7%, 10-year note payable. She would make monthly payments of $1,000 per month for 10 years.

Required

1. Prepare the journal entry to reflect the initial $86,000 investment under each of the options (*a*), (*b*), and (*c*).
2. Evaluate the three proposals for expansion, providing the pros and cons of each option.
3. Which option do you recommend Santana adopt? Explain.

GL GENERAL LEDGER PROBLEM

Available in Connect

connect ACCOUNTING

The following General Ledger assignments highlight the impact, or lack thereof, on financial statements from equity-based transactions.

GL 11-1 General Ledger assignment 11-1 is adapted from Problem 11-2A, including beginning equity balances. Prepare journal entries related to treasury stock, cash dividends, and net income. Then, prepare the statement of retained earnings and the stockholders' equity section of the balance sheet.

GL 11-2 General Ledger assignment 11-2 is adapted from Problem 11-4A, including beginning and ending equity balances. Prepare journal entries related to cash dividends and stock dividends. Calculate the number of shares outstanding, the amount of net income, and the amount of retained earnings to be capitalized as a result of the stock dividend, if any.

Beyond the Numbers

REPORTING IN ACTION

C2 A1 A4

APPLE

BTN 11-1 Refer to **Apple**'s financial statements in Appendix A to answer the following.

1. How many shares of common stock are issued and outstanding at September 28, 2013, and September 29, 2012? How do these numbers compare with the basic weighted-average common shares outstanding at September 28, 2013, and September 29, 2012?
2. What is the book value of its entire common stock at September 28, 2013?
3. What is the total amount of cash dividends paid to common stockholders for the years ended September 28, 2013, and September 29, 2012?
4. Identify and compare basic EPS amounts across fiscal years 2013, 2012, and 2011. Identify and comment on any notable changes.
5. How many shares does Apple hold in treasury stock, if any, as of September 28, 2013, and September 29, 2012?

Fast Forward

6. Access Apple's financial statements for fiscal years ending after September 28, 2013, from its website (**Apple.com**) or the SEC's EDGAR database (**www.SEC.gov**). Has the number of common shares outstanding increased since that date? Has the company increased the total amount of cash dividends paid compared to the total amount for fiscal year 2013?

BTN 11-2 Key comparative figures for **Apple** and **Google** follow.

COMPARATIVE ANALYSIS
A1 A2 A3 A4

APPLE
GOOGLE

Key Figures	Apple	Google
Net income (in millions)	$ 37,037	$ 12,920
Cash dividends declared per common share	$ 11.40	$ —
Common shares outstanding (in millions)	899.213	279.325
Weighted-average common shares outstanding (in millions)	925.331	273.518
Market value (price) per share	$ 477.25	$ 560.92
Equity applicable to common shares (in millions)	$123,549	$ 87,309

Required

1. Compute the book value per common share for each company using these data.
2. Compute the basic EPS for each company using these data.
3. Compute the dividend yield for each company using these data. Does the dividend yield of either of the companies characterize it as an income or growth stock? Explain.
4. Compute, compare, and interpret the price-earnings ratio for each company using these data.

BTN 11-3 Harriet Moore is an accountant for New World Pharmaceuticals. Her duties include tracking research and development spending in the new product development division. Over the course of the past six months, Harriet has noticed that a great deal of funds have been spent on a particular project for a new drug. She hears "through the grapevine" that the company is about to patent the drug and expects it to be a major advance in antibiotics. Harriet believes that this new drug will greatly improve company performance and will cause the company's stock to increase in value. Harriet decides to purchase shares of New World in order to benefit from this expected increase.

ETHICS CHALLENGE
C3

Required

What are Harriet's ethical responsibilities, if any, with respect to the information she has learned through her duties as an accountant for New World Pharmaceuticals? What are the implications of her planned purchase of New World shares?

BTN 11-4 Teams are to select an industry, and each team member is to select a different company in that industry. Each team member then is to acquire the selected company's financial statements (or Form 10-K) from the SEC site (**www.SEC.gov**). Use these data to identify basic EPS. Use the financial press (or **finance.yahoo.com**) to determine the market price of this stock, and then compute the pricc-earnings ratio. Communicate with teammates via a meeting, e-mail, or telephone to discuss the meaning of this ratio, how companies compare, and the industry norm. The team must prepare a single memorandum reporting the ratio for each company and identifying the team conclusions or consensus of opinion. The memorandum is to be duplicated and distributed to the instructor and teammates.

COMMUNICATING IN PRACTICE
A1 A2

Hint: Make a transparency of each team's memo for a class discussion.

BTN 11-5 Access the February 24, 2014, filing of the 2013 calendar-year 10-K report of **McDonald's**, (ticker MCD) from **www.SEC.gov**.

TAKING IT TO THE NET
C1 C3

Required

1. Review McDonald's balance sheet and identify how many classes of stock it has issued.
2. What are the par values, number of authorized shares, and issued shares of the classes of stock you identified in part 1?
3. Review its statement of cash flows and identify what total amount of cash it paid in 2013 to purchase treasury stock.
4. What amount did McDonald's pay out in common stock cash dividends for 2013?

TEAMWORK IN ACTION

P3

Hint: Instructor should be sure each team accurately completes part 1 before proceeding.

BTN 11-6 This activity requires teamwork to reinforce understanding of accounting for treasury stock.

1. Write a brief team statement (*a*) generalizing what happens to a corporation's financial position when it engages in a stock "buyback" and (*b*) identifying reasons why a corporation would engage in this activity.
2. Assume that an entity acquires 100 shares of its $100 par value common stock at a cost of $134 cash per share. Discuss the entry to record this acquisition. Next, assign *each* team member to prepare *one* of the following entries (assume each entry applies to all shares):
   - **a.** Reissue treasury shares at cost.
   - **b.** Reissue treasury shares at $150 per share.
   - **c.** Reissue treasury shares at $120 per share; assume the paid-in capital account from treasury shares has a $1,500 balance.
   - **d.** Reissue treasury shares at $120 per share; assume the paid-in capital account from treasury shares has a $1,000 balance.
   - **e.** Reissue treasury shares at $120 per share; assume the paid-in capital account from treasury shares has a zero balance.
3. In sequence, each member is to present his/her entry to the team and explain the *similarities* and *differences* between that entry and the previous entry.

ENTREPRENEURIAL DECISION

C2 P2

BTN 11-7 Assume that **Alibaba Group** decides to launch a new website to market discount bookkeeping services to consumers. This chain, named Aladin, requires $500,000 of start-up capital. The founder contributes $375,000 of personal assets in return for 15,000 shares of common stock, but he must raise another $125,000 in cash. There are two alternative plans for raising the additional cash. *Plan A* is to sell 3,750 shares of common stock to one or more investors for $125,000 cash. *Plan B* is to sell 1,250 shares of cumulative preferred stock to one or more investors for $125,000 cash (this preferred stock would have a $100 par value, an annual 8% dividend rate, and be issued at par).

1. If the new business is expected to earn $72,000 of after-tax net income in the first year, what rate of return on beginning equity will the founder earn under each alternative plan? Which plan will provide the higher expected return?
2. If the new business is expected to earn $16,800 of after-tax net income in the first year, what rate of return on beginning equity will the founder earn under each alternative plan? Which plan will provide the higher expected return?
3. Analyze and interpret the differences between the results for parts 1 and 2.

HITTING THE ROAD

A1 A2 A3

BTN 11-8 Review 30 to 60 minutes of financial news programming on television. Take notes on companies that are catching analysts' attention. You might hear reference to over- and undervaluation of firms and to reports about PE ratios, dividend yields, and earnings per share. Be prepared to give a brief description to the class of your observations.

GLOBAL DECISION

A1 C3

Samsung

BTN 11-9 Financial information for **Samsung** (www.Samsung.com) follows (drawn from its financial statements and footnotes):

Net income less dividends available to preferred shares (in millions)	₩ 25,893,396
Cash dividends declared for common stock (in millions)	₩ 1,806,629
Cash dividends declared per common share	₩ 14,300
Number of common shares outstanding (in millions)*	130.915
Weighted average common shares outstanding (in millions)	130.880
Equity applicable to common shares (in millions)†	₩149,896,543

*Computed as 147.299 mil. issued shares less 16.384 mil. treasury shares.

†Computed as ₩150,016,010 total equity less ₩119,467 preferred stock.

Required

1. Compute book value per share for Samsung.
2. Compute earnings per share (EPS) for Samsung.
3. Compare Samsung's dividends per share with its EPS. Is Samsung paying out a large or small amount of its income as dividends? Explain.

ANSWERS TO MULTIPLE CHOICE QUIZ

1. e; Entry to record this stock issuance is:

Cash (6,000 × $8)	48,000	
Common Stock (6,000 × $5)		30,000
Paid-In Capital in Excess of Par Value, Common Stock		18,000

2. b; $75,000/19,000 shares = $3.95 per share
3. d; Preferred stock = 5,000 × $100 = $500,000
   Book value per share = ($2,000,000 − $500,000)/50,000 shares = $30 per common share
4. a; $0.81/$45.00 = 1.8%
5. c; Earnings per share = $3,500,000/700,000 shares = $5 per share
   PE ratio = $85/$5 = 17.0

chapter 12

Reporting Cash Flows

Chapter Preview

BASICS OF CASH FLOW REPORTING	CASH FLOWS FROM OPERATING	CASH FLOWS FROM INVESTING	CASH FLOWS FROM FINANCING
C1 Purpose, measurement, and classification Noncash activities **P1** Format and preparation	**P2** Indirect and direct methods of reporting Illustration of indirect method Summary of indirect method adjustments	**P3** Three-stage process of analysis Analyzing noncurrent assets Analyzing other assets	**P3** Three-stage process of analysis Analyzing noncurrent liabilities Analyzing equity Overall summary using T-accounts **A1** Analyzing cash

Learning Objectives

CONCEPTUAL

C1 Distinguish between operating, investing, and financing activities, and describe how noncash investing and financing activities are disclosed.

ANALYTICAL

A1 Analyze the statement of cash flows and apply the cash flow on total assets ratio.

PROCEDURAL

P1 Prepare a statement of cash flows.

P2 Compute cash flows from operating activities using the indirect method.

P3 Determine cash flows from both investing and financing activities.

P4 *Appendix 12A*—Illustrate use of a spreadsheet to prepare a statement of cash flows.

P5 *Appendix 12B*—Compute cash flows from operating activities using the direct method.

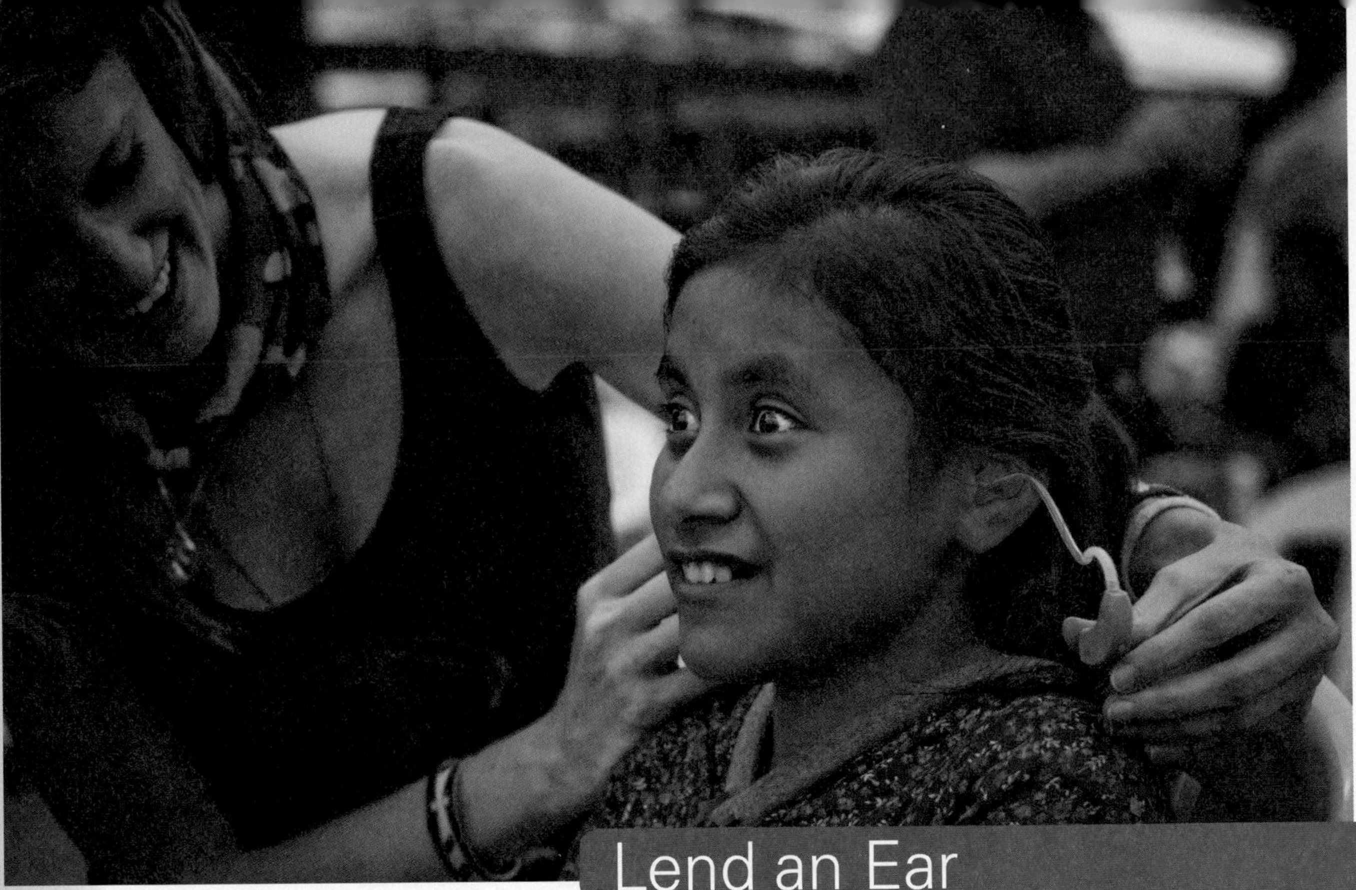

Courtesy of Bridget Hilton

Lend an Ear

LOS ANGELES—"To have never heard music, laughter, nature—that's unimaginable for me," explains Bridget Hilton. "I'm inspired to enable people to have that joy in their lives." That inspiration led Bridget, along with Joe Huff, to launch **LSTN (LSTNheadphones.com)**, a social enterprise "making headphones that sounded good, looked good, and were doing good!" Bridget explains that "we set forth on a mission that would set us apart—we'd produce great headphones made from reclaimed wood and, for every pair sold, LSTN would help restore hearing to a person in need."

"Consider your social values"
—Bridget Hilton

To make her mission a reality, Bridget had to learn to run a manufacturing business with little cash. First, she set up what she says are "the two most important things—a manufacturer and a charity partner." However, cash shortage was still a problem. In response, Bridget "launched the site as a pre-order—in this day and age, you can launch a company with next to no money."

Bridget admits that as business grew and revenue flowed in, it was hard to find the cash from operations to expand. Many entrepreneurs turn to external cash financing in such cases. However, Bridget tightened her belt and focused on a lean operation. "Keep the spending down as long as possible. You don't need an office right away, or T-shirts with your logo, big events, a super fancy website, a bunch of employees, etc.," insists Bridget. "Work out of your house and coffee shops, use your network as much as possible, and put your head down and work hard. If you have a physical product, buy or make as little as possible (a minimum viable product) and test it to see if people even want it before you dump all your money into inventory."

Bridget monitors and controls cash flows for each of her operating, investing, and financing activities. "Being frugal will help you not only financially, but it will also force you to be creative," insists Bridget. Yet it is the mission that inspires her. "I love my company and what I do, so working is exciting." Even her analysis of LSTN's statement of cash flows, and its individual inflows and outflows, is embraced as it helps her stay on track.

To date, Bridget has successfully controlled cash outflows while growing cash inflows. She relies on cash flow information to make important business decisions, but never loses touch with her mission. "I recently returned from a trip to Peru," says Bridget. "When I saw the faces that lit up when children connected and communicated with their families, I lost it. It was truly life changing . . . to even change one person's life through our business proved that our plan was working."

Sources: *LSTN's website,* January 2015; *Trend Hunter,* August 2012; *Upstart,* May 2014; *SocialEarth,* August 2012; *Women 2.0,* January 2014

BASICS OF CASH FLOW REPORTING

This section describes the basics of cash flow reporting, including its purpose, measurement, classification, format, and preparation.

Purpose of the Statement of Cash Flows

The purpose of the **statement of cash flows** is to report cash receipts (inflows) and cash payments (outflows) during a period. This includes separately identifying the cash flows related to operating, investing, and financing activities. It is the detailed disclosure of individual sources and uses of cash that makes this statement useful to users. Information in this statement helps users answer questions such as these:

Point: Internal users rely on the statement of cash flows to make investing and financing decisions. External users rely on this statement to assess the amount and timing of a company's cash flows.

- What explains the change in the cash balance?
- Where does a company spend its cash?
- How does a company receive its cash?
- Why do income and cash flows differ?
- How much is paid in dividends?
- Is there a cash shortage?

Importance of Cash Flows

Information about cash flows can influence decision makers in important ways. For instance, we look more favorably at a company that is financing its expenditures with cash from operations than one that does it by selling its assets. Information about cash flows helps users decide whether a company has enough cash to pay its existing debts as they mature. It is also relied upon to evaluate a company's ability to meet unexpected obligations and pursue unexpected opportunities. External information users, especially, want to assess a company's ability to take advantage of new business opportunities. Internal users such as managers use cash flow information to plan day-to-day operating activities and make long-term investment decisions.

Bloomberg via Getty Images

Macy's striking turnaround is an example of how analysis and management of cash flows can lead to improved financial stability. Several years ago Macy's obtained temporary protection from bankruptcy. It desperately needed to improve its cash flows, and did so by engaging in aggressive cost-cutting measures. As a result, Macy's annual cash flow rose to $210 million, up from a negative cash flow of $38.9 million in the prior year. Macy's eventually met its financial obligations and then successfully merged with **Federated Department Stores**.

The case of **W. T. Grant Co.** is a classic example of the importance of cash flow information in predicting a company's future performance and financial strength. Grant reported net income of more than $40 million per year for three consecutive years. At that same time, it was experiencing an alarming decrease in cash provided by operations. For instance, net cash outflow was more than $90 million by the end of that three-year period. Grant soon went bankrupt. Users who relied solely on Grant's income numbers were unpleasantly surprised. This reminds us that cash flows as well as income statement and balance sheet information are crucial in business decisions.

Decision Insight

Do You Know Your Cash Flows? "A lender must have a complete understanding of a borrower's cash flows to assess both the borrowing needs and repayment sources. This requires information about the major types of cash inflows and outflows. I have seen many companies, whose financial statements indicate good profitability, experience severe financial problems because the owners or managers lacked a good understanding of cash flows."—Mary E. Garza, **Bank of America** ■

Cash Equivalents

Measurement of Cash Flows

Cash flows are defined to include both *cash* and *cash equivalents*. The statement of cash flows explains the difference between the beginning and ending balances of cash and cash equivalents. We continue to use the phrases *cash flows* and the *statement of cash flows,* but remember that both phrases refer to cash *and* cash equivalents.

Recall that a cash equivalent must satisfy two criteria: (1) be readily convertible to a known amount of cash and (2) be sufficiently close to its maturity so its market value is unaffected by interest rate changes. In most cases, a debt security must be within three months of its maturity to satisfy these criteria. Companies must disclose and follow a clear policy for determining cash and cash equivalents and apply it consistently from period to period. **American Express**, for example, defines its cash equivalents as "time deposits and other highly liquid investments with original maturities of 90 days or less."

Classification of Cash Flows

C1 Distinguish between operating, investing, and financing activities, and describe how noncash investing and financing activities are disclosed.

Since cash and cash equivalents are combined, the statement of cash flows does not report transactions between cash and cash equivalents, such as cash paid to purchase cash equivalents and cash received from selling cash equivalents. However, all other cash receipts and cash payments are classified and reported on the statement in one of three categories—operating, investing, or financing activities. Individual cash receipts and payments for each of these three categories are labeled to identify their originating transactions or events. A net cash inflow (source) occurs when the receipts in a category exceed the payments. A net cash outflow (use) occurs when the payments in a category exceed the receipts.

Operating Activities **Operating activities** include those transactions and events that determine net income. Examples are the production and purchase of inventory, the sale of goods and services to customers, and the expenditures to operate the business. Not all items in income, such as unusual gains and losses, are operating activities (we discuss these exceptions later). Exhibit 12.1 lists the more common cash inflows and outflows from operating activities.

EXHIBIT 12.1

Cash Flows from Operating Activities

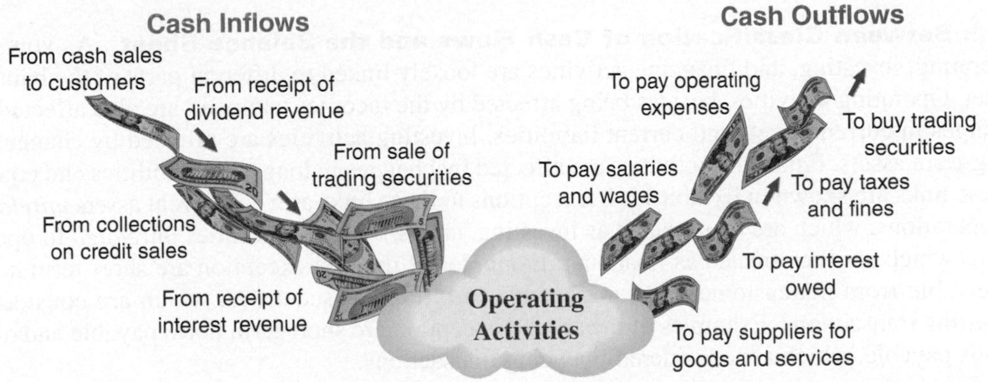

Investing Activities **Investing activities** generally include those transactions and events that affect long-term assets—namely, the purchase and sale of long-term assets. They also include (1) the purchase and sale of short-term investments in the securities of other entities, *except* trading securities, and (2) lending and collecting money for notes receivable. Exhibit 12.2 lists examples of cash flows from investing activities. Cash from collecting the principal amounts of notes that result from a loan to another party are classified as investing. However, the FASB requires that the collection of interest on notes be reported as an operating activity; also, if a note results from sales to customers, it is classified as operating.

Point: The FASB requires that *cash dividends received* and *cash interest received* be reported as operating activities.

EXHIBIT 12.2

Cash Flows from Investing Activities

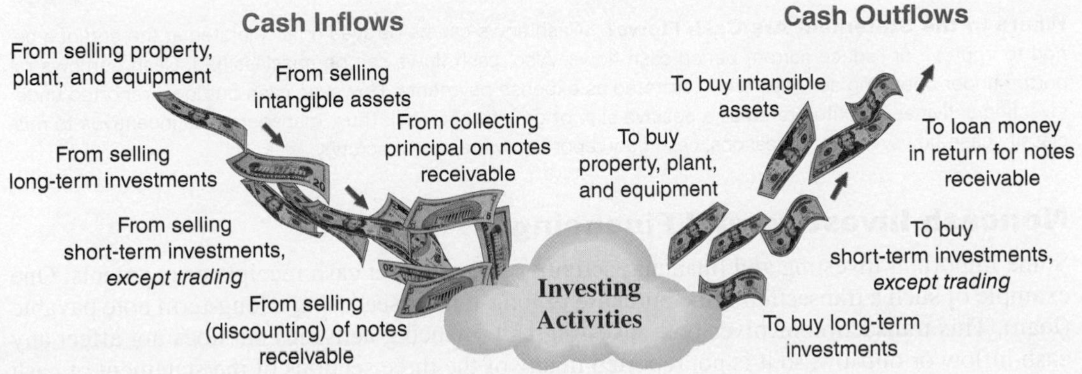

Financing Activities **Financing activities** include those transactions and events that affect long-term liabilities and equity. Examples are (1) obtaining cash from issuing debt and repaying the amounts borrowed and (2) receiving cash from or distributing cash to owners. These activities involve transactions with a company's owners and creditors. They also involve borrowing and repaying principal amounts relating to both short- and long-term debt. GAAP requires that payments of interest expense be classified as operating activities. Exhibit 12.3 lists examples of cash flows from financing activities.

Point: Interest payments on a loan are classified as operating activities, but payments of loan principal are financing activities.

EXHIBIT 12.3
Cash Flows from Financing Activities

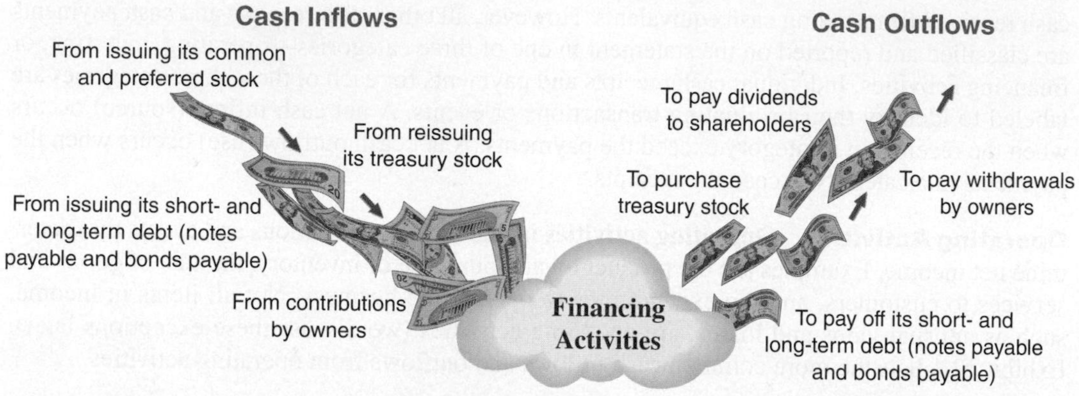

Link Between Classification of Cash Flows and the Balance Sheet As you see, operating, investing, and financing activities are loosely linked to different parts of the balance sheet. Operating activities, besides being affected by the income statement, are also affected by changes in current assets and current liabilities. Investing activities are affected by changes in long-term assets. Financing activities are affected by changes in long-term liabilities and equity. These links are shown in Exhibit 12.4. Exceptions to these links are: (1) current assets *unrelated* to operations, which are then treated as investing, and (2) current liabilities *unrelated* to operations, which are then treated as financing. Examples of the first exception are short-term notes receivable from noncustomers and marketable (not trading) securities, which are considered investing transactions. Examples of the second exception are short-term notes payable and dividends payable, which are considered financing transactions.

EXHIBIT 12.4
Linkage of Cash Flow Classifications to the Balance Sheet

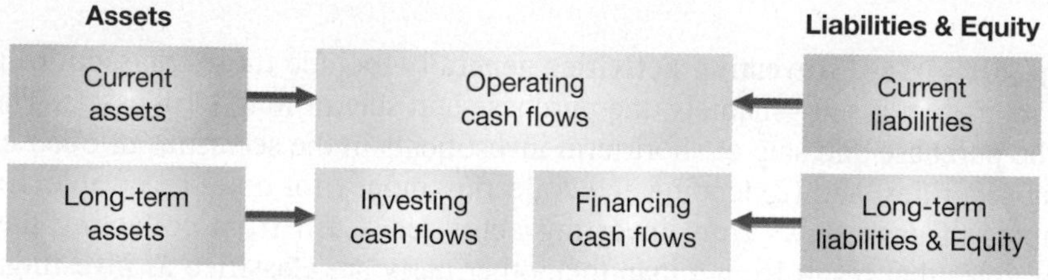

Decision Insight

Where in the Statement Are Cash Flows? Cash flows can be delayed or accelerated at the end of a period to improve or reduce current period cash flows. Also, cash flows can be misclassified. Cash outflows reported under operating activities are interpreted as expense payments. However, cash outflows reported under investing activities are interpreted as a positive sign of growth potential. Thus, managers face incentives to misclassify cash flows. For these reasons, cash flow reporting warrants our scrutiny. ■

Noncash Investing and Financing

Some important investing and financing activities do not affect cash receipts or payments. One example of such a transaction is the purchase of long-term assets using a long-term note payable (loan). This transaction involves both investing and financing activities but does not affect any cash inflow or outflow, so it is not reported in any of the three sections of the statement of cash flows. Such transactions are reported at the bottom of the statement of cash flows or in a note to the statement because of their importance and the *full-disclosure principle.* Exhibit 12.5 lists transactions commonly disclosed as noncash investing and financing activities.

EXHIBIT 12.5

Examples of Noncash Investing and Financing Activities

- Retirement of debt by issuing equity stock.
- Conversion of preferred stock to common stock.
- Lease of assets in a capital lease transaction.
- Purchase of long-term assets by issuing a note or bond.
- Exchange of noncash assets for other noncash assets.
- Purchase of noncash assets by issuing equity or debt.

Format of the Statement of Cash Flows

P1 Prepare a statement of cash flows.

A statement of cash flows must report information about a company's cash receipts and cash payments during the period. Exhibit 12.6 shows the usual format. A company must report cash flows from three activities: operating, investing, and financing. The statement then shows the net increase or decrease from those activities. Finally, it explains how transactions and events impact the prior period-end cash balance to produce its current period-end balance. Any noncash investing and financing transactions are disclosed in a note disclosure or separate schedule.

EXHIBIT 12.6

Format of the Statement of Cash Flows

COMPANY NAME
Statement of Cash Flows
For *period* Ended *date*

Cash flows from operating activities	
[Compute operating cash flows using indirect or direct method]	
Net cash provided (used) by operating activities	$ #
Cash flows from investing activities	
[List of individual inflows and outflows]	
Net cash provided (used) by investing activities	#
Cash flows from financing activities	
[List of individual inflows and outflows]	
Net cash provided (used) by financing activities	#
Net increase (decrease) in cash	$ #
Cash (and equivalents) balance at prior period-end	#
Cash (and equivalents) balance at current period-end	$ #

Separate schedule or note disclosure of any noncash investing and financing transactions is required.

Point: Positive cash flows for a section are titled net cash "provided by" or "from." Negative cash flows are labeled as net cash "used by."

Decision Maker

Entrepreneur You are considering purchasing a start-up business that recently reported a $110,000 annual net loss and a $225,000 annual net cash inflow. How are these results possible? ■ [Answers follow the chapter's Summary.]

Preparing the Statement of Cash Flows

Preparing a statement of cash flows involves five steps, as shown in Exhibit 12.7.

1. Compute the net increase or decrease in cash.
2. Compute and report the net cash provided or used by operating activities (using either the direct or indirect method; both are explained).
3. Compute and report the net cash provided or used by investing activities.
4. Compute and report the net cash provided or used by financing activities.
5. Compute the net cash flow by combining net cash provided or used by operating, investing, and financing activities, and then *prove it* by adding it to the beginning cash balance to show that it equals the ending cash balance.

Point: View the change in cash as a *target* number (or check figure) that we will fully explain and prove in the statement of cash flows.

EXHIBIT 12.7

Five Steps in Preparing the Statement of Cash Flows

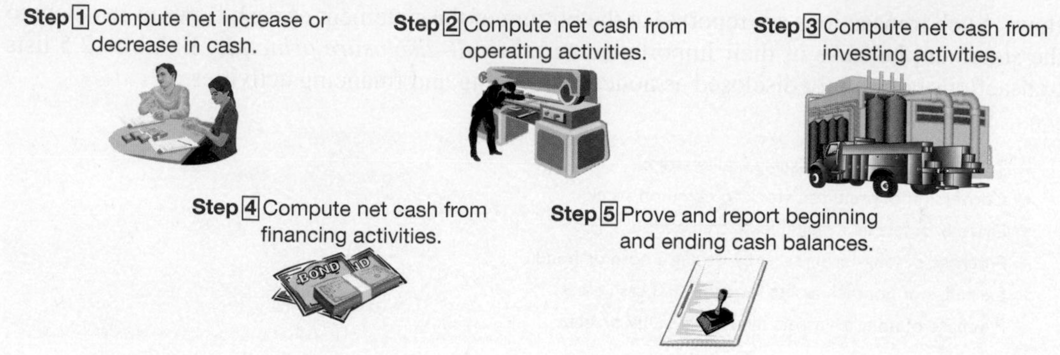

Computing the net increase or net decrease in cash is a simple but crucial computation. It equals the current period's cash balance minus the prior period's cash balance. This is the *bottom-line* figure for the statement of cash flows and is a check on accuracy.

Analyzing the Cash Account A company's cash receipts and cash payments are recorded in the Cash account in its general ledger. The Cash account is therefore a natural place to look for information about cash flows from operating, investing, and financing activities. To illustrate, see the summarized Cash T-account of Genesis, Inc., in Exhibit 12.8. The Cash account increased $5,000, from $12,000 to $17,000. Individual cash transactions are summarized in this Cash account according to the major types of cash receipts and cash payments. For instance, only the total of cash receipts from all customers is listed. Individual cash transactions underlying these totals can number in the thousands. Accounting software is available to provide summarized cash accounts.

EXHIBIT 12.8

Summarized Cash Account

Accounting System:

File Edit Maintain Tasks Analysis Options Reports Window Help

Cash

Balance, Dec. 31, 2014	12,000		
Receipts from customers	570,000	Payments for inventory	319,000
Receipts from asset sales	2,000	Payments for wages and operating expenses	218,000
Receipts from stock issuance ..	15,000	Payments for interest	8,000
		Payments for taxes	5,000
		Payments for notes retirement	18,000
		Payments for dividends	14,000
Balance, Dec. 31, 2015	17,000		

1 Cash change

Sales Purchases General Ledger Payroll Inventory Company Analysis

The statement of cash flows summarizes and classifies the transactions that led to the $5,000 increase in the Cash account. Preparing a statement of cash flows from Exhibit 12.8 requires determining whether an individual cash inflow or outflow is an operating, investing, or financing activity, and then listing each by activity. However, preparing the statement of cash flows from an analysis of the summarized Cash account has two limitations. First, most companies have many individual cash receipts and payments, making it difficult to review them all. Accounting software minimizes this burden, but it is still a task requiring professional judgment for many transactions. Second, the Cash account does not usually carry an adequate description of each cash transaction, making assignment of all cash transactions according to activity difficult.

Analyzing Noncash Accounts A second approach to preparing the statement of cash flows is analyzing noncash accounts. This approach uses the fact that when a company records cash inflows and outflows with debits and credits to the Cash account (see Exhibit 12.8), it also records credits and debits in noncash accounts (reflecting double-entry accounting). Many of these noncash accounts are balance sheet accounts—for instance, from the sale of land for cash. Others are revenue and expense accounts that are closed to equity. For instance, the sale of services for cash yields a credit to Services Revenue that is closed to Retained Earnings for a corporation. In sum, *all cash transactions eventually affect noncash balance sheet accounts*. Thus, we can determine cash inflows and outflows by analyzing changes in noncash balance sheet accounts.

Exhibit 12.9 uses the accounting equation to show the relation between the Cash account and the noncash balance sheet accounts. This exhibit starts with the accounting equation (at the top). It is then expanded in line (2) to separate cash from noncash asset accounts. To isolate cash on one side of the equation, line (3) shows noncash asset accounts being subtracted from both sides of the equation. Cash now equals the sum of the liability and equity accounts *minus* the noncash asset accounts. Line (4) points out that *changes* on one side of the accounting equation equal *changes* on the other side. It shows that we can explain changes in cash by analyzing changes in the noncash accounts consisting of liability accounts, equity accounts, and noncash asset accounts. By analyzing noncash balance sheet accounts and any related income statement accounts, we can prepare a statement of cash flows.

EXHIBIT 12.9

Relation between Cash and Noncash Accounts

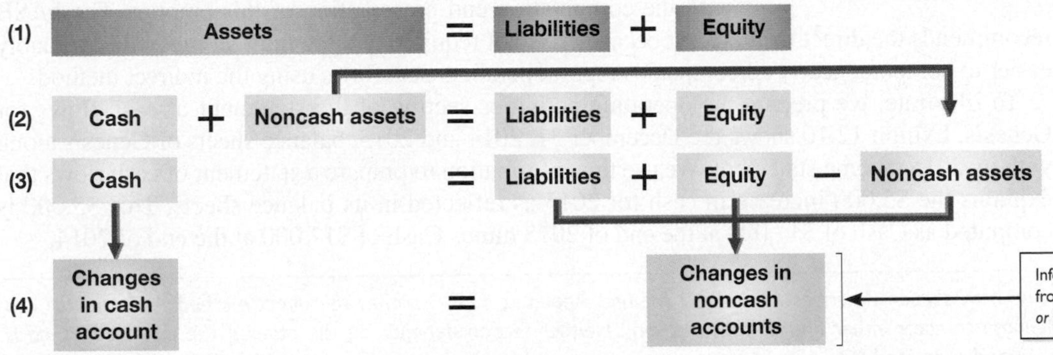

Information on changes in cash is obtained from analyzing *either* the Cash account *or* the noncash accounts.

Information to Prepare the Statement Information to prepare the statement of cash flows usually comes from three sources: (1) comparative balance sheets, (2) the current income statement, and (3) additional information. Comparative balance sheets are used to compute changes in noncash accounts from the beginning to the end of the period. The current income statement is used to help compute cash flows from operating activities. Additional information often includes details on transactions and events that help explain both the cash flows and noncash investing and financing activities.

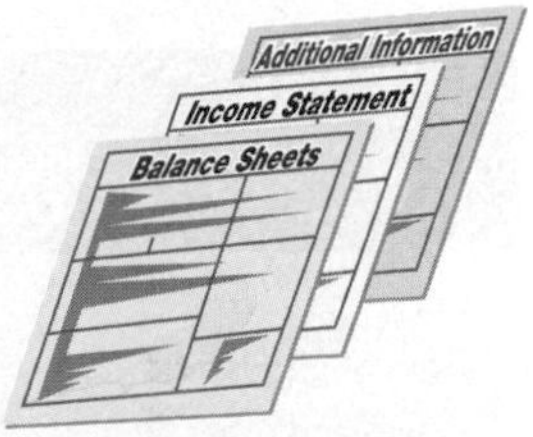

NEED-TO-KNOW 12-1

Classifying Cash Flows

C1

Classify each of the following cash flows as operating, investing, or financing activities.

____ **a.** Purchase equipment for cash
____ **b.** Cash payment of wages
____ **c.** Issuance of stock for cash
____ **d.** Receipt of cash dividends from investments
____ **e.** Cash collections from customers
____ **f.** Note payable issued for cash
____ **g.** Cash paid for utilities
____ **h.** Cash paid to acquire investments
____ **i.** Cash paid to retire debt
____ **j.** Cash received as interest on investments
____ **k.** Cash received from selling investments
____ **l.** Cash received from a bank loan

QC1

Solution

a. Investing **b.** Operating **c.** Financing **d.** Operating **e.** Operating **f.** Financing **g.** Operating **h.** Investing **i.** Financing **j.** Operating **k.** Investing **l.** Financing

Do More: QS 12-1, QS 12-2, E 12-1

CASH FLOWS FROM OPERATING

Indirect and Direct Methods of Reporting

Cash flows provided (used) by operating activities are reported in one of two ways: the *direct method* or the *indirect method.* **These two different methods apply only to the operating activities section.**

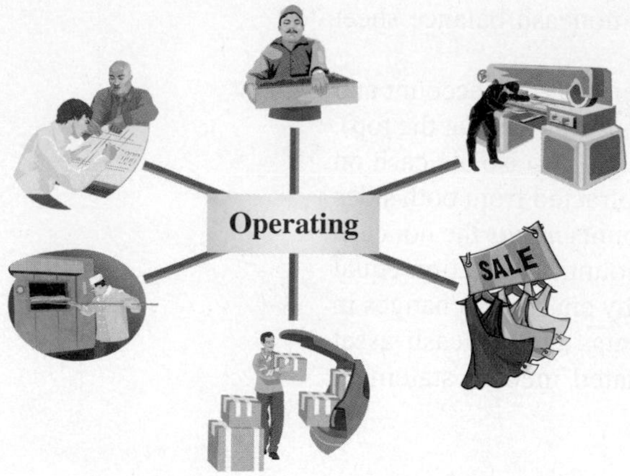

The **direct method** separately lists each major item of operating cash receipts (such as cash received from customers) and each major item of operating cash payments (such as cash paid for inventory). The cash payments are subtracted from cash receipts to determine the net cash provided (used) by operating activities.

The **indirect method** reports net income and then adjusts it for items necessary to obtain net cash provided or used by operating activities. It does *not* report individual items of cash inflows and cash outflows from operating activities. Instead, the indirect method reports the necessary adjustments to reconcile net income to net cash provided or used by operating activities. **The net cash amount provided by operating activities is *identical* under both the direct and indirect methods.** This equality always exists. The difference in these methods is with the computation and presentation of this amount. The FASB recommends the direct method, but because it is not required and the indirect method is arguably easier to compute, nearly all companies report operating cash flows using the indirect method.

To illustrate, we prepare the operating activities section of the statement of cash flows for Genesis. Exhibit 12.10 shows the December 31, 2014 and 2015, balance sheets of Genesis along with its 2015 income statement. We use this information to prepare a statement of cash flows that explains the $5,000 increase in cash for 2015 as reflected in its balance sheets. This $5,000 is computed as Cash of $17,000 at the end of 2015 minus Cash of $12,000 at the end of 2014.

The next section describes the indirect method. Appendix 12B describes the direct method. An instructor can choose to cover either one or both methods. Neither section depends on the other. If the indirect method is skipped, then read Appendix 12B and return to the section (five pages ahead) titled "Cash Flows from Investing."

EXHIBIT 12.10

Financial Statements

GENESIS
Income Statement
For Year Ended December 31, 2015

Sales		$590,000
Cost of goods sold	$300,000	
Wages and other operating expenses	216,000	
Interest expense	7,000	
Depreciation expense	24,000	(547,000)
		43,000
Other gains (losses)		
Loss on sale of plant assets	(6,000)	
Gain on retirement of notes	16,000	10,000
Income before taxes		53,000
Income taxes expense		(15,000)
Net income		$ 38,000

Additional information for 2015

a. The accounts payable balances result from inventory purchases.

b. Purchased $60,000 in plant assets by issuing $60,000 of notes payable.

c. Sold plant assets with a book value of $8,000 (original cost of $20,000 and accumulated depreciation of $12,000) for $2,000 cash, yielding a $6,000 loss.

d. Received $15,000 cash from issuing 3,000 shares of common stock.

e. Paid $18,000 cash to retire notes with a $34,000 book value, yielding a $16,000 gain.

f. Declared and paid cash dividends of $14,000.

GENESIS
Balance Sheets
December 31, 2015 and 2014

	2015	2014	Change
Assets			
Current assets			
Cash	$ 17,000	$ 12,000	**$ 5,000 Increase**
Accounts receivable	60,000	40,000	20,000 Increase
Inventory	84,000	70,000	14,000 Increase
Prepaid expenses	6,000	4,000	2,000 Increase
Total current assets	167,000	126,000	
Long-term assets			
Plant assets	250,000	210,000	40,000 Increase
Accumulated depreciation	(60,000)	(48,000)	12,000 Increase
Total assets	$357,000	$288,000	
Liabilities			
Current liabilities			
Accounts payable	$ 35,000	$ 40,000	$ 5,000 Decrease
Interest payable	3,000	4,000	1,000 Decrease
Income taxes payable	22,000	12,000	10,000 Increase
Total current liabilities	60,000	56,000	
Long-term notes payable	90,000	64,000	26,000 Increase
Total liabilities	150,000	120,000	
Equity			
Common stock, $5 par	95,000	80,000	15,000 Increase
Retained earnings	112,000	88,000	24,000 Increase
Total equity	207,000	168,000	
Total liabilities and equity	$357,000	$288,000	

Applying the Indirect Method of Reporting

Net income is computed using accrual accounting, which recognizes revenues when earned and expenses when incurred. Revenues and expenses do not necessarily reflect the receipt and payment of cash. The indirect method of computing and reporting net cash flows from operating activities involves adjusting the net income figure to obtain the net cash provided or used by operating activities. This includes subtracting noncash increases from net income and adding noncash charges back to net income.

P2 Compute cash flows from operating activities using the indirect method.

To illustrate, the indirect method begins with Genesis's net income of $38,000 and adjusts it to obtain net cash provided by operating activities of $20,000. Exhibit 12.11 shows the results of the indirect method of reporting operating cash flows, which adjusts net income for two types of adjustments. There are ① adjustments to income statement items that neither provide nor use cash and ② adjustments to reflect changes in balance sheet current assets and current liabilities (linked to operating activities). This section describes each of these adjustments.

EXHIBIT 12.11

Operating Activities Section—Indirect Method

GENESIS
Statement of Cash Flows—Operating Section under Indirect Method
For Year Ended December 31, 2015

	Cash flows from operating activities		
	Net income		$ 38,000
	Adjustments to reconcile net income to net cash provided by operating activities		
①	Income statement items not affecting cash		
	Depreciation expense	24,000	
	Loss on sale of plant assets	6,000	
	Gain on retirement of notes	(16,000)	
②	Changes in current assets and liabilities		
	Increase in accounts receivable	(20,000)	
	Increase in inventory	(14,000)	
	Increase in prepaid expenses	(2,000)	
	Decrease in accounts payable	(5,000)	
	Decrease in interest payable	(1,000)	
	Increase in income taxes payable	10,000	
	Net cash provided by operating activities		**$20,000**

① Adjustments for Income Statement Items Not Affecting Cash The income statement usually includes some expenses and losses that do not reflect cash outflows. Examples are depreciation, amortization, depletion, bad debts expense, loss from an asset sale, and loss from retirement of notes payable. When there are expenses and losses that do not reflect cash outflows, the indirect method for reporting operating cash flows requires the following adjustment:

Expenses and losses with no cash outflows are added back to net income.

To see the logic of this adjustment, recall that items such as depreciation, amortization, and depletion have *no* cash effect, and adding them back cancels their deductions. To see the logic for losses, consider that items such as a plant asset sale and a notes retirement are usually recorded by recognizing the cash, removing all plant asset or notes accounts, and recording any loss or gain. The cash received or paid is part of either investing or financing cash flows. *No* operating cash flow effect occurs, and adding it back to net income cancels the deduction.

Similarly, when net income includes revenues that do not reflect cash inflows, the indirect method for reporting operating cash flows requires the following adjustment:

Revenues and gains with no cash inflows are subtracted from net income.

We apply these adjustments to the income statement items in Exhibit 12.10 that do not affect cash.

Point: An income statement reports revenues, gains, expenses, and losses on an accrual basis. The statement of cash flows reports cash received and cash paid for operating, financing, and investing activities.

Depreciation. Depreciation expense is Genesis's only operating item that has no effect on cash flows. We must add back the $24,000 depreciation expense to net income when computing cash provided by operating activities. Adding it back cancels the expense. (We later explain that any cash outflow to acquire a plant asset is reported as an investing activity.)

Loss on sale of plant assets. Genesis reports a $6,000 loss on sale of plant assets as part of net income. This loss is a proper deduction in computing income, but it is *not part of operating activities*. Instead, a sale of plant assets is part of investing activities. Thus, the $6,000 nonoperating loss is added back to net income (see Exhibit 12.11). Adding it back cancels the loss. We later explain how to report the cash inflow from the asset sale in investing activities.

Gain on retirement of debt. A $16,000 gain on retirement of debt is properly included in net income, but it is *not part of operating activities*. This means the $16,000 nonoperating gain must be subtracted from net income to obtain net cash provided by operating activities (see Exhibit 12.11). Subtracting it cancels the recorded gain. We later describe how to report the cash outflow to retire debt.

These three adjustments to net income for "items not affecting cash" are shown as follows in the operating section:

Net income	$ 38,000
Adjustments to reconcile net income to net cash provided by operating activities	
Income statement items not affecting cash	
Depreciation expense	24,000
Loss on sale of plant assets	6,000
Gain on retirement of notes	(16,000)

② Adjustments for Changes in Current Assets and Current Liabilities This section describes adjustments for changes in current assets and current liabilities.

Adjustments for changes in current assets. Decreases in current assets require the following adjustment:

Reconstructed Entry		
Cash	#	
Current Asset		#

Decreases in current assets are added to net income.

Increases in current assets require the following adjustment:

Reconstructed Entry		
Current Asset	#	
Cash		#

Increases in current assets are subtracted from net income.

Adjustments for changes in current liabilities. Increases in current liabilities require the following adjustment to net income when computing operating cash flows:

Reconstructed Entry		
Cash	#	
Current Liabilities		#

Increases in current liabilities are added to net income.

Conversely, when current liabilities decrease, the following adjustment is required:

Reconstructed Entry		
Current Liabilities	#	
Cash		#

Decreases in current liabilities are subtracted from net income.

To illustrate, we apply these adjustment rules to the three noncash current assets and three current liabilities in Exhibit 12.10, which are then reported as follows in the operating section:

Net income	$ 38,000
Adjustments to reconcile net income to net cash provided by operating activities	
Increase in accounts receivable	(20,000)
Increase in inventory	(14,000)
Increase in prepaid expenses	(2,000)
Decrease in accounts payable	(5,000)
Decrease in interest payable	(1,000)
Increase in income taxes payable	10,000

Following is an explanation, including T-account analysis, for how these adjustments result in cash receipts and cash payments.

Accounts receivable. Following the rule above, the $20,000 increase in the current asset of accounts receivable is subtracted from income. This increase implies that Genesis collects less cash than is reported in sales. To see this it is helpful to use *account analysis.* This involves setting up a T-account and reconstructing its major entries to compute cash receipts or payments as follows.

Point: Operating activities are typically those that determine income, which are often reflected in changes in current assets and current liabilities.

Numbers in black are taken from Exhibit 12.10. The red number is the computed (plug) figure.

Accounts Receivable			
Bal., Dec. 31, 2014	40,000		
Sales	590,000	**Cash receipts =**	**570,000**
Bal., Dec. 31, 2015	60,000		

We see that sales are $20,000 greater than cash receipts. This $20,000—reflected in the increase in Accounts Receivable—is subtracted from net income when computing cash provided by operating activities.

Inventory. The $14,000 increase in inventory is subtracted from income. This increase implies that Genesis had greater cash purchases than cost of goods sold, as reflected in the following account analysis:

Inventory			
Bal., Dec. 31, 2014	70,000		
Purchases =	**314,000**	Cost of goods sold	300,000
Bal., Dec. 31, 2015	84,000		

Prepaid expenses. The $2,000 increase in prepaid expense is subtracted from income, implying that Genesis's cash payments exceed its recorded prepaid expenses and is reflected in the following T-account:

Prepaid Expenses			
Bal., Dec. 31, 2014	4,000		
Cash payments =	**218,000**	Wages and other operating exp.	216,000
Bal., Dec. 31, 2015	6,000		

Accounts payable. The $5,000 decrease in the current liability for accounts payable is subtracted from income. This decrease implies that cash payments to suppliers exceed purchases, which is reflected in the following T-account:

Accounts Payable			
		Bal., Dec. 31, 2014	40,000
Cash payments =	**319,000**	Purchases	314,000
		Bal., Dec. 31, 2015	35,000

Interest payable. The $1,000 decrease in interest payable is subtracted from income. This decrease indicates that cash paid for interest exceeds interest expense, which is reflected in the following T-account:

Interest Payable			
		Bal., Dec. 31, 2014	4,000
Cash paid for interest =	**8,000**	Interest expense	7,000
		Bal., Dec. 31, 2015	3,000

Income taxes payable. The $10,000 increase in income taxes payable is added to income. This increase implies that reported income taxes exceed the cash paid for taxes, which is reflected in the following T-account:

Income Taxes Payable			
		Bal., Dec. 31, 2014	12,000
Cash paid for taxes =	5,000	Income taxes expense	15,000
		Bal., Dec. 31, 2015	22,000

Summary Adjustments for Operating Activities—Indirect Method

Exhibit 12.12 summarizes the adjustments to net income when computing net cash provided or used by operating activities under the indirect method.

EXHIBIT 12.12

Summary of Adjustments for Operating Activities—Indirect Method

Net Income (or Loss)

① Adjustments for operating items not providing or using cash

+Noncash expenses and losses

Examples: Expenses for depreciation, depletion, and amortization; losses from disposal of long-term assets and from retirement of debt

−Noncash revenues and gains

Examples: Earnings from equity-method investments; gains from disposal of long-term assets and from retirement of debt

② Adjustments for changes in current assets and current liabilities

+Decrease in noncash current operating asset

−Increase in noncash current operating asset

+Increase in current operating liability

−Decrease in current operating liability

Net cash provided (used) by operating activities

Decision Insight

How Much Cash Is in Income? The difference between net income and operating cash flows can be large and sometimes reflects on the quality of earnings. This bar chart shows the net income and operating cash flows of three companies. Operating cash flows can be either higher or lower than net income. ■

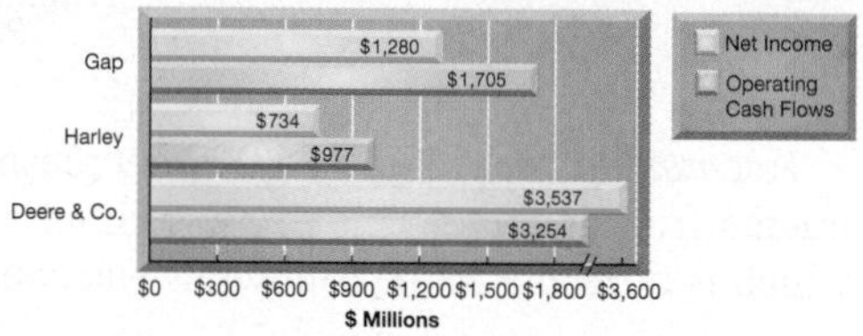

NEED-TO-KNOW 12-2

Reporting Operating Cash Flows (Indirect)

P2

A company's current-year income statement and selected balance sheet data at December 31 of the current and prior years follow. Prepare the cash flows from operating activities section only of its statement of cash flows using the indirect method for the current year.

Income Statement
For Current Year Ended December 31

Sales revenue	$120
Expenses	
Cost of goods sold	50
Depreciation expense	30
Salaries expense	17
Interest expense	3
Net income	$ 20

Selected Balance Sheet Accounts

At December 31	Current Yr	Prior Yr
Accounts receivable	$12	$10
Inventory	6	9
Accounts payable	7	11
Salaries payable	8	3
Interest payable	1	0

Solution

Cash Flows from Operating Activities—Indirect Method For Current Year Ended December 31		
Cash flows from operating activities		
Net income		$20
Adjustments to reconcile net income to net cash provided by operating activities		
Income statement items not affecting cash		
Depreciation expense	$30	
Changes in current assets and current liabilities		
Increase in accounts receivable	(2)	
Decrease in inventory	3	
Decrease in accounts payable	(4)	
Increase in salaries payable	5	
Increase in interest payable	1	33
Net cash provided by operating activities		$53

Do More: QS 12-3, QS 12-4, E 12-4, E 12-5, E 12-6

QC2

CASH FLOWS FROM INVESTING

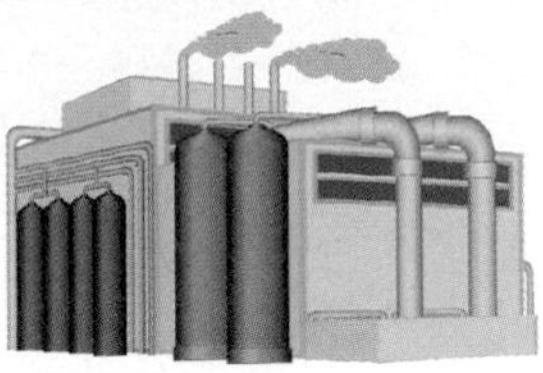

The third major step in preparing the statement of cash flows is to compute and report cash flows from investing activities. We normally do this by identifying changes in (1) all noncurrent asset accounts and (2) the current accounts for both notes receivable and investments in securities (excluding trading securities). We then analyze changes in these accounts to determine their effect, if any, on cash and report the cash flow effects in the investing activities section of the statement of cash flows. **Reporting of investing activities is identical under the direct method and indirect method.**

Three-Stage Process of Analysis

P3 Determine cash flows from both investing and financing activities.

Information to compute cash flows from investing activities is usually taken from beginning and ending balance sheets and the income statement. We use a three-stage process to determine cash provided or used by investing activities: (1) identify changes in investing-related accounts, (2) explain these changes using reconstruction analysis, and (3) report their cash flow effects.

Analyzing Noncurrent Assets

Information about the Genesis transactions provided earlier reveals that the company both purchased and sold plant assets during the period. Both transactions are investing activities and are analyzed for their cash flow effects in this section.

Plant Asset Transactions The *first stage* in analyzing the Plant Assets account and its related Accumulated Depreciation account is to identify any changes in these accounts from comparative balance sheets in Exhibit 12.10. This analysis reveals a $40,000 increase in plant assets from $210,000 to $250,000 and a $12,000 increase in accumulated depreciation from $48,000 to $60,000.

The *second stage* is to explain these changes. Items *b* and *c* of the additional information in Exhibit 12.10 affect plant assets. Recall that the Plant Assets account is affected by both asset purchases and sales; its Accumulated Depreciation account is normally increased from depreciation and decreased from the removal of accumulated depreciation in asset sales. To explain changes in these accounts and to identify their cash flow effects, we prepare *reconstructed entries* from prior transactions; *they are not the actual entries by the preparer.*

Point: Investing activities include (1) purchasing and selling long-term assets, (2) lending and collecting on notes receivable, and (3) purchasing and selling short-term investments other than cash equivalents and trading securities.

Point: Financing and investing info is available in ledger accounts to help explain changes in comparative balance sheets. Post references lead to relevant entries and explanations.

To illustrate, item *b* reports that Genesis purchased plant assets of $60,000 by issuing $60,000 in notes payable to the seller. The reconstructed entry for analysis of item *b* follows.

Reconstruction	Plant Assets	60,000	
	Notes Payable		60,000

Next, item *c* reports that Genesis sold plant assets costing $20,000 (with $12,000 of accumulated depreciation) for $2,000 cash, resulting in a $6,000 loss. The reconstructed entry for analysis of item *c* follows.

Reconstruction	**Cash**	**2,000**	
	Accumulated Depreciation	12,000	
	Loss on Sale of Plant Assets	6,000	
	Plant Assets		20,000

Point: When determining cash flows from investing, T-account analysis is key to reconstructing accounts and amounts.

We also reconstruct the entry for Depreciation Expense from the income statement. Depreciation expense results in no cash flow effect.

Reconstruction	Depreciation Expense	24,000	
	Accumulated Depreciation		24,000

These three reconstructed entries are reflected in the following plant asset and related T-accounts.

Plant Assets

Bal., Dec. 31, 2014	210,000		
Purchase	**60,000**	**Sale**	**20,000**
Bal., Dec. 31, 2015	250,000		

Accumulated Depreciation—Plant Assets

		Bal., Dec. 31, 2014	48,000
Sale	**12,000**	**Depr. expense**	**24,000**
		Bal., Dec. 31, 2015	60,000

Example: If a plant asset costing $40,000 with $37,000 of accumulated depreciation is sold at a $1,000 loss, what is the cash flow? What is the cash flow if this asset is sold at a gain of $3,000? *Answers:* +$2,000; +$6,000.

This reconstruction analysis is complete in that the change in plant assets from $210,000 to $250,000 is fully explained by the $60,000 purchase and the $20,000 sale. Also, the change in accumulated depreciation from $48,000 to $60,000 is fully explained by depreciation expense of $24,000 and the removal of $12,000 in accumulated depreciation from the asset sale.

The *third stage* in analyzing the Plant Assets account looks back at the reconstructed entries to identify any cash flows. The identified cash flow effect is reported in the investing section of the statement as follows:

Cash flows from investing activities	
Cash received from sale of plant assets	$2,000

The $60,000 purchase described in item *b* and financed by issuing notes is a noncash investing and financing activity. It is reported in a note or in a separate schedule to the statement as follows:

Noncash investing and financing activity	
Purchased plant assets with issuance of notes	$60,000

Analyzing Additional Assets

Genesis did not have any additional noncurrent assets (or nonoperating current assets) and, therefore, we have no additional investing transactions to analyze. If other investing assets did exist, we would identify and report the investing cash flows using the same three-stage process illustrated for plant assets.

Use the following information to determine this company's cash flows from investing activities.

a. A factory with a book value of $100 and an original cost of $800 was sold at a loss of $10.

b. Paid $70 cash for new equipment.

c. Long-term stock investments were sold for $20 cash, yielding a loss of $4.

d. Sold land costing $175 for $160 cash, yielding a loss of $15.

NEED-TO-KNOW 12-3

Reporting Investing Cash Flows

P3

Solution

Cash flows from investing activities	
Cash received from sale of factory*	$ 90
Cash paid for new equipment	(70)
Cash received from sale of long-term investments	20
Cash received from sale of land	160
Net cash provided by investing activities	$200

*Cash received from sale of factory = Book value − Loss = $100 − $10 = $90

Do More: QS 12-5, QS 12-6, QS 12-9, E 12-7

QC3

CASH FLOWS FROM FINANCING

The fourth major step in preparing the statement of cash flows is to compute and report cash flows from financing activities. We normally do this by identifying changes in all noncurrent liability accounts (including the current portion of any notes and bonds) and the equity accounts. These accounts include long-term debt, notes payable, bonds payable, common stock, and retained earnings. Changes in these accounts are then analyzed using available information to determine their effect, if any, on cash. Results are reported in the financing activities section of the statement. **Reporting of financing activities is identical under the direct method and indirect method.**

Three-Stage Process of Analysis

We again use a three-stage process to determine cash provided or used by financing activities: (1) identify changes in financing-related accounts, (2) explain these changes using reconstruction analysis, and (3) report their cash flow effects.

Analyzing Noncurrent Liabilities

Information about Genesis provided earlier reveals two transactions involving noncurrent liabilities. We analyzed one of those, the $60,000 issuance of notes payable to purchase plant assets. This transaction is reported as a significant noncash investing and financing activity in a footnote or a separate schedule to the statement of cash flows. The other remaining transaction involving noncurrent liabilities is the cash retirement of notes payable.

Point: Financing activities generally refer to changes in the noncurrent liability and the equity accounts. Examples are (1) receiving cash from issuing debt or repaying amounts borrowed and (2) receiving cash from or distributing cash to owners.

Notes Payable Transactions The *first stage* in analysis of notes is to review the comparative balance sheets from Exhibit 12.10. This analysis reveals an increase in notes payable from $64,000 to $90,000.

The *second stage* explains this change. Item *e* of the additional information in Exhibit 12.10 reports that notes with a carrying value of $34,000 are retired for $18,000 cash, resulting in a $16,000 gain. The reconstructed entry for analysis of item *e* follows:

Reconstruction	Notes Payable	34,000	
	Gain on retirement of debt		16,000
	Cash		**18,000**

This entry reveals an $18,000 cash outflow for retirement of notes and a $16,000 gain from comparing the notes payable carrying value to the cash received. This gain does not reflect any cash inflow or outflow. Also, item *b* of the additional information reports that Genesis purchased plant assets costing $60,000 by issuing $60,000 in notes payable to the seller. We reconstructed this entry when analyzing investing activities: It showed a $60,000 increase to notes payable that is reported as a noncash investing and financing transaction. The Notes Payable account is explained by these reconstructed entries as follows:

Notes Payable			
		Bal., Dec. 31, 2014	64,000
Retired notes	**34,000**	**Issued notes**	**60,000**
		Bal., Dec. 31, 2015	90,000

The *third stage* is to report the cash flow effect of the notes retirement in the financing section of the statement as follows:

Cash flows from financing activities	
Cash paid to retire notes	$(18,000)

Analyzing Equity

The Genesis information reveals two transactions involving equity accounts. The first is the issuance of common stock for cash. The second is the declaration and payment of cash dividends. We analyze both.

Common Stock Transactions The *first stage* in analyzing common stock is to review the comparative balance sheets from Exhibit 12.10, which reveal an increase in common stock from $80,000 to $95,000.

The *second stage* explains this change. Item *d* of the additional information in Exhibit 12.10 reports that 3,000 shares of common stock are issued at par for $5 per share. The reconstructed entry for analysis of item *d* follows:

Reconstruction	**Cash**	**15,000**	
	Common Stock		15,000

This entry reveals a $15,000 cash inflow from stock issuance and is reflected in (and explains) the Common Stock account as follows:

Common Stock	
	Bal., Dec. 31, 2014 80,000
	Issued stock 15,000
	Bal., Dec. 31, 2015 95,000

The *third stage* discloses the cash flow effect from stock issuance in the financing section of the statement as follows:

Cash flows from financing activities	
Cash received from issuing stock	$15,000

Retained Earnings Transactions The *first stage* in analyzing the Retained Earnings account is to review the comparative balance sheets from Exhibit 12.10. This reveals an increase in retained earnings from $88,000 to $112,000.

The *second stage* explains this change. Item *f* of the additional information in Exhibit 12.10 reports that cash dividends of $14,000 are paid. The reconstructed entry follows:

Reconstruction	Retained Earnings	14,000	
	Cash		**14,000**

This entry reveals a $14,000 cash outflow for cash dividends. Also see that the Retained Earnings account is impacted by net income of $38,000. (Net income was analyzed under the operating section of the statement of cash flows.) The reconstructed Retained Earnings account follows:

Retained Earnings			
		Bal., Dec. 31, 2014	88,000
Cash dividend	**14,000**	**Net income**	**38,000**
		Bal., Dec. 31, 2015	112,000

The *third stage* reports the cash flow effect from the cash dividend in the financing section of the statement as follows:

Cash flows from financing activities	
Cash paid for dividends	$(14,000)

Point: Financing activities not affecting cash flow include *declaration* of a cash dividend, *declaration* of a stock dividend, issuance of a stock dividend, and a stock split.

We now have identified and explained all of the Genesis cash inflows and cash outflows and one noncash investing and financing transaction.

Proving Cash Balances

The fifth and final step in preparing the statement is to report the beginning and ending cash balances and prove that the *net change in cash* is explained by operating, investing, and financing cash flows. This step is shown here for Genesis.

Net cash provided by operating activities	$20,000
Net cash provided by investing activities	2,000
Net cash used in financing activities	(17,000)
Net increase in cash	**$ 5,000**
Cash balance at 2014 year-end	12,000
Cash balance at 2015 year-end	$17,000

The preceding table shows that the $5,000 net increase in cash, from $12,000 at the beginning of the period to $17,000 at the end, is reconciled by net cash flows from operating ($20,000 inflow), investing ($2,000 inflow), and financing ($17,000 outflow) activities. This is formally reported at the bottom of the complete statement of cash flows as shown in Exhibit 12.13.

Global: There are no requirements to separate domestic and international cash flows, leading some users to ask, "Where in the world is cash flow?"

Decision Maker

Reporter Management is in labor contract negotiations and grants you an interview. It highlights a recent $600,000 net loss that involves a $930,000 extraordinary loss and a total net cash outflow of $550,000 (which includes net cash outflows of $850,000 for investing activities and $350,000 for financing activities). What is your assessment of this company? ■ [Answers follow the chapter's Summary.]

EXHIBIT 12.13

Complete Statement of Cash Flows—Indirect Method

GENESIS Statement of Cash Flows For Year Ended December 31, 2015		
Cash flows from operating activities		
Net income	$ 38,000	
Adjustments to reconcile net income to net cash provided by operating activities		
Income statement items not affecting cash		
Depreciation expense	24,000	
Loss on sale of plant assets	6,000	
Gain on retirement of notes	(16,000)	
Changes in current assets and liabilities		
Increase in accounts receivable	(20,000)	
Increase in inventory	(14,000)	
Increase in prepaid expenses	(2,000)	
Decrease in accounts payable	(5,000)	
Decrease in interest payable	(1,000)	
Increase in income taxes payable	10,000	
Net cash provided by operating activities		$20,000
Cash flows from investing activities		
Cash received from sale of plant assets	2,000	
Net cash provided by investing activities		2,000
Cash flows from financing activities		
Cash received from issuing stock	15,000	
Cash paid to retire notes	(18,000)	
Cash paid for dividends	(14,000)	
Net cash used in financing activities		(17,000)
Net increase in cash		$ 5,000
Cash balance at prior year-end		12,000
Cash balance at current year-end		$17,000

Point: Refer to Exhibit 12.10 and identify the $5,000 change in cash. This change is what the statement of cash flows explains; it serves as a check.

Point: The statement of cash flows is usually the last prepared of the four required financial statements.

NEED-TO-KNOW 12-4

Reporting Financing Cash Flows

P3

Use the following information to determine this company's cash flows from financing activities.

a. Issued common stock for $40 cash.

b. Paid $70 cash to retire a note payable at its $70 maturity value.

c. Paid cash dividend of $15.

d. Paid $5 cash to acquire its treasury stock.

Solution

Cash flows from financing activities	
Cash received from issuance of common stock	$ 40
Cash paid to settle note payable	(70)
Cash paid for dividend	(15)
Cash paid to acquire treasury stock	(5)
Net cash used by financing activities	$(50)

Do More: QS 12-9, QS 12-10, QS 12-13, E 12-8

OVERALL SUMMARY USING T-ACCOUNTS

A statement of cash flows is prepared by analyzing changes in noncash balance sheet accounts. Exhibit 12.14 uses T-accounts to summarize how changes in Genesis's noncash balance sheet accounts affect its cash inflows and outflows (dollar amounts in thousands). The top of the exhibit shows the company's Cash T-account, and the lower part shows T-accounts for its remaining balance sheet accounts. We see that the $20,000 net cash provided by operating activities and the $5,000 net increase in cash shown in the Cash T-account agree with the same figures in the statement of cash flows in Exhibit 12.13.

We explain Exhibit 12.14 in five parts (amounts in $ thousands):

a. Entry (1) records $38 net income in the credit side of the Retained Earnings account and the debit side of the Cash account. This $38 net income in the Cash T-account is adjusted until it reflects the $5 net increase in cash.

b. Entries (2) through (4) add the $24 depreciation and $6 loss on asset sale to net income, and subtract the $16 gain on retirement of notes.

c. Entries (5) through (10) adjust net income for changes in current asset and current liability accounts.

d. Entry (11) records the noncash investing and financing transaction involving a $60 purchase of assets by issuing $60 of notes.

e. Entries (12) and (13) record the $15 stock issuance and the $14 dividend.

EXHIBIT 12.14

Balance Sheet T-Accounts to Explain the Change in Cash ($ thousands)

Cash

(1) Net income	38		
(2) Depreciation	24	(4) Gain on retirement of notes	16
(3) Loss on sale of plant assets	6		
(10) Increase in income taxes payable	10	(5) Increase in accounts receivable	20
		(6) Increase in inventory	14
		(7) Increase in prepaid expanse	2
		(8) Decrease in accounts payable	5
		(9) Decrease in interest payable	1
Net cash provided by operating activities	20		
(3) Cash received from sale of plant assets	2	(4) Cash paid to retire notes	18
(12) Cash received from issuing stock	15	(13) Cash paid for dividends	14
Net increase in cash	5		

Data to prepare statement of cash flows

Accounts Receivable

Beg.	40		
(5)	20		
End.	60		

Inventory

Beg.	70		
(6)	14		
End.	84		

Prepaid Expenses

Beg.	4		
(7)	2		
End.	6		

Plant Assets

Beg.	210		
		(3)	20
(11)	60		
End.	250		

Accumulated Depreciation

		Beg.	48
(3)	12	(2)	24
		End.	60

Accounts Payable

		Beg.	40
(8)	5		
		End.	35

Interest Payable

		Beg.	4
(9)	1		
		End.	3

Income Taxes Payable

		Beg.	12
		(10)	10
		End.	22

Long-Term Notes Payable

		Beg.	64
(4)	34		
		(11)	60
		End.	90

Common Stock

		Beg.	80
		(12)	15
		End.	95

Retained Earnings

		Beg.	88
		(1)	38
(13)	14		
		End.	112

GLOBAL VIEW

The statement of cash flows, which explains changes in cash (including cash equivalents) from period to period, is required under both U.S. GAAP and IFRS. This section discusses similarities and differences between U.S. GAAP and IFRS in reporting that statement.

Samsung

Reporting Cash Flows from Operating Both U.S. GAAP and IFRS permit the reporting of cash flows from operating activities using either the direct or indirect method. Further, the basic requirements underlying the application of both methods are fairly consistent across these two accounting systems. Appendix A shows that **Samsung** reports its cash flows from operating activities using the indirect method, and in a manner similar to that explained in this chapter. Further, the definition of cash and cash equivalents is roughly similar for U.S. GAAP and IFRS.

There are, however, some differences between U.S. GAAP and IFRS in reporting operating cash flows. We mention two of the more notable. First, U.S. GAAP requires that cash inflows from interest revenue and dividend revenue be classified as operating, whereas IFRS permits classification under operating or investing provided that this classification is consistently applied across periods. Samsung reports its cash from interest received under operating, consistent with U.S. GAAP (no mention is made of any dividends received). Second, U.S. GAAP requires cash outflows for interest expense be classified as operating, whereas IFRS again permits classification under operating or financing provided that it is consistently applied across periods. (Some believe that interest payments, like dividend payments, are better classified as financing because they represent payments to financiers.) Samsung reports cash outflows for interest under operating, which is consistent with U.S. GAAP and acceptable under IFRS.

Reporting Cash Flows from Investing and Financing U.S. GAAP and IFRS are broadly similar in computing and classifying cash flows from investing and financing activities. A quick review of these two sections for **Samsung**'s statement of cash flows shows a structure similar to that explained in this chapter. One notable exception is that U.S. GAAP requires that cash outflows for income tax be classified as operating, whereas IFRS permits the splitting of those cash flows among operating, investing, and financing depending on the sources of that tax. Samsung reports its cash outflows for income tax under operating, which is similar to U.S. GAAP.

Sustainability and Accounting **LSTN**, as introduced in this chapter's opening feature, places an emphasis on being a socially conscious and environmentally friendly alternative within the luxury headphone market. LSTN partners with The Starkey Hearing Foundation "to provide hearing for children in deaf schools," explains Bridget Hilton, its founder. "Ninety-five percent of children in deaf schools worldwide can be helped . . . [and] eighty percent of those people live in developing countries." LSTN also recognizes the need to work within the local markets so that its successes are sustainable. Our hearing products and services "will not undercut the local economies—these are basic senses that everyone on earth should be able to experience," explains Bridget. "To me, success in business is doing something you love while being financially secure." That is something we all hope is sustainable.

For every purchase, LSTN helps restore hearing to a person in need through the Starkey Hearing Foundation.

Courtesy of Bridget Hilton

Decision Analysis — Cash Flow Analysis

A1 Analyze the statement of cash flows and apply the cash flow on total assets ratio.

Analyzing Cash Sources and Uses

Most managers stress the importance of understanding and predicting cash flows for business decisions. Creditors evaluate a company's ability to generate cash before deciding whether to lend money. Investors also assess cash inflows and outflows before buying and selling stock. Information in the statement of cash flows helps address these and other questions such as (1) How much cash is generated from or used in operations? (2) What expenditures are made with cash from operations? (3) What is the source of cash for debt payments? (4) What is the source of cash for distributions to owners? (5) How is the increase in investing activities financed? (6) What is the source of cash for new plant assets? (7) Why is cash flow from operations different from income? (8) How is cash from financing used?

To effectively answer these questions, it is important to separately analyze investing, financing, and operating activities. To illustrate, consider data from three different companies in Exhibit 12.15. These companies operate in the same industry and have been in business for several years.

EXHIBIT 12.15

Cash Flows of Competing Companies

($ thousands)	BMX	ATV	Trex
Cash provided (used) by operating activities	$90,000	$40,000	$(24,000)
Cash provided (used) by investing activities			
Proceeds from sale of plant assets			26,000
Purchase of plant assets	(48,000)	(25,000)	
Cash provided (used) by financing activities			
Proceeds from issuance of debt			13,000
Repayment of debt	(27,000)		
Net increase (decrease) in cash	$15,000	$15,000	$ 15,000

Each company generates an identical $15,000 net increase in cash, but its sources and uses of cash flows are very different. BMX's operating activities provide net cash flows of $90,000, allowing it to purchase plant assets of $48,000 and repay $27,000 of its debt. ATV's operating activities provide $40,000 of cash flows, limiting its purchase of plant assets to $25,000. Trex's $15,000 net cash increase is due to selling plant assets and incurring additional debt. Its operating activities yield a net cash outflow of $24,000. Overall, analysis of these cash flows reveals that BMX is more capable of generating future cash flows than is ATV or Trex.

Decision Insight

Free Cash Flows Many investors use cash flows to value company stock. However, cash-based valuation models often yield different stock values due to differences in measurement of cash flows. Most models require cash flows that are "free" for distribution to shareholders. These *free cash flows* are defined as cash flows available to shareholders after operating asset reinvestments and debt payments. Knowledge of the statement of cash flows is key to proper computation of free cash flows. A company's growth and financial flexibility depend on adequate free cash flows. ■

Point: CFO (Cash flow from operations)
Less: Capital Expenditures
Less: Debt Repayments
= FCF (free cash flows)

Cash Flow on Total Assets

Cash flow information has limitations, but it can help measure a company's ability to meet its obligations, pay dividends, expand operations, and obtain financing. Users often compute and analyze a cash-based ratio similar to return on total assets except that its numerator is net cash flows from operating activities. The **cash flow on total assets** ratio is shown in Exhibit 12.16.

EXHIBIT 12.16

Cash Flow on Total Assets

$$\textbf{Cash flow on total assets} = \frac{\textbf{Cash flow from operations}}{\textbf{Average total assets}}$$

This ratio reflects actual cash flows and is not affected by accounting income recognition and measurement. It can help business decision makers estimate the amount and timing of cash flows when planning and analyzing operating activities.

To illustrate, the 2013 cash flow on total assets ratio for **Nike** is 18.3%—see Exhibit 12.17. Is an 18.3% ratio good or bad? To answer this question, we compare this ratio with the ratios of prior years (we could also compare its ratio with those of its competitors and the market). Nike's cash flow on total assets ratio

EXHIBIT 12.17

Nike's Cash Flow on Total Assets

Year	Cash Flow on Total Assets	Return on Total Assets
2013	18.3%	15.0%
2012	12.5	14.6
2011	12.3	14.5
2010	22.9	13.8
2009	13.5	11.6

for several prior years is in the second column of Exhibit 12.17. Results show that its 18.3% return is its second highest return over the past five years. This is probably reflective of the recent recessionary period.

As an indicator of *earnings quality,* some analysts compare the cash flow on total assets ratio to the return on total assets ratio. Nike's return on total assets is provided in the third column of Exhibit 12.17. Nike's cash flow on total assets ratio exceeds its return on total assets in three of the five years, leading some analysts to infer that Nike's earnings quality is good for that period because much of its earnings are realized in the form of cash.

Point: Cash flow ratios are often used by financial analysts.

Decision Insight

Cash Flow Ratios Analysts use various other cash-based ratios, including the following two:

(1) $$\textbf{Cash coverage of growth} = \frac{\textbf{Operating cash flow}}{\textbf{Cash outflow for plant assets}}$$

where a low ratio (less than 1) implies cash inadequacy to meet asset growth, whereas a high ratio implies cash adequacy for asset growth.

(2) $$\textbf{Operating cash flow to sales} = \frac{\textbf{Operating cash flow}}{\textbf{Net sales}}$$

When this ratio substantially and consistently differs from the operating income to net sales ratio, the risk of accounting improprieties increases.

Point: The following ratio helps assess whether operating cash flow is adequate to meet long-term obligations:

Cash coverage of debt = Cash flow from operations ÷ Noncurrent liabilities.

A low ratio suggests a higher risk of insolvency; a high ratio suggests a greater ability to meet long-term obligations.

NEED-TO-KNOW

COMPREHENSIVE

Preparing Statement of Cash Flows—Indirect *and* Direct Methods

Umlauf's comparative balance sheets, income statement, and additional information follow.

UMLAUF COMPANY
Balance Sheets
December 31, 2015 and 2014

	2015	2014
Assets		
Cash	$ 43,050	$ 23,925
Accounts receivable	34,125	39,825
Inventory	156,000	146,475
Prepaid expenses	3,600	1,650
Total current assets	236,775	211,875
Equipment	135,825	146,700
Accum. depreciation—Equipment	(61,950)	(47,550)
Total assets	$310,650	$311,025
Liabilities		
Accounts payable	$ 28,800	$ 33,750
Income taxes payable	5,100	4,425
Dividends payable	0	4,500
Total current liabilities	33,900	42,675
Bonds payable	0	37,500
Total liabilities	33,900	80,175
Equity		
Common stock, $10 par	168,750	168,750
Retained earnings	108,000	62,100
Total liabilities and equity	$310,650	$311,025

UMLAUF COMPANY
Income Statement
For Year Ended December 31, 2015

Sales		$446,100
Cost of goods sold	$222,300	
Other operating expenses	120,300	
Depreciation expense	25,500	(368,100)
		78,000
Other gains (losses)		
Loss on sale of equipment	3,300	
Loss on retirement of bonds	825	(4,125)
Income before taxes		73,875
Income taxes expense		(13,725)
Net income		$ 60,150

Additional Information

a. Equipment costing $21,375 with accumulated depreciation of $11,100 is sold for cash.
b. Equipment purchases are for cash.
c. Accumulated Depreciation is affected by depreciation expense and the sale of equipment.
d. The balance of Retained Earnings is affected by dividend declarations and net income.
e. All sales are made on credit.
f. All inventory purchases are on credit.
g. Accounts Payable balances result from inventory purchases.
h. Prepaid expenses relate to "other operating expenses."

Required

1. Prepare a statement of cash flows using the indirect method for year 2015.

2.[B] Prepare a statement of cash flows using the direct method for year 2015.

PLANNING THE SOLUTION

- Prepare two blank statements of cash flows with sections for operating, investing, and financing activities using the (1) indirect method format and (2) direct method format.
- Compute the cash paid for equipment and the cash received from the sale of equipment using the additional information provided along with the amount for depreciation expense and the change in the balances of equipment and accumulated depreciation. Use T-accounts to help chart the effects of the sale and purchase of equipment on the balances of the Equipment account and the Accumulated Depreciation account.
- Compute the effect of net income on the change in the Retained Earnings account balance. Assign the difference between the change in retained earnings and the amount of net income to dividends declared. Adjust the dividends declared amount for the change in the Dividends Payable balance.
- Compute cash received from customers, cash paid for inventory, cash paid for other operating expenses, and cash paid for taxes as illustrated in the chapter.
- Enter the cash effects of reconstruction entries to the appropriate section(s) of the statement.
- Total each section of the statement, determine the total net change in cash, and add it to the beginning balance to get the ending balance of cash.

SOLUTION

Supporting computations for cash receipts and cash payments.

(1) *Cost of equipment sold	$ 21,375
Accumulated depreciation of equipment sold	(11,100)
Book value of equipment sold	10,275
Loss on sale of equipment	(3,300)
Cash received from sale of equipment	$ 6,975
Cost of equipment sold	$ 21,375
Less decrease in the Equipment account balance	(10,875)
Cash paid for new equipment	$ 10,500
(2) Loss on retirement of bonds	$ 825
Carrying value of bonds retired	37,500
Cash paid to retire bonds	$ 38,325
(3) Net income	$ 60,150
Less increase in retained earnings	45,900
Dividends declared	14,250
Plus decrease in dividends payable	4,500
Cash paid for dividends	$ 18,750
(4)[B] Sales	$ 446,100
Add decrease in accounts receivable	5,700
Cash received from customers	$451,800
(5)[B] Cost of goods sold	$ 222,300
Plus increase in inventory	9,525
Purchases	231,825
Plus decrease in accounts payable	4,950
Cash paid for inventory	$236,775
(6)[B] Other operating expenses	$ 120,300
Plus increase in prepaid expenses	1,950
Cash paid for other operating expenses	$122,250
(7)[B] Income taxes expense	$ 13,725
Less increase in income taxes payable	(675)
Cash paid for income taxes	$ 13,050

* Supporting T-account analysis for part 1 follows:

Equipment			
Bal., Dec. 31, 2014	146,700		
Cash purchase	10,500	Sale	21,375
Bal., Dec. 31, 2015	135,825		

Accumulated Depreciation—Equipment			
		Bal., Dec. 31, 2014	47,550
Sale	11,100	Depr. expense	25,500
		Bal., Dec. 31, 2015	61,950

1. Indirect method:

UMLAUF COMPANY
Statement of Cash Flows (Indirect Method)
For Year Ended December 31, 2015

Cash flows from operating activities		
Net income	$60,150	
Adjustments to reconcile net income to net cash provided by operating activities		
Income statement items not affecting cash		
Depreciation expense	25,500	
Loss on sale of plant assets	3,300	
Loss on retirement of bonds	825	
Changes in current assets and current liabilities		
Decrease in accounts receivable	5,700	
Increase in inventory	(9,525)	
Increase in prepaid expenses	(1,950)	
Decrease in accounts payable	(4,950)	
Increase in income taxes payable	675	
Net cash provided by operating activities		$79,725
Cash flows from investing activities		
Cash received from sale of equipment	6,975	
Cash paid for equipment	(10,500)	
Net cash used in investing activities		(3,525)
Cash flows from financing activities		
Cash paid to retire bonds payable	(38,325)	
Cash paid for dividends	(18,750)	
Net cash used in financing activities		(57,075)
Net increase in cash		$19,125
Cash balance at prior year-end		23,925
Cash balance at current year-end		$43,050

2.[B] Direct method (Appendix 12B):

UMLAUF COMPANY
Statement of Cash Flows (Direct Method)
For Year Ended December 31, 2015

Cash flows from operating activities		
Cash received from customers	$451,800	
Cash paid for inventory	(236,775)	
Cash paid for other operating expenses	(122,250)	
Cash paid for income taxes	(13,050)	
Net cash provided by operating activities		$79,725
Cash flows from investing activities		
Cash received from sale of equipment	6,975	
Cash paid for equipment	(10,500)	
Net cash used in investing activities		(3,525)
Cash flows from financing activities		
Cash paid to retire bonds payable	(38,325)	
Cash paid for dividends	(18,750)	
Net cash used in financing activities		(57,075)
Net increase in cash		$19,125
Cash balance at prior year-end		23,925
Cash balance at current year-end		$43,050

APPENDIX

Spreadsheet Preparation of the Statement of Cash Flows

12A

This appendix explains how to use a spreadsheet (work sheet) to prepare the statement of cash flows under the indirect method.

P4 Illustrate use of a spreadsheet to prepare a statement of cash flows.

Preparing the Indirect Method Spreadsheet Analyzing noncash accounts can be challenging when a company has a large number of accounts and many operating, investing, and financing transactions. A *spreadsheet,* also called *work sheet* or *working paper,* can help us organize the information needed to prepare a statement of cash flows. A spreadsheet also makes it easier to check the accuracy of our work. To illustrate, we return to the comparative balance sheets and income statement shown in Exhibit 12.10. We use the following identifying letters *a* through *g* to code changes in accounts, and letters *h* through *m* for additional information, to prepare the statement of cash flows:

a. Net income is $38,000.
b. Accounts receivable increase by $20,000.
c. Inventory increases by $14,000.
d. Prepaid expenses increase by $2,000.
e. Accounts payable decrease by $5,000.
f. Interest payable decreases by $1,000.
g. Income taxes payable increase by $10,000.
h. Depreciation expense is $24,000.
i. Plant assets costing $20,000 with accumulated depreciation of $12,000 are sold for $2,000 cash. This yields a loss on sale of assets of $6,000.
j. Notes with a book value of $34,000 are retired with a cash payment of $18,000, yielding a $16,000 gain on retirement.
k. Plant assets costing $60,000 are purchased with an issuance of notes payable for $60,000.
l. Issued 3,000 shares of common stock for $15,000 cash.
m. Paid cash dividends of $14,000.

Exhibit 12A.1 shows the indirect method spreadsheet for Genesis. We enter both beginning and ending balance sheet amounts on the spreadsheet. We also enter information in the Analysis of Changes columns (keyed to the additional information items *a* through *m*) to explain changes in the accounts and determine the cash flows for operating, investing, and financing activities. Information about noncash investing and financing activities is reported near the bottom.

Entering the Analysis of Changes on the Spreadsheet The following sequence of procedures is used to complete the spreadsheet after the beginning and ending balances of the balance sheet accounts are entered:

① Enter net income as the first item in the statement of cash flows section for computing operating cash inflow (debit) and as a credit to Retained Earnings.

② In the statement of cash flows section, adjustments to net income are entered as debits if they increase cash flows and as credits if they decrease cash flows. Applying this same rule, adjust net income for the change in each noncash current asset and current liability account related to operating activities. For each adjustment to net income, the offsetting debit or credit must help reconcile the beginning and ending balances of a current asset or current liability account.

③ Enter adjustments to net income for income statement items not providing or using cash in the period. For each adjustment, the offsetting debit or credit must help reconcile a noncash balance sheet account.

④ Adjust net income to eliminate any gains or losses from investing and financing activities. Because the cash from a gain must be excluded from operating activities, the gain is entered as a credit in the operating activities section. Losses are entered as debits. For each adjustment, the related debit and/or credit must help reconcile balance sheet accounts and involve reconstructed entries to show the cash flow from investing or financing activities.

⑤ After reviewing any unreconciled balance sheet accounts and related information, enter the remaining reconciling entries for investing and financing activities. Examples are purchases of plant assets,

Point: Analysis of the changes on the spreadsheet are summarized here:
1. Cash flows from operating activities generally affect net income, current assets, and current liabilities.
2. Cash flows from investing activities generally affect noncurrent asset accounts.
3. Cash flows from financing activities generally affect noncurrent liability and equity accounts.

EXHIBIT 12A.1

Spreadsheet for Preparing Statement of Cash Flows—Indirect Method

	A	B	C	D	E	F	G
1	**GENESIS**						
2	**Spreadsheet for Statement of Cash Flows—Indirect Method**						
3	**For Year Ended December 31, 2015**						
4		**Dec. 31,**		**Analysis of Changes**			**Dec. 31,**
5		**2014**		**Debit**		**Credit**	**2015**
6	**Balance Sheet—Debit Bal. Accounts**						
7	Cash	$ 12,000					$ 17,000
8	Accounts receivable	40,000	*(b)*	$ 20,000			60,000
9	Inventory	70,000	*(c)*	14,000			84,000
10	Prepaid expenses	4,000	*(d)*	2,000			6,000
11	Plant assets	210,000	*(k1)*	60,000	*(i)*	$ 20,000	250,000
12		$336,000					$417,000
13	**Balance Sheet—Credit Bal. Accounts**						
14	Accumulated depreciation	$ 48,000	*(i)*	12,000	*(h)*	24,000	$ 60,000
15	Accounts payable	40,000	*(e)*	5,000			35,000
16	Interest payable	4,000	*(f)*	1,000			3,000
17	Income taxes payable	12,000			*(g)*	10,000	22,000
18	Notes payable	64,000	*(j)*	34,000	*(k2)*	60,000	90,000
19	Common stock, $5 par value	80,000			*(l)*	15,000	95,000
20	Retained earnings	88,000	*(m)*	14,000	*(a)*	38,000	112,000
21		$336,000					$417,000
22	**Statement of Cash Flows**						
23	Operating activities						
24	Net income		*(a)*	38,000			
25	Increase in accounts receivable				*(b)*	20,000	
26	Increase in inventory				*(c)*	14,000	
27	Increase in prepaid expenses				*(d)*	2,000	
28	Decrease in accounts payable				*(e)*	5,000	
29	Decrease in interest payable				*(f)*	1,000	
30	Increase in income taxes payable		*(g)*	10,000			
31	Depreciation expense		*(h)*	24,000			
32	Loss on sale of plant assets		*(i)*	6,000			
33	Gain on retirement of notes				*(j)*	16,000	
34	Investing activities						
35	Receipts from sale of plant assets		*(i)*	2,000			
36	Financing activities						
37	Payment to retire notes				*(j)*	18,000	
38	Receipts from issuing stock		*(l)*	15,000			
39	Payment of cash dividends				*(m)*	14,000	
40							
41	**Noncash Investing and Financing Activities**						
42	Purchase of plant assets with notes		*(k2)*	60,000	*(k1)*	60,000	
				$317,000		$317,000	

issuances of long-term debt, stock issuances, and dividend payments. Some of these may require entries in the noncash investing and financing section of the spreadsheet (reconciled).

⑥ Check accuracy by totaling the Analysis of Changes columns and by determining that the change in each balance sheet account has been explained (reconciled).

We illustrate these steps in Exhibit 12A.1 for Genesis:

Step	Entries
①	*(a)*
②	*(b)* through *(g)*
③	*(h)*
④	*(i)* through *(j)*
⑤	*(k)* through *(m)*

Since adjustments *i, j,* and *k* are more challenging, we show them in the following debit and credit format. These entries are for purposes of our understanding; they are *not* the entries actually made in the journals. Changes in the Cash account are identified as sources or uses of cash.

i.	Cash—Receipt from sale of plant assets **(source of cash)**	2,000	
	Loss from sale of plant assets	6,000	
	Accumulated depreciation	12,000	
	Plant assets		20,000
	To describe sale of plant assets.		
j.	Notes payable	34,000	
	Cash—Payments to retire notes **(use of cash)**		18,000
	Gain on retirement of notes		16,000
	To describe retirement of notes.		
k1.	Plant assets	60,000	
	Cash—Purchase of plant assets financed by notes		60,000
	To describe purchase of plant assets.		
k2.	Cash—Purchase of plant assets financed by notes	60,000	
	Notes payable		60,000
	To issue notes for purchase of assets.		

APPENDIX

Direct Method of Reporting Operating Cash Flows 12B

P5 Compute cash flows from operating activities using the direct method.

We compute cash flows from operating activities under the direct method by adjusting accrual-based income statement items to the cash basis. The usual approach is to adjust income statement accounts related to operating activities for changes in their related balance sheet accounts as follows:

Revenue or expense + or − Adjustments for changes in related balance sheet accounts = Cash receipts or cash payments

The framework for reporting cash receipts and cash payments for the operating section of the cash flow statement under the direct method is presented in Exhibit 12B.1. We consider cash receipts first and then cash payments.

EXHIBIT 12B.1

Major Classes of Operating Cash Flows

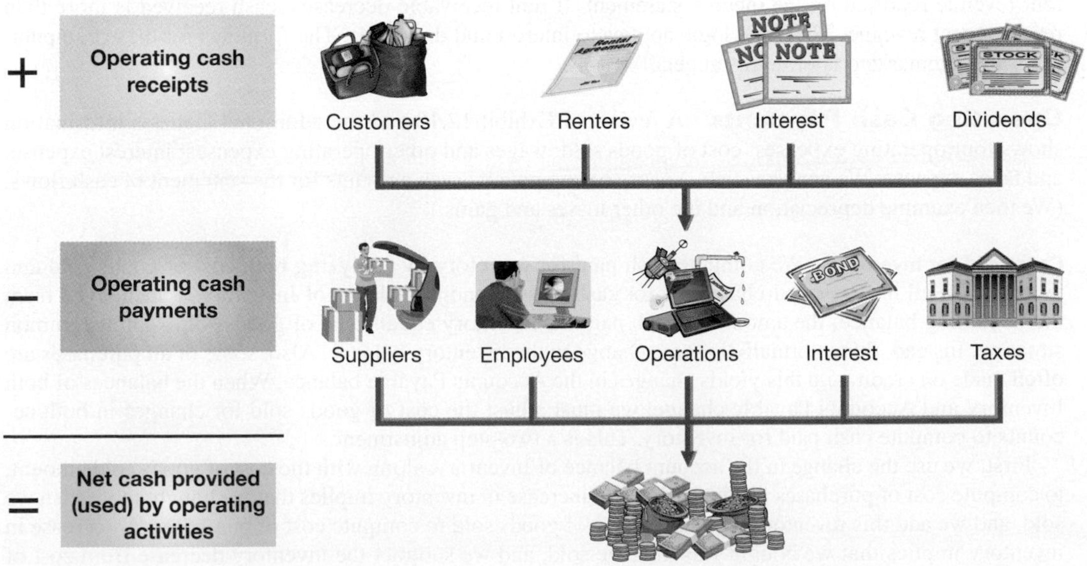

Operating Cash Receipts A review of Exhibit 12.10 and the additional information reported by Genesis suggests only one potential cash receipt: sales to customers. This section, therefore, starts with sales to customers as reported on the income statement and then adjusts it as necessary to obtain cash received from customers to report on the statement of cash flows.

Cash Received from Customers If all sales are for cash, the amount received from customers equals the sales reported on the income statement. When some or all sales are on account, however, we must adjust the amount of sales for the change in Accounts Receivable. It is often helpful to use *account analysis* to do this. This usually involves setting up a T-account and reconstructing its major entries, with emphasis on cash receipts and payments.

Point: An accounts receivable increase implies that cash received from customers is less than sales (the converse is also true).

To illustrate, we use a T-account that includes accounts receivable balances for Genesis on December 31, 2014 and 2015. The beginning balance is $40,000 and the ending balance is $60,000. Next, the income statement shows sales of $590,000, which we enter on the debit side of this account. We now can reconstruct the Accounts Receivable account to determine the amount of cash received from customers as follows:

Reconstructed Entry

Cash	570,000	
Accts Recble.	20,000	
Sales		590,000

Accounts Receivable

Bal., Dec. 31, 2014	40,000		
Sales	590,000	**Cash receipts =**	**570,000**
Bal., Dec. 31, 2015	60,000		

Example: If the ending balance of Accounts Receivable is $20,000 (instead of $60,000), what is cash received from customers? *Answer:* $610,000

This T-account shows that the Accounts Receivable balance begins at $40,000 and increases to $630,000 from sales of $590,000, yet its ending balance is only $60,000. This implies that cash receipts from customers are $570,000, computed as $40,000 + $590,000 − [?] = $60,000. This computation can be rearranged to express cash received as equal to sales of $590,000 minus a $20,000 increase in accounts receivable. This computation is summarized as a general rule in Exhibit 12B.2. Genesis reports the $570,000 cash received from customers as a cash inflow from operating activities.

EXHIBIT 12B.2

Formula to Compute Cash Received from Customers—Direct Method

Cash received from customers = Sales **+ Decrease** in accounts receivable **or** **− Increase** in accounts receivable

Other Cash Receipts While Genesis's cash receipts are limited to collections from customers, we often see other types of cash receipts, most commonly cash receipts involving rent, interest, and dividends. We compute cash received from these items by subtracting an increase in their respective receivable or adding a decrease. For instance, if rent receivable increases in the period, cash received from renters is less than rent revenue reported on the income statement. If rent receivable decreases, cash received is more than reported rent revenue. The same logic applies to interest and dividends. The formulas for these computations are summarized later in this appendix.

Point: Net income is measured using accrual accounting. Cash flows from operations are measured using cash basis accounting.

Operating Cash Payments A review of Exhibit 12.10 and the additional Genesis information shows four operating expenses: cost of goods sold; wages and other operating expenses; interest expense; and taxes expense. We analyze each expense to compute its cash amounts for the statement of cash flows. (We then examine depreciation and the other losses and gains.)

Cash Paid for Inventory We compute cash paid for inventory by analyzing both cost of goods sold and inventory. If all inventory purchases are for cash and the ending balance of Inventory is unchanged from the beginning balance, the amount of cash paid for inventory equals cost of goods sold—an uncommon situation. Instead, there normally is some change in the Inventory balance. Also, some or all purchases are often made on credit, and this yields changes in the Accounts Payable balance. When the balances of both Inventory and Accounts Payable change, we must adjust the cost of goods sold for changes in both accounts to compute cash paid for inventory. This is a two-step adjustment.

First, we use the change in the account balance of Inventory, along with the cost of goods sold amount, to compute cost of purchases for the period. An increase in inventory implies that we bought more than we sold, and we add this inventory increase to cost of goods sold to compute cost of purchases. A decrease in inventory implies that we bought less than we sold, and we subtract the inventory decrease from cost of goods sold to compute purchases. We illustrate the *first step* by reconstructing the Inventory account of Genesis:

Inventory			
Bal., Dec. 31, 2014	70,000		
Purchases =	**314,000**	Cost of goods sold	300,000
Bal., Dec. 31, 2015	84,000		

The beginning balance is $70,000, and the ending balance is $84,000. The income statement shows that cost of goods sold is $300,000, which we enter on the credit side of this account. With this information, we determine the amount for cost of purchases to be $314,000. This computation can be rearranged to express cost of purchases as equal to cost of goods sold of $300,000 plus the $14,000 increase in inventory.

The second step uses the change in the balance of Accounts Payable, and the amount of cost of purchases, to compute cash paid for inventory. A decrease in accounts payable implies that we paid for more goods than we acquired this period, and we would then add the accounts payable decrease to cost of purchases to compute cash paid for inventory. An increase in accounts payable implies that we paid for less than the amount of goods acquired, and we would subtract the accounts payable increase from purchases to compute cash paid for inventory. The *second step* is applied to Genesis by reconstructing its Accounts Payable account:

Accounts Payable			
		Bal., Dec. 31, 2014	40,000
Cash payments =	**319,000**	Purchases	314,000
		Bal., Dec. 31, 2015	35,000

Reconstructed Entry

COGS.	300,000	
Inventory	14,000	
Accounts Payable. .	5,000	
Cash		319,000

Its beginning balance of $40,000 plus purchases of $314,000 minus an ending balance of $35,000 yields cash paid of $319,000 (or $40,000 + $314,000 − [?] = $35,000). Alternatively, we can express cash paid for inventory as equal to purchases of $314,000 plus the $5,000 decrease in accounts payable. The $319,000 cash paid for inventory is reported on the statement of cash flows as a cash outflow under operating activities.

Example: If the ending balances of Inventory and Accounts Payable are $60,000 and $50,000, respectively (instead of $84,000 and $35,000), what is cash paid for inventory? *Answer:* $280,000

We summarize this two-step adjustment to cost of goods sold to compute cash paid for inventory in Exhibit 12B.3.

EXHIBIT 12B.3

Two Steps to Compute Cash Paid for Inventory—Direct Method

Step 1

Purchases = Cost of goods sold + **Increase** in inventory **or** − **Decrease** in inventory

Step 2

Cash paid for inventory = Purchases + **Decrease** in accounts payable **or** − **Increase** in accounts payable

Cash Paid for Wages and Operating Expenses (Excluding Depreciation) The income statement of Genesis shows wages and other operating expenses of $216,000 (see Exhibit 12.10). To compute cash paid for wages and other operating expenses, we adjust this amount for any changes in their related balance sheet accounts. We begin by looking for any prepaid expenses and accrued liabilities related to wages and other operating expenses in the balance sheets of Genesis in Exhibit 12.10. The balance sheets show prepaid expenses but no accrued liabilities. Thus, the adjustment is limited to the change in prepaid expenses. The amount of adjustment is computed by assuming that all cash paid for wages and other operating expenses is initially debited to Prepaid Expenses. This assumption allows us to reconstruct the Prepaid Expenses account:

Prepaid Expenses			
Bal., Dec. 31, 2014	4,000		
Cash payments =	**218,000**	Wages and other operating exp.	216,000
Bal., Dec. 31, 2015	6,000		

Reconstructed Entry

Wages and Other Expenses.	216,000	
Prepaid Expenses . .	2,000	
Cash		218,000

Point: A decrease in prepaid expenses implies that reported expenses include an amount(s) that did not require a cash outflow in the period.

Prepaid expenses increase by $2,000 in the period, meaning that cash paid for wages and other operating expenses exceeds the reported expense by $2,000. Alternatively, we can express cash paid for wages and other operating expenses as equal to its reported expenses of $216,000 plus the $2,000 increase in prepaid expenses.[1]

Exhibit 12B.4 summarizes the adjustments to wages (including salaries) and other operating expenses. The Genesis balance sheet did not report accrued liabilities, but we include them in the formula to explain the adjustment to cash when they do exist. A decrease in accrued liabilities implies that we paid cash for more goods or services than received this period, so we add the decrease in accrued liabilities to the expense amount to obtain cash paid for these goods or services. An increase in accrued liabilities implies that we paid cash for less than what was acquired, so we subtract this increase in accrued liabilities from the expense amount to get cash paid.

EXHIBIT 12B.4

Formula to Compute Cash Paid for Wages and Operating Expenses—Direct Method

Cash paid for wages and other operating expenses	=	Wages and other operating expenses	+ **Increase** in prepaid expenses or − **Decrease** in prepaid expenses	+ **Decrease** in accrued liabilities or − **Increase** in accrued liabilities

Cash paid for interest and income taxes Computing operating cash flows for interest and taxes is similar to that for operating expenses. Both require adjustments to their amounts reported on the income statement for changes in their related balance sheet accounts. We begin with the Genesis income statement showing interest expense of $7,000 and income taxes expense of $15,000. To compute the cash paid, we adjust interest expense for the change in interest payable and then the income taxes expense for the change in income taxes payable. These computations involve reconstructing both liability accounts:

Reconstructed Entry

Int. Expense	7,000	
Int. Payable	1,000	
Cash		8,000

Interest Payable			
		Bal., Dec. 31, 2014	4,000
Cash paid for interest =	**8,000**	Interest expense	7,000
		Bal., Dec. 31, 2015	3,000

Reconstructed Entry

Inc. Tax Exp.	15,000	
Inc. Tax Pay. . . .		10,000
Cash		5,000

Income Taxes Payable			
		Bal., Dec. 31, 2014	12,000
Cash paid for taxes =	**5,000**	Income taxes expense	15,000
		Bal., Dec. 31, 2015	22,000

These accounts reveal cash paid for interest of $8,000 and cash paid for income taxes of $5,000. The formulas to compute these amounts are in Exhibit 12B.5. Both of these cash payments are reported as operating cash outflows on the statement of cash flows.

EXHIBIT 12B.5

Formulas to Compute Cash Paid for Both Interest and Taxes—Direct Method

Cash paid for interest	= Interest expense	+ **Decrease** in interest payable or − **Increase** in interest payable
Cash paid for taxes	= Income taxes expense	+ **Decrease** in income taxes payable or − **Increase** in income taxes payable

Analyzing Additional Expenses, Gains, and Losses Genesis has three additional items reported on its income statement: depreciation, loss on sale of assets, and gain on retirement of debt. We must consider each for its potential cash effects.

[1] The assumption that all cash payments for wages and operating expenses are initially debited to Prepaid Expenses is not necessary for our analysis to hold. If cash payments are debited directly to the expense account, the total amount of cash paid for wages and other operating expenses still equals the $216,000 expense plus the $2,000 increase in prepaid expenses (which arise from end-of-period adjusting entries).

Depreciation Expense Depreciation expense is $24,000. It is often called a *noncash expense* because depreciation has no cash flows. Depreciation expense is an allocation of an asset's depreciable cost. The cash outflow with a plant asset is reported as part of investing activities when it is paid for. Thus, depreciation expense is *never* reported on a statement of cash flows using the direct method; nor is depletion or amortization expense.

Loss on Sale of Assets Sales of assets frequently result in gains and losses reported as part of net income, but the amount of recorded gain or loss does *not* reflect any cash flows in these transactions. Asset sales result in cash inflow equal to the cash amount received, regardless of whether the asset was sold at a gain or a loss. This cash inflow is reported under investing activities. Thus, the loss or gain on a sale of assets is *never* reported on a statement of cash flows using the direct method.

Gain on Retirement of Debt Retirement of debt usually yields a gain or loss reported as part of net income, but that gain or loss does *not* reflect cash flow in this transaction. Debt retirement results in cash outflow equal to the cash paid to settle the debt, regardless of whether the debt is retired at a gain or loss. This cash outflow is reported under financing activities; the loss or gain from retirement of debt is *never* reported on a statement of cash flows using the direct method.

Point: The direct method is usually viewed as *user friendly* because less accounting knowledge is required to understand and use it.

Summary of Adjustments for Direct Method Exhibit 12B.6 summarizes common adjustments for net income to yield net cash provided (used) by operating activities under the direct method.

EXHIBIT 12B.6

Summary of Selected Adjustments for Direct Method

Item	From Income Statement	Adjustments to Obtain Cash Flow Numbers	
Receipts			
From sales	Sales Revenue	+Decrease in Accounts Receivable −Increase in Accounts Receivable	
From rent	Rent Revenue	+Decrease in Rent Receivable −Increase in Rent Receivable	
From interest	Interest Revenue	+Decrease in Interest Receivable −Increase in Interest Receivable	
From dividends	Dividend Revenue	+Decrease in Dividends Receivable −Increase in Dividends Receivable	
Payments			
To suppliers	Cost of Goods Sold	+Increase in Inventory −Decrease in Inventory	+Decrease in Accounts Payable −Increase in Accounts Payable
For operations	Operating Expense	+Increase in Prepaids −Decrease in Prepaids	+Decrease in Accrued Liabilities −Increase in Accrued Liabilities
To employees	Wages (Salaries) Expense	+Decrease in Wages (Salaries) Payable −Increase in Wages (Salaries) Payable	
For interest	Interest Expense	+Decrease in Interest Payable −Increase in Interest Payable	
For taxes	Income Tax Expense	+Decrease in Income Tax Payable −Increase in Income Tax Payable	

Direct Method Format of Operating Activities Section Exhibit 12B.7 shows the Genesis statement of cash flows using the direct method. Major items of cash inflows and cash outflows are listed separately in the operating activities section. The format requires that operating cash outflows be subtracted from operating cash inflows to get net cash provided (used) by operating activities.

The FASB recommends that the operating activities section of the statement of cash flows be reported using the direct method, which is considered more useful to financial statement users. *However, the FASB requires a reconciliation of net income to net cash provided (used) by operating activities when the direct method is used* (which can be reported in the notes). This reconciliation follows the preparation of the operating activities section of the statement of cash flows using the indirect method.

Point: Some preparers argue that it is easier to prepare a statement of cash flows using the indirect method. This likely explains its greater frequency in financial statements.

IFRS

Currently, U.S. GAAP and IFRS allow cash flows from operating activities to be reported using either the indirect method or the direct method. The IASB and FASB are working on joint guidance that would require the direct method for the operating section with the indirect method's operating section disclosed in the footnotes. Stay tuned . . . ■

EXHIBIT 12B.7

Statement of Cash Flows—Direct Method

GENESIS
Statement of Cash Flows
For Year Ended December 31, 2015

Cash from operating	Cash flows from operating activities		
	Cash received from customers	$570,000	
	Cash paid for inventory	(319,000)	
	Cash paid for wages and other operating expenses	(218,000)	
	Cash paid for interest	(8,000)	
	Cash paid for taxes	(5,000)	
	Net cash provided by operating activities		$20,000
Cash from investing	Cash flows from investing activities		
	Cash received from sale of plant assets	2,000	
	Net cash provided by investing activities		2,000
Cash from financing	Cash flows from financing activities		
	Cash received from issuing stock	15,000	
	Cash paid to retire notes	(18,000)	
	Cash paid for dividends	(14,000)	
	Net cash used in financing activities		(17,000)
Cash proved	Net increase in cash		$ 5,000
	Cash balance at prior year-end		12,000
	Cash balance at current year-end		$17,000

NEED-TO-KNOW 12-5

Reporting Operating Cash Flows (Direct)

P5

A company's current-year income statement and selected balance sheet data at December 31 of the current and prior years follow. Prepare the cash flows from operating activities section only of its statement of cash flows using the direct method for the current year.

Income Statement
For Current Year Ended December 31

Sales revenue	$120
Expenses	
Cost of goods sold	50
Depreciation expense	30
Salaries expense	17
Interest expense	3
Net income	$ 20

Selected Balance Sheet Accounts

At December 31	Current Yr	Prior Yr
Accounts receivable	$12	$10
Inventory	6	9
Accounts payable	7	11
Salaries payable	8	3
Interest payable	1	0

Solution

Cash Flows from Operating Activities—Direct Method
For Current Year Ended December 31

Cash flows from operating activities*		
Cash received from customers	$118	
Cash paid for inventory	(51)	
Cash paid for salaries	(12)	
Cash paid for interest	(2)	
Net cash provided by operating activities		$53

*Supporting computations:
Cash received from customers = Sales of $120 − Accounts Receivable increase of $2.
Cash paid for inventory = COGS of $50 − Inventory decrease of $3 + Accounts Payable decrease of $4.
Cash paid for salaries = Salaries Expense of $17 − Salaries Payable increase of $5.
Cash paid for interest = Interest Expense of $3 − Interest Payable increase of $1.

Do More: QS 12-12, QS 12-13, QS 12-14, E 12-12, E 12-14, E 12-15, E 12-16

QC4

Summary

C1 Distinguish between operating, investing, and financing activities, and describe how noncash investing and financing activities are disclosed. The purpose of the statement of cash flows is to report major cash receipts and cash payments relating to operating, investing, or financing activities. Operating activities include transactions and events that determine net income. Investing activities include transactions and events that mainly affect long-term assets. Financing activities include transactions and events that mainly affect long-term liabilities and equity. Noncash investing and financing activities must be disclosed in either a note or a separate schedule to the statement of cash flows. Examples are the retirement of debt by issuing equity and the exchange of a note payable for plant assets.

A1 Analyze the statement of cash flows and apply the cash flow on total assets ratio. To understand and predict cash flows, users stress identification of the sources and uses of cash flows by operating, investing, and financing activities. Emphasis is on operating cash flows since they derive from continuing operations. The cash flow on total assets ratio is defined as operating cash flows divided by average total assets. Analysis of current and past values for this ratio can reflect a company's ability to yield regular and positive cash flows. It is also viewed as a measure of earnings quality.

P1 Prepare a statement of cash flows. Preparation of a statement of cash flows involves five steps: (1) Compute the net increase or decrease in cash; (2) compute net cash provided or used by operating activities (*using either the direct or indirect method*); (3) compute net cash provided or used by investing activities; (4) compute net cash provided or used by financing activities; and (5) report the beginning and ending cash balances and prove that the ending cash balance is explained by net cash flows. Noncash investing and financing activities are also disclosed.

P2 Compute cash flows from operating activities using the indirect method. The indirect method for reporting net cash provided or used by operating activities starts with net income and then adjusts it for three items: (1) changes in noncash current assets and current liabilities related to operating activities, (2) revenues and expenses not providing or using cash, and (3) gains and losses from investing and financing activities.

P3 Determine cash flows from both investing and financing activities. Cash flows from both investing and financing activities are determined by identifying the cash flow effects of transactions and events affecting each balance sheet account related to these activities. All cash flows from these activities are identified when we can explain changes in these accounts from the beginning to the end of the period.

P4A Illustrate use of a spreadsheet to prepare a statement of cash flows. A spreadsheet is a useful tool in preparing a statement of cash flows. Six key steps (see Appendix 12A) are applied when using the spreadsheet to prepare the statement.

P5B Compute cash flows from operating activities using the direct method. The direct method for reporting net cash provided or used by operating activities lists major operating cash inflows less cash outflows to yield net cash inflow or outflow from operations.

Guidance Answers to Decision Maker

Entrepreneur Several factors might explain an increase in net cash flows when a net loss is reported, including (1) early recognition of expenses relative to revenues generated (such as research and development), (2) cash advances on long-term sales contracts not yet recognized in income, (3) issuances of debt or equity for cash to finance expansion, (4) cash sale of assets, (5) delay of cash payments, and (6) cash prepayment on sales. Analysis needs to focus on the components of both the net loss and the net cash flows and their implications for future performance.

Reporter Your initial reaction based on the company's $600,000 loss with a $550,000 decrease in net cash is not positive. However, closer scrutiny reveals a more positive picture of this company's performance. Cash flow from operating activities is $650,000, computed as [?] − $850,000 − $350,000 = $(550,000). You also note that net income *before* the extraordinary loss is $330,000, computed as [?] − $930,000 = $(600,000).

Key Terms

Cash flow on total assets
Direct method
Financing activities
Indirect method
Investing activities
Operating activities
Statement of cash flows

Multiple Choice Quiz

Answers at end of chapter

1. A company uses the indirect method to determine its cash flows from operating activities. Use the following information to determine its net cash provided or used by operating activities.

Net income	$15,200
Depreciation expense	10,000
Cash payment on note payable	8,000
Gain on sale of land	3,000
Increase in inventory	1,500
Increase in accounts payable	2,850

   a. $23,550 used by operating activities
   b. $23,550 provided by operating activities
   c. $15,550 provided by operating activities
   d. $42,400 provided by operating activities
   e. $20,850 provided by operating activities

2. A machine with a cost of $175,000 and accumulated depreciation of $94,000 is sold for $87,000 cash. The amount reported as a source of cash under cash flows from investing activities is
   a. $81,000.
   b. $6,000.
   c. $87,000.
   d. Zero; this is a financing activity.
   e. Zero; this is an operating activity.

3. A company settles a long-term note payable plus interest by paying $68,000 cash toward the principal amount and $5,440 cash for interest. The amount reported as a use of cash under cash flows from financing activities is
   a. Zero; this is an investing activity.
   b. Zero; this is an operating activity.
   c. $73,440.
   d. $68,000.
   e. $5,440.

4. The following information is available regarding a company's annual salaries and wages. What amount of cash is paid for salaries and wages?

Salaries and wages expense	$255,000
Salaries and wages payable, prior year-end	8,200
Salaries and wages payable, current year-end	10,900

   a. $252,300 **b.** $257,700 **c.** $255,000 **d.** $274,100 **e.** $235,900

5. The following information is available for a company. What amount of cash is paid for inventory for the current year?

Cost of goods sold	$545,000
Inventory, prior year-end	105,000
Inventory, current year-end	112,000
Accounts payable, prior year-end	98,500
Accounts payable, current year-end	101,300

   a. $545,000 **b.** $554,800 **c.** $540,800 **d.** $535,200 **e.** $549,200

A(B) *Superscript letter A (B) denotes assignments based on Appendix 12A (12B).*
Icon denotes assignments that involve decision making.

Discussion Questions

1. What is the reporting purpose of the statement of cash flows? Identify at least two questions that this statement can answer.
2. What are some investing activities reported on the statement of cash flows?
3. What are some financing activities reported on the statement of cash flows?
4. Describe the direct method of reporting cash flows from operating activities.
5. When a statement of cash flows is prepared using the direct method, what are some of the operating cash flows?
6. Describe the indirect method of reporting cash flows from operating activities.
7. Where on the statement of cash flows is the payment of cash dividends reported?
8. Assume that a company purchases land for $1,000,000, paying $400,000 cash and borrowing the remainder with a long-term note payable. How should this transaction be reported on a statement of cash flows?
9. On June 3, a company borrows $200,000 cash by giving its bank a 90-day, interest-bearing note. On the statement of cash flows, where should this be reported?
10. If a company reports positive net income for the year, can it also show a net cash outflow from operating activities? Explain.
11. Is depreciation a source of cash flow?

12. Refer to **Apple**'s statement of cash flows in Appendix A. (*a*) Which method is used to compute its net cash provided by operating activities? (*b*) Its balance sheet shows an increase in accounts (trade) receivable from September 29, 2012, to September 28, 2013; why is this increase in accounts (trade) receivable subtracted when computing net cash provided by operating activities for the fiscal year ended September 28, 2013?

APPLE

13. Refer to **Google**'s statement of cash flows in Appendix A. What are its cash flows from financing activities for the year ended December 31, 2013? List the items and amounts.

GOOGLE

14. Refer to **Samsung**'s 2013 statement of cash flows in Appendix A. List its cash flows from operating activities, investing activities, and financing activities.

Samsung

15. Refer to **Samsung**'s statement of cash flows in Appendix A. What investing activities result in cash outflows for the year ended December 31, 2013? List items and amounts.

Samsung

connect

QUICK STUDY

QS 12-1
Transaction classification by activity C1

Classify the following cash flows as either operating, investing, or financing activities.

____ **1.** Sold long-term investments for cash.
____ **2.** Received cash payments from customers.
____ **3.** Paid cash for wages and salaries.
____ **4.** Purchased inventories for cash.
____ **5.** Paid cash dividends.
____ **6.** Issued common stock for cash.
____ **7.** Received cash interest on a note.
____ **8.** Paid cash interest on outstanding notes.
____ **9.** Received cash from sale of land at a loss.
____ **10.** Paid cash for property taxes on building.

QS 12-2
Statement of cash flows
P1

Label the following headings, line items, and notes with the numbers *1* through *13* according to their sequential order (from top to bottom) for presentation of the statement of cash flows.

____ **a.** "Cash flows from investing activities" title
____ **b.** "For *period* Ended *date*" heading
____ **c.** "Cash flows from operating activities" title
____ **d.** Company name
____ **e.** Schedule or note disclosure of noncash investing and financing transactions
____ **f.** "Statement of Cash Flows" heading
____ **g.** Net increase (decrease) in cash . . . . $ #
____ **h.** Net cash provided (used) by operating activities . . . . $ #
____ **i.** Cash (and equivalents) balance at prior period-end . . . . . $ #
____ **j.** Net cash provided (used) by financing activities . . . . $ #
____ **k.** "Cash flows from financing activities" title
____ **l.** Net cash provided (used) by investing activities . . . . $ #
____ **m.** Cash (and equivalents) balance at current period-end . . . $ #

QS 12-3
Indirect: Computing cash flows from operations
P2

For each of the following three separate cases X, Y and Z, compute cash flows from operations using the indirect method. The list includes all balance sheet accounts related to cash from operating activities.

	Case X	Case Y	Case Z
Net income	$ 4,000	$100,000	$72,000
Depreciation expense	30,000	8,000	24,000
Accounts receivable increase (decrease)	40,000	20,000	(4,000)
Inventory increase (decrease)	(20,000)	(10,000)	10,000
Accounts payable increase (decrease)	24,000	(22,000)	14,000
Accrued liabilities increase (decrease)	(44,000)	12,000	(8,000)

QS 12-4
Indirect: Computing cash from operations P2

Use the following information to determine this company's cash flows from operating activities using the indirect method.

MOSS COMPANY
Selected Balance Sheet Information
December 31, 2015 and 2014

	2015	2014
Current assets		
Cash	$84,650	$26,800
Accounts receivable	25,000	32,000
Inventory	60,000	54,100
Current liabilities		
Accounts payable	30,400	25,700
Income taxes payable	2,050	2,200

MOSS COMPANY
Income Statement
For Year Ended December 31, 2015

Sales		$515,000
Cost of goods sold		331,600
Gross profit		183,400
Operating expenses		
Depreciation expense	$ 36,000	
Other expenses	121,500	157,500
Income before taxes		25,900
Income taxes expense		7,700
Net income		$ 18,200

The following information is necessary to answer QS 12-5 and QS 12-6.

QS 12-5
Indirect: Computing investing cash flows
P2

The plant assets section of the comparative balance sheets of Anders Company is reported below.

Anders Company
Comparative Balance Sheets

	2015	2014
Plant assets		
Equipment	$ 180,000	$270,000
Accum. Depr.—Equipment	(100,000)	(210,000)
Equipment, net	$ 80,000	$ 60,000
Buildings	$ 380,000	$400,000
Accum. Depr.—Buildings	(100,000)	(285,000)
Buildings, net	$ 280,000	$115,000

Refer to the balance sheet data above from Anders Company. During 2015, equipment with a book value of $40,000 and an original cost of $210,000 was sold at a loss of $3,000.

1. How much cash did Anders receive from the sale of equipment?
2. How much depreciation expense was recorded on equipment during 2015?
3. What was the cost of new equipment purchased by Anders during 2015?

QS 12-6
Indirect: Computing investing cash flows
P2

Refer to the balance sheet data above from Anders Company. During 2015, a building with a book value of $70,000 and an original cost of $300,000 was sold at a gain of $60,000.

1. How much cash did Anders receive from the sale of the building?
2. How much depreciation expense was recorded on buildings during 2015?
3. What was the cost of buildings purchased by Anders during 2015?

QS 12-7
Computing cash from asset sales
P3

The following selected information is from Ellerby Company's comparative balance sheets.

At December 31	2015	2014
Furniture	$132,000	$ 184,500
Accumulated depreciation—Furniture	(88,700)	(110,700)

The income statement reports depreciation expense for the year of $18,000. Also, furniture costing $52,500 was sold for its book value. Compute the cash received from the sale of furniture.

QS 12-8
Computing cash flows from investing
P3

Compute cash flows from investing activities using the following company information.

Sale of short-term investments	$ 6,000
Cash collections from customers	16,000
Purchase of used equipment	5,000
Depreciation expense	2,000

QS 12-9
Computing financing cash flows
P3

The following selected information is from Princeton Company's comparative balance sheets.

At December 31	2015	2014
Common stock, $10 par value	$105,000	$100,000
Paid-in capital in excess of par	567,000	342,000
Retained earnings	313,500	287,500

The company's net income for the year ended December 31, 2015, was $48,000.

1. Compute the cash received from the sale of its common stock during 2015.
2. Compute the cash paid for dividends during 2015.

QS 12-10
Computing cash flows from financing
P3

Compute cash flows from financing activities using the following company information.

Additional short-term borrowings	$20,000
Purchase of short-term investments	5,000
Cash dividends paid	16,000
Interest paid	8,000

QS 12-11
Indirect: Computing cash from operations
P2

Use the following balance sheets and income statement to answer QS 12-11 through QS 12-16.

CRUZ, INC.
Comparative Balance Sheets
December 31, 2015

	2015	2014
Assets		
Cash	$ 94,800	$ 24,000
Accounts receivable, net	41,000	51,000
Inventory	85,800	95,800
Prepaid expenses	5,400	4,200
Total current assets	227,000	175,000
Furniture	109,000	119,000
Accum. depreciation—Furniture	(17,000)	(9,000)
Total assets	$319,000	$285,000
Liabilities and Equity		
Accounts payable	$ 15,000	$ 21,000
Wages payable	9,000	5,000
Income taxes payable	1,400	2,600
Total current liabilities	25,400	28,600
Notes payable (long-term)	29,000	69,000
Total liabilities	54,400	97,600
Equity		
Common stock, $5 par value	229,000	179,000
Retained earnings	35,600	8,400
Total liabilities and equity	$319,000	$285,000

CRUZ, INC.
Income Statement
For Year Ended December 31, 2015

Sales		$488,000
Cost of goods sold		314,000
Gross profit		174,000
Operating expenses		
Depreciation expense	$37,600	
Other expenses	89,100	126,700
Income before taxes		47,300
Income taxes expense		17,300
Net income		$ 30,000

Required

Use the indirect method to prepare the cash provided or used from operating activities section only of the statement of cash flows for this company.

QS 12-12
Computing cash from asset sales
P3

Refer to the data in QS 12-11.
Furniture costing $55,000 is sold at its book value in 2015. Acquisitions of furniture total $45,000 cash, on which no depreciation is necessary because it is acquired at year-end. What is the cash inflow related to the sale of furniture?

QS 12-13
Computing financing cash outflows
P3

Refer to the data in QS 12-11.

1. Assume that all common stock is issued for cash. What amount of cash dividends is paid during 2015?
2. Assume that no additional notes payable are issued in 2015. What cash amount is paid to reduce the notes payable balance in 2015?

QS 12-14[B]
Direct: Computing cash received from customers
P5

Refer to the data in QS 12-11.

1. How much cash is received from sales to customers for year 2015?
2. What is the net increase or decrease in cash for year 2015?

QS 12-15[B]
Direct: Computing operating cash outflows
P5

Refer to the data in QS 12-11.

1. How much cash is paid to acquire inventory during year 2015?
2. How much cash is paid for "other expenses" during year 2015? (*Hint:* Examine prepaid expenses and wages payable.)

QS 12-16[B]
Direct: Computing cash from operations
P5

Refer to the data in QS 12-11.
Use the direct method to prepare the cash provided or used from operating activities section only of the statement of cash flows for this company.

QS 12-17
Analyses of sources and uses of cash
A1

Financial data from three competitors in the same industry follow.

1. Which of the three competitors is in the strongest position as shown by its statement of cash flows?
2. Analyze and compare the strength of Moore's cash flow on total assets ratio to that of Sykes.

	A	B	C	D
1	($ thousands)	Moore	Sykes	Kritch
2	Cash provided (used) by operating activities	$ 70,000	$ 60,000	$ (24,000)
3	Cash provided (used) by investing activities			
4	Proceeds from sale of operating assets			26,000
5	Purchase of operating assets	(28,000)	(34,000)	
6	Cash provided (used) by financing activities			
7	Proceeds from issuance of debt			23,000
8	Repayment of debt	(6,000)		
9	Net increase (decrease) in cash	$ 36,000	$ 26,000	$ 25,000
10				
11	Average total assets	$790,000	$625,000	$300,000

QS 12-18A
Noncash accounts on a spreadsheet
P4

When a spreadsheet for a statement of cash flows is prepared, all changes in noncash balance sheet accounts are fully explained on the spreadsheet. Explain how these noncash balance sheet accounts are used to fully account for cash flows on a spreadsheet.

QS 12-19
Indirect: Preparation of statement of cash flows
P1 P2 P3

Use the following financial statements and additional information to (1) prepare a statement of cash flows for the year ended December 31, 2016, using the *indirect method,* and (2) analyze and briefly discuss the statement prepared in part 1 with special attention to operating activities and to the company's cash level.

MONTGOMERY INC.
Comparative Balance Sheets
December 31, 2016 and 2015

	2016	2015
Assets		
Cash	$ 30,400	$ 30,550
Accounts receivable, net	10,050	12,150
Inventory	90,100	70,150
Total current assets	130,550	112,850
Equipment	49,900	41,500
Accum. depreciation—Equipment	(22,500)	(15,300)
Total assets	$157,950	$139,050
Liabilities and Equity		
Accounts payable	$ 23,900	$ 25,400
Salaries payable	500	600
Total current liabilities	24,400	26,000
Equity		
Common stock, no par value	110,000	100,000
Retained earnings	23,550	13,050
Total liabilities and equity	$157,950	$139,050

MONTGOMERY INC.
Income Statement
For Year Ended December 31, 2016

Sales		$45,575
Cost of goods sold		(18,950)
Gross profit		26,625
Operating expenses		
Depreciation expense	$7,200	
Other expenses	5,550	
Total operating expense		12,750
Income before taxes		13,875
Income tax expense		3,375
Net income		$10,500

Additional Information

a. No dividends are declared or paid in 2016.

b. Issued additional stock for $10,000 cash in 2016.

c. Purchased equipment for cash in 2016; no equipment was sold in 2016.

QS 12-20
International cash flow disclosures
C1

Answer each of the following questions related to international accounting standards.

1. Which method, indirect or direct, is acceptable for reporting operating cash flows under IFRS?

2. For each of the following four cash flows, identify whether it is reported under the operating, investing, or financing section (or some combination) within the indirect format of the statement of cash flows reported under IFRS and under U.S. GAAP.

Cash Flow Source	US GAAP Reporting	IFRS Reporting
a. Interest paid		
b. Dividends paid		
c. Interest received		
d. Dividends received		

connect

EXERCISES

Exercise 12-1
Indirect: Cash flow classification C1

The following transactions and events occurred during the year. Assuming that this company uses the *indirect method* to report cash provided by operating activities, indicate where each item would appear on its statement of cash flows by placing an *x* in the appropriate column.

	Statement of Cash Flows			Noncash Investing and Financing Activities	Not Reported on Statement or in Notes
	Operating Activities	Investing Activities	Financing Activities		
a. Declared and paid a cash dividend	____	____	____	____	____
b. Recorded depreciation expense	____	____	____	____	____
c. Paid cash to settle long-term note payable	____	____	____	____	____
d. Prepaid expenses increased in the year	____	____	____	____	____
e. Accounts receivable decreased in the year	____	____	____	____	____
f. Purchased land by issuing common stock	____	____	____	____	____
g. Inventory increased in the year	____	____	____	____	____
h. Sold equipment for cash, yielding a loss	____	____	____	____	____
i. Accounts payable decreased in the year	____	____	____	____	____
j. Income taxes payable increased in the year	____	____	____	____	____

Exercise 12-2
Indirect: Reporting cash flows from operations
P2

Hampton Company reports the following information for its recent calendar year. Prepare the operating activities section of the statement of cash flows for Hampton Company using the *indirect method.*

Income Statement Data		Selected Year-End Balance Sheet Data	
Sales	$160,000	Accounts receivable increase	$10,000
Expenses		Inventory decrease	16,000
Cost of goods sold	100,000	Salaries payable increase	1,000
Salaries expense	24,000		
Depreciation expense	12,000		
Net income	$ 24,000		

Exercise 12-3
Indirect: Reporting and interpreting cash flows from operations
P2

Arundel Company disclosed the following information for its recent calendar year.

Income Statement Data		Selected Year-End Balance Sheet Data	
Revenues	$100,000	Accounts receivable decrease	$24,000
Expenses		Purchased a machine for cash	10,000
Salaries expense	84,000	Salaries payable increase	18,000
Utilities expense	14,000	Other accrued liabilities decrease	8,000
Depreciation expense	14,600		
Other expenses	3,400		
Net loss	$(16,000)		

Required

1. Prepare the operating activities section of the statement of cash flows using the *indirect method.*
2. What were the major reasons that this company was able to report a net loss but positive cash flow from operations?
3. Of the potential causes of differences between cash flow from operations and net income, which are the most important to investors?

Exercise 12-4
Indirect: Cash flows from operating activities
P2

The following income statement and information about changes in noncash current assets and current liabilities are reported.

SONAD COMPANY Income Statement For Year Ended December 31, 2015		
Sales		$1,828,000
Cost of goods sold		991,000
Gross profit		837,000
Operating expenses		
Salaries expense	$245,535	
Depreciation expense	44,200	
Rent expense	49,600	
Amortization expenses—Patents	4,200	
Utilities expense	18,125	361,660
		475,340
Gain on sale of equipment		6,200
Net income		$ 481,540

Changes in current asset and current liability accounts for the year that relate to operations follow.

Accounts receivable	$30,500 increase	Accounts payable	$12,500 decrease
Inventory	25,000 increase	Salaries payable	3,500 decrease

Required

Prepare only the cash flows from operating activities section of the statement of cash flows using the *indirect method*.

Exercise 12-5
Indirect: Cash flows from operating activities
P2

Fitz Company reports the following information. Use the *indirect method* to prepare only the operating activities section of its statement of cash flows for the year ended December 31, 2015.

Selected 2015 Income Statement Data		Selected Year-End 2015 Balance Sheet Data	
Net income	$374,000	Accounts receivable decrease	$17,100
Depreciation expense	44,000	Inventory decrease	42,000
Amortization expense	7,200	Prepaid expenses increase	4,700
Gain on sale of plant assets	6,000	Accounts payable decrease	8,200
		Salaries payable increase	1,200

Exercise 12-6
Indirect: Cash flow from operations
P2

Salud Company reports the following information. Use the *indirect method* to prepare only the operating activities section of its statement of cash flows for the year ended December 31, 2015.

Selected 2015 Income Statement Data		Selected Year-End 2015 Balance Sheet Data	
Net income	$400,000	Accounts receivable increase	$40,000
Depreciation expense	80,000	Prepaid expenses decrease	12,000
Gain on sale of machinery	20,000	Accounts payable increase	6,000
		Wages payable decrease	2,000

Exercise 12-7
Cash flows from investing activities
P3

Use the following information to determine this company's cash flows from investing activities.

a. Equipment with a book value of $65,300 and an original cost of $133,000 was sold at a loss of $14,000.

b. Paid $89,000 cash for a new truck.

c. Sold land costing $154,000 for $198,000 cash, yielding a gain of $44,000.

d. Long-term investments in stock were sold for $60,800 cash, yielding a gain of $4,150.

Exercise 12-8
Cash flows from financing activities
P3

Use the following information to determine this company's cash flows from financing activities.

a. Net income was $35,000.
b. Issued common stock for $64,000 cash.
c. Paid cash dividend of $14,600.
d. Paid $50,000 cash to settle a note payable at its $50,000 maturity value.
e. Paid $12,000 cash to acquire its treasury stock.
f. Purchased equipment for $39,000 cash.

Exercise 12-9
Indirect: Statement of cash flows under IFRS
P1

Peugeot S.A. reports the following financial information for the year ended December 31, 2011 (euros in millions). Prepare its statement of cash flows under the *indirect method*. (*Hint:* Each line item below is titled, and any necessary parentheses added, as it is reported in the statement of cash flows.)

Net income	€ 784	Cash paid for purchases of treasury stock	€ (199)
Depreciation and amortization	3,037	Cash paid for other financing activities	(2,282)
Gains on disposals and other	(883)	Cash from disposal of plant assets and intangibles	189
Net increase in current operating assets	(1,183)	Cash paid for plant assets and intangibles	(3,921)
Cash paid for dividends	(290)	Cash and cash equivalents, December 31, 2010	10,442

Exercise 12-10
Analyses of cash flow on total assets A1

A company reported average total assets of $1,240,000 in 2014 and $1,510,000 in 2015. Its net operating cash flow was $102,920 in 2014 and $138,920 in 2015. Calculate its cash flow on total assets ratio for both years. Comment on the results and any change in performance.

Exercise 12-11
Indirect: Preparation of statement of cash flows
P1 P2 P3 A1

The following financial statements and additional information are reported.

IKIBAN INC.
Comparative Balance Sheets
June 30, 2015 and 2014

	2015	2014
Assets		
Cash	$ 87,500	$ 44,000
Accounts receivable, net	65,000	51,000
Inventory	63,800	86,500
Prepaid expenses	4,400	5,400
Total current assets	220,700	186,900
Equipment	124,000	115,000
Accum. depreciation—Equipment	(27,000)	(9,000)
Total assets	$317,700	$292,900
Liabilities and Equity		
Accounts payable	$ 25,000	$ 30,000
Wages payable	6,000	15,000
Income taxes payable	3,400	3,800
Total current liabilities	34,400	48,800
Notes payable (long term)	30,000	60,000
Total liabilities	64,400	108,800
Equity		
Common stock, $5 par value	220,000	160,000
Retained earnings	33,300	24,100
Total liabilities and equity	$317,700	$292,900

IKIBAN INC.
Income Statement
For Year Ended June 30, 2015

Sales		$678,000
Cost of goods sold		411,000
Gross profit		267,000
Operating expenses		
Depreciation expense	$58,600	
Other expenses	67,000	
Total operating expenses		125,600
		141,400
Other gains (losses)		
Gain on sale of equipment		2,000
Income before taxes		143,400
Income taxes expense		43,890
Net income		$ 99,510

Additional Information

a. A $30,000 note payable is retired at its $30,000 carrying (book) value in exchange for cash.
b. The only changes affecting retained earnings are net income and cash dividends paid.

Check (*b*) Cash paid for dividends, $90,310

c. New equipment is acquired for $57,600 cash.
d. Received cash for the sale of equipment that had cost $48,600, yielding a $2,000 gain.
e. Prepaid Expenses and Wages Payable relate to Other Expenses on the income statement.
f. All purchases and sales of inventory are on credit.

(*d*) Cash received from equip. sale, $10,000

Required

1. Prepare a statement of cash flows for the year ended June 30, 2015, using the *indirect method.*
2. Compute the company's cash flow on total assets ratio for its fiscal year 2015.

Exercise 12-12[B]
Direct: Preparation of statement of cash flows
P1 P3 P5

Refer to the information in Exercise 12-11. Using the *direct method,* prepare the statement of cash flows for the year ended June 30, 2015.

Exercise 12-13
Indirect: Cash flows spreadsheet
P4

Complete the following spreadsheet in preparation of the statement of cash flows. (The statement of cash flows is not required.) Prepare the spreadsheet as in Exhibit 12A.1; report operating activities under the *indirect method.* Identify the debits and credits in the Analysis of Changes columns with letters that correspond to the following transactions and events *a* through *h.*

a. Net income for the year was $100,000.
b. Dividends of $80,000 cash were declared and paid.
c. Scoreteck's only noncash expense was $70,000 of depreciation.
d. The company purchased plant assets for $70,000 cash.
e. Notes payable of $20,000 were issued for $20,000 cash.
f. Change in accounts receivable.
g. Change in inventory.
h. Change in accounts payable.

	A	B	C	D	E	F	G
1	SCORETECK CORPORATION						
2	Spreadsheet for Statement of Cash Flows—Indirect Method						
3	For Year Ended December 31, 2015						
4				Analysis of Changes			
5		Dec. 31, 2014		Debit		Credit	Dec. 31, 2015
6	**Balance Sheet—Debit Bal. Accounts**						
7	Cash	$ 80,000					$ 60,000
8	Accounts receivable	120,000					190,000
9	Inventory	250,000					230,000
10	Plant assets	600,000					670,000
11		$1,050,000					$1,150,000
12	**Balance Sheet—Credit Bal. Accounts**						
13	Accumulated depreciation	$ 100,000					$ 170,000
14	Accounts payable	150,000					140,000
15	Notes payable	370,000					390,000
16	Common stock	200,000					200,000
17	Retained earnings	230,000					250,000
18		$1,050,000					$1,150,000
19	**Statement of Cash Flows**						
20	Operating activities						
21	Net income						
22	Increase in accounts receivable						
23	Decrease in inventory						
24	Decrease in accounts payable						
25	Depreciation expense						
26	Investing activities						
27	Cash paid to purchase plant assets						
28	Financing activities						
29	Cash paid for dividends						
30	Cash from issuance of notes						
31							

Exercise 12-14[B]
Direct: Cash flow classification
C1 P5

The following transactions and events occurred during the year. Assuming that this company uses the *direct method* to report cash provided by operating activities, indicate where each item would appear on the statement of cash flows by placing an *x* in the appropriate column.

	Statement of Cash Flows			Noncash Investing and Financing Activities	Not Reported on Statement or in Notes
	Operating Activities	Investing Activities	Financing Activities		
a. Retired long-term notes payable by issuing common stock	____	____	____	____	____
b. Paid cash to acquire inventory	____	____	____	____	____
c. Sold inventory for cash	____	____	____	____	____
d. Paid cash dividend that was declared in a prior period	____	____	____	____	____
e. Accepted six-month note receivable in exchange for plant assets	____	____	____	____	____
f. Recorded depreciation expense	____	____	____	____	____
g. Paid cash to acquire treasury stock	____	____	____	____	____
h. Collected cash from sales	____	____	____	____	____
i. Borrowed cash from bank by signing a nine-month note payable	____	____	____	____	____
j. Paid cash to purchase a patent	____	____	____	____	____

Exercise 12-15[B]
Direct: Computation of cash flows
P5

For each of the following three separate cases, use the information provided about the calendar-year 2016 operations of Sahim Company to compute the required cash flow information.

Case X: Compute cash received from customers:	
Sales	$515,000
Accounts receivable, December 31, 2015	27,200
Accounts receivable, December 31, 2016	33,600
Case Y: Compute cash paid for rent:	
Rent expense	$139,800
Rent payable, December 31, 2015	7,800
Rent payable, December 31, 2016	6,200
Case Z: Compute cash paid for inventory:	
Cost of goods sold	$525,000
Inventory, December 31, 2015	158,600
Accounts payable, December 31, 2015	66,700
Inventory, December 31, 2016	130,400
Accounts payable, December 31, 2016	82,000

Exercise 12-16[B]
Direct: Cash flows from operating activities P5

Refer to the information about Sonad Company in Exercise 12-4. Use the *direct method* to prepare only the cash provided or used by operating activities section of the statement of cash flows for this company.

Exercise 12-17[B]
Direct: Preparation of statement of cash flows and supporting note
P1 P3 P5

Use the following information about the cash flows of Ferron Company to prepare a complete statement of cash flows (*direct method*) for the year ended December 31, 2015. Use a note disclosure for any noncash investing and financing activities.

Cash and cash equivalents balance, December 31, 2014	$ 40,000
Cash and cash equivalents balance, December 31, 2015	148,000
Cash received as interest	3,500
Cash paid for salaries	76,500

[continued on next page]

[continued from previous page]

Bonds payable retired by issuing common stock (no gain or loss on retirement)	185,500
Cash paid to retire long-term notes payable	100,000
Cash received from sale of equipment	60,250
Cash received in exchange for six-month note payable	35,000
Land purchased by issuing long-term note payable	105,250
Cash paid for store equipment	24,750
Cash dividends paid	10,000
Cash paid for other expenses	20,000
Cash received from customers	495,000
Cash paid for inventory	254,500

Exercise 12-18[B]
Direct: Preparation of statement of cash flows from Cash T-account
P1 P3 P5

The following summarized Cash T-account reflects the total debits and total credits to the Cash account of Thomas Corporation for calendar-year 2015.

1. Use this information to prepare a complete statement of cash flows for year 2015. The cash provided or used by operating activities should be reported using the *direct method.*
2. Refer to the statement of cash flows prepared for part 1 to answer the following questions *a* through *d*: (*a*) Which section—operating, investing, or financing—shows the largest cash (i) inflow and (ii) outflow? (*b*) What is the largest individual item among the investing cash outflows? (*c*) Are the cash proceeds larger from issuing notes or issuing stock? (*d*) Does the company have a net cash inflow or outflow from borrowing activities?

Accounting System:
File Edit Maintain Tasks Analysis Options Reports Window Help

Cash			
Balance, Dec. 31, 2014	333,000		
Receipts from customers	5,000,000	Payments for inventory	2,590,000
Receipts from dividends	208,400	Payments for wages	550,000
Receipts from land sale	220,000	Payments for rent	320,000
Receipts from machinery sale	710,000	Payments for interest	218,000
Receipts from issuing stock	1,540,000	Payments for taxes	450,000
Receipts from borrowing	3,600,000	Payments for machinery	2,236,000
		Payments for long-term investments	1,260,000
		Payments for note payable	386,000
		Payments for dividends	500,000
		Payments for treasury stock	218,000
Balance, Dec. 31, 2015	$?		

Sales Purchases General Ledger Payroll Inventory Company Analysis

connect

PROBLEM SET A

Problem 12-1A
Indirect: Computing cash flows from operations
P2

Lansing Company's 2015 income statement and selected balance sheet data (for current assets and current liabilities) at December 31, 2014 and 2015, follow.

LANSING COMPANY
Income Statement
For Year Ended December 31, 2015

Sales revenue		$97,200
Expenses		
Cost of goods sold		42,000
Depreciation expense		12,000
Salaries expense		18,000
Rent expense		9,000
Insurance expense		3,800
Interest expense		3,600
Utilities expense		2,800
Net income		$ 6,000

LANSING COMPANY
Selected Balance Sheet Accounts

At December 31	2015	2014
Accounts receivable	$5,600	$5,800
Inventory	1,980	1,540
Accounts payable	4,400	4,600
Salaries payable	880	700
Utilities payable	220	160
Prepaid insurance	260	280
Prepaid rent	220	180

Required

Prepare the cash flows from operating activities section only of the company's 2015 statement of cash flows using the *indirect method.*

Check Cash from operating activities, $17,780

Problem 12-2A[B]
Direct: Computing cash flows from operations
P5

Refer to the information in Problem 12-1A.

Required

Prepare the cash flows from operating activities section only of the company's 2015 statement of cash flows using the *direct method.*

Problem 12-3A
Indirect: Statement of cash flows
A1 P1 P2 P3

Forten Company, a merchandiser, recently completed its calendar-year 2015 operations. For the year, (1) all sales are credit sales, (2) all credits to Accounts Receivable reflect cash receipts from customers, (3) all purchases of inventory are on credit, (4) all debits to Accounts Payable reflect cash payments for inventory, and (5) Other Expenses are paid in advance and are initially debited to Prepaid Expenses. The company's income statement and balance sheets follow.

FORTEN COMPANY
Comparative Balance Sheets
December 31, 2015 and 2014

	2015	2014
Assets		
Cash	$ 49,800	$ 73,500
Accounts receivable	65,810	50,625
Inventory	275,656	251,800
Prepaid expenses	1,250	1,875
Total current assets	392,516	377,800
Equipment	157,500	108,000
Accum. depreciation—Equipment	(36,625)	(46,000)
Total assets	$513,391	$439,800
Liabilities and Equity		
Accounts payable	$ 53,141	$114,675
Short-term notes payable	10,000	6,000
Total current liabilities	63,141	120,675
Long-term notes payable	65,000	48,750
Total liabilities	128,141	169,425
Equity		
Common stock, $5 par value	162,750	150,250
Paid-in capital in excess of par, common stock	37,500	0
Retained earnings	185,000	120,125
Total liabilities and equity	$513,391	$439,800

FORTEN COMPANY
Income Statement
For Year Ended December 31, 2015

Sales		$582,500
Cost of goods sold		285,000
Gross profit		297,500
Operating expenses		
Depreciation expense	$ 20,750	
Other expenses	132,400	153,150
Other gains (losses)		
Loss on sale of equipment		(5,125)
Income before taxes		139,225
Income taxes expense		24,250
Net income		$114,975

Additional Information on Year 2015 Transactions

a. The loss on the cash sale of equipment was $5,125 (details in *b*).
b. Sold equipment costing $46,875, with accumulated depreciation of $30,125, for $11,625 cash.
c. Purchased equipment costing $96,375 by paying $30,000 cash and signing a long-term note payable for the balance.
d. Borrowed $4,000 cash by signing a short-term note payable.
e. Paid $50,125 cash to reduce the long-term notes payable.
f. Issued 2,500 shares of common stock for $20 cash per share.
g. Declared and paid cash dividends of $50,100.

Required

Check Cash from operating activities, $40,900

1. Prepare a complete statement of cash flows; report its operating activities using the *indirect method.* Disclose any noncash investing and financing activities in a note.

Analysis Component

2. Analyze and discuss the statement of cash flows prepared in part 1, giving special attention to the wisdom of the cash dividend payment.

Refer to the information reported about Forten Company in Problem 12-3A.

Problem 12-4A[A]
Indirect: Cash flows spreadsheet
P1 P2 P3 P4

Required

Prepare a complete statement of cash flows using a spreadsheet as in Exhibit 12A.1; report its operating activities using the *indirect method*. Identify the debits and credits in the Analysis of Changes columns with letters that correspond to the following list of transactions and events.

a. Net income was $114,975.
b. Accounts receivable increased.
c. Inventory increased.
d. Prepaid expenses decreased.
e. Accounts payable decreased.
f. Depreciation expense was $20,750.
g. Sold equipment costing $46,875, with accumulated depreciation of $30,125, for $11,625 cash. This yielded a loss of $5,125.
h. Purchased equipment costing $96,375 by paying $30,000 cash and **(i.)** by signing a long-term note payable for the balance.
j. Borrowed $4,000 cash by signing a short-term note payable.
k. Paid $50,125 cash to reduce the long-term notes payable.
l. Issued 2,500 shares of common stock for $20 cash per share.
m. Declared and paid cash dividends of $50,100.

Check Analysis of Changes column totals, $600,775

Refer to Forten Company's financial statements and related information in Problem 12-3A.

Problem 12-5A[B]
Direct: Statement of cash flows P1 P3 P5

Required

Prepare a complete statement of cash flows; report its operating activities according to the *direct method*. Disclose any noncash investing and financing activities in a note.

Check Cash used in financing activities, $(46,225)

Golden Corp., a merchandiser, recently completed its 2015 operations. For the year, (1) all sales are credit sales, (2) all credits to Accounts Receivable reflect cash receipts from customers, (3) all purchases of inventory are on credit, (4) all debits to Accounts Payable reflect cash payments for inventory, (5) Other Expenses are all cash expenses, and (6) any change in Income Taxes Payable reflects the accrual and cash payment of taxes. The company's balance sheets and income statement follow.

Problem 12-6A
Indirect: Statement of cash flows
P1 P2 P3

GOLDEN CORPORATION
Comparative Balance Sheets
December 31, 2015 and 2014

	2015	2014
Assets		
Cash	$ 164,000	$107,000
Accounts receivable	83,000	71,000
Inventory	601,000	526,000
Total current assets	848,000	704,000
Equipment	335,000	299,000
Accum. depreciation—Equipment	(158,000)	(104,000)
Total assets	$1,025,000	$899,000
Liabilities and Equity		
Accounts payable	$ 87,000	$ 71,000
Income taxes payable	28,000	25,000
Total current liabilities	115,000	96,000
Equity		
Common stock, $2 par value	592,000	568,000
Paid-in capital in excess of par value, common stock	196,000	160,000
Retained earnings	122,000	75,000
Total liabilities and equity	$1,025,000	$899,000

GOLDEN CORPORATION
Income Statement
For Year Ended December 31, 2015

Sales		$1,792,000
Cost of goods sold		1,086,000
Gross profit		706,000
Operating expenses		
Depreciation expense	$ 54,000	
Other expenses	494,000	548,000
Income before taxes		158,000
Income taxes expense		22,000
Net income		$ 136,000

Additional Information on Year 2015 Transactions

a. Purchased equipment for $36,000 cash.

b. Issued 12,000 shares of common stock for $5 cash per share.

c. Declared and paid $89,000 in cash dividends.

Required

Check Cash from operating activities, $122,000

Prepare a complete statement of cash flows; report its cash inflows and cash outflows from operating activities according to the *indirect method.*

Problem 12-7A[A]
Indirect: Cash flows spreadsheet
P1 P2 P3 P4

Refer to the information reported about Golden Corporation in Problem 12-6A.

Required

Prepare a complete statement of cash flows using a spreadsheet as in Exhibit 12A.1; report operating activities under the *indirect method.* Identify the debits and credits in the Analysis of Changes columns with letters that correspond to the following list of transactions and events.

a. Net income was $136,000.

b. Accounts receivable increased.

c. Inventory increased.

d. Accounts payable increased.

e. Income taxes payable increased.

f. Depreciation expense was $54,000.

g. Purchased equipment for $36,000 cash.

h. Issued 12,000 shares at $5 cash per share.

i. Declared and paid $89,000 of cash dividends.

Check Analysis of Changes column totals, $481,000

Problem 12-8A[B]
Direct: Statement of cash flows
P1 P3 P5

Refer to Golden Corporation's financial statements and related information in Problem 12-6A.

Required

Prepare a complete statement of cash flows; report its cash flows from operating activities according to the *direct method.*

Check Cash used in financing activities, $(29,000)

PROBLEM SET B

Problem 12-1B
Indirect: Computing cash flows from operations
P2

Salt Lake Company's 2015 income statement and selected balance sheet data (for current assets and current liabilities) at December 31, 2014 and 2015, follow.

SALT LAKE COMPANY
Income Statement
For Year Ended December 31, 2015

Sales revenue	$156,000
Expenses	
Cost of goods sold	72,000
Depreciation expense	32,000
Salaries expense	20,000
Rent expense	5,000
Insurance expense	2,600
Interest expense	2,400
Utilities expense	2,000
Net income	$ 20,000

SALT LAKE COMPANY
Selected Balance Sheet Accounts

At December 31	2015	2014
Accounts receivable	$3,600	$3,000
Inventory	860	980
Accounts payable	2,400	2,600
Salaries payable	900	600
Utilities payable	200	0
Prepaid insurance	140	180
Prepaid rent	100	200

Required

Prepare the cash flows from operating activities section only of the company's 2015 statement of cash flows using the *indirect method*.

Check Cash from operating activities, $51,960

Problem 12-2B[B]
Direct: Computing cash flows from operations
P5

Refer to the information in Problem 12-1B.

Required

Prepare the cash flows from operating activities section only of the company's 2015 statement of cash flows using the *direct method*.

Problem 12-3B
Indirect: Statement of cash flows
A1 P1 P2 P3

Gazelle Corporation, a merchandiser, recently completed its calendar-year 2015 operations. For the year, (1) all sales are credit sales, (2) all credits to Accounts Receivable reflect cash receipts from customers, (3) all purchases of inventory are on credit, (4) all debits to Accounts Payable reflect cash payments for inventory, and (5) Other Expenses are paid in advance and are initially debited to Prepaid Expenses. The company's balance sheets and income statement follow.

GAZELLE CORPORATION
Comparative Balance Sheets
December 31, 2015 and 2014

	2015	2014
Assets		
Cash	$123,450	$ 61,550
Accounts receivable	77,100	80,750
Inventory	240,600	250,700
Prepaid expenses	15,100	17,000
Total current assets	456,250	410,000
Equipment	262,250	200,000
Accum. depreciation—Equipment	(110,750)	(95,000)
Total assets	$607,750	$515,000
Liabilities and Equity		
Accounts payable	$ 17,750	$102,000
Short-term notes payable	15,000	10,000
Total current liabilities	32,750	112,000
Long-term notes payable	100,000	77,500
Total liabilities	132,750	189,500
Equity		
Common stock, $5 par	215,000	200,000
Paid-in capital in excess of par, common stock	30,000	0
Retained earnings	230,000	125,500
Total liabilities and equity	$607,750	$515,000

GAZELLE CORPORATION
Income Statement
For Year Ended December 31, 2015

Sales		$1,185,000
Cost of goods sold		595,000
Gross profit		590,000
Operating expenses		
Depreciation expense	$ 38,600	
Other expenses	362,850	
Total operating expenses		401,450
		188,550
Other gains (losses)		
Loss on sale of equipment		(2,100)
Income before taxes		186,450
Income taxes expense		28,350
Net income		$ 158,100

Additional Information on Year 2015 Transactions

a. The loss on the cash sale of equipment was $2,100 (details in *b*).
b. Sold equipment costing $51,000, with accumulated depreciation of $22,850, for $26,050 cash.
c. Purchased equipment costing $113,250 by paying $43,250 cash and signing a long-term note payable for the balance.
d. Borrowed $5,000 cash by signing a short-term note payable.
e. Paid $47,500 cash to reduce the long-term notes payable.
f. Issued 3,000 shares of common stock for $15 cash per share.
g. Declared and paid cash dividends of $53,600.

Required

Check Cash from operating activities, $130,200

1. Prepare a complete statement of cash flows; report its operating activities using the *indirect method.* Disclose any noncash investing and financing activities in a note.

Analysis Component

2. Analyze and discuss the statement of cash flows prepared in part 1, giving special attention to the wisdom of the cash dividend payment.

Problem 12-4B[A]
Indirect: Cash flows spreadsheet
P1 P2 P3 P4

Refer to the information reported about Gazelle Corporation in Problem 12-3B.

Required

Prepare a complete statement of cash flows using a spreadsheet as in Exhibit 12A.1; report its operating activities using the *indirect method.* Identify the debits and credits in the Analysis of Changes columns with letters that correspond to the following list of transactions and events.

a. Net income was $158,100.
b. Accounts receivable decreased.
c. Inventory decreased.
d. Prepaid expenses decreased.
e. Accounts payable decreased.
f. Depreciation expense was $38,600.
g. Sold equipment costing $51,000, with accumulated depreciation of $22,850, for $26,050 cash. This yielded a loss of $2,100.
h. Purchased equipment costing $113,250 by paying $43,250 cash and **(i.)** by signing a long-term note payable for the balance.
j. Borrowed $5,000 cash by signing a short-term note payable.
k. Paid $47,500 cash to reduce the long-term notes payable.
l. Issued 3,000 shares of common stock for $15 cash per share.
m. Declared and paid cash dividends of $53,600.

Check Analysis of Changes column totals, $681,950

Problem 12-5B[B]
Direct: Statement of cash flows
P1 P3 P5

Check Cash used in financing activities, $(51,100)

Refer to Gazelle Corporation's financial statements and related information in Problem 12-3B.

Required

Prepare a complete statement of cash flows; report its operating activities according to the *direct method.* Disclose any noncash investing and financing activities in a note.

Problem 12-6B
Indirect: Statement of cash flows
P1 P2 P3

Satu Company, a merchandiser, recently completed its 2015 operations. For the year, (1) all sales are credit sales, (2) all credits to Accounts Receivable reflect cash receipts from customers, (3) all purchases of inventory are on credit, (4) all debits to Accounts Payable reflect cash payments for inventory, (5) Other Expenses are cash expenses, and (6) any change in Income Taxes Payable reflects the accrual and cash payment of taxes. The company's income statement and balance sheets follow.

SATU COMPANY
Comparative Balance Sheets
December 31, 2015 and 2014

	2015	2014
Assets		
Cash	$ 58,750	$ 28,400
Accounts receivable	20,222	25,860
Total current assets	78,972	54,260
Inventory	165,667	140,320
Equipment	107,750	77,500
Accum. depreciation—Equipment	(46,700)	(31,000)
Total assets	$305,689	$241,080
Liabilities and Equity		
Accounts payable	$ 20,372	$157,530
Income taxes payable	2,100	6,100
Total current liabilities	22,472	163,630
Equity		
Common stock, $5 par value	40,000	25,000
Paid-in capital in excess of par, common stock	68,000	20,000
Retained earnings	175,217	32,450
Total liabilities and equity	$305,689	$241,080

SATU COMPANY
Income Statement
For Year Ended December 31, 2015

Sales		$750,800
Cost of goods sold		269,200
Gross profit		481,600
Operating expenses		
Depreciation expense	$ 15,700	
Other expenses	173,933	189,633
Income before taxes		291,967
Income taxes expense		89,200
Net income		$202,767

Additional Information on Year 2015 Transactions

a. Purchased equipment for $30,250 cash.
b. Issued 3,000 shares of common stock for $21 cash per share.
c. Declared and paid $60,000 of cash dividends.

Required

Prepare a complete statement of cash flows; report its cash inflows and cash outflows from operating activities according to the *indirect method.*

Check Cash from operating activities, $57,600

Problem 12-7B[A]
Indirect: Cash flows spreadsheet
P1 P2 P3 P4

Refer to the information reported about Satu Company in Problem 12-6B.

Required

Prepare a complete statement of cash flows using a spreadsheet as in Exhibit 12A.1; report operating activities under the *indirect method.* Identify the debits and credits in the Analysis of Changes columns with letters that correspond to the following list of transactions and events.

a. Net income was $202,767.
b. Accounts receivable decreased.
c. Inventory increased.
d. Accounts payable decreased.
e. Income taxes payable decreased.
f. Depreciation expense was $15,700.
g. Purchased equipment for $30,250 cash.
h. Issued 3,000 shares at $21 cash per share.
i. Declared and paid $60,000 of cash dividends.

Check Analysis of Changes column totals, $543,860

Problem 12-8B[B]
Direct: Statement of cash flows
P1 P3 P5

Refer to Satu Company's financial statements and related information in Problem 12-6B.

Required

Prepare a complete statement of cash flows; report its cash flows from operating activities according to the *direct method.*

Check Cash provided by financing activities, $3,000

SERIAL PROBLEM

Business Solutions

(Indirect)

P1 P2 P3

(This serial problem began in Chapter 1 and continues through most of the book. If previous chapter segments were not completed, the serial problem can begin at this point. It is helpful, but not necessary, to use the Working Papers that accompany the book.)

SP 12 Santana Rey, owner of Business Solutions, decides to prepare a statement of cash flows for her business. (Although the serial problem allowed for various ownership changes in earlier chapters, we will prepare the statement of cash flows using the following financial data.)

BUSINESS SOLUTIONS
Comparative Balance Sheets
December 31, 2015, and March 31, 2016

	Mar. 31, 2016	Dec. 31, 2015
Assets		
Cash	$ 68,057	$48,372
Accounts receivable	22,867	5,668
Inventory	704	0
Computer supplies	2,005	580
Prepaid insurance	1,110	1,665
Prepaid rent	825	825
Total current assets	95,568	57,110
Office equipment	8,000	8,000
Accumulated depreciation—Office equipment	(800)	(400)
Computer equipment	20,000	20,000
Accumulated depreciation—Computer equipment	(2,500)	(1,250)
Total assets	$120,268	$83,460
Liabilities and Equity		
Accounts payable	$ 0	$ 1,100
Wages payable	875	500
Unearned computer service revenue	0	1,500
Total current liabilities	875	3,100
Equity		
Common stock	98,000	73,000
Retained earnings	21,393	7,360
Total liabilities and equity	$120,268	$83,460

BUSINESS SOLUTIONS
Income Statement
For Three Months Ended March 31, 2016

Computer services revenue		$25,307
Net sales		18,693
Total revenue		44,000
Cost of goods sold	$14,052	
Depreciation expense—Office equipment	400	
Depreciation expense—Computer equipment	1,250	
Wages expense	3,250	
Insurance expense	555	
Rent expense	2,475	
Computer supplies expense	1,305	
Advertising expense	600	
Mileage expense	320	
Repairs expense—Computer	960	
Total expenses		25,167
Net income		$18,833

Required

Prepare a statement of cash flows for Business Solutions using the *indirect method* for the three months ended March 31, 2016. Recall that owner Santana Rey contributed $25,000 to the business in exchange for additional stock in the first quarter of 2016 and has received $4,800 in cash dividends.

Check Cash flows used by operations: $(515)

GENERAL LEDGER PROBLEM

Available in Connect

connect ACCOUNTING

The following General Ledger assignments highlight the impact, or lack thereof, on the statement of cash flows from summary journal entries derived from consecutive trial balances. Prepare summary journal entries reflecting changes in consecutive trial balances. Then prepare the statement of cash flows (direct method) from those entries. Finally, prepare the reconciliation to the indirect method for net cash provided (used) by operating activities.

GL 12-1 General Ledger assignment based on Exercise 12-11

GL 12-2 General Ledger assignment based on Problem 12-3

GL 12-3 General Ledger assignment based on Problem 12-6

Beyond the Numbers

REPORTING IN ACTION
A1
APPLE

BTN 12-1 Refer to **Apple**'s financial statements in Appendix A to answer the following.

1. Is Apple's statement of cash flows prepared under the direct method or the indirect method? How do you know?
2. For each fiscal year 2013, 2012, and 2011, is the amount of cash provided by operating activities more or less than the cash paid for dividends?
3. What is the largest amount in reconciling the difference between net income and cash flow from operating activities in fiscal 2013? In fiscal 2012? In fiscal 2011?
4. Identify the largest cash inflow and cash outflow for investing *and* for financing activities in fiscal 2013 and in fiscal 2012.

Fast Forward

5. Obtain Apple's financial statements for a fiscal year ending after September 28, 2013, from either its website (Apple.com) or the SEC's database (www.SEC.gov). Since September 28, 2013, what are Apple's largest cash outflows and cash inflows in the investing and in the financing sections of its statement of cash flows?

COMPARATIVE ANALYSIS
A1
APPLE
GOOGLE

BTN 12-2 Key figures for **Apple** and **Google** follow.

($ millions)	Apple			Google		
	Current Year	1 Year Prior	2 Years Prior	Current Year	1 Year Prior	2 Years Prior
Operating cash flows	$ 53,666	$ 50,856	$ 37,529	$ 18,659	$16,619	$14,565
Total assets.	207,000	176,064	116,371	110,920	93,798	72,574

Required

1. Compute the recent two years' cash flow on total assets ratios for Apple and Google.
2. What does the cash flow on total assets ratio measure?
3. Which company has the highest cash flow on total assets ratio for the periods shown?
4. Does the cash flow on total assets ratio reflect on the quality of earnings? Explain.

ETHICS CHALLENGE
C1 A1

BTN 12-3 Katie Murphy is preparing for a meeting with her banker. Her business is finishing its fourth year of operations. In the first year, it had negative cash flows from operations. In the second and third years, cash flows from operations were positive. However, inventory costs rose significantly in year 4, and cash flows from operations will probably be down 25%. Murphy wants to secure a line of credit from her banker as a financing buffer. From experience, she knows the banker will scrutinize operating cash flows for years 1 through 4 and will want a projected number for year 5. Murphy knows that a steady progression upward in operating cash flows for years 1 through 4 will help her case. She decides to use her discretion as owner and considers several business actions that will turn her operating cash flow in year 4 from a decrease to an increase.

Required

1. Identify two business actions Murphy might take to improve cash flows from operations.
2. Comment on the ethics and possible consequences of Murphy's decision to pursue these actions.

COMMUNICATING IN PRACTICE
C1

BTN 12-4 Your friend, Diana Wood, recently completed the second year of her business and just received annual financial statements from her accountant. Wood finds the income statement and balance sheet informative but does not understand the statement of cash flows. She says the first section is especially confusing because it contains a lot of additions and subtractions that do not make sense to her. Wood adds, "The income statement tells me the business is more profitable than last year and that's most important. If I want to know how cash changes, I can look at comparative balance sheets."

Required

Write a half-page memorandum to your friend explaining the purpose of the statement of cash flows. Speculate as to why the first section is so confusing and how it might be rectified.

TAKING IT TO THE NET

A1

BTN 12-5 Access the March 31, 2014, filing of the 10-K report (for year ending December 31, 2013) of **Mendocino Brewing Company, Inc.** (ticker: MENB), at www.SEC.gov.

Required

1. Does Mendocino Brewing use the direct or indirect method to construct its consolidated statement of cash flows?
2. For the year ended December 31, 2013, what is the largest item in reconciling the net income to net cash provided by operating activities?
3. In the recent two years, has the company been more successful in generating operating cash flows or in generating net income? Identify the figures to support the answer.
4. In the year ended December 31, 2013, what was the largest cash outflow for investing activities *and* for financing activities?
5. What item(s) does Mendocino Brewing report as supplementary cash flow information?
6. Does Mendocino Brewing report any noncash financing activities for 2013? Identify them, if any.

TEAMWORK IN ACTION

C1 A1 P2 P5

BTN 12-6 Team members are to coordinate and independently answer one question within each of the following three sections. Team members should then report to the team and confirm or correct teammates' answers.

1. Answer *one* of the following questions about the statement of cash flows.
   - **a.** What are this statement's reporting objectives?
   - **b.** What two methods are used to prepare it? Identify similarities and differences between them.
   - **c.** What steps are followed to prepare the statement?
   - **d.** What types of analyses are often made from this statement's information?
2. Identify and explain the adjustment from net income to obtain cash flows from operating activities using the indirect method for *one* of the following items.
   - **a.** Noncash operating revenues and expenses.
   - **b.** Nonoperating gains and losses.
   - **c.** Increases and decreases in noncash current assets.
   - **d.** Increases and decreases in current liabilities.

3.[B] Identify and explain the formula for computing cash flows from operating activities using the direct method for *one* of the following items.
   - **a.** Cash receipts from sales to customers.
   - **b.** Cash paid for inventory.
   - **c.** Cash paid for wages and operating expenses.
   - **d.** Cash paid for interest and taxes.

Note: For teams of more than four, some pairing within teams is necessary. Use as an in-class activity or as an assignment. If used in class, specify a time limit on each part. Conclude with reports to the entire class, using team rotation. Each team can prepare responses on a transparency.

ENTREPRENEURIAL DECISION

C1 A1

BTN 12-7 Review the chapter's opener involving **LSTN** and its entrepreneurial owner, Bridget Hilton.

Required

1. In a business such as LSTN, monitoring cash flow is always a priority. Even though it is off to a successful start and is growing with a positive net income, explain how cash flow can lag behind net income.
2. LSTN is a privately owned company. What are potential sources of financing for its future expansion?

BTN 12-8 Jenna and Matt Wilder are completing their second year operating Mountain High, a downhill ski area and resort. Mountain High reports a net loss of $(10,000) for its second year, which includes an $85,000 extraordinary loss from fire. This past year also involved major purchases of plant assets for renovation and expansion, yielding a year-end total asset amount of $800,000. Mountain High's net cash outflow for its second year is $(5,000); a summarized version of its statement of cash flows follows:

C1 A1

Net cash flow provided by operating activities	$295,000
Net cash flow used by investing activities	(310,000)
Net cash flow provided by financing activities	10,000

Required

Write a one-page memorandum to the Wilders evaluating Mountain High's current performance and assessing its future. Give special emphasis to cash flow data and their interpretation.

HITTING THE ROAD

C1

BTN 12-9 Visit **The Motley Fool**'s website (**Fool.com**). Enter the *Fool's School* (at *Fool.com/School*). Identify and select the link "How to Value Stocks." (This site might ask you to register with your email address; registration had been free and did grant access to articles on the site.)

Required

1. Click on "Introduction to Valuation Methods," and then "Cash-Flow-Based Valuations." How does the Fool's school define cash flow? What is the school's reasoning for this definition?
2. Per the school's instruction, why do analysts focus on earnings before interest and taxes (EBIT)?
3. Visit other links at this website that interest you such as "How to Read a Balance Sheet," or find out what the "Fool's Ratio" is. Write a half-page report on what you find.

GLOBAL DECISION

C1

Samsung
APPLE
GOOGLE

BTN 12-10 Key comparative information for **Samsung** (**www.Samsung.com**), which is a leading manufacturer of electronic consumer products, follows.

(₩ in millions)	Current Year	1 Year Prior	2 Years Prior
Operating cash flows	₩ 46,707,440	₩ 37,972,809	₩ 22,917,901
Total assets	214,075,018	181,071,570	155,800,263

Required

1. Compute the recent two years' cash flow on total assets ratio for Samsung.
2. How does Samsung's ratio compare to **Apple**'s and **Google**'s ratios from BTN 12-2?

ANSWERS TO MULTIPLE CHOICE QUIZ

1. b;

Net income	$15,200
Depreciation expense	10,000
Gain on sale of land	(3,000)
Increase in inventory	(1,500)
Increase in accounts payable	2,850
Net cash provided by operations	$23,550

2. c; Cash received from sale of machine is reported as an investing activity.
3. d; FASB requires cash interest paid to be reported under operating.
4. a; Cash paid for salaries and wages = $255,000 + $8,200 − $10,900 = $252,300
5. e; Increase in inventory = $112,000 − $105,000 = $7,000
   Increase in accounts payable = $101,300 − $98,500 = $2,800
   Cash paid for inventory = $545,000 + $7,000 − $2,800 = $549,200

chapter 13

Analysis of Financial Statements

Chapter Preview

BASICS OF ANALYSIS	HORIZONTAL ANALYSIS	VERTICAL ANALYSIS	RATIO ANALYSIS AND REPORTING
C1 Analysis: Its purpose, building blocks, and information needs	P1 Application of:	P2 Application of:	P3 Liquidity and efficiency
C2 Standards for comparisons, and analysis tools	Comparative balance sheets	Common-size balance sheet	Solvency
	Comparative income statements	Common-size income statement	Profitability
	Trend analysis	Common-size graphics	Market prospects
			A1 Analysis reports

Learning Objectives

CONCEPTUAL

C1 Explain the purpose and identify the building blocks of analysis.

C2 Describe standards for comparisons in analysis.

ANALYTICAL

A1 Summarize and report results of analysis.

A2 *Appendix 13A*—Explain the form and assess the content of a complete income statement.

PROCEDURAL

P1 Explain and apply methods of horizontal analysis.

P2 Describe and apply methods of vertical analysis.

P3 Define and apply ratio analysis.

CD1 WENN/Newscom

In Search of Truth

ALEXANDRIA, VA—In Shakespeare's Elizabethan comedy *As You Like It,* only the fool could speak truthfully to the king without getting his head lopped off. Inspired by Shakespeare's stage character, Tom and David Gardner vowed to become modern-day fools who tell it like it is. With under $10,000 in start-up money, the brothers launched **The Motley Fool (Fool.com).** And befitting of a Shakespearean play, the two say they are "dedicated to educating, amusing, and enriching individuals in search of the truth."

The Gardners do not fear the wrath of any king, real or fictional. They are intent on exposing the truth, as they see it, "that the financial world preys on ignorance and fear." As Tom explains, "There is such a great need in the general populace for financial information." Who can argue, given their brilliant success through practically every medium, including their website, radio shows, newspaper columns, online store, investment newsletters, and global expansion.

"The Motley Fool . . . is similar to what goes on in a library"

—Tom Gardner

Despite the brothers' best efforts, however, ordinary people still do not fully use information available in financial statements. For instance, discussions keep appearing on The Motley Fool's online bulletin board that can be easily resolved using reliable and published accounting data. So, it would seem that the Fools must continue their work of "educating and enriching" individuals and showing them the advantages of financial statement analysis.

Following The Motley Fool's objectives, this chapter introduces horizontal and vertical analyses—tools used to reveal crucial trends and insights from financial information. It also expands on ratio analysis, which gives insight into a company's financial condition and performance. By arming ourselves with the information contained in this chapter and the investment advice of The Motley Fool, *we* can be sure to not play the fool in today's financial world.

Sources: *Motley Fool website,* January 2015; *Washington Business Journal,* January 2011; *What to Do with Your Money Now,* June 2002; *USA Weekend,* July 2004; *Washington Post,* November 2007; *Money After 40,* April 2007

BASICS OF ANALYSIS

C1 Explain the purpose and identify the building blocks of analysis.

Financial statement analysis applies analytical tools to general-purpose financial statements and related data for making business decisions. It involves transforming accounting data into more useful information. Financial statement analysis reduces our reliance on hunches, guesses, and intuition as well as our uncertainty in decision making. It does not lessen the need for expert judgment; instead, it provides us an effective and systematic basis for making business decisions. This section describes the purpose of financial statement analysis, its information sources, the use of comparisons, and some issues in computations.

Purpose of Analysis

Internal users of accounting information are those involved in strategically managing and operating the company. They include managers, officers, internal auditors, consultants, budget directors, and market researchers. The purpose of financial statement analysis for these users is to provide strategic information to improve company efficiency and effectiveness in providing products and services.

Point: Financial statement analysis tools are also used for personal financial investment decisions.

External users of accounting information are *not* directly involved in running the company. They include shareholders, lenders, directors, customers, suppliers, regulators, lawyers, brokers, and the press. External users rely on financial statement analysis to make better and more informed decisions in pursuing their own goals.

Point: Financial statement analysis is a topic on the CPA, CMA, CIA, and CFA exams.

We can identify other uses of financial statement analysis. Shareholders and creditors assess company prospects to make investing and lending decisions. A board of directors analyzes financial statements in monitoring management's decisions. Employees and unions use financial statements in labor negotiations. Suppliers use financial statement information in establishing credit terms. Customers analyze financial statements in deciding whether to establish supply relationships. Public utilities set customer rates by analyzing financial statements. Auditors use financial statements in assessing the "fair presentation" of their clients' financial results. Analyst services such as **Dun & Bradstreet**, **Moody's**, and **Standard & Poor's** use financial statements in making buy-sell recommendations and in setting credit ratings. The common goal of these users is to evaluate company performance and financial condition. This includes evaluating (1) past and current performance, (2) current financial position, and (3) future performance and risk.

Building Blocks of Analysis

Financial statement analysis focuses on one or more elements of a company's financial condition or performance. Our analysis emphasizes four areas of inquiry—with varying degrees of importance. These four areas are described and illustrated in this chapter and are considered the *building blocks* of financial statement analysis:

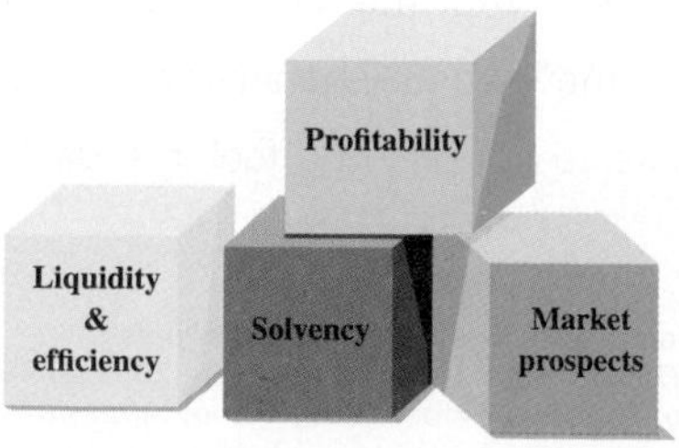

- **Liquidity** and **efficiency**—ability to meet short-term obligations and to efficiently generate revenues.
- **Solvency**—ability to generate future revenues and meet long-term obligations.
- **Profitability**—ability to provide financial rewards sufficient to attract and retain financing.
- **Market prospects**—ability to generate positive market expectations.

Applying the building blocks of financial statement analysis involves determining (1) the objectives of analysis and (2) the relative emphasis among the building blocks. We distinguish among these four building blocks to emphasize the different aspects of a company's financial condition or performance, yet we must remember that these areas of analysis are interrelated. For instance, a company's operating performance is affected by the availability of financing and short-term liquidity conditions. Similarly, a company's credit standing is not limited to satisfactory short-term liquidity but depends also on its profitability and efficiency in using assets. Early in our analysis, we need to determine the relative emphasis of each building block. Emphasis and analysis can later change as a result of evidence collected.

Decision Insight

Chips and Brokers The phrase *blue chips* refers to stock of big, profitable companies. The phrase, comes from poker, where the most valuable chips are blue. The term *brokers* refers to those who execute orders to buy or sell stock. The term comes from wine retailers—individuals who broach (break) wine casks. ■

Information for Analysis

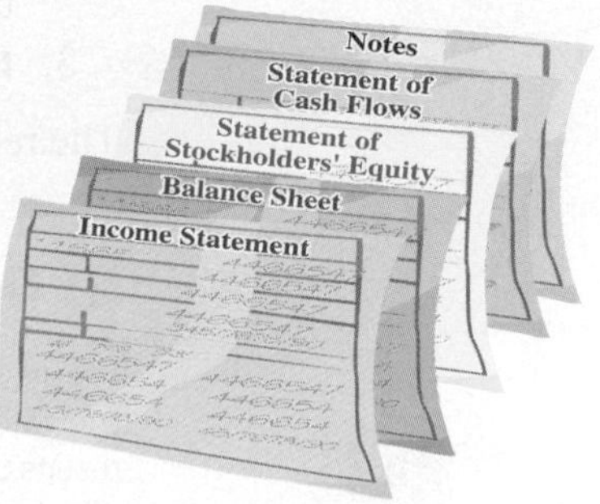

Some users, such as managers and regulatory authorities, are able to receive special financial reports prepared to meet their analysis needs. However, most users must rely on **general-purpose financial statements** that include the (1) income statement, (2) balance sheet, (3) statement of stockholders' equity (or statement of retained earnings), (4) statement of cash flows, and (5) notes to these statements.

Financial reporting refers to the communication of financial information useful for making investment, credit, and other business decisions. Financial reporting includes not only general-purpose financial statements but also information from SEC 10-K or other filings, press releases, shareholders' meetings, forecasts, management letters, auditors' reports, and webcasts.

Management's Discussion and Analysis (MD&A) is one example of useful information outside traditional financial statements. **Apple**'s MD&A (available at **Investor.Apple.com** and 'Item 7' in the annual report), for example, begins with an overview, followed by critical accounting policies and estimates. It then discusses operating results followed by financial condition (liquidity, capital resources, and cash flows). The final few parts discuss legal proceedings, market risk of financial instruments, and risks from interest rate and foreign currency fluctuations. The MD&A is an excellent starting point in understanding a company's business activities.

Decision Insight

Analysis Online Many websites offer free access and screening of companies by key numbers such as earnings, sales, and book value. For instance, **Investor's Business Daily** has information for more than 10,000 stocks (**www.investors.com**). ■

Standards for Comparisons

C2 Describe standards for comparisons in analysis.

When interpreting measures from financial statement analysis, we need to decide whether the measures indicate good, bad, or average performance. To make such judgments, we need standards (benchmarks) for comparisons that include the following:

- *Intracompany*—The company under analysis can provide standards for comparisons based on its own prior performance and relations between its financial items. Apple's current net income, for instance, can be compared with its prior years' net income and in relation to its revenues or total assets.
- *Competitor*—One or more direct competitors of the company being analyzed can provide standards for comparisons. **Coca-Cola**'s profit margin, for instance, can be compared with **PepsiCo**'s profit margin.
- *Industry*—Industry statistics can provide standards of comparisons. Such statistics are available from services such as Dun & Bradstreet, Standard & Poor's, and Moody's.
- *Guidelines (rules of thumb)*—General standards of comparisons can develop from experience. Examples are the 2:1 level for the current ratio or 1:1 level for the acid-test ratio. Guidelines, or rules of thumb, must be carefully applied because context is crucial.

All of these comparison standards are useful when properly applied, yet measures taken from a selected competitor or group of competitors are often best. Intracompany and industry measures are also important. Guidelines or rules of thumb should be applied with care, and then only if they seem reasonable given past experience and industry norms.

Point: Each chapter's *Reporting in Action* problems engage students in *intracompany* analysis, whereas *Comparative Analysis* problems require competitor analysis (Apple vs. Google vs. Samsung).

Tools of Analysis

Three of the most common tools of financial statement analysis are

1. **Horizontal analysis**—comparison of a company's financial condition and performance across time.
2. **Vertical analysis**—comparison of a company's financial condition and performance to a base amount.
3. **Ratio analysis**—measurement of key relations between financial statement items.

The remainder of this chapter describes these analysis tools and how to apply them.

Decision Insight

QC1

Fraud Fighters. Horizontal, vertical, and ratio analysis tools can uncover fraud by identifying amounts out of line with expectations. One can then follow up and ask questions that can either identify a logical reason for such results or confirm/raise suspicions of fraud. Many past fraud schemes could have been identified much earlier had people applied these tools and pressured management for explanations. ■

HORIZONTAL ANALYSIS

P1 Explain and apply methods of horizontal analysis.

Analysis of any single financial number is of limited value. Instead, much of financial statement analysis involves identifying and describing relations between numbers, groups of numbers, and changes in those numbers. Horizontal analysis refers to examination of financial statement data *across time*. (The term *horizontal analysis* arises from the left-to-right [or right-to-left] movement of our eyes as we review comparative financial statements across time.)

Comparative Statements

Comparing amounts for two or more successive periods often helps in analyzing financial statements. **Comparative financial statements** facilitate this comparison by showing financial amounts in side-by-side columns on a single statement, called a *comparative format*. Using figures from **Apple**'s financial statements, this section explains how to compute dollar changes and percent changes for comparative statements.

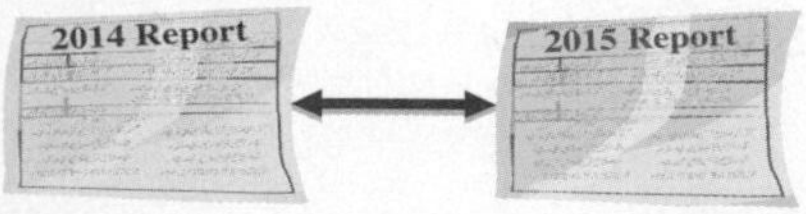

Computation of Dollar Changes and Percent Changes Comparing financial statements over relatively short time periods—two to three years—is often done by analyzing changes in line items. A change analysis usually includes analyzing absolute dollar amount changes and percent changes. Both analyses are relevant because dollar changes can yield large percent changes inconsistent with their importance. For instance, a 50% change from a base figure of $100 is less important than the same percent change from a base amount of $100,000 in the same statement. Reference to dollar amounts is necessary to retain a proper perspective and to assess the importance of changes. We compute the *dollar change* for a financial statement item as follows:

Example: Which is a more significant change, a 70% increase on a $1,000 expense or a 30% increase on a $400,000 expense? *Answer:* The 30% increase.

$$\textbf{Dollar change} = \textbf{Analysis period amount} - \textbf{Base period amount}$$

Analysis period is the point or period of time for the financial statements under analysis, and *base period* is the point or period of time for the financial statements used for comparison purposes. The prior year is commonly used as a base period. We compute the *percent change* by dividing the dollar change by the base period amount and then multiplying this quantity by 100 as follows:

$$\textbf{Percent change (\%)} = \frac{\textbf{Analysis period amount} - \textbf{Base period amount}}{\textbf{Base period amount}} \times 100$$

We can always compute a dollar change, but we must be aware of a few rules in working with percent changes. To illustrate, look at four separate cases in this chart:

Case	Analysis Period	Base Period	Change Analysis: Dollar	Change Analysis: Percent
A	$ 1,500	$(4,500)	$ 6,000	—
B	(1,000)	2,000	(3,000)	—
C	8,000	—	8,000	—
D	0	10,000	(10,000)	(100%)

When a negative amount appears in the base period and a positive amount in the analysis period (or vice versa), we cannot compute a meaningful percent change; see cases A and B. Also, when no value is in the base period, no percent change is computable; see case C. Finally, when an item has a value in the base period and zero in the analysis period, the decrease is 100 percent; see case D.

It is common when using horizontal analysis to compare amounts to either average or median values from prior periods (average and median values smooth out erratic or unusual fluctuations).[1] We also commonly round percents and ratios to one or two decimal places, but practice on this matter is not uniform. Computations are as detailed as necessary, which is judged by whether rounding potentially affects users' decisions. Computations should not be excessively detailed so that important relations are not lost among a mountain of decimal points and digits.

Example: When there is a value in the base period and zero in the analysis period, the decrease is 100%. Why isn't the reverse situation an increase of 100%? *Answer:* A 100% increase of zero is still zero.

Comparative Balance Sheets Comparative balance sheets consist of balance sheet amounts from two or more balance sheet dates arranged side by side. The usefulness of this method of analysis is often improved by showing each item's dollar change and percent change to highlight large changes.

Analysis of comparative financial statements begins by focusing on items that show large dollar or percent changes. We then try to identify the reasons for these changes and, if possible, determine whether they are favorable or unfavorable. We also follow up on items with small changes when we expected the changes to be large.

Point: Spreadsheet programs can help with horizontal, vertical, and ratio analyses, including graphical depictions of financial relations.

Exhibit 13.1 shows comparative balance sheets for Apple Inc. (Nasdaq: AAPL). A few items stand out on the asset side. Apple's inventories show a substantial 123.0% increase. While some of this increase can be explained by growth in operations as evidenced by a 9.2% increase in sales, the bulk of this increased inventory seems inefficient (with increased risks from obsolescence and consumer fads). Other notable increases occur with (1) short-term (and long-term) securities and cash, reflecting Apple's success but also a limited vision for reinvestment; (2) goodwill and property, plant and equipment, reflecting Apple's continued growth; and (3) accounts receivable, which warrants attention as it exceeds the growth in sales. Its sizable total asset growth of 17.6% must be accompanied by future income to validate Apple's asset reinvestments. Some of Apple's shareholders are concerned about its growing assets and declining return on assets.

Point: Business consultants use comparative statement analysis to provide management advice.

On Apple's financing side, we see the 17.6% increase is driven by a 44.2% increase in liabilities (equity increased only 4.5%). The largest increase is due to issuance of long-term debt, followed by various increases in current liabilities. We also see a 2.9% growth ($2,967) in retained earnings, which is much less than its $37,037 in net income. This is in part due to cash dividends and stock repurchases.

Comparative Income Statements Comparative income statements are prepared similarly to comparative balance sheets. Amounts for two or more periods are placed side by side, with additional columns for dollar and percent changes. Exhibit 13.2 shows Apple's comparative income statements.

Apple reports substantial sales growth of 9.2% in 2013. This finding helps support management's 17.6% growth in assets as reflected in the comparative balance sheets. The 21.4% growth in cost of sales with only a 9.2% sales increase raises a concern with Apple's control over its

Point: Percent change can also be computed by dividing the current period by the prior period and subtracting 1.0. For example, the 9.2% sales increase in Exhibit 13.2 is computed as: ($170,910/$156,508) − 1.

[1] *Median* is the middle value in a group of numbers. For instance, if five prior years' incomes are (in 000s) $15, $19, $18, $20, and $22, the median value is $19. When there are two middle numbers, we can take their average. For instance, if four prior years' sales are (in 000s) $84, $91, $96, and $93, the median is $92 (computed as the average of $91 and $93).

EXHIBIT 13.1

Comparative Balance Sheets

APPLE

APPLE INC.
Comparative Balance Sheets
September 28, 2013 and September 29, 2012

(in millions)	2013	2012	Dollar Change	Percent Change
Assets				
Cash and cash equivalents	$ 14,259	$ 10,746	$ 3,513	32.7%
Short-term marketable securities	26,287	18,383	7,904	43.0
Accounts receivable, net	13,102	10,930	2,172	19.9
Inventories	1,764	791	973	123.0
Deferred tax assets	3,453	2,583	870	33.7
Vendor non-trade receivables	7,539	7,762	(223)	(2.9)
Other current assets	6,882	6,458	424	6.6
Total current assets	73,286	57,653	15,633	27.1
Long-term marketable securities	106,215	92,122	14,093	15.3
Property, plant and equipment, net	16,597	15,452	1,145	7.4
Goodwill	1,577	1,135	442	38.9
Acquired intangible assets, net	4,179	4,224	(45)	(1.1)
Other assets	5,146	5,478	(332)	(6.1)
Total assets	$207,000	$176,064	$30,936	17.6
Liabilities				
Accounts payable	$22,367	$21,175	$1,192	5.6%
Accrued expenses	13,856	11,414	2,442	21.4
Deferred revenue	7,435	5,953	1,482	24.9
Total current liabilities	43,658	38,542	5,116	13.3
Deferred revenue—noncurrent	2,625	2,648	(23)	(0.9)
Long-term debt	16,960	—	16,960	—
Other noncurrent liabilities	20,208	16,664	3,544	21.3
Total liabilities	83,451	57,854	25,597	44.2
Stockholders' Equity				
Common stock	19,764	16,422	3,342	20.4
Retained earnings	104,256	101,289	2,967	2.9
Accumulated other comprehensive income	(471)	499	(970)	—
Total stockholders' equity	123,549	118,210	5,339	4.5
Total liabilities and stockholders' equity	$207,000	$176,064	$30,936	17.6

EXHIBIT 13.2

Comparative Income Statements

APPLE

APPLE INC.
Comparative Income Statements
For Years Ended September 28, 2013, and September 29, 2012

(in millions, except per share)	2013	2012	Dollar Change	Percent Change
Net sales	$170,910	$156,508	$14,402	9.2%
Cost of sales	106,606	87,846	18,760	21.4
Gross margin	64,304	68,662	(4,358)	(6.3)
Research and development	4,475	3,381	1,094	32.4
Selling, general and administrative	10,830	10,040	790	7.9
Total operating expenses	15,305	13,421	1,884	14.0
Operating income	48,999	55,241	(6,242)	(11.3)
Other income, net	1,156	522	634	121.5
Income before provision for income taxes	50,155	55,763	(5,608)	(10.1)
Provision for income taxes	13,118	14,030	(912)	(6.5)
Net income	$ 37,037	$ 41,733	(4,696)	(11.3)
Basic earnings per share	$ 40.03	$ 44.64	($4.61)	(10.3)
Diluted earnings per share	$ 39.75	$ 44.15	($4.40)	(10.0)

costs of sales. Similarly, we see a 14.0% increase in operating expenses, which exceeds the 9.2% sales growth (not good news). However, much of this is due to increased research and development costs, from which management hopes to reap future rewards. Apple reports a decline of 11.3% in net income, which is again mainly attributed to the 21.4% growth in cost of sales.

Trend Analysis

Trend analysis, also called *trend percent analysis* or *index number trend analysis,* is a form of horizontal analysis that can reveal patterns in data across successive periods. It involves computing trend percents for a series of financial numbers and is a variation on the use of percent changes. The difference is that trend analysis does not subtract the base period amount in the numerator. To compute trend percents, we do the following:

1. Select a *base period* and assign each item in the base period a weight of 100%.
2. Express financial numbers as a percent of their base period number.

Point: *Index* refers to the comparison of the analysis period to the base period. Percents determined for each period are called *index numbers.*

Specifically, a *trend percent,* also called an *index number,* is computed as follows:

$$\textbf{Trend percent (\%)} = \frac{\textbf{Analysis period amount}}{\textbf{Base period amount}} \times 100$$

To illustrate trend analysis, we use the Apple data shown in Exhibit 13.3.

EXHIBIT 13.3

Sales and Expensess

(in millions)	2013	2012	2011	2010	2009
Net sales	$170,910	$156,508	$108,249	$65,225	$42,905
Cost of sales	106,606	87,846	64,431	39,541	25,683
Operating expenses	15,305	13,421	10,028	7,299	5,482

These data are from Apple's current and prior financial statements. The base period is 2009 and the trend percent is computed in each subsequent year by dividing that year's amount by its 2009 amount. For instance, the revenue trend percent for 2013 is 398.3%, computed as $170,910/$42,905. The trend percents—using the data from Exhibit 13.3—are shown in Exhibit 13.4.

Point: Trend analysis expresses a percent of base, not a percent of change.

EXHIBIT 13.4

Trend Percents for Sales and Expenses

	2013	2012	2011	2010	2009
Net sales	398.3%	364.8%	252.3%	152.0%	100.0%
Cost of sales	415.1	342.0	250.9	154.0	100.0
Operating expenses	279.2	244.8	182.9	133.1	100.0

Graphical depictions often aid analysis of trend percents. Exhibit 13.5 shows the trend percents from Exhibit 13.4 in a *line graph,* which can help us identify trends and detect changes in direction or magnitude. It reveals that the trend line for revenue consistently exceeds that for both operating expenses and for cost of sales (except for 2010 and 2013). The marked increase in cost of sales in 2013 is concerning for Apple because its long-run profitability will suffer if those costs are not controlled. The trend line for operating expenses is encouraging because it lags revenue growth for each year from 2010–2013; however, the 2013 cost of sales reflects a marked rise in its trend line and exceeds that for net sales, which is worrying.

EXHIBIT 13.5

Trend Percent Lines for Sales and Expenses of Apple

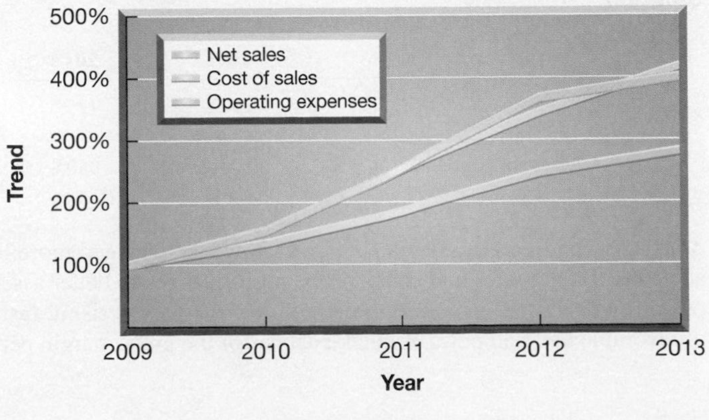

EXHIBIT 13.6

Revenue Trend Percent Lines—Apple, Google and Samsung

APPLE
GOOGLE
Samsung

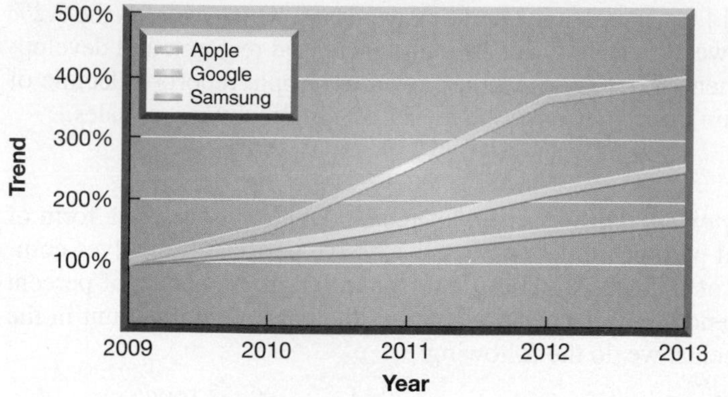

Exhibit 13.6 compares Apple's revenue trend line to that of **Google** and **Samsung** for this same period. Apple is able to grow its revenue in each year relative to its base year. In this respect Apple outperforms its competitors, although both Google and Samsung performed well over this same period of time. These data indicate that Apple's products and services have met with great consumer acceptance.

Trend analysis of financial statement items can include comparisons of relations between items on different financial statements. For instance, Exhibit 13.7 compares Apple's revenue and total assets. The rate of increase in total assets (435.8%) is more than the increase in revenues (398.3%) since 2009. Is this result favorable or not? The answer is that Apple was *less* efficient in using its assets in 2013 versus 2009. Management has not generated revenues sufficient to compensate for the asset growth.

EXHIBIT 13.7

Sales and Asset Data for Apple

(in millions)	2013	2009	Trend Percent (2013 vs. 2009)
Net sales	$170,910	$42,905	398.3%
Total assets	207,000	47,501	435.8

Overall we must remember that an important role of financial statement analysis is identifying questions and areas of interest, which often direct us to important factors bearing on a company's future. Accordingly, financial statement analysis should be seen as a continuous process of refining our understanding and expectations of company performance and financial condition.

Decision Maker

Auditor Your tests reveal a 3% increase in sales from $200,000 to $206,000 and a 4% decrease in expenses from $190,000 to $182,400. Both changes are within your "reasonableness" criterion of ±5%, and thus you don't pursue additional tests. The audit partner in charge questions your lack of follow-up and mentions the *joint relation* between sales and expenses. To what is the partner referring? ■ [Answers follow the chapter's Summary.]

NEED-TO-KNOW 13-1

Horizontal Analysis

P1

Compute trend percents for the following accounts, using 2012 as the base year (round percents to whole numbers). State whether the situation as revealed by the trends appears to be favorable or unfavorable for each account.

($ millions)	2015	2014	2013	2012
Sales	$500	$350	$250	$200
Cost of goods sold.	400	175	100	50

Solution

($ millions)	2015	2014	2013	2012
Sales	250% ($500/$200)	175% ($350/$200)	125% ($250/$200)	100% ($200/$200)
Cost of goods sold.	800% ($400/$50)	350% ($175/$50)	200% ($100/$50)	100% ($50/$50)

Analysis: The trend in sales is favorable; however, we need more information about economic conditions such as inflation rates and competitors' performances to better assess it. Cost of sales is also rising (as expected with increasing sales); however, cost of sales is rising faster than the increase in sales, which is unfavorable and bad news. A quick analysis of the gross margin percentage would highlight this concern.

Do More: QS 13-3, QS 13-4, E 13-3

VERTICAL ANALYSIS

Vertical analysis is a tool to evaluate individual financial statement items or a group of items in terms of a specific base amount. We usually define a key aggregate figure as the base, which for an income statement is usually revenue and for a balance sheet is usually total assets. This section explains vertical analysis and applies it to **Apple**. (The term *vertical analysis* arises from the up-down [or down-up] movement of our eyes as we review common-size financial statements. Vertical analysis is also called *common-size analysis.*)

P2 Describe and apply methods of vertical analysis.

Common-Size Statements

The comparative statements in Exhibits 13.1 and 13.2 show the change in each item over time, but they do not emphasize the relative importance of each item. We use **common-size financial statements** to reveal changes in the relative importance of each financial statement item. All individual amounts in common-size statements are redefined in terms of common-size percents. A *common-size percent* is measured by dividing each individual financial statement amount under analysis by its base amount:

Income Statement	
Sales	10,000
Expenses	6,000
Income	4,000

$$\textbf{Common-size percent (\%)} = \frac{\textbf{Analysis amount}}{\textbf{Base amount}} \times 100$$

Common-Size Balance Sheets Common-size statements express each item as a percent of a *base amount,* which for a common-size balance sheet is usually total assets. The base amount is assigned a value of 100%. (This implies that the total amount of liabilities plus equity equals 100% since this amount equals total assets.) We then compute a common-size percent for each asset, liability, and equity item using total assets as the base amount. When we present a company's successive balance sheets in this way, changes in the mixture of assets, liabilities, and equity are apparent.

Point: The *base* amount in common-size analysis is an *aggregate* amount from that period's financial statement.

Exhibit 13.8 shows common-size comparative balance sheets for Apple. Some relations that stand out on both a magnitude and percentage basis include (1) a 2.3% point increase in short-term securities, which equates to a $7,904 million increase; (2) a new issuance of $16,960 million in long-term debt; and (3) a 7.1% decrease in retained earnings, which equates to a $2,967 million decrease. The lack of substantial change in the balance sheet suggests a mature company, but with some lack of focus as evidenced by the increasing amount in short- and long-term securities. This buildup in securities is a concern as the return on securities is historically smaller than the return on operating assets from successful reinvestment. Time will tell whether Apple can continue to generate sufficient revenue and income from its growing asset base.

Point: Common-size statements often are used to compare two or more companies in the same industry.

Point: Common-size statements are also useful in comparing firms that report in different currencies.

Common-Size Income Statements Analysis also benefits from use of a common-size income statement. Revenue is usually the base amount, which is assigned a value of 100%. Each common-size income statement item appears as a percent of revenue. If we think of the 100% revenue amount as representing one sales dollar, the remaining items show how each revenue dollar is distributed among costs, expenses, and income.

Exhibit 13.9 shows common-size comparative income statements for each dollar of Apple's revenue. The past two years' common-size numbers are similar with a few exceptions. One important exception is the decrease of 5.0 cents in net income per each net sales dollar—evidenced by the decrease in income as a percent of net sales from 26.7% to 21.7%. This implies that management is *not* effectively controlling costs. Much of this is attributed to the rise in cost of sales from 56.1% to 62.4% as a percent of net sales. In sum, analysis here shows that common-size percents for successive income statements can uncover potentially important changes in a company's cost management. (Evidence of no changes, especially when changes are expected, is also informative.)

Global: International companies sometimes disclose "convenience" financial statements, which are statements translated in other languages and currencies. However, these statements rarely adjust for differences in accounting principles across countries.

Common-Size Graphics

Two of the most common tools of common-size analysis are trend analysis of common-size statements and graphical analysis. The trend analysis of common-size statements is similar to that of comparative statements discussed under vertical analysis. It is not illustrated here because the only difference is the substitution of common-size percents for trend percents. Instead, this

EXHIBIT 13.8

Common-Size Comparative Balance Sheets

APPLE

APPLE INC.
Common-Size Comparative Balance Sheets
September 28, 2013, and September 29, 2012

(in millions)	2013	2012	Common-Size Percents* 2013	Common-Size Percents* 2012
Assets				
Cash and cash equivalents	$ 14,259	$ 10,746	6.9%	6.1%
Short-term marketable securities	26,287	18,383	12.7	10.4
Accounts receivable, net	13,102	10,930	6.3	6.2
Inventories	1,764	791	0.9	0.4
Deferred tax assets	3,453	2,583	1.7	1.5
Vendor non-trade receivables	7,539	7,762	3.6	4.4
Other current assets	6,882	6,458	3.3	3.7
Total current assets	73,286	57,653	35.4	32.7
Long-term marketable securities	106,215	92,122	51.3	52.3
Property, plant and equipment, net	16,597	15,452	8.0	8.8
Goodwill	1,577	1,135	0.8	0.6
Acquired intangible assets, net	4,179	4,224	2.0	2.4
Other assets	5,146	5,478	2.5	3.1
Total assets	$207,000	$176,064	100.0%	100.0%
Liabilities				
Accounts payable	$ 22,367	$ 21,175	10.8%	12.0%
Accrued expenses	13,856	11,414	6.7	6.5
Deferred revenue	7,435	5,953	3.6	3.4
Total current liabilities	43,658	38,542	21.1	21.9
Deferred revenue—noncurrent	2,625	2,648	1.3	1.5
Long-term debt	16,960	0	8.2	0.0
Other noncurrent liabilities	20,208	16,664	9.8	9.5
Total liabilities	83,451	57,854	40.3	32.9
Stockholders' Equity				
Common stock	19,764	16,422	9.5	9.3
Retained earnings	104,256	101,289	50.4	57.5
Accumulated other comprehensive income	(471)	499	(0.2)	0.3
Total stockholders' equity	123,549	118,210	59.7	67.1
Total liabilities and stockholders' equity	$207,000	$176,064	100.0%	100.0%

* Percents are rounded to tenths and thus may not exactly sum to totals and subtotals.

EXHIBIT 13.9

Common-Size Comparative Income Statements

APPLE

APPLE INC.
Common-Size Comparative Income Statements
For Years Ended September 28, 2013, and September 29, 2012

(in millions)	2013	2012	Common-Size Percents* 2013	Common-Size Percents* 2012
Net sales	$170,910	$156,508	100.0%	100.0%
Cost of sales	106,606	87,846	62.4	56.1
Gross margin	64,304	68,662	37.6	43.9
Research and development	4,475	3,381	2.6	2.2
Selling, general and administrative	10,830	10,040	6.3	6.4
Total operating expenses	15,305	13,421	9.0	8.6
Operating income	48,999	55,241	28.7	35.3
Other income, net	1,156	522	0.7	0.3
Income before provision for income taxes	50,155	55,763	29.3	35.6
Provision for income taxes	13,118	14,030	7.7	9.0
Net income	$ 37,037	$ 41,733	21.7%	26.7%

* Percents are rounded to tenths and thus may not exactly sum to totals and subtotals.

section discusses graphical analysis of common-size statements.

An income statement readily lends itself to common-size graphical analysis. This is so because revenues affect nearly every item in an income statement. Exhibit 13.10 shows Apple's 2013 common-size income statement in graphical form. This pie chart highlights the contribution of each cost component of net sales for net income (for this graph, "other income, net" is included in selling, general, administrative, and other costs).

EXHIBIT 13.10

Common-Size Graphic of Income Statement

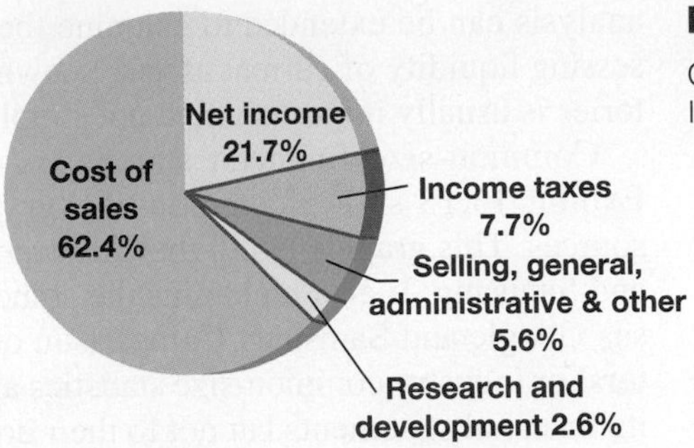

Exhibit 13.11 previews more complex graphical analyses available and the insights they provide. The data for this exhibit are taken from Apple's *Segments* footnote. Apple reports six operating segments for 2013: (1) Americas, (2) Europe, (3) China, (4) Japan, (5) Asia Pacific, and (6) Retail.

EXHIBIT 13.11

Sales and Operating Income Margin Breakdown by Segment

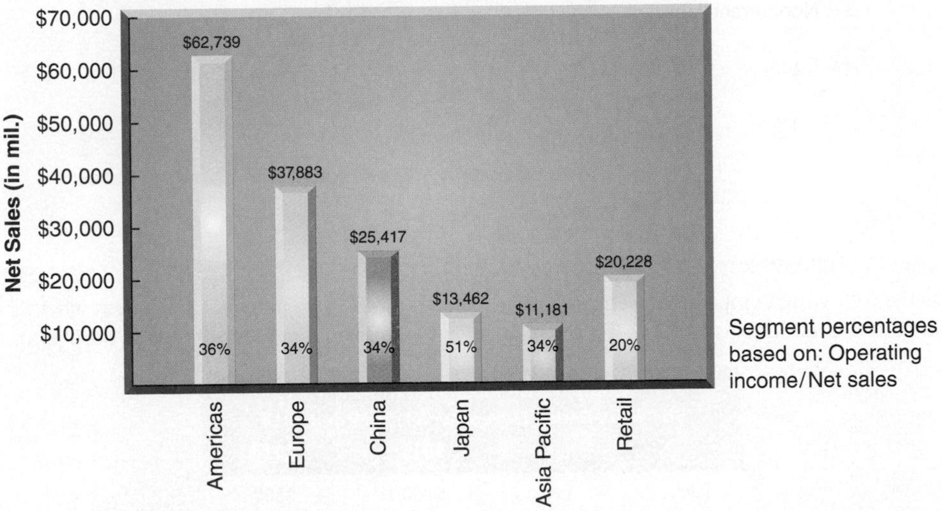

The bars in Exhibit 13.11 show the level of net sales for each of the six reportable segments of Apple. Its Americas segment generates $62,739 million of its total net sales, which is roughly 37% of its total sales. The five other bars show the level of sales generated from each of the other international segments, including its retail segment. At the bottom of each bar is that segment's operating income margin, defined as segment operating income divided by segment net sales. The Americas segment yields a 36% operating income margin; margins for the other five segments are shown at the bottom of each of the other segment bars. This type of graphic presentation can lead to questions about the profitability of each segment and discussion of potential expansions into the more lucrative segments. For example, the Japan segment yields an operating margin of 51%. A natural question for management is what potential is there to further expand sales into the Japan segment and maintain the similar operating margin? This type of analysis can help users in determining strategic plans and actions.

Graphical analysis is also useful in identifying (1) sources of financing including the distribution among current liabilities, noncurrent liabilities, and equity capital and (2) focuses of investing activities, including the distribution among current and noncurrent assets. To illustrate, Exhibit 13.12 shows a common-size graphical display of Apple's assets. Common-size balance sheet

EXHIBIT 13.12

Common-Size Graphic of Asset Components

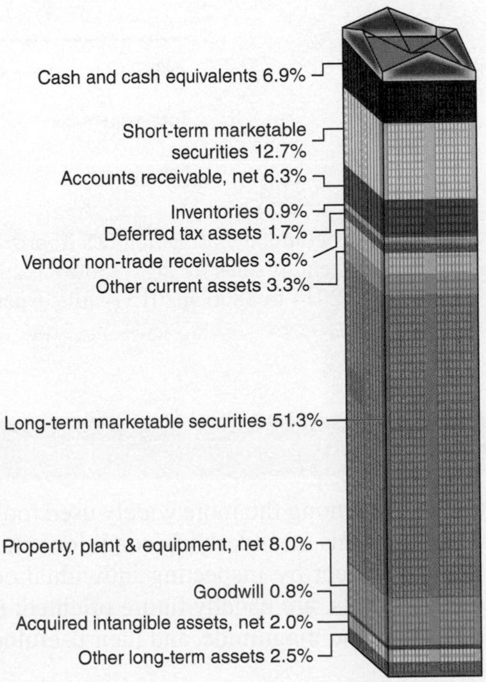

analysis can be extended to examine the composition of these subgroups. For instance, in assessing liquidity of current assets, knowing what proportion of *current* assets consists of inventories is usually important, and not simply what proportion inventories are of *total* assets.

Common-size financial statements are also useful in comparing different companies. Exhibit 13.13 shows common-size graphics of Apple, Google, and Samsung on financing sources. This graphic highlights the larger percent of equity financing for Google versus Apple and Samsung. It also highlights the somewhat larger noncurrent (debt) financing of Apple versus Google and Samsung. Comparison of a company's common-size statements with competitors' or industry common-size statistics alerts us to differences in the structure or distribution of its financial statements but not to their dollar magnitude.

EXHIBIT 13.13

Common-Size Graphic of Financing Sources—Competitor Analysis

APPLE
GOOGLE
Samsung

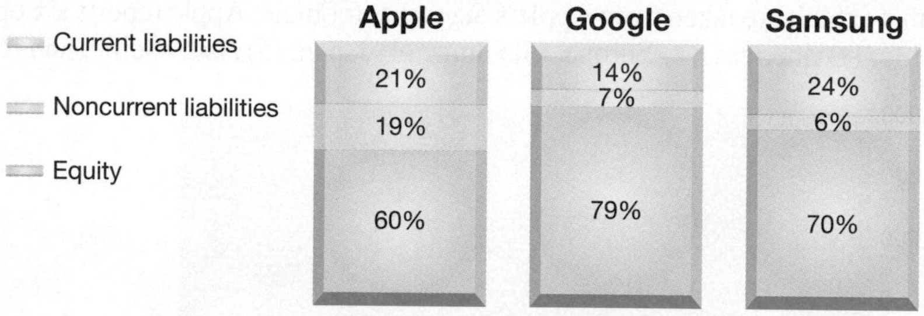

NEED-TO-KNOW 13-2

Vertical Analysis
P2

Express the following comparative income statements in common-size percents and assess whether or not this company's situation has improved in the most recent year (round percents to whole numbers).

Comparative Income Statements For Years Ended December 31, 2015 and 2014	2015	2014
Sales	$800	$500
Total expenses	560	400
Net income	$240	$100

Solution

	2015	2014
Sales	100% ($800/$800)	100% ($500/$500)
Total expenses	70% ($560/$800)	80% ($400/$500)
Net income	30%	20%

Do More: QS 13-5, E 13-4, E 13-6

QC2

Analysis: This company's situation has improved. This is evident from its substantial increase in net income as a percent of sales for 2015 (30%) relative to 2014 (20%). Further, the company's sales increased from $500 in 2014 to $800 in 2015 (while expenses declined as a percent of sales from 80% to 70%).

RATIO ANALYSIS

P3 Define and apply ratio analysis.

Ratios are among the more widely used tools of financial analysis because they provide clues to and symptoms of underlying conditions. A ratio can help us uncover conditions and trends difficult to detect by inspecting individual components making up the ratio. Ratios, like other analysis tools, are usually future oriented; that is, they are often adjusted for their probable future trend and magnitude, and their usefulness depends on skillful interpretation.

A ratio expresses a mathematical relation between two quantities. It can be expressed as a percent, rate, or proportion. For instance, a change in an account balance from $100 to $250 can be expressed as (1) 150% increase, (2) 2.5 times, or (3) 2.5 to 1 (or 2.5:1). Computation of a ratio is a simple arithmetic operation, but its interpretation is not. To be meaningful, a ratio must refer to an economically important relation. For example, a direct and crucial relation exists between an item's sales price and its cost. Accordingly, the ratio of cost of goods sold to sales is meaningful. In contrast, no obvious relation exists between freight costs and the balance of long-term investments.

This section describes an important set of financial ratios and their application. The selected ratios are organized into the four building blocks of financial statement analysis: (1) liquidity and efficiency, (2) solvency, (3) profitability, and (4) market prospects. All of these ratios were explained at relevant points in prior chapters. The purpose here is to organize and apply them under a summary framework. We use four common standards, in varying degrees, for comparisons: intracompany, competitor, industry, and guidelines.

Point: Some sources for industry norms are *Annual Statement Studies* by Robert Morris Associates, *Industry Norms & Key Business Ratios* by Dun & Bradstreet, *Standard & Poor's Industry Surveys*, and Reuters.com/finance.

Liquidity and Efficiency

Liquidity refers to the availability of resources to meet short-term cash requirements. It is affected by the timing of cash inflows and outflows along with prospects for future performance. Analysis of liquidity is aimed at a company's funding requirements. *Efficiency* refers to how productive a company is in using its assets. Efficiency is usually measured relative to how much revenue is generated from a certain level of assets.

Both liquidity and efficiency are important and complementary. If a company fails to meet its current obligations, its continued existence is doubtful. Viewed in this light, all other measures of analysis are of secondary importance. Although accounting measurements assume the company's continued existence, our analysis must always assess the validity of this assumption using liquidity measures. Moreover, inefficient use of assets can cause liquidity problems. A lack of liquidity often precedes lower profitability and fewer opportunities. It can foretell a loss of owner control. To a company's creditors, lack of liquidity can yield delays in collecting interest and principal payments or the loss of amounts due them. A company's customers and suppliers of goods and services also are affected by short-term liquidity problems. Implications include a company's inability to execute contracts and potential damage to important customer and supplier relationships. This section describes and illustrates key ratios relevant to assessing liquidity and efficiency.

Working Capital and Current Ratio The amount of current assets less current liabilities is called **working capital,** or *net working capital.* A company needs adequate working capital to meet current debts, to carry sufficient inventories, and to take advantage of cash discounts. A company that runs low on working capital is less likely to meet current obligations or to continue operating. When evaluating a company's working capital, we must not only look at the dollar amount of current assets less current liabilities, but also at their ratio. The *current ratio* is defined as follows (see Chapter 3 for additional explanation):

$$\textbf{Current ratio} = \frac{\textbf{Current assets}}{\textbf{Current liabilities}}$$

Drawing on information in Exhibit 13.1, **Apple**'s working capital and current ratio for both 2013 and 2012 are shown in Exhibit 13.14. Also, **Google** (4.58), **Samsung** (2.16), and the industry's current ratio (2.5) are shown in the margin. Apple's 2013 ratio (1.68) is lower than competitors' ratios, but it is not in danger of defaulting on loan payments. A high current ratio suggests a strong liquidity position and an ability to meet current obligations. A company can, however, have a current ratio that is too high. An excessively high current ratio means that the company has invested too much in current assets compared to its current obligations.

EXHIBIT 13.14

Apple's Working Capital and Current Ratio

(in millions)	2013	2012
Current assets	$ 73,286	$ 57,653
Current liabilities	43,658	38,542
Working capital	**$29,628**	**$19,111**
Current ratio		
$73,286/$43,658 =	**1.68 to 1**	
$57,653/$38,542 =		**1.50 to 1**

Current ratio
Google = 4.58
Samsung = 2.16
Industry = 2.5

An excessive investment in current assets is not an efficient use of funds because current assets normally generate a low return on investment (compared with long-term assets).

Many users apply a guideline of 2:1 (or 1.5:1) for the current ratio in helping evaluate a company's debt-paying ability. A company with a 2:1 or higher current ratio is generally thought to be a good credit risk in the short run. Such a guideline or any analysis of the current ratio must recognize at least three additional factors: (1) type of business, (2) composition of current assets, and (3) turnover rate of current asset components.

Type of business. A service company that grants little or no credit and carries few inventories can probably operate on a current ratio of less than 1:1 if its revenues generate enough cash to pay its current liabilities. On the other hand, a company selling high-priced clothing or furniture requires a higher ratio because of difficulties in judging customer demand and cash receipts. For instance, if demand falls, inventory may not generate as much cash as expected. Accordingly, analysis of the current ratio should include a comparison with ratios from successful companies in the same industry and from prior periods. We must also recognize that a company's accounting methods, especially choice of inventory method, affect the current ratio. For instance, when costs are rising, a company using LIFO tends to report a smaller amount of current assets than when using FIFO.

Point: When a firm uses LIFO in a period of rising costs, the standard for an adequate current ratio usually is lower than if it used FIFO.

Composition of current assets. The composition of a company's current assets is important to an evaluation of short-term liquidity. For instance, cash, cash equivalents, and short-term investments are more liquid than accounts and notes receivable. Also, short-term receivables normally are more liquid than inventory. Cash, of course, can be used to immediately pay current debts. Items such as accounts receivable and inventory, however, normally must be converted into cash before payment is made. An excessive amount of receivables and inventory weakens a company's ability to pay current liabilities. The acid-test ratio (see below) can help with this assessment.

Turnover rate of assets. Asset turnover measures a company's efficiency in using its assets. One relevant measure of asset efficiency is the revenue generated. A measure of total asset turnover is revenues divided by total assets, but evaluation of turnover for individual assets is also useful. We discuss both receivables turnover and inventory turnover next.

Decision Maker

Banker A company requests a one-year, $200,000 loan for expansion. This company's current ratio is 4:1, with current assets of $160,000. Key competitors carry a current ratio of about 1.9:1. Using this information, do you approve the loan application? Does your decision change if the application is for a 10-year loan? ■ [Answers follow the chapter's Summary.]

Acid-Test Ratio Quick assets are cash, short-term investments, and current receivables. These are the most liquid types of current assets. The *acid-test ratio,* also called *quick ratio,* and introduced in Chapter 4, reflects on a company's short-term liquidity.

$$\text{Acid-test ratio} = \frac{\text{Cash + Short-term investments + Current receivables}}{\text{Current liabilities}}$$

Apple's acid-test ratio is computed in Exhibit 13.15. Apple's 2013 acid-test ratio (1.23) is lower than that for Google (4.25) and Samsung (1.37), but is greater than the 1:1 common guideline for

EXHIBIT 13.15
Acid-Test Ratio

(in millions)	2013	2012
Cash and equivalents	$14,259	$10,746
Short-term securities	26,287	18,383
Current receivables	13,102	10,930
Total quick assets	$53,648	$40,059
Current liabilities	$43,658	$38,542
Acid-test ratio		
$53,648/$43,658	1.23 to 1	
$40,059/$38,542		1.04 to 1

Acid-test ratio
Google = 4.25
Samsung = 1.37
Industry = 0.9

an acceptable acid-test ratio. The ratio for Apple is also greater than the 0.9 industry norm; thus, we are not concerned. As with analysis of the current ratio, we need to consider other factors. For instance, the frequency with which a company converts its current assets into cash affects its working capital requirements. This implies that analysis of short-term liquidity should also include an analysis of receivables and inventories, which we consider next.

Global: Ratio analysis helps overcome currency translation problems, but it does *not* overcome differences in accounting principles.

Accounts Receivable Turnover We can measure how frequently a company converts its receivables into cash by computing the *accounts receivable turnover*. This ratio is defined as follows (see Chapter 7 for additional explanation).

$$\textbf{Accounts receivable turnover} = \frac{\textbf{Net sales}}{\textbf{Average accounts receivable, net}}$$

Short-term receivables from customers are often included in the denominator along with accounts receivable. Also, accounts receivable turnover is more precise if credit sales are used for the numerator, but external users generally use net sales (or net revenues) because information about credit sales is typically not reported. Apple's 2013 accounts receivable turnover is computed as follows ($ millions).

Point: Some users prefer using gross accounts receivable (before subtracting the allowance for doubtful accounts) to avoid the influence of a manager's bad debts estimate.

$$\frac{\$170{,}910}{(\$10{,}930 + \$13{,}102)/2} = 14.2 \text{ times}$$

Accounts receivable turnover
Google = 7.1
Samsung = 8.4
Industry = 5.0

Apple's value of 14.2 exceeds that of both Google's 7.1 and Samsung's 8.4. Accounts receivable turnover is high when accounts receivable are quickly collected. A high turnover is favorable because it means the company need not commit large amounts of funds to accounts receivable. However, an accounts receivable turnover can be too high; this can occur when credit terms are so restrictive that they negatively affect sales volume.

Point: Ending accounts receivable can be substituted for the average balance in computing accounts receivable turnover if the difference between ending and average receivables is small.

Inventory Turnover How long a company holds inventory before selling it will affect working capital requirements. One measure of this effect is *inventory turnover,* also called *merchandise turnover* or *merchandise inventory turnover,* which is defined as follows (see Chapter 5 for additional explanation).

$$\textbf{Inventory turnover} = \frac{\textbf{Cost of goods sold}}{\textbf{Average inventory}}$$

Using Apple's cost of goods sold and inventories information, we compute its inventory turnover for 2013 as follows (if the beginning and ending inventories for the year do not represent the usual inventory amount, an average of quarterly or monthly inventories can be used).

$$\frac{\$106{,}606}{(\$791 + \$1{,}764)/2} = 83.45 \text{ times}$$

Inventory turnover
Google = 55.55
Samsung = 7.47
Industry = 7.0

Apple's inventory turnover of 83.45 is more than Google's 55.55 and Samsung's 7.47, and the industry's 7.0. A company with a high turnover requires a smaller investment in inventory than one producing the same sales with a lower turnover. Inventory turnover can be too high, however, if the inventory a company keeps is so small that it restricts sales volume.

Days' Sales Uncollected Accounts receivable turnover provides insight into how frequently a company collects its accounts. Days' sales uncollected is one measure of this activity, which is defined as follows (Chapter 6 provides additional explanation).

$$\textbf{Days' sales uncollected} = \frac{\textbf{Accounts receivable, net}}{\textbf{Net sales}} \times \textbf{365}$$

Any short-term notes receivable from customers are normally included in the numerator.

Rita Qian/AFP/Getty Images

Apple's 2013 days' sales uncollected follows.

Days' sales uncollected
Google = 54.2
Samsung = 44.5

$$\frac{\$13{,}102}{\$170{,}910} \times 365 = 28.0 \text{ days}$$

Both Google's days' sales uncollected of 54.2 days and Samsung's 50.7 days are more than the 28.0 days for Apple. Days' sales uncollected is more meaningful if we know company credit terms. A rough guideline states that days' sales uncollected should not exceed $1\frac{1}{3}$ times the days in its (1) credit period, *if* discounts are not offered or (2) discount period, *if* favorable discounts are offered.

Days' Sales in Inventory *Days' sales in inventory* is a useful measure in evaluating inventory liquidity. Days' sales in inventory is linked to inventory in a way that days' sales uncollected is linked to receivables. We compute days' sales in inventory as follows (Chapter 5 provides additional explanation).

$$\textbf{Days' sales in inventory} = \frac{\textbf{Ending inventory}}{\textbf{Cost of goods sold}} \times \textbf{365}$$

Apple's days' sales in inventory for 2013 follows.

Days' sales in inventory
Google = 6.0
Samsung = 50.7
Industry = 35

$$\frac{\$1{,}764}{\$106{,}606} \times 365 = 6.0 \text{ days}$$

Point: *Average collection period* is estimated by dividing 365 by the accounts receivable turnover ratio. For example, 365 divided by an accounts receivable turnover of 6.1 indicates a 60-day average collection period.

If the products in Apple's inventory are in demand by customers, this formula estimates that its inventory will be converted into receivables (or cash) in 6.0 days. If all of Apple's sales were credit sales, the conversion of inventory to receivables in 6.0 days *plus* the conversion of receivables to cash in 28.0 days implies that inventory will be converted to cash in about 34.0 days (6.0 + 28.0).

Total Asset Turnover *Total asset turnover* reflects a company's ability to use its assets to generate sales and is an important indication of operating efficiency. The definition of this ratio follows (Chapter 8 offers additional explanation).

$$\textbf{Total asset turnover} = \frac{\textbf{Net sales}}{\textbf{Average total assets}}$$

Apple's total asset turnover of 0.89 for 2013 follows, which is greater than that for Google (0.58) but less than that for Samsung (1.16).

Total asset turnover
Google = 0.58
Samsung = 1.16
Industry = 1.2

$$\frac{\$170{,}910}{(\$176{,}064 + \$207{,}000)/2} = 0.89 \text{ times}$$

Solvency

Solvency refers to a company's long-run financial viability and its ability to cover long-term obligations. All of a company's business activities—financing, investing, and operating—affect its solvency. Analysis of solvency is long term and uses less precise but more encompassing measures than liquidity. One of the most important components of solvency analysis is the composition of a company's capital structure. *Capital structure* refers to a company's financing sources. It ranges from relatively permanent equity financing to riskier or more temporary short-term financing. Assets represent security for financiers, ranging from loans secured by specific assets to the assets available as general security to unsecured creditors. This section describes the tools of solvency analysis. Our analysis focuses on a company's ability to both meet its obligations and provide security to its creditors *over the long run*. Indicators of

this ability include *debt* and *equity* ratios, the relation between *pledged assets and secured liabilities,* and the company's capacity to earn sufficient income to *pay fixed interest charges*.

Debt and Equity Ratios One element of solvency analysis is to assess the portion of a company's assets contributed by its owners and the portion contributed by creditors. This relation is reflected in the debt ratio (also described in Chapter 2). The *debt ratio* expresses total liabilities as a percent of total assets. The **equity ratio** provides complementary information by expressing total equity as a percent of total assets. **Apple**'s debt and equity ratios follow.

Point: For analysis purposes, noncontrolling interest is usually included in equity.

(in millions)	2013	Ratios	
Total liabilities	$ 83,451	40.3%	[Debt ratio]
Total equity	123,549	59.7	[Equity ratio]
Total liabilities and equity	$207,000	100.0%	

Debt ratio :: Equity ratio
Google = 21.3% :: 78.7%
Samsung = 29.9% :: 70.1%
Industry = 35% :: 65%

Apple's financial statements reveal more equity than debt. A company is considered less risky if its capital structure (equity and long-term debt) contains more equity. One risk factor is the required payment for interest and principal when debt is outstanding. Another factor is the greater the stockholder financing, the more losses a company can absorb through equity before the assets become inadequate to satisfy creditors' claims. From the stockholders' point of view, if a company earns a return on borrowed capital that is higher than the cost of borrowing, the difference represents increased income to stockholders. The inclusion of debt is described as *financial leverage* because debt can have the effect of increasing the return to stockholders. Companies are said to be highly leveraged if a large portion of their assets is financed by debt.

Point: Bank examiners from the FDIC and other regulatory agencies use debt and equity ratios to monitor compliance with regulatory capital requirements imposed on banks and S&Ls.

Debt-to-Equity Ratio The ratio of total liabilities to equity is another measure of solvency. We compute the ratio as follows (Chapter 10 offers additional explanation).

$$\textbf{Debt-to-equity ratio} = \frac{\textbf{Total liabilities}}{\textbf{Total equity}}$$

Apple's debt-to-equity ratio for 2013 is

$$\$83,451/\$123,549 = 0.68$$

Debt-to-equity
Google = 0.27
Samsung = 0.43
Industry = 0.6

Apple's 0.68 debt-to-equity ratio is higher than that of Samsung (0.43) and Google (0.27), and greater than the industry ratio of 0.6. Consistent with our inferences from the debt ratio, Apple's capital structure has less debt than equity, which helps limit risk. Recall that debt must be repaid with interest, while equity does not. These debt requirements can be burdensome when the industry and/or the economy experience a downturn. A larger debt-to-equity ratio also implies less opportunity to expand through use of debt financing.

Times Interest Earned The amount of income before deductions for interest expense and income taxes is the amount available to pay interest expense. The following *times interest earned* ratio reflects the creditors' risk of loan repayments with interest (see Chapter 9 for additional explanation).

Point: The times interest earned ratio and the debt and equity ratios are of special interest to bank lending officers.

$$\textbf{Times interest earned} = \frac{\textbf{Income before interest expense and income taxes}}{\textbf{Interest expense}}$$

The larger this ratio, the less risky is the company for creditors. One guideline says that creditors are reasonably safe if the company earns its fixed interest expense two or more times each year. Apple's times interest earned ratio follows. Apple's 369.8 result suggests that its creditors have little risk of nonrepayment.

Times interest earned
Google = 184.2
Samsung = 76.3

$$\frac{\$37{,}037 + \$136 + \$13{,}118}{\$136} = 369.8 \text{ times}$$

Decision Insight

Bears and Bulls A *bear market* is a declining market. The phrase comes from bear-skin jobbers who often sold the skins before the bears were caught. The term *bear* was then used to describe investors who sold shares they did not own in anticipation of a price decline. A *bull market* is a rising market. This phrase comes from the once popular sport of bear and bull baiting. The term *bull* came to mean the opposite of *bear.* ■

Profitability

We are especially interested in a company's ability to use its assets efficiently to produce profits (and positive cash flows). *Profitability* refers to a company's ability to generate an adequate return on invested capital. Return is judged by assessing earnings relative to the level and sources of financing. Profitability is also relevant to solvency. This section describes key profitability measures and their importance to financial statement analysis.

Profit Margin A company's operating efficiency and profitability can be expressed by two components. The first is *profit margin,* which reflects a company's ability to earn net income from sales (Chapter 3 offers additional explanation). It is measured by expressing net income as a percent of sales (*sales* and *revenues* are similar terms). Apple's profit margin follows.

Profit margin
Google = 21.6%
Samsung = 13.3%
Industry = 11%

$$\textbf{Profit margin} = \frac{\textbf{Net income}}{\textbf{Net sales}} = \frac{\$37{,}037}{\$170{,}910} = 21.7\%$$

To evaluate profit margin, we must consider the industry. For instance, an appliance company might require a profit margin between 10% and 15%, whereas a retail supermarket might require a profit margin of 1% or 2%. Both profit margin and *total asset turnover* make up the two basic components of operating efficiency. These ratios reflect on management because managers are ultimately responsible for operating efficiency. The next section explains how we use both measures to analyze return on total assets.

Return on Total Assets *Return on total assets* is defined as follows.

$$\textbf{Return on total assets} = \frac{\textbf{Net income}}{\textbf{Average total assets}}$$

Apple's 2013 return on total assets is

Return on total assets
Google = 12.6%
Samsung = 15.4%
Industry = 9%

$$\frac{\$37{,}037}{(\$176{,}064 + \$207{,}000)/2} = 19.3\%$$

Point: Many analysts add back *Interest expense × (1 − Tax rate)* to net income in computing return on total assets.

Apple's 19.3% return on total assets is higher than that for many businesses and is higher than Google's 12.6%, Samsung's 15.4%, and the industry's 9% return. We also should evaluate any trend in the rate of return.

The following equation shows the important relation between profit margin, total asset turnover, and return on total assets.

Profit margin × Total asset turnover = Return on total assets

or

$$\frac{\text{Net income}}{\text{Net sales}} \times \frac{\text{Net sales}}{\text{Average total assets}} = \frac{\text{Net income}}{\text{Average total assets}}$$

Both profit margin and total asset turnover contribute to overall operating efficiency, as measured by return on total assets. If we apply this formula to Apple, we get

$$21.7\% \times 0.89 = 19.3\% \text{ (with rounding)}$$

Google: 21.6% × 0.58 = 12.6%
Samsung: 13.3% × 1.16 = 15.4%
(with rounding)

This analysis shows that Apple's superior return on assets versus that of both Google and Samsung is driven by its higher profit and, in the case of Google, also by its better asset turnover.

Return on Common Stockholders' Equity Perhaps the most important goal in operating a company is to earn net income for its owner(s). *Return on common stockholders' equity* measures a company's success in reaching this goal and is defined as follows.

$$\text{Return on common stockholders' equity} = \frac{\text{Net income} - \text{Preferred dividends}}{\text{Average common stockholders' equity}}$$

Apple's 2013 return on common stockholders' equity is computed as follows:

$$\frac{\$37{,}037 - \$0}{(\$118{,}210 + \$123{,}549)/2} = 30.6\%$$

Return on common equity
Google = 16.2%
Samsung = 22.5%
Industry = 15%

The denominator in this computation is the book value of common equity (noncontrolling interest is often included in common equity for this ratio). In the numerator, the dividends on cumulative preferred stock are subtracted whether they are declared or are in arrears. If preferred stock is noncumulative, its dividends are subtracted only if declared. Apple's return on common stockholders' equity (30.6%) is superior to Google's 16.2% and Samsung's 22.5%.

Decision Insight

Wall Street *Wall Street* is synonymous with financial markets, but its name comes from the street location of the original New York Stock Exchange. The street's name derives from stockades built by early settlers to protect New York from pirate attacks. ■

Market Prospects

Market measures are useful for analyzing corporations with publicly traded stock. These market measures use stock price, which reflects the market's (public's) expectations for the company. This includes expectations of both company return and risk—as the market perceives it.

Price-Earnings Ratio Computation of the *price-earnings ratio* follows (Chapter 11 provides additional explanation).

$$\text{Price-earnings ratio} = \frac{\text{Market price per common share}}{\text{Earnings per share}}$$

Point: PE ratio can be viewed as an indicator of the market's expected growth and risk for a stock. High expected risk suggests a low PE ratio. High expected growth suggests a high PE ratio.

Predicted earnings per share for the next period is often used in the denominator of this computation. Reported earnings per share for the most recent period is also commonly used. In both cases, the ratio is used as an indicator of the future growth and risk of a company's earnings as perceived by the stock's buyers and sellers.

The market price of Apple's common stock at the start of fiscal year 2014 was $477.25. Using Apple's $40.03 basic earnings per share, we compute its price-earnings ratio as follows (some analysts compute this ratio using the median of the low and high stock price).

PE (year-end)
Google = 30.5
Samsung = 6.9

$$\frac{\$477.25}{\$40.03} = 11.9$$

Point: Some investors avoid stocks with high PE ratios under the belief they are "overpriced." Alternatively, some investors *sell these stocks short*—hoping for price declines.

Apple's price-earnings ratio is less than that for Google, but it is higher than that for Samsung and near the norm for this period.

Dividend Yield *Dividend yield* is used to compare the dividend-paying performance of different investment alternatives. We compute dividend yield as follows (Chapter 11 offers additional explanation).

$$\textbf{Dividend yield} = \frac{\textbf{Annual cash dividends per share}}{\textbf{Market price per share}}$$

Apple's dividend yield, based on its fiscal year-end market price per share of $477.25 and its $11.40 cash dividends per share, is computed as follows.

Dividend yield
Google = 0.0%
Samsung = 1.0%

$$\frac{\$11.40}{\$477.25} = 2.4\%$$

Point: Corporate PE ratios and dividend yields are found in daily stock market quotations listed in *The Wall Street Journal, Investor's Business Daily,* or other publications and web services.

Some companies, such as Google, do not declare and pay dividends because they wish to reinvest the cash to grow their businesses in the hope of generating greater future earnings and dividends.

Summary of Ratios

Exhibit 13.16 summarizes the major financial statement analysis ratios illustrated in this chapter and throughout the book. This summary includes each ratio's title, its formula, and the purpose for which it is commonly used.

Decision Insight

Ticker Prices *Ticker prices* refer to a band of moving data on a monitor carrying up-to-the-minute stock prices. The phrase comes from *ticker tape,* a 1-inch-wide strip of paper spewing stock prices from a printer that ticked as it ran. Most of today's investors have never seen actual ticker tape, but the phrase survives. ■

© Comstock Images/Jupiter Images

EXHIBIT 13.16

Financial Statement Analysis Ratios*

Ratio	Formula	Measure of
Liquidity and Efficiency		
Current ratio	$= \frac{\text{Current assets}}{\text{Current liabilities}}$	Short-term debt-paying ability
Acid-test ratio	$= \frac{\text{Cash + Short-term investments + Current receivables}}{\text{Current liabilities}}$	Immediate short-term debt-paying ability
Accounts receivable turnover	$= \frac{\text{Net sales}}{\text{Average accounts receivable, net}}$	Efficiency of collection
Inventory turnover	$= \frac{\text{Cost of goods sold}}{\text{Average inventory}}$	Efficiency of inventory management
Days' sales uncollected	$= \frac{\text{Accounts receivable, net}}{\text{Net sales}} \times 365$	Liquidity of receivables
Days' sales in inventory	$= \frac{\text{Ending inventory}}{\text{Cost of goods sold}} \times 365$	Liquidity of inventory
Total asset turnover	$= \frac{\text{Net sales}}{\text{Average total assets}}$	Efficiency of assets in producing sales
Solvency		
Debt ratio	$= \frac{\text{Total liabilities}}{\text{Total assets}}$	Creditor financing and leverage
Equity ratio	$= \frac{\text{Total equity}}{\text{Total assets}}$	Owner financing
Debt-to-equity ratio	$= \frac{\text{Total liabilities}}{\text{Total equity}}$	Debt versus equity financing
Times interest earned	$= \frac{\text{Income before interest expense and income taxes}}{\text{Interest expense}}$	Protection in meeting interest payments
Profitability		
Profit margin ratio	$= \frac{\text{Net income}}{\text{Net sales}}$	Net income in each sales dollar
Gross margin ratio	$= \frac{\text{Net sales} - \text{Cost of goods sold}}{\text{Net sales}}$	Gross margin in each sales dollar
Return on total assets	$= \frac{\text{Net income}}{\text{Average total assets}}$	Overall profitability of assets
Return on common stockholders' equity	$= \frac{\text{Net income} - \text{Preferred dividends}}{\text{Average common stockholders' equity}}$	Profitability of owner investment
Book value per common share	$= \frac{\text{Shareholders' equity applicable to common shares}}{\text{Number of common shares outstanding}}$	Liquidation at reported amounts
Basic earnings per share	$= \frac{\text{Net income} - \text{Preferred dividends}}{\text{Weighted-average common shares outstanding}}$	Net income per common share
Market Prospects		
Price-earnings ratio	$= \frac{\text{Market price per common share}}{\text{Earnings per share}}$	Market value relative to earnings
Dividend yield	$= \frac{\text{Annual cash dividends per share}}{\text{Market price per share}}$	Cash return per common share

* Additional ratios also examined in previous chapters included credit risk ratio; plant asset useful life; plant asset age; days' cash expense coverage; cash coverage of growth; cash coverage of debt; free cash flow; cash flow on total assets; and payout ratio.

NEED-TO-KNOW 13-3

Ratio Analysis

P3

For each ratio listed, identify whether the change in ratio value from 2014 to 2015 is regarded as favorable or unfavorable.

Ratio	2015	2014	Ratio	2015	2014
1. Profit margin	6%	8%	4. Accounts receivable turnover	8.8	9.4
2. Debt ratio	50%	70%	5. Basic earnings per share	$2.10	$2.00
3. Gross margin	40%	36%	6. Inventory turnover	3.6	4.0

Solution

Ratio	2015	2014	Change
1. Profit margin ratio.	6%	8%	Unfavorable
2. Debt ratio	50%	70%	Favorable
3. Gross margin ratio	40%	36%	Favorable
4. Accounts receivable turnover.	8.8	9.4	Unfavorable
5. Basic earnings per share	$2.10	$2.00	Favorable
6. Inventory turnover	3.6	4.0	Unfavorable

Do More: QS 13-6, E 13-7, E 13-8, E 13-9, E 13-10, E 13-11, P 13-4

QC3

GLOBAL VIEW

The analysis and interpretation of financial statements is, of course, impacted by the accounting system in effect. This section discusses similarities and differences for analysis of financial statements when prepared under U.S. GAAP vis-à-vis IFRS.

Horizontal and Vertical Analyses Horizontal and vertical analyses help eliminate many differences between U.S. GAAP and IFRS when analyzing and interpreting financial statements. Financial numbers are converted to percentages that are, in the best-case scenario, consistently applied across and within periods. This enables users to effectively compare companies across reporting regimes. However, when fundamental differences in reporting regimes impact financial statements, such as with certain recognition rule differences, the user must exercise caution when drawing conclusions. Some users will reformulate one set of numbers to be more consistent with the other system to enable comparative analysis. This reformulation process is covered in advanced courses. The important point is that horizontal and vertical analyses help strip away differences between the reporting regimes, but several key differences sometimes remain and require adjustment of the numbers.

Ratio Analysis Ratio analysis of financial statement numbers has many of the advantages and disadvantages of horizontal and vertical analyses discussed above. Importantly, ratio analysis is useful for business decisions, with some possible changes in interpretation depending on what is and what is not included in accounting measures across U.S. GAAP and IFRS. Still, we must take care in drawing inferences from a comparison of ratios across reporting regimes because what a number measures can differ across regimes. **Piaggio**, which manufactures two-, three- and four-wheel vehicles and is Europe's leading manufacturer of motorcycles and scooters, offers the following example of its own ratio analysis applied to its financing objectives: "The object of capital management . . . , [and] consistent with others in the industry, the Company monitors capital on the basis of a total liabilities to equity ratio. This ratio is calculated as total liabilities divided by equity."

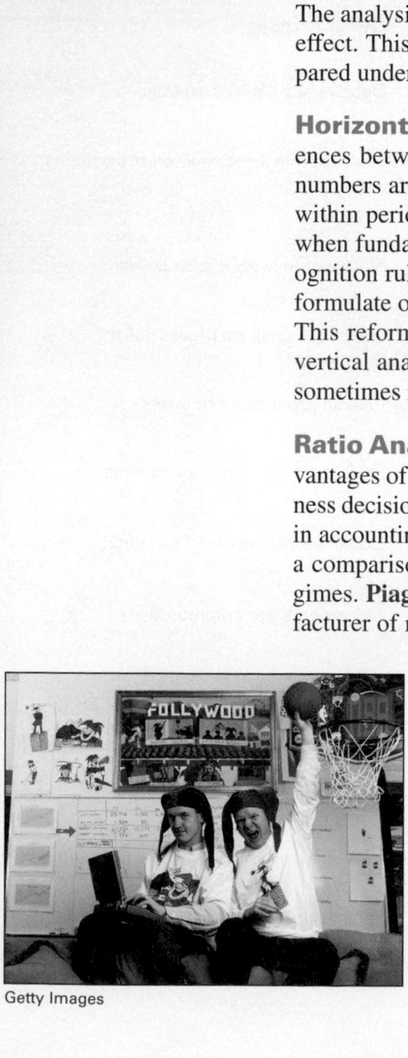

Getty Images

Sustainability and Accounting **The Motley Fool**, as introduced in this chapter's opening feature, emphasizes the importance of a sustainable and vibrant work environment. The Gardners wrote, "Sustainable advantage will not always be easy. That's one of the reasons that we value discussion in The Motley Fool . . . When determining a subjective attribute like sustainable advantage, we should all be interested in discovery." Morgan Housel, a Fool employee, explains that. "At the Motley Fool, we observe that the best . . . culture [is] built on trust and respect" (*USA Today,* April 2014). Thus, sustainability at the Fool means a dynamic, energetic, questioning workforce to analyze and interpret the information conveyed through financial reports.

Decision Insight

Not Created Equal Financial regulation has several goals. Two of them are to ensure adequate accounting disclosure and to strengthen corporate governance. For disclosure purposes, companies must now provide details of related-party transactions and material off-balance-sheet agreements. This is motivated by several major frauds. For corporate governance, the CEO and CFO must now certify the fairness of financial statements and the effectiveness of internal controls. Yet, concerns remain. A study reports that 23% of management and administrative employees observed activities that posed a conflict of interest in the past year (KPMG 2009). Another 12% witnessed the falsifying or manipulating of accounting information. The bottom line: All financial statements are not of equal quality. ■

Analysis Reporting — Decision Analysis

A1 Summarize and report results of analysis.

Understanding the purpose of financial statement analysis is crucial to the usefulness of any analysis. This understanding leads to efficiency of effort, effectiveness in application, and relevance in focus. The purpose of most financial statement analyses is to reduce uncertainty in business decisions through a rigorous and sound evaluation. A *financial statement analysis report* helps by directly addressing the building blocks of analysis and by identifying weaknesses in inference by requiring explanation: It forces us to organize our reasoning and to verify its flow and logic. A report also serves as a communication link with readers, and the writing process reinforces our judgments and vice versa. Finally, the report helps us (re) evaluate evidence and refine conclusions on key building blocks. A good analysis report usually consists of six sections:

1. **Executive summary**—brief focus on important analysis results and conclusions.
2. **Analysis overview**—background on the company, its industry, and its economic setting.
3. **Evidential matter**—financial statements and information used in the analysis, including ratios, trends, comparisons, statistics, and all analytical measures assembled; often organized under the building blocks of analysis.
4. **Assumptions**—identification of important assumptions regarding a company's industry and economic environment, and other important assumptions for estimates.
5. **Key factors**—list of important favorable and unfavorable factors, both quantitative and qualitative, for company performance; usually organized by areas of analysis.
6. **Inferences**—forecasts, estimates, interpretations, and conclusions drawing on all sections of the report.

We must remember that the user dictates relevance, meaning that the analysis report should include a brief table of contents to help readers focus on those areas most relevant to their decisions. All irrelevant matter must be eliminated. For example, decades-old details of obscure transactions and detailed miscues of the analysis are irrelevant. Ambiguities and qualifications to avoid responsibility or hedging inferences must be eliminated. Finally, writing is important. Mistakes in grammar and errors of fact compromise the report's credibility.

Decision Insight

Short Selling *Short selling* refers to selling stock before you buy it. Here's an example: You borrow 100 shares of Nike stock, sell them at $40 each, and receive money from their sale. You then wait. You hope that Nike's stock price falls to, say, $35 each and you can replace the borrowed stock for less than you sold it for, reaping a profit of $5 each less any transaction costs. ■

NEED-TO-KNOW
COMPREHENSIVE

Use the following financial statements of Precision Co. to complete these requirements.

1. Prepare comparative income statements showing the percent increase or decrease for year 2015 in comparison to year 2014.
2. Prepare common-size comparative balance sheets for years 2015 and 2014.

3. Compute the following ratios as of December 31, 2015, or for the year ended December 31, 2015, and identify its building block category for financial statement analysis.

a. Current ratio
b. Acid-test ratio
c. Accounts receivable turnover
d. Days' sales uncollected
e. Inventory turnover
f. Debt ratio
g. Debt-to-equity ratio
h. Times interest earned
i. Profit margin ratio
j. Total asset turnover
k. Return on total assets
l. Return on common stockholders' equity

PRECISION COMPANY
Comparative Income Statements
For Years Ended December 31, 2015 and 2014

	2015	2014
Sales	$2,486,000	$2,075,000
Cost of goods sold	1,523,000	1,222,000
Gross profit	963,000	853,000
Operating expenses		
Advertising expense	145,000	100,000
Sales salaries expense	240,000	280,000
Office salaries expense	165,000	200,000
Insurance expense	100,000	45,000
Supplies expense	26,000	35,000
Depreciation expense	85,000	75,000
Miscellaneous expenses	17,000	15,000
Total operating expenses	778,000	750,000
Operating income	185,000	103,000
Interest expense	44,000	46,000
Income before taxes	141,000	57,000
Income taxes	47,000	19,000
Net income	$ 94,000	$ 38,000
Earnings per share	$ 0.99	$ 0.40

PRECISION COMPANY
Comparative Balance Sheets
December 31, 2015 and 2014

	2015	2014
Assets		
Current assets		
Cash	$ 79,000	$ 42,000
Short-term investments	65,000	96,000
Accounts receivable, net	120,000	100,000
Merchandise inventory	250,000	265,000
Total current assets	514,000	503,000
Plant assets		
Store equipment, net	400,000	350,000
Office equipment, net	45,000	50,000
Buildings, net	625,000	675,000
Land	100,000	100,000
Total plant assets	1,170,000	1,175,000
Total assets	$1,684,000	$1,678,000
Liabilities		
Current liabilities		
Accounts payable	$ 164,000	$ 190,000
Short-term notes payable	75,000	90,000
Taxes payable	26,000	12,000
Total current liabilities	265,000	292,000
Long-term liabilities		
Notes payable (secured by mortgage on buildings)	400,000	420,000
Total liabilities	665,000	712,000
Stockholders' Equity		
Common stock, $5 par value	475,000	475,000
Retained earnings	544,000	491,000
Total stockholders' equity	1,019,000	966,000
Total liabilities and equity	$1,684,000	$1,678,000

PLANNING THE SOLUTION

- Set up a four-column income statement; enter the 2015 and 2014 amounts in the first two columns and then enter the dollar change in the third column and the percent change from 2014 in the fourth column.
- Set up a four-column balance sheet; enter the 2015 and 2014 year-end amounts in the first two columns and then compute and enter the amount of each item as a percent of total assets.

- Compute the required ratios using the data provided. Use the average of beginning and ending amounts when appropriate (see Exhibit 13.16 for definitions).

SOLUTION

1.

PRECISION COMPANY
Comparative Income Statements
For Years Ended December 31, 2015 and 2014

	2015	2014	Increase (Decrease) in 2015 Amount	Increase (Decrease) in 2015 Percent
Sales	$2,486,000	$2,075,000	$411,000	19.8%
Cost of goods sold	1,523,000	1,222,000	301,000	24.6
Gross profit	963,000	853,000	110,000	12.9
Operating expenses				
Advertising expense	145,000	100,000	45,000	45.0
Sales salaries expense	240,000	280,000	(40,000)	(14.3)
Office salaries expense	165,000	200,000	(35,000)	(17.5)
Insurance expense	100,000	45,000	55,000	122.2
Supplies expense	26,000	35,000	(9,000)	(25.7)
Depreciation expense	85,000	75,000	10,000	13.3
Miscellaneous expenses	17,000	15,000	2,000	13.3
Total operating expenses	778,000	750,000	28,000	3.7
Operating income	185,000	103,000	82,000	79.6
Interest expense	44,000	46,000	(2,000)	(4.3)
Income before taxes	141,000	57,000	84,000	147.4
Income taxes	47,000	19,000	28,000	147.4
Net income	$ 94,000	$ 38,000	$ 56,000	147.4
Earnings per share	$ 0.99	$ 0.40	$ 0.59	147.5

2.

PRECISION COMPANY
Common-Size Comparative Balance Sheets
December 31, 2015 and 2014

	December 31 2015	December 31 2014	Common-Size Percents 2015*	Common-Size Percents 2014*
Assets				
Current assets				
Cash	$ 79,000	$ 42,000	4.7%	2.5%
Short-term investments	65,000	96,000	3.9	5.7
Accounts receivable, net	120,000	100,000	7.1	6.0
Merchandise inventory	250,000	265,000	14.8	15.8
Total current assets	514,000	503,000	30.5	30.0
Plant assets				
Store equipment, net	400,000	350,000	23.8	20.9
Office equipment, net	45,000	50,000	2.7	3.0
Buildings, net	625,000	675,000	37.1	40.2
Land	100,000	100,000	5.9	6.0
Total plant assets	1,170,000	1,175,000	69.5	70.0
Total assets	$1,684,000	$1,678,000	100.0	100.0

[continued on next page]

[continued from previous page]

Liabilities				
Current liabilities				
Accounts payable	$ 164,000	$ 190,000	9.7%	11.3%
Short-term notes payable	75,000	90,000	4.5	5.4
Taxes payable	26,000	12,000	1.5	0.7
Total current liabilities	265,000	292,000	15.7	17.4
Long-term liabilities				
Notes payable (secured by mortgage on buildings)	400,000	420,000	23.8	25.0
Total liabilities	665,000	712,000	39.5	42.4
Stockholders' Equity				
Common stock, $5 par value	475,000	475,000	28.2	28.3
Retained earnings	544,000	491,000	32.3	29.3
Total stockholders' equity	1,019,000	966,000	60.5	57.6
Total liabilities and equity	$1,684,000	$1,678,000	100.0	100.0

* Columns do not always exactly add to 100 due to rounding.

3. Ratios for 2015:

a. Current ratio: $514,000/$265,000 = 1.9:1 (liquidity and efficiency)
b. Acid-test ratio: ($79,000 + $65,000 + $120,000)/$265,000 = 1.0:1 (liquidity and efficiency)
c. Average receivables: ($120,000 + $100,000)/2 = $110,000
Accounts receivable turnover: $2,486,000/$110,000 = 22.6 times (liquidity and efficiency)
d. Days' sales uncollected: ($120,000/$2,486,000) × 365 = 17.6 days (liquidity and efficiency)
e. Average inventory: ($250,000 + $265,000)/2 = $257,500
Inventory turnover: $1,523,000/$257,500 = 5.9 times (liquidity and efficiency)
f. Debt ratio: $665,000/$1,684,000 = 39.5% (solvency)
g. Debt-to-equity ratio: $665,000/$1,019,000 = 0.65 (solvency)
h. Times interest earned: $185,000/$44,000 = 4.2 times (solvency)
i. Profit margin ratio: $94,000/$2,486,000 = 3.8% (profitability)
j. Average total assets: ($1,684,000 + $1,678,000)/2 = $1,681,000
Total asset turnover: $2,486,000/$1,681,000 = 1.48 times (liquidity and efficiency)
k. Return on total assets: $94,000/$1,681,000 = 5.6% or 3.8% × 1.48 = 5.6% (profitability)
l. Average total common equity: ($1,019,000 + $966,000)/2 = $992,500
Return on common stockholders' equity: $94,000/$992,500 = 9.5% (profitability)

APPENDIX

13A Sustainable Income

A2 Explain the form and assess the content of a complete income statement.

When a company's revenue and expense transactions are from normal, continuing operations, a simple income statement is usually adequate. When a company's activities include income-related events not part of its normal, continuing operations, it must disclose information to help users understand these events and predict future performance. To meet these objectives, companies separate the income statement into continuing operations, discontinued segments, extraordinary items, comprehensive income, and earnings per share. For illustration, Exhibit 13A.1 shows such an income statement for ComUS. These separate distinctions help us measure *sustainable income,* which is the income level most likely to continue into the future. Sustainable income is commonly used in PE ratios and other market-based measures of performance.

Continuing Operations The first major section (①) shows the revenues, expenses, and income from continuing operations. Users especially rely on this information to predict future operations. Many

EXHIBIT 13A.1

Income Statement (all-inclusive) for a Corporation

ComUS Income Statement For Year Ended December 31, 2015			
①	Net sales		$8,478,000
	Operating expenses		
	Cost of goods sold	$5,950,000	
	Depreciation expense	35,000	
	Other selling, general and administrative expenses	515,000	
	Interest expense	20,000	
	Total operating expenses		(6,520,000)
	Other gains (losses)		
	Loss on plant relocation		(45,000)
	Gain on sale of surplus land		72,000
	Income from continuing operations before taxes		1,985,000
	Income taxes expense		(595,500)
	Income from continuing operations		1,389,500
②	**Discontinued segment**		
	Income from operating Division A (net of $180,000 taxes)	420,000	
	Loss on disposal of Division A (net of $66,000 tax benefit)	(154,000)	266,000
	Income before extraordinary items		1,655,500
③	**Extraordinary items**		
	Gain on land expropriated by state (net of $85,200 taxes)	198,800	
	Loss from earthquake damage (net of $270,000 tax benefit)	(630,000)	(431,200)
	Net income		$1,224,300
④	**Earnings per common share (200,000 outstanding shares)**		
	Income from continuing operations		$ 6.95
	Discontinued operations		1.33
	Income before extraordinary items		8.28
	Extraordinary items		(2.16)
	Net income (basic earnings per share)		$ 6.12

users view this section as the most important. Earlier chapters explained the items comprising income from continuing operations.

Discontinued Segments A **business segment** is a part of a company's operations that serves a particular line of business or class of customers. A segment has assets, liabilities, and financial results of operations that can be distinguished from those of other parts of the company. A company's gain or loss from selling or closing down a segment is separately reported. Section ② of Exhibit 13A.1 reports both (1) income from operating the discontinued segment for the current period prior to its disposal and (2) the loss from disposing of the segment's net assets. The income tax effects of each are reported separately from the income taxes expense in section ①.

Extraordinary Items Section ③ reports **extraordinary gains and losses,** which are those that are *both unusual* and *infrequent.* An **unusual gain or loss** is abnormal or otherwise unrelated to the company's regular activities and environment. An **infrequent gain or loss** is not expected to recur given the company's operating environment. Reporting extraordinary items in a separate category helps users predict future performance, absent the effects of extraordinary items. Items usually considered extraordinary include (1) expropriation (taking away) of property by a foreign government, (2) condemning of property by a domestic government body, (3) prohibition against using an asset by a newly enacted law, and (4) losses and gains from an unusual and infrequent calamity ("act of God"). Items *not* considered extraordinary include (1) write-downs of inventories and write-offs of receivables, (2) gains and losses from disposing of segments, and (3) financial effects of labor strikes.

Gains and losses that are neither unusual nor infrequent are reported as part of continuing operations. Gains and losses that are *either* unusual *or* infrequent, but *not* both, are reported as part of continuing operations *but* after the normal revenues and expenses.

Decision Maker

Small Business Owner You own an orange grove near Jacksonville, Florida. A bad frost destroys about one-half of your oranges. You are currently preparing an income statement for a bank loan. Can you claim the loss of oranges as extraordinary? ■ [Answers follow the chapter's Summary.]

Earnings per Share The final section ④ of the income statement in Exhibit 13A.1 reports earnings per share for each of the three subcategories of income (continuing operations, discontinued segments, and extraordinary items) when they exist. Earnings per share is discussed in Chapter 11.

Changes in Accounting Principles The *consistency concept* directs a company to apply the same accounting principles across periods. Yet a company can change from one acceptable accounting principle (such as FIFO, LIFO, or weighted-average) to another as long as the change improves the usefulness of information in its financial statements. A footnote would describe the accounting change and why it is an improvement.

Point: Changes in principles are sometimes required when new accounting standards are issued.

Changes in accounting principles require retrospective application to prior periods' financial statements. *Retrospective application* involves applying a different accounting principle to prior periods as if that principle had always been used. Retrospective application enhances the consistency of financial information between periods, which improves the usefulness of information, especially with comparative analyses. Accounting standards also require that *a change in depreciation, amortization, or depletion method for long-term operating assets is accounted for as a change in accounting estimate*—that is, prospectively over current and future periods. This reflects the notion that an entity should change its depreciation, amortization, or depletion method only with changes in estimated asset benefits, the pattern of benefit usage, or information about those benefits.

QC4

Summary

C1 Explain the purpose and identify the building blocks of analysis. The purpose of financial statement analysis is to help users make better business decisions. Internal users want information to improve company efficiency and effectiveness in providing products and services. External users want information to make better and more informed decisions in pursuing their goals. The common goals of all users are to evaluate a company's (1) past and current performance, (2) current financial position, and (3) future performance and risk. Financial statement analysis focuses on four "building blocks" of analysis: (1) liquidity and efficiency—ability to meet short-term obligations and efficiently generate revenues; (2) solvency—ability to generate future revenues and meet long-term obligations; (3) profitability—ability to provide financial rewards sufficient to attract and retain financing; and (4) market prospects—ability to generate positive market expectations.

C2 Describe standards for comparisons in analysis. Standards for comparisons include (1) intracompany—prior performance and relations between financial items for the company under analysis; (2) competitor—one or more direct competitors of the company; (3) industry—industry statistics; and (4) guidelines (rules of thumb)—general standards developed from past experiences and personal judgments.

A1 Summarize and report results of analysis. A financial statement analysis report is often organized around the building blocks of analysis. A good report separates interpretations and conclusions of analysis from the information underlying them. An analysis report often consists of six sections: (1) executive summary, (2) analysis overview, (3) evidential matter, (4) assumptions, (5) key factors, and (6) inferences.

A2A Explain the form and assess the content of a complete income statement. An income statement has four *potential* sections: (1) continuing operations, (2) discontinued segments, (3) extraordinary items, and (4) earnings per share.

P1 Explain and apply methods of horizontal analysis. Horizontal analysis is a tool to evaluate changes in data across time. Two important tools of horizontal analysis are comparative statements and trend analysis. Comparative statements show amounts for two or more successive periods, often with changes disclosed in both absolute and percent terms. Trend analysis is used to reveal important changes occurring from one period to the next.

P2 Describe and apply methods of vertical analysis. Vertical analysis is a tool to evaluate each financial statement item or group of items in terms of a base amount. Two tools of vertical analysis are common-size statements and graphical analyses. Each item in common-size statements is expressed as a percent of a base amount. For the balance sheet, the base amount is usually total assets, and for the income statement, it is usually sales.

P3 Define and apply ratio analysis. Ratio analysis provides clues to and symptoms of underlying conditions. Ratios, properly interpreted, identify areas requiring further investigation. A ratio expresses a mathematical relation between two quantities such as a percent, rate, or proportion. Ratios can be organized into the building blocks of analysis: (1) liquidity and efficiency, (2) solvency, (3) profitability, and (4) market prospects.

Guidance Answers to Decision Maker

Auditor The *joint relation* referred to is the combined increase in sales and the decrease in expenses yielding more than a 5% increase in income. Both *individual* accounts (sales and expenses) yield percent changes within the ±5% acceptable range. However, a joint analysis suggests a different picture. For example, consider a joint analysis using the profit margin ratio. The client's profit margin is 11.46% ($206,000 − $182,400/$206,000) for the current year compared with 5.0% ($200,000 − $190,000/$200,000) for the prior year—yielding a 129% increase in profit margin! This is what concerns the partner, and it suggests expanding audit tests to verify or refute the client's figures.

Banker Your decision on the loan application is positive for at least two reasons. First, the current ratio suggests a strong ability to meet short-term obligations. Second, current assets of $160,000 and a current ratio of 4:1 imply current liabilities of $40,000 (one-fourth of current assets) and a working capital excess of $120,000. This working capital excess is 60% of the loan amount. However, if the application is for a 10-year loan, our decision is less optimistic. The current ratio and working capital suggest a good safety margin, but indications of inefficiency in operations exist. In particular, a 4:1 current ratio is more than double its key competitors' ratio. This is characteristic of inefficient asset use.

Small Business Owner The frost loss is probably not extraordinary. Jacksonville experiences enough recurring frost damage to make it difficult to argue this event is both unusual and infrequent. Still, you want to highlight the frost loss and hope the bank views this uncommon event separately from continuing operations.

Key Terms

Business segment
Common-size financial statement
Comparative financial statements
Efficiency
Equity ratio
Extraordinary gains and losses
Financial reporting
Financial statement analysis
General-purpose financial statements
Horizontal analysis
Infrequent gain or loss
Liquidity
Market prospects
Profitability
Ratio analysis
Solvency
Unusual gain or loss
Vertical analysis
Working capital

Multiple Choice Quiz

Answers at end of chapter

1. A company's sales in 2014 were $300,000 and in 2015 were $351,000. Using 2014 as the base year, the sales trend percent for 2015 is:
a. 17% **c.** 100% **e.** 48%
b. 85% **d.** 117%

Use the following information for questions 2 through 5.

GALLOWAY COMPANY
Balance Sheet
December 31, 2015

Assets	
Cash	$ 86,000
Accounts receivable	76,000
Merchandise inventory	122,000
Prepaid insurance	12,000
Long-term investments	98,000
Plant assets, net	436,000
Total assets	$830,000
Liabilities and Equity	
Current liabilities	$124,000
Long-term liabilities	90,000
Common stock	300,000
Retained earnings	316,000
Total liabilities and equity	$830,000

2. What is Galloway Company's current ratio?
a. 0.69
b. 1.31
c. 3.88
d. 6.69
e. 2.39

3. What is Galloway Company's acid-test ratio?
a. 2.39
b. 0.69
c. 1.31
d. 6.69
e. 3.88

4. What is Galloway Company's debt ratio?
a. 25.78%
b. 100.00%
c. 74.22%
d. 137.78%
e. 34.74%

5. What is Galloway Company's equity ratio?
a. 25.78%
b. 100.00%
c. 34.74%
d. 74.22%
e. 137.78%

A Superscript letter A denotes assignments based on Appendix 13A.
Icon denotes assignments that involve decision making.

Discussion Questions

1. Explain the difference between financial reporting and financial statements.
2. What is the difference between comparative financial statements and common-size comparative statements?
3. Which items are usually assigned a 100% value on (*a*) a common-size balance sheet and (*b*) a common-size income statement?
4. What three factors would influence your evaluation as to whether a company's current ratio is good or bad?
5. Suggest several reasons why a 2:1 current ratio might not be adequate for a particular company.
6. Why is working capital given special attention in the process of analyzing balance sheets?
7. What does the number of days' sales uncollected indicate?
8. What does a relatively high accounts receivable turnover indicate about a company's short-term liquidity?
9. Why is a company's capital structure, as measured by debt and equity ratios, important to financial statement analysts?
10. How does inventory turnover provide information about a company's short-term liquidity?
11. What ratios would you compute to evaluate management performance?
12. Why would a company's return on total assets be different from its return on common stockholders' equity?
13. Where on the income statement does a company report an unusual gain not expected to occur more often than once every two years or so?
14. Refer to **Apple**'s financial statements in Appendix A. Compute its profit margin for the years ended September 28, 2013, and September 29, 2012. **APPLE**
15. Refer to **Google**'s financial statements in Appendix A to compute its equity ratio as of December 31, 2013, and December 31, 2012. **GOOGLE**
16. Refer to **Samsung**'s financial statements in Appendix A. Compute its debt ratio as of December 31, 2013, and December 31, 2012. **Samsung**
17. Use **Samsung**'s financial statements in Appendix A to compute its return on total assets for fiscal year ended December 31, 2013. **Samsung**

connect

QUICK STUDY

QS 13-1
Financial reporting
C1

Which of the following items *a* through *i* are part of financial reporting but are *not* included as part of general-purpose financial statements?

____ **a.** Income statement
____ **b.** Balance sheet
____ **c.** Prospectus
____ **d.** Financial statement notes
____ **e.** Company news releases
____ **f.** Statement of cash flows
____ **g.** Stock price information and analysis
____ **h.** Statement of shareholders' equity
____ **i.** Management discussion and analysis of financial performance

QS 13-2
Standard of comparison
C2

Identify which standard of comparison, (*a*) intracompany, (*b*) competitor, (*c*) industry, or (*d*) guidelines, is best described by each of the following.

______ **1.** Is often viewed as the best standard of comparison.
______ **2.** Rules of thumb developed from past experiences.
______ **3.** Provides analysis based on a company's prior performance.
______ **4.** Compares a company against industry statistics.

QS 13-3
Horizontal analysis
P1

Compute the annual dollar changes and percent changes for each of the following accounts.

	2015	2014
Short-term investments	$374,634	$234,000
Accounts receivable	97,364	101,000
Notes payable	0	88,000

QS 13-4
Trend percents
P1

Use the following information for Tide Corporation to determine the 2014 and 2015 trend percents for net sales using 2014 as the base year.

($ thousands)	2015	2014
Net sales	$801,810	$453,000
Cost of goods sold	392,887	134,088

QS 13-5
Common-size analysis P2

Refer to the information in QS 13-4. Use that information for Tide Corporation to determine the 2014 and 2015 common-size percents for cost of goods sold using net sales as the base.

QS 13-6
Ratio interpretation
P3

For each ratio listed, identify whether the change in ratio value from 2014 to 2015 is usually regarded as favorable or unfavorable.

Ratio	2015	2014	Ratio	2015	2014
____ 1. Profit margin	9%	8%	____ 5. Accounts receivable turnover	5.5	6.7
____ 2. Debt ratio	47%	42%	____ 6. Basic earnings per share	$1.25	$1.10
____ 3. Gross margin	34%	46%	____ 7. Inventory turnover	3.6	3.4
____ 4. Acid-test ratio	1.00	1.15	____ 8. Dividend yield	2.0%	1.2%

QS 13-7
Analysis of short-term financial condition
A1

The following information is available for Morgan Company and Parker Company, similar firms operating in the same industry. Write a half-page report comparing Morgan and Parker using the available information. Your discussion should include their ability to meet current obligations and to use current assets efficiently.

	A	B	C	D	E	F	G	H
1			Morgan				Parker	
2		2015	2014	2013		2015	2014	2013
3	Current ratio	1.7	1.6	2.1		3.2	2.7	1.9
4	Acid-test ratio	1.0	1.1	1.2		2.8	2.5	1.6
5	Accounts receivable turnover	30.5	25.2	29.2		16.4	15.2	16.0
6	Merchandise inventory turnover	24.2	21.9	17.1		14.5	13.0	12.6
7	Working capital	$70,000	$58,000	$52,000		$131,000	$103,000	$78,000
8								

Team Project: Assume that the two companies apply for a one-year loan from the team. Identify additional information the companies must provide before the team can make a loan decision.

QS 13-8^A
Error adjustments
A2

A review of the notes payable files discovers that three years ago the company reported the entire $1,000 cash payment (consisting of $800 principal and $200 interest) toward an installment note payable as interest expense. This mistake had a material effect on the amount of income in that year. How should the correction be reported in the current-year financial statements?

QS 13-9
International ratio analysis
C2

Answer each of the following related to international accounting and analysis.

a. Identify a limitation to using ratio analysis when examining companies reporting under different accounting systems such as IFRS versus U.S. GAAP.

b. Identify an advantage to using horizontal and vertical analyses when examining companies reporting under different currencies.

connect

EXERCISES

Exercise 13-1
Building blocks of analysis
C1

Match the ratio to the building block of financial statement analysis to which it best relates.

A. Liquidity and efficiency **B.** Solvency **C.** Profitability **D.** Market prospects

____ **1.** Equity ratio
____ **2.** Return on total assets
____ **3.** Dividend yield
____ **4.** Book value per common share
____ **5.** Days' sales in inventory
____ **6.** Accounts receivable turnover
____ **7.** Debt-to-equity
____ **8.** Times interest earned
____ **9.** Gross margin ratio
____ **10.** Acid-test ratio

Exercise 13-2
Identifying financial ratios
C2

Identify which of the following six metrics *a* through *f* best completes questions *1* through *3* below.

a. Days' sales uncollected
b. Accounts receivable turnover
c. Working capital
d. Return on total assets
e. Total asset turnover
f. Profit margin

1. Which two ratios are key components in measuring a company's operating efficiency? ______ ______ Which ratio summarizes these two components? ______
2. What measure reflects the difference between current assets and current liabilities? ______
3. Which two short-term liquidity ratios measure how frequently a company collects its accounts? ______ ______

Exercise 13-3
Computation and analysis of trend percents
P1

Compute trend percents for the following accounts, using 2011 as the base year (round the percents to whole numbers). State whether the situation as revealed by the trends appears to be favorable or unfavorable for each account.

	2015	2014	2013	2012	2011
Sales	$282,880	$270,800	$252,600	$234,560	$150,000
Cost of goods sold	128,200	122,080	115,280	106,440	67,000
Accounts receivable	18,100	17,300	16,400	15,200	9,000

Exercise 13-4
Common-size percent computation and interpretation
P2

Express the following comparative income statements in common-size percents and assess whether or not this company's situation has improved in the most recent year (round the percents to one decimal).

GOMEZ CORPORATION
Comparative Income Statements
For Years Ended December 31, 2015 and 2014

	2015	2014
Sales	$740,000	$625,000
Cost of goods sold	560,300	290,800
Gross profit	179,700	334,200
Operating expenses	128,200	218,500
Net income	$ 51,500	$115,700

Exercise 13-5
Determination of income effects from common-size and trend percents
P1 P2

Common-size and trend percents for Rustynail Company's sales, cost of goods sold, and expenses follow. Determine whether net income increased, decreased, or remained unchanged in this three-year period.

	Common-Size Percents			Trend Percents		
	2015	2014	2013	2015	2014	2013
Sales	100.0%	100.0%	100.0%	105.4%	104.2%	100.0%
Cost of goods sold	63.4	61.9	59.1	113.1	109.1	100.0
Total expenses	15.3	14.8	15.1	106.8	102.1	100.0

Exercise 13-6
Common-size percents
P2

Simon Company's year-end balance sheets follow. Express the balance sheets in common-size percents. Round amounts to the nearest one-tenth of a percent. Analyze and comment on the results.

At December 31	2015	2014	2013
Assets			
Cash	$ 31,800	$ 35,625	$ 37,800
Accounts receivable, net	89,500	62,500	50,200
Merchandise inventory	112,500	82,500	54,000
Prepaid expenses	10,700	9,375	5,000
Plant assets, net	278,500	255,000	230,500
Total assets	$523,000	$445,000	$377,500
Liabilities and Equity			
Accounts payable	$129,900	$ 75,250	$ 51,250
Long-term notes payable secured by mortgages on plant assets	98,500	101,500	83,500
Common stock, $10 par value	163,500	163,500	163,500
Retained earnings	131,100	104,750	79,250
Total liabilities and equity	$523,000	$445,000	$377,500

Exercise 13-7
Liquidity analysis
P3

Refer to Simon Company's balance sheets in Exercise 13-6. Analyze its year-end short-term liquidity position at the end of 2015, 2014, and 2013 by computing (1) the current ratio and (2) the acid-test ratio. Comment on the ratio results. (Round ratio amounts to two decimals.)

Exercise 13-8
Liquidity analysis and interpretation
P3

Refer to the Simon Company information in Exercise 13-6. The company's income statements for the years ended December 31, 2015 and 2014, follow. Assume that all sales are on credit and then compute: (1) days' sales uncollected, (2) accounts receivable turnover, (3) inventory turnover, and (4) days' sales in inventory. Comment on the changes in the ratios from 2014 to 2015. (Round amounts to one decimal.)

For Year Ended December 31	2015		2014	
Sales		$673,500		$532,000
Cost of goods sold	$411,225		$345,500	
Other operating expenses	209,550		134,980	
Interest expense	12,100		13,300	
Income taxes	9,525		8,845	
Total costs and expenses		642,400		502,625
Net income		$ 31,100		$ 29,375
Earnings per share		$ 1.90		$ 1.80

Exercise 13-9
Risk and capital structure analysis
P3

Refer to the Simon Company information in Exercises 13-6 and 13-8. Compare the company's long-term risk and capital structure positions at the end of 2015 and 2014 by computing these ratios: (1) debt and equity ratios—percent rounded to one decimal, (2) debt-to-equity ratio—rounded to two decimals, and (3) times interest earned—rounded to one decimal. Comment on these ratio results.

Exercise 13-10
Efficiency and profitability analysis
P3

Refer to Simon Company's financial information in Exercises 13-6 and 13-8. Evaluate the company's efficiency and profitability by computing the following for 2015 and 2014: (1) profit margin ratio—percent rounded to one decimal, (2) total asset turnover—rounded to one decimal, and (3) return on total assets—percent rounded to one decimal. Comment on these ratio results.

Exercise 13-11
Profitability analysis
P3

Refer to Simon Company's financial information in Exercises 13-6 and 13-8. Additional information about the company follows. To help evaluate the company's profitability, compute and interpret the following ratios for 2015 and 2014: (1) return on common stockholders' equity—percent rounded to one decimal, (2) price-earnings ratio on December 31—rounded to one decimal, and (3) dividend yield—percent rounded to one decimal.

Common stock market price, December 31, 2015	$30.00
Common stock market price, December 31, 2014	28.00
Annual cash dividends per share in 2015	0.29
Annual cash dividends per share in 2014	0.24

Exercise 13-12
Analysis of efficiency and financial leverage
A1

Roak Company and Clay Company are similar firms that operate in the same industry. Clay began operations in 2013 and Roak in 2010. In 2015, both companies pay 7% interest on their debt to creditors. The following additional information is available.

	Roak Company			Clay Company		
	2015	2014	2013	2015	2014	2013
Total asset turnover	3.1	2.8	3.0	1.7	1.5	1.1
Return on total assets	9.0%	9.6%	8.8%	5.9%	5.6%	5.3%
Profit margin ratio	2.4%	2.5%	2.3%	2.8%	3.0%	2.9%
Sales	$410,000	$380,000	$396,000	$210,000	$170,000	$110,000

Write a half-page report comparing Roak and Clay using the available information. Your analysis should include their ability to use assets efficiently to produce profits. Also comment on their success in employing financial leverage in 2015.

Exercise 13-13A
Income statement categories
A2

In 2015, Randa Merchandising, Inc., sold its interest in a chain of wholesale outlets, taking the company completely out of the wholesaling business. The company still operates its retail outlets. A listing of the major sections of an income statement follows:

A. Income (loss) from continuing operations
B. Income (loss) from operating, or gain (loss) from disposing, a discontinued segment
C. Extraordinary gain (loss)

Indicate where each of the following income-related items for this company appears on its 2015 income statement by writing the letter of the appropriate section in the blank beside each item.

Section	Item	Debit	Credit
______	1. Net sales		$2,900,000
______	2. Gain on state's condemnation of company property (net of tax)		230,000
______	3. Cost of goods sold	$1,480,000	
______	4. Income taxes expense	217,000	
______	5. Depreciation expense	232,500	
______	6. Gain on sale of wholesale business segment (net of tax)		775,000
______	7. Loss from operating wholesale business segment (net of tax)	444,000	
______	8. Salaries expense	640,000	

Exercise 13-14A
Income statement presentation A2

Use the financial data for Randa Merchandising, Inc., in Exercise 13-13 to prepare its income statement for calendar year 2015. (Ignore the earnings per share section.)

Exercise 13-15
Ratio analysis under different currencies
P3

Nintendo Company, Ltd., reports the following financial information as of, or for the year ended, March 31, 2013. Nintendo reports its financial statements in both Japanese yen and U.S. dollars as shown (amounts in millions).

Current assets	¥1,192,250	$12,683,516
Total assets	1,447,878	15,402,966
Current liabilities	194,475	2,068,887
Net sales	635,422	6,759,818
Net income	7,099	75,527

1. Compute Nintendo's current ratio, net profit margin, and sales-to-total-assets using the financial information reported in (a) yen and (b) dollars. Round amounts to two decimals.
2. What can we conclude from a review of the results for part 1?

connect

PROBLEM SET A

Problem 13-1A
Calculation and analysis of trend percents
A1 P1

Selected comparative financial statements of Haroun Company follow.

HAROUN COMPANY
Comparative Income Statements
For Years Ended December 31, 2015–2009

($ thousands)	2015	2014	2013	2012	2011	2010	2009
Sales	$1,694	$1,496	$1,370	$1,264	$1,186	$1,110	$928
Cost of goods sold	1,246	1,032	902	802	752	710	586
Gross profit	448	464	468	462	434	400	342
Operating expenses	330	256	234	170	146	144	118
Net income	$ 118	$ 208	$ 234	$ 292	$ 288	$ 256	$224

HAROUN COMPANY
Comparative Balance Sheets
December 31, 2015–2009

($ thousands)	2015	2014	2013	2012	2011	2010	2009
Assets							
Cash	$ 58	$ 78	$ 82	$ 84	$ 88	$ 86	$ 89
Accounts receivable, net	490	514	466	360	318	302	216
Merchandise inventory	1,838	1,364	1,204	1,032	936	810	615
Other current assets	36	32	14	34	28	28	9
Long-term investments	0	0	0	146	146	146	146
Plant assets, net	2,020	2,014	1,752	944	978	860	725
Total assets	$4,442	$4,002	$3,518	$2,600	$2,494	$2,232	$1,800
Liabilities and Equity							
Current liabilities	$1,220	$1,042	$ 718	$ 614	$ 546	$ 522	$ 282
Long-term liabilities	1,294	1,140	1,112	570	580	620	400
Common stock	1,000	1,000	1,000	850	850	650	650
Other paid-in capital	250	250	250	170	170	150	150
Retained earnings	678	570	438	396	348	290	318
Total liabilities and equity	$4,442	$4,002	$3,518	$2,600	$2,494	$2,232	$1,800

Required

1. Compute trend percents for all components of both statements using 2009 as the base year. (Round percents to one decimal.)

Check (1) 2015, Total assets trend, 246.8%

Analysis Component

2. Analyze and comment on the financial statements and trend percents from part 1.

Problem 13-2A
Ratios, common-size statements, and trend percents
P1 P2 P3

Selected comparative financial statements of Korbin Company follow.

KORBIN COMPANY
Comparative Income Statements
For Years Ended December 31, 2015, 2014, and 2013

	2015	2014	2013
Sales	$555,000	$340,000	$278,000
Cost of goods sold	283,500	212,500	153,900
Gross profit	271,500	127,500	124,100
Selling expenses	102,900	46,920	50,800
Administrative expenses	50,668	29,920	22,800
Total expenses	153,568	76,840	73,600
Income before taxes	117,932	50,660	50,500
Income taxes	40,800	10,370	15,670
Net income	$ 77,132	$ 40,290	$ 34,830

KORBIN COMPANY
Comparative Balance Sheets
December 31, 2015, 2014, and 2013

	2015	2014	2013
Assets			
Current assets	$ 52,390	$ 37,924	$ 51,748
Long-term investments	0	500	3,950
Plant assets, net	100,000	96,000	60,000
Total assets	$152,390	$134,424	$115,698
Liabilities and Equity			
Current liabilities	$ 22,800	$ 19,960	$ 20,300
Common stock	72,000	72,000	60,000
Other paid-in capital	9,000	9,000	6,000
Retained earnings	48,590	33,464	29,398
Total liabilities and equity	$152,390	$134,424	$115,698

Required

1. Compute each year's current ratio. (Round ratio amounts to one decimal.)
2. Express the income statement data in common-size percents. (Round percents to two decimals.)
3. Express the balance sheet data in trend percents with 2013 as the base year. (Round percents to two decimals.)

Check (3) 2015, Total assets trend, 131.71%

Analysis Component

4. Comment on any significant relations revealed by the ratios and percents computed.

Problem 13-3A
Transactions, working capital, and liquidity ratios
P3

Plum Corporation began the month of May with $700,000 of current assets, a current ratio of 2.50:1, and an acid-test ratio of 1.10:1. During the month, it completed the following transactions (the company uses a perpetual inventory system).

May	2	Purchased $50,000 of merchandise inventory on credit.
	8	Sold merchandise inventory that cost $55,000 for $110,000 cash.
	10	Collected $20,000 cash on an account receivable.
	15	Paid $22,000 cash to settle an account payable.
	17	Wrote off a $5,000 bad debt against the Allowance for Doubtful Accounts account.
	22	Declared a $1 per share cash dividend on its 50,000 shares of outstanding common stock.

Check May 22: Current ratio, 2.19; Acid-test ratio, 1.11

26 Paid the dividend declared on May 22.
27 Borrowed $100,000 cash by giving the bank a 30-day, 10% note.
28 Borrowed $80,000 cash by signing a long-term secured note.
29 Used the $180,000 cash proceeds from the notes to buy new machinery.

May 29: Current ratio, 1.80; Working capital, $325,000

Required

Prepare a table showing Plum's (1) current ratio, (2) acid-test ratio, and (3) working capital after each transaction. Round ratios to two decimals.

Problem 13-4A
Calculation of financial statement ratios
P3

Selected year-end financial statements of Cabot Corporation follow. (All sales were on credit; selected balance sheet amounts at December 31, 2014, were inventory, $48,900; total assets, $189,400; common stock, $90,000; and retained earnings, $22,748.)

CABOT CORPORATION
Income Statement
For Year Ended December 31, 2015

Sales	$448,600
Cost of goods sold	297,250
Gross profit	151,350
Operating expenses	98,600
Interest expense	4,100
Income before taxes	48,650
Income taxes	19,598
Net income	$ 29,052

CABOT CORPORATION
Balance Sheet
December 31, 2015

Assets		Liabilities and Equity	
Cash	$ 10,000	Accounts payable	$ 17,500
Short-term investments	8,400	Accrued wages payable	3,200
Accounts receivable, net	29,200	Income taxes payable	3,300
Notes receivable (trade)*	4,500	Long-term note payable, secured by mortgage on plant assets	63,400
Merchandise inventory	32,150	Common stock	90,000
Prepaid expenses	2,650	Retained earnings	62,800
Plant assets, net	153,300	Total liabilities and equity	$240,200
Total assets	$240,200		

* These are short-term notes receivable arising from customer (trade) sales.

Required

Compute the following: (1) current ratio, (2) acid-test ratio, (3) days' sales uncollected, (4) inventory turnover, (5) days' sales in inventory, (6) debt-to-equity ratio, (7) times interest earned, (8) profit margin ratio, (9) total asset turnover, (10) return on total assets, and (11) return on common stockholders' equity. Round to one decimal place; for part 6, round to two decimals.

Check Acid-test ratio, 2.2 to 1; Inventory turnover, 7.3

Problem 13-5A
Comparative ratio analysis A1 P3

Summary information from the financial statements of two companies competing in the same industry follows.

	Barco Company	Kyan Company
Data from the current year-end balance sheets		
Assets		
Cash	$ 19,500	$ 34,000
Accounts receivable, net	37,400	57,400
Current notes receivable (trade)	9,100	7,200
Merchandise inventory	84,440	132,500
Prepaid expenses	5,000	6,950
Plant assets, net	290,000	304,400
Total assets	$445,440	$542,450
Liabilities and Equity		
Current liabilities	$ 61,340	$ 93,300
Long-term notes payable	80,800	101,000
Common stock, $5 par value	180,000	206,000
Retained earnings	123,300	142,150
Total liabilities and equity	$445,440	$542,450

	Barco Company	Kyan Company
Data from the current year's income statement		
Sales	$770,000	$880,200
Cost of goods sold	585,100	632,500
Interest expense	7,900	13,000
Income tax expense	14,800	24,300
Net income	162,200	210,400
Basic earnings per share	4.51	5.11
Cash dividends per share	3.81	3.93
Beginning-of-year balance sheet data		
Accounts receivable, net	$ 29,800	$ 54,200
Current notes receivable (trade)	0	0
Merchandise inventory	55,600	107,400
Total assets	398,000	382,500
Common stock, $5 par value	180,000	206,000
Retained earnings	98,260	93,666

Required

Check (1) Kyan: Accounts receivable turnover, 14.8; Inventory turnover, 5.3

(2) Barco: Profit margin, 21.1%; PE, 16.6

1. For both companies compute the (*a*) current ratio, (*b*) acid-test ratio, (*c*) accounts (including notes) receivable turnover, (*d*) inventory turnover, (*e*) days' sales in inventory, and (*f*) days' sales uncollected. Identify the company you consider to be the better short-term credit risk and explain why. Round to one decimal place.
2. For both companies compute the (*a*) profit margin ratio, (*b*) total asset turnover, (*c*) return on total assets, and (*d*) return on common stockholders' equity. Assuming that each company's stock can be purchased at $75 per share, compute their (*e*) price-earnings ratios and (*f*) dividend yields. Round to one decimal place. Identify which company's stock you would recommend as the better investment and explain why.

Problem 13-6A[A]
Income statement computations and format
A2

Selected account balances from the adjusted trial balance for Olinda Corporation as of its calendar year-end December 31, 2015, follow.

	Debit	Credit
a. Interest revenue		$ 14,000
b. Depreciation expense—Equipment	$ 34,000	
c. Loss on sale of equipment	25,850	
d. Accounts payable		44,000
e. Other operating expenses	106,400	
f. Accumulated depreciation—Equipment		71,600
g. Gain from settlement of lawsuit		44,000
h. Accumulated depreciation—Buildings		174,500
i. Loss from operating a discontinued segment (pretax)	18,250	
j. Gain on insurance recovery of tornado damage (pretax and extraordinary)		29,120
k. Net sales		998,500
l. Depreciation expense—Buildings	52,000	
m. Correction of overstatement of prior year's sales (pretax)	16,000	
n. Gain on sale of discontinued segment's assets (pretax)		34,000
o. Loss from settlement of lawsuit	23,750	
p. Income taxes expense	?	
q. Cost of goods sold	482,500	

Required

Answer each of the following questions by providing supporting computations.

1. Assume that the company's income tax rate is 30% for all items. Identify the tax effects and after-tax amounts of the four items labeled pretax.
2. What is the amount of income from continuing operations before income taxes? What is the amount of the income taxes expense? What is the amount of income from continuing operations?
3. What is the total amount of after-tax income (loss) associated with the discontinued segment?
4. What is the amount of income (loss) before the extraordinary items?
5. What is the amount of net income for the year?

Check (3) $11,025
(4) $243,425
(5) $263,809

PROBLEM SET B

Problem 13-1B
Calculation and analysis of trend percents
A1 P1

Selected comparative financial statements of Tripoly Company follow.

TRIPOLY COMPANY
Comparative Income Statements
For Years Ended December 31, 2015–2009

($ thousands)	2015	2014	2013	2012	2011	2010	2009
Sales	$560	$610	$630	$680	$740	$770	$860
Cost of goods sold	276	290	294	314	340	350	380
Gross profit	284	320	336	366	400	420	480
Operating expenses	84	104	112	126	140	144	150
Net income	$200	$216	$224	$240	$260	$276	$330

TRIPOLY COMPANY
Comparative Balance Sheets
December 31, 2015–2009

($ thousands)	2015	2014	2013	2012	2011	2010	2009
Assets							
Cash	$ 44	$ 46	$ 52	$ 54	$ 60	$ 62	$ 68
Accounts receivable, net	130	136	140	144	150	154	160
Merchandise inventory	166	172	178	180	186	190	208
Other current assets	34	34	36	38	38	40	40
Long-term investments	36	30	26	110	110	110	110
Plant assets, net	510	514	520	412	420	428	454
Total assets	$920	$932	$952	$938	$964	$984	$1,040
Liabilities and Equity							
Current liabilities	$148	$156	$186	$190	$210	$260	$280
Long-term liabilities	92	120	142	148	194	214	260
Common stock	160	160	160	160	160	160	160
Other paid-in capital	70	70	70	70	70	70	70
Retained earnings	450	426	394	370	330	280	270
Total liabilities and equity	$920	$932	$952	$938	$964	$984	$1,040

Required

1. Compute trend percents for all components of both statements using 2009 as the base year. (Round percents to one decimal.)

Check (1) 2015, Total assets trend, 88.5%

Analysis Component

2. Analyze and comment on the financial statements and trend percents from part 1.

Problem 13-2B
Ratios, common-size statements, and trend percents
P1 P2 P3

Selected comparative financial statement information of Bluegrass Corporation follows.

BLUEGRASS CORPORATION Comparative Income Statements For Years Ended December 31, 2015, 2014, and 2013	2015	2014	2013
Sales	$198,800	$166,000	$143,800
Cost of goods sold	108,890	86,175	66,200
Gross profit	89,910	79,825	77,600
Selling expenses	22,680	19,790	18,000
Administrative expenses	16,760	14,610	15,700
Total expenses	39,440	34,400	33,700
Income before taxes	50,470	45,425	43,900
Income taxes	6,050	5,910	5,300
Net income	$ 44,420	$ 39,515	$ 38,600

BLUEGRASS CORPORATION Comparative Balance Sheets December 31, 2015, 2014, and 2013	2015	2014	2013
Assets			
Current assets	$ 54,860	$ 32,660	$ 36,300
Long-term investments	0	1,700	10,600
Plant assets, net	112,810	113,660	79,000
Total assets	$167,670	$148,020	$125,900
Liabilities and Equity			
Current liabilities	$ 22,370	$ 19,180	$ 16,500
Common stock	46,500	46,500	37,000
Other paid-in capital	13,850	13,850	11,300
Retained earnings	84,950	68,490	61,100
Total liabilities and equity	$167,670	$148,020	$125,900

Required

1. Compute each year's current ratio. (Round ratio amounts to one decimal.)
2. Express the income statement data in common-size percents. (Round percents to two decimals.)
3. Express the balance sheet data in trend percents with 2013 as the base year. (Round percents to two decimals.)

Check (3) 2015, Total assets trend, 133.18%

Analysis Component

4. Comment on any significant relations revealed by the ratios and percents computed.

Problem 13-3B
Transactions, working capital, and liquidity ratios P3

Koto Corporation began the month of June with $300,000 of current assets, a current ratio of 2.5:1, and an acid-test ratio of 1.4:1. During the month, it completed the following transactions (the company uses a perpetual inventory system).

Check June 3: Current ratio, 2.88; Acid-test ratio, 2.40

June 1 Sold merchandise inventory that cost $75,000 for $120,000 cash.
3 Collected $88,000 cash on an account receivable.
5 Purchased $150,000 of merchandise inventory on credit.
7 Borrowed $100,000 cash by giving the bank a 60-day, 10% note.
10 Borrowed $120,000 cash by signing a long-term secured note.
12 Purchased machinery for $275,000 cash.
15 Declared a $1 per share cash dividend on its 80,000 shares of outstanding common stock.
19 Wrote off a $5,000 bad debt against the Allowance for Doubtful Accounts account.
22 Paid $12,000 cash to settle an account payable.
30 Paid the dividend declared on June 15.

June 30: Working capital, $(10,000); Current ratio, 0.97

Required

Prepare a table showing the company's (1) current ratio, (2) acid-test ratio, and (3) working capital after each transaction. Round ratios to two decimals.

Problem 13-4B
Calculation of financial statement ratios
P3

Selected year-end financial statements of Overton Corporation follow. (All sales were on credit; selected balance sheet amounts at December 31, 2014, were inventory, $17,400; total assets, $94,900; common stock, $35,500; and retained earnings, $18,800.)

OVERTON CORPORATION
Income Statement
For Year Ended December 31, 2015

Sales	$315,500
Cost of goods sold	236,100
Gross profit	79,400
Operating expenses	49,200
Interest expense	2,200
Income before taxes	28,000
Income taxes	4,200
Net income	$ 23,800

OVERTON CORPORATION
Balance Sheet
December 31, 2015

Assets		**Liabilities and Equity**	
Cash	$ 6,100	Accounts payable	$ 11,500
Short-term investments	6,900	Accrued wages payable	3,300
Accounts receivable, net	12,100	Income taxes payable	2,600
Notes receivable (trade)*	3,000	Long-term note payable, secured by mortgage on plant assets	30,000
Merchandise inventory	13,500		
Prepaid expenses	2,000	Common stock, $5 par value	35,000
Plant assets, net	73,900	Retained earnings	35,100
Total assets	$117,500	Total liabilities and equity	$117,500

* These are short-term notes receivable arising from customer (trade) sales.

Required

Compute the following: (1) current ratio, (2) acid-test ratio, (3) days' sales uncollected, (4) inventory turnover, (5) days' sales in inventory, (6) debt-to-equity ratio, (7) times interest earned, (8) profit margin ratio, (9) total asset turnover, (10) return on total assets, and (11) return on common stockholders' equity. Round to one decimal place; for part 6, round to two decimals.

Check Acid-test ratio, 1.6 to 1; Inventory turnover, 15.3

Problem 13-5B
Comparative ratio analysis A1 P3

Summary information from the financial statements of two companies competing in the same industry follows.

	Fargo Company	Ball Company
Data from the current year-end balance sheets		
Assets		
Cash	$ 20,000	$ 36,500
Accounts receivable, net	77,100	70,500
Current notes receivable (trade)	11,600	9,000
Merchandise inventory	86,800	82,000
Prepaid expenses	9,700	10,100
Plant assets, net	176,900	252,300
Total assets	$382,100	$460,400
Liabilities and Equity		
Current liabilities	$ 90,500	$ 97,000
Long-term notes payable	93,000	93,300
Common stock, $5 par value	133,000	141,000
Retained earnings	65,600	129,100
Total liabilities and equity	$382,100	$460,400

	Fargo Company	Ball Company
Data from the current year's income statement		
Sales	$393,600	$667,500
Cost of goods sold	290,600	480,000
Interest expense	5,900	12,300
Income tax expense	5,700	12,300
Net income	33,850	61,700
Basic earnings per share	1.27	2.19
Beginning-of-year balance sheet data		
Accounts receivable, net	$ 72,200	$ 73,300
Current notes receivable (trade)	0	0
Merchandise inventory	105,100	80,500
Total assets	383,400	443,000
Common stock, $5 par value	133,000	141,000
Retained earnings	49,100	109,700

Required

Check (1) Fargo: Accounts receivable turnover, 4.9; Inventory turnover, 3.0

(2) Ball: Profit margin, 9.2%; PE, 11.4

1. For both companies compute the (*a*) current ratio, (*b*) acid-test ratio, (*c*) accounts (including notes) receivable turnover, (*d*) inventory turnover, (*e*) days' sales in inventory, and (*f*) days' sales uncollected. Identify the company you consider to be the better short-term credit risk and explain why. Round to one decimal place.
2. For both companies compute the (*a*) profit margin ratio, (*b*) total asset turnover, (*c*) return on total assets, and (*d*) return on common stockholders' equity. Assuming that each company paid cash dividends of $1.50 per share and each company's stock can be purchased at $25 per share, compute their (*e*) price-earnings ratios and (*f*) dividend yields. Round to one decimal place; for part *b*, round to two decimals. Identify which company's stock you would recommend as the better investment and explain why.

Problem 13-6B^A
Income statement computations and format
A2

Selected account balances from the adjusted trial balance for Harbor Corp. as of its calendar year-end December 31, 2015, follow.

	Debit	Credit
a. Accumulated depreciation—Buildings		$ 400,000
b. Interest revenue		20,000
c. Net sales		2,640,000
d. Income taxes expense	$?	
e. Loss on hurricane damage (pretax and extraordinary)	64,000	
f. Accumulated depreciation—Equipment		220,000
g. Other operating expenses	328,000	
h. Depreciation expense—Equipment	100,000	
i. Loss from settlement of lawsuit	36,000	
j. Gain from settlement of lawsuit		68,000
k. Loss on sale of equipment	24,000	
l. Loss from operating a discontinued segment (pretax)	120,000	
m. Depreciation expense—Buildings	156,000	
n. Correction of overstatement of prior year's expense (pretax)		48,000
o. Cost of goods sold	1,040,000	
p. Loss on sale of discontinued segment's assets (pretax)	180,000	
q. Accounts payable		132,000

Required

Answer each of the following questions by providing supporting computations.

1. Assume that the company's income tax rate is 25% for all items. Identify the tax effects and after-tax amounts of the four items labeled pretax.
2. What is the amount of income from continuing operations before income taxes? What is the amount of income taxes expense? What is the amount of income from continuing operations?
3. What is the total amount of after-tax income (loss) associated with the discontinued segment?
4. What is the amount of income (loss) before the extraordinary items?
5. What is the amount of net income for the year?

Check (3) $(225,000)
(4) $558,000
(5) $510,000

SERIAL PROBLEM
Business Solutions
P3

(This serial problem began in Chapter 1 and continues through most of the book. If previous chapter segments were not completed, the serial problem can begin at this point. It is helpful, but not necessary, to use the Working Papers that accompany the book.)

SP 13 Use the following selected data from Business Solutions's income statement for the three months ended March 31, 2016, and from its March 31, 2016, balance sheet to complete the requirements below: computer services revenue, $25,307; net sales (of goods), $18,693; total sales and revenue, $44,000; cost of goods sold, $14,052; net income, $18,833; quick assets, $90,924; current assets, $95,568; total assets, $120,268; current liabilities, $875; total liabilities, $875; and total equity, $119,393.

Required

1. Compute the gross margin ratio (both with and without services revenue) and net profit margin ratio (round the percent to one decimal).
2. Compute the current ratio and acid-test ratio (round to one decimal).
3. Compute the debt ratio and equity ratio (round the percent to one decimal).
4. What percent of its assets are current? What percent are long term (round the percent to one decimal)?

Beyond the Numbers

REPORTING IN ACTION
A1 P1 P2

APPLE

BTN 13-1 Refer to **Apple**'s financial statements in Appendix A to answer the following.

1. Using fiscal 2011 as the base year, compute trend percents for fiscal years 2011, 2012, and 2013 for net sales, cost of sales, operating income, other income (expense) net, provision for income taxes, and net income. (Round percents to one decimal.)
2. Compute common-size percents for fiscal years 2012 and 2013 for the following categories of assets: (*a*) total current assets, (*b*) property, plant and equipment, net, and (*c*) goodwill plus acquired intangible assets, net. (Round percents to one decimal.)
3. Comment on any notable changes across the years for the income statement trends computed in part 1 and the balance sheet percents computed in part 2.

Fast Forward

4. Access Apple's financial statements for fiscal years ending after September 28, 2013, from its website (Apple.com) or the SEC database (www.SEC.gov). Update your work for parts 1, 2, and 3 using the new information accessed.

COMPARATIVE ANALYSIS
C2 P2

APPLE
GOOGLE

BTN 13-2 Key figures for **Apple** and **Google** follow.

($ millions)	Apple	Google
Cash and equivalents	$ 14,259	$18,898
Accounts receivable, net	13,102	8,882
Inventories	1,764	426
Retained earnings	104,256	61,262
Cost of sales	106,606	25,858
Revenues	170,910	59,825
Total assets	207,000	110,920

Required

1. Compute common-size percents for each of the companies using the data provided. (Round percents to one decimal.)
2. Which company retains a higher portion of cumulative net income in the company?
3. Which company has a higher gross margin ratio on sales?
4. Which company holds a higher percent of its total assets as inventory?

ETHICS CHALLENGE
A1

BTN 13-3 As Beacon Company controller, you are responsible for informing the board of directors about its financial activities. At the board meeting, you present the following information.

	2015	2014	2013
Sales trend percent	147.0%	135.0%	100.0%
Selling expenses to sales	10.1%	14.0%	15.6%
Sales to plant assets ratio	3.8 to 1	3.6 to 1	3.3 to 1
Current ratio	2.9 to 1	2.7 to 1	2.4 to 1
Acid-test ratio	1.1 to 1	1.4 to 1	1.5 to 1
Inventory turnover	7.8 times	9.0 times	10.2 times
Accounts receivable turnover	7.0 times	7.7 times	8.5 times
Total asset turnover	2.9 times	2.9 times	3.3 times
Return on total assets	10.4%	11.0%	13.2%
Return on stockholders' equity	10.7%	11.5%	14.1%
Profit margin ratio	3.6%	3.8%	4.0%

After the meeting, the company's CEO holds a press conference with analysts in which she mentions the following ratios.

	2015	2014	2013
Sales trend percent	147.0%	135.0%	100.0%
Selling expenses to sales	10.1%	14.0%	15.6%
Sales to plant assets ratio	3.8 to 1	3.6 to 1	3.3 to 1
Current ratio	2.9 to 1	2.7 to 1	2.4 to 1

Required

1. Why do you think the CEO decided to report 4 ratios instead of the 11 prepared?
2. Comment on the possible consequences of the CEO's reporting of the ratios selected.

COMMUNICATING IN PRACTICE

A1 P3

BTN 13-4 Each team is to select a different industry, and each team member is to select a different company in that industry and acquire its financial statements. Use those statements to analyze the company, including at least one ratio from each of the four building blocks of analysis. When necessary, use the financial press to determine the market price of its stock. Communicate with teammates via a meeting, e-mail, or telephone to discuss how different companies compare to each other and to industry norms. The team is to prepare a single one-page memorandum reporting on its analysis and the conclusions reached.

TAKING IT TO THE NET

P3

BTN 13-5 Access the February 21, 2014, filing of the December 31, 2013, 10-K report of **The Hershey Company** (ticker HSY) at www.SEC.gov and complete the following requirements.

Required

Compute or identify the following profitability ratios of Hershey for its years ending December 31, 2013, *and* December 31, 2012. Interpret its profitability using the results obtained for these two years.

1. Profit margin ratio (round the percent to one decimal).
2. Gross profit ratio (round the percent to one decimal).
3. Return on total assets (round the percent to one decimal). (Total assets at year-end 2011 were $4,407,094 in thousands.)
4. Return on common stockholders' equity (round the percent to one decimal). (Total shareholders' equity at year-end 2011 was $880,943 in thousands.)
5. Basic net income per common share (round to the nearest cent).

TEAMWORK IN ACTION

P1 P2 P3

BTN 13-6 A team approach to learning financial statement analysis is often useful.

Required

1. Each team should write a description of horizontal and vertical analysis that all team members agree with and understand. Illustrate each description with an example.
2. *Each* member of the team is to select *one* of the following categories of ratio analysis. Explain what the ratios in that category measure. Choose one ratio from the category selected, present its formula, and explain what it measures.
   - **a.** Liquidity and efficiency
   - **b.** Solvency
   - **c.** Profitability
   - **d.** Market prospects
3. Each team member is to present his or her notes from part 2 to teammates. Team members are to confirm or correct other teammates' presentations.

Hint: Pairing within teams may be necessary for part 2. Use as an in-class activity or as an assignment. Consider presentations to the entire class using team rotation with transparencies.

ENTREPRENEURIAL DECISION

A1 P1 P2 P3

BTN 13-7 Assume that David and Tom Gardner of **The Motley Fool** (Fool.com) have impressed you since you first heard of their rather improbable rise to prominence in financial circles. You learn of a staff opening at The Motley Fool and decide to apply for it. Your resume is successfully screened from the thousands received and you advance to the interview process. You learn that the interview consists of analyzing the following financial facts and answering analysis questions below. (The data are taken from a small merchandiser in outdoor recreational equipment.)

	2015	2014	2013
Sales trend percents	137.0%	125.0%	100.0%
Selling expenses to sales	9.8%	13.7%	15.3%
Sales to plant assets ratio	3.5 to 1	3.3 to 1	3.0 to 1
Current ratio	2.6 to 1	2.4 to 1	2.1 to 1
Acid-test ratio	0.8 to 1	1.1 to 1	1.2 to 1
Merchandise inventory turnover	7.5 times	8.7 times	9.9 times
Accounts receivable turnover	6.7 times	7.4 times	8.2 times
Total asset turnover	2.6 times	2.6 times	3.0 times
Return on total assets	8.8%	9.4%	11.1%
Return on equity	9.75%	11.50%	12.25%
Profit margin ratio	3.3%	3.5%	3.7%

Required

Use these data to answer each of the following questions with explanations.

1. Is it becoming easier for the company to meet its current liabilities on time and to take advantage of any available cash discounts? Explain.
2. Is the company collecting its accounts receivable more rapidly? Explain.
3. Is the company's investment in accounts receivable decreasing? Explain.
4. Is the company's investment in plant assets increasing? Explain.
5. Is the owner's investment becoming more profitable? Explain.
6. Did the dollar amount of selling expenses decrease during the three-year period? Explain.

HITTING THE ROAD

C1 P3

BTN 13-8 You are to devise an investment strategy to enable you to accumulate $1,000,000 by age 65. Start by making some assumptions about your salary. Next compute the percent of your salary that you will be able to save each year. If you will receive any lump-sum monies, include those amounts in your calculations. Historically, stocks have delivered average annual returns of 10–11%. Given this history, you should probably not assume that you will earn above 10% on the money you invest. It is not necessary to specify exactly what types of assets you will buy for your investments; just assume a rate you expect to earn. Use the future value tables in Appendix B to calculate how your savings will grow. Experiment a bit with your figures to see how much less you have to save if you start at, for example, age 25 versus age 35 or 40. (For this assignment, do not include inflation in your calculations.)

GLOBAL DECISION

A1

Samsung
APPLE
GOOGLE

BTN 13-9 **Samsung** (www.Samsung.com), which is a leading manufacturer of consumer electronic products, along with **Apple** and **Google**, are competitors in the global marketplace. Key figures for Samsung follow (in KRW millions).

Cash and equivalents	₩ 16,284,780	Cost of sales	₩137,696,309
Accounts receivable, net	27,875,934	Revenues	228,692,667
Inventories	19,134,868	Total assets	214,075,018
Retained earnings	148,600,282		

Required

1. Compute common-size percents for Samsung using the data provided. (Round percents to one decimal.)
2. Compare the results with Apple and Google from BTN 13-2.

ANSWERS TO MULTIPLE CHOICE QUIZ

1. d; ($351,000/$300,000) × 100 = 117%
2. e; ($86,000 + $76,000 + $122,000 + $12,000)/$124,000 = 2.39
3. c; ($86,000 + $76,000)/$124,000 = 1.31
4. a; ($124,000 + $90,000)/$830,000 = 25.78%
5. d; ($300,000 + $316,000)/$830,000 = 74.22%

chapter 14

Managerial Accounting Concepts and Principles

Chapter Preview

MANAGERIAL ACCOUNTING BASICS	MANAGERIAL COST CONCEPTS	REPORTING
C1 Purpose of managerial accounting Nature of managerial accounting Managerial decisions Fraud and ethics in managerial accounting	**C2** Types of cost classifications **C3** Identification of cost classifications Cost concepts for service companies	**C4** Manufacturer costs Balance sheet **P1** Income statement **C5** Flow of activities **P2** Schedule of cost of goods manufactured **C6** Managerial accounting trends **A1** Inventory analysis

Learning Objectives

CONCEPTUAL

C1 Explain the purpose and nature of, and the role of ethics in, managerial accounting.

C2 Describe accounting concepts useful in classifying costs.

C3 Define product and period costs and explain how they impact financial statements.

C4 Explain how balance sheets and income statements for manufacturing, merchandising, and service companies differ.

C5 Explain manufacturing activities and the flow of manufacturing costs.

C6 Describe trends in managerial accounting.

ANALYTICAL

A1 Assess raw materials inventory management using raw materials inventory turnover and days' sales in raw materials inventory.

PROCEDURAL

P1 Compute cost of goods sold for a manufacturer and for a merchandiser.

P2 Prepare a schedule of cost of goods manufactured and explain its purpose and links to financial statements.

Courtesy of SunSaluter

Follow the Sun

CALGARY, CANADA—As a child, Eden Full experimented with solar electricity, starting with a desktop solar car she built from a kit as a 10-year-old. In high school, Eden tinkered with how to arrange solar panels to generate the most electricity. "I found that to get the most electricity, you have to face your solar panels toward the sun," says Eden. Thus was born the SunSaluter, Eden's invention that uses a water filtration system to automatically rotate solar panels to follow the sun's path each day.

"If it's beneficial and sustainable, you have to keep pushing"

—Eden Full

Like most successful entrepreneurs, Eden is finding success by creating a niche. While solar tracking is not a novel idea, Eden notes that "solar trackers can be expensive, many require electricity, and they often involve complex mechanisms prone to failure. A lot of technologies fail simply because they are too complicated." Because Eden's product does not use electricity, and it creates clean filtered water while it also produces solar electricity, its use has great potential benefit in developing countries. "When I realized I could invent a technology for social good, I fell in love with tinkering with something that mattered," she says.

With her product and a desire to change the world, Eden started her company, **SunSaluter.** Though still small, her company generates enough revenue to cover its costs. Eden stresses it is good to start a business when one is young. Risk is low, and "if the owners are passionate about their idea, someone will provide financing." In addition to passion and seed money, aspiring entrepreneurs need to understand basic managerial principles, cost classifications, and cost flows. Managerial accounting information enables Eden to plan and control costs and make good decisions. But, as Eden notes, "innovators must execute what they plan to do," and information on costs can help owners see if their plans are working.

Eden notes that it took her a while to "understand how to develop a realistic product with market potential." While financial success ultimately rests on monitoring and controlling operations, Eden measures success by more than just profits. "Anything that provides economic value should have a positive social impact," claims Eden. "You have to think about long-term returns." Eden offers sound advice for aspiring entrepreneurs: "Find your passion. But, no matter what your dream is, there will be tough days. Don't give up." And, of course, follow the sun.

Sources: *SunSaluter website,* January 2015; *Conscious Magazine; Entrepreneur.com,* April 18, 2013; *Carbon Talks,* www.carbontalks.ca/innovator-profile/eden-full; *EnergyMatters.com,* June 10, 2011; *NPR,* December 2012

MANAGERIAL ACCOUNTING BASICS

Managerial accounting is an activity that provides financial and nonfinancial information to an organization's managers. Managers include, for example, employees in charge of a company's divisions; the heads of marketing, information technology, and human resources; and top-level managers such as the chief executive officer (CEO) and chief financial officer (CFO). To do their jobs, such managers need more than just the general-purpose financial statements provided by the financial accounting system. This section explains the purpose of managerial accounting (also called *management accounting*) and compares it with financial accounting.

Purpose of Managerial Accounting

C1

Explain the purpose and nature of, and the role of ethics in, managerial accounting.

The purpose of managerial accounting is to provide useful information to managers of an organization. Managerial accounting helps managers with three key tasks: (1) determining the costs of an organization's products and services, (2) planning future activities, and (3) comparing actual results to planned results. For example, managerial accounting information can help the marketing manager decide whether to advertise on social media such as **Twitter**; it also can help the information technology manager decide whether to buy new computers. Managerial accounting information also helps the CEO decide which divisions to expand and which to eliminate.

Point: Costs are important to managers because they impact both the financial position and profitability of a business. Managerial accounting assists in analysis, planning, and control of costs.

The remainder of this book looks carefully at how managerial accounting information is gathered and how managers use it. We begin by showing how the managerial accounting system collects cost information and assigns it to an organization's products and services. Information about such costs is important for many decisions that managers make, such as predicting the future costs of a product or service. Predicted costs are used in product pricing, profitability analysis, and in deciding whether to make or buy a product or component. More generally, much of managerial accounting involves gathering information about costs for planning and control decisions.

Planning is the process of setting goals and making plans to achieve them. Companies make long-term strategic plans that usually span a 5- to 10-year horizon. Strategic plans usually set a firm's long-term direction based on opportunities such as new products, new markets, and capital investments. A strategic plan's goals and objectives are broadly defined given its long-term orientation. With long-term plans in place, companies then set short-term plans, which are more operational in nature. Short-term plans translate the strategic plan into actions, and they are more concrete and consist of better-defined objectives and goals. A short-term plan often covers a one-year period that, when translated in monetary terms, is known as a budget.

Control is the process of monitoring planning decisions and evaluating an organization's activities and employees. It includes the measurement and evaluation of actions, processes, and outcomes. Feedback provided by the control function allows managers to revise their plans. Measurement of actions and processes also allows managers to take corrective actions to obtain better outcomes. For example, managers periodically compare actual results with planned results. Exhibit 14.1 portrays the important management functions of planning and control. In later chapters, we explain how managers also use this information to direct and improve business operations.

EXHIBIT 14.1

Planning and Control (including monitoring and feedback)

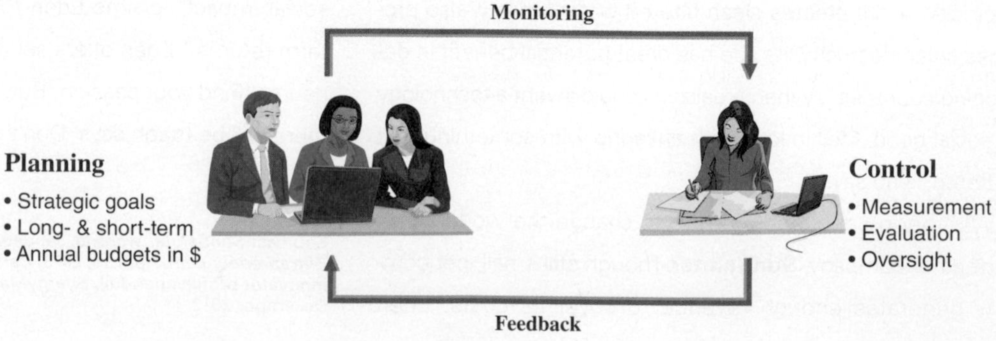

Nature of Managerial Accounting

Managerial accounting differs from financial accounting. We discuss seven key differences in this section, as summarized in Exhibit 14.2.

EXHIBIT 14.2

Key Differences between Managerial Accounting and Financial Accounting

	Financial Accounting	Managerial Accounting
1. Users	External: Investors, creditors, and others outside of the managers of the organization	Internal: Managers, employees, and decision makers inside the organization
2. Purpose of information	Help external users make investment, credit, and other decisions	Help managers make planning and control decisions
3. Flexibility of reporting	Structured and often controlled by GAAP	Relatively flexible (no GAAP constraints)
4. Timeliness of information	Often available only after an audit is complete	Available quickly without the need to wait for an audit
5. Time dimension	The past; historical information with some predictions	The future; many projections and estimates, with some historical information
6. Focus of information	The whole organization	An organization's projects, processes, and divisions
7. Nature of information	Monetary information	Mostly monetary; but also nonmonetary information

Users and Decision Makers Companies accumulate, process, and report financial accounting and managerial accounting information for different groups of decision makers. Financial accounting information is provided primarily to external users including investors, creditors, analysts, and regulators. External users rarely have a major role in managing a company's daily activities. Managerial accounting information, in contrast, is provided primarily to internal users who are responsible for making and implementing decisions about a company's business activities.

Point: It is desirable to accumulate certain information for management reports in a database separate from financial accounting records.

Purpose of Information Investors, creditors, and other external users of financial accounting information must often decide whether to invest in or lend to a company. If they have already done so, they must decide whether to continue owning the company or carrying the loan. Internal decision makers must plan a company's future. They seek to take advantage of opportunities or to overcome obstacles. They also try to control activities. Managerial accounting information helps internal users make both planning and control decisions.

Flexibility of Practice External users compare companies by using financial reports, and they need protection against false or misleading information. Thus, financial accounting relies on accepted principles that are enforced through an extensive set of rules and guidelines, or GAAP. Internal users need managerial accounting information for planning and controlling their company's activities rather than for external comparisons. Internal users require different types of information, depending on the activity and the type of organization. Thus, managerial accounting systems are flexible and differ across companies. The design of a company's managerial accounting system depends largely on the nature of the business and the arrangement of its internal operations. Managers can decide for themselves what information they want and how they want it reported. Even within a single company, different managers often design their own systems to meet their special needs. The important question a manager must ask is whether the information being collected and reported is useful for planning, decision making, and control purposes.

Point: The *Institute of Management Accountants* issues statements that govern the practice of managerial accounting. Accountants who pass a qualifying exam are awarded the CMA.

Timeliness of Information Formal financial statements reporting past transactions and events are not immediately available to outside parties. Independent certified public accountants often must *audit* a company's financial statements before providing them to external users. Thus, because audits often take several weeks to complete, financial reports to outsiders usually are not available until well after the period-end. However, managers can quickly obtain managerial accounting information. External auditors need not review it. Estimates and projections are acceptable. To get information quickly, managers often accept less precision in reports. As an example, an early internal report to management prepared right after the year-end could report net income for the year between $4.2 and $4.8 million. An audited income statement could later show net income for the year at $4.6 million. The internal report is not precise, but its information can be more useful because it is available earlier.

Point: Financial statements are usually issued several weeks after the period-end. GAAP requires the reporting of important events that occur while the statements are being prepared. These events are called *subsequent events.*

Internal auditing plays an important role in managerial accounting. Internal auditors evaluate the flow of information not only inside but also outside the company. Managers are responsible for preventing and detecting fraudulent activities in their companies.

Time Dimension To protect external users from false expectations, financial reports deal primarily with results of both past activities and current conditions. While some predictions such as service lives and salvage values of plant assets are necessary, financial accounting avoids predictions whenever possible. In contrast, managerial accounting regularly includes predictions of conditions and events. As an example, one important managerial accounting report is a budget, which predicts revenues, expenses, and other items. If managerial accounting reports were restricted to the past and present, managers would be less able to plan activities and less effective in managing and evaluating current activities.

EXHIBIT 14.3

Focus of External Reports

Reports to external users focus on company as a whole

Focus of Information Companies often organize into divisions and departments, but investors rarely can buy shares in one division or department. Nor do creditors lend money to a company's single division or department. Instead, they own shares in or make loans to the entire company. Financial accounting focuses primarily on a company as a whole as depicted in Exhibit 14.3.

The focus of managerial accounting is different. While top-level managers are responsible for managing the whole company, most other managers are responsible for much smaller sets of activities. These middle-level and lower-level managers need managerial accounting reports dealing with specific activities, projects, and subdivisions for which they are responsible. For instance, division sales managers are directly responsible only for the results achieved in their divisions. Accordingly, to improve performance, they need only information about results achieved in their own divisions. This information includes the level of success achieved by each individual, product, or department in each division of the whole company as depicted in Exhibit 14.4.

EXHIBIT 14.4

Focus of Internal Reports

Reports to internal users focus on company units and divisions

Nature of Information Both financial and managerial accounting systems report monetary information. Managerial accounting systems also report considerable nonmonetary information. Monetary information is an important part of managerial decisions, and nonmonetary information also plays a crucial role, especially when monetary effects are difficult to measure. Common examples of nonmonetary information include customer and employee satisfaction data, the percentage of on-time deliveries, and product defect rates.

James Startt/Agence Zoom/Getty Images

Managerial Decision Making

Although there are differences between financial and managerial accounting, the two are not entirely separate. Some similar information is useful to both external and internal users. For instance, information about costs of manufacturing products is useful to all users in making decisions. Also, both financial and managerial accounting affect people's actions. For example, **Trek**'s sales compensation plan affects the behavior of its salesforce when selling its manufactured bikes. Trek also must estimate the effects of promotions on buying patterns of customers. These estimates impact the equipment purchase decisions for manufacturing and can affect the supplier selection criteria established by purchasing. Thus, financial and managerial accounting systems do more than measure; they also affect people's decisions and actions.

Fraud and Ethics in Managerial Accounting

Fraud, and the role of ethics in reducing fraud, are important factors in running business operations. Fraud involves the use of one's job for personal gain through the deliberate misuse of the employer's assets. Examples include theft of the employer's cash or other assets, overstating reimbursable expenses, payroll schemes, and financial statement fraud. Three factors must exist for a person to commit fraud: opportunity, financial pressure, and rationalization. This is known as the *fraud triangle.* Fraud affects all business and it is costly: A 2014 *Report to the Nation* from the Association of Certified Fraud Examiners (ACFE) estimates the average U.S. business loses 5% of its annual revenues to fraud.

The most common type of fraud, where employees steal or misuse the employer's resources, results in an average loss of $130,000 per occurrence. For example, in a billing fraud, an employee sets up a bogus supplier. The employee then prepares bills from the supplier and pays these bills from the employer's checking account. The employee cashes the checks sent to the bogus supplier and uses them for his or her own personal benefit. An organization's best chance to minimize fraud is through reducing opportunities for employees to commit fraud.

Implications for Managerial Accounting Fraud increases a business's costs, and an important goal of managerial accounting is accurate cost information. Left undetected, inflated costs can result in poor pricing decisions, an improper product mix, and faulty performance evaluations. All of these can lead to poor financial results for the company. Management can develop accounting systems to closely track costs and identify deviations from expected amounts. In addition, managers rely on an **internal control system** to monitor and control business activities. An internal control system is the policies and procedures managers use to:

- Ensure reliable accounting.
- Protect assets.
- Urge adherence to company policies.
- Promote efficient operations.

Combating fraud and other dilemmas requires ethics in accounting. **Ethics** are beliefs that distinguish right from wrong. They are accepted standards of good and bad behavior. Identifying the ethical path can be difficult. The **Institute of Management Accountants (IMA),** the professional association for management accountants, has issued a code of ethics to help accountants involved in solving ethical dilemmas. The IMA's Statement of Ethical Professional Practice requires that management accountants be competent, maintain confidentiality, act with integrity, and communicate information in a fair and credible manner.

The IMA provides a "road map" for resolving ethical conflicts. It suggests that an employee follow the company's policies on how to resolve such conflicts. If the conflict remains unresolved, an employee should contact the next level of management (such as the immediate supervisor) who is not involved in the ethical conflict.

Point: The IMA also issues the Certified Management Accountant (CMA) and the Certified Financial Manager (CFM) certifications. Employees with the CMA or CFM certifications typically earn higher salaries than those without.

Point: The **Sarbanes-Oxley Act** requires each issuer of securities to disclose whether it has adopted a code of ethics for its senior officers and the content of that code.

Decision Ethics

Production Manager You invite three friends to a restaurant. When the dinner check arrives, David, a self-employed entrepreneur, picks it up saying, "Here, let me pay. I'll deduct it as a business expense on my tax return." Denise, a salesperson, takes the check from David's hand and says, "I'll put this on my company's credit card. It won't cost us anything." Derek, a factory manager for a company, laughs and says, "Neither of you understands. I'll put this on my company's credit card and call it overhead on a cost-plus contract my company has with a client." (*A cost-plus contract means the company receives its costs plus a percent of those costs.*) Adds Derek, "That way, my company pays for dinner *and* makes a profit." Who should pay the bill? Why? ■ [Answers follow the chapter's Summary.]

QC1

MANAGERIAL COST CONCEPTS

C2 Describe accounting concepts useful in classifying costs.

Because managers use costs for many different purposes, organizations classify costs in different ways (that is, different costs for different purposes). This section explains common ways to classify costs and links them to managerial decisions. We illustrate these cost classifications with Rocky Mountain Bikes, a manufacturer of bicycles.

Types of Cost Classifications

Fixed versus Variable At a basic level, a cost can be classified by how it behaves with changes in the volume of activity. Thus, a cost can be classified as fixed or variable. A **fixed cost** does not change with changes in the volume of activity (within a range of activity known as an activity's *relevant range*). For example, straight-line depreciation on equipment is a fixed cost. A **variable cost** changes in proportion to changes in the volume of activity. Sales commissions computed as a percent of sales revenue are variable costs. Additional examples of fixed and variable costs for a bike manufacturer are provided in Exhibit 14.5. Classification of costs as fixed or variable is helpful in cost-volume-profit analyses and short-term decision making. We discuss these in Chapters 18 and 24.

EXHIBIT 14.5

Fixed and Variable Costs

Fixed Cost: Rent for Rocky Mountain Bikes' building is $22,000, and it doesn't change with the number of bikes produced.

Variable Cost: Cost of bicycle tires is variable with the number of bikes produced—this cost is $15 per pair.

Direct versus Indirect A cost is often traced to a **cost object,** which is a product, process, department, or customer to which costs are assigned. **Direct costs** are traceable to a single cost object. **Indirect costs** cannot be easily and cost-beneficially traced to a single cost object. Assuming the cost object is a bicycle, Rocky Mountain Bikes will first identify the costs that can be directly traced to bicycles. The direct costs traceable to a bicycle as a cost object would include direct material and direct labor costs used in its production. Such direct costs include wheels, brakes, chains, and seat, plus the wages and benefits of the employees who work directly on making the bike.

What are indirect costs associated with bicycles? One example is the salary of the supervisor. She monitors the production process and other factory activities, but she does not actually work on producing any bikes. Thus, her salary cannot be directly traced to bikes. Likewise, depreciation (other than the units-of-production method) on manufacturing warehouses cannot be traced to individual bikes. Another example is a maintenance department that provides services to two or more departments of a company making bicycles and strollers. If the cost object is the bicycle, the wages of the maintenance department employees who clean the factory area every night would be indirect costs. Exhibit 14.6 identifies more examples of direct and indirect costs when the cost object is a bicycle.

Decision Maker

Entrepreneur You wish to trace as many of your assembly department's direct costs as possible. You can trace 90% of them in an economical manner. To trace the other 10%, you need sophisticated and costly accounting software. Do you purchase this software? ■ [Answers follow the chapter's Summary.]

EXHIBIT 14.6

Direct and Indirect Costs for a Bicycle

Direct Costs (for bicycle)		Indirect Costs (for bicycle)	
• Tires	• Frames	• Factory accounting	• Factory light and heat
• Seats	• Chains	• Factory administration	• Factory intranet
• Handlebars	• Brakes	• Factory rent	• Insurance on factory
• Bike maker wages	• Bike maker benefits	• Factory manager's salary	• Factory equipment depreciation*

* For all depreciation methods other than units-of-production.

C3 Define product and period costs and explain how they impact financial statements.

Product versus Period Costs All production (or factory) costs are product costs. **Product costs** are those production costs necessary to create a product and consist of: direct materials, direct labor, and factory overhead. Overhead refers to production costs other than direct materials and direct labor. Product costs are capitalized as inventory during and after completion of the products; they are recorded as cost of goods sold when those products are sold.

Period costs are non-production costs and are usually more associated with activities linked to a time period than with completed products. Common examples of period costs include salaries of the sales staff, wages of maintenance workers, advertising expenses, and depreciation on office furniture and equipment. Period costs are expensed in the period when incurred either as selling expenses or as general and administrative expenses.

A distinction between product and period costs is important because period costs are expensed when incurred and reported on the income statement whereas product costs are capitalized as inventory on the balance sheet until that inventory is sold. An ability to understand and identify product costs and period costs is crucial to using and interpreting a *schedule of cost of goods manufactured,* described later in this chapter.

Point: Product costs are either in the income statement as part of cost of goods sold or in the balance sheet as inventory. Period costs appear only on the income statement under operating expenses.

Exhibit 14.7 shows the different effects of product and period costs. Period costs flow directly to the current income statement as expenses. They are not reported as assets. Product costs are

EXHIBIT 14.7

Period and Product Costs in Financial Statements

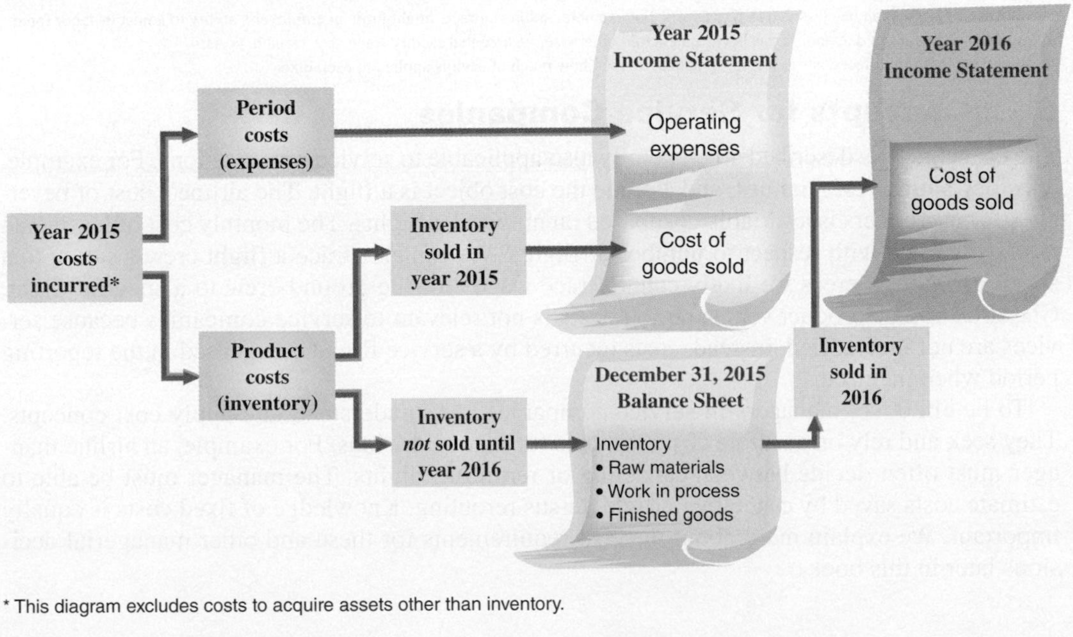

Point: For a team approach to identifying period and product costs, see *Teamwork in Action* in the *Beyond the Numbers* section.

* This diagram excludes costs to acquire assets other than inventory.

first assigned to inventory. Their final treatment depends on when inventory is sold or disposed of. Product costs assigned to finished goods that are sold in year 2015 are reported on the 2015 income statement as cost of goods sold. Product costs assigned to unsold inventory are carried forward on the balance sheet at the end of year 2015. If this inventory is sold in year 2016, product costs assigned to it are reported as cost of goods sold in that year's income statement.

Exhibit 14.8 summarizes typical managerial decisions for common cost classifications.

EXHIBIT 14.8

Summary of Cost Classifications and Example Managerial Decisions

Point: In subsequent chapters, we discuss some other ways to classify costs. The three cost classifications presented here are the foundation.

Costs Classified As	Example Managerial Decision
Variable or Fixed	How many units must we sell to break even? What will profit be if we raise the selling price? Should we add a new line of business?
Direct or Indirect	How well did our departments perform?
Product or Period	What is the cost of our inventory? Are selling expenses too high?

Identification of Cost Classifications

It is important to understand that a cost can be classified using any one (or combination) of the three different means described here. Understanding how to classify costs in several different ways enables managers to use cost information for a variety of decisions. Factory rent, for instance, is classified as a *product* cost; it is *fixed* with respect to the number of units produced, and it is *indirect* with respect to the product. Potential multiple classifications are shown in Exhibit 14.9 using different cost items incurred in manufacturing mountain bikes. The finished bike is the cost object. Proper allocation of these costs and the managerial decisions based on cost data depend on a correct cost classification.

EXHIBIT 14.9

Examples of Multiple Cost Classifications

Cost Item	Fixed or Variable	Direct or Indirect	Product or Period
Bicycle tires and wheels.	Variable	Direct	Product
Wages of assembly worker*	Variable	Direct	Product
Advertising	Fixed	Indirect	Period
Production manager's salary	Fixed	Indirect	Product
Office depreciation	Fixed	Indirect	Period
Factory depreciation (straight-line).	Fixed	Indirect	Product
Oil and grease applied to gears/chains**.	Variable	Indirect	Product
Sales commissions	Variable	Indirect	Period

*In some cases wages can be classified as fixed costs. For example, union contracts might limit an employer's ability to adjust its labor force in response to changes in demand. In this book, unless told otherwise, assume that factory wages are variable costs.
**Oil and grease are indirect costs as it is not practical to track how much of each is applied to each bike.

Cost Concepts for Service Companies

Justin Sullivan/Getty Images

Service Costs

- Beverages and snacks
- Cleaning fees
- Pilot and copilot salaries
- Attendant salaries
- Fuel and oil costs
- Travel agent fees
- Ground crew salaries

The cost concepts described are generally also applicable to service organizations. For example, consider **Southwest Airlines**, and assume the cost object is a flight. The airline's cost of beverages for passengers is a variable cost based on number of flights. The monthly cost of leasing an aircraft is fixed with respect to number of flights. We can also trace a flight crew's salary to a specific flight whereas we likely cannot trace wages for the ground crew to a specific flight. Classification as product versus period costs is not relevant to service companies because services are not inventoried. Instead, costs incurred by a service firm are expensed in the reporting period when incurred.

To be effective, managers in service companies must understand and apply cost concepts. They seek and rely on accurate cost estimates for many decisions. For example, an airline manager must often decide between canceling or rerouting flights. The manager must be able to estimate costs saved by canceling a flight versus rerouting. Knowledge of fixed costs is equally important. We explain more about the cost requirements for these and other managerial decisions later in this book.

Following are selected costs of a company that manufactures computer chips. Classify each as either a product cost or a period cost. Then classify each of the product costs as direct material, direct labor, or overhead.

NEED-TO-KNOW 14-1

Cost Classification

C2 C3

QC2

Do More: QS 14-4, QS 14-5, E 14-5

1. Plastic boards used to mount chips
2. Advertising costs
3. Factory maintenance workers' salaries
4. Real estate taxes paid on the sales office
5. Real estate taxes paid on the factory
6. Factory supervisor salary
7. Depreciation on factory equipment
8. Assembly worker hourly pay to make chips

Solution

	Product Costs			Period Cost
	Direct Material	Direct Labor	Overhead	
1. Plastic boards used to mount chips	X			
2. Advertising costs				X
3. Factory maintenance workers' salaries			X	
4. Real estate taxes paid on the sales office				X
5. Real estate taxes paid on the factory			X	
6. Factory supervisor salary			X	
7. Depreciation on factory equipment			X	
8. Assembly worker hourly pay to make chips		X		

REPORTING

Companies with manufacturing activities differ from both merchandising and service companies. The main difference between merchandising and manufacturing companies is that merchandisers buy goods ready for sale while manufacturers produce goods from materials and labor. **Amazon.com** is an example of a merchandising company. It buys and sells goods without physically changing them. **Adidas** is primarily a manufacturer of shoes, apparel, and accessories. It purchases materials such as leather, cloth, dye, plastic, rubber, glue, and laces and then uses employees' labor to convert these materials to products. Southwest Airlines is a service company that transports people and items. Some companies have several types of activities. For example, **Best Buy** is a merchandiser that also provides services via its Geek Squad.

The next section discusses costs for manufacturing companies. We then discuss the reporting of activities for manufacturing, merchandising, and service companies. Importantly, as these types of organizations have different kinds of costs and they classify costs in different ways, their accounting reports will also differ in some respects.

Manufacturers' Costs

Direct Materials **Direct materials** are tangible components of a finished product. **Direct material costs** are the expenditures for direct materials that are separately and readily traced through the manufacturing process to finished goods. Examples of direct materials in manufacturing a mountain bike include its tires, seat, frame, pedals, brakes, cables, gears, and handlebars. The chart in the margin shows that direct materials generally make up about 45% of manufacturing costs in today's products, but this amount varies across industries and companies.

Typical Manufacturing Costs in Today's Products

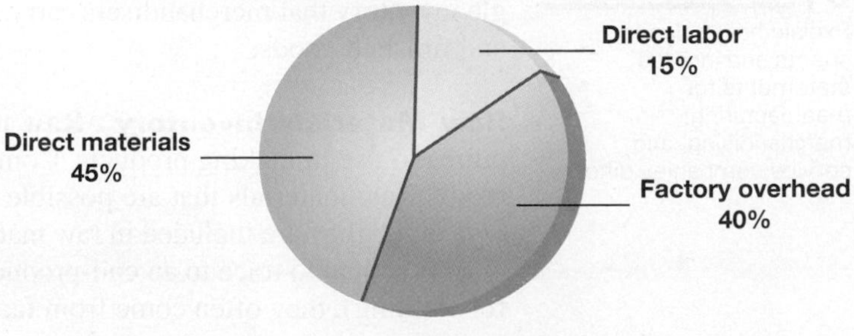

Point: Direct material and direct labor costs increase with increases in production volume and are called *variable costs.* Overhead can be both variable and fixed. When overhead costs vary with production, they are called *variable overhead.* When overhead costs don't vary with production, they are called *fixed overhead.*

Direct Labor **Direct labor** refers to the efforts of employees who physically convert materials to finished product. **Direct labor costs** are the wages and salaries for direct labor that are separately and readily traced through the manufacturing process to finished goods. Examples of direct labor in manufacturing a mountain bike include operators directly involved in converting raw materials into finished products (welding, painting, forming) and assembly workers who attach materials such as tires, seats, pedals, and brakes to the bike frames.

Point: All factory costs, other than direct materials and direct labor, are classified as Factory Overhead.

Factory Overhead **Factory overhead,** also called *manufacturing overhead,* consists of all manufacturing costs that are not direct materials or direct labor. **Factory overhead costs** cannot be separately or readily traced to finished goods. Thus, all factory overhead costs are considered indirect costs. These costs include indirect materials, **indirect labor**, and other costs not directly traceable to the product. **Indirect materials** are materials used in manufacturing and become part of the final product, but they are *not* clearly identified with specific product units. Often, direct materials are classified as indirect materials when their costs are low. Examples include screws and nuts used in assembling mountain bikes, and staples and glue used in manufacturing shoes. Applying the *materiality principle,* companies may decide it does not make economic sense to individually trace costs of each of these materials to individual products. For example, keeping detailed records of the amount of glue used to manufacture one shoe is not cost-beneficial.

Indirect labor costs refer to the costs of workers who assist in or supervise the manufacturing process. Examples include costs for employees who maintain the manufacturing equipment and salaries of production supervisors. Those workers do not assemble products. These costs are not linked to specific units of product, though they are indirectly related to production. Overtime premiums paid to direct laborers are also included in overhead because overtime is due to delays, interruptions, or constraints not necessarily identifiable to a specific product or batches of product.

Factory overhead costs also include maintenance of the mountain bike factory, supervision of its employees, repairing manufacturing equipment, factory utilities (water, gas, electricity), factory manager's salary, factory rent, depreciation on factory buildings and equipment, factory insurance, property taxes on factory buildings and equipment, and factory accounting and legal services. Factory overhead does *not* include selling and administrative expenses because they are not incurred in manufacturing products. These expenses are *period costs,* and they are recorded as expenses on the income statement when incurred.

EXHIBIT 14.10

Prime and Conversion Costs and Their Makeup

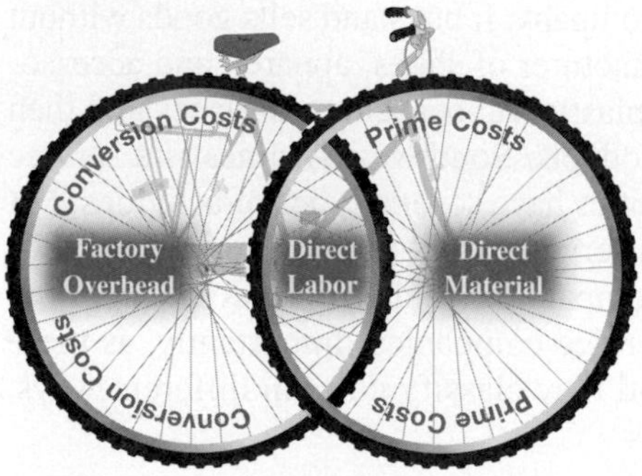

Prime costs = Direct materials + Direct labor.
Conversion costs = Direct labor + Factory overhead.

Prime and Conversion Costs Direct material costs and direct labor costs are also called **prime costs**—expenditures directly associated with the manufacture of finished goods. Direct labor costs and overhead costs are called **conversion costs**—expenditures incurred in the process of converting raw materials to finished goods. Direct labor costs are considered both prime costs and conversion costs. Exhibit 14.10 conveys the relation between prime and conversion costs and their components of direct material, direct labor, and factory overhead.

Balance Sheet

C4 Explain how balance sheets and income statements for manufacturing, merchandising, and service companies differ.

Manufacturers carry several unique assets and usually have three inventories instead of the single inventory that merchandisers carry. The three inventories are raw materials, work in process, and finished goods.

Raw Materials Inventory **Raw materials inventory** refers to the goods a company acquires to use in making products. Companies use raw materials in two ways: directly and indirectly. Raw materials that are possible and practical to trace to an end-product are called *direct materials;* they are included in raw materials inventory. Raw materials that are either impossible or impractical to trace to an end-product are classified as indirect materials (such as solder used for welding); they often come from factory supplies or raw materials inventory.

Work in Process Inventory Another inventory held by manufacturers is **work in process inventory,** also called *goods in process inventory.* It consists of products in the process of being manufactured but not yet complete. The amount of work in process inventory depends on the type of production process. If the time required to produce a unit of product is short, the work in process inventory is likely small; but if weeks or months are needed to produce a unit, the work in process inventory is usually larger.

Marco Prosch/Getty Images

Finished Goods Inventory A third inventory owned by a manufacturer is **finished goods inventory,** which consists of completed products ready for sale. This inventory is similar to merchandise inventory owned by a merchandising company.

Balance Sheets for Merchandising and Service Companies The current assets section of the balance sheet will look different for merchandising and service companies as compared to manufacturing companies. A merchandiser will report only merchandise inventory rather than the three types of inventory reported by a manufacturer. A service company's balance sheet does not have any inventory held for sale. Exhibit 14.11 shows the current assets section of the balance sheet for a manufacturer, a merchandiser, and a service company. Note that the manufacturer, Rocky Mountain Bikes, shows three different inventories. The merchandiser, Tele-Mart, shows one inventory, and the service provider, Northeast Air, shows no inventory of goods for sale.

Manufacturers also often own unique plant assets such as small tools, factory buildings, factory equipment, and patents to manufacture products. Merchandisers and service providers also typically own fixed assets.

EXHIBIT 14.11

Balance Sheets for Manufacturer, Merchandiser, and Service Provider

ROCKY MOUNTAIN BIKES Balance Sheet (partial) December 31, 2015	
Assets	
Current assets	
Cash	$11,000
Accounts receivable, net	30,150
Raw materials inventory	9,000
Work in process inventory	7,500
Finished goods inventory	10,300
Factory supplies	350
Prepaid insurance	300
Total current assets	$68,600

TELE-MART (Merchandiser) Balance Sheet (partial) December 31, 2015	
Assets	
Current assets	
Cash	$11,000
Accounts receivable, net	30,150
Merchandise inventory	21,000
Supplies	350
Prepaid insurance	300
Total current assets	$62,800

NORTHEAST AIR (Service Provider) Balance Sheet (partial) December 31, 2015	
Assets	
Current assets	
Cash	$11,000
Accounts receivable, net	30,150
Supplies	350
Prepaid insurance	300
Total current assets	$41,800

Income Statement

P1 Compute cost of goods sold for a manufacturer, and for a merchandiser.

The main difference between the income statement of a manufacturer and that of a merchandiser involves the items making up cost of goods sold. In this section, we look at how manufacturers determine and report cost of goods sold.

Cost of Goods Sold In earlier chapters, you studied how merchandisers report cost of goods sold. Exhibit 14.12 compares the components of cost of goods sold for a merchandiser with those for a manufacturer. To determine its cost of goods sold, a *merchandiser* adds cost of goods purchased to beginning merchandise inventory and then subtracts ending merchandise inventory. To determine its cost of goods sold, a *manufacturer* adds cost of goods manufactured to beginning finished goods inventory and then subtracts ending finished goods inventory.

In computing cost of goods sold, a merchandiser uses *merchandise* inventory while a manufacturer uses *finished goods* inventory. A manufacturer's inventories of raw materials and work in process are not included in finished goods because they are not available for

EXHIBIT 14.12

Cost of Goods Sold Computation

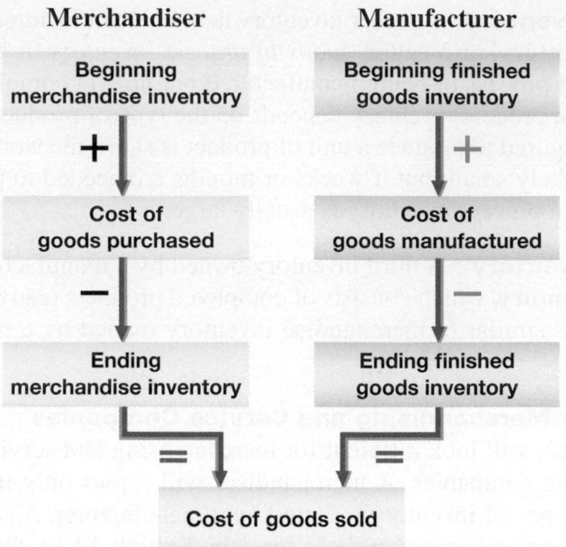

sale. A manufacturer also shows cost of goods *manufactured* instead of cost of goods *purchased.* This difference occurs because a manufacturer produces its goods instead of purchasing them ready for sale. The Cost of Goods Sold sections for both a merchandiser (Tele-Mart) and a manufacturer (Rocky Mountain Bikes) are shown in Exhibit 14.13 to highlight these differences. The remaining income statement sections are similar for merchandisers and manufacturers.

EXHIBIT 14.13

Cost of Goods Sold for a Merchandiser and Manufacturer

Merchandising Company (Tele-Mart)	
Cost of goods sold	
Beginning *merchandise* inventory	$ 14,200
Cost of merchandise *purchased*	234,150
Goods available for sale	248,350
Less ending *merchandise* inventory	12,100
Cost of goods sold	$236,250

Manufacturing Company (Rocky Mtn. Bikes)	
Cost of goods sold	
Beginning *finished goods* inventory	$ 11,200
Cost of goods *manufactured**	170,500
Goods available for sale	181,700
Less ending *finished goods* inventory	10,300
Cost of goods sold	$171,400

* Cost of goods manufactured is reported in the income statement of Exhibit 14.14.

Although the cost of goods sold computations are similar, the numbers in these computations reflect different activities. A merchandiser's cost of goods purchased is the cost of buying products to be sold. A manufacturer's cost of goods manufactured is the sum of direct materials, direct labor, and factory overhead costs incurred in producing products.

Income Statement for Service Company Since a service provider does not make or buy inventory to be sold, it does not report cost of goods manufactured or cost of goods sold. Instead, its operating expenses include all of the costs it incurred in providing its service. Southwest Airlines, for example, reports large operating expenses for employee pay and benefits, fuel and oil, and depreciation.

Reporting Performance Exhibit 14.14 shows the income statement for Rocky Mountain Bikes. Its operating expenses include selling expenses and general and administrative expenses, which include salaries for those business functions as well as depreciation for related equipment. Operating expenses do not include manufacturing costs such as factory workers' wages and depreciation of production equipment and the factory buildings. These manufacturing costs are reported as part of cost of goods manufactured and included in cost of goods sold. This exhibit also shows the income statement for Tele-Mart (merchandiser) and Northeast Air (service provider). Note that Tele-Mart reports *cost of merchandise purchased* instead of cost of goods manufactured. Tele-Mart reports its operating expenses like those of the manufacturing company. Finally, the income statement for Northeast Air shows only operating expenses.

Point: Manufacturers treat costs such as depreciation and rent as product costs if they are related to manufacturing.

EXHIBIT 14.14

Income Statements for Manufacturer, Merchandiser, and Service Provider

ROCKY MOUNTAIN BIKES (Manufacturer) Income Statement For Year Ended December 31, 2015		
Sales		$310,000
Cost of goods sold		
Finished goods inventory, Dec. 31, 2014	$ 11,200	
Cost of goods manufactured (from Exhibit 14.16)	170,500	
Goods available for sale	181,700	
Less finished goods inventory, Dec. 31, 2015	10,300	
Cost of goods sold		171,400
Gross profit		138,600
Operating expenses		
Selling expenses	38,150	
General and administrative expenses	21,750	
Total operating expenses		59,900
Income before income taxes		78,700
Income tax expense		32,600
Net income		$ 46,100

TELE-MART (Merchandiser) Income Statement For Year Ended December 31, 2015		
Sales		$345,000
Cost of goods sold		
Merchandise inventory, Dec. 31, 2014	$ 14,200	
Cost of merchandise purchased	234,150	
Goods available for sale	248,350	
Merchandise inventory, Dec. 31, 2015	12,100	
Cost of goods sold		236,250
Gross profit		108,750
Operating expenses		
Selling expenses	38,150	
General and administrative expenses	21,750	
Total operating expenses		59,900
Income before income taxes		48,850
Income tax expense		20,235
Net income		$ 28,615

NORTHEAST AIR (Service Provider) Income Statement For Year Ended December 31, 2015		
Service revenue		$425,000
Operating expenses		
Salaries and wages	$127,750	
Fuel and oil	159,375	
Maintenance and repairs	29,750	
Rent	42,500	
Depreciation	14,000	
General and admin. expenses	20,000	
Total operating expenses		393,375
Income before income taxes		31,625
Income tax expense		13,100
Net income		$ 18,525

NEED-TO-KNOW 14-2

Organization Costs and Types

C4

Indicate whether the following financial statement items apply to a manufacturer, a merchandiser, or a service provider. Some items apply to more than one type of organization.

_______ **1.** Merchandise inventory
_______ **2.** Finished goods inventory
_______ **3.** Cost of goods sold
_______ **4.** Operating expenses
_______ **5.** Cost of goods manufactured
_______ **6.** Supplies inventory

Solution

	Manufacturer	Merchandiser	Service Provider
1. Merchandise inventory		✓	
2. Finished goods inventory	✓		
3. Cost of goods sold	✓	✓	
4. Operating expenses	✓	✓	✓
5. Cost of goods manufactured	✓		
6. Supplies inventory	✓	✓	✓

Do More: E 14-7

QC3

Flow of Manufacturing Activities

C5 Explain manufacturing activities and the flow of manufacturing costs.

In addition to income statements and balance sheets, manufacturing companies typically prepare additional reports to help managers plan and control the manufacturing process. In order to understand these reports, we must first understand the flow of manufacturing activities and costs. Exhibit 14.15 shows the flow of manufacturing activities and the cost flows of those activities. As you can see (across the top row), the activities flow consists of *materials activity* followed by *production activity* followed by *sales activity*. The boxes below those activities show the costs for each activity and how costs flow across the three manufacturing activities. We explain further in this section.

EXHIBIT 14.15

Activities and Cost Flows in Manufacturing

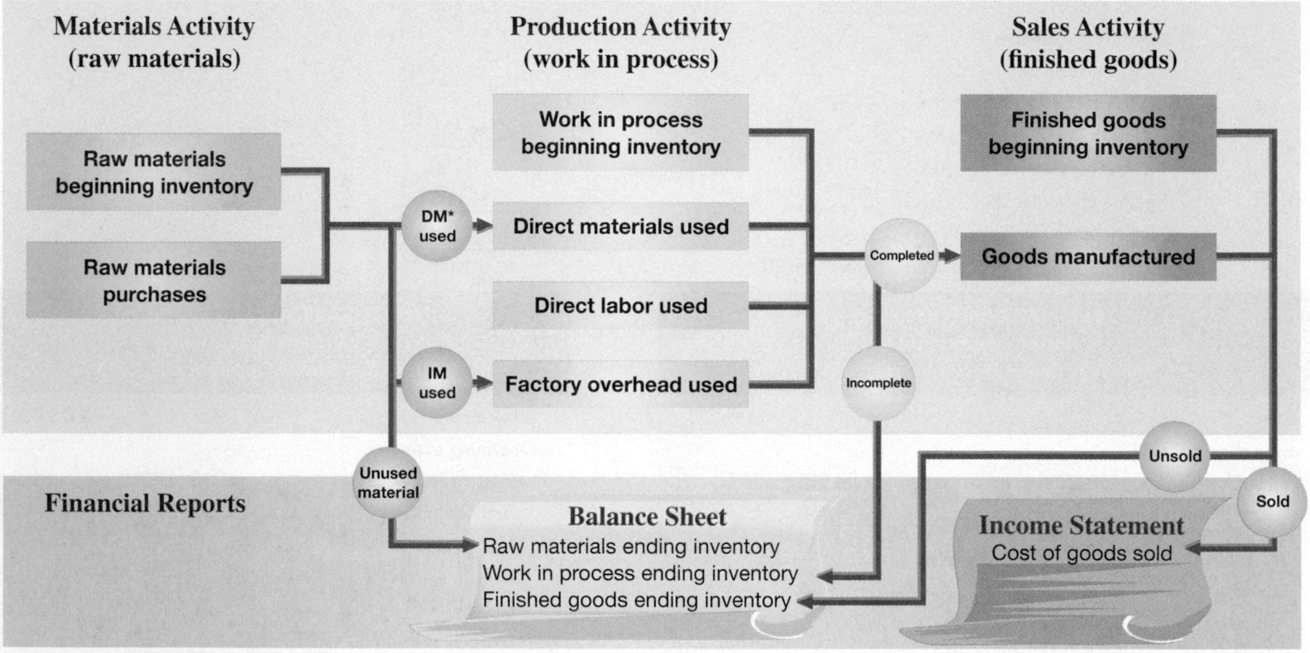

* DM = direct materials, IM = indirect materials.

Point: Knowledge of managerial accounting provides us a means of measuring manufacturing costs and is a sound foundation for studying advanced business topics.

Materials Activity The far left side of Exhibit 14.15 shows the flow of raw materials. Manufacturers usually start a period with some beginning raw materials inventory left over from the previous period. The company then acquires additional raw materials in the current period. Adding these purchases to beginning inventory gives *total raw materials available for use* in production. These raw materials are then either used in production in the current period or remain in inventory at the end of the period for use in future periods.

Production Activity The middle section of Exhibit 14.15 describes production activity. Four factors come together in production: beginning work in process inventory, raw materials, direct labor, and overhead. *Beginning work in process inventory* consists of partially complete products from the previous period. To the beginning work in process inventory are added direct materials, direct labor, and manufacturing overhead.

The production activity that takes place in the period from those inputs results in products that are either finished or remain unfinished. The cost of finished products makes up the **cost of goods manufactured** for the current period. The cost of goods manufactured is the total cost of making and finishing products in the period. That amount is included on the income statement in the computation of cost of goods sold, as we showed in Exhibit 14.14. Unfinished products are identified as *ending work in process inventory*. The cost of unfinished products consists of raw materials, direct labor, and factory overhead, and is reported on the current period's balance sheet. The costs of both finished goods manufactured and work in process are *product costs.*

Sales Activity The far right side of Exhibit 14.15 shows what happens to the finished goods: The company combines the beginning inventory of finished goods with the newly completed units (goods manufactured). Together, they make up *total finished goods available for sale* in the current period. These goods now are ready for sales activity. As they are sold, the cost of finished products sold is reported on the income statement as cost of goods sold. The cost of any finished products not sold in the period is reported as a current asset, *finished goods inventory,* on the current period's balance sheet.

Schedule of Cost of Goods Manufactured

P2 Prepare a schedule of cost of goods manufactured and explain its purpose and links to financial statements.

Managers of manufacturing firms typically analyze product costs in detail. Such analysis can help managers make better decisions about materials, labor, and overhead in order to reduce the cost of goods manufactured and maximize the company's profits. A company's manufacturing activities are described in a separate report, called a **schedule of cost of goods manufactured.** (It is also called a *manufacturing statement,* a *statement of cost of goods manufactured,* or a similar term.) By whatever name, the schedule of cost of goods manufactured summarizes the types and amounts of costs incurred in a company's manufacturing process. Exhibit 14.16 shows the schedule of cost of goods manufactured for Rocky Mountain Bikes. The schedule is divided into four parts: *direct materials, direct labor, overhead,* and *computation of cost of goods manufactured.* The schedule of cost of goods manufactured is completed in the following steps.

① Compute direct materials used. Add the beginning raw materials inventory of $8,000 to the current period's purchases of $86,500. This yields $94,500 of total raw materials available for use. A physical count of inventory shows $9,000 of ending raw materials inventory. If $94,500 of materials were available for use, and $9,000 of materials remains in inventory, then $85,500 of materials were used in the period. (*Note:* All raw materials are direct materials for Rocky Mountain Bikes.)

Raw Materials Inventory

Beg. bal.	8,000		
Purch.	86,500		
		Mtls. used	85,500
End. bal.	9,000		

② Compute direct labor costs used. Rocky Mountain Bikes had total direct labor costs of $60,000 for the period. This amount includes payroll taxes and fringe benefits.

EXHIBIT 14.16

Schedule of Cost of Goods Manufactured

ROCKY MOUNTAIN BIKES
Schedule of Cost of Goods Manufactured
For Year Ended December 31, 2015

①	**Direct materials**			
	Raw materials inventory, Dec. 31, 2014	$ 8,000		
	Raw materials purchases	86,500		
	Raw materials available for use	94,500		
	Less raw materials inventory, Dec. 31, 2015	9,000		
	Direct materials used		$ 85,500	
②	**Direct labor**		60,000	
③	**Factory overhead**			
	Indirect labor	9,000		
	Factory supervision	6,000		
	Factory utilities	2,600		
	Repairs—Factory equipment	2,500		
	Property taxes—Factory building	1,900		
	Factory supplies used	600		
	Factory insurance expired	1,100		
	Depreciation expense—Small tools	200		
	Depreciation expense—Factory equipment	3,500		
	Depreciation expense—Factory building	1,800		
	Amortization expense—Patents (on factory equipment)	800		
	Total factory overhead		30,000	
④	Total manufacturing costs			$175,500
	Add work in process inventory, Dec. 31, 2014			2,500
	Total cost of work in process			178,000
	Less work in process inventory, Dec. 31, 2015			7,500
	Cost of goods manufactured			$170,500

Point: Manufacturers sometimes report variable and fixed overhead separately in the schedule of cost of goods manufactured to provide more information to managers about cost behavior.

③ Compute total factory overhead costs used. The statement lists each important factory overhead item and its cost. All of these costs are indirectly related to manufacturing activities. In addition, period expenses, such as selling expenses and other costs not related to manufacturing activities, are *not* reported on this statement. Total factory overhead cost for the period is $30,000. Some companies report only *total* factory overhead on the schedule of cost of goods manufactured and attach a separate schedule listing individual overhead costs.

④ Compute the *cost of goods manufactured.* Total manufacturing costs for the period are $175,500 ($85,500 + $60,000 + $30,000), the sum of direct materials used and direct labor and overhead costs incurred. This amount is added to beginning work in process inventory. This gives the total work in process during the period of $178,000 ($175,500 + $2,500). A physical count shows $7,500 of work in process inventory remains at the end of the period. We then compute the current period's cost of goods manufactured of $170,500 by taking the $178,000 total work in process and subtracting the $7,500 cost of ending work in process inventory. The cost of goods manufactured amount is also called *net cost of goods manufactured* or *cost of goods completed.*

Work in Process Inventory

Beg. bal. 2,500	
Mfg. costs 175,500	
	COG Mfg. 170,500
End. bal. 7,500	

Using the Schedule of Cost of Goods Manufactured Management uses information in the schedule of cost of goods manufactured to plan and control the company's manufacturing activities. To provide timely information for decision making, the statement is often prepared monthly, weekly, or even daily. In anticipation of release of its much-hyped iPad, **Apple** grew its inventory of critical components, and its finished goods inventory. The schedule of cost of goods manufactured contains information useful to external users, but it is not a general-purpose financial statement. Companies rarely publish this schedule because managers view this information as proprietary and potentially harmful to the company if released to competitors.

Jin Lee/Bloomberg/Getty Images

Manufacturing Cost Flows across Accounting Reports The previous section showed manufacturing activities and cost flows and their reporting in the schedule of cost of goods manufactured. This cost information is also used to complete the financial statements at the end of an accounting period. Exhibit 14.17 summarizes how product costs flow through the accounting system: Direct materials, direct labor, and overhead costs are summarized in the schedule of cost of goods manufactured; then the amount of the cost of goods manufactured from that statement is used to compute cost of goods sold on the income statement. Physical counts determine the dollar amounts of ending raw materials inventory and work in process inventory, and those amounts are included on the end-of-period balance sheet. (*Note:* This exhibit shows only partial reports.)

EXHIBIT 14.17

Manufacturing Cost Flows across Accounting Reports

ROCKY MOUNTAIN BIKES
Schedule of Cost of Goods Manufactured For Year Ended December 31, 2015

Direct materials used*	$ 85,500
Direct labor used	60,000
Factory overhead**	30,000
Total manuf. costs	175,500
Beg. work in process	2,500
Total work in process	178,000
End. work in process	(7,500)
Cost of goods manuf.	**$170,500**

*Direct materials used is computed in Exhibit 14.16.
** Overhead items are listed in Exhibit 14.16.

ROCKY MOUNTAIN BIKES
Income Statement
For Year Ended December 31, 2015

Sales	$310,000
Cost of goods sold	
Beg. finished goods	11,200
Cost of goods manuf.	**170,500**
End. finished goods	(10,300)
Cost of goods sold	171,400
Gross profit	138,600
Operating expenses	59,900
Income before tax	$ 78,700

ROCKY MOUNTAIN BIKES
Balance Sheet–PARTIAL
December 31, 2015

Cash	$11,000
Accounts receivable, net	30,150
Raw materials inventory	**9,000**
Work in process inventory	**7,500**
Finished goods inventory	**10,300**
Factory supplies	350
Prepaid insurance	300
Total current assets	$68,600

NEED-TO-KNOW 14-3

Key Cost Measures

P1 P2

Compute the following three measures using the information below.

_______ **1.** Cost of materials used

_______ **2.** Cost of goods manufactured

_______ **3.** Cost of goods sold

Beginning raw materials inventory	$15,500	Ending raw materials inventory	$10,600
Beginning work in process inventory	29,000	Ending work in process inventory	44,000
Beginning finished goods inventory	24,000	Ending finished goods inventory	37,400
Raw materials purchased	66,000	Direct labor used	38,000
Total factory overhead used	80,000		

Do More: QS 14-8, QS 14-9, QS 14-10, E 14-8, E 14-11

QC4

Solution

1. $70,900 **2.** $173,900 **3.** $160,500

Raw Materials Inventory

Begin. Inv.	15,500		
Purchases	66,000		
Avail for use	81,500	**Matls used**	**70,900**
End. Inv.	10,600		

Work in Process Inventory

Begin. Inv.	29,000		
Materials	70,900		
Labor	38,000		
Overhead	80,000		
Avail for mfg.	217,900	**Cost of goods mfg**	**173,900**
End. Inv.	44,000		

Finished Goods Inventory

Begin. Inv.	24,000		
Cost of goods mfg	173,900		
Avail for sale	197,900	**Cost of goods sold**	**160,500**
End. Inv.	37,400		

Trends in Managerial Accounting

C6 Describe trends in managerial accounting.

The analytical tools and techniques of managerial accounting have always been useful, and their relevance and importance continue to increase. This is so because of changes in the business environment. This section describes some of these changes and their impact on managerial accounting.

Customer Orientation There is an increased emphasis on *customers* as the most important constituent of a business. Customers expect to derive a certain value for the money they spend to buy products and services. Specifically, they expect that their suppliers will offer them the right service (or product) at the right time and the right price. This implies that companies accept the notion of **customer orientation,** which means that employees understand the changing needs and wants of their customers and align their management and operating practices accordingly.

Global Economy Our *global economy* expands competitive boundaries and provides customers more choices. The global economy also produces changes in business activities. One notable case that reflects these changes in customer demand and global competition is auto manufacturing. The top three Japanese auto manufacturers (**Honda**, **Nissan**, and **Toyota**) once controlled more than 40% of the U.S. auto market. Customers perceived that Japanese auto manufacturers provided value not available from other manufacturers. Many European and North American auto manufacturers responded to this challenge and regained much of the lost market share.

E-Commerce People have become increasingly interconnected via smartphones, text messaging, and other electronic applications. Consumers thus expect and demand to be able to buy items electronically, whenever and wherever they want. Many businesses have enhanced their websites to allow for online transactions. Online sales now make up about 6% of total retail sales.

Service Economy Businesses that provide services, such as telecommunications and health care, constitute an ever-growing part of our economy. In developed economies like the United States, service businesses typically account for over 60% to 70% of total economic activity.

Point: Goals of a TQM process include reduced waste, better inventory control, fewer defects, and continuous improvement. Just-in-time concepts have similar goals.

Companies must be alert to these and other factors. Many companies have responded by adopting the **lean business model,** whose goal is to *eliminate waste* while "satisfying the customer" and "providing a positive return" to the company.

"My boss wants us to appeal to a younger and hipper crowd. So, I'd like to get a tattoo that says-- 'Accounting rules!'"

Lean Practices **Continuous improvement** rejects the notions of "good enough" or "acceptable" and challenges employees and managers to continuously experiment with new and improved business practices. This has led companies to adopt practices such as total quality management (TQM) and just-in-time (JIT) manufacturing. The philosophy underlying both practices is continuous improvement; the difference is in the focus.

Total quality management focuses on quality improvement and applies this standard to all aspects of business activities. In doing so, managers and employees seek to uncover waste in business activities including accounting activities such as payroll and disbursements. To encourage an emphasis on quality, the U.S. Congress established the Malcolm Baldrige National Quality Award (MBNQA). Entrants must conduct a thorough analysis and evaluation of their business using guidelines from the Baldrige committee. **Ritz Carlton Hotel** is a recipient of the Baldrige award in the service category. The company applies a core set of values, collectively called *The Gold Standards,* to improve customer service.

Just-in-time manufacturing is a system that acquires inventory and produces only when needed. An important aspect of JIT is that companies manufacture products only after they receive an order (a *demand-pull* system) and then deliver the customer's requirements on time. This means that processes must be aligned to eliminate any delays and inefficiencies including inferior inputs and outputs. Companies must also establish good relations and communications with their suppliers. On the downside, JIT is more susceptible to disruption than traditional systems. As one example, several **General Motors** plants were temporarily shut down due to a strike at an assembly division; the plants supplied components *just in time* to the assembly division.

Point: The time between buying raw materials and selling finished goods is called *throughput time.*

Value Chain The **value chain** refers to the series of activities that add value to a company's products or services. Exhibit 14.18 illustrates a possible value chain for a retail cookie company. Companies can use lean practices across the value chain to increase efficiency and profits.

EXHIBIT 14.18

Typical Value Chain (Cookie Retailer)

Implications for Managerial Accounting Adopting the lean business model can be challenging because to foster its implementation, all systems and procedures that a company follows must be realigned. Managerial accounting has an important role to play by providing accurate cost and performance information. Companies must understand the nature and sources of cost and must develop systems that capture costs accurately. Developing such a system is important to measuring the "value" provided to customers. The price that customers pay for acquiring goods and services is an important determinant of value. In turn, the costs a company incurs are key determinants of price. All else being equal, the better a company is at controlling its costs, the better its performance.

Corporate Social Responsibility In addition to maximizing shareholder value, when making decisions corporations often must consider the demands of other stakeholders, including employees, suppliers, and society in general. **Corporate social responsibility (CSR)** is a concept that goes beyond just following the law. For example, to reduce its impact on the environment, **Three Twins Ice Cream** uses only cups and spoons made from organic ingredients. **United By Blue**, an apparel and jewelry company, removes one pound of trash from waterways for every product sold. Companies like **Microsoft**, **Google**, and **Walt Disney**, ranked at the top of large multinational companies in terms of CSR, report progress on their CSR goals on their company websites.

Decision Insight

Balanced Scorecard The *balanced scorecard* aids continuous improvement by augmenting financial measures with information on the "drivers" (indicators) of future financial performance along four dimensions: (1) *financial*—profitability and risk, (2) *customer*—value creation and product and service differentiation, (3) *internal business processes*—business activities that create customer and owner satisfaction, and (4) *learning and growth*—organizational change, innovation, and growth. ■

GLOBAL VIEW

Managerial accounting is more flexible than financial accounting and does not follow a set of strict rules. However, many international businesses use the managerial accounting concepts and principles described in this chapter.

Customer Focus **Nestlé**, one of the world's leading nutrition and wellness companies, adopts a customer focus and strives to understand its customers' tastes. For example, Nestlé employees spent three days living with people in Lima, Peru, to understand their motivations, routines, buying habits, and everyday lives. This allowed Nestlé to adjust its products to suit local tastes.

Reporting Manufacturing Activities Nestlé must classify and report costs. In reporting inventory, Nestlé includes direct production costs, production overhead, and factory depreciation. A recent Nestlé annual report shows the following:

(in millions of Swiss francs)	Ending Inventory	Beginning Inventory
Raw materials, work in progress, and sundry supplies	3,499	3,815
Finished goods	5,138	5,302

Nestlé managers use this information, along with the more detailed information found in a schedule of cost of goods manufactured, to plan and control manufacturing activities.

Sustainability and Accounting Nestlé's version of corporate social responsibility focuses on sustainability. The company seeks to increase shareholder value by reducing water usage, improving farmers' operations, and enhancing children's nutrition in developing countries. Eden Full, founder of this chapter's opening company **SunSaluter**, designed her company around the development of sustainable energy and water conservation.

Courtesy of SunSaluter

Raw Materials Inventory Turnover and Days' Sales in Raw Materials Inventory — Decision Analysis

Managerial accounting information helps business managers perform detailed analyses that are not readily available to external users of accounting information. Inventory management is one example. Using publicly available financial statements, an external user can compute the *inventory turnover* ratio. However, a managerial accountant can go much further.

A1 Assess raw materials inventory management using raw materials inventory turnover and days' sales in raw materials inventory.

Raw Materials Inventory Turnover

A business manager can assess how effectively a company manages its *raw materials* inventory by computing the **raw materials inventory turnover** ratio as shown in Exhibit 14.19.

EXHIBIT 14.19 Raw Materials Inventory Turnover

Raw materials inventory turnover = Raw materials used/Average raw materials inventory

This ratio reveals how many times a company turns over (uses in production) its raw materials inventory during a period. Generally, a high ratio of raw materials inventory turnover is preferred, as long as raw materials inventory levels are adequate to meet demand. To illustrate, Rocky Mountain Bikes reports direct (raw) materials used of $85,500 for a year, with a beginning raw materials inventory of $8,000 and an ending raw materials inventory of $9,000 (see Exhibit 14.16). Raw materials inventory turnover for Rocky Mountain Bikes for that year is computed as in Exhibit 14.20.

EXHIBIT 14.20

Raw Materials Inventory Turnover Computed

Raw materials inventory turnover = $85,500/[($8,000 + $9,000)/2] = 10.06 (rounded).

Days' Sales in Raw Materials Inventory

To further assess raw materials inventory management, a manager can measure the adequacy of raw materials inventory to meet production demand. **Days' sales in raw materials inventory** reveals how much raw materials inventory is available in terms of the number of days' sales. It is a measure of how long it takes raw materials to be used in production. It is defined and computed for Rocky Mountain Bikes in Exhibit 14.21.

EXHIBIT 14.21

Days' Sales in Raw Materials Inventory Turnover

Days' sales in raw materials inventory = Ending raw materials inventory/Raw materials used × 365

= $9,000/$85,500 × 365 = 38.4 days (rounded)

This computation suggests that it will take 38 days for Rocky Mountain Bikes' raw materials inventory to be used in production. Assuming production needs can be met, companies usually prefer a *lower* number of days' sales in raw materials inventory. Just-in-time manufacturing techniques can be useful in lowering days' sales in raw materials inventory; for example, **Dell** keeps less than seven days of production needs in raw materials inventory for most of its computer components.

NEED-TO-KNOW

COMPREHENSIVE

The following account balances and other information are from SUNN Corporation's accounting records for year-end December 31, 2015. Use this information to prepare (1) a table listing factory overhead costs, (2) a schedule of cost of goods manufactured (show only the total factory overhead cost), and (3) an income statement.

Advertising expense	$ 85,000	Work in process inventory, Dec. 31, 2014	$ 8,000
Amortization expense—Factory patents	16,000	Work in process inventory, Dec. 31, 2015	9,000
Bad debts expense	28,000	Income taxes	53,400
Depreciation expense—Office equipment	37,000	Indirect labor	26,000
Depreciation expense—Factory building	133,000	Interest expense	25,000
Depreciation expense—Factory equipment	78,000	Miscellaneous expense	55,000
Direct labor	250,000	Property taxes on factory equipment	14,000
Factory insurance used up	62,000	Raw materials inventory, Dec. 31, 2014	60,000
Factory supervisor salary	74,000	Raw materials inventory, Dec. 31, 2015	78,000
Factory supplies used	21,000	Raw materials purchases	313,000
Factory utilities	115,000	Repairs expense—Factory equipment	31,000
Finished goods inventory, Dec. 31, 2014	15,000	Salaries expense	150,000
Finished goods inventory, Dec. 31, 2015	12,500	Sales	1,630,000

PLANNING THE SOLUTION

- Analyze the account balances and select those that are part of factory overhead costs.
- Arrange these costs in a table that lists factory overhead costs for the year.

- Analyze the remaining costs and select those related to production activity for the year; selected costs should include the materials and work in process inventories and direct labor.
- Prepare a schedule of cost of goods manufactured for the year showing the calculation of the cost of materials used in production, the cost of direct labor, and the total factory overhead cost. When presenting overhead cost on this statement, report only total overhead cost from the table of overhead costs for the year. Show the costs of beginning and ending work in process inventory to determine cost of goods manufactured.
- Organize the remaining revenue and expense items into the income statement for the year. Combine cost of goods manufactured from the schedule of cost of goods manufactured with the finished goods inventory amounts to compute cost of goods sold for the year.

SOLUTION

SUNN CORPORATION
Factory Overhead Costs
For Year Ended December 31, 2015

Amortization expense—Factory patents	$ 16,000
Depreciation expense—Factory building	133,000
Depreciation expense—Factory equipment	78,000
Factory insurance used up	62,000
Factory supervisor salary	74,000
Factory supplies used	21,000
Factory utilities	115,000
Indirect labor	26,000
Property taxes on factory equipment	14,000
Repairs expense—Factory equipment	31,000
Total factory overhead	$570,000

SUNN CORPORATION
Schedule of Cost of Goods Manufactured
For Year Ended December 31, 2015

Direct materials	
Raw materials inventory, Dec. 31, 2014	$ 60,000
Raw materials purchase	313,000
Raw materials available for use	373,000
Less raw materials inventory, Dec. 31, 2015	78,000
Direct materials used	295,000
Direct labor	250,000
Factory overhead	570,000
Total manufacturing costs	1,115,000
Add work in process inventory, Dec. 31, 2014	8,000
Total cost of work in process	1,123,000
Less work in process inventory, Dec. 31, 2015	9,000
Cost of goods manufactured	$1,114,000

SUNN CORPORATION
Income Statement
For Year Ended December 31, 2015

Sales		$1,630,000
Cost of goods sold		
Finished goods inventory, Dec. 31, 2014	$ 15,000	
Cost of goods manufactured	1,114,000	
Goods available for sale	1,129,000	
Less finished goods inventory, Dec. 31, 2015	12,500	
Cost of goods sold		1,116,500
Gross profit		513,500
Operating expenses		
Advertising expense	85,000	
Bad debts expense	28,000	
Depreciation expense—Office equipment	37,000	
Interest expense	25,000	
Miscellaneous expense	55,000	
Salaries expense	150,000	
Total operating expenses		380,000
Income before income taxes		133,500
Income taxes		53,400
Net income		$ 80,100

Raw Materials Inventory

12/31/2014 60,000	
Purch. 313,000	
Avail. 373,000	
	Dir. Mtls. Used 295,000
12/31/2015 78,000	

Work in Process Inventory

12/31/2014 8,000	
Dir. Mtls. Used 295,000	
Dir. Labor 250,000	
FOH 570,000	
Avail. 1,123,000	
	COGM 1,114,000
12/31/2015 9,000	

Finished Goods Inventory

12/31/2014 15,000	
COGM 1,114,000	
Avail. 1,129,000	
	COGS 1,116,500
12/31/2015 12,500	

Summary

C1 Explain the purpose and nature of, and the role of ethics in, managerial accounting. The purpose of managerial accounting is to provide useful information to management and other internal decision makers. It does this by collecting, managing, and reporting both monetary and nonmonetary information in a manner useful to internal users. Major characteristics of managerial accounting include (1) focus on internal decision makers, (2) emphasis on planning and control, (3) flexibility, (4) timeliness, (5) reliance on forecasts and estimates, (6) focus on segments and projects, and (7) reporting both monetary and nonmonetary information. Ethics are beliefs that distinguish right from wrong. Ethics can be important in reducing fraud in business operations.

C2 Describe accounting concepts useful in classifying costs. We can classify costs as (1) fixed vs. variable, (2) direct vs. indirect, and (3) product vs. period. A cost can be classified in more than one way, depending on the purpose for which the cost is being determined. These classifications help us understand cost patterns, analyze performance, and plan operations.

C3 Define product and period costs and explain how they impact financial statements. Costs that are capitalized because they are expected to have future value are called *product costs;* costs that are expensed are called *period costs.* This classification is important because it affects the amount of costs expensed in the income statement and the amount of costs assigned to inventory on the balance sheet. Product costs are commonly made up of direct materials, direct labor, and overhead. Period costs include selling and administrative expenses.

C4 Explain how balance sheets and income statements for manufacturing, merchandising, and service companies differ. The main difference is that manufacturers usually carry three inventories on their balance sheets—raw materials, work in process, and finished goods—instead of one inventory that merchandisers carry. Service company balance sheets do not include inventories of items for sale. The main difference between income statements of manufacturers and merchandisers is the items making up cost of goods sold. A merchandiser uses merchandise inventory and the cost of goods purchased to compute cost of goods sold; a manufacturer uses finished goods inventory and the cost of goods manufactured to compute cost of goods sold. A service company's income statement does not include cost of goods sold.

C5 Explain manufacturing activities and the flow of manufacturing costs. Manufacturing activities consist of materials, production, and sales activities. The materials activity consists of the purchase and issuance of materials to production. The production activity consists of converting materials into finished goods. At this stage in the process, the materials, labor, and overhead costs have been incurred and the schedule of cost of goods manufactured is prepared. The sales activity consists of selling some or all of finished goods available for sale. At this stage, the cost of goods sold is determined.

C6 Describe trends in managerial accounting. Important trends in managerial accounting include an increased focus on satisfying customers, the impact of a global economy, and the growing presence of e-commerce and service-based businesses. The lean business model, designed to eliminate waste and satisfy customers, can be useful in responding to recent trends. Concepts such as total quality management, just-in-time production, and the value chain often aid in application of the lean business model.

A1 Assess raw materials inventory management using raw materials inventory turnover and days' sales in raw materials inventory. A high raw materials inventory turnover suggests a business is more effective in managing its raw materials inventory. We use days' sales in raw materials inventory to assess the likelihood of production being delayed due to inadequate levels of raw materials. We prefer a high raw materials inventory turnover ratio and a small number of days' sales in raw materials inventory, provided that raw materials inventory levels are adequate to keep production steady.

P1 Compute cost of goods sold for a manufacturer and for a merchandiser. A manufacturer adds beginning finished goods inventory to cost of goods manufactured and then subtracts ending finished goods inventory to get cost of goods sold. A merchandiser adds beginning merchandise inventory to cost of goods purchased and then subtracts ending merchandise inventory to get cost of goods sold.

P2 Prepare a schedule of cost of goods manufactured and explain its purpose and links to financial statements. This schedule reports the computation of cost of goods manufactured for the period. It begins by showing the period's costs for direct materials, direct labor, and overhead and then adjusts these numbers for the beginning and ending inventories of the work in process to yield cost of goods manufactured.

Guidance Answers to Decision Maker and Decision Ethics

Production Manager It appears that all three friends want to pay the bill with someone else's money. David is using money belonging to the tax authorities, Denise is taking money from her company, and Derek is defrauding the client. To prevent such practices, companies have internal audit mechanisms. Many companies also adopt ethical codes of conduct to help guide employees. We must recognize that some entertainment expenses are justifiable and even encouraged. For example, the tax law allows certain deductions for entertainment that have a business purpose. Corporate policies also sometimes allow and encourage reimbursable spending for social activities, and contracts can include entertainment as allowable costs. Nevertheless, without further details, payment for this bill should be made from personal accounts.

Entrepreneur Tracing all costs directly to cost objects is always desirable, but you need to be able to do so in an economically feasible manner. In this case, you are able to trace 90% of the assembly department's direct costs. It may not be economical to spend more money on a new software to trace the final 10% of costs. You need to make a cost-benefit trade-off. If the software offers benefits beyond tracing the remaining 10% of the assembly department's costs, your decision should consider this.

Key Terms

Continuous improvement
Control
Conversion costs
Corporate social responsibility (CSR)
Cost object
Cost of goods manufactured
Customer orientation
Days' sales in raw materials inventory
Direct costs
Direct labor
Direct labor costs
Direct materials
Direct material costs
Ethics
Factory overhead
Factory overhead costs
Finished goods inventory
Fixed cost
Indirect costs
Indirect labor
Indirect labor costs
Indirect materials
Institute of Management Accountants (IMA)
Internal control system
Just-in-time (JIT) manufacturing
Lean business model
Managerial accounting
Period costs
Planning
Prime costs
Product costs
Raw materials inventory
Raw materials inventory turnover
Schedule of cost of goods manufactured
Total quality management (TQM)
Value chain
Variable cost
Work in process inventory

Multiple Choice Quiz

Answers at end of chapter

1. Continuous improvement
a. Is used to reduce inventory levels.
b. Is applicable only in service businesses.
c. Rejects the notion of "good enough."
d. Is used to reduce ordering costs.
e. Is applicable only in manufacturing businesses.

2. A direct cost is one that is
a. Variable with respect to the cost object.
b. Traceable to the cost object.
c. Fixed with respect to the cost object.
d. Allocated to the cost object.
e. A period cost.

3. Costs that are incurred as part of the manufacturing process, but are not clearly traceable to the specific unit of product or batches of product, are called
a. Period costs.
b. Factory overhead.
c. Variable costs.
d. Operating expenses.
e. Fixed costs.

4. The three major cost components of manufacturing a product are
a. Direct materials, direct labor, and factory overhead.
b. Period costs, product costs, and conversion costs.
c. Indirect labor, indirect materials, and fixed expenses.
d. Variable costs, fixed costs, and period costs.
e. Overhead costs, fixed costs, and direct costs.

5. A company reports the following for the current year.

Finished goods inventory, beginning year	$6,000
Finished goods inventory, ending year	3,200
Cost of goods sold	7,500

Its cost of goods manufactured for the current year is
a. $1,500.
b. $1,700.
c. $7,500.
d. $2,800.
e. $4,700.

Icon denotes assignments that involve decision making.

Discussion Questions

1. Describe the managerial accountant's role in business planning, control, and decision making.

2. Distinguish between managerial and financial accounting on
a. Users and decision makers. **b.** Purpose of information.
c. Flexibility of practice. **d.** Time dimension.
e. Focus of information. **f.** Nature of information.

3. Identify the usual changes that a company must make when it adopts a customer orientation.

4. Distinguish between direct labor and indirect labor.

5. Distinguish between (*a*) factory overhead and (*b*) selling and administrative overhead.

6. Distinguish between direct material and indirect material.

7. What product cost is listed as both a prime cost and a conversion cost?
8. Assume that we tour **Samsung**'s factory where it makes its products. List three direct costs and three indirect costs that we are likely to see.
9. Should we evaluate a production manager's performance on the basis of operating expenses? Why?
10. Explain why knowledge of cost behavior is useful in product performance evaluation.
11. Explain why product costs are capitalized but period costs are expensed in the current accounting period.
12. Explain how business activities and inventories for a manufacturing company, a merchandising company, and a service company differ.
13. Why does managerial accounting often involve working with numerous predictions and estimates?
14. How do an income statement and a balance sheet for a manufacturing company and a merchandising company differ?
15. Besides inventories, what other assets often appear on manufacturers' balance sheets but not on merchandisers' balance sheets?
16. Why does a manufacturing company require three different inventory categories?
17. Manufacturing activities of a company are described in the ________. This schedule summarizes the types and amounts of costs incurred in its manufacturing ________.
18. What are the three categories of manufacturing costs?
19. List several examples of factory overhead.
20. List the four components of a schedule of cost of goods manufactured and provide specific examples of each for **Apple**.
21. Prepare a proper title for the annual schedule of cost of goods manufactured of **Google**. Does the date match the balance sheet or income statement? Why?
22. Describe the relations among the income statement, the schedule of cost of goods manufactured, and a detailed listing of factory overhead costs.
23. Define and describe two measures to assess raw materials inventory management.
24. Can management of a company such as **Apple** use cycle time and cycle efficiency as useful measures of performance? Explain.
25. Access **Dell**'s annual report (10-K) for the fiscal year ended February 1, 2013, at the SEC's EDGAR database (SEC.gov) or its website (Dell.com). From its financial statement notes, identify the titles and amounts of its inventory components.

connect

QUICK STUDY

QS 14-1
Managerial accounting versus financial accounting C1

Identify whether each description most likely applies to managerial or financial accounting.

______ 1. Its primary users are company managers.
______ 2. Its information is often available only after an audit is complete.
______ 3. Its primary focus is on the organization as a whole.
______ 4. Its principles and practices are very flexible.

QS 14-2
Fixed and variable costs C2

A cell phone company offers two different plans. Plan A costs $80 per month for unlimited talk and text. Plan B costs $0.20 per minute plus $0.10 per text message sent. You need to purchase a plan for your 14-year-old sister. Your sister currently uses 1,700 minutes and sends 1,600 texts each month.

1. What is your sister's total cost under each of the two plans?
2. Suppose your sister doubles her monthly usage to 3,400 minutes and sends 3,200 texts. What is your sister's total cost under each of the two plans?

QS 14-3
Direct and indirect costs C2

Diez Company produces sporting equipment, including leather footballs. Identify each of the following costs as direct or indirect. The cost object is a football produced by Diez.

______ 1. Electricity used in the production plant.
______ 2. Labor used on the football production line.
______ 3. Salary of manager who supervises the entire plant.
______ 4. Depreciation on equipment used to produce footballs.
______ 5. Leather used to produce footballs.

QS14-4
Classifying product costs C2

Identify each of the following costs as either direct materials, direct labor, or factory overhead. The company manufactures tennis balls.

______ 1. Rubber used to form the cores
______ 2. Factory maintenance
______ 3. Wages paid to assembly workers
______ 4. Glue used in binding rubber cores to felt covers
______ 5. Depreciation—Factory equipment
______ 6. Cans to package the balls

QS 14-5
Product and period costs
C3

Identify each of the following costs as either a product cost or a period cost.

_______ **1.** Factory maintenance
_______ **2.** Sales commissions
_______ **3.** Depreciation—Factory equipment
_______ **4.** Depreciation—Office equipment
_______ **5.** Rent on factory building
_______ **6.** Interest expense
_______ **7.** Office manager salary
_______ **8.** Indirect materials used in making goods

QS 14-6
Inventory reporting for manufacturers
C4

Compute ending work in process inventory for a manufacturer with the following information.

Raw materials purchased	$124,800
Raw materials used in production	74,300
Direct labor used	55,000
Total factory overhead	95,700
Work in process inventory, beginning of year	26,500
Cost of goods manufactured	221,800

QS 14-7
Cost of goods sold
P1

Compute cost of goods sold for 2015 using the following information.

Finished goods inventory, Dec. 31, 2014	$345,000
Work in process inventory, Dec. 31, 2014	83,500
Work in process inventory, Dec. 31, 2015	72,300
Cost of goods manufactured, 2015	918,700
Finished goods inventory, Dec. 31, 2015	283,600

QS 14-8
Cost of goods sold
P1

Compute cost of goods sold using the following information:

Finished goods inventory, beginning	$ 500
Cost of goods manufactured	4,000
Finished goods inventory, ending	750

QS 14-9
Manufacturing cost flows
C5

Compute the total manufacturing cost for a manufacturer with the following information for the month.

Raw materials purchased	$32,400
Raw materials used in production	53,750
Direct labor used	12,000
Factory supervisor salary	8,000
Salesperson commissions	6,200
Depreciation expense—Factory building	3,500
Depreciation expense—Delivery equipment	2,200
Indirect materials	1,250

QS 14-10
Cost of goods manufactured
P2

Prepare the 2015 schedule of cost of goods manufactured for Barton Company using the following information.

Direct materials	$190,500
Direct labor	63,150
Factory overhead costs	24,000
Work in process, Dec. 31, 2014	157,600
Work in process, Dec. 31, 2015	142,750

QS 14-11
Direct materials used
P2

Use the following information to compute the cost of direct materials used for the current year.

	January 1	December 31
Inventories		
Raw materials inventory	$ 6,000	$7,500
Work in process inventory	12,000	9,000
Finished goods inventory	8,500	5,500
Activity during current year		
Materials purchased		$123,500
Direct labor		94,000
Factory overhead		39,000

QS 14-12
Trends in managerial accounting
C6

Match each concept with its best description by entering its letter in the blank.

_____ **1.** Just-in-time manufacturing
_____ **2.** Continuous improvement
_____ **3.** Customer orientation
_____ **4.** Total quality management

A. Focuses on quality throughout the production process.
B. Flexible product designs can be modified to accommodate customer choices.
C. Every manager and employee constantly looks for ways to improve company operations.
D. Inventory is acquired or produced only as needed.

QS 14-13
Direct materials used
C5

Nestlé reports beginning raw materials inventory of 3,815 and ending raw materials inventory of 3,499 (both numbers in millions of Swiss francs). If Nestlé purchased 13,860 (in millions of Swiss francs) of raw materials during the year, what is the amount of raw materials it used during the year?

QS 14-14
Raw materials inventory management A1

Nestlé reports beginning raw materials inventory of 3,815 and ending raw materials inventory of 3,499 (both numbers in millions of Swiss francs). Assume Nestlé purchased 13,860 and used 14,176 (both amounts in millions of Swiss francs) in raw materials during the year. Compute raw materials inventory turnover and the number of days' sales in raw materials inventory.

connect

EXERCISES

Exercise 14-1
Sources of accounting information
C1

Both managerial accounting and financial accounting provide useful information to decision makers. Indicate in the following chart the most likely source of information for each business decision.

Business Decision	Primary Information Source: Managerial	Primary Information Source: Financial
1. Determine whether to lend to a company	____	____
2. Evaluate a purchasing department's performance	____	____
3. Report financial performance to board of directors	____	____
4. Estimate product cost for a new line of shoes	____	____
5. Plan the budget for next quarter	____	____
6. Measure profitability of an individual store	____	____
7. Prepare financial reports according to GAAP	____	____
8. Determine location and size for a new plant	____	____

Exercise 14-2
Cost classification
C2

Listed here are product costs for the production of soccer balls. Classify each cost (a) as either variable or fixed and (b) as either direct or indirect. What patterns do you see regarding the relation between costs classified in these two ways?

Product Cost	Variable or Fixed		Direct or Indirect	
	Variable	Fixed	Direct	Indirect
1. Leather covers for soccer balls	____	____	____	____
2. Annual flat fee paid for office security	____	____	____	____
3. Coolants for machinery	____	____	____	____
4. Wages of assembly workers	____	____	____	____
5. Lace to hold leather together	____	____	____	____
6. Taxes on factory	____	____	____	____
7. Machinery depreciation (straight-line)	____	____	____	____

Exercise 14-3
Cost classifications for a service provider
C2

TechPro offers instructional courses in e-commerce website design. The company holds classes in a building that it owns. Classify each of TechPro's costs below as (a) variable or fixed and (b) direct or indirect. Assume the cost object is an individual class.

______ **1.** Depreciation on classroom building
______ **2.** Monthly Internet connection cost
______ **3.** Instructional manuals for students
______ **4.** Travel expenses for salesperson
______ **5.** Depreciation on computers used for classes
______ **6.** Instructor wage (per class)

Exercise 14-4
Cost classifications for a service company
C2

Listed below are costs of providing an airline service. Classify each cost as (a) either variable or fixed, and (b) either direct or indirect. Consider the cost object to be a flight.

Cost	Variable or Fixed		Direct or Indirect	
	Variable	Fixed	Direct	Indirect
1. Advertising	____	____	____	____
2. Beverages and snacks	____	____	____	____
3. Regional vice-president salary	____	____	____	____
4. Depreciation on ground equipment	____	____	____	____
5. Fuel and oil used in planes	____	____	____	____
6. Flight attendant salaries	____	____	____	____
7. Pilot salaries	____	____	____	____
8. Maintenance worker wages	____	____	____	____
9. Customer service salaries	____	____	____	____

Exercise 14-5
Classifying manufacturing costs
C3

Some costs related to **Apple**'s iPad are listed below. Classify each cost as either direct materials, direct labor, factory overhead, selling expenses, or general and administrative expenses.

______ **1.** Display screen
______ **2.** Assembly-line supervisor salary
______ **3.** Wages for assembly workers
______ **4.** Salary of the chief executive officer
______ **5.** Glue to hold iPad cases together
______ **6.** Uniforms provided for each factory worker
______ **7.** Wages for retail store worker
______ **8.** Depreciation (straight-line) on robotic equipment used in assembly

Exercise 14-6
Cost classification
C3

Georgia Pacific, a manufacturer, incurs the following costs. (1) Classify each cost as either a product or a period cost. If a product cost, identify it as direct materials, direct labor, or factory overhead, and then as a prime and/or conversion cost. (2) Classify each product cost as either a direct cost or an indirect cost using the product as the cost object.

	Product Cost						
	Prime		Conversion				
Cost	Direct Materials	Direct Labor	Direct Labor	Overhead	Period Cost	Direct Cost	Indirect Cost
1. Factory utilities	____	____	____	____	____	____	____
2. Advertising	____	____	____	____	____	____	____
3. Amortization of patents on factory machine	____	____	____	____	____	____	____
4. State and federal income taxes	____	____	____	____	____	____	____
5. Office supplies used	____	____	____	____	____	____	____
6. Insurance on factory building	____	____	____	____	____	____	____
7. Wages to assembly workers	____	____	____	____	____	____	____

Exercise 14-7
Balance sheet identification and preparation
C4

Current assets for two different companies at fiscal year-end 2015 are listed here. One is a manufacturer, Rayzer Skis Mfg., and the other, Sunrise Foods, is a grocery distribution company. (1) Identify which set of numbers relates to the manufacturer and which to the merchandiser. (2) Prepare the current asset section for each company from this information. Discuss why the current asset section for these two companies is different.

Account	Company 1	Company 2
Cash	$ 7,000	$ 5,000
Raw materials inventory	—	42,000
Merchandise inventory	45,000	—
Work in process inventory	—	30,000
Finished goods inventory	—	50,000
Accounts receivable, net	62,000	75,000
Prepaid expenses	1,500	900

Exercise 14-8
Cost of goods manufactured and cost of goods sold computation
P1 P2

Using the following data, compute (1) the cost of goods manufactured and (2) the cost of goods sold for both Garcon Company and Pepper Company for the year ended December 31, 2015.

	Garcon Company	Pepper Company
Beginning finished goods inventory	$12,000	$16,450
Beginning work in process inventory	14,500	19,950
Beginning raw materials inventory	7,250	9,000
Rental cost on factory equipment	27,000	22,750
Direct labor	19,000	35,000
Ending finished goods inventory	17,650	13,300
Ending work in process inventory	22,000	16,000
Ending raw materials inventory	5,300	7,200
Factory utilities	9,000	12,000
Factory supplies used	8,200	3,200
General and administrative expenses	21,000	43,000
Indirect labor	1,250	7,660
Repairs—Factory equipment	4,780	1,500
Raw materials purchases	33,000	52,000
Selling expenses	50,000	46,000
Sales	195,030	290,010
Cash	20,000	15,700
Factory equipment, net	212,500	115,825
Accounts receivable, net	13,200	19,450

Check Garcon COGS, $91,030

Exercise 14-9
Prepare financial statements for a manufacturer C4 P2

Use the data in Exercise 14-8 to prepare an income statement and the current assets section of the balance sheet for each company. Ignore income taxes.

Exercise 14-10
Cost classification C2

Refer to the data in Exercise 14-8. Compute the total (1) prime costs and (2) conversion costs for each company.

Exercise 14-11
Cost of goods sold computation P1

Compute cost of goods sold for each of these two companies for the year ended December 31, 2015.

	A	B	C
1–2		Unimart	Precision Manufacturing
3	Beginning inventory		
4	Merchandise	$275,000	
5	Finished goods		$450,000
6	Cost of purchases	500,000	
7	Cost of goods manufactured		900,000
8	Ending inventory		
9	Merchandise	115,000	
10	Finished goods		375,000
11			

Check Unimart COGS, $660,000

Exercise 14-12
Components of accounting reports P2

For each of the following accounts for a manufacturing company, place a ✓ in the appropriate column indicating that it appears on the balance sheet, the income statement, the schedule of cost of goods manufactured, and/or a detailed listing of factory overhead costs. *Assume that the income statement shows the calculation of cost of goods sold and the schedule of cost of goods manufactured shows only the total amount of factory overhead.* (An account can appear on more than one report.)

	A	B	C	D	E
1–2	Account	Balance Sheet	Income Statement	Sched. of Cost of Goods Manuf'd.	Overhead Report
3	Accounts receivable				
4	Computer supplies used (office)				
5	Beginning finished goods inventory				
6	Beginning work in process inventory				
7	Cash				
8	Depreciation expense—Factory building				
9	Depreciation expense—Office building				
10	Direct labor				
11	Ending work in process inventory				
12	Ending raw materials inventory				
13	Factory maintenance wages				
14	Income taxes				
15	Insurance on factory building				
16	Property taxes on factory building				
17	Raw materials purchases				
18	Sales				
19					

Exercise 14-13
Preparation of schedule of cost of goods manufactured P2

Given the following selected account balances of Delray Mfg. prepare its schedule of cost of goods manufactured for the year ended December 31, 2015. Include a listing of the individual overhead account balances in this schedule.

Sales	$1,250,000	Repairs—Factory equipment	$ 5,250
Raw materials inventory, Dec. 31, 2014	37,000	Rent cost of factory building	57,000
Work in process inventory, Dec. 31, 2014	53,900	Advertising expense	94,000
Finished goods inventory, Dec. 31, 2014	62,750	General and administrative expenses	129,300
Raw materials purchases	175,600	Raw materials inventory, Dec. 31, 2015	42,700
Direct labor	225,000	Work in process inventory, Dec. 31, 2015	41,500
Factory computer supplies used	17,840	Finished goods inventory, Dec. 31, 2015	67,300
Indirect labor	47,000		

Check Cost of goods manufactured, $534,390

Exercise 14-14
Income statement preparation P2

Use the information in Exercise 14-13 to prepare an income statement for Delray Mfg. (a manufacturer). Assume that its cost of goods manufactured is $534,390.

Exercise 14-15
Schedule of cost of goods manufactured and cost of goods sold P1 P2

Beck Manufacturing reports the information below for 2015. Using this information:

1. Prepare the schedule of cost of goods manufactured for the year.
2. Compute cost of goods sold for the year.

Raw Materials Inventory

Begin. Inv.	10,000		
Purchases	45,000		
Avail for Use	55,000	Matls used	46,500
End. Inv.	8,500		

Work in Process Inventory

Begin. Inv.	14,000		
Materials	46,500		
Direct labor	27,500		
Overhead	55,000		
Avail for mfg.	143,000	Cost of goods mfg	131,000
End. Inv.	12,000		

Finished Goods Inventory

Begin. Inv.	16,000		
Cost of goods mfg	131,000		
Avail for sale	147,000	Cost of goods sold	129,000
End. Inv.	18,000		

Exercise 14-16
Cost flows in manufacturing
C5

The following chart shows how costs flow through a business as a product is manufactured. Some boxes in the flowchart show cost amounts. Compute the cost amounts for the boxes that contain question marks.

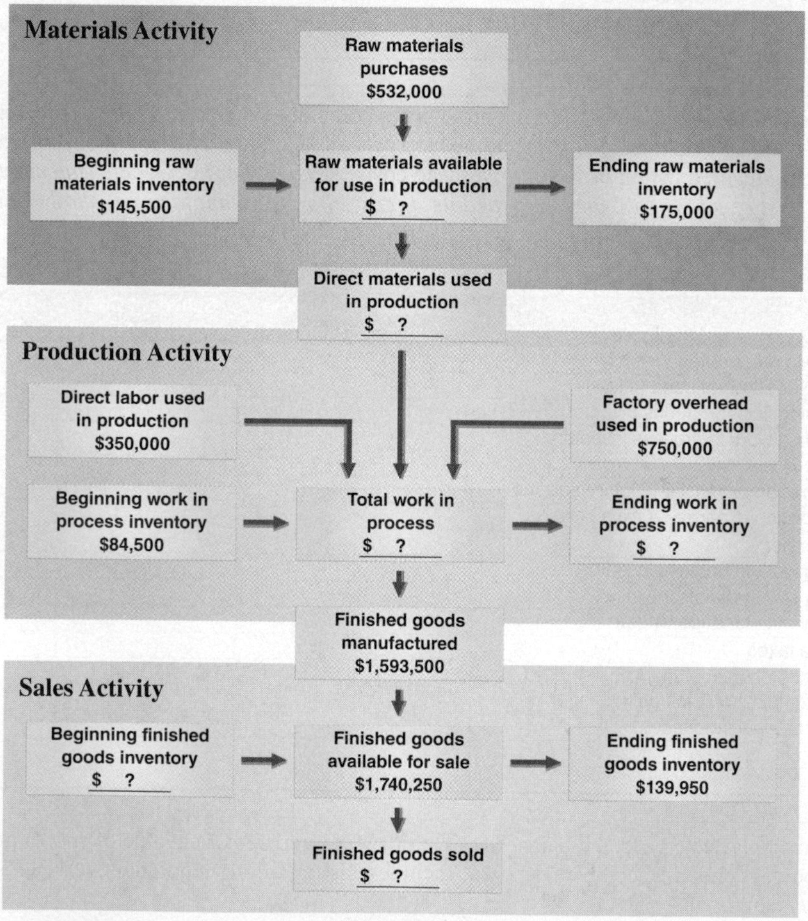

Exercise 14-17
Lean business concepts
C6

Many fast-food restaurants compete on lean business concepts. Match each of the following activities at a fast-food restaurant with the lean business concept it strives to achieve. Some activities might relate to more than one lean business concept.

_____ **1.** Courteous employees
_____ **2.** Food produced to order
_____ **3.** Clean tables and floors
_____ **4.** Orders filled within three minutes
_____ **5.** Standardized food making processes
_____ **6.** New product development

a. Just-in-time (JIT)
b. Continuous improvement (CI)
c. Total quality management (TQM)

PROBLEM SET A

Problem 14-1A
Cost computation, classification, and analysis
C2 C3

Listed here are the total costs associated with the 2015 production of 1,000 drum sets manufactured by TrueBeat. The drum sets sell for $500 each.

Costs	Variable or Fixed: Variable	Variable or Fixed: Fixed	Product or Period: Product	Product or Period: Period
1. Plastic for casing—$17,000	$17,000	___	$17,000	___
2. Wages of assembly workers—$82,000	___	___	___	___
3. Property taxes on factory—$5,000	___	___	___	___
4. Accounting staff salaries—$35,000	___	___	___	___
5. Drum stands (1,000 stands purchased)—$26,000	___	___	___	___
6. Rent cost of equipment for sales staff—$10,000	___	___	___	___
7. Upper management salaries—$125,000	___	___	___	___
8. Annual flat fee for factory maintenance service—$10,000	___	___	___	___
9. Sales commissions—$15 per unit	___	___	___	___
10. Machinery depreciation, straight-line—$40,000	___	___	___	___

Required

1. Classify each cost and its amount as (*a*) either variable or fixed and (*b*) either product or period. (The first cost is completed as an example.)
2. Compute the manufacturing cost per drum set.

Check (1) Total variable production cost, $125,000

Analysis Component

3. Assume that 1,200 drum sets are produced in the next year. What do you predict will be the total cost of plastic for the casings and the per unit cost of the plastic for the casings? Explain.
4. Assume that 1,200 drum sets are produced in the next year. What do you predict will be the total cost of property taxes and the per unit cost of the property taxes? Explain.

Problem 14-2A
Classifying costs
C2 C3

The following calendar year-end information is taken from the December 31, 2015, adjusted trial balance and other records of Leone Company.

Advertising expense	$ 28,750	Miscellaneous production costs	$ 8,425
Depreciation expense—Office equipment	7,250	Office salaries expense	63,000
Depreciation expense—Selling equipment	8,600	Raw materials purchases	925,000
Depreciation expense—Factory equipment	33,550	Rent expense—Office space	22,000
Factory supervision	102,600	Rent expense—Selling space	26,100
Factory supplies used	7,350	Rent expense—Factory building	76,800
Factory utilities	33,000	Maintenance expense—Factory equipment	35,400
Direct labor	675,480	Sales	4,462,500
Indirect labor	56,875	Sales salaries expense	392,560

Required

1. Identify and classify each of the costs above as either a product or period cost.
2. Classify each of the product costs as either direct materials, direct labor, or factory overhead.
3. Classify each of the period costs as either selling or general and administrative expenses.

Problem 14-3A
Schedule of cost of goods manufactured and income statement; inventory analysis
P2 A1

Using the data from Problem 14-2A and the inventory information for Leone Company below, complete the requirements below. Assume income tax expense is $233,725 for the year.

Inventories	
Raw materials, December 31, 2014	$166,850
Raw materials, December 31, 2015	182,000
Work in process, December 31, 2014	15,700
Work in process, December 31, 2015	19,380
Finished goods, December 31, 2014	167,350
Finished goods, December 31, 2015	136,490

Required

Check (1) Cost of goods manufactured, $1,935,650

1. Prepare the company's 2015 schedule of cost of goods manufactured.
2. Prepare the company's 2015 income statement that reports separate categories for (*a*) selling expenses and (*b*) general and administrative expenses.

Analysis Component

3. Compute the (*a*) inventory turnover, defined as cost of goods sold divided by average inventory, and (*b*) days' sales in inventory, defined as 365 times ending inventory divided by cost of goods sold, for both its raw materials inventory and its finished goods inventory. (To compute turnover and days' sales in inventory for raw materials, use raw materials used rather than cost of goods sold.) Discuss some possible reasons for differences between these ratios for the two types of inventories. Round answers to one decimal place.

Problem 14-4A
Ending inventory computation and evaluation
C4

Nazaro's Boot Company makes specialty boots for the rodeo circuit. On December 31, 2014, the company had (*a*) 300 pairs of boots in finished goods inventory and (*b*) 1,200 heels at a cost of $8 each in raw materials inventory. During 2015, the company purchased 35,000 additional heels at $8 each and manufactured 16,600 pairs of boots.

Required

Check (1) Ending (heel) inventory, 3,000 units; $24,000

1. Determine the unit and dollar amounts of raw materials inventory in heels at December 31, 2015.

Analysis Component

2. Write a one-half page memorandum to the production manager explaining why a just-in-time inventory system for heels should be considered. Include the amount of working capital that can be reduced at December 31, 2015, if the ending heel raw material inventory is cut by half.

Problem 14-5A
Inventory computation and reporting
C4 P1

Shown here are annual financial data at December 31, 2015, taken from two different companies.

	Music World Retail	Wave-Board Manufacturing
Beginning inventory		
Merchandise	$200,000	
Finished goods		$500,000
Cost of purchases	300,000	
Cost of goods manufactured		875,000
Ending inventory		
Merchandise	175,000	
Finished goods		225,000

Required

Check (1) Wave-Board's cost of goods sold, $1,150,000

1. Compute the cost of goods sold section of the income statement at December 31, 2015, for each company. Include the proper title and format in the solution.
2. Write a half-page memorandum to your instructor (*a*) identifying the inventory accounts and (*b*) describing where each is reported on the income statement and balance sheet for both companies.

PROBLEM SET B

Problem 14-1B
Cost computation, classification, and analysis
C2 C3

Listed here are the total costs associated with the 2015 production of 15,000 Blu-ray Discs (BDs) manufactured by Maxwell. The BDs sell for $18 each.

Costs	Variable or Fixed: Variable	Variable or Fixed: Fixed	Product or Period: Product	Product or Period: Period
1. Plastic for BDs—$1,500	$1,500		$1,500	
2. Wages of assembly workers—$30,000				
3. Cost of factory rent—$6,750				
4. Systems staff salaries—$15,000				
5. Labeling—$0.25 per BD				
6. Cost of office equipment rent—$1,050				
7. Upper management salaries—$120,000				
8. Annual fixed fee for cleaning service—$4,520				
9. Sales commissions—$0.50 per BD				
10. Machinery depreciation, straight-line—$18,000				

Required

1. Classify each cost and its amount as (*a*) either variable or fixed and (*b*) either product or period. (The first cost is completed as an example.)
2. Compute the manufacturing cost per BD.

Check (2) Total variable production cost, $35,250

Analysis Component

3. Assume that 10,000 BDs are produced in the next year. What do you predict will be the total cost of plastic for the BDs and the per unit cost of the plastic for the BDs? Explain.
4. Assume that 10,000 BDs are produced in the next year. What do you predict will be the total cost of factory rent and the per unit cost of the factory rent? Explain.

Problem 14-2B
Classifying costs
C2 C3

The following calendar year-end information is taken from the December 31, 2015, adjusted trial balance and other records of Best Bikes.

Advertising expense	$ 20,250	Miscellaneous production costs	$ 8,440
Depreciation expense—Office equipment	8,440	Office salaries expense	70,875
Depreciation expense—Selling equipment	10,125	Raw materials purchases	894,375
Depreciation expense—Factory equipment	35,400	Rent expense—Office space	23,625
Factory supervision	121,500	Rent expense—Selling space	27,000
Factory supplies used	6,060	Rent expense—Factory building	93,500
Factory utilities	37,500	Maintenance expense—Factory equipment	30,375
Direct labor	562,500	Sales	4,942,625
Indirect labor	59,000	Sales salaries expense	295,300

Required

1. Identify and classify each of the costs above as either a product or period cost.
2. Classify each of the product costs as either direct materials, direct labor, or factory overhead.
3. Classify each of the period costs as either selling or general and administrative expenses.

Problem 14-3B
Schedule of cost of goods manufactured and income statement; analysis of inventories
P2 A1

Using the information from Problem 14-2B and the inventory information for Best Bikes below, complete the requirements below. Assume income tax expense is $136,700 for the year.

Inventories	
Raw materials, December 31, 2014	$ 40,375
Raw materials, December 31, 2015	70,430
Work in process, December 31, 2014	12,500
Work in process, December 31, 2015	14,100
Finished goods, December 31, 2014	177,200
Finished goods, December 31, 2015	141,750

Required

1. Prepare the company's 2015 schedule of cost of goods manufactured.
2. Prepare the company's 2015 income statement that reports separate categories for (*a*) selling expenses and (*b*) general and administrative expenses.

Check (1) Cost of goods manufactured, $1,816,995

Analysis Component

3. Compute the (*a*) inventory turnover, defined as cost of goods sold divided by average inventory, and (*b*) days' sales in inventory, defined as 365 times ending inventory divided by cost of goods sold, for both its raw materials inventory and its finished goods inventory. (To compute turnover and days' sales in inventory for raw materials, use raw materials used rather than cost of goods sold.) Discuss some possible reasons for differences between these ratios for the two types of inventories. Round answers to one decimal place.

Problem 14-4B
Ending inventory computation and evaluation C4

Racer's Edge makes specialty skates for the ice skating circuit. On December 31, 2014, the company had (*a*) 1,500 skates in finished goods inventory and (*b*) 2,500 blades at a cost of $20 each in raw materials inventory. During 2015, Racer's Edge purchased 45,000 additional blades at $20 each and manufactured 20,750 pairs of skates.

Required

Check (1) Ending (blade) inventory, 6,000 units; $120,000

1. Determine the unit and dollar amounts of raw materials inventory in blades at December 31, 2015.

Analysis Component

2. Write a one-half page memorandum to the production manager explaining why a just-in-time inventory system for blades should be considered. Include the amount of working capital that can be reduced at December 31, 2015, if the ending blade raw materials inventory is cut in half.

Problem 14-5B
Inventory computation and reporting
C4 P1

Shown here are annual financial data at December 31, 2015, taken from two different companies.

	TeeMart (Retail)	Aim Labs (Manufacturing)
Beginning inventory		
Merchandise	$100,000	
Finished goods		$300,000
Cost of purchases	250,000	
Cost of goods manufactured		586,000
Ending inventory		
Merchandise	150,000	
Finished goods		200,000

Required

Check (1) TeeMart cost of goods sold, $200,000

1. Compute the cost of goods sold section of the income statement at December 31, 2015, for each company. Include the proper title and format in the solution.
2. Write a half-page memorandum to your instructor (*a*) identifying the inventory accounts and (*b*) identifying where each is reported on the income statement and balance sheet for both companies.

SERIAL PROBLEM
Business Solutions
C2 C4 P2

(This serial problem begins in Chapter 1 and continues through most of the book. If previous chapter segments were not completed, the serial problem can begin at this point. It is helpful, but not necessary, to use the Working Papers that accompany the book.)

SP 14 Santana Rey, owner of Business Solutions, decides to diversify her business by also manufacturing computer workstation furniture.

Required

1. Classify the following manufacturing costs of Business Solutions as either (*a*) variable or fixed and (*b*) direct or indirect.

	Variable or Fixed		Direct or Indirect	
Product Costs	Variable	Fixed	Direct	Indirect
1. Monthly flat fee to clean workshop	____	____	____	____
2. Laminate coverings for desktops	____	____	____	____
3. Taxes on assembly workshop	____	____	____	____
4. Glue to assemble workstation component parts	____	____	____	____
5. Wages of desk assembler	____	____	____	____
6. Electricity for workshop	____	____	____	____
7. Depreciation on tools	____	____	____	____

2. Prepare a schedule of cost of goods manufactured for Business Solutions for the month ended January 31, 2016. Assume the following manufacturing costs:
   Direct materials: $2,200
   Factory overhead: $490
   Direct labor: $900
   Beginning work in process: none (December 31, 2015)
   Ending work in process: $540 (January 31, 2016)
   Beginning finished goods inventory: none (December 31, 2015)
   Ending finished goods inventory: $350 (January 31, 2016)
3. Prepare the cost of goods sold section of a partial income statement for Business Solutions for the month ended January 31, 2016.

Check (3) COGS, $2,700

Beyond the Numbers

REPORTING IN ACTION
C1

APPLE

BTN 14-1 Managerial accounting is more than recording, maintaining, and reporting financial results. Managerial accountants must provide managers with both financial and nonfinancial information including estimates, projections, and forecasts. An important estimate for **Apple** is its reserve for warranty claims, and the company must provide shareholders information on these estimates.

Required

1. Access and read Apple's "Warranty costs" section of the "Critical Accounting Policies and Estimates" footnote to its financial statements, from Appendix A. How does management establish and adjust the warranty reserve? What are some of the effects if the company's actual results differ from its estimates?
2. What is the management accountant's role in determining those estimates?
3. What are some factors that could impact the warranty accrual in a given year?

Fast Forward

4. Access **Apple**'s annual report for a fiscal year ending after September 28, 2013, from either its website [Apple.com] or the SEC's EDGAR database [SEC.gov]. Answer the questions in parts 1, 2, and 3 after reading the current "Critical Accounting Policies and Estimates." Identify any major changes.

COMPARATIVE ANALYSIS
C2

APPLE
GOOGLE

BTN 14-2 Both **Apple** and **Google** have audit committees as part of their boards of directors. Access each company's website (investor.apple.com or investor.google.com) and read about the purpose of the audit committee.

Required

1. From Apple's website, select Leadership & Governance, Committee Charters, and Audit and Finance. What is the purpose of Apple's audit committee?
2. From Google's website, select Corporate Governance, Board Committees, and Audit. What is the purpose of Google's audit committee?
3. Based on your answers to parts *1* and *2*, how would management accountants be involved in assisting the audit committee in carrying out its responsibilities?

ETHICS CHALLENGE
C1 C3

BTN 14-3 Assume that you are the managerial accountant at Infostore, a manufacturer of hard drives, CDs, and DVDs. Its reporting year-end is December 31. The chief financial officer is concerned about having enough cash to pay the expected income tax bill because of poor cash flow management. On November 15, the purchasing department purchased excess inventory of CD raw materials in anticipation of rapid growth of this product beginning in January. To decrease the company's tax liability, the chief financial officer tells you to record the purchase of this inventory as part of supplies and expense it in the current year; this would decrease the company's tax liability by increasing expenses.

Required

1. In which account should the purchase of CD raw materials be recorded?
2. How should you respond to this request by the chief financial officer?

COMMUNICATING IN PRACTICE

C6

BTN 14-4 Write a one-page memorandum to a prospective college student about salary expectations for graduates in business. Compare and contrast the expected salaries for accounting (including different subfields such as public, corporate, tax, audit, and so forth), marketing, management, and finance majors. Prepare a graph showing average starting salaries (and those for experienced professionals in those fields if available). To get this information, stop by your school's career services office; libraries also have this information. The website JobStar.org (click on "Salary Info") also can get you started.

TAKING IT TO THE NET

C1

BTN 14-5 Managerial accounting professionals follow a code of ethics. As a member of the Institute of Management Accountants, the managerial accountant must comply with Standards of Ethical Conduct.

Required

1. Identify, print, and read the *Statement of Ethical Professional Practice* posted at www.IMAnet.org. (Under "Resources and Publications" select "Ethics Center," and then select "IMA Statement of Ethical Professional Practice.")
2. What four overarching ethical principles underlie the IMA's statement?
3. Describe the courses of action the IMA recommends in resolving ethical conflicts.

TEAMWORK IN ACTION

C5 P2

BTN 14-6 The following calendar-year information is taken from the December 31, 2015, adjusted trial balance and other records of Dahlia Company.

Advertising expense	$ 19,125	Direct labor	$ 650,750
Depreciation expense—Office equipment	8,750	Indirect labor	60,000
Depreciation expense—Selling equipment	10,000	Miscellaneous production costs	8,500
Depreciation expense—Factory equipment	32,500	Office salaries expense	100,875
Factory supervision	122,500	Raw materials purchases	872,500
Factory supplies used	15,750	Rent expense—Office space	21,125
Factory utilities	36,250	Rent expense—Selling space	25,750
Inventories		Rent expense—Factory building	79,750
Raw materials, December 31, 2014	177,500	Maintenance expense—Factory equipment	27,875
Raw materials, December 31, 2015	168,125	Sales	3,275,000
Work in process, December 31, 2014	15,875	Sales discounts	57,500
Work in process, December 31, 2015	14,000	Sales salaries expense	286,250
Finished goods, December 31, 2014	164,375		
Finished goods, December 31, 2015	129,000		

Required

1. *Each* team member is to be responsible for computing **one** of the following amounts. You are not to duplicate your teammates' work. Get any necessary amounts from teammates. Each member is to explain the computation to the team in preparation for reporting to class.
   - **a.** Materials used.
   - **b.** Factory overhead.
   - **c.** Total manufacturing costs.
   - **d.** Total cost of work in process.
   - **e.** Cost of goods manufactured.
2. Check your cost of goods manufactured with the instructor. If it is correct, proceed to part 3.
3. *Each* team member is to be responsible for computing **one** of the following amounts. You are not to duplicate your teammates' work. Get any necessary amounts from teammates. Each member is to explain the computation to the team in preparation for reporting to class.
   - **a.** Net sales.
   - **b.** Cost of goods sold.
   - **c.** Gross profit.
   - **d.** Total operating expenses.
   - **e.** Net income or loss before taxes.

Point: Provide teams with transparencies and markers for presentation purposes.

BTN 14-7 Eden Full of **SunSaluter** must understand manufacturing costs to effectively operate and succeed as a profitable and efficient business.

ENTREPRENEURIAL DECISION

C1 C2 C6

Required

1. What are the three main categories of manufacturing costs Eden must monitor and control? Provide examples of each.
2. What are four goals of a total quality management process? How can SunSaluter use TQM to improve its business activities?

BTN 14-8 Visit your favorite fast-food restaurant. Observe its business operations.

HITTING THE ROAD

C1 C2

Required

1. Describe all business activities from the time a customer arrives to the time that customer departs.
2. List all costs you can identify with the separate activities described in part 1.
3. Classify each cost from part 2 as fixed or variable, and explain your classification.

BTN 14-9 Access **Samsung**'s 2013 annual report from its website (www.samsung.com). Like **Apple**, Samsung offers warranties on its products.

GLOBAL DECISION

C1

Samsung

APPLE

Required

1. Access and read footnote 18, "Provisions," included in Samsung's 2013 annual report. What amount of warranty expense did Samsung record during 2013? What amount of warranty claims did Samsung pay in 2013?
2. Access and read information on Apple's accrued warranty in footnote 10 of its 2013 annual report. What amount of warranty expense did Apple record during 2013? What amount of warranty claims did Apple pay in 2013?
3. Using your answer from parts 1 and 2, which company was more accurate in estimating warranty claims for 2013?

ANSWERS TO MULTIPLE CHOICE QUIZ

1. c
2. b
3. b
4. a
5. e; Beginning finished goods + Cost of goods manufactured (COGM) − Ending finished goods = Cost of goods sold
   $6,000 + COGM − $3,200 = $7,500
   COGM = $4,700

chapter 15

Job Order Costing and Analysis

Chapter Preview

JOB ORDER COSTING	JOB ORDER COST FLOWS AND REPORTS	ADJUSTING FACTORY OVERHEAD AND PRICING
Cost accounting system C1 Job order production Comparing job order and process operations Production activities in job order costing Cost flows C2 Job cost sheet	P1 Materials cost flows and documents P2 Labor cost flows and documents P3 Overhead cost flows and recording applied overhead Recording actual overhead Summary of cost flows Schedule of cost of goods manufactured	Overhead T-account and actual vs applied overhead P4 Underapplied or overapplied overhead A1 Pricing services

Learning Objectives

CONCEPTUAL

C1 Describe important features of job order production.

C2 Explain job cost sheets and how they are used in job order costing.

ANALYTICAL

A1 Apply job order costing in pricing services.

PROCEDURAL

P1 Describe and record the flow of materials costs in job order costing.

P2 Describe and record the flow of labor costs in job order costing.

P3 Describe and record the flow of overhead costs in job order costing.

P4 Determine adjustments for overapplied and underapplied factory overhead.

Courtesy of Quintin Middleton

Sharpest Knife in the Shed

ST. STEPHEN, SC—Growing up, Quintin Middleton was fascinated by swords. "It all started with the movies . . . *Star Wars* and *He-Man*," laughs Quintin. Working part-time at a knife shop to help pay for his study of aircraft mechanics at a local technical school, Quintin decided he wanted to make knives. But not just any knives. Quintin makes handmade culinary knives of the very highest quality. Although his business, **Middleton Made Knives (Middletonmadeknives.com)**, is young and small, Quintin has sold his knives to chefs of both local and national renown. One top chef, Craig Deihl, says buying one of Quintin's knives "is like buying a tailored suit. Everything is made to order, and Quintin gives personalized attention."

Quintin uses direct labor (his own!) in making knives. He begins with only the highest-quality raw materials, including high-carbon steel, stainless steel, and exotic woods for the handles. His production process is labor-intensive; every step, from knife design to grinding the edges, is done by hand. Quintin keeps his overhead costs low by working out of a 12-by-16-foot storage shed in his backyard. "I also keep fixed costs low by not stocking inventory," explains Quintin, who makes his knives to order. Quintin uses a job order costing system—the topic of this chapter—to track his costs and to make quick business decisions regarding costs and selling prices. In Quintin's case, he separately tracks the costs of making each special-order knife and the costs of making each group ("job lot") of standard knives. Job order costing enables entrepreneurs like Quintin to better isolate costs and avoid the runaway costs often experienced by start-ups that fail to use such costing techniques.

Like many entrepreneurs who build their own businesses, Quintin started with little more than a dream. He used his own money to buy his equipment. Although not a chef, he wanted to make knives for chefs, and after many rejections he "finally made a knife that [a top chef] liked." Quintin's dream continues to grow with his business. Someday he hopes to have a small knife "factory," with about 10 employees. Expanding his business will increase Quintin's materials, labor, and overhead costs, and he will need to rely even more on accurate cost information to succeed.

"Passion creates quality"

—Quintin Middleton

Quintin notes that "to succeed in any business you need a great product." In Quintin's case that means constantly striving to make better knives. In addition to a passion for quality, persistence is critical, believes Quintin, and he encourages young entrepreneurs to believe in themselves. "Follow your great ideas, and always have a plan," says Quintin.

Sources: *Middleton Made Knives website,* January 2015; *The Local Palate,* July 8, 2013; *The Post and Courier,* September 29, 2012; *Entrepreneur.com,* September 28, 2011

JOB ORDER COSTING

This section describes a cost accounting system, job order production and costing, and contrasts job order production with process operations.

Cost Accounting System

Point: Cost accounting systems accumulate costs and then assign them to products and services.

Companies use cost accounting systems to generate timely and accurate cost information. A **cost accounting system** records manufacturing activities using a *perpetual* inventory system, which continuously updates records for costs of materials, work in process, and finished goods inventories. A cost accounting system also provides timely information about inventories and manufacturing costs per unit of product. This is especially helpful for managers' efforts to control costs and determine selling prices.

C1 Describe important features of job order production.

The two basic types of cost accounting systems are *job order costing* and *process costing*. In the next section we differentiate between job order operations and process operations. We then describe job order costing in this chapter and process costing in the next chapter.

Job Order Production

Many companies produce products individually designed to meet the needs of a specific customer. Each customized product is manufactured separately and its production is called **job order production,** or *job order manufacturing* (also called *customized production,* which is the production of products in response to special orders). Examples of such products or services include special-order machines, a factory building, custom jewelry, wedding invitations, tattoos, and audits by an accounting firm. The production activities for a customized product represent a **job.**

Maddie Meyer/Getty Images

A key feature of job order production is the diversity, often called *heterogeneity,* of the products produced. That is, each customer order differs from another customer order in some important respect. These differences can be large or small. For example, **Nike** allows custom orders over the Internet, enabling customers to select materials and colors and to personalize their shoes with letters and numbers.

When a job involves producing more than one unit of a custom product, it is often called a **job lot.** Products produced as job lots could include benches for a church, imprinted T-shirts for a 10K race or company picnic, or advertising signs for a chain of stores. Although these orders involve more than one unit, the volume of production is typically low, such as 50 benches, 200 T-shirts, or 100 signs.

Comparing Job Order and Process Operations

Point: Many professional examinations, including the CPA and CMA exams, require knowledge of job order and process costing.

Process operations, also called *process manufacturing* or *process production,* is the mass production of products in a continuous flow of steps. Unlike job order production, where every product differs depending on customer needs, process operations are designed to mass-produce large quantities of identical products. For example, each year **Penn** makes millions of tennis balls, and **The Hershey Company** produces over a billion pounds of chocolate.

Exhibit 15.1 lists important features of job order and process operations. Both types of operations are used by manufacturers and also by service companies. Movies made by **Walt Disney** and financial audits done by **KPMG** are examples of job order service operations. Order processing in large mail-order firms like **L.L. Bean** is an example of a process service operation.

EXHIBIT 15.1

Comparing Job Order and Process Operations

Job Order Operations	Process Operations
• Custom orders	• Repetitive procedures
• Heterogeneous products and services	• Homogeneous products and services
• Low production volume	• High production volume
• High product flexibility	• Low product flexibility
• Low to medium standardization	• High standardization

Production Activities in Job Order Costing

An overview of job order production activity and cost flows is shown in Exhibit 15.2. This exhibit shows the March production activity of Road Warriors, which installs entertainment systems and security devices in cars and trucks. The company customizes any vehicle by adding speakers, amplifiers, video systems, alarms, and reinforced exteriors.

EXHIBIT 15.2

Job Order Production Activities and Cost Flows

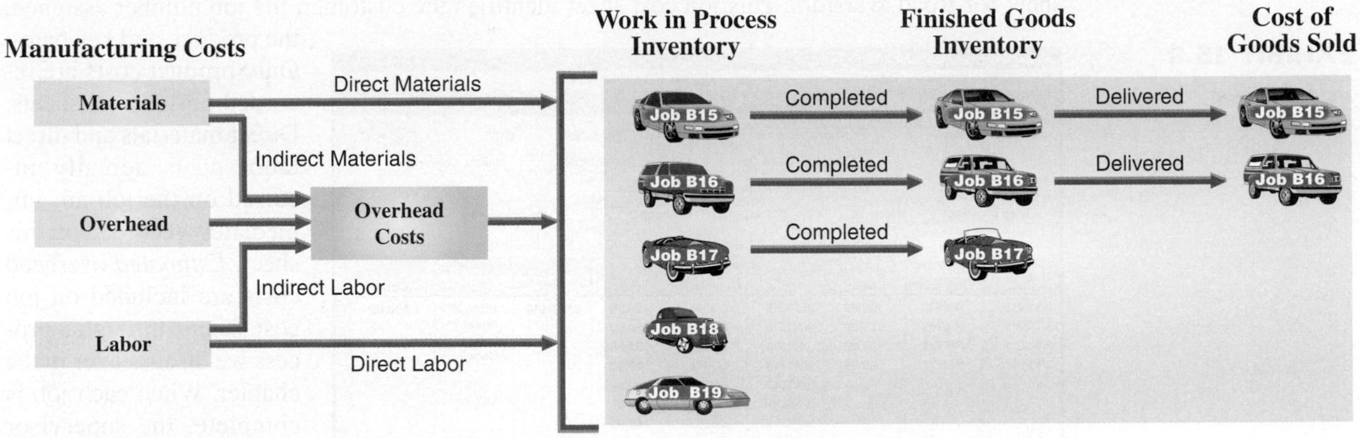

Job order production for Road Warriors requires materials, labor, and overhead costs. Recall that direct materials are used in manufacturing and can be clearly identified with a particular job. Similarly, direct labor is effort devoted to a particular job. Overhead costs support production of more than one job. Common overhead items are depreciation on factory buildings and equipment, factory supplies (indirect materials), supervision and maintenance (indirect labor), cleaning, and utilities.

Point: Factory insurance and property taxes are included in overhead.

Exhibit 15.2 shows that materials, labor, and overhead are added to Jobs B15, B16, B17, B18, and B19, which were started during the month (March). Alarm systems are added to Jobs B15 and B16; Job B17 receives a high-end audio and video entertainment system. Road Warriors completed Jobs B15, B16, and B17 in March and delivered Jobs B15 and B16 to customers. At the end of March, Jobs B18 and B19 remain in work in process inventory and Job B17 is in finished goods inventory.

Decision Insight

Target Costing Many producers determine a target cost for their jobs. Target cost is determined as follows: Expected selling price − Desired profit = Target cost. If the projected target cost of the job as determined by job costing is too high, the producer can apply *value engineering,* which is a method of determining ways to reduce job cost until the target cost is met. ■

Cost Flows

Because they are product costs, manufacturing costs flow through inventory accounts (Raw Materials Inventory, Work in Process Inventory, and Finished Goods Inventory) until the related goods are sold. While a job is being produced, its accumulated costs are kept in **Work in Process Inventory.** When a job is finished, its accumulated costs are transferred from Work in Process Inventory to **Finished Goods Inventory.** When a finished job is delivered to a customer, its accumulated costs are transferred from Finished Goods Inventory to Cost of Goods Sold.

These general ledger inventory accounts, however, do not provide enough detail for managers of job order operations to plan and control production activities. Managers need to know the costs of each individual job (or job lot). Subsidiary records store this information about the manufacturing costs for each individual job. The next section describes the use of these subsidiary records.

Job Cost Sheet

C2 Explain job cost sheets and how they are used in job order costing.

A major aim of a **job order costing system** is to determine the cost of producing each job or job lot. In the case of a job lot, the system also aims to compute the cost per unit. The accounting system must include separate records for each job to accomplish this, and it must capture information about costs incurred and charge these costs to each job.

A **job cost sheet** is a separate record maintained for each job. Exhibit 15.3 shows a job cost sheet for Road Warriors. This job cost sheet identifies the customer, the job number assigned, the product, and key dates. Only product costs are recorded on job cost sheets. Direct materials and direct labor costs actually incurred on the job are immediately recorded on this sheet. *Estimated* overhead costs are included on job cost sheets, through a process we discuss later in the chapter. When each job is complete, the supervisor enters the date of completion, records any remarks, and signs the sheet. The balance in the Work in Process Inventory account at any point in time is the sum of the costs on job cost sheets for all jobs that are not yet complete. The balance in the Finished Goods Inventory account at any point in time is the sum of the costs on job cost sheets for all jobs that *are* complete and awaiting sale. The balance in Cost of Goods Sold is the sum of all job sheets for jobs that have been sold and delivered to the customer. Managers use job cost sheets to monitor costs incurred to date and to predict and control costs for each job. In the next section we use Road Warriors' production and sales activity for March to illustrate job order costing and the use of job cost sheets.

EXHIBIT 15.3

Job Cost Sheet

Accounting System: Exhibit 15-3

File Edit Maintain Tasks Analysis Options Reports Window Help

Road Warriors, Los Angeles, California — **JOB COST SHEET**

Customer's Name	Carroll Connor	Job No.	B15
Address	1542 High Point Dr.	City & State	Malibu, California
Job Description	Level 1 Alarm System on Ford Expedition		
Date promised	March 15	Date started	March 3
Date completed	March 11		

Direct Materials			Direct Labor			Overhead		
Date	Requisition	Cost	Date	Time Ticket	Cost	Date	Rate	Cost
3/3/2015	R-4698	100.00	3/3/2015	L-3393	120.00	3/11/2015	160% of Direct Labor Cost	1,600.00
3/7/2015	R-4705	225.00	3/4/2015	L-3422	150.00			
3/9/2015	R-4725	180.00	3/5/2015	L-3456	180.00			
3/10/2015	R-4777	95.00	3/8/2015	L-3479	60.00			
			3/9/2015	L-3501	90.00			
			3/10/2015	L-3535	240.00			
			3/11/2015	L-3559	160.00			
	Total	600.00		Total	1,000.00		Total	1,600.00

REMARKS: Completed job on March 11, and shipped to customer on March 15. Met all specifications and requirements.

SUMMARY:	
Materials	600.00
Labor	1,000.00
Overhead	1,600.00
Total cost	3,200.00

Signed: *C. Luther, Supervisor*

Point: Documents (electronic and paper) are crucial in a job order system. The job cost sheet is the cornerstone. Understanding it aids in grasping concepts of capitalizing product costs and product cost flow.

QC1

JOB ORDER COST FLOWS AND REPORTS

The previous section provided an overview of job order costing. Next we look at job order costing in more detail, including the source documents for each cost flow. In this example, Road Warriors begins the month (March) with $1,000 in Raw Materials Inventory and nothing in the Work in Process Inventory or Finished Goods Inventory accounts.

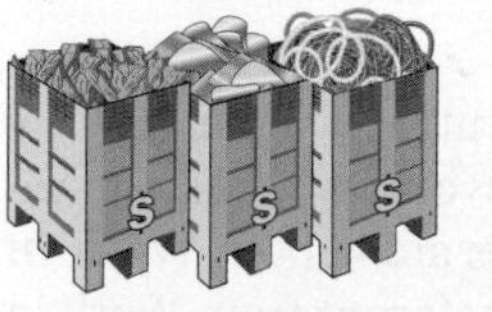

Materials

Materials Cost Flows and Documents

P1 Describe and record the flow of materials costs in job order costing.

This section focuses on the flow of materials costs and the related documents in a job order costing system. We begin analysis of the flow of materials costs by examining Exhibit 15.4. When materials are first received from suppliers, the employees count and inspect them and record the items' quantity and cost on a receiving report. The **receiving report** serves as the *source document* for recording materials received in both a materials ledger card and in the general ledger. In nearly all job order cost systems, **materials ledger cards** (or electronic files) are perpetual records that are updated each time materials are purchased and each time materials are issued for use in production.

Point: Some companies certify certain suppliers based on the quality of their materials. Goods received from these suppliers are not always inspected by the purchaser to save costs.

To illustrate the purchase of materials, Road Warriors acquired $2,750 of materials on credit on March 4, 2015. These include both direct and indirect materials. This purchase is recorded as shown below. After this entry is recorded, each individual materials ledger card is updated to

EXHIBIT 15.4

Materials Cost Flows

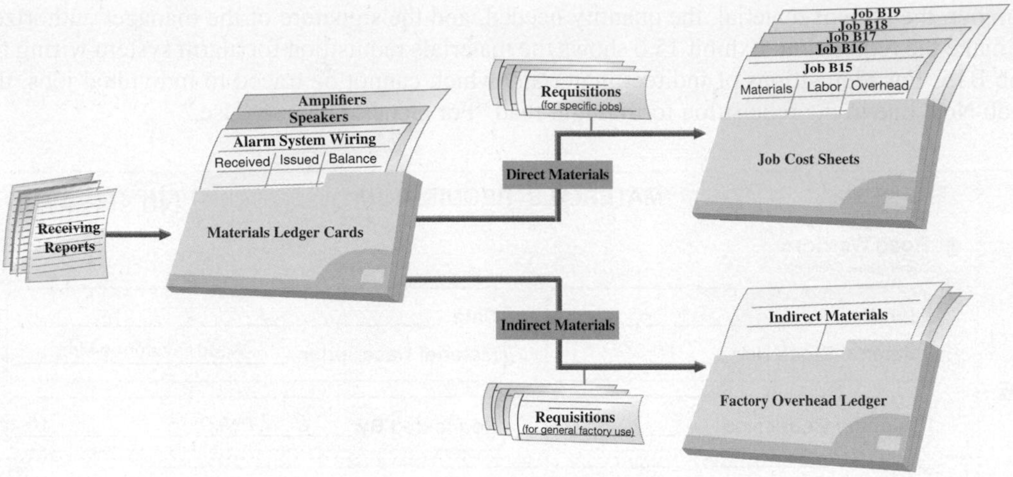

reflect the added materials. In addition, the entry is posted to the Raw Materials Inventory and Accounts Payable general ledger accounts.

Mar. 4	Raw Materials Inventory	2,750	
	Accounts Payable		2,750
	To record purchase of materials for production.		

Assets = Liabilities + Equity
+2,750 +2,750

Exhibit 15.4 shows that materials can be requisitioned for use either on a specific job (direct materials) or as overhead (indirect materials). Direct materials include costs, such as alarm system wiring, that are easily traced to individual jobs. Indirect materials include costs, such as those for screws, that are not easily traced to jobs. Cost of direct materials flows from the materials ledger card to the job cost sheets. The cost of indirect materials flows from the materials ledger card to the Indirect Materials account in the factory overhead ledger, which is a subsidiary ledger controlled by the Factory Overhead account in the general ledger. The factory overhead ledger includes all of the individual overhead costs.

Exhibit 15.5 shows a materials ledger card for one type of material received and issued by Road Warriors. The card identifies the item as alarm system wiring and shows the item's stock number, its location in the storeroom, information about the maximum and minimum quantities that should be available, and the reorder quantity. For example, two units of alarm system wiring were purchased on March 4, 2015, as evidenced by receiving report C-7117. After this purchase the company has three units of alarm system wiring on hand. Materials ledger cards would also be updated for each of the other materials purchased.

When materials are needed in production, a production manager prepares a **materials requisition** and sends it to the materials manager. For direct materials, the requisition shows the job

EXHIBIT 15.5

Materials Ledger Card

MATERIALS LEDGER CARD

Road Warriors
Los Angeles, California

Item	Alarm system wiring	Stock No.	M–347	Location in Storeroom	Bin 137
Maximum quantity	5 units	Minimum quantity	1 unit	Quantity to reorder	2 units

	Received				Issued				Balance		
Date	Receiving Report Number	Units	Unit Price	Total Price	Requisition Number	Units	Unit Price	Total Price	Units	Unit Price	Total Price
									1	225.00	225.00
3/4/2015	C-7117	2	225.00	450.00					3	225.00	675.00
3/7/2015					R–4705	1	225.00	225.00	2	225.00	450.00

number, the type of material, the quantity needed, and the signature of the manager authorized to make the requisition. Exhibit 15.6 shows the materials requisition for alarm system wiring for Job B15. For requisitions of indirect materials, which cannot be traced to individual jobs, the "Job No." line in the requisition form might read "For General Factory Use."

EXHIBIT 15.6

Materials Requisition

MATERIALS REQUISITION No. R–4705

Road Warriors
Los Angeles, California

Job No. B15	**Date** 3/7/2015
Material Stock No. M–347	**Material Description** Alarm system wiring
Quantity Requested 1	**Requested By** C. Luther
Quantity Provided 1	**Date Provided** 3/7/2015
Filled By M. Bateman	**Material Received By** C. Luther
Remarks	

Requisitions are often accumulated and recorded in one journal entry. The frequency of entries depends on the job, the industry, and management procedures. In this example, Road Warriors records materials requisitions at the end of each week. These materials requisitions are shown below.

Direct materials—requisitioned for specific jobs	
Job B15	$ 600
Job B16	300
Job B17	500
Job B18	150
Job B19	250
Total direct materials	**$1,800**
Indirect materials—requisitioned for general factory use	550
Total	$ 2,350

The use of direct materials for the week (including alarm system wiring for Job B15) yields the following entry.

Assets = Liabilities + Equity
+1,800
−1,800

Mar. 7	Work in Process Inventory	1,800	
	Raw Materials Inventory		1,800
	To record use of direct materials.		

This entry is posted both to general ledger accounts and to subsidiary records. Posting to subsidiary records includes debits to job cost sheets and credits to materials ledger cards. Exhibit 15.7 shows the postings to general ledger accounts (Work in Process Inventory and Raw Materials Inventory) and to the job cost sheets (subsidiary records). The Raw Materials Inventory account began the month with $1,000 of beginning inventory; it was increased for the March 7 purchase of $2,750. The $1,800 cost of materials used reduces Raw Materials Inventory and increases Work in Process Inventory. Note that the total amount of direct materials used so far ($1,800) is reflected in Work in Process Inventory and in the job cost sheets. Later we show the accounting for indirect materials. At this point, it is important only to know that requisitions of indirect materials do not directly impact Work in Process Inventory.

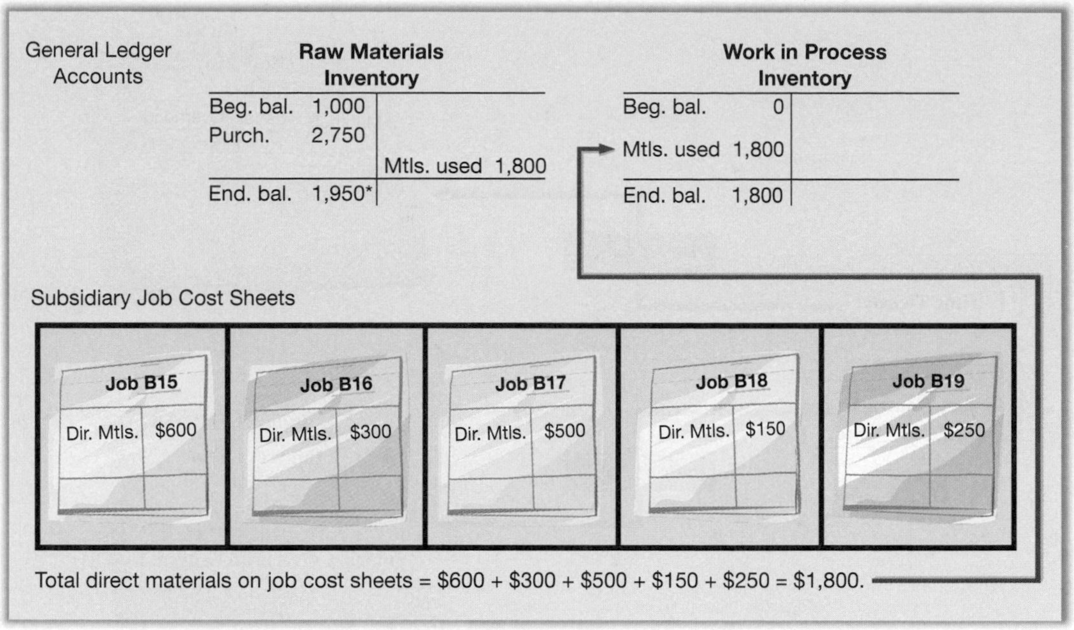

* Equals total amount from all materials ledger cards (not shown in this exhibit).

EXHIBIT 15.7

Posting Direct Materials Used to the General Ledger and Job Cost Sheets

NEED-TO-KNOW 15-1

Recording Direct Materials

P1

A manufacturing company purchased $1,200 of materials (on account) for use in production. The company used $200 of direct materials on Job 1 and $350 of direct materials on Job 2. Prepare journal entries to record these two transactions.

Solution

Raw Materials Inventory	1,200	
Accounts Payable		1,200
To record purchase of materials on account.		
Work in Process Inventory	550	
Raw Materials Inventory		550
To record use of direct materials in production.		

Do More: QS 15-4, E 15-8

Labor Cost Flows and Documents

P2 Describe and record the flow of labor costs in job order costing.

Labor

Labor is the next manufacturing cost to account for. Exhibit 15.8 shows that factory labor costs are classified as either direct or indirect. Direct labor costs flow to individual job cost sheets. To assign direct labor costs to individual jobs, companies use **time tickets** to track how each employee's time is used. Employees fill out time tickets to record how much time they spent on each job. For many companies, this process is automated: Employees swipe electronic identification badges, and a computer system assigns employees' hours worked to individual jobs. An employee who works on several jobs during a day completes separate time tickets for each job. In all cases, supervisors check and approve the accuracy of time tickets.

Point: Many employee fraud schemes involve payroll, including overstated hours on time tickets.

Indirect labor includes factory costs like supervisor salaries and maintenance worker wages. These costs cannot be assigned directly to individual jobs. Instead, the company determines the amounts of supervisor salaries from their salary contracts and the amounts of maintenance worker wages from time tickets, and classifies those costs as overhead. These costs flow to the factory overhead ledger. Later in the chapter we show how these overhead costs are allocated to specific jobs.

EXHIBIT 15.8

Labor Cost Flows

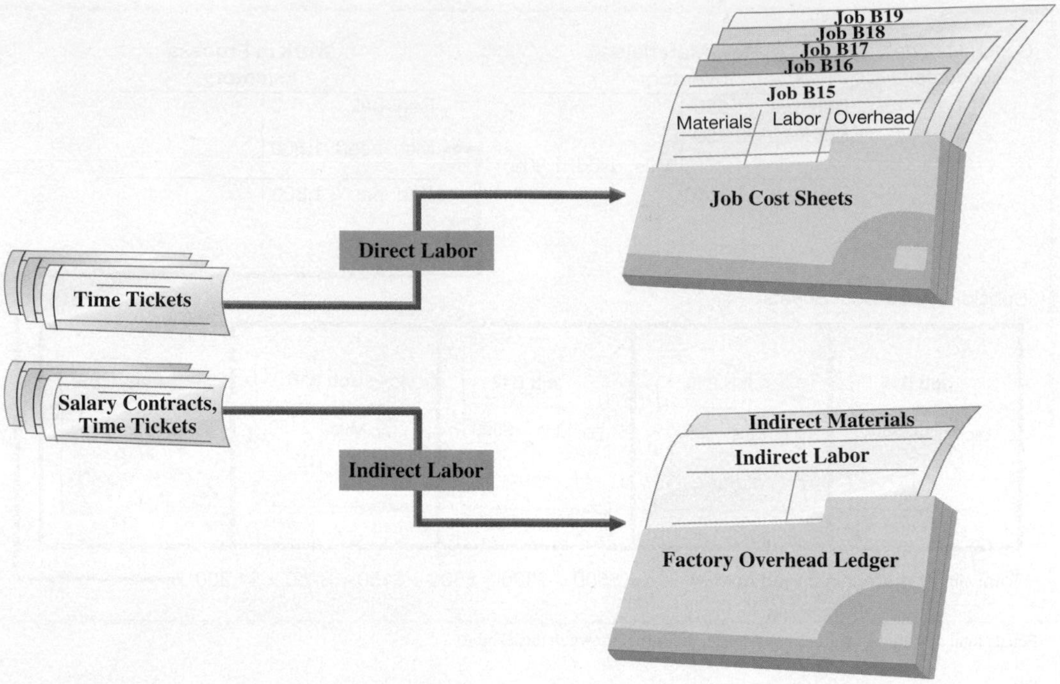

Exhibit 15.9 shows a time ticket reporting the time a Road Warrior employee spent working on Job B15. The employee's supervisor signed the ticket to confirm its accuracy. The hourly rate and total labor cost are computed after the time ticket is turned in.

EXHIBIT 15.9

Time Ticket

Road Warriors
Los Angeles, California

No. L–3479

TIME TICKET **Date** March 8 **20** 15

Employee Name	Employee Number	Job No.
T. Zeller	3969	B15

TIME AND RATE INFORMATION:

Start Time	Finish Time	Elapsed Time	Hourly Rate
9:00	12:00	3.0	$20.00
Approved By C. Luther		**Total Cost**	$60.00

Remarks

Time tickets are often accumulated and recorded in one journal entry. The frequency of these entries varies across companies. In this example, Road Warriors journalizes direct labor monthly. During March, Road Warriors' factory payroll costs total $5,300. Of this amount, $4,200 can be traced directly to jobs, and the remaining $1,100 is classified as indirect labor, as shown below.

Direct labor—traceable to specific jobs	
Job B15	$ 1,000
Job B16	800
Job B17	1,100
Job B18	700
Job B19	600
Total direct labor	**$4,200**
Indirect labor	1,100
Total	$ 5,300

The following entry records direct labor for the month, based on all the direct labor time tickets for the month.

Mar. 31	Work in Process Inventory	4,200	
	Factory Wages Payable........................		4,200
	To record direct labor used for the month.		

Assets = Liabilities + Equity
+4,200 +4,200

This entry is posted to the general ledger accounts, Work in Process Inventory and Factory Wages Payable (or Cash, if paid), and to individual job cost sheets. Exhibit 15.10 shows these postings. Time tickets are used to determine how much of the monthly total direct labor cost ($4,200) to assign to specific jobs. This total matches the amount of direct labor posted to the Work in Process Inventory general ledger account. After this entry is posted, the balance in Work in Process Inventory is $6,000, consisting of $1,800 of direct materials and $4,200 of direct labor. Later we show the accounting for indirect labor. At this point it is important only to know that the use of indirect labor does not impact Work in Process Inventory.

EXHIBIT 15.10

Posting Direct Labor to General Ledger and Job Cost Sheets

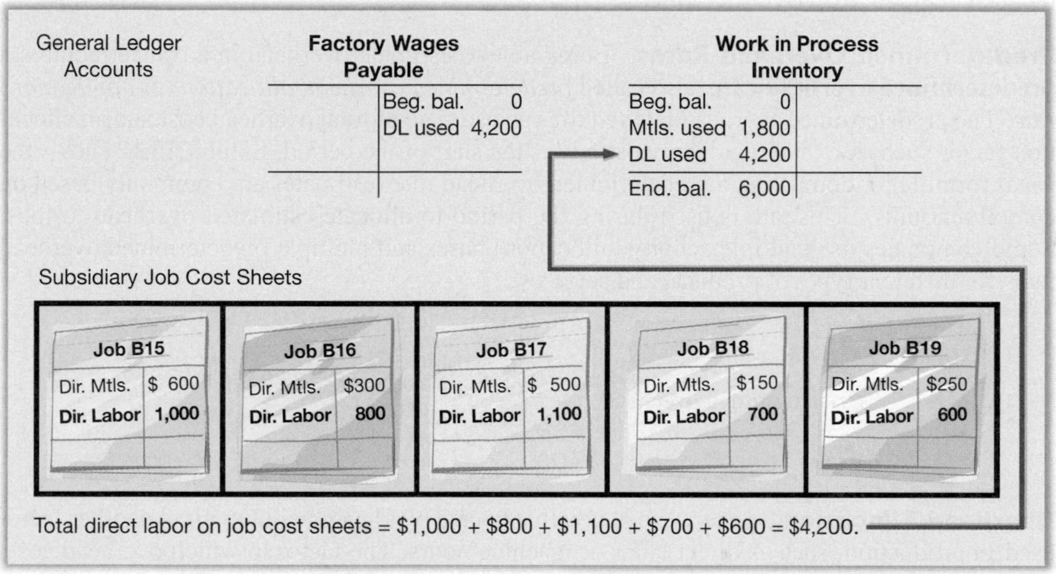

NEED-TO-KNOW 15-2

Recording Direct Labor

P2

A manufacturing company used $5,400 of direct labor in production activities in May. Of this amount, $3,100 of direct labor was used on Job A1 and $2,300 of direct labor was used on Job A2. Prepare the journal entry to record direct labor used.

Solution

Work in Process Inventory..	5,400	
Factory Wages Payable..		5,400
To record direct labor used in production.		

Do More: QS 15-5, E 15-9

Overhead Cost Flows and Recording Applied Overhead

P3

Describe and record the flow of overhead costs in job order costing.

We turn now to overhead costs. Unlike direct materials and direct labor, overhead costs cannot be traced directly to individual jobs. Instead, the accounting for overhead costs follows the four-step process shown in Exhibit 15.11. Overhead accounting requires managers to first estimate what total overhead costs will be for the coming period. We cannot wait until the end of a period to allocate overhead to jobs, because a job order costing system uses perpetual inventory records that require

Overhead

EXHIBIT 15.11

Four-Step Process for Overhead

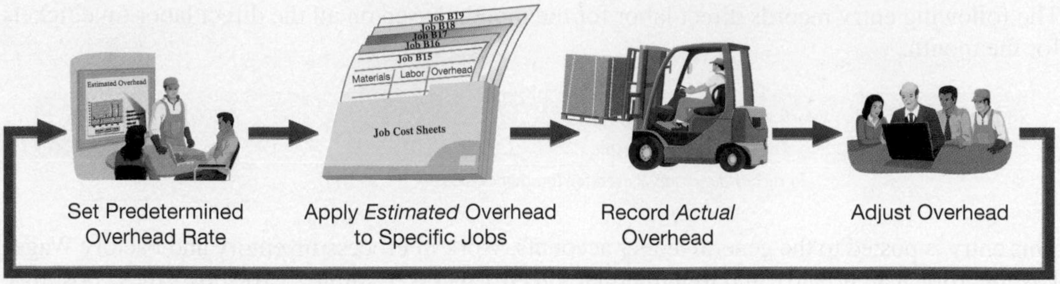

up-to-date costs. This estimated overhead cost, even if it is not exactly precise, is needed to estimate a job's total costs before its completion. Such estimated costs are useful for managers in many decisions, including setting prices and identifying costs that are out of control. At the end of the year, the company adjusts its estimated overhead to the actual amount of overhead incurred for that year, and then considers whether to change its predetermined overhead rate for the next year. We discuss each of these steps below.

Predetermined Overhead Rates Being able to estimate overhead in advance requires a **predetermined overhead rate,** also called *predetermined overhead allocation* (or *application*) *rate.* The predetermined overhead rate requires an estimate of total overhead cost and an allocation factor such as total direct labor cost *before* the start of the period. Exhibit 15.12 shows the usual formula for computing a predetermined overhead rate (estimates are commonly based on annual amounts). This rate is used during the period to allocate estimated overhead to jobs. Some companies use multiple activity (allocation) bases and multiple predetermined overhead rates for different types of products and services.

Point: Predetermined overhead rates can be estimated using mathematical equations, statistical analysis, or professional experience.

EXHIBIT 15.12

Predetermined Overhead Rate Formula

$$\text{Predetermined overhead rate} = \frac{\text{Estimated}}{\text{overhead costs}} \div \frac{\text{Estimated}}{\text{activity base}}$$

© Royalty-Free/Corbis

Overhead Allocation Bases We generally allocate overhead by linking it to another factor used in production, such as direct labor or machine hours. The factor to which overhead costs are linked is known as the *activity (or allocation) base.* The allocation should reflect a "cause and effect" relation between the base and overhead costs. A manager must think carefully about how many and which activity bases to use. This managerial decision influences the accuracy with which overhead costs are allocated to individual jobs. In turn, the cost of individual jobs might impact a manager's decisions for pricing or performance evaluation.

Recording Applied Overhead To illustrate, Road Warriors applies (also termed *allocates, assigns,* or *charges*) overhead by linking it to direct labor. At the start of the current year, management estimates total direct labor costs of $125,000 and total overhead costs of $200,000. Using these estimates, management computes its predetermined overhead rate as 160% of direct labor cost ($200,000 ÷ $125,000). Earlier we showed that Road Warriors used $4,200 of direct labor in March. We then use the predetermined overhead rate of 160% to allocate $6,720 (equal to $4,200 × 1.60) of overhead. The entry to record this allocation is:

Point: Factory Overhead is a temporary account that holds costs. The Factory Overhead account is closed to zero at the end of the year.

Mar. 31	Work in Process Inventory	6,720	
	Factory Overhead		6,720
	To apply overhead at 160% of direct labor.		

Then, overhead is allocated to each individual job based on the amount of the activity base that job used (in this example, direct labor). Exhibit 15.13 shows these calculations for Road Warriors' March production activity.

EXHIBIT 15.13

Allocating Overhead to Specific Jobs

Job	Direct Labor Cost	Predetermined Overhead Rate*	Allocated Overhead
B15	$1,000	1.6	$1,600
B16	800	1.6	1,280
B17	1,100	1.6	1,760
B18	700	1.6	1,120
B19	600	1.6	960
Total	$4,200		$6,720

*160% of direct labor cost

After overhead is journalized in the general journal and the amounts of overhead to allocate to each job are determined (Exhibit 15.13), postings to general ledger accounts and to individual job cost sheets follow, as in Exhibit 15.14.

EXHIBIT 15.14

Posting Overhead to General Ledger and Job Cost Sheets

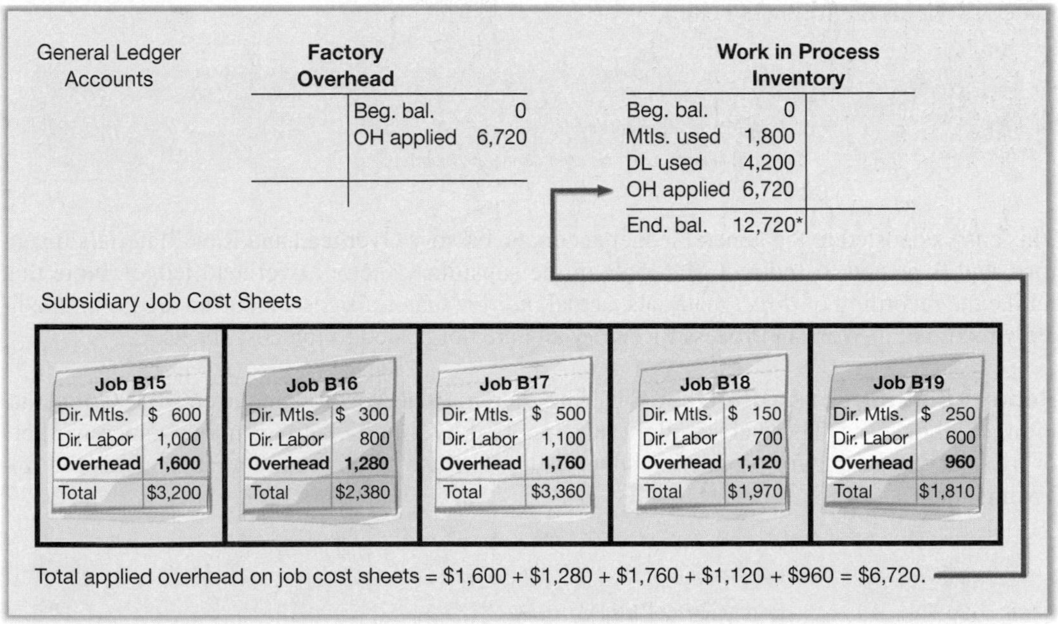

* Total product costs assigned to jobs = $3,200 + $2,380 + $3,360 + $1,970 + $1,810 = $12,720, equal to the ending balance in Work in Process Inventory in the general ledger.

At this point, estimated (allocated) overhead has been posted to general ledger accounts and to individual job cost sheets. In addition, we verified that the balance in the Work in Process Inventory account equals the sum of the accumulated balances in the job cost sheets. In the next section we discuss how to record *actual* overhead.

NEED-TO-KNOW 15-3

Recording Applied Overhead

P3

A manufacturing company estimates it will incur $240,000 of overhead costs in the next year. The company allocates overhead using machine hours, and estimates it will use 1,600 machine hours in the next year. During the month of June, the company used 80 machine hours on Job 1 and 70 machine hours on Job 2.

1. Compute the predetermined overhead rate to be used to apply overhead during the year.
2. Determine how much overhead should be applied to Job 1 and to Job 2 for June.
3. Prepare the journal entry to record overhead applied for June.

Solution

1. $240,000/1,600 = $150 per machine hour.
2. 80 × $150 = $12,000 applied to Job 1; 70 × $150 = $10,500 applied to Job 2.
3.

Work in Process Inventory..	22,500	
Factory Overhead..		22,500
To record applied overhead.		

QC2

Do More: QS 15-6, QS 15-8, QS 15-11, E 15-10

Recording Actual Overhead

Point: Companies also incur *nonmanufacturing* costs, such as advertising, salesperson's salaries, and depreciation on assets not used in production. These types of costs are not considered overhead, but instead are treated as period costs and charged directly to the income statement. These period costs can be relevant to managers' pricing decisions.

Factory overhead includes all factory costs other than direct materials and direct labor. Two sources of overhead costs are *indirect* materials and *indirect* labor. These costs are recorded from materials requisition forms for indirect materials and from salary contracts or time tickets for indirect labor. Two other sources of overhead are (1) vouchers authorizing payment for factory items such as supplies or utilities and (2) adjusting journal entries for costs such as depreciation on factory assets.

Factory overhead usually contains many different costs. These costs are recorded with debits to the Factory Overhead general ledger account, and with credits to various accounts. Next we show how to record journal entries for actual overhead costs. While journal entries for different types of overhead costs might be recorded with varying frequency, in our example we assume these entries are each made at the end of the month.

Recording Indirect Materials Used During March, Road Warriors incurred $550 of actual indirect materials costs, as supported by materials requisitions. The use of these indirect materials yields the following entry.

Mar. 31	Factory Overhead	550	
	Raw Materials Inventory		550
	To record indirect materials used during the month.		

This entry is posted to the general ledger accounts, Factory Overhead and Raw Materials Inventory, and is posted to Indirect Materials in the subsidiary factory overhead ledger. Note that unlike the recording of *direct* materials, actual *indirect* materials costs incurred are not immediately recorded in Work in Process Inventory and are not posted to job cost sheets.

Recording Indirect Labor Used During March, Road Warriors incurred $1,100 of actual indirect labor costs. These costs might be supported by time tickets for maintenance workers or by salary contracts for production supervisors. The use of this indirect labor yields the following entry.

Mar. 31	Factory Overhead	1,100	
	Factory Wages Payable		1,100
	To record indirect labor used during the month.		

This entry is posted to the general ledger accounts, Factory Overhead and Factory Wages Payable, and is posted to Indirect Labor in the subsidiary factory overhead ledger. Note that unlike the recording of *direct* labor, actual *indirect* labor costs incurred are not recorded immediately in Work in Process Inventory and are not posted to job cost sheets.

Recording Other Overhead Costs During March, Road Warriors incurred $5,270 of actual other overhead costs. These costs could include items such as factory building rent, depreciation on the factory building, factory utilities, and other such costs indirectly related to production activities. These costs are recorded with debits to Factory Overhead and credits to other accounts such as Cash, Accounts Payable, Utilities Payable, and Accumulated Depreciation—Factory Equipment. The entry to record these other overhead costs for March is as follows.

Mar. 31	Factory Overhead	5,270	
	Accumulated Depreciation—Factory Equipment		2,400
	Rent Payable		1,620
	Utilities Payable		250
	Prepaid Insurance		1,000
	To record actual overhead costs for the month.		

This entry is posted to the general ledger account, Factory Overhead, and is posted to separate accounts for each of the overhead items in the subsidiary factory overhead ledger. Note that actual overhead costs incurred are not recorded in Work in Process Inventory and are not posted to job cost sheets. Only applied overhead is recorded in Work in Process Inventory and posted to job cost sheets.

NEED-TO-KNOW 15-4

Recording Actual Overhead

P3

A manufacturing company used $400 of indirect materials and $2,000 of indirect labor during the month. The company also incurred $1,200 of depreciation on factory equipment, $500 of depreciation on office equipment, and $300 of factory utilities. Prepare the journal entry to record actual factory overhead costs incurred during the month.

Solution

Factory Overhead	3,900	
Raw Materials Inventory		400
Factory Wages Payable		2,000
Accumulated Depreciation—Factory Equipment*		1,200
Utilities Payable		300
To record actual overhead costs used in production.		

*Depreciation on office equipment is a period cost and is excluded from factory overhead.

QC3

Do More: QS 15-7, E 15-10

Summary of Cost Flows

In this section we summarize the flow of costs. Exhibit 15.15 shows how costs for a manufacturing company flow to its financial statements.

EXHIBIT 15.15

Cost Flows and Reports

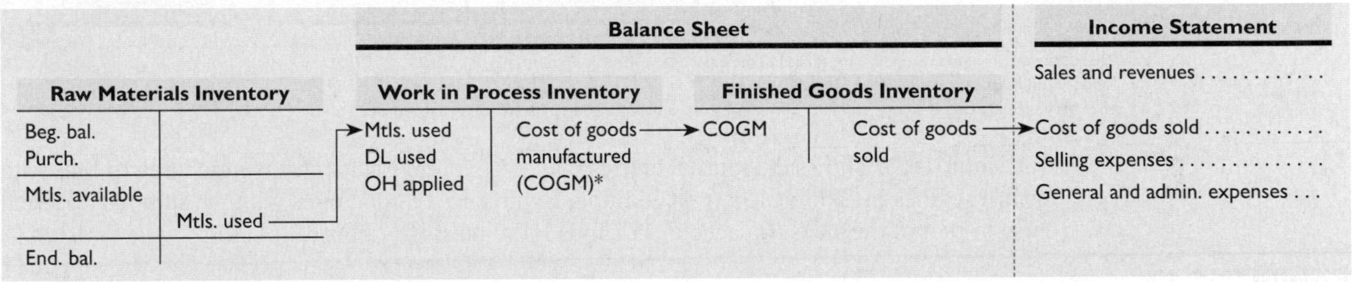

*Reported on the schedule of cost of goods manufactured.

Exhibit 15.15 shows that direct materials used, direct labor used, and factory overhead applied flow through the Work in Process Inventory and Finished Goods balance sheet accounts. The cost of goods manufactured (COGM) is computed and shown on the schedule of cost of goods manufactured. When goods are sold, their costs are transferred from Finished Goods Inventory to the income statement as cost of goods sold.

Period costs do not impact inventory accounts. As a result, they do not impact cost of goods sold, and they are not reported on the schedule of cost of goods manufactured. They are reported on the income statement as operating expenses.

We next show the flow of costs and their reporting for our Road Warriors example. The upper part of Exhibit 15.16 shows the flow of Road Warriors' product costs through general ledger accounts. Arrow lines are numbered to show the flows of costs for March. Each numbered cost flow reflects journal entries made in March. The lower part of Exhibit 15.16 shows summarized job cost sheets and their status at the end of March. The sum of costs assigned to the two jobs in process ($1,970 + $1,810) equals the $3,780 balance in Work in Process Inventory. Also, costs assigned to Job B17 equal the $3,360 balance in Finished Goods Inventory. These balances in Work in Process Inventory and Finished Goods Inventory are reported on the end-of-period balance sheet. The sum of costs assigned to Jobs B15 and B16 ($3,200 + $2,380) equals the $5,580 balance in Cost of Goods Sold. This amount is reported on the income statement for the period.

EXHIBIT 15.16

Job Order Cost Flows and Ending Job Cost Sheets

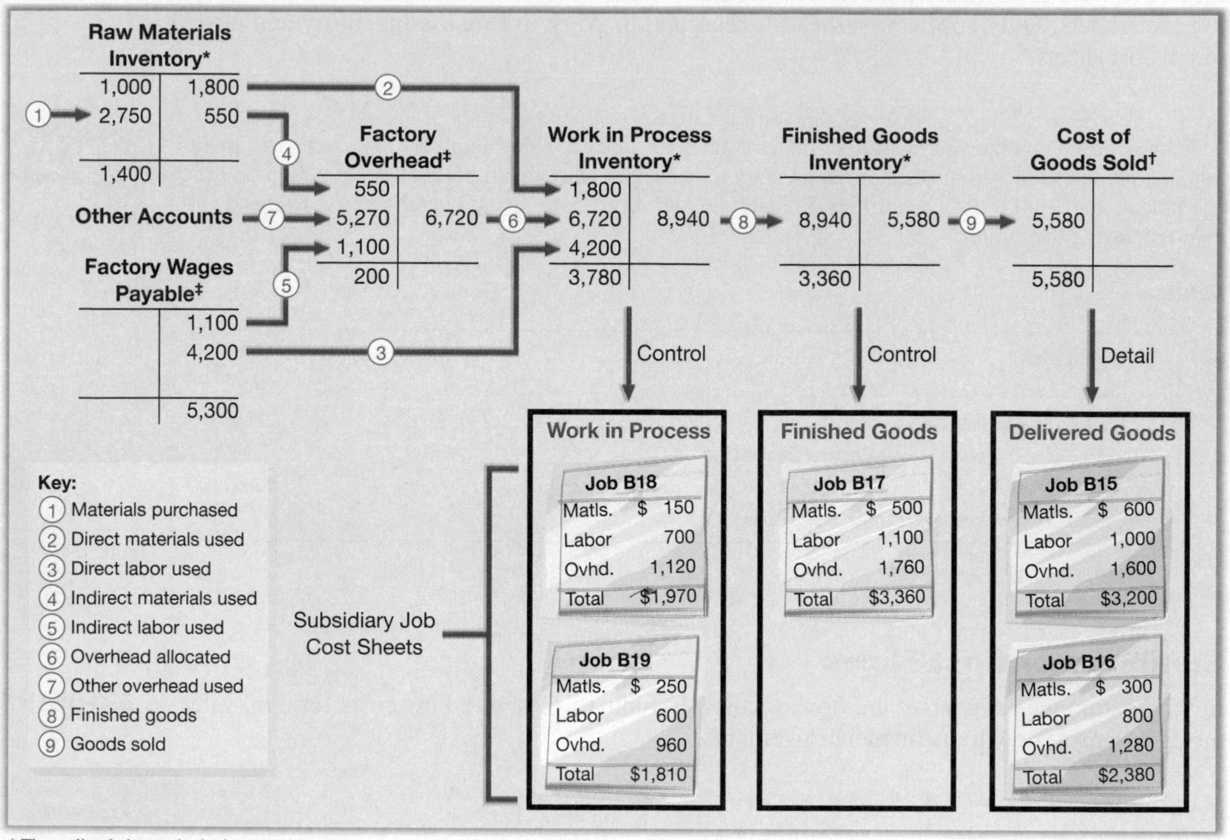

* The ending balances in the inventory accounts are carried to the balance sheet.

† The Cost of Goods Sold balance is carried to the income statement.

‡ Factory Overhead is considered a temporary account; when these costs are allocated to jobs, its balance is reduced.

Exhibit 15.17 shows the journal entries made in March. Each entry is numbered to link with the arrow lines in Exhibit 15.16. In addition, Exhibit 15.17 concludes with the summary journal entry to record the sales (on account) of Jobs B15 and B16.

EXHIBIT 15.17

Entries for Job Order Production Costs*

①	Raw Materials Inventory	2,750	
	Accounts Payable		2,750
	Acquired raw materials.		
②	Work in Process Inventory	1,800	
	Raw Materials Inventory		1,800
	To assign costs of direct materials used.		
③	Work in Process Inventory	4,200	
	Factory Wages Payable		4,200
	To assign costs of direct labor used.		
④	Factory Overhead	550	
	Raw Materials Inventory		550
	To record use of indirect materials.		
⑤	Factory Overhead	1,100	
	Factory Wages Payable		1,100
	To record indirect labor costs.		
⑥	Work in Process Inventory	6,720	
	Factory Overhead		6,720
	To apply overhead at 160% of direct labor.		
⑦	Factory Overhead	5,270	
	Cash (and other accounts)		5,270
	To record factory overhead costs such as insurance, utilities, rent, and depreciation.		
⑧	Finished Goods Inventory	8,940	
	Work in Process Inventory		8,940
	To record completion of Jobs B15, B16, and B17.		
⑨	Cost of Goods Sold	5,580	
	Finished Goods Inventory		5,580
	To record cost of goods sold for Jobs B15 and B16.		
⑩	Accounts Receivable	7,780	
	Sales		7,780
	To record sale of Jobs B15 and B16.		

* Exhibit 15.17 provides summary journal entries. *Actual* overhead is debited to Factory Overhead. *Applied* overhead is credited to Factory Overhead.

Schedule of Cost of Goods Manufactured

We end the Road Warriors example with the schedule of cost of goods manufactured in Exhibit 15.18. This schedule is similar to the one reported in the previous chapter, with one key difference: *Total manufacturing costs includes overhead applied rather than actual overhead costs.* In this example, actual overhead costs were $6,920, while applied overhead was $6,720. We discuss how to account for this difference in the next section.

Work in Process Inventory		
Beg. bal.	0	
Mtls. used	1,800	
DL used	4,200	
OH applied	6,720	
Ttl mfg. costs	12,720	
		COGM 8,940
End. bal.	3,780	

EXHIBIT 15.18

Schedule of Cost of Goods Manufactured

ROAD WARRIORS Schedule of Cost of Goods Manufactured For the Month of March, 2015	
Direct materials used	$ 1,800
Direct labor used	4,200
Factory overhead applied*	6,720
Total manufacturing costs	$12,720
Add: Work in process, March 1, 2015	0
Total cost of work in process	12,720
Less: Work in process, March 31, 2015	3,780
Cost of goods manufactured	$ 8,940

* Actual overhead = $6,920. Overhead is $200 underapplied.

ADJUSTING FACTORY OVERHEAD

Refer to the debits in the Factory Overhead account in Exhibit 15.16 (or Exhibit 15.17). The total cost of factory overhead incurred during March is $6,920 ($550 + $5,270 + $1,100). The $6,920 of actual overhead costs does not equal the $6,720 of overhead applied to work in process inventory (see ⑥). This leaves a debit balance of $200 in the Factory Overhead account. Companies usually wait until the end of the year to adjust the Factory Overhead account for differences between actual and applied overhead. We show how this is done in the next section.

Factory Overhead T-Account

EXHIBIT 15.19

Factory Overhead T-account

Factory Overhead	
Actual amounts	Applied amounts

Exhibit 15.19 shows a Factory Overhead T-account. The company applies overhead (credits the Factory Overhead account) using a predetermined rate estimated at the beginning of the year. During the year, the company records actual overhead costs with debits to the Factory Overhead account. Exhibit 15.20 shows what to do when, at year-end, actual overhead does not equal applied overhead. First, we determine whether the applied overhead is more or less than the actual overhead:

- When *less* overhead is applied than is actually incurred, the remaining debit balance in the Factory Overhead account is called **underapplied overhead.**
- When *more* overhead is applied than is actually incurred, the resulting credit balance in the Factory Overhead account is called **overapplied overhead.**

When overhead is underapplied, it means that individual jobs have not been charged enough overhead during the year, and cost of goods sold for the year is too low. When overhead is overapplied, it means that jobs have been charged too much overhead during the year, and cost of goods sold is too high. In either case, a journal entry is needed to adjust Factory Overhead and Cost of Goods Sold. Exhibit 15.20 summarizes this entry.

EXHIBIT 15.20
Adjusting Factory Overhead

Overhead Costs	Factory Overhead Balance Is	Overhead Is	Journal Entry Required		
Actual > Applied	Debit	Underapplied	Cost of Goods Sold	#	
			Factory Overhead		#
Actual < Applied	Credit	Overapplied	Factory Overhead	#	
			Cost of Goods Sold		#

P4 Determine adjustments for overapplied and underapplied factory overhead.

Underapplied or Overapplied Overhead

To illustrate, assume that Road Warriors applied $200,000 of overhead to jobs during 2015. This equals the amount of overhead that management estimated in advance for the year. We further assume that Road Warriors incurred a total of $200,480 of actual overhead costs during 2015. Thus, at the end of the year, the Factory Overhead account has a debit balance of $480.

Example: If we do not adjust for underapplied overhead, will net income be overstated or understated? *Answer:* Overstated.

The $480 debit balance reflects manufacturing costs not assigned to jobs. This means that the balances in Work in Process Inventory, Finished Goods Inventory, and Cost of Goods Sold do not include all production costs incurred. The required journal entry depends on whether the difference (under- or overapplied) is material. When the underapplied overhead amount is immaterial, it is closed to the Cost of Goods Sold account with the following adjusting entry.

Dec. 31	Cost of Goods Sold	480	
	Factory Overhead		480
	To adjust for underapplied overhead costs.		

The $480 debit (increase) to Cost of Goods Sold reduces income by $480. After this entry, the Factory Overhead account has a zero balance. (When the underapplied or overapplied overhead is material, the amount is normally allocated to the Cost of Goods Sold, Finished Goods Inventory, and Work in Process Inventory accounts. This process is covered in advanced courses.) We treat overapplied overhead at the end of the period in the same way we treat underapplied overhead, except that we debit Factory Overhead and credit Cost of Goods Sold for the amount.

NEED-TO-KNOW 15-5

Adjusting Overhead
P4

A manufacturing company applied $300,000 of overhead to its jobs during the year. For the independent scenarios below, prepare the journal entry to adjust over- or underapplied overhead. Assume the adjustment amounts are not material.

1. Actual overhead costs incurred during the year equal $305,000.
2. Actual overhead costs incurred during the year equal $298,500.

Solution

1.

Cost of Goods Sold	5,000	
Factory Overhead..		5,000
To close underapplied overhead to Cost of Goods Sold.		

2.

Factory Overhead...	1,500	
Cost of Goods Sold		1,500
To close overapplied overhead to Cost of Goods Sold.		

Do More: QS 15-9, QS 15-10, E 15-11, E 15-12

Job Order Costing of Services

The principle of customization also applies to service companies. Most service companies meet customers' needs by performing a custom service for a specific customer. Examples of such services include an accountant auditing a client's financial statements, an interior designer remodeling an office, a wedding consultant planning and supervising a reception, and a lawyer defending a client. Whether the setting is manufacturing or services, job order operations involve meeting the needs of customers by producing or performing custom jobs. We show an example of job order costing for an advertising service in the Decision Analysis section of this chapter.

Decision Maker

Management Consultant One of your tasks is to control and manage costs for a consulting company. At the end of a recent month, you find that three consulting jobs were completed and two are 60% complete. Each unfinished job is estimated to cost $10,000 and to earn a revenue of $12,000. You are unsure how to recognize work in process inventory and record costs and revenues. Do you recognize any inventory? If so, how much? How much revenue is recorded for unfinished jobs this month? ■ [Answers follow the chapter's Summary.]

GLOBAL VIEW

Porsche AG manufactures high-performance cars. Each car is built according to individual customer specifications. Customers can use the Internet to place orders for their dream cars. Porsche employs just-in-time inventory techniques to ensure a flexible production process that can respond rapidly to customer orders. For a recent year, Porsche reported €33,781 million in costs of materials and €9,038 million in personnel costs, which helped generate €57,081 million in revenue.

Sean Gallup/Getty Images

Sustainability and Accounting **Porsche**'s sustainability efforts extend beyond its manufacturing operations to event management. Each year when the company sponsors a professional tennis tournament, it uses a Porsche Cayenne Hybrid to shuttle players to and from the venue. In addition, the company sells event tickets that include public transportation, thus reducing the number of distinct journeys to the venue by about 30%. In addition, **Middleton Made Knives** applies sustainablity through Quintin Middleton's choice of materials. The steel used for his knife blades can be recycled, and new trees can be planted to supply the wood for his knife blades.

Pricing for Services — Decision Analysis

A1 Apply job order costing in pricing services.

The chapter described job order costing mainly using a manufacturing setting. However, these concepts and procedures are applicable to a service setting. Consider AdWorld, an advertising agency that develops Web-based ads for small firms. Each of its customers has unique requirements, so costs for each individual job must be tracked separately.

AdWorld uses two types of labor: Web designers ($65 per hour) and computer staff ($50 per hour). It also incurs overhead costs that it assigns using two different predetermined overhead allocation rates: $125 per designer hour and $96 per staff hour. For each job, AdWorld must estimate the number of designer and staff hours needed. Then total costs pertaining to each job are determined using the procedures in the chapter. [*Note:* Most service firms have neither the raw materials inventory nor finished goods inventory. Such firms do typically have inventories of supplies, and they can have work in process inventory (services in process inventory).]

To illustrate, a manufacturer of golf balls requested a quote from AdWorld for an advertising engagement. AdWorld estimates that the job will require 43 designer hours and 61 staff hours, with the following total estimated cost for this job.

Direct Labor		
Designers (43 hours × $65)	$ 2,795	
Staff (61 hours × $50)	3,050	
Total direct labor		$ 5,845
Overhead		
Designer related (43 hours × $125)	5,375	
Staff related (61 hours × $96)	5,856	
Total overhead		11,231
Total estimated job cost		$17,076

AdWorld can use this cost information to help determine the price quote for the job (see *Decision Maker,* **Sales Manager,** below).

Another source of information that AdWorld must consider is the market, that is, how much competitors will quote for this job. Competitor information is often unavailable; therefore, AdWorld's managers must use estimates based on their assessment of the competitive environment.

Decision Maker

Sales Manager As AdWorld's sales manager, assume that you estimate costs pertaining to a proposed job as $17,076. Your normal pricing policy is to apply a markup of 18% from total costs. However, you learn that three other agencies are likely to bid for the same job, and that their quotes will range from $16,500 to $22,000. What price should you quote? What factors other than cost must you consider? ■ [Answers follow the chapter's Summary.]

NEED-TO-KNOW

COMPREHENSIVE

The following information reflects Walczak Company's job order production activities for May.

Raw materials purchases	$16,000
Factory payroll cost	15,400
Overhead costs incurred	
Indirect materials	5,000
Indirect labor	3,500
Other factory overhead	9,500

Walczak's predetermined overhead rate is 150% of direct labor cost. Costs are allocated to the three jobs worked on during May as follows.

	Job 401	Job 402	Job 403
Work in process inventory, April 30			
Direct materials	$3,600		
Direct labor	1,700		
Applied overhead	2,550		
Costs during May			
Direct materials	3,550	$3,500	$1,400
Direct labor	5,100	6,000	800
Applied overhead	?	?	?
Status on May 31	**Finished (sold)**	**Finished (unsold)**	**In process**

Required

1. Determine the total cost of:
   a. The April 30 inventory of jobs in process.
   b. Materials (direct and indirect) used during May.
   c. Labor (direct and indirect) used during May.
   d. Factory overhead incurred and applied during May and the amount of any over- or underapplied overhead on May 31.
   e. The total cost of each job as of May 31, the May 31 inventories of both work in process and finished goods, and the cost of goods sold during May.
2. Prepare summarized journal entries for the month to record:
   a. Materials purchases (on credit), direct materials used in production, direct labor used in production, and overhead applied.
   b. Actual overhead costs, including indirect materials, indirect labor, and other overhead costs.
   c. Transfer of each completed job to the Finished Goods Inventory account.
   d. Cost of goods sold.
   e. The sale (on account) of Job 401 for $35,000.
   f. Removal of any underapplied or overapplied overhead from the Factory Overhead account. (Assume the amount is not material.)
3. Prepare a schedule of cost of goods manufactured for May.

PLANNING THE SOLUTION

- Determine the cost of the April 30 work in process inventory by totaling the materials, labor, and applied overhead costs for Job 401.
- Compute the cost of materials used and labor by totaling the amounts assigned to jobs and to overhead.
- Compute the total overhead incurred by summing the amounts for the three components. Compute the amount of applied overhead by multiplying the total direct labor cost by the predetermined overhead rate. Compute the underapplied or overapplied amount as the difference between the actual cost and the applied cost.
- Determine the total cost charged to each job by adding the costs incurred in April (if any) to the cost of materials, labor, and overhead applied during May.
- Group the costs of the jobs according to their completion status.
- Record the direct materials costs assigned to the three jobs.
- Transfer costs of Jobs 401 and 402 from Work in Process Inventory to Finished Goods.
- Record the costs of Job 401 as cost of goods sold.
- Record the sale (on account) of Job 401 for $35,000.
- On the schedule of cost of goods manufactured, remember to include the beginning and ending work in process inventories and to use applied rather than actual overhead.

SOLUTION

1. Total cost of
   a. April 30 inventory of jobs in process (Job 401).

Direct materials	$3,600
Direct labor	1,700
Applied overhead	2,550
Total cost	$7,850

   b. Materials used during May.

Direct materials	
Job 401	$ 3,550
Job 402	3,500
Job 403	1,400
Total direct materials	8,450
Indirect materials	5,000
Total materials used	$13,450

c. Labor used during May.

Direct labor	
Job 401	$ 5,100
Job 402	6,000
Job 403	800
Total direct labor	11,900
Indirect labor	3,500
Total labor used	$15,400

d. Factory overhead incurred in May.

Actual overhead	
Indirect materials	$ 5,000
Indirect labor	3,500
Other factory overhead	9,500
Total actual overhead	18,000
Overhead applied (150% × $11,900)	17,850
Underapplied overhead	$ 150

e. Total cost of each job.

	401	402	403
Work in process, April 30			
Direct materials	$ 3,600		
Direct labor	1,700		
Applied overhead*	2,550		
Cost incurred in May			
Direct materials (from part b)	3,550	$ 3,500	$1,400
Direct labor	5,100	6,000	800
Applied overhead*	7,650	9,000	1,200
Total costs	$24,150	$18,500	$3,400

* Equals 150% of the direct labor cost.

Total cost of the May 31 inventory of work in process (Job 403) = $3,400

Total cost of the May 31 inventory of finished goods (Job 402) = $18,500

Total cost of goods sold during May (Job 401) = $24,150

2. Journal entries.

a. Record raw materials purchases, direct materials used, direct labor used, and overhead applied.

Raw Materials Inventory	16,000	
Accounts Payable		16,000
To record materials purchases.		
Work in Process Inventory	8,450	
Raw Materials Inventory		8,450
To assign direct materials to jobs.		
Work in Process Inventory	11,900	
Factory Payroll Payable		11,900
To assign direct labor to jobs.		
Work in Process Inventory	17,850	
Factory Overhead		17,850
To apply overhead to jobs.		

b. Record actual overhead costs.

Factory Overhead	5,000	
Raw Materials Inventory		5,000
To record indirect materials.		
Factory Overhead	3,500	
Factory Payroll Payable		3,500
To record indirect labor.		
Factory Overhead	9,500	
Cash		9,500
To record other actual factory overhead.		

c. Transfer of completed jobs to Finished Goods Inventory.

Finished Goods Inventory	42,650	
Work in Process Inventory		42,650
To record completion of jobs ($24,150 for Job 401 + $18,500 for Job 402).		

d. Record cost of job sold.

Cost of Goods Sold	24,150	
Finished Goods Inventory		24,150
To record costs for sale of Job 401.		

e. Record sales for job sold.

Accounts Receivable	35,000	
Sales		35,000
To record sale of Job 401.		

f. Close overhead to cost of goods sold.

Cost of Goods Sold	150	
Factory Overhead		150
To assign underapplied overhead to Cost of Goods Sold.		

3.

WALCZAK COMPANY
Schedule of Cost of Goods Manufactured
For Month Ended May 31

Direct materials	$ 8,450
Direct labor	11,900
Factory overhead applied*	17,850
Total manufacturing costs	38,200
Add: Work in process, April 30	7,850
Total cost of work in process	46,050
Less: Work in process, May 31	3,400
Cost of goods manufactured	$42,650

* Actual overhead = $18,000. Overhead is $150 underapplied.

Summary

C1 Describe important features of job order production. Certain companies called *job order manufacturers* produce custom-made products for customers. These customized products are produced in response to a customer's orders. A job order manufacturer produces products that usually are different and, typically, produced in low volumes. The production systems of job order companies are flexible and are not highly standardized.

C2 Explain job cost sheets and how they are used in job order costing. In a job order costing system, the costs of producing each job are accumulated on a separate job cost sheet. Costs of direct materials, direct labor, and overhead applied are accumulated separately on the job cost sheet and then added to determine the total cost of a job. Job cost sheets for jobs in process, finished jobs, and jobs sold make up subsidiary records controlled by general ledger accounts.

A1 Apply job order costing in pricing services. Job order costing can usefully be applied to a service setting. The resulting job cost estimate can then be used to help determine a price for services.

P1 Describe and record the flow of materials costs in job order costing. Costs of direct materials flow to the Work in Process Inventory account and to job cost sheets. Costs of indirect materials flow to the Factory Overhead account and to the factory overhead subsidiary ledger. Receiving reports evidence the purchase of raw materials, and requisition forms evidence the use of materials in production.

P2 Describe and record the flow of labor costs in job order costing. Costs of direct labor flow to the Work in Process Inventory account and to job cost sheets. Costs of indirect labor flow to the Factory Overhead account and to the factory overhead subsidiary ledger. Time tickets document the use of labor.

P3 Describe and record the flow of overhead costs in job order costing. Overhead costs are charged to jobs using a predetermined overhead rate. Actual overhead costs incurred are accumulated in the Factory Overhead account that controls the subsidiary factory overhead ledger.

P4 Determine adjustments for overapplied and underapplied factory overhead. At the end of each year, the Factory Overhead account usually has a residual debit (underapplied overhead) or credit (overapplied overhead) balance. Assuming the balance is not material, it is transferred to Cost of Goods Sold, and the Factory Overhead account is closed.

Guidance Answers to Decision Maker

Management Consultant Service companies (such as this consulting firm) do not recognize work in process inventory or finished goods inventory—an important difference between service and manufacturing companies. For the two jobs that are 60% complete, you could recognize revenues and costs at 60% of the total expected amounts. This means you could recognize revenue of \$7,200 (0.60 × \$12,000) and costs of \$6,000 (0.60 × \$10,000), yielding net income of \$1,200 from each job.

Sales Manager The price based on AdWorld's normal pricing policy is \$20,150 (\$17,076 × 1.18), which is within the price range offered by competitors. One option is to apply normal pricing policy and quote a price of \$20,150. On the other hand, assessing the competition, particularly in terms of their service quality and other benefits they might offer, would be useful. Although price is an input customers use to select suppliers, factors such as quality and timeliness (responsiveness) of suppliers are important. Accordingly, your price can reflect such factors.

Key Terms

Cost accounting system
Finished Goods Inventory
Job
Job cost sheet
Job lot
Job order costing system
Job order production
Materials ledger card
Materials requisition
Overapplied overhead
Predetermined overhead rate
Process operations
Receiving report
Target cost
Time ticket
Underapplied overhead
Work in Process Inventory

Multiple Choice Quiz

Answers at end of chapter

1. A company's predetermined overhead allocation rate is 150% of its direct labor costs. How much overhead is applied to a job that requires total direct labor costs of \$30,000?
   a. \$15,000 **b.** \$30,000 **c.** \$45,000 **d.** \$60,000 **e.** \$75,000
2. A company's cost accounting system uses direct labor costs to apply overhead to work in process and finished goods inventories. Its production costs for the period are: direct materials, \$45,000; direct labor, \$35,000; and overhead applied, \$38,500. What is its predetermined overhead allocation rate?
   a. 10% **b.** 110% **c.** 86% **d.** 91% **e.** 117%
3. A company's ending inventory of finished goods has a total cost of \$10,000 and consists of 500 units. If the overhead applied to these goods is \$4,000, and the predetermined overhead rate is 80% of direct labor costs, how much direct materials cost was incurred in producing these 500 units?
   a. \$10,000 **b.** \$6,000 **c.** \$ 4,000 **d.** \$5,000 **e.** \$1,000
4. A company's Work in Process Inventory T-account follows.

Work in Process Inventory

Beginning balance	9,000		
Direct materials	94,200		
Direct labor	59,200	Cost of goods manufactured	?
Overhead applied	31,600		
Ending balance	17,800		

The Cost of Goods Manufactured is

a. $193,000 **c.** $185,000 **e.** $176,200
b. $211,800 **d.** $144,600

5. At the end of its current year, a company learned that its overhead was underapplied by $1,500 and that this amount is not considered material. Based on this information, the company should

a. Close the $1,500 to Finished Goods Inventory.
b. Close the $1,500 to Cost of Goods Sold.
c. Carry the $1,500 to the next period.
d. Do nothing about the $1,500 because it is not material and it is likely that overhead will be overapplied by the same amount next year.
e. Carry the $1,500 to the income statement as "Other Expense."

Icon denotes assignments that involve decision making.

Discussion Questions

1. Why must a company estimate the amount of factory overhead assigned to individual jobs or job lots?

2. The chapter used a percent of labor cost to assign factory overhead to jobs. Identify another factor (or base) a company might reasonably use to assign overhead costs.

3. What information is recorded on a job cost sheet? How do management and employees use job cost sheets?

4. In a job order costing system, what records serve as a subsidiary ledger for Work in Process Inventory? For Finished Goods Inventory?

5. What journal entry is recorded when a materials manager receives a materials requisition and then issues materials (both direct and indirect) for use in the factory?

6. How does the materials requisition help safeguard a company's assets?

7. **Samsung** uses a "time ticket" for some employees. How are time tickets used in job order costing?

Samsung

8. What events cause debits to be recorded in the Factory Overhead account? What events cause credits to be recorded in the Factory Overhead account?

9. **Google** applies overhead to product costs. What account(s) is(are) used to eliminate overapplied or underapplied overhead from the Factory Overhead account, assuming the amount is not material?

GOOGLE

10. Assume that **Apple** produces a batch of 1,000 iPhones. Does it account for this as 1,000 individual jobs or as a job lot? Explain (consider costs and benefits).

APPLE

11. Why must a company use predetermined overhead rates when using job order costing?

12. How would a hospital apply job order costing? Explain.

13. **Harley-Davidson** manufactures 30 custom-made, luxury-model motorcycles. Does it account for these motorcycles as 30 individual jobs or as a job lot? Explain.

14. Assume **Sprint** will install and service a server to link all of a customer's employees' smartphones to a centralized company server, for an up-front flat price. How can Sprint use a job order costing system?

connect

QUICK STUDY

QS 15-1
Jobs and job lots
C1

Determine which of the following are most likely to be considered as a job and which as a job lot.

______ **1.** Hats imprinted with company logo.
______ **2.** Little League trophies.
______ **3.** A hand-crafted table.
______ **4.** A 90-foot motor yacht.
______ **5.** Wedding dresses for a chain of stores.
______ **6.** A custom-designed home.

QS 15-2
Documents in job order costing
P1 P2 P3

The left column lists the titles of documents and accounts used in job order costing. The right column presents short descriptions of the purposes of the documents. Match each document in the left column to its numbered description in the right column.

A. Time ticket
B. Materials ledger card
C. Voucher
D. Factory Overhead account
E. Materials requisition

______ **1.** Shows amount of time an employee works on a job.
______ **2.** Accumulates the cost of incurred overhead and the overhead cost assigned to specific jobs.
______ **3.** Perpetual inventory record of raw materials received, used, and available for use.
______ **4.** Shows amount approved for payment of an overhead or other cost.
______ **5.** Communicates the need for materials to complete a job.

QS 15-3
Job cost sheets C2

Clemens Cars' job cost sheet for Job A40 shows that the cost to add security features to a car was $10,500. The car was delivered to the customer, who paid $14,900 in cash for the added features. What journal entries should Clemens record for the completion and delivery of Job A40?

QS 15-4
Direct materials journal entries P1

During the current month, a company that uses job order costing purchases $50,000 in raw materials for cash. It then uses $12,000 of raw materials indirectly as factory supplies and uses $32,000 of raw materials as direct materials. Prepare journal entries to record these three transactions.

QS 15-5
Direct labor journal entries P2

During the current month, a company that uses job order costing incurred a monthly factory payroll of $180,000. Of this amount, $40,000 is classified as indirect labor and the remainder as direct. Prepare journal entries to record these transactions.

QS 15-6
Factory overhead rates P3

A company incurred the following manufacturing costs this period: direct labor, $468,000; direct materials, $390,000; and factory overhead, $117,000. Compute its overhead cost as a percent of (1) direct labor and (2) direct materials. Express your answers as percents, rounded to the nearest whole number.

QS 15-7
Factory overhead journal entries P3

During the current month, a company that uses job order costing incurred a monthly factory payroll of $175,000. Of this amount, $44,000 is classified as indirect labor and the remainder as direct labor for the production of Job 65A. Factory overhead is applied at 90% of direct labor. Prepare the journal entry to apply factory overhead to this job.

QS 15-8
Predetermined overhead rate P3

At the beginning of a year, a company predicts total direct materials costs of $900,000 and total overhead costs of $1,170,000. If the company uses direct materials costs as its activity base to allocate overhead, what is the predetermined overhead rate it should use during the year?

QS 15-9
Entry for over- or underapplied overhead P4

A company's Factory Overhead T-account shows total debits of $624,000 and total credits of $646,000 at the end of the year. Prepare the journal entry to close the balance in the Factory Overhead account to Cost of Goods Sold.

QS 15-10
Entry for over- or underapplied overhead P4

A company allocates overhead at a rate of 150% of direct labor cost. Actual overhead cost for the current period is $950,000, and direct labor cost is $600,000. Prepare the journal entry to close over- or underapplied overhead to Cost of Goods Sold.

QS 15-11
Applied overhead P3

On March 1 a dressmaker starts work on three custom-designed wedding dresses. The company uses job order costing and applies overhead to each job (dress) at the rate of 40% of direct materials costs. During the month, the jobs used direct materials as shown below. Compute the amount of overhead applied to each of the three jobs.

	Job 1	Job 2	Job 3
Direct materials used	$5,000	$7,000	$1,500

QS 15-12
Manufacturing cost flows P1 P2 P3

Refer to the information in QS 15-11. During the month, the jobs used direct labor as shown below. Jobs 1 and 3 are not finished by the end of March, and Job 2 is finished but not sold by the end of March. (1) Determine the amounts of direct materials, direct labor, and factory overhead applied that would be reported on job cost sheets for each of the three jobs for March. (2) Determine the total dollar amount of Work in Process Inventory at the end of March. (3) Determine the total dollar amount of Finished Goods Inventory at the end of March. Assume the company has no beginning Work in Process or Finished Goods inventories.

	Job 1	Job 2	Job 3
Direct labor used	$9,000	$4,000	$3,000

QS 15-13
Job order costing of services A1

An advertising agency is estimating costs for advertising a music festival. The job will require 200 direct labor hours at a cost of $50 per hour. Overhead costs are applied at a rate of $65 per direct labor hour. What is the total estimated cost for this job?

QS 15-14
Job order production
C1

Refer to this chapter's Global View. **Porsche AG** is the manufacturer of the Porsche automobile line. Does Porsche produce in jobs or in job lots? Explain.

connect

EXERCISES

Exercise 15-1
Job order production
C1

Match each of the terms/phrases numbered *1* through *5* with the best definition on the right.

_______ **1.** Cost accounting system
_______ **2.** Target cost
_______ **3.** Job lot
_______ **4.** Job
_______ **5.** Job order production

a. Production of products in response to customer orders.
b. Production activities for a customized product.
c. A system that records manufacturing costs using a perpetual inventory system.
d. The expected selling price of a job minus its desired profit.
e. Production of more than one unit of a custom product.

Exercise 15-2
Job cost computation
C2

The following information is from the materials requisitions and time tickets for Job 9-1005 completed by Great Bay Boats. The requisitions are identified by code numbers starting with the letter Q and the time tickets start with W. At the start of the year, management estimated that overhead cost would equal 110% of direct labor cost for each job. Determine the total cost on the job cost sheet for Job 9-1005.

Date	Document	Amount
7/1/2015	Q-4698	$1,250
7/1/2015	W-3393	600
7/5/2015	Q-4725	1,000
7/5/2015	W-3479	450
7/10/2015	W-3559	300

Exercise 15-3
Analysis of cost flows
C2 P1 P2 P3

As of the end of June, the job cost sheets at Racing Wheels, Inc., show the following total costs accumulated on three custom jobs.

	Job 102	Job 103	Job 104
Direct materials	$15,000	$33,000	$27,000
Direct labor	8,000	14,200	21,000
Overhead applied	4,000	7,100	10,500

Job 102 was started in production in May and the following costs were assigned to it in May: direct materials, $6,000; direct labor, $1,800; and overhead, $900. Jobs 103 and 104 are started in June. Overhead cost is applied with a predetermined rate based on direct labor cost. Jobs 102 and 103 are finished in June, and Job 104 is expected to be finished in July. No raw materials are used indirectly in June. Using this information, answer the following questions. (Assume this company's predetermined overhead rate did not change across these months.)

1. What is the cost of the raw materials requisitioned in June for each of the three jobs?
2. How much direct labor cost is incurred during June for each of the three jobs?
3. What predetermined overhead rate is used during June?
4. How much total cost is transferred to finished goods during June?

Check (4) $81,300

Exercise 15-4
Overhead rate; costs assigned to jobs
P3

In December 2014, Shire Computer's management establishes the 2015 predetermined overhead rate based on direct labor cost. The information used in setting this rate includes estimates that the company will incur $747,500 of overhead costs and $575,000 of direct labor cost in year 2015. During March 2015, Shire began and completed Job No. 13-56.

Check (2) $22,710

1. What is the predetermined overhead rate for 2015?
2. Use the information on the following job cost sheet to determine the total cost of the job.

JOB COST SHEET

Customer's Name: Keiser Co. Job No. 13-56

Job Description: 5 plasma monitors—61 inch

	Direct Materials		Direct Labor		Overhead Costs Applied	
Date	**Requisition No.**	**Amount**	**Time-Ticket No.**	**Amount**	**Rate**	**Amount**
Mar. 8	4-129	$5,000	T-306	$ 700		
Mar. 11	4-142	7,020	T-432	1,250		
Mar. 18	4-167	3,330	T-456	1,250		
Totals						

Exercise 15-5
Analysis of costs assigned to work in process
P3

Lorenzo Company uses a job order costing system that charges overhead to jobs on the basis of direct material cost. At year-end, the Work in Process Inventory account shows the following.

	A	B	C	D	E
1		Work in Process Inventory			
2		Acct. No. 121			
3	Date	Explanation	Debit	Credit	Balance
4	2015				
5	Dec. 31	Direct materials cost	1,500,000		1,500,000
6	31	Direct labor cost	300,000		1,800,000
7	31	Overhead applied	600,000		2,400,000
8	31	To finished goods		2,350,000	50,000
9					

1. Determine the predetermined overhead rate used (based on direct material cost).
2. Only one job remained in work in process inventory at December 31, 2015. Its direct materials cost is $30,000. How much direct labor cost and overhead cost are assigned to this job?

Check (2) Direct labor cost, $8,000

Exercise 15-6
Recording product costs
P1 P2 P3

Starr Company reports the following information for August.

Raw materials purchased on account	$76,200
Direct materials used in production	$48,000
Factory wages earned (direct labor)	$15,350
Overhead rate	120% of direct labor cost

Prepare journal entries to record the following events.

1. Raw materials purchased.
2. Direct materials used in production.
3. Direct labor used in production.
4. Applied overhead.

Exercise 15-7
Cost flows in a job order costing system
P1 P2 P3 P4

The following information is available for Lock-Tite Company, which produces special-order security products and uses a job order costing system.

	April 30	May 31
Inventories		
Raw materials	$43,000	$ 52,000
Work in process	10,200	21,300
Finished goods	63,000	35,600
Activities and information for May		
Raw materials purchases (paid with cash)		210,000
Factory payroll (paid with cash)		345,000
Factory overhead		
Indirect materials		15,000
Indirect labor		80,000
Other overhead costs		120,000
Sales (received in cash)		1,400,000
Predetermined overhead rate based on direct labor cost		70%

Compute the following amounts for the month of May.

1. Cost of direct materials used.
2. Cost of direct labor used.
3. Cost of goods manufactured.
4. Cost of goods sold.*
5. Gross profit.
6. Overapplied or underapplied overhead.

*Do not consider any underapplied or overapplied overhead.

Check (3) $625,400

Exercise 15-8
Journal entries for materials P1

Use information in Exercise 15-7 to prepare journal entries for the following events for the month of May.

1. Raw materials purchases for cash.
2. Direct materials usage.
3. Indirect materials usage.

Exercise 15-9
Journal entries for labor P2

Use information in Exercise 15-7 to prepare journal entries for the following events for the month of May.

1. Direct labor usage.
2. Indirect labor usage.
3. Total payroll paid in cash.

Exercise 15-10
Journal entries for overhead P3

Use information in Exercise 15-7 to prepare journal entries for the following events for the month of May.

1. Incurred other overhead costs (record credit to Other Accounts).
2. Application of overhead to work in process.

Exercise 15-11
Adjusting factory overhead P4

Refer to information in Exercise 15-7. Prepare the journal entry to allocate (close) overapplied or underapplied overhead to Cost of Goods Sold.

Exercise 15-12
Adjusting factory overhead P4

Record the journal entry to close over- or underapplied factory overhead to Cost of Goods Sold for each of the two companies below.

	Storm Concert Promotions	Valle Home Builders
Actual indirect materials costs	$22,000	$ 12,500
Actual indirect labor costs	46,000	46,500
Other overhead costs	17,000	47,000
Overhead applied	88,200	105,200

Exercise 15-13
Recording events in job order costing
P1 P2 P3 P4

Using Exhibit 15.17 as a guide, prepare summary journal entries to record the following transactions and events *a* through *g* for a company in its first month of operations.

a. Raw materials purchased on account, $90,000.

b. Direct materials used in production, $36,500. Indirect materials used in production, $19,200.

c. Paid cash for factory payroll, $50,000. Of this total, $38,000 is for direct labor and $12,000 is for indirect labor.

d. Paid cash for other actual overhead costs, $11,475.

e. Applied overhead at the rate of 125% of direct labor cost.

f. Transferred cost of jobs completed to finished goods, $56,800.

g. Sold jobs on account for $82,000. The jobs had a cost of $56,800.

Exercise 15-14
Factory overhead computed, applied, and adjusted
P3 P4

In December 2014, Custom Mfg. established its predetermined overhead rate for jobs produced during 2015 by using the following cost predictions: overhead costs, $750,000, and direct labor costs, $625,000. At year-end 2015, the company's records show that actual overhead costs for the year are $830,000. Actual direct labor cost had been assigned to jobs as follows.

Jobs completed and sold	$513,750
Jobs in finished goods inventory	102,750
Jobs in work in process inventory	68,500
Total actual direct labor cost	$685,000

1. Determine the predetermined overhead rate for 2015.

2. Set up a T-account for Factory Overhead and enter the overhead costs incurred and the amounts applied to jobs during the year using the predetermined overhead rate.

3. Determine whether overhead is overapplied or underapplied (and the amount) during the year.

4. Prepare the adjusting entry to allocate any over- or underapplied overhead to Cost of Goods Sold.

Check (3) $8,000 underapplied

Exercise 15-15
Factory overhead computed, applied, and adjusted
P3 P4

In December 2014, Infodeo established its predetermined overhead rate for movies produced during 2015 by using the following cost predictions: overhead costs, $1,680,000, and direct labor costs, $480,000. At year-end 2015, the company's records show that actual overhead costs for the year are $1,652,000. Actual direct labor cost had been assigned to jobs as follows.

Movies completed and released	$425,000
Movies still in production	50,000
Total actual direct labor cost	$475,000

1. Determine the predetermined overhead rate for 2015.

2. Set up a T-account for overhead and enter the overhead costs incurred and the amounts applied to movies during the year using the predetermined overhead rate.

3. Determine whether overhead is overapplied or underapplied (and the amount) during the year.

4. Prepare the adjusting entry to allocate any over- or underapplied overhead to Cost of Goods Sold.

Check (3) $10,500 overapplied

Exercise 15-16
Overhead rate calculation, allocation, and analysis
P3

Moonrise Bakery applies factory overhead based on direct labor costs. The company incurred the following costs during 2015: direct materials costs, $650,000; direct labor costs, $3,000,000; and factory overhead costs applied, $1,800,000.

1. Determine the company's predetermined overhead rate for 2015.

2. Assuming that the company's $71,000 ending Work in Process Inventory account for 2015 had $20,000 of direct labor costs, determine the inventory's direct materials costs.

3. Assuming that the company's $490,000 ending Finished Goods Inventory account for 2015 had $250,000 of direct materials costs, determine the inventory's direct labor costs and its overhead costs.

Check (3) $90,000 overhead costs

Exercise 15-17
Manufacturing cost flows
P1 P2 P3

Custom Cabinetry has one job in process (Job 120) as of June 30; at that time, its job cost sheet reports direct materials of $6,000, direct labor of $2,800, and applied overhead of $2,240. Custom Cabinetry applies overhead at the rate of 80% of direct labor cost. During July, Job 120 is sold (on account) for $22,000, Job 121 is started and completed, and Job 122 is started and still in process at the end of the month. Custom Cabinetry incurs the following costs during July.

July Product Costs	Job 120	Job 121	Job 122	Total
Direct materials	$1,000	$6,000	$2,500	$9,500
Direct labor	2,200	3,700	2,100	8,000
Overhead applied	?	?	?	?

1. Prepare journal entries for the following in July.
   a. Direct materials used in production.
   b. Direct labor used in production.
   c. Overhead applied.
   d. The sale of Job 120.
   e. Cost of goods sold for Job 120.

2. Compute the July 31 balances of the Work in Process Inventory and the Finished Goods Inventory general ledger accounts.

Exercise 15-18
Job order costing for services
A1

Hansel Corporation has requested bids from several architects to design its new corporate headquarters. Frey Architects is one of the firms bidding on the job. Frey estimates that the job will require the following direct labor.

	A	B	C
1	Labor	Estimated Hours	Hourly Rate
2	Architects	150	$300
3	Staff	300	75
4	Clerical	500	20
5			

Frey applies overhead to jobs at 175% of direct labor cost. Frey would like to earn at least $80,000 profit on the architectural job. Based on past experience and market research, it estimates that the competition will bid between $285,000 and $350,000 for the job.

1. What is Frey's estimated cost of the architectural job?
2. What bid would you suggest that Frey submit?

Check (1) $213,125

Exercise 15-19
Direct materials journal entries P1

A recent balance sheet for **Porsche AG** shows beginning raw materials inventory of €83 million and ending raw materials inventory of €85 million. Assume the company purchased raw materials (on account) for €3,108 million during the year. (1) Prepare journal entries to record (a) the purchase of raw materials and (b) the use of raw materials in production. (2) What do you notice about the € amounts in your journal entries?

connect

PROBLEM SET A

Problem 15-1A
Production costs computed and recorded; reports prepared
C2 P1 P2 P3 P4

Marcelino Co.'s March 31 inventory of raw materials is $80,000. Raw materials purchases in April are $500,000, and factory payroll cost in April is $363,000. Overhead costs incurred in April are: indirect materials, $50,000; indirect labor, $23,000; factory rent, $32,000; factory utilities, $19,000; and factory equipment depreciation, $51,000. The predetermined overhead rate is 50% of direct labor cost. Job 306 is sold for $635,000 cash in April. Costs of the three jobs worked on in April follow.

	Job 306	Job 307	Job 308
Balances on March 31			
Direct materials	$ 29,000	$ 35,000	
Direct labor	20,000	18,000	
Applied overhead	10,000	9,000	
Costs during April			
Direct materials	135,000	220,000	$100,000
Direct labor	85,000	150,000	105,000
Applied overhead	?	?	?
Status on April 30	Finished (sold)	Finished (unsold)	In process

Required

1. Determine the total of each production cost incurred for April (direct labor, direct materials, and applied overhead), and the total cost assigned to each job (including the balances from March 31).
2. Prepare journal entries for the month of April to record the following.
   a. Materials purchases (on credit).
   b. Direct materials used in production.
   c. Direct labor paid and assigned to Work in Process Inventory.
   d. Indirect labor paid and assigned to Factory Overhead.
   e. Overhead costs applied to Work in Process Inventory.
   f. Actual overhead costs incurred, including indirect materials. (Factory rent and utilities are paid in cash.)
   g. Transfer of Jobs 306 and 307 to Finished Goods Inventory.
   h. Cost of goods sold for Job 306.
   i. Revenue from the sale of Job 306.
   j. Assignment of any underapplied or overapplied overhead to the Cost of Goods Sold account. (The amount is not material.)
3. Prepare a schedule of cost of goods manufactured.
4. Compute gross profit for April. Show how to present the inventories on the April 30 balance sheet.

Check (2*j*) $5,000 underapplied

(3) Cost of goods manufactured, $828,500

Analysis Component

5. The over- or underapplied overhead is closed to Cost of Goods Sold. Discuss how this adjustment impacts business decision making regarding individual jobs or batches of jobs.

Problem 15-2A
Source documents, journal entries, overhead, and financial reports
P1 P2 P3 P4

Bergamo Bay's computer system generated the following trial balance on December 31, 2015. The company's manager knows something is wrong with the trial balance because it does not show any balance for Work in Process Inventory but does show a balance for the Factory Overhead account. In addition, the accrued factory payroll (Factory Payroll Payable) has not been recorded.

	Debit	Credit
Cash	$170,000	
Accounts receivable	75,000	
Raw materials inventory	80,000	
Work in process inventory	0	
Finished goods inventory	15,000	
Prepaid rent	3,000	
Accounts payable		$ 17,000
Notes payable		25,000
Common stock		50,000
Retained earnings		271,000
Sales		373,000
Cost of goods sold	218,000	
Factory overhead	115,000	
Operating expenses	60,000	
Totals	$736,000	$736,000

After examining various files, the manager identifies the following six source documents that need to be processed to bring the accounting records up to date.

Materials requisition 21-3010:	$10,200 direct materials to Job 402
Materials requisition 21-3011:	$18,600 direct materials to Job 404
Materials requisition 21-3012:	$5,600 indirect materials
Labor time ticket 6052:	$36,000 direct labor to Job 402
Labor time ticket 6053:	$23,800 direct labor to Job 404
Labor time ticket 6054:	$8,200 indirect labor

Jobs 402 and 404 are the only units in process at year-end. The predetermined overhead rate is 200% of direct labor cost.

Required

1. Use information on the six source documents to prepare journal entries to assign the following costs.
   a. Direct materials costs to Work in Process Inventory.
   b. Direct labor costs to Work in Process Inventory.
   c. Overhead costs to Work in Process Inventory.
   d. Indirect materials costs to the Factory Overhead account.
   e. Indirect labor costs to the Factory Overhead account.
2. Determine the revised balance of the Factory Overhead account after making the entries in part 1. Determine whether there is any under- or overapplied overhead for the year. Prepare the adjusting entry to allocate any over- or underapplied overhead to Cost of Goods Sold, assuming the amount is not material.
3. Prepare a revised trial balance.
4. Prepare an income statement for 2015 and a balance sheet as of December 31, 2015.

Check (2) $9,200 underapplied overhead

(3) T. B. totals, $804,000

(4) Net income, $85,800

Analysis Component

5. Assume that the $5,600 on materials requisition 21-3012 should have been direct materials charged to Job 404. Without providing specific calculations, describe the impact of this error on the income statement for 2015 and the balance sheet at December 31, 2015.

Problem 15-3A
Source documents, journal entries, and accounts in job order costing
P1 P2 P3

Widmer Watercraft's predetermined overhead rate for 2015 is 200% of direct labor. Information on the company's production activities during May 2015 follows.

a. Purchased raw materials on credit, $200,000.
b. Materials requisitions record use of the following materials for the month.

Job 136	$ 48,000
Job 137	32,000
Job 138	19,200
Job 139	22,400
Job 140	6,400
Total direct materials	128,000
Indirect materials	19,500
Total materials used	$147,500

c. Paid $15,000 cash to a computer consultant to reprogram factory equipment.
d. Time tickets record use of the following labor for the month. These wages were paid in cash.

Job 136	$ 12,000
Job 137	10,500
Job 138	37,500
Job 139	39,000
Job 140	3,000
Total direct labor	102,000
Indirect labor	24,000
Total	$126,000

e. Applied overhead to Jobs 136, 138, and 139.
f. Transferred Jobs 136, 138, and 139 to Finished Goods.
g. Sold Jobs 136 and 138 on credit at a total price of $525,000.

h. The company incurred the following overhead costs during the month (credit Prepaid Insurance for expired factory insurance).

Depreciation of factory building	$68,000
Depreciation of factory equipment	36,500
Expired factory insurance	10,000
Accrued property taxes payable	35,000

i. Applied overhead at month-end to the Work in Process Inventory account (Jobs 137 and 140) using the predetermined overhead rate of 200% of direct labor cost.

Required

1. Prepare a job cost sheet for each job worked on during the month. Use the following simplified form.

Job No. ________	
Materials	$ ________
Labor	________
Overhead.	________
Total cost	$ ________

Check (2*e*) Cr. Factory Overhead, $177,000

2. Prepare journal entries to record the events and transactions *a* through *i*.

3. Set up T-accounts for each of the following general ledger accounts, each of which started the month with a zero balance: Raw Materials Inventory; Work in Process Inventory; Finished Goods Inventory; Factory Overhead; Cost of Goods Sold. Then post the journal entries to these T-accounts and determine the balance of each account.

Check (4) Finished Goods Inventory, $139,400

4. Prepare a report showing the total cost of each job in process and prove that the sum of their costs equals the Work in Process Inventory account balance. Prepare similar reports for Finished Goods Inventory and Cost of Goods Sold.

Problem 15-4A
Overhead allocation and adjustment using a predetermined overhead rate
P3 P4

In December 2014, Learer Company's manager estimated next year's total direct labor cost assuming 50 persons working an average of 2,000 hours each at an average wage rate of $25 per hour. The manager also estimated the following manufacturing overhead costs for 2015.

Indirect labor	$ 319,200
Factory supervision	240,000
Rent on factory building	140,000
Factory utilities	88,000
Factory insurance expired	68,000
Depreciation—Factory equipment	480,000
Repairs expense—Factory equipment	60,000
Factory supplies used	68,800
Miscellaneous production costs	36,000
Total estimated overhead costs	$1,500,000

At the end of 2015, records show the company incurred $1,520,000 of actual overhead costs. It completed and sold five jobs with the following direct labor costs: Job 201, $604,000; Job 202, $563,000; Job 203, $298,000; Job 204, $716,000; and Job 205, $314,000. In addition, Job 206 is in process at the end of 2015 and had been charged $17,000 for direct labor. No jobs were in process at the end of 2014. The company's predetermined overhead rate is based on direct labor cost.

Required

1. Determine the following.
   a. Predetermined overhead rate for 2015.
   b. Total overhead cost applied to each of the six jobs during 2015.
   c. Over- or underapplied overhead at year-end 2015.
2. Assuming that any over- or underapplied overhead is not material, prepare the adjusting entry to allocate any over- or underapplied overhead to Cost of Goods Sold at the end of 2015.

Check (1*c*) 12,800 underapplied
(2) Cr. Factory Overhead $12,800

Problem 15-5A
Production transactions, subsidiary records, and source documents
P1 P2 P3 P4

Sager Company manufactures variations of its product, a technopress, in response to custom orders from its customers. On May 1, the company had no inventories of work in process or finished goods but held the following raw materials.

Material M	200 units @ $250 =	$50,000
Material R	95 units @ 180 =	17,100
Paint	55 units @ 75 =	4,125
Total cost		$71,225

On May 4, the company began working on two technopresses: Job 102 for Worldwide Company and Job 103 for Reuben Company.

Required

Using Exhibit 15.3 as a guide, prepare Job cost sheets for Jobs 102 and 103. Using Exhibit 15.5 as a guide, prepare materials ledger cards for Material M, Material R, and paint. Enter the beginning raw materials inventory dollar amounts for each of these materials on their respective ledger cards. Then, follow the instructions in this list of activities.

a. Purchased raw materials on credit and recorded the following information from receiving reports and invoices.

   Receiving Report No. 426, Material M, 250 units at $250 each.
   Receiving Report No. 427, Material R, 90 units at $180 each.

   Instructions: Record these purchases with a single journal entry. Enter the receiving report information on the materials ledger cards.

b. Requisitioned the following raw materials for production.

   Requisition No. 35, for Job 102, 135 units of Material M.
   Requisition No. 36, for Job 102, 72 units of Material R.
   Requisition No. 37, for Job 103, 70 units of Material M.
   Requisition No. 38, for Job 103, 38 units of Material R.
   Requisition No. 39, for 15 units of paint.

   Instructions: Enter amounts for direct materials requisitions on the materials ledger cards and the job cost sheets. Enter the indirect material amount on the materials ledger card. Do not record a journal entry at this time.

c. Received the following employee time tickets for work in May.

   Time tickets Nos. 1 to 10 for direct labor on Job 102, $90,000.
   Time tickets Nos. 11 to 30 for direct labor on Job 103, $65,000.
   Time tickets Nos. 31 to 36 for equipment repairs, $19,250.

   Instructions: Record direct labor from the time tickets on the job cost sheets. Do not record a journal entry at this time.

d. Paid cash for the following items during the month: factory payroll, $174,250, and miscellaneous overhead items, $102,000. Use the time tickets to record the total direct and indirect labor costs.
Instructions: Record these payments with journal entries.

e. Finished Job 102 and transferred it to the warehouse. The company assigns overhead to each job with a predetermined overhead rate equal to 80% of direct labor cost.
Instructions: Enter the allocated overhead on the cost sheet for Job 102, fill in the cost summary section of the cost sheet, and then mark the cost sheet "Finished." Prepare a journal entry to record the job's completion and its transfer to Finished Goods.

f. Delivered Job 102 and accepted the customer's promise to pay $400,000 within 30 days.
Instructions: Prepare journal entries to record the sale of Job 102 and the cost of goods sold.

g. Applied overhead to Job 103 based on the job's direct labor to date.
Instructions: Enter overhead on the job cost sheet but do not make a journal entry at this time.

Check (*h*) Dr. Work in Process Inventory, $71,050

h. Recorded the total direct and indirect materials costs as reported on all the requisitions for the month.
Instructions: Prepare a journal entry to record these costs.

Check Balance in Factory Overhead, $1,625 Cr., overapplied

i. Recorded the total overhead costs applied to jobs.
Instructions: Prepare a journal entry to record the allocation of these overhead costs.

j. Compute the balance in the Factory Overhead account as of the end of May.

PROBLEM SET B

Problem 15-1B
Production costs computed and recorded; reports prepared
C2 P1 P2 P3 P4

Perez Mfg.'s August 31 inventory of raw materials is $150,000. Raw materials purchases in September are $400,000, and factory payroll cost in September is $232,000. Overhead costs incurred in September are: indirect materials, $30,000; indirect labor, $14,000; factory rent, $20,000; factory utilities, $12,000; and factory equipment depreciation, $30,000. The predetermined overhead rate is 50% of direct labor cost. Job 114 is sold for $380,000 cash in September. Costs for the three jobs worked on in September follow.

	Job 114	Job 115	Job 116
Balances on August 31			
Direct materials	$ 14,000	$ 18,000	
Direct labor	18,000	16,000	
Applied overhead	9,000	8,000	
Costs during September			
Direct materials	100,000	170,000	$ 80,000
Direct labor	30,000	68,000	120,000
Applied overhead	?	?	?
Status on September 30	Finished (sold)	Finished (unsold)	In process

Required

1. Determine the total of each production cost incurred for September (direct labor, direct materials, and applied overhead), and the total cost assigned to each job (including the balances from August 31).
2. Prepare journal entries for the month of September to record the following.
   a. Materials purchases (on credit).
   b. Direct materials used in production.
   c. Direct labor paid and assigned to Work in Process Inventory.
   d. Indirect labor paid and assigned to Factory Overhead.
   e. Overhead costs applied to Work in Process Inventory.
   f. Actual overhead costs incurred, including indirect materials. (Factory rent and utilities are paid in cash.)
   g. Transfer of Jobs 114 and 115 to the Finished Goods Inventory.
   h. Cost of Job 114 in the Cost of Goods Sold account.
   i. Revenue from the sale of Job 114.
   j. Assignment of any underapplied or overapplied overhead to the Cost of Goods Sold account. (The amount is not material.)

Check (2*j*) $3,000 overapplied

3. Prepare a schedule of cost of goods manufactured.
4. Compute gross profit for September. Show how to present the inventories on the September 30 balance sheet.

(3) Cost of goods manufactured, $500,000

Analysis Component

5. The over- or underapplied overhead adjustment is closed to Cost of Goods Sold. Discuss how this adjustment impacts business decision making regarding individual jobs or batches of jobs.

Problem 15-2B
Source documents, journal entries, overhead, and financial reports
P1 P2 P3 P4

Cavallo Mfg.'s computer system generated the following trial balance on December 31, 2015. The company's manager knows that the trial balance is wrong because it does not show any balance for Work in Process Inventory but does show a balance for the Factory Overhead account. In addition, the accrued factory payroll (Factory Payroll Payable) has not been recorded.

	Debit	Credit
Cash	$ 64,000	
Accounts receivable	42,000	
Raw materials inventory	26,000	
Work in process inventory	0	
Finished goods inventory	9,000	
Prepaid rent	3,000	
Accounts payable		$ 10,500
Notes payable		13,500
Common stock		30,000
Retained earnings		87,000
Sales		180,000
Cost of goods sold	105,000	
Factory overhead	27,000	
Operating expenses	45,000	
Totals	$321,000	$321,000

After examining various files, the manager identifies the following six source documents that need to be processed to bring the accounting records up to date.

Materials requisition 94-231:	$4,600 direct materials to Job 603
Materials requisition 94-232:	$7,600 direct materials to Job 604
Materials requisition 94-233:	$2,100 indirect materials
Labor time ticket 765:	$5,000 direct labor to Job 603
Labor time ticket 766:	$8,000 direct labor to Job 604
Labor time ticket 777:	$3,000 indirect labor

Jobs 603 and 604 are the only units in process at year-end. The predetermined overhead rate is 200% of direct labor cost.

Required

1. Use information on the six source documents to prepare journal entries to assign the following costs.
   a. Direct materials costs to Work in Process Inventory.
   b. Direct labor costs to Work in Process Inventory.
   c. Overhead costs to Work in Process Inventory.
   d. Indirect materials costs to the Factory Overhead account.
   e. Indirect labor costs to the Factory Overhead account.

Check (2) $6,100 underapplied overhead

2. Determine the revised balance of the Factory Overhead account after making the entries in part 1. Determine whether there is under- or overapplied overhead for the year. Prepare the adjusting entry to allocate any over- or underapplied overhead to Cost of Goods Sold, assuming the amount is not material.

(3) T. B. totals, $337,000

3. Prepare a revised trial balance.

(4) Net income, $23,900

4. Prepare an income statement for 2015 and a balance sheet as of December 31, 2015.

Analysis Component

5. Assume that the $2,100 indirect materials on materials requisition 94-233 should have been direct materials charged to Job 604. Without providing specific calculations, describe the impact of this error on the income statement for 2015 and the balance sheet at December 31, 2015.

Problem 15-3B
Source documents, journal entries, and accounts in job order costing
P1 P2 P3

Starr Mfg.'s predetermined overhead rate is 200% of direct labor. Information on the company's production activities during September 2015 follows.

a. Purchased raw materials on credit, $125,000.

b. Materials requisitions record use of the following materials for the month.

Job 487	$30,000
Job 488	20,000
Job 489	12,000
Job 490	14,000
Job 491	4,000
Total direct materials	80,000
Indirect materials	12,000
Total materials used	$92,000

c. Paid $11,000 cash for miscellaneous factory overhead costs.

d. Time tickets record use of the following labor for the month. These wages are paid in cash.

Job 487	$ 8,000
Job 488	7,000
Job 489	25,000
Job 490	26,000
Job 491	2,000
Total direct labor	68,000
Indirect labor	16,000
Total	$84,000

e. Allocated overhead to Jobs 487, 489, and 490.

f. Transferred Jobs 487, 489, and 490 to Finished Goods.

g. Sold Jobs 487 and 489 on credit for a total price of $340,000.

h. The company incurred the following overhead costs during the month (credit Prepaid Insurance for expired factory insurance).

Depreciation of factory building	$37,000
Depreciation of factory equipment	21,000
Expired factory insurance	7,000
Accrued property taxes payable	31,000

i. Applied overhead at month-end to the Work in Process Inventory account (Jobs 488 and 491) using the predetermined overhead rate of 200% of direct labor cost.

Required

1. Prepare a job cost sheet for each job worked on in the month. Use the following simplified form.

Job No. ________	
Materials	$ ________
Labor	________
Overhead	________
Total cost	$ ________

2. Prepare journal entries to record the events and transactions *a* through *i*.

3. Set up T-accounts for each of the following general ledger accounts, each of which started the month with a zero balance: Raw Materials Inventory, Work in Process Inventory, Finished Goods Inventory, Factory Overhead, Cost of Goods Sold. Then post the journal entries to these T-accounts and determine the balance of each account.

4. Prepare a report showing the total cost of each job in process and prove that the sum of their costs equals the Work in Process Inventory account balance. Prepare similar reports for Finished Goods Inventory and Cost of Goods Sold.

Check (2*e*) Cr. Factory Overhead, $118,000
(3) Finished Goods Inventory, $92,000 bal.

Problem 15-4B
Overhead allocation and adjustment using a predetermined overhead rate
P3 P4

In December 2014, Pavelka Company's manager estimated next year's total direct labor cost assuming 50 persons working an average of 2,000 hours each at an average wage rate of $15 per hour. The manager also estimated the following manufacturing overhead costs for 2015.

Indirect labor	$159,600
Factory supervision	120,000
Rent on factory building.	70,000
Factory utilities	44,000
Factory insurance expired	34,000
Depreciation—Factory equipment	240,000
Repairs expense—Factory equipment	30,000
Factory supplies used	34,400
Miscellaneous production costs	18,000
Total estimated overhead costs	$750,000

At the end of 2015, records show the company incurred $725,000 of actual overhead costs. It completed and sold five jobs with the following direct labor costs: Job 625, $354,000; Job 626, $330,000; Job 627, $175,000; Job 628, $420,000; and Job 629, $184,000. In addition, Job 630 is in process at the end of 2015 and had been charged $10,000 for direct labor. No jobs were in process at the end of 2014. The company's predetermined overhead rate is based on direct labor cost.

Required

1. Determine the following.

a. Predetermined overhead rate for 2015.

b. Total overhead cost applied to each of the six jobs during 2015.

c. Over- or underapplied overhead at year-end 2015.

2. Assuming that any over- or underapplied overhead is not material, prepare the adjusting entry to allocate any over- or underapplied overhead to Cost of Goods Sold at the end of year 2015.

Check (1*c*) $11,500 overapplied
(2) Dr. Factory Overhead, $11,500

Problem 15-5B
Production transactions, subsidiary records, and source documents
P1 P2 P3 P4

King Company produces variations of its product, a megatron, in response to custom orders from its customers. On June 1, the company had no inventories of work in process or finished goods but held the following raw materials.

Material M	120 units @ $200 =	$24,000
Material R	80 units @ 160 =	12,800
Paint	44 units @ 72 =	3,168
Total cost		$39,968

On June 3, the company began working on two megatrons: Job 450 for Encinita Company and Job 451 for Fargo, Inc.

Required

Using Exhibit 15.3 as a guide, prepare job cost sheets for Jobs 450 and 451. Using Exhibit 15.5 as a guide, prepare materials ledger cards for Material M, Material R, and paint. Enter the beginning raw materials inventory dollar amounts for each of these materials on their respective ledger cards. Then, follow instructions in this list of activities.

a. Purchased raw materials on credit and recorded the following information from receiving reports and invoices.

> Receiving Report No. 20, Material M, 150 units at $200 each.
> Receiving Report No. 21, Material R, 70 units at $160 each.

Instructions: Record these purchases with a single journal entry. Enter the receiving report information on the materials ledger cards.

b. Requisitioned the following raw materials for production.

> Requisition No. 223, for Job 450, 80 units of Material M.
> Requisition No. 224, for Job 450, 60 units of Material R.
> Requisition No. 225, for Job 451, 40 units of Material M.
> Requisition No. 226, for Job 451, 30 units of Material R.
> Requisition No. 227, for 12 units of paint.

Instructions: Enter amounts for direct materials requisitions on the materials ledger cards and the job cost sheets. Enter the indirect material amount on the materials ledger card. Do not record a journal entry at this time.

c. Received the following employee time tickets for work in June.

> Time tickets Nos. 1 to 10 for direct labor on Job 450, $40,000.
> Time tickets Nos. 11 to 20 for direct labor on Job 451, $32,000.
> Time tickets Nos. 21 to 24 for equipment repairs, $12,000.

Instructions: Record direct labor from the time tickets on the job cost sheets. Do not record a journal entry at this time.

d. Paid cash for the following items during the month: factory payroll, $84,000, and miscellaneous overhead items, $36,800. Use the time tickets to record the total direct and indirect labor costs.

Instructions: Record these payments with journal entries.

e. Finished Job 450 and transferred it to the warehouse. The company assigns overhead to each job with a predetermined overhead rate equal to 70% of direct labor cost.

Instructions: Enter the allocated overhead on the cost sheet for Job 450, fill in the cost summary section of the cost sheet, and then mark the cost sheet "Finished." Prepare a journal entry to record the job's completion and its transfer to Finished Goods.

f. Delivered Job 450 and accepted the customer's promise to pay $290,000 within 30 days.

Instructions: Prepare journal entries to record the sale of Job 450 and the cost of goods sold.

g. Applied overhead cost to Job 451 based on the job's direct labor used to date.

Instructions: Enter overhead on the job cost sheet but do not make a journal entry at this time.

Check (*h*) Dr. Work in Process Inventory, $38,400

h. Recorded the total direct and indirect materials costs as reported on all the requisitions for the month.

Instructions: Prepare a journal entry to record these.

i. Recorded the total overhead costs applied to jobs.
Instructions: Prepare a journal entry to record the allocation of these overhead costs.

j. Compute the balance in the Factory Overhead account as of the end of June.

Check Balance in Factory Overhead, $736 Cr., overapplied

SERIAL PROBLEM

Business Solutions

P1 P2 P3

(This serial problem began in Chapter 1 and continues through most of the book. If previous chapter segments were not completed, the serial problem can begin at this point. It is helpful, but not necessary, to use the Working Papers that accompany the book.)

SP 15 The computer workstation furniture manufacturing that Santana Rey started in January is progressing well. As of the end of June, Business Solutions's job cost sheets show the following total costs accumulated on three furniture jobs.

	Job 602	Job 603	Job 604
Direct materials	$1,500	$3,300	$2,700
Direct labor	800	1,420	2,100
Overhead	400	710	1,050

Job 602 was started in production in May, and these costs were assigned to it in May: direct materials, $600; direct labor, $180; and overhead, $90. Jobs 603 and 604 were started in June. Overhead cost is applied with a predetermined rate based on direct labor costs. Jobs 602 and 603 are finished in June, and Job 604 is expected to be finished in July. No raw materials are used indirectly in June. (Assume this company's predetermined overhead rate did not change over these months).

Required

1. What is the cost of the raw materials used in June for each of the three jobs and in total?
2. How much total direct labor cost is incurred in June?
3. What predetermined overhead rate is used in June?
4. How much cost is transferred to Finished Goods Inventory in June?

Check (1) Total materials, $6,900

(3) 50%

GENERAL LEDGER PROBLEM

Available in Connect

The **General Ledger** tool in *Connect* automates several of the procedural steps in accounting so that the financial professional can focus on the impacts of each transaction on various reports and performance measures.

GL 15-1 General Ledger assignment GL 15-1, based on Problem 15-1A, focuses on transactions related to job-order costing. Prepare summary journal entries to record the cost of jobs and their flow through the manufacturing environment. Then prepare a schedule of cost of goods manufactured and a partial income statement.

Beyond the Numbers

REPORTING IN ACTION

C1

APPLE

BTN 15-1 Apple's financial statements and notes in Appendix A provide evidence of growth potential in its sales.

Required

1. Identify at least two types of costs that will predictably increase as a percent of sales with growth in sales.
2. Explain why you believe the types of costs identified for part 1 will increase, and describe how you might assess Apple's success with these costs. (*Hint:* You might consider the gross margin ratio.)

Fast Forward

3. Access Apple's annual report for a fiscal year ending after September 28, 2013, from its website [Apple.com] or the SEC's EDGAR database [www.SEC.gov]. Review and report its growth in sales along with its cost and income levels (including its gross margin ratio).

COMPARATIVE ANALYSIS

C1

APPLE
GOOGLE

BTN 15-2 Manufacturers and merchandisers can apply just-in-time (JIT) to their inventory management. Both **Apple** and **Google** want to know the impact of a JIT inventory system for their operating cash flows. Review each company's statement of cash flows in Appendix A to answer the following.

Required

1. Identify the impact on operating cash flows (increase or decrease) for changes in inventory levels (increase or decrease) for both companies for each of the three most recent years.
2. What impact would a JIT inventory system have on both Apple's and Google's operating income? Link the answer to your response for part 1.
3. Would the move to a JIT system have a one-time or recurring impact on operating cash flow?

ETHICS CHALLENGE

P3

BTN 15-3 An accounting professional requires at least two skill sets. The first is to be technically competent. Knowing how to capture, manage, and report information is a necessary skill. Second, the ability to assess manager and employee actions and biases for accounting analysis is another skill. For instance, knowing how a person is compensated helps anticipate information biases. Draw on these skills and write a half-page memo to the financial officer on the following practice of allocating overhead.

Background: Assume that your company sells portable housing to both general contractors and the government. It sells jobs to contractors on a bid basis. A contractor asks for three bids from different manufacturers. The combination of low bid and high quality wins the job. However, jobs sold to the government are bid on a cost-plus basis. This means price is determined by adding all costs plus a profit based on cost at a specified percent, such as 10%. You observe that the amount of overhead allocated to government jobs is higher than that allocated to contract jobs. These allocations concern you and motivate your memo.

Point: Students could compare responses and discuss differences in concerns with allocating overhead.

COMMUNICATING IN PRACTICE

C1 C2

BTN 15-4 Assume that you are preparing for a second interview with a manufacturing company. The company is impressed with your credentials but has indicated that it has several qualified applicants. You anticipate that in this second interview, you must show what you offer over other candidates. You learn the company currently uses a periodic inventory system and is not satisfied with the timeliness of its information and its inventory management. The company manufactures custom-order holiday decorations and display items. To show your abilities, you plan to recommend that it use a cost accounting system.

Required

In preparation for the interview, prepare notes outlining the following:

1. Your cost accounting system recommendation and why it is suitable for this company.
2. A general description of the documents that the proposed cost accounting system requires.
3. How the documents in part 2 facilitate the operation of the cost accounting system.

Point: Have students present a mock interview, one assuming the role of the president of the company and the other the applicant.

TAKING IT TO THE NET

C1

BTN 15-5 Many contractors work on custom jobs that require a job order costing system.

Required

Access the website <u>AMSI.com</u>; click on "Construction Management Software," and then on "STARBUILDER." Prepare a one-page memorandum for the CEO of a construction company providing information about the job order costing software this company offers. Would you recommend that the company purchase this software?

TEAMWORK IN ACTION

C1

BTN 15-6 Consider the activities undertaken by a medical clinic in your area.

Required

1. Do you consider a job order costing system appropriate for the clinic?
2. Identify as many factors as possible to lead you to conclude that it uses a job order system.

ENTREPRENEURIAL DECISION

C1 C2

BTN 15-7 Refer to the chapter opener regarding Quintin Middleton and his company, **Middleton Made Knives**. All successful businesses track their costs, and it is especially important for start-up businesses to monitor and control costs.

Required

1. Assume that Middleton Made Knives uses a job order costing system. For the basic cost category of direct materials, explain how a job cost sheet for Middleton Made Knives would differ from a job cost sheet for a service company.
2. For the basic cost categories of direct labor and overhead, provide examples of the types of costs that would fall into each category for Middleton Made Knives.

HITTING THE ROAD

C2 P1 P2 P3

BTN 15-8 Job order costing is frequently used by home builders.

Required

1. You (or your team) are to prepare a job cost sheet for a single-family home under construction. List four items of both direct materials and direct labor. Explain how you think overhead should be applied.
2. Contact a builder and compare your job cost sheet to this builder's job cost sheet. If possible, speak to that company's accountant. Write your findings in a short report.

GLOBAL DECISION

C1

APPLE

Samsung

BTN 15-9 **Apple** and **Samsung** are competitors in the global marketplace. Apple's and Samsung's financial statements are in Appendix A.

Required

1. Determine the change in Apple's and Samsung's inventories for the most recent year reported. Then identify the impact on net resources generated by operating activities (increase or decrease) for the change in inventory level (increase or decrease) for Apple and Samsung for that same year.
2. How would the move to a just-in-time (JIT) system likely impact future operating cash flows and operating income?
3. Would a move to a JIT system likely impact Apple more than it would Samsung? Explain.

ANSWERS TO MULTIPLE CHOICE QUIZ

1. c; $30,000 × 150% = $45,000
2. b; $38,500/$35,000 = 110%
3. e; Direct materials + Direct labor + Overhead = Total cost;
   Direct materials + ($4,000/.80) + $4,000 = $10,000
   Direct materials = $1,000
4. e; $9,000 + $94,200 + $59,200 + $31,600 − Finished goods = $17,800
   Thus, finished goods = $176,200
5. b

chapter 16

Process Costing and Analysis

Chapter Preview

PROCESS OPERATIONS	PROCESS COSTING ILLUSTRATION	ACCOUNTING AND REPORTING
C1 Organization of process operations	**C3** Overview of GenX Company	**P1** Accounting for materials
A1 Process cost vs. job order systems	Physical flow of units	**P2** Accounting for labor
C2 Equivalent units (EUP)	Computing EUP	**P3** Accounting for overhead
	Cost per EUP	**P4** Accounting for transfers
	Cost reconciliation	**A2** Hybrid costing system
	Process cost summary	**C4** *Appendix:* FIFO method

Learning Objectives

CONCEPTUAL

C1 Explain process operations and the way they differ from job order operations.

C2 Define and compute equivalent units and explain their use in process costing.

C3 Describe accounting for production activity and preparation of a process cost summary using weighted average.

C4 *Appendix 16A*—Describe accounting for production activity and preparation of a process cost summary using FIFO.

ANALYTICAL

A1 Compare process costing and job order costing.

A2 Explain and illustrate a hybrid costing system.

PROCEDURAL

P1 Record the flow of materials costs in process costing.

P2 Record the flow of labor costs in process costing.

P3 Record the flow of factory overhead costs in process costing.

P4 Record the transfer of goods across departments, to Finished Goods Inventory, and to Cost of Goods Sold.

©Nathan Skid/Crain Communications, Inc.

Mixing It Up

MADISON HEIGHTS, MI—Like many small businesses, **Kar's Nuts (karsnuts.com)** started at home, where Sue Kar roasted peanuts to sell at nearby Tiger Stadium. From humble beginnings, the company now has the country's best-selling branded trail mix, Sweet 'n Salty Mix. Kar's CEO and family-owner Nick Nicolay notes that "Sweet 'n Salty is our flagship item, and we sell over 15 million pounds of it each year."

Unlike products made in job order operations, Kar's operates a continuous production line that runs around the clock, processing over 26 million pounds of different trail mixes during the year. High production volumes are characteristic of products made in process operations. This operation requires production managers to track costs differently than in job order systems, and Kar's relies on a process costing system to monitor and control its costs. These systems track the costs of each process, which in Kar's case include roasting, blending, and packaging.

"We roast around the clock . . . the demand is there"
—Nick Nicolay

Each of Kar's processes adds direct materials costs. In the roasting department, thousand-pound supersacks of peanuts and sunflower kernels are roasted and then transferred to the blending department. "We're choosy with ingredients, and use only jumbo peanuts because they taste better," says Nick. In the blending department, direct materials like dark chocolate chunks, raisins, and various berries are blended with the roasted nuts.

Like many process operations, Kar's relies heavily on automation. Much of the work is done by machines, including roasters, conveyors, bucket elevators, and robots. The overhead costs of running the machines must be carefully monitored and (as in job order costing) allocated. In process costing, overhead costs are allocated to individual processes, such as roasting, blending, and packaging, rather than to individual jobs. With costly raw materials and overhead costs, Nick and his production managers must be adept at interpreting process cost summary reports to monitor and control costs.

While Kar's has been in business for many years, Nick stresses the need for the company to remain entrepreneurial and creative: "Coming up with innovative, new products can be challenging. No one's creating new fruits or nuts, so our charge is to take what's out there and continue to come up with unique, tasty, healthy combinations to meet new demand." A 30-minute internal meeting was the genesis of the idea for Sweet 'n Salty. According to Nicolay, "We thought a sweet and salty trail mix would be a good alternative to candy bars in vending machines in the summertime. . . . But it quickly became more than a seasonal item." Likewise, Kar's developed Second Nature, a line focused on meeting trends toward even healthier snacks. "We saw that consumers wanted a more premium, upscale, healthy eating option, and we responded with this line of mixes that includes all-natural ingredients," says Nick.

Nick encourages young entrepreneurs to "enjoy what you do and work hard." Though he started as a banker, Nick realized that "snack food is in my family's blood," and he made the move to Kar's. Now, the company boasts yearly sales of over $90 million, and Nick has plans for his products to be sold in nearly all the top grocery stores in the United States within the next few years. "There is a lot of geography left," notes Nick.

Source: *Kar's Nuts website,* January 2015; *mlbiz.com,* October 9, 2013; *plantemoran.com,* October 16, 2013; *Crain's Detroit Business,* May 5, 2013

PROCESS OPERATIONS

C1 Explain process operations and the way they differ from job order operations.

In the previous chapter we described differences in job order and process operations and illustrated job order costing. Recall that job order operations involve individual, customized jobs, with little standardization of work activities. **Process operations** involve the mass production of similar products in a continuous flow of sequential processes. A key feature of process operations is the high level of standardization needed if the system is to produce large volumes of products. Thus, process operations use a standardized process to make similar products; job order operations use a customized process to make unique products.

Penn, a maker of tennis balls, reflects a process operation. Tennis players want every tennis ball to be the same in terms of bounce, playability, and durability. This uniformity requires Penn to use a production process that can repeatedly make large volumes of tennis balls to the same specifications. Such a process is unlike job order operations, where customers want products or services customized to their individual needs. Process operations also extend to services, such as mail sorting in large post offices and order processing in retailers like **Amazon.com**. Other companies using process operations include:

Company*	Product	Company	Product
Kellogg	Cereals	Heinz	Ketchup
Pfizer	Pharmaceuticals	Mars	M&Ms
Procter & Gamble	Household products	Hershey	Chocolate
Coca-Cola	Soft drinks	Suja	Organic juice

*For virtual tours of process operations visit PennRacquet.com/video.html (tennis balls) and Hersheys.com/ads-and-videos/how-we-make-chocolate.aspx (chocolate).

Organization of Process Operations

Each of these products involves operations having a series of repetitive *processes,* or steps, resulting in a noncustomized product or service. A production operation that makes tennis balls, for instance, might include the three steps shown in Exhibit 16.1. Understanding such processes for companies with process operations is crucial for measuring their costs. Increasingly, process operations use machines and automation to control product quality and reduce manufacturing costs.

EXHIBIT 16.1

Process Operations: Making of Tennis Balls

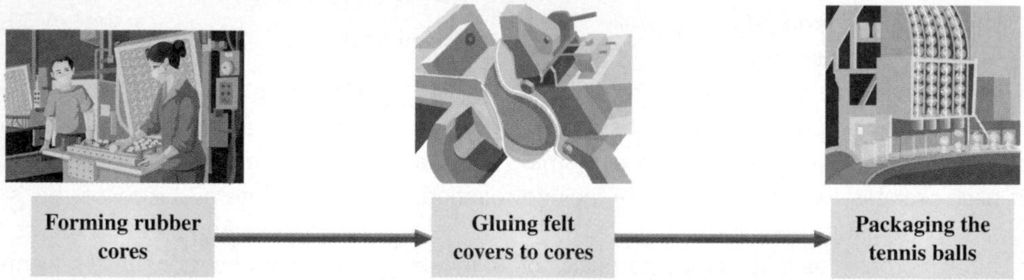

In a process operation, each process is identified as a separate *production department, workstation,* or *work center.* With the exception of the first process or department, each receives the output from the prior department as a partially processed product. Depending on the nature of the process, each process applies direct labor, overhead, and, perhaps, additional direct materials to move the product toward completion. Only the final process or department in the series produces finished goods ready for sale to customers. In Exhibit 16.1, the first step in tennis ball production involves cutting rubber into pellets and forming the core of each ball. These rubber cores are passed to the second department, where felt is cut into covers and glued to the rubber cores. The completed tennis balls are then passed to the final department for quality checks and packaging.

Tracking costs for several related departments can seem complex. Yet because process costing procedures are applied to *the activity of each department or process separately,* we need to consider only one process at a time. This simplifies the procedures. In addition, as we will show in this chapter, many of the journal entries in a process costing system are like those in a job order costing system.

Comparing Process and Job Order Costing Systems

A1 Compare process costing and job order costing.

Both **job order costing systems** and **process costing systems** track direct materials, direct labor, and overhead costs. The measurement focus in a job order costing system is on the individual job or batch, whereas in a process costing system, it is on the individual process. Regardless of the measurement focus, we are ultimately interested in determining the cost per unit of product (or service) resulting from either system.

While both measure costs per unit, these two accounting systems differ in terms of how they do so. A job order system measures cost per unit upon completion of a job, by dividing the total cost for that job by the number of units in that job. As we showed in the previous chapter, job cost sheets accumulate the costs for each job. In a job order system, the cost object is a job. A process costing system measures unit costs at the end of a period (for example, a month) by combining the costs per equivalent unit (explained in the next section) from each separate department. In process costing, the cost object is the process. Differences in the way these two systems apply materials, labor, and overhead costs are highlighted in Exhibit 16.2.

Point: The cost object in a job order system is the specific job; the cost object in a process costing system is the process.

QC1

EXHIBIT 16.2

Cost Flows: Comparing Job Order and Process Costing Systems

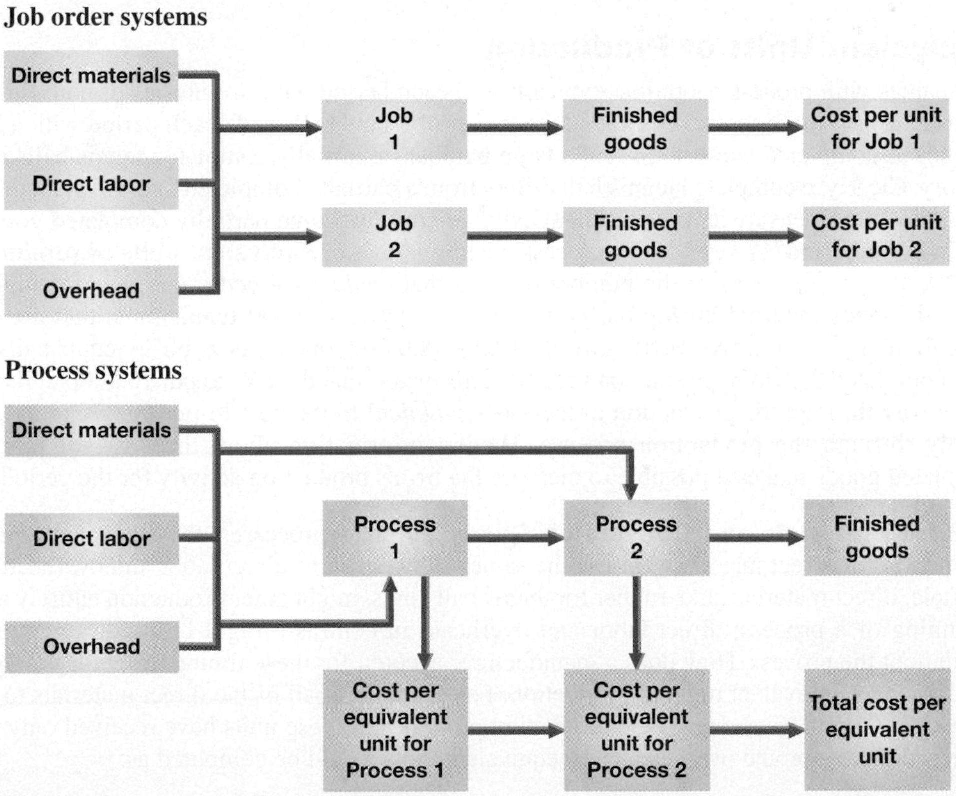

Transferring Costs across Departments A key difference between job order and process costing arises with respect to work in process inventory: Job order costing often uses *only one* Work in Process Inventory account; the balance in this account agrees with the accumulated balances across all the job cost sheets for the jobs still in process. Process costing, however, uses *separate* Work in Process Inventory accounts for each department. When the production process is complete in process costing, the completed goods and the accumulated costs are transferred from the Work in Process Inventory account for the final department in the series of processes to the Finished Goods Inventory account. Exhibit 16.3 summarizes the journal entries to capture this flow of costs for a tennis ball manufacturer.

EXHIBIT 16.3

Flow of Costs through Separate Work in Process Accounts

Work in Process Inventory—Felt department	##	
Work in Process Inventory—Core department		##
To transfer costs of partially completed goods to the next department.		
Finished Goods Inventory	##	
Work in Process Inventory—Felt department		##
To transfer costs of completed products to finished goods.		

NEED-TO-KNOW 16-1

Job Order vs. Process Costing Systems

C1 A1

Do More: QS 16-1, QS 16-2, E 16-1, E 16-2

QC2

Complete the following table with either a yes or no regarding the attributes of job order and process costing systems.

	Job Order	Process
Uses direct materials, direct labor, and overhead costs	a.	e.
Uses job cost sheets to accumulate costs	b.	f.
Typically uses several Work in Process Inventory accounts	c.	g.
Yields a cost per unit of product	d.	h.

Solution

a. yes **b.** yes **c.** no **d.** yes **e.** yes **f.** no **g.** yes **h.** yes

Equivalent Units of Production

C2

Define and compute equivalent units and explain their use in process costing.

Companies with process operations typically end each period with inventories of both finished goods and work in process. For example, a maker of tennis balls ends each period with a large number of completed tennis balls and a large number of partially completed tennis balls in inventory. Clearly, a completed tennis ball differs from a partially completed one. How, then, does a manufacturer measure its production activity when it has some partially completed goods at the end of a period? A key idea in process costing is that of **equivalent units of production (EUP),** a term that refers to the number of units that *could have been* started and completed given the costs incurred during the period. For example, 100,000 tennis balls that are 60% through the production process is equivalent to 60,000 (100,000 units × 60%) tennis balls that have completed the entire production process. This means that the cost to put 100,000 units 60% of the way through the production process is *equivalent to* the cost to put 60,000 units completely through the production process. Having information about the costs of partially completed goods makes it possible to measure the firm's production activity for the period.

EUP for Materials and Conversion Costs In many processes, the equivalent units of production for direct materials are not the same with respect to direct labor and overhead. For example, direct materials, like rubber for tennis ball cores, might enter production entirely at the beginning of a process; direct labor and overhead, in contrast, might be used continuously throughout the process. How does a manufacturer account for these timing differences? Again, by measuring equivalent units of production. For example, if all of the direct materials to produce 10,000 units have entered the production process, but those units have received only 20% of their direct labor and overhead costs, equivalent units would be computed as:

EUP for direct materials	= 10,000 × 100%	=	10,000
EUP for direct labor	= 10,000 × 20%	=	2,000
EUP for overhead	= 10,000 × 20%	=	2,000

As discussed in a previous chapter, direct labor and factory overhead can be classified as *conversion costs*—that is, as costs of converting direct materials into finished products. Many businesses with process operations compute **conversion cost per equivalent unit,** which is the combined costs of direct labor and factory overhead per equivalent unit. If, as shown in the example above, direct labor and overhead enter the production process at the same rate, it is convenient to combine them and focus on them, together, as conversion costs. In addition, advances in technology

Point: When overhead is applied based on direct labor cost, the percentage of completion for direct labor and overhead will be the same.

enable companies to automate their production processes and reduce direct labor costs. For these reasons, many companies with process operations use the categories of direct materials and conversion costs both for accounting and decision-making purposes. We illustrate this in the next section.

Weighted Average versus FIFO As we will show later, there are different ways to compute the number of equivalent units. These methods make different assumptions about how costs flow. The **weighted-average method** combines units and costs *across two periods* in computing equivalent units. The **FIFO method** computes equivalent units based only on production activity in the *current period.* The objectives, concepts, and journal entries (but not amounts) are the same under the weighted-average and FIFO methods; the computations of equivalent units differ. While the FIFO method is generally considered to be more precise than the weighted-average method, it requires more calculations. Often, the differences between the two methods are not large. When using a just-in-time inventory system, these different methods will yield very similar results because inventories are immaterial. **In this chapter we assume the weighted-average method for inventory costs and illustrate the FIFO method in the appendix.**

PROCESS COSTING ILLUSTRATION

In this section we provide a step-by-step illustration of process costing. Each process (or department) in a process operation follows these steps:

C3 Describe accounting for production activity and preparation of a process cost summary using weighted average.

1. Determine the physical flow of units.
2. Compute the equivalent units of production.
3. Compute the cost per equivalent unit of production.
4. Assign and reconcile costs.

The next section shows these steps for the first of two sequential processes used by a company to produce one of its products.

Overview of GenX Company's Process Operation

The GenX Company produces an organic trail mix called FitMix. Its target customers are active people who are interested in fitness and the environment. GenX sells FitMix to wholesale distributors, who in turn sell it to retailers. FitMix is manufactured in a continuous, two-process operation (roasting and blending), shown in Exhibit 16.4.

EXHIBIT 16.4

GenX's Process Operation

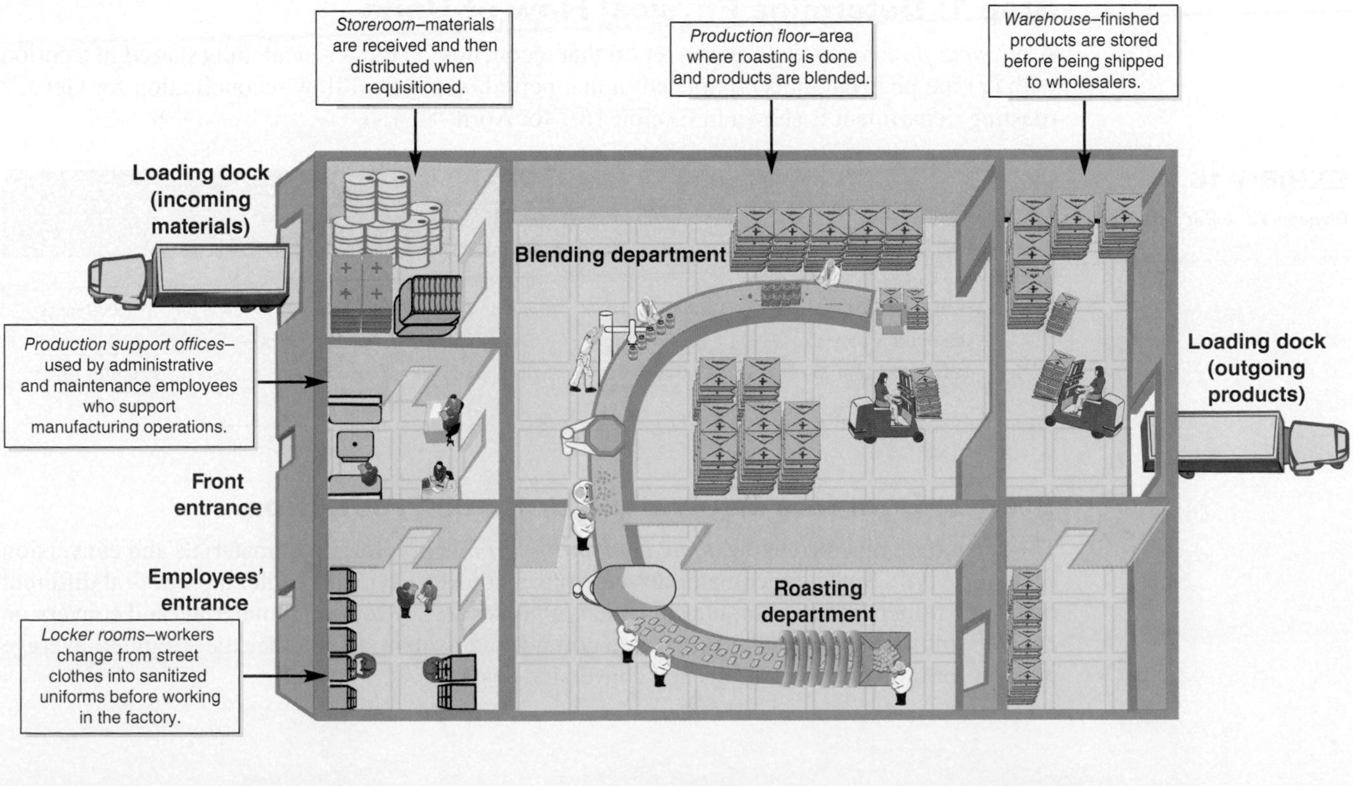

In the first process (roasting department), GenX roasts, oils, and salts organically grown peanuts. These peanuts are then passed to the blending department, the second process. In the blending department, machines blend organic chocolate pieces and organic dried fruits with the peanuts from the first process. The blended mix is then inspected and packaged for delivery. In both departments, direct materials enter production at the beginning of the process, while conversion costs occur continuously throughout each department's processing. Exhibit 16.5 presents production data (in units) for GenX's roasting department. This exhibit includes the percentage of completion for both materials and conversion; for example, beginning work in process inventory is 100% complete with respect to materials but only 65% complete with respect to conversion.

EXHIBIT 16.5

Production Data (in units) for Roasting Department

		Percentage of Completion	
Roasting Department	**Units**	**Direct Materials**	**Conversion**
Beginning work in process inventory (March 31)	30,000	100%	65%
Units started this period	+90,000	—	—
Units completed and transferred out	−100,000	100%	100%
Ending work in process inventory (April 30)	20,000	100%	25%

Exhibit 16.6 presents production cost data for GenX's roasting department. We will use the data in Exhibits 16.5 and 16.6 to illustrate the four-step approach to process costing.

EXHIBIT 16.6

Roasting Department Production Cost Data

GenX—Roasting Department		
Beginning work in process inventory (March 31)		
Direct materials costs	$ 81,000	
Conversion costs	108,900	$189,900
Costs during the current period (April)		
Direct materials costs	279,000	
Direct labor costs*	171,000	
Factory overhead costs applied (120% of direct labor)*	205,200	655,200
Total production costs		$845,100

*Total conversion costs for the month equal $376,200 ($171,000 + $205,200).

Step 1: Determine Physical Flow of Units

A *physical flow reconciliation* is a report that reconciles (1) the physical units started in a period with (2) the physical units completed in that period. A physical flow reconciliation for GenX's roasting department is shown in Exhibit 16.7 for April.

EXHIBIT 16.7

Physical Flow Reconciliation

GenX—Roasting Department			
Units to Account For		**Units Accounted For**	
Beginning work in process inventory	30,000 units	Units completed and transferred out	100,000 units
Units started this period	90,000 units	Ending work in process inventory	20,000 units
Total units to account for	**120,000 units**	Total units accounted for	**120,000 units**

(reconciled)

Step 2: Compute Equivalent Units of Production

The second step is to compute *equivalent units of production* for direct materials and conversion costs for April. Since direct materials and conversion costs typically enter a process at different rates, departments must compute equivalent units separately for direct materials and conversion costs. Exhibit 16.8 shows the formula to compute equivalent units under the weighted-average method for both direct materials and conversion costs.

EXHIBIT 16.8
Computing EUP—Weighted-Average Method

Equivalent units of production (EUP)	=	Number of whole units completed and transferred to next department*	+	Number of equivalent units in ending work in process inventory

*Or transferred to finished goods inventory.

For GenX's roasting department, we must convert the 120,000 physical units measure to *equivalent units* based on how each input has been used. The roasting department fully completed its work on 100,000 units, and partially completed its work on 20,000 units (from Exhibit 16.5). Equivalent units are computed by multiplying the number of units accounted for (from Step 1) by the percentage of completion for each input—see Exhibit 16.9.

EXHIBIT 16.9
Equivalent Units of Production—Weighted Average

GenX—Roasting Department		
Equivalent Units of Production	Direct Materials	Conversion
Equivalent units completed and transferred out (100,000 × 100%)	100,000 EUP	100,000 EUP
Equivalent units for ending work in process		
Direct materials (20,000 × 100%).............................	20,000 EUP	
Conversion (20,000 × 25%)		5,000 EUP
Equivalent units of production	120,000 EUP	105,000 EUP

The first row of Exhibit 16.9 reflects units transferred out in April. The roasting department entirely completed its work on the 100,000 units transferred out. These units have 100% of the materials and conversion required, or 100,000 equivalent units of each input (100,000 × 100%).

GenX ended the month with 20,000 partially completed units. For direct materials, the units in ending work in process inventory include all materials required, so there are 20,000 equivalent units (20,000 × 100%) of materials in the unfinished physical units. Regarding conversion, the units in ending work in process inventory include 25% of the conversion required, which implies 5,000 equivalent units of conversion (20,000 × 25%).

The final row reflects the total equivalent units of production, which is whole units of product that could have been manufactured with the amount of inputs used to create some complete and some incomplete units. For GenX, the amount of inputs used to produce 100,000 complete units and to start 20,000 additional units is equivalent to the amount of direct materials in 120,000 whole units and the amount of conversion in 105,000 whole units.

Ken Whitmore/Stone/Getty Images

NEED-TO-KNOW 16-2

EUP—Direct Materials and Conversion (Weighted Average)
C2

A department began the month with 8,000 units in work in process inventory. These units were 100% complete with respect to direct materials and 40% complete with respect to conversion. During the current month, the department started 56,000 units and completed 58,000 units. Ending work in process inventory includes 6,000 units, 100% complete with respect to direct materials and 70% complete with respect to conversion. Use the weighted-average method of process costing to:

1. Compute the department's equivalent units of production for the month for direct materials.

2. Compute the department's equivalent units of production for the month for conversion.

Solution

1. EUP for materials = 58,000 + (6,000 × 100%) = 64,000 EUP

2. EUP for conversion = 58,000 + (6,000 × 70%) = 62,200 EUP

Do More: QS 16-5, QS 16-6, QS 16-10, E 16-4, E 16-8

QC3

Step 3: Compute Cost per Equivalent Unit

Under the weighted-average method, the computation of EUP does not separate the units in beginning inventory from those started this period, as shown above. Similarly, the weighted-average method combines the costs of beginning work in process inventory with the costs incurred in the current period. This total cost is then divided by the equivalent units of production (from step 2), to compute the average cost per equivalent unit. This process is illustrated in

Point: The weighted-average method mixes production activity and costs across two periods.

Point: Managers can examine changes in monthly costs per equivalent unit to help control the production process.

Exhibit 16.10. For direct materials, the cost averages $3.00 per EUP. For conversion, the cost per equivalent unit averages $4.62 per unit.

EXHIBIT 16.10

Cost per Equivalent Unit of Production—Weighted Average

GenX—Roasting Department Cost per Equivalent Unit of Production	Direct Materials	Conversion
Costs of beginning work in process inventory***	$ 81,000	$108,900
Costs incurred this period***	279,000	376,200**
Total costs	$360,000	$485,100
÷ Equivalent units of production (from step 2)	120,000 EUP	105,000 EUP
= Cost per equivalent unit of production	$3.00 per EUP*	$4.62 per EUP†

*$360,000 ÷ 120,000 EUP **$171,000 + $205,200 †$485,100 ÷ 105,000 EUP *** From Exhibit 16.6

Step 4: Assign and Reconcile Costs

The EUP from step 2 and the cost per EUP from step 3 are used in step 4 to assign costs to (a) units that the roasting department completed and transferred to the blending department (100,000 units), and (b) units that remain in process in the roasting department (20,000 units). This is illustrated in Exhibit 16.11.

EXHIBIT 16.11

Report of Costs Accounted For—Weighted Average

GenX—Roasting Department		
Cost of units completed and transferred to blending dept.		
Direct materials (100,000 EUP × $3.00 per EUP)	$300,000	
Conversion (100,000 EUP × $4.62 per EUP)	462,000	
Cost of units completed this period		$762,000
Cost of ending work in process inventory		
Direct materials (20,000 EUP × $3.00 per EUP)	60,000	
Conversion (5,000 EUP × $4.62 per EUP)	23,100	
Cost of ending work in process inventory		83,100
Total costs accounted for		**$845,100**

Cost of Units Completed and Transferred The 100,000 units completed and transferred to the blending department required 100,000 EUP of direct materials and 100,000 EUP of conversion. Thus, we assign $300,000 (100,000 EUP × $3.00 per EUP) of direct materials cost to those units. Similarly, we assign $462,000 (100,000 EUP × $4.62 per EUP) of conversion to those units. The total cost of the 100,000 completed and transferred units is $762,000 ($300,000 + $462,000) and their average cost per unit is $7.62 ($762,000 ÷ 100,000 units).

Cost of Units for Ending Work in Process There are 20,000 incomplete units in work in process inventory at period-end. For direct materials, those units have 20,000 EUP of material (from step 2) at a cost of $3.00 per EUP (from step 3), which yields the materials cost of work in process inventory of $60,000 (20,000 EUP × $3.00 per EUP). For conversion, the in-process units reflect 5,000 EUP (from step 2). Using the $4.62 conversion cost per EUP (from step 3) we obtain conversion costs for in-process inventory of $23,100 (5,000 EUP × $4.62 per EUP). Total cost of work in process inventory at period-end is $83,100 ($60,000 + $23,100).

As a check, management verifies that total costs assigned to units completed and transferred plus the costs of units in process (from Exhibit 16.11) equal the costs incurred by production. Exhibit 16.12 shows the costs incurred by production this period. We then reconcile the *costs accounted for* in Exhibit 16.11 with the *costs to account for* in Exhibit 16.12.

EXHIBIT 16.12

Report of Costs to Account For—Weighted Average

GenX—Roasting Department		
Cost of beginning work in process inventory		
Direct materials	$ 81,000	
Conversion	108,900	$ 189,900
Cost incurred this period		
Direct materials	279,000	
Conversion	376,200	655,200
Total costs to account for		**$845,100**

The roasting department manager is responsible for $845,100 in costs: $189,000 from beginning work in process plus $655,200 of materials and conversion incurred in the period. At period-end, that manager must show where these costs are assigned. The roasting department manager reports that $83,100 are assigned to units in process and $762,000 are assigned to units transferred out to the blending department (per Exhibit 16.11). The sum of these amounts equals $845,100. Thus, the total *costs to account for* equal the total *costs accounted for* (minor differences can sometimes occur from rounding).

NEED-TO-KNOW 16-3

Cost per EUP—Conversion, with Transfer

C3

A department began the month with conversion costs of $65,000 in its beginning work in process inventory. During the current month, the department incurred $55,000 of conversion costs. Equivalent units of production for conversion for the month was 15,000 units. The department completed and transferred 12,000 units to the next department. The department uses the weighted-average method of process costing.

1. Compute the department's cost per equivalent unit for conversion for the month.

2. Compute the department's conversion cost of units transferred to the next department for the month.

Solution

1. ($65,000 + $55,000)/15,000 units = $8.00 per EUP for conversion

2. 12,000 units × $8.00 = $96,000 conversion cost transferred to next department

Do More: QS 16-11, QS 16-13, E 16-6

QC4

Process Cost Summary

An important managerial accounting report for a process costing system is the **process cost summary** (also called *production report*), which is prepared separately for each process or production department. Three reasons for the summary are to (1) help department managers control and monitor their departments, (2) help factory managers evaluate department managers' performances, and (3) provide cost information for financial statements. A process cost summary achieves these purposes by describing the costs charged to each department, reporting the equivalent units of production achieved by each department, and determining the costs assigned to each department's output. For our purposes, it is prepared using a combination of Exhibits 16.7, 16.9, 16.10, 16.11, and 16.12.

Point: The key report in a job order costing system is a job cost sheet, which reports manufacturing costs per job. A process cost summary reports manufacturing costs per equivalent unit of a process or department.

The process cost summary for the roasting department is shown in Exhibit 16.13. The report is divided into three sections. Section ① lists the total costs charged to the department, including direct materials and conversion costs incurred, as well as the cost of the beginning work in process inventory. Section ② describes the equivalent units of production for the department. Equivalent units for materials and conversion are in separate columns. It also reports direct materials and conversion costs per equivalent unit. Section ③ allocates total costs among units worked on in the period. The $762,000 is the total cost of the 100,000 units transferred out of the roasting department to the blending department. The $83,100 is the cost of the 20,000 partially completed units in ending inventory in the roasting department. The assigned costs are then added to show that the total $845,100 cost charged to the roasting department in section ① is now assigned to the units in section ③.

EXHIBIT 16.13

Process Cost Summary (Weighted-Average)

GenX COMPANY—ROASTING DEPARTMENT
Process Cost Summary (Weighted-Average Method)
For Month Ended April 30, 2015

① **Costs Charged to Production**

Costs of beginning work in process		
Direct materials	$ 81,000	
Conversion	108,900	$ 189,900
Costs incurred this period		
Direct materials	279,000	
Conversion	376,200	655,200
Total costs to account for		$845,100

② **Unit Information**

Units to account for:		Units accounted for:	
Beginning work in process	30,000	Completed and transferred out	100,000
Units started this period	90,000	Ending work in process	20,000
Total units to account for	120,000	Total units accounted for	120,000

Equivalent Units of Production (EUP)	**Direct Materials**	**Conversion**
Units completed and transferred out (100,000 × 100%)	100,000 EUP	100,000 EUP
Units of ending work in process		
Direct materials (20,000 × 100%)	20,000 EUP	
Conversion (20,000 × 25%)		5,000 EUP
Equivalent units of production	120,000 EUP	105,000 EUP

Cost per EUP	**Direct Materials**	**Conversion**
Costs of beginning work in process	$ 81,000	$108,900
Costs incurred this period	279,000	376,200
Total costs	$360,000	$485,100
÷EUP	120,000 EUP	105,000 EUP
Cost per EUP	$3.00 per EUP	$4.62 per EUP

③ **Cost Assignment and Reconciliation**

Costs transferred out (cost of goods manufactured)		
Direct materials (100,000 EUP × $3.00 per EUP)	$300,000	
Conversion (100,000 EUP × $4.62 per EUP)	462,000	$ 762,000
Costs of ending work in process		
Direct materials (20,000 EUP × $3.00 per EUP)	60,000	
Conversion (5,000 EUP × $4.62 per EUP)	23,100	83,100
Total costs accounted for		$845,100

(reconciled)

ACCOUNTING AND REPORTING FOR PROCESS COSTING

In this section we illustrate the journal entries to account for the operations of a process manufacturer. We continue to focus on GenX Company's roasting department. Exhibit 16.14 illustrates the flow of costs for GenX. Materials, labor, and overhead costs flow into the manufacturing processes. GenX keeps separate Work in Process Inventory accounts for the roasting and blending departments; when goods are packaged and ready for sale, their costs are transferred to the Finished Goods Inventory account.

Like a job order costing system, a process costing system relies on source documents. For example, *materials requisitions* are used to signal the use of direct and indirect materials. *Time tickets* are used to record the use of direct and indirect labor. While some companies might combine direct labor and overhead into conversion costs when computing costs per equivalent unit (as we showed previously), labor and overhead costs are accounted for separately within the company's accounts. In addition, since overhead costs typically cannot be tied to individual processes, but rather benefit all processes or departments, most companies use a single Factory Overhead account to accumulate actual and applied overhead costs.

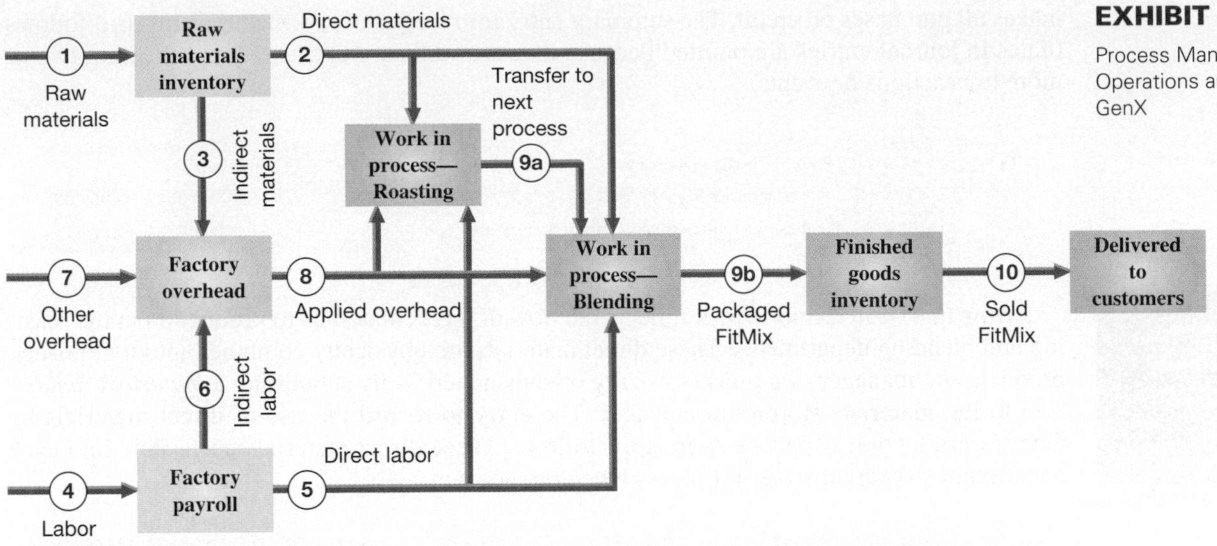

EXHIBIT 16.14

Process Manufacturing Operations and Costs: GenX

As with job order costing, process manufacturers must allocate, or apply, overhead to processes. This requires such companies to find good *allocation bases,* such as direct labor hours or machine hours used. With increasing automation, companies with process operations use fewer direct labor hours and thus are more likely to use machine hours to allocate overhead.

For some companies, a single allocation base will not provide good overhead allocations. For example, direct labor cost might be a good allocation base for GenX's roasting department, but not for its blending department, depending on the amounts of direct labor used in each of those departments. As a result, a process manufacturer can use different overhead allocation rates for different production departments. However, all applied overhead is credited to a single Factory Overhead account.

Exhibit 16.15 presents cost data for GenX. Roasting department costs are from Exhibit 16.6. We use these data next to show the journal entries in a process costing system.

EXHIBIT 16.15

Cost Data—GenX

Raw materials inventory (March 31)	$100,000
Beginning work in process inventories (March 31)	
Work in process—Roasting	$189,900
Work in process—Blending	151,688
Materials purchased (on account)	$400,000
Materials requisitions during April	
Direct materials—Roasting	$279,000
Direct materials—Blending	102,000
Indirect materials	71,250
Factory payroll for April	
Direct labor—Roasting	$171,000
Direct labor—Blending	183,160
Indirect labor	78,350
Other actual overhead costs during April	
Insurance expense—Factory	$ 11,930
Utilities payable—Factory	7,945
Depreciation expense—Factory equipment	220,650
Other (paid in cash)	21,875

Accounting for Materials Costs

P1 Record the flow of materials costs in process costing.

In Exhibit 16.14, arrow line ① reflects the arrival of materials at GenX's factory. These materials include organic peanuts, chocolate pieces, dried fruits, oil, salt, and packaging. They also include supplies for the production support office. GenX uses a perpetual inventory system and makes all purchases on credit. The summary entry for receipts of raw materials in April follows (dates in journal entries are omitted because they are summary entries, often reflecting two or more transactions or events).

Assets = Liabilities + Equity
+400,000 +400,000

①	Raw Materials Inventory	400,000	
	Accounts Payable		400,000
	Acquired materials on credit for factory use.		

Natalia Kolesnikova/AFP/Getty Images

Arrow line ② in Exhibit 16.14 reflects the flow of direct materials to production in the roasting and blending departments. These direct materials are physically combined into the finished product. The manager of a process usually obtains materials by submitting a *materials requisition* to the materials storeroom manager. The entry to record the use of direct materials by GenX's production departments in April follows. These direct materials costs flow into each department's separate Work in Process Inventory account.

Assets = Liabilities + Equity
+279,000
+102,000
−381,000

②	Work in Process—Roasting	279,000	
	Work in Process—Blending	102,000	
	Raw Materials Inventory		381,000
	To assign costs of direct materials used in production.		

Example: What types of materials might the flow of arrow line ③ in Exhibit 16.14 reflect? *Answer:* Goggles, gloves, protective clothing, oil, salt, and cleaning supplies.

In Exhibit 16.14, arrow line ③ reflects the flow of indirect materials from the storeroom to factory overhead. These materials are not clearly linked with any specific production process or department but are used to support overall production activity. As these costs cannot be linked directly to either the roasting or blending departments, they are recorded in GenX's single Factory Overhead account. The following entry records the cost of indirect materials used by GenX in April.

③	Factory Overhead	71,250	
	Raw Materials Inventory		71,250
	To record indirect materials used in April.		

Accounting for Labor Costs

P2
Record the flow of labor costs in process costing.

Exhibit 16.14 shows GenX's factory payroll costs as reflected in arrow line ④. Exhibit 16.15 shows costs of $171,000 for roasting department direct labor, $183,160 for blending department direct labor, and $78,350 for indirect labor. This total payroll of $432,510 is a product cost, and it is allocated to either Work in Process Inventory or Factory Overhead, as we show next.

Time reports from the production departments and the production support office trigger payroll entries. (For simplicity, we do not separately identify withholdings and additional payroll taxes for employees.) In a process operation, the direct labor of a production department includes all labor used exclusively by that department. This is the case even if the labor is not applied to the product itself. If a production department in a process operation, for instance, has a full-time manager and a full-time maintenance worker, their salaries are direct labor costs of that process and are not factory overhead.

Arrow line ⑤ in Exhibit 16.14 shows GenX's use of direct labor. The following entry then records direct labor used. These direct labor costs flow into each department's separate Work in Process Inventory account.

Assets = Liabilities + Equity
+171,000 +354,160
+183,160

⑤	Work in Process Inventory—Roasting	171,000	
	Work in Process Inventory—Blending	183,160	
	Factory Payroll Payable		354,160
	To record direct labor used in production.		

Arrow line ⑥ in Exhibit 16.14 reflects GenX's indirect labor costs. These employees provide clerical, maintenance, and other services that help production in both the roasting and blending departments. For example, they order materials, deliver them to the factory floor, repair equipment, operate and program computers used in production, keep payroll and other production records, clean up, and move goods across departments. The following entry records these indirect labor costs.

Point: A department's indirect labor cost might include an allocated portion of the salary of a manager who supervises two or more departments. Allocation of costs between departments is discussed in a later chapter.

⑥	Factory Overhead	78,350	
	Factory Payroll Payable		78,350
	To record indirect labor as overhead.		

After GenX posts these entries for direct and indirect labor, the Factory Payroll Payable account has a balance of \$432,510 (\$354,160 + \$78,350). The entry below shows the payment of this total payroll. After this entry, the Factory Payroll Payable account has a zero balance.

④	Factory Payroll Payable..........................	432,510	
	Cash		432,510
	To record factory wages for April.		

Assets = Liabilities + Equity
−432,510 −432,510

Accounting for Factory Overhead

P3 Record the flow of factory overhead costs in process costing.

Overhead costs other than indirect materials and indirect labor are reflected by arrow line ⑦ in Exhibit 16.14. These overhead items include the costs of insuring production assets, renting the factory building, using factory utilities, and depreciating factory equipment not directly related to a specific process. The following entry records these other overhead costs for April.

⑦	Factory Overhead	262,400	
	Prepaid Insurance		11,930
	Utilities Payable		7,945
	Cash		21,875
	Accumulated Depreciation—Factory Equipment ...		220,650
	To record other overhead costs incurred in April.		

Applying Overhead to Work in Process Recall that companies use *predetermined overhead rates* to apply overhead. These rates are estimated at the beginning of a period and used to apply overhead during the period. The application of overhead allows managers to obtain up-to-date estimates of the costs of their processes during the period. This is important for process costing, where goods are transferred across departments before the entire production process is complete.

Point: The time it takes to process (cycle) products through a process is sometimes used to allocate costs.

Arrow line ⑧ in Exhibit 16.14 reflects the application of factory overhead to the two production departments. Factory overhead is applied to processes by relating overhead cost to another variable such as direct labor hours or machine hours used. In many situations, a single allocation basis such as direct labor hours (or a single rate for the entire plant) fails to provide useful allocations. As a result, management may use different rates for different production departments. In our example, GenX applies overhead on the basis of direct labor cost as shown in Exhibit 16.16.

EXHIBIT 16.16
Applying Factory Overhead

Production Department	Direct Labor Cost	Predetermined Rate	Overhead Applied
Roasting	\$171,000	120%	\$205,200
Blending	183,160	120	219,792
Total............			\$424,992

GenX records its applied overhead with the following entry.

(8)	Work in Process Inventory—Roasting	205,200	
	Work in Process Inventory—Blending	219,792	
	Factory Overhead		424,992
	Applied overhead costs to production departments at 120% of direct labor cost.		

Decision Ethics

Budget Officer You are working to identify the direct and indirect costs of a new processing department that has several machines. This department's manager instructs you to classify a majority of the costs as indirect to take advantage of the direct labor-based overhead allocation method so it will be charged a lower amount of overhead (because of its small direct labor cost). This would penalize other departments with higher allocations. It also will cause the performance ratings of managers in these other departments to suffer. What action do you take? ■ [Answers follow the chapter's Summary.]

NEED-TO-KNOW 16-4

Overhead Rate and Costs

P1 P2 P3

Tower Mfg. estimates it will incur $200,000 of total overhead costs during 2015. Tower allocates overhead based on machine hours; it estimates it will use a total of 10,000 machine hours during 2015. During February 2015, the assembly department of Tower Mfg. uses 375 machine hours. In addition, Tower incurred actual overhead costs as follows during February: indirect materials, $1,800; indirect labor, $5,700; depreciation on factory equipment, $8,000; factory utilities, $500.

1. Compute the company's predetermined overhead rate for 2015.
2. Prepare journal entries to record (a) overhead applied for the assembly department for the month and (b) actual overhead costs used during the month.

Solution

1. Predetermined overhead rate = Estimated overhead costs ÷ Estimated activity base = $200,000/10,000 = $20 per machine hour.

2a.

Work in Process Inventory—Assembly	7,500	
Factory Overhead		7,500
To record applied overhead (375 hours × $20 per hour).		

2b.

Factory Overhead	16,000	
Raw Materials Inventory		1,800
Factory Payroll Payable		5,700
Accumulated Depreciation—Factory Equipment		8,000
Utilities Payable		500
To record actual overhead.		

Do More: QS 16-25, E 16-23, E 16-25

QC5

Accounting for Transfers

P4 Record the transfer of goods across departments, to Finished Goods Inventory, and to Cost of Goods Sold.

Assets = Liabilities + Equity
+762,000
−762,000

Transfers across Departments Arrow line (9a) in Exhibit 16.14 reflects the transfer of units from the roasting department to the blending department. The process cost summary for the roasting department (Exhibit 16.13) shows that the 100,000 units transferred to the blending department are assigned a cost of $762,000. The entry to record this transfer follows.

(9a)	Work in Process Inventory—Blending	762,000	
	Work in Process Inventory—Roasting		762,000
	To record the transfer of 100,000 units from the roasting department to the blending department.		

Units and costs *transferred out* of the roasting department are *transferred into* the blending department. Exhibit 16.17 shows this transfer using T-accounts for the separate Work in Process Inventory accounts (first in units and then in dollars).

EXHIBIT 16.17

Production and Cost Activity—Transfer to Blending Department

Roasting Department—Units		
Beg. inv.	30,000 units	
Started	90,000 units	
Total	120,000 units	**100,000 units transferred out** → Blending Dept.
End. inv.	20,000 units	

Blending Department—Units		
Beg. inv.	12,000 units	
Transferred in	**100,000 units**	
Total	112,000 units	97,000 units transferred to Finished Goods
End. inv.	15,000 units	

WIP—Roasting Dept.		
Beg. inv.*	189,900	
DM	279,000	
Conv.	376,200	
Total	**845,100**	**762,000 Transferred out** → WIP—Blending Dept.
End. Inv.	83,100	

*$81,000 direct materials + $108,900 conversion

WIP—Blending Dept.		
Beg. inv.†	151,688	
Transferred in	**762,000**	
DM	102,000	
Conv.	402,952	
Total	**1,418,640**	

†$91,440 transferred-in + $10,000 DM + $50,248 conversion

As Exhibit 16.17 shows, the blending department began the month with 12,000 units in beginning inventory, with a related cost of $151,688. In computing its production activity and costs, the blending department must also consider the units and costs transferred in from the roasting department, as shown in Exhibit 16.17. The 100,000 units transferred in from the roasting department, and their related costs of $762,000, are added to the blending department's number of units and separate Work in Process (WIP) Inventory account.

The blending department then adds additional direct materials and conversion costs. The blending department incurred direct materials costs of $102,000 and conversion costs of $402,952 during the month. (Although not illustrated here, the concepts and methods used in this second department would be similar to those we showed in detail for the first department.)

Accounting for Transfer to Finished Goods Arrow line (9b) in Exhibit 16.14 reflects the transfer of units and their related costs from the blending department to finished goods inventory. At the end of the month, the blending department transferred 97,000 completed units, with a related cost of $1,262,940, to finished goods. The entry to record this transfer follows.

(9b)	Finished Goods Inventory	1,262,940	
	Work in Process Inventory—Blending		1,262,940
	To record transfer of completed goods.		

Assets = Liabilities + Equity
+1,262,940
−1,262,940

Accounting for Transfer to Cost of Goods Sold Arrow line (10) reflects the sale of finished goods. Assume that GenX sold 106,000 units of FitMix this period, and that its beginning finished goods inventory was 26,000 units with a cost of $338,520. Also assume that its ending finished goods inventory consists of 20,000 units at a cost of $260,400. Using this information, cost of goods sold is computed as in Exhibit 16.18.

Finished Goods Inventory		
Beg. bal.	338,520	
COGM	1,262,940	
Avail.	1,601,460	**COGS 1,341,060**
End. bal.	260,400	

EXHIBIT 16.18

Cost of Goods Sold

Beginning finished goods inventory	$ 338,520
+ Cost of goods manufactured this period	1,262,940
= Cost of goods available for sale	1,601,460
− Ending finished goods inventory	260,400
= Cost of goods sold	$1,341,060

The summary entry to record cost of goods sold for this period follows:

Assets	= Liabilities	+ Equity
−1,341,060		−1,341,060

(10)	Cost of Goods Sold	1,341,060	
	Finished Goods Inventory		1,341,060
	To record cost of goods sold for April.		

Trends in Process Operations

Some recent trends in process operations are discussed in the following paragraphs.

Process Design Management concerns with production efficiency can lead companies to entirely reorganize production processes. For example, instead of producing different types of computers in a series of departments, a separate work center for each computer can be established in one department. The process cost system is then changed to account for each work center's costs.

Just-in-Time Production Companies are increasingly adopting just-in-time techniques. With a just-in-time inventory system, inventory levels can be minimal. If raw materials are not ordered or received until needed, a Raw Materials Inventory account might be unnecessary. Instead, materials cost is immediately debited to the Work in Process Inventory account. Similarly, a Finished Goods Inventory account may not be needed. Instead, cost of finished goods may be immediately debited to the Cost of Goods Sold account.

Automation Companies are increasingly automating their production processes and using robots. For example, **Volkswagen** recently began using robots on tasks that are hard for humans to perform. This automation resulted in reduced direct labor costs and a healthier workforce.

Continuous Processing In some companies, materials move continuously through the manufacturing process. **Pepsi Bottling** uses a process in which inventory moves continuously through the system. In these cases, a **materials consumption report** summarizes the materials used and replaces materials requisitions.

Services Service-based businesses are increasingly prevalent. For routine, standardized services like oil changes and simple tax returns, computing costs based on the process is simpler and more useful than a cost per individual job. More complex service companies use process departments to perform specific tasks for consumers. Hospitals, for example, have radiology and physical therapy facilities, each with special equipment and trained employees. When patients need services, they are processed through departments to receive prescribed care.

Customer Orientation Focus on customer orientation also leads to improved processes. A manufacturer of control devices improved quality and reduced production time by forming teams to study processes and suggest improvements. An ice cream maker studied customer tastes to develop a more pleasing ice cream texture.

GLOBAL VIEW

As part of a series of global environmental goals, **Anheuser-Busch InBev** set targets to reduce its water usage. The company uses massive amounts of water in beer production and in its cleaning and cooling processes. To meet these goals, the company followed recent trends in process operations. These included extensive redesign of production processes and the use of advanced technology to increase efficiency at wastewater treatment plants. As a result water usage decreased by almost 37 percent in its global operations.

Sustainability and Accounting As society becomes more attuned to health issues, businesses must respond. As described in the opener to this chapter, **Kar's Nuts** met demand for healthier snacks by offering trail mixes based on all-natural ingredients. The company also takes precautions to ensure its production process is allergen-free. For example, when transitioning its production line from products with allergens, such as wheat, workers perform a detailed cleaning of all conveyors and packaging equipment. These cleaning efforts add costs but help Kar's fulfill its obligations to its customers and ensure a sustainable product and business.

Hybrid Costing System — Decision Analysis

A2 Explain and illustrate a hybrid costing system.

This chapter explained the process costing system and contrasted it with the job order costing system. Many organizations use a *hybrid system* that contains features of both process and job order operations. A recent survey of manufacturers revealed that a majority use hybrid systems (also called *operation cost systems*).

To illustrate, consider a car manufacturer's assembly line. On one hand, the line resembles a process operation in that the assembly steps for each car are nearly identical. On the other hand, the specifications of most cars have several important differences. At the **Ford** Mustang plant, each car assembled on a given day can be different from the previous car and the next car. This means that the costs of materials (subassemblies or components) for each car can differ. Accordingly, while the conversion costs (direct labor and overhead) can be accounted for using a process costing system, the component costs (direct materials) are accounted for using a job order system (separately for each car or type of car).

A hybrid system of processes requires a *hybrid costing system* to properly cost products or services. In the Ford plant, the assembly costs per car are readily determined using process costing. The costs of additional components can then be added to the assembly costs to determine each car's total cost (as in job order costing). To illustrate, consider the following information for a daily assembly process at Ford.

Assembly process costs	
Direct materials	$10.6 million
Conversion costs	$12.0 million
Number of cars assembled	1,000
Costs of three different types of steering wheels	$240, $330, $480
Costs of three different types of seats	$620, $840, $1,360

The assembly process costs $22,600 per car. Depending on the type of steering wheel and seats the customer requests, the cost of a car can range from $23,460 to $24,440 (a $980 difference).

Today companies are increasingly trying to standardize processes while attempting to meet individual customer needs. To the extent that differences among individual customers' requests are large, understanding the costs to satisfy those requests is important. Thus, monitoring and controlling both process and job order costs are important.

Decision Ethics

Entrepreneur You operate a process production company making similar products for three different customers. One customer demands 100% quality inspection of products at your location before shipping. The added costs of that inspection are spread across all customers, not just the one demanding it. If you charge the added costs to that customer, you could lose that customer and experience a loss. Moreover, your other two customers have agreed to pay 110% of full costs. What actions (if any) do you take? ■ [Answers follow the chapter's Summary.]

NEED-TO-KNOW

COMPREHENSIVE 1

Weighted-Average Method

Pennsylvania Company produces a product that passes through two processes: grinding and mixing. Information related to its grinding department manufacturing activities for July follows. The company uses the weighted-average method of process costing.

Grinding Department	
Raw Materials	
Beginning inventory	$100,000
Raw materials purchased on credit	211,400
Direct materials used	(190,000)
Indirect materials used	(51,400)
Ending inventory	$ 70,000
Factory Payroll	
Direct labor incurred	$ 55,500
Indirect labor incurred	50,625
Total payroll	$106,125
Factory Overhead	
Indirect materials used	$ 51,400
Indirect labor used	50,625
Other overhead costs	71,725
Total factory overhead incurred	$173,750
Factory Overhead Applied	
Overhead applied (200% of direct labor)	$111,000

Grinding Department	
Beginning work in process inventory (units)	5,000
Percentage completed—Materials	100%
Percentage completed—Conversion	70%
Beginning work in process inventory (costs)	
Direct materials used	$ 20,000
Direct labor incurred	9,600
Overhead applied (200% of direct labor)	19,200
Total costs of beginning work in process	$ 48,800
Units started this period	20,000
Units transferred to mixing this period	17,000
Ending work in process inventory (units)	8,000
Percentage completed—Materials	100%
Percentage completed—Conversion	20%

Required

Complete the requirements below for the grinding department.

1. Prepare a physical flow reconciliation for July.
2. Compute the equivalent units of production in July for direct materials and conversion.
3. Compute the costs per equivalent units of production in July for direct materials and conversion.
4. Prepare a report of costs accounted for and a report of costs to account for.

PLANNING THE SOLUTION

- Track the physical flow to determine the number of units completed in July.
- Compute the equivalent units of production for direct materials and conversion.
- Compute the costs per equivalent unit of production with respect to direct materials and conversion, and determine the cost per unit for each.
- Compute the total cost of the goods transferred to mixing by using the equivalent units and unit costs. Determine (a) the cost of the beginning work in process inventory, (b) the materials and conversion costs added to the beginning work in process inventory, and (c) the materials and conversion costs added to the units started and completed in the month.

SOLUTION

1. Physical flow reconciliation.

Units to Account For		Units Accounted For	
Beginning work in process inventory	5,000 units	Units completed and transferred out	17,000 units
Units started this period	20,000 units	Ending work in process inventory	8,000 units
Total units to account for	**25,000 units**	Total units accounted for	**25,000 units**

reconciled

2. Equivalent units of production (Weighted-average).

Equivalent Units of Production	Direct Materials	Conversion
Equivalent units completed and transferred out ...	17,000 EUP	17,000 EUP
Equivalent units in ending work in process		
Direct materials (8,000 × 100%)	8,000 EUP	
Conversion (8,000 × 20%)		1,600 EUP
Equivalent units of production	25,000 EUP	18,600 EUP

3. Costs per equivalent unit of production (Weighted-average).

Costs per Equivalent Unit of Production	Direct Materials	Conversion
Costs of beginning work in process	$ 20,000	$ 28,800
Costs incurred this period	190,000	166,500*
Total costs	$210,000	$195,300
÷ Equivalent units of production (from part 2)	25,000 EUP	18,600 EUP
= Costs per equivalent unit of production	$8.40 per EUP	$10.50 per EUP

*Direct labor of $55,500 + overhead applied of $111,000

4. Reports of costs accounted for and of costs to account for (Weighted-average).

Report of Costs Accounted For		
Cost of units transferred out (cost of goods manufactured)		
Direct materials ($8.40 per EUP × 17,000 EUP)	$142,800	
Conversion ($10.50 per EUP × 17,000 EUP)	178,500	
Cost of units completed this period		$ 321,300
Cost of ending work in process inventory		
Direct materials ($8.40 per EUP × 8,000 EUP)	67,200	
Conversion ($10.50 per EUP × 1,600 EUP)	16,800	
Cost of ending work in process inventory		84,000
Total costs accounted for		**$405,300**

Report of Costs to Account For		
Cost of beginning work in process inventory		
Direct materials	$ 20,000	
Conversion	28,800	$ 48,800
Cost incurred this period		
Direct materials	190,000	
Conversion	166,500	356,500
Total costs to account for		**$405,300**

reconciled

NEED-TO-KNOW
COMPREHENSIVE 2
FIFO Method

Refer to the information given for the weighted-average method version of this Comprehensive Need-To-Know. For the grinding department, complete requirements 1 through 4 using the FIFO method. (Round the cost per equivalent unit of conversion to two decimal places.)

SOLUTION

1. Physical flow reconciliation (FIFO).

Units to Account For		Units Accounted For	
Beginning work in process inventory	5,000 units	Units completed and transferred out	17,000 units
Units started this period	20,000 units	Ending work in process inventory	8,000 units
Total units to account for	**25,000 units**	Total units accounted for	**25,000 units**

reconciled

2. Equivalent units of production (FIFO).

Equivalent Units of Production	Direct Materials	Conversion
(a) Equivalent units complete beginning work in process		
Direct materials (5,000 × 0%)	0 EUP	
Conversion (5,000 × 30%)		1,500 EUP
(b) Equivalent units started and completed	12,000 EUP	12,000 EUP
(c) Equivalent units in ending work in process		
Direct materials (8,000 × 100%)	8,000 EUP	
Conversion (8,000 × 20%)		1,600 EUP
Equivalent units of production	20,000 EUP	15,100 EUP

3. Costs per equivalent unit of production (FIFO).

Costs per Equivalent Unit of Production	Direct Materials	Conversion
Costs incurred this period	$190,000	$166,500
÷ Equivalent units of production (from part 2)	20,000 EUP	15,100 EUP
= Costs per equivalent unit of production	$9.50 per EUP	$11.03 per EUP**

*Direct labor of $55,500 plus overhead applied of $111,000 **Rounded

4. Reports of costs accounted for and of costs to account for (FIFO).

Report of Costs Accounted For		
Cost of units transferred out (cost of goods manufactured)		
Cost of beginning work in process inventory		$ 48,800
Cost to complete beginning work in process		
Direct materials ($9.50 per EUP × 0 EUP)	$ 0	
Conversion ($11.03 per EUP × 1,500 EUP)	16,545	16,545
Cost of units started and completed this period		
Direct materials ($9.50 per EUP × 12,000 EUP)	114,000	
Conversion ($11.03 per EUP × 12,000 EUP)	132,360	246,360
Total cost of units finished this period		311,705
Cost of ending work in process inventory		
Direct materials ($9.50 per EUP × 8,000 EUP)	76,000	
Conversion ($11.03 per EUP × 1,600 EUP)	17,648	
Total cost of ending work in process inventory		93,648
Total costs accounted for		**$405,353**
Report of Costs to Account For		
Cost of beginning work in process inventory		
Direct materials	$ 20,000	
Conversion	28,800	$ 48,800
Costs incurred this period		
Direct materials	190,000	
Conversion	166,500	356,500
Total costs to account for		**$405,300**

reconciled (with $53 rounding difference)

NEED-TO-KNOW

COMPREHENSIVE 3

Journal Entries for Process Costing

Garcia Manufacturing produces a product that passes through a molding process and then through an assembly process. Partial information related to its manufacturing activities for July follows.

Direct materials		**Factory Overhead Applied**	
Raw materials purchased on credit	$400,000	Molding (150% of direct labor)	$ 63,000
Direct materials used—Molding	190,000	Assembly (200% of direct labor)	110,750
Direct materials used—Assembly	88,600	Total factory overhead applied	$173,750
Direct Labor		**Cost Transfers**	
Direct labor—Molding	$ 42,000	From molding to assembly	$277,200
Direct labor—Assembly	55,375	From assembly to finished goods	578,400
Factory Overhead (Actual costs)		From finished goods to cost of goods sold	506,100
Indirect materials used	$ 51,400		
Indirect labor used	50,625		
Other overhead costs	71,725		
Total factory overhead incurred	$173,750		

Required

Prepare summary journal entries to record the transactions and events of July for: (a) raw materials purchases, (b) direct materials usage, (c) indirect materials usage, (d) direct labor usage, (e) indirect labor usage, (f) other overhead costs (credit Other Accounts), (g) application of overhead to the two departments, (h) transfer of partially completed goods from molding to assembly, (i) transfer of finished goods out of assembly, and (j) the cost of goods sold.

SOLUTION

Summary journal entries for the transactions and events in July.

	Account	Debit	Credit
a.	Raw Materials Inventory	400,000	
	Accounts Payable		400,000
	To record raw materials purchases.		
b.	Work in Process Inventory—Molding	190,000	
	Work in Process Inventory—Assembly	88,600	
	Raw Materials Inventory		278,600
	To record direct materials usage.		
c.	Factory Overhead	51,400	
	Raw Materials Inventory		51,400
	To record indirect materials usage.		
d.	Work in Process Inventory—Molding	42,000	
	Work in Process Inventory—Assembly	55,375	
	Factory Payroll Payable		97,375
	To record direct labor usage.		
e.	Factory Overhead	50,625	
	Factory Payroll Payable		50,625
	To record indirect labor usage.		
f.	Factory Overhead	71,725	
	Other Accounts		71,725
	To record other overhead costs.		
g.	Work in Process Inventory—Molding	63,000	
	Work in Process Inventory—Assembly	110,750	
	Factory Overhead		173,750
	To record application of overhead.		
h.	Work in Process Inventory—Assembly	277,200	
	Work in Process Inventory—Molding		277,200
	To record transfer of partially completed goods from molding to assembly.		
i.	Finished Goods Inventory	578,400	
	Work in Process Inventory—Assembly		578,400
	To record transfer of finished goods out of assembly.		
j.	Cost of Goods Sold	506,100	
	Finished Goods Inventory		506,100
	To record cost of goods sold.		

APPENDIX

16A FIFO Method of Process Costing

The FIFO method of process costing assigns costs to units assuming a first-in, first-out flow of product. The key difference between the FIFO and weighted-average methods lies in the treatment of beginning work in process inventory. Under the weighted-average method, the number of units and the costs in beginning work in process inventory are combined with production activity in the current period to compute

C4 *Appendix*—Describe accounting for production activity and preparation of a process cost summary using FIFO.

costs per equivalent unit. Thus, the weighted-average method combines production activity across two periods.

The FIFO method, in contrast, focuses on production activity *in the current period only*. The FIFO method assumes that the units that were in process at the beginning of the period are completed during the current period. Thus, under the FIFO method equivalent units of production are computed as shown in Exhibit 16A.1.

EXHIBIT 16A.1

Computing EUP—FIFO Method

Equivalent units of production (EUP)	=	Number of equivalent units needed to complete beginning work in process inventory	+	Number of whole units started, completed, and transferred to the next department*	+	Number of equivalent units in ending work in process inventory

*Or to Finished Goods Inventory

In computing cost per equivalent unit, the FIFO method ignores the cost of beginning work in process inventory. Instead, FIFO uses *only the costs incurred in the current period*, as shown in Exhibit 16A.2.

EXHIBIT 16A.2

Cost per EUP—FIFO Method

$$\text{Cost per EUP (FIFO)} = \frac{\text{Manufacturing costs added during the current period}}{\text{Equivalent units of production during current period}}$$

We use the data in Exhibit 16A.3 to illustrate the FIFO method for GenX's roasting department.

EXHIBIT 16A.3

Production Data—Roasting Department

GenX—Roasting Department

Beginning work in process inventory (March 31)	
Units of product	30,000 units
Percentage of completion—Direct materials	100%
Percentage of completion—Conversion costs	65%
Direct materials costs	$ 81,000
Conversion costs	$108,900
Activities during the current period (April)	
Units started this period	90,000 units
Units transferred out (completed)	100,000 units
Direct materials costs	$279,000
Direct labor costs	$171,000
Factory overhead costs applied (120% of direct labor)	$205,200
Ending work in process inventory (April 30)	
Units of product	20,000 units
Percentage of completion—Direct materials	100%
Percentage of completion—Conversion	25%

Exhibit 16A.3 shows selected information from GenX's roasting department for the month of April. Accounting for a department's activity for a period includes four steps: (1) determine physical flow, (2) compute equivalent units, (3) compute cost per equivalent unit, and (4) determine cost assignment and reconciliation. This appendix describes each of these steps using the FIFO method for process costing.

Step 1: Determine Physical Flow of Units A *physical flow reconciliation* is a report that reconciles (1) the physical units started in a period with (2) the physical units completed in that period. The physical flow reconciliation for GenX's roasting department is shown in Exhibit 16A.4 for April.

EXHIBIT 16A.4

Physical Flow Reconciliation

GenX—Roasting Department

Units to Account For		Units Accounted For	
Beginning work in process inventory	30,000 units	Units completed and transferred out	100,000 units
Units started this period	90,000 units	Ending work in process inventory	20,000 units
Total units to account for	**120,000 units**	Total units accounted for	**120,000 units**

reconciled

Step 2: Compute Equivalent Units of Production—FIFO Exhibit 16A.4 shows that the roasting department completed 100,000 units during the month. The FIFO method assumes that the units in beginning inventory were the first units completed during the month. Thus, FIFO assumes that of the 100,000 completed units, 30,000 consist of units in beginning work in process inventory that were completed during the month. This means that 70,000 (100,000 − 30,000) units were both started and completed during the month. This also means that 20,000 units were started but not completed during the month (90,000 units started − 70,000 units started and completed). Exhibit 16A.5 shows how units flowed through the roasting department, assuming FIFO.

EXHIBIT 16A.5

FIFO—Flow of Units

Roasting Department—Units		
Beg. inv.	30,000	→ 30,000 Completed and transferred out
Started	90,000	70,000 Started and completed
Total	120,000	
		100,000 Transferred out
End. inv.	20,000	

In computing the equivalent units of production, the roasting department must consider these three distinct groups of units:

- Units in beginning work in process inventory (30,000).
- Units started and completed during the month (70,000).
- Units in ending work in process inventory (20,000).

GenX's roasting department then computes equivalent units of production under FIFO as shown in Exhibit 16A.6. We compute EUP for each of the three distinct groups of units, and sum them to find total EUP.

EXHIBIT 16A.6

Equivalent Units of Production—FIFO

GenX—Roasting Department Equivalent Units of Production	Direct Materials	Conversion
(a) Equivalent units to complete beginning work in process		
Direct materials (30,000 × 0%)	0 EUP	
Conversion (30,000 × 35%)		10,500 EUP
(b) Equivalent units started and completed*	70,000 EUP	70,000 EUP
(c) Equivalent units in ending work in process		
Direct materials (20,000 × 100%)	20,000 EUP	
Conversion (20,000 × 25%)		5,000 EUP
Equivalent units of production	90,000 EUP	85,500 EUP

*Units completed this period	100,000 units
Less units in beginning work in process	30,000 units
Units started and completed this period	70,000 units

Direct Materials To calculate the equivalent units of production for direct materials, we start with the equivalent units in beginning work in process inventory. We see that beginning work in process inventory was 100% complete with respect to materials; no materials were needed to complete these units. Thus, this group of units required 0 EUP during the month. Next, we consider the units started and completed during the month. In terms of direct materials, the 70,000 units started and completed during the month received 100% of their materials during the month. Thus, EUP for this group is 70,000 units (70,000 × 100%). Finally, we consider the units in ending work in process inventory. The roasting department started but *did not* complete 20,000 units during the month. This group received all of its materials during the month. Thus, EUP for this group is 20,000 units (20,000 × 100%). The sum of the EUP for these three distinct groups of units is 90,000 (computed as 0 + 70,000 + 20,000), which is the total number of equivalent units of production for direct materials during the month.

Conversion To calculate the equivalent units of production for conversion, we start by determining the percentage of conversion costs needed to complete the beginning work in process inventory. As Exhibit 16A.3 shows, the beginning work in process inventory of 30,000 units was 65% complete with respect to conversion. Thus, this group of units required an additional 35% of conversion costs during the period to complete those units (100% − 65%), or 10,500 EUP (30,000 × 35%). Next, we consider the units started and completed during the month. The units started and completed during the month incurred 100% of their conversion costs during the month. Thus, EUP for this group is 70,000 units (70,000 × 100%). Finally, we consider the units in ending work in process inventory. The ending work in process inventory incurred 25% of its conversion costs (see Exhibit 16A.3) during the month. Thus, EUP for this group is 5,000 units (20,000 × 25%). The sum of the EUP for these three distinct groups of units is 85,500 (computed as 10,500 + 70,000 + 5,000). Thus, the roasting department's equivalent units of production for conversion for the month is 85,500 units.

NEED-TO-KNOW 16-5

EUP—Direct Materials and Conversion (FIFO)

C4

A department began the month with 50,000 units in work in process inventory. These units were 60% complete with respect to direct materials and 40% complete with respect to conversion. During the month the department started 286,000 units; 220,000 of these units were completed during the month. The remaining 66,000 units are in ending work in process inventory, 80% complete with respect to direct materials and 30% complete with respect to conversion. Use the FIFO method of process costing to:

1. Compute the department's equivalent units of production for the month for direct materials.
2. Compute the department's equivalent units of production for the month for conversion.

Solution

Do More: QS 16-14, QS 16-15, E 16-5, E 16-10

1. EUP for materials = (50,000 × 40%) + (220,000 × 100%) + (66,000 × 80%) = 292,800 EUP
2. EUP for conversion = (50,000 × 60%) + (220,000 × 100%) + (66,000 × 30%) = 269,800 EUP

Step 3: Compute Cost per Equivalent Unit—FIFO To compute cost per equivalent unit, we take the direct materials and conversion costs added in April and divide by the equivalent units of production from step 2. Exhibit 16A.7 illustrates these computations.

EXHIBIT 16A.7

Cost per Equivalent Unit of Production—FIFO

GenX—Roasting Department		
Cost per Equivalent Unit of Production	**Direct Materials**	**Conversion**
Costs incurred this period (from Exhibit 16A.3)	$279,000	$376,200
÷ Equivalent units of production (from step 2)	90,000 EUP	85,500 EUP
Cost per equivalent unit of production	$3.10 per EUP	$4.40 per EUP

It is essential to compute costs per equivalent unit for *each* input because production inputs are added at different times in the process. The FIFO method computes the cost per equivalent unit based solely on this period's EUP and costs (unlike the weighted-average method, which adds in the costs of the beginning work in process inventory).

NEED-TO-KNOW 16-6

Cost per EUP—Direct Materials and Conversion (FIFO)

C4

A department started the month with beginning work in process inventory of $130,000 ($90,000 for direct materials and $40,000 for conversion). During the month, the department incurred additional direct materials costs of $700,000 and conversion costs of $500,000. Assume that equivalent units for the month were computed as 250,000 for materials and 200,000 for conversion.

1. Compute the department's cost per equivalent unit of production for the month for direct materials.
2. Compute the department's cost per equivalent unit of production for the month for conversion.

Solution

Do More: QS 16-15, QS 16-17, E 16-7

1. Cost per EUP of materials = $700,000/250,000 = $2.80
2. Cost per EUP of conversion = $500,000/200,000 = $2.50

Step 4: Assign and Reconcile Costs The equivalent units determined in step 2 and the cost per equivalent unit computed in step 3 are both used to assign costs (1) to units that the production department completed and transferred to the blending department and (2) to units that remain in process at period-end.

In Exhibit 16A.8, under the section for cost of units transferred out, we see that the cost of units completed in April includes the $189,900 cost carried over from March for work already applied to the 30,000 units that make up beginning work in process inventory, plus the $46,200 incurred in April to complete those units. This section also includes the $525,000 of cost assigned to the 70,000 units started and completed this period. Thus, the total cost of goods manufactured in April is $761,100. The average cost per unit for goods completed in April is $7.611 ($761,100 ÷ 100,000 completed units).

EXHIBIT 16A.8

Report of Costs Accounted For—FIFO

Cost of units transferred out (cost of goods manufactured)		
Cost of beginning work in process inventory		$ 189,900
Cost to complete beginning work in process		
Direct materials ($3.10 per EUP × 0 EUP)	$ 0	
Conversion ($4.40 per EUP × 10,500 EUP)	46,200	46,200
Cost of units started and completed this period		
Direct materials ($3.10 per EUP × 70,000 EUP)	217,000	
Conversion ($4.40 per EUP × 70,000 EUP)	308,000	525,000
Total cost of units finished this period		761,100
Cost of ending work in process inventory		
Direct materials ($3.10 per EUP × 20,000 EUP)	62,000	
Conversion ($4.40 per EUP × 5,000 EUP)	22,000	
Total cost of ending work in process inventory		84,000
Total costs accounted for		**$845,100**

The computation for cost of ending work in process inventory is in the lower part of Exhibit 16A.8. That cost of $84,000 ($62,000 + $22,000) also is the ending balance for the Work in Process Inventory—Roasting account.

The roasting department manager verifies that the total costs assigned to units transferred out and units still in process equal the total costs incurred by production. We reconcile the costs accounted for (in Exhibit 16A.8.) to the costs that production was charged for as shown in Exhibit 16A.9.

EXHIBIT 16A.9

Report of Costs to Account For—FIFO

Cost of beginning work in process inventory		
Direct materials	$ 81,000	
Conversion	108,900	$ 189,900
Costs incurred this period		
Direct materials	279,000	
Conversion	376,200	655,200
Total costs to account for		**$845,100**

The roasting department production manager is responsible for $845,100 in costs: $189,900 that had been assigned to the department's work in process inventory as of April 1 plus $655,200 of costs the department incurred in April. At period-end, the manager must identify where those costs were assigned. The production manager can report that $761,100 of cost was assigned to units completed in April and $84,000 was assigned to units still in process at period-end.

Process Cost Summary The final report is the process cost summary, which summarizes key information from previous exhibits. Reasons for the summary are to (1) help managers control and monitor costs, (2) help upper management assess department manager performance, and (3) provide cost information for financial reporting. The process cost summary, using FIFO, for GenX's roasting department is in Exhibit 16A.10. Section ⟨1⟩ lists the total costs charged to the department, including direct materials and conversion costs incurred, as well as the cost of the beginning work in process inventory. Section ⟨2⟩ describes the equivalent units of production for the department. Equivalent units for conversion are in separate columns. It also reports direct materials and conversion costs per equivalent unit. Section ⟨3⟩ allocates total costs among units worked on in the period.

EXHIBIT 16A.10
Process Cost Summary (FIFO)

GenX COMPANY— ROASTING DEPARTMENT
Process Cost Summary (FIFO Method)
For Month Ended April 30, 2015

①	**Costs charged to production**		
	Costs of beginning work in process inventory		
	Direct materials	$ 81,000	
	Conversion	108,900	$ 189,900
	Costs incurred this period		
	Direct materials	279,000	
	Conversion	376,200	655,200
	Total costs to account for		**$845,100**

②	**Unit information**			
	Units to account for		Units accounted for	
	Beginning work in process	30,000	Transferred out	100,000
	Units started this period	90,000	Ending work in process	20,000
	Total units to account for	120,000	Total units accounted for	120,000

	Equivalent units of production	**Direct Materials**	**Conversion**
	Equivalent units to complete beginning work in process		
	Direct materials (30,000 × 0%)	0 EUP	
	Conversion (30,000 × 35%)		10,500 EUP
	Equivalent units started and completed	70,000 EUP	70,000 EUP
	Equivalent units in ending work in process		
	Direct materials (20,000 × 100%)	20,000 EUP	
	Conversion (20,000 × 25%)		5,000 EUP
	Equivalent units of production	90,000 EUP	85,500 EUP

	Cost per equivalent unit of production	**Direct Materials**	**Conversion**
	Costs incurred this period	$279,000	$376,200
	÷ Equivalent units of production	90,000 EUP	85,500 EUP
	Cost per equivalent unit of production	$3.10 per EUP	$4.40 per EUP

③	**Cost assignment and reconciliation**		
	(cost of units completed and transferred out)		
	Cost of beginning work in process		$ 189,900
	Cost to complete beginning work in process		
	Direct materials ($3.10 per EUP × 0 EUP)	$ 0	
	Conversion ($4.40 per EUP × 10,500 EUP)	46,200	46,200
	Cost of units started and completed this period		
	Direct materials ($3.10 per EUP × 70,000 EUP)	217,000	
	Conversion ($4.40 per EUP × 70,000 EUP)	308,000	525,000
	Total cost of units finished this period		761,100
	Cost of ending work in process		
	Direct materials ($3.10 per EUP × 20,000 EUP)	62,000	
	Conversion ($4.40 per EUP × 5,000 EUP)	22,000	
	Total cost of ending work in process		84,000
	Total costs accounted for		**$845,100**

(Total costs to account for and total costs accounted for: reconciled)

Decision Maker

Cost Manager As cost manager for an electronics manufacturer, you apply a process costing system using FIFO. Your company plans to adopt a just-in-time system and eliminate inventories. What is the impact of the use of FIFO (versus the weighted-average method) given these plans? ■ [Answers follow the chapter's Summary.]

Summary

C1 Explain process operations and the way they differ from job order operations. Process operations produce large quantities of similar products or services by passing them through a series of processes, or steps, in production. Like job order operations, they combine direct materials, direct labor, and overhead in the operations. Unlike job order operations that assign the responsibility for each job to a manager, process operations assign the responsibility for each *process* to a manager.

C2 Define and compute equivalent units and explain their use in process costing. Equivalent units of production measure the activity of a process as the number of units that would be completed in a period if all effort had been applied to units that were started and finished. This measure of production activity is used to compute the cost per equivalent unit and to assign costs to finished goods and work in process inventory. To compute equivalent units, determine the number of units that would have been finished if all materials (or conversion) had been used to produce units that were started and completed during the period. The costs incurred by a process are divided by its equivalent units to yield cost per equivalent unit.

C3 Describe accounting for production activity and preparation of a process cost summary using weighted average. A process cost summary reports on the activities of a production process or department for a period. It describes the costs charged to the department, the equivalent units of production for the department, and the costs assigned to the output. The report aims to (1) help managers control their departments, (2) help factory managers evaluate department managers' performances, and (3) provide cost information for financial statements. A process cost summary includes the physical flow of units, equivalent units of production, costs per equivalent unit, and a cost reconciliation. It reports the units and costs to account for during the period and how they were accounted for during the period. In terms of units, the summary includes the beginning work in process inventory and the units started during the month. These units are accounted for in terms of the goods completed and transferred out, and the ending work in process inventory. With respect to costs, the summary includes materials and conversion costs assigned to the process during the period. It shows how these costs are assigned to goods completed and transferred out, and to ending work in process inventory.

C4 *Appendix*—Describe accounting for production activity and preparation of a process cost summary using FIFO. The FIFO method for process costing is applied and illustrated to (1) report the physical flow of units, (2) compute the equivalent units of production, (3) compute the cost per equivalent unit of production, and (4) assign and reconcile costs.

A1 Compare process costing and job order costing. Process and job order manufacturing operations are similar in that both combine materials, and conversion to produce products or services. They differ in the way they are organized and managed. In job order operations, the job order costing system assigns product costs to specific jobs. In process operations, the process costing system assigns product costs to specific processes. The total costs associated with each process are then divided by the number of units passing through that process to get cost per equivalent unit. The costs per equivalent unit for all processes are added to determine the total cost per unit of a product or service.

A2 Explain and illustrate a hybrid costing system. A hybrid costing system contains features of both job order and process costing systems. Generally, certain direct materials are accounted for by individual products as in job order costing, but direct labor and overhead costs are accounted for similar to process costing.

P1 Record the flow of materials costs in process costing. Materials purchased are debited to a Raw Materials Inventory account. As direct materials are issued to processes, they are separately accumulated in a Work in Process Inventory account for that process. As indirect materials are used their costs are debited to Factory Overhead.

P2 Record the flow of labor costs in process costing. Direct labor costs are assigned to the Work in Process Inventory account pertaining to each process. As indirect labor is used its cost is debited to Factory Overhead.

P3 Record the flow of factory overhead costs in process costing. Actual overhead costs are recorded as debits to the Factory Overhead account. Estimated overhead costs are allocated, using a predetermined overhead rate, to the different processes. This allocated amount is credited to the Factory Overhead account and debited to the Work in Process Inventory account for each separate process.

P4 Record the transfer of goods across departments, to Finished Goods Inventory, and to Cost of Goods Sold. As units are passed through processes, their accumulated costs are transferred across separate Work in Process Inventory accounts for each process. As units complete the final process and are eventually sold, their accumulated cost is transferred to Finished Goods Inventory and finally to Cost of Goods Sold.

Guidance Answers to Decision Maker and Decision Ethics

Budget Officer By instructing you to classify a majority of costs as indirect, the manager is passing some of his department's costs to a common overhead pool that other departments will partially absorb. Since overhead costs are allocated on the basis of direct labor for this company and the new department has a relatively low direct labor cost, the new department will be assigned less overhead. Such action suggests unethical behavior by this manager. You must object to such reclassification. If this manager refuses to comply, you must inform someone in a more senior position.

Entrepreneur By spreading the added quality-related costs across three customers, the entrepreneur is probably trying to remain competitive with respect to the customer that demands the

100% quality inspection. Moreover, the entrepreneur is partly covering the added costs by recovering two-thirds of them from the other two customers who are paying 110% of total costs. This act likely breaches the trust placed by the two customers in this entrepreneur's application of its costing system. The costing system should be changed, and the entrepreneur should consider renegotiating the pricing and/or quality test agreement with this one customer (at the risk of losing this currently loss-producing customer).

Cost Manager Differences between the FIFO and weighted-average methods are greatest when large work in process inventories exist and when costs fluctuate. The method used if inventories are eliminated does not matter; both produce identical costs.

Key Terms

Conversion cost per equivalent unit
Equivalent units of production (EUP)
FIFO method
Job order costing system
Materials consumption report
Process costing system
Process cost summary
Process operations
Weighted-average method

Multiple Choice Quiz

Answers at end of chapter

1. Equivalent units of production are equal to
a. Physical units that were completed this period from all effort being applied to them.
b. The number of units introduced into the process this period.
c. The number of finished units actually completed this period.
d. The number of units that could have been started and completed given the cost incurred.
e. The number of units in the process at the end of the period.

2. Recording the cost of raw materials purchased for use in a process costing system includes a
a. Credit to Raw Materials Inventory.
b. Debit to Work in Process Inventory.
c. Debit to Factory Overhead.
d. Credit to Factory Overhead.
e. Debit to Raw Materials Inventory.

3. The production department started the month with a beginning work in process inventory of $20,000. During the month, it was assigned the following costs: direct materials, $152,000; direct labor, $45,000; overhead applied at the rate of 40% of direct labor cost. Inventory with a cost of $218,000 was transferred to finished goods. The ending balance of work in process inventory is
a. $330,000.
b. $ 17,000.
c. $220,000.
d. $112,000.
e. $118,000.

4. A company's beginning work in process inventory consists of 10,000 units that are 20% complete with respect to conversion costs. A total of 40,000 units are completed this period. There are 15,000 units in work in process, one-third complete for conversion, at period-end. The equivalent units of production (EUP) with respect to conversion at period-end, assuming the weighted-average method, are
a. 45,000 EUP.
b. 40,000 EUP.
c. 5,000 EUP.
d. 37,000 EUP.
e. 43,000 EUP.

5. Assume the same information as in question 4. Also assume that beginning work in process had $6,000 in conversion cost and that $84,000 in conversion is added during this period. What is the cost per EUP for conversion?
a. $0.50 per EUP
b. $1.87 per EUP
c. $2.00 per EUP
d. $2.10 per EUP
e. $2.25 per EUP

[A] *Superscript letter A denotes assignments based on Appendix 16A.*
Icon denotes assignments that involve decision making.

Discussion Questions

1. What is the main factor for a company in choosing between the job order costing and process costing systems? Give two likely applications of each system.

2. The focus in a job order costing system is the job or batch. Identify the main focus in process costing.

3. Can services be delivered by means of process operations? Support your answer with an example.

4. Are the journal entries that match cost flows to product flows in process costing primarily the same or much different than those in job order costing? Explain.

5. Identify the control document for materials flow when a materials requisition slip is not used.

6. Explain in simple terms the notion of equivalent units of production (EUP). Why is it necessary to use EUP in process costing?

7. What are the two main inventory methods used in process costing? What are the differences between these methods?

8. Why is it possible for direct labor in process operations to include the labor of employees who do not work directly on products or services?

9. Assume that a company produces a single product by processing it first through a single production department. Direct labor costs flow through what accounts in this company's process cost system?

10. At the end of a period, what balance should remain in the Factory Overhead account?

11. Is it possible to have under- or overapplied overhead costs in a process costing system? Explain.

12. Explain why equivalent units of production for both direct labor and overhead can be the same as, and why they can be different from, equivalent units for direct materials.

13. Companies such as **Samsung** apply process operations. List the four steps in accounting for production activity in a reporting period (for process operations). **Samsung**

14. Companies such as **Apple** commonly prepare a process cost summary. What purposes does a process cost summary serve? **APPLE**

15. Are there situations where **Google** can use process costing? Identify at least one and explain it. **GOOGLE**

16. **Samsung** produces digital televisions with a multiple process production line. Identify and list some of its production processing steps and departments. **Samsung**

connect

QUICK STUDY

QS 16-1
Process vs. job order operations C1

For each of the following products and services, indicate whether it is more likely produced in a process operation or in a job order operation.

_____ **1.** Tennis courts
_____ **2.** Organic juice
_____ **3.** Audit of financial statements
_____ **4.** Luxury yachts
_____ **5.** Vanilla ice cream
_____ **6.** Tennis balls

QS 16-2
Process vs. job order costing
A1

Label each statement below as either true ("T") or false ("F").

_____ **1.** The cost per equivalent unit is computed as the total costs of a process divided by the number of equivalent units passing through that process.
_____ **2.** Service companies are not able to use process costing.
_____ **3.** Costs per job are computed in both job order and process costing systems.
_____ **4.** Job order and process operations both combine materials, labor, and overhead in producing products or services.

QS 16-3
Process vs. job order operations
C1

For each of the following products and services, indicate whether it is more likely produced in a process operation or a job order operation.

_____ **1.** Beach toys
_____ **2.** Concrete swimming pool
_____ **3.** iPhones
_____ **4.** Wedding reception
_____ **5.** Custom suits
_____ **6.** Juice
_____ **7.** Tattoos
_____ **8.** Guitar picks

QS 16-4
Physical flow reconciliation
C2

The following refers to units processed in Sunflower Printing's binding department in March. Prepare a physical flow reconciliation.

	Units of Product	Percent of Conversion Added
Beginning work in process..........	150,000	80%
Goods started..................	310,000	100
Goods completed	340,000	100
Ending work in process............	120,000	25

QS 16-5
Weighted average: Computing equivalent units of production C2

Refer to QS 16-4. Compute the total equivalent units of production with respect to conversion for March using the weighted-average inventory method.

QS 16-6A
FIFO: Computing equivalent units C4

Refer to QS 16-4. Compute the total equivalent units of production with respect to conversion for March using the FIFO inventory method.

QS 16-7
Weighted average: Cost per EUP C3

A production department's beginning inventory cost includes $394,900 of conversion costs. This department incurs an additional $907,500 in conversion costs in the month of March. Equivalent units of production for conversion total 740,000 for March. Calculate the cost per equivalent unit of conversion using the weighted-average method.

QS 16-8
Weighted average: Computing equivalent units of production C2

The following refers to units processed by an ice cream maker in July. Compute the total equivalent units of production with respect to conversion for July using the weighted-average inventory method.

	Gallons of Product	Percent of Conversion Added
Beginning work in process	320,000	25%
Goods started	620,000	100
Goods completed	680,000	100
Ending work in process	260,000	75

QS 16-9A
FIFO: Computing equivalent units C4

Refer to QS 16-8 and compute the total equivalent units of production with respect to conversion for July using the FIFO inventory method.

QS 16-10
Weighted average: Equivalent units of production C2

The following information applies to QS 16-10 through QS 16-17.

The Carlberg Company has two manufacturing departments, assembly and painting. The assembly department started 10,000 units during November. The following production activity unit and cost information refers to the assembly department's November production activities.

Assembly Department	Units	Percent of Direct Materials Added	Percent of Conversion Added
Beginning work in process	2,000	60%	40%
Units transferred out	9,000	100%	100%
Ending work in process	3,000	80%	30%

Beginning work in process inventory—Assembly dept.	$1,581 (includes $996 for direct materials and $585 for conversion)
Costs added during the month:	
Direct materials	$10,404
Conversion	$12,285

Required

Calculate the assembly department's equivalent units of production for materials and for conversion for November. Use the weighted-average method.

QS 16-11
Weighted average: Cost per EUP C2

Refer to the information in QS 16-10. Calculate the assembly department's cost per equivalent unit of production for materials and for conversion for November. Use the weighted-average method.

QS 16-12
Weighted average: Assign costs to output C3

Refer to the information in QS 16-10. Assign costs to the assembly department's output—specifically, the units transferred out to the painting department and the units that remain in process in the assembly department at month-end. Use the weighted-average method.

QS 16-13
Weighted average: Journal entry to transfer costs P4

Refer to the information in QS 16-10. Prepare the November 30 journal entry to record the transfer of units (and costs) from the assembly department to the painting department. Use the weighted-average method.

QS 16-14A
FIFO: Equivalent units of production C4

Refer to the information in QS 16-10. Calculate the assembly department's equivalent units of production for materials and for conversion for November. Use the FIFO method.

QS 16-15A
FIFO: Cost per EUP C4

Refer to the information in QS 16-10. Calculate the assembly department's cost per equivalent unit of production for materials and for conversion for November. Use the FIFO method.

QS 16-16A
FIFO: Assign costs to output C4

Refer to the information in QS 16-10. Assign costs to the assembly department's output—specifically, the units transferred out to the painting department and the units that remain in process in the assembly department at month-end. Use the FIFO method.

QS 16-17A
FIFO: Journal entry to transfer costs C4 P4

Refer to the information in QS 16-10. Prepare the November 30 journal entry to record the transfer of units (and costs) from the assembly department to the painting department. Use the FIFO method.

QS 16-18
Weighted average: Computing equivalent units and cost per EUP (direct materials)
C2 C3

The Plastic Flowerpots Company has two manufacturing departments, molding and packaging. At the beginning of the month, the molding department has 2,000 units in inventory, 70% complete as to materials. During the month, the molding department started 18,000 units. At the end of the month, the molding department had 3,000 units in ending inventory, 80% complete as to materials. Units completed in the molding department are transferred into the packaging department.

Cost information for the molding department for the month follows:

Beginning work in process inventory (direct materials). . . .	$ 1,200
Direct materials added during the month.	27,900

Using the weighted-average method, compute the molding department's (a) equivalent units of production for materials and (b) cost per equivalent unit of production for materials for the month. (Round to two decimal places.)

QS 16-19
Weighted average: Assigning costs to output
C3

Refer to information in QS 16-18. Using the weighted-average method, assign direct materials costs to the molding department's output—specifically, the units transferred out to the packaging department and the units that remain in process in the molding department at month-end.

QS 16-20
Transfer of costs; ending WIP balances
C3

Azule Co. manufactures in two sequential processes, cutting and binding. The two departments report the information below for a recent month. Determine the ending balances in the Work in Process Inventory accounts of each department.

	Cutting	Binding
Beginning work in process		
Transferred in from cutting dept.		$ 1,200
Direct materials.	$ 845	1,926
Conversion.	2,600	3,300
Costs added during March		
Direct materials.	$ 8,240	$ 6,356
Conversion.	11,100	18,575
Transferred in from cutting dept.		15,685
Transferred to finished goods		30,000

QS 16-21^A
FIFO: Computing equivalent units and cost per EUP (direct materials)
C4

BOGO Inc. has two sequential processing departments, roasting and mixing. At the beginning of the month, the roasting department has 2,000 units in inventory, 70% complete as to materials. During the month, the roasting department started 18,000 units. At the end of the month, the roasting department had 3,000 units in ending inventory, 80% complete as to materials.

Cost information for the roasting department for the month is as follows:

Beginning work in process inventory (direct materials)	$ 2,170
Direct materials added during the month	27,900

Using the FIFO method, compute the roasting department's (a) equivalent units of production for materials and (b) cost per equivalent unit of production for materials for the month.

QS 16-22^A
FIFO: Assigning costs to output C4

Refer to QS 16-21. Using the FIFO method, assign direct materials costs to the roasting department's output—specifically, the units transferred out to the mixing department and the units that remain in process in the roasting department at month-end.

QS 16-23
Recording costs of materials P1

Hotwax makes surfboard wax in a single operation. This period, Hotwax purchased $62,000 in raw materials. Its production department requisitioned $50,000 of those materials for use in production. Prepare journal entries to record its (1) purchase of raw materials and (2) requisition of direct materials.

QS 16-24
Recording costs of labor
P2

Prepare journal entries to record the following production activities for Hotwax.

1. Incurred direct labor of $125,000 (credit Factory Payroll Payable).
2. Incurred indirect labor of $10,000 (credit Factory Payroll Payable).
3. Total factory payroll of $135,000 was paid in cash.

QS 16-25
Recording costs of factory overhead
P1 P3

Prepare journal entries to record the following production activities for Hotwax.

1. Requisitioned $9,000 of indirect materials for use in production of surfboard wax.
2. Incurred $156,000 overhead costs (credit "Other accounts").
3. Applied overhead at the rate of 140% of direct labor costs. Direct labor costs were $125,000.

QS 16-26
Recording transfer of costs to finished goods
P4

Hotwax completed products costing $275,000 and transferred them to finished goods. Prepare its journal entry to record the transfer of units from production to finished goods inventory.

QS 16-27
Process cost summary
C3

Anheuser-Busch InBev is attempting to reduce its water usage. How could a company manager use a process cost summary to determine if the program to reduce water usage is successful?

connect

EXERCISES

Exercise 16-1
Matching of product to cost accounting system
C1

For each of the following products and services, indicate whether it is more likely produced in a process operation or in a job order operation.

____ **1.** Beach towels	____ **5.** Designed patio	____ **9.** Concrete swimming pools
____ **2.** Bolts and nuts	____ **6.** Door hardware	____ **10.** Custom tailored dresses
____ **3.** Lawn chairs	____ **7.** Cut flower arrangements	____ **11.** Grand pianos
____ **4.** Headphones	____ **8.** House paints	____ **12.** Table lamps

Exercise 16-2
Compare process and job order operations
C1

Label each item *a* through *h* below as a feature of either a job order or process operation.

_____ **a.** Heterogeneous products and services
_____ **b.** Custom orders
_____ **c.** Low production volume
_____ **d.** Routine, repetitive procedures
_____ **e.** Focus on individual batch
_____ **f.** Low product standardization
_____ **g.** Low product flexibility
_____ **h.** Focus on standardized units

Exercise 16-3
Terminology in process costing
C1 A1 P1 P2 P3

Match each of the following items A through G with the best numbered description of its purpose.

A. Factory Overhead account
B. Process cost summary
C. Equivalent units of production
D. Work in Process Inventory account
E. Raw Materials Inventory account
F. Materials requisition
G. Finished Goods Inventory account

_____ **1.** Notifies the materials manager to send materials to a production department.
_____ **2.** Holds costs of indirect materials, indirect labor, and similar costs until assigned to production.
_____ **3.** Holds costs of direct materials, direct labor, and applied overhead until products are transferred from production to finished goods (or another department).
_____ **4.** Standardizes partially completed units into equivalent completed units.
_____ **5.** Holds costs of finished products until sold to customers.
_____ **6.** Describes the activity and output of a production department for a period.
_____ **7.** Holds costs of materials until they are used in production or as factory overhead.

Exercise 16-4
Weighted average: Equivalent units computed
C2

The production department in a process manufacturing system completed 80,000 units of product and transferred them to finished goods during a recent period. Of these units, 24,000 were in process at the beginning of the period. The other 56,000 units were started and completed during the period. At period-end, 16,000 units were in process. Compute the department's equivalent units of production with respect to direct materials under each of three separate assumptions, using the weighted average method:

1. All direct materials are added to products when processing begins.
2. Beginning inventory is 40% complete as to materials and conversion costs. Ending inventory is 75% complete as to materials and conversion costs.
3. Beginning inventory is 60% complete as to materials and 40% complete as to conversion costs. Ending inventory is 30% complete as to materials and 60% complete as to conversion costs.

Check (3) EUP for materials, 84,800

Exercise 16-5[A]
FIFO: Equivalent units computed C4

Refer to the information in Exercise 16-4 and complete the requirements for each of the three separate assumptions using the FIFO method for process costing.

Check (3) EUP for materials, 70,400

Exercise 16-6
Weighted average: Cost per EUP and costs assigned to output
C2

The Fields Company has two manufacturing departments, forming and painting. The company uses the weighted-average method of process costing. At the beginning of the month, the forming department has 25,000 units in inventory, 60% complete as to materials and 40% complete as to conversion costs. The beginning inventory cost of $60,100 consisted of $44,800 of direct material costs and $15,300 of conversion cost.

During the month, the forming department started 300,000 units. At the end of the month, the forming department had 30,000 units in ending inventory, 80% complete as to materials and 30% complete as to conversion. Units completed in the forming department are transferred to the painting department.

Cost information for the forming department is as follows:

Beginning work in process inventory	$ 60,100
Direct materials added during the month	1,231,200
Conversion added during the month	896,700

1. Calculate the equivalent units of production for the forming department.
2. Calculate the costs per equivalent unit of production for the forming department.
3. Using the weighted-average method, assign costs to the forming department's output—specifically, its units transferred to painting and its ending work in process inventory.

Exercise 16-7^A
FIFO: Costs per EUP
C4

Refer to the information in Exercise 16-6. Assume that Fields uses the FIFO method of process costing.

1. Calculate the equivalent units of production for the forming department.
2. Calculate the costs per equivalent unit of production for the forming department.

Exercise 16-8
Weighted average: Computing equivalent units of production
C2

During April, the production department of a process manufacturing system completed a number of units of a product and transferred them to finished goods. Of these transferred units, 60,000 were in process in the production department at the beginning of April and 240,000 were started and completed in April. April's beginning inventory units were 60% complete with respect to materials and 40% complete with respect to conversion. At the end of April, 82,000 additional units were in process in the production department and were 80% complete with respect to materials and 30% complete with respect to conversion.

1. Compute the number of units transferred to finished goods.
2. Compute the number of equivalent units with respect to both materials used and conversion used in the production department for April using the weighted-average method.

Check (2) EUP for materials, 365,600

Exercise 16-9
Weighted average: Costs assigned to output and inventories C2

The production department described in Exercise 16-8 had $850,368 of direct materials and $649,296 of conversion costs charged to it during April. Also, its beginning inventory of $167,066 consists of $118,472 of direct materials cost and $48,594 of conversion costs.

1. Compute the direct materials cost and the conversion cost per equivalent unit for the department.
2. Using the weighted-average method, assign April's costs to the department's output—specifically, its units transferred to finished goods and its ending work in process inventory.

Check (1) $2.65 per EUP of direct materials

Exercise 16-10^A
FIFO: Computing equivalent units of production C4

Refer to the information in Exercise 16-8 to compute the number of equivalent units with respect to both materials used and conversion costs in the production department for April using the FIFO method.

Exercise 16-11^A
FIFO: Costs assigned to output C4 P4

Refer to the information in Exercise 16-9 and complete its parts 1 and 2 using the FIFO method.

Exercise 16-12
Weighted average: Completing a process cost summary
C3

The following partially completed process cost summary describes the July production activities of Ashad Company. Its production output is sent to its warehouse for shipping. All direct materials are added to products when processing begins. Beginning work in process inventory is 20% complete with respect to conversion. Prepare its process cost summary using the weighted-average method.

Equivalent Units of Production	**Direct Materials**	**Conversion**
Units transferred out	32,000 EUP	32,000 EUP
Units of ending work in process	2,500 EUP	1,500 EUP
Equivalent units of production	34,500 EUP	33,500 EUP
Costs per EUP	**Direct Materials**	**Conversion**
Costs of beginning work in process	$ 18,550	$ 2,280
Costs incurred this period	357,500	188,670
Total costs	$376,050	$190,950
Units in beginning work in process (all completed during July)		2,000
Units started this period		32,500
Units completed and transferred out		32,000
Units in ending work in process		2,500

Exercise 16-13^A
FIFO: Completing a process cost summary
C3 C4

Refer to the information in Exercise 16-12. Prepare a process cost summary using the FIFO method. (Round cost per equivalent unit calculations to two decimal places.)

Exercise 16-14
Production cost flow and measurement; journal entries
P1 P2 P3 P4

Pro-Weave manufactures stadium blankets by passing the products through a weaving department and a sewing department. The following information is available regarding its June inventories:

	Beginning Inventory	Ending Inventory
Raw materials inventory	$ 120,000	$ 185,000
Work in process inventory—Weaving	300,000	330,000
Work in process inventory—Sewing	570,000	700,000
Finished goods inventory	1,266,000	1,206,000

The following additional information describes the company's manufacturing activities for June:

Raw materials purchases (on credit)	$ 500,000
Factory payroll cost (paid in cash)	3,060,000
Other factory overhead cost (Other Accounts credited)	156,000
Materials used	
Direct—Weaving	$ 240,000
Direct—Sewing	75,000
Indirect	120,000
Labor used	
Direct—Weaving	$1,200,000
Direct—Sewing	360,000
Indirect	1,500,000
Overhead rates as a percent of direct labor	
Weaving	80%
Sewing	150%
Sales (on credit)	$4,000,000

Required

1. Compute the (a) cost of products transferred from weaving to sewing, (b) cost of products transferred from sewing to finished goods, and (c) cost of goods sold.
2. Prepare journal entries dated June 30 to record (a) goods transferred from weaving to sewing, (b) goods transferred from sewing to finished goods, and (c) sale of finished goods.

Check (1*c*) Cost of goods sold $3,275,000

Exercise 16-15
Recording product costs
P1 P2 P3

Refer to the information in Exercise 16-14. Prepare journal entries dated June 30 to record: (a) raw materials purchases, (b) direct materials usage, (c) indirect materials usage, (d) direct labor usage, (e) indirect labor usage, (f) other overhead costs, (g) overhead applied, and (h) payment of total payroll costs.

Exercise 16-16
Weighted average: Process cost summary units and costs C3

Elliott Company produces large quantities of a standardized product. The following information is available for its production activities for March.

Units	
Beginning work in process inventory	2,000
Started	20,000
Ending work in process inventory	5,000
Status of ending work in process inventory	
Materials—Percent complete	100%
Conversion—Percent complete	35%

Costs		
Beginning work in process inventory		
Direct materials	$2,500	
Conversion	6,360	$ 8,860
Direct materials added		168,000
Direct labor added		199,850
Overhead applied (140% of direct labor)		279,790
Total costs to account for		$656,500
Ending work in process inventory		$ 84,110

Check Cost per equivalent unit: materials, $7.75; conversion, $25.92

Prepare a process cost summary report for this company, showing costs charged to production, unit cost information, equivalent units of production, cost per EUP, and its cost assignment and reconciliation. Use the weighted-average method.

Exercise 16-17
Weighted average: Process cost summary
C3

Oslo Company produces large quantities of a standardized product. The following information is available for its production activities for May.

Units	
Beginning work in process inventory	4,000
Started	12,000
Ending work in process inventory	3,000
Status of ending work in process inventory	
Materials—Percent complete	100%
Conversion—Percent complete	25%

Costs		
Beginning work in process inventory		
Direct materials	$2,880	
Conversion	5,358	$ 8,238
Direct materials added		197,120
Direct labor added		123,680
Overhead applied (90% of direct labor)		111,312
Total costs to account for		$440,350
Ending work in process inventory		$ 50,610

Check (1) Cost per equivalent unit: materials, $12.50; conversion, $17.48

Prepare a process cost summary report for this company, showing costs charged to production, unit cost information, equivalent units of production, cost per EUP, and its cost assignment and reconciliation. Use the weighted-average method.

Exercise 16-18A
FIFO: Equivalent units
C4 P4

RSTN Co. produces its product through two sequential processing departments. Direct materials and conversion are added to the product evenly throughout the process. The company uses monthly reporting periods for its process costing system. During October, the company finished and transferred 150,000 units of its product to Department 2. Of these units, 30,000 were in process at the beginning of the month and 120,000 were started and completed during the month. The beginning work in process inventory was 30% complete. At the end of the month, the work in process inventory consisted of 20,000 units that were 80% complete. Compute the number of equivalent units of production for October. Use the FIFO method.

Check (1) 157,000 EUP

Exercise 16-19
Production cost flows
P1 P2 P3 P4

The flowchart below shows the August production activity of the punching and bending departments of Wire Box Company. Use the amounts shown on the flowchart to compute the missing numbers identified by question marks.

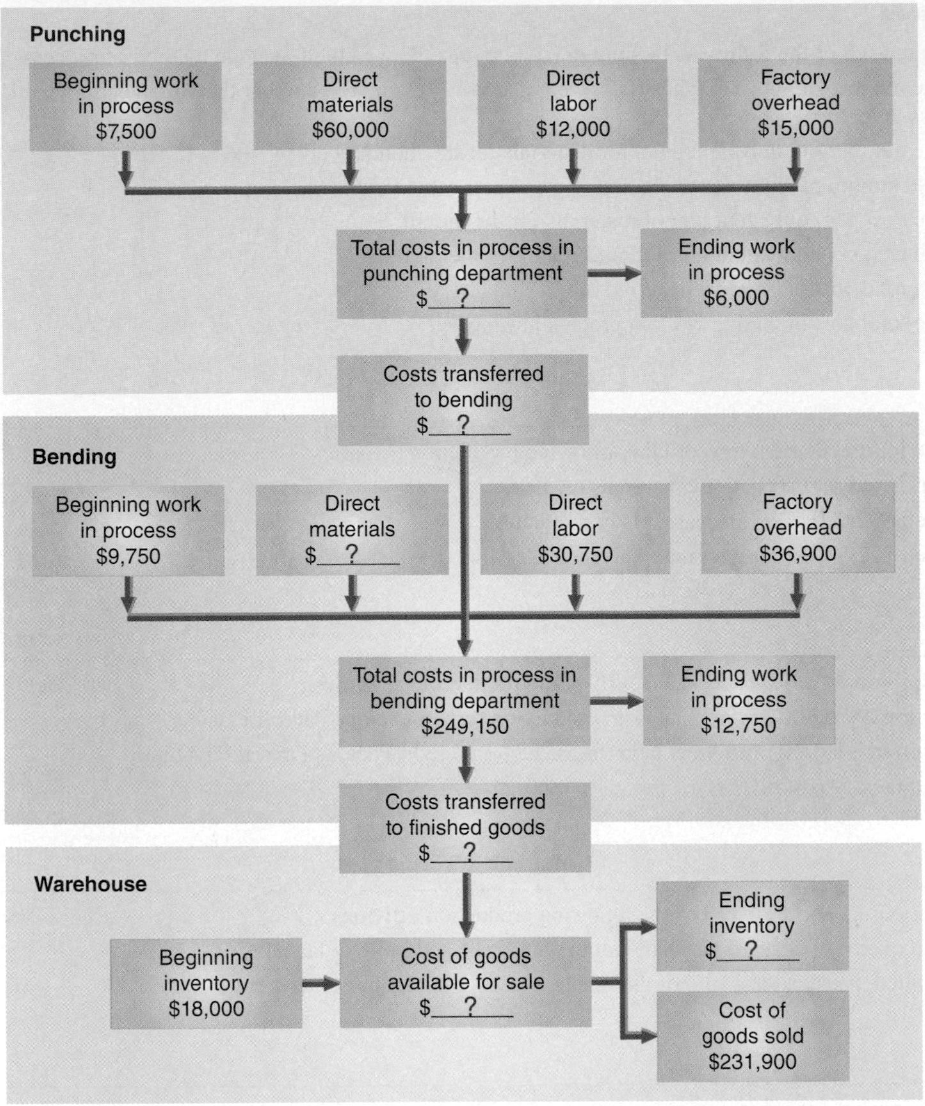

Exercise 16-20
Weighted average: Process cost summary
C3

Hi-Test Company uses the weighted-average method of process costing to assign production costs to its products. Information for September follows. Assume that all materials are added at the beginning of its production process, and that conversion costs are added uniformly throughout the process.

Work in process inventory, September 1 (2,000 units, 100% complete with respect to direct materials, 80% complete with respect to direct labor and overhead; includes $45,000 of direct material cost, $25,600 in direct labor cost, $30,720 overhead cost)	$101,320
Units started in April	28,000
Units completed and transferred to finished goods inventory	23,000
Work in process inventory, September 30 (? units, 100% complete with respect to direct materials, 40% complete with respect to direct labor and overhead)	$?
Costs incurred in September	
Direct materials	$375,000
Conversion	$341.000

Required

Compute each of the following, assuming Hi-Test uses the weighted-average method of process costing.

1. The number of physical units that were transferred out and the number that are in ending work in process inventory.
2. The number of equivalent units for materials for the month.
3. The number of equivalent units for conversion for the month.
4. The cost per equivalent unit of materials for the month.
5. The cost per equivalent unit for conversion for the month.
6. The total cost of goods transferred out.
7. The total cost of ending work in process inventory.

Exercise 16-21
Recording costs of materials
P1

Prepare journal entries to record the following production activities.

1. Purchased $80,000 of raw materials on credit.
2. Used $42,000 of direct materials in production.
3. Used $22,500 of indirect materials in production.

Exercise 16-22
Recording costs of labor
P2

Prepare journal entries to record the following production activities.

1. Incurred $75,000 of direct labor in production (credit Factory Payroll Payable).
2. Incurred $20,000 of indirect labor in production (credit Factory Payroll Payable).
3. Paid factory payroll.

Exercise 16-23
Recording overhead costs P3

Prepare journal entries to record the following production activities.

1. Paid overhead costs (other than indirect materials and indirect labor) of $38,750.
2. Applied overhead at 110% of direct labor costs. Direct labor costs were $75,000.

Exercise 16-24
Recording cost of completed goods P4

Prepare journal entries to record the following production activities.

1. Transferred completed goods from the Assembly department to finished goods inventory. The goods cost $135,600.
2. Sold $315,000 of goods on credit. Their cost is $175,000.

Exercise 16-25
Recording cost flows in a process cost system
P1 P2 P3 P4

Laffer Lumber produces bagged bark for use in landscaping. Production involves packaging bark chips in plastic bags in a bagging department. The following information describes production operations for October.

	A	B
1		Bagging
2		Department
3	Direct materials used	$ 522,000
4	Direct labor used	$ 130,000
5	Predetermined overhead rate (based on direct labor)	175%
6	Goods transferred from bagging to finished goods	$(595,000)
7		

The company's revenue for the month totaled $950,000 from credit sales, and its cost of goods sold for the month is $540,000. Prepare summary journal entries dated October 31 to record its October production activities for (1) direct material usage, (2) direct labor incurred (3) overhead allocation, (4) goods transfer from production to finished goods, and (5) credit sales.

Check (3) Cr. Factory Overhead, $227,500

Exercise 16-26
Interpretation of journal entries in process costing
P1 P2 P3 P4

The following journal entries are recorded in Kiesha Co.'s process costing system. Kiesha produces apparel and accessories. Overhead is applied to production based on direct labor cost for the period. Prepare a brief explanation (including any overhead rates applied) for each journal entry *a* through *j*.

a.	Raw Materials Inventory	52,000	
	Accounts Payable		52,000
b.	Work in Process Inventory	42,000	
	Raw Materials Inventory		42,000
c.	Work in Process Inventory	32,000	
	Factory Payroll Payable		32,000
d.	Factory Overhead	6,000	
	Factory Payroll Payable		6,000
e.	Factory Overhead	12,000	
	Cash		12,000
f.	Factory Overhead	10,000	
	Raw Materials Inventory		10,000
g.	Factory Payroll Payable	38,000	
	Cash		38,000
h.	Work in Process Inventory	33,600	
	Factory Overhead		33,600
i.	Finished Goods Inventory	88,000	
	Work in Process Inventory		88,000
j.	Accounts Receivable	250,000	
	Sales		250,000
	Cost of Goods Sold	100,000	
	Finished Goods Inventory		100,000

Exercise 16-27
Hybrid costing system
A2

Explain a hybrid costing system. Identify a product or service operation that might well fit a hybrid costing system.

connect

PROBLEM SET A

Problem 16-1A
Production cost flow and measurement; journal entries
P1 P2 P3 P4

Sierra Company manufactures woven blankets and accounts for product costs using process costing. The company uses a single processing department. The following information is available regarding its May inventories.

	Beginning Inventory	Ending Inventory
Raw materials inventory	$ 60,000	$ 92,500
Work in process inventory	435,000	515,000
Finished goods inventory	633,000	605,000

The following additional information describes the company's production activities for May.

Raw materials purchases (on credit)	$ 250,000
Factory payroll cost (paid in cash)	1,530,000
Other overhead cost (Other Accounts credited)	87,000
Materials used	
Direct	$ 157,500
Indirect	60,000
Labor used	
Direct	$ 780,000
Indirect	750,000
Overhead rate as a percent of direct labor	115%
Sales (on credit)	$2,500,000

Required

1. Compute the cost of (a) products transferred from production to finished goods, and (b) goods sold.
2. Prepare summary journal entries dated May 31 to record the following production activities during May: (a) raw materials purchases, (b) direct materials usage, (c) indirect materials usage, (d) direct labor costs incurred, (e) indirect labor costs incurred, (f) payment of factory payroll, (g) other overhead costs, (h) overhead applied, (i) goods transferred from production to finished goods, and (j) sale of finished goods.

Check (1*b*) Cost of goods sold, $1,782,500

Problem 16-2A
Weighted average: Cost per equivalent unit; costs assigned to products
C2 C3

Victory Company uses weighted-average process costing to account for its production costs. Conversion cost is added evenly throughout the process. Direct materials are added at the beginning of the process. During November, the company transferred 700,000 units of product to finished goods. At the end of November, the work in process inventory consists of 180,000 units that are 30% complete with respect to conversion. Beginning inventory had $420,000 of direct materials and $139,000 of conversion cost. The direct material cost added in November is $2,220,000, and the conversion cost added is $3,254,000. Beginning work in process consisted of 60,000 units that were 100% complete with respect to direct materials and 80% complete with respect to conversion. Of the units completed, 60,000 were from beginning work in process and 640,000 units were started and completed during the period.

Required

1. Determine the equivalent units of production with respect to (a) direct materials and (b) conversion.
2. Compute both the direct material cost and the conversion cost per equivalent unit.
3. Compute the direct material cost and the conversion cost assigned to (a) units completed and transferred out, and (b) ending work in process inventory.

Check (2) Conversion cost per equivalent unit, $4.50
(3b) $783,000

Analysis Component

4. The company sells and ships all units to customers as soon as they are completed. Assume that an error is made in determining the percentage of completion for units in ending inventory. Instead of being 30% complete with respect to labor, they are actually 60% complete. Write a one-page memo to the plant manager describing how this error affects its November financial statements.

Problem 16-3A
Weighted average: Process cost summary; equivalent units
C2 C3 P4

Fast Co. produces its product through a single processing department. Direct materials are added at the start of production, and conversion costs are added evenly throughout the process. The company uses monthly reporting periods for its weighted-average process costing system. The Work in Process Inventory account has a balance of $84,300 as of October 1, which consisted of $17,100 of direct materials and $67,200 of conversion costs.

During the month the company incurred the following costs:

Direct materials	$144,400
Conversion.	862,400

During October, the company started 140,000 units and transferred 150,000 units to finished goods. At the end of the month, the work in process inventory consisted of 20,000 units that were 80% complete with respect to conversion costs.

Required

1. Prepare the company's process cost summary for October using the weighted-average method.
2. Prepare the journal entry dated October 31 to transfer the cost of the completed units to finished goods inventory.

Check (1) Costs transferred out to finished goods, $982,500

Problem 16-4A
Weighted average: Process cost summary, equivalent units, cost estimates
C2 C3 P4

Tamar Co. manufactures a single product in one department. All direct materials are added at the beginning of the manufacturing process. Conversion costs are added evenly throughout the process. During May, the company completed and transferred 22,200 units of product to finished goods inventory. Its 3,000 units of beginning work in process consisted of $19,800 of direct materials and $221,940 of conversion costs. It has 2,400 units (100% complete with respect to direct materials and 80% complete with respect to conversion) in process at month-end. During the month, $496,800 of direct material costs and $2,165,940 of conversion costs were charged to production.

Required

1. Prepare the company's process cost summary for May using the weighted-average method.
2. Prepare the journal entry dated May 31 to transfer the cost of completed units to finished goods inventory.

Check (1) EUP for conversion, 24,120
(2) Cost transferred out to finished goods, $2,664,000

Analysis Components

3. The costing process depends on numerous estimates.
   a. Identify two major estimates that determine the cost per equivalent unit.
   b. In what direction might you anticipate a bias from management for each estimate in part 3a (assume that management compensation is based on maintaining low inventory amounts)? Explain your answer.

Problem 16-5A^A
FIFO: Process cost summary; equivalent units; cost estimates
C3 C4 P4

Refer to the data in Problem 16-4A. Assume that Tamar uses the FIFO method to account for its process costing system. The following additional information is available:

- Beginning work in process consisted of 3,000 units that were 100% complete with respect to direct materials and 40% complete with respect to conversion.
- Of the 22,200 units completed, 3,000 were from beginning work in process. The remaining 19,200 were units started and completed during May.

Required

1. Prepare the company's process cost summary for May using FIFO.
2. Prepare the journal entry dated May 31 to transfer the cost of completed units to finished goods inventory.

Check (1) EUP for conversion, 22,920
(2) Cost transferred out to finished goods, $2,667,840

Problem 16-6A^A
FIFO: Costs per equivalent unit; costs assigned to products
C2 C4

During May, the production department of a process manufacturing system completed a number of units of a product and transferred them to finished goods. Of these transferred units, 37,500 were in process in the production department at the beginning of May and 150,000 were started and completed in May. May's beginning inventory units were 60% complete with respect to materials and 40% complete with respect to conversion. At the end of May, 51,250 additional units were in process in the production department and were 60% complete with respect to materials and 20% complete with respect to conversion. The production department had $505,035 of direct materials and $396,568 of conversion cost charged to it during May. Its beginning inventory included $74,075 of direct materials cost and $28,493 of conversion cost.

1. Compute the number of units transferred to finished goods.
2. Compute the number of equivalent units with respect to both materials used and conversion used in the production department for May using the FIFO method.
3. Compute the direct materials cost and the conversion cost per equivalent unit for the department.
4. Using the FIFO method, assign May's costs to the units transferred to finished goods and assign costs to its ending work in process inventory.

Check (2) EUP for materials, 195,750

Problem 16-7A^A
FIFO: Process cost summary, equivalent units, cost estimates
C2 C3 C4 P4

Dengo Co. makes a trail mix in two departments: roasting and blending. Direct materials are added at the beginning of each process, and conversion costs are added evenly throughout each process. The company uses the FIFO method of process costing. During October, the roasting department completed and transferred 22,200 units to the blending department. Of the units completed, 3,000 were from beginning inventory and the remaining 19,200 were started and completed during the month. Beginning work in process was 100% complete with respect to direct materials and 40% complete with respect to conversion. The company has 2,400 units (100% complete with respect to direct materials and 80% complete with respect to conversion) in process at month-end. Information on the roasting department's costs of beginning work in process inventory and costs added during the month follows.

Cost	Direct Materials	Conversion
Of beginning work in process inventory.........	$ 9,900	$ 110,970
Added during the month.....................	248,400	1,082,970

Required

1. Prepare the roasting department's process cost summary for October using the FIFO method.
2. Prepare the journal entry dated October 31 to transfer the cost of completed units to the blending department.

Check (1) EUP for conversion, 22,920
(2) Cost transferred out to blending, $1,333,920

Analysis Component

3. The company provides incentives to department managers by paying monthly bonuses based on their success in controlling costs per equivalent unit of production. Assume that a production department underestimates the percentage of completion for units in ending inventory with the result that its equivalent units of production for October are understated. What impact does this error have on the October bonuses paid to that department's managers? What impact, if any, does this error have on November bonuses?

PROBLEM SET B

Problem 16-1B
Production cost flow and measurement; journal entries
P1 P2 P3 P4

Dream Toys Company manufactures video game consoles and accounts for product costs using process costing. The company uses a single processing department. The following information is available regarding its June inventories.

	Beginning Inventory	Ending Inventory
Raw materials inventory	$ 72,000	$110,000
Work in process inventory	156,000	250,000
Finished goods inventory	160,000	198,000

The following additional information describes the company's production activities for June.

Raw materials purchases (on credit)	$200,000
Factory payroll cost (paid in cash)	400,000
Other overhead cost (Other Accounts credited)	170,500
Materials used	
Direct	$120,000
Indirect	42,000
Labor used	
Direct	$350,000
Indirect	50,000
Overhead rate as a percent of direct labor	75%
Sales (on credit)	$1,000,000

Required

Check (1*b*) Cost of goods sold, $600,500

1. Compute the cost of (a) products transferred from production to finished goods, and (b) goods sold.
2. Prepare journal entries dated June 30 to record the following production activities during June: (a) raw materials purchases, (b) direct materials usage, (c) indirect materials usage, (d) direct labor costs, (e) indirect labor costs, (f) payment of factory payroll (g) other overhead costs, (h) overhead applied, (i) goods transferred from production to finished goods, and (j) sale of finished goods.

Problem 16-2B
Weighted average:
Cost per equivalent unit; costs assigned to products
C2 C3

Abraham Company uses process costing to account for its production costs. Conversion is added evenly throughout the process. Direct materials are added at the beginning of the process. During September, the production department transferred 80,000 units of product to finished goods. Beginning work in process consisted of 2,000 units that were 100% complete with respect to direct materials and 85% complete with respect to conversion. Of the units completed, 2,000 were from beginning work in process and 78,000 units were started and completed during the period. Beginning work in process had $58,000 of direct materials and $86,400 of conversion cost. At the end of September, the work in process inventory consists of 8,000 units that are 25% complete with respect to conversion. The direct materials cost added in September is $712,000, and conversion cost added is $1,980,000. The company uses the weighted-average method.

Required

1. Determine the equivalent units of production with respect to (a) conversion and (b) direct materials.

Check (2) Conversion cost per equivalent unit, $25.20

(3*b*) $120,400

2. Compute both the conversion cost and the direct materials cost per equivalent unit.
3. Compute both conversion cost and direct materials cost assigned to (a) units completed and transferred out and (b) ending work in process inventory.

Analysis Component

4. The company sells and ships all units to customers as soon as they are completed. Assume that an error is made in determining the percentage of completion for units in ending inventory. Instead of being 25% complete with respect to conversion, they are actually 75% complete. Write a one-page memo to the plant manager describing how this error affects its September financial statements.

Problem 16-3B
Weighted average: Process cost summary; equivalent units
C2 C3 P4

Braun Company produces its product through a single processing department. Direct materials are added at the beginning of the process. Conversion costs are added to the product evenly throughout the process. The company uses monthly reporting periods for its weighted-average process costing. The Work in Process Inventory account had a balance of $21,300 on November 1, which consisted of $6,800 of direct materials and $14,500 of conversion costs.

During the month the company incurred the following costs:

Direct materials	$ 116,400
Conversion.	1,067,000

During November, the company finished and transferred 100,000 units of its product to finished goods. At the end of the month, the work in process inventory consisted of 12,000 units that were 100% complete with respect to direct materials and 25% complete with respect to conversion.

Required

1. Prepare the company's process cost summary for November using the weighted-average method.
2. Prepare the journal entry dated November 30 to transfer the cost of the completed units to finished goods inventory.

Check (1) Cost transferred out to finished goods, $1,160,000

Problem 16-4B
Weighted average: Process cost summary; equivalent units; cost estimates
C2 C3 P4

Switch Co. manufactures a single product in one department. Direct labor and overhead are added evenly throughout the process. Direct materials are added as needed. The company uses monthly reporting periods for its weighted-average process costing. During January, Switch completed and transferred 220,000 units of product to finished goods inventory. Its 10,000 units of beginning work in process consisted of $7,500 of direct materials and $49,850 of conversion. In process at month-end are 40,000 units (50% complete with respect to direct materials and 30% complete with respect to conversion). During the month, the company used direct materials of $112,500 in production, and incurred conversion costs of $616,000.

Required

1. Prepare the company's process cost summary for January using the weighted-average method.
2. Prepare the journal entry dated January 31 to transfer the cost of completed units to finished goods inventory.

Check (1) EUP for conversion, 232,000
(2) Cost transferred out to finished goods, $741,400

Analysis Components

3. The cost accounting process depends on several estimates.
   a. Identify two major estimates that affect the cost per equivalent unit.
   b. In what direction might you anticipate a bias from management for each estimate in part 3a (assume that management compensation is based on maintaining low inventory amounts)? Explain your answer.

Problem 16-5B[A]
FIFO: Process cost summary; equivalent units; cost estimates
C3 C4 P4

Refer to the information in Problem 16-4B. Assume that Switch uses the FIFO method to account for its process costing system. The following additional information is available.

- Beginning work in process consists of 10,000 units that were 75% complete with respect to direct materials and 60% complete with respect to conversion.
- Of the 220,000 units completed, 10,000 were from beginning work in process; the remaining 210,000 were units started and completed during January.

Required

1. Prepare the company's process cost summary for January using FIFO. Round cost per EUP to three decimal places.
2. Prepare the journal entry dated January 31 to transfer the cost of completed units to finished goods inventory.

Check (1) Conversion EUP, 226,000
(2) Cost transferred out, $743,554

Problem 16-6B^A
FIFO: Costs per equivalent unit; costs assigned to products
C2 C4

During May, the production department of a process manufacturing system completed a number of units of a product and transferred them to finished goods. Of these transferred units, 62,500 were in process in the production department at the beginning of May and 175,000 were started and completed in May. May's beginning inventory units were 40% complete with respect to materials and 80% complete with respect to conversion. At the end of May, 76,250 additional units were in process in the production department and were 80% complete with respect to materials and 20% complete with respect to conversion. The production department had $683,750 of direct materials and $446,050 of conversion cost charged to it during May. Its beginning inventory included $99,075 of direct materials cost and $53,493 of conversion cost.

1. Compute the number of units transferred to finished goods.
2. Compute the number of equivalent units with respect to both materials used and conversion used in the production department for May using the FIFO method.
3. Compute the direct materials cost and the conversion cost per equivalent unit for the department.
4. Using the FIFO method, assign May's costs to the units transferred to finished goods and assign costs to its ending work in process inventory.

Check (2) EUP for materials, 273,500

Problem 16-7B^A
FIFO: Process cost summary, equivalent units, cost estimates
C2 C3 C4 P4

Belda Co. makes organic juice in two departments: cutting and blending. Direct materials are added at the beginning of each process, and conversion costs are added evenly throughout each process. The company uses the FIFO method of process costing. During March, the cutting department completed and transferred 220,000 units to the blending department. Of the units completed, 10,000 were from beginning inventory and the remaining 210,000 were started and completed during the month. Beginning work in process was 75% complete with respect to direct materials and 60% complete with respect to conversion. The company has 40,000 units (50% complete with respect to direct materials and 30% complete with respect to conversion) in process at month-end. Information on the cutting department's costs of beginning work in process inventory and costs added during the month follows.

Cost	Direct Materials	Conversion
Of beginning work in process inventory	$ 16,800	$ 97,720
Added during the month	223,200	1,233,960

Required

1. Prepare the cutting department's process cost summary for March using the FIFO method.
2. Prepare the journal entry dated March 31 to transfer the cost of completed units to the blending department.

Check (1) EUP for conversion, 226,000
(2) Cost transferred out, $1,486,960

Analysis Component

3. The company provides incentives to department managers by paying monthly bonuses based on their success in controlling costs per equivalent unit of production. Assume that the production department overestimates the percentage of completion for units in ending inventory with the result that its equivalent units of production for March are overstated. What impact does this error have on bonuses paid to the managers of the production department? What impact, if any, does this error have on these managers' April bonuses?

SERIAL PROBLEM
Business Solutions
C1 A1

(This serial problem began in Chapter 1 and continues through most of the book. If previous chapter segments were not completed, the serial problem can begin at this point.)

SP 16 The computer workstation furniture manufacturing that Santana Rey started is progressing well. At this point, Santana is using a job order costing system to account for the production costs of this product line. Santana has heard about process costing and is wondering whether process costing might be a better method for her to keep track of and monitor her production costs.

Required

1. What are the features that distinguish job order costing from process costing?
2. Do you believe that Santana should continue to use job order costing or switch to process costing for her workstation furniture manufacturing? Explain.

COMPREHENSIVE PROBLEM

Major League Bat Company

Weighted average: Review of Chapters 2, 4, 14, 16

CP 16 Major League Bat Company manufactures baseball bats. In addition to its work in process inventories, the company maintains inventories of raw materials and finished goods. It uses raw materials as direct materials in production and as indirect materials. Its factory payroll costs include direct labor for production and indirect labor. All materials are added at the beginning of the process, and conversion costs are applied uniformly throughout the production process.

Required

You are to maintain records and produce measures of inventories to reflect the July events of this company. Set up the following general ledger accounts and enter the June 30 balances: Raw Materials Inventory, $25,000; Work in Process Inventory, $8,135 ($2,660 of direct materials and $5,475 of conversion); Finished Goods Inventory, $110,000; Sales, $0; Cost of Goods Sold, $0; Factory Payroll Payable, $0; and Factory Overhead, $0.

1. Prepare journal entries to record the following July transactions and events.
   a. Purchased raw materials for $125,000 cash (the company uses a perpetual inventory system).
   b. Used raw materials as follows: direct materials, $52,440; and indirect materials, $10,000.
   c. Recorded factory payroll payable costs as follows: direct labor, $202,250; and indirect labor, $25,000.
   d. Paid factory payroll cost of $227,250 with cash (ignore taxes).
   e. Incurred additional factory overhead costs of $80,000 paid in cash.
   f. Allocated factory overhead to production at 50% of direct labor costs.

Check (1*f*) Cr. Factory Overhead, $101,125

2. Information about the July inventories follows. Use this information with that from part 1 to prepare a process cost summary, assuming the weighted-average method is used.

Check (2) EUP for conversion, 14,200

Units	
Beginning inventory	5,000 units
Started	14,000 units
Ending inventory	8,000 units
Beginning inventory	
Materials—Percent complete	100%
Conversion—Percent complete	75%
Ending inventory	
Materials—Percent complete	100%
Conversion—Percent complete	40%

3. Using the results from part 2 and the available information, make computations and prepare journal entries to record the following:
   g. Total costs transferred to finished goods for July (label this entry g).
   h. Sale of finished goods costing $265,700 for $625,000 in cash (label this entry h).

(3*g*) $271,150

4. Post entries from parts 1 and 3 to the ledger accounts set up at the beginning of the problem.

5. Compute the amount of gross profit from the sales in July. (*Note:* Add any underapplied overhead to, or deduct any overapplied overhead from, the cost of goods sold. Ignore the corresponding journal entry.)

GENERAL LEDGER PROBLEM

Available in Connect

connect ACCOUNTING

The **General Ledger** tool in *Connect* automates several of the procedural steps in accounting so that the financial professional can focus on the impacts of each transaction on various reports and performance measures.

GL 16-1 General Ledger assignment GL 16-1, based on Problem 16-1A, focuses on transactions related to process costing. Prepare summary journal entries to record the cost of units manufactured and their flow through the manufacturing environment. Then prepare a schedule of cost of goods manufactured and a partial income statement.

Beyond the Numbers

REPORTING IN ACTION

C2

APPLE

BTN 16-1 **Apple** reports in notes to its financial statements that, in addition to its products sold, it includes the following costs (among others) in cost of sales: customer shipping and handling expenses and warranty expenses.

Required

1. Why do you believe Apple includes these costs in its cost of sales?
2. What effect does this cost accounting policy for its cost of sales have on Apple's financial statements and any analysis of those statements? Explain.

Fast Forward

3. Access Apple's financial statements for the years after September 28, 2013, from its website (**Apple.com**) or the SEC's EDGAR website (**SEC.gov**). Review its footnote relating to Summary of Significant Accounting Policies. Has Apple changed its policy with respect to what costs are included in the cost of sales? Explain.

COMPARATIVE ANALYSIS

C1

APPLE
GOOGLE

BTN 16-2 Manufacturers such as **Apple** and **Google** usually work to maintain a high-quality and low-cost operation. One ratio routinely computed for this assessment is the cost of goods sold divided by total expenses. A decline in this ratio can mean that the company is spending too much on selling and administrative activities. An increase in this ratio beyond a reasonable level can mean that the company is not spending enough on selling activities. (Assume for this analysis that total expenses equal the cost of goods sold plus total operating expenses.)

Required

1. For Apple and Google refer to Appendix A and compute the ratios of cost of goods sold to total expenses for their two most recent fiscal years. (Record answers as percents, rounded to one decimal.)
2. Comment on the similarities or differences in the ratio results across both years between the companies.

ETHICS CHALLENGE

C1

BTN 16-3 Many accounting and accounting-related professionals are skilled in financial analysis, but most are not skilled in manufacturing. This is especially the case for process manufacturing environments (for example, a bottling plant or chemical factory). To provide professional accounting and financial services, one must understand the industry, product, and processes. We have an ethical responsibility to develop this understanding before offering services to clients in these areas.

Required

Write a one-page action plan, in memorandum format, discussing how you would obtain an understanding of key business processes of a company that hires you to provide financial services. The memorandum should specify an industry, a product, and one selected process and should draw on at least one reference, such as a professional journal or industry magazine.

COMMUNICATING IN PRACTICE

A1 C1 P1 P2

BTN 16-4 You hire a new assistant production manager whose prior experience is with a company that produced goods to order. Your company engages in continuous production of homogeneous products that go through various production processes. Your new assistant e-mails you questioning some cost classifications on an internal report—specifically why the costs of some materials that do not actually become part of the finished product, including some labor costs not directly associated with producing the product, are classified as direct costs. Respond to this concern via memorandum.

TAKING IT TO THE NET

C1

BTN 16-5 Many companies acquire software to help them monitor and control their costs and as an aid to their accounting systems. One company that supplies such software is **proDacapo** (**prodacapo.com**). There are many other such vendors. Access proDacapo's website, click on "Products," then click on "Prodacapo Process Management," and review the information displayed.

Required

How is process management software helpful to businesses? Explain with reference to costs, efficiency, and examples, if possible.

BTN 16-6 The purpose of this team activity is to ensure that each team member understands process operations and the related accounting entries. Find the activities and flows identified in Exhibit 16.14 with numbers ①–⑩. Pick a member of the team to start by describing activity number ① in this exhibit, then verbalizing the related journal entry, and describing how the amounts in the entry are computed. The other members of the team are to agree or disagree; discussion is to continue until all members express understanding. Rotate to the next numbered activity and next team member until all activities and entries have been discussed. If at any point a team member is uncertain about an answer, the team member may pass and get back in the rotation when he or she can contribute to the team's discussion.

TEAMWORK IN ACTION

C1 P1 P2 P3 P4

BTN 16-7 This chapter's opener featured Nick Nicolay and his company **Kar's Nuts**.

ENTREPRENEURIAL DECISION

C3 A2

Required

1. Kar's Nuts uses three processes: roasting, blending, and packaging. What are some benefits of using separate process cost summary reports for each process?
2. Nick tries to order raw materials just-in-time for their use in production. How does holding raw materials inventories increase costs? If the items are not used in production, how can they impact profits? Explain.
3. Suppose Kar's Nuts decides to allow customers to make their own unique trail mix flavors. Why might the company then use a hybrid costing system?

BTN 16-8 In process costing, the process is analyzed first and then a unit measure is computed in the form of equivalent units for direct materials, conversion (direct labor and overhead), and both types of costs combined. The same analysis applies to both manufacturing and service processes.

HITTING THE ROAD

C2

Required

Visit your local **U.S. Mail** center. Look into the back room, and you will see several ongoing processes. Select one process, such as sorting, and list the costs associated with this process. Your list should include materials, labor, and overhead; be specific. Classify each cost as fixed or variable. At the bottom of your list, outline how overhead should be assigned to your identified process. The following format (with an example) is suggested.

Point: The class can compare and discuss the different processes studied and the answers provided.

		Conversion			
Cost Description	Direct Material	Direct Labor	Overhead	Variable Cost	Fixed Cost
Manual sorting		X		X	
⋮					
Overhead allocation suggestions:					

BTN 16-9 **Samsung**, **Apple**, and **Google** are competitors in the global marketplace. Selected data for Samsung follow.

GLOBAL DECISION

C1

Samsung
APPLE
GOOGLE

(billions of Korean won)	Current Year	Prior Year
Cost of goods sold	₩137,696.3	₩126,651.9
Operating expenses	54,211.3	45,402.3
Total expenses	₩191,907.6	₩172,054.2

Required

1. Review the discussion of the importance of the cost of goods sold divided by total expenses ratio in BTN 16-2. Compute the cost of goods sold to total expenses ratio for Samsung for the two years of data provided. (Record answers as percents, rounded to one decimal.)
2. Comment on the similarities or differences in the ratio results calculated in part 1 and in BTN 16-2 across years and companies. (Record answers as percents, rounded to one decimal.)

ANSWERS TO MULTIPLE CHOICE QUIZ

1. d
2. e
3. b; $20,000 + $152,000 + $45,000 + $18,000 − $218,000 = $17,000
4. a; 40,000 + (15,000 × 1/3) = 45,000 EUP
5. c; ($6,000 + $84,000) ÷ 45,000 EUP = $2 per EUP

chapter 17

Activity-Based Costing and Analysis

Chapter Preview

ASSIGNING OVERHEAD COSTS	APPLYING ACTIVITY-BASED COSTING	ASSESSING ACTIVITY-BASED COSTING
C1 Alternative methods **P1** Single plantwide overhead rate method **P2** Multiple departmental overhead rate method **A1** Assessing plantwide and departmental rate methods **C2** Activity-based costing rates and methods	**P3** Step 1 Identify activities and their costs Step 2 Trace overhead costs to cost pools Step 3 Determine activity rates Step 4 Assign overhead costs to cost objects	**A2** Advantages of activity-based costing Disadvantages of activity-based costing Activity-based costing for service providers **C3** Types of activities

Learning Objectives

CONCEPTUAL

C1 Distinguish between the plantwide overhead rate method, the departmental overhead rate method, and the activity-based costing method.

C2 Explain cost flows for activity-based costing.

C3 Describe the four types of activities that cause overhead costs.

ANALYTICAL

A1 Identify and assess advantages and disadvantages of the plantwide overhead and departmental overhead rate methods.

A2 Identify and assess advantages and disadvantages of activity-based costing.

PROCEDURAL

P1 Allocate overhead costs to products using the plantwide overhead rate method.

P2 Allocate overhead costs to products using the departmental overhead rate method.

P3 Allocate overhead costs to products using activity-based costing.

© Robert Gallagher/Forbes Magazine/Forbes Collection/Corbis Outline

Juicin' Profits

SAN DIEGO—Chance encounters sometimes lead to great opportunities. "I was just into eating healthy food, surfing, and doing a lot of yoga," says Eric Ethans. Stressed out from law school, Annie Lawless devoted herself to teaching yoga and making fresh juices. "I would bring juice to yoga classes, and people started to buy it," says Annie. One day, Eric strode into Annie's yoga class carrying his own homemade juice. "We became instant best friends, talking about all things juice and health-related," says Annie. Together, these best friends started **Suja Juice Co. (Sujajuice.com)**, a maker of cold-pressed juices made from organic fruits and vegetables.

> *"Do what you love and learn all you can about it"*
>
> **—Annie Lawless**

The duo started small, making juices in Ethans's beach bungalow and selling mainly to Annie's yoga class. Then they started a home-delivery service for their juices, and demand skyrocketed. Ethans found himself delivering juice via his skateboard, sometimes at night. Former customer (and company co-founder) James Brennan recalls, "One day Eric rode up on his skateboard and dropped the juice, shattering glass everywhere. I said, 'Eric, what's your plan here? If you ever really want to do something with this, let me know.'" Eric and Annie, exhausted after working so much and making little profit, asked Brennan to join their venture. In turn, Brennan introduced them to Jeff Church, a serial entrepreneur and now company CEO.

Making cold-pressed juice begins with organic fruits and vegetables, grown on the company's own farms, and cut and inspected by trained chefs. To extend the shelf life of its juices, the company relies on expensive high-pressure processing instead of pasteurization or the use of chemical preservatives. "People don't want the additives and concentrates we grew up with," notes Brennan, "they want things that are organic and natural and raw." Making Suja's juices is expensive, and the use of costly raw materials and overhead costs require company managers to understand product costs.

While Eric and Annie focus mainly on developing new juices, they understand that overhead cost allocation is vital for managerial decisions such as product pricing and product mix. Overhead costs, such as plant maintenance, supervision, and clean-up costs, must be allocated to products. In smaller businesses with few product lines, a single plantwide overhead allocation rate is often sufficient. But, as businesses grow and offer more diverse product lines, more sophisticated costing techniques are often needed. The departmental overhead rate method improves upon the plantwide rate method by using more than one overhead allocation rate. Activity-based costing (ABC), which focuses on the activities that cause costs, can help managers monitor and control overhead costs and ensure product quality. ABC can be especially useful in companies like Suja, where different product lines require different processes and varying levels of overhead.

So far, Suja's recipe is clearly working. Founded in 2012, the company generated sales of $17 million in 2013 and about $50 million in 2014. "I don't think anyone here thought this was going to be as big as it is," says Eric. "I would have been happy even if it was much smaller." Still, the owners are planning for even more rapid growth. "Natural cold-pressed organic juices—this is the hottest beverage market on the planet right now," says Brennan. In addition to stressing the importance of partnering with experienced and talented mentors, Annie encourages young entrepreneurs to "constantly push forward and never settle. Put in the extra work to make things extraordinary."

Sources: *Suja Juice Co. website,* January 2015; *Forbes,* February 10, 2014; *San Diego Business Journal,* May 20, 2013; *Livetheprocess.com; Wellandgoodnyc.com,* December 31, 2013

ASSIGNING OVERHEAD COSTS

C1

Distinguish between the plantwide overhead rate method, the departmental overhead rate method, and the activity-based costing method.

Managerial activities such as product pricing, product mix decisions, and cost control depend on accurate product cost information. Distorted product cost information can result in poor decisions. Knowing accurate costs for producing, delivering, and servicing products helps managers set a price to cover product costs and yield a profit.

In competitive markets, price is established through the forces of supply and demand. In these situations, managers must understand product costs to assess whether the market price is high enough to justify the cost of entering the market. Disparities between market prices and producer costs give managers insight into their efficiency relative to competitors.

Product costs consist of direct materials, direct labor, and overhead (indirect costs). Since the physical components of a product (direct materials) and the work of making a product (direct labor) can be traced to units of output, the assignment of costs of these factors is usually straightforward. Overhead costs, however, are not directly related to production volume and therefore cannot be traced to units of product in the same way that direct materials and direct labor can.

Point: Evidence suggests overhead costs have steadily increased while direct labor costs have steadily decreased as a percentage of total manufacturing costs over recent decades. This puts greater importance on accurate cost allocations.

For example, we can trace the cost of putting tires on a car because we know there is a logical relation between the number of cars produced and the number of tires needed for each car. The cost to heat an automobile manufacturing factory, however, is not readily linked to the number of cars made. Consequently, we must use an allocation system to assign overhead costs such as utilities and factory maintenance. This chapter introduces three methods of overhead allocation: (1) the single plantwide overhead rate method, (2) the departmental overhead rate method, and (3) the activity-based costing method.

Alternative Methods of Overhead Allocation

Exhibit 17.1 summarizes some key features of these three alternative methods. Both the *plantwide overhead rate method* and the *departmental overhead rate method* use volume-based measures such as direct labor hours, direct labor dollars, or machine hours to allocate overhead costs to products. These methods differ in that the plantwide method uses a single rate for allocating overhead costs, and the departmental rate method uses at least two rates. The departmental method arguably provides more accurate cost allocations than the single rate allocations of the plantwide method. In contrast, *activity-based costing* focuses on activities and the costs of carrying out activities. Rates based on these activities are then used to assign overhead to products in proportion to the amount of activity required to produce them. Activity-based costing typically uses more overhead allocation rates than the plantwide and departmental methods.

EXHIBIT 17.1

Overhead Cost Allocation Methods

Allocation Method	Overhead Allocations Based on	Overhead Allocation Rates Based on
Plantwide rate	One rate	Volume-based measures such as direct labor hours or machine hours
Departmental rate	Two or more rates	Volume-based measures such as direct labor hours or machine hours
Activity-based costing	At least two (but often many) rates	Activities that drive costs, such as number of batches of product produced

Plantwide Overhead Rate Method

P1

Allocate overhead costs to products using the plantwide overhead rate method.

The first method of allocating overhead costs to products is known as the *single plantwide overhead rate method,* or simply the *plantwide overhead rate method.*

Cost Flows under Plantwide Overhead Rate Method For the plantwide overhead rate method, the target of the cost assignment, or **cost object,** is the unit of product—see Exhibit 17.2. The overhead rate is determined using volume-related measures such as direct labor hours, direct labor cost dollars, or machine hours, which are readily available in most manufacturing settings. In some industries, overhead costs are closely related to these volume-related measures. In such cases it is logical to use this method to assign overhead costs to products.

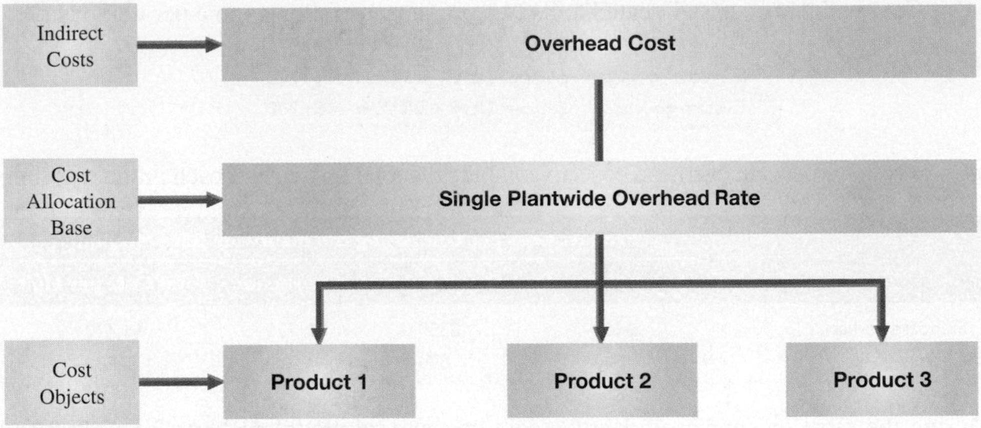

EXHIBIT 17.2

Plantwide Overhead Rate Method

Applying the Plantwide Overhead Rate Method Under the single plantwide overhead rate method, total budgeted overhead costs are combined into one overhead cost pool. This cost pool is then divided by the chosen allocation base, such as total direct labor hours, to arrive at a single plantwide overhead rate. This rate then is applied to assign costs to all products based on their usage of the allocation base.

To illustrate, consider data from KartCo, a go-kart manufacturer that produces both standard and custom go-karts for amusement parks. The standard go-kart is a basic model sold primarily to amusement parks that service county and state fairs. Custom go-karts are produced for theme parks who want unique go-karts that coordinate with their respective themes.

Assume that KartCo applies the plantwide overhead rate method and uses direct labor hours (DLH) as its overhead allocation base. KartCo's budgeted DLH information is in Exhibit 17.3.

EXHIBIT 17.3

KartCo's Budgeted Direct Labor Hours

	Number of Units	Direct Labor Hours per Unit	Total Direct Labor Hours
Standard go-kart . . .	5,000	15	75,000
Custom go-kart	1,000	25	25,000
Total			100,000

KartCo's budgeted overhead cost information is in Exhibit 17.4. Its overhead cost consists of indirect labor and factory utilities.

EXHIBIT 17.4

KartCo's Budgeted Overhead Cost

	Budgeted Cost
Indirect labor cost	$4,000,000
Factory utilities	800,000
Total budgeted overhead cost	$4,800,000

The single plantwide overhead rate for KartCo is computed as follows.

$$\text{Plantwide overhead rate} = \text{Total budgeted overhead cost} \div \text{Total budgeted direct labor hours}$$
$$= \$4{,}800{,}000 \div 100{,}000 \text{ DLH}$$
$$= \$48 \text{ per DLH}$$

This plantwide overhead rate is then used to allocate overhead cost to products based on the number of direct labor hours required to produce each unit as follows.

$$\text{Overhead allocated to each product unit} = \text{Plantwide overhead rate} \times \text{DLH per unit}$$

For KartCo, overhead cost is allocated to its two products as follows (on a per unit basis).

Standard go-kart:	$48 per DLH × 15 DLH = $ 720
Custom go-kart:	$48 per DLH × 25 DLH = $1,200

KartCo uses these per unit overhead costs to compute the total unit cost of each product as follows.

	Product Cost per Unit Using the Plantwide Rate Method			
	Direct Materials	Direct Labor	Overhead	Total Cost per Unit
Standard go-kart	$400	$350	$ 720	$1,470
Custom go-kart	600	500	1,200	2,300

© Getty Images

During the most recent period, KartCo sold its standard model go-karts for $2,000 and its custom go-karts for $3,500. A recent report from its marketing staff indicates that competitors are selling go-karts similar to KartCo's standard model for as low as $1,200. KartCo management knows the company must be competitive, but management is concerned that meeting this lower price would result in a loss of $270 ($1,200 − $1,470) on each standard go-kart sold.

In the case of its custom go-kart, KartCo has been swamped with orders and cannot meet demand. Accordingly, management is considering dropping the standard model and concentrating on the custom model. Yet management recognizes that its pricing and cost decisions are influenced by its cost allocations. Thus, before making any strategic decisions, management has directed its cost analysts to further review production costs for both the standard and custom go-kart models. To pursue this analysis, the cost analysts first turned to the departmental overhead rate method.

Departmental Overhead Rate Method

P2

Allocate overhead costs to products using the departmental overhead rate method.

Many companies have several departments that produce various products and consume overhead resources in substantially different ways. Under such circumstances, use of a single plantwide overhead rate can produce cost assignments that fail to accurately reflect the cost to manufacture a specific product. In these cases, use of multiple overhead rates can result in better overhead cost allocations and improve management decisions.

Cost Flows under Departmental Overhead Rate Method The *departmental overhead rate method* uses a different overhead rate for each production department. This is usually done through a four-step process (see Exhibit 17.5):

1. Assign overhead costs to departmental *cost pools.*
2. Select an allocation base for each department.
3. Compute overhead allocation rates for each department.
4. Use departmental overhead rates to assign overhead costs to cost objects (products).

EXHIBIT 17.5

Departmental Overhead Rate Method

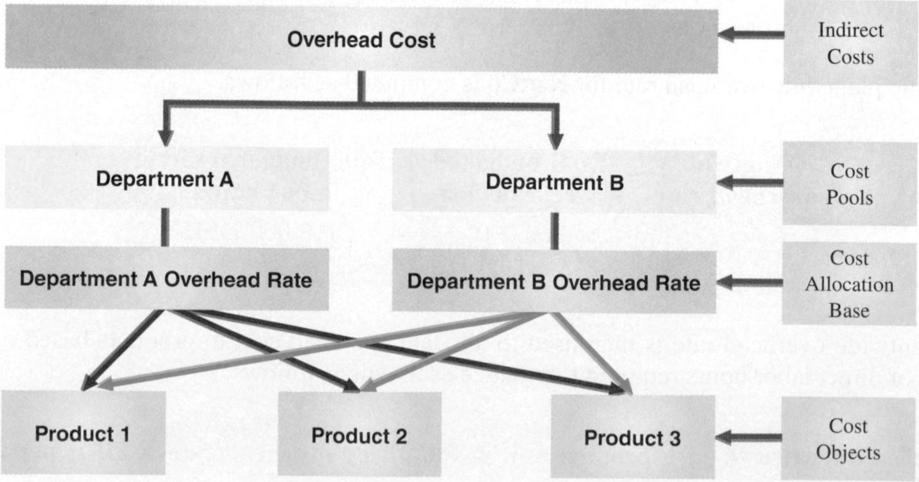

Exhibit 17.5 shows that under the departmental overhead rate method, overhead costs are first determined separately for each production department. Next, an overhead rate is computed for each production department to allocate the overhead costs of each department to products passing through that department. The departmental overhead rate method allows each department to have its own overhead rate and its own allocation base. For example, an assembly department can use direct labor hours to allocate its overhead cost while a machining department can use machine hours as its base.

Applying the Departmental Overhead Rate Method To illustrate the departmental overhead rate method, let's return to KartCo. KartCo has two production departments, the machining department and the assembly department. The first step requires that KartCo assign its $4,800,000 overhead cost to its two production departments. KartCo determines from an analysis of its indirect labor and factory utilities that $4,200,000 of overhead costs are traceable to its machining department and the remaining $600,000 are traceable to its assembly department.

The second step requires each department to determine an allocation base. For KartCo, the machining department uses machine hours (MH) as a base for allocating its overhead; the assembly department uses direct labor hours (DLH) as the base for allocating its overhead. The relevant information for KartCo's machining and assembly departments is in Exhibit 17.6.

Point: In some cases it is difficult for companies to trace overhead costs to distinct departments as some overhead costs can be common to several departments. In these cases, companies must allocate overhead to departments applying reasonable allocation bases.

EXHIBIT 17.6

Allocation Information for Machining and Assembly Departments

	Number of Units	Machining Department		Assembly Department	
		Hours per Unit	Total Hours	Hours per Unit	Total Hours
Standard go-kart	5,000	10 MH per unit	50,000 MH	5 DLH per unit	25,000 DLH
Custom go-kart	1,000	20 MH per unit	20,000 MH	5 DLH per unit	5,000 DLH
Totals			70,000 MH		30,000 DLH

In step three, each department computes its own overhead rate using the following formula.

$$\text{Departmental overhead rate} = \frac{\text{Total budgeted departmental overhead cost}}{\text{Total amount of departmental allocation base}}$$

KartCo's departmental overhead rates are computed as follows.

$$\text{Machining department overhead rate} = \frac{\$4{,}200{,}000}{70{,}000\text{ MH}} = \$60\text{ per MH}$$

$$\text{Assembly department overhead rate} = \frac{\$600{,}000}{30{,}000\text{ DLH}} = \$20\text{ per DLH}$$

Step four is to apply overhead costs to each product based on departmental overhead rates. For KartCo, since each standard go-kart requires 10 MH from the machining department and five DLH from the assembly department, the overhead cost allocated to each standard go-kart is $600 from the machining department (10 MH × $60 per MH) and $100 from the assembly department (5 DLH × $20 per DLH). The same procedure is applied for its custom go-kart. The allocation of overhead costs to KartCo's standard and custom go-karts is summarized in Exhibit 17.7.

EXHIBIT 17.7

Overhead Allocation Using Departmental Overhead Rates

	Departmental Overhead Rate	Standard Go-Kart		Custom Go-Kart	
		Hours per Unit	Overhead Allocated	Hours per Unit	Overhead Allocated
Machining department	$60 per MH	10 MH per unit	$600	20 MH per unit	$1,200
Assembly department	$20 per DLH	5 DLH per unit	100	5 DLH per unit	100
Totals			$700		$1,300

Point: Total budgeted overhead costs are the same under both the plantwide and departmental rate methods.

Allocated overhead costs vary depending upon the allocation methods used. Exhibit 17.8 summarizes and compares the allocated overhead costs for standard and custom go-karts under the single plantwide overhead rate and the departmental overhead rate methods. The overhead cost allocated to each standard go-kart decreased from $720 under the plantwide overhead rate method to $700 under the departmental overhead rate method, whereas overhead cost allocated to each custom go-kart increased from $1,200 to $1,300. These differences occur because the custom go-kart requires more hours in the machining department (20 MH) than the standard go-kart requires (10 MH).

EXHIBIT 17.8

Comparison of Plantwide Overhead Rate and Departmental Overhead Rate Methods

Overhead per Unit Using:	Standard Go-Kart	Custom Go-Kart
Plantwide overhead rate method	$720	$1,200
Departmental overhead rate method.........	$700	$1,300

Compared to the plantwide overhead rate method, the departmental overhead rate method usually results in more accurate overhead allocations. When cost analysts are able to logically trace overhead costs to different cost allocation bases, costing accuracy is improved. For KartCo, using the multiple departmental overhead rate method yields the following total costs per unit.

	Product Cost per Unit Using Departmental Rate Method			
	Direct Materials	Direct Labor	Overhead	Total Cost per Unit
Standard go-kart..........	$400	$350	$ 700	$1,450
Custom go-kart	600	500	1,300	2,400

These costs per unit under the departmental overhead rate method are different from those under the plantwide overhead rate method. Further, this information suggests that KartCo management seriously review future production for its standard go-kart product. Specifically, these cost data imply that KartCo cannot make a profit on its standard go-kart if it meets competitors' $1,200 price.

NEED-TO-KNOW 17-1

Plantwide and Departmental Rate Methods

P1 P2

A manufacturer reports the following budgeted data for its two production departments.

	Machining	Assembly
Manufacturing overhead costs...............	$600,000	$300,000
Machine hours to be used (MH)	20,000	0
Direct labor hours to be used (DLH).........	20,000	5,000

1. What is the company's single plantwide overhead rate based on direct labor hours?
2. What are the company's departmental overhead rates if the machining department assigns overhead based on machine hours and the assembly department assigns overhead based on direct labor hours?
3. Using the departmental overhead rates from part 2, how much overhead should be assigned to a job that uses 16 machine hours in the machining department and 5 direct labor hours in the assembly department?

Solution

1. Plantwide overhead rate $= \dfrac{\$600{,}000 + \$300{,}000}{20{,}000 \text{ DLH} + 5{,}000 \text{ DLH}} = \dfrac{\$900{,}000}{25{,}000 \text{ DLH}} = \$36$ per direct labor hour
2. Machining department rate $= \dfrac{\$600{,}000}{20{,}000 \text{ MH}} = \$30$ per machine hour

   Assembly department rate $= \dfrac{\$300{,}000}{5{,}000 \text{ DLH}} = \$60$ per direct labor hour
3. Overhead assigned to job = (16 MH × $30 per MH) + (5 DLH × $60 per DLH) = $780

Do More: QS 17-3, QS 17-4, QS 17-5, E 17-1

Assessing the Plantwide and Departmental Overhead Rate Methods

A1 Identify and assess advantages and disadvantages of the plantwide overhead and departmental overhead rate methods.

The plantwide and departmental overhead rate methods have three key advantages: (1) They are based on readily available information, like direct labor hours. (2) They are easy to implement. (3) They are consistent with GAAP and can be used for external reporting needs. Both suffer from an important disadvantage, in that overhead costs are frequently too complex to be explained by one factor like direct labor hours or machine hours. Further, technological advances often lower direct labor costs as a percentage of total manufacturing costs, meaning direct labor hours might not be a good allocation base.

Plantwide Overhead Rate Method The usefulness of overhead allocations based on the single plantwide overhead rate for managerial decisions depends on two critical assumptions: (1) overhead costs change with the allocation base (such as direct labor hours); and (2) all products use overhead costs in the same proportions.

The reasonableness of these assumptions varies. For companies that manufacture few products or whose operations are labor-intensive, the single plantwide method can yield reasonably useful information for managerial decisions. However, for companies with many different products or those with products that use overhead costs in very different ways, the assumptions of the single plantwide rate are not reasonable. When overhead costs, like machinery depreciation, bear little if any relation to direct labor hours used, allocating overhead cost using a single plantwide overhead rate based on direct labor hours can distort product cost and lead to poor managerial decisions. Despite such shortcomings, some companies continue to use the plantwide method for its simplicity.

Departmental Overhead Rate Method The departmental overhead rate method is more refined than the plantwide overhead rate method, but it too can distort product costs. The departmental overhead rate method assumes that different products are similar in volume, complexity, and batch size, and that departmental overhead costs are directly proportional to the department allocation base (such as direct labor hours and machine hours for KartCo). When products differ in batch size and complexity, they usually consume different amounts of overhead costs. This is likely the case for KartCo with its high-volume standard model and its low-volume custom model built to customer specifications. In addition, since the departmental overhead rate method still allocates overhead costs based on measures closely related to production volume, it also fails to accurately assign many overhead costs, like machine depreciation or utility costs, that are not driven by production volume.

The next section describes the activity-based costing method, which is designed to overcome some of the limitations of the plantwide and departmental overhead rate methods.

Decision Ethics

Department Manager Three department managers jointly decide to hire a consulting firm for advice on increasing departmental effectiveness and efficiency. The consulting firm spends 50% of its efforts on department "A" and 25% on each of the other two departments. The manager for department "A" suggests that the three departments equally share the consulting fee. As a manager of one of the other two departments, do you believe equal sharing is fair? ■ [Answers follow the chapter's Summary.]

Activity-Based Costing Rates and Method

C2 Explain cost flows for activity-based costing.

Activity-based costing (ABC) attempts to more accurately assign overhead costs to the users of overhead by focusing on *activities*. Unlike the plantwide rate method, ABC uses more than a single rate. Unlike the departmental rate method, ABC focuses on activities rather than departments. In the next section we illustrate the activity-based costing method of assigning overhead costs.

Cost Flows under Activity-Based Costing Method The basic principle underlying activity-based costing is that an **activity,** which is a task, operation, or procedure, is what causes costs to be incurred. For example, cutting raw materials consumes labor and machine hours.

© Bloomberg via Getty Images

Likewise, warehousing products consumes resources (costs) such as employee time for driving a forklift, the electricity to power the forklift, and the wear and tear on a forklift. Also, training employees drives costs such as fees or salaries paid to trainers and the training supplies required. Generally, all activities of an organization can be linked to use of resources. An **activity cost pool** is a collection of costs that are related to the same or similar activity. Pooling costs to determine an **activity overhead (pool) rate** for all costs incurred by the same activity reduces the number of cost assignments required.

There are four basic steps to the ABC method (see Exhibit 17.9):

1. Identify activities and the overhead costs they cause.
2. Trace overhead costs to activity cost pools.
3. Compute overhead allocation rates for each activity.
4. Use the activity overhead rates to assign overhead costs to cost objects (products).

EXHIBIT 17.9

Activity-Based Costing Method

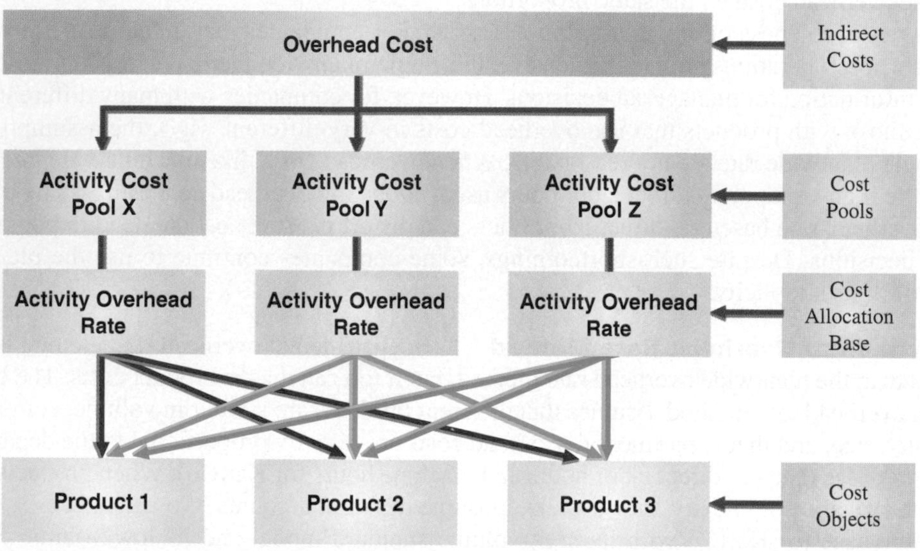

To reduce the total number of activities that must be assigned costs, similar activities (those caused by the same factor) are grouped into activity cost *pools*. For example, handling raw materials requires several activities, including wages of receiving department employees, wages of forklift employees who move materials, and depreciation on forklifts. These activities can be grouped into a single cost pool since they are all caused by the amount of materials moved. Next we apply the ABC method to KartCo.

QC1

APPLYING ACTIVITY-BASED COSTING

© JoeFox Karting/Alamy

Activity-based costing accumulates overhead costs into activity cost pools and then uses activity rates to allocate those costs to products. This involves four steps: (1) identify activities and the costs they cause; (2) trace overhead costs to activity cost pools; (3) determine an activity rate for each activity cost pool; and (4) allocate overhead costs to products using those activity rates. To illustrate, let's return to KartCo and apply steps 1 through 4.

Step 1: Identify Activities and the Costs They Cause

Step 1 in applying ABC is to identify activities and the costs they cause. This is commonly done through discussions with employees in production departments and through reviews of production activities. The more activities that ABC tracks, the more accurately overhead costs are assigned. However, tracking too many activities makes the system cumbersome and costly to maintain. It is often necessary to reduce the number of activities tracked by combining similar activities. An activity can also involve several related tasks. The aim of this first step is to understand actions performed in the organization that drive costs.

KartCo has total overhead costs of $4,800,000 consisting of $4,000,000 indirect labor costs and $800,000 factory utilities costs. Details gathered by KartCo about its overhead costs are shown in Exhibit 17.10. Column totals for indirect labor and factory utilities correspond to amounts in Exhibit 17.4. Activity-based costing provides more detail about the activities and the costs they cause than is provided from traditional costing methods.

P3

Allocate overhead costs to products using activity-based costing.

EXHIBIT 17.10

KartCo Overhead Cost Details

Activity	Indirect Labor	Factory Utilities	Total Overhead
Machine setup	$ 700,000	—	$ 700,000
Machine repair	1,300,000	—	1,300,000
Factory maintenance	800,000	—	800,000
Engineer salaries	1,200,000	—	1,200,000
Assembly line power	—	$600,000	600,000
Heating and lighting	—	200,000	200,000
Totals	$4,000,000	$800,000	$4,800,000

Step 2: Trace Overhead Costs to Activity Cost Pools

Step 2 in applying ABC is to assign activities and their overhead costs to activity cost pools. Overhead costs are commonly accumulated by each department in a traditional accounting system. Instead of combining costs from different activities into one plantwide pool or multiple departmental pools, ABC focuses on activities as the cost object in the first step of cost assignment. We are then able to *trace* costs to a cost object and then combine activities that are used by products in similar ways to reduce the number of cost allocations.

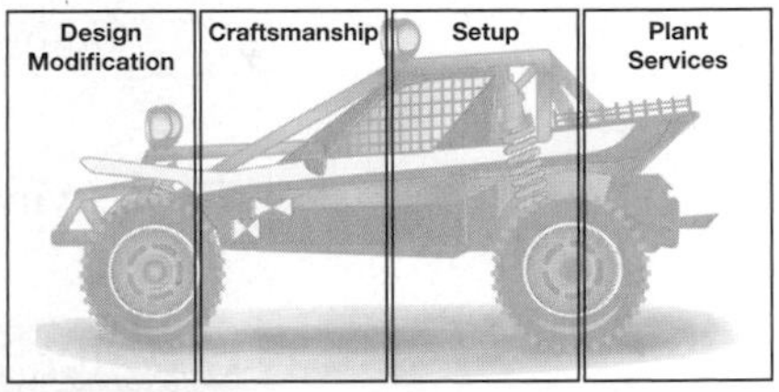

After a review and analysis of its activities, KartCo management assigns its overhead costs into its four activity cost pools: craftsmanship, setup, design modification, and plant services (see Exhibit 17.11). To assign costs to pools, management looks for costs that are caused by similar activities.

EXHIBIT 17.11

Assigning Overhead to Activity Cost Pools

Activity Pools	Activity Cost	Pool Cost
Craftsmanship		
Assembly line power	$ 600,000	$ 600,000
Setup		
Machine setup	700,000	
Machine repair	1,300,000	2,000,000
Design modification		
Engineer salaries	1,200,000	1,200,000
Plant services		
Factory maintenance	800,000	
Heating and lighting	200,000	1,000,000
Total overhead cost		$4,800,000

Exhibit 17.11 shows that $600,000 of overhead costs are assigned to the craftsmanship cost pool; $2,000,000 to the setup cost pool; $1,200,000 to the design-modification cost pool; and $1,000,000 to the plant services cost pool. This reduces the potential number of overhead rates from six (one for each of its six activities) to four (one for each activity pool).

Step 3: Determine Activity Rates

Step 3 is to compute activity rates used to assign overhead costs to final cost objects such as products. Proper determination of activity rates depends on (1) proper identification of the factor that drives the cost in each activity cost pool and (2) proper measures of activities.

The factor that drives cost, or **activity cost driver,** is that activity causing costs in the pool to be incurred. For KartCo's overhead, craftsmanship costs are mainly driven by the direct labor

© AP Images/Christof Stache

hours used to assemble products; setup costs are driven by the number of batches produced; design-modification costs are driven by the number of new designs; and plant service costs are driven by the square feet of building space occupied. These activity cost drivers serve as the allocation base for each activity cost pool. KartCo then determines an expected activity level for each activity pool, as shown below.

Activity Cost Pool	Activity Driver (# of)	Expected Activity Level
Craftsmanship	Direct labor hours	30,000 DLH
Setup	Batches	200 batches
Design modification	Designs	10 design modifications
Plant services	Square feet	20,000 square feet

In general, cost pool activity rates are computed as:

Cost pool activity rate = Overhead costs assigned to pool ÷ Expected activity level

For KartCo, the activity rate for the craftsmanship cost pool is computed as:

Craftsmanship cost pool activity rate = \$600,000 ÷ 30,000 DLH = \$20 per DLH

The activity rate computations for KartCo are summarized in Exhibit 17.12.

EXHIBIT 17.12

Activity Rates for KartCo

Activity Cost Pools	Activity Driver	Overhead Costs Assigned to Pool	÷ Expected Activity Level	= Activity Rate
Craftsmanship	DLH	\$ 600,000	30,000 DLH	\$20 per DLH
Setup	Batches	2,000,000	200 batches	\$10,000 per batch
Design modification	Number of designs	1,200,000	10 designs	\$120,000 per design
Plant services	Square feet	1,000,000	20,000 sq. ft.	\$50 per sq. ft.

Step 4: Assign Overhead Costs to Cost Objects

Step 4 is to assign overhead costs in each activity cost pool to final cost objects using activity rates. To do this, overhead costs are allocated to products based on the *actual* levels of activities used.

For KartCo, overhead costs in each pool are allocated to the standard go-karts and the custom go-karts using the activity rates from Exhibit 17.12. The actual activities used by each product line and the overhead costs allocated to standard and custom go-karts under ABC for KartCo are summarized in Exhibit 17.13. To illustrate, of the \$600,000 of overhead costs in the craftsmanship cost pool, \$500,000 is allocated to standard go-karts as follows.

Overhead from craftsmanship pool allocated to standard go-kart	=	**Activities consumed**	×	**Activity rate**
	=	25,000 DLH	×	\$20 per DLH
	=	\$500,000		

Point: In ABC, overhead is allocated based on the actual level of activities used, multiplied by a predetermined activity rate for each cost pool.

We know that standard go-karts require 25,000 direct labor hours and the activity rate for craftsmanship is \$20 per direct labor hour. Multiplying the number of direct labor hours by the activity rate yields the craftsmanship costs assigned to standard go-karts (\$500,000). Custom go-karts consumed 5,000 direct labor hours, so we assign \$100,000 (5,000 DLH × \$20 per DLH) of craftsmanship costs to that product line. We similarly allocate overhead of setup, design modification, and plant services pools to each type of go-kart.

EXHIBIT 17.13

Overhead Allocated to Go-Karts for KartCo

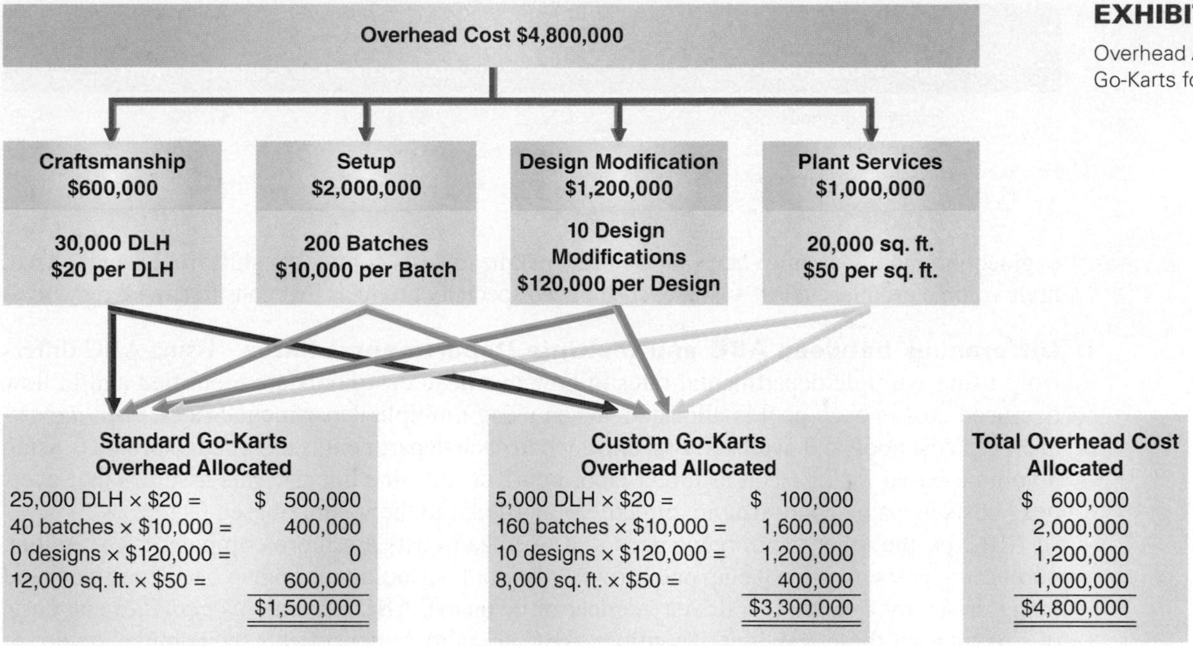

In assigning overhead costs to products, KartCo assigned no design-modification costs to standard go-karts because standard go-karts are sold as "off-the-shelf" items. Using ABC, a total of $1,500,000 of overhead costs is allocated to standard go-karts and a total of $3,300,000 is allocated to custom go-karts. While the total overhead cost allocated ($4,800,000) is the same as under the plantwide and departmental rate methods, the amounts allocated to the two product lines differ.

Overhead cost per unit is computed by dividing total overhead cost allocated to each product line by the number of product units. KartCo's overhead cost per unit for its standard and custom go-karts is computed and shown in Exhibit 17.14.

EXHIBIT 17.14

Overhead Cost per Unit for Go-Karts Using ABC

	(A) Total Overhead Cost Allocated	(B) Units Produced	(A ÷ B) Overhead Cost per Unit
Standard go-kart	$1,500,000	5,000 units	$ 300 per unit
Custom go-kart	3,300,000	1,000 units	$3,300 per unit

Total cost per unit for KartCo using ABC for its two products follows.

	Direct Materials	Direct Labor	Overhead	Total Cost per Unit
Standard go-kart ...	$400	$350	$ 300	$1,050
Custom go-kart	600	500	3,300	4,400

Assuming that ABC more accurately assigns costs, we now are able to help KartCo's management understand how its competitors can sell their standard models at $1,200 and why KartCo is flooded with orders for custom go-karts. Specifically, if the cost to produce a standard go-kart is $1,050, as shown above (and not $1,470 as computed using the plantwide rate or $1,450 computed using departmental rates), a profit of $150 ($1,200 − $1,050) occurs on each standard unit sold at the competitive $1,200 market price. Further, selling its custom go-kart at $3,500 is a mistake by KartCo management because it is losing $900 ($3,500 − $4,400) on each custom go-kart sold. That is, KartCo has underpriced its custom go-kart relative to its production costs and competitors' prices, which explains why the company has more custom orders than it can supply.

Point: Accurately assigning costs to products is key to setting many product prices. If product costs are inaccurate and result in prices that are too low, the company loses money on each item sold. Likewise, if product prices are improperly set too high, the company loses business to competitors. ABC can be used to more accurately set prices.

Exhibit 17.15 summarizes overhead allocation per go-kart under the single plantwide rate method, multiple departmental rate method, and ABC. Overhead cost allocated to standard go-karts is much less under ABC than under either of the volume-based costing methods. One reason for this difference is the large design-modification costs that were spread over all go-karts under both the plantwide rate and the departmental rate methods even though standard go-karts require no

EXHIBIT 17.15

Comparison of Overhead Allocations by Method

Overhead Cost Allocation Method	Overhead Cost per Go-Kart: Standard Go-Kart	Overhead Cost per Go-Kart: Custom Go-Kart
Plantwide method	$720	$1,200
Departmental method	700	1,300
Activity-based costing	300	3,300

engineering modification. When ABC is used, overhead costs commonly shift from standardized, high-volume products to low-volume, customized specialty products that consume more resources.

Differences between ABC and Multiple Departmental Rates Using ABC differs from using multiple departmental rates in how overhead cost pools are identified and in how overhead cost in each pool is allocated. When using multiple departmental rates, each *department* is a cost pool, and overhead cost allocated to each department is assigned to products using a volume-based factor (such as direct labor hours or machine hours). This assumes that overhead costs in each department are directly proportional to the volume-based factor.

ABC, on the other hand, recognizes that overhead costs are more complex. For example, purchasing costs might make up one activity cost pool, spanning more than one department and being driven by a single cost driver (number of invoices). ABC emphasizes *activities* and costs of carrying out these activities. Therefore, ABC arguably better reflects the complex nature of overhead costs and how these costs are used in making products.

Decision Maker

Entrepreneur You are the entrepreneur of a start-up pharmaceutical company. You are assigning overhead to product units based on machine hours in the packaging area. Profits are slim due to increased competition. One of your larger overhead costs is $10,000 for cleaning and sterilization that occurs each time the packaging system is converted from one product to another. These overhead costs average $0.10 per product unit. Can you reduce cleaning and sterilizing costs by reducing the number of units produced? If not, what should you do to control these overhead costs? ■ [Answers follow the chapter's Summary.]

NEED-TO-KNOW 17-2

Activity-Based Costing

P3

A manufacturer makes two types of snowmobiles, Basic and Deluxe, and reports the following data to be used in applying activity-based costing. The company budgets production of 6,000 Basic snowmobiles and 2,000 Deluxe snowmobiles.

Activity Cost Pool	Activity Cost Driver	Cost Assigned to Pool	Basic	Deluxe
Machine setup	Number of setups	$ 150,000	200 setups	300 setups
Materials handling	Number of parts	250,000	10 parts per unit	20 parts per unit
Machine depreciation	Machine hours (MH)	720,000	1 MH per unit	1.5 MH per unit
Total		$1,120,000		

1. Compute overhead activity rates for each cost pool using ABC.
2. Compute the total amount of overhead cost to be allocated to each of the company's product lines using ABC.
3. Compute the overhead cost per unit for each product line using ABC.

Solution

1. $$\text{Machine setup activity rate} = \frac{\$150{,}000}{200 + 300} = \$300 \text{ per machine setup}$$

$$\text{Materials handling activity rate} = \frac{\$250{,}000}{60{,}000 + 40{,}000^{*}} = \$2.50 \text{ per part}$$

*(6,000 units × 10 parts per unit for Basic, 2,000 units × 20 parts per unit for Deluxe)

$$\text{Machine depreciation activity rate} = \frac{\$720{,}000}{6{,}000 + 3{,}000^{**}} = \$80 \text{ per machine hour}$$

**(6,000 units × 1 MH per unit for Basic, 2,000 units × 1.5 MH per unit for Deluxe)

2.

Activity Cost Pool	Activity Pool Rate	Basic		Deluxe	
Machine setup	$300 per setup	$300 × 200 =	$ 60,000	$300 × 300 =	$ 90,000
Materials handling. . .	$2.50 per part	$2.50 × 6,000 × 10 =	150,000	$2.50 × 2,000 × 20 =	100,000
Machine depreciation	$80 per MH	$80 × 6,000 × 1 =	480,000	$80 × 2,000 × 1.5 =	240,000
Totals			$690,000		$430,000

3. Basic snowmobile overhead cost per unit $= \frac{\$690{,}000}{6{,}000} = \$115$ per unit

Deluxe snowmobile overhead cost per unit $= \frac{\$430{,}000}{2{,}000} = \$215$ per unit

QC2

Do More: QS 17-8, QS 17-9, QS 17-10, E 17-2, E 17-11, E 17-12

ASSESSING ACTIVITY-BASED COSTING

While activity-based costing can improve the accuracy of overhead cost allocations to products, it too has limitations. This section describes the major advantages and disadvantages of activity-based costing.

A2 Identify and assess advantages and disadvantages of activity-based costing.

Advantages of Activity-Based Costing

More Accurate Overhead Cost Allocation Companies have typically used either a plantwide overhead rate or multiple departmental overhead rates because these methods are more straightforward than ABC and are acceptable under GAAP for external reporting. Under these traditional systems, overhead costs are pooled in a few large pools and are spread uniformly across high- and low-volume products. With ABC, overhead costs are grouped into activity pools. There are usually more activity pools under ABC than cost pools under traditional costing, which usually increases costing accuracy. More important is that overhead costs in each ABC pool are caused by a single activity. This means that overhead costs in each activity pool are allocated to products based on the cost of resources consumed by a product (input) rather than on how many units are produced (output). In sum, overhead cost allocation under ABC is more accurate because (1) there are more cost pools, (2) costs in each pool are more similar, and (3) allocation is based on activities that cause overhead costs.

Point: ABC is not acceptable under GAAP for external financial reporting.

Point: ABC can allocate the selling and administrative costs expensed by GAAP to activities; such costs can include marketing costs, costs to process orders, and costs to process customer returns.

More Effective Overhead Cost Control Using the plantwide or departmental rate methods, companies usually allocate overhead costs to products based on either direct labor hours or machine hours. Such allocation typically leads management to focus attention on direct labor cost or machine hours. Yet, direct labor or machine hours are often not the cause of overhead costs and often not even linked with these volume-related measures. As we saw with KartCo, design modifications markedly affect its overhead costs. Consequently, a plantwide overhead rate or departmental overhead rate based on direct labor or machine hours can mislead managers, preventing effective control of overhead costs and leading to product mispricing. ABC, on the other hand, can be used to identify activities that can benefit from process improvement. ABC can also help managers effectively control overhead costs by focusing on processes or activities such as setups, order processing, and design modifications instead of focusing only on direct labor or machine hours. For KartCo, identification of large design-modification costs would allow managers to work on ways to improve this process. Besides controlling overhead costs, KartCo's better assignment of overhead costs (particularly design-modification costs) for its go-karts helps its managers make better production and pricing decisions.

Focus on Relevant Factors Basing cost assignment on activities is not limited to determining product costs. ABC can be used to assign costs to any cost object that is of management interest. For instance, a marketing manager often wants to determine the profitability of various market segments. Activity-based costing can be used to accurately assign costs of shipping, advertising, order-taking, and customer service that are unrelated to sales and costs of products sold. Such an activity-based analysis can reveal to the marketing department some customers that are better left to the competition if they consume a larger amount of marketing resources than the gross profit generated by sales to

Point: Many companies use ABC techniques for these types of special projects even if they don't use ABC in determining overall product costs.

© Getty Images

those customers. Generally, ABC provides better customer profitability information by including all resources consumed to serve a customer. This allows managers to make better pricing decisions on custom orders and to better manage customers by focusing on those that are most profitable.

Better Management of Activities Being competitive requires that managers be able to use resources efficiently. Understanding how costs are incurred is a first step toward controlling costs. One important contribution of ABC is helping managers identify the causes of costs, that is, the activities driving them. **Activity-based management (ABM)** is an outgrowth of ABC that draws on the link between activities and cost incurrence for better management. Activity-based management can be useful in distinguishing **value-added activities,** which add value to a product, from *non-value-added activities,* which do not. For KartCo, its value-added activities include machining, assembly, and the costs of engineering design changes. Its non-value-added activity is machine repair. The way to control a cost requires changing how much of an activity is performed.

Decision Insight

The ABCs of Decisions Business managers must make long-term strategic decisions, day-to-day operating decisions, and decisions on the type of financing the business needs. Survey evidence suggests that managers find ABC more useful in making strategic, operating, and financing decisions than non-ABC methods. ■

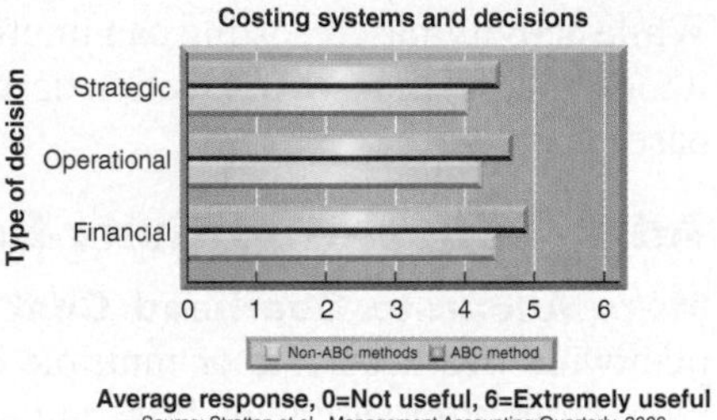

Costs of Quality A focus on the costs of activities, via ABC and ABM, lends itself to assessments of the **costs of quality.** These costs refer to costs resulting from manufacturing defective products or providing services that do not meet customer expectations. Exhibit 17.16 summarizes the typical costs of quality. These costs can be summarized in a **cost of quality report,** which lists the costs of quality activities by category. A focus on activities and quality costs can lead to higher quality and lower costs.

EXHIBIT 17.16

Types of Quality Costs

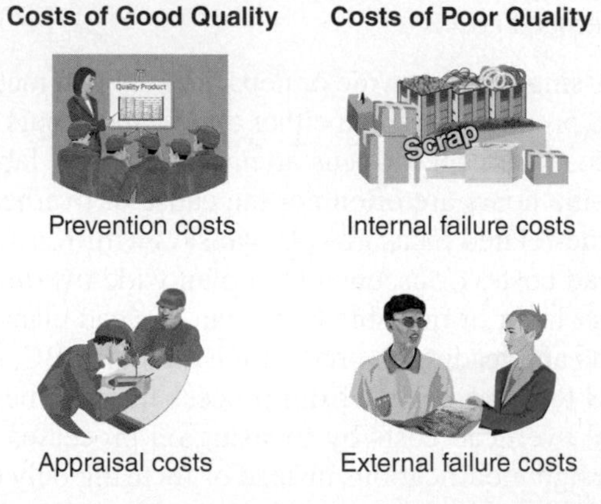

Cost of Quality Report	Cost
Prevention	
Training....................	$ 22,000
Appraisal	
Inspecting materials...........	37,500
Testing finished goods.........	14,200
Internal failure	
Rework.....................	8,250
Scrap......................	11,750
External failure	
Warranty claims..............	45,700
Total cost of quality.........	$139,400

Point: Prevention and appraisal costs are usually considered value-added costs, while internal and external costs are considered non-value-added costs.

Prevention and *appraisal costs* are incurred before a good or service is provided to a customer. The purpose of these costs is to reduce the chance the customer is provided a defective good or service. These are the costs of trying to ensure that only good-quality items are produced. Prevention activities focus on quality training and improvement programs to ensure quality is built into the product or service. Common appraisal costs include the costs of inspections to ensure that materials and supplies meet specifications and inspections of finished goods.

Internal and external failure costs are the costs of making poor-quality items. *Internal failure costs* are incurred after a company has manufactured a defective product but before that product has been delivered to a customer. Internal failure costs include the costs of reworking products, reinspecting reworked products, and scrap.

Finally, *external failure costs* are incurred after a customer has been provided a defective product or service. Examples of this type of cost include costs of warranty repairs and costs of recalling products. This category also includes lost profits due to dissatisfied customers buying from other companies.

Disadvantages of Activity-Based Costing

Costs to Implement and Maintain ABC Designing and implementing an activity-based costing system requires management commitment and financial resources. For ABC to be effective, a thorough analysis of cost activities must be performed and appropriate cost pools must be determined. Collecting and analyzing cost data is expensive and so is maintaining an ABC system. While technology, such as bar coding, has made it possible for many companies to use ABC, it is still too costly for some. Managers must weigh the cost of implementing and maintaining an ABC system against the potential benefits of ABC in light of company circumstances.

Uncertainty with Decisions Remains As with all cost information, managers must interpret ABC data with caution in making decisions. In the KartCo case, given the huge design-modification costs for custom go-karts determined under the ABC system, a manager might be tempted to decline some custom go-kart orders to save overhead costs. However, in the short run, some or all of the design-modification costs cannot be saved even if some custom go-kart orders are rejected. Managers must examine carefully the controllability of costs before making decisions.

ABC for Service Providers

Although we've shown how to use ABC in a manufacturing setting, ABC also applies to service providers. The only requirements for ABC are the existence of costs and demand for reliable cost information. **First Tennessee National Corporation**, a bank, applied ABC and found that 30% of its certificate of deposit (CD) customers provided nearly 90% of its profits from CDs. Further, 30% of the bank's CD customers were actually losing money for the bank. The bank's management used ABC to correct the problem and increase profits. Laboratories performing medical tests, accounting and law offices, and advertising agencies are other examples of service firms that can benefit from ABC. (Refer to this chapter's Decision Analysis for an example of applying ABC to assess customer profitability and this chapter's Comprehensive Need-To-Know for an example of applying ABC to a law firm.)

Types of Activities

C3 Describe the four types of activities that cause overhead costs.

Activities causing overhead costs can be separated into four levels of types of activities: (1) **unit-level activities,** (2) **batch-level activities,** (3) **product-level activities,** and (4) **facility-level activities.** These four activities are described as follows.

Activity Levels

Unit-level activities are performed on each product unit. For example, the machining department needs electricity to power the machinery to produce each unit of product. Unit-level costs tend to change with the number of units produced.

Batch-level activities are performed only on each batch or group of units. For example, machine setup is needed only for each batch regardless of the units in that batch, and customer order processing must be performed for each order regardless of the number of units ordered. Batch-level costs do not vary with the number of units, but instead vary with the number of batches.

Product-level activities are performed on each product line and are not affected by either the numbers of units or batches. For example, product design is needed only for each product line. Product-level costs do not vary with the number of units or batches produced.

Facility-level activities are performed to sustain facility capacity as a whole and are not caused by any specific product. For example, rent and factory maintenance costs are incurred no matter what is being produced. Facility-level costs do not vary with what is manufactured, how many batches are produced, or the output quantity.

In the KartCo example, the craftsmanship pool reflects unit-level costs, the setup pool reflects batch-level costs, the design-modification pool reflects product-level costs, and plant services reflect facility-level costs.

Exhibit 17.17 shows additional examples of activities commonly found within each of the four activity levels. This is not a complete list, but reviewing it can help in understanding this hierarchy of production activities. This list also includes common measures used to reflect the specific activity identified. Knowing this hierarchy can help us simplify and understand activity-based costing.

EXHIBIT 17.17

Examples of Activities by Activity Level

QC3

Activity Level	Examples of Activity	Activity Driver (Measure)
Unit level	Cutting parts	Machine hours
	Assembling components	Direct labor hours
	Printing checks	Number of checks
Batch level	Calibrating machines	Number of batches
	Receiving shipments	Number of orders
	Sampling product quality	Number of lots produced
Product level	Designing modifications	Change requests
	Organizing production	Engineering hours
	Controlling inventory	Parts per product
Facility level	Cleaning workplace	Square feet of floors*
	Providing electricity	Kilowatt hours*
	Providing personnel support	Number of employees*

* Facility-level costs are not traceable to individual product lines, batches, or units. They are normally assigned to units using a unit-level driver such as direct labor hours or machine hours even though they are caused by another activity.

GLOBAL VIEW

© Robert Gallagher/Forbes Magazine/ Forbes Collection/Corbis Outline

Toyota Motor Corporation pioneered *lean manufacturing,* which focuses on eliminating waste while satisfying customers. Many lean manufacturers embrace **lean accounting,** which has two key components. First, the company applies lean thinking to eliminate waste in its accounting process. Second, instead of focusing on cost allocation methods such as activity-based costing, the company develops alternative performance measures that better reflect the benefits of manufacturing process changes. Examples include the percentage of products produced without defects, the percentage of ontime deliveries, and the level of sales per employee.

Sustainability and Accounting **Suja Juice Co.** also relies on lean techniques. The company must use extremely fresh raw materials, thus it employs just-in-time inventory management. Likewise, its finished product has a limited shelf life, so managers must carefully monitor sales demand to ensure that no juice is wasted.

Decision Analysis — Customer Profitability

Are all customers equal? To help answer this, let's return to the KartCo case and assume that costs of providing customer support (such as delivery, installation, and warranty work) are related to the distance a technician must travel to provide services. Also assume that, as a result of applying activity-based costing, KartCo plans to sell its standard go-kart for $1,200 per unit. If the annual cost of customer services is expected to be $250,000 and the distance traveled by technicians is 100,000 miles annually, KartCo would want to link the cost of customer services with individual customers to make efficient marketing decisions.

Using these data, an activity rate of $2.50 per mile ($250,000/100,000 miles) is computed for assigning customer service costs to individual customers. For KartCo, it would compute a typical customer profitability report for one of its customers, Six Flags, as follows.

Customer Profitability Report—Six Flags		
Sales (10 standard go-karts × $1,200)		$12,000
Less: Product costs		
Direct materials (10 go-karts × $400 per go-kart)	$4,000	
Direct labor (10 go-karts × $350 per go-kart)	3,500	
Overhead (10 go-karts × $300 per go-kart, Exhibit 17.14)	3,000	10,500
Product profit margin		1,500
Less: Customer service costs (200 miles × $2.50 per mile)		500
Customer profit margin		$ 1,000

Analysis indicates that a total profit margin of $1,000 is generated from this customer. The management of KartCo can see that if this customer requires service technicians to travel more than 600 miles ($1,500 ÷ $2.50 per mile), the sale of 10 standard go-karts to this customer would be unprofitable. ABC encourages management to consider all resources consumed to serve a customer, not just manufacturing costs that are the focus of traditional costing methods.

NEED-TO-KNOW

COMPREHENSIVE

Silver Law Firm provides litigation and mediation services to a variety of clients. Attorneys keep track of the time they spend on each case, which is used to charge fees to clients at a rate of $300 per hour. A management advisor commented that activity-based costing might prove useful in evaluating the costs of its legal services, and the firm has decided to evaluate its fee structure by comparing ABC to its alternative cost allocations. The following data relate to a typical month at the firm. During a typical month the firm handles seven mediation cases and three litigation cases.

	Activity Driver	Total Amount	Consumption by Service Type: Litigation	Consumption by Service Type: Mediation	Activity Cost
Providing legal advice	Billable hours	200	75	125	$30,000
Overhead costs					
Internal support departments					
Preparing documents	Documents	30	16	14	$ 4,000
Occupying office space	Billable hours	200	75	125	1,200
Heating and lighting of office	Billable hours	200	75	125	350
External support departments					
Registering court documents	Documents	30	16	14	1,250
Retaining consultants (investigators, psychiatrists)	Court dates	6	5	1	10,000
Using contract services (couriers, security guards)	Court dates	6	5	1	5,000
Total overhead costs					$21,800

Required

1. Determine the cost of providing legal services to each type of case using activity-based costing (ABC).
2. Determine the cost of each type of case using a single plantwide rate for nonattorney costs based on billable hours.
3. Determine the cost of each type of case using multiple departmental overhead rates for the internal support department (based on number of documents) and external support department (based on billable hours).
4. Compare and discuss the costs assigned under each method for management decisions.

PLANNING THE SOLUTION

- Compute pool rates and assign costs to cases using ABC.
- Compute costs for the cases using the volume-based methods and discuss differences between these costs and the costs computed using ABC.

SOLUTION

1. We need to set up activity pools and compute pool rates for ABC. All activities except "occupying office space" and "heating and lighting" are unit-level activities (meaning they are traceable to the individual cases handled by the law firm). "Preparing documents" and "registering documents" are both driven by the number of documents associated with each case. We can therefore combine these activities and their costs into a single pool, which we call "clerical support." Similarly, "retaining consultants" and "using services" are related to the number of times the attorneys must go to court (court dates). We combine these activities and their costs into another activity cost pool labeled "litigation support." The costs associated with occupying office space and the heating and lighting are facility-level activities and are not traceable to individual cases. Yet they are costs that must be covered by fees charged to clients. We assign these costs using a convenient base—in this example we use the number of billable hours, which attorneys record for each client. Providing legal advice is the direct labor for a law firm.

Activity Pool	Activity Cost	Pool Cost	Activity Driver	Pool Rate (Pool Cost ÷ Activity Driver)
Providing legal advice	$30,000	$30,000	200 billable hours	$150 per billable hour
Clerical support				
Preparing documents	4,000			
Registering documents	1,250	5,250	30 documents	$175 per document
Litigation support				
Retaining consultants	10,000			
Using services	5,000	15,000	6 court dates	$2,500 per court date
Facility costs				
Occupying office space	1,200			
Heating and lighting	350	1,550	200 billable hours	$7.75 per billable hour

We next determine the cost of providing each type of legal service as shown in the following table. Specifically, the pool rates from above are used to assign costs to each type of service provided by the law firm. Since litigation consumed 75 billable hours of attorney time, we assign $11,250 (75 billable hours × $150 per billable hour) of the cost of providing legal advice to this type of case. Mediation required 125 hours of attorney time, so $18,750 (125 billable hours × $150 per billable hour) of the cost to provide legal advice is assigned to mediation cases. Clerical support costs $175 per document, so the costs associated with activities in this cost pool are assigned to litigation cases (16 documents × $175 per document = $2,800) and mediation cases (14 documents × $175 per document = $2,450). The costs of activities in the litigation support and the facility cost pools are similarly assigned to the two case types.

We compute the total cost of litigation ($27,131.25) and mediation ($24,668.75) and divide these totals by the number of cases of each type to determine the average cost of each case type: $9,044 for litigation and $3,524 for mediation. This analysis shows that charging clients $300 per billable hour without regard to the type of case results in litigation clients being charged less than the cost to provide that service ($7,500 versus $9,044).

	Pool Rate	Litigation		Mediation	
Providing legal advice.	$150 per billable hour	75 hours	$11,250.00	125 hours	$18,750.00
Clerical support.	$175 per document	16 docs	2,800.00	14 docs	2,450.00
Litigation support	$2,500 per court date	5 court dates	12,500.00	1 court date	2,500.00
Facility costs	$7.75 per billable hour	75 hours	581.25	125 hours	968.75
Total cost.			$27,131.25		$24,668.75
÷ Number of cases.			3 cases		7 cases
Average cost per case.			**$9,044**		**$3,524**
Average fee per case.			**$7,500***		**$5,357†**

* (75 billable hours × $300 per hour) ÷ 3 cases † (125 billable hours × $300 per hour) ÷ 7 cases

2. The cost of each type of case using a single plantwide rate for nonattorney costs (that is, all costs except for those related to providing legal advice) based on billable hours is as follows.

Total overhead cost/Total billable hours = $21,800/200 billable hours = $109 per hour

We then determine the cost of providing each type of legal service as follows.

		Litigation		Mediation	
Providing legal advice.	$150 per billable hour	75 hours	$11,250	125 hours	$18,750
Overhead (from part 2)	$109 per billable hour	75 hours	8,175	125 hours	13,625
Total cost.			$19,425		$32,375
÷ Number of cases.			3 cases		7 cases
Average cost per case.			**$6,475**		**$4,625**
Average fee per case. . . . . (from part 1)			**$7,500**		**$5,357**

3. The cost of each type of case using multiple departmental overhead rates for the internal support department (based on number of documents) and external support department (based on billable hours) is determined as follows.

		Departmental Cost	Base	Departmental Rate (Departmental Cost ÷ Base)
Internal support departments				
Preparing documents.	$ 4,000			
Occupying office space	1,200			
Heating and lighting of office . . .	350	$ 5,550	30 documents	$185 per document
External support departments				
Registering documents	1,250			
Retaining consultants	10,000			
Using contract services.	5,000	16,250	200 billable hours	$81.25 per hour

The departmental overhead rates computed above are used to assign overhead costs to the two types of legal services. For the internal support department we use the overhead rate of $185 per document to assign $2,960 ($185 × 16 documents) to litigation and $2,590 ($185 × 14 documents) to mediation. For the external support department we use the overhead rate of $81.25 per hour to assign $6,093.75 ($81.25 × 75 hours) to litigation and $10,156.25 ($81.25 × 125 hours) to mediation. As shown below, the resulting average costs of litigation cases and mediation cases are $6,768 and $4,499, respectively. Using this method of cost assignment, it *appears* that the fee of $300 per billable hour is adequate to cover costs associated with each case.

		Litigation		Mediation	
Attorney fees.	$150 per billable hour	75 hours	$11,250.00	125 hours	$18,750.00
Internal support.	$185 per document	16 documents	2,960.00	14 documents	2,590.00
External support	$81.25 per hour	75 hours	6,093.75	125 hours	10,156.25
Total cost.			$20,303.75		$31,496.25
÷ Number of cases.			3 cases		7 cases
Average cost per case. . .			**$6,768**		**$4,499**
Average fee per case. . . . (from part 1)			**$7,500**		**$5,357**

4. A comparison and discussion of the costs assigned under each method follows.

	Method of Assigning Overhead Costs		
Average Cost per Case	**Activity-Based Costing**	**Plantwide Overhead Rate**	**Departmental Overhead Rates**
Litigation cases.	$9,044	$6,475	$6,768
Mediation cases	3,524	4,625	4,499

The departmental and plantwide overhead rate methods assign overhead on the basis of volume-related measures (billable hours and document filings). Litigation costs *appear* profitable under these methods, because the average costs are below the average revenue of $7,500. ABC, however, focuses attention on activities that drive costs. A large part of overhead costs was for consultants and contract services, which were unrelated to the number of cases, but related to the type of cases consuming those resources. Using ABC, the costs shift from the high-volume cases (mediation) to the low-volume cases (litigation). When the firm considers the consumption of resources for these cases using ABC, it finds that the fees charged to litigate cases is insufficient (average revenue of $7,500 versus average cost of $9,044). The law firm is charging too little for the complex cases that require litigation.

Summary

C1 Distinguish between the plantwide overhead rate method, the departmental overhead rate method, and the activity-based costing method. Overhead costs can be assigned to cost objects using a plantwide rate that combines all overhead costs into a single rate, usually based on direct labor hours, machine hours, or direct labor cost. Multiple departmental overhead rates that include overhead costs traceable to departments are used to allocate overhead based on departmental functions. ABC links overhead costs to activities and assigns overhead based on how much of each activity is required for a product.

C2 Explain cost flows for activity-based costing. With ABC, overhead costs are first traced to the activities that cause them, and then cost pools are formed combining costs caused by the same activity. Overhead rates based on these activities are then used to assign overhead to products in proportion to the amount of activity required to produce them.

C3 Describe the four types of activities that cause overhead costs. The four types of activities that cause overhead costs are: (1) unit-level activities, (2) batch-level activities, (3) product-level activities, and (4) facility-level activities. Unit-level activities are performed on each unit, batch-level activities are performed only on each group of units, and product-level activities are performed only on each product line. Facility-level activities are performed to sustain facility capacity and are not caused by any specific product. Understanding these types of activities can help in applying activity-based costing.

A1 Identify and assess advantages and disadvantages of the plantwide overhead and departmental overhead rate methods. A single plantwide overhead rate is a simple way to assign overhead cost. A disadvantage is that it can inaccurately assign costs when costs are caused by multiple factors and when different products consume different amounts of inputs. Overhead costing accuracy is improved by use of multiple departmental rates because differences across departmental functions can be linked to costs incurred in departments. Yet, accuracy of cost assignment with departmental rates suffers from the same problems associated with plantwide rates because activities required for each product are not identified with costs of providing those activities.

A2 Identify and assess advantages and disadvantages of activity-based costing. ABC improves product costing accuracy and draws management attention to relevant factors to control. The cost of constructing and maintaining an ABC system can sometimes outweigh its value.

P1 Allocate overhead costs to products using the plantwide overhead rate method. The plantwide overhead rate equals total budgeted overhead divided by budgeted plant volume, the latter often measured in direct labor hours or machine hours. This rate multiplied by the number of direct labor hours (or machine hours) required for each product provides the overhead assigned to each product.

P2 Allocate overhead costs to products using the departmental overhead rate method. When using multiple departmental rates, overhead costs must first be traced to each department and then divided by the measure of output for that department to yield the departmental overhead rate. Overhead is applied to products using this rate as products pass through each department.

P3 Allocate overhead costs to products using activity-based costing. With ABC, overhead costs are matched to activities that cause them. If there is more than one cost with the same activity, these costs are combined into pools. An overhead rate for each pool is determined by dividing total cost for that pool by its activity measure. Overhead costs are assigned to products by multiplying the ABC pool rate by the amount of the activity required for each product.

Guidance Answers to Decision Maker and Decision Ethics

Department Manager When dividing a bill, common sense suggests fairness. That is, if one department consumes more services than another, we attempt to share the bill in proportion to consumption. Equally dividing the bill among the number of departments is fair if each consumed equal services. This same notion applies in assigning costs to products and services. For example, dividing overhead costs by the number of units is fair if all products consumed overhead in equal proportion.

Entrepreneur Cleaning and sterilizing costs are not directly related to the volume of product manufactured. Thus, changing the number of units produced does not necessarily reduce these costs. Further, expressing costs of cleaning and sterilizing on a per unit basis is often misleading for the person responsible for controlling costs. Costs of cleaning and sterilizing are related to changing from one product line to another. Consequently, the way to control those costs is to control the number of times the packaging system has to be changed for a different product line. Thus, efficient product scheduling would help reduce those overhead costs and improve profitability.

Key Terms

Activity
Activity-based costing (ABC)
Activity-based management (ABM)
Activity cost driver
Activity cost pool
Activity overhead (pool) rate
Batch-level activities
Cost object
Cost of quality report
Costs of quality
Facility-level activities
Lean accounting
Product-level activities
Unit-level activities
Value-added activities

Multiple Choice Quiz

Answers at end of chapter

1. In comparison to a traditional cost system, and when there are batch-level or product-level costs, an activity-based costing system usually:
a. Shifts costs from low-volume to high-volume products.
b. Shifts costs from high-volume to low-volume products.
c. Shifts costs from standardized to specialized products.
d. Shifts costs from specialized to standardized products.

2. Which of the following statements is (are) true?
a. An activity-based costing system is generally easier to implement and maintain than a traditional costing system.
b. One of the goals of activity-based management is the elimination of waste by allocating costs to products that waste resources.
c. Activity-based costing uses a number of activity cost pools, each of which is allocated to products on the basis of direct labor hours.
d. Activity rates in activity-based costing are computed by dividing costs from the first-stage allocations by the activity measure for each activity cost pool.

3. All of the following are examples of batch-level activities except:
a. Purchase order processing.
b. Setting up equipment.
c. Clerical activity associated with processing purchase orders to produce an order for a standard product.
d. Employee recreational facilities.

4. A company has two products: A and B. It uses activity-based costing and prepares the following analysis showing budgeted cost and activity for each of its three activity cost pools.

Activity Cost Pool	Budgeted Overhead Cost	Budgeted Activity		
		Product A	Product B	Total
Activity 1	$ 80,000	200	800	1,000
Activity 2	58,400	1,000	500	1,500
Activity 3	360,000	600	5,400	6,000

Annual production and sales level of Product A is 18,188 units, and the annual production and sales level of Product B is 31,652 units. The approximate overhead cost per unit of Product B under activity-based costing is:
a. $2.02 **c.** $12.87
b. $5.00 **d.** $22.40

5. A company uses activity-based costing to determine the costs of its two products: A and B. The budgeted cost and activity for each of the company's three activity cost pools follow.

Activity Cost Pool	Budgeted Cost	Budgeted Activity		
		Product A	Product B	Total
Activity 1	$19,800	800	300	1,100
Activity 2	16,000	2,200	1,800	4,000
Activity 3	14,000	400	300	700

The activity rate under the activity-based costing method for Activity 3 is.
a. $4.00 **c.** $18.00
b. $8.59 **d.** $20.00

Icon denotes assignments that involve decision making.

Discussion Questions

1. Why are overhead costs allocated to products and not traced to products as direct materials and direct labor are?

2. What are three common methods of assigning overhead costs to a product?

3. Why are direct labor hours and machine hours commonly used as the bases for overhead allocation?

4. What are the advantages of using a single plantwide overhead rate?

5. The usefulness of a single plantwide overhead rate is based on two assumptions. What are those assumptions?
6. What is a cost object?
7. Explain why a single plantwide overhead rate can distort the cost of a particular product.
8. Why are multiple departmental overhead rates more accurate for product costing than a single plantwide overhead rate?
9. In what way are departmental overhead rates similar to a single plantwide overhead rate? How are they different?
10. Why is overhead allocation under ABC usually more accurate than either the plantwide overhead allocation method or the departmental overhead allocation method?
11. **Google** reports costs in financial statements. If plantwide overhead rates are allowed for reporting costs to external users, why might a company choose to use a more complicated and more expensive method for assigning overhead costs to products? **GOOGLE**
12. What is the first step in applying activity-based costing?
13. What is an activity cost driver?
14. **Apple**'s production requires activities. What are value-added activities? **APPLE**
15. What are the four activity levels associated with activity-based costing? Define each.
16. **Samsung** is a manufacturer. "Activity-based costing is only useful for manufacturing companies." Is this a true statement? Explain. **Samsung**
17. **Apple** must assign overhead costs to its products. Activity-based costing is generally considered more accurate than other methods of assigning overhead. If this is so, why don't all manufacturing companies use it? **APPLE**

connect

QUICK STUDY

QS 17-1
Overhead cost allocation methods
C1

In the blank next to each of the following terms, place the letter *A* through *D* that corresponds to the description of that term. Some letters are used more than once.

______ 1. Activity-based costing
______ 2. Plantwide overhead rate method
______ 3. Departmental overhead rate method

A. Uses more than one rate to allocate overhead costs to products.
B. Uses only volume-based measures such as direct labor hours to allocate overhead costs to products.
C. Typically uses the most overhead allocation rates.
D. Focuses on the costs of carrying out activities.

QS 17-2
Cost allocation methods
C1

1. Which costing method assumes all products use overhead costs in the same proportions?
   a. Activity-based costing
   b. Plantwide overhead rate method
   c. Departmental overhead rate method
   d. All cost allocation methods
2. Which of the following would usually *not* be used in computing plantwide overhead rates?
   a. Direct labor hours
   b. Number of quality inspections
   c. Direct labor dollars
   d. Machine hours
3. With ABC, overhead costs should be traced to which cost object first?
   a. Units of product
   b. Departments
   c. Activities
   d. Product batches

QS 17-3
Plantwide rate method
P1

A manufacturer uses machine hours to assign overhead costs to products. Budgeted information for the next year follows. Compute the plantwide overhead rate for the next year based on machine hours.

Budgeted factory overhead costs	$544,000
Budgeted machine hours	6,400

QS 17-4
Compute plantwide overhead rates
P1

Rafner Manufacturing identified the following budgeted data in its two production departments.

	Assembly	Finishing
Manufacturing overhead costs	$1,200,000	$600,000
Direct labor hours	12,000 DLH	20,000 DLH
Machine hours	6,000 MH	16,000 MH

1. What is the company's single plantwide overhead rate based on direct labor hours?
2. What is the company's single plantwide overhead rate based on machine hours? (Round your answer to two decimal places.)

QS 17-5
Compute departmental overhead rates P2

Refer to the information in QS 17-4. What are the company's departmental overhead rates if the assembly department assigns overhead based on direct labor hours and the finishing department assigns overhead based on machine hours?

QS 17-6
Advantages of plantwide and departmental rate methods A1

List the three main advantages of the plantwide and departmental overhead rate methods.

QS 17-7
Costing terminology C2

In the blank next to the following terms, place the letter *A* through *D* corresponding to the best description of that term.

______ **1.** Activity	**A.** Measurement associated with an activity.
______ **2.** Activity driver	**B.** A group of costs that have the same activity drivers.
______ **3.** Cost object	**C.** Anything to which costs will be assigned.
______ **4.** Cost pool	**D.** A task that causes a cost to be incurred.

QS 17-8
Computing activity rates P3

A manufacturer uses activity-based costing to assign overhead costs to products. Budgeted information for selected activities for next year follows. Form two cost pools and compute activity rates for each of the cost pools.

Activity	Expected Cost	Cost Driver	Expected Usage of Cost Driver
Purchasing	$135,000	Purchase orders	4,500 purchase orders
Cleaning factory..........	32,000	Square feet	5,000 square feet
Providing utilities	65,000	Square feet	5,000 square feet

---

QS 17-9
Assigning costs using ABC P3

Aziz Company sells two types of products, Basic and Deluxe. The company provides technical support for users of its products, at an expected cost of $250,000 per year. The company expects to process 10,000 customer service calls per year.

1. Determine the company's cost of technical support per customer service call.
2. During the month of January, Aziz received 550 calls for customer service on its Deluxe model and 250 calls for customer service on its Basic model. Assign technical support costs to each model using activity-based costing (ABC).

QS 17-10
Computing activity rates P3

A company uses activity-based costing to determine the costs of its three products: A, B, and C. The budgeted cost and cost driver activity for each of the company's three activity cost pools follow. Compute the activity rates for each of the company's three activities.

		Budgeted Activity of Cost Driver		
Activity Cost Pool	**Budgeted Cost**	**Product A**	**Product B**	**Product C**
Activity 1	$140,000	20,000	9,000	6,000
Activity 2	$ 90,000	8,000	15,000	7,000
Activity 3	$ 82,000	1,625	1,000	2,500

QS 17-11
Multiple choice overhead questions A2

1. If management wants the most accurate product cost, which of the following costing methods should be used?
   a. Volume-based costing using departmental overhead rates
   b. Volume-based costing using a plantwide overhead rate
   c. Normal costing using a plantwide overhead rate
   d. Activity-based costing
2. Which costing method tends to overstate the cost of high-volume products?
   a. Traditional volume-based costing
   b. Activity-based costing
   c. Job order costing
   d. Differential costing
3. Disadvantages of activity-based costing include
   a. It is not acceptable under GAAP for external reporting.
   b. It can be costly to implement.
   c. It can be used in an activity-based management.
   d. Both a. and b.

QS 17-12
Costs of quality
A2

A list of activities that generate quality costs is provided below. For each activity, indicate whether it relates to a prevention activity (P), appraisal activity (A), internal failure activity (I), or external failure activity (E).

a. Inspecting raw materials
b. Training workers in quality techniques
c. Collecting data on a manufacturing process
d. Overtime labor to rework products
e. Cost of additional materials to rework a product
f. Inspecting finished goods inventory
g. Scrapping defective goods
h. Lost sales due to customer dissatisfaction

QS 17-13
Identify activity levels
C3

Classify each of the following activities as unit level (U), batch level (B), product level (P), or facility level (F) for a manufacturer of organic juices.

_____ 1. Cutting fruit
_____ 2. Developing new types of juice
_____ 3. Blending fruit into juice
_____ 4. Receiving fruit shipments
_____ 5. Cleaning blending machines

QS 17-14
Identify activity levels
C3

Classify each of the following activities as unit level (U), batch level (B), product level (P), or facility level (F) for a manufacturer of trail mix.

_____ 1. Roasting peanuts
_____ 2. Cleaning roasting machines
_____ 3. Sampling product quality
_____ 4. Providing utilities for factory
_____ 5. Calibrating mixing machines

QS 17-15
Lean accounting and ABC
A2

Toyota embraces lean techniques, including lean accounting. What are the two key components of lean accounting?

connect

EXERCISES

Exercise 17-1
Compute plantwide overhead rates
P1

Xie Company identified the following activities, costs, and activity drivers for 2015. The company manufactures two types of go-karts: Deluxe and Basic.

Activity	Expected Costs	Expected Activity
Handling materials	$625,000	100,000 parts
Inspecting product	900,000	1,500 batches
Processing purchase orders	105,000	700 orders
Paying suppliers	175,000	500 invoices
Insuring the factory	300,000	40,000 square feet
Designing packaging	75,000	2 models

Required

1. Compute a single plantwide overhead rate assuming that the company assigns overhead based on 125,000 budgeted direct labor hours.
2. In January 2015 the Deluxe model required 2,500 direct labor hours, and the Standard model required 6,000 direct labor hours. Assign overhead costs to each model using the single plantwide overhead rate.

Exercise 17-2
Compute overhead rates under ABC P3

Refer to the information in Exercise 17-1. Compute the activity rate for each activity, assuming the company uses activity-based costing.

Exercise 17-3
Assigning costs using ABC
P3

Refer to the information in Exercise 17-1. Assume that the following information is available for the company's two products for the first quarter of 2015.

	Deluxe Model	Basic Model
Production volume.	10,000 units	30,000 units
Parts required	20,000 parts	30,000 parts
Batches made.	250 batches	100 batches
Purchase orders	50 orders	20 orders
Invoices	50 invoices	10 invoices
Space occupied	10,000 square feet	7,000 square feet
Models	1 model	1 model

Required

Compute activity rates for each activity and assign overhead costs to each product model using activity-based costing (ABC). What is the overhead cost per unit of each model?

Exercise 17-4
Plantwide overhead rate
P1

Textra Plastics produces parts for a variety of small machine manufacturers. Most products go through two operations, molding and trimming, before they are ready for packaging. Expected costs and activities for the molding department and for the trimming department for 2015 follow.

	Molding	Trimming
Direct labor hours.	52,000 DLH	48,000 DLH
Machine hours	30,500 MH	3,600 MH
Overhead costs	$730,000	$590,000

Data for two special order parts to be manufactured by the company in 2015 follow:

	Part A27C	Part X82B
Number of units	9,800 units	54,500 units
Machine hours		
Molding	5,100 MH	1,020 MH
Trimming	2,600 MH	650 MH
Direct labor hours		
Molding	5,500 DLH	2,150 DLH
Trimming	700 DLH	3,500 DLH

Required

1. Compute the plantwide overhead rate using direct labor hours as the base.
2. Determine the overhead cost assigned to each product line using the plantwide rate computed in requirement 1.

Exercise 17-5
Departmental overhead rates
P2

Refer to the information in Exercise 17-4.

Required

1. Compute a departmental overhead rate for the molding department based on machine hours and a department overhead rate for the trimming department based on direct labor hours.
2. Determine the total overhead cost assigned to each product line using the departmental overhead rates from requirement 2.
3. Determine the overhead cost per unit for each product line using the departmental rate.

Exercise 17-6
Assigning overhead costs using the plantwide rate and departmental rate methods
P1 P2

Laval produces lamps and home lighting fixtures. Its most popular product is a brushed aluminum desk lamp. This lamp is made from components shaped in the fabricating department and assembled in its assembly department. Information related to the 35,000 desk lamps produced annually follow.

Direct materials	$280,000
Direct labor	
Fabricating department (7,000 DLH × $20 per DLH)	$140,000
Assembly department (16,000 DLH × $29 per DLH)	$464,000
Machine hours	
Fabricating department	15,040 MH
Assembly department	21,000 MH

Expected overhead cost and related data for the two production departments follow.

	Fabricating	Assembly
Direct labor hours	75,000 DLH	125,000 DLH
Machine hours	80,000 MH	62,500 MH
Overhead cost	$300,000	$200,000

Required

1. Determine the plantwide overhead rate for Laval using direct labor hours as a base.
2. Determine the total manufacturing cost per unit for the aluminum desk lamp using the plantwide overhead rate.
3. Compute departmental overhead rates based on machine hours in the fabricating department and direct labor hours in the assembly department.
4. Use departmental overhead rates from requirement 3 to determine the total manufacturing cost per unit for the aluminum desk lamps.

Check (2) $26.90 per unit

Check (4) $27.60 per unit

Exercise 17-7
Using the plantwide overhead rate to assess prices
P1

Way Cool produces two different models of air conditioners. The company produces the mechanical systems in their components department. The mechanical systems are combined with the housing assembly in its finishing department. The activities, costs, and drivers associated with these two manufacturing processes and the production support process follow.

Process	Activity	Overhead Cost	Driver	Quantity
Components	Changeover	$ 500,000	Number of batches	800
	Machining	279,000	Machine hours	6,000
	Setups	225,000	Number of setups	120
		$1,004,000		
Finishing	Welding	$ 180,300	Welding hours	3,000
	Inspecting	210,000	Number of inspections	700
	Rework	75,000	Rework orders	300
		$ 465,300		
Support	Purchasing	$ 135,000	Purchase orders	450
	Providing space	32,000	Number of units	5,000
	Providing utilities	65,000	Number of units	5,000
		$ 232,000		

Additional production information concerning its two product lines follows.

	Model 145	Model 212
Units produced	1,500	3,500
Welding hours	800	2,200
Batches	400	400
Number of inspections	400	300
Machine hours	1,800	4,200
Setups	60	60
Rework orders	160	140
Purchase orders	300	150

Required

1. Using a plantwide overhead rate based on machine hours, compute the overhead cost per unit for each product line.
2. Determine the total cost per unit for each product line if the direct labor and direct materials costs per unit are $250 for Model 145 and $180 for Model 212.
3. If the market price for Model 145 is $820 and the market price for Model 212 is $480, determine the profit or loss per unit for each model. Comment on the results.

Check (3) Model 212, $(40.26) per unit loss

Exercise 17-8
Using departmental overhead rates to assess prices
P2

Refer to the information in Exercise 17-7 to answer the following requirements.

Required

1. Determine departmental overhead rates and compute the overhead cost per unit for each product line. Base your overhead assignment for the components department on machine hours. Use welding hours to assign overhead costs to the finishing department. Assign costs to the support department based on number of purchase orders.
2. Determine the total cost per unit for each product line if the direct labor and direct materials costs per unit are $250 for Model 145 and $180 for Model 212.
3. If the market price for Model 145 is $820 and the market price for Model 212 is $480, determine the profit or loss per unit for each model. Comment on the results.

Check (3) Model 212, $(20.38) per unit loss

Exercise 17-9
Using ABC to assess prices
P3

Refer to the information in Exercise 17-7 to answer the following requirements.

Required

1. Using ABC, compute the overhead cost per unit for each product line.
2. Determine the total cost per unit for each product line if the direct labor and direct materials costs per unit are $250 for Model 145 and $180 for Model 212.
3. If the market price for Model 145 is $820 and the market price for Model 212 is $480, determine the profit or loss per unit for each model. Comment on the results.

Check (3) Model 212, $34.88 per unit profit

Exercise 17-10
Using ABC for strategic decisions
P1 P3

Consider the following data for two products of Gitano Manufacturing.

	Overhead Cost	Product A	Product B
Number of units produced		10,000 units	2,000 units
Direct labor cost (@$24 per DLH)		0.20 DLH per unit	0.25 DLH per unit
Direct materials cost		$2 per unit	$3 per unit
Activity			
Machine setup	$121,000		
Materials handling	48,000		
Quality control inspections	80,000		
	$249,000		

Required

1. Using direct labor hours as the basis for assigning overhead costs, determine the total production cost per unit for each product line.

Check (2) Product B, $26.10 per unit profit

2. If the market price for Product A is $20 and the market price for Product B is $60, determine the profit or loss per unit for each product. Comment on the results.
3. Consider the following additional information about these two product lines. If ABC is used for assigning overhead costs to products, what is the cost per unit for Product A and for Product B?

	Product A	Product B
Number of setups required for production	10 setups	12 setups
Number of parts required	1 part/unit	3 parts/unit
Inspection hours required	40 hours	210 hours

(4) Product B, ($24.60) per unit loss

4. Determine the profit or loss per unit for each product. Should this information influence company strategy? Explain.

Exercise 17-11
Activity-based costing and overhead cost allocation
P3

The following is taken from Ronda Co.'s internal records of its factory with two production departments. The cost driver for indirect labor and supplies is direct labor costs, and the cost driver for the remaining overhead items is number of hours of machine use. Compute the total amount of overhead cost allocated to Department 1 using activity-based costing.

	Direct Labor	Machine Use Hours
Department 1	$18,800	2,000
Department 2	13,200	1,200
Totals	$32,000	3,200
Factory overhead costs		
Rent and utilities		$12,200
Indirect labor		5,400
General office expense		4,000
Depreciation—Equipment		3,000
Supplies		2,600
Total factory overhead		$27,200

Check Dept. 1 allocation, $16,700

Exercise 17-12
Activity-based costing rates and allocations
P3

A company has two products: standard and deluxe. The company expects to produce 36,375 standard units and 62,240 deluxe units. It uses activity-based costing and has prepared the following analysis showing budgeted cost and cost driver activity for each of its three activity cost pools.

		Budgeted Activity of Cost Driver	
Activity Cost Pool	Budgeted Cost	Standard	Deluxe
Activity 1	$93,000	2,500	5,250
Activity 2	$92,000	4,500	5,500
Activity 3	$87,000	3,000	2,800

Required

1. Compute overhead rates for each of the three activities.
2. What is the expected overhead cost per unit for the standard units?
3. What is the expected overhead cost per unit for the deluxe units?

Exercise 17-13
Using ABC in a service company
P3

Cardiff and Delp is an architectural firm that provides services for residential construction projects. The following data pertain to a recent reporting period.

	Activities	Costs
Design department		
Client consultation	1,500 contact hours	$270,000
Drawings	2,000 design hours	115,000
Modeling	40,000 square feet	30,000
Project management department		
Supervision	600 days	$120,000
Billings	8 jobs	10,000
Collections	8 jobs	12,000

Required

1. Using ABC, compute the firm's activity overhead rates. Form activity cost pools where appropriate.
2. Assign costs to a 9,200-square-foot job that requires 450 contact hours, 340 design hours, and 200 days to complete.

Check (2) $150,200

Exercise 17-14
Activity-based costing
P3 A2

Glassworks Inc. produces two types of glass shelving, rounded edge and squared edge, on the same production line. For the current period, the company reports the following data.

	Rounded Edge	Squared Edge	Total
Direct materials	$19,000	$ 43,200	$ 62,200
Direct labor	12,200	23,800	36,000
Overhead (300% of direct labor cost)	36,600	71,400	108,000
Total cost	$67,800	$138,400	$206,200
Quantity produced	10,500 ft.	14,100 ft.	
Average cost per ft. (rounded)	$ 6.46	$ 9.82	

Glassworks's controller wishes to apply activity-based costing (ABC) to allocate the $108,000 of overhead costs incurred by the two product lines to see whether cost per foot would change markedly from that reported above. She has collected the following information.

Overhead Cost Category (Activity Cost Pool)	Cost
Supervision	$ 5,400
Depreciation of machinery	56,600
Assembly line preparation	46,000
Total overhead	$108,000

She has also collected the following information about the cost drivers for each category (cost pool) and the amount of each driver used by the two product lines.

Overhead Cost Category (Activity Cost Pool)	Driver	Usage		
		Rounded Edge	Squared Edge	Total
Supervision	Direct labor cost ($)	$12,200	$23,800	$36,000
Depreciation of machinery	Machine hours	500 hours	1,500 hours	2,000 hours
Assembly line preparation	Setups (number)	40 times	210 times	250 times

Required

1. Assign these three overhead cost pools to each of the two products using ABC.
2. Determine average cost per foot for each of the two products using ABC.
3. Compare the average cost per foot under ABC with the average cost per foot under the current method for each product. Explain why a difference between the two cost allocation methods exists.

Check (2) Rounded edge, $5.19; Squared edge, $10.76

Exercise 17-15
Activity-based costing
P3

Surgery Center is an outpatient surgical clinic that was profitable for many years, but Medicare has cut its reimbursements by as much as 40%. As a result, the clinic wants to better understand its costs. It decides to prepare an activity-based cost analysis, including an estimate of the average cost of both general surgery and orthopedic surgery. The clinic's three activity cost pools and their cost drivers follow.

Activity Cost Pool	Cost	Cost Driver	Driver Quantity
Professional salaries	$1,600,000	Professional hours	10,000
Patient services and supplies	27,000	Number of patients	600
Building cost	150,000	Square feet	1,500

The two main surgical units and their related data follow.

Service	Hours	Square Feet*	Patients
General surgery	2,500	600	400
Orthopedic surgery	7,500	900	200

* Orthopedic surgery requires more space for patients, supplies, and equipment.

Required

1. Compute the cost per cost driver for each of the three activity cost pools.
2. Use the results from part 1 to allocate costs to both the general surgery and the orthopedic surgery units. Compute total cost and average cost per patient for both the general surgery and the orthopedic surgery units.

Check (2) Average cost of general (orthopedic) surgery, $1,195 ($6,495) per patient

Exercise 17-16
Comparing costs under ABC to traditional plantwide overhead rate
P1 P3 A1 A2

Smythe Crystal makes fine tableware in its Ireland factory. The following data are taken from its production plans for the year.

Direct labor costs	€5,870,000
Setup costs	630,000

	Wineglasses	Commemorative Vases
Expected production	211,000 units	17,000 units
Direct labor hours required	254,000 DLH	16,400 DLH
Machine setups required	200 setups	800 setups

Required

1. Determine the setup cost per unit for the wineglasses and for the commemorative vases if setup costs are assigned using a single plantwide overhead rate based on direct labor hours.
2. Determine setup costs per unit for the wineglasses and for the commemorative vases if the setup costs are assigned based on the number of setups.
3. Which method is better for assigning costs to each product? Explain.

Check (2) Vases, €29.65 per unit

Exercise 17-17
Identify activity levels
C3

Identify each of the following activities as unit level (U), batch level (B), product level (P), or facility level (F) to indicate the way each is incurred with respect to production.

______ **1.** Paying real estate taxes on the factory building
______ **2.** Attaching labels to collars of shirts
______ **3.** Redesigning a bicycle seat in response to customer feedback
______ **4.** Cleaning the assembly department
______ **5.** Polishing of gold wedding rings
______ **6.** Mixing of bread dough in a commercial bakery
______ **7.** Sampling cookies to determine quality

Exercise 17-18
Activity classification
C3

Following are activities in providing medical services at Healthsmart Clinic.

A. Registering patients
B. Cleaning beds
C. Stocking examination rooms
D. Washing linens
E. Ordering medical equipment
F. Heating the clinic
G. Providing security services
H. Filling prescriptions

Required

1. Classify each activity as unit level (U), batch level (B), product level (P), or facility level (F).
2. Identify an activity driver that might be used to measure these activities at the clinic.

connect

PROBLEM SET A

Problem 17-1A
Comparing costs using ABC with the plantwide overhead rate
P1 P3 A1 A2

The following data are for the two products produced by Tadros Company.

	Product A	Product B
Direct materials	$15 per unit	$24 per unit
Direct labor hours	0.3 DLH per unit	1.6 DLH per unit
Machine hours	0.1 MH per unit	1.2 MH per unit
Batches	125 batches	225 batches
Volume	10,000 units	2,000 units
Engineering modifications	12 modifications	58 modifications
Number of customers	500 customers	400 customers
Market price	$30 per unit	$120 per unit

The company's direct labor rate is $20 per direct labor hour (DLH). Additional information follows.

	Costs	Driver
Indirect manufacturing		
Engineering support	$24,500	Engineering modifications
Electricity	34,000	Machine hours
Setup costs	52,500	Batches
Nonmanufacturing		
Customer service	81,000	Number of customers

Required

1. Compute the manufacturing cost per unit using the plantwide overhead rate based on direct labor hours. What is the gross profit per unit?
2. How much gross profit is generated by each customer of Product A using the plantwide overhead rate? How much gross profit is generated by each customer of Product B using the plantwide overhead rate? What is the cost of providing customer service to each customer? What information is provided by this comparison?
3. Determine the manufacturing cost per unit of each product line using ABC. What is the gross profit per unit?
4. How much gross profit is generated by each customer of Product A using ABC? How much gross profit is generated by each customer of Product B using ABC? Is the gross profit per customer adequate?
5. Which method of product costing gives better information to managers of this company? Explain why.

Check (1) Product A, $26.37 per unit cost

(3) Product A, $24.30 per unit cost

Problem 17-2A
Assessing impacts of using a plantwide overhead rate versus ABC
A1 A2

Xylon Company manufactures custom-made furniture for its local market and produces a line of home furnishings sold in retail stores across the country. The company uses traditional volume-based methods of assigning direct materials and direct labor to its product lines. Overhead has always been assigned by using a plantwide overhead rate based on direct labor hours. In the past few years, management has seen its line of retail products continue to sell at high volumes, but competition has forced it to lower prices on these items. The prices are declining to a level close to its cost of production.

Meanwhile, its custom-made furniture is in high demand and customers have commented on its favorable (lower) prices compared to its competitors. Management is considering dropping its line of retail products and devoting all of its resources to custom-made furniture.

Required

1. What reasons could explain why competitors are forcing the company to lower prices on its high-volume retail products?
2. Why do you believe the company charges less for custom-order products than its competitors?
3. Does a company's costing method have any effect on its pricing decisions? Explain.
4. Aside from the differences in volume of output, what production differences do you believe exist between making custom-order furniture and mass-market furnishings?
5. What information might the company obtain from using ABC that it might not obtain using volume-based costing methods?

Problem 17-3A
Applying activity-based costing
P1 P3 A1 A2 C3

Craft Pro Machining produces machine tools for the construction industry. The following details about overhead costs were taken from its company records.

Production Activity	Indirect Labor	Indirect Materials	Other Overhead
Grinding	$320,000		
Polishing		$135,000	
Product modification	600,000		
Providing power			$255,000
System calibration	500,000		

Additional information on the drivers for its production activities follows.

Grinding	13,000 machine hours
Polishing	13,000 machine hours
Product modification	1,500 engineering hours
Providing power	17,000 direct labor hours
System calibration	400 batches

Required

1. Classify each activity as unit level, batch level, product level, or facility level.
2. Compute the activity overhead rates using ABC. Form cost pools as appropriate.
3. Determine overhead costs to assign to the following jobs using ABC.

	Job 3175	Job 4286
Number of units	200 units	2,500 units
Machine hours	550 MH	5,500 MH
Engineering hours	26 eng. hours	32 eng. hours
Batches	30 batches	90 batches
Direct labor hours	500 DLH	4,375 DLH

Check (4) Job 3175, $373.25 per unit

4. What is the overhead cost per unit for Job 3175? What is the overhead cost per unit for Job 4286?
5. If the company used a plantwide overhead rate based on direct labor hours, what is the overhead cost for each unit of Job 3175? Of Job 4286?
6. Compare the overhead costs per unit computed in requirements 4 and 5 for each job. Which method more accurately assigns overhead costs?

Problem 17-4A
Evaluating product line costs and prices using ABC
P3

Bright Day Company produces two beverages, Hi-Voltage and EasySlim. Data about these products follow.

	Hi-Voltage	EasySlim
Production volume	12,500 bottles	180,000 bottles
Liquid materials	1,400 gallons	37,000 gallons
Dry materials	620 pounds	12,000 pounds
Bottles	12,500 bottles	180,000 bottles
Labels	3 labels per bottle	1 label per bottle
Machine setups	500 setups	300 setups
Machine hours	200 MH	3,750 MH

Additional data from its two production departments follow.

Department	Driver	Cost
Mixing department		
Liquid materials	Gallons	$ 2,304
Dry materials	Pounds	6,941
Utilities	Machine hours	1,422
Bottling department		
Bottles	Units	$77,000
Labeling	Labels per bottle	6,525
Machine setup	Setups	20,000

Required

1. Determine the cost of each product line using ABC.
2. What is the cost per bottle for Hi-Voltage? What is the cost per bottle of EasySlim? (*Hint:* Your answer should draw on the total cost for each product line computed in requirement 1.)
3. If Hi-Voltage sells for $3.75 per bottle, how much profit does the company earn per bottle of Hi-Voltage that it sells?
4. What is the minimum price that the company should set per bottle of EasySlim? Explain.

Check (3) $2.22 profit per bottle

Problem 17-5A
Pricing analysis with ABC and a plantwide overhead rate
A1 A2 P1 P3

Sara's Salsa Company produces its condiments in two types: Extra Fine for restaurant customers and Family Style for home use. Salsa is prepared in department 1 and packaged in department 2. The activities, overhead costs, and drivers associated with these two manufacturing processes and the company's production support activities follow.

Process	Activity	Overhead Cost	Driver	Quantity
Department 1	Mixing	$ 4,500	Machine hours	1,500
	Cooking	11,250	Machine hours	1,500
	Product testing	112,500	Batches	600
		$128,250		
Department 2	Machine calibration	$250,000	Production runs	400
	Labeling	12,000	Cases of output	120,000
	Defects	6,000	Cases of output	120,000
		$268,000		
Support	Recipe formulation	$ 90,000	Focus groups	45
	Heat, lights, and water	27,000	Machine hours	1,500
	Materials handling	65,000	Container types	8
		$182,000		

Additional production information about its two product lines follows.

	Extra Fine	Family Style
Units produced	20,000 cases	100,000 cases
Batches	200 batches	400 batches
Machine hours	500 MH	1,000 MH
Focus groups	30 groups	15 groups
Container types	5 containers	3 containers
Production runs	200 runs	200 runs

Required

1. Using a plantwide overhead rate based on cases, compute the overhead cost that is assigned to each case of Extra Fine Salsa and each case of Family Style Salsa.
2. Using the plantwide overhead rate, determine the total cost per unit for the two products if the direct materials and direct labor cost is $6 per case of Extra Fine and $5 per case of Family Style.
3. If the market price of Extra Fine Salsa is $18 per case and the market price of Family Style Salsa is $9 per case, determine the gross profit per case for each product. What might management conclude about each product line?
4. Using ABC, compute the total cost per case for each product type if the direct labor and direct materials cost is $6 per case of Extra Fine and $5 per case of Family Style.
5. If the market price is $18 per case of Extra Fine and $9 per case of Family Style, determine the gross profit per case for each product. How should management interpret the market prices given your computations?
6. Would your pricing analysis be improved if the company used departmental rates based on machine hours in department 1 and number of cases in department 2, instead of ABC? Explain.

Check (2) Cost per case: Extra Fine, $10.82; Family Style, $9.82

(4) Cost per case: Extra Fine, $20.02; Family Style, $7.98

PROBLEM SET B

Problem 17-1B
Comparing costs using ABC with the plantwide overhead rate
A1 A2 P1 P3

Wade Company makes two distinct products with the following information available for each.

	Standard	Deluxe
Direct materials	$4 per unit	$8 per unit
Direct labor hours	4 DLH per unit	5 DLH per unit
Machine hours	3 MH per unit	3 MH per unit
Batches	175 batches	75 batches
Volume	40,000 units	10,000 units
Engineering modifications	50 modifications	25 modifications
Number of customers	1,000 customers	1,000 customers
Market price	$92 per unit	$125 per unit

The company's direct labor rate is $20 per direct labor hour (DLH). Additional information follows.

	Costs	Driver
Indirect manufacturing		
Engineering support	$ 56,250	Engineering modifications
Electricity	112,500	Machine hours
Setup costs	41,250	Batches
Nonmanufacturing		
Customer service	250,000	Number of customers

Required

1. Compute the manufacturing cost per unit using the plantwide overhead rate based on machine hours. What is the gross profit per unit?
2. How much gross profit is generated by each customer of the standard product using the plantwide overhead rate? How much gross profit is generated by each customer of the deluxe product using the plantwide overhead rate? What is the cost of providing customer service to each customer? What information is provided by this comparison?
3. Determine the manufacturing cost per unit of each product line using ABC. What is the gross profit per unit?
4. How much gross profit is generated by each customer of the standard product using ABC? How much gross profit is generated by each customer of the deluxe product using ABC? Is the gross profit per customer adequate?
5. Which method of product costing gives better information to managers of this company? Explain.

Check (1) Gross profit per unit: Standard, $3.80; Deluxe, $12.80

(3) Gross profit per unit: Standard, $4.09; Deluxe, $11.64

Problem 17-2B
Assessing impacts of using a plantwide overhead rate versus ABC
A1 A2

Midwest Paper produces cardboard boxes. The boxes require designing, cutting, and printing. (The boxes are shipped flat and customers fold them as necessary.) Midwest has a reputation for providing high-quality products and excellent service to customers, who are major U.S. manufacturers. Costs are assigned to products based on the number of machine hours required to produce them.

Three years ago, a new marketing executive was hired. She suggested the company offer custom design and manufacturing services to small specialty manufacturers. These customers required boxes for their products and were eager to have Midwest as a supplier. Within one year Midwest found that it was so busy with orders from small customers, it had trouble supplying boxes to all its customers on a timely basis. Large, long-time customers began to complain about slow service, and several took their business elsewhere. Within another 18 months, Midwest was in financial distress with a backlog of orders to be filled.

Required

1. What do you believe are the major costs of making its boxes? How are those costs related to the volume of boxes produced?
2. How did Midwest's new customers differ from its previous customers?
3. Would the unit cost to produce a box for new customers be different from the unit cost to produce a box for its previous customers? Explain.
4. Could Midwest's fate have been different if it had used ABC for determining the cost of its boxes?
5. What information would have been available with ABC that might have been overlooked using a traditional volume-based costing method?

Problem 17-3B
Applying activity-based costing
P1 P3 A1 A2 C3

Ryan Foods produces gourmet gift baskets that it distributes online as well as from its small retail store. The following details about overhead costs are taken from its records.

Production Activity	Indirect Labor	Indirect Materials	Other Overhead
Wrapping	$300,000	$200,000	
Assembling	400,000		
Product design	180,000		
Obtaining business licenses			$100,000
Cooking	150,000	120,000	

Additional information on the drivers for its production activities follows.

Wrapping	100,000 units
Assembling	20,000 direct labor hours
Product design	3,000 design hours
Obtaining business licenses	20,000 direct labor hours
Cooking	1,000 batches

Required

1. Classify each activity as unit level, batch level, product level, or facility level.
2. Compute the activity overhead rates using ABC. Form cost pools as appropriate.
3. Determine the overhead cost to assign to the following jobs using ABC.

	Holiday Basket	Executive Basket
Number of units	8,000 units	1,000 units
Direct labor hours	2,000 DLH	500 DLH
Design hours	40 design hours	40 design hours
Batches	80 batches	200 batches

Check (4) Holiday Basket, $14.25 per unit

(5) Holiday Basket, $18.13 per unit

4. What is the overhead cost per unit for the Holiday Basket? What is the overhead cost per unit for the Executive Basket?
5. If the company used a plantwide overhead rate based on direct labor hours, what is the overhead cost for each Holiday Basket unit? What would be the overhead cost for each Executive Basket unit if a single plantwide overhead rate is used?
6. Compare the costs per unit computed in requirements 4 and 5 for each job. Which cost assignment method provides the most accurate cost? Explain.

Problem 17-4B
Evaluating product line costs and prices using ABC
P3

Mathwerks produces two electronic, handheld educational games: *Fun with Fractions* and *Count Calculus*. Data on these products follow.

	Fun with Fractions	*Count Calculus*
Production volume	150,000 units	10,000 units
Components	450,000 parts	100,000 parts
Direct labor hours	15,000 DLH	2,000 DLH
Packaging materials	150,000 boxes	10,000 boxes
Shipping cartons	100 units per carton	25 units per carton
Machine setups	52 setups	52 setups
Machine hours	5,000 MH	2,000 MH

Additional data from its two production departments follow.

Department	Driver	Cost
Assembly department		
Component cost	Parts	$495,000
Assembly labor	Direct labor hours	244,800
Maintenance	Machine hours	100,800
Wrapping department		
Packaging materials	Boxes	$460,800
Shipping	Cartons	27,360
Machine setup	Setups	187,200

Required

1. Using ABC, determine the cost of each product line.
2. What is the cost per unit for *Fun with Fractions*? What is the cost per unit of *Count Calculus*?
3. If *Count Calculus* sells for $59.95 per unit, how much profit does the company earn per unit of *Count Calculus* sold?
4. What is the minimum price that the company should set per unit of *Fun with Fractions*? Explain.

Check (3) $32.37 profit per unit

Problem 17-5B
Pricing analysis with ABC and a plantwide overhead rate
A1 A2 P1 P3

Tent Pro produces two lines of tents sold to outdoor enthusiasts. The tents are cut to specifications in department A. In department B the tents are sewn and folded. The activities, costs, and drivers associated with these two manufacturing processes and the company's production support activities follow.

Process	Activity	Overhead Cost	Driver	Quantity
Department A	Pattern alignment	$ 64,400	Batches	560
	Cutting	50,430	Machine hours	12,300
	Moving product	100,800	Moves	2,400
		$215,630		
Department B	Sewing	$327,600	Direct labor hours	4,200
	Inspecting	24,000	Inspections	600
	Folding	47,880	Units	22,800
		$399,480		
Support	Design	$280,000	Modification orders	280
	Providing space	51,600	Square feet	8,600
	Materials handling	184,000	Square yards	920,000
		$515,600		

Additional production information on the two lines of tents follows.

	Pup Tent	Pop-Up Tent
Units produced	15,200 units	7,600 units
Moves	800 moves	1,600 moves
Batches	140 batches	420 batches
Number of inspections	240 inspections	360 inspections
Machine hours	7,000 MH	5,300 MH
Direct labor hours	2,600 DLH	1,600 DLH
Modification orders	70 modification orders	210 modification orders
Space occupied	4,300 square feet	4,300 square feet
Material required	450,000 square yards	470,000 square yards

Required

1. Using a plantwide overhead rate based on direct labor hours, compute the overhead cost that is assigned to each pup tent and each pop-up tent.
2. Using the plantwide overhead rate, determine the total cost per unit for the two products if the direct materials and direct labor cost is $25 per pup tent and $32 per pop-up tent.
3. If the market price of the pup tent is $65 and the market price of the pop-up tent is $200, determine the gross profit per unit for each tent. What might management conclude about the pup tent?
4. Using ABC, compute the total cost per unit for each tent if the direct labor and direct materials cost is $25 per pup tent and $32 per pop-up tent.
5. If the market price is $65 per pup tent and $200 per pop-up tent, determine the gross profit per unit for each tent. Comment on the results.
6. Would your pricing analysis be improved if the company used, instead of ABC, departmental rates determined using machine hours in department A and direct labor hours in department B? Explain.

Check (4) Pup tent, $58.46 per unit cost

SERIAL PROBLEM
Business Solutions
P3

(This serial problem began in Chapter 1 and continues through most of the book. If previous chapter segments were not completed, the serial problem can begin at this point. It is helpful, but not necessary, to use the Working Papers that accompany the book.)

SP 17 After reading an article about activity-based costing in a trade journal for the furniture industry, Santana Rey wondered if it was time to critically analyze overhead costs at Business Solutions. In a recent month, Santana found that setup costs, inspection costs, and utility costs made up most of its overhead. Additional information about overhead follows.

Activity	Cost	Driver
Setting up machines	$20,000	25 batches
Inspecting components	$ 7,500	5,000 parts
Providing utilities	$10,000	5,000 machine hours

Overhead has been applied to output at a rate of 50% of direct labor costs. The following data pertain to Job 615.

Direct materials	$2,500
Direct labor	$3,500
Batches	2 batches
Number of parts	400 parts
Machine hours	600 machine hours

Required

1. Classify each of its three overhead activities as unit level, batch level, product level, or facility level.
2. What is the total cost of Job 615 if Business Solutions applies overhead at 50% of direct labor cost?
3. What is the total cost of Job 615 if Business Solutions uses activity-based costing?
4. Which approach to assigning overhead gives a better representation of the costs incurred to produce Job 615? Explain.

Beyond the Numbers

REPORTING IN ACTION

C3 A2

APPLE

GOOGLE

BTN 17-1 Refer to financial statements of **Apple (Apple.com)** and **Google (Google.com)** to answer the following.

Required

1. Identify at least two activities at Apple and at Google that cause costs to be incurred. Do you believe these companies should be concerned about controlling costs of the activities you identified? Explain.
2. Would you classify Apple and Google as service, merchandising, or manufacturing companies? Explain.
3. Is activity-based costing useful for companies such as Apple and Google? Explain.

COMPARATIVE ANALYSIS

C2 A2

APPLE

GOOGLE

BTN 17-2 **Apple** and **Google** are competitors in the sales of electronic devices. Compare these companies' income statements and answer the following.

Required

1. Which company has a higher ratio of costs, defined as cost of goods sold plus total operating expenses, to revenues? Use the two most recent years' income statements from Appendix A. Show your analysis.
2. How might the use of activity-based costing help the less competitive company become *more* competitive?
3. Assume Apple is considering opening a new retail store. What are the activities associated with opening a new retail store?

BTN 17-3 In conducting interviews and observing factory operations to implement an activity-based costing system, you determine that several activities are unnecessary or redundant. For example, warehouse personnel were inspecting purchased components as they were received at the loading dock. Later that day, the components were inspected again on the shop floor before being installed in the final product. Both of these activities caused costs to be incurred but were not adding value to the product. If you include this observation in your report, one or more employees who perform inspections will likely lose their jobs.

ETHICS CHALLENGE

A2 C3

Required

1. As a plant employee, what is your responsibility to report your findings to superiors?
2. Should you attempt to determine if the redundancy is justified? Explain.
3. What is your responsibility to the employees whose jobs will likely be lost because of your report?
4. What facts should you consider before making your decision to report or not?

BTN 17-4 The chief executive officer (CEO) of your company recently returned from a luncheon meeting where activity-based costing was presented and discussed. Though her background is not in accounting, she has worked for the company for 15 years and is thoroughly familiar with its operations. Her impression of the presentation about ABC was that it was just another way of dividing up total overhead cost and that the total would still be the same "no matter how you sliced it."

COMMUNICATING IN PRACTICE

A2

Required

Write a memorandum to the CEO, no more than one page, explaining how ABC is different from traditional volume-based costing methods. Also, identify its advantages and disadvantages vis-à-vis traditional methods. Be sure it is written to be understandable to someone who is not an accountant.

BTN 17-5 Accounting professionals who work for private companies often obtain the Certified Management Accountant (CMA) designation to indicate their proficiency in several business areas in addition to managerial accounting. The CMA examination is administered by the Institute of Management Accountants (IMA).

TAKING IT TO THE NET

A2

Required

Go to the IMA website (**IMAnet.org**) and determine which parts of the CMA exam likely cover activity-based costing. A person planning to become a CMA should take what college course work?

BTN 17-6 Observe the operations at your favorite fast-food restaurant.

TEAMWORK IN ACTION

C2 C3

Required

1. How many people does it take to fill a typical order of sandwich, beverage, and one side order?
2. Describe the activities involved in its food service process.
3. What costs are related to each activity identified in requirement 2?

BTN 17-7 **Suja Juice Co.** has expanded its product offerings to include many varieties of cold-pressed organic juices. Company founders know that financial success depends on cost control as well as revenue generation.

ENTREPRENEURIAL DECISION

C3

Required

1. If Suja Juice Co. wanted to expand its product line to include organic energy bars, what activities would it need to perform that are not required for its current product lines?
2. Related to part 1, should the additional overhead costs related to new product lines be shared by existing product lines? Explain your reasoning.

HITTING THE ROAD

C2 C3

BTN 17-8 Visit and observe the processes of three different fast-food restaurants—these visits can be done as individuals or as teams. The objective of activity-based costing is to accurately assign costs to products and to improve operational efficiency.

Required

1. Individuals (or teams) can be assigned to each of three different fast-food establishments. Make a list of the activities required to process an order of a sandwich, beverage, and one side order at each restaurant. Record the time required for each process, from placing the order to receiving the completed order.
2. What activities do the three establishments have in common? What activities are different across the establishments?
3. Is the number of activities related to the time required to process an order? Is the number of activities related to the price charged to customers? Explain both.
4. Make recommendations for improving the processes you observe. Would your recommendations increase or decrease the cost of operations?

GLOBAL DECISION

C3

Samsung
APPLE

BTN 17-9 Visit the websites and review the financial statements for **Apple** (**Apple.com**) and **Samsung** (**Samsung.com**). Each of these companies sells electronic devices like smartphones in global markets.

Required

1. For Apple in 2013, what are the largest three geographic markets in which it sells products? What is the amount (in millions of dollars) of sales in each market?
2. For Samsung in 2013, what are the largest three geographic markets in which it sells products? What is the amount (in millions of Korean won) of sales in each market? (Use "revenue from external customers.")
3. How would customer service activities differ across different geographic markets?

ANSWERS TO MULTIPLE CHOICE QUIZ

1. b; Under traditional costing methods, overhead costs are allocated to products on the basis of some measure of volume such as direct labor hours or machine hours. This results in much of the overhead cost being allocated to high-volume products. In contrast, under activity-based costing, some overhead costs are allocated on the basis of batch-level or product-level activities. This change in allocation bases results in shifting overhead costs from high-volume products to low-volume products.
2. d; Generally, an activity-based costing system is more difficult to implement and maintain than a traditional costing system (thus answer **a** is false). Instead of eliminating waste by allocating costs to products that waste resources, activity-based management is a management approach that focuses on managing activities as a means of eliminating waste and reducing delays and defects (thus answer **b** is false). Instead of using a single allocation base (such as direct labor hours), activity-based costing uses a number of allocation bases for assigning costs to products (thus answer **c** is false). Answer **d** is true.
3. d; Batch-level activities are activities that are performed each time a batch of goods is handled or processed, regardless of how many units are in a batch. Further, the amount of resources consumed depends on the number of batches rather than on the number of units in the batch. Worker recreational facilities relate to the organization as a whole rather than to specific batches and, as such, are not considered to be batch level. On the other hand, purchase order processing, setting up equipment, and the clerical activities described are activities that are performed each time a batch of goods is handled or processed, and, as such, are batch-level activities.

4. c;

	(A) Activity Rate (Budgeted overhead cost ÷ Budgeted activity)	(B) Actual Activity	(A × B) Overhead Cost Applied to Production
Activity 1	(\$80,000 ÷ 1,000) = \$80.00	800	\$ 64,000
Activity 2	(\$58,400 ÷ 1,500) = \$38.93*	500	19,465
Activity 3	(\$360,000 ÷ 6,000) = \$60.00	5,400	324,000
Total overhead cost per unit for Product B			\$407,465
Divided by number of units produced			÷ 31,652
Overhead cost per unit of Product B			\$ 12.87

*rounded

5. d; The activity rate for Activity 3 is determined as follows:

Budgeted cost	÷	Budgeted activity	=	Activity rate
\$14,000	÷	700	=	\$20

chapter 18

Cost Behavior and Cost-Volume-Profit Analysis

Chapter Preview

IDENTIFYING COST BEHAVIOR	MEASURING COST BEHAVIOR	CONTRIBUTION MARGIN AND BREAK-EVEN ANALYSIS	APPLYING COST-VOLUME-PROFIT ANALYSIS
C1 Fixed costs Variable costs Mixed costs Step-wise costs and relevant range Curvilinear costs	P1 Scatter diagrams High-low method Least-squares regression Comparison of cost estimation methods	A1 Computing contribution margin P2 Computing break-even Computing margin of safety P3 Preparing a cost-volume-profit chart Impact of estimates on break-even analysis	C2 Computing income from sales and costs Computing sales for target income Sensitivity analysis P4 Computing multi-product break-even A2 Analyzing sales with operating leverage

Learning Objectives

CONCEPTUAL

C1 Describe different types of cost behavior in relation to production and sales volume.

C2 Describe several applications of cost-volume-profit analysis.

ANALYTICAL

A1 Compute the contribution margin and describe what it reveals about a company's cost structure.

A2 Analyze changes in sales using the degree of operating leverage.

PROCEDURAL

P1 Determine cost estimates using the scatter diagram, high-low, and regression methods of estimating costs.

P2 Compute the break-even point for a single product company.

P3 Graph costs and sales for a single product company.

P4 Compute the break-even point for a multiproduct company.

Courtesy of Fast Yeti Tees

Find the Yeti

COLUMBIA, MO—After finishing his marketing degree and obtaining over 13 years of professional marketing and design experience, Reid Lyle needed a change. "I wanted to produce creative quality products with talented, genuine people in a business that I could actually influence for the better" says Reid. Reid, along with partners Ryan Montgomery and Jordan Roudenis, opened a custom T-shirt shop, **Fast Yeti Custom Tees** (**fastyetitees.com**).

"We all contributed to every aspect of starting this business" says Reid. That includes brainstorming to find a name for their company. The trio came up with a mythical character, Freddie the Yeti, who allegedly trekked from the Ozark Mountains to convince the group to start a business. "Fast Yeti is memorable and fun," says Reid. "It's interesting. It raises questions." During the week, Freddie roams the streets of Columbia, and customers who capture a photo of him receive a discount on merchandise. "A common misconception is that he's a human wearing a costume," jokes Ryan. "It's a real yeti."

"The T-shirt is the epitome of creativity."

—Reid Lyle

While humor is a large part of their business, the owners have a serious focus on providing high-quality products to meet customer demands. "Everyone has a favorite T-shirt," says Reid. "We want to be the shop that designs and sells it." Jordan, the company's production manager, says he "is very particular about how I do things. If I mess up, I fix it and try not to let it happen again. I try to perfect what I do."

Operating at a small scale, in a highly competitive industry, requires the owners to understand and control their costs. Successful entrepreneurs must understand cost behavior to succeed. Identifying fixed and variable costs is key to understanding break-even points determining the amount of sales required to make a target income, key topics in this chapter. In addition to selling custom T-shirts, Fast Yeti also sells custom hats and polo shirts. Understanding multiproduct break-even points and sales mix is important in companies with diverse product lines. Contribution margin income statements, which separate fixed and variable costs, enable entrepreneurs to quickly see how changes in selling prices, variable costs, or fixed costs impact profit. Understanding contribution margins and cost-volume-profit analyses enables small businesses to profit and grow.

Reid, Ryan, and Jordan agree that young entrepreneurs should follow their passion and "make it happen." "We all are interested in apparel, humor, and design," says Reid. "Still, we all had to strip out old carpet and make our own shelves to get this store opened." While still a young company, the trio is seeing their hard work rewarded with increasing sales. "We work hard," says Ryan, "but it's really fun." And, if you see a yeti roaming around . . . take a photo.

Sources: *Fast Yeti Custom Tees website,* January 2015; *Columbia Missourian,* May 14, 2014; *Columbia Daily Tribune,* June 16, 2014

IDENTIFYING COST BEHAVIOR

Planning a company's future activities and events is crucial to successful management. One of the first steps in planning is to predict the volume of activity, the costs to be incurred, sales to be made, and profit to be earned. An important tool in such planning is **cost-volume-profit (CVP) analysis,** which helps managers predict how changes in costs and sales levels affect profit. In its basic form, CVP analysis involves computing the sales level at which a company neither earns an income nor incurs a loss, called the *break-even point.* For this reason, this basic form of cost-volume-profit analysis is often called *break-even analysis.*

Managers use variations of CVP analysis to answer questions like:

- How much does income increase if we install a new machine to reduce labor costs?
- What is the change in income if selling prices decline and sales volume increases?
- How will income change if we change the sales mix of our products or services?
- What sales volume is needed to earn a target income?

Consequently, cost-volume-profit analysis is useful in a wide range of business decisions.

The concept of *relevant range* is important to classifying costs for CVP analysis. The **relevant range of operations** is the normal operating range for a business. Except for unusually good or bad times, management typically plans for operations within a range of volume neither close to zero nor at maximum capacity. The relevant range excludes extremely high or low operating levels that are unlikely to recur. CVP analysis requires management to classify costs as either *fixed* or *variable* with respect to production or sales volume, within the relevant range of operations. The remainder of this section discusses concepts of cost behavior as they relate to CVP analysis.

Fixed Costs

C1 Describe different types of cost behavior in relation to production and sales volume.

Fixed costs remain unchanged despite variations in the volume of activity within a relevant range. For example, $32,000 in monthly rent paid for a factory building remains the same whether the factory operates with a single eight-hour shift or around the clock with three shifts. This means that rent cost is the same each month at any level of output from zero to the plant's full productive capacity. Common examples of fixed costs include depreciation, property taxes, office salaries, and many service department costs.

Be sure to realize that the idea of fixed cost not changing as the level of production changes applies to the *total* dollar amount. It does not apply to the per unit amount. Rather, the fixed cost *per unit* of output decreases as volume increases. For instance, if 200 units are produced when monthly rent is $32,000, the average rent cost per unit is $160 (computed as $32,000/200 units). When production increases to 1,000 units per month, the average rent cost per unit decreases to $32 (computed as $32,000/1,000 units).

When production volume and costs are graphed, units of product are usually plotted on the *horizontal axis* and dollars of cost are plotted on the *vertical axis.* Fixed costs then are represented as a horizontal line because they remain constant at all levels of production. To illustrate, the top graph in Exhibit 18.1 shows that fixed costs remain at $32,000 at all production levels up to the company's monthly capacity of 2,000 units of output. The bottom graph in Exhibit 18.1 shows that fixed costs per unit fall as production levels increase. This drop in costs per unit as production levels increase is known as *economies of scale.* The *relevant range* for fixed costs in Exhibit 18.1 is 0 to 2,000 units. If the relevant range changes (that is, production capacity extends beyond this range), the amount of fixed costs will likely change.

gerenme/Vetta/Getty Images

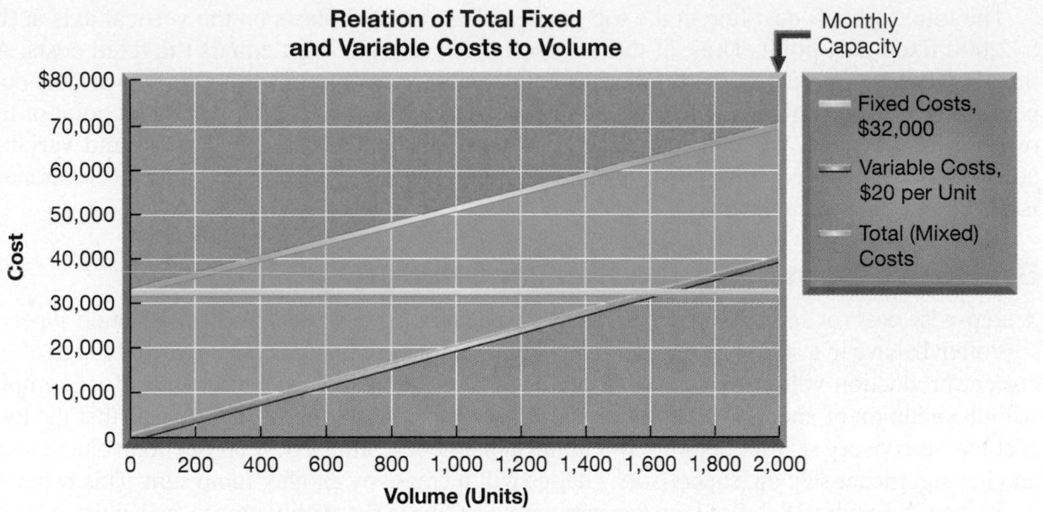

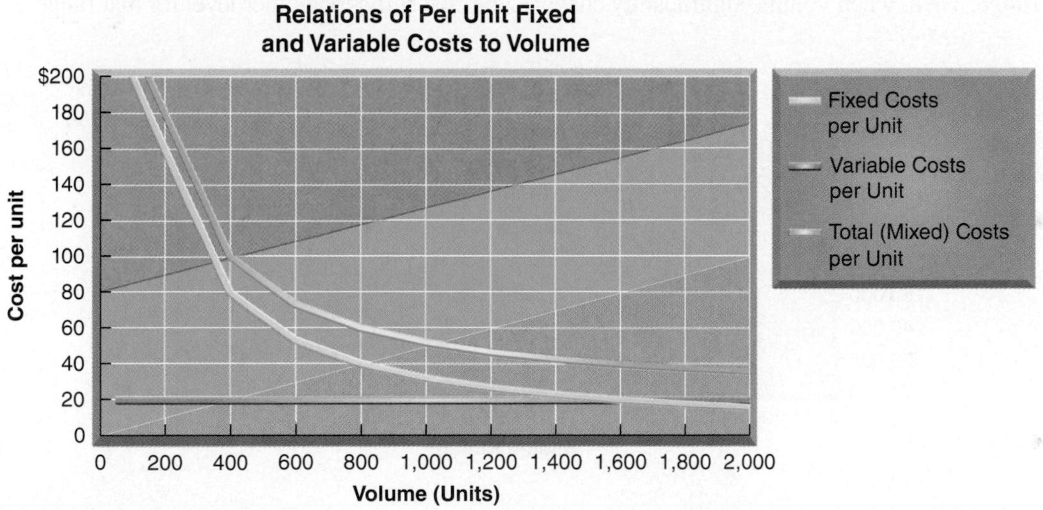

EXHIBIT 18.1

Relations of Total and Per Unit Costs to Volume

Example: If the fixed cost line in Exhibit 18.1 is shifted upward, does the total cost line shift up, down, or remain in the same place? *Answer:* It shifts up by the same amount.

Example: If the level of fixed costs in Exhibit 18.1 changes, does the slope of the total cost line change? *Answer:* No, the slope doesn't change. The total cost line is simply shifted upward or downward.

Variable Costs

Variable costs change in proportion to changes in volume of activity. The direct materials cost of a product is one example of a variable cost. If one unit of product requires materials costing $20, total materials costs are $200 when 10 units of product are manufactured, $400 for 20 units, $600 for 30 units, and so on. In addition to direct materials, common variable costs include direct labor (if employees are paid per unit), sales commissions, shipping costs, and some overhead costs.

Point: Fixed costs are constant in total but vary (decline) per unit as more units are produced. Variable costs vary in total but are fixed per unit.

Notice that variable cost *per unit* remains constant but the *total* amount of variable cost changes with the level of production. When variable costs are plotted on a graph of cost and volume, they appear as a straight line starting at the zero cost level. This straight line is upward (positive) sloping. The line rises as volume of activity increases. A variable cost line using a $20 per unit cost is graphed in Exhibit 18.1. The bottom graph in Exhibit 18.1 shows that variable cost per unit is constant as production levels change.

Mixed Costs

Are costs either fixed or variable? No—another category, **mixed costs,** includes both fixed and variable cost components. For example, compensation for sales representatives often includes a fixed monthly salary and a variable commission based on sales. Utilities can also be considered a mixed cost; even if no units are produced, it is not likely a manufacturing plant will use no electricity or water. Like a fixed cost, a mixed cost is greater than zero when volume is zero; but unlike a fixed cost, it increases steadily in proportion to increases in volume.

The total (mixed) cost line in the top graph in Exhibit 18.1 starts on the vertical axis at the \$32,000 fixed cost point. Thus, at the zero volume level, total cost equals the fixed costs. As the activity level increases, the total cost line increases at an amount equal to the variable cost per unit. This line is highest when the volume of activity is at 2,000 units (the end point of the relevant range). In CVP analysis, mixed costs should be separated into fixed and variable components. The fixed component is added to other fixed costs, and the variable component is added to other variable costs.

Step-wise Costs and the Relevant Range

A **step-wise cost** (or *stair-step cost*) reflects a step pattern in costs. Salaries of production supervisors often behave in a step-wise manner in that their salaries are fixed within a *relevant range* of the current production volume. However, if production volume expands significantly (for example, with the addition of another shift), additional supervisors must be hired. This means that the total cost for supervisory salaries goes up by a lump-sum amount. Similarly, if production volume takes another significant step up, supervisory salaries will increase by another lump sum. This behavior is graphed in Exhibit 18.2. See how the step-wise cost line is flat within ranges, called the *relevant range*. Then, when volume significantly changes, the cost shifts to another level for that range.

EXHIBIT 18.2

Step-wise and Curvilinear Costs

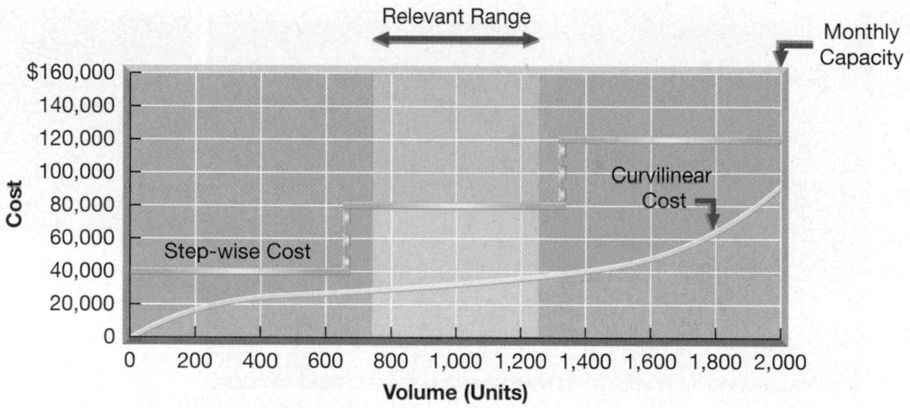

In CVP analysis, a step-wise cost is usually treated as either a fixed cost or a variable cost. This treatment involves manager judgment and depends on the width of the relevant range and the expected volume. To illustrate, suppose after the production of every 25 snowboards, an operator lubricates the finishing machine. The cost of this lubricant reflects a step-wise pattern. Also, suppose that after the production of every 1,000 units, the snowboard cutting tool is replaced. Again, this is a step-wise cost. Note that the relevant range of 25 snowboards is much narrower than the relevant range of 1,000 snowboards. Some managers might treat the lubricant cost as a variable cost and the cutting tool cost as a fixed cost.

Point: Computer spreadsheets are important and effective tools for CVP analysis and for analyzing alternative "what-if" strategies.

Curvilinear Costs

As shown earlier, variable costs increase at a constant rate as the volume of activity increases. For example, a salesperson's commission of 7% of sales volume would increase at a constant rate as sales volume increases. **Curvilinear costs** also increase as volume increases, but at a nonconstant rate. The curved line in Exhibit 18.2 shows a curvilinear cost beginning at zero (when production is zero) and increasing at different rates as volume increases.

An example of a curvilinear cost is total direct labor cost when workers are paid by the hour. For example, a company might add new employees assigned to specialize in certain tasks. When production levels are relatively low, adding those specialized employees often yields more output. This is reflected in a flatter slope in the curvilinear cost graph in Exhibit 18.2. At some point, however, adding still more employees creates inefficiencies (they get in each other's way); this inefficiency is reflected in a steeper slope for the curvilinear cost graph. In CVP analysis, curvilinear costs are often treated as variable costs, within a relevant range. This is reasonable for most types of curvilinear costs.

Determine whether each of the following is best described as a fixed, variable, mixed, step-wise, or curvilinear cost with respect to product units.

NEED-TO-KNOW 18-1

Classifying Costs

C1

	Type of Cost
Rubber used to manufacture tennis balls	a. ______
Depreciation (straight-line method)	b. ______
Electricity usage	c. ______
Supervisory salaries	d. ______
A salesperson's commission is 7% for sales of up to $100,000, and 10% of sales for sales above $100,000	e. ______

Solution

a. variable **b.** fixed **c.** mixed **d.** fixed* **e.** curvilinear

*If more shifts are added, then supervisory salaries behave like a step-wise cost with respect to the number of shifts.

Do More: QS 18-1, QS 18-2, E 18-1, E 18-2, E 18-3

QC1

MEASURING COST BEHAVIOR

P1 Determine cost estimates using the scatter diagram, high-low, and regression methods of estimating costs.

Identifying and measuring cost behavior requires careful analysis and judgment. An important part of this process is to identify costs that can be classified as either fixed or variable, which often requires analysis of past cost behavior. A goal of classifying costs is to develop a *cost equation*. The cost equation expresses total costs as a function of fixed costs plus variable cost per unit. Three methods are commonly used to analyze past costs: scatter diagrams, the high-low method, and least-squares regression. Each method is discussed in this section using the unit and cost data shown in Exhibit 18.3, which are taken from a start-up company that uses units produced as the activity base in estimating cost behavior.

EXHIBIT 18.3

Data for Estimating Cost Behavior

Month	Units Produced	Total Cost
January	27,500	$21,500
February	17,500	20,500
March	25,000	25,000
April	35,000	21,500
May	47,500	25,500
June	22,500	18,500
July	30,000	23,500
August	52,500	28,500
September	37,500	26,000
October	67,500	29,000
November	62,500	31,000
December	57,500	26,000

Scatter Diagrams

Scatter diagrams display past cost and unit data in graphical form. In preparing a scatter diagram, units are plotted on the horizontal axis, and costs are plotted on the vertical axis. Each individual point on a scatter diagram reflects the cost and number of units for a prior period. In Exhibit 18.4, the prior 12 months' costs and numbers of units are graphed. Each point reflects total costs incurred and units produced for one of those months. For instance, the point labeled March had units produced of 25,000 and costs of $25,000.

The **estimated line of cost behavior** is drawn on a scatter diagram to reflect the relation between cost and unit volume. This line best visually "fits" the points in a scatter diagram. Fitting this line demands judgment, or can be done with spreadsheet software, as we illustrate

EXHIBIT 18.4

Scatter Diagram

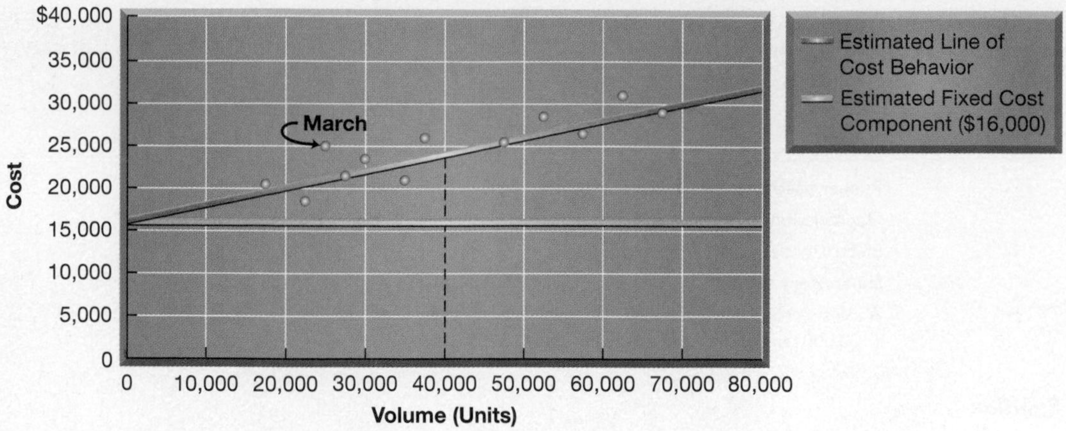

in this chapter's Appendix. The line drawn in Exhibit 18.4 intersects the vertical axis at approximately $16,000, which reflects fixed cost. To compute variable cost per unit, or the slope, we perform three steps. First, we select any two points on the horizontal axis (units), say 0 and 40,000. Second, we draw a vertical line from each of these points to intersect the estimated line of cost behavior. The point on the vertical axis (cost) corresponding to the 40,000 units point that intersects the estimated line is roughly $24,000. Similarly, the cost corresponding to zero units is $16,000 (the fixed cost point). Third, we compute the slope of the line, or variable cost, as the change in cost divided by the change in units. Exhibit 18.5 shows this computation.

EXHIBIT 18.5

Variable Cost per Unit (Scatter Diagram)

$$\frac{\textbf{Change in cost}}{\textbf{Change in units}} = \frac{\$24{,}000 - \$16{,}000}{40{,}000 - 0} = \frac{\$8{,}000}{40{,}000} = \$0.20 \text{ per unit}$$

Example: In Exhibits 18.4 and 18.5, if units are projected at 30,000, what is the predicted cost? *Answer:* Approximately $22,000.

Variable cost is $0.20 per unit. Thus, the cost equation that management will use to estimate costs for different unit levels is **$16,000 plus $0.20 per unit produced**.

High-Low Method

The **high-low method** is a way to estimate the cost equation using just two points: the highest and lowest volume levels. The high-low method follows these steps:

Step 1: Identify the highest and lowest volume levels. It is important to note that these might not be the highest or lowest levels of *costs*.

Step 2: Compute the slope (variable cost per unit) using the high and low activity levels.

Step 3: Compute the total fixed costs by computing the total variable cost at either the high or low activity level, and then subtracting that amount from the total cost at that activity level.

We illustrate the high-low method next.

Step 1: In our case, the lowest number of units is 17,500, and the highest is 67,500. The costs corresponding to these unit volumes are $20,500 and $29,000, respectively (see the data in Exhibit 18.3).

Step 2: The variable cost per unit is calculated using a simple formula: change in cost divided by the change in units. Using the data from the high and low unit volumes, this results in a slope, or variable cost per unit, of $0.17 as computed in Exhibit 18.6.

EXHIBIT 18.6

Variable Cost per Unit (High-Low Method)

$$\frac{\textbf{Change in cost}}{\textbf{Change in units}} = \frac{\$29{,}000 - \$20{,}500}{67{,}500 - 17{,}500} = \frac{\$8{,}500}{50{,}000} = \$0.17 \text{ per unit}$$

Step 3: To estimate the fixed cost for the high-low method, we use the knowledge that total cost equals fixed cost plus variable cost per unit times the number of units. Then we pick either the high or low point to determine the fixed cost. This computation is shown in Exhibit 18.7—where we use the high point (67,500 units) in determining the fixed cost of $17,525. (Use of the low point yields the same fixed cost estimate.)

EXHIBIT 18.7

Determining Fixed Costs (High-Low Method)

Total cost	=	**Fixed cost + (Variable cost per unit × Units)**
$29,000	=	Fixed cost + ($0.17 per unit × 67,500 units)
$29,000	=	Fixed cost + $11,475
		Fixed cost = $17,525

Thus, the cost equation from the high-low method is **$17,525 plus $0.17 per unit produced**. This cost equation differs slightly from that determined from the scatter diagram method. A weakness of the high-low method is that it ignores all cost points except the highest and lowest volume levels.

Example: Using information from Exhibit 18.6, what is the amount of fixed cost at the low level of volume? *Answer:* $17,525, computed as $29,000 − ($0.17 × 17,500 units).

Least-Squares Regression

Least-squares regression is a statistical method for identifying cost behavior. For our purposes, we use the cost equation estimated from this method but leave the computational details for more advanced courses. Such computations for least-squares regression are readily done using most spreadsheet programs or calculators. We illustrate this using Excel in this chapter's Appendix. Using least-squares regression, the cost equation for the data presented in Exhibit 18.3 is **$16,947 plus $0.19 per unit produced**; that is, the fixed cost is estimated as $16,947 and the variable cost at $0.19 per unit.

Comparison of Cost Estimation Methods

The three cost estimation methods result in slightly different estimates of fixed and variable costs as summarized in Exhibit 18.8. Estimates from the scatter diagram, unless done with spreadsheet software, are based on a visual fit of the cost line and are subject to interpretation. Estimates from the high-low method use only two sets of values corresponding to the lowest and highest unit volumes. Sometimes these two extreme activity levels do not reflect the more usual conditions likely to recur. Estimates from least-squares regression use a statistical technique and all available data points.

EXHIBIT 18.8

Comparison of Cost Estimation Methods

Estimation Method	Fixed Cost	Variable Cost
Scatter diagram	$16,000	$0.20 per unit
High-low method	17,525	0.17 per unit
Least-squares regression	16,947	0.19 per unit

We must remember that all three methods use *past data.* Thus, cost estimates resulting from these methods are only as good as the data used for estimation. Managers must establish that the data are reliable in deriving cost estimates for the future. If the data are reliable, the use of more data points, as in the regression or scatter diagram methods, should yield more accurate estimates than the high-low method. However, the high-low method is easier to apply and thus might be useful for obtaining a quick cost equation estimate.

NEED-TO-KNOW 18-2

High-Low Method

P1

Using the information below, apply the high-low method to determine the *cost equation* (total fixed costs plus variable costs per unit).

Activity Level	Units Produced	Total Cost
Lowest	1,600	$ 9,800
Highest	4,000	17,000

Solution

The variable cost per unit is computed as: [$17,000 − $9,800]/[4,000 units − 1,600 units] = $3 per unit. Total fixed costs using the lowest activity level is computed from the following equation: $9,800 = Fixed costs + ($3 × 1,600 units); thus, fixed costs = $5,000. This implies the cost equation is **$5,000 plus $3 per unit produced.** We can prove the accuracy of this cost equation at either the highest or lowest point shown here.

Do More: QS 18-3, E 18-6

QC2

Highest point:
Total cost = $5,000 + ($3 per unit × 4,000 units)
= $5,000 + $12,000
= $17,000

Lowest point:
Total cost = $5,000 + ($3 per unit × 1,600 units)
= $5,000 + $4,800
= $9,800

CONTRIBUTION MARGIN AND BREAK-EVEN ANALYSIS

In this section we introduce the concept of *contribution margin,* the key measure in cost-volume-profit analysis. We also discuss break-even analysis, an important special case of cost-volume-profit analysis.

Contribution Margin and Its Measures

A1 Compute the contribution margin and describe what it reveals about a company's cost structure.

CVP analysis requires managers to classify costs as being fixed or variable with respect to volume of activity. In manufacturing companies, volume of activity usually refers to the number of units produced. We then classify a cost as either fixed or variable, depending on whether total cost changes as the number of units produced changes. Once we classify costs by behavior, we can then compute a product's contribution margin. **Contribution margin per unit,** or *unit contribution margin,* is the amount by which a product's unit selling price exceeds its total variable cost per unit. This amount contributes to covering fixed costs and generating profits. Exhibit 18.9 shows the formula used to calculate contribution margin per unit.

EXHIBIT 18.9
Contribution Margin per Unit

Contribution margin per unit = Selling price per unit − Total variable cost per unit

Another way to calculate contribution margin is as a ratio. The **contribution margin ratio,** which is the percent of a unit's selling price that exceeds total unit variable cost, is also useful for business decisions. It can be interpreted as the percent of each sales dollar that remains after deducting the total unit variable cost. Exhibit 18.10 shows the formula for the contribution margin ratio.

EXHIBIT 18.10
Contribution Margin Ratio

$$\textbf{Contribution margin ratio} = \frac{\textbf{Contribution margin per unit}}{\textbf{Selling price per unit}}$$

AP Images/Skip Peterson

To illustrate the use of contribution margin, let's consider Rydell, which sells footballs for $100 each and incurs variable costs of $70 per football sold. Its fixed costs are $24,000 per month with monthly capacity of 1,800 units (footballs). Rydell's contribution margin per unit is $30, which is computed as follows.

Selling price per unit	$100
Variable cost per unit	70
Contribution margin per unit	$ 30

Thus, at a selling price of $100 per unit, Rydell covers its variable costs and makes $30 per football to contribute to fixed costs and profit. Rydell's contribution margin ratio is 30%, computed as $30/$100. A contribution margin ratio of 30% implies that for each $1 in sales, Rydell has $0.30 that contributes to fixed cost and profit. Next we show how to use these contribution margin measures in break-even analysis.

Decision Maker

Sales Manager You are evaluating orders from two customers but can accept only one of the orders because of your company's limited capacity. The first order is for 100 units of a product with a contribution margin ratio of 60% and a selling price of $1,000 per unit. The second order is for 500 units of a product with a contribution margin ratio of 20% and a selling price of $800 per unit. The incremental fixed costs are the same for both orders. Which order do you accept? ■ [Answers follow the chapter's Summary.]

Computing the Break-Even Point

P2

Compute the break-even point for a single product company.

The **break-even point** is the sales level at which a company neither earns a profit nor incurs a loss. The concept of break-even applies to nearly all organizations, activities, and events. A key concern when launching a project is whether it will break even—that is, whether sales will at least cover total costs. The break-even point can be expressed in either units or dollars of sales.

Point: Selling prices and variable costs are usually expressed in per unit amounts. Fixed costs are usually expressed in total amounts.

To illustrate break-even analysis, let's again look at Rydell, which sells footballs for $100 per unit and incurs $70 of variable costs per unit sold. Its fixed costs are $24,000 per month. We compute the break-even point using the formula in Exhibit 18.11. This formula uses the contribution margin per unit (calculated above), which for Rydell is $30 ($100 − $70). From this we can compute the break-even sales volume in units as follows:

EXHIBIT 18.11

Formula for Computing Break-Even Sales (in Units)

$$\textbf{Break-even point in units} = \frac{\textbf{Fixed costs}}{\textbf{Contribution margin per unit}}$$
$$= \$24{,}000/\$30$$
$$= 800 \text{ units per month}$$

If Rydell sells 800 units, its profit will be zero. Profit increases or decreases by $30 for every unit sold above or below that break-even point; if Rydell sells 801 units, profit will equal $30. We also can calculate the break-even point in dollars. Also called *break-even sales dollars,* it uses the contribution margin ratio to determine the required sales dollars needed for the company to break even. Exhibit 18.12 shows the formula and Rydell's break-even point in dollars:

EXHIBIT 18.12

Formula for Computing Break-Even Sales (in Dollars)

$$\textbf{Break-even point in dollars} = \frac{\textbf{Fixed costs}}{\textbf{Contribution margin ratio}}$$
$$= \$24{,}000/30\%$$
$$= \$24{,}000/0.30$$
$$= \$80{,}000 \text{ of monthly sales}$$

Point: Even if a company operates at a level above its break-even point, management may decide to stop operating because it is not earning a reasonable return on investment.

To verify that Rydell's monthly break-even point equals $80,000 (or 800 units), we prepare a simplified income statement in Exhibit 18.13. It shows that the $80,000 revenue from sales of 800 units exactly equals the sum of variable and fixed costs.

EXHIBIT 18.13

Contribution Margin Income Statement for Break-Even Sales

RYDELL COMPANY
Contribution Margin Income Statement (at Break-Even)
For Month Ended January 31, 2015

Sales (800 units at $100 each)	$80,000
Variable costs (800 units at $70 each)	56,000
Contribution margin	24,000
Fixed costs	24,000
Net income	$ 0

Point: A contribution margin income statement is also referred to as a ***variable costing income statement.*** This differs from the traditional ***absorption costing*** approach where all product costs are assigned to units sold and to units in ending inventory. Recall that variable costing expenses all fixed product costs. Thus, income for the two approaches differs depending on the level of finished goods inventory; the lower inventory is, the more similar the two approaches are. GAAP requires financial statements for external users be prepared using absorption costing.

The statement in Exhibit 18.13 is called a *contribution margin income statement.* It differs in format from a conventional income statement in two ways. First, it separately classifies costs and expenses as variable or fixed. Second, it reports contribution margin (Sales − Variable costs). We will use the contribution margin income statement format in this chapter's assignment materials because of its usefulness in CVP analysis.

Computing the Margin of Safety

All companies wish to sell more than the break-even number of units. The excess of expected sales over the break-even sales level is called a company's **margin of safety,** the amount that sales can drop before the company incurs a loss. It is often expressed in dollars or as a percent of the expected sales level.

To illustrate, recall that Rydell's break-even point in dollars is $80,000. If its expected sales are $100,000, the margin of safety is $20,000 (= $100,000 − $80,000). As a percent, the margin of safety is 20% of expected sales as shown in Exhibit 18.14.

EXHIBIT 18.14

Computing Margin of Safety (in Percent)

$$\textbf{Margin of safety (in percent)} = \frac{\textbf{Expected sales} - \textbf{Break-even sales}}{\textbf{Expected sales}}$$

$$= \frac{\$100{,}000 - \$80{,}000}{\$100{,}000}$$

$$= \$20{,}000/\$100{,}000$$

$$= 20\%$$

Management must assess whether the margin of safety is adequate in light of factors such as sales variability, competition, consumer tastes, and economic conditions.

NEED-TO-KNOW 18-3

Contribution Margin, Break-Even Point, Margin of Safety

A1 P2

A manufacturer predicts fixed costs of $400,000 for the next year. Its one product sells for $170 per unit, and it incurs variable costs of $150 per unit. The company predicts total sales of 25,000 units for the next year.

1. Compute the contribution margin per unit.
2. Compute the break-even point (in units).
3. Compute the margin of safety (in dollars).

Solution

1. Contribution margin per unit = $170 − $150 = $20
2. Break-even point = $400,000/$20 = 20,000 units
3. Margin of safety = [25,000 × $170] − [20,000 × $170] = $850,000

Do More: QS 18-5, QS 18-6, QS 18-10, E 18-8, E 18-9, E 18-16

Preparing a Cost-Volume-Profit Chart

P3 Graph costs and sales for a single product company.

Point: CVP charts can also be drawn with computer programs.

Exhibit 18.15 is a graph of Rydell's cost-volume-profit relations. This graph is called a **cost-volume-profit (CVP) chart,** or a *break-even chart* or *break-even graph.* The horizontal axis is the number of units produced and sold, and the vertical axis is dollars of sales and costs. The lines in the chart depict both sales and costs at different output levels.

We follow three steps to prepare a CVP chart:

1. Plot fixed costs on the vertical axis ($24,000 for Rydell). Draw a horizontal line at this level to show that fixed costs remain unchanged regardless of output volume (drawing this fixed cost line is not essential to the chart).
2. Draw the total (variable plus fixed) cost line for a relevant range of volume levels. This line starts at the fixed costs level on the vertical axis because total costs equal fixed costs

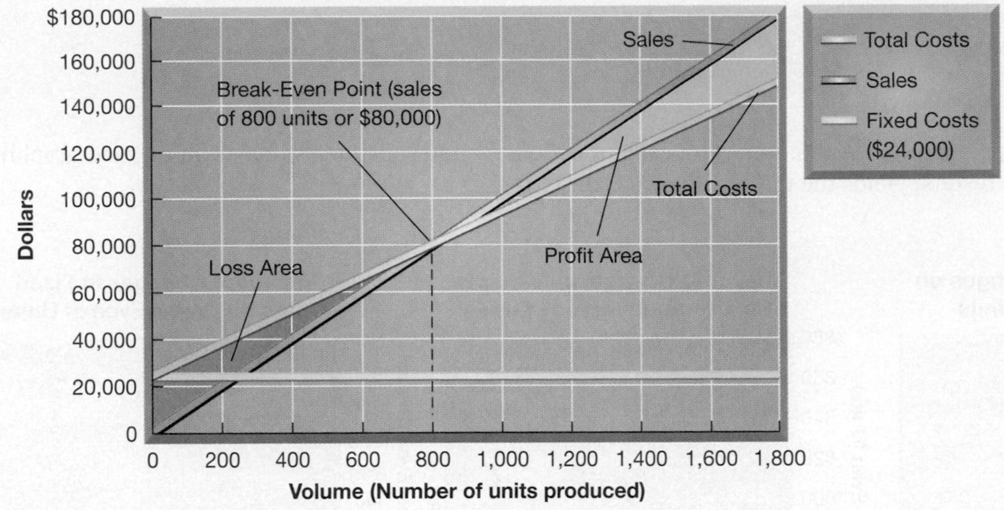

EXHIBIT 18.15

Cost-Volume-Profit Chart

at zero volume. The slope of the total cost line equals the variable cost per unit ($70). To draw the line, compute the total costs for any volume level, and connect this point with the vertical axis intercept ($24,000). Do not draw this line beyond the productive capacity for the planning period (1,800 units for Rydell).

3. Draw the sales line. Start at the origin (zero units and zero dollars of sales) and make the slope of this line equal to the selling price per unit ($100). To draw the line, compute dollar sales for any volume level and connect this point with the origin. Do not extend this line beyond the productive capacity. Total sales will be highest at maximum capacity.

Point: CVP analysis is often based on *sales volume*, using either units sold or dollar sales. Other output measures, such as the number of units produced, can also be used.

The total cost line and the sales line intersect at 800 units in Exhibit 18.15, which is the break-even point—the point where total dollar sales of $80,000 equals the sum of both fixed and variable costs ($80,000). (Note that 800 units is the same result we calculated earlier using the formula in Exhibit 18.11.)

On either side of the break-even point, the vertical distance between the sales line and the total cost line at any specific volume reflects the profit or loss expected at that point. At volume levels to the left of the break-even point, this vertical distance is the amount of the expected loss because the total costs line is above the total sales line. At volume levels to the right of the break-even point, the vertical distance represents the expected profit because the total sales line is above the total cost line.

Example: In Exhibit 18.15, the sales line intersects the total cost line at 800 units. At what point would the two lines intersect if selling price is increased by 20% to $120 per unit? *Answer:* $24,000/($120 − $70) = 480 units

Working with Changes in Estimates

QC3

Because CVP analysis uses estimates, knowing how changes in those estimates impact break-even is useful. For example, a manager might form three estimates for each of the components of break-even: optimistic, most likely, and pessimistic. Then ranges of break-even points in units can be computed, using the formula from Exhibit 18.11. To illustrate, assume Rydell's managers provide the set of estimates in Exhibit 18.16.

EXHIBIT 18.16

Alternative Estimates for Break-Even Analysis

	Selling Price per Unit	Variable Cost per Unit	Total Fixed Costs
Optimistic	$105	$68	$21,000
Most likely	100	70	24,000
Pessimistic	95	72	27,000

If, for example, Rydell's managers believe they can raise the selling price of a football to $105, without any change in unit variable or total fixed costs, then the revised contribution margin per football is $35 ($105 − $70), and the revised break-even in units follows in Exhibit 18.17.

EXHIBIT 18.17

Revised Break-Even in Units

$$\text{Revised break-even point in units} = \frac{\$24{,}000}{\$35} = 686 \text{ units (rounded)}$$

EXHIBIT 18.18

Break-Even Points for Alternative Estimates

Repeating this calculation using each of the other eight separate estimates above, and graphing the results, yields the three graphs in Exhibit 18.18.

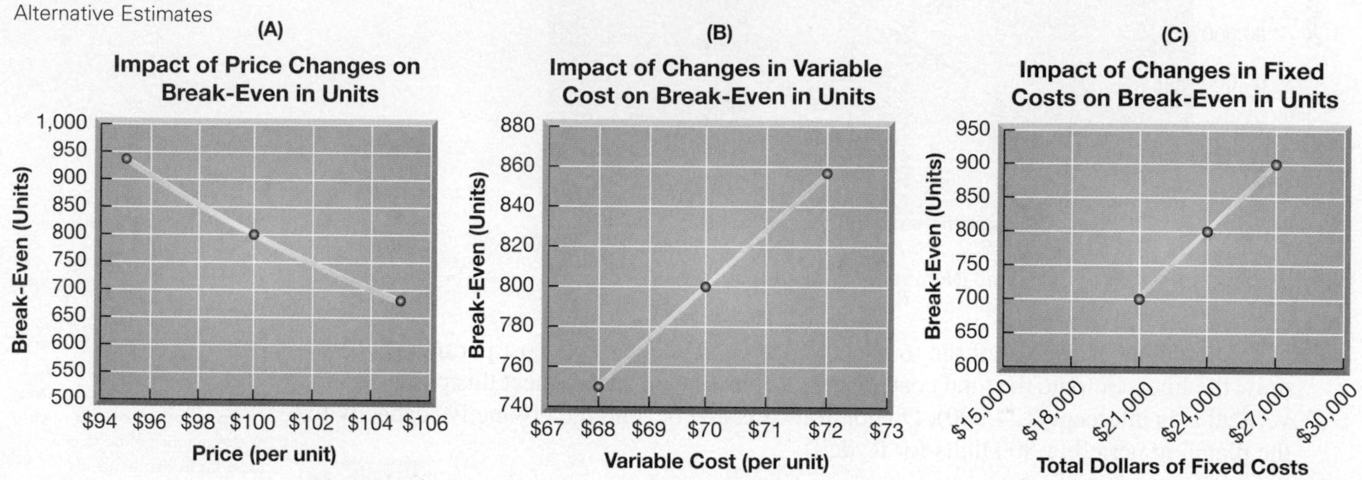

These graphs show how changes in selling prices, variable costs, and fixed costs impact break-even. When selling prices can be increased without impacting unit variable costs or total fixed costs, break-even decreases (graph A). When competition reduces selling prices, and the company cannot reduce costs, break-even increases (graph A). Increases in either variable (graph B) or fixed costs (graph C), if they cannot be passed on to customers via higher selling prices, will increase break-even. If costs can be reduced and selling prices held constant, the break-even point decreases.

Point: This analysis changed only one estimate at a time; managers can examine how combinations of changes in estimates will impact break-even.

Decision Ethics

Supervisor Your team is conducting a cost-volume-profit analysis for a new product. Different sales projections have different incomes. One member suggests picking numbers yielding favorable income because any estimate is "as good as any other." Another member points to a diagram of 20 months' production on a comparable product and suggests dropping unfavorable data points for cost estimation. What do you do? ■ [Answers follow the chapter's Summary.]

APPLYING COST-VOLUME-PROFIT ANALYSIS

Managers consider a variety of strategies in planning business operations. Cost-volume-profit analysis is useful in helping managers evaluate the likely effects of these strategies.

Computing Income from Sales and Costs

C2 Describe several applications of cost-volume-profit analysis.

An important question managers often ask is "What is the predicted income from a predicted level of sales?" To answer this, we look at four variables in CVP analysis—sales, variable costs, contribution margin, and fixed costs. Exhibit 18.19 shows these variables and their relations to income (pretax). We use these relations to compute expected income from predicted sales and cost levels.

EXHIBIT 18.19

Income Relations in CVP Analysis

Sales
− Variable costs
Contribution margin
− Fixed costs
Income (pretax)

To illustrate, let's assume that Rydell's management expects to sell 1,500 units in January 2015. What is the amount of income if this sales level is achieved? Using the calculation format in Exhibit 18.19, we compute Rydell's expected income in Exhibit 18.20.

EXHIBIT 18.20

Computing Expected Pretax Income from Expected Sales

RYDELL COMPANY Contribution Margin Income Statement For Month Ended January 31, 2015	
Sales (1,500 units at $100 each)	$150,000
Variable costs (1,500 units at $70 each)	105,000
Contribution margin	45,000
Fixed costs	24,000
Income (pretax)	$ 21,000

This income amount can also be computed as (units sold × contribution margin per unit) − fixed costs, or (1,500 × $30) − $24,000. The $21,000 income is pretax. To find the amount of *after-tax* income from selling 1,500 units, management must apply the proper tax rate. Assume that the tax rate is 25%. Then we can prepare a projected after-tax income statement, shown in Exhibit 18.21. We can also compute pretax income as after-tax income divided by (1 − tax rate); for Rydell, this is $15,750/(1 − 0.25), or $21,000.

Point: 1,500 units of sales is 700 units above Rydell's break-even point. Income can also be computed as 700 units × $30 contribution margin per unit.

EXHIBIT 18.21

Computing Expected After-Tax Income from Expected Sales

RYDELL COMPANY Contribution Margin Income Statement For Month Ended January 31, 2015	
Sales (1,500 units at $100 each)	$150,000
Variable costs (1,500 units at $70 each)	105,000
Contribution margin	45,000
Fixed costs	24,000
Pretax income	21,000
Income taxes (25%)	5,250
Net income (after tax)	$ 15,750

Management then assesses whether this income is an adequate return on assets invested. Management should also consider whether sales and income can be increased by raising or lowering prices. CVP analysis is a good tool for addressing these kinds of "what-if" questions.

Computing Sales for a Target Income

Many companies' annual plans are based on certain income targets (sometimes called *budgets*). Rydell's income target for this year is to increase income by 10% over the prior year. When prior year income is known, Rydell easily computes its target income. CVP analysis helps to determine the sales level needed to achieve the target income. Planning for the year is then based on this level.

We use the formula shown in Exhibit 18.22 to compute sales for a target income (pretax). To illustrate, Rydell has monthly fixed costs of $24,000 and a 30% contribution margin ratio. Assume that it sets a target monthly income of $12,000. Using the formula in Exhibit 18.22, we find that Rydell needs $120,000 of sales to produce a $12,000 pretax target income.

EXHIBIT 18.22

Computing Sales (Dollars) for a Target Income

$$\textbf{Dollar sales at target income} = \frac{\textbf{Fixed costs} + \textbf{Target income}}{\textbf{Contribution margin ratio}}$$

$$= \frac{\$24{,}000 + \$12{,}000}{30\%} = \$120{,}000$$

Point: Break-even is a special case of the formulas in Exhibits 18.22 and 18.23; simply set target income to $0 and the formulas reduce to those in Exhibits 18.11 and 18.12.

Alternatively, we can compute *unit sales* instead of dollar sales. To do this, we substitute *contribution margin per unit* for the contribution margin ratio in the denominator. This gives the number of units to sell to reach the target income. Exhibit 18.23 illustrates this for Rydell. The two computations in Exhibits 18.22 and 18.23 are equivalent because sales of 1,200 units at $100 per unit equal $120,000 of sales.

EXHIBIT 18.23

Computing Sales (Units) for a Target Income

$$\text{Unit sales at target income} = \frac{\text{Fixed costs} + \text{Target income}}{\text{Contribution margin per unit}}$$

$$= \frac{\$24{,}000 + \$12{,}000}{\$30} = 1{,}200 \text{ units}$$

We can also use the contribution margin income statement approach to compute sales for a target income, in two steps.

Step 1: Insert the fixed costs ($24,000) and the target profit level ($12,000) into a contribution margin income statement, as shown in Exhibit 18.24. To cover its fixed costs of $24,000 and yield target income of $12,000, Rydell must generate a contribution margin of $36,000 (computed as $24,000 plus $12,000).

Step 2: Enter $36,000 in the contribution margin row as step 2. With a contribution margin ratio of 30%, sales must be $120,000, computed as $36,000/0.30, to yield a contribution margin of $36,000. We enter $120,000 in the sales row of the contribution margin income statement and solve for variable costs of $84,000 (computed as $120,000 − $36,000). At a selling price of $100 per unit, Rydell must sell 1,200 units ($120,000/$100) to earn a target income of $12,000.

EXHIBIT 18.24

Using the Contribution Margin Income Statement to Find Target Sales

RYDELL COMPANY
Contribution Margin Income Statement
For Month Ended January 31, 2015

	Step 1	Step 2
Sales	?	$120,000
Variable costs	?	84,000
Contribution margin	?	36,000
Fixed costs	24,000	24,000
Target income	$12,000	$ 12,000

$24,000 + $12,000 → Contribution margin (36,000); $36,000/0.30 → Sales ($120,000)

NEED-TO-KNOW 18-4

Contribution Margin and Target Income

A1 C2

A manufacturer predicts fixed costs of $502,000 for the next year. Its one product sells for $180 per unit, and it incurs variable costs of $126 per unit. Its target (pretax) income is $200,000.

1. Compute the contribution margin ratio.
2. Compute the dollar sales needed to yield the target income.
3. Compute the unit sales needed to yield the target income.

Solution

1. Contribution margin ratio = [$180 − $126]/$180 = 30%
2. Dollar sales at target income = [$502,000 + $200,000]/0.30 = $2,340,000
3. Unit sales at target income = [$502,000 + $200,000]/[$180 − $126] = 13,000 units

Do More: QS 18-9, QS 18-13, E 18-12, E 18-17

Using Sensitivity Analysis

Earlier we showed how changing one of the estimates in a CVP analysis impacts break-even. We can also examine strategies that impact several estimates in the CVP analysis. For instance, we might want to know what happens to income if we automate a currently manual process. We can use *sensitivity analysis* to predict income if we can describe how these changes affect a company's fixed costs, variable costs, selling price, and volume. CVP analyses based on different estimates can be useful to management in planning business strategy. We provide examples next.

Buy a New Machine Assume Rydell is considering buying a new machine that would increase monthly fixed costs from $24,000 to $30,000 and would decrease variable costs by $10 per unit (from $70 per unit to $60 per unit). Recall from Exhibit 18.12 that Rydell's break-even point in dollars is currently $80,000. Management needs to know how the new machine would affect Rydell's break-even point in dollars. If Rydell maintains its selling price of $100 per unit, its contribution margin per unit will increase to $40—computed as the sales price of $100 per unit minus the (new) variable costs of $60 per unit. With this new machine, the revised contribution margin ratio per unit is 40% (computed as $40/$100). Rydell's revised break-even point in dollars would be $75,000, as computed in Exhibit 18.25. The new machine would lower Rydell's break-even point by $5,000, or 50 units, per month. The revised margin of safety increases to 25%, computed as ($100,000 − $75,000)/$100,000.

EXHIBIT 18.25

Revised Break-Even

$$\textbf{Revised break-even point in dollars} = \frac{\textbf{Revised fixed costs}}{\textbf{Revised contribution margin ratio}} = \frac{\$30{,}000}{40\%} = \$75{,}000$$

Increase Advertising Instead of buying a new machine, Rydell's advertising manager suggests increasing advertising instead. She believes that an increase of $3,000 in the monthly advertising budget will increase sales by $25,000 per month (at a selling price of $100 per unit). The contribution margin will continue to be $30 per unit. Recall from Exhibit 18.14 that the company's margin of safety was 20% when Rydell's expected sales level was $100,000. Management wants to know how a new advertising campaign would affect Rydell's break-even point and margin of safety. With the advertising campaign, Rydell's revised break-even point in dollars is $90,000, as computed in Exhibit 18.26.

EXHIBIT 18.26

Revised Break-Even (in dollars)

$$\textbf{Revised break-even point in dollars} = \frac{\textbf{Revised fixed costs}}{\textbf{Revised contribution margin ratio}} = \frac{\$27{,}000}{30\%} = \$90{,}000$$

The revised margin of safety is then computed as shown in Exhibit 18.27. Without considering other factors, the advertising campaign would increase Rydell's margin of safety from 20% (see Exhibit 18.14) to 28%.

QC4

EXHIBIT 18.27

Revised Margin of Safety (in percent)

$$\textbf{Revised margin of safety (in percent)} = \frac{\textbf{Expected sales} - \textbf{Break-even sales}}{\textbf{Expected sales}}$$

$$= \frac{\$125{,}000 - \$90{,}000}{\$125{,}000} = 28\%$$

Computing a Multiproduct Break-Even Point

P4 Compute the break-even point for a multiproduct company.

So far we have looked only at cases where the company sells a single product or service. However, many companies sell multiple products or services, and we can modify the CVP analysis for use in these cases. An important assumption in a multiproduct setting is that the sales mix of different products is known and remains constant during the planning period. **Sales mix** is the ratio (proportion) of the sales volumes for the various products. For instance, if a company normally sells 10,000 footballs, 5,000 softballs, and 4,000 basketballs per month, its sales mix can be expressed as 10:5:4 for footballs, softballs, and basketballs.

In multiproduct CVP analysis, we estimate the break-even point by using a **composite unit,** which summarizes the sales mix and contribution margins of each product. Multiproduct CVP analysis treats this composite unit as a single product. To illustrate, let's look at Hair-Today, a styling salon that offers three cuts: basic, ultra, and budget in the ratio of 4 basic units to 2 ultra units to 1 budget unit (expressed as 4:2:1). Management wants to estimate its break-even point for next year. Unit selling prices for these three cuts are basic, \$20; ultra, \$32; and budget, \$16. Using the 4:2:1 sales mix, the selling price of a composite unit of the three products is computed as follows.

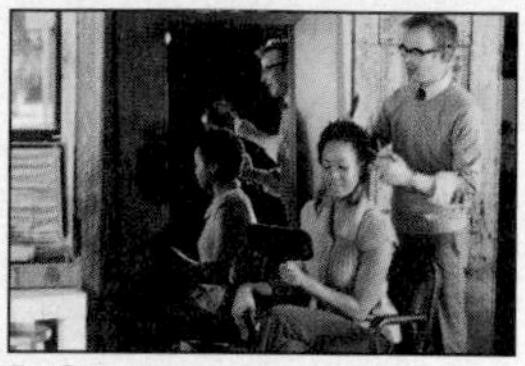
E+/Getty Images

Selling price per composite unit	
4 units of basic @ \$20 per unit	\$ 80
2 units of ultra @ \$32 per unit	64
1 unit of budget @ \$16 per unit	16
Selling price of a composite unit	**\$160**

Hair-Today's fixed costs are \$192,000 per year, and its unit variable costs of the three products are basic, \$13; ultra, \$18; and budget, \$8. Variable costs for a composite unit of these products follow.

Variable costs per composite unit	
4 units of basic @ \$13 per unit	\$52
2 units of ultra @ \$18 per unit	36
1 unit of budget @ \$8 per unit	8
Variable costs of a composite unit	**\$96**

We calculate the contribution margin for a *composite unit* using essentially the same formula used earlier (see Exhibit 18.9), as shown in Exhibit 18.28:

EXHIBIT 18.28

Contribution Margin per Composite Unit

$$\text{Contribution margin per composite unit} = \text{Selling price per composite unit} - \text{Variable cost per composite unit}$$

$$\$64 = \$160 - \$96$$

We then use the contribution margin per composite unit to determine Hair-Today's break-even point in composite units in Exhibit 18.29.

EXHIBIT 18.29

Break-Even Point in Composite Units

$$\text{Break-even point in composite units} = \frac{\text{Fixed costs}}{\text{Contribution margin per composite unit}}$$

$$= \frac{\$192{,}000}{\$64} = 3{,}000 \text{ composite units}$$

This computation implies that Hair-Today breaks even when it sells 3,000 composite units. To determine how many units of each product it must sell to break even, we use the expected sales mix of 4:2:1 and multiply the number of units of each product in the composite by 3,000 as follows.

Point: The break-even point in dollars for Exhibit 18.29 is $192,000/($64/$160) = $480,000.

Basic:	4 × 3,000	12,000 units
Ultra:	2 × 3,000	6,000 units
Budget:	1 × 3,000	3,000 units
		21,000 units

Point: Each composite unit represents 7 haircuts. Total haircuts at the break-even point equal 21,000 (3,000 composite units × 7 haircuts per composite unit).

Exhibit 18.30 verifies the results for composite units by showing Hair-Today's sales and costs at this break-even point using a forecasted contribution margin income statement.

EXHIBIT 18.30

Multiproduct Break-Even Income Statement

HAIR-TODAY
Forecasted Contribution Margin Income Statement (at Break-Even)

	Basic	Ultra	Budget	Total
Sales				
Basic (12,000 @ $20)	$240,000			
Ultra (6,000 @ $32)		$192,000		
Budget (3,000 @ $16)			$48,000	
Total sales				$480,000
Variable costs				
Basic (12,000 @ $13)	156,000			
Ultra (6,000 @ $18)		108,000		
Budget (3,000 @ $8)			24,000	
Total variable costs				288,000
Contribution margin	$ 84,000	$ 84,000	$24,000	192,000
Fixed costs				192,000
Net income				$ 0

A CVP analysis using composite units can be used to answer a variety of planning questions. Once a product mix is set, all answers are based on the assumption that the mix remains constant at all relevant sales levels as other factors in the analysis do. If the sales mix changes, it is likely that the break-even point will change also. For example, if Hair-Today sells more ultra cuts and fewer basic cuts, its break-even point will decrease. We can vary the sales mix to see what happens under alternative strategies.

Point: Enterprise resource planning (ERP) systems can quickly generate multiproduct break-even analyses.

Decision Maker

Entrepreneur A CVP analysis indicates that your start-up, which markets electronic products, will break even with the current sales mix and price levels. You have a target income in mind. What analysis might you perform to assess the likelihood of achieving this income? ■ [Answers follow the chapter's Summary.]

NEED-TO-KNOW 18-5

Contribution Margin and Break-Even Point, Composite Units

P4

The sales mix of a company's two products, X and Y, is 2:1. Unit variable costs for both products are $2, and unit selling prices are $5 for X and $4 for Y. The company has $640,000 of fixed costs.

1. What is the contribution margin per composite unit?
2. What is the break-even point in composite units?
3. How many units of X and how many units of Y will be sold at the break-even point?

Solution

1.

Selling price of a composite unit	
2 units of X @ $5 per unit	$10
1 unit of Y @ $4 per unit	4
Selling price of a composite unit	$14

Variable costs of a composite unit	
2 units of X @ $2 per unit	$4
1 unit of Y @ $2 per unit	2
Variable costs of a composite unit	$6

Do More: QS 18-14, E 18-21, E 18-23

QC5

Therefore, the contribution margin per composite unit is $8.

2. The break-even point in composite units = $640,000/$8 = 80,000 units.

3. At break-even, the company will sell 160,000 units (80,000 × 2) of X and 80,000 units of Y (80,000 × 1).

Making Assumptions in Cost-Volume-Profit Analysis

CVP analysis assumes that costs can be classified as variable or fixed. CVP analysis also assumes that selling prices per unit, variable costs per unit, and total fixed costs are all held constant. Further, multiproduct CVP analysis assumes a constant sales mix. If the expected costs and sales behavior differ from the assumptions, the results of CVP analysis can be limited. While the behavior of individual costs and sales may not be perfectly consistent with CVP assumptions, we can still perform useful analyses in spite of these assumptions' limitations, for reasons we describe next.

Summing Costs Offsets Individual Deviations Deviations from assumptions with individual costs are often minor when these costs are summed. That is, individual variable cost items may not be perfectly variable, but when we sum these variable costs, their individual deviations can offset each other. This means the assumption of variable cost behavior can be proper for total variable costs. Similarly, an assumption that total fixed costs are constant can be proper even when individual fixed cost items are not exactly constant.

CVP Applies to a Relevant Range of Operations Sales, variable costs, and fixed costs often are reasonably reflected in straight lines on a graph when the assumptions are applied over a relevant range. The validity of assuming that a specific cost is fixed or variable is more acceptable when operations are within the relevant range. As shown in Exhibit 18.2, a curvilinear cost can be treated as variable and linear if the relevant range covers volumes where it has a nearly constant slope. If the normal range of activity changes, some costs might need reclassification.

CVP Analysis Yields Estimates CVP analysis yields approximate answers to questions about costs, volumes, and profits. These answers do not have to be precise because the analysis makes rough estimates about the future. As long as managers understand that CVP analysis gives estimates, it can be a useful tool for starting the planning process. Other qualitative factors also must be considered.

GLOBAL VIEW

Survey evidence shows that many German companies have elaborate and detailed cost accounting systems. Over 90 percent of companies surveyed report their systems focus on *contribution margin.* This focus helps German companies like **Volkswagen** control costs and plan their production levels. Recently, Volkswagen announced it expects its Spanish brand *SEAT* to break even within five years. For 2012, the *SEAT* brand lost €156 million on revenue of €6.485 billion.

Sustainability and Accounting **Volkswagen** (VW) is regarded as the most sustainable automotive group in the Dow Jones Sustainability Index—in part because of its efforts to embrace opportunities and manage risks deriving from economic, environmental, and social developments. The company recently entered a long-term contract to buy wind-generated power for several of its Mexican manufacturing facilities. VW expects the use of wind power not only to reduce its carbon emissions but also to save $3.5 million per year in electric utility costs. Smaller companies can also make a difference. **Fast Yeti Custom Tees**, this chapter's feature company, buys its T-shirts from suppliers with good environmental practices. All of the company's shirts are made from 100% cotton, a natural and renewable fiber.

Degree of Operating Leverage — Decision Analysis

A2 Analyze changes in sales using the degree of operating leverage.

CVP analysis is especially useful when management begins the planning process and wishes to predict outcomes of alternative strategies. These strategies can involve changes in selling prices, fixed costs, variable costs, sales volume, and product mix. Managers are interested in seeing the effects of changes in some or all of these factors.

One goal of all managers is to get maximum benefits from their fixed costs. Managers would like to use 100% of their output capacity so that fixed costs are spread over the largest number of units. This would decrease fixed cost per unit and increase income. The extent, or relative size, of fixed costs in the total cost structure is known as **operating leverage.** Companies having a higher proportion of fixed costs in their total cost structure are said to have higher operating leverage. An example of this is a company that chooses to automate its processes instead of using direct labor, increasing its fixed costs and lowering its variable costs.

A useful managerial measure to help assess the effect of changes in the level of sales on income is the **degree of operating leverage (DOL),** calculated as shown in Exhibit 18.31.

EXHIBIT 18.31 Degree of Operating Leverage

DOL = Total contribution margin (in dollars)/Pretax income

To illustrate, let's return to Rydell Company and assume it sells 1,200 footballs. At this sales level, its contribution margin (in dollars) and pretax income are computed as:

Sales (1,200 × $100)	$120,000
Variable costs (1,200 × $70)	84,000
Contribution margin	**36,000**
Fixed costs	24,000
Income (pretax)	**$ 12,000**

Rydell's degree of operating leverage (DOL) is then computed as shown in Exhibit 18.32.

EXHIBIT 18.32 Rydell's Degree of Operating Leverage

DOL = Total contribution margin (in dollars)/Pretax income
DOL = $36,000/$12,000 = 3.0

We then can use DOL to measure the effect of changes in the level of sales on pretax income. For example, if Rydell expects sales can either increase or decrease by 10%, and these changes would be within Rydell's relevant range, we can compute the change in pretax income using DOL as shown in Exhibit 18.33.

EXHIBIT 18.33 Impact of Change in Sales on Income

Change in income (%) = DOL × Change in sales (%)
= 3.0 × 10%
= 30%

Thus, if Rydell's sales *increase* by 10%, its income will increase by $3,600 (computed as $12,000 × 30%), to $15,600. If, instead, Rydell's sales decrease by 10%, its net income will decrease by $3,600, to $8,400. We can prove these results with contribution margin income statements, as shown below.

	Current	Sales Increase by 10%	Sales Decrease by 10%
Sales	$120,000	$132,000	$108,000
Variable costs	84,000	92,400	75,600
Contribution margin	$ 36,000	$ 39,600	$ 32,400
Fixed costs	24,000	24,000	24,000
Target (pretax) income	$ 12,000	$ 15,600	$ 8,400

NEED-TO-KNOW

COMPREHENSIVE

Sport Caps Co. manufactures and sells caps for different sporting events. The fixed costs of operating the company are $150,000 per month, and the variable costs are $5 per cap. The caps are sold for $8 per unit. The fixed costs provide a production capacity of up to 100,000 caps per month.

Required

1. Use the formulas in the chapter to compute the following:
   a. Contribution margin per cap.
   b. Break-even point in terms of the number of caps produced and sold.
   c. Amount of income at 30,000 caps sold per month (ignore taxes).
   d. Amount of income at 85,000 caps sold per month (ignore taxes).
   e. Number of caps to be produced and sold to provide $60,000 of income (pretax).
2. Draw a CVP chart for the company, showing cap output on the horizontal axis. Identify (*a*) the break-even point and (*b*) the amount of pretax income when the level of cap production is 70,000. (Omit the fixed cost line.)
3. Use the formulas in the chapter to compute the
   a. Contribution margin ratio.
   b. Break-even point in terms of sales dollars.
   c. Amount of income at $250,000 of sales per month (ignore taxes).
   d. Amount of income at $600,000 of sales per month (ignore taxes).
   e. Dollars of sales needed to provide $60,000 of pretax income.

PLANNING THE SOLUTION

- Identify the formulas in the chapter for the required items expressed in units and solve them using the data given in the problem.
- Draw a CVP chart that reflects the facts in the problem. The horizontal axis should plot the volume in units up to 100,000, and the vertical axis should plot the total dollars up to $800,000. Plot the total cost line as upward sloping, starting at the fixed cost level ($150,000) on the vertical axis and increasing until it reaches $650,000 at the maximum volume of 100,000 units. Verify that the break-even point (where the two lines cross) equals the amount you computed in part 1.
- Identify the formulas in the chapter for the required items expressed in dollars and solve them using the data given in the problem.

SOLUTION

1. a. Contribution margin per cap = Selling price per unit − Variable cost per unit
= $8 − $5 = $3

b. Break-even point in caps $= \dfrac{\text{Fixed costs}}{\text{Contribution margin per cap}} = \dfrac{\$150{,}000}{\$3} = \underline{\underline{50{,}000 \text{ caps}}}$

c. Income at 30,000 caps sold = (Units × Contribution margin per unit) − Fixed costs
= (30,000 × $3) − $150,000 = $(60,000) loss

d. Income at 85,000 caps sold = (Units × Contribution margin per unit) − Fixed costs
= (85,000 × $3) − $150,000 = $105,000 profit

e. Units needed for $60,000 income $= \dfrac{\text{Fixed costs + Target income}}{\text{Contribution margin per cap}}$

$= \dfrac{\$150{,}000 + \$60{,}000}{\$3} = 70{,}000 \text{ caps}$

2. CVP chart.

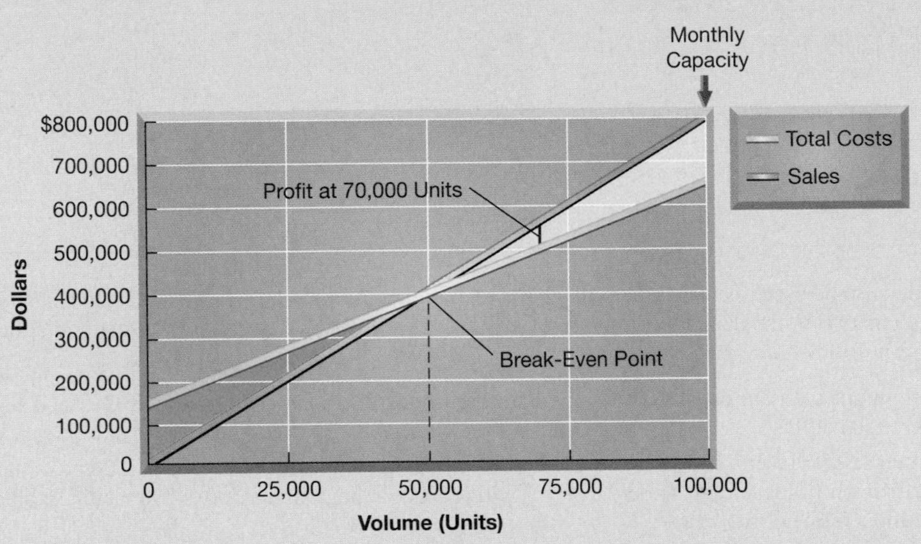

3. a. Contribution margin ratio $= \dfrac{\text{Contribution margin per unit}}{\text{Selling price per unit}} = \dfrac{\$3}{\$8} = 0.375, \text{ or } 37.5\%$

b. Break-even point in dollars $= \dfrac{\text{Fixed costs}}{\text{Contribution margin ratio}} = \dfrac{\$150{,}000}{37.5\%} = \$400{,}000$

c. Income at sales of $250,000 = (Sales × Contribution margin ratio) − Fixed costs
= ($250,000 × 37.5%) − $150,000 = $(56,250) loss

d. Income at sales of $600,000 = (Sales × Contribution margin ratio) − Fixed costs
= ($600,000 × 37.5%) − $150,000 = $75,000 income

e. Dollars of sales to yield $60,000 pretax income $= \dfrac{\text{Fixed costs + Target pretax income}}{\text{Contribution margin ratio}}$

$= \dfrac{\$150{,}000 + \$60{,}000}{37.5\%} = \$560{,}000$

APPENDIX

Using Excel to Estimate Least-Squares Regression 18A

Microsoft Excel® and other spreadsheet software can be used to perform least-squares regressions to identify cost behavior. In Excel, the INTERCEPT and SLOPE functions are used. The following screen shot reports the data from Exhibit 18.3 in cells Al through C13 and shows the cell contents to find the intercept (cell B15) and slope (cell B16). Cell B15 uses Excel to find the intercept from a least-squares regression of total cost (shown as C2:C13 in cell B15) on units produced (shown as B2:B13 in cell B15). Spreadsheet software is useful in understanding cost behavior when many data points (such as monthly total costs and units produced) are available.

	A	B	C
1	Month	Units Produced	Total Cost
2	January	27,500	$21,500
3	February	17,500	20,500
4	March	25,000	25,000
5	April	35,000	21,500
6	May	47,500	25,500
7	June	22,500	18,500
8	July	30,000	23,500
9	August	52,500	28,500
10	September	37,500	26,000
11	October	67,500	29,000
12	November	62,500	31,000
13	December	57,500	26,000
14			Result
15	**Intercept**	=INTERCEPT(C2:C13, B2:B13)	$16,947.17
16	**Slope**	=SLOPE(C2:C13, B2:B13)	$ 0.1930
17			

Excel can also be used to create scatter diagrams such as that in Exhibit 18.4. In contrast to visually drawing a line that "fits" the data, Excel more precisely fits the regression line. To draw a scatter diagram with a line of fit, follow these steps:

1. Highlight the data cells you wish to diagram; in this example, start from cell C13 and highlight through cell B2.
2. Then select "Insert" and "Scatter" from the drop-down menus. Selecting the chart type in the upper left corner of the choices under "Scatter" will produce a diagram that looks like that in Exhibit 18.4, without a line of fit.
3. To add a line of fit (also called a trend line), select "Layout" and "Trendline" from the drop-down menus. Selecting "Linear Trendline" will produce a diagram that looks like that in Exhibit 18.4, including the line of fit.

APPENDIX

18B Variable Costing and Performance Reporting

This chapter showed the usefulness of *contribution margin,* or selling price minus variable costs, in CVP analysis. The contribution margin income statement introduced in this chapter is also known as a **variable costing income statement.** In **variable costing,** only costs that change in total with changes in production levels are included in product costs. These costs include direct materials, direct labor, and *variable* overhead costs. Thus, under variable costing, *fixed* overhead costs are excluded from product costs. As we showed in this chapter, a variable costing approach can be useful in many managerial analyses and decisions.

The variable costing method is not allowed, however, for external financial reporting. Instead, GAAP requires **absorption costing.** Under absorption costing, product costs include direct materials, direct labor, *and all overhead,* both variable and fixed. Managers can use variable costing information for internal decision making, but they must use absorption costing for external reporting purposes.

Exhibit 18B.1 shows product cost per unit computations for both absorption and variable costing.

EXHIBIT 18B.1

Unit Cost Computation

	Absorption Costing	Variable Costing
Direct materials cost per unit	$ 4	$ 4
Direct labor cost per unit	8	8
Overhead cost		
Variable overhead cost per unit	3	3
Fixed overhead cost per unit	10	—
Total product cost per unit	$25	$15

Summary

C1 Describe different types of cost behavior in relation to production and sales volume. Cost behavior is described in terms of how its amount changes in relation to changes in volume of activity within a relevant range. Fixed costs remain constant to changes in volume. Total variable costs change in direct proportion to volume changes. Mixed costs display the effects of both fixed and variable components. Step-wise costs remain constant over a small volume range, then change by a lump sum and remain constant over another volume range, and so on. Curvilinear costs change in a nonlinear relation to volume changes.

C2 Describe several applications of cost-volume-profit analysis. Cost-volume-profit analysis can be used to predict what can happen under alternative strategies concerning sales volume, selling prices, variable costs, or fixed costs. Applications include "what-if" analysis, computing sales for a target income, and break-even analysis.

A1 Compute the contribution margin and describe what it reveals about a company's cost structure. Contribution margin per unit is a product's selling price less its total variable costs. Contribution margin ratio is a product's contribution margin per unit divided by its selling price. Unit contribution margin is the amount received from each sale that contributes to fixed costs and income. The contribution margin ratio reveals what portion of each sales dollar is available as contribution to fixed costs and income.

A2 Analyze changes in sales using the degree of operating leverage. The extent, or relative size, of fixed costs in a company's total cost structure is known as *operating leverage.* One tool useful in assessing the effect of changes in sales on income is the degree of operating leverage, or DOL. DOL is the ratio of the contribution margin divided by pretax income. This ratio can be used to determine the expected percent change in income given a percent change in sales.

P1 Determine cost estimates using the scatter diagram, high-low, and regression methods of estimating costs. Three different methods used to estimate costs are the scatter diagram, the high-low method, and least-squares regression. All three methods use past data to estimate costs. Cost estimates from a scatter diagram are based on a visual fit of the cost line. Estimates from the high-low method are based only on costs corresponding to the lowest and highest sales. The least-squares regression method is a statistical technique and uses all data points.

P2 Compute the break-even point for a single product company. A company's break-even point for a period is the sales volume at which total revenues equal total costs. To compute a break-even point in terms of sales units, we divide total fixed costs by the contribution margin per unit. To compute a break-even point in terms of sales dollars, divide total fixed costs by the contribution margin ratio.

P3 Graph costs and sales for a single product company. The costs and sales for a company can be graphically illustrated using a CVP chart. In this chart, the horizontal axis represents the number of units sold and the vertical axis represents dollars of sales or costs. Straight lines are used to depict both costs and sales on the CVP chart.

P4 Compute the break-even point for a multiproduct company. CVP analysis can be applied to a multiproduct company by expressing sales volume in terms of composite units. A composite unit consists of a specific number of units of each product in proportion to their expected sales mix. Multiproduct CVP analysis treats this composite unit as a single product.

Guidance Answers to Decision Maker and Decision Ethics

Sales Manager The contribution margin per unit for the first order is $600 (60% of $1,000); the contribution margin per unit for the second order is $160 (20% of $800). You are likely tempted to accept the first order based on its high contribution margin per unit, but you must compute the total contribution margin based on the number of units sold for each order. Total contribution margin is $60,000 ($600 per unit × 100 units) and $80,000 ($160 per unit × 500 units) for the two orders, respectively. The second order provides the largest return in absolute dollars and is the order you would accept. Another factor to consider in your selection is the potential for a long-term relationship with these customers including repeat sales and growth.

Supervisor Your dilemma is whether to go along with the suggestions to "manage" the numbers to make the project look like it will achieve sufficient profits. You should not succumb to these suggestions. Many people will likely be affected negatively if you manage the predicted numbers and the project eventually is unprofitable. Moreover, if it does fail, an investigation would likely reveal that data in the proposal were "fixed" to make it look good. Probably the only benefit from managing the numbers is the short-term payoff of pleasing those who proposed the product. One way to deal with this dilemma is to prepare several analyses showing results under different assumptions and then let senior management make the decision.

Entrepreneur You must first compute the level of sales required to achieve the desired net income. Then you must conduct sensitivity analysis by varying the price, sales mix, and cost estimates. Results from the sensitivity analysis provide information you can use to assess the possibility of reaching the target sales level. For instance, you might have to pursue aggressive marketing strategies to push the high-margin products, or you might have to cut prices to increase sales and profits, or another strategy might emerge.

Key Terms

Absorption costing
Break-even point
Composite unit
Contribution margin per unit
Contribution margin ratio
Cost-volume-profit (CVP) analysis
Cost-volume-profit (CVP) chart
Curvilinear cost
Degree of operating leverage (DOL)
Estimated line of cost behavior
High-low method
Least-squares regression
Margin of safety
Mixed cost
Operating leverage
Relevant range of operations
Sales mix
Scatter diagram
Step-wise cost
Variable costing
Variable costing income statement

Multiple Choice Quiz

Answers at end of chapter

1. A company's only product sells for $150 per unit. Its variable costs per unit are $100, and its fixed costs total $75,000. What is its contribution margin per unit?
   a. $50 **b.** $250 **c.** $100 **d.** $150 **e.** $25
2. Using information from question 1, what is the company's contribution margin ratio?
   a. 66⅔% **b.** 100% **c.** 50% **d.** 0% **e.** 33⅓%
3. Using information from question 1, what is the company's break-even point in units?
   a. 500 units **b.** 750 units **c.** 1,500 units **d.** 3,000 units **e.** 1,000 units
4. A company's forecasted sales are $300,000 and its sales at break-even are $180,000. Its margin of safety in dollars is
   a. $180,000. **b.** $120,000. **c.** $480,000. **d.** $60,000. **e.** $300,000.
5. A product sells for $400 per unit and its variable costs per unit are $260. The company's fixed costs are $840,000. If the company desires $70,000 pretax income, what is the required dollar sales?
   a. $2,400,000 **b.** $200,000 **c.** $2,600,000 **d.** $2,275,000 **e.** $1,400,000

A *Superscript letter A denotes assignments based on Appendix 18A.*
Icon denotes assignments that involve decision making.

Discussion Questions

1. What is a variable cost? Identify two variable costs.
2. When output volume increases, do variable costs per unit increase, decrease, or stay the same within the relevant range of activity? Explain.
3. When output volume increases, do fixed costs per unit increase, decrease, or stay the same within the relevant range of activity? Explain.
4. How is cost-volume-profit analysis useful?
5. How do step-wise costs and curvilinear costs differ?
6. Describe the contribution margin ratio in layperson's terms.
7. Define and explain the *contribution margin ratio.*
8. Define and describe *contribution margin per unit.*
9. In performing CVP analysis for a manufacturing company, what simplifying assumption is usually made about the volume of production and the volume of sales?
10. What two arguments tend to justify classifying all costs as either fixed or variable even though individual costs might not behave exactly as classified?
11. How does assuming that operating activity occurs within a relevant range affect cost-volume-profit analysis?
12. List three methods to measure cost behavior.
13. How is a scatter diagram used to identify and measure the behavior of a company's costs?
14. In cost-volume-profit analysis, what is the estimated profit at the break-even point?
15. Assume that a straight line on a CVP chart intersects the vertical axis at the level of fixed costs and has a positive slope that rises with each additional unit of volume by the amount of the variable costs per unit. What does this line represent?
16. **Apple** has both fixed and variable costs. Why are fixed costs depicted as a horizontal line on a CVP chart? **APPLE**
17. Each of two similar companies has sales of $20,000 and total costs of $15,000 for a month. Company A's total costs include $10,000 of variable costs and $5,000 of fixed costs. If Company B's total costs include $4,000 of variable costs and $11,000 of fixed costs, which company will enjoy more profit if sales double?
18. ________ of ________ reflects expected sales in excess of the level of break-even sales.

19. **Google** produces tablet computers for sale. Identify some of the variable and fixed product costs associated with that production. [*Hint:* Limit costs to product costs.] **GOOGLE**

20. Should **Apple** use single product or multiproduct break-even analysis? Explain. **APPLE**

21. **Samsung** is thinking of expanding sales of its most popular smartphone model by 65%. Should we expect its variable and fixed costs for this model to stay within the relevant range? Explain. **Samsung**

connect

QUICK STUDY

QS 18-1
Cost behavior identification C1

Listed here are four series of separate costs measured at various volume levels. Examine each series and identify whether it is best described as a fixed, variable, step-wise, or curvilinear cost. (It can help to graph the cost series.)

Volume (Units)	Series 1	Series 2	Series 3	Series 4
0	$ 0	$450	$ 800	$100
100	800	450	800	105
200	1,600	450	800	120
300	2,400	450	1,600	145
400	3,200	450	1,600	190
500	4,000	450	2,400	250
600	4,800	450	2,400	320

QS 18-2
Cost behavior identification
C1

Determine whether each of the following is best described as a fixed, variable, or mixed cost with respect to product units.

______ **1.** Rubber used to manufacture athletic shoes.
______ **2.** Maintenance of factory machinery.
______ **3.** Packaging expense.
______ **4.** Wages of an assembly-line worker paid on the basis of acceptable units produced.
______ **5.** Factory supervisor's salary.
______ **6.** Taxes on factory building.
______ **7.** Depreciation expense of warehouse.

QS 18-3
Cost behavior estimation—high-low method
P1

The following information is available for a company's maintenance cost over the last seven months. Using the high-low method, estimate both the fixed and variable components of its maintenance cost.

Month	Maintenance Hours	Maintenance Cost
June..............	9	$5,450
July	18	6,900
August	12	5,100
September	15	6,000
October..........	21	6,900
November	24	8,100
December	6	3,600

QS 18-4
Cost behavior estimation—scatter diagram
P1

This scatter diagram reflects past maintenance hours and their corresponding maintenance costs.

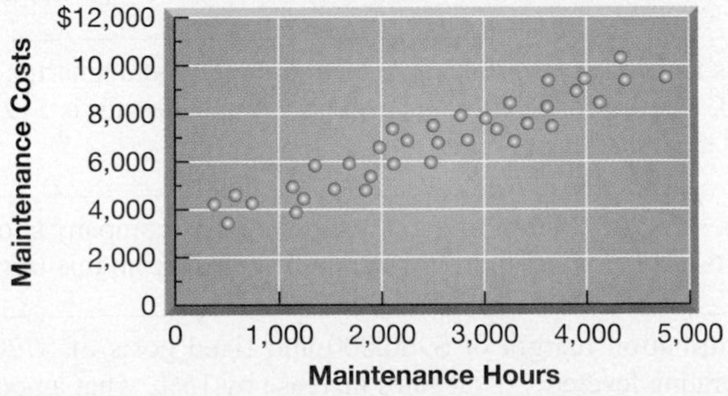

1. Draw an estimated line of cost behavior.
2. Estimate the fixed and variable components of maintenance costs.

QS 18-5
Contribution margin ratio
A1

Compute and interpret the contribution margin ratio using the following data: sales, $5,000; total variable cost, $3,000.

QS 18-6
Contribution margin per unit and break-even units P2

SBD Phone Company sells its waterproof phone case for $90 per unit. Fixed costs total $162,000, and variable costs are $36 per unit. Determine the (1) contribution margin per unit and (2) break-even point in units.

QS 18-7
Assumptions in CVP analysis C2

SBD Phone Company sells its waterproof phone case for $90 per unit. Fixed costs total $162,000, and variable costs are $36 per unit. How will the break-even point in units change in response to each of the following independent changes in selling price per unit, variable cost per unit, or total fixed costs? Use I for increase and D for decrease. (It is not necessary to compute new break-even points.)

Change	Break-Even in Units Will
1. Total fixed costs to $190,000	________
2. Variable costs to $34 per unit.........	________
3. Selling price per unit to $80	________
4. Variable costs to $67 per unit.........	________
5. Total fixed costs to $150,000	________
6. Selling price per unit to $120	________

QS 18-8
Contribution margin ratio and break-even dollars P2

SBD Phone Company sells its waterproof phone case for $90 per unit. Fixed costs total $162,000, and variable costs are $36 per unit. Determine the (1) contribution margin ratio and (2) break-even point in dollars.

QS 18-9
CVP analysis and target income P2

SBD Phone Company sells its waterproof phone case for $90 per unit. Fixed costs total $162,000, and variable costs are $36 per unit. Compute the units of product that must be sold to earn pretax income of $200,000. (Round to the nearest whole unit.)

QS 18-10
Computing break-even P2

Zhao Co. has fixed costs of $354,000. Its single product sells for $175 per unit, and variable costs are $116 per unit. Determine the break-even point in units.

QS 18-11
Margin of safety P2

Zhao Co. has fixed costs of $354,000. Its single product sells for $175 per unit, and variable costs are $116 per unit. If the company expects sales of 10,000 units, compute its margin of safety (a) in dollars and (b) as a percent of expected sales.

QS 18-12
Contribution margin income statement P2

Zhao Co. has fixed costs of $354,000. Its single product sells for $175 per unit, and variable costs are $116 per unit. The company expects sales of 10,000 units. Prepare a contribution margin income statement for the year ended December 31, 2015.

QS 18-13
Target income C2

Zhao Co. has fixed costs of $354,000. Its single product sells for $175 per unit, and variable costs are $116 per unit. Compute the level of sales in units needed to produce a target (pretax) income of $118,000.

QS 18-14
Multiproduct break-even P4

US-Mobile manufactures and sells two products, tablet computers and smartphones, in the ratio of 5:3. Fixed costs are $105,000, and the contribution margin per composite unit is $125. What number of each type of product is sold at the break-even point?

QS 18-15
CVP graph P3

Corme Company expects sales of $34 million (400,000 units). The company's total fixed costs are $17.5 million and its variable costs are $35 per unit. Prepare a CVP chart from this information.

QS 18-16
Operating leverage analysis A2

Singh Co. reports a contribution margin of $960,000 and fixed costs of $720,000. (1) Compute the company's degree of operating leverage. (2) If sales increase by 15%, what amount of income will Singh Co. report?

QS 18-17
Contribution margin
A1

A recent income statement for **Volkswagen** reports the following (in € millions). Assume 75 percent of the cost of sales and 75 percent of the selling and administrative costs are variable costs, and the remaining 25 percent of each is fixed. Compute the contribution margin (in € millions). (Round computations using percentages to the nearest whole euro.)

Sales	€126,875
Cost of sales	105,431
Selling and administrative expenses	15,500

connect

EXERCISES

Exercise 18-1
Cost behavior in graphs
C1

Following are five graphs representing various cost behaviors. (1) Identify whether the cost behavior in each graph is mixed, step-wise, fixed, variable, or curvilinear. (2) Identify the graph (by number) that best illustrates each cost behavior: (a) Factory policy requires one supervisor for every 30 factory workers; (b) real estate taxes on factory; (c) electricity charge that includes the standard monthly charge plus a charge for each kilowatt hour; (d) commissions to salespersons; and (e) costs of hourly paid workers that provide substantial gains in efficiency when a few workers are added but gradually smaller gains in efficiency when more workers are added.

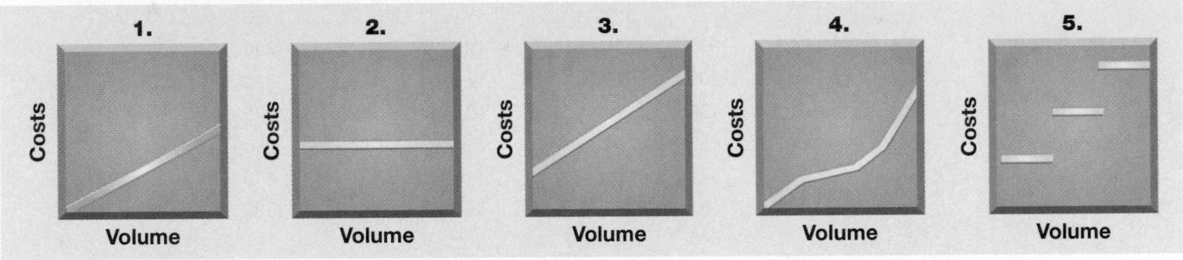

Exercise 18-2
Cost behavior defined
C1

The left column lists several cost classifications. The right column presents short definitions of those costs. In the blank space beside each of the numbers in the right column, write the letter of the cost best described by the definition.

A. Total cost
B. Mixed cost
C. Variable cost
D. Curvilinear cost
E. Step-wise cost
F. Fixed cost

_____ **1.** This cost is the combined amount of all the other costs.
_____ **2.** This cost remains constant over a limited range of volume; when it reaches the end of its limited range, it changes by a lump sum and remains at that level until it exceeds another limited range.
_____ **3.** This cost has a component that remains the same over all volume levels and another component that increases in direct proportion to increases in volume.
_____ **4.** This cost increases when volume increases, but the increase is not constant for each unit produced.
_____ **5.** This cost remains constant over all volume levels within the productive capacity for the planning period.
_____ **6.** This cost increases in direct proportion to increases in volume; its amount is constant for each unit produced.

Exercise 18-3
Cost behavior identification
C1

Following are five series of costs *A* through *E* measured at various volume levels. Examine each series and identify which is fixed, variable, mixed, step-wise, or curvilinear.

	A	B	C	D	E	F
	Volume (Units)	**Series A**	**Series B**	**Series C**	**Series D**	**Series E**
1	0	$ 0	$2,500	$ 0	$1,000	$5,000
2	400	3,600	3,100	6,000	1,000	5,000
3	800	7,200	3,700	6,600	2,000	5,000
4	1,200	10,800	4,300	7,200	2,000	5,000
5	1,600	14,400	4,900	8,200	3,000	5,000
6	2,000	18,000	5,500	9,600	3,000	5,000
7	2,400	21,600	6,100	13,500	4,000	5,000

Exercise 18-4
Measurement of cost behavior using a scatter diagram
P1

A company reports the following information about its sales and its cost of sales. Each unit of its product sells for $500. Use these data to prepare a scatter diagram. Draw an estimated line of cost behavior and determine whether the cost appears to be variable, fixed, or mixed.

Period	Sales	Cost of Sales	Period	Sales	Cost of Sales
1	$22,500	$15,150	4	$11,250	$ 8,250
2	17,250	11,250	5	13,500	9,000
3	15,750	10,500	6	18,750	14,250

Exercise 18-5
Scatter diagram and measurement of cost behavior
P1

Use the following information about sales and costs to prepare a scatter diagram. Draw a cost line that reflects the behavior displayed by this cost. Determine whether the cost is variable, step-wise, fixed, mixed, or curvilinear.

Period	Sales	Costs	Period	Sales	Costs
1	$760	$590	9	$580	$390
2	800	560	10	320	240
3	200	230	11	240	230
4	400	400	12	720	550
5	480	390	13	280	260
6	620	550	14	440	410
7	680	590	15	380	260
8	540	430			

Exercise 18-6
Cost behavior estimation—scatter diagram and high-low
P1

Felix & Co. reports the following information about its sales and cost of sales. Draw an estimated line of cost behavior using a scatter diagram, and compute fixed costs and variable costs per unit sold. Then use the high-low method to estimate the fixed and variable components of the cost of sales.

Period	Units Sold	Cost of Sales	Period	Units Sold	Cost of Sales
1	0	$2,500	6	2,000	$5,500
2	400	3,100	7	2,400	6,100
3	800	3,700	8	2,800	6,700
4	1,200	4,300	9	3,200	7,300
5	1,600	4,900	10	3,600	7,900

Exercise 18-7A
Measurement of cost behavior using regression P1

Refer to the information from Exercise 18-6. Use spreadsheet software to use ordinary least-squares regression to estimate the cost equation, including fixed and variable cost amounts.

Exercise 18-8
Contribution margin
A1

A jeans maker is designing a new line of jeans called Slims. The jeans will sell for $205 per pair and cost $164 per pair in variable costs to make.

1. Compute the contribution margin per pair.
2. Compute the contribution margin ratio.
3. Describe what the contribution margin ratio reveals about this new jeans line.

Exercise 18-9
Contribution margin and break-even P2

Blanchard Company manufactures a single product that sells for $180 per unit and whose total variable costs are $135 per unit. The company's annual fixed costs are $562,500. Use this information to compute the company's (a) contribution margin, (b) contribution margin ratio, (c) break-even point in units, and (d) break-even point in dollars of sales.

Exercise 18-10
CVP chart P3

Blanchard Company manufactures a single product that sells for $180 per unit and whose total variable costs are $135 per unit. The company's annual fixed costs are $562,500. Prepare a CVP chart for the company.

Exercise 18-11
Income reporting and break-even analysis C2

Blanchard Company manufactures a single product that sells for $180 per unit and whose total variable costs are $135 per unit. The company's annual fixed costs are $562,500.

1. Prepare a contribution margin income statement for Blanchard Company showing sales, variable costs, and fixed costs at the break-even point.
2. If the company's fixed costs increase by $135,000, what amount of sales (in dollars) is needed to break even? Explain.

Exercise 18-12
Computing sales to achieve target income C2

Blanchard Company manufactures a single product that sells for $180 per unit and whose total variable costs are $135 per unit. The company's annual fixed costs are $562,500. Management targets an annual pretax income of $1,012,500. Assume that fixed costs remain at $562,500. Compute the (1) unit sales to earn the target income and (2) dollar sales to earn the target income.

Exercise 18-13
Forecasted income statement C2

Blanchard Company manufactures a single product that sells for $180 per unit and whose total variable costs are $135 per unit. The company's annual fixed costs are $562,500. The sales manager predicts that annual sales of the company's product will soon reach 40,000 units and its price will increase to $200 per unit. According to the production manager, the variable costs are expected to increase to $140 per unit but fixed costs will remain at $562,500. The income tax rate is 20%. What amounts of pretax and after-tax income can the company expect to earn from these predicted changes? (*Hint:* Prepare a forecasted contribution margin income statement as in Exhibit 18.21.)

Check Forecasted after-tax income, $1,470,000

Exercise 18-14
Predicting sales and variable costs using contribution margin C2

Bloom Company management predicts that it will incur fixed costs of $160,000 and earn pretax income of $164,000 in the next period. Its expected contribution margin ratio is 25%. Use this information to compute the amounts of (1) total dollar sales and (2) total variable costs.

Exercise 18-15
Computation of variable and fixed costs C2

Cooper Company expects to sell 200,000 units of its product next year, which would generate total sales of $17 million. Management predicts that pretax net income for next year will be $1,250,000 and that the contribution margin per unit will be $25. Use this information to compute next year's total expected (a) variable costs and (b) fixed costs.

Exercise 18-16
Break-even P2

Hudson Co. reports the contribution margin income statement for 2015 below. Using this information, compute Hudson Co.'s (1) break-even point in units and (2) break-even point in sales dollars.

HUDSON CO.
Contribution Margin Income Statement
For Year Ended December 31, 2015

Sales (9,600 units at $225 each)	$2,160,000
Variable costs (9,600 units at $180 each)	1,728,000
Contribution margin	$ 432,000
Fixed costs	324,000
Pretax income	$ 108,000

Exercise 18-17
Target income and margin of safety (in dollars) C2

Refer to the information in Exercise 18-16.

1. Assume Hudson Co. has a target pretax income of $162,000 for 2016. What amount of sales (in dollars) is needed to produce this target income?
2. If Hudson achieves its target pretax income for 2016, what is its margin of safety (in percent)? (Round to one decimal place.)

Exercise 18-18
Sensitivity analysis C2

Refer to the information in Exercise 18-16. Assume the company is considering investing in a new machine that will increase its fixed costs by $40,500 per year and decrease its variable costs by $9 per unit. Prepare a forecasted contribution margin income statement for 2016 assuming the company purchases this machine.

Exercise 18-19
Sensitivity analysis C2

Refer to the information in Exercise 18-16. If the company raises its selling price to $240 per unit, compute its (1) contribution margin per unit, (2) contribution margin ratio, (3) break-even point in units, and (4) break-even point in sales dollars.

Exercise 18-20
Sensitivity analysis C2

Refer to the information in Exercise 18-16. The marketing manager believes that increasing advertising costs by $81,000 in 2016 will increase the company's sales volume to 11,000 units. Prepare a forecasted contribution margin income statement for 2016 assuming the company incurs the additional advertising costs.

Exercise 18-21
Predicting unit and dollar sales C2

Nombre Company management predicts $390,000 of variable costs, $430,000 of fixed costs, and a pretax income of $155,000 in the next period. Management also predicts that the contribution margin per unit will be $9. Use this information to compute the (1) total expected dollar sales for next period and (2) number of units expected to be sold next period.

Exercise 18-22
CVP analysis using composite units P4

Check (3) 1,000 composite units

Handy Home sells windows and doors in the ratio of 8:2 (windows:doors). The selling price of each window is $200 and of each door is $500. The variable cost of a window is $125 and of a door is $350. Fixed costs are $900,000. Use this information to determine the (1) selling price per composite unit, (2) variable costs per composite unit, (3) break-even point in composite units, and (4) number of units of each product that will be sold at the break-even point.

Exercise 18-23
CVP analysis using composite units P4

R&R Tax Service offers tax and consulting services to individuals and small businesses. Data for fees and costs of three types of tax returns follow. R&R provides services in the ratio of 5:3:2 (easy, moderate, business). Fixed costs total $18,000 for the tax season. Use this information to determine the (1) selling price per composite unit, (2) variable costs per composite unit, (3) break-even point in composite units, and (4) number of units of each product that will be sold at the break-even point.

Type of Return	Fee Charged	Variable Cost per Return
Easy (Form 1040EZ)	$ 50	$ 30
Moderate (Form 1040)	125	75
Business	275	100

Exercise 18-24
Operating leverage computed and applied A2

Company A is a manufacturer with current sales of $6,000,000 and a 60% contribution margin. Its fixed costs equal $2,600,000. Company B is a consulting firm with current service revenues of $4,500,000 and a 25% contribution margin. Its fixed costs equal $375,000. Compute the degree of operating leverage (DOL) for each company. Identify which company benefits more from a 20% increase in sales and explain why.

Exercise 18-25
Degree of operating leverage A2

Refer to the information in Exercise 18-16.

1. Compute the company's degree of operating leverage for 2015.
2. If sales decrease by 5% in 2016, what will be the company's pretax income?
3. Assume sales for 2016 decrease by 5%. Prepare a contribution margin income statement for 2016.

connect

PROBLEM SET A

Problem 18-1A
Contribution margin income statement and contribution margin ratio
A1

The following costs result from the production and sale of 1,000 drum sets manufactured by Tight Drums Company for the year ended December 31, 2015. The drum sets sell for $500 each. The company has a 25% income tax rate.

Variable production costs	
Plastic for casing	$ 17,000
Wages of assembly workers	82,000
Drum stands	26,000
Variable selling costs	
Sales commissions	15,000
Fixed manufacturing costs	
Taxes on factory	5,000
Factory maintenance	10,000
Factory machinery depreciation	40,000
Fixed selling and administrative costs	
Lease of equipment for sales staff	10,000
Accounting staff salaries	35,000
Administrative management salaries	125,000

Required

1. Prepare a contribution margin income statement for the company.
2. Compute its contribution margin per unit and its contribution margin ratio.

Check (1) Net income, $101,250

Analysis Component

3. Interpret the contribution margin and contribution margin ratio from part 2.

Problem 18-2A
Scatter diagram and cost behavior estimation
P1

Alden Co.'s monthly sales and cost data for its operating activities of the past year follow. Management wants to use these data to predict future fixed and variable costs.

Month	Sales	Total Cost	Month	Sales	Total Cost
1	$320,000	$160,000	7	$340,000	$220,000
2	160,000	100,000	8	280,000	160,000
3	280,000	220,000	9	80,000	64,000
4	200,000	100,000	10	160,000	140,000
5	300,000	230,000	11	100,000	100,000
6	200,000	120,000	12	110,000	80,000

Required

1. Prepare a scatter diagram for these data with sales volume (in $) plotted on the horizontal axis and total cost plotted on the vertical axis.
2. Estimate both the variable costs per sales dollar and the total monthly fixed costs using the high-low method. Draw the total costs line on the scatter diagram in part 1.
3. Use the estimated line of cost behavior and results from part 2 to predict future total costs when sales volume is (a) $200,000 and (b) $300,000.

Check (2) Variable costs, $0.60 per sales dollar; fixed costs, $16,000

Problem 18-3A
CVP analysis and charting P2 P3

Praveen Co. manufactures and markets a number of rope products. Management is considering the future of Product XT, a special rope for hang gliding, that has not been as profitable as planned. Since Product XT is manufactured and marketed independently of the other products, its total costs can be precisely measured. Next year's plans call for a $200 selling price per 100 yards of XT rope. Its fixed costs for the year are expected to be $270,000, up to a maximum capacity of 700,000 yards of rope. Forecasted variable costs are $140 per 100 yards of XT rope.

Required

Check (1*a*) Break-even sales, 4,500 units

1. Estimate Product XT's break-even point in terms of (a) sales units and (b) sales dollars.
2. Prepare a CVP chart for Product XT like that in Exhibit 18.15. Use 7,000 units (700,000 yards/100 yards) as the maximum number of sales units on the horizontal axis of the graph, and $1,400,000 as the maximum dollar amount on the vertical axis.
3. Prepare a contribution margin income statement showing sales, variable costs, and fixed costs for Product XT at the break-even point.

Problem 18-4A
Break-even analysis; income targeting and forecasting
C2 P2 A1

Astro Co. sold 20,000 units of its only product and incurred a $50,000 loss (ignoring taxes) for the current year as shown here. During a planning session for year 2016's activities, the production manager notes that variable costs can be reduced 50% by installing a machine that automates several operations. To obtain these savings, the company must increase its annual fixed costs by $200,000. The maximum output capacity of the company is 40,000 units per year.

ASTRO COMPANY Contribution Margin Income Statement For Year Ended December 31, 2015	
Sales	$1,000,000
Variable costs	800,000
Contribution margin	200,000
Fixed costs	250,000
Net loss	$ (50,000)

Required

1. Compute the break-even point in dollar sales for year 2015.
2. Compute the predicted break-even point in dollar sales for year 2016 assuming the machine is installed and there is no change in the unit selling price.
3. Prepare a forecasted contribution margin income statement for 2016 that shows the expected results with the machine installed. Assume that the unit selling price and the number of units sold will not change, and no income taxes will be due.
4. Compute the sales level required in both dollars and units to earn $200,000 of target pretax income in 2016 with the machine installed and no change in unit sales price. Round answers to whole dollars and whole units.
5. Prepare a forecasted contribution margin income statement that shows the results at the sales level computed in part 4. Assume no income taxes will be due.

Check (3) Net income, $150,000

(4) Required sales, $1,083,333 or 21,667 units (both rounded)

Problem 18-5A
Break-even analysis, different cost structures, and income calculations
C2 A1 P4

Henna Co. produces and sells two products, T and O. It manufactures these products in separate factories and markets them through different channels. They have no shared costs. This year, the company sold 50,000 units of each product. Sales and costs for each product follow.

	Product T	Product O
Sales	$2,000,000	$2,000,000
Variable costs	1,600,000	250,000
Contribution margin	400,000	1,750,000
Fixed costs	125,000	1,475,000
Income before taxes	275,000	275,000
Income taxes (32% rate)	88,000	88,000
Net income	$ 187,000	$ 187,000

Required

1. Compute the break-even point in dollar sales for each product. (Round the answer to whole dollars.)
2. Assume that the company expects sales of each product to decline to 30,000 units next year with no change in unit selling price. Prepare forecasted financial results for next year following the format of the contribution margin income statement as just shown with columns for each of the two products (assume a 32% tax rate). Also, assume that any loss before taxes yields a 32% tax benefit.
3. Assume that the company expects sales of each product to increase to 60,000 units next year with no change in unit selling price. Prepare forecasted financial results for next year following the format of the contribution margin income statement shown with columns for each of the two products (assume a 32% tax rate).

Check (2) After-tax income: T, $78,200; O, $(289,000)

(3) After-tax income: T, $241,400; O, $425,000

Analysis Component

4. If sales greatly decrease, which product would experience a greater loss? Explain.
5. Describe some factors that might have created the different cost structures for these two products.

Problem 18-6A
Analysis of price, cost, and volume changes for contribution margin and net income
P2 A1

This year Burchard Company sold 40,000 units of its only product for $25 per unit. Manufacturing and selling the product required $200,000 of fixed manufacturing costs and $325,000 of fixed selling and administrative costs. Its per unit variable costs follow.

Material	$8.00
Direct labor (paid on the basis of completed units)	5.00
Variable overhead costs	1.00
Variable selling and administrative costs	0.50

Next year the company will use new material, which will reduce material costs by 50% and direct labor costs by 60% and will not affect product quality or marketability. Management is considering an increase in the unit selling price to reduce the number of units sold because the factory's output is nearing its annual output capacity of 45,000 units. Two plans are being considered. Under plan 1, the company will keep the selling price at the current level and sell the same volume as last year. This plan will increase income because of the reduced costs from using the new material. Under plan 2, the company will increase the selling price by 20%. This plan will decrease unit sales volume by 10%. Under both plans 1 and 2, the total fixed costs and the variable costs per unit for overhead and for selling and administrative costs will remain the same.

Required

1. Compute the break-even point in dollar sales for both (a) plan 1 and (b) plan 2.
2. Prepare a forecasted contribution margin income statement with two columns showing the expected results of plan 1 and plan 2. The statements should report sales, total variable costs, contribution margin, total fixed costs, income before taxes, income taxes (30% rate), and net income.

Check (1) Break-even: Plan 1, $750,000; Plan 2, $700,000

(2) Net income: Plan 1, $122,500; Plan 2, $199,500

Problem 18-7A
Break-even analysis with composite units
P4

Patriot Co. manufactures and sells three products: red, white, and blue. Their unit selling prices are red, $20; white, $35; and blue, $65. The per unit variable costs to manufacture and sell these products are red, $12; white, $22; and blue, $50. Their sales mix is reflected in a ratio of 5:4:2 (red:white:blue). Annual fixed costs shared by all three products are $250,000. One type of raw material has been used to manufacture all three products. The company has developed a new material of equal quality for less cost. The new material would reduce variable costs per unit as follows: red, by $6; white, by $12; and blue, by $10. However, the new material requires new equipment, which will increase annual fixed costs by $50,000. (Round answers to whole composite units.)

Required

1. If the company continues to use the old material, determine its break-even point in both sales units and sales dollars of each individual product.
2. If the company uses the new material, determine its new break-even point in both sales units and sales dollars of each individual product.

Check (1) Old plan break-even, 2,050 composite units (rounded)

(2) New plan break-even, 1,364 composite units (rounded)

Analysis Component

3. What insight does this analysis offer management for long-term planning?

PROBLEM SET B

Problem 18-1B
Contribution margin income statement and contribution margin ratio
A1

The following costs result from the production and sale of 12,000 CD sets manufactured by Gilmore Company for the year ended December 31, 2015. The CD sets sell for $18 each. The company has a 25% income tax rate.

Variable manufacturing costs	
Plastic for CD sets	$ 1,500
Wages of assembly workers	30,000
Labeling	3,000
Variable selling costs	
Sales commissions	6,000
Fixed manufacturing costs	
Rent on factory	6,750
Factory cleaning service	4,520
Factory machinery depreciation	20,000
Fixed selling and administrative costs	
Lease of office equipment	1,050
Systems staff salaries	15,000
Administrative management salaries	120,000

Required

Check (1) Net income, $6,135

1. Prepare a contribution margin income statement for the company.
2. Compute its contribution margin per unit and its contribution margin ratio.

Analysis Component

3. Interpret the contribution margin and contribution margin ratio from part 2.

Problem 18-2B
Scatter diagram and cost behavior estimation
P1

Sun Co.'s monthly sales and cost data for its operating activities of the past year follow. Management wants to use these data to predict future fixed and variable costs. (Dollar amounts are in thousands.)

Month	Sales	Total Cost	Month	Sales	Total Cost
1	$195	$ 97	7	$145	$ 93
2	125	87	8	185	105
3	105	73	9	135	85
4	155	89	10	85	58
5	95	81	11	175	95
6	215	110	12	115	79

Required

1. Prepare a scatter diagram for these data with sales volume (in $) plotted on the horizontal axis and total costs plotted on the vertical axis.

Check (2) Variable costs, $0.40 per sales dollar; fixed costs, $24,000

2. Estimate both the variable costs per sales dollar and the total monthly fixed costs using the high-low method. Draw the total costs line on the scatter diagram in part 1.
3. Use the estimated line of cost behavior and results from part 2 to predict future total costs when sales volume is (a) $100 and (b) $170.

Problem 18-3B
CVP analysis and charting
P2 P3

Hip-Hop Co. manufactures and markets several products. Management is considering the future of one product, electronic keyboards, that has not been as profitable as planned. Since this product is manufactured and marketed independently of the other products, its total costs can be precisely measured. Next year's plans call for a $350 selling price per unit. The fixed costs for the year are expected to be $42,000, up to a maximum capacity of 700 units. Forecasted variable costs are $210 per unit.

Required

1. Estimate the keyboards' break-even point in terms of (a) sales units and (b) sales dollars.
2. Prepare a CVP chart for keyboards like that in Exhibit 18.15. Use 700 keyboards as the maximum number of sales units on the horizontal axis of the graph, and $250,000 as the maximum dollar amount on the vertical axis.
3. Prepare a contribution margin income statement showing sales, variable costs, and fixed costs for keyboards at the break-even point.

Check (1) Break-even sales, 300 units

Problem 18-4B
Break-even analysis; income targeting and forecasting
C2 P2 A1

Rivera Co. sold 20,000 units of its only product and incurred a $50,000 loss (ignoring taxes) for the current year as shown here. During a planning session for year 2016's activities, the production manager notes that variable costs can be reduced 50% by installing a machine that automates several operations. To obtain these savings, the company must increase its annual fixed costs by $150,000. The maximum output capacity of the company is 40,000 units per year.

RIVERA COMPANY Contribution Margin Income Statement For Year Ended December 31, 2015	
Sales	$750,000
Variable costs	600,000
Contribution margin	150,000
Fixed costs	200,000
Net loss	$ (50,000)

Required

1. Compute the break-even point in dollar sales for year 2015.
2. Compute the predicted break-even point in dollar sales for year 2016 assuming the machine is installed and no change occurs in the unit selling price. (Round the change in variable costs to a whole number.)
3. Prepare a forecasted contribution margin income statement for 2016 that shows the expected results with the machine installed. Assume that the unit selling price and the number of units sold will not change, and no income taxes will be due.
4. Compute the sales level required in both dollars and units to earn $200,000 of target pretax income in 2016 with the machine installed and no change in unit sales price. (Round answers to whole dollars and whole units.)
5. Prepare a forecasted contribution margin income statement that shows the results at the sales level computed in part 4. Assume no income taxes will be due.

Check (3) Net income, $100,000

(4) Required sales, $916,667 or 24,445 units (both rounded)

Problem 18-5B
Break-even analysis, different cost structures, and income calculations
C2 P4 A1

Stam Co. produces and sells two products, BB and TT. It manufactures these products in separate factories and markets them through different channels. They have no shared costs. This year, the company sold 50,000 units of each product. Sales and costs for each product follow.

	Product BB	Product TT
Sales	$800,000	$800,000
Variable costs	560,000	100,000
Contribution margin	240,000	700,000
Fixed costs	100,000	560,000
Income before taxes	140,000	140,000
Income taxes (32% rate)	44,800	44,800
Net income	$ 95,200	$ 95,200

Required

1. Compute the break-even point in dollar sales for each product. (Round the answer to the next whole dollar.)
2. Assume that the company expects sales of each product to decline to 33,000 units next year with no change in the unit selling price. Prepare forecasted financial results for next year following the format

Check (2) After-tax income: BB, $39,712; TT, $(66,640)

of the contribution margin income statement as shown here with columns for each of the two products (assume a 32% tax rate, and that any loss before taxes yields a 32% tax benefit).

(3) After-tax income: BB, $140,896; TT, $228,480

3. Assume that the company expects sales of each product to increase to 64,000 units next year with no change in the unit selling prices. Prepare forecasted financial results for next year following the format of the contribution margin income statement as shown here with columns for each of the two products (assume a 32% tax rate).

Analysis Component

4. If sales greatly increase, which product would experience a greater increase in profit? Explain.

5. Describe some factors that might have created the different cost structures for these two products.

Problem 18-6B
Analysis of price, cost, and volume changes for contribution margin and net income
A1 P2

This year Best Company earned a disappointing 5.6% after-tax return on sales (net income/sales) from marketing 100,000 units of its only product. The company buys its product in bulk and repackages it for resale at the price of $20 per unit. Best incurred the following costs this year.

Total variable unit costs	$800,000
Total variable packaging costs	$100,000
Fixed costs	$950,000
Income tax rate	25%

The marketing manager claims that next year's results will be the same as this year's unless some changes are made. The manager predicts the company can increase the number of units sold by 80% if it reduces the selling price by 20% and upgrades the packaging. This change would increase variable packaging costs by 20%. Increased sales would allow the company to take advantage of a 25% quantity purchase discount on the cost of the bulk product. Neither the packaging change nor the volume discount would affect fixed costs, which provide an annual output capacity of 200,000 units.

Required

Check (1*b*) Break-even sales for new strategy, $1,727,273 (rounded)

1. Compute the break-even point in dollar sales under the (a) existing business strategy and (b) new strategy that alters both unit selling price and variable costs. (Round answers to the next whole dollar.)

(2) Net income: Existing strategy, $112,500; new strategy, $475,500

2. Prepare a forecasted contribution margin income statement with two columns showing the expected results of (a) the existing strategy and (b) changing to the new strategy. The statements should report sales, total variable costs (unit and packaging), contribution margin, fixed costs, income before taxes, income taxes, and net income. Also determine the after-tax return on sales for these two strategies.

Problem 18-7B
Break-even analysis with composite units
P4

Milano Co. manufactures and sells three products: product 1, product 2, and product 3. Their unit selling prices are product 1, $40; product 2, $30; and product 3, $20. The per unit variable costs to manufacture and sell these products are product 1, $30; product 2, $15; and product 3, $8. Their sales mix is reflected in a ratio of 6:4:2. Annual fixed costs shared by all three products are $270,000. One type of raw material has been used to manufacture products 1 and 2. The company has developed a new material of equal quality for less cost. The new material would reduce variable costs per unit as follows: product 1 by $10 and product 2 by $5. However, the new material requires new equipment, which will increase annual fixed costs by $50,000.

Required

Check (1) Old plan break-even, 1,875 composite units

1. If the company continues to use the old material, determine its break-even point in both sales units and sales dollars of each individual product.

(2) New plan break-even, 1,429 composite units (rounded)

2. If the company uses the new material, determine its new break-even point in both sales units and sales dollars of each individual product. (Round to the next whole unit.)

Analysis Component

3. What insight does this analysis offer management for long-term planning?

SERIAL PROBLEM
Business Solutions
P4

(This serial problem began in Chapter 1 and continues through most of the book. If previous chapter segments were not completed, the serial problem can begin at this point. It is helpful, but not necessary, to use the working papers that accompany the book.)

SP 18 Business Solutions sells upscale modular desk units and office chairs in the ratio of 3:2 (desk unit:chair). The selling prices are $1,250 per desk unit and $500 per chair. The variable costs are $750 per desk unit and $250 per chair. Fixed costs are $120,000.

Required

1. Compute the selling price per composite unit.
2. Compute the variable costs per composite unit.
3. Compute the break-even point in composite units.
4. Compute the number of units of each product that would be sold at the break-even point.

Check (3) 60 composite units

Beyond the Numbers

REPORTING IN ACTION
C1
APPLE

BTN 18-1 **Apple** offers extended service contracts that provide repair coverage for its products. As you complete the following requirements, assume that Apple's repair services department uses many of the company's existing resources such as its facilities, repair machinery, and computer systems.

Required

1. Identify several of the variable, mixed, and fixed costs that Apple's repair services department is likely to incur in carrying out its services.
2. Assume that Apple's repair service revenues are expected to grow by 25% in the next year. How would we expect the costs identified in part 1 to change, if at all?
3. Based on the answer to part 2, can Apple use the contribution margin ratio to predict how income will change in response to increases in Apple's repair service revenues?

COMPARATIVE ANALYSIS
P2 A2
APPLE
GOOGLE

BTN 18-2 Both **Apple** and **Google** sell electronic devices like phones and computers, and each of these companies has a different product mix.

Required

1. Assume the following data are available for both companies. Compute each company's break-even point in unit sales. (Each company sells many devices at many different selling prices, and each has its own variable costs. This assignment assumes an *average* selling price per unit and an *average* cost per item.)

	Apple	Google
Average selling price per unit sold.	$550 per unit	$470 per unit
Average variable cost per unit sold.	$250 per unit	$270 per unit
Total fixed costs ($ in millions).	$36,000	$10,000

2. If unit sales were to decline, which company would experience the larger decline in operating profit? Explain.

ETHICS CHALLENGE
C1

BTN 18-3 Labor costs of an auto repair mechanic are seldom based on actual hours worked. Instead, the amount paid a mechanic is based on an industry average of time estimated to complete a repair job. The repair shop bills the customer for the industry average amount of time at the repair center's billable cost per hour. This means a customer can pay, for example, $120 for two hours of work on a car when the actual time worked was only one hour. Many experienced mechanics can complete repair jobs faster than the industry average. The average data are compiled by engineering studies and surveys conducted in the auto repair business. Assume that you are asked to complete such a survey for a repair center. The survey calls for objective input, and many questions require detailed cost data and analysis. The mechanics and owners know you have the survey and encourage you to complete it in a way that increases the average billable hours for repair work.

Required

Write a one-page memorandum to the mechanics and owners that describes the direct labor analysis you will undertake in completing this survey.

COMMUNICATING IN PRACTICE

C2

BTN 18-4 Several important assumptions underlie CVP analysis. Assumptions often help simplify and focus our analysis of sales and costs. A common application of CVP analysis is as a tool to forecast sales, costs, and income.

Required

Assume that you are actively searching for a job. Prepare a half-page report identifying (1) three assumptions relating to your expected revenue (salary) and (2) three assumptions relating to your expected costs for the first year of your new job. Be prepared to discuss your assumptions in class.

TAKING IT TO THE NET

C1

BTN 18-5 Access and review the entrepreneurial information at **Business Owner's Toolkit [Toolkit.com].** Access and review its *New Business Cash Needs Checklist* (or similar worksheets related to controls of cash and costs) under the "Start Up" link. (Look under the heading "Free Startup Downloads.")

Required

Write a half-page report that describes the information and resources available at the Business Owner's Toolkit to help the owner of a start-up business to control and monitor its cash flows and costs.

TEAMWORK IN ACTION

C2

BTN 18-6 A local movie theater owner explains to you that ticket sales on weekends and evenings are strong, but attendance during the weekdays, Monday through Thursday, is poor. The owner proposes to offer a contract to the local grade school to show educational materials at the theater for a set charge per student during school hours. The owner asks your help to prepare a CVP analysis listing the cost and sales projections for the proposal. The owner must propose to the school's administration a charge per child. At a minimum, the charge per child needs to be sufficient for the theater to break even.

Required

Your team is to prepare two separate lists of questions that enable you to complete a reliable CVP analysis of this situation. One list is to be answered by the school's administration, the other by the owner of the movie theater.

ENTREPRENEURIAL DECISION

C1 A1

BTN 18-7 **Fast Yeti Custom Tees**, launched by entrepreneurs Reid Lyle, Jordan Roudenis, and Ryan Montgomery, produces apparel products. The company has a diverse product line of T-shirts, hats, and polo shirts.

Required

1. Identify at least two fixed costs that will not change regardless of how many T-shirts Fast Yeti produces.
2. How could overly optimistic sales estimates potentially hurt Fast Yeti's business?
3. Explain how cost-volume-profit analysis can help Reid, Jordan, and Ryan manage Fast Yeti.

HITTING THE ROAD

P4

BTN 18-8 Multiproduct break-even analysis is often viewed differently when actually applied in practice. You are to visit a local fast-food restaurant and count the number of items on the menu. To apply multiproduct break-even analysis to the restaurant, similar menu items must often be fit into groups. A reasonable approach is to classify menu items into approximately five groups. We then estimate average selling price and average variable cost to compute average contribution margin. (*Hint:* For fast-food restaurants, the highest contribution margin is with its beverages, at about 90%.)

Required

1. Prepare a one-year multiproduct break-even analysis for the restaurant you visit. Begin by establishing groups. Next, estimate each group's volume and contribution margin. These estimates are necessary to compute each group's contribution margin. Assume that annual fixed costs in total are $500,000 per year. (*Hint:* You must develop your own estimates on volume and contribution margin for each group to obtain the break-even point and sales.)
2. Prepare a one-page report on the results of your analysis. Comment on the volume of sales necessary to break even at a fast-food restaurant.

BTN 18-9 Access and review **Samsung**'s website (**www.samsung.com**) to answer the following questions.

GLOBAL DECISION

P4

Samsung

Required

1. Do you believe that Samsung's managers use single product CVP analysis or multiproduct break-even analysis? Explain.
2. How does the addition of a new product line affect Samsung's CVP analysis?

ANSWERS TO MULTIPLE CHOICE QUIZ

1. a; $150 − $100 = $50
2. e; ($150 − $100)/$150 = 33⅓%
3. c; $75,000/$50 CM per unit = 1,500 units
4. b; $300,000 − $180,000 = $120,000
5. c; Contribution margin ratio = ($400 − $260)/$400 = 0.35
   Targeted sales = ($840,000 + $70,000)/0.35 = $2,600,000

chapter 19

Variable Costing and Analysis

Chapter Preview

VARIABLE COSTING AND ABSORPTION COSTING

Absorption costing

Variable costing

P1 Computing unit costs

INCOME REPORTING IMPLICATIONS

P2 When production equals sales

When production exceeds sales

When production is less than sales

Income reporting

P3 Converting income under variable costing to absorption costing

COMPARING VARIABLE COSTING AND ABSORPTION COSTING

C1 Planning production

P4 Setting prices

Controlling costs

CVP analysis

Limitations of variable costing

Variable costing for services

A1 Pricing special orders with variable costing

Learning Objectives

CONCEPTUAL

C1 Describe how absorption costing can result in overproduction.

ANALYTICAL

A1 Use variable costing in pricing special orders.

PROCEDURAL

P1 Compute unit cost under both absorption and variable costing.

P2 Prepare and analyze an income statement using absorption costing and using variable costing.

P3 Convert income under variable costing to the absorption cost basis.

P4 Determine product selling price based on absorption costing.

NEW YORK—Shazi Visram grew up in Alabama, and she felt entrepreneurship was her calling. "I always knew that I wanted to be my own boss," recalls Shazi. "I had this idea to make baby food the way moms would." However, entrepreneurship had its challenges. "There was an evening when I got to the subway with nothing in my wallet but maxed out credit cards and no way to pay for my ride home," admits Shazi. "The path of entrepreneurship isn't smooth . . . it's a rollercoaster!" From these modest beginnings, Shazi created **Happy Family Brands (HappyBabyFood.com)**, which is committed to quality foods for the entire family.

"We are an authentic mom-run company; we are real people behind this business who care about the quality of our products," explains Shazi. "I made the first recipes in my kitchen, using the best organic ingredients. Then, I subjected these recipes to the critics; hundreds of babies, including my own!" Along the way, Shazi set up an accounting system to measure, track, summarize, and report on operations. An important part of this accounting system is a focus on variable costs and product contribution margins. "We are a small business with a big vision and a big heart," says Shazi. "Quality is of the utmost concern," explains Shazi.

"We've grown exponentially . . . now we're in over 17,000 stores," says Shazi. "What's important [in both business and accounting] is . . . being adaptable!" A variable costing approach allows Shazi to adapt to changing market conditions and unique opportunities.

Shazi's company is riding high, and she recently sold a large portion of her company to Danone, a multinational corporation based in France. "Our mission is to remove toxins from children's lives. With a mission that big, we need our company to be as big as possible," says Shazi. "What an incredible opportunity to build a meaningful brand," says Shazi. "[We] make a difference in a child's life." Shazi adds, "We have been really blessed!"

Courtesy of Happy Family Brands

Happy Times

"We let our investors see, and share, our passion"

—Shazi Visram

Sources: *Happy Family Brands website,* January 2015; *Inc.,* August 2011, March 2012, and September 2013; *New Hope 360,* March 2011; *FOXBusiness,* November 2011

INTRODUCING VARIABLE COSTING AND ABSORPTION COSTING

Product costs consist of direct materials, direct labor, and overhead. Direct materials and direct labor costs are those that can be identified and traced to the product(s). Overhead, which consists of costs such as electricity, equipment depreciation, and supervisor salaries, is not traceable to the product. Overhead costs must be allocated to products.

There are a variety of costing methods for identifying and allocating overhead costs to products. A prior chapter focused on *how* to allocate overhead costs to products. This chapter focuses on *what* overhead costs are included in product costs.

Under the traditional costing approach, *all* manufacturing costs are assigned to products. Those costs consist of direct materials, direct labor, and manufacturing overhead, both variable and fixed. This traditional approach is referred to as **absorption costing** (also called *full costing*), which assumes that products *absorb* all costs incurred to produce them. While widely used for external financial reporting (GAAP), this costing method can result in misleading product cost information for managers' business decisions.

Under **variable costing,** only costs that change in total with changes in production level are included in product costs. Those consist of direct materials, direct labor, and variable manufacturing overhead. Fixed manufacturing overhead does not change with changes in production and, thus, it is excluded from product costs under variable costing. Instead, fixed overhead is treated as a *period cost,* meaning it is expensed in the period when it is incurred.

Point: Under variable costing, fixed overhead is expensed at the time the units are produced. Under absorption costing, fixed overhead is expensed at the time the units are sold (as a component of cost of goods sold).

Exhibit 19.1 compares the absorption and variable costing methods. Under both methods, direct materials, direct labor, and variable overhead are included in product costs. The key difference between the methods lies in their treatment of *fixed* overhead costs—such costs are included in product costs under absorption costing but included in period expenses under variable costing. Recall that product costs are included in inventory until the goods are sold, at which time they are included in cost of goods sold. Period expenses are reported as expenses immediately in the period in which they are incurred.

EXHIBIT 19.1

Absorption versus Variable Costing

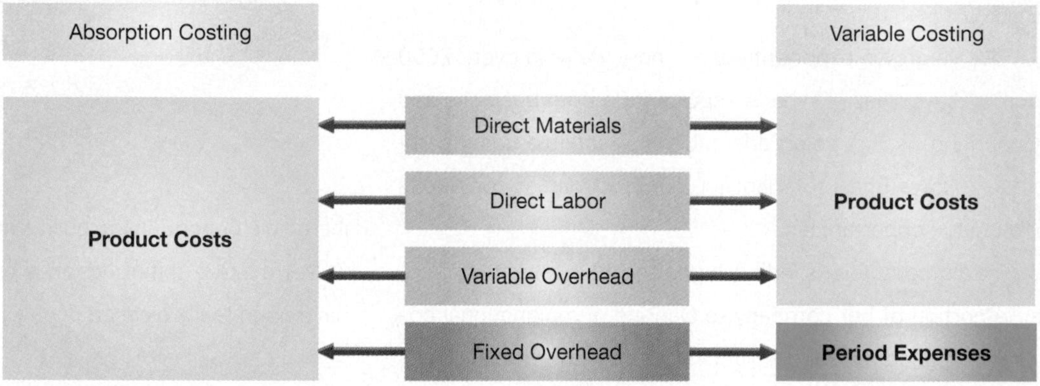

Exhibit 19.1 helps us understand when the absorption and variable costing methods will yield different income amounts over a period. In particular, differences in income resulting from the alternative costing methods will be *small* when:

- Fixed overhead is small as a percentage of total manufacturing costs.
- Inventory levels are low. As more companies adopt lean techniques, including just-in-time manufacturing, inventory levels fall. Lower inventory levels reduce income differences between absorption and variable costing.
- Inventory turnover is rapid. The more quickly inventory turns over, the more product costs are included in cost of goods sold, relative to the product costs that remain in inventory.
- The period of analysis is long. For example, different costing methods might yield very different income numbers over a quarter or year, but these differences will decrease as income is compared over longer periods.

Computing Unit Cost

P1 Compute unit cost under both absorption and variable costing.

To illustrate the difference between absorption costing and variable costing, let's consider the product cost data in Exhibit 19.2 from IceAge, a skate manufacturer.

EXHIBIT 19.2

Summary Product Cost Data

Direct materials cost	$4 per unit
Direct labor cost	$8 per unit
Overhead cost	
Variable overhead cost	$ 180,000
Fixed overhead cost	600,000
Total overhead cost	$ 780,000
Expected units produced	60,000 units

©TOSHIFUMI KITAMURA/AFP/Getty Images

Drawing on the product cost data, Exhibit 19.3 shows the product cost per unit computations for both absorption and variable costing. These computations are shown both in a tabular format (left side of exhibit) and a visual format (right side of exhibit). For absorption costing, the product cost per unit is $25, which consists of $4 in direct materials, $8 in direct labor, $3 in variable overhead ($180,000/60,000 units), and $10 in fixed overhead ($600,000/60,000 units).

For variable costing, the product cost per unit is $15, which consists of $4 in direct materials, $8 in direct labor, and $3 in variable overhead. Fixed overhead costs of $600,000 are treated as a period cost and are recorded as expense in the period incurred. *The difference between the two costing methods is the exclusion of fixed overhead from product costs for variable costing.*

EXHIBIT 19.3

Unit Cost Computation

	Product Cost per Unit	
	Absorption Costing	Variable Costing
Direct materials	$ 4	$ 4
Direct labor	8	8
Overhead costs		
Variable overhead	3	3
Fixed overhead	10	—
Total product cost per unit	$25	$15

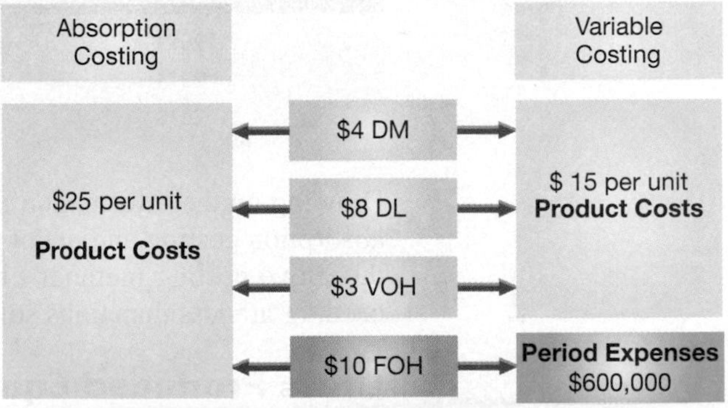

NEED-TO-KNOW 19-1

Computing Product Cost per Unit

P1

A manufacturer reports the following data.

Direct materials cost	$6 per unit	Variable overhead	$220,000 per year
Direct labor cost	$14 per unit	Fixed overhead	$680,000 per year
Expected units produced	20,000 units		

1. Compute the total product cost per unit under absorption costing.
2. Compute the total product cost per unit under variable costing.

Solution

Per Unit Costs	(1) Absorption Costing	(2) Variable Costing
Direct materials	$ 6	$ 6
Direct labor	14	14
Variable overhead ($220,000/20,000)	11	11
Fixed overhead ($680,000/20,000)*	34	—
Total product cost per unit	$65	$31

*Not included in product costs under variable costing.

Do More: QS 19-1, QS 19-2, E 19-1, E 19-2

QC1

INCOME REPORTING IMPLICATIONS

The prior section showed how the different treatment of fixed overhead costs leads to different product costs per unit under absorption and variable costing. This section shows the implications of this difference for income reporting.

To illustrate the income reporting implications, we return to IceAge Company. Below are the manufacturing cost data for IceAge as well as additional data on selling and administrative expenses. Assume that IceAge's variable costs per unit are constant and that its annual fixed costs remain unchanged during the three-year period 2013 through 2015.

Manufacturing Costs		Selling and Administrative Expenses	
Direct materials cost..........	$4 per unit	Variable....................	$2 per unit
Direct labor cost.............	$8 per unit	Fixed.......................	$200,000 per year
Variable overhead cost.........	$3 per unit		
Fixed overhead cost...........	$600,000 per year		

The reported sales and production information for IceAge follows. Its sales price was a constant $40 per unit over this time period. We see that the units produced equal those sold for 2013, exceed those sold for 2014, and are less than those sold for 2015. IceAge began 2013 with no units in beginning inventory.

	Units Produced	Units Sold	Units in Ending Inventory
2013	60,000	60,000	0
2014	60,000	40,000	20,000
2015	60,000	80,000	0

Drawing on the information above, we next prepare income statements for IceAge both under absorption costing and under variable costing. Our purpose is to highlight differences between these two costing methods under three different cases: when units produced are equal to, exceed, or are less than units sold.

P2 Prepare and analyze an income statement using absorption costing and using variable costing.

Units Produced Equal Units Sold

Exhibit 19.4 presents the 2013 income statement for both costing methods (2014 and 2015 statements will follow). The income statement under variable costing (on the right) is referred to as the **contribution margin income statement.** Contribution margin is the excess of sales over variable costs. This margin contributes to covering all fixed costs and earning income. Under

EXHIBIT 19.4

Income for 2013—Quantity Produced Equals Quantity Sold*

Point: Contribution margin (Sales − Variable expenses) is different from gross margin (Sales − Cost of sales).

A performance report that excludes fixed expenses and net income is a *contribution margin report.* Its bottom line is contribution margin.

ICEAGE COMPANY
Income Statement (Absorption Costing)
For Year Ended December 31, 2013

Sales† (60,000 × $40)	$2,400,000
Cost of goods sold (60,000 × $25**) ..	1,500,000
Gross margin	900,000
Selling and administrative expenses [$200,000 + (60,000 × $2)]......	320,000
Net income	$ 580,000

* ($4 DM + $8 DL + $3 VOH)
** ($4 DM + $8 DL + $3 VOH + $10 FOH)
† Units produced equal 60,000; units sold equal 60,000.

ICEAGE COMPANY
Income Statement (Variable Costing)
For Year Ended December 31, 2013

Sales† (60,000 × $40)		$2,400,000
Variable expenses		
Variable production costs (60,000 × $15*)	$900,000	
Variable selling and administrative expenses (60,000 × $2)....	120,000	1,020,000
Contribution margin.........		1,380,000
Fixed expenses		
Fixed overhead	600,000	
Fixed selling and administrative expenses...	200,000	800,000
Net income................		$ 580,000

variable costing, expenses are grouped according to cost behavior—variable or fixed, and production or nonproduction. Under the traditional format of absorption costing, expenses are grouped according to function but not separated into variable and fixed components.

Exhibit 19.4 reveals that *reported income is identical under absorption costing and variable costing when the number of units produced equals the number of units sold.* Because variable costing results in expensing of fixed manufacturing overhead based on the number of units produced (60,000 × $10), and absorption costing results in expensing of fixed manufacturing overhead based on the number of units sold (also 60,000 × $10), the net income is the same under either method when units produced equals units sold.

Exhibit 19.5 reorganizes the information from Exhibit 19.4 to show the assignment of costs to different expenses and assets under both absorption costing and variable costing. In this year, there are no units in ending inventory, so the finished goods inventory is $0 under both methods. When quantity produced equals quantity sold, there is no difference in total expenses reported on the income statement. Yet, there is a difference in what categories receive those costs. Absorption costing assigns $1,500,000 to cost of goods sold compared to $900,000 for variable costing. The $600,000 difference is a period cost for variable costing.

Point: Contribution margin income statements prepared under variable costing are useful in performing cost-volume-profit analyses.

EXHIBIT 19.5

Production Cost Assignment for 2013

Absorption Costing		For Year 2013
Beginning finished goods inventory		$ 0
Cost of goods manufactured		
Direct materials	$240,000	
Direct labor	480,000	
Variable manufacturing overhead	180,000	
Fixed manufacturing overhead	600,000	1,500,000
Cost of goods available for sale		1,500,000
Less: Ending finished goods inventory		0
Cost of goods sold		$1,500,000

Variable Costing		For Year 2013
Beginning finished goods inventory		$ 0
Cost of goods manufactured		
Direct materials	$240,000	
Direct labor	480,000	
Variable manufacturing overhead	180,000	
Fixed manufacturing overhead	0	900,000
Cost of goods available for sale		900,000
Less: Ending finished goods inventory		0
Cost of goods sold		900,000
Period costs		
Fixed manufacturing overhead		600,000
Total costs		$1,500,000

Decision Insight

Manufacturing Margin Some managers compute **manufacturing margin** (also called *production margin*), which is sales less variable production costs. Some managers also require that internal income statements show this amount to highlight the impact of variable product costs on income. The contribution margin section of IceAge's variable costing income statement would appear as follows (compare this to Exhibit 19.4).

Sales	$2,400,000
Variable production costs	900,000
Manufacturing margin	1,500,000
Variable selling & admin. exp.	120,000
Contribution margin	$1,380,000

©Steve Mason/Getty Images

Units Produced Exceed Units Sold

Exhibit 19.6 shows absorption costing and variable costing income statements for 2014. In 2014, 60,000 units were produced, which is the same as in 2013. However, only 40,000 units were sold, which means 20,000 units remain in ending inventory.

The income statements reveal that for 2014, income is $320,000 under absorption costing. Under variable costing, income is $120,000, which is $200,000 less than under absorption costing. The cause of this $200,000 difference is due to the different treatment of fixed overhead under the two costing methods. Because variable costing expenses fixed manufacturing overhead (FOH) based on the number of units produced (60,000 × $10), and absorption costing

EXHIBIT 19.6

Income for 2014—Quantity Produced Exceeds Quantity Sold

ICEAGE COMPANY Income Statement (Absorption Costing) For Year Ended December 31, 2014	
Sales† (40,000 × $40)	$1,600,000
Cost of goods sold (40,000 × $25**) . . .	1,000,000
Gross margin	600,000
Selling and administrative expenses [$200,000 + (40,000 × $2)]	280,000
Net income	$ 320,000

* ($4 DM + $8 DL + $3 VOH)
** ($4 DM + $8 DL + $3 VOH + $10 FOH)
† Units produced equal 60,000; units sold equal 40,000.

ICEAGE COMPANY Income Statement (Variable Costing) For Year Ended December 31, 2014		
Sales† (40,000 × $40)		$1,600,000
Variable expenses		
Variable production costs (40,000 × $15*)	$600,000	
Variable selling and administrative expenses (40,000 × $2). . . .	80,000	680,000
Contribution margin		920,000
Fixed expenses		
Fixed overhead	600,000	
Fixed selling and administrative expense	200,000	800,000
Net income		$ 120,000

expenses FOH based on the number of units sold (40,000 × $10), net income is lower under variable costing by $200,000 (20,000 units × $10).

Under variable costing, the entire $600,000 fixed overhead cost is treated as an expense in computing 2014 income. Under absorption costing, the fixed overhead cost is allocated to each unit of product at the rate of $10 per unit (from Exhibit 19.3). When production exceeds sales by 20,000 units (60,000 versus 40,000), the $200,000 ($10 × 20,000 units) of fixed overhead cost allocated to these 20,000 units is included in the cost of ending inventory (see Exhibit 19.7). This means that $200,000 of fixed overhead cost incurred in 2014 is not expensed until future years, when it is reported in cost of goods sold as those products are sold. Consequently, income for 2014 under absorption costing is $200,000 higher than income under variable costing. Even though sales (of 40,000 units) and the number of units produced (totaling 60,000) are the same under both costing methods, net income differs greatly due to the treatment of fixed overhead.

EXHIBIT 19.7

Production Cost Assignment for 2014

Absorption Costing		For Year 2014
Beginning finished goods inventory		$ 0
Cost of goods manufactured		
Direct materials	$240,000	
Direct labor	480,000	
Variable manufacturing overhead	180,000	
Fixed manufacturing overhead	600,000	1,500,000
Cost of goods available for sale		1,500,000
Less: Ending finished goods inventory . . .		500,000*
Cost of goods sold		$1,000,000

* 20,000 units × $25 per unit
** 20,000 units × $15 per unit

Variable Costing		For Year 2014
Beginning finished goods inventory		$ 0
Cost of goods manufactured		
Direct materials	$240,000	
Direct labor	480,000	
Variable manufacturing overhead	180,000	
Fixed manufacturing overhead	0	900,000
Cost of goods available for sale		900,000
Less: Ending finished goods inventory . .		300,000**
Cost of goods sold		600,000
Period costs		
Fixed manufacturing overhead		600,000
Total costs		$1,200,000

Exhibit 19.7 reorganizes the information from Exhibit 19.6 to show the assignment of costs to different expenses and assets under both absorption costing and variable costing. When quantity produced exceeds quantity sold, there is a difference in total expenses. Under absorption costing, cost of goods sold is $200,000 lower than the total costs ($1,200,000) under variable costing. As a result, income (and ending finished goods inventory) under absorption costing is $200,000 greater than under variable costing because of the fixed overhead cost allocated to ending inventory (asset) under absorption costing.

Units Produced Are Less Than Units Sold

Exhibit 19.8 shows absorption costing and variable costing income statements for 2015. In 2015, IceAge produced 60,000 units and sold 80,000 units. Thus, IceAge produced 20,000 units fewer than it sold. This means IceAge sold all that it produced during the period, and it sold all of its beginning finished goods inventory. IceAge's income is $840,000 under absorption costing, but it is $1,040,000 under variable costing.

Point: IceAge can sell more units than it produced in 2015 because of inventory carried over from 2014.

EXHIBIT 19.8

Income for 2015—Quantity Produced Is Less Than Quantity Sold

ICEAGE COMPANY
Income Statement (Absorption Costing)
For Year Ended December 31, 2015

Sales† (80,000 × $40)	$3,200,000
Cost of goods sold (80,000 × $25*)	2,000,000
Gross margin	1,200,000
Selling and administrative expenses [$200,000 + (80,000 × $2)]	360,000
Net income	$ 840,000

* ($4 DM + $8 DL + $3 VOH)
** ($4 DM + $8 DL + $3 VOH + $10 FOH)
† Units produced equal 60,000; units sold equal 80,000.

ICEAGE COMPANY
Income Statement (Variable Costing)
For Year Ended December 31, 2015

Sales† (80,000 × $40)		$3,200,000
Variable expenses		
Variable production costs (80,000 × $15**)	$1,200,000	
Variable selling and administrative expenses (80,000 × $2)	160,000	1,360,000
Contribution margin		1,840,000
Fixed expenses		
Fixed overhead	600,000	
Fixed selling and administrative expense	200,000	800,000
Net income		$1,040,000

The cause of this $200,000 income difference lies with the treatment of fixed overhead. Beginning inventory in 2015 under absorption costing included $200,000 of fixed overhead cost incurred in 2014, which is assigned to cost of goods sold in 2015 under absorption costing. Because variable costing expenses fixed manufacturing overhead (FOH) based on the number of units produced (60,000 × $10), and absorption costing expenses FOH based on the number of units sold (80,000 × $10), net income is higher under variable costing by $200,000 (20,000 units × $10).

Exhibit 19.9 reorganizes the information from Exhibit 19.8 to show the assignment of costs to different expenses and assets under both absorption costing and variable costing. When quantity produced is less than quantity sold, there is a difference in total costs assigned.

EXHIBIT 19.9

Production Cost Assignment for 2015

Absorption Costing		For Year 2015
Beginning finished goods inventory		$ 500,000*
Cost of goods manufactured		
Direct materials	$240,000	
Direct labor	480,000	
Variable manufacturing overhead	180,000	
Fixed manufacturing overhead	600,000	1,500,000
Cost of goods available for sale		2,000,000
Less: Ending finished goods inventory		0
Cost of goods sold		$2,000,000

* 20,000 units × $25 per unit
** 20,000 units × $15 per unit

Variable Costing		For Year 2015
Beginning finished goods inventory		$ 300,000**
Cost of goods manufactured		
Direct materials	$240,000	
Direct labor	480,000	
Variable manufacturing overhead	180,000	
Fixed manufacturing overhead	0	900,000
Cost of goods available for sale		1,200,000
Less: Ending finished goods inventory		0
Cost of goods sold		1,200,000
Period costs		
Fixed manufacturing overhead		600,000
Total costs		$1,800,000

Specifically, ending inventory in 2014 under absorption costing was $500,000 (20,000 units × $25) whereas it was only $300,000 (20,000 units × $15) under variable costing—see Exhibit 19.7. Consequently, when that inventory is sold in 2015, that $200,000 difference in ending inventory is included in cost of goods sold under absorption costing. Thus, the 2015 income under absorption costing is $200,000 less than the income under variable costing. That inventory cost difference flows through cost of goods sold and then to income.

Summarizing Income Reporting

Income reported under both variable costing and absorption costing for the years 2013 through 2015 for IceAge is summarized in Exhibit 19.10. We see that total income is $1,740,000 for this time period for *both* methods. Further, income under absorption costing and that under variable costing differ whenever the quantity produced and the quantity sold differ. These differences in income are due to the different timing with which fixed overhead costs are reported in income under the two methods. Specifically, *income under absorption costing is higher when more units are produced relative to units sold and is lower when fewer units are produced than are sold.*

EXHIBIT 19.10

Summary of Income Reporting

	Units Produced	Units Sold	Income under Absorption Costing	Income under Variable Costing	Income Differences
2013	60,000	60,000	$ 580,000	$ 580,000	$ 0
2014	60,000	40,000	320,000	120,000	200,000
2015	60,000	80,000	840,000	1,040,000	(200,000)
Totals	180,000	180,000	$1,740,000	$1,740,000	$ 0

Point: In our illustration the company produces the same number of units (60,000) each year. We provide an example with varying yearly production levels in the Comprehensive Need-To-Know at the end of the chapter.

In our illustration using IceAge, the total number of units produced over 2013–2015 was exactly equal to the number of units sold over that period. This meant that the difference between absorption costing income and variable costing income for the *total* three-year period is zero. In reality, it is unusual for production and sales quantities to exactly equal each other over such a short period of time. This means that we normally continue to see differences in income for these two methods extending over several years.

NEED-TO-KNOW 19-2

Computing Income under Absorption and Variable Costing

P2

ZBest Mfg. reports the following data for 2015.

Direct materials cost.....	$6 per unit	Units produced	20,000 units
Direct labor cost........	$11 per unit	Units sold	14,000 units
Variable overhead cost ...	$3 per unit	Variable selling and administrative expenses ..	$2 per unit
Fixed overhead	$680,000 per year	Fixed selling and administrative expenses....	$112,000 per year
Sales price	$80 per unit		

1. Prepare an income statement for 2015 under absorption costing.
2. Prepare an income statement for 2015 under variable costing.

Solution

ZBEST MFG.
Income Statement (Absorption Costing)
For Year Ended December 31, 2015

Sales (14,000 × $80)	$1,120,000
Cost of goods sold (14,000 × $54)*...	756,000
Gross margin	364,000
Selling and admin. expenses [$112,000 + (14,000 × $2)]	140,000
Net income......................	$ 224,000

* $6 DM + $11 DL + $3 VOH + $20 FOH ($680,000/20,000) = $54 per unit
** 14,000 × $2 per unit.
† $6 DM + $11 DL + $3 VOH = $20 per unit

The difference in income between the two methods ($204,000) can be computed as the 6,000 units added to ending inventory × $34 FOH per unit.

ZBEST MFG.
Income Statement (Variable Costing)
For Year Ended December 31, 2015

Sales (14,000 × $80)		$1,120,000
Variable expenses		
Variable production costs (14,000 × $20)†	$280,000	
Variable selling and admin. expenses**........	28,000	308,000
Contribution margin..........		812,000
Fixed expenses		
Fixed overhead	680,000	
Fixed selling and admin. expenses	112,000	792,000
Net income.................		$ 20,000

Do More: QS 19-3, QS 19-4, E 19-3, E 19-4, E 19-5.

QC2

Converting Income under Variable Costing to Absorption Costing

P3 Convert income under variable costing to the absorption cost basis.

Companies commonly use variable costing for internal reporting and business decisions, and they use absorption costing for external reporting and tax reporting. For companies concerned about the cost of maintaining two costing systems, it is comforting to know that we can readily convert reports under variable costing to those using absorption costing.

Income under variable costing is restated to that under absorption costing by adding the fixed overhead cost in ending inventory and subtracting the fixed overhead cost in beginning inventory. Exhibit 19.11 shows the formula for this calculation.

EXHIBIT 19.11
Formula to Convert Variable Costing Income to Absorption Costing

$$\text{Income under absorption costing} = \text{Income under variable costing} + \text{Fixed overhead cost in ending inventory} - \text{Fixed overhead cost in beginning inventory}$$

Using IceAge's data, in 2014, absorption costing income was $200,000 higher than variable costing income. The $200,000 difference was because the fixed overhead cost incurred in 2014 was allocated to the 20,000 units of ending inventory under absorption costing (and not expensed in 2014 under absorption costing). On the other hand, the $200,000 fixed overhead costs (along with all other fixed costs) were expensed in 2014 under variable costing.

Exhibit 19.12 shows the computations for restating income under the two costing methods. To restate variable costing income to absorption costing income for 2014, we must add back the **fixed overhead cost deferred in** (ending) **inventory.** Similarly, to restate variable costing income to absorption costing income for 2015, we must deduct the **fixed overhead cost recognized from** (beginning) **inventory,** which was incurred in 2014, but expensed in the 2015 cost of goods sold when the inventory was sold.

EXHIBIT 19.12
Converting Variable Costing Income to Absorption Costing Income

	2013	2014	2015
Variable costing income (Exhibit 19.10)	$580,000	$120,000	$1,040,000
Add: Fixed overhead cost deferred in ending inventory (20,000 × $10)	0	200,000	0
Less: Fixed overhead cost recognized from beginning inventory (20,000 × $10)	0	0	(200,000)
Absorption costing income	$580,000	$320,000	$ 840,000

COMPARING VARIABLE COSTING AND ABSORPTION COSTING

This section compares the roles of absorption and variable costing in managers' business decisions.

Planning Production

C1 Describe how absorption costing can result in overproduction.

Production planning is an important managerial function. Producing too much leads to excess inventory, which in turn leads to higher storage and financing costs, and to greater risk of product obsolescence. On the other hand, producing too little can lead to lost sales and customer dissatisfaction.

Production levels should be based on reliable sales forecasts. However, overproduction and inventory buildup can occur because of how managers are evaluated and rewarded. For instance, many companies link manager bonuses to income computed under absorption costing because this is how income is reported to shareholders (per GAAP).

To illustrate how a reward system can lead to overproduction under absorption costing, let's use IceAge's 2013 data with one change: assume that its manager decides to produce 100,000 units instead of 60,000. Since only 60,000 units are sold, the 40,000 units of excess production will be stored in ending finished goods inventory.

The left side of Exhibit 19.13 shows the unit cost when 60,000 units are produced (same as Exhibit 19.3). The right side shows unit cost when 100,000 units are produced. The exhibit is prepared under absorption costing for 2013.

EXHIBIT 19.13

Unit Cost under Absorption Costing for Different Production Levels

Absorption Costing When 60,000 Units Are Produced		Absorption Costing When 100,000 Units Are Produced	
Direct materials cost	$ 4 per unit	Direct materials cost	$ 4 per unit
Direct labor cost	8 per unit	Direct labor cost	8 per unit
Variable overhead cost	3 per unit	Variable overhead cost	3 per unit
Total variable cost	15 per unit	Total variable cost	15 per unit
Fixed overhead ($600,000/60,000 units)	10 per unit	Fixed overhead ($600,000/100,000 units)	6 per unit
Total product cost	$25 per unit	Total product cost	$21 per unit

Total production cost *per unit* is $4 less when 100,000 units are produced. Specifically, cost per unit is $21 when 100,000 units are produced versus $25 per unit at 60,000 units. The reason for this difference is because the company is spreading the $600,000 fixed overhead cost over more units when 100,000 units are produced than when 60,000 units are produced.

The difference in cost per unit impacts income reporting. Exhibit 19.14 presents the 2013 income statement under absorption costing for the two alternative production levels.

EXHIBIT 19.14

Income under Absorption Costing for Different Production Levels

ICEAGE COMPANY
Income Statement (Absorption Costing)
For Year Ended December 31, 2013
[60,000 Units Produced; 60,000 Units Sold]

Sales (60,000 × $40)		$2,400,000
Cost of goods sold (60,000 × $25)		1,500,000
Gross margin		900,000
Selling and administrative expenses		
Variable (60,000 × $2)	$120,000	
Fixed	200,000	320,000
Net income		$ 580,000

ICEAGE COMPANY
Income Statement (Absorption Costing)
For Year Ended December 31, 2013
[100,000 Units Produced; 60,000 Units Sold]

Sales (60,000 × $40)		$2,400,000
Cost of goods sold (60,000 × $21)		1,260,000
Gross margin		1,140,000
Selling and administrative expenses		
Variable (60,000 × $2)	$120,000	
Fixed	200,000	320,000
Net income		$ 820,000

Common sense suggests that because the company's variable cost per unit, total fixed costs, and sales are identical in both cases, merely producing more units and creating excess ending inventory should not increase income. Yet, as we see in Exhibit 19.14, income under absorption costing is $240,000 greater if management produces 40,000 more units than necessary and builds up ending inventory. The reason is that $240,000 of fixed overhead (40,000 units × $6) is assigned to ending inventory instead of being expensed as cost of goods sold in 2013. This shows that under absorption costing, a manager can report increased income merely by producing more and disregarding whether the excess units can be sold or not.

Manager bonuses are tied to income computed under absorption costing for many companies. Accordingly, these managers may be enticed to increase production that increases income and their bonuses. This incentive problem encourages inventory buildup, which leads to increased costs in storage, financing, and obsolescence. If the excess inventory is never sold, it will be disposed of at a loss.

The manager incentive problem can be avoided when income is measured using variable costing. To illustrate, Exhibit 19.15 reports income under variable costing for the same production levels used in Exhibit 19.14. This demonstrates that managers cannot increase income under variable costing by merely increasing production without increasing sales.

Why is income under absorption costing affected by the production level when that for variable costing is not? The answer lies in the different treatment of fixed overhead costs for the two methods. Under absorption costing, fixed overhead *per unit* is lower when 100,000 units are produced than when 60,000 units are produced, and then fixed overhead cost is allocated to more units—recall Exhibit 19.13. If those excess units produced are not sold, the fixed overhead cost allocated to those units is not expensed until a future period when those units are sold.

EXHIBIT 19.15

Income under Variable Costing for Different Production Levels

ICEAGE COMPANY Income Statement (Variable Costing) For Year Ended December 31, 2013 [60,000 Units Produced; 60,000 Units Sold]		
Sales (60,000 × $40)		$2,400,000
Variable expenses		
Variable production costs (60,000 × $15)	$900,000	
Variable selling and administrative expenses (60,000 × $2)	120,000	1,020,000
Contribution margin		1,380,000
Fixed expenses		
Fixed overhead	600,000	
Fixed selling and administrative expense	200,000	800,000
Net income		$ 580,000

ICEAGE COMPANY Income Statement (Variable Costing) For Year Ended December 31, 2013 [100,000 Units Produced; 60,000 Units Sold]		
Sales (60,000 × $40)		$2,400,000
Variable expenses		
Variable production costs (60,000 × $15)	$900,000	
Variable selling and administrative expenses (60,000 × $2)	120,000	1,020,000
Contribution margin		1,380,000
Fixed expenses		
Fixed overhead	600,000	
Fixed selling and administrative expenses	200,000	800,000
Net income		$ 580,000

Reported income under variable costing, on the other hand, is not affected by production level changes because *all* fixed production costs are expensed in the year when incurred. Under variable costing, companies increase reported income by selling more units—it is not possible to increase income just by producing more units and creating excess inventory.

Decision Ethics

Production Manager Your company produces and sells MP3 players. Due to competition, your company projects sales to be 35% less than last year. In a recent meeting, the CEO expressed concern that top executives may not receive bonuses because of the expected sales decrease. The controller suggests that if the company continues to produce as many units as last year, reported income might achieve the level for bonuses to be paid. Should your company produce excess inventory to maintain income? What ethical issues arise? ■ [Answers follow the chapter's Summary.]

Setting Prices

P4 Determine product selling price based on absorption costing.

Setting prices for products and services is one of the more complex and important managerial decisions. Although many factors impact pricing, cost is a crucial factor. Cost information from both absorption costing and variable costing can aid managers in pricing.

Over the long run, prices must be high enough to cover all costs, including variable costs and fixed costs, and still provide an acceptable return to owners. For this purpose, absorption cost information is useful because it reflects the full costs that sales must exceed for the company to be profitable. We can use a three-step process to determine product selling prices:

Step 1: Determine the product cost per unit using absorption costing.

Step 2: Determine the target *markup* on product cost per unit.

Step 3: Add the target markup to the product cost to find the target selling price.

To illustrate, consider IceAge. Under absorption costing, its product cost is $25 per unit (from Exhibit 19.3). IceAge's management must then determine a target markup on this product cost. This target markup could be based on industry averages, prices that have been charged in the past, or other information. In addition, this markup must be set high enough to cover selling and administrative expenses (both variable and fixed) that are excluded from product costs. In this example, IceAge targets a markup of 60% of absorption cost. With that information, the company computes a target selling price as in Exhibit 19.16.

EXHIBIT 19.16

Determining Selling Price with Absorption Costing

Step 1	Absorption cost per unit (from Exhibit 19.3)	$25
Step 2	Target markup per unit ($25 × 60%)	15
Step 3	Target selling price per unit	$40

IceAge can use this target selling price as a starting point in setting prices. Management must also consider the level of competition in its industry and customer preferences. If customers are not willing to pay $40 per unit, IceAge must either lower its target markup or find ways to reduce its costs.

While absorption cost information is useful in setting long-run prices, it can lead to misleading decisions in analyzing special orders. We show how variable cost information can be used to analyze special order decisions in the Decision Analysis at the end of the chapter.

Controlling Costs

Every company strives to control costs to be competitive. An effective cost control practice is to hold managers responsible only for their **controllable costs.** A cost is controllable if a manager has the power to determine or at least markedly affect the amount incurred. **Uncontrollable costs** are not within the manager's control or influence. For example, direct materials cost is controllable by a production supervisor. On the other hand, costs related to production capacity are not controllable by that supervisor as that supervisor does not have authority to change factory size or add new machinery. Generally, variable production costs and fixed production costs are controlled at different levels of management. Similarly, variable selling and administrative costs are usually controlled at a level of management different from that which controls fixed selling and administrative costs.

Under absorption costing, both variable production costs and fixed production costs are included in product cost. This makes it difficult to evaluate the effectiveness of cost control by different levels of managers. Variable costing separates the variable costs from fixed costs and, therefore, makes it easier to identify and assign control over costs.

Decisions to change a company's fixed costs are usually assigned to higher-level managers. This is different from most variable costs that are assigned to lower-level managers and supervisors. When we separately report variable and fixed cost elements, as is done with an income statement in the **contribution format,** it highlights the impact of each cost element for income. This makes it easier for us to identify problem areas and to take cost control measures by appropriate levels of management. This approach is also useful in evaluating the performance of managers of different segments within a company.

Decision Maker

Internal Auditor Your company uses absorption costing for preparing its GAAP-based income statement and balance sheet. Management is disappointed because its external auditors are requiring it to write off an inventory amount because it exceeds what the company could reasonably sell in the foreseeable future. Why would management produce more than it sells? Why would management be disappointed about the write-off? ■ [Answers follow the chapter's Summary.]

CVP Analysis

The previous chapter discussed cost-volume-profit (CVP) analysis for making managerial decisions. If the income statement is prepared under variable costing and presented in the contribution format, the data needed for CVP analysis are readily available. However, if the income statement is prepared under absorption costing, the data needed for CVP analysis are not readily available. Thus, if absorption costing is used, substantial effort is needed to reclassify cost data in order to conduct CVP analysis.

Limitations of Reports Using Variable Costing

An important generally accepted accounting principle is that of matching. Most managers interpret the matching principle as expensing all manufacturing costs, both variable and fixed, in the period when the related product is sold rather than when costs are incurred. Thus, and despite the many useful applications and insights provided by variable cost reports, *absorption costing is the only acceptable basis for external reporting under both U.S. GAAP and IFRS.* Also, as we discussed, top executives are often awarded bonuses based on income computed using absorption costing. For income tax purposes, absorption costing is the only acceptable basis for filings with the Internal Revenue Service (IRS) under the Tax Reform Act of 1986. These realities contribute to the widespread use of absorption costing by companies.

QC3

Variable Costing for Service Firms

Although this chapter's examples used data for a manufacturer, variable costing also applies to service companies. Since service companies do not produce inventory, the differences in income from absorption and variable costing shown for a manufacturer do not apply. Still, a focus on variable costs can be useful in managerial decisions for service firms. One example is "special order" pricing for airlines when they sell tickets a day or so before a flight at deeply discounted prices. Provided the discounted price exceeds variable costs, such sales increase contribution margin and net income.

GLOBAL VIEW

U.S. multinational companies must change their business processes when moving their operations to international locations. These changes can impact the company's cost structure. For example, both **McDonald's** and **Yum Brands** offer delivery services in major international cities like Beijing (China) and Seoul (South Korea). Cities like these are heavily populated and real estate costs are high. These factors discourage the building of drive-through facilities, which would increase fixed overhead costs. Fixed overhead costs also fall as these companies process more orders over the Internet and thus build fewer call centers. As fixed overhead costs decrease, the difference in net income that would result from applying variable costing versus absorption costing also decreases.

Sustainability and Accounting **Happy Family Brands**'s focus on sustainability extends beyond organic raw materials to the packaging of its products. Many of the company's packaging materials are made from recyclable materials. Such materials increase variable costs but are consistent with the company's philosophy.

©Krzysztof Dydynski/Getty Images/Lonely Planet Images

Pricing Special Orders — Decision Analysis

A1 Use variable costing in pricing special orders.

Over the long run, prices must cover all fixed and variable costs. Over the short run, however, fixed production costs such as the cost to maintain plant capacity do not change with changes in production levels. With excess capacity, increases in production levels would increase variable production costs, but not fixed costs. This implies that while managers try to maintain the long-run price on existing orders, which covers all production costs, managers should accept special orders *provided the special order price exceeds variable cost.*

To illustrate, let's return to the data of IceAge Company. Recall that its variable production cost per unit is $15 and its total production cost per unit is $25 (at production level of 60,000 units). Assume that it receives a special order for 1,000 pairs of skates at an offer price of $22 per pair from a foreign skating school. This special order will not affect IceAge's regular sales and its plant has excess capacity to fill the order.

Drawing on absorption costing information, we observe that cost is $25 per unit and that the special order price is $22 per unit. These data would suggest that management reject the order as it would lose $3,000, computed as 1,000 units at $3 loss per pair ($22 − $25).

However, closer analysis suggests that this order should be accepted. This is because the $22 order price exceeds the $15 variable cost of the product. Specifically, Exhibit 19.17 reveals that the incremental revenue from accepting the order is $22,000 (1,000 units at $22 per unit), whereas the incremental production cost of the order is $15,000 (1,000 units at $15 per unit) and the incremental variable selling and administrative cost is $2,000 (1,000 units at $2 per unit). Thus, both its contribution margin and net income would increase by $5,000 from accepting the order. Variable costing reveals this profitable opportunity while absorption costing hides it.

Point: Use of relevant costs in special order and other managerial decisions is covered more extensively in a later chapter.

EXHIBIT 19.17

Computing Incremental Income for a Special Order

Rejecting Special Order		Accepting Special Order	
Incremental sales	$ 0	Incremental sales (1,000 × $22)	$22,000
Incremental costs	0	Incremental costs	
		Variable production cost (1,000 × $15)	15,000
		Variable selling and admin. expense (1,000 × $2)	2,000
Incremental income	$ 0	Incremental income................................	$ 5,000

The reason for increased income from accepting the special order lies in the different behavior of variable and fixed production costs. We see that if the order is rejected, only variable costs are saved. Fixed costs, on the other hand, do not change in the short run regardless of rejecting or accepting this order. Since incremental revenue from the order exceeds incremental costs (only variable cost in this case), accepting the special order increases company income.

Point: Fixed overhead costs won't increase when these additional units are sold because the company already has the capacity.

NEED-TO-KNOW

COMPREHENSIVE

Navaroli Company began operations on January 5, 2014. Cost and sales information for its first two calendar years of operations are summarized below.

Manufacturing costs		Production and sales data	
Direct materials..................	$80 per unit	Units produced, 2014	200,000 units
Direct labor......................	$120 per unit	Units sold, 2014................	140,000 units
Factory overhead costs for the year		Units in ending inventory, 2014 ...	60,000 units
Variable overhead	$30 per unit	Units produced, 2015	80,000 units
Fixed overhead................	$14,000,000	Units sold, 2015................	140,000 units
Nonmanufacturing costs		Units in ending inventory, 2015 ...	0 units
Variable selling and administrative ...	$10 per unit	Sales price per unit	$600 per unit
Fixed selling and administrative	$ 8,000,000		

Required

1. Prepare an income statement for the company for 2014 under absorption costing.
2. Prepare an income statement for the company for 2014 under variable costing.
3. Explain the source(s) of the difference in reported income for 2014 under the two costing methods.
4. Prepare an income statement for the company for 2015 under absorption costing.
5. Prepare an income statement for the company for 2015 under variable costing.
6. Prepare a schedule to convert variable costing income to absorption costing income for each of the years 2014 and 2015. Use the format in Exhibit 19.12.

PLANNING THE SOLUTION

- Set up a table to compute the unit cost under the two costing methods (refer to Exhibit 19.3).
- Prepare an income statement under both of the two costing methods (refer to Exhibit 19.6).
- Consider differences in the treatment of fixed production costs for the income statement to answer requirements 3 and 6.

SOLUTION

Before the income statement for 2014 is prepared, unit costs for 2014 are computed under the two costing methods as follows.

	Production Cost Per Unit	
	Absorption Costing	Variable Costing
Direct materials	$ 80	$ 80
Direct labor	120	120
Overhead		
Variable overhead	30	30
Fixed overhead*	70	—
Total production cost per unit	$300	$230

*Fixed overhead per unit = $14,000,000 ÷ 200,000 units = $70 per unit.

1. Absorption costing income statement for 2014.

NAVAROLI COMPANY Income Statement (Absorption Costing) For Year Ended December 31, 2014	
Sales (140,000 × $600)	$84,000,000
Cost of goods sold (140,000 × $300)	42,000,000
Gross margin	42,000,000
Selling and administrative expenses ($1,400,000 + $8,000,000)	9,400,000
Net income	$32,600,000

2. Variable costing income statement for 2014.

NAVAROLI COMPANY Income Statement (Variable Costing) For Year Ended December 31, 2014		
Sales (140,000 × $600)		$84,000,000
Variable expenses		
Variable production costs (140,000 × $230)	$32,200,000	
Variable selling and administrative costs	1,400,000	33,600,000
Contribution margin		50,400,000
Fixed expenses		
Fixed overhead	14,000,000	
Fixed selling and administrative	8,000,000	22,000,000
Net income		$28,400,000

3. Income under absorption costing is $4,200,000 more than that under variable costing even though sales are identical for each. This difference is due to the different treatment of fixed overhead cost. Under variable costing, the entire $14,000,000 of fixed overhead is expensed on the 2014 income statement. However, under absorption costing, $70 of fixed overhead cost is allocated to each of the 200,000 units produced. Since there were 60,000 units unsold at year-end, $4,200,000 (60,000 units × $70 per unit) of fixed overhead cost allocated to these units will be carried on its balance sheet in ending inventory. Consequently, reported income under absorption costing is $4,200,000 higher than variable costing income for the current period.

Before the income statement for 2015 is prepared, unit costs for production in 2015 are computed under the two costing methods as follows.

	Production Cost Per Unit	
	Absorption Costing	Variable Costing
Direct materials	$ 80	$ 80
Direct labor	120	120
Overhead		
Variable overhead	30	30
Fixed overhead*	175	—
Total production cost	$405	$230

*Fixed overhead per unit = $14,000,000/80,000 units = $175 per unit.

4. Absorption costing income statement for 2015.

NAVAROLI COMPANY Income Statement (Absorption Costing) For Year Ended December 31, 2015		
Sales (140,000 × $600)		$84,000,000
Cost of goods sold		
From beginning inventory (60,000 × $300)	$18,000,000	
Produced during the year (80,000 × $405)	32,400,000	50,400,000
Gross margin		33,600,000
Selling and administrative expenses ($1,400,000 + $8,000,000)		9,400,000
Net income		$24,200,000

5. Variable costing income statement for 2015.

NAVAROLI COMPANY Income Statement (Variable Costing) For Year Ended December 31, 2015		
Sales (140,000 × $600)		$84,000,000
Variable expenses		
Variable production costs (140,000 × $230)	$32,200,000	
Variable selling and administrative costs	1,400,000	33,600,000
Contribution margin		50,400,000
Fixed expenses		
Fixed overhead	14,000,000	
Fixed selling and administrative	8,000,000	22,000,000
Net income		$28,400,000

6. Conversion of variable costing income to absorption costing income.

	2014	2015
Variable costing income	$28,400,000	$28,400,000
Add: Fixed overhead cost deferred in ending inventory (60,000 × $70)	4,200,000	0
Less: Fixed overhead cost recognized from beginning inventory (60,000 × $70)	0	(4,200,000)
Absorption costing income	$32,600,000	$24,200,000

Point: Total income across the two years equals $56,800,000 under both costing methods. This is because the total number of units produced over these two years equals the total number of units sold over these two years.

Summary

C1 Describe how absorption costing can result in overproduction. Under absorption costing, fixed overhead costs are allocated to all units including both units sold and units in ending inventory. Consequently, expenses associated with the fixed overhead allocated to ending inventory are deferred to a future period. As a result, the larger ending inventory is, the more overhead cost is deferred to the future, and the greater current period income is.

A1 Use variable costing in pricing special orders. Over the short run, fixed production costs such as cost of maintaining plant capacity do not change with changes in production levels. When there is excess capacity, increases in production levels would only increase variable costs. Thus, managers should accept special orders as long as the order price is greater than the variable cost. This is because accepting the special order would increase only variable costs.

P1 Compute unit cost under both absorption and variable costing. Absorption cost per unit includes direct materials, direct labor, and *all* overhead, whereas variable cost per unit includes direct materials, direct labor, and only *variable* overhead.

P2 Prepare and analyze an income statement using absorption costing and using variable costing. The variable costing income statement differs from the absorption costing income statement in that it classifies expenses based on cost behavior rather than function. Instead of gross margin, the variable costing income statement shows contribution margin. This contribution margin format focuses attention on the relation between costs and sales that is not evident from the absorption costing format. Under absorption costing, some fixed overhead cost is allocated to ending inventory and is carried on the balance sheet to the next period. However, all fixed costs are expensed in the period incurred under variable costing. Consequently, absorption costing income is generally greater than variable costing income if units produced exceed units sold, and conversely.

P3 Convert income under variable costing to the absorption cost basis. Variable costing income can be adjusted to absorption costing income by adding the fixed cost allocated to ending inventory and subtracting the fixed cost previously allocated to beginning inventory.

P4 Determine product selling price based on absorption costing. Target selling prices can be determined by adding a markup to the total product cost under absorption costing. The markup should be enough to cover selling and administrative expenses, provide for a target profit, and yield a competitive price.

Guidance Answers to Decision Maker and Decision Ethics

Production Manager Under absorption costing, fixed production costs are spread over all units produced. Thus, fixed cost for each unit will be lower if more units are produced because the fixed cost is spread over more units. This means the company can increase income by producing excess units even if sales remain constant. With sales lagging, producing excess inventory leads to increased financing cost and inventory obsolescence. Also, producing excess inventory to meet income levels for bonuses harms company owners and is unethical. You must discuss this with the appropriate managers.

Internal Auditor If manager bonuses are tied to income, they would have incentives to increase income for personal gain. If absorption costing is used to determine income, management can reduce current period expenses (and raise income) with overproduction, which shifts fixed production costs to future periods. This decision fails to consider whether there is a viable market for all units that are produced. If there is not, an auditor can conclude that the inventory does not have "future economic value" and pressure management to write it off. Such a write-off reduces income by the cost of the excess inventory.

Key Terms

Absorption costing (also called **full costing**)
Contribution format
Contribution margin income statement
Controllable costs
Fixed overhead cost deferred in inventory
Fixed overhead cost recognized from inventory
Manufacturing margin
Uncontrollable costs
Variable costing (also called **direct** or **marginal costing**)

Multiple Choice Quiz

Answers at end of chapter

Answer questions 1 and 2 using the following company data.

Units produced	1,000
Variable costs	
Direct materials	$3 per unit
Direct labor	$5 per unit
Variable overhead	$3 per unit
Variable selling and administrative	$1 per unit
Fixed overhead	$3,000 total
Fixed selling and administrative	$1,000 total

1. Product cost per unit under absorption costing is:
a. $11 **b.** $12 **c.** $14 **d.** $15 **e.** $16

2. Product cost per unit under variable costing is:
a. $11 **b.** $12 **c.** $14 **d.** $15 **e.** $16

3. Under variable costing, which costs are included in product cost?
a. All variable product costs, including direct materials, direct labor, and variable overhead.
b. All variable and fixed allocations of product costs, including direct materials, direct labor, and both variable and fixed overhead.
c. All variable product costs except for variable overhead.
d. All variable and fixed allocations of product costs, except for both variable and fixed overhead.

4. The difference between product cost per unit under absorption costing as compared to that under variable costing is:
a. Direct materials and direct labor.
b. Fixed and variable portions of overhead.
c. Fixed overhead only.
d. Variable overhead only.

5. When production exceeds sales, which of the following is true?
a. No change occurs to inventories for either absorption costing or variable costing methods.
b. Use of absorption costing produces a higher net income than the use of variable costing.
c. Use of absorption costing produces a lower net income than the use of variable costing.
d. Use of absorption costing causes inventory value to decrease more than it would through the use of variable costing.

Icon denotes assignments that involve decision making.

Discussion Questions

1. What costs are normally included in product costs under variable costing?

2. What costs are normally included in product costs under absorption costing?

3. When units produced exceed units sold for a reporting period, would income under variable costing be greater than, equal to, or less than income under absorption costing? Explain.

4. Describe how the following items are computed: *a.* Gross margin, and *b.* Contribution margin.

5. How can absorption costing lead to incorrect short-run pricing decisions?

6. What conditions must exist to achieve accurate short-run pricing decisions using variable costing?

7. Describe the usefulness of variable costing for controlling company costs.

8. Describe how use of absorption costing in determining income can lead to overproduction and a buildup of inventory. Explain how variable costing can avoid this same problem.

9. What are the major limitations of variable costing?

10. **Google** uses variable costing for several business decisions. How can variable costing income statements be converted to absorption costing?

GOOGLE

11. Explain how contribution margin analysis is useful for managerial decisions and performance evaluations.

12. **Samsung**'s managers rely on reports of variable costs. How can variable costing reports prepared using the contribution margin format help managers in computing break-even volume in units?

Samsung

13. Assume that **Apple** has received a special order from a retailer for 1,000 specially outfitted iPads. This is a one-time order, which will not require any additional capacity or fixed costs. What should Apple consider when determining a selling price for these iPads?

APPLE

14. How can **Samsung** use variable costing to help better understand its operations and to make better pricing decisions?

Samsung

connect

QUICK STUDY

QS 19-1
Computing unit cost under absorption costing P1

Vijay Company reports the following information regarding its production costs. Compute its production cost per unit under absorption costing.

Direct materials	$10 per unit
Direct labor	$20 per unit
Overhead costs for the year	
Variable overhead	$10 per unit
Fixed overhead	$160,000
Units produced	20,000 units

QS 19-2
Computing unit cost under variable costing P1

Refer to Vijay Company's data in QS 19-1. Compute its production cost per unit under variable costing.

QS 19-3
Variable costing income statement P2

Aces Inc., a manufacturer of tennis rackets, began operations this year. The company produced 6,000 rackets and sold 4,900. Each racket was sold at a price of $90. Fixed overhead costs are $78,000 and fixed selling and administrative costs are $65,200. The company also reports the following per unit costs for the year. Prepare an income statement under variable costing.

Variable production costs	$25.00
Variable selling and administrative expenses	2.00

QS 19-4
Absorption costing income statement P2

Aces Inc., a manufacturer of tennis rackets, began operations this year. The company produced 6,000 rackets and sold 4,900. Each racket was sold at a price of $90. Fixed overhead costs are $78,000 and fixed selling and administrative costs are $65,200. The company also reports the following per unit costs for the year. Prepare an income statement under absorption costing.

Variable production costs	$25.00
Variable selling and administrative expenses	2.00

QS 19-5
Absorption costing and gross margin P2

Ramort Company reports the following cost data for its single product. The company regularly sells 20,000 units of its product at a price of $60 per unit. Compute gross margin under absorption costing.

Direct materials	$10 per unit
Direct labor	$12 per unit
Overhead costs for the year	
Variable overhead	$3 per unit
Fixed overhead per year	$40,000
Selling and adminstrative costs for the year	
Variable	$2 per unit
Fixed	$65,200
Normal production level (in units)	20,000 units

QS 19-6
Absorption costing and gross margin P2

Refer to the information about Ramort Company in QS 19-5. If Ramort doubles its production to 40,000 units while sales remain at the current 20,000-unit level, by how much would the company's gross margin increase or decrease under absorption costing?

QS 19-7
Variable costing and contribution margin P2

Refer to the information about Ramort Company in QS 19-5. Compute contribution margin under variable costing.

QS 19-8
Variable costing and contribution margin P2

Refer to the information about Ramort Company in QS 19-5. If Ramort doubles its production to 40,000 units while sales remain at the current 20,000-unit level, by how much would the company's contribution margin increase or decrease under variable costing?

QS 19-9
Computing manufacturing margin P2

D'Souza Company sold 10,000 units of its product at a price of $80 per unit. Total variable cost is $50 per unit, consisting of $40 in variable production cost and $10 in variable selling and administrative cost. Compute the manufacturing (production) margin for the company under variable costing.

QS 19-10
Computing contribution margin P2

D'Souza Company sold 10,000 units of its product at a price of $80 per unit. Total variable cost is $50 per unit, consisting of $40 in variable production cost and $10 in variable selling and administrative cost. Compute the contribution margin.

QS 19-11
Converting variable costing income to absorption costing P3

Diaz Company reports the following variable costing income statement for its single product. This company's sales totaled 50,000 units, but its production was 80,000 units. It had no beginning finished goods inventory for the current period.

DIAZ COMPANY Income Statement (Variable Costing)	
Sales (50,000 units × $60 per unit)	$3,000,000
Variable expenses	
Variable manufacturing expense (50,000 units × $28 per unit)	1,400,000
Variable selling and admin. expense (50,000 units × $5 per unit)	250,000
Total variable expenses	1,650,000
Contribution margin	1,350,000
Fixed expenses	
Fixed overhead	320,000
Fixed selling and administrative expense	160,000
Total fixed expenses	480,000
Net income	$ 870,000

1. Convert this company's variable costing income statement to an absorption costing income statement.
2. Explain the difference in income between the variable costing and absorption costing income statement.

QS 19-12
Converting variable costing income to absorption costing income P3

Ming Company had net income of $772,200 based on variable costing. Beginning and ending inventories were 7,800 units and 5,200 units, respectively. Assume the fixed overhead per unit was $3.00 for both the beginning and ending inventory. What is net income under absorption costing?

QS 19-13
Converting variable costing income to absorption costing income P3

Mortech had net income of $250,000 based on variable costing. Beginning and ending inventories were 50,000 units and 48,000 units, respectively. Assume the fixed overhead per unit was $0.75 for both the beginning and ending inventory. What is net income under absorption costing?

QS 19-14
Converting variable costing income to absorption costing income P3

Hong Co. had net income of $386,100 under variable costing. Beginning and ending inventories were 2,600 units and 3,900 units, respectively. Fixed overhead cost was $4.00 per unit for both the beginning and ending inventory. What is net income under absorption costing?

QS 19-15
Converting variable costing income to absorption costing income P3

E-Com had net income of $130,000 under variable costing. Beginning and ending inventories were 1,200 units and 4,900 units, respectively. Fixed overhead cost was $2.50 per unit for both the beginning and ending inventory. What is net income under absorption costing?

QS 19-16
Absorption costing and overproduction
C1

Under absorption costing a company had the following per unit costs when 10,000 units were produced.

Direct labor	$ 2
Direct material	3
Variable overhead	4
Total variable cost	9
Fixed overhead ($50,000/10,000 units)	5
Total production cost per unit	$14

1. Compute the company's total production cost per unit if 12,500 units had been produced.
2. Why might a manager of a company using absorption costing produce more units than can currently be sold?

QS 19-17
Absorption costing and product pricing
P4

A manufacturer reports the following information on its product. Compute the target selling price per unit under absorption costing.

Direct materials cost	$50 per unit
Direct labor cost	$12 per unit
Variable overhead cost	$6 per unit
Fixed overhead cost	$2 per unit
Target markup	40%

QS 19-18
Special order pricing
A1

Li Company produces a product that sells for $84 per unit. A customer contacts Li and offers to purchase 2,000 units of its product at a price of $68 per unit. Variable production costs with this order would be $30 per unit, and variable selling expenses would be $18 per unit. Assuming that this special order would not require any additional fixed costs, and that Li has sufficient capacity to produce the product without affecting regular sales, explain to Li's management why it might be a good decision to accept this special order.

connect

EXERCISES

Exercise 19-1
Computing unit and inventory costs under absorption costing
P1

Trio Company reports the following information for the current year, which is its first year of operations.

Direct materials	$15 per unit
Direct labor	$16 per unit
Overhead costs for the year	
Variable overhead	$ 80,000 per year
Fixed overhead	$160,000 per year
Units produced this year	20,000 units
Units sold this year	14,000 units
Ending finished goods inventory in units	6,000 units

1. Compute the cost per unit using absorption costing.
2. Determine the cost of ending finished goods inventory using absorption costing.
3. Determine the cost of goods sold using absorption costing.

Check (1) Absorption cost per unit, $43

Exercise 19-2
Computing unit and inventory costs under variable costing P2

Refer to the information in Exercise 19-1. Assume instead that Trio Company uses variable costing.

1. Compute the cost per unit using variable costing.
2. Determine the cost of ending finished goods inventory using variable costing.
3. Determine the cost of goods sold using variable costing.

Check (1) Variable cost per unit, $35

Exercise 19-3
Income reporting under absorption costing and variable costing
P2

Sims Company, a manufacturer of tablet computers, began operations on January 1, 2015. Its cost and sales information for this year follows.

Manufacturing costs	
Direct materials	$40 per unit
Direct labor	$60 per unit
Overhead costs for the year	
Variable overhead	$3,000,000
Fixed overhead	$7,000,000
Selling and administrative costs for the year	
Variable	$ 770,000
Fixed	$4,250,000
Production and sales for the year	
Units produced	100,000 units
Units sold	70,000 units
Sales price per unit	$350 per unit

Check (1) Variable costing income, $3,380,000

1. Prepare an income statement for the year using variable costing.
2. Prepare an income statement for the year using absorption costing.
3. Under what circumstance(s) is reported income identical under both absorption costing and variable costing?

Exercise 19-4
Variable costing income statement
P2

Kenzi Kayaking, a manufacturer of kayaks, began operations this year. During this first year, the company produced 1,050 kayaks and sold 800 at a price of $1,050 each. At this first year-end, the company reported the following income statement information using absorption costing.

Sales (800 × $1,050)	$840,000
Cost of goods sold (800 × $500)	400,000
Gross margin	440,000
Selling and administrative expenses	230,000
Net income	$210,000

Additional Information

a. Production cost per kayak totals $500, which consists of $400 in variable production cost and $100 in fixed production cost—the latter amount is based on $105,000 of fixed production costs allocated to the 1,050 kayaks produced.
b. The $230,000 in selling and administrative expense consists of $75,000 that is variable and $155,000 that is fixed.

1. Prepare an income statement for the current year under variable costing.
2. Explain the difference in income between the variable costing and absorption costing income statement.

Exercise 19-5
Absorption costing and variable costing income statements
P2

Rey Company's single product sells at a price of $216 per unit. Data for its single product for its first year of operations follow. Prepare an income statement for the year assuming (a) absorption costing and (b) variable costing.

Direct materials	$20 per unit
Direct labor	$28 per unit
Overhead costs	
Variable overhead	$ 6 per unit
Fixed overhead per year	$160,000 per year
Selling and administrative expenses	
Variable	$ 18 per unit
Fixed	$200,000 per year
Units produced (and sold)	20,000 units

Exercise 19-6
Absorption costing income statement
P2

Hayek Bikes prepares the income statement under variable costing for its managerial reports, and it prepares the income statement under absorption costing for external reporting. For its first month of operations, 375 bikes were produced and 225 were sold; this left 150 bikes in ending inventory. The income statement information under variable costing follows.

Sales (225 × $1,600)	$360,000
Variable production cost (225 × $625)	140,625
Variable selling and administrative expenses (225 × $65)	14,625
Contribution margin	204,750
Fixed overhead cost	56,250
Fixed selling and administrative expense	75,000
Net income	$ 73,500

1. Prepare this company's income statement for its first month of operations under absorption costing.
2. Explain the difference in income between the variable costing and absorption costing income statement.

Exercise 19-7
Income reporting under absorption costing and variable costing
P2

Oak Mart, a producer of solid oak tables, reports the following data from its second year of business.

Sales price per unit	$320 per unit	Manufacturing costs this year	
Units produced this year	115,000 units	Direct materials	$40 per unit
Units sold this year	118,000 units	Direct labor	$62 per unit
Units in beginning-year inventory	3,000 units	Overhead costs this year	
Beginning inventory costs		Variable overhead	$3,220,000
Variable (3,000 units × $135)	$405,000	Fixed overhead	$7,400,000
Fixed (3,000 units × $80)	240,000	Selling and adminstrative costs this year	
Total	$645,000	Variable	$1,416,000
		Fixed	4,600,000

1. Prepare the current year income statement for the company using variable costing.
2. Prepare the current year income statement for the company using absorption costing.
3. Explain any difference between the two income numbers under the two costing methods in parts 1 and 2.

Check (2) Absorption costing income, $8,749,000

Exercise 19-8
Contribution margin format income statement
P2

Polarix is a retailer of ATVs (all-terrain vehicles) and accessories. An income statement for its Consumer ATV Department for the current year follows. ATVs sell for $3,800 each. Variable selling expenses are $270 per ATV. The remaining selling expenses are fixed. Administrative expenses are 40% variable and 60% fixed. The company does not manufacture its own ATVs; it purchases them from a supplier for $1,830 each.

POLARIX
Income Statement—Consumer ATV Department
For Year Ended December 31, 2015

Sales		$646,000
Cost of goods sold		311,100
Gross margin		334,900
Operating expenses		
Selling expenses	$135,000	
Administrative expenses	59,500	194,500
Net income		$140,400

1. Prepare an income statement for this current year using the contribution margin format.
2. For each ATV sold during this year, what is the contribution toward covering fixed expenses and earning income?

Check (2) $1,560

Exercise 19-9
Income statement under absorption costing and variable costing
P1 P2

Cool Sky reports the following costing data on its product for its first year of operations. During this first year, the company produced 44,000 units and sold 36,000 units at a price of $140 per unit.

Manufacturing costs	
Direct materials per unit	$60
Direct labor per unit	$22
Variable overhead per unit	$8
Fixed overhead for the year	$528,000
Selling and administrative costs	
Variable selling and administrative cost per unit	$11
Fixed selling and administrative cost per year	$105,000

1. Assume the company uses absorption costing.
a. Determine its product cost per unit.
b. Prepare its income statement for the year under absorption costing.
2. Assume the company uses variable costing.
a. Determine its product cost per unit.
b. Prepare its income statement for the year under variable costing.

Check (1a) Absorption cost per unit, $102

(2a) Variable cost per unit, $90

Exercise 19-10
Computing absorption costing income
P3

A manufacturer reports the information below for three recent years. Compute income for each of the three years using absorption costing.

	Year 1	Year 2	Year 3
Variable costing income	$110,000	$114,400	$118,950
Beginning finished goods inventory (units)	0	1,200	700
Ending finished goods inventory (units)	1,200	700	800
Fixed manufacturing overhead per unit	$ 2.50	$ 2.50	$ 2.50

Exercise 19-11
Absorption costing and product pricing
P4

Sirhuds Inc., a maker of smartwatches, reports the information below on its product. The company uses absorption costing and has a target markup of 40% of absorption cost per unit. Compute the target selling price per unit under absorption costing.

Direct materials cost	$100 per unit
Direct labor cost	$30 per unit
Variable overhead cost	$8 per unit
Fixed overhead cost	$600,000 per year
Variable selling and administrative expenses	$3 per unit
Fixed selling and administrative expenses	$120,000 per year
Expected production (and sales)	50,000 units per year

Exercise 19-12
Absorption costing and overproduction
C1

Jacquie Inc. reports the following annual cost data for its single product.

Normal production and sales level	60,000 units
Sales price	$56.00 per unit
Direct materials	$9.00 per unit
Direct labor	$6.50 per unit
Variable overhead	$11.00 per unit
Fixed overhead	$720,000 in total

If Jacquie increases its production to 80,000 units, while sales remain at the current 60,000-unit level, by how much would the company's gross margin increase or decrease under absorption costing? Assume the company has idle capacity to double current production.

Exercise 19-13
Variable cost analysis for a services company
A1

Grand Garden is a luxury hotel with 150 suites. Its regular suite rate is $250 per night per suite. The hotel's cost per night is $140 per suite and consists of the following.

Variable direct labor and materials cost	$ 30
Fixed cost	110
Total cost per night per suite	$140

The hotel manager received an offer to hold the local Bikers' Club annual meeting at the hotel in March, which is the hotel's low season with an occupancy rate of under 50%. The Bikers' Club would reserve 50 suites for three nights if the hotel could offer a 50% discount, or a rate of $125 per night. The hotel manager is inclined to reject the offer because the cost per suite per night is $140. Prepare an analysis of this offer for the hotel manager. Explain (with supporting computations) whether the offer from the Bikers' Club should be accepted or rejected.

Exercise 19-14
Variable cost analysis for a services company
A1

Empire Plaza Hotel is a luxury hotel with 400 rooms. Its regular room rate is $300 per night per room. The hotel's cost is $165 per night per room and consists of the following.

Variable direct labor and materials cost	$ 40
Fixed cost	125
Total cost per night per room...........	$165

The hotel manager received an offer to hold the Junior States of America (JSA) convention at the hotel in February, which is the hotel's low season with an occupancy rate of under 45%. JSA would reserve 100 rooms for four nights if the hotel could offer a 50% discount, or a rate of $150 per night. The hotel manager is inclined to reject the offer because the cost per room per night is $165. Prepare an analysis of this offer for the hotel manager. Explain (with supporting computations) whether the offer from JSA should be accepted or rejected.

Exercise 19-15
Variable costing for services
A1

MidCoast Airlines provides charter airplane services. In October of this year, the company was operating at 60% of its capacity when it received a bid from the local community college. The college was organizing a Washington, D.C., trip for its international student group. The college budgeted only $30,000 for round-trip airfare. MidCoast Airlines normally charges between $50,000 and $60,000 for such service. MidCoast determined its cost for the round-trip flight to Washington to be $44,000, which consists of the following:

Variable cost......................	$15,000
Fixed cost (allocated)...............	29,000
Total cost.........................	$44,000

Although the manager at MidCoast supports the college's educational efforts, she could not justify accepting the $30,000 bid for the trip given the projected $14,000 loss. Still, she decides to consult with you, an independent financial consultant. Do you believe the airline should accept the bid from the college? Prepare a memorandum, with supporting computations, explaining why or why not.

Exercise 19-16
Analyzing income growth
P2

A recent annual report for **McDonald**'s reports the following operating income for its United States and Europe geographic segments:

In $ millions	2013	2012
United States	$3,779	$3,750
Europe	3,371	3,196

Required

1. Is operating income growing faster in the United States or in the Europe segment? Explain.
2. Is the difference in operating income growth due to the use of different costing methods (absorption or variable costing) in the two geographic segments? Explain.

PROBLEM SET A

Problem 19-1A
Variable costing income statement and conversion to absorption costing income (two consecutive years)
P2 P3

Dowell Company produces a single product. Its income statements under absorption costing for its first two years of operation follow.

	2014	2015
Sales ($46 per unit)	$920,000	$1,840,000
Cost of goods sold ($31 per unit)	620,000	1,240,000
Gross margin	300,000	600,000
Selling and administrative expenses	290,000	340,000
Net income	$ 10,000	$ 260,000

Additional Information

a. Sales and production data for these first two years follow.

	2014	2015
Units produced	30,000	30,000
Units sold	20,000	40,000

b. Variable cost per unit and total fixed costs are unchanged during 2014 and 2015. The company's $31 per unit product cost consists of the following.

Direct materials	$ 5
Direct labor	9
Variable overhead	7
Fixed overhead ($300,000/30,000 units)	10
Total product cost per unit	$31

c. Selling and administrative expenses consist of the following.

	2014	2015
Variable selling and administrative expenses ($2.50 per unit)	$ 50,000	$100,000
Fixed selling and administrative expenses	240,000	240,000
Total selling and administrative expenses	$290,000	$340,000

Required

Check (1) 2014 net loss, $(90,000)

1. Prepare income statements for the company for each of its first two years under variable costing.
2. Explain any difference between the absorption costing income and the variable costing income for these two years.

Problem 19-2A
Variable costing income statement and conversion to absorption costing income
P2 P3

Trez Company began operations this year. During this first year, the company produced 100,000 units and sold 80,000 units. The absorption costing income statement for this year follows.

Sales (80,000 units × $50 per unit)		$4,000,000
Cost of goods sold		
Beginning inventory	$ 0	
Cost of goods manufactured (100,000 units × $30 per unit)	3,000,000	
Cost of goods available for sale	3,000,000	
Ending inventory (20,000 × $30)	600,000	
Cost of goods sold		2,400,000
Gross margin		1,600,000
Selling and administrative expenses		530,000
Net income		$1,070,000

Additional Information

a. Selling and administrative expenses consist of $350,000 in annual fixed expenses and $2.25 per unit in variable selling and administrative expenses.

b. The company's product cost of $30 per unit is computed as follows.

Direct materials	$5 per unit
Direct labor	$14 per unit
Variable overhead	$2 per unit
Fixed overhead ($900,000/100,000 units)	$9 per unit

Required

1. Prepare an income statement for the company under variable costing.
2. Explain any difference between the income under variable costing (from part 1) and the income reported above.

Check (1) Variable costing income, $890,000

Problem 19-3A
Income reporting, absorption costing, and managerial ethics
P2 C1

Blazer Chemical produces and sells an ice-melting granular used on roadways and sidewalks in winter. It annually produces and sells about 100 tons of its granular. In its nine-year history, the company has never reported a net loss. However, because of this year's unusually mild winter, projected demand for its product is only 60 tons. Based on its predicted production and sales of 60 tons, the company projects the following income statement (under absorption costing).

Sales (60 tons at $21,000 per ton)	$1,260,000
Cost of goods sold (60 tons at $16,000 per ton)	960,000
Gross margin	300,000
Selling and administrative expenses	318,600
Net loss	$ (18,600)

Its product cost information follows and consists mainly of fixed cost because of its automated production process requiring expensive equipment.

Variable direct labor and material costs per ton	$ 3,500
Fixed cost per ton ($750,000 ÷ 60 tons)	12,500
Total product cost per ton	$16,000

Selling and administrative expenses consist of variable selling and administrative expenses of $310 per ton and fixed selling and administrative expenses of $300,000 per year. The company's president is concerned about the adverse reaction from its creditors and shareholders if the projected net loss is reported. The operations manager mentions that since the company has large storage capacity, it can report a net income by keeping its production at the usual 100-ton level even though it expects to sell only 60 tons. The president was puzzled by the suggestion that the company can report income by producing more without increasing sales.

Required

1. Can the company report a net income by increasing production to 100 tons and storing the excess production in inventory? Your explanation should include an income statement (using absorption costing) based on production of 100 tons and sales of 60 tons.
2. Should the company produce 100 tons given that projected demand is 60 tons? Explain, and also refer to any ethical implications of such a managerial decision.

PROBLEM SET B

Problem 19-1B
Variable costing income statement and conversion to absorption costing income (two consecutive years)
P2 P3

Azule Company produces a single product. Its income statements under absorption costing for its first two years of operation follow.

	2014	2015
Sales ($35 per unit)	$1,925,000	$2,275,000
Cost of goods sold ($26 per unit)	1,430,000	1,690,000
Gross margin	495,000	585,000
Selling and administrative expenses	465,000	495,000
Net income	$ 30,000	$ 90,000

Additional Information

a. Sales and production data for these first two years follow:

	2014	2015
Units produced	60,000	60,000
Units sold	55,000	65,000

b. Its variable cost per unit and total fixed costs are unchanged during 2014 and 2015. Its $26 per unit product cost consists of the following.

Direct materials	$ 4
Direct labor	6
Variable overhead	8
Fixed overhead ($480,000/60,000 units)	8
Total product cost per unit	$26

c. Its selling and administrative expenses consist of the following.

	2014	2015
Variable selling and administrative expenses ($3 per unit)	$165,000	$195,000
Fixed selling and administrative expenses	300,000	300,000
Total selling and administrative expenses	$465,000	$495,000

Required

Check (1) 2014 net loss, $(10,000)

1. Prepare this company's income statements under variable costing for each of its first two years.

2. Explain any difference between the absorption costing income and the variable costing income for these two years.

Problem 19-2B
Variable costing income statement and conversion to absorption costing income
P2 P3

E'Lonte Company began operations this year. During this first year, the company produced 300,000 units and sold 250,000 units. Its income statement under absorption costing for this year follows.

Sales (250,000 units × $18 per unit)		$4,500,000
Cost of goods sold		
Beginning inventory	$ 0	
Cost of goods manufactured (300,000 units × $7.50 per unit)	2,250,000	
Cost of goods available for sale	2,250,000	
Ending inventory (50,000 × $7.50)	375,000	
Cost of goods sold		1,875,000
Gross margin		2,625,000
Selling and administrative expenses		2,200,000
Net income		$ 425,000

Additional Information

a. Selling and administrative expenses consist of $1,200,000 in annual fixed expenses and $4 per unit in variable selling and administrative expenses.

b. The company's product cost of $7.50 per unit is computed as follows.

Direct materials	$2.00 per unit
Direct labor	$2.40 per unit
Variable overhead	$1.60 per unit
Fixed overhead ($450,000/300,000 units)	$1.50 per unit

Required

Check (1) Variable costing income, $350,000

1. Prepare the company's income statement under variable costing.

2. Explain any difference between the company's income under variable costing (from part 1) and the income reported above.

Problem 19-3B
Income reporting, absorption costing, and managerial ethics
P2 C1

Chem-Melt produces and sells an ice-melting granular used on roadways and sidewalks in winter. The company annually produces and sells about 300,000 pounds of its granular. In its ten-year history, the company has never reported a net loss. Because of this year's unusually mild winter, projected demand for its product is only 250,000 pounds. Based on its predicted production and sales of 250,000 pounds, the company projects the following income statement under absorption costing.

Sales (250,000 lbs. at $8 per lb.)	$2,000,000
Cost of goods sold (250,000 lbs. at $6.80 per lb.)	1,700,000
Gross margin	300,000
Selling and administrative expenses	450,000
Net loss	$ (150,000)

Its product cost information follows and consists mainly of fixed production cost because of its automated production process requiring expensive equipment.

Variable direct labor and materials costs per pound	$2.00
Fixed production cost per pound ($1,200,000/250,000 lbs.)	4.80
Total product cost per pound	$6.80

The company's selling and administrative expenses are all fixed. The president is concerned about the adverse reaction from its creditors and shareholders if the projected net loss is reported. The controller suggests that since the company has large storage capacity, it can report a net income by keeping its production at the usual 300,000-pound level even though it expects to sell only 250,000 pounds. The president was puzzled by the suggestion that the company can report a profit by producing more without increasing sales.

Required

1. Can the company report a net income by increasing production to 300,000 pounds and storing the excess production in inventory? Your explanation should include an income statement (using absorption costing) based on production of 300,000 pounds and sales of 250,000 pounds.
2. Should the company produce 300,000 pounds given that projected demand is 250,000 pounds? Explain, and also refer to any ethical implications of such a managerial decision.

SERIAL PROBLEM

Business Solutions
P2 P3

(This serial problem began in Chapter 1 and continues through most of the book. If previous chapter segments were not completed, the serial problem can begin at this point. It is helpful, but not necessary, to use the Working Papers that accompany the book.)

SP 19 Santana Rey expects sales of her line of computer workstation furniture to equal 300 workstations (at a sales price of $3,000) for 2016. The workstations' manufacturing costs include the following.

Direct materials	$800 per unit
Direct labor	$400 per unit
Variable overhead	$100 per unit
Fixed overhead	$24,000 per year

The selling expenses related to these workstations follow.

Variable selling expenses	$50 per unit
Fixed selling expenses	$4,000 per year

Santana is considering how many workstations to produce in 2016. She is confident that she will be able to sell any workstations in her 2016 ending inventory during 2017. However, Santana does not want to overproduce as she does not have sufficient storage space for many more workstations.

Required

1. Compute Business Solutions's absorption costing income assuming
   a. 300 workstations are produced.
   b. 320 workstations are produced.

[continued on next page]

2. Compute Business Solutions's variable costing income assuming
   a. 300 workstations are produced.
   b. 320 workstations are produced.
3. Explain to Santana any differences in the income figures determined in parts 1 and 2. How should Santana use the information from parts 1 and 2 to help make production decisions?

Beyond the Numbers

REPORTING IN ACTION
P2
APPLE

BTN 19-1 **Apple**'s ending inventory amounts (in $ millions) are shown below:

	2013	2012	2011
Ending inventory	$1,764	$791	$776

Required

1. Assume Apple uses variable costing for some of its internal reports. For each of the years 2013 and 2012, would net income based on variable costing be higher, lower, or no different from net income based on absorption costing? Explain.
2. Assume Apple is considering implementing a just-in-time (JIT) inventory system. Would a JIT system increase, decrease, or have no effect on differences in net income between absorption costing and variable costing? Explain.

COMPARATIVE ANALYSIS
P2
APPLE
GOOGLE

BTN 19-2 **Apple** offers repair service on its products. Assume that **Google** wants to offer in-home and online services for computer repair and support.

Required

1. What are some of the costs that Google must consider when deciding to offer these additional computer services? Are these costs different from what Apple must consider when offering additional new types of repair and support services?
2. Would variable or absorption costing be more useful to Google in analyzing whether repair and support services are profitable?

ETHICS CHALLENGE
C1

BTN 19-3 FDP Company produces a variety of home security products. Gary Price, the company's president, is concerned with the fourth quarter market demand for the company's products. Unless something is done in the last two months of the year, the company is likely to miss its earnings expectation of Wall Street analysts. Price still remembers when FDP's earnings were below analysts' expectation by two cents a share three years ago, and the company's share price fell 19% the day earnings were announced. In a recent meeting, Price told his top management that something must be done quickly. One proposal by the marketing vice president was to give a deep discount to the company's major customers to increase the company's sales in the fourth quarter. The company controller pointed out that while the discount could increase sales, it may not help the bottom line; to the contrary, it could lower income. The controller said, "Since we have enough storage capacity, we might simply increase our production in the fourth quarter to increase our reported profit."

Required

1. Gary Price is not sure how the increase in production without a corresponding increase in sales could help boost the company's income. Explain to Price how reported income varies with respect to production level.
2. Is there an ethical concern in this situation? If so, which parties are affected? Explain.

COMMUNICATING IN PRACTICE
P3

BTN 19-4 Mertz Chemical has three divisions. Its consumer product division faces strong competition from companies overseas. During its recent teleconference, Ryan Peterson, the consumer product division manager, reported that his division's sales for the current year were below its break-even point. However, when the division's annual reports were received, Billie Mertz, the company president, was surprised that the consumer product division actually reported a profit of $264,000. How could this be possible?

Required

Assume that you work in the corporate controller's office. Write a half-page memorandum to the president explaining how the division can report income even if its sales are below the break-even point.

TAKING IT TO THE NET
P2

BTN 19-5 This chapter discussed the variable costing method and how to use variable costing information to make various business decisions. We also can find several websites on variable costing and its business applications.

Required

1. Review the website of **Value Based Management** at **ValueBasedManagement.net.** Identify and print the site page on the topic of variable costing (**valuebasedmanagement.net/methods_variable_costing.html**).
2. What other phrases are used in practice for *variable costing*?
3. According to this website, what are the consequences of variable costing for profit calculation?

TEAMWORK IN ACTION
P4

BTN 19-6 This chapter identified several decision contexts in which managers use product cost information.

Required

Break into teams and identify at least one specific decision context in which absorption costing information is more relevant than variable costing information and at least one decision context in which variable costing information is more relevant than absorption costing. Be prepared to discuss your answers in class.

ENTREPRENEURIAL DECISION
P3

BTN 19-7 **Happy Family Brands**, which was launched by entrepreneur Shazi Visram, produces high-quality organic foods for babies, young children, and adults.

Required

1. The founder of Happy Family Brands uses variable costing in her business decisions. If Happy Family Brands used absorption costing, would you expect the company's income to be more, less than, or about the same as its income measured under variable costing? Explain.

HITTING THE ROAD
A1

BTN 19-8 Visit a local hotel and observe its daily operating activities. The costs associated with some of its activities are variable while others are fixed with respect to occupancy levels.

Required

1. List cost items that are likely variable for the hotel.
2. List cost items that are likely fixed for the hotel.
3. Compare the fixed cost items with variable cost items. Rank costs within each category based on your perception of which ones you believe are the larger.
4. Based on your observations and the answers to parts 1 through 3, explain why many hotels offer discounts as high as 50% or more during their low occupancy season.

GLOBAL DECISION
P2

Samsung
APPLE

BTN 19-9 Assume that **Samsung** (**Samsung.com**) is considering offering a service similar to **Apple**'s iTunes music download store. However, instead of developing the division internally, Samsung is considering buying a company that already offers such services.

Required

Would absorption or variable costing be most useful to Samsung in evaluating whether to acquire an existing business that provides services similar to iTunes? Explain.

ANSWERS TO MULTIPLE CHOICE QUIZ

1. c; \$14, computed as \$3 + \$5 + \$3 + (\$3,000/1,000 units).
2. a; \$11, computed as \$3 + \$5 + \$3 (consisting of all variable product costs).
3. a
4. c
5. b

chapter 20

Master Budgets and Performance Planning

Chapter Preview

BUDGET PROCESS AND ADMINISTRATION

C1 Budgeting as a management tool

Benefits of budgeting

Budgeting and human behavior

Budget reporting and timing

Budget committee

THE MASTER BUDGET

C2 Budget components

P1 Operating budgets—including sales; production; selling; administrative

Direct materials budget

Direct labor budget

Factory overhead budget

Capital expenditures budget

P2 Cash budget

BUDGETED FINANCIAL STATEMENTS

P3 Budgeted income statement

Budgeted balance sheet

Using the master budget

A1 Activity-based budgeting

P4 *Appendix:* Master budget—merchandiser

Learning Objectives

CONCEPTUAL

C1 Describe the benefits of budgeting and the process of budget administration.

C2 Describe a master budget and the process of preparing it.

ANALYTICAL

A1 Analyze expense planning using activity-based budgeting.

PROCEDURAL

P1 Prepare the operating budget components of a master budget—for a manufacturing company.

P2 Prepare a cash budget.

P3 Prepare budgeted financial statements.

P4 *Appendix 20A*—Prepare each component of a master budget and link each to the budgeting process—for a merchandising company.

MONTERREY, MEXICO—To fulfill requirements for his high school degree, Daniel Gómez Iñiguez completed a project on how to make biodiesel fuel from vegetable oil and animal fats. "Searching the Internet, I realized it is real easy to make biodiesel at your home," explains Daniel. As Daniel's interest in making biodiesel grew, he expanded his knowledge by taking college courses on biodiesel production and joining an informal biodiesel club. His efforts led to connections with three partners—Guillermo Colunga, Antonio Lopez, and Maurico Pareja—and the group started **Solben**, a company that sells technology for biodiesel production.

Like most entrepreneurs, the partners faced challenges in getting their business going. "We regularly entered entrepreneurship competitions, knowing we had no chance to win," admits Daniel. "The competitions wanted business plans and budgets, and we didn't have those. But we learned something every time." This continual learning enabled the company to find a niche by developing technology that can be effective in a developing economy. "Large plants are costly to build and expensive to operate," says Daniel, "but most homegrown systems produce low-quality fuel. Our system makes high-quality fuel, even at small volumes, and it is modular, so the plant can grow as demand grows."

As Solben grew, budgeting and the budgeting process became increasingly important. Daniel explains that budgets help formalize business plans and goals and help direct and monitor employees. Budgeted income statements enable managers to assess how changes in materials, labor, and overhead impact the bottom line. As Solben expanded its sales and its work force grew, the partners began developing more formal plans and budgets. "Budgeting gives us a plan of where we want to go," asserts Daniel. "Still, we must never stop learning and adapting our plans." Although budgets are expressed in monetary terms, Daniel says that "money is not the only way to measure success. Success is based on the number of people you can impact in a positive way."

Daniel offers advice for budding entrepreneurs. "Do something you are really passionate about. And don't be afraid of failure. Failure is positive if you learn from it. Always keep learning." In Solben's case, this emphasis on learning has led to sales of over $3 million in a recent year, and an over 85 percent share of Mexico's market for biodiesel technology production. And, the company continues to plan for more growth—into the United States and ultimately a listing on the Mexican stock exchange.

Courtesy of Daniel E. Gómez Iñiguez and Solben

Full of Energy

"Success is a path . . . you determine how long it is"

—Daniel Gómez Iñiguez

Sources: *Solben website,* January 2015; *billionsuccess.com* interview, July 21, 2012; *Mother Nature Network,* April 27, 2012; *news.niagara.edu,* November 15, 2012

BUDGET PROCESS AND ADMINISTRATION

C1

Describe the benefits of budgeting and the process of budget administration.

Budgeting as a Management Tool

An important management objective in large companies is to ensure that activities of all departments contribute to meeting the company's overall goals. This requires coordination. Budgeting helps to achieve this coordination. The budgeting process coordinates the activities of various departments to meet the company's overall goals.

Most companies prepare long-term strategic plans spanning 5 to 10 years. They then fine-tune them in medium-term and short-term plans. Long-term strategic plans provide a road map for the future about potential opportunities such as new products, markets, and investments. Medium- and short-term plans are more operational and translate strategic plans into actions. These action plans are fairly concrete and consist of defined objectives and goals.

Short-term financial plans are called *budgets* and typically cover a one-year period. A **budget** is a formal statement of a company's future plans. It is usually expressed in monetary terms because the economic or financial aspects of the business are the primary factors driving management's decisions. All managers should be involved in **budgeting,** the process of planning future business actions and expressing them as formal plans. Managers who participate in a budgeting process increase the likelihood of both personal and company success.

Benefits of Budgeting

Budgets help fulfill the key managerial functions of planning and controlling. There are several benefits to having a written budget:

- A budget focuses on the future opportunities and threats to the organization. This focus on the future is important, because the daily pressures of operating an organization can divert management's attention to planning. The budgeting system counteracts this tendency by formalizing the planning process and demanding input. Budgeting makes planning an explicit management responsibility.
- The control function requires management to evaluate (benchmark) operations against some norm. Since budgeted performance takes into account important company, industry, and economic factors, a comparison of actual to budgeted performance provides an effective monitoring and control system. This evaluation assists management in identifying problems and taking corrective actions if necessary.
- An important management objective in large companies is to ensure that the activities of all departments contribute to meeting the company's overall goals. This requires coordination. Budgeting helps to achieve this coordination across departments.
- A written budget is an effective way to communicate management's specific action plans to all employees. When plans are not written down, conversations can lead to uncertainty and confusion among employees.
- Budgets can be used to motivate employees. Budgeted performance levels can provide goals for employees to attain or even exceed. Many companies provide incentives, like cash bonuses, for employee performance that meets or exceeds budget goals.

Decision Insight

Incentive Pay Budgets are important in determining managers' pay. A recent survey shows that 82% of large companies tie managers' bonus payments to beating budget goals. For these companies, bonus payments are frequently more than 20% of total manager pay. ■

Budgeting and Human Behavior

Budgets provide standards for evaluating performance and can affect the attitudes of employees evaluated by them. Budgeting can be used to create a positive effect on employees' attitudes, but it can also create negative effects if not properly applied. Budgeted levels of performance, for instance, must be realistic to avoid discouraging employees. Personnel who will be evaluated should be consulted and involved in preparing the budget to increase their commitment to meeting it. Performance evaluations must allow the affected employees to explain the reasons for apparent performance deficiencies.

The budgeting process has three important guidelines:

1. Employees affected by a budget should be consulted when it is prepared (*participatory budgeting*).
2. Goals reflected in a budget should be attainable.
3. Evaluations should be made carefully with opportunities to explain differences between actual and budgeted amounts.

Budgeting can be a positive motivating force when these guidelines are followed.

Managers must also be aware of potential negative outcomes of budgeting. Under participatory budgeting, some employees might understate sales budgets and overstate expense budgets to allow themselves a cushion, or *budgetary slack,* to aid in meeting targets. For some businesses, pressure to meet budgeted results might lead employees to engage in unethical behavior or commit fraud. Finally, some employees might always spend their budgeted amounts, even on unnecessary items, to ensure their budgets aren't reduced for the next period.

Example: Assume a company's sales force receives a bonus when sales exceed the budgeted amount. How would this arrangement affect the participatory sales forecasts? *Answer:* Sales reps may understate their budgeted sales.

Budget Reporting and Timing

The budget period usually coincides with the accounting period. Most companies prepare at least an annual budget, which reflects the objectives for the next year. To provide specific guidance, the annual budget usually is separated into quarterly or monthly budgets. These short-term budgets allow management to periodically evaluate performance and take corrective action.

Companies Using Rolling Budgets

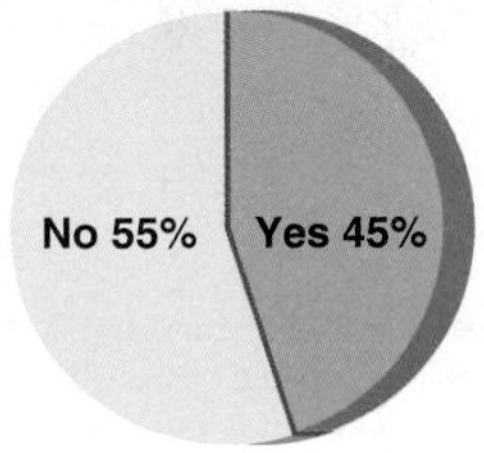

The time period required for the annual budgeting process can vary considerably. Large, complex organizations usually require a longer time to prepare their budgets than do smaller organizations. This is so because considerable effort is required to coordinate the different units (departments) within large organizations.

Many companies apply **continuous budgeting** by preparing **rolling budgets.** As each monthly or quarterly budget period goes by, these companies revise their entire set of budgets for the months or quarters remaining and add new monthly or quarterly budgets to replace the ones that have lapsed. Thus, at any point in time, monthly or quarterly budgets are available for the next 12 months or four quarters. Exhibit 20.1 shows rolling budgets prepared at the end of five consecutive periods. The first set (at top) is prepared in December 2014 and covers the four calendar quarters of 2015. In March 2015, the company prepares another rolling budget for the next four quarters through March 2016. This same process is repeated every three months. As a result, management is continuously planning ahead.

Exhibit 20.1 reflects an annual budget composed of four quarters, prepared four times per year using the most recent information available. When continuous budgeting is not used, the fourth-quarter budget is nine months old and perhaps out of date when applied.

EXHIBIT 20.1

Rolling Budgets

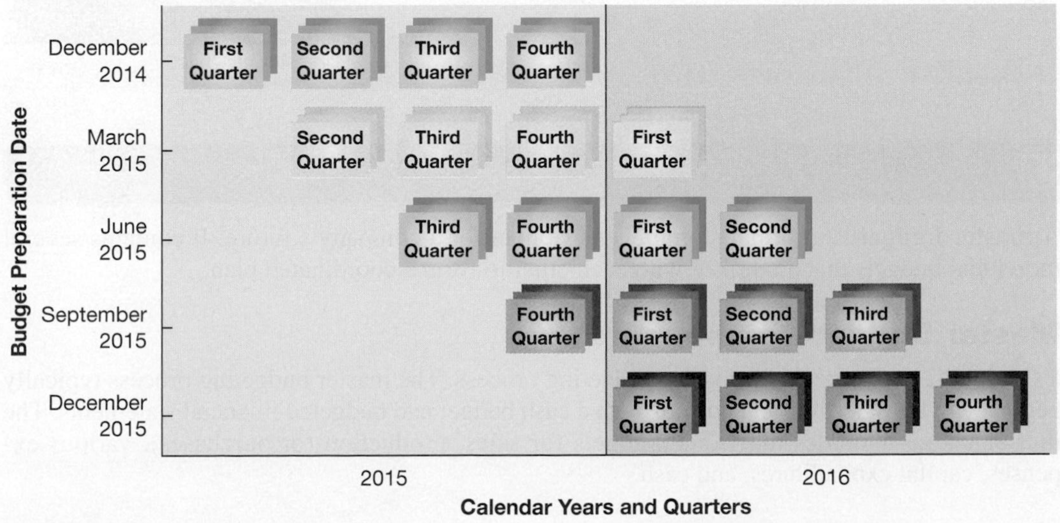

Decision Insight

Budget Calendar Many companies use long-range operating budgets. For large companies, three groups usually determine or influence the budgets: creditors, directors, and management. All three are interested in the companies' future cash flows and earnings. The annual budget process often begins six months or more before the budget is due to the board of directors. When rolling budgets are used, directors must be aware that management's updated budgets might be used to mask poor performance. ■

Budget Committee

The task of preparing a budget should not be the sole responsibility of any one department. Similarly, the budget should not be simply handed down as top management's final word. Instead, budget figures and budget estimates developed through a *bottom-up* process usually are more useful. This includes, for instance, involving the sales department in preparing sales estimates. Likewise, the production department should have initial responsibility for preparing its own expense budget. Without active employee involvement in preparing budget figures, there is a risk these employees will feel that the numbers fail to reflect their special problems and needs.

Although most budgets should be developed using a bottom-up process, the budgeting system requires central guidance. This guidance is supplied by a budget committee of department heads and other executives responsible for seeing that budgeted amounts are realistic and coordinated. If a department submits initial budget figures that do not reflect efficient performance, the budget committee should return them with explanatory comments on how to improve them. Then the originating department must either adjust its proposals or explain why they are acceptable. Communication between the originating department and the budget committee should continue as needed to ensure that both parties accept the budget as reasonable, attainable, and desirable.

Point: In a large company, developing a budget through a bottom-up process can involve hundreds of employees and take several weeks to finalize.

Decision Insight

Strategic Planning Most companies allocate dollars based on budgets submitted by department managers. These managers verify the numbers and monitor the budget. Managers must remember, however, that a budget is judged by its success in helping achieve the company's mission. One analogy is that a hiker must know the route to properly plan a hike and monitor hiking progress. ■

Pixland/AGE fotostock

THE MASTER BUDGET

C2 Describe a master budget and the process of preparing it.

A **master budget** is a formal, comprehensive plan for a company's future. It contains several individual budgets that are linked with each other to form a coordinated plan.

Master Budget Components

Exhibit 20.2 summarizes the master budgeting process. The master budgeting process typically begins with the sales budget and ends with a cash budget and budgeted financial statements. The master budget includes individual budgets for sales, production (or purchases), various expenses, capital expenditures, and cash.

EXHIBIT 20.2

Master Budget Process for a Manufacturer

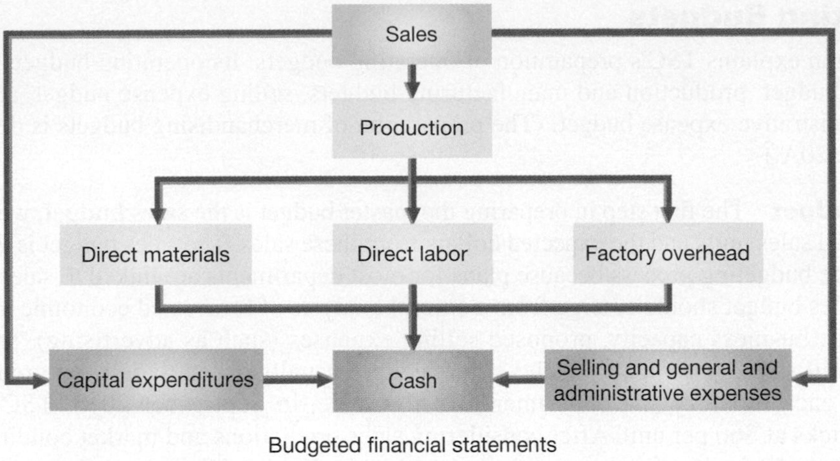

The usual number and types of budgets included in a master budget depend on the company's size and complexity. A manufacturer's master budget should include, at a minimum, several operating budgets (shown in yellow in Exhibit 20.2), a capital expenditures budget, and a cash budget. Managers also often express the expected financial results of these planned activities with a budgeted balance sheet and a budgeted income statement. Some budgets require the input of other budgets. For example, direct materials and direct labor budgets cannot be prepared until a production budget is prepared. A company cannot plan its production until it prepares a sales budget.

Point: Merchandisers prepare *merchandise purchase* budgets instead of the operating budgets in Exhibit 20.2.

The rest of this chapter explains how Toronto Sticks Company (TSC), a manufacturer of youth hockey sticks, prepares its master budget. Its master budget includes operating, capital expenditures, and cash budgets for each month in each quarter. It also includes a budgeted income statement for each quarter and a budgeted balance sheet as of the last day of each quarter. We show how TSC prepares budgets for October, November, and December 2015. Exhibit 20.3 presents TSC's balance sheet at the start of this budgeting period, which we often refer to as we prepare the component budgets.

Courtesy of JJW Images

EXHIBIT 20.3

Balance Sheet Prior to the Budgeting Periods

TORONTO STICKS COMPANY
Balance Sheet
September 30, 2015

Assets		
Cash		$ 20,000
Accounts receivable		25,200
Raw materials inventory (178 pounds @ $20)		3,560
Finished goods inventory (1,010 units @ $17)		17,170
Equipment*	$200,000	
Less: Accumulated depreciation	36,000	164,000
Total assets		$229,930
Liabilities and Equity		
Liabilities		
Accounts payable	$ 7,060	
Income taxes payable (due 10/31/2015)	20,000	
Note payable	10,000	$ 37,060
Stockholders' equity		
Common stock	150,000	
Retained earnings	42,870	192,870
Total liabilities and equity		$229,930

* Equipment is depreciated on a straight-line basis over 10 years (salvage value is $20,000).

P1

Prepare the operating budget components of a master budget—for a manufacturing company.

Operating Budgets

This section explains TSC's preparation of operating budgets. Its operating budgets consist of the sales budget, production and manufacturing budgets, selling expense budget, and general and administrative expense budget. (The preparation of merchandising budgets is described in Appendix 20A.)

Sales Budget The first step in preparing the master budget is the **sales budget,** which shows the planned sales units and the expected dollars from these sales. The sales budget is the starting point in the budgeting process because plans for most departments are linked to sales.

The sales budget should emerge from a careful analysis of forecasted economic and market conditions, business capacity, proposed selling expenses (such as advertising), and predictions of unit sales. A company's sales personnel are usually asked to develop predictions of sales for each territory and department. To illustrate, in September 2015, TSC sold 700 hockey sticks at $60 per unit. After considering sales predictions and market conditions, TSC prepares its sales budget for the next three months (see Exhibit 20.4). Note that the sales budget in Exhibit 20.4 includes forecasts of both unit sales and unit prices. Some sales budgets are expressed only in total sales dollars, but most are more detailed. Management finds it useful to know budgeted units and unit prices for many different products, regions, departments, and sales representatives.

EXHIBIT 20.4

Sales Budget

	A	B	C	D	E
1	TORONTO STICKS COMPANY				
2	Sales Budget				
3	October 2015–December 2015				
4		October	November	December	Totals
5	Budgeted sales (units)	1,000	800	1,400	3,200
6	Selling price per unit	× $ 60	× $ 60	× $ 60	× $ 60
7	Total budgeted sales (dollars)	$60,000	$48,000	$84,000	$192,000
8					

Decision Maker

Entrepreneur You run a start-up that manufactures designer clothes. Business is seasonal, and fashions and designs quickly change. How do you prepare reliable annual sales budgets? ■ [Answers follow the chapter's Summary.]

Production Budget A manufacturer prepares a **production budget,** which shows the number of units to be produced in a period. The production budget is based on the unit sales projected in the sales budget, along with inventory considerations. Manufacturers often determine a certain amount of **safety stock,** a quantity of inventory that provides protection against lost sales caused by unfulfilled demands from customers or delays in shipments from suppliers. Exhibit 20.5 shows the general computation of the production required for a period. ***A production budget does not show costs; it is always expressed in units of product.***

EXHIBIT 20.5

Computing Production Requirements

Budgeted ending inventory (units of safety stock) + **Budgeted sales units for the period (from the sales budget)** = **Required units needed for the period** − **Number of units in beginning inventory** = **Total units to be produced in the period**

In a *safety stock inventory system,* companies maintain sufficient inventory to reduce the risk and cost of running short. This practice requires enough production or purchases to satisfy the budgeted sales amounts. To illustrate, after assessing the cost of keeping inventory along with the risk and cost of inventory shortages, TSC decided that the number of units in its finished goods inventory at each month-end should equal 90% of next month's predicted sales. For example, inventory at the end of October should equal 90% of budgeted November sales, and so on. This information along with knowledge of 1,010 units in inventory at September 30 (see Exhibit 20.3) allows the company to prepare the production budget shown in Exhibit 20.6. The

Example: Under a JIT system, how will a sales budget differ from a merchandise purchases or production budget? *Answer:* The two budgets will be similar because future inventory should be near zero.

EXHIBIT 20.6

Production Budget

	A	B	C	D
1	TORONTO STICKS COMPANY			
2	Production Budget			
3	October 2015–December 2015			
4		October	November	December
5	Next month's budgeted sales (units) from Sales Budget*	800	1,400	900
6	Ratio of inventory to future sales	× 90%	× 90%	× 90%
7	Budgeted ending inventory (units)	720	1,260	810
8	Add: Budgeted sales (units)	1,000	800	1,400
9	Required units of available production	1,720	2,060	2,210
10	Deduct: Beginning inventory (units)	1,010**	720	1,260
11	Units to be produced	710	1,340	950
12				

*From Sales Budget (Exhibit 22.4); January budgeted sales of 900 units from next quarter's sales budget.
**October's beginning inventory (1,010 units) is inconsistent with company policy.

actual number of units of ending inventory at September 30 is not consistent with TSC's policy. This is not uncommon, as sales forecasts are uncertain and production can sometimes be disrupted.

Courtesy of JJW Images

The first three lines of TSC's production budget determine the budgeted ending inventories (in units). Budgeted unit sales are then added to the budgeted ending inventory to give the required units of production. We then subtract beginning inventory to determine the budgeted number of units to be produced. The information about units to be produced provides the basis for *manufacturing budgets* for the production costs of those units—direct materials, direct labor, and overhead.

Decision Insight

Just-in-Time Inventory Systems Managers of *just-in-time* (JIT) inventory systems use sales budgets for short periods (often as few as one or two days) to order just enough merchandise or materials to satisfy the immediate sales demand. This keeps the amount of inventory to a minimum (or zero in an ideal situation). A JIT system minimizes the costs of maintaining inventory, but it is practical only if customers are content to order in advance or if managers can accurately determine short-term sales demand. Suppliers also must be able and willing to ship small quantities regularly and promptly. ■

Point: Accurate estimates of future sales are crucial in a JIT system.

NEED-TO-KNOW 20-1

Production Budget

P1

A manufacturing company predicts sales of 220 units for May and 250 units for June. The company wants each month's ending inventory to equal 30% of next month's predicted unit sales. Beginning inventory for May is 66 units. Compute the company's budgeted production in units for May.

Solution

Production Budget	Units
Budgeted ending inventory for May (250 × 30%)	75
Plus: Budgeted sales for May	220
Required units of available production	295
Less: Beginning inventory	(66)
Total units to be produced	229

QC1

Do More: QS 20-12, QS 20-16, QS 20-17, E 20-3, E 20-10, E 20-11

Direct Materials Budget The **direct materials budget** shows the budgeted costs for the direct materials that will need to be purchased to satisfy the estimated production for the period. Whereas the production budget shows *units* to be produced, the direct materials budget translates the units to be produced into budgeted *costs*. (The same is true for the other two manufacturing budgets that we will discuss below—the direct labor budget and the factory overhead budget).

To develop a direct materials budget, companies need the following inputs:

- Number of units to produce (from the production budget).
- Materials requirements per unit—How many units (pounds, gallons, etc.) of direct materials go into each unit of finished product?
- Budgeted ending inventory (in units) of direct materials—As with finished goods, most companies maintain a safety stock of materials to ensure that production can continue.
- Beginning inventory (in units) of direct materials.
- Cost per unit of direct materials.

Using these inputs the company can then prepare a direct materials budget. As an example, Exhibit 20.7 shows the direct materials budget for TSC. This budget begins with the budgeted production, taken directly from the production budget. Next, TSC needs to know the amount of direct materials needed for each of the units to be produced—in this case, half a pound (.5) of wood. With these two inputs we can now compute the amount of direct materials needed for production. For example, to produce 710 hockey sticks in October, TSC will need 355 pounds of wood (710 units × 0.5 lbs. = 355 lbs.).

EXHIBIT 20.7

Direct Materials Budget

	A	B	C	D
1	TORONTO STICKS COMPANY			
2	Direct Materials Budget			
3	October 2015–December 2015			
4		October	November	December
5	Budgeted production units*	710	1,340	950
6	Materials requirements per unit	× 0.5	× 0.5	× 0.5
7	Materials needed for production (pounds)	355	670	475
8	Add: Budgeted ending inventory (pounds)	335	237.5	247.5**
9	Total materials requirements (pounds)	690	907.5	722.5
10	Deduct: Beginning inventory (pounds)	(178)	(335)	(237.5)
11	Materials to be purchased (pounds)	512	572.5	485.0
12				
13	Material price per pound	$ 20	$ 20	$ 20
14	Total cost of direct materials purchases	$10,240	$11,450	$9,700
15				

*From Production Budget (Exhibit 20.6)
**Computed from January 2016 production requirements, assumed to be 990 units.

The company then needs to consider its safety stock of direct materials. TSC has determined that it wants to have a safety stock of direct materials on hand at the end of each month to complete 50% of the budgeted units to be produced in the next month. Since TSC expects to produce 1,340 units in November, requiring 670 pounds of materials, it needs ending inventory of direct materials of 335 pounds (50% × 670) at the end of October. TSC's total direct materials requirement for October is therefore 690 pounds (355 + 335).

TSC already has 178 pounds of direct materials in its beginning inventory (refer to Exhibit 20.3). TSC deducts the amount of direct materials that were in beginning inventory from the total materials requirements for the month. For October, the calculation is 690 pounds − 178 pounds, resulting in the need for 512 pounds of direct materials to be purchased in October.

The direct materials budget next translates the *pounds* of direct materials to be purchased into budgeted *costs*. TSC estimates that the cost of direct materials will be $20 per pound over the quarter. At $20 per pound, purchasing 512 pounds of direct materials for October production will cost $10,240 (computed as $20 × 512). Similar calculations are done to compute the cost of direct materials purchases for November ($11,450) and December ($9,700). (For December, assume the budgeted ending inventory of direct materials, based on January's production requirements, is 247.5 pounds). (*Note*: If the company expects direct materials costs to change in the future, it can easily work those changes into the direct materials budget. For example, if it expected the price of wood to jump to $25 per pound in December—say, because a long-term contract with the supplier was about to expire—it could simply change that number in the direct materials budget.)

Direct Labor Budget The **direct labor budget** shows the budgeted costs for the direct labor that will be needed to satisfy the estimated production for the period. Because there is no "inventory" of labor, the direct labor budget is easier to prepare than the direct materials budget. TSC's direct labor budget is shown in Exhibit 20.8. Fifteen minutes of labor time (a quarter of an hour) is required to produce one unit. Labor is paid at the rate of $12 per hour. Budgeted labor hours are computed by multiplying the budgeted production level for each month by one-quarter (0.25) of an hour. Direct labor cost is then computed by multiplying budgeted labor hours by the labor rate of $12 per hour.

Point: A quarter of an hour can be expressed as 0.25 hours.

EXHIBIT 20.8

Direct Labor Budget

	A	B	C	D
1	TORONTO STICKS COMPANY			
2	Direct Labor Budget			
3	October 2015–December 2015			
4		October	November	December
5	Budgeted production (units)*	710	1,340	950
6	Labor requirements per unit (hours)	× 0.25	× 0.25	× 0.25
7	Total labor hours needed	177.5	335	237.5
8				
9	Labor rate (per hour)	$ 12	$ 12	$ 12
10	Labor dollars	$2,130	$4,020	$2,850
11				

*From Production Budget (Exhibit 20.6)

As before, estimated changes in direct labor costs can be easily shown in the budgeting process. Companies thus can ensure the right amount of labor for periods in which production is expected to change or to take into account expected changes in hourly labor rates.

NEED-TO-KNOW 20-2

Direct Materials and Direct Labor Budgets

P1

A manufacturing company budgets production of 800 units during June and 900 units during July. Each unit of finished goods requires 2 pounds of direct materials, at a cost of $8 per pound. The company maintains an inventory of direct materials equal to 10% of next month's budgeted production. Beginning direct materials inventory for June is 160 pounds. Each finished unit requires 1 hour of direct labor at the rate of $14 per hour. Compute the budgeted (a) cost of direct materials purchases for June and (b) direct labor cost for June.

Solution

a.

Direct Materials Budget	
Budgeted production (units)	800
Materials requirements per unit (lbs.)	× 2
Materials needed for production (lbs.)	1,600
Add: Budgeted ending inventory (lbs.)	180*
Total materials requirements (lbs.)	1,780
Less: Beginning inventory (lbs.)	(160)
Materials to be purchased (lbs.)	1,620
Material price per pound	$ 8
Total cost of direct materials purchases	$12,960

*900 units × 2 lbs. per unit × 10% = 180 lbs.

b.

Direct Labor Budget	
Budgeted production (units)	800
Labor requirements per unit (hours)	× 1
Total direct labor hours needed	800
Labor rate (per hour)	$ 14
Direct labor cost (June)	$11,200

Do More: QS 20-7, QS 20-8, QS 20-13, QS 20-14, E 20-4, E 20-5, E 20-8

Factory Overhead Budget The **factory overhead budget** shows the budgeted costs for factory overhead that will be needed to complete the estimated production for the period. TSC's factory overhead budget is shown in Exhibit 20.9. TSC separates variable and fixed overhead costs in its overhead budget, as do many companies.

EXHIBIT 20.9

Factory Overhead Budget

	A	B	C	D
1	TORONTO STICKS COMPANY			
2	Factory Overhead Budget			
3	October 2015–December 2015			
4		October	November	December
5	Budgeted production (units)*	710	1,340	950
6	Variable factory overhead rate	× $ 2.50	× $ 2.50	× $ 2.50
7	Budgeted variable overhead	1,775	3,350	2,375
8	Budgeted fixed overhead	1,500	1,500	1,500
9	Budgeted total overhead	$3,275	$4,850	$3,875
10				

*From Production Budget (Exhibit 20.6)

Point: Companies can use scatter diagrams, the high-low method, or regression analysis to classify overhead costs as fixed or variable.

Separating variable and fixed overhead costs enables companies to more closely estimate changes in overhead costs as production volume varies. The variable portion of overhead is assigned at the rate of $2.50 per unit of production. This predetermined overhead rate might be based on inputs such as direct materials costs, machine hours, direct labor hours, or other activity measures. TSC's fixed overhead consists entirely of depreciation on manufacturing equipment. From Exhibit 20.3, this is computed as $18,000 per year [($200,000 − $20,000)/10 years], or $1,500 per month ($18,000/12 months). This fixed portion stays constant at $1,500 per month.

The budget in Exhibit 20.9 is in condensed form; most overhead budgets are more detailed, listing each overhead cost item. Other costs included on overhead budgets commonly include supervisor salaries, indirect materials, indirect labor, utilities, and maintenance of manufacturing equipment. We explain these more detailed overhead budgets in the next chapter.

Product Cost Per Unit With the information from the three manufacturing budgets (direct materials, direct labor, and factory overhead), we can compute TSC's product cost per unit. This is useful in computing cost of goods sold and preparing a budgeted income statement, as we show later. For budgeting purposes, TSC assumes it will normally produce 3,000 units of product each quarter, yielding fixed overhead of $1.50 per unit. TSC's other product costs are all variable. Exhibit 20.10 summarizes the product cost per unit calculation.

EXHIBIT 20.10

Product Cost Per Unit

Product Cost	Per Unit
Direct materials: ½ pound of materials × $20 per pound of materials	$10.00
Direct labor: 0.25 hours of direct labor × $12 per hour of direct labor	3.00
Variable overhead (given)	2.50
Fixed overhead ($4,500 total fixed overhead per quarter/3,000 units of expected production per quarter	1.50
Total product cost per unit*	$17.00

*At the normal production level of 3,000 units per quarter.

Selling Expense Budget The **selling expense budget** is an estimate of the types and amounts of selling expenses expected during the budget period. It is usually prepared by the vice president of marketing or an equivalent sales manager. Budgeted selling expenses are based on the sales budget, plus a fixed amount of sales manager salaries.

Point: Other common selling expenses include advertising, delivery expenses, and marketing expenses.

To illustrate, TSC's selling expense budget is in Exhibit 20.11. The firm's selling expenses consist of commissions paid to sales personnel and a $2,000 monthly salary paid to the sales manager. Sales commissions equal 10% of total sales and are paid in the month sales occur. Sales commissions are variable with respect to sales volume, but the sales manager's salary is fixed. No advertising expenses are budgeted for this particular quarter.

EXHIBIT 20.11
Selling Expense Budget

	A	B	C	D	E
1		TORONTO STICKS COMPANY			
2		Selling Expense Budget			
3		October 2015–December 2015			
4		October	November	December	Totals
5	Budgeted sales*	$60,000	$48,000	$ 84,000	$192,000
6	Sales commission percent	× 10%	× 10%	× 10%	× 10%
7	Sales commissions	6,000	4,800	8,400	19,200
8	Salary for sales manager	2,000	2,000	2,000	6,000
9	Total selling expenses	$ 8,000	$ 6,800	$ 10,400	$ 25,200
10					

*From Sales Budget (Exhibit 20.4)

Example: If TSC expects a 12% sales commission will result in budgeted sales of $220,000 for the quarter, what is the total amount of selling expenses for the quarter? *Answer:* $32,400.

General and Administrative Expense Budget The **general and administrative expense budget** plans the predicted operating expenses not included in the selling expenses or manufacturing budgets. The office manager responsible for general administration often is responsible for preparing the general and administrative expense budget.

Exhibit 20.12 shows TSC's general and administrative expense budget. It includes salaries of $54,000 per year, or $4,500 per month (paid each month when they are earned). Insurance, taxes, and depreciation on nonmanufacturing assets are other common examples of general and administrative expenses.

Point: Some companies combine selling and general administrative expenses into a single budget.

EXHIBIT 20.12
General and Administrative Expense Budget

	A	B	C	D	E
1		TORONTO STICKS COMPANY			
2		General and Administrative Expense Budget			
3		October 2015–December 2015			
4		October	November	December	Totals
5	Administrative salaries	$4,500	$4,500	$4,500	$13,500
6	Total general and administrative expenses	$4,500	$4,500	$4,500	$13,500
7					

Decision Insight

No Biz Like Snow Biz Ski resorts' costs of making snow are in the millions of dollars for equipment alone. Snowmaking involves spraying droplets of water into the air, causing them to freeze and come down as snow. Making snow can cost more than $2,000 an hour. Snowmaking accounts for 40 to 50 percent of the budgeted costs for many ski resorts. ■

Gail Shotlander/Getty Images

Example: In Exhibit 20.12, how would a rental agreement of $5,000 per month plus 1% of sales affect the general and administrative expense budget? (Budgeted sales are in Exhibit 20.4.) *Answer: Rent expense:* Oct. = $5,600; Nov. = $5,480; Dec. = $5,840; Total = $16,920; *Revised total general and administrative expenses:* Oct. = $10,100; Nov. = $9,980; Dec. = $10,340; Total = $30,420.

NEED-TO-KNOW 20-3
Selling and General and Administrative Expense Budgets
P1

A manufacturing company budgets sales of $70,000 during July. It pays sales commissions of 5% of sales and also pays a sales manager a salary of $3,000 per month. Other monthly costs include depreciation on office equipment ($500), insurance expense ($200), advertising ($1,000), and office manager salary of $2,500 per month. For the month of July, compute the total (a) budgeted selling expense and (b) budgeted general and administrative expense.

Solution

a. Total budgeted selling expense = ($70,000 × 5%) + $3,000 + $1,000 = $7,500
b. Total budgeted general and administrative expense = $500 + $200 + $2,500 = $3,200

Do More: QS 20-5, QS 20-11

QC2

At this point we have illustrated how a manufacturing company prepares its operating budgets. Information from these operating budgets is useful in preparing the capital expenditures budget, the cash budget, and budgeted financial statements, as we show next.

Capital Expenditures Budget The **capital expenditures budget** shows dollar amounts estimated to be spent to purchase additional plant assets the company will use to carry out its budgeted business activities. It also shows any amounts expected to be received from plant asset disposals, as companies replace old assets with new ones. Thus, the capital expenditures budget shows the company's expected investing activities in plant assets. It is usually prepared after the operating budgets. Since a company's plant assets determine its productive capacity, this budget is usually affected by long-range plans for the business. Yet the process of preparing other budgets can reveal that the company requires more (or less) capacity, which implies more (or less) plant assets.

Capital budgeting is the process of evaluating and planning for capital (plant asset) expenditures. This is an important management task because these expenditures often involve long-run commitments of large amounts, affect predicted cash flows, and impact future debt and equity financing. This means that the capital expenditures budget is often linked with management's evaluation of the company's ability to take on more debt. We describe capital budgeting in a later chapter.

TSC does not anticipate disposal of any plant assets through December 2015, but it does plan to acquire additional equipment for $25,000 cash near the end of December 2015. This is the only budgeted capital expenditure from October 2015 through December 2015. Thus, no separate budget is shown. TSC's cash budget will reflect this $25,000 planned expenditure.

Cash Budget

P2 Prepare a cash budget.

After developing budgets for sales, manufacturing costs, expenses, and capital expenditures, the next step is to prepare the **cash budget,** which shows expected cash inflows and outflows during the budget period. The cash budget is especially important because it helps the company maintain a cash balance necessary to meet ongoing obligations. Most companies set an amount of cash they want to have on hand. By preparing a cash budget, management can prearrange loans to cover anticipated cash shortages before they are needed. A cash budget also helps management avoid a cash balance that is too large. Too much cash is undesirable because it earns a relatively low (if any) return. Exhibit 20.13 shows the general formula for the cash budget.

EXHIBIT 20.13

General Formula for Cash Budget

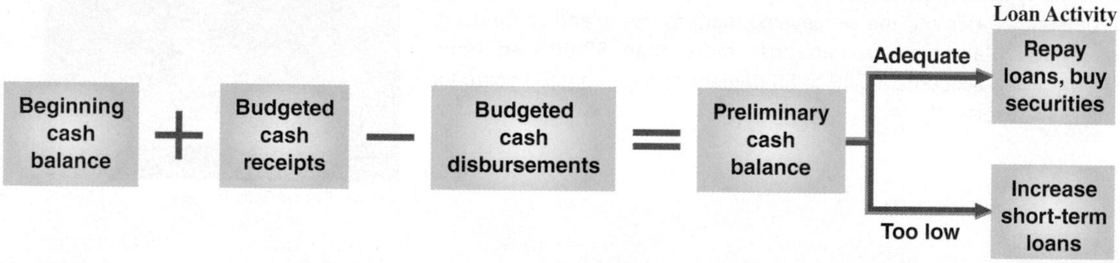

When preparing a cash budget, we add expected cash receipts to the beginning cash balance and deduct expected cash disbursements. If the expected (preliminary) cash balance is too low, additional cash requirements appear in the budget as planned increases from short-term loans. If the preliminary cash balance exceeds the balance the company wants to maintain, the excess is used to repay loans (if any) or to acquire short-term investments. Information for preparing the cash budget is mainly taken from the operating and capital expenditures budgets. Preparing the cash budget typically requires the preparation of other supporting schedules; we show the first of these, a schedule of cash receipts from sales, next.

Cash Receipts from Sales Managers use the sales budget, combined with knowledge about how frequently customers pay on credit sales, to budget monthly cash receipts. To illustrate, Exhibit 20.14 presents TSC's schedule of budgeted cash receipts.

EXHIBIT 20.14

Computing Budgeted Cash Receipts from Sales

	A	B	C	D	E
1	TORONTO STICKS COMPANY				
2	Schedule of Cash Receipts from Sales				
3	October 2015–December 2015				
4		September	October	November	December
5	Sales*	$42,000	$60,000	$48,000	$84,000
6	Less: Ending accounts receivable (60%)	25,200**	36,000	28,800	50,400
7	Cash receipts from				
8	Cash sales (40% of sales)		24,000	19,200	33,600
9	Collections of prior month's receivables		25,200	36,000	28,800
10	Total cash receipts		$49,200	$55,200	$62,400
11					

*From Sales Budget (Exhibit 20.4)
**Accounts receivable balance from September 30 balance sheet (Exhibit 20.3)

We begin with reference to TSC's budgeted sales (Exhibit 20.4). Analysis of past sales indicates that 40% of the firm's sales are for cash. The remaining 60% are credit sales; these customers are expected to pay in full in the month following the sales. We now can compute the budgeted cash receipts from customers, as shown in Exhibit 20.14. October's budgeted cash receipts consist of $24,000 from expected cash sales ($60,000 × 40%) plus the anticipated collection of $25,200 of accounts receivable from the end of September.

Cash Payments for Materials Managers use the beginning balance sheet (Exhibit 20.3) and the direct materials budget (Exhibit 20.7) to help prepare a schedule of cash disbursements for materials. Managers must also know *how* TSC purchases direct materials (pay cash or on account), and for credit purchases, how quickly TSC pays. TSC's materials purchases are entirely on account. It makes full payment during the month following its purchases. Using this information, the schedule of cash payments for materials is shown in Exhibit 20.15.

EXHIBIT 20.15

Computing Cash Payments for Materials Purchases

	A	B	C	D
1	TORONTO STICKS COMPANY			
2	Schedule of Cash Payments for Direct Materials			
3	October 2015–December 2015			
4		October	November	December
5	Materials purchases*	$10,240	$11,450	$ 9,700
6	Cash disbursements for			
7	Current month purchases (0%)	0	0	0
8	Prior month purchases (100%)	7,060**	10,240	11,450
9	Total cash disbursements for direct materials	$ 7,060	$10,240	$11,450
10				

*From Direct Materials Budget (Exhibit 20.7)
**Accounts payable balance from September 30 balance sheet (Exhibit 20.3)

The schedule above can be modified for alternative payment timing. For example, if Toronto Sticks Company paid for 20% of its purchases in the month of purchase, and paid the remaining 80% of a month's purchases in the following month, its cash disbursements in December would equal $11,100, computed as (20% × $9,700) plus (80% × $11,450).

Preparing the Cash Budget Managing cash flows is vital for a company's success. The cash budget is useful in this regard because it summarizes many other budgets in terms of their effects on cash. To prepare the cash budget, TSC's managers use the budgets and other schedules listed below.

1. Cash receipts from sales (Exhibit 20.14).
2. Cash payments for direct materials (Exhibit 20.15).
3. Cash payments for direct labor (Exhibit 20.8).
4. Cash payments for variable overhead (Exhibit 20.9).
5. Cash payments for selling expenses (Exhibit 20.11).
6. Cash payments for general and administrative expenses (Exhibit 20.12).

Note that the *fixed overhead* assigned to depreciation in the factory overhead budget (Exhibit 20.9) does not require a cash payment. Therefore, it is not included in the cash budget. Other types of fixed overhead—such as payments for property taxes and insurance—*are* included if they require cash payments.

Additional information is typically needed to prepare the cash budget. For TSC, this additional information includes:

1. Income taxes payable (from the beginning balance sheet, Exhibit 20.3).
2. Expected dividend payments: TSC plans to pay $3,000 of cash dividends in the second month of each quarter.
3. Loan activity: TSC's managers want to maintain a minimum cash balance of $20,000 at each month-end. This is important, as it helps ensure TSC maintains enough liquidity to pay its bills as they come due.

Courtesy of JJW Images

Exhibit 20.16 shows the full cash budget for TSC. The company begins October with $20,000 in cash. To this is added $49,200 in expected cash receipts from sales (from Exhibit 20.14). We next subtract expected cash payments for direct materials, direct labor, overhead, selling expenses, and general and administrative expenses. Income taxes of $20,000 were due as of the end of September 30, 2015, and payable in October. We next discuss TSC's loan activity, including any interest payments.

EXHIBIT 20.16

Cash Budget

	A	B	C	D
1	**TORONTO STICKS COMPANY**			
2	**Cash Budget**			
3	**October 2015–December 2015**			
4		**October**	**November**	**December**
5	Beginning cash balance	$20,000	$20,000	$38,881
6	**Add:** Cash receipts from customers (Exhibit 20.14)	49,200	55,200	62,400
7	Total cash available	69,200	75,200	101,281
8	**Less:** Cash payments for			
9	Direct materials (Exhibit 20.15)	7,060	10,240	11,450
10	Direct labor (Exhibit 20.8)	2,130	4,020	2,850
11	Variable overhead (Exhibit 20.9)	1,775	3,350	2,375
12	Sales commissions (Exhibit 20.11)	6,000	4,800	8,400
13	Sales salaries (Exhibit 20.11)	2,000	2,000	2,000
14	General and administrative expenses (Exhibit 20.12)	4,500	4,500	4,500
15	Income taxes payable (Exhibit 20.3)	20,000		
16	Dividends		3,000	
17	Interest on bank loan			
18	October ($10,000 × 1%)*	100		
19	November ($4,365 × 1%)**		44	
20	Purchase of equipment			25,000
21	Total cash disbursements	43,565	31,954	56,575
22	Preliminary cash balance	$25,635	$43,246	$44,706
23	**Loan activity**			
24	Additional loan from bank			
25	Repayment of loan to bank	5,635	4,365	
26	Ending cash balance	$20,000	$38,881	$44,706
27	Loan balance, end of month	$ 4,365	$ 0	$ 0
28				

* Beginning loan balance (note payable) from Exhibit 20.3 ** Rounded to the nearest dollar.

Loan Activity TSC has an agreement with its bank that promises additional loans at each month-end, if necessary, so that the company keeps a minimum cash balance of $20,000. If the cash balance exceeds $20,000 at a month-end, TSC uses the excess to repay loans. If the cash balance is less than $20,000 at month-end, the bank loans TSC the difference.

At the end of each month, TSC pays the bank interest on any outstanding loan amount, at the monthly rate of 1% of the beginning balance of these loans. For October, this payment is 1% of the $10,000 note payable amount reported in the balance sheet of Exhibit 20.3. For November, TSC expects to pay interest of $44, computed as 1% of the $4,365 expected loan balance at October 31. No interest is budgeted for December because the company expects to repay the loans in full at the end of November. Exhibit 20.16 shows that the October 31 cash balance increases to $25,635 (before any loan-related activity). This amount is more than the $20,000 minimum. Thus, TSC will pay off a portion of its outstanding loan. At the end of November, TSC's cash balance is sufficient to pay off its remaining loan balance. Had TSC's preliminary cash balance been below the $20,000 minimum in any month, TSC would have increased its loan from the bank so that the ending cash balance was $20,000. We show an example of this situation in Need-To-Know Comprehensive 2 at the end of this chapter.

Decision Insight

Cash Cushion Why do some companies maintain a minimum cash balance even when the budget shows extra cash is not needed? For example, Apple's cash and short-term investments balance is over $40 billion. According to Apple's CEO, Tim Cook, the cushion provides "flexibility and security," important in navigating uncertain economic times. A cash cushion also enables companies to jump on new ventures or acquisitions that may present themselves. ■

Kevork Djansezian/Getty Images

BUDGETED FINANCIAL STATEMENTS

One of the final steps in the budgeting process is summarizing the financial statement effects. We next illustrate TSC's budgeted income statement and budgeted balance sheet.

P3 Prepare budgeted financial statements.

Budgeted Income Statement

The **budgeted income statement** is a managerial accounting report showing predicted amounts of sales and expenses for the budget period. It summarizes the income effects of the budgeted activities. Information needed to prepare a budgeted income statement is primarily taken from already-prepared budgets. The volume of information summarized in the budgeted income statement is so large for some companies that they often use spreadsheets to accumulate the budgeted transactions and classify them by their effects on income.

We condense TSC's budgeted income statement and show it in Exhibit 20.17. All information in this exhibit is taken from the component budgets we've examined in this chapter. Also, we now can predict the amount of income tax expense for the quarter, computed as 40% of the budgeted pretax income. For TSC, these taxes are not payable until January 31, 2016. Thus, these taxes are not shown on the October–December 2015 cash budget in Exhibit 20.16, but they are included on the December 31, 2015, balance sheet (shown next).

Point: Lenders often require potential borrowers to provide cash budgets, budgeted income statements, and budgeted balance sheets, as well as data on past performance.

EXHIBIT 20.17 Budgeted Income Statement

TORONTO STICKS COMPANY
Budgeted Income Statement
For Three Months Ended December 31, 2015

Sales (Exhibit 20.4, 3,200 units @ $60)		$192,000
Cost of goods sold (3,200 units @ $17)*		54,400
Gross profit		137,600
Operating expenses		
Sales commissions (Exhibit 20.11)	$19,200	
Sales salaries (Exhibit 20.11)	6,000	
Administrative salaries (Exhibit 20.12)	13,500	
Interest expense (Exhibit 20.16)	144	38,844
Income before income taxes		98,756
Income tax expense ($98,756 × 40%)**		39,502
Net income		$ 59,254

*$17 product cost per unit from Exhibit 20.10 **Rounded to the nearest dollar

Budgeted Balance Sheet

The final step in preparing the master budget is summarizing the company's financial position. The **budgeted balance sheet** shows predicted amounts for the company's assets, liabilities, and equity as of the end of the budget period. TSC's budgeted balance sheet in Exhibit 20.18 is prepared using information from the other budgets. The sources of amounts are reported in the notes to the budgeted balance sheet.

EXHIBIT 20.18

Budgeted Balance Sheet

TORONTO STICKS COMPANY
Budgeted Balance Sheet
December 31, 2015

Assets		
Cash[a]		$ 44,706
Accounts receivable[b]		50,400
Raw materials inventory[c]		4,950
Finished goods inventory[d]		13,770
Equipment[e]	$225,000	
Less: Accumulated depreciation[f]	40,500	184,500
Total assets		$298,326
Liabilities and Equity		
Liabilities		
Accounts payable[g]	$ 9,700	
Income taxes payable[h]	39,502	$ 49,202
Stockholders' equity		
Common stock[i]	150,000	
Retained earnings[j]	99,124	249,124
Total liabilities and equity		$298,326

[a] Ending balance for December from the cash budget (in Exhibit 20.16).
[b] 60% of $84,000 sales budgeted for December from the sales budget (in Exhibit 20.4).
[c] 247.5 pounds of raw materials in budgeted ending inventory at the budgeted cost of $20 per unit (direct materials budget, Exhibit 20.7).
[d] 810 units in budgeted finished goods inventory (Exhibit 20.6) at the budgeted cost of $17 per unit (Exhibit 20.10).
[e] September 30 balance of $200,000 from the beginning balance sheet in Exhibit 20.3 plus $25,000 cost of new equipment from the cash budget in Exhibit 20.16.
[f] September 30 balance of $36,000 from the beginning balance sheet in Exhibit 20.3 plus $4,500 depreciation expense from the factory overhead budget in Exhibit 20.9.
[g] Budgeted cost of materials purchases for December from Exhibit 20.7, to be paid in January.
[h] Income tax expense from the budgeted income statement for the fourth quarter in Exhibit 20.17, to be paid in January.
[i] Unchanged from the beginning balance sheet in Exhibit 20.3.
[j] September 30 balance of $42,870 from the beginning balance sheet in Exhibit 20.3 plus budgeted net income of $59,254 from the budgeted income statement in Exhibit 20.17 minus budgeted cash dividends of $3,000 from the cash budget in Exhibit 20.16.

Using the Master Budget

For a master budget to be useful, managers must employ it in their planning and controlling activities. With respect to *planning,* the master budget is clearly a plan for future activities. In addition, any stage in the master budgeting process might reveal undesirable outcomes. The new information can cause management to change its decisions. For example, an early version of the cash budget could show an insufficient amount of cash unless cash outlays are reduced. This information could yield a reduction in planned equipment purchases. Likewise, a budgeted balance sheet might reveal too much debt from too many planned equipment purchases; the company could reduce its planned equipment purchases and thus reduce its need for borrowing.

QC3

In *controlling* operations, managers typically compare actual results to budgeted results. Differences between actual and budgeted results are called *variances.* Management examines variances, particularly large ones, to identify areas for improvement and take corrective action. We discuss variances in more detail in the next chapter.

GLOBAL VIEW

Royal Philips Electronics of the Netherlands is a diversified company. Preparing budgets and evaluating progress helps the company achieve its goals. In a recent annual report the company reports that it budgets sales to grow at a faster pace than overall economic growth. Based on this sales target, company managers prepare detailed operating, capital expenditure, and financial budgets.

Budgeted and actual results of companies that do global business are impacted by changes in foreign currency exchange rates. While most of Royal Philips's cash disbursements are in euros, the company's sales are in euros, U.S. dollars, Chinese yuan, Brazilian real, and other currencies. Forecasting future exchange rates and their impact on sales budgets is difficult. In addition, global economic and political uncertainties add to budgeting challenges.

Sustainability and Accounting **Solben**, this chapter's opener company, is focused on alternative fuels. According to the U.S. Department of Energy, burning biodiesel instead of petroleum diesel reduces tailpipe emissions and is better for the environment. Daniel Gómez Iñiguez, one of Solben's founders, notes that "the benefits of biodiesel technology extend beyond earth-friendly fuel. Our plants can be built in remote locations, and thus create local jobs. Companies like ours can have a global impact, and be an example of how socially responsible businesses can also be profitable." The sustainability of Solben's operations, and operations like it, is arguably one path to making business accountable.

Steve McAlister/The Image Bank/Getty Images

Activity-Based Budgeting — Decision Analysis

A1 Analyze expense planning using activity-based budgeting.

Activity-based budgeting (ABB) is a budget system based on expected activities. Knowledge of expected activities and their levels for the budget period enables management to plan for resources required to perform the activities. Exhibit 20.19 contrasts a traditional budget with an activity-based budget for a company's accounting department. Traditional budgeting systems list items such as salaries, supplies, equipment, and utilities. With a traditional budget, management often makes across-the-board budget cuts or increases. For example, management might decide that each of the line items in the traditional budget must be cut by 5%. This might not be a good strategic decision. In contrast, ABB requires management to list activities performed by, say, the accounting department such as auditing, tax reporting, financial reporting, and cost accounting. An understanding of the resources required to perform the activities, the costs associated with these resources, and the way resource use changes with changes in activity levels allows management to better assess how expenses will change to accommodate changes in activity levels. Moreover, by knowing the relation between activities and costs, management can attempt to reduce costs by eliminating nonvalue-added activities.

EXHIBIT 20.19 Activity-Based Budgeting versus Traditional Budgeting (for an accounting department)

Traditional Budget		Activity-Based Budget	
Salaries	$152,000	Auditing	$ 58,000
Supplies	22,000	Tax reporting	71,000
Depreciation	36,000	Financial reporting	63,000
Utilities	14,000	Cost accounting	32,000
Total	$224,000	Total	$224,000

Decision Maker

Environmental Manager You hold the new position of environmental control manager for a chemical company. You are asked to develop a budget for your job and identify job responsibilities. How do you proceed? ■ [Answers follow the chapter's Summary.]

NEED-TO-KNOW

COMPREHENSIVE 1

Master Budget—Manufacturer

Payne Company's management asks you to prepare its master budget using the following information. The budget is to cover the months of April, May, and June of 2015.

PAYNE COMPANY
Balance Sheet
March 31, 2015

Assets			**Liabilities and Equity**		
Cash	$ 50,000		Accounts payable	$ 63,818	
Accounts receivable	175,000		Short-term notes payable	12,000	
Raw materials inventory	30,798*		Total current liabilities		$ 75,818
Finished goods inventory	96,600**		Long-term note payable		200,000
Total current assets		$352,398	Total liabilities		275,818
Equipment	480,000		Common stock	435,000	
Less: Accumulated depreciation	(90,000)		Retained earnings	31,580	
Equipment, net		390,000	Total stockholders' equity		466,580
Total assets		$742,398	Total liabilities and equity		$742,398

*2,425 pounds @$12.70, rounded to nearest whole dollar **8,400 units @ $11.50 per unit

Additional Information

a. Sales for March total 10,000 units. Expected sales (in units) are: 10,500 (April), 9,500 (May), 10,000 (June), and 10,500 (July). The product's selling price is $25 per unit.

b. Company policy calls for a given month's ending finished goods inventory to equal 80% of the next month's expected unit sales. The March 31 finished goods inventory is 8,400 units, which complies with the policy. The product's manufacturing cost is $11.50 per unit, including per unit costs of $6.35 for materials (.5 lbs. at $12.70 per lb.), $3.75 for direct labor (1/4 hour × $15 direct labor rate per hour), $0.90 for variable overhead, and $0.50 for fixed overhead. Fixed overhead consists entirely of $5,000 of monthly depreciation expense. Company policy also calls for a given month's ending raw materials inventory to equal 50% of next month's expected materials needed for production. The March 31 inventory is 2,425 units of materials, which complies with the policy. The company expects to have 2,100 units of materials inventory on June 30.

c. Sales representatives' commissions are 12% of sales and are paid in the month of the sales. The sales manager's monthly salary will be $3,500 in April and $4,000 per month thereafter.

d. Monthly general and administrative expenses include $8,000 administrative salaries and 0.9% monthly interest on the long-term note payable.

e. The company expects 30% of sales to be for cash and the remaining 70% on credit. Receivables are collected in full in the month following the sale (none is collected in the month of the sale).

f. All direct materials purchases are on credit, and no payables arise from any other transactions. One month's purchases are fully paid in the next month. Materials cost $12.70 per pound.

g. The minimum ending cash balance for all months is $50,000. If necessary, the company borrows enough cash using a short-term note to reach the minimum. Short-term notes require an interest payment of 1% at each month-end (before any repayment). If the ending cash balance exceeds the minimum, the excess will be applied to repaying the short-term notes payable balance.

h. Dividends of $100,000 are to be declared and paid in May.

i. No cash payments for income taxes are to be made during the second calendar quarter. Income taxes will be assessed at 35% in the quarter.

j. Equipment purchases of $55,000 are scheduled for June.

Required

Prepare the following budgets and other financial information as required:

1. Sales budget, including budgeted sales for July.

2. Production budget.

3. Direct materials budget. Round costs of materials purchases to the nearest dollar.

4. Direct labor budget.

5. Factory overhead budget.
6. Selling expense budget.
7. General and administrative expense budget.
8. Expected cash receipts from customers and the expected June 30 balance of accounts receivable.
9. Expected cash payments for purchases and the expected June 30 balance of accounts payable.
10. Cash budget.
11. Budgeted income statement, budgeted statement of retained earnings, and budgeted balance sheet.

SOLUTION

1.

	A	B	C	D	E
1	**Sales Budget**	**April**	**May**	**June**	**Quarter**
2	Projected unit sales	10,500	9,500	10,000	
3	Selling price per unit	× $ 25	× $ 25	× $ 25	
4	Projected sales	$262,500	$237,500	$250,000	$750,000
5					

2.

	A	B	C	D	E
1	**Production Budget**	**April**	**May**	**June**	**Quarter**
2	Next period's unit sales (part I)	9,500	10,000	10,500	
3	Ending inventory percent	× 80%	× 80%	× 80%	
4	Desired ending inventory	7,600	8,000	8,400	
5	Current period's unit sales (part I)	10,500	9,500	10,000	
6	Required units of available production	18,100	17,500	18,400	
7	Less: Beginning inventory	8,400	7,600	8,000	
8	Total units to be produced	9,700	9,900	10,400	
9					

3.

	A	B	C	D
1	**Direct Materials Budget**	**April**	**May**	**June**
2	Budgeted production (units) (part 2)	9,700	9,900	10,400
3	Materials requirements per unit (pounds)	× 0.5	× 0.5	× 0.5
4	Materials needed for production (pounds)	4,850	4,950	5,200
5	Add: Budgeted ending inventory (pounds)	2,475	2,600	2,100
6	Total material requirements (pounds)	7,325	7,550	7,300
7	Deduct: Beginning inventory (pounds)	2,425	2,475	2,600
8	Materials to be purchased (pounds)	4,900	5,075	4,700
9				
10	Materials price per pound	$ 12.70	$ 12.70	$ 12.70
11	Total cost of direct materials purchases	$62,230	$64,453*	$59,690
12				

*Rounded to nearest dollar

4.

	A	B	C	D
1	**Direct Labor Budget**	**April**	**May**	**June**
2	Budgeted production (units) (part 2)	9,700	9,900	10,400
3	Labor requirements per unit (hours)	× 0.25	× 0.25	× 0.25
4	Total labor hours needed	2,425	2,475	2,600
5				
6	Labor rate (per hour)	$ 15	$ 15	$ 15
7				
8	Total direct labor cost	$36,375	$37,125	$39,000
9				

5.

	A	B	C	D
1	**Factory Overhead Budget**	**April**	**May**	**June**
2	Budgeted production (units) (part 2)	9,700	9,900	10,400
3	Variable factory overhead rate	× $ 0.90	× $ 0.90	× $ 0.90
4	Budgeted variable overhead	8,730	8,910	9,360
5	Budgeted fixed overhead	5,000	5,000	5,000
6	Budgeted total overhead	$13,730	$13,910	$14,360
7				

6.

	A	B	C	D	E
1	**Selling Expense Budget**	**April**	**May**	**June**	**Quarter**
2	Budgeted sales (part 1)	$262,500	$237,500	$250,000	$750,000
3	Commission percent	× 12%	× 12%	× 12%	× 12%
4	Sales commissions	31,500	28,500	30,000	90,000
5	Manager's salary	3,500	4,000	4,000	11,500
6	Budgeted selling expenses	$ 35,000	$ 32,500	$ 34,000	$101,500
7					

7.

	A	B	C	D	E
1	**General and Administrative Expense Budget**	**April**	**May**	**June**	**Quarter**
2	Administrative salaries	$8,000	$8,000	$8,000	$24,000
3	Interest on long-term note				
4	payable (0.9% × $200,000)	1,800	1,800	1,800	5,400
5	Budgeted general and administrative expenses	$9,800	$9,800	$9,800	$29,400
6					

8.

	A	B	C	D	E
1	**Schedule of Cash Receipts**	**April**	**May**	**June**	**Quarter**
2	Budgeted sales (part 1)	$262,500	$237,500	$250,000	
3	Ending accounts receivable (70%)	$183,750	$166,250	$175,000	
4	Cash receipts				
5	Cash sales (30% of budgeted sales)	$ 78,750	$ 71,250	$ 75,000	$225,000
6	Collections of prior month's receivables	175,000*	183,750	166,250	525,000
7	Total cash to be collected	$253,750	$255,000	$241,250	$750,000
8					

*Accounts receivable balance from March 31 balance sheet

9.

	A	B	C	D	E
1	**Schedule of Cash Payments for Materials**	**April**	**May**	**June**	**Quarter**
2	Cash payments (equal to prior month's				
3	materials purchases)	$63,818*	$62,230	$64,453	$190,501
4	Expected June 30 balance of accounts				
5	payable (June purchases)			$59,690	
6					

*Accounts payable balance from March 31 balance sheet

10.

	A	B	C	D
1	**Cash Budget**	**April**	**May**	**June**
2	Beginning cash balance	$ 50,000	$137,907	$142,342
3	Cash receipts from customers (part 8)	253,750	255,000	241,250
4	Total cash available	303,750	392,907	383,592
5	Cash disbursements			
6	Payments for materials (part 9)	63,818	62,230	64,453
7	Payments for direct labor (part 4)	36,375	37,125	39,000
8	Payments for variable overhead (part 5)	8,730	8,910	9,360
9	Sales commissions (part 6)	31,500	28,500	30,000
10	Salaries			
11	Sales (part 6)	3,500	4,000	4,000
12	Administrative (part 7)	8,000	8,000	8,000
13	Dividends		100,000	
14	Interest on long-term note (part 7)	1,800	1,800	1,800
15	Interest on bank loan			
16	October ($12,000 × 1%)	120		
17	Purchase of equipment			55,000
18	Total cash disbursements	153,843	250,565	211,613
19	Preliminary cash balance	$149,907	$142,342	$171,979
20	Additional loan from bank			
21	Repayment of loan to bank	12,000	0	0
22	Ending cash balance	$137,907	$142,342	$171,979
23	Loan balance, end of month	$ 0	$ 0	$ 0
24				

11.

PAYNE COMPANY
Budgeted Income Statement
For Quarter Ended June 30, 2015

Sales (part 1)		$750,000
Cost of goods sold (30,000 @ $11.50)		345,000
Gross profit		405,000
Operating expenses		
Sales commissions (part 6)	$90,000	
Sales salaries (part 6)	11,500	
Administrative salaries (part 7)	24,000	
Interest on long-term note (part 7)	5,400	
Interest on short-term notes (part 10)	120	
Total operating expenses		131,020
Income before income taxes		273,980
Income taxes (35%)		95,893
Net income		$178,087

PAYNE COMPANY
Budgeted Statement of Retained Earnings
For Quarter Ended June 30, 2015

Beginning retained earnings (given)	$ 31,580
Net income	178,087
	209,667
Less: Cash dividends (part 10)	100,000
Ending retained earnings	$109,667

PAYNE COMPANY
Budgeted Balance Sheet
June 30, 2015

Assets		
Cash (part 10)	$171,979	
Accounts receivable (part 8)	175,000	
Raw materials inventory (2,100 pounds @$12.70)*	26,671	
Finished goods inventory (8,400 units @$11.50)	96,600	
Total current assets		$470,250
Equipment (Mar. 31 bal. plus purchase)	535,000	
Less: Accumulated depreciation (Mar. 31 bal. plus depreciation expense)	105,000	430,000
Total assets		$900,250

Liabilities and Equity		
Accounts payable (part 9)	$ 59,690	
Income taxes payable	95,893	
Total current liabilities		$155,583
Long-term note payable (Mar. 31 bal.)		200,000
Total liabilities		355,583
Common stock (Mar. 31 bal.)	435,000	
Retained earnings	109,667	
Total stockholders' equity		544,667
Total liabilities and equity		$900,250

*Plus $1 rounding difference

NEED-TO-KNOW

COMPREHENSIVE 2

Master Budget—Merchandiser

Wild Wood Company's management asks you to prepare its master budget using the following information. The budget is to cover the months of April, May, and June of 2015.

WILD WOOD COMPANY
Balance Sheet
March 31, 2015

Assets	
Cash	$ 50,000
Accounts receivable	175,000
Inventory	126,000
Total current assets	351,000
Equipment, gross	480,000
Accumulated depreciation	(90,000)
Equipment, net	390,000
Total assets	$741,000

Liabilities and Equity	
Accounts payable	$156,000
Short-term notes payable	12,000
Total current liabilities	168,000
Long-term note payable	200,000
Total liabilities	368,000
Common stock	235,000
Retained earnings	138,000
Total stockholders' equity	373,000
Total liabilities and equity	$741,000

Additional Information

a. Sales for March total 10,000 units. Each month's sales are expected to exceed the prior month's results by 5%. The product's selling price is $25 per unit.

b. Company policy calls for a given month's ending inventory to equal 80% of the next month's expected unit sales. The March 31 inventory is 8,400 units, which complies with the policy. The purchase price is $15 per unit.

c. Sales representatives' commissions are 12.5% of sales and are paid in the month of the sales. The sales manager's monthly salary will be $3,500 in April and $4,000 per month thereafter.

d. Monthly general and administrative expenses include $8,000 administrative salaries, $5,000 depreciation, and 0.9% monthly interest on the long-term note payable.

e. The company expects 30% of sales to be for cash and the remaining 70% on credit. Receivables are collected in full in the month following the sale (none is collected in the month of the sale).

f. All merchandise purchases are on credit, and no payables arise from any other transactions. One month's purchases are fully paid in the next month.

g. The minimum ending cash balance for all months is $50,000. If necessary, the company borrows enough cash using a short-term note to reach the minimum. Short-term notes require an interest payment of 1% at each month-end (before any repayment). If the ending cash balance exceeds the minimum, the excess will be applied to repaying the short-term notes payable balance.

h. Dividends of $100,000 are to be declared and paid in May.

i. No cash payments for income taxes are to be made during the second calendar quarter. Income taxes will be assessed at 35% in the quarter.

j. Equipment purchases of $55,000 are scheduled for June.

Required

Prepare the following budgets and other financial information as required:

1. Sales budget, including budgeted sales for July.
2. Purchases budget.
3. Selling expense budget.
4. General and administrative expense budget.
5. Expected cash receipts from customers and the expected June 30 balance of accounts receivable.
6. Expected cash payments for purchases and the expected June 30 balance of accounts payable.
7. Cash budget.
8. Budgeted income statement, budgeted statement of retained earnings, and budgeted balance sheet.

PLANNING THE SOLUTION

- The sales budget shows expected sales for each month in the quarter. Start by multiplying March sales by 105% and then do the same for the remaining months. July's sales are needed for the purchases budget. To complete the budget, multiply the expected unit sales by the selling price of $25 per unit.
- Use these results and the 80% inventory policy to budget the size of ending inventory for April, May, and June. Add the budgeted sales to these numbers and subtract the actual or expected beginning inventory for each month. The result is the number of units to be purchased each month. Multiply these numbers by the per unit cost of $15. Find the budgeted cost of goods sold by multiplying the unit sales in each month by the $15 cost per unit. Compute the cost of the June 30 ending inventory by multiplying the expected units available at that date by the $15 cost per unit.
- The selling expense budget has only two items. Find the amount of the sales representatives' commissions by multiplying the expected dollar sales in each month by the 12.5% commission rate. Then include the sales manager's salary of $3,500 in April and $4,000 in May and June.
- The general and administrative expense budget should show three items. Administrative salaries are fixed at $8,000 per month, and depreciation is $5,000 per month. Budget the monthly interest expense on the long-term note by multiplying its $200,000 balance by the 0.9% monthly interest rate.
- Determine the amounts of cash sales in each month by multiplying the budgeted sales by 30%. Add to this amount the credit sales of the prior month (computed as 70% of prior month's sales). April's cash receipts from collecting receivables equals the March 31 balance of $175,000. The expected June 30 accounts receivable balance equals 70% of June's total budgeted sales.
- Determine expected cash payments on accounts payable for each month by making them equal to the merchandise purchases in the prior month. The payments for April equal the March 31 balance of

accounts payable shown on the beginning balance sheet. The June 30 balance of accounts payable equals merchandise purchases for June.

- Prepare the cash budget by combining the given information and the amounts of cash receipts and cash payments on account that you computed. Complete the cash budget for each month by either borrowing enough to raise the preliminary balance to the minimum or paying off short-term debt as much as the balance allows without falling below the minimum. Show the ending balance of the short-term note in the budget.
- Prepare the budgeted income statement by combining the budgeted items for all three months. Determine the income before income taxes and multiply it by the 35% rate to find the quarter's income tax expense.
- The budgeted statement of retained earnings should show the March 31 balance plus the quarter's net income minus the quarter's dividends.
- The budgeted balance sheet includes updated balances for all items that appear in the beginning balance sheet and an additional liability for unpaid income taxes. Amounts for all asset, liability, and equity accounts can be found either in the budgets, other calculations, or by adding amounts found there to the beginning balances.

SOLUTION

1.

	A	B	C	D	E
1	**Calculation of Unit Sales**	**April**	**May**	**June**	**July**
2	Prior period's unit sales	10,000	10,500	11,025	11,576
3	Plus 5% growth*	500	525	551	579
4	Projected unit sales	10,500	11,025	11,576	12,155
5					

*Rounded to nearest whole unit

	A	B	C	D	E
1	**Sales Budget**	**April**	**May**	**June**	**Quarter**
2	Projected unit sales	10,500	11,025	11,576	
3	Selling price per unit	× $ 25	× $ 25	× $ 25	
4	Projected sales	$262,500	$275,625	$289,400	$827,525
5					

2.

	A	B	C	D	E
1	**Purchases Budget**	**April**	**May**	**June**	**Quarter**
2	Next period's unit sales (part 1)	11,025	11,576	12,155	
3	Ending inventory percent	× 80%	× 80%	× 80%	
4	Desired ending inventory (units)	8,820	9,261	9,724	
5	Current period's unit sales (part 1)	10,500	11,025	11,576	
6	Units to be available	19,320	20,286	21,300	
7	Less: Beginning inventory (units)	8,400	8,820	9,261	
8	Units to be purchased	10,920	11,466	12,039	
9	Budgeted cost per unit	× $ 15	× $ 15	× $ 15	
10	Budgeted purchases	$163,800	$171,990	$180,585	$516,375
11					

3.

	A	B	C	D	E
1	**Selling Expense Budget**	**April**	**May**	**June**	**Quarter**
2	Budgeted sales (part 1)	$262,500	$275,625	$289,400	$827,525
3	Commission percent	× 12.5%	× 12.5%	× 12.5%	× 12.5%
4	Sales commissions*	32,813	34,453	36,175	103,441
5	Manager's salary	3,500	4,000	4,000	11,500
6	Budgeted selling expenses*	$ 36,313	$ 38,453	$ 40,175	$114,941
7					

*Rounded to the nearest dollar

4.

	A	B	C	D	E
1	**General and Administrative Expense Budget**	**April**	**May**	**June**	**Quarter**
2	Administrative salaries	$ 8,000	$ 8,000	$ 8,000	$24,000
3	Depreciation	5,000	5,000	5,000	15,000
4	Interest on long-term note payable (0.9% × $200,000)	1,800	1,800	1,800	5,400
5	Budgeted expenses	$14,800	$14,800	$14,800	$44,400
6					

5.

	A	B	C	D	E
1	**Schedule of Cash Receipts from Sales**	**April**	**May**	**June**	**Quarter**
2	Budgeted sales (part 1)	$262,500	$275,625	$289,400	
3	Ending accounts receivable (70%)	$183,750	$192,938	$202,580	
4	Cash receipts				
5	Cash sales (30% of budgeted sales)	$ 78,750	$ 82,687	$ 86,820	$248,257
6	Collections of prior month's receivables	175,000*	183,750	192,938	551,688
7	Total cash to be collected	$253,750	$266,437	$279,758	$799,945
8					

*March 31 Accounts Receivable balance (from Balance Sheet)

6.

	A	B	C	D	E
1	**Schedule of Cash Payments to Suppliers**	**April**	**May**	**June**	**Quarter**
2	Cash payments (equal to prior month's				
3	purchases)	$156,000*	$163,800	$171,990	$491,790
4	Expected June 30 balance of accounts				
5	payable (June purchases)			$180,585	
6					

*March 31 Accounts Payable balance (from Balance Sheet)

7.

	A	B	C	D
1	**Cash Budget**	**April**	**May**	**June**
2	Beginning cash balance	$ 50,000	$ 89,517	$ 50,000
3	Cash receipts (part 5)	253,750	266,437	279,758
4	Total cash available	303,750	355,954	329,758
5	Cash payments			
6	Payments for merchandise (part 6)	156,000	163,800	171,990
7	Sales commissions (part 3)	32,813	34,453	36,175
8	Salaries			
9	Sales (part 3)	3,500	4,000	4,000
10	Administrative (part 4)	8,000	8,000	8,000
11	Interest on long-term note (part 4)	1,800	1,800	1,800
12	Dividends		100,000	
13	Equipment purchase			55,000
14	Interest on short-term notes			
15	April ($12,000 × 1%)	120		
16	June ($6,099 × 1%)			61
17	Total cash payments	202,233	312,053	277,026
18	Preliminary balance	101,517	43,901	52,732
19	Loan activity			
20	Additional loan		6,099	
21	Loan repayment	(12,000)		(2,732)
22	Ending cash balance	$ 89,517	$ 50,000	$ 50,000
23	Ending short-term notes	$ 0	$ 6,099	$ 3,367
24				

8.

WILD WOOD COMPANY
Budgeted Income Statement
For Quarter Ended June 30, 2015

Sales (part 1)		$827,525
Cost of goods sold*		496,515
Gross profit		331,010
Operating expenses		
Sales commissions (part 3)	$103,441	
Sales salaries (part 3)	11,500	
Administrative salaries (part 4)	24,000	
Depreciation (part 4)	15,000	
Interest on long-term note (part 4)	5,400	
Interest on short-term notes (part 7)	181	
Total operating expenses		159,522
Income before income taxes		171,488
Income taxes (35%)		60,021
Net income		$111,467

*33,101 units sold @ $15 per unit

WILD WOOD COMPANY
Budgeted Statement of Retained Earnings
For Quarter Ended June 30, 2015

Beginning retained earnings (Mar. 31 bal.)	$138,000
Net income	111,467
	249,467
Less: Cash dividends (Mar. 31 bal.)	100,000
Ending retained earnings	$149,467

WILD WOOD COMPANY
Budgeted Balance Sheet
June 30, 2015

Assets			**Liabilities and Equity**		
Cash (part 7)	$ 50,000		Accounts payable (part 6)	$180,585	
Accounts receivable (part 5)	202,580		Short-term notes payable (part 7)	3,367	
Inventory (9,724 units @ $15 each)	145,860		Income taxes payable	60,021	
Total current assets		$398,440	Total current liabilities		$243,973
			Long-term note payable (Mar. 31 bal.)		200,000
			Total liabilities		443,973
Equipment (Mar. 31 bal. plus purchase)	535,000		Common stock (Mar. 31 bal.)	235,000	
Less: Accumulated depreciation			Retained earnings	149,467	
(Mar. 31 bal. plus depreciation expense)	105,000	430,000	Total stockholders' equity		384,467
Total assets		$828,440	Total liabilities and equity		$828,440

APPENDIX

Merchandise Purchases Budget 20A

Exhibit 20A.1 shows the master budget sequence for a merchandiser. Unlike a manufacturing company, a merchandiser must prepare a merchandise purchases budget rather than a production budget. In addition, a merchandiser does not prepare direct materials, direct labor, or factory overhead budgets. In this appendix we show the merchandise purchases budget for Hockey Den (HD), a retailer of hockey sticks.

P4 Prepare each component of a master budget and link each to the budgeting process—for a merchandising company.

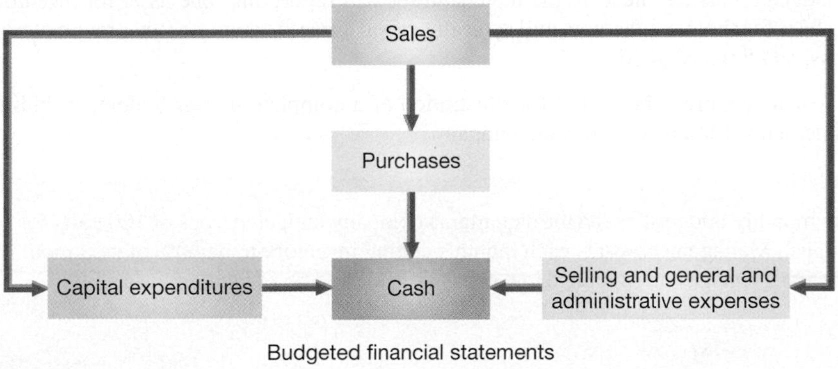

EXHIBIT 20A.1
Master Budget Sequence—Merchandiser

Merchandise purchases budget preparation. Toronto Sticks Company is an exclusive supplier of hockey sticks to Hockey Den, meaning that the companies rely on the same budgeted sales figures (Exhibit 20.4) in preparing budgets. A merchandiser usually expresses a **merchandise purchases budget** in both units and dollars. Exhibit 20A.2 shows the general layout for this budget in equation form. If this formula is expressed in units and only one product is involved, we can compute the number of dollars of inventory to be purchased for the budget by multiplying the units to be purchased by the cost per unit.

Budgeted ending merchandise inventory + **Budgeted sales for the period** − **Budgeted beginning merchandise inventory** = **Merchandise inventory to be purchased**

EXHIBIT 20A.2
General Formula for Merchandise Purchases Budget

To illustrate, after assessing the cost of keeping inventory along with the risk and cost of inventory shortages, HD decided that the number of units in its inventory at each month-end should equal 90% of next month's predicted sales. For example, inventory at the end of October should equal 90% of budgeted November sales, and the November ending inventory should equal 90% of budgeted December sales, and so on. Also, HD expects the September 2015 per unit purchase cost of $60 to remain unchanged through January 2016. This information along with knowledge of 1,010 units in inventory at September 30 (given) allows the company to prepare the merchandise purchases budget shown in Exhibit 20A.3.

EXHIBIT 20A.3

Merchandise Purchases Budget

	A	B	C	D
1	HOCKEY DEN			
2	Merchandise Purchases Budget			
3	October 2015–December 2015			
4		October	November	December
5	Next month's budgeted sales (units)	800	1,400	900
6	Ratio of inventory to future sales	× 90%	× 90%	× 90%
7	Budgeted ending inventory (units)	720	1,260	810
8	Add: Budgeted sales (units)	1,000	800	1,400
9	Required units of available merchandise	1,720	2,060	2,210
10	Deduct: Beginning inventory (units)	1,010*	720	1,260
11	Total units to be purchased	710	1,340	950
12				
13	Budgeted cost per unit	$ 60	$ 60	$ 60
14	Budgeted cost of merchandise purchases	$42,600	$80,400	$57,000
15				

*Does not comply with company policy.

The first three lines of HD's merchandise purchases budget determine the required ending inventories (in units). Budgeted unit sales are then added to the desired ending inventory to give the required units of available merchandise. We then subtract beginning inventory to determine the budgeted number of units to be purchased. The last line is the budgeted cost of the purchases, computed by multiplying the number of units to be purchased by the predicted cost per unit.

Other Master Budget Differences—Merchandiser vs. Manufacturer In addition to preparing a purchases budget instead of production, direct materials, direct labor, and overhead budgets, other key differences in master budgets for merchandisers include:

1. Depreciation expense is included in the general and administrative expense budget of the merchandiser. For the manufacturer, depreciation on manufacturing assets is included in the factory overhead budget and treated as a product cost.
2. The budgeted balance sheet for the merchandiser will report only one asset for inventory. The balance sheet for the manufacturer will typically report three inventory assets: raw materials, work in process, and finished goods.

See Need-To-Know Comprehensive 2 for illustration of a complete master budget, including budgeted financial statements, for a merchandising company.

NEED-TO-KNOW 20-4

Merchandise Purchases Budget

P4

In preparing monthly budgets for the third quarter, a company budgeted sales of 120 units for July and 140 units for August. Management wants each month's ending inventory to be 60% of next month's sales. The June 30 inventory consists of 72 units. How many units should be purchased in July?

Solution

Purchases Budget	July
Next month's budgeted sales (units)	140
Ratio of inventory to future sales	× 60%
Budgeted ending inventory (units)	84
Add: Budgeted sales (units)	+120
Required units of available merchandise	204
Deduct: Beginning inventory (units)	− 72
Units to be purchased	132

Do More: QS 20-28, QS 20-29, QS 20-30, E 20-23

Summary

C1 Describe the benefits of budgeting and the process of budget administration. Planning is a management responsibility of critical importance to business success. Budgeting is the process management uses to formalize its plans. Budgeting promotes management analysis and focuses its attention on the future. Budgeting also provides a basis for evaluating performance, serves as a source of motivation, is a means of coordinating activities, and communicates management's plans and instructions to employees. Budgeting is a detailed activity that requires administration. At least three aspects are important: budget committee, budget reporting, and budget timing. A budget committee oversees the budget preparation. The budget period pertains to the time period for which the budget is prepared such as a year or month.

C2 Describe a master budget and the process of preparing it. A master budget is a formal overall plan for a company. It consists of plans for business operations and capital expenditures, plus the financial results of those activities. The budgeting process begins with a sales budget. Based on expected sales volume, companies can budget production and manufacturing costs, selling expenses, and administrative expenses. Next, the capital expenditures budget is prepared, followed by the cash budget and budgeted financial statements. Merchandisers must budget merchandise purchases instead of manufacturing costs.

A1 Analyze expense planning using activity-based budgeting. Activity-based budgeting requires management to identify activities performed by departments, plan necessary activity levels, identify resources required to perform these activities, and budget the resources.

P1 Prepare the operating budget components of a master budget—for a manufacturing company. From budgeted sales a manufacturer prepares a *production budget.* A *manufacturing budget* shows the budgeted production costs for direct materials, direct labor, and overhead. *Selling* and *general and administrative expense* budgets complete the operating budgets of the master budget.

P2 Prepare a cash budget. The cash budget shows expected cash inflows and outflows during a budgeting period. This budget helps management maintain the company's desired cash balance.

P3 Prepare budgeted financial statements. The operating budgets, capital expenditures budget, and cash budget contain much of the information to prepare a budgeted income statement for the budget period and a budgeted balance sheet at the end of the budget period. Budgeted financial statements show the expected financial consequences of the planned activities described in the budgets.

P4A Prepare each component of a master budget and link each to the budgeting process—for a merchandising company. The term *master budget* refers to a collection of individual component budgets. Each component budget is designed to guide persons responsible for activities covered by that component. A master budget must reflect the components of a company and their interaction in pursuit of company goals.

Guidance Answers to Decision Maker

Entrepreneur You must deal with two issues. First, because fashions and designs frequently change, you cannot heavily rely on previous budgets. As a result, you must carefully analyze the market to understand what designs are in vogue. This will help you plan the product mix and estimate demand. The second issue is the budgeting period. An annual sales budget may be unreliable because tastes can quickly change. Your best bet might be to prepare monthly and quarterly sales budgets that you continuously monitor and revise.

Environmental Manager You are unlikely to have data on this new position to use in preparing your budget. In this situation, you can use activity-based budgeting. This requires developing a list of activities to conduct, the resources required to perform these activities, and the expenses associated with these resources. You should challenge yourself to be absolutely certain that the listed activities are necessary and that the listed resources are required.

Key Terms

Activity-based budgeting (ABB)
Budget
Budgeted balance sheet
Budgeted income statement
Budgeting
Capital expenditures budget
Cash budget
Continuous budgeting
Direct labor budget
Direct materials budget
Factory overhead budget
General and administrative expense budget
Master budget
Merchandise purchases budget
Production budget
Rolling budgets
Safety stock
Sales budget
Selling expense budget

Multiple Choice Quiz

Answers at end of chapter

1. A plan that reports the units of merchandise to be produced by a manufacturing company during the budget period is called a
   a. Capital expenditures budget.
   b. Cash budget.
   c. Production budget.
   d. Manufacturing budget.
   e. Sales budget.

2.A A hardware store has budgeted sales of $36,000 for its power tool department in July. Management wants to have $7,000 in power tool inventory at the end of July. Its beginning inventory of power tools is expected to be $6,000. What is the budgeted dollar amount of merchandise purchases?
   a. $36,000
   b. $43,000
   c. $42,000
   d. $35,000
   e. $37,000

3. A store has the following budgeted sales for the next five months.

May	$210,000
June	186,000
July	180,000
August	220,000
September	240,000

Cash sales are 25% of total sales and all credit sales are expected to be collected in the month following the sale. The total amount of cash expected to be received from customers in September is

a. $240,000 **c.** $60,000 **e.** $220,000
b. $225,000 **d.** $165,000

4. A plan that shows the expected cash inflows and cash outflows during the budget period, including receipts from loans needed to maintain a minimum cash balance and repayments of such loans, is called

a. A rolling budget. **d.** A cash budget.
b. An income statement. **e.** An operating budget.
c. A balance sheet.

5. The following sales are predicted for a company's next four months.

	September	October	November	December
Unit sales	480	560	600	480

Each month's ending inventory of finished goods should be 30% of the next month's sales. At September 1, the finished goods inventory is 140 units. The budgeted production of units for October is

a. 572 units. **c.** 548 units. **e.** 180 units.
b. 560 units. **d.** 600 units.

A Superscript letter A denotes assignments based on Appendix 20A, which relates to budgets for merchandising companies.
Icon denotes assignments that involve decision making.

Discussion Questions

1. Identify at least three roles that budgeting plays in helping managers control and monitor a business.
2. What two common benchmarks can be used to evaluate actual performance? Which of the two is generally more useful?
3. What is the benefit of continuous budgeting?
4. Identify three usual time horizons for short-term planning and budgets.
5. Why should each department participate in preparing its own budget?
6. How does budgeting help management coordinate and plan business activities?
7. Why is the sales budget so important to the budgeting process?
8. What is a selling expense budget? What is a capital expenditures budget?
9. Budgeting promotes good decision making by requiring managers to conduct ______ and by focusing their attention on the ______.
10. **Google** prepares a cash budget. What is a cash budget? Why must operating budgets and the capital expenditures budget be prepared before the cash budget? **GOOGLE**
11. **Apple** regularly uses budgets. What is the difference between a production budget and a manufacturing budget? **APPLE**
12. Would a manager of an **Apple** retail store participate more in budgeting than a manager at the corporate offices? Explain. **APPLE**
13. Does the manager of a **Samsung** distribution center participate in long-term budgeting? Explain. **Samsung**
14. Assume that **Samsung**'s consumer electronics division is charged with preparing a master budget. Identify the participants—for example, the sales manager for the sales budget—and describe the information each person provides in preparing the master budget. **Samsung**

connect

QUICK STUDY

QS 20-1
Budget motivation C1

The motivation of employees is one goal of budgeting. Identify three guidelines that organizations should follow if budgeting is to serve effectively as a source of motivation for employees.

QS 20-2
Budgeting process C1

Good management includes good budgeting. (1) Explain why the bottom-up approach to budgeting is considered a more successful management technique than a top-down approach. (2) Provide an example of implementation of the bottom-up approach to budgeting.

QS 20-3
Components of a master budget C2

Identify which of the following sets of items are necessary components of the master budget.

_______ **1.** Operating budgets, historical income statement, and budgeted balance sheet.
_______ **2.** Prior sales reports, capital expenditures budget, and financial budgets.
_______ **3.** Sales budget, operating budgets, and historical financial budgets.
_______ **4.** Operating budgets, financial budgets, and capital expenditures budget.

QS 20-4
Sales budget P1

Grace manufactures and sells miniature digital cameras for $250 each. 1,000 units were sold in May, and management forecasts 4% growth in unit sales each month. Determine (a) the number of units of camera sales and (b) the dollar amount of camera sales for the month of June.

QS 20-5
Selling expense budget P1

Zilly Co. predicts sales of $400,000 for June. Zilly pays a sales manager a monthly salary of $6,000 and a commission of 8% of sales dollars. Prepare a selling expense budget for the month of June.

QS 20-6
Cash budget P2

Liza's predicts sales of $40,000 for May and $52,000 for June. Assume 60% of Liza's sales are for cash. The remaining 40% are credit sales; these customers pay in the month following the sale. Compute the budgeted cash receipts for June.

QS 20-7
Manufacturing: Direct materials budget P1

Zortek Corp. budgets production of 400 units in January and 200 units in February. Each finished unit requires five pounds of raw material Z, which costs $2 per pound. Each month's ending inventory of raw materials should be 40% of the following month's budgeted production. The January 1 raw materials inventory has 130 pounds of Z. Prepare a direct materials budget for January.

QS 20-8
Manufacturing: Direct labor budget P1

Tora Co. plans to produce 1,020 units in July. Each unit requires two hours of direct labor. The direct labor rate is $20 per hour. Prepare a direct labor budget for July.

QS 20-9
Sales budget P1

Scora, Inc., is preparing its master budget for the quarter ending March 31. It sells a single product for $50 per unit. Budgeted sales for the next four months follow. Prepare a sales budget for the months of January, February, and March.

	January	February	March	April
Sales in units	1,200	2,000	1,600	1,400

QS 20-10
Cash receipts budget P2

X-Tel budgets sales of $60,000 for April, $100,000 for May, and $80,000 for June. In addition, sales are 40% cash and 60% on credit. All credit sales are collected in the month following the sale. The April 1 balance in accounts receivable is $15,000. Prepare a schedule of budgeted cash receipts for April, May, and June.

QS 20-11
Selling expense budget P1

X-Tel budgets sales of $60,000 for April, $100,000 for May, and $80,000 for June. In addition, sales commissions are 10% of sales dollars and the company pays a sales manager a salary of $6,000 per month. Sales commissions and salaries are paid in the month incurred. Prepare a selling expense budget for April, May, and June.

QS 20-12
Manufacturing: Production budget P1

Champ, Inc., predicts the following sales in units for the coming three months:

	May	June	July
Sales in units	180	200	240

Each month's ending inventory of finished units should be 60% of the next month's sales. The April 30 finished goods inventory is 108 units. Compute Champ's budgeted production (in units) for May.

QS 20-13
Manufacturing: Direct materials budget
P1

Miami Solar manufactures solar panels for industrial use. The company budgets production of 5,000 units (solar panels) in July and 5,300 units in August. Each unit requires 3 pounds of direct materials, which cost $6 per pound. The company's policy is to maintain direct materials inventory equal to 30% of the next month's direct materials requirement. As of June 30, the company has 4,500 pounds of direct materials in inventory, which complies with the policy. Prepare a direct materials budget for July.

QS 20-14
Manufacturing: Direct labor budget P1

Miami Solar budgets production of 5,000 solar panels in July. Each unit requires 4 hours of direct labor at a rate of $16 per hour. Prepare a direct labor budget for July.

QS 20-15
Manufacturing: Factory overhead budget P1

Miami Solar budgets production of 5,300 solar panels for August. Each unit requires 4 hours of direct labor at a rate of $16 per hour. Variable factory overhead is budgeted to be 70% of direct labor cost, and fixed factory overhead is $180,000 per month. Prepare a factory overhead budget for August.

QS 20-16
Manufacturing: Production budget
P1

Atlantic Surf manufactures surfboards. The company's sales budget for the next three months is shown below. In addition, company policy is to maintain finished goods inventory equal (in units) to 40% of the next month's unit sales. As of June 30, the company has 1,600 finished surfboards in inventory, which complies with the policy. Prepare a production budget for the months of July and August.

	July	August	September
Sales (in units)	4,000	6,500	3,500

QS 20-17
Manufacturing: Production budget
P1

Forrest Company manufactures phone chargers and has a JIT policy that ending inventory must equal 10% of the next month's sales. It estimates that October's actual ending inventory will consist of 40,000 units. November and December sales are estimated to be 400,000 and 350,000 units, respectively. Compute the number of units to be produced that would appear on the company's production budget for the month of November.

QS 20-18
Manufacturing: Factory overhead budget P1

Hockey Pro budgets production of 3,900 hockey pucks during May. The company assigns variable overhead at the rate of $1.50 per unit. Fixed overhead equals $46,000 per month. Prepare a factory overhead budget for May.

QS 20-19
Cash receipts P2

Music World reports the following sales forecast: August, $150,000; September, $170,000. Cash sales are normally 40% of total sales and all credit sales are expected to be collected in the month following the date of sale. Prepare a schedule of cash receipts for September.

QS 20-20
Cash receipts, with uncollectible accounts
P2

The Guitar Shoppe reports the following sales forecast: August, $150,000; September, $170,000. Cash sales are normally 40% of total sales, 55% of credit sales are collected in the month following sale, and the remaining 5% of credit sales are written off as uncollectible. Prepare a schedule of cash receipts for September.

QS 20-21
Cash receipts, with uncollectible accounts P2

Wells Company reports the following sales forecast: September, $55,000; October, $66,000; and November, $80,000. All sales are on account. Collections of credit sales are received as follows: 25% in the month of sale, 60% in the first month after sale, and 10% in the second month after sale. 5% of all credit sales are written off as uncollectible. Prepare a schedule of cash receipts for November.

QS 20-22
Computing budgeted accounts receivable
P2

Lighthouse Company anticipates total sales for June and July of $420,000 and $398,000, respectively. Cash sales are normally 60% of total sales. Of the credit sales, 20% are collected in the same month as the sale, 70% are collected during the first month after the sale, and the remaining 10% are collected in the second month. Determine the amount of accounts receivable reported on the company's budgeted balance sheet as of July 31.

QS 20-23
Budgeted loan activity
P2

Messers Company is preparing a cash budget for February. The company has $20,000 cash at the beginning of February and anticipates $75,000 in cash receipts and $100,250 in cash disbursements during February. What amount, if any, must the company borrow during February to maintain a $5,000 cash balance? The company has no loans outstanding on February 1.

QS 20-24
Cash budget
P2

Use the following information to prepare a cash budget for the month ended on March 31 for Gado Company. The budget should show expected cash receipts and cash disbursements for the month of March and the balance expected on March 31.

a. Beginning cash balance on March 1, $72,000.
b. Cash receipts from sales, $300,000.
c. Budgeted cash disbursements for purchases, $140,000.
d. Budgeted cash disbursements for salaries, $80,000.
e. Other budgeted cash expenses, $45,000.
f. Cash repayment of bank loan, $20,000.

QS 20-25
Budgeted financial statements
P3

Following are selected accounts for a company. For each account, indicate whether it will appear on a budgeted income statement (BIS) or a budgeted balance sheet (BBS). If an item will not appear on either budgeted financial statement, label it NA.

Sales	______	Interest expense on note payable	______
Office salaries expense	______	Cash dividends paid	______
Accumulated depreciation	______	Bank loan owed	______
Amortization expense	______	Cost of goods sold	______

QS 20-26[A]
Merchandising: Cash disbursements for merchandise P4

Gordands purchased $600,000 of merchandise in August and expects to purchase $720,000 in September. Merchandise purchases are paid as follows: 25% in the month of purchase and 75% in the following month. Compute cash disbursements for merchandise for September.

QS 20-27[A]
Merchandising: Cash disbursements for merchandise P4

Meyer Co. forecasts merchandise purchases of $15,800 in January, $18,600 in February, and $20,200 in March; 40% of purchases are paid in the month of purchase and 60% are paid in the following month. At December 31 of the prior year, the balance of accounts payable (for December purchases) is $22,000. Prepare a schedule of cash disbursements for merchandise for each of the months of January, February, and March.

QS 20-28[A]
Merchandising: Computing purchases
P4

Raider-X Company forecasts sales of 18,000 units for April. Beginning inventory is 3,000 units. The desired ending inventory is 30% higher than the beginning inventory. How many units should Raider-X purchase in April?

QS 20-29[A]
Merchandising: Computing purchases
P4

Lexi Company forecasts unit sales of 1,040,000 in April, 1,220,000 in May, 980,000 in June, and 1,020,000 in July. Beginning inventory on April 1 is 280,000 units, and the company wants to have 30% of next month's sales in inventory at the end of each month. Prepare a merchandise purchases budget for the months of April, May, and June.

QS 20-30[A]
Merchandising: Purchases budget P4

Montel Company's July sales budget calls for sales of $600,000. The store expects to begin July with $50,000 of inventory and to end the month with $40,000 of inventory. Gross margin is typically 40% of sales. Determine the budgeted cost of merchandise purchases for July.

QS 20-31
Activity-based budgeting
A1

Activity-based budgeting is a budget system based on *expected activities.* (1) Describe activity-based budgeting, and explain its preparation of budgets. (2) How does activity-based budgeting differ from traditional budgeting?

QS 20-32
Operating budgets
P1

Royal Philips Electronics of the Netherlands reports sales of €25,400 million for a recent year. Assume that the company expects sales growth of 3 percent for the next year. Also assume that selling expenses are typically 20 percent of sales, while general and administrative expenses are 4 percent of sales.

1. Compute budgeted sales for the next year.
2. Assume budgeted sales for next year is €26,000 million, and then compute budgeted selling expenses and budgeted general and administrative expenses for the next year.

connect

EXERCISES

Exercise 20-1
Budget consequences
C1

Participatory budgeting can sometimes lead to negative consequences. From the following list of outcomes that can arise from participatory budgeting, identify those with potentially *negative* consequences.

_____ **a.** Budgetary slack will not be available to meet budgeted results.
_____ **b.** Employees might understate expense budgets.
_____ **c.** Employees might commit unethical or fraudulent acts to meet budgeted results.
_____ **d.** Employees set sales targets too high.
_____ **e.** Employees always spend budgeted amounts, even if on unnecessary items.
_____ **f.** Employees might understate sales budgets and overstate expense budgets.

Exercise 20-2
Master budget definitions
C2

Match the definitions 1 through 9 with the term or phrase *a* through *i*.

A. Budget
B. Merchandise purchases budget
C. Cash budget
D. Safety stock
E. Budgeted income statement
F. General and administrative expense budget
G. Sales budget
H. Master budget
I. Budgeted balance sheet

_____ **1.** A comprehensive business plan that includes specific plans for expected sales, the units of product to be produced, the merchandise or materials to be purchased, the expenses to be incurred, the long-term assets to be purchased, and the amounts of cash to be borrowed or loans to be repaid, as well as a budgeted income statement and balance sheet.
_____ **2.** A quantity of inventory or materials over the minimum to reduce the risk of running short.
_____ **3.** A plan showing the units of goods to be sold and the sales to be derived; the usual starting point in the budgeting process.
_____ **4.** An accounting report that presents predicted amounts of the company's revenues and expenses for the budgeting period.
_____ **5.** An accounting report that presents predicted amounts of the company's assets, liabilities, and equity balances at the end of the budget period.
_____ **6.** A plan that shows the units or costs of merchandise to be purchased by a merchandising company during the budget period.
_____ **7.** A formal statement of a company's future plans, usually expressed in monetary terms.
_____ **8.** A plan that shows predicted operating expenses not included in the selling expenses budget.
_____ **9.** A plan that shows the expected cash inflows and cash outflows during the budget period, including receipts from any loans needed to maintain a minimum cash balance and repayments of such loans.

Exercise 20-3
Manufacturing: Production budget
P1

Hospitable Co. provides the following sales forecast for the next four months:

	April	May	June	July
Sales (units)	500	580	540	620

The company wants to end each month with ending finished goods inventory equal to 25% of next month's sales. Finished goods inventory on April 1 is 190 units. Assume July's budgeted production is 540 units. Prepare a production budget for the months of April, May, and June.

Exercise 20-4
Manufacturing: Direct materials budget P1

Refer to the information in Exercise 20-3. In addition, each finished unit requires five pounds of raw materials and the company wants to end each month with raw materials inventory equal to 30% of next month's production needs. Beginning raw materials inventory for April was 663 pounds. Assume direct materials cost $4 per pound. Prepare a direct materials budget for April, May, and June.

Exercise 20-5
Manufacturing: Direct labor budget P1

The production budget for Manner Company shows units to be produced as follows: July, 620; August, 680; September, 540. Each unit produced requires two hours of direct labor. The direct labor rate is currently $20 per hour but is predicted to be $21 per hour in September. Prepare a direct labor budget for the months July, August, and September.

Exercise 20-6
Manufacturing: Direct materials budget P1

Rida, Inc., a manufacturer in a seasonal industry, is preparing its direct materials budget for the second quarter. It plans production of 240,000 units in the second quarter and 52,500 units in the third quarter. Raw material inventory is 43,200 pounds at the beginning of the second quarter. Other information follows. Prepare a direct materials budget for the second quarter.

Direct materials	Each unit requires 0.60 pounds of a key raw material, priced at $175 per pound. The company plans to end each quarter with an ending inventory of materials equal to 30% of next quarter's budgeted materials requirements.

Exercise 20-7
Manufacturing: Direct labor and factory overhead budgets P1

Addison Co. budgets production of 2,400 units during the second quarter. In addition, information on its direct labor and its variable and fixed overhead is shown below. For the second quarter, prepare (1) a direct labor budget and (2) a factory overhead budget.

Direct labor	Each finished unit requires 4 direct labor hours, at a cost of $9 per hour.
Variable overhead.	Applied at the rate of $11 per direct labor hour
Fixed overhead	Budgeted at $450,000 per quarter

Exercise 20-8
Manufacturing: Direct materials budget P1

Rad Co. provides the following sales forecast and production budget for the next four months:

	April	May	June	July
Sales (units)	500	580	530	600
Budgeted production (units)	442	570	544	540

The company plans for finished goods inventory of 120 units at the end of June. In addition, each finished unit requires 5 pounds of raw materials and the company wants to end each month with raw materials inventory equal to 30% of next month's production needs. Beginning raw materials inventory for April was 663 pounds. Each finished unit requires 0.50 hours of direct labor at the rate of $16 per hour. The company budgets variable overhead at the rate of $20 per direct labor hour and budgets fixed overhead of $8,000 per month. Prepare a raw materials budget for April, May, and June.

Exercise 20-9
Manufacturing: Direct labor and factory overhead budgets P1

Refer to Exercise 20-8. For April, May, and June, prepare (1) a direct labor budget and (2) a factory overhead budget.

Exercise 20-10
Manufacturing: Production budget P1

Blue Wave Co. predicts the following unit sales for the coming four months: September, 4,000 units; October, 5,000 units; November, 7,000 units; and December, 7,600 units. The company's policy is to maintain finished goods inventory equal to 60% of the next month's sales. At the end of August, the company had 2,400 finished units on hand. Prepare a production budget for each of the months of September, October, and November.

Exercise 20-11
Manufacturing: Production budget P1

Tyler Co. predicts the following unit sales for the next four months: April, 3,000 units; May, 4,000 units; June, 6,000 units; and July, 2,000 units. The company's policy is to maintain finished goods inventory equal to 30% of the next month's sales. At the end of March, the company had 900 finished units on hand. Prepare a production budget for each of the months of April, May, and June.

Exercise 20-12
Manufacturing: Preparing production budgets (for two periods)
P1
Check Second quarter production, 480,000 units

Electro Company manufactures an innovative automobile transmission for electric cars. Management predicts that ending finished goods inventory for the first quarter will be 75,000 units. The following unit sales of the transmissions are expected during the rest of the year: second quarter, 450,000 units; third quarter, 525,000 units; and fourth quarter, 475,000 units. Company policy calls for the ending finished goods inventory of a quarter to equal 20% of the next quarter's budgeted sales. Prepare a production budget for both the second and third quarters that shows the number of transmissions to manufacture. Ending inventory for the first quarter does not comply with company policy.

Exercise 20-13
Manufacturing: Direct materials budget P1

Electro Company budgets production of 450,000 transmissions in the second quarter and 520,000 transmissions in the third quarter. Each transmission requires 0.80 pounds of a key raw material. Electro Company aims to end each quarter with an ending inventory of direct materials equal to 20% of next quarter's budgeted materials requirements. Beginning inventory of this raw material is 72,000 pounds. Direct materials cost $1.70 per pound. Prepare a direct materials budget for the second quarter.

Exercise 20-14
Manufacturing: Direct labor budget P1

Branson Belts makes hand-crafted belts. The company budgets production of 4,500 belts during the second quarter. Each belt requires 4 direct labor hours, at a cost of $12 per hour. Prepare a direct labor budget for the second quarter.

Exercise 20-15
Manufacturing: Direct materials, direct labor, and overhead budgets
P1

MCO Leather Goods manufactures leather purses. Each purse requires 2 pounds of direct materials at a cost of $4 per pound and 0.8 direct labor hours at a rate of $16 per hour. Variable manufacturing overhead is charged at a rate of $2 per direct labor hour. Fixed manufacturing overhead is $10,000 per month. The company's policy is to end each month with direct materials inventory equal to 40% of the next month's materials requirement. At the end of August the company had 3,680 pounds of direct materials in inventory. The company's production budget reports the following. Prepare budgets for September *and* October for (1) direct materials, (2) direct labor, and (3) factory overhead.

Production Budget	September	October	November
Units to be produced	4,600	6,200	5,800

Exercise 20-16
Manufacturing: Direct materials, direct labor, and overhead budgets
P1

Ornamental Sculptures Mfg. manufactures garden sculptures. Each sculpture requires 8 pounds of direct materials at a cost of $3 per pound and 0.5 direct labor hours at a rate of $18 per hour. Variable manufacturing overhead is charged at a rate of $3 per direct labor hour. Fixed manufacturing overhead is $4,000 per month. The company's policy is to maintain direct materials inventory equal to 20% of the next month's materials requirement. At the end of March the company had 5,280 pounds of direct materials in inventory. The company's production budget reports the following. Prepare budgets for March *and* April for (1) direct materials, (2) direct labor, and (3) factory overhead.

Production Budget	March	April	May
Units to be produced	3,300	4,600	4,800

Exercise 20-17
Preparation of cash budgets (for three periods)
P2

Kayak Co. budgeted the following cash receipts (excluding cash receipts from loans received) and cash disbursements (excluding cash disbursements for loan principal and interest payments) for the first three months of next year.

	Cash Receipts	Cash Disbursements
January	$525,000	$475,000
February.........	400,000	350,000
March	450,000	525,000

According to a credit agreement with the company's bank, Kayak promises to have a minimum cash balance of $30,000 at each month-end. In return, the bank has agreed that the company can borrow up to $150,000 at an annual interest rate of 12%, paid on the last day of each month. The interest is computed based on the beginning balance of the loan for the month. The company repays loan principal with available cash on the last day of each month. The company has a cash balance of $30,000 and a loan balance of $60,000 at January 1. Prepare monthly cash budgets for each of the first three months of next year.

Check January ending cash balance, $30,000

Exercise 20-18
Budgeted cash receipts
P2

Jasper Company has sales on account and for cash. Specifically, 70% of its sales are on account and 30% are for cash. Credit sales are collected in full in the month following the sale. The company forecasts sales of $525,000 for April, $535,000 for May, and $560,000 for June. The beginning balance of accounts receivable is $400,000 on April 1. Prepare a schedule of budgeted cash receipts for April, May, and June.

Exercise 20-19
Cash budget
P2

Karim Corp. requires a minimum $8,000 cash balance. If necessary, loans are taken to meet this requirement at a cost of 1% interest per month (paid monthly). Any excess cash is used to repay loans at month-end. The cash balance on July 1 is $8,400 and the company has no outstanding loans. Forecasted cash receipts (other than for loans received) and forecasted cash payments (other than for loan or interest payments) follow. Prepare a cash budget for July, August, and September. Round interest payments to the nearest whole dollar.

	July	August	September
Cash receipts	$20,000	$26,000	$40,000
Cash disbursements	28,000	30,000	22,000

Exercise 20-20
Cash budget
P2

Foyert Corp. requires a minimum $30,000 cash balance. If necessary, loans are taken to meet this requirement at a cost of 1% interest per month (paid monthly). Any excess cash is used to repay loans at month-end. The cash balance on October 1 is $30,000 and the company has an outstanding loan of $10,000. Forecasted cash receipts (other than for loans received) and forecasted cash payments (other than for loan or interest payments) follow. Prepare a cash budget for October, November, and December. Round interest payments to the nearest whole dollar.

	October	November	December
Cash receipts	$110,000	$80,000	$100,000
Cash disbursements	120,000	75,000	80,000

Exercise 20-21
Manufacturing: Cash budget
P2

Use the following information to prepare the September cash budget for PTO Manufacturing Co. The following information relates to expected cash receipts and cash disbursements for the month ended September 30.

a. Beginning cash balance, September 1, $40,000.
b. Budgeted cash receipts from sales in September, $255,000.
c. Raw materials are purchased on account. Purchase amounts are: August (actual), $80,000, and September (budgeted), $110,000. Payments for direct materials are made as follows: 65% in the month of purchase and 35% in the month following purchase.
d. Budgeted cash disbursements for direct labor in September, $40,000.
e. Budgeted depreciation expense for September, $4,000.
f. Other cash expenses budgeted for September, $60,000.
g. Accrued income taxes payable in September, $10,000.
h. Bank loan interest payable in September, $1,000.

Exercise 20-22
Manufacturing: Cash budget
P2

Mike's Motors Corp. manufactures motors for dirt bikes. The company requires a minimum $30,000 cash balance at each month-end. If necessary, the company takes a loan to meet this requirement, at a cost of 2% interest per month (paid at the end of each month). Any cash balance above $30,000 at month-end is used to repay loans. The cash balance on July 1 is $34,000, and the company has no outstanding loans at that time. Forecasted cash receipts and forecasted cash payments (other than for loan activity) are as follows. Prepare a cash budget for July, August, and September.

	Cash Receipts	Cash Disbursements
July	$ 85,000	$113,000
August	111,000	99,900
September	150,000	127,400

Exercise 20-23[A]
Merchandising:
Preparation of purchases budgets (for three periods)
P4

Walker Company prepares monthly budgets. The current budget plans for a September ending inventory of 30,000 units. Company policy is to end each month with merchandise inventory equal to a specified percent of budgeted sales for the following month. Budgeted sales and merchandise purchases for the next three months follow.

1. Prepare the merchandise purchases budget for the months of July, August, and September.
2. Compute the ratio of ending inventory to the next month's sales for each budget prepared in part 1.
3. How many units are budgeted for sale in October?

	Sales (Units)	Purchases (Units)
July	180,000	200,250
August	315,000	308,250
September	270,000	259,500

Exercise 20-24[A]
Merchandising:
Preparation of a cash budget
P4

Use the following information to prepare the July cash budget for Acco Co. It should show expected cash receipts and cash disbursements for the month and the cash balance expected on July 31.

a. Beginning cash balance on July 1: $50,000.
b. Cash receipts from sales: 30% is collected in the month of sale, 50% in the next month, and 20% in the second month after sale (uncollectible accounts are negligible and can be ignored). Sales amounts are: May (actual), $1,720,000; June (actual), $1,200,000; and July (budgeted), $1,400,000.
c. Payments on merchandise purchases: 60% in the month of purchase and 40% in the month following purchase. Purchases amounts are: June (actual), $700,000; and July (budgeted), $750,000.
d. Budgeted cash disbursements for salaries in July: $275,000.
e. Budgeted depreciation expense for July: $36,000.
f. Other cash expenses budgeted for July: $200,000.
g. Accrued income taxes due in July: $80,000.
h. Bank loan interest paid in July: $6,600.

Check Ending cash balance, $122,400

Exercise 20-25[A]
Merchandising:
Preparing a budgeted income statement and balance sheet
P4

Use the information in Exercise 20-24 and the following additional information to prepare a budgeted income statement for the month of July and a budgeted balance sheet for July 31.

a. Cost of goods sold is 55% of sales.
b. Inventory at the end of June is $80,000 and at the end of July is $60,000.
c. Salaries payable on June 30 are $50,000 and are expected to be $60,000 on July 31.
d. The equipment account balance is $1,600,000 on July 31. On June 30, the accumulated depreciation on equipment is $280,000.
e. The $6,600 cash payment of interest represents the 1% monthly expense on a bank loan of $660,000.
f. Income taxes payable on July 31 are $30,720, and the income tax rate applicable to the company is 30%.
g. The only other balance sheet accounts are: Common Stock, with a balance of $600,000 on June 30; and Retained Earnings, with a balance of $964,000 on June 30.

Check Net income, $71,680; Total assets, $2,686,400

Exercise 20-26[A]
Merchandising:
Computing budgeted cash payments for purchases P4

Hardy Company's cost of goods sold is consistently 60% of sales. The company plans to carry ending merchandise inventory for each month equal to 20% of the next month's budgeted cost of goods sold. All merchandise is purchased on credit, and 50% of the purchases made during a month is paid for in that month. Another 35% is paid for during the first month after purchase, and the remaining 15% is paid for during the second month after purchase. Expected sales are: August (actual), $325,000; September (actual), $320,000; October (estimated), $250,000; and November (estimated), $310,000. Use this information to determine October's expected cash payments for purchases.

Check Budgeted purchases: August, $194,400; October, $157,200

Exercise 20-27[A]
Merchandising:
Computing budgeted purchases and cost of goods sold P4

Quick Dollar Company purchases all merchandise on credit. It recently budgeted the following month-end accounts payable balances and merchandise inventory balances. Cash payments on accounts payable during each month are expected to be: May, $1,600,000; June, $1,490,000; July, $1,425,000; and August, $1,495,000. Use the available information to compute the budgeted amounts of (1) merchandise purchases for June, July, and August and (2) cost of goods sold for June, July, and August.

[continued on next page]

	Accounts Payable	Merchandise Inventory
May 31	$150,000	$250,000
June 30	200,000	400,000
July 31	235,000	300,000
August 31	195,000	330,000

Check June purchases, $1,540,000; June cost of goods sold, $1,390,000

Exercise 20-28[A]
Merchandising: Computing budgeted accounts payable and purchases—sales forecast in dollars P4

Big Sound, a merchandising company specializing in home computer speakers, budgets its monthly cost of goods sold to equal 70% of sales. Its inventory policy calls for ending inventory in each month to equal 20% of the next month's budgeted cost of goods sold. All purchases are on credit, and 25% of the purchases in a month is paid for in the same month. Another 60% is paid for during the first month after purchase, and the remaining 15% is paid for in the second month after purchase. The following sales budgets are set: July, $350,000; August, $290,000; September, $320,000; October, $275,000; and November, $265,000.

Compute the following: (1) budgeted merchandise purchases for July, August, September, and October; (2) budgeted payments on accounts payable for September and October; and (3) budgeted ending balances of accounts payable for September and October. (*Hint:* For part *1,* refer to Exhibits 22A.2 and 22A.3 for guidance, but note that budgeted sales are in dollars for this assignment.)

Check July purchases, $236,600; Sept. payments on accts. pay., $214,235

Exercise 20-29[A]
Merchandising: Budgeted cash disbursements
P4

Hector Company reports the following sales and purchases data. Payments for purchases are made in the month after purchase. Selling expenses are 10% of sales, administrative expenses are 8% of sales, and both are paid in the month of sale. Rent expense of $7,400 is paid monthly. Depreciation expense is $2,300 per month. Prepare a schedule of budgeted cash disbursements for August and September.

	July	August	September
Sales	$50,000	$72,000	$66,000
Purchases	14,400	19,200	21,600

Exercise 20-30[A]
Merchandising: Cash budget
P4

Castor, Inc., is preparing its master budget for the quarter ended June 30. Budgeted sales and cash payments for merchandise for the next three months follow:

Budgeted	April	May	June
Sales	$32,000	$40,000	$24,000
Cash payments for merchandise.........	20,200	16,800	17,200

Sales are 50% cash and 50% on credit. All credit sales are collected in the month following the sale. The March 30 balance sheet includes balances of $12,000 in cash, $12,000 in accounts receivable, $11,000 in accounts payable, and a $2,000 balance in loans payable. A minimum cash balance of $12,000 is required. Loans are obtained at the end of any month when a cash shortage occurs. Interest is 1% per month based on the beginning of the month loan balance and is paid at each month-end. If an excess balance of cash exists, loans are repaid at the end of the month. Operating expenses are paid in the month incurred and consist of sales commissions (10% of sales), shipping (2% of sales), office salaries ($5,000 per month), and rent ($3,000 per month). Prepare a cash budget for each of the months of April, May, and June (round all dollar amounts to the nearest whole dollar).

Exercise 20-31[A]
Merchandising: Cash budget
P4

Kelsey is preparing its master budget for the quarter ended September 30. Budgeted sales and cash payments for merchandise for the next three months follow:

Budgeted	July	August	September
Sales	$64,000	$80,000	$48,000
Cash payments for merchandise.........	40,400	33,600	34,400

Sales are 20% cash and 80% on credit. All credit sales are collected in the month following the sale. The June 30 balance sheet includes balances of $15,000 in cash; $45,000 in accounts receivable; $4,500 in accounts payable; and a $5,000 balance in loans payable. A minimum cash balance of $15,000 is required. Loans are obtained at the end of any month when a cash shortage occurs. Interest is 1% per month based on the beginning of the month loan balance and is paid at each month-end. If an excess balance of cash exists, loans are repaid at the end of the month. Operating expenses are paid in the month incurred and consist of sales commissions (10% of sales), office salaries ($4,000 per month), and rent ($6,500 per month). (1) Prepare a cash receipts budget for July, August, and September. (2) Prepare a cash budget for each of the months of July, August, and September. (Round all dollar amounts to the nearest whole dollar.)

Exercise 20-32A
Merchandising:
Budgeted balance sheet
P4

The following information is available for Zetrov Company:

a. The cash budget for March shows an ending bank loan of $10,000 and an ending cash balance of $50,000.

b. The sales budget for March indicates sales of $140,000. Accounts receivable are expected to be 70% of the current-month sales.

c. The merchandise purchases budget indicates that $89,000 in merchandise will be purchased on account in March. Purchases on account are paid 100% in the month following the purchase. Ending inventory for March is predicted to be 600 units at a cost of $35 each.

d. The budgeted income statement for March shows net income of $48,000. Depreciation expense of $1,000 and $26,000 in income tax expense were used in computing net income for March. Accrued taxes will be paid in April.

e. The balance sheet for February shows equipment of $84,000 with accumulated depreciation of $46,000, common stock of $25,000, and ending retained earnings of $8,000. There are no changes budgeted in the Equipment or Common Stock accounts.

Prepare a budgeted balance sheet for March.

Exercise 20-33A
Merchandising:
Budgeted income statement
P4

Fortune, Inc., is preparing its master budget for the first quarter. The company sells a single product at a price of $25 per unit. Sales (in units) are forecasted at 45,000 for January, 55,000 for February, and 50,000 for March. Cost of goods sold is $14 per unit. Other expense information for the first quarter follows. Prepare a budgeted income statement for this first quarter.

Commissions	8% of sales dollars
Rent	$14,000 per month
Advertising	15% of sales dollars
Office salaries	$75,000 per month
Depreciation	$40,000 per month
Interest	15% annually on a $250,000 note payable
Tax rate	30%

Exercise 20-34
Activity-based budgeting
A1

Render Co. CPA is preparing activity-based budgets for 2015. The partners expect the firm to generate billable hours for the year as follows:

Data entry	2,200 hours
Auditing	4,800 hours
Tax	4,300 hours
Consulting	750 hours

The company pays $10 per hour to data-entry clerks, $40 per hour to audit personnel, $50 per hour to tax personnel, and $50 per hour to consulting personnel. Prepare a schedule of budgeted labor costs for 2015 using activity-based budgeting.

connect

PROBLEM SET A

Problem 20-1A
Manufacturing: Preparing production and manufacturing budgets
C2 P1

Black Diamond Company produces snow skis. Each ski requires 2 pounds of carbon fiber. The company's management predicts that 5,000 skis and 6,000 pounds of carbon fiber will be in inventory on June 30 of the current year and that 150,000 skis will be sold during the next (third) quarter. A set of two skis sells for $300. Management wants to end the third quarter with 3,500 skis and 4,000 pounds of carbon fiber in inventory. Carbon fiber can be purchased for $15 per pound. Each ski requires 0.5 hours of direct labor at $20 per hour. Variable overhead is applied at the rate of $8 per direct labor hour. The company budgets fixed overhead of $1,782,000 for the quarter.

Required

1. Prepare the third-quarter production budget for skis.
2. Prepare the third-quarter direct materials (carbon fiber) budget; include the dollar cost of purchases.
3. Prepare the direct labor budget for the third quarter.
4. Prepare the factory overhead budget for the third quarter.

Check (1) Units manuf., 148,500; (2) Cost of carbon fiber purchases, $4,425,000

Problem 20-2A
Manufacturing: Cash budget
P2

Built-Tight is preparing its master budget for the quarter ended September 30, 2015. Budgeted sales and cash payments for product costs for the quarter follow:

	A	B	C	D
1		July	August	September
2	Budgeted sales	$64,000	$80,000	$48,000
3	Budgeted cash payments for			
4	Direct materials	16,160	13,440	13,760
5	Direct labor	4,040	3,360	3,440
6	Factory overhead	20,200	16,800	17,200
7				

Sales are 20% cash and 80% on credit. All credit sales are collected in the month following the sale. The June 30 balance sheet includes balances of $15,000 in cash; $45,000 in accounts receivable; $4,500 in accounts payable; and a $5,000 balance in loans payable. A minimum cash balance of $15,000 is required. Loans are obtained at the end of any month when a cash shortage occurs. Interest is 1% per month based on the beginning of the month loan balance and is paid at each month-end. If an excess balance of cash exists, loans are repaid at the end of the month. Operating expenses are paid in the month incurred and consist of sales commissions (10% of sales), office salaries ($4,000 per month), and rent ($6,500 per month).

1. Prepare a cash receipts budget for July, August, and September.
2. Prepare a cash budget for each of the months of July, August, and September. (Round amounts to the dollar.)

Problem 20-3A
Manufacturing: Preparation and analysis of budgeted income statements
P3

Merline Manufacturing makes its product for $75 per unit and sells it for $150 per unit. The sales staff receives a 10% commission on the sale of each unit. Its December income statement follows.

MERLINE MANUFACTURING Income Statement For Month Ended December 31, 2015		
Sales		$2,250,000
Cost of goods sold		1,125,000
Gross profit		1,125,000
Operating expenses		
Sales commissions (10%)	225,000	
Advertising	250,000	
Store rent	30,000	
Administrative salaries	45,000	
Depreciation—Office equipment	50,000	
Other expenses	10,000	
Total expenses		610,000
Net income		$ 515,000

Management expects December's results to be repeated in January, February, and March of 2016 without any changes in strategy. Management, however, has an alternative plan. It believes that unit sales will increase at a rate of 10% *each* month for the next three months (beginning with January) if the item's selling price is reduced to $125 per unit and advertising expenses are increased by 15% and remain at that level for all three months. The cost of its product will remain at $75 per unit, the sales staff will continue to earn a 10% commission, and the remaining expenses will stay the same.

Required

Check (1) Budgeted net income: January, $196,250; February, $258,125; March, $326,187

1. Prepare budgeted income statements for each of the months of January, February, and March that show the expected results from implementing the proposed changes. Use a three-column format, with one column for each month.

Analysis Component

2. Use the budgeted income statements from part 1 to recommend whether management should implement the proposed changes. Explain.

Problem 20-4A
Manufacturing:
Preparation of a complete master budget
P1 P2 P3

The management of Zigby Manufacturing prepared the following estimated balance sheet for March, 2015:

ZIGBY MANUFACTURING
Estimated Balance Sheet
March 31, 2015

Assets		Liabilities and Equity	
Cash	$ 40,000	Accounts payable	$ 200,500
Accounts receivable	342,248	Short-term notes payable	12,000
Raw materials inventory	98,500	Total current liabilities	212,500
Finished goods inventory	325,540	Long-term note payable	500,000
Total current assets	806,288	Total liabilities	712,500
Equipment, gross	600,000	Common stock	335,000
Accumulated depreciation	(150,000)	Retained earnings	208,788
Equipment, net	450,000	Total stockholders' equity	543,788
Total assets	$1,256,288	Total liabilities and equity	$1,256,288

To prepare a master budget for April, May, and June of 2015, management gathers the following information:

a. Sales for March total 20,500 units. Forecasted sales in units are as follows: April, 20,500; May, 19,500; June, 20,000; and July, 20,500. Sales of 240,000 units are forecasted for the entire year. The product's selling price is $23.85 per unit and its total product cost is $19.85 per unit.

b. Company policy calls for a given month's ending raw materials inventory to equal 50% of the next month's materials requirements. The March 31 raw materials inventory is 4,925 units, which complies with the policy. The expected June 30 ending raw materials inventory is 4,000 units. Raw materials cost $20 per unit. Each finished unit requires 0.50 units of raw materials.

c. Company policy calls for a given month's ending finished goods inventory to equal 80% of the next month's expected unit sales. The March 31 finished goods inventory is 16,400 units, which complies with the policy.

d. Each finished unit requires 0.50 hours of direct labor at a rate of $15 per hour.

e. Overhead is allocated based on direct labor hours. The predetermined variable overhead rate is $2.70 per direct labor hour. Depreciation of $20,000 per month is treated as fixed factory overhead.

f. Sales representatives' commissions are 8% of sales and are paid in the month of the sales. The sales manager's monthly salary is $3,000.

g. Monthly general and administrative expenses include $12,000 administrative salaries and 0.9% monthly interest on the long-term note payable.

h. The company expects 30% of sales to be for cash and the remaining 70% on credit. Receivables are collected in full in the month following the sale (none is collected in the month of the sale).

i. All raw materials purchases are on credit, and no payables arise from any other transactions. One month's raw materials purchases are fully paid in the next month.

j. The minimum ending cash balance for all months is $40,000. If necessary, the company borrows enough cash using a short-term note to reach the minimum. Short-term notes require an interest payment of 1% at each month-end (before any repayment). If the ending cash balance exceeds the minimum, the excess will be applied to repaying the short-term notes payable balance.

k. Dividends of $10,000 are to be declared and paid in May.

l. No cash payments for income taxes are to be made during the second calendar quarter. Income tax will be assessed at 35% in the quarter and paid in the third calendar quarter.

m. Equipment purchases of $130,000 are budgeted for the last day of June.

Required

Prepare the following budgets and other financial information as required. All budgets and other financial information should be prepared for the second calendar quarter, except as otherwise noted below. Round calculations up to the nearest whole dollar, except for the amount of cash sales, which should be rounded down to the nearest whole dollar.

1. Sales budget.
2. Production budget.
3. Raw materials budget.
4. Direct labor budget.
5. Factory overhead budget.
6. Selling expense budget.
7. General and administrative expense budget.
8. Cash budget.
9. Budgeted income statement for the entire second quarter (not for each month separately).
10. Budgeted balance sheet as of the end of the second calendar quarter.

Check (2) Units to produce: April, 19,700; May, 19,900
(3) Cost of raw materials purchases, April, $198,000
(5) Total overhead cost, May, $46,865
(8) Ending cash balance: April, $83,346; May, $124,295
(10) Budgeted total assets, June 30: $1,299,440

Problem 20-5A[A]
Merchandising:
Preparation and analysis of purchases budgets
P4

Keggler's Supply is a merchandiser of three different products. The company's February 28 inventories are footwear, 20,000 units; sports equipment, 80,000 units; and apparel, 50,000 units. Management believes that excessive inventories have accumulated for all three products. As a result, a new policy dictates that ending inventory in any month should equal 30% of the expected unit sales for the following month. Expected sales in units for March, April, May, and June follow.

	Budgeted Sales in Units			
	March	April	May	June
Footwear	15,000	25,000	32,000	35,000
Sports equipment	70,000	90,000	95,000	90,000
Apparel	40,000	38,000	37,000	25,000

Required

1. Prepare a merchandise purchases budget (in units) for each product for each of the months of March, April, and May.

Check (1) March budgeted purchases: Footwear, 2,500; Sports equip., 17,000; Apparel, 1,400

Analysis Component

2. The purchases budgets in part 1 should reflect fewer purchases of all three products in March compared to those in April and May. What factor caused fewer purchases to be planned? Suggest business conditions that would cause this factor to both occur and impact the company in this way.

Problem 20-6A[A]
Merchandising:
Preparation of cash budgets (for three periods)
P4

During the last week of August, Oneida Company's owner approaches the bank for a $100,000 loan to be made on September 2 and repaid on November 30 with annual interest of 12%, for an interest cost of $3,000. The owner plans to increase the store's inventory by $80,000 during September and needs the loan to pay for inventory acquisitions. The bank's loan officer needs more information about Oneida's ability to repay the loan and asks the owner to forecast the store's November 30 cash position. On September 1, Oneida is expected to have a $5,000 cash balance, $159,100 of net accounts receivable, and $125,000 of accounts payable. Its budgeted sales, merchandise purchases, and various cash disbursements for the next three months follow.

	A	B	C	D
1	Budgeted Figures*	September	October	November
2	Sales	$250,000	$375,000	$400,000
3	Merchandise purchases	240,000	225,000	200,000
4	Cash disbursements			
5	Payroll	20,000	22,000	24,000
6	Rent	10,000	10,000	10,000
7	Other cash expenses	35,000	30,000	20,000
8	Repayment of bank loan			100,000
9	Interest on the bank loan			3,000
10				

*Operations began in August; August sales were $215,000 and purchases were $125,000.

The budgeted September merchandise purchases include the inventory increase. All sales are on account. The company predicts that 25% of credit sales is collected in the month of the sale, 45% in the month following the sale, 20% in the second month, 9% in the third, and the remainder is uncollectible. Applying these percents to the August credit sales, for example, shows that $96,750 of the $215,000 will be collected in September, $43,000 in October, and $19,350 in November. All merchandise is purchased on credit; 80% of the balance is paid in the month following a purchase, and the remaining 20% is paid in the second month. For example, of the $125,000 August purchases, $100,000 will be paid in September and $25,000 in October.

Check Budgeted cash balance: September, $99,250; October, $69,500; November, $22,600

Required

Prepare a cash budget for September, October, and November for Oneida Company. Show supporting calculations as needed.

Problem 20-7A[A]
Merchandising: Preparation and analysis of cash budgets with supporting inventory and purchases budgets
P4

Aztec Company sells its product for $180 per unit. Its actual and budgeted sales follow.

	Units	Dollars
April (actual)	4,000	$ 720,000
May (actual)	2,000	360,000
June (budgeted)	6,000	1,080,000
July (budgeted)	5,000	900,000
August (budgeted)	3,800	684,000

All sales are on credit. Recent experience shows that 20% of credit sales is collected in the month of the sale, 50% in the month after the sale, 28% in the second month after the sale, and 2% proves to be uncollectible. The product's purchase price is $110 per unit. All purchases are payable within 12 days. Thus, 60% of purchases made in a month is paid in that month and the other 40% is paid in the next month. The company has a policy to maintain an ending monthly inventory of 20% of the next month's unit sales plus a safety stock of 100 units. The April 30 and May 31 actual inventory levels are consistent with this policy. Selling and administrative expenses for the year are $1,320,000 and are paid evenly throughout the year in cash. The company's minimum cash balance at month-end is $100,000. This minimum is maintained, if necessary, by borrowing cash from the bank. If the balance exceeds $100,000, the company repays as much of the loan as it can without going below the minimum. This type of loan carries an annual 12% interest rate. On May 31, the loan balance is $25,000, and the company's cash balance is $100,000. (Round amounts to the nearest dollar.)

Required

Check (1) Cash collections: June, $597,600; July, $820,800

(3) Budgeted purchases: May, $308,000; June, $638,000

1. Prepare a table that shows the computation of cash collections of its credit sales (accounts receivable) in each of the months of June and July.
2. Prepare a table that shows the computation of budgeted ending inventories (in units) for April, May, June, and July.
3. Prepare the merchandise purchases budget for May, June, and July. Report calculations in units and then show the dollar amount of purchases for each month.

4. Prepare a table showing the computation of cash payments on product purchases for June and July.
5. Prepare a cash budget for June and July, including any loan activity and interest expense. Compute the loan balance at the end of each month.

(5) Budgeted ending loan balance: June, $43,650; July, $0

Analysis Component

6. Refer to your answer to part 5. Aztec's cash budget indicates the company will need to borrow more than $18,000 in June. Suggest some reasons that knowing this information in May would be helpful to management.

Problem 20-8A[A]
Merchandising:
Preparation of a complete master budget P4

Near the end of 2015, the management of Dimsdale Sports Co., a merchandising company, prepared the following estimated balance sheet for December 31, 2015.

DIMSDALE SPORTS COMPANY
Estimated Balance Sheet
December 31, 2015

Assets			**Liabilities and Equity**		
Cash	$ 36,000		Accounts payable	$360,000	
Accounts receivable	525,000		Bank loan payable	15,000	
Inventory	150,000		Taxes payable (due 3/15/2016)	90,000	
Total current assets		$ 711,000	Total liabilities		$ 465,000
Equipment	540,000		Common stock	472,500	
Less: Accumulated depreciation	67,500		Retained earnings	246,000	
Equipment, net		472,500	Total stockholders' equity		718,500
Total assets		$1,183,500	Total liabilities and equity		$1,183,500

To prepare a master budget for January, February, and March of 2016, management gathers the following information.

a. Dimsdale Sports's single product is purchased for $30 per unit and resold for $55 per unit. The expected inventory level of 5,000 units on December 31, 2015, is more than management's desired level for 2016, which is 20% of the next month's expected sales (in units). Expected sales are: January, 7,000 units; February, 9,000 units; March, 11,000 units; and April, 10,000 units.

b. Cash sales and credit sales represent 25% and 75%, respectively, of total sales. Of the credit sales, 60% is collected in the first month after the month of sale and 40% in the second month after the month of sale. For the December 31, 2015, accounts receivable balance, $125,000 is collected in January and the remaining $400,000 is collected in February.

c. Merchandise purchases are paid for as follows: 20% in the first month after the month of purchase and 80% in the second month after the month of purchase. For the December 31, 2015, accounts payable balance, $80,000 is paid in January and the remaining $280,000 is paid in February.

d. Sales commissions equal to 20% of sales are paid each month. Sales salaries (excluding commissions) are $60,000 per year.

e. General and administrative salaries are $144,000 per year. Maintenance expense equals $2,000 per month and is paid in cash.

f. Equipment reported in the December 31, 2015, balance sheet was purchased in January 2015. It is being depreciated over eight years under the straight-line method with no salvage value. The following amounts for new equipment purchases are planned in the coming quarter: January, $36,000; February, $96,000; and March, $28,800. This equipment will be depreciated under the straight-line method over eight years with no salvage value. A full month's depreciation is taken for the month in which equipment is purchased.

g. The company plans to acquire land at the end of March at a cost of $150,000, which will be paid with cash on the last day of the month.

h. Dimsdale Sports has a working arrangement with its bank to obtain additional loans as needed. The interest rate is 12% per year, and interest is paid at each month-end based on the beginning balance. Partial or full payments on these loans can be made on the last day of the month. The company has agreed to maintain a minimum ending cash balance of $25,000 in each month.

i. The income tax rate for the company is 40%. Income taxes on the first quarter's income will not be paid until April 15.

Required

Prepare a master budget for each of the first three months of 2016; include the following component budgets (show supporting calculations as needed, and round amounts to the nearest dollar):

1. Monthly sales budgets (showing both budgeted unit sales and dollar sales).
2. Monthly merchandise purchases budgets.
3. Monthly selling expense budgets.
4. Monthly general and administrative expense budgets.
5. Monthly capital expenditures budgets.
6. Monthly cash budgets.
7. Budgeted income statement for the entire first quarter (not for each month).
8. Budgeted balance sheet as of March 31, 2016.

Check (2) Budgeted purchases: January, $114,000; February, $282,000
(3) Budgeted selling expenses: January, $82,000; February, $104,000
(6) Ending cash bal.: January, $30,100; February, $210,300
(8) Budgeted total assets at March 31, $1,568,650

PROBLEM SET B

Problem 20-1B
Manufacturing: Preparing production and manufacturing budgets
C2 P1

NSA Company produces baseball bats. Each bat requires 3 pounds of aluminum alloy. Management predicts that 8,000 bats and 15,000 pounds of aluminum alloy will be in inventory on March 31 of the current year and that 250,000 bats will be sold during this year's second quarter. Bats sell for $80 each. Management wants to end the second quarter with 6,000 finished bats and 12,000 pounds of aluminum alloy in inventory. Aluminum alloy can be purchased for $4 per pound. Each bat requires 0.5 hours of direct labor at $18 per hour. Variable overhead is applied at the rate of $12 per direct labor hour. The company budgets fixed overhead of $1,776,000 for the quarter.

Required

1. Prepare the second-quarter production budget for bats.
2. Prepare the second-quarter direct materials (aluminum alloy) budget; include the dollar cost of purchases.
3. Prepare the direct labor budget for the second quarter.
4. Prepare the factory overhead budget for the second quarter.

Check (1) Units manuf., 248,000
(2) Cost of materials purchases, $2,964,000

Problem 20-2B
Manufacturing: Cash budget
P2 A1

A1 Manufacturing is preparing its master budget for the quarter ended September 30, 2015. Budgeted sales and cash payments for product costs for the quarter follow.

	A	B	C	D
1		July	August	September
2	Budgeted sales	$63,400	$80,600	$48,600
3	Budgeted cash payments for			
4	Direct materials	12,480	9,900	10,140
5	Direct labor	10,400	8,250	8,450
6	Factory overhead	18,720	14,850	15,210
7				

Sales are 20% cash and 80% on credit. All credit sales are collected in the month following the sale. The June 30 balance sheet includes balances of $12,900 in cash; $47,000 in accounts receivable; $5,100 in accounts payable; and a $2,600 balance in loans payable. A minimum cash balance of $12,600 is required. Loans are obtained at the end of any month when a cash shortage occurs. Interest is 1% per month based on the beginning of the month loan balance and is paid at each month-end. If an excess balance of cash exists, loans are repaid at the end of the month. Operating expenses are paid in the month incurred and consist of sales commissions (10% of sales), office salaries ($4,600 per month), and rent ($7,100 per month).

1. Prepare a cash receipts budget for July, August, and September.
2. Prepare a cash budget for each of the months of July, August, and September. (Round amounts to the dollar.)

Problem 20-3B
Manufacturing:
Preparation and analysis of budgeted income statements P3

HCS Mfg. makes its product for $60 and sells it for $130 per unit. The sales staff receives a 10% commission on the sale of each unit. Its June income statement follows.

HCS MFG. Income Statement For Month Ended June 30, 2015	
Sales	$1,300,000
Cost of goods sold	600,000
Gross profit	700,000
Operating expenses	
Sales commissions (10%)	130,000
Advertising	200,000
Store rent	24,000
Administrative salaries	40,000
Depreciation—Office equipment	50,000
Other expenses	12,000
Total expenses	456,000
Net income	$ 244,000

Management expects June's results to be repeated in July, August, and September without any changes in strategy. Management, however, has another plan. It believes that unit sales will increase at a rate of 10% *each* month for the next three months (beginning with July) if the item's selling price is reduced to $115 per unit and advertising expenses are increased by 25% and remain at that level for all three months. The cost of its product will remain at $60 per unit, the sales staff will continue to earn a 10% commission, and the remaining expenses will stay the same.

Required

1. Prepare budgeted income statements for each of the months of July, August, and September that show the expected results from implementing the proposed changes. Use a three-column format, with one column for each month.

Check Budgeted net income: July, $102,500; August, $150,350; September, $202,985

Analysis Component

2. Use the budgeted income statements from part 1 to recommend whether management should implement the proposed plan. Explain.

Problem 20-4B
Manufacturing:
Preparation of a complete master budget
P1 P2 P3

The management of Nabar Manufacturing prepared the following estimated balance sheet for June, 2015:

NABAR MANUFACTURING Estimated Balance Sheet June 30, 2015			
Assets		**Liabilities and Equity**	
Cash	$ 40,000	Accounts payable	$ 51,400
Accounts receivable	249,900	Income taxes payable	10,000
Raw materials inventory	35,000	Short-term notes payable	24,000
Finished goods inventory	241,080	Total current liabilities	85,400
Total current assets	565,980	Long-term note payable	300,000
Equipment, gross	720,000	Total liabilities	385,400
Accumulated depreciation	(240,000)	Common stock	600,000
Equipment, net	480,000	Retained earnings	60,580
		Total stockholders' equity	660,580
Total assets	$1,045,980	Total liabilities and equity	$1,045,980

To prepare a master budget for July, August, and September of 2015, management gathers the following information:

a. Sales were 20,000 units in June. Forecasted sales in units are as follows: July, 21,000; August, 19,000; September, 20,000; October, 24,000. The product's selling price is $17 per unit and its total product cost is $14.35 per unit.

b. Company policy calls for a given month's ending finished goods inventory to equal 70% of the next month's expected unit sales. The June 30 finished goods inventory is 16,800 units, which does not comply with the policy.

c. Company policy calls for a given month's ending raw materials inventory to equal 20% of the next month's materials requirements. The June 30 raw materials inventory is 4,375 units (which also fails to meet the policy). The budgeted September 30 raw materials inventory is 1,980 units. Raw materials cost $8 per unit. Each finished unit requires 0.50 units of raw materials.

d. Each finished unit requires 0.50 hours of direct labor at a rate of $16 per hour.

e. Overhead is allocated based on direct labor hours. The predetermined variable overhead rate is $2.70 per direct labor hour. Depreciation of $20,000 per month is treated as fixed factory overhead.

f. Monthly general and administrative expenses include $9,000 administrative salaries and 0.9% monthly interest on the long-term note payable.

g. Sales representatives' commissions are 10% of sales and are paid in the month of the sales. The sales manager's monthly salary is $3,500 per month.

h. The company expects 30% of sales to be for cash and the remaining 70% on credit. Receivables are collected in full in the month following the sale (none are collected in the month of the sale).

i. All raw materials purchases are on credit, and no payables arise from any other transactions. One month's raw materials purchases are fully paid in the next month.

j. Dividends of $20,000 are to be declared and paid in August.

k. Income taxes payable at June 30 will be paid in July. Income tax expense will be assessed at 35% in the quarter and paid in October.

l. Equipment purchases of $100,000 are budgeted for the last day of September.

m. The minimum ending cash balance for all months is $40,000. If necessary, the company borrows enough cash using a short-term note to reach the minimum. Short-term notes require an interest payment of 1% at each month-end (before any repayment). If the ending cash balance exceeds the minimum, the excess will be applied to repaying the short-term notes payable balance.

Required

Prepare the following budgets and other financial information as required. All budgets and other financial information should be prepared for the third calendar quarter, except as otherwise noted below. Round calculations to the nearest whole dollar.

1. Sales budget.
2. Production budget.
3. Raw materials budget.
4. Direct labor budget.
5. Factory overhead budget.
6. Selling expense budget.
7. General and administrative expense budget.
8. Cash budget.
9. Budgeted income statement for the entire quarter (not for each month separately).
10. Budgeted balance sheet as of September 30, 2015.

Check (2) Units to produce: July, 17,500; August, 19,700
(3) Cost of raw materials purchases, July, $50,760
(5) Total overhead cost, August, $46,595
(8) Ending cash balance: July, $96,835; August, $141,180
(10) Budgeted total assets, Sept. 30: $1,054,920

Problem 20-5B^A
Merchandising: Preparation and analysis of purchases budgets
P4

H20 Sports Company is a merchandiser of three different products. The company's March 31 inventories are water skis, 40,000 units; tow ropes, 90,000 units; and life jackets, 150,000 units. Management believes that excessive inventories have accumulated for all three products. As a result, a new policy dictates that ending inventory in any month should equal 10% of the expected unit sales for the following month. Expected sales in units for April, May, June, and July follow.

Budgeted Sales in Units	April	May	June	July
Water skis	70,000	90,000	130,000	100,000
Tow ropes	100,000	90,000	110,000	100,000
Life jackets	160,000	190,000	200,000	120,000

Required

1. Prepare a merchandise purchases budget (in units) for each product for each of the months of April, May, and June.

Check (1) April budgeted purchases: Water skis, 39,000; Tow ropes, 19,000; Life jackets, 29,000

Analysis Component

2. The purchases budgets in part 1 should reflect fewer purchases of all three products in April compared to those in May and June. What factor caused fewer purchases to be planned? Suggest business conditions that would cause this factor to both occur and affect the company as it has.

Problem 20-6B[A]
Merchandising:
Preparation of cash budgets (for three periods)
P4

During the last week of March, Sony Stereo's owner approaches the bank for an $80,000 loan to be made on April 1 and repaid on June 30 with annual interest of 12%, for an interest cost of $2,400. The owner plans to increase the store's inventory by $60,000 in April and needs the loan to pay for inventory acquisitions. The bank's loan officer needs more information about Sony Stereo's ability to repay the loan and asks the owner to forecast the store's June 30 cash position. On April 1, Sony Stereo is expected to have a $3,000 cash balance, $135,000 of accounts receivable, and $100,000 of accounts payable. Its budgeted sales, merchandise purchases, and various cash disbursements for the next three months follow.

	A	B	C	D
1	Budgeted Figures*	April	May	June
2	Sales	$220,000	$300,000	$380,000
3	Merchandise purchases	210,000	180,000	220,000
4	Cash disbursements			
5	Payroll	16,000	17,000	18,000
6	Rent	6,000	6,000	6,000
7	Other cash expenses	64,000	8,000	7,000
8	Repayment of bank loan			80,000
9	Interest on the bank loan			2,400
10				

*Operations began in March; March sales were $180,000 and purchases were $100,000.

The budgeted April merchandise purchases include the inventory increase. All sales are on account. The company predicts that 25% of credit sales is collected in the month of the sale, 45% in the month following the sale, 20% in the second month, 9% in the third, and the remainder is uncollectible. Applying these percents to the March credit sales, for example, shows that $81,000 of the $180,000 will be collected in April, $36,000 in May, and $16,200 in June. All merchandise is purchased on credit; 80% of the balance is paid in the month following a purchase and the remaining 20% is paid in the second month. For example, of the $100,000 March purchases, $80,000 will be paid in April and $20,000 in May.

Required

Prepare a cash budget for April, May, and June for Sony Stereo. Show supporting calculations as needed.

Check Budgeted cash balance: April, $53,000; May, $44,000; June, $34,800

Problem 20-7B[A]
Merchandising:
Preparation and analysis of cash budgets with supporting inventory and purchases budgets
P4

Connick Company sells its product for $22 per unit. Its actual and budgeted sales follow.

	Units	Dollars
January (actual)	18,000	$396,000
February (actual)	22,500	495,000
March (budgeted)	19,000	418,000
April (budgeted)	18,750	412,500
May (budgeted)	21,000	462,000

All sales are on credit. Recent experience shows that 40% of credit sales is collected in the month of the sale, 35% in the month after the sale, 23% in the second month after the sale, and 2% proves to be uncollectible. The product's purchase price is $12 per unit. All purchases are payable within 21 days. Thus, 30% of purchases made in a month is paid in that month and the other 70% is paid in the next month. The company has a policy to maintain an ending monthly inventory of 20% of the next month's unit sales plus a safety stock of 100 units. The January 31 and February 28 actual inventory levels are consistent with this policy. Selling and administrative expenses for the year are $1,920,000 and are paid evenly throughout the year in cash. The company's minimum cash balance for month-end is $50,000. This minimum is maintained, if necessary, by borrowing cash from the bank. If the balance exceeds $50,000, the company repays as much of the loan as it can without going below the minimum. This type of loan carries an annual 12% interest rate. At February 28, the loan balance is $12,000, and the company's cash balance is $50,000.

Required

Check (1) Cash collections: March, $431,530; April, $425,150

(3) Budgeted purchases: February, $261,600; March, $227,400

(5) Ending cash balance: March, $58,070; April, $94,920

1. Prepare a table that shows the computation of cash collections of its credit sales (accounts receivable) in each of the months of March and April.
2. Prepare a table showing the computations of budgeted ending inventories (units) for January, February, March, and April.
3. Prepare the merchandise purchases budget for February, March, and April. Report calculations in units and then show the dollar amount of purchases for each month.
4. Prepare a table showing the computation of cash payments on product purchases for March and April.
5. Prepare a cash budget for March and April, including any loan activity and interest expense. Compute the loan balance at the end of each month.

Analysis Component

6. Refer to your answer to part 5. Connick's cash budget indicates whether the company must borrow additional funds at the end of March. Suggest some reasons that knowing the loan needs in advance would be helpful to management.

Problem 20-8B^A
Merchandising: Preparation of a complete master budget
P4

Near the end of 2015, the management of Isle Corp., a merchandising company, prepared the following estimated balance sheet for December 31, 2015.

ISLE CORPORATION
Estimated Balance Sheet
December 31, 2015

Assets			Liabilities and Equity		
Cash	$ 36,000		Accounts payable	$360,000	
Accounts receivable	525,000		Bank loan payable	15,000	
Inventory	150,000		Taxes payable (due 3/15/2016)	90,000	
Total current assets		$ 711,000	Total liabilities		$ 465,000
Equipment	540,000		Common stock	472,500	
Less: Accumulated depreciation	67,500		Retained earnings	246,000	
Equipment, net		472,500	Total stockholders' equity		718,500
Total assets		$1,183,500	Total liabilities and equity		$1,183,500

To prepare a master budget for January, February, and March of 2016, management gathers the following information.

a. Isle Corp.'s single product is purchased for $30 per unit and resold for $45 per unit. The expected inventory level of 5,000 units on December 31, 2015, is more than management's desired level for 2016, which is 25% of the next month's expected sales (in units). Expected sales are: January, 6,000 units; February, 8,000 units; March, 10,000 units; and April, 9,000 units.

b. Cash sales and credit sales represent 25% and 75%, respectively, of total sales. Of the credit sales, 60% is collected in the first month after the month of sale and 40% in the second month after the month of sale. For the $525,000 accounts receivable balance at December 31, 2015, $315,000 is collected in January 2014 and the remaining $210,000 is collected in February 2016.

c. Merchandise purchases are paid for as follows: 20% in the first month after the month of purchase and 80% in the second month after the month of purchase. For the $360,000 accounts payable balance at December 31, 2015, $72,000 is paid in January 2016 and the remaining $288,000 is paid in February 2016.

d. Sales commissions equal to 20% of sales are paid each month. Sales salaries (excluding commissions) are $90,000 per year.

e. General and administrative salaries are $144,000 per year. Maintenance expense equals $3,000 per month and is paid in cash.

f. Equipment reported in the December 31, 2015, balance sheet was purchased in January 2015. It is being depreciated over eight years under the straight-line method with no salvage value. The following amounts for new equipment purchases are planned in the coming quarter: January, $72,000; February, $96,000; and March, $28,800. This equipment will be depreciated using the straight-line method over eight years with no salvage value. A full month's depreciation is taken for the month in which equipment is purchased.

g. The company plans to acquire land at the end of March at a cost of $150,000, which will be paid with cash on the last day of the month.

h. Isle Corp. has a working arrangement with its bank to obtain additional loans as needed. The interest rate is 12% per year, and interest is paid at each month-end based on the beginning balance. Partial or full payments on these loans can be made on the last day of the month. Isle has agreed to maintain a minimum ending cash balance of $36,000 in each month.

i. The income tax rate for the company is 40%. Income taxes on the first quarter's income will not be paid until April 15.

Required

Prepare a master budget for each of the first three months of 2016; include the following component budgets (show supporting calculations as needed, and round amounts to the nearest dollar):

1. Monthly sales budgets (showing both budgeted unit sales and dollar sales).
2. Monthly merchandise purchases budgets.
3. Monthly selling expense budgets.
4. Monthly general and administrative expense budgets.
5. Monthly capital expenditures budgets.
6. Monthly cash budgets.
7. Budgeted income statement for the entire first quarter (not for each month).
8. Budgeted balance sheet as of March 31, 2016.

Check (2) Budgeted purchases: January, $90,000; February, $255,000
(3) Budgeted selling expenses: January, $61,500; February, $79,500
(6) Ending cash bal.: January, $182,850; February, $107,850
(8) Budgeted total assets at March 31, $1,346,875

SERIAL PROBLEM

Business Solutions

P3

(This serial problem began in Chapter 1 and continues through most of the book. If previous chapter segments were not completed, the serial problem can begin at this point. It is helpful, but not necessary, to use the Working Papers that accompany the book.)

SP 20 Santana Rey expects second-quarter 2016 sales of her new line of computer furniture to be the same as the first quarter's sales (reported below) without any changes in strategy. Monthly sales averaged 40 desk units (sales price of $1,250) and 20 chairs (sales price of $500).

BUSINESS SOLUTIONS
Segment Income Statement*
For Quarter Ended March 31, 2016

Sales†	$180,000
Cost of goods sold‡	115,000
Gross profit	65,000
Expenses	
Sales commissions (10%)	18,000
Advertising expenses	9,000
Other fixed expenses	18,000
Total expenses	45,000
Net income	$ 20,000

* Reflects revenue and expense activity only related to the computer furniture segment.
† Revenue: (120 desks × $1,250) + (60 chairs × $500) = $150,000 + $30,000 = $180,000
‡ Cost of goods sold: (120 desks × $750) + (60 chairs × $250) + $10,000 = $115,000

Santana Rey believes that sales will increase each month for the next three months (April, 48 desks, 32 chairs; May, 52 desks, 35 chairs; June, 56 desks, 38 chairs) *if* selling prices are reduced to $1,150 for desks and $450 for chairs, and advertising expenses are increased by 10% and remain at that level for all three months. The products' variable cost will remain at $750 for desks and $250 for chairs. The sales staff will continue to earn a 10% commission, the fixed manufacturing costs per month will remain at $10,000, and other fixed expenses will remain at $6,000 per month.

Required

Check (1) Budgeted income (loss): April, $(660); May, $945

1. Prepare budgeted income statements for each of the months of April, May, and June that show the expected results from implementing the proposed changes. Use a three-column format, with one column for each month.
2. Use the budgeted income statements from part 1 to recommend whether Santana Rey should implement the proposed changes. Explain.

Beyond the Numbers

REPORTING IN ACTION

P2

APPLE

BTN 20-1 Financial statements often serve as a starting point in formulating budgets. Review **Apple**'s financial statements in Appendix A to determine its cash paid for acquisitions of property, plant, and equipment in the current year and the budgeted cash needed for such acquisitions in the next year.

Required

1. Which financial statement reports the amount of cash paid for acquisitions of property, plant, and equipment? Explain where on the statement this information is reported.
2. Indicate the amount of cash (a) paid for acquisitions of property and equipment in the year ended September 28, 2013, and (b) to be paid (budgeted for) next year under the assumption that annual acquisitions of property and equipment equal 20% of the prior year's net income.

Fast Forward

3. Access Apple's financial statements for a year ending after September 28, 2013, from either its website [Apple.com] or the SEC's EDGAR database [www.SEC.gov]. Compare your answer for part 2 with actual cash paid for acquisitions of property and equipment for that fiscal year. Compute the error, if any, in your estimate. Speculate as to why cash paid for acquisitions of property and equipment was higher or lower than your estimate.

COMPARATIVE ANALYSIS

P2

APPLE

GOOGLE

BTN 20-2 One source of cash savings for a company is improved management of inventory. To illustrate, assume that **Apple** and **Google** both have $1 billion per month in sales of one model of smartphone in Canada, and both forecast this level of sales per month for the next 24 months. Also assume that both Apple and Google have a 20% contribution margin, their fixed costs are equal, and that cost of goods sold is the only variable cost. Assume that the main difference between Apple and Google is the distribution system. Apple uses a just-in-time system and requires ending inventory of only 10% of next month's sales in inventory at each month-end. However, Google is building an improved distribution system and currently requires 30% of next month's sales in inventory at each month-end.

Required

1. Compute the amount by which Google can reduce its inventory level if it can match Apple's system of maintaining an inventory equal to 10% of next month's sales. (*Hint:* Focus on the facts given and only on the Canadian market.)
2. Explain how the analysis in part 1 that shows ending inventory levels for both the 30% and 10% required inventory policies can help justify a just-in-time inventory system. Assume a 15% interest cost for resources that are tied up in ending inventory.

ETHICS CHALLENGE

C1

BTN 20-3 Both the budget process and budgets themselves can impact management actions, both positively and negatively. For instance, a common practice among not-for-profit organizations and government agencies is for management to spend any amounts remaining in a budget at the end of the budget period, a practice often called "use it or lose it." The view is that if a department manager does not spend the budgeted amount, top management will reduce next year's budget by the amount not spent. To avoid losing budget dollars, department managers often spend all budgeted amounts regardless of the value added to products or services. All of us pay for the costs associated with this budget system.

Required

Write a half-page report to a local not-for-profit organization or government agency offering a solution to the "use it or lose it" budgeting problem.

BTN 20-4 The sales budget is usually the first and most crucial of the component budgets in a master budget because all other budgets usually rely on it for planning purposes.

COMMUNICATING IN PRACTICE

C2

Required

Assume that your company's sales staff provides information on expected sales and selling prices for items making up the sales budget. Prepare a one-page memorandum to your supervisor outlining concerns with the sales staff's input in the sales budget when its compensation is at least partly tied to these budgets. More generally, explain the importance of assessing any potential bias in information provided to the budget process.

BTN 20-5 Access information on e-budgets through **The Manage Mentor** website (**themanagementor.com/kuniverse/kmailers_universe/finance_kmailers/cfa/budgeting2.htm**). Read the information provided.

TAKING IT TO THE NET

C1

Required

1. Assume the role of a senior manager in a large, multidivision company. What are the benefits of using e-budgets?
2. As a senior manager, what concerns do you have with the concept and application of e-budgets?

BTN 20-6 Your team is to prepare a budget report outlining the costs of attending college (full-time) for the next two semesters (30 hours) or three quarters (45 hours). This budget's focus is solely on attending college; do not include personal items in the team's budget. Your budget must include tuition, books, supplies, club fees, food, housing, and all costs associated with travel to and from college. This budgeting exercise is similar to the initial phase in activity-based budgeting. Include a list of any assumptions you use in completing the budget. Be prepared to present your budget in class.

TEAMWORK IN ACTION

A1

BTN 20-7 **Solben** sells technology to use in the production of biodiesel. Company founder Daniel Gómez Iñiguez stresses the importance of planning and budgeting for business success.

ENTREPRENEURIAL DECISION

C1

Required

1. How can budgeting help Daniel efficiently develop and operate his business?
2. Daniel plans to expand his business. How can a budget be useful in expanding a business's operations?

BTN 20-8 To help understand the factors impacting a sales budget, you are to visit three businesses with the same ownership or franchise membership. Record the selling prices of two identical products at each location, such as regular and premium gas sold at **Chevron** stations. You are likely to find a difference in prices for at least one of the three locations you visit.

HITTING THE ROAD

C2 P1

Required

1. Identify at least three external factors that must be considered when setting the sales budget. (*Note:* There is a difference between internal and external factors that impact the sales budget.)
2. What factors might explain any differences identified in the prices of the businesses you visited?

BTN 20-9 Access **Samsung**'s income statement (in Appendix A) for the business year 2013.

GLOBAL DECISION

P1

Samsung

Required

1. Is Samsung's selling and administrative expenses budget likely to be an important budget in its master budgeting process? Explain.
2. Identify three types of expenses that would be reported as selling and administrative expenses on Samsung's income statement.
3. Who likely has the initial responsibility for Samsung's selling and administrative expense budget? Explain.

ANSWERS TO MULTIPLE CHOICE QUIZ

1. c
2. e; Budgeted purchases = $36,000 + $7,000 − $6,000 = $37,000
3. b; Cash collected = 25% of September sales + 75% of August sales = (0.25 × $240,000) + (0.75 × $220,000) = $225,000
4. d
5. a; 560 units + (0.30 × 600 units) − (0.30 × 560 units) = 572 units

chapter 21

Flexible Budgets and Standard Costs

Chapter Preview

FIXED BUDGET REPORTS	FLEXIBLE BUDGET REPORTS	MATERIALS AND LABOR STANDARDS	OVERHEAD STANDARDS AND VARIANCES
Fixed budget performance report Fixed budget reports for evaluation	Purpose P1 Preparation Flexible budget performance report	C1 Identifying standard costs Setting standard costs C2 Cost variance analysis Cost variance computation P2 Materials and labor variances	Flexible overhead budget Setting overhead standards P3 Computing overhead variances A1 Sales variances P4 Overhead variances P5 Standard cost entries

Learning Objectives

CONCEPTUAL

C1 Define *standard costs* and explain how standard cost information is useful for management by exception.

C2 Describe cost variances and what they reveal about performance.

ANALYTICAL

A1 Analyze changes in sales from expected amounts.

PROCEDURAL

P1 Prepare a flexible budget and interpret a flexible budget performance report.

P2 Compute materials and labor variances.

P3 Compute overhead controllable and volume variances.

P4 *Appendix 21A*—Compute overhead spending and efficiency variances.

P5 *Appendix 21A*—Prepare journal entries for standard costs and account for price and quantity variances.

Courtesy of Niner Bikes

Roll On

FORT COLLINS, CO—Avid mountain biker Chris Sugai was looking for a better bike. "I wanted a higher-end bike, one that was better at climbing, braking, and descending. I noticed that no one was making it, so I decided to do it." Chris and his company, **Niner Bikes (www.ninerbikes.com)**, staked their future on 29-inch-wheel bikes, a radical departure from the more standard 26-inch wheel. "Everyone thought we were crazy," laughs Chris, "but we're convinced the 29-inch wheel gives the best ride quality." Apparently, many customers agree, as evidenced by the company's over 400% increase in sales over the past few years.

"Great products come from great people"

—Chris Sugai

Chris considers Niner Bikes to be a "virtual company." The company does much of its work online via Google Docs. The company collects new product ideas from customer chat rooms, and an engineering and design team uses software to perform virtual testing and simulation. The resulting information is shared electronically with a marketing team to develop graphics. "I need to get the best people possible, and I can't force them to move to a certain location. With Skype, iPads, and cell phones, I don't need to. I'm very much for freedom and allowing people to work how they work best."

Manufacturers like Niner Bikes must control materials, labor, and overhead costs. Determining standard costs helps. Since Niner Bikes makes only bikes with 29-inch wheels, it is able to better understand how design elements and bike components work together, enabling the company to develop very precise manufacturing specifications and standards. "We are able to focus on the minutest details. We just spent four hours talking about a cable routing system for braking." This attention to detail, and analysis of any variances in the actual manufacturing process from standards, helps Chris keep the manufacturing process on track.

Materials price and quantity variances are important in controlling the costs of expensive raw materials like carbon steel. Chris stresses the need for "precise specifications and controls; we don't use any material that does not meet our requirements." Unfavorable materials price variances could result from rising raw materials prices, which might cause the company to consider alternative suppliers or to raise its selling prices.

From sales of $2.7 million in 2009 to over $14 million currently, Niner Bikes has seen rapid growth. When production activity changes so rapidly, budgets can quickly become outdated. The use of flexible budgets, which reflect budgeted costs at several different production levels, can be useful in analyzing performance and making business decisions. While attention to budgeting, standard costs, and variances is important, Chris encourages potential entrepreneurs to build a business they are passionate about and to give back. "Part of our company's mission statement is to give back to the community that makes what we do possible. Helping organizations that support the development and maintenance of bike trails is important for our company and the right thing to do."

Sources: *Niner Bikes website,* January 2015; *Wired.com,* September 10, 2012; Interbike interview, http://vimeo.com/ninerbikes/; *Northern Colorado Business Report,* August 20, 2013

Section 1—Flexible Budgets

To monitor and control operations, companies exercise budgetary control and require budget reports. **Budgetary control** refers to management's use of budgets to see that planned objectives are met. **Budget reports** contain relevant information that compares actual results to planned activities. Budget reports are sometimes viewed as progress reports, or *report cards,* on management's performance in achieving planned objectives. These reports can be prepared at any time and for any period. Three common periods for a budget report are a month, quarter, and year.

Point: Budget reports are often used to determine bonuses of managers.

The budgetary control process involves at least four steps: (1) develop the budget from planned objectives, (2) compare actual results to budgeted amounts and analyze any differences, (3) take corrective and strategic actions, and (4) establish new planned objectives and prepare a new budget. Exhibit 21.1 shows this continual process of budgetary control. Budget reports and related documents are effective tools for managers to obtain the greatest benefits from this budgetary process.

EXHIBIT 21.1

Process of Budgetary Control

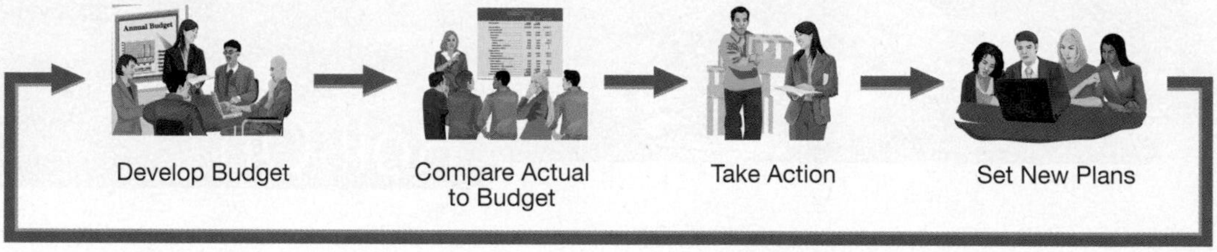

Because budgets are the main vehicle by which companies monitor and control operations, we need to look at them in some detail. As we showed in the previous chapter, a *master budget* is based on a predicted level of activity, such as sales volume, for the budget period. In preparing a master budget, two alternative approaches can be used: *fixed budgeting* or *flexible budgeting*. A **fixed budget,** also called a *static budget,* is based on a single predicted amount of sales or other activity measure. A **flexible budget,** also called a *variable budget,* is based on several different amounts of sales. As we will show in this section, a flexible budget is more useful than a fixed budget when the actual level of sales activity differs from the level of sales activity predicted at the beginning of the period. We look first at fixed budgets; understanding the limitations of fixed budgets better enables us to appreciate the benefits of flexible budgets later.

FIXED BUDGET REPORTS

Fixed Budget Performance Report

One use of a budget is to compare actual results with planned activities. Information useful for this analysis is often presented in a *performance report* that shows budgeted amounts, actual amounts, and *variances* (differences between budgeted and actual amounts). In a fixed budget control system, the master budget is based on a *single prediction* for sales volume, and the budgeted amount for each cost essentially assumes that a specific (or *fixed*) amount of sales will occur.

We illustrate fixed budget performance reports with Optel, which manufactures eyeglasses, frames, contact lenses, and related supplies. For 2015, Optel based its fixed budget on a prediction of 10,000 (composite) units of sales; costs also were budgeted based on 10,000 composite units of sales. Exhibit 21.2 shows a **fixed budget performance report,** a report that compares actual results with the results expected under a fixed budget. As the report shows, Optel's actual sales for the year were 12,000 composite units. In addition, Optel produced 12,000 composite units during the year (its inventory level did not change). The final column in the performance report shows the differences (variances) between the budgeted and actual amounts for each budget item.

EXHIBIT 21.2

Fixed Budget Performance Report

OPTEL Fixed Budget Performance Report For Month Ended January 31, 2015	Fixed Budget	Actual Results	Variances*
Sales (in units)	10,000	12,000	
Sales (in dollars)	$100,000	$125,000	$25,000 F
Cost of goods sold			
Direct materials	10,000	13,000	3,000 U
Direct labor	15,000	20,000	5,000 U
Overhead			
Factory supplies	2,000	2,100	100 U
Utilities	3,000	4,000	1,000 U
Depreciation—machinery	8,000	8,000	0
Supervisory salaries	11,000	11,000	0
Selling expenses			
Sales commissions	9,000	10,800	1,800 U
Shipping expenses	4,000	4,300	300 U
General and administrative expenses			
Office supplies	5,000	5,200	200 U
Insurance expenses	1,000	1,200	200 U
Depreciation—office equipment	7,000	7,000	0
Administrative salaries	13,000	13,000	0
Total expenses	88,000	99,600	11,600 U
Income from operations	$ 12,000	$ 25,400	$13,400 F

* F = Favorable variance; U = Unfavorable variance.

This type of performance report designates differences between budgeted and actual results as *variances*. We use the letters *F* and *U* to describe the variances, with meanings as follows:

F = **Favorable variance** When compared to budget, the actual cost or revenue contributes to a *higher* income. That is, actual revenue is higher than budgeted revenue, or actual cost is lower than budgeted cost.

U = **Unfavorable variance** When compared to budget, the actual cost or revenue contributes to a *lower* income; actual revenue is lower than budgeted revenue, or actual cost is higher than budgeted cost.

Example: How is it that the favorable sales variance in Exhibit 21.2 is linked with so many unfavorable cost and expense variances? *Answer:* Costs have increased with the increase in sales.

This convention is common in practice and is used throughout this chapter.

Budget Reports for Evaluation

A primary use of budget reports is as a tool for management to monitor and control operations. From the fixed budget performance report in Exhibit 21.2, Optel's management might raise questions such as:

- Why is actual income from operations $13,400 higher than budgeted?
- Is manufacturing using too much direct material?
- Is manufacturing using too much direct labor?
- Why are sales commissions higher than budgeted?
- Why are so many of the variances unfavorable?

The performance report in Exhibit 21.2 will not be very useful in answering these types of questions. This is because it is not based on an "apples to apples" comparison. That is, the budgeted dollar amounts are based on 10,000 units of sales, but the actual dollar amounts are based on

12,000 units of sales. Clearly, the costs to make 12,000 units will be greater than the costs to make 10,000 units, so it is no surprise that Optel's total expense variance is unfavorable. In addition, the costs in Exhibit 21.2 with the highest unfavorable variances (direct materials, direct labor, and sales commissions) are typically considered *variable* costs, which increase directly with sales activity. In general, the fixed budget performance report is not very useful in analyzing performance when actual sales differ from predicted sales. In the next section we show how a flexible budget can be useful in analyzing performance.

Decision Insight

Cruise Control Budget reporting and evaluation are used at service providers such as **Royal Caribbean Cruises Ltd.** It regularly prepares performance plans and budget requests for its fleet of cruise ships, which describe performance goals, measure outcomes, and analyze variances. ■

Melanie Stetson Freeman/The Christian Science Monitor/Getty Images

FLEXIBLE BUDGET REPORTS

Purpose of Flexible Budgets

To help address limitations with the fixed budget performance report, particularly from the effects of changes in sales volume, management can use a flexible budget. Since flexible budgets vary by level of activity, they are useful both before and after the period's activities are complete.

A flexible budget prepared before the period is often based on several levels of activity. Budgets for those different levels can provide a "what-if" look at operations. The different levels often include both a best-case and worst-case scenario. This allows management to make adjustments to avoid or lessen the effects of the worst-case scenario.

A flexible budget prepared after the period helps management evaluate past performance. It is especially useful for such an evaluation because it reflects budgeted revenues and costs based on the actual level of activity. Thus, the flexible budget gives an "apples to apples" comparison because the budgeted activity level is the same as the actual activity level. With a flexible budget, comparisons of actual results with budgeted performance are likely to be able to identify the causes of any differences. Such information can help managers focus attention on real problem areas and implement corrective actions.

Preparation of Flexible Budgets

P1 Prepare a flexible budget and interpret a flexible budget performance report.

A flexible budget is designed to reveal the effects of different activity levels on revenues and costs. To prepare a flexible budget, management must classify costs as variable or fixed, within a relevant range. Recall that the total amount of a variable cost changes in direct proportion to a change in activity level. The total amount of fixed cost remains unchanged regardless of changes in the level of activity within a relevant (normal) operating range.

When we create the numbers in a flexible budget, we express each variable cost in one of two ways: either as (1) a constant amount per unit of sales or as (2) a percentage of a sales dollar. In the case of a fixed cost, we express its budgeted amount as the total amount expected to occur at any sales volume within the relevant range.

Point: The usefulness of a flexible budget depends on valid classification of variable and fixed costs. Some costs are mixed and must be analyzed to determine their variable and fixed portions.

Exhibit 21.3 shows a set of flexible budgets for Optel for January 2015. Seven of its expenses are classified as variable costs. Optel expects these costs to change in total as sales change. Its remaining five expenses are fixed costs. These classifications result from management's investigation of each expense. Variable and fixed expense categories are *not* the same for every company, and we must avoid drawing conclusions from specific cases. For example, depending on the nature of a company's operations, office supplies expense can be either fixed or variable with respect to sales.

EXHIBIT 21.3

Flexible Budgets

OPTEL
Flexible Budgets
For Month Ended January 31, 2015

	Flexible Budget		Flexible Budget for Unit Sales of		
	Variable Amount per Unit	Total Fixed Cost	10,000	12,000	14,000
Sales	$10.00		$100,000	$120,000	$140,000
Variable costs					
Direct materials	1.00		10,000	12,000	14,000
Direct labor	1.50		15,000	18,000	21,000
Factory supplies	0.20		2,000	2,400	2,800
Utilities	0.30		3,000	3,600	4,200
Sales commissions	0.90		9,000	10,800	12,600
Shipping expenses	0.40		4,000	4,800	5,600
Office supplies	0.50		5,000	6,000	7,000
Total variable costs	4.80		48,000	57,600	67,200
Contribution margin	$ 5.20		$ 52,000	$ 62,400	$ 72,800
Fixed costs					
Depreciation—machinery		$ 8,000	8,000	8,000	8,000
Supervisory salaries		11,000	11,000	11,000	11,000
Insurance expense		1,000	1,000	1,000	1,000
Depreciation—office equipment		7,000	7,000	7,000	7,000
Administrative salaries		13,000	13,000	13,000	13,000
Total fixed costs		$40,000	40,000	40,000	40,000
Income from operations			$ 12,000	$ 22,400	$ 32,800

The layout for the flexible budgets in Exhibit 21.3 follows a *contribution margin format*—beginning with sales followed by variable costs and then fixed costs. Both the expected individual and total variable costs are reported and then subtracted from sales. Sales minus variable costs equals contribution margin. The expected amounts of fixed costs are listed next, followed by the expected income from operations before taxes.

Example: Using Exhibit 21.3, what is the budgeted income from operations for unit sales of (a) 11,000 and (b) 13,000? *Answers:* $17,200 for unit sales of 11,000; $27,600 for unit sales of 13,000.

The first column of numbers in Exhibit 21.3 shows the variable costs per unit for each of Optel's variable costs. The second column of numbers shows Optel's fixed costs, which won't change as sales volume changes. The third, fourth, and fifth number columns show the flexible budget amounts computed for three different sales volumes. For instance, the third number column's flexible budget is based on 10,000 units. In this column, total variable costs for each of Optel's seven variable costs are computed as the variable cost per unit (from column 1) multiplied by 10,000 units. Also, the total fixed costs in this column are the same as those in the second number column.

Overall, the numbers in the third number column of Exhibit 21.3 are the same as those in the fixed budget of Exhibit 21.2 because the expected sales volume (10,000 units) is the same for both budgets. In addition, the flexible budget in Exhibit 21.3 reports budgeted costs for activity levels of 12,000 and 14,000 units. Note that the total variable costs increase as the activity levels increase, but the total fixed costs stay unchanged as activity increases. A flexible budget like that in Exhibit 21.3 can be useful to management in planning operations. In addition, as we will show in the next section, a flexible budget is particularly useful in analyzing performance when actual sales volume differs from that predicted by a fixed budget.

Point: Flexible budgeting allows a budget to be prepared at the *actual* output level. Performance reports are then prepared comparing the flexible budget to actual revenues and costs.

Flexible Budget Performance Report

Recall that Optel's actual sales volume for January was 12,000 units. This sales volume is 2,000 units more than the 10,000 units originally predicted in the fixed budget. So, when management evaluates Optel's performance, it needs a flexible budget showing actual and budgeted dollar amounts at 12,000 units.

A **flexible budget performance report** compares actual performance and budgeted performance based on actual sales volume (or other activity level). This report directs management's attention to those costs or revenues that differ substantially from budgeted amounts. In Optel's case, we prepare this report after January's sales volume is known to be 12,000 units. Exhibit 21.4 shows Optel's flexible budget performance report for January. The flexible budget report shows a favorable net income variance of $3,000. Management then uses this report to investigate variances and evaluate Optel's performance. Quite often management will focus on large variances. This report shows a $5,000 favorable variance in total dollar sales. Because actual and budgeted volumes are both 12,000 units, the $5,000 sales variance must have resulted from a higher than expected selling price. Management would like to determine if the conditions that resulted in higher selling prices are likely to continue.

EXHIBIT 21.4

Flexible Budget Performance Report

OPTEL
Flexible Budget Performance Report
For Month Ended January 31, 2015

	Flexible Budget (12,000 units)	Actual Results (12,000 units)	Variances*
Sales	$120,000	$125,000	**$5,000 F**
Variable costs			
Direct materials	12,000	13,000	**1,000 U**
Direct labor	18,000	20,000	**2,000 U**
Factory supplies	2,400	2,100	**300 F**
Utilities	3,600	4,000	**400 U**
Sales commissions	10,800	10,800	**0**
Shipping expenses	4,800	4,300	**500 F**
Office supplies	6,000	5,200	**800 F**
Total variable costs	57,600	59,400	**1,800 U**
Contribution margin	62,400	65,600	**3,200 F**
Fixed costs			
Depreciation—machinery	8,000	8,000	**0**
Supervisory salaries	11,000	11,000	**0**
Insurance expense	1,000	1,200	**200 U**
Depreciation—office equipment	7,000	7,000	**0**
Administrative salaries	13,000	13,000	**0**
Total fixed costs	40,000	40,200	**200 U**
Income from operations	$ 22,400	$ 25,400	**$3,000 F**

* F = Favorable variance; U = Unfavorable variance.

The other variances in Exhibit 21.4 also direct management's attention to areas where corrective actions can help control Optel's operations. For example, both the direct materials and direct labor variances are relatively large and unfavorable. On the other hand, relatively large favorable variances are observed for shipping expenses and office supplies. Management will try to determine the causes for these variances, both favorable and unfavorable, and make changes to Optel's operations if needed.

In addition to analyzing variances using a flexible budget performance report, management can also take a more detailed approach based on a *standard cost* system. We illustrate this form of variance analysis next in the Standard Costs section of this chapter.

Decision Maker

Entrepreneur The heads of both the strategic consulting and tax consulting divisions of your financial services firm complain to you about the unfavorable variances on their performance reports. "We worked on more consulting assignments than planned. It's not surprising our costs are higher than expected. To top it off, this report characterizes our work as *poor*!" How do you respond? ■ [Answers follow the chapter's Summary.]

A manufacturing company reports the fixed budget and actual results for the past year as shown below. The company's fixed budget assumes a selling price of $40 per unit. The fixed budget is based on 20,000 units of sales, and the actual results are based on 24,000 units of sales. Prepare a flexible budget performance report for the past year.

NEED-TO-KNOW 21-1

Flexible Budget

P1

	Fixed Budget (20,000 units)	Actual Results (24,000 units)
Sales	$800,000	$972,000
Variable costs*	160,000	240,000
Fixed costs	500,000	490,000

*Budgeted variable cost per unit = $160,000/20,000 = $8.00

Solution

Flexible Budget Performance Report

	Flexible Budget (24,000 units)	Actual Results (24,000 units)	Variances
Sales	$960,000*	$972,000	$12,000 F
Variable costs	192,000**	240,000	48,000 U
Contribution margin	768,000	732,000	36,000 U
Fixed costs	500,000	490,000	10,000 F
Income from operations	$268,000	$242,000	$26,000 U

*24,000 × $40 **24,000 × $8

Do More: QS 21-1, QS 21-2, QS 21-3, QS 21-4, E 21-3, E 21-4

QC1

Section 2—Standard Costs

C1

Define *standard costs* and explain how standard cost information is useful for management by exception.

In this section we show how *standard costs* can be used in a flexible budgeting system to enable management to better understand the reasons for variances. **Standard costs** are preset costs for delivering a product or service under normal conditions. These costs are established by personnel, engineering, and accounting studies using past experiences and data. Standard costs vary across companies. Management can use standard costs to assess the reasonableness of actual costs incurred for producing the product or providing the service. When actual costs vary from standard costs, management follows up to identify potential problems and take corrective actions. **Management by exception** means that managers focus attention on the most significant differences between actual costs and standard costs and give less attention to areas where performance is reasonably close to standard. Management by exception is especially useful when directed at controllable items, enabling top management to affect the actions of lower-level managers responsible for the company's revenues and costs.

Standard costs are often used in preparing budgets because they are the anticipated costs incurred under normal conditions. Terms such as *standard materials cost, standard labor cost,* and *standard overhead cost* are often used to refer to amounts budgeted for direct materials, direct labor, and overhead.

Point: Business practice often uses the word *budget* when speaking of total amounts and *standard* when discussing per unit amounts.

While many managers use standard costs to investigate manufacturing costs, standard costs can also help control *nonmanufacturing* costs. Companies providing services instead of products can also benefit from the use of standard costs. For example, while quality medical service is paramount, efficiency in providing that service is also important to medical professionals. The use of budgeting and standard costing is touted as an effective means to control and monitor medical costs, especially overhead.

MATERIALS AND LABOR STANDARDS

This section explains how to set direct materials and direct labor standards and how to prepare a standard cost card.

Identifying Standard Costs

Managerial accountants, engineers, personnel administrators, and other managers combine their efforts to set standard costs. To identify standards for direct labor costs, we can conduct time and motion studies for each labor operation in the process of providing a product or service. From these studies, management can learn the best way to perform the operation and then set the standard labor time required for the operation under normal conditions. Similarly, standards for direct materials are set by studying the quantity, grade, and cost of each material used. (Standards for overhead costs are explained later in the chapter.)

Example: What factors might be considered when deciding whether to revise standard costs? *Answer:* Changes in the processes and/or resources needed to carry out the processes.

Regardless of the care used in setting standard costs and in revising them as conditions change, actual costs frequently differ from standard costs. For instance, the actual quantity of material used can differ from the standard, or the price paid per unit of material can differ from the standard. Quantity and price differences from standard amounts can also occur for labor. That is, the actual labor time and actual labor rate can vary from what was expected.

Decision Insight

Cruis'n Standards The **Corvette** consists of hundreds of parts for which engineers set standards. Various types of labor are also involved in its production, including machining, assembly, painting, and welding, and standards are set for each. Actual results are periodically compared with standards to assess performance. ■

Car Culture/Getty Images

Setting Standard Costs

To illustrate the setting of standard costs, we consider baseball bats manufactured by ProBat. Its engineers have determined that manufacturing one bat requires 0.90 kilograms (kg) of high-grade wood. They also expect some loss of material as part of the process because of inefficiencies and waste. This results in adding an *allowance* of 0.10 kg, making the standard requirement 1.0 kg of wood for each bat.

The 0.90 kg portion is called an *ideal standard;* it is the quantity of material required if the process is 100% efficient without any loss or waste. Reality suggests that some loss of material usually occurs with any process. The standard of 1.0 kg is known as the *practical standard,* the quantity of material required under normal application of the process. Most companies use practical rather than ideal standards.

Point: Companies promoting continuous improvement strive to achieve ideal standards by eliminating inefficiencies and waste.

ProBat needs to develop standard costs for direct materials, direct labor, and overhead. For direct materials and direct labor, ProBat must develop standard quantities and standard prices. For overhead, ProBat must consider the activities that drive overhead costs.

- High-grade wood can be purchased at a standard price of $25 per kg. The purchasing department sets this price as the expected price for the budget period. To determine this price, the purchasing department considers factors such as the quality of materials, future economic conditions, supply factors (shortages and excesses), and any available discounts.
- The engineers also decide that two hours of labor time (after including allowances) are required to manufacture a bat. The wage rate is $20 per hour (better-than-average skilled labor is required).
- ProBat assigns all overhead at the rate of $10 per labor hour.

The standard costs of direct materials, direct labor, and overhead for one bat are shown in Exhibit 21.5 in what is called a *standard cost card.* These standard cost amounts are then used to prepare manufacturing budgets for a budgeted level of production.

EXHIBIT 21.5

Standard Cost Card

STANDARD COST CARD

Production factor	Standard Quantity	Standard Cost per Unit	Total Standard Cost
Direct materials (wood)	1 kg	$25 per kg	$25
Direct labor	2 hours	$20 per hour	40
Overhead	2 labor hours	$10 per hour	20
		Total	$85

COST VARIANCE ANALYSIS

C2 Describe cost variances and what they reveal about performance.

Knowing the standard costs they expect, companies have a way to monitor and analyze differences from the standards. A **cost variance,** also simply called a *variance,* is the difference between actual and standard costs. Cost variances can be favorable (F) or unfavorable (U). If actual cost is less than standard cost, the variance is considered favorable. If actual costs are greater than standard costs, the variance is unfavorable.[1] This section discusses cost variance analysis.

Exhibit 21.6 shows the flow of events in **variance analysis:** (1) preparing a standard cost performance report, (2) computing and analyzing variances, (3) identifying questions and their explanations, and (4) taking corrective and strategic actions. These variance analysis steps are interrelated and are frequently applied in good organizations.

EXHIBIT 21.6

Variance Analysis

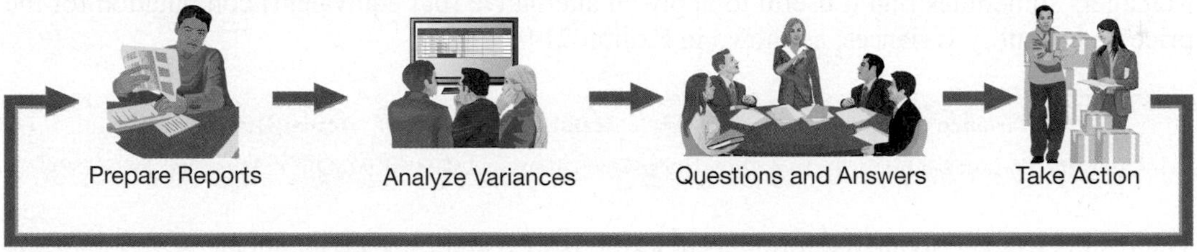

Cost Variance Computation

Management needs information about the factors causing a cost variance, but first it must properly compute the variance. In its most simple form, a cost variance (CV) is computed as shown in Exhibit 21.7.

EXHIBIT 21.7

Cost Variance Formulas

Cost Variance (CV) = **Actual Cost** (AC) − **Standard Cost** (SC)

where:

Actual Cost (AC) = **Actual Quantity** (AQ) × **Actual Price** (AP)

Standard Cost (SC) = **Standard Quantity** (SQ) × **Standard Price** (SP)

A cost variance is further defined by its components. Actual quantity (AQ) is the input (material or labor) used to manufacture the quantity of output. Standard quantity (SQ) is the standard input for the quantity of output. For example, if ProBat's actual output is 500 bats, its standard quantity of direct labor is 1,000 hours (500 bats × 2 hours per bat). Actual price (AP) is the actual amount paid to acquire the input (material or labor), and standard price (SP) is the standard price.

[1] Short-term favorable variances can sometimes lead to long-term unfavorable variances. For instance, if management spends less than the budgeted amount on maintenance or insurance, the performance report would show a favorable variance. Cutting these expenses can lead to major losses in the long run if machinery wears out prematurely or insurance coverage proves inadequate.

Two main factors cause a cost variance:

1. The difference between actual price per unit of input and standard price per unit of input results in a **price** (or rate) **variance**
2. The difference between actual quantity of input used and standard quantity of input used results in a **quantity** (or usage or efficiency) **variance.**

To assess the impacts of these two factors in a cost variance, we use the formulas in Exhibit 21.8.

EXHIBIT 21.8

Price Variance and Quantity Variance Formulas

Actual Cost AQ × AP — AQ × SP — **Standard Cost** SQ × SP

Price Variance (AQ × AP) − (AQ × SP)

Quantity Variance (AQ × SP) − (SQ × SP)

Cost Variance

Exhibit 21.8 illustrates three important general rules in computing cost variances:

1. In computing a price variance, the quantity (actual) is held constant.
2. In computing a quantity variance, the price (standard) is held constant.
3. The cost variance, or total variance, is the sum of the price and quantity variances.

Managers sometimes find it useful to apply an alternative (but equivalent) computation for the price and quantity variances, as shown in Exhibit 21.9.

EXHIBIT 21.9

Alternative Price Variance and Quantity Variance Formulas

Price Variance (PV) = [**Actual Price** (AP) − **Standard Price** (SP)] × **Actual Quantity** (AQ)

Quantity Variance (QV) = [**Actual Quantity** (AQ) − **Standard Quantity** (SQ)] × **Standard Price** (SP)

The results from applying the formulas in Exhibits 21.8 and 21.9 are identical.

Computing Materials and Labor Variances

P2 Compute materials and labor variances.

We illustrate the computation of the materials and labor cost variances using data from G-Max, a company that makes specialty golf equipment and accessories for individual customers. This company has set the following standard quantities and costs for direct materials and direct labor per unit for one of its handcrafted golf clubheads:

Direct materials (0.5 lb. per unit at $20 per lb.)	$10.00
Direct labor (1 hr. per unit at $8 per hr.)	8.00
Total standard direct cost per unit	$18.00

Kristjan Maack/Getty Images/Nordic Photos

Materials Cost Variances During May 2015, G-Max budgeted to produce 4,000 clubheads (units). It actually produced only 3,500 units. It used 1,800 pounds of direct materials (titanium) costing $21 per pound, meaning its total direct materials cost was $37,800. To produce 3,500 units, G-Max should have used 1,750 pounds of direct materials (3,500 × 0.5 lb. per unit). This information allows us to compute both actual and standard direct materials costs for G-Max's 3,500 units and its total direct materials cost variance as follows:

Direct Materials	Quantity	Price per Unit	Cost
Actual cost	1,800 lbs.	@ $21.00 per lb. =	$37,800
Standard cost	1,750 lbs.*	@ $20.00 per lb. =	35,000
Direct materials cost variance (unfavorable)		=	$ 2,800

*Standard quantity = 3,500 units × 0.5 lb. per unit

Management would like to determine if this unfavorable cost variance is due to unfavorable quantity or price variances, or both. To better isolate the causes of this $2,800 unfavorable total direct materials cost variance, the materials price and quantity variances for these G-Max clubheads are computed and shown in Exhibit 21.10.

EXHIBIT 21.10

Materials Price and Quantity Variances*

Actual Cost		Standard Cost
AQ × AP	AQ × SP	SQ × SP
1,800 lbs. × $21.00	1,800 lbs. × $20.00	1,750 lbs. × $20.00
$37,800	$36,000	$35,000

$1,800 U — **Price Variance** $37,800 − $36,000

$1,000 U — **Quantity Variance** $36,000 − $35,000

$2,800 U — **Total Direct Materials Variance** $1,800 U + $1,000 U

*AQ is actual quantity; AP is actual price; SP is standard price; SQ is standard quantity allowed for actual output.

We now can see the two components of the $2,800 unfavorable variance: The $1,800 unfavorable price variance results from paying $1 more per pound than the standard price, computed as 1,800 lbs. × $1. G-Max also used 50 pounds more materials than the standard quantity (1,800 actual pounds −1,750 standard pounds). The $1,000 unfavorable quantity variance is computed as [(1,800 actual lbs. − 1,750 standard lbs.) × $20 standard price per lb.]. Detailed price and quantity variances allow management to ask the responsible individuals for explanations and corrective actions.

Example: Identify at least two factors that might have caused the unfavorable quantity variance and the unfavorable price variance in Exhibit 21.10. *Answer:* Poor quality materials or untrained workers for the former; poor price negotiation or higher-quality materials for the latter.

Evaluating Materials Variances The purchasing department is usually responsible for the price paid for materials. Responsibility for explaining the price variance in this case rests with the purchasing manager if a price higher than standard caused the variance. The production department is usually responsible for the amount of material used. In this case the production manager is responsible for explaining why the process used more than the standard amount of materials.

Variance analysis presents challenges. For instance, the production department could have used more than the standard amount of material because the materials' quality did not meet specifications and led to excessive waste. In this case, the purchasing manager is responsible for explaining why inferior materials were acquired. However, if analysis shows that waste was due to inefficiencies, not poor-quality material, the production manager is responsible for explaining what happened.

© ColorBlind Images/Corbis

In evaluating price variances, managers must recognize that a favorable price variance can indicate a problem with poor product quality. **Redhook Ale**, a microbrewery in the Pacific Northwest, can probably save 10% to 15% in material prices by buying six-row barley malt instead of the better two-row from Washington's Yakima valley. Attention to quality, however, has helped Redhook Ale increase its sales. Purchasing activities are judged on both the quality of the materials and the purchase price variance.

NEED-TO-KNOW 21-2

Direct Materials Variances

P2

A manufacturing company reports the following for one of its products. Compute the direct materials (*a*) price variance and (*b*) quantity variance and indicate whether they are favorable or unfavorable.

Direct materials standard	8 pounds at $6 per pound
Actual direct materials used	83,000 pounds @ $5.80 per pound
Actual finished units produced	10,000

Solution

a. Price variance = (Actual quantity × Actual price) − (Actual quantity × Standard price)
= (83,000 × $5.80) − (83,000 × $6) = $16,600 favorable

b. Quantity variance = (Actual quantity × Standard price) − (Standard quantity* × Standard price)
= (83,000 × $6) − (80,000 × $6) = $18,000 unfavorable

*Standard quantity = 10,000 units × 8 standard pounds per unit = 80,000 pounds

Do More: QS 21-8, E 21-9, E 21-11, E 21-12, E 21-13

Labor Cost Variances Labor cost for a specific product or service depends on the number of hours worked (quantity) and the wage rate paid to employees (price). To illustrate, G-Max's direct labor standard for 3,500 units of its handcrafted clubheads is one direct labor hour per unit, or 3,500 hours at $8 per hour. But because only 3,400 hours at $8.30 per hour were actually used to complete the units, the actual and standard direct labor costs are

Direct Labor	Quantity	Rate per Hour	Cost
Actual cost	3,400 hrs.	@ $8.30 per hr. =	$28,220
Standard cost	3,500 hrs.*	@ $8.00 per hr. =	28,000
Direct labor cost variance (unfavorable)		=	$ 220

*Standard quantity = 3,500 units × 1 standard DLH per unit

This analysis shows that actual cost is merely $220 over the standard; that small difference might suggest no immediate concern. The direct labor cost variance can be divided into price and quantity variances, which are almost always called *rate* and *efficiency* variances. Computing both the labor rate and efficiency variances reveals a different picture, however, as shown in Exhibit 21.11.

EXHIBIT 21.11

Labor Rate and Efficiency Variances*

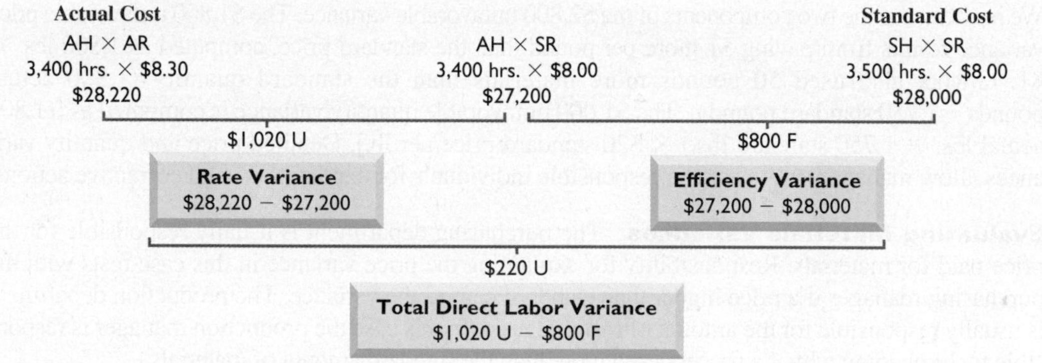

* Here, we employ hours (H) for quantity (Q), and the wage rate (R) for price (P). Thus: AH is actual direct labor hours: AR is actual wage rate; SH is standard direct labor hours allowed for actual output; SR is standard wage rate.

Example: Compute the rate variance and the efficiency variance for Exhibit 21.11 if 3,700 actual hours are used at an actual price of $7.50 per hour. *Answer:* $1,850 favorable labor rate variance and $1,600 unfavorable labor efficiency variance.

Evaluating Labor Variances Exhibit 21.11 shows that the total unfavorable labor cost variance results from an $800 favorable efficiency variance and a $1,020 unfavorable rate variance. The favorable efficiency variance results from using 100 fewer direct labor (3,400 actual DLH − 3,500 standard DLH) hours than standard for the units produced. The unfavorable rate variance results from paying a wage rate that is $0.30 per hour higher ($8.30 actual rate − $8.00 standard rate) than standard. The personnel administrator or the production manager needs to explain why the wage rate is higher than expected. The production manager should also explain how the labor hours were reduced. If this experience can be repeated and transferred to other departments, more savings are possible.

One possible explanation of these labor rate and efficiency variances is the use of workers with different skill levels. If this is the reason, senior management must discuss the implications with the production manager who has the responsibility to assign workers to tasks with the appropriate skill level. In this case, an investigation might show that higher-skilled workers were used to produce 3,500 units of hand-crafted clubheads. As a result, fewer labor hours might be required for the work, but the wage rate paid these workers is higher than standard because of their greater skills. The effect of this strategy is a higher than standard total cost, which would require actions to remedy the situation or adjust the standard.

Decision Maker

Production Manager You receive the manufacturing variance report for June and discover a large unfavorable labor efficiency (quantity) variance. What factors do you investigate to identify its possible causes? ■ [Answers follow the chapter's Summary.]

The following information is available for York Company. Compute the direct labor rate and efficiency variances.

NEED-TO-KNOW 21-3

Direct Labor Variances

P2

Actual direct labor cost (6,250 hours @ $13.10 per hour)	$81,875
Standard direct labor hours per unit	2.0 hours
Standard rate per hour	$13.00
Actual production (units)	2,500 units
Budgeted production (units)	3,000 units

Solution

Total standard hours	= 2,500 × 2.0 = 5,000
Rate variance	= ($13.10 − $13.00) × 6,250 = $625 unfavorable
Efficiency variance	= (6,250 − 5,000) × $13.00 = $16,250 unfavorable

Do More: QS 21-11, E 21-10, E 21-11, E 21-12, E 21-16

QC2

OVERHEAD STANDARDS AND VARIANCES

In previous chapters we showed how companies can use *predetermined overhead rates* to allocate overhead costs to products or services. In a standard costing system this allocation is done using the *standard* amount of the overhead allocation base, such as standard labor hours or standard machine hours. Next we show how to use standard costs to develop flexible overhead budgets.

Flexible Overhead Budgets

Standard overhead costs are the overhead amounts expected to occur at a certain activity level. Unlike direct materials and direct labor, overhead includes fixed costs and variable costs. This requires management to classify overhead costs as fixed or variable (within a relevant range), and to develop a flexible budget for overhead costs.

To illustrate, the first two number columns of Exhibit 21.12 show the overhead cost structure to develop G-Max's flexible overhead budgets for May 2015. At the beginning of the year, G-Max predicted variable overhead costs of $1.00 per unit (clubhead), comprised of $0.40 per unit for indirect labor, $0.30 per unit for indirect materials, $0.20 per unit for power and lights, and $0.10 per unit for factory maintenance. In addition, G-Max predicts monthly fixed overhead of $4,000.

Point: With increased automation, machine hours are frequently used in applying overhead instead of labor hours.

With these variable and fixed overhead cost amounts, G-Max can prepare flexible overhead budgets at various capacity levels (four right-most number columns in Exhibit 21.12). At its maximum capacity (100% column), G-Max could produce 5,000 clubheads. At 70% of maximum capacity, G-Max could produce 3,500 (computed as 5,000 × 70%) clubheads. Recall that total variable costs will increase as production activity increases, but total fixed costs will not change as production activity changes. At 70% capacity, variable overhead costs are budgeted at $3,500 (3,500 × $1.00), while at 100% capacity variable costs are budgeted at $5,000 (5,000 × $1.00). At all capacity levels, fixed overhead costs are budgeted at $4,000 per month.

Halfdark/Getty Images

Setting Overhead Standards

To allocate overhead costs to products or services, management needs to establish the standard overhead cost rate. To do that, management must determine (1) an allocation base and (2) a predicted activity level.

Allocation Base The allocation base is some measure of input that management believes is related to overhead costs. Examples include direct labor hours or machine hours. In this section

EXHIBIT 21.12
Flexible Overhead Budgets

G-MAX
Flexible Overhead Budgets
For Month Ended May 31, 2015

	Flexible Budget		Flexible Budget at Capacity Level of			
	Variable Amount per Unit	Total Fixed Cost	70%	80%	90%	100%
Production (in units)	1 unit		3,500	**4,000**	4,500	5,000
Factory overhead						
Variable costs						
Indirect labor	$0.40/unit		$1,400	**$1,600**	$1,800	$2,000
Indirect materials	0.30/unit		1,050	**1,200**	1,350	1,500
Power and lights	0.20/unit		700	**800**	900	1,000
Maintenance	0.10/unit		350	**400**	450	500
Total variable overhead costs	$1.00/unit		3,500	**4,000**	4,500	5,000
Fixed costs (per month)						
Building rent		$1,000	1,000	**1,000**	1,000	1,000
Depreciation—machinery		1,200	1,200	**1,200**	1,200	1,200
Supervisory salaries		1,800	1,800	**1,800**	1,800	1,800
Total fixed overhead costs		$4,000	4,000	**4,000**	4,000	4,000
Total factory overhead			$7,500	**$8,000**	$8,500	$9,000
Standard direct labor hours 1 hr./unit			3,500 hrs.	**4,000 hrs.**	4,500 hrs.	5,000 hrs.
Predetermined overhead rate per standard direct labor hour				**$ 2.00**		

Point: According to the U.S. Federal Reserve Board, U.S. businesses operated at an average capacity level of 80.1% between 1972 and 2013. Average capacity usage levels ranged from 78.7% for manufacturing businesses to 87.4% for mining companies.

Example: What would G-Max's standard overhead rate per unit be if management expected to operate at 70% capacity? At 100% capacity? *Answer:* At 70% capacity, the standard overhead rate is $2.14 per unit (rounded), computed as $7,500/3,500 direct labor hours. At 100% capacity, the standard overhead rate per unit is $1.80 ($9,000/5,000).

we assume that G-Max uses direct labor hours as an allocation base, and it has a standard of one direct labor hour per finished unit.

Predicted Activity Level When choosing the predicted activity level, management considers many factors. The level could be set at 100% of capacity, but this is rare. Difficulties in scheduling work, equipment breakdowns, and insufficient product demand typically cause the activity level to be less than full capacity. Also, good long-run management practices usually call for some excess plant capacity, to allow for special opportunities and demand changes. G-Max managers predicted an 80% activity level for May, or a production volume of 4,000 clubheads.

Standard Overhead Rate At the predicted activity level of 4,000 units, the flexible budget in Exhibit 21.12 predicts total overhead of $8,000. At this activity level of 4,000 units, G-Max's standard direct labor hours is 4,000 hours (4,000 units × 1 direct labor hour per unit). G-Max's standard overhead rate is then computed as:

$$\textbf{Standard overhead rate} = \frac{\textbf{Total overhead cost at predicted activity level}}{\textbf{Total direct labor hours at predicted activity level}}$$

$$= \frac{\$8{,}000}{4{,}000} = \$2 \text{ per direct labor hour}$$

This standard overhead rate will be used in computing overhead cost variances, as we show next, and in recording journal entries in a standard cost system, which we show in the appendix to this chapter.

Decision Insight

Measuring Up In the spirit of continuous improvement, competitors compare their processes and performance standards against benchmarks established by industry leaders. Those that use **benchmarking** include Jiffy Lube, All Tune and Lube, and SpeeDee Oil Change and Tune-Up. ■

Computing Overhead Cost Variances

P3

Compute overhead controllable and volume variances.

When standard costs are used, the cost accounting system applies overhead to the units produced using the predetermined standard overhead rate. The standard overhead applied is based on the predetermined overhead rate (at the predicted activity level) and the standard number of hours that *should have been used,* based on the actual production. Actual overhead incurred might be different from the overhead cost applied for a period, and management will again use *variance analysis*. The difference between the total overhead cost applied to products and the total overhead cost actually incurred is called an **overhead cost variance** (total overhead variance), which is defined in Exhibit 21.13.

EXHIBIT 21.13

Overhead Cost Variance

Overhead cost variance (OCV) = Actual overhead incurred (AOI) − Standard overhead applied (SOA)

To illustrate, G-Max produced 3,500 units during the month, which should have used 3,500 direct labor hours. Recall that management expected to produce 4,000 units during the month; thus G-Max operated below its expected level. From Exhibit 21.12, G-Max's predetermined overhead rate at the predicted capacity level of 4,000 units was $2.00 per direct labor hour, so the standard overhead applied is $7,000 (computed as 3,500 direct labor hours × $2.00). Additional data from cost reports show that the actual overhead cost incurred in the month is $7,650. Using the formula in Exhibit 21.13, we find that G-Max's total overhead variance is $650, computed as:

Actual total overhead (given)	$7,650
Standard overhead applied (3,500 DLH × $2.00 per DLH)	7,000
Total overhead variance (unfavorable)	$ 650

This variance is unfavorable: G-Max's actual overhead was higher than it should have been based on budgeted amounts.

Overhead Controllable and Volume Variances To help identify factors causing the overhead cost variance, managers separate out the *overhead controllable* and *overhead volume variances,* as illustrated in Exhibit 21.14. The results provide information useful for taking strategic actions to improve company performance.

EXHIBIT 21.14

Framework for Understanding Total Overhead Variance

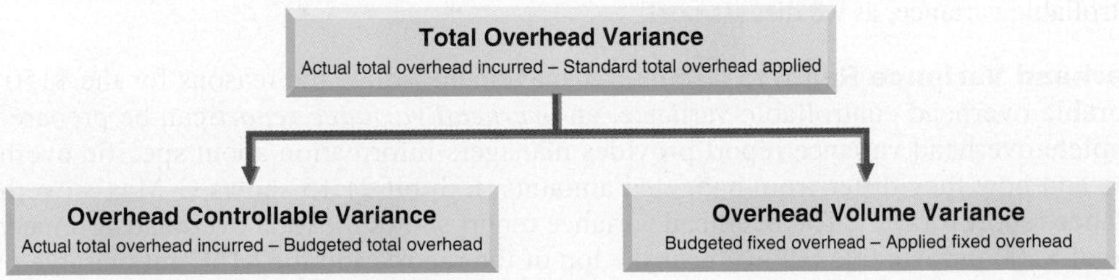

The **controllable variance** is the difference between actual overhead costs incurred and the budgeted overhead costs based on a flexible budget. The controllable variance is so named because it refers to activities usually under management control. Since G-Max only produced 3,500 units during the month, we need to compare the *actual* overhead costs to make 3,500 units to the *budgeted* cost to make 3,500 units.

Point: The budgeted overhead cost is from a flexible budget.

A **volume variance** occurs when there is a difference between the actual volume of production and the standard volume of production. The volume variance is based solely on *fixed* overhead. The budgeted fixed overhead amount is the same regardless of the volume of production (within the relevant range). The applied fixed overhead is based, however, on the standard direct labor hours allowed for the actual volume of production. When a company operates at a capacity level different from what it expected, a volume variance will exist. We next compute the controllable and volume variances for G-Max.

The flexible budget in Exhibit 21.12 shows budgeted factory overhead of $7,500 at the production volume of 3,500 units. The controllable variance is computed as:

Overhead Controllable Variance	
Actual total overhead (given)	$7,650
Budgeted total overhead (from flexible budget)	7,500
Controllable variance (unfavorable)	$ 150

Next, we compute the volume variance. G-Max's budgeted fixed overhead at the predicted capacity level for the month (4,000 units) was $4,000. Recall from Exhibit 21.12 that G-Max's predetermined fixed overhead rate at the predicted capacity level of 4,000 units was $1 per direct labor hour. Thus, G-Max's applied fixed overhead was $3,500, computed as 3,500 direct labor hours × $1.00 per unit. G-Max's volume variance is computed as:

Overhead Volume Variance	
Budgeted fixed overhead (at predicted capacity)	$4,000
Applied fixed overhead (3,500 DLH × $1.00 per DLH)	3,500
Volume variance (unfavorable)	$ 500

Analyzing Overhead Controllable and Volume Variances How should the top management of G-Max interpret the unfavorable overhead controllable and volume variances? An unfavorable volume variance means that the company did not reach its predicted operating level. In this case, 80% of manufacturing capacity was budgeted but only 70% was used. Management needs to know why the actual level of production differs from the expected level. The main purpose of the volume variance is to identify what portion of the total overhead variance is caused by failing to meet the expected production level. Often the reasons for failing to meet this expected production level are due to factors, for example customer demand, that are beyond employees' control. This information permits management to focus on explanations for the controllable variance, as we discuss next.

Overhead Variance Reports To help management isolate the reasons for the $150 unfavorable overhead controllable variance, an *overhead variance report* can be prepared. A complete overhead variance report provides managers information about specific overhead costs and how they differ from budgeted amounts. Exhibit 21.15 shows G-Max's overhead variance report for May. The overhead variance report shows the total overhead volume variance of $500 unfavorable (shown near the top of the report) and the $150 unfavorable overhead controllable variance (shown at the bottom right of the report). The detailed listing of individual overhead costs reveals the following: (1) Fixed overhead costs and variable factory maintenance costs were incurred as expected. (2) Costs for indirect labor and power and lights were higher than expected. (3) Indirect materials cost was less than expected. Management can use the variance overhead report to identify the individual overhead costs it wants to investigate.

Appendix 21A describes an expanded analysis of overhead variances.

EXHIBIT 21.15

Overhead Variance Report

G-MAX
Overhead Variance Report
For Month Ended May 31, 2015

Overhead Volume Variance

Expected production level	80% of capacity (4,000 units)
Production level achieved	70% of capacity (3,500 units)
Budgeted fixed overhead (4,000 DLH × $1.00)	$4,000
Fixed overhead applied (3,500 DLH × $1.00)	$3,500
Volume variance	**$ 500 (unfavorable)**

Overhead Controllable Variance	Flexible Budget	Actual Results	Variances*
Variable overhead costs			
Indirect labor	$1,400	$1,525	$125 U
Indirect materials	1,050	1,025	25 F
Power and lights	700	750	50 U
Maintenance	350	350	0
Total variable overhead costs	3,500	3,650	150 U
Fixed overhead costs			
Building rent	1,000	1,000	0
Depreciation—machinery	1,200	1,200	0
Supervisory salaries	1,800	1,800	0
Total fixed overhead costs	4,000	4,000	0
Total overhead costs	$7,500	$7,650	$150 U

Total overhead variance = $650 unfavorable

* F = Favorable variance; U = Unfavorable variance.

NEED-TO-KNOW 21-4

Overhead Variances

P3

A manufacturing company uses standard costs and reports the information below for January. The company uses machine hours to allocate overhead, and the standard is two machine hours per finished unit. Compute the total overhead cost variance, overhead controllable variance, and overhead volume variance for January. Indicate whether each variance is favorable or unfavorable.

Predicted activity level	1,500 units
Variable overhead rate budgeted	$2.50 per machine hour
Fixed overhead budgeted	$6,000 per month ($2.00 per machine hour at predicted activity level)
Actual activity level	1,800 units
Actual overhead costs	$15,800

Solution

Total overhead cost variance	
Actual total overhead cost (given)	$15,800
Standard overhead applied (1,800 × 2 × $4.50)	16,200
Total overhead variance (favorable)	$ 400

Overhead controllable variance	
Actual total overhead cost (given)	$15,800
Flexible budget total overhead (1,800 × 2 × $2.50) + $6,000	15,000
Overhead controllable variance (unfavorable)	$ 800

Overhead volume variance	
Budgeted fixed overhead	$ 6,000
Applied fixed overhead (1,800 × 2 × $2)	7,200
Overhead volume variance (favorable)	$ 1,200

Do More: QS 21-13, QS 21-14, QS 21-15, E 21-17, E 21-19, E 21-20

QC3

GLOBAL VIEW

BMW, a German automobile manufacturer, uses concepts of standard costing and variance analysis. Production begins with huge rolls of steel and aluminum, which are then cut and pressed by large machines. Material must meet high quality standards, and the company sets standards for each of its machine operations. In the assembly department, highly trained employees complete the assembly of the painted car chassis, often to customer specifications. Again, BMW sets standards for how much labor should be used and monitors its employee performance. The company then computes and analyzes materials price and quantity variances and labor rate and efficiency variances and takes action as needed. Like most manufacturers, BMW uses *practical standards* and thus must address waste of raw materials in its production process. In a recent year, BMW used over 3 million tons of steel, plastic, and aluminum to make over 1.8 million cars. Of the 665,000 tons of these raw materials wasted in production, over 98% are recyclable.

Sustainability and Accounting **Niner Bikes** employs standard cost principles in making bikes. But, founder and CEO Chris Sugai offers flexible work schedules for his employees and insists that employees stay home after they or their spouses give birth. These benefits are costly, but they allow Chris to sustain a loyal workforce.

Decision Analysis — Sales Variances

A1 Analyze changes in sales from expected amounts.

This chapter explained the computation and analysis of cost variances. A similar variance analysis can be applied to sales. For this analysis, the budgeted amount of unit sales is the predicted activity level, and the budgeted selling price can be treated as a "standard" price. To illustrate, consider the following sales data from G-Max for two of its golf products, Excel golf balls and Big Bert drivers.

	Budgeted	Actual
Sales of Excel golf balls (units)	1,000 units	1,100 units
Sales price per Excel golf ball	$10	$10.50
Sales of Big Bert drivers (units)	150 units	140 units
Sales price per Big Bert driver	$200	$190

Using this information, we compute both the *sales price variance* and the *sales volume variance* as shown in Exhibit 21.16. The total sales price variance is $850 unfavorable, and the total sales volume variance is $1,000 unfavorable. However, further analysis of these total sales variances reveals that both the sales price and sales volume variances for Excel golf balls are favorable, while both variances are unfavorable for the Big Bert driver.

EXHIBIT 21.16

Computing Sales Variances*

Excel Golf Balls	Actual Results AS × AP	Flexible Budget AS × BP	Fixed Budget BS × BP
Sales dollars (balls)	(1,100 × $10.50) **$11,550**	(1,100 × $10) **$11,000**	(1,000 × $10) **$10,000**

	Sales Price Variance (AS × AP) − (AS × BP)	Sales Volume Variance (AS × BP) − (BS × BP)
Excel Golf Balls	$550 F	$1,000 F

Big Bert Drivers	Actual Results AS × AP	Flexible Budget AS × BP	Fixed Budget BS × BP
Sales dollars (drivers)	(140 × $190) **$26,600**	(140 × $200) **$28,000**	(150 × $200) **$30,000**

	Sales Price Variance (AS × AP) − (AS × BP)	Sales Volume Variance (AS × BP) − (BS × BP)
Big Bert Drivers	$1,400 U	$2,000 U
Total	**$850 U**	**$1,000 U**

* AS = actual sales units; AP = actual sales price; BP = budgeted sales price; BS = budgeted sales units (fixed budget).

Managers use sales variances for planning and control purposes. G-Max sold 90 combined total units (both balls and drivers) more than budgeted, yet its total sales price and sales volume variances are unfavorable. The unfavorable sales price variance is due mainly to a decrease in the selling price of Big

Bert drivers by $10 per unit. Management must assess whether this price decrease will continue. Likewise, the unfavorable sales volume variance is due to G-Max selling fewer Big Bert drivers (140) than was budgeted (150). Management must assess whether this decreased demand for Big Bert drivers will persist.

Overall, management can use the detailed sales variances to examine what caused the company to sell more golf balls and fewer drivers. Managers can also use this information to evaluate and even reward salespeople. Extra compensation is paid to salespeople who contribute to a higher profit margin.

Decision Maker

Sales Manager The current performance report reveals a large favorable sales volume variance but an unfavorable sales price variance. You did not expect to see a large increase in sales volume. What steps do you take to analyze this situation? ■ [Answers follow the chapter's Summary.]

NEED-TO-KNOW

COMPREHENSIVE

Pacific Company provides the following information about its budgeted and actual results for June 2015. Although the expected June volume was 25,000 units produced and sold, the company actually produced and sold 27,000 units as detailed here:

	Budget (25,000 units)	Actual (27,000 units)
Selling price	$5.00 per unit	$141,210
Variable costs (per unit)		
Direct materials	1.24 per unit	$30,800
Direct labor	1.50 per unit	37,800
Factory supplies*	0.25 per unit	9,990
Utilities*	0.50 per unit	16,200
Selling costs	0.40 per unit	9,180
Fixed costs (per month)		
Depreciation—machinery*	$3,750	$3,710
Depreciation—factory building*	2,500	2,500
General liability insurance	1,200	1,250
Property taxes on office equipment	500	485
Other administrative expense	750	900

* Indicates factory overhead item; $0.75 per unit or $3 per direct labor hour for variable overhead, and $0.25 per unit or $1 per direct labor hour for fixed overhead.

Standard costs based on expected output of 25,000 units:

	Standard Quantity	Total Cost
Direct materials, 4 oz. per unit @ $0.31/oz.	100,000 oz.	$31,000
Direct labor, 0.25 hrs. per unit @ $6.00/hr.	6,250 hrs.	37,500
Overhead, 6,250 standard hours × $4.00 per DLH		25,000

Actual costs incurred to produce 27,000 units:

	Actual Quantity	Total Cost
Direct materials, 110,000 oz. @ $0.28/oz.	110,000 oz.	$30,800
Direct labor, 5,400 hrs. @ $7.00/hr.	5,400 hrs.	37,800
Overhead ($9,990 + $16,200 + $3,710 + $2,500)		32,400

Required

1. Prepare June flexible budgets showing expected sales, costs, and net income assuming 20,000, 25,000, and 30,000 units of output produced and sold.
2. Prepare a flexible budget performance report that compares actual results with the amounts budgeted if the actual volume of 27,000 units had been expected.
3. Apply variance analysis for direct materials and direct labor.
4. Compute the total overhead variance, and the overhead controllable and overhead volume variances.
5. Compute spending and efficiency variances for overhead. (Refer to Appendix 21A.)
6. Prepare journal entries to record standard costs, and price and quantity variances, for direct materials, direct labor, and factory overhead. (Refer to Appendix 21A.)

PLANNING THE SOLUTION

- Prepare a table showing the expected results at the three specified levels of output. Compute the variable costs by multiplying the per unit variable costs by the expected volumes. Include fixed costs at the given amounts. Combine the amounts in the table to show total variable costs, contribution margin, total fixed costs, and income from operations.
- Prepare a table showing the actual results and the amounts that should be incurred at 27,000 units. Show any differences in the third column and label them with an *F* for favorable if they increase income or a *U* for unfavorable if they decrease income.
- Using the chapter's format, compute these total variances and the individual variances requested:
  - Total materials variance (including the direct materials quantity variance and the direct materials price variance).
  - Total direct labor variance (including the direct labor efficiency variance and rate variance).
  - Total overhead variance (including both controllable and volume overhead variances and their component variances). Variable overhead is applied at the rate of $3.00 per direct labor hour. Fixed overhead is applied at the rate of $1.00 per direct labor hour.

SOLUTION

1.

PACIFIC COMPANY
Flexible Budgets
For Month Ended June 30, 2015

	Flexible Budget		Flexible Budget for Unit Sales of		
	Variable Amount per Unit	Total Fixed Cost	20,000	25,000	30,000
Sales	$5.00		$100,000	$125,000	$150,000
Variable costs					
Direct materials	1.24		24,800	31,000	37,200
Direct labor	1.50		30,000	37,500	45,000
Factory supplies	0.25		5,000	6,250	7,500
Utilities	0.50		10,000	12,500	15,000
Selling costs	0.40		8,000	10,000	12,000
Total variable costs	3.89		77,800	97,250	116,700
Contribution margin	$1.11		22,200	27,750	33,300
Fixed costs					
Depreciation—machinery		$3,750	3,750	3,750	3,750
Depreciation—factory building		2,500	2,500	2,500	2,500
General liability insurance		1,200	1,200	1,200	1,200
Property taxes on office equipment		500	500	500	500
Other administrative expense		750	750	750	750
Total fixed costs		$8,700	8,700	8,700	8,700
Income from operations			$ 13,500	$ 19,050	$ 24,600

2.

PACIFIC COMPANY
Flexible Budget Performance Report
For Month Ended June 30, 2015

	Flexible Budget	Actual Results	Variance**
Sales (27,000 units)	$135,000	$141,210	**$6,210 F**
Variable costs			
Direct materials	33,480	30,800	**2,680 F**
Direct labor	40,500	37,800	**2,700 F**
Factory supplies*	6,750	9,990	**3,240 U**
Utilities*	13,500	16,200	**2,700 U**
Selling costs	10,800	9,180	**1,620 F**
Total variable costs	105,030	103,970	**1,060 F**
Contribution margin	29,970	37,240	**7,270 F**
Fixed costs			
Depreciation—machinery*	3,750	3,710	**40 F**
Depreciation—factory building*	2,500	2,500	**0**
General liability insurance	1,200	1,250	**50 U**
Property taxes on office equipment	500	485	**15 F**
Other administrative expense	750	900	**150 U**
Total fixed costs	8,700	8,845	**145 U**
Income from operations	$ 21,270	$ 28,395	**$7,125 F**

* Indicates factory overhead item ** Abbreviations: F = Favorable variance; U = Unfavorable variance.

3. Variance analysis of materials and labor costs.

Direct materials cost variances

Actual cost	110,000 oz. @ $0.28	$30,800
Standard cost	108,000 oz. @ $0.31	33,480
Direct materials cost variance (favorable)		$ 2,680

Price and quantity variances (based on formulas in Exhibit 21.10):

Actual Cost		Standard Cost
AQ × AP	AQ × SP	SQ* × SP
110,000 oz. × $0.28	110,000 oz. × $0.31	108,000 oz. × $0.31
$30,800	$34,100	$33,480

$3,300 F — **Price Variance**

$620 U — **Quantity Variance**

$2,680 F — **Total Direct Materials Variance**

*SQ = 27,000 actual units of output × 4 oz. standard quantity rate per unit

Direct labor cost variances

Actual cost	5,400 hrs. @ $7.00	$37,800
Standard cost	6,750 hrs. @ $6.00	40,500
Direct labor cost variance (favorable)		$ 2,700

Rate and efficiency variances (based on formulas in Exhibit 21.11):

Actual Cost		Standard Cost
AH × AR	AH × SR	SH** × SR
5,400 hrs. × $7	5,400 hrs. × $6	6,750 hrs. × $6
$37,800	$32,400	$40,500

$5,400 U — **Rate Variance**

$8,100 F — **Efficiency Variance**

$2,700 F — **Total Direct Labor Variance**

**SH = 27,000 actual units of output × 0.25 standard DLH per unit.

4. Total, controllable, and volume variances for overhead.

Total overhead cost variance	
Total overhead cost incurred . . . . (given)	$32,400
Total overhead applied . . . . (27,000 units × .25 DLH per unit × $4 per DLH)	27,000
Overhead cost variance (unfavorable)	$ 5,400
Controllable variance	
Total overhead cost incurred (given)	$32,400
Budgeted overhead (from flexible budget for 27,000 units)	26,500
Controllable variance (unfavorable)	$ 5,900
Volume variance	
Budgeted fixed overhead (at predicted capacity)	$ 6,250
Applied fixed overhead (6,750 standard DLH × $1.00 fixed overhead rate per DLH)	6,750
Volume variance (favorable)	$ 500

5. Variable overhead spending variance, variable overhead efficiency variance, fixed overhead spending variance, and fixed overhead volume variance. (See Appendix 21A.)

Variable overhead variance *(factory supplies and utilities)*

Variable overhead cost incurred	($9,990 + $16,200)	$26,190
Variable overhead cost applied	6,750 hrs. @ $3/hr.	20,250
Variable overhead cost variance (unfavorable)		$ 5,940

Spending and efficiency variances (based on formulas in Exhibit 21A.2):

Actual Overhead		**Applied Overhead**
AH × AVR	AH × SVR	SH × SVR
	5,400 × $3	6,750 × $3
$26,190	$16,200	$20,250

$9,990 U — **Spending Variance**

$4,050 F — **Efficiency Variance**

$5,940 U — **Total Variable Overhead Variance**

Fixed overhead variance *(depreciation on machinery and building)*

Fixed overhead cost incurred	($3,710 + $2,500)	$ 6,210
Fixed overhead cost applied	6,750 hrs. @ $1/hr.	6,750
Fixed overhead cost variance (favorable)		$ 540

Spending and volume variances (based on formulas in Exhibit 21A.2):

Actual Overhead	**Budgeted Overhead**	**Applied Overhead**
		6,750 × $1
$6,210	$6,250	$6,750

$40 F — **Spending Variance**

$500 F — **Volume Variance**

$540 F — **Total Fixed Overhead Variance**

We can also compute:

Controllable variance: $5,900 U (both spending variances plus variable overhead efficiency variance)

Volume variance: 500 F (identified as above)

6. Journal entries under a standard cost system. (Refer to Appendix 21A.)

Work in Process Inventory	33,480	
Direct Materials Quantity Variance	620	
Direct Materials Price Variance		3,300
Raw Materials Inventory		30,800
Work in Process Inventory	40,500	
Direct Labor Rate Variance	5,400	
Direct Labor Efficiency Variance		8,100
Factory Payroll Payable		37,800
Work in Process Inventory*	27,000	
Variable Overhead Spending Variance	9,990	
Variable Overhead Efficiency Variance		4,050
Fixed Overhead Spending Variance		40
Fixed Overhead Volume Variance		500
Factory Overhead**		32,400

* Overhead applied = 6,750 standard DLH × $4 per DLH
** Overhead incurred = $9,990 + $16,200 + $3,710 + $2,500

APPENDIX

Expanded Overhead Variances and Standard Cost Accounting System

21A

P4 Compute overhead spending and efficiency variances.

Expanded Overhead Variances Similar to analysis of direct materials and direct labor, overhead variances can be more completely analyzed. Exhibit 21A.1 shows an expanded framework for understanding these component overhead variances.

This framework uses classifications of overhead costs as either variable or fixed. Within those two classifications are further types of variances—spending, efficiency, and volume variances. We looked at the latter in the body of the chapter.

A **spending variance** occurs when management pays an amount different from the standard price to acquire an item. For instance, the actual wage rate paid to indirect labor might be higher than the standard rate. Similarly, actual supervisory salaries might be different than expected. Spending variances such as these cause management to investigate the reasons that the amount paid differs from the standard. Both variable and fixed overhead costs can yield their own spending variances.

EXHIBIT 21A.1

Expanded Framework for Total Overhead Variance

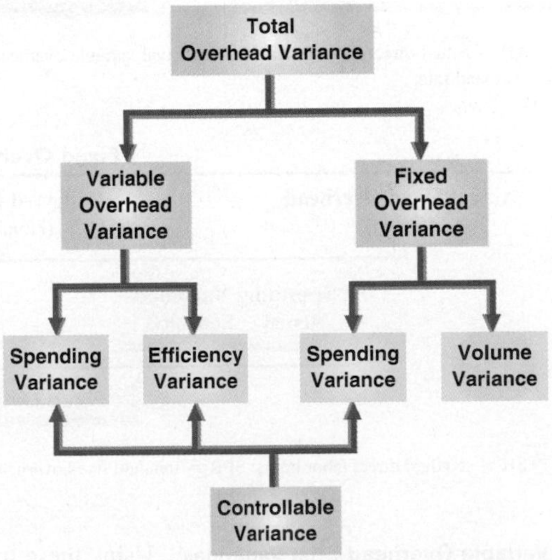

Analyzing variable overhead also includes computing an **efficiency variance,** which occurs when standard direct labor hours (the allocation base) expected for actual production differ from the actual direct labor hours used. This efficiency variance reflects on the cost-effectiveness in using the overhead allocation base (such as direct labor).

Exhibit 21A.1 shows that we can combine the variable overhead spending variance, the fixed overhead spending variance, and the variable overhead efficiency variance to get the controllable variance.

Computing Variable and Fixed Overhead Cost Variances To illustrate the computation of more detailed overhead cost variances, we return to the G-Max data. We know that G-Max produced 3,500 units when

4,000 units were budgeted. Additional data from cost reports (from Exhibit 21.15) show that the actual overhead cost incurred is $7,650 (the variable portion of $3,650 and the fixed portion of $4,000). Recall from Exhibit 21.12 that each unit requires one hour of direct labor, that variable overhead is applied at a rate of $1.00 per direct labor hour, and that the predetermined fixed overhead rate is $1.00 per direct labor hour. Using this information, we can compute overhead variances for both variable and fixed overhead as follows:

Variable Overhead Variance	
Actual variable overhead (given)	$3,650
Applied variable overhead (3,500 units × 1 standard DLH × $1.00 VOH rate per DLH)	3,500
Variable overhead variance (unfavorable)	$ 150

Fixed Overhead Variance	
Actual fixed overhead (given)	$4,000
Applied fixed overhead (3,500 units × 1 standard DLH × $1.00 FOH rate per DLH)	3,500
Fixed overhead variance (unfavorable)	$ 500

Management should seek to determine the causes of these unfavorable variances and take corrective action. To help better isolate the causes of these variances, more detailed overhead variances can be used, as shown in the next section.

Expanded Overhead Variance Formulas Exhibit 21A.2 shows formulas to use in computing detailed overhead variances that can better identify reasons for variable and fixed overhead variances.

EXHIBIT 21A.2

Variable and Fixed Overhead Variances

Variable Overhead Variance*

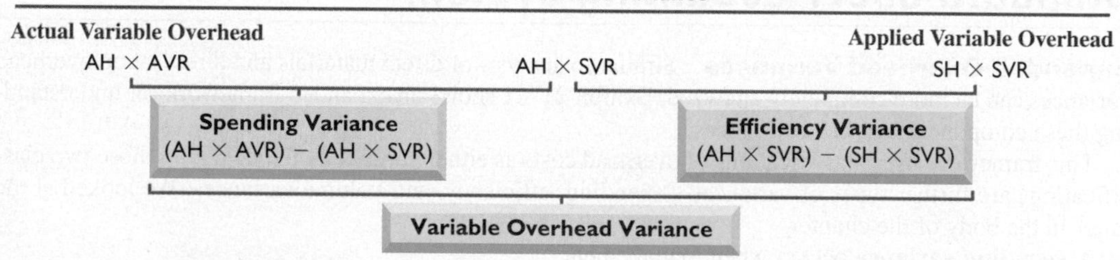

* AH = actual direct labor hours; AVR = actual variable overhead rate; SH = standard direct labor hours; SVR = standard variable overhead rate.

Fixed Overhead Variance**

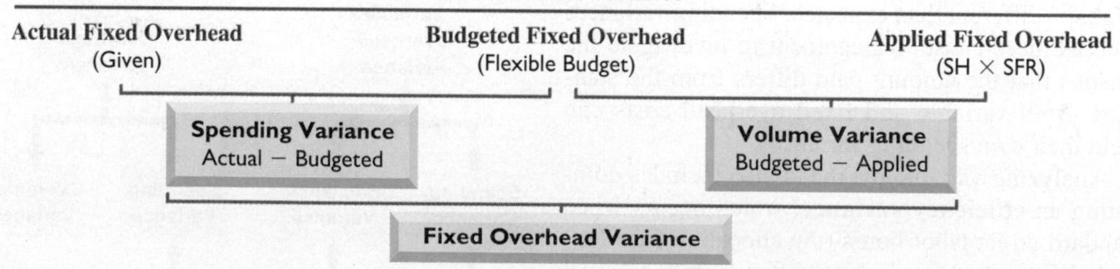

**SH = standard direct labor hours; SFR = standard fixed overhead rate.

Variable Overhead Cost Variances Using these formulas, Exhibit 21A.3 offers insight into the causes of G-Max's $150 unfavorable variable overhead cost variance. Recall that G-Max applies overhead based on direct labor hours as the allocation base. We know that it used 3,400 direct labor hours to produce 3,500 units. This compares favorably to the standard requirement of 3,500 direct labor hours at one labor hour per unit. At a standard variable overhead rate of $1.00 per direct labor hour, this should have resulted in variable overhead costs of $3,400 (middle column of Exhibit 21A.3).

EXHIBIT 21A.3

Computing Variable Overhead Cost Variances

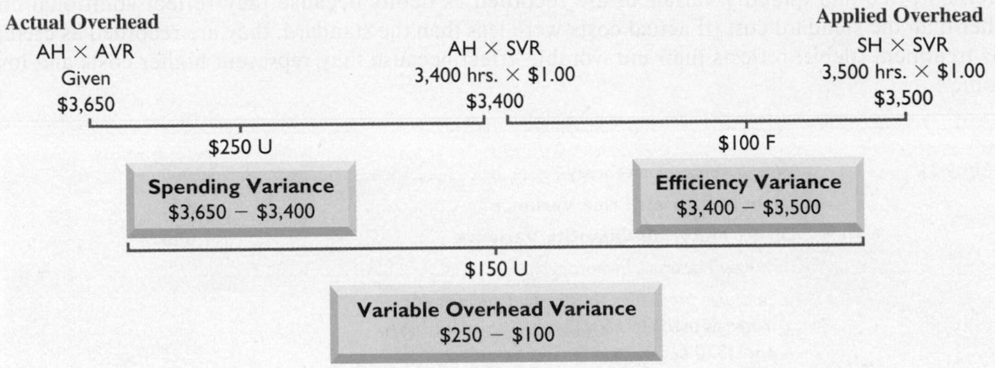

G-Max's cost records, however, report actual variable overhead of $3,650, or $250 higher than expected. This means G-Max has an unfavorable variable overhead spending variance of $250 ($3,650 − $3,400). On the other hand, G-Max used 100 fewer labor hours than expected to make 3,500 units, and its actual variable overhead is lower than its applied variable overhead. Thus, G-Max has a favorable variable overhead efficiency variance of $100 ($3,400 − $3,500).

Fixed Overhead Cost Variances Exhibit 21A.4 provides insight into the causes of G-Max's $500 unfavorable fixed overhead variance. G-Max reports that it incurred $4,000 in actual fixed overhead; this amount equals the budgeted fixed overhead for May at the expected production level of 4,000 units (see Exhibit 21.12). Thus, the fixed overhead spending variance is zero, suggesting good control of fixed overhead costs. G-Max's budgeted fixed overhead application rate is $1 per hour ($4,000/4,000 direct labor hours), but the actual production level is only 3,500 units.

Using this information, we can compute the fixed overhead volume variance shown in Exhibit 21A.4. The applied fixed overhead is computed by multiplying 3,500 standard hours allowed for the actual production by the $1 fixed overhead allocation rate. The volume variance of $500 occurs because 500 fewer units are produced than budgeted; namely, 80% of the manufacturing capacity is budgeted but only 70% is used. Management needs to know why the actual level of production differs from the expected level.

EXHIBIT 21A.4

Computing Fixed Overhead Cost Variances

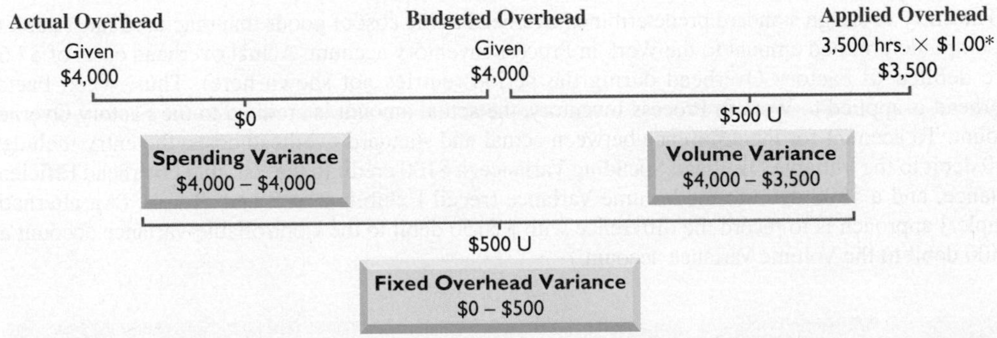

*3,500 units × 1 DLH per unit × $1.00 FOH rate per DLH

P5 Prepare journal entries for standard costs and account for price and quantity variances.

Standard Cost Accounting System We have shown how companies use standard costs in management reports. Most standard cost systems also record these costs and variances in accounts. This practice simplifies recordkeeping and helps in preparing reports. Although we do not need knowledge of standard cost accounting practices to understand standard costs and their use, we must know how to interpret the accounts in which standard costs and variances are recorded. The entries in this section briefly illustrate the important aspects of this process for G-Max's standard costs and variances for May.

The first of these entries records standard materials cost incurred in May in the Work in Process Inventory account. This part of the entry is similar to the usual accounting entry, but the amount of the debit equals the standard cost ($35,000) instead of the actual cost ($37,800). This entry credits Raw Materials Inventory for actual cost. The difference between standard and actual direct materials costs is recorded with debits to two separate materials variance accounts (recall Exhibit 21.10). Both the materials price and quantity variances are recorded as debits because they reflect additional costs higher than the standard cost (if actual costs were less than the standard, they are recorded as credits). This treatment (debit) reflects their unfavorable effect because they represent higher costs and lower income.

May 31	Work in Process Inventory	35,000	
	Direct Materials Price Variance*	**1,800**	
	Direct Materials Quantity Variance	**1,000**	
	Raw Materials Inventory		37,800
	To charge production for standard quantity of materials used (1,750 lbs.) at the standard price ($20 per lb.), and to record material price and material quantity variances.		

* Many companies record the materials price variance when materials are purchased. For simplicity, we record both the materials price and quantity variances when materials are issued to production.

The second entry debits Work in Process Inventory for the standard labor cost of the goods manufactured during May ($28,000). Actual labor cost ($28,220) is recorded with a credit to the Factory Payroll Payable account. The difference between standard and actual labor costs is explained by two variances (see Exhibit 21.11). The direct labor rate variance is unfavorable and is debited to that account. The direct labor efficiency variance is favorable and that account is credited. The direct labor efficiency variance is favorable because it represents a lower cost and a higher net income.

May 31	Work in Process Inventory	28,000	
	Direct Labor Rate Variance	**1,020**	
	Direct Labor Efficiency Variance		**800**
	Factory Payroll Payable		28,220
	To charge production with 3,500 standard hours of direct labor at the standard $8 per hour rate, and to record the labor rate and efficiency variances.		

The entry to assign standard predetermined overhead to the cost of goods manufactured must debit the $7,000 predetermined amount to the Work in Process Inventory account. Actual overhead costs of $7,650 were debited to Factory Overhead during the period (entries not shown here). Thus, when Factory Overhead is applied to Work in Process Inventory, the actual amount is credited to the Factory Overhead account. To account for the difference between actual and standard overhead costs, the entry includes a $250 debit to the Variable Overhead Spending Variance, a $100 credit to the Variable Overhead Efficiency Variance, and a $500 debit to the Volume Variance (recall Exhibits 21A.3 and 21A.4). (An alternative [simpler] approach is to record the difference with a $150 debit to the Controllable Variance account and a $500 debit to the Volume Variance account.)

May 31	Work in Process Inventory	7,000	
	Volume Variance	**500**	
	Variable Overhead Spending Variance	**250**	
	Variable Overhead Efficiency Variance		**100**
	Factory Overhead		7,650
	To apply overhead at the standard rate of $2 per standard direct labor hour (3,500 hours), and to record overhead variances.		

Point: If variances are material they can be allocated between Work in Process Inventory, Finished Goods Inventory, and Cost of Goods Sold. This closing process is explained in advanced courses.

The balances of these different variance accounts accumulate until the end of the accounting period. As a result, the unfavorable variances of some months can offset the favorable variances of other months.

These ending variance account balances, which reflect results of the period's various transactions and events, are closed at period-end. If the amounts are *immaterial,* they are added to or subtracted from the balance of the Cost of Goods Sold account. This process is similar to that shown in the job order costing chapter for eliminating an underapplied or overapplied balance in the Factory Overhead account. (*Note:* These variance balances, which represent differences between actual and standard costs, must be added to or subtracted from the materials, labor, and overhead costs recorded. In this way, the recorded costs equal the actual costs incurred in the period; a company must use actual costs in external financial statements prepared in accordance with generally accepted accounting principles.)

Standard Costing Income Statement In addition to the reports discussed in this chapter, management can use a **standard costing income statement** to summarize company performance for a period. This income statement reports sales and cost of goods sold at their standard amounts, and then lists the individual sales and cost variances to compute gross profit at actual cost. Exhibit 21A.5 provides an example. Unfavorable variances are added to cost of goods sold at standard cost; favorable variances are subtracted from cost of goods sold at standard cost.

EXHIBIT 21A.5

Standard Costing Income Statement

G-MAX
Standard Costing Income Statement
For Year Ended December 31, 2015

Sales revenue (at standard)			•••••
Sales price variance		•••	
Sales volume variance		•••	•••
Sales revenue (actual)			•••••
Cost of goods sold (at standard)		•••••	
Manufacturing cost variances			
Direct materials price variance	•••		
Direct materials quantity variance	•••		
Direct labor rate variance	•••		
Direct labor efficiency variance	•••		
Variable overhead spending variance	•••		
Variable overhead efficiency variance	•••		
Fixed overhead spending variance	•••		
Fixed overhead volume variance	•••		
Total manufacturing cost variances		•••	
Cost of goods sold (actual)			•••••
Gross profit			••••
Selling expenses			•••
General and administrative expenses			•••
Income from operations			•••••

Add unfavorable variances; subtract favorable variances.

NEED-TO-KNOW 21-5

Recording Variances

P4

A company uses a standard cost accounting system. Prepare the journal entry to record these direct materials variances:

Direct materials cost actually incurred	$73,200
Direct materials quantity variance (favorable)	3,800
Direct materials price variance (unfavorable)	1,300

Solution

Work in Process Inventory	75,700	
Direct Materials Price Variance	1,300	
Direct Materials Quantity Variance		3,800
Raw Materials Inventory		73,200

Do More: QS 21-17, E 21-14

Summary

C1 Define *standard costs* and explain how standard cost information is useful for management by exception. Standard costs are the normal costs that should be incurred to produce a product or perform a service. They should be based on a careful examination of the processes used to produce a product or perform a service as well as the quantities and prices that should be incurred in carrying out those processes. On a performance report, standard costs (which are flexible budget amounts) are compared to actual costs, and the differences are presented as variances. Standard cost accounting provides management information about costs that differ from budgeted (expected) amounts. Performance reports disclose the costs or areas of operations that have significant variances from budgeted amounts. This allows managers to focus more attention on the exceptions and less attention on areas proceeding normally.

C2 Describe cost variances and what they reveal about performance. Management can use variances to monitor and control activities. Total cost variances can be broken into price and quantity variances to direct management's attention to those responsible for quantities used and prices paid.

A1 Analyze changes in sales from expected amounts. Actual sales can differ from budgeted sales, and managers can investigate this difference by computing both the sales price and sales volume variances. The *sales price variance* refers to that portion of total variance resulting from a difference between actual and budgeted selling prices. The *sales volume variance* refers to that portion of total variance resulting from a difference between actual and budgeted sales quantities.

P1 Prepare a flexible budget and interpret a flexible budget performance report. A flexible budget expresses variable costs in per unit terms so that it can be used to develop budgeted amounts for any volume level within the relevant range. Thus, managers compute budgeted amounts for evaluation after a period for the volume that actually occurred. To prepare a flexible budget, we express each variable cost as a constant amount per unit of sales (or as a percent of sales dollars). In contrast, the budgeted amount of each fixed cost is expressed as a total amount expected to occur at any sales volume within the relevant range. The flexible budget is then determined using these computations and amounts for fixed and variable costs at the expected sales volume.

P2 Compute materials and labor variances. Materials and labor variances are due to differences between the actual costs incurred and the budgeted costs. The price (or rate) variance is computed by comparing the actual cost with the flexible budget amount that should have been incurred to acquire the actual quantity of resources. The quantity (or efficiency) variance is computed by comparing the flexible budget amount that should have been incurred to acquire the actual quantity of resources with the flexible budget amount that should have been incurred to acquire the standard quantity of resources.

P3 Compute overhead controllable and volume variances. Overhead variances are due to differences between the actual overhead costs incurred and the overhead applied to production. The overhead controllable variance equals the actual overhead minus the budgeted overhead, based on a flexible budget. The volume variance equals the budgeted fixed overhead minus the applied fixed overhead.

P4A Compute overhead spending and efficiency variances. An overhead spending variance occurs when management pays an amount different from the standard price to acquire an item. An overhead efficiency variance occurs when the standard amount of the allocation base to assign overhead differs from the actual amount of the allocation base used.

P5A Prepare journal entries for standard costs and account for price and quantity variances. When a company records standard costs in its accounts, the standard costs of direct materials, direct labor, and overhead are debited to the Work in Process Inventory account. Based on an analysis of the material, labor, and overhead costs, each quantity variance, price variance, volume variance, and controllable variance is recorded in a separate account. At period-end, if the variances are not material, they are debited (if unfavorable) or credited (if favorable) to the Cost of Goods Sold account.

Guidance Answers to Decision Maker

Entrepreneur From the complaints, this performance report appears to compare actual results with a fixed budget. This comparison is useful in determining whether the amount of work actually performed was more or less than planned, but it is not useful in determining whether the divisions were more or less efficient than planned. If the two consulting divisions worked on more assignments than expected, some costs will certainly increase. Therefore, you should prepare a flexible budget using the actual number of consulting assignments and then compare actual performance to the flexible budget.

Production Manager As production manager, you should investigate the causes for any labor-related variances although you may not be responsible for them. An unfavorable labor efficiency variance occurs because more labor hours than standard were used during the period. There are at least three possible reasons for this: (1) materials quality could be poor, resulting in more labor consumption due to rework; (2) unplanned interruptions (strike, breakdowns, accidents) could have occurred during the period; and (3) a different labor mix might have occurred for a strategic reason such as to expedite orders. This new labor mix could have consisted of a larger proportion of untrained labor, which resulted in more labor hours.

Sales Manager The unfavorable sales price variance suggests that actual prices were lower than budgeted prices. As the sales manager, you want to know the reasons for a lower than expected price. Perhaps your salespeople lowered the price of certain products by offering quantity discounts. You then might want to know what prompted them to offer the quantity discounts (perhaps competitors were offering discounts). You want to break the sales volume variance into both the sales mix and sales quantity variances. You could find that although the sales quantity variance is favorable, the sales mix variance is not. Then you need to investigate why the actual sales mix differs from the budgeted sales mix.

Key Terms

Benchmarking
Budget report
Budgetary control
Controllable variance
Cost variance
Efficiency variance
Favorable variance
Fixed budget
Fixed budget performance report
Flexible budget
Flexible budget performance report
Management by exception
Overhead cost variance
Price variance
Quantity variance
Spending variance
Standard costing income statement
Standard costs
Unfavorable variance
Variance analysis
Volume variance

Multiple Choice Quiz

Answers at end of chapter

1. A company predicts its production and sales will be 24,000 units. At that level of activity, its fixed costs are budgeted at $300,000, and its variable costs are budgeted at $246,000. If its activity level declines to 20,000 units, what will be its fixed costs and its variable costs?

a. Fixed, $300,000; variable, $246,000
b. Fixed, $250,000; variable, $205,000
c. Fixed, $300,000; variable, $205,000
d. Fixed, $250,000; variable, $246,000
e. Fixed, $300,000; variable, $300,000

2. Using the following information about a single product company, compute its total actual cost of direct materials used.

- Direct materials standard cost: 5 lbs. × $2 per lb. = $10.
- Total direct materials cost variance: $15,000 unfavorable.
- Actual direct materials used: 300,000 lbs.
- Actual units produced: 60,000 units.

a. $585,000 **c.** $300,000 **e.** $615,000
b. $600,000 **d.** $315,000

3. A company uses four hours of direct labor to produce a product unit. The standard direct labor cost is $20 per hour. This period the company produced 20,000 units and used 84,160 hours of direct labor at a total cost of $1,599,040. What is its labor rate variance for the period?

a. $83,200 F **c.** $84,160 F **e.** $960 F
b. $84,160 U **d.** $83,200 U

4. A company's standard for a unit of its single product is $6 per unit in variable overhead (4 hours × $1.50 per hour). Actual data for the period show variable overhead costs of $150,000 and production of 24,000 units. Its total variable overhead cost variance is

a. $6,000 F **c.** $114,000 U **e.** $0
b. $6,000 U **d.** $114,000 F

5. A company's standard for a unit of its single product is $4 per unit in fixed overhead ($24,000 total/6,000 units budgeted). Actual data for the period show total actual fixed overhead of $24,100 and production of 4,800 units. Its volume variance is

a. $4,800 U **c.** $100 U **e.** $4,900 U
b. $4,800 F **d.** $100 F

A Superscript letter A denotes assignments based on Appendix 21A.
Icon denotes assignments that involve decision making.

Discussion Questions

1. What limits the usefulness to managers of fixed budget performance reports?

2. Identify the main purpose of a flexible budget for managers.

3. Prepare a flexible budget performance report title (in proper form) for Spalding Company for the calendar year 2015. Why is a proper title important for this or any report?

4. What type of analysis does a flexible budget performance report help management perform?

5. In what sense can a variable cost be considered constant?

6. What department is usually responsible for a direct labor rate variance? What department is usually responsible for a direct labor efficiency variance? Explain.

7. What is a price variance? What is a quantity variance?
8. What is the purpose of using standard costs?
9. **Google** monitors its fixed overhead. In an analysis of fixed overhead cost variances, what is the volume variance?
10. What is the predetermined standard overhead rate? How is it computed?
11. In general, variance analysis is said to provide information about ________ and ________ variances.
12. **Samsung** monitors its overhead. In an analysis of overhead cost variances, what is the controllable variance and what causes it?
13. What are the relations among standard costs, flexible budgets, variance analysis, and management by exception?
14. How can the manager of advertising sales at **Google** use flexible budgets to enhance performance?
15. Is it possible for a retail store such as **Apple** to use variances in analyzing its operating performance? Explain.
16. Assume that **Samsung** is budgeted to operate at 80% of capacity but actually operates at 75% of capacity. What effect will the 5% deviation have on its controllable variance? Its volume variance?

GOOGLE GOOGLE APPLE Samsung Samsung

connect

QUICK STUDY

QS 21-1
Flexible budget performance report P1

Beech Company produced and sold 105,000 units of its product in May. For the level of production achieved in May, the budgeted amounts were: sales, $1,300,000; variable costs, $750,000; and fixed costs, $300,000. The following actual financial results are available for May. Prepare a flexible budget performance report for May.

	Actual
Sales (105,000 units)	$1,275,000
Variable costs	712,500
Fixed costs	300,000

QS 21-2
Flexible budget P1

Based on predicted production of 24,000 units, a company anticipates $300,000 of fixed costs and $246,000 of variable costs. If the company actually produces 20,000 units, what are the flexible budget amounts of fixed and variable costs?

QS 21-3
Flexible budget P1

Brodrick Company expects to produce 20,000 units for the year ending December 31. A flexible budget for 20,000 units of production reflects sales of $400,000; variable costs of $80,000; and fixed costs of $150,000. If the company instead expects to produce and sell 26,000 units for the year, calculate the expected level of income from operations.

QS 21-4
Flexible budget performance report P1

Refer to information in QS 21-3. Assume that actual sales for the year are $480,000, actual variable costs for the year are $112,000, and actual fixed costs for the year are $145,000. Prepare a flexible budget performance report for the year.

QS 21-5
Standard cost card C1

BatCo makes metal baseball bats. Each bat requires 1 kg of aluminum at $18 per kg and 0.25 direct labor hours at $20 per hour. Overhead is assigned at the rate of $40 per direct labor hour. What amounts would appear on a standard cost card for BatCo?

QS 21-6
Cost variances C2

Refer to information in QS 21-5. Assume the actual cost to manufacture one metal bat was $40. Compute the cost variance and classify it as favorable or unfavorable.

QS 21-7
Management by exception C1

Managers use *management by exception* for control purposes.
1. Describe the concept of management by exception.
2. Explain how standard costs help managers apply this concept to monitor and control costs.

QS 21-8
Materials variances P2

Tercer reports the following on one of its products. Compute the direct materials price and quantity variances.

Direct materials standard (4 lbs. @ $2/lb.)	$8 per finished unit
Actual direct materials used	300,000 lbs.
Actual finished units produced	60,000 units
Actual cost of direct materials used	$535,000

QS 21-9
Materials cost variances
P2

For the current period, Kayenta Company's manufacturing operations yield a $4,000 unfavorable price variance on its direct materials usage. The actual price per pound of material is $78; the standard price is $77.50 per pound. How many pounds of material were used in the current period?

QS 21-10
Materials cost variances
P2

Juan Company's output for the current period was assigned a $150,000 standard direct materials cost. The direct materials variances included a $12,000 favorable price variance and a $2,000 favorable quantity variance. What is the actual total direct materials cost for the current period?

QS 21-11
Direct labor variances
P2

The following information describes a company's usage of direct labor in a recent period. Compute the direct labor rate and efficiency variances for the period.

Actual direct labor hours used	65,000
Actual direct labor rate per hour	$15
Standard direct labor rate per hour	$14
Standard direct labor hours for units produced	67,000

QS 21-12
Labor cost variances
P2

Frontera Company's output for the current period results in a $20,000 unfavorable direct labor rate variance and a $10,000 unfavorable direct labor efficiency variance. Production for the current period was assigned a $400,000 standard direct labor cost. What is the actual total direct labor cost for the current period?

QS 21-13
Controllable overhead variance P3

Fogel Co. expects to produce 116,000 units for the year. The company's flexible budget for 116,000 units of production shows variable overhead costs of $162,400 and fixed overhead costs of $124,000. For the year, the company incurred actual overhead costs of $262,800 while producing 110,000 units. Compute the controllable overhead variance.

QS 21-14
Controllable overhead variance
P3

AirPro Corp. reports the following for November. Compute the controllable overhead variance for November.

Actual total factory overhead incurred	$28,175
Standard factory overhead:	
Variable overhead	$3.10 per unit produced
Fixed overhead	
($12,000/12,000 predicted units to be produced)	$1 per unit
Predicted units to produce	12,000 units
Actual units produced	9,800 units

QS 21-15
Volume variance P3

Refer to information in QS 21-14. Compute the overhead volume variance for November.

QS 21-16
Overhead cost variances
P3

Alvarez Company's output for the current period yields a $20,000 favorable overhead volume variance and a $60,400 unfavorable overhead controllable variance. Standard overhead applied to production for the period is $225,000. What is the actual total overhead cost incurred for the period?

QS 21-17ᴬ
Preparing overhead entries P5

Refer to the information in QS 21-16. Alvarez records standard costs in its accounts. Prepare the journal entry to charge overhead costs to the Work in Process Inventory account and to record any variances.

QS 21-18
Total variable overhead cost variance
P3

Mosaic Company applies overhead using machine hours and reports the following information. Compute the total variable overhead cost variance.

Actual machine hours used	4,700 hours
Standard machine hours (for actual production)	5,000 hours
Actual variable overhead rate per hour	$4.15
Standard variable overhead rate per hour	$4.00

QS 21-19[A]
Overhead spending and efficiency variances P4

Refer to the information from QS 21-18. Compute the variable overhead spending variance and the variable overhead efficiency variance.

QS 21-20
Computing sales price and volume variances A1

Farad, Inc., specializes in selling used SUVs. During the month, the dealership sold 50 trucks at an average price of $9,000 each. The budget for the month was to sell 45 trucks at an average price of $9,500 each. Compute the dealership's sales price variance and sales volume variance for the month.

QS 21-21
Sales variances A1

In a recent year, **BMW** sold 216,944 of its 1 Series cars. Assume the company expected to sell 225,944 of these cars during the year. Also assume the budgeted sales price for each car was $30,000, and the actual sales price for each car was $30,200. Compute the sales price variance and the sales volume variance.

connect

EXERCISES

Exercise 21-1
Classification of costs as fixed or variable
P1

JPAK Company manufactures and sells mountain bikes. It normally operates eight hours a day, five days a week. Using this information, classify each of the following costs as fixed or variable. If additional information would affect your decision, describe the information.

____ **a.** Bike frames	____ **e.** Bike tires	____ **i.** Office supplies
____ **b.** Screws for assembly	____ **f.** Gas used for heating	____ **j.** Depreciation on tools
____ **c.** Repair expense for tools	____ **g.** Incoming shipping expenses	____ **k.** Management salaries
____ **d.** Direct labor	____ **h.** Taxes on property	

Exercise 21-2
Preparation of flexible budgets
P1

Tempo Company's fixed budget (based on sales of 7,000 units) for the first quarter of calendar year 2015 reveals the following. Prepare flexible budgets following the format of Exhibit 21.3 that show variable costs per unit, fixed costs, and three different flexible budgets for sales volumes of 6,000, 7,000, and 8,000 units.

	Fixed Budget	
Sales (7,000 units)		$2,800,000
Cost of goods sold		
Direct materials	$280,000	
Direct labor	490,000	
Production supplies	175,000	
Plant manager salary	65,000	1,010,000
Gross profit		1,790,000
Selling expenses		
Sales commissions	140,000	
Packaging	154,000	
Advertising	125,000	419,000
Administrative expenses		
Administrative salaries	85,000	
Depreciation—office equip.	35,000	
Insurance	20,000	
Office rent	36,000	176,000
Income from operations		$1,195,000

Check Income (at 6,000 units), $972,000

Exercise 21-3
Preparation of a flexible budget performance report
P1

Solitaire Company's fixed budget performance report for June follows. The $315,000 budgeted expenses include $294,000 variable expenses and $21,000 fixed expenses. Actual expenses include $27,000 fixed expenses. Prepare a flexible budget performance report showing any variances between budgeted and actual results. List fixed and variable expenses separately.

	Fixed Budget	Actual Results	Variances
Sales (in units)	8,400	10,800	
Sales (in dollars)	$420,000	$540,000	$120,000 F
Total expenses	315,000	378,000	63,000 U
Income from operations	$105,000	$162,000	$ 57,000 F

Check Income variance, $21,000 F

Exercise 21-4
Preparation of a flexible budget performance report
P1

Bay City Company's fixed budget performance report for July follows. The $647,500 budgeted total expenses include $487,500 variable expenses and $160,000 fixed expenses. Actual expenses include $158,000 fixed expenses. Prepare a flexible budget performance report that shows any variances between budgeted results and actual results. List fixed and variable expenses separately.

	Fixed Budget	Actual Results	Variances
Sales (in units)	7,500	7,200	
Sales (in dollars)	$750,000	$737,000	$13,000 U
Total expenses	647,500	641,000	6,500 F
Income from operations	$102,500	$ 96,000	$ 6,500 U

Check Income variance, $4,000 F

Exercise 21-5
Standard costs
C1

Match the terms *a–e* with their correct definition 1–5.

a. Standard cost card
b. Management by exception
c. Standard cost
d. Ideal standard
e. Practical standard

____ **1.** Quantity of input required under normal conditions.
____ **2.** Quantity of input required if a production process is 100% efficient.
____ **3.** Managing by focusing on large differences from standard costs.
____ **4.** Record that accumulates standard cost information.
____ **5.** Preset cost for delivering a product or service under normal conditions.

Exercise 21-6
Analyzing variances
C1

Resset Co. provides the following results of April's operations: F indicates favorable and U indicates unfavorable. Applying the management by exception approach, which of the variances are of greatest concern? Why?

Direct materials price variance	$ 300 F
Direct materials quantity variance	3,000 U
Direct labor rate variance	100 U
Direct labor efficiency variance	2,200 F
Controllable overhead variance	400 U
Fixed overhead volume variance	500 F

Exercise 21-7
Cost variances
C2

Presented below are terms preceded by letters *a* through *j* and a list of definitions 1 through 10. Enter the letter of the term with the definition, using the space preceding the definition.

a. Fixed budget
b. Standard costs
c. Price variance
d. Quantity variance
e. Volume variance
f. Controllable variance
g. Cost variance
h. Flexible budget
i. Variance analysis
j. Management by exception

____ **1.** The difference between actual and budgeted sales or cost caused by the difference between the actual price per unit and the budgeted price per unit.
____ **2.** A planning budget based on a single predicted amount of sales or production volume; unsuitable for evaluations if the actual volume differs from the predicted volume.
____ **3.** Preset costs for delivering a product, component, or service under normal conditions.
____ **4.** A process of examining the differences between actual and budgeted sales or costs and describing them in terms of the amounts that resulted from price and quantity differences.
____ **5.** The difference between the total budgeted overhead cost and the overhead cost that was allocated to products using the predetermined fixed overhead rate.
____ **6.** A budget prepared based on predicted amounts of revenues and expenses corresponding to the actual level of output.
____ **7.** The difference between actual and budgeted cost caused by the difference between the actual quantity and the budgeted quantity.
____ **8.** The combination of both overhead spending variances (variable and fixed) and the variable overhead efficiency variance.
____ **9.** A management process to focus on significant variances and give less attention to areas where performance is close to the standard.
____ **10.** The difference between actual cost and standard cost, made up of a price variance and a quantity variance.

Exercise 21-8
Standard unit cost; total cost variance
C2

A manufactured product has the following information for June.

	Standard	Actual
Direct materials	(6 lbs. @ $8 per lb.)	48,500 lbs. @ $8.10 per lb.
Direct labor	(2 hrs. @ $16 per hr.)	15,700 hrs. @ $16.50 per hr.
Overhead	(2 hrs. @ $12 per hr.)	$198,000
Units manufactured		8,000

Compute the (1) standard cost per unit and (2) total cost variance for June. Indicate whether the cost variance is favorable or unfavorable.

Exercise 21-9
Direct materials variances P2

Refer to the information in Exercise 21-8 and compute the (1) direct materials price and (2) direct materials quantity variances. Indicate whether each variance is favorable or unfavorable.

Exercise 21-10
Direct labor variances
P2

Refer to the information in Exercise 21-8 and compute the (1) direct labor rate and (2) direct labor efficiency variances. Indicate whether each variance is favorable or unfavorable.

Exercise 21-11
Direct materials and direct labor variances
P2

Hutto Corp. has set the following standard direct materials and direct labor costs per unit for the product it manufactures.

Direct materials (15 lbs. @ $4 per lb.)	$60
Direct labor (3 hrs. @ $15 per hr.)	45

During May the company incurred the following actual costs to produce 9,000 units.

Direct materials (138,000 lbs. @ $3.75 per lb.)	$517,500
Direct labor (31,000 hrs. @ $15.10 per hr.)	468,100

Compute the (1) direct materials price and quantity variances and (2) direct labor rate and efficiency variances. Indicate whether each variance is favorable or unfavorable.

Exercise 21-12
Direct materials and direct labor variances
P2

Reed Corp. has set the following standard direct materials and direct labor costs per unit for the product it manufactures.

Direct materials (10 lbs. @ $3 per lb.)	$30
Direct labor (4 hrs. @ $6 per hr.)	24

During June the company incurred the following actual costs to produce 9,000 units.

Direct materials (92,000 lbs. @ $2.95 per lb.)	$271,400
Direct labor (37,600 hrs. @ $6.05 per hr.)	227,480

Compute the (1) direct materials price and quantity variances and (2) direct labor rate and efficiency variances. Indicate whether each variance is favorable or unfavorable.

Exercise 21-13
Computation and interpretation of materials variances P2

Check Price variance, $2,200 U

Hart Company made 3,000 bookshelves using 22,000 board feet of wood costing $266,200. The company's direct materials standards for one bookshelf are 8 board feet of wood at $12 per board foot.

1. Compute the direct materials price and quantity variances incurred in manufacturing these bookshelves.

2. Interpret the direct materials variances.

Exercise 21-14^A
Materials variances recorded and closed
P5

Refer to Exercise 21-13. Hart Company records standard costs in its accounts and its materials variances in separate accounts when it assigns materials costs to the Work in Process Inventory account.

1. Show the journal entry that both charges the direct materials costs to the Work in Process Inventory account and records the materials variances in their proper accounts.
2. Assume that Hart's materials variances are the only variances accumulated in the accounting period and that they are immaterial. Prepare the adjusting journal entry to close the variance accounts at period-end.
3. Identify the variance that should be investigated according to the management by exception concept. Explain.

Check (2) Cr. to Cost of Goods Sold, $21,800

Exercise 21-15
Direct materials and direct labor variances
P2

The following information describes production activities of Mercer Manufacturing for the year:

Actual direct materials used	16,000 lbs. at $4.05 per lb.
Actual direct labor used	5,545 hours for a total of $105,355
Actual units produced	30,000

Budgeted standards for each unit produced are 0.50 pounds of direct material at $4.00 per pound and 10 minutes of direct labor at $20 per hour.

1. Compute the direct materials price and quantity variances.
2. Compute the direct labor rate and efficiency variances. Indicate whether each variance is favorable or unfavorable.

Exercise 21-16
Computation and interpretation of labor variances P2

After evaluating Null Company's manufacturing process, management decides to establish standards of 3 hours of direct labor per unit of product and $15 per hour for the labor rate. During October, the company uses 16,250 hours of direct labor at a $247,000 total cost to produce 5,600 units of product. In November, the company uses 22,000 hours of direct labor at a $335,500 total cost to produce 6,000 units of product.

1. Compute the direct labor rate variance, the direct labor efficiency variance, and the total direct labor cost variance for each of these two months.
2. Interpret the October direct labor variances.

Check (1) October rate variance, $3,250 U

Exercise 21-17
Computation of total variable and fixed overhead variances
P3

Sedona Company set the following standard costs for one unit of its product for 2015.

Direct material (20 lbs. @ $2.50 per lb.)	$ 50
Direct labor (10 hrs. @ $8.00 per hr.)	80
Factory variable overhead (10 hrs. @ $4.00 per hr.)	40
Factory fixed overhead (10 hrs. @ $1.60 per hr.)	16
Standard cost	$186

The $5.60 ($4.00 + $1.60) total overhead rate per direct labor hour is based on an expected operating level equal to 75% of the factory's capacity of 50,000 units per month. The following monthly flexible budget information is also available.

	A	B	C	D
1		Operating Levels (% of capacity)		
2	Flexible Budget	70%	75%	80%
3	Budgeted output (units)	35,000	37,500	40,000
4	Budgeted labor (standard hours)	350,000	375,000	400,000
5	Budgeted overhead (dollars)			
6	Variable overhead	$1,400,000	$1,500,000	$1,600,000
7	Fixed overhead	600,000	600,000	600,000
8	Total overhead	$2,000,000	$2,100,000	$2,200,000
9				

During the current month, the company operated at 70% of capacity, employees worked 340,000 hours, and the following actual overhead costs were incurred.

Variable overhead costs	$1,375,000
Fixed overhead costs	628,600
Total overhead costs	$2,003,600

Check (2) Variable overhead cost variance, $25,000 F

1. Show how the company computed its predetermined overhead application rate per hour for total overhead, variable overhead, and fixed overhead.
2. Compute the total variable and total fixed overhead variances.

Exercise 21-18A
Computation and interpretation of overhead spending, efficiency, and volume variances P4

Refer to the information from Exercise 21-17. Compute and interpret the following.

1. Variable overhead spending and efficiency variances.
2. Fixed overhead spending and volume variances.
3. Controllable variance.

Check (1) Variable overhead: Spending, $15,000 U; Efficiency, $40,000 F

Exercise 21-19
Computation of total overhead rate and total overhead variance P3

World Company expects to operate at 80% of its productive capacity of 50,000 units per month. At this planned level, the company expects to use 25,000 standard hours of direct labor. Overhead is allocated to products using a predetermined standard rate based on direct labor hours. At the 80% capacity level, the total budgeted cost includes $50,000 fixed overhead cost and $275,000 variable overhead cost. In the current month, the company incurred $305,000 actual overhead and 22,000 actual labor hours while producing 35,000 units.

Check (1) Variable overhead rate, $11.00 per hour

1. Compute the overhead application rate for total overhead.
2. Compute the total overhead variance.

Exercise 21-20
Computation of volume and controllable overhead variances P3

Refer to the information from Exercise 21-19. Compute the (1) overhead volume variance and (2) overhead controllable variance.

Check (2) $14,375 U

Exercise 21-21
Overhead controllable and volume variances; overhead variance report P3

James Corp. applies overhead on the basis of direct labor hours. For the month of May, the company planned production of 8,000 units (80% of its production capacity of 10,000 units) and prepared the following overhead budget:

Overhead Budget	Operating Level 80%
Production in units	8,000
Standard direct labor hours	24,000
Budgeted overhead	
Variable overhead costs	
Indirect materials	$15,000
Indirect labor	24,000
Power	6,000
Maintenance	3,000
Total variable costs	48,000
Fixed overhead costs	
Rent of factory building	15,000
Depreciation—machinery	10,000
Supervisory salaries	19,400
Total fixed costs	44,400
Total overhead costs	$92,400

During May, the company operated at 90% capacity (9,000 units) and incurred the following actual overhead costs:

Overhead costs	
Indirect materials	$15,000
Indirect labor	26,500
Power	6,750
Maintenance	4,000
Rent of factory building	15,000
Depreciation—machinery	10,000
Supervisory salaries	22,000
Total actual overhead costs	$99,250

1. Compute the overhead controllable variance.
2. Compute the overhead volume variance.
3. Prepare an overhead variance report at the actual activity level of 9,000 units.

Exercise 21-22
Overhead controllable and volume variances; overhead variance report
P3

Blaze Corp. applies overhead on the basis of direct labor hours. For the month of March, the company planned production of 8,000 units (80% of its production capacity of 10,000 units) and prepared the following budget:

Overhead Budget	Operating Level 80%
Production in units	8,000
Standard direct labor hours	32,000
Budgeted overhead	
Variable overhead costs	
Indirect materials	$10,000
Indirect labor	16,000
Power	4,000
Maintenance	2,000
Total variable costs	32,000
Fixed overhead costs	
Rent of factory building	12,000
Depreciation—machinery	20,000
Taxes and insurance	2,400
Supervisory salaries	13,600
Total fixed costs	48,000
Total overhead costs	$80,000

During March, the company operated at 90% capacity (9,000 units), and it incurred the following actual overhead costs:

Overhead costs	
Indirect materials	$10,000
Indirect labor	16,000
Power	4,500
Maintenance	3,000
Rent of factory building	12,000
Depreciation—machinery	19,200
Taxes and insurance	3,000
Supervisory salaries	14,000
Total actual overhead costs	$81,700

1. Compute the overhead controllable variance.
2. Compute the overhead volume variance.
3. Prepare an overhead variance report at the actual activity level of 9,000 units.

Exercise 21-23
Computing and interpreting sales variances A1

Comp Wiz sells computers. During May 2015, it sold 350 computers at a $1,200 average price each. The May 2015 fixed budget included sales of 365 computers at an average price of $1,100 each.

1. Compute the sales price variance and the sales volume variance for May 2015.
2. Interpret the findings.

connect

PROBLEM SET A

Phoenix Company's 2015 master budget included the following fixed budget report. It is based on an expected production and sales volume of 15,000 units.

Problem 21-1A
Preparation and analysis of a flexible budget
P1

PHOENIX COMPANY Fixed Budget Report For Year Ended December 31, 2015		
Sales		$3,000,000
Cost of goods sold		
Direct materials	$975,000	
Direct labor	225,000	
Machinery repairs (variable cost)	60,000	
Depreciation—plant equipment (straight-line)	300,000	
Utilities ($45,000 is variable)	195,000	
Plant management salaries	200,000	1,955,000
Gross profit		1,045,000
Selling expenses		
Packaging	75,000	
Shipping	105,000	
Sales salary (fixed annual amount)	250,000	430,000
General and administrative expenses		
Advertising expense	125,000	
Salaries	241,000	
Entertainment expense	90,000	456,000
Income from operations		$ 159,000

Required

1. Classify all items listed in the fixed budget as variable or fixed. Also determine their amounts per unit or their amounts for the year, as appropriate.

Check (2) Budgeted income at 16,000 units, $260,000

2. Prepare flexible budgets (see Exhibit 21.3) for the company at sales volumes of 14,000 and 16,000 units.
3. The company's business conditions are improving. One possible result is a sales volume of 18,000 units. The company president is confident that this volume is within the relevant range of existing capacity. How much would operating income increase over the 2015 budgeted amount of $159,000 if this level is reached without increasing capacity?

(4) Potential operating loss, $(144,000)

4. An unfavorable change in business is remotely possible; in this case, production and sales volume for 2015 could fall to 12,000 units. How much income (or loss) from operations would occur if sales volume falls to this level?

Problem 21-2A
Preparation and analysis of a flexible budget performance report
P1 P2 A1

Refer to the information in Problem 21-1A. Phoenix Company's actual income statement for 2015 follows.

PHOENIX COMPANY Statement of Income from Operations For Year Ended December 31, 2015		
Sales (18,000 units)		$3,648,000
Cost of goods sold		
Direct materials	$1,185,000	
Direct labor	278,000	
Machinery repairs (variable cost)	63,000	
Depreciation—plant equipment	300,000	
Utilities (fixed cost is $147,500)	200,500	
Plant management salaries	210,000	2,236,500
Gross profit		1,411,500
Selling expenses		
Packaging	87,500	
Shipping	118,500	
Sales salary (annual)	268,000	474,000
General and administrative expenses		
Advertising expense	132,000	
Salaries	241,000	
Entertainment expense	93,500	466,500
Income from operations		$ 471,000

Required

1. Prepare a flexible budget performance report for 2015.

Analysis Component

2. Analyze and interpret both the (a) sales variance and (b) direct materials cost variance.

Check (1) Variances: Fixed costs, $36,000 U; Income, $9,000 F

Problem 21-3A
Flexible budget preparation; computation of materials, labor, and overhead variances; and overhead variance report

P1 P2 P3 C2

Antuan Company set the following standard costs for one unit of its product.

Direct materials (6 lbs. @ $5 per lb.)	$ 30
Direct labor (2 hrs. @ $17 per hr.)	34
Overhead (2 hrs. @ $18.50 per hr.)	37
Total standard cost	$101

The predetermined overhead rate ($18.50 per direct labor hour) is based on an expected volume of 75% of the factory's capacity of 20,000 units per month. Following are the company's budgeted overhead costs per month at the 75% capacity level.

Overhead Budget (75% Capacity)		
Variable overhead costs		
Indirect materials	$ 45,000	
Indirect labor	180,000	
Power	45,000	
Repairs and maintenance	90,000	
Total variable overhead costs		$360,000
Fixed overhead costs		
Depreciation—building	24,000	
Depreciation—machinery	80,000	
Taxes and insurance	12,000	
Supervision	79,000	
Total fixed overhead costs		195,000
Total overhead costs		$555,000

The company incurred the following actual costs when it operated at 75% of capacity in October.

Direct materials (91,000 lbs. @ $5.10 per lb.)		$ 464,100
Direct labor (30,500 hrs. @ $17.25 per hr.)		526,125
Overhead costs		
Indirect materials	$ 44,250	
Indirect labor	177,750	
Power	43,000	
Repairs and maintenance	96,000	
Depreciation—building	24,000	
Depreciation—machinery	75,000	
Taxes and insurance	11,500	
Supervision	89,000	560,500
Total costs		$1,550,725

Required

1. Examine the monthly overhead budget to (a) determine the costs per unit for each variable overhead item and its total per unit costs, and (b) identify the total fixed costs per month.
2. Prepare flexible overhead budgets (as in Exhibit 21.12) for October showing the amounts of each variable and fixed cost at the 65%, 75%, and 85% capacity levels.
3. Compute the direct materials cost variance, including its price and quantity variances.

Check (2) Budgeted total overhead at 13,000 units, $507,000

(3) Materials variances: Price, $9,100 U; Quantity, $5,000 U

(4) Labor variances: Rate, $7,625 U; Efficiency, $8,500 U

4. Compute the direct labor cost variance, including its rate and efficiency variances.
5. Prepare a detailed overhead variance report (as in Exhibit 21.15) that shows the variances for individual items of overhead.

Problem 21-4A
Computation of materials, labor, and overhead variances
P2 P3

Trico Company set the following standard unit costs for its single product.

Direct materials (30 lbs. @ $4 per lb.)	$120
Direct labor (5 hrs. @ $14 per hr.)	70
Factory overhead—variable (5 hrs. @ $8 per hr.)	40
Factory overhead—fixed (5 hrs. @ $10 per hr.)	50
Total standard cost	$280

The predetermined overhead rate is based on a planned operating volume of 80% of the productive capacity of 60,000 units per quarter. The following flexible budget information is available.

	Operating Levels		
	70%	80%	90%
Production in units	42,000	48,000	54,000
Standard direct labor hours	210,000	240,000	270,000
Budgeted overhead			
Fixed factory overhead	$2,400,000	$2,400,000	$2,400,000
Variable factory overhead	$1,680,000	$1,920,000	$2,160,000

During the current quarter, the company operated at 90% of capacity and produced 54,000 units of product; actual direct labor totaled 265,000 hours. Units produced were assigned the following standard costs:

Direct materials (1,620,000 lbs. @ $4 per lb.)	$ 6,480,000
Direct labor (270,000 hrs. @ $14 per hr.)	3,780,000
Factory overhead (270,000 hrs. @ $18 per hr.)	4,860,000
Total standard cost	$15,120,000

Actual costs incurred during the current quarter follow:

Direct materials (1,615,000 lbs. @ $4.10 per lb.)	$ 6,621,500
Direct labor (265,000 hrs. @ $13.75 per hr.)	3,643,750
Fixed factory overhead costs	2,350,000
Variable factory overhead costs	2,200,000
Total actual costs	$14,815,250

Check (1) Materials variances: Price, $161,500 U; Quantity, $20,000 F
(2) Labor variances: Rate, $66,250 F; Efficiency, $70,000 F

Required

1. Compute the direct materials cost variance, including its price and quantity variances.
2. Compute the direct labor cost variance, including its rate and efficiency variances.
3. Compute the overhead controllable and volume variances.

Problem 21-5A[A]
Expanded overhead variances
P4

Refer to information in Problem 21-4A.

Required

Compute these variances: (a) variable overhead spending and efficiency, (b) fixed overhead spending and volume, and (c) total overhead controllable.

Problem 21-6A^A
Materials, labor, and overhead variances recorded and analyzed
C1 P5

Boss Company's standard cost accounting system recorded this information from its December operations.

Standard direct materials cost	$100,000
Direct materials quantity variance (unfavorable)	3,000
Direct materials price variance (favorable)	500
Actual direct labor cost	90,000
Direct labor efficiency variance (favorable)	7,000
Direct labor rate variance (unfavorable)	1,200
Actual overhead cost	375,000
Volume variance (unfavorable)	12,000
Controllable variance (unfavorable)	9,000

Required

1. Prepare December 31 journal entries to record the company's costs and variances for the month. (Do not prepare the journal entry to close the variances.)

Check (1) Dr. Work in Process Inventory (for overhead), $354,000

Analysis Component

2. Identify the variances that would attract the attention of a manager who uses management by exception. Explain what action(s) the manager should consider.

PROBLEM SET B

Problem 21-1B
Preparation and analysis of a flexible budget
P1 A1

Tohono Company's 2015 master budget included the following fixed budget report. It is based on an expected production and sales volume of 20,000 units.

TOHONO COMPANY Fixed Budget Report For Year Ended December 31, 2015		
Sales		$3,000,000
Cost of goods sold		
Direct materials	$1,200,000	
Direct labor	260,000	
Machinery repairs (variable cost)	57,000	
Depreciation—machinery (straight-line)	250,000	
Utilities (25% is variable cost)	200,000	
Plant manager salaries	140,000	2,107,000
Gross profit		893,000
Selling expenses		
Packaging	80,000	
Shipping	116,000	
Sales salary (fixed annual amount)	160,000	356,000
General and administrative expenses		
Advertising	81,000	
Salaries	241,000	
Entertainment expense	90,000	412,000
Income from operations		$ 125,000

Required

1. Classify all items listed in the fixed budget as variable or fixed. Also determine their amounts per unit or their amounts for the year, as appropriate.
2. Prepare flexible budgets (see Exhibit 21.3) for the company at sales volumes of 18,000 and 24,000 units.
3. The company's business conditions are improving. One possible result is a sales volume of 28,000 units. The company president is confident that this volume is within the relevant range of existing capacity. How much would operating income increase over the 2015 budgeted amount of $125,000 if this level is reached without increasing capacity?
4. An unfavorable change in business is remotely possible; in this case, production and sales volume for 2015 could fall to 14,000 units. How much income (or loss) from operations would occur if sales volume falls to this level?

Check (2) Budgeted income at 24,000 units, $372,400

(4) Potential operating loss, $(246,100)

Problem 21-2B
Preparation and analysis of a flexible budget performance report
P1 A1

Refer to the information in Problem 21-1B. Tohono Company's actual income statement for 2015 follows.

TOHONO COMPANY Statement of Income from Operations For Year Ended December 31, 2015		
Sales (24,000 units)		$3,648,000
Cost of goods sold		
Direct materials	$1,400,000	
Direct labor	360,000	
Machinery repairs (variable cost)	60,000	
Depreciation—machinery	250,000	
Utilities (variable cost, $64,000)	218,000	
Plant manager salaries	155,000	2,443,000
Gross profit		1,205,000
Selling expenses		
Packaging	90,000	
Shipping	124,000	
Sales salary (annual)	162,000	376,000
General and administrative expenses		
Advertising expense	104,000	
Salaries	232,000	
Entertainment expense	100,000	436,000
Income from operations		$ 393,000

Required

Check (1) Variances: Fixed costs, $45,000 U; Income, $20,600 F

1. Prepare a flexible budget performance report for 2015.

Analysis Component

2. Analyze and interpret both the (a) sales variance and (b) direct materials cost variance.

Problem 21-3B
Flexible budget preparation; computation of materials, labor, and overhead variances; and overhead variance report
P1 P2 P3 C2

Suncoast Company set the following standard costs for one unit of its product.

Direct materials (4.5 lbs. @ $6 per lb.)	$27
Direct labor (1.5 hrs. @ $12 per hr.)	18
Overhead (1.5 hrs. @ $16 per hr.)	24
Total standard cost	$69

The predetermined overhead rate ($16.00 per direct labor hour) is based on an expected volume of 75% of the factory's capacity of 20,000 units per month. Following are the company's budgeted overhead costs per month at the 75% capacity level.

Overhead Budget (75% Capacity)		
Variable overhead costs		
Indirect materials	$22,500	
Indirect labor	90,000	
Power	22,500	
Repairs and maintenance	45,000	
Total variable overhead costs		$180,000
Fixed overhead costs		
Depreciation—building	24,000	
Depreciation—machinery	72,000	
Taxes and insurance	18,000	
Supervision	66,000	
Total fixed overhead costs		180,000
Total overhead costs		$360,000

The company incurred the following actual costs when it operated at 75% of capacity in December.

Direct materials (69,000 lbs. @ $6.10 per lb.)		$ 420,900
Direct labor (22,800 hrs. @ $12.30 per hr.)		280,440
Overhead costs		
Indirect materials	$21,600	
Indirect labor	82,260	
Power	23,100	
Repairs and maintenance	46,800	
Depreciation—building	24,000	
Depreciation—machinery	75,000	
Taxes and insurance	16,500	
Supervision	66,000	355,260
Total costs		$1,056,600

Required

1. Examine the monthly overhead budget to (a) determine the costs per unit for each variable overhead item and its total per unit costs, and (b) identify the total fixed costs per month.
2. Prepare flexible overhead budgets (as in Exhibit 21.12) for December showing the amounts of each variable and fixed cost at the 65%, 75%, and 85% capacity levels.
3. Compute the direct materials cost variance, including its price and quantity variances.
4. Compute the direct labor cost variance, including its rate and efficiency variances.
5. Prepare a detailed overhead variance report (as in Exhibit 21.15) that shows the variances for individual items of overhead.

Check (2) Budgeted total overhead at 17,000 units, $384,000

(3) Materials variances: Price, $6,900 U; Quantity, $9,000 U

(4) Labor variances: Rate, $6,840 U; Efficiency, $3,600 U

Problem 21-4B
Computation of materials, labor, and overhead variances
P2 P3

Kryll Company set the following standard unit costs for its single product.

Direct materials (25 lbs. @ $4 per lb.)	$100
Direct labor (6 hrs. @ $8 per hr.)	48
Factory overhead—variable (6 hrs. @ $5 per hr.)	30
Factory overhead—fixed (6 hrs. @ $7 per hr.)	42
Total standard cost	$220

The predetermined overhead rate is based on a planned operating volume of 80% of the productive capacity of 60,000 units per quarter. The following flexible budget information is available.

	Operating Levels		
	70%	80%	90%
Production in units	42,000	48,000	54,000
Standard direct labor hours	252,000	288,000	324,000
Budgeted overhead			
Fixed factory overhead	$2,016,000	$2,016,000	$2,016,000
Variable factory overhead	1,260,000	1,440,000	1,620,000

During the current quarter, the company operated at 70% of capacity and produced 42,000 units of product; direct labor hours worked were 250,000. Units produced were assigned the following standard costs:

Direct materials (1,050,000 lbs. @ $4 per lb.)	$4,200,000
Direct labor (252,000 hrs. @ $8 per hr.)	2,016,000
Factory overhead (252,000 hrs. @ $12 per hr.)	3,024,000
Total standard cost	$9,240,000

Actual costs incurred during the current quarter follow:

Direct materials (1,000,000 lbs. @ $4.25 per lb.)	$4,250,000
Direct labor (250,000 hrs. @ $7.75 per hr.)	1,937,500
Fixed factory overhead costs	1,960,000
Variable factory overhead costs	1,200,000
Total actual costs	$9,347,500

Check (1) Materials variances: Price, $250,000 U; Quantity, $200,000 F (2) Labor variances: Rate, $62,500 F; Efficiency, $16,000 F

Required

1. Compute the direct materials cost variance, including its price and quantity variances.
2. Compute the direct labor cost variance, including its rate and efficiency variances.
3. Compute the total overhead controllable and volume variances.

Problem 21-5B^A
Expanded overhead variances
P4

Refer to information in Problem 21-4B.

Required

Compute these variances: (a) variable overhead spending and efficiency, (b) fixed overhead spending and volume, and (c) total overhead controllable.

Problem 21-6B^A
Materials, labor, and overhead variances recorded and analyzed
C1 P5

Kenya Company's standard cost accounting system recorded this information from its June operations.

Standard direct materials cost	$130,000
Direct materials quantity variance (favorable)	5,000
Direct materials price variance (favorable)	1,500
Actual direct labor cost	65,000
Direct labor efficiency variance (favorable)	3,000
Direct labor rate variance (unfavorable)	500
Actual overhead cost	250,000
Volume variance (unfavorable)	12,000
Controllable variance (unfavorable)	8,000

Check (1) Dr. Work in Process Inventory (for overhead), $230,000

Required

1. Prepare journal entries dated June 30 to record the company's costs and variances for the month. (Do not prepare the journal entry to close the variances.)

Analysis Component

2. Identify the variances that would attract the attention of a manager who uses management by exception. Describe what action(s) the manager should consider.

SERIAL PROBLEM
Business Solutions
P1

(This serial problem began in Chapter 1 and continues through most of the book. If previous chapter segments were not completed, the serial problem can begin at this point. It is helpful, but not necessary, to use the working papers that accompany the book.)

SP 21 Business Solutions's second quarter 2016 fixed budget performance report for its computer furniture operations follows. The $156,000 budgeted expenses include $108,000 in variable expenses for desks and $18,000 in variable expenses for chairs, as well as $30,000 fixed expenses. The actual expenses include $31,000 fixed expenses. Prepare a flexible budget performance report that shows any variances between budgeted results and actual results. List fixed and variable expenses separately.

	Fixed Budget	Actual Results	Variances
Desk sales (in units)	144	150	
Chair sales (in units)	72	80	
Desk sales	$180,000	$186,000	$6,000 F
Chair sales	36,000	41,200	5,200 F
Total expenses	156,000	163,880	7,880 U
Income from operations	$ 60,000	$ 63,320	$3,320 F

Check Variances: Fixed expenses, $1,000 U

Beyond the Numbers

REPORTING IN ACTION
C1
APPLE

BTN 21-1 Analysis of flexible budgets and standard costs emphasizes the importance of a similar unit of measure for meaningful comparisons and evaluations. When **Apple** compiles its financial reports in compliance with GAAP, it applies the same unit of measurement, U.S. dollars, for most measures of business operations. One issue for Apple is how best to adjust account values for its subsidiaries that compile financial reports in currencies other than the U.S. dollar.

Required

1. Read Apple's Note 1 in Appendix A and identify the financial statement where it reports the annual adjustment for foreign currency translation for subsidiaries that do not use the U.S. dollar as their functional currency.
2. Translating financial statements requires the use of a currency exchange rate. For each of the following financial statement items, explain the exchange rate the company would apply to translate into U.S. dollars.
   a. Cash
   b. Sales revenue
   c. Property, plant and equipment

COMPARATIVE ANALYSIS
A1
APPLE
GOOGLE

BTN 21-2 The usefulness of budgets, variances, and related analyses often depends on the accuracy of management's estimates of future sales activity.

Required

1. Identify and record the prior three years' sales (in dollars) for **Apple** and **Google** using their financial statements in Appendix A.
2. Using the data in part *1,* predict both companies' sales activity for the next two to three years. (If possible, compare your predictions to actual sales figures for those years.)

ETHICS CHALLENGE
C1

BTN 21-3 Setting materials, labor, and overhead standards is challenging. If standards are set too low, companies might purchase inferior products and employees might not work to their full potential. If standards are set too high, companies could be unable to offer a quality product at a profitable rate and employees could be overworked. The ethical challenge is to set a high but reasonable standard. Assume that as a manager you are asked to set the standard materials price and quantity for the new 1,000 CKB Mega-Max chip, a technically advanced product. To properly set the price and quantity standards, you assemble a team of specialists to provide input.

Required

Identify four types of specialists that you would assemble to provide information to help set the materials price and quantity standards. Briefly explain why you chose each individual.

COMMUNICATING IN PRACTICE
P5 C2

BTN 21-4 The reason we use the words *favorable* and *unfavorable* when evaluating variances is made clear when we look at the closing of accounts. To see this, consider that (1) all variance accounts are closed at the end of each period (temporary accounts), (2) a favorable variance is always a credit balance, and (3) an unfavorable variance is always a debit balance. Write a half-page memorandum to your instructor with three parts that answer the three following requirements. (Assume that variance accounts are closed to Cost of Goods Sold.)

Required

1. Does Cost of Goods Sold increase or decrease when closing a favorable variance? Does gross margin increase or decrease when a favorable variance is closed to Cost of Goods Sold? Explain.

2. Does Cost of Goods Sold increase or decrease when closing an unfavorable variance? Does gross margin increase or decrease when an unfavorable variance is closed to Cost of Goods Sold? Explain.
3. Explain the meaning of a favorable variance and an unfavorable variance.

TAKING IT TO THE NET

C1

BTN 21-5 Access **iSixSigma**'s website (iSixSigma.com) to search for and read information about *benchmarking* to complete the following requirements. (*Hint:* Look in the "dictionary" link.)

Required

1. Write a one-paragraph explanation (in layperson's terms) of benchmarking.
2. How does standard costing relate to benchmarking?

TEAMWORK IN ACTION

C2

BTN 21-6 Many service industries link labor rate and time (quantity) standards with their processes. One example is the standard time to board an aircraft. The reason time plays such an important role in the service industry is that it is viewed as a competitive advantage: best service in the shortest amount of time. Although the labor rate component is difficult to observe, the time component of a service delivery standard is often readily apparent—for example, "Lunch will be served in less than five minutes, or it is free."

Required

Break into teams and select two service industries for your analysis. Identify and describe all the time elements each industry uses to create a competitive advantage.

ENTREPRENEURIAL DECISION

C1 C2

BTN 21-7 **Niner Bikes**, as discussed in the chapter opener, uses a costing system with standard costs for direct materials, direct labor, and overhead costs. Two comments frequently are mentioned in relation to standard costing and variance analysis: "Variances are not explanations" and "Management's goal is not to minimize variances."

Required

Write a short memo to Chris Sugai, Niner Bikes' president, (no more than one page) interpreting these two comments in the context of his business.

HITTING THE ROAD

C1

BTN 21-8 Training employees to use standard amounts of materials in production is common. Typically, large companies invest in this training but small organizations do not. One can observe these different practices in a trip to two different pizza businesses. Visit both a local pizza business and a national pizza chain business and then complete the following.

Required

1. Observe and record the number of raw material items used to make a typical cheese pizza. Also observe how the person making the pizza applies each item when preparing the pizza.
2. Record any differences in how items are applied between the two businesses.
3. Estimate which business is more profitable from your observations. Explain.

BTN 21-9 Access the annual report of Samsung (at samsung.com) for the year ended December 31, 2013. The usefulness of its budgets, variances, and related analyses depends on the accuracy of management's estimates of future sales activity.

GLOBAL DECISION

A1

Samsung

Required

1. Identify and record the prior two years' sales (in ₩ millions) for Samsung from its income statement.
2. Using the data in part *1*, predict sales activity for Samsung for the next two years. Explain your prediction process.

ANSWERS TO MULTIPLE CHOICE QUIZ

1. c; Fixed costs remain at \$300,000; Variable costs = (\$246,000/24,000 units) × 20,000 units = \$205,000
2. e; Budgeted direct materials + Unfavorable variance = Actual cost of direct materials used; or, 60,000 units × \$10 per unit = \$600,000 + \$15,000 U = \$615,000
3. c; (AH × AR) − (AH × SR) = \$1,599,040 − (84,160 hours × \$20 per hour) = \$84,160 F
4. b; Actual variable overhead − Variable overhead applied to production = Variable overhead cost variance; or \$150,000 − (96,000 hours × \$1.50 per hour) = \$6,000 U
5. a; Budgeted fixed overhead − Fixed overhead applied to production = Volume variance; or \$24,000 − (4,800 units × \$4 per unit) = \$4,800 U

chapter 22

Performance Measurement and Responsibility Accounting

Chapter Preview

DECENTRALIZATION	RESPONSIBILITY ACCOUNTING	PROFIT CENTERS	INVESTMENT CENTERS
Advantages Disadvantages Performance evaluation	Controllable versus uncontrollable costs Responsibility accounting system P1 Responsibility accounting report	C1 Direct and indirect expenses P2 Allocation of indirect expenses P3 Departmental income statements Departmental contribution to overhead	A1 ROI and residual income A2 Margin and turnover A3 Nonfinancial performance measures A4 Cycle time C2 Transfer pricing C3 Joint costs allocation

Learning Objectives

CONCEPTUAL

C1 Distinguish between direct and indirect expenses and identify bases for allocating indirect expenses to departments.

C2 *Appendix 22A*—Explain transfer pricing and methods to set transfer prices.

C3 *Appendix 22B*—Describe allocation of joint costs across products.

ANALYTICAL

A1 Analyze investment centers using return on investment and residual income.

A2 Analyze investment centers using profit margin and investment turnover.

A3 Analyze investment centers using the balanced scorecard.

A4 Compute cycle time and cycle efficiency, and explain their importance to production management.

PROCEDURAL

P1 Prepare a responsibility accounting report using controllable costs.

P2 Allocate indirect expenses to departments.

P3 Prepare departmental income statements and contribution reports.

Saving Troubled Waters

PHILADELPHIA—Brian Linton has a passion for oceans. Growing up in Singapore, Brian spent time scuba diving and tending to his 30 fish tanks. Traveling the world enabled Brian to see the "good, the bad, and the ugly of oceans and waterways." Combining his love of the water with an entrepreneurial spirit, Brian started his company **United By Blue** **(UnitedByBlue.com),** an apparel and jewelry company that removes one pound of trash in oceans and waterways for every product sold. As Brian notes, the company's unique business model was driven by "a quest for concrete ways to contribute to real and significant conservation efforts."

Building off Brian's college experiences selling jewelry he imported from Thailand, United By Blue sells men's and women's clothing, bags, and jewelry. The company uses organic cotton and creative designs to make products that elicit a fun vibe associated with oceans and harbor villages. Offering a diverse product line requires Brian to pay attention to cost management and departmental profits. The Sand Shack, a product in the company's jewelry department, "is a line of jewelry with chunky turquoise stones that generates much of the profits the company runs on," says Brian. His managers monitor direct, indirect, and controllable costs; allocate indirect costs to departments; and "measure return on investment (ROI)," explains Brian.

"Do the dirty work yourself"
—Brian Linton

While focusing on controlling costs, United By Blue also strives to remove plastic from its packaging. "The number one material we collect during cleanups is plastic debris. We try to eliminate as much plastic as we can from our supply chain," says Brian. Apparel tags are made from biodegradable substances, infused with flower seeds. T-shirts are packaged in banana fiber paper. "We use things that go back to the earth in a very natural way and actually grow life." While these materials are more costly than plastic, they better fit the company's philosophy and, Brian believes, help generate new business. "We have customers that double their orders the next season because of the cleanups," Brian notes.

As United By Blue continues to grow, Brian focuses on financial *and* nonfinancial performance measures. From $330,000 in 2010, revenues have grown to over $2 million in 2013. A focus on departmental contribution margins enables the company to operate efficiently to finance future growth. Likewise, more revenues mean the company collects more trash, over 170,000 pounds through early 2014 and a goal of over a million pounds. As company founder and chief trash collector, this nonfinancial indicator measures progress toward Brian's vision of "doing the most good possible."

Brian encourages young entrepreneurs to "leave a positive impact on this world" by focusing on what you love. "My heart is in the ocean, so whatever I am doing is going to be in that realm. Whatever your passion is, leave that positive impact."

Sources: *United By Blue website,* January 2015; *Philly.com,* September 5, 2013; *Bloomberg Businessweek,* January 9, 2012; *businessinterviews.com,* interview, September 2014; *Philadelphia Magazine,* July 2011; *PRweb.com,* January 2012

DECENTRALIZATION

Companies are divided into smaller units, called *divisions, segments, departments,* or *subunits,* when they become too large to be managed effectively as a single unit. In these **decentralized organizations,** decisions are made by managers throughout the company rather than by a few top executives. Common ways to decentralize organizations are by geography or product line (also called *brand*). For example, **LinkedIn** organizes its operations into three geographic segments: North America, Europe, and Asia-Pacific. **Callaway Golf** organizes its operations around two product lines, golf balls and golf clubs, and **Kraft Foods Group (Kraft)** organizes its operations around six product lines.

In this section we discuss the motivation for and the advantages and disadvantages of decentralization. In later sections of this chapter we discuss performance measurement in decentralized organizations.

Advantages of Decentralization

Many companies are so large and complex that they are broken into separate divisions for efficiency and/or effectiveness purposes. Divisions then are usually organized into separate departments. Each department is often placed under the direction of a manager. Providing lower-level managers with decision-making authority offers several advantages:

- Lower-level managers have timely access to detailed information about their departments. This enables these managers to better oversee and control their departments' operations.
- Providing lower-level managers with authority to make day-to-day decisions for their departments enables top-level managers to focus more on long-term strategy for the entire organization.
- Managing a division can be good training for employees who later might be promoted to top-level management.
- Having decision-making authority often boosts employee morale and retention.

Disadvantages of Decentralization

Decentralization has potential disadvantages which organizations should consider:

- Because they are so focused on their own departments, department managers might make decisions that do not reflect the organization's overall strategy.
- When an organization has several departments, the decisions of individual departments might conflict with one another.
- Departments might duplicate certain activities (for example, payroll accounting or purchasing); such duplication increases costs. In many decentralized organizations, activities like payroll, purchasing, and other administrative functions are *centralized* to reduce costs.

Performance Evaluation

When a company is decentralized, managers need to know how each department is performing. The accounting system must supply information about resources used and outputs achieved by each department. This requires a system to measure and accumulate revenue and expense information for each department.

Departmental information is prepared for internal managers to help control operations, appraise performance, allocate resources, and plan strategy. If a department is highly profitable, management may decide to expand its operations; if a department is performing poorly, information about revenues or expenses can suggest useful changes. Departmental information is rarely distributed publicly, because of its potential usefulness to competitors.

Financial information used to evaluate a department depends on whether it is evaluated as a cost center, profit center, or investment center.

- A **cost center** incurs costs without directly generating revenues. The manufacturing departments of a manufacturer and its service departments, such as accounting, advertising, and purchasing, are all cost centers. **Kraft**'s Delaware manufacturing plant is a cost center.

- A **profit center** generates revenues and incurs costs. Product lines and selling departments are often evaluated as profit centers. Kraft's Kool-Aid and Capri Sun drinks are examples of profit centers. A profit center manager would not have the authority to make significant investing decisions, such as the decision to build a new manufacturing plant.
- An **investment center** generates revenues and incurs costs, and its manager is also responsible for the investments made in operating assets. For example, the manager of Kraft's beverage division has the authority to make decisions such as building a new manufacturing plant.

Evaluation of managers' performance depends on whether they are responsible for cost centers, profit centers, or investment centers. Cost center managers are evaluated on their ability to control costs. Profit center managers are judged on their ability to generate revenues in excess of the profit center's costs. Investment center managers are evaluated on their use of investment-center assets to generate income. In the remainder of this chapter we discuss alternative ways to measure performance for these different types of departments.

RESPONSIBILITY ACCOUNTING

P1 Prepare a responsibility accounting report using controllable costs.

A **responsibility accounting system** can be set up to control costs and evaluate managers' performance by assigning costs to the managers responsible for controlling them. We discuss responsibility accounting and cost control in this section.

Controllable versus Uncontrollable Costs

We often evaluate a manager's performance using responsibility accounting reports that describe a department's activities in terms of whether a cost is controllable. **Controllable costs** are those for which a manager has the power to determine or at least significantly affect the amount incurred. **Uncontrollable costs** are not within the manager's control or influence. For example, department managers often have little or no control over depreciation expense because they cannot affect the amount of equipment assigned to their departments. Also, department managers rarely control their own salaries. However, they can control or influence items such as the cost of supplies used in their department. When evaluating managers' performances, we should use data reflecting their departments' outputs along with their controllable costs and expenses.

Point: *Cost* refers to a monetary outlay to acquire some resource that has a future benefit. *Expense* usually refers to an expired cost.

Distinguishing between controllable and uncontrollable costs depends on the particular manager and time period under analysis. For example, the cost of property insurance is usually not controllable at the department manager's level, but it is controllable by the executive responsible for obtaining the company's insurance coverage. Likewise, this executive does not control expenses resulting from insurance policies already in force. However, when a policy expires, this executive can renegotiate a replacement policy and then controls these costs. Therefore, all costs are controllable at some management level if the time period is sufficiently long. We must use good judgment in identifying controllable costs.

QC1

Responsibility Accounting System

A responsibility accounting system uses the concept of controllable costs to assign managers the responsibility for costs and expenses under their control. Prior to each reporting period, a company prepares plans that identify costs and expenses under each manager's control. These **responsibility accounting budgets** are typically based on the flexible budgeting approach we showed in the previous chapter. However, a responsibility accounting budget includes only controllable costs.

A responsibility accounting system also involves performance reports. A **responsibility accounting performance report** reports actual expenses that a manager is responsible for and their budgeted amounts. Management's analysis of differences between budgeted and actual amounts often results in corrective or strategic managerial actions. Upper-level management uses performance reports to evaluate the effectiveness of lower-level managers in keeping costs within budgeted amounts.

Point: Responsibility accounting does not place blame. Instead, responsibility accounting is used to identify opportunities for improving performance.

EXHIBIT 22.1

Organizational Responsibility Chart

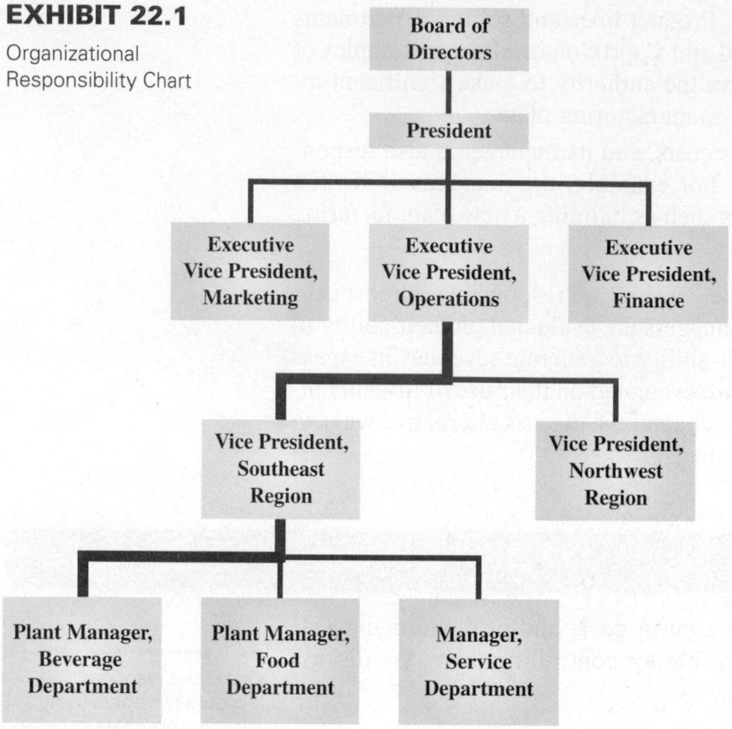

A responsibility accounting system recognizes that control over costs and expenses belongs to several levels of management. We illustrate this in the organization chart in Exhibit 22.1. The lines in this chart connecting the managerial positions reflect channels of authority. For example, the three department managers (beverage, food, and service) in this company are responsible for controllable costs incurred in their departments. These department managers report to the vice president (VP) of the Southeast region, and thus these same costs are subject to the overall control of this VP. Similarly, the costs of the Southeast region are reported to and subject to the control of the executive vice president (EVP) of operations, the president, and, ultimately, the board of directors.

Responsibility Accounting Report

Exhibit 22.2 shows summarized performance reports for the three management levels identified in Exhibit 22.1. The beverage department is a cost center, and its manager is responsible for controlling costs. Exhibit 22.2 shows that costs under the control of the beverage department plant manager are totaled and included among the controllable costs of the VP of the Southeast region. Costs under the control of this VP are totaled and included among

EXHIBIT 22.2

Responsibility Accounting Performance Reports

Executive Vice President, Operations	For July		
Controllable Costs	**Budgeted Amount**	**Actual Amount**	**Over (Under) Budget**
Salaries, VPs	$ 80,000	$ 80,000	$ 0
Quality control costs	21,000	22,400	1,400
Office costs	29,500	28,800	(700)
Southeast region	**276,700**	**279,500**	**2,800**
Northwest region	390,000	380,600	(9,400)
Totals	$ 797,200	$ 791,300	$ (5,900)

Vice President, Southeast Region	For July		
Controllable Costs	**Budgeted Amount**	**Actual Amount**	**Over (Under) Budget**
Salaries, department managers	$ 75,000	$ 76,500	$ 1,500
Depreciation	10,600	10,600	0
Insurance	6,800	6,300	(500)
Beverage department	**79,600**	**79,900**	**300**
Food department	61,500	64,200	2,700
Service department	43,200	42,000	(1,200)
Totals	**$276,700**	**$279,500**	**$2,800**

Plant Manager, Beverage Department	For July		
Controllable Costs	**Budgeted Amount**	**Actual Amount**	**Over (Under) Budget**
Direct materials	$ 51,600	$ 52,500	$ 900
Direct labor	20,000	19,600	(400)
Overhead	8,000	7,800	(200)
Totals	**$ 79,600**	**$ 79,900**	**$ 300**

the controllable costs of the EVP of operations. In this way, responsibility accounting reports provide relevant information for each management level. (If the VP and EVP are responsible for more than just costs, the responsibility accounting system will be expanded, as we show later in this chapter.)

The number of controllable costs reported varies across management levels. At lower levels, managers have limited responsibility and thus few controllable costs. Responsibility and control broaden for higher-level managers; therefore, their reports span a wider range of costs. However, reports to higher-level managers usually are summarized because: (1) lower-level managers are often responsible for these detailed costs, and (2) detailed reports can obscure the broader issues facing the top managers of an organization.

Point: Responsibility accounting usually divides a company into subunits, or *responsibility centers.* A center manager is evaluated on how well the center performs, as reported in responsibility accounting reports.

PROFIT CENTERS

When departments are organized as profit centers, responsibility accounting focuses on how well each department controlled costs *and* generated revenues. This information leads to **departmental income statements** as a common way to report profit center performance. When a company computes departmental profits, it confronts some accounting challenges that involve allocating expenses across departments. We next illustrate these allocations and departmental income reporting.

Direct and Indirect Expenses

C1 Distinguish between direct and indirect expenses and identify bases for allocating indirect expenses to departments.

Direct expenses are costs readily traced to a department because they are incurred for that department's sole benefit. They require no allocation across departments. For example, the salary of an employee who works in only one department is a direct expense of that one department. Direct expenses are often, but not always, controllable costs.

Indirect expenses are costs that are incurred for the joint benefit of more than one department; they cannot be readily traced to only one department. For example, if two or more departments share a single building, all enjoy the benefits of the expenses for rent, heat, and light. Likewise, the *operating departments* that perform an organization's main functions, for example manufacturing and selling, benefit from the work of *service departments.* Service departments, like payroll and human resource management, do not generate revenues, but their support is crucial for the operating departments' success.

When we need information about departmental profits, indirect expenses are allocated across departments benefiting from them. Ideally, we allocate indirect expenses by using a cause-effect relation. When we cannot identify cause-effect relations, we allocate each indirect expense on a basis approximating the relative benefit each department receives.

Illustration of Indirect Expense Allocation To illustrate how to allocate an indirect expense, we consider a retail store that hires an outside company to provide cleaning services. Management allocates this cost across the store's three departments according to the floor space each occupies. Costs of cleaning services for a recent month are $800. Exhibit 22.3 shows the square feet of floor space each department occupies. The store computes the percent of total square feet allotted to each department and uses the percentages to allocate the $800 cost.

Specifically, because the jewelry department occupies 60% of the floor space, 60% of the total $800 cost is assigned to it. The same procedure is applied to the other departments. When

EXHIBIT 22.3

Indirect Expense Allocation

Department	Department Square Feet	Percent of Total Square Feet	Cost Allocated to Department
Jewelry	2,400	60%	$480
Watch repair	600	15	120
China and silver	1,000	25	200
Totals	4,000	100%	$800

the allocation process is complete, these and other allocated costs are deducted from the gross profit for each department to determine net income for each.

Allocation of Indirect Expenses

P2 Allocate indirect expenses to departments.

We've just seen one example of how to allocate indirect expenses across departments—by percentage of floor space for cleaning services. Many other bases exist for allocating indirect expenses. This section describes how to identify appropriate allocation bases.

No standard rule identifies the best basis because expense allocation involves several factors, and the relative importance of these factors varies across departments and organizations. Judgment is required, and people do not always agree. Employee morale suffers when allocations are perceived as unfair. Thus, it is important to carefully design and explain the allocation of service department costs.

Purestock/SuperStock

Point: Some companies ask supervisors to estimate time spent supervising specific departments for purposes of expense allocation.

Wages and Salaries Employee wages and salaries can be either direct or indirect expenses. If their time is spent entirely in one department, their wages are direct expenses of that department. However, if employees work for the benefit of more than one department, their wages are indirect expenses and must be allocated across the departments benefited. An employee's contribution to a department usually depends on the number of hours worked in contributing to that department. Thus, a reasonable basis for allocating employee wages and salaries is the *relative amount of time spent in each department.* In the case of a supervisor who manages more than one department, recording the time spent in each department may not always be practical. Instead, a company can allocate the supervisor's salary to departments on the basis of the number of employees or the amount of sales in each department.

Rent and Related Expenses Rent expense for a building is reasonably allocated to a department on the basis of floor space it occupies. Location can often make some floor space more valuable than other space. Ground floor retail space, for instance, is often more valuable than basement or upper-floor space because all customers pass departments near the entrance but fewer go beyond the first floor. Thus, the allocation method can charge departments that occupy more valuable space a higher expense per square foot.

When no precise measures of floor space values exist, basing allocations on data such as customer traffic and real estate assessments is helpful. When a company owns its building, its expenses for depreciation, taxes, insurance, and other related building expenses are allocated like rent expense.

Advertising Expenses Effective advertising of a department's products increases its sales and customer traffic. Moreover, advertising products for some departments usually helps other departments' sales because customers also often buy unadvertised products. Thus, many stores treat advertising as an indirect expense allocated on the basis of each department's proportion of total sales. For example, a department with 10% of a store's total sales is assigned 10% of advertising expense. Another method is to analyze each advertisement to compute the web/newspaper space or TV/radio time devoted to the products of a department and charge that department for the proportional costs of advertisements. Management must consider whether this more detailed and costly method is justified.

Equipment and Machinery Depreciation Depreciation on equipment and machinery used in only one department is a direct expense of that department. Depreciation on equipment and machinery used by more than one department is an indirect expense to be allocated across departments. Accounting for each department's depreciation expense requires a company to keep records showing which departments use specific assets. The number of hours that a department uses equipment and machinery is a reasonable basis for allocating depreciation.

Utilities Expenses Utilities expenses such as heating and lighting are usually allocated on the basis of floor space occupied by departments. This practice assumes their use is uniform across departments. When this is not so, a more involved allocation can be necessary, although there is often a trade-off between the usefulness of more precise allocations and the effort to compute them. Manufacturers often allocate electricity cost to departments on the basis of the machine hours used or the horsepower of equipment located in each department.

Service Department Expenses To generate revenues, operating departments require support services provided by departments such as personnel, payroll, and purchasing. Such service departments are typically evaluated as *cost centers* because they do not produce revenues. A departmental accounting system can accumulate and report costs incurred by each service department for this purpose. The system then allocates a service department's expenses to operating departments benefiting from them. Exhibit 22.4 shows some commonly used bases for allocating service department expenses to operating departments. In the next section we illustrate how to allocate costs to operating departments.

EXHIBIT 22.4

Bases for Allocating Service Department Expenses

Service Department	Common Allocation Bases
Office expenses	Number of employees or sales in each department
Personnel expenses	Number of employees in each department
Payroll expenses	Number of employees in each department
Purchasing costs	Dollar amounts of purchases or number of purchase orders processed
Maintenance expenses	Square feet of floor space occupied

Departmental Income Statements

P3 Prepare departmental income statements and contribution reports.

An income statement can be prepared for each operating department once expenses have been assigned to it. Its expenses include both direct expenses and its share of indirect expenses. For this purpose, it is useful to compile all expenses incurred in service departments before assigning those expenses to operating departments. We illustrate the steps to prepare departmental income statements using **A-1 Hardware** and its five departments. Two of them (office and purchasing) are service departments; the other three (hardware, housewares, and appliances) are operating (selling) departments. Allocating costs to operating departments and preparing departmental income statements involves four steps.

Step 1: Accumulating revenues and direct expenses by department.

Step 2: Allocating indirect expenses across departments.

Step 3: Allocating service department expenses to operating departments.

Step 4: Preparing departmental income statements.

Exhibit 22.5 summarizes these steps in preparing departmental performance reports for cost centers and profit centers (links to the steps are coded with circled numbers *1* through *4*). A-1 Hardware's service departments (general office and purchasing) are cost centers, so their performance will be based on how well they controlled total service department expenses. The company's operating departments (hardware, housewares, and appliances) are profit centers, and their performance will be based on how well they generated departmental net income.

Point: Operating departments generate revenues. Service departments do not generate revenues.

Step 1: Step 1 accumulates revenues and direct expenses in departmental accounts for each department. As cost centers, the service departments do not generate revenues. Direct expenses

EXHIBIT 22.5

Departmental Performance Reporting

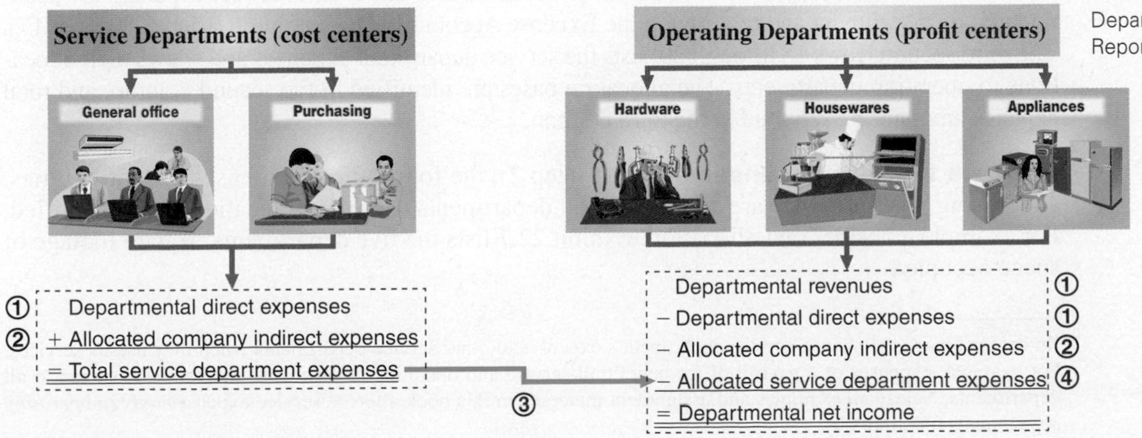

Point: We sometimes allocate service department costs across other service departments before allocating them to operating departments. This "step-wise" process is covered in advanced courses.

for all five departments include salaries, wages, and other expenses that each department incurs but does not share with any other department.

Step 2: Step 2 allocates indirect company expenses across all service and operating departments. Indirect expenses can include items such as depreciation, rent, advertising, and any other expenses that cannot be directly assigned to a department. Indirect expenses are first recorded in *company* accounts. Then, an allocation base is identified for each expense, and costs are allocated using a *departmental expense allocation spreadsheet,* described next.

Step 3: Step 3 allocates service department expenses to operating departments. Service department expenses typically are not allocated to other service departments.[1] Exhibit 22.6 shows the use of a departmental allocation spreadsheet. It uses various allocation bases to allocate all of the direct and indirect expenses of service departments to operating departments. After this allocation, no expenses remain in the service departments, as shown in row 21 of Exhibit 22.6.

EXHIBIT 22.6

Departmental Expense Allocation Spreadsheet

	A		B	C	D	E	F	G
1								
2	A-1 HARDWARE							
3	Departmental Expense Allocations For Year Ended December 31, 2015							
4								
5				Allocation of Expenses to Departments				
6			Expense Account Balance	General Office Dept.	Purchasing Dept.	Hardware Dept.	Housewares Dept.	Appliances Dept.
7		Allocation Base						
8	**Direct expenses**							
9	Salaries expense	Payroll records	$51,900	$13,300	$8,200	$15,600	$ 7,000	$ 7,800
10	Depreciation—Equipment	Depreciation records	1,500	500	300	400	100	200
11	Supplies expense	Requisitions	900	200	100	300	200	100
12	**Indirect expenses**							
13	Rent expense	Amount and value of space	12,000	600	600	4,860	3,240	2,700
14	Utilities expense	Floor space	2,400	300	300	810	540	450
15	Advertising expense	Sales	1,000			500	300	200
16	Insurance expense	Value of insured assets	2,500	400	200	900	600	400
17	Total department expenses		72,200	15,300	9,700	23,370	11,980	11,850
18	**Service department expenses**							
19	General office department	Sales		(15,300)		7,650	4,590	3,060
20	Purchasing department	Purchase orders			(9,700)	3,880	2,630	3,190
21	**Total expenses allocated to operating departments**		$72,200	$ 0	$ 0	$34,900	$19,200	$18,100
22								

Computations for steps 2 and 3 are commonly made using a departmental expense allocation spreadsheet.

Accumulate Revenues and Direct Expenses First, direct and indirect expenses are accumulated by department and reported in the Expense Account Balance column (rows 8 through 17). The third section (rows 18 through 20) lists the service department expenses and shows their allocations to operating departments. The allocation bases are identified in the second column, and total expense amounts are reported in the third column.

Allocate Indirect Expenses Second (step 2), the four indirect expenses of rent, utilities, advertising, and insurance are allocated to all departments using the allocation bases identified. For example, consider rent allocation. Exhibit 22.7 lists the five departments' square footage of space occupied.

[1]In some cases we allocate a service department's expenses to other service departments when they use its services. For example, expenses of a payroll office benefit all service and operating departments and can be assigned to all departments. Nearly all examples and assignment materials in this book allocate service expenses *only to operating departments* for simplicity.

EXHIBIT 22.7

Departments' Allocation Bases

Department	Floor Space (Square Feet)	Value of Insured Assets ($)	Sales ($)	Number of Purchase Orders*
General office	1,500	$ 38,000		—
Purchasing	1,500	19,000		—
Hardware	4,050	85,500	$119,500	394
Housewares	2,700	57,000	71,700	267
Appliances	2,250	38,000	47,800	324
Total	12,000	$237,500	$239,000	985

*Purchasing department tracks purchase orders by department.

The two service departments (office and purchasing) occupy 25% of the total space (3,000 sq. feet/12,000 sq. feet). However, they are located near the back of the building, which is of lower value than space near the front that is occupied by operating departments. Management estimates that space near the back accounts for $1,200 (10%) of the total rent expense of $12,000. Exhibit 22.8 shows how we allocate the $1,200 rent expense between these two service departments in proportion to their square footage. The calculations in Exhibit 22.8 show a simple rule for cost allocations:

EXHIBIT 22.8

Allocating Indirect (Rent) Expense to Service Departments

Department	Square Feet	Percent of Total	Allocated Cost*
General office	1,500	50.0%	$ 600
Purchasing	1,500	50.0	600
Totals	3,000	100.0%	$1,200

*See row 13 of departmental expense allocation spreadsheet (Exhibit 22.6).

Allocated cost = Percentage of allocation base × Total cost to allocate

We then have the remaining amount of $10,800 ($12,000 − $1,200) of rent expense to allocate to the three operating departments, as shown in Exhibit 22.9.

EXHIBIT 22.9

Allocating Indirect (Rent) Expense to Operating Departments

Department	Square Feet	Percent of Total	Allocated Cost*
Hardware	4,050	45.0%	$ 4,860
Housewares	2,700	30.0	3,240
Appliances	2,250	25.0	2,700
Totals	9,000	100.0%	$10,800

*See row 13 of departmental expense allocation spreadsheet (Exhibit 22.6).

We continue step 2 by allocating the $2,400 of utilities expense to all departments based on the square footage occupied, as shown in Exhibit 22.10.

EXHIBIT 22.10

Allocating Indirect (Utilities) Expense to All Departments

Department	Square Feet	Percent of Total	Allocated Cost*
General office	1,500	12.50%	$ 300
Purchasing	1,500	12.50	300
Hardware	4,050	33.75	810
Housewares	2,700	22.50	540
Appliances	2,250	18.75	450
Totals	12,000	100.00%	$2,400

*See row 14 of departmental expense allocation spreadsheet (Exhibit 22.6).

Exhibit 22.11 shows the allocation of $1,000 of advertising expense to the three operating departments on the basis of sales dollars. We exclude the service departments from this allocation because they do not generate sales.

EXHIBIT 22.11

Allocating Indirect (Advertising) Expense to Operating Departments

Department	Sales	Percent of Total	Allocated Cost*
Hardware	$119,500	50.0%	$ 500
Housewares	71,700	30.0	300
Appliances	47,800	20.0	200
Totals	$239,000	100.0%	$1,000

*See row 15 of departmental expense allocation spreadsheet (Exhibit 22.6).

Finally, to complete step 2 we allocate insurance expense to each service and operating department, as shown in Exhibit 22.12.

EXHIBIT 22.12

Allocating Indirect (Insurance) Expense to All Departments

Department	Value of Insured Assets	Percent of Total	Allocated Cost*
General office	$ 38,000	16.0%	$ 400
Purchasing	19,000	8.0	200
Hardware	85,500	36.0	900
Housewares	57,000	24.0	600
Appliances	38,000	16.0	400
Total	$237,500	100.0%	$2,500

*See row 16 of departmental expense allocation spreadsheet (Exhibit 22.6).

Allocate Service Department Expenses Third (step 3), total expenses of the two service departments are allocated to the three operating departments. Exhibit 22.13 shows the allocation of total general office expenses ($15,300) to operating departments.

EXHIBIT 22.13

Allocating Service Department (General Office) Expenses to Operating Departments

Department	Sales	Percent of Total	Allocated Cost*
Hardware	$119,500	50.0%	$ 7,650
Housewares	71,700	30.0	4,590
Appliances	47,800	20.0	3,060
Total	$239,000	100.0%	$15,300

*See row 19 of departmental expense allocation spreadsheet (Exhibit 22.6).

Exhibit 22.14 shows the allocation of total purchasing department expenses ($9,700) to operating departments.

EXHIBIT 22.14

Allocating Service Department (Purchasing) Expenses to Operating Departments

Department	Number of Purchase Orders	Percent of Total	Allocated Cost*
Hardware	394	40.00%	$3,880
Housewares	267	27.11	2,630
Appliances	324	32.89	3,190
Total	985	100.00%	$9,700

*See row 20 of departmental expense allocation spreadsheet (Exhibit 22.6).

Step 4: The departmental expense allocation spreadsheet can now be used to prepare departmental performance reports. The general office and purchasing departments are cost centers, and their managers will be evaluated on their control of costs, as we showed in Exhibit 22.2.

Exhibit 22.15 shows income statements for A-1 Hardware's three operating departments. This exhibit uses the spreadsheet (in Exhibit 22.6) for its operating expenses; information on sales and cost of goods sold comes from departmental records.

EXHIBIT 22.15

Departmental Income Statements (Operating Departments)

A-1 HARDWARE
Departmental Income Statements
For Year Ended December 31, 2015

	Hardware Department	Housewares Department	Appliances Department	Combined	
Sales	$119,500	$71,700	$47,800	$239,000	
Cost of goods sold	73,800	43,800	30,200	147,800	
Gross profit	45,700	27,900	17,600	91,200	
Operating expenses					
Salaries expense	15,600	7,000	7,800	30,400	Direct expenses
Depreciation expense—Equipment	400	100	200	700	Direct expenses
Supplies expense	300	200	100	600	Direct expenses
Rent expense	4,860	3,240	2,700	10,800	Allocated indirect expenses
Utilities expense	810	540	450	1,800	Allocated indirect expenses
Advertising expense	500	300	200	1,000	Allocated indirect expenses
Insurance expense	900	600	400	1,900	Allocated indirect expenses
Share of general office expenses	7,650	4,590	3,060	15,300	Allocated service department expenses
Share of purchasing expenses	3,880	2,630	3,190	9,700	Allocated service department expenses
Total operating expenses	34,900	19,200	18,100	72,200	
Operating income (loss)	**$10,800**	**$8,700**	**$ (500)**	**$19,000**	

Higher-level managers can use departmental income statements to determine which of a company's departments are most profitable. After considering all costs, A-1 Hardware's hardware department is its most profitable. As such, the company might attempt to expand its hardware department.

Example: If the $15,300 general office expenses in Exhibit 22.6 are allocated equally across departments, what is income for the hardware department and for the combined company? *Answer:* Hardware income, $13,350; combined income, $19,000.

Departmental Contribution to Overhead

Exhibit 22.15 shows that the appliances department reported an operating loss of $(500). Should this department be eliminated? We must be careful when indirect expenses are a large portion of total expenses and when weaknesses in assumptions and decisions in allocating indirect expenses can markedly affect income. Also, operating department managers might have no control over the level of service department services they use. In these and other cases, we might better evaluate profit center performance using the **departmental contribution to overhead,** a measure of the amount of sales less *direct* expenses. A department's contribution is said to be "to overhead" because of the practice of considering all indirect expenses as overhead. Thus, the excess of a department's sales over direct expenses is a contribution toward at least a portion of its total overhead.

The upper half of Exhibit 22.16 shows a departmental contribution to overhead, as part of an expanded income statement. This format is common when reporting departmental contributions to overhead.

Using the information in Exhibits 22.15 and 22.16, we can evaluate the profitability of the three profit centers. For instance, let's compare the performance of the appliances department as described in these two exhibits. Exhibit 22.15 shows a $500 loss resulting from this department's operations. Yet Exhibit 22.16 shows a $9,500 positive contribution to overhead. The difference arises because the loss includes allocated indirect expenses while the contribution to overhead does not. The contribution of the appliances department is not as large as those of the other selling departments, but a $9,500 contribution to overhead is better than a $500 loss. This tells us that the appliances department is not a money loser. On the contrary, it is contributing $9,500 toward defraying total indirect expenses of $40,500.

EXHIBIT 22.16

Departmental Contribution to Overhead

A-1 HARDWARE
Income Statement Showing Departmental Contribution to Overhead
For Year Ended December 31, 2015

	Hardware Department	Housewares Department	Appliances Department	Combined
Sales	$119,500	$ 71,700	$47,800	$239,000
Cost of goods sold	73,800	43,800	30,200	147,800
Gross profit	45,700	27,900	17,600	91,200
Direct expenses				
Salaries expense	15,600	7,000	7,800	30,400
Depreciation expense—Equipment	400	100	200	700
Supplies expense	300	200	100	600
Total direct expenses	16,300	7,300	8,100	31,700
Departmental contributions to overhead	**$29,400**	**$20,600**	**$ 9,500**	**$59,500**
Indirect expenses				
Rent expense				10,800
Utilities expense				1,800
Advertising expense				1,000
Insurance expense				1,900
General office department expense				15,300
Purchasing department expense				9,700
Total indirect expenses				40,500
Operating income				**$ 19,000**

Point: Operating income is the same in Exhibits 22.15 and 22.16. The method of reporting indirect expenses in Exhibit 22.16 does not change total income but does identify each operating department's contribution to overhead.

Behavioral Aspects of Departmental Performance Reports An organization must consider potential effects on employee behavior from departmental income statements and contribution to overhead reports. These include:

- Indirect expenses are typically uncontrollable costs for a department manager. Thus departmental contribution to overhead might be a better way to evaluate department manager performance. Including uncontrollable costs in performance evaluation is inconsistent with responsibility accounting and can reduce department manager morale.
- On the other hand, including indirect expenses in the department manager's performance evaluation can lead the manager to be more careful in using service departments, which can reduce the organization's costs.
- Some companies allocate *budgeted* service department costs rather than actual service department costs. In this way, operating departments are not held responsible for excessive costs from service departments, and service departments are more likely to try to control their costs.

QC2

EVALUATING INVESTMENT CENTER PERFORMANCE

We now come to the third type of responsibility center, the investment center. This section introduces both financial and nonfinancial measures of investment center performance.

Financial Performance Evaluation Measures

A1 Analyze investment centers using return on investment and residual income.

Investment center managers are typically evaluated using performance measures that combine income and assets. These measures include return on investment, residual income, profit margin, and investment turnover. Consider the following data for ZTel, a company that operates two divisions: LCD and S-Phone. The LCD division manufactures liquid crystal display (LCD) touch-screen monitors and sells them for use in computers, cellular phones, and other products. The S-Phone division sells smartphones. Exhibit 22.17 shows current-year income and assets for those divisions.

EXHIBIT 22.17

Investment Center Income and Assets

	LCD Division	S-Phone Division
Investment center income......................	$ 526,500	$ 417,600
Investment center average invested assets.........	2,500,000	1,850,000

Investment Center Return on Investment One measure to evaluate division performance is the investment center **return on investment (ROI),** commonly called *return on assets* (ROA). This measure is computed as follows:

$$\text{Return on investment} = \frac{\text{Investment center income}}{\text{Investment center average invested assets}}$$

The return on investment for the LCD division is 21% (rounded), computed as \$526,500/\$2,500,000. The S-Phone division's return on investment is 23% (rounded), computed as \$417,600/\$1,850,000. ZTel's management can use ROI as part of its performance evaluation for its investment center managers. For example, the actual ROI can be compared to a targeted ROI or to the ROI for similar departments at competing businesses.

princigalli/iStock/360/Getty Images

Investment Center Residual Income Another way to evaluate division performance is to compute investment center **residual income,** which is computed as follows:

$$\text{Residual income} = \text{Investment center income} - \text{Target investment center income}$$

Assume ZTel's top management sets target income at 8% of investment center assets. For an investment center, this target is typically the cost of obtaining financing. Applying this target rate using the data from Exhibit 22.17 yields the residual income for ZTel's divisions shown in Exhibit 22.18.

EXHIBIT 22.18

Investment Center Residual Income

	LCD Division	S-Phone Division
Investment center income......................	$526,500	$417,600
Less: Target investment center income		
$2,500,000 × 8%..........................	200,000	
$1,850,000 × 8%..........................		148,000
Investment center residual income..............	$326,500	$269,600

Notice that residual income is expressed in dollars, not as a percentage. The LCD division produced more dollars of residual income than the S-Phone division. Ztel's management can use residual income, along with ROI, to evaluate investment center manager performance.

Using residual income to evaluate division performance encourages division managers to accept all opportunities that return more than the target income, thus increasing company value. For example, the S-Phone division might (mistakenly) not want to accept a new customer that will provide a 15% return on investment, since that will reduce the S-Phone division's overall return on investment (23% as shown above). However, the S-Phone division should accept this opportunity because the new customer would increase residual income by providing income above the target income of 8% of invested assets.

NEED-TO-KNOW 22-1

Return on Investment
A1

Do More: QS 22-9, QS 22-10, E 22-8, E 22-9, E 22-10

The media division of a company reports income of \$600,000, average invested assets of \$7,500,000, and a target income of 6% of invested assets. Compute the division's (a) return on investment and (b) residual income.

Solution

a. \$600,000/\$7,500,000 = 8%
b. \$600,000 − (\$7,500,000 × 6%) = \$150,000

Issues in Computing Return on Investment and Residual Income Evaluations of investment center performance using return on investment and residual income can be affected by how a company answers the questions below:

1. How do you compute *average* invested assets? It is common to compute the average by adding the year's beginning amount of invested assets to the year's ending amount of invested assets, and dividing that sum by 2. Averages based on monthly or quarterly asset amounts are also acceptable.
2. How do you measure invested assets? It is common to measure invested assets using their *net* book values. For example, depreciable assets would be measured at their cost minus accumulated depreciation. As net book value declines over a depreciable asset's useful life, the result is that return on investment and residual income would increase over that asset's life. This might cause managers not to invest in new assets. In addition, in measuring invested assets, companies commonly exclude assets that are not used in generating investment center income, such as land held for resale.
3. How do you measure investment center income? It is common to exclude both interest expense and tax expense from investment center income. Interest expense reflects a company's financing decisions, and tax expense is typically considered outside the control of an investment center manager. Excluding interest and taxes in these calculations enables more meaningful comparisons of return on investment and residual income across investment centers and companies.

Point: *Economic Value Added* (EVA®), developed and trademarked by Stern, Stewart, and Co., is an approach to address issues in computing residual income. This method uses a variety of adjustments to compute income, assets, and the target rate.

Decision Insight

In-the-Money Executive pay is often linked to performance measures. Bonus payments are often based on exceeding a target return on investment or certain balanced scorecard indicators. Stock awards, such as stock options and restricted stock, reward executives when their company's stock price rises. The goal of bonus plans and stock awards is to encourage executives to make decisions that increase company performance and value. ■

A2 Analyze investment centers using profit margin and investment turnover.

Investment Center Profit Margin and Investment Turnover We can further examine investment center (division) performance by splitting return on investment into two measures—profit margin and investment turnover, as follows.

$$\textbf{Return on investment} = \textbf{Profit margin} \times \textbf{Investment turnover}$$

$$\frac{\text{Investment center income}}{\text{Investment center average assets}} = \frac{\text{Investment center income}}{\text{Investment center sales}} \times \frac{\text{Investment center sales}}{\text{Investment center average assets}}$$

Profit margin measures the income earned per dollar of sales. As learned in an earlier chapter, profit margin for the entire organization is calculated as net income divided by sales. In analyzing investment center performance, we typically use a measure of income *before* tax. Thus, for an investment center, profit margin is computed as investment center income divided by investment center sales. Likewise, **investment turnover** measures how efficiently an investment center generates sales from its invested assets. It is calculated as investment center sales divided by investment center average assets. Profit margin is expressed as a percent, while investment turnover is interpreted as the number of times assets were converted into sales. Higher profit margin and higher investment turnover indicate better performance.

Point: This partitioning of return on investment is sometimes referred to as DuPont analysis.

To illustrate, consider **Walt Disney Co.**, which reports in Exhibit 22.19 results for two of its operating divisions: Media Networks and Parks and Resorts.

EXHIBIT 22.19
Walt Disney Division Sales, Income, and Assets

($ millions)	Media Networks	Parks and Resorts
Sales	$20,356	$14,089
Income	6,818	2,220
Average invested assets	28,644	21,504

Profit margin and investment turnover for these two divisions are computed and shown in Exhibit 22.20:

EXHIBIT 22.20
Walt Disney Division Profit Margin and Investment Turnover

($ millions)	Media Networks	Parks and Resorts
Profit margin		
$6,818/$20,356	33.49%	
$2,220/$14,089		15.76%
Investment turnover		
$20,356/$28,644	0.71	
$14,089/$21,504		0.66
Return on investment		
33.49% × 0.71	23.78%	
15.76% × 0.66		10.40%

Disney's Media Networks division generates 33.49 cents of profit for every dollar of sales, while its Parks and Resorts division generates 15.76 cents of profit per dollar of sales. The Media Networks division (0.71 investment turnover) is slightly more efficient than the Parks and Resorts division (0.66 investment turnover) in using assets. Top management can use profit margin and investment turnover to evaluate the performance of division managers. The measures can also aid management when considering further investment in its divisions. As a result of both a much higher profit margin and more rapid investment turnover, the Media Networks division's return on investment (23.78%) is much greater than that of the Parks and Resorts division (10.40%).

Decision Maker

Division Manager You manage a division in a highly competitive industry. You will receive a cash bonus if your division achieves an ROI above 12%. Your division's profit margin is 7%, equal to the industry average, and your division's investment turnover is 1.5. What actions can you take to increase your chance of receiving the bonus? ■ [Answers follow the chapter's Summary.]

NEED-TO-KNOW 22-2
Margin, Turnover, and Return
A2

A division reports sales of $50,000, income of $2,000, and average invested assets of $10,000. Compute the division's (a) profit margin, (b) investment turnover, and (c) return on investment.

Solution

a. $2,000/$50,000 = 4%
b. $50,000/$10,000 = 5
c. $2,000/$10,000 = 20%

Do More: QS 22-12, E 22-10, E 22-11, E 22-13

Nonfinancial Performance Evaluation Measures

A3 Analyze investment centers using the balanced scorecard.

Evaluating performance solely on financial measures such as return on investment or residual income has limitations. For example, some investment center managers might forgo profitable opportunities to keep their return on investment high. Also, residual income is less useful when comparing investment centers of different size. And, both return on investment and residual income can encourage managers to focus too heavily on short-term financial goals.

In response to these limitations, companies consider nonfinancial measures. For example, a delivery company such as **FedEx** might track the percentage of on-time deliveries. The percentage of defective tennis balls manufactured can be used to assess performance of **Penn**'s production managers. **Walmart**'s credit card screens commonly ask customers at checkout whether the cashier was friendly or the store was clean. This kind of information can help division managers run their divisions and help top management evaluate division manager performance. A popular measure that uses some nonfinancial indicators is the balanced scorecard.

Balanced Scorecard The **balanced scorecard** is a system of performance measures, including nonfinancial measures, used to assess company and division manager performance. The balanced scorecard requires managers to think of their company from four perspectives:

1. **Customer:** What do customers think of us?
2. **Internal processes:** Which of our operations are critical to meeting customer needs?
3. **Innovation and learning:** How can we improve?
4. **Financial:** What do our owners think of us?

Point: One survey indicates that nearly 60% of global companies use some form of a balanced scorecard.

The balanced scorecard collects information on several key performance indicators within each of the four perspectives. These key indicators vary across companies. Exhibit 22.21 lists some common performance indicators used in the balanced scorecard.

EXHIBIT 22.21
Balanced Scorecard Performance Indicators

Customer	Internal Processes	Innovation/Learning	Financial
• Customer satisfaction rating	• Defect rates	• Employee satisfaction	• Net income
• # of new customers acquired	• Cycle time	• Employee turnover	• ROI
• % of on-time deliveries	• Product costs	• $ spent on training	• Sales growth
• % of sales from new products	• Labor hours per order	• # of new products	• Cash flow
• Time to fill orders	• Production days without an accident	• # of patents	• Residual income
• % of sales returned		• $ spent on research	• Stock price

After selecting key performance indicators, companies collect data on each indicator and compare actual amounts to expected amounts to assess performance. For example, a company might have a goal of filling 98% of customer orders within two hours. Balanced scorecard reports are often presented in graphs or tables that can be updated frequently. Such timely information aids division managers in their decisions and can be used by top management to evaluate division manager performance.

Exhibit 22.22 is an example of balanced scorecard reporting on the customer perspective for an Internet retailer. This scorecard reports that the retailer is getting 62% of its potential customers successfully through the checkout process, and that 2.2% of all orders are returned. The *color* of the arrows in the right-most column reveals whether the company is exceeding its goal (green), barely meeting the goal (yellow), or not meeting the goal (red). The *direction* of the arrows

EXHIBIT 22.22
Balanced Scorecard Reporting: Internet Retailer

Customer Perspective	Actual	Goal
Checkout success	62%	↑
Orders returned	2.2%	↓
Customer satisfaction rating	9.5	↑
Number of customer complaints	142	↓

reveals any trend in performance: an upward arrow indicates improvement, a downward arrow indicates declining performance, and an arrow pointing sideways indicates no change. A review of these arrows' color and direction suggests the retailer is meeting or exceeding its goals on checkout success, orders returned, and customer satisfaction. Further, checkout success and customer satisfaction are improving. The red arrow shows the company has received more customer complaints than was hoped for; however, the number of customer complaints is declining. A manager would combine this information with similar information on the internal process, innovation and learning, and financial perspectives to get an overall view of division performance.

Decision Maker

Center Manager Your center's usual return on total assets is 19%. You are considering two new investments for your center. The first requires a $250,000 average investment and is expected to yield annual net income of $50,000. The second requires a $1 million average investment with an expected annual net income of $175,000. Do you pursue either? ■ [Answers follow the chapter's Summary.]

GLOBAL VIEW

L'Oréal is an international cosmetics company incorporated in France. With multiple brands and operations in over 100 countries, the company uses concepts of departmental accounting and controllable costs to evaluate performance. For example, for 2012 the company reports the following for the major divisions in its cosmetics branch:

Division	Operating Profit (€ millions)		
Consumer products	€2,051		
Professional products	615		
Luxury products	1,077		
Active cosmetics	311	€4,054	← Similar to "Departmental contributions to overhead" in Exhibit 22.16
Nonallocated costs		(577)	
Cosmetics branch total		€3,477	← Similar to "Operating income" in Exhibit 22.16

For L'Oréal, nonallocated costs include costs that are not controllable by division managers, including fundamental research and development and costs of service operations like insurance and banking. Excluding noncontrollable costs enables L'Oréal to prepare more meaningful division performance evaluations.

Sustainability and Accounting **Kraft**'s cream cheese-making process generates a lot of a by-product called whey. Kraft recently retrofitted a manufacturing plant to convert whey into energy. Here, a "digestion" system converts whey into a biogas, which is then used to create steam to power manufacturing machines. In this way, the company has converted a by-product into a source of sustainable energy and yielded cost savings. **United By Blue**, this chapter's feature company, uses recyclable packaging and eliminates as much plastic as possible from its supply chain. Although they add costs, company founder Brian Linton believes these sustainability efforts increase customer loyalty and sales.

Cycle Time and Cycle Efficiency — Decision Analysis

A4 Compute cycle time and cycle efficiency, and explain their importance to production management.

Manufacturing companies commonly use nonfinancial measures to evaluate the performance of their production processes. For example, as lean manufacturing practices help companies move toward just-in-time manufacturing, it is important for these companies to reduce the time to manufacture their products and to improve manufacturing efficiency. One metric that measures that time element is **cycle time (CT)**, which describes the time it takes to produce a product or service. It is defined in Exhibit 22.23.

EXHIBIT 22.23 Cycle Time

Cycle time = Process time + Inspection time + Move time + Wait time

Process time is the time spent producing the product. *Inspection time* is the time spent inspecting (1) raw materials when received, (2) work in process while in production, and (3) finished goods prior to shipment. *Move time* is the time spent moving (1) raw materials from storage to production and (2) work in process from one factory location to another factory location. *Wait time* is the time that an order or job sits with no production applied to it. Wait time can be due to order delays, bottlenecks in production, or poor scheduling.

Process time is considered **value-added time:** it is the only activity in cycle time that adds value to the product from the customer's perspective. The other three time activities are considered **non-value-added time:** they add no value to the customer.

Companies strive to reduce non-value-added time to improve **cycle efficiency (CE),** which is a measure of production efficiency. Cycle efficiency is the ratio of value-added time to total cycle time, as shown in Exhibit 22.24.

EXHIBIT 22.24

Cycle Efficiency

$$\text{Cycle efficiency} = \frac{\text{Value-added time}}{\text{Cycle time}}$$

To illustrate, assume that Rocky Mountain Bikes receives and produces an order for 500 Tracker mountain bikes. Assume that it took the following times to produce this order.

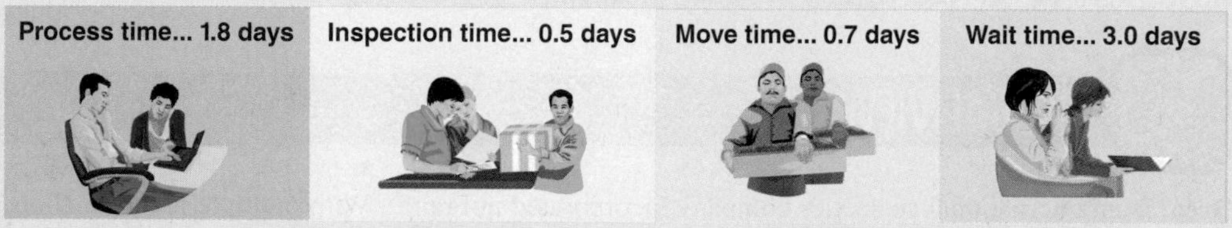

In this case, cycle time is 6.0 days (1.8 + 0.5 + 0.7 + 3.0 days). Also, cycle efficiency is 0.3, or 30%, computed as 1.8 days divided by 6.0 days. This means that Rocky Mountain Bikes' value-added time (its process time, or time spent working on the product) is 30%. The other 70% is spent on non-value-added activities.

If a company has a CE of 1, it means that its time is spent entirely on value-added activities. If the CE is low, the company should evaluate its production process to see if it can identify ways to reduce non-value-added activities. The 30% CE for Rocky Mountain Bikes is low, and its management should look for ways to reduce non-value-added activities.

NEED-TO-KNOW

COMPREHENSIVE

Management requests departmental income statements for Gamer's Haven, a computer store that has five departments. Three are operating departments (hardware, software, and repairs) and two are service departments (general office and purchasing).

	General Office	Purchasing	Hardware	Software	Repairs
Sales	—	—	$960,000	$600,000	$840,000
Cost of goods sold	—	—	500,000	300,000	200,000
Direct expenses					
Payroll	$60,000	$45,000	80,000	25,000	325,000
Depreciation	6,000	7,200	33,000	4,200	9,600
Supplies	15,000	10,000	10,000	2,000	25,000

The departments incur several indirect expenses. To prepare departmental income statements, the indirect expenses must be allocated across the five departments. Then the expenses of the two service departments must be allocated to the three operating departments. Total cost amounts and the allocation bases for each indirect expense follow.

Indirect Expense	Total Cost	Allocation Basis
Rent	$150,000	Square footage occupied
Utilities	50,000	Square footage occupied
Advertising	125,000	Dollars of sales
Insurance	30,000	Value of assets insured
Service departments		
General office	?	Number of employees
Purchasing	?	Dollars of cost of goods sold

The following additional information is needed for indirect expense allocations.

Department	Square Feet	Sales	Insured Assets	Employees	Cost of Goods Sold
General office	500		$ 60,000		
Purchasing	500		72,000		
Hardware	4,000	$ 960,000	330,000	5	$ 500,000
Software	3,000	600,000	42,000	5	300,000
Repairs	2,000	840,000	96,000	10	200,000
Totals	10,000	$2,400,000	$600,000	20	$1,000,000

Required

1. Prepare a departmental expense allocation spreadsheet for Gamer's Haven.

2. Prepare a departmental income statement reporting net income for each operating department and for all operating departments combined.

PLANNING THE SOLUTION

- Set up and complete four tables to allocate the indirect expenses—one each for rent, utilities, advertising, and insurance.
- Allocate the departments' indirect expenses using a spreadsheet like the one in Exhibit 22.6. Enter the given amounts of the direct expenses for each department. Then enter the allocated amounts of the indirect expenses that you computed.
- Complete two tables for allocating the general office and purchasing department costs to the three operating departments. Enter these amounts on the spreadsheet and determine the total expenses allocated to the three operating departments.
- Prepare departmental income statements like the one in Exhibit 22.15. Show sales, cost of goods sold, gross profit, individual expenses, and net income for each of the three operating departments and for the combined company.

SOLUTION

Allocations of the four indirect expenses across the five departments.

Rent	Square Feet	Percent of Total	Allocated Cost
General office	500	5.0%	$ 7,500
Purchasing	500	5.0	7,500
Hardware	4,000	40.0	60,000
Software	3,000	30.0	45,000
Repairs	2,000	20.0	30,000
Totals	10,000	100.0%	$150,000

Utilities	Square Feet	Percent of Total	Allocated Cost
General office	500	5.0%	$ 2,500
Purchasing	500	5.0	2,500
Hardware	4,000	40.0	20,000
Software	3,000	30.0	15,000
Repairs	2,000	20.0	10,000
Totals	10,000	100.0%	$50,000

Advertising	Sales Dollars	Percent of Total	Allocated Cost
Hardware	$ 960,000	40.0%	$ 50,000
Software	600,000	25.0	31,250
Repairs	840,000	35.0	43,750
Totals	$2,400,000	100.0%	$125,000

Insurance	Assets Insured	Percent of Total	Allocated Cost
General office	$ 60,000	10.0%	$ 3,000
Purchasing	72,000	12.0	3,600
Hardware	330,000	55.0	16,500
Software	42,000	7.0	2,100
Repairs	96,000	16.0	4,800
Totals	$600,000	100.0%	$30,000

1. Allocations of service department expenses to the three operating departments.

General Office Allocations to	Employees	Percent of Total	Allocated Cost
Hardware	5	25.0%	$23,500
Software	5	25.0	23,500
Repairs	10	50.0	47,000
Totals	20	100.0%	$94,000

Purchasing Allocations to	Cost of Goods Sold	Percent of Total	Allocated Cost
Hardware	$ 500,000	50.0%	$37,900
Software	300,000	30.0	22,740
Repairs	200,000	20.0	15,160
Totals	$1,000,000	100.0%	$75,800

GAMER'S HAVEN
Departmental Expense Allocations
For Year Ended December 31, 2015

	Allocation Base	Expense Account Balance	General Office Dept.	Purchasing Dept.	Hardware Dept.	Software Dept.	Repairs Dept.
Direct Expenses							
Payroll		$ 535,000	$ 60,000	$ 45,000	$ 80,000	$ 25,000	$ 325,000
Depreciation		60,000	6,000	7,200	33,000	4,200	9,600
Supplies		62,000	15,000	10,000	10,000	2,000	25,000
Indirect Expenses							
Rent	Square ft.	150,000	7,500	7,500	60,000	45,000	30,000
Utilities	Square ft.	50,000	2,500	2,500	20,000	15,000	10,000
Advertising	Sales	125,000	—	—	50,000	31,250	43,750
Insurance	Assets	30,000	3,000	3,600	16,500	2,100	4,800
Total expenses		**1,012,000**	**94,000**	**75,800**	269,500	124,550	448,150
Service Department Expenses							
General office	Employees		**(94,000)**		23,500	23,500	47,000
Purchasing	Goods sold			**(75,800)**	37,900	22,740	15,160
Total expenses allocated to operating departments		**$1,012,000**	**$ 0**	**$ 0**	**$330,900**	**$170,790**	**$510,310**

2. Departmental income statements.

GAMER'S HAVEN
Departmental Income Statements
For Year Ended December 31, 2015

	Hardware	Software	Repairs	Combined
Sales	$ 960,000	$ 600,000	$ 840,000	$2,400,000
Cost of goods sold	500,000	300,000	200,000	1,000,000
Gross profit	460,000	300,000	640,000	1,400,000
Expenses				
Payroll	80,000	25,000	325,000	430,000
Depreciation	33,000	4,200	9,600	46,800
Supplies	10,000	2,000	25,000	37,000
Rent	60,000	45,000	30,000	135,000
Utilities	20,000	15,000	10,000	45,000
Advertising	50,000	31,250	43,750	125,000
Insurance	16,500	2,100	4,800	23,400
Share of general office	23,500	23,500	47,000	94,000
Share of purchasing	37,900	22,740	15,160	75,800
Total expenses	330,900	170,790	510,310	1,012,000
Operating income	**$129,100**	**$129,210**	**$129,690**	**$ 388,000**

APPENDIX

Transfer Pricing

22A

C2 Explain transfer pricing and methods to set transfer prices.

Divisions in decentralized companies sometimes do business with one another. For example, a separate division of **Harley-Davidson** manufactures its plastic and fiberglass parts used in the company's motorcycles. **Anheuser-Busch**'s metal container division makes cans and lids used in its brewing operations, and also sells cans and lids to soft-drink companies. A division of **Prince** produces strings used in tennis rackets made by Prince and other manufacturers. The price used to record transfers of goods across divisions of the same company is called the **transfer price.** Transfer prices can be used in cost, profit, and investment centers. Determining how to set transfer prices is the focus of this appendix.

In decentralized organizations, division managers have input on or decide transfer prices. Since these transfers are not with customers outside the company, the transfer price has no direct impact on the company's overall profits. However, transfer prices can impact performance evaluations and, if set incorrectly, lead to bad decisions.

Point: Transfer pricing can impact company profits when divisions are located in countries with different tax rates; this is covered in advanced courses.

Alternative Transfer Prices The top portion of Exhibit 22A.1 reports data on the LCD division of ZTel. That division manufactures liquid crystal display (LCD) touch-screen monitors for use in ZTel's S-Phone division's smartphones. The monitors can also be used in other products. The LCD division can sell its monitors to the S-Phone division as well as to buyers other than S-Phone. Likewise, the S-Phone division can purchase monitors from suppliers other than LCD.

EXHIBIT 22A.1

LCD Division Manufacturing Information—Monitors

Production capacity	100,000 units
Selling price per unit to outside customers	$80
Variable manufacturing costs per unit	$40
Fixed manufacturing costs	$2,000,000

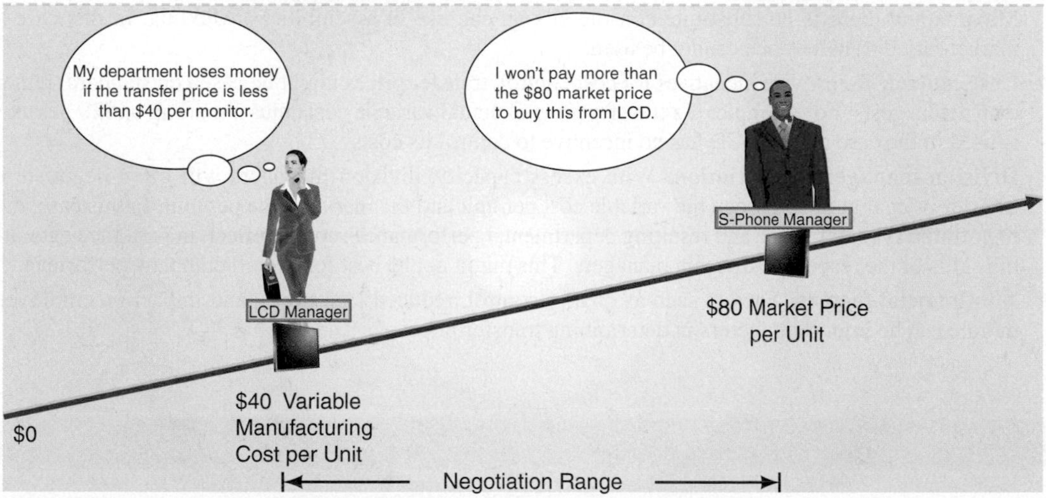

The bottom portion of Exhibit 22A.1 reveals the range of transfer prices for transfers of monitors from LCD to S-Phone. As you can see, the transfer price can reasonably range from $40 (the variable manufacturing cost per unit) to $80 (the cost of buying the monitor from an outside supplier). The manager of LCD wants to report a divisional profit. Thus, this manager will not accept a transfer price less than $40; a price less than $40 would cause the division to lose money on each monitor transferred. The LCD manager will consider transfer prices of only $40 or more. On the other hand, the S-Phone division manager also wants to report a divisional profit. Thus, this manager will not pay more than $80 per monitor because similar monitors can be bought from outside suppliers at that price. The S-Phone manager will consider transfer prices of only $80 or less.

As any transfer price between $40 and $80 per monitor is possible, how does ZTel determine the transfer price? The answer depends in part on whether the LCD division has excess capacity to manufacture monitors.

No Excess Capacity If the LCD division can sell every monitor it produces (100,000 units) at a market price of $80 per monitor, LCD managers would not accept any transfer price less than $80 per monitor. This is a **market-based transfer price**—one based on the market price of the good or service being transferred. Any transfer price less than $80 would cause the LCD division managers to incur an unnecessary *opportunity cost* that would lower the division's income and hurt its managers' performance evaluation.

Typically, a division operating at full capacity will sell to external customers rather than sell internally. Still, the market-based transfer price of $80 can be considered the maximum possible transfer price when there is excess capacity, which is the case we consider next.

Excess Capacity Now assume that the LCD division has excess capacity. For example, the LCD division might currently be producing only 80,000 units. Because LCD has $2,000,000 of fixed manufacturing costs, both the LCD division and the top management of ZTel prefer that the S-Phone division purchases its monitors from LCD. For example, if S-Phone purchases its monitors from an outside supplier at the market price of $80 each, LCD manufactures no units. Then, LCD reports a division loss equal to its fixed costs, and ZTel overall reports a lower net income as its costs are higher. Consequently, with excess capacity, LCD should accept any transfer price of $40 per unit or greater, and S-Phone should purchase monitors from LCD. This will allow LCD to recover some (or all) of its fixed costs and increase ZTel's overall profits.

For example, if a transfer price of $50 per monitor is used, the S-Phone manager is pleased to buy from LCD, since that price is below the market price of $80. For each monitor transferred from LCD to S-Phone at $50, the LCD division receives a *contribution margin* of $10 (computed as $50 transfer price less $40 variable cost) to contribute toward recovering its fixed costs. This form of transfer pricing is called **cost-based transfer pricing.** Under this approach the transfer price might be based on variable costs, total costs, or variable costs plus a markup. Determining the transfer price under excess capacity is complex and is covered in advanced courses.

Transfer Pricing Approaches Used by Companies

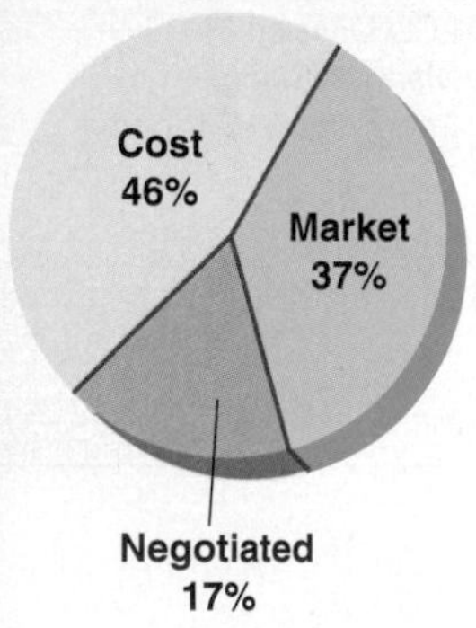

Additional Issues in Transfer Pricing Several additional issues arise in determining transfer prices which include the following:

- **No market price exists.** Sometimes there is no market price for the product being transferred. The product might be a key component that requires additional conversion costs at the next stage and is not easily replicated by an outside company. For example, there is no market for a console for a **Nissan** Maxima and there is no substitute console Nissan can use in assembling a Maxima. In this case a market-based transfer price cannot be used.
- **Cost control.** To provide incentives for cost control, transfer prices might be based on standard, rather than actual costs. For example, if a transfer price of actual variable costs plus a markup of $20 per unit is used in the case above, LCD has no incentive to control its costs.
- **Division managers' negotiation.** With excess capacity, division managers will often negotiate a transfer price that lies between the variable cost per unit and the market price per unit. In this case, the **negotiated transfer price** and resulting departmental performance reports reflect, in part, the negotiating skills of the respective division managers. This might not be best for overall company performance.
- **Nonfinancial factors.** Factors such as quality control, reduced lead times, and impact on employee morale can be important factors in determining transfer prices.

APPENDIX

22B Joint Costs and Their Allocation

C3 Describe allocation of joint costs across products.

Most manufacturing processes involve **joint costs,** which refer to costs incurred to produce or purchase two or more products at the same time. For example, a sawmill company incurs joint costs when it buys logs that it cuts into lumber as shown in Exhibit 22B.1. The joint costs include the logs (raw material) and their being cut (conversion) into boards classified as Clear, Select, No. 1 Common, No. 2 Common, No. 3 Common, and other types of lumber and by-products. After the logs are cut into boards, any further processing costs on the boards are not joint costs.

When a joint cost is incurred, a question arises as to whether to allocate it to different products resulting from it. The answer is that when management wishes to estimate the costs of individual products, joint costs are included and must be allocated to these joint products. However, when management needs information to help decide whether to sell a product at a certain point in the production process or to process it further, the joint costs are ignored. (We study this sell-or-process-further decision in a later chapter.)

Financial statements prepared according to GAAP must assign joint costs to products. To do this, management must decide how to allocate joint costs across products benefiting from these costs. If some products are sold and others remain in inventory, allocating joint costs involves assigning costs to both cost of goods sold and ending inventory.

EXHIBIT 22B.1

Joint Products from Logs

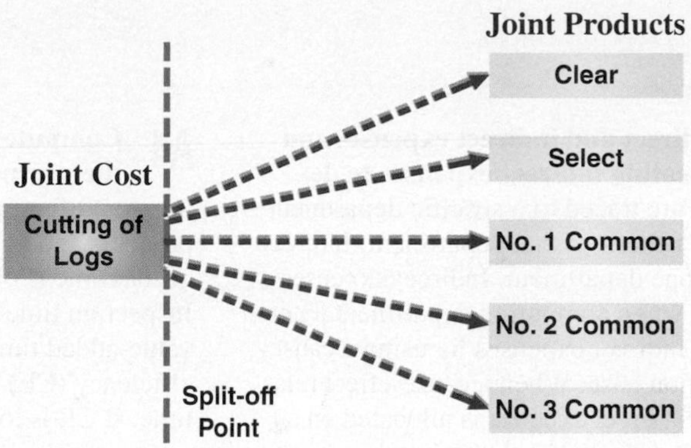

The two usual methods to allocate joint costs are the (1) *physical basis* and (2) *value basis.* The physical basis typically involves allocating a joint cost using physical characteristics such as the ratio of pounds, cubic feet, or gallons of each joint product to the total pounds, cubic feet, or gallons of all joint products flowing from the cost. This method is not preferred because the resulting cost allocations do not reflect the relative market values the joint cost generates. The preferred approach is the value basis, which allocates a joint cost in proportion to the sales value of the output produced by the process at the "split-off point"; see Exhibit 22B.1. The split-off point is the point at which separate products can be identified.

Physical Basis Allocation of Joint Costs To illustrate the physical basis of allocating a joint cost, we consider a sawmill that bought logs for $30,000. When cut, these logs produce 100,000 board feet of lumber in the grades and amounts shown in Exhibit 22B.2. The logs produce 20,000 board feet of No. 3 Common lumber, which is 20% of the total. With physical allocation, the No. 3 Common lumber is assigned 20% of the $30,000 cost of the logs, or $6,000 ($30,000 × 20%). Because this low-grade lumber sells for $4,000, this allocation gives a $2,000 loss from its production and sale. The physical basis for allocating joint costs does not reflect the extra value flowing into some products or the inferior value flowing into others. That is, the portion of a log that produces Clear and Select grade lumber is worth more than the portion used to produce the three grades of common lumber, but the physical basis fails to reflect this.

EXHIBIT 22B.2

Allocating Joint Costs on a Physical Basis

Grade of Lumber	Board Feet Produced	Percent of Total	Allocated Cost	Sales Value	Gross Profit
Clear and Select.	10,000	10.0%	$ 3,000	$12,000	$ 9,000
No. 1 Common	30,000	30.0	9,000	18,000	9,000
No. 2 Common	40,000	40.0	12,000	16,000	4,000
No. 3 Common	20,000	20.0	6,000	4,000	(2,000)
Totals	100,000	100.0%	$30,000	$50,000	$20,000

Value Basis Allocation of Joint Costs Exhibit 22B.3 illustrates the value basis method of allocation. It determines the percents of the total costs allocated to each grade by the ratio of each grade's sales value at the split-off point to the total sales value of $50,000 (sales value is the unit selling price multiplied by the number of units produced). The Clear and Select lumber grades receive 24% of the total cost ($12,000/$50,000) instead of the 10% portion using a physical basis. The No. 3 Common lumber receives only 8% of the total cost, or $2,400, which is much less than the $6,000 assigned to it using the physical basis.

EXHIBIT 22B.3

Allocating Joint Costs on a Value Basis

Grade of Lumber	Sales Value	Percent of Total	Allocated Cost	Gross Profit
Clear and Select	$12,000	24.0%	$ 7,200	$ 4,800
No. 1 Common.	18,000	36.0	10,800	7,200
No. 2 Common.	16,000	32.0	9,600	6,400
No. 3 Common.	4,000	8.0	2,400	1,600
Totals.	$50,000	100.0%	$30,000	$20,000

An outcome of value basis allocation is that *each* grade produces exactly the same 40% gross profit at the split-off point. This 40% rate equals the gross profit rate from selling all the lumber made from the $30,000 logs for a combined price of $50,000. It is this closer matching of cost and revenues that makes the value basis allocation of joint costs the preferred method.

Example: Refer to Exhibit 22B.3. If the sales value of Clear and Select lumber is changed to $10,000, what is the revised ratio of the market value of No. 1 Common to the total? *Answer:* $18,000/$48,000 = 37.5%

Summary

C1 Distinguish between direct and indirect expenses and identify bases for allocating indirect expenses to departments. Direct expenses are traced to a specific department and are incurred for the sole benefit of that department. Indirect expenses benefit more than one department. Indirect expenses are allocated to departments when computing departmental net income. Ideally, we allocate indirect expenses by using a cause-effect relation for the allocation base. When a cause-effect relation is not identifiable, each indirect expense is allocated on a basis reflecting the relative benefit received by each department.

C2 Explain transfer pricing and methods to set transfer prices. Transfer prices are used to record transfers of items between divisions of the same company. Transfer prices can be based on costs or market prices, or can be negotiated by division managers.

C3 Describe allocation of joint costs across products. A joint cost refers to costs incurred to produce or purchase two or more products at the same time. When income statements are prepared, joint costs are usually allocated to the resulting joint products using either a physical or value basis.

A1 Analyze investment centers using return on investment and residual income. A financial measure often used to evaluate an investment center manager is the *return on investment,* also called *return on assets.* This measure is computed as the center's income divided by the center's average total assets. Residual income, computed as investment center income minus a target income is an alternative financial measure of investment center performance.

A2 Analyze investment centers using profit margin and investment turnover. Return on investment can also be computed as profit margin times investment turnover. Profit margin (equal to income/sales) measures the income earned per dollar of sales, and investment turnover (equal to sales/assets) measures how efficiently a division uses its assets.

A3 Analyze investment centers using the balanced scorecard. A balanced scorecard uses a combination of financial and nonfinancial measures to evaluate performance. Customer, internal process, and innovation and learning are the three primary perspectives of nonfinancial measures used in balanced scorecards.

A4 Compute cycle time and cycle efficiency, and explain their importance to production management. It is important for companies to reduce the time to produce their products and to improve manufacturing efficiency. One measure of that time is cycle time (CT), defined as Process time + Inspection time + Move time + Wait time. Process time is value-added time; the others are non-value-added time. Cycle efficiency (CE) is the ratio of value-added time to total cycle time. If CE is low, management should evaluate its production process to see if it can reduce non-value-added activities.

P1 Prepare a responsibility accounting report using controllable costs. Responsibility accounting systems provide information for evaluating the performance of department managers. A responsibility accounting system's performance reports for evaluating department managers should include only the expenses (and revenues) that each manager controls.

P2 Allocate indirect expenses to departments. Indirect expenses include items like depreciation, rent, advertising, and other expenses that cannot be assigned directly to departments. Indirect expenses are recorded in company accounts, an allocation base is identified for each expense, and costs are allocated to departments. Departmental expense allocation spreadsheets are often used in allocating indirect expenses to departments.

P3 Prepare departmental income statements and contribution reports. Each profit center (department) is assigned its expenses to yield its own income statement. These costs include its direct expenses and its share of indirect expenses. The departmental income statement lists its revenues and costs of goods sold to determine gross profit. Its operating expenses (direct expenses and its indirect expenses allocated to the department) are deducted from gross profit to yield departmental net income. The departmental contribution report is similar to the departmental income statement in terms of computing the gross profit for each department. Then the direct operating expenses for each department are deducted from gross profit to determine the contribution generated by each department. Indirect operating expenses are deducted *in total* from the company's combined contribution.

Guidance Answers to Decision Maker

Division Manager Your division's ROI without further action is 10.5% (equal to 7% × 1.5). In a highly competitive industry, it is difficult to increase profit margins by raising prices. Your division might be better able to control its costs to increase its profit margin. In addition, you might engage in a marketing program to increase sales without increasing your division's invested assets. Investment turnover and thus ROI will increase if the marketing campaign attracts customers.

Center Manager We must first realize that the two investment opportunities are not comparable on the basis of absolute dollars of income or on assets. For instance, the second investment provides a higher income in absolute dollars but requires a higher investment. Accordingly, we need to compute return on investment for each alternative: (1) $50,000 ÷ $250,000 = 20%, and (2) $175,000 ÷ $1 million = 17.5%. Alternative 1 has the higher return and is preferred over alternative 2. Do you pursue one, both, or neither? Because alternative 1's return is higher than the center's usual return of 19%, it should be pursued, assuming its risks are acceptable. Also, since alternative 1 requires a small investment, top management is likely to be more agreeable to pursuing it. Alternative 2's return is lower than the usual 19% and is not likely to be acceptable.

Key Terms

Balanced scorecard
Controllable costs
Cost-based transfer pricing
Cost center
Cycle efficiency (CE)
Cycle time (CT)
Decentralized organization
Departmental contribution to overhead
Departmental income statements
Direct expenses
Indirect expenses
Investment center
Investment turnover
Joint cost
Market-based transfer price
Negotiated transfer price
Non-value-added time
Profit center
Profit margin
Residual income
Responsibility accounting budget
Responsibility accounting performance report
Responsibility accounting system
Return on investment
Transfer price
Uncontrollable costs
Value-added time

Multiple Choice Quiz

Answers at end of chapter

1. A retailer has three departments—housewares, appliances, and clothing—and buys advertising that benefits all departments. Advertising expense is $150,000 for the year, and departmental sales for the year follow: housewares, $356,250; appliances, $641,250; and clothing, $427,500. How much advertising expense is allocated to appliances if allocation is based on departmental sales?

a. $37,500
b. $67,500
c. $45,000
d. $150,000
e. $641,250

2. Indirect expenses

a. Cannot be readily traced to one department.
b. Are allocated to departments based on the relative benefit each department receives.
c. Are the same as uncontrollable expenses.
d. *a*, *b*, and *c* above are all true.
e. *a* and *b* above are true.

3. A division reports the information below. What is the division's investment (asset) turnover?

Sales	$500,000
Income	75,000
Average assets	200,000

a. 37.5%
b. 15
c. 2.5
d. 2.67
e. 4

4. A company operates three retail departments as profit centers, and the following information is available for each. Which department has the largest dollar amount of departmental contribution to overhead, and what is the dollar amount contributed?

Department	Sales	Cost of Goods Sold	Direct Expenses	Allocated Indirect Expenses
X	$500,000	$350,000	$50,000	$40,000
Y	200,000	75,000	20,000	50,000
Z	350,000	150,000	75,000	10,000

a. Department Y, $55,000
b. Department Z, $125,000
c. Department X, $500,000
d. Department Z, $200,000
e. Department X, $60,000

5. Using the data in question 4, Department X's contribution to overhead as a percentage of sales is

a. 20%
b. 30%
c. 12%
d. 48%
e. 32%

A(B) *Superscript letter A (B) denotes assignments based on Appendix 22A (22B).*
[icon] Icon denotes assignments that involve decision making.

Discussion Questions

1. Why are many companies divided into departments?

2. What is the difference between operating departments and service departments?

3. [icon] What are controllable costs?

4. Controllable and uncontrollable costs must be identified with a particular _____ and a definite _____ period.

5. [icon] Why should managers be closely involved in preparing their responsibility accounting budgets?

6. [icon] What are two main goals in managerial accounting for reporting on and analyzing departments?

7. [icon] Is it possible to evaluate a cost center's profitability? Explain.

8. What is the difference between direct and indirect expenses?

9. Suggest a reasonable basis for allocating each of the following indirect expenses to departments: (a) salary of a supervisor who manages several departments, (b) rent, (c) heat, (d) electricity for lighting, (e) janitorial services, (f) advertising, (g) expired insurance on equipment, and (h) property taxes on equipment.

10. **Samsung** has many departments. How is a department's contribution to overhead measured? **Samsung**

11. **Google** aims to give its managers timely cost reports. In responsibility accounting, who receives timely cost reports and specific cost information? Explain. **GOOGLE**

12.[A] What is a transfer price? Under what conditions is a market-based transfer price most likely to be used?

13.[B] What is a joint cost? How are joint costs usually allocated among the products produced from them?

14.[B] Give two examples of products with joint costs.

15. Each **Apple** retail store has several departments. Why is it useful for its management to (a) collect accounting information about each department and (b) treat each department as a profit center? **APPLE**

16. **Apple** delivers its products to locations around the world. List three controllable and three uncontrollable costs for its delivery department. **APPLE**

17. Define and describe *cycle time* and identify the components of cycle time.

18. Explain the difference between value-added time and non-value-added time.

19. Define and describe *cycle efficiency*.

20. Can management of a company such as **Samsung** use cycle time and cycle efficiency as useful measures of performance? Explain. **Samsung**

connect

QUICK STUDY

QS 22-1
Allocating costs to departments
P1

Macee Department Store has three departments, and it conducts advertising campaigns that benefit all departments. Advertising costs are $100,000 this year, and departmental sales for this year follow. How much advertising cost is allocated to each department if the allocation is based on departmental sales?

Department	Sales
Department 1	$220,000
Department 2	400,000
Department 3	180,000

QS 22-2
Allocating costs to departments
P1

Mervon Company has two operating departments: mixing and bottling. Mixing has 300 employees and occupies 22,000 square feet. Bottling has 200 employees and occupies 18,000 square feet. Indirect factory costs for the current period follow: administrative, $160,000; and maintenance, $200,000. Administrative costs are allocated to operating departments based on the number of workers. Determine the administrative costs allocated to each operating department.

QS 22-3
Allocating costs to departments P1

Mervon Company has two operating departments: mixing and bottling. Mixing has 300 employees and occupies 22,000 square feet. Bottling has 200 employees and occupies 18,000 square feet. Indirect factory costs for the current period follow: administrative, $160,000; and maintenance, $200,000. If the maintenance costs are allocated to operating departments based on square footage, determine the amount of maintenance costs allocated to each operating department.

QS 22-4
Allocation and measurement terms
C1

In each blank next to the following terms, place the identifying letter of its best description.

1. ______ Cost center
2. ______ Investment center
3. ______ Departmental accounting system
4. ______ Operating department
5. ______ Profit center
6. ______ Responsibility accounting system
7. ______ Service department

A. Incurs costs without directly yielding revenues.
B. Provides information used to evaluate the performance of a department.
C. Holds manager responsible for revenues, costs, and investments.
D. Engages directly in manufacturing or in making sales directly to customers.
E. Does not directly manufacture products but contributes to profitability of the entire company.
F. Incurs costs and also generates revenues.
G. Provides information used to evaluate the performance of a department manager.

QS 22-5
Basis for cost allocation
C1

For each of the following types of indirect expenses and service department expenses, identify one allocation basis that could be used to distribute it to the departments indicated.

_______ **1.** Computer service expenses of production scheduling for operating departments.
_______ **2.** General office department expenses of the operating departments.
_______ **3.** Maintenance department expenses of the operating departments.
_______ **4.** Electric utility expenses of all departments.

QS 22-6
Responsibility accounting terms
C1

In each blank next to the following terms, place the identifying letter of its best description.

_______ **1.** Indirect expenses	**A.** Costs not within a manager's control or influence
_______ **2.** Controllable costs	**B.** Costs that can be readily traced to a department
_______ **3.** Direct expenses	**C.** Cost that a manager has the ability to affect
_______ **4.** Uncontrollable costs	**D.** Costs incurred for the joint benefit of more than one department

QS 22-7
Rent expense allocated to departments
P2

Car Mart pays $130,000 rent each year for its two-story building. The space in this building is occupied by five departments as specified here.

Paint department	1,440 square feet of first-floor space
Engine department	3,360 square feet of first-floor space
Window department	2,016 square feet of second-floor space
Electrical department	960 square feet of second-floor space
Accessory department	1,824 square feet of second-floor space

The company allocates 65% of total rent expense to the first floor and 35% to the second floor, and then allocates rent expense for each floor to the departments occupying that floor on the basis of space occupied. Determine the rent expense to be allocated to each department. (Round percents to the nearest one-tenth and dollar amounts to the nearest whole dollar.)

Check Allocated to paint dept., $25,350

QS 22-8
Departmental contribution to overhead
P3

Use the information in the following table to compute each department's contribution to overhead (both in dollars and as a percent). Which department contributes the largest dollar amount to total overhead? Which contributes the highest percent (as a percent of sales)? Round percents to one decimal.

	Dept. A	Dept. B	Dept. C
Sales	$53,000	$180,000	$84,000
Cost of goods sold	34,185	103,700	49,560
Gross profit	18,815	76,300	34,440
Total direct expenses	3,660	37,060	7,386
Contribution to overhead	$ _______	$ _______	$ _______
Contribution percent (of sales).........	_______ %	_______ %	_______ %

QS 22-9
Computing return on investment
A1

Compute return on investment for each of the divisions below (each is an investment center). Comment on the relative performance of each investment center.

Investment Center	Net Income	Average Assets	Return on Investment
Cameras and camcorders	$4,500,000	$20,000,000	_______
Phones and communications.........	1,500,000	12,500,000	_______
Computers and accessories	800,000	10,000,000	_______

QS 22-10
Computing residual income A1

Refer to information in QS 22-9. Assume a target income of 12% of average invested assets. Compute residual income for each division.

QS 22-11
Performance measures
A1 A2

Fill in the blanks in the schedule below for two separate investment centers A and B. Round answers to the nearest whole percent.

	Investment Center A	Investment Center B
Sales	$______	$10,400,000
Net income	$ 352,000	$______
Average invested assets	$1,400,000	______
Profit margin	8%	______%
Investment turnover	______	1.5
Return on investment	______%	12%

QS 22-12
Computing profit margin and investment turnover
A2

A company's shipping division (an investment center) has sales of $2,420,000, net income of $516,000, and average invested assets of $2,250,000. Compute the division's profit margin and investment turnover.

QS 22-13
Performance measures—balanced scorecard
A3

Classify each of the performance measures below into the most likely balanced scorecard perspective it relates to. Label your answers using *C* (customer), *P* (internal process), *I* (innovation and growth), or *F* (financial).

______ **1.** Customer wait time
______ **2.** Number of days of employee absences
______ **3.** Profit margin
______ **4.** Number of new products introduced
______ **5.** Change in market share
______ **6.** Employee training sessions attended
______ **7.** Length of time raw materials are in inventory
______ **8.** Customer satisfaction index

QS 22-14
Performance measures—balanced scorecard
A3

Walt Disney reports the following information for its two Parks and Resorts divisions.

	U.S.		International	
	Current year	Prior year	Current year	Prior year
Hotel occupancy rates	81%	82%	85%	88%

Assume Walt Disney uses a balanced scorecard and sets a target of 85% occupancy in its resorts. Using Exhibit 22.22 as a guide, show how the company's performance on hotel occupancy would appear on a balanced scorecard report.

QS 22-15
Manufacturing cycle time and efficiency
A4

Compute and interpret (*a*) manufacturing cycle time and (*b*) manufacturing cycle efficiency using the following information from a manufacturing company.

Process time	15 minutes
Inspection time	2 minutes
Move time	6.4 minutes
Wait time	36.6 minutes

QS 22-16A
Determining transfer prices without excess capacity C2

The windshield division of Fast Car Co. makes windshields for use in Fast Car's assembly division. The windshield division incurs variable costs of $200 per windshield and has capacity to make 500,000 windshields per year. The market price is $450 per windshield. The windshield division incurs total fixed costs of $3,000,000 per year. If the windshield division is operating at full capacity, what transfer price should be used on transfers between the windshield and assembly divisions? Explain.

QS 22-17A
Determining transfer prices with excess capacity C2

The windshield division of Fast Car Co. makes windshields for use in Fast Car's assembly division. The windshield division incurs variable costs of $200 per windshield and has capacity to make 500,000 windshields per year. The market price is $450 per windshield. The windshield division incurs total fixed costs of $3,000,000 per year. If the windshield division has excess capacity, what is the range of possible transfer prices that could be used on transfers between the windshield and assembly divisions? Explain.

QS 22-18B
Joint cost allocation C3

A company purchases a 10,020 square-foot commercial building for $325,000 and spends an additional $50,000 to divide the space into two separate rental units and prepare it for rent. Unit A, which has the desirable location on the corner and contains 3,340 square feet, will be rented for $1.00 per square foot. Unit B contains 6,680 square feet and will be rented for $0.75 per square foot. How much of the joint cost should be assigned to Unit B using the value basis of allocation?

QS 22-19
Return on investment A1

For a recent year **L'Oréal** reported operating profit of €3,385 (in millions) for its cosmetics division. Total assets were €12,888 (in millions) at the beginning of the year and €13,099 (in millions) at the end of the year. Compute return on investment for the year. State your answer as a percent, rounded to one decimal.

connect

EXERCISES

Exercise 22-1
Responsibility accounting report
P1

Marvin Dinardo manages an auto dealership's service department. Costs and expenses for a recent quarter for his department follows. List the controllable costs that would appear on a responsibility accounting report for the service department.

Costs and expenses	
Cost of parts sold	$30,000
Building depreciation (allocated)	9,300
Manager's salary	12,000
Supplies	15,900
Utilities (allocated)	4,400
Wages	16,000

Exercise 22-2
Departmental expense allocation-spreadsheet
P2

Marathon Running Shop has two service departments (advertising and administrative) and two operating departments (shoes and clothing). During 2015, the departments had the following direct expenses and occupied the following amount of floor space.

Department	Direct Expenses	Square Feet
Advertising	$ 18,000	1,120
Administrative	25,000	1,400
Shoes	103,000	7,140
Clothing	15,000	4,340

The advertising department developed and distributed 120 advertisements during the year. Of these, 90 promoted shoes and 30 promoted clothing. The store sold $350,000 of merchandise during the year. Of this amount, $273,000 is from the shoes department, and $77,000 is from the clothing department. The utilities expense of $64,000 is an indirect expense to all departments. Prepare a departmental expense allocation spreadsheet for Marathon Running Shop. The spreadsheet should assign (1) direct expenses to each of the four departments, (2) the $64,000 of utilities expense to the four departments on the basis of floor space occupied, (3) the advertising department's expenses to the two operating departments on the basis of the number of ads placed that promoted a department's products, and (4) the administrative department's expenses to the two operating departments based on the amount of sales. Provide supporting computations for the expense allocations.

Check Total expenses allocated to shoes dept., $177,472

Exercise 22-3
Service department expenses allocated to operating departments P2

The following is a partially completed lower section of a departmental expense allocation spreadsheet for Cozy Bookstore. It reports the total amounts of direct and indirect expenses allocated to its five departments. Complete the spreadsheet by allocating the expenses of the two service departments (advertising and purchasing) to the three operating departments.

	A		B	C	D	E	F	G
1				Allocation of Expenses to Departments				
2								
3			Expense Account					
4		Allocation Base	Balance	Advertising Dept.	Purchasing Dept.	Books Dept.	Magazines Dept.	Newspapers Dept.
5	Total department expenses..........		$698,000	$24,000	$34,000	$425,000	$90,000	$125,000
6	**Service department expenses**							
7	Advertising department............	Sales		?		?	?	?
8	Purchasing department............	Purch. orders			?	?	?	?
9	Total expenses allocated to							
10	operating departments.............		?	$ 0	$ 0	?	?	?

Advertising and purchasing department expenses are allocated to operating departments on the basis of dollar sales and purchase orders, respectively. Information about the allocation bases for the three operating departments follows.

Department	Sales	Purchase Orders
Books	$495,000	516
Magazines	198,000	360
Newspapers	207,000	324
Total	$900,000	1,200

Check Total expenses allocated to books dept., $452,820

Exercise 22-4
Indirect payroll expense allocated to departments
P2

Jessica Porter works in both the jewelry department and the hosiery department of a retail store. Porter assists customers in both departments and arranges and stocks merchandise in both departments. The store allocates Porter's $30,000 annual wages between the two departments based on a sample of the time worked in the two departments. The sample is obtained from a diary of hours worked that Porter kept in a randomly chosen two-week period. The diary showed the following hours and activities spent in the two departments. Allocate Porter's annual wages between the two departments.

Selling in jewelry department	51 hours
Arranging and stocking merchandise in jewelry department	6 hours
Selling in hosiery department	12 hours
Arranging and stocking merchandise in hosiery department	7 hours
Idle time spent waiting for a customer to enter one of the selling departments	4 hours

Check Assign $7,500 to hosiery

Exercise 22-5
Departmental expense allocations
P2

Woh Che Co. has four departments: materials, personnel, manufacturing, and packaging. In a recent month, the four departments incurred three shared indirect expenses. The amounts of these indirect expenses and the bases used to allocate them follow.

Indirect Expense	Cost	Allocation Base
Supervision	$ 82,500	Number of employees
Utilities	50,000	Square feet occupied
Insurance	22,500	Value of assets in use
Total	$155,000	

Departmental data for the company's recent reporting period follow.

Department	Employees	Square Feet	Asset Values
Materials	27	25,000	$ 6,000
Personnel	9	5,000	1,200
Manufacturing	63	55,000	37,800
Packaging	51	15,000	15,000
Total	150	100,000	$60,000

1. Use this information to allocate each of the three indirect expenses across the four departments.
2. Prepare a summary table that reports the indirect expenses assigned to each of the four departments.

Check (2) Total of $29,600 assigned to materials dept.

Exercise 22-6
Departmental contribution report
P3

Below are departmental income statements for a guitar manufacturer. The manufacturer is considering dropping its electric guitar department since it has a net loss. The company classifies advertising, rent, and utilities expenses as indirect.

WHOLESALE GUITARS
Departmental Income Statements
For Year Ended December 31, 2015

	Acoustic	Electric
Sales	$112,500	$105,500
Cost of goods sold	55,675	66,750
Gross profit	56,825	38,750
Operating expenses		
Advertising expense	8,075	6,250
Depreciation expense—equipment	10,150	9,000
Salaries expense	17,300	13,500
Supplies expense	2,030	1,700
Rent expense	6,105	5,950
Utilities expense	3,045	2,550
Total operating expenses	46,705	38,950
Net income (loss)	**$ 10,120**	**($200)**

1. Prepare a departmental contribution report that shows each department's contribution to overhead.
2. Based on contribution to overhead, should the electric guitar department be eliminated?

Exercise 22-7
Departmental income statement and contribution to overhead
P3

Jansen Company reports the following for its ski department for the year 2015. All of its costs are direct, except as noted.

Sales	$605,000
Cost of goods sold	425,000
Salaries	112,000 ($15,000 is indirect)
Utilities	14,000 ($3,000 is indirect)
Depreciation	42,000 ($10,000 is indirect)
Office expenses	20,000 (all indirect)

Prepare a (1) departmental income statement for 2015 and (2) departmental contribution to overhead report for 2015. (3) Based on these two performance reports, should Jansen eliminate the ski department?

Exercise 22-8
Investment center analysis A1

You must prepare a return on investment analysis for the regional manager of Fast & Great Burgers. This growing chain is trying to decide which outlet of two alternatives to open. The first location (A) requires a $1,000,000 average investment and is expected to yield annual net income of $160,000. The second location (B) requires a $600,000 average investment and is expected to yield annual net income of $108,000. Compute the return on investment for each Fast & Great Burgers alternative and then make your recommendation in a half-page memorandum to the regional manager. (The chain currently generates an 18% return on total assets.)

Exercise 22-9
Computing return on investment and residual income; investing decision
A1

Megamart, a retailer of consumer goods, provides the following information on two of its departments (each considered an investment center).

Investment Center	Sales	Income	Average Invested Assets
Electronics	$40,000,000	$2,880,000	$16,000,000
Sporting goods	20,000,000	2,040,000	12,000,000

1. Compute return on investment for each department. Using return on investment, which department is most efficient at using assets to generate returns for the company?
2. Assume a target income level of 12% of average invested assets. Compute residual income for each department. Which department generated the most residual income for the company?
3. Assume the electronics department is presented with a new investment opportunity that will yield a 15% return on investment. Should the new investment opportunity be accepted? Explain.

Exercise 22-10
Computing margin and turnover; department efficiency A2

Refer to information in Exercise 22-9. Compute profit margin and investment turnover for each department. Which department generates the most net income per dollar of sales? Which department is most efficient at generating sales from average invested assets?

Exercise 22-11
Return on investment
A1 A2

Kraft Foods Group reports the following for two of its divisions for a recent year. All numbers are in millions of dollars.

($ millions)	Beverage Division	Cheese Division
Invested assets, beginning	$2,662	$4,455
Invested assets, ending	2,593	4,400
Sales	2,681	3,925
Operating income	349	634

For each division, compute (1) return on investment, (2) profit margin, and (3) investment turnover for the year. Round answers to two decimal places.

Exercise 22-12
Residual income A1

Refer to the information in Exercise 22-11. Assume that each of the company's divisions has a required rate of return of 7%. Compute residual income for each division.

Exercise 22-13
Profit margin A2

Apple Inc. reports the following for three of its geographic segments for a recent year. All numbers are in millions of dollars.

($ millions)	Americas	Europe	China
Operating income	$22,817	$13,025	$ 8,541
Sales	62,739	37,883	25,417

Compute profit margin for each division. Express answers as percentages, rounded to one decimal place.

Exercise 22-14
Return on investment
A1 A2

ZNet Co. is a web-based retail company. The company reports the following for 2015.

Sales	$ 5,000,000
Operating income	1,000,000
Average invested assets	12,500,000

The company's CEO believes that sales for 2016 will increase by 20%, and both profit margin (%) and the level of average invested assets will be the same as for 2015.

1. Compute return on investment for 2015.
2. Compute profit margin for 2015.
3. If the CEO's forecast is correct, what will return on investment equal for 2016?
4. If the CEO's forecast is correct, what will investment turnover equal for 2016?

Exercise 22-15
Performance measures—balanced scorecard
A3

USA Airlines uses the following performance measures. Classify each of the performance measures below into the most likely balanced scorecard perspective it relates to. Label your answers using *C* (customer), *P* (internal process), *I* (innovation and growth), or *F* (financial).

______ **1.** Cash flow from operations
______ **2.** Number of reports of mishandled or lost baggage
______ **3.** Percentage of on-time departures
______ **4.** On-time flight percentage
______ **5.** Percentage of ground crew trained
______ **6.** Return on investment
______ **7.** Market value
______ **8.** Accidents or safety incidents per mile flown
______ **9.** Customer complaints
______ **10.** Flight attendant training sessions attended
______ **11.** Time airplane is on ground between flights
______ **12.** Airplane miles per gallon of fuel
______ **13.** Revenue per seat
______ **14.** Cost of leasing airplanes

Exercise 22-16
Manufacturing cycle time and efficiency
A4

Oakwood Company produces maple bookcases to customer order. It received an order from a customer to produce 5,000 bookcases. The following information is available for the production of the bookcases.

Process time.	6.0 days	Move time	3.2 days
Inspection time	0.8 days	Wait time	5.0 days

1. Compute the company's manufacturing cycle time.
2. Compute the company's manufacturing cycle efficiency. Interpret your answer.
3. Oakwood believes it can reduce move time by 1.2 days and wait time by 2.8 days by adopting lean manufacturing techniques. Compute the company's manufacturing cycle efficiency assuming the company's predictions are correct.

Check (2) Manufacturing cycle efficiency, 0.40

Exercise 22-17
Manufacturing cycle time and efficiency
A4

Best Ink produces ink-jet printers for personal computers. It received an order for 500 printers from a customer. The following information is available for this order.

Process time.	16.0 hours	Move time	9.0 hours
Inspection time	3.5 hours	Wait time	21.5 hours

1. Compute the company's manufacturing cycle time.
2. Compute the company's manufacturing cycle efficiency. Interpret your answer.
3. Assume that Best Ink wishes to increase its manufacturing cycle efficiency to 0.80. What are some ways that it can accomplish this?

Exercise 22-18^A
Determining transfer prices
C2

The trailer division of Baxter Bicycles makes bike trailers that attach to bicycles and can carry children or cargo. The trailers have a retail price of $200 each. Each trailer incurs $80 of variable manufacturing costs. The trailer division has capacity for 40,000 trailers per year and incurs fixed costs of $1,000,000 per year.

1. Assume the assembly division of Baxter Bicycles wants to buy 15,000 trailers per year from the trailer division. If the trailer division can sell all of the trailers it manufactures to outside customers, what price should be used on transfers between Baxter Bicycles' divisions? Explain.
2. Assume the trailer division currently only sells 20,000 trailers to outside customers, and the assembly division wants to buy 15,000 trailers per year from the trailer division. What is the range of acceptable prices that could be used on transfers between Baxter Bicycles' divisions? Explain.
3. Assume transfer prices of either $80 per trailer or $140 per trailer are being considered. Comment on the preferred transfer prices from the perspectives of the trailer division manager, the assembly division manager, and the top management of Baxter Bicycles.

Exercise 22-19B
Joint real estate costs assigned C3

Check Total Hilltop cost, $3,000,000

Heart & Home Properties is developing a subdivision that includes 600 home lots. The 450 lots in the Canyon section are below a ridge and do not have views of the neighboring canyons and hills; the 150 lots in the Hilltop section offer unobstructed views. The expected selling price for each Canyon lot is $55,000 and for each Hilltop lot is $110,000. The developer acquired the land for $4,000,000 and spent another $3,500,000 on street and utilities improvements. Assign the joint land and improvement costs to the lots using the value basis of allocation and determine the average cost per lot.

Exercise 22-20B
Joint product costs assigned
C3

Check (2) Inventory cost, $2,268

Pirate Seafood Company purchases lobsters and processes them into tails and flakes. It sells the lobster tails for $21 per pound and the flakes for $14 per pound. On average, 100 pounds of lobster are processed into 52 pounds of tails and 22 pounds of flakes, with 26 pounds of waste. Assume that the company purchased 2,400 pounds of lobster for $4.50 per pound and processed the lobsters with an additional labor cost of $1,800. No materials or labor costs are assigned to the waste. If 1,096 pounds of tails and 324 pounds of flakes are sold, what is (1) the allocated cost of the sold items and (2) the allocated cost of the ending inventory? The company allocates joint costs on a value basis. (Round the dollar cost per pound to the nearest thousandth.)

Exercise 22-21
Profit margin and investment turnover
A2

L'Oréal reports the following for a recent year for the major divisions in its cosmetics branch.

(€ millions)	Sales	Income	Total Assets End of Year	Total Assets Beginning of Year
Professional products	€ 2,717	€ 552	€ 2,624	€ 2,516
Consumer products	9,530	1,765	5,994	5,496
Luxury products	4,507	791	3,651	4,059
Active cosmetics	1,386	278	830	817
Total	€18,140	€3,386	€13,099	€12,888

1. Compute profit margin for each division. State your answers as percents, rounded to two decimal places. Which L'Oréal division has the highest profit margin?
2. Compute investment turnover for each division. Round your answers to two decimal places. Which L'Oréal division has the best investment turnover?

connect

PROBLEM SET A

Problem 22-1A
Responsibility accounting performance reports; controllable and budgeted costs
P1

Billie Whitehorse, the plant manager of Travel Free's Indiana plant, is responsible for all of that plant's costs other than her own salary. The plant has two operating departments and one service department. The camper and trailer operating departments manufacture different products and have their own managers. The office department, which Whitehorse also manages, provides services equally to the two operating departments. A budget is prepared for each operating department and the office department. The company's responsibility accounting system must assemble information to present budgeted and actual costs in performance reports for each operating department manager and the plant manager. Each performance report includes only those costs that a particular operating department manager can control: raw materials, wages, supplies used, and equipment depreciation. The plant manager is responsible for the department managers' salaries, utilities, building rent, office salaries other than her own, and other office costs plus all costs controlled by the two operating department managers. The annual departmental budgets and actual costs for the two operating departments follow.

	Budget			Actual		
	Campers	Trailers	Combined	Campers	Trailers	Combined
Raw materials	$195,000	$275,000	$ 470,000	$194,200	$273,200	$ 467,400
Employee wages	104,000	205,000	309,000	106,600	206,400	313,000
Dept. manager salary	43,000	52,000	95,000	44,000	53,500	97,500
Supplies used	33,000	90,000	123,000	31,700	91,600	123,300
Depreciation—Equip.	60,000	125,000	185,000	60,000	125,000	185,000
Utilities	3,600	5,400	9,000	3,300	5,000	8,300
Building rent	5,700	9,300	15,000	5,300	8,700	14,000
Office department costs	68,750	68,750	137,500	67,550	67,550	135,100
Totals	$513,050	$830,450	$1,343,500	$512,650	$830,950	$1,343,600

The office department's annual budget and its actual costs follow.

	Budget	Actual
Plant manager salary	$ 80,000	$ 82,000
Other office salaries	32,500	30,100
Other office costs	25,000	23,000
Totals	$137,500	$135,100

Required

1. Prepare responsibility accounting performance reports like those in Exhibit 22.2 that list costs controlled by the following:
   a. Manager of the camper department.
   b. Manager of the trailer department.
   c. Manager of the Indiana plant.

   In each report, include the budgeted and actual costs and show the amount that each actual cost is over or under the budgeted amount.

Check (1*a*) $500 total over budget

(1*c*) Indiana plant controllable costs, $1,900 total under budget

Analysis Component

2. Did the plant manager or the operating department managers better manage costs? Explain.

Problem 22-2A
Allocation of building occupancy costs to departments
P2

National Bank has several departments that occupy both floors of a two-story building. The departmental accounting system has a single account, Building Occupancy Cost, in its ledger. The types and amounts of occupancy costs recorded in this account for the current period follow.

Depreciation—Building	$18,000
Interest—Building mortgage	27,000
Taxes—Building and land	9,000
Gas (heating) expense	3,000
Lighting expense	3,000
Maintenance expense	6,000
Total occupancy cost	$66,000

The building has 4,000 square feet on each floor. In prior periods, the accounting manager merely divided the $66,000 occupancy cost by 8,000 square feet to find an average cost of $8.25 per square foot and then charged each department a building occupancy cost equal to this rate times the number of square feet that it occupied.

Diane Linder manages a first-floor department that occupies 1,000 square feet, and Juan Chiro manages a second-floor department that occupies 1,800 square feet of floor space. In discussing the departmental reports, the second-floor manager questions whether using the same rate per square foot for all departments makes sense because the first-floor space is more valuable. This manager also references a recent real estate study of average local rental costs for similar space that shows first-floor space worth $30 per square foot and second-floor space worth $20 per square foot (excluding costs for heating, lighting, and maintenance).

Required

1. Allocate occupancy costs to the Linder and Chiro departments using the current allocation method.
2. Allocate the depreciation, interest, and taxes occupancy costs to the Linder and Chiro departments in proportion to the relative market values of the floor space. Allocate the heating, lighting, and maintenance costs to the Linder and Chiro departments in proportion to the square feet occupied (ignoring floor space market values).

Check (1) Total allocated to Linder and Chiro, $23,100; (2) total occupancy cost to Linder, $9,600

Analysis Component

3. Which allocation method would you prefer if you were a manager of a second-floor department? Explain.

Problem 22-3A
Departmental income statements; forecasts
P3

Williams Company began operations in January 2015 with two operating (selling) departments and one service (office) department. Its departmental income statements follow.

WILLIAMS COMPANY Departmental Income Statements For Year Ended December 31, 2015	Clock	Mirror	Combined
Sales	$130,000	$55,000	$185,000
Cost of goods sold	63,700	34,100	97,800
Gross profit	66,300	20,900	87,200
Direct expenses			
Sales salaries	20,000	7,000	27,000
Advertising	1,200	500	1,700
Store supplies used	900	400	1,300
Depreciation—Equipment	1,500	300	1,800
Total direct expenses	23,600	8,200	31,800
Allocated expenses			
Rent expense	7,020	3,780	10,800
Utilities expense	2,600	1,400	4,000
Share of office department expenses	10,500	4,500	15,000
Total allocated expenses	20,120	9,680	29,800
Total expenses	43,720	17,880	61,600
Net income	$ 22,580	$ 3,020	$ 25,600

Williams plans to open a third department in January 2016 that will sell paintings. Management predicts that the new department will generate $50,000 in sales with a 55% gross profit margin and will require the following direct expenses: sales salaries, $8,000; advertising, $800; store supplies, $500; and equipment depreciation, $200. It will fit the new department into the current rented space by taking some square footage from the other two departments. When opened the new painting department will fill one-fifth of the space presently used by the clock department and one-fourth used by the mirror department. Management does not predict any increase in utilities costs, which are allocated to the departments in proportion to occupied space (or rent expense). The company allocates office department expenses to the operating departments in proportion to their sales. It expects the painting department to increase total office department expenses by $7,000. Since the painting department will bring new customers into the store, management expects sales in both the clock and mirror departments to increase by 8%. No changes for those departments' gross profit percents or their direct expenses are expected except for store supplies used, which will increase in proportion to sales.

Required

Prepare departmental income statements that show the company's predicted results of operations for calendar year 2016 for the three operating (selling) departments and their combined totals. (Round percents to the nearest one-tenth and dollar amounts to the nearest whole dollar.)

Check 2016 forecasted combined net income (sales), $43,472 ($249,800)

Problem 22-4A
Departmental contribution to income
P3

Vortex Company operates a retail store with two departments. Information about those departments follows.

	Department A	Department B
Sales	$800,000	$450,000
Cost of goods sold	497,000	291,000
Direct expenses		
Salaries	125,000	88,000
Insurance	20,000	10,000
Utilities	24,000	14,000
Depreciation	21,000	12,000
Maintenance	7,000	5,000

The company also incurred the following indirect costs.

Salaries	$36,000
Insurance	6,000
Depreciation	15,000
Office expenses	50,000

Indirect costs are allocated as follows: salaries on the basis of sales; insurance and depreciation on the basis of square footage; and office expenses on the basis of number of employees. Additional information about the departments follows.

Department	Square footage	Number of employees
A	28,000	75
B	12,000	50

Required

1. For each department, determine the departmental contribution to overhead and the departmental net income.
2. Should Department B be eliminated? Explain.

Check (1) Dept. A net income, $38,260

Problem 22-5A[B]
Allocation of joint costs
C3

Georgia Orchards produced a good crop of peaches this year. After preparing the following income statement, the company believes it should have given its No. 3 peaches to charity and saved its efforts.

GEORGIA ORCHARDS
Income Statement
For Year Ended December 31, 2015

	No. 1	No. 2	No. 3	Combined
Sales (by grade)				
No. 1: 300,000 lbs. @ $1.50/lb	$450,000			
No. 2: 300,000 lbs. @ $1.00/lb		$300,000		
No. 3: 750,000 lbs. @ $0.25/lb			$ 187,500	
Total sales				$937,500
Costs				
Tree pruning and care @ $0.30/lb	90,000	90,000	225,000	405,000
Picking, sorting, and grading @ $0.15/lb	45,000	45,000	112,500	202,500
Delivery costs	15,000	15,000	37,500	67,500
Total costs	150,000	150,000	375,000	675,000
Net income (loss)	$300,000	$150,000	$(187,500)	$262,500

In preparing this statement, the company allocated joint costs among the grades on a physical basis as an equal amount per pound. The company's delivery cost records show that $30,000 of the $67,500 relates to crating the No. 1 and No. 2 peaches and hauling them to the buyer. The remaining $37,500 of delivery costs is for crating the No. 3 peaches and hauling them to the cannery.

Required

1. Prepare reports showing cost allocations on a sales value basis to the three grades of peaches. Separate the delivery costs into the amounts directly identifiable with each grade. Then allocate any shared delivery costs on the basis of the relative sales value of each grade.
2. Using your answers to part 1, prepare an income statement using the joint costs allocated on a sales value basis.

Check (1) $129,600 tree pruning and care costs allocated to No. 2

(2) Net income from No. 1 & No. 2 peaches, $140,400 & $93,600

Analysis Component

3. Do you think delivery costs fit the definition of a joint cost? Explain.

PROBLEM SET B

Problem 22-1B
Responsibility accounting performance reports; controllable and budgeted costs
P1

Britney Brown, the plant manager of LMN Co.'s Chicago plant, is responsible for all of that plant's costs other than her own salary. The plant has two operating departments and one service department. The refrigerator and dishwasher operating departments manufacture different products and have their own managers. The office department, which Brown also manages, provides services equally to the two operating departments. A monthly budget is prepared for each operating department and the office department. The company's responsibility accounting system must assemble information to present budgeted and actual costs in performance reports for each operating department manager and the plant manager. Each performance report includes only those costs that a particular operating department manager can control: raw materials, wages, supplies used, and equipment depreciation. The plant manager is responsible for the department managers' salaries, utilities, building rent, office salaries other than her own, and other office costs plus all costs controlled by the two operating department managers. The April departmental budgets and actual costs for the two operating departments follow.

	Budget			Actual		
	Refrigerators	Dishwashers	Combined	Refrigerators	Dishwashers	Combined
Raw materials	$400,000	$200,000	$ 600,000	$385,000	$202,000	$ 587,000
Employee wages	170,000	80,000	250,000	174,700	81,500	256,200
Dept. manager salary	55,000	49,000	104,000	55,000	46,500	101,500
Supplies used	15,000	9,000	24,000	14,000	9,700	23,700
Depreciation—Equip.	53,000	37,000	90,000	53,000	37,000	90,000
Utilities	30,000	18,000	48,000	34,500	20,700	55,200
Building rent	63,000	17,000	80,000	65,800	16,500	82,300
Office department costs	70,500	70,500	141,000	75,000	75,000	150,000
Totals	$856,500	$480,500	$1,337,000	$857,000	$488,900	$1,345,900

The office department's budget and its actual costs for April follow.

	Budget	Actual
Plant manager salary	$ 80,000	$ 85,000
Other office salaries	40,000	35,200
Other office costs	21,000	29,800
Totals	$141,000	$150,000

Required

1. Prepare responsibility accounting performance reports like those in Exhibit 22.2 that list costs controlled by the following:
   a. Manager of the refrigerator department.
   b. Manager of the dishwasher department.
   c. Manager of the Chicago plant.

   In each report, include the budgeted and actual costs for the month and show the amount by which each actual cost is over or under the budgeted amount.

Check (1*a*) $11,300 total under budget

(1*c*) Chicago plant controllable costs, $3,900 total over budget

Analysis Component

2. Did the plant manager or the operating department managers better manage costs? Explain.

Problem 22-2B
Allocation of building occupancy costs to departments
P2

Harmon's has several departments that occupy all floors of a two-story building that includes a basement floor. Harmon rented this building under a long-term lease negotiated when rental rates were low. The departmental accounting system has a single account, Building Occupancy Cost, in its ledger. The types and amounts of occupancy costs recorded in this account for the current period follow.

Building rent	$400,000
Lighting expense	25,000
Cleaning expense	40,000
Total occupancy cost	$465,000

The building has 7,500 square feet on each of the upper two floors but only 5,000 square feet in the basement. In prior periods, the accounting manager merely divided the $465,000 occupancy cost by 20,000 square feet to find an average cost of $23.25 per square foot and then charged each department a building occupancy cost equal to this rate times the number of square feet that it occupies.

Jordan Style manages a department that occupies 2,000 square feet of basement floor space. In discussing the departmental reports with other managers, she questions whether using the same rate per square foot for all departments makes sense because different floor space has different values. Style checked a recent real estate report of average local rental costs for similar space that shows first-floor space worth $40 per square foot, second-floor space worth $20 per square foot, and basement space worth $10 per square foot (excluding costs for lighting and cleaning).

Required

1. Allocate occupancy costs to Style's department using the current allocation method.
2. Allocate the building rent cost to Style's department in proportion to the relative market value of the floor space. Allocate to Style's department the lighting and cleaning costs in proportion to the square feet occupied (ignoring floor space market values). Then, compute the total occupancy cost allocated to Style's department.

Check Total costs allocated to Style's dept., (1) $46,500; (2) Total occupancy cost to Style $22,500

Analysis Component

3. Which allocation method would you prefer if you were a manager of a basement department?

Problem 22-3B
Departmental income statements; forecasts
P3

Bonanza Entertainment began operations in January 2015 with two operating (selling) departments and one service (office) department. Its departmental income statements follow.

BONANZA ENTERTAINMENT
Departmental Income Statements
For Year Ended December 31, 2015

	Movies	Video Games	Combined
Sales	$600,000	$200,000	$800,000
Cost of goods sold	420,000	154,000	574,000
Gross profit	180,000	46,000	226,000
Direct expenses			
Sales salaries	37,000	15,000	52,000
Advertising	12,500	6,000	18,500
Store supplies used	4,000	1,000	5,000
Depreciation—Equipment	4,500	3,000	7,500
Total direct expenses	58,000	25,000	83,000
Allocated expenses			
Rent expense	41,000	9,000	50,000
Utilities expense	7,380	1,620	9,000
Share of office department expenses	56,250	18,750	75,000
Total allocated expenses	104,630	29,370	134,000
Total expenses	162,630	54,370	217,000
Net income (loss)	$ 17,370	$ (8,370)	$ 9,000

The company plans to open a third department in January 2016 that will sell compact discs. Management predicts that the new department will generate $300,000 in sales with a 35% gross profit margin and will require the following direct expenses: sales salaries, $18,000; advertising, $10,000; store supplies, $2,000; and equipment depreciation, $1,200. The company will fit the new department into the current rented space by taking some square footage from the other two departments. When opened, the new compact disc department will fill one-fourth of the space presently used by the movie department and one-third of the space used by the video game department. Management does not predict any increase in utilities costs, which are allocated to the departments in proportion to occupied space (or rent expense). The company allocates office department expenses to the operating departments in proportion to their sales. It expects the compact disc department to increase total office department expenses by $10,000. Since the compact disc department will bring new customers into the store, management expects sales in both the movie and video game departments to increase by 8%. No changes for those departments' gross profit percents or for their direct expenses are expected, except for store supplies used, which will increase in proportion to sales.

Required

Check 2016 forecasted Movies net income (sales), $52,450 ($648,000)

Prepare departmental income statements that show the company's predicted results of operations for calendar year 2016 for the three operating (selling) departments and their combined totals. (Round percents to the nearest one-tenth and dollar amounts to the nearest whole dollar.)

Problem 22-4B
Departmental contribution to income
P3

Sadar Company operates a store with two departments: videos and music. Information about those departments follows.

	Videos Department	Music Department
Sales	$370,500	$279,500
Cost of goods sold	320,000	175,000
Direct expenses		
Salaries	35,000	25,000
Maintenance	12,000	10,000
Utilities	5,000	4,500
Insurance	4,200	3,700

The company also incurred the following indirect costs.

Advertising	$15,000
Salaries	27,000
Office expenses	3,200

Indirect costs are allocated as follows: advertising on the basis of sales; salaries on the basis of number of employees; and office expenses on the basis of square footage. Additional information about the departments follows.

Department	Square footage	Number of employees
Videos	5,000	3
Music	3,000	2

Required

Check (1) Music dept. net income, $42,850

1. For each department, determine the departmental contribution to overhead and the departmental net income.
2. Should the video department be eliminated? Explain.

Problem 22-5B[B]
Allocation of joint costs
C3

Rita and Rick Redding own and operate a tomato grove. After preparing the following income statement, Rita believes they should have offered the No. 3 tomatoes to the public for free and saved themselves time and money.

RITA AND RICK REDDING
Income Statement
For Year Ended December 31, 2015

	No. 1	No. 2	No. 3	Combined
Sales (by grade)				
No. 1: 500,000 lbs. @ $1.80/lb	$900,000			
No. 2: 400,000 lbs. @ $1.25/lb		$500,000		
No. 3: 100,000 lbs. @ $0.40/lb			$ 40,000	
Total sales				$1,440,000
Costs				
Land preparation, seeding, and cultivating @ $0.70/lb	350,000	280,000	70,000	700,000
Harvesting, sorting, and grading @ $0.04/lb.	20,000	16,000	4,000	40,000
Delivery costs	10,000	7,000	3,000	20,000
Total costs	380,000	303,000	77,000	760,000
Net income (loss)	$520,000	$197,000	$(37,000)	$ 680,000

In preparing this statement, Rita and Rick allocated joint costs among the grades on a physical basis as an equal amount per pound. Also, their delivery cost records show that $17,000 of the $20,000 relates to crating the No. 1 and No. 2 tomatoes and hauling them to the buyer. The remaining $3,000 of delivery costs is for crating the No. 3 tomatoes and hauling them to the cannery.

Required

1. Prepare reports showing cost allocations on a sales value basis to the three grades of tomatoes. Separate the delivery costs into the amounts directly identifiable with each grade. Then allocate any shared delivery costs on the basis of the relative sales value of each grade. (Round percents to the nearest one-tenth and dollar amounts to the nearest whole dollar.)
2. Using your answers to part 1, prepare an income statement using the joint costs allocated on a sales value basis.

Check (1) $1,120 harvesting, sorting and grading costs allocated to No. 3

(2) Net income from No. 1 & No. 2 tomatoes, $426,569 & $237,151

Analysis Component

3. Do you think delivery costs fit the definition of a joint cost? Explain.

SERIAL PROBLEM

Business Solutions

A3

(This serial problem began in Chapter 1 and continues through most of the book. If previous chapter segments were not completed, the serial problem can begin at this point. It is helpful, but not necessary, to use the Working Papers that accompany the book.)

SP 22 Santana Rey's two departments, computer consulting services and computer workstation furniture manufacturing, have each been profitable. Santana has heard of the balanced scorecard and wants you to provide details on how it could be used to measure performance of her departments.

Required

1. Explain the four performance perspectives included in a balanced scorecard.
2. For each of the four performance perspectives included in a balanced scorecard, provide examples of measures Santana could use to measure performance of her departments.

Beyond the Numbers

REPORTING IN ACTION

C1

APPLE

BTN 22-1 Review **Apple**'s income statement in Appendix A and identify its revenues for the years ended September 28, 2013, September 29, 2012, and September 24, 2011. For the year ended September 28, 2013, Apple reports the following product revenue mix. (Assume that its product revenue mix is the same for each of the three years reported when answering the requirements.)

iPhone	iPad and iPod	Mac	iTunes, Software and Services, and Accessories
53%	21%	13%	13%

Required

1. Compute the amount of revenue from each of its product lines for the years ended September 28, 2013, September 29, 2012, and September 24, 2011.
2. If Apple wishes to evaluate each of its product lines, how can it allocate its operating expenses to each of them to determine each product line's profitability?

Fast Forward

3. Access Apple's annual report for a fiscal year ending after September 28, 2013, from its website (**Apple.com**) or the SEC's EDGAR database (**www.SEC.gov**). Locate its table of "Net Sales by Product" in the footnotes. How has its product mix changed from 2013?

COMPARATIVE ANALYSIS

A2

APPLE

GOOGLE

BTN 22-2 **Apple** and **Google** compete in several product categories. Sales, income, and asset information is provided for fiscal year 2013 for each company below.

(in millions)	Apple	Google
Sales	$170,910	$ 59,825
Net income	37,037	12,920
Invested assets, beginning of year	176,064	93,798
Invested assets, end of year	207,000	110,920

Required

1. Compute profit margin for each company.
2. Compute investment turnover for each company.

Analysis Component

3. Using your answers to the questions above, compare the companies' performance for the year.

ETHICS CHALLENGE

P3

BTN 22-3 Super Security Co. offers a range of security services for athletes and entertainers. Each type of service is considered within a separate department. Marc Pincus, the overall manager, is compensated partly on the basis of departmental performance by staying within the quarterly cost budget. He often revises operations to make sure departments stay within budget. Says Pincus, "I will not go over budget even if it means slightly compromising the level and quality of service. These are minor compromises that don't significantly affect my clients, at least in the short term."

Required

1. Is there an ethical concern in this situation? If so, which parties are affected? Explain.
2. Can Marc Pincus take action to eliminate or reduce any ethical concerns? Explain.
3. What is Super Security's ethical responsibility in offering professional services?

COMMUNICATING IN PRACTICE

P2

BTN 22-4 Improvement Station is a national home improvement chain with more than 100 stores throughout the country. The manager of each store receives a salary plus a bonus equal to a percent of the store's net income for the reporting period. The following net income calculation is on the Denver store manager's performance report for the recent monthly period.

Sales	$2,500,000
Cost of goods sold	800,000
Wages expense	500,000
Utilities expense	200,000
Home office expense	75,000
Net income	$ 925,000
Manager's bonus (0.5%)	$ 4,625

In previous periods, the bonus had also been 0.5%, but the performance report had not included any charges for the home office expense, which is now assigned to each store as a percent of its sales.

Required

Assume that you are the national office manager. Write a half-page memorandum to your store managers explaining why home office expense is in the new performance report.

TAKING IT TO THE NET

P2

BTN 22-5 This chapter described and used spreadsheets to prepare various managerial reports (see Exhibit 22-6). You can download from websites various tutorials showing how spreadsheets are used in managerial accounting and other business applications.

Required

1. Link to the website Lacher.com. Select "Table of Contents" under "Microsoft Excel Examples." Identify and list three tutorials for review.
2. Describe in a half-page memorandum to your instructor how the applications described in each tutorial are helpful in business and managerial decision making.

TEAMWORK IN ACTION

P1

APPLE

Samsung

BTN 22-6 **Apple** and **Samsung** compete across the world in several markets.

Required

1. Design a three-tier responsibility accounting organizational chart assuming that you have available internal information for both companies. Use Exhibit 22.1 as an example. The goal of this assignment is to design a reporting framework for the companies; numbers are not required. Limit your reporting framework to sales activity only.
2. Explain why it is important to have similar performance reports when comparing performance within a company (and across different companies). Be specific in your response.

ENTREPRENEURIAL DECISION

P3

BTN 22-7 Brian Linton's company, **United By Blue**, sells jewelry and apparel. His company plans for continued expansion into other types of products.

Required

1. How can United By Blue use departmental income statements to assist in understanding and controlling operations?
2. Are departmental income statements always the best measure of a department's performance? Explain.
3. Provide examples of nonfinancial performance indicators United By Blue might use as part of a balanced scorecard system of performance evaluation.

HITTING THE ROAD

C1 P1

BTN 22-8 Visit a local movie theater and check out both its concession area and its showing areas. The manager of a theater must confront questions such as:

- How much return do we earn on concessions?
- What types of movies generate the greatest sales?
- What types of movies generate the greatest net income?

Required

Assume that you are the new accounting manager for a 16-screen movie theater. You are to set up a responsibility accounting reporting framework for the theater.

1. Recommend how to segment the different departments of a movie theater for responsibility reporting.
2. Propose an expense allocation system for heat, rent, insurance, and maintenance costs of the theater.

GLOBAL DECISION

P3

Samsung

BTN 22-9 Selected product data from **Samsung (www.samsung.com)** follow.

Product Segment for Year Ended (billions of Korean won)	Net Sales		Operating Income	
	Dec. 31, 2013	Dec. 31, 2012	Dec. 31, 2013	Dec. 31, 2012
Consumer electronics	₩ 50,332	₩ 51,105	₩ 1,673	₩ 2,324
IT and mobile communications	138,817	105,845	24,958	19,418

Required

1. Compute the percentage growth in net sales for each product line from fiscal year 2012 to 2013. Round percents to one decimal.
2. Which product line's net sales grew the fastest?
3. Which segment was the most profitable?
4. How can Samsung's managers use this information?

ANSWERS TO MULTIPLE CHOICE QUIZ

1. b; [$641,250/($356,250 + $641,250 + $427,500)] × $150,000 = $67,500
2. d;
3. c; $500,000/200,000 = 2.5
4. b;

	Department X	Department Y	Department Z
Sales	$500,000	$200,000	$350,000
Cost of goods sold	350,000	75,000	150,000
Gross profit	150,000	125,000	200,000
Direct expenses	50,000	20,000	75,000
Departmental contribution to overhead	$100,000	$105,000	$125,000

5. a; $100,000/$500,000 = 20%

chapter 23

Relevant Costing for Managerial Decisions

Chapter Preview

DECISIONS AND INFORMATION	DECISION SCENARIOS
Decision making	**A1** Additional business
C1 Relevant costs and benefits	Make or buy
P1 Identify relevant costs	Scrap or rework
	Sell or process further
	Sales mix selection
	Segment elimination
	Keep or replace
	A2 Determine selling price

Learning Objectives

CONCEPTUAL

C1 Describe the importance of relevant costs for short-term decisions.

ANALYTICAL

A1 Evaluate short-term managerial decisions using relevant costs.

A2 Determine product selling price based on total costs.

PROCEDURAL

P1 Identify relevant costs and apply them to managerial decisions.

Courtesy of Charlie's Brownies

Sweet Success

"Put all of your love into your product"

—Charlie Fyffe

LOS ANGELES—Noticing long lines and an inadequate supply of sweets to satisfy his high school friends' cravings, Charlie Fyffe began making brownies and selling them at school. His brownies were an instant hit, and as his clientele and passion for baking grew, so did his desire to start his own business. "I started **Charlie's Brownies** (**CharliesBrownies.com**) because sweets make people happy and baking is a fun industry," explains Charlie. "I developed a quality original recipe and started selling brownies in simple cake boxes. Staying simple and consistent opened the door to a viable business."

After six months of professional baking classes to sharpen his skills, Charlie turned to the business side. "I had a lot to learn," admits Charlie. "I read entrepreneurial books and did internships to learn how to run a business. Becoming an entrepreneur was hard work, but it allows me a life of freedom outside the cubicle and the opportunity to pursue my dreams and visions." Charlie had to learn how to use accounting information to make important business decisions. For example, attention to contribution margins enables Charlie to decide if adding new product lines, like vegan and gluten-free brownies, would increase profits. Focusing on contribution margins, his own and his competition's, also helps Charlie decide whether to eliminate certain products because they are not profitable.

Charlie applies high standards to his production process. Unlike some companies that can rework substandard materials into a viable product, Charlie explains that "raw materials that don't meet our standards never enter the baking process." Further, although expensive, exotic ingredients like "pink Himalayan salt and organic coconut palm sugar create a pop and that undeniable urge to eat another brownie. You can't help but to want another one!" Charlie has also managed to control overhead costs by doing much of the baking, marketing, and delivery himself. "I do whatever it takes to get the job done" he says. "There is never a dull moment!"

Much of Charlie's Brownies business is done online. To meet Charlie's goal of developing the company into a "nationwide and global Brownie Experience," he must focus on relevant costs to help him make good decisions. Determining the optimal sales mix requires Charlie to understand product contribution margins. Charlie sees farmers' markets and retail distribution as central to his vision and explains that "we need to upgrade our space and add to our capacity." The decision to keep or replace equipment is common in growing businesses and assessing relevant costs helps Charlie with this and other key managerial decisions.

Charlie advises young entrepreneurs to follow their passion. "Hang out with other overachievers and young entrepreneurs to stay one step ahead," he says. "Stay focused, work hard, and seek guidance from other successful businesspeople." Sounds like a recipe for success.

Sources: *Charlie's Brownies website,* January 2015; *JaredSurnamer.com,* August 2011; *PopularFinesse.tumblr.com,* October 2011; *Twentity.com,* February 2011

This chapter focuses on methods that use accounting information to make several important managerial decisions. Most of these involve short-term decisions. This differs from methods used for longer-term managerial decisions that are described in the first section of this chapter and in several other chapters of this book.

DECISIONS AND INFORMATION

This section explains how managers make decisions and the information relevant to those decisions.

Decision Making

Managerial decision making involves five steps: (1) define the decision task, (2) identify alternative courses of action, (3) collect relevant information and evaluate each alternative, (4) select the preferred course of action, and (5) analyze and assess decisions made. These five steps are illustrated in Exhibit 23.1.

EXHIBIT 23.1

Managerial Decision Making

Both managerial and financial accounting information play an important role in most management decisions. The accounting system is expected to provide primarily *financial* information such as performance reports and budget analyses for decision making. *Nonfinancial* information is also relevant, however; it includes information on environmental effects, political sensitivities, and social responsibility.

Relevant Costs and Benefits

C1 Describe the importance of relevant costs for short-term decisions.

Most financial measures of revenues and costs from accounting systems are based on historical costs. Although historical costs are important and useful for many tasks such as product pricing and the control and monitoring of business activities, their use can lead to incorrect decisions in some instances. Instead, an analysis of *relevant costs,* or *avoidable costs,* is especially useful in managers' short-term decisions. Three types of costs are pertinent to our discussion of relevant costs: sunk costs, out-of-pocket costs, and opportunity costs.

A *sunk cost* arises from a past decision and cannot be avoided or changed; it is irrelevant to future decisions. An example is the cost of computer equipment previously purchased by a company. This cost is not relevant to the decision of whether to replace the computer equipment. Likewise, depreciation of the original cost of plant (and intangible) assets are sunk costs. Most of a company's allocated costs, including fixed overhead items such as depreciation and administrative expenses, are sunk costs.

An *out-of-pocket cost* requires a future outlay of cash and is relevant for current and future decision making. These costs are usually the direct result of management's decisions. For instance, future purchases of computer equipment involve out-of-pocket costs. The cost of future computer purchases is relevant to the decision of whether to replace the computer equipment.

An *opportunity cost* is the potential benefit lost by taking a specific action when two or more alternative choices are available. An example is a student giving up wages from a job to attend summer school. The forgone wages should be considered as part of the total cost of attending summer school. Companies continually must choose from alternative courses of action. For instance, a company making standardized products might be approached by a customer to supply a special (nonstandard) product. A decision to accept or reject the special order must consider not only the profit to be made from the special order but also the profit given up by devoting time and resources to this order instead of pursuing an alternative project. The profit given up is an opportunity cost. Consideration of opportunity costs is important. Although opportunity costs are not entered in accounting records, they are relevant to many managerial decisions.

In sum, the relevant costs in making decisions are the **incremental costs,** also called *differential costs,* which are the additional costs incurred if a company pursues a certain course of action.

Besides relevant costs, management must also consider the relevant benefits associated with a decision. **Relevant benefits** refer to the additional or *incremental* revenue generated by selecting a particular course of action over another. In making decisions, managers should focus on those for which the relevant benefits exceed the relevant costs. As we will show, however, managers must also consider qualitative factors that are not easily expressed in terms of costs and benefits.

MANAGERIAL DECISION SCENARIOS

A1 Evaluate short-term managerial decisions using relevant costs.

Managers experience many different scenarios that require analyzing alternative actions and making a decision. We describe several different types of decision scenarios in this section. We set these tasks in the context of FasTrac, a manufacturer of exercise equipment and supplies. *We treat each of these decision tasks as separate from each other.*

Additional Business

FasTrac is operating at its normal level of 80% of full capacity. At this level, it produces and sells approximately 100,000 units of product annually. Its per unit and annual total sales and costs are shown in the contribution margin income statement in Exhibit 23.2. Its normal selling price is $10.00 per unit, and each unit sold generates $1.00 per unit of operating income.

EXHIBIT 23.2

Selected Operating Income Data

FASTRAC
Contribution Margin Income Statement
For Year Ended December 31, 2015

	Per Unit	Annual Total
Sales (100,000 units)	$10.00	$1,000,000
Variable costs		
Direct materials	(3.50)	(350,000)
Direct labor	(2.20)	(220,000)
Variable overhead	(0.50)	(50,000)
Selling expenses	(1.40)	(140,000)
Contribution margin	2.40	240,000
Fixed costs		
Fixed overhead	0.60	60,000
Administrative expenses	0.80	80,000
Operating income	$ 1.00	$ 100,000

A current buyer of FasTrac's products wants to purchase additional units of its product and export them to another country. This buyer offers to buy 10,000 units of the product at $8.50 per unit, or $1.50 less than the current price. The offer price is low, but FasTrac is considering the proposal because this sale would be several times larger than any single previous sale and it would use idle capacity. Also, the units will be exported, so this new business will not affect current sales.

To determine whether to accept or reject this order, management needs to know whether accepting the offer will increase net income. The analysis in Exhibit 23.3 shows that if management relies incorrectly on per unit historical costs, it would reject the sale because the selling price ($8.50) per unit is less than the total historical costs per unit ($9.00), and it thus yields a loss.

EXHIBIT 23.3

Analysis of Additional Business Using Historical Costs

Additional Business	Per Unit	Total
Sales (10,000 additional units)	$ 8.50	$ 85,000
Total costs and expenses (historical)	(9.00)	(90,000)
Operating loss	$(0.50)	$(5,000)

P1 Identify relevant costs and apply them to managerial decisions.

To correctly make its decision, FasTrac must analyze the costs of this potential new business differently. The $9.00 historical cost per unit is not necessarily the incremental cost of this order. The following information regarding the order is available:

- The variable manufacturing costs to produce this order will be the same as for FasTrac's normal business—$3.50 per unit for direct materials, $2.20 per unit for direct labor, and $0.50 per unit for variable overhead.
- Selling expenses for this order will be $0.20 per unit, which is less than the selling expenses of FasTrac's normal business.
- Fixed overhead expenses will not change regardless of whether this order is accepted.
- This order will incur *incremental* administrative expenses of $1,000 for clerical work. These are additional fixed costs due to this order.

We use this information to determine whether FasTrac should accept this new business. The analysis of relevant benefits and costs in Exhibit 23.4 suggests that the additional business should be accepted. It would yield $20,000 of additional pretax income. More generally, FasTrac would increase its income with any price that exceeded $6.50 per unit ($65,000 incremental cost/10,000 additional units). The key point is that *management must not blindly use historical costs, especially allocated overhead costs.* Instead, management must focus on the incremental costs to be incurred if the additional business is accepted.

EXHIBIT 23.4

Analysis of Additional Business Using Relevant Costs

FASTRAC
Contribution Margin Income Statement (for special order)
For Year Ended December 31, 2015

	Per Unit	Annual Total
Sales (10,000 units)	$8.50	$85,000
Variable costs		
Direct materials	(3.50)	(35,000)
Direct labor	(2.20)	(22,000)
Variable overhead	(0.50)	(5,000)
Selling expenses	(0.20)	(2,000)
Contribution margin	2.10	21,000
Fixed costs		
Fixed overhead	—	—
Administrative expenses	(0.10)	(1,000)
Operating income (incremental)	$2.00	$20,000

Point: The income statement in Exhibit 23.4 is based on the incremental revenues and costs of the special order.

Other Factors An analysis of the incremental costs pertaining to the additional volume is always relevant for this type of decision. We must proceed cautiously, however, when the additional volume approaches or exceeds the factory's existing available capacity. If the additional volume requires the company to expand its capacity by obtaining more equipment, more space, or more personnel, the incremental costs could quickly exceed the incremental revenue. Another cautionary note is the effect on existing sales. All new units of the extra business will be sold outside FasTrac's normal domestic sales channels. If accepting additional business would cause existing sales to decline, this information must be included in our analysis. The contribution margin lost from a decline in sales is an opportunity cost. The company must also consider whether this customer is really a one-time customer. If not, can the company continue to offer this low price in the long run?

Example: Exhibit 23.4 uses quantitative information. Suggest some qualitative factors to be considered when deciding whether to accept this project. *Answer:* (1) Impact on relationships with other customers and (2) improved relationship with customer buying additional units.

NEED-TO-KNOW 23-1

Special Order

A1

A company receives a special order for 200 units that requires stamping the buyer's name on each unit, yielding an additional fixed cost of $400 to its normal costs. Without the order, the company is operating at 75% of capacity and produces 7,500 units of product at the costs below. The company's normal selling price is $22 per unit.

Direct materials	$37,500
Direct labor	60,000
Overhead (30% variable)	20,000
Selling expenses (60% variable)	25,000

The sales price for the special order is $18 per unit. The special order will not affect normal unit sales and will not increase fixed overhead or fixed selling expenses. Variable selling expenses on the special order are reduced to one-half the normal amount. Should the company accept the special order?

Solution

Incremental variable costs per unit for this order of 200 units are computed as follows:

Direct materials ($37,500/7,500)	$ 5.00
Direct labor ($60,000/7,500)	8.00
Variable overhead [(0.30 × $20,000)/7,500]	0.80
Variable selling expenses [(0.60 × $25,000 × 0.5)/7,500]	1.00
Total incremental variable costs per unit	$14.80

QC1

The contribution margin from the special order is $640, computed as [($18.00 − $14.80) × 200]. This will cover the incremental fixed costs of $400 and yield incremental income of $240. The offer should be accepted.

Do More: QS 23-6, E 23-2, E 23-3

Decision Maker

Partner You are a partner in a small accounting firm that specializes in keeping the books and preparing taxes for clients. A local restaurant is interested in obtaining these services from your firm. Identify factors that are relevant in deciding whether to accept the engagement. ■ [Answers follow the chapter's Summary.]

Make or Buy

The managerial decision to make or buy a component is common. For example, **Apple** buys the component parts for its electronic products, but it could consider making these components in its own manufacturing facilities. This decision depends on incremental costs. We return to FasTrac to illustrate. FasTrac currently buys part 417, a component of the main product it sells, for $1.20 per unit. FasTrac has excess productive capacity, and management is wondering whether the company should make part 417 instead of buy it. FasTrac estimates that making part 417 would incur variable costs of $0.45 for direct materials and $0.50 for direct labor. FasTrac's normal predetermined overhead application rate is 100% of direct labor cost. If management *incorrectly* relies on this historical overhead rate, it will prepare the analysis in Exhibit 23.5.

EXHIBIT 23.5

Make or Buy Analysis Using Historical Costs

(per unit)	Make	Buy
Direct materials	$0.45	—
Direct labor	0.50	—
Overhead costs (using historical rate)	**0.50**	—
Purchase price	—	$1.20
Total costs	$1.45	$1.20

Using the data in Exhibit 23.5, management would mistakenly believe that the cost to make the component part is $1.45 per unit and conclude that the company is better off buying the part at $1.20 per unit. This analysis is flawed, however, because it uses the historical predetermined overhead rate.

As we explained earlier, only *incremental* overhead costs are relevant to this make or buy decision. Incremental overhead costs might include, for example, additional power for operating machines, extra supplies, added cleanup costs, materials handling, and quality control. Assume that management computes an *incremental overhead rate* of $0.20 per unit if it makes the part. We can then prepare a per unit analysis, using relevant costs, as shown in Exhibit 23.6.

EXHIBIT 23.6

Make or Buy Analysis Using Relevant Costs

(per unit)	Make	Buy
Direct materials	$0.45	—
Direct labor	0.50	—
Overhead costs (using incremental rate)	**0.20**	—
Purchase price	—	$1.20
Total costs	$1.15	$1.20

Exhibit 23.6 shows that the relevant cost to make part 417 is $1.15. Based on this analysis, it is cheaper to make the part than to buy it. We can see that if incremental overhead costs are less than $0.25 per unit, the total cost of making the part will be less than the purchase price of $1.20 per unit.

Other Factors While our analysis suggests it is cheaper to make part 417, FasTrac must also consider several nonfinancial factors in the make or buy decision. These factors might include product quality, timeliness of delivery (especially in a just-in-time setting), reactions of customers and suppliers, and other intangibles like employee morale and workload. It must also consider whether making the part requires incremental fixed costs to expand plant capacity. When these additional factors are considered, small cost differences might not matter.

NEED-TO-KNOW 23-2

Make or Buy

A1

A company currently pays $5 per unit to buy a key part for a product it manufactures. The company believes it can make the part for $1.50 per unit for direct materials and $2.50 per unit for direct labor. The company allocates overhead costs at the rate of 50% of direct labor. Incremental overhead costs to make this part are $0.75 per unit. Should the company make or buy the part?

Solution

(per unit)	Make	Buy
Direct materials	$1.50	—
Direct labor	2.50	—
Overhead	0.75	—
Cost to buy the part	—	$5.00
Total	$4.75	$5.00

The company should make the part because the cost to make it is less than the cost to buy it.

Do More: QS 23-7, QS 23-8, E 23-4, E 23-5

Decision Insight

Make or Buy IT Companies apply make or buy decisions to their services. Many now outsource their information technology activities. Information technology companies provide infrastructure and services to enable businesses to focus on their key activities. It is argued that outsourcing saves money and streamlines operations, and without the headaches. ■

Scrap or Rework

Manufacturing processes sometimes yield defective products. In such cases, managers must make a decision on whether to scrap or rework products in process. Two points are important here. First, costs already incurred in manufacturing the defective units are sunk and not relevant. Second, we must consider opportunity costs—reworking the defective products uses productive capacity that could be devoted to normal operations.

To illustrate, assume that FasTrac has 10,000 defective units of a product that have already cost $1 per unit to manufacture. These units can be sold as is (as scrap) for $0.40 each, or they can be reworked for $0.80 per unit and then sold for their full price of $1.50 each. Should FasTrac sell the units as scrap or rework them?

The $1 per unit manufacturing cost already incurred is irrelevant. Further, if FasTrac is operating near its maximum capacity, reworking the defects means that FasTrac is unable to manufacture 10,000 *new* units with an incremental cost of $1 per unit and a selling price of $1.50 per unit, meaning it incurs an *opportunity cost* of $0.50 per unit ($1.50 selling price − $1.00 incremental cost). Our analysis is then reflected in Exhibit 23.7.

EXHIBIT 23.7

Scrap or Rework Analysis

	Scrap	Rework
Sale of scrapped/reworked units (10,000 units)	$ 4,000	$ 15,000*
Less out-of-pocket costs to rework defects ($0.80 per unit)		(8,000)
Less opportunity cost of not making new units ($0.50 per unit)		**(5,000)**
Incremental net income	**$4,000**	**$ 2,000**

*10,000 × $1.50

Scrapping the units would yield incremental income of $4,000; reworking the units would yield only $2,000 of income. Based on this analysis, the defective units should be scrapped and sold as is for $0.40 each. If we had failed to include the opportunity costs of $5,000, the rework option would have shown an income of $7,000 instead of $2,000, mistakenly making reworking appear more favorable than scrapping.

Sell or Process Further

Some companies must decide whether to sell partially completed products as is or to process them further for sale as other products. For example, a peanut grower could sell its peanut harvest as is, or it could process peanuts into other products such as peanut butter, trail mix, and candy. The decision depends on the incremental costs and benefits of further processing, as we show next.

To illustrate, suppose that FasTrac has 40,000 units of partially finished Product Q. It has already spent $30,000 to manufacture these 40,000 units. FasTrac can sell the 40,000 units to another manufacturer as raw material for $50,000. Alternatively, it can process them further and produce finished Products X, Y, and Z. Processing the units further will cost an additional $80,000 and will yield total revenues of $150,000. FasTrac must decide whether the added revenues from selling finished Products X, Y, and Z exceed the costs of finishing them.

Exhibit 23.8 presents the analysis.

EXHIBIT 23.8

Sell or Process Further Analysis

	Sell as Product Q	Process Further into Products X, Y, and Z
Incremental revenue	$50,000	$150,000
Incremental cost	—	(80,000)
Incremental income	$50,000	$ 70,000

The analysis shows that the incremental income from processing further ($70,000) is greater than the incremental income ($50,000) from selling Product Q as is. Therefore, FasTrac should process further; by doing so, it will earn an additional $20,000 of income ($70,000 − $50,000).

Notice that the $30,000 of previously incurred manufacturing costs are *excluded* from the analysis. These costs are sunk, and they are not relevant to the decision. The incremental revenue from selling Product Q as is ($50,000) is properly included. It is the opportunity cost associated with processing further.

NEED-TO-KNOW 23-3

Sell or Process Further

A1

For each of the two independent scenarios below, determine whether the company should sell the partially completed product as is or process it further into other saleable products.

1. $10,000 of manufacturing costs have been incurred to produce Product Alpha. Alpha can be sold as is for $30,000 or processed further into two separate products. The further processing will cost $15,000, and the resulting products can be sold for total revenues of $60,000.
2. $5,000 of manufacturing costs have been incurred to produce Product Delta. Delta can be sold as is for $150,000 or processed further into two separate products. The further processing will cost $75,000, and the resulting products can be sold for total revenues of $200,000.

Solution

1.

Alpha	Sell As Is	Process Further
Incremental revenue	$30,000	$60,000
Incremental cost	—	(15,000)
Incremental income	$30,000	$45,000

Alpha should be processed further; doing so will yield an extra $15,000 ($45,000 − $30,000) of income.

2.

Delta	Sell As Is	Process Further
Incremental revenue	$150,000	$200,000
Incremental cost	—	(75,000)
Incremental income	$150,000	$125,000

QC2

Do More: QS 23-4, QS 23-10, QS 23-11, E 23-8

Delta should be sold as is; doing so will yield an extra $25,000 ($150,000 − $125,000) of income.

Sales Mix Selection When Resources Are Constrained

Point: A method called *linear programming* is useful for finding the optimal sales mix for several products subject to many market and production constraints. This method is described in advanced courses.

When a company sells a mix of products, some are likely to be more profitable than others. Management concentrates sales efforts on more profitable products. If production facilities or other factors are limited, producing more of one product usually requires producing less of others. In this case, management must identify the most profitable combination, or *sales mix,* of products. To identify the best sales mix, management focuses on the *contribution margin per unit of scarce resource.*

To illustrate, assume that FasTrac makes and sells two products, A and B. The same machines are used to produce both products. A and B have the following selling prices and variable costs per unit:

(per unit)	Product A	Product B
Selling price	$5.00	$7.50
Variable costs.........	3.50	5.50

FasTrac has an existing capacity of 100,000 machine hours per year. In addition, Product A uses 1 machine hour per unit while Product B uses 2 machine hours per unit. With limited resources, FasTrac should focus its productive capacity on the product that yields the highest contribution margin per machine hour, until market demand for that product is satisfied. Exhibit 23.9 shows the relevant analysis.

EXHIBIT 23.9

Sales Mix Analysis

	Product A	Product B
Selling price per unit	$5.00	$7.50
Variable costs per unit	3.50	5.50
Contribution margin per unit (a)	$1.50	$2.00
Machine hours per unit (b)	1.0	2.0
Contribution margin per machine hour (a) ÷ (b)	**$1.50**	**$1.00**

Exhibit 23.9 shows that although Product B has a higher contribution margin per *unit,* Product A has a higher contribution margin per *machine hour*. In this case, FasTrac should produce as much of Product A as possible, up to the market demand. For example, if the demand for Product A is unlimited, FasTrac should produce 100,000 units of Product A and none of Product B. This sales mix would yield a contribution margin of $150,000 per year, the maximum the company could make subject to its resource constraint.

If demand for Product A is limited—say, to 80,000 units—FasTrac will begin by producing those 80,000 units. This production level would leave 20,000 machine hours to devote to production of Product B. FasTrac would use these remaining machine hours to produce 10,000 units (20,000 machine hours/2 machine hours per unit) of Product B. This sales mix would yield the contribution margin shown in Exhibit 23.10.

EXHIBIT 23.10

Contribution Margin from Sales Mix, with Resource Constraint

	Contribution Margin	Machine Hours Used
Product A (80,000 × $1.50 per unit)	$120,000	80,000
Product B (10,000 × $2.00 per unit)	20,000	20,000
Total	$140,000	100,000

With limited demand for Product A, the optimal sales mix yields a contribution margin of $140,000, the best the company can do subject to its resource constraint and market demand. In general, if demand for products is limited, management should produce its most profitable product (per unit of scarce resource) up to the point of total demand (or its capacity constraint). It then uses remaining capacity to produce its next most profitable product.

Point: FasTrac might consider buying more machines to reduce the constraint on production. A strategy designed to reduce the impact of constraints or bottlenecks on production is called the *theory of constraints.*

NEED-TO-KNOW 23-4

Sales Mix with Constrained Resources

A1

A company produces two products, Gamma and Omega. Gamma sells for $10 per unit and Omega sells for $12.50 per unit. Variable costs are $7 per unit of Gamma and $8 per unit of Omega. The company has a capacity of 5,000 machine hours per month. Gamma uses 1 machine hour per unit, and Omega uses 3 machine hours per unit.

1. Compute the contribution margin per machine hour for each product.
2. Assume demand for Gamma is limited to 3,800 units per month. How many units of Gamma and Omega should the company produce, and what will be the total contribution margin from this sales mix?

Solution

1.

	Gamma	Omega
Selling price per unit	$10.00	$12.50
Variable costs per unit	7.00	8.00
Contribution margin per unit	$ 3.00	$ 4.50
Machine hours per unit	1	3
Contribution margin per machine hour	$ 3.00	$ 1.50

2. The company will begin by producing Gamma to meet the market demand of 3,800 units. This production level will consume 3,800 machine hours, leaving 1,200 machine hours to produce Omega. With 1,200 machine hours, the company can produce 400 units (1,200 machine hours/3 machine hours per unit) of Omega. The total contribution margin from this sales mix is:

Gamma	3,800 units × $3.00 per unit =	$11,400
Omega	400 units × $4.50 per unit =	1,800
Total		$13,200

Do More: QS 23-12, E 23-9

Decision Insight

Companies such as **Gap**, **Abercrombie & Fitch**, and **American Eagle** must continuously monitor and manage the sales mix of their product lists. Selling their products worldwide further complicates their decision process. The contribution margin of each product is crucial to their product mix strategies. ■

BananaStock/Punchstock

Segment Elimination

When a segment, division, or store is performing poorly, management must consider eliminating it. As we showed in a previous chapter, determining a segment's *contribution to overhead* is an important first step in this analysis. Segments with revenues less than direct costs are candidates for elimination. However, contribution to overhead is not sufficient for this decision. Instead, we must further classify the segment's expenses as avoidable or unavoidable. **Avoidable expenses** are amounts the company would not incur if it eliminated the segment. **Unavoidable expenses** are amounts that would continue even if the segment was eliminated.

Example: How can insurance be classified as either avoidable or unavoidable? *Answer:* It depends on whether the assets insured can be removed and the premiums canceled.

To illustrate, FasTrac is considering eliminating its treadmill division, which reported a $500 operating loss for the recent year, as shown in Exhibit 23.11. From Exhibit 23.11, we see that the treadmill division contributes $9,700 to recovery of overhead costs. The next step is to classify the division's costs as either avoidable or unavoidable. Variable costs, such as cost of goods sold and

EXHIBIT 23.11

Classification of Segment Operating Expenses for Analysis

Treadmill Division	Total	Avoidable Expenses	Unavoidable Expenses
Sales	$47,800		
Cost of goods sold	30,000	$30,000	
Gross profit	17,800		
Direct expenses			
Wages expense	7,900	7,900	
Depreciation expense—Equipment	200		$ 200
Total direct expenses	8,100		
Departmental contribution to overhead	$ 9,700		
Indirect expenses			
Rent and utilities expense	3,150		3,150
Advertising expense	400	400	
Insurance expense	400	300	100
Share of office department expenses	3,060	2,200	860
Share of purchasing department expenses	3,190	1,000	2,190
Total indirect expenses	10,200		
Operating income (loss)	$ (500)		
Total avoidable expenses		$41,800	
Total unavoidable expenses			$6,500

Point: The analysis is summarized as:

Sales	$47,800
Avoidable expenses	(41,800)
Reduction in income	$ 6,000

Because sales > avoidable expenses, do *not* eliminate division.

wages expense, are avoidable. In addition, some of the division's indirect expenses are avoidable; for example, if the treadmill division were eliminated, FasTrac could reduce its overall advertising expense by $400 and its overall insurance expense by $300. In addition, FasTrac could avoid office department expenses of $2,200 and purchasing expenses of $1,000 if the treadmill division were eliminated. It is important to realize that these *avoidable* expenses would not be allocated to other divisions of the company; rather, these expenses would be eliminated. Unavoidable expenses, however, will be reallocated to other divisions if the treadmill division is eliminated.

FasTrac's analysis shows that it can avoid a total of $41,800 of expenses if it eliminates the treadmill division. However, because this division's sales are $47,800, eliminating the division would reduce FasTrac's income by $6,000 ($47,800 − $41,800). Based on this analysis, FasTrac should not eliminate its treadmill division. *Our decision rule is that a segment is a candidate for elimination if its revenues are less than its avoidable expenses.* Avoidable expenses can be viewed as the costs to generate this segment's revenues.

Other Factors When considering elimination of a segment, we must assess its impact on other segments. A segment could be unprofitable on its own, but it might still contribute to other segments' revenues and profits. It is possible then to continue a segment even when its revenues are less than its avoidable expenses. Similarly, a profitable segment might be discontinued if its space, assets, or staff can be more profitably used by expanding existing segments or by creating new ones. Our decision to keep or eliminate a segment requires a more complex analysis than simply looking at a segment's performance report.

Example: Give an example of a segment that a company might profitably use to attract customers even though it might incur a loss. *Answer:* Warranty and post-sales services.

NEED-TO-KNOW 23-5

Segment Elimination

A1

A bike maker is considering eliminating its tandem bike division because it operates at a loss of $6,000 per year. Sales for the year total $40,000, and the company reports the costs for this division as shown below. Should the tandem bike division be eliminated?

	Avoidable Expenses	Unavoidable Expenses
Cost of goods sold	$30,000	$ —
Direct expenses	8,000	—
Indirect expenses	2,500	3,000
Service department costs	250	2,250
Total	$40,750	$5,250

Solution

Total avoidable costs of $40,750 are greater than the division's sales of $40,000, suggesting the division should be eliminated. Other factors might be relevant, since the shortfall in sales ($750) is low. For example, are sales expected to increase in the future? Does the sale of tandem bikes help sales of other types of products?

Do More: QS 23-13, QS 23-14, E 23-10

Keep or Replace Equipment

Businesses periodically must decide whether to keep using equipment or replace it. Advances in technology typically mean newer equipment can operate more efficiently and at lower cost than older equipment. If the reduction in *variable* manufacturing costs with the new equipment is greater than its net purchase price, the equipment should be replaced. In this setting, the net purchase price of the equipment is its total cost minus any trade-in allowance or cash receipt for the old equipment.

For example, FasTrac has a piece of manufacturing equipment with a book value (cost minus accumulated depreciation) of $20,000 and a remaining useful life of four years. At the end of four years the equipment will have a salvage value of zero. The market value of the equipment is currently $25,000.

FasTrac can purchase a new machine for $100,000 and receive $25,000 in return for trading in its old machine. The new machine will reduce FasTrac's variable manufacturing costs by $18,000 per year over the four-year life of the new machine. FasTrac's incremental analysis is shown in Exhibit 23.12.

EXHIBIT 23.12

Keep or Replace Analysis

	Increase or (Decrease) in Net Income
Cost to buy new machine	$(100,000)
Cash received to trade in old machine	25,000
Reduction in variable manufacturing costs	72,000*
Total increase (decrease) in net income	$ (3,000)

*18,000 × 4 years

QC3

The analysis in Exhibit 23.12 shows that FasTrac should not replace the old equipment with this newer version as it will decrease income by $3,000. Note, the book value of the old equipment ($20,000) is not relevant to this analysis. Book value is a sunk cost, and it cannot be changed regardless of whether FasTrac keeps or replaces this equipment.

GLOBAL VIEW

Courtesy of Charlie's Brownies

Heinz India Private Limited, headquartered in India, is a maker of ketchup, energy drinks, and other products. The company recently decided to eliminate several unprofitable segments, including those that made biscuits and ready-to-eat packaged foods, in order to focus on more profitable segments. Analyses of avoidable and unavoidable expenses, along with consideration of these segments' potential impact on other segments, support such decisions.

Sustainability and Accounting Charlie Fyffe of **Charlie's Brownies** strives to reduce the impact his company has on the environment while also growing sales. Unlike companies that make brownies with animal fats, Charlie makes his brownies entirely from plant-based, organic raw materials. The use of such materials enables Charlie to expand his sales to customers who follow vegan diets.

Decision Analysis — Setting Product Price

A2 Determine product selling price based on total costs.

Relevant costs are useful to management in determining prices for special short-term decisions. But longer run pricing decisions of management need to cover both variable and fixed costs, and yield a profit.

There are several methods to help management in setting prices. The *cost-plus* methods are probably the most common, where management adds a **markup** to cost to reach a target price. We will describe the **total cost method,** where management sets price equal to the product's total costs plus a desired profit on the product. This is a four-step process:

1. Determine total costs.

   Total costs = Production (direct materials, direct labor, and overhead) costs + Nonproduction (selling and administrative) costs

2. Determine total cost per unit.

   Total cost per unit = Total costs ÷ Total units expected to be produced and sold

3. Determine the dollar markup per unit.

   Markup per unit = Total cost per unit × Markup percentage

   where Markup percentage = Desired profit/Total costs

4. Determine selling price per unit.

   Selling price per unit = Total cost per unit + Markup per unit

To illustrate, consider a company that produces MP3 players. The company desires a 20% return on its assets of $1,000,000, and it expects to produce and sell 10,000 players. The following additional company information is available:

Variable costs (per unit)	
Production costs	$44
Nonproduction costs	6
Fixed costs (in dollars)	
Overhead	$140,000
Nonproduction	60,000

We apply our four-step process to determine price.

1. Total costs = Production costs + Nonproduction costs
   = [($44 × 10,000 units) + $140,000] + [($6 × 10,000 units) + $60,000]
   = $700,000
2. Total cost per unit = Total costs/Total units expected to be produced and sold
   = $700,000/10,000
   = $70
3. Markup per unit = Total cost per unit × (Desired profit/Total costs)
   = $70 × [(20% × $1,000,000)/$700,000]
   = $20
4. Selling price per unit = Total cost per unit + Markup per unit
   = $70 + $20
   = $90

To verify that our price yields the $200,000 desired profit (20% × $1,000,000), we compute the following simplified income statement using the information above.

Sales ($90 × 10,000)		$900,000
Expenses		
Variable ($50 × 10,000)		500,000
Fixed ($140,000 + $60,000)		200,000
Income		$200,000

Companies use cost-plus pricing as a starting point for determining selling prices. Many factors determine price, including consumer preferences and competition.

NEED-TO-KNOW

COMPREHENSIVE

Determine the appropriate action in each of the following managerial decision situations.

1. Packer Company is operating at 80% of its manufacturing capacity of 100,000 product units per year. A chain store has offered to buy an additional 10,000 units at $22 each and sell them to customers so as not to compete with Packer Company. The following data are available.

Costs at 80% Capacity	Per Unit	Total
Direct materials	$ 8.00	$ 640,000
Direct labor	7.00	560,000
Overhead (fixed and variable)	12.50	1,000,000
Totals	$27.50	$2,200,000

In producing 10,000 additional units, fixed overhead costs would remain at their current level but incremental variable overhead costs of $3 per unit would be incurred. Should the company accept or reject this order?

2. Green Company uses Part JR3 in manufacturing its products. It has always purchased this part from a supplier for $40 each. It recently upgraded its own manufacturing capabilities and has enough excess capacity (including trained workers) to begin manufacturing Part JR3 instead of buying it. The company prepares the following cost projections of making the part, assuming that overhead is allocated to the part at the normal predetermined rate of 200% of direct labor cost.

Direct materials	$11
Direct labor	15
Overhead (fixed and variable) (200% of direct labor)	30
Total	$56

The required volume of output to produce the part will not require any incremental fixed overhead. Incremental variable overhead cost will be $17 per unit. Should the company make or buy this part?

3. Gold Company's manufacturing process causes a relatively large number of defective parts to be produced. The defective parts can be (a) sold for scrap, (b) melted to recover the recycled metal for reuse, or (c) reworked to be good units. Reworking defective parts reduces the output of other good units because no excess capacity exists. Each unit reworked means that one new unit cannot be produced. The following information reflects 500 defective parts currently available.

Proceeds of selling as scrap	$2,500
Additional cost of melting down defective parts	400
Cost of purchases avoided by using recycled metal from defects	4,800
Cost to rework 500 defective parts	
Direct materials	0
Direct labor	1,500
Incremental overhead	1,750
Cost to produce 500 new parts	
Direct materials	6,000
Direct labor	5,000
Incremental overhead	3,200
Selling price per good unit	40

Should the company melt the parts, sell them as scrap, or rework them?

PLANNING THE SOLUTION

- Determine whether Packer Company should accept the additional business by finding the incremental costs of materials, labor, and overhead that will be incurred if the order is accepted. Omit fixed costs that the order will not increase. If the incremental revenue exceeds the incremental cost, accept the order.
- Determine whether Green Company should make or buy the component by finding the incremental cost of making each unit. If the incremental cost exceeds the purchase price, the component should be purchased. If the incremental cost is less than the purchase price, make the component.
- Determine whether Gold Company should sell the defective parts, melt them down and recycle the metal, or rework them. To compare the three choices, examine all costs incurred and benefits received from the alternatives in working with the 500 defective units versus the production of 500 new units. For the scrapping alternative, include the costs of producing 500 new units and subtract the $2,500 proceeds from selling the old ones. For the melting alternative, include the costs of melting the defective units, add the net cost of new materials in excess over those obtained from recycling, and add the direct labor and overhead costs. For the reworking alternative, add the costs of direct labor and incremental overhead. Select the alternative that has the lowest cost. The cost assigned to the 500 defective units is sunk and not relevant in choosing among the three alternatives.

SOLUTION

1. This decision involves accepting additional business. Since current unit costs are $27.50, it appears initially as if the offer to sell for $22 should be rejected, but the $27.50 cost includes fixed costs. When the analysis includes only *incremental* costs, the per unit cost is as shown in the following table. The offer should be accepted because it will produce $4 of additional profit per unit (computed as $22 price less $18 incremental cost), which yields a total profit of $40,000 for the 10,000 additional units.

Direct materials	$ 8.00
Direct labor	7.00
Variable overhead (given)	3.00
Total incremental cost	$18.00

2. For this make or buy decision, the analysis must not include the $13 nonincremental overhead per unit ($30 − $17). When only the $17 incremental overhead is included, the relevant unit cost of manufacturing the part is shown in the following table. It would be better to continue buying the part for $40 instead of making it for $43.

Direct materials	$11.00
Direct labor	15.00
Variable overhead	17.00
Total incremental cost	$43.00

3. The goal of this scrap or rework decision is to identify the alternative that produces the greatest net benefit to the company. To compare the alternatives, we determine the net cost of obtaining 500 marketable units as follows:

Incremental Cost to Produce 500 Marketable Units	Sell As Is	Melt and Recycle	Rework Units
Direct materials			
New materials	$ 6,000	$6,000	
Recycled metal materials		(4,800)	
Net materials cost		1,200	
Melting costs		400	
Total direct materials cost	6,000	1,600	
Direct labor	5,000	5,000	$1,500
Incremental overhead	3,200	3,200	1,750
Cost to produce 500 marketable units	14,200	9,800	3,250
Less proceeds of selling defects as scrap	(2,500)		
Opportunity costs*			5,800
Net cost	$11,700	$9,800	$9,050

* The $5,800 opportunity cost is the lost contribution margin from not being able to produce and sell 500 units because of reworking, computed as ($40 − [$14,200/500 units]) × 500 units.

The incremental cost of 500 marketable parts is smallest if the defects are reworked.

Summary

C1 Describe the importance of relevant costs for short-term decisions. A company must rely on relevant costs pertaining to alternative courses of action rather than historical costs. Out-of-pocket expenses and opportunity costs are relevant because these are avoidable; sunk costs are irrelevant because they result from past decisions and are therefore unavoidable. Managers must also consider the relevant benefits associated with alternative decisions.

A1 Evaluate short-term managerial decisions using relevant costs. Relevant costs are useful in making decisions such as to accept additional business, make or buy, and sell as is or process further. For example, the relevant factors in deciding whether to produce and sell additional units of product are incremental costs and incremental revenues from the additional volume.

A2 Determine product selling price based on total costs. Product selling price is estimated using total production and nonproduction costs plus a markup. Price is set to yield management's desired profit for the company.

P1 Identify relevant costs and apply them to managerial decisions. Several illustrations apply relevant costs to managerial decisions, such as whether to accept additional business; make or buy; scrap or rework products; sell products or process them further; or eliminate a segment and how to select the best sales mix.

Guidance Answer to Decision Maker

Partner You should identify the differences between existing clients and this potential client. A key difference is that the restaurant business has additional inventory components (groceries, vegetables, meats, etc.) and is likely to have a higher proportion of depreciable assets. These differences imply that the partner must spend more hours auditing the records and understanding the business, regulations, and standards that pertain to the restaurant business. Such differences suggest that the partner must use a different "formula" for quoting a price to this potential client vis-à-vis current clients.

Key Terms

Avoidable expense
Incremental cost
Markup
Relevant benefits
Total cost method
Unavoidable expense

Multiple Choice Quiz

Answers at end of chapter

1. A company inadvertently produced 3,000 defective MP3 players. The players cost $12 each to produce. A recycler offers to purchase the defective players as they are for $8 each. The production manager reports that the defects can be corrected for $10 each, enabling them to be sold at their regular market price of $19 each. The company should:
   a. Correct the defect and sell them at the regular price.
   b. Sell the players to the recycler for $8 each.
   c. Sell 2,000 to the recycler and repair the rest.
   d. Sell 1,000 to the recycler and repair the rest.
   e. Throw the players away.
2. A company's productive capacity is limited to 480,000 machine hours. Product X requires 10 machine hours to produce; Product Y requires 2 machine hours to produce. Product X sells for $32 per unit and has variable costs of $12 per unit; Product Y sells for $24 per unit and has variable costs of $10 per unit. Assuming that the company can sell as many of either product as it produces, it should:
   a. Produce X and Y in the ratio of 57% and 43%.
   b. Produce X and Y in the ratio of 83% X and 17% Y.
   c. Produce equal amounts of Product X and Product Y.
   d. Produce only Product X.
   e. Produce only Product Y.
3. A company receives a special one-time order for 3,000 units of its product at $15 per unit. The company has excess capacity and it currently produces and sells the units at $20 each to its regular customers. Production costs are $13.50 per unit, which includes $9 of variable costs. To produce the special order, the company must incur additional fixed costs of $5,000. Should the company accept the special order?
   a. Yes, because incremental revenue exceeds incremental costs.
   b. No, because incremental costs exceed incremental revenue.
   c. No, because the units are being sold for $5 less than the regular price.
   d. Yes, because incremental costs exceed incremental revenue.
   e. No, because incremental costs exceed $15 per unit when total costs are considered.
4. A cost that cannot be changed because it arises from a past decision and is irrelevant to future decisions is
   a. An uncontrollable cost.
   b. An out-of-pocket cost.
   c. A sunk cost.
   d. An opportunity cost.
   e. An incremental cost.
5. The potential benefit of one alternative that is lost by choosing another is known as
   a. An alternative cost.
   b. A sunk cost.
   c. A differential cost.
   d. An opportunity cost.
   e. An out-of-pocket cost.

Icon denotes assignments that involve decision making.

Discussion Questions

1. Identify the five steps involved in the managerial decision-making process.
2. Is nonfinancial information ever useful in managerial decision making?
3. What is a relevant cost? Identify the two types of relevant costs.
4. Why are sunk costs irrelevant in deciding whether to sell a product in its present condition or to make it into a new product through additional processing?
5. Identify some qualitative factors that should be considered when making managerial decisions.
6. **Google** has many types of costs. What is an out-of-pocket cost? What is an opportunity cost? Are opportunity costs recorded in the accounting records?

GOOGLE

7. **Samsung** must confront sunk costs. Why are sunk costs irrelevant in deciding whether to sell a product in its present

Samsung

condition or to make it into a new product through additional processing?

8. Identify the incremental costs incurred by **Apple** for shipping one additional iPod from a warehouse to a retail store along with the store's normal order of 75 iPods. **APPLE**

9. **Apple** is considering eliminating one of its stores in a large U.S. city. What are some factors that it should consider in making this decision? **APPLE**

10. Assume that **Samsung** manufactures and sells 60,000 units of a product at $11,000 per unit in domestic markets. It costs $6,000 per unit to manufacture ($4,000 variable cost per unit, $2,000 fixed cost per unit). Can you describe a situation under which the company is willing to sell an additional 8,000 units of the product in an international market at $5,000 per unit? **Samsung**

connect

QUICK STUDY

QS 23-1
Identification of relevant costs
P1

Helix Company has been approached by a new customer to provide 2,000 units of its regular product at a special price of $6 per unit. The regular selling price of the product is $8 per unit. Helix is operating at 75% of its capacity of 10,000 units. Identify whether the following costs are relevant to Helix's decision as to whether to accept the order at the special selling price. No additional fixed manufacturing overhead will be incurred because of this order. The only additional selling expense on this order will be a $0.50 per unit shipping cost. There will be no additional administrative expenses because of this order. Place an X in the appropriate column to identify whether the cost is relevant or irrelevant to accepting this order.

Item	Relevant	Not relevant
a. Selling price of $6.00 per unit	______	______
b. Direct materials cost of $1.00 per unit	______	______
c. Direct labor of $2.00 per unit	______	______
d. Variable manufacturing overhead of $1.50 per unit	______	______
e. Fixed manufacturing overhead of $0.75 per unit	______	______
f. Regular selling expenses of $1.25 per unit	______	______
g. Additional selling expenses of $0.50 per unit	______	______
h. Administrative expenses of $0.60 per unit	______	______

QS 23-2
Analysis of relevant costs A1

Refer to the data in QS 23-1. Based on financial considerations alone, should Helix accept this order at the special price? Explain.

QS 23-3
Identification of relevant nonfinancial factors P1

Refer to QS 23-1 and QS 23-2. What nonfinancial factors should Helix consider before accepting this order? Explain.

QS 23-4
Sell or process
P1 A1

Garcia Company has 10,000 units of its product that were produced last year at a total cost of $150,000. The units were damaged in a rainstorm because the warehouse where they were stored developed a leak in the roof. Garcia can sell the units as is for $2 each or it can repair the units at a total cost of $18,000 and then sell them for $5 each. Should Garcia sell the units as is or repair them and then sell them? Explain.

QS 23-5
Relevant costs
C1

Label each of the following statements as either true ("T") or false ("F").

1. Relevant costs are also known as unavoidable costs.
2. Incremental costs are also known as differential costs.
3. An out-of-pocket cost requires a current and/or future outlay of cash.
4. An opportunity cost is the potential benefit that is lost by taking a specific action when two or more alternative choices are available.
5. A sunk cost will change with a future course of action.

QS 23-6
Decision to accept additional business A1

Radar Company sells bikes for $300 each. The company currently sells 3,750 bikes per year and could make as many as 5,000 bikes per year. The bikes cost $225 each to make; $150 in variable costs per bike and $75 of fixed costs per bike. Radar received an offer from a potential customer who wants to buy 750 bikes for $250 each. Incremental fixed costs to make this order are $50,000. No other costs will change if this order is accepted. Compute Radar's additional income (ignore taxes) if it accepts this order.

QS 23-7
Make or buy
A1

Kando Company incurs a $9 per unit cost for Product A, which it currently manufactures and sells for $13.50 per unit. Instead of manufacturing and selling this product, the company can purchase Product B for $5 per unit and sell it for $12 per unit. If it does so, unit sales would remain unchanged and $5 of the $9 per unit costs assigned to Product A would be eliminated. Should the company continue to manufacture Product A or purchase Product B for resale?

QS 23-8
Make or buy
A1

Xia Co. currently buys a component part for $5 per unit. Xia believes that making the part would require $2.25 per unit of direct materials and $1.00 per unit of direct labor. Xia allocates overhead using a predetermined overhead rate of 200% of direct labor cost. Xia estimates an incremental overhead rate of $0.75 per unit to make the part. Should Xia make or buy the part?

QS 23-9
Scrap or rework
A1

Signal mistakenly produced 1,000 defective cell phones. The phones cost $60 each to produce. A salvage company will buy the defective phones as they are for $30 each. It would cost Signal $80 per phone to rework the phones. If the phones are reworked, Signal could sell them for $120 each. Assume there is no opportunity cost associated with reworking the phones. Compute the incremental net income from reworking the phones.

QS 23-10
Sell or process further
A1

Holmes Company produces a product that can either be sold as is or processed further. Holmes has already spent $50,000 to produce 1,250 units that can be sold now for $67,500 to another manufacturer. Alternatively, Holmes can process the units further at an incremental cost of $250 per unit. If Holmes processes further, the units can be sold for $375 each. Compute the incremental income if Holmes processes further.

QS 23-11
Sell or process further A1

A company has already incurred $5,000 of costs in producing 6,000 units of Product XY. Product XY can be sold as is for $15 per unit. Instead, the company could incur further processing costs of $8 per unit and sell the resulting product for $21 per unit. Should the company sell Product XY as is or process it further?

QS 23-12
Selection of sales mix
A1

Excel Memory Company can sell all units of computer memory X and Y that it can produce, but it has limited production capacity. It can produce two units of X per hour *or* three units of Y per hour, and it has 4,000 production hours available. Contribution margin is $5 for Product X and $4 for Product Y. What is the most profitable sales mix for this company?

QS 23-13
Segment elimination
A1

A guitar manufacturer is considering eliminating its electric guitar division because its $76,000 expenses are higher than its $72,000 sales. The company reports the following expenses for this division. Should the division be eliminated?

	Avoidable Expenses	Unavoidable Expenses
Cost of goods sold	$56,000	
Direct expenses	9,250	$1,250
Indirect expenses	470	1,600
Service department costs	6,000	1,430

QS 23-14
Segment elimination
A1

A division of a large company reports the information shown below for a recent year. Variable costs and direct fixed costs are avoidable, and 40% of the indirect fixed costs are avoidable. Based on this information, should the division be eliminated?

	Total
Sales	$200,000
Variable costs..........	145,000
Fixed costs	
Direct..............	30,000
Indirect.............	50,000
Operating loss	$ (25,000)

QS 23-15
Keep or replace decision
A1

Rory Company has a machine with a book value of $75,000 and a remaining five-year useful life. A new machine is available at a cost of $112,500, and Rory can also receive $60,000 for trading in its old machine. The new machine will reduce variable manufacturing costs by $13,000 per year over its five-year useful life. Should the machine be replaced?

connect

EXERCISES

Exercise 23-1
Relevant costs
C1

Fill in each of the blanks below with the correct term.

1. A ______ arises from a past decision and cannot be avoided or changed; it is irrelevant to future decisions.
2. ______ refer to the incremental revenue generated from taking one particular action over another.
3. Relevant costs are also known as ______.
4. An ______ requires a future outlay of cash and is relevant for current and future decision making.
5. An ______ is the potential benefit lost by taking a specific action when two or more alternative choices are available.

Exercise 23-2
Accept new business or not
A1

Farrow Co. expects to sell 150,000 units of its product in the next period with the following results.

Sales (150,000 units)	$2,250,000
Costs and expenses	
Direct materials	300,000
Direct labor	600,000
Overhead	150,000
Selling expenses	225,000
Administrative expenses	385,500
Total costs and expenses	1,660,500
Net income	$ 589,500

The company has an opportunity to sell 15,000 additional units at $12 per unit. The additional sales would not affect its current expected sales. Direct materials and labor costs per unit would be the same for the additional units as they are for the regular units. However, the additional volume would create the following incremental costs: (1) total overhead would increase by 15% and (2) administrative expenses would increase by $64,500. Prepare an analysis to determine whether the company should accept or reject the offer to sell additional units at the reduced price of $12 per unit.

Check Income increase, $3,000

Exercise 23-3
Accept new business or not
A1

Goshford Company produces a single product and has capacity to produce 100,000 units per month. Costs to produce its current sales of 80,000 units follow. The regular selling price of the product is $100 per unit. Management is approached by a new customer who wants to purchase 20,000 units of the product for $75 per unit. If the order is accepted, there will be no additional fixed manufacturing overhead, and no additional fixed selling and administrative expenses. The customer is not in the company's regular selling territory, so there will be a $5 per unit shipping expense in addition to the regular variable selling and administrative expenses.

	Per Unit	Costs at 80,000 Units
Direct materials	$12.50	$1,000,000
Direct labor	15.00	1,200,000
Variable manufacturing overhead	10.00	800,000
Fixed manufacturing overhead	17.50	1,400,000
Variable selling and administrative expenses	14.00	1,120,000
Fixed selling and administrative expenses	13.00	1,040,000
Totals	$82.00	$6,560,000

1. Determine whether management should accept or reject the new business.
2. What nonfinancial factors should management consider when deciding whether to take this order?

Check (1) Additional volume effect on net income, $370,000

Exercise 23-4
Make or buy decision
A1

Check $9,500 increased costs to buy

Gilberto Company currently manufactures 65,000 units per year of one of its crucial parts. Variable costs are $1.95 per unit, fixed costs related to making this part are $75,000 per year, and allocated fixed costs are $62,000 per year. Allocated fixed costs are unavoidable whether the company makes or buys the part. Gilberto is considering buying the part from a supplier for a quoted price of $3.25 per unit guaranteed for a three-year period. Should the company continue to manufacture the part, or should it buy the part from the outside supplier? Support your answer with analyses.

Exercise 23-5
Make or buy
A1

Check Increased cost to make, $3,000

Gelb Company currently manufactures 40,000 units per year of a key component for its manufacturing process. Variable costs are $1.95 per unit, fixed costs related to making this component are $65,000 per year, and allocated fixed costs are $58,500 per year. The allocated fixed costs are unavoidable whether the company makes or buys this component. The company is considering buying this component from a supplier for $3.50 per unit. Should it continue to manufacture the component, or should it buy this component from the outside supplier? Support your decision with analysis of the data provided.

Exercise 23-6
Scrap or rework
A1

A company must decide between scrapping or reworking units that do not pass inspection. The company has 22,000 defective units that cost $6 per unit to manufacture. The units can be sold as is for $2.50 each, or they can be reworked for $4.50 each and then sold for the full price of $8.50 each. If the units are sold as is, the company will be able to build 22,000 replacement units at a cost of $6 each, and sell them at the full price of $8.50 each. (1) What is the incremental income from selling the units as scrap? (2) What is the incremental income from reworking and selling the units? (3) Should the company sell the units as scrap or rework them?

Exercise 23-7
Scrap or rework A1

Check Incremental net income of reworking, $(6,000)

Varto Company has 7,000 units of its sole product in inventory that it produced last year at a cost of $22 each. This year's model is superior to last year's and the 7,000 units cannot be sold at last year's regular selling price of $35 each. Varto has two alternatives for these items: (1) they can be sold to a wholesaler for $8 each, or (2) they can be reworked at a cost of $125,000 and then sold for $25 each. Prepare an analysis to determine whether Varto should sell the products as is or rework them and then sell them.

Exercise 23-8
Sell or process further
A1

Cobe Company has already manufactured 28,000 units of Product A at a cost of $28 per unit. The 28,000 units can be sold at this stage for $700,000. Alternatively, the units can be further processed at a $420,000 total additional cost and be converted into 5,600 units of Product B and 11,200 units of Product C. Per unit selling price for Product B is $105 and for Product C is $70. Prepare an analysis that shows whether the 28,000 units of Product A should be processed further or not.

Exercise 23-9
Sales mix determination and analysis
A1

Colt Company owns a machine that can produce two specialized products. Production time for Product TLX is two units per hour and for Product MTV is five units per hour. The machine's capacity is 2,750 hours per year. Both products are sold to a single customer who has agreed to buy all of the company's output up to a maximum of 4,700 units of Product TLX and 2,500 units of Product MTV. Selling prices and variable costs per unit to produce the products follow. Determine (1) the company's most profitable sales mix and (2) the contribution margin that results from that sales mix.

	Product TLX	Product MTV
Selling price per unit	$15.00	$9.50
Variable costs per unit	4.80	5.50

Check (2) $55,940

Exercise 23-10
Analysis of income effects from eliminating departments
A1

Suresh Co. expects its five departments to yield the following income for next year.

	A	B	C	D	E	F	G
1		Dept. M	Dept. N	Dept. O	Dept. P	Dept. T	Total
2	Sales	$63,000	$35,000	$56,000	$42,000	$ 28,000	$224,000
3	Expenses						
4	Avoidable	9,800	36,400	22,400	14,000	37,800	120,400
5	Unavoidable	51,800	12,600	4,200	29,400	9,800	107,800
6	Total expenses	61,600	49,000	26,600	43,400	47,600	228,200
7	Net income (loss)	$ 1,400	$(14,000)	$29,400	$(1,400)	$ (19,600)	$ (4,200)
8							

Recompute and prepare the departmental income statements (including a combined total column) for the company under each of the following separate scenarios: Management (1) eliminates departments with expected net losses, and (2) eliminates departments with sales dollars that are less than avoidable expenses. Explain your answers to parts 1 and 2.

Check Total income (loss) (1) $(21,000), (2) $7,000

Exercise 23-11
Sales mix
A1

Childress Company produces three products, K1, S5, and G9. Each product uses the same type of direct material. K1 uses 4 pounds of the material, S5 uses 3 pounds of the material, and G9 uses 6 pounds of the material. Demand for all products is strong, but only 50,000 pounds of material are available. Information about the selling price per unit and variable cost per unit of each product follows. Orders for which product should be produced and filled first, then second, and then third? Support your answer.

	K1	S5	G9
Selling price	$160	$112	$210
Variable costs	96	85	144

Check K1 contribution margin per pound, $16

Exercise 23-12
Keep or replace
A1

Xinhong Company is considering replacing one of its manufacturing machines. The machine has a book value of $45,000 and a remaining useful life of 5 years, at which time its salvage value will be zero. It has a current market value of $52,000. Variable manufacturing costs are $36,000 per year for this machine. Information on two alternative replacement machines follows. Should Xinhong keep or replace its manufacturing machine? If the machine should be replaced, which alternative new machine should Xinhong purchase?

	Alternative A	Alternative B
Cost	$115,000	$125,000
Variable manufacturing costs per year	19,000	15,000

Exercise 23-13
Income analysis of eliminating departments
A1

Marinette Company makes several products, including canoes. The company has been experiencing losses from its canoe segment and is considering dropping that product line. The following information is available regarding its canoe segment. Should management discontinue the manufacturing of canoes? Support your decision.

MARINETTE COMPANY Income Statement—Canoe Segment		
Sales		$2,000,000
Variable costs		
Direct materials	$450,000	
Direct labor	500,000	
Variable overhead	300,000	
Variable selling and administrative	200,000	
Total variable costs		1,450,000
Contribution margin		550,000
Fixed costs		
Direct	375,000	
Indirect	300,000	
Total fixed costs		675,000
Net income		$ (125,000)

Check Income impact if canoe segment dropped, $(175,000)

connect

PROBLEM SET A

Problem 23-1A
Analysis of income effects of additional business
A1

Jones Products manufactures and sells to wholesalers approximately 400,000 packages per year of underwater markers at $6 per package. Annual costs for the production and sale of this quantity are shown in the table.

Direct materials	$ 576,000
Direct labor	144,000
Overhead	320,000
Selling expenses	150,000
Administrative expenses	100,000
Total costs and expenses	$1,290,000

A new wholesaler has offered to buy 50,000 packages for $5.20 each. These markers would be marketed under the wholesaler's name and would not affect Jones Products's sales through its normal channels. A study of the costs of this additional business reveals the following:

- Direct materials costs are 100% variable.
- Per unit direct labor costs for the additional units would be 50% higher than normal because their production would require overtime pay at 1½ times the usual labor rate.
- Twenty-five percent of the normal annual overhead costs are fixed at any production level from 350,000 to 500,000 units. The remaining 75% of the annual overhead cost is variable with volume.
- Accepting the new business would involve no additional selling expenses.
- Accepting the new business would increase administrative expenses by a $5,000 fixed amount.

Required

Prepare a three-column comparative income statement that shows the following:

1. Annual operating income without the special order (column 1).
2. Annual operating income received from the new business only (column 2).
3. Combined annual operating income from normal business and the new business (column 3).

Check Operating income: (1) $1,110,000 (2) $126,000

Problem 23-2A
Analysis of income effects of additional business
P1 A1

Calla Company produces skateboards that sell for $50 per unit. The company currently has the capacity to produce 90,000 skateboards per year, but is selling 80,000 skateboards per year. Annual costs for 80,000 skateboards follow.

Direct materials	$ 800,000
Direct labor	640,000
Overhead	960,000
Selling expenses	560,000
Administrative expenses	480,000
Total costs and expenses	$3,440,000

A new retail store has offered to buy 10,000 of its skateboards for $45 per unit. The store is in a different market from Calla's regular customers and would not affect regular sales. A study of its costs in anticipation of this additional business reveals the following:

- Direct materials and direct labor are 100% variable.
- Thirty percent of overhead is fixed at any production level from 80,000 units to 90,000 units; the remaining 70% of annual overhead costs are variable with respect to volume.
- Selling expenses are 60% variable with respect to number of units sold, and the other 40% of selling expenses are fixed.
- There will be an additional $2 per unit selling expense for this order.
- Administrative expenses would increase by a $1,000 fixed amount.

Required

1. Prepare a three-column comparative income statement that reports the following:
   a. Annual income without the special order.
   b. Annual income from the special order.
   c. Combined annual income from normal business and the new business.
2. Should Calla accept this order? What nonfinancial factors should Calla consider? Explain.

Check (1*b*) Added income from order, $123,000

Analysis Component

3. Assume that the new customer wants to buy 15,000 units instead of 10,000 units—it will only buy 15,000 units or none and will not take a partial order. Without any computations, how does this change your answer for part 2?

Problem 23-3A
Make or buy
P1 A1

Haver Company currently produces component RX5 for its sole product. The current cost per unit to manufacture the required 50,000 units of RX5 follows.

Direct materials	$ 5.00
Direct labor	8.00
Overhead	9.00
Total cost per unit	$22.00

Direct materials and direct labor are 100% variable. Overhead is 80% fixed. An outside supplier has offered to supply the 50,000 units of RX5 for $18.00 per unit.

Required

1. Determine whether the company should make or buy the RX5.
2. What factors besides cost must management consider when deciding whether to make or buy RX5?

Check (1) Incremental cost to make RX5, $740,000

Problem 23-4A
Sell or process
P1 A1

Harold Manufacturing produces denim clothing. This year, it produced 5,000 denim jackets at a manufacturing cost of $45 each. These jackets were damaged in the warehouse during storage. Management investigated the matter and identified three alternatives for these jackets.

1. Jackets can be sold to a secondhand clothing shop for $6 each.
2. Jackets can be disassembled at a cost of $32,000 and sold to a recycler for $12 each.
3. Jackets can be reworked and turned into good jackets. However, with the damage, management estimates it will be able to assemble the good parts of the 5,000 jackets into only 3,000 jackets. The remaining pieces of fabric will be discarded. The cost of reworking the jackets will be $102,000, but the jackets can then be sold for their regular price of $45 each.

Required

Which alternative should Harold choose? Show analysis for each alternative.

Check Incremental income for alternative 2, $28,000

Problem 23-5A
Analysis of sales mix strategies
A1

Edgerron Company is able to produce two products, G and B, with the same machine in its factory. The following information is available.

	Product G	Product B
Selling price per unit	$120	$160
Variable costs per unit	40	90
Contribution margin per unit	$ 80	$ 70
Machine hours to produce 1 unit	0.4 hours	1.0 hours
Maximum unit sales per month	600 units	200 units

The company presently operates the machine for a single eight-hour shift for 22 working days each month. Management is thinking about operating the machine for two shifts, which will increase its productivity by another eight hours per day for 22 days per month. This change would require $15,000 additional fixed costs per month.

Required

1. Determine the contribution margin per machine hour that each product generates.
2. How many units of Product G and Product B should the company produce if it continues to operate with only one shift? How much total contribution margin does this mix produce each month?
3. If the company adds another shift, how many units of Product G and Product B should it produce? How much total contribution margin would this mix produce each month? Should the company add the new shift? Explain.
4. Suppose that the company determines that it can increase Product G's maximum sales to 700 units per month by spending $12,000 per month in marketing efforts. Should the company pursue this strategy and the double shift? Explain.

Check Units of Product G: (2) 440 (3) 600

Problem 23-6A
Analysis of possible elimination of a department
A1

Elegant Decor Company's management is trying to decide whether to eliminate Department 200, which has produced losses or low profits for several years. The company's 2015 departmental income statements show the following.

ELEGANT DECOR COMPANY
Departmental Income Statements
For Year Ended December 31, 2015

	Dept. 100	Dept. 200	Combined
Sales	$436,000	$290,000	$726,000
Cost of goods sold	262,000	207,000	469,000
Gross profit	174,000	83,000	257,000
Operating expenses			
Direct expenses			
Advertising	17,000	12,000	29,000
Store supplies used	4,000	3,800	7,800
Depreciation—Store equipment	5,000	3,300	8,300
Total direct expenses	26,000	19,100	45,100
Allocated expenses			
Sales salaries	65,000	39,000	104,000
Rent expense	9,440	4,720	14,160
Bad debts expense	9,900	8,100	18,000
Office salary	18,720	12,480	31,200
Insurance expense	2,000	1,100	3,100
Miscellaneous office expenses	2,400	1,600	4,000
Total allocated expenses	107,460	67,000	174,460
Total expenses	133,460	86,100	219,560
Net income (loss)	$ 40,540	$ (3,100)	$ 37,440

In analyzing whether to eliminate Department 200, management considers the following:

a. The company has one office worker who earns $600 per week, or $31,200 per year, and four salesclerks who each earn $500 per week, or $26,000 per year for each salesclerk.

b. The full salaries of two salesclerks are charged to Department 100. The full salary of one salesclerk is charged to Department 200. The salary of the fourth clerk, who works half-time in both departments, is divided evenly between the two departments.

c. Eliminating Department 200 would avoid the sales salaries and the office salary currently allocated to it. However, management prefers another plan. Two salesclerks have indicated that they will be quitting soon. Management believes that their work can be done by the other two clerks if the one office worker works in sales half-time. Eliminating Department 200 will allow this shift of duties. If this change is implemented, half the office worker's salary would be reported as sales salaries and half would be reported as office salary.

d. The store building is rented under a long-term lease that cannot be changed. Therefore, Department 100 will use the space and equipment currently used by Department 200.

e. Closing Department 200 will eliminate its expenses for advertising, bad debts, and store supplies; 70% of the insurance expense allocated to it to cover its merchandise inventory; and 25% of the miscellaneous office expenses presently allocated to it.

Required

1. Prepare a three-column report that lists items and amounts for (a) the company's total expenses (including cost of goods sold)—in column 1, (b) the expenses that would be eliminated by closing Department 200—in column 2, and (c) the expenses that will continue—in column 3.

2. Prepare a forecasted annual income statement for the company reflecting the elimination of Department 200 assuming that it will not affect Department 100's sales and gross profit. The statement should reflect the reassignment of the office worker to one-half time as a salesclerk.

Check (1) Total expenses: (*a*) $688,560, (*b*) $284,070

(2) Forecasted net income without Department 200, $31,510

Analysis Component

3. Reconcile the company's combined net income with the forecasted net income assuming that Department 200 is eliminated (list both items and amounts). Analyze the reconciliation and explain why you think the department should or should not be eliminated.

PROBLEM SET B

Problem 23-1B
Analysis of income effects of additional business
A1

Windmire Company manufactures and sells to local wholesalers approximately 300,000 units per month at a sales price of $4 per unit. Monthly costs for the production and sale of this quantity follow.

Direct materials	$384,000
Direct labor	96,000
Overhead	288,000
Selling expenses	120,000
Administrative expenses	80,000
Total costs and expenses	$968,000

A new out-of-state distributor has offered to buy 50,000 units next month for $3.44 each. These units would be marketed in other states and would not affect Windmire's sales through its normal channels. A study of the costs of this new business reveals the following:

- Direct materials costs are 100% variable.
- Per unit direct labor costs for the additional units would be 50% higher than normal because their production would require overtime pay at 1½ times their normal rate to meet the distributor's deadline.
- Twenty-five percent of the normal annual overhead costs are fixed at any production level from 250,000 to 400,000 units. The remaining 75% is variable with volume.
- Accepting the new business would involve no additional selling expenses.
- Accepting the new business would increase administrative expenses by a $4,000 fixed amount.

Required

Prepare a three-column comparative income statement that shows the following:

1. Monthly operating income without the special order (column 1).

2. Monthly operating income received from the new business only (column 2).

3. Combined monthly operating income from normal business and the new business (column 3).

Check Operating income: (1) $232,000, (2) $44,000

Problem 23-2B
Analysis of income effects of additional business
P1 A1

Mervin Company produces circuit boards that sell for $8 per unit. It currently has capacity to produce 600,000 circuit boards per year, but is selling 550,000 boards per year. Annual costs for the 550,000 circuit boards follow.

Direct materials	$ 825,000
Direct labor	1,100,000
Overhead	1,375,000
Selling expenses	275,000
Administrative expenses	550,000
Total costs and expenses	$4,125,000

An overseas customer has offered to buy 50,000 circuit boards for $6 per unit. The customer is in a different market from Mervin's regular customers and would not affect regular sales. A study of its costs in anticipation of this additional business reveals the following:

- Direct materials and direct labor are 100% variable.
- Twenty percent of overhead is fixed at any production level from 550,000 units to 600,000 units; the remaining 80% of annual overhead costs are variable with respect to volume.
- Selling expenses are 40% variable with respect to number of units sold, and the other 60% of selling expenses are fixed.
- There will be an additional $0.20 per unit selling expense for this order.
- Administrative expenses would increase by a $700 fixed amount.

Required

1. Prepare a three-column comparative income statement that reports the following:

a. Annual income without the special order.

b. Annual income from the special order.

c. Combined annual income from normal business and the new business.

2. Should management accept the order? What nonfinancial factors should Mervin consider? Explain.

Check (1*b*) Additional income from order, $4,300

Analysis Component

3. Assume that the new customer wants to buy 100,000 units instead of 50,000 units—it will only buy 100,000 units or none and will not take a partial order. Without any computations, how does this change your answer in part 2?

Problem 23-3B
Make or buy
P1 A1

Alto Company currently produces component TH1 for its sole product. The current cost per unit to manufacture its required 400,000 units of TH1 follows.

Direct materials	$1.20
Direct labor	1.50
Overhead...................	6.00
Total cost per unit	$8.70

Direct materials and direct labor are 100% variable. Overhead is 75% fixed. An outside supplier has offered to supply the 400,000 units of TH1 for $4 per unit.

Required

Check (1) Incremental cost to make TH1, $1,680,000

1. Determine whether management should make or buy the TH1.

2. What factors besides cost must management consider when deciding whether to make or buy TH1?

Problem 23-4B
Sell or process
P1 A1

Micron Manufacturing produces electronic equipment. This year, it produced 7,500 oscilloscopes at a manufacturing cost of $300 each. These oscilloscopes were damaged in the warehouse during storage and, while usable, cannot be sold at their regular selling price of $500 each. Management has investigated the matter and has identified three alternatives for these oscilloscopes.

1. They can be sold to a wholesaler for $75 each.

2. They can be disassembled at a cost of $400,000 and the parts sold to a recycler for $130 each.

3. They can be reworked and turned into good units. The cost of reworking the units will be $3,200,000, after which the units can be sold at their regular price of $500 each.

Required

Check Incremental income for alternative 2, $575,000

Which alternative should management pursue? Show analysis for each alternative.

Problem 23-5B
Analysis of sales mix strategies
A1

Sung Company is able to produce two products, R and T, with the same machine in its factory. The following information is available.

	Product R	Product T
Selling price per unit	$60	$80
Variable costs per unit	20	45
Contribution margin per unit	$40	$35
Machine hours to produce 1 unit	0.4 hours	1.0 hours
Maximum unit sales per month	550 units	175 units

The company presently operates the machine for a single eight-hour shift for 22 working days each month. Management is thinking about operating the machine for two shifts, which will increase its productivity by another eight hours per day for 22 days per month. This change would require $3,250 additional fixed costs per month.

Required

1. Determine the contribution margin per machine hour that each product generates.
2. How many units of Product R and Product T should the company produce if it continues to operate with only one shift? How much total contribution margin does this mix produce each month?
3. If the company adds another shift, how many units of Product R and Product T should it produce? How much total contribution margin would this mix produce each month? Should the company add the new shift? Explain.
4. Suppose that the company determines that it can increase Product R's maximum sales to 675 units per month by spending $4,500 per month in marketing efforts. Should the company pursue this strategy and the double shift? Explain.

Check Units of Product R: (2) 440 (3) 550

Problem 23-6B
Analysis of possible elimination of a department
A1

Esme Company's management is trying to decide whether to eliminate Department Z, which has produced low profits or losses for several years. The company's 2015 departmental income statements show the following.

ESME COMPANY
Departmental Income Statements
For Year Ended December 31, 2015

	Dept. A	Dept. Z	Combined
Sales	$700,000	$175,000	$875,000
Cost of goods sold	461,300	125,100	586,400
Gross profit	238,700	49,900	288,600
Operating expenses			
Direct expenses			
Advertising	27,000	3,000	30,000
Store supplies used	5,600	1,400	7,000
Depreciation—Store equipment	14,000	7,000	21,000
Total direct expenses	46,600	11,400	58,000
Allocated expenses			
Sales salaries	70,200	23,400	93,600
Rent expense	22,080	5,520	27,600
Bad debts expense	21,000	4,000	25,000
Office salary	20,800	5,200	26,000
Insurance expense	4,200	1,400	5,600
Miscellaneous office expenses	1,700	2,500	4,200
Total allocated expenses	139,980	42,020	182,000
Total expenses	186,580	53,420	240,000
Net income (loss)	$ 52,120	$ (3,520)	$ 48,600

In analyzing whether to eliminate Department Z, management considers the following items:

a. The company has one office worker who earns $500 per week or $26,000 per year and four salesclerks who each earn $450 per week or $23,400 per year for each salesclerk.

b. The full salaries of three salesclerks are charged to Department A. The full salary of one salesclerk is charged to Department Z.

c. Eliminating Department Z would avoid the sales salaries and the office salary currently allocated to it. However, management prefers another plan. Two salesclerks have indicated that they will be quitting soon. Management believes that their work can be done by the two remaining clerks if the one office worker works in sales half-time. Eliminating Department Z will allow this shift of duties. If this change is implemented, half the office worker's salary would be reported as sales salaries and half would be reported as office salary.

d. The store building is rented under a long-term lease that cannot be changed. Therefore, Department A will use the space and equipment currently used by Department Z.

e. Closing Department Z will eliminate its expenses for advertising, bad debts, and store supplies; 65% of the insurance expense allocated to it to cover its merchandise inventory; and 30% of the miscellaneous office expenses presently allocated to it.

Required

Check (1) Total expenses: (*a*) $826,400, (*b*) $181,960

1. Prepare a three-column report that lists items and amounts for (a) the company's total expenses (including cost of goods sold)—in column 1, (b) the expenses that would be eliminated by closing Department Z—in column 2, and (c) the expenses that will continue—in column 3.

(2) Forecasted net income without Department Z, $55,560

2. Prepare a forecasted annual income statement for the company reflecting the elimination of Department Z assuming that it will not affect Department A's sales and gross profit. The statement should reflect the reassignment of the office worker to one-half time as a salesclerk.

Analysis Component

3. Reconcile the company's combined net income with the forecasted net income assuming that Department Z is eliminated (list both items and amounts). Analyze the reconciliation and explain why you think the department should or should not be eliminated.

SERIAL PROBLEM

Business Solutions

A1

(This serial problem began in Chapter 1 and continues through most of the book. If previous chapter segments were not completed, the serial problem can begin at this point. It is helpful, but not necessary, to use the Working Papers that accompany the book.)

SP 23 Santana Rey has found that her line of computer desks and chairs has become very popular and she is finding it hard to keep up with demand. She knows that she cannot fill all of her orders for both items, so she decides she must determine the optimal sales mix given the resources she has available. Information about the desks and chairs follows.

	Desks	Chairs
Selling price per unit	$1,125	$375
Variable costs per unit	500	200
Contribution margin per unit	$ 625	$175
Direct labor hours per unit	5 hours	4 hours
Expected demand for next quarter	175 desks	50 chairs

Santana has determined that she only has 1,015 direct labor hours available for the next quarter and wants to optimize her contribution margin given the limited number of direct labor hours available.

Required

Determine the optimal sales mix and the contribution margin the business will earn at that sales mix.

Beyond the Numbers

REPORTING IN ACTION
P1 C1

APPLE

BTN 23-1 **Apple** currently chooses to buy (mainly from suppliers located in Asia)—rather than make—nearly all of its manufactured products. Assume you have been asked to analyze whether Apple should instead make its products.

Required

1. Provide examples of relevant costs that Apple should consider in this make or buy decision.
2. Provide examples of qualitative (nonfinancial) factors Apple should consider in this decision.

COMPARATIVE ANALYSIS
A1

APPLE
GOOGLE

BTN 23-2 **Apple** and **Google** sell a variety of products, including smartphones and tablet computers. Some products are more profitable than others. Teams of employees in each company make advertising, investment, and product mix decisions. A certain portion of advertising for both companies is on a local basis to a target audience.

Required

1. Contact the local newspaper and ask the approximate cost of ad space (for example, cost of one page or one-half page of advertising) for a company's product or group of products (such as Apple iPads).
2. Estimate how many products this advertisement must sell to justify its cost. Begin by taking the product's sales price advertised for each company and assume a 20% contribution margin.
3. Prepare a half-page memorandum explaining the importance of effective advertising when making a product mix decision. Be prepared to present your ideas in class.

ETHICS CHALLENGE
A1

BTN 23-3 Bert Asiago, a salesperson for Convertco, received an order from a potential new customer for 50,000 units of Convertco's single product at a price $25 below its regular selling price of $65. Asiago knows that Convertco has the capacity to produce this order without affecting regular sales. He has spoken to Convertco's controller, Bia Morgan, who has informed Asiago that at the $40 selling price, Convertco will not be covering its variable costs of $42 for the product, and she recommends the order not be accepted. Asiago knows that variable costs include his sales commission of $4 per unit. If he accepts a $2 per unit commission, the sale will produce a contribution margin of zero. Asiago is eager to get the new customer because he believes that this could lead to the new customer becoming a regular customer.

Required

1. Determine the contribution margin per unit on the order as determined by the controller.
2. Determine the contribution margin per unit on the order as determined by Asiago if he takes the lower commission.
3. Do you recommend Convertco accept the special order? What factors must management consider?

COMMUNICATING IN PRACTICE
P1

BTN 23-4 Assume that you work for Greeble's Department Store, and your manager requests that you outline the pros and cons of discontinuing its hardware department. That department appears to be generating losses, and your manager believes that discontinuing it will increase overall store profits.

Required

Prepare a memorandum to your manager outlining what Greeble's management should consider when trying to decide whether to discontinue its hardware department.

TAKING IT TO THE NET

A1

BTN 23-5 Many companies must determine whether to internally produce their component parts or to outsource them. Further, some companies now outsource key components or business processes to international providers. Access the website sourcingmag.com and review the available information on business process outsourcing (click on "What is BPO?").

Required

1. According to this website, what is business process outsourcing?
2. What types of processes are commonly outsourced, according to this website?
3. What are some of the benefits of business process outsourcing?

TEAMWORK IN ACTION

P1

BTN 23-6 Break into teams and identify costs that an airline such as **Delta Airlines** would incur on a flight from Green Bay to Minneapolis. (1) Identify the individual costs as variable or fixed. (2) Assume that Delta is trying to decide whether to drop this flight because it seems to be unprofitable. Determine which costs are likely to be saved if the flight is dropped. Set up your answer in the following format.

Cost	Variable or Fixed	Cost Saved if Flight Is Dropped	Rationale

ENTREPRENEURIAL DECISION

A1

BTN 23-7 Charlie Fyffe of **Charlie's Brownies** makes brownies and other sweets. Charlie must decide on the best sales mix for his products. Assume that his company has a capacity of 400 hours of processing time available each month and it makes two types of brownies, Deluxe and Premium. Information on these foods follows.

	Deluxe	Premium
Selling price per carton	$70	$90
Variable costs per carton	$40	$50
Processing minutes per carton	60 minutes	120 minutes

Required

1. Assume the markets for both cartons of brownies are unlimited. How many Deluxe cartons and how many Premium cartons should the company make each month? Explain. How much total contribution margin does this mix produce each month?
2. Assume the market for the Deluxe carton is limited to 60 cartons per month, with no market limit for the Premium cartons. How many Deluxe cartons and how many Premium cartons should the company make each month? Explain. How much total contribution margin does this mix produce each month?

HITTING THE ROAD

P1

BTN 23-8 Restaurants often add and remove menu items. Visit a restaurant and identify a new food item. Make a list of costs that the restaurant must consider when deciding whether to add that new item. Also, make a list of nonfinancial factors that the restaurant must consider when adding that item.

GLOBAL DECISION

C1

Samsung

BTN 23-9 Access **Samsung**'s 2013 Corporate Sustainability Report, from its website www.samsung.com. Identify and read the section "Social Responsibility: Making Contributions Around the Globe."

Required

Samsung's 2013 Corporate Sustainability Report notes that the company spent 245 billion Korean won in 2012 for programs devoted to better health and education for children. Why would a company like Samsung pursue such a costly program?

ANSWERS TO MULTIPLE CHOICE QUIZ

1. a; Reworking provides incremental revenue of \$11 per unit (\$19 − \$8); it costs \$10 to rework them. The company is better off by \$1 per unit when it reworks these products and sells them at the regular price.

2. e; Product X has a \$2 contribution margin per machine hour [(\$32 − \$12)/10 MH]; Product Y has a \$7 contribution margin per machine hour [(\$24 − \$10)/2 MH]. It should produce as much of Product Y as possible.

3. a; Total revenue from the special order = 3,000 units × \$15 per unit = \$45,000; total costs for the special order = (3,000 units × \$9 per unit) + \$5,000 = \$32,000. Net income from the special order = \$45,000 − \$32,000 = \$13,000. Thus, yes, it should accept the order.

4. c

5. d

chapter 24

Capital Budgeting and Investment Analysis

Chapter Preview

NONPRESENT VALUE METHODS

P1 Payback period

P2 Accounting rate of return

PRESENT VALUE METHODS

P3 Net present value

P4 Internal rate of return

COMPARISON AND ANALYSIS

Comparison of methods

A1 Break-even time

Learning Objectives

ANALYTICAL

A1 Analyze a capital investment project using break-even time.

PROCEDURAL

P1 Compute payback period and describe its use.

P2 Compute accounting rate of return and explain its use.

P3 Compute net present value and describe its use.

P4 Compute internal rate of return and explain its use.

Courtesy of Adafruit Industries

High Energy

"We put our heart and soul into it . . . every day"

—Limor Fried

NEW YORK—Studying computer science and electrical engineering, Limor Fried used the skills she learned in class to make electrical devices like MP3 players, synthesizers, and toys. Thinking others might like her designs, she posted instructions for her projects on her website. Inundated with requests to sell her designs as project kits, Limor invested her tuition money in a large quantity of parts and began designing. The result is her company **Adafruit Industries**, which now boasts sales of over $22 million per year.

Adafruit started small, with one employee (Limor) operating out of her dorm room. "The company took off," says Limor, "because we sold learning projects that you would actually use or want to keep." Projects like MintyBoost (a mobile-device charger assembled from an Altoids tin and electronic components), a set of bicycle lights that spell out words and draw symbols as you ride, and a mini-electric guitar are both fun to make and fun to use. "The idea is that people will learn a little about electronics by assembling the kits, and, in the end have a handmade good that is also useful."

Limor uses accounting information to make business decisions. She priced her kits to yield about a $10 contribution margin per kit. These profits enabled her to hire more employees and expand her business. Focusing on contribution margins enables Adafruit to add more-profitable products and eliminate less-profitable products. In addition to profits, Limor must consider qualitative factors in her decisions, and she focuses on customer satisfaction. "Everything is designed to be painless," says Ada. "I spend a lot of time thinking about how customers will interact with products, and we always give good documentation."

In addition to short-term decisions involving sales mix, Limor had to confront decisions regarding capital investments. Recently, the company moved from a small loft into a 12,000-square-foot industrial space. The industrial-grade power supply in this new space enabled investments in large equipment, enabling faster production. Net present value calculations, based on the cost of this new equipment and the future cash flows from additional sales, support such decisions. "It's a new chapter in our business," exclaims Limor. "I think we can quadruple our current size."

For Limor, though, business is not just about making more profit. She is passionate about education, and in particular about encouraging young women to pursue engineering and related technical fields. "It is possible to help people all while running a business," she says. Limor encourages young entrepreneurs to "go for it." "Entrepreneurship is cool," says Limor. "It's about freedom, the ability to do great work with great people for great customers. It's hard to do this if you are working for someone else."

Sources: *Adafruit Industries website,* January 2015; *Entrepreneur.com,* December 18, 2012; *New York Times,* November 15, 2007

Capital budgeting is the process of analyzing alternative long-term investments and deciding which assets to acquire or sell. Common examples of capital budgeting decisions include buying a machine or a building or acquiring an entire company. An objective for these decisions is to earn a satisfactory return on investment.

Capital budgeting decisions require careful analysis because they are usually the most difficult and risky decisions that managers make. These decisions are difficult because they require predicting events that will not occur until well into the future. Many of these predictions are tentative and potentially unreliable. Specifically, a capital budgeting decision is risky because (1) the outcome is uncertain, (2) large amounts of money are usually involved, (3) the investment involves a long-term commitment, and (4) the decision could be difficult or impossible to reverse, no matter how poor it turns out to be. Risk is especially high for investments in technology due to innovations and uncertainty.

Managers use several methods to evaluate capital budgeting decisions. Nearly all of these methods involve predicting future cash inflows and cash outflows of proposed investments, assessing the risk of and returns on those cash flows, and then choosing the investments to make. Management often restates future cash flows in terms of their present value. This approach applies the time value of money: A dollar today is worth more than a dollar tomorrow. Similarly, a dollar tomorrow is worth less than a dollar today. The process of restating future cash flows in terms of their present value is called *discounting*. The time value of money is important when evaluating capital investments, but managers sometimes apply evaluation methods that ignore present value. This chapter describes four methods for comparing alternative investments.

Point: The nature of capital spending has changed with the business environment. Budgets for information technology have increased from about 25% of corporate capital spending 20 years ago to an estimated 35% today.

METHODS NOT USING TIME VALUE OF MONEY

All investments, whether they involve the purchase of a machine or another long-term asset, are expected to produce net cash flows. *Net cash flow* is cash inflows minus cash outflows. Sometimes managers perform simple analyses of the financial feasibility of an investment's net cash flow without using the time value of money. This section explains two of the most common methods in this category: (1) payback period and (2) accounting rate of return.

Payback Period

P1 Compute payback period and describe its use.

An investment's **payback period (PBP)** is the expected amount of time to recover the initial investment amount. Managers prefer investing in assets with shorter payback periods to reduce the risk of an unprofitable investment over the long run. Acquiring assets with short payback periods reduces a company's risk from potentially inaccurate long-term predictions of future cash flows.

Computing Payback Period with Even Cash Flows To illustrate use of the payback period for an investment with even cash flows, we look at data from FasTrac, a manufacturer of exercise equipment and supplies. (*Even cash flows* are cash flows that are the same each and every year; *uneven cash flows* are cash flows that are not all equal in amount.) FasTrac is considering several different capital investments, one of which is to purchase a machine to use in manufacturing a new product. This machine costs $16,000 and is expected to have an eight-year life with no salvage value. Management predicts this machine will produce 1,000 units of product each year and that the new product will be sold for $30 per unit. Exhibit 24.1 shows the expected net income and expected annual net cash flows for this asset over its life.

Point: Annual net cash flow in Exhibit 24.1 equals net income plus depreciation (a noncash expense).

The amount of net cash flow from the machinery is computed by subtracting expected cash outflows from expected cash inflows. The Expected Net Cash Flow column of Exhibit 24.1 excludes all noncash revenues and expenses. Depreciation is FasTrac's only noncash item. Alternatively, managers can adjust the projected net income for revenue and expense items that do not affect cash flows. For FasTrac, this means taking the $2,100 net income and adding back the $2,000 depreciation, to yield $4,100 of net cash flow.

EXHIBIT 24.1

Cash Flow Analysis

FASTRAC
Cash Flow Analysis—Machinery Investment
January 15, 2015

	Expected Net Income	Expected Net Cash Flow
Annual sales of new product	$30,000	$30,000
Deduct annual expenses		
Cost of materials, labor, and overhead (except depreciation)	15,500	15,500
Depreciation—Machinery	2,000	
Additional selling and administrative expenses	9,500	9,500
Annual pretax income	3,000	
Income taxes (30%)	900	900
Annual net income	$ 2,100	
Annual net cash flow		**$ 4,100**

The formula for computing the payback period of an investment that yields even net cash flows is in Exhibit 24.2.

EXHIBIT 24.2

Payback Period Formula with Even Cash Flows

$$\textbf{Payback period} = \frac{\textbf{Cost of investment}}{\textbf{Annual net cash flow}}$$

The payback period reflects the amount of time for the investment to generate enough net cash flow to return (or pay back) the cash initially invested to purchase it. FasTrac's payback period for this machine is just under four years:

$$\text{Payback period} = \frac{\$16{,}000}{\$4{,}100} = 3.9 \text{ years}$$

The initial investment is fully recovered in 3.9 years, or just before reaching the halfway point of this machine's useful life of eight years.

Example: If an alternative machine (with different technology) yields a payback period of 3.5 years, which one does a manager choose? *Answer:* The alternative (3.5 is less than 3.9).

Decision Insight

e-Payback Health care providers are increasingly using electronic systems to improve their operations. With *e-charting,* doctors' orders and notes are saved electronically. Such systems allow for more personalized care plans, more efficient staffing, and reduced costs. Investments in such systems must be evaluated on the basis of payback periods and other financial measures. ■

Tetra Images/Getty Images

Computing Payback Period with Uneven Cash Flows Computing the payback period in the prior section assumed even net cash flows. What happens if the net cash flows are uneven? In this case, the payback period is computed using the *cumulative total of net cash flows.* The word *cumulative* refers to the addition of each period's net cash flows as we progress through time. To illustrate, consider data for another investment that FasTrac is considering. This machine is predicted to generate uneven net cash flows over the next eight years. The relevant data and payback period computation are shown in Exhibit 24.3.

Year 0 refers to the period of initial investment in which the $16,000 cash outflow occurs at the end of year 0 to acquire the machinery. By the end of year 1, the cumulative net cash flow is reduced to $(13,000), computed as the $(16,000) initial cash outflow plus year 1's $3,000 cash inflow. This process continues throughout the asset's life. The cumulative net cash flow amount changes from negative to positive in year 5. Specifically, at the end of year 4, the cumulative net cash flow is $(1,000). As soon as FasTrac receives net cash inflow of $1,000 during the fifth year,

Example: Find the payback period in Exhibit 24.3 if net cash flows for the first 4 years are: Year 1 = $6,000; Year 2 = $5,000; Year 3 = $4,000; Year 4 = $3,000. *Answer:* 3.33 years

EXHIBIT 24.3

Payback Period Calculation with Uneven Cash Flows

Period*	Expected Net Cash Flows	Cumulative Net Cash Flows
Year 0	$(16,000)	$(16,000)
Year 1	3,000	(13,000)
Year 2	4,000	(9,000)
Year 3	4,000	(5,000)
Year 4	4,000	**(1,000)**
Year 5	**5,000**	**4,000**
Year 6	3,000	7,000
Year 7	2,000	9,000
Year 8	2,000	11,000

Payback occurs between years 4 and 5.

Payback period = 4 years + $1,000/$5,000 of year 5 = 4.2 years

* All cash inflows and outflows occur uniformly during years 1 through 8.

it has fully recovered the $16,000 initial investment. If we assume that cash flows are received uniformly *within* each year, receipt of the $1,000 occurs about one-fifth (0.20) of the way through the fifth year. This is computed as $1,000 divided by year 5's total net cash flow of $5,000, or 0.20. This yields a payback period of 4.2 years, computed as 4 years plus 0.20 of year 5.

Using the Payback Period Companies like short payback periods to increase return and reduce risk. The more quickly a company receives cash, the sooner it is available for other uses and the less time it is at risk of loss. A shorter payback period also improves the company's ability to respond to unanticipated changes and lowers its risk of having to keep an unprofitable investment.

Payback period should never be the only consideration in evaluating investments because it ignores at least three important factors. First, it fails to reflect differences in the timing of net cash flows within the payback period. In Exhibit 24.3, FasTrac's net cash flows in the first five years were $3,000, $4,000, $4,000, $4,000, and $5,000. If another investment had predicted cash flows of $9,000, $3,000, $2,000, $1,800, and $1,000 in these five years, its payback period would also be 4.2 years, but this second alternative could be more desirable because it returns cash more quickly. Second, payback period ignores *all* cash flows after the point where an investment's costs are fully recovered. For example, one investment might pay back its cost in 3 years but stop producing cash after 4 years. A second investment might require 5 years to pay back its cost yet continue to produce net cash flows for another 15 years. A focus on only the payback period would mistakenly lead management to choose the first investment over the second. Third, payback period ignores the time value of money.

NEED-TO-KNOW 24-1

Payback Period

P1

A company is considering purchasing equipment costing $75,000. Future annual net cash flows from this equipment are $30,000, $25,000, $15,000, $10,000, and $5,000. Cash flows occur uniformly during the year. What is this investment's payback period?

Solution

Period	Expected Net Cash Flows	Cumulative Net Cash Flows
Year 0..........	$(75,000)	$(75,000)
Year 1..........	30,000	(45,000)
Year 2..........	25,000	(20,000)
Year 3..........	15,000	(5,000)
Year 4..........	10,000	5,000
Year 5..........	5,000	10,000

Payback period = 3.5 years, computed as 3 + $5,000/$10,000

QC1

Do More: QS 24-1, QS 24-5, E 24-1, E 24-3, E 24-5

Accounting Rate of Return

P2 Compute accounting rate of return and explain its use.

The **accounting rate of return** is the percentage accounting return on annual average investment. It is called an "accounting" return because it is based on net income, rather than on cash flows. It is computed by dividing a project's after-tax net income by the average amount invested in it. To illustrate, we return to FasTrac's $16,000 machinery investment described in

Exhibit 24.1. We first compute (1) the after-tax net income and (2) the average amount invested. The $2,100 after-tax net income is already available from Exhibit 24.1.

If a company uses straight-line depreciation, we can find the average amount invested by using the formula in Exhibit 24.4. Because FasTrac uses straight-line depreciation, its average amount invested for the eight years equals the sum of the book value at the beginning of the asset's investment period and the book value at the end of its investment period, divided by 2, as shown in Exhibit 24.4.

Point: Amount invested includes all costs that must be incurred to get the asset in its location and ready for use.

EXHIBIT 24.4

Computing Average Amount Invested under Straight-Line Depreciation

$$\textbf{Annual average investment (straight-line case only)} = \frac{\textbf{Beginning book value + Ending book value}}{\textbf{2}}$$

$$= \frac{\$16{,}000 + \$0}{2} = \$8{,}000$$

If an investment has a salvage value, the average amount invested when using straight-line depreciation is computed as (Beginning book value + Salvage value)/2.

If a company uses a depreciation method other than straight-line, for example MACRS for tax purposes, the calculation of average book value is more complicated. In this case, the book value of the asset is computed for *each year* of its life. The general formula for the annual average investment is shown in Exhibit 24.5.

EXHIBIT 24.5

General Formula for Average Amount Invested

$$\textbf{Annual average investment (general case)} = \frac{\textbf{Sum of individual years' average book values}}{\textbf{Number of years of the planned investment}}$$

Once we determine the annual after-tax net income and the annual average amount invested, the accounting rate of return is computed as shown in Exhibit 24.6.

EXHIBIT 24.6

Accounting Rate of Return Formula

$$\textbf{Accounting rate of return} = \frac{\textbf{Annual after-tax net income}}{\textbf{Annual average investment}}$$

$$= \frac{\$2{,}100}{\$8{,}000} = 26.25\%$$

FasTrac management must decide whether a 26.25% accounting rate of return is satisfactory. To make this decision, we must factor in the investment's risk. For instance, we cannot say an investment with a 26.25% return is preferred over one with a lower return unless we consider any differences in risk. When comparing investments with similar lives and risk, a company will prefer the investment with the higher accounting rate of return.

Using the Accounting Rate of Return The accounting rate of return should never be the only consideration in evaluating investments because it has at least two important limitations: First, an asset's net income may vary from year to year. In this case, the accounting rate of return will also vary across years, and the project might appear desirable in some years and not in others. Second, the accounting rate of return ignores the time value of money.

NEED-TO-KNOW 24-2

Accounting Rate of Return

P2

The following data relate to a company's decision on whether to purchase a machine:

Cost	$180,000
Salvage value	15,000
Annual after-tax net income	40,000

Assume net cash flows occur uniformly over each year and the company uses straight-line depreciation. What is the machine's accounting rate of return?

QC2

Solution

Annual average investment = ($180,000 + $15,000)/2 = $97,500
Accounting rate of return = $40,000/$97,500 = 41% (rounded)

Do More: QS 24-6, QS 24-7, E 24-7, E 24-8

METHODS USING TIME VALUE OF MONEY

Methods Using Time Value of Money

This section describes two methods that help managers with capital budgeting decisions and that use the time value of money: (1) net present value and (2) internal rate of return. *(To apply these methods, you need a basic understanding of the concept of present value. An expanded explanation of present value concepts is in Appendix B near the end of the book. You can use the present value tables at the end of Appendix B to solve many of this chapter's assignments that use the time value of money.)*

Net Present Value

P3 Compute net present value and describe its use.

Net present value analysis applies the time value of money to future cash inflows and cash outflows so management can evaluate a project's benefits and costs at one point in time. Specifically, **net present value (NPV)** is computed by discounting the future net cash flows from the investment at the project's required rate of return and then subtracting the initial amount invested. A company's required return, often called its *hurdle rate,* is typically its **cost of capital,** which is an average of the rate the company must pay to its long-term creditors and shareholders. (Computation of the cost of capital is covered in advanced courses.)

To illustrate, let's return to FasTrac's proposed machinery purchase described in Exhibit 24.1. Does this machine provide a satisfactory return while recovering the amount invested? Recall that the machine requires a $16,000 investment and is expected to provide $4,100 annual net cash inflows for the next eight years. If we assume that net cash inflows from this machine are received at each year-end and that FasTrac requires a 12% annual return, net present value can be computed as in Exhibit 24.7.

Point: The assumption of end-of-year cash flows simplifies computations and is common in practice.

EXHIBIT 24.7

Net Present Value Calculation with Equal Cash Flows

	Net Cash Flows*	Present Value of 1 at 12%**	Present Value of Net Cash Flows
Year 1	$ 4,100	0.8929	$ 3,661
Year 2	4,100	0.7972	3,269
Year 3	4,100	0.7118	2,918
Year 4	4,100	0.6355	2,606
Year 5	4,100	0.5674	2,326
Year 6	4,100	0.5066	2,077
Year 7	4,100	0.4523	1,854
Year 8	4,100	0.4039	1,656
Totals	$32,800		20,367
Amount invested (at year 0)			**(16,000)**
Net present value			**$ 4,367**

* Cash flows occur at the end of each year.
** Present value of 1 factors are taken from Table B.1 in Appendix B.

Example: What is the net present value in Exhibit 24.7 if a 10% return is applied? *Answer:* $5,873

Cost of Capital by Industry

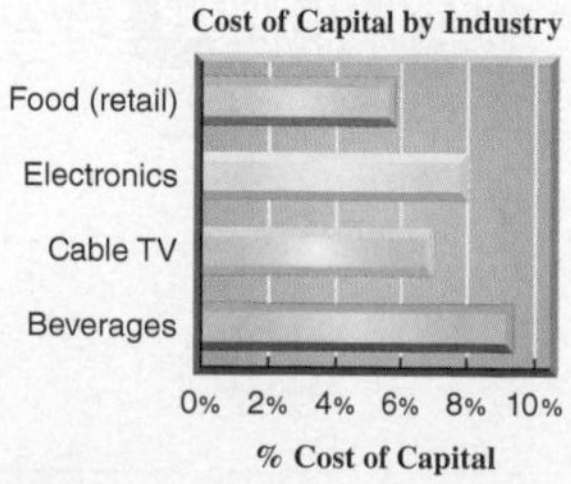

Source: www.stern.nyu.edu/adamordoran, data as of January 2014.

The first number column of Exhibit 24.7 shows the annual net cash flows. Present value of 1 factors, also called *discount factors,* are shown in the second column. Taken from Table B.1 in Appendix B, they assume that net cash flows are received at each year-end. *(To simplify present value computations and for assignment material at the end of this chapter, we assume that net cash flows are received at each year-end.)* Annual net cash flows from the first column of Exhibit 24.7 are multiplied by the discount factors in the second column to give present values of annual net cash flows shown in the third column. These annual amounts are summed to yield the total present value of net cash flows ($20,367). The last three lines of this exhibit show the final NPV computations. The asset's $16,000 initial cost is deducted from the $20,367 total present value of all future net cash flows to give this asset's NPV of $4,367. Thus, the present value of this machine's future net cash flows exceeds the initial $16,000 investment by $4,367. FasTrac should invest in this machine.

Net Present Value Decision Rule The decision rule in applying NPV is as follows: When an asset's expected future cash flows yield a *positive* net present value when discounted at the required rate of return, the asset should be acquired. This decision rule is reflected in the graphic below. When comparing several investment opportunities of similar cost and risk, we prefer the one with the highest positive net present value.

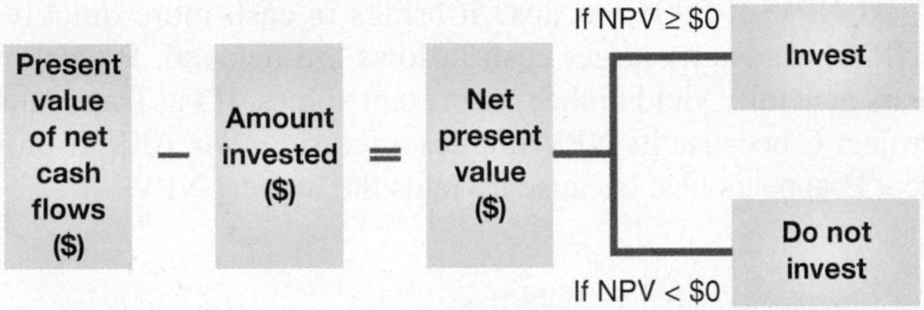

Simplifying Computations The computations in Exhibit 24.7 use separate present value of 1 factors for each of the eight years. Each year's net cash flow is multiplied by its present value of 1 factor to determine its present value. The individual present values for each of the eight net cash flows are added to give the asset's total present value. This computation can be simplified if annual net cash flows are equal in amount. A series of cash flows of equal dollar amount is called an **annuity.** One way is to use Table B.3, which gives the present value of 1 to be received periodically for a number of periods. To determine the present value of these eight annual receipts discounted at 12%, go down the 12% column of Table B.3 to the factor on the eighth line. This cumulative discount factor, also known as an *annuity* factor, is 4.9676. We then compute the $20,367 present value for these eight annual $4,100 receipts, computed as 4.9676 × $4,100.

Example: Why does the net present value of an investment increase when a lower discount rate is used? *Answer:* The present value of net cash flows increases.

Another way to simplify present value calculations, whether net cash flows are equal in amount or not, is to use a calculator with compound interest functions or a spreadsheet program. We show how to use Excel functions to compute net present value in this chapter's appendix. Whatever procedure you use, it is important to understand the concepts behind these computations.

Decision Ethics

Systems Manager Top management adopts a policy requiring purchases in excess of $5,000 to be submitted with cash flow projections to the cost analyst for capital budget approval. As systems manager, you want to upgrade your computers at a $25,000 cost. You consider submitting several orders all under $5,000 to avoid the approval process. You believe the computers will increase profits and wish to avoid a delay. What do you do? ■ [Answers follow the chapter's Summary.]

Uneven Cash Flows Net present value analysis can also be applied when net cash flows are uneven (unequal). To illustrate, assume that FasTrac can choose only one capital investment from among Projects A, B, and C. Each project requires the same $12,000 initial investment. Future net cash flows for each project are shown in the first three number columns of Exhibit 24.8.

EXHIBIT 24.8

Net Present Value Calculation with Uneven Cash Flows

	Net Cash Flows			Present Value of 1 at 10%	Present Value of Net Cash Flows		
	A	B	C		A	B	C
Year 1	$ 5,000	$ 8,000	$ 1,000	0.9091	$ 4,546	$ 7,273	$ 909
Year 2	5,000	5,000	5,000	0.8264	4,132	4,132	4,132
Year 3	5,000	2,000	9,000	0.7513	3,757	1,503	6,762
Totals	$15,000	$15,000	$15,000		12,435	12,908	11,803
Amount invested					(12,000)	(12,000)	(12,000)
Net present value					**$ 435**	**$ 908**	**$ (197)**

Example: If 12% is the required return in Exhibit 24.8, which project is preferred? *Answer:* Project B. Net present values are: A = $10; B = $553; C = $(715).

Example: Will the rankings of Projects A, B, and C change with the use of different discount rates, assuming the same rate is used for all projects? *Answer:* No; only the NPV amounts will change.

The three projects in Exhibit 24.8 have the same expected total net cash flows of $15,000. Project A is expected to produce equal amounts of $5,000 each year. Project B is expected to produce a larger amount in the first year. Project C is expected to produce a larger amount in the third year. The fourth column of Exhibit 24.8 shows the present value of 1 factors from Table B.1 assuming 10% required return.

Computations in the right-most columns show that Project A has a $435 positive NPV. Project B has the largest NPV of $908, because it brings in cash more quickly. Project C has a $(197) *negative* NPV because its larger cash inflows are delayed. Projects with higher cash flows in earlier years generally yield higher net present values. If FasTrac requires a 10% return, it should reject Project C because its NPV implies a return *under* 10%. If only one project can be accepted, Project B appears best because it yields the highest NPV.

NEED-TO-KNOW 24-3

Net Present Value

P3

A company is considering two potential projects. Each project requires a $20,000 initial investment and is expected to generate end-of-period annual cash flows as shown below. Assuming a discount rate of 10%, compute the net present value of each project.

	Net Cash Inflows			
	Year 1	Year 2	Year 3	Total
Project A	$12,000	$8,500	$ 4,000	$24,500
Project B	4,500	8,500	13,000	26,000

Solution

Net present values are computed as follows:

		Project A		Project B	
Year	Present Value of 1 at 10%	Net Cash Flows	Present Value of Net Cash Flows	Net Cash Flows	Present Value of Net Cash Flows
1	0.9091	$12,000	$10,909	$ 4,500	$ 4,091
2	0.8264	8,500	7,024	8,500	7,024
3	0.7513	4,000	3,005	13,000	9,767
Totals		$24,500	$20,938	$26,000	$20,882
Amount invested			(20,000)		(20,000)
Net present value			$ 938		$ 882

Do More: QS 24-2, QS 24-8, QS 24-9, QS 24-11, E 24-2, E 24-6, E 24-9

QC3

Salvage Value FasTrac predicted the $16,000 machine to have zero salvage value at the end of its useful life (recall Exhibit 24.1). In many cases, assets are expected to have salvage values. If so, this amount is an additional net cash inflow expected to be received at the end of the final year of the asset's life. All other computations remain the same. For example, the net present value of the $16,000 investment that yields $4,100 of net cash flows for eight years is $4,367, as shown in Exhibit 24.7. If that machine is expected to have a $1,500 salvage value at the end of its eight-year life, the present value of this salvage amount is $606 (computed as $1,500 × 0.4039). The net present value of the machine, including the present value of its expected salvage amount, is $4,973 (computed as $4,367 + $606).

Accelerated Depreciation Depreciation computations also affect net present value analysis. FasTrac computes depreciation using the straight-line method. Accelerated depreciation is also commonly used, especially for income tax purposes. Accelerated depreciation produces larger depreciation deductions in the early years of an asset's life and smaller deductions in later years. This pattern results in smaller income tax payments in early years and larger payments in later years. Accelerated depreciation does not change the basics of a present value analysis, but it can change the result. Using accelerated depreciation for tax reporting affects the NPV of an asset's cash flows because it produces larger net cash inflows in the early years of the asset's life and smaller ones in later years. Being able to use accelerated depreciation for tax reporting always makes an investment more desirable because early cash flows are more valuable than later ones.

Point: Tax savings from depreciation is called *depreciation tax shield.*

Comparing Positive NPV Projects In deciding whether to make a capital investment, we invest if the NPV is positive; we do not invest if the NPV is negative. When considering several projects of similar investment amounts and risk levels, we can compare the different projects' NPVs and rank them on the basis of their NPVs. However, if the amount invested differs substantially across projects, the NPV is of limited value for comparison purposes. One way to compare projects, especially when a company cannot fund all positive net present value projects, is to use the **profitability index,** which is computed as:

Example: When is it appropriate to use different discount rates for different projects? *Answer:* When risk levels are different.

$$\textbf{Profitability index} = \frac{\textbf{Present value of net cash flows}}{\textbf{Investment}}$$

Exhibit 24.9 illustrates the computation of the profitability index for three potential investments.

EXHIBIT 24.9

Profitability Index

	Investment		
	1	2	3
Present value of net cash flows (a)	$900,000	$375,000	$270,000
Amount invested (b)	750,000	250,000	300,000
Profitability index (a)/(b)	1.2	1.5	0.90

A profitability index less than 1 indicates an investment with a *negative* net present value. These potential investments, like Investment 3 in Exhibit 24.9, are eliminated from further consideration. Both Investments 1 and 2 have profitability indexes greater than 1, thus they have positive net present values. For example, Investment 1's NPV equals $150,000 (computed as $900,000 − $750,000); Investment 2's NPV equals $125,000 (computed as $375,000 − $250,000). Ideally, the company would accept all positive NPV projects, but if forced to choose, it should select the project with the higher profitability index. Thus, Investment 2 would be ranked ahead of Investment 1, based on its higher profitability index.

Inflation Large price-level increases should be considered in NPV analyses. Discount rates should already include inflation forecasts. Net cash flows can be adjusted for inflation by using *future value* computations. For example, if the expected net cash inflow in year 1 is $4,100 and 5% inflation is expected, then the expected net cash inflow in year 2 is $4,305, computed as $4,100 × 1.05 (1.05 is the future value of $1 [Table B.2] for one period with a 5% rate).

Internal Rate of Return

P4 Compute internal rate of return and explain its use.

Another means to evaluate capital investments is to use the **internal rate of return (IRR),** which equals the discount rate that yields an NPV of zero for an investment. This means that if we compute the total present value of a project's net cash flows using the IRR as the discount rate and then subtract the initial investment from this total present value, we get a zero NPV.

To illustrate, we use the data for FasTrac's Project A from Exhibit 24.8 to compute its IRR. Below is the two-step process for computing IRR with even cash flows.

Step 1: **Compute the present value factor for the investment project.**

$$\textbf{Present value factor} = \frac{\textbf{Amount invested}}{\textbf{Net cash flows}} = \frac{\$12{,}000}{\$5{,}000} = 2.4000$$

Step 2: **Identify the discount rate (IRR) yielding the present value factor.**

Search Table B.3 for a present value factor of 2.4000 in the three-year row (equaling the 3-year project duration). The 12% discount rate yields a present value factor of 2.4018. This implies that the IRR is approximately 12%.

When cash flows are equal, as with Project A, we compute the present value factor by dividing the initial investment by its annual net cash flows. We then use an annuity table to determine the discount rate equal to this present value factor. For FasTrac's Project A, we look across the three-period row of Table B.3 and find that the discount rate corresponding to the present value factor of 2.4000 roughly equals the 2.4018 value for the 12% rate.* This row of Table B.3 is reproduced here:

Present Value of an Annuity of 1 for Three Periods	Discount Rate				
Periods	1%	5%	10%	12%	15%
3	2.9410	2.7232	2.4869	**2.4018**	2.2832

The 12% rate is the project's IRR. A more precise IRR estimate can be computed using an Excel function, as we show in this chapter's appendix.

Uneven Cash Flows If net cash flows are uneven, it is best to use either a calculator or spreadsheet software to compute the IRR. However, we can also use trial and error to compute the IRR. We do this by selecting any reasonable discount rate and computing the NPV. If the amount is positive (negative), we recompute the NPV using a higher (lower) discount rate. We continue these steps until we reach a point where two consecutive computations result in NPVs having different signs (positive and negative). Because the NPV is zero using IRR, we know that the IRR lies between these two discount rates. We can then estimate its value.

Decision Insight

CEO-IRR A survey reported that 41% of top managers would reject a project with an internal rate of return *above* the cost of capital *if* the project would cause the firm to miss its earnings forecast. The roles of benchmarks and manager compensation plans must be considered in capital budgeting decisions. ■

Robert Kirk/Stockbyte/Getty Images

Use of Internal Rate of Return When we use the IRR to evaluate a project, we compare it to a predetermined **hurdle rate,** which is a minimum acceptable rate of return. The decision rule using IRR is applied as follows.

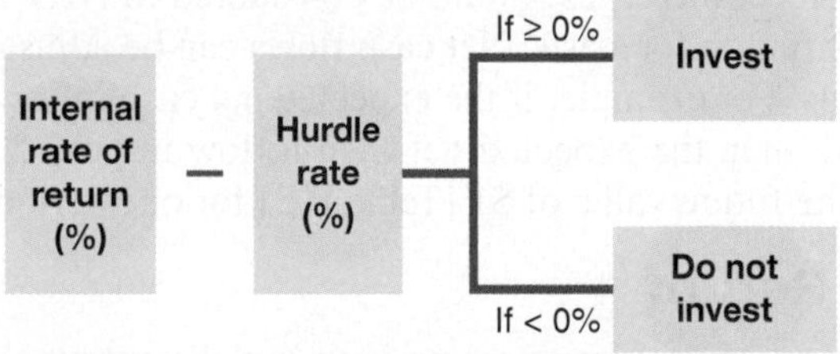

Example: How can management evaluate the risk of an investment? *Answer:* It must assess the uncertainty of future cash flows.

Top management selects the hurdle rate to use in evaluating capital investments. If the IRR is higher than the hurdle rate, the investment is made.

Comparing Projects Using IRR Multiple projects are often ranked by the extent to which their IRR exceeds the hurdle rate. The hurdle rate for individual projects is often different,

* Since the present value factor of 2.4000 is not exactly equal to the 12% factor of 2.4018, we can more precisely estimate the IRR as follows:

Discount Rate	Present Value Factor from Table B.3
12%	2.4018
15%	2.2832
	0.1186 = difference

$$\text{Then, IRR} = 12\% + \left[(15\% - 12\%) \times \frac{2.4018 - 2.4000}{0.1186}\right] = \underline{\underline{12.05\%}}$$

depending on the risk involved. IRR is not subject to the limitations of NPV when comparing projects with different amounts invested because the IRR is expressed as a percent rather than as a dollar value in NPV.

Decision Maker

Entrepreneur You are developing a new product and you use a 12% discount rate to compute its NPV. Your banker, from whom you hope to obtain a loan, expresses concern that your discount rate is too low. How do you respond? ■ [Answers follow the chapter's Summary.]

NEED-TO-KNOW 24-4

Internal Rate of Return

P4

A machine costing $58,880 is expected to generate net cash flows of $8,000 per year for each of the next 10 years.

1. Compute the machine's internal rate of return (IRR).

2. If a company's hurdle rate is 6.5%, use IRR to determine whether the company should purchase this machine.

Solution

1. Amount invested/net cash flows = $58,880/$8,000 = 7.36. Scanning the "Periods equal 10" row in Table B.3 for a present value factor near 7.36 indicates the IRR is 6%.

2. The machine should not be purchased because its IRR (6%) is less than the company's hurdle rate (6.5%).

Do More: QS 24-3, QS 24-13, E 24-13, E 24-14

Comparison of Capital Budgeting Methods

We explained four methods that managers use to evaluate capital investment projects. How do these methods compare with each other? Exhibit 24.10 addresses that question. Neither the payback period nor the accounting rate of return considers the time value of money. On the other hand, both the net present value and the internal rate of return do.

EXHIBIT 24.10

Comparing Capital Budgeting Methods

	Payback Period	Accounting Rate of Return	Net Present Value	Internal Rate of Return
Measurement basis	• Cash flows	• Accrual income	• Cash flows	• Cash flows
Measurement unit	• Years	• Percent	• Dollars	• Percent
Strengths	• Easy to understand • Allows comparison of projects	• Easy to understand • Allows comparison of projects	• Reflects time value of money • Reflects varying risks over project's life	• Reflects time value of money • Allows comparisons of dissimilar projects
Limitations	• Ignores time value of money • Ignores cash flows after payback period	• Ignores time value of money • Ignores annual rates over life of project	• Difficult to compare dissimilar projects	• Ignores varying risks over life of project

The payback period is probably the simplest method. It gives managers an estimate of how soon they will recover their initial investment. Managers sometimes use this method when they have limited cash to invest and a number of projects to choose from. The accounting rate of return yields a percent measure computed using accrual income instead of cash flows. The accounting rate of return is an average rate for the entire investment period. Net present value considers all estimated net cash flows for the project's expected life. It can be applied to even and uneven cash flows and can reflect changes in the level of risk over a project's life. Since NPV yields a dollar measure, comparing projects of unequal sizes is more difficult. The profitability index, based on each project's net present value, can be used in this case. The internal rate of return considers all cash flows from a project. It is readily computed when the cash flows are even but requires some trial and error or use of a computer estimation when cash flows are uneven. Because the IRR is a percent measure, it is readily used to compare projects with different investment amounts. However, IRR does not reflect changes in risk over a project's life.

Decision Insight

And the Winner Is . . . How do we choose among the methods for evaluating capital investments? Management surveys consistently show the internal rate of return (IRR) as the most popular method followed by the payback period and net present value (NPV). Few companies use the accounting rate of return (ARR), but nearly all use more than one method. ■

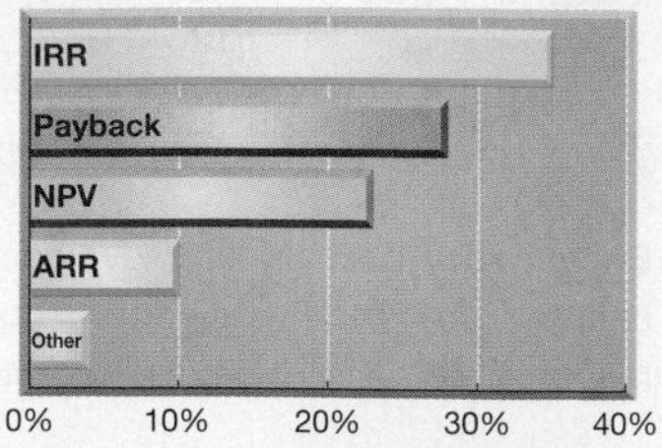

Company Usage of Capital Budgeting Methods

GLOBAL VIEW

Siemens AG is a global electrical engineering and electronics company headquartered in Germany. Recently, the company announced plans to invest £160 million to build a wind turbine plant in the United Kingdom. Net present value analyses support such decisions. In this case, Siemens foresees strong future cash flows based on increased demand for clean sources of energy, like wind power.

Sustainability and Accounting Net present value calculations extend to investments in sustainable energy sources like solar power. Predicting the future benefits of solar panel installations, in terms of reduced energy costs, is challenging for several reasons. First, the amount of solar energy that can be produced depends on geographic location, with locations nearer the equator typically better. Second, south-facing roofs are better able to capture solar energy than other orientations. Third, cost savings from solar energy require predictions of the future costs of other sources of power, which can be volatile. While challenging, these factors must be considered when performing a net present value calculation on a potential investment in solar power.

Sustainability extends beyond natural resources. **Adafruit**'s founder Limor Fried invests in programs to educate future engineers and entrepreneurs. In this way Limor is helping to develop and sustain the human capital that will benefit society in the future.

Decision Analysis Break-Even Time

A1 Analyze a capital investment project using break-even time.

The first section of this chapter explained several methods to evaluate capital investments. Break-even time of an investment project is a variation of the payback period method that overcomes the limitation of not using the time value of money. **Break-even time (BET)** is a time-based measure used to evaluate a capital investment's acceptability. Its computation yields a measure of expected time, reflecting the time period until the *present value* of the net cash flows from an investment equals the initial cost of the investment. In basic terms, break-even time is computed by restating future cash flows in terms of present values and then determining the payback period using these present values.

To illustrate, we return to the FasTrac case described in Exhibit 24.1 involving a $16,000 investment in machinery. The annual net cash flows from this investment are projected at $4,100 for eight years. Exhibit 24.11 shows the computation of break-even time for this investment decision.

EXHIBIT 24.11

Break-Even Time Analysis*

Year	Cash Flows	Present Value of 1 at 10%	Present Value of Cash Flows	Cumulative Present Value of Cash Flows
0	$(16,000)	1.0000	$(16,000)	$(16,000)
1	4,100	0.9091	3,727	(12,273)
2	4,100	0.8264	3,388	(8,885)
3	4,100	0.7513	3,080	(5,805)
4	4,100	0.6830	2,800	(3,005)
5	4,100	0.6209	2,546	**(459)**
6	4,100	0.5645	2,314	**1,855**
7	4,100	0.5132	2,104	3,959
8	4,100	0.4665	1,913	5,872

* The time of analysis is the start of year 1 (same as end of year 0). All cash flows occur at the end of each year.

The right-most column of this exhibit shows that break-even time is between 5 and 6 years, or about 5.2 years—also see margin graph (where the line crosses the zero point). This is the time the project takes to break even after considering the time value of money (recall that the payback period computed without considering the time value of money was 3.9 years). We interpret this as cash flows earned after 5.2 years contribute to a positive net present value that, in this case, eventually amounts to $5,872.

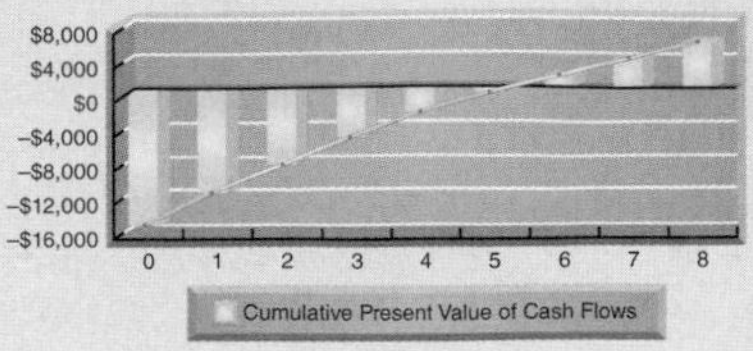

Break-even time is a useful measure for managers because it identifies the point in time when they can expect the cash flows to begin to yield net positive returns. Managers expect a positive net present value from an investment if break-even time is less than the investment's estimated life. The method allows managers to compare and rank alternative investments, giving the project with the shortest break-even time the highest rank.

Decision Maker

Investment Manager Management asks you, the investment manager, to evaluate three alternative investments. Investment recovery time is crucial because cash is scarce. The time value of money is also important. Which capital budgeting method(s) do you use to assess the investments? ■ [Answers follow the chapter's Summary.]

NEED-TO-KNOW

COMPREHENSIVE

White Company can invest in one of two projects, TD1 or TD2. Each project requires an initial investment of $101,250 and produces the year-end cash inflows shown in the following table.

	Net Cash Flows	
	TD1	TD2
Year 1	$ 20,000	$ 40,000
Year 2	30,000	40,000
Year 3	70,000	40,000
Totals	$120,000	$120,000

Required

1. Compute the payback period for both projects. Which project has the shortest payback period?
2. Assume that the company requires a 10% return from its investments. Compute the net present value of each project.
3. Drawing on your answers to parts 1 and 2, determine which project, if any, should be chosen.
4. Compute the internal rate of return for project TD2. Based on its internal rate of return, should project TD2 be chosen?

PLANNING THE SOLUTION

- Compute the payback period for the series of unequal cash flows (Project TD1) and for the series of equal cash flows (Project TD2).
- Compute White Company's net present value of each investment using a 10% discount rate.
- Use the payback and net present value rules to determine which project, if any, should be selected.
- Compute the internal rate of return for the series of equal cash flows (Project TD2) and determine whether that internal rate of return is greater than the company's 10% discount rate.

SOLUTION

1. The payback period for a project with a series of equal cash flows is computed as follows:

$$\text{Payback period} = \frac{\text{Cost of investment}}{\text{Annual net cash flow}}$$

For project TD2, the payback period equals 2.53 (rounded), computed as $101,250/$40,000. This means that the company expects to recover its investment in Project TD2 after approximately two and one-half years of its three-year life.

Next, determining the payback period for a series of unequal cash flows (as in Project TD1) requires us to compute the cumulative net cash flows from the project at the end of each year. Assuming the cash outflow for Project TD1 occurs at the end of year 0, and cash inflows occur continuously over years 1, 2, and 3, the payback period calculation follows.

TD1:

Period	Expected Net Cash Flows	Cumulative Net Cash Flows
0	$(101,250)	$(101,250)
1	20,000	(81,250)
2	30,000	(51,250)
3	70,000	18,750

The cumulative net cash flow for Project TD1 changes from negative to positive in year 3. As cash flows are received continuously, the point at which the company has recovered its investment into year 3 is 0.27 (rounded), computed as $18,750/$70,000. This means that the payback period for TD1 is 2.27 years, computed as 2 years plus 0.27 of year 3.

2. TD1:

	Net Cash Flows	Present Value of 1 at 10%	Present Value of Net Cash Flows
Year 1	$ 20,000	0.9091	$ 18,182
Year 2	30,000	0.8264	24,792
Year 3	70,000	0.7513	52,591
Totals	$120,000		95,565
Amount invested			(101,250)
Net present value			**$ (5,685)**

TD2:

	Net Cash Flows	Present Value of 1 at 10%	Present Value of Net Cash Flows
Year 1	$ 40,000	0.9091	$ 36,364
Year 2	40,000	0.8264	33,056
Year 3	40,000	0.7513	30,052
Totals	$120,000		99,472
Amount invested			(101,250)
Net present value			**$ (1,778)**

3. White Company should not invest in either project. Both are expected to yield a negative net present value, and it should invest only in positive net present value projects. Although the company expects to recover its investment from both projects before the end of these projects' useful lives, the projects are not acceptable after considering the time value of money.

4. To compute Project TD2's internal rate of return, we first compute a present value factor as follows:

$$\text{Present value factor} = \frac{\text{Amount invested}}{\text{Net cash flow}} = \$101{,}250/\$40{,}000 = 2.5313 \text{ (rounded)}$$

Then, we search Table B.3 for the discount rate that corresponds to the present value factor of 2.5313 for three periods. From Table B.3, this discount rate is 9%. Project TD2's internal rate of return of 9% is below this company's hurdle rate of 10%. Thus, Project TD2 should *not* be chosen.

APPENDIX

Using Excel to Compute Net Present Value and Internal Rate of Return

24A

Computing present values and internal rates of return for projects with uneven cash flows is tedious and error prone. These calculations can be performed simply and accurately by using functions built into Excel. Many calculators and other types of spreadsheet software can perform them too. To illustrate, consider FasTrac, a company that is considering investing in a new machine with the expected cash flows shown in the following spreadsheet. Cash outflows are entered as negative numbers, and cash inflows are entered as positive numbers. Assume FasTrac requires a 12% annual return, entered as 0.12 in cell C1.

	A	B	C	D
1	**Annual discount rate**		**0.12**	
2	**Initial investment, made at beginning of period 1**		**-16000**	
3	**Annual cash flows received at end of period:**			
4		**1**	**3000**	
5		**2**	**4000**	
6		**3**	**4000**	
7		**4**	**4000**	
8		**5**	**5000**	
9		**6**	**3000**	
10		**7**	**2000**	
11		**8**	**2000**	
12				
13			**=NPV(C1,C4:C11)+C2**	
14				
15			**=IRR(C2:C11)**	
16				

To compute the net present value of this project, the following is entered into cell C13:

=NPV(C1,C4:C11)+C2

This instructs Excel to use its NPV function to compute the present value of the cash flows in cells C4 through C11, using the discount rate in cell C1, and then add the amount of the (negative) initial investment. For this stream of cash flows and a discount rate of 12%, the net present value is $1,326.03.

To compute the internal rate of return for this project, the following is entered into cell C15:

=IRR(C2:C11)

This instructs Excel to use its IRR function to compute the internal rate of return of the cash flows in cells C2 through C11. By default, Excel starts with a guess of 10%, and then uses trial and error to find the IRR. The IRR equals 14% for this project.

Summary

A1 Analyze a capital investment project using break-even time. Break-even time (BET) is a method for evaluating capital investments by restating future cash flows in terms of their present values (discounting the cash flows) and then calculating the payback period using these present values of cash flows.

P1 Compute payback period and describe its use. One way to compare potential investments is to compute and compare their payback periods. The payback period is an estimate of the expected time before the cumulative net cash inflow from the investment equals its initial cost. A payback period analysis fails to reflect risk of the cash flows, differences in the timing of cash flows within the payback period, and cash flows that occur after the payback period.

P2 Compute accounting rate of return and explain its use. A project's accounting rate of return is computed by dividing the expected annual after-tax net income by the average amount of investment in the project. When the net cash flows are received evenly throughout each period and straight-line depreciation is used, the average investment is computed as the average of the investment's initial book value and its salvage value.

P3 Compute net present value and describe its use. An investment's net present value is determined by predicting the future cash flows it is expected to generate, discounting them at a rate that represents an acceptable return, and then by subtracting the investment's initial cost from the sum of the present values. This technique can deal with any pattern of expected cash flows and applies a superior concept of return on investment.

P4 Compute internal rate of return and explain its use. The internal rate of return (IRR) is the discount rate that results in a zero net present value. When the cash flows are equal, we can compute the present value factor corresponding to the IRR by dividing the initial investment by the annual cash flows. We then use the annuity tables to determine the discount rate corresponding to this present value factor.

Guidance Answers to Decision Maker and Decision Ethics

Systems Manager Your dilemma is whether to abide by rules designed to prevent abuse or to bend them to acquire an investment that you believe will benefit the firm. You should not pursue the latter action because breaking up the order into small components is dishonest and there are consequences of being caught at a later stage. Develop a proposal for the entire package and then do all you can to expedite its processing, particularly by pointing out its benefits. When faced with controls that are not working, there is rarely a reason to overcome its shortcomings by dishonesty. A direct assault on those limitations is more sensible and ethical.

Entrepreneur The banker is probably concerned because new products are risky and should therefore be evaluated using a higher rate of return. You should conduct a thorough technical analysis and obtain detailed market data and information about any similar products available in the market. These factors might provide sufficient information to support the use of a lower return. You must convince yourself that the risk level is consistent with the discount rate used. You should also be confident that your company has the capacity and the resources to handle the new product.

Investment Manager You should probably focus on either the payback period or break-even time because both the time value of money and recovery time are important. Break-even time method is superior because it accounts for the time value of money, which is an important consideration in this decision.

Key Terms

Accounting rate of return
Annuity
Break-even time (BET)
Capital budgeting
Cost of capital
Hurdle rate
Internal rate of return (IRR)
Net present value (NPV)
Payback period (PBP)
Profitability index

Multiple Choice Quiz

Answers at end of chapter

1. The minimum acceptable rate of return for an investment decision is called the
   a. Hurdle rate of return.
   b. Payback rate of return.
   c. Internal rate of return.
   d. Average rate of return.
   e. Maximum rate of return.
2. A corporation is considering the purchase of new equipment costing $90,000. The projected after-tax annual net income from the equipment is $3,600, after deducting $30,000 depreciation. Assume that revenue is to be received at each year-end, and the machine has a useful life of three years with zero salvage value. Management requires a 12% return on its investments. What is the net present value of this machine?
   a. $ 60,444
   b. $ 80,700
   c. $(88,560)
   d. $ 90,000
   e. $ (9,300)
3. A disadvantage of using the payback period to compare investment alternatives is that it
   a. Ignores cash flows beyond the payback period.
   b. Cannot be used to compare alternatives with different initial investments.
   c. Cannot be used when cash flows are not uniform.
   d. Involves the time value of money.
   e. Cannot be used if a company records depreciation.
4. A company is considering the purchase of equipment for $270,000. Projected annual cash inflow from this equipment is $61,200 per year. The payback period is:
   a. 0.2 years
   b. 5.0 years
   c. 4.4 years
   d. 2.3 years
   e. 3.9 years
5. A company buys a machine for $180,000 that has an expected life of nine years and no salvage value. The company expects an annual net income (after taxes of 30%) of $8,550. What is the accounting rate of return?
   a. 4.75%
   b. 42.75%
   c. 2.85%
   d. 9.50%
   e. 6.65%

Icon denotes assignments that involve decision making.

Discussion Questions

1. Capital budgeting decisions require careful analysis because they are generally the ______________ and ________ decisions that management faces.
2. What is capital budgeting?
3. Identify four reasons that capital budgeting decisions by managers are risky.
4. Identify two disadvantages of using the payback period for comparing investments.
5. Why is an investment more attractive to management if it has a shorter payback period?
6. What is the average amount invested in a machine during its predicted five-year life if it costs $200,000 and has a $20,000 salvage value? Assume that net income is received evenly throughout each year and straight-line depreciation is used.
7. If the present value of the expected net cash flows from a machine, discounted at 10%, exceeds the amount to be invested, what can you say about the investment's expected rate of return? What can you say about the expected rate of return if the present value of the net cash flows, discounted at 10%, is less than the investment amount?
8. Why is the present value of $100 that you expect to receive one year from today worth less than $100 received today? What is the present value of $100 that you expect to receive one year from today, discounted at 12%?
9. If a potential investment's internal rate of return is above the company's hurdle rate, should the investment be made?
10. **Google** managers must select depreciation methods. Why does the use of the accelerated depreciation method (instead of straight-line) for income tax reporting increase an investment's value?
11. The management of **Samsung** is planning to invest in a new companywide computerized inventory tracking system. What makes this potential investment risky?
12. The management of **Google** is planning to acquire new equipment to manufacture tablet computers. What are some of the costs and benefits that would be included in Google's analysis?
13. **Apple** is considering expanding a store. Identify three methods management can use to evaluate whether to expand.

GOOGLE

Samsung

GOOGLE

APPLE

connect

QUICK STUDY

QS 24-1
Payback period P1

Park Co. is considering an investment that requires immediate payment of $27,000 and provides expected cash inflows of $9,000 annually for four years. What is the investment's payback period?

QS 24-2
Net present value P3

Park Co. is considering an investment that requires immediate payment of $27,000 and provides expected cash inflows of $9,000 annually for four years. If Park Co. requires a 10% return on its investments, what is the net present value of this investment? (Round your calculations to the nearest dollar.)

QS 24-3
Internal rate of return P4

Park Co. is considering an investment that requires immediate payment of $27,000 and provides expected cash inflows of $9,000 annually for four years. Assume Park Co. requires a 10% return on its investments. Based on its internal rate of return, should Park Co. make the investment?

QS 24-4
Analyzing payback periods P1

Howard Co. is considering two alternative investments. The payback period is 3.5 years for Investment A and 4 years for Investment B. (1) If management relies on the payback period, which investment is preferred? (2) Why might Howard's analysis of these two alternatives lead to the selection of B over A?

QS 24-5
Payback period P1

Project A requires a $280,000 initial investment for new machinery with a five-year life and a salvage value of $30,000. The company uses straight-line depreciation. Project A is expected to yield annual net income of $20,000 per year for the next five years. Compute Project A's payback period.

QS 24-6
Accounting rate of return
P2

Project A requires a $280,000 initial investment for new machinery with a five-year life and a salvage value of $30,000. The company uses straight-line depreciation. Project A is expected to yield annual net income of $20,000 per year for the next five years. Compute Project A's accounting rate of return. Express your answer as a percentage, rounded to two decimal places.

QS 24-7
Computation of accounting rate of return
P2

Peng Company is considering an investment expected to generate an average net income after taxes of $1,950 for three years. The investment costs $45,000 and has an estimated $6,000 salvage value. Compute the accounting rate of return for this investment; assume the company uses straight-line depreciation. Express your answer as a percentage, rounded to two decimal places.

QS 24-8
Net present value P3

Peng Company is considering an investment expected to generate an average net income after taxes of $1,950 for three years. The investment costs $45,000 and has an estimated $6,000 salvage value. Assume Peng requires a 15% return on its investments. Compute the net present value of this investment. (Round each present value calculation to the nearest dollar.)

QS 24-9
Computation of net present value P3

If Quail Company invests $50,000 today, it can expect to receive $10,000 at the end of each year for the next seven years, plus an extra $6,000 at the end of the seventh year. What is the net present value of this investment assuming a required 10% return on investments? (Round present value calculations to the nearest dollar.)

QS 24-10
Profitability index
P3

Yokam Company is considering two alternative projects. Project 1 requires an initial investment of $400,000 and has a present value of cash flows of $1,100,000. Project 2 requires an initial investment of $4 million and has a present value of cash flows of $6 million. Compute the profitability index for each project. Based on the profitability index, which project should the company prefer? Explain.

QS 24-11
Net present value
P3

Following is information on an investment considered by Hudson Co. The investment has zero salvage value. The company requires a 12% return from its investments. Compute this investment's net present value.

	Investment A1
Initial investment	($200,000)
Expected net cash flows in year:	
1	100,000
2	90,000
3	75,000

QS 24-12
Net present value, with salvage value P3

Refer to the information in QS 24-11 and instead assume the investment has a salvage value of $20,000. Compute the investment's net present value.

QS 24-13
Internal rate of return P4

A company is considering investing in a new machine that requires a cash payment of $47,947 today. The machine will generate annual cash flows of $21,000 for the next three years. What is the internal rate of return if the company buys this machine?

QS 24-14
Net present value P3

A company is considering investing in a new machine that requires a cash payment of $47,947 today. The machine will generate annual cash flows of $21,000 for the next three years. Assume the company uses an 8% discount rate. Compute the net present value of this investment. (Round your answer to the nearest dollar.)

QS 24-15
Computation of break-even time
A1

Heels, a shoe manufacturer, is evaluating the costs and benefits of new equipment that would custom fit each pair of athletic shoes. The customer would have his or her foot scanned by digital computer equipment; this information would be used to cut the raw materials to provide the customer a perfect fit. The new equipment costs $90,000 and is expected to generate an additional $35,000 in cash flows for five years. A bank will make a $90,000 loan to the company at a 10% interest rate for this equipment's purchase. Use the following table to determine the break-even time for this equipment. (Round the present value of cash flows to the nearest dollar.)

Year	Cash Flows*	Present Value of 1 at 10%	Present Value of Cash Flows	Cumulative Present Value of Cash Flows
0	$(90,000)	1.0000	______	______
1	35,000	0.9091	______	______
2	35,000	0.8264	______	______
3	35,000	0.7513	______	______
4	35,000	0.6830	______	______
5	35,000	0.6209	______	______

* All cash flows occur at year-end.

QS 24-16
Capital budgeting methods P1 P3

Siemens AG invests €80 million to build a manufacturing plant to build wind turbines. The company predicts net cash flows of €16 million per year for the next eight years. Assume the company requires an 8% rate of return from its investments.

1. What is the payback period of this investment?
2. What is the net present value of this investment?

connect

EXERCISES

Exercise 24-1
Payback period computation; uneven cash flows P1
Check 3.08 years

Beyer Company is considering the purchase of an asset for $180,000. It is expected to produce the following net cash flows. The cash flows occur evenly throughout each year. Compute the payback period for this investment (round years to two decimals).

	Year 1	Year 2	Year 3	Year 4	Year 5	Total
Net cash flows	$60,000	$40,000	$70,000	$125,000	$35,000	$330,000

Exercise 24-2
Net present value P3

Refer to the information in Exercise 24-1 and assume that Beyer requires a 10% return on its investments. Compute the net present value of this investment. (Round to the nearest dollar.) Should Beyer accept the investment?

Exercise 24-3
Payback period computation; straight-line depreciation
P1

A machine can be purchased for $150,000 and used for five years, yielding the following net incomes. In projecting net incomes, straight-line depreciation is applied, using a five-year life and a zero salvage value. Compute the machine's payback period (ignore taxes). (Round the payback period to three decimals.)

	Year 1	Year 2	Year 3	Year 4	Year 5
Net income	$10,000	$25,000	$50,000	$37,500	$100,000

Exercise 24-4
Payback period; accelerated depreciation
P1
Check 2.265 years

Refer to the information in Exercise 24-3 and assume instead that double-declining depreciation is applied. Compute the machine's payback period (ignore taxes). (Round the payback period to three decimals.)

Exercise 24-5
Payback period computation; even cash flows
P1

Compute the payback period for each of these two separate investments (round the payback period to two decimals):

a. A new operating system for an existing machine is expected to cost $520,000 and have a useful life of six years. The system yields an incremental after-tax income of $150,000 each year after deducting its straight-line depreciation. The predicted salvage value of the system is $10,000.

b. A machine costs $380,000, has a $20,000 salvage value, is expected to last eight years, and will generate an after-tax income of $60,000 per year after straight-line depreciation.

Exercise 24-6
Net present value P3

Refer to the information in Exercise 24-5. Assume the company requires a 10% rate of return on its investments. Compute the net present value of each potential investment. (Round to the nearest dollar.)

Exercise 24-7
Accounting rate of return P2

A machine costs $700,000 and is expected to yield an after-tax net income of $52,000 each year. Management predicts this machine has a 10-year service life and a $100,000 salvage value, and it uses straight-line depreciation. Compute this machine's accounting rate of return.

Exercise 24-8
Payback period and accounting rate of return on investment
P1 P2

B2B Co. is considering the purchase of equipment that would allow the company to add a new product to its line. The equipment is expected to cost $360,000 with a 12-year life and no salvage value. It will be depreciated on a straight-line basis. The company expects to sell 144,000 units of the equipment's product each year. The expected annual income related to this equipment follows. Compute the (1) payback period and (2) accounting rate of return for this equipment.

Sales	$225,000
Costs	
Materials, labor, and overhead (except depreciation on new equipment)	120,000
Depreciation on new equipment	30,000
Selling and administrative expenses	22,500
Total costs and expenses	172,500
Pretax income	52,500
Income taxes (30%)	15,750
Net income	$ 36,750

Check (1) 5.39 years (2) 20.42%

Exercise 24-9
Computing net present value P3

After evaluating the risk of the investment described in Exercise 24-8, B2B Co. concludes that it must earn at least an 8% return on this investment. Compute the net present value of this investment. (Round the net present value to the nearest dollar.)

Exercise 24-10
NPV and profitability index
P3

Following is information on two alternative investments being considered by Jolee Company. The company requires a 10% return from its investments.

	Project A	Project B
Initial investment	$(160,000)	$(105,000)
Expected net cash flows in year:		
1	40,000	32,000
2	56,000	50,000
3	80,295	66,000
4	90,400	72,000
5	65,000	24,000

For each alternative project compute the (a) net present value, and (b) profitability index. (Round your answers in part *b* to two decimal places.) If the company can only select one project, which should it choose? Explain.

Exercise 24-11
Net present value, profitability index
P3

Following is information on two alternative investments being considered by Tiger Co. The company requires a 4% return from its investments.

	Project X1	Project X2
Initial investment	($80,000)	($120,000)
Expected net cash flows in year:		
1	25,000	60,000
2	35,500	50,000
3	60,500	40,000

Compute each project's (a) net present value and (b) profitability index. (Round present value calculations to the nearest dollar and round the profitability index to two decimal places.) If the company can choose only one project, which should it choose? Explain.

Exercise 24-12
Net present value, profitability index P3

Refer to the information in Exercise 24-11 and instead assume the company requires a 12% return on its investments. Compute each project's (a) net present value and (b) profitability index. (Round present value calculations to the nearest dollar.) Express the profitability index as a percentage (rounded to two decimal places). If the company can choose only one project, which should it choose? Explain.

Exercise 24-13^A
Internal rate of return P4

Refer to the information in Exercise 24-11. Create an Excel spreadsheet to compute the internal rate of return for each of the projects. Based on internal rate of return, determine whether the company should accept either of the two projects.

Exercise 24-14
Computation and interpretation of net present value and internal rate of return
P3 P4

Phoenix Company can invest in each of three cheese-making projects: C1, C2, and C3. Each project requires an initial investment of $228,000 and would yield the following annual cash flows.

	C1	C2	C3
Year 1	$ 12,000	$ 96,000	$180,000
Year 2	108,000	96,000	60,000
Year 3	168,000	96,000	48,000
Totals	$288,000	$288,000	$288,000

(1) Assuming that the company requires a 12% return from its investments, use net present value to determine which projects, if any, should be acquired. (2) Using the answer from part 1, explain whether the internal rate of return is higher or lower than 12% for Project C2.

Exercise 24-15^A
Using Excel to compute IRR P4

Refer to the information in Exercise 24-10. Create an Excel spreadsheet to compute the internal rate of return for each of the projects. Round the percentage return to two decimals.

Exercise 24-16
Comparison of payback and BET
P1 A1

This chapter explained two methods to evaluate investments using recovery time, the payback period and break-even time (BET). Refer to QS 24-15 and (1) compute the recovery time for both the payback period and break-even time, (2) discuss the advantage(s) of break-even time over the payback period, and (3) list two conditions under which payback period and break-even time are similar.

connect

PROBLEM SET A

Problem 24-1A
Computation of payback period, accounting rate of return, and net present value
P1 P2 P3

Factor Company is planning to add a new product to its line. To manufacture this product, the company needs to buy a new machine at a $480,000 cost with an expected four-year life and a $20,000 salvage value. All sales are for cash, and all costs are out-of-pocket, except for depreciation on the new machine. Additional information includes the following.

Expected annual sales of new product	$1,840,000
Expected annual costs of new product	
Direct materials	480,000
Direct labor	672,000
Overhead (excluding straight-line depreciation on new machine)	336,000
Selling and administrative expenses	160,000
Income taxes	30%

Required

1. Compute straight-line depreciation for each year of this new machine's life. (Round depreciation amounts to the nearest dollar.)
2. Determine expected net income and net cash flow for each year of this machine's life. (Round answers to the nearest dollar.)
3. Compute this machine's payback period, assuming that cash flows occur evenly throughout each year. (Round the payback period to two decimals.)

Check (4) 21.56%

(5) $107,356

4. Compute this machine's accounting rate of return, assuming that income is earned evenly throughout each year. (Round the percentage return to two decimals.)
5. Compute the net present value for this machine using a discount rate of 7% and assuming that cash flows occur at each year-end. (*Hint:* Salvage value is a cash inflow at the end of the asset's life. Round the net present value to the nearest dollar.)

Problem 24-2A
Analysis and computation of payback period, accounting rate of return, and net present value P1 P2 P3

Most Company has an opportunity to invest in one of two new projects. Project Y requires a $350,000 investment for new machinery with a four-year life and no salvage value. Project Z requires a $350,000 investment for new machinery with a three-year life and no salvage value. The two projects yield the following predicted annual results. The company uses straight-line depreciation, and cash flows occur evenly throughout each year.

	Project Y	Project Z
Sales	$350,000	$280,000
Expenses		
Direct materials	49,000	35,000
Direct labor	70,000	42,000
Overhead including depreciation	126,000	126,000
Selling and administrative expenses	25,000	25,000
Total expenses	270,000	228,000
Pretax income	80,000	52,000
Income taxes (30%)	24,000	15,600
Net income	$ 56,000	$ 36,400

Required

1. Compute each project's annual expected net cash flows. (Round the net cash flows to the nearest dollar.)
2. Determine each project's payback period. (Round the payback period to two decimals.)
3. Compute each project's accounting rate of return. (Round the percentage return to one decimal.)
4. Determine each project's net present value using 8% as the discount rate. For part 4 only, assume that cash flows occur at each year-end. (Round the net present value to the nearest dollar.)

Check For Project Y: (2) 2.44 years, (3) 32%

(4) $125,286

Analysis Component

5. Identify the project you would recommend to management and explain your choice.

Problem 24-3A
Computation of cash flows and net present values with alternative depreciation methods
P3

Manning Corporation is considering a new project requiring a $90,000 investment in test equipment with no salvage value. The project would produce $66,000 of pretax income before depreciation at the end of each of the next six years. The company's income tax rate is 40%. In compiling its tax return and computing its income tax payments, the company can choose between the two alternative depreciation schedules shown in the table.

	Straight-Line Depreciation	MACRS Depreciation*
Year 1	$ 9,000	$18,000
Year 2	18,000	28,800
Year 3	18,000	17,280
Year 4	18,000	10,368
Year 5	18,000	10,368
Year 6	9,000	5,184
Totals	$90,000	$90,000

* The modified accelerated cost recovery system (MACRS) for depreciation is discussed in Chapter 8.

Required

1. Prepare a five-column table that reports amounts (assuming use of straight-line depreciation) for each of the following for each of the six years: (a) pretax income before depreciation, (b) straight-line depreciation expense, (c) taxable income, (d) income taxes, and (e) net cash flow. Net cash flow equals the amount of income before depreciation minus the income taxes. (Round answers to the nearest dollar.)
2. Prepare a five-column table that reports amounts (assuming use of MACRS depreciation) for each of the following for each of the six years: (a) pretax income before depreciation, (b) MACRS depreciation expense, (c) taxable income, (d) income taxes, and (e) net cash flow. Net cash flow equals the income amount before depreciation minus the income taxes. (Round answers to the nearest dollar.)
3. Compute the net present value of the investment if straight-line depreciation is used. Use 10% as the discount rate. (Round the net present value to the nearest dollar.)
4. Compute the net present value of the investment if MACRS depreciation is used. Use 10% as the discount rate. (Round the net present value to the nearest dollar.)

Check Net present value: (3) $108,518 (4) $110,303

Analysis Component

5. Explain why the MACRS depreciation method increases this project's net present value.

Problem 24-4A
Computing net present value of alternate investments
P3

Interstate Manufacturing is considering either replacing one of its old machines with a new machine or having the old machine overhauled. Information about the two alternatives follows. Management requires a 10% rate of return on its investments.

Alternative 1: Keep the old machine and have it overhauled. If the old machine is overhauled, it will be kept for another five years and then sold for its salvage value.

Cost of old machine	$112,000
Cost of overhaul	150,000
Annual expected revenues generated	95,000
Annual cash operating costs after overhaul	42,000
Salvage value of old machine in 5 years	15,000

Alternative 2: Sell the old machine and buy a new one. The new machine is more efficient and will yield substantial operating cost savings with more product being produced and sold.

Cost of new machine	$300,000
Salvage value of old machine now	29,000
Annual expected revenues generated	100,000
Annual cash operating costs	32,000
Salvage value of new machine in 5 years	20,000

Required

1. Determine the net present value of alternative 1.
2. Determine the net present value of alternative 2.
3. Which alternative do you recommend that management select? Explain.

Check (1) Net present value of alternative 1, $60,226

Problem 24-5A
Payback period, break-even time, and net present value
P1 A1

Sentinel Company is considering an investment in technology to improve its operations. The investment will require an initial outlay of $250,000 and will yield the following expected cash flows. Management requires investments to have a payback period of three years, and it requires a 10% return on investments.

Period	Cash Flow
1	$ 47,000
2	52,000
3	75,000
4	94,000
5	125,000

Required

Check (1) Payback period, 3.8 years

1. Determine the payback period for this investment. (Round the answer to one decimal.)
2. Determine the break-even time for this investment. (Round the answer to one decimal.)
3. Determine the net present value for this investment.

Analysis Component

4. Should management invest in this project? Explain.

Problem 24-6A
Payback period, break-even time, and net present value
P1 A1

Lenitnes Company is considering an investment in technology to improve its operations. The investment will require an initial outlay of $250,000 and will yield the following expected cash flows. Management requires investments to have a payback period of three years, and it requires a 10% return on its investments.

Period	Cash Flow
1	$125,000
2	94,000
3	75,000
4	52,000
5	47,000

Required

Check (1) Payback period, 2.4 years

1. Determine the payback period for this investment. (Round the answer to one decimal.)
2. Determine the break-even time for this investment. (Round the answer to one decimal.)
3. Determine the net present value for this investment.

Analysis Component

4. Should management invest in this project? Explain.
5. Compare your answers for parts 1 through 4 with those for Problem 24-5A. What are the causes of the differences in results and your conclusions?

PROBLEM SET B

Problem 24-1B
Computation of payback period, accounting rate of return, and net present value
P1 P2 P3

Cortino Company is planning to add a new product to its line. To manufacture this product, the company needs to buy a new machine at a $300,000 cost with an expected four-year life and a $20,000 salvage value. All sales are for cash and all costs are out-of-pocket, except for depreciation on the new machine. Additional information includes the following.

Expected annual sales of new product	$1,150,000
Expected annual costs of new product	
Direct materials	300,000
Direct labor	420,000
Overhead (excluding straight-line depreciation on new machine)	210,000
Selling and administrative expenses	100,000
Income taxes	30%

Required

1. Compute straight-line depreciation for each year of this new machine's life. (Round depreciation amounts to the nearest dollar.)
2. Determine expected net income and net cash flow for each year of this machine's life. (Round answers to the nearest dollar.)
3. Compute this machine's payback period, assuming that cash flows occur evenly throughout each year. (Round the payback period to two decimals.)

Check (4) 21.88%

4. Compute this machine's accounting rate of return, assuming that income is earned evenly throughout each year. (Round the percentage return to two decimals.)

(5) $70,915

5. Compute the net present value for this machine using a discount rate of 7% and assuming that cash flows occur at each year-end. (*Hint:* Salvage value is a cash inflow at the end of the asset's life.)

Problem 24-2B
Analysis and computation of payback period, accounting rate of return, and net present value
P1 P2 P3

Aikman Company has an opportunity to invest in one of two projects. Project A requires a $240,000 investment for new machinery with a four-year life and no salvage value. Project B also requires a $240,000 investment for new machinery with a three-year life and no salvage value. The two projects yield the following predicted annual results. The company uses straight-line depreciation, and cash flows occur evenly throughout each year.

	Project A	Project B
Sales	$250,000	$200,000
Expenses		
Direct materials	35,000	25,000
Direct labor	50,000	30,000
Overhead including depreciation	90,000	90,000
Selling and administrative expenses	18,000	18,000
Total expenses	193,000	163,000
Pretax income	57,000	37,000
Income taxes (30%)	17,100	11,100
Net income	$ 39,900	$ 25,900

Required

1. Compute each project's annual expected net cash flows. (Round net cash flows to the nearest dollar.)
2. Determine each project's payback period. (Round the payback period to two decimals.)
3. Compute each project's accounting rate of return. (Round the percentage return to one decimal.)
4. Determine each project's net present value using 8% as the discount rate. For part 4 only, assume that cash flows occur at each year-end. (Round net present values to the nearest dollar.)

Check For Project A: (2) 2.4 years (3) 33.3% (4) $90,879

Analysis Component

5. Identify the project you would recommend to management and explain your choice.

Problem 24-3B
Computation of cash flows and net present values with alternative depreciation methods
P3

Grossman Corporation is considering a new project requiring a $30,000 investment in an asset having no salvage value. The project would produce $12,000 of pretax income before depreciation at the end of each of the next six years. The company's income tax rate is 40%. In compiling its tax return and computing its income tax payments, the company can choose between two alternative depreciation schedules as shown in the table.

	Straight-Line Depreciation	MACRS Depreciation*
Year 1	$ 3,000	$ 6,000
Year 2	6,000	9,600
Year 3	6,000	5,760
Year 4	6,000	3,456
Year 5	6,000	3,456
Year 6	3,000	1,728
Totals	$30,000	$30,000

* The modified accelerated cost recovery system (MACRS) for depreciation is discussed in Chapter 8.

Required

1. Prepare a five-column table that reports amounts (assuming use of straight-line depreciation) for each of the following items for each of the six years: (a) pretax income before depreciation, (b) straight-line depreciation expense, (c) taxable income, (d) income taxes, and (e) net cash flow. Net cash flow equals the amount of income before depreciation minus the income taxes. (Round answers to the nearest dollar.)
2. Prepare a five-column table that reports amounts (assuming use of MACRS depreciation) for each of the following items for each of the six years: (a) pretax income before depreciation, (b) MACRS depreciation expense, (c) taxable income, (d) income taxes, and (e) net cash flow. Net cash flow equals the amount of income before depreciation minus the income taxes. (Round answers to the nearest dollar.)

Check Net present value: (3) $10,041 (4) $10,635

3. Compute the net present value of the investment if straight-line depreciation is used. Use 10% as the discount rate. (Round the net present value to the nearest dollar.)
4. Compute the net present value of the investment if MACRS depreciation is used. Use 10% as the discount rate. (Round the net present value to the nearest dollar.)

Analysis Component

5. Explain why the MACRS depreciation method increases the net present value of this project.

Problem 24-4B
Computing net present value of alternate investments
P3

Archer Foods has a freezer that is in need of repair and is considering whether to replace the old freezer with a new freezer or have the old freezer extensively repaired. Information about the two alternatives follows. Management requires a 10% rate of return on its investments.

Alternative 1: Keep the old freezer and have it repaired. If the old freezer is repaired, it will be kept for another eight years and then sold for its salvage value.

Cost of old freezer	$75,000
Cost of repair	50,000
Annual expected revenues generated	63,000
Annual cash operating costs after repair	55,000
Salvage value of old freezer in 8 years	3,000

Alternative 2: Sell the old freezer and buy a new one. The new freezer is larger than the old one and will allow the company to expand its product offerings, thereby generating more revenues. Also, it is more energy efficient and will yield substantial operating cost savings.

Cost of new freezer	$150,000
Salvage value of old freezer now	5,000
Annual expected revenues generated	68,000
Annual cash operating costs	30,000
Salvage value of new freezer in 8 years	8,000

Required

Check (1) Net present value of alternative 1, $(5,921)

1. Determine the net present value of alternative 1.
2. Determine the net present value of alternative 2.
3. Which alternative do you recommend that management select? Explain.

Problem 24-5B
Payback period, break-even time, and net present value
P1 A1

Aster Company is considering an investment in technology to improve its operations. The investment will require an initial outlay of $800,000 and yield the following expected cash flows. Management requires investments to have a payback period of two years, and it requires a 10% return on its investments.

Period	Cash Flow
1	$300,000
2	350,000
3	400,000
4	450,000

Required

Check (1) Payback period, 2.4 years

1. Determine the payback period for this investment.
2. Determine the break-even time for this investment.
3. Determine the net present value for this investment.

Analysis Component

4. Should management invest in this project? Explain.

Problem 24-6B
Payback period, break-even time, and net present value
P1 A1

Retsa Company is considering an investment in technology to improve its operations. The investment will require an initial outlay of $800,000 and will yield the following expected cash flows. Management requires investments to have a payback period of two years, and it requires a 10% return on its investments.

Period	Cash Flow
1	$450,000
2	400,000
3	350,000
4	300,000

Required

1. Determine the payback period for this investment. (Round the answer to one decimal.)
2. Determine the break-even time for this investment. (Round the answer to one decimal.)
3. Determine the net present value for this investment.

Check (1) Payback period, 1.9 years

Analysis Component

4. Should management invest in this project? Explain.
5. Compare your answers for parts 1 through 4 with those for Problem 24-5B. What are the causes of the differences in results and your conclusions?

SERIAL PROBLEM
Business Solutions
P1 P2

(This serial problem began in Chapter 1 and continues through most of the book. If previous chapter segments were not completed, the serial problem can begin at this point. It is helpful, but not necessary, to use the Working Papers that accompany the book.)

SP 24 Santana Rey is considering the purchase of equipment for Business Solutions that would allow the company to add a new product to its computer furniture line. The equipment is expected to cost $300,000 and to have a six-year life and no salvage value. It will be depreciated on a straight-line basis. Business Solutions expects to sell 100 units of the equipment's product each year. The expected annual income related to this equipment follows.

Sales	$375,000
Costs	
Materials, labor, and overhead (except depreciation)	200,000
Depreciation on new equipment	50,000
Selling and administrative expenses	37,500
Total costs and expenses	287,500
Pretax income	87,500
Income taxes (30%)	26,250
Net income	$ 61,250

Required

Compute the (1) payback period and (2) accounting rate of return for this equipment. (Record answers as percents, rounded to one decimal.)

Beyond the Numbers

REPORTING IN ACTION
P3
APPLE

BTN 24-1 Assume **Apple** invested $2.12 billion to expand its manufacturing capacity. Assume that these assets have a 10-year life and that Apple requires a 10% internal rate of return on these assets.

Required

1. What is the amount of annual cash flows that Apple must earn from these projects to have a 10% internal rate of return? (*Hint:* Identify the 10-period, 10% factor from the present value of an annuity table, and then divide $2.12 billion by this factor to get the annual cash flows necessary.)

Fast Forward

2. Access Apple's financial statements for fiscal years ended after September 28, 2013, from its website (**Apple.com**) or the SEC's website (**SEC.gov**).

a. Determine the amount that Apple invested in capital assets for the most recent year. (*Hint:* Refer to the statement of cash flows.)

b. Assume a 10-year life and a 10% internal rate of return. What is the amount of cash flows that Apple must earn on these new projects?

COMPARATIVE ANALYSIS

P3 P4

APPLE
GOOGLE

BTN 24-2 Assume that **Google** invests $2.42 billion in capital expenditures, including $1.08 billion related to manufacturing capacity. Assume that these projects have a seven-year life and that management requires a 15% internal rate of return on those projects.

Required

1. What is the amount of annual cash flows that Google must earn from those expenditures to achieve a 15% internal rate of return? (*Hint:* Identify the seven-period, 15% factor from the present value of an annuity table and then divide $1.08 billion by the factor to get the annual cash flows required.)

2. BTN 24-1 must be completed to answer part 2. How does your answer to part 1 compare to **Apple**'s required cash flows determined in BTN 24-1? What does this imply about each company's cash flow requirements for these types of projects?

ETHICS CHALLENGE

P3

BTN 24-3 A consultant commented that "too often the numbers look good but feel bad." This comment often stems from estimation error common to capital budgeting proposals that relate to future cash flows. Three reasons for this error often exist. First, reliably predicting cash flows several years into the future is very difficult. Second, the present value of cash flows many years into the future (say, beyond 10 years) is often very small. Third, it is difficult for personal biases and expectations not to unduly influence present value computations.

Required

1. Compute the present value of $100 to be received in 10 years assuming a 12% discount rate.

2. Why is understanding the three reasons mentioned for estimation errors important when evaluating investment projects? Link this response to your answer for part 1.

COMMUNICATING IN PRACTICE

P1 P2 P3 P4

BTN 24-4 Payback period, accounting rate of return, net present value, and internal rate of return are common methods to evaluate capital investment opportunities. Assume that your manager asks you to identify the type of measurement basis and unit that each method offers and to list the advantages and disadvantages of each. Present your response in memorandum format of less than one page.

TAKING IT TO THE NET

P1 P3

BTN 24-5 Capital budgeting is an important topic, and there are websites designed to help people understand the methods available. Access **TeachMeFinance.com**'s capital budgeting web page (**teachmefinance.com/capitalbudgeting.html**). This web page contains an example of a capital budgeting case involving a $15,000 initial cash outflow.

Required

Compute the payback period and the net present value (assuming a 10% required rate of return) of the following investment—assume that its cash flows occur at year-end. Compared to the example case at the website, the larger cash inflows in the example below occur in the later years of the project's life. Is this investment acceptable based on the application of these two capital budgeting methods? Explain.

Year	Cash Flow
0	$(15,000)
1	1,000
2	2,000
3	3,000
4	6,000
5	7,000

TEAMWORK IN ACTION
P1 P3

BTN 24-6 Break into teams and identify four reasons that an international airline such as **Southwest** or **Delta** would invest in a project when its direct analysis using both payback period and net present value indicate it to be a poor investment. (*Hint:* Think about qualitative factors.) Provide an example of an investment project that supports your answer.

ENTREPRENEURIAL DECISION
P1 P2 P3 P4

BTN 24-7 Read the chapter opener about Limor Fried and her company, **Adafruit Industries**. Suppose Limor's business continues to grow, and she builds a massive new manufacturing facility and warehousing center to make her business more efficient and reduce costs.

Required

1. What are some of the management tools that Limor can use to evaluate whether the new manufacturing facility and warehousing center will be a good investment?
2. What information does Limor need to use the tools that you identified in your answer to part 1?
3. What are some of the advantages and disadvantages of each tool identified in your answer to part 1?

HITTING THE ROAD
P3

BTN 24-8 Visit or call a local auto dealership and inquire about leasing a car. Ask about the down payment and the required monthly payments. You will likely find the salesperson does not discuss the cost to purchase this car but focuses on the affordability of the monthly payments. This chapter gives you the tools to compute the cost of this car using the lease payment schedule in present dollars and to estimate the profit from leasing for an auto dealership.

Required

1. Compare the cost of leasing the car to buying it in present dollars using the information from the dealership you contact. (Assume you will make a final payment at the end of the lease and then own the car.)
2. Is it more costly to lease or buy the car? Support your answer with computations.

GLOBAL DECISION
P3 P4

Samsung

BTN 24-9 **Samsung**'s annual report includes information about its debt and interest rates. Its annual report reveals that Samsung recently issued bonds with an interest rate of 4.1%.

Required

Explain how Samsung would use that 4.1% rate to evaluate its investments in capital projects.

ANSWERS TO MULTIPLE CHOICE QUIZ

1. a
2. e;

	Net Cash Flow	Present Value of an Annuity of 1 at 12%	Present Value of Cash Flows
Years 1–3	$3,600 + $30,000	2.4018	$ 80,700
Amount invested			(90,000)
Net present value . . .			$ (9,300)

3. a
4. c; Payback = $270,000/$61,200 per year = 4.4 years.
5. d; Accounting rate of return = $8,550/[($180,000 + $0)/2] = 9.5%.

appendix A

Financial Statement Information

This appendix includes financial information for (1) **Apple**, (2) **Google**, and (3) **Samsung**. Apple states that it designs, manufactures, and markets mobile communication and media devices, personal computers, and portable digital music players, and sells a variety of related software, services, peripherals, networking solutions, and third-party digital content and applications; it competes with both Google and Samsung in the United States and globally. The information in this appendix is taken from their annual 10-K reports (or annual report for Samsung) filed with the SEC or other regulatory agency. An **annual report** is a summary of a company's financial results for the year along with its current financial condition and future plans. This report is directed to external users of financial information, but it also affects the actions and decisions of internal users.

A company often uses an annual report to showcase itself and its products. Many annual reports include photos, diagrams, and illustrations related to the company. The primary objective of annual reports, however, is the financial section, which communicates much information about a company, with most data drawn from the accounting information system. The layout of an annual report's financial section is fairly established and typically includes the following:

- Letter to Shareholders
- Financial History and Highlights
- Management Discussion and Analysis
- Management's Report on Financial Statements and on Internal Controls
- Report of Independent Accountants (Auditor's Report) and on Internal Controls
- Financial Statements
- Notes to Financial Statements
- List of Directors and Officers

This appendix provides the financial statements for Apple (plus selected notes), Google, and Samsung. The appendix is organized as follows:

APPLE
GOOGLE
Samsung

Many assignments at the end of each chapter refer to information in this appendix. We encourage readers to spend time with these assignments; they are especially useful in showing the relevance and diversity of financial accounting and reporting.

Special note: The SEC maintains the EDGAR (**E**lectronic **D**ata **G**athering, **A**nalysis, and **R**etrieval) database at **www.SEC.gov** for U.S. filers. The **Form 10-K** is the annual report form for most companies. It provides electronically accessible information. The **Form 10-KSB** is the annual report form filed by small businesses. It requires slightly less information than the Form 10-K. One of these forms must be filed within 90 days after the company's fiscal year-end. (Forms 10-K405, 10-KT, 10-KT405, and 10-KSB405 are slight variations of the usual form due to certain regulations or rules.)

Apple Inc.
CONSOLIDATED BALANCE SHEETS
(In millions, except number of shares which are reflected in thousands)

	September 28, 2013	September 29, 2012
ASSETS:		
Current assets:		
Cash and cash equivalents	$ 14,259	$ 10,746
Short-term marketable securities	26,287	18,383
Accounts receivable, less allowances of $99 and $98, respectively	13,102	10,930
Inventories	1,764	791
Deferred tax assets	3,453	2,583
Vendor non-trade receivables	7,539	7,762
Other current assets	6,882	6,458
Total current assets	73,286	57,653
Long-term marketable securities	106,215	92,122
Property, plant and equipment, net	16,597	15,452
Goodwill	1,577	1,135
Acquired intangible assets, net	4,179	4,224
Other assets	5,146	5,478
Total assets	$ 207,000	$ 176,064
LIABILITIES AND SHAREHOLDERS' EQUITY:		
Current liabilities:		
Accounts payable	$ 22,367	$ 21,175
Accrued expenses	13,856	11,414
Deferred revenue	7,435	5,953
Total current liabilities	43,658	38,542
Deferred revenue – non-current	2,625	2,648
Long-term debt	16,960	0
Other non-current liabilities	20,208	16,664
Total liabilities	83,451	57,854
Commitments and contingencies		
Shareholders' equity:		
Common stock, no par value; 1,800,000 shares authorized; 899,213 and 939,208 shares issued and outstanding, respectively	19,764	16,422
Retained earnings	104,256	101,289
Accumulated other comprehensive income/(loss)	(471)	499
Total shareholders' equity	123,549	118,210
Total liabilities and shareholders' equity	$ 207,000	$ 176,064

See accompanying Notes to Consolidated Financial Statements.

Apple Inc.
CONSOLIDATED STATEMENTS OF OPERATIONS
(In millions, except number of shares which are reflected in thousands and per share amounts)

Years ended	September 28, 2013	September 29, 2012	September 24, 2011
Net sales	$ 170,910	$ 156,508	$ 108,249
Cost of sales	106,606	87,846	64,431
Gross margin	64,304	68,662	43,818
Operating expenses:			
Research and development	4,475	3,381	2,429
Selling, general and administrative	10,830	10,040	7,599
Total operating expenses	15,305	13,421	10,028
Operating income	48,999	55,241	33,790
Other income/(expense), net	1,156	522	415
Income before provision for income taxes	50,155	55,763	34,205
Provision for income taxes	13,118	14,030	8,283
Net income	$ 37,037	$ 41,733	$ 25,922
Earnings per share:			
Basic	$ 40.03	$ 44.64	$ 28.05
Diluted	$ 39.75	$ 44.15	$ 27.68
Shares used in computing earnings per share:			
Basic	925,331	934,818	924,258
Diluted	931,662	945,355	936,645
Cash dividends declared per common share	$ 11.40	$ 2.65	$ 0.00

Apple Inc.
CONSOLIDATED STATEMENTS OF COMPREHENSIVE INCOME
(In millions)

Years ended	September 28, 2013	September 29, 2012	September 24, 2011
Net income	$ 37,037	$ 41,733	$ 25,922
Other comprehensive income/(loss):			
Change in foreign currency translation, net of tax effects of $35, $13 and $18, respectively	(112)	(15)	(12)
Change in unrecognized gains/losses on derivative instruments:			
Change in fair value of derivatives, net of tax benefit/(expense) of $(351), $73 and $(50),respectively	522	(131)	92
Adjustment for net losses/(gains) realized and included in net income, net of tax expense/(benefit) of $255, $220 and $(250), respectively	(458)	(399)	450
Total change in unrecognized gains/losses on derivative instruments, net of tax	64	(530)	542
Change in unrealized gains/losses on marketable securities:			
Change in fair value of marketable securities, net of tax benefit/(expense) of $458, $(421) and $17, respectively	(791)	715	29
Adjustment for net losses/(gains) realized and included in net income, net of tax expense/(benefit) of $82, $68 and $(40), respectively	(131)	(114)	(70)
Total change in unrealized gains/losses on marketable securities, net of tax	(922)	601	(41)
Total other comprehensive income/(loss)	(970)	56	489
Total comprehensive income	$ 36,067	$ 41,789	$ 26,411

See accompanying Notes to Consolidated Financial Statements.

Apple Inc.
CONSOLIDATED STATEMENTS OF SHAREHOLDERS' EQUITY
(In millions, except number of shares which are reflected in thousands)

	Common Stock Shares	Common Stock Amount	Retained Earnings	Accumulated Other Comprehensive Income/(Loss)	Total Shareholders' Equity
Balances as of September 25, 2010	915,970	$ 10,668	$ 37,169	$ (46)	$ 47,791
Net income	0	0	25,922	0	25,922
Other comprehensive income/(loss)	0	0	0	489	489
Share-based compensation	0	1,168	0	0	1,168
Common stock issued under stock plans, net of shares withheld for employee taxes	13,307	561	(250)	0	311
Tax benefit from equity awards, including transfer pricing adjustments	0	934	0	0	934
Balances as of September 24, 2011	929,277	13,331	62,841	443	76,615
Net income	0	0	41,733	0	41,733
Other comprehensive income/(loss)	0	0	0	56	56
Dividends and dividend equivalent rights declared	0	0	(2,523)	0	(2,523)
Share-based compensation	0	1,740	0	0	1,740
Common stock issued under stock plans, net of shares withheld for employee taxes	9,931	200	(762)	0	(562)
Tax benefit from equity awards, including transfer pricing adjustments	0	1,151	0	0	1,151
Balances as of September 29, 2012	939,208	16,422	101,289	499	118,210
Net income	0	0	37,037	0	37,037
Other comprehensive income/(loss)	0	0	0	(970)	(970)
Dividends and dividend equivalent rights declared	0	0	(10,676)	0	(10,676)
Repurchase of common stock	(46,976)	0	(22,950)	0	(22,950)
Share-based compensation	0	2,253	0	0	2,253
Common stock issued under stock plans, net of shares withheld for employee taxes	6,981	(143)	(444)	0	(587)
Tax benefit from equity awards, including transfer pricing adjustments	0	1,232	0	0	1,232
Balances as of September 28, 2013	899,213	$ 19,764	$ 104,256	$ (471)	$ 123,549

See accompanying Notes to Consolidated Financial Statements.

Apple Inc.
CONSOLIDATED STATEMENTS OF CASH FLOWS
(In millions)

Years ended	September 28, 2013	September 29, 2012	September 24, 2011
Cash and cash equivalents, beginning of the year	$ 10,746	$ 9,815	$ 11,261
Operating activities:			
Net income	37,037	41,733	25,922
Adjustments to reconcile net income to cash generated by operating activities:			
Depreciation and amortization	6,757	3,277	1,814
Share-based compensation expense	2,253	1,740	1,168
Deferred income tax expense	1,141	4,405	2,868
Changes in operating assets and liabilities:			
Accounts receivable, net	(2,172)	(5,551)	143
Inventories	(973)	(15)	275
Vendor non-trade receivables	223	(1,414)	(1,934)
Other current and non-current assets	1,080	(3,162)	(1,391)
Accounts payable	2,340	4,467	2,515
Deferred revenue	1,459	2,824	1,654
Other current and non-current liabilities	4,521	2,552	4,495
Cash generated by operating activities	53,666	50,856	37,529
Investing activities:			
Purchases of marketable securities	(148,489)	(151,232)	(102,317)
Proceeds from maturities of marketable securities	20,317	13,035	20,437
Proceeds from sales of marketable securities	104,130	99,770	49,416
Payments made in connection with business acquisitions, net	(496)	(350)	(244)
Payments for acquisition of property, plant and equipment	(8,165)	(8,295)	(4,260)
Payments for acquisition of intangible assets	(911)	(1,107)	(3,192)
Other	(160)	(48)	(259)
Cash used in investing activities	(33,774)	(48,227)	(40,419)
Financing activities:			
Proceeds from issuance of common stock	530	665	831
Excess tax benefits from equity awards	701	1,351	1,133
Taxes paid related to net share settlement of equity awards	(1,082)	(1,226)	(520)
Dividends and dividend equivalent rights paid	(10,564)	(2,488)	0
Repurchase of common stock	(22,860)	0	0
Proceeds from issuance of long-term debt, net	16,896	0	0
Cash generated by/(used in) financing activities	(16,379)	(1,698)	1,444
Increase/(decrease) in cash and cash equivalents	3,513	931	(1,446)
Cash and cash equivalents, end of the year	$ 14,259	$ 10,746	$ 9,815
Supplemental cash flow disclosure:			
Cash paid for income taxes, net	$ 9,128	$ 7,682	$ 3,338

See accompanying Notes to Consolidated Financial Statements.

APPLE INC.
SELECTED NOTES TO CONSOLIDATED FINANCIAL STATEMENTS

Basis of Presentation and Preparation

The Company's fiscal year is the 52- or 53-week period that ends on the last Saturday of September. The Company's fiscal years 2013, 2012 and 2011 ended on September 28, 2013, September 29, 2012 and September 24, 2011, respectively. An additional week is included in the first fiscal quarter approximately every six years to realign fiscal quarters with calendar quarters. Fiscal year 2012 spanned 53 weeks, with a 14th week included in the first quarter of 2012. Fiscal years 2013 and 2011 spanned 52 weeks each. Unless otherwise stated, references to particular years, quarters, months and periods refer to the Company's fiscal years ended in September and the associated quarters, months and periods of those fiscal years.

Revenue Recognition

Net sales consist primarily of revenue from the sale of hardware, software, digital content and applications, peripherals, and service and support contracts. The Company recognizes revenue when persuasive evidence of an arrangement exists, delivery has occurred, the sales price is fixed or determinable, and collection is probable. Product is considered delivered to the customer once it has been shipped and title and risk of loss have been transferred. For most of the Company's product sales, these criteria are met at the time the product is shipped. For online sales to individuals, for some sales to education customers in the U.S., and for certain other sales, the Company defers revenue until the customer receives the product because the Company retains a portion of the risk of loss on these sales during transit. The Company recognizes revenue from the sale of hardware products, software bundled with hardware that is essential to the functionality of the hardware, and third-party digital content sold on the iTunes Store in accordance with general revenue recognition accounting guidance. The Company recognizes revenue in accordance with industry specific software accounting guidance for the following types of sales transactions: (i) standalone sales of software products, (ii) sales of software upgrades and (iii) sales of software bundled with hardware not essential to the functionality of the hardware.

For the sale of most third-party products, the Company recognizes revenue based on the gross amount billed to customers because the Company establishes its own pricing for such products, retains related inventory risk for physical products, is the primary obligor to the customer and assumes the credit risk for amounts billed to its customers. For third-party applications sold through the App Store and Mac App Store and certain digital content sold through the iTunes Store, the Company does not determine the selling price of the products and is not the primary obligor to the customer. Therefore, the Company accounts for such sales on a net basis by recognizing in net sales only the commission it retains from each sale. The portion of the gross amount billed to customers that is remitted by the Company to third-party app developers and certain digital content owners is not reflected in the Company's Consolidated Statements of Operations.

The Company records deferred revenue when it receives payments in advance of the delivery of products or the performance of services. This includes amounts that have been deferred for unspecified and specified software upgrade rights and non-software services that are attached to hardware and software products. The Company sells gift cards redeemable at its retail and online stores, and also sells gift cards redeemable on the iTunes Store for the purchase of digital content and software. The Company records deferred revenue upon the sale of the card, which is relieved upon redemption of the card by the customer. Revenue from AppleCare service and support contracts is deferred and recognized over the service coverage periods. AppleCare service and support contracts typically include extended phone support, repair services, web-based support resources and diagnostic tools offered under the Company's standard limited warranty.

The Company records reductions to revenue for estimated commitments related to price protection and other customer incentive programs. For transactions involving price protection, the Company recognizes revenue net of the estimated amount to be refunded. For the Company's other customer incentive programs, the estimated cost of these programs is recognized at the later of the date at which the Company has sold the product or the date at which the program is offered. The Company also records reductions to revenue for expected future product returns based on the Company's historical experience. Revenue is recorded net of taxes collected from customers that are remitted to governmental authorities, with the collected taxes recorded as current liabilities until remitted to the relevant government authority.

Shipping Costs

For all periods presented, amounts billed to customers related to shipping and handling are classified as revenue, and the Company's shipping and handling costs are included in cost of sales.

Warranty Expense

The Company generally provides for the estimated cost of hardware and software warranties at the time the related revenue is recognized. The Company assesses the adequacy of its pre-existing warranty liabilities and adjusts the amounts as necessary based on actual experience and changes in future estimates.

Apple Inc. Notes—continued

Software Development Costs

Research and development costs are expensed as incurred. Development costs of computer software to be sold, leased, or otherwise marketed are subject to capitalization beginning when a product's technological feasibility has been established and ending when a product is available for general release to customers. In most instances, the Company's products are released soon after technological feasibility has been established. Costs incurred subsequent to achievement of technological feasibility were not significant, and software development costs were expensed as incurred during 2013, 2012 and 2011.

Advertising Costs

Advertising costs are expensed as incurred and included in selling, general and administrative expenses. Advertising expense was $1.1 billion, $1.0 billion and $933 million for 2013, 2012 and 2011, respectively.

Earnings Per Share

Basic earnings per share is computed by dividing income available to common shareholders by the weighted-average number of shares of common stock outstanding during the period. Diluted earnings per share is computed by dividing income available to common shareholders by the weighted-average number of shares of common stock outstanding during the period increased to include the number of additional shares of common stock that would have been outstanding if the potentially dilutive securities had been issued.

Cash Equivalents and Marketable Securities

All highly liquid investments with maturities of three months or less at the date of purchase are classified as cash equivalents. The Company's marketable debt and equity securities have been classified and accounted for as available-for-sale. Management determines the appropriate classification of its investments at the time of purchase and reevaluates the designations at each balance sheet date. The Company classifies its marketable debt securities as either short-term or long-term based on each instrument's underlying contractual maturity date. Marketable debt securities with maturities of 12 months or less are classified as short-term and marketable debt securities with maturities greater than 12 months are classified as long-term. The Company classifies its marketable equity securities, including mutual funds, as either short-term or long-term based on the nature of each security and its availability for use in current operations. The Company's marketable debt and equity securities are carried at fair value, with the unrealized gains and losses, net of taxes, reported as a component of shareholders' equity. The cost of securities sold is based upon the specific identification method.

Accounts Receivable (Trade Receivables)

The Company has considerable trade receivables outstanding with its third-party cellular network carriers, wholesalers, retailers, value-added resellers, small and mid-sized businesses, and education, enterprise and government customers. The Company's cellular network carriers accounted for 68% and 66% of trade receivables as of September 28, 2013 and September 29, 2012, respectively. The additions and write-offs to the Company's allowance for doubtful accounts during 2013, 2012 and 2011 were not significant.

Allowance for Doubtful Accounts

The Company records its allowance for doubtful accounts based upon its assessment of various factors. The Company considers historical experience, the age of the accounts receivable balances, credit quality of the Company's customers, current economic conditions, and other factors that may affect customers' ability to pay.

Inventories

Inventories are stated at the lower of cost, computed using the first-in, first-out method, or market. If the cost of the inventories exceeds their market value, provisions are made currently for the difference between the cost and the market value.

Inventories	2013	2012
Components	$ 683	$124
Finished goods	1,081	667
Total inventories	$1,764	$791

Property, Plant and Equipment

Property, plant and equipment are stated at cost. Depreciation is computed by use of the straight-line method over the estimated useful lives of the assets, which for buildings is the lesser of 30 years or the remaining life of the underlying building; between two to five years for machinery and equipment, including product tooling and manufacturing process equipment; and the shorter of lease terms or ten years for leasehold improvements. The Company capitalizes eligible costs to acquire or develop internal-use software that are incurred subsequent to the preliminary project stage. Capitalized costs related to internal-use software are amortized using the straight-line method over the estimated useful lives of the assets, which range from three to five years. Depreciation and amortization expense on property and equipment was $5.8 billion, $2.6 billion and $1.6 billion during 2013, 2012 and 2011, respectively.

Property, Plant and Equipment	2013	2012
Land and buildings	$ 3,309	$ 2,439
Machinery, equipment and internal-use software	21,242	15,984
Leasehold improvements	3,968	3,464
Gross property, plant and equipment	28,519	21,887
Accumulated depreciation and amortization	(11,922)	(6,435)
Net property, plant and equipment	$16,597	$15,452

Apple Inc. Notes—continued

Long-Lived Assets Including Goodwill and Other Acquired Intangible Assets

The Company reviews property, plant and equipment, inventory component prepayments, and certain identifiable intangibles, excluding goodwill, for impairment. Long-lived assets are reviewed for impairment whenever events or changes in circumstances indicate the carrying amount of an asset may not be recoverable. Recoverability of these assets is measured by comparison of their carrying amounts to future undiscounted cash flows the assets are expected to generate. If property, plant and equipment, inventory component prepayments, and certain identifiable intangibles are considered to be impaired, the impairment to be recognized equals the amount by which the carrying value of the assets exceeds its fair value. The Company did not record any significant impairments during 2013, 2012 and 2011.

The Company does not amortize goodwill and intangible assets with indefinite useful lives, rather such assets are required to be tested for impairment at least annually or sooner whenever events or changes in circumstances indicate that the assets may be impaired. The Company performs its goodwill and intangible asset impairment tests in the fourth quarter of each year. The Company did not recognize any impairment charges related to goodwill or indefinite lived intangible assets during 2013, 2012 and 2011. The Company established reporting units based on its current reporting structure. For purposes of testing goodwill for impairment, goodwill has been allocated to these reporting units to the extent it relates to each reporting unit. In 2013 and 2012, the Company's goodwill was allocated to the Americas and Europe reportable operating segments.

The Company amortizes its intangible assets with definite useful lives over their estimated useful lives and reviews these assets for impairment. The Company is currently amortizing its acquired intangible assets with definite useful lives over periods typically from three to seven years.

Goodwill and Other Intangible Assets

The Company's acquired intangible assets with definite useful lives primarily consist of patents and licenses and are amortized over periods typically from three to seven years. The following table summarizes the components of gross and net intangible asset balances as of September 28, 2013 (in millions):

	Gross Carrying Amount	Accumulated Amortization	Net Carrying Amount
Definite lived and amortizable acquired intangible assets	$ 6,081	$ (2,002)	$ 4,079
Indefinite lived and non-amortizable trademarks	100	0	100
Total acquired intangible assets	$ 6,181	$ (2,002)	$ 4,179

The Company's gross carrying amount of goodwill was $1.6 billion and $1.1 billion as of September 28, 2013 and September 29, 2012, respectively. The Company did not have any goodwill impairment during 2013, 2012 or 2011. Amortization expense related to acquired intangible assets was $960 million, $605 million and $192 million in 2013, 2012 and 2011, respectively.

Fair Value Measurements

The Company applies fair value accounting for all financial assets and liabilities and non-financial assets and liabilities that are recognized or disclosed at fair value in the financial statements on a recurring basis. The Company defines fair value as the price that would be received from selling an asset or paid to transfer a liability in an orderly transaction between market participants at the measurement date. When determining the fair value measurements for assets and liabilities, which are required to be recorded at fair value, the Company considers the principal or most advantageous market in which the Company would transact and the market-based risk measurements or assumptions that market participants would use in pricing the asset or liability, such as risks inherent in valuation techniques, transfer restrictions and credit risk. Fair value is estimated by applying the following hierarchy, which prioritizes the inputs used to measure fair value into three levels and bases the categorization within the hierarchy upon the lowest level of input that is available and significant to the fair value measurement:

Level 1—Quoted prices in active markets for identical assets or liabilities.

Level 2—Observable inputs other than quoted prices in active markets for identical assets and liabilities, quoted prices for identical or similar assets or liabilities in inactive markets, or other inputs that are observable or can be corroborated by observable market data for substantially the full term of the assets or liabilities.

Level 3—Inputs that are generally unobservable and typically reflect management's estimate of assumptions that market participants would use in pricing the asset or liability.

The Company's valuation techniques used to measure the fair value of money market funds and certain marketable equity securities were derived from quoted prices in active markets for identical assets or liabilities. The valuation techniques used to measure the fair value of all other financial instruments, all of which have counterparties with high credit ratings, were valued based on quoted market prices or model driven valuations using significant inputs

Apple Inc. Notes—continued

derived from or corroborated by observable market data. In accordance with the fair value accounting requirements, companies may choose to measure eligible financial instruments and certain other items at fair value. The Company has not elected the fair value option for any eligible financial instruments.

Accrued Warranty and Indemnification

The Company offers a basic limited parts and labor warranty on its hardware products. The basic warranty period for hardware products is typically one year from the date of purchase by the end-user. The Company also offers a 90-day basic warranty for its service parts used to repair the Company's hardware products. The Company provides currently for the estimated cost that may be incurred under its basic limited product warranties at the time related revenue is recognized. Factors considered in determining appropriate accruals for product warranty obligations include the size of the installed base of products subject to warranty protection, historical and projected warranty claim rates, historical and projected cost-per-claim, and knowledge of specific product failures that are outside of the Company's typical experience. The Company assesses the adequacy of its pre-existing warranty liabilities and adjusts the amounts as necessary based on actual experience and changes in future estimates. The following table shows changes in the Company's accrued warranties and related costs for 2013, 2012 and 2011 (in millions):

	2013	2012	2011
Beginning accrued warranty and related costs	$ 1,638	$ 1,240	$ 761
Cost of warranty claims	(3,703)	(1,786)	(1,147)
Accruals for product warranty	5,032	2,184	1,626
Ending accrued warranty and related costs	$ 2,967	$ 1,638	$ 1,240

Accrued Expenses	2013	2012
Accrued warranty and related costs	$ 2,967	$ 1,638
Accrued taxes	1,200	1,535
Deferred margin on component sales	1,262	1,492
Accrued marketing and selling expenses	1,291	910
Accrued compensation and employee benefits	959	735
Other current liabilities	6,177	5,104
Total accrued expenses	$13,856	$11,414

Non-Current Liabilities	2013	2012
Deferred tax liabilities	$16,489	$13,847
Other non-current liabilities	3,719	2,817
Total other non-current liabilities	$20,208	$16,664

Long-Term Debt

In May 2013, the Company issued floating- and fixed-rate notes with varying maturities for an aggregate principal amount of $17.0 billion (collectively the "Notes"). The Notes are senior unsecured obligations, and interest is payable in arrears, quarterly for the floating-rate notes and semi-annually for the fixed-rate notes. As of September 28, 2013, the fair value of the Company's Notes, based on Level 2 inputs, was $15.9 billion.

Segment Information and Geographic Data

The following table shows information by operating segment for 2013, 2012 and 2011 (in millions):

	2013	2012	2011
Americas:			
Net sales	$62,739	$57,512	$38,315
Operating income	$22,817	$23,414	$13,111
Europe:			
Net sales	$37,883	$36,323	$27,778
Operating income	$13,025	$14,869	$11,209
Greater China:			
Net sales	$25,417	$22,533	$12,690
Operating income	$ 8,541	$ 9,843	$ 5,246
Japan:			
Net sales	$13,462	$10,571	$ 5,437
Operating income	$ 6,819	$ 5,861	$ 2,415
Rest of Asia Pacific:			
Net sales	$11,181	$10,741	$ 9,902
Operating income	$ 3,753	$ 4,253	$ 4,004
Retail:			
Net sales	$20,228	$18,828	$14,127
Operating income	$ 4,025	$ 4,613	$ 3,075

GOOGLE

Google Inc.
CONSOLIDATED BALANCE SHEETS
(In millions, except share and par value amounts which are reflected in thousands, and par value per share amounts)

As of December 31	2012	2013
Assets		
Current assets:		
Cash and cash equivalents	$ 14,778	$ 18,898
Marketable securities	33,310	39,819
Total cash, cash equivalents, and marketable securities (including securities loaned of $3,160 and $5,059)	48,088	58,717
Accounts receivable, net of allowance of $581 and $631	7,885	8,882
Inventories	505	426
Receivable under reverse repurchase agreements	700	100
Deferred income taxes, net	1,144	1,526
Income taxes receivable, net	0	408
Prepaid revenue share, expenses and other assets	2,132	2,827
Total current assets	60,454	72,886
Prepaid revenue share, expenses and other assets, non-current	2,011	1,976
Non-marketable equity investments	1,469	1,976
Property and equipment, net	11,854	16,524
Intangible assets, net	7,473	6,066
Goodwill	10,537	11,492
Total assets	$ 93,798	$ 110,920
Liabilities and Stockholders' Equity		
Current liabilities:		
Accounts payable	$ 2,012	$ 2,453
Short-term debt	2,549	3,009
Accrued compensation and benefits	2,239	2,502
Accrued expenses and other current liabilities	3,258	3,755
Accrued revenue share	1,471	1,729
Securities lending payable	1,673	1,374
Deferred revenue	895	1,062
Income taxes payable, net	240	24
Total current liabilities	14,337	15,908
Long-term debt	2,988	2,236
Deferred revenue, non-current	100	139
Income taxes payable, non-current	2,046	2,638
Deferred income taxes, net, non-current	1,872	1,947
Other long-term liabilities	740	743
Commitments and contingencies		
Stockholders' equity:		
Convertible preferred stock, $0.001 par value per share, 100,000 shares authorized; no shares issued and outstanding	0	0
Class A and Class B common stock and additional paid-in capital, $0.001 par value per share: 12,000,000 shares authorized (Class A 9,000,000, Class B 3,000,000); 329,979 (Class A 267,448, Class B 62,531) and par value of $330 (Class A $267, Class B $63) and 335,832 (Class A 279,325, Class B 56,507) and par value of $336 (Class A $279, Class B $57) shares issued and outstanding	22,835	25,922
Class C capital stock, $0.001 par value per share: 3,000,000 shares authorized; no shares issued and outstanding	0	0
Accumulated other comprehensive income	538	125
Retained earnings	48,342	61,262
Total stockholders' equity	71,715	87,309
Total liabilities and stockholders' equity	$ 93,798	$ 110,920

See accompanying notes.

Google Inc.
CONSOLIDATED STATEMENTS OF INCOME
(In millions, except per share amounts)

Year Ended December 31	**2011**	**2012**	**2013**
Revenues:			
Google (advertising and other)	$37,905	$46,039	$55,519
Motorola Mobile (hardware and other)	0	4,136	4,306
Total revenues	$37,905	$50,175	$59,825
Costs and expenses:			
Cost of revenues—Google (advertising and other) [1]	13,188	17,176	21,993
Cost of revenues—Motorola Mobile (hardware and other)[1]	0	3,458	3,865
Research and development[1]	5,162	6,793	7,952
Sales and marketing[1]	4,589	6,143	7,253
General and administrative[1]	2,724	3,845	4,796
Charge related to the resolution of Department of Justice investigation	500	0	0
Total costs and expenses	26,163	37,415	45,859
Income from operations	11,742	12,760	13,966
Interest and other income, net	584	626	530
Income from continuing operations before income taxes	12,326	13,386	14,496
Provision for income taxes	2,589	2,598	2,282
Net income from continuing operations	$ 9,737	$10,788	$12,214
Net income (loss) from discontinued operations	0	(51)	706
Net income	$ 9,737	$10,737	$12,920
Net income (loss) per share of Class A and Class B common stock—basic:			
Continuing operations	$ 30.17	$ 32.97	$ 36.70
Discontinued operations	0.00	(0.16)	2.12
Net income (loss) per share of Class A and Class B common stock—basic	$ 30.17	$ 32.81	$ 38.82
Net income (loss) per share of Class A and Class B common stock—diluted:			
Continuing operations	$ 29.76	$ 32.46	$ 36.05
Discontinued operations	0.00	(0.15)	2.08
Net income (loss) per share of Class A and Class B common stock—diluted	$ 29.76	$ 32.31	$ 38.13
[1]Includes stock-based compensation expense as follows:			
Cost of revenues—Google (advertising and other)	$ 249	$ 359	$ 469
Cost of revenues—Motorola Mobile (hardware and other)	0	14	18
Research and development	1,061	1,325	1,717
Sales and marketing	361	498	578
General and administrative	303	453	486
	$ 1,974	$ 2,649	$ 3,268

See accompanying notes.

GOOGLE

GOOGLE

Google Inc.
CONSOLIDATED STATEMENTS OF STOCKHOLDERS' EQUITY
(In millions, except for share amounts which are reflected in thousands)

	Class A and Class B Common Stock and Additional Paid-In Capital		Accumulated Other Comprehensive Income	Retained Earnings	Total Stockholders' Equity
	Shares	Amount			
Balance at January 1, 2011	321,301	$ 18,235	$ 138	$ 27,868	$ 46,241
Common stock issued	3,594	621	0	0	621
Stock-based compensation expense		1,974	0	0	1,974
Stock-based compensation tax benefits		60	0	0	60
Tax withholding related to vesting of restricted stock units		(626)	0	0	(626)
Net income		0	0	9,737	9,737
Other comprehensive income		0	138	0	138
Balance at December 31, 2011	324,895	20,264	276	37,605	58,145
Common stock issued	5,084	736	0	0	736
Stock-based compensation expense		2,692	0	0	2,692
Stock-based compensation tax benefits		166	0	0	166
Tax withholding related to vesting of restricted stock units		(1,023)	0	0	(1,023)
Net income		0	0	10,737	10,737
Other comprehensive income		0	262	0	262
Balance at December 31, 2012	329,979	22,835	538	48,342	71,715
Common stock issued	5,853	1,174	0	0	1,174
Stock-based compensation expense		3,343	0	0	3,343
Stock-based compensation tax benefits		449	0	0	449
Tax withholding related to vesting of restricted stock units		(1,879)	0	0	(1,879)
Net income		0	0	12,920	12,920
Other comprehensive income		0	(413)	0	(413)
Balance at December 31, 2013	335,832	$ 25,922	$ 125	$ 61,262	$ 87,309

Google Inc.
CONSOLIDATED STATEMENTS OF COMPREHENSIVE INCOME
(In millions)

Year Ended December 31	2011	2012	2013
Net income	$9,737	$10,737	$12,920
Other comprehensive income (loss):			
Change in foreign currency translation adjustment	(107)	75	89
Available-for-sale investments:			
Change in net unrealized gains	348	493	(392)
Less: reclassification adjustment for net gains included in net income	(115)	(216)	(162)
Net change (net of tax effect of $54, $68, $212)	233	277	(554)
Cash flow hedges:			
Change in unrealized gains	39	47	112
Less: reclassification adjustment for gains included in net income	(27)	(137)	(60)
Net change (net of tax effect of $2, $53, $30)	12	(90)	52
Other comprehensive income (loss)	138	262	(413)
Comprehensive income	$9,875	$10,999	$12,507

See accompanying notes.

Google Inc.
CONSOLIDATED STATEMENTS OF CASH FLOWS
(In millions)

Year Ended December 31	2011	2012	2013
Operating activities			
Net income	$ 9,737	$ 10,737	$ 12,920
Adjustments:			
Depreciation and amortization of property and equipment	1,396	1,988	2,781
Amortization of intangible and other assets	455	974	1,158
Stock-based compensation expense	1,974	2,692	3,343
Excess tax benefits from stock-based award activities	(86)	(188)	(481)
Deferred income taxes	343	(266)	(437)
Impairment of equity investments	110	0	0
Gain on divestiture of businesses	0	(188)	(700)
Other	6	(28)	106
Changes in assets and liabilities, net of effects of acquisitions:			
Accounts receivable	(1,156)	(787)	(1,307)
Income taxes, net	731	1,492	401
Inventories	(30)	301	(234)
Prepaid revenue share, expenses and other assets	(232)	(833)	(696)
Accounts payable	101	(499)	605
Accrued expenses and other liabilities	795	762	713
Accrued revenue share	259	299	254
Deferred revenue	162	163	233
Net cash provided by operating activities	14,565	16,619	18,659
Investing activities			
Purchases of property and equipment	(3,438)	(3,273)	(7,358)
Purchases of marketable securities	(61,672)	(33,410)	(45,444)
Maturities and sales of marketable securities	48,746	35,180	38,314
Investments in non-marketable equity investments	(428)	(696)	(569)
Cash collateral related to securities lending	(354)	(334)	(299)
Investments in reverse repurchase agreements	5	45	600
Proceeds from divestiture of businesses	0	0	2,525
Acquisitions, net of cash acquired, and purchases of intangibles and other assets	(1,900)	(10,568)	(1,448)
Net cash used in investing activities	(19,041)	(13,056)	(13,679)
Financing activities			
Net payments related to stock-based award activities	(5)	(287)	(781)
Excess tax benefits from stock-based award activities	86	188	481
Proceeds from issuance of debt, net of costs	10,905	16,109	10,768
Repayments of debt	(10,179)	(14,781)	(11,325)
Net cash provided by (used in) financing activities	807	1,229	(857)
Effect of exchange rate changes on cash and cash equivalents	22	3	(3)
Net increase (decrease) in cash and cash equivalents	(3,647)	4,795	4,120
Cash and cash equivalents at beginning of period	13,630	9,983	14,778
Cash and cash equivalents at end of period	$ 9,983	$ 14,778	$ 18,898
Supplemental disclosures of cash flow information			
Cash paid for taxes	$ 1,471	$ 2,034	$ 1,932
Cash paid for interest	$ 40	$ 74	$ 72
Non-cash investing and financing activities:			
Receipt of Arris shares in connection with divestiture of Motorola Home	$ 0	$ 0	$ 175
Fair value of stock-based awards assumed in connection with acquisition of Motorola	$ 0	$ 41	$ 0
Property under capital lease	$ 0	$ 0	$ 258

See accompanying notes.

GOOGLE

Samsung Electronics Co., Ltd. and its subsidiaries
CONSOLIDATED STATEMENTS OF FINANCIAL POSITION

(In millions of Korean won)	**December 31, 2013**	**December 31, 2012**
	KRW	KRW
Assets		
Current assets		
Cash and cash equivalents	16,284,780	18,791,460
Short-term financial instruments	36,722,702	17,397,937
Available-for-sale financial assets	1,488,527	1,258,874
Trade and other receivables	27,875,934	26,674,596
Advances	1,928,188	1,674,428
Prepaid expenses	2,472,950	2,262,234
Inventories	19,134,868	17,747,413
Other current assets	2,135,589	1,462,075
Assets held for sale	2,716,733	—
Total current assets	110,760,271	87,269,017
Non-current assets		
Available-for-sale financial assets	6,238,380	5,229,175
Associates and joint ventures	6,422,292	8,785,489
Property, plant and equipment	75,496,388	68,484,743
Intangible assets	3,980,600	3,729,705
Long-term prepaid expenses	3,465,783	3,515,479
Deferred income tax assets	4,621,780	2,516,080
Other non-current assets	3,089,524	1,541,882
Total assets	214,075,018	181,071,570
Liabilities and Equity		
Current liabilities		
Trade and other payables	17,633,705	16,889,350
Short-term borrowings	6,438,517	8,443,752
Advances received	1,706,313	1,517,672
Withholdings	1,176,046	966,374
Accrued expenses	11,344,530	9,495,156
Income tax payable	3,386,018	3,222,934
Current portion of long-term borrowings and debentures	2,425,831	999,010
Provisions	6,736,476	5,054,853
Other current liabilities	467,973	343,951
Total current liabilities	51,315,409	46,933,052
Non-current liabilities		
Long-term trade and other payables	1,053,756	1,165,881
Debentures	1,311,068	1,829,374
Long-term borrowings	985,117	3,623,028
Net defined benefit liabilities	1,854,902	1,729,939
Deferred income tax liabilities	6,012,371	3,429,467
Provisions	460,924	408,529
Other non-current liabilities	1,065,461	472,094
Total liabilities	64,059,008	59,591,364
Equity attributable to owners of the parent		
Preferred stock	119,467	119,467
Common stock	778,047	778,047
Share premium	4,403,893	4,403,893
Retained earnings	148,600,282	119,985,689
Other components of equity	(9,459,073)	(8,193,044)
Non-controlling interests	5,573,394	4,386,154
Total equity	150,016,010	121,480,206
Total liabilities and equity	214,075,018	181,071,570

The accompanying notes are an integral part of these consolidated financial statements.

SAMSUNG

Samsung Electronics Co., Ltd. and its subsidiaries
CONSOLIDATED STATEMENTS OF INCOME

(In millions of Korean won)

For the year ended December 31,	2013	2012
	KRW	KRW
Revenue	228,692,667	201,103,613
Cost of sales	137,696,309	126,651,931
Gross profit	90,996,358	74,451,682
Selling and administrative expenses	54,211,345	45,402,344
Operating profit	36,785,013	29,049,338
Other non-operating income	2,429,551	1,552,989
Other non-operating expense	1,614,048	1,576,025
Share of profit of associates and joint ventures	504,063	986,611
Finance income	8,014,672	7,836,554
Finance costs	7,754,972	7,934,450
Profit before income tax	38,364,279	29,915,017
Income tax expense	7,889,515	6,069,732
Profit for the year	**30,474,764**	**23,845,285**
Profit attributable to owners of the parent	29,821,215	23,185,375
Profit attributable to non-controlling interests	653,549	659,910
Earnings per share for profit attributable to owners of the parent (in Korean Won)		
—Basic	197,841	154,020
—Diluted	197,800	153,950

Samsung Electronics Co., Ltd. and its subsidiaries
CONSOLIDATED STATEMENTS OF COMPREHENSIVE INCOME

(In millions of Korean won)

For the year ended December 31,	2013	2012
	KRW	KRW
Profit for the year	30,474,764	23,845,285
Other comprehensive income		
Items not to be reclassified subsequently to profit or loss:		
Remeasurement of net defined benefit liabilities, net of tax	(213,113)	(504,120)
Items to be reclassified subsequently to profit or loss:		
Changes in value of available-for-sale financial assets, net of tax	186,480	962,184
Share of other comprehensive income (loss) of associates and joint ventures, net of tax	20,756	(350,491)
Foreign currency translation, net of tax	(1,000,961)	(1,824,653)
Other comprehensive loss for the year, net of tax	(1,006,838)	(1,717,080)
Total comprehensive income for the year	29,467,926	22,128,205
Comprehensive income attributable to:		
Owners of the parent	28,837,590	21,499,343
Non-controlling interests	630,336	628,862

The accompanying notes are an integral part of these consolidated financial statements.

Samsung Electronics Co., Ltd. and its subsidiaries
CONSOLIDATED STATEMENTS OF CHANGES IN EQUITY

(In millions of Korean won)	Preferred stock	Common stock	Share premium	Retained earnings	Other components of equity	Equity attributable to owners of the parent	Noncontrolling interests	Total
Balance at January 1, 2012	119,467	778,047	4,403,893	97,622,872	(5,833,896)	97,090,383	4,223,247	101,313,630
Profit for the year	—	—	—	23,185,375	—	23,185,375	659,910	23,845,285
Changes in value of available-for-sale financial assets, net of tax	—	—	—	—	960,688	960,688	1,496	962,184
Share of other comprehensive loss of associates and joint ventures, net of tax	—	—	—	—	(350,491)	(350,491)	—	(350,491)
Foreign currency translation, net of tax	—	—	—	—	(1,789,877)	(1,789,877)	(34,776)	(1,824,653)
Remeasurement of net defined benefit liabilities, net of tax	—	—	—	—	(506,351)	(506,351)	2,231	(504,120)
Total comprehensive income (loss)	—	—	—	23,185,375	(1,686,031)	21,499,344	628,861	22,128,205
Dividends	—	—	—	(827,501)	—	(827,501)	(373,632)	(1,201,133)
Capital transaction under common control	—	—	—	—	(1,089,835)	(1,089,835)	(104,395)	(1,194,230)
Changes in consolidated entities	—	—	—	—	—	—	12,844	12,844
Disposal of treasury stock	—	—	—	—	455,377	455,377	—	455,377
Stock option activities	—	—	—	—	(33,071)	(33,071)	—	(33,071)
Others	—	—	—	4,943	(5,588)	(645)	(771)	(1,416)
Total transactions with owners	—	—	—	(822,558)	(673,117)	(1,495,675)	(465,954)	(1,961,629)
Balance at December 31, 2012	119,467	778,047	4,403,893	119,985,689	(8,193,044)	117,094,052	4,386,154	121,480,206
Profit for the year	—	—	—	29,821,215	—	29,821,215	653,549	30,474,764
Changes in value of available-for-sale financial assets, net of tax	—	—	—	—	187,477	187,477	(997)	186,480
Share of other comprehensive income (loss) of associates and joint ventures, net of tax	—	—	—	—	20,949	20,949	(193)	20,756
Foreign currency translation, net of tax	—	—	—	—	(986,691)	(986,691)	(14,270)	(1,000,961)
Remeasurement of net defined benefit liabilities, net of tax	—	—	—	—	(205,360)	(205,360)	(7,753)	(213,113)
Total comprehensive income (loss)	—	—	—	29,821,215	(983,625)	28,837,590	630,336	29,467,926
Dividends	—	—	—	(1,206,622)	—	(1,206,622)	(42,155)	(1,248,777)
Capital transaction under common control	—	—	—	—	(312,959)	(312,959)	600,042	287,083
Changes in consolidated entities	—	—	—	—	—	—	(918)	(918)
Disposal of treasury stock	—	—	—	—	41,817	41,817	—	41,817
Stock option activities	—	—	—	—	(11,999)	(11,999)	—	(11,999)
Others	—	—	—	—	737	737	(65)	672
Total transactions with owners	—	—	—	(1,206,622)	(282,404)	(1,489,026)	556,904	(932,122)
Balance at December 31, 2013	119,467	778,047	4,403,893	148,600,282	(9,459,073)	144,442,616	5,573,394	150,016,010

The accompanying notes are an integral part of these consolidated financial statements.

Samsung Electronics Co., Ltd. and its subsidiaries
CONSOLIDATED STATEMENTS OF CASH FLOWS

(In millions of Korean won)

For the year ended December 31,	2013	2012
	KRW	KRW
Cash flows from operating activities		
Profit for the year	30,474,764	23,845,285
Adjustments	23,804,832	22,759,559
Changes in operating assets and liabilities	(1,313,245)	(5,777,949)
Cash flows from operating activities	52,966,351	40,826,895
Interest received	1,034,074	789,397
Interest paid	(434,857)	(576,379)
Dividend received	592,217	1,112,940
Income tax paid	(7,450,345)	(4,180,044)
Net cash generated from operating activities	46,707,440	37,972,809
Cash flows from investing activities		
Net increase in short-term financial instruments	(19,391,643)	(5,965,611)
Net decrease (increase) in short-term available-for-sale financial assets	33,663	(589,072)
Proceeds from disposal of long-term available-for-sale financial assets	1,691,463	106,208
Acquisition of long-term available for-sale financial assets	(1,531,356)	(870,249)
Proceeds from disposal of associates and joint ventures	240	41,091
Acquisition of associates and joint ventures	(181,307)	(279,022)
Disposal of property and equipment	377,445	644,062
Purchases of property and equipment	(23,157,587)	(22,965,271)
Disposal of intangible assets	4,562	61,497
Purchases of intangible assets	(934,743)	(650,884)
Cash outflows from business combination	(167,155)	(464,279)
Others	(1,490,601)	(390,024)
Net cash used in investing activities	(44,747,019)	(31,321,554)
Cash flows from financing activities		
Net repayment of short-term borrowings	(1,861,536)	(800,579)
Disposal of treasury stock	34,390	88,473
Proceeds from long-term borrowings and debentures	26,672	1,862,256
Repayment of long-term borrowings and debentures	(1,368,436)	(522,899)
Payment of dividends	(1,249,672)	(1,265,137)
Net increase (decrease) in noncontrolling interests	281,551	(1,200,134)
Others	—	(26,488)
Net cash used in financing activities	(4,137,031)	(1,864,508)
Effect of exchange rate changes on cash and cash equivalents	(330,070)	(687,048)
Net increase (decrease) in cash and cash equivalents	**(2,506,680)**	**4,099,699**
Cash and cash equivalents		
Beginning of the year	18,791,460	14,691,761
End of the year	16,284,780	18,791,460

The accompanying notes are an integral part of these consolidated financial statements.

SAMSUNG

appendix B

Time Value of Money

Appendix Preview

PRESENT AND FUTURE VALUE CONCEPTS	VALUE OF A SINGLE AMOUNT	VALUE OF AN ANNUITY
C1 Time is money and the concept of interest	P1 Present value of a single amount P2 Future value of a single amount	P3 Present value of an annuity P4 Future value of an annuity

Learning Objectives

CONCEPTUAL

C1 Describe the earning of interest and the concepts of present and future values.

PROCEDURAL

P1 Apply present value concepts to a single amount by using interest tables.

P2 Apply future value concepts to a single amount by using interest tables.

P3 Apply present value concepts to an annuity by using interest tables.

P4 Apply future value concepts to an annuity by using interest tables.

PRESENT AND FUTURE VALUE CONCEPTS

The old saying "Time is money" reflects the notion that as time passes, the values of our assets and liabilities change. This change is due to *interest,* which is a borrower's payment to the owner of an asset for its use. The most common example of interest is a savings account asset. As we keep a balance of cash in the account, it earns interest that the financial institution pays us. An example of a liability is a car loan. As we carry the balance of the loan, we accumulate interest costs on it. We must ultimately repay this loan with interest.

C1 Describe the earning of interest and the concepts of present and future values.

Present and future value computations enable us to measure or estimate the interest component of holding assets or liabilities over time. The present value computation is important when we want to know the value of future-day assets *today.* The future value computation is important when we want to know the value of present-day assets *at a future date.* The first section focuses on the present value of a single amount. The second section focuses on the future value of a single amount. Then both the present and future values of a series of amounts (called an *annuity*) are defined and explained.

Decision Insight

What's Five Million Worth? A maintenance worker duped out of a $5 million scratch-off ticket got his winnings seven years later. Robert Miles bought the ticket in 2006 at a convenience store where the owner and his two sons convinced Miles the ticket was worth $5,000 and paid him $4,000 for it. The brothers waited until 2012 to claim the jackpot, prompting an investigation, which uncovered the fraud. The $5 million will be paid to Miles as a $250,000 annuity over 20 years or as a lump-sum payment of $3,210,000, which results in about $2,124,378 after taxes. ■

PRESENT VALUE OF A SINGLE AMOUNT

We graphically express the present value, called *p*, of a single future amount, called *f*, that is received or paid at a future date in Exhibit B.1.

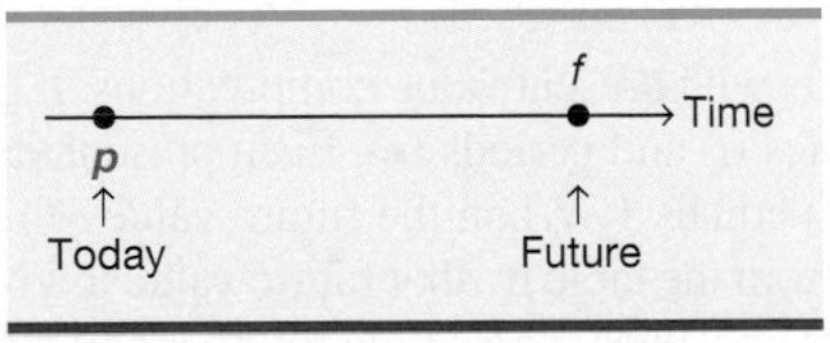

EXHIBIT B.1 Present Value of a Single Amount Diagram

P1 Apply present value concepts to a single amount by using interest tables.

The formula to compute the present value of a single amount is shown in Exhibit B.2, where p = present value (PV); f = future value (FV); i = rate of interest per period; and n = number of periods. (Interest is also called the *discount,* and an interest rate is also called the *discount rate.*)

EXHIBIT B.2 Present Value of a Single Amount Formula

$$p = \frac{f}{(1 + i)^n}$$

To illustrate present value concepts, assume that we need $220 one period from today. We want to know how much we must invest now, for one period, at an interest rate of 10% to provide for this $220. For this illustration, the *p*, or present value, is the unknown amount—the specifics are shown graphically as follows:

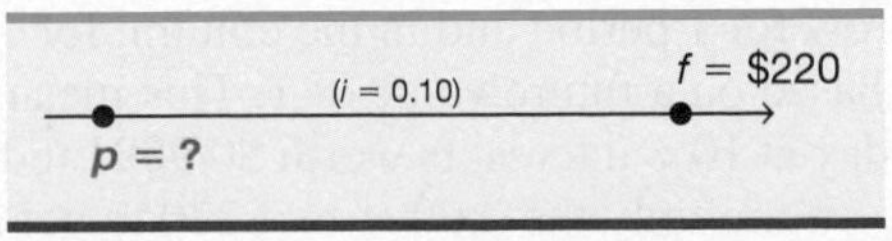

Conceptually, we know *p* must be less than $220. This is obvious from the answer to this question: Would we rather have $220 today or $220 at some future date? If we had $220 today, we could invest it and see it grow to something more than \$220 in the future. Therefore, we would prefer the \$220 today. This means that if we were promised \$220 in the future, we would take less than \$220 today. But how much less? To answer that question, we compute an estimate of the present value of the \$220 to be received one period from now using the formula in Exhibit B.2 as follows:

$$p = \frac{f}{(1 + i)^n} = \frac{\$220}{(1 + 0.10)^1} = \$200$$

Point: The FV factor when n = 2 and i = 10%, is 1.2100. Its reciprocal, 0.8264, is the PV factor when n = 2 and i = 10%.

We interpret this result to say that given an interest rate of 10%, we are indifferent between \$200 today or \$220 at the end of one period.

We can also use this formula to compute the present value for *any number of periods.* To illustrate, consider a payment of \$242 at the end of two periods at 10% interest. The present value of this \$242 to be received two periods from now is computed as follows:

$$p = \frac{f}{(1 + i)^n} = \frac{\$242}{(1 + 0.10)^2} = \$200$$

Together, these results tell us we are indifferent between \$200 today, or \$220 one period from today, or \$242 two periods from today given a 10% interest rate per period.

The number of periods (n) in the present value formula does not have to be expressed in years. Any period of time such as a day, a month, a quarter, or a year can be used. Whatever period is used, the interest rate (i) must be compounded for the same period. This means that if a situation expresses n in months and i equals 12% per year, then i is transformed into interest earned per month (or 1%). In this case, interest is said to be *compounded monthly.* For example, the present value of \$1 when n is 12 months and i is 12% compounded monthly follows:

$$p = \frac{1}{(1 + .01)^{12}} = \$0.8874$$

A present value table helps us with present value computations. It gives us present values (factors) for a variety of both interest rates (i) and periods (n). Each present value in a present value table assumes that the future value (f) equals 1. When the future value (f) is different from 1, we simply multiply the present value (p) from the table by that future value to give us the estimate. The formula used to construct a table of present values for a single future amount of 1 is shown in Exhibit B.3.

EXHIBIT B.3

Present Value of 1 Formula

$$p = \frac{1}{(1 + i)^n}$$

This formula is identical to that in Exhibit B.2 except that f equals 1. Table B.1 at the end of this appendix is such a present value table. It is often called a **present value of 1 table**. A present value table involves three factors: p, i, and n. Knowing two of these three factors allows us to compute the third. (A fourth is f, but as already explained, we need only multiply the 1 used in the formula by f.) To illustrate the use of a present value table, consider three cases.

Case 1 (solve for p when knowing i and n). To show how we use a present value table, let's look again at how we estimate the present value of \$220 (the f value) at the end of one period ($n = 1$) where the interest rate (i) is 10%. To solve this case, we go to the present value table (Table B.1) and look in the row for 1 period and in the column for 10% interest. Here we find a present value (p) of 0.9091 based on a future value of 1. This means, for instance, that \$1 to be received one period from today at 10% interest is worth \$0.9091 today. Since the future value in this case is not \$1 but \$220, we multiply the 0.9091 by \$220 to get an answer of \$200.

Case 2 (solve for n when knowing p and i). To illustrate, assume a \$100,000 future value (f) that is worth \$13,000 today (p) using an interest rate of 12% (i) but where n is unknown. In particular, we want to know how many periods (n) there are between the present value and the future value. To put this in context, it would fit a situation in which we want to retire with \$100,000 but currently have only \$13,000 that is earning a 12% return and we will be unable to save any additional money. How long will it be before we can retire? To answer this, we go to Table B.1 and look in the 12% interest column. Here we find a column of present values (p) based on a future value of 1. To use the present value table for this solution, we must divide \$13,000 (p) by \$100,000 (f), which equals 0.1300. This is necessary because *a present value table defines* f *equal to 1, and* p *as a fraction of 1.* We look for a value nearest to 0.1300 (p), which we find in the row for 18 periods (n). This means that the present value of \$100,000 at the end of 18 periods at 12% interest is \$13,000; alternatively stated, we must work 18 more years.

Case 3 (solve for i when knowing p and n). In this case, we have, say, a \$120,000 future value (f) worth \$60,000 today (p) when there are nine periods (n) between the present and future values, but the interest rate is unknown. As an example, suppose we want to retire with \$120,000 in nine years, but we have only \$60,000 and we will be unable to save any additional money. What interest rate must we earn to retire with \$120,000 in nine years? To answer this, we go to the present value table (Table B.1) and look in the row for nine periods. To use the present value table, we must divide \$60,000 (p) by \$120,000 (f), which equals 0.5000. Recall that this step is necessary because a present value table defines f equal to 1 and p as a fraction of 1. We look for a value in the row for nine periods that is nearest to 0.5000 (p), which we find in the column for 8% interest (i). This means that the present value of \$120,000 at the end of nine periods at 8% interest is \$60,000 or, in our example, we must earn 8% annual interest to retire in nine years.

NEED-TO-KNOW B-1

Present Value of Single Amount

P1

A company is considering an investment expected to yield \$70,000 after six years. If this company demands an 8% return, how much is it willing to pay for this investment today?

Solution

\$70,000 × 0.6302 = \$44,114 (using PV factor from Table B.1, $i = 8\%$, $n = 6$).

FUTURE VALUE OF A SINGLE AMOUNT

P2

Apply future value concepts to a single amount by using interest tables.

We must modify the formula for the present value of a single amount to obtain the formula for the future value of a single amount. In particular, we multiply both sides of the equation in Exhibit B.2 by $(1 + i)^n$ to get the result shown in Exhibit B.4.

EXHIBIT B.4

Future Value of a Single Amount Formula

$$f = p \times (1 + i)^n$$

The future value (f) is defined in terms of p, i, and n. We can use this formula to determine that \$200 (p) invested for 1 (n) period at an interest rate of 10% (i) yields a future value of \$220 as follows:

$$\begin{aligned} f &= p \times (1 + i)^n \\ &= \$200 \times (1 + 0.10)^1 \\ &= \$220 \end{aligned}$$

This formula can also be used to compute the future value of an amount for *any number of periods* into the future. To illustrate, assume that \$200 is invested for three periods at 10%. The future value of this \$200 is \$266.20, computed as follows:

Point: The FV factor in Table B2 when n = 3 and i = 10% is 1.3310.

$$\begin{aligned} f &= p \times (1 + i)^n \\ &= \$200 \times (1 + 0.10)^3 \\ &= \$200 \times 1.3310 \\ &= \$266.20 \end{aligned}$$

A future value table makes it easier for us to compute future values (f) for many different combinations of interest rates (i) and time periods (n). Each future value in a future value table assumes the present value (p) is 1. As with a present value table, if the future amount is something other than 1, we simply multiply our answer by that amount. The formula used to construct a table of future values (factors) for a single amount of 1 is in Exhibit B.5.

EXHIBIT B.5

Future Value of 1 Formula

$$f = (1 + i)^n$$

Table B.2 at the end of this appendix shows a table of future values for a current amount of 1. This type of table is called a **future value of 1 table.**

Point:
1/PV factor = FV factor.
1/FV factor = PV factor.

There are some important relations between Tables B.1 and B.2. In Table B.2, for the row where $n = 0$, the future value is 1 for each interest rate. This is so because no interest is earned when time does not pass. We also see that Tables B.1 and B.2 report the same information but in a different manner. In particular, one table is simply the *reciprocal* of the other. To illustrate this inverse relation, let's say we invest $100 for a period of five years at 12% per year. How much do we expect to have after five years? We can answer this question using Table B.2 by finding the future value (f) of 1, for five periods from now, compounded at 12%. From that table we find $f = 1.7623$. If we start with $100, the amount it accumulates to after five years is $176.23 ($100 × 1.7623). We can alternatively use Table B.1. Here we find that the present value (p) of 1, discounted five periods at 12%, is 0.5674. Recall the inverse relation between present value and future value. This means that $p = 1/f$ (or equivalently, $f = 1/p$). We can compute the future value of $100 invested for five periods at 12% as follows: f = $100 × (1/0.5674) = $176.24 (which equals the $176.23 just computed, except for a 1 cent rounding difference).

A future value table involves three factors: f, i, and n. Knowing two of these three factors allows us to compute the third. To illustrate, consider these three possible cases.

Case 1 (solve for f when knowing i and n). Our preceding example fits this case. We found that $100 invested for five periods at 12% interest accumulates to $176.24.

Case 2 (solve for n when knowing f and i). In this case, we have, say, $2,000 ($p$) and we want to know how many periods (n) it will take to accumulate to $3,000 ($f$) at 7% interest ($i$). To answer this, we go to the future value table (Table B.2) and look in the 7% interest column. Here we find a column of future values (f) based on a present value of 1. To use a future value table, we must divide $3,000 ($f$) by $2,000 ($p$), which equals 1.500. This is necessary because *a future value table defines* p *equal to 1, and* f *as a multiple of 1.* We look for a value nearest to 1.50 (f), which we find in the row for six periods (n). This means that $2,000 invested for six periods at 7% interest accumulates to $3,000.

Case 3 (solve for i when knowing f and n). In this case, we have, say, $2,001 ($p$), and in nine years ($n$) we want to have $4,000 ($f$). What rate of interest must we earn to accomplish this? To answer that, we go to Table B.2 and search in the row for nine periods. To use a future value table, we must divide $4,000 ($f$) by $2,001 ($p$), which equals 1.9990. Recall that this is necessary because a future value table defines p equal to 1 and f as a multiple of 1. We look for a value nearest to 1.9990 (f), which we find in the column for 8% interest (i). This means that $2,001 invested for nine periods at 8% interest accumulates to $4,000.

NEED-TO-KNOW B-2

Future Value of Single Amount

P2

Assume that you win a $150,000 cash sweepstakes today. You decide to deposit this cash in an account earning 8% annual interest, and you plan to quit your job when the account equals $555,000. How many years will it be before you can quit working?

Solution

$555,000/$150,000 = 3.7000 (the future value factor)

Table B.2 shows this value is not achieved until reaching 17 years at 8% interest.

PRESENT VALUE OF AN ANNUITY

An *annuity* is a series of equal payments occurring at equal intervals. One example is a series of three annual payments of $100 each. An *ordinary annuity* is defined as equal end-of-period payments at equal intervals. An ordinary annuity of $100 for three periods and its present value (p) are illustrated in Exhibit B.6.

P3 Apply present value concepts to an annuity by using interest tables.

EXHIBIT B.6

Present Value of an Ordinary Annuity Diagram

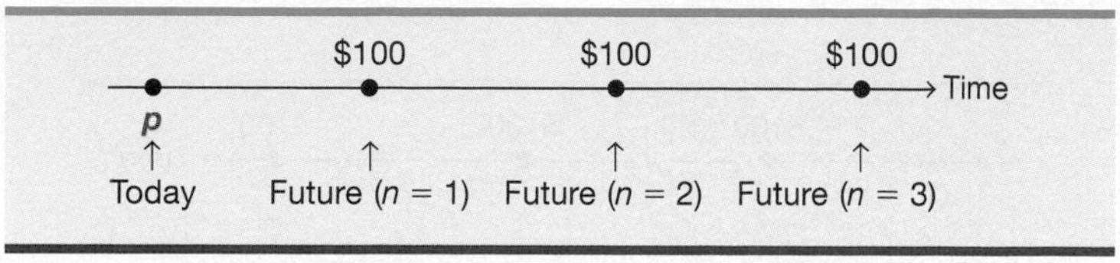

One way to compute the present value of an ordinary annuity is to find the present value of each payment using our present value formula from Exhibit B.3. We then add each of the three present values. To illustrate, let's look at three $100 payments at the end of each of the next three periods with an interest rate of 15%. Our present value computations are

$$p = \frac{\$100}{(1 + 0.15)^1} + \frac{\$100}{(1 + 0.15)^2} + \frac{\$100}{(1 + 0.15)^3} = \$228.32$$

This computation is identical to computing the present value of each payment (from Table B.1) and taking their sum or, alternatively, adding the values from Table B.1 for each of the three payments and multiplying their sum by the $100 annuity payment.

A more direct way is to use a present value of annuity table. Table B.3 at the end of this appendix is one such table. This table is called a **present value of an annuity of 1 table**. If we look at Table B.3 where $n = 3$ and $i = 15\%$, we see the present value is 2.2832. This means that the present value of an annuity of 1 for three periods, with a 15% interest rate, equals 2.2832.

A present value of an annuity formula is used to construct Table B.3. It can also be constructed by adding the amounts in a present value of 1 table. To illustrate, we use Tables B.1 and B.3 to confirm this relation for the prior example:

From Table B.1		From Table B.3	
$i = 15\%, n = 1$	0.8696		
$i = 15\%, n = 2$	0.7561		
$i = 15\%, n = 3$	0.6575		
Total	2.2832	$i = 15\%, n = 3$	2.2832

Point: Excel functions follow:
= −PV (rate, periods, payment)
= −PV (0.15, 3, 100)
= $228.32

We can also use business calculators or spreadsheet programs to find the present value of an annuity.

Decision Insight

Count Your Blessings "I don't have good luck—I'm blessed," proclaimed Andrew "Jack" Whittaker, a sewage treatment contractor, after winning the largest ever undivided jackpot in a U.S. lottery. Whittaker had to choose between $315 million in 30 annual installments or $170 million in one lump sum ($112 million after-tax). ■

NEED-TO-KNOW B-3

Present Value of an Annuity

P3

A company is considering an investment that would produce payments of $10,000 every six months for three years. The first payment would be received in six months. If this company requires an 8% annual return, what is the maximum amount it is willing to pay for this investment today?

Solution

$10,000 × 5.2421 = $52,421 is the maximum (using PV of annuity factor from Table B.3, $i = 4\%$, $n = 6$).

FUTURE VALUE OF AN ANNUITY

P4 Apply future value concepts to an annuity by using interest tables.

The future value of an *ordinary annuity* is the accumulated value of each annuity payment with interest as of the date of the final payment. To illustrate, let's consider the earlier annuity of three annual payments of \$100. Exhibit B.7 shows the point in time for the future value (f). The first payment is made two periods prior to the point when future value is determined, and the final payment occurs on the future value date.

EXHIBIT B.7

Future Value of an Ordinary Annuity Diagram

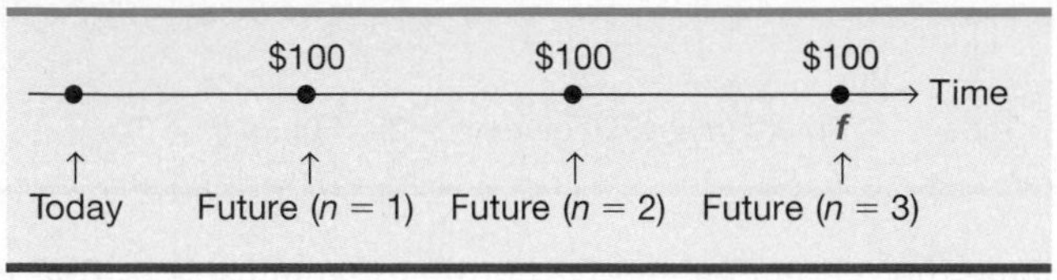

Point: An ordinary annuity is a series of equal cash flows, with the payment at the *end* of each period.

One way to compute the future value of an annuity is to use the formula to find the future value of *each* payment and add them. If we assume an interest rate of 15%, our calculation is

$$f = \$100 \times (1 + 0.15)^2 + \$100 \times (1 + 0.15)^1 + \$100 \times (1 + 0.15)^0 = \$347.25$$

This is identical to using Table B.2 and summing the future values of each payment, or adding the future values of the three payments of 1 and multiplying the sum by \$100.

A more direct way is to use a table showing future values of annuities. Such a table is called a **future value of an annuity of 1 table**. Table B.4 at the end of this appendix is one such table. Note that in Table B.4 when $n = 1$, the future values equal 1 ($f = 1$) for all rates of interest. This is so because such an annuity consists of only one payment and the future value is determined on the date of that payment—no time passes between the payment and its future value. The future value of an annuity formula is used to construct Table B.4. We can also construct it by adding the amounts from a future value of 1 table. To illustrate, we use Tables B.2 and B.4 to confirm this relation for the prior example:

From Table B.2		From Table B.4	
$i = 15\%, n = 0$	1.0000		
$i = 15\%, n = 1$	1.1500		
$i = 15\%, n = 2$	1.3225		
Total	3.4725	$i = 15\%, n = 3$	3.4725

Point: Excel functions follow:
= −FV (rate, periods, payment)
= −FV (0.15, 3, 100)
= \$347.25

Note that the future value in Table B.2 is 1.0000 when $n = 0$, but the future value in Table B.4 is 1.0000 when $n = 1$. Is this a contradiction? No. When $n = 0$ in Table B.2, the future value is determined on the date when a single payment occurs. This means that no interest is earned because no time has passed, and the future value equals the payment. Table B.4 describes annuities with equal payments occurring at the end of each period. When $n = 1$, the annuity has one payment, and its future value equals 1 on the date of its final and only payment. Again, no time passes between the payment and its future value date.

NEED-TO-KNOW B-4

Future Value of an Annuity

P4

A company invests \$45,000 per year for five years at 12% annual interest. Compute the value of this annuity investment at the end of five years.

Solution

\$45,000 × 6.3528 = \$285,876 (using the FV of annuity factor from Table B.4, $i = 12\%$, $n = 5$).

Summary

C1 Describe the earning of interest and the concepts of present and future values. Interest is payment by a borrower to the owner of an asset for its use. Present and future value computations are a way for us to estimate the interest component of holding assets or liabilities over a period of time.

P1 Apply present value concepts to a single amount by using interest tables. The present value of a single amount received at a future date is the amount that can be invested now at the specified interest rate to yield that future value.

P2 Apply future value concepts to a single amount by using interest tables. The future value of a single amount invested at a specified rate of interest is the amount that would accumulate by the future date.

P3 Apply present value concepts to an annuity by using interest tables. The present value of an annuity is the amount that can be invested now at the specified interest rate to yield that series of equal periodic payments.

P4 Apply future value concepts to an annuity by using interest tables. The future value of an annuity invested at a specific rate of interest is the amount that would accumulate by the date of the final payment.

connect

QUICK STUDY

QS B-1 Identifying interest rates in tables C1

Assume that you must make two-year-ahead future value estimates using the *future value of 1 table* (Table B.2). Which interest rate column *and* number-of-periods row do you use when working with the following rates?

1. 8% annual rate, compounded quarterly
2. 12% annual rate, compounded annually
3. 6% annual rate, compounded semiannually
4. 12% annual rate, compounded monthly (the answer for number-of-periods in part 4 is not shown in Table B.2)

QS B-2 Interest rate on an investment P1

Ken Francis is offered the possibility of investing $2,745 today and in return to receive $10,000 after 15 years. What is the annual rate of interest for this investment? (Use Table B.1.)

QS B-3 Number of periods of an investment P1

Megan Brink is offered the possibility of investing $6,651 today at 6% interest per year in a desire to accumulate $10,000. How many years must Brink wait to accumulate $10,000? (Use Table B.1.)

QS B-4 Present value of an amount P1

Flaherty is considering an investment that, if paid for immediately, is expected to return $140,000 five years from now. If Flaherty demands a 9% return, how much is she willing to pay for this investment?

QS B-5 Future value of an amount P2

CII, Inc., invests $630,000 in a project expected to earn a 12% annual rate of return. The earnings will be reinvested in the project each year until the entire investment is liquidated 10 years later. What will the cash proceeds be when the project is liquidated?

QS B-6 Present value of an annuity P3

Beene Distributing is considering a project that will return $150,000 annually at the end of each year for the next six years. If Beene demands an annual return of 7% and pays for the project immediately, how much is it willing to pay for the project?

QS B-7 Future value of an annuity P4

Claire Fitch is planning to begin an individual retirement program in which she will invest $1,500 at the end of each year. Fitch plans to retire after making 30 annual investments in the program earning a return of 10%. What is the value of the program on the date of the last payment (30 years from the present)?

connect

EXERCISES

Exercise B-1
Present value of an amount P1

Mike Derr Company expects to earn 10% per year on an investment that will pay $606,773 six years from now. Use Table B.1 to compute the present value of this investment. (Round the amount to the nearest dollar.)

Exercise B-2
Present value of an amount P1

On January 1, 2015, a company agrees to pay $20,000 in three years. If the annual interest rate is 10%, determine how much cash the company can borrow with this agreement.

Exercise B-3
Number of periods of an investment P2

Tom Thompson expects to invest $10,000 at 12% and, at the end of a certain period, receive $96,463. How many years will it be before Thompson receives the payment? (Use Table B.2.)

Exercise B-4
Interest rate on an investment P2

Bill Padley expects to invest $10,000 for 25 years, after which he wants to receive $108,347. What rate of interest must Padley earn? (Use Table B.2.)

Exercise B-5
Future value of an amount P2

Mark Welsch deposits $7,200 in an account that earns interest at an annual rate of 8%, compounded quarterly. The $7,200 plus earned interest must remain in the account 10 years before it can be withdrawn. How much money will be in the account at the end of 10 years?

Exercise B-6
Future value of an amount P2

Catten, Inc., invests $163,170 today earning 7% per year for nine years. Use Table B.2 to compute the future value of the investment nine years from now. (Round the amount to the nearest dollar.)

Exercise B-7
Interest rate on an investment P3

Jones expects an immediate investment of $57,466 to return $10,000 annually for eight years, with the first payment to be received one year from now. What rate of interest must Jones earn? (Use Table B.3.)

Exercise B-8
Number of periods of an investment P3

Keith Riggins expects an investment of $82,014 to return $10,000 annually for several years. If Riggins earns a return of 10%, how many annual payments will he receive? (Use Table B.3.)

Exercise B-9
Present value of an annuity P3

Dave Krug finances a new automobile by paying $6,500 cash and agreeing to make 40 monthly payments of $500 each, the first payment to be made one month after the purchase. The loan bears interest at an annual rate of 12%. What is the cost of the automobile?

Exercise B-10
Present values of annuities
P3

C&H Ski Club recently borrowed money and agrees to pay it back with a series of six annual payments of $5,000 each. C&H subsequently borrows more money and agrees to pay it back with a series of four annual payments of $7,500 each. The annual interest rate for both loans is 6%.

1. Use Table B.1 to find the present value of these two separate annuities. (Round amounts to the nearest dollar.)
2. Use Table B.3 to find the present value of these two separate annuities. (Round amounts to the nearest dollar.)

Exercise B-11
Present value with semiannual compounding
C1 P3

Otto Co. borrows money on April 30, 2015, by promising to make four payments of $13,000 each on November 1, 2015; May 1, 2016; November 1, 2016; and May 1, 2017.

1. How much money is Otto able to borrow if the interest rate is 8%, compounded semiannually?
2. How much money is Otto able to borrow if the interest rate is 12%, compounded semiannually?
3. How much money is Otto able to borrow if the interest rate is 16%, compounded semiannually?

Exercise B-12
Present value of bonds
P1 P3

Spiller Corp. plans to issue 10%, 15-year, $500,000 par value bonds payable that pay interest semiannually on June 30 and December 31. The bonds are dated December 31, 2015, and are issued on that date. If the market rate of interest for the bonds is 8% on the date of issue, what will be the total cash proceeds from the bond issue?

Exercise B-13
Present value of an amount and of an annuity
P1 P3

Compute the amount that can be borrowed under each of the following circumstances:

1. A promise to repay $90,000 seven years from now at an interest rate of 6%.
2. An agreement made on February 1, 2015, to make three separate payments of $20,000 on February 1 of 2016, 2017, and 2018. The annual interest rate is 10%.

Exercise B-14
Interest rate on an investment P4

Algoe expects to invest $1,000 annually for 40 years to yield an accumulated value of $154,762 on the date of the last investment. For this to occur, what rate of interest must Algoe earn? (Use Table B.4.)

Exercise B-15
Number of periods of an investment P4

Steffi Derr expects to invest $10,000 annually that will earn 8%. How many annual investments must Derr make to accumulate $303,243 on the date of the last investment? (Use Table B.4.)

Exercise B-16
Future value of an annuity P4

Kelly Malone plans to have $50 withheld from her monthly paycheck and deposited in a savings account that earns 12% annually, compounded monthly. If Malone continues with her plan for two and one-half years, how much will be accumulated in the account on the date of the last deposit?

Exercise B-17
Future value of an amount plus an annuity
P2 P4

Starr Company decides to establish a fund that it will use 10 years from now to replace an aging production facility. The company will make a $100,000 initial contribution to the fund and plans to make quarterly contributions of $50,000 beginning in three months. The fund earns 12%, compounded quarterly. What will be the value of the fund 10 years from now?

Exercise B-18
Practical applications of the time value of money
P1 P2 P3 P4

a. How much would you have to deposit today if you wanted to have $60,000 in four years? Annual interest rate is 9%.

b. Assume that you are saving up for a trip around the world when you graduate in two years. If you can earn 8% on your investments, how much would you have to deposit today to have $15,000 when you graduate?

c. Would you rather have $463 now or $1,000 ten years from now? Assume that you can earn 9% on your investments.

d. Assume that a college parking sticker today costs $90. If the cost of parking is increasing at the rate of 5% per year, how much will the college parking sticker cost in eight years?

e. Assume that the average price of a new home is $158,500. If new homes are increasing at a rate of 10% per year, how much will a new home cost in eight years?

f. An investment will pay you $10,000 in 10 years, and it will also pay you $400 at the end of *each* of the next 10 years (years 1 thru 10). If the annual interest rate is 6%, how much would you be willing to pay today for this type of investment?

g. A college student is reported in the newspaper as having won $10,000,000 in the Kansas State Lottery. However, as is often the custom with lotteries, she does *not* actually receive the entire $10 million now. Instead she will receive $500,000 at the end of the year for *each* of the next 20 years. If the annual interest rate is 6%, what is the present value (today's amount) that she won? (Ignore taxes.)

Exercise B-19
Using present and future value tables
C1 P1 P2 P3 P4

For each of the following situations, identify (1) the case as either (*a*) a present or a future value and (*b*) a single amount or an annuity, (2) the table you would use in your computations (but do not solve the problem), and (3) the interest rate and time periods you would use.

a. You need to accumulate $10,000 for a trip you wish to take in four years. You are able to earn 8% compounded semiannually on your savings. You plan to make only one deposit and let the money accumulate for four years. How would you determine the amount of the one-time deposit?

b. Assume the same facts as in part (*a*) except that you will make semiannual deposits to your savings account.

c. You want to retire after working 40 years with savings in excess of $1,000,000. You expect to save $4,000 a year for 40 years and earn an annual rate of interest of 8%. Will you be able to retire with more than $1,000,000 in 40 years? Explain.

d. A sweepstakes agency names you a grand prize winner. You can take $225,000 immediately or elect to receive annual installments of $30,000 for 20 years. You can earn 10% annually on any investments you make. Which prize do you choose to receive?

TABLE B.1*

Present Value of 1

$$p = 1/(1 + i)^n$$

	Rate											
Periods	1%	2%	3%	4%	5%	6%	7%	8%	9%	10%	12%	15%
1	0.9901	0.9804	0.9709	0.9615	0.9524	0.9434	0.9346	0.9259	0.9174	0.9091	0.8929	0.8696
2	0.9803	0.9612	0.9426	0.9246	0.9070	0.8900	0.8734	0.8573	0.8417	0.8264	0.7972	0.7561
3	0.9706	0.9423	0.9151	0.8890	0.8638	0.8396	0.8163	0.7938	0.7722	0.7513	0.7118	0.6575
4	0.9610	0.9238	0.8885	0.8548	0.8227	0.7921	0.7629	0.7350	0.7084	0.6830	0.6355	0.5718
5	0.9515	0.9057	0.8626	0.8219	0.7835	0.7473	0.7130	0.6806	0.6499	0.6209	0.5674	0.4972
6	0.9420	0.8880	0.8375	0.7903	0.7462	0.7050	0.6663	0.6302	0.5963	0.5645	0.5066	0.4323
7	0.9327	0.8706	0.8131	0.7599	0.7107	0.6651	0.6227	0.5835	0.5470	0.5132	0.4523	0.3759
8	0.9235	0.8535	0.7894	0.7307	0.6768	0.6274	0.5820	0.5403	0.5019	0.4665	0.4039	0.3269
9	0.9143	0.8368	0.7664	0.7026	0.6446	0.5919	0.5439	0.5002	0.4604	0.4241	0.3606	0.2843
10	0.9053	0.8203	0.7441	0.6756	0.6139	0.5584	0.5083	0.4632	0.4224	0.3855	0.3220	0.2472
11	0.8963	0.8043	0.7224	0.6496	0.5847	0.5268	0.4751	0.4289	0.3875	0.3505	0.2875	0.2149
12	0.8874	0.7885	0.7014	0.6246	0.5568	0.4970	0.4440	0.3971	0.3555	0.3186	0.2567	0.1869
13	0.8787	0.7730	0.6810	0.6006	0.5303	0.4688	0.4150	0.3677	0.3262	0.2897	0.2292	0.1625
14	0.8700	0.7579	0.6611	0.5775	0.5051	0.4423	0.3878	0.3405	0.2992	0.2633	0.2046	0.1413
15	0.8613	0.7430	0.6419	0.5553	0.4810	0.4173	0.3624	0.3152	0.2745	0.2394	0.1827	0.1229
16	0.8528	0.7284	0.6232	0.5339	0.4581	0.3936	0.3387	0.2919	0.2519	0.2176	0.1631	0.1069
17	0.8444	0.7142	0.6050	0.5134	0.4363	0.3714	0.3166	0.2703	0.2311	0.1978	0.1456	0.0929
18	0.8360	0.7002	0.5874	0.4936	0.4155	0.3503	0.2959	0.2502	0.2120	0.1799	0.1300	0.0808
19	0.8277	0.6864	0.5703	0.4746	0.3957	0.3305	0.2765	0.2317	0.1945	0.1635	0.1161	0.0703
20	0.8195	0.6730	0.5537	0.4564	0.3769	0.3118	0.2584	0.2145	0.1784	0.1486	0.1037	0.0611
25	0.7798	0.6095	0.4776	0.3751	0.2953	0.2330	0.1842	0.1460	0.1160	0.0923	0.0588	0.0304
30	0.7419	0.5521	0.4120	0.3083	0.2314	0.1741	0.1314	0.0994	0.0754	0.0573	0.0334	0.0151
35	0.7059	0.5000	0.3554	0.2534	0.1813	0.1301	0.0937	0.0676	0.0490	0.0356	0.0189	0.0075
40	0.6717	0.4529	0.3066	0.2083	0.1420	0.0972	0.0668	0.0460	0.0318	0.0221	0.0107	0.0037

*Used to compute the present value of a known future amount. For example: How much would you need to invest today at 10% compounded semiannually to accumulate $5,000 in 6 years from today? Using the factors of n = 12 and i = 5% (12 semiannual periods and a semiannual rate of 5%), the factor is 0.5568. You would need to invest $2,784 today ($5,000 × 0.5568).

TABLE B.2**

Future Value of 1

$$f = (1 + i)^n$$

	Rate											
Periods	1%	2%	3%	4%	5%	6%	7%	8%	9%	10%	12%	15%
0	1.0000	1.0000	1.0000	1.0000	1.0000	1.0000	1.0000	1.0000	1.0000	1.0000	1.0000	1.0000
1	1.0100	1.0200	1.0300	1.0400	1.0500	1.0600	1.0700	1.0800	1.0900	1.1000	1.1200	1.1500
2	1.0201	1.0404	1.0609	1.0816	1.1025	1.1236	1.1449	1.1664	1.1881	1.2100	1.2544	1.3225
3	1.0303	1.0612	1.0927	1.1249	1.1576	1.1910	1.2250	1.2597	1.2950	1.3310	1.4049	1.5209
4	1.0406	1.0824	1.1255	1.1699	1.2155	1.2625	1.3108	1.3605	1.4116	1.4641	1.5735	1.7490
5	1.0510	1.1041	1.1593	1.2167	1.2763	1.3382	1.4026	1.4693	1.5386	1.6105	1.7623	2.0114
6	1.0615	1.1262	1.1941	1.2653	1.3401	1.4185	1.5007	1.5869	1.6771	1.7716	1.9738	2.3131
7	1.0721	1.1487	1.2299	1.3159	1.4071	1.5036	1.6058	1.7138	1.8280	1.9487	2.2107	2.6600
8	1.0829	1.1717	1.2668	1.3686	1.4775	1.5938	1.7182	1.8509	1.9926	2.1436	2.4760	3.0590
9	1.0937	1.1951	1.3048	1.4233	1.5513	1.6895	1.8385	1.9990	2.1719	2.3579	2.7731	3.5179
10	1.1046	1.2190	1.3439	1.4802	1.6289	1.7908	1.9672	2.1589	2.3674	2.5937	3.1058	4.0456
11	1.1157	1.2434	1.3842	1.5395	1.7103	1.8983	2.1049	2.3316	2.5804	2.8531	3.4785	4.6524
12	1.1268	1.2682	1.4258	1.6010	1.7959	2.0122	2.2522	2.5182	2.8127	3.1384	3.8960	5.3503
13	1.1381	1.2936	1.4685	1.6651	1.8856	2.1329	2.4098	2.7196	3.0658	3.4523	4.3635	6.1528
14	1.1495	1.3195	1.5126	1.7317	1.9799	2.2609	2.5785	2.9372	3.3417	3.7975	4.8871	7.0757
15	1.1610	1.3459	1.5580	1.8009	2.0789	2.3966	2.7590	3.1722	3.6425	4.1772	5.4736	8.1371
16	1.1726	1.3728	1.6047	1.8730	2.1829	2.5404	2.9522	3.4259	3.9703	4.5950	6.1304	9.3576
17	1.1843	1.4002	1.6528	1.9479	2.2920	2.6928	3.1588	3.7000	4.3276	5.0545	6.8660	10.7613
18	1.1961	1.4282	1.7024	2.0258	2.4066	2.8543	3.3799	3.9960	4.7171	5.5599	7.6900	12.3755
19	1.2081	1.4568	1.7535	2.1068	2.5270	3.0256	3.6165	4.3157	5.1417	6.1159	8.6128	14.2318
20	1.2202	1.4859	1.8061	2.1911	2.6533	3.2071	3.8697	4.6610	5.6044	6.7275	9.6463	16.3665
25	1.2824	1.6406	2.0938	2.6658	3.3864	4.2919	5.4274	6.8485	8.6231	10.8347	17.0001	32.9190
30	1.3478	1.8114	2.4273	3.2434	4.3219	5.7435	7.6123	10.0627	13.2677	17.4494	29.9599	66.2118
35	1.4166	1.9999	2.8139	3.9461	5.5160	7.6861	10.6766	14.7853	20.4140	28.1024	52.7996	133.1755
40	1.4889	2.2080	3.2620	4.8010	7.0400	10.2857	14.9745	21.7245	31.4094	45.2593	93.0510	267.8635

**Used to compute the future value of a known present amount. For example: What is the accumulated value of $3,000 invested today at 8% compounded quarterly for 5 years? Using the factors of n = 20 and i = 2% (20 quarterly periods and a quarterly interest rate of 2%), the factor is 1.4859. The accumulated value is $4,457.70 ($3,000 × 1.4859).

$$p = \left[1 - \frac{1}{(1+i)^n}\right] / i$$

TABLE B.3[†]

Present Value of an Annuity of 1

	Rate											
Periods	1%	2%	3%	4%	5%	6%	7%	8%	9%	10%	12%	15%
1	0.9901	0.9804	0.9709	0.9615	0.9524	0.9434	0.9346	0.9259	0.9174	0.9091	0.8929	0.8696
2	1.9704	1.9416	1.9135	1.8861	1.8594	1.8334	1.8080	1.7833	1.7591	1.7355	1.6901	1.6257
3	2.9410	2.8839	2.8286	2.7751	2.7232	2.6730	2.6243	2.5771	2.5313	2.4869	2.4018	2.2832
4	3.9020	3.8077	3.7171	3.6299	3.5460	3.4651	3.3872	3.3121	3.2397	3.1699	3.0373	2.8550
5	4.8534	4.7135	4.5797	4.4518	4.3295	4.2124	4.1002	3.9927	3.8897	3.7908	3.6048	3.3522
6	5.7955	5.6014	5.4172	5.2421	5.0757	4.9173	4.7665	4.6229	4.4859	4.3553	4.1114	3.7845
7	6.7282	6.4720	6.2303	6.0021	5.7864	5.5824	5.3893	5.2064	5.0330	4.8684	4.5638	4.1604
8	7.6517	7.3255	7.0197	6.7327	6.4632	6.2098	5.9713	5.7466	5.5348	5.3349	4.9676	4.4873
9	8.5660	8.1622	7.7861	7.4353	7.1078	6.8017	6.5152	6.2469	5.9952	5.7590	5.3282	4.7716
10	9.4713	8.9826	8.5302	8.1109	7.7217	7.3601	7.0236	6.7101	6.4177	6.1446	5.6502	5.0188
11	10.3676	9.7868	9.2526	8.7605	8.3064	7.8869	7.4987	7.1390	6.8052	6.4951	5.9377	5.2337
12	11.2551	10.5753	9.9540	9.3851	8.8633	8.3838	7.9427	7.5361	7.1607	6.8137	6.1944	5.4206
13	12.1337	11.3484	10.6350	9.9856	9.3936	8.8527	8.3577	7.9038	7.4869	7.1034	6.4235	5.5831
14	13.0037	12.1062	11.2961	10.5631	9.8986	9.2950	8.7455	8.2442	7.7862	7.3667	6.6282	5.7245
15	13.8651	12.8493	11.9379	11.1184	10.3797	9.7122	9.1079	8.5595	8.0607	7.6061	6.8109	5.8474
16	14.7179	13.5777	12.5611	11.6523	10.8378	10.1059	9.4466	8.8514	8.3126	7.8237	6.9740	5.9542
17	15.5623	14.2919	13.1661	12.1657	11.2741	10.4773	9.7632	9.1216	8.5436	8.0216	7.1196	6.0472
18	16.3983	14.9920	13.7535	12.6593	11.6896	10.8276	10.0591	9.3719	8.7556	8.2014	7.2497	6.1280
19	17.2260	15.6785	14.3238	13.1339	12.0853	11.1581	10.3356	9.6036	8.9501	8.3649	7.3658	6.1982
20	18.0456	16.3514	14.8775	13.5903	12.4622	11.4699	10.5940	9.8181	9.1285	8.5136	7.4694	6.2593
25	22.0232	19.5235	17.4131	15.6221	14.0939	12.7834	11.6536	10.6748	9.8226	9.0770	7.8431	6.4641
30	25.8077	22.3965	19.6004	17.2920	15.3725	13.7648	12.4090	11.2578	10.2737	9.4269	8.0552	6.5660
35	29.4086	24.9986	21.4872	18.6646	16.3742	14.4982	12.9477	11.6546	10.5668	9.6442	8.1755	6.6166
40	32.8347	27.3555	23.1148	19.7928	17.1591	15.0463	13.3317	11.9246	10.7574	9.7791	8.2438	6.6418

[†]Used to calculate the present value of a series of equal payments made at the end of each period. For example: What is the present value of $2,000 per year for 10 years assuming an annual interest rate of 9%. For (n = 10, i = 9%), the PV factor is 6.4177. $2,000 per year for 10 years is the equivalent of $12,835 today ($2,000 × 6.4177).

$$f = [(1+i)^n - 1]/i$$

TABLE B.4[‡]

Future Value of an Annuity of 1

	Rate											
Periods	1%	2%	3%	4%	5%	6%	7%	8%	9%	10%	12%	15%
1	1.0000	1.0000	1.0000	1.0000	1.0000	1.0000	1.0000	1.0000	1.0000	1.0000	1.0000	1.0000
2	2.0100	2.0200	2.0300	2.0400	2.0500	2.0600	2.0700	2.0800	2.0900	2.1000	2.1200	2.1500
3	3.0301	3.0604	3.0909	3.1216	3.1525	3.1836	3.2149	3.2464	3.2781	3.3100	3.3744	3.4725
4	4.0604	4.1216	4.1836	4.2465	4.3101	4.3746	4.4399	4.5061	4.5731	4.6410	4.7793	4.9934
5	5.1010	5.2040	5.3091	5.4163	5.5256	5.6371	5.7507	5.8666	5.9847	6.1051	6.3528	6.7424
6	6.1520	6.3081	6.4684	6.6330	6.8019	6.9753	7.1533	7.3359	7.5233	7.7156	8.1152	8.7537
7	7.2135	7.4343	7.6625	7.8983	8.1420	8.3938	8.6540	8.9228	9.2004	9.4872	10.0890	11.0668
8	8.2857	8.5830	8.8923	9.2142	9.5491	9.8975	10.2598	10.6366	11.0285	11.4359	12.2997	13.7268
9	9.3685	9.7546	10.1591	10.5828	11.0266	11.4913	11.9780	12.4876	13.0210	13.5795	14.7757	16.7858
10	10.4622	10.9497	11.4639	12.0061	12.5779	13.1808	13.8164	14.4866	15.1929	15.9374	17.5487	20.3037
11	11.5668	12.1687	12.8078	13.4864	14.2068	14.9716	15.7836	16.6455	17.5603	18.5312	20.6546	24.3493
12	12.6825	13.4121	14.1920	15.0258	15.9171	16.8699	17.8885	18.9771	20.1407	21.3843	24.1331	29.0017
13	13.8093	14.6803	15.6178	16.6268	17.7130	18.8821	20.1406	21.4953	22.9534	24.5227	28.0291	34.3519
14	14.9474	15.9739	17.0863	18.2919	19.5986	21.0151	22.5505	24.2149	26.0192	27.9750	32.3926	40.5047
15	16.0969	17.2934	18.5989	20.0236	21.5786	23.2760	25.1290	27.1521	29.3609	31.7725	37.2797	47.5804
16	17.2579	18.6393	20.1569	21.8245	23.6575	25.6725	27.8881	30.3243	33.0034	35.9497	42.7533	55.7175
17	18.4304	20.0121	21.7616	23.6975	25.8404	28.2129	30.8402	33.7502	36.9737	40.5447	48.8837	65.0751
18	19.6147	21.4123	23.4144	25.6454	28.1324	30.9057	33.9990	37.4502	41.3013	45.5992	55.7497	75.8364
19	20.8109	22.8406	25.1169	27.6712	30.5390	33.7600	37.3790	41.4463	46.0185	51.1591	63.4397	88.2118
20	22.0190	24.2974	26.8704	29.7781	33.0660	36.7856	40.9955	45.7620	51.1601	57.2750	72.0524	102.4436
25	28.2432	32.0303	36.4593	41.6459	47.7271	54.8645	63.2490	73.1059	84.7009	98.3471	133.3339	212.7930
30	34.7849	40.5681	47.5754	56.0849	66.4388	79.0582	94.4608	113.2832	136.3075	164.4940	241.3327	434.7451
35	41.6603	49.9945	60.4621	73.6522	90.3203	111.4348	138.2369	172.3168	215.7108	271.0244	431.6635	881.1702
40	48.8864	60.4020	75.4013	95.0255	120.7998	154.7620	199.6351	259.0565	337.8824	442.5926	767.0914	1,779.0903

[‡]Used to calculate the future value of a series of equal payments made at the end of each period. For example: What is the future value of $4,000 per year for 6 years assuming an annual interest rate of 8%. For (n = 6, i = 8%), the FV factor is 7.3359. $4,000 per year for 6 years accumulates to $29,343.60 ($4,000 × 7.3359).

appendix C

Investments and International Operations

Appendix Preview

BASICS OF INVESTMENTS	NONINFLUENTIAL INVESTMENTS	INFLUENTIAL INVESTMENTS
C1 Motivation for investments	P1 Trading securities	P4 Securities with significant influence
Short-term versus long-term	P2 Held-to-maturity securities	C2 Securities with controlling influence
Classification and reporting	P3 Available-for-sale securities	A1 Analyze components of return on assets
Accounting basics		

Learning Objectives

CONCEPTUAL

C1 Distinguish between debt and equity securities and between short-term and long-term investments.

C2 Describe how to report equity securities with controlling influence.

C3 *Appendix C-A*—Explain foreign exchange rates and record transactions listed in a foreign currency.

ANALYTICAL

A1 Compute and analyze the components of return on total assets.

PROCEDURAL

P1 Account for trading securities.

P2 Account for held-to-maturity securities.

P3 Account for available-for-sale securities.

P4 Account for equity securities with significant influence.

BASICS OF INVESTMENTS

C1 Distinguish between debt and equity securities and between short-term and long-term investments.

In prior chapters we discussed the reporting of both equity (common and preferred stock) and debt (bonds and notes) from the seller's (also called *issuer* or *investee*) standpoint. This appendix explains the reporting of both equity and debt from the buyer's (also called *investor*) standpoint. The first section of this appendix describes the motivation for investments, the distinction between short- and long-term investments, and the different classes of investments.

Motivation for Investments

Companies make investments for at least three reasons. First, companies transfer *excess cash* into investments to produce higher income. Second, some entities, such as mutual funds and pension funds, are set up to produce income from investments. Third, companies make investments for strategic reasons. Examples are investments in competitors, suppliers, and even customers. Exhibit C.1 shows short-term (S-T) and long-term (L-T) investments as a percent of total assets for several companies.

EXHIBIT C.1

Investments of Selected Companies

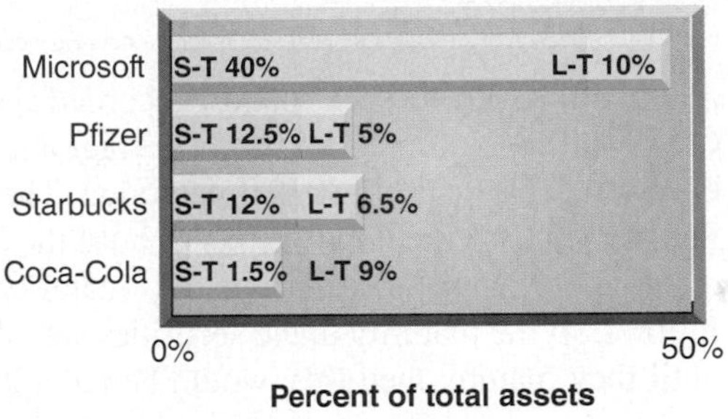

Short-Term Investments Cash equivalents are investments that are both readily converted to known amounts of cash and mature within three months. Many investments, however, mature between 3 and 12 months. These investments are **short-term investments,** also called *temporary investments* and *marketable securities*. Specifically, short-term investments are securities that (1) management intends to convert to cash within one year or the operating cycle, whichever is longer, and (2) are readily convertible to cash. Short-term investments are reported under current assets and serve a purpose similar to cash equivalents.

Long-Term Investments **Long-term investments** in securities are defined as those securities that are not readily convertible to cash or are not intended to be converted into cash in the short term. Long-term investments can also include funds earmarked for a special purpose, such as bond sinking funds and investments in land or other assets not used in the company's operations. Long-term investments are reported in the noncurrent section of the balance sheet, often in its own separate line titled *Long-Term Investments*.

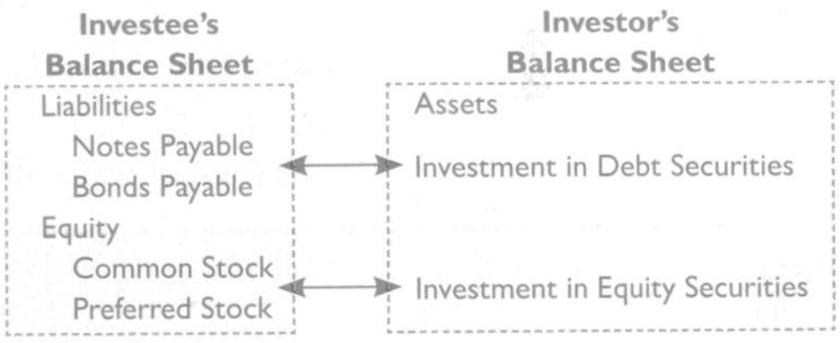

Debt Securities versus Equity Securities Investments in securities can include both debt and equity securities. *Debt securities* reflect a creditor relationship such as investments in notes, bonds, and certificates of deposit; they are issued by governments, companies, and individuals. *Equity securities* reflect an owner relationship such as shares of stock issued by companies.

Classification and Reporting

Accounting for investments in securities depends on three factors: (1) security type, either debt or equity, (2) the company's intent to hold the security either short term or long term, and (3) the company's (investor's) percentage of ownership in the other company's (investee's) equity securities. Exhibit C.2 identifies five classes of securities using these three factors. It describes each of these five classes of securities and the standard reporting required under each class.

Scott Olson/Getty Images

Debt Securities: Accounting Basics

This section explains the accounting basics for *debt securities,* including that for acquisition, disposition, and any interest.

EXHIBIT C.2

Investments in Securities

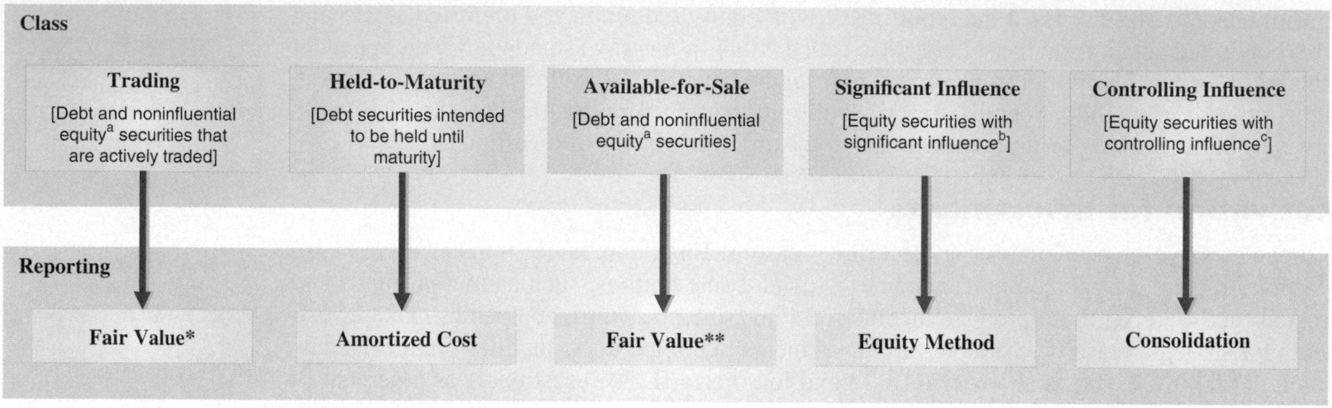

[a] Holding less than 20% of voting stock (equity securities only). [b] Holding 20% or more, but not more than 50%, of voting stock. [c] Holding more than 50% of voting stock.
* Unrealized gains and losses reported on the income statement.
**Unrealized gains and losses reported in the equity section of the balance sheet and in comprehensive income.

Acquisition. Debt securities are recorded at cost when purchased. To illustrate, assume that Music City paid $29,500 plus a $500 brokerage fee on September 1, 2014, to buy Dell's 7%, two-year bonds payable with a $30,000 par value. The bonds pay interest semiannually on August 31 and February 28. Music City intends to hold the bonds until they mature on August 31, 2016; consequently, they are classified as held-to-maturity (HTM) securities. The entry to record this purchase follows. (If the maturity of the securities was short term, and management's intent was to hold them until they mature, then they would be recorded in the Short-Term Investments—HTM account.)

Assets	= Liabilities	+ Equity
+30,000		
−30,000		

2014			
Sept. 1	Long-Term Investments—HTM (Dell)	30,000	
	Cash		30,000
	Purchased bonds to be held to maturity.		

Interest earned. Interest revenue for investments in debt securities is recorded when earned. To illustrate, on December 31, 2014, at the end of its accounting period, Music City accrues interest receivable as follows.

Assets	= Liabilities	+ Equity
+700		+700

Dec. 31	Interest Receivable	700	
	Interest Revenue		700
	Accrued interest earned ($30,000 × 7% × 4/12).		

The $700 interest earned from September 1 to December 31 is computed as "Principal × Annual rate × Fraction of year" (shown above), which also equals 4/6 of the semiannual cash receipt of interest. Music City's financial statements at December 31, 2014, report the interest revenue and the investment as shown in Exhibit C.3.

EXHIBIT C.3

Financial Statement Presentation of Debt Securities

On the income statement for year 2014:	
Interest revenue	**$ 700**
On the December 31, 2014, balance sheet:	
Long-term investments—Held-to-maturity securities (at amortized cost)	**$30,000**

On February 28, 2015, Music City records receipt of semiannual interest.

Assets	= Liabilities	+ Equity
+1,050		+350
−700		

Point: Feb. 28 entry reflects 4 months interest earned and accrued in 2014 and 2 months earned in 2015.

Feb. 28	Cash	1,050	
	Interest Receivable*		700
	Interest Revenue**		350
	Received six months' interest on Dell bonds.		

*$30,000 × 7% × 4/12 **$30,000 × 7% × 2/12

Disposition. When the bonds mature, the proceeds (not including the interest entry) are recorded as:

2016			
Aug. 31	Cash	30,000	
	Long-Term Investments—HTM (Dell)...........		30,000
	Received cash from matured bonds.		

Assets = Liabilities + Equity
+30,000
−30,000

The cost of a debt security can be either higher or lower than its maturity value. When the investment is long term, the difference between cost and maturity value is amortized over the remaining life of the security. We assume for ease of computations that the cost of a long-term debt security equals its maturity value.

Example: What is cost per share? *Answer:* Cost per share is the total cost of acquisition, including broker fees, divided by number of shares acquired.

Equity Securities: Accounting Basics

This section explains the accounting basics for *equity securities,* including that for acquisition, dividends, and disposition.

Acquisition. Equity securities are recorded at cost when acquired, including commissions or brokerage fees paid. To illustrate, assume that Music City purchases 1,000 shares of Intex common stock at par value for $86,000 on October 10, 2014. It records this purchase of available-for-sale (AFS) securities as follows.

Oct. 10	Long-Term Investments—AFS (Intex)	86,000	
	Cash		86,000
	Purchased 1,000 shares of Intex.		

Assets = Liabilities + Equity
+86,000
−86,000

Dividend earned. Any cash dividends received are credited to Dividend Revenue and reported in the income statement. To illustrate, on November 2, Music City receives a $1,720 quarterly cash dividend on the Intex shares, which it records as:

Nov. 2	Cash	1,720	
	Dividend Revenue		1,720
	Received dividend of $1.72 per share.		

Assets = Liabilities + Equity
+1,720 +1,720

Disposition. When the securities are sold, sale proceeds are compared with the cost, and any gain or loss is recorded. To illustrate, on December 20, Music City sells 500 of the Intex shares for $45,000 cash and records this sale as:

Dec. 20	Cash	45,000	
	Long-Term Investments—AFS (Intex)		43,000
	Gain on Sale of Long-Term Investments		2,000
	Sold 500 Intex shares ($86,000 × 500/1,000).		

Assets = Liabilities + Equity
+45,000 +2,000
−43,000

REPORTING OF NONINFLUENTIAL INVESTMENTS

Companies must value and report most noninfluential investments at *fair value.* The exact reporting requirements depend on whether the investments are classified as (1) trading, (2) held-to-maturity, or (3) available-for-sale.

Trading Securities

P1 Account for trading securities.

Trading securities are *debt and equity securities* that the company intends to actively manage and trade for profit. Frequent purchases and sales are expected and are made to earn profits on short-term price changes. Trading securities are *always* reported as current assets.

Valuing and reporting trading securities. The entire portfolio of trading securities is reported at its fair value; this requires a "fair value adjustment" from the cost of the portfolio. The term *portfolio* refers to a group of securities. **Any unrealized gain (or loss) from a change in the fair value of the portfolio of trading securities is reported on the income statement.** Most users believe accounting reports are more useful when changes in fair value for trading securities are reported in income.

Point: *Unrealized gain (or loss)* refers to a change in fair value that is not yet realized through actual sale.

Point: Fair Value Adj. is a balance sheet account with either a debit bal. (Fair Value > Cost) or credit bal. (Fair Value < Cost).

To illustrate, TechCom's portfolio of trading securities had a total cost of $11,500 and a fair value of $13,000 on December 31, 2014, the first year it held trading securities. The difference between the $11,500 cost and the $13,000 fair value reflects a $1,500 gain. It is an unrealized gain because it is not yet confirmed by actual sales. The fair value adjustment for trading securities is recorded with an adjusting entry at the end of each period to equal the difference between the portfolio's cost and its fair value. TechCom records this gain as follows.

Assets	=	Liabilities	+	Equity
+1,500				+1,500

Dec. 31	Fair Value Adjustment—Trading	1,500	
	Unrealized Gain—Income		1,500
	To reflect an unrealized gain in fair values of trading securities.		

This adjustment can also be determined using our "3-Step Adjusting Process" from Chapter 3.

Unadj. bal. is rarely $0; it is $0 here because it's the first year.

Step 1: Determine what unadjusted balance equals: Fair Value Adj—Trading = $0.

Step 2: Determine what adjusted balance should equal: Fair Value Adj—Trading = $1,500 Dr. Explanation: $13,000 fair value > $11,500 cost, thus the Fair Value Adj—Trading requires a $1,500 debit so securities are at fair value.

Step 3: Record the $1,500 adjusting entry to get from Step 1 to Step 2. Explanation: This implies a $1,500 debit to Fair Value Adj—Trading (and the Unrealized Gain).

Example: If TechCom's trading securities have a cost of $14,800 and a fair value of $16,100 at Dec. 31, 2015, its adjusting entry is
Unreal. Loss—Inc. . . . 200
FV Adj.—Trading. . . 200
This is computed as:
$1,500 Beg. Dr. bal. + $200 Cr. = $1,300 End. Dr. bal.

The **unrealized gain (or loss)** is reported in the Other Revenues and Gains (or Expenses and Losses) section on the income statement. Unrealized Gain (or Loss)—Income is a *temporary* account that is closed to Income Summary at the end of each period. Fair Value Adjustment—Trading is a *permanent* account, which adjusts the reported value of the trading securities portfolio from its prior period fair value to the current period fair value. The total cost of the trading securities portfolio is maintained in one account, and the fair value adjustment is recorded in a separate account. For example, TechCom's investment in trading securities is reported in the current assets section of its balance sheet as follows.

ST Investments–Trading

1/1/2014	0	
Purch.	11,500	
12/31/2014	11,500	

Fair Value Adj.–Trading

1/1/2014	0	
Adj.	**1,500**	
12/31/2014	1,500	

Current Assets		
Short-term investments—Trading (at cost)	$11,500	
Fair Value adjustment—Trading	1,500	
Short-term investments—Trading (at fair value)		$13,000
or simply		
Short-term investments—Trading (at fair value; cost is $11,500)		$13,000

Selling trading securities. When individual trading securities are sold, the difference between the net proceeds (sale price less fees) and the cost of the individual trading securities that are sold is recognized as a gain or a loss. **Any prior period fair value adjustment to the portfolio is *not* used to compute the gain or loss from sale of individual trading securities.** This is because the balance in the Fair Value Adjustment account is for the entire portfolio, not individual securities. For example, if TechCom sold some of its trading securities that had cost $1,000 for $1,200 cash on January 9, 2015, it would record the following.

Point: Reporting securities at fair value is referred to as *mark-to-market* accounting.

Assets	=	Liabilities	+	Equity
+1,200				+200
−1,000				

Jan. 9	Cash	1,200	
	Short-Term Investments—Trading		1,000
	Gain on Sale of Short-Term Investments		200
	Sold trading securities costing $1,000 for $1,200 cash.		

A gain is reported in the Other Revenues and Gains section on the income statement, whereas a loss is shown in Other Expenses and Losses. When the period-end fair value adjustment for the portfolio of trading securities is computed, it excludes the cost and fair value of any securities sold.

NEED-TO-KNOW C-1

Trading Securities

P1

Berkshire Co. purchases investments in trading securities at a cost of $130 on December 15, 2015. (This is its first and only purchase of such securities.) On December 28, Berkshire received a $15 cash dividend from the stock purchased on December 15. At December 31, 2015, the trading securities had a fair value of $140.

a. Prepare the December 15 acquisition entry for the trading securities' portfolio.

b. Prepare the December 28 receipt of cash dividends entry for the trading securities' portfolio.

c. Prepare the December 31 year-end adjusting entry for the trading securities' portfolio.

d. Explain how each account in entry *c* is reported in financial statements.

e. Prepare the January 3, 2016, entry when a portion of its trading securities (that had originally cost $33) is sold for $36.

Solution

a.

Dec. 15	Short-Term Investments—Trading	130	
	Cash		130
	To record purchase of trading securities.		

b.

Dec. 28	Cash	15	
	Dividend Revenue.		15
	To record dividend received on trading securities.		

c.

Dec. 31	Fair Value Adjustment—Trading	10	
	Unrealized Gain—Income		10
	To record unrealized gain in fair value of trading securities.		

Fair Value Adj.–Trading

Unadj.	0	
Adj.	10	
12/31/2015	10	

d. **(i)** The $10 debit in the Fair Value Adjustment—Trading account is an adjunct asset account in the balance sheet. It increases the $130 balance of the Short-Term Investment—Trading account to its $140 fair value.

(ii) The $10 credit for Unrealized Gain is reported in the Other Revenues and Gains section of the income statement.

e.

Jan. 3	Cash	36	
	Gain on Sale of Short-Term Investments		3
	Short-Term Investments—Trading		33
	To record sale of trading securities.		

Do More: QS C-3, QS C-4, QS C-5, E C-2, E C-3

QC1

Held-to-Maturity Securities

P2

Account for held-to-maturity securities.

Held-to-maturity (HTM) securities are *debt* securities a company intends and is able to hold until maturity. They are reported in current assets if their maturity dates are within one year or the operating cycle, whichever is longer. HTM securities are reported in long-term assets when the maturity dates extend beyond one year or the operating cycle, whichever is longer. All HTM securities are recorded at cost when purchased, and interest revenue is recorded when earned.

The portfolio of HTM securities is usually reported at (amortized) cost, which is explained in advanced courses. There is no fair value adjustment to the portfolio of HTM securities—neither to the short-term nor long-term portfolios. The basics of accounting for HTM securities were described earlier in this appendix.

Point: Only debt securities can be classified as *held-to-maturity;* equity securities have no maturity date.

Decision Maker

Money Manager You expect interest rates to sharply fall within a few weeks and remain at this lower rate. What is your strategy for holding investments in fixed-rate bonds and notes? ■ [Answers follow the appendix's Summary.]

NEED-TO-KNOW C-2

Held-to-Maturity Securities

P2

Prepare journal entries to record the following transactions involving the short-term securities investments of LA Life.

a. On May 14, paid $100 cash to purchase Muni's 90-day short-term debt securities ($100 principal), dated May 15, that pay 8% interest (categorized as held-to-maturity securities).

b. On November 16, received a check from Muni in payment of the principal and 90 days' interest on the debt securities purchased in transaction *a*.

Solution

a.

May 14	Short-Term Investments—HTM (Muni)	100	
	Cash		100
	Purchased 90-day, 8% debt securities.		

b.

Nov. 16	Cash	102	
	Short-Term Investments—HTM (Muni)		100
	Interest Revenue		2
	Collected $100 principal plus interest of $100 × 8% × 90/360.		

Do More: QS C-6, E C-4

QC2

Available-for-Sale Securities

P3 Account for available-for-sale securities.

Available-for-sale (AFS) securities are *debt and equity securities* not classified as trading or held-to-maturity securities. AFS securities are purchased to yield interest, dividends, or increases in fair value. They are not actively managed like trading securities. If the intent is to sell AFS securities within the longer of one year or operating cycle, they are classified as short-term investments. Otherwise, they are classified as long-term investments.

Valuing and reporting available-for-sale securities. As with trading securities, companies adjust the cost of the portfolio of AFS securities to reflect changes in fair value. This is done with a fair value adjustment to its total portfolio cost. However, any unrealized gain or loss for the portfolio of AFS securities is *not* reported on the income statement. Instead, it is reported in the equity section of the balance sheet (and is part of *comprehensive income,* explained later). To illustrate, assume that Music City had no prior period investments in available-for-sale securities other than those purchased in the current period. Exhibit C.4 shows both the cost and fair value of those investments on December 31, 2014, the end of its reporting period.

EXHIBIT C.4

Cost and Fair Value of Available-for-Sale Securities

	Cost	Fair Value	Unrealized Gain (Loss)
Improv bonds	$30,000	$29,050	$ (950)
Intex common stock, 500 shares	43,000	45,500	2,500
Total	$73,000	$74,550	$1,550

Example: If fair value in Exhibit C.4 is $70,000 (instead of $74,550), what entry is made? *Answer:*
Unreal. Loss—Equity 3,000
FV Adj.—AFS 3,000

The year-end adjusting entry to record the fair value of these investments follows.

Assets = Liabilities + Equity
+1,550 +1,550

Dec. 31	Fair Value Adjustment—Available-for-Sale (LT)	1,550	
	Unrealized Gain—Equity		1,550
	To record adjustment to fair value of available-for-sale securities.		

Point: Unrealized Loss—Equity and Unrealized Gain—Equity are *permanent* (balance sheet) equity *accounts.*

Exhibit C.5 shows the December 31, 2014, balance sheet presentation—it assumes these investments are long term, but they can also be short term. It is also common to combine the cost of investments with the balance in the Fair Value Adjustment account and report the net as a single amount.

EXHIBIT C.5

Balance Sheet Presentation of Available-for-Sale Securities

Assets		
Long-term investments—Available-for-sale (at cost)	$73,000	
Fair value adjustment—Available-for-sale	1,550	
Long-term investments—Available-for-sale (at fair value)		$74,550
or simply		
Long-term investments—Available-for-sale (at fair value; cost is $73,000)		$74,550
Equity		
... consists of usual equity accounts ...		
Add unrealized gain on available-for-sale securities*		$ 1,550

Reconciled

* Often included under the caption Accumulated Other Comprehensive Income.

LT Investments–AFS

1/1/2014	0	
Purch.	73,000	
12/31/2014	73,000	

Fair Value Adj.–AFS (LT)

1/1/2014	0	
Adj.	**1,550**	
12/31/2014	1,550	

Point: Income is increased by selling AFS securities with unrealized gains; income is reduced by selling those with unrealized losses.

Let's extend this illustration and assume that at the end of its next calendar year (December 31, 2015), Music City's portfolio of long-term AFS securities has an $81,000 cost and an $82,000 fair value. It records the adjustment to fair value as follows.

Dec. 31	Unrealized Gain—Equity	550	
	Fair Value Adjustment—Available-for-Sale (LT)		550
	To record adjustment to fair value of available-for-sale securities.		

Assets = Liabilities + Equity
−550 −550

The effects of the 2014 and 2015 securities transactions are reflected in the following T-accounts.

Unrealized Gain—Equity

Adj. 12/31/15	550	Bal. 12/31/14	1,550
		Bal. 12/31/15	**1,000**

Fair Value Adjustment—Available-for-Sale (LT)

Bal. 12/31/14	1,550	Adj. 12/31/15	550
Bal. 12/31/15	**1,000**		

Amounts reconcile.

Example: If cost is $83,000 and fair value is $82,000 at Dec. 31, 2015, it records the following adjustment:
Unreal. Gain—Equity 1,550
Unreal. Loss—Equity 1,000
FV Adj.—AFS 2,550

This adjustment can also be determined using our "3-Step Adjusting Process."

Step 1: Determine what unadjusted balance equals: Fair Value Adj—AFS = $1,550 Dr.

Step 2: Determine what adjusted balance should equal: Fair Value Adj—AFS = $1,000 Dr.
Explanation: $82,000 fair value > $81,000 cost, thus the Fair Value Adj—Trading requires a $1,000 debit so securities are at fair value.

Step 3: Record the $550 adjusting entry to get from Step 1 to Step 2.
Explanation: This implies a $550 credit to Fair Value Adj—AFS (and reduction of Unrealized Gain).

Selling available-for-sale securities. Accounting for the sale of individual AFS securities is identical to that described for the sale of trading securities. When individual AFS securities are sold, the difference between the cost of the individual securities sold and the net proceeds (sale price less fees) is recognized as a gain or loss.

Point: Fair Value Adj.—AFS is a permanent account, shown as a deduction or addition to the investment account.

Alert *Both U.S. GAAP (and IFRS) permit companies to use fair value in reporting financial assets (referred to as the fair value option). This option allows companies to report any financial asset at fair value and recognize value changes in income. This method was previously reserved only for trading securities, but is now an option for available-for-sale and held-to-maturity securities (and other "financial assets and liabilities" such as accounts and notes receivable, accounts and notes payable, and bonds). U.S. standards also set a three-level system to determine fair value:*
—Level 1: Use quoted market values.
—Level 2: Use observable values from related assets or liabilities.
—Level 3: Use unobservable values from estimates or assumptions.
To date, a fairly small set of companies has chosen to broadly apply the fair value option—but, we continue to monitor its use ...

NEED-TO-KNOW C-3

Available-for-Sale Securities

P3

Gard Company completes the following selected transactions related to its short-term investments.

May 8 Purchased 300 shares of FedEx stock as a short-term investment in available-for-sale securities at $40 per share plus $975 in broker fees.

Sept. 2 Sold 100 shares of its investment in FedEx stock at $47 per share and held the remaining 200 shares; broker's commission was $225.

Oct. 2 Purchased 400 shares of Ajay stock for $60 per share plus $1,600 in commissions. The stock is held as a short-term investment in available-for-sale securities.

Required

1. Prepare journal entries for the above transactions.
2. Prepare an adjusting journal entry as of December 31, if the fair values of the equity securities held by Gard are $48 per share for FedEx and $55 per share for Ajay. (This year is the first year Gard Company acquired short-term investments.)

Solution

1.

May 8	Short-Term Investments—AFS (FedEx)	12,975	
	Cash		12,975
	Purchased FedEx stock; (300 sh. × $40) + $975.		
Sept. 2	Cash	4,475	
	Gain on Sale of Short-Term Investment		150
	Short-Term Investments—AFS (FedEx)		4,325
	Sold FedEx shares; original cost is ($12,975 × 100/300)		
Oct. 2	Short-Term Investments—AFS (Ajay)	25,600	
	Cash		25,600
	Purchased Ajay shares; (400 sh. × $60) + $1,600.		

ST Investments–AFS

1/1/2014	0		
5/8/2014	12,975		
		9/2/2014	4,325
10/2/2014	25,600		
12/31/2014	34,250		

Fair Value Adj.–AFS (ST)

1/1/2014	0		
		Adj.	**2,650**
		12/31/2014	2,650

2. Computation of unrealized gain or loss follows.

Short-Term Investments in Available-for-Sale Securities	Shares	Cost per Share	Total Cost	Fair Value per Share	Total Fair Value	Unrealized Gain (Loss)
FedEx	200	$43.25	$ 8,650	$48.00	$ 9,600	
Ajay	400	64.00	25,600	55.00	22,000	
Totals			$34,250		$31,600	$(2,650)

The adjusting entry follows:

Dec. 31	Unrealized Loss—Equity	2,650	
	Fair Value Adjustment—Available-for-Sale (ST)		2,650
	To reflect an unrealized loss in fair values.		

Do More: QS C-7, QS C-8, QS C-9, QS C-10, E C-5, E C-7, E C-8, E C-10

QC3

REPORTING OF INFLUENTIAL INVESTMENTS

Investment in Securities with Significant Influence

P4

Account for equity securities with significant influence.

A long-term investment classified as **equity securities with significant influence** implies that the investor can exert significant influence over the investee. An investor that owns 20% or more (but not more than 50%) of a company's voting stock is usually presumed to have a significant influence over the investee. In some cases, however, the 20% test of significant influence is overruled by other, more persuasive, evidence. This evidence can either lower the 20% requirement or increase it. The **equity method** of accounting and reporting is used for long-term investments in equity securities with significant influence, which is explained in this section.

Long-term investments in equity securities with significant influence are recorded at cost when acquired. To illustrate, Micron Co. records the purchase of 3,000 shares (30%) of Star Co. common stock at a total cost of $70,650 on January 1, 2014, as follows.

Jan. 1	Long-Term Investments—Star	70,650	
	Cash		70,650
	To record purchase of 3,000 Star shares.		

Assets = Liabilities + Equity
+70,650
−70,650

The investee's (Star) earnings increase both its net assets and the claim of the investor (Micron) on the investee's net assets. Thus, when the investee reports its earnings, the investor records its share of those earnings in its investment account. To illustrate, assume that Star reports net income of $20,000 for 2014. Micron then records its 30% share of those earnings as follows.

Dec. 31	Long-Term Investments—Star	6,000	
	Earnings from Long-Term Investment		6,000
	To record 30% equity in investee earnings.		

Assets = Liabilities + Equity
+6,000 +6,000

The debit reflects the increase in Micron's equity in Star. The credit reflects 30% of Star's net income. Earnings from Long-Term Investment is a *temporary* account (closed to Income Summary at each period-end) and is reported on the investor's (Micron's) income statement. If the investee incurs a net loss instead of a net income, the investor records its share of the loss and reduces (credits) its investment account. The investor closes this earnings or loss account to Income Summary.

The receipt of cash dividends is not revenue under the equity method because the investor has already recorded its share of the investee's earnings. Instead, cash dividends received by an investor from an investee are viewed as a conversion of one asset to another; that is, dividends reduce the balance of the investment account. To illustrate, Star declares and pays $10,000 in cash dividends on its common stock. Micron records its 30% share of these dividends received on January 9, 2015, as:

Jan. 9	Cash	3,000	
	Long-Term Investments—Star		3,000
	To record share of dividend paid by Star.		

Assets = Liabilities + Equity
+3,000
−3,000

The book value of an investment under the equity method equals the cost of the investment plus (minus) the investor's equity in the *undistributed* (*distributed*) earnings of the investee. Once Micron records these transactions, its Long-Term Investments account appears as in Exhibit C.6.

EXHIBIT C.6

Investment in Star Common Stock (Ledger Account)

Long-Term Investment—Star			
1/1/2014 Investment acquisition	70,650		
12/31/2014 Share of earnings	6,000		
12/31/2014 Balance	76,650		
		1/9/2015 Share of dividend	3,000
1/9/2015 Balance	73,650		

Micron's account balance on January 9, 2015, for its investment in Star is $73,650. This is the investment's cost *plus* Micron's equity in Star's earnings since its purchase *less* Micron's equity in Star's cash dividends since its purchase. When an investment in equity securities is sold, the gain or loss is computed by comparing proceeds from the sale with the book value of

Point: Security prices are sometimes listed in fractions. For example, a debt security with a price of $22\frac{1}{4}$ is the same as $22.25.

the investment on the date of sale. If Micron sells its Star stock for $80,000 on January 10, 2015, it records the sale as:

Assets	= Liabilities	+ Equity
+80,000		+6,350
−73,650		

Jan. 10	Cash	80,000	
	Long-Term Investments—Star		73,650
	Gain on Sale of Investment		6,350
	Sold 3,000 shares of stock for $80,000.		

Investment in Securities with Controlling Influence

C2 Describe how to report equity securities with controlling influence.

A long-term investment classified as **equity securities with controlling influence** implies that the investor can exert a controlling influence over the investee. An investor who owns more than 50% of a company's voting stock has control over the investee. This investor can dominate all other shareholders in electing the corporation's board of directors and has control over the investee's management. In some cases, controlling influence can extend to situations of less than 50% ownership. Exhibit C.7 summarizes the accounting for investments in equity securities based on an investor's ownership in the stock.

EXHIBIT C.7

Accounting for Equity Investments by Percent of Ownership

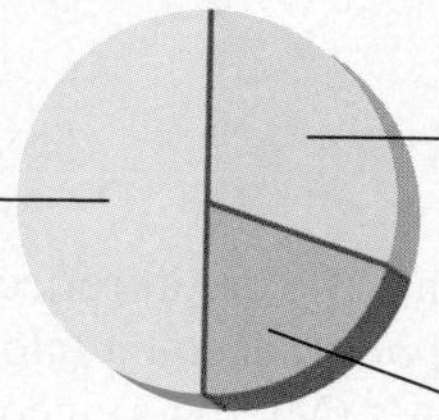

The *equity method with consolidation* is used to account for long-term investments in equity securities with controlling influence. The investor reports *consolidated financial statements* when owning such securities. The controlling investor is called the **parent,** and the investee is called the **subsidiary.** Many companies are parents with subsidiaries. Examples are (1) **Gap Inc.**, the parent of Gap, Old Navy, and Banana Republic; and (2) **Brunswick**, the parent of Mercury Marine, Sea Ray, and U.S. Marine. A company owning all the outstanding stock of a subsidiary can, if it desires, take over the subsidiary's assets, retire the subsidiary's stock, and merge the subsidiary into the parent. However, there often are financial, legal, and tax advantages if a business operates as a parent controlling one or more subsidiaries. When a company operates as a parent with subsidiaries, each entity maintains separate accounting records. From a legal viewpoint, the parent and each subsidiary are separate entities with all rights, duties, and responsibilities of individual companies.

Consolidated financial statements show the financial position, results of operations, and cash flows of all entities under the parent's control, including all subsidiaries. These statements are prepared as if the business were organized as one entity. The parent uses the equity method in its accounts, but the investment account is *not* reported on the parent's financial statements. Instead, the individual assets and liabilities of the parent and its subsidiaries are combined on one balance sheet. Their revenues and expenses also are combined on one income statement, and their cash flows are combined on one statement of cash flows. The procedures for preparing consolidated financial statements are in advanced courses.

IFRS

Unlike U.S. GAAP, IFRS requires uniform accounting policies be used throughout the group of consolidated subsidiaries. Also, unlike U.S. GAAP, IFRS offers no detailed guidance on valuation procedures. ■

Accounting Summary for Investments in Securities

Exhibit C.8 summarizes the standard accounting for investments in securities. Recall that many investment securities are classified as either short term or long term depending on management's intent and ability to convert them in the future. Understanding the accounting for these investments enables us to draw better conclusions from financial statements in making business decisions.

EXHIBIT C.8

Accounting for Investments in Securities

Classification	Accounting
Short-Term Investment in Securities	
Held-to-maturity (debt) securities	**Cost** (without any discount or premium amortization)
Trading (debt and equity) securities	**Fair value** (with fair value adjustment to income)
Available-for-sale (debt and equity) securities	**Fair value** (with fair value adjustment to equity)
Long-Term Investment in Securities	
Held-to-maturity (debt) securities	**Cost** (with any discount or premium amortization)
Available-for-sale (debt and equity) securities	**Fair value** (with fair value adjustment to equity)
Equity securities with significant influence	Equity method
Equity securities with controlling influence	Equity method (with consolidation)

Comprehensive Income **Comprehensive income** is defined as all changes in equity during a period except those from owners' investments and dividends. Specifically, comprehensive income is computed by adding or subtracting *other comprehensive income* to net income:

Net income	$ #
Other comprehensive income	#
Comprehensive income	$ #

Other comprehensive income includes unrealized gains and losses on available-for-sale securities, foreign currency translation adjustments, and certain pension adjustments. (*Accumulated other comprehensive income* is defined as the cumulative impact of *other comprehensive income.*)

Comprehensive income is reported in financial statements in one of two ways (which reflects new FASB guidance):

1. On a separate *statement of comprehensive income* that immediately follows the income statement.
2. On the lower section of the income statement (as a single continuous *statement of income and comprehensive income*).

Point: Some users believe that since AFS securities are not actively traded, reporting fair value changes in income would unnecessarily increase income variability and decrease usefulness.

Option 1 is the most common. **Google**, for example, reports a statement of comprehensive income following its income statement. Shown here is an abbreviated version of the Google statement:

GOOGLE

Net income	**$12,920**
Available-for-sale investments, net of tax	(554)
Foreign currency translation from consolidation	89
Cash flow hedges, net of tax	52
Other comprehensive income	(413)
Total comprehensive income	**$12,507**

(Other comprehensive income — bracketing the three components and their total)

Option 2 adds the components of other comprehensive income to net income on the bottom of the income statement to compute a continuous statement of income and comprehensive income. There is no difference in the numbers; it is simply a matter of how those numbers are presented. A third option, which is no longer generally acceptable by itself, was to include the components of other comprehensive income and its total along with the total of comprehensive income in the statement of equity.

QC4

GLOBAL VIEW

This section discusses similarities and differences for the accounting and reporting of investments when financial statements are prepared under U.S. GAAP vis-à-vis IFRS.

Accounting for Noninfluential Securities The accounting for noninfluential securities is broadly similar between U.S. GAAP and IFRS. *Trading securities* are accounted for using fair values with unrealized gains and losses reported in net income as fair values change. *Available-for-sale securities* are accounted for using fair values with unrealized gains and losses reported in other comprehensive income as fair values change (and later in net income when realized). *Held-to-maturity securities* are accounted for using amortized cost. Similarly, companies have the option under both systems to apply the fair value option for available-for-sale and held-to-maturity securities. Also, both systems review held-to-maturity securities for impairment. There are some differences in terminology under IFRS: (1) trading securities are commonly referred to as *financial assets at fair value through profit and loss,* and (2) available-for-sale securities are commonly referred to as *available-for-sale financial assets.* **NOKIA** reports the following categories for noninfluential securities: (1) ***Financial assets at fair value through profit or loss,*** consisting of financial assets held for trading and financial assets designated upon initial recognition as at fair value through profit or loss, and (2) ***Available-for-sale financial assets,*** which are measured at fair value.

Accounting for Influential Securities The accounting for influential securities is broadly similar across U.S. GAAP and IFRS. Specifically, under the *equity method,* the share of investee's net income is reported in the investor's income in the same period the investee earns that income; also, the investment account equals the acquisition cost plus the share of investee income less the share of investee dividends (minus amortization of excess on purchase price above fair value of identifiable, limited-life assets). Under the *consolidation method,* investee and investor revenues and expenses are combined, absent intercompany transactions, and subtracting noncontrolling interests. Also, nonintercompany assets and liabilities are similarly combined (eliminating the need for an investment account), and noncontrolling interests are subtracted from equity. There are some differences in terminology: (1) U.S. GAAP companies commonly refer to earnings from long-term investments as *equity in earnings of affiliates* whereas IFRS companies commonly use *equity in earnings of associated (or associate) companies,* and (2) U.S. GAAP companies commonly refer to noncontrolling interests in consolidated subsidiaries as *minority interests* whereas IFRS companies commonly use *noncontrolling interests.*

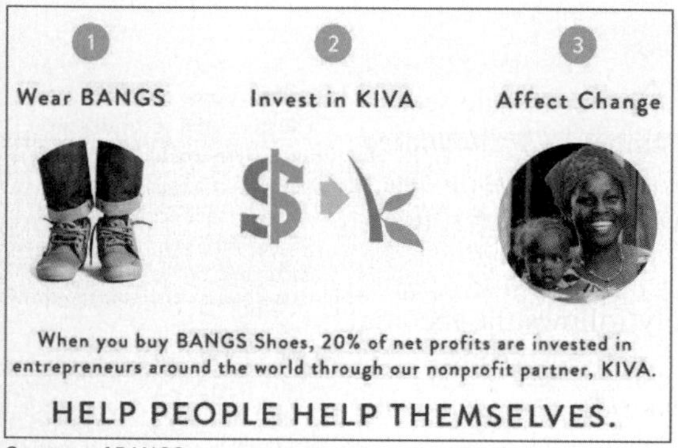

Courtesy of BANGS

Sustainability and Accounting Hannah Davis, the founder of **BANGS Shoes**, is a social entrepreneur. "There is one reason I consciously decide to stick with the turbulent journey of launching a social enterprise, and that reason is people," explains Hannah. "The really important part about BANGS is that we only invest in sustainable methods of change . . . If you give a man a fish, he eats for a day. If you teach a man to fish, he eats for a lifetime—and that's the BANGS mentality." The graphic in the margin identifies the model of sustainability that BANGS utilizes and its motto: *Help People Help Themselves.*

Decision Analysis — Components of Return on Total Assets

A1 Compute and analyze the components of return on total assets.

A company's **return on total assets** (or simply *return on assets*) is important in assessing financial performance. The return on total assets can be separated into two components, profit margin and total asset turnover, for additional analyses. Exhibit C.9 shows how these two components determine return on total assets.

EXHIBIT C.9

Components of Return on Total Assets

Return on total assets = Profit margin × Total asset turnover

$$\frac{\text{Net income}}{\text{Average total assets}} = \frac{\text{Net income}}{\text{Net sales}} \times \frac{\text{Net sales}}{\text{Average total assets}}$$

Profit margin reflects the percent of net income in each dollar of net sales. Total asset turnover reflects a company's ability to produce net sales from total assets. All companies desire a high return on total assets. By considering these two components, we can often discover strengths and weaknesses not revealed by return on total assets alone. This improves our ability to assess future performance and company strategy.

To illustrate, consider return on total assets and its components for **Gap Inc.** in Exhibit C.10.

EXHIBIT C.10

Gap's Components of Return on Total Assets

Fiscal Year	Return on Total Assets	=	Profit Margin	×	Total Asset Turnover
2014	16.7%	=	7.9%	×	2.11
2013*	15.0	=	7.3	×	2.06
2012	11.5	=	5.7	×	2.01
2011	16.0	=	8.2	×	1.95
2010	14.1	=	7.7	×	1.83

* 2013 sales and income data scaled by 52/53 due to the 53-week year.

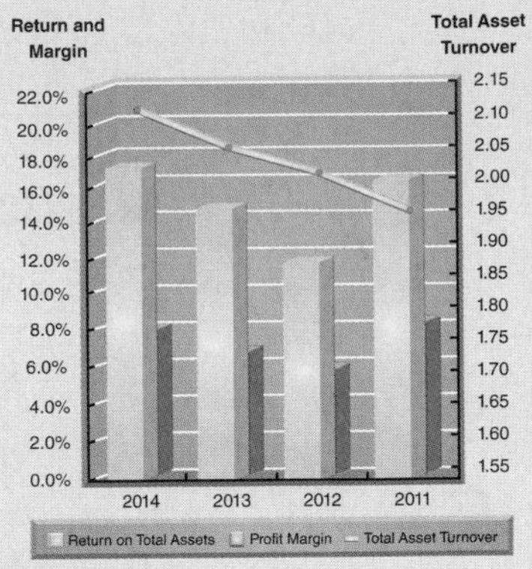

At least three findings emerge. First, Gap's return on total assets improved over the past few years from 11.5% in 2012 to 16.7% in 2014. Second, total asset turnover has improved over this period, from 1.83 to 2.11. Third, Gap's profit margin dipped in 2012, but has otherwise stayed between 7.3% and 8.2%. These components reveal the dual role of profit margin and total asset turnover in determining return on total assets. They also reveal that the driver of Gap's recent improvement in return on total assets is both total asset turnover and profit margin.

Generally, if a company is to maintain or improve its return on total assets, it must meet any decline in either profit margin or total asset turnover with an increase in the other. If not, return on assets will decline. Companies consider these components in planning strategies. A component analysis can also reveal where a company is weak and where changes are needed, especially in a competitor analysis. If asset turnover is lower than the industry norm, for instance, a company should focus on raising asset turnover at least to the norm. The same applies to profit margin.

Decision Maker

Retailer You are an entrepreneur and owner of a retail sporting goods store. The store's recent annual performance reveals (industry norms in parentheses): return on total assets = 11% (11.2%); profit margin = 4.4% (3.5%); and total asset turnover = 2.5 (3.2). What does your analysis of these figures reveal? ■ [Answers follow the appendix's Summary.]

NEED-TO-KNOW

COMPREHENSIVE

The following transactions relate to Brown Company's long-term investments. Brown did not own any long-term investments prior to these transactions. Show (1) the necessary journal entries and (2) the relevant portions of each year's balance sheet and income statement that reflect these transactions for both years.

2014

Sept.	9	Purchased 1,000 shares of Packard, Inc., common stock for $80,000 cash. These shares represent 30% of Packard's outstanding shares.
Oct.	2	Purchased 2,000 shares of AT&T common stock for $60,000 cash as a long-term investment. These shares represent less than a 1% ownership in AT&T.
	17	Purchased as a long-term investment 1,000 shares of Apple Computer common stock for $40,000 cash. These shares are less than 1% of Apple's outstanding shares.
Nov.	1	Received $5,000 cash dividend from Packard.
	30	Received $3,000 cash dividend from AT&T.
Dec.	15	Received $1,400 cash dividend from Apple.
	31	Packard's net income for this year is $70,000.
	31	Fair values for the investments in equity securities are Packard, $84,000; AT&T, $48,000; and Apple Computer, $45,000.
	31	For preparing financial statements, note the following post-closing account balances: Common Stock, $500,000, and Retained Earnings, $350,000.

2015

Jan.	1	Sold Packard, Inc., shares for $108,000 cash.
May	30	Received $3,100 cash dividend from AT&T.
June	15	Received $1,600 cash dividend from Apple.
Aug.	17	Sold the AT&T stock for $52,000 cash.
	19	Purchased 2,000 shares of Coca-Cola common stock for $50,000 cash as a long-term investment. The stock represents less than a 5% ownership in Coca-Cola.
Dec.	15	Received $1,800 cash dividend from Apple.
	31	Fair values of the investments in equity securities are Apple, $39,000, and Coca-Cola, $48,000.
	31	For preparing financial statements, note the following post-closing account balances: Common Stock, $500,000, and Retained Earnings, $410,000.

PLANNING THE SOLUTION

- Account for the investment in Packard under the equity method.
- Account for the investments in AT&T, Apple, and Coca-Cola as long-term investments in available-for-sale securities.

- Prepare the information for the two years' balance sheets by including the relevant asset and equity accounts, and the two years' income statements by identifying the relevant revenues, earnings, gains, and losses.

SOLUTION

1. Journal entries for 2014.

Sept. 9	Long-Term Investments—Packard	80,000	
	Cash		80,000
	Acquired 1,000 shares, representing a 30% equity in Packard.		
Oct. 2	Long-Term Investments—AFS (AT&T)	60,000	
	Cash		60,000
	Acquired 2,000 shares as a long-term investment in available-for-sale securities.		
Oct. 17	Long-Term Investments—AFS (Apple)	40,000	
	Cash		40,000
	Acquired 1,000 shares as a long-term investment in available-for-sale securities.		
Nov. 1	Cash	5,000	
	Long-Term Investments—Packard.............		5,000
	Received dividend from Packard.		
Nov. 30	Cash	3,000	
	Dividend Revenue..........................		3,000
	Received dividend from AT&T.		
Dec. 15	Cash	1,400	
	Dividend Revenue..........................		1,400
	Received dividend from Apple.		
Dec. 31	Long-Term Investments—Packard	21,000	
	Earnings from Investment (Packard)		21,000
	To record 30% share of Packard's annual earnings of $70,000.		
Dec. 31	Unrealized Loss—Equity	7,000	
	Fair Value Adjustment—Available-for-Sale (LT)* ...		7,000
	To record change in fair value of long-term available-for-sale securities.		

LT Investments–AFS

1/1/2014	0	
10/2/2014	60,000	
10/17/2014	40,000	
12/31/2014	100,000	

Fair Value Adj.–AFS (LT)

1/1/2014	0		
		Adj.	**7,000**
		12/31/2014	7,000

* Fair value adjustment computations:

	Cost	Fair Value	Unrealized Gain (Loss)
AT&T	$ 60,000	$48,000	$(12,000)
Apple	40,000	45,000	5,000
Total	$100,000	$93,000	$ (7,000)

Required balance of the Fair Value Adjustment—Available-for-Sale (LT) account (credit)............	$(7,000)
Existing balance	0
Necessary adjustment (credit)	$(7,000)

2. The December 31, 2014, selected balance sheet items appear as follows.

Assets	
Long-term investments	
Available-for-sale securities (at fair value; cost is $100,000)	$ 93,000
Investment in equity securities	96,000
Total long-term investments	189,000
Stockholders' Equity	
Common stock	500,000
Retained earnings..	350,000
Unrealized loss—Equity	(7,000)

The relevant income statement items for the year ended December 31, 2014, follow.

Dividend revenue	$ 4,400
Earnings from investment	21,000

1. Journal entries for 2015.

Jan. 1	Cash	108,000	
	Long-Term Investments—Packard		96,000
	Gain on Sale of Long-Term Investments		12,000
	Sold 1,000 shares for cash.		
May 30	Cash	3,100	
	Dividend Revenue		3,100
	Received dividend from AT&T.		
June 15	Cash	1,600	
	Dividend Revenue		1,600
	Received dividend from Apple.		
Aug. 17	Cash	52,000	
	Loss on Sale of Long-Term Investments	8,000	
	Long-Term Investments—AFS (AT&T)		60,000
	Sold 2,000 shares for cash.		
Aug. 19	Long-Term Investments—AFS (Coca-Cola)	50,000	
	Cash		50,000
	Acquired 2,000 shares as a long-term investment in available-for-sale securities.		
Dec. 15	Cash	1,800	
	Dividend Revenue		1,800
	Received dividend from Apple.		
Dec. 31	Fair Value Adjustment—Available-for-Sale (LT)*	4,000	
	Unrealized Loss—Equity		4,000
	To record change in fair value of long-term available-for-sale securities.		

LT Investments–AFS

1/1/2015 100,000	
	8/17/2015 60,000
8/19/2015 50,000	
12/31/2015 90,000	

Fair Value Adj.–AFS (LT)

	1/1/2015 7,000
Adj. 4,000	
	12/31/2015 3,000

* Fair value adjustment computations:

	Cost	Fair Value	Unrealized Gain (Loss)
Apple	$40,000	$39,000	$(1,000)
Coca-Cola	50,000	48,000	(2,000)
Total	$90,000	$87,000	$(3,000)

Required balance of the Fair Value Adjustment—Available-for-Sale (LT) account (credit)	$(3,000)
Existing balance (credit)	(7,000)
Necessary adjustment (debit)	$ 4,000

2. The December 31, 2015, balance sheet items appear as follows.

Assets	
Long-term investments	
Available-for-sale securities (at fair value; cost is $90,000)	$ 87,000
Stockholders' Equity	
Common stock	500,000
Retained earnings	410,000
Unrealized loss—Equity	(3,000)

The relevant income statement items for the year ended December 31, 2015, follow.

Dividend revenue	$ 6,500
Gain on sale of long-term investments	12,000
Loss on sale of long-term investments	(8,000)

APPENDIX

C-A Investments in International Operations

Many entities from small entrepreneurs to large corporations conduct business internationally. Some entities' operations occur in so many different countries that the companies are called **multinationals.** Many of us think of **Coca-Cola** and **McDonald's**, for example, as primarily U.S. companies, but most of their sales occur outside the United States. Exhibit C-A.1 shows the percent of international sales and income for selected U.S. companies. Managing and accounting for multinationals present challenges. This section describes some of these challenges and how to account for and report these activities.

EXHIBIT C-A.1

International Sales and Income as a Percent of Their Totals

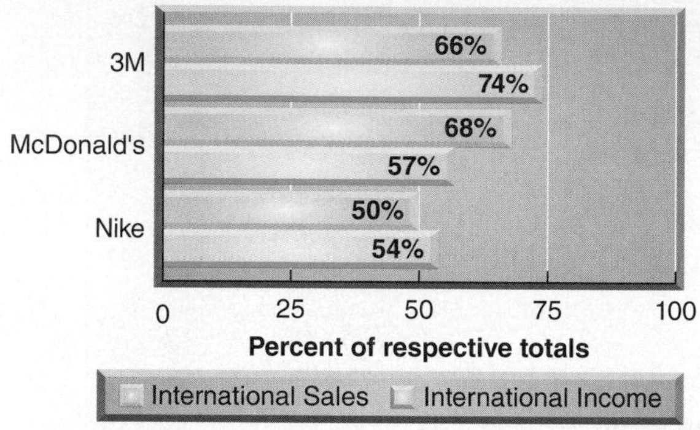

Two major accounting challenges that arise when companies have international operations relate to transactions that involve more than one currency. The first is to account for sales and purchases listed in a foreign currency. The second is to prepare consolidated financial statements with international subsidiaries. For ease in this discussion, we use companies with a U.S. base of operations and assume the need to prepare financial statements in U.S. dollars. This means the *reporting currency* of these companies is the U.S. dollar.

Point: Transactions *listed* or *stated* in a foreign currency are said to be *denominated* in that currency.

C3 Explain foreign exchange rates and record transactions listed in a foreign currency.

Exchange Rates between Currencies Markets for the purchase and sale of foreign currencies exist all over the world. In these markets, U.S. dollars can be exchanged for Canadian dollars, British pounds, Japanese yen, euros, or any other legal currencies. The price of one currency stated in terms of another currency is called a **foreign exchange rate.** Exhibit C-A.2 lists recent exchange rates for selected currencies. The exchange rate for British pounds and U.S. dollars is $1.8980, meaning 1 British pound could be purchased for $1.8980. On that same day, the exchange rate between Mexican pesos and U.S. dollars is $0.0925, or 1 Mexican peso can be purchased for $0.0925. Exchange rates fluctuate due to changing economic and political conditions, including the supply and demand for currencies and expectations about future events.

Point: To convert currency, see XE.com

EXHIBIT C-A.2

Foreign Exchange Rates for Selected Currencies*

Source (unit)	Price in $U.S.	Source (unit)	Price in $U.S.
Britain (pound)	$1.8980	Canada (dollar)	$0.9793
Mexico (peso)	0.0925	Japan (yen)	0.0090
Taiwan (dollar)	0.0305	Europe (euro)	1.2920

* Rates will vary over time based on economic, political, and other changes.

Decision Insight

Greek Haircut Investors in government debt securities in the eurozone are wary of the heightened default risk with securities issued by certain eurozone member nations. For example, a few years ago, buyers of certain Greek bonds were repaid only 30% of principal because of the government's inability to honor its full obligation on the bonds.

Glow Images

Sales and Purchases Listed in a Foreign Currency When a U.S. company makes a credit sale to an international customer, accounting for the sale and the account receivable is straightforward if sales terms require the international customer's payment in U.S. dollars. If sale terms require (or allow) payment in a foreign currency, however, the U.S. company must account for the sale and the account receivable in a different manner.

Sales in a Foreign Currency To illustrate, consider the case of the U.S.-based manufacturer Boston Company, which makes credit sales to London Outfitters, a British retail company. A sale occurs on December 12, 2014, for a price of £10,000 with payment due on February 10, 2015. Boston Company keeps its accounting records in U.S. dollars. To record the sale, Boston Company must translate the sales price from pounds to dollars. This is done using the exchange rate on the date of the sale. Assuming the exchange rate on December 12, 2014, is $1.80, Boston records this sale as follows.

Dec. 12	Accounts Receivable—London Outfitters	18,000	
	Sales*		18,000
	To record a sale at £10,000, when the exchange rate equals $1.80. * (£10,000 × $1.80/£)		

Assets = Liabilities + Equity
+18,000 +18,000

When Boston Company prepares its annual financial statements on December 31, 2014, the current exchange rate is $1.84. Thus, the current dollar value of Boston Company's receivable is $18,400 (£10,000 × $1.84/£). This amount is $400 higher than the amount recorded on December 12. Accounting principles require a receivable to be reported in the balance sheet at its current dollar value. Thus, Boston Company must make the following entry to record the increase in the dollar value of this receivable at year-end.

Dec. 31	Accounts Receivable—London Outfitters	400	
	Foreign Exchange Gain		400
	To record the increased value of the British pound for the receivable.		

Assets = Liabilities + Equity
+400 +400

On February 10, 2015, Boston Company receives London Outfitters's payment of £10,000. It immediately exchanges the pounds for U.S. dollars. On this date, the exchange rate for pounds is $1.78. Thus, Boston Company receives only $17,800 (£10,000 × $1.78/£). It records the cash receipt and the loss associated with the decline in the exchange rate as follows.

Point: Foreign exchange gains are credits, and foreign exchange losses are debits.

Feb. 10	Cash	17,800	
	Foreign Exchange Loss	600	
	Accounts Receivable—London Outfitters		18,400
	Received foreign currency payment of an account and converted it into dollars.		

Assets = Liabilities + Equity
+17,800 −600
−18,400

Gains and losses from foreign exchange transactions are accumulated in the Foreign Exchange Gain (or Loss) account. After year-end adjustments, the balance in the Foreign Exchange Gain (or Loss) account is reported on the income statement and closed to the Income Summary account.

Purchases in a Foreign Currency Accounting for credit purchases from an international seller is similar to the case of a credit sale to an international customer. In particular, if the U.S. company is required to make payment in a foreign currency, the account payable must be translated into dollars before the U.S. company can record it. If the exchange rate is different when preparing financial statements and when paying for the purchase, the U.S. company must recognize a foreign exchange gain or loss at those dates. To illustrate, assume NC Imports, a U.S. company, purchases products costing €20,000 (euros) from Hamburg Brewing on January 15, when the exchange rate is $1.20 per euro. NC records this transaction as follows.

Example: Assume that a U.S. company makes a credit purchase from a British company for £10,000 when the exchange rate is $1.62. At the balance sheet date, this rate is $1.72. Does this imply a gain or loss for the U.S. company? *Answer:* A loss.

Jan. 15	Inventory	24,000	
	Accounts Payable—Hamburg Brewing		24,000
	To record a €20,000 purchase when exchange rate is $1.20 (€20,000 × $1.20/€).		

Assets = Liabilities + Equity
+24,000 +24,000

NC Imports makes payment in full on February 14 when the exchange rate is $1.25 per euro, which is recorded as follows.

Feb. 14	Accounts Payable—Hamburg Brewing	24,000	
	Foreign Exchange Loss	1,000	
	Cash		25,000
	To record cash payment toward €20,000 account when exchange rate is $1.25 (€20,000 × $1.25/€).		

Assets = Liabilities + Equity
−25,000 −24,000 −1,000

Decision Insight

Global Greenback What do changes in foreign exchange rates mean? A decline in the price of the U.S. dollar against other currencies usually yields increased international sales for U.S. companies, without hiking prices or cutting costs, and puts them on a stronger competitive footing abroad. At home, they can raise prices without fear that foreign rivals will undercut them. ■

Google reported $75 million in other comprehensive income as a result of consolidating the non-U.S. dollar financial statements of its subsidiaries.

Consolidated Statements with International Subsidiaries A second challenge in accounting for international operations involves preparing consolidated financial statements when the parent company has one or more international subsidiaries. Consider a U.S.-based company that owns a controlling interest in a French subsidiary. The reporting currency of the U.S. parent is the dollar. The French subsidiary maintains its financial records in euros. Before preparing consolidated statements, the parent must translate financial statements of the French company into U.S. dollars. After this translation is complete (including that for accounting differences), it prepares consolidated statements the same as for domestic subsidiaries. Procedures for translating an international subsidiary's account balances depend on the nature of the subsidiary's operations. The process requires the parent company to select appropriate foreign exchange rates and to apply those rates to the foreign subsidiary's account balances, and report the change as a component of other comprehensive income. This is described in advanced courses.

Global: A weaker U.S. dollar often increases global sales for U.S. companies.

Decision Maker

Entrepreneur Assume that **Ben & Jerry's** purchases milk from dairies in both the U.S. and Canada. The price of the Canadian dollar in terms of the U.S. dollar jumps from US$0.70 to US$0.80. Is the ice cream maker now more or less likely to buy milk from Canadian or U.S. suppliers? ■ [Answers follow the appendix's Summary.]

Summary

C1 Distinguish between debt and equity securities and between short-term and long-term investments. *Debt securities* reflect a creditor relationship and include investments in notes, bonds, and certificates of deposit. *Equity securities* reflect an owner relationship and include shares of stock issued by other companies. Short-term investments in securities are current assets that meet two criteria: (1) They are expected to be converted into cash within one year or the current operating cycle of the business, whichever is longer, and (2) they are readily convertible to cash, or *marketable*. All other investments in securities are long term. Long-term investments also include assets not used in operations and those held for special purposes, such as land for expansion. Investments in securities are classified into one of five groups: (1) trading securities, which are always short-term; (2) debt securities held-to-maturity; (3) debt and equity securities available-for-sale; (4) equity securities in which an investor has a significant influence over the investee; and (5) equity securities in which an investor has a controlling influence over the investee.

C2 Describe how to report equity securities with controlling influence. If an investor owns more than 50% of another company's voting stock and controls the investee, the investor's financial reports are prepared on a consolidated basis. These reports are prepared as if the company were organized as one entity.

C3A Explain foreign exchange rates and record transactions listed in a foreign currency. A foreign exchange rate is the price of one currency stated in terms of another. An entity with transactions in a foreign currency when the exchange rate changes between the transaction dates and their settlement will experience exchange gains or losses. When a company makes a credit sale to a foreign customer and sales terms call for payment in a foreign currency, the company must translate the foreign currency into dollars to record the receivable. If the exchange rate changes before payment is received, exchange gains or losses are recognized in the year they occur. The same treatment is used when a company makes a credit purchase from a foreign supplier and is required to make payment in a foreign currency.

A1 Compute and analyze the components of return on total assets. Return on total assets has two components: profit margin and total asset turnover. A decline in one component must be met with an increase in another if return on assets is to be maintained. Component analysis is helpful in assessing company performance compared to that of competitors and its own past.

P1 Account for trading securities. Investments are initially recorded at cost, and any dividend or interest from these investments is recorded in the income statement. Investments classified as trading securities are reported at fair value. Unrealized gains and losses on trading securities are reported in income. When investments are sold, the difference between the net proceeds from the sale and the cost of the securities is recognized as a gain or loss.

P2 Account for held-to-maturity securities. Debt securities held-to-maturity are reported at cost when purchased. Interest revenue is recorded as it accrues. The cost of long-term held-to-maturity securities is adjusted for the amortization of any difference between cost and maturity value.

P3 Account for available-for-sale securities. Debt and equity securities available-for-sale are recorded at cost when purchased. Available-for-sale securities are reported at their fair values on the balance sheet with unrealized gains or losses shown in the equity section. Gains and losses realized on the sale of these investments are reported in the income statement.

P4 Account for equity securities with significant influence. The equity method is used when an investor has a significant influence over an investee. This usually exists when an investor owns 20% or more of the investee's voting stock but not more than 50%. The equity method means an investor records its share of investee earnings with a debit to the investment account and a credit to a revenue account. Dividends received reduce the investment account balance.

Guidance Answers to Decision Maker

Money Manager If you have investments in fixed-rate bonds and notes when interest rates fall, the value of your investments increases. This is so because the bonds and notes you hold continue to pay the same (high) rate while the market is demanding a new lower interest rate. Your strategy is to continue holding your investments in bonds and notes, and, potentially, to increase these holdings through additional purchases.

Retailer Your store's return on assets is 11%, which is similar to the industry norm of 11.2%. However, disaggregation of return on assets reveals that your store's profit margin of 4.4% is much higher than the norm of 3.5%, but your total asset turnover of 2.5 is much lower than the norm of 3.2. These results suggest that, as compared with competitors, you are less efficient in using assets. You need to focus on increasing sales or reducing assets. You might consider reducing prices to increase sales, provided such a strategy does not reduce your return on assets. For instance, you could reduce your profit margin to 4% to increase sales. If total asset turnover increases to more than 2.75 when profit margin is lowered to 4%, your overall return on assets is improved.

Entrepreneur You are now less likely to buy Canadian milk products because it takes more U.S. money to buy a Canadian dollar (and milk). For instance, the purchase of milk from a Canadian dairy with a $1,000 (Canadian dollars) price would have cost the U.S. company $700 (U.S. dollars, computed as C$1,000 × US$0.70) before the rate change, and $800 (US dollars, computed as C$1,000 × US$0.80) after the rate change.

Key Terms

Available-for-sale (AFS) securities
Comprehensive income
Consolidated financial statements
Equity method
Equity securities with controlling influence
Equity securities with significant influence
Foreign exchange rate
Held-to-maturity (HTM) securities
Long-term investments
Multinational
Other comprehensive income
Parent
Return on total assets
Short-term investments
Subsidiary
Trading securities
Unrealized gain (loss)

Multiple Choice Quiz

Answers at end of appendix

1. A company purchased $30,000 of 5% bonds for investment purposes on May 1. The bonds pay interest on February 1 and August 1. The amount of interest revenue accrued at December 31 (the company's year-end) is:
a. $1,500
b. $1,375
c. $1,000
d. $625
e. $300

2. Earlier this period, Amadeus Co. purchased its only available-for-sale investment in the stock of Bach Co. for $83,000. The period-end fair value of this stock is $84,500. Amadeus records a:
a. Credit to Unrealized Gain—Equity for $1,500.
b. Debit to Unrealized Loss—Equity for $1,500.
c. Debit to Investment Revenue for $1,500.
d. Credit to Fair Value Adjustment—Available-for-Sale for $3,500.
e. Credit to Cash for $1,500.

3. Mozart Co. owns 35% of Melody Inc. Melody pays $50,000 in cash dividends to its shareholders for the period. Mozart's entry to record the Melody dividend includes a:
a. Credit to Investment Revenue for $50,000.
b. Credit to Long-Term Investments for $17,500.
c. Credit to Cash for $17,500.
d. Debit to Long-Term Investments for $17,500.
e. Debit to Cash for $50,000.

4. A company has net income of $300,000, net sales of $2,500,000, and total assets of $2,000,000. Its return on total assets equals:
a. 6.7%
b. 12.0%
c. 8.3%
d. 80.0%
e. 15.0%

5. A company had net income of $80,000, net sales of $600,000, and total assets of $400,000. Its profit margin and total asset turnover are:

	Profit Margin	Total Asset Turnover
a.	1.5%	13.3
b.	13.3%	1.5
c.	13.3%	0.7
d.	7.0%	13.3
e.	10.0%	26.7

[A] *Superscript A denotes assignments based on Appendix C-A.*

Icon denotes assignments that involve decision making.

Discussion Questions

1. Under what two conditions should investments be classified as current assets?
2. On a balance sheet, what valuation must be reported for short-term investments in trading securities?
3. If a short-term investment in available-for-sale securities costs $10,000 and is sold for $12,000, how should the difference between these two amounts be recorded?
4. Identify the three classes of noninfluential and two classes of influential investments in securities.
5. Under what conditions should investments be classified as current assets? As long-term assets?
6. For investments in available-for-sale securities, how are unrealized (holding) gains and losses reported?
7. If a company purchases its only long-term investments in available-for-sale debt securities this period and their fair value is below cost at the balance sheet date, what entry is required to recognize this unrealized loss?
8. On a balance sheet, what valuation must be reported for debt securities classified as available-for-sale?
9. Under what circumstances are long-term investments in debt securities reported at cost and adjusted for amortization of any difference between cost and maturity value?
10. In accounting for investments in equity securities, when should the equity method be used?
11. Under what circumstances does a company prepare consolidated financial statements?

12.[A] What are two major challenges in accounting for international operations?

13.[A] Assume a U.S. company makes a credit sale to a foreign customer that is required to make payment in its foreign currency. In the current period, the exchange rate is $1.40 on the date of the sale and $1.30 on the date the customer pays the receivable. Will the U.S. company record an exchange gain or loss?

14.[A] If a U.S. company makes a credit sale to a foreign customer required to make payment in U.S. dollars, can the U.S. company have an exchange gain or loss on this sale?

15. Refer to **Apple**'s statement of comprehensive income in Appendix A. What is the amount of foreign currency translation adjustment for the year ended September 28, 2013? Is this adjustment an unrealized gain or an unrealized loss? **APPLE**

16. Refer to **Google**'s statement of comprehensive income. What was the amount of its 2013 *change in net unrealized gains* for its AFS investments? **GOOGLE**

17. Refer to the income statement of **Samsung** in Appendix A. How can you tell that it uses the consolidated method of accounting? **Samsung**

connect

QUICK STUDY

QS C-1
Distinguishing between short- and long-term investments
C1

Which of the following statements *a* through *g* are true of long-term investments?

____ **a.** They are held as an investment of cash available for current operations.
____ **b.** They can include funds earmarked for a special purpose, such as bond sinking funds.
____ **c.** They can include investments in trading securities.
____ **d.** They can include debt securities held-to-maturity.
____ **e.** They are always easily sold and therefore qualify as being marketable.
____ **f.** They can include debt and equity securities available-for-sale.
____ **g.** They can include bonds and stocks not intended to serve as a ready source of cash.

QS C-2
Distinguishing between debt and equity securities
C1

A solar company invests in the following securities. Identify those investments as either an investment in debt (D) securities or equity (E) securities.

____ **a.** U.S. treasury bonds	____ **e.** IBM Corporate notes	____ **i.** Chicago municipal bonds
____ **b.** Google stock	____ **f.** German government bonds	____ **j.** Apple stock
____ **c.** Certificate of deposit	____ **g.** Amazon stock	____ **k.** David Bowie bonds
____ **d.** Apple bonds	____ **h.** Costco corporate notes	____ **l.** Facebook stock

QS C-3
Short-term equity investments P1

On April 18, Riley Co. made a short-term investment in 300 common shares of XLT Co. The purchase price is $42 per share and the broker's fee is $250. The intent is to actively manage these shares for profit. On May 30, Riley Co. receives $1 per share from XLT in dividends. Prepare the April 18 and May 30 journal entries to record these transactions.

Prepare Hertog Company's journal entries to reflect the following transactions for the current year.

May 7 Purchases 200 shares of Kraft stock as a short-term investment in trading securities at a cost of $50 per share plus $300 in broker fees.

June 6 Sells 200 shares of its investment in Kraft stock at $56 per share. The broker's commission on this sale is $150.

QS C-4 Recording trading securities P1

Kitty Company began operations in 2014 and maintains short-term investments in trading securities. The year-end cost and fair values for its portfolio of these investments follow. Prepare journal entries to record each December 31 year-end fair value adjustment for these securities.

QS C-5 Multiyear fair value adjustments to trading securities P1

Portfolio of Trading Securities	Cost	Fair Value
December 31, 2014	$37	$35
December 31, 2015	42	46
December 31, 2016	60	69
December 31, 2017	56	55

On February 1, 2015, Garzon purchased 6% bonds issued by PBS Utilities at a cost of $40,000, which is their par value. The bonds pay interest semiannually on July 31 and January 31. For 2015, prepare entries to record Garzon's July 31 receipt of interest and its December 31 year-end interest accrual.

QS C-6 Debt securities transactions P2

Journ Co. purchased short-term investments in available-for-sale securities at a cost of $50,000 on November 25, 2015. At December 31, 2015, these securities had a fair value of $47,000. This is the first and only time the company has purchased such securities.

1. Prepare the December 31, 2015, year-end adjusting entry for the securities' portfolio.
2. For each account in the entry for part 1, explain how it is reported in financial statements.
3. Prepare the April 6, 2016, entry when Journ sells one-half of these securities for $26,000.

QS C-7 Available-for-sale securities P3

Hiker Company completes the following transactions during the current year. Prepare the May 9 and June 2 journal entries and the December 31 adjusting entry. This is the first and only time the company purchased such securities.

May 9 Purchases 200 shares of Higo stock as a short-term investment in available-for-sale securities at a cost of $25 per share plus $150 in broker fees.

June 2 Sells 100 shares of its investment in Higo stock at $28 per share. The broker's commission on this sale is $90.

Dec. 31 The closing market price (fair value) of the Higo stock is $23 per share.

QS C-8 Available-for-sale securities P3

During the current year, Reed Consulting Group acquired long-term available-for-sale securities at a $70,000 cost. At its December 31 year-end, these securities had a fair value of $58,000. This is the first and only time the company purchased such securities.

1. Prepare the necessary year-end adjusting entry related to these securities.
2. Explain how each account used in part 1 is reported in the financial statements.

QS C-9 Recording fair value adjustment for securities P3

On May 20, 2015, Montero Co. paid $1,000,000 to acquire 25,000 common shares (10%) of ORD Corp. as a long-term investment. On August 5, 2016, Montero sold one-half of these shares for $625,000. What valuation method should be used to account for this stock investment? Prepare entries to record both the acquisition and the sale of these shares.

QS C-10 Recording long-term equity securities P3

Montero Co. holds 100,000 common shares (40%) of ORD Corp. as a long-term investment. ORD Corp. paid a $100,000 dividend on November 1, 2015, and reported a net income of $700,000 for 2015. Prepare Montero's entries to record (*a*) the receipt of the dividend and (*b*) the December 31, 2015, year-end adjustment required for the investment account.

QS C-11 Equity method transactions P4

QS C-12
Describing investments in securities
C2

Complete the following descriptions by filling in the blanks.

1. Equity securities giving an investor significant influence are accounted for using the ______ ______.
2. Available-for-sale debt securities are reported on the balance sheet at ______ ______.
3. Trading securities are classified as ______ assets.
4. Accrual of interest on bonds held as long-term investments requires a credit to ______ ______.
5. The controlling investor (more than 50% ownership) is called the ______, and the investee company is called the ______.

QS C-13
Equity securities with controlling influence
C2

Complete the following descriptions by filling in the blanks.

1. The controlling investor is called the ______, and the investee is called the ______.
2. A long-term investment classified as equity securities with controlling influence implies that the investor can exert a ______ influence over the investee.

QS C-14
Return on total assets
A1

The return on total assets is the focus of analysts, creditors, and other users of financial statements.

1. How is the return on total assets computed?
2. What does this important ratio reflect?

QS C-15
Component return on total assets A1

Return on total assets can be separated into two important components.

1. Write the formula to separate the return on total assets into its two basic components.
2. Explain how these components of the return on total assets are helpful to financial statement users for business decisions.

QS C-16^A^
Foreign currency transactions C3

A U.S. company sells a product to a British company with the transaction listed in British pounds. On the date of the sale, the transaction total of $14,500 is billed as £10,000, reflecting an exchange rate of 1.45 (that is, $1.45 per pound). Prepare the entry to record (1) the sale and (2) the receipt of payment in pounds when the exchange rate is 1.35.

QS C-17^A^
Foreign currency transactions C3

On March 1, 2015, a U.S. company made a credit sale requiring payment in 30 days from a Malaysian company, Hamac Sdn. Bhd., in 20,000 Malaysian ringgits. Assuming the exchange rate between Malaysian ringgits and U.S. dollars is $0.4538 on March 1 and $0.4899 on March 31, prepare the entries to record the sale on March 1 and the cash receipt on March 31.

QS C-18
International accounting for investments
P1

The **Carrefour Group** reports the following description of its trading securities (titled "financial assets reported at fair value in the income statement").

> These are financial assets held by the Group in order to make a short-term profit on the sale. These assets are valued at their fair value with variations in value recognized in the income statement.

Carrefour's financial statements report €7 million in unrealized gains and €26 million in unrealized losses, both included in the fair value of those financial assets held for trading. What amount of these unrealized gains and unrealized losses, if any, are reported in its income statement? Explain.

connect

EXERCISES

Exercise C-1
Debt and equity securities and short- and long-term investments
C1

Complete the following descriptions by filling in the blanks.

1. Debt securities reflect a ______ relationship such as investments in notes, bonds, and certificates of deposit.
2. Equity securities reflect an ______ relationship such as shares of stock issued by companies.
3. Short-term investments are securities that (1) management intends to convert to cash within ____ ____ or the ____ ____, whichever is longer, and (2) are readily convertible to ____.
4. Long-term investments in securities are defined as those securities that are ____ ____ convertible to cash or are ____ ____ to be converted into cash in the short term.

Exercise C-2
Accounting for short-term trading securities
P1

Prepare journal entries to record the following transactions involving the short-term securities investments of Duke Co., all of which occurred during year 2015.

a. On March 22, purchased 1,000 shares of RIP Company stock at $10 per share plus an $80 brokerage fee. These shares are categorized as trading securities.

b. On September 1, received a $1.00 per share cash dividend on the RIP Company stock purchased in transaction *a*.

c. On October 8, sold 500 shares of RIP Co. stock for $15 per share, less a $50 brokerage fee.

(*c*) Dr. Cash $7,450

Exercise C-3
Accounting for trading securities
P1

Brooks Co. purchases various investments in trading securities at a cost of $66,000 on December 27, 2015. (This is its first and only purchase of such securities.) At December 31, 2015, these securities had a fair value of $72,000.

1. Prepare the December 31, 2015, year-end adjusting entry for the trading securities' portfolio.

2. Explain how each account in the entry of part 1 is reported in financial statements.

3. Prepare the January 3, 2016, entry when Brooks sells a portion of its trading securities (that had originally cost $33,000) for $35,000.

Check (3) Gain, $2,000

Exercise C-4
Accounting for short-term held-to-maturity securities
P2

Prepare journal entries to record the following transactions involving the short-term securities investments of Natura Co., all of which occurred during year 2015.

a. On June 15, paid $1,000,000 cash to purchase Remedy's 90-day short-term debt securities ($1,000,000 principal), dated June 15, that pay 10% interest (categorized as held-to-maturity securities).

b. On September 16, received a check from Remedy in payment of the principal and 90 days' interest on the debt securities purchased in transaction *a*.

Exercise C-5
Accounting for short-term available-for-sale securities
P3

Prepare journal entries to record the following transactions involving the short-term securities investments of Krum Co., all of which occurred during year 2015.

a. On August 1, paid $450,000 cash to purchase Houtte's 9% debt securities ($450,000 principal), dated July 30, 2015, and maturing January 30, 2016 (categorized as available-for-sale securities).

b. On October 30, received a check from Houtte for 90 days' interest on the debt securities purchased in transaction *a*.

Exercise C-6
Transactions in short-term and long-term investments
P1 P2 P3

Prepare journal entries to record the following transactions involving both the short-term and long-term investments of Cancun Corp., all of which occurred during calendar-year 2015. Use the account Short-Term Investments for any transactions that you determine are short term.

a. On February 15, paid $160,000 cash to purchase American General's 90-day short-term notes at par, which are dated February 15 and pay 10% interest (classified as held-to-maturity).

b. On March 22, bought 700 shares of Fran Industries common stock at $51 cash per share plus a $150 brokerage fee (classified as long-term available-for-sale securities).

c. On May 15, received a check from American General in payment of the principal and 90 days' interest on the notes purchased in transaction *a*.

d. On July 30, paid $100,000 cash to purchase MP3 Electronics's 8% notes at par, dated July 30, 2015, and maturing on January 30, 2016 (classified as trading securities).

e. On September 1, received a $1.00 per share cash dividend on the Fran Industries common stock purchased in transaction *b*.

f. On October 8, sold 350 shares of Fran Industries common stock for $64 cash per share, less a $125 brokerage fee.

g. On October 30, received a check from MP3 Electronics for three months' interest on the notes purchased in transaction *d*.

Exercise C-7
Adjusting available-for-sale securities to fair value
P3

On December 31, 2015, Reggit Company held the following short-term investments in its portfolio of available-for-sale securities. Reggit had no short-term investments in its prior accounting periods. Prepare the December 31, 2015, adjusting entry to report these investments at fair value.

Available-for-Sale Securities	Cost	Fair Value
Verrizano Corporation bonds payable	$89,600	$91,600
Preble Corporation notes payable	70,600	62,900
Lucerne Company common stock	86,500	83,100

Check Unrealized loss, $9,100

Exercise C-8
Fair value adjustment to available-for-sale securities
P3

On December 31, 2015, Lujack Co. held the following short-term available-for-sale securities. Lujack had no short-term investments prior to the current period. Prepare the December 31, 2015, year-end adjusting entry to record the fair value adjustment for these securities.

Available-for-Sale Securities	Cost	Fair Value
Nintendo Co. common stock	$44,450	$48,900
Atlantic bonds payable	49,000	47,000
Kellogg Co. notes payable	25,000	23,200
McDonald's Corp. common stock	46,300	44,800

Exercise C-9
Fair value adjustment to available-for-sale securities
P3

Prescrip Co. began operations in 2014. The cost and fair values for its long-term investments portfolio in available-for-sale securities are shown below. Prepare Prescrip's December 31, 2015, adjusting entry to reflect any necessary fair value adjustment for these investments.

Portfolio of Available-for-Sale Securities	Cost	Fair Value
December 31, 2014	$120,483	$118,556
December 31, 2015	60,120	90,271

Exercise C-10
Multiyear fair value adjustments to available-for-sale securities
P3

Ticker Services began operations in 2013 and maintains long-term investments in available-for-sale securities. The year-end cost and fair values for its portfolio of these investments follow. Prepare journal entries to record each year-end fair value adjustment for these securities.

Portfolio of Available-for-Sale Securities	Cost	Fair Value
December 31, 2013	$372,000	$360,860
December 31, 2014	428,500	455,800
December 31, 2015	600,200	700,500
December 31, 2016	876,900	780,200

Exercise C-11
Classifying investments in securities; recording fair values
C1 P2 P3 P4

Information regarding Carperk Company's individual investments in securities during its calendar-year 2015, along with the December 31, 2015, fair values, follows.

a. Investment in Brava Company bonds: $420,500 cost, $457,000 fair value. Carperk intends to hold these bonds until they mature in 2020.

b. Investment in Baybridge common stock: 29,500 shares; $362,450 cost; $391,375 fair value. Carperk owns 32% of Baybridge's voting stock and has a significant influence over Baybridge.

c. Investment in Buffa common stock: 12,000 shares; $165,500 cost; $178,000 fair value. This investment amounts to 3% of Buffa's outstanding shares, and Carperk's goal with this investment is to earn dividends over the next few years.

d. Investment in Newton common stock: 3,500 shares; $90,300 cost; $88,625 fair value. Carperk's goal with this investment is to reap an increase in fair value of the stock over the next three to five years. Newton has 30,000 common shares outstanding.

e. Investment in Farmers common stock: 16,300 shares; $100,860 cost; $111,210 fair value. This stock is marketable and is held as an investment of cash available for operations.

Required

1. Identify whether each investment should be classified as a short-term or long-term investment. For each long-term investment, indicate in which of the long-term investment classifications it should be placed.

2. Prepare a journal entry dated December 31, 2015, to record the fair value adjustment of the long-term investments in available-for-sale securities. Carperk had no long-term investments prior to year 2015.

Check (2) Unrealized gain, $10,825

Exercise C-12
Securities transactions; equity method
P4

Prepare journal entries to record the following transactions and events of Kodax Company.

2015

Jan. 2 Purchased 30,000 shares of Grecco Co. common stock for $408,000 cash plus a broker's fee of $3,000 cash. Grecco has 90,000 shares of common stock outstanding and its policies will be significantly influenced by Kodax.
Sept. 1 Grecco declared and paid a cash dividend of $1.50 per share.
Dec. 31 Grecco announced that net income for the year is $486,900.

2016

June 1 Grecco declared and paid a cash dividend of $2.10 per share.
Dec. 31 Grecco announced that net income for the year is $702,750.
Dec. 31 Kodax sold 10,000 shares of Grecco for $320,000 cash.

Exercise C-13
Equity securities with controlling influence
C2

Complete the following descriptions by filling in the blanks.

1. Consolidated ______ ______ show the financial position, results of operations, and cash flows of all entities under the parent's control, including all subsidiaries.

2. The equity method with ______ is used to account for long-term investments in equity securities with controlling influence.

Exercise C-14
Return on total assets
A1

The following information is available from the financial statements of Regae Industries. Compute Regae's return on total assets for 2015 and 2016. (Round returns to one-tenth of a percent.) Comment on the company's efficiency in using its assets in 2015 and 2016.

	A	B	C	D
1		2014	2015	2016
2	Total assets, December 31	$210,000	$340,000	$770,000
3	Net income	30,200	38,400	60,300
4				

Exercise C-15[A]
Foreign currency transactions
C3

Leigh of New York sells its products to customers in the United States and the United Kingdom. On December 16, 2015, Leigh sold merchandise on credit to Bronson Ltd. of London at a price of 17,000 pounds. The exchange rate on that day for £1 was $1.4583. On December 31, 2015, when Leigh prepared its financial statements, the rate was £1 for $1.4382. Bronson paid its bill in full on January 15, 2016, at which time the exchange rate was £1 for $1.4482. Leigh immediately exchanged the 17,000 pounds for U.S. dollars. Prepare Leigh's journal entries on December 16, December 31, and January 15 (round to the nearest dollar).

Exercise C-16[A]
Computing foreign exchange gains and losses on receivables
C3

On May 8, 2015, Jett Company (a U.S. company) made a credit sale to Lopez (a Mexican company). The terms of the sale required Lopez to pay 800,000 pesos on February 10, 2016. Jett prepares quarterly financial statements on March 31, June 30, September 30, and December 31. The exchange rates for pesos during the time the receivable is outstanding follow.

May 8, 2015	$0.1323
June 30, 2015	0.1352
September 30, 2015	0.1368
December 31, 2015	0.1335
February 10, 2016	0.1386

Compute the foreign exchange gain or loss that Jett should report on each of its quarterly income statements for the last three quarters of 2015 and the first quarter of 2016. Also compute the amount reported on Jett's balance sheets at the end of each of its last three quarters of 2015.

Exercise C-17
International accounting for investments
P3

The **Carrefour Group** reports the following description of its financial assets available-for-sale.

> Assets available for sale are . . . valued at fair value. Unrealized . . . gains or losses are recorded as shareholders' equity until they are sold.

Carrefour's financial statements report €18 million in *net* unrealized losses (net of unrealized gains), which are included in the fair value of its available-for-sale securities reported on the balance sheet.

1. What amount of the €18 million net unrealized losses, if any, is reported in the income statement? Explain.
2. If the €18 million net unrealized losses are not reported in the income statement, in which statement are they reported, if any? Explain.

connect

PROBLEM SET A

Problem C-1A
Recording transactions and fair value adjustments for trading securities
P1

Carlsville Company, which began operations in 2015, invests its idle cash in trading securities. The following transactions are from its short-term investments in trading securities.

2015

Jan. 20	Purchased 800 shares of Ford Motor Co. at $26 per share plus a $125 commission.
Feb. 9	Purchased 2,200 shares of Lucent at $44.25 per share plus a $578 commission.
Oct. 12	Purchased 750 shares of Z-Seven at $7.50 per share plus a $200 commission.
Dec. 31	Fair value of the short-term investments in trading securities is $130,000.

2016

Apr. 15	Sold 800 shares of Ford Motor Co. at $29 per share less a $285 commission.
July 5	Sold 750 shares of Z-Seven at $10.25 per share less a $102.50 commission.
July 22	Purchased 1,600 shares of Hunt Corp. at $30 per share plus a $444 commission.
Aug. 19	Purchased 1,800 shares of Donna Karan at $18.25 per share plus a $290 commission.
Dec. 31	Fair value of the short-term investments in trading securities is $160,000.

2017

Feb. 27	Purchased 3,400 shares of HCA at $34 per share plus a $420 commission.
Mar. 3	Sold 1,600 shares of Hunt at $25 per share less a $250 commission.
June 21	Sold 2,200 shares of Lucent at $42 per share less a $420 commission.
June 30	Purchased 1,200 shares of Black & Decker at $47.50 per share plus a $595 commission.
Nov. 1	Sold 1,800 shares of Donna Karan at $18.25 per share less a $309 commission.
Dec. 31	Fair value of the short-term investments in trading securities is $180,000.

Check Dec. 31, 2016
Cr. Fair Value Adjustment—Trading $24,834

Required

Prepare journal entries to record these short-term investment activities for the years shown. On December 31 of each year, prepare the adjusting entry to record any necessary fair value adjustment for the portfolio of trading securities.

Problem C-2A
Recording, adjusting, and reporting short-term available-for-sale securities
P3

Rose Company had no short-term investments prior to year 2015. It had the following transactions involving short-term investments in available-for-sale securities during 2015.

Apr. 16	Purchased 4,000 shares of Gem Co. stock at $24.25 per share plus a $180 brokerage fee.
May 1	Paid $100,000 to buy 13-week U.S. Treasury bills (debt securities): $100,000 principal amount, 6% interest, securities dated May 1 and maturing July 31 with $1,500 in interest revenue.
July 7	Purchased 2,000 shares of PepsiCo stock at $49.25 per share plus a $175 brokerage fee.
20	Purchased 1,000 shares of Xerox stock at $16.75 per share plus a $205 brokerage fee.
31	Received a check for principal and accrued interest on the U.S. Treasury bills that matured on July 31.
Aug. 15	Received an $0.85 per share cash dividend on the Gem Co. stock.
28	Sold 2,000 shares of Gem Co. stock at $30 per share less a $225 brokerage fee.
Oct. 1	Received a $1.90 per share cash dividend on the PepsiCo shares.
Dec. 15	Received a $1.05 per share cash dividend on the remaining Gem Co. shares.
31	Received a $1.30 per share cash dividend on the PepsiCo shares.

Required

1. Prepare journal entries to record the preceding transactions and events.
2. Prepare a table to compare the year-end cost and fair values of Rose's short-term investments in available-for-sale securities. The year-end fair values per share are: Gem Co., $26.50; PepsiCo, $46.50; and Xerox, $13.75.
3. Prepare an adjusting entry, if necessary, to record the year-end fair value adjustment for the portfolio of short-term investments in available-for-sale securities.

Check (2) Cost = $164,220

(3) Dr. Unrealized Loss—Equity $4,470

Analysis Component

4. Explain the balance sheet presentation of the fair value adjustment for Rose's short-term investments.
5. How do these short-term investments affect Rose's (*a*) income statement for year 2015 and (*b*) the equity section of its balance sheet at year-end 2015?

Problem C-3A
Recording, adjusting, and reporting long-term available-for-sale securities
P3

Grass Security, which began operations in 2015, invests in long-term available-for-sale securities. Following is a series of transactions and events determining its long-term investment activity.

2015

Jan. 20	Purchased 1,000 shares of Johnson & Johnson at $20.50 per share plus a $240 commission.
Feb. 9	Purchased 1,200 shares of Sony at $46.20 per share plus a $225 commission.
June 12	Purchased 1,500 shares of Mattel at $27.00 per share plus a $195 commission.
Dec. 31	Per share fair values for stocks in the portfolio are Johnson & Johnson, $21.50; Mattel, $30.90; Sony, $38.

2016

Apr. 15	Sold 1,000 shares of Johnson & Johnson at $23.50 per share less a $525 commission.
July 5	Sold 1,500 shares of Mattel at $23.90 per share less a $235 commission.
July 22	Purchased 600 shares of Sara Lee at $22.50 per share plus a $480 commission.
Aug. 19	Purchased 900 shares of Eastman Kodak at $17 per share plus a $198 commission.
Dec. 31	Per share fair values for stocks in the portfolio are: Kodak, $19.25; Sara Lee, $20.00; Sony, $35.00.

2017

Feb. 27	Purchased 2,400 shares of Microsoft at $67.00 per share plus a $525 commission.
June 21	Sold 1,200 shares of Sony at $48.00 per share less an $880 commission.
June 30	Purchased 1,400 shares of Black & Decker at $36.00 per share plus a $435 commission.
Aug. 3	Sold 600 shares of Sara Lee at $16.25 per share less a $435 commission.
Nov. 1	Sold 900 shares of Eastman Kodak at $22.75 per share less a $625 commission.
Dec. 31	Per share fair values for stocks in the portfolio are: Black & Decker, $39.00; Microsoft, $69.00.

Required

1. Prepare journal entries to record these transactions and events and any year-end fair value adjustments to the portfolio of long-term available-for-sale securities.
2. Prepare a table that summarizes the (*a*) total cost, (*b*) total fair value adjustment, and (*c*) total fair value of the portfolio of long-term available-for-sale securities at each year-end.
3. Prepare a table that summarizes (*a*) the realized gains and losses and (*b*) the unrealized gains or losses for the portfolio of long-term available-for-sale securities at each year-end.

Check (2*b*) Fair Value Adj. bal.: 12/31/15, $3,650 Cr.; 12/31/16; $13,818 Cr.

(3*b*) Unrealized Gain at 12/31/2017, $8,040

Problem C-4A
Accounting for long-term investments in securities; with and without significant influence
P3 P4

Selk Steel Co., which began operations on January 4, 2015, had the following subsequent transactions and events in its long-term investments.

2015

Jan. 5	Selk purchased 60,000 shares (20% of total) of Kildaire's common stock for $1,560,000.
Oct. 23	Kildaire declared and paid a cash dividend of $3.20 per share.
Dec. 31	Kildaire's net income for 2015 is $1,164,000, and the fair value of its stock at December 31 is $30.00 per share.

2016

Oct. 15 Kildaire declared and paid a cash dividend of $2.60 per share.
Dec. 31 Kildaire's net income for 2016 is $1,476,000, and the fair value of its stock at December 31 is $32.00 per share.

2017

Jan. 2 Selk sold all of its investment in Kildaire for $1,894,000 cash.

Part 1

Assume that Selk has a significant influence over Kildaire with its 20% share of stock.

Required

1. Prepare journal entries to record these transactions and events for Selk.
2. Compute the carrying (book) value per share of Selk's investment in Kildaire common stock as reflected in the investment account on January 1, 2017.
3. Compute the net increase or decrease in Selk's equity from January 5, 2015, through January 2, 2017, resulting from its investment in Kildaire.

Check (2) Carrying value per share, $29

Part 2

Assume that although Selk owns 20% of Kildaire's outstanding stock, circumstances indicate that it does not have a significant influence over the investee and that it is classified as an available-for-sale security investment.

Required

1. Prepare journal entries to record the preceding transactions and events for Selk. Also prepare an entry dated January 2, 2017, to remove any balance related to the fair value adjustment.
2. Compute the cost per share of Selk's investment in Kildaire common stock as reflected in the investment account on January 1, 2017.
3. Compute the net increase or decrease in Selk's equity from January 5, 2015, through January 2, 2017, resulting from its investment in Kildaire.

(1) 1/2/2017 Dr. Unrealized Gain—Equity $360,000

(3) Net increase, $682,000

Problem C-5A
Long-term investment transactions; unrealized and realized gains and losses
C2 P3 P4

Stoll Co.'s long-term available-for-sale portfolio at December 31, 2014, consists of the following.

Available-for-Sale Securities	Cost	Fair Value
40,000 shares of Company A common stock	$535,300	$490,000
7,000 shares of Company B common stock	159,380	154,000
17,500 shares of Company C common stock	662,750	640,938

Stoll enters into the following long-term investment transactions during year 2015.

Jan. 29 Sold 3,500 shares of Company B common stock for $79,188 less a brokerage fee of $1,500.
Apr. 17 Purchased 10,000 shares of Company W common stock for $197,500 plus a brokerage fee of $2,400. The shares represent a 30% ownership in Company W.
July 6 Purchased 4,500 shares of Company X common stock for $126,562 plus a brokerage fee of $1,750. The shares represent a 10% ownership in Company X.
Aug. 22 Purchased 50,000 shares of Company Y common stock for $375,000 plus a brokerage fee of $1,200. The shares represent a 51% ownership in Company Y.
Nov. 13 Purchased 8,500 shares of Company Z common stock for $267,900 plus a brokerage fee of $2,450. The shares represent a 5% ownership in Company Z.
Dec. 9 Sold 40,000 shares of Company A common stock for $515,000 less a brokerage fee of $4,100.

The fair values of its investments at December 31, 2015, are: B, $81,375; C, $610,312; W, $191,250; X, $118,125; Y, $531,250; and Z, $278,800.

Required

1. Determine the amount Stoll should report on its December 31, 2015, balance sheet for its long-term investments in available-for-sale securities.
2. Prepare any necessary December 31, 2015, adjusting entry to record the fair value adjustment for the long-term investments in available-for-sale securities.
3. What amount of gains or losses on transactions relating to long-term investments in available-for-sale securities should Stoll report on its December 31, 2015, income statement?

Check (2) Cr. Unrealized Loss—Equity, $20,002

Problem C-6A^A
Foreign currency transactions
C3

Doering Company, a U.S. corporation with customers in several foreign countries, had the following selected transactions for 2015 and 2016.

2015

Apr. 8 Sold merchandise to Salinas & Sons of Mexico for $5,938 cash. The exchange rate for pesos is $0.1043 on this day.
July 21 Sold merchandise on credit to Sumito Corp. in Japan. The price of 1.5 million yen is to be paid 120 days from the date of sale. The exchange rate for yen is $0.0094 on this day.
Oct. 14 Sold merchandise for 19,000 pounds to Smithers Ltd. of Great Britain, payment in full to be received in 90 days. The exchange rate for pounds is $1.4566 on this day.
Nov. 18 Received Sumito's payment in yen for its July 21 purchase and immediately exchanged the yen for dollars. The exchange rate for yen is $0.0092 on this day.
Dec. 20 Sold merchandise for 17,000 ringgits to Hamid Albar of Malaysia, payment in full to be received in 30 days. On this day, the exchange rate for ringgits is $0.4501.
Dec. 31 Recorded adjusting entries to recognize exchange gains or losses on Doering's annual financial statements. Rates for exchanging foreign currencies on this day follow.

Pesos (Mexico)	$0.1055	Pounds (Britain)	$1.4620
Yen (Japan)	0.0093	Ringgits (Malaysia)	0.4456

2016

Jan. 12 Received full payment in pounds from Smithers for the October 14 sale and immediately exchanged the pounds for dollars. The exchange rate for pounds is $1.4699 on this day.
Jan. 19 Received Hamid Albar's full payment in ringgits for the December 20 sale and immediately exchanged the ringgits for dollars. The exchange rate for ringgits is $0.4420 on this day.

Required

1. Prepare journal entries for the Doering transactions and adjusting entries (round amounts to the nearest dollar).
2. Compute the foreign exchange gain or loss to be reported on Doering's 2015 income statement.

Check (2) 2015 total foreign exchange loss, $274

Analysis Component

3. What actions might Doering consider to reduce its risk of foreign exchange gains or losses?

PROBLEM SET B

Problem C-1B
Recording transactions and fair value adjustments for trading securities
P1

Harris Company, which began operations in 2015, invests its idle cash in trading securities. The following transactions relate to its short-term investments in its trading securities.

2015

Mar. 10 Purchased 2,400 shares of AOL at $59.15 per share plus a $1,545 commission.
May 7 Purchased 5,000 shares of MTV at $36.25 per share plus a $2,855 commission.
Sept. 1 Purchased 1,200 shares of UPS at $57.25 per share plus a $1,250 commission.
Dec. 31 Fair value of the short-term investments in trading securities is $380,000.

2016

Apr. 26 Sold 5,000 shares of MTV at $34.50 per share less a $2,050 commission.
Apr. 27 Sold 1,200 shares of UPS at $60.50 per share less an $1,788 commission.
June 2 Purchased 3,600 shares of SPW at $172 per share plus a $3,250 commission.
June 14 Purchased 900 shares of Walmart at $50.25 per share plus a $1,082 commission.
Dec. 31 Fair value of the short-term investments in trading securities is $828,000.

2017

Jan. 28 Purchased 2,000 shares of PepsiCo at $43 per share plus a $2,890 commission.
Jan. 31 Sold 3,600 shares of SPW at $168 per share less a $2,040 commission.
Aug. 22 Sold 2,400 shares of AOL at $56.75 per share less a $2,480 commission.
Sept. 3 Purchased 1,500 shares of Vodaphone at $40.50 per share plus a $1,680 commission.
Oct. 9 Sold 900 shares of Walmart at $53.75 per share less a $1,220 commission.
Dec. 31 Fair value of the short-term investments in trading securities is $140,000.

Required

Check Dec. 31, 2016 Dr. Fair Value Adjustment—Trading $33,298

Prepare journal entries to record these short-term investment activities for the years shown. On December 31 of each year, prepare the adjusting entry to record any necessary fair value adjustment for the portfolio of trading securities.

Problem C-2B
Recording, adjusting, and reporting short-term available-for-sale securities
P3

Slip Systems had no short-term investments prior to 2015. It had the following transactions involving short-term investments in available-for-sale securities during 2015.

Feb.	6	Purchased 3,400 shares of Nokia stock at $41.25 per share plus a $3,000 brokerage fee.
	15	Paid $20,000 to buy six-month U.S. Treasury bills (debt securities): $20,000 principal amount, 6% interest, securities dated February 15.
Apr.	7	Purchased 1,200 shares of Dell Co. stock at $39.50 per share plus a $1,255 brokerage fee.
June	2	Purchased 2,500 shares of Merck stock at $72.50 per share plus a $2,890 brokerage fee.
	30	Received a $0.19 per share cash dividend on the Nokia shares.
Aug.	11	Sold 850 shares of Nokia stock at $46 per share less a $1,050 brokerage fee.
	16	Received a check for principal and accrued interest on the U.S. Treasury bills purchased February 15.
	24	Received a $0.10 per share cash dividend on the Dell shares.
Nov.	9	Received a $0.20 per share cash dividend on the remaining Nokia shares.
Dec.	18	Received a $0.15 per share cash dividend on the Dell shares.

Required

1. Prepare journal entries to record the preceding transactions and events.

Check (2) Cost = $340,232

2. Prepare a table to compare the year-end cost and fair values of the short-term investments in available-for-sale securities. The year-end fair values per share are: Nokia, $40.25; Dell, $40.50; and Merck, $59.

(3) Dr. Unrealized Loss—Equity, $41,494

3. Prepare an adjusting entry, if necessary, to record the year-end fair value adjustment for the portfolio of short-term investments in available-for-sale securities.

Analysis Component

4. Explain the balance sheet presentation of the fair value adjustment to Slip's short-term investments.
5. How do these short-term investments affect (*a*) its income statement for year 2015 and (*b*) the equity section of its balance sheet at the 2015 year-end?

Problem C-3B
Recording, adjusting, and reporting long-term available-for-sale securities
P3

Paris Enterprises, which began operations in 2015, invests in long-term available-for-sale securities. Following is a series of transactions and events involving its long-term investment activity.

2015

Mar. 10	Purchased 1,200 shares of Apple at $25.50 per share plus $800 commission.
Apr. 7	Purchased 2,500 shares of Ford at $22.50 per share plus $1,033 commission.
Sept. 1	Purchased 600 shares of Polaroid at $47.00 per share plus $890 commission.
Dec. 31	Per share fair values for stocks in the portfolio are: Apple, $27.50; Ford, $21.00; Polaroid, $49.00.

2016

Apr. 26	Sold 2,500 shares of Ford at $20.50 per share less a $1,207 commission.
June 2	Purchased 1,800 shares of Duracell at $19.25 per share plus a $1,050 commission.
June 14	Purchased 1,200 shares of Sears at $21 per share plus a $280 commission.
Nov. 27	Sold 600 shares of Polaroid at $51 per share less an $845 commission.
Dec. 31	Per share fair values for stocks in the portfolio are: Apple, $29.00; Duracell, $18.00; Sears, $23.00.

2017

Jan. 28	Purchased 1,000 shares of Coca-Cola Co. at $40 per share plus a $1,480 commission.
Aug. 22	Sold 1,200 shares of Apple at $21.50 per share less a $1,850 commission.
Sept. 3	Purchased 3,000 shares of Motorola at $28 per share plus a $780 commission.
Oct. 9	Sold 1,200 shares of Sears at $24.00 per share less a $599 commission.
Oct. 31	Sold 1,800 shares of Duracell at $15.00 per share less an $898 commission.
Dec. 31	Per share fair values for stocks in the portfolio are: Coca-Cola, $48.00; Motorola, $24.00.

Required

1. Prepare journal entries to record these transactions and events and any year-end fair value adjustments to the portfolio of long-term available-for-sale securities.
2. Prepare a table that summarizes the (*a*) total cost, (*b*) total fair value adjustment, and (*c*) total fair value for the portfolio of long-term available-for-sale securities at each year-end.
3. Prepare a table that summarizes (*a*) the realized gains and losses and (*b*) the unrealized gains or losses for the portfolio of long-term available-for-sale securities at each year-end.

Check (2*b*) Fair Value Adj. bal.: 12/31/15, $2,873 Cr.; 12/31/16, $2,220 Dr.

(3*b*) Unrealized Loss at 12/31/2017, $6,260

Problem C-4B
Accounting for long-term investments in securities; with and without significant influence
P3 P4

Brinkley Company, which began operations on January 3, 2015, had the following subsequent transactions and events in its long-term investments.

2015

Jan. 5 Brinkley purchased 20,000 shares (25% of total) of Bloch's common stock for $200,500.
Aug. 1 Bloch declared and paid a cash dividend of $1.05 per share.
Dec. 31 Bloch's net income for 2015 is $82,000, and the fair value of its stock is $11.90 per share.

2016

Aug. 1 Bloch declared and paid a cash dividend of $1.35 per share.
Dec. 31 Bloch's net income for 2016 is $78,000, and the fair value of its stock is $13.65 per share.

2017

Jan. 8 Brinkley sold all of its investment in Bloch for $375,000 cash.

Part 1

Assume that Brinkley has a significant influence over Bloch with its 25% share.

Required

1. Prepare journal entries to record these transactions and events for Brinkley.
2. Compute the carrying (book) value per share of Brinkley's investment in Bloch common stock as reflected in the investment account on January 7, 2017.
3. Compute the net increase or decrease in Brinkley's equity from January 5, 2015, through January 8, 2017, resulting from its investment in Bloch.

Check (2) Carrying value per share, $9.63

Part 2

Assume that although Brinkley owns 25% of Bloch's outstanding stock, circumstances indicate that it does not have a significant influence over the investee and that it is classified as an available-for-sale security investment.

Required

1. Prepare journal entries to record these transactions and events for Brinkley. Also prepare an entry dated January 8, 2017, to remove any balance related to the fair value adjustment.
2. Compute the cost per share of Brinkley's investment in Bloch common stock as reflected in the investment account on January 7, 2017.
3. Compute the net increase or decrease in Brinkley's equity from January 5, 2015, through January 8, 2017, resulting from its investment in Bloch.

(1) 1/8/2017 Dr. Unrealized Gain—Equity $72,500

(3) Net increase, $222,500

Problem C-5B
Long-term investment transactions; unrealized and realized gains and losses
C2 P3 P4

Troyer's long-term available-for-sale portfolio at December 31, 2014, consists of the following.

Available-for-Sale Securities	Cost	Fair Value
27,500 shares of Company R common stock	$559,125	$599,063
8,500 shares of Company S common stock	308,380	293,250
11,000 shares of Company T common stock	147,295	151,800

Troyer enters into the following long-term investment transactions during year 2015.

Jan. 13 Sold 2,125 shares of Company S stock for $72,250 less a brokerage fee of $1,195.
Mar. 24 Purchased 15,500 shares of Company U common stock for $282,875 plus a brokerage fee of $1,980. The shares represent a 62% ownership interest in Company U.
Apr. 5 Purchased 42,500 shares of Company V common stock for $133,875 plus a brokerage fee of $1,125. The shares represent a 10% ownership in Company V.
Sept. 2 Sold 11,000 shares of Company T common stock for $156,750 less a brokerage fee of $2,700.
Sept. 27 Purchased 2,500 shares of Company W common stock for $50,500 plus a brokerage fee of $1,050. The shares represent a 25% ownership interest in Company W.
Oct. 30 Purchased 5,000 shares of Company X common stock for $48,750 plus a brokerage fee of $1,170. The shares represent a 13% ownership interest in Company X.

The fair values of its investments at December 31, 2015, are: R, $568,125; S, $210,375; U, $272,800; V, $134,938; W, $54,689; and X, $45,625.

Required

1. Determine the amount Troyer should report on its December 31, 2015, balance sheet for its long-term investments in available-for-sale securities.

2. Prepare any necessary December 31, 2015, adjusting entry to record the fair value adjustment of the long-term investments in available-for-sale securities.

Check (2) Dr. Unrealized Loss—Equity, $16,267; Cr. Fair Value Adjustment—AFS (LT), $45,580

3. What amount of gains or losses on transactions relating to long-term investments in available-for-sale securities should Troyer report on its December 31, 2015, income statement?

Problem C-6B[A]
Foreign currency transactions
C3

Datamix, a U.S. corporation with customers in several foreign countries, had the following selected transactions for 2015 and 2016.

2015

May 26 Sold merchandise for 6.5 million yen to Fuji Company of Japan, payment in full to be received in 60 days. On this day, the exchange rate for yen is $0.0093.
June 1 Sold merchandise to Fordham Ltd. of Great Britain for $64,800 cash. The exchange rate for pounds is $1.4498 on this day.
July 25 Received Fuji's payment in yen for its May 26 purchase and immediately exchanged the yen for dollars. The exchange rate for yen is $0.0092 on this day.
Oct. 15 Sold merchandise on credit to Martinez Brothers of Mexico. The price of 378,000 pesos is to be paid 90 days from the date of sale. On this day, the exchange rate for pesos is $0.1020.
Dec. 6 Sold merchandise for 250,000 yuans to Chi-Ying Company of China, payment in full to be received in 30 days. The exchange rate for yuans is $0.1439 on this day.
Dec. 31 Recorded adjusting entries to recognize exchange gains or losses on Datamix's annual financial statements. Rates of exchanging foreign currencies on this day follow.

Yen (Japan)	$0.0094	Pesos (Mexico)	$0.1060
Pounds (Britain)	1.4580	Yuans (China)	0.1450

2016

Jan. 5 Received Chi-Ying's full payment in yuans for the December 6 sale and immediately exchanged the yuans for dollars. The exchange rate for yuans is $0.1580 on this day.
Jan. 13 Received full payment in pesos from Martinez for the October 15 sale and immediately exchanged the pesos for dollars. The exchange rate for pesos is $0.1039 on this day.

Required

1. Prepare journal entries for the Datamix transactions and adjusting entries.

2. Compute the foreign exchange gain or loss to be reported on Datamix's 2015 income statement.

Check (2) 2015 total foreign exchange gain, $1,137

Analysis Component

3. What actions might Datamix consider to reduce its risk of foreign exchange gains or losses?

SERIAL PROBLEM
Business Solutions
P1

(This serial problem began in Chapter 1 and continues through most of the book. If previous chapter segments were not completed, the serial problem can begin at this point. It is helpful, but not necessary, to use the Working Papers that accompany the book.)

SP C While reviewing the March 31, 2016, balance sheet of Business Solutions, Santana Rey notes that the business has built a large cash balance of $68,057. Its most recent bank money market statement shows that the funds are earning an annualized return of 0.75%. S. Rey decides to make several investments with the desire to earn a higher return on the idle cash balance. Accordingly, in April 2016, Business Solutions makes the following investments in trading securities:

Apr. 16 Purchases 400 shares of Johnson & Johnson stock at $50 per share plus a $300 commission.
Apr. 30 Purchases 200 shares of Starbucks Corporation at $22 per share plus a $250 commission.

On June 30, 2016, the per share market price (fair value) of the Johnson & Johnson shares is $55 and the Starbucks shares is $19.

Required

1. Prepare journal entries to record the April purchases of trading securities by Business Solutions.
2. On June 30, 2016, prepare the adjusting entry to record any necessary fair value adjustment to its portfolio of trading securities.

GENERAL LEDGER PROBLEM

Available in Connect

connect ACCOUNTING

The following General Ledger assignments focus on the account for investments in available-for-sale securities and equity method investments.

GL C-1 General Ledger assignment C-1 is adapted from Problem C-2A. Prepare journal entries related to short-term investments in available-for-sale securities, including the adjustment to fair value, if necessary.

GL C-2 General Ledger assignment C-2 is adapted from Problem C-5A. Prepare journal entries related to long-term investments transactions and the related realized and unrealized gains.

Beyond the Numbers

REPORTING IN ACTION
C3 A1
APPLE

BTN C-1 Refer to **Apple**'s financial statements in Appendix A to answer the following.

1. Are its financial statements consolidated? How can you tell?
2. What is the amount of *comprehensive income* for the year ended September 28, 2013?
3. Does it have any foreign operations? How can you tell?
4. Compute its return on total assets for the year ended September 28, 2013.

Fast Forward

5. Access Apple's annual report for a fiscal year ending after September 28, 2013, from either its website (Apple.com) or the SEC's database (www.SEC.gov). Recompute its return on total assets for the years subsequent to September 28, 2013.

COMPARATIVE ANALYSIS
A1
APPLE
GOOGLE

BTN C-2 Key figures for **Apple** and **Google** follow.

	Apple			Google		
($ millions)	Current Year	1 Year Prior	2 Years Prior	Current Year	1 Year Prior	2 Years Prior
Net income	$ 37,037	$ 41,733	$ 25,922	$ 12,920	$10,737	$ 9,737
Net sales	170,910	156,508	108,249	59,825	50,175	37,905
Total assets.	207,000	176,064	116,371	110,920	93,798	72,574

Required

1. Compute return on total assets for Apple and Google for the two most recent years.
2. Separate the return on total assets computed in part 1 into its components for both companies and both years according to the formula in Exhibit C.9.
3. Which company has the highest total return on assets? The highest profit margin? The highest total asset turnover? What does this comparative analysis reveal? (Assume an industry average of 10.0% for return on assets.)

ETHICS CHALLENGE

P2 P3

BTN C-3 Kasey Hartman is the controller for Wholemart Company, which has numerous long-term investments in debt securities. Wholemart's investments are mainly in five-year bonds. Hartman is preparing its year-end financial statements. In accounting for long-term debt securities, she knows that each long-term investment must be designated as a held-to-maturity or an available-for-sale security. Interest rates rose sharply this past year, causing the portfolio's fair value to substantially decline. The company does not intend to hold the bonds for the entire five years. Hartman also earns a bonus each year, which is computed as a percent of net income.

Required

1. Will Hartman's bonus depend in any way on the classification of the debt securities? Explain.
2. What criteria must Hartman use to classify the securities as held-to-maturity or available-for-sale?
3. Is there likely any company oversight of Hartman's classification of the securities? Explain.

COMMUNICATING IN PRACTICE

P4

BTN C-4 Assume that you are Jolee Company's accountant. Company owner Mary Jolee has reviewed the 2015 financial statements you prepared and questions the $6,000 loss reported on the sale of its investment in Kemper Co. common stock. Jolee acquired 50,000 shares of Kemper's common stock on December 31, 2013, at a cost of $500,000. This stock purchase represented a 40% interest in Kemper. The 2014 income statement reported that earnings from all investments were $126,000. On January 3, 2015, Jolee Company sold the Kemper stock for $575,000. Kemper did not pay any dividends during 2014 but reported a net income of $202,500 for that year. Mary Jolee believes that because the Kemper stock purchase price was $500,000 and was sold for $575,000, the 2015 income statement should report a $75,000 gain on the sale.

Required

Draft a half-page memorandum to Mary Jolee explaining why the $6,000 loss on sale of Kemper stock is correctly reported.

TAKING IT TO THE NET

C1

BTN C-5 Access the July 30, 2013, 10-K filing (for year-end June 30, 2013) of **Microsoft** (MSFT) at www.SEC.gov. Review its note 4, "Investments."

Required

1. How does the "cost-basis" total amount for its investments as of June 30, 2013, compare to the prior year-end amount?
2. Identify at least eight types of short-term investments held by Microsoft as of June 30, 2013.
3. What were Microsoft's unrealized gains and its unrealized losses from its investments for 2013?
4. Was the cost or fair value ("recorded basis") of the investments higher as of June 30, 2013?

TEAMWORK IN ACTION

C1 C2 P1 P2 P3 P4

BTN C-6 Each team member is to become an expert on a specific classification of long-term investments. This expertise will be used to facilitate other teammates' understanding of the concepts and procedures relevant to the classification chosen.

1. Each team member must select an area for expertise by choosing one of the following classifications of long-term investments.
   a. Held-to-maturity debt securities
   b. Available-for-sale debt and equity securities
   c. Equity securities with significant influence
   d. Equity securities with controlling influence
2. Learning teams are to disburse and expert teams are to be formed. Expert teams are made up of those who select the same area of expertise. The instructor will identify the location where each expert team will meet.
3. Expert teams will collaborate to develop a presentation based on the following requirements. Students must write the presentation in a format they can show to their learning teams in part 4.

Requirements for Expert Presentation

a. Write a transaction for the acquisition of this type of investment security. The transaction description is to include all necessary data to reflect the chosen classification.
b. Prepare the journal entry to record the acquisition.

   [*Note:* The expert team on equity securities with controlling influence will substitute requirements (*d*) and (*e*) with a discussion of the reporting of these investments.]
c. Identify information necessary to complete the end-of-period adjustment for this investment.
d. Assuming that this is the only investment owned, prepare any necessary year-end entries.
e. Present the relevant balance sheet section(s).

4. Re-form learning teams. In rotation, experts are to present to their teams the presentations they developed in part 3. Experts are to encourage and respond to questions.

ENTREPRENEURIAL DECISION

C3

BTN C-7[A] Refer to the Sustainability and Accounting feature in this appendix about Hannah Davis and her company, **BANGS**. Assume that the company must acquire the Japanese rights to the website BANGS, which will then be branded with its shoes for sale in Japan. Assume the company acquires those rights on January 1, 2015, from a Japanese distributor and agrees to pay 12,000,000 yen per year for those rights. Quarterly payments are due March 31, June 30, September 30, and December 31 each year. On January 1, 2015, the yen is worth $0.00891.

Required

1. Prepare the journal entry to record the Internet rights purchased on January 1, 2015.
2. Prepare the journal entries to record the payments on March 31, June 30, September 30, and December 31, 2015. The value of the yen on those dates follows.

March 31	$0.00893
June 30	0.00901
September 30	0.00902
December 31	0.00897

3. How can the company protect itself from unanticipated gains and losses from currency translation if all of the payments are specified to be paid in yen?

HITTING THE ROAD

C3

BTN C-8[A] Assume that you are planning a spring break trip to Europe. Identify three locations where you can find exchange rates for the dollar relative to the euro or other currencies.

GLOBAL DECISION

A1

Samsung
APPLE
GOOGLE

BTN C-9 Samsung, Apple, and Google are competitors in the global marketplace. Following are selected data from each company.

Key Figure	Samsung (Korean won millions) Current Year	One Year Prior	Two Years Prior	Apple Current Year	Apple Prior Year	Google Current Year	Google Prior Year
Net income	₩30,474,764	₩ 23,845,285	₩13,759,043	—	—	—	—
Net sales	228,692,667	201,103,613	165,001,771	—	—	—	—
Total assets	214,075,018	181,071,570	155,800,263	—	—	—	—
Profit margin	?	?	—	21.7%	26.7%	21.6%	21.4%
Total asset turnover	?	?	—	0.89	1.07	0.58	0.60

Required

1. Compute Samsung's return on total assets, and its components of profit margin and total asset turnover, for the most recent two years using the data provided.
2. Which of these three companies has the highest return on total assets? Highest profit margin? Highest total asset turnover? Interpret these results for the (*a*) current year and (*b*) prior year.

ANSWERS TO MULTIPLE CHOICE QUIZ

1. d; $\$30,000 \times 5\% \times 5/12 = \$625$
2. a; Unrealized gain = $\$84,500 - \$83,000 = \$1,500$
3. b; $\$50,000 \times 35\% = \$17,500$
4. e; $\$300,000/\$2,000,000 = 15\%$
5. b; Profit margin = $\$80,000/\$600,000 = 13.3\%$
   Total asset turnover = $\$600,000/\$400,000 = 1.5$

Index

Chart of Accounts

Following is a typical chart of accounts, which is used in several assignments. Each company has its own unique set of accounts and numbering system. *An asterisk denotes a contra account.

Assets

Current Assets

101 Cash
102 Petty cash
103 Cash equivalents
104 Short-term investments
105 Fair value adjustment, _______ securities (S-T)
106 Accounts receivable
107 Allowance for doubtful accounts*
108 Legal fees receivable
109 Interest receivable
110 Rent receivable
111 Notes receivable
119 Merchandise inventory (or Inventory)
120 _________ inventory
121 _________ inventory
124 Office supplies
125 Store supplies
126 _______ supplies
128 Prepaid insurance
129 Prepaid interest
131 Prepaid rent
132 Raw materials inventory
133 Work in process inventory, _______
134 Work in process inventory, _______
135 Finished goods inventory

Long-Term Investments

141 Long-term investments
142 Fair value adjustment, _______ securities (L-T)
144 Investment in _______
145 Bond sinking fund

Plant Assets

151 Automobiles
152 Accumulated depreciation—Automobiles*
153 Trucks
154 Accumulated depreciation—Trucks*
155 Boats
156 Accumulated depreciation—Boats*
157 Professional library
158 Accumulated depreciation—Professional library*
159 Law library
160 Accumulated depreciation—Law library*
161 Furniture
162 Accumulated depreciation—Furniture*
163 Office equipment
164 Accumulated depreciation—Office equipment*
165 Store equipment
166 Accumulated depreciation—Store equipment*
167 _______ equipment
168 Accumulated depreciation—_______ equipment*
169 Machinery
170 Accumulated depreciation—Machinery*
173 Building _______
174 Accumulated depreciation—Building _______*
175 Building _______
176 Accumulated depreciation—Building _______*
179 Land improvements _______
180 Accumulated depreciation—Land improvements _______*
181 Land improvements _______
182 Accumulated depreciation—Land improvements _______*
183 Land

Natural Resources

185 Mineral deposit
186 Accumulated depletion—Mineral deposit*

Intangible Assets

191 Patents
192 Leasehold
193 Franchise
194 Copyrights
195 Leasehold improvements
196 Licenses
197 Accumulated amortization—_______*

Liabilities

Current Liabilities

201 Accounts payable
202 Insurance payable
203 Interest payable
204 Legal fees payable
207 Office salaries payable
208 Rent payable
209 Salaries payable
210 Wages payable
211 Accrued payroll payable
212 Factory payroll payable
214 Estimated warranty liability
215 Income taxes payable
216 Common dividend payable
217 Preferred dividend payable
218 State unemployment taxes payable
219 Employee federal income taxes payable
221 Employee medical insurance payable
222 Employee retirement program payable
223 Employee union dues payable
224 Federal unemployment taxes payable
225 FICA taxes payable
226 Estimated vacation pay liability

Unearned Revenues

230 Unearned consulting fees
231 Unearned legal fees
232 Unearned property management fees
233 Unearned _______ fees
234 Unearned _______ fees
235 Unearned janitorial revenue
236 Unearned _______ revenue
238 Unearned rent

Notes Payable

240 Short-term notes payable
241 Discount on short-term notes payable*
245 Notes payable
251 Long-term notes payable
252 Discount on long-term notes payable*

Long-Term Liabilities

253 Long-term lease liability
255 Bonds payable
256 Discount on bonds payable*
257 Premium on bonds payable
258 Deferred income tax liability

Equity

Owner's Equity

301 _____________, Capital
302 _____________, Withdrawals
303 _____________, Capital
304 _____________, Withdrawals
305 _____________, Capital
306 _____________, Withdrawals

Paid-In Capital

307 Common stock, $ _______ par value
308 Common stock, no-par value
309 Common stock, $ _______ stated value
310 Common stock dividend distributable
311 Paid-in capital in excess of par value, Common stock
312 Paid-in capital in excess of stated value, No-par common stock

313 Paid-in capital from retirement of common stock
314 Paid-in capital, Treasury stock
315 Preferred stock
316 Paid-in capital in excess of par value, Preferred stock

Retained Earnings

318 Retained earnings
319 Cash dividends (or Dividends)
320 Stock dividends

Other Equity Accounts

321 Treasury stock, Common*
322 Unrealized gain—Equity
323 Unrealized loss—Equity

Revenues

401 ______________ fees earned
402 ______________ fees earned
403 ______________ revenues
404 Revenues
405 Commissions earned
406 Rent revenue (or Rent earned)
407 Dividends revenue (or Dividends earned)
408 Earnings from investment in _______
409 Interest revenue (or Interest earned)
410 Sinking fund earnings
413 Sales
414 Sales returns and allowances*
415 Sales discounts*

Cost of Sales

Cost of Goods Sold

502 Cost of goods sold
505 Purchases
506 Purchases returns and allowances*
507 Purchases discounts*
508 Transportation-in

Manufacturing

520 Raw materials purchases
521 Freight-in on raw materials
530 Direct labor
540 Factory overhead
541 Indirect materials
542 Indirect labor
543 Factory insurance expired
544 Factory supervision
545 Factory supplies used
546 Factory utilities
547 Miscellaneous production costs
548 Property taxes on factory building
549 Property taxes on factory equipment
550 Rent on factory building
551 Repairs, factory equipment
552 Small tools written off
560 Depreciation of factory equipment
561 Depreciation of factory building

Standard Cost Variances

580 Direct material quantity variance
581 Direct material price variance
582 Direct labor quantity variance
583 Direct labor price variance
584 Factory overhead volume variance
585 Factory overhead controllable variance

Expenses

Amortization, Depletion, and Depreciation

601 Amortization expense—_______
602 Amortization expense—_______
603 Depletion expense—_______
604 Depreciation expense—Boats
605 Depreciation expense—Automobiles
606 Depreciation expense—Building _______
607 Depreciation expense—Building _______
608 Depreciation expense—Land improvements _______
609 Depreciation expense—Land improvements _______
610 Depreciation expense—Law library
611 Depreciation expense—Trucks
612 Depreciation expense—_______ equipment
613 Depreciation expense—_______ equipment
614 Depreciation expense—_______
615 Depreciation expense—_______

Employee-Related Expenses

620 Office salaries expense
621 Sales salaries expense
622 Salaries expense
623 _______ wages expense
624 Employees' benefits expense
625 Payroll taxes expense

Financial Expenses

630 Cash over and short
631 Discounts lost
632 Factoring fee expense
633 Interest expense

Insurance Expenses

635 Insurance expense—Delivery equipment
636 Insurance expense—Office equipment
637 Insurance expense—_______

Rental Expenses

640 Rent expense
641 Rent expense—Office space
642 Rent expense—Selling space
643 Press rental expense
644 Truck rental expense
645 _______ rental expense

Supplies Expenses

650 Office supplies expense
651 Store supplies expense
652 _______ supplies expense
653 _______ supplies expense

Miscellaneous Expenses

655 Advertising expense
656 Bad debts expense
657 Blueprinting expense
658 Boat expense
659 Collection expense
661 Concessions expense
662 Credit card expense
663 Delivery expense
664 Dumping expense
667 Equipment expense
668 Food and drinks expense
671 Gas and oil expense
672 General and administrative expense
673 Janitorial expense
674 Legal fees expense
676 Mileage expense
677 Miscellaneous expenses
678 Mower and tools expense
679 Operating expense
680 Organization expense
681 Permits expense
682 Postage expense
683 Property taxes expense
684 Repairs expense—_______
685 Repairs expense—_______
687 Selling expense
688 Telephone expense
689 Travel and entertainment expense
690 Utilities expense
691 Warranty expense
692 _______ expense
695 Income taxes expense

Gains and Losses

701 Gain on retirement of bonds
702 Gain on sale of machinery
703 Gain on sale of investments
704 Gain on sale of trucks
705 Gain on _______
706 Foreign exchange gain or loss
801 Loss on disposal of machinery
802 Loss on exchange of equipment
803 Loss on exchange of _______
804 Loss on sale of notes
805 Loss on retirement of bonds
806 Loss on sale of investments
807 Loss on sale of machinery
808 Loss on _______
809 Unrealized gain—Income
810 Unrealized loss—Income
811 Impairment gain
812 Impairment loss

Clearing Accounts

901 Income summary
902 Manufacturing summary

SELECTED TRANSACTIONS AND RELATIONS

① Merchandising Transactions Summary—Perpetual Inventory System

	Merchandising Transactions	Merchandising Entries	Dr.	Cr.
Purchases	Purchasing merchandise for resale.	• Merchandise Inventory	#	
		Cash or Accounts Payable		#
	Paying freight costs on purchases; FOB shipping point.	• Merchandise Inventory	#	
		Cash		#
	Paying within discount period.	• Accounts Payable	#	
		Merchandise Inventory		#
		Cash		#
	Recording purchase returns or allowances.	• Cash or Accounts Payable	#	
		Merchandise Inventory		#
Sales	Selling merchandise.	• Cash or Accounts Receivable	#	
		Sales		#
		• Cost of Goods Sold	#	
		Merchandise Inventory		#
	Receiving payment within discount period.	• Cash	#	
		Sales Discounts	#	
		Accounts Receivable		#
	Granting sales returns or allowances.	• Sales Returns and Allowances	#	
		Cash or Accounts Receivable		#
		• Merchandise Inventory	#	
		Cost of Goods Sold		#
	Paying freight costs on sales; FOB destination.	• Delivery Expense	#	
		Cash		#

	Merchandising Events	Adjusting and Closing Entries	Dr.	Cr.
Adjusting	Adjusting due to shrinkage (occurs when recorded amount larger than physical inventory).	Cost of Goods Sold	#	
		Merchandise Inventory		#
Closing	Closing temporary accounts with credit balances.	Sales	#	
		Income Summary		#
	Closing temporary accounts with debit balances.	Income Summary	#	
		Sales Returns and Allowances		#
		Sales Discounts		#
		Cost of Goods Sold		#
		Delivery Expense		#
		"Other Expenses"		#

② Merchandising Cash Flows

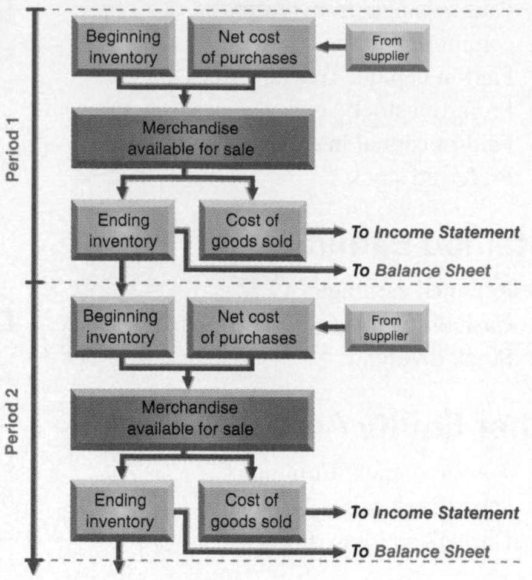

③ Credit Terms and Amounts

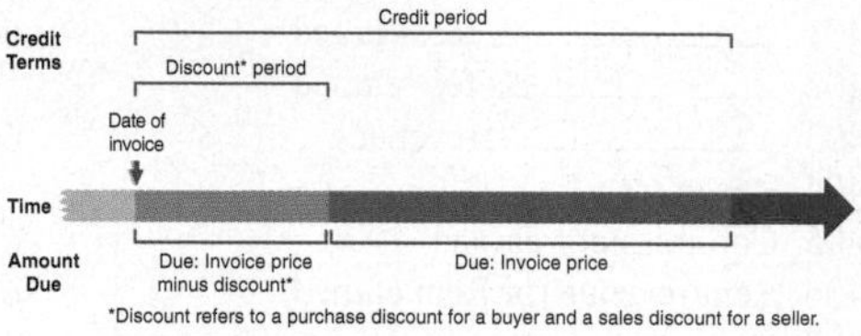

④ Bad Debts Estimation

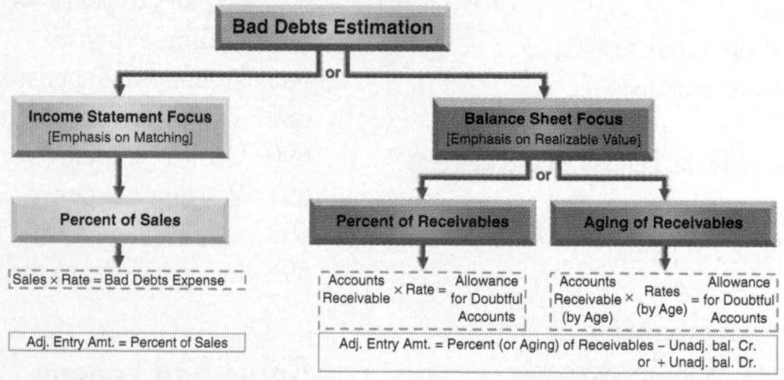

⑤ Bond Valuation

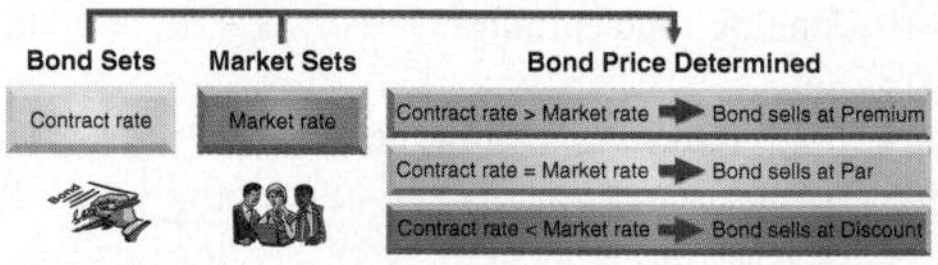

⑥ Stock Transactions Summary

	Stock Transactions	Stock Entries	Dr.	Cr.
Issue Common Stock	Issue par value common stock at par (par stock recorded at par).	Cash	#	
		Common Stock		#
	Issue par value common stock at premium (par stock recorded at par).	Cash	#	
		Common Stock		#
		Paid-In Capital in Excess of Par Value, Common Stock		#
	Issue no-par value common stock (no-par stock recorded at amount received).	Cash	#	
		Common Stock		#
	Issue stated value common stock at stated value (stated stock recorded at stated value).	Cash	#	
		Common stock		#
	Issue stated value common stock at premium (stated stock recorded at stated value).	Cash	#	
		Common stock		#
		Paid-In Capital in Excess of Stated Value, Common Stock		#
Issue Preferred Stock	Issue par value preferred stock at par (par stock recorded at par).	Cash	#	
		Preferred Stock		#
	Issue par value preferred stock at premium (par stock recorded at par).	Cash	#	
		Preferred Stock		#
		Paid-In Capital in Excess of Par Value, Preferred Stock		#
Reacquire Common Stock	Reacquire its own common stock (treasury stock recorded at cost).	Treasury Stock, Common	#	
		Cash		#
Reissue Common Stock	Reissue its treasury stock at cost (treasury stock removed at cost).	Cash	#	
		Treasury Stock, Common		#
	Reissue its treasury stock above cost (treasury stock removed at cost).	Cash	#	
		Treasury Stock, Common		#
		Paid-In Capital, Treasury		#
	Reissue its treasury stock below cost (treasury stock removed at cost; if paid-in capital is insufficient to cover amount below cost, retained earnings is debited for remainder).	Cash	#	
		Paid-In Capital, Treasury	#	
		Treasury Stock, Common		#
		Retained Earnings (if necessary)	#	

⑦ Dividend Transactions

Account Affected	Type of Dividend: Cash Dividend	Stock Dividend	Stock Split
Cash	Decrease	—	—
Common Stock	—	Increase	—
Retained Earnings	Decrease	Decrease	—

⑧ A Rose by Any Other Name

The same financial statement sometimes receives different titles. Following are some of the more common aliases.*

Balance Sheet	Statement of Financial Position Statement of Financial Condition
Income Statement	Statement of Income Operating Statement Statement of Operations Statement of Operating Activity Earnings Statement Statement of Earnings Profit and Loss (P&L) Statement
Statement of Cash Flows	Statement of Cash Flow Cash Flows Statement Statement of Changes in Cash Position Statement of Changes in Financial Position
Statement of Stockholders' Equity	Statement of Shareholders' Equity Statement of Changes in Shareholders' Equity Statement of Stockholders' Equity and Comprehensive Income Statement of Changes in Owner's Equity Statement of Changes in Owner's Capital Statement of Changes in Capital Accounts

* The term **Consolidated** often precedes or follows these statement titles to reflect the combination of different entities, such as a parent company and its subsidiaries.

MANAGERIAL ANALYSES AND REPORTS

① Cost Types

Variable costs: Total cost changes in proportion to volume of activity
Fixed costs: Total cost does not change in proportion to volume of activity
Mixed costs: Cost consists of both a variable and a fixed element

② Cost Sources

Direct materials: Raw materials costs directly linked to finished product
Direct labor: Employee costs directly linked to finished product
Overhead: Production costs indirectly linked to finished product

③ Costing Systems

Job order costing: Costs assigned to each unique unit or batch of units
Process costing: Costs assigned to similar products that are mass-produced in a continuous manner

④ Costing Ratios

Contribution margin ratio = (Net sales − Variable costs)/Net sales
Predetermined overhead rate = Estimated overhead costs/Estimated activity base
Break-even point in units = Total fixed costs/Contribution margin per unit

⑤ Planning and Control Metrics

Cost variance = Actual cost − Standard (budgeted) cost
Sales (revenue) variance = Actual sales − Standard (budgeted) sales

⑥ Capital Budgeting

Payback period = Time expected to recover investment cost
Accounting rate of return = Expected annual net income/Average annual investment
Net present value (NPV) = Present value of future cash flows − Investment cost
NPV rule: 1. Compute net present value (NPV in $)
2. If NPV ≥ 0, then accept project; If NPV < 0, then reject project
Internal rate of return rule: 1. Compute internal rate of return (IRR in %)
2. If IRR ≥ hurdle rate, accept project; If IRR < hurdle rate, reject project

⑦ Costing Terminology

Relevant range: Organization's normal range of operating activity.
Direct cost: Cost incurred for the benefit of one cost object.
Indirect cost: Cost incurred for the benefit of more than one cost object.
Product cost: Cost that is necessary and integral to finished products.
Period cost: Cost identified more with a time period than with finished products.
Overhead cost: Cost not separately or directly traceable to a cost object.
Relevant cost: Cost that is pertinent to a decision.
Opportunity cost: Benefit lost by choosing an action from two or more alternatives.
Sunk cost: Cost already incurred that cannot be avoided or changed.
Standard cost: Cost computed using standard price and standard quantity.
Budget: Formal statement of an organization's future plans.
Break-even point: Sales level at which an organization earns zero profit.
Incremental cost: Cost incurred only if the organization undertakes a certain action.
Transfer price: Price on transactions between divisions within a company.

⑧ Standard Cost Variances

Total materials variance = Materials price variance + Materials quantity variance

Total labor variance = Labor (rate) variance + Labor efficiency (quantity) variance

Total overhead variance = Overhead controllable variance + Fixed overhead volume variance

Overhead controllable variance = Actual total overhead − Budgeted total overhead per flexible budget

Fixed overhead volume variance = Budgeted fixed overhead − Applied fixed overhead

Variable overhead variance = Variable overhead spending variance + Variable overhead efficiency variance
Fixed overhead variance = Fixed overhead spending variance + Fixed overhead volume variance
} = Total overhead variance

Materials price variance = [AQ × AP] − [AQ × SP]

Materials quantity variance = [AQ × SP] − [SQ × SP]

Labor (rate) variance = [AH × AR] − [AH × SR]

Labor efficiency (quantity) variance = [AH × SR] − [SH × SR]

Variable overhead spending variance = [AH × AVR] − [AH × SVR]
Variable overhead efficiency variance = [AH × SVR] − [SH × SVR]
Fixed overhead spending variance = Actual fixed overhead − Budgeted fixed overhead

where AQ is Actual Quantity of materials; AP is Actual Price of materials; AH is Actual Hours of labor; AR is Actual Rate of wages; AVR is Actual Variable Rate of overhead; SQ is Standard Quantity of materials; SP is Standard Price of materials; SH is Standard Hours of labor; SR is Standard Rate of wages; SVR is Standard Variable Rate of overhead.

⑨ Sales Variances

Sales price variance = [AS × AP] − [AS × BP]

Sales volume variance = [AS × BP] − [BS × BP]

where AS = Actual Sales units; AP = Actual sales Price; BP = Budgeted sales Price; BS = Budgeted Sales units (fixed budget)

Schedule of Cost of Goods Manufactured
For *period* Ended *date*

Direct materials	
Raw materials inventory, Beginning	$ #
Raw materials purchases	#
Raw materials available for use	#
Raw materials inventory, Ending	(#)
Direct materials used	#
Direct labor	#
Overhead costs	
Total overhead costs	#
Total manufacturing costs	#
Add work in process inventory, Beginning	#
Total cost of work in process	#
Deduct work in process inventory, Ending	(#)
Cost of goods manufactured	$ #

Contribution Margin Income Statement
For *period* Ended *date*

Net sales (revenues)	$ #
Total variable costs	#
Contribution margin	#
Total fixed costs	#
Net income (pretax)	$ #

Flexible Budget
For *period* Ended *date*

	Flexible Budget: Variable Amount per Unit	Flexible Budget: Fixed Cost	Flexible Budget for Unit Sales of #
Sales (revenues)	$ #		$ #
Variable costs			
Examples: Direct materials, Direct labor, Other variable costs	#		#
Total variable costs	#		#
Contribution margin	$ #		#
Fixed costs			
Examples: Depreciation, Manager		$ #	#
salaries, Administrative salaries		#	#
Total fixed costs		$ #	#
Income from operations			$ #

Budget Performance Report*
For *period* Ended *date*

	Budget	Actual Performance	Variances[†]
Sales: In units	#	#	
In dollars	$ #	$ #	$ # F or U
Cost of sales			
Direct costs	#	#	# F or U
Indirect costs	#	#	# F or U
Selling expenses			
Examples: Commissions	#	#	# F or U
Shipping expenses	#	#	# F or U
General and administrative expenses			
Examples: Administrative salaries	#	#	# F or U
Total expenses	$ #	$ #	$ # F or U
Income from operations	$ #	$ #	$ # F or U

*[†] F = Favorable variance; U = Unfavorable variance. * Applies to both flexible and fixed budgets.*

Master Budget Sequence

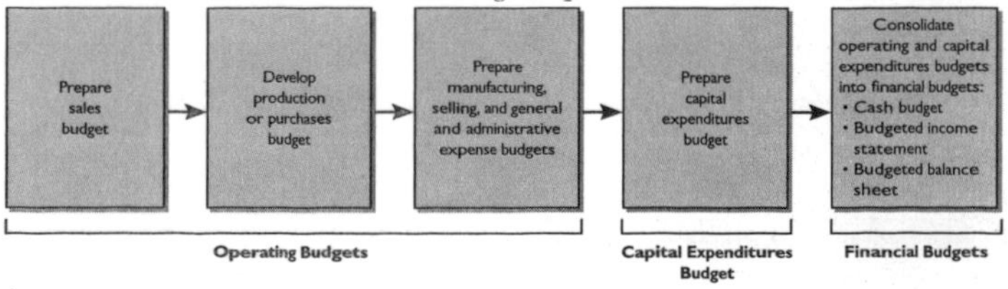

FUNDAMENTALS

① Accounting Equation

Assets		=	Liabilities		+	Equity	
↑ Debit for increases	↓ Credit for decreases		↓ Debit for decreases	↑ Credit for increases		↓ Debit for decreases	↑ Credit for increases

Equity: Contributed Capital* + Retained Earnings

Retained Earnings: Common Stock − Dividends + Revenues − Expenses

Common Stock		Dividends		Revenues		Expenses	
Dr. for decreases	↑ Cr. for increases	↑ Dr. for increases	Cr. for decreases	Dr. for decreases	↑ Cr. for increases	↑ Dr. for increases	Cr. for decreases

[shaded box] Indicates normal balance.

*Includes common stock and any preferred stock.

② Accounting Cycle

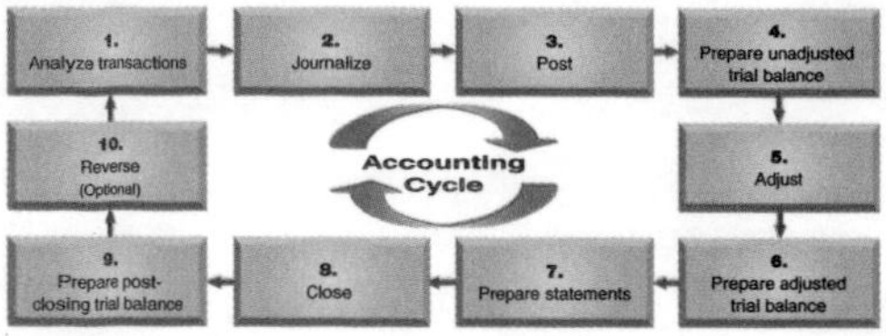

③ Adjustments and Entries

Type	Adjusting Entry	
Prepaid Expenses	Dr. Expense	Cr. Asset*
Unearned Revenues	Dr. Liability	Cr. Revenue
Accrued Expenses	Dr. Expense	Cr. Liability
Accrued Revenues	Dr. Asset	Cr. Revenue

*For depreciation, credit Accumulated Depreciation (contra asset).

④ 4-Step Closing Process

1. Transfer revenue and gain account balances to Income Summary.
2. Transfer expense and loss account balances to Income Summary.
3. Transfer Income Summary balance to Retained Earnings.
4. Transfer Dividends balance to Retained Earnings.

⑤ Accounting Concepts

Characteristics	Assumptions	Principles	Constraints
Relevance	Business entity	Measurement (historical cost)	Cost-benefit
Reliability	Going concern	Revenue recognition	Materiality
Comparability	Monetary unit	Expense recognition	Industry practice
Consistency	Periodicity	Full disclosure	Conservatism

⑥ Ownership of Inventory

	Ownership Transfers To Buyer When Good Are	Transportation Costs Paid By
FOB Shipping Point	Shipped	Buyer
FOB Destination	Received by Buyer	Seller

⑦ Inventory Costing Methods

- Specific identification
- First-in, first-out (FIFO)
- Weighted-average
- Last-in, first-out (LIFO)

⑧ Depreciation and Depletion

Straight-line: $\dfrac{\text{Cost} - \text{Salvage value}}{\text{Useful life in periods}}$

Units-of-production: $\dfrac{\text{Cost} - \text{Salvage value}}{\text{Useful life in units}} \times \text{Units produced in current period}$

Declining-balance: Rate* $\times$ Beginning-of-period book value

*Rate is often double the straight-line rate, or $2 \times (1/\text{Useful life})$

Depletion: $\dfrac{\text{Cost} - \text{Salvage value}}{\text{Total capacity in units}} \times \text{Units extracted in current period}$

⑨ Interest Computation

Interest = Principal (face) $\times$ Rate $\times$ Time

⑩ Accounting for Investment Securities

Classification*	Accounting
Short-Term Investment in Securities	
Held-to-maturity (debt) securities	**Cost** (without any discount or premium amortization)
Trading (debt and equity) securities	**Fair value** (with fair value adjustment to income)
Available-for-sale (debt and equity) securities	**Fair value** (with fair value adjustment to equity)
Long-Term Investment in Securities	
Held-to-maturity (debt) securities	**Cost** (with any discount or premium amortization)
Available-for-sale (debt and equity) securities	**Fair value** (with fair value adjustment to equity)
Equity securities with significant influence	Equity method
Equity securities with controlling influence	Equity method (with consolidation)

*A *fair value option* allows companies to report HTM and AFS securities much like trading securities.

ANALYSES

① Liquidity and Efficiency

Measure	Page
Current ratio $= \dfrac{\text{Current assets}}{\text{Current liabilities}}$	pp. 125 & 595
Working capital = Current assets − Current liabilities	p. 595
Acid-test ratio $= \dfrac{\text{Cash} + \text{Short-term investments} + \text{Current receivables}}{\text{Current liabilities}}$	pp. 183 & 596
Accounts receivable turnover $= \dfrac{\text{Net sales}}{\text{Average accounts receivable, net}}$	pp. 327 & 597
Credit risk ratio $= \dfrac{\text{Allowance for doubtful accounts}}{\text{Accounts receivable, net}}$	p. 327
Inventory turnover $= \dfrac{\text{Cost of goods sold}}{\text{Average inventory}}$	pp. 229 & 597
Days' sales uncollected $= \dfrac{\text{Accounts receivable, net}}{\text{Net sales}} \times 365^*$	pp. 285 & 597
Days' sales in inventory $= \dfrac{\text{Ending inventory}}{\text{Cost of goods sold}} \times 365^*$	pp. 229 & 598
Total asset turnover $= \dfrac{\text{Net sales}}{\text{Average total assets}}$	pp. 367 & 598
Plant asset useful life $= \dfrac{\text{Plant asset cost}}{\text{Depreciation expense}}$	p. 367
Plant asset age $= \dfrac{\text{Accumulated depreciation}}{\text{Depreciation expense}}$	p. 368
Days' cash expense coverage $= \dfrac{\text{Cash and cash equivalents}}{\text{Average daily cash expenses}}$	p. 270

*360 days is also commonly used.

② Solvency

Measure	Page
Debt ratio $= \dfrac{\text{Total liabilities}}{\text{Total assets}}$ Equity ratio $= \dfrac{\text{Total equity}}{\text{Total assets}}$	pp. 76 & 599
Debt-to-equity $= \dfrac{\text{Total liabilities}}{\text{Total equity}}$	pp. 452 & 599
Times interest earned $= \dfrac{\text{Income before interest expense and income taxes}}{\text{Interest expense}}$	pp. 406 & 599
Cash coverage of growth $= \dfrac{\text{Cash flow from operations}}{\text{Cash outflow for plant assets}}$	p. 548
Cash coverage of debt $= \dfrac{\text{Cash flow from operations}}{\text{Total noncurrent liabilities}}$	p. 548

③ Profitability

Measure	Page
Profit margin ratio $= \dfrac{\text{Net income}}{\text{Net sales}}$	p. 125
Gross margin ratio $= \dfrac{\text{Net sales} - \text{Cost of goods sold}}{\text{Net sales}}$	p. 184
Return on total assets $= \dfrac{\text{Net income}}{\text{Average total assets}}$	p. 600
= Profit margin ratio $\times$ Total asset turnover	p. 601
Return on common stockholders' equity $= \dfrac{\text{Net income} - \text{Preferred dividends}}{\text{Average common stockholders' equity}}$	p. 601
Book value per common share $= \dfrac{\text{Stockholders' equity applicable to common shares}}{\text{Number of common shares outstanding}}$	p. 504
Basic earnings per share $= \dfrac{\text{Net income} - \text{Preferred dividends}}{\text{Weighted-average common shares outstanding}}$	p. 502
Cash flow on total assets $= \dfrac{\text{Cash flow from operations}}{\text{Average total assets}}$	p. 547
Payout ratio $= \dfrac{\text{Cash dividends declared on common stock}}{\text{Net income}}$	p. 503

④ Market

Measure	Page
Price-earnings ratio $= \dfrac{\text{Market value (price) per share}}{\text{Earnings per share}}$	pp. 503 & 601
Dividend yield $= \dfrac{\text{Annual cash dividends per share}}{\text{Market price per share}}$	pp. 503 & 602
Residual income = Income − Target income	p. 983